Emon

415 - 268 - 1144

415 - 897 - 4776

408 - 998 - 2565

Modern Patent Law Precedent

Dictionary of Key Terms and Concepts

FOURTH EDITION

Modern Patent Law Precedent

Dictionary of Key Terms and Concepts

FOURTH EDITION

by
Irwin M. Aisenberg

GLASSER LEGALWORKS

ISBN: 1-888075-91-0

Glasser LegalWorks
150 Clove Road
Little Falls, New Jersey 07424

Printed in the United States of America

Contents

Special Notice

In response to readers' suggestions, this edition of Patent Law Precedent now contains parallel citations to federal reporters, in addition to the U.S.P.Q. citations. The Publisher hopes this will be helpful to users of the book.

About the Author

Irwin M. Aisenberg is a partner in the Washington, DC law firm of Jacobson, Price, Holman & Stern. An active patent practitioner for over 40 years and former patent examiner, Mr. Aisenberg has written widely over the years on aspects of patent prosecution, claims and litigation. He served on the Editorial Advisory boards of a leading patent law publication and is a member of the District of Columbia and American Bar Associations as well as the American Intellectual Property Law Association and the International Association for the Protection of Industrial Property.

Introduction

Patent law is increasingly driven by the rapid pace of technological change and the necessity of fitting a traditional body of law and doctrine to ever-new and novel applications. This phenomenon has been paralleled by an increase in the economic importance of patents. In this environment, even the most experienced patent professionals can find themselves swimming in a flood of precedent they are obliged to know and respect.

Some patent attorneys try to keep current with evolving case law by reading advance sheets as they are published. Of these, a small number maintain systematic card files of salient points of law. Even so, while working on their own cases, many practitioners find it difficult to maintain a broad general view.

Consequently, a reference work is needed that will provide a quick, up-to-date point of access to the burgeoning body of case law. This book, which is based on many years of compilation, is just such a tool. It is a handy desk reference with immediate and easy access to relevant cases.

The book is designed to be useful in a number of ways. These include: ascertaining basic prevailing practice and doctrines, addressing issues while preparing responses to Office Actions of the United States Patent and Trademark Office (PTO), addressing litigation issues, and accessing precedent while drafting appeal briefs. Modern Patent Law Precedent may also serve as a supplemental reference for teaching patent law and practice and as a handbook for both patent practitioners and others who are concerned with patent rights.

The goal of patent law is deceptively simple. As the opinion of *In re Ruschig, Aumuller, Korger, Wagner, Scholz, and Bänder*, 343 F.2d 965, 145 U.S.P.Q. 274 (C.C.P.A. 1965) states (at 286):

The basic principle of the patent system is to protect inventions which meet the statutory requirements. Valuable inventions should be given protection of value in the real world of business and the courts.

The inherent tensions in the patent system, however, immediately introduce complications:

The public purpose on which the patent law rests requires the granting of claims commensurate in scope with the invention disclosed. This requires as much the granting of broad claims on broad inventions as it does granting of specific claims on more specific inventions. It is neither contemplated by the public purpose of the patent laws nor required by the statute that an inventor shall be forced to accept claims narrower than his invention in order to secure allowance of his patent. *In re Sus and Schaefer*, 306 F.2d 494, 134 U.S.P.Q. 301, 304 (C.C.P.A. 1962).

In theory, the ideal patent would depend on a perfect fit between the claims and the invention. To achieve or to scrutinize this fit, however, patent professionals are obliged to apply an enormous amount of scientific, technical, and legal learning.

The book places considerable emphasis on diverse issues that arise before the United States Patent and Trademark Office during prosecution of applications for letters patent, as well as extensive material even more relevant to patent litigation.

The text is primarily composed of language from cited opinions or close paraphrases thereof. The evaluation and interpretation of these opinions, however, necessarily depends upon the actual facts and issues of each case, upon the nature of the proceeding, and upon the tribunal in which the case was heard. Factors relating to prosecution of an application for letters patent, reexamination, preliminary or permanent injunctions, summary judgments, directed verdicts, JNOV, and appeals may all significantly influence the relevance of reported statements. The advice of *In re Ruscetta and Jenny*, 255 F.2d 687, 118 U.S.P.Q. 101, 103 (C.C.P.A. 1958), is pertinent:

> Undue liberties should not be taken with a court decision, which should be construed in accord with the precise issue before the court. A fertile source of error in patent law is the misapplication of a sound legal principle established in one case to another case in which the facts are essentially different and the principle has no application whatsoever.

Users of this work will be accorded fast and easy access to a vast array of precedent, including that which may bear precisely on the factual details of their own work.

In addition to the discussion of individual terms, the system of cross references in this book is a quick guide through the maze of interrelated issues and concepts. Many of these interconnections are far from obvious. For example, a practitioner who begins by looking up the entry for Estoppel will immediately find access to a network of cases dealing with such related topics as Assignor Estoppel, Collateral Estoppel, File Wrapper, Marking, and Prosecution History. This is only one indication of the flexibility of approach we have created for this text.

The fourth edition adds to both the key word entries and the crossreferences, as well updating to include decisions published through the end of 1998.

How To Use This Book

The words and phrases covered in this book have been drawn from a variety of sources: (1) key terms from the United States Code; (2) particular terms that have sometimes raised problems in claims challenged by PTO Examiners; (3) terms of art; and (4) general legal concepts as they apply to patent law. In addition, the book includes a variety of scientific and technical entries.

Entries keyed to statutory provisions refer to related concepts. Title 35 of the United States Code is the basic patent statute. Section 100 (35 U.S.C. §100), for instance, refers to such terms as Art, Composition, Invention, Manufacture, Material, Method, New Use, Patent, and Process. Section 102 refers to Invention, Novelty, On Sale, Printed Publication, and Public Use. Section 103 refers to Obviousness, Ordinary Skill, Prior Art, and Subject Matter as a Whole. These key terms all have appropriate entries, along with others corresponding to further sections of Title 35.

Drawing upon practical experience, this work also contains entries for particular words found in claims that have sometimes been challenged by PTO Examiners. These terms include About, Acid, Adapted, Alkyl, An, Approximately, Aromatic, Automatic, Comprise, Consisting, Effective, and Substantially. Most of these entries assume some familiarity with patent law and practice.

In addition to terms used in the statute or in actual claims, the text also discusses numerous terms of art, such as Abandoned Experiment, All Claims Rule, Allowed Application, Analogous Art, Antecedent Basis, Anticipation, Markush, Overclaiming, Reference, and Restriction.

The book also discusses such legal concepts as Abuse of Discretion, Action, Administrative Regularity, Antitrust, Applicant's Rights, Best Evidence, Consent Judgment, Damages, Estoppel, Fraud on a Patent, JNOV, Preliminary Injunction, Privilege, and Summary Judgment.

The preceding paragraphs merely indicate the framework on which this text was created. Repeatedly faced issues, such as Breadth, Combining References, Double Patenting, Enablement, Indefiniteness, Reduction to Practice, and Support are also included, along with numerous other relevant considerations.

Related entries are cross-referenced. Cited text, therefore, does not necessarily include the particular word or expression under which it is found. The entry for Attorney leads to Advice of Counsel, Affidavit, Attorney's Fees, Billings, Conclusions, Conduct, Disqualification, Docket Number, Opinion, Privilege, Work Product Doctrine. The entry for Breadth leads to Indefiniteness, Inoperative Embodiments, Overclaiming, 35 U.S.C. §112. Such cross-referencing facilitates finding pertinent text from published cases.

Under each entry cases are cited in chronological order and thus reflect, in some instances, historical development or changes. When more than one case is excerpted under a particular heading, an earlier holding may even be reversed by a later holding. All entries under any heading of interest should be considered in making an evaluation of current practice.

Whenever any issue is being researched and relevant material is found in language cited in this work, it is always necessary to refer to text of the cited case to make certain that the facts adequately correspond to those of the matter involved. If not, the cited case may refer to others which are even more pertinent. In addition, the cited case should be Shepardized to make certain that the precedent relied upon has not been modified or even reversed.

In evaluating any statement taken from a court's opinion, the opinion should be reviewed to obtain an understanding of the context in which the statement was made. Due consideration should be accorded the nature of the involved proceeding (ex parte, interference, de novo, judgment after trial, appeal, infringement, validity, declaratory judgment, summary judgment) and the nature of the issue (one under the exclusive jurisdiction of the Federal Circuit or one decided under regional circuit precedent).

A. *See also* **Indefinite Article, One.**

The express language "described in a printed publication" does not preclude the use of more than one reference; "a printed publication" can include two or more printed publications. *In re Foster,* 343 F.2d 980, 145 U.S.P.Q. 166, 173 (C.C.P.A. 1965).

☞

In patent parlance "a" or "an" can mean one or more. *North American Vaccine Inc. v. American Cyanamid Co.*, 7 F.3d 1571, 28 U.S.P.Q.2d 1333, 1336 (Fed. Cir. 1993).

☞

Patent parlance construes "a" to connote "one or more," yet holding that "there is no indication in the patent specification that the inventors here intended it to have other than its normal singular meaning." *AbTox Inc. v. Exitron Corp.*, 122 F.3d 1019, 43 U.S.P.Q.2d 1545, 1548 (Fed. Cir. 1997).

☞

While the article "a" can mean "one or more," the court must look to the patent specification and history to determine whether the "inventors here intended it to have other than its normal singular meaning." *Regents of the University of California v. Oncor Inc.*, 44 U.S.P.Q.2d 1321, 1324 (Cal. 1997).

Abandoned. *See also* **Abandoned Application, Abandoned Experiment, Abandonment of Contest, 35 U.S.C. §102(g).**

The junior party in an interference was almost continuously active in pursuing the commercialization of the process of the counts. Except for the period from 1959 to 1964, during which no government funds were allocated for the purpose of testing any bactericide, neither the junior party nor his supervisor gave up on the invention of the counts. Neither the pertinent case law nor a rule of reason would dictate that, under these circumstances, there was an abandonment of the invention by the junior party during this period. *Spiner and Hoffman v. Pierce*, 177 U.S.P.Q. 709, 712 (PO Bd. Pat. Int. 1972).

☞

Subject matter once abandoned may not lawfully be resurrected and recaptured in a later-filed patent application. *USM Corp. v. SPS Technologies, Inc.*, 514 F.Supp. 213, 211 U.S.P.Q. 112, 134 (Ill. 1981).

☞

An invention may be regarded as abandoned, suppressed, or concealed if, within a reasonable time after the invention was reduced to practice, the inventor took no steps to make the invention publicly known. Factors supporting a finding of abandonment, concealment, or suppression include not filing a patent application, not publicly disseminating documents describing the invention, and not publicly using the invention. Although not filing a patent application within a reasonable time after reduction to practice may negate a 35 U.S.C. §102(g) defense, it is only one factor. Not filing or delaying the filing of a patent application may support a conclusion of suppression or concealment. However, it is not clear that failure to file a patent application would show abandonment. In fact, there simply is no requirement to file a patent application if a party is not seeking protection of the patent laws. *Oak Industries, Inc. v. Zenith Electronics Corp.*, 726 F. Supp. 1525, 14 U.S.P.Q.2d 1417, 1422, 1423 (Ill. 1989).

Abandoned Application. *See also* **Abandoned, Abandoned Experiment, Abandonment, Patent Application, Revival, Unintentional Abandonment.**

Since the disclosure in an abandoned application was referred to in an issued patent, it became part of the patent disclosure. Any reference to a disclosure which is available to the public is permissible. *In re Heritage*, 182 F.2d 639, 86 U.S.P.Q. 160, 164 (C.C.P.A. 1950).

ω

A disclosure in an abandoned application for a patent does not constitute such evidence of prior knowledge as will bar the allowance of a subsequent application. An abandoned application is merely evidence of the conception of the invention it discloses. *In re Schlittler and Uffer*, 234 F.2d 882, 110 U.S.P.Q. 304, 306 (C.C.P.A. 1956).

ω

Already-abandoned applications less than twenty years old can be incorporated by reference to the same extent as copending applications. Both types are open to the public upon the referencing application issuing as a patent. *In re Fouche*, 439 F.2d 1237, 169 U.S.P.Q. 429, 431 n.1 (C.C.P.A. 1971).

ω

Abandoned patent applications are statutorily exempt from the necessity of disclosure under FOIA. The language in 35 U.S.C. §122 creating confidentiality speaks of "applications for patents." The language is broad enough to include all categories of applications (pending, abandoned, and granted) that would appear to be in keeping with the legislative intent of Congress. Where the concept of an abandoned application has been published or practiced so as to become "prior art", 35 U.S.C. §122 would not prevent a litigant in a suit over the validity of a patent from discovering any relevant and material abandoned patent applications. *Sears v. Gottschalk, Commissioner of Patents*, 502 F.2d 122, 183 U.S.P.Q. 134, 137, 140 (4th Cir. 1974).

ω

An abandoned U.S.A. application (by a different and unrelated inventive entity) is not made available as a reference as of its filing date when a subsequently-filed counterpart foreign application is published. *Ex parte Smolka and Schwuger,* 207 U.S.P.Q. 232, 234 (PTO Bd. App. 1980).

ω

An abandoned patent application, with which there is no copendency, is not regarded as a constructive reduction to practice. *In re Costello and McClean*, 717 F.2d 1346, 219 U.S.P.Q. 389 (Fed. Cir. 1983).

Abandoned Experiment

The fact that a patent application was made, as a matter of law, constitutes a constructive reduction to practice and negates any theory of abandoned experiment. *Ampex Corp. v. Memorex Corp.*, 205 U.S.P.Q. 794, 797 (Cal. 1980).

Abandonment. *See also* **Abandoned Application, Continuing Application, Dedication to the Public, Pendency, Revival, Unintentional Abandonment, Withdraw from Issue.**

A patentee may claim the whole or only a part of his invention. If he only claims a part, he is presumed to have abandoned the residue to the public. *McLain v. Ortmayer*, 141 U.S. 419 (1891).

ᴕ

Neither commercial use nor the filing of an application for letters patent is required to preclude abandonment of an invention that has been reduced to practice. *Corona Cord Tire Co. v. Dovan Chemical Corp.*, 276 U.S. 358, 1928 C.D. 253 (1928).

ᴕ

Abandonment is of two general types, actual and constructive. Actual abandonment is divided into two categories, express and implied. When there is a hiatus between the issuance of a patent and the subsequent filing (by the same inventor) of an application claiming subject matter disclosed, but not claimed, in the patent, neither the fact that there is a hiatus nor its length is significant as long as the application was filed within the one-year statutory grace period allowed by 35 U.S.C. §102(b). *In re Gibbs and Griffin*, 437 F.2d 486, 168 U.S.P.Q. 578, 581 (C.C.P.A. 1971).

ᴕ

A separate claim embodying a figure of the drawings was treated as unnecessary because it was merely descriptive of the use to be made of the patented device. Under these circumstances cancellation of the claim should not be considered an abandonment of the embodiment of the invention that it had described. *Olympic Fastening Systems, Inc. v. Textron Inc.*, 504 F.2d 609, 183 U..S.P.Q. 449, 452 (6th Cir. 1974).

ᴕ

A delay in filing a patent application of more than 17 months after reducing the invention to practice was not regarded as unreasonable (raising an inference of intent to suppress) in view of continued activities to within six months of the filing date. *D'Silva v. Drabek*, 214 U.S.P.Q. 556 (PTO Bd. Pat. Int. 1981).

ᴕ

A delay of approximately 51 months was unreasonably long and sufficient to give rise to an inference of an intent to abandon, suppress, or conceal the invention. An inference of suppression or concealment may be overcome with evidence that the reason for the delay was to perfect the invention. When, however, the delay is caused by working on refinements and improvements that are not elected in the final patent application, the delay will not be excused. Further, when the activities that caused the delay go to commercialization of the invention, the delay will not be excused. *Lutzker v. Plet*, 843 F.2d 1364, 6 U.S.P.Q.2d 1370 (Fed. Cir. 1988).

ϖ

Actual abandonment under 35 U.S.C. §102(c) requires that the inventor *intend* to abandon the invention, and intent can be implied from the inventor's conduct with respect to the invention. Such intent to abandon an invention will not be imputed, and every reasonable doubt should be resolved in favor of the inventor. *Ex parte Dunne*, 20 U.S.P.Q.2d 1479, 1480 (B.P.A.I. 1991).

Abandonment of Contest.

When a party to an interference files an abandonment of the contest, concedes priority, or disclaims the subject matter of an interference count, he stands in the same position as he would had there been an award of priority adverse to him with respect to the interference count. An adverse award of priority bars an applicant from obtaining a claim not patentably distinct from the subject matter awarded his adversary. *In re Fenn*, 315 F.2d 949, 137 U.S.P.Q. 367, 368 (C.C.P.A. 1963).

Abbreviated New Drug Application. *See also* ANDA, Exclusivity, Hatch-Waxman Amendments.

The Drug Price Competition and Patent Term Restoration Act, Pub. L. No. 98-417, 98 Stat. 1585 (1984), is generally known as the Hatch Waxman Amendments to the Federal Food, Drug, and Cosmetic Act, 21 U.S.C. §§301 et seq. The purpose of this legislation was to increase competition in the drug industry by facilitating the approval of generic copies of drugs. Rather than complete the full NDA process, generic copiers could proceed via an Abbreviated New Drug Application (ANDA), which required merely reference to the safety and effectiveness status submitted by the "pioneer" drug manufacturer, along with submission of manufacturing and bioequivalence data for the generic copy. *Mead Johnson Pharmaceutical Group v. Bowen*, 838 F.2d 1332, 6 U.S.P.Q.2d 1565 (D.C. Cir. 1988).

About. *See also* Approximately, Substantially.

Claims having the expression "at least about" were held to be invalid for indefiniteness. This holding was further supported by the fact that nothing in the specification, prosecution history, or prior art provides any indication as to what range of specific activity is covered by the term "about" and by the fact that no expert testified as to a definite meaning for the term in the context of the prior art. The holding that the term "about" renders claims indefinite should not be understood as ruling out any and all uses of this term in patent claims. It may be acceptable in appropriate fact situations. *Amgen Inc. v. Chugai Pharmaceutical Co. Ltd.*, 927 F.2d 1200, 18 U.S.P.Q.2d 1016, 1030, 1031 (Fed. Cir. 1991).

ϖ

There is simply no basis for interpreting the phrase "about 40:1" to encompass the 162:1 ratio. That would imply an expansion of the term "about" to encompass over a fourfold increase in the specified mumerical ratio and thus would ignore the ordinary meaning of that term. According to Webster's Third New International Dictionary, the term means: "3 a: with some approach to exactness in quantity, number, or time: APPROXIMATELY. . . ." *Conopco Inc. v. May Department Stores Co.*, 46 F.3d 1556, 32 U.S.P.Q.2d 1225, 1227 (Fed. Cir. 1994).

ᛦ

The word "about" in a later added claim can broaden an original disclosure that indicates to one skilled in the art that his or her invention is to a precise, not an approximate, amount, range, or limit. Under such circumstances, the term "about" in the later added claim is new matter and may not receive the benefit of an earlier filing date. The meaning of the word "about" is dependent on the facts of a case, the nature of the invention, and the knowledge imparted by the totality of the earlier disclosure to those skilled in the art. *Eiselstein v. Frank*, 52 F.3d 1035, 34 U.S.P.Q.2d 1467, 1471 (Fed. Cir. 1995).

ᛦ

Precedent illustrates the fact-dependency of determinations of the technologic scope of "about" and similar terms, depending on their contexts and the precision or significance of the measurements used. *Modine Manufacturing Co. v. U.S. International Trade Commission*, 75 F.3d 1545, 37 U.S.P.Q.2d 1609, 1615 (Fed. Cir. 1996).

Abstract.

The abstract is embraced by the word "specification" for the purposes of a rejection under 35 U.S.C. §112, first paragraph. *In re Armbruster*, 512 F.2d 676, 185 U.S.P.Q. 152 (C.C.P.A. 1975).

ᛦ

An abstract of the disclosure is not to be used to interpret claims. *Trilogy Communications Inc. v. Comm Scope Co.*, 754 F. Supp. 468, 18 U.S.P.Q.2d 1177, 1207 (N.C. 1990).

Abstract Idea.

Every discovery is not embraced within the statutory terms of 35 U.S.C. §101. Excluded from such patent protection are laws of nature, physical phenomena, and abstract ideas. A principle, in the abstract, is a fundamental truth, an original cause, a motive; these cannot be patented, and no one can claim in any of them an exclusive right. A new mineral discovered in the earth or a new plant found in the wild is not patentable subject matter. Likewise, Einstein could not patent his celebrated law that $E = mc^2$; nor could Newton have patented the law of gravity. Such discoveries are "manifestations of . . . nature, free to all men and reserved exclusively to none." *Diamond v. Diehr and Lutton*, 450 U.S. 175, 209 U.S.P.Q. 1, 7 (1981).

Abuse of Administrative Proceedings. *See* **Noerr-Pennington Doctrine.**

Abuse of Discretion.

The grant or denial of either a motion for a new trial or a motion to amend the judgment must be reviewed on the basis of a determination of whether the district court abused its discretion. Abuse of discretion may obtain when a court ruling reflects an erroneous application or interpretation of law, or shows a clear error of judgment, or is based on clearly erroneous factual findings. *Richardson v. Suzuki Motor Co.*, 868 F.2d 1226, 9 U.S.P.Q.2d 1913, 1928 (Fed. Cir. 1989); *Seattle Box Co. v. Industrial Crating & Packing, Inc.*, 756 F.2d 1574, 225 U.S.P.Q. 357, 363 (Fed. Cir. 1985).

ᚥ

Abuse of discretion may be found when a district court's decision is clearly unreasonable, the decision is based on an error of law, the court's findings of fact are clearly erroneous, or the record contains no evidence upon which the court rationally could have based its decision. *Gerritsen v. Shirai*, 979 F.2d 1524, 24 U.S.P.Q.2d 1912, 1916 (Fed. Cir. 1992); *Adelberg Laboratories Inc. v. Miles Inc.*, 921 F.2d 1267, 17 U.S.P.Q.2d 1111, 1113 (Fed. Cir. 1990).

ᚥ

Discretion "is abused if the record contains no basis on which the district court rationally could have made its decision or if the judicial action is arbitrary, fanciful or clearly unreasonable." *Imagineering Inc. v. Van Klassens Inc.*, 53 F.3d 1260, 34 U.S.P.Q.2d 1526, 1531 (Fed. Cir. 1995).

ᚥ

It is an abuse of discretion for a trial court to refuse to allow a party to introduce prior art produced within thirty days of the trial, if the opposing party had an opportunity to review the documents and to produce rebuttal evidence. *Donelly Corp. v. Gentex Corp.*, 913 F.Supp. 1014, 37 U.S.P.Q.2d 1146, 1149 (Mich. 1995).

Accelerated Reentry Theory.

By infringing upon plaintiff's patent for two and a half years prior to its expiration date, defendant gained a foothold in the market for the infringing products that it would not otherwise have enjoyed had it waited until the patent expired to begin its sales. Accordingly, patentee is entitled to compensation, not for defendant's post-expiration sales per se, but for the "accelerated reentry" into the market that defendant enjoyed as a result of its pre-expiration infringement. Thus, damages based upon the defendant's accelerated reentry are actually compensation for the defendant's past infringement, not its post-expiration conduct. *Amsted Industries Inc. v. National Castings Inc.*, 16 U.S.P.Q.2d 1737, 1752, 1753 (Ill. 1990).

Acceptability. *See* **Availability.**

Acceptable Substitute. *See* **Substitute, Two-Supplier Market.**

Access.

Since the disclosure in an abandoned application was referred to in an issued patent, it became part of the patent disclosure. *In re Heritage*, 182 F.2d 639, 86 U.S.P.Q. 160, 164 (C.C.P.A. 1950).

Accessible to the Public. *See* **Thesis.**

Accessory. *See also* **Entire-Market-Value Rule.**

Even though the prod of a crossbow can be separated from the stock and it may be possible for some people to fire an arrow from the prod (minus the stock), the prod alone does not qualify as a "complete basic operable bow." The owner's manual (shipped with every crossbow) clearly explains how the prod is to be mounted on the stock and drawn and shot only after it has been secured to the stock. In interpreting a license agreement under established facts, the stock of the crossbow is not properly regarded as an accessory. *Allan Archery Inc. v. Precision Shooting Equipment Inc.*, 865 F.2d 896, 9 U.S.P.Q.2d 1728 (7th Cir. 1989).

Accidental.

Since the prior art Aureomycin fermentation broths and antibiotics contained insufficient tetracycline to be of any benefit to mankind, they do not, as a matter of law, negate the validity of tetracycline patent claims. The prior existence of tetracycline and Aureomycin in trace amounts, unrecognized and of no use, does not invalidate the patent. *Chas. Pfizer & Co., Inc. v. Barry-Martin Pharmaceuticals, Inc.*, 241 F.Supp. 191, 145 U.S.P.Q. 29, 32 (Fla. 1965).

ϖ

An accidental or unappreciated duplication of an invention does not defeat the patent right of one who, though later in time, was first to recognize that which constitutes the inventive subject matter. *Silvestri and Johnson v. Grant and Alburn*, 496 F.2d 593, 181 U.S.P.Q. 706, 708 (C.C.P.A. 1974).

ϖ

An accidental or unwitting duplication of an invention cannot constitute anticipation. *In re Felton,* 484 F.2d 495, 179 U.S.P.Q. 295 (C.C.P.A. 1973); *In re Marshall*, 578 F.2d 301, 198 U.S.P.Q. 344 (C.C.P.A. 1978).

Accumulation.

The mere accumulation of patents, no matter how many, is not in and of itself illegal. *In re Reclosable Plastic Bags*, 192 U.S.P.Q. 674, 679 (U.S. Intl. Trade Commn. 1977).

Accuracy. *See also* **Particularity.**

An invention must be capable of accurate definition, and it must be accurately defined, to be patentable. *United Carbon Co. v. Binney & Smith Co.*, 317 U.S. 228, 55 U.S.P.Q. 381, 386 (1942).

ϖ

A specification disclosure that contains a teaching of the manner and process of making and using the invention in terms that correspond in scope to those used in describing and defining the subject matter sought to be patented must be taken as in compliance with the enabling requirement of the first paragraph of 35 U.S.C. §112 unless there is reason to doubt the objective truth of the statements contained therein that must be relied on for enabling support. Assuming that sufficient reason for such doubt does exist, a rejection for failure to teach how to make and/or use will be proper on that basis. In any event, it is incumbent on the Patent Office, whenever a rejection on this basis is made, to explain why it doubts the truth or accuracy of any statement in a supporting disclosure and to back up assertions of its own with acceptable evidence or reasoning that is inconsistent with the contested statement. Otherwise, there would be no need for the applicant to go to the trouble and expense of supporting his presumptively accurate disclosure. *In re Marzocchi and Horton*, 439 F.2d 220, 169 U.S.P.Q. 367 (C.C.P.A. 1971).

ω

The basis of the district court's holding that the claims are indefinite is that "they do not disclose how infringement may be avoided because antibody affinity cannot be estimated with any consistency." Even if the district court's finding and support of this holding—that "there is no standard set of experimental conditions which are used to estimate affinities"—is accurate, under the law pertaining to indefiniteness—"if the claims, read in the light of specification, reasonably apprise those skilled in the art both of the utilization and scope of the invention, and if the language is as precise as the subject matter permits, the courts can demand no more"—the claims clearly are definite. The evidence of record indisputably shows that calculating affinity was known in the art at the time of filing and, notwithstanding the fact that those calculations are not precise, or "standard," the claims, read in the light of the specification, reasonably apprise those skilled in the art and are as precise as the subject matter permits. *Hybritech Inc. v. Monoclonal Antibodies, Inc.*, 802 F.2d 1367, 231 U.S.P.Q. 81 (Fed. Cir. 1986).

Acid.

Although there are undoubtedly a large number of acids that come within the scope of "organic and inorganic acids," the expression is not for that reason indefinite. There is no reason to believe that the public would be confused as to what subject matter is circumscribed by that expression in the claim. *In re Skoll*, 523 F.2d 1392, 187 U.S.P.Q. 481 (C.C.P.A. 1975).

Acquiescence.

A patentee moved to dissolve an interference on the ground that his patent claims had not been copied by an applicant prior to one year from the date on which his patent was granted. The Examiner's decision to deny the motion was reversed by the Commissioner, on petition. The interference was dissolved, and the applicant subsequently canceled the claims corresponding to the interference counts. The applicant subsequently urged he had timely copied the claims in order to overcome the patent as a reference in ex parte prosecution. The applicant was required to reassert the patent claims, and the interference was reinstated. The Commissioner decided (on petition) that the applicant was bound by the Commissioner's prior decision, from which no appeal was taken. From the applicant's cancellation of claims and failure to appeal, it was concluded that applicant has acquiesced in the prior decision and the applicant was estopped, on the ground of res judicata, from raising the question of whether he had originally copied the patent claims in timely fashion. *Rubenstein v. Schmidt*, 145 U.S.P.Q. 613 (Comm'r Patents 1965).

ϖ

Long continued public acquiescence in the monopoly created by a patent claim furnishes a valid basis of reinforcement for the statutory presumption of the patent's validity for purposes of a preliminary injunction. *Eli Lilly & Co., Inc. v. Generix Drug Sales, Inc.*, 460 F.2d 1096, 174 U.S.P.Q. 65, 69 (5th Cir. 1972).

ϖ

After the PTO holds that an amendment to the specification involves "new matter," the filing of a continuing application that includes the amendatory material and designating the application as a cip application constitutes an acquiesence in the PTO's conclusion that the amendment contained new matter. *Max Daetwyler Corp. v. Input Graphics, Inc.*, 608 F. Supp. 1549, 226 U.S.P.Q. 393 (Pa. 1985).

Action. *See* **Appeal, Arbitration, Bifurcation, Declaratory Judgment, Directed Verdict, JNOV, Preliminary Injunction, Summary Judgment.**

Active Inducement. *See* **Inducement.**

Active Ingredient. *See* **Ingredient.**

Actively Induce. *See* **Induce.**

Actual Controversy.

In the context of patent litigation, "actual controversy" means trhat the declaratory plaintiff must have a reasonable apprehension that its present or foreseeable actions could constitute patent infringement and lead to a suit by the patent owner. *Turbocare Division of Demag Delaval Turbomachinery Corp. v. General Electric Co.*, 40 U.S.P.Q.2d 1795, 1797 (Mass. 1996).

ϖ

A declaratory plaintiff may establish an actual controversy by averring: (1) that it holds a recognized interest in a patent that could be adversely affected by an action brought under 35 U.S.C. §256, and (2) another party with a right to bring an action under 35 U.S.C. §256 has created in the declaratory plaintiff a reasonable apprehension that it will do so. *Fina Oil and Chemical Co. V. Ewen*, 123 F.3d 1466, 43 U.S.P.Q.2d 1935, 1939 (Fed. Cir. 1997).

Adapted.

The claims require that the claimed compositions be "adapted for application to the human skin." This characterization imposes a limitation in the claims that cannot be ignored in considering the patentability of the claims. There is no disclosure in the references that would have motivated the worker in the art to modify the compositions disclosed in the references to include a cosmetic oil carrier and/or to render the compositions of the references suitable for application to the skin. *Ex parte Conner*, 215 U.S.P.Q. 384 (PTO Bd. App. 1981).

Adequacy. *See* **Sufficiency of Disclosure.**

Adhesive.

Defendant's use of 100% synthetic resin adhesive is insufficient to remove it from the purview of claims calling for a "rubbery base" adhesive or a "rubber-resin type" adhesive. *Minnesota Mining and Manufacturing Company v. Neisner Brothers, Inc.*, 101 F.Supp. 926, 92 U.S.P.Q. 272, 274 (Ill. 1951).

ϖ

A totally new and surprising beneficial result must be taken fully into account pursuant to the Congressional mandate for considering the invention "as a whole." *Ex parte Leonard and Brandes*, 187 U.S.P.Q. 122, 123 (PTO Bd. App. 1974).

Adjustability.

The provision of adjustability, where needed, is not a patentable advance. *In re Stevens*, 212 F.2d 197, 101 U.S.P.Q. 284, 285 (C.C.P.A. 1954).

Administration. *See* **Enablement, Mode of Administration.**

Administrative Correctness.

The presumption of validity is based on the presumption of administrative correctness of actions of the agency charged with examination of patentability. The government agency is presumed to have done its job. *Applied Materials Inc. v. Advanced Semiconductor Materials*, 40 U.S.P.Q.2d 1481, 1485 (Fed. Cir. 1996).

Administrative Procedure Act[1] (A.P.A.). *See also* **5 U.S.C. §553.**

Judicial review of an agency's action is not to be had under the Administrative Procedure Act [5 U.S.C. §701(a)(2)] when the involved statute is drawn so that a court would have no meaningful standard against which to judge the agency's exercise of discretion. In such a case, the statute (law) can be taken to have "committed" the decision making to the agency's judgment absolutely. *Southern Research Institute v. Griffin Corp.*, 938 F.2d 1761, 19 U.S.P.Q.2d 1761, 1765 (llth Cir. 1991).

---

[1]See *In re Zurko*, 142 F.3d 1447, 46 U.S.P.Q.2d 1691 (Fed. Cir. 1998—*in banc*).

Administrative Regularity. *See also* **Presumption, Presumption of Administrative Regularity, Search Record.**

A patent shall be presumed valid. The burden of establishing invalidity of a patent rests on the party asserting it. That burden never shifts. When no prior art other than that which was considered by the PTO Examiner is relied on by an attacker, he has the added burden of overcoming the deference that is due to a qualified government agency presumed to have properly done its job, which includes one or more Examiners who are assumed to have expertise in interpreting the references and to be familiar from their work with the level of skill in the art and whose duty it is to issue only valid patents. When an attacker produces prior art or other evidence not considered in the PTO, there is no reason to defer to the PTO so far as its effect on validity is concerned. New prior art not before the PTO may so clearly invalidate a patent that the burden is fully sustained merely by proving its existence and applying the proper law, but that has no effect on the presumption or on who has burden of proof. They are static and in reality different expressions of the same thing. Neither does the standard of proof change; it must be by clear and convincing evidence or its equivalent, by whatever form of words may be expressed. When new evidence touching validity of the patent not considered by the PTO is relied on, the tribunal considering it is not faced with having to disagree with the PTO or with deferring to its judgment or with taking its expertise into account. The evidence may, therefore, carry more weight and go further toward sustaining the attacker's unchanging burden. *American Hoist & Derrick Co. v. Sowa Sons, Inc.*, 725 F.2d 1350, 220 U.S.P.Q. 763 (Fed. Cir. 1984).

ω

The plaintiff in an action brought pursuant to 35 U.S.C. §145 has a heavy burden. Because the Patent Office is an expert body preeminently qualified to determine questions of this kind, its conclusions are entitled to a broad presumption of validity. In these circumstances, the court is authorized to reverse the decision only if the Patent Office did not have a rational basis for its conclusions or if the plaintiff presented new evidence that led to a thorough conviction that the plaintiff should prevail. In trials de novo under §145, great weight attaches to the expertise of the Patent Office, and its findings will not be overtuned unless new evidence is introduced that carries the thorough conviction that the Patent Office erred. Based upon the opinion testimony of an independent expert, the court was satisfied that the only way one would reach the plaintiff's claimed alloy composition from the reference disclosure was by experimentation. The testimony offered on behalf of the plaintiff at the trial was uncontradicted by the defendant. The court found that testimony to be very persuasive, and the court concluded that the plaintiff demonstrated by clear and convincing evidence that the determination by the Board of Appeals was in error. *Titanium Metals Corp. of America v. Mossinghoff*, 603 F. Supp. 87, 225 U.S.P.Q. 673 (D.C. 1984).

Admission.

A reference patent issued on an application filed the same day as appellant's application was regarded as prior art with respect to subject matter therein admitted by appellant to be prior art. *In re Hellsund*, 474 F.2d 1307, 177 U.S.P.Q. 170, 173 (C.C.P.A. 1973).

ω

Valid prior art may be created by the admissions of the parties. *In re Fout, Mishkin, and Roychoudhury,* 675 F.2d 297, 213 U.S.P.Q. 532 (C.C.P.A. 1982).

ᴥ

37 C.F.R. §1.106(c) appears to open reexamination proceedings to any and all issues affecting patentability so long as there is a related admission. However, construing the rule in light of the statute and other implementing rules, reexamination is specifically restricted to a consideration of patents and printed publications. (New or amended claims are also examined for compliance with 35 U.S.C. §§112 and 132.) For an admission to form some or all of the basis for a prior art rejection in reexamination proceedings, such admission must necessarily relate to patents or printed publications. Otherwise, patentees or patent owners would be able to circumvent the restrictive nature of the statute by making admissions relating to prior public use, sale, abandonment, etc., issues that were never intended to be resolved by way of reexamination. *Ex parte Horton*, 226 U.S.P.Q. 697 (B.P.A.I. 1985).

ᴥ

Statements of fact contained in a brief may be considered admissions of the party in the discretion of the district court. *The Heil Company v. Snyder Industries Inc.*, 763 F. Supp. 422, 18 U.S.P.Q.2d 2022, 2027 (Neb. 1991).

Admission to Practice before the PTO.

The *General Requirements* for the April 1993 examination listed three ways to qualify for the examination. An applicant (1) could have a bachelor's degree in a scientific subject; (2) could have a bachelor's degree in a nonscientific subject and a required number of hours in scientific classes (including 24 credit hours of physics) or practical experience or both; or (3) could successfully complete the Engineer-in-Training ("EIT") examination. *Premysler v. Lehman*, 33 U.S.P.Q.2d 1859, 1860 (D.C. 1994).

ADR. *See* Alternative Dispute Resolution.

Advance the Art. *See also* Improvement.

The facts that a process may not be an advancement in the art, may be a simpler process than a prior art process, or may produce an impure material, even if correct, do not necessarily make it obvious. *See Demaco Corp. v. Von Langsdorff Licensing Ltd.*, 851 F.2d 1387, 7 U.S.P.Q.2d 1222, 1225 (Fed. Cir.), *cert. denied*, 488 U.S. 956 (1988).

Advantage. *See also* "All Advantages" Rule, Benefit, Better, Improvement, Inherent, Progress, Properties, Unexpected Results.

There is no need for a claim to recite a result that inherently occurs through other claim limitations. The Board refused to consider the clarity of film and the degree of substitution obtained by appellant's process because the claims were not directed to a process yielding a film and did not recite the degree of substitution. There can be no doubt from the record that these advantages accrue from the claimed process, and they are not required to be recited in the claims. *In re Estes*, 420 F.2d 1397, 164 U.S.P.Q. 519, 521 (C.C.P.A. 1970).

ᴡ

In the absence of a showing that either of the differences between the claimed and reference products is of any practical advantage, the attempt to overcome prima facie obviousness failed. *In re D'Ancicco, Collings, and Shine*, 439 F.2d 1244, 169 U.S.P.Q. 303, 306 (C.C.P.A. 1971).

ᴡ

By disclosing a device that inherently performs a function, operates according to a theory, or has an advantage, a patent applicant necessarily discloses that function, theory, or advantage even though he says nothing concerning it. The application may be later amended to recite the function, theory, or advantage without introducing prohibited new matter. *In re Smythe and Shamos*, 480 F.2d 1376, 178 U.S.P.Q. 279 (C.C.P.A. 1973).

ᴡ

To establish non-obviousness, advantages relied upon must stem from limitations in the claims. When claims do not require such limitations, the advantages are not regarded as commensurate with the scope of the claims. *In re Altenpohl*, 500 F.2d 1151, 183 U.S.P.Q. 38 (C.C.P.A. 1974).

ᴡ

Advantages not set forth in the specification are of little weight in assessing the validity of an invention. *Westwood Chemical, Inc. v. United States*, 525 F.2d 1367, 186 U.S.P.Q. 383, 392 (Ct. Cl. 1975).

ᴡ

Treating an advantage as the invention disregards the statutory requirement that the invention be viewed "as a whole," ignores the problem recognition element, and injects an improper "obvious to try" consideration. *Jones v. Hardy*, 727 F.2d 1524, 220 U.S.P.Q. 1021, 1026 (Fed. Cir. 1984).

ᴡ

Advantages or "sales pitch features" do not belong in claims. The sole function of claims is to point out distinctly the process, machine, manufacture, or composition of matter that is patented, not its advantages. *Preemption Devices, Inc. v. Minnesota Mining & Manufacturing Co.*, 732 F.2d 903, 221 U.S.P.Q. 841, 844 (Fed. Cir. 1984).

ᴡ

An action in the district court under 35 U.S.C. §145 is a proceeding de novo and, while it is limited to the invention claimed in the PTO, the court may consider any additional competent evidence that a plaintiff neither intentionally nor negligently failed to submit to the PTO. The presumption of correctness that attaches to the decision of the Commissioner is a rebuttable presumption that may be overcome by the introduction of evidence (at a trial under 35 U.S.C. §145) that is of such character and amount as to carry a thorough conviction of error. At such a trial the plaintiff and defendant may present evidence on any issue properly before the court. This additional evidence may include testimony of expert witnesses and inventors skilled in the art, and evidence of commercial success. In making its determination of non-obviousness, the court recognized the non-analogous nature of one reference, the lack of teaching or suggestion in the prior art of the useful advantage of a flexible track incapable of self-support, and the commercial success of the highly flexible Hot Wheels trackway-toy vehicle combination covered by the plaintiff's Reissue Application. The fact that the claimed invention seemed simple and, when viewed in hindsight, appeared to be obvious was not enough to negate invention. *Lemelson v. Mossinghoff*, 225 U.S.P.Q. 1063 (D.C. 1985).

ω

Advantages described in the body of the specification, if not included in the claims, are not per se limitations of the claimed invention. *Vehicular Technologies Corp. v. Titan Wheel International Inc.*, 141 F.3d 1084, 46 U.S.P.Q.2d 1257, 1266 *dissent* (Fed. Cir. 1998).

Adverse Party.

In an interference proceeding wherein the only issue on appeal from a BPAI decision is the patentability of claims of the winning party, the losing party (which properly challenged that patentability during the *inter partes* proceedings below) is an "adverse" party in light of the Board's final judgment. *Wu v. Wang*, 129 F.3d 1237, 44 U.S.P.Q.2d 1641, 1644 (Fed. Cir. 1997).

Advertising.

Advertising that one's product is covered by a patent or pending application when in fact it is not, or not yet, may be tortious and may be grounds for a counterclaim in a suit for infringement, but it is not a legally sufficient affirmative defense. *National Presto Industries Inc. v. Black & Decker (U.S.) Inc.*, 760 F. Supp. 699, 19 U.S.P.Q.2d 1457, 1459 (Ill. 1991).

ω

The defendant's invoices bearing the legend: THIS PRODUCT IS PRODUCED UNDER US PATENT #4,566,294 constitute a "use in advertising" within the meaning of 35 U.S.C. §292. *Accent Designs Inc. v. Jan Jewelry Designs*, 827 F.Supp. 957, 30 U.S.P.Q.2d 1734, 1741 (N.Y. 1993).

ω

When plaintiff alleges that defendant has sold an infringing product, "a patent infringement occurs where allegedly infringing sales are made." When no sales of an accused product have occurred, promotion and advertising of the product in Massachusetts is an "infringing activity" or "offending act". *Hologic Inc. v. Lunar Corp.*, 36 U.S.P.Q.2d 1182, 1187 (Mass. 1995).

Advice of Counsel. *See also* **Opinion of Counsel.**

In order to negate the attorney-client privilege, a party seeking to obtain information that may arguably be privileged must establish that the client seeking to invoke the privilege consulted and obtained the advice of counsel for the purpose of conducting fraudulent activities. The person seeking to negate the privilege must make out a prima facie case of fraud. The alleged fraudulent activities must be of such a serious nature as to warrant the obviation of the privilege.

The work-product privilege protects (from discovery) materials prepared in anticipation of litigation. The mere likelihood of litigation in the future is insufficient for invoking the privilege. Rather, the probability of litigation must be substantial and the commencement of the litigation imminent. Materials that are prepared in the ordinary course of business do not fall within the work-product exception. While all documents generated in the patent application process may not be protected from discovery, in any given situation there can be documents that do in fact fall within the work product privilege. *Stauffer Chemical Co. v. Monsanto Co.*, 623 F. Supp. 148, 227 U.S.P.Q. 401 (Mo. 1985).

ω

An aggressive strategy may or may not be a factor in a decision to deny or award increased damages. An "aggressive strategy" unsupported by any competent advice of counsel, thorough investigation of validity and infringement, discovery of more pertinent uncited prior art, or similar factors, is the type of activity the reference in the patent law to increased damages seeks to prevent. An alleged infringer who intentionally blinds himself to the facts and law, continues to infringe, and employs the judicial process with no solidly based expectation of success can hardly be surprised when his infringement is found to have been willful. Willfulness of infringement relates to the accused infringer's conduct in the marketplace. Because that conduct may be seen as producing an unnecessary and outcome-certain lawsuit, it may make the case so exceptional as to warrant attorney's fees under 35 U.S.C. §285. Similarly, bad faith displayed in pretrial and trial stages, by counsel or party, may render the case exceptional under §285. When a court declines to award attorney's fees on the basis of a determination that a case is not exceptional, the fact findings underlying that determination are reviewed under the clearly erroneous standard. When the determination is that a case is exceptional, the election to grant or deny attorney's fees is reviewed under the abuse of discretion standard. *Kloster Speedsteel A.B. v. Crucible Inc.*, 793 F.2d 1565, 230 U.S.P.Q. 81 (Fed. Cir. 1986).

ω

Where a potential infringer has actual notice of the patent rights of another, it has an affirmative duty of due care. That affirmative duty normally entails obtaining competent legal advice before the initiation of any possible infringing activity. Proof of reliance upon competent legal advice is an important element of a defense to a willful infringement claim. In response to a request for discovery, a putative infringer must elect whether it intends to introduce (at trial) evidence that it relied upon advice of counsel. If it chooses to invoke the attorney-client privilege to prevent discovery of the items sought, it will be precluded from introducing the opinions or testimony of its counsel as evidence that it satisfied its affirmative duty of due care to determine that no infringement existed or that it did not act willfully. If the putative infringer intends to use such privileged material at trial, the patentee is entitled to examine the privileged documents as a part of pretrial discovery. *Columbia Cascade Co. v. Interplay Design Ltd.*, 17 U.S.P.Q.2d 1882, 1884 (Or. 1990).

ω

Because defendant made a tactical decision during the liability phase of a bifurcated patent infringement action to withhold its privileged evidence of the patent advice it received from counsel, the court refused to allow defendant to introduce such evidence during the damages phase. On redirect, however, the court allowed defendant's patent counsel to testify that he gave defendant oral opinions on whether its proposed design infringed the patents. No evidence was presented as to that opinion's content. Although absence of proof of advice of counsel can give rise to an inference against an infringer, the court drew no such inference in this case. In most cases defendants enter no advice-of-counsel proof. Here, however, defendant strenuously sought to introduce its advice-of-counsel evidence. *Micro Motion Inc. v. Exac Corp.*, 761 F. Supp. 1420, 19 U.S.P.Q.2d 1001, 1016 (Cal. 1991).

ᵹ

If a party asserts as an essential element (in his defense) reliance upon the advice of counsel, the party waives the attorney-client privilege with respect to all documents and communications to or from counsel concerning the transaction for which counsel's advice was sought, together with all documents and communications relating to the subject matter of the attorney's advice. By raising the defense of equitable estoppel in a declaratory judgment action, plaintiff has waived the attorney-client privilege as to the patent in suit. *Sig Swiss Industrial Co. v. Fres-Co System USA Inc.*, 22 U.S.P.Q.2d 1601, 1602, 1603 (Pa. 1992).

ᵹ

Some courts have found that the invocation of the advice of counsel defense waives both the attorney-client privilege and work product immunity. *Mushroom Associates v. Monterey Mushrooms Inc.*, 24 U.S.P.Q.2d 1767, 1770 (Cal. 1992).

ᵹ

Advice of counsel alone cannot be used as a shield irrespective of the nature and timing of that advice in the context of surrounding circumstances. *In re Hayes Microcomputer Products Inc. Patent Litigation*, 982 F.2d 1527, 25 U.S.P.Q.2d 1241, 1254 (Fed. Cir. 1992).

ᵹ

The assertion of an advice of counsel defense to willful infringement was a subject-matter waiver of the attorney-client privilege (including any evidence relating to infringement, validity, and/or enforceability that was communicated between attorney and client throughout the entire time period of the alleged willful infringement) and a waiver of the work-product privilege with respect to the subject matter of the asserted defense up to the time that the law suit was filed. *Dunhall Pharmaceuticals Inc. v. Discus Dental Inc.*, 994 F. Supp. 1202, 994 F. Supp. 1202, 46 U.S.P.Q.2d 1365, 1369 (Cal. 1998).

Advisory.

The view that a jury verdict on non-obviousness is at best advisory would make charades of motions for directed verdict or JNOV under Fed. R. Civ. P. 50 in patent cases. These motions apply only to binding jury verdicts. Moreover, use of an advisory jury is limited to actions not triable of right by a jury. All fact findings of a jury are non-advisory, unless made in an area expressly removed from jury verdict. A jury may decide the questions of anticipation and obviousness, either as separate special verdicts or en route to a verdict on the question of validity, which may also be decided by the jury. No warrant appears for distinguishing the submission of legal questions to a jury in patent cases from such submissions routinely made in other types of cases. So long as the Seventh Amendment stands, the right to a jury trial should not be rationed, nor should particular issues in particular types of cases be treated differently from similar issues in other types of cases. When the judgment arises from a jury verdict, the reviewing court applies the reasonable jury/substantial evidence standard: A standard gives greater deference to the judgment simply because appellate review is more limited, compared with review of a trial judge's decision. The appellate court's function is exhausted when the evidentiary basis of the jury's verdict becomes apparent, it being immaterial that the court might draw a contrary inference or feel that another conclusion is more reasonable. *Richardson v. Suzuki Motor Co., Ltd.*, 868 F.2d 1226, 9 U.S.P.Q .2d 1913 (Fed. Cir. 1989).

Affidavit. *See also* **Antedating a Reference, 37 C.F.R. §1.107(b), Comparative Test Data, Declaration, Evidence.**

If the appellants wished to object to the Board's statement and to question the correctness of the facts contained therein, they should have requested the Board to cite its authority for the statement. If the cited authority was based upon facts within the personal knowledge of the Board, the appellants should have proceeded under Rules 66 and 76 of the Patent Office and called for an affidavit of the Board. The appellants would then have been in a position to contradict or explain the Board's statement. In the absence of such request, the appellants may not be heard to challenge a statement made in the Board's opinion. The statement of the Board must therefore be accepted as correct. *In re Selmi and Altenburger*, 156 F.2d 96, 70 U.S.P.Q. 197 (C.C.P.A. 1946).

ω

Affidavit evidence admitted in a protested reissue proceeding is treated in the same manner as if it had been submitted in ex parte proceedings before the PTO. Such evidence has been held to be competent to the extent that it refers to matters known to or observed by the affiant prior to or contemporaneous with the actual reduction to practice by another in an interference, where it was offered as evidence of the level of knowledge in the art at the time the invention was made. *In re Farrenkopf and Usategui Gomez, and Travenol Laboratories, Inc., Intervenor*, 713 F.2d 714, 219 U.S.P.Q. 1, 6 (Fed. Cir. 1983).

ω

Where affidavits are proffered as evidence on a motion for summary judgment, in support of or in opposition to the essential elements of a claim, the Court must be satisfied that such affidavits meet the standards set forth in Rule (Fed.R.Civ.P.) 56(e), as well as relevant evidentiary standards. Although expert witnesses are permitted to offer an opinion on the ultimate issue in the case pursuant to Fed.R. Evid. 704(a), the Court may exclude the expert testimony if such opinions are nothing more than legal conclusions. *Ciba-Geigy Corp. v. Crompton & Knowles Corp.*, 22 U.S.P.Q.2d 1761, 1763 (Pa. 1991).

ω

A rejection on the ground of anticipation by each of two abstracts (published more than one year prior to the filing date) was affirmed because appellants' evidence was insufficient to rebut the prima facie case that the two abstracts were enabling and therefore prior art, because appellants conceded that all limitations in the claims were inherent in the two abstracts, and because the anticipation findings were not otherwise tainted by legal error. In response to appellants' challenge of each of the abstracts as nonenabling, the Examiner explained his position without establishing the state of the art or providing citation of any substantiating documentation. The procedures established by 37 C.F.R. §1.107(b) (1993) expressly entitle an applicant, on mere request, to an Examiner affidavit that provides such citation. Appellants' failure to avail themselves of this procedure waived any right thereto under well established rules of law. *In re Sun*, 31 U.S.P.Q.2d 1451, 1454, 1455 (Fed. Cir. 1993—*unpublished*).

ω

Affidavits and other materials submitted for the first time to a district court in support of objections to a Magistrate Judge's Report and Recommendation should not be considered. *Maitland Co. Inc. v. Terra First Inc.*, 33 U.S.P.Q.2d 1882, 1884 (S.C. 1994).

ω

Uncontroverted affidavits may be treated as true. *Western Water Management Inc. v. Brown*, 40 F.3d 105, 33 U.S.P.Q.2d 2014, 2016 (5th Cir. 1994).

Affirm.

A "court of appeals may affirm the judgment of a district court on any ground, including grounds not relied upon by the district court." *Athletic Alternatives Inc. v. Prince Manufacturing Inc.*, 73 F.3d 1573, 37 U.S.P.Q.2d 1365, 1374 (Fed. Cir. 1996).

Affirmative Defense.

An unnecessary ruling on an affirmative defense is not the same as the necessary resolution of a counterclaim for a declaratory judgment. *Cardinal Chemical Co. v. Morton International Inc.*, 113 S.Ct. 1967, 26 U.S.P.Q.2d 1721, 1726 (S.Ct. 1993).

ω

Failure to raise an affirmative defense generally results in the waiver of that defense, unless amendment is allowed. Leave to amend may be denied on the basis of undue delay, bad faith, or prejudice to the opposing party. *PreVent Inc. v. WNCK Inc.*, 33 U.S.P.Q.2d 1701, 1702 (Penn. 1994).

ω

"An unnecessary ruling on an affirmative defense is not the same as the necessary resolution of a counterclaim for a declaratory judgment." *Multiform Desiccants Inc. v. Medzam Ltd.*, 133 F.3d 1473, 45 U.S.P.Q.2d 1429, 1435 (Fed. Cir. 1998).

Agency Interpretation

Deference to an agency interpretation is required if Congress has not "directly spoken to the precise question at issue" and if the agency interpretation is reasonable. *Mova Pharmaceutical Corp. v. Shalala*, 41 U.S.P.Q.2d 2012 (D.C. 1997).

Agent.

A patent attorney does not enter into an agency relationship with an inventor for purposes of what is disclosed in the inventor's patent application. The inventor never authorizes his patent attorney to "act on his behalf" with respect to disclosing the invention. The patent attorney's authority does not include inventing, i.e., either supplementing or supplanting the inventor's knowledge of his own invention. The information disclosed in the inventor's patent application must be that which is actually known to him. *Glaxo Inc. v. Novopharm Ltd.*, 52 F.3d 1043, 34 U.S.P.Q.2d 1565, 1571 (Fed. Cir. 1995).

Age of Reference. *See* **Date.**

Agreement to Assign.

Even where there is a clear oral agreement to assign a patent, to establish standing in a case under the Patent Act, the party must have and actual assignment in writing. *Dynamic Manufacturing Inc. v. Craze*, 46 U.S.P.Q.2d 1548, 1555 (Va. 1998).

Aggregation. *See also* **Obviousness, 35 U.S.C. §103.**

The term "aggregation" appears to be used by the courts in either one of two different ways. It is applied in one sense to a device having two or more unrelated, independent units or elements, each of which performs its function separately, uninfluenced by and indifferent to the action of the other units. There is no essential or inherent correlation, or cooperation, or coordination of elements which mutually contribute to a common purpose or result, other than mere convenience due to juxtaposition or collection of the units in a common setting. It is applied in another sense (almost invariably preceded by a deprecating adjective as, for example, "mere aggregation") to devices which really appear to be a combination of two or more units coacting or cooperating in the full sense of the term, but which the court regarded as not displaying the exercise of invention because no new or unexpected result was produced by the combination. It seems to us that the former is the correct use of the term. In the latter case, such a device should properly be regarded as an unpatentable combination, and not as an aggregation. [The term has also been applied to claims which enumerate elements without defining a relationship between the elements or how they are connected to each other.] *In re Worrest*, 201 F.2d 930, 96 U.S.P.Q. 381, 385 (C.C.P.A. 1953).

ᛉ

When an applicant produces a new and useful result by carrying forward features selected from cited prior art and incorporates them into a single structure wherein such features perform their usual functions unmodified by the presence of other features, there is no novel combination but only an aggregation of old elements that does not constitute a patentable invention. *In re Carter*, 212 F.2d 189, 101 U.S.P.Q. 290, 293 (C.C.P.A. 1954).

ᛉ

An aggregation of old components in an apparatus in which these components perform no function or operation different from that theretofore performed by them in a prior similar apparatus lacks invention and is not patentable. *Chemical Construction Corp. v. Jones & Laughlin Steel Corp.*, 311 F.2d 367, 136 U.S.P.Q. 150, 154 (3d Cir. 1962).

ϖ

Whatever meaning might be attributed to "aggregation", it has become a term of art in patent law to connote something which is not patentable. The test for the presence or absence of "invention", and along with it the subsidiary question of whether a device or process is or is not an "aggregation", or a "combination", or an "unpatentable combination" for want of "invention", was replaced by the statutory test of 35 U.S.C. §103. *In re Gustafson*, 331 F.2d 905, 141 U.S.P.Q. 585, 588, 589 (C.C.P.A. 1964).

Aggressive.

An aggressive strategy may or may not be a factor in a decision to deny or award increased damages. An "aggressive strategy" unsupported by any competent advice of counsel, thorough investigation of validity and infringement, discovery of more pertinent uncited prior art, or similar factors, is the type of activity the reference in the patent law to increased damages seeks to prevent. An alleged infringer who intentionally blinds himself to the facts and law, continues to infringe, and employs the judicial process with no solidly based expectation of success, can hardly be surprised when his infringement is found to have been willful. Willfulness of infringement relates to the accused infringer's conduct in the marketplace. Because that conduct may be seen as producing an unnecessary and outcome-certain lawsuit, it may make the case so exceptional as to warrant attorney's fees under 35 U.S.C. §285. Similarly, bad faith displayed in pretrial and trial stages, by counsel or party, may render the case exceptional under §285. When a court declines to award attorney's fees on the basis of a determination that a case is not exceptional, the fact findings underlying that determination are reviewed under the clearly erroneous standard. When the determination is that a case is exceptional, the election to grant or deny attorney's fees is reviewed under the abuse of discretion standard. *Kloster Speedsteel A.B. v. Crucible Inc.*, 793 F.2d 1565, 230 U.S.P.Q. 81 (Fed. Cir. 1986).

Agreement.

The Supreme Court held that a license agreement that promised not to challenge the validity of a patent was void and unenforceable because it contravened the strong federal policy in favor of the full and free use of ideas in the public domain. Six circuits have ruled that consent judgments of validity and infringement are enforceable despite the Supreme Court's holding in *Lear* [395 U.S. 653, 162 U.S.P.Q. 1 (1969)]. *Foster v. Hallco Manufacturing Co., Inc.*, 14 U.S.P.Q.2d 1746, 1747 (Or. 1990).

Agreement to Assign.

An agreement to assign a patent when issued constitutes an executory contract to assign the invention upon the happening of a later event, i.e., the issuance of the patent, and thus does not constitute a sale at the time of the execution of the agreement. *Bell Intercontinental Corp. v. United States*, 381 F.2d 1004, 152 U.S.P.Q. 182, 191 (Ct. Cl. 1966).

Algorithm. *See also* **Computer-Arts Invention, Mathematical Equation, Mathematical Formula, Program.**

A claimed invention (considered as a whole) that does not preempt a mathematical formula, an involved algorithm, or a program per se, and that is within the tech-nologically useful art of controlling and optimizing a system of manufacturing plants to a particular end use, is a statutory "process" within the purview of 35 U.S.C. §101. *In re Deutsch,* 553 F.2d 689, 193 U.S.P.Q. 645, 649 (C.C.P.A. 1977).

ᛦ

Over-concentration on the word algorithm alone may mislead. The Supreme Court in *Benson* [409 U.S. 63, 175 U.S.P.Q. 548 (1972)] carefully supplied a definition of the particular algorithm before it, i.e., a procedure for solving a given type of mathematical problem. The broader definition of algorithm, according to *Webster's New Collegiate Dictionary* (1976), is "a step-by-step procedure for solving a problem or accomplishing some end." It would be unnecessarily detrimental to our patent system to deny inventors patent protection on the sole ground that their contribution could be broadly termed an algorithm. *In re Chatfield,* 545 F.2d 152, 191 U.S.P.Q. 730, 734 (C.C.P.A. 1976), *cert. denied,* 434 U.S. 875, 195 U.S.P.Q. 465 (1977).

ᛦ

Determination of whether a claim preempts nonstatutory subject matter as a whole, in the light of *Benson* [409 U.S. 63, 175 U.S.P.Q. 548 (1972)], requires a two-step analysis. First, it must be determined whether the claim directly or indirectly recites an *algorithm* as defined in *Benson*; for a claim that fails even to recite an algorithm clearly cannot wholly preempt an algorithm. Second, the claim must be further analyzed to ascertain whether in its entirety it wholly preempts that algorithm. The preferred definition of *algorithm* in the computer art is: "A fixed step-by-step procedure for accomplishing a given result; usually a simplified procedure for solving a complex problem, also a full statement of a finite number of steps." C. Sippl & C. Sippl, *Computer Dictionary and Handbook* (1972). *In re Freeman,* 573 F.2d 1237, 197 U.S.P.Q. 464, 471 (C.C.P.A. 1978).

ᛦ

Once a mathematical algorithm has been found, the claim as a whole must be further analyzed. If it appears that the mathematical algorithm is implemented in a specific manner to define structural relationships between the physical elements of the claim (in apparatus claims) or to refine or limit claim steps (in process claims), the claim, being otherwise statutory, passes muster under 35 U.S.C. §101. *In re Walter,* 618 F.2d 758, 205 U.S.P.Q. 397, 407 (C.C.P.A. 1980).

ᛦ

If a mathematical algorithm is merely presented and solved by a claimed invention and is not applied in any other manner to physical elements or process steps, no amount of post-solution activity will render the claim statutory; nor is it saved by a preamble merely reciting the field of use of the mathematical algorithm. If, however, the claimed invention produces a physical thing, the fact that it is represented in numerical form does not render the claim nonstatutory. *Ex parte Head,* 214 U.S.P.Q. 551 (PTO Bd. App. 1981).

ᛦ

A computer algorithm, as opposed to a mathematical algorithm, is patentable subject matter. *Paine, Webber, Jackson & Curtis, Inc. v. Merrill Lynch, Pierce, Fenner & Smith, Inc. v. Dean Witter Reynolds, Inc.*, 564 F. Supp. 1358, 218 U.S.P.Q. 212, 218 (Del. 1983).

Ꮹ

According to the *Freeman-Walter-Abele* test for statutory subject matter, it is first determined whether a mathematical algorithm is recited directly or indirectly in the claim. If so, it is next determined whether the claimed invention as a whole is no more than the algorithm itself; that is, whether the claim is directed to a mathematical algorithm that is not applied to or limited by physical elements or process steps. Such claims are nonstatutory. However, when the mathematical algorithm is applied to one or more steps of an otherwise statutory process claim, or one or more elements of an otherwise statutory apparatus claim, the requirements of 35 U.S.C. §101 are met. *Arrhythmia Research Technology Inc. v. Corazonix Corp.*, 958 F.2d 1053, 22 U.S.P.Q.2d 1033, 1037 (Fed. Cir. 1992).

Ꮹ

Steps, such as "computing," "determining," "cross-correlating," "comparing," "selecting," "initializing," "testing," "modifying," and "identifying," have implicitly been found to recite the solving of a mathematical algorithm. *In re Warmerdam*, 33 F.3d 1354, 31 U.S.P.Q.2d 1754, 1758 (Fed. Cir. 1994).

Alien.

An alien corporation may be sued in any district under 28 U.S.C. §1391(d), which applies to all federal actions, including patent infringement suits. *Brunswick Corporation v. Suzuki Motor Company, Ltd.*, 575 F.Supp. 1412, 220 U.S.P.Q. 822, 831 (Wis. 1983).

Ꮹ

In all federal actions against aliens, the applicable venue provision is 28 U.S.C. §1391(d), which provides that "[a]n alien may be sued in any district." In federal question cases, due process requires only sufficient contacts with the United States as a whole rather than with any particular state. *Miller Pipeline Corp. v. British Gas plc*, 901 F.Supp. 1416, 38 U.S.P.Q.2d 1010, 1012, 1014 (Ind. 1995).

Alkaryl. *See* Aryl.

Alkyl.

A rejection of claims as failing to define the invention properly and based on the phrases "substituted mononuclear and polynuclear homocyclic compounds," "alkyl," "ester," and "heterocyclic and aromatic compounds being free of substituents containing aliphatic hydroxyl and amino groups," in process claims was reversed. *Ex parte Westfahl*, 136 U.S.P.Q. 265 (PTO Bd. App. 1962).

Alkylene. *See* Ethylene.

"All Advantages" Rule.

The panel majority holds that the advantages mentioned in the specification, although not included in the claims, must be possessed by an accused device before there can be a finding of infringement by equivalency. *Vehicular Technologies Corp. v. Titan Wheel International Inc.*, 141 F.3d 1084, 46 U.S.P.Q.2d 1257, 1264 *dissent* (Fed. Cir. 1998).

All-Claims Rule.

The all-claims rule (that a patent is invalid for failure to name proper inventors unless the inventorship entity named is that of the true original inventors of every claim in a patent containing more than one claim) was not uniformly accepted as "the substantive law" before the 1984 Act. *SmithKline Diagnostics, Inc. v. Helena Laboratories Corp.*, 859 F.2d 878, 8 U.S.P.Q.2d 1468 (Fed. Cir. 1988).

All Defenses. *See* 19 U.S.C. §1337(c).

Allegation. *See also* Assertion, Statement.

A finding of a new fact, supporting an alternative ground for sustaining an Examiner's rejection, and based on apparently nothing more than a bare allegation of scientific fact, does everything but cry out for an opportunity to respond. Appellant challenged the Board's assertion with an allegation of his own to the contrary and supported his assertion with an affidavit opinion of an acknowledged expert in the art. Appellant's response was more than mere "argument"; it was a direct challenge to a finding of fact made for the first time by the Board and included with it some evidence in the nature of rebuttal. It was thus entitled to more serious consideration. *In re Moore*, 444 F.2d 572, 170 U.S.P.Q. 260, 263 (C.C.P.A. 1971).

ϖ

Under challenge the absence of support for an Examiner's statement may be critical. *In re Mochel*, 470 F.2d 638, 176 U.S.P.Q. 194, 196 (C.C.P.A. 1972).

ϖ

No weight can be accorded to an allegation or assertion by the PTO without foundation in the record upon which the involved position can be based. *In re Noznick, Tatter, and Obenauf*, 478 F.2d 1260, 178 U.S.P.Q. 43 (C.C.P.A. 1973).

ϖ

Inherency may not be established by probabilities or possibilities. The mere fact that a certain thing may result from a given set of circumstances is not sufficient. Although an applicant may be required to prove that the subject matter shown to be in prior art does not possess characteristics relied upon where an Examiner has reason to believe that a functional limitation asserted to be critical for establishing novelty in the claimed subject matter may, in fact, be an inherent characteristic of the prior art, the Examiner must provide some evidence or scientific reasoning to establish the reasonableness of the belief that the functional limitation is an inherent characteristic of the prior art before the applicant can be put through this burdensome task. *Ex parte Skinner*, 2 U.S.P.Q.2d 1788 (B.P.A.I. 1986).

All-Elements Rule.

Infringement requires that each element of a claim or its substantial equivalent be found in an accused device. In the all-elements rule, element is used in the sense of a limitation of a claim; it may be used to mean a single limitation, but it also has been used to mean a series of limitations that, taken together, make up a component of the claimed invention. *Corning Glass Works v. Sumitomo Electric U.S.A. Inc.*, 868 F.2d 1251, 9 U.S.P.Q.2d 1962 (Fed. Cir. 1989).

ω

To establish infringement of a patent, every limitation set forth in a claim must be found in an accused product or process exactly, or by a substantial equivalent. A more precise name for this rule would be the all limitations rule. *Johnston v. IVAC Corp.*, 885 F.2d 1574, 12 U.S.P.Q.2d 1382, 1384 (Fed. Cir. 1989).

ω

The doctrine of equivalents is not a license to ignore or "erase...structural and functional limitations of the claim," limitations "on which the public is entitled to rely in avoiding infringement." As a corollary to the "all limitations" rule, "the concept of equivalency cannot embrace a structure that is specifically excluded from the scope of the claims." *Athletic Alternatives Inc. v. Prince Manufacturing Inc.*, 73 F.3d 1573, 37 U.S.P.Q.2d 1365, 1373 (Fed. Cir. 1996).

All-Limitations Rule. *See* **All-Elements Rule.**

Allowed Application. *See* **Withdraw from Issue.**

Allowed Claim.

Although certain of the involved claims were formerly allowed in appellant's parent application, the question of patentability of appealed claims must be decided on the merits and not on the basis of holdings made in some other application. *In re Boileau*, 168 F.2d 753, 78 U.S.P.Q. 146, 148 (C.C.P.A. 1948).

ω

Allowability of an appealed claim is not controlled by the fact that similar claims have been allowed in the Patent Office since an appealed claim must be patentable in its own right. However, similar claims allowed by the Patent Office tribunals furnish evidence of what features those tribunals regard as patentable. It is proper, and sometimes necessary, to consider allowed claims in order to fully determine the views of the Board and of the Examiner. *In re Schechter and LaForge*, 205 F.2d 185, 98 U.S.P.Q. 144, 150 (C.C.P.A. 1953).

ω

Allowed claims cannot, by construction, be read to cover what was eliminated from a patent by a claim canceled during prosecution. This rule is applicable not only when the canceled claim is broader than those allowed but also when the canceled claim is narrower. *Chemical Construction Corp. v. Jones & Laughlin Steel Corp.*, 311 F.2d 367, 136 U.S.P.Q. 150, 155 (3d Cir. 1962).

Alloy.

Patentability of an alloy on the basis of new proportions of old elements requires that the new proportions give a new result; either a new metal or an old metal with new characteristics which result in entirely new, or substantially enhanced, qualities of utility. *Becket v. Coe*, 98 F.2d 332, 38 U.S.P.Q. 26, 30 (App DC 1938).

ʊ

The mere fact that a claim covers a large, or even an unlimited number of products, does not necessarily establish that it is too broad. Claims are commonly allowed for alloys or mixtures that permit substantial variations in the proportions of two or more ingredients. Theoretically, an infinite number of products may be produced falling within the scope of such a claim. In the case of alloys or mixtures, however, it is generally apparent how a product of any desired proportions may be produced, and, since the properties of the aggregate ordinarily vary in accordance with the proportions of the ingredients, the characteristics of any aggregate covered by the claim can generally be predicted with reasonable certainty if the properties of typical aggregates are known. *In re Cavallito and Gray*, 282 F.2d 363, 127 U.S.P.Q. 202, 204, 205 (C.C.P.A. 1960).

ʊ

Reliance on component proportions in an antecedent application was in issue for purpose of overcoming an intervening reference. *Eiselstein v. Frank*, 52 F.3d 1035, 34 U.S.P.Q.2d 1467, 1470, 1471 (Fed. Cir. 1995).

Alteration. *See* **Modification.**

Alternative. *See also* **Interchangeable, Optionally, Zero.**

Patentability of a product claim is not precluded merely because the claim recites alternatively used or interchangeable parts. *In re Worrest*, 201 F.2d 930, 96 U.S.P.Q. 381 (C.C.P.A. 1953).

ʊ

Alternative expressions do not necessarily render the boundaries of a claimed invention undeterminable. Expressions, such as "made entirely or in part of" (which is to say "made at least partially of"), "one or several pieces" (which is to say "at least one piece"), and "iron, steel or any other magnetic material," accurately determine the boundaries of pro-tection involved. *In re Gaubert*, 524 F.2d 1222, 187 U.S.P.Q. 664, 667, 668 (C.C.P.A. 1975).

ʊ

The mere use of an alternative expression in a claim is not fatal. *Ex parte Head*, 214 U.S.P.Q. 551 (PTO Bd. App. 1981).

ʊ

The metes and bounds of claims are not rendered unclear merely because of the presence of alternative language. *Ex parte Holt*, 19 U.S.P.Q.2d 1211, 1214 (B.P.A.I. 1991).

Alternative Dispute Resolution.

When parties to an ADR process have a legitimate secrecy interest that would be harmed if an outsider were allowed to intervene and the outsider's need for information does not outweigh existing privacy concerns, there are several reasons why the specter of collateral estoppel does not loom as large as it might in other situations. First, as a condition of participating in ADR, each party has surrendered its right to appeal the decision of the special master. More importantly, the ethic of ADR is often different from that of litigation. There is an emphasis on compromise, of each side softening its positions in order to meet in the middle. Each concession must be understood in the context of those of the other party. The series of positions each party takes and the decisions of the special master must be looked at as an integrated whole. Therefore, the rationale which drives issue-by-issue collateral estoppel is not wholly applicable. *Haworth Inc. v. Steelcase Inc.*, 26 U.S.P.Q.2d 1152, 1153 (Mich. 1993).

Ambiguity. *See also* **Claim Construction, Deference, Indefiniteness, Overclaiming, 35 U.S.C. §112, Vague.**

When a term of an interference count, as used in the art, has several possible meanings, it is, to that extent, ambiguous. It is thus necessary to look at the patent in which the count originated in order to determine the intended meaning of the term. *Bethell and Hadley v. Koch, Robinson, and Wiley,* 427 F.2d 1372, 166 U.S.P.Q. 199, 201 (C.C.P.A. 1970).

ʊ

Where a latent ambiguity is alleged to exist in an interference count, a literal application of the rule that "only in the case where a count is ambiguous should resort be had to the patent where it originated" prevents the court from looking to the specification even to determine whether there is an ambiguity, let alone to resolve the meaning of the count for purposes of the interference. *Stansbury v. Bond,* 482 F.2d 968, 179 U.S.P.Q. 88, 92 (C.C.P.A. 1973).

ʊ

Lack of antecedent basis in a claim could render it invalid under 35 U.S.C. §112, second paragraph, and correction of such a defect by reissue should not have to depend on difference in scope of the claim. Inasmuch as 35 U.S.C. §251 is a remedial provision, which should be liberally construed, a patentee should be allowed to correct an error or ambiguity in a claim without having to rely on implication or litigation. Lack of antecedent basis in a claim is a proper ground for reissue under 35 U.S.C. §251. *In re Altenpohl,* 500 F.2d 1151, 183 U.S.P.Q. 38, 43 (C.C.P.A. 1974).

ʊ

While there does not appear to be any ambiguity in the language used by the drafters, the test is whether the contractor, who realistically had to acquiesce in the government's proffered form, could reasonably construe it that way. This rule places the risk of ambiguity, lack of clarity, and absence of proper warning on the drafting party that could have forestalled the controversy; it pushes the drafters toward improving contractual forms; and it saves contractors from hidden traps not of their own making. *Lockheed Aircraft Corp. v. United States*, 190 U.S.P.Q. 134, 154 (Ct. Cl. 1976).

ᐜ

In an interference, determination of the existence of an ambiguity requires consideration of both the language of the counts and the reasonableness of arguments indicating that the language of the counts has different meanings. Resort to a patent or application disclosure has the limited purpose of resolving an ambiguity—not of creating one. *Kroekel v. Shah*, 558 F.2d 29, 194 U.S.P.Q. 544, 546, 547 (C.C.P.A. 1977).

ᐜ

If a claim is subject to two interpretations, and one interpretation would render the claim unpatentable over the prior art, the proper course of action is for the Examiner to enter two rejections: (1) a rejection based on indefiniteness under 35 U.S.C. §112, second paragraph, and (2) a rejection over the prior art based on the interpretation of the claims which renders the prior art applicable. *Ex parte Ionescu*, 222 U.S.P.Q. 537, 540 (PTO Bd. App. 1984).

ᐜ

Interference counts are given the broadest reasonable interpretation possible, and resort to the specification is necessary only when there are ambiguities inherent in the claim language or obvious from arguments of counsel. If there is such ambiguity, resort must be had to the specification of the patent from which the copied claim came. *DeGeorge v. Bernier*, 768 F.2d 1318, 226 U.S.P.Q. 758 (Fed. Cir. 1985).

Ambiguous.

A patent claim may be interpreted only as broadly as its unambiguous scope. *Ethicon Endo-Surgery Inc. v. United States Surgical Corp.*, 40 U.S.P.Q.2d 1019, 1026 (Fed. Cir. 1996).

"Ambush" Theory

The critical issue is "whether the plaintiff in the earlier-filed declaratory judgment action misled the defendant into believing that their dispute could be resolved amicably so that the plaintiff could win the race to the courthouse..." *Comtec Information Systems Inc. v. Monarch Marking Systems Inc.*, 42 U.S.P.Q.2d 1951, 1953 (R.I. 1997).

Amelioration.

Amelioration of the symptoms or even cure of cancer is no longer considered to be "incredible." Nonetheless, decisional law would seem to indicate that the utility in question is sufficiently unusual to justify an Examiner's requiring substantiating evidence. This may be in the form of animal tests that constitute recognized screening procedures with clear relevance to utility in humans. The specification of appellant's parent application sets forth several animal tests on numerous types of specific cancers as well as in vitro studies, both of which are asserted to be predictive with regard to utility in humans. The Examiner has not challenged the evidence presented in a single, relevant, material respect. There is only the blanket statement of lack of "patentable utility" per se. In fact, the only specific comments the Examiner has directed toward appellant's evidence are with regard to the breadth of the types of tumor against which the claimed compounds have been shown to be active. The appealed claims are drawn to compounds and not to a method of treatment. Generally speaking, utility in treating a single disease is an adequate basis for the patentability of a pharmaceutical compound under 35 U.S.C. §101. *Ex parte Krepelka*, 231 U.S.P.Q. 746 (B.P.A.I. 1986).

Amend[2]. *See* **Leave to amend, Rule 13(f).**

Amend Complaint.

In determining whether to grant leave to amend, a trial court should take into account the possibility of prejudice to the adverse party if leave were granted. If a ground for rejecting the amendment is delay, the delay must be "undue." *Tenneco Resins, Inc. v. Reeves Bros., Inc.*, 752 F.2d 630, 634-35, 224 U.S.P.Q. 536 (Fed. Cir. 1985).

Amended Pleading.

An amended pleading adding plaintiffs appropriately relates back to the date of filing where it "relates to the same conduct, transaction, or occurrence set forth in the original pleading." *MDS Associates v. U.S.*, 31 Fed.Cl. 389, 32 U.S.P.Q.2d 1784, 1789 (U.S. Ct. Fed. Cl. 1994).

Amending Answer.

Leave to amend is not appropriately granted when the amendment is futile. An amendment is considered futile if it could not survive a motion to dismiss or a motion for summary judgment. *Black & Decker Inc. v. Greenfield Industries Inc.*, 22 U.S.P.Q.2d 1637, 1638 (Md. 1991).

Amendment. *See also* **Amend, Competitor's Product.**

Although the opinion of the Examiner is to be given great weight on the question of what constitutes new matter in an amendment to an application for patent, an amendment made more than one year after the invention went on sale does not disqualify applicant where the amendment was clarifying in its form and effect rather than new matter. *Milgo Electronics Corp. v. United Telecommunications, Inc,* 189 U.S.P.Q. 160, 169 (Kan. 1976).

ω

When claims are amended during reexamination (following a rejection based on prior art), the claims are not deemed substantively changed as a matter of law. There is no per se rule. To determine whether a claim change is substantive, it is necessary to analyze the claims of the original and the reexamined patents in light of the particular facts, including the prior art, the prosecution history, other claims, and any other pertinent information. When the issue is the doctrine of equivalents or substantive change on reexamination, the mere amendment of a claim does not act as a per se estoppel. *The Laitram Corp. v. NEC Corp.*, 952 F.2d 1357, 21 U.S.P.Q.2d 1276, 1280 (Fed. Cir. 1991).

ω

---

[2]*See Total Containment Inc. v. Environ Products Inc.*, 34 U.S.P.Q.2d 1254, 1255 (Pa. 1995)

An applicant may insert clarifying language in a claim to meet an Examiner's objection without thereby accepting the Examiner's position that the change is substantive. *Tennant Co. v. Hako Minuteman Inc.*, 22 U.S.P.Q.2d 1161, 1168 (Ill. 1991).

ω

When a claim is amended, but the prosecution history does not reveal the reason for the change, it should be presumed that there was "a substantial reason related to patentability for including the limiting element added by amendment." *Hilton Davis Chemical Co. v. Warner-Jenkinson Co.*, 43 U.S.P.Q.2d 1152, 1153 (Fed. Cir. 1997).

ω

When an applicant disagrees with an Examiner's prior art rejection and fails to prevail by argument, he has two choices: either to amend the claim or to appeal the rejection. He may not both make the amendment and then challenge its necessity in a subsequent infringement action on the allowed claim. *Bai v. L&L Wings, Inc.*, 48 U.S.P.Q.2d 1674, 1678 (Fed. Cir. 1998).

Amendment after Final.

An Examiner only permits After Final Amendments upon "a showing of good and sufficient reasons why they are necessary and were not earlier presented." A refusal to permit such an amendment is not a rejection on the merits and leaves the application in the same status it was in after the final rejection. *Waldemar Link, GmbH & Co. v. Osteonics Corp.*, 32 F.3d 556, 31 U.S.P.Q.2d 1855, 1858 (Fed. Cir. 1994).

ω

Amend Pleadings.

Four factors that are to be taken into consideration before granting a party leave to amend pleadings: (1) undue delay; (2) bad faith or dilatory motive; (3) futility of amendment, and (4) prejudice to opposing party. *Qualcomm Inc. v. Motorola Inc.*, 989 F. Supp. 1048, 45 U.S.P.Q.2d 1472, 1473 (Cal. 1997).

Amount. *See also* Effective.

Proportions need not be recited in composition claims when they are not critical to the disclosed and claimed invention. Failure to recite proportions in such claims does not subject them to rejection for indefiniteness. *In re Conley, Catherwood, and Lloyd*, 490 F.2d 972, 180 U.S.P.Q. 454, 456 (C.C.P.A. 1974).

An. *See* Indefinite Article.

Analog. *See also* Chlorine Analog, Relationship, Structural Similarity.

A disclosure of a particular, significant usefulness for claimed compounds that was not known or obvious in the art is adequate consideration for a patent grant on the compounds, where the prior art previously was unaware of any usefulness for the class of compounds to which the claimed compounds belong. *In re Stemniski,* 444 F.2d 581, 170 U.S.P.Q. 343, 348 (C.C.P.A. 1971).

ᆩ

A newly discovered activity of a claimed novel compound that bears no material relationship to the activity disclosed for prior art analogs is clear evidence, not to be ignored, of the non-obviousness of the claimed invention. *In re Albrecht,* 514 F.2d 1389, 185 U.S.P.Q. 585, 590 (C.C.P.A. 1975).

ᆩ

One who claims a compound, per se, which is structurally similar to a prior-art compound must rebut the presumed expectation that the structurally similar compounds have similar properties. *In re Wilder,* 563 F.2d 457, 195 U.S.P.Q. 426, 429 (C.C.P.A. 1977).

ᆩ

When chemical compounds have "very close" structural similarities and similar utilities, without more, a prima facie case may be made. When such "close" structural similarity to prior art compounds is shown, in accordance with established precedents, the burden of coming forward shifts to the applicant, and evidence affirmatively supporting non-obviousness is required. Generalization should be avoided insofar as specific chemical structures are alleged to be prima facie obvious one from the other. There must be adequate prior-art support for involved structural changes in order to complete the PTO's prima facie case and shift the burden of going forward to the applicant. The mere fact that it is possible to find two isolated disclosures that might be combined in such a way to produce a new compound does not necessarily render such production obvious unless the art also contains something to suggest the desirability of the proposed combination. In the absence of such a reference suggestion, there is inadequate support for the position that the required modification would prima facie have been obvious.

Even though it may not be inconceivable to substitute sulfur for oxygen to obtain compounds having the same expected properties, that is not the standard; the standard is whether it would have been obvious in terms of 35 U.S.C. §103. *In re Grabiak,* 769 F.2d 729, 226 U.S.P.Q. 870 (Fed. Cir. 1985).

Analogous Art. *See also* **Double Use, Problem, Relevant Art.**

A reference cited from alleged non-analogous art is a proper reference if the disclosure thereof suggests doing that which the applicant has relied upon to endow his claims with patentable distinction. *In re Weiskopf,* 210 F.2d 287, 100 U.S.P.Q. 383, 385 (C.C.P.A. 1954).

ᆩ

The rationale behind the rule precluding rejections based on a combination of teachings of references from non-analogous arts is the realization that an inventor could not possibly be aware of every teaching in every art. The inventor is presumed to have knowledge of prior art in the field of his endeavor and in analogous arts. If a reference is not within the field of the inventor's endeavor, it may still be regarded as within analogous art if the reference is reasonably pertinent to the particular problem with which the inventor was involved. *In re Wood and Eversole*, 599 F.2d 1032, 202 U.S.P.Q. 171, 174 (C.C.P.A. 1979).

ω

While the diverse Patent Office classification of the references is some evidence of "non-analogy", and cross-references in the official search notes is some evidence of "analogy", the similarities and differences in structure and function of the inventions disclosed in the references carry far greater weight. *In re Mlot-Fijalkowski*, 676 F.2d 666, 213 U.S.P.Q. 713, 715 n.5 (C.C.P.A. 1982).

ω

The scope of the prior art is that art that would have been considered by those endeavoring to solve the problem that the patent in-suit allegedly solves. *Atlas Powder Company v. E.I. duPont de Nemours and Company*, 588 F.Supp. 1455, 221 U.S.P.Q. 426, 431 (Tex. 1983).

ω

To decide whether prior art in an analogous field is pertinent, the problems confronting a person skilled in the subject art must be considered to decide whether such a person would have looked to art in other fields of endeavor to solve those problems. It is a question of fact for a jury to decide whether another field of art is sufficiently analogous to the art with which each patent is concerned that a person with a problem in the latter field would look to the former field to adopt solutions to the problem devised there. If the reference is not within the field of the inventor's endeavor, one looks at whether the field of the reference is reasonably pertinent to the problem the inventor is trying to solve. *Lacotte v. Thomas*, 758 F.2d 611, 225 U.S.P.Q. 633 (Fed. Cir. 1985).

ω

An action in the district court under 35 U.S.C. §145 is a proceeding de novo and, while it is limited to the invention claimed in the PTO, the court may consider any additional competent evidence that a plaintiff neither intentionally nor negligently failed to submit to the PTO. The presumption of correctness that attaches to the decision of the Commissioner is a rebuttable presumption that may be overcome by the introduction of evidence (at a trial under 35 U.S.C. §145) that is of such character and amount as to carry a thorough conviction of error. At such a trial the plaintiff and defendant may present evidence on any issue properly before the court. This additional evidence may include testimony of expert witnesses and inventors skilled in the art, as well as evidence of commercial success. In making its determination of non-obviousness, the court recognized the non-analogous nature of one reference, the lack of teaching or suggestion in the prior art of the useful advantage of a flexible track incapable of self-support, and the commercial success of the highly flexible Hot Wheels trackway toy-vehicle combination covered by plaintiff's Reissue Application. The fact that the claimed invention seemed simple and, when viewed in hindsight, appeared to be obvious was not enough to negate invention. *Lemelson v. Mossinghoff*, 225 U.S.P.Q. 1063 (D.C. 1985).

ω

A reference is not available under 35 U.S.C. §103 if it is not within the field of the inventor's endeavor and was not directly pertinent to the particular problem with which the inventor was involved. *King Instrument Corp. v. Otari Corp.*, 767 F.2d 853, 226 U.S.P.Q. 402 (Fed. Cir. 1985).

ᴕ

If a reference is not within the field of the inventor's endeavor, one looks at whether the field of the reference is reasonably pertinent to the problem the inventor is trying to solve. *Ryco Inc. v. Ag-Bag Corp.*, 857 F.2d 1418, 8 U.S.P.Q.2d 1323 (Fed. Cir. 1988).

ᴕ

Two criteria for determining whether prior art is analogous are: (1) whether the art is from the same field of endeavor, regardless of the problem addressed, and (2) if the reference is not within the field of the inventor's endeavor, whether the reference is still reasonably pertinent to the particular problem with which the inventor is involved. *In re Clay*, 966 F.2d 656, 23 U.S.P.Q.2d 1058, 1060 (Fed. Cir. 1992).

ᴕ

References that are not within the field of the inventor's endeavor may be relied on in a patentability determination, and thus are described as "analogous art,", when a person of ordinary skill would reasonably have consulted those references and applied their teachings in seeking a solution to the problem that the inventor was attempting to solve. *Heidelberger Druckmaschinen AG v. Hantscho Commercial Products Inc.*, 21 F.3d 1068, 30 U.S.P.Q.2d 1377, 1379 (Fed. Cir. 1994); *In re GPAC Inc.*, 57 F.3d 1573, 35 U.S.P.Q.2d 1116, 1120 (Fed. Cir. 1995).

Analogue. *See* **Analog, Chlorine Analog.**

Analogy Process[3]. *See also* **Method of Making, Method of Use.**

The use of a previously-unknown microorganism strain to produce an antibiotic previously produced by other strains of the same microorganism is not obvious because the process as a whole could not be obvious to anyone in the absence of the new strain. *In re Mancy, Florent, and Preud'Homme*, 499 F.2d 1289, 182 U.S.P.Q. 303, 305 (C.C.P.A. 1974).

ᴕ

Process claims cannot be rejected simply because they recite use of new materials in an old process. *Ex parte MacAdams, Wu, and Joyner*, 206 U.S.P.Q. 445, 447 (PTO Bd. App. 1978).

ᴕ

Although the claimed reaction had not previously been conducted with the particular starting material involved, the Examiner maintained that a chemist of ordinary skill

---

[3]"[T]here are not '*Durden* obviousness rejections' or '*Albertson* obviousness rejections,' but rather only [35 U.S.C.] 103 obviousness rejections." *In re Brouwer*, 77 F.3d 422, 37 U.S.P.Q.2d 1663, 1666 (Fed. Cir. 1996). In a Notice issued on February 28, 1996, the PTO announced that henceforth it would analyze process claims in accordance with *Ochiai* and *Brouwer* decisions of the Federal Circuit, and treat as material limitations any recitations in process claims of the use of nonobvious starting materials or the making of nonobvious products. *AIPLA BULLETIN*, 36, 1997 Annual meeting Issue.

would have realized that the reference reaction was applicable to that starting material. The claims were actually directed to a new use of a novel starting material for the involved reaction, as the identified starting material had not previously been used in the claimed process. *Ex parte Klioze,* 220 U.S.P.Q. 91 (PTO Bd. App. 1983).

ʊ

Although an otherwise old process becomes a new process when a previously unknown starting material is used in it and is subjected to a conventional manipulation or reaction to produce a product that may also be new, albeit the expected result of what is done, it does not necessarily mean that the whole process has become non-obvious in the sense of 35 U.S.C. §103. In short, a new process may still be obvious, even when considered "as a whole," notwithstanding the fact that the specific starting material or resulting product, or both, are not to be found in the prior art. *In re Durden,* 763 F.2d 1406, 226 U.S.P.Q. 359 (Fed. Cir. 1985).

ʊ

An otherwise old process wherein a previously unknown starting material is used to make a novel final product is patentable when prior art fails to suggest the final product or the use of the specific starting material in the claimed process. *In re Ochiai,* 71 F.3d 1565, 37 U.S.P.Q.2d 1127, 1131 (Fed. Cir. 1995).

Analysis. *See* **Claim Analysis/Limitations.**

Analytical Approach. *See* **Royalty.**

Ancillary Jurisdiction.

A federal district court may excercise ancillary jurisdiction over a non-federal matter (such as a settlement agreement) (1) if the issues presented are "factually interdependent" with a federal matter before the court (federal courts have jurisdiction to consider ancillary non-federal claims when the non-federal and federal matters "derive from a common nucleus of operative fact") and (2) as needed to manage its proceedings, vindicate its authority, and effectuate its decrees. To bring a settlement agreement under this inherent court power, an order or judgment of the court must incorporate the settlement agreement such that a breach of the agreement also violates the court's decree. *National Presto Industries Inc. v. Dazey Corp.,* 107 F.3d 1576, 42 U.S.P.Q.2d 1070 (Fed. Cir. 1997).

ANDA. *See also* **Abbreviated New Drug Application, Exclusivity.**

An ANDA applicant need provide certification, pursuant to 21 U.S.C. §355(j)(2)(A)(vii), only for patents listed by an NDA applicant in its application and subsequently by the FDA in the Orange Book. *Abbott Laboratories v. Zenith Laboratories Inc.,* 35 U.S.P.Q.2d 1161, 1168 (Ill. 1995).

ʊ

The Uraguay Round Agreements Act (URAA) works no change on the definition of infringement under 35 U.S.C. §271(e)(2) and has no effect on the statutory provisions relating to FDA approval of ANDAs that are triggered by that act of infringement. *DuPont*

Merck Pharmaceutical Co. v. Bristol-Myers Squibb Co., 62 F.3d 1397, 35 U.S.P.Q.2d 1718, 1722 (Fed. Cir. 1995).

ᛒ

Inclusion of a paragraph IV certification (that the patent on a drug "is invalid or that it will not be infringed by the manufacture, use, or sale of the new drug" for which an ANDA is submitted) in an ANDA is deemed as an act of infringement. Although the manufacture, use, or sale of a patented drug is not an act of infringement to the extent it is necessary for the preparation and submission of an ANDA, once it is clear that a party (seeking approval of an ANDA) wants to market a patented drug prior to the expiration of the patent, the patent owner can seek to prevent approval of the ANDA by bringing a patent infringement suit. While it is pending such suit can have the effect of barring ANDA approval for two and a half years. *Bristol-Myers Squibb Co. v. Royce Laboratories Inc.*, 69 F.3d 1130, 36 U.S.P.Q.2d 1641, 1643 (Fed. Cir. 1995).

ᛒ

The FDA determined that "Congress intended that an ANDA applicant need consult only the Orange Book to determine the existence of an applicable patent claiming the listed drug or a use of the listed drug." *Abbott Laboratories v. Zenith Laboratories Inc.*, 36 U.S.P.Q.2d 1801, 1808 (Ill. 1995).

ᛒ

Once a patent infringement suit is filed against the first ANDA applicant, "the [FDA] approval [of the generic drug] shall be made effective upon the expiration of the 30-month period beginning on the date of the receipt [of the required notice to patent owners] or such shorter or longer period as the court may order because either party to the action failed to reasonably cooperate in expediting the action [with certain enumerated exceptions] . . ." *Mova Pharmaceutical Corp. v. Shalala*, 41 U.S.P.Q.2d 2012 (D.C. 1997).

ᛒ

Defendant's ANDA filing constituted a willful infringement since it was not made on a reasonable basis, causing the case to be an "exceptional" one and making it appropriate for an award of attorney's fees to plaintiffs. In filing its paragraph IV certification along with its ANDA, defendant represented that "in the opinion of the applicant and to the best of its knowledge" the famotidine patent was invalid. However, the patent law imposes an affirmative duty of due care on one making such an assertion, and this standard is applied in determining whether one, such as the defendant, had an objective good faith basis for such action. *Yamanouchi Pharmaceutical Co. v. Danbury Pharmacal Inc.*, 48 U.S.P.Q.2d 1741, 1748 (N.Y. 1998).

Animal. *See* **Life Form, Standard Experimental Animal.**

Animal Tests. *See also* **Human Use.**

Although animal tests did not include control animals to which no test compound was administered, larger doses of the test compound successfully inhibited pregnancy is some groups of animals, while sufficiently small doses were partially or totally unsuccessful in preventing pregnancy in other groups of animals. In this kind of testing the appearance of pregnancy in the latter groups of animals corresponds, in effect, to the result achieved by the presence of a control. *Campbell and Babcock v. Wettstein, Anner, Wieland, and Heusler*, 476 F.2d 642, 177 U.S.P.Q. 376, 380 (C.C.P.A. 1973).

ω

Pharmacological testing of animals is a screening procedure for testing new drugs for practical utility. This in vivo testing is but an intermediate link in a screening chain that may eventually lead to the use of a drug as a therapeutic agent in humans. *Cross v. Iizuka*, 753 F.2d 1040, 224 U.S.P.Q. 739 (Fed. Cir. 1985).

ω

Amelioration of the symptoms or even cure of cancer is no longer considered to be "incredible." Nonetheless, decisional law would seem to indicate that the utility in question is sufficiently unusual to justify an Examiner's requiring substantiating evidence. This may be in the form of animal tests that constitute recognized screening procedures with clear relevance to utility in humans. The specification of appellant's parent application sets forth several animal tests on numerous types of specific cancers as well as in vitro studies, both of which are asserted to be predictive with regard to utility in humans. The Examiner has not challenged the evidence presented in a single, relevant, material respect. There is only the blanket statement of lack of "patentable utility" per se. In fact, the only specific comments the Examiner has directed toward appellant's evidence are with regard to the breadth of the types of tumor against which the claimed compounds have been shown to be active. The appealed claims are drawn to compounds and not to a method of treatment. Generally speaking, utility in treating a single disease is an adequate basis for the patentability of a pharmaceutical compound under 35 U.S.C. §101. *Ex parte Krepelka*, 231 U.S.P.Q. 746 (B.P.A.I. 1986).

Annul.

In the interest of protecting the public from the monopoly of a patent procured by fraud, such patent should be annulled, and the only means by which this can be conclusively accomplished is in a direct proceeding brought by the government. *United States v. SafT-Boom Corp.*, 431 F.2d 737, 167 U.S.P.Q. 195 (8th Cir. 1970).

Annulment. *See* Revocation.

Another. *See also* Applicant's Own Work, Entity.

The significant words in 35 U.S.C. §102(a) are "known and used by others...before the invention thereof by the applicant," and the parallel words in 35 U.S.C. §102(e) are "application for patent by another...before the invention thereof by the applicant" (emphasis court's). The real issue is whether all the evidence, including the references, truly shows knowledge by another prior to the time appellants made their invention or whether it shows the contrary. *In re Land and Rogers*, 368 F.2d 866, 151 U.S.P.Q. 621, 632 (C.C.P.A. 1966).

ω

Even though an application and a patent have been conceived by different inventive entities, the 35 U.S.C. §102(e) exclusion for a patent granted to "another" is not necessarily satisfied when they share one or more persons as joint inventors. *Applied Materials Inc. v. Gemini Research Corp.*, 835 F.2d 279, 15 U.S.P.Q.2d 1816, 1818 (Fed. Cir. 1988).

ᚱ

In determining whether prior work is in fact by "another," the theory of the inventorship entity must be applied. The sole work of one person is usable against the joint work of that person with another. Similarly, the joint work of two or more persons is usable against the sole work of either and against the joint work of any other inventorship entity. *De Graffenried v. U.S.*, 20 Cl. Ct. 458, 16 U.S.P.Q.2d 1321, 1328 (Cl. Ct. 1990).

ᚱ

An inventive entity of a patent with three inventors is "another" within the meaning of 35 U.S.C. §102(e) vis-a-vis an inventive entity comprised of two inventors, one of which is common to both inventive entities. The patent is thus available as prior art under 35 U.S.C. §102(e), (f) and (g) for purposes of 35 U.S.C. §103. *Ex parte DesOrneaux*, 25 U.S.P.Q.2d 2040, 2043 (B.P.A.I. 1992).

Antecedent Basis. *See also* Support.

A term in a claim lacks an antecedent, in violation of proper practice, when the term does not appear in the specification. *In re Menough*, 324 F.2d 1011, 139 U.S.P.Q. 278 (C.C.P.A. 1963).

ᚱ

Lack of antecedent basis in a claim could render it invalid under 35 U.S.C. §112, second paragraph, and correction of such a defect by reissue should not have to depend on difference in scope of the claim. Inasmuch as 35 U.S.C. §251 is a remedial provision, which should be liberally construed, a patentee should be allowed to correct an error or ambiguity in a claim without having to rely on implication or litigation. Lack of antecedent basis in a claim is a proper ground for reissue under 35 U.S.C. §251. *In re Altenpohl*, 500 F.2d 1151, 183 U.S.P.Q. 38, 43 (C.C.P.A. 1974).

Antecedent Support. *See also* Support.

While the particular words quoted may not appear as such in the specification, the meaning thereof by other words is clearly present and constitutes adequate antecedent basis for the words in fact used. *Ex parte Siegmund and Cole*, 156 U.S.P.Q. 477 (PTO Bd. App. 1967).

ᚱ

The claimed invention does not have to be described in ipsis verbis in order to satisfy the description requirement of 35 U.S.C. §112. The burden of showing that the claimed invention is not described in the specification rests on the PTO in the first instance, and it is up to the PTO to give reasons why a description not in ipsis verbis is insufficient. *In re Wertheim*, 541 F.2d 257, 191 U.S.P.Q. 90 (C.C.P.A. 1976).

ᚱ

The expressions "free of bleaching agent comprising an alkaline earth metal being capable of releasing hypochlorite or hypobromite in an aqueous solution" and "a non-reducing saccharide" find no support in the specification. They thus do not comply with the description requirement of the first paragraph of 35 U.S.C. §112. The fact that no compounds of this nature are taught to be present in the examples of this case is an insufficient basis for the limitations introduced into the claims when (1) quite evidently the presence of a bleaching agent is not intended to be excluded from the claim composition and, in fact, is intended to be present as an ingredient, and (2) nowhere is it indicated that only non-reducing sugars are intended to be within the scope of saccharides as broadly disclosed. That sucrose is a nonreducing sugar does not entitle appellant to claim a genus of which sucrose is a member. *Ex parte Pearson,* 230 U.S.P.Q. 711 (B.P.A.I. 1985).

Antedating a Reference. *See also* 37 C.F.R. §1.131.

Applicants' own British application (from which priority rights were claimed) was published more than a year prior to the filing of a continuation-in-part (cip) application. With regard to subject matter added to cip, the published British application was a statutory bar, which could not be antedated. *In re Ruscetta and Jenny,* 255 F.2d 687, 118 U.S.P.Q. 101, 104 (C.C.P.A. 1958).

ɷ

While a species may be patentably distinct from a genus, when an earlier disclosed species is broadly the same invention as the genus, the requirement of 35 U.S.C. §119 that only "the same invention" (in the later application as is shown in the earlier) will obtain the benefit of the earlier filing date is satisfied for the purpose of overcoming references. *In re Ziegler, Breil, Holzkamp, and Martin,* 347 F.2d 642, 146 U.S.P.Q. 76, 82 (C.C.P.A. 1966).

ɷ

An antedating affidavit establishing conception and reduction to practice commensurate in scope with a reference disclosure and at a date prior to the effective date of the reference is adequate to overcome the reference as prior art. *In re Stryker,* 435 F.2d 1340, 168 U.S.P.Q. 372 (C.C.P.A. 1971).

ɷ

An anticipatory disclosure, not a statutory bar, may be removed as a reference against a generic claim by a Rule 131 affidavit showing prior reduction to practice of as much of the claimed invention as the reference shows. When that species of the generic invention that has been completed prior to the effective date of the reference would make obvious to one of ordinary skill in the art the species disclosed in the reference, the reference may be said to have been "indirectly antedated." All that is required is to establish that facts set out in an affidavit are such as "would persuade one of ordinary skill in the art to a reasonable certainty that the applicant possessed so much of the invention as to encompass the reference disclosure." *In re Schaub, Bernady, and Weiss,* 537 F.2d 509, 190 U.S.P.Q. 324 (C.C.P.A. 1976).

ɷ

The function of the description requirement is to ensure that the inventor had possession (as of the filing date of the application relied on) of the specific subject matter later claimed by him; how the specification accomplishes this is not material. It is not necessary that the application describe the claim limitations exactly, but only so clearly that persons of ordinary skill in the art will recognize from the disclosure that appellants invented processes including those limitations. *In re Wertheim,* 541 F.2d 257, 191 U.S.P.Q. 90 (C.C.P.A. 1976).

ᙡ

An application was prepared in the Netherlands and sent to a related party in interest in the United States, where it was received on July 15, 1974. A corresponding Netherlands patent application was filed on October 9, 1974. The U.S. application was filed within a year (August 6, 1975) under the International Convention, claiming the benefit of the Netherlands filing date under 35 U.S.C. §119. Confronted with rejections of claims based on a publication received by the PTO on October 7, 1974 (two days prior to the priority date), an attempt was made to antedate, and thus remove, the reference as prior art by filing declarations under 37 C.F.R. §1.131 (Rule 131). As no actual reduction to practice of the invention and no constructive reduction to practice prior to the date of the reference was shown, it was essential under Rule 131(b) to show conception in this country (prior to the reference) coupled with "due diligence from said date to . . . the filing of the application." Even though the PTO accepted July 15, 1974, the date of receipt in the United States of the draft application, as a conception date, the noted due diligence was still required even though there was only a two-day period between the effective date of the reference and the filing date. *In re Mulder and Wulms,* 716 F.2d 1542, 219 U.S.P.Q. 189 (Fed. Cir. 1983).

ᙡ

When (a) the effective date of a reference (not a statutory bar) is between an applicant's foreign priority date and his actual filing date in the United States, (b) the priority-based application adequately discloses all subject matter for which the reference is relied upon, and (c) the application filed in the United States has an expanded disclosure and commensurate claims, applicant should divide his generic claim into two claims: (a) one limited to the subject matter supported by the priority-based application (for which reliance on the priority application cannot be denied) and (b) the other directed to the rest of the subject matter supported by the Convention application in the United States. *In re Gosteli,* 872 F.2d 1008, 10 U.S.P.Q.2d 1614, 1616 (Fed. Cir. 1989).

ᙡ

An affidavit may not be used in a reexamination proceeding to swear behind a United States patent claiming the same invention. MPEP 706.02(b)(4) (6th ed. 1997). *Slip Track Systems Inc. v. Metal Lite Inc.,* 48 U.S.P.Q.2d 1055, 1056 (Fed. Cir. 1998).

Antibody.

Although the technique underlying hybridoma technology is well recognized, the results obtained by its use are clearly unpredictable. Hybridoma technology is an empirical art in which the routineer is unable to foresee what particular antibodies will be produced and which specific surface antigens will be recognized by them. Only by actually carrying out the requisite steps can the nature of the monoclonal antibodies be determined and ascertained; no "expected" results can thus be said to be present. Hence, it may be "obvious to try" the Kohler-Milstein technique as applied to malignant renal cells, but such is not the standard under which obviousness under 35 U.S.C. §103 must be established. *Ex parte Old*, 229 U.S.P.Q. 196 (B.P.A.I. 1985).

ᛒ

The basis of the district court's holding that the claims are indefinite is that "they do not disclose how infringement may be avoided because antibody affinity cannot be estimated with any consistency." Even if the district court's finding and support of this holding—that "there is no standard set of experimental conditions which are used to estimate affinities"—is accurate, under the law pertaining to indefiniteness—"if the claims, read in the light of specification, reasonably apprise those skilled in the art both of the utilization and scope of the invention, and if the language is as precise as the subject matter permits, the courts can demand no more"—the claims clearly are definite. The evidence of record indisputably shows that calculating affinity was known in the art at the time of filing, and notwithstanding the fact that those calculations are not precise, or "standard," the claims, read in the light of the specification, reasonably apprise those skilled in the art and are as precise as the subject matter permits. *Hybritech Inc. v. Monoclonal Antibodies, Inc.*, 802 F.2d 1367, 231 U.S.P.Q. 81 (Fed. Cir. 1986).

Anticipation. *See also* Accidental, 37 C.F.R. §1.108, Duplication, Enabling Disclosure, Free, Generic Claim, Inherency, Natural Product, Novelty, Orientation During Operation, Prior Art, Prior Invention, Pure, Unrecognized, 35 U.S.C. §101, 35 U.S.C. §102.

Prior accidental production of the same thing, where character and function are not recognized, does not anticipate. *Ralph W. McKee and Harold Perpall v. Graton & Knight Co.*, 87 F.2d 262, 32 U.S.P.Q. 89, 91 (4th Cir. 1937).

ᛒ

Everyone is charged with knowledge of prior patents, and the failure of a patentee to properly exploit his invention does not furnish grounds for the subsequent granting of another patent on substantially the same invention. *In re Coey and Petersen*, 190 F.2d 347, 90 U.S.P.Q. 216 (C.C.P.A. 1951).

ᛒ

A design patent can anticipate a claim in a utility application. *In re Pio*, 217 F.2d 956, 104 U.S.P.Q. 177 (C.C.P.A. 1954).

ᛒ

Experimental use and abandoned experiments are not available as evidence of anticipation. *Lyon v. Bausch & Lomb Optical Co.*, 224 F.2d 530, 106 U.S.P.Q. 1 (2d Cir. 1955).

ᛒ

A generic claim cannot be allowed when prior art discloses a species falling within the claimed genus; whatever would infringe if subsequent will anticipate if prior. *In re Slayter*, 276 F.2d 408, 125 U.S.P.Q. 345 (C.C.P.A. 1960).

ᛒ

A foreign patent cannot be used to anticipate an application in the United States by another until the specification disclosing the invention is available to the public. *Ex parte Gruschwitz and Fritz,* 138 U.S.P.Q. 505 (PTO Bd. App. 1961).

ᴡ

This doctrine infers a lack of novelty in a product under 35 U.S.C. §101 when a comparable process for making a product is found to exist in prior art. In this case the claimed product (if produced by the reference process) was produced in such minuscule amounts and under such conditions that its presence was undetectable. Under the circumstances, the reference is not an anticipation. *In re Seaborg,* 328 F.2d 996, 140 U.S.P.Q. 662 (C.C.P.A. 1964).

ᴡ

It is irrelevant that appellant (a party to an interference) never referred to or appreciated the support material to be *eta*-alumina or to contain *eta*-alumina *by that name.* However, it is fatal to appellant's case that he did not recognize (until after his interference opponent's filing date) that his "ammonia-aged" catalyst *"contained any different form of alumina at all!"* (Emphasis in original.) The count calls for a particular form of alumina. Appellant's failure to recognize that he had produced a new form, regardless of what he called it, is indicative that he never conceived the invention prior to his opponent's filing date. *Heard v. Burton, Kaufman, Lefrancois, and Riblett,* 333 F.2d 239, 142 U.S.P.Q. 97, 100 (C.C.P.A. 1964). See *Sulkowski v. Houlihan,* 179 U.S.P.Q. 685, 686 (PTO Bd. Pat. Int. 1973).

ᴡ

There is no conception or reduction to practice of a new form of an otherwise old composition of matter where there has been no recognition or appreciation of the existence of the new form. *Silvestri and Johnson v. Grant and Alburn,* 496 F.2d 593, 181 U.S.P.Q. 706, 708 (C.C.P.A. 1974).

ᴡ

A rejection under 35 U.S.C. §102 cannot be overcome by showing unexpected results or teaching away in the art; these are relevant only to an obviousness rejection. *In re Malagari,* 499 F.2d 1297, 182 U.S.P.Q. 549 (C.C.P.A. 1974).

ᴡ

A printed publication can constitute an anticipation of a claimed compound even though it fails to disclose how to make or use the compound and it indicates that the compound is "without effect" or "without activity", if (subsequent to the effective date of the reference and prior to the effective date of an application claiming the compound) a further reference teaches how the compound may be made. *In re Samour,* 571 F.2d 559, 197 U.S.P.Q. 1, 3, 4 (C.C.P.A. 1978).

ᴡ

An accidental or unwitting duplication of an invention cannot constitute anticipation. *In re Felton,* 484 F.2d 495, 179 U.S.P.Q. 295 (C.C.P.A. 1973); *In re Marshall,* 578 F.2d 301, 198 U.S.P.Q. 344 (C.C.P.A. 1978).

ᴡ

A party asserting that a patent claim is anticipated under 35 U.S.C. §102 must demonstrate, among other things, identity of invention. Identity of invention is a question of fact, and one who seeks such a finding must show that each element of the claim in issue is found, either expressly described or under principles of inherency, in a single prior-art reference, or that the claimed invention was previously known or embodied in a single prior-art device or practice. Preliminary to this determination is construction of the claims to determine their meaning in light of the specification and prosecution history, which construction is a matter of law for the court. *Kalman v. Kimberly-Clark Corp.*, 713 F.2d 760, 218 U.S.P.Q. 781, 789 (Fed. Cir. 1983).

ᚥ

Though anticipation is the epitome of obviousness, they are separate and distinct concepts. *Jones v. Hardy,* 727 F.2d 1524, 220 U.S.P.Q. 1021, 1025 (Fed. Cir. 1984).

ᚥ

A Gebrauchsmuster (GM) is a limited type of West German patent. Such a patent only "anticipates" a U.S. patent to the extent of the claims of the GM. Thus, if the claims of the GM do not disclose the invention of the American patent but the drawing or specification of the GM do disclose the invention, the American patent is not anticipated by the GM. The specifications and drawings in the GM can only be considered under 35 U.S.C. §102(b) to the extent that they help to explain the claims of the GM. *Max Daetwyler Corp. v. Input Graphics, Inc.,* 583 F. Supp. 446, 222 U.S.P.Q. 150 (Pa. 1984).

ᚥ

When claim interpretation is required to resolve an issue of anticipation, it is a question of law. *Loctite Corp. v. Ultraseal Ltd.,* 781 F.2d 861, 228 U.S.P.Q. 90 (Fed. Cir. 1985).

ᚥ

A reference that discloses a process does not have to recognize a particular inherent property of any aspect of that process to negate validity of a claim to the process. *Verdegaal Brothers Inc. v. Union Oil Company of California,* 814 F.2d 628, 2 U.S.P.Q.2d 1051 (Fed. Cir. 1987).

ᚥ

Under the current statute the test for anticipation is: "that which would literally infringe if later in time anticipates if earlier than the date of invention." Since the 1952 Act "anticipation" is a restricted term of art in patent law meaning that the claimed invention lacks novelty. *Lewmar Marine Inc. v. Barient Inc.,* 827 F.2d 744, 3 U.S.P.Q.2d 1766 (Fed. Cir. 1987).

ᚥ

To find anticipation of claims, the prior-art embodiments must possess the properties expressly recited in the claims. Property limitations can serve to distinguish claimed subject matter from other products. Identity of invention is a question of fact, and a challenger must show that each element of a claim is found in a prior patent or publication, either expressly or under principles of inherency. To establish anticipation, however, it is not necessary to prove that prior artisans were aware that their products possessed the recited properties. *E.I. du Pont de Nemours & Co. v. Phillips Petroleum Co.*, 849 F.2d 1430, 7 U.S.P.Q.2d 1129 (Fed. Cir. 1988).

ᛠ

A jury may decide the questions of anticipation and obviousness, either as separate special verdicts or en route to a verdict on the question of validity, which may also be decided by the jury. No warrant appears for distinguishing the submission of legal questions to a jury in patent cases from such submissions routinely made in other types of cases. So long as the Seventh Amendment stands, the right to a jury trial should not be rationed, nor should particular issues in particular types of cases be treated differently from similar issues in other types of cases. When the judgment arises from a jury verdict, the reviewing court applies the reasonable jury/substantial evidence standard, a standard that gives greater deference to the judgment simply because appellate review is more limited, compared with review of a trial judge's decision. The appellate court's function is exhausted when the evidentiary basis of the jury's verdict becomes apparent, it being immaterial that the court might draw a contrary inference or feel that another conclusion is more reasonable. *Richardson v. Suzuki Motor Co., Ltd.*, 868 F.2d 1226, 9 U.S.P.Q.2d 1913, 1919 (Fed. Cir. 1989).

ᛠ

A party claiming anticipation under 35 U.S.C. §102 because of prior use is put to "the strictest of proofs." Because of the unsatisfactory character of mere oral testimony to prove an anticipation, a party attempting to establish an anticipation has the burden of doing so by "clear and satisfactory evidence." *Trend Products Co. v. Metro Industries, Inc.*, 10 U.S.P.Q.2d 1531, 1538 (Cal. 1989).

ᛠ

When a claimed invention is not identically disclosed in a reference, and instead requires picking and choosing among a number of different options disclosed by the reference, then the reference does not anticipate. *Mendenhall v. Astec Industries, Inc.*, 13 U.S.P.Q.2d 1913, 1928 (Tenn. 1988), *aff'd*, 13 U.S.P.Q.2d 1956 (Fed. Cir. 1989).

ᛠ

A party claiming anticipation under 35 U.S.C. §102(g) must show by clear and convincing evidence prior invention and that the invention was not abandoned, suppressed, or concealed. The standard necessarily follows from the rule that the burden of proving patent invalidity is at all times on the party challenging the patent, and never shifts. *Oak Industries, Inc. v. Zenith Electronics Corp.*, 726 F. Supp. 1525, 14 U.S.P.Q.2d 1417, 1420 (Ill. 1989).

ᛠ

For a prior-art reference to anticipate, every element of the claimed invention must be identically shown in a single reference. These elements must be arranged as in the claim under review, but this is not an "ipsissimis verbis" test. Anticipation is a fact question subject to review under the clearly erroneous standard. Even though the disclosed and prior-art structures are not identical, a claim may nonetheless be anticipated. While a means-plus-function limitation may appear to include all means capable of achieving the desired function, the statute requires that it be "construed to cover the corresponding structure, material, or acts described in the specification and equivalents thereof." *In re Bond,* 910 F.2d 831, 15 U.S.P.Q.2d 1566, 1567, 1568 (Fed. Cir. 1990).

ᅇ

Although references cannot be combined for purposes of anticipation, additional references may be used to interpret an allegedly anticipating reference and shed light on what it would have meant to those skilled in the art at the time of the invention. *Studiengesellschaft Kohle, m.b.H. v. Dart Indus., Inc.,* 726 F.2d 724, 726-27, 220 U.S.P.Q. 841, 842 (Fed. Cir. 1984). Anticipation by inherency requires that "the missing descriptive matter is necessarily present in the thing described in the reference, and that it would be so recognized by persons of ordinary skill." *Continental Can Co. USA Inc. v. Monsanto Co.,* 948 F.2d 1264, 1268, 20 U.S.P.Q.2d 1746, 1749 (Fed. Cir. 1991).

ᅇ

Anticipation can occur when a claimed limitation is "inherent" or otherwise implicit in the relevant reference. *Standard Havens Products Inc. v. Gencor Industries Inc.,* 953 F.2d 1360, 21 U.S.P.Q.2d 1321, 1328 (Fed. Cir. 1991).

ᅇ

A party asserting that a patent claim is anticipated under 35 U.S.C. §102 "must demonstrate...identity of invention." *Minnesota Mining and Manufacturing Co. v. Johnson & Johnson Orthopaedics Inc.,* 976 F.2d 1558, 24 U.S.P.Q.2d 1321, 1326 (Fed. Cir. 1992).

ᅇ

Evidence may be introduced to overcome a rejection under 35 U.S.C. §102, e.g., evidence demonstrating that an applied reference is nonenabling, to show that a recited characteristic is not inherent in a prior art article, or to show that an applied reference is not actually valid *prior* art under 35 U.S.C. §102. *Ex parte Lee,* 31 U.S.P.Q.2d 1105, 1110 *dissent* n.1 (B.P.A.I. 1993).

ᅇ

Extrinsic evidence may be considered to explain, but not expand on, the meaning of an anticipatory reference. The Court may look to extrinsic evidence to learn how the person of ordinary skill would interpret an anticipatory reference. Extrinsic evidence may be used "where the common knowledge of technologists is not recorded in the reference; that is, where technological facts are known to those in the field of the invention, albeit not known to judges." *Ciba-Geigy Corp. v. Alza Corp.,* 864 F.Supp. 429, 33 U.S.P.Q.2d 1018, 1023 (N.J. 1994).

ᅇ

Anticipation requires identity of invention. The claimed invention, as described in appropriately construed claims, must be the same as that of the reference in order to anticipate. *Glaverbel Société Anonyme v. Northlake Marketing & Supply Inc.,* 45 F.3d 1550, 33 U.S.P.Q.2d 1496, 1498 (Fed. Cir. 1995).

ᅇ

A reference anticipates a claim if it discloses the claimed invention "such that a skilled artisan could take its teachings in *combination with his own knowledge of the* particular art and be in possession of the invention." *In re Graves*, 69 F.3d 1147, 36 U.S.P.Q.2d 1697, 1701 (Fed. Cir. 1995).

ᴡ

"[A]ny degree of physical difference, however slight, invalidates claims of anticipation". *Ultradent Products Inc. v. Life-Like Cosmetics Inc.*, 39 U.S.P.Q.2d 1969, 1980 (Utah 1996).

ᴡ

See *In re Graves*, 69 F.3d 1147, 1152, 36 U.S.P.Q.2d 1697, 1701 (Fed. Cir. 1995) (prior art reference disclosing a system for testing the integrity of electrical interconnections that did not specifically disclose simultaneous monitoring of output points still anticipated claimed invention if simultaneous monitoring is within the knowledge of a skilled artisan); *In re Donohue*, 766 F.2d 531, 533, 226 U.S.P.Q. 619, 621 (Fed. Cir. 1985) (prior art anticipates a claim if it discloses the claimed invention such that a skilled artisan could take its teachings and his own knowledge to possess the claimed invention). *Fenton Golf Trust v. Cobra Golf Inc.*, 48 U.S.P.Q.2d 1198, 1201 (Ill. 1998).

Antigen.

Although the technique underlying hybridoma technology is well recognized, the results obtained by its use are clearly unpredictable. Hybridoma technology is an empirical art in which the routineer is unable to foresee what particular antibodies will be produced and which specific surface antigens will be recognized by them. Only by actually carrying out the requisite steps can the nature of the monoclonal antibodies be determined and ascertained; no "expected" results can thus be said to be present. Hence, it may be "obvious to try" the Kohler-Milstein technique as applied to malignant renal cells, but such is not the standard under which obviousness under 35 U.S.C. §103 must be established. *Ex parte Old*, 229 U.S.P.Q. 196 (B.P.A.I. 1985).

Antitrust. *See also* Accumulation, Dividing Markets, Division of Markets, Grant Backs, Misuse, Price Fixing, Restraint of Trade, Sherman Act.

An agreement among competitors not to license others unless both agree is not a per se violation of the Sherman Act, 15 U.S.C. §1. There is no evidence of any illegal agreement to fix prices, allocate markets, or engage in predatory pricing. The mere fact that two competitors enter into a contractual arrangement to share (to the exclusion of the others) the rights derived from a patent as well as expenses connected thereto is insufficient to trigger per se liability. *Polysius Corp. v. Fuller Co.*, 709 F. Supp. 560, 10 U.S.P.Q.2d 1417 (Pa. 1989).

ᴡ

When a patent owner uses his patent rights not only as a shield to protect his invention, but as a sword to eviscerate competition unfairly, that owner may be found to have abused the grant and may become liable for antitrust violations when sufficient power in the relevant market is present. Therefore, patent owners may incur antitrust liability for enforcement of a patent known to be obtained through fraud or known to be invalid, where license of a patent compels the purchase of unpatented goods, or where there is an overall scheme to use the patent to violate antitrust laws. The danger of disturbing the complementary balance struck by Congress is great when a court is asked to preliminarily enjoin conduct affecting patent and antitrust rights. A preliminary injunction entered without a sufficient factual basis and findings, though intended to maintain the status quo, can offend the public policies embodied in both the patent and antitrust laws. *Atari Games Corp. v. Nintendo of America Inc.*, 897 F.2d 1572, 14 U.S.P.Q.2d 1034, 1037 (Fed. Cir. 1990).

ϖ

As long as a patent holder uses his patents in a lawful manner, he will not violate the antitrust laws, and a court's instruction to a jury to that effect is neither improper nor prejudicial. *Lightwave Technologies Inc. v. Corning Glass Works*, 19 U.S.P.Q.2d 1838, 1844 (N.Y. 1991).

ϖ

"[T]he fact that [an antitrust counterclaim for damages] might have been asserted . . . in a prior suit . . . does not mean that the failure to do so renders the prior judgment res judicata as respects it." A claim that patent infringement litigation violated an antitrust statute is a permissive, not a mandatory, counterclaim in a patent infringement case, and is not barred in a subsequent suit by failure to raise it in the infringement suit. "In a case involving a fraudulently obtained patent, that which immunized the predatory behavior from antitrust liability (the patent) is, in effect, a nullity because of the underlying fraud." *Hydranautics v. FilmTec Corp.*, 70 F.3d 533, 36 U.S.P.Q.2d 1773, 1775, 1777 (9th Cir. 1995).

ϖ

Courts have consistently recognized an implied and limited "patent" exception to the antitrust laws. *BEAL Corp. Liquidating Trust v. Valleylab Inc.*, 40 U.S.P.Q.2d 1072, 1076 (Colo. 1996).

ϖ

A counterclain for treble damages under the antitrust laws is permissive in nature, so that failure by a defendant to plead it in a prior patent suit does not bar a subsequent independent suit by him under the antitrust laws. *Longwood Manufacturing Corp. v. Wheelabrator Clean Water Systems Inc.*, 40 U.S.P.Q.2d 1638, 1639 (Mc. 1996).

ϖ

"[T]here is an obvious tension between the patent laws and the antitrust laws" since "[o]ne body of law protects monploy power while the other seeks to proscribe it." *DiscoVision Associates v. Disc Manufacturing Inc.*, 42 U.S.P.Q.2d 1749, 1756 (Del. 1997)

ϖ

A patentee who brings an infringement suit may be subject to antitrust liability for the anti-competitive effects of that suit if the alleged infringer (the antitrust plaintiff) proves (1) that the asserted patent was obtained through knowing and willful fraud within the meaning of *Walker Process Equipment, Inc. v. Food Machinery & Chemical Corp.*, 382 U.S. 172, 177, 147 U.S.P.Q.2d 404, 407 (1965), or (2) that the infringement suit was "a mere sham to cover what is actually nothing more than an attempt to interfere directly with the business relationships of a competitor." *Nobelpharma AB v. Implant Innovations Inc.*, 129 F.3d 1463, 44 U.S.P.Q.2d 1705, 1711 (Fed. Cir. 1997).

ϖ

Antitrust claims are compulsory counterclaims under Rule (FRCP) 13(a) if the antitrust claim arises out of the same transaction or occurrence as the original claim. Whether conduct in procuring or enforcing a patent is sufficient to strip a patentee of its immunity from the antitrust laws is to be decided as a question of Federal Circuit law. This conclusion applies equally to all antitrust claims premised on the bringing of a patent infringement suit. *Nobelpharma AB v. Implant Innovations Inc.*, 141 F.3d 1059, 46 U.S.P.Q.2d 1097, 1104 (Fed. Cir. 1998).

ϖ

Under the *Noerr-Pennington* doctrine, "[t]hose who petition government for redress are generally immune from antitrust liability." Given this broad immunity, a litigant may only proceed with antitrust counterclaims which are based upon the filing of a lawsuit if it "pierces" the presumption that a patent infringement suit is brought in good faith. *Mitek Surgical Products Inc. v. Arthrex Inc.*, 49 U.S.P.Q.2d 1275, 1282 (Utah 1998).

Any Other.

Alternative expressions do not necessarily render the boundaries of a claimed invention undeterminable. Expressions, such as "made entirely or in part of" (which is to say "made at least partially of"), "one or several pieces" (the same as "at least one piece"), and "iron, steel or any other magnetic material," accurately determine the boundaries of protection involved. *In re Gaubert,* 524 F.2d 1222, 187 U.S.P.Q. 664, 667, 668 (C.C.P.A. 1975).

A.P.A. *See* Administrative Procedure Act.

Apostille.

On October 15, 1981, the Hague Convention Abolishing the Requirement of Legalization for Foreign Public Documents entered into force between the United States and 28 foreign countries that are parties to the Convention. The Convention applies to any document submitted to the U.S. Patent and Trademark Office for filing or recording, which is sworn to or acknowledged by a notary public in any one of the member countries. The Convention abolishes the certification of the authority of the notary public in a member country by a diplomatic or consular officer of the United States and substitutes certification by a special certification, or apostille, executed by an officer of the member country. Accordingly, the PTO will accept for filing or recording a document sworn to or acknowledged before a notary public in a member country if the document bears, or has appended to it, an apostille certifying the notary's authority. The requirement for a diplomatic or consular certificate, specified in 37 C.F.R. §1.66 and note 1 of 37 C.F.R. §3.45, will not apply to a document sworn to or acknowledged before a notary public in a member country if an apostille is used. 1013 O.G. 3, Dec. 1, 1981 (Commissioner's Notice, Nov. 5, 1981).

Apparatus. *See also* Aggregation, Device, Machine, Manufacture, Old Combination, Product, Reduction in Elements.

Claims to a method were held to be patentably indistinct from claims to apparatus for performing the method. *In re Abernathy,* 118 F.2d 358, 49 U.S.P.Q. 82 (C.C.P.A. 1941).

ϖ

In order to be patentable, claims drawn to structure (rather than to method) must distinguish from the prior art by structural limitations. *In re Stattmann,* 146 F.2d 290, 64 U.S.P.Q. 245, 247 (C.C.P.A. 1944).

ʊ

Apparatus claims must distinguish from applied prior art by structural limitations, and cannot be allowed because of functions not necessarily produced by the recited apparatus. *In re Gartner and Roeber,* 223 F.2d 502, 106 U.S.P.Q. 273, 275 (C.C.P.A. 1955).

ʊ

The law does not require that a machine, to be patentable must act on physical substances. *In re Prater and Wei,* 415 F.2d 1378, 159 U.S.P.Q. 583, 592 (C.C.P.A. 1968).

ʊ

A party cannot escape infringement by producing all essential parts of a patented machine in the United States and shipping them in a form which contemplates minor final assembly in a foreign market. *The Laitram Corporation v. Deepsouth Packing Co., Inc.,* 443 F.2d 936, 170 U.S.P.Q. 196, 197 (5th Cir. 1971).

ʊ

Apparatus claims cover what a device is, not what a device does. An invention need not operate differently from the prior art to be patentable, but need only be unobviously different. *Hewlett-Packard Co. v. Bausch & Lomb Inc.,* 909 F.2d 1464, 15 U.S.P.Q.2d 1525, 1528 (Fed. Cir. 1990).

Appeal. *See also* 37 C.F.R. §1.192(c)(5), Reasons for Appeal.

When the Board of Appeals reverses all grounds of rejection with regard to a particular claim, that claim will not be considered by the CCPA on appeal to that court on other issues. *In re Launder and Hosmer,* 222 F.2d 371, 105 U.S.P.Q. 446, 447 (C.C.P.A. 1955).

ʊ

The solicitor's reliance on an allegedly standard textbook on chemistry (not previously of record) as further support for the Patent Office position illustrates a growing tendency on the part of appellants and the Patent Office alike to impair the clear and specific language of 35 U.S.C. §144, which requires an appeal to be determined "on the evidence produced before the Patent Office." *In re Cofer,* 354 F.2d 664, 148 U.S.P.Q. 268, 272 (C.C.P.A. 1966).

ʊ

The PTO cannot appeal from a decision of the BPAI reversing an Examiner's ground of rejection. *Holmes, Faber, Boykin, and Francis v. Kelley, Hornberger, and Strief,* 586 F.2d 234, 199 U.S.P.Q. 778 (C.C.P.A. 1978).

ʊ

In view of the PTO's failure to challenge the sufficiency of the appellants' rebuttal evidence prior to appeal (when the appellants could no longer offer evidence), the Board's decision was vacated and the case remanded to afford the appellants the opportunity to submit objective evidence of unexpected results. *In re De Blauwe*, 736 F.2d 699, 222 U.S.P.Q. 191 (Fed. Cir. 1984).

ᵥ

The function of an appeal from a district court's findings is to show that those findings are clearly erroneous or, if correct, cannot support the district court's legal conclusion. *Fromson v. Western Litho Plate Supply Co.*, 853 F.2d 1568, 7 U.S.P.Q.2d 1606 (Fed. Cir. 1988).

ᵥ

The public responsibility of the PTO requires attentive performance of all aspects of the patent examination function. The PTO is charged with the duty of examining the claims contained in a patent application, including review by the BPAI when an appeal is taken under 35 U.S.C. §134. It is not only unfair to the applicant, it is also inefficient to decline to review claims that are properly appealed and reasonably argued before the Board. *In re Beaver*, 893 F.2d 329, 13 U.S.P.Q.2d 1409, 1411 (Fed. Cir. 1989).

ᵥ

An appellate court lacks jurisdiction to consider an issue where the notice of appeal did not mention any intention to appeal from the relevant order. An appellate court has before it only that part of the judgment designated in the notice of appeal and, even under a liberal construction, cannot review an issue that is plainly absent from the notice. Where the appellant specifies a judgment or a part thereof, an appellate court has no jurisdiction to review other judgments or issues that are not expressly referred to and that are not impliedly intended for appeal. *Durango Associates Inc. v. Reflange Inc.*, 912 F.2d 1423, 15 U.S.P.Q.2d 1910, 1912 (Fed. Cir. 1990).

ᵥ

The statute governing reexamination provides that a patent owner may appeal an adverse reexamination finding to the CAFC. 35 U.S.C. §306. However, the district court has no power to review a PTO finding favorable to the patent owner at the behest of a patent challenger. *E.I. du Pont de Nemours & Co. V. Cetus Corp.*, 19 U.S.P.Q.2d 1174, 1181 (Cal. 1990).

ᵥ

Given the difficulty of showing reversible error in discretionary rulings, counsel should be particularly cautious about filing an appeal that challenges them. There are two distinct (though, in practice, often related) senses in which an appeal may be frivolous. First, where an appeal is taken in a case where "the judgment by the tribunal below was so plainly correct and the legal authority contrary to appellant's position so clear that there really is no appealable issue," the appeal is held to be "frivolous as filed." "Second, even in cases in which genuinely appealable issues may exist, so that the taking of an appeal is not frivolous, the appellant's misconduct in arguing the appeal may be such as to justify holding the appeal to be 'frivolous as argued.'" Sanctionable conduct has been held to include (though is by no means limited to) seeking to relitigate issues already finally adjudicated, failing to explain how the trial court erred or to present clear and cogent arguments for reversal, rearguing frivolous positions for which sanctions had already been imposed in the trial forum, failing to cite authority and ignoring opponent's cited authority, citing irrelevant or inapplicable authority, distorting cited authority by omitting language from quotations, making irrelevant and illogical arguments, and misrepresenting facts or law to the court. *State Industries Inc. v. Mor-Flo Industries Inc.*, 20 U.S.P.Q.2d 1738, 1742, 1743 (Fed. Cir. 1991).

ʊ

Applicants for patents, or applicants for renewal of patents, may appeal a decision of the BPAI in one of two ways. They may appeal on the record to the CAFC, or they may appeal de novo to the U.S. District Court for the District of Columbia. If an applicant chooses the latter avenue of appeal, "[a]ll the expenses of the proceedings shall be paid by the applicant." These expenses must be paid—win, lose, or draw. An applicant is, however, only responsible for those expenses that are reasonable. *Sandvik Aktiebolag v. Samuels*, 20 U.S.P.Q.2d 1879 (D.C. 1991).

Appellate Court.

An appellate court will consider an issue not presented below only if: (i) the issue involves a pure question of law and refusal to consider it would result in a miscarriage of justice; (ii) the proper resolution is beyond any doubt, (iii) the appellant had no opportunity to raise the objection at the district court level; (iv) the issue presents "significant questions of general impact or of great public concern[;]" or (v) the interest of substantial justice is at stake. *L.E.A. Dynatech Inc v. Allina*, 49 F.3d 1527, 33 U.S.P.Q.2d 1839, 1843 (Fed. Cir. 1995).

Appellee

Appellees do not select the issues to be appealed. Appellees are at a procedural disadvantage in appeals because they can neither file reply briefs nor choose when to appeal. Avoidance of piecemeal litigation and conservation of judicial resources are less implicated when the party against whom waiver is asserted is the appellee. *Laitram Corp. v. NEC Corp.*, 42 U.S.P.Q.2d 1897, 1902 (Fed. Cir. 1997).

Applicant. *See also* **Conduct, Inventor.**

Because Congress provided for the correction of innocent error in stating an inventive entity when an application is filed, there is no reason to discriminate against the correction of the same innocent error involving sole inventors and their assignees. *A.F. Stoddard & Co. Ltd. v. Dann, Commissioner of Patents*, 564 F.2d 556, 195 U.S.P.Q. 97 (D.C. Cir. 1977).

ʊ

The negligence of his attorney does not excuse applicant's duty to exercise due diligence. An applicant has the duty to make sure his application is being prosecuted. Applicant's lack of due diligence over a two and one-half year period overcame and superseded any negligence of his attorney. The delay was not unavoidable because, had applicant exercised the due care of a reasonably prudent person, he would have been able to act to correct the situation in a timely fashion. *Douglas v. Manbeck*, 21 U.S.P.Q.2d 1697, 1700 (Pa. 1991).

ʊ

This statute (35 U.S.C. §115) creates no duty between the patent applicant and the purported inventor. Instead, because the Patent and Trademark Office's interest is in rewarding the true inventor with the issuance of a letter patent, the sole duty created is between the applicant and the Office. Breach of this duty results in the patent being "unauthorized by law and void..." *The University of Colorado Foundation v. American Cyanamid*, 880 F.Supp. 1387, 35 U.S.P.Q.2d 1737, 1745 (Colo. 1995).

Applicant's Own Work. *See also* **Applicant's Publication, Disclosure Without Claiming, Mosaic.**

D and N jointly filed an application for a combination invention on June 1, 1973 (subsequently issued as U.S.P. 3,842,678 on October 22, 1974). Applicant D was the sole applicant of an application (S.N. 952,695) for reissue of U.S.P. 3,964,519 (issued on an application filed November 18, 1974), claiming a subcombination that was fully disclosed, but not claimed, in U.S.P. 3,842,678. In the prosecution of the reissue application, D presented his own Declaration that a drawing of the subcombination invention (dated March 15, 1973) established conception prior to June 1, 1973, and that the subcombination was a sole invention originally conceived by D and described to patent counsel prior to June 1, 1973, to enable counsel to satisfy the requirements of 35 U.S.C. §112 in drafting the joint application. The joint patent was used as a reference against the reissue application, even though it was silent with regard to who invented the subcombination. There was no basis to presume that the subcombination was the invention of D and N jointly or of either of them. The joint patent of D and N, having been issued less than one year before the filing date of D's original patent application, is only available as a reference if the pertinent disclosure is not the sole work of D. An applicant's own work, even though publicly disclosed prior to his application, may not be used against him as a reference, absent a time bar to his application. In spite of the fact that a completed invention requires both conception and reduction to practice, there is no requirement that the inventor be the one to reduce the invention to practice so long as reduction to practice is done on his behalf. *In re DeBaun,* 687 F.2d 459, 214 U.S.P.Q. 933 (C.C.P.A. 1982).

ϖ

The appellant had filed (with his application) a Declaration in which he acknowledged his coauthorship of a paper (published less than a year earlier) and further stated unequivocally that he was the sole inventor of the subject matter disclosed in that publication. Unlike the filing of a patent application, the publication of an article is not a constructive reduction to practice of the subject matter described therein. Therefore, disclosure in a publication does not prove that any "invention" within the meaning of 35 U.S.C. §102(g) has ever been made by anyone. Since §102(g) is predicated on the invention having been made in this country by another, nothing short of an actual or constructive reduction to practice could provide a valid basis for the rejection. Even though a printed publication, which describes the subject matter of a claimed invention and is published before an application is filed, may raise a substantial question whether the applicant is the inventor, coauthors of the publication may not be presumed to be coinventors merely from the fact of coauthorship. The appellant's Declaration that he was the sole inventor and that the coauthors "were students working under the direction and supervision of the inventor" was accepted as a sufficient showing to establish that the subject disclosure was his original work, and his alone. *In re Katz*, 687 F.2d 450, 215 U.S.P.Q. 14 (C.C.P.A. 1982).

ᘒ

A patent on an antecedent application was section (35 U.S.C.) 102(b) prior art with respect to a continuation-in-part application filed more than one year after the patent (a "printed publication") issued. *Chester v. Miller*, 906 F.2d 1574, 15 U.S.P.Q.2d 1333, 1336 (Fed. Cir. 1990).

Applicant's Publication. *See also* Applicant's Own Work.

The patentability of subject matter disclosed and claimed for the first time in a cip more than one year after publication of subject matter in the parent application is subject to statutory bar preclusions even when the publication is that of applicant's own foreign counterpart application. The parent application cannot be used to antedate the publication. *In re Ruscetta and Jenny*, 255 F.2d 687, 118 U.S.P.Q. 101, 104 (C.C.P.A. 1958).

Applicant's Rights. *See also* Comparative Testing, Promote Progress, 35 U.S.C. §132.

The public purpose on which the patent law rests requires the granting of claims commensurate in scope with the invention disclosed. This requires as much the granting of broad claims on broad inventions as it does the granting of specific claims on more specific inventions. It is neither contemplated by the public purpose of the patent laws nor required by the statute that an inventor shall be forced to accept claims narrower than his invention in order to secure allowance of his patent. *In re Sus and Schaefer*, 306 F.2d 494, 134 U.S.P.Q. 301, 304 (C.C.P.A. 1962).

ᘒ

The basic principle of the patent system is to protect inventions that meet the statutory requirements. Valuable inventions should be given protection of value in the real world of business and the courts. *In re Ruschig, Aumüller, Korger, Wagner, Scholz, and Bänder*, 343 F.2d 965, 145 U.S.P.Q. 274, 286 (C.C.P.A. 1965).

ᘒ

The PTO, in discharging its duties to the public, has commendably required applicants for patents to provide an adequate quid pro quo in exchange for the monopoly sought. It should be equally alert in protecting the rights of applicants who have legally and properly established such a right. To do otherwise would be to enrich the public unjustly at the expense of the inventor, a result Congress could not have intended. *In re Herr*, 377 F.2d 610, 153 U.S.P.Q. 548, 549 (C.C.P.A. 1967).

ᘒ

It is for the inventor to decide what bounds of protection he will seek. Applicant's right to retreat to an otherwise patentable species is not precluded merely because he erroneously thought he was first with the genus when he filed. *In re Johnson and Farnham*, 558 F.2d 1008, 194 U.S.P.Q. 187, 196 (C.C.P.A. 1977).

ᘒ

An applicant has a right to have each claim examined on the merits and in a form which he considers to define his invention best. In drawing priorities between the Commissioner (as administrator) and the applicant (as beneficiary of his statutory rights), the statutory rights are paramount. A rejection under 35 U.S.C. §121 violates the basic right of the applicant to claim his invention as he chooses. *In re Weber, Soder, and Boksay*, 580 F.2d 455, 198 U.S.P.Q. 328, 331, 332 (C.C.P.A. 1978).

ᚒ

The public responsibility of the PTO requires attentive performance of all aspects of the patent examination function. The PTO is charged with the duty of examining the claims contained in a patent application, including review by the BPAI when an appeal is taken under 35 U.S.C. §134. It is not only unfair to the applicant, it is also inefficient to decline to review claims that are properly appealed and reasonably argued before the Board. *In re Beaver*, 893 F.2d 329, 13 U.S.P.Q.2d 1409, 1411 (Fed. Cir. 1989).

ᚒ

The act of invention itself vests an inventor with a common law or "natural" right to make, use, and sell his or her invention absent conflicting patent rights in others (and, in certain circumstances, may similarly vest such rights in an employer of the inventor). *Arachnid Inc. v. Merit Industries Inc.*, 939 F.2d 1574, 19 U.S.P.Q.2d 1513, 1516 (Fed. Cir. 1991).

Application. *See also* Abandoned Application, Continuation Application, Continuation-in-Part Application, Continuing Application, Disclosure, Patent Application, Pending Application, Specification.

Where an applicant files an application with a set of claims and with an accompanying instruction to the PTO to cancel all of those claims, without the substitution of new claims, the applicant has not fulfilled the requirements of 35 U.S.C. §112, paragraph 2, and is not entitled to a filing date until at least one claim has been submitted. A submission to the PTO which fails to meet the requirements of 35 U.S.C. §112 also fails to meet the definition of "application" in 35 U.S.C. §111, and is not an "application" entitled to a filing date of a parent application under 35 U.S.C. §120. *Baxter International Inc. v. McGaw Inc.*, 149 F.3d 1321, 47 U.S.P.Q.2d 1225, 1234 (Fed. Cir. 1998).

Apprehension

A "patentee's refusal to give assurances that it will not enforce its patent . . . is not dispositive". *CAE Screenplates Inc. v. Beloit Corp.*, 45 U.S.P.Q.2d 1895, 1901 (Va 1997).

ᚒ

Patentee's refusal to give assurances that it will not enforce patent is relevant to court's determination of reasonable apprehension. *Progressive Technology in Lighting Inc. v. Lumatech Corp.*, 45 U.S.P.Q.2d 1928, 1933 (Mich. 1998).

Appropriate. *See also* **Appropriation.**

One who appropriates the teachings of a patent may not deny the utility of the invention. *Tapco Products Co. v. Van Mark Products Corp.*, 446 F.2d 420, 170 U.S.P.Q. 550 (6th Cir. 1971).

ϖ

The claimed composition rapidly cures at room temperature, whereas the accused counterpart rapidly cures only at 90°C. It was precisely because of that difference that the district court found that the claimed invention and the accused counterpart do not perform in substantially the same way. That finding, however, would allow the difference itself to dictate a finding of no equivalents; if that were the law, one could never infringe by equivalents. The analysis must go further, and the question the district court should consider on remand is this: Given the difference, would the accused composition at 90°C and the claimed invention at room temperature perform substantially the same function (e.g., filling the pores of the treated material with solid material) in substantially the same way (e.g., by rapidly curing in the absence but not in the presence of oxygen) to give substantially the same results (e.g., a filled material)? There are limitations to the doctrine of equivalents. The doctrine has been judicially devised to do equity in situations where there is no literal infringement but liability is nevertheless appropriate to prevent what is in essence a pirating of the patentee's invention. Concommitently, two policy-oriented limitations, applied as questions of law, have developed. First, the doctrine will not extend to an infringing device within the public domain, i.e., found in the prior art at the time the patent issued; second, prosecution history estoppel will not allow the patentee to recapture through equivalents certain coverage given up during prosecution. *Loctite Corp. v. Ultraseal Ltd.*, 781 F.2d 861, 228 U.S.P.Q. 90 (Fed. Cir. 1985).

ϖ

Evidence of independent development is highly relevant to refute a patent owner's contention that the doctrine of equivalents applies because the accused infringer copied (intentially appropriated) the substance of the claimed invention. *Hilton Davis Chemical Co. v. Warner-Jenkinson Co. Inc.*, 62 F.3d 1512, 35 U.S.P.Q.2d 1641, 1647 (Fed. Cir. 1995).

ϖ

A finding that a claimed invention has or has not been appropriated by an alleged infringer may carry substantial weight in a court's analysis of all the evidence bearing on the obvious-nonobvious issue. *Nordberg Inc. v. Telsmith Inc.*, 801 F.Supp. 1252, 36 U.S.P.Q.2d 1577, 1600 (Wis. 1995).

Appropriation. *See also* **Fraud on a Patent, Pirating, Post Employment Invention, Reverse Doctrine of Equivalents, Trailer Clause.**

Bona fide attempts to design a non-infringing product are one of the beneficial results of the incentive-to-disclose system established by the patent statute. Bona fides of such attempts, however, are not governed solely by whether the words of a patent claim can be literally read on the newly designed product. The matter is not one for semantic antics alone. An infringer appropriates an invention, not words; hence, the doctrine of equivalents. At the same time, the words of a claim may be so limited by the file history or by the prior art as to define an invention that was not appropriated; hence, the doctrine of estoppel. *Caterpillar Tractor Co. v. Berco, S.A.*, 714 F.2d 1110, 219 U.S.P.Q. 185 (Fed. Cir. 1983).

ᴕ

The doctrine of equivalents allows a finding of infringement when an accused product and claimed invention perform substantially the same function in substantially the same way to yield substantially the same result. Where defendant has appropriated the material features of a patent in suit, infringement will be found even when those features have been supplemented and modified to such an extent that the defendant may be entitled to a patent for the improvement. It is not a requirement of equivalents that those skilled in the art know of the equivalence when the patent application is filed or the patent issues. *Atlas Powder Co. v. E.I. du Pont de Nemours Co.*, 750 F.2d 1569, 224 U.S.P.Q. 409 (Fed. Cir. 1984).

ᴕ

It is not required that those skilled in the art knew, at the time the patent application was filed, of the asserted equivalent means of performing the claimed functions; that equivalence is determined as of the time infringement takes place. Infringement will be found when the material features of a patent have been appropriated, even when those features have been patentably improved. *Texas Instruments, Inc. v. U.S. International Trade Commission*, 805 F.2d 1558, 231 U.S.P.Q. 833 (Fed. Cir. 1986).

ᴕ

If, in the eye of any ordinary observer, giving such attention as a purchaser usually gives, two designs are substantially the same and the resemblance is such as to deceive such an observer (inducing him to purchase one supposing it to be the other), the first one patented is infringed by the other. In addition to overall similarity of designs, the accused device must appropriate the novelty in the patented device that distinguishes it from the prior art. *Avia Group International, Inc. v. L.A. Gear California, Inc.*, 853 F.2d 1557, 7 U.S.P.Q.2d 1548 (Fed. Cir. 1988).

ᴕ

A corporate assignee of a patent application may be ordered to assign to the original holder of trade secrets all rights to a patent application based thereon. When an employee has acquired patents on inventions developed by his former employer, the courts will hold the wrongdoer to be a constructive trustee of the property misappropriated and will order a conveyance by the wrongdoer to the former employer. The courts are not powerless to redress wrongful appropriation of intellectual property by those subject to the court's jurisdiction. *Richardson v. Suzuki Motor Co., Ltd.*, 868 F.2d 1226, 9 U.S.P.Q.2d 1913 (Fed. Cir. 1989).

Approved Product. *See* **Product.**

Approximately. *See also* **About, Substantially.**

The use of such terms as *about* and *approximately* does not subject the claims to a rejection as failing to define the invention with the required particularity. It is clear from the specification that the temperatures modified by the quoted terms are not critical in the sense that a few degrees more or less than the stated temperature would have any effect. *Ex parte Shelton,* 92 U.S.P.Q. 374, 375 (PTO Bd. App. 1950).

ᚥ

The descriptive word about is not indefinite. Its meaning is not broad and arbitrary. The term is clear, but flexible, and is deemed to be similar in meaning to terms, such as approximately or nearly. *Ex parte Eastwood, Brindle and Kolb,* 163 U.S.P.Q. 316 (PTO Bd. App. 1968).

ᚥ

A range of proportions disclosed in an application is not rendered indefinite when qualified by *approximately* in claims. *Ex parte Shea,* 171 U.S.P.Q. 383 (PTO Bd. App. 1970).

ᚥ

The use of the words substantially and approximately in a claim does not necessarily render it vague and therefore invalid under 35 U.S.C. §112. *H.M. Chase Corp. v. Idaho Potato Processors, Inc.,* 185 U.S.P.Q. 106, 116, 529 P.2d 1270 (Idaho 1974).

Aralkyl. *See* **Aryl.**

Arbitration.

The validity of a U.S. patent is not arbitrable. *N.V. Maatschappij Voor Industriele Waarden v. A. O. Smith Corp.,* 532 F.2d 874, 190 U.S.P.Q. 385, 386 (2d Cir. 1976).

ᚥ

The denial of a stay to permit arbitration is appealable because it is an interlocutory order refusing an injunction under 28 U.S.C. §1292(a)(1). Denials of stays to permit arbitration are final and appealable decisions. *Rhone-Poulenc Specialties Chimique v. SCM Corp.,* 769 F.2d 1569, 226 U.S.P.Q. 873, 874 (Fed. Cir. 1985).

ᚥ

A party to an international transaction will be required to honor its agreement to arbitrate disputes involving statutory claims under U.S. law when the arbitration agreement reaches the statutory issues and when there are no legal constraints external to the agreement that foreclose arbitration of such claims. *Farrel Corp. v. International Trade Commission,* 20 U.S.P.Q. 2d 1912, 1913, 1915 (Fed. Cir. 1991).

ᚥ

"Manifest disregard of the law" by arbitrators is a judicially-created ground for vacating their arbitration award. *Willemijn Houdstermaatschappij BV v. Standard Microsystems Corp.,* 39 U.S.P.Q.2d 1528, 1531 (N.Y. 1996).

Argument. *See also* **Assertion, Challenge.**

Due process requires that an applicant be given notice of the reasons his claims are rejected and why arguments upon which he relies are deemed lacking in merit. This principle is the essence of 35 U.S.C. §132 and should guide the proceedings of the Board of Appeals as well. *Ex parte Hageman,* 179 U.S.P.Q. 747, 751 (PTO Bd. App. 1972).

ω

Argument of counsel cannot take the place of evidence lacking in the record. *In re Scarborough,* 500 F.2d 560, 182 U.S.P.Q. 298, 302 (C.C.P.A. 1974).

ω

Mere lawyer's arguments and conclusory statements in the specification, unsupported by objective evidence, are insufficient to establish unexpected results. *In re Wood, Whittaker, Stirling, and Ohta,* 582 F.2d 638, 199 U.S.P.Q. 137, 140 (C.C.P.A. 1978).

ω

As arguments relating to patentability have been presented without regard to any particular claim, all claims on appeal stand or fall with appealed Claim 1. Mere unsupported arguments cannot take the place of evidence and may be accorded little or no weight. Arguments that are not supported by any evidence or that are not presented below (even if supported by evidence) will not be considered on appeal. *In re Wiseman and Kovac,* 596 F.2d 1019, 201 U.S.P.Q. 658, 661 (C.C.P.A. 1979).

ω

When an article is said to achieve unexpected (i.e., superior) results, those results must logically be shown as superior compared to the results achieved with other articles. Moreover, an applicant relying on comparative tests to rebut a prima facie case of obviousness must compare his claimed invention to the closest prior art. In the absence of comparative test data, assertions of unexpected results constitute mere argument; conclusory statements in the specification cannot establish patentability. *In re De Blauwe,* 736 F.2d 699, 222 U.S.P.Q. 191 (Fed. Cir. 1984).

ω

"[A]rguments made during prosecution regarding the meaning of a claim term are relevant to the interpretation of that term in every claim of the patent absent a clear indication to the contrary. *Digital Biometrics Inc. v. Identix Inc.,* 149 F.3d 1335, 47 U.S.P.Q.2d 1418, 1427 (Fed. Cir. 1998).

Arise under Patent Laws.

Every case involving patent issues is not a "civil action arising under an Act of Congress relating to patents," as set forth in 28 U.S.C. §1338(a). Actions to enforce patent license agreements are not within exclusive federal jurisdiction notwithstanding the availability of the invalidity defense. *Kysor Industrial Corp. v. Pet,* 459 F.2d 1010, 173 U.S.P.Q. 642, 643 (6th Cir. 1972).

ω

Asserting a defense of patent invalidity does not convert an action for breach of contract to one arising under the patent laws. *Wham-O Manufacturing Co. v. All-American Yo-Yo Corp.,* 377 F. Supp. 993, 181 U.S.P.Q. 320, 321 (N.Y. 1973).

ω

There are two types of cases that may be said to "arise under" the patent laws for purposes of 28 U.S.C. §1338. First, a suit arises under the law that creates the cause of action. Although this creation test may be helpful in identifying many cases that come within the court's jurisdiction, it has limited value in identifying those that do not. Second, a case arises under the patent laws if the plaintiff seeks to vindicate a right or interest "that would be defeated by one or sustained by an opposite construction" of the patent laws. *Christianson v. Colt Industries Operating Corp.*, 798 F.2d 1051, 230 U.S.P.Q. 840 (7th Cir. 1986).

ᚹ

A cause of action will arise under federal patent law when it involves the validity, scope or infringement of a patent. When patent issues are merely implicated incidentally in a cause of action federal courts do not have jurisdiction of the case pursuant to 28 U.S.C. §1338. *Kaufman Malchman & Kirby P.C. v. Hasbro Inc.*, 897 F.Supp. 719, 37 U.S.P.Q.2d 1458, 1459 (N.Y. 1995).

ᚹ

At least two doctrines restrict the reach of "arising under" jurisdiction under 28 USC §§1331 and 1338(a). Under the first, the "well-pleaded complaint" rule, "whether a claim 'arises under' patent law 'must be determined from what necessarily appears in the plaintiff's statement of his own claim in the bill or declaration, unaided by anything alleged in anticipation or avoidance of defenses which it is thought the defendant may interpose.'" *Christianson v. Colt Indus. Operating Corp*, 486 U.S. 800, 809, 7 U.S.P.Q.2d 1109 (1988) [quoting *Taylor v. Anderson*, 234 U.S. 74, 75-76 (1914)]. Under the second, "a claim supported by alternative theories in the complaint may not form the basis for 28 U.S.C. §1338(a) jurisdiction unless patent law is essential to each of those theories." *Hunter Douglas Inc. v. Harmonic Design Inc.*, 47 U.S.P.Q.2d 1769, 1770, 1773 (Fed. Cir. 1998).

Aromatic.

A rejection of claims as failing to define the invention properly and based on the phrases "substituted mononuclear and polynuclear homocyclic compounds," "alkyl," "ester," and "heterocyclic and aromatic compounds being free of substituents containing aliphatic hydroxyl and amino groups," in process claims, was reversed. *Ex parte West-fahl*, 136 U.S.P.Q. 265 (PTO Bd. App. 1962).

Art. *See also* Analogous Art, Apparatus, Article, Composition, Compound, Machine, Manufacture, Method, Prior Art, Process, Product, Same Art, Skilled in the Art, Skill of the Art, State of the Art.

A process is a mode of treatment of certain materials to produce a given result. It is an act, or a series of acts, performed upon the subject matter to be transformed and reduced to a different state or thing. If new and useful, it is just as patentable as a piece of machinery. In the language of the patent law, it is an art. The machinery pointed out as being suitable to perform the process may or may not be new or patentable, while the process itself may be altogether new and produce an entirely new result. The process requires that certain things be done with certain substances, and in a certain order; but the tools to be used in doing this may be of secondary consequence. *Cochrane v. Deener,* 94 U.S. 780 (1876).

ʊ

Patent protection for a process disclosed as being a sequence or combination of steps capable of performance without human intervention and directed to an industrial technology (a "useful art" within the intendment of the Constitution) is not precluded by the mere fact that the process could alternatively be carried out by mental steps. *In re Prater and Wei,* 415 F.2d 1378, 159 U.S.P.Q. 583, 593 (C.C.P.A. 1968).

Article[4]. *See also* **Apparatus, Composition, Compound, Device, Gene, Indefinite Article, Machine, Manufacture, Product.**

The method of manufacture may be relevant to the patentability of claims drawn to articles. *In re Epple and Kaiser,* 477 F.2d 582, 177 U.S.P.Q. 696 (C.C.P.A. 1973).

Aryl.

While the term "aryl and substituted aryl radicals" is a broad term, it is not objectionable for this reason alone if the term (1) is supported by the specification, and (2) it properly defines the novel subject matter described in the specification. *In re Sus and Schaefer,* 306 F.2d 494, 134 U.S.P.Q. 301, 304 (C.C.P.A. 1962).

ʊ

A rejection of claims as failing to define the invention properly and based on the phrases "substituted mononuclear and polynuclear homocyclic compounds," "alkyl," "ester," and "heterocyclic and aromatic compounds being free of substituents containing aliphatic hydroxyl and amino groups," in process claims, was reversed. *Ex parte Westfahl,* 136 U.S.P.Q. 265 (PTO Bd. App. 1962).

ʊ

Although various authorities may place a slightly different interpretation on the meaning of "aryl," when used in conjunction with "aralkyl" and "alkaryl," those in the art readily appreciate the total scope of the subject matter defined. Likewise, "heterocyclic" has an art-recognized meaning. Neither of such terms is indefinite. *Ex parte Scherberich and Pfeifer,* 201 U.S.P.Q. 397 (PTO Bd. App. 1977).

As a Whole. *See* **Whole.**

Assembly. *See* **Kit.**

---

[4]*See* Kelly, Patrick D., "Old Drug, New Use: Article Of Manufacture Claims," BIO/TECHNOLOGY, Vol. 11, pp 839 and 840, July 1993, which refers directly to claim 18 of USP 5,011,853 and to claim 7 of USP 5,208,031, as well as to claim 7 of USP 4,988,710, which reads (in part): "An article of manufacture comprising packaging material and a pharmaceutical agent contained within the packaging material, wherein the pharmaceutical agent . . . , and wherein the packaging material comprises a label which indicates that the pharmaceutical agent can be used for reducing neurotoxic brain damage that might otherwise be caused by at least one cholinesterase inhibitor, . . .

Assertion. *See also* **Allegation, Argument, Assumption, Challenge, Conclusion, Conjecture, Convince, Credibility, Deem, Fact, Generality, Speculation, Statement, Statement by the Board, Statement in Disclosure, Statement in the Specification, Truth.**

A showing of superiority over prior art requires evidence of comparative testing in the record and not mere assertions by counsel in briefs. *In re Swentzel,* 219 F.2d 216, 104 U.S.P.Q. 343 (C.C.P.A. 1955).

ω

Assertions made by appellant's counsel that have not been disputed by the Examiner or the Board and are not contradicted by record evidence or prior art must be accorded due weight. *In re Sporck,* 301 F.2d 686, 133 U.S.P.Q. 360, 363 (C.C.P.A. 1962).

ω

Section 112 of 35 U.S.C. does not require that a specification convince persons skilled in the art that assertions therein are correct. *In re Robins,* 429 F.2d 452, 166 U.S.P.Q. 552 (C.C.P.A. 1970).

ω

A specification disclosure that contains a teaching of the manner and process of making and using the invention in terms that correspond in scope to those used in describing and defining the subject matter sought to be patented must be taken as in compliance with the enabling requirement of the first paragraph of 35 U.S.C. §112 unless there is reason to doubt the objective truth of the statements contained therein that must be relied on for enabling support. Assuming that sufficient reason for such doubt does exist, a rejection for failure to teach how to make and/or use will be proper on that basis. In any event, it is incumbent on the Patent Office, whenever a rejection on this basis is made, to explain why it doubts the truth or accuracy of any statement in a supporting disclosure and to back up assertions of its own with acceptable evidence or reasoning that is inconsistent with the contested statement. Otherwise, there would be no need for the applicant to go to the trouble and expense of supporting his presumptively accurate disclosure. *In re Marzocchi and Horton,* 439 F.2d 220, 169 U.S.P.Q. 367 (C.C.P.A. 1971).

ω

The primary contention of the PTO is that reasonable basis exists for doubting that all of the compounds encompassed by a claim have the asserted utility. Adequate support for the PTO's assertions is an essential requirement for sustaining a rejection on this basis. *In re Gardner,* 475 F.2d 1389, 177 U.S.P.Q. 396, 397 (C.C.P.A. 1973).

ω

The assertion that the references contained no suggestion of a compatibility problem is confirmed by the references. Moreover, nothing is found in the references to support the PTO's mere assertion that there really is no such problem, but it would be obvious how to solve it if it existed. *In re Rice,* 481 F.2d 1316, 178 U.S.P.Q. 478 (C.C.P.A. 1973).

ω

The correctness of an assertion in the specification may always be challenged, but only if there is sound basis therefor. Mere surmise, speculation, and conjecture are insufficient to refute an explicit teaching about operability. An appellant's assertion must be accepted in the absence of factual evidence (not merely unsupported skepticism) to the contrary. *Ex parte Dunn and Mathis,* 181 U.S.P.Q. 652, 653 (PO Bd. App. 1973).

ᚳ

Any assertion by the PTO that the enabling disclosure is not commensurate in scope with the protection sought must be supported by evidence or reasoning substantiating the doubts so expressed. *In re Dinh-Nguyen and Stenhagen,* 492 F.2d 856, 181 U.S.P.Q. 46 (C.C.P.A. 1974).

ᚳ

Section 112 of 35 U.S.C. does not require that a specification convince persons skilled in the art that assertions therein are correct. *In re Armbruster,* 512 F.2d 676, 185 U.S.P.Q. 152 (C.C.P.A. 1975).

ᚳ

The PTO's brief does not take issue with the appellant's assertion that the 35 U.S.C. §102 rejection is not before the court. When appellant's counsel repeated this assertion at oral argument, the assistant solicitor did not object. Thus, the PTO has abandoned §102 as a basis for rejecting Claim 11. *In re Hayashibara and Sugimoto,* 525 F.2d 1062, 188 U.S.P.Q. 4 (C.C.P.A. 1975).

ᚳ

The PTO has not challenged the appellants' assertion that their 1953 application enabled those skilled in the art in 1953 to make and use "a solid polymer" as claimed. The appellants disclosed, as the only then-existing way to make such a polymer, a method of making the crystalline form. To say now that the appellants should have disclosed in 1953 the amorphous form (which did not exist until 1962) would be to impose an impossible burden on inventors and thus on the patent system. There cannot, in an effective patent system, be such a burden placed on the right to broad claims. To restrict the appellants to the crystalline form disclosed, under such circumstances, would be a poor way to stimulate invention and, particularly, to encourage its early disclosure. To demand such restriction is merely to state a policy against broad protection for pioneer inventions, a policy both shortsighted and unsound from the standpoint of promoting progress in the useful arts, which is the constitutional purpose of the patent laws. *In re Hogan and Banks,* 559 F.2d 595, 194 U.S.P.Q. 527 (C.C.P.A. 1977).

ᚳ

A showing of superiority over prior art requires evidence of comparative testing in the record and not mere assertions by counsel in briefs. *In re Holladay,* 584 F.2d 384, 199 U.S.P.Q. 516, 518 (C.C.P.A. 1978).

ᚳ

There is no requirement in 35 U.S.C. §112, or anywhere else in the patent law, that a specification must convince persons skilled in the art that the assertions in the specification are correct. In examining a patent application, the PTO is required to assume that the specification complies with the enablement provisions of §112 unless it has "acceptable evidence or reasoning" to suggest otherwise. The PTO must thus provide reasons supported by the record as a whole why the specification is not enabling. Then and only then does the burden shift to the applicant to show that one of ordinary skill in the art could have practiced the claimed invention without undue experimentation. A patent specification must be enabling as to "the invention" as set forth in the claims. Thus, a disclosure may be insufficient for one claim but sufficient for another. *Gould v. Mossinghoff,* 229 U.S.P.Q. 1 (D.C. 1985).

Assignee. *See also* **Agreement to Assign, Assignee Estoppel, Assignment, Assignor, Best Efforts, Exclusive License, Royalty.**

A transfer by a patentee of the exclusive right to make, use, and sell the invention throughout the United States "is an assignment, properly speaking, and vests in the assignee a title in so much of the patent itself, with a right to sue infringers . . . in the name of the assignee alone." *Waterman v. Mackenzie,* 138 U.S. 252, 255 (1891).

ᚐ

Under the Patent Office Rules an assignee of the entire interest is entitled to control the prosecution of an application, but the assignee of only a part interest is not. *Ex parte Harrison,* 1925 C.D. 122, 123 (Comm'r Patents 1924).

ᚐ

The assignee of two parties in a multiparty interference must make an election between the applications of those parties even when the status of one of the applications is under attack by an adversary, unless the assignee can demonstrate its inability to obtain facts upon which to base an election. *Young v. Young, Baker, and Canaday v. Giffard,* 119 U.S.P.Q. 470, 471 (Comm'r Patents 1955).

ᚐ

An enlarged reissue patent filed by an assignee is issued to the inventor. *In re Schuyler,* 119 U.S.P.Q. 97, 98 (Comm'r Patents 1957).

ᚐ

The earlier of two commonly assigned copending applications by different inventive entities is prior art with regard to the later-filed application unless there is a disclaimer by the applicant of the earlier-filed application of the subject matter claimed in the later-filed application or the applicant of the later-filed application establishes a date of invention prior to the filing of the earlier-filed application. *Pierce v. Watson, Commissioner of Patents,* 275 F.2d 890, 124 U.S.P.Q. 356, 357 (D.C. Cir. 1960).

ᚐ

Proof of the authority of anyone signing on behalf of an assignee corporation must be provided in order for the PTO to accept an abandonment of the application after the issue fee is paid and a patent number and an issue date are assigned. *Schmidt v. Reynolds, Commissioner of Patents,* 140 U.S.P.Q. 118, 119, 1964 C.D. 1 (D.C. 1963).

ᚐ

The assignee of two copending applications of different inventors has the duty to disclose to the PTO the first of the two inventors with regard to commonly claimed subject matter and to abandon the application to the later inventor. *Ampex Corp. v. Memorex Corp.*, 205 U.S.P.Q. 794, 797 (Cal. 1980).

ʊ

Between the time of an invention and the issuance of a patent thereon, rights in the invention may be assigned, and legal title to the ensuing patent will pass to the assignee upon grant of the patent. If an assignment of rights in an invention is made prior to the existence of the invention, this may be viewed as an assignment of an expectant interest (future goods or after acquired property). An assignment of an expectant interest in personal property can be a valid assignment. In such a situation, the assignee holds at most an equitable title. Once the invention is made and an application for patent is filed, however, legal title to the rights accruing thereunder would be in the assignee (subject to the rights of a subsequent purchaser under 35 U.S.C. §261), and the inventor-assignor would have nothing remaining to assign. *FilmTec Corp. v. Allied-Signal Inc.*, 939 F.2d 1568, 19 U.S.P.Q.2d 1508, 1511 (Fed. Cir. 1991).

Assignee Estoppel.

Assignee estoppel prevents an assignee from representing the validity of and defending a patent to the world, and then asserting its worthlessness to its assignor when it is asked to pay for the rights it has purchased and used. Under a contrary rule " . . . the buyer of a patent could obtain its benefits and control it and refuse to pay the agreed consideration. The transaction is a 'bargain and sale' of its subject matter and the amount agreed to must be paid." *Sybron Transition Corp. v. Nixon, Hargrave, Devans & Doyle*, 770 F.Supp. 803, 21 U.S.P.Q.2d 1515, 1517, 1521, 1522 (N.Y. 1991).

Assignment. *See also* **Assignee, Assignor, Champerty, Expectant Interest, Record, Sale.**

Between the time of an invention and the issuance of a patent, rights in an invention may be assigned, and legal title to an ensuing patent will pass to the assignee upon grant of the patent. *Gayler v. Wilder*, 51 U.S. 477, 493 (1850).

ʊ

A patentee or his assigns may, by an instrument in writing, assign, grant, and convey, first, the whole patent, comprising the exclusive right to make, use, and vend the invention throughout the United States; or, second, an undivided part or share of that exclusive right; or, third, the exclusive right under the patent within or throughout a specified part of the United States. A transfer of either of these three kinds of interests is an assignment, properly speaking, and vests in the assignee a title in so much of the patent itself, with a right to sue infringers: in the second case, jointly with the assignor; in the first and third cases, in the name of the assignee alone. Any assignment or transfer, short of one of these, is a mere license, giving the licensee no title in the patent and no right to sue at law in his own name for an infringement. *Waterman v. Mackenzie*, 138 U.S. 252, 255 (1891).

ʊ

One who is employed to make an invention and then succeeds during his term of service in accomplishing that task is bound to assign to his employer any patent obtained. The reason is that he has only produced that which he was employed to invent. His invention is the precise subject of the contract of employment. A term of the agreement necessarily is that what he is paid to produce belongs to his paymaster. On the other hand, if the employment be general, albeit it covers a field of labor and effort in the performance of which the employee conceived the invention for which he obtained a patent, the contract is not so broadly construed as to require an assignment of the patent. *United States v. Dubilier Condensor Corp.,* 289 U.S. 178, 17 U.S.P.Q. 154, 158 (1933).

ம

When an applicant files two applications containing the same subject matter and makes a full assignment of one of the applications, the applicant conclusively elects to give preference to the assigned application and to assert in the unassigned application only such portion, if any, of the invention as is special thereto. *Ex parte Ferla,* 65 U.S.P.Q. 285, 286 (PO Bd. App. 1944).

ம

A copending reference patent was issued to a different inventor on an application filed on the same date and refers to the subject application. The Patent Office tribunals stated that the subject application is presumed to be owned by the assignee of the copending reference patent. Since that statement was not controverted, it was accepted as correct. *In re Keim and Thompson,* 229 F.2d 466, 108 U.S.P.Q. 330, 331 (C.C.P.A. 1956).

ம

An employee not specifically hired to invent who perfects an invention on company time and with company assistance cannot be compelled to assign to his employer a patent obtained on the invention. *Banner Metals, Inc. v. Lockwood,* 125 U.S.P.Q. 29, 35, 178 Cal. App. 2d 643, (Cal. 1960).

ம

The monopoly granted by the patent laws cannot be divided into parts, except as authorized by those laws. The patentee may assign (1) the whole patent, (2) an undivided part or share of that patent, or (3) the exclusive right under the patent "to the whole or any specified part of the United States. Any assignment or transfer, short of these, is a mere license, giving the licensee no title in the patent, and no right to sue at law in his own name for an infringement." In accordance with these principles an exclusive license to make, use, and vend is in the same category as an assignment on the theory that the licensor holds title to the patent in trust for such licensee. Even though the exclusive license is restricted to a specified territory or covers less than the full life of the patent, this still remains true. *Channel Master Corp. v. JFD Electronics Corp.,* 260 F. Supp. 568, 151 U.S.P.Q. 498, 500 (N.Y. 1966).

ம

A patent confers upon the owner the right to exclude others from making, using, or selling the invention during the life of the patent; in order that a transfer constitute a sale, there must be a grant of all substantial rights of value in the patent. The transfer of anything less is a license that conveys no proprietary interest to the licensee. Whether a transfer constitutes a sale or license is determined by the substance of the transaction, and a transfer will suffice as a sale if it appears from the agreement and surrounding circumstances that the parties intended that the patentee surrender all his substantial rights to the invention. The question does not depend upon the labels or the terminology used in the agreement; hence, the fact that an agreement is termed a license and that the parties are referred to as licensor and licensee is not decisive. Nor is the question governed by the method of payment, and it is, therefore, immaterial that payment is based on a percentage of sales or profits, or on an amount per unit manufactured. Moreover, clauses in an agreement permitting termination by the grantor upon the occurrence of stated conditions or events will not preclude the transaction from being considered a sale; such clauses are uniformly treated as conditions subsequent. The fact that the grantee has the right to terminate the agreement at will does not defeat a sale. *Bell Intercontinental Corp. v. United States*, 381 F.2d 866, 152 U.S.P.Q. 182, 184 (Ct. Cl. 1966).

ᗡ

An agreement entitled "Exclusive License Agreement" granted licensee an exclusive right to make, to sell, and to use a patented invention in return for a specified royalty of the licensee's gross income. The licensor reserved to itself a lien upon the licenses granted and could terminate the agreement upon default by the licensee. The licensor retained legal title to the patents and retained a right to recapture the patents in the event of default of payment. An agreement that grants an exclusive license to make, to sell, and to use is a sale of the patent even if it is called a license. The fact that compensation is to be paid by a percentage of the gross licensed income or the existence of a term for recapture of the patents in default of payment does not convert an otherwise valid assignment into a license. *Transducer Patents Co. v. Renegotiation Board*, 485 F.2d 26, 179 U.S.P.Q. 398, 399 (9th Cir. 1973).

ᗡ

A transfer of the rights to make, use, and vend amounts to a transfer of all substantial rights to a patent, and has consistently been deemed to be a sale. Examples of substantial rights retained by a transferor include the right to terminate the agreement with or without cause; the right to grant a non-exclusive license to another firm and to compel the transferee to sublicense another; and the right to prohibit assignment of the agreement without the transferor's written consent. An obligation on the licensee to use its best efforts to promote the sale of products manufactured under the patents and the requirement that the licensee utilize appropriate accounting methods and permit the licensor access to the licensee's books of accounts are simply provisions included to protect the licensor to compensation under the agreement. Such provisions provide security for the transferor, but do not preclude transfer of ownership. *Newton Insert Co. v. Commissioner of Internal Revenue*, 181 U.S.P.Q. 765, 771 (U.S.T.C. 1974).

ᗡ

The motive or purpose of a patent assignment is irrelevant to the assignee's standing to enforce the assigned patent. Even a motive solely and expressly to facilitate litigation "is of no concern to the defendant and does not bear on the effectiveness of the assignment." *Discovery Rights, Inc. v. Avon Prods., Inc.*, 182 U.S.P.Q. 396, 398 (N.D. Ill. 1974).

ᗡ

If an assignee conveys to another in writing the whole patent, comprising the exclusive right to make, use, and sell the invention throughout the United States, or conveys an undivided part or share of that exclusive right, or transfers the exclusive right under the patent within and throughout a specified part of the United States, then the transfer will be properly characterized as an assignment. *Sanofi, S.A. v. Med-Tech Veterinarian Products, Inc.*, 565 F. Supp. 931, 220 U.S.P.Q. 416, 419 (N.J. 1983).

ω

Although the formal written assignment occurred after the critical date, the district court held that, even if there were an earlier oral agreement, an assignment or sale of the rights in the invention and potential patent rights is not a sale of "the invention" within the meaning of 35 U.S.C. §102(b). *Moleculon Research Corp. v. CBS, Inc.*, 793 F.2d 1261, 229 U.S.P.Q. 805 (Fed. Cir. 1986).

ω

A basic distinction between the transfer of a license and the transfer of a patent is whether the transferee has received the right to sue for infringement. If such a right to sue for infringement is transferred, the transferee has received an assignment. If no such right to sue is transferred, the transferee has received a license. In co-owner situations, the right to sue independently for infringement cannot be inferred; all co-owners must join in a patent infringement suit. Thus, one co-owner cannot sue independently for infringement or compel other co-owners to join in such a suit absent an agreement among all co-owners permitting him to do so. *Eickmeyer v. United States,* 10 Cl. Ct. 598, 231 U.S.P.Q. 820, 821, 822 (1986).

ω

A corporate assignee of a patent application may be ordered to assign to the original holder of trade secrets all rights to the patent application based thereon. When an employee has acquired patents on inventions developed by his former employer, the courts will hold the wrongdoer to be a constructive trustee of the misappropriated property and will order a conveyance by the wrongdoer to the former employer. The courts are not powerless to redress wrongful appropriation of intellectual property by those subject to the court's jurisdiction. *Richardson v. Suzuki Motor Co., Ltd.,* 868 F.2d 1226, 9 U.S.P.Q.2d 1913 (Fed. Cir. 1989).

ω

Employment, salary, and bonuses are valid consideration for an assignment. To hold that fear of their loss constitutes duress or intimidation would undermine every assignment by an employee-inventor. *Shamrock Technologies Inc. v. Medical Sterilization Inc.,* 903 F.2d 789, 14 U.S.P.Q.2d 1728, 1733 (Fed. Cir. 1990).

ω

When a legal title holder of a patent transfers title to a third-party purchaser for value without notice of an outstanding equitable claim or title, the purchaser takes the entire ownership of the patent, free of any prior equitable encumbrance. This is an application of the common law bona-fide-purchaser-for-value rule. Going a step further, 35 U.S.C. §261 adopts the principle of the real property recording acts and provides that the bona fide purchaser for value cuts off the rights of a prior assignee who has failed to record the prior assignment in the PTO by the dates specified in the statute. The statute is intended to cut off prior *legal* interests, which the common law rule did not. Both the common law rule and the statute contemplate that the subsequent purchaser is exactly that—a transferee who pays valuable consideration and is without notice of the prior transfer. *FilmTec Corp. v. Allied-Signal Inc.*, 939 F.2d 1568, 19 U.S.P.Q.2d 1508, 1512 (Fed. Cir. 1991).

ω

An assignment of a right of action for past infringements must be express and cannot be inferred from an assignment of a patent itself. *Arachnid Inc. v. Merit Industries Inc.*, 939 F.2d 1574, 19 U.S.P.Q.2d 1513, 1517 (Fed. Cir. 1991).

ω

The right to sue for past infringement may be assigned after a patent has expired, and the assignee of such a right can maintain an infringement suit in its own name. ("An assignment of a patent after it expires is a nullity with respect to the transfer of a grant but will operate to transfer to the assignee the right to sue for past infringements.") *Valmet Paper Machinery Inc. v. Beloit Corp.*, 868 F.Supp. 1085, 32 U.S.P.Q.2d 1794, 1796 (Wis. 1994).

ω

An assignment is effective only if it is in writing. *Procter & Gamble Co. v. Paragon Trade Brands Inc.*, 917 F.Supp. 305, 38 U.S.P.Q.2d 1678, 1681 (Del. 1995).

ω

The right to sue for prior infringement is not transferred unless the assignment agreement manifests an intent to transfer this right. *Minco Inc. v. Combustion Engineering Inc.*, 40 U.S.P.Q.2d 1001, 1006 (Fed. Cir. 1996).

ω

The general rule is that a corporation that purchases the assets of another does not thereby assume the obligations of its predecessor. *Horphag Research Ltd. v. Consac Industries Inc.*, 42 U.S.P.Q.2d 1567, 1570 (Fed. Cir. 1997).

ω

Nunc pro tunc assignments are not sufficient to confer retroactive standing. As a general matter, parties should possess patent rights before seeking to have them vindicated in court. *Enzo APA & Son Inc. v. Geapag A.G.*, 134 F.3d 1090, 45 U.S.P.Q.2d 1368, 1371 (Fed. Cir. 1998).

Assignment of Claims Act.

The Assignment of Claims Act of 1940, 31 U.S.C. §3727 (1988), (the "Act") has been interpreted as applying to assignments in patent cases only with respect to the right to recover for past infringement of the patent. Regarding the Act's predecessor statute, 31 U.S.C. §203, the Supreme Court set forth the following purposes for the Anti-Assignment Act: 1) to prevent the trafficking of claims by persons of influence who might improperly urge them upon officers of the Government; 2) to prevent the potential of multiple payment of claims by the Government, to eliminate the potential necessity of reviewing any alleged assignments, and to allow it to deal solely with the original claimant; and 3) to preserve the Government's defenses against the transferor, which may be inapplicable to a transferee. *MDS Associates v. U.S.*, 31 Fed.Cl. 389, 32 U.S.P.Q.2d 1784, 1787 (U.S. Ct.Fed.Cl. 1994).

Assignor.

An assignor is entitled to intervene as of right as of Fed. R. Civ. P. 24(a)(2) after a decision of the district court granting summary judgment (on the ground of patent invalidity) in favor of a putative infringer, from which the plaintiff assignee decided not to appeal. The inventor-assignor both knew of, and was actively involved in, the litigation prior to the granting of summary judgment. As of the time the assignee decided not to appeal, its representation of the assignor's interest became inadequate; even prior to that time the assignor satisfied the other requirements for intervention as of right. *The Triax Company v. TRW, Inc.*, 724 F.2d 1224, 221 U.S.P.Q. 1133, 1135 (6th Cir. 1984).

ᵀᴼ

In seeking to establish noninfringement (rather than invalidity), the assignor may use "the state of the art . . . to construe and narrow the claims of the patent, conceding [its] validity." *Total Containment Inc. v. Environ Products Inc.*, 33 U.S.P.Q.2d 1316, 1317 (Pa. 1994).

Assignor Estoppel.

The court, faced with the issue of whether the doctrine of assignor estoppel bars a party from seeking reexamination of a patent, reasoned that, because the doctrine of assignor estoppel is an equitable doctrine and the reexamination provisions are statutory mandates, the conflict between the two should be resolved in favor of the statute, and the motion to stay pending the reexamination outcome should be granted. *Vitronics Corp. v. Conceptronic Inc.*, 44 U.S.P.Q.2d 1536, 1538 (N.H. 1977).

ᵀᴼ

An assignor can be estopped from challenging the validity of the assigned patent when the assignor is sued by the assignee for infringement of the assigned patent. This estoppel bars only the assignor (and those in privity with the assignor), leaving everyone else free to try to invalidate the patent. The estoppel is, however, limited by allowing the assignor to present evidence of the state of the art for the sole purpose of construing and narrowing the claims of the patent. This accommodation permits the assignor to defend against the infringement suit by attempting to show that the accused device falls outside the proper scope of the claims of the patented suit, yet prevents the assignor from attacking the patent's validity. The scope of the right conveyed in an assignment of patent rights before the granting of the patent is much less certainly defined than that of a granted patent, and the question of the extent of the estoppel against the assignor of such an inchoate right is more difficult to determine than in a case of the patent assigned after its granting. *Diamond Scientific Co. v. Ambico Inc.*, 848 F.2d 1220, 6 U.S.P.Q.2d 2028 (Fed. Cir. 1988).

ᵀᴼ

Assignor estoppel is an equitable doctrine that precludes one who has assigned his right to a patent or a patent application from later contending that what he assigned was invalid or a nullity. In this case the inventor signed a declaration attesting to his belief in the patentability of the patented invention. *Hexcel Corp. v. Advanced Textiles Inc.*, 716 F. Supp. 974, 12 U.S.P.Q.2d 1390, 1391, 1392 (Tex. 1989).

ᶺ

It is at best incongruous to suppose that the equitable doctrine of assignor estoppel can never be applied to an equitable defense. The premise of the doctrine, prevention of unfairness and injustice, is not removed upon the mere denomination of a defense as "equitable." *Shamrock Technologies Inc. v. Medical Sterilization Inc.*, 903 F.2d 789, 14 U.S.P.Q.2d 1728, 1733 (Fed. Cir. 1990).

ᶺ

The public policy favoring allowing a licensee to contest the validity of a patent is not present in an assignment situation. Unlike the licensee, who without *Lear* [395 U.S. 653, 670, 162 U.S.P.Q. 1 (1969)] might be forced to continue to pay for a potentially invalid patent, the assignor who would challenge the patent has already been fully paid for the patent rights. *Acoustical Design Inc. v. Control Electronics Co.*, 932 F.2d 939, 18 U.S.P.Q.2d 1707, 1710 (Fed. Cir. 1991).

ᶺ

Privity, like the doctrine of assignor estoppel itself, is determined upon a balance of the equities. If an inventor assigns his invention to his employer, company A, and leaves to join company B, whether company B is in privity and thus bound by the doctrine will depend on the equities dictated by the relationship between the inventor and company B in light of the act of infringement. The closer that relationship, the more the equities will favor applying the doctrine to company B. *Intel Corp. v. International Trade Commission*, 946 F.2d 821, 20 U.S.P.Q.2d 1161, 1174 (Fed. Cir. 1991).

ᶺ

An assignor defendant may submit evidence to help properly construe or narrow claims of an assigned patent, while estopped to challenge their validity. Unlike assignment of a patent, a party's representations upon assignment of an application are not as clearly bounded. *Q.G. Products Inc. v. Shorty Inc.*, 992 F.2d 1211, 26 U.S.P.Q.2d 1778, 1780 (Fed. Cir. 1993).

ᶺ

"Assignor estoppel is an equitable doctrine that prevents one who has assigned the rights to a patent (or patent application) from later contending that what was assigned is a nullity. The estoppel also operates to bar other parties in privity with the assignor, such as a corporation founded by the assignor." A determination whether assignor estoppel applies in a particular case requires a balancing of the equities between the parties. That determination is a matter committed to the sound discretion of the trial court. *Carroll Touch Inc. v. Electro Mechanical Systems Inc.*, 3 F.3d 404, 27 U.S.P.Q.2d 1836, 1841 (Fed. Cir. 1993).

ᶺ

An assignee may not use the equitable doctrine of assignor estoppel to circumvent statutory law. *Total Containment Inc. v. Environ Products Inc.*, 34 U.S.P.Q.2d 1254, 1255 (Pa. 1995).

ω

In patent infringement litigation, no weight need be given to an opinion of invalidity of the inventor/assignor, who is not a defendant nor in privity with a defendant, since he is estopped from challenging the validity of the assigned patent. *Total Containment Inc. v. Buffalo Environmental Products Corp.*, 35 U.S.P.Q.2d 1385, 1394 (Va. 1995).

ω

Without exceptional circumstances (such as an express reservation by the assignor of the right to challenge the validity of the patent or an express waiver by the assignee of the right to assert assignor estoppel), one who assigns a patent surrenders with that assignment the right to later challenge the validity of the assigned patent. *Mentor Graphics Corp. v. Quickturn Design Systems Inc.*, 150 F.3d 1374, 47 U.S.P.Q.2d 1683, 1686 (Fed. Cir. 1998).

Assignor Intervention.

In a patent infringement suit by the assignee, the defendant prevailed in a motion for summary judgment for patent invalidity, and the assignee decided not to appeal. The inventor (assignor) knew of and was actively involved in the litigation prior to the granting of summary judgment. The district court denied his motion to intervene for the purpose of appealing from the adverse summary judgment holding. Because a final judgment declaring the patents at issue invalid meant that the inventor would no longer be entitled to receive any royalties on these patents and would be collaterally estopped from seeking damages from other potential infringers of the patents (because there could be no infringement of an invalid patent), the only way he could protect his interest effectively would be to seek appellate review of the district court's decision on summary judgment. The assignee's decision not to file a notice of appeal left the inventor without a mechanism to seek appellate review of the summary judgment of the district court declaring the two patents invalid. The denial of the inventor's motion to intervene impairs and impedes his ability to protect his interest in the patent. The inventor had an interest in the property or transaction that was the subject matter of the litigation, and the parties already in litigation could not adequately protect his interest. The inventor thus satisfied the criteria that warrant intervention as of right, and the motion to intervene was timely. *The Triax Company v. TRW, Inc.*, 724 F.2d 1224, 221 U.S.P.Q. 1133 (6th Cir. 1984).

Assistant.

The work of an assistant, working under the supervision and direction of an inventor, inures to the benefit of the inventor. Such assistant is a proper corroborating witness. It is not material as a matter of law that the inventor was not present at all experiments and tests made for him by his assistant. *Damaskus v. Homon and Neutlings*, 141 U.S.P.Q. 923, 925 (PO Bd. Pat. Int. 1964).

Associate. *See* **Foreign Associate.**

Assumption. *See also* **Assertion.**

A rejection under 35 U.S.C. §103 is not properly based on what are at best speculative assumptions as to the meaning of asserted claims. *In re Steele, Mills, and Leis,* 305 F.2d 859, 134 U.S.P.Q. 292, 295 (C.C.P.A. 1962).

ᛡ

An argument that process claims encompass inoperative embodiments on the premise of unrealistic or vague assumptions is not a valid basis for rejection. *In re Geerdes,* 491 F.2d 1260, 180 U.S.P.Q. 789, 793 (C.C.P.A. 1974).

ᛡ

An Examiner's burden of supporting his holding of unpatentability is not met by "assuming" the presence of a component that is missing from applied art. *Ex parte Wolters and Kuypers,* 214 U.S.P.Q. 735, 737 (PTO Bd. App. 1979).

Assurance. *See* **Examination, Examiner's Opinion.**

At. *See* **Process Parameter.**

ATCC. *See* **Deposit.**

At Least. *See also* **A, Open-Ended Claim.**

A claim calling for "means responsive to flow through one of said inlet orifices" reads on means responsive to flow through two orifices because flow through two includes flow through one. As the claim does not say "only one," it must be construed as meaning "at least one." *In re Teague,* 254 F.2d 145, 117 U.S.P.Q. 284, 289 (C.C.P.A. 1958).

ᛡ

The scope of a claim is definite when each recited limitation is definite. The use of "at least" does not justify a rejection of claims for indefiniteness under the second paragraph of 35 U.S.C. §112. *In re Fisher,* 427 F.2d 833, 166 U.S.P.Q. 18, 23 (C.C.P.A. 1970).

ᛡ

The difference between "at least one" and "a plurality" is a de minimis obvious variation. *In re Deters,* 515 F.2d 1152, 185 U.S.P.Q. 644, 648 (C.C.P.A. 1975).

ᛡ

Alternative expressions do not necessarily render the boundaries of a claimed invention undeterminable. Expressions, such as "made entirely or in part of" (which is to say "made at least partially of"), "one or several pieces" (the same as "at least one piece"), and "iron, steel or any other magnetic material," accurately determine the boundaries of protection involved. *In re Gaubert,* 524 F.2d 1222, 187 U.S.P.Q. 664, 667, 668 (C.C.P.A. 1975).

At Most. *See* **Up To.**

Atomic Energy Act of 1946. *See* **Development.**

Atomic Energy Commission.

The language in 42 U.S.C. §2182 limiting review to the CCPA was intended to establish an exclusive forum for review of decisions of the Board of Patent Interferences. *UMC Industries, Inc. v. Seaborg,* 439 F.2d 953, 169 U.S.P.Q. 325, 326 (9th Cir. 1971).

Attorney. *See also* **Advice of Counsel, Affidavit, Argument, Attorney's Fees, Billing, Conclusions, Conduct, Counsel, Discretion, Disqualification, Docket Number, Inconsistent, Opinion, Opinion of Counsel, Patent Attorney, Privilege, Work-Product Doctrine.**

The general rule is that a party to litigation cannot avoid the consequences of the acts or omissions of its freely selected attorney. *Link v. Wabash R.R.,* 370 U.S. 626, 633, 634 (1962).

ω

An attorney is charged with the responsibility of getting patent claims which are commensurate with his client's invention. *Ex parte Bielstein,* 135 U.S.P.Q. 402, 404 (PO Bd. App. 1962).

ω

An attorney's affidavit was not accepted as adequate proof that the person who signed a Declaration had authority to act for and bind the assignee company. *Schmidt v. Reynolds,* 140 U.S.P.Q. 118, 119, 1964 C.D. 1 (D.C. 1963).

ω

Although an attorney may be deposed and required to disclose what he knows about the subject matter, he cannot be required to disclose his mental impressions, conclusions, opinions, or legal theories concerning the litigation. He may be required to refer to his file to refresh his recollection, but he cannot be compelled to state why he amended the claims or what he meant by this or that word or phrase; that would require him to express an opinion, one of the exceptions provided for by Fed. R. Civ. P. 26(b)(3). *MacLaren v. B-I-W Group, Inc.,* 180 U.S.P.Q. 387, 388 (Va. 1973).

ω

Section 118 of 35 U.S.C. was not intended to permit patent attorneys to sign patent applications on behalf of missing individual clients. The language "sufficient proprietary interest in the matter justifying such action" means that a person filing the application must have such an interest as to be able to participate in the grant of a patent issued on the basis of an application filed pursuant to §118. In order to participate in the grant of the patent, a person must be able to enforce or require enforcement of a patent grant. Examples of such a person are exclusive licensees or trustees in bankruptcy. The PTO will accept a proposed application under 35 U.S.C. §118 and Rule 47(b) signed by a registered patent attorney when the application is owned by an assignee of the inventor when the assignee is a juristic entity, such as a corporation or a government agency. *In re Striker,* 182 U.S.P.Q. 507, 508 (PO Solicitor 1973).

ᛒ

In an interference between an application with joint inventors and a sole application of one of the two joint inventors the attorney who prepared the application for the joint inventors was disqualified as having a conflict in interest. *Isaacs v. Isaacs and Stern,* 183 U.S.P.Q. 790 (PTO Bd. Pat. Int. 1974).

ᛒ

When an attorney has intentionally misrepresented facts to his client and the client has justifiably relied on those misrepresentations to his detriment, the client may be permitted to avoid the consequences of the acts or omissions of the attorney. When the client has not misbehaved and opponents in litigation have not been harmed, the "vindication of the judicial process" does not require punishing the client instead of the attorney. *Jackson v. Washington Monthly Co.,* 569 F.2d 119, 122, 123 (D.C. Cir. 1977).

ᛒ

Plaintiff-inventor is "bound by the acts" of his lawyer-agent since he voluntarily chose him as his representative and cannot avoid the consequences of his acts or omissions. *Smith v. Diamond,* 209 U.S.P.Q. 1091, 1093 (D.C. 1981).

ᛒ

Absent extraordinary circumstances or compelling reasons, an attorney who participates in a case should not be called as a witness. *Liqui-Box Corp. v. Reid Valve Co. Inc.,* 16 U.S.P.Q.2d 1074, 1075 (Pa. 1989).

ᛒ

In a civil action under 35 U.S.C. §145 in which plaintiff seeks to set aside a BPAI decision affirming an Examiner's final rejection of claims in plaintiff's reissue patent application, the court refused to exclude the testimony of a patent law expert with regard to relevant matters, but did exclude any exposition or opinion as to legal issues in the case or patent law generally. *Ely v. Manbeck,* 17 U.S.P.Q.2d 1252, 1254 (D.C. 1990).

Attorney-Client Privilege. *See also* **Advice of Counsel, Conduit Theory, Foreign Associate, Patentanwaltzskandidat, Patentassessor, Privilege.**

Plaintiff's production of certain documents related to the prosecution of his patent constitutes a waiver of the attorney-client privilege with respect to all documents related to prosecution of the patent, even those which constitute "work product." *Bowmar Instrument Corp. v. Texas Instruments Incorporated,* 196 U.S.P.Q. 199, 201 (Ind. 1977).

ᛒ

The fact that a communication contains technical information does not automatically preclude application of the privilege. If the primary purpose of the document is to solicit legal advice based on that information, the privilege applies. *Crane Co. v. The Goodyear Tire & Rubber Company,* 204 U.S.P.Q. 502 (Ohio 1979).

ᛒ

The documents are summaries of conferences between counsel representing plaintiff during the prosecution of the patent in suit and of an employee of plaintiff who participated in the prosecution of the patent in suit. The matters contained in the documents relate to legal advice and assistance in connection with the renewed prosecution of plaintiff's patent application and are of the type encompassed within the attorney-client privilege. *Rohm & Haas Co. v. Dawson Chemical Co., Inc.*, 214 U.S.P.Q. 56, 58 (Tex. 1981).

ω

Attorney-client privilege is applicable to corporate clients. Essential elements of this privilege are outlined in VIII *Wigmore on Evidence* 2292 (McNaughten Rev. 1961):

(1) Where legal advice of any kind is sought, (2) from a professional legal advisor in his capacity as such, (3) the communications relating to that purpose, (4) made in confidence, (5) by the client, (6) are at his instance permanently protected, (7) from disclosure by himself or by the legal advisor, (8) except the protection be waived.

The burden of establishing the elements of attorney-client privilege falls squarely upon the party asserting the privilege. The mere existence of an attorney-client privilege does not raise a presumption of confidentiality. As a general rule, no communications from patent agents, whether American or foreign, are subject to an attorney-client privilege in the United States. However, in certain instances, courts have given deference to foreign statutes and applied the principle of comity if the foreign law is not contrary to the public policy of the forum. Committing fraud during the prosecution of an application before the PTO can negate attorney-client privilege; a prima facie showing that the lawyer's advice was designed to serve his client in the furtherance of its wrongful conduct is necessary to vitiate attorney client privilege. *Detection Systems, Inc. v. Pittway Corp.*, 96 F.R.D. 152, 220 U.S.P.Q. 716 (N.Y. 1982).

ω

Inequitable conduct may be sufficient to render a patent unenforceable, but that standard is not a test for piercing the attorney-client privilege.

The protection afforded confidential communications between a patent attorney and his client is forfeited upon a prima facie showing that the communications were made in the furtherance of a fraud upon the PTO. The mere allegation of fraud, however, is not sufficient to terminate the attorney-client privilege. Prima facie evidence of fraud, not mere suspicion of fraud, is required to abrogate the privilege. *Research Corp. v. Gourmet's Delight Mushroom Co., Inc.*, 560 F. Supp. 811, 219 U.S.P.Q. 1023, 1024, 1025 (Pa. 1983).

ω

The defendant's use of its patent counsel's opinions to prove reliance in connection with another issue waives the attorney-client privilege and places those opinions in issue. The plaintiff is entitled to discover the pertinent attorney-client documents. *Southwire Co. v. Essex Group, Inc.*, 570 F. Supp. 643, 219 U.S.P.Q. 1053, 1059 (Ill. 1983).

ω

In order to negate the attorney-client privilege, a party seeking to obtain information that may arguably be privileged must establish that the client seeking to invoke the privilege consulted and obtained the advice of counsel for the purpose of conducting fraudulent activities. The person seeking to negate the privilege must make out a prima facie case of fraud. The alleged fraudulent activities must be of such a serious nature as to warrant the obviation of the privilege. *Stauffer Chemical Co. v. Monsanto Co.*, 623 F. Supp. 148, 227 U.S.P.Q. 401 (Mo. 1985).

ᚦ

Where the question is not whether a patent is enforceable, but whether the protective shield of the attorney-client privilege may be pierced, the patentee's conduct must be measured against the traditional standard for fraud, which in a patent action, equates to a prima facie showing of (1) a knowing, willful, and intentional act of misrepresentation or omission before the PTO (2) that is material and (3) that the PTO relied upon in deciding to issue the patent. The attorney-client privilege is "designed to secure the client's confidence in the secrecy of his communications." Yet the privilege is not absolute and can be waived. Two basic elements are given play in deciding whether the client has waived the privilege: the client's intent to waive the privilege, which may be implied from the circumstances, and considerations of fairness and consistency. Fairness prevents a party from disclosing facts beneficial to its position while refusing to disclose, on the ground of privilege, related facts adverse to its position. A mere denial of intent, without more, is insufficient to constitute a waiver. On the other hand, when state of mind is an issue in a case, a party should not be permitted to testify about its state of mind at the time an allegedly privileged communication occurred without pointing to nonprivileged evidence to substantiate its claim or allowing the opposition to discover the privileged communication. Although communications between a client and his attorney for the purpose of seeking professional advice are generally privileged and not subject to disclosure, it is also well established that a client may intentionally waive its privilege by, for example, disclosing a privileged communication or asserting reliance upon the advice of counsel as an essential element of its defense. In such situations, the client waives the privilege with respect to the subject matter of the advice disclosed or asserted as a defense. *General Electric Co. v. Hoechst Celanese Corp.*, 740 F. Supp. 305, 15 U.S.P.Q.2d 1673, 1676, 1679, 1687 (Del. 1990).

ᚦ

A party that withholds material information from counsel in seeking an opinion as to potential infringement cannot subsequently assert good faith reliance on that opinion in defense to a claim of willful infringement. Moreover, a patentee is entitled to call to the stand the attorney who provided the opinion and to examine him as to the information that defendant provided to him in seeking his counsel. *Amsted Industries Inc. v. National Castings Inc.*, 16 U.S.P.Q.2d 1737, 1742 (Ill. 1990).

ᚦ

The attorney-client privilege applies to invention disclosures that communicate technical information from an inventor to a corporate patent attorney, where the attorney uses the documents "not only as an aid in preparing patent applications, but to help him render opinions with regard to patentability of the invention. . . ." *W.R. Grace & Co.-Conn. v. Viskase Corp.*, 21 U.S.P.Q.2d 1121, 1122 (Ill. 1991).

ᗡ

The "subject matter" to which waiver of attorney-client privilege attaches (through the voluntary decision of a party and its counsel to invoke the advice of counsel defense) reaches all issues related to validity, enforceability, and infringement, but not any other theoretically independent potential bases for defending the case. *McCormick-Morgan Inc. v. Teledyne Industries Inc.*, 765 F. Supp. 611, 21 U.S.P.Q.2d 1412, 1417 (Cal. 1991).

ᗡ

If a party asserts as an essential element (in his defense) reliance upon the advice of counsel, the party waives the attorney-client privilege with respect to all documents and communications to or from counsel concerning the transaction for which counsel's advice was sought, together with all documents and communications relating to the subject matter of the attorney's advice. By raising the defense of equitable estoppel in a declaratory judgment action, plaintiff has waived the attorney-client privilege as to the patent in suit. *Sig Swiss Industrial Co. v. Fres-Co System USA Inc.*, 22 U.S.P.Q.2d 1601, 1602, 1603 (Pa. 1992).

ᗡ

The attorney-client privilege applies to confidential communications with patent agents acting under the authority and control of counsel. The courts are split as to whether the attorney-client privilege should be available equally to communications of registered United States patent agents and registered United States patent attorneys, in order not to frustrate the congressional scheme of providing registration of both. Communications between attorneys and foreign patent agents may be privileged under certain circumstances. *Stryker Corp. v. Intermedics Orthopedics Inc.*, 145 F.R.D. 298, 24 U.S.P.Q.2d 1676, 1680 (N.Y. 1992).

ᗡ

Some courts have found that the invocation of the advice of counsel defense waives both the attorney-client privilege and work product immunity. *Mushroom Associates v. Monterey Mushrooms Inc.*, 24 U.S.P.Q.2d 1767, 1770 (Cal. 1992).

ᗡ

Helping an inventor prepare a patent application and prosecute a patent can involve at least some work that is fairly characterized as lawyering. The communications from inventor to patent lawyer, even those that are entirely technical, remain presumptively protected by the attorney-client privilege. *Advanced Cardiovascular Systems Inc. v. C.R. Bard Inc.*, 144 F.R.D. 372, 25 U.S.P.Q.2d 1354, 1356, 1359 (Cal. 1992).

ᗡ

The factors for determining whether a communication should be protected from disclosure by the attorney-client privilege are: (1) whether the asserted holder of the privilege is or has sought to become a client; (2) whether the person to whom the communication was made is a member of the bar and is acting as a lawyer in connection with the communication; (3) whether the communication relates to a fact of which the attorney was informed by the client in confidence for the purpose of obtaining legal advice; and (4) whether the privilege has been claimed and not waived. *Rohm and Haas Co. v. Brotech Corp.*, 815 F.Supp. 793, 26 U.S.P.Q.2d 1800, 1802 (Del. 1993).

ω

The attorney-client privilege attaches to draft patent applications. *Ball Corp. v. American National Can Co.*, 27 U.S.P.Q.2d 1958, 1959 (Ind. 1993).

ω

Once a defendant asserts that he is faced with a dilemma of choosing between waiving attorney-client privilege in order to protect itself from a willfulness finding (in which case it may risk prejudicing itself on the question of liability) and maintaining the privilege (in which case it may risk being found to be a willful infringer if liability is found), a trial court should inspect the defendant's attorney-client documents *in camera* to ascertain that the dilemma is legitimate. If the dilemma is real, bifurcation of the willfulness issue is an appropriate way to proceed. *Neorx Corp. v. Immunomedics Inc.*, 28 U.S.P.Q.2d 1395, 1396 (N.J. 1993).

ω

In patent matters, confidential communications between attorney and client for the purpose of securing legal advice concerning preparation or prosecution of a patent application are protected, whether the attorney is employed as outside counsel, in-house counsel, or as a member of the Patent Department. *Conner Peripherals Inc. v. Western Digital Corp.*, 31 U.S.P.Q.2d 1042, 1044 (Cal. 1993).

ω

In asserting their affirmative defenses of laches and estoppel, the defendants have waived their attorney-client privilege regarding the opinions of counsel on the validity and enforceability of the patents at issue. *THK America Inc. v. NSK Co. Ltd.*, 157 FRD 637, 33 U.S.P.Q.2d 1248, 1259 (Ill. 1993).

ω

Courts have followed three general approaches in deciding whether the inadvertent production of a document that contains a confidential attorney-client communication waives the privilege. Some courts have found that inadvertently producing the document does waive the privilege. These courts follow a traditional view expressed by Wigmore that any disclosure of a privileged communication is a waiver, no matter what precautions were taken to avoid it. Other courts have looked to the general circumstances surrounding the disclosure of the documents to determine whether finding a waiver would be fair and reasonable. Those courts consider factors, such as the reasonableness of the precautions taken to prevent inadvertent disclosure, the number of inadvertent disclosures, the extent of the disclosure, measures taken to rectify the disclosure, any delay in taking those measures and whether the overriding interests of justice would or would not be served by relieving a party of its error. Still other courts have found that the mere inadvertent production of documents by counsel does not waive the privilege. These cases look to the factual basis for the claim the disclosure was inadvertent to determine whether the client intended to disclose the document or communication, whether the disclosure was inadvertent, or whether the disclosure was unintentional but was so negligent or reckless that a court should deem it intentional. *Berg Electronics Inc. v. Molex Inc.*, 875 F.Supp. 261, 34 U.S.P.Q.2d 1315, 1316 (Del. 1995).

ᛡ

Attorney-client privilege is not limited to actions taken and advice obtained in the shadow of litigation. Persons seek legal advice and assistance in order to meet legal requirements and to plan their conduct; such steps serve the public interest in achieving compliance with law and facilitate the administration of justice, and indeed may avert litigation. *In re University of California,* 40 U.S.P.Q.2d 1784, 1788 (Fed. Cir. 1996).

ᛡ

"Consultation with counsel during patent prosecution meets the criteria of compliance with law and meeting the legal requirements, thereby reducing or avoiding litigation, and is within the scope of the subject matter that is subject to the attorney-client privilege." *In re Regents of the University of California*, 101 F.3d 1386, 1391 [40 U.S.P.Q.2d 1784] (Fed. Cir. 1996). *Bristol-Meyers Squibb Co. v. Rhône-Poulenc Rorer Inc.*, 44 U.S.P.Q.2d 1463, 1465 (N.Y. 1997).

ᛡ

The attorney-client privilege protects confidential disclosures by a client to an attorney made in order to obtain legal assistance. The privilege attaches, not to the information itself, but to the communication of the information. The attorney-client privilege is broader than the work product doctrine insofar as it extends, in the patent context, beyond communications made in anticipation of litigation, to cover consultations during prosecution of patent applications. However, in refusing to answer deposition questions, a party may not rely on generalized assertions of attorney-client privilege but must make reference to specific privileged communications that would be revealed. *Bristol-Myers Squibb Co. v. Rhône-Poulenc Rorer Inc.*, 45 U.S.P.Q.2d 1775, 1779 (N.Y. 1998).

ᛡ

The attorney/client privilege is dispelled when a *prima facie* showing of fraud has been made. *Bristol-Myers Squibb Co. v. Rhône-Poulenc Rorer Inc.*, 48 U.S.P.Q.2d 1817, 1823 (N.Y. 1998).

Attorney Disqualification.

Under the peripheral representation standard an attorney previously associated with a firm that handled matters substantially related to those in which the attorney's disqualification is sought may avoid disqualification by showing that he had no personal involvement in the matters. *Atasi Corp. v. Seagate Technology,* 847 F.2d 826, 6 U.S.P.Q.2d 1955 (Fed. Cir. 1988).

Attorney's Docket Number. *See* **Docket Number.**

Attorney's Fees. *See also* **Bad Faith, Billing Rate, Exceptional, In-House Counsel, Legal Fees, Lodestar, 28 U.S.C. §1920.**

When the plaintiff knew or should have known that the patent upon which suit was based was invalid, granting reasonable attorney's fees is in order. Such reasonable attorney's fees may be based on the number of hours expended and the usual hourly charges of the defendant's attorney for the type of services rendered in preparation for and defense of the lawsuit and appeal. *Townsend Co. v. M.S.L. Industries,* 150 U.S.P.Q. 237, 239 (Ill. 1966).

ᴡ

A patent applicant has a duty to the PTO to make a full and fair disclosure of all facts that may affect the patentability of his invention. A breach of that duty prevents the PTO from properly performing its function of preventing the issuance of unlawful patent monopolies. A patent applicant's breach of duty to the PTO is relevant in determining not only the validity of his patent, but also his good faith in maintaining a subsequent infringement action. An applicant's fraud on the PTO is enough standing alone to convert his later infringement action into an exceptional case within the meaning of 35 U.S.C. §285. But conduct short of fraud and in excess of simply negligence is also an adequate foundation for deciding that a patent action is exceptional. Such conduct is a serious breach of the patentee's duty to the PTO. The party who succeeds in invalidating the unlawful patent performs an invaluable public service. It is appropriate under such circumstances to reward the prevailing party by giving him attorney's fees for his efforts, and it is equally appropriate to penalize in the same measure the patentee who obtained the patent by his wrongdoing. *Monolith Portland Midwest Co. v. Kaiser Aluminum & Chemical Corp.,* 407 F.2d 288, 160 U.S.P.Q. 577, 581 (9th Cir. 1969).

ᴡ

The defendant had knowledge of plaintiff's pending patent application as early as 1958. In 1962, the defendant received a notice of patent infringement from the plaintiff's attorney. Having had knowledge of the plaintiff's patent application while it was on file, and having received actual notice of infringement after the issuance of the patent, the defendant's infringement is deemed to be deliberate, unconscionable, willful, and in bad faith. The defendant acquired this information from the plaintiff and, in utilizing the information, breached a confidential relationship that existed. Furthermore, after acquiring knowledge of the otherwise secret patent application and secret information, defendant deliberately and willfully undertook to infringe upon the device disclosed in the application and to duplicate the information disclosed by the plaintiff. These acts of the defendant present special circumstances under which an award of reasonable attorney's fees, costs, and interest is warranted. *Holmes v. The Thew Shovel Company,* 162 U.S.P.Q. 559, 566 (Ohio 1969).

ᴡ

Under 35 U.S.C. §285 the defendants are only entitled to an award of attorney's fees in connection with the patent claims. The hours expended preparing a claim for attorney's fees must be excluded. *Chromalloy American Corp. v. Alloy Surfaces Co., Inc.,* 353 F. Supp. 429, 176 U.S.P.Q. 508, 510 (Del. 1973).

ᴡ

Lawyers qualified and experienced in patent and trade secret litigation are in a branch of legal service recognized by judges handling such cases as involving special highly developed skills and deserve a substantial compensation above hourly rates, whether fixed by the court or by contract with clients. *Molinaro v. Burnbaum,* 201 U.S.P.Q. 150, 154 (Mass. 1978).

ᴡ

The award of attorney's fees under 35 U.S.C. §285 is compensatory rather than punitive. The party who succeeds in invalidating an unlawful patent performs a valuable public service, and it is appropriate under such circumstances to reward the prevailing party by giving him attorney's fees for his efforts. *Plastic Container Corp. v. Continential Plastics of Oklahoma, Inc.*, 515 F. Supp. 834, 214 U.S.P.Q. 543, 547, 548 (Okla. 1981).

ϖ

The cost of preparing papers and making submissions relating to attorney's fees is included in the allowance for attorney's fees and expenses. *Berkeley Park Clothes, Inc. v. Firma Schaeffer-Homberg GmbH*, 217 U.S.P.Q. 388, 392 (N.J. 1981).

ϖ

If a patent holder or licensee takes the draconian step of notifying the trade that a competitor's product infringes its patent, the patent holder should be responsible for attorney's fees if he is clearly in error and if he has failed to consult competent counsel. *Machinery Corporation of America v. Gullfiber A.B.*, 225 U.S.P.Q. 743 (Pa. 1984).

ϖ

In order to support an award of attorney's fees in a patent case, there must be a showing of conduct that is unfair, in bad faith, inequitable, or unconscionable. In view of defendant's willful infringement, this case involves those elements set out above and is an exceptional case, thereby entitling plaintiff to an award of its attorney's fees. Plaintiff is also entitled to prejudgment interest based upon the damages found or assessed in the second phase of this trial. *Great Northern Corp. v. Davis Core & Pad Co.*, 226 U.S.P.Q. 540 (Ga. 1985).

ϖ

Only after the prevailing party has established the exceptional nature of the case by clear and convincing evidence should a district court exercise its discretion to award attorney's fees. *Machinery Corp. of America v. Gullfiber AB*, 774 F.2d 467, 227 U.S.P.Q. 368, 371 (Fed. Cir. 1985).

ϖ

Even an exceptional case does not require the award of attorney's fees in all circumstances. Many factors could affect this result. The trial judge is in the best position to weigh considerations, such as the closeness of the case, the tactics of counsel, the conduct of the parties, and any other factors that may contribute to a fair allocation of the burdens of litigation as between winner and loser. The court's choice of discretionary ruling should be in furtherance of the policies of the laws that are being enforced, as informed by the court's familiarity of the matter in litigation and the interest of justice. Appellate review to the court's exercise of discretion in this matter cannot be provided in the absence of some explanation of the court's reasoning. *S.C. Johnson & Son, Inc. v. Carter-Wallace, Inc.*, 781 F.2d 198, 228 U.S.P.Q. 367, 369 (Fed. Cir. 1986).

ϖ

An aggressive strategy may or may not be a factor in a decision to deny or award increased damages. An "aggressive strategy" unsupported by any competent advice of counsel, thorough investigation of validity and infringement, discovery of more pertinent uncited prior art, or similar factors, is the type of activity the reference in the patent law to increased damages seeks to prevent. An alleged infringer who intentionally blinds himself to the facts and law, continues to infringe, and employs the judicial process with no solidly based expectation of success, can hardly be surprised when his infringement is found to have been willful. Willfulness of infringement relates to the accused infringer's conduct in the marketplace. Because that conduct may be seen as producing an unnecessary and outcome-certain lawsuit, it may make the case so exceptional as to warrant attorney's fees under 35 U.S.C. §285. Similarly, bad faith displayed in pretrial and trial stages by counsel or party may render the case exceptional under §285. When a court declines to award attorney's fees on the basis of a determination that a case is not exceptional, the fact findings underlying that determination are reviewed under the clearly erroneous standard. When the determination is that a case is exceptional, the election to grant or deny attorney's fees is reviewed under the abuse-of-discretion standard. *Kloster Speedsteel A.B. v. Crucible Inc.*, 793 F.2d 1565, 230 U.S.P.Q. 81 (Fed. Cir. 1986).

ϖ

Under 35 U.S.C. §285 a party awarded attorney's fees may also recover disbursements, which include such expenses as travel, copying, and telephone charges. *Padco Inc. v. Nowell Companies,* 13 U.S.P.Q.2d 1607, 1615 (Wis. 1988).

ϖ

The court may use actual billings as a basis for determining the amount to be awarded as reasonable attorney's fees. Further, the court may accept as reasonable the number of hours actually expended by counsel, provided the expenditure of time is supported by the complexity and length of the litigation. Similarly, if actual billing rates are within the range of fees charged by other patent lawyers in the locale involved, these rates are also considered reasonable. The term attorney's fees, as used in 35 U.S.C. §285, includes disbursements incurred in connection with the legal services rendered. It is proper to include in the award of attorney's fees the attorney's time expended in connection with the plantiff's claim for attorney's fees. The right to attorney's fees and proof of the amount thereof are integral parts of the case. *Trend Products Co. v. Metro Industries,* 10 U.S.P.Q.2d 1539, 1541 (Cal. 1989).

ϖ

The district court's inherent equitable power and informed discretion remain available in determining the level of exceptionality arising out of an offender's particular conduct, and in then determining, in light of that conduct, the compensatory question of the award under §285, including the amount of attorney's fees and the rate of prejudgment interest, if any, on the award. Since the defendant's willful infringement made it necessary for the plaintiffs to bring this suit, an award of prejudgment interest is proper to compensate the plaintiffs fully for the expenses they incurred during litigation. *Water Technologies Corp. v. Calco Ltd.*, 714 F. Supp. 899, 11 U.S.P.Q.2d 1410, 1415 (Ill. 1989).

ϖ

Disregard for the opinion of a sales engineer with neither an aerodynamic nor a legal background and who was thus not qualified to make either a technical or legal determination of infringement does not justify an award of treble damages or attorney's fees.

Uniroyal Inc. v. Rudkin-Wiley Corp., 721 F. Supp. 128, 13 U.S.P.Q.2d 1192, 1201 (Conn. 1989).

ω

While the decision to award attorney's fees is discretionary with the trial judge, the finding that a case is "exceptional" is a finding of fact reviewable under the clearly erroneous standard. Among the types of conduct that can form a basis for finding a case exceptional are willful infringement, inequitable conduct before the PTO, misconduct during litigation, vexatious or unjustified litigation, and frivolous suit. Such conduct must be supported by clear and convincing evidence. The trial judge's failure to take into account the particular misconduct involved in determining the amount of attorney's fees is an abuse of discretion. Commentators seem to suggest that the correct approach is either to deny attorney's fees entirely or to grant fees only to the extent that a party "prevails." When the sole basis for imposing attorney's fees is "gross injustice," and one party prevails on some claims in issue while the other party prevails on other claims, this fact should be taken into account when determining the amount of fees under §285. In other words, the amount of fees awarded to the "prevailing party" should bear some relation to the extent to which that party actually prevailed. Failure of the district court to take into account this factor in assessing fees in the present case constituted an abuse of discretion. *Beckman Instruments Inc. v. LKB Produkter A.B.*, 892 F.2d 1547, 13 U.S.P.Q.2d 1301, 1304, 1306, 1307 (Fed. Cir. 1989).

ω

Although the case was held to be "exceptional" because of the patentee's inequitable conduct in the prosecution of the patent in suit, the court refused to grant attorney's fees because, at a time when the patent was presumed to be valid, the defendant, without a substantial basis for believing the patent to be invalid, embarked on its course of action without regard to the patent laws. A prevailing alleged infringer should be awarded attorney's fees only when it would be unjust not to make such an award. Here, there is no injustice in denying defendant an award of counsel fees. *Hoffmann-La Roche Inc. v. Lemmon Co.*, 13 U.S.P.Q.2d 1224, 1229 (Pa. 1989), vacated and remanded, 906 F.2d 684, 15 U.S.P.Q.2d 1363 (Fed. Cir. 1990).

ω

The fact that a number of different attorneys were involved in different stages of the litigation does not mean that there was an unreasonable duplication of effort for the purpose of reducing attorney's fees. However, overhead charges for such items as secretarial services, word processing equipment, library services, and general office staff are generally considered as part of an attorney's overhead and are usually deleted from awards made to attorneys under 35 U.S.C. §285. *Howes v. Medical Components Inc.*, 741 F. Supp. 528, 17 U.S.P.Q.2d 1591, 1595, 1596 (Pa. 1990).

ω

An attorney's fee determination should not result in a second major litigation. *Slimfold Manufacturing Co. Inc. v. Kinkead Industries Inc.*, 932 F.2d 1453, 18 U.S.P.Q.2d 1842, 1848 (Fed. Cir. 1991).

ω

Attorney fee awards to prevailing parties in patent cases are oftentimes substantial. In a patent defense case, an attorney's fee award was $580,183.50, and an expenses award was $83,421.91; $1.95 million in attorney's fees, costs, and expenses were awarded in another patent case. *Automotive Products plc v. Tilton Engineering Inc.*, 855 F.Supp. 1101, 33 U.S.P.Q.2d 1065, 1098 (Cal. 1994).

ᅟᗡ

A successful plaintiff, who demonstrates a wilful violation and proves itself entitled to attorney's fees in the district court proceedings, may nevertheless be compelled to bear the expense of a related appeal unless it can make a separate showing that the appeal itself is exceptional. The Court addressed the amount of attorney's fees and stated that partners would be awarded no more than $200 per hour with the exception of lead counsel, who would be awarded $250 per hour. Associates would be billed at a rate not to exceed $135 per hour, and paralegals and law clerks at a rate not to exceed $50 per hour. *Stryker Corp. v. Intermedics Orthopedics Inc.*, 42 U.S.P.Q.2d 1935, 1937, 1938 (N.Y. 1997).

ᗡ

"[A]ttorney fees for appellate work is not the exclusive domain of an appellate court." "Where a lawsuit consists of related claims, a plaintiff who has won substantial relief should not have his attorney fee reduced simply because the district court did not adopt each contention raised." *Concept Design Electronics and Manufacturing Inc. v. Duplitronics Inc.*, 79 F.3d 1167, 43 U.S.P.Q.2d 1112, 1113, 1114 (Fed. Cir. 1996 - *unpublished*).

Attorney's File.

Although an attorney may be deposed and required to disclose what he knows about the subject matter, he cannot be required to disclose his mental impressions, conclusions, opinions, or legal theories concerning the litigation. He may be required to refer to his file to refresh his recollection, but he cannot be compelled to state why he amended the claims or what he meant by this or that word or phrase; that would require him to express an opinion, one of the exceptions provided for in Fed. R. Civ. P. 26(b)(3). *MacLaren v. B-l-W Group Inc.*, 180 U.S.P.Q. 387 (Va. 1973).

Attorney's Lien.

Since a retaining lien never affects the rights of ownership (but only the right of possession), a retaining lien is an insufficient interest in a patent or application to warrant recordation. The retaining lien exists regardless of recordation and stays in place until discharged. An attorney's retaining lien cannot affect the title of the patent or invention to which it relates. Moreover, notice is not required to protect an attorney's retaining lien against assignment by the client or attachment by the client's creditors. *In re Refusal of Assignment Branch to Record Attorney's Lien,* 8 U.S.P.Q.2d 1446 (Comm'r Patents & Trademarks 1988).

Attorney's Opinion. *See* **Opinion, Opinion of Counsel.**

Aukerman Presumption

As plaintiff either knew or should have known of the accused infringer's allegedly infringing activities six or more years prior to filing suit, the accused infringer was entitled to the benefit of a presumption of unreasonable delay and prejudice, the two critical factual predicates for the application of the equitable bar of laches. *Hall v. Aqua Queen Manufacturing Inc.*, 93 F.3d 1548, 39 U.S.P.Q.2d 1925 (Fed. Cir. 1996)

Auslegeschrift.

When the prosecution of an application before the Examiner in Germany terminates with a formal indication that the case is considered allowable and the specification issues in printed form, the rights that come into being on the date of publication of the allowed application are the full patent rights. The published allowed application is equivalent to a patent with respect to the existence and exercise, by the owner, of the rights of a patentee and the invention can properly be said to have been patented from the date of the publication.

This event in the German practice represents the conclusion of the prosecution of the application before the Examiner, the formal indication by the Examiner that the case is considered allowable, a time for paying a "publication" fee (which may be accepted late), and the publication (which can be postponed) of the application with issuance of the specification in printed form. According to the German law, the publication of the allowed application at this time confers and marks the beginning of the exclusive rights that are conferred by a patent. The rights that come into being on the date of publication of the allowed application are the full patent rights. Acts of making, using, selling, etc., by others of the subject matter protected after the date of this publication constitute acts of infringement in the same manner and to the same extent as if the formal order of granting a patent had been executed, and suits for infringement may be initiated and prosecuted by the owner of the rights. *Ex parte Maino Des Granges*, 862 O.G. 657, 658, 659 (PTO Bd. App. 1968). *See also Ex parte Gruschwitz and Fritz*, 138 U.S.P.Q. 505 (PO Bd. App. 1961).

Authenticate.

In attempting to establish an earlier date for reduction to practice, a junior party in an interference was unable to identify the person who labeled the container of a critical starting material, did not have personal knowledge as to whether the material was in the same form as it was when the container was labeled, and did not analyze a sample from the container prior to using the material therein. The contents of the container were thus not adequately authenticated. *Castro and Marsh v. Moller, Muhlhausen, and Hauptmann*, 182 U.S.P.Q. 502 (PTO Bd. Pat. Int. 1973).

Authoritative Opinion. *See also* Opinion.

While courts have recognized that good faith reliance on an "authoritative" opinion of counsel may be a defense to a charge of willful infringement, conclusory statements (without supporting reasons) do not constitute an "authoritative opinion" upon which good faith reliance may be founded. *Fromson v. RVP Chemical Corp.,* 15 U.S.P.Q.2d 1689, 1699 (Wis. 1990).

Authority. *See also* Challenge.

An attorney's affidavit was not accepted as adequate proof that the person who signed a Declaration had authority to act for and bind the assignee company. *Schmidt v. Reynolds,* 140 U.S.P.Q. 118, 119, 1964 C.D. 1 (D.C. 1963).

Authority of the Commissioner.

The Commissioner lacks authority to reopen the reexamination proceeding after receipt of the Federal Circuit's mandate affirming the Examiner's rejection of all claims since the case is no longer considered pending. See MPEP §1216.06 (5th ed., rev. 12, July 1989) under "Office Procedure Following Decision by the Federal Circuit," subheading "1. All claims rejected;" *Morganroth v. Quigg,* 885 F.2d 843, 12 U.S.P.Q.2d 1125, 1128 (Fed. Cir. 1989) (Commissioner does not have authority to revive application abandoned by termination of proceedings resulting from a failure to appeal a final district court judgment); *In re Jones,* 542 F.2d 65, 191 U.S.P.Q. 249, 252 (C.C.P.A. 1976) ("receipt of the mandate by the PTO terminated proceedings in the case"); *In re Willis,* 537 F.2d 513, 190 U.S.P.Q. 327, 329 (C.C.P.A. 1976) ("When, on January 12, 1976, our mandate was received in the PTO, no claims having been allowed, the appealed application suffered its demise."); *Continental Can Co. v. Schuyler,* 326 F. Supp. 283, 168 U.S.P.Q. 625 (D.C. 1970) ("where rejection of all claims is affirmed by the Court of Customs and Patent Appeals, the responsibility is upon the plaintiff to stay the Court's judgment if the pendency of the application is to be preserved"). Petitioner's relief, if any, lies in a motion for the Federal Circuit to withdraw its mandate, not with the Commissioner. *See Jones,* 542 F.2d at 68, 191 U.S.P.Q. at 252 (CCPA "has the power, in the interest of justice, to recall its mandate in an appropriate case, and this power should be exercised sparingly and only upon a showing of good cause"). *In re Eckerle,* 1115 O.G. 6 (Comm'r Patents & Trademarks 1990).

Authorship. *See* Coauthor.

Automate.

It is not "invention" broadly to provide a mechanical or automatic means to replace manual activity that has accomplished the same result. *In re Venner and Bowser,* 262 F.2d 91, 120 U.S.P.Q. 192, 194 (C.C.P.A. 1958).

Automatic.

The mere statement that a device is to be operated automatically instead of by hand, without a claim specifying any particular automatic mechanism, is not the statement of an invention. *In re Rundell,* 48 F.2d 958, 9 U.S.P.Q. 220 (C.C.P.A. 1931).

Availability. *See also* **Thesis.**

When foreign publications were relied upon to establish what was known at the time of applicant's filing date, the PTO questioned the availability of the publications in the United States. Section 112 simply requires that a disclosure of an invention enable any man skilled in the relevant art to make and use it. No mention of convenience is made. Thus, even if the origin of the material is in Australia, this is merely a matter of degree of convenience and not a matter of lack of availability. *In re Metcalfe and Lowe,* 410 F.2d 1378, 161 U.S.P.Q. 789, 791 (C.C.P.A. 1969).

ɷ

The court is unpersuaded by the defendant's arguments that a non-infringing device's "availability" suffices for accepted "acceptability" as a substitute under the Panduit test. More than speculation that the non-infringing device "could have been used" in North or South America during the relevant period must be shown to overturn the Master's finding of fact on the non-infringing device as an acceptable substitute. *T.D. Williamson Inc. v. Laymon,* 723 F. Supp. 587, 13 U.S.P.Q.2d 1417, 1423 (Okla. 1989).

Availability of Prior Art.

The differences between the prior art and the invention defined by the asserted claims, the availability of that art to all workers in the field, the failure of established competitors in a highly competitive market to make the invention despite the incentive to do so, the admittedly unobvious performance benefits realized through the claimed invention, the impressive commercial success of the claimed product, the praise of independent commentators, and the forbearance of competitors from infringing the patent all go to confirm that the claimed invention was not obvious at the time it was made to a person of ordinary skill in the art. *S.C. Johnson & Son, Inc. v. Carter-Wallace, Inc.,* 614 F. Supp. 1278, 225 U.S.P.Q. 1022 (N.Y. 1985).

Avoid. *See also* **Exclude, Teach Away From.**

Appellant's claimed method involves doing what the reference tries to avoid. Appellant has invented a method for producing small wire or ribbon of 55-Nitinol when the prior art strongly suggests that such a method would produce carbon contamination and unacceptable results. This is the very antithesis of obviousness. The prior art of record does not teach or even hint at appellant's discovery that 55-Nitinol is essentially inert to graphite, and this explains the successful performance of the claimed method. *In re Buehler,* 515 F.2d 1134, 185 U.S.P.Q. 781 (C.C.P.A. 1975).

Avoiding Infringement.

The mere fact that an accused infringer has made a significant improvement over a patented invention does not avoid infringement when making or selling any device that satisfies all of the limitations of a valid patent claim. *Berkley Park Clothes, Inc. v. Firma Schaffer-Homberg GmbH,* 217 U.S.P.Q. 388 (N.J. 1981).

Awards. *See* **Secondary Considerations.**

Key Terms and Concepts

Backfiring.

Phrases in claims referring back to the description and drawing, such as "substantially as described" or "as herein shown and described" were once customary in claims in the days of the central definition. Expressions referring back to the disclosure are sometimes referred to by patent authors as "backfiring" expressions. *Ex parte Fressola*, 27 U.S.P.Q.2d 1608, 1610 (B.P.A.I. 1993).

Bacteria.

A description of several newly discovered strains of bacteria (having one particularly desirable metabolic property in terms of the conventionally measured culture characteristics and a number of metabolic and physiological properties) does not enable one of ordinary skill in the relevant art independently to discover additional strains having the same specific, desirable metabolic property (i.e., the production of a particular antibiotic). A verbal description of a new species does not enable one of ordinary skill in the relevant art to obtain strains of that species over and above the specific strains made available through deposit in one of the recognized culture depositories. *Ex parte Jackson, Theriault, Sinclair, Fager, and Karwowski*, 217 U.S.P.Q. 804, 806 (PTO Bd. App. 1982).

Bad Faith. *See also* **Exceptional, Inequitable Conduct, Spurious, 35 U.S.C. §285.**

The plaintiff was induced to accept the terms of a compromise settlement offer by representations that this litigation and its consequential legal expenses would be at an end. The promised bargain was not realized by the plaintiff because of the Asgrow Companies' most immediate collateral attack upon the consent judgment once it was approved and entered by this court. As a direct result, the plaintiff sustained unforeseen legal expenses in seeking to preserve and enforce the settlement agreement to which the Asgrow Companies had silently acquiesced during negotiations and hearings prior to entry of the final order. The conduct of the Asgrow Companies demonstrates sufficient bad faith to warrant an award of attorney's fees to the plaintiff. *Research Corp. v. Pfister Associated Growers, Inc.*, 318 F. Supp. 1405, 168 U.S.P.Q. 206 (Ill. 1970).

ᛦ

Bad faith on the part of a patentee is not a requirement of an estoppel defense. All that is required is that the patentee conduct itself in such a way as to induce the belief that it has abandoned its claim, regardless of its good or bad faith. *Adelberg Laboratories Inc. v. Miles Inc.*, 921 F.2d 1267, 17 U.S.P.Q.2d 1111, 1116 (Fed. Cir. 1990).

ᛦ

In order to support a 35 U.S.C. §285 award based on bad faith, a verdict form need not specifically ask whether a patentee asserted its rights in bad faith so long as the verdict form yields sufficient evidence from which the court may infer bad faith. A verdict form does not yield sufficient evidence as to bad faith unless the information it contains can be said to establish bad faith by clear and convincing evidence. *Manildra Milling Corp. v. Ogilvie Mills Inc.*, 878 F.Supp. 1417, 30 U.S.P.Q.2d 1020, 1023 (Kan. 1993).

ɷ

Bad faith is used in referring to misconduct in the prosecution of or litigation over a patent. Such conduct includes inequitable conduct during patent prosecution, bringing vexatious or unjustified suits, attorney or client misconduct during litigation, or unnecessarily prolonging litigation. These acts by themselves, however, are not sufficient for an increased damages award under 35 U.S.C. §284 because they are not related to the underlying act of infringement and say nothing about the culpability of the infringer. Only a culpable infringer can be held liable for increased damages, not an innocent one. In an initial determination of culpability, and thus liability for increased damages, "bad faith" properly refers to an infringer's failure to meet his affiormative duty to use due care in avoiding infringement of another's patent rights. *Jurgens v. CBK Ltd.*, 80 F.3d 1566, 38 U.S.P.Q.2d 1397, 1400 (Fed. Cir. 1996).

Bald. *See* **Hair Growth.**

Bankruptcy.

Whether an action is by or against a debtor is determined by the debtor's status at the time the action was begun, not by who was ahead when a bankruptcy petition was filed. So far as the literal meaning of 11 U.S.C. §362(a)(1) is concerned, a federal district court may proceed to decision on a declaratory judgment action brought by a petitioner in bankruptcy as if no bankruptcy proceeding were pending. *In re Mahurkar Double Lumen Hemodialysis Catheter Patent Litigation*, 23 U.S.P.Q.2d 1903, 1908 (Ill. 1992).

ɷ

Although the Bankruptcy Code is silent on the question of appellate standing, this court has held that the "person aggrieved" test, derived from the Bankruptcy Act of 1898, governs appellate standing under the code. *Everex Systems Inc. v. Cadtrak Corp.*, 39 U.S.P.Q.2d 1518, 1520 (9th Cir. 1996).

Basic Invention or Patent. *See also* **Pioneer Invention.**

What were once referred to as "basic inventions" have led to "basic patents," which amounted to real incentives, not only to invention and its disclosure, but to its prompt, early disclosure. *In re Hogan and Banks*, 559 F.2d 595, 194 U.S.P.Q. 527, 537 (C.C.P.A. 1977).

Batchelder Doctrine. *See* **New Matter, Reduction in Scope.**

Bayh-Dole Act. *See* **35 U.S.C. §202(c)(7)(B).**

Beauty.

Utility under 35 U.S.C. §103 can reside in beauty and/or increasing visual appeal. *Ex parte Contrael, Stahlhut, and Trippeer,* 174 U.S.P.Q. 61 (PTO Bd. App. 1971).

Bench Test.

To establish reduction to practice, test data must be such as to indicate that the invention worked as intended in practical use. This may be done in several ways. The invention may be tested under actual conditions of use. The invention may be given bench tests that fully duplicate each and every condition of actual use. Finally, in some cases, bench tests may be performed that do not duplicate all of the conditions of actual use. In order to show reduction to practice based on such tests, the evidence must establish such a relationship between the test conditions and the intended functional setting of the invention. *White v. Lemmerman,* 341 F.2d 110, 144 U.S.P.Q. 409, 411 (C.C.P.A. 1965).

Benefit. *See also* **Advantage.**

An inventor is entitled to all of the benefits of his invention, even though they were greater than he believed. *Tapco Products Co. v. Van Mark Products Corp.,* 446 F.2d 420, 170 U.S.P.Q. 550 (6th Cir. 1971).

ϖ

The mere lack of literal support in a parent application for a claim limitation is not enough to carry the PTO's initial burden to establish that the applicant is not entitled to the benefit of the filing date of such parent application. *In re Voss,* 557 F.2d 812, 194 U.S.P.Q. 267, 271 (C.C.P.A. 1977).

Benzene.

Even though pyridine and benzene are similar in many respects, the effect of their interchange in the instant complex nucleus could hardly be foretold, considering that there is little predictability in the subject art. *Ex parte Koo,* 150 U.S.P.Q. 131, 132 (PO Bd. App. 1965).

Benzyl.

A single benzene ring, such as that of benzylthiocyanate, is not equivalent to a double-condensed benzene ring, such as that in naphthylmethylthiocyanate. *In re Jones,* 149 F.2d 501, 65 U.S.P.Q. 480, 481 (C.C.P.A. 1945).

Benzyl vs. Phenyl.

Even though the issue was one of reforming an interference, it appears from the wording of the opinion that unwarranted weight may have inadvertently been accorded to testimony that only established obviousness to try. An expert testified that it would be obvious for someone testing or making the phenyl-substituted compounds also to make and test the benzyl substituted compounds. Nothing in the opinion appears to address the issue as to whether either the benzyl- or phenyl-subgenus would have been obvious (as a whole) prior to testing that particular subgenus. *Winter v. Banno,* 229 U.S.P.Q. 212 (B.P.A.I. 1985).

Best Efforts.

An implied obligation to exploit a licensed patent is not binding on an exclusive licensee if its observance would prevent the licensee from meeting market competition with a reasonable chance of success. *William Hodges & Co., Inc. v. Sterwood Corp.*, 348 F.Supp. 383, 176 U.S.P.Q. 49, 57 (N.Y. 1972).

ᘐ

A court will imply a duty on the part of an exclusive licensee to exploit the subject matter of the license with due diligence or with best efforts, where such covenant is essential as a matter of equity, and in such circumstances the implied obligation must conform to what the court may assume would have been the agreement of the parties if the situation had been anticipated and provided for. Where the parties have considered the matter, however, and deliberately omitted any obligation on the part of the exclusive licensee to exploit the subject matter of the license with due diligence, where it is unnecessary to imply such obligation in order to give effect to the terms of the contract, the obligation will not be implied. *Willis Brothers, Inc. v. Ocean Scallops, Inc.*, 356 F. Supp. 1151, 176 U.S.P.Q. 53, 56 (N.C. 1972).

ᘐ

While the phrase "best efforts" is often used to describe the extent of the implied undertaking by an exclusive licensee, this has properly been termed an "extravagant" phrase. A more accurate description of the obligation owed would be the exercise of "due diligence" or "reasonable efforts." It would be inherently unfair to place the productiveness of the licensed property solely within the control of the licensee, thereby putting the licensor at his mercy, without imposing a reciprocal obligation on the licensee. *Permanence Corp. v. Kennametal Inc.*, 908 F.2d 98, 15 U.S.P.Q.2d 1550, 1552 (6th Cir. 1990).

ᘐ

A best efforts clause is inferred in a license agreement only if it is necessary to prevent the contract from failing for lack of mutuality or, otherwise, to achieve the clear intentions of the parties derived from their express agreement. *Beraha v. Baxter Health Care Corp.*, 956 F.2d 1436, 22 U.S.P.Q.2d 1100, 1105 (7th Cir. 1992).

Best Evidence.

The best evidence of unexpected beneficial properties of a claimed intermediate is evidence of unexpected advantageous properties of the final product derived from the claimed intermediate. *Deutsche Gold-Und Silber Scheideanstalt Vormals Roessler v. Commissioner of Patents*, 251 F. Supp. 624, 148 U.S.P.Q. 412 (D.C. 1966).

Best Mode.[1] *See also* Production Detail.

The "best mode disclosure requirement prevents the simultaneous enjoyment of both patent and trade secrecy protection for a single invention." *Picard v. United Aircraft Corp.*, 128 F.2d 632, 53 U.S.P.Q. 563 (2d Cir.), *cert. denied*, 317 U.S. 651, 55 U.S.P.Q. 493 (1942).

ᘐ

---

[1]See *Nobelpharma AB v. Implant Innovations Inc.*, 129 F.3d 1463, 44 U.S.P.Q.2d 1705 (Fed. Cir. 1997)

Best Mode

The sole purpose of the best mode requirement is to restrain inventors from applying for patents while, at the same time, concealing from the public preferred embodiments of their invention that they have in fact conceived. An inventor is in compliance with the best mode requirement if he does not conceal what he feels is a preferred embodiment of his invention. *In re Gay,* 309 F.2d 769, 135 U.S.P.Q. 311, 315 (C.C.P.A. 1962).

ᛒ

A patentee must disclose the best method known to him to carry out the invention. Even if there is a better method, his failure to disclose it will not invalidate his patent if he does not know of it or if he does not appreciate that it is the best method. It is enough that he act in good faith in his patent disclosure. On the other hand, if he knows at the time the application is filed of a better method to practice the invention and knows it to be the best method, it would make no difference whether or not he was the discoverer of that method. *Engelhard Industries, Inc. v. Sel-Rex Corp.,* 253 F. Supp. 832, 149 U.S.P.Q. 607, 611 (N.J. 1966).

ᛒ

An inventor is in compliance with the best mode requirement if he does not conceal what he feels is a preferred embodiment of his invention. There is no statutory basis for reading into the best mode portion a requirement that the mode disclosed be in fact the optimum mode for carrying out the invention. *In re Bosy,* 360 F.2d 972, 149 U.S.P.Q. 789 (C.C.P.A. 1966).

ᛒ

The absence of a specific working example is not necessarily evidence that the best mode has not been disclosed, nor is the presence of one evidence that it has. An inventor may represent his contemplated best mode just as well by a preferred range of conditions or group of reactants as by a working example that employs unitary values of each variable involved. *In re Honn and Sims,* 364 F.2d 454, 150 U.S.P.Q. 652 (C.C.P.A. 1966).

ᛒ

With regard to its description of the claimed invention, the patent fails to set forth the best mode contemplated by the inventor. Although the preferred composition was known prior to the effective filing date of the parent application, it was effectively obscured in both the parent application and the patent in suit. Rather than disclose its specific recipe, plaintiff merely included the elements of the preferred composition within the series of broad ranges claimed by the patent in suit, which ranges extended beyond the area representing significant technological advancement. The patent in suit is invalid for failing to comply with the requirements of 35 U.S.C. §112. *Indiana General Corp. v. Krystinel Corp.,* 297 F. Supp. 427, 161 U.S.P.Q. 82, 91, 92 (N.Y. 1968).

ᛒ

The best mode provision of 35 U.S.C. §112 has been held to require only that the inventor set forth in the specification the mode that he considers the best at the time of filing his application. Applicant does not have the burden of updating a pending application as he discovers more practicable means of implementing his invention, so long as such improvements are covered by the specification and claims of his application. Also, on filing a continuing application, there is no need to present a better mode of practicing the invention discovered subsequent to his initial filing date. *Sylgab Steel & Wire Corp. v. Imoco-Gateway Corp.*, 357 F. Supp. 657, 178 U.S.P.Q. 22, 23 (Ill. 1973).

ᛞ

Failure to set forth any mode is equivalent to non-enablement; the best mode provision is directed to a different type of situation. *In re Glass*, 492 F.2d 1228, 181 U.S.P.Q. 31, 35 (C.C.P.A. 1974).

ᛞ

Issues with respect to the best mode requirement are concerned with acts of disclosure or concealment of certain subject matter by the inventor during the preparation of a patent application. The essence of the requirement is not that the best mode, as such, be set forth in the specification, but that the best mode known to the inventor at the time of the execution of the application be included therein. *Ex parte Richter*, 185 U.S.P.Q. 380, 381 (PO Bd. App. 1974).

ᛞ

The best mode requirement only requires disclosure of methods the inventor has reduced to practice; it does not require the disclosure of a system that, at the time of the filing date, was only theoretical. *Columbia Broadcasting System, Inc. v. Zenith Radio Corp.*, 391 F. Supp. 780, 185 U.S.P.Q. 662, 671 (Ill. 1975).

ᛞ

Failure to set forth the best mode contemplated by an inventor of carrying out his invention need not rise to the level of active concealment or grossly inequitable conduct in order to warrant invalidation of a patent. *Union Carbide Corp. v. Borg-Warner Corp.*, 550 F.2d 355, 193 U.S.P.Q. 1, 8 (6th Cir. 1977).

ᛞ

Since the inventors had full knowledge of a specific arrangement to be used in practicing their process, but failed to disclose the same in their patent, instead disclosing a blank box described as "conventional," the patent fails to comply with the best mode require-ments of 35 U.S.C. §112. *Thyssen Plastik Anger KG v. Induplas, Inc.*, 195 U.S.P.Q. 534, 538 (P.R. 1977)

ᛞ

In the absence of any cause to suspect the inventor of concealing pertinent information he may have possessed, a rejection for failure to disclose his best mode was not sustained. *Ex parte Krenzer*, 199 U.S.P.Q. 227, 229 (PTO Bd. App. 1978).

ᛞ

There is no objective standard by which to judge the adequacy of a best mode disclosure. Only evidence of concealment (accidental or intentional) is to be considered. That evidence, in order to result in affirmance of a best mode rejection, must tend to show that the quality of an applicant's best mode disclosure is so poor as to effectively result in concealment. *In re Sherwood*, 613 F.2d 809, 204 U.S.P.Q. 537, 544 (C.C.P.A. 1980).

ᛞ

The best mode that must be disclosed is the best mode known to the inventor. *Railroad Dynamics, Inc. v. A. Stucki Co.*, 579 F. Supp. 353, 218 U.S.P.Q. 618 (Pa. 1983).

ʊ

In evaluating the quality of an applicant's best mode disclosure, the court should read into the specification any information that is "known to those having ordinary skill in the art." Thus, a failure to disclose all of the information in possession of the inventor is not fatal when the application of routine skill in the art would allow practice of the invention. *H.H. Robertson Co. v. Barger Metal Fabricating Co.*, 225 U.S.P.Q. 1191 (Ohio 1984).

ʊ

Not complying with the best mode requirement amounts to concealing the preferred mode contemplated by the applicant at the time of filing. Only evidence of concealment (accidental or intention) is to be considered. That evidence, in order to result in affirmance of a best mode rejection, must tend to show that the quality of an applicant's best mode disclosure is so poor as to effectively result in concealment. The purpose of the best mode requirement is to restrain inventors from applying for patents while, at the same time, concealing from the public preferred embodiments of their inventions that they in fact have conceived. Compliance with the best mode requirement exists when an inventor discloses his preferred embodiment. *DeGeorge v. Bernier*, 768 F.2d 1318, 226 U.S.P.Q. 758 (Fed. Cir. 1985).

ʊ

The fact that the specification is devoid of a working example is without significance. Examples are not necessary. While a full example may have provided additional useful information, one possessed of knowledge of one skilled in this art could practice the invention without the exercise of an undue amount of experimentation. With respect to the best mode rejection, we find no evidence of concealment and are unable to agree with the Examiner that the quality of the appellants' disclosure is so lacking as to effectively result in concealment. *Ex parte Nardi and Simier*, 229 U.S.P.Q. 79 (B.P.A.I. 1986).

ʊ

Proof that an applicant knew of and concealed a better mode than that disclosed is required to establish failure to satisfy the best-mode requirement. *Hybritech Inc. v. Abbott Laboratories*, 4 U.S.P.Q.2d 1001 (Cal. 1987).

ʊ

Although a trade name alone may be inappropriate in a best mode disclosure when suitable substitutes are unavailable, here, commercial substitutes were readily available in the prior art and the trade name is mere surplusage - an addition to the generic description. Contrary to the district court's conclusion, patentee's disclosure was not an attempt to conceal its cleaning fluid formula; it disclosed the contents of the fluid as "a nonresidue detergent solution," the same solution as the surgical detergent solution used in the prior art. *Randomex Inc. v. Scopus Corp.*, 849 F.2d 585, 7 U.S.P.Q.2d 1050, 1054 (Fed. Cir. 1988).

ʊ

The best mode requirement mandates disclosure by the inventor not simply of generic information for carrying out the invention, but also of the best mode contemplated by the inventor. *Scripps Clinic and Research Foundation v. Genentech Inc.*, 707 F. Supp. 1547, 11 U.S.P.Q.2d 1187, 1192 (Cal. 1989).

ထ

Absent inequitable conduct, a best mode defense only affects those claims covering subject matter the practice of which has not been disclosed in compliance with the best mode requirement. *See Northern Telecom, Inc. v. Datapoint Corp.*, 908 F.2d 931, 15 U.S.P.Q.2d 1321, 1328 (Fed. Cir.), *cert. denied*, 111 S. Ct. 296 (1990).

ထ

The intentional withholding of the best mode and the disclosure of a fictitious, inoperative mode constitute inequitable conduct in connection with the prosecution of a patent. *Consolidated Aluminum Corp. v. Foseco International Ltd.*, 910 F.2d 804, 15 U.S.P.Q.2d 1481, 1483 (Fed. Cir. 1990).

ထ

A proper best mode analysis has two components. The first is whether, at the time the inventor filed his patent application, he knew of a mode of practicing his invention that he considered to be better than any other. This part of the inquiry is wholly subjective and resolves whether the inventor must disclose any facts in addition to those for enablement. If the inventor, in fact, contemplated such a preferred mode, the second part of the analysis compares what he knew with what he disclosed: Is the disclosure adequate to enable one skilled in the art to practice the best mode, or, in other words, has the inventor "concealed" his best mode from the "public"? Assessing the adequacy of the disclosure, as opposed to its necessity, is largely an objective inquiry that depends upon the scope of the claimed invention and the level of skill in the art. An inventor need not disclose manufacturing data or the requirements of a particular customer when that information is not a part of the best mode of practicing the claimed invention, but the converse is also true. Whether characterizable as "manufacturing data," "customer requirements," or even "trade secrets," information necessary to practice the best mode simply must be disclosed. *Chemcast Corp. v. Arco Industries Corp.*, 913 F.2d 923, 16 U.S.P.Q.2d 1033, 1036, 1037, 1038 (Fed. Cir. 1990).

ထ

The alleged invalidity of a patent for failure to disclose the best mode contemplated for carrying out the invention was considered without merit because dozens of subsequent patents cite that patent and its method as prior art, and this attests to the ability of others to learn from the patent. *Allied-Signal Inc. v. Field Tec Corp.*, 17 U.S.P.Q.2d 1692, 1694 (Cal. 1990).

ထ

The best mode requirement does not require the inventor to disclose production details as long as the best means of achieving the inventive results are disclosed. Nor must all operating conditions be recited, as long as one of ordinary skill in the art would know how to select operating conditions to achieve the desired result. Nor should a patent be invalidated for a violation of the best mode requirement if the results desired can readily be achieved by other conventional means and if the undisclosed information was conventional and well known in the art as of the date of the invention. *Juno Lighting Inc. v. Cooper Industries Inc.*, 17 U.S.P.Q.2d 1802, 1803 (Ill. 1990).

ᚔ

A best mode of disclosure may be adequate even though it does not make it possible for skilled workers to duplicate the inventor's best mode. *Scripps Clinic & Research v. Genentech*, 18 U.S.P.Q.2d 1001 (Fed. Cir. 1991).

ᚔ

The best mode requirement is a safeguard against the possible selfish desire on the part of some people to obtain patent protection without making a full disclosure. The requirement does not permit an inventor to disclose only what is known to be the second-best embodiment, retaining the best. The fundamental issue that should be addressed is whether there was evidence to show that the quality of an applicant's best mode disclosure is so poor as to effectively result in concealment. If deposit is the only way to comply with the best mode requirement, the deposit must be made. 52 Fed. Reg. 34,080, 34,086 (Sept. 8, 1987). *Amgen Inc. v. Chugai Pharmaceutical Co. Ltd.*, 927 F.2d 1200, 18 U.S.P.Q.2d 1016, 1025 (Fed. Cir. 1991).

ᚔ

There is no mechanical rule that a best mode violation occurs because the inventor failed to disclose particular manufacturing procedures beyond the information sufficient for enablement. One must look at the scope of the invention, the skill of the art, the evidence as to the inventor's belief, and all of the circumstances in order to evaluate whether the inventor's failure to disclose particulars of manufacture gives rise to an inference that he concealed information that one of ordinary skill in the art would not know. When missing information on manufacturing was well known to those of skill in the art, its specific disclosure is not required. Any process of manufacture requires the selection of specific steps and materials over others. The best mode does not necessarily cover each of these selections. To so hold would turn a patent specification into a detailed production schedule, which is not its function. *Wahl Instruments Inc. v. Acvious Inc.*, 950 F.2d 1575, 21 U.S.P.Q.2d 1123, 1127, 1128 (Fed. Cir. 1991).

ᚔ

The proposition that failure to disclose the best mode results in inequitable conduct is legally incorrect. Inequitable conduct requires an intent to deceive as well as a threshold level of materiality. *In re Hayes Microcomputer Products Inc. Patent Litigation*, 982 F.2d 1527, 25 U.S.P.Q.2d 1241, 1255 (Fed. Cir. 1992).

ᚔ

The best mode of practicing the invention known to the patent owner at the time of filing the original United States application included a trade secret process, which was not disclosed in the patent and has intentionally been kept as a trade secret. Such failure to disclose the best mode is in violation of 35 U.S.C. §112, and makes the patentee's claim unenforceable. *Katrapat A.G. v. Advanced Machine and Engineering Co.*, 28 U.S.P.Q.2d 1270, 1279 (Ill. 1993).

ᚔ

No Federal Circuit decision has explicitly addressed whether an applicant filing a continuation or continuation-in-part application under 35 U.S.C. §120 must disclose a best mode arrived at after the initial application was filed {see 2 Donald Chisum, *Patents* §7.05[2], at 7-151 to -152 (1993)}. *Transco Products Inc. v. Performance Contracting Inc.*, 821 F.Supp. 537, 28 U.S.P.Q.2d 1739, 1747 (Ill. 1993).

ω

Knowledge of officials of an inventor's assignee (directly connected to an application for patent) is not imputed to the inventor for purposes of finding a best mode violation, even though the assignee (not the inventor individually) both directed the patent prosecution and enjoyed the monopoly the issued patent provided. *Glaxo Inc. v. Novopharm Ltd.*, 830 F.Supp. 871, 29 U.S.P.Q.2d 1126, 1134 (N.C. 1993).

ω

Because CPC (the assignee) was primarily involved in the preparation and filing of the patent application, the purpose of the statute would not be served merely by looking to Edwards' intent at the time the application was filed. The Court must instead consider information available to Edwards (the inventor) and additional information available to his agent, CPC, at the time they applied for the patent, even though there was no evidence to suggest that Edwards was even aware of the additional information. *CPC International Inc. v. Archer Daniels Midland Co.*, 831 F.Supp. 1091, 30 U.S.P.Q.2d 1427, 1441 (Del 1993).

ω

The relevant date for evaluating a best mode disclosure in a continuing application is the date of the parent application in which the claimed subject matter is adequately disclosed. *Transco Products Inc. v. Performance Contracting Inc.*, 38 F.3d 551, 32 U.S.P.Q.2d 1077, 1083 (Fed. Cir. 1994).

ω

While the best mode requirement may not be met *solely* by reference to the prior art, a high level of skill in the art combined with implicit disclosure of the best mode by the terms of the patent is sufficient. *Wang Laboratories Inc. v. Mitsubishi Electronics America Inc.*, 32 U.S.P.Q.2d 1641, 1645 (Cal. 1994).

ω

If an inventor files a continuation application, it serves the ends of both 35 U.S.C. §§112 and 120 to require the inventor to disclose any best mode information not known at the time of filing the original application, but learned before the filing of the Continuation-In-Part Application. *Applied Materials Inc. v. Advanced Semiconductor Materials America Inc.*, 32 U.S.P.Q.2d 1865, 1881 (Cal. 1994).

ω

A proper "best mode" analysis involves a two-part test: (1) whether the inventors "knew of a mode of practicing [their] claimed invention that [they] considered to be better than any other . . . ;" and (2) whether the inventors' disclosure in the patent reflects what they knew - that is, whether their "disclosure [is] adequate to enable one skilled in the art to practice the best mode. . . ." *Automotive Products plc v. Tilton Engineering Inc.*, 855 F.Supp. 1101, 33 U.S.P.Q.2d 1065, 1086 (Cal. 1994).

ω

Separating scenarios in which employers unintentionally isolate inventors from relevant research from instances in which employers deliberately set out to screen inventors from research, and finding a best mode violation in the latter case, would ignore the very words of 35 U.S.C. §112, first paragraph, and the case law as it has developed, which consistently has analyzed the best mode requirement in terms of knowledge of and concealment by the inventor. Congress was aware of the differences between inventors and assignees, *see* 35 U.S.C. §§100(d) and 152, and it specifically limited the best mode required to that contemplated by the inventor. The law "does not permit using *imputed knowledge*" in a best mode defense. *Glaxo Inc. v. Novopharm Ltd.*, 52 F.3d 1043, 34 U.S.P.Q.2d 1565, 1571 (Fed. Cir. 1995).

ॐ

"[S]upplier/trade name information must be provided only when a skilled artisan could not practice the best mode of the claimed invention absent this information." Because the composition of Sil-42 perlite was not defined in the literature (it was a trade secret) or disclosed in the specification, supplier/trade name information alone may not have satisfied the PTO's guidelines. Failure to find intentional concealment does not preclude a finding that the best mode requirement has been violated. The second inquiry concerning best mode compliance is an objective one, relating to whether the inventor objectively enabled his best mode of practicing the claimed invention. Inquiry into an intent to conceal, being subjective, is inconsistent with the objective nature of the second aspect of best mode compliance; it is not part of that analysis. In addition, intentional concealment of a best mode coupled with disclosure of a false mode of practicing an invention may constitute inequitable conduct rendering a patent unenforceable. *United States Gypsum Co. v. National Gypsum Co.*, 74 F.3d 1209, 37 U.S.P.Q.2d 1388, 1392, 1393 (Fed. Cir. 1996).

ॐ

"The best mode inquiry is directed to what the applicant regards as his invention, which in turn is measured by the claims." "Unclaimed subject matter is not subject to the disclosure requirements of 35 U.S.C. §112." *Zygo Corp v. Wyko Corp.*, 79 F.3d 1563, 38 U.S.P.Q.2d 1281, 1284 (Fed. Cir. 1996).

ॐ

The point in time at which we measure the adequacy of the disclosure for a best mode inquiry in the context of a patent with a priority claim under 35 U.S.C. §119 is the filing date of the foreign application. *Lenzing Aktiengesellschaft v. Courtaulds Fibers Inc.*, 119 F.3d 16, 44 U.S.P.Q.2d 1832, 1834 (Fed. Cir. 1997 - *unpublished*).

ॐ

Where and invention relates only to a part of, or one aspect of, a device, an applicant is not required to disclose a nonclaimed element necessary to the operation of the invention to which the patent is directed. *Applied Medical Resources Corp. v. United States Surgical Corp.*, 147 F.3d 1374, 47 U.S.P.Q.2d 1289, 1291 (Fed. Cir. 1998).

Better. *See also* **Advantage, Improvement.**

To be patentable, an invention need not advance the art in the sense that it be shown to be better than that which came before. *Ex parte Maxey and Harrington,* 177 U.S.P.Q. 468 (PTO Bd. App. 1972).

Bias.

Of all the charges that might be leveled against one sworn to administer justice and to discharge and perform all the duties incumbent upon him faithfully and impartially, a charge of bias must be deemed at or near the very top in terms of seriousness, for bias kills the very soul of judging—fairness. *Pac-Tec Inc. v. Amerace Corp.,* 903 F.2d 796, 14 U.S.P.Q.2d 1871, 1877 (Fed. Cir. 1990).

Bidder. *See* **Second Lowest Bidder.**

Bifurcation.

Bifurcation of an appeal based on different "legal claims" is inappropriate. The language of 28 U.S.C. §1295(a)(2) discusses jurisdiction over an appeal "in a case," not over an appeal from decision of "a claim." This strongly suggests that appeals of different parts of a single case should not go to different courts. A bifurcated appeal of the different legal claims raised in any one case would result in an inefficient commitment of the limited resources of the federal appellate courts. *United States v. Hohri,* 482 U.S. 64, 69 n.3 (1987).

ϖ

Patent cases often present circumstances uniquely favoring bifurcation of the liability and damage issues. Even where bifurcation is found to promote judicial economy, however, separate trials may not be ordered if bifurcation would result in unnecessary delays, additional expense, or some other form of prejudice. An overlapping of issues is significant to a decision regarding bifurcation. Perhaps the most important consideration for a court ruling on a motion to bifurcate is whether separate trials would unduly prejudice the nonmoving party. *Willemijn Houdstermaatschaapij B.V. v. Apollo Computer Inc.,* 707 F. Supp. 1429, 13 U.S.P.Q.2d 1001, 1003, 1004 (Del. 1989).

ϖ

Bifurcation is warranted when the issues are particularly complex and/or the proof of damages is essentially independent of the proof of liability. Bifurcating trial does not require bifurcating discovery. *Air-Shields Inc. v. The BOC Group,* 23 U.S.P.Q.2d 1955, 1956, 1968 (Md. 1992).

ϖ

Once a defendant asserts that he is faced with a dilemma of choosing between waiving attorney-client privilege in order to protect itself from a willfulness finding (in which case it may risk prejudicing itself on the question of liability) and maintaining the privilege (in which case it may risk being found to be a willful infringer if liability is found), a trial court should inspect the defendant's attorney-client documents *in camera* to ascertain that the dilemma is legitimate. If the dilemma is real, bifurcation of the willfulness issue is an appropriate way to proceed. *Neorx Corp. v. Immunomedics Inc.,* 28 U.S.P.Q.2d 1395, 1396 (N.J. 1993).

ϖ

Historically, courts have found it worthwhile to hold separate trials on liability and damage issues in patent cases. They have also apparently found it can be more efficient to defer discovery and trial on damage issues until after liability has been resolved at trial and on appeal. The opinions in *Underwater Devices* [717 F.2d 1380, 219 U.S.P.Q. 569 (Fed. Cir. 1983)], *Crucible* [793 F.2d 1565, 230 U.S.P.Q. 81 (Fed. Cir. 1986), *cert. denied*, 479 U.S. 1034 (1987)], and *Quantum* [940 F.2d 642, 643-44 (Fed. Cir. 1991)] have shifted the focus of most bifurcation motions in patent cases from a technique to reduce the inefficiencies in litigation by trying issues separately to a way to minimized potential prejudice in a single trial by staying discovery. *The Johns Hopkins University v. CellPro*, 160 F.R.D. 30, 34 U.S.P.Q.2d 1276, 1279, 1280 (Del. 1995).

ω

The courts have recognized that it would be manifestly unfair to allow a defendant to argue in the liability phase that it did not rely on the opinions of counsel, while precluding discovery as to those opinions, and later argue in the damages phase that its actions were not willful based on those same opinions. *Fuji Machine Manufacturing v. Hover-Davis Inc.* 45 U.S.P.Q.2d 1158, 1160 (N.Y. 1997).

ω

In the normal case separate trial of issues is seldom required, but in a patent infringe-ment suit considerations exist which suggest that efficient judicial administration would be served by separate trials on the issues of liability and damages. The trial of the damages question in such a suit is often difficult and expensive, while being easily severed from the trial of the questions of validity and infringement of the patent. A preliminary finding on the question of liability may well make unnecessary the damages inquiry, and thus result in substantial saving of time of the Court and counsel and reduction of expense to the parties. Moreover, separate trial of the issue of liability may present counsel the opportunity to obtain final settlement of that issue or appeal without having reached the often time-consuming and difficult damages question. *Princeton Biochemicals Inc. v. Beckman Instruments Inc.*, 180 F.R.D. 254, 45 U.S.P.Q.2d 1757, 1759 (N.J. 1997).

Billing.

The lodestar method allows courts to adjust attorney's fees upward or downwward to reflect such facts as quality of representation and the degree of success achieved by the prevailing party. *Padco Inc. v. Nowell Companies*, 13 U.S.P.Q.2d 1607, 1615 (Wis. 1988).

Billing Rate.

If it appears (in determining attorney's fees) that the hourly rate charged is within a range normally charged for the defense of a patent infringement suit by attorneys of comparable experience and expertise, the court will look no further. Only if the evidence reveals that the rate actually charged is abnormally high or abnormally low will the court base an attorney's fee award on an hourly rate at variance with the bill for legal services that was actually rendered to the client. *Chromalloy American Corp. v. Alloy Surfaces Co.*, 353 F. Supp. 429, 176 U.S.P.Q. 508, 510 (Del. 1973).

Bioisosterism.

In attempting to predict the biological activities of a drug, a skilled medicinal chemist would not proceed randomly but would base his attempts on the available knowledge of prior research techniques and on literature used in his field. One such technique is "bioisosteric replacement," or the theory of bioisosterism, where the substitution of one atom or group of atoms for another atom or group of atoms having similar size, shape, and electron density provides molecules having the same type of biological activity. Application of this technique led to a holding of obviousness of a new use of a known compound. *In re Merck & Co.*, 800 F.2d 1091, 231 U.S.P.Q. 375 (Fed. Cir. 1986).

Biotechnology. *See also* Deposit.

The appealed claims are directed to a new human cell line and the hybridomas resulting from its fusion with lymphoid cells. The new cell line was developed by mutagenesis and selection from a known cell line by procedures that fill 12 pages of specification. Because of the uncertainties of reproducibility that inhere in such processes, at least in the present state of biotechnology, this invention is of the class covered by the deposit requirement. The inventor filed an application for a patent prior to depositing his new cell line with the American Type Culture Collection (ATCC). 35 U.S.C. §112, first paragraph, does not require the transfer of a sample of the invention to an independent depository prior to the filing date of the patent application. The requirements of PTO access to a sample of the cell line during pendency, and public access after grant, were made by the procedures that were followed. The deposit with the ATCC, which was made after filing but prior to issuance of his patent, and which is referred to in his specification, meets the statutory requirements. *In re Lundak,* 773 F.2d 1216, 227 U.S.P.Q. 90 (Fed. Cir. 1985).

ᴔ

Although the level of skill in the art of producing monoclonal antibodies had progressed to the point where a method had been used to produce numerous monoclonal antibodies specific to a variety of antigens and one may have approached the project with a reasonable expectation of success, it was not established that the claimed products would be "obvious" from prior-art teachings. The mere statement that the method of making the products would be obvious and that there would be a reasonable expectation of success reflects the regularly rejected obvious-to-try standard. *Ex parte Erlich,* 3 U.S.P.Q.2d 1011 (B.P.A.I. 1986).

ᴔ

Biological materials need not be deposited when the invention can be practiced without undue experimentation from biological materials available in prior art. *Hybritech Inc. v. Abbott Laboratories,* 4 U.S.P.Q.2d 1001 (Cal. 1987).

Blameless Ignorance. *See* Unknowable.

Block.

The fact that there was a technological block in the practical implementation of a concept that those skilled in the art had failed to eliminate is strongly supportive of lack of obviousness. *Kaiser Industries Corp. v. Jones & Laughlin Steel Corp.*, 181 U.S.P.Q. 193, 203 (Pa. 1974).

Block Diagram.

Even if the specification does not particularly identify each of the elements represented by the blocks or the relationship therebetween, and even if the specification does not specify particular apparatus intended to carry out each function, functional-type block diagrams (a group of rectangles representing the elements of a system, functionally labeled and interconnected by lines), together with their accompanying description, are sufficient to enable a person skilled in the art to practice the claimed invention. Functional-type block diagrams may be acceptable and, in fact, preferable when they serve in conjunction with the rest of the specification to enable a person skilled in the art to practice the claimed invention with only a reasonable degree of routine operation. *Ex parte Billottet and Fechner,* 192 U.S.P.Q. 413 (PTO Bd. App. 1976).

ᚥ

Since the inventors had full knowledge of a specific arrangement to be used in practicing their process, but failed to disclose the same in their patent, instead disclosing a blank box described as "conventional," the patent fails to comply with the best-mode requirements of 35 U.S.C. §112. *Thyssen Plastik Anger KC v. Induplas, Inc.,* 195 U.S.P.Q. 534, 538 (P.R. 1977).

ᚥ

Employment of block diagrams and descriptions of their functions is not fatal under 35 U.S.C. §112, first paragraph, provided that the represented structure is conventional and can be determined without undue experimentation. *Hirschfeld v. Banner,* 462 F. Supp. 135, 200 U.S.P.Q. 276, 281 (D.C. 1978).

Blonder-Tongue Doctrine. *See also* Relitigating Invalidity.

Once a court determines a patent is invalid in a proceeding where the patent owner had a full and fair opportunity to adjudicate, the patent owner is precluded from relitigating the validity of the patent against all others. The Supreme Court thus eliminated the mutuality requirement in the use of collateral estoppel in cases finding patent invalidity. *Blonder-Tongue v. University Foundation,* 402 U.S. 313, 169 U.S.P.Q. 513 (1971). *But see Blumcraft of Pittsburgh v. Kawneer Company, Inc.,* 174 U.S.P.Q. 14, 15 (Ga. 1972).

ᚥ

The guidelines suggested by the Supreme Court for reaching a result permitting relitigation are replete with qualifying words making a patentee's burden onerous. In effect, a patentee must persuade a second trial court "that the entire proceedings were seriously defective." In order to show that a prior judgment is not binding for want of essential evidence, a patentee must fulfill the two criteria of the Supreme Court's test. It must persuade the second court that the additional evidence was crucial to a proper resolution in the first tribunal and that the patentee bore no responsibility for the absence of the evidence in the prior trial. *Kaiser Industries Corp. v. Jones & Laughlin Steel Corp.,* 515 F.2d 964, 185 U.S.P.Q. 343, 355, 358 (3d Cir. 1975).

ᚥ

Even where the Federal Circuit has confirmed an ITC determination of patent invalidity, *Blonder-Tongue* does not apply in an infringement setting. *In re Convertible Rowing Exercizer Patent Litigation*, 721 F.Supp. 596, 12 U.S.P.Q.2d 1275, 1280, 1281 (Del. 1989).

ᴡ

A jury determination of patent validity and willful infringement (confirmed by the CAFC) is not affected in any way by a subsequent determination (on reexamination by the PTO) that the patent is invalid. *Standard Havens Products Inc. v. Gencor Industries Inc.*, 810 F.Supp. 1072, 25 U.S.P.Q.2d 1949, 1951 (Mo. 1993).

Blueprint.

In determining validity of a patent claim, it is not enough to show that each of the components of the claim was known and had been used in other similar systems. Guided by the defendants, the court below treated each reference as teaching one or more of the specific components for use in the patented system, although the patented system did not then exist. Thus, the court reconstructed the patented system, using the blueprint of the patent claims. This is legal error. *Interconnect Planning Corp. v. Feil*, 774 F.2d 1132, 227 U.S.P.Q. 543, 548 (Fed. Cir. 1985).

ᴡ

To combine references (A) and (B) properly to reach the conclusion that the subject matter of a patent would have been obvious, case law requires that there must be some teaching, suggestion, or inference in either reference (A) or (B), or both, or knowledge generally available to one of ordinary skill in the relevant art, that would lead one skilled in the art to combine the relevant teachings of references (A) and (B). Consideration must be given to teachings in the references that would have led one skilled in the art away from the claimed invention. A claim cannot properly be used as a blueprint for abstracting individual teachings from references. *Ashland Oil, Inc. v. Delta Resins & Refractories, Inc.*, 776 F.2d 281, 227 U.S.P.Q. 657 (Fed. Cir. 1985).

ᴡ

Presuming arguendo that the references show the elements or concepts urged, the Examiner presented no line of reasoning as to why the artisan reviewing only the collective teachings of the references would have found it obvious to selectively pick and choose various elements and/or concepts from the several references relied on to arrive at the claimed invention. In the instant application, the Examiner has done little more than cite references to show that one or more elements or some combinations thereof, when each is viewed in a vacuum, is known. The claimed invention, however, is clearly directed to a combination of elements. That is to say, the appellant does not claim that he has invented one or more new elements, rather, he has presented claims to a new combination of elements. To support the conclusion that the claimed combination is directed to obvious subject matter, either the references must expressly or impliedly suggest the claimed combination or the Examiner must present a convincing line of reasoning as to why the artisan would have found the claimed invention to have been obvious in light of the teachings of the references. The Board found nothing in the references that would expressly or impliedly teach or suggest the modifications urged by the Examiner. Additionally, the Board found no line of reasoning in the answer as to why the artisan would have found the modifications urged by the Examiner to have been obvious. Based upon the record, the artisan would not have found it obvious to selectively pick and choose elements or concepts from the various references so as to arrive at the claimed invention without using the claims as a guide. *Ex parte Clapp,* 227 U.S.P.Q. 972 (B.P.A.I. 1985).

Board (Board of Appeals). *See also* BPAI.

If appellants wished to object to the Board's statement and to question the correctness of the facts contained therein, they should have requested the Board to cite its authority for the statement. If the cited authority was based upon facts within the personal knowledge of the Board, appellants should have proceeded under Rules 66 and 76 of the Patent Office and called for an affidavit of the Board. Appellants would then have been in a position to contradict or explain the Board's statement. In the absence of such request, appellants may not be heard to challenge a statement made in the Board's opinion. The statement of the Board must therefore be accepted as correct. *In re Selmi and Altenburger,* 156 F.2d 96, 70 U.S.P.Q. 197 (C.C.P.A. 1946).

ω

Evidence from a purported expert, who has expressed an expert opinion, is accorded more weight than an unsupported opinion of the Board on a highly technical subject on which the primary Examiner (presumed to be specializing in the relevant art) expressed no opinion. *In re Ehringer,* 347 F.2d 612, 146 U.S.P.Q. 31 (C.C.P.A. 1965).

ω

It is improper for the Examiner to direct the Board's attention to a reference that was not relied upon as part of the rejection of claims. *Ex parte Titone,* 177 U.S.P.Q. 731, 733 (PO Bd. App. 1971).

Board (Constitution).

The proper forum in which to settle the question of the legality of the Board's constitution is the district court (by mandamus) with appeal to the court of appeals. *In re Wiechert,* 370 F.2d 927, 152 U.S.P.Q. 247 (C.C.P.A. 1967).

Bond.

The bond provided for in §337(g)(3) [19 U.S.C. §1337(g)(3)] was prescribed by the Secretary of the Treasury in the amount of 100 percent of the value of the articles concerned, f.o.b. foreign port, to offset any competitive advantage resulting from the unfair acts of importation or sale of the infringing articles. *In re Reclosable Plastic Bags,* 192 U.S.P.Q. 674, 681 (U.S. Intl. Trade Commn. 1977).

Borcherdt Doctrine.

Where the disclosure of an application gives two materials or operations as equivalents, such disclosure alone may be sufficient for the rejection of a claim specific to one equivalent where the other appears in the prior art. *In re Borcherdt, Hamblet, and Webb*, 197 F.2d 550, 94 U.S.P.Q. 175, 177 (C.C.P.A. 1952); significantly limited by *In re Ruff and Dukeshire*, 256 F.2d 590, 118 U.S.P.Q. 340 (C.C.P.A. 1958).

Bounds. *See also* Definiteness, Substituted.

A determination by the Patent Office that earlier, separate claims encompass a "plurality of different inventions" cannot serve, under 35 U.S.C. §112, as the basis for a rejection of a later combined claim. An applicant is free under that provision to set the metes and bounds of "his invention" as he sees them. *In re Wolfrum and Gold*, 486 F.2d 588, 179 U.S.P.Q. 620, 622 (C.C.P.A. 1973).

℧

To determine whether claim language is definite, the claims must be examined to see whether the metes and bounds of the subject invention can be adequately determined from the claim language. In this examination of the claims, effect must be given to all limitations. When those skilled in the art would have no trouble in ascertaining whether a particular embodiment is encompassed by claim language, the claim satisfies the definition requirement. The mere fact that a claim is broad does not make it indefinite. The scope of a claim is definite when each of the limitations recited therein is definite. *In re Goffe*, 526 F.2d 1393, 188 U.S.P.Q. 131 (C.C.P.A. 1975).

℧

The second paragraph of 35 U.S.C. §112 merely requires that an applicant set out and circumscribe a particular area with a reasonable degree of precision and particularity such that the metes and bounds of the claimed invention are reasonably set forth. *Ex parte Head,* 214 U.S.P.Q. 551, 552 (PTO Bd. App. 1981).

Boykin Act.

The Boykin Act, Pub. L. No. 89-690, ch. 910, 60 Stat. 940 (1946), relates to situations in which foreign applications were filed or in which a disclosure was made to the government of the United States pursuant to an agreement between the U.S. government and the government of a foreign country. *In re McIntosh*, 230 F.2d 615, 109 U.S.P.Q. 101, 104 (C.C.P.A. 1956).

BPAI (Board of Patent Appeals and Interferences). *See also* Board, 37 C.F.R. §1.192(c)(5), 37 C.F.R. §1.196(b), Expanded Panel.

The PTO cannot appeal from a decision of the BPAI reversing an Examiner's ground of rejection. *Holmes, Faber, Boykin, and Francis v. Kelley, Hornberger, and Strief,* 586 F.2d 234, 199 U.S.P.Q. 778 (C.C.P.A. 1978).

℧

The government has no right to review an Examiner or Board decision favorable to the patent owner. *Syntex (U.S.A.) Inc. v. U.S Patent and Trademark Office,* 882 F.2d 1570, 11 U.S.P.Q.2d 1866, 1869, 1871 (Fed. Cir. 1989).

℧

Once the oral hearing provided for by 37 C.F.R. §1.194 is held, ordinarily the only order of business left is the Board's decision. It is manifestly inappropriate, and contrary to the orderly course of business, for an appellant to file a paper in an apparent attempt to get the "last word," setting forth his perception of the substance of the oral hearing, and to enter into a rehash of the arguments of record. Nor is it appropriate to attempt, in such a paper, to present answers to questions presented by the panel, the answers to which were not forthcoming at the hearing or were not fully answered to appellant's satisfaction. Nor is it appropriate to amplify positions that could have been presented at oral hearing. Of course, during the oral hearing, the panel may well deem it necessary, or otherwise desirable, for an appellant to present a subsequent paper regarding a matter raised at the hearing. *Ex parte Cillario*, 14 U.S.P.Q.2d 1079 (B.P.A.I. 1989).

ϖ

Where the CAFC has addressed a point of law in a published opinion, its decision is controlling over the BPAI. Similarly controlling are decisions considered to be binding precedent by the CAFC (i.e., decisions of the former Court of Claims and the former CCPA, as well as the former Customs Court). In those relatively rare cases where the CAFC has not addressed an issue, but there is "authorized published" Board precedent, that published Board precedent is binding on panels of the Board and Examiners in the Patent Examining Corps. Generally, the Board authorizes publication of its opinions only in those instances in which the opinion is (1) consistent with other decisions that have been rendered by the Board and (2) consistent with binding precedent of the CAFC. In most instances a "published" Board opinion will be one that (1) significantly adds to the body of law by addressing a substantive legal point not specifically previously addressed by the CAFC, or (2) discusses proper procedure within or interpretation of a rule of the PTO, or (3) informs the patent bar and examining corps how the Board is interpreting prior court or Board decisions as they relate to particular factual situations before the Board. A published Board opinion may be overruled only by the Board sitting en banc or by an expanded panel of the Board (i.e., one with more than three members). Un-published Board opinions, except as they may be the "law of the case," may not be binding precedent since the opinions are often fact driven by the specific facts present in the appeal before the Board. Generally, unless the facts in a succeeding case are "on all fours" with or substantially the same as the facts in the preceding appeal, the opinion in the preceding unpublished appeal decision may not be controlling in a succeeding appeal. Of course, previously decided points of law must be followed unless overruled, and the application of the law to particular facts must be consistent from case to case. *Ex parte Holt*, 19 U.S.P.Q.2d 1211, 1214 (B.P.A.I. 1991).

ϖ

The Board does not allow claims; it merely decides whether, based on evidence before it, a rejection is proper or not. The Board has limited authority under 37 C.F.R. §1.196 to enter a rejection of the claims, make a recommendation that previously allowed claims be rejected, and make a recommendation that a claim be allowed if certain additions to the record are made. The Board is without authority to "allow" a claim. A reversal of an Examiner's rejection normally results in an allowance of the claims involved. However, the Examiner is not required to allow a claim where there is a change in the record of the application. The presentation of new evidence, such as newly discovered prior art, on an applicant's submission of claims broader in scope than the claims whose rejection was reversed renders the Board's decision moot. *Ex parte Alpha Industries Inc.*, 22 U.S.P.Q.2d 1851, 1857 (B.P.A.I. 1992).

ᴆ

That part of the Examiner's "objection" which centers on description, enablement and best mode concerns the correspondence of the specification to the statutory requirements set forth in 35 U.S.C. §112 and is within the jurisdiction of the BPAI . However, that part of the "objection" which relates to the Examiner's desire for information concerning (a) an explanation of the "gist" of the invention, (b) the phenotypic characteristics of the parent plants and the inheritability thereof, and (c) the goals sought to be achieved by the inventors relates solely to the ease and accuracy of the examination process and the ability of the Examiner to obtain sufficient information therefrom to examine the application effectively. It concerns either the rules of practice or established customs and practices. It is outside the jurisdiction of the BPAI. *Ex parte C*, 27 U.S.P.Q.2d 1492, 1494 (B.P.A.I. 1992).

ᴆ

When an applicant files a notice of appeal *after* filing a Rule (37 C.F.R. §) 197(b) request and *before* the Board has rendered its decision in response to that request, *and* when no appealable decision exists when the applicant files the notice of appeal, the mere filing of the notice does not deprive the Board of jurisdiction to render its reconsideration decision, and the applicant has filed the notice "within the time prescribed by law." The CAFC, however, cannot exercise jurisdiction over the appeal before the Board enters its reconsideration decision on the Rule 197(b) request. *In re Graves*, 69 F.3d 1147, 36 U.S.P.Q.2d 1697, 1699 (Fed. Cir. 1995).

ᴆ

The Board is required to set forth in its opinions specific findings of fact and conclusions of law adequate to form a basis for CAFC review. *Gechter v. Davidson*, 116 F.3d 1454, 43 U.S.P.Q.2d 1030, 1035 (Fed. Cir. 1997).

Breadth. *See also* **At Least, Bounds, Commensurate in Scope, Generic, Indefiniteness, Inoperative Embodiments, Open-Ended Claim, Overclaiming, Scope, Substituted, Sufficiency of Disclosure, Support, Undue Breadth, 35 U.S.C. §112.**

The claimed use of a solvent may be regarded as in the nature of a manipulative expedient. A number of solvents of widely different chemical structure and solvent action are disclosed. With knowledge that what is desired is a solvent that dissolves the starting materials but has little solvent action on the adduct, the average chemist can readily select many solvents other than those specifically named. Under these particular circumstances, the claims are not rejectable for undue breadth in use of the term "an organic solvent." *Ex parte Dubbs and Stevens*, 119 U.S.P.Q. 440, 441 (PO Bd. App. 1958).

ᴆ

The mere fact that a claim covers a large, or even an unlimited number of products, does not necessarily establish that it is too broad. Claims are commonly allowed for alloys or mixtures that permit substantial variations in the proportions of two or more ingredients. Theoretically, an infinite number of products may be produced falling within the scope of such a claim. The same principles should apply to claims covering a wide range of distinct chemical compounds. However, because of the proportion of unknown compounds, it would ordinarily be necessary to give many more examples and much more specific information than would be necessary in the case of an alloy or a mixture.

The appealed claim covers a very large number of chemical compounds that may be developed in the future and that will possess the novel structure defined by the claim. Due to the nature of the chemical compounds and chemical processes, it is conceivable that an almost infinite number of compounds may be developed by chemists if they have before them the teachings that appellants assert to be new in this field; namely, the particular structure and molecular arrangement of their new compounds. It is proper for the PTO to examine such assertions of patentability with great care but, when that has been done, the standards by which the ultimate determination of patentability or unpatentability should be made are those standards that Congress has provided in the patent statutes. In the final analysis, the Board's holding appears to be that, as a matter of law, 19 examples are not enough to support a claim embracing many thousands of compounds. The sufficiency of a disclosure depends not on the number but, rather, on the nature of the claimed compounds per se and the nature of the supporting disclosures. If a claim covers compounds that are closely related, a comparatively limited disclosure may be sufficient to support it. If, however, the claim covers compounds that are related only in some structural respects, a more extensive supporting disclosure may be necessary to support it. Moreover, the selection of the examples and other exemplary material used as the disclosure to support a claim must be adequately representative of the area covered by it. *In re Cavallito and Gray,* 282 F.2d 363, 127 U.S.P.Q. 202, 204, 205, 206, 209 (C.C.P.A. 1960).

ω

The public purpose on which the patent law rests requires the granting of claims commensurate in scope with the invention disclosed. This requires as much the granting of broad claims on broad inventions as it does granting of specific claims on more specific inventions. It is neither contemplated by the public purpose of the patent laws nor required by the statute that an inventor shall be forced to accept claims narrower than his invention in order to secure allowance of his patent. *In re Sus and Schaefer,* 306 F.2d 494, 134 U.S.P.Q. 301, 304 (C.C.P.A. 1962).

ω

Since it is conventional to prepare quaternary ammonium derivatives of tertiary amines that have therapeutic utility, the recitation in a product claim of "quaternary ammonium salts" is not too broad. *Ex parte Biel,* 137 U.S.P.Q. 315, 317 (PO Bd. App. 1962).

ω

Appellant has described his invention as comprehending the use therein of any inorganic salt capable of performing a specific function in a specific combination, and he has specifically disclosed four such salts that are capable of performing his function. The claims are not "unduly broad" merely because one skilled in the art may not know offhand which inorganic salts are capable of so functioning. Nothing is found in patent law that requires the appellant to discover which of all salts have the specified properties and which will function properly in his combination. The invention description clearly indicates that any inorganic salt that has such properties is usable in his combination. *In re Fuetterer,* 319 F.2d 259, 138 U.S.P.Q. 217, 223 (C.C.P.A. 1963).

ϖ

As azo dyes are well known, the expression "an organic azo dyestuff residue" is not unduly broad in the definition of a claimed dyestuff when the structure of the azo component is not critical. *In re Riat, DeMontmollin, and Koller,* 327 F.2d 685, 140 U.S.P.Q. 471, 472, 473 (C.C.P.A. 1964).

ϖ

A claim, the terms of which are clearly and precisely stated and easily understood, cannot, under the guise of interpretation, be expanded by the specification either to cover an alleged infringing article or to make the claim so broad that the prior art will invalidate it. *Turbo Machine Co. v. Proctor & Schwartz, Inc.,* 241 F. Supp. 723, 145 U.S.P.Q. 327, 330 (Pa. 1965).

ϖ

When a claim is not limited to a structure essential to accomplish the advantage claimed for the invention, the claim does not satisfy the requirement of "particularly pointing out and distinctly claiming the subject matter which the applicant regards as his invention." *Murton v. Ladd,* 352 F.2d 942, 146 U.S.P.Q. 699, 700 (D.C. Cir. 1965).

ϖ

The main difficulty with broad claims is not that the claim is so broad as to be indefinite, like infinity, but that such a broad claim is quite likely to be either anticipated under 35 U.S.C. §102 or rendered obvious under 35 U.S.C. §103. *Clinical Products Ltd v. Brenner,* 255 F. Supp. 131, 149 U.S.P.Q. 475, 477 (D.C. 1966).

ϖ

The Examiner's reference to specific ethers not mentioned in the specification and his unsupported suggestion or implication that these ethers might not produce the desired product of the claimed reaction provides no convincing evidence of undue breadth of the description of the ether. *Ex parte Argabright and Hall,* 161 U.S.P.Q. 703, 704 (PO Bd. App. 1967).

ϖ

Failure of claims to specify the ring positions of substituents does not warrant a rejection on grounds of undue breadth when the disclosure shows that position is unimportant to the utility of claimed mixtures. A rejection due to undue breadth must be based on a discrepency between scope of disclosure and scope of claim. *In re Steinhauer and Valenta,* 410 F.2d 411, 161 U.S.P.Q. 595, 599 (C.C.P.A. 1969).

ϖ

Where the chemical identity of a material is not critical, there is no reason why an applicant should not be permitted to define that material partly in terms of its physical properties or in terms of the function that it performs. *In re Metcalfe and Lowe,* 410 F.2d 1378, 161 U.S.P.Q. 789, 793 (C.C.P.A. 1969).

ϖ

Claims are too broad and indefinite when they call for "an effective amount" of a designated component without specifying what the intended effect is. Claims are also too broad and incomplete when they specify up to about a designated percent by weight of a specified component because they read on compositions totally lacking that component. *Ex parte Dobson, Jacob, and Herschler,* 165 U.S.P.Q. 29, 30 (PO Bd. App. 1969).

ʊ

A rejection of claims under 35 U.S.C. §112 as being broader than the invention clearly described in the specification is really an assertion that the specification is insufficient to support claims of the breadth sought and is, therefore, a rejection under the first paragraph of §112.

In the absence of convincing evidence of the criticality of limitations that are not in claims, such limitations are not regarded as essential for patentability. *In re Wakefield and Foster,* 422 F.2d 897, 164 U.S.P.Q. 636 (C.C.P.A. 1970).

ʊ

There is no magical relation between the number of representative examples and the breadth of the claim; the number and variety of examples are irrelevant if the disclosure is "enabling" and sets forth the "best mode" contemplated.

Section 112 of 35 U.S.C. §does not permit an Examiner to study a disclosure, to formulate a conclusion as to what he (the Examiner) regards as the broadest invention supported by the disclosure, and then to determine that the claims are broader than the Examiner's conception of what "the invention" is. The first sentence of the second paragraph of §112 is essentially a requirement for precision and definiteness of claim language. If the scope of subject matter embraced by a claim is clear, and if the applicant has not otherwise indicated that he intends the claims to be of a different scope, then the claim does particularly point out and distinctly claim the subject matter that the applicant regards as his invention. *In re Borkowski and Van Venrooy,* 422 F.2d 904, 164 U.S.P.Q. 642 (C.C.P.A. 1970).

ʊ

The failure to apply the terms of a statutory section to the facts of a rejection illustrates the problems arising from use of the characterizations "too broad" or "undue breadth" because of the fact that these terms have no fixed meaning in patent law and mean different things to different people. *In re Frilette and Weisz,* 423 F.2d 1397, 165 U.S.P.Q. 259, 262 n.4 (C.C.P.A. 1970).

ʊ

An inventor should be allowed to dominate future patentable inventions of others where those inventions are based in some way on his teachings. Such improvements, while unobvious from his teachings, are still within his contribution, since the improvement is made possible by his work. It is equally apparent, however, that he must not be permitted to achieve this dominance by claims that are insufficiently supported and hence not in compliance with the first paragraph of 35 U.S.C. §112. That paragraph requires that the scope of the claims must bear a reasonable correlation to the scope of enablement provided by the specification to persons of ordinary skill in the art. In cases involving predictable factors, such as mechanical or electrical elements, a single embodiment provides broad enablement in the sense that, once imagined, other embodiments can be made without difficulty and their performance characteristics predicted by resort to known scientific laws. In cases involving unpredictable factors, such as most chemical reactions and physiological activity, the scope of enablement obviously varies inversely with the degree of unpredictability of the factors involved. *In re Fisher,* 427 F.2d 833, 166 U.S.P.Q. 18 (C.C.P.A. 1970).

ᛏ

Claims need not recite limitations that deal with factors that must be presumed to be within the level of ordinary skill in the art, where one of ordinary skill in the art, to whom the specification and claims are directed, would consider such factors obvious. *In re Skrivan,* 427 F.2d 801, 166 U.S.P.Q. 85 (C.C.P.A. 1970).

ᛏ

Claim language is accorded its broadest possible meaning in the absence of special definitions. An immense scope of claims is not, by itself, grounds for rejection. The ability of the Examiner to enumerate radicals encompassed by the claim language points up the weakness of the indefiniteness argument. Giving the language its broadest possible meaning, the breadth of the claim is indeed immense. However, breadth is not indefiniteness.

When a specification contains a statement of the invention that is as broad as the broadest claims and the sufficiency of the specification to satisfy the best-mode requirement of 35 U.S.C. §112 and to enable one skilled in the art to practice the invention as broadly as it is claimed has not been questioned, a rejection under the first paragraph of §112 does not lie. *In re Robins,* 429 F.2d 452, 166 U.S.P.Q. 552 (C.C.P.A. 1970).

ᛏ

Claims may be too broad "to the point of invalidity" by reason of reading on significant numbers of inoperative embodiments. However, many patented claims read on a vast number of inoperative embodiments in the trivial sense that they can and do omit "factors which must be presumed to be within the level of ordinary skill in the art" and, therefore, read on embodiments in which such factors may be included in such a manner as to make the embodiments inoperative. There is nothing wrong with this so long as it would be obvious to one of ordinary skill in the relevant art how to include those factors in such a manner as to make the embodiment operative rather than inoperative. The mere possibility of inclusion of inoperative subject matter does not prevent allowance of broad claims. *In re Cook and Merigold,* 439 F.2d 730, 169 U.S.P.Q. 298, 302 (C.C.P.A. 1971).

ᛏ

It has never been contended that appellants, when they included the disputed term in their specification, intended only to indicate a single compound. Accepting, therefore, that the term is a generic one, its recitation must be taken as an assertion by the appellants that all of the "considerable number of compounds" that are included within the generic term would, as a class, be operative to produce the asserted enhancement of adhesion characteristics. The only relevant concern of the Patent Office under these circumstances should be over the truth of any such assertion. The first paragraph of 35 U.S.C. §112 requires nothing more than objective enablement. How such a teaching is set forth, either by the use of illustrative examples or by broad terminology, is of no importance. *In re Marzocchi and Horton*, 439 F.2d 220, 169 U.S.P.Q. 367 (C.C.P.A. 1971).

ᵈ

If those skilled in the art can tell whether any particular embodiment is or is not within the scope of a claim, the claim fulfills its purpose as a definition. *In re Miller*, 441 F.2d 689, 169 U.S.P.Q. 597, 599 (C.C.P.A. 1971).

ᵈ

While claims as broad as appellant's claims must necessarily read on many chemicals, the operativeness of which the applicant has not individually verified, and while it might well have been reasonable for the Examiner or the Board to have demanded specific proof from the appellant that this or that class of compounds embraced by the claims really could be used in the disclosed manner, the filing of the solicitor's brief is far too late a point in prosecution to inform an applicant of what additional working examples are thought to be needed to support his claim. *In re Barr, Williams, and Whitmore*, 444 F.2d 588, 170 U.S.P.Q. 330, 338 (C.C.P.A. 1971).

ᵈ

The second paragraph of 35 U.S.C. §112 requires an applicant to "particularly point out and distinctly claim the subject matter sought to be patented." When the scope of the invention sought to be patented is unclear from the language of the claim, a second paragraph rejection lies. *In re Wiggins, James, and Gittos*, 488 F.2d 538, 179 U.S.P.Q. 421, 423 (C.C.P.A. 1973).

ᵈ

Even if the claims were broad enough to include resins that could not be used to produce the invention, that fact does not render appellant's claims too vague with reference to future enterprise. The claims per force will inform potential inventors that any plastic resin that does work to produce the appellant's wheel is covered by the patent. Viewed from the perspective of a potential inventor, challenged "relative" expressions are regarded as sufficiently narrow to define the wheel adequately, for the claims, when read together with the specification, have a very low degree of variation. The objections to the claims as too indefinite do not appear to raise the specter of unwitting infringement by future innovators. Rather, the claims seem broad enough "to permit reasonable tolerance in commercial practice of inventions...," a breadth that is acceptable. *Charvat v. Commissioner of Patents*, 503 F.2d 138, 182 U.S.P.Q. 577, 587 (D.C. Cir. 1974).

ᵈ

To provide effective incentives, claims must adequately protect inventors. To demand that the first to disclose shall limit his claims to what he has found will work or to materials that meet the guidelines specified for "preferred" materials in a process would not serve the constitutional purpose of promoting progress in the useful arts. *In re Goffe*, 542 F.2d 564, 191 U.S.P.Q. 429, 431 (C.C.P.A. 1976).

ᵈ

The PTO has not challenged the appellants' assertion that their 1953 application enabled those skilled in the art in 1953 to make and use "a solid polymer" as called for by their claim. The appellants disclosed, as the only then-existing way to make such a polymer, a method of making the crystalline form. To say now that the appellants should have disclosed in 1953 the amorphous form (which did not exist until 1962) would be to impose an impossible burden on inventors and thus on the patent system. There cannot, in an effective patent system, be such a burden placed on the right to broad claims. To restrict appellants to the crystalline form disclosed, under such circumstances, would be a poor way to stimulate invention, and particularly to encourage its early disclosure. To demand such restriction is merely to state a policy against broad protection for pioneer inventions, a policy both shortsighted and unsound from the standpoint of promoting progress in the useful arts, which is the constitutional purpose of the patent laws. *In re Hogan and Banks,* 559 F.2d 595, 194 U.S.P.Q. 527 (C.C.P.A. 1977).

ω

Breadth alone does not constitute indefiniteness when applied to phrases or terms, such as "organic basic nitrogen compound having at least a hydrogen atom attached to the basic nitrogen atom", "aryl", "aralkyl", "alkaryl" and "heterocyclic". Only appellants may determine what constitutes their invention. *Ex parte Scherberich and Pfeifer,* 201 U.S.P.Q. 397, 398, 399 (PTO Bd. App. 1977).

ω

Section 112 of 35 U.S.C. does not permit an Examiner to determine whether claims satisfy the requirements by studying the disclosure, formulating a conclusion as to what he (the Examiner) regards as the broadest invention supported by the disclosure, and then determining whether the claims are broader than the Examiner's concept of what "the invention" is. *In re Ehrreich and Avery,* 590 F.2d 902, 200 U.S.P.Q. 504, 508 (C.C.P.A. 1979).

ω

It is not necessary to describe in the specification all possible forms in which a claimed limitation may be reduced to practice. *Stevenson v. International Trade Commission,* 612 F.2d 546, 204 U.S.P.Q. 276, 283 (C.C.P.A. 1979).

ω

The Examiner reasoned that, because of the breadth of the invention, a large number of examples (50 to 100) would be required to enable one of ordinary skill in the art to make and use the invention. 35 U.S.C. §112, first paragraph. Although working examples are desirable in complex technology and detailed examples can satisfy the statutory enablement requirement, examples are not required to satisfy §112, first paragraph. The Examiner's statement that "nearly universal applicability" alleged for the invention necessitated numerous examples was erroneous. Although the invention is applicable to a large variety of embodiments, the Examiner offered no reason why these different compounds would require different techniques or process parameters. *In re Strahilevitz,* 668 F.2d 1229, 212 U.S.P.Q. 561, 563 (C.C.P.A. 1982).

ω

Once the best mode contemplated by the inventor is presented, he is entitled to claim every form in which the invention may be used and to obtain all benefits therefrom regardless whether those forms are mentioned in the patent or whether the inventor was aware of them. *The Magnavox Company v. Mattel, Inc.*, 216 U.S.P.Q. 28, 57 (Ill. 1982).

ω

The scope of a patent's claims determines what infringes the patent; it is no measure of what it discloses. A patent discloses only that which it describes, whether specifically or in general terms, so as to convey intelligence to one capable of understanding. *In re Benno*, 768 F.2d 1340, 226 U.S.P.Q. 683, 686 (Fed. Cir. 1985).

ω

Literal infringement requires that an accused device embody every element of a claim as properly interpreted. If the claim describes a combination of functions, and each function is performed by a means described in the specification or an equivalent of such means, then literal infringement holds. When a claimed invention is a novel combination of steps, all possible methods of carrying out each step of the combination are not required to be described in the specification. Correctly construed claims cover "equivalents" of the described embodiments. The purpose is to grant an inventor of a combination invention a fair scope that is not dependent on a catalog of alternative embodiments in the specification. The court has cautioned against limiting the claimed invention to preferred embodiments or specific examples in the specification. The details of performing each step need not be included in the claims unless required to distinguish the claimed invention from the prior art, or otherwise to specifically point out and distinctly claim the invention. Claims should be read in a way that avoids enabling an infringer to "practice a fraud on a patent."

It is not required that those skilled in the art knew, at the time the patent application was filed, of the asserted equivalent means of performing the claimed functions; that equivalence is determined as of the time infringement takes place. Infringement will be found when the material features of a patent have been appropriated, even when those features have been patentably improved. *Texas Instruments, Inc. v. U.S. International Trade Commission*, 805 F.2d 1558, 231 U.S.P.Q. 833 (Fed. Cir. 1986).

ω

The claims were intended to cover the use of the invention with various types of automobiles. That a particular chair of the claims may fit within some automobiles and not others is of no moment. The phrase "so dimensioned" is as accurate as the subject matter permits, automobiles being of various sizes. As long as those of ordinary skill in the art realize that the dimensions could be easily obtained, 35 U.S.C. §112, second paragraph, requires nothing more. The patent law does not require that all possible lengths corresponding to the spaces in hundreds of different automobiles be listed in the patent, let alone that they be listed in the claims. *Orthokinetics Inc. v. Safety Travel Chairs Inc.*, 806 F.2d 1565, 1 U.S.P.Q.2d 1081 (Fed. Cir. 1986).

Brevet Octroyé.

In Belgium a decree, which does not expressly grant specific rights but merely certifies that an application for letters patent complies with formal requirements, is issued on the "brevet octroyé date. Although the expression may properly be translated "patent granted", such is not within the meaning of 35 U.S.C. §102. The word "patented" as used in 35 U.S.C. §§102(a) and 102(b) is limited to patents which are available to the public. *In re Ekenstam*, 256 F.2d 321, 118 U.S.P.Q. 349 (C.C.P.A. 1958).

Brief. *See also* **37 C.F.R. §1.192(c)(5).**

A party wishing to file a CD-ROM counterpart brief must seek consent of the other parties before submitting a CD-ROM brief to the CAFC. Consent of the other parties will be a substantial factor in considering whether to grant leave. On the other hand, prejudice to another party could be an important factor in denying leave. Additionally, a party must seek leave of the court to file a CD-ROM brief and must provide information both to the court and to the other parties about the computer equipment needed to view the CD-ROM brief. Finally, the filing party must submit a motion for leave at the same time or before it submits twelve copies of the CD-ROM brief. *Yukiyo Ltd. v. Watanabe*, 111 F.3d 883, 42 U.S.P.Q.2d 1474, 1476 (Fed. Cir. 1997).

Broad. *See* **Breadth.**

Broaden. *See also* **Late Claiming.**

A long delay in adding broadened claims to a patent application warrants an inference that such claims were added as an afterthought and not as a logical development of the original application. Where the subject matter of the later claims was in public use more than one year before such claims were first introduced, such claims are invalid. *Honeywell Inc. v. Sperry Rand Corp.*, 180 U.S.P.Q. 673, 704 (Minn. 1973).

ᚹ

There is nothing wrong with broadening claims to cover competitive devices about which the applicant's assignee learns after the application is filed, so long as the claims are supported by the specification and drawings; however, such broadening is viewed critically by the courts. *Micro-Acoustics Corp. v. Bose Corp.*, 493 F. Supp. 356, 207 U.S.P.Q. 378, 387 (N.Y. 1980).

ᚹ

The determination of whether claims have been enlarged is a matter of claim construction and is treated as a question of law. The doctrine of equivalents cannot be used to enlarge the scope of the claims. The test to determine whether a claim has been impermissibly broadened during reexamination is the same as that used to determine whether a claim has been impermissibly broadened during reissue. "An amended or new claim is enlarged if it includes within its scope any subject matter that would not have infringed the original patent." *Thermalloy Inc. v. Aavid Engineering Inc.*, 39 U.S.P.Q.2d 1457, 1460, 1462 (N.H. 1996).

Broadened Reissue.

This appeal is from a decision of the PTO Board of Appeals rejecting claims of a reissue application on the ground that a broadening reissue application that was filed within two years of the patent issue date (but was erroneously filed by the assignee) could not be corrected by a Declaration of the inventor filed more than two years after the patent issue date. The CAFC reversed. Recognizing that all of the provisions of a unified statute must he read in harmony, the portion of 35 U.S.C. §251 that requires that a broadening reissue application must be signed by the inventor does not mean that an error in compliance with §251 is insulated from the remedial ruling of *Stoddard* [564 F.2d 556, 195 U.S.P.Q. 97 (D.C. Cir. 1977)] or the statutory provision for the correction of error. The purpose of the reissue statute is to remedy errors. Reissue is remedial in nature and is based on fundamental principles of equity and fairness. These fundamental principles must not be forgotten in implementation of the statute. *In re Bennett*, 766 F.2d 524, 226 U.S.P.Q. 413 (Fed. Cir. 1985).

Broadening Claim.

"[C]laims in an application which are broader than the applicant's disclosure are not allowable." *Reiffin v. Microsoft Corp.*, 48 U.S.P.Q.2d 1274, 1277 (Cal. 1998).

Brown Bag Sales. *See also* **Plant Variety Protection Act.**

Farmers often place harvested planting seed in plain brown bags for sale to other farmers. Therefore, "brown bag sales" refers to the sale of harvested seed from one farmer to another for planting future crops. *Asgrow Seed Co. v. Winterboer*, 982 F.2d 486, 25 U.S.P.Q.2d 1202, 1203 (Fed. Cir. 1992).

Budapest Treaty.

Reliance upon Rule 11.3(b) of the Budapest Treaty as authorizing the international depository authority to provide samples of the present deposits once a patent is issued is misplaced. This rule comes into operation only after a patent has been granted. It has no bearing on the present issue where a patent application is pending before the PTO with a pending rejection of claims under 35 U.S.C. §112, first paragraph, for lack of enablement. Rules pertaining to the issue of deposits of biological material have recently come into force for all applications filed in the PTO on or after January 1, 1990. These rules provide an orderly procedure for these issues to be raised and resolved. *Ex parte Hildebrand*, 15 U.S.P.Q.2d 1662, 1664 (B.P.A.I. 1990).

Burden. *See also* **Administrative Regularity, Copying Claims, Persuasion, Presumption of Validity, Proof.**

The burden is on an applicant for a patent to prove entitlement to a patent. The mere fact that such applicant uses broad or generic terminology in his original disclosure does not necessarily entitle him to claim the subject matter broadly. *Ex parte Dubbs and Stevens*, 119 U.S.P.Q. 440, 442 (PO Bd. App. 1958).

ω

Once the Examiner cites prior art showing a general reaction to be old, the burden is on the applicant to present "reason or authority for believing" that a particular group on the starting material in the claimed process would take place in or affect the basic reaction disclosed in the cited prior art. *In re Ross and Davis*, 305 F.2d 878, 134 U.S.P.Q. 320, 322 (C.C.P.A. 1962).

ω

In an interference between a patentee and a reissue applicant, the junior party patentee had the burden of proving priority by a preponderance of the evidence. *Poage v. Dyer*, 184 U.S.P.Q. 223, 225 (PO Bd. Pat. Int. 1974).

ᚳ

The mere lack of literal support in a parent application for a claim limitation is not enough to carry the PTO's initial burden to establish that the applicant is not entitled to the benefit of the filing date of such parent application. *In re Voss*, 557 F.2d 812, 194 U.S.P.Q. 267, 271 (C.C.P.A. 1977).

ᚳ

The PTO has not challenged the appellants' assertion that their 1953 application enabled those skilled in the art in 1953 to make and use "a solid polymer" as called for by their claim. The appellants disclosed, as the only then-existing way to make such a polymer, a method of making the crystalline form. To say now that the appellants should have disclosed in 1953 the amorphous form (which did not exist until 1962) would be to impose an impossible burden on inventors and thus on the patent system. There cannot, in an effective patent system, be such a burden placed on the right to broad claims. To restrict the appellants to the crystalline form disclosed, under such circumstances, would be a poor way to stimulate invention, and particularly to encourage its early disclosure. To demand such restriction is merely to state a policy against broad protection for pioneer inventions, a policy both shortsighted and unsound from the standpoint of promoting progress in the useful arts, which is the constitutional purpose of the patent laws. *In re Hogan and Banks*, 559 F.2d 595, 194 U.S.P.Q. 527 (C.C.P.A. 1977).

ᚳ

The burden of showing that the claimed invention is not described in the application rests on the PTO in the first instance, and it is up to the PTO to give reasons why a description not in ipsis verbis is insufficient. *In re Edwards, Rice, and Soulen*, 568 F.2d 1349, 196 U.S.P.Q. 465, 469 (C.C.P.A. 1978).

ᚳ

Section 282 of 35 U.S.C. mandates not only a presumption shifting the burden of going forward in a purely procedural sense, but also places the burden of persuasion on the party who asserts that a patent is invalid. The burden of persuasion is and remains always upon the party asserting invalidity, whether the most pertinent prior art was or was not considered by the Examiner. Mere failure to cite certain prior art does not necessarily mean that it was not considered by the Examiner, who may have considered it unworthy of citation. Though the presumption of validity remains in existence until rebutted and the burden of persuasion continues throughout the litigation on him who asserts invalidity, the burden of persuasion may be more easily carried by evidence consisting of more pertinent prior art than that considered by the Examiner. *Solder Removal Co. v. U.S. International Trade Commission*, 582 F.2d 628, 199 U.S.P.Q. 129, 133 (C.C.P.A. 1978).

ᚳ

The PTO must have adequate support for its challenge to the credibility of applicant's statements as to utility. Only then does the burden shift to appellant to provide rebuttal evidence. *In re Bundy*, 642 F.2d 430, 209 U.S.P.Q. 48, 51 (C.C.P.A. 1981).

ᚳ

As the burden of proving invalidity is with the party attacking validity, evidence educed in connection with a motion for preliminary relief must be considered in this light. A patentee retains the burden of showing a reasonable likelihood that an attack on its patent's validity would fail. This does not change the immutable allocation to the challenger of the burden of proving invalidity, but rather reflects the rule that the burden is always on the movant to demonstrate entitlement to preliminary relief. Such entitlement, however, is determined in the context of the presumptions and burdens that would inhere at trial on the merits. *H. Robertson Co. v. United Steel Deck, Inc.*, 820 F.2d 384, 2 U.S.P.Q.2d 1926 (Fed. Cir. 1987).

ω

The burden on one who appeals the grant of a motion for JNOV is to show that the jury's factual findings were supported by at least substantial evidence and the legal conclusions made by the jury can be supported by those findings. Substantial evidence is such relevant evidence from the record, taken as a whole, as might be accepted by a reasonable mind as adequate to support the finding under review. *Vieau v. Japax Inc.*, 823 F.2d 1510, 3 U.S.P.Q.2d 1094 (Fed. Cir. 1987).

ω

To the extent reliance is placed on evidence previously considered by the PTO, there is "the added burden of overcoming the deference that is due to a qualified government agency presumed to have properly done its job, which includes...Examiners who are assumed to have some expertise in interpreting the references and to be familiar from their work with the level of skill in the art and whose duty it is to issue only valid patents." *Sonoco Products Co. v. Mobil Oil Corp.*, 15 U.S.P.Q.2d 1186, 1191 (S.C. 1989).

ω

Where the parties' applications were not copending, the junior party has the burden of proving priority and/or derivation by clear and convincing evidence, evidence that produces in the mind of the trier of fact an abiding conviction that the truth of the factual contention is "highly probable." *English v. Ausnit*, 38 U.S.P.Q.2d 1625, 1630 (B.P.A.I. 1993).

ω

A patent infringement plaintiff bears a significant pre-filing investigation burden before asserting a patent claim, and such burden cannot be fulfilled by merely filing suit on a suspicion of infringement and then asking for discovery to prove up the suspicions. "To fulfill his duty, an attorney must investigate the fact, examine the law, and then decide whether the Complaint is justified." *Nasatka v. Delta Scientific Corp.*, 34 U.S.P.Q.2d 1649, 1652 (Va. 1994).

ω

The patentee bears the burden of proving that its (claim or infringement) interpretation would not ensnare prior art. *Sage Products Inc. v. Devon Industries Inc.*, 880 F.Supp. 718, 35 U.S.P.Q.2d 1321, 1328 (Cal. 1994).

Bursting Bubble.

Under the "bursting bubble" theory, a presumption is not merely rebuttable, but completely vanishes upon the introduction of evidence sufficient to support a finding of the nonexistence of the presumed fact. *A.C. Aukerman Co. v. R.L. Chaides Construction Co.*, 960 F.2d 1020, 22 U.S.P.Q.2d 1321, 1332 (Fed. Cir. 1992).

Business. *See also* **Method of Doing Business, Transacting Business.**

The basic principle of the patent system is to protect inventions which meet the statutory requirements. Valuable inventions should be given protection of value in the real world of business and the courts. *In re Ruschig, Aumüller, Korger, Wagner, Scholz, and Bänder*, 343 F.2d 965, 145 U.S.P.Q. 274, 286 (C.C.P.A. 1965).

Business Activity. *See also* **Transacting Business.**

Substantial business activity, beyond mere solicitation, by a distributor of an alien corporation on that corporation's behalf can be sufficient to provide in personam jurisdiction over the alien corporation. Such activities were sufficiently important to the alien corporation that, if the distributor were not performing them, the alien corporation would have to do so itself—as it in fact did on two occasions. *Nippon Electric Co. Ltd. v. American Broadcasting Companies*, 204 U.S.P.Q. 496, 497 (N.Y. 1978).

But-For Rule or Test.

In determining materiality, three different tests have been used. The first is the objective but-for test, i.e., the misrepresentation was so material that, but for the misrepresentation, the patent not only would not have been issued but should not have been issued. The second is the subjective but-for test, i.e., the misrepresentation caused the Examiner to approve the application for a patent when he would not otherwise have done so. Thus, the subjective does not permit the reviewing court to conclude that, notwithstanding the misrepresentation, the patent was properly issued. The third test has been labeled the "but it might have been" test, i.e., the misrepresentation in the course of the patent prosecution might have influenced the Examiner. *Plastic Container Corp. v. Continental Plastics of Oklahoma, Inc.*, 607 F.2d 885, 203 U.S.P.Q. 27 (10th Cir. 1979).

ω

In a challenge to the validity of a patent because of fraud or inequitable conduct in its procurement, two elements must be shown: (1) there must be a knowing, willful, and intentional act of misrepresentation to the PTO, and (2) the misrepresentation to the PTO must be material. A misrepresentation is material if the patent would not have issued but for the omission. The burden of proof is by clear and convincing evidence. To hold that an antitrust suit might reach an otherwise valid patent merely because the patent was procured with less than the highest degree of candor and fiduciary duty would chill the disclosure of inventions through obtaining a patent due to fear of the vexatious or punitive consequences of antitrust suits. The but-for standard of materiality properly balances the competing policies of the antitrust and patent laws. *United States v. Ciba-Geigy Corp.*, 508 F. Supp. 1157, 211 U.S.P.Q. 529 (N.J. 1979).

ω

In order to recover lost profits rather than merely a reasonable royalty in a patent infringement action, the patent holder must demonstrate that but for the infringement, he would have made sales that the infringer made. No presumption operates in the patent holder's favor that he would have made the sales in question. The patent holder must advance affirmative proof of the demand for his patented product in the marketplace, the absence of acceptable non-infringing substitutes, and his production and marketing capacity to meet the demand. Yet, the but-for rule necessarily expresses a hypothesis. Neither the trial court nor the appellate court can demand absolute proof that purchasers of the infringing product would have bought the patent holder's product instead. It is impossible and therefore unnecessary for the patent holder to negate every possibility that the purchasers might not have bought another product. The plaintiff's burden of proof is not absolute, but rather one of reasonable probability. *Milgo Electronic Corp. v. United Business Communications, Inc.*, 623 F.2d 645, 206 U.S.P.Q. 481 (10th Cir. 1980).

ω

In addition to requiring that a nondisclosed prior art reference be material in a strict but-for sense, the failure to cite the prior art must be done with a "specific intent" to defraud. Without a showing of willful and intentional fraud, no antitrust liability can be sustained. A good faith judgment not to cite the prior art to the PTO, even if erroneous, does not constitute fraud. *Oetiker v. Jurid Werke GmbH*, 556 F.2d 1, 209 U.S.P.Q. 809 (D.C. 1981).

ω

Inequitable conduct requires proof by clear and convincing evidence of a threshold degree of materiality of nondisclosed or false information. That threshold can be established by any of four tests: (1) objective but for; (2) subjective but for; (3) but it may have been; and (4) 37 C.F.R. §1.56(a), i.e., whether there is a substantial likelihood that a reasonable Examiner would have considered the omitted or false information important in deciding whether to allow the application to issue as a patent. The PTO standard is the appropriate starting point because it is the broadest and most closely aligned with how one ought to conduct business with the PTO. Inequitable conduct also requires proof of a threshold intent. Proof of deliberate scheming is not needed; gross negligence is sufficient. *J. P. Stevens & Co., Inc. v. Lex Tex, Ltd., Inc.*, 747 F.2d 1553, 223 U.S.P.Q. 1089, 1092 (Fed. Cir. 1984).

ω

The patentee's burden in demonstrating an absence of acceptable substitutes is not stringent. The patent holder does not need to negate all possibilities that a purchaser might have bought a different product or might have foregone the purchase altogether. The but-for rule only requires the patentee to provide proof to a reasonable probability that the sale would have been made but for the infringement. *T. D. Williamson Inc. v. Laymon*, 723 F. Supp. 587, 13 U.S.P.Q.2d 1417, 1427 (Okla. 1989).

Buyer. *See* **Purchaser.**

By Hand.

The inclusion in a patent of a claim to a process that may be performed by a person, but that also is capable of being performed by a machine, is not fatal to patentability. The presence of the steps of correlating and combining, which a machine is capable of doing, does not invalidate a patent. *Alco Standard Corp. v. Tennessee Valley Authority*, 808 F.2d 1490, 1 U.S.P.Q.2d 1337, 1341 (Fed. Cir. 1986).

Key Terms and Concepts

C

CAFC (Court of Appeals for the Federal Circuit). *See also* **Federal Circuit, Jurisdiction of the CAFC, Standard of Review, Summary Judgment.**

As a foundation for decisions in the CAFC, the court deemed it fitting, necessary, and proper to adopt an established body of law as precedent. That body of law represented by the holdings of the CCPA announced before the close of business on September 30, 1982, was regarded as most applicable to the areas of law within the substantitive jurisdiction of the CAFC. That body of law was thus adopted by the CAFC. *South Corp. v. United States,* 690 F.2d 1368, 215 U.S.P.Q. 657 (Fed. Cir. 1982).

ω

The CAFC does not sit to judge the character of district court judges, nor does it have the authority to order assignment of a case to a different judge on remand. Unlike other Circuit Courts of Appeal, the CAFC has no direct supervisory authority over district courts. *Petersen Manufacturing Co., Inc. v. Central Purchasing, Inc.,* 740 F.2d 1541, 222 U.S.P.Q. 562, 570 (Fed. Cir. 1984).

ω

A decision by the CAFC that the district court erred in setting aside a finding of the master will necessarily make a contrary finding by the district court ineffectual. The CAFC evaluates the district court's decision on an objection to the master's report, not the district court's substitute finding. Upholding the district court ruling that the master's finding was clearly erroneous does not ipso facto uphold a substitute finding by the district court. The latter is subject to review in accordance with Rule 52(a). The CAFC must review, as a matter of law, the correctness of the district court's setting aside any factual finding by the master and, if that is upheld, review any substitute or additional findings of the district court under the "clearly erroneous" standard of Rule 52(a). *Milliken Research Corporation v. Dan River, Inc.,* 739 F.2d 587, 222 U.S.P.Q. 571, 576 (Fed. Cir. 1984).

ω

The CAFC does not review findings of the U.S. International Trade Commission under the clearly erroneous standard applicable to the findings of a district court, as provided in Fed. R. Civ. P. 52(a). The CAFC reviews the factual findings of the Commission to determine whether they are unsupported by substantial evidence and is not bound by the Commission's legal conclusions. *American Hospital Supply Corp. v. Travenol Laboratories, Inc.,* 745 F.2d 1, 223 U.S.P.Q. 577 (Fed. Cir. 1984).

ω

Although an obviousness determination per se is a question of law that the CAFC reviews de novo, it is based upon underlying factual inquiries concerning the claimed invention, and the prior art, which predicate findings by the BPAI, are binding on the

CAFC unless shown to be clearly erroneous. *In re Kulling*, 897 F.2d 1147, 14 U.S.P.Q.2d 1056, 1057 (Fed. Cir. 1990).

ᛟ

A federal court exercising patent jurisdiction is bound by the substantive patent law of the Federal Circuit. *ALM Surgical Equipment Inc. v. Kirschner Medical Corp.*, 15 U.S.P.Q.2d 1241, 1251 (S.C. 1990).

ᛟ

When the *Graham* factual underpinnings have been genuinely disputed, the CAFC presumes that the jury resolved them in favor of the verdict winner. In the absence of a proper motion for directed verdict during the trial below, the sole question for review is whether the factual story told to the jury by the verdict winner (assuming that the jury correctly believed it) supports the legal conclusion of non-obviousness. *Jurgens v. McKasy*, 927 F.2d 1552, 18 U.S.P.Q.2d 1031, 1036 (Fed. Cir. 1991).

ᛟ

The CAFC does not vacate and remand for new trial a judgment rendered on a jury verdict when no motions for directed verdict, JNOV, or new trial were made in the district court and when appellant has not demonstrated that prejudicial legal error occurred in the conduct of the trial. *Acoustical Design Inc. v. Control Electronics Co.*, 932 F.2d 939, 18 U.S.P.Q.2d 1707, 1709 (Fed. Cir. 1991).

ᛟ

The sufficiency of the evidence cannot be reviewed on appeal after a jury verdict absent some post-verdict disposition, either by a deferred ruling or upon a post-verdict motion. *Biodex Corp. v. Loredan Biomedical Inc.*, 946 F.2d 850, 20 U.S.P.Q.2d 1252, 1261 (Fed. Cir. 1991).

ᛟ

In reviewing procedural matters that are not unique to patent law, the CAFC applies the law of the regional circuit where appeals from the particular district court would normally lie. *Beech Aircraft Corp. v. EDO Corp.*, 990 F.2d 1237, 26 U.S.P.Q.2d 1572, 1580 (Fed. Cir. 1993).

ᛟ

In cases where the Federal Circuit has appellate jurisdiction, that jurisdiction extends to appeals from appealable orders in ancillary discovery proceedings. *Dorf & Stanton Communications Inc. v. Molson Breweries*, 34 U.S.P.Q.2d 1856, 1857 (2d Cir. 1995).

ᛟ

The importance of uniformity in the treatment of a given patent is an independent reason to allocate all issues of construction to the court. It was just for the sake of such desirable uniformity that Congress created the Court of Appeals for the Federal Circuit as an exclusive appellate court for patent cases, observing that increased uniformity would "strengthen the United States patent system in such a way as to foster technological growth and industrial innovation." *Markman v. Westview Instruments Inc.*, 116 S.Ct. 1384, 38 U.S.P.Q.2d 1461, 1470, 1471 (S.Ct. 1996).

ᛟ

Prior decisions of a panel of the CAFC are binding precedent on subsequent panels unless and until overturned in banc. *Texas Instruments Inc. v. Cypress Semiconductor Corp.*, 39 U.S.P.Q.2d 1492, 1500 (Fed. Cir. 1996).

ᚥ

The Administrative Procedure Act, in 5 U.S.C. §559, permits, and *stare decisis* warrants continued application of the clearly erroneous standard in review of PTO fact findings by the CAFC. *In re Zurko*, 142 F.3d 1447, 46 U.S.P.Q.2d 1691, 1693 (Fed. Cir. 1998—*in banc*).

Can. *See also* Label License.

Although the applicant's disclosure provided details as to how some 150 specifically named compounds "were prepared" or "can be prepared," a rejection based on undue breadth and speculation was affirmed because the only compounds actually tested that demonstrated the particular disclosed pharmacological properties were far more limited in structure than those claimed. *In re Surrey,* 370 F.2d 349, 151 U.S.P.Q. 724 (C.C.P.A. 1966).

ᚥ

The solicitor would have us read "must" for "may". Although it is common practice in drafting patent applications to use "may" in a mandatory sense, it should be interpreted in this case as illustrative and not as limiting because the originally-filed claims (part of the original disclosure) recite "a diamine" without further limitation. *In re DiLeone and Lucas*, 436 F.2d 1404, 168 U.S.P.Q. 592, 594 (C.C.P.A. 1971).

Canceled Claims. *See also* Reassert Cancelled Subject Matter, Recapture.

Allowed claims cannot, by construction, be read to cover subject matter eliminated by canceling other claims. This rule is applicable not only when the canceled claims are broader than those allowed, but also when the canceled claims are narrower. *Chemical Construction Corp. v. Jones & Laughlin Steel Corp.*, 311 F.2d 367, 136 U.S.P.Q. 150, 155 (3d Cir. 1962).

ᚥ

Claims canceled during patent reexamination cannot be asserted in a pending application. *Ex parte Morimoto*, 18 U.S.P.Q.2d 1540 (B.P.A.I. 1991).

Canceled Subject Matter. *See also* Reassert Cancelled Subject Matter, Recapture, 35 U.S.C. §154.

Subject matter canceled from the specification of an application that subsequently issues as a patent and thus does not appear in the issued patent is not prior art with regard to an application that has an effective filing date prior to the issuance of the patent. Whether that subject matter is prior art as of the date on which the patent issued was not determined. *Ex parte Stalego*, 839 O.G. 828, 829, 830 (PO Bd. App. 1966).

ᚥ

Subject matter initially disclosed in, but subsequently canceled from, the specification (prior to issuance) of a copending patent of another can be considered as part of the stock of public knowledge on the date of issuance of the copending patent. Prior to that date the most the canceled portions of the specification could be used for would be as evidence of conception. *Ex parte Thelin,* 152 U. S. P. Q. 624, 625, 626 (PO Bd. App. 1966).

Cancellation. *See also* Revocation.

An Examiner's requirement to cancel the drawing and a portion of the specification is a petitionable matter. It is not appealable to the Board of Appeals. *Ex parte Wolf,* 65 U.S.P.Q. 527 (PO Bd. App. 1945).

ω

The disclosure is sufficient to satisfy the statutory requirements with respect to how to use even though a significant part of it may be of a questionable nature. With respect to the latter it is within the discretion of the Examiner to require cancellation of alternative uses disclosed in a specification. *In re Gottlieb,* 328 F.2d 1016, 140 U.S.P.Q. 665 (C.C.P.A. 1964).

ω

A patentee moved to dissolve an interference on the ground that his patent claims had not been copied by an applicant prior to one year from the date on which his patent was granted. The Examiner's decision to deny the motion was reversed by the Commissioner on petition. The interference was dissolved, and the applicant subsequently canceled the claims corresponding to the interference counts. The applicant subsequently urged he had timely copied the claims in order to overcome the patent as a reference in ex parte prosecution. The applicant was required to reassert the patent claims, and the interference was reinstated. The Commissioner decided (on petition) that the applicant was bound by the Commissioner's prior decision, from which no appeal was taken. From the applicant's cancellation of claims and failure to appeal, it was concluded that applicant has acquiesced in the prior decision and applicant was estopped, on the ground of res judicata, from raising the question of whether he had originally copied the patent claims in timely fashion. *Rubenstein v. Schmidt,* 145 U.S.P.Q. 613 (Comm'r Patents 1965).

ω

Subject matter canceled from the specification of an application prior to its issuance as a patent is not available prior art against a copending application. *Ex parte Stalego,* 154 U.S.P.Q. 52 (Bd. App. 1966).

ω

In the interest of protecting the public from the monopoly of a patent procured by fraud, such patent should be annulled, and the only means by which this can be conclusively accomplished is in a direct proceeding brought by the government. *United States v. Saf-T-Boom Corp.,* 431 F.2d 737, 167 U.S.P.Q. 195 (8th Cir. 1970).

ω

A separate claim embodying Figure 4 was treated as unnecessary because it was merely descriptive of the use to be made of the patent device. Under these circumstances the cancellation of Claim 18 should not be considered an abandonment of the embodiment of the invention that it had described. *Olympic Fastening Systems, Inc. v. Textron Inc.*, 504 F.2d 609, 183 U.S.P.Q. 449, 452 (6th Cir. 1974).

ω

The Primary Examiner objected to the words "and anti-tumour" and required either "cancellation of said term or proof that the instant compound is safe, reliable and effective for the utility set forth...." Considerable evidence was adduced, which the ÜCommissioner concedes is sufficient to support a conclusion that the compound has anti-tumour effect in treating certain tumours. The Primary Examiner adhered to his requirement that the phrase be stricken because it was broader than the proof offered in support. The Commissioner went beyond his interpretation of the disputed words to reject amending language that would restrict the assertion to those uses supported by the proof. Such amendment would not be objectionable "new matter." "Amendments to specifications for the purpose of clarity and definiteness are permissible." *Helms Products, Inc. v. Lake Shore Manufacturing Co.*, 227 F.2d 677, 107 U.S.P.Q. 313, 314 (7th Cir. 1955). *See also Aerosol Research Co. v. Scovill Manufacturing Co.*, 334 F.2d 751, 141 U.S.P.Q. 758 (7th Cir. 1964). Cancellation of the words "and anti-tumour" by the Patent Office was arbitrary and capricious. The cancellation requirement is set aside with leave to the Commissioner to allow an amendment restricting the specification to assertions that are supported by applicants' proof. *Rhone Poulenc S.A. v. Dann*, 507 F.2d 261, 184 U.S.P.Q. 196 (4th Cir. 1974).

ω

A sufficient disclosure with respect to one use is all that is required for compliance with statutory requirements. It is within the Examiner's discretion, if he deems it appropriate, to require cancellation of alternate uses disclosed in a specification. *Ex parte Richter*, 185 U.S.P.Q. 380 (Bd. App. 1974).

ω

Claims canceled during the year subsequent to the issuance of the patent (from which they were copied) could be relied upon to avoid the R.S. 4903 bar in view of the words "for the first time." Thus, regardless of whether the cancellation of claims might have been relevant to the application of the equitable doctrine of *Chapman v. Wintroath*, 252 U.S. 126 (1920), such cancellation is not relevant to the application of its statutory successor. The second paragraph of R.S. 4903, as amended, was codified in its present form in 1952 as the second paragraph of 35 U.S.C. §135, later designated paragraph (b). No substantial change was intended by the changes in language. The words "prior to" in the present code clearly point to a "critical date" prior to which the copier had to be claiming the invention, whether or not the claims were subsequently canceled. No language is found in §135(b), or any of its predecessor statutes, that requires restricting cancellation of claims to cancellation after the patent (from which they are copied) issues. *Corbett v. Chisholm and Schrenk*, 568 F.2d 759, 196 U.S.P.Q. 337 (C.C.P.A. 1977).

ω

A petition was filed in response to a requirement to cancel from the specification all assertions pertaining to cancer utility. The Examiner took the position that the recitation in the specification of a broad genus (e.g., malignant tumors) without specific examples of human and animal in vivo and additional in vitro data does not meet minimum standards. Reference to utility as an antitumor agent in a warm-blooded animal afflicted by malignant tumors was not regarded by the Examiner as believable on its face to those of ordinary skill in the art in view of contemporary knowledge in the art. The Examiner does not need to provide reasons why this speculative assertion should not be believed. The mere fact that the art of cancer chemotherapy is highly unpredictable places the burden on applicants to provide a basis for believing the speculative statements that they choose to place in the specification in the form of a positive assertion. The ignorance of the PTO and the applicants in not being able to provide a scientific reason why the assertion is not sound is not a justification for permitting such an assertion to be made in a patent document where those of ordinary skill in this art would not accept it as believable on its face without some data or other evidence to support it. The PTO does not want to spend the time or resources that may be necessary to provide a scientifically reasoned opinion as to why the speculative statements would not be believed by a person skilled in the art. *In re Application of Hozumi*, 226 U.S.P.Q. 353 (Commr. Patents & Trademarks 1985).

Cancellation from Disclosure.

The application stood in condition for allowance and ready for the issuance of a patent grant except for the presence in the specification disclosure of certain asserted utilities that the Examiner believed to be too speculative, i.e., not believable on their face to those of ordinary skill in the art in view of the contemporary knowledge of the art. While it may be clear that workers in this art had shown that some cancers can be treated successfully in some patients, the effective treatment of various forms of malignant tumors remains a highly unpredictable art. Under these circumstances, the Examiner does not need to provide reasons why this speculative assertion should not be believed. The mere fact that the art of cancer chemotherapy is highly unpredictable places the burden on applicants to provide a basis for believing the speculative statements that they chose to place in the specification in the form of a positive assertion. *In re Application of Hozumi*, 226 U.S.P.Q. 353 (Comm'r Patents & Trademarks 1985).

Cancelled Claims. *See* Canceled Claims.

Cancer.

That claimed compounds actually inhibit the growth of a transplanted cancer strain is sufficient to satisfy the express language of 35 U.S.C. §101 and is in harmony with the basic constitutional concept of promoting the progress of science and the useful arts. *In re Bergel and Stock,* 292 F.2d 955, 130 U.S.P.Q. 206, 209 (C.C.P.A. 1961).

ω

A demonstration that a compound has desirable or beneficial properties in the prevention, alleviation, or cure of some disease in experimental animals does not necessarily mean that the compound will have the same properties when used with humans. However, this is by no means support for the position that such evidence is not relevant to human utility. Evidence showing substantial activity against experimental tumors in mice in tests customarily used for the screening of anti-cancer agents of potential utility in the treatment of humans is relevant to utility in humans and is not to be disregarded. *In re Jolles,* 628 F.2d 1322, 206 U.S.P.Q. 885, 890 (C.C.P.A. 1980).

ᖬ

The application stood in condition for allowance and ready for the issuance of a patent grant except for the presence in the specification disclosure of certain asserted utilities that the Examiner believed to be too speculative, i.e., not believable on their face to those of ordinary skill in the art in view of the contemporary knowledge of the art. While it may be clear that workers in this art had shown that some cancers can be treated successfully in some patients, the effective treatment of various forms of malignant tumors remains a highly unpredictable art. Under these circumstances, the Examiner does not need to provide reasons why this speculative assertion should not be believed. The mere fact that the art of cancer chemotherapy is highly unpredictable places the burden on applicants to provide a basis for believing the speculative statements that they chose to place in the specification in the form of a positive assertion.

A petition was filed in response to a requirement to cancel from the specification all assertions pertaining to cancer utility. The Examiner took the position that the recitation in the specification of a broad genus (e.g., malignant tumors) without specific examples of human and animal in vivo and additional in vitro data does not meet minimum standards. Reference to utility as an antitumor agent in a warm-blooded animal afflicted by malignant tumors was not regarded by the Examiner as believable on its face to those of ordinary skill in the art in view of contemporary knowledge in the art. The Examiner does not need to provide reasons why this speculative assertion should not be believed. The mere fact that the art of cancer chemotherapy is highly unpredictable places the burden on applicants to provide a basis for believing the speculative statements that they choose to place in the specification in the form of a positive assertion. The ignorance of the PTO and the applicants in not being able to provide a scientific reason why the assertion is not sound is not a justification for permitting such an assertion to be made in a patent document where those of ordinary skill in this art would not accept it as believable on its face without some data or other evidence to support it. The PTO does not want to spend the time or resources that may be necessary to provide a scientifically reasoned opinion as to why the speculative statements would not be believed by a person skilled in the art *In re Application of Hozumi,* 226 U.S.P.Q. 353 (Commr. Patents & Trademarks 1985).

ᖬ

Amelioration of the symptoms or even cure of cancer is no longer considered to be "incredible." Nonetheless, decisional law would seem to indicate that the utility in question is sufficiently unusual to justify an Examiner's requiring substantiating evidence. This may be in the form of animal tests that constitute recognized screening procedures with clear relevance to utility in humans. The specification of the appellant's parent application sets forth several animal tests on numerous types of specific cancers as well as in vitro studies, both of which are asserted to be predictive with regard to utility in humans. The Examiner has not challenged the evidence presented in a single, relevant, material respect. There is only the blanket statement of lack of "patentable utility" per se. In fact, the only specific comments the Examiner has directed toward the appellant's evidence are with regard to the breadth of the types of tumor against which the claimed compounds have been shown to be active. The appealed claims are drawn to compounds and not to a method of treatment. Generally speaking, utility in treating a single disease is adequate basis for the patentability of a pharmaceutical compound under 35 U.S.C. §101. *Ex parte Krepelka,* 231 U.S.P.Q. 746 (B.P.A.I. 1986).

ᚹ

Claims were rejected because they encompassed the treatment of humans and the only tests disclosed in the specification were in vitro studies and animal tests. The Examiner did not raise any specific challenge to the tests reported with respect to their acceptance in the art as being predictive of efficacy in treating humans or in any other respect; she merely took the position that such tests are inherently incapable of supporting claims that could read on treatment of humans. The claims are limited to the treatment of a single type of cancer or, more precisely, a single closely related group of cancers, and the evidence relates to that type of cancer. The Examiner has not replied to appellant's argument based on the similarity between the claimed compound and a known effective compound in both structure and in vivo test results. The rejection was reversed. *Ex parte Chwang,* 231 U.S.P.Q. 751 (B.P.A.I. 1986).

ᚹ

The "contemporary knowledge in the art" has far advanced since the days when any statement of utility in treating cancer was per se "incredible." The medical treatment of a specific cancer is not such an inherently unbelievable undertaking and does not involve such implausible scientific principles as to be considered incredible. *Ex parte Rubin,* 5 U.S.P.Q.2d 1461 (B.P.A.I. 1987).

ᚹ

Some amount and type of evidence is required to provide reasonable support for assertions of usefulness of compositions and processes for treating cancer. *Ex parte Stevens,* 16 U.S.P.Q.2d 1379, 1380 (B.P.A.I. 1990).

ᚹ

The purpose of treating cancer with chemical compounds does not suggest an inherently unbelievable undertaking or involve implausible scientific principles. *In re Brana,* 51 F.3d 1560, 34 U.S.P.Q.2d 1436, 1441 (Fed. Cir. 1995).

ᚹ

Whatever might have been the case earlier in the 20th Century, in 1992 (when applicants filed their application) the notion that a chemical compound may be useful in treating cancer was not inherently incredible. *Ex parte Bhide,* 42 U.S.P.Q.2d 1441, 1447 (B.P.A.I. 1996).

Candor. *See also* **Conduct, Duty to Disclose, Inequitable Conduct.**

An applicant's knowledge of a fact as to which he knows the Patent Office is ignorant or mistaken and which would be material under the theory he knows the Patent Office is applying would impose an obligation of candor. *University of Illinois Foundation v. Blonder-Tongue Laboratories, Inc.,* 422 F.2d 769, 164 U.S.P.Q. 545, 550 (7th Cir. 1970).

ᚹ

Patent applicants are held to a high standard of conduct before the PTO due in part to the Office's inability to verify independently many of the representations made to it. This is particularly true when the representations pertain to the results of tests or experiments conducted by applicants. Since patent Examiners are not equipped to perform their own tests and experiments, they must rely upon the candor and good faith of the applicants in reporting such results. Some courts have been particularly vigilant in requiring patent applicants to disclose all pertinent test results, including those that are unfavorable. *Grefco Inc. v. Kewanee Industries, Inc.*, 499 F. Supp. 844, 208 U.S.P.Q. 218 (Del. 1980).

ω

Although inequitable conduct amounting to gross negligence may support a finding that the patentee breached its duty of candor to the Patent Office, such finding will not support a Sherman Act claim. A patentee's breach of duty of frank disclosure does not answer the question of whether applicant engaged in willful and knowing misrepresentation of material facts. A Sherman Act cause of action is not established when an applicant obtains a patent on an "obvious" invention or when a patentee fails to disclose nonrelevant prior art. *Jackson Jordan, Inc. v. Plasser American Corp.*, 219 U.S.P.Q. 922, 933 (Va. 1983).

ω

The reason for high standards of conduct and candor before the PTO is the ex parte nature of the proceedings there. The PTO and the applicant for a patent are more fiduciaries than antagonists. A duty of candor attaches to an application for a patent and to the extent and nature of the information provided in connection therewith. However, the duty of candor is not without bounds; it does not extend to adversarial proceedings. *United Sweetener U.S.A. Inc. v. The Nutrasweet Company*, 760 F. Supp. 400, 19 U.S.P.Q.2d 1561, 1577 (Del. 1991).

ω

The duty of candor extends to withholding unfavorable test data even when such data may be incomplete and even when it is subsequently shown to be irrelevant. *Imperial Chemical Industries PLC v. Barr Laboratories*, 87 Civ. 7833, 22 U.S.P.Q.2d 1906, 1910 (N.Y. 1992).

ω

There is no presumption of the inventor's knowledge of material prior art in connection with the duty of candor. *Code Alarm Inc. v. Electromotive Technologies Corp.*, 26 U.S.P.Q.2d 1561, 1563 (Mich. 1992).

ω

The duty of candor owed the PTO being uncompromising, it would deal a deathblow to that duty if direct proof of wrongful intent were required. *Williams Service Group Inc. v. O.B. Cannon & Son Inc.*, 33 U.S.P.Q.2d 1705, 1732 n.15 (Pa. 1994).

Can Label. *See* **Label License.**

Can License. *See* **Label License.**

Canon 4.

A factor to be considered when determining whether there has been a breach of Canon 4 ("A lawyer should preserve the confidences and secrets of a client.") is whether matters embraced within a pending suit are substantially related to matters or a cause of action for which the attorney previously represented the moving party. Support for the position that the two actions are not substantially related is found in the fact that the U.S. Patent and Trademark Office assigned different classifications to the two patents in question. The argument that the subjects of the two lawsuits are substantially related because they both involve infringements of patents on "agricultural products" was regarded as unpersuasive. *Yetter Manufacturing Co. v. Hiniker Co., Inc.*, 213 U.S.P.Q. 119, 121 (Minn. 1981).

Capability.

There is nothing in the statutes or the case law which makes "that which is within the capabilities of one skilled in the art" synonymous with obviousness. *Ex parte Gerlach and Woerner*, 212 U.S.P.Q. 471 (PTO Bd. App. 1980).

Capital Asset.

A patent application is an assignable property right, but not a depreciable asset. When a patent is issued, depreciation may be taken over its life. The application, which was sold, constituted a capital asset. A patent is intangible property whose value is protected by a government-imposed monopoly for a period of time over which its development costs are normally depreciable. Because it constitutes depreciable property when used in the operation of a business, it does not qualify as a capital asset under section 1221 (Internal Revenue Code of 1954), but, if held for more than six months, its sale or exchange may result in capital gain under section 1231. *United States Mineral Products Co. v. Commissioner of Internal Revenue*, 52 T.C. 177, 162 U.S.P.Q. 480, 491, 493 (U.S.T.C. 1969).

ω

Since a transfer of patents in return for 80 percent of the income generated by their use was found to be a purchase of capital assets with a determinable useful life, the purchaser was entitled to deduct the percentage payments, but only as depreciation of the cost of the patents. *Newton Insert Co. v. Commissioner of Internal Revenue*, 181 U.S.P.Q. 765, 772 (U.S.T.C. 1974).

Capital Gains.

The transfer of all substantial rights to a patent by a holder is considered the sale or exchange of a capital asset held for more than six months, even though the payment therefor is not made at the time of the transfer, but is made periodically later over a period of time. *Puschelberg v. United States*, 330 F.2d 56, 141 U.S.P.Q. 323 (6th Cir. 1964).

ω

It has been held that for capital gain purposes the patent grant may be separated into different fields of application and each field transferred to a different transferee, with each transfer qualifying separately as a sale. To like effect, capital gain effect has been allowed for a transfer limited to one industrial use only; for a transfer of only one of the claims in the general patent; and for a transfer limiting the use of the patent to a particular territory or industry. The "substantial right" in a patent, the retention of which by the grantor will preclude a sale, has reference to the substantial property right in a patent (i.e., the right to exclude others from making, using, or selling under the patent grant) not to the grantor's contractual right to obtain future payments in return for his conveyance of that property right. *Bell Intercontinental Corp. v. United States*, 381 F.2d 1004, 152 U.S.P.Q. 182, 187 (Ct. Cl. 1966).

ᅲ

Patent rights are intangible property rights, the transfer of which may qualify as a sale for capital gains purposes. The precise form and terminology of the transfer are not controlling, so long as it transfers exclusive rights for the full life of the patent. For capital gains purposes, the nylon rights, considered independently, were proper subjects for a sale. For such purposes, patent rights are divisible between different industries and different industrial products. *E.I. du Pont de Nemours & Co. v. United States*, 432 F.2d 1052, 167 U.S.P.Q. 321, 322, 324 (3d Cir. 1970).

ᅲ

The patent application was not depreciable property. The proceeds of the sale were entitled to capital gains treatment. *Davis v. Commissioner of Internal Revenue*, 491 F.2d 709, 181 U.S.P.Q. 552 (6th Cir. 1974).

ᅲ

Section 1235 (Internal Revenue Code of 1954) was enacted to clarify the tax treatment of percentage payments to inventors and their financial backers and to allow persons whose efforts led to the development of valuable inventions capital gains treatment on the sale or assignment of the underlying patents, regardless of the mode of payment involved and whether the inventor was in the business of inventing. The substance of the provisions is that a transfer shall be deemed a sale or exchange of a capital asset held for more than six months—and, consequently, result in a long-term capital gain—where enumerated conditions are met. *Newton Insert Co. v. Commissioner of Internal Revenue*, 181 U.S.P.Q. 765, 773 (U.S.T.C. 1974).

Carrier.

A composition composed of an old (known) chemical compound and a diluent (solvent) is patentably indistinct from the compound itself, notwithstanding the express designation of the composition as a plant stimulant composition. *Ex parte Billman*, 71 U.S.P.Q. 253, 254 (PO Bd. App. 1946).

ᅲ

Claims to a resin per se are not directed to the same invention as patent claims to a hair-setting composition comprising the resin dispersed in a solvent. *In re Walles, Tousignant, and Houtman*, 366 F.2d 786, 151 U.S.P.Q. 185, 189 (C.C.P.A. 1966).

ᅲ

The patentability of a composition comprising a known compound and a carrier is not precluded, particularly when claims define the amount or concentration of the compound, are limited to dosage units or specified dosage forms, or otherwise distinguish over prior-art teachings. *In re Wiggins*, 397 F.2d 356, 158 U.S.P.Q. 199 (C.C.P.A. 1968).

ᅲ

The mere recitation of a new use for an old composition does not render the composition patentable anew. There is nothing in the reference, however, which teaches that the known compound may be combined with a finely-divided inert insoluble solid-carrier vehicle. The carriers recited in the claims are those conventionally employed, and the disclosure teaches that compounds having algaecidal and herbicidal properties are usually blended with a solid or liquid carrier vehicle. As the reference does not teach that the known compound has algaecidal and/or herbicidal properties, there is simply no motivation to combine the known compound with conventional herbicidal carriers. There is nothing in the record that establishes the obviousness of mixing the known compound with a finely divided inert insoluble solid-carrier vehicle for any purpose whatsoever. Merely establishing that the particular compound is a known compound and that the carrier vehicles are conventional is not sufficient to render the claimed composition unpatentable. There must be some suggestion in the art to combine these materials for some purpose to support a holding of obviousness. *Ex parte Erdmann, Schneider, and Koch*, 194 U.S.P.Q. 96 (PTO Bd. App. 1975).

Case.

There are two types of cases that may be said to "arise under" the patent laws for purposes of 28 U.S.C. §1338. First, a suit arises under the law that creates the cause of action. Although this creation test may be helpful in identifying many cases that come within the court's jurisdiction, it has limited value in identifying those that do not. Second, a case arises under the patent laws if the plaintiff seeks to vindicate a right or interest "that would be defeated by one or sustained by an opposite construction" of the patent laws. *Christianson v. Colt Industries Operating Corp.*, 798 F.2d 1051, 230 U.S.P.Q. 840 (7th Cir. 1986).

ᴛᴐ

Undue liberties should not be taken with court decisions, which should be construed in accord with the precise issue before the court. A fertile source of error in patent law is the misapplication of a sound legal principle established in one case to another case in which the facts are essentially different and the principle has no application whatsoever. *In re Ruscetta and Jenny*, 255 F.2d 687, 118 U.S.P.Q. 101, 103 (C.C.P.A. 1958).

Case Law. *See* **Case.**

Case or Controversy. *See also* **Declaratory Judgment, Moot.**

In an action by a nonmanufacturer potential licensor seeking a declaratory judgment of patent invalidity, the case or controversy requirement of article III, section 2, of the Constitution is satisfied:

(1) (a) when a defendant's conduct has created on the part of the declaratory plaintiff a reasonable apprehension that it will face an infringement suit if a potential licensee of plaintiff commences the activity in question; or

(b) when there is an unwillingness on the part of a potential licensee-manufacturer to enter into a licensing agreement with a declaratory plaintiff and to manufacture the device, and a substantial factor in that unwillingness is an apprehension on the part of the potential licensee manufacturer, caused by defendant's conduct, that it will itself face an infringement suit if it commences manufacture; and

(2) (a) when plaintiff's licensee-manufacturer has actually manufactured rhe accused device; or

(b) it is probable that a potential licensee-manufacturer will commence manufacture, assuming the consumation of a licensing agreement between the licensor and the potential licensee-manufacturer, and assuming judicial elimination of the prospect of an infringement suit by defendant.

Research Institute for Medicine and Chemistry Inc. v. Wisconsin Alumni Research Foundation Inc., 647 F. Supp. 761, 1 U.S.P.Q.2d 1929 (Wis. 1986).

ᛦ

A declaratory judgment counterclaim by a licensee lacks the prerequisites for a case or controversy when the licensor unequivocally declares that it will never terminate the agreement for default or failure to perform. Such promise insulates the defendant from a patent infringement suit because a licensee cannot be sued for infringement. *Schwarzkopf Development Corp. v. Ti Coating Inc.*, 7 U.S.P.Q.2d 1557 (N.Y. 1988).

ᛦ

Because plaintiff has already expressed its intent to enforce its patent and because defendant clearly intends to file an NDA and has conducted clinical tests at substantial cost for that purpose, defendant has met the "meaningful preparation" requirement and shown that a real case and controversy exists necessary to permit the court to hear a declaratory judgment action. Those who seriously wish to practice an art facially preempted by a (pharmaceutical use) patent are permitted to test the patent's validity before completing the arduous task of obtaining administrative approval without requiring the court to participate in speculation as to the potential infringement of a product whose final formulation has not yet been settled. *Farmaceutisk Laboratorium Ferring A/S v. Solvay Pharmaceuticals Inc.*, 25 U.S.P.Q.2d 1344, 1350, 1352 (Ga. 1992).

ᛦ

A justifiable controversy exists with respect to a declaratory judgment counterclaim asserting the invalidity of all of a patentee's claims in response to an accusation in a complaint that asserts infringement of less than all of the claims where the declaratory judgment plaintiff is able to meet both the case or controversy requirements for all of the claims. *Petersen Manufacturing Co. Inc. v. Adjustable Clamp Co. Inc.*, 30 U.S.P.Q 2d 1193, 1200 (Ill. 1993).

ᛦ

Declaratory judgment plaintiff's actions in developing Perfluoron and in taking steps to obtain FDA approval sufficiently demonstrate plaintiff's intent to try to bring Perfluoron to market in some form. While plaintiff may not have the present ability to market Perfluoron, it has embarked on a protracted and costly process of obtaining regulatory approval. Plaintiff's conduct thus evinces the kind of "concrete steps" or "meaningful preparation" needed to establish an actual controversy under "all the circumstances." *Infinitech Inc. v. Vitrophage Inc.*, 30 U.S.P.Q.2d 1201, 1205 (Ill. 1994).

ᛒ

Jurisdiction over plaintiff's declaratory judgment action was based on (i) defendant's threat to bring patent infringement suits against generic drug manufacturers who attempt to market their products during the Delta period (creating a reasonable apprehension that plaintiff would face an infringement suit on amending its ANDA to include paragraph IV certification) and (ii) plaintiff's having spent much money in preparation for the potentially infringing activity of submitting ANDA's. *DuPont Merck Pharmaceutical Co. v. Bristol-Myers Squibb Co.*, 62 F.3d 1397, 35 U.S.P.Q.2d 1718, 1721, 1722 (Fed. Cir. 1995).

ᛒ

Defendant's expenditure of $1 million in preparing to market Captopril, including costs for performing in vivo and in vitro tests and other research necessary to obtain FDA approval of its ANDA, satisfies the investment requirement and qualifies defendant to operate under the "safe harbor" of URAA. *Bristol-Myers Squibb Co. v. Royce Laboratories Inc.*, 36 U.S.P.Q.2d 1637, 1640 n.7 (Fla. 1995), *rev'd* 69 F.3d 1397, 36 U.S.P.Q.2d 1641 (Fed. Cir. 1995).

ᛒ

State and federal claims are said to form part of the same case or controversy when such claims arise from "a common nucleus of operative facts" such that a plaintiff "would ordinarily be expected to try them all in a single judicial proceeding." *Qualcomm Inc. v. Motorola Inc.*, 989 F. Supp. 1048, 45 U.S.P.Q.2d 1472, 1474 (Cal. 1997).

Catalysis.[1] *See also* Catalyst.

The fact that the patents in suit involve catalytic behavior, which is inherently unpredictable, reinforces the normal presumption of validity. *Mobil Oil Corp. v. W.R. Grace & Co.*, 367 F. Supp. 207, 180 U.S.P.Q. 418, 452 (Conn. 1973).

ᛒ

Catalytic effects are a particularly unpredictable aspect of the art of chemistry. *In re Slocombe*, 510 F.2d 1398, 184 U.S.P.Q. 740, 744 (C.C.P.A. 1975).

ᛒ

Lack of obviousness to one having ordinary skill in the art is buttressed by the fact that the claimed invention is a catalytic process. The unpredictability of catalytic phenomena has long been recognized. A successfully catalyzed process depends not only on the particular catalyst that may be employed but also on the environment within which the catalysis is accomplished. The adequacy of any showing of equivalency must be scrutinized especially carefully where it is alleged to have been obvious to substitute one starting material for another in a catalytic process. *In re Mercier,* 515 F.2d 1161, 185 U.S.P.Q. 774 (C.C.P.A. 1975).

ᛒ

---

[1]*See In re Robins*, 429 F.2d 452, 166 U.S.P.Q. 552 (C.C.P.A. 1970).

The peculiar degree of unpredictability associated with the art of catalysis does not translate into a requirement that an enabling disclosure provide an exhaustive listing of all possible treating steps and agents that could be used in the recited process without affecting the stated objective of producing the desired catalyst. *Ex parte Vollheim, Troger, and Lippert,* 191 U.S.P.Q. 407 (PTO Bd. App. 1975).

Catalyst.

The mere fact that a known compound is a catalyst does not render "obvious" later discovered catalytic activity of a distinctly different compound notwithstanding close structural similarity. Catalytic action cannot be forecast by chemical composition, for such action is not understood and is not known except by actual test. *Corona Cord Tire Co. v. Dovan Chemical Corp.,* 276 U.S. 358, 1928 C.D. 253 (1928).

ω

The known similarity between two materials may be such that when one of them is found to be a suitable catalyst for certain purposes, it will suggest the probability that the other will also be suitable. The question whether substitution of one for the other is obvious must be determined on the basis of the circumstances of each case, especially the extent to which similarity and equivalence between the substances involved are recognized in the prior art. *In re Doumani and Huffman,* 281 F.2d 215, 126 U.S.P.Q. 408 (C.C.P.A. 1960).

ω

A properly constructed patent claiming a chemical catalyst system looks not only at the components of the system but also at the reaction or reactions catalyzed and at the reaction products. The basic question is whether the accused operation employs a catalyst system that is substantially equivalent to that disclosed in the patent. First, the components of each system; second, the particular chemical reactions catalyzed (that is, the particular monomer polymerized); and, third, the reaction product (the particular polymer) produced must be considered. No one similarity or difference is determinative. *Ziegler v. Phillips Petroleum Co.,* 483 F.2d 858, 177 U.S.P.Q. 481, 491 (5th Cir. 1973).

ω

Where intricate questions of chemistry are involved, which are peculiarly within the particular competence of the Patent Office, the presumption of validity should be weighed with great care. This is especially true where catalysts are involved because of their known unpredictability under modified changes in their environmental use. *Mobil Oil Corp. v. W. R. Grace Co.,* 367 F. Supp. 207, 180 U.S.P.Q. 418, 430 (Conn. 1973).

ω

In an unpredictable art, does 35 U.S.C. §112 require disclosure of a test with every species covered by a claim? To require such a complete disclosure would apparently necessitate a patent application with thousands of examples or a disclosure with thousands of catalysts along with information as to whether each exhibits catalytic behavior resulting in the production of the desired products. More importantly, such a requirement would force an inventor seeking adequate patent protection to carry out a prohibitive number of actual experiments. This would tend to discourage inventors from filing patent applications in an unpredictable area since the patent claims would have to be limited to those embodiments that are expressly disclosed. A potential infringer could readily avoid "literal" infringement of such claims by merely finding another analogous catalyst complex that could be used in forming the same products. *In re Angstadt and Griffin,* 537 F.2d 498, 190 U.S.P.Q. 214, 218 (C.C.P.A. 1976).

ᚥ

A chemical catalyst and the use of that catalyst are the same invention, and only one patent may be granted for a single invention. *Studiengesellschaft Kohle mbH v. Eastman Kodak Co.,* 450 F. Supp. 1211, 197 U.S.P.Q. 164, 175 (Tex. 1977).

Cause. *See also* Good Cause, Order to Show Cause, Principle, Source.

Patentability may be predicated on discovering the cause of a problem even though, once that cause is known, the solution is brought about by obvious means. Such causes may often be classed as laws of nature or their effects. *In re Bergy, Coats, and Malik,* 596 F.2d 952, 201 U.S.P.Q. 352, 365 (C.C.P.A. 1979).

ᚥ

Patentability may exist in the discovery of the cause of a defect in an existing machine or process and applying a remedy therefor even though, after the cause is understood, the remedy would be obvious. *In re Wiseman and Kovac,* 596 F.2d 1019, 201 U.S.P.Q. 658, 661 (C.C.P.A. 1979).

CCPA. *See also* Pendency.

A decision of the CCPA, reversing the Patent Office Board of Appeals in a patent case, does not constitute a holding that the application contains patentable subject matter or that it is "allowable" and does not direct the Patent Office to issue a patent. All the CCPA does is pass on the propriety of rejections brought before it for review. *In re Citron,* 326 F.2d 418, 140 U.S.P.Q. 220, 221 (C.C.P.A. 1964).

ᚥ

The United States Court of Customs and Patent Appeals (CCPA) had an inherent power to review any action of the Board that affected its appellate jurisdiction. Both 28 U.S.C. §1542 and 35 U.S.C. §141 limit the jurisdiction of the CCPA to appeals of "decisions" of the Board. The Board's authority to make such decisions is set forth in 35 U.S.C. §7. The CCPA, however, had the right to determine whether the Board properly refused to make such decisions in its statutory capacity. To hold otherwise would be to confer upon the Board the power to control the subject matter jurisdiction of the CCPA. *In re Haas,* 486 F.2d 1053, 179 U.S.P.Q. 623 (C.C.P.A. 1973).

ᚥ

When there is an inconsistency between the MPEP and a ruling of the CCPA, the PTO Board of Appeals will follow the ruling of its reviewing court (the CCPA) with which the manual is at variance. *Ex parte Hartmann,* 186 U.S.P.Q. 366, 367 (PTO Bd. App. 1974).

ᚥ

Because obviousness is a legal conclusion based on factual evidence, the proper issue before the court was whether the International Trade Commission erred, as a matter of law, in holding that patent claims were invalid under 35 U.S.C. §103. In deciding this issue, the court makes "an independent determination as to the legal conclusions and inferences which should be drawn from [the findings of fact]." *Stevenson v. International Trade Commission,* 612 F.2d 546, 204 U.S.P.Q. 276, 279 (C.C.P.A. 1979).

CD-ROM.

A party wishing to file a CD-ROM counterpart brief must seek consent of the other parties before submitting a CD-ROM brief to the CAFC. Consent of the other parties will be a substantial factor in considering whether to grant leave. On the other hand, prejudice to another party could be an important factor in denying leave. Additionally, a party must seek leave of the court to file a CD-ROM brief and must provide information both to the court and to the other parties about the computer equipment needed to view the CD-ROM brief. Finally, the filing party must submit a motion for leave at the same time or before it submits twelve copies of the CD-ROM brief. *Yukiyo Ltd. v. Watanabe,* 111 F.3d 883, 42 U.S.P.Q.2d 1474, 1476 (Fed. Cir. 1997).

ω

The CAFC encourages the filing of CD-ROM briefs, provided that the opposing party will not be prejudiced by such a filing. *In re Berg,* 43 U.S.P.Q.2d 1703, 1704 (Fed. Cir. 1997—*unpublished*).

Cease and Desist Letter.

In the context of an action for non-infringement in copyright or patent cases, the sending of a cease and desist letter to the alleged infringer is alone insufficient to establish the minimum contacts necessary for personal jurisdiction. *Modern Computer Corp. v. Ma,* 862 F.Supp. 938, 32 U.S.P.Q.2d 1586, 1590 (N.Y. 1994).

Cell Line. *See also* Deposit of Cell Line.

The appealed claims are directed to a new human cell line and the hybridomas resulting from its fusion with lymphoid cells. The new cell line was developed by muta-genesis and selection from a known cell line by procedures that fill 12 pages of specification. Because of the uncertainties of reproducibility that inhere in such processes, at least in the present state of biotechnology, this invention is of the class covered by the deposit requirement. The inventor filed an application for a patent prior to depositing his new cell line with the American Type Culture Collection (ATCC). 35 U.S.C. §112, first paragraph, does not require the transfer of a sample of the invention to an independent depository prior to the filing date of the patent application. The requirements of PTO access to a sample of the cell line during pendency, and public access after grant, were made by the procedures that were followed. The deposit with the ATCC, which was made after filing but prior to issuance of his patent, and that is referred to in his specification, meets the statutory requirements. *In re Lundak,* 773 F.2d 1216, 227 U.S.P.Q. 90 (Fed. Cir. 1985).

ω

The P388 and L1210 cell lines, though technically labeled tumor models, were originally derived from lymphocytic leukemias in mice. Therefore, these cell lines represent actual specific lymphocytic tumors; these models will produce this particular disease once implanted in mice. If applicants were required to wait until an animal actually developed this specific tumor before testing the effectiveness of a compound against the tumor *in vivo*, as would be implied from the Commissioner's argument, there would be no effective way to test compounds *in vivo* on a large scale. These tumor models represent a specific disease against which the claimed compounds are alleged to be effective. *In re Brana*, 51 F.3d 1560, 34 U.S.P.Q.2d 1436, 1440 (Fed. Cir. 1995).

Central Definition.

Phrases in claims referring back to the description and drawing, such as "substantially as described" or "as herein shown and described" were once customary in claims in the days of the central definition. *Ex parte Fressola*, 27 U.S.P.Q.2d 1608, 1610 (B.P.A.I. 1993).

Certainty.

The term "experimentation" implies that the success of the particular activity is uncertain. The basic policy of the Patent Act is to encourage disclosure of inventions and thereby to promote progress in the useful arts. To require disclosures in patent applications to transcend the level of knowledge of those skilled in the art would stifle the disclosure of inventions in fields we understand imperfectly, like catalytic chemistry. The certainty that the law requires in patents is not greater than is reasonable, having regard for their subject matter. *In re Angstadt and Griffin*, 537 F.2d 498, 190 U.S.P.Q. 214, 219 (C.C.P.A. 1976).

ω

Where there has been a failure to use reasonable efforts to commercialize, damages are often not susceptible of certain proof. A lesser degree of certainty is required in such cases. *Bailey v. Chattem, Inc.*, 684 F.2d 386, 215 U.S.P.Q. 671, 679 (6th Cir. 1982).

Certificate of Correction.[2]

A petition for a Certificate of Correction under Rule 322 (37 C.F.R. §1.322) to delete specific trademarks from an issued patent was filed by the owner of the trademarks, not the patentee. The petitioner asserted that section 608.01(v) of the MPEP places upon the Examiner the affirmative duty of ensuring the proper use of trademarks; that prior practice has been to regard the misuse of a trademark in a patent as a mistake on the part of the Patent Office; and that a literal reading of Rule 322 and of the corresponding section of the statute would indicate that petitioner is entitled to the requested relief. The petition was granted. *In re Johnson*, 146 U.S.P.Q. 547 (Commr. Patents 1965).

ω

A district court, in an infringement action, has jurisdiction under 35 U.S.C. §256 to review the propriety of the issuance by the Patent Office of a Certificate of Correction

---

[2] See *Carnegie Mellon University v. Schwartz*, 41 U.S.P.Q.2d 1623 (3d Cir. 1997).

removing a named applicant as a joint inventor. *Borden, Inc. v. Occidental Petroleum Corp.*, 381 F. Supp. 1178, 182 U.S.P.Q. 472, 493 (Tex. 1974).

ω

Omission of a reference to an earlier application on which priority is based is a mistake "of a minor character," which is correctable by a request for a Certificate of Correction under 37 C.F.R. §1.323. *In re Lambrech,* 202 U.S.P.Q. 620, 622 (Comm'r Patents & Trademarks 1976).

ω

The Solicitor's Office has the ultimate responsibility for the issuance or denial of requests for Certificates of Correction. A request that broadens claims is beyond that permitted under 35 U.S.C. §255 and 37 C.F.R. §1.323 (Rule 323), which statute and regulation have been uniformly limited to minor clerical errors that do not affect the scope of the claimed subject matter. Because improper requests for Certificates of Correction had been granted, the Certificate of Correction Branch was authorized to issue a Certificate of Correction under 37 C.F.R. §1.322(a) vacating all previous certificates. *In re Shirouchi and Urade,* 204 U.S.P.Q. 511, 512 (PTO Solicitor 1978).

ω

Where a proposed correction involves a change in claim scope, the reissue statute is controlling, not the provisions of law governing Certificates of Correction. *In re Arnott,* 19 U.S.P.Q.2d 1049, 1054 (Commr. Patents & Trademarks 1991).

ω

Congress did not intend that third parties have the right to judicial review of Certificates of Correctioin issued by the PTO. *Hallmark Cards Inc. v. Lehman*, 959 F.Supp. 539, 42 U.S.P.Q.2d 1134 (D.C. 1997).

Certification.

A patentee's motion for class certification on the issue of infringement was denied, although it was denied without prejudice with regard to certification under Fed. R. Civ. P. 23(b)(3). A class of defendants was certified pursuant to Fed. R. Civ. P. 23(b)(2) with regard to questions of validity and enforceability. *Webcraft Technologies, Inc. v. Alden Press, Inc.,* 228 U.S.P.Q. 182, 186 (Ill. 1985).

ω

A failure to enter a judgment at this time (allowing an intermediate appeal) would with certainty extend the plaintiff's patent coverage for months beyond its expiration. There is clearly a danger of hardship or injustice in delaying the entry of judgment pursuant to the Court's earlier orders. *Glaxo Inc. v. Boehringer Ingelheim Corp.*, 41 U.S.P.Q.2d 1795 (Conn. 1997).

ω

It is within the Court's discretion whether to certify an order, but "the rule of interlocutory appeals is to be applied 'sparingly and only in exceptional cases' in furtherance of the longstanding federal policy against piecemeal appeals." The party seeking certification bears the burden to show the presence of "exceptional circumstances where considerations of judicial economy and fairness demand interlocutory review of an order." *Mont-Bell Co. Ltd. v. Mountain Hardwear Inc.*, 44 U.S.P.Q.2d 1568, 1577 (Cal. 1997).

21 C.F.R. §314.107(c)(1).

The FDA's successful-defense requirement is inconsistent with the unambiguously expressed intent of Congress. The rule is gravely inconsistent with the text and structure of the statute. Nor can the FDA show that the successful-defense requirement is needed to avoid "a result demonstrably at odds with the intentions of [section 355(j)(5)(B)(iv)'s] drafters." *Mova Pharmaceutical Corp. v. Shalala*, 140 F.3d 1060, 46 U.S.P.Q.2d 1385, 1392 (D.C. Cir. 1998).

37 C.F.R. §1.14(b). *See* 35 U.S.C. §122.

37 C.F.R. §1.28(c)

Rule 28(c) [37 C.F.R. §1.28(c)] must be read in conjunction with the deadlines set forth in 37 C.F.R. §1.317 for correcting the payment of an insufficient issue fee. Pursuant to §1.317(c), a good-faith error in claiming small-entity status, and in paying a small-entity issue fee, must be corrected no later than one year and three months after the date of the notice of allowance, or within three months of the PTO's denial of a timely petition to accept late payment due to unavoidable delay. *DH Technology Inc. v. Synergystex International Imc.*, 40 U.S.P.Q.2d 1754, 1761 (Cal. 1996).

37 C.F.R. §1.47

Both parts of Rule 47 and the sections of the patent statute upon which they are based leave the determination of the sufficiency of a showing in a particular case up to the discretion of the Commissioner. The consideration of such showings has been delegated to the Office of the Solicitor. An action by the Office of the Solicitor in such matters is not reviewable by a Primary Examiner. *Fryer v. Tachikawa*, 179 U.S.P.Q. 381, 382 (PO Bd. Pat. Intf. 1972).

37 C.F.R. §1.47(b)

The fact that an application under Rule 47(b) is a reissue application does not justify grant of a reissue patent to the assignee of the original patent. *In re Schuyler*, 119 U.S.P.Q. 97, 98 (Comm'r 1957).

ω

The Patent Office will accept a proposed application under 35 U.S.C. §118 and Rule 47(b) signed by a registered patent attorney when the application is owned by an assignee of the inventor and the assignee is a juristic entity, such as a corporation or a government agency. *In re Striker*, 182 U.S.P.Q. 507, 508 (PO Solicitor 1973).

37 C.F.R. §1.52

The practice of accepting applications (in which the specification is a photocopy) for filing should not be followed except upon a showing which would satisfy the requirement of Rule 183 (37 C.F.R. §1.183) for a waiver of the requirement of Rule 52 that the application papers be "legibly written or printed in permanent ink". *In re Application Papers Filed Mar. 27, 1963*, 138 U.S.P.Q. 393 (Comm'r 1963).

37 C.F.R. §1.53(e)

Section 26, Title 35 U.S.C., permits the patent commissioner to accept provisionally a defectively-executed document. Under the authority of the latter section, the Patent Office has promulgated Rule 53(a) [now Rule 53(e)], which reflects the attitude that minor technical defects in a patent application should not affect the effective filing date. The provisional acceptance of a "Declaration and Power of Attorney" in which the applicant fails to state his citizenship is not beyond the scope of discretion conferred on the Patent Office under 35 U.S.C. §26. *Autovox, S.p.A. v. Lenco Italiana, S.p.A.*, 210 U.S.P.Q. 277, 278 (Ill. 1980).

37 C.F.R. §1.55

The burden on an interference opponent in challenging compliance with Rule 55 is not sustained by showing that there are differences between the provisional application relied upon and the provisional as printed in the British patent. *Farthing v. Boardman*, 139 U.S.P.Q. 450, 453 (PO Bd. Pat. Intf. 1962).

37 C.F.R. §1.56

If previously undisclosed information as to commercial use is found "material to the examination" under 37 C.F.R. §1.56(a), action must be taken under 37 C.F.R. §1.56(d) "if it is established by clear and convincing evidence that any fraud was practiced or attempted or that there was any violation of the duty of disclosure through bad faith or gross negligence." *In re Goldman*, 205 U.S.P.Q. 1086, 1088 (Comm'r 1980).

ω

The invocation of 37 C.F.R. §1.56(d) with respect to a reissue application is clearly contemplated and surely permitted by PTO regulations. *Digital Equipment Corporation v. Parker v. Computer Operations, Inc.*, 487 F.Supp. 1104, 206 U.S.P.Q. 428, 434 (Mass. 1980).

37 C.F.R. §1.66. *See* Apostille.

37 C.F.R. §1.71(b)

There is no statutory antecedent basis for the "specific embodiment" requirement of Rule 71(b) except insofar as it implements the first paragraph of 35 U.S.C. §112. The terms "specific embodiment" of Rule 71(b) and the "best mode contemplated" of 35 U.S.C. §112 are not equated. If by "specific embodiment" is meant a working example, then the same is not required where sufficient working procedure has been set forth. *In re Long*, 368 F.2d 892, 151 U.S.P.Q. 640, 642 (C.C.P.A. 1966).

ᗡ

Rule 71(b) does not require, in examples, some data on which to base an evaluation of the invention's usefulness. All that is required of the specification is that it enables a person skilled in the art to which it pertains to practice the invention. *In re Bartholome, Lehrer, and Schierwater*, 386 F.2d 1019, 156 U.S.P.Q. 20, 22 (C.C.P.A. 1967).

ᗡ

Noncompliance with a requirement of Rule 71(b) which goes only to a matter of form in the written description is subject to review by petition to the Commissioner rather than rejection of the claims and enforcement of the law through appeals to the Board and the Court. *In re Newton*, 414 F.2d 1400, 163 U.S.P.Q. 34, 40 (C.C.P.A. 1969).

ᗡ

A specification need be no more specific under Rule 71(b) than is required by the enablement provision of 35 U.S.C. §112. The test is whether there is sufficient working procedure for one skilled in the art to practice the claimed invention without undue experimentation. *In re Stephens, Benvau, and Benvau*, 529 F.2d 1343, 188 U.S.P.Q. 659, 661 (C.C.P.A. 1976).

37 C.F.R. §1.75(d). *See also* Ipsis Verbis.

Even though a term is used in an original claim, if it has no antecedent basis in the specification, the requirements of Rule 75(d) are missing. *Ex parte Bonnefoy*, 156 U.S.P.Q. 423, 426 (PO Bd. App. 1967).

37 C.F.R. §1.78(c). *See* Conflicting Claims.

37 C.F.R. §1.81.

The requirement for a drawing, when the nature of the case admits thereof, is statutory. Rule 81, based thereon, states that the drawing must be filed with the application. Where claims are drawn to an article or device, the general rule is that the case admits of drawings, and illustration is necessary under the statute to complete the application. When the claimed invention resides in properties or characteristics incapable of illustration, or in the composition used in making a product, the practice contemplates acceptance of the application without a drawing. *In re Hacklander*, 122 U.S.P.Q. 278, 279 (Comm'r 1956).

37 C.F.R. §1.84.

The Rules of Practice of the Patent Office have always contained rigid standards for patent drawings, and strict adherence to the requirements of the rules has been enforced. Furthermore, the Office has always frowned upon the filing of unnecessary sheets of drawings. *In re Taggart*, 115 U.S.P.Q. 413, 414 (Comm'r 1957).

ᗡ

When a drawing is described in an application, the application is not complete unless the described drawing, prepared in accordance with the standards and requirements of Rule 84, accompanies the papers (Rule 81). As mounted photographs are not the drawings required by the rules, the originally filed papers are not considered a proper complete application. *In re Incomplete Application filed November 28, 1958*, 123 U.S.P.Q. 70 (Comm'r 1959).

37 C.F.R. §1.106.

It is incumbent upon the Patent Office in the first instance to set forth clearly why it regards a claim to be anticipated, obvious or otherwise defective. *In re Mullin, Wetherby, and Chevalier*, 481 F.2d 1333, 179 U.S.P.Q. 97, 100 (C.C.P.A. 1973).

37 C.F.R. §1.107(b). *See also* Affidavit.

A rejection on the ground of anticipation by each of two abstracts (published more than one year prior to the filing date) was affirmed because appellants' evidence was insufficient to rebut the prima facie case that the two abstracts were enabling and therefore prior art, because appellants conceded that all limitations in the claims were inherent in the two abstracts, and because the anticipation findings were not otherwise tainted by legal error. In response to appellants' challenge of each of the abstracts as nonenabling, the Examiner explained his position without establishing the state of the art or providing citation of any substantiating documentation. The procedures established by 37 C.F.R. §1.107(b) (1993) expressly entitle an applicant, on mere request, to an Examiner affidavit that provides such citation. Appellants' failure to avail themselves of this procedure waived any right thereto under well established rules of law. *In re Sun*, 31 U.S.P.Q.2d 1451, 1454, 1455 (Fed. Cir. 1993—*unpublished*).

37 C.F.R. §1.108.

Section 122 (Title 35 U.S.C.) and 37 C.F.R. §§1.14(b) and 1.108 are not unconstitutional. *Sears v. Gottschalk*, 502 F.2d 122, 183 U.S.P.Q. 134, 139 (4th Cir. 1974).

37 C.F.R. §1.131. *See also* Antedating a Reference.

When a reference is not a statutory bar, Rule 131 provides a procedure by which an applicant is permitted to show that his date of invention was earlier than the date of the reference. All an applicant has to show is priority with respect to so much of the claimed invention as the reference happens to show. When he has done that, he has disposed of the reference. The rule must be construed in accord with the rights given to inventors by statute, and this excludes a construction permitting the further use of a reference as a ground of rejection after all pertinent subject matter in it has been antedated to the satisfaction of the Patent Office. *In re Stempel*, 241 F.2d 755, 113 U.S.P.Q. 77, 81 (C.C.P.A. 1957).

ᛒ

The claims on appeal were first supported by and made in an application filed nearly two years after publication of the British priority specification, fully disclosing the invention as applied to a species within the generic claims. The disclosure of a species in a reference is sufficient to prevent a later applicant from obtaining generic claims, unless the reference can be overcome. The British specification, published more than a year prior to filing the generic disclosure, is clearly a statutory bar to the granting of the generic claims. *In re Ruscetta and Jenny,* 255 F.2d 687, 118 U.S.P.Q. 101, 104 (C.C.P.A. 1958).

ᛠ

Where it can be concluded that facts, offered in a Rule 131 affidavit in support of a general allegation of conception and reduction to practice of the invention, would persuade one of ordinary skill in the art to a reasonable certainty that the applicant possessed so much of the invention as to encompass the reference disclosure, then that showing should be accepted as establishing *prima facie* a case of inventorship prior to the reference, sufficient for the purpose of overcoming the reference in an ex parte case. Upon satisfying that test, species of the reference falling within the claim may be antedated indirectly. *In re Clarke*, 356 F.2d 987, 148 U.S.P.Q. 665, 670 (C.C.P.A. 1966).

ᛠ

An effective affidavit under Rule 131 can establish a reduction to practice of a claimed invention based on an embodiment of such invention other than one which is described in the subject application. Once a reference is antedated by an affidavit under Rule 131, the reference is also antedated with regard to claims for obvious variations therefrom. *In re Dardick*, 496 F.2d 1234, 181 U.S.P.Q. 834, 838, 839 (C.C.P.A. 1974); *see also In re Spiller*, 500 F.2d 1170, 182 U.S.P.Q. 614 (C.C.P.A. 1974).

ᛠ

A reduction to practice of an adjacent homologue of a compound disclosed in a reference was sufficient to overcome the reference. *In re Schaub*, Bernady, and Weiss, 537 F.2d 509, 190 U.S.P.Q. 324, 326 (C.C.P.A. 1976).

ᛠ

The purpose of filing a 131 affidavit is not to demonstrate prior invention per se, but merely to antedate the effective date of a reference. Although the test for sufficiency of an affidavit under Rule 131(b) parallels that for determining priority of invention in an interference under 35 U.S.C. §102(g), it does not follow that Rule 131 practice is controlled by interference law. Thus, "the 'conception' and 'reduction to practice' which must be established under the rule need not be the same as what is required in the 'interference' sense of those terms." *In re Eickmeyer*, 602 F.2d 974, 202 U.S.P.Q. 655, 660 (C.C.P.A. 1979).

ᛠ

Section 119 (35 U.S.C.) is a patent-saving provision for the benefit of applicants, and an applicant is entitled to rely on it as a constructive reduction to practice to overcome the date of a reference under Rule 131. As entitlement to a foreign filing date can completely overcome a reference, it can provide the constructive reduction to practice element of proof required by Rule 131. It is a statutory priority right which cannot be interfered with by a construction placed on a PTO rule. *In re Mulder and Wulms*, 716 F.2d 1542, 219 U.S.P.Q. 189, 193 (Fed. Cir. 1983).

ᛠ

All the evidence must be considered in its entirety, including Rule 131 declarations and accompanying exhibits, records, and "notes." An accompanying exhibit need not support all of the claimed limitations but, rather, a missing feature may be supplied by the declaration itself. It is entirely appropriate to rely on a showing of facts set forth in a Rule 131 declaration to establish conception of the invention prior to the effective date of a reference. Failure to give probative weight to a Rule 131 declaration constitutes reversable error. *Ex parte Ovshinsky,* 10 U.S.P.Q.2d 1075 (B.P.A.I. 1989).

ᗡ

A losing party to an interference, on showing that the invention now claimed is not "substantially the same" as that of the lost count, may employ the procedures of Rule 131 in order to antedate the filing date of the interfering application. The lost count of the interference is not prior art against a different invention, for prior art in the sense of 35 U.S.C. §102(g) cannot be the basis of a 35 U.S.C. §102(a) rejection, the invention not being publicly known or used. The law developed in our Rule 131 cases has little bearing on the law relating to interference practice. *In re Zletz,* 893 F.2d 319, 13 U.S.P.Q.2d 1320, 1323 (Fed. Cir. 1989).

ᗡ

Where an interference has been declared, a preliminary statement alleging invention prior to the date of a reference can be accepted as a substitute for an affidavit under Rule 131, making out a prima facie case of prior invention justifying the setting of a testimony period to take proofs. The test for sufficiency of a Rule 131 affidavit is parallel to (albeit not identical to) that for determining priority under 35 U.S.C. §102(g). *Goutzoulis v. Athale,* 15 U.S.P.Q.2d 1461, 1464 (Commr. Patents & Trademarks 1990).

ᗡ

In concluding that an obviousness analysis was proper under Rule 131, the court ruled that "[c]ertainly appellants should not be required to submit facts under Rule 131 showing that they reduced to practice that which is obvious...for the purpose of antedating a reference." *Tronzo v. Biomet Inc.,* 950 F.Supp. 1142, 41 U.S.P.Q.2d 1403 (Fla. 1996)

37 C.F.R. §1.132. *See also* Comparative Test Data.

While appellants certainly did not isolate every possible variable and demonstrate that substitution of their surfactants invariably led to a superior result, their showing was adequate for an ex parte case absent any reason to expect a different result with some other set of variables. Although objective comparisons are generally to be preferred to subjective comparisons, the latter cannot be completely ignored. Subjective comparisons are not, for that reason alone, entitled to little weight where the Patent Office has not suggested a practicable objective standard for measuring the same variable. *In re Saunders and Gemeinhardt,* 444 F.2d 599, 170 U.S.P.Q. 213, 218, 219 (C.C.P.A. 1971).

ᗡ

There is no requirement that superiority over prior art be disclosed in the application; it is enough if the basic property or utility (in which the advantage resides) is disclosed. Affidavit evidence may not be disregarded simply because of the broad scope of the claims in the original application. *In re Slocombe*, 510 F.2d 1398, 184 U.S.P.Q. 740, 743, 744 (C.C.P.A. 1975).

ဃ

When a reference publication is coauthored by an applicant and others, submission of "disclaiming affidavits or declarations by the other authorsto support appellant's position that he is, in fact, the sole inventor of the subject matter described in the article and claimed herein" would have ended the inquiry, but are not required by the statute or by Rule 132. What is required is a reasonable showing supporting the basis for the applicant's position. *In re Katz*, 687 F.2d 450, 215 U.S.P.Q. 14, 18 (C.C.P.A. 1982).

ဃ

An affiant must review references as they are combined (not individually) to establish the *prima facie* case of obviousness. The references need not be capable of being physically combined. *Ex parte GPAC Inc.*, 29 U.S.P.Q.2d 1401, 1406 (B.P.A.I. 1993).

37 C.F.R. §1.141.

Rejection of all species claims under Rule 141 to force an election of a preferred species is improper. *Ex parte Crigler*, 125 U.S.P.Q. 448, 454 (PO Bd. App. 1959).

37 C.F.R. §1.146. *See also* Election of Species.

Under Rule 146 an Examiner must require an election of species if no generic claim is allowable and the claimed species are considered patentably distinct. *Ex parte Crigler*, 125 U.S.P.Q. 448, 454 (PO Bd. App. 1959).

37 C.F.R. §1.183.

When conflicting decisions are rendered on different applications having claims to substantially the same invention, the possibility of discriminatory rulings by the Board of Appeals is a relevant consideration for the Commissioner to weigh in determining whether relief should be granted under Rule 183. He must then balance that determination against the Patent Office's interest in the finality of the Board of Appeals decisions to determine whether justice requires some relief. *Mobil Oil Corporation v. Dann*, 421 F.Supp. 995, 197 U.S.P.Q. 59, 61 (D.C. 1976).

37 C.F.R. §1.191(c).

37 C.F.R. §1.191(c) provides that jurisdiction over an application vests in the BPAI when the application is transmitted to the BPAI. However, this provision does not create jurisdiction, it merely specifies timing. *Ex parte Lemoine*, 46 U.S.P.Q.2d 1432, 1434 (B.P.A.I. 1995—*unpublished*).

37 C.F.R. §1.192(c)(5).

Section 1.192(c)(5) of 37 C.F.R. requires appellant to perform two affirmative acts in his brief in order to have the separate patentability of a plurality of claims subject to the same rejection considered. The appellant must: (1) state that the claims do not stand or fall together and (2) present arguments why the claims subject to the same rejection are separately patentable. Where the appellant does neither, it is appropriate for the Examiner and the Board to rely upon the presumption created by the words of the rule and to treat all claims as standing or falling together. Where, however, the appellant (1) omits the statement required by 37 C.F.R. §1.192(c)(5), yet presents arguments in the argument section of his brief, or (2) includes the statement required by 37 C.F.R. §1.192(c)(5) to the effect that one or more claims do not stand or fall with the rejection of the other claims, yet does not offer arguments in support in the argument section of the brief, it is imperative that the inconsistency apparent on the face of the brief be resolved. A brief evidencing either form of inconsistency is not in compliance with 37 C.F.R. §1.192. When appellant presents a brief having either form of inconsistency, the Examiner invokes the presumption of 37 C.F.R. §1.192(c)(5), and when appellant allows the Examiner's invocation of the presumption to go unchallenged by petition under 37 C.F.R. §1.181, the BPAI will simply decide the appeal and will decline to consider the patentability of the claims separately in reaching its decision. *Ex parte Schier,* 21 U.S.P.Q.2d 1016, 1018, 1019 (B.P.A.I. 1991).

ϖ

When a brief on appeal to the BPAI omits the statement required by 37 C.F.R. §1.192(c)(5), yet presents arguments in the argument section, it is not in compliance with 37 C.F.R. §1.192(c). Appellant will be notified of the reasons for noncompliance and provided with a period of one month within which to file an amended brief. If appellant does not file an amended brief within the one-month period, or files an amended brief that does not overcome all the reasons for noncompliance stated in the notification, the appeal will be dismissed. In any instance where an Examiner and appellant engage in an interchange over such compliance, the BPAI will treat the matter as one within the jurisdiction of the Examiner, requiring an appellant dissatisfied with the Examiner's holding to seek relief by way of petition under 37 C.F.R. §1.181, rather than by way of appeal under 37 C.F.R. §1.191. *Ex parte Ohsumi,* 21 U.S.P.Q.2d 1020, 1023 (B.P.A.I. 1991).

37 C.F.R. §1.193(a).

When an Examiner's answer states a new ground of rejection, appellant may file a reply thereto that includes any amendment or material appropriate to the new ground, including the addition of claims without canceling a corresponding number of claims. (See MPEP §1208.03.) *Ex parte Abseck and Rehheld,* 133 U.S.P.Q. 411, 412 (PO Supervisory Examiner 1960).

37 C.F.R. §1.196(b).

The authority of the B.P.A.I. is limited by 35 U.S.C. §7(b) to "review adverse decisions of Examiners upon applications for patents. . . ." No authority is granted to that body to review favorable decisions. To the extent that Rule 196(b) is inconsistent with the statute, it must fall. *Watson, Commissioner of Patents v. Bruns,* 239 F.2d 948, 111 U.S.P.Q. 325 (D.C. Cir. 1956).

ϖ

While the general rule has been that the reopening of prosecution before the Examiner provided by Rule 196(b) extends only to the new ground of rejection, there are many cases in which the "amendment or showing of facts not previously of record" which an applicant is entitled to present will also affect and require reconsideration of an affirmed ground of rejection. Where an affidavit had been presented to and was refused consideration by the Board as having been belatedly filed, such affidavit warranted consideration by the Examiner with regard to both the new ground of rejection and the affirmed ground of rejection. *Ex parte Depoorter*, 163 U.S.P.Q. 510, 512 (PO Director 1965).

ᴡ

The proper forum in which to settle the question of the legality of the Board's constitution is the district court (by mandamus) with appeal to the court of appeals. *In re Wichert*, 370 F.2d 927, 152 U.S.P.Q. 247 (C.C.P.A. 1967).

ᴡ

Effective August 20, 1989, 37 C.F.R. §1.196(b) was amended to provide that a new ground of rejection pursuant to the rule is not considered final for the purpose of judicial review under 35 U.S.C. §141 or §145. *Ex parte Kranz*, 19 U.S.P.Q.2d 1216, 1219 (B.P.A.I. 1990).

37 C.F.R. §1.291.

Proceedings on reissue applications are open to the public. 37 C.F.R. §1.11(b). Hence, counsel for defendants may attend the hearing before the BPAI and listen to applicant's argument, even though he cannot otherwise participate in the hearing. Although a court ordered that "plaintiff allow defendants to participate in all phases of the reissue proceedings before the Patent Office," the order is not directed to the PTO. Indeed, the doctrine of separation of powers precludes applying the order against the PTO. Rule 291 (37 C.F.R. §1.291) has the force and effect of law and does not permit defendants in an infringement litigation proceeding to participate in plaintiff's oral argument (in the prosecution of his reissue application) before the BPAI. *In re Blaese*, 19 U.S.P.Q.2d 1232, 1235 (Comm'r Patents & Trademarks 1991).

37 C.F.R. §1.292.

Rule 292 does not expressly preclude a public use proceeding involving a reissue application. *Goodyear v. Brush*, 104 U.S.P.Q. 346, 347 (Comm'r 1954).

37 C.F.R. §1.312.

An applicant, who succeeds in having the rejection of a generic claim reversed on appeal, can ask for entry of species claims under Rule 312. *Ex parte Ulfstedt and Bengtsson*, 109 U.S.P.Q. 458, 459 (PO Supervisory Ex'r 1956).

37 C.F.R. §1.313.

Abandonment of an allowed application by an assignee after the application is allowed, the final fee is paid, and a number has been assigned to the patent is contrary to 37

C.F.R §1.313 in the absence of a showing of an extraordinary situation justifying waiver of that rule under the provisions of 37 C.F.R. §1.183. *Schmidt v. Reynolds,* 1964 C.D. 1, 140 U.S.P.Q. 118 (D.C. 1963).

37 C.F.R. §1.322.

A petition for a Certificate of Correction under Rule 322 to delete specific trademarks from an issued patent was filed by the owner of the trademarks, not the patentee. The petitioner asserted that section 608.01(v) of the MPEP places upon the Examiner the affirmative duty of ensuring the proper use of trademarks; that prior practice has been to regard the misuse of a trademark in a patent as a mistake on the part of the Patent Office; and that a literal reading of Rule 322 and of the corresponding section of the statute would indicate that petitioner is entitled to the requested relief. The petition was granted. *In re Johnson,* 146 U.S.P.Q. 547 (Comm'r Patents 1965).

37 C.F.R. §1.323.

The prior granting of a patentee's Request for a Certificate of Correction was vacated "on motion of the Office" under the authority of 37 C.F.R. §1.322(a) because the proposed corrections were beyond those permitted under 35 U.S.C. §255 and 37 C.F.R. §1.323, which statute and regulation have been uniformly limited to minor clerical errors which do not affect the scope of the claimed subject matter. *In re Shirouchi and Urade,* 204 U.S.P.Q. 511, 512 (PTO Solicitor 1978).

37 C.F.R. §1.530(a).

In accordance with 37 C.F.R. §1.530(a), a patentee is barred from communication with the PTO during the three-month statutory period during which the PTO is required to decide whether any substantial new question of patentability is raised by a reexamination request. The PTO must rely solely on the representations of the person who requested reexamination, without opportunity for any explanation or correction by the patentee. The reexamination statute does not prohibit such participation. The provision of 37 C.F.R. §1.530(a) that bars threshold participation by the patent holder is within tolerable limits of the authority delegated to the PTO by Congress in enacting the reexamination statute, and does not violate the due process clause. *Patlex Corp. v. Mossinghoff,* 771 F.2d 480, 226 U.S.P.Q. 985 (Fed. Cir. 1985).

37 C.F.R. §1.607(a).

Pursuant to 37 C.F.R. §1.607(a) an applicant may request an interference by presenting a proposed count and at least one claim corresponding to the proposed count, and, where the claim does not correspond exactly to the proposed count, by explaining why such claim corresponds to the proposed count. *Brooks v. Street,* 16 U.S.P.Q.2d 1374 (B.P.A.I. 1990).

37 C.F.R. §1.608(b).

The purpose of 37 C.F.R. §1.608(b) is to minimize the expense of an interference to a patentee. *Holmwood v. Cherpeck,* 2 U.S.P.Q.2d 1942, 1944 (B.P.A.I. 1986).

The determination whether a party seeking to initiate an interference has shown "good cause" for his failure to present the additional evidence at the time of his initial submission is a matter within the discretion of the Board. *Huston v. Ladner*, 973 F.2d 1564, 23 U.S.P.Q.2d 1910, 1912 (Fed. Cir. 1992).

37 C.F.R. §1.633. *See also* Motion.

After an Examiner-in-Chief (EIC) has ruled on a preliminary motion brought under 37 C.F.R. §1.633 (1989), further consideration of the matter raised in the motion may be pursued in different ways, depending on the procedural circumstances. If a show-cause order has issued, an interference party may request a final hearing that may address all issues specified in 37 C.F.R. §1.655(b) that were previously decided by the EIC. Such issues include §1.633 preliminary motions, whether denied or granted. A party can also request reconsideration of any §1.633 motion that did not result in a show-cause order. However, such a request must be made within 14 days from the date of the decision. *Chester v. Miller,* 906 F.2d 1574, 15 U.S.P.Q.2d 1333, 1338 (Fed. Cir. 1990).

37 C.F.R. §1.633(a). *See also* Motion.

The PTO had good reason to promulgate a new rule in light of the new practice in which patentability of claims can be considered during the motion period of an interference. *Rowe v. Dror*, 112 F.3d 473, 42 U.S.P.Q.2d 1550, 1554 n.2 (Fed. Cir. 1997).

37 C.F.R. §1.640(b)(1)(1992). *See* Supplemental Preliminary Statement.

37 C.F.R. §1.644(a)(2).

Parties in interference are advised to file petitions under 37 C.F.R. §1.644(a)(2) within 15 days after entry of the Board's final decision and also to include, as part of the petition or in a separate paper, a request for an extension of time to seek judicial review. *Goutzoulis v. Athale*, 15 U.S.P.Q.2d 1461, 1464 (Comm'r Patents & Trademarks 1990).

37 C.F.R. §1.662(c).

Rule 1.662(c) as promulgated by the Commissioner under 35 U.S.C. §6(a) is valid. *Guinn v. Kopf*, 40 U.S.P.Q.2d 1157, 1160 (Fed. Cir. 1996).

37 C.F.R. §1.671(e).

The purpose of 37 C.F.R. §1.671(e)—i.e., to provide notice to an opponent when an affidavit (or declaration) is relied on so that the opponent will have an opportunity to cross-examine the affiant, if desired, or to present rebuttal evidence—would be frustrated if a party were permitted to rely on a declaration without introducing the declaration into evidence in the manner provided for by the rule. *Grose v. Plank,* 15 U.S.P.Q.2d 1338, 1341 (B.P.A.I. 1990).

Challenge. *See also* **Assertion, Credibility, Incorporate by Reference, Rebuttal Evidence, Statement in the Specification.**

If the appellants wished to object to the Board's statement and to question the correctness of the facts contained therein, they should have requested the Board to cite its authority for the statement. If the cited authority was based upon facts within the personal knowledge of the Board, appellants should have proceeded under Rules 66 and 76 of the Patent Office {see 37 C.F.R. §1.107(B)(1994)} and called for an affidavit of the Board. The appellants would then have been in a position to contradict or explain the Board's statement. In the absence of such request, the appellants may not be heard to challenge a statement made in the Board's opinion. The statement of the Board must therefore be accepted as correct. *In re Selmi and Altenburger,* 156 F.2d 96, 70 U.S.P.Q. 197 (C.C.P.A. 1946).

ᛒ

A copending reference patent issued to a different inventor on an application filed on the same date and refers to the subject application. The Patent Office tribunals stated that the subject application is presumed to be owned by the assignee of the copending reference patent. Since that statement was not controverted, it was accepted as correct. *In re Keim and Thompson,* 229 F.2d 466, 108 U.S.P.Q. 330, 331 (C.C.P.A. 1956).

ᛒ

As there was nothing in the record to controvert a statement in appellant's affidavit, the statement was accepted as accurate. *In re Nathan, Hogg, and Schneider*, 328 F.2d 1005, 140 U.S.P.Q. 601, 604 (C.C.P.A. 1964).

ᛒ

The appellant with the assistance of his assignee prepared and inserted in the application two series of photomicrographs together with extensive descriptions of them for the purpose of showing how the invention differs from the prior filaments in an extensively developed art. The court took the position that this would not have been done unless the photomicrographs in fact showed persons of ordinary skill in the art what the appellant asserted they show and was unwilling to give credence to a contrary opinion expressed by the Board as the basis of the rejection that it originated sua sponte. *In re Ehringer,* 347 F.2d 612, 146 U.S.P.Q. 31, 35 (C.C.P.A. 1965).

ᛒ

An unsupported, but unchallenged, statement by an Examiner may be accepted as factual. *In re Eskild and Houghton,* 387 F.2d 987, 156 U.S.P.Q. 208, 209 (C.C.P.A. 1968).

ᛒ

Despite appellants' specific request for evidence of the factual basis for the Board's decision, the Board has provided no such evidence. *In re Kamal and Rogier,* 398 F.2d 867, 158 U.S.P.Q. 320, 323 (C.C.P.A. 1968).

ᛒ

An unchallenged conclusion by the Board of what would have been *prima facie* obvious is accepted as true in the absence of evidence of unexpected results or other evidence of unobviousness. *In re Cother,* 437 F.2d 1399, 168 U.S.P.Q. 773, 777 (C.C.P.A. 1971).

ᗡ

Ordinarily, citation by the Board of a new reference and reliance thereon to support a rejection will be considered as tantamount to assertion of a new ground of rejection. This will not be the case, however, where such a reference is a standard work, cited only to support a fact judicially noticed and where the fact so noticed plays a minor role, serving only "to 'fill in the gaps' which might exist in the evidentiary showing made by the Examiner to support a particular ground for rejection." Under such circumstances an applicant must be given the opportunity to challenge either the correctness of the fact asserted or the notoriety or repute of the reference cited in support of the assertion. A challenge to the Board's judicial notice must contain adequate information or argument so that on its face it creates a reasonable doubt regarding the circumstances justifying the judicial notice. *In re Boon,* 439 F.2d 724, 169 U.S.P.Q. 231, 234 (C.C.P.A. 1971).

ᗡ

When an Examiner sets forth reasonable grounds in support of his conclusion that an applicant's claims may read on inoperative subject matter [other than subject matter inoperative only in the sense of *In re Skrivan,* 427 F.2d 801, 166 U.S.P.Q. 85, 88 (C.C.P.A. 1970)], it becomes incumbent upon the applicant either to reasonably limit his claims to the approximate area where operativeness has not been challenged or to rebut the Examiner's challenge either by the submission of representative evidence or by persuasive arguments based on known laws of physics and chemistry. *In re Cook and Merigold,* 439 F.2d 730, 169 U.S.P.Q. 298, 302 (C.C.P.A. 1971).

ᗡ

A finding of a new fact, supporting an alternative ground for sustaining an Examiner's rejection, and based on apparently nothing more than a bare allegation of scientific fact, does everything but cry out for an opportunity to respond. Appellant challenged the Board's assertion with an allegation of his own to the contrary and supported his assertion with an affidavit opinion of an acknowledged expert in the art. Appellant's response was more than mere "argument"; it was a direct challenge to a finding of fact made for the first time by the Board and included with it some evidence in the nature of rebuttal. It was thus entitled to more serious consideration. *In re Moore,* 444 F.2d 572, 170 U.S.P.Q. 260, 263 (C.C.P.A. 1971).

ᗡ

Under challenge the absence of support for an Examiner's statement may be critical. *In re Mochel,* 470 F.2d 638, 176 U.S.P.Q. 194, 196 (C.C.P.A. 1972).

ᗡ

If an applicant fails to challenge an Examiner's conclusion regarding enablement or fails to do so in a timely manner, the rejection stands. *In re Eynde, Pollet, and de Cat,* 480 F.2d 1364, 178 U.S.P.Q. 470, 474 (C.C.P.A. 1973).

ᗡ

Because the Examiner advanced a reasonable basis for questioning the adequacy of the disclosure, it was incumbent on appellant to rebut that challenge. More specifically, the applicant had the burden of supplying adequate information on which the Examiner could base a finding of whether the challenge was correct. Ordinarily that requires factual support as to what would be required or what was actually done in carrying out the invention, material particularly within the power of the applicant to provide. *In re Doyle,* 482 F.2d 1385, 179 U.S.P.Q. 227, 232 (C.C.P.A. 1973).

ᛟ

The PTO must have adequate support for its challenge to the credibility of the applicant's statements as to utility. Only then does the burden shift to the appellant to provide rebuttal evidence. *In re Bundy,* 642 F.2d 430, 209 U.S.P.Q. 48, 51 (C.C.P.A. 1981).

ᛟ

Prevailing practice represents a reasonable attempt by the PTO to accommodate potential conflicts between trial schedules and patent reexamination proceedings for the agency. Challenge provisions of reexamination procedures were found to be constitutional. *Patlex Corp. v. Mossinghoff,* 585 F. Supp. 713, 220 U.S.P.Q. 342 (Pa. 1983).

ᛟ

In view of the PTO's failure to challenge the sufficiency of the appellants' rebuttal evidence prior to appeal (when the appellants could no longer offer evidence), the Board's decision was vacated and the case remanded to afford the appellants the opportunity to submit objective evidence of unexpected results. *In re De Blauwe,* 736 F.2d 699, 222 U.S.P.Q. 191 (Fed. Cir. 1984).

ᛟ

Amelioration of the symptoms or even cure of cancer is no longer considered to be "incredible." Nonetheless, decisional law would seem to indicate that the utility in question is sufficiently unusual to justify an Examiner's requiring substantiating evidence. Substantiating evidence may be in the form of animal tests that constitute recognized screening procedures with clear relevance to utility in humans. The specification of the appellant's parent application sets forth several animal tests on numerous types of specific cancers as well as in vitro studies, both of which are asserted to be predictive with regard to utility in humans. The Examiner has not challenged the evidence presented in a single, relevant, material respect. There is only the blanket statement of lack of "patentable utility" per se. In fact, the only specific comments the Examiner has directed toward the appellant's evidence are with regard to the breadth of the types of tumor against which the claimed compounds have been shown to be active. The appealed claims are drawn to compounds and not to a method of treatment. Generally speaking, utility in treating a single disease is an adequate basis for the patentability of a pharmaceutical compound under 35 U.S.C. §101. *Ex parte Krepelka,* 231 U.S.P.Q. 746 (B.P.A.I. 1986).

ᛟ

Claims were rejected because they encompassed the treatment of humans and the only tests disclosed in the specification were in vitro studies and animal tests. The Examiner did not raise any specific challenge to the tests reported, with respect to their acceptance in the art as being predictive of efficacy in treating humans or in any other respect; she merely took the position that such tests are inherently incapable of supporting claims that could read on treatment of humans. The claims are limited to the treatment of a single type of cancer or, more precisely, a single closely related group of cancers, and the evidence relates to that type of cancer. The Examiner has not replied to appellant's argument based on the similarity between the claimed compound and a known effective compound in both structure and in vivo test results. The rejection was reversed. *Ex parte Chwang*, 231 U.S.P.Q. 751 (B.P.A.I. 1986).

ᵭ

The Examiner's failure to provide objective evidence to support a challenged officially noticed fact constitutes clear and reversible error. *Ex parte Natale*, 11 U.S.P.Q.2d 1222, 1226 (B.P.A.I. 1989).

ᵭ

The Supreme Court held that a license agreement that promised not to challenge the validity of a patent was void and unenforceable because it contravened the strong federal policy in favor of the full and free use of ideas in the public domain. Six circuits have ruled that consent judgments of validity and infringement are enforceable despite the Supreme Court's holding in *Lear* [395 U.S. 653, 162 U.S.P.Q. 1 (1969)]. *Foster v. Hallco Manufacturing Co., Inc.*, 14 U.S.P.Q.2d 1746, 1747 (Or. 1990).

ᵭ

The expertise of a deciding official is not legally relevant to the merits of any decision and is not subject to challenge. There can be no challenge to the authority of the Commissioner to decide a petition in person. *In re Arnott*, 19 U.S.P.Q.2d 1049, 1052 (Comm'r Patents & Trademarks 1991).

ᵭ

A rejection on the ground of anticipation by each of two abstracts (published more than one year prior to the filing date) was affirmed because appellants' evidence was insufficient to rebut the prima facie case that the two abstracts were enabling and therefore prior art, because appellants conceded that all limitations in the claims were inherent in the two abstracts, and because the anticipation findings were not otherwise tainted by legal error. In response to appellants' challenge of each of the abstracts as nonenabling, the Examiner explained his position without establishing the state of the art or providing citation of any substantiating documentation. The procedures established by 37 C.F.R. §1.107(b) (1993) expressly entitle an applicant, on mere request, to an Examiner affidavit that provides such citation. Appellants' failure to avail themselves of this procedure waived any right thereto under well established rules of law. *In re Sun*, 31 U.S.P.Q.2d 1451, 1454, 1455 (Fed. Cir. 1993—*unpublished*).

Champerty.

The motive or purpose of a patent assignment is irrelevant to the assignee's standing to enforce the assigned patent. Even a motive solely and expressly to facilitate litigation "is of no concern to the defendant and does not bear on the effectiveness of the assignment." *Discovery Rights, Inc. v. Avon Prods., Inc.*, 182 U.S.P.Q. 396, 398 (N.D. Ill. 1974).

ᵭ

An assignment of a 5 percent interest in order to facilitate infringement suits in the assignee's name as surrogate plaintiff while the assignor remains outside the litigation as the real party in interest is champertous and therefore void. *Refac International Ltd. v. Lotus Development Corp.*, 131 F.R.D. 56, 15 U.S.P.Q.2d 1747, 1748 (N.Y. 1990).

Chance. *See* **Accidental.**

Change. *See also* **Adjustability, Automate, Color, Compactness, Difference, Duplication of Parts, Form, Making Integral, Material, Mechanize, Negative Rules of Invention, Obviousness, Portable, Proportions, Purity, Rearranging Parts, Reduction in Steps, Reversal of Parts, Separable, Shade, Shape, Size, Strength, Structural Difference, Substitution of Equivalents, Weight.**

The law has other tests of invention than subtle conjecture of what might have been seen and yet was not. It regards a change as evidence of novelty, and the acceptance and utility of change as further evidence, even as a demonstration. Nor does it detract from its merit that it is the result of experiment and not the instant and perfect product of inventive power. A patentee may be baldly empirical, seeing nothing beyond his experiments and the result; yet, if he has added a new and valuable article to the world's utilities, he is entitled to the rank and protection of an inventor. It is certainly not necessary that he understand or be able to state the scientific principles underlying his invention, and it is immaterial whether he can stand a successful examination as to the speculative ideas involved. *Diamond Rubber Co. v. Consolidated Rubber Tire Co.*, 220 U.S. 428, 435 (1911).

ω

Although the patentee had merely changed the pitch of the Fourdrinier wire of a paper-making machine, the change in pitch was regarded as directed toward a wholly different object from that of the prior art. *Eibel Process Co. v. Minnesota & Ontario Paper Co.*, 261 U.S. 45, 67 (1923).

ω

One alleging a critical difference (that is, a difference in kind as distinguished from a difference in degree) growing out of claimed proportions of ingredients must establish such criticalness by proof. *In re Waite and Allport,* 168 F.2d 104, 77 U.S.P.Q. 586, 591 (C.C.P.A. 1948).

ω

Patentability is gauged not only by the extent or simplicity of physical changes, but also by the perception of the necessity or desirability of making such changes to produce a new result. When viewed after disclosure, the changes may seem simple and such as should have been obvious to those in the field. However, this does not necessarily negative invention or patentability. The conception of a new and useful improvement must be considered along with the actual means of achieving it in determining the presence or absence of invention. The discovery of a problem calling for an improvement is often a very essential element in an invention correcting such a problem. Though the problem, once realized, may be solved by use of old and known elements, this does not necessarily negative patentability.

Although the physical means of accomplishing the appellant's improvement and its new and useful results are simple, the conception of so improving on the prior art devices would not be obvious to those skilled in the art. *In re Bisley,* 197 F.2d 355, 94 U.S.P.Q. 80, 86, 87 (C.C.P.A. 1952).

ʊ

Under some circumstances, changes in temperature, in concentration, or in both, may impart patentability to a process if the particular ranges claimed produce a new and unexpected result that is different in kind and not merely in degree from the results of the prior art. Such ranges are termed "critical" ranges, and the applicant has the burden of proving such criticality. Where the general conditions of a claim are disclosed in prior art, it is not inventive merely to discover the optimum or workable ranges by routine experimentation. *In re Aller, Lacey, and Hall,* 220 F.2d 454, 105 U.S.P.Q. 233, 235 (C.C.P.A. 1955).

ʊ

In judging what requires uncommon ingenuity, the best standard is what common ingenuity has failed to contrive. Once a problem has been solved, it may be easy to see how prior-art references can be modified and manipulated to reconstruct the solution. The change may be simple and, by hindsight, seem obvious. However, the simplicity of new inventions is oftentimes the very thing that is not obvious before they are made. *In re Sporck,* 301 F.2d 686, 133 U.S.P.Q. 360, 363 (C.C.P.A. 1962).

ʊ

The change in a lower limit of a range in a continuing application can be, but is not necessarily, fatal to relying on the filing date of the parent application for the invention claimed in the continuing application. *Synthetic Industries (Texas) Inc. v. Forta Fiber, Inc.,* 590 F. Supp. 1574, 224 U.S.P.Q. 955 (Pa. 1984).

ʊ

Changes from prior art, whether minor or not, must be evaluated in terms of the whole invention, including whether the prior art provides any teaching or suggestion to one of ordinary skill in the art to make the changes that would produce the patentee's method and device. *Northern Telecom Inc. v. Datapoint Corp.,* 908 F.2d 931, 15 U.S.P.Q.2d 1321, 1324 (Fed. Cir. 1990).

ʊ

A change of words does not always mean change of scope. The question of whether the claims have been materially or substantially enlarged must be determined upon the claim as a whole. *Anderson v. International Engineering and Manufacturing Inc.,* 48 U.S.P.Q.2d 1631, 1634 (Fed. Cir. 1998).

Change in Form. *See also* **Form.**

The mere change in form without any corresponding change in function is not a patentable difference. *In re Launder and Hosmer,* 222 F.2d 371, 105 U.S.P.Q. 446, 450 (C.C.P.A. 1955).

ʊ

Where the claimed product and that of the art have the same utility, any change in the form, purity, color, stability or any of the other characteristics of the claimed product does not render the product patentable. *Ex parte Hartop*, 139 U.S.P.Q. 525, 527 (PO Bd. App. 1962).

ᚥ

There is no conception or reduction to practice of a new form of an otherwise old composition where there has been no recognition or appreciation of the existence of the new form. *Silvestri and Johnson v. Grant and Alburn*, 496 F.2d 593, 181 U.S.P.Q. 706, 708 (C.C.P.A. 1974).

ᚥ

Infringement is not avoided by a mere reversal or transposition of parts or components, or a mere change in form without a change in function. *Corning Class Works v. Sumitomo Electric USA Inc.*, 671 F. Supp. 1369, 5 U.S.P.Q.2d 1545 (N.Y. 1987).

Characteristic. *See also* **Properties.**

Although the Board described one of appellant's key discoveries as merely an "obviously desirable" characteristic, this would not make appellant's invention, considered as a whole, obvious. Obviousness is not to be determined on the basis of purpose alone. *In re Saether,* 492 F.2d 849, 181 U.S.P.Q. 36, 39 (C.C.P.A. 1974).

ᚥ

Where the Patent Office has reason to believe that a functional limitation asserted to be critical for establishing novelty in the claimed subject matter may, in fact, be an inherent characteristic of the prior art, it possesses the authority to require the applicant to prove that the subject matter shown to be in the prior art does not possess the characteristic relied on. *In re Best, Bolton, and Shaw*, 562 F.2d 1252, 195 U.S.P.Q. 430, 433 (C.C.P.A. 1977).

Characteristics. *See* **Product by Properties.**

Check. *See* **Unsigned Check.**

Chemical. *See also* **Combining Steps, Composition, Compound, Empirical, Properties, Reduction in Steps.**

The patentability of a new chemical structure is independent of how it is made. *See, e.g, In re Hoeksema,* 332 F.2d 374, 141 U.S.P.Q. 733, 736 (C.C.P.A. 1964) (product patentable, although the process was unpatentable for obviousness).

ᚥ

The first paragraph of 35 U.S.C. §112 requires that the scope of the claims bear a reasonable correlation to the scope of enablement provided by the specification to persons of ordinary skill in the art. In cases involving predictable factors, such as mechanical or electrical elements, a single embodiment provides broad enablement in the sense that, once imagined, other embodiments can be made without difficulty and their performance characteristics predicted by resort to known scientific laws. In cases involving unpredictable factors, such as most chemical reactions and physiological activity, the scope of enablement obviously varies inversely with the degree of unpredictability of the factors involved. *In re Fisher,* 427 F.2d 833, 166 U.S.P.Q. 18, 24 (C.C.P.A. 1970).

ω

In its early development, the doctrine of equivalents generally was applied in cases involving the equivalence of devices having mechanical components. Today, however, the same principles are applied to compositions of matter where there is equivalence between chemical ingredients. *Ziegler v. Phillips Petroleum Co.,* 483 F.2d 858, 177 U.S.P.Q. 481, 487 (5th Cir. 1973).

ω

Where intricate questions of chemistry are involved, which are peculiarly within the particular competence of the Patent Office, the presumption of validity should be weighed with great care. This is especially true where catalysts are involved because of their known unpredictability under modified changes in their environmental use. *Mobil Oil Corp. v. W. R. Grace & Co.,* 367 F. Supp. 207, 180 U.S.P.Q. 418, 430 (Conn. 1973).

ω

The unpredictability noted in the decision of the Board was in the admittedly chemical fact that the "properties of 'polymerizable materials' can vary over a wide range," but no reasons were given to appellant by the Patent Office for the alleged failure—or at least uncertainty—of the class of "polymerizable materials" to work in the claimed process to controvert the statement in appellant's application that his invention, in its broader aspects, is applicable to other polymers. Even in cases involving the unpredictable world of chemistry, such reasons are required. *In re Bowen,* 492 F.2d 859, 181 U.S.P.Q. 48, 50, 51 (C.C.P.A. 1974).

ω

Although there is a vast amount of knowledge about general relationships in the chemical arts, chemistry is still largely empirical, and there is often great difficulty in predicting precisely how a given compound will behave. *In re Carleton,* 599 F.2d 1021, 202 U.S.P.Q. 165, 170 (C.C.P.A. 1979).

ω

A process patent in a chemical field that has not been developed creates a monopoly of knowledge that should be granted only if clearly commanded by the statute. This is because such patents may engross unknown and perhaps unknowable areas and may confer power "to block off whole areas of scientific development, without compensating benefit to the public." *Ex parte Kranz,* 19 U.S.P.Q.2d 1216, 1219 (B.P.A.I. 1990).

ω

The scope of enablement under the first paragraph of 35 U.S.C. §112 varies with the degree of complexity of the subject matter involved. However, there is no distinction in law as to the enablement or description requirements of the first paragraph of 35 U.S.C. §112 based on whether the subject matter is chemical or nonchemical. *Ex parte DesOrneaux,* 25 U.S.P.Q.2d 2040, 2043 (B.P.A.I. 1992).

Chemical Obviousness.

The problem of "obviousness" under 35 U.S.C. §103 in determining the patentability of a new and useful chemical compound, or, as it is sometimes called, the problem of "chemical obviousness" is not really a problem in chemistry or pharmacology or in any related field of science, such as biology, biochemistry, pharmacodynamics, ecology, or others yet to be conceived. It is a problem of patent law. *In re Papesch,* 315 F.2d 381, 137 U.S.P.Q. 43 (C.C.P.A. 1963).

Chemical Reaction. *See also* **Combining Steps, Reduction in Steps.**

An inventor should be allowed to dominate future patentable inventions of others where those inventions are based in some way on his teachings. Such improvements, while unobvious from his teachings, are still within his contribution, since the improvement is made possible by his work. It is equally apparent, however, that he must not be permitted to achieve this dominance by claims that are insufficiently supported and hence not in compliance with the first paragraph of 35 U.S.C. §112. That paragraph requires that the scope of the claims must bear a reasonable correlation to the scope of enablement provided by the specification to persons of ordinary skill in the art. In cases involving predictable factors, such as mechanical or electrical elements, a single embodiment provides broad enablement in the sense that, once imagined, other embodiments can be made without difficulty and their performance characteristics predicted by resort to known scientific laws. In cases involving unpredictable factors, such as most chemical reactions and physiological activity, the scope of enablement obviously varies inversely with the degree of unpredictability of the factors involved. *In re Fisher,* 427 F.2d 833, 166 U.S.P.Q. 18 (C.C.P.A. 1970).

Chemical Theory. *See also* **Theory.**

When the PTO seeks to rely upon a chemical theory in establishing a *prima facie* case of obviousness, it must provide evidentiary support for the existence and meaning of that theory. *In re Grose and Flanigen,* 592 F.2d 1161, 201 U.S.P.Q. 57, 63 (C.C.P.A. 1979).

Chemistry. *See* **Empirical.**

Chicken Egg.[3]

Chlorine.

Where there is a difference in the structural formulae of the prior art dyes over the dyes defined by the appealed claims and, as a result, the properties imparted to the various dyes are such that those produced according to the present invention possess properties that are important when the dyes are used for their intended purpose, as distinguished from deficiencies noted in the prior art dyes, the claims may well be considered patentable over the references on which they were rejected. The presence of

---

[3] See claims 1 to 4 of United States Patent No. 5,246,717.

the additional chlorine atom in the claimed dyes is thus of significance, and the results produced amount to more than a mere difference in degree. *Ex parte Carson*, 78 U.S.P.Q. 93, 94 (PO Bd. App. 1948).

Chlorine Analog.

The mere fact that it is possible to find two isolated disclosures that might be combined in such a way to produce a new compound does not necessarily render such production obvious unless the art also contains something to suggest the desirability of the proposed combination. *In re Bergel and Stock*, 292 F.2d 955, 130 U.S.P.Q. 206, 208 (C.C.P.A. 1961).

Choice. *See* **Design Choice, Optimize, Purpose.**

cip. *See* **Continuation-in-Part Application.**

Circumstances.

The mere fact that certain things may result from a given set of circumstances is not sufficient basis on which to sustain a rejection under 35 U.S.C. §103. *Ex parte Seiler and Seiler*, 215 U.S.P.Q. 742, 743 (PTO Bd. App. 1982).

Circumstantial Evidence.

Direct infringement may be proven by circumstantial evidence. *Total Containment Inc. v. Buffalo Environmental Products Corp.*, 35 U.S.P.Q.2d 1385, 1389 (Va. 1995).

Citation of References. *See* **Duty to Disclose.**

Citizenship.

While 35 U.S.C. §115 requires the filing of a statement of citizenship and of an oath that the inventor believes himself to be the actual inventor of the device, the provisional acceptance of a Declaration and Power of Attorney in which the applicant fails to state his citizenship is not beyond the scope of discretion conferred on the Patent Office under 35 U.S.C. §26. *Autovox, S.p.A. v. Lenco Italiana [sic], S.p.A.*, 210 U.S.P.Q. 277, 278 (Ill. 1980).

Civil Action.

A party dissatisfied with a decision of the Board of Patent Interference on a question of priority of invention between conflicting patent applications may pursue a civil action against the other parties to the interference proceeding. This action is not a standard civil action; it is more in the nature of a review of an administrative proceeding with inherent limitations on the issues that may be raised in the original claim or by counterclaim. Cases under 35 U.S.C. §146 are limited to a review of the administrative proceedings in the Patent Office supplemented by additional evidence and testimony only insofar as it relates to contentions advanced below. *Montecatini Edison, S.p.A. v. Ziegler,* 172 U.S.P.Q. 519, 520 (D.C. 1972).

ω

Every case involving patent issues is not a "civil action arising under an Act of Congress relating to patents," as set forth in 28 U.S.C. §1338(a). Actions to enforce patent license agreements are not within exclusive federal jurisdiction notwithstanding the availability of the invalidity defense. *Kysor Industrial Corp. v. Pet,* 459 F.2d 1010, 173 U.S.P.Q. 642, 643 (6th Cir. 1972).

Claim. *See also* **Allowed Claim, Antecedent Basis, Breadth, Cancellation, Claim Construction, Claim Limitation, Claims, Class, Competitor's Product, Copying Claims, Count, Definition, Dependent Claim, Independent Claim, Intent to Claim, Invention, Judicial Redrafting, Language, Means Plus Function, Multiplicity, Original Claims, Priority, Product by Process, Product by Properties, Rejected Claim, Result, Rule 8, Symbols, Written Description.**

A patentee may claim the whole or only a part of his invention. If he only describes and claims a part, he is presumed to have abandoned the residue to the public. *McClain v. Ortmayer,* 141 U.S. 419 (1891).

ω

Allowability of an appealed claim is not controlled by the fact that similar claims have been allowed in the Patent Office since an appealed claim must be patentable in its own right. However, similar claims allowed by the Patent Office tribunals furnish evidence of what features those tribunals regard as patentable. It is proper, and sometimes necessary, to consider allowed claims in order to fully determine the views of the Board and of the Examiner. *In re Schechter and LaForge,* 205 F.2d 185, 98 U.S.P.Q. 144, 150 (C.C.P.A. 1953).

ω

A particular feature upon which patentability is predicated not only must be disclosed in the specification but also must be brought out or recited in the claims. *In re Ruse,* 220 F.2d 459, 105 U.S.P.Q. 237, 241 (C.C.P.A. 1955).

ω

Patentability of claims depends on whether the claims adequately recite features upon which patentability is predicated, assuming that such features are patentable. When claims to a device fail to define inventive features adequately by proper limitations, they are not allowable even though the device supports patentable claims. *In re Lander and Hosmer,* 222 F.2d 371, 105 U.S.P.Q. 446 (C.C.P.A. 1955).

ω

Claims are read in the light of the disclosure of the specification on which they are based, not in a vacuum. *In re Dean,* 291 F.2d 947, 130 U.S.P.Q. 107, 110 (C.C.P.A. 1961).

ω

One does not look to claims to find out how to practice the inventions they define, but, rather, to the specification. *In re Rainer, Redding, Hitov, Sloan, and Stewart,* 305 F.2d 505, 134 U.S.P.Q. 343, 346 (C.C.P.A. 1962).

ᙡ

While claims of a patent limit the invention, and specifications cannot be utilized to expand the patent monopoly, it is fundamental that claims are to be construed in the light of the specifications and both are to be read with a view to ascertain the invention. *United States v. Adams,* 383 U.S. 39, 148 U.S.P.Q. 479, 482 (1966).

ᙡ

A claim is a group of words defining only the boundary of the patent monopoly. It may not describe any physical thing, and indeed may encompass physical things not yet dreamed of. *In re Vogel and Vogel,* 422 F.2d 438, 164 U.S.P.Q. 619, 622 (C.C.P.A. 1970).

ᙡ

Section 112 does not require that the claims define the invention, whatever that would mean. The second paragraph of that section requires that the claims define "the subject matter which the applicant regards as his invention." The meaning of this provision is simply that an applicant is required to set definite boundaries on the patent protection sought. What the applicant does not regard as an element of his invention need not be specified in claims. *In re Wakefield and Foster,* 422 F.2d 897, 164 U.S.P.Q. 636 (C.C.P.A. 1970).

ᙡ

Significant evidence, if not the best evidence, of the scope of any one claim is the language employed in other claims. *Bethell and Hadley v. Koch, Robinson, and Wiley,* 427 F.2d 1372, 166 U.S.P.Q. 199, 201 (C.C.P.A. 1970).

ᙡ

Since the claims are the sole measure of the monopoly granted by the patent and the claims are "means-plus-function" claims, it was error to rely on a function of the patented device not mentioned in the claims. *Burgess & Associates, Inc. v. Klingensmith,* 487 F.2d 321, 180 U.S.P.Q. 115, 117 (9th Cir. 1973).

ᙡ

It is not a function of the claims to specifically exclude either possible inoperative substances or ineffective reactant proportions. *In re Dinh-Nguven and Stenhagen,* 492 F.2d 856, 181 U.S.P.Q. 46 (C.C.P.A. 1974).

ᙡ

Each claim of a patent is to be considered as setting forth a complete and independent invention. A patent attorney almost always presents to the Patent Office a set of claims, each differing in scope, one from the other, and usually running from the broadest permissible definition of the invention to a very specific definition of the invention. *Westwood Chemical, Inc. v. United States,* 525 F.2d 1367, 186 U.S.P.Q. 383, 387 (Ct. Cl. 1975).

ᙡ

To provide effective incentives, claims must adequately protect inventors. To demand that the first to disclose shall limit his claims to what he has found will work or to materials that meet the guidelines specified for "preferred" materials in a process would not serve the constitutional purpose of promoting progress in the useful arts. *In re Goffe,* 542 F.2d 564, 191 U.S.P.Q. 429, 431 (C.C.P.A. 1976).

ω

Product claims meet the requirements of the first paragraph of 35 U.S.C. §112 when the specification contains a description of the products, the claims are of a similar scope, and the disclosure does not fail to teach one of ordinary skill in the art how to make and use any of the claimed products. *In re Priest,* 582 F.2d 33, 199 U.S.P.Q. 11, 15 (C.C.P.A. 1978).

ω

There is nothing in the statutes or the case law which makes "that which is within the capabilities of one skilled in the art" synonymous with obviousness. *Ex parte Gerlach and Woerner,* 212 U.S.P.Q. 471 (PTO Bd. App. 1980).

ω

The two principles:

a. the claims measure the invention, and
b. claims are to be interpreted "in the light of the specifications and both are to be read with a view to ascertaining the invention,"

are not irreconcilable. The specifications are not to be used to expand the claims to cover advances clearly not claimed, but they should be considered to explain ambiguous claims or to limit overbroad claims. Although an invention on which a patentee is entitled to claim a monopoly is strictly limited to that which is properly disclosed in the file wrapper, overly technical interpretation of claim language is disfavored:

> Patents are to be liberally construed so as to secure to an inventor the real invention which he intends to secure by his patent, and the specification may be referred to in order to explain any ambiguity in the claim and to limit the claim, but the specification is never available to expand the claim. The claims must be read in the light of the disclosure...[T]he claims wherever possible are to be construed so as to cover the real invention as found in the specification and drawings, and this is particularly so in the case of a meritorious invention. 4 Deller's Walker on Patents §246 (2d ed. 1965).

Stewart-Warner Corp. v. The City of Pontiac, Michigan, 717 F.2d 269, 219 U.S.P.Q. 1162, 1168, 1169 (6th Cir. 1983).

ω

When not all claims are asserted to be invalid for anticipation or obviousness, the patent cannot be held invalid on either ground. Each claim must be presumed valid independently of the validity of any other claim. A court must limit its decision to the claims before it.

Advantages or "sales pitch features" do not belong in claims, the sole function of which is to point out distinctly the process, machine, manufacture, or composition of matter that is patented, not its advantages. *Preemption Devices, Inc. v. Minnesota Mining & Manufacturing Co.*, 732 F.2d 903, 221 U.S.P.Q. 841, 843, 844 (Fed. Cir. 1984).

ω

Claims must be evaluated separately, rather than as a single unit of claims tied together or "in tandem." *Milliken Research Corp. v. Dan River, Inc.*, 739 F.2d 587, 222 U.S.P.Q. 571, 576 (Fed. Cir. 1984).

ω

The rejection of a claim to a chemical compound (of a specified structure "where R_1, R_2, R_4, R_6, R_7, R_8, R_9, R_{10}, R_{11}, n and q are defined in the specification") under the second paragraph of 35 U.S.C. §112 was reversed. The absence of the definitions of the symbols in the claim itself may be objectionable. *Ex parte Moon*, 224 U.S.P.Q. 519 (PTO Bd. App. 1984).

ω

The contention that a claimed configuration would be obvious from a reference claim on which it reads is a non sequitur. According to such reasoning Morse's telegraph patent would have made the Telex obvious. The scope of a patent's claims determines what infringes the patent; it is no measure of what it discloses. A patent discloses only that which it describes, whether specifically or in general terms, so as to convey intelligence to one capable of understanding. *In re Benno*, 768 F.2d 1340, 226 U.S.P.Q. 683 (Fed. Cir. 1985).

ω

The district court employed two measures impermissible in law: (1) it required that Claim 1 "describe" the invention, which is the role of the disclosure portion of the specification, not the role of the claims; and (2) it applied the "full, clear, concise, and exact" requirement of the first paragraph of 35 U.S.C. §112 to the claim, when that paragraph only applies to the disclosure portion of the specification, not to the claims. The district court spoke inappropriately of the indefiniteness of the "patent," and it did not review the claim for indefiniteness under the second paragraph of 112. A decision on whether a claim is invalid under 112 requires a determination of whether those skilled in the art would understand what is claimed when the claim is read in the light of the specification. *Orthokinetics Inc. v. Safety Travel Chairs Inc.*, 806 F.2d 1565, 1 U.S.P.Q.2d 1081 (Fed. Cir. 1986).

ω

The sole function of claims is to delineate the scope of protection afforded by a patent, not to describe what the patentee has invented. *Alco Standard Corp. v. Tennessee Valley Authority*, 808 F.2d 1490, 1 U.S.P.Q.2d 1337 (Fed. Cir. 1986).

ω

Claims need not be limited to exemplification or preferred embodiments in order to satisfy enablement requirements. *Ex parte Gould*, 6 U.S.P.Q.2d 1680 (B.P.A.I. 1987).

ω

It is a claim that defines the "actual" invention, not the other way around. *See E.I. du Pont de Nemours & Co. v. Phillips Petroleum Co.*, 849 F.2d 1430, 7 U.S.P.Q.2d 1129, 1131 (Fed. Cir.), ccrt. denied, 109 S. Ct. 542 (1988).

ᅟ ᴡ

Where a specification does not require a limitation, that limitation should not be read from the specification into the claims. *Intel Corp. v. International Trade Commission*, 946 F.2d 821, 20 U.S.P.Q.2d 1161, 1174 (Fed. Cir. 1991).

ᴡ

Modern claim practice requires that the claims stand alone to define the invention. Incorporation into the claims by express reference to the specification and/or drawings is not permitted except in very limited circumstances. *Ex parte Fressola*, 27 U.S.P.Q.2d 1608, 1609 (B.P.A.I. 1993).

ᴡ

Each claim of a patent constitutes a separate invention and gives rise to separate rights. *Cyrix Corp. v. Intel Corp.*, 846 F.Supp. 522, 32 U.S.P.Q.2d 1890, 1901 (Tex. 1994).

ᴡ

A patent applicant is entitled to a reasonable degree of latitude in complying with the second paragraph of 35 U.S.C. §112, and the Examiner may not dictate the literal terms of the claims for the stated purpose of facilitating a search of the prior art. Just how an applicant must comply with the second paragraph of 35 U.S.C. §112, within reason, is within applicant's discretion. *Ex parte Tanksley*, 37 U.S.P.Q.2d 1382, 1386 (B.P.A.I. 1994).

ᴡ

The "claims" as used in (35 U.S.C.) §134 is a reference to the repeated "claim for a patent" as used in (35 U.S.C.) §132 rather than a reference to a particular claim "of an application." So long as the applicant has twice been denied a patent, an appeal may be filed. *Ex parte Lemoine*, 46 U.S.P.Q.2d 1420, 1423 (B.P.A.I. 1994).

ᴡ

The meaning of a term used in a patent claim is a question of law for the court, not a question of fact for the jury, and on appeal is decided de novo when there is a disputed question requiring interpretation of claim terms. *National Presto Industries Inc. v. The West Bend Co.*, 76 F.3d 1185, 37 U.S.P.Q.2d 1685, 1687 (Fed. Cir. 1996).

ᴡ

Drafting or amending claims to encompass existing technology, including a competitor's product, is a perfectly acceptable use of the patent system and is a form of reasonable "commercial gamesmanship." *Ford Motor Co. v. Lemelson*, 40 U.S.P.Q.2d 1349, 1361 (Nev. 1996).

Claim Analysis/Limitations.

The claimed invention must be viewed as a whole. The district court appeared to distill the invention down to a "gist" or "core," a superficial mode of analysis that disregards elements of the whole. It disregarded express claim limitations. *Bausch & Lomb, Inc. v. Barnes-Hind/Hydrocurve, Inc.*, 796 F.2d 443, 230 U.S.P.Q. 416 (Fed. Cir. 1986).

Claim Construction. *See also* **Claim Differentiation, Claim Interpretation, Claim Limitation, Construction of Claims, Fair Notice Function, Judicial Redrafting, Lexicographer, Prosecution History, Redrafting Claims.**

In patents for combinations of mechanisms, limitations and provisos imposed by the inventor, especially such as were introduced into an application after it had been persistently rejected, must be strictly construed against the inventor and in favor of the public, and looked upon as in the nature of disclaimers. *Sargent v. Hall & Safe Lock Co.*, 114 U.S. 63 (1885).

ω

The claim is a statutory requirement, prescribed for the very purpose of making a patentee define precisely what his invention is; it is unjust to the public, as well as an evasion of the law, to construe it in a manner different from the plain import of its terms. *White v. Dunbar*, 119 U.S. 47, 52 (1886).

ω

A patentee cannot successfully contend that his patent shall be construed as if it still contained the claims that were rejected and withdrawn. *Royer v. Coup*, 146 U.S. 524 (1892).

ω

Where an applicant acquiesces in the rejection of claims by the Patent Office or in a construction that narrows or restricts them, and where the elements that go to make up the combination of the claim are mentioned specifically and by reference letters, leaving no room for questions as to what was intended, the claim must be confined and restricted to the particular device described. *Lehigh Valley Railway Co. v. Kearney*, 158 U.S. 461 (1895).

ω

A claim in a patent (as allowed) must be read and interpreted with reference to claims that have been canceled or rejected, and the claims allowed cannot (by construction) be read to cover what was thus eliminated from the patent. A patentee may not, by resort to the doctrine of equivalents, give to an allowed claim a scope that it might have had without the amendments, the cancellation of which amounts to a disclaimer. *The Schriber-Schroth Company v. The Cleveland Trust Company*, 311 U.S. 211, 47 U.S.P.Q. 345, 349 (1940).

ω

Claims are read in the light of the disclosure of the specification on which they are based, not in a vacuum. *In re Dean*, 291 F.2d 947, 130 U.S.P.Q. 107, 110 (C.C.P.A. 1961).

ω

Allowed claims cannot, by construction, be read to cover subject matter eliminated by canceling other claims. This rule is applicable not only when the canceled claims are broader than those allowed, but also when the canceled claims are narrower. *Chemical*

Construction Corp. v. Jones & Laughlin Steel Corp., 311 F.2d 367, 136 U.S.P.Q. 150, 155 (3d Cir. 1962).

ᛒ

Unpatented claims are given the broadest reasonable interpretation consistent with the specification during the examination of a patent application, since the applicant may then amend his claims, the thought being to reduce the possibility that, after the patent is granted, the claims may be interpreted as giving broader coverage than is justified. Prior to the grant of a patent, an applicant should not have limitations of the specification read into a claim where no express statement of the limitation is included in the claim. *In re Prater and Wei*, 415 F.2d 1393, 162 U.S.P.Q. 541, 550, 551 (C.C.P.A. 1969).

ᛒ

Claims subject to examination are given their broadest reasonable interpretation consistent with the specification, and limitations appearing in the specification are not to be read into the claims. When an application is pending in the PTO, the applicant has the ability to correct errors in claim language and adjust the scope of claim protection as needed. This opportunity is not available in an infringement action in a district court. A district court may find it necessary to interpret claims to protect only that which constitutes patentable subject matter in order to do justice between the parties. The same policies warranting the PTO's approach to claim interpretation when an original application is involved have been held applicable to reissue proceedings because the reissue provision, 35 U.S.C. §251, permits amendment to the claims to avoid prior art. The reasons underlying the PTO's interpretation of the claims in reissue proceedings justify using the same approach in reexamination proceedings. *In re Yamamoto*, 740 F.2d 1569, 222 U.S.P.Q. 934, 936, 937 (C.C.P.A. 1984).

ᛒ

A claim is construed in the light of the claim language, the other claims, the prior art, the prosecution history, and the specification, not in light of an accused device. Claims are not construed "to cover" or "not to cover" an accused device. That procedure would make infringement a matter of judicial whim. It is only after the claims have been construed without reference to an accused device that the claims, as so construed, are applied to the accused device to determine infringement.

If everything in the specification were required to be read into the claims, or if structural claims were to be limited to devices operated precisely as a specification-described embodiment is operated, there would be no need for claims. Nor could an applicant, regardless of the prior art, claim more broadly than that embodiment. Nor would a basis remain for the statutory necessity that an applicant conclude his specification with "claims particularly pointing out and distinctly claiming the subject matter which the applicant regards as his invention."

It is settled law that, when a patent claim does not contain a certain limitation and another claim does, that limitation cannot be read into the former claim in determining either validity or infringement. *SRI International v. Matsushita Electric Corp. of America*, 775 F.2d 1107, 227 U.S.P.Q. 577 (Fed. Cir. 1985).

ᛒ

The court clearly looked to what was defined by the claim and interpreted it in the light of the disclosure upon which the claim was based. The court did not expand the meaning of comprises to include further limitations required by the reference. *Ashland Oil, Inc. v. Delta Resins & Refractories, Inc.*, 776 F.2d 281, 227 U.S.P.Q. 657 (Fed. Cir. 1985).

ᘂ

Claims are construed as they would be by those skilled in the art. That the specific examples set forth in the patent occur at room temperature does not mean that the claims are imbued with a room temperature limitation. Generally, particular limitations or embodiments appearing in the specification will not be read into the claims. *Loctite Corp. v. Ultraseal Ltd.*, 781 F.2d 861, 228 U.S.P.Q. 90 (Fed. Cir. 1985).

ᘂ

Disputed issues, such as the meaning of a term, should be construed by resort to extrinsic evidence, such as the specification, other claims, and the prosecution history. *Bausch & Lomb, Inc. v. Barnes-Hind/Hydrocurve, Inc.*, 796 F.2d 443, 230 U.S.P.Q. 416 (Fed. Cir. 1986).

ᘂ

According to the Examiner, the definition comes full circle and raises the specter that the claims embrace compounds containing a never-ending substituent group. This claim construction, though literal, is not reasonable and is not how a person having ordinary skill would view the claims. The only reasonable construction precludes never-ending substituent groups. The Examiner's claim construction, though possible, is not reasonable and is incorrect. *Ex parte Breuer,* 1 U.S.P.Q.2d 1906, 1907 (B.P.A.I. 1986).

ᘂ

No matter how clear a claim appears to be, lurking in the background are documents that may completely disrupt initial views on its meaning. *Tandon Corp. v. U.S. International Trade Commission,* 831 F.2d 1017, 4 U.S.P.Q.2d 1283 (Fed. Cir. 1987).

ᘂ

Having construed the claims one way for determining their validity, it is axiomatic that the claims must be construed in the same way for infringement. *W. L. Gore & Associates Inc. v. Garlock Inc.*, 842 F.2d 1275, 6 U.S.P.Q.2d 1277 (Fed. Cir. 1988).

ᘂ

The claims of a patent provide the concise formal definition of the invention. One must look to the wording of claims to determine whether there has been infringement. Courts can neither broaden nor narrow the claims to give a patentee something different from what he has set forth. No matter how great the temptation of fairness or policy making, courts do not rework claims; they only interpret them. Courts cannot alter what the patentee has chosen to claim as his invention. Generally, particular limitations or embodiments appearing in the specification are not to be read into the claims. It is entirely proper to use the specification to interpret what a patentee means by a word or phrase in the claims, but this is not to be confused with adding an extraneous limitation appearing in the specification, which is improper. By "extraneous" is meant a limitation read into a claim from the specification wholly apart from any need to interpret what the patentee meant by particular words or phrases in the claim. Where a specification does not require a limitation, that limitation should not be read from the specification to the claims. *E.I. du Pont de Nemours & Co. v. Phillips Petroleum Co.*, 849 F.2d 1430, 7 U.S.P.Q.2d 1129 (Fed. Cir. 1988).

ᙡ

The scope of patent claims must be narrowly construed in fields of technology where the outcome of substitutions are unpredictable. What constitutes equivalence must be determined against the context of the patent, prior art, and the particular circumstances of the case. Consideration must be given to the purpose for which an ingredient is used in the patent, the qualities it has when combined with other ingredients, and the function that it is intended to perform. *Genentech Inc. v. The Wellcome Foundation Ltd.*, 14 U.S.P.Q.2d 1363, 1371 (Del. 1990).

ᙡ

When the meaning of a term in a claim is disputed, underlying factual questions may arise, and claim construction is properly left to the jury under appropriate instructions. *Howes v. Medical Components Inc.*, 741 F. Supp. 528, 16 U.S.P.Q.2d 1671, 1679 (Pa. 1990).

ᙡ

Improper claim construction can distort an entire infringement analysis. Claim interpretation is a question of law. While a factual dispute over the meaning of terms in a claim may arise, when there is no assertion that the words on which the issue of infringement turns have anything other than their common, ordinary meaning, proper interpretation of a claim is a question of law, freely reviewable on appeal. *Key Manufacturing Group Inc. v. Microdot Inc.*, 925 F.2d 1444, 17 U.S.P.Q.2d 1806, 1809 (Fed. Cir. 1991).

ᙡ

What is claimed is what is *defined by the claim taken as a whole*, every limitation being material. That is the fundamental rule of claim construction. *General Foods Corp. v. Studiengesellschaft Kohle mbH*, 972 F.2d 1272, 23 U.S.P.Q.2d 1839, 1845 (Fed. Cir. 1992).

ᙡ

Classic issues of claim construction (i.e., what do the claims mean) are issues of law. They are for the court to decide and explicate on the record. *Genentech Inc. v. The Wellcome Foundation Ltd.*, 29 F.3d 1555, 31 U.S.P.Q.2d 1161, 1165 (Fed. Cir. 1994).

ᙡ

Claims should be construed as one skilled in the art would construe them. *Magnesystems Inc. v. Nikken Inc.*, 34 U.S.P.Q.2d 1112, 1115 (Cal. 1994).

ᙡ

The testimony of experts concerning claim construction "is evidence of the construction of the claims as they would be construed by those skilled in the art." *International Rectifier Corp. v. SGS-Thomson Microelectronics Inc.*, 38 U.S.P.Q.2d 1083, 1102 (Cal. 1994).

ᙡ

Claim Construction

The terms, claim construction and claim interpretation, mean one and the same thing in patent law. The reason that the courts construe patent claims as a matter of law and should not give such task to the jury as a factual matter is straightforward: It has long been and continues to be a fundamental principle of American law that "the construction of a written evidence is exclusively with the court." ("Ambiguity, undue breadth, vagueness, and triviality are matters that go to claim *validity* for failure to comply with 35 U.S.C. §112-§2, not to interpretation or construction.") But, the dissent explains: the distinction between "construction" and "interpretation" reflects the difference between the "meaning" of a term and its "legal effect"; "interpretation" relates to meaning, whereas ascertainment of legal operation or effect is sometimes called "construction." *Markman v. Westview Instruments Inc.*, 52 F.3d 967, 34 U.S.P.Q.2d 1321, 1326, 1328, 1335, 1347 (Fed. Cir. 1995); *confirmed,* 38 U.S.P.Q.2d 1461 (S.Ct. 1996); *see* Manak, "Confusion In The Law Of Patent Infringement: The Federal Circuit's Decisions in Markman and Hilton Davis", *BIOTECH Patent News*, Vol. 9, No. 10, October 1995.

ᴡ

The rule against enlargement of claim scope during claim construction is well settled. *Hilton Davis Chemical Co. v. Warner-Jenkinson Co. Inc.*, 62 F.3d 1512, 35 U.S.P.Q.2d 1641, 1653 (Fed. Cir. 1995).

ᴡ

When the body of a claim (having a preamble) references and/or further limits an element set forth in the preamble, the preamble imposes a limitation on the scope of the claim. *Derman v. PC Guardian*, 37 U.S.P.Q.2d 1733, 1734 (Fed. Cir. 1995), unpublished, not citable as precedent.

ᴡ

Markman [52 F.3d 967, 34 U.S.P.Q.2d 1321 (Fed. Cir.)(en banc), *cert. granted*, 116 S.Ct. 40 (1995)] appears to leave a district court with three options: (1) interpret the claims on the paper record, if possible; (2) hold a separate bench trial to resolve the disputes surrounding claim interpretation before trial; or (3) wait until the actual trial and rule on the claim interpretation issues just prior to instructing the jury. *Moll v. Northern Telecom Inc.*, 37 U.S.P.Q.2d 1839, 1842 (Pa. 1995).

ᴡ

"To ascertain the meaning of claims, we consider three sources: The claims, the specification, and the prosecution history." "Expert testimony, including evidence of how those skilled in the art would interpret the claims, may also be used." *Ethicon EndoSurgery v. United States Surgical Corp.*, 900 F. Supp. 172, 38 U.S.P.Q.2d 1385, 1387 (Ohio 1995).

ᴡ

The construction of a patent, including terms of art within its claim, is exclusively within the province of the court. *Markman v. Westview Instruments Inc.*, 116 S.Ct. 1384, 38 U.S.P.Q.2d 1461, 1462 (S.Ct. 1996).

ᴡ

The determination of whether claims have been enlarged is a matter of claim construction and is treated as a question of law. The test to determine whether a claim has been impermissibly broadened during reexamination is the same as that used to determine whether a claim has been impermissibly broadened during reissue. "An amended or new claim is enlarged if it includes within its scope any subject matter that would not have infringed the original patent." *Thermalloy Inc. v. Aavid Engineering Inc.*, 39 U.S.P.Q.2d 1457, 1460 (N.H. 1996).

ω

"Extrinsic evidence (such as expert testimony) may be considered, *if needed* to assist in determining the meaning or scope of technical terms in the claims." *Vitronics Corp. v. Conceptronic Inc.*, 39 U.S.P.Q.2d 1573, 1577 (Fed. Cir. 1996).

ω

Claim construction may use prosecution history differently than prosecution history estoppel does. However, the scope of the doctrine of equivalents is very closely related to both the claim construction and the prosecution history. *James River Corp. of Virginia v. Hallmark Cards Inc.*, 43 U.S.P.Q.2d 1422, 1424 (Wis. 1997).

ω

The PTO applies to verbiage of a proposed claim the broadest reasonable meaning of the words in their ordinary usage as they would be understood by one of ordinary skill in the art, taking into account whatever enlightenment by way of definitions or otherwise that may be afforded by the written description contained in the applicant's specification. *In re Morris*, 127 F.3d 1048, 44 U.S.P.Q.2d 1023, 1027 (Fed. Cir. 1997).

ω

When intrinsic evidence is unambiguous, it is improper for a court to rely on extrinsic evidence, such as expert testimony, for purposes of claim construction. The rationale for this rule is that:

> [t]he claims, specification, and file history, rather than extrinsic evidence, constitute the public record of the patentee's claim, a record upon which the public is entitled to rely. In other words, competitors are entitled to review the public record, apply the established rules of claim construction, ascertain the scope of the patentee's claimed invention and, thus, design around the claimed invention. Allowing the public record to be altered or changed by extrinsic evidence..., such as expert testimony, would make this right meaningless. The same holds true whether it is the patentee or the alleged infringer who seeks to alter the scope of the claims. *Vitronics Corp. v. Conceptronic, Inc.*, 90 F.3d 1576, 1583, 39 U.S.P.Q.2d 1573, 1577.

Bell & Howell Document Management Products Co. v. Altek Systems, 132 F.3d 701, 45 U.S.P.Q.2d 1033, 1037, 1038 (Fed. Cir. 1997).

ω

When the specification explains and defines a term used in the claims, without ambiguity or incompleteness, there is no need to search further for the meaning of the term. *Multiform Desiccants Inc. v. Medzam Ltd.*, 133 F.3d 1473, 45 U.S.P.Q.2d 1429, 1433 (Fed. Cir. 1998).

℧

The totality of claim construction is a legal question to be decided by the judge. "[T]reating interpretive issues as *purely legal* will promote (though not guarantee) intra-jurisdictional certainty through the application of *stare decisis* on those questions not yet subject to interjurisdictional uniformity under the authority of the single appeals court." *Cybor Corp. v. FAS Technologies Inc.*, 138 F.3d 1448, 46 U.S.P.Q.2d 1169, 1173 (Fed. Cir. 1998), but see opinion of J. Rader, 1189.

℧

"While . . . claims are to be interpreted in light of the specification and with a view to ascertaining the invention, it does not follow that limitations from the specification may be read into the claims." The specification can supply understanding of unclear terms, but should never trump the clear meaning of the claim terms. *Comark Communications Inc. v. Harris Corp.*, 48 U.S.P.Q.2d 1001, 1005 (Fed. Cir. 1998).

Claim Differentiation. *See also* Claim Construction.

The theory of claim differentiation is that anything recited in a dependent claim cannot be included in its independent claim. *Plasser American Corp. v. Canron Inc.*, 546 F. Supp. 589, 217 U.S.P.Q. 823, 834 (S.C. 1980).

℧

Practice has long recognized that "claims may be multiplied . . . to define the metes and bounds of the invention in a variety of different ways." Thus, two claims that read differently can cover the same subject matter.

There is presumed to be a difference in meaning and scope when different words or phrases are used in separate claims. To the extent that the absence of such difference in meaning and scope would make a claim superfluous, the doctrine of claim differentiation states the presumption that the difference between claims is significant. *Tandon Corp. v. U.S. International Trade Commission*, 831 F.2d 1017, 4 U.S.P.Q.2d 1283 (Fed. Cir. 1987).

℧

The judicially developed guide to claim interpretation known as claim differentiation cannot override the statute. A means-plus-function limitation is not made open-ended by the presence of another claim specifically claiming the disclosed structure that underlies the means clause or an equivalent of that structure. One cannot escape the mandate of 35 U.S.C. §112, sixth paragraph, by merely adding a claim or claims specifically reciting such structure or structures. Different structures are not ipso facto equivalent merely because they perform the same function. To so hold would effectively eliminate the statutory restriction of the sixth paragraph of 35 U.S.C. §112. *The Laitram Corp. v. Rexnord Inc.*, 939 F.2d 1533, 19 U.S.P.Q.2d 1367, 1371 (Fed. Cir. 1991).

℧

The doctrine of claim differentiation "cannot overshadow the express and contrary intentions of the patent draftsman". *O.I. Corp. v. Tekmar Co.*, 42 U.S.P.Q.2d 1777, 1781 (Fed. Cir. 1997).

ω

The presumption that separate claims have different scope "is a guide, not a rigid rule." *ATD Corp. v. Lydall Inc.*, 48 U.S.P.Q.2d 1321, 1325 (Fed. Cir. 1998).

Claim Format.

Modern claim practice is an end result of over 155 years of evolution since the first requirement for a claim was enacted in the Patent Act of 1836. While claim practice has undergone significant changes since that time, it appears that Office practice has always required claims to be submitted in single sentence format. *In re Fressola*, 22 U.S.P.Q.2d 1828, 1830 (Comm'r Patents and Trademarks 1992).

Claim Interpretation. *See also* Claim Construction, Redundant.

Unpatented claims are accorded the broadest reasonable interpretation consistent with the specification. *In re Barr, Williams, and Whitmore*, 444 F.2d 588, 170 U.S.P.Q. 330, 335 (C.C.P.A. 1971).

ω

An interpretation of a claim which limits it to the relationship disclosed in the specification is consistent with the principle that, where susceptible to more than one construction, that one will be adopted which will preserve to the patentee his actual invention. *Leesona Corporation v. United States*, 185 U.S.P.Q. 156, 164 (U.S. Ct. Cl. 1975).

ω

When a patentee is aware that the Examiner allowed claims on the basis of a particular interpretation, his acceptance of the patent under such circumstances precludes him from obtaining a claim construction that would resurrect subject matter surrendered during prosecution of his application. *Hughes Aircraft Co. v. United States*, 717 F.2d 1351, 219 U.S.P.Q. 473, 481 (Fed. Cir. 1983).

ω

In patent law, a word means nothing outside of the claim and the description in the specification. A disregard of claim limitations renders a claim examination in the PTO meaningless.

Claim interpretation—in light of the specification, claim language, other claims, and prosecution history—is a matter of law and will normally control the remainder of the decisional process. *Panduit Corp. v. Dennison Manufacturing Co.*, 810 F.2d 1561, 1 U.S.P.Q.2d 1593 (Fed. Cir. 1987).

ω

The claims of a patent provide the concise formal definition of the invention. One must look to the wording of claims to determine whether there has been infringement. Courts can neither broaden nor narrow the claims to give a patentee something different from what he has set forth. No matter how great the temptation of fairness or policy making, courts do not rework claims; they only interpret them. Courts cannot alter what the patentee has chosen to claim as his invention. Generally, particular limitations or embodiments appearing in the specification are not to be read into the claims. It is entirely proper to use the specification to interpret what a patentee means by a word or phrase in the claims, but this is not to be confused with adding an extraneous limitation appearing in the specification, which is improper. By "extraneous" is meant a limitation read into a claim from the specification wholly apart from any need to interpret what the patentee meant by particular words or phrases in the claim. Where a specification does not require a limitation, that limitation should not be read from the specification to the claims. *E.I. du Pont de Nemours & Co. v. Phillips Petroleum Co.*, 849 F.2d 1430, 7 U.S.P.Q.2d 1129 (Fed. Cir. 1988).

ᴡ

A general rule of interpretation is that words in a claim will be given their ordinary and accustomed meaning, unless it appears that the inventor used them differently. *Casler v. United States*, 15 Cl. Ct. 717, 9 U.S.P.Q.2d 1753 (1988).

ᴡ

The general proposition that a court may not redraft a claim for purposes of avoiding a defense of anticipation does not apply where "extraneous" limitations from the specification are not being read into the claim wholly apart from any need to interpret what the patentee meant by particular words or phrases in the claim. When the question is what effect to give to words in a claim, it is entirely proper to use the specification to interpret what the patentee meant by a word or phrase in the claim. *Corning Glass Works v. Sumitomo Electric U.S.A. Inc.*, 868 F.2d 1251, 9 U.S.P.Q. 1962 (Fed. Cir. 1989).

ᴡ

Where no underlying fact issue must be resolved, claim interpretation is a question of law. Thus, a mere dispute over a meaning of a term does not itself create an issue of fact. This is true even where the meaning cannot be determined without resort to the specification, the prosecution history or other extrinsic evidence provided that, upon consideration of the entirety of such evidence, the court concludes that there is no genuine underlying issue of material fact. *Johnston v. IVAC Corp.*, 885 F.2d 1574, 12 U.S.P.Q.2d 1382, 1385 (Fed. Cir. 1989).

ᴡ

During patent examination the pending claims must be interpreted as broadly as their terms reasonably allow. When the applicant states the meaning that the claimed terms are intended to have, the claims are examined with that meaning, in order to achieve complete exploration of the applicant's invention and its relation to the prior art. Before an application is granted, there is no reason to read into the claim the limitations of the specification. The reason is simply that, during patent prosecution when claims can be amended, ambiguity should be recognized, scope and breadth of language explored, and clarification imposed. The issued claims are the measure of the protected right. An essential purpose of patent examination is to fashion claims that are precise, clear, correct, and unambiguous. Only in this way can uncertainties of claimed scope be removed, as much as possible, during the administrative process. Thus, the inquiry during examination is patentability of the invention as "the applicant regards" it; and, if the claims do not particularly point out and distinctly claim, in the words of 35 U.S.C. §112, that which examination shows the applicant is entitled to claim as his invention, the appropriate PTO action is to reject the claims for that reason. A claim that reads on subject matter beyond the applicant's invention fails to comply with 112. *In re Zletz*, 893 F.2d 319, 13 U.S.P.Q.2d 1320, 1322 (Fed. Cir. 1989).

ᛒ

Although claim interpretation is a question of law, expert testimony is admissible to give an opinion on the ultimate question of infringement. *Symbol Technologies Inc. v. Opticon Inc.*, 935 F.2d 1569, 19 U.S.P.Q.2d 1241, 1245 (Fed. Cir. 1991).

ᛒ

A factual dispute is "genuine" when the evidence is such that a reasonable jury could return a verdict for the non-movant. Thus, although the interpretation of claims is a question of law, when it is necessary to resolve disputed issues of fact in the course of interpreting the claims, summary disposition is improper. *The Laitram Corp. v. NEC Corp.*, 952 F.2d 1357, 21 U.S.P.Q.2d 1276, 1281 (Fed. Cir. 1991).

ᛒ

Claim interpretation is a question of law amenable to summary judgment. Disagreement over the meaning of a term within a claim does not necessarily create a genuine issue of material fact. Terms in a claim are given their ordinary meaning to one of skill in the art unless it appears from the patent and file history that the terms were used differently by the inventors. *Intellicall Inc. v. Phonometrics Inc.*, 952 F.2d 1384, 21 U.S.P.Q.2d 1383, 1386 (Fed. Cir. 1992).

ᛒ

In making an analysis of claim limitations in this case, the Court distinguished between a) interpreting a statute and contract in light of their clear provisions and b) conducting an infringement analysis or determining priority in an interference. *Filmtec Corp. v. Hydranautics*, 982 F.2d 1546, 25 U.S.P.Q.2d 1283, 1289 n.5 (Fed. Cir. 1992).

ᛒ

If complex scientific principles are involved, a court may hear the testimony of experts in the art to see how they would interpret a claim. *Powell v. Iolab Corp.*, 32 U.S.P.Q.2d 1579, 1581 (Cal. 1994).

ᛒ

The terms, claim construction and claim interpretation, mean one and the same thing in patent law. The reason that the courts construe patent claims as a matter of law and should not give such task to the jury as a factual matter is straightforward: It has long been and continues to be a fundamental principle of American law that "the construction of a and continues to be a fundamental principle of American law that "the construction of a written evidence is exclusively with the court." ("Ambiguity, undue breadth, vagueness, and triviality are matters that go to claim *validity* for failure to comply with 35 U.S.C. §112-§2, not to interpretation or construction.") But, the dissent explains: the distinction between "construction" and "interpretation" reflects the difference between the "meaning" of a term and its "legal effect"; "interpretation" relates to meaning, whereas ascertainment of legal operation or effect is sometimes called "construction". *Markman v. Westview Instruments Inc.*, 52 F.3d 967, 34 U.S.P.Q.2d 1321, 1326, 1328, 1335, 1347 (Fed. Cir. 1995).

ω

The patentee bears the burden of proving that its (claim or infringement) interpretation would not ensnare prior art. *Sage Products Inc. v. Devon Industries Inc.*, 880 F.Supp. 718, 35 U.S.P.Q.2d 1321, 1328 (Cal. 1994).

ω

A patent's title is an interpretative aid. *Exxon Chemical Patents Inc. v. Lubrizol Corp.*, 64 F.3d 1553, 35 U.S.P.Q.2d 1801, 1804 (Fed. Cir. 1995).

ω

A patent claim may be interpreted only as broadly as its unambiguous scope. *Ethicon Endo-Surgery Inc. v. United States Surgical Corp.*, 40 U.S.P.Q.2d 1019, 1026 (Fed. Cir. 1996).

ω

The fact that claims receive their broadest reasonable meaning during the patent examination process does not relieve the PTO of its essential task of examining the entire patent disclosure to discern the meaning of claim words and phrases. *Rowe v. Dror*, 112 F.3d 473, 42 U.S.P.Q.2d 1550, 1555 (Fed. Cir. 1997).

ω

"A trial court may exercise its discretion to interpret the claims at a time when the parties have presented a full picture of the claimed invention and the prior art." *Toter Inc. v. City of Visalia*, 44 U.S.P.Q.2d 1312 (Cal. 1997).

ω

The focus in construing disputed terms in claim language is not the subjective intent of the parties to the patent contract when they used a particular term. Rather the focus is on the objective test of what one of ordinary skill in the art at the time of the invention would have understood the term to mean. Where there is an equal choice between a broader and narrower meaning of a claim, and there is an enabling disclosure that indicates that the applicant is at least entitled to a claim having the narrower meaning, we consider the notice function of the claim to be best served by adopting the narrower meaning. *Regents of the University of California v. Oncor Inc.*, 44 U.S.P.Q.2d 1321, 1325, 1326 (Cal. 1997).

ω

In a proceeding in the PTO, drawings "may be used like the written specifications to provide evidence relevant to claim interpretation." 1 No. 8 MLRPAT 8 (1993). *Mentor Graphics Corp. v. Quickturn Design Systems Inc.*, 44 U.S.P.Q.2d 1621, 1625 (Oreg. 1997).

ω

"[A]rguments made during prosecution regarding the meaning of a claim term are relevant to the interpretation of that term in every claim of the patent absent a clear indication to the contrary. *Digital Biometrics Inc. v. Identix Inc.*, 149 F.3d 1335, 47 U.S.P.Q.2d 1418, 1427 (Fed. Cir. 1998).

ϖ

The interpretation to be given a term can only be determined and confirmed with a full understanding of what the inventors actually invented and intended to envelop with the claim. The construction that stays true to the claim language and most naturally aligns with the patent's description of the invention will be, in the end, the correct construction. A claim construction is persuasive, not because it follows a certain rule, but because it defines terms in the context of the whole patent. Any interpretation that is provided or disavowed in the prosecution history also shapes the claim scope. *Renishaw plc v. Marposs Societa' per Azioni*, 48 U.S.P.Q.2d 1117, 1121 n.3, 1122 (Fed. Cir. 1998).

Claim Language. *See also* Lexicographer.

If patent claims, read in the light of the specification, reasonably apprise one skilled in the art of the utilization and scope of the invention and if the language is as precise as the subject matter permits, the patent should not be deemed invalid for indefiniteness. A patentee is required to draft the patent specification and claims as precisely as the subject matter permits, and failure to do so may result in invalidation. Absolute specificity and precision, however, are not required. The claims need only go so far as to apprise one reasonably skilled in the area of the true teaching of the invention. Mere breadth of a claim does not in itself cause invalidation. As long as the meaning of the claims is clear in light of the specification and accompanying drawings, breadth merely enhances the risk that the claim will be found invalid. *Andco Environmental Processes, Inc. v. Niagara Environmental Associates, Inc.*, 220 U.S.P.Q. 468 (N.Y. 1983).

ϖ

The basis of the district court's holding that the claims are indefinite is that "they do not disclose how infringement may be avoided because antibody affinity cannot be estimated with any consistency." Even if the district court's finding and support of this holding—that "there is no standard set of experimental conditions which are used to estimate affinities"—is accurate, under the law pertaining to indefiniteness—"if the claims, read in the light of the specification, reasonably apprise those skilled in the art both of the utilization and scope of the invention, and if the language is as precise as the subject matter permits, the courts can demand no more"—the claims clearly are definite. The evidence of record indisputably shows that calculating affinity was known in the art at the time of filing, and notwithstanding the fact that those calculations are not precise, or "standard," the claims, read in the light of the specification, reasonably apprise those skilled in the art and are as precise as the subject matter permits. *Hybritech Inc. v. Monoclonal Antibodies, Inc.*, 802 F.2d 1367, 231 U.S.P.Q. 81 (Fed. Cir. 1986).

ϖ

The claims were intended to cover the use of the invention with various types of automobiles. That a particular chair of the claims may fit within some automobiles and not others is of no moment. The phrase "so dimensioned" is as accurate as the subject matter permits, automobiles being of various sizes. As long as those of ordinary skill in the art realize that the dimensions could be easily obtained, 35 U.S.C. §112, second paragraph, requires nothing more. The patent law does not require that all possible lengths corresponding to the spaces in hundreds of different automobiles be listed in the patent, let alone that they be listed in the claims. *Orthokinetics Inc. v. Safety Travel Chairs Inc.*, 806 F.2d 1565, 1 U.S.P.Q.2d 1081 (Fed. Cir. 1986).

ω

Language specifically suggested by the PTO for inclusion in claims is entitled to a strong presumption of validity under 35 U.S.C. §§112 and 282. *American Dental Association Health Foundation v. Bisco Inc.*, 24 U.S.P.Q.2d 1524, 1529 (Ill. 1992).

Claim Limitation. *See also* **Breadth, Limitation, Narrowing Claim, New Matter, Restriction.**

In patents for combinations of mechanisms, limitations and provisos imposed by the inventor, especially such as were introduced into an application after it had been persistently rejected, must be strictly construed against the inventor and in favor of the public, and looked upon as in the nature of disclaimers. *Sargent v. Hall & Safe Lock Co.*, 114 U.S. 63 (1885).

ω

An applicant has a right to submit claims of varying scope. The practice of holding a limitation in a claim as not being critical, merely because it was omitted from other claims, is clearly not proper. *Ex parte Seavey*, 125 U.S.P.Q. 454, 457 (PO Bd. App. 1959).

ω

Claims need not recite limitations that deal with factors that must be presumed to be within the level of ordinary skill in the art, where one of ordinary skill in the art, to whom the specification and claims are directed, would consider such factors obvious. *In re Skrivan*, 427 F.2d 801, 166 U.S.P.Q. 85 (C.C.P.A. 1970).

ω

The change in a lower limit of a range in a continuing application can be, but is not necessarily, fatal to relying on the filing date of the parent application for the invention claimed in the continuing application. *Synthetic Industries (Texas) Inc. v. Forta Fiber, Inc.*, 590 F. Supp. 1574, 224 U.S.P.Q. 955 (Pa. 1984).

ω

The terms in the preamble to a claim are deemed limitations in the claims only where necessary to give meaning to the claim and properly define the invention. *Lemelson v. U.S.*, 6 U.S.P.Q.2d 1657, 1671 (U.S. Cl. Ct. 1988).

Claim of Priority. *See* **Priority, 35 U.S.C. §119.**

Claim Preclusion.

A "claim" rests on a particular factual transaction or series thereof on which a suit is brought. An assertion of invalidity of a patent by an alleged infringer is not a claim, but a defense to the patent owner's claim. While defenses to a claim are extinguished by application of the doctrine of claim preclusion, the facts related to the defense do not in themselves constitute the transaction or "claim." In a declaratory judgment action, invalidity is but an anticipatory defense, and the claim of the declaratory judgment suit is based on the facts related to the patent owner's charge of infringement. *Foster v. Hallco Manufacturing Co. Inc.*, 947 F.2d 469, 20 U.S.P.Q.2d 1241, 1248, 1249 (Fed. Cir. 1991).

ᛟ

A dismissal with prejudice before an issue or claim has been decided in an adversarial setting constitutes a final judgment barring relitigation for the purposes of claim preclusion but not for issue preclusion. *InterDigital Technology Corp. v. OKI America Inc.*, 866 F.Supp. 212, 32 U.S.P.Q.2d 1850, 1852 (Pa. 1994).

ᛟ

Claim preclusion may be invoked by a corporate parent following a final judgment against its wholly owned subsidiary. A party may not split a cause of action into separate grounds of recovery and raise the separate grounds in successive lawsuits; instead, a party must raise (in a single lawsuit) all the grounds of recovery arising from a single transaction or series of transactions that can be brought together. "[C]laim splitting cannot be justified on the ground that the two actions are based on different legal theories". *Mars Inc. v. Nippon Conlux Kabushiki-Kaisha*, 58 F.3d 616, 35 U.S.P.Q.2d 1311, 1313, 1314 (Fed. Cir. 1995).

ᛟ

With respect to patent litigation the CAFC was unpersuaded "that an 'infringement claim,' for purposes of claim preclusion, embraces more than the specific devices before the court in the first suit." "It is not every case in which a litigant has had 'one bite at the cherry' that the law forbids another. Thus, it is not every such case in which the policy of stopping litigation outweighs that of showing the truth." *Kearns v. General Motors Corp.*, 39 U.S.P.Q.2d 1949, 1952 (Fed. Cir. 1996).

Claim Reconstruction. *See also* Retrospective Reconstruction.

It is impermissible within the framework of 35 U.S.C. §103 to pick and choose from any one reference only so much of it as will support a given position to the exclusion of other parts necessary to the full appreciation of what such reference fairly suggests to one skilled in the art. *Bausch & Lomb, Inc. v. Barnes-Hind/Hydrocurve, Inc.*, 796 F.2d 443, 230 U.S.P.Q. 416 (Fed. Cir. 1986).

Claims. *See also* Unnecessary.

Section 1.192(c)(5) of 37 C.F.R. requires appellant to perform two affirmative acts in his brief in order to have the separate patentability of a plurality of claims subject to the same rejection considered. The appellant must (1) state that the claims do not stand or fall together and (2) present arguments why the claims subject to the same rejection are separately patentable. Where the appellant does neither, it is appropriate for the Examiner and the Board to rely upon the presumption created by the words of the rule and to treat all claims as standing or falling together. Where, however, the appellant (1) omits the statement required by 37 C.F.R. §1.192(c)(5), yet presents arguments in the argument section of his brief, or (2) includes the statement required by 37 C.F.R. §1.192(c)(5) to the effect that one or more claims do not stand or fall with the rejection of the other claims, yet does not offer arguments in support in the argument section of the brief, it is imperative that the inconsistency apparent on the face of the brief be resolved. A brief evidencing either form of inconsistency is not in compliance with 37 C.F.R. §1.192. When appellant presents a brief having either form of inconsistency, the Examiner invokes the presumption of 37 C.F.R. §1.192(c)(5), and appellant allows the Examiner's invocation of the presumption to go unchallenged by petition under 37 C.F.R. §1.181, the BPAI will simply decide the appeal and will decline to consider the patentability of the claims separately in reaching its decision. *Ex parte Schier,* 21 U.S.P.Q.2d 1016, 1018, 1019 (B.P.A.I. 1991).

ω

When a brief on appeal to the BPAI omits the statement required by 37 C.F.R. §1.192(c)(5), yet presents arguments in the argument section, it is not in compliance with 37 C.F.R. §1.192(c). Appellant will be notified of the reasons for noncompliance and provided with a period of one month within which to file an amended brief. If appellant does not file an amended brief within the one-month period, or files an amended brief that does not overcome all the reasons for noncompliance stated in the notification, the appeal will be dismissed. In any instance where an Examiner and appellant engage in an interchange over such compliance, the BPAI will treat the matter as one within the jurisdiction of the Examiner, requiring an appellant dissatisfied with the Examiner's holding to seek relief by way of petition under 37 C.F.R. §1.181, rather than by way of appeal under 37 C.F.R. §1.191. *Ex parte Ohsumi,* 21 U.S.P.Q.2d 1020, 1023 (B.P.A.I. 1991).

Claims Corresponding to Count.

When an interference is declared between a patent and an application, the PTO rules require that "all claims in the application and patent which define the same patentable invention as a count shall be designated to correspond to the count." A party to an interference, who has failed to timely contest the designation of claims corresponding to a count, has not conceded that claims corresponding to a count are anticipated or made obvious by the prior art when the subject matter of the count is determined to be unpatentable for obviousness. The PTO must determine, based on the actual prior art, whether claims not corresponding exactly to the count are unpatentable. A party to an interference proceeding should be permitted to argue separately the patentability of claims designated as corresponding substantially to a count, just as a party would be permitted to do in an *ex parte* prosecution and appeal. If a party chooses not to argue the claims separately, they would stand or fall together. *In re Van Geuns,* 988 F.2d 1181, 26 U.S.P.Q.2d 1057, 1060 (Fed. Cir. 1993).

Claims Court. *See* Eminent Domain.

Claims of Same Scope. *See* Multiplicity.

Claim Splitting.

"[C]laim splitting cannot be justified on the ground that the two actions are based on different legal theories". *Mars Inc. v. Nippon Conlux Kabushiki-Kaisha*, 58 F.3d 616, 35 U.S.P.Q.2d 1311, 1313, 1314 (Fed. Cir. 1995).

ω

A main purpose of the general rule against claim splitting "is to protect the defendant from being harassed by repetitive actions based on the same claim." If a defendant chooses not to make the objection that another action based on the same claim is pending, that defendant has waived his protective aspect of res judicata and acquiesces to the splitting of the claim. *Klipsch Inc. v. WWR Technology Inc.*, 127 F.3d 729, 44 U.S.P.Q.2d 1588, 1592 (8th Cir. 1997).

Claims Suggested for Interference.

The PTO, having insisted that appellant should have copied claims, must show, in support of that contention, that appellant had support for the claims in his application. *In re Ogiue*, 517 F.2d 382, 186 U.S.P.Q. 227, 233 (C.C.P.A. 1975).

ω

Normally when a claim is suggested to an applicant for purposes of interference and the applicant refuses to make it, such refusal constitutes a concession that the subject matter of the claim was the prior invention of another in this country, and thus is prior art against the applicant under 35 U.S.C. §102(g)/103. However, if the applicant's disclosure does not support the suggested claim, there is no such disclaimer, and the suggested claim is not prior art. *Ex parte Cullis*, 11 U.S.P.Q.2d 1876, 1878 (B.P.A.I. 1989).

Class.[4] *See also* Certification, Field of Search, Promoting Progress, Statutory Class.

While processes and products are separate categories of invention, it is not inconsistent to state that a process and product may present identical issues concerning, for example, their obviousness. *Westwood Chemical, Inc. v. United States*, 525 F.2d 1367, 186 U.S.P.Q. 383, 393 (Ct. Cl. 1975).

Class Action.

There is nothing inherent in patent litigation to prevent the application of Fed. R. Civ. P. 23. In view of the uniqueness and complexity of patent litigation, however, injecting additional complications should be avoided. Class actions, therefore, should be permitted

---

[4] The fact that a dependent claim is in a different statutory class from the independent claim from which it depends does not, in itself, render the dependent claim improper. Thus, if Claim 1 recites a specific product, a claim for the method of making the product of Claim 1 in a particular manner would be a proper dependent claim, since it could not be infringed without infringing Claim 1. Similarly, if Claim 1 recites a method of making a product, a claim for a product made by the method of Claim 1 could be a proper dependent claim. On the other hand, if Claim 1 recites a method of making a specified product, a claim to the product set forth in Claim 1 would not be a proper dependent claim if the product might be made in other ways. [*Commissioner's Notice*, 942 O.G. 15, June 8, 1966—MPEP §608.01(n)].

only after the closest scrutiny and after unequivocal determination that a class action should be the most efficacious, advantageous manner in pursuing the suit. The proponent of a class action bears the burden of showing that the requirements of Rule 23 have been met. *Webcraft Technologies, Inc. v. Alden Press, Inc.*, 228 U.S.P.Q. 182, 183 (Ill. 1985).

℧

A class action for infringement against purchasers, users, and sellers of patented products may be maintained under Fed. R. Civ. P. 23(b)(1)(A). *Standal's Patents Ltd. v. Weyerhauser Co.*, 2 U.S.P.Q.2d 1185, 1190 (Or. 1986).

Clarification.

An amendment is best characterized as a clarification, not an avoidance of the prior art.

[W]hen claim changes or arguments are made in order to more particularly point out the applicant's invention, the purpose is to impart precision, not to overcome prior art. . . . Such prosecution is not presumed to raise and estoppel, but is reviewed on its facts, with the guidance of precedent.

Pall Corp. v. Micron Separations, Inc., 66 F.3d 1211, 1220 , 36 U.S.P.Q.2d 1050 (Fed. Cir. 1995); *James River Corp. of Virginia v. Hallmark Cards Inc.*, 43 U.S.P.Q.2d 1422, 1430, 1431 (Wis. 1997).

Classification. *See also* Classified, Field of Search, Search Record, Statutory Class.

The court stated that it would hesitate to sustain a requirement for division (restriction) solely upon the ground that the different alleged inventions received separate classification in the Patent Office, even though it has been a consistent policy of the courts to recognize that a certain discretion should be and is lodged in the tribunals of the Patent Office relative to the question of division. *In re Young, Young, and Guest,* 173 F.2d 239, 81 U.S.P.Q. 139, 142 (C.C.P.A. 1949).

℧

Separate classification is not necessarily controlling on the question of division (restriction). *Ex parte Musselman,* 94 U.S.P.Q. 212, 213 (PO Bd. App. 1949).

℧

The validity of a patent is strengthened where the principal references urged against the patent are within the classifications noted as searched (in the patent file wrapper), but with the asserted references not noted as pertinent. *Calico Scallop Corp. v. Willis Brothers, Inc.,* 171 U.S.P.Q. 476, 478 (N.C. 1971).

℧

When particular prior art is classified within a class searched by the Examiner, it is presumed that the Examiner considered the art and discarded it as being no more pertinent than that cited by him. *Panduit Corp. v. Burndy Corp.*, 517 F.2d 535, 186 U.S.P.Q. 75, 77 (7th Cir. 1975).

ᛤ

The fact that various groups of compounds (within the scope of a Markush claim) are classified in different subclasses does not mean that it would be repugnant to accepted principles of scientific classification to associate them together as a genus; on the contrary, the fact that all of the claimed compounds share a common cinnamonitrile group and have the capability to dye polyester fibers suggests that it would not be repugnant to scientific classification to associate them together as a genus. *Ex parte Brouard, Leroy, and Stiot*, 201 U.S.P.Q. 538, 540 (PTO Bd. App. 1976).

ᛤ

As all of the claimed compounds are dyes and are coumarin compounds (i.e., have a single structural similarity), the claimed compounds all belong to a subgenus that is not repugnant to scientific classification. Under these circumstances, the claimed compounds are part of a single invention; the requisite "unity of invention" is thus satisfied. *In re Harnisch*, 631 F.2d 716, 206 U.S.P.Q. 300, 305 (C.C.P.A. 1980).

ᛤ

A factor to be considered when determining whether there has been a breach of Canon 4 ("A lawyer should preserve the confidences and secrets of a client.") is whether matters embraced within a pending suit are substantially related to matters or a cause of action for which the attorney previously represented the moving party. Support for the position that the two actions are not substantially related is found in the fact that the U.S. Patent and Trademark Office assigned different classifications to the two patents in question. The argument that the subjects of the two lawsuits are substantially related because they both involve infringements of patents on "agricultural products" was regarded as unpersuasive. *Yetter Manufacturing Co. v. Hiniker Co., Inc.*, 213 U.S.P.Q. 119, 121 (Minn. 1981).

ᛤ

While the diverse Patent Office classification of the references is some evidence of "non-analogy", and cross-references in the official search notes is some evidence of "analogy", the similarities and differences in structure and function of the inventions disclosed in the references carry far greater weight. *In re Mlot-Fijalkowski*, 676 F.2d 666, 213 U.S.P.Q. 713, 715 n.5 (C.C.P.A. 1982).

ᛤ

Reference in a file wrapper to a patent classification area does not compel an inference that the Examiner considered and rejected all prior art in that classification. There simply are too many patents within each patent classification area to assume that an Examiner will consider carefully every patent within a given classification. *Manufacturing Research Corp. v. Graybar Electric Co., Inc.*, 679 F.2d 1355, 215 U.S.P.Q. 29, 35 (11th Cir. 1982).

ᛤ

Classification of plants involves a number of descending categories, each being a subdivision of the one preceding it. Those categories are: Kingdom, Division, Class,

Order, Family, Genus, Species, Variety (also called "cultivar"), Form, and Individual. *Imazio Nursery Inc. v. Dania Greenhouse*, 29 U.S.P.Q.2d 1217, 1220 (Cal. 1992).

Classified. *See also* Classification, Concealment, Search Record.

Classified documents whose security classification was not removed until after the invention of the patent in suit are not prior publications or evidence of prior knowledge as they are not "public" within the meaning of 35 U.S.C. §102(a). These principles are not altered merely because the patentees had a security clearance where there is no evidence of actual knowledge by the patentees of that prior secret work. The mere fact that an individual had a security clearance does not justify the conclusion that he had, or could have had, access to specific secret information. *Del Mar Engineering Laboratories v. United States*, 524 F.2d 1178, 186 U.S.P.Q. 42, 45 (Ct. Cl. 1975).

ᴡ

Reports that are classified at the time a patent issues are not prior art within the meaning of 35 U.S.C. §102 or 103. *Lockheed Aircraft Corp. v. United States*, 190 U.S.P.Q. 134, 142 (Ct. Cl. 1976).

Clayton Act.

The misuse of a patent does not depend on a showing that an improper tying provision of a license may have a substantial effect on competition as is required to establish liability under section 3 of the Clayton Act, 15 U.S.C. §14. *The Duplan Corp. v. Deering Milliken, Inc.*, 444 F. Supp. 648, 197 U.S.P.Q. 342, 385, 386 (S.C. 1977).

Clean Hands.

Courts require clean hands only where unconscionable act has immediate and necessary relation to the equity sought in respect of the matter of litigation. *Xilinx Inc. v. Altera Corp.*, 33 U.S.P.Q.2d 1149, 1153 (Cal. 1994).

Cleaning Composition.

Declaration evidence showed greater-than-additive cleaning performance resulting from the combination of zeolites with a variety of auxiliary builders, in the face of diminished (less than additive) depletion of calcium ions for the combination. The Board agreed that the results for some of the combinations tested for cleaning performance are "better than would be expected." A greater-than-expected result is an evidentiary factor pertinent to the legal conclusion of obviousness vel non of the claims at issue. The Board concluded that the evidence demonstrated synergism "to some degree" with respect to cleaning performance, but observed that appellant's claims were not limited to those specific cobuilders and detergent compositions for which data showing synergism had been submitted. The Board also held that this result, even if unexpected, was not "sufficient to overcome the prima facie case of obviousness established by the prior art."

The court could discern no *prima facie* teaching of the prior art with respect to these compositions of components. The PTO failed to point out any reference that suggests combining a known builder with zeolite, or that this combination would produce a greater-than-additive effect in cleaning performance. The PTO failed to establish a *prima facie* case of obviousness with respect to those claims that require the presence of an auxiliary builder. The Board observed that the combination of zeolite and cobuilder were not, in most instances as reported in the Declaration, superior in cleaning performance to the auxiliary builder alone. This is not the test. In view of the evidence of a result greater than additive, evidencing some unobvious results in the combination of components where the one component is in itself more active than the other is not controlling. The specification teaches that a broad range of surfactants may be used in combination with zeolite plus auxiliary builders. In the absence of prior art suggesting or otherwise making these compositions obvious to one of ordinary skill in the art, there is inadequate support for the PTO's rejection of these claims. The burden on this point has not shifted to the applicant. *In re Corkill*, 771 F.2d 1496, 226 U.S.P.Q. 1005 (Fed. Cir. 1985).

Clear and Convincing.

The "clear and convincing" standard is an intermediate standard between "beyond a reasonable doubt" and a "perponderance of the evidence", evidence which produces in the mind of the factfinder an abiding conviction that the truth of a factual contention is "highly probable." *Buildex Inc. v Kason Indus., Inc.*, 849 F.2d 1461, 1463, 7 U.S.P.Q.2d 1325 (Fed. Cir. 1988).

ʊ

Clear and convincing evidence has been described as evidence that produces in the mind of the trier of fact "an abiding conviction" that the truth of the factual contentions is "highly probable." *Sonoco Products Co. v. Mobil Oil Corp.*, 15 U.S.P.Q.2d 1186, 1191 (S.C. 1989).

Clear Error.

Where a trial judge's finding is based on his decision to credit the testimony of one of two or more witnesses, each of whom has told a coherent and facially plausible story that is not contradicted by extrinsic evidence, that finding, if not internally inconsistent, can virtually never be clear error. *State Industries Inc. v. Mor-Flo Industries Inc.*, 20 U.S.P.Q.2d 1738, 1741 (Fed. Cir. 1991).

Clearly Erroneous.

"A finding is 'clearly erroneous' when although there is evidence to support it, the reviewing court on the entire evidence is left with the definite and firm conviction that a mistake has been committed." *Stryker Corp. v. Intermedics Orthopedics Inc.*, 40 U.S.P.Q.2d 1065, 1068 (Fed. Cir. 1996).

ʊ

The Administrative Procedure Act, in 5 U.S.C. §559, permits, and *stare decisis* warrants continued application of the clearly erroneous standard in review of PTO fact findings by the CAFC. *In re Zurko*, 142 F.3d 1447, 46 U.S.P.Q.2d 1691, 1693 (Fed. Cir. 1998 — *in banc*).

Clemens Test. *See* **Prior Work.**

Clinical Testing.

It is not proper for the Patent Office to require clinical testing in humans to rebut a prima facie case for lack of utility when the pertinent references that establish the prima facie case show in vitro tests and when they do not show in vivo tests employing standard experimental animals. *In re Langer,* 503 F.2d 1380, 183 U.S.P.Q. 288, 297 (C.C.P.A. 1974).

Cloud.

Even though substantially identical language appears in the claims of issued patents and even though the rejection on breadth may cast a cloud on appellant's parent patent, such does not justify reversal of the Examiner's adverse holding. *Ex parte Frey, Hepp, and Morey,* 69 U.S.P.Q. 623, 624 (PO Bd. App. 1946).

Coauthor.

Authorship of an article by itself does not raise a presumption of inventorship with respect to subject matter disclosed in the article. Coauthors may not be presumed to be coinventors merely from the fact of coauthorship. The content and nature of the printed publication, as well as the circumstances surrounding its publication, not merely its authorship, must be considered. Although disclaiming affidavits or declarations by the other authors would end any inquiry, they are not required by the statute or by Rule 132. What is required is a reasonable showing supporting the basis for the applicant's position. *In re Katz,* 687 F.2d 450, 215 U.S.P.Q. 14, 18 (C.C.P.A. 1982).

Coauthors of Publication. *See* **Applicant's Publication, Coauthor.**

Coercion. *See* **Misuse.**

Coined Name.

When a product can be properly defined by its empirical formula together with its physical and chemical characteristics and infrared absorption spectra, it is improper, also, to include claims that define the product by its method of preparation or only by a coined name. As the coined name is not art recognized, product claims that define the product only by the coined name (failing to recite the empirical formula coupled with the chemical and physical characteristics and infrared absorption spectra necessary to identify the product properly) do not adequately define the invention. *Ex parte Brian, Radley, Curtis, and Elson,* 118 U.S.P.Q. 242, 244, 245 (PO Bd. App. 1958).

ω

The use of a coined name to designate a product made by the process defined in a claim does not render the claim indefinite or as failing to point out the invention with requisite particularity. It is relatively immaterial what the product is called in such a process claim as long as it is not misleading or misdescriptive. *Ex parte Brockmann and Bohne,* 127 U.S.P.Q. 57, 60 (PO Bd. App. 1959).

Coinventor.[5] *See also* Co-Owner, Joint Inventors.

A prior contribution of another employee of plaintiff was not prior art, but was adequate to qualify the employee as a coinventor and thus justify granting a motion for conversion by the plaintiff in an infringement action. *Norton Co. v. Carborundum Co.,* 397 F. Supp. 639, 186 U.S.P.Q. 189, 196 (Mass. 1975).

ʊ

The issuance of a patent constitutes notice to the world of its existence. Patent indexes are published weekly, and patent records are readily available to the public. A coinventor is put on constructive notice when a patent issues without listing him as an inventor. A belated inventorship contest can be barred by laches. *Advanced Cardiovascular Systems Inc. v. SciMed Life Systems Inc.,* 20 U.S.P.Q.2d 1870, 1872 (Minn. 1991).

ʊ

A co-inventor need not make a contribution to every claim of a patent. A contribution to one claim is enough. Thus, the critical question for joint conception is who conceived, as that term is used in the patent law, the subject matter of the claim at issue. *Ethicon Inc. v. United States Surgical Corp.,* 135 F.3d 1456, 45 U.S.P.Q.2d 1545, 1548 (Fed. Cir. 1998).

Collaboration.

A joint invention is the product of *collaboration* of the inventive endeavors of two or more persons *working toward the same end* and producing an invention by their *aggregate* efforts. To constitute a joint invention, it is necessary that each of the inventors work on the same subject matter and make some contribution to the inventive thought and to the final result. Each needs to perform but a part of the task if an invention emerges from all of the steps taken together. It is not necessary that the entire inventive concept should occur to each of the joint inventors, or that two should physically work on the project together. One may take a step at one time, another an approach at different times. One may do more of the experimental work while another makes suggestions from time to time. The fact that each of the inventors plays a different role and that the contribution of one may not be as great as that of another does not detract from the fact that the invention is joint if each makes some original contribution, though partial, to the final solution of the problem. *Kimberly-Clark Corp. v. The Procter & Gamble Distributing Co. Inc.,* 972 F.2d 911, 23 U.S.P.Q.2d 1921, 1925, 1926 (Fed. Cir. 1992).

Collateral Attack.

Misrepresentation by a reference patentee to overcome a rejection based on lack of enablement does not provide a basis for precluding availability of the reference patent and raises issues that are not properly considered in an ex parte proceeding in which the reference patentee is not a party. *In re Ludovici and Meola,* 482 F.2d 958, 179 U.S.P.Q. 84, 88 (C.C.P.A. 1973).

---

[5] See dissent in *Ethicon Inc. v. United States Surgical Corp.,* 135 F.3d 1456, 45 U.S.P.Q.2d 1545, 1555 (Fed. Cir. 1998).

Collateral Estoppel. *See also* **Blonder-Tongue Doctrine, Issue Preclusion.**

A patentee moved to dissolve an interference on the ground that his patent claims had not been copied by an applicant prior to one year from the date on which his patent was granted. The Examiner's decision to deny the motion was reversed by the Commissioner, on petition. The interference was dissolved, and the applicant subsequently canceled the claims corresponding to the interference counts. The applicant subsequently urged that he had timely copied the claims in order to overcome the patent as a reference in ex parte prosecution. The applicant was required to reassert the patent claims, and the interference was reinstated. The Commissioner decided (on petition) that the applicant was bound by the Commissioner's prior decision, from which no appeal was taken. From the applicant's cancellation of claims and failure to appeal, it was concluded that applicant had acquiesced in the prior decision and applicant was estopped, on the ground of res judicata, from raising the question of whether he had originally copied the patent claims in timely fashion. *Rubenstein v. Schmidt,* 145 U.S.P.Q. 613 (Comm'r Patents 1965).

ω

When a patent is found invalid or unenforceable in one action, the patentee is collaterally estopped from claiming that the patent is valid or enforceable in another action if the patentee had a full and fair opportunity, procedurally, substantively, and evidentially, to fully litigate the validity of its patent in the prior suit. *Blonder-Tongue Laboratories, Inc. v. University of Illinois Foundation,* 402 U.S. 313, 169 U.S.P.Q. 513, 521 (1971).

ω

In determining the applicability of the estoppel, the first consideration is whether the issue of invalidity common to each action is substantially identical. The issues litigated, not the specific claims around which the issues were framed, are determinative. Only by focusing on the issues, and examining the substance of those issues, can a second court ascertain whether the patentee had the requisite full and fair chance to litigate the validity of his patent in the first suit. By the same token, only by using this approach can an attempt to relitigate the prior decision be revealed. Limiting the application of an estoppel only to specific claims seems to be much too mechanical and ignores the practicalities of patent practice. Collateral estoppel may apply to nonlitigated claims. *Westwood Chemical, Inc. v. United States,* 525 F.2d 1367, 186 U.S.P.Q. 383, 387 (Ct. Cl. 1975).

ω

The public interest in granting valid patents outweighs the public interest underlying collateral estoppel and res judicata, particularly where the issue presented is not substantially identical to that previously decided. *In re Oelrich and Divigard,* 666 F.2d 578, 212 U.S.P.Q. 323, 325 n.2 (C.C.P.A. 1981).

ω

In a prior infringement suit against a different defendant, the validity of plaintiff's patent was upheld, but the claims were narrowly construed. The narrow construction of the claims in the previous litigation was held to bind plaintiff in this action under collateral estoppel principles. *A. B. Dick Co. v. Burroughs Corp.,* 550 F.2d 1065, 218 U.S.P.Q. 90, 94 (Ill. 1982).

ω

The doctrines of *res judicata* and collateral estoppel have been developed to protect litigants from the expense and vexation attending multiple law suits and to conserve judicial resources. They are fully applicable to the patent area. *Shelcore, Inc. v. CBS, Inc.*, 220 U.S.P.Q. 459, 463 (N.J. 1983).

ᛟ

"The requirement that a finding be 'necessary' to a judgment [for collateral estoppel to apply] does not mean that the finding must be so crucial that, without it, the judgment could not stand." *Mother's Restaurant, Inc. v. Mama's Pizza, Inc*, 723 F.2d 1566, 1571, 221 U.S.P.Q. 394, 398 (Fed. Cir. 1983).

ᛟ

Collateral estoppel precludes a party from relitigating issues previously decided in other actions where the following criteria are met: "(1) the issue is identical to one decided in the first action; (2) the issue was actually litigated in the first action; (3) resolution of the issue was essential to a final judgment in the first action; and (4) plaintiff had a full and fair opportunity to litigate the issue in the first action." *A.B. Dick Co. v. Burroughs Corp.*, 713 F.2d 700, 704, 218 U.S.P.Q. 965, 967 (Fed. Cir. 1983), *cert. denied*, 464 U.S. 1042 (1984).

ᛟ

The appellant was initially the senior party and subsequently the losing party in an interference in which the winning party prevailed on the basis of a Convention filing in a foreign country. The Board held that the appellant's claims were not patentably distinct from the subject matter defined by the counts lost in the inteference. The issue here was not obviousness under 35 U.S.C. §103 or so-called interference estoppel. Rather, the Board relied on the more general principle of res judicata and collateral estoppel wherein a judgment previously rendered bars consideration of questions of fact or mixed questions of fact and law that were, or should have been, resolved in earlier litigation. An interference should settle all issues that are decided or that could have been decided. When an applicant loses an interference, the applicant is not entitled to a patent containing claims corresponding to the count or claims that are not patentably distinct from the count. *Ex parte Tytgat, Clerbois, and Noel*, 225 U.S.P.Q. 907 (PTO Bd. App. 1985).

ᛟ

In denying a motion for summary judgment, a district court held that the Examiner's final office action (rejecting all of the patent claims in now terminated reissue/reexamination proceedings) is not entitled to a preclusive effect in that court based on the doctrine of collateral estoppel. *E.I. du Pont de Nemours & Co. v. Phillips Petroleum Co.*, 656 F. Supp. 1343, 2 U.S.P.Q.2d 1545, 1550 (Del. 1987).

ᛟ

A district court held a patent invalid under the doctrine of collateral estoppel because the CCPA affirmed a rejection of the claims of a parent application. The district court erred in not giving proper weight to the patent's presumption of validity. 35 U.S.C. §282 (1982). The presumption of validity carries with it the assumption that evidence considered by the PTO (when granting the patent) was material. In considering a summary judgment motion (in which the facts must be construed in a light most favorable to the non-moving party), the record must show conclusively that the evidence (introduced by the patentee) was immaterial. *Applied Materials Inc. v. Gemini Research Corp.*, 835 F.2d 279, 5 U.S.P.Q.2d 1127, 1129 (Fed. Cir. 1987).

ʊ

Nothing in *Blonder-Tongue*, 402 U.S. 313, 169 U.S.P.Q. 513 (1971), indicates that timing of the decision giving rise to estoppel is critical or that the plea of that defense cannot thereafter be timely made at any stage of the affected proceedings. Raising the issue of estoppel for the first time in a reply brief on appeal was considered timely. *Dana Corp. v. NOK Inc.*, 882 F.2d 505, 11 U.S.P.Q.2d 1883, 1884 (Fed. Cir. 1989).

ʊ

Where a prior adjudication was by a foreign nation's court applying its patent law to its patents, the barriers to reliance on the foreign judgment for collateral estoppel purposes become almost insurmountable. Differences in the law of the two nations and in the detailed language of the patent are emphasized to avoid issue preclusion in a patent case pending in this country even where the invention, the technological and economic competition between the parties, and the consequences of the judgments are for all practical purposes the same. Even if the court in this country were to apply collateral estoppel to certain factual findings made by a British court as opposed to importing its legal conclusions wholesale, it is not clear that trial time would be significantly shortened. Furthermore, the Federal Circuit's reluctance to give collateral estoppel effect to foreign judgments would seem to apply to foreign findings of fact insofar as those findings involve mixed questions of fact and foreign law. It is a quiddity of our law that a well and thoroughly reasoned decision reached by a highly skilled and scientifically informed justice of the Patent Court, Chancery Division, in the High Court of Justice of Great Britain after four weeks of trial must be ignored, and essentially the same issues with the same evidence must now be retried by American jurors with no background in science or patents, whose average formal education will be no more than high school. This curious event is the result of the world's chauvinistic view of patents. *Cuno Inc. v. Pall Corp.*, 729 F. Supp. 234, 14 U.S.P.Q.2d 1815, 1819 (N.Y. 1989).

ʊ

After a patentee prevailed in an infringement action based on his Canadian patent, he initiated an infringement action against the same party with regard to the same product based on his corresponding U.S. patent. Although a court may not say that a U.S. patent is valid and infringed because a corresponding Canadian patent is valid and infringed, it is commonplace for courts in the United States to employ issue preclusion (collateral estoppel) even when claim preclusion is unavailable. When a foreign court renders judgment on a question of fact with significance in each system of law, there is no reason not to take over that decision. *Vas-Cath Inc. v. Mahurkar*, 745 F. Supp. 517, 17 U.S.P.Q.2d 1353, 1359 (Ill. 1990).

ʊ

Once an issue is actually and necessarily determined by a court of competent jurisdiction, that determination is conclusive in subsequent suits based on a different cause of action involving a party to the prior litigation. *In re Convertible Rowing Exerciser Patent Litigation*, 814 F.Supp. 1197, 26 U.S.P.Q.2d 1677, 1680 (Del. 1993).

ʊ

The principle of collateral estoppel, also called issue preclusion, protects a defendant from the burden of litigating an issue that has been fully and fairly tried in a prior action and decided against the plaintiff. The defendant must show that, in the prior action, the party against whom estoppel is sought had a full and fair opportunity to litigate the issue; the issue was actually litigated; the controlling facts and applicable legal rules were the same in both actions; resolution of the particular issue was essential to the final judgment in the first action; and the identical issue was decided in the first action. *Comair Rotron Inc. v. Nippon Densan Corp.*, 49 F.3d 1535, 33 U.S.P.Q.2d 1929, 1930 (Fed. Cir. 1995).

ϖ

"Collateral estoppel is inapplicable when there has been a subsequent modification of the *significant facts or a change or development in the controlling legal principles, statute or case law, which may have the effect of making the first determination obsolete or erroneous, at least for future purposes.*" Prior decisions generally act as collateral estoppel; however, "where the situation is vitally altered between the time of the first judgment and the second, the prior determination is not conclusive... [and] a judicial declaration intervening between the two proceedings may so change the legal atmosphere as to render the rule of collateral estoppel inapplicable." *Al-Site Corp. v. VSI International Inc.*, 36 U.S.P.Q.2d 1054, 1055, 1056 (Fla. 1995).

ϖ

Collateral estoppel based on default judgments is undesirable. *Artmatic USA Cosmetics v. Maybelline Co.*, 906 F.Supp. 850, 38 U.S.P.Q.2d 1037, 1041 (N.Y. 1995).

ϖ

Application of collateral estoppel to a legal action based on an equitable determination does not violate Seventh Amendment right to a jury trial. *Texas Instruments Inc. v. Cypress Semiconductor Corp.*, 90 F.3d 1558, 39 U.S.P.Q.2d 1492, 1501 n.10 (Fed. Cir. 1996).

Collateral Order Doctrine. ***See also*** **Interlocutory Order.**

There is a "small class" of decisions that, although not final in the sense that they terminate the litigation, are reviewable because they "finally determine claims of right separable from and collateral to, rights asserted in the action, too important to be denied review and too independent of the cause itself to require that appellate consideration be deferred until the whole case is adjudicated." For appealability, an order a) must "conclusively determine the disputed question", b) must "resolve an important issue completely separate from the merits of the action", and c) must be "effectively unreviewable on appeal from a final judgment." *Emerson Electric Co. v. Daviol Inc.*, 88 F.3d 1051, 39 U.S.P.Q.2d 1474, 1475 (Fed. Cir. 1996).

Color.

Where a claimed product and that of a reference have the same utility, any change in the form, purity, color, or any of the other characteristics of the claimed product does not render the product patentable. Not only do the asserted color and stability changes in appellant's product appear as inherent properties in the pure crystalline form but also, because these differences do not change the utility of the product, patentability is not conferred thereon. *Ex parte Hartop,* 139 U.S.P.Q. 525, 527 (PO Bd. App. 1963).

ꞷ

Although the exact color or shade of the claimed isomer was unpredictable, it was not unexpected; it was a shade somewhere in the family of reddish tints encompassed by a reference disclosure. Absolute predictability is not the law. *In re Crounse,* 363 F.2d 881, 150 U.S.P.Q. 554, 557 (C.C.P.A. 1966).

Combination. *See also* **Aggregation, Combination Invention, Combination of Elements, Combining References, Combining Steps, New Combination, Old Combination, Packaging Material, Recipe, Selection.**

In a patentable combination of old elements, all the constituents must enter into it such that each qualifies every other. It must either form a new machine of a distinct character and function or produce a result due to the joint and cooperating action of all the elements, which is not the mere adding together of separate contributions. Otherwise, it is only a mechanical juxtaposition and not a vital union. *Pickering v. McCullough,* 104 U.S. (14 Otto) 310, 318 (1881).

ꞷ

In patents for combinations of mechanisms, limitations and provisos imposed by the inventor, especially such as were introduced into an application after it had been persistently rejected, must be strictly construed against the inventor and in favor of the public, and looked upon as in the nature of disclaimers. *Sargent v. Hall & Safe Lock Co.,* 114 U.S. 63 (1885).

ꞷ

Although the patentee had merely changed the pitch of the Fourdrinier wire of a paper-making machine, the change in pitch was regarded as directed toward a wholly different object from that of the prior art. *Eibel Process Co. v. Minnesota & Ontario Paper Co.,* 261 U.S. 45, 67 (1923).

ꞷ

If an applicant has taken one feature from one patented device and another feature from another patented device and combined them, and has produced no results other than were produced by the original devices in their individual operation, then he has invented nothing. *Hugh W. Batcheller v. Henry Cole Co.,* 7 F. Supp. 898, 22 U.S.P.Q. 354, 357 (Mass. 1934).

ꞷ

A combination of a device and the material upon which the device works is not patentable. *In re Hodler,* 73 F.2d 507, 23 U.S.P.Q. 317 (C.C.P.A. 1934).

ꞷ

Where a class of materials that does not pertain to the essence of the invention is claimed, the need for the precise definition of that class is not so pressing. *Ex parte Dubbs and Stevens,* 119 U.S.P.Q. 440, 441 (PO Bd. App. 1958).

ꞷ

The mere fact that it is possible to find two isolated disclosures that might be combined in such a way to produce a new compound does not necessarily render such production obvious unless the art also contains something to suggest the desirability of the proposed combination. *In re Bergel and Stock,* 292 F.2d 955, 130 U.S.P.Q. 206. (C.C.P.A. 1961).

ʊ

The word "combination" in 35 U.S.C. §112 includes "not only a combination of mechanical elements, but also a combination of substances in a composition claim, or steps in a process claim." All elements of a combination can be claimed in terms of what they do as well as in terms of what they are. *In re Fuetterer,* 319 F.2d 259, 138 U.S.P.Q. 217, 222 (C.C.P.A. 1963).

ʊ

One element of a combination claim, though an old element, may serve to distinguish from the art by making a new combination, and the same is true of the recitation of this old feature when taken in conjunction with the other recited features. *In re Civitello,* 339 F.2d 243, 144 U.S.P.Q. 10, 13 (C.C.P.A. 1964).

ʊ

From the standpoint of patent law, a composition of matter is, as stated in *Robinson on Patents* §193 (1890):

> ...always a true combination. Each of its ingredients is itself a means whose operative forces manifest themselves through the chemical or mechanical properties by which it is distinguished.... It differs from all other combinations in that its ingredients, or elemental means, when once united in the combination, often become individually undiscernible by human sense, and can be recovered and distinguished only by the destruction of the combination as a whole.

The character of a new composition of individually old substances cannot, therefore, be determined from an examination of its component elements alone. It must be judged rather by the intrinsic attributes of the composition as a new combination. See *Robinson on Patents* §194 (1890). *In re Henderson,* 348 F.2d 550, 146 U.S.P.Q. 372, 373 (C.C.P.A. 1965).

ʊ

Claims to a resin per se are not directed to the same invention as patent claims to a hair-setting composition comprising the resin dispersed in a solvent. *In re Walles, Tousignant, and Houtman,* 366 F.2d 786, 151 U.S.P.Q. 185, 189 (C.C.P.A. 1966).

ʊ

In cases of inventions for combinations (and this includes chemical compositions) the elements thereof need not be so precisely defined. *Ex parte Dobson, Jacob, and Herschler,* 165 U.S.P.Q. 29 (PTO Bd. App. 1969).

ʊ

The word combination includes not only a combination of mechanical elements but also a combination of substances in a composition claim, or steps in a process claim. All "compositions of matter" are combinations if they consist of two more substances in some degree of corelationship. Chemical compounds are clearly included as one kind of composition of matter. *In re Barr, Williams, and Whitmore,* 444 F.2d 588, 170 U.S.P.Q. 330 (C.C.P.A. 1971).

ᴡ

It is always possible to put something into a combination to render it inoperative. It is not the function of claims to exclude all such matters, but to point out what the combination is. *In re Anderson,* 471 F.2d 1237, 176 U.S.P.Q. 331, 335 (C.C.P.A. 1973).

ᴡ

When a patent claims only a combination, no element thereof (not separately patented) is entitled to patent protection. *Biuro Projektow Zaklodow Przerobki Mechanicznej Wegla "Separator" v. UOP, Inc.,* 203 U.S.P.Q. 175, 179 (Ill. 1979).

ᴡ

An applicant is entitled to the benefit of the filing dates of respective parent applications when the present application has not combined bits and pieces of previously disclosed and claimed subject matter, but has consolidated the two parent disclosures into a single unitary concept. *Ex parte Janin,* 209 U.S.P.Q. 761, 764 (PTO Bd. App. 1979).

ᴡ

The "evidence" was that use of vertical heights for range finding, use of multiple elements on a site, and use of circular apertures were each known in the art, but the court concluded that the prior art lacked any teaching or suggestion to combine the separate features in a manner permitting use of circular apertures for simultaneous range finding and aiming. Obviousness cannot be established by combining the teachings of the prior art to produce the claimed invention, absent some teaching, suggestion, or incentive supporting the combination. *Carela v. Starlight Archery,* 804 F.2d 135, 231 U.S.P.Q. 644 (Fed. Cir. 1986).

ᴡ

Literal infringement requires that an accused device embody every element of a claim as properly interpreted. If the claim describes a combination of functions, and each function is performed by a means described in the specification or an equivalent of such means, then literal infringement holds. When a claimed invention is a novel combination of steps, all possible methods of carrying out each step of the combination are not required to be described in the specification. Correctly construed claims cover "equivalents" of the described embodiments. The purpose is to grant an inventor of a combination invention a fair scope that is not dependent on a catalog of alternative embodiments in the specification. The court has cautioned against limiting the claimed invention to preferred embodiments or specific examples in the specification. The details of performing each step need not be included in the claims unless required to distinguish the claimed invention from the prior art, or otherwise to specifically point out and distinctly claim the invention. Claims should be read in a way that avoids enabling an infringer to "practice a fraud on a patent."

It is not required that those skilled in the art knew, at the time the patent application was filed, of the asserted equivalent means of performing the claimed functions; that equivalence is determined as of the time infringement takes place. Infringement will be found when the material features of a patent have been appropriated, even when those features have been patentably improved. *Texas Instruments, Inc. v. U.S. International Trade Commission*, 805 F.2d 1558, 231 U.S.P.Q. 833 (Fed. Cir. 1986).

ϖ

The motivation to make a specific structure is not abstract, but practical, and is always related to the properties or uses one skilled in the art would expect the structure to have if made. The critical inquiry is whether there is something in the prior art as a whole to suggest the desirability, and thus the obviousness, of making the combination. *In re Newell*, 891 F.2d 899, 13 U.S.P.Q.2d 1248, 1250 (Fed. Cir. 1989).

ϖ

When a claimed invention is not identically disclosed in a reference, and instead requires picking and choosing among a number of different options disclosed by the reference, then the reference does not anticipate. *Mendenhall v. Astec Industries, Inc.*, 13 U.S.P.Q.2d 1913, 1928 (Tenn. 1988), *aff'd*, 13 U.S.P.Q.2d 1956 (Fed. Cir. 1989).

ϖ

Where the invention is a combination of elements, an undisclosed prior art reference that contains more of the combined elements than the disclosed references is not cumulative simply because various elements of the invention appear in other disclosed references. *Semiconductor Energy Laboratory Co. v. Samsung Electronics Co.*, 4 F. Supp. 2d 477, 46 U.S.P.Q.2d 1874, 1878 (Va. 1998).

Combination Invention.

The fact that a patent specifically discloses and claims a combination of features previously used in two separate devices is not fatal to patentability. A basic issue is whether applied references, alone or in any combination, suggest the claimed invention as a solution to the specific problem solved. The claimed invention achieved new and unexpected results nowhere suggested in the prior art, and that achievement was overlooked. The district court erroneously focused its inquiry "solely on the product created, rather than on the obviousness or non-obviousness of its creation." The initial inquiry should be directed to the vantage point of attacking the problem solved by the invention at the time the invention was made. When prior art itself does not suggest or render "obvious" the claimed solution to that problem, the art involved does not satisfy the criteria of 35 U.S.C. §103 for precluding patentability. *Lindemann Maschinenfabrik GmbH v. American Hoist and Derrick Co.*, 730 F.2d 1452, 221 U.S.P.Q. 481 (Fed. Cir. 1984).

ϖ

Declaration evidence showed greater-than-additive cleaning performance resulting from the combination of zeolites with a variety of auxiliary builders, in the face of diminished (less than additive) depletion of calcium ions for the combination. The Board agreed that the results for some of the combinations tested for cleaning performance are "better than would be expected." A greater-than-expected result is an evidentiary factor pertinent to the legal conclusion of obviousness vel non of the claims at issue. The Board concluded that the evidence demonstrated synergism "to some degree" with respect to cleaning performance, but observed that appellant's claims were not limited to those specific cobuilders and detergent compositions for which data showing synergism had been submitted. The Board also held that this result, even if unexpected, was not "sufficient to overcome the *prima facie* case of obviousness established by the prior art."

The court could discern no prima facie teaching of the prior art with respect to these compositions of components. The PTO failed to point out any reference that suggests combining a known builder with zeolite, or that this combination would produce a greater-than-additive effect in cleaning performance. The PTO failed to establish a *prima facie* case of obviousness with respect to those claims that require the presence of an auxiliary builder. The Board observed that the combination of zeolite and cobuilder were not, in most instances as reported in the Declaration, superior in cleaning performance to the auxiliary builder alone. This is not the test. In view of the evidence of a result greater than additive, evidencing some unobvious results in the combination of components where the one component is in itself more active than the other is not controlling. The specification teaches that a broad range of surfactants may be used in combination with zeolite plus auxiliary builders. In the absence of prior art suggesting or otherwise making these compositions obvious to one of ordinary skill in the art, there is inadequate support for the PTO's rejection of these claims. The burden on this point has not shifted to the applicant. *In re Corkill,* 771 F.2d 1496, 226 U.S.P.Q. 1005 (Fed. Cir. 1985).

ᛒ

Presuming arguendo that the references show the elements or concepts urged, the Examiner presented no line of reasoning as to why the artisan reviewing only the collective teachings of the references would have found it obvious to selectively pick and choose various elements and/or concepts from the several references relied on to arrive at the claimed invention. In the instant application, the Examiner has done little more than cite references to show that one or more elements or some combinations thereof, when each is viewed in a vacuum, is known. The claimed invention, however, is clearly directed to a combination of elements. That is to say, the appellant does not claim that he has invented one or more new elements but has presented claims to a new combination of elements. To support the conclusion that the claimed combination is directed to obvious subject matter, either the references must expressly or impliedly suggest the claimed combination or the Examiner must present a convincing line of reasoning as to why the artisan would have found the claimed invention to have been obvious in light of the teachings of the references. The Board found nothing in the references that would expressly or impliedly teach or suggest the modifications urged by the Examiner. Additionally, the Board found no line of reasoning in the answer as to why the artisan would have found the modifications urged by the Examiner to have been obvious. Based upon the record, the artisan would not have found it obvious to selectively pick and choose elements or concepts from the various references so as to arrive at the claimed invention without using the claims as a guide. *Ex parte Clapp,* 227 U.S.P.Q. 972 (B.P.A.I. 1985).

ᛒ

Although each of the references does teach in general what the Examiner asserts it teaches, the rejection under 35 U.S.C. §103 fails because there is no concept in any of the art relied upon, either express or implied, of providing a composition that includes both interferon and a tyrosinase inhibitor. None of the art teaches increasing the effectiveness of interferon. Also, none of the art teaches inhibiting the patient's serum tyrosinase as it increases concomitantly with the interferon treatment. *Ex parte Rubin*, 5 U.S.P.Q.2d 1461 (B.P.A.I. 1987).

Combination of Elements. *See also* **Combination, Combining References, Prior Art Anagrams.**

In every mechanical combination, whether patentable or not, the function of the combination is bound to be the "sum of the old function of the individual elements." Mechanical elements can do no more than contribute to the combination the mechanical functions of which they are inherently capable. The patentability of combinations has always depended on the unobviousness of the combination per se. *In re Menough*, 324 F.2d 1011, 139 U.S.P.Q. 278, 281 (C.C.P.A. 1963).

ω

Casting an invention as "a combination of old elements" leads improperly to an analysis of the claimed invention by the parts, not by the whole. The critical inquiry is whether there is something in the prior art as a whole to suggest the desirability, and thus the obviousness, of making the combination. A traditional problem with focusing on a patent as a combination of old elements is the attendant notion that patentability is undeserving without some "synergistic" or "different" effect. Here, the district court spoke of the need for "a new and useful result." Such tests for patentability have been soundly rejected by this court. Though synergism is relevant when present, its "absence has no place in evaluating the evidence on obviousness." *Custom Accessories Inc. v. Jeffrey-Allan Industries, Inc.*, 807 F.2d 955, 1 U.S.P.Q.2d 1196 (Fed. Cir. 1986).

Combining. *See also* **Mental Steps.**

The inclusion in a patent of a claim to a process that may be performed by a person, but that also is capable of being performed by a machine, is not fatal to patentability. The presence of the steps of correlating and combining, which a machine is capable of doing, does not invalidate a patent. *Alco Standard Corp. v. Tennessee Valley Authority*, 808 F.2d 1490, 1 U.S.P.Q.2d 1337, 1341 (Fed. Cir. 1986).

Combining Priority Applications.

An applicant cannot combine multiple priority applications to obtain an earlier filing date for an individual claim. *Studiengesellschaft Kohle m.b.H. v. Shell Oil Co.*, 112 F.3d 1561, 42 U.S.P.Q.2d 1674, 1676 (Fed. Cir. 1997).

Combining References. *See also* **Analogous Art, Combination Invention, Combining Steps, Destroy, Hindsight, Motivation, Piecemeal, Prima Facie, Problem, Retrospective Reconstruction, Same Art.**

When a person, having the references before him and not being cognizant of applicant's disclosure, would not be informed that a problem (solved by applicant's claimed invention) ever existed, such references (which never recognized the problem) could not have suggested its solution. The references were thus improperly combined since there is no suggestion in either of them that they can be combined to produce the result obtained by the claimed invention. *In re Shaffer,* 229 F.2d 476, 108 U.S.P.Q. 326, 329 (C.C.P.A. 1956).

ω

The mere fact that it is possible to find two isolated disclosures that might be combined in such a way as to produce a new compound does not necessarily render such production obvious unless the art also contains something to suggest the desirability of the proposed combination. *In re Bergel,* 292 F.2d 955, 130 U.S.P.Q. 206, 208 (C.C.P.A. 1961).

ω

The test for combining references is not what the individual references themselves suggest, but rather what the combination of disclosures, taken as a whole, would suggest to one of ordinary skill in the art. Any judgment on obviousness is in a sense necessarily a reconstruction based upon hindsight reasoning, but so long as it takes into account only knowledge that was within the level of ordinary skill at the time the claimed invention was made and does not include knowledge gleaned only from applicant's disclosure, such a reconstruction is proper. *In re McLaughlin,* 443 F.2d 1392, 170 U.S.P.Q. 209, 212 (C.C.P.A. 1971).

ω

A basic mandate inherent in 35 U.S.C. §103 is that "a piecemeal reconstruction of prior art patents in the light of appellants' disclosure" shall not be the basis for a holding of obviousness. *In re Kamm and Young,* 452 F.2d 1052, 172 U.S.P.Q. 298, 301 (C.C.P.A. 1972).

ω

References cannot properly be combined with each other when such would result in destroying that on which the invention of one of the references is based. *Ex parte Hartmann,* 186 U.S.P.Q. 366, 367 (PTO Bd. App. 1974).

ω

Although references may be combined to show that a claim is unpatentable, they may not be combined indiscriminately. To determine whether a combination of references is proper, the following criterion is often used: namely, whether the prior art suggests doing what an applicant has done. It is not enough for a valid rejection to view the prior art in retrospect once an applicant's disclosure is known. *In re Skoll,* 523 F.2d 1392, 187 U.S.P.Q. 481, 484 (C.C.P.A. 1975).

ω

There must be some logical reason apparent from positive, concrete evidence of record that justifies a combination of primary and secondary references. *In re Regel, Buchel, and Plempel,* 526 F.2d 1399, 188 U.S.P.Q. 136, 139 (C.C.P.A. 1975).

ω

A reference must not be considered in a vacuum, but against the background of the other references of record that may disprove theories and speculations in a reference, or reveal previously undiscovered or unappreciated problems. The question in a 35 U.S.C. §103 case is what the references would collectively suggest to one of ordinary skill in the art. It is only by proceeding in this manner that we may fairly determine the scope and content of the prior art according to the mandate of *Graham v. John Deere Co.* [383 U.S. 1, 17, 148 U.S.P.Q. 459, 467 (1966)]. Therefore, combining the references would not have rendered obvious the particle-size limitation or the particular volume-percent limitation, and certainly not the subject matter as a whole, which encompasses these limitations. *In re Ehrreich and Avery,* 590 F.2d 902, 200 U.S.P.Q. 504 (C.C.P.A. 1979).

ʊ

The person of ordinary skill in the art at the time of the patentee's invention is presumed to have before him all of the relevant prior art. In this particular case the available art shows each of the elements of the claims in suit. Armed with this information, would it then be non-obvious to this person of ordinary skill in the art to coordinate these elements in the same manner as the claims in suit? The difficulty that attaches to all honest attempts to answer this question can be attributed to the strong temptation to rely on hindsight while undertaking this evaluation. It is wrong to use the patent in suit as a guide through the maze of prior art references, combining the right references in the right way so as to achieve the results of the claims in suit. Monday morning quarterbacking is quite improper when resolving the question of non-obviousness in a court of law. *Orthopaedic Equipment Co. v. United States,* 702 F.2d 1005, 217 U.S.P.Q. 193 (Fed. Cir. 1983).

ʊ

The law does not require an express suggestion in a prior-art reference to make a claimed combination obvious. The proper test is whether the references, taken as a whole, would suggest the invention of one of ordinary skill in the art. *Milliken Research Corp. v. Dan River, Inc.,* 739 F.2d 587, 222 U.S.P.Q. 571, 583 (Fed. Cir. 1984).

ʊ

In the absence of evidence that suggests the desirability of combining references in a proposed manner, such combination is not available to preclude patentability under 35 U.S.C. §103. *King Instrument Corp. v. Otari Corp.,* 767 F.2d 853, 226 U.S.P.Q. 402 (Fed. Cir. 1985).

ʊ

In determining validity of a patent claim, it is not enough to show that each of the components of the claim was known and had been used in other similar systems. Guided by the defendants, the court below treated each reference as teaching one or more of the specific components for use in the patented system, although the patented system did not then exist. Thus, the court reconstructed the patented system, using the blueprint of the patent claims. This is legal error. *Interconnect Planning Corp. v. Feil,* 774 F.2d 1132, 227 U.S.P.Q. 543, 548 (Fed. Cir. 1985).

ʊ

To combine references (A) and (B) properly to reach the conclusion that the subject matter of a patent would have been obvious, case law requires that there must be some teaching, suggestion, or inference in either reference (A) or (B), or both, or knowledge generally available to one of ordinary skill in the relevant art that would lead one skilled in the art to combine the relevant teachings of references (A) and (B). Consideration must be given to teachings in the references that would have led one skilled in the art away from the claimed invention. A claim cannot properly be used as a blueprint for extracting individual teachings from references. *Ashland Oil, Inc. v. Delta Resins & Refractories, Inc.*, 776 F.2d 281, 227 U.S.P.Q. 657 (Fed. Cir. 1985).

ᛦ

Presuming arguendo that the references show the elements or concepts urged, the Examiner presented no line of reasoning as to why the artisan reviewing only the collective teachings of the references would have found it obvious to selectively pick and choose various elements and/or concepts from the several references relied on to arrive at the claimed invention. In the instant application, the Examiner has done little more than cite references to show that one or more elements or some combinations thereof, when each is viewed in a vacuum, is known. The claimed invention, however, is clearly directed to a combination of elements. That is to say, the appellant does not claim that he has invented one or more new elements but has presented claims to a new combination of elements. To support the conclusion that the claimed combination is directed to obvious subject matter, either the references must expressly or impliedly suggest the claimed combination or the Examiner must present a convincing line of reasoning as to why the artisan would have found the claimed invention to have been obvious in light of the teachings of the references. The Board found nothing in the references that would expressly or impliedly teach or suggest the modifications urged by the Examiner. Additionally, the Board found no line of reasoning in the answer as to why the artisan would have found the modifications urged by the Examiner to have been obvious. Based upon the record, the artisan would not have found it obvious to selectively pick and choose elements or concepts from the various references so as to arrive at the claimed invention without using the claims as a guide. *Ex parte Clapp*, 227 U.S.P.Q. 972 (B.P.A.I. 1985).

ᛦ

There was "evidence" that use of vertical heights for range finding, use of multiple elements on a site, and use of circular apertures were each known in the art, but the prior art lacked any teaching or suggestion to combine the separate features in a manner permitting use of circular apertures for simultaneous range finding and aiming. Obviousness cannot be established by combining the teachings of the prior art to produce the claimed invention, absent some teaching, suggestion, or incentive supporting the combination. *Carela v. Starlight Archery*, 804 F.2d 135, 231 U.S.P.Q. 644 (Fed. Cir. 1986).

ᛦ

To combine references to reach a conclusion that claimed subject matter would have been obvious, case law requires that there must be some teaching, suggestion, or inference in either reference, or in both, or knowledge generally available that would have led one of ordinary skill in the relevant art to combine the relevant teachings of the references. When the incentive to combine the teachings of the references is not readily apparent, it is the duty of the Examiner to explain why a combination of the reference teachings is proper. Absent such reasons or incentives, the teachings of the references are not combinable. *Ex parte Skinner,* 2 U.S.P.Q.2d 1788 (B.P.A.I. 1986).

ത

Elements of separate prior patents cannot be combined when there is no suggestion of such combination anywhere in those patents. *Panduit Corp. v. Dennison Manufacturing Co.,* 810 F.2d 1561, 1 U.S.P.Q.2d 1593 (Fed. Cir. 1987).

ത

Although the fact that each of the three components of the composition used in the claimed method was conventionally employed in the art for treating cooling water systems, to employ these components in combination for their known functions and to optimize the amount of each additive were not regarded as obvious. Obviousness cannot be established by combining the teachings of the prior art to produce a claimed invention, absent some teaching, suggestion, or incentive supporting the combination. At best, in view of the prior art, one skilled in the art might find it obvious to try various combinations of these known scale and corrosion prevention agents. This is not the standard of 35 U.S.C. §103. *In re Geiger,* 815 F.2d 686, 2 U.S.P.Q.2d 1276 (Fed. Cir. 1987).

ത

When prior art references require a selective combination to render obvious a subsequent invention, there must be some reason for the combination other than the hindsight gleaned from the invention itself. Something in the prior art as a whole must suggest the desirability, and thus the obviousness, of making the combination. It is impermissible to use the claims as a frame and the prior art references as a mosaic to piece together a facsimile of the claimed invention. *Uniroyal Inc. v. Rudkin-Wiley Corp.,* 837 F.2d 1044, 5 U.S.P.Q.2d 1434 (Fed. Cir. 1988).

ത

There must be some logical reason apparent from positive, concrete evidence of record that justifies a combination of primary and secondary references. *In re Laskowski,* 871 F.2d 115, 10 U.S.P.Q.2d 1397 (Fed. Cir. 1989).

ത

Providing substitution on a ring of a herbicidally active compound by finding another herbicidally active compound with the same ring and desired optional constituents is not enough to preclude patentability of a claimed herbicide. In the chemical arts the mere fact that it is possible to find two isolated disclosures that might be combined in such a way to produce a new compound does not necessarily render such production obvious unless the art also contains something to suggest the desirability of the proposed combination. In the absence of an express or implied suggestion in at least one of the references that the specifically claimed substitution would be desirable for herbicide compounds other than those of the specific class disclosed in one reference, patentability is not precluded. The mere fact that both references originate from the herbicide art does not provide any teaching or suggestion to combine them. Nor does the fact that both references concern compounds containing a specific ring suggest that substituents suitable in one case would be expected to be suitable in the other. *In re Levitt,* 11 U.S.P.Q.2d 1315, 1316 (Fed. Cir. 1989—unpublished).

ω

Where claimed subject matter has been rejected as obvious in view of a combination of prior-art references, a proper analysis under 35 U.S.C. §103 requires, inter alia, consideration of two factors: (1) whether the prior art would have suggested to those of ordinary skill in the art that they should make the claimed composition or device, or carry out the claimed process; and (2) whether the prior art would also have revealed that, in so making or carrying out, those of ordinary skill would have a reasonable expectation of success. Both the suggestion and the reasonable expectation of success must be founded in the prior art, not in the applicant's disclosure. *In re Vaeck,* 947 F.2d 488, 20 U.S.P.Q.2d 1438, 1442 (Fed. Cir. 1991).

ω

Before the PTO may combine the disclosures of two or more prior art references in order to establish *prima facie* obviousness, there must be some suggestion for doing so, found either in the references themselves or in the knowledge generally available to one of ordinary skill in the art. *In re Jones,* 958 F.2d 347, 21 U.S.P.Q.2d 1941, 1943 (Fed. Cir. 1992).

ω

The question in design cases, as distinguished from utility or "mechanical" cases, is "not whether the references sought to be combined are in analogous arts in the mechanical sense, but whether they are so related that the appearance of certain ornamental features in one would suggest the application of those features to the other." *Ex parte Pappas,* 23 U.S.P.Q.2d 1636, 1638 (B.P.A.I. 1992).

ω

The fact that the Examiner's conclusion of obviousness can be seen to be proper when based upon fewer references than relied upon in the rejection does not necessarily amount to a new ground of rejection. *Ex parte Raychem Corp.,* 25 U.S.P.Q.2d 1265, 1272 (B.P.A.I. 1992).

ω

Motivation for combining teachings of various references need not be explicitly found in the references themselves. The Examiner may provide an explanation based on logic and sound scientific reasoning that will support a holding of obviousness. However, an Examiner's mere assertion that one of ordinary skill in the relevant art would have been able to arrive at a claimed invention because he had the necessary skills to carry out the requisite process steps is an inappropriate standard for obviousness. *Ex parte Levengood,* 28 U.S.P.Q.2d 1300, 1301 (B.P.A.I. 1993).

ω

If the invention is different from what is disclosed in one reference, but the differences are such that combination with another reference would lead to what is claimed, the obviousness question then requires inquiry as to whether there is reason, suggestion, or motivation to make that combination. Such a suggestion may come expressly from the references themselves. It may come from knowledge of those skilled in the art that certain references, or disclosures in the references, are known to be of special interest or importance in the particular field. It may also come from the nature of a problem to be solved, leading inventors to look to references relating to possible solutions to that problem. *Pro-Mold and Tool Co. v. Great Lakes Plastics Inc.*, 75 F.3d 1568, 37 U.S.P.Q.2d 1626, 1630 (Fed. Cir. 1996).

ϖ

Even when a claimed invention only involves the physical insertion of one reference's component into another reference's composite, such simplicity alone is not determinative of obviousness. *See In re Oetiker*, 977 F.2d 1443, 1447, 24 U.S.P.Q.2d 1443, 1446 (Fed. Cir. 1992)("Simplicity is not inimical to patentability." *The Gentry Gallery Inc. v. The Berkline Corp.*, 134 F.3d 1473, 45 U.S.P.Q.2d 1498, 1502 (Fed. Cir. 1998).

ϖ

Three possible sources for a motivation to combine references are: the nature of the problem to be solved, the teachings of the prior art, and the knowledge of persons of ordinary skill in the art. *In re Rouffet*, 149 F.3d 1350, 47 U.S.P.Q.2d 1453, 1458 (Fed. Cir. 1998).

Combining Steps.

To select the best steps of prior-art processes and combine them into a single method is not inventive when the combination is such as would be obvious to the skilled worker in the art and the result achieved is such as would be expected therefrom. *In re Petersen*, 223 F.2d 508, 106 U.S.P.Q. 281 (C.C.P.A. 1955).

ϖ

It is logical and reasonable to infer that one teaching a chemical reaction process would set out the least number of reactions thought necessary to accomplish the desired objective. Thus, one skilled in the art who reads the teaching would have to presume that, if the reactants were not combined in the manner shown, some adverse side reaction or no reaction at all would occur. *In re Freed*, 425 F.2d 785, 165 U.S.P.Q. 570, 572 (C.C.P.A. 1970).

Comity.

Federal courts are obliged to give comity to state courts and not to assume expertise where none may lie. *Loral Fairchild Corp. v. Matsushita Electric Industrial Co. Ltd.*, 840 F.Supp. 211, 31 U.S.P.Q.2d 1499, 1504 (Cal. 1994).

ϖ

Principles of international comity, or mutual respect of sovereigns, direct that United States courts, when possible, should recognize and enforce foreign judgments. *Glaverbel Societe Anonyme v. Northlake Marketing & Supply Inc.*, 48 U.S.P.Q.2d 1344, 1346 (Fed. Cir. 1998).

Commensurate. *See also* **Commensurate in Scope, Evidence Commensurate with Claimed Scope.**

An attorney is charged with the responsibility of getting patent claims which are commensurate with his client's invention. *Ex parte Bielstein*, 135 U.S.P.Q. 402, 404 (PO Bd. App. 1962).

ᚖ

The application and the claims affirmatively set up an equivalence between crabgrass and all other "undesired vegetation" insofar as the herbicidal effectiveness of the instant compounds is concerned. The Examiner cited no art, and the Board referred to none, that would show that proof of criticality with respect to crabgrass was insufficient with respect to other undesired vegetation. *In re Lemin*, 332 F.2d 839, 141 U.S.P.Q. 814, 816 (C.C.P.A. 1964).

ᚖ

Even if proof of utility of the claimed invention as an anti-arthritic agent for humans is lacking, there remains the proven utility as an anti-arthritic agent for lower animals. Having found that the claimed composition has utility as contemplated in the specification, 35 U.S.C. §101 is satisfied, and it is unnecessary to decide whether it is in fact useful for the other purposes indicated in the specification as possibilities. *In re Malachowski*, 530 F.2d 1402, 189 U.S.P.Q. 432, 435 (C.C.P.A. 1976).

ᚖ

As appellant had not provided a sufficient basis upon which to reasonably extrapolate the reported results to a reasonable number of liquid crystal polymers encompassed by appealed claims, the probative value of the evidence was not regarded as reasonably commensurate in scope with the degree of protection sought. *Ex parte George*, 21 U.S.P.Q.2d 1058, 1062 (B.P.A.I. 1991).

Commensurate in Scope. *See also* **Objective Enablement, Scope, Support.**

The public purpose on which the patent law rests requires the granting of claims commensurate in scope with the invention disclosed. This requires as much the granting of broad claims on broad inventions as it does granting of specific claims on more specific inventions. It is neither contemplated by the public purpose of the patent laws nor required by the statute that an inventor shall be forced to accept claims narrower than his invention in order to secure allowance of his patent. *In re Sus and Schaefer*, 306 F.2d 494, 134 U.S.P.Q. 301, 304 (C.C.P.A. 1962).

ᚖ

The discovery does not appear to be of such a "speculative," abstruse, or esoteric nature that it must inherently be considered unbelievable, "incredible," or "factually misleading." Nor does operativeness appear "unlikely" or an assertion thereof appear to run counter "to what would be believed would happen by the ordinary person" in the art. Nor does the field of endeavor appear to be one where "little of a successful nature has been developed" or one that "from common knowledge has long been the subject matter of much humbuggery and fraud." Nor has the Examiner provided evidence inconsistent with the assertions and evidence of operativeness presented by the appellant. To the contrary, the appellant's assertions of usefulness in his specification appear to be believable on their face and straightforward, at least in the absence of reason or authority in variance. *In re Gazave,* 379 F.2d 973, 154 U.S.P.Q. 92, 96 (C.C.P.A. 1967).

ᚳ

A single species reduction to practice may be adequate to overcome a reference showing of a genus when novel properties are attributable to a specific component of the species. *In re DaFano,* 392 F.2d 280, 157 U.S.P.Q. 192, 196 (C.C.P.A. 1968).

ᚳ

The first paragraph of 35 U.S.C. §112 requires that the scope of the claims bear a reasonable correlation to the scope of enablement provided by the specification to persons of ordinary skill in the art. In cases involving predictable factors, such as mechanical or electrical elements, a single embodiment provides broad enablement in the sense that, once imagined, other embodiments can be made without difficulty and their performance characteristics predicted by resort to known scientific laws. In cases involving unpredictable factors, such as most chemical reactions and physiological activity, the scope of enablement obviously varies inversely with the degree of unpredictability of the factors involved. *In re Fisher,* 427 F.2d 833, 166 U.S.P.Q. 18, 24 (C.C.P.A. 1970).

ᚳ

An antedating affidavit establishing conception and reduction to practice commensurate in scope with a reference disclosure and at a date prior to the effective date of the reference is adequate to overcome the reference as prior art. *In re Stryker,* 435 F.2d 1340, 168 U.S.P.Q. 372 (C.C.P.A. 1971).

ᚳ

The relevant inquiry under the how-to-make requirement of paragraph one of 35 U.S.C. §112 is whether the scope of enablement provided to one of ordinary skill in the art by the disclosure is commensurate in scope with the protection sought by the claims. *In re Cescon,* 474 F.2d 1331, 177 U.S.P.Q. 264, 267 (C.C.P.A. 1973).

ᚳ

Any assertion by the PTO that the enabling disclosure is not commensurate in scope with the protection sought must be supported by evidence or reasoning substantiating the doubts so expressed. *In re Dinh-Nguyen and Stenhagen,* 492 F.2d 856, 181 U.S.P.Q. 46 (C.C.P.A. 1974).

ᚳ

To establish non-obviousness, advantages relied upon must stem from limitations in the claims. When claims do not require such limitations, the advantages are not regarded as commensurate with the scope of the claims. *In re Altenpohl,* 500 F.2d 1151, 183 U.S.P.Q. 38 (C.C.P.A. 1974).

ᚳ

In an unpredictable art, does 35 U.S.C. §112 require disclosure of a test with every species covered by a claim? To require such a complete disclosure would apparently necessitate a patent application with thousands of examples or a disclosure with thousands of catalysts along with information as to whether each exhibits catalytic behavior resulting in the production of the desired products. More importantly, such a requirement would force an inventor seeking adequate patent protection to carry out a prohibitive number of actual experiments. This would tend to discourage inventors from filing patent applications in an unpredictable area since the patent claims would have to be limited to those embodiments that are expressly disclosed. A potential infringer could readily avoid "literal" infringement of such claims by merely finding another analogous catalyst complex that could be used in forming the same products. *In re Angstadt and Griffin*, 537 F.2d 498, 190 U.S.P.Q. 214, 218 (C.C.P.A. 1976).

ᚥ

Objective evidence of non-obviousness must be commensurate in scope with the claims that the evidence is offered to support. *In re Greenfield and DuPont*, 571 F.2d 1185, 197 U.S.P.Q. 227, 230 (C.C.P.A. 1978); *In re Clemens, Hurwitz, and Walker*, 622 F.2d 1029, 206 U.S.P.Q. 289, 296 (C.C.P.A. 1980).

ᚥ

Early filing of an application with its disclosure of novel compounds which possess significant therapeutic use is to be encouraged. Requiring specific testing of thousands of analogs encompassed by the present claim in order to satisfy the how-to-use requirement of 35 U.S.C. §112 would delay disclosure and frustrate, rather than further, the interests of the public. *In re Bundy*, 642 F.2d 430, 209 U.S.P.Q. 48, 52 (C.C.P.A. 1981).

ᚥ

The question is not whether evidence of commercial success is "commensurate in scope with the claims," but whether the evidence is relevant to the question of non-obviousness. *E.I. du Pont deNemours & Co. v. Phillips Petroleum Co.*, 656 F. Supp, 1343, 2 U.S.P.Q.2d 1545 (Del. 1987).

ᚥ

The scope of enablement must be commensurate with the scope of the claims. *Ex parte Sizto*, 9 U.S.P.Q.2d 2081 (B.P.A.I. 1988).

ᚥ

Objective evidence of non-obviousness must be commensurate in scope with the claims that the evidence is offered to support. By the same token, the appellant is not required to test each and every species within the scope of the appealed claims and compare same with the closest prior art species. Rather, patentability is established by a showing of unexpected superiority for representative compounds within the scope of the appealed claims. What is representative is a factual question that is decided on a case-by-case basis. Here, we find that: (1) the narrow subgenus of compounds defined in the claim embraces only four species or a physiologically acceptable salt of those species; (2) the four species defined by the claim are closely related isomers; and (3) the evidence presented in the declaration irrefutably establishes that one of the claimed species possesses unexpectedly superior results compared with the closest prior art compound. On these facts, the declaration showing is adequately representative and rebuts the prima facie case of obviousness of the claim. We note the Examiner's speculation that the declaration evidence may reflect only an anomalous "interaction" between the 2-methyl propyl group and the 2-methylphenyl group that causes an unexpected and surprising increase in potency for the claimed species. This speculation, however, is not supported by any facts of record or by sound scientific reasoning. *Ex parte Winters*, 11 U.S.P.Q.2d 1387, 1388 (B.P.A.I. 1989).

ϖ

Evidence presented to overcome a *prima facie* case of obviousness has to be commensurate with the scope of the claims in support of which the evidence is offered. *General Electric Co. v. Hoechst Celanese Corp.*, 683 F. Supp. 305, 16 U.S.P.Q.2d 1977, 1989 (Del. 1990).

ϖ

There must be a reasonable correlation between the scope of the exclusive right granted to a patent applicant and the scope of enablement set forth in the patent application. *Ex parte Maizel*, 27 U.S.P.Q.2d 1662, 1665 (B.P.A.I. 1992).

ϖ

A holding that comparative test data were unpersuasive "because it only compares one species and...is not commensurate with the scope of the claims" was reversed because provided evidence of unexpected superiority was based on representative compounds which differ only by a methyl versus hydrogen substituent at the very point of structural distinction relied upon. *Ex parte Casagrande, Montanari, and Santangelo*, 36 U.S.P.Q.2d 1860 (B.P.A.I. 1995—unpublished).

Commerce Clause.

"[T]he Commerce Clause...precludes the application of a state statute to commerce that takes place wholly outside the State's borders, whether or not the commerce has effects within the State." *Automotive Products plc v. Tilton Engineering Inc.*, 855 F. Supp. 1101, 33 U.S.P.Q.2d 1065, 1077 (Cal. 1993).

Commercialize. *See also* Duty to Use.

The junior party in an interference was almost continuously active in pursuing the commercialization of the process of the counts. Except for the period from 1959 to 1964, wherein no government funds were allocated for the purpose of testing any bactericide, neither the junior party nor his supervisor gave up on the invention of the counts. Neither the pertinent case law nor a rule of reason would dictate that, under these circumstances, there was an abandonment of the invention by the junior party during this period. *Spiner and Hoffman v. Pierce*, 177 U.S.P.Q. 709, 712 (PO Bd. Pat. Int. 1972).

ϖ

Where there has been a failure to use reasonable efforts to commercialize, damages are often not susceptible of certain proof. A lesser degree of certainty is required in such cases. *Bailey v. Chattem, Inc.*, 684 F.2d 386, 215 U.S.P.Q. 671, 679 (6th Cir. 1982).

Commercial Marketing.

The issue is whether permission for commercial marketing or use of Opticrom 4% on October 3, 1984, or Intal Nebulizer Solution on January 19, 1985, represents the first permitted commercial marketing or use of the product within the meaning of 156(a)(5)(A).

By the explicit terms of the statute, the term product, as it relates to a human drug product, means the active ingredient of a new drug. The active ingredient in both of the approved products is cromolyn sodium. As noted in the FDA letters, the active ingredient had been approved for commercial marketing in 1973 and 1983, both prior to the approval of Opticrom 4% and Intal Nebulizer Solution for commercial marketing under 21 U.S.C. 355. Applying the explicit language of this statute to the facts: The permission for commercial marketing or use of the product after such regulatory review period was not the first permitted commercial marketing or use of the product under the provision of law under which the regulatory review occurred.

There is no basis in the statutory language for making a distinction between the content of a "product" vis-a-vis an "approved product." An approved product is a product that has been approved by the FDA for commercial marketing or use. The statute is explicit in defining the meaning of product in §156(f); the statute does not state that the product referred to in paragraphs (4) and (5) is the approved product. Thus, the statute itself clearly dictates that the product referred to in paragraphs (4) and (5) be defined in the manner required in §156(f). *In re Fisons Pharmaceuticals Ltd.*, 231 U.S.P.Q. 305 (Comm'r Patents & Trademarks 1986).

Commercial Success. *See also* Secondary Considerations.

The provided figures do not indicate whether sales came at the expense of existing products. They are not related in any way to the total market. For all the record shows, the sales may be the result of advertising or other extraneous factors not related to claim limitations. No nexus between commercial success and the merits of the invention has been established. *In re Noznick, Tatter, and Obenauf,* 478 F.2d 1260, 178 U.S.P.Q. 43 (C.C.P.A. 1973).

ᵀᵂ

"[C]ommercial success is strong evidence of utility and patentability, especially in the absence of other competing devices; and where followed by defendant's copying the patented device as closely as possible...is sufficient to establish utility." 1 A. Deller, *Deller's Walker on Patents* §87, at 497 (2d ed. 1965). *Wilden Pump & Engineering Co. v. Pressed & Welded Products Co.*, 655 F.2d 984, 213 U.S.P.Q. 282, 285 (9th Cir. 1981).

ᵀᵂ

Evidence that patentee had captured between 2 and 5 percent of the U.S. market over five years, had a generally upward sales trend, and had machines that were usually priced above those of its competitors indicates a successful company, but is hardly the evidence of a long-awaited breakthrough rapidly penetrating an expectant market required for an indirect signpost of unusual commercial success that sometimes accompanies a patent owner's case on validity and which has some relevance on the question of obviousness. *Colortronic Reinhard & Co., K.G. v. Plastic Controls, Inc.*, 668 F.2d 1, 213 U.S.P.Q. 801, 806 (1st Cir. 1981).

ᵀᵂ

The mere existence of commercial success is not sufficient to include a holding of obviousness; the commercial success must be shown to result from the nature and acceptance of the invention rather than some relatively unrelated fact, such as marketing. In this particular case there was not particular evidence of market share, of growth in market share, of replacing earlier units sold by others, or of dollar amounts, and no evidence of nexus between sales and the merits of the invention. *Kansas Jack, Inc. v. Kuhn*, 719 F.2d 1144, 219 U.S.P.Q. 857 (Fed. Cir. 1983).

ᚳ

A showing of commercial success of a claimed invention, whenever such success occurs, is relevant in resolving the issue of nonobviousness. *Lindemann Maschinenfabrik GmbH v. American Hoist & Derrick Co.*, 730 F.2d 1452, 1461, 221 U.S.P.Q. 481, 487 (Fed. Cir. 1984).

ᚳ

An action in the district court under 35 U.S.C. §145 is a proceeding *de novo* and, while it is limited to the invention claimed in the PTO, the court may consider any additional competent evidence that a plaintiff neither intentionally nor negligently failed to submit to the PTO. The presumption of correctness that attaches to the decision of the Commissioner is a rebuttable presumption that may be overcome by the introduction of evidence (at a trial under 35 U.S.C. §145) that is of such character and amount as to carry a thorough conviction of error. At such a trial the plaintiff and defendant may present evidence on any issue properly before the court. This additional evidence may include testimony of expert witnesses and inventors skilled in the art, and evidence of commercial success. In making its determination of non-obviousness, the court recognized the non-analogous nature of one reference, the lack of teaching or suggestion in the prior art of the useful advantage of a flexible track incapable of self-support, and the commercial success of the highly flexible Hot Wheels trackway toy-vehicle combination covered by plaintiff's Reissue Application. The fact that the claimed invention seemed simple and, when viewed in hindsight, appeared to be obvious was not enough to negate invention. *Lemelson v. Mossinghoff*, 225 U.S.P.Q. 1063 (D.C. 1985).

ᚳ

The court found that "the commercial success of the kits may well be attributed to the business expertise and acumen of the plaintiff's personnel, together with its capital base and marketing abilities" and later that "where commercial success is based on the sudden availability of starting materials, in this instance, the availability of monoclonal antibodies as a result of the Kohler and Milstein discovery, business acumen, marketing ability, and capital sources, no causal relationship is proven."

The undisputed evidence is that Hybritech's diagnostic kits had a substantial market impact. The first diagnostic kit sales, occurring in mid 1981, were $7 million in just over one year; sales in 1980 were non-existent. Competing with products from industry giants, Hybritech's HCG kit became the market leader with roughly 25 percent of the market at the expense of market shares of the other companies. Hybritech's other kits, indisputably embodying the invention claimed in the 110 patent, obtained similar substantial market positions.

With respect to the objective indicia of non-obviousness, while there is evidence that marketing and financing played a role in the success of Hybritech's kits, as they do with any product, it is clear to us on the entire record that the commercial success here was due to the merits of the claimed invention. It cannot be argued on this record that Hybritech's success would have been as great and as prolonged, as admittedly it has been, if that success were not due to the merits of the invention. The evidence is that these kits compete successfully with numerous others for the trust of persons who have to make fast, accurate, and safe diagnoses. This is not the kind of merchandise that can be sold by advertising hyperbole. H*ybritech Inc. v. Monoclonal Antibodies, Inc.*, 802 F.2d 1367, 231 U.S.P.Q. 81 (Fed. Cir. 1986).

ω

Because plaintiffs failed to present and support contentions of commercial success or copying during PTO proceedings, and have not set forth any reasons for this omission, they are precluded from presenting such evidence over defendant's objection in an action under 35 U.S.C. §145. *MacKay v. Quigg*, 641 F. Supp. 567, 231 U.S.P.Q. 907, 909 (D.C. 1986).

ω

Objective evidence of non-obviousness includes commercial success, long felt but unresolved need, failure of others, and copying. When present, such objective evidence must be considered. It can be the most probative evidence of non-obviousness in the record, and it enables the district court to avert the trap of hindsight. On the other hand, the absence of objective evidence does not preclude a holding of non-obviousness because such evidence is not a requirement for patentability. *Custom Accessories Inc. v. Jeffrey-Allan Industries Inc.*, 807 F.2d 955, 1 U.S.P.Q.2d 1196 (Fed. Cir. 1986).

ω

The commercial success of a patented invention is clearly important. That evidence of such success is "secondary" in time does not mean that it is secondary in importance. Evidence of secondary considerations may often be the most probative and cogent evidence in the record. *Trustwall Systems Corp. v. Hydro-Air Engineering Inc.*, 813 F.2d 1207, 2 U.S.P.Q.2d 1034 (Fed. Cir. 1987).

ω

The question is not whether evidence of commercial success is "commensurate in scope with the claims," but rather whether the evidence is relevant to the question of non-obviousness. *E.I. du Pont de Nemours & Co. v. Phillips Petroleum Co.*, 656 F. Supp. 1343, 2 U.S.P.Q.2d 1545 (Del. 1987).

ω

The only evidence of record concerning commercial success comprises a statement by the inventor in a 35 U.S.C. §1.131 affidavit that more than 5,000 lures "constructed according to the disclosure and claims of my patent application" have been sold. The affidavit statement does not reflect the time period during which the lures were sold or the average number of product sales per unit of time that would normally be expected in the marketplace under consideration. Accordingly it cannot be determined whether the lure, in fact, has been commercially successful. Further, the inventor's statement that his commercial lure is "constructed according to the disclosure and claims of my patent application" does not constitute probative evidence that the lure that has been sold corresponds to the lure defined by the appealed claims or that whatever commercial success may have occurred is attributable to the construction defined by the appealed claims. In short, a nexus between the claimed invention and the alleged success has not been established. Such a nexus must be established before consideration of commercial success becomes relevant to the issue of obviousness versus non-obviousness. *Ex parte Standish,* 10 U.S.P.Q.2d 1454 (B.P.A.I. 1988).

ᚹ

The evidence of commercial success consisted solely of the number of units sold. There was no evidence of market share, of growth in market share, of replacing earlier units sold by others, or of dollar amounts, and no evidence of a nexus between sales and the merits of the invention. Under such circumstances, consideration of the totality of the evidence, including that relating to commercial success, does not require a holding that the invention would have been non-obvious to one skilled in the art at the time it was made. *American Standard Inc. v. Pfizer Inc.,* 722 F. Supp. 86, 14 U.S.P.Q.2d 1673, 1715 (Del. 1989).

ᚹ

When the PTO issues a patent because the Examiner did not consider prior art teaching the very technique essential to the claimed invention... it is not unusual to see astute businessmen capitalize on it by erecting a temporarily successful licensing program thereon. Such programs are not infallible guides to patentability. They sometimes succeed because they are mutually beneficial to the licensed group or because of business judgments that it is cheaper to take licenses than to defend infringement suits, or for other reasons unrelated to the unobviousness of the licensed subject matter. Such a "secondary consideration" must be carefully appraised as to its evidentiary value. *Ex parte GPAC Inc.,* 29 U.S.P.Q.2d 1401, 1407 (B.P.A.I. 1993).

ᚹ

When a patented device is a commercial product, there is an inference that its commercial success is due to the patented device itself, absent a showing to the contrary. *See, e.g., Hughes Tool Co. v. Dresser Indus., Inc.,* 816 F.2d 1549, 1556, 2 U.S.P.Q.2d 1396, 1402 (Fed. Cir.), *cert denied,* 484 U.S. 914 (1987), as interpretted in the unpublished (not citable as precedent) opinion for *Comair Rotron Inc. v. Matsushita Electric Corp. of America,* 33 U.S.P.Q.2d 1785, 1788 (Fed. Cir. 1994).

ᚹ

A patentee asserting commercial success of non-obviousness must demonstrate a sufficient relationship between the commercial success and the patented invention such that the success can be attributed to the invention. *Alpex Computer Corp. v. Nintendo Co. Ltd.,* 86 Civ. 1749, 34 U.S.P.Q.2d 1167, 1190 (N.Y. 1994).

ᚹ

A patentee need not show that all possible embodiments within the claims were successfully commercialized in order to rely on the success in the marketplace of the embodiment that was commercialized. *Applied Materials Inc. v. Advanced Semiconductor Materials*, 40 U.S.P.Q.2d 1481, 1486 (Fed. Cir. 1996).

ᚎ

Evidence related solely to the number of units sold provides a very weak showing of commercial success, if any. Mere sales figures do not establish a substantial share of any definable market or a nexus between sales and the patented invention. *In re Huang*, 40 U.S.P.Q.2d 1685, 1689 (Fed. Cir. 1996).

ᚎ

When a patentee can demonstrate commercial success, usually shown by significant sales in a relevant market, and that the successful product is the invention disclosed and claimed in the patent, it is presumed that the commercial success is due to the patented invention. If a patentee makes the requisite showing of nexus between commercial success and the patented invention, the burden shifts to the challenger to prove that the commercial success is instead due to other factors extraneous to the patented invention, such as advertising or superior workmanship. *J.T. Eaton & Co. v. Atlantic Paste & Glue Co.*, 106 F.3d 1563, 41 U.S.P.Q.2d 1641 (Fed. Cir. 1997).

ᚎ

Evidence of secondary considerations, including evidence of unexpected results and commercial success, are but a part of the "totality of the evidence" that is used to reach the ultimate conclusion of obviousness. The existence of such evidence, however, does not control the obviousness determination. *Richardson-Vicks Inc. v. The Upjohn Co.*, 122 F.3d 1476, 44 U.S.P.Q.2d 1181, 1187 (Fed. Cir. 1997).

Commercial Use.

The question whether suppression or concealment under 35 U.S.C. §102(g) is negated ought to be determined by asking whether the public has gained knowledge of the invention that will ensure its preservation in the public domain. When commercial use does not convey knowledge of the invention to the public, it does not negate a legal conclusion of concealing the invention within the meaning of §102(g). *Palmer and Taylor v. Dudzik*, 481 F.2d 1377, 178 U.S.P.Q. 608, 616 (C.C.P.A. 1973).

Commissioner. *See also* **Authority of the Commissioner.**

The Commissioner is not bound by a BPAI decision that an applicant is entitled to a patent. Only a court can order the Commissioner to act, not the BPAI. Even though Board members serve an essential function, they are but Examiner-employees of the PTO, and the ultimate authority regarding the granting of patents lies with the Commissioner. If the BPAI rejects an application, the Commissioner can control the PTO's position in any appeal through the Solicitor of the PTO; the BPAI cannot demand that the Solicitor attempt to sustain the Board's position. Conversely, if the BPAI approves an application, the Commissioner has the option of refusing to sign a patent; an action which would be subject to a mandamus action by the applicant. *In re Alappat*, 33 F.3d 1526, 31 U.S.P.Q.2d 1545, 1550 (Fed. Cir. 1994).

Commissioner's Authority.

When a three-member panel of the BPAI has rendered its decision, the Commissioner has authority to constitute a new panel for the purposes of reconsideration. *In re Alappat*, 33 F.3d 1526, 31 U.S.P.Q.2d 1545, 1546 (Fed. Cir. 1994).

Commissioner's Decision. *See* **Standard.**

The appropriate standard of review of a Commissioner's decision is set out at §706(2)(A) of the APA, 5 U.S.C. §706(2)(A). That standard requires the Court to "hold unlawful and set aside agency action, findings, and conclusions found to be arbitrary, capricious, an abuse of discretion or otherwise not in accordance with law." The standard is a narrow one: a court may not "substitute its judgment for that of the agency," but rather must uphold the agency's decision if "the agency's path may reasonably be discerned." *Unisys Corp. v. Commissioner of Patents and Trademarks*, 39 U.S.P.Q.2d 1842, 1844 (D.C. 1993).

Commonality.

The fact that some of the same evidence is relevant to both the legal and equitable claims is not enough to establish "commonality." *Avco Corp. v.* PPG Industries Inc., 867 F.Supp. 84, 34 U.S.P.Q.2d 1026, 1037 n.12 (Mass. 1994).

Common Assignee. *See* **Double Patenting.**

Common Law Right.

An inventor has a common law right to make, use, and vend his invention. *Joy Technologies v. Quigg,* 12 U.S.P.Q.2d 1112, 1115 (D.C. 1989).

Common Practice.

Even though the Examiner cited no art to illustrate what he had alleged to be "common practice," the court accepted the statement as factual and agreed with the Examiner's holding of obviousness since appellants raised no challenge to the statements. *In re Eskild and Houghton,* 387 F.2d 987, 156 U.S.P.Q. 208, 209 (C.C.P.A. 1968).

Common Properties. *See also* **Impetus.**

The present compounds have many significant properties as dyes in common with the prior art compounds, in addition to a close similarity in chemical structure. Both sets of compounds have the property of being wool dyes and both result in dyeings on wool fabrics which are fast to washing and fulling. The additional ability of the subject compounds to dye cotton is not sufficient to render the subject matter as a whole unobvious. *In re De Montmollin and Riat,* 344 F.2d 976, 145 U.S.P.Q. 416, 417 (C.C.P.A. 1965); *but see In re Murch,* 464 F.2d 1051, 175 U.S.P.Q. 89, 92 (C.C.P.A. 1972).

Communication of Conception.

To establish derivation, "[c]ommunication of a complete conception must be sufficient to enable one of ordinary skill in the art to construct and successfully operate the invention." *Gambro Lundia AB v. Baxter Healthcare Corp.*, 110 F.3d 1573, 42 U.S.P.Q.2d 1378, 1382 (Fed. Cir. 1997).

Compactness.

Patentability may not be predicated upon mere compactness or size. *In re Myers*, 104 F.2d 391, 42 U.S.P.Q. 32, 35 (C.C.P.A. 1939).

Comparable.

The record must establish how close the values for melt index and density of copolymers need to be in order for the copolymers to be considered "comparable." If it is intended that comparisons are to be made between resins having the same or equivalent melt index and density, the claims should use such language. The claims cannot leave to surmise and conjecture the specific properties to be compared and how "comparable" their values need to be when determining infringement and dominance issues. *Ex parte Anderson*, 21 U.S.P.Q.2d 1241, 1250 (B.P.A.I. 1991).

Comparative Test Data. *See also* 37 C.F.R. §1.132, Commensurate in Scope, Evidence Commensurate with Claimed Scope.

When a chemical compound coming within a broad or general class (disclosed in a prior art reference) is inoperative for the purposes claimed by an applicant against whom the reference is cited, operativeness of a different chemical compound (even though included in the same broad or general class) for the purposes claimed by the applicant is unexpected and therefore patentable over such reference. *Douglas Aircraft Company, Inc. v. Mueller*, 194 F.Supp. 268, 130 U.S.P.Q. 426, 430 (D.C. 1961).

ᛟ

Even though the application made no mention of the separation of hypotensive and tranquilizing activity, the advantage of minimized hypotensive activity would inherently flow from the indicated use of the compounds as tranquilizers. When claimed compounds are used for their disclosed tranquilizer activity, they are better insofar as they minimize the side effects of hypotensive activity. The latter undisclosed property must thus be considered in determining patentability of the claimed compounds. *In re Zenitz*, 333 F.2d 924, 142 U.S.P.Q. 158, 161 (C.C.P.A. 1964).

ᛟ

A comparison of products of a claimed process to products of prior-art processes seriatim relates to the question whether, at the time of the claimed invention, it would have been obvious to those skilled in the art to have combined the prior-art processes in the manner set forth by the Examiner, and the superiority of products of the claimed process to products of each of the prior-art processes is highly relevant to that question. *In re Tiffin and Erdman*, 443 F.2d 394, 170 U.S.P.Q. 88, 93 (C.C.P.A. 1971).

ᛟ

A basic property or utility relied upon must be disclosed in the application in order for affidavit evidence of unexpected properties to be offered. *In re Davies and Hopkins*, 475 F.2d 667, 177 U.S.P.Q. 381, 385 (C.C.P.A. 1973).

ᛒ

An applicant relying upon a comparative showing to rebut a *prima facie* case must compare his claimed invention with the closest prior art. *In re Merchant*, 575 F.2d 865, 197 U.S.P.Q. 785 (C.C.P.A. 1978).

ᛒ

When two pieces of prior art are in fact equally close to the claimed invention, there is no logical reason for requiring an applicant to make a comparison with one instead of the other. Practical considerations favor allowing the applicant to choose between them. Prior art devices are sometimes unavailable for testing. They may be disclosed in "paper patents" on inventions that have never been reduced to practice. Where the applicant uncovers a piece of prior art actually used in the real world and establishes that its teachings are equal to the relevant disclosure in a paper patent relied upon in the Examiner's rejection, it would be unfair not to permit the applicant to make his comparison with the commercially used piece of prior art. *In re Holladay*, 584 F.2d 384, 199 U.S.P.Q. 516, 518 (C.C.P.A. 1978).

ᛒ

Appellants may show improved results for their claimed compounds in comparison with compounds that are even more closely related than those of the prior art relied upon by the Examiner in order to rebut a *prima facie* case. *Ex parte Vanderhye*, 217 U.S.P.Q. 266 (PTO Bd. App. 1982).

ᛒ

Presented comparative test data established that the claimed compound yielded superior results, exhibiting selectivity factors at least five times greater than those of the closest prior art compounds. The claimed compound is novel. That its superior activity in corn and soybeans is a new and unexpected property was confirmed by the allowance of the method claims to its use on corn and soybeans. The grant of method claims is persuasive of the compound's non-obviousness. *Papesch* [315 F.2d 381, 137 U.S.P.Q. 43 (C.C.P.A. 1963)] held that a compound can be patented on the basis of its properties; it did not hold that those properties must produce superior results in every environment in which the compound may be used. To be patentable, a compound need not excel over prior art compounds in all common properties. Evidence that a compound is unexpectably superior in one of a spectrum of common properties can be enough to rebut a prima facie case of obviousness. *In re Chupp*, 816 F.2d 643, 2 U.S.P.Q.2d 1437 (Fed. Cir. 1987).

ᛒ

Declaration evidence of unexpected results is not negated by an Examiner's assertion that such results are inherent. *Ex parte Ohsaka*, 2 U.S.P.Q.2d 1461 (B.P.A.I. 1987).

ᛒ

It is immaterial whether phenomena just outside of claim limits are qualitatively different from that which is claimed. A patentee is not required to show that some technological discontinuity exists between a claimed invention and subject matter just outside of the claims, but only that the claimed subject matter would have been non-obvious in view of the prior art. *Andrew Corp. v. Gabriel Electronics, Inc.*, 847 F.2d 819, 6 U.S.P.Q.2d 2010 (Fed. Cir. 1988).

ω

Objective evidence of non-obviousness must be commensurate in scope with the claims that the evidence is offered to support. By the same token, the appellant is not required to test each and every species within the scope of the appealed claims and compare same with the closest prior art species. Rather, patentability is established by a showing of unexpected superiority for representative compounds within the scope of the appealed claims. What is representative is a factual question that is decided on a case-by-case basis. Here, we find that: (1) the narrow subgenus of compounds defined in the claim embraces only four species or a physiologically acceptable salt of those species; (2) the four species defined by the claim are closely related isomers; and (3) the evidence presented in the Declaration irrefutably establishes that one of the claimed species possesses unexpectedly superior results compared with the closest prior art compound. On these facts, the declaration showing is adequately representative and rebuts the *prima facie* case of obviousness of the claim. We note the Examiner's speculation that the declaration evidence may reflect only an anomalous "interaction" between the 2-methylpropyl group and the 2-methylphenyl group that causes an unexpected and suprising increase in potency for the claimed species. This speculation, however, is not supported by any facts of record or by sound scientific reasoning. *Ex parte Winters*, 11 U.S.P.Q.2d 1387 (B.P.A.I. 1989).

Comparative Testing.

An applicant has the absolute right to decline to do work suggested by the PTO, and to withdraw claims that have been presented for examination, without incurring liability for inequitable conduct. *Scripps Clinic & Research Foundation v. Genentech Inc.*, 927 F.2d 1565, 18 U.S.P.Q.2d 1001, 1015 (Fed. Cir. 1991).

Comparing. *See also* Mental Steps.

Steps, such as "computing," "determining," "cross-correlating," "comparing," "selecting," "initializing," "testing," "modifying," and "identifying," have implicitly been found to recite the solving of a mathematical algorithm. *In re Warmerdam*, 33 F.3d 1354, 31 U.S.P.Q.2d 1754, 1758 (Fed. Cir. 1994).

Compensation Base. *See* Entire Market Value Rule.

Competing Device. *See* Discriminatory Licensing, Two-Supplier Market.

Competitor's Product.

It is not "improper to amend or insert claims intended to cover a competitor's product the applicant's attorney has learned about during the prosecution of a patent application." *Ford Motor Co. v. Lemelson*, 42 U.S.P.Q.2d 1706, 1710 (Nev. 1997).

Complaint. *See also* **Well-Pleaded Complaint.**

A complaint that conforms to Form 16 contained in the Appendix of Forms to the Federal Rules of Civil Procedure is "sufficient under the rules" to apprise defendants of the nature of the asserted claim. Fed. R. Civ. P. 84. *Ingersoll-Rand Co. v. Joy Manufacturing Co.*, 185 U.S.P.Q. 21 (Ga. 1975).

ᛒ

The complaint "should contain either direct or indirect allegations, from which inferences can be made, on every material point necessary to sustain recovery on any legal theory." *Cobe Laboratories Inc. v. Baxter Healthcare Corp.*, 34 U.S.P.Q.2d 1472, 1473 (Colo. 1994).

ᛒ

If the complaint fails to state a claim, the court should grant leave to amend unless it appears beyond a doubt the plaintiff would not be entitled to relief under any set of facts proved. *Amylin Pharmaceuticals Inc. v. University of Minnesota*, 45 U.S.P.Q.2d 1949, 1952 (Cal. 1998).

Complete. *See also* **Subcombination.**

An entire article is of record in appellant's parent application, which is in the PTO's possession, and appellant requested that such article be considered in arriving at a decision on his present application. The fact that only the first page of the article was physically inserted into the record as an attachment to appellant's brief to the Board and the Board did not actually consider the article or mention it is immaterial, since evidence need not be physically introduced and also considered by a PTO tribunal to be considered "evidence produced before the Patent and Trademark Office". [There are thus limitations to any requirement that each file wrapper must be complete in itself.] *In re Hutton*, 568 F.2d 1355, 196 U.S.P.Q. 676 (C.C.P.A. 1978).

Component. *See also* **Element, Ingredient.**

Although a combination patent covers only the totality of the elements in the patent claims and no element, separately viewed, is within the grant, one who sells components, knowing them to be especially made or especially adapted for use in an infringement of such patent, is, at the very least, liable as a contributory infringer of such patent under 35 U.S.C. §271(a). *Bliss & Laughlin Industries, Inc. v. Bil-Jax, Inc.*, 356 F. Supp. 577, 176 U.S.P.Q. 119, 122 (Ohio 1972).

Composition. *See also* **Adapted, Combination, Compound, DNA, Element, Gene, Microorganism, Pharmaceutical, Product, Radical, Recipe.**

A claim to an old composition is not imparted with novelty by recitation therein of a new use of the composition. *In re Thuau,* 135 F.2d 344, 57 U.S.P.Q. 324, 325 (C.C.P.A. 1943).

ᛒ

A composition composed of an old (known) chemical compound and a diluent (solvent) is patentably indistinct from the compound itself, notwithstanding the express designation of the composition as a plant stimulant composition. *Ex parte Billman*, 71 U.S.P.Q. 253, 254 (PO Bd. App. 1946).

ᛒ

While the ingredients in the reference and in the claimed compositions are the same, the proportioning thereof is so different that the resulting compositions exhibit distinct and unrelated functions. It is not enough that the ingredients be identical. They must be similarly proportioned, or substantially similarly proportioned, so that the functions thereof are inherently the same. *Ex parte Ritchie*, 92 U.S.P.Q. 381, 382 (PO Bd. App. 1950).

ᛒ

When a composition is found to be inoperative for the purpose disclosed, it would be unobvious to one skilled in the art to expect that a particular composition having (as the essential component) a different chemical compound, but from the same general class, would possess the necessary properties and therefore be operative for the same purpose. *Douglas Aircraft Co., Inc. v. Mueller*, 194 F. Supp. 268, 130 U.S.P.Q. 426, 430 (D.C. 1961).

ᛒ

From the standpoint of patent law, a composition of matter is, as stated in *Robinson on Patents* §193 (1890):

> . . . always a true combination. Each of its ingredients is itself a means whose operative forces manifest themselves through the chemical or mechanical properties by which it is distinguished. . . . It differs from all other combinations in that its ingredients, or elemental means, when once united in the combination, often become individually undiscernible by human sense, and can be recovered and distinguished only by the destruction of the combination as a whole.

At least in the patent law context, a composition is necessarily a complete and separate entity whose existence as such entity is distinct from the substances of which it is composed. The character of a new composition of individually old substances cannot, therefore, be determined from an examination of its component elements alone. It must be judged rather by the intrinsic attributes of the composition as a new combination. See *Robinson on Patents* §194. *In re Henderson*, 348 F.2d 550, 146 U.S.P.Q. 372, 373 (C.C.P.A. 1965).

ᛒ

Claims to a resin per se are not directed to the same invention as patent claims to a hair-setting composition comprising the resin dispersed in a solvent. *In re Walles, Tousignant, and Houtman*, 366 F.2d 786, 151 U.S.P.Q. 185, 189 (C.C.P.A. 1966).

ᛒ

The patentability of a composition comprising a known compound and a carrier is not precluded, particularly when claims define the amount or concentration of the compound, are limited to dosage units or specified dosage forms, or otherwise distinguish over prior art teachings. *In re Wiggins*, 397 F.2d 356, 158 U.S.P.Q. 199 (C.C.P.A. 1968).

ᛒ

The word combination includes not only a combination of mechanical elements but also a combination of substances in a combination claim, or steps in a process claim. All "compositions of matter" are "combinations" if they consist of two or more substances in some degree of correlationship. Chemical compounds are clearly included as one kind of "composition of matter." A radical constituting an element of a claimed chemical compound is an "element in a claim for a combination" within the meaning of 35 U.S.C. §112, third paragraph. *In re Barr, Williams, and Whitmore*, 444 F.2d 588, 170 U.S.P.Q. 330, 336 (C.C.P.A. 1971).

ω

Proportions need not be recited in composition claims when they are not critical to the disclosed and claimed invention. Failure to recite proportions in such claims does not subject them to rejection for indefiniteness. *In re Conley, Catherwood, and Lloyd*, 490 F.2d 972, 180 U.S.P.Q. 454, 456 (C.C.P.A. 1974).

ω

Terms that merely set forth an intended use for, or a property inherent in, an otherwise old composition do not differentiate a claimed composition from those known to the prior art. *In re Pearson*, 494 F.2d 1399, 181 U.S.P.Q. 641 (C.C.P.A. 1974).

ω

The mere recitation of a new use for an old composition does not render the composition patentable anew. There is nothing in the reference, however, that teaches that the known compound may be combined with a finely divided inert insoluble solid-carrier vehicle. The carriers recited in the claims are those conventionally employed, and the disclosure teaches that compounds having algaecidal and herbicidal properties are usually blended with a solid or liquid carrier vehicle. As the reference does not teach that the known compound has algaecidal and/or herbicidal properties, there is simply no motivation to combine the known compound with conventional herbicidal carriers. There is nothing in the record that establishes the obviousness of mixing the known compound with a finely divided inert insoluble solid-carrier vehicle for any purpose whatsoever. Merely establishing that the particular compound is a known compound and that the carrier vehicles are conventional is not sufficient to render the claimed composition unpatentable. There must be some suggestion in the art to combine these materials for some purpose to support a holding of obviousness. *Ex parte Erdmann, Schneider, and Koch*, 194 U.S.P.Q. 96 (PTO Bd. App. 1975).

ω

A microorganism, which is not a hitherto unknown natural phenomenon, but a non-naturally occurring manufacture or composition of matter, a product of human ingenuity having a distinctive name, character, and use, plainly qualifies as patentable subject matter. *Diamond, Commissioner of Patents and Trademarks v. Chakrabarty*, 447 U.S. 303, 206 U.S.P.Q. 193, 197 (1980).

ω

Although each of the references does teach in general what the Examiner asserts it teaches, the rejection under 35 U.S.C. §103 fails because there is no concept in any of the art relied upon, either express or implied, of providing a composition that includes both interferon and a tyrosinase inhibitor. None of the art teaches increasing the effectiveness of interferon. Also, none of the art teaches inhibiting the patient's serum tyrosinase as it increases concomitantly with the interferon treatment. *Ex parte Rubin*, 5 U.S.P.Q.2d 1461 (B.P.A.I. 1987).

ထ

A claim to a pharmaceutical composition comprising an effective amount of a specified compound and suitable carrier adequately sets forth the use to comply with requirements of 35 U.S.C. §112. The recitation of a more specific use in composition claims calling for "an effective amount" is not necessary; claims are read in the light of the specification on which they are based, and the specification must provide essential particulars. *Ex parte Skuballa*, 12 U.S.P.Q.2d 1570, 1571 (B.P.A.I. 1989).

ထ

A composition is not merely a recipe of components and proportions of ingredients from which it is prepared when there is any interaction between such ingredients. *Exxon Chemical Patents Inc. v. Lubrizol Corp.*, 64 F.3d 1553, 35 U.S.P.Q.2d 1801, 1804 (Fed. Cir. 1995).

Compound. *See also* **Free, Gene, Name, Product, Properties, Pure, Structural Obviousness, Structural Similarity, Structure, Synthesis, Synthetic, Unity of Invention, Unrecognized, 35 U.S.C. §103.**

As two claims do not use exactly the same terminology to define the structural formula of the compounds, which is stated to be that of one or the other of the claims, the allowance of both claims is not objectionable since there is no unreasonable multiplicity of claims. *Ex parte Scott*, 54 U.S.P.Q. 148, 149 (PO Bd. App. 1941).

ထ

The mere fact that it is possible to find two isolated disclosures that might be combined in such a way to produce a new compound does not necessarily render such production obvious unless the art also contains something to suggest the desirability of the proposed combination. *In re Bergel*, 292 F.2d 955, 130 U.S.P.Q. 206, 208 (C.C.P.A. 1961).

ထ

When a chemical compound falling within a broad or general class (disclosed in a prior-art reference) is inoperative for the purposes claimed by an applicant against whom the reference is cited, operativeness of a different chemical compound (even though included in the same broad or general class) for the purposes claimed by the applicant is unexpected and therefore patentable over such reference. *Douglas Aircraft Co., Inc. v. Mueller*, 194 F. Supp 268, 130 U.S.P.Q. 426, 430 (D.C. 1961).

ထ

Product claims have practical advantages over method-of-use claims from the standpoint of protection. Where we are concerned with new compounds in which non-obvious properties have been found, the properties being inherent in the compounds, one could even say it is "somewhat irrational" to say the "invention" is not in the compounds. The basic principle of the patent system is to protect inventions that meet the statutory requirements. Valuable inventions should be given protection of value in the real world of business and the courts. *In re Ruschig, Aumüller, Korger, Wagner, Scholz, and Bänder,* 343 F.2d 965, 145 U.S.P.Q. 274 (C.C.P.A. 1965).

ϖ

Names and structural formulae are not chemical compounds, but mere designations therefor. When a claimed invention is a group of compounds, the obviousness or unobviousness of the compounds is in issue. Certainly, the structure and/or name of a compound might well be suggested when the compound itself is not. *In re Krazinski, Shepherd, and Taft,* 347 F.2d 656, 146 U.S.P.Q. 25, 28 (C.C.P.A. 1965).

ϖ

All "compositions of matter" are "combinations" if they consist of two or more substances in some degree of correlationship. Chemical compounds are clearly included as one kind of "composition of matter." A radical constituting an element of a claimed chemical compound is an "element in a claim for a combination" within the meaning of 35 U.S.C. §112, third paragraph. *In re Barr, Williams, and Whitmore,* 444 F.2d 588, 170 U.S.P.Q. 330, 336 (C.C.P.A. 1971).

ϖ

One who claims a compound, per se, that is structurally similar to a prior-art compound must rebut the presumed expectation that the structurally similar compounds have similar properties. *In re Wilder,* 563 F.2d 457, 195 U.S.P.Q. 426, 429 (C.C.P.A. 1977).

ϖ

When chemical compounds have "very close" structural similarities and similar utilities, without more, a *prima facie* case may be made. When such "close" structural similarity to prior art compounds is shown, in accordance with established precedents, the burden of coming forward shifts to the applicant, and evidence affirmatively supporting obviousness is required. Generalization should be avoided insofar as specific chemical structures are alleged to be *prima facie* obvious one from the other. There must be adequate prior art support for involved structural changes to complete the PTO's prima facie case and shift the burden of going forward to the applicant. The mere fact that it is possible to find two isolated disclosures that might be combined in such a way to produce a new compound does not necessarily render such production obvious unless the art also contains something to suggest the desirability of the proposed combination. In the absence of such a reference suggestion, there is inadequate support for the position that the required modification would *prima facie* have been obvious. *In re Grabiak,* 769 F.2d 729, 226 U.S.P.Q. 870 (Fed. Cir. 1985).

ϖ

The test of whether a particular compound described in the prior art may be relied upon to show that claimed subject matter would have been obvious is whether the prior art provides an enabling disclosure with respect to the disclosed prior art compound. No evidence was offered to show an enabling disclosure for the reference structure, while uncontroverted testimony showed the reference structure to be a hypothetical structure. *Ashland Oil, Inc. v. Delta Resins & Refractories, Inc.,* 776 F.2d 281, 227 U.S.P.Q. 657 (Fed. Cir. 1985).

ϖ

Amelioration of the symptoms or even cure of cancer is no longer considered to be "incredible." Nonetheless, decisional law would seem to indicate that the utility in question is sufficiently unusual to justify an Examiner's requiring substantiating evidence. Substantiating evidence may be in the form of animal tests that constitute recognized screening procedures with clear relevance to utility in humans. The specification of appellant's parent application sets forth several animal tests on numerous types of specific cancers as well as in vitro studies, both of which are asserted to be predictive with regard to utility in humans. The Examiner has not challenged the evidence presented in a single, relevant, material respect. There is only the blanket statement of lack of "patentable utility" per se. In fact, the only specific comments the Examiner has directed toward appellant's evidence are with regard to the breadth of the types of tumor against which the claimed compounds have been shown to be active. The appealed claims are drawn to compounds and not to a method of treatment. Generally speaking, utility in treating a single disease is adequate basis for the patentability of a pharmaceutical compound under 35 U.S.C. §101. *Ex parte Krepelka*, 231 U.S.P.Q. 746 (B.P.A.I. 1986).

ω

For a chemical compound to be obvious, the prior art must teach an obvious method of making that compound. Even when the prior art does teach an obvious method for making the compound, such compound is not obvious when the properties of the compound are not obvious. Chemical compounds and their properties are inseparable, and there is no basis in law for ignoring any property in making a comparison. When a superior property of a new drug has led to its acceptance in the medical community, the compound's superior property is a "significant enough contribution to be deserving of a patent." *Ortho Pharmaceutical Corp. v. Smith*, 15 U.S.P.Q.2d 1856, 1862 (Pa. 1990).

ω

A gene, being a chemical compound, could be defined "by its method of preparation, its physical or chemical properties, or whatever characteristics sufficiently distinguished it [from other materials]." *Ex parte Deuel*, 33 U.S.P.Q.2d 1445, 1448 (B.P.A.I. 1993), *reversed* 51 F.3d 1552, 34 U.S.P.Q.2d 1210 (Fed. Cir. 1995).

Compounding. *See* Enablement.

Comprise. *See also* Contain.

The absence of any particular art that necessitates restriction of the claims to "consisting essentially of" terminology and in the absence of some cogent reason to question the objective enablement provided by the disclosure in the application, a rejection of comprising claims (permitting the use of additional steps and/or additional treating agents that could yield results other than those desired) is improper.

Claims were rejected because the term comprising permits the use of additional steps and/or additional treating agents that could yield results other than those desired; limiting the claims to "consist essentially of" the recited steps was recommended since the claimed subject matter related to the highly unpredictable and empirical art of catalysis. The rejection under 35 U.S.C. §112, first paragraph, was not sustained. The rejection is improper in the absence of any prior art that necessitates restriction of the claims to the suggested terminology and in the absence of some cogent reason to question the objective enablement provided by the disclosure in the application. *Ex parte Vollheim, Troger, and Lippert*, 191 U.S.P.Q. 407 (PTO Bd. App. 1975).

ω

The court clearly looked to what was defined by the claim and interpreted it in the light of the disclosure upon which the claim was based. The court did not expand the meaning of comprises to include further limitations required by the reference. *Ashland Oil, Inc. v. Delta Resins & Refractories, Inc.*, 776 F.2d 281, 227 U.S.P.Q. 657 (Fed. Cir. 1985).

ω

The word "comprising" means the recited elements are only a part of the device; therefore, the claim is open. *Berenter v. Quigg*, 737 F. Supp. 5, 14 U.S.P.Q.2d 1175 (D.C. 1988).

Comprising. *See also* **Comprise, Contain.**

A group of Primary Examiners of the Patent Office adopted a code of terms for use in compositions to aid uniformity of practice, which regarded:

1. "comprising" and "comprising essentially" as leaving a claim open for inclusion of unspecified ingredients, even in major amounts;
2. "consisting of" as closing a claim to inclusion of materials other than those recited except for impurities ordinarily associated therewith; and
3. recital of "essentially" along with "consisting of" as rendering a claim open only for inclusion of unspecified ingredients that do not materially affect the basic and novel characteristics of the composition.

Ex parte David and Tuukkanen, 80 U.S.P.Q. 448, 450 (PO Bd. App. 1949).

ω

Claims to a process that "comprises" specified steps may not be held to exclude the use of additional steps to those set out therein. *In re Reid*, 179 F.2d 998, 84 U.S.P.Q. 478, 480 (C.C.P.A. 1950).

ω

Claims stand rejected for the reason that recitation of the term "comprising" permits the use of additional steps and/or additional treating agents which could yield results other than those desired. Notwithstanding the fact that the claimed subject matter relates to the highly unpredictable and empirical art of catalysis, there is no justification to force limitation of claims to a process "which consists essentially of" the recited steps in the absence of any prior art which necessitates restriction of the claims to the suggested terminology, and in the absence of some cogent reason to question the objective enablement provided by the disclosure in the supporting application. *Ex parte Vollheim, Troger, and Lippert*, 191 U.S.P.Q. 407, 408 (PTO Bd. App. 1975).

ω

In patent law parlance, the terms "including" and "comprising" in a patent claim are synonymous. Claims containing those terms do not exclude any materials or processes not recited therein. *Gould v. Mossinghoff,* 215 U.S.P.Q. 310, 313 (D.C. 1982).

ਠ

"Comprising" leaves a claim open for inclusion of unspecified ingredients; "consisting essentially of " restricts the inclusion of unspecified ingredients to those ingredients that do not materially affect basic and novel characteristics of the claimed subject matter. *General Electric Co. v. Hoechst Celanese Corp.,* 683 F. Supp. 305, 16 U.S.P.Q.2d 1977, 1979 (Del. 1990).

Compulsory Counterclaim.

In determining whether a claim is a compulsory counterclaim, courts should ask: (1) whether the issues of fact and law raised by the claim and counterclaim largely are the same; (2) whether *res judicata* would bar a subsequent suit on defendant's claim absent the compulsory counterclaim rule; (3) whether substantially the same evidence will support or refute plaintiff's claim as well as defendant's counterclaim; and (4) whether there is any logical relationship between the claim and the counterclaim. There is an exception to Rule 13(a) for antitrust counterclaims in which the gravamen is a patent infringement lawsuit initiated by the counterclaim defendant. *Tank Insulation International Inc. v. Insultherm Inc.,* 104 F.3d 83, 41 U.S.P.Q.2d 1545 (5th Cir. 1997).

Compulsory License.

A compulsory license, which may arise from a refusal to enjoin, is fundamentally at odds with the right of exclusion built into our patent system. *Odetics Inc. v. Storage Technology Corp.,* 47 U.S.P.Q.2d 1573, 1585 (Va. 1998).

Compulsory Licensing.

Compulsory licensing of patents by the courts for patent misuse is a permissible remedy in antitrust cases. *American Cyanamid Co. v. Federal Trade Commission,* 363 F.2d 757, 150 U.S.P.Q. 135, 145 (6th Cir. 1966).

Computer. *See also* Program.

Record-keeping machine systems are clearly within the "technological arts." Such machine systems, which comprise programmed digital computers, are statutory subject matter under the provisions of 35 U.S.C. §101, and "claims defining them must be judged for patentability in light of the prior art." *In re Johnston,* 502 F.2d 765, 183 U.S.P.Q. 172, 183, 184 (C.C.P.A. 1974).

ਠ

A computer operating pursuant to software *may* represent patentable subject matter, provided that the claimed subject matter meets all of the other requirements of Title 35 (U.S.C.) *In re Alappat,* 33 F.3d 1526, 31 U.S.P.Q.2d 1545, 1558 (Fed. Cir. 1994).

Computer-Arts Invention.[6] *See also* **Algorithm, Computer, Computer Program.**

Claims to a method, which really defined a mathematical formula that had no substantial practical application except in connection with a digital computer, were denied because the resulting patent would wholly preempt the mathematical formula and would be a patent on the algorithm itself. *Gottschalk v. Benson*, 409 U.S. 63, 175 U.S.P.Q. 673, 676 (1972).

ϖ

There is no different standard with regard to 35 U.S.C. §112 for computer-arts inventions. The statutory provision for means-plus-function terminology does not add any additional description requirement to that set forth in the first paragraph of §112. *In re Knowlton*, 481 F.2d 1357, 178 U.S.P.Q. 486 (C.C.P.A. 1973).

ϖ

A rejection under the second paragraph of 35 U.S.C. §112 (based on failure to disclose the detailed internal structure of a computer as programmed) cannot stand where there is adequate description in the specification to satisfy the first paragraph of 35 U.S.C. §112, regarding means plus-function recitations in the claims that are not, per se, challenged for being unclear. It is the *claims* that define the invention. The claims describe an apparatus, *not* a program. How appellant "perceives his invention" is irrelevant to a rejection under 35 U.S.C. §101. Neither the Board nor the Solicitor may extract that part of the claimed invention that he deems to be novel and test only that part to determine whether it belongs to one of the statutory classes of patentable subject matter. It is the *claimed subject matter as a whole* that must be subjected to this test. *In re Noll*, 545 F.2d 141, 191 U.S.P.Q. 721, 725, 727 (C.C.P.A. 1976).

ϖ

Claims were allowed to a method for operating a computing machine system for an interval and accumulating resource use data for that operating interval. Periodically, the processing operation was halted, and the use data were analyzed. That analysis determined the priorities, and consequent resource access, for the next period of operation. The processing operation was resumed for another period of time, use data accumulated, the operation halted, data analyzed, priorities and access determined and assigned, and so on, repetitively. The net effect was an overall gain in operating efficiency (i.e., an increased "throughput"). The claims, analyzed as a whole, simply define a novel method for operating a particular machine system in a particular mode. The method is claimed in a series of discrete method steps of the type one might expect to find governing the operation of a system of noncomputing machines (e.g., a milling machine system). The claimed process does not end with a solution of a particular equation, as in *Christensen* [178 U.S.P.Q. 35 (C.C.P.A. 1973)]. Nor are the claims so "abstract and sweeping" as

---

[6](i) A computer or other programmable apparatus whose actions are directed by a computer program or other form of "software" is a statutory "machine"; (ii) a computer-readable memory that can be used to direct a computer to function in a particular manner when used by the computer is a statutory "article of manufacture"; and (iii) a series of specific operational steps to be performed on or with the aid of a computer is a statutory "process". Bruce A. Lehman, Commissioner of Patents and Trademarks, Proposed Examination Guidelines for Computer-Implemented Inventions, May 30, 1995. See PTCJ, Vol. 50, No. 1232, pp. 164 and 165, June 8, 1995.

those in *Benson* [409 U.S. 63, 175 U.S.P.Q. 673 (1972)], being limited to the particular operation of a computing machine system as specified in the claims. *In re Chatfield*, 545 F.2d 152, 191 U.S.P.Q. 730, 732, 736 (C.C.P.A. 1976).

ᚲ

If allowance of a method claim is proscribed by *Benson* [409 U.S. 63, 175 U.S.P.Q. 673 (1972)], it would be anomalous to grant a claim to apparatus encompassing any and every "means for" practicing that very method. A claim drawn to a new, useful, and unobvious apparatus, specifying what the apparatus is, and not merely what it does, would not, on the other hand, be rejectable on the sole ground that the only presently known use for that apparatus is the practice of an unpatentable method. A claim to a new, useful, and unobvious computer, describing that computer in truly structural terms, would not be rejectable on the ground that the only known use for that computer is the performance of unpatentable methods of calculation. To assert the contrary, on a "pre-empt an unpatentable method" theory, would be to deny the incentive of the patent system for research and development in the field of computer-building technology. *In re Freeman*, 573 F.2d 1237, 197 U.S.P.Q. 464, 472 (C.C.P.A. 1978).

ᚲ

A problem arises in computer-arts inventions when structure and apparatus claims are defined only as a "means for" performing specified functions. If the functionally defined disclosed means and their equivalents are so broad that they encompass any and every means for performing the recited functions, the apparatus claim is an attempt to exalt form over substance since the claim is really to the method or series of functions itself. In computer-related inventions, the recited means often perform the function of "number crunching" (solving mathematical algorithms and making calculations). In such cases, the burden must be placed on the applicant to demonstrate that the claims are truly drawn to specific apparatus distinct from other apparatus capable of performing the identical functions. When this burden is not discharged, the apparatus claims will be treated as if they are drawn to the method or process that encompasses all of the claimed "means." *In re Walter*, 618 F.2d 758, 205 U.S.P.Q. 397 (C.C.P.A. 1980).

ᚲ

If no *Benson* [409 U.S. 63, 175 U.S.P.Q. 673 (1972)] algorithm exists, the product of a computer program (even one for a highly useful business method that would be unpatentable if done by hand) is irrelevant, and the analysis should focus on the operation of the program on the computer. Claims to a method of operation on a computer to effectuate a business activity were held to be directed to statutory subject matter. *Paine, Webber, Jackson & Curtis, Inc. v. Merrill, Lynch, Pierce, Fenner & Smith, Inc. v. Dean Witter Reynolds, Inc.*, 564 F. Supp. 1358, 218 U.S.P.Q. 212, 220 (Del. 1983).

Computer Program. *See also* Computer-Arts Invention, Program.

Patent property rights may not be secured on mathematical equations. A method claim in which the point of novelty is a mathematical equation to be solved as the final step of the method is not directed to a statutory method. *In re Christensen*, 478 F.2d 1392, 178 U.S.P.Q. 35, 37 (C.C.P.A. 1973).

ᚲ

When the challenged subject matter is a computer program that implements a claimed device or method, enablement is determined from the viewpoint of a skilled programmer using the knowledge and skill with which such a person is charged. The amount of disclosure that will enable practice of an invention that utilizes a computer program may vary according to the nature of the invention, the role of the program in carrying it out, and the complexity of the contemplated programming, all from the viewpoint of the skilled programmer. *Northern Telecom Inc. v. Datapoint Corp.*, 908 F.2d 931, 15 U.S.P.Q.2d 1321, 1329 (Fed. Cir. 1990).

ω

The Commissioner now states "that computer programs embodied in a tangible medium, such as floppy diskettes, are patentable subject matter under 35 U.S.C. §101 and must be examined under 35 U.S.C. §§102 and 103." The printed matter doctrine is not applicable. *In re Beauregard*, 53 F.3d 1583, 35 U.S.P.Q.2d 1383, 1384 (Fed. Cir. 1995).

Computing. *See also* Mental Steps.

Steps, such as "computing", "determining", "cross-correlating", "comparing", "selecting", "initializing", "testing", "modifying", and "identifying", have implicitly been found to recite the solving of a mathematical algorithm. *In re Warmerdam*, 33 F.3d 1354, 31 U.S.P.Q.2d 1754, 1758 (Fed. Cir. 1994).

Conceal. *See also* Concealment.

A court may find that an invention was abandoned, suppressed, or concealed if, within a reasonable time after the invention was reduced to practice, the inventor took no steps to make the invention publicly known. Factors supporting a finding of abandonment, concealment, or suppression include not filing a patent application, not publicly disseminating documents describing the invention, and not publicly using the invention. Although not filing a patent application within a reasonable time after reduction to practice may negate a 35 U.S.C. §102(g) defense, it is only one factor. It appears that not filing or delaying the filing of a patent application may support a conclusion of suppression or concealment. However, it is not clear that failure to file a patent application would show abandonment. In fact, there simply is no requirement to file a patent application if a party is not seeking protection of the patent laws. *Oak Industries, Inc. v. Zenith Electronics Corp.*, 726 F. Supp. 1525, 14 U.S.P.Q.2d 1417, 1422, 1423 (Ill. 1989).

Concealed Disclosure.

Validity was denied by a memo that was admittedly not prior art, notwithstanding the fact that the contents of such memo had been concealed by the alleged infringer. *Newell Companies v. Kenney Manufacturing Co.*, 606 F. Supp. 1282, 226 U.S.P.Q. 157 (R.I. 1985).

Concealment. *See also* **Best Mode, Delay, Fraudulent Concealment, Suppression, 35 U.S.C. §102(g).**

Each case involving suppression or concealment must be considered on its own particular set of facts. The length of time from reduction to practice to filing an application for a patent is not determinative. Mere delay, without more, is not sufficient to establish suppression or concealment. However, one who delays filing his application does so at the peril of a finding of suppression or concealment due to the circumstances surrounding the delay. Thus, when the delay period is determined to be "unreasonable," there is a basis for inferring an intent to suppress. The activities of an inventor during the delay period (e.g., taking steps to improve or perfect the invention after it has been reduced to practice) may well excuse the delay and, thereby, support a finding that it was "reasonable." Spurring into filing an application for a patent by knowledge of another's entry into the field (e.g., by issuance of a patent) is not essential to a finding of suppression or concealment. Establishing an intent to suppress by record evidence, coupled with a delay in filing an application for patent, can support a finding of suppression for purposes of 35 U.S.C. §102(g). *Young v. Dworkin,* 489 F.2d 1277, 180 U.S.P.Q. 388, 391, 392 (C.C.P.A. 1974).

ϖ

The fact of security classification should not be regarded per se as a suppression and concealment; rather, it should be viewed as but one fact in the totality of particular facts applicable to the specific situation under consideration. *Del Mar Engineering Laboratories v. United States,* 524 F.2d 1178, 186 U.S.P.Q. 42, 47 (Ct. Cl. 1975).

ϖ

Dismantling an actual reduction to practice in September 1968, preparing a patent disclosure during June and July 1969, and deciding to file a patent application in April 1970 do not lead to the conclusion that the invention was abandoned, suppressed, or concealed after the actual reduction to practice. *Cochran v. Kresock,* 530 F.2d 385, 188 U.S.P.Q. 553, 558 (C.C.P.A. 1976).

ϖ

To amount to a loss of right to a patent in favor of a later inventor, suppression or concealment must be deliberate or intentional. However, excessive or unreasonable delay gives rise to an inference of intent to suppress or conceal, and the burden shifts to the first inventor to explain the delay by showing that there was no intent to suppress or conceal. Delay may be excused by activities of the inventor or his assignee during the delay period. Activity directed toward perfecting an invention justifies delay in filing a patent application. *English v. Heredero,* 200 U.S.P.Q. 597, 600 (PTO Bd. Pat. Int. 1978).

ϖ

There is no justification for not applying the suppression and concealment doctrine [codified in 35 U.S.C. §102(g)] in a case involving an ex parte application for a patent. Were an applicant granted a patent on claims to obvious variations of the invention of the counts, which he lost in an interference because of his suppression and concealment, the public policy underlying the suppression and concealment doctrine would clearly be frustrated. The rights of the de jure first inventor would clearly not be commensurate with the scope of the benefits to the public resulting from the disclosure of his invention. *In re Suska,* 589 F.2d 527, 200 U.S.P.Q. 497, 499 (C.C.P.A. 1979).

ʊ

Considering the nature of the invention in issue and the fact that it constituted part of a generic concept, a period of eight months until the filing of a patent application therefor was not considered to be per se of such length as to infer suppression or concealment. *Ginos and Cotzias v. Nedelec, Frechet, and Dumont,* 220 U.S.P.Q. 831, 836 (PTO Bd. Pat. Int. 1983).

ʊ

A junior party is not precluded from asserting abandonment, suppression, or concealment because he did not previously raise the issue via a motion to dissolve under 37 C.F.R. §1.231(a)(1). Abandonment, suppression, or concealment is inappropriate for consideration by the Primary Examiner, to whom motions under 37 C.F.R. §1.231 are addressed, because it cannot arise unless and until a prior actual reduction to practice has been established. Since the senior party, by definition, is the party who first started his invention on the path to public disclosure by filing a patent application, a charge of abandonment, suppression, or concealment cannot be sustained against him if the charge is based solely on an unexplained delay between actual reduction to practice and filing when there is no evidence either of specific intent or that the senior party was spurred into filing his application by knowledge of the opponent's activities. *Connin v. Andrews,* 223 U.S.P.Q. 243, 249, 250 (PTO Bd. Pat. Int. 1984).

ʊ

The fact that the specification is devoid of a working example is without significance. Examples are not necessary. While a full example may have provided additional useful information, one possessed of knowledge of one skilled in this art could practice the invention without the exercise of an undue amount of experimentation. With respect to the best-mode rejection, we find no evidence of concealment and are unable to agree with the Examiner that the quality of the appellants' disclosure is so lacking as to effectively result in concealment. *Ex parte Nardi and Simier,* 229 U.S.P.Q. 79 (B.P.A.I. 1986).

ʊ

If a junior party relies on an actual reduction to practice and if a hiatus in time between the date for its asserted reduction to practice and the filing of its application is unreasonably long, the hiatus may give rise to an inference that the junior party suppressed or concealed the invention. A hiatus of at least 33 months is sufficiently long to justify raising the question of suppression or concealment. The Examiner-in-Chief (EIC) has authority to raise sua sponte that question and to issue a show-cause order thereon. The mere fact that an EIC issues an order to show cause on a question of suppression or concealment is normally a sufficient reason to permit an applicant to file additional evidence in response thereto. *Holmwood v. Cherpeck,* 2 U.S.P.Q.2d 1942, 1944, 1945 (B.P.A.I. 1986).

ʊ

Proof that an applicant knew of and concealed a better mode than that disclosed is required to establish failure to satisfy the best mode requirement. *Hybritech Inc. v. Abbott Laboratories,* 4 U.S.P.Q.2d 1001 (Cal. 1987).

ϖ

Mere concealment of an invention (at least until an application for patent is filed) is normal behavior for a cautious inventor and is not reprehensible. *National Presto Industries Inc. v. Black & Decker (U.S.) Inc.*, 760 F. Supp. 699, 19 U.S.P.Q.2d 1457, 1459 (Ill. 1991).

Concentration.

Under some circumstances, changes in temperature, in concentration, or in both, may impart patentability to a process if the particular ranges claimed produce a new and unexpected result that is different in kind and not merely in degree from the results of the prior art. Such ranges are termed "critical" ranges, and the applicant has the burden of proving such criticality. Where the general conditions of a claim are disclosed in prior art, it is not inventive merely to discover the optimum or workable ranges by routine experimentation. *In re Aller, Lacey, and Hall,* 220 F.2d 454, 105 U.S.P.Q. 233, 235 (C.C.P.A. 1955).

Concept.

Although each of the references does teach in general what the Examiner asserts it teaches, the rejection under 35 U.S.C. §103 fails because there is no concept in any of the art relied upon, either express or implied, of providing a composition that includes both interferon and a tyrosinase inhibitor. None of the art teaches increasing the effectiveness of interferon. Also, none of the art teaches inhibiting the patient's serum tyrosinase as it increases concomitantly with the interferon treatment. *Ex parte Rubin,* 5 U.S.P.Q.2d 1461 (B.P.A.I. 1987).

Conception. *See also* Abandoned Application, Communication of Conception, Corroboration, Derivation, Introduction, Name, Rule of Reason, Simultaneous Conception and Reduction to Practice.

Patentability is gauged not only by the extent or simplicity of physical changes, but also by the perception of the necessity or desirability of making such changes to produce a new result. When viewed after disclosure, the changes may seem simple and such as should have been obvious to those in the field. However, this does not necessarily negative invention or patentability. The conception of a new and useful improvement must be considered along with the actual means of achieving it in determining the presence or absence of invention. The discovery of a problem calling for an improvement is often a very essential element in an invention correcting such a problem. Though the problem, once realized, may be solved by use of old and known elements, this does not necessarily negative patentability. *In re Bisley,* 197 F.2d 355, 94 U.S.P.Q. 80, 86 (C.C.P.A. 1952).

ϖ

Before enactment of the Patent Act of 1952, prior knowledge (in order to defeat a claim for a patent) had to be knowledge of a complete and operative device, as distinguished from knowledge of a conception only. When individuals in this country have full knowledge of a device being successfully used abroad before its invention by a patentee, there is no such prior knowledge in this country as would invalidate the patent. Knowledge of a conception that has not been reduced to practice can be no more effective than knowledge in this country of a conception that has been reduced to practice aboard. Knowledge of a prior conception of an invention in this country is not enough to defeat claims of a subsequent inventor. *In re Schlittler and Uffer,* 234 F.2d 882, 110 U.S.P.Q. 304, 306 (C.C.P.A. 1956).

ᖡ

The conception of an invention consists in the complete performance of the mental part of the inventive act. All that remains to be accomplished, in order to perfect the act or instrument, belongs to the department of construction, not invention. It is therefore the formation, in the mind of the inventor, of a definite and permanent idea of the complete and operative invention as it is thereafter to be applied in practice. *Jacobs v. Sohl,* 280 F.2d 140, 126 U.S.P.Q. 399, 402 (C.C.P.A. 1960).

ᖡ

It is irrelevant that appellant (a party to an interference) never referred to or appreciated the support material to be *eta*-alumina or to contain *eta*-alumina *by that name.* However, it is fatal to appellant's case that he did not recognize (until after his interference opponent's filing date) that his "ammonia-aged" catalyst "*contained any different form of alumina at all!*" (Emphasis in original.) The count calls for a particular form of alumina. Appellant's failure to recognize that he had produced a new form, regardless of what he called it, is indicative that he never conceived the invention prior to his opponent's filing date. *Heard v. Burton, Kaufman, Lefrancois, and Riblett,* 333 F.2d 239, 142 U.S.P.Q. 97, 100 (C.C.P.A. 1964). See *Sulkowski v. Houlihan,* 179 U.S.P.Q. 685 (PO Bd. Pat. Intf. 1973).

ᖡ

The invention being a method of treating the human body to effect a lifting of the mood, conception thereof is a far different thing from merely thinking of the use of the compound. There must be some concomitant reasonable understanding or appreciation of the fact that the compound would work and in what way. *Biel v. Chessin,* 347 F.2d 898, 146 U.S.P.Q. 293, 296 (C.C.P.A. 1965).

ᖡ

Subject matter initially disclosed in, but subsequently canceled from, the specification (prior to issuance) of a copending patent of another can be considered as part of the stock of public knowledge on the date of issuance of the copending patent. Prior to that date the most the canceled portions of the specification could be used for would be as evidence of conception. *Ex parte Thelin,* 152 U. S. P. Q. 624, 625, 626 (PO Bd . App. 1966).

ᖡ

A memorandum disclosing a process meeting the terms of an interference count and introduced into the United States prior to filing the party's priority application in England was regarded as adequate to establish conception in this country prior to the effective filing date of the priority application. *Lassman v. Brossi, Gerecke, and Kyburz,* 159 U.S.P.Q. 182, 184 (PO Bd. Pat. Int. 1967).

ᛒ

A conception is not necessarily complete merely because it can be read on the terms of an interference count. *Meitzner and Oline v. Corte and Meyer,* 410 F.2d 433, 161 U.S.P.Q. 599, 602 (C.C.P.A. 1969).

ᛒ

Neither conception nor reduction to practice can be established nunc pro tunc. *Langer and Tornqvist v. Kaufman and McMullen,* 465 F.2d 915, 175 U.S.P.Q. 172, 174 (C.C.P.A. 1972).

ᛒ

The question of whether the mental formulation of an invention rises to the level of conception goes to whether the inventor has also conceived the means of putting that formulation in the hands of the public where no more than routine skill would be required to do so. The extent of testing or other research done after the mental formulation of an invention is not a reliable indicator that prior conception is precluded. *Rey-Bellet and Spiegelberg v. Engelhardt v. Schindler,* 493 F.2d 1380, 181 U.S.P.Q. 453, 457, 458 (C.C.P.A. 1974).

ᛒ

There is no conception or reduction to practice of a new form of an otherwise old composition of matter where there has been no recognition or appreciation of the existence of the new form. *Silvestri and Johnson v. Grant and Alburn,* 496 F.2d 593, 181 U.S.P.Q. 706, 708 (C.C.P.A. 1974).

ᛒ

Introduction into the United States of a disclosure (in Dutch) is adequate to establish conception in this country even if the disclosure is not translated into English or even read. *Clevenger v. Kooi,* 190 U.S.P.Q. 188, 192 (PTO Bd. Pat. Int. 1974).

ᛒ

When one of two joint applicants files an application that is copending with an application subsequently filed by the joint applicants, and the two applications become involved in an interference, the junior party has the burden of proof by a preponderance of the evidence that the invention was jointly conceived. *Linkow v. Linkow and Edelman,* 517 F.2d 1370, 186 U.S.P.Q. 223, 225 (C.C.P.A. 1975).

ᛒ

A party to an interference alleged that the process invention (which he made abroad) was conceived by the introduction (by an acquaintance) into this country of knowledge (in the form of a written explanation) of the invention (of the interference count) and of products made by the process count. The written explanation (in Spanish) and the products were brought to an exhibition in Atlantic City and then shown to people in Charlotte. The bringing of the explanation (which apparently lacked complete enablement) and products into the United States did not in and of itself constitute such an introduction of the invention into this country as would support a finding of conception and actual reduction to practice since the acquaintance had only a general understanding of the invention and was not aware of all of the subject matter set forth in the count. Knowledge in this country of the invention by an agent of the inventor is not equivalent to an introduction of the invention into this country "in the absence of a disclosure to others or reduction of the invention to practice by [the agent] within a reasonable time." *Tapia v. Micheletti v. Wignall, Shelton, and Klee,* 202 U.S.P.Q. 123, 124, 125 (PTO Bd. Pat. Int. 1976).

ᚱ

The law does not require that every element of the counts be conceived; the test of conception is whether the disclosure by the inventor(s) was such that no extensive research or experimentation would be required for one of ordinary skill in the art to construct the invention in issue based upon that disclosure. *Vancil and Jenkins v. Arata,* 202 U.S.P.Q. 58, 60 (PTO Bd. Pat. Int. 1977).

ᚱ

Evidence of conception, naming only inventor included in the true inventive entity, inures to the benefit of and serves as evidence of conception by the complete inventive entity, whether initially thought to be joint inventors or only considered to be such at a later time, upon a change of inventorship during prosecution. *Haskell, Hench, and Yates v. Colebourne, Rolfe, McAloon, and Orton,* 671 F.2d 1362, 213 U.S.P.Q. 192, 195 (C.C.P.A. 1982).

ᚱ

Section 102(g) of 35 U.S.C. is usually applied in the context of a priority contest rather than in the context of prior art to defeat the invention of another. In those instances where §102(g) is invoked arguing prior art, the invention must be completed, and until complete, no prior art exists; mere conception is simply insufficient. *Rohm & Haas Co. v. Dawson Chemical Co., Inc.,* 557 F. Supp, 739, 217 U.S.P.Q. 515, 566 (Tex. 1983).

ᚱ

Section 119 (35 U.S.C.) is a patent-saving provision for the benefit of applicants, and an applicant is entitled to rely on it as a constructive reduction to practice to overcome the date of a reference under 37 C.F.R. §1.131. As entitlement to a foreign filing date can completely overcome a reference, it can provide the constructive reduction to practice element of proof required by 37 C.F.R. §1.131. It is a statutory priority right which cannot be interfered with by a construction placed on a PTO rule. It may be possible to couple conception in the United States with diligence to a constructive reduction to practice abroad to overcome an intervening reference. *In re Mulder and Wulms,* 716 F.2d 1542, 219 U.S.P.Q. 189, 193 (Fed. Cir. 1983).

ᚱ

The date a draft application (originating in a foreign country) is introduced into this country by way of counsel may be taken as the date of conception of the invention in this country. *Ex parte Hachiken and Ogino,* 223 U.S.P.Q. 879, 880 (PTO Bd. App. 1984).

ᚱ

After the complete performance of the mental part of the inventive act, all that remains to be accomplished, in order to perfect the acts or instrument, belongs to the department of construction, not invention. It is therefore the formation, in the mind of the inventor of a definite and permanent idea of the complete and operative invention, as it is thereafter to be applied in practice, that constitutes an available conception, within the patent law. *Coleman v. Dines,* 754 F.2d 353, 224 U.S.P.Q. 857 (Fed. Cir. 1985).

ω

Conception is the "formation in the mind of the inventor, of a definite and permanent idea of the complete and operative invention, as it is hereafter to be applied in practice." *Hybritech Inc. v. Monoclonal Antibodies, Inc.,* 802 F.2d 1367, 231 U.S.P.Q. 81 (Fed. Cir. 1986).

ω

Conception is the "formation in the mind of the inventor, of a definite and permanent idea of a complete and operative invention, as it is hereafter to be applied in practice." The idea must be of specific means, not just a desirable end or result, and must be sufficiently complete so as to enable anyone of ordinary skill in the art to reduce the concept to practice. 3 D. Chisum, *Patents* §10.03 at 10-45 (1989).

In certain unusual cases, an inventor may be unable to establish a complete conception of a given subject matter prior to reduction to practice, and the work of conception must be considered to proceed simultaneously with the work of reduction to practice. The mental formulation of an invention is deemed "complete" if the inventor has conceived the means of putting that formulation in the hands of the public where no more than routine skill would be required to do so. *Amgen Inc. v. Chugai Pharmaceutical Co., Ltd.,* 13 U.S.P.Q.2d 1737, 1759, 1760 (Mass. 1989).

ω

Conception requires both the idea of the invention's structure and possession of an operative method of making it. In some instances, an inventor is unable to establish a conception until he has reduced the invention to practice by a successful experiment. This situation results in simultaneous conception and reduction to practice. A gene is a chemical compound, albeit a complex one, and conception of a chemical compound requires that the inventor be able to define it so as to distinguish it from other materials and to describe how to obtain it. Conception does not occur unless one has a mental picture of the structure of the chemical or is able to define it by its method of preparation, its physical or chemical properties, or whatever characteristics sufficiently distinguish it. It is not sufficient to define it solely by its principal biological property (e.g., encoding human erythropoietin) because an alleged conception having no more specificity than that is simply a wish to know the identity of any material with that biological property. When an inventor is unable to envision the detailed constitution of a gene so as to distinguish it from other materials, as well as to describe a method for obtaining it, conception has not been achieved until reduction to practice has occurred—that is, until after the gene has been isolated. *Amgen Inc. v. Chugai Pharmaceutical Co. Ltd.,* 927 F.2d 1200, 18 U.S.P.Q.2d 1016, 1020, 1021 (Fed. Cir. 1991).

ω

Conception must take place in the United States, or in lieu thereof, it must have been brought to this country or must have been communicated to someone in this country. If an invention is reduced to practice in a foreign country and knowledge of the invention was brought into this country and disclosed to others, the inventor can derive no benefit from the work done abroad, and such knowledge is merely evidence of conception of the invention. However, the nature of the work abroad might be important in determining the identity of the invention or whether the inventor had any concept of it or not, but it is incumbent upon the inventor to prove that the invention was introduced into the United States. Introduction of the invention into this country on behalf of the inventor must be judged by what knowledge was imparted to others and by the items brought into the United States. For a compound, conception requires both the idea of the invention's structure and possession of an operative method of making it. When an inventor is unable to envision the detailed constitution of a gene so as to distinguish it from other materials, as well as a method for obtaining it, conception is not achieved until reduction to practice has occurred—i.e., until after the gene has been isolated. It is not sufficient to define the recombinant molecule by its principal biological property because an alleged conception having no more specificity than that is simply a wish to know the identity of any material with that biological property. Conception of an invention must have been manifested or proved by means of exterior acts or declarations (disclosures). *Colbert v. Lofdahl*, 21 U.S.P.Q.2d 1068, 1071 (B.P.A.I. 1991).

ω

Evidence of conception, naming only one of the inventive entity, inures to the benefit of and serves as evidence of conception by the entire inventive entity. *Staehelin v. Secher*, 24 U.S.P.Q.2d 1513, 1522 (B.P.A.I. 1992).

ω

Conception of a substance claimed *per se* without reference to a process requires conception of its structure, name, formula, or definitive chemical or physical properties. *Fiers v. Revel*, 984 F.2d 1164, 25 U.S.P.Q.2d 1601, 1605 (Fed. Cir. 1993).

ω

The law of conception is comprised of two elements. The first element relates to the state of mind of the inventor—whether he had a definite and permanent idea of the complete and operative invention. This element is subjective; so long as the idea is sufficiently defined and preserved, the law does not require that the inventor's idea be reasonable, scientifically accurate, or capable of being proved. The second element asks whether the inventor's idea, as defined and preserved, enables one of ordinary skill in the art to reduce the invention to practice. This element is objective. *Burroughs Wellcome Co. v. Barr Laboratories Inc.*, 829 F.Supp. 1200, 29 U.S.P.Q.2d 1721, 1730 (N.C. 1993).

ω

An inventor's belief that his invention will work or his reasons for chosing a particular approach are irrelevant to conception. An enabling draft patent application is sufficient to corroborate conception. One need not necessarily meet the enablement standard of 35 U.S.C. §112 to prove conception. The question is not whether the inventors reasonably believed that the inventions would work for their intended purpose, but whether the inventors had formed the idea of their use for that purpose in sufficiently final form that only the exercise or ordinary skill remained to reduce it to practice. *Burroughs Wellcome Co. v. Barr Laboratories Inc.*, 40 F.3d 1223, 32 U.S.P.Q.2d 1915, 1920, 1921, 1922 (Fed. Cir. 1994).

ᛦ

Corroborating evidence must be in the form of (a) the testimony of non-inventors who, from discussions with the alleged inventors, understood the claimed invention at the time it purportedly was conceived or (b) from documents created at the time of the alleged conception that show the alleged invention. *Sturtevant v. Van Remortel*, 38 U.S.P.Q.2d 1134, 1138 (N.Y. 1995).

Concession. *See also* Claims Suggested for Interference, Disclaimer, Lost Count.

When a party to an interference files an abandonment of the contest, concedes priority, or disclaims the subject matter of an interference count, he stands in the same position as he would had there been an award of priority adverse to him with respect to the interference count. An adverse award of priority bars an applicant from obtaining a claim not patentably distinct from the subject matter awarded his adversary. *In re Fenn*, 315 F.2a 949, 137 U.S.P.Q. 367, 368 (C.C.P.A. 1963).

ᛦ

Under the proper circumstances, a concession of priority or disclaimer of an interference count renders that count available with the same effect as a prior-art reference disclosing such subject matter, and the count may be combined with other prior art to show lack of patentable distinction between the count and appealed claims. The legislative history of 35 U.S.C. §102 and §103 makes it clear that the "prior art," which §103 requires to be compared with "the subject matter sought to be patented" in a given situation, refers to at least the statutory prior-art material named in §102. The subject matter of a count lost in an interference by concession of priority must be regarded as made in this country by another before the losing party's invention thereof. That subject matter is prior art within the meaning of 35 U.S.C. §103, and in accordance with that provision, the losing party may not obtain any claim that distinguishes over that prior art only in matters that would have been obvious to one having ordinary skill in the art *at the time the losing party's invention was made*. That analysis, however, does not completely dispose of the issue since it requires a finding that the subject matter of the count was invented before the subject matter of the present claims. A concession of priority with regard to the subject matter defined by an interference count does not extend to distinctly different subject matter later claimed by the losing party to an interference in which the count was in issue. *In re Yale, Sowinski, and Bernstein*, 347 F.2d 995, 146 U.S.P.Q. 400, 403 (C.C.P.A. 1965).

ᛦ

An applicant who refuses to copy claims (he could have copied) suggested by an Examiner for interference purposes suffers the same consequences that would have befallen him had he entered the interference and either conceded priority of invention in the subject matter or lost priority on evidence of prior inventorship by another in this country of the subject matter of the claims. *In re Ogiue*, 517 F.2d 1382, 186 U.S.P.Q. 227, 234 (C.C.P.A. 1975).

ᛦ

Absent evidence of where an invention was made, conceding priority of the subject matter of an interference count is an admission that such subject matter is the prior invention of another in this country under section 102(g) (Title 35) and thus *prior art* under 35 U.S.S. §103. An invention apparently made outside of the United States is not accorded the same effective date as a reference as it would have had, had it been made in this country. *In re McKellin, Mageli, and D'Angelo*, 529 F.2d 1324, 188 U.S.P.Q. 428, 434, 435 (C.C.P.A. 1976).

Conclusion.

Although an attorney may be deposed and required to disclose what he knows about the subject matter, he cannot be required to disclose his mental impressions, conclusions, opinions, or legal theories concerning the litigation. He may be required to refer to his file to refresh his recollection, but he cannot be compelled to state why he amended the claims or what he meant by this or that word or phrase; that would require him to express an opinion, one of the exceptions provided for in Fed. R. Civ. P. 26(b)(3). *MacLaren v. B-l-W Group Inc.*, 180 U.S.P.Q. 387 (Va. 1973).

ω

Prima facie obviousness is a legal conclusion, not a fact. Facts established by rebuttal evidence must be evaluated along with the facts on which the earlier conclusion was based, not against the conclusion itself. Though the tribunal must begin anew, a final finding of obviousness may of course be reached, but such finding will rest upon evaluation of all facts in evidence, uninfluenced by any earlier conclusion reached by an earlier Board upon a different record. *In re Rinehart*, 531 F.2d 1048, 189 U.S.P.Q. 143, 147 (C.C.P.A. 1976).

ω

A mere conclusory statement of expectancy (without evidence or reasoning) does not provide adequate basis for upholding a Board decision. *In re Nolan*, 553 F.2d 1261, 193 U.S.P.Q. 641, 644, 645 (C.C.P.A. 1977).

ω

Affidavits regarding the use of a particular reference as prior art were regarded as of limited probative value since they set forth mere conclusions therein without cogent, supporting reasons. None of the affiants state any facts that differentiate the properties of the respective compounds. If, as affiants stated, "no reasonable interpretation" can equate the two, affiants should have submitted factual substantiation of that contention. The affidavits fail to offer the bases upon which their conclusions are built. *In re Grunwell and Petrow*, 609 F.2d 486, 203 U.S.P.Q. 1055, 1059 (C.C.P.A. 1979).

Conclusory. *See* **Examiner's Opinion, Statement.**

Concurrent. *See* **Simultaneous.**

Concurrent Litigation.

With regard to the issue of enjoining the prosecution of concurrent litigation, it is not controlling whether plaintiff is likely to succeed on the merits. Instead, a primary question is whether the issues and parties are such that the disposition of one case would be dispositive of the other. *Katz v. Lear Siegler Inc.*, 909 F.2d 1459, 15 U.S.P.Q.2d 1554, 1557 (Fed. Cir. 1990).

Condensate.

Defining a claimed product as the acid phosphate of the condensation product of formaldehyde and a salt of a certain compound does not make the claim a product-by-process claim. *In re Steppan, Rebenstock, and Neugebauer*, 394 F.2d 1013, 156 U.S.P.Q. 143 (C.C.P.A. 1967).

Conditions. *See also* Reacting.

The fact that claims recite a condition without reciting each and every step necessary to obtain that condition does not render the claims indefinite. *In re Alul and McEwan*, 468 F.2d 939, 175 U.S.P.Q. 700, 704 (C.C.P.A. 1972).

ᙡ

It is not a function of the claims to specifically exclude either possible inoperative conditions or ineffective reactant proportions. *Ex parte Vollheim, Kroger, and Lippert*, 191 U.S.P.Q. 407, 408 (PTO Bd. App. 1975).

ᙡ

With few exceptions, any conditions which are not in their very nature illegal with regard to this kind of property, imposed by a patentee and agreed to by a licensee for the right to manufacture or use or sell a patented article, will be upheld by the courts. A patentee may grant a license "upon any condition the performance of which is reasonably within the reward which the patentee by the grant of the patent is entitled to secure". *Mallinckrodt Inc. v. Medipart Inc.*, 976 F.2d 700, 24 U.S.P.Q.2d 1173, 1176 (Fed. Cir. 1992).

Conduct. *See also* Candor, Duty to Disclose, Gross Negligence, Inequitable Conduct, New Trial.

Participants in proceedings before the PTO are held to high standards of conduct because of the ex parte nature of such proceedings and because of the Examiner's relative inability to test the veracity of certain representations made to him. *Grefco, Inc. v. Kewanee Industries, Inc.*, 499 F. Supp. 844, 208 U.S.P.Q. 218, 233 (Del. 1980).

ᙡ

Because of limitations on the time and facilities available to the PTO to search for prior art relevant to pending applications for patent or to conduct tests to check assertions of efficacy or superiority, the PTO must rely heavily on the representations of patent applicants. Every patent applicant has an "uncompromising duty" to report to the PTO all facts affecting the patentability of the inventions claimed, to ensure that any "patent monopoly spring from backgrounds free of fraud or other inequitable conduct." Patent applicants must show "the highest degree of candor and good faith." They stand before the PTO in a confidential relationship and owe the obligation of frank and truthful disclosure. The patent system could not function successfully if applicants were allowed to approach the PTO as an arm's length adversary. The duty of candor applies equally to the applicant and his attorney, even where a foreign attorney has primary responsibility for the prosecution of the application and acts only through a corresponding attorney in the United States. Thus, it constitutes fraud or inequitable conduct for a foreign attorney to withhold from his U.S. correspondent information as to prior art more relevant than that cited by the PTO. *Gemveto Jewelry Co. v. Lambert Bros., Inc.*, 542 F. Supp. 933, 216 U.S.P.Q. 976, 980, 981 (N.Y. 1982).

ω

A very important policy consideration is to discourage all manner of dishonest conduct in dealing with the PTO. At the same time, the basic policy underlying the patent system is to encourage the disclosure of inventions through issuance of patents. Another policy of the system is to stimulate the investment of risk capital in the commercialization of useful patentable inventions so that the public gets some benefit from them, which may not occur in the absence of some patent protection. Being faced with questions of both socioeconomic policy on the one hand and morals or ethics on the other, neither category should be so emphasized as to forget the other. *Rohm & Haas Co. v. Crystal Chemical Co.*, 722 F.2d 1156, 220 U.S.P.Q. 289, 301 (Fed. Cir. 1983).

ω

The duty of due care normally requires a party to obtain legal advice before initiating or continuing an operation that might result in infringement. Failure to obtain an opinion of counsel is one of the factors supporting a finding of willfulness. This principle, which addresses the conduct of an accused willful infringer, is part of the substantive law of patents and is not merely a procedural housekeeping rule. A federal court exercising patent jurisdiction is bound by the substantive patent law of the Federal Circuit. When an infringer fails to introduce (at trial) an opinion of counsel pertaining to the activity in question, an adverse inference may be drawn against the infringer that any legal advice obtained regarding the activity in question was unfavorable to the infringer. *ALM Surgical Equipment Inc. v. Kirschner Medical Corp.*, 15 U.S.P.Q.2d 1241, 1251 (S.C. 1990).

Conduit Theory.

As a general rule, the attorney-client privilege does not apply to communications of largely factual information to be disclosed in the patent application process because the element of confidentiality is lacking; the attorney serves only "as a conduit for factual information" and "not . . . primarily as a lawyer." However, even under the conduit theory a communication containing considerable factual and technical information may be privileged if it constitutes legal advice or a request for legal advice. *Ami/Rec-Pro Inc. v. Illinois Tool Works Inc.*, 46 U.S.P.Q.2d 1369, 1370 (Ill. 1998).

Confidentiality.

The language in 35 U.S.C. §122 creating confidentiality speaks of "applications for patents." The language is broad enough to include all categories of applications (pending, abandoned, and granted), including those that would appear to be the legislative intent of Congress. *Sears v. Gottschalk, Commissioner of Patents*, 502 F.2d 122, 183 U.S.P.Q. 134, 137 (4th Cir. 1974).

ῶ

Although 35 U.S.C. §122 provides that the Patent Office shall maintain the confidentiality of a patent application, that prohibition is not binding on a district court, which may order release of the material where a movant's need for the material outweighs the applicant's interest in the confidentiality of its application. *Paper Converting Machine Company v. Magna-Graphics Corporation*, 207 U.S.P.Q. 1136 (Wisc. 1980).

ῶ

Confidentiality was found to be implicit in an inventor's confidential demonstration of his invention to close colleagues in a personal and informal setting. *Nordberg Inc. v. Telsmith Inc.*, 881 F.Supp. 1252, 36 U.S.P.Q.2d 1577, 1607 (Wis. 1995).

ῶ

While denying plaintiff's motion for a protective order, the court granted infringement defendant's discovery with regard to plaintiff's pending and abandoned patent applications that are directly relevant to the subject matter in issue. *Central Sprinkler Co. v. Grinnell Corp.*, 897 F.Supp. 225, 37 U.S.P.Q.2d 1208, 1211 (Pa. 1995).

Confidentiality Agreement.

Although there may not have been a confidentiality agreement in place between the patent owner and noncompany people involved in testing more than a year prior to filing the patent application, three test analysts testified that it was their practice to inform the noncompany people at the test site that the patent owner's equipment was experimental and confidential. Each of them also made clear by his testimony that his work with the equipment during the critical period was directed toward working the bugs out of an experimental machine that had not been refined to the point where it was ready for commercial use. *Schrag v. Strosser*, 21 U.S.P.Q.2d 1025, 1029 (B.P.A.I. 1991).

Confidential Relationship.

Having had knowledge of the contents of plaintiff's patent applications while these applications were on file and having received actual notice of infringement of claims after a patent issued, defendant's infringement of such claims is deemed to be deliberate, unconscionable, willful, and in bad faith. Defendant acquired this information from the plaintiff and, in utilizing the information, breached a confidential relationship that existed. Furthermore, after acquiring knowledge of these otherwise secret patent applications and secret information, defendant deliberately and willfully undertook to infringe upon the device disclosed in the applications and to duplicate the information disclosed by the plaintiff. These acts of the defendant present special circumstances under which an award of reasonable attorney's fees, costs, and interest is warranted. *Holmes v. The Thew Shovel Company*, 305 F. Supp. 139, 162 U.S.P.Q. 559, 566 (Ohio 1969).

ῶ

"The only distinction between the rules of discovery in the ordinary fraud case and those in the confidential relationship category is that in the latter situation the duty to investigate may arise later by reason of the fact the plaintiff is entitled to rely upon the assumption his fiduciary is acting in his behalf...." *Center for Neurologic Study v. Kohne,* 49 U.S.P.Q.2d 1040, 1047 (Cal. Super. Ct. 1998).

Conflicting Claims.

Section 1.78(c) of 37 C.F.R. was promulgated for the purpose of providing a "basis for requiring a determination of priority without an interference by the common owner of a plurality of applications, or patent and applications, containing conflicting claims." The Examiner requested, under threat of abandonment of the application, that petitioners state which inventive entity is the prior inventor of the subject matter of allegedly conflicting claims and that petitioners' assignee limit the claims of the other application accordingly. Section 1.78(c) sets forth the requirement that petitioners state which named inventor is the prior inventor. The regulation does not provide that, upon threat of abandonment of their application, petitioners may be required to state which inventive entity is the prior inventor of the subject matter of conflicting claims, MPEP §804.03 to the contrary notwithstanding. If the petitioners did not believe there were conflicting claims, their only available response was to state who was the prior inventor of their respective inventions. Section 1.78(c) clearly provides that petitioners have the right to explain "that no conflict exists in fact." Although the regulations do not define "conflicting claims," MPEP §804.03 uses this term to describe "a single inventive concept [claimed by different inventive entities], including variations of the same concept each of which would be obvious in view of the other." It is incum bent upon an Examiner, in making a request pursuant to 37 C.F.R. §1.78(c), to specify the "subject matter" so that an applicant can name the prior inventor thereof. *Margolis, Rushmore, Liu, and Anderson v. Banner,* 599 F.2d 435, 202 U.S.P.Q. 365, 371 (C.C.P.A. 1979).

Conflict of Interest.

In an interference between an application having joint inventors and a sole application of one of the two joint inventors, the attorney who prepared the application for the joint inventors was disqualified as having a conflict in interest. *Isaacs v. Isaacs and Stern,* 183 U.S.P.Q. 790, 791 (PTO Bd. Pat. Int. 1974).

ϖ

In determining whether there is a conflict of interest, foreign patent agents or attorneys are not clients of a U.S. patent attorney; the clients are the individual inventors or their assignees. *Strojirenstvi v. Toyoda,* 2 U.S.P.Q.2d 1222, 1223 (Comm'r Patents & Trademarks 1986).

Conflict Preemption.

[The patent laws], like other laws of the United States enacted pursuant to constitutional authority, are the supreme law of the land. When state law touches upon the area of these federal statutes, it is "familiar doctrine" that the federal policy "may not be set at naught, or its benefits denied" by the state law. This is true even if the state law is enacted in the exercise of otherwise undoubted state power. *Hunter Douglas Inc. v. Harmonic Design Inc.,* 962 F.Supp. 1249, 42 U.S.P.Q.2d 1629, 1632 (Cal. 1997)

Confusing.

There is nothing vague or confusing about a claim when, in the light of the specification and drawings, the disclosure makes the invention sufficiently clear to enable a mechanic skilled in the involved art to construct and use the claimed subject matter. *The Tillotson Manufacturing Company v. Textron, Inc.*, 337 F.2d 833, 143 U.S.P.Q. 268, 274 (6th Cir. 1964).

Confusion.

The "actual confusion" evidence, like the expert's evidence, was *not* submitted to show that the confusion was caused by ornamental features, but rather to show that the overall designs are similar. *OddzOn Products Inc. v. Just Toys Inc.*, 122 F.3d 1396, 43 U.S.P.Q.2d 1641, 1648 (Fed. Cir. 1997).

Congressional Hearing.

No basis is found for a holding that a violation of any duty of candor before a congressional committee would render a patent unenforceable. Congressional hearings are not ex parte proceedings at which members of Congress depend on the frankness or integrity of a particular witness to receive the full scope of information pertinent to the merits of a proposed piece of legislation. In addition, an adversarial method of interrogating witnesses is permitted at congressional committee hearings. *United Sweetener U.S.A. Inc. v. The Nutrasweet Company,* 760 F. Supp. 400, 19 U.S.P.Q.2d 1561, 1578 (Del. 1991).

Conjecture. *See also* Argument, Assertion.

The law has other tests of invention than subtle conjecture of what might have been seen and yet was not. It regards a change as evidence of novelty, and the acceptance and utility of change as further evidence, even as a demonstration. Nor does it detract from its merit that it is the result of experiment and not the instant and perfect product of inventive power. A patentee may be baldly empirical, seeing nothing beyond his experiments and the result; yet, if he has added a new and valuable article to the world's utilities, he is entitled to the rank and protection of an inventor. It is certainly not necessary that he understand or be able to state the scientific principles underlying his invention, and it is immaterial whether he can stand a successful examination as to the speculative ideas involved. *Diamond Rubber Co.v. Consolidated Rubber Tire Co.*, 220 U.S. 428, 435 (1911).

ϖ

The Board's challenged speculation on allegedly obvious methods that could be used to make the claimed compounds was inadequate. Since it had not been established that methods for making the compound named in the reference were known or described in that reference, it cannot be said that the reference would have placed the public in possession of the invention. *In re Coker, Phillips, and Miller,* 463 F.2d 1344, 175 U.S.P.Q. 26, 28, 29 (C.C.P.A. 1972).

ϖ

When the Examiner alleged that providing additional means to cause oscillation was conventionally done by mixing conductive carrier particles with toner particles to form a developer, the alleged conventionality was successfully challenged. *In re Rarey and Kennedy,* 480 F.2d 1345, 178 U.S.P.Q. 463, 468 (C.C.P.A. 1973).

ᴡ

A fertile imagination does not make a claimed invention obvious. *In re Way*, 514 F.2d 1057, 185 U.S.P.Q. 580, 584 (C.C.P.A. 1975).

ᴡ

In the reduction to practice of an invention, certainty is required rather than conjecture, even though the conjecture may have some plausible scientific basis to rest upon. *Taylor v. Brackman,* 208 U.S.P.Q. 275, 281 (PTO Bd. Pat. Int. 1979).

Consent Decree.

A consent decree that adjudicates only the validity of a patent and does not adjudicate the question of infringement will not be res judicata even on the question of validity of the patent in a later suit by one of the parties to the consent decree. *Nina Footwear Co., Inc. v. J. C. Penney Co., Inc.,* 199 U.S.P.Q. 577, 578 (N.Y. 1978).

ᴡ

In patent cases consent decrees entered in settlement of an infringement action are entitled to res judicata effect. *American Equipment Corp. v. Wikomi Manufacturing Co.,* 630 F.2d 544, 208 U.S.P.Q. 465 (7th Cir. 1980).

ᴡ

While a consent decree is not a decision on the merits pursuant to consideration by the court of the prior art, a consent decree is a "decision on the merits" as to the parties of the litigation. *In re Johnson*, 230 U.S.P.Q. 240, 241 (Comm'r 1984).

ᴡ

Consent decrees are entered into by parties to a case after careful negotiation has produced agreement on their precise terms. The parties waive their right to litigate the issues involved in the case and thus save themselves the time, expense, and inevitable risk of litigation. Naturally, the agreement reached normally embodies a compromise; in exchange for the saving of cost and elimination of risk, the parties each gave up something they might have won had they proceeded with the litigation. Thus, the decree itself cannot be said to have a purpose; rather, the parties have purposes, generally opposed to each other, and the resultant decree embodies as much of those opposing purposes as the respective parties have the bargaining power and skill to achieve. A consent decree may well require of a party more than is required by law; a consent decree may also fix greater limits on a party than are set by the law. In either instance, it would be unfair for a court to modify a consent decree based on a negotiated compromise. *W. L. Gore & Associates Inc. v. C. R. Bard Inc.,* 761 F. Supp. 376, 19 U.S.P.Q.2d 1621, 1624, 1625 (N.J. 1991).

ᴡ

The U.S. Supreme Court abrogated licensee estoppel, thus permitting challenges to validity to proceed not only in the typical situation involving the grant of a license after a patent issues, but also in the case of a preissuance licensee. Principles of res judicata, however, bar a licensee's challenge to the validity of a patent when prior litigation was terminated by a consent decree that, by its terms, acknowledged the patent's validity. *Foster v. Hallco Manufacturing Co. Inc.*, 947 F.2d 469, 20 U.S.P.Q.2d 1241, 1245, 1247 (Fed. Cir. 1991).

ᛟ

Consent decrees possess "the same force with regard to res judicata and collateral estoppel as a judgment entered after a trial on the merits." When a consent decree is ambiguous, a court may look at extrinsic evidence in order to resolve that ambiguity. *Surgical Laser Technologies Inc. v. Heraeus Laseronics Inc.*, 34 U.S.P.Q.2d 1226, 1231, 1232 (Pa. 1995).

Consent Judgment.

Although consent judgments may, in rare cases, be denied res judicata effect, "judicial decrees disposing of issues cannot be treated as idle ceremonies without denigrating the judicial process." *Wallace Clarke & Co. v. Acheson Industries, Inc.*, 532 F.2d 846, 190 U.S.P.Q. 321 (2d Cir. 1976).

ᛟ

Where it appears on appeal that the controversy has become entirely moot, it is the duty of the appellate court to set aside the decree below and to remand the cause with directions to dismiss. This case did not become moot on appeal; rather a consent judgment was entered pursuant to a settlement agreement entered into by the parties. The agreed settlement and entry of consent judgment mooted any possibility of pursuing an appeal and foreclosed the appellate court from obtaining jurisdiction. *Gould v. Control Laser Corp.*, 866 F.2d 1391, 9 U.S.P.Q.2d 1718 (Fed. Cir. 1989).

ᛟ

A consent judgment previously entered into has res judicata effect and is binding on the parties as to the issue of the validity of the involved patent. A party to the consent judgment is precluded from contesting the validity of the patent and remains bound to the terms of the consent judgment even if the PTO rejects the claims of the patent on reexamination or a court finds the patent to be invalid. This result is consistent with the public policies of encouraging early and vigorous tests of patent validity, conservation of judicial time, and limitations on excessive litigation. A motion to modify the consent judgment to escrow royalty payments is not well taken. *Glasstech Inc. v. A.B. Kyro OY*, 11 U.S.P.Q.2d 1703, 1707 (Ill. 1989).

ᛟ

The Supreme Court held that a license agreement that promised not to challenge the validity of a patent was void and unenforceable because it contravened the strong federal policy in favor of the full and free use of ideas in the public domain. Six circuits have ruled that a consent judgment of validity and infringement is enforceable despite the Supreme Court's holding in *Lear* [395 U.S. 653, 162 U.S.P.Q. 1 (1969)]. *Foster v. Hallco Manufacturing Co.*, 14 U.S.P.Q.2d 1746, 1747 (Or. 1990).

ᛟ

Even though a consent judgment does not constitute a prior adjudication of a patent's validity, it nevertheless indicates the patent's validity because of the infringing party's acquiescence. *California Medical Products Inc. v. Emergency Medical Products Inc.*, 796 F.Supp. 640, 24 U.S.P.Q.2d 1205, 1207 (R.I. 1992).

ᙡ

"[A] party may expressly reserve in a consent judgment the right to relitigate some or all issues that would have otherwise been barred between the same parties." The scope of a consent decree or judgment "is limited to its terms and...should not be strained." *Scosche Industries Inc. v. Visor Gear Inc.*, 121 F.3d 675, 43 U.S.P.Q.2d 1659, 1662 (Fed. Cir. 1997).

Consent Order.

A consent order embodying a settlement between parties is a final judgment; it is accompanied by finality as stark as an adjudication after full trial. When litigation is ended by the deliberate choice of the parties, a movant's burden for modification of a consent order is particularly heavy. Still, modification of a consent order is not precluded in appropriately exceptional circumstances. It must be shown that "absent such relief an extreme and unexpected hardship will result." The equities presented by the facts of the particular case must be examined. *W.L. Gore & Associates Inc. v. C.R. Bard Inc.*, 977 F.2d 558, 24 U.S.P.Q.2d 1451, 1453 (Fed. Cir. 1992).

ᙡ

The International Trade Commission rules in effect before, during, and after enactment of the OTCA [Omnibus Trade and Competitiveness Act of 1988, Pub. L. No. 100-418 (1988)(amending 19 U.S.C. §1337)] provided that consent orders could be enforced by civil penalties. *San Huan New Materials High Tech Inc. v. ITC*, 48 U.S.P.Q.2d 1865, 1871 (Fed. Cir. 1998).

Consist.

The use of the words "consists of" in the description of the organic phosphorous compound additive does not limit the patentee's right to bring an action alleging that use of a compound not expressly included in the description infringes under the doctrine of equivalents. *Acme Resin Corp. v. Ashland Oil Inc.*, 20 U.S.P.Q.2d 1305, 1309 (Ohio 1991).

Consisting.

A group of Primary Examiners of the Patent Office adopted a code of terms for use in compositions to aid uniformity of practice, which regarded:

1. "comprising" and "comprising essentially" as leaving a claim open for inclusion of unspecified ingredients, even in major amounts;
2. "consisting of" as closing a claim to inclusion of materials other than those recited except for impurities ordinarily associated therewith; and
3. recital of "essentially" along with "consisting of" as rendering a claim open only for inclusion of unspecified ingredients that do not materially affect the basic and novel characteristics of the composition.

Ex parte Davis and Tuukkanen, 80 U.S.P.Q. 448, 450 (PO Bd. App. 1949).

ᙡ

The word *consisting* means that the claim covers devices having recited elements and no more; therefore, the claim is closed. *Berenter v. Quigg,* 737 F. Supp. 5, 14 U.S.P.Q.2d 1175 (D.C. 1988).

Consisting Essentially of. *See also* **Comprise, Consisting.**

A claim to a product "consisting essentially of" enumerated components adequately distinguishes the product over reference products that require at least one additional component. *In re Garnero,* 412 F.2d 276, 162 U.S.P.Q. 221, 223 (C.C.P.A. 1969).

ω

In the absence of any evidence that a third component was being excluded by the "essentially consisting of" language, those words are not read as meaning "consisting solely of" or "consisting exclusively of." Rather, the most logical construction of the phrase would be to read it as limiting the claimed catalyst to one in which both specified elements are necessarily present. *Ziegler v. Phillips Petroleum Co.,* 483 F.2d 858, 177 U.S.P.Q. 481, 494 (5th Cir. 1973).

ω

This phrase denotes a partially closed claim. A process which includes additional features that are not limitations of a partially closed claim will infringe that claim unless the additional features materially affect the basic and novel characteristics of the claimed process. *Atlas Powder Co. v. E.I. DuPont De Nemours & Co.,* 750 F.2d 1569, 1573-74, 224 U.S.P.Q. 409, 412 (Fed. Cir. 1984); *In re Herz,* 537 F.2d 549, 551-52, 190 U.S.P.Q. 461, 463 (C.C.P.A. 1976).

ω

The phrase "consisting essentially of" is a term of art having an accepted meaning in chemical patent practice. Its use leaves a claim open for inclusion of unspecified ingredients that do not materially affect the basic and novel characteristics of a claimed composition. *Carter-Wallace, Inc. v. The Gillette Company,* 531 F. Supp. 840, 211 U.S.P.Q. 499, 527 n.29 (Mass. 1981).

ω

A patentee is not barred by file wrapper estoppel from asserting the doctrine of equivalents because the claims in suit were amended by insertion of the "consisting essentially of" language. The fact that claims are narrowed does not always mean that the doctrine of file history estoppel completely prohibits a patentee from recapturing some of what was originally claimed. *Syntex (U.S.A.) Inc. v. Paragon Optical Inc.,* 7 U.S.P.Q.2d 1001 (Ariz. 1987).

ω

Although "consisting essentially of" is typically used and defined in the context of compositions of matter, there is nothing intrinsically wrong with the use of such language as a modifier of method steps. Accordingly, the language "consisting essentially of," when used as a modifier of method steps, renders the claim open only to the inclusion of steps that do not materially affect the basic and novel characteristics of the claimed method. To determine the steps included versus excluded by this language, the claim must be read in the light of the specification. It is applicant's burden to establish that a step practiced in a prior art method is excluded from his claim by "consisting essentially of" language. An applicant who has not clearly limited his claims is in a weak position to assert a narrow construction. In the absence of any evidence that a third component was being excluded by the "consisting essentially of" language, those words are not read as meaning "consisting solely of" or "consisting exclusively of." *Ex parte Hoffman*, 12 U.S.P.Q.2d 1061, 1063, 1064 (B.P.A.I. 1989).

ω

"Comprising" leaves a claim open for inclusion of unspecified ingredients; "consisting essentially of" restricts the inclusion of unspecified ingredients to those ingredients that do not materially affect basic and novel characteristics of the claimed subject matter. *General Electric Co. v. Hoechst Celanese Corp.*, 683 F. Supp. 305, 16 U.S.P.Q.2d 1977, 1979 (Del. 1990).

ω

Typically, "consisting essentially of" precedes a list of ingredients in a composition claim or a series of steps in a process claim. By using the term "consisting essentially of," the drafter signals that the invention necessarily includes the listed ingredients and is open to unlisted ingredients that do not materially affect the basic and novel properties of the invention. A "consisting essentially of" claim occupies a middle ground between closed claims that are written in a "consisting of" format and fully open claims that are drafted in a "comprising" format. *See Ex parte Davis*, 80 U.S.P.Q. 448, 449-50 (Pat. Off. Bd. App. 1948); *Manual of Patent Examining Procedure* §2111.03 (6th ed. 1997). *PPG Industries Inc. v. Guardian Industries Corp.*, 48 U.S.P.Q.2d 1351, 1353 (Fed. Cir. 1998).

Consolidation.

Fed. R. Civ. P. 42(a) allows a court to consolidate actions involving common questions of law or fact and to order joint hearings of any or all matters at issue. The decision is left to the sound discretion of the trial judge and may be appropriate in patent infringement actions involving the same patents and multiple defendants. Cases can be consolidated solely for pretrial matters. *Sage Products Inc. v. Devon Industries Inc.*, 148 F.R.D. 213, 28 U.S.P.Q.2d 1149, 1150 (Ill. 1993).

Consonance.

With regard to double patenting, 35 U.S.C. §121 (1988) will not apply to remove the parent as a reference where the principle of consonance is violated. Consonance requires that the line of demarcation between the "independent and distinct inventions" that prompted the restriction requirement be maintained. Though the claims may be amended, they may not be so amended as to bring them back over the line imposed in the restriction requirement. Where that line is crossed, the prohibition of the third sentence of 35 U.S.C. §121 does not apply. The judicially created doctrine of obviousness-type double patenting applies when two applications or patents, not drawn to precisely the same invention, are "drawn to inventions so very much alike as to render one obvious in view of the other and to effectively extend the life of the patent that would have the earlier of the two issue dates." *Symbol Technologies Inc. v. Opticon Inc.*, 935 F.2d 1569, 19 U.S.P.Q.2d 1241, 1249 (Fed. Cir. 1991).

Conspiracy to Infringe.

District courts have recognized, albeit implicitly, a cause of action for conspiracy to infringe a patent. *Ernster v. Ralston Purina Co.*, 740 F. Supp. 724, 16 U.S.P.Q.2d 1222, 1224 (Mo. 1990).

Constitutional Question.

"[C]ourts should not, unless compelled, decide constitutional questions." *Transmatic Inc. v. Gulton Industries Inc.*, 53 F.3d 1270, 35 U.S.P.Q.2d 1035, 1042 (Fed. Cir. 1995).

Construct.

Although a close relationship exists between a DNA construct and the protein it encodes, the two are not equal. The count specifically defines a DNA construct, not the protein that is produced by expression from the construct. The specific elements enumerated in the count that necessarily must be included in any DNA construct within the count are a DNA sequence coding for the secretory leader, a processing signal sequence, and a human IGF-I. *Genentech Inc. v. Chiron Corp.*, 112 F.3d 495, 42 U.S.P.Q.2d 1608, 1613 (Fed. Cir. 1997).

Construction. *See also* Claim Construction, Claim Interpretation, Construe, Preamble, Remedial Statute.

A claim to structure having two orifices and means responsive to flow through one of the orifices reads on means responsive to flow through each orifice; as the claim does not specify "only one," it must be construed as meaning "at least one." *In re Teague*, 254 F.2d 145, 117 U.S.P.Q. 284, 289 (C.C.P.A. 1958).

ϖ

The claims of a patent are to be construed in light of the specification, and both are to be read with a view to ascertaining the invention. In interpreting a patent claim, resort may be had to the prior state of the art, to the specification, and, when related claims have been rejected by the Patent Office, to the file wrapper history. *Dale Electronics, Inc. v. R. C. L. Electronics*, Inc., 178 U.S.P.Q. 525, 536 (N.H. 1972).

ϖ

Patent claims are construed in the light of the description and to cover the real invention found in the specification and drawings. Although the specification and drawings cannot enlarge the scope of a claim, they may give the claim such limitation and definition as are necessary to make its abstract words descriptive of a specific invention. A patent is not limited to the preferred embodiments shown in the specification. The claims delineate the scope of protection afforded by a patent, not the specific embodiments shown in patent drawings. *Ziegler v. Phillips Petroleum Co.*, 483 F.2d 858, 177 U.S.P.Q. 481, 487, 488 (5th Cir. 1973).

ϖ

The specification must be read in the light of physical and practical reality. The fact that certain methods of disclosed administration may not be conveniently employed on certain animals or fish docs not invalidate the entire teaching of utility. *Ex parte Kenaga*, 190 U.S.P.Q. 346, 348 (PTO Bd. App. 1974).

℧

Indiscriminate reliance on definitions found in dictionaries can often produce absurd results. One need not arbitrarily pick and choose from the various accepted definitions of a word to decide which meaning was intended as the word is used in a given claim. The subject matter, the context, and so on will more often than not lead to the correct conclusion. Rather than looking to a dictionary, look to the art or technology to which the claimed subject matter pertains. In doing so, give due consideration to the interpretation that one of ordinary skill in the art would give the terminology in question. *In re Salem, Butterworth, and Ryan*, 553 F.2d 676, 193 U.S.P.Q. 513, 518 (C.C.P.A. 1977).

℧

The specifications are not to be used to expand the claims to cover advances clearly not claimed, but they should be considered to explain ambiguous claims or to limit overbroad claims. Although the invention on which a patentee is entitled to claim a monopoly is strictly limited to that which is properly disclosed in the file wrapper, overly technical interpretation of claim language is disfavored. [See 4 A. Deller, *Deller's Walker on Patents* §246 (2d ed. 1965).] *Stewart-Warner Corp. v. The City of Pontiac, Michigan*, 717 F.2d 269, 219 U.S.P.Q. 1162, 1168 (6th Cir. 1983).

℧

"The law governing interpretation of written instruments establishes that the *subjective intent* of a party is of no moment in ascertaining the meaning of the words used in the instruments. . . . Although Civil Code §1636 provides that a contract must be interpreted to give effect to the 'mutual intention' of the parties as it existed at the time of contracting, it is well settled that the correct approach is to avoid the terminology of 'intention' and look for the *expressed intent* under an *objective standard*." *International Rectifier Corp. v. SGS-Thomson Microelectronics Inc.*, 38 U.S.P.Q.2d 1083, 1101 (Cal. 1994).

℧

Neither the Supreme Court nor the Federal Circuit have determined whether the construction of a means-plus-function claim is a question of law or fact. *Contempo Tobacco Products Inc. v. McKinnie*, 45 U.S.P.Q.2d 1969, 1974 (Ill. 1997).

Construction of Claims. *See also* Claim Construction, Construction, Count.

To interpret means-plus-function claims, one must resort to the last paragraph of 35 U.S.C. §112. The statute expressly states that the patentee is entitled to a claim covering equivalents as well as the specified "structure, material or act." Such a patent claim is construed to cover both the disclosed structure and equivalents thereof. To interpret means-plus-function limitations as limited to a particular means set forth in the specification would be to nullify the provision of §112 requiring that the limitation "shall be construed to cover the structure described in the specification and equivalents thereof." In construing a means-plus-function claim, a number of factors may be considered, including the language of the claim, the patent specification, the prosecution history of the patent, other claims in the patent, and expert testimony. Once such factors are weighed, the scope of the means claim may be determined. *Palumbo v. Don-Joy Co.*, 762 F.2d 969, 226 U.S.P.Q. 5 (Fed. Cir. 1985).

ᙡ

In reexamination proceedings in which the PTO is considering the patentability of claims of an expired patent that are not subject to amendment, a policy of liberal claim construction may properly and should be applied. Such a policy favors a construction of a patent claim that will render it valid (i.e., a narrow construction) over a broad construction that would render it invalid. *Ex parte Papst-Motoren*, 1 U.S.P.Q.2d 1655, 1657 (B.P.A.I. 1986).

ᙡ

Having construed the claims one way for determining their validity, it is axiomatic that the claims must be construed in the same way for infringement. *W. L. Gore & Associates Inc. v. Garlock Inc.*, 842 F.2d 1275, 6 U.S.P.Q.2d 1277 (Fed. Cir. 1988).

Constructive.

The MPEP contains some mandatory language. For the most part, however, the MPEP only suggests or authorizes procedures for patent Examiners to follow. For example, MPEP §707.03(d) provides that Examiners "should allow claims which define the patentable novelty with a reasonable degree of particularity and distinctness." The section further provides, "the Examiner's action should be constructive in nature. . . ." The decision as to what is "reasonable" and "constructive" under the circumstances is necessarily a matter of the Examiner's discretion and judgment. The Forward to the Fifth Edition of the MPEP, dated August 1983, states that the MPEP "contains instructions to examiners," but "does not have the force of law or the force of the Patent Rules of Practice in Title 37, Code of Federal Regulations." The MPEP does not eliminate a patent Examiner's discretion when examining patent applications. Rather, the MPEP is merely part of the overall scheme providing for discretionary examination of patent applications. *Chamberlin v. Isen*, 779 F.2d 522, 228 U.S.P.Q. 369, 372 (9th Cir. 1985).

Constructive Notice.[7]

Constructive Reduction to Practice. *See also* 35 U.S.C. §119.

A proposed amendment (including a new specification and drawing corresponding to those later filed as parts of a copending, but later-filed, application) was refused entry because the substance thereof had not been required and contained new matter not

---

[7]Constructive notice is not limited to the notice provided by a recording system, such as 35 U.S.C. §261. Rather,

> constructive notice may be based on any fact within the knowledge, or means of knowledge, of the purchaser of the unrecorded assignment, and which fact should logically lead him, upon inquiry, to a knowledge of the existence and purport of that assignment itself.

A. Walker, *Walker on Patents* §281 (4th ed. 1904).

supported by the original disclosure. While the proposed substitute specification and drawing (which were identical to those of a subsequently filed application) were physically part of the record of the previously filed application, they never formed part of the official disclosure of that application. The added subject matter has an effective date only as of the filing date of the subsequently filed application. *In re McIntosh,* 230 F.2d 615, 109 U.S.P.Q. 101, 103 (C.C.P.A. 1956).

ᙡ

When an interference count is directed solely to compounds without limitation as to use, to require that the parent application (for purposes of a constructive reduction to practice) disclose the same utility as the involved application would effectively be reading a "use" limitation into the count. Where an interference count does not specify any particular use, proof of substantial utility for any purpose is sufficient to establish either actual or constructive reduction to practice. *Biel v. Coan,* 130 U.S.P.Q. 241, 242 (PO Bd. Pat. Int. 1959).

ᙡ

For an application to be entitled to the benefit of the date of a previously filed copending application, such application must contain a written description of the invention claimed in the second application that complies with the first requirement of the first paragraph of 35 U.S.C. §112. However, the invention claimed in the later application does not have to be described (in the parent application) in ipsis verbis in order to satisfy the description requirement of §112. The question in cases in which the parent application does not contain language contained in the claims of the later application is whether the language that is contained in the parent application is the legal equivalent of the claim language, in the sense that the "necessary and only reasonable construction to be given the disclosure [in the parent application] by one skilled in the art" is the same as the construction that such person would give the language in the claims of the later application (emphasis in original). *Wagoner and Protzman v. Barger and Haggerty,* 463 F.2d 1377, 175 U.S.P.Q. 85, 86 (C.C.P.A. 1972).

ᙡ

The fact that a patent application was made, as a matter of law, constitutes a constructive reduction to practice and negates any theory of abandoned experiment. *Ampex Corp. v. Memorex Corp.,* 205 U.S.P.Q. 794, 797 (Cal. 1980).

ᙡ

An abandoned patent application, with which there is no copendency, is not regarded as a constructive reduction to practice. *In re Costello and McClean,* 717 F.2d 1346, 219 U.S.P.Q. 389 (Fed. Cir. 1983).

ᙡ

The PTO argued that a prefiling deposit with an independent depository, referred to in the specification at the time of filing, was essential to ensure that the disclosure was enabling as of the filing date, which in turn was required so that the filing date might be taken as the date of constructive reduction to practice. The PTO asserted that a post-filing deposit is barred as "new matter," as is the insertion in the specification of reference to such deposit. Constructive reduction to practice, however, does not turn on the question of who has possession of a sample, and thus it does not turn on the inclusion or absence, in the specification as filed, of the name and address of who will have possession of the sample on grant of the patent. The specification, as filed, thus met the requirements of constructive reduction to practice, and the insertion of depository data after filing is not "new matter" under 35 U.S.C. §132. *In re Lundak*, 773 F.2d 1216, 227 U.S.P.Q. 90 (Fed. Cir. 1985).

ω

Actual reduction to practice requires that the claimed invention work for its intended purpose, and, as has long been the law, constructive reduction to practice occurs when a patent application on the claimed invention is filed. *Hybritech Inc. v. Monoclonal Antibodies, Inc.*, 802 F.2d 1367, 231 U.S.P.Q. 81 (Fed. Cir. 1986).

Constructive Trustee.

When an employee has acquired patents on inventions developed by his former employer, the courts will hold the wrongdoer to be a constructive trustee of the property misappropriated and will order a conveyance by the wrongdoer to the former employer. *Richardson v. Suzuki Motor Co., Ltd.*, 868 F.2d 1226, 9 U.S.P.Q.2d 1913 (Fed. Cir. 1989).

Construe.

Paragraph 6 of 35 U.S.C. §112 cannot be ignored when a claim is before the PTO any more than when it is before the courts in an issued patent. *In re Iwahashi*, 888 F.2d 1370, 1375 n.1, 12 U.S.P.Q.2d 1908, 1912 n.1 (Fed. Cir. 1989).

ω

The Supreme Court used the terms "construed" or "cover" around 1952 when referring to post-issuance matters in court (e.g., validity or infringement), and not to interpretation of claims by the PTO in a patentability determination. It is thus reasonable to conclude that a 1952 statute that used either of those terms referred only to matters in court, not in the PTO. Since the last clause of 35 U.S.C. §112's final paragraph used (a) "construed" and (b) "covered" in the same phrase "construed to cover", it must have referred only to infringement cases in court. *Ex parte Isaksen*, 23 U.S.P.Q.2d 1001, 1011 (B.P.A.I. 1991).

Consultant. *See* Expert.

Contain. *See also* Comprising.

The term "containing" in its general usage is intended to allow for substances in a claimed composition other than those specifically named. Such a term does not broaden a claim or a count to include ingredients that would change the nature or intent of the invention. However, restricting the general meaning of or placing a limitation on such terms as "containing," "comprising," and the like is not without precedent. *Price v. Vandenberg v. Bailey*, 174 U.S.P.Q. 42, 43 (PO Bd. Pat. Int. 1971).

Contemplate. *See also* **Assertion.**

The test under 35 U.S.C. §103 is not what "one might contemplate." The proper test is whether the references, taken as a whole, would suggest the invention to one of ordinary skill in the art. *Medtronic, Inc. v. Cardiac Pacemakers, Inc.*, 421 F.2d 1563, 220 U.S.P.Q. 97, 110 (Fed. Cir. 1983).

Contemporaneous Independent Invention.

Because Title 35 provides for interference proceedings, it implicitly recognizes that contemporaneous independent invention may not alone show obviousness. *Monarch Knitting Machinery Corp. v. Sulzer Morat GmbH*, 139 F.3d 877, 45 U.S.P.Q.2d 1977, 1983 (Fed. Cir. 1998).

Contempt.

When a suit is settled and a judgment entered permanently enjoining defendant from further infringement, defendant's intended act, if not already consummated, to import unlicensed tetracycline is a civil contempt of the court's order that must be punished unless it is found that enforcement of the order would thwart justice and perpetrate a wrong. *Charles Pfizer Co., Inc. v. Davis-Edwards Pharmacal Corp.*, 267 F. Supp. 42, 152 U.S.P.Q. 803, 804 (N.Y. 1967).

ω

Having enjoined an infringer, a patent owner who is confronted with another possible infringement by that party in the form of a modified device will very likely seek to invoke the power of the court to punish the adjudged infringer for contempt in violating the court's injunctive order. While the patent owner could institute a separate suit to enjoin the modified device, the advantages to proceeding on a motion to hold his adversary in contempt are substantial. The adjudged infringer is already under the jurisdiction of the court and may be summoned to appear to respond on the merits, the contempt motion being merely part of the original action. An enjoined party under a narrow decree will not be permitted to escape on a purely "in rem" theory that only a particular device is prohibited where it is evident that the modifications do not avoid infringement and were made for the purpose of evasion of the court's order. The standard is whether the differences between the two devices are merely colorable. *KSM Fastening Systems, Inc. v. H. A. Jones Co., Inc.*, 776 F.2d 1522, 227 U.S.P.Q. 676, 677, 679 (Fed. Cir. 1985).

ω

A distinction between civil and criminal contempt lies in what the court primarily seeks to accomplish by imposing sentence in the proceedings. A civil contempt sanction is remedial and for the benefit of the complainant, while a criminal contempt sentence is punitive, intended to vindicate the authority of the court. Judicial sanctions in criminal contempt proceedings may, in a proper case, be employed for either or both of two purposes: to coerce the defendant to comply with the court's order, and to compensate the complainant for losses sustained. Where compensation is intended, a fine is imposed, payable to the complainant. Such a fine must be based upon evidence of the complainant's actual loss. Although a fine payable to the court is normally punitive, it is also remedial when the defendant can avoid paying the fine simply by performing the affirmative act required by the court's order. Because criminal contempt is intended to vindicate the authority of the court, it cannot be purged by any act of the contemnor. It is unconditional since it penalizes yesterday's defiance rather than seeking to coerce tomorrow's compliance. It cannot be ended or shortened by any act by the defendant. *Spindelfabrik Suessen-Schurr, Stahlecker & Grill GmbH v. Schubert & Salzer Maschinenfabrik Aktiengesellschaft*, 903 F.2d 1568, 14 U.S.P.Q.2d 1913, 1921, 1922 (Fed. Cir. 1990).

ϖ

A court has the inherent power to hold a party in civil contempt in order to enforce compliance with an order of the court or to compensate for losses or damages. However, this power may be exercised only if (1) the accused party had actual knowledge of the order, (2) the order is clear and unambiguous, and (3) proof of noncompliance is clear and convincing. *Bulk Store Structures Ltd. v. Campcore Inc.*, 16 U.S.P.Q.2d 2029, 2033 (N.Y. 1990).

ϖ

In deciding whether to conduct contempt proceedings, a trial court must act expeditiously to protect litigants from continuing infringements after adjudication. Further, a trial court may act expeditiously to enforce its orders in the face of conduct ignoring judicial authority. *Lund Industries Inc. v. GO Industries Inc.*, 938 F.2d 1273, 19 U.S.P.Q.2d 1383, 1385 (Fed. Cir. 1991).

ϖ

"In deciding whether to conduct contempt proceedings, a trial court must act expeditiously to protect litigants from continuing infringements after an adjudication. Further, a trial court may act expeditiously to enforce its orders in the face of conduct ignoring judicial authority. "Infringement is the *sine qua non* of violation of an injunction against infringements." *Additive Controls and Measurement Systems Inc. v. Flowdata Inc.*, 32 U.S.P.Q.2d 1747, 1753 (Tex. 1994).

ϖ

To show contempt, a patent owner must prove by clear and convincing evidence that "the modified device falls within the admitted or adjudicated scope of the claims and is, therefore, an infringement". A trial court may decide contempt motions "on affidavits and exhibits without the formalities of a full trial". *Arbek Manufacturing Inc. v. Moazzam*, 55 F.3d 1567, 34 U.S.P.Q.2d 1670, 1671 (Fed. Cir. 1995).

ϖ

Contempt is not a sword for wounding a former infringer who has made a goodfaith effort to modify a previously adjudged or admitted infringing device to remain in the marketplace. Moreover, in balancing protection for the patentee and for the former infringer, "...if there are substantial open issues with respect to infringement to be tried, contempt proceedings are inappropriate. The presence of such disputed issues creates a fair ground for doubt that the decree has been violated." *Pirkle v. Ogontz Controls Co.*, 39 U.S.P.Q.2d 1317, 1318 (Pa. 1996).

ϖ

Non-parties may be held in contempt if they "either abet the defendant, or [are] legally identified with him." They are also subject to contempt sanctions if they act with an enjoined party to bring about a result forbidden by the injunction, but only if they are aware of the injunction and know that their acts violate the injunction. *Additive Controls & Measurement Systems Inc. v. Flowdata Inc.*, 47 U.S.P.Q.2d 1906, 1909, 1911 (Fed. Cir. 1998).

Context. *See* **Teach Away From.**

Continuation Application. *See also* **Continuing Application, Continuity, Recapture.**

An applicant has a right to file a continuation application (following an adverse Board of Appeals decision) within the time allowed for further appeal. He has the further right to have such continuation application examined. A holding of res judicata without reliance on any other ground of rejection is not an examination on the merits of the application and may not be used in such a situation. *In re Kaghan, Schmitt, and Kay*, 387 F.2d 398, 156 U.S.P.Q. 130, 132 (C.C.P.A. 1967).

ᙒ

Representing an application to be a continuation application when it is, in fact, a continuation-in-part application is not necessarily material to the Examiner's subjective decision to allow claims therein. *Langer and Tornqvist v. Kaufman and McMullen*, 465 F.2d 915, 175 U.S.P.Q. 172, 176 (C.C.P.A. 1972).

ᙒ

A pending utility application can be amended by filing a continuing plant application when the parent application contains a written description of the subject matter claimed in the continuing application. The deposit of a culture of the claimed microfungi in a public depository complies with the accepted procedure for meeting the requirements of 35 U.S.C. §112 and §162. *Ex parte Solomons and Scammell*, 201 U.S.P.Q. 42, 43 (PTO Bd. App. 1978).

ᙒ

A nonreissue continuation application may be based on a pending reissue application if no statutory bar exists. The basic requirements of §120 are copendency, continuity of disclosure and inventorship, and reference to the earlier application. Additionally, the continuing application must contain a specific reference to the earlier-filed application. There is no reason that a barrier to the patentability of claims in a parent (reissue) application that is unrelated to the date of constructive reduction to practice necessarily precludes claims in a later application from receiving the benefit of the parent's filing date. As stated in *Godfrey v. Eames*, [68 U.S. 317 (1863)], which involved only regular, nonreissue applications, two applications (parent and continuing) "are to be considered as parts of the same transaction, and both as constituting one continuous application, within the meaning of the law." *In re Bauman*, 683 F.2d 405, 214 U.S.P.Q. 585 (C.C.P.A. 1982).

ᙒ

An objection to a disclosure as a "continuation" is a petitionable matter and not subject to appeal. *Ex parte George*, 230 U.S.P.Q. 575 (B.P.A.I. 1984).

ᙒ

A parent application and a continuation thereof constitute one continuous application. To the extent that an applicant submits material in an initial patent application, the applicant cannot be found to have omitted that material from the continuation application. *Beckman Instruments, Inc. v. LKB Produkter A.B.*, 5 U.S.P.Q.2d 1462 (Md. 1987).

ʊ

Section 120 (35 U.S.C.) neither establishes nor implies a requirement that a continuation application must be identical to the original application in all respects. As long ago explained in *Godfrey v. Eames*, 68 U.S. (1 Wall.) 317, 324-25 (1863):

> A change in the specification as filed in the first instance, or the subsequent filing of a new one, whereby a patent is still sought for the substance of the invention as originally claimed, or a part of it, cannot in any wise affect the sufficiency of the original application or the legal consequences flowing from it. To produce that result the new or amended application must be intended to serve as the basis of the patent for a distinct and different invention, and one not contemplated by the specification, as submitted at the outset.

Transco Products Inc. v. Performance Contracting Inc., 821 F.Supp. 537, 28 U.S.P.Q.2d 1739, 1748 (Ill. 1993).

Continuation-in-Part (cip) Application. *See also* Continuation Application, Recapture.

The term "continuation" apparently was first used as applying to an application in which the prosecution of an earlier application was continued. Sometimes, however, in filing such second application, the applicant adds to the disclosure of the earlier application some additional disclosure, and the term "continuation-in-part" was used to identify the relation between these two applications. This latter term, however, has come to be used in a similar and different sense; namely, in referring to a second application that discloses subject matter taken from the first (to which extent it could be called a division) and additional subject matter not disclosed in the first. In no case should an application be called a continuation-in-part of an earlier application where the one has a different specific disclosure from the other and they are merely related in the sense that both are species of a broader invention, and, hence, if broad claims are presented in the latter application, they will read on the earlier. Whether a later application is either a continuation or a continuation-in-part of an earlier application should be determined (as is the question whether a second application is a division of an earlier one) by the disclosure and not by the claims. *In re Klein,* 5 U.S.P.Q. 259 (Commr. Patents 1930).

ʊ

The claims on appeal were first supported by and made in an application filed nearly two years after publication of the British priority specification, fully disclosing the invention as applied to a species within the generic claims. The disclosure of a species in a reference is sufficient to prevent a later applicant from obtaining generic claims, unless the reference can be overcome. The British specification, published more than a year prior to filing the generic disclosure, is clearly a statutory bar to the granting of the generic claims. *In re Ruscetta and Jenny,* 255 F.2d 687, 118 U.S.P.Q. 101, 104 (C.C.P.A. 1958).

ᵡ

Claims to compounds in a cip application that are identical to claims in the parent application are entitled to the benefit of the filing date of the parent application even though the utility of the compounds set forth in the cip application is different from that indicated in the parent application, as long as there is common inventorship, cross-reference required by 35 U.S.C. §120, and disclosure in the parent application complying with the first paragraph of 35 U.S.C. §112. *In re Kirchner,* 305 F.2d 897, 134 U.S.P.Q. 324, 330 (C.C.P.A. 1962).

ᵡ

To obtain the benefit of the filing date of a parent application for subject matter claimed in a cip, the parent application must satisfy the description requirement of the statute with regard to that subject matter. Neither a specific example falling within the scope of (but not commensurate in scope with) nor a disclosure generic to such subject matter will suffice. In either or both cases publication of the applicant's own foreign application more than a year prior to the filing date of the cip serves as a statutory bar. *In re Lukach, Olson, and Spurlin,* 440 F.2d 1263, 169 U.S.P.Q. 795, 796, 797 (C.C.P.A. 1971).

ᵡ

If an application discloses a new composition of matter and describes a utility of it sufficiently to satisfy 35 U.S.C. §112, a later-filed cip application may claim the date of the first application even though the later application is supported with an additional (but not contradictory) utility not included in the first application. Section 120 requires only that the "invention" (which is the new composition of matter in se), and not either the statement of utility, nor the manner in which the cip application otherwise complies with the requirement of §112, be identical. *Carter-Wallace, Inc. v. Davis-Edwards Pharmacal Corp.,* 341 F. Supp. 1303, 173 U.S.P.Q. 65, 104 (N.Y. 1972).

ᵡ

A continuation-in-part of two parent applications is entitled to the benefit of the filing dates of the respective parent applications even though support for the subject matter of one claim is dependent upon the combined disclosures of both parent applications. *Ex parte Janin,* 209 U.S.P.Q. 761, 764 (PTO Bd. App. 1979).

ᵡ

A cip application is an application that is filed during the pendency of an application filed earlier by the same inventor (i.e., the parent application), disclosing some subject matter common to the parent application, as well as some subject matter not common to and not supported by the parent application. The cip application may or may not claim the new subject matter. Although a cip application discloses subject matter not found in the parent application, one or more of its claims may be directed solely to subject matter disclosed in the parent application. In such cases, the effective filing date for the cip claims that are supported in the parent application is the filing date of the parent application. *Rohm & Haas Co. v. Dawson Chemical Co., Inc.*, 557 F. Supp. 739, 217 U.S.P.Q. 515, 533 (Tex. 1983).

℧

An invention claimed in a cip, which is not patentably distinct from that claimed in a patent issued on the parent application, may not be salvageable with a terminal disclaimer if the invention claimed in the issued patent was on sale more than one year prior to the filing date of the cip. The on-sale bar cannot be overcome by a terminal disclaimer. *Gemveto Jewelry Co. v. Jeff Cooper Inc.*, 368 F. Supp. 319, 219 U.S.P.Q. 806 (N.Y. 1983).

℧

The filing of a cip application raises an irrebuttable presumption that the cip application adds new subject matter. An applicant's filing of a cip application estops the applicant from arguing that the cip application does not disclose new subject matter or that the subject matter was inherent in an earlier application. *Litton Systems, Inc. v. Whirlpool Corp.*, 728 F.2d 1423, 221 U.S.P.Q. 97 (Fed. Cir. 1984).

℧

The filing of a cip application to overcome a PTO rejection does not give rise to an irrebutable presumption of acquiesence in the rejection. Whether claims are entitled to the cip application's filing date or that of a parent application becomes important when an intervening event occurs that will invalidate the claims under 35 U.S.C. §102 if they are only accorded the latter filing date. *Pennwalt Corp. v. Akzona Inc.*, 740 F.2d 1573, 222 U.S.P.Q. 833, 836 (Fed. Cir. 1984).

℧

The change in a lower limit of a range in a continuing application can be, but is not necessarily, fatal to relying on the filing date of the parent application for the invention claimed in a continuing application. *Synthetic Industries (Texas) Inc. v. Forta Fiber, Inc.*, 590 F. Supp. 1574, 224 U.S.P.Q. 955 (Pa. 1984).

℧

The filing of a cip application to overcome a PTO rejection does not give rise to an irrebuttable presumption of acquiescence in the rejection. Whether claims are entitled to a cip application's filing date or that of a parent application becomes important when an intervening event occurs that will invalidate the claims under 35 U.S.C. §102 if they are only accorded the latter filing date. When a cip is filed subsequent to receipt of a new matter rejection, the applicant may be estopped from arguing that the cip application only added subject matter that was inherent in the parent application. *Foseco International Ltd. v. Fireline, Inc.*, 607 F. Supp. 1537, 226 U.S.P.Q. 33 (Ohio 1984).

℧

The mere designation of a continuing application as a continuation-in-part application may preclude obtaining the benefit of the filing date of a copending parent application whether or not added text is actually objectionable new matter under the statute. *Litton Systems, Inc. v. Whirlpool Corp.*, 728 F.2d 1423, 221 U.S.P.Q. 97 (Fed. Cir. 1984).

℧

The filing date of a copending parent application is the effective date for claims in a second application drawn to subject matter that is also disclosed in the parent application, as well as for claims (added through amendment) that define subject matter that is deemed "inherent" to the parent application. Relying on the PTO Manual of Patent Examining Procedure (MPEP) definition of a cip application, the *Litton* court [in *Litton Systems, Inc. v. Whirlpool Corp.*, 728 F.2d 1423, 221 U.S.P.Q. 97 (Fed. Cir. 1984)] held that the filing of a cip application raises an irrebuttable presumption that the cip application adds new subject matter. An applicant's filing of a cip application, therefore, estops the applicant from arguing that the cip application does not disclose new subject matter or that the subject matter was inherent in an earlier application. *Foseco International Ltd. v. Fireline, Inc.*, 607 F. Supp. 1537, 224 U.S.P.Q. 888 (Ohio 1984).

ω

After the PTO holds that an amendment to the specification involves new matter, the filing of a continuing application that includes the amendatory material and designating the application as a continuation-in-part (cip) application constitutes an acquiesence in the PTO's conclusion that the amendment contained new matter. *Max Daetwyler Corp. v. Input Graphics, Inc.*, 608 F. Supp. 1549, 226 U.S.P.Q. 393 (Pa. 1985).

ω

Since there was no final rejection on insufficiency of disclosure in the prosecution of the previously-filed (parent) application, the filing of a cip (with an amplified disclosure) was not an admission that the parent's disclosure was insufficient. When a patent issues on a cip application and a claim thereof is determined to be limited to the filing date of the cip application because the disclosure of the parent application is insufficient to support such claim, a corresponding foreign publication (patent) that is substantially the same as the parent application is also insufficient to anticipate the claim under 35 U.S.C. §102(b). The correct role of the foreign publication in such case is as a reference under 35 U.S.C. §103. *Paperless Accounting, Inc. v. Bay Area Rapid TransitSystem*, 804 F.2d 659, 231 U.S.P.Q. 649, 652, 653 (Fed. Cir. 1986).

ω

When a patent issues on an application that is a continuation-in-part of a parent application, the prosecution history of the parent application and the construction of a term contained in claims of the parent application are relevant to an understanding of the same term as it is used in claims of the patent issuing on the cip application. *Jonsson v. The Stanley Works*, 903 F.2d 812, 14 U.S.P.Q.2d 1863, 1869 (Fed. Cir. 1990).

ω

A cip application has the benefit of the effective filing date of its parent application as to all subject matter common to both applications. *Stranco Inc. v. Atlantes Chemical Systems Inc.*, 15 U.S.P.Q.2d 1704, 1713 (Tex. 1990).

Continuing Application. *See also* **Continuation Application, Continuation-in-Part Application, Division, Recapture.**

If the present appellants had not filed continuing applications, the only filing date involved would be that of the 1953 application. To judge the 1971 application in isolation would have a chilling effect upon the right of applicants to file continuations. The 24 years of pendency herein may be decried, but a limit upon continuing applications is a matter of policy for the Congress. As presently constituted, the law as set forth in 35 U.S.C. §§112 and 120 is the same for all applications, whether of long or short pendency. *In re Hogan and Banks,* 559 F.2d 595, 194 U.S.P.Q. 527 (C.C.P.A. 1977).

ʊ

An applicant, under the statutes, is entitled as a matter of right to amend his pending utility application by filing a continuing plant application. *Ex parte Solomons and Scammell,* 201 U.S.P.Q. 42 (PTO Bd. App. 1978).

ʊ

Where the basic process and claimed improvement are disclosed in each of several parent applications and it is only in considering the basic starting materials that it is necessary to direct attention to the different parent applications for adequate support, a continuing application is entitled to the benefit of the filing dates of the respective parent applications. The subject continuing application has not combined bits and pieces of previously disclosed and claimed subject matter, but has consolidated two parent disclosures into a single unitary concept. *Ex parte Janin,* 209 U.S.P.Q. 761, 764 (PTO Bd. App. 1979).

ʊ

The Commissioner reviewed a decision of the Group Director denying the applicant's design application the benefit of the filing date of a utility application, of which the design application was a purported cip. No art rejection on an intervening reference was made. The Commissioner held that the decision by the Group Director (denying continuation status) is reversed without prejudice to a later consideration of the issue in a proper forum. *In re Corba,* 212 U.S.P.Q. 825 (Comm'r Patents 1981).

ʊ

The statement that parent and continuing applications are considered "parts of the same transaction, and . . . as constituting one continuous application" does not necessarily mean that a continuing application must be based on an application upon which a valid patent could have issued. There is no reason that a barrier to the patentability of claims in a parent application that is unrelated to the date of constructive reduction to practice necessarily precludes claims in a later application from receiving the benefit of the parent's filing date. *In re Bauman,* 683 F.2d 405, 214 U.S.P.Q. 585, 588 (C.C.P.A. 1982).

ʊ

Section 120 (35 U.S.C.) plainly allows continuation, divisional, and continuation-in-part applications to be filed and afforded the filing date of the parent application even though there is not complete identity of inventorship between the parent and subsequent applications. D. Chisum, *Patents* §13.07 (1955). *In re Chu,* 66 F.3d 292, 36 U.S.P.Q.2d 1089, 1093 (Fed. Cir. 1995).

ʊ

An abusive continuing application practice is challenged because of prejudice imposed upon all manufacturers or users of related products. *Ford Motor Co. v. Lemelson,* 40 U.S.P.Q.2d 1349, 1362 (Nev. 1996).

Continuity.

The doctrine of continuity holds that a second application should be considered a continuation of a first application and entitled to the filing date of the first application where a patent is still sought for the substance of the originally claimed invention. In order for the doctrine to be applicable, it is necessary that the description in both applications be sufficient to support the claims. *Bersworth v. Watson*, 159 F. Supp 12, 116 U.S.P.Q. 87 (D.C. 1956).

ω

In order for a patent to be entitled to the filing date of the first application in a chain of applications of which it is a part, it must be shown that, as to the inventions claimed, there has been continuous disclosure through the chain of applications, without hiatus. Such hiatus does not result from cancellation of relevant disclosure from one of the applications in the chain, since such disclosure can be reinstated in that application during the life thereof. A hiatus occurs when an application (in the chain) is filed without such relevant disclosure. *Lemelson v. TRW, Inc.*, 760 F.2d 1254, 225 U.S.P.Q. 697 (Fed. Cir. 1985).

Continuity of Disclosure.

Entitlement to a filing date does not extend to subject matter which is not disclosed, but would be obvious over what is expressly disclosed. It extends only to that which is disclosed. A prior application itself must describe an invention, and do so in sufficient detail that one skilled in the art can clearly conclude that the inventor invented the claimed invention as of the filing date sought. *Lockwood v. American Airlines Inc.*, 41 U.S.P.Q.2d 1961 (Fed. Cir. 1997).

Continuous Activity.

Because public policy favors early disclosure, the law is reluctant to displace an inventor who was the first to disclose his invention to the public. To satisfy the reasonable diligence requirement of 35 U.S.C. §102(g), the work relied on must ordinarily be directly related to reduction to practice of the invention of the counts in issue in an interference. During the critical period there must be "reasonably continuous activity." *Griffith v. Kanamaru*, 231 U.S.P.Q. 892, 893 (B.P.A.I. 1986).

Contract.[8] *See also* State Law, United States Government.

Notwithstanding an agreement not to infringe the plaintiff's patents (avoiding any need for plaintiff to resort to a patent infringement suit) until such time as there is an adjudication determining that the patents are invalid or that the life of the patents has expired, defendants are free to seek an independent determination of the validity of

---

[8] Title to intellectual property in research and development contract—see *Beech Aircraft Corp. v. EDO Corp.*, 990 F.2d 1237, 26 U.S.P.Q.2d 1572, 1575 (Fed. Cir. 1993).

plaintiff's patents. The agreement was entered into for valuable consideration and should be respected by the parties and enforced by the courts until there is such an adjudication. The agreement does not require plaintiff to prove the validity of the patents to be entitled to enforcement of the agreement by the court. *The Battelle Development Corp. v. Angevine-Funke, Inc.*, 165 U.S.P.Q. 776, 778 (Ohio 1970).

ω

Claims of defendants' violation of the terms of an agreement by their alleged sale and manufacture of plastic hoops arise under general principles of contract law. The fact that the manufacture and sale of these hoops may also be an infringement of the plaintiff's patent does not alter this conclusion. Defendants have agreed that plaintiff's patent is valid and infringed by the manufacture and sale of the hoops in question. As a result, a determination of the merits, in the first instance, requires an analysis of the agreement and not an analysis of the validity and infringement of the patent. Nor can the defendants turn this matter into one arising under the patent laws of the United States by asserting the invalidity defense. *Wham-O Manufacturing Co. v. All-American Yo-Yo Corp.*, 377 F. Supp. 993, 181 U.S.P.Q. 320, 321 (N.Y. 1973).

ω

A patent is not a contract. A patent is "*a grant*...of the right to exclude others from making, using or selling the invention throughout the United States," 35 U.S.C. §154 (emphasis added). A patent has "the attributes of personal *property*," 35 U.S.C. §261 (emphasis added). *In re Yardley*, 493 F.2d 1389, 181 U.S.P.Q. 331, 335 (C.C.P.A. 1974).

ω

Since *Lear, Inc. v. Adkins*, 395 U.S. 653, 162 U.S.P.Q. 1 (1969), state courts have passed upon the defense of patent validity in breach of contract cases. *Consolidated Kinetics Corp. v. Marshall, Weil, and Pauley*, 182 U.S.P.Q. 434, 435, 436, 521 P.2d 1209, (Wash. Ct. App. 1974).

ω

The Examiner's notion about the United States granting a contract is inapt. The government grants only a right to exclude. There is no other agreement. While a patent has often been likened to a contract on the theory that it is issued in exchange for the disclosure of the invention (the consideration), the analogy is inexact. A patent is a statutory right. It is granted to whoever fulfills the conditions, 35 U.S.C. §101, unless fraud has been committed. *In re Breslow*, 616 F.2d 516, 205 U.S.P.Q. 221, 224 (C.C.P.A. 1980).

ω

A patent is a written contract between an inventor and the government. The consideration given on the part of the inventor to the government is the disclosure of his invention. The consideration on the part of the government given to the patentee for such disclosure is a monopoly for 17 years of the invention disclosed to the extent of the claims allowed in the patent. The interpretation of patent claims is conducted according to the same general rules of construction as other contracts. *Amgen Inc. v. Chugai Pharmaceutical Co.*, 706 F. Supp. 94, 9 U.S.P.Q.2d 1833 (Mass. 1989).

ω

As a matter of law, the issuance of a patent by the PTO does not create a contractual relationship between that office and the patentee. *Constant v. United States,* 929 F.2d 654, 18 U.S.P.Q.2d 1298, 1299 (Fed. Cir. 1991).

ʊ

[I]t is the duty of every contracting party to learn and know [the contract's] contents before he signs and delivers it. He owes this duty to the other party to the contract, because the latter may, and probably will, pay his money and shape his action in reliance upon the agreement. He owes it to the public, which, as a matter of public policy treats the written contract as a conclusive answer to the question, what was the agreement? *Bradley v. Chiron*, 45 U.S.P.Q.2d 1819, 1823 (Fed. Cir. 1998).

Contractual Relations.

The elements of intentional interference with contractual relations are: (1) a valid contract between the plaintiff and a third party; (2) the defendant's knowledge of this contract; (3) the defendant's intentional acts to induce a breach or disruption of the contractual relationship; and (4) resulting damage. *Litton Systems Inc. v. Honeywell Inc.*, 39 U.S.P.Q.2d 1321, 1330 (Fed. Cir. 1996).

Contradict.

If the appellants wished to object to the Board's statement and to question the correctness of the facts contained therein, they should have requested the Board to cite its author-ity for the statement. If the cited authority was based upon facts within the personal knowledge of the Board, the appellants should have proceeded under Rules 66 and 76 of the Patent Office and called for an affidavit of the Board. The appellants would then have been in a position to contradict or explain the Board's statement. In the absence of such request, the appellants may not be heard to challenge a statement made in the Board's opinion. The statement of the board must therefore be accepted as correct. *In re Selmi and Altenburger,* 156 F.2d 96, 70 U.S.P.Q. 197 (C.C.P.A. 1946).

Contrary. *See* Teach Away From.

Contributing Cause.

That the unexpectedly superior activity or property of an end product has to do with a pharmaceutical utility is an insufficient justification for precluding a determination that the claimed intermediate is the contributing cause of the end product's unexpectedly superior activity or property. Although the action of many pharmaceuticals, as well as many chemical compounds, is "unpredictable" and "generally highly specific," such factors will be reflected in the evidence required to meet the contributing-cause test. In order to establish that the claimed intermediate is the contributing cause of the unexpectedly superior activity or property of the end product, an applicant must identify the cause of the unexpectedly superior activity or property (compared to the prior art) in the end product and establish a nexus for that cause between the intermediate and the end product. *In re Magerlein,* 602 F.2d 366, 202 U.S.P.Q. 473, 479 (C.C.P.A. 1979).

Contributory Infringement. *See also* **Component, Induce, Reconstruction, Repair, Replacement.**

A completed act of infringement is not necessary to afford ground of relief in an action for contributory infringement; threatened infringement is sufficient. *Graham Paper Company v. International Paper Company*, 46 F.2d 881, 8 U.S.P.Q. 463, 468 (8th Cir. 1931).

ω

The presence or absence of the element of substantial noninfringing use is significant principally in determining whether there is an intention to infringe. The absence of a substantial noninfringing use, of course, warrants the inference of an intention to infringe. As to situations in which intention is clearly established by other evidence, there is some indication that suitability for noninfringing use is no defense. *Fromberg, Inc. v. Thornhill*, 315 F.2d 407, 137 U.S.P.Q. 84, 89 n.20 (5th Cir. 1963).

ω

A supplier of replacement parts specially designed for use in the repair of infringing articles is liable for contributory infringement. *Aro Manufacturing Co., Inc. v. Convertible Top Replacement Co., Inc.*, 377 U.S. 476, 141 U.S.P.Q. 681, 686 (1964).

ω

Section 271(c) of 35 U.S.C. prohibits the "sale," whether or not domestic, of an "apparatus for use in [the domestic practice] of a patented process" where the seller knows that the apparatus will reach domestic markets and there will be found "especially adapted for an infringement" of the patent. 35 U.S.C. §271(b) and (c) was meant to confirm the principle of contributory infringement based upon aiding and abetting a direct infringer. The foreign manufacture of patented devices for ultimate sale in the United States is thus in conflict with the statue's purpose. *Engineered Sports Products v. Brunswick Corp.*, 362 F. Supp. 722, 179 U.S.P.Q. 486, 489 (Utah 1973).

ω

A patent holder must establish acts of direct infringement before liability for inducement or contributory infringement can be found. In order to establish inducement to infringe a method patent, plaintiffs have the burden of showing that defendant encouraged others, through its literature, to take each and every step of the method. *Plastering Development Center, Inc. v. Perma Glas-Mesh Corp.*, 371 F. Supp. 939, 179 U.S.P.Q. 838, 845, 846 (Ohio 1973).

ω

An inducement under 35 U.S.C. §271(b), like a direct infringement under §271(a), does not require a specific intent. *Hauni Werke Koerber & Co., KG. v. Molins Limited*, 183 U.S.P.Q. 168, 171 (Va. 1974).

ω

The manufacture and sale of an unpatented component of a combination patent is not a direct infringement under 35 U.S.C. §271(a). A purchaser buys the use of a whole combination, and repair or replacement of a worn out part is but an exercise of the right "to give duration to that which he owns, or has a right to use as a whole." Maintenance of the use of the whole of the patented combination through replacement of a spent, unpatented element does not constitute reconstruction. Reconstruction of a patented entity, comprised of unpatented elements, is limited to such a true reconstruction of the entity as to, in fact, make a new article after the entity (viewed as a whole) has become spent. This is true even where the replacement part is not a staple article or commodity of commerce suitable for substantial use other than as part of the patented invention. *Biuro Projektow Zaklodow Przerobki Mechanicznej Wegla "Separator" v. UOP, Inc.*, 203 U.S.P.Q. 175, 179 (Ill. 1979).

ᚩ

The owner of a patent on a chemical process is not guilty of patent misuse and therefore barred from seeking relief against contributory infringement of its patent rights if it exploits the patent only in conjunction with the sale of an unpatented article that constitutes a material part of the invention and is not suited for commercial use outside the scope of the patent claims. *Dawson Chemical Co. v. Rohm & Haas Co.*, 448 U.S. 176, 206 U.S.P.Q. 385, 389, 407 (1980).

ᚩ

Unlike direct infringement, which must take place within the United States, contributory infringement under 35 U.S.C. §271(b) or (c) does not require any activity by the contributory infringer in this country, as long as the direct infringement occurs here. *Nippon Electric Glass Co., Ltd. v. Sheldon*, 489 F. Supp. 119, 209 U.S.P.Q. 1023, 1025, 1026 (N.Y. 1980).

ᚩ

A U.S. process patent may only be infringed by processes carried out in the United States. A product made by a process does not infringe a patent on that process. The defendant's manufacturing activities in Italy, followed by sales in the United States, were not regarded as sufficient grounds for patent infringement. The defendant could not be guilty of contributory infringement in the absence of some direct infringement of the patent. The plaintiff asserted that the defendant had induced others to perform the third step of a patented process; however, no argument was made that anyone in the United States had engaged in the first two steps of the patent process. The plaintiff therefore failed to state a claim for infringement of the patent because a patent for a method or process is not infringed unless all of the steps or stages of the process are used. *University Patents Inc. v. Questor Corp.*, 517 F. Supp. 676, 213 U.S.P.Q. 711 (Colo. 1981).

ᚩ

The plaintiff alleged that the defendants, knowing that the grant of a patent was imminent, "flooded the market with infringing products with the knowledge, belief or expectation that a substantial portion if not all of said cookies would be the subject of infringing retail sales to the public after the patent issued." The case involved the same risk of harm to the patentee as the cases that applied the common law doctrine of contributory infringement. The defendants had allegedly evaded an action for direct infringement by rushing shipments to retailers, and the plaintiff had no practical remedy for the direct infringement. The doctrine of contributory infringement was developed to protect against these very acts. Under the circumstances, the legislative intent to codify the common law rule was held to be best effectuated by allowing the count to remain.

Such a conclusion is not without some support in reported cases. Several other courts have concluded that liability for inducement under 271(b) can be based on preissuance activities. *The Procter & Gamble Company v. Nabisco Brands, Inc.*, 604 F. Supp. 1485, 225 U.S.P.Q. 929 (Del. 1985).

ᴡ

A patent owner's unrestricted sales of a machine useful only in performing a patented process and producing a patented product "plainly indicate that the grant of a license should be inferred." Absent any circumstances tending to show the contrary, the patent owner's customers enjoy an implied license under the patent. Absent direct infringement of the patent claims by those customers, sales of essential elements by another to the same customers can be neither contributory infringement nor inducement of infringement. *Met-Coil Systems Corp. v. Korners Unlimited, Inc.*, 803 F.2d 684, 231 U.S.P.Q. 474, 476, 477 (Fed. Cir. 1986).

ᴡ

Corporate officers who actively aid and abet their corporation's infringement may be personally liable for inducing infringement under 35 U.S.C. §271(b) regardless of whether the corporation is the alter ego of the corporate officer. *Orthokinetics Inc, v. Safety Travel Chairs Inc.*, 806 F.2d 1565, 1 U.S.P.Q.2d 1081, 1090 (Fed. Cir. 1986).

ᴡ

A person may be liable under 35 U.S.C. §271(b) or §271(c) for actions constituting patent infringement but that occurred prior to the date of patent issuance. To establish such liability, the patent holder or his successor in interest must make three showings: (1) It must be demonstrated that the challenged party acted knowingly to induce infringement under §271(b) or to contribute to infringement under §271(c) by selling either a material component of the patented product or a material apparatus for use in practicing a patented process. (2) It must be shown that the party's act culminated in a direct infringement of the patent. (3) It must be demonstrated that the eventual direct infringement occurred within the statutory 17-year life of the patent. If these three showings are made, the complaint in infringement will not be dismissed solely because the challenged actions occurred prior to the date the patent was issued. *Mixing Equipment Co., Inc. v. Innova-Tech, Inc.*, 2 U.S.P.Q.2d 1212 (Pa. 1986).

ᴡ

Liability for contributory infringement under 35 U.S.C. §271(c) is limited to occurrences subsequent to actual knowledge of the patent involved. *Mendenhall v. Astec Industries, Inc.*, 14 U.S.P.Q.2d 1134, 1137 (Tenn. 1988), *aff'd*, 14 U.S.P.Q.2d 1140 (Fed. Cir. 1989).

ᴡ

Failure to raise the issue of knowledge of contributory infringement does not bar consideration of this question for the first time on appeal. *Trell v. Marlee Electronic Corp.*, 912 F.2d 1443, 16 U.S.P.Q.2d 1059, 1063 (Fed. Cir. 1990).

ᴡ

Contributory infringement liability is not meant for situations where noninfringing uses are common as opposed to farfetched, illusory, impractical or merely experimental. 4 Chisum *Patents*, 17.03 [3], at 17-62 (1993). *D.O.C.C. Inc. v. Spintech Inc.*, 93 Civ. 4679, 36 U.S.P.Q.2d 1145, 1155 (N.Y. 1994).

ω

Direct infringement must be pleaded in the complaint in order to state a claim for inducement of infringement and contributory infringement. *Fuji Machine Manufacturing Co. v. Hover-Davis Inc.*, 40 U.S.P.Q.2d 1313, 1315 (N.Y. 1996).

Control.

Although there was no control group of animals to which no test compound was administered, documentary exhibits showing that larger doses successfully inhibited pregnancy in some groups of animals, while sufficiently small doses were partially or totally unsuccessful in preventing pregnancy in other groups of animals, effectively established the other groups of animals as a control group. *Campbell and Babcock v. Wettstein, Anner, Wieland, and Hensler,* 476 F.2d 642, 177 U.S.P.Q. 376, 380 (C.C.P.A. 1973).

ω

"Control" with respect to the production of documents is defined "not only as possession, but as the legal right to obtain the documents requested upon demand." *Cochran Consulting Inc. v. Uwatec USA Inc.*, 41 U.S.P.Q.2d 1161 (Fed. Cir. 1996)

Control of Unpatented Goods. *See also* Misuse.

Through restrictions on the use of his claimed process, a holder of a process patent may exert control over the end product, particularly when the claims of the patent are directed to the only process by which a certain product may be produced commercially. The patentee can, for example, refuse to allow the use of his process at all and thus keep the product produced by that process off the market. One court has held that he may limit the number of articles produced by his process because this is a valid exercise of his process patent rather than an invalid attempt to limit the sale of the unpatented article. *Ethyl Corp. v. Hercules Powder Co.*, 232 F. Supp. 453, 139 U.S.P.Q. 471, 474 (Del. 1963).

ω

It is patent misuse for the holder of a process patent to use license agreements to impose territorial restrictions on sales of unpatented products. However, 35 U.S.C. §271(c) and (d) appears to permit the owner of a patented method to monopolize and reserve to himself sale of unpatented *nonstaple* products that are materially component parts of his patented process. *Robintech, Inc. v. Chemidus Wavin Limited*, 628 F.2d 142, 205 U.S.P.Q. 873, 877 (D.C. Cir. 1980).

Controversy. *See also* Actual Controversy, Case or Controversy, Declaratory Judgment.

There is an obvious distinction between the alleged injury of a party threatened with a lawsuit for infringement and the alleged injury of a patent holder. In a typical patent case brought under the Declaratory Judgment Act, 28 U.S.C. §2201, the plaintiff asserts his intent and ability to produce a product, which defendant contends is a patent infringement. Courts find a justiciable controversy because to do otherwise would leave the plaintiff no option but to produce the products and be sued for infringement. The patent holder, on the other hand, is injured only if actual infringement occurs. His remedy is provided in 35 U.S.C. §271. *D. G. Rung Industries, Inc. v. Tinnerman,* 626 F. Supp. 1062, 229 U.S.P.Q. 930, 932 (Wash. 1986).

ω

A declaratory judgment plaintiff must establish an actual controversy on the "totality of the circumstances." In cases involving a declaratory judgment of patent non-infringement or invalidity, the test for determining whether an actual controversy exists is two-pronged. First, the accused infringer must have actually produced or prepared to produce an allegedly infringing product. The first prong "looks to the accused infringer's conduct and ensures that the controversy is sufficiently real and substantial." Second, the patent holder's conduct must create an objectively reasonable apprehension on the part of the accused infringer that the patent holder will initiate suit if the allegedly infringing activity continues. Application of the rule of law requiring that jurisdictional facts (sufficient to support declaratory judgment jurisdiction) be alleged in a well-pleaded complaint does not conclude the inquiry since facts sufficient to vest jurisdiction initially may remain immutable where no justiciable controversy survives. "Article III of the Constitution requires that there be a live case or controversy at the time that a federal court decides the case." Moreover, "[a]n actual controversy must be extant at all stages of review, not merely at the time the complaint is filed." *Spectronics Corp. v. H. B. Fuller Co. Inc.,* 940 F.2d 631, 19 U.S.P.Q.2d 1545, 1547, 1548 (Fed. Cir. 1991).

ω

A patent owner's willingness and capacity to enforce its patent rights is pertinent to the inquiry for an actual controversy. However, litigation against unrelated third parties by the patent owner does not give plaintiff in a declaratory judgment action reason to fear litigation. *West Interactive Corp. v. First Data Resources Inc.,* 972 F.2d 1295, 23 U.S.P.Q.2d 1927, 1930 (Fed. Cir. 1992).

ω

"The requirement of actual controversy encompasses concepts such as ripeness, standing, and the prohibition against advisory judicial rulings". *BP Chemicals Ltd. v. Union Carbide Corp.,* 4 F.3d 975, 977, 28 U.S.P.Q.2d 1124 (Fed. Cir. 1993).

ω

The declaratory judgment plaintiff's actions in developing Perfluoron and in taking steps to obtain FDA approval sufficiently demonstrate its intent to try to bring Perfluoron to market in some form. While it may not have the present ability to market Perfluoron, it has embarked upon a protracted and costly process of obtaining regulatory approval. Its conduct thus evinces the kind of "concrete steps" or "meaningful preparation" needed to establish an actual controversy under "all the circumstances". *Infinitech Inc. v. Vitrophage Inc.,* 842 F.Supp. 1201, 30 U.S.P.Q.2d 1201, 1205 (Ill. 1994).

ω

"[O]ne who may become liable for infringement should not be subject to manipulation by a patentee who uses careful phrases in order to avoid explicit threats." However, where all that is present is negotiation unaccompanied by threats of legal action, the setting is not sufficiently adverse to create a justiciable controversy. *EMC Corp. v. Norand Corp.*, 89 F.3d 807, 39 U.S.P.Q.2d 1451, 1454 (Fed. Cir. 1996).

ᗡ

The court declined to create a per se rule that an actual controversy (in a declaratory judgment action) predicated only on inducing infringement may exist only if direct infringement has already occurred. *Fina Research S.A. v. Baroid Ltd.*, 141 F.3d 1479, 46 U.S.P.Q.2d 1461, 1467 (Fed. Cir. 1998).

Convenience.

When foreign publications were relied upon to establish what was known at the time of the applicant's filing date, the PTO questioned the availability of the publications in the U.S. Section 112 of 35 U.S.C. §simply requires that a disclosure of an invention enable any man skilled in the relevant art to make and use it. No mention of convenience is made. Thus, even if the origin of the material is in Australia, this is merely a matter of degree of convenience and not a matter of lack of availability. *In re Metcalfe and Lowe*, 410 F.2d 1378, 161 U.S.P.Q. 789, 791 (C.C.P.A. 1969).

Convention. *See* 35 U.S.C. §119.

Conventional.

The court was not prepared to take judicial notice that the dependent claims add only conventional elements commonly known. *In re Flint*, 411 F.2d 1353, 162 U.S.P.Q. 228, 230 (C.C.P.A. 1969).

ᗡ

Whether a term used in a claim is conventional is not necessarily controlling on the question of indefiniteness. *In re Mercier*, 515 F.2d 780, 185 U.S.P.Q. 773, 780 (C.C.P.A. 1975).

ᗡ

The mere recitation of a new use for an old composition does not render the composition patentable anew. There is nothing in the reference, however, that teaches that the known compound may be combined with a finely divided inert insoluble solid-carrier vehicle. The carriers recited in the claims are those conventionally employed, and the disclosure teaches that compounds having algaecidal and herbicidal properties are usually blended with a solid or liquid carrier vehicle. As the reference does not teach that the known compound has algaecidal and/or herbicidal properties, there is simply no motivation to combine the known compound with conventional herbicidal carriers. There is nothing in the record that establishes the obviousness of mixing the known compound with a finely divided inert insoluble solid-carrier vehicle for any purpose whatsoever. Merely establishing that the particular compound is a known compound and that the carrier vehicles are conventional is not sufficient to render the claimed composition unpatentable. There must be some suggestion in the art to combine these materials for some purpose to support a holding of obviousness. *Ex parte Erdmann, Schneider, and Koch*, 194 U.S.P.Q. 96 (PTO Bd. App. 1975).

ω

Since the inventors had full knowledge of a specific arrangement to be used in practicing their process, but failed to disclose the same in their patent, instead disclosing a blank box described as "conventional," the patent fails to comply with the best-mode requirements of 35 U.S.C. §112. *Thyssen Plastik Anger KG v. Induplas, Inc.*, 195 U.S.P.Q. 534, 538 (P.R. 1977).

ω

Employment of block diagrams and descriptions of their functions is not fatal under 35 U.S.C. §112, first paragraph, provided that the represented structure is conventional and can be determined without undue experimentation. *Hirschfeld v. Banner*, 462 F. Supp. 135, 200 U.S.P.Q. 276, 281 (D.C. 1978).

Conversion. *See also* Inventorship, Sole, 35 U.S.C. §116, 35 U.S.C. §256.

A district court, in an infringement action, has jurisdiction under 35 U.S.C. §256 to review the propriety of the issuance by the Patent Office of a Certificate of Correction removing a named applicant as a joint inventor. A Certificate of Correction (removing the name of an applicant as a joint inventor) issued by the U.S. Patent Office was held to be invalid, as the applicant was properly named as a joint inventor in the issued patent. *Borden, Inc. v. Occidental Petroleum Corp.*, 381 F. Supp. 1178, 182 U.S.P.Q. 472, 493 (Tex. 1974).

ω

A prior contribution of another employee of plaintiff was not prior art, but was adequate to qualify the employee as a coinventor and thus justify granting a motion for conversion by the plaintiff in an infringement action. *Norton Co. v. Carborundum Co.*, 397 F. Supp. 639, 186 U.S.P.Q. 189, 196 (Mass. 1975).

ω

35 U.S.C. §116 and 37 C.F.R. §1.45 are remedial in nature and should be liberally construed so that "errors" may be readily corrected. *In re Russell, Jarrett, Bruno, and Remper*, 193 U.S.P.Q. 680, 681, 682 (Comm'r Patents & Trademarks 1975).

ω

Congress having provided for the correction of innocent error in stating inventive entity when an application is filed, there is no reason to discriminate against the correction of the same innocent error involving sole inventors and their assignees. *A. F. Stoddard & Company Ltd. v. Dann, Commissioner of Patents*, 564 F.2d 556, 195 U.S.P.Q. 97 (D.C. Cir. 1977).

ω

A declaration in support of converting a cip application from two inventors to three inventors is not defective merely because the parent application was not similarly converted. *Weil v. Fritz, Evans, and Cooke*, 572 F.2d 856, 196 U.S.P.Q. 600, 606 (C.C.P.A. 1978).

ᚳ

The factual resolutions to be made on this issue are whether any incorrect statement as to inventorship was made with a deceptive intent, whether the amendment correcting the statement was diligently made, and whether any advantage was intended or secured by the applicant by the incorrect statement. *SAB Industri AB v. The Bendix Corporation*, 199 U.S.P.Q. 95, 104 (Va. 1978).

ᚳ

The court questioned whether the inventorship of a great-grandparent application was effectively amended by the PTO's acquiescence in accepting the sole inventorship of the grandparent application. It further questioned whether the great-grandparent application was amended nunc pro tunc by the submission of copies of the Rule 45 (37 C.F.R. §1.45) papers. *In re Herschler,* 591 F.2d 693, 200 U.S.P.Q. 711, 716 (C.C.P.A. 1979).

ᚳ

As noted by Paul T. Meiklejohn in his article entitled: "Misjoinder, Non Joinder and Whatever—*Stoddard v. Dann*" in the August 1978 issue of the Journal of the Patent Office Society:

The holding in *Stoddard* [*A. F. Stoddard & Co. v. Dann*, 564 F.2d 556, 195 U.S.P.Q. 97 (D.C. Cir. 1977)] is an extremely limited one. It would apply only when (a) a sole actual inventor is to be substituted for a sole original signatory who is not an inventor of that subject matter, (b) the sole original signatory is a true party in interest in the application, (c) the inventorship error was made innocently and without deceptive intent, and (d) the error was corrected by diligent action upon its discovery.

In re Shibata, 203 U.S.P.Q. 780, 782 (Commr. Patents & Trademarks 1979).

ᚳ

In enacting 35 U.S.C. §256, Congress intended it to be broadly remedial, to correct inadvertent mistakes in naming or failing to name inventors. Section 116 (35 U.S.C.) is the counterpart of §256, the former being for correction of applications, and the latter being for correction of issued patents. These provisions are "remedial in nature and as such should be liberally construed in order that 'errors' may be readily rectified." *Racal-Vadic, Inc. v. Universal Data Systems*, 207 U.S.P.Q. 902, 929 (Ala. 1980).

ᚳ

The primary reason that a party is required to act diligently to correct the misjoinder of inventors in an interference context is so that his opponent will know the correct name of the party's inventive entity and thereby know whom the party can or cannot rely upon as a corroborating witness for conception, reduction to practice, and so on. *Fisher and Speer v. Gardiner and Aymami*, 215 U.S.P.Q. 620, 623 (PTO Bd. Pat. Int. 1981).

ᚳ

35 U.S.C. §116, together with 35 U.S.C. §256 with which it should be read, was added to the law in the 1952 revision for the purpose of removing technical grounds for attacking the validity of patents by reason of the erroneous naming of inventors, on which point the prior law was very strict. As such a liberalizing provision, it should be given a liberal construction in favor of applicants, permitting them to make such changes as more thorough consideration of the facts may show to be necessary in order to comply accurately with the law in naming inventors. *Kahl v. Scoville,* 219 U.S.P.Q. 725, 728 (PTO Bd. Pat. Int. 1982).

ᵡ

A coinventor who is not acknowledged in an issued patent must establish that omission of his name was due to inadvertent error to obtain relief from a court under 35 U.S.C. §256. *Dee v. Aukerman,* 625 F.Supp. 1427, 228 U.S.P.Q. 600, 603 (Ohio 1986).

ᵡ

Correction of the named inventors in a patent is provided for in 35 U.S.C. §256. *Akiebolag v. Waukesha Cutting Tools Inc.,* 640 F. Supp. 1139, 1 U.S.P.Q.2d 2002 (Wis. 1986).

ᵡ

The statute governing conversion (35 U.S.C. §116, third paragraph) is remedial in nature and must be liberally construed. This is especially true in view of the intervening statutory expansion in the definition of joint inventorship. Furthermore, for a party to convert, the fact of joint inventorship need not be conclusively proved. Conversely, it stands to reason, that a party (opposing conversion) in an interference bears the burden of going forward with the evidence once a *prima facie* case of joint inventorship has been established. *Chai v. Frame,* 10 U.S.P.Q.2d 1460 (B.P.A.I. 1988).

ᵡ

A deliberate act can be an error susceptible to correction under either 35 U.S.C. §116 or 35 U.S.C. §256. Furthermore, an error may include mistakes in legal judgment as to who should be named or whether or not there was a joint invention. The amendment of inventors to create identity of inventive entities prior to amendment of the filing date is not without precedent. *The Upjohn Company v. Medtron Laboratories, Inc.,* 751 F. Supp. 416, 17 U.S.P.Q.2d 1268, 1277 (N.Y. 1990).

ᵡ

A claim of misjoinder or nonjoinder of inventors of a patent must be proved by clear and convincing evidence. *The Boots Co. plc v. Analgesic Associates,* 91 Civ. 2739, 26 U.S.P.Q.2d 1144, 1145 (N.Y. 1993).

ᵡ

There have been occasions when the PTO has waived the requirement of its Rules 48 and 324 (37 C.F.R. §§1.48 and 1.324) for a statement signed by all originally named inventors, any added inventors, and any deleted inventors in connection with any change in inventorship in an application or a patent. One purpose of the statement is to assist the PTO in determining whether the error in not naming all correct inventors occurred "without any deceptive intention". A waiver will not be considered by the PTO unless the facts of record "unequivocally support" the correction sought. *Davis v. Uke*, 27 U.S.P.Q.2d 1180, 1184 (PTO Comm'r 1993).

ᛦ

Neither 35 U.S.C. §256 nor 37 C.F.R. §1.324 requires that an omitted inventor of an issued patent must diligently bring a lawsuit to correct inventorship or be forever barred from doing so. *Stark v. Advanced Magnetics Inc.*, 29 F.3d 1570, 31 U.S.P.Q.2d 1290, 1294 (Fed. Cir. 1994).

ᛦ

Summary judgment for conversion was denied to those claiming to be inventors of an invention claimed in a patent issued on an application filed in the names of other applicants. *The University of Colorado Foundation v. American Cyanamid*, 880 F.Supp. 1387, 35 U.S.P.Q.2d 1737, 1743 (Colo. 1995).

ᛦ

The common law bona fide purchaser for value rule provides an affirmative defense to patent infringement and conversion claims. *Heidelberg Harris Inc. v. Loebach*, 43 U.S.P.Q.2d 1049, 1052 (N.H. 1997).

Conversion (*in situ* or *in vivo*). *See also* Metabolite, Pro-Drug.

Under the boiler treating conditions employed by defendant, Sequestrol 60 dissociates to produce about 90% by weight of thiourea in the free or uncombined form, and some formaldehyde. Plaintiff's patent claimed a chemical process for cleaning industrial steam generating boilers by using thiourea. Sequestrol 60 does the same work, is employed in the same way, and accomplishes the same result as thiourea. Its use for treating boilers was held to be the equivalent and an infringement of plaintiff's claimed use of a thiourea solution. *Chemical Cleaning, Inc. v. The Dow Chemical Company*, 379 F.2d 294, 155 U.S.P.Q. 49, 50 (5th Cir. 1967).

ᛦ

The substituted compound dissociated in operation to form the claimed compound which, in turn, performed its intended function—acting as a sequestering agent for copper. *Chemical Cleaning Corp. v. Dow Chemical Co.*, 379 F.2d 294, 155 U.S.P.Q. 49 (5th Cir. 1967), *cert. denied*, 389 U.S. 1040, 156 U.S.P.Q. 719 (1968).

ᛦ

A substituted compound—an oil-in-water emulsifier—converted *in situ* to the claimed compound—a water-in-oil emulsifier—which, in turn, performed its intended function—forming an emulsion between oil and water. *Atlas Powder Co. v. E.I. DuPont de Nemours & Co.*, 588 F.Supp. 1455, 221 U.S.P.Q. 426 (N.D. Tex. 1983, *aff'd* 750 F.2d 1569, 224 U.S.P.Q. 409 (Fed. Cir. 1984).

ᛦ

The substituted compound converted *in vivo* to the claimed compounds which, in turn, performed their intended function—contraception. *Ortho Pharmaceutical Corp. v.*

Smith, 18 U.S.P.Q.2d 1977 (Pa. 1990), *aff'd*, 959 F.2d 936, 22 U.S.P.Q.2d 1119 (Fed. Cir. 1992).

ω

The doctrine of equivalents has been applied to find infringement in situations involving *in situ* or *in vivo* conversions when a substituted compound or ingredient converts *in vivo* or *in situ* to a compound or ingredient called for by a patent claim, and performs the same function as that of the claimed product. *Zenith Laboratories Inc. v. Bristol-Myers Squibb Co.*, 19 F.3d 1418, 30 U.S.P.Q.2d 1285, 1291 (Fed. Cir. 1994).

ω

Tacrine hydrochloride is converted *in vivo* to the hydroxy-tacrine of the '286 claims. *In vivo* conversion into the drug named in the claims is direct infringement. Since the registered product would directly infringe the claims during use, the product is covered by the claims and qualifies the claims for extension. The distinction drawn by the panel majority leads to the curious result that the '286 claims would be infringed for all purposes of Title 35 U.S.C except for §156. This result is not supported by the law of claiming, of infringement, or of term extension. *Hoechst-Roussel Pharmaceuticals Inc. v. Lehman*, 42 U.S.P.Q.2d 1220, *concurring opinion* 1227 (Fed. Cir. 1997).

Conveyance.

When an employee has acquired patents on inventions developed by his former employer, the courts will hold the wrongdoer to be a constructive trustee of the property misappropriated and will order a conveyance by the wrongdoer to the former employer. *Richardson v. Suzuki Motor Co., Ltd.*, 868 F.2d 1226, 9 U.S.P.Q.2d 1913 (Fed. Cir. 1989).

Convince.

Section 112 of 35 U.S.C. does not require that a specification convince persons skilled in the art that assertions therein are correct. *In re Robins*, 429 F.2d 452, 166 U.S.P.Q. 552 (C.C.P.A. 1970).

ω

The disclosure need not convince one skilled in the art that assertions therein are correct. *Kaiser Industries Corp. v. Jones & Laughlin Steel Corp.*, 181 U.S.P.Q. 193, 209 (Pa. 1974); *In re Armbruster*, 512 F.2d 676, 185 U.S.P.Q. 152, 153 (C.C.P.A. 1975).

ω

There is no requirement in 35 U.S.C. §112, or anywhere else in the patent law, that a specification must convince persons skilled in the art that the assertions in the specification are correct. In examining a patent application, the PTO is required to assume that the specification complies with the enablement provisions of §112 unless it has "acceptable evidence or reasoning" to suggest otherwise. The PTO must thus provide reasons supported by the record as a whole why the specification is not enabling. Then and only then does the burden shift to the applicant to show that one of ordinary skill in the art could have practiced the claimed invention without undue experimentation. A patent specification must be enabling as to "the invention" as set forth in the claims. Thus, a disclosure may be insufficient for one claim but sufficient for another. *Gould v. Mossinghoff*, 229 U.S.P.Q. 1 (D.C. 1985).

Convoyed Sale. *See also* **Entire Market Value Rule.**

It is not the physical joinder or separation of contested items that determines their inclusion in or exclusion from a compensation base, so much as their financial and marketing dependence on the patented item under standard marketing procedures for goods in question. *Leesona Corp. v. United States*, 599 F.2d 958, 974, 202 U.S.P.Q. 424, 439 (Ct. Cl.), *cert. denied*, 444 U.S. 991, 204 U.S.P.Q. 252 (1979).

ϖ

Lost sales of collateral items in proving damages for patent infringement. *Rite-Hite Corp. v. Kelley Co. Inc.*, 35 U.S.P.Q.2d 1065, 1096 (Fed. Cir. 1995).

Co-Owner.

Adoption of amended Fed. R. Civ. P. 19 in 1966 makes inappropriate any contention that patent co-owners are per se indispensable in infringement suits. *Catanzaro v. International Telephone & Telegraph Corp.*, 378 F. Supp. 203, 183 U.S.P.Q. 273, 274 (Del. 1974).

ϖ

"[O]ne co-owner has the right to impede the other co-owner's ability to sue infringers by refusing to voluntarily join in such a suit." This rule finds support in 35 U.S.C. §262. This freedom to exploit the patent without the duty to account to other co-owners also allows co-owners to freely license others to exploit the patent without the consent of other co-owners. Thus, the congressional policy expressed by section 262 is that patent co-owners are "at the mercy of each other." *Ethicon Inc. v. United States Surgical Corp.*, 135 F.3d 1456, 45 U.S.P.Q.2d 1545, 1554 (Fed. Cir. 1998).

Coparty.

A party is generally not aggrieved by, and thus lacks standing to appeal from, a judgment rendered against a coparty. "[A] party may only appeal to protect its own interests, and not those of a coparty." *Penda Corp. v. U.S.*, 44 F.3d 967, 33 U.S.P.Q.2d 1200, 1203 (Fed. Cir. 1994).

Copending Patent.

When a patent is issued, it constitutes evidence that everything disclosed by it was known by others in this country at least as early as the filing date of the application on which the patent issued. *In re Beck, Siebel, and Bosskuhler*, 155 F.2d 398, 69 U.S.P.Q. 520, 523 (C.C.P.A. 1946).

ϖ

A copending reference patent was issued to a different inventor on an application filed on the same date and refers to the subject application. The Patent Office tribunals stated that the subject application is presumed to be owned by the assignee of the copending reference patent. Since that statement was not controverted, it was accepted as correct. *In re Keim and Thompson*, 229 F.2d 466, 108 U.S.P.Q. 330, 331 (C.C.P.A. 1956).

ᵹ

A U.S. patent speaks for all it discloses as of its filing date, even when used in combination with other references. Section 103 of 35 U.S.C. is in pari materia with 35 U.S.C. §102(e), and the latter section was intended to enact the rule of *Milburn Co. v. Davis-Bournonville Co.*, 270 U.S. 390 (1926). *In re Zenitz*, 333 F.2d 924, 142 U.S.P.Q. 158, 159 (C.C.P.A. 1964).

ᵹ

Claims to a composition were held unpatentable (based on double patenting) over claims in applicant's copending patent to the essential component of the composition, on which patentability of the composition claims was dependent. The use and advantages (properties) of the essential component disclosed in the patent were relied upon. *In re Higgins and Le Suer*, 369 F.2d 414, 152 U.S.P.Q. 103, 105 (C.C.P.A. 1966).

ᵹ

Subject matter canceled from the specification of an application that subsequently issues as a patent and thus does not appear in the issued patent is not prior art with regard to an application that has an effective filing date prior to the issuance of the patent. Whether that subject matter is prior art as of the date on which the patent issued was not determined. *Ex parte Stalego*, 839 O.G. 828, 829, 830 (PO Bd. App. 1966).

ᵹ

A reference patent issued on an application filed the same day as appellant's application was regarded as prior art with respect to subject matter therein admitted by appellant to be prior art. *In re Hellsund*, 474 F.2d 1307, 177 U.S.P.Q. 170, 173 (C.C.P.A. 1973).

ᵹ

A patent does not show, as of its filing date, what is known generally to "any person skilled in the art". *In re Glass*, 492 F.2d 1228, 181 U.S.P.Q. 31, 34 (C.C.P.A. 1974).

ᵹ

A patent issued after the appellant's filing date cannot be relied upon as evidence that appellant's specification was enabling. *In re Scarborough*, 500 F.2d 560, 182 U.S.P.Q. 298, 299 (C.C.P.A. 1974).

ᵹ

A concurrently filed commonly assigned copending patent of a different inventive entity that makes reference to the subject application and acknowledges the invention disclosed and claimed therein was held to be unavailable as prior art since the knowledge of the patentee relied upon was derived from applicants. *In re Bulloch and Kim*, 604 F.2d 1362, 203 U.S.P.Q. 171, 173, 174, 175 (C.C.P.A. 1979).

ᵹ

When a reference patent issues on a continuation-in-part (cip) application and the filing date of the parent application is being relied upon by the PTO, the type of new matter added to the cip application must be inquired into. If such new matter is critical to the patentability of the claimed invention, a patent could not have issued on the earlier-filed application, and the theory of Patent Office delay is not applicable. It is at this point in the analysis that 35 U.S.C. §120 enters the picture, for the phrase in §102(e), "on an *application for patent*," necessarily invokes §120 rights of priority for prior copending applications (emphasis in original). If the PTO wishes to utilize (against an applicant) a part of that patent disclosure found in an application filed earlier than the date of the application that became the patent, it must demonstrate that the earlier-filed application contains §120/§112 support for the invention claimed in the reference patent. If a patent could not theoretically have issued the day the application was filed, it is not entitled to be used against another as "secret prior art," the rationale of *Milburn* [270 U.S. 390 (1926)] being inapplicable. *In re Wertheim and Mishkin,* 646 F.2d 527, 209 U.S.P.Q. 554, 563, 564 (C.C.P.A. 1981).

ω

Copending issued patents, originally cited by the Examiner as 35 U.S.C. §102(e)/§103 prior art against the claims, cannot be relied upon as evidence of enablement if the appellant wishes to retain the benefit of his parent application's filing date. *In re Strahilevitz,* 668 F.2d 1229, 212 U.S.P.Q. 561, 564 (C.C.P.A. 1982).

Copending Reference. *See also* Copending Patent.

A patent issued on an application pending in the Patent Office at the time another application is filed constitutes part of the prior art available in the prosecution of the other application. *Hazeltine Research, Inc. v. Brenner,* 382 U.S. 252, 147 U.S.P.Q. 429, 430, 431 (1965).

Copy.

To copy the principle or mode of operation described is an infringement, although such copy is totally unlike the original in form or proportions. *Blumenthal v. Barber-Colman Holdings Corp.,* 62 F.3d 1433, 38 U.S.P.Q.2d 1031, 1036 (Fed. Cir. 1995).

Copying. *See also* Copying Claims, Secondary Considerations.

The use of an invention by another who has been trying to develop a similar product is evidence of the validity of a patent. *Neff Instrument Corporation v. Cohu Electronics, Inc.,* 298 F.2d 82, 132 U.S.P.Q. 98, 101 n.11 (9th Cir. 1961).

ω

To allow a State, by use of its law of unfair competition, to prevent the copying of an article which represents too slight an advance to be patented would be to permit the State to block off from the public something which federal law has said belongs to the public. *Sears, Roebuck & Co. v. Stiffel Company,* 376 U.S. 225, 140 U.S.P.Q. 524 (1964).

ω

Neither *Sears, Roebuck & Co. v. Stiffel Co.,* 376 U.S. 225, 140 U.S.P.Q. 524 (1964), nor *Compco Corp. v. Day-Brite Lighting, Inc.,* 376 U.S. 234, 140 U.S.P.Q. 528 (1964), support a contention that, absent federal protection by design patent, copyright or trademark, the mere act of copying is not actionable. *Loctite Corporation v. B. Jadow and Sons, Inc.*, 177 U.S.P.Q. 410, 412 (N.Y. 1973).

ᛒ

Copying a patented invention suggests that there was significant innovation in the invention. It further suggests that the invention is significantly useful so that competitors must react in some way if they are to remain in business. While neither of these inferences can be considered in connection with the threshold question of obviousness, both are significant secondary indicators and are relevant to a finding of non-obviousness. *Systematic Tool & Machine Co. v. Walter Kidde & Co., Inc.*, 390 F. Supp. 178, 185 U.S.P.Q. 281, 293 (Pa. 1975).

ᛒ

The conclusion of non-obviousness is buttressed by evidence relative to secondary tests, which include commercial success, filling a long-felt need, failure of others to develop the invention, and copying by others. *Scholl, Inc. v. S.S. Kresge Co.*, 193 U.S.P.Q. 695, 705 (Ill. 1977).

ᛒ

Evidence that an infringing device was copied from a patented device may provide evidence of non-obviousness of the patented device. *Railroad Dynamics, Inc. v. A. Stucki Co.*, 579 F. Supp. 353, 218 U.S.P.Q. 618, 628 (Pa. 1983).

ᛒ

Objective evidence of non-obviousness includes commercial success, long-felt but unresolved need, failure of others, and copying. When present, such objective evidence must be considered. It can be the most probative evidence of non-obviousness in the record, and enables the district court to avert the trap of hindsight. On the other hand, the absence of objective evidence does not preclude a holding of non-obviousness because such evidence is not a requirement for patentability. *Custom Accessories Inc. v. Jeffrey-Allan Industries Inc.*, 807 F.2d 955, 1 U.S.P.Q.2d 1196 (Fed. Cir. 1986).

ᛒ

Copying the claimed invention, rather than one in the public domain, is indicative of non-obviousness. *Specialty Composites v. Cabot Corp.*, 845 F.2d 981, 6 U.S.P.Q.2d 1601 (Fed. Cir. 1988).

ᛒ

Copying of a design is perhaps one of the most probative and compelling arguments that the design is novel and unique. *Benchcraft Inc. v. Broyhill Furniture Industries, Inc.*, 681 F. Supp. 1190, 7 U.S.P.Q.2d 1257 (Miss. 1988).

ᛒ

Because copying can be motivated by lack of concern for patent property, contempt for the specific patent in question, or inability to enforce patent rights, "more than the mere fact of the copying by an accused infringer is needed to make that action significant to a determination of the obviousness issue." *Dotolo v. Quigg*, 12 U.S.P.Q.2d 1032, 1038 (D.C. 1989).

ᛒ

Rather than supporting a conclusion of obviousness, copying could have occurred out of a lack of concern for patent property, in which case it weighs neither for nor against the nonobviousness of a specific patent. It may have occurred out of contempt for the specific patent in question, only arguably demonstrating obviousness, or for the ability or willingness of the patentee (financially or otherwise) to enforce the patent right, which would call for deeper inquiry. Even widespread copying could weigh toward opposite conclusions, depending on the attitudes existing toward patent property and the accepted practices in the industry in question. It is simplistic to assert that copying per se should bolster the validity of a patent. *Ex parte GPAC Inc.*, 29 U.S.P.Q.2d 1401, 1408 (B.P.A.I. 1993).

Copying Claims. *See also* **Copying, Refusing to Copy Claims.**

The key to determining whether a disclosure supports a claim for interference purposes is whether the disclosure teaches the gist of the invention defined by the claim. While all limitations of a claim must be considered in deciding what invention is defined, it is futile merely to compare quantitatively range limits and numbers set out in counts with range limits and numbers disclosed in an allegedly supporting specification. Closer scrutiny is required to get at the essence of what invention the count purports to define. *Hall v. Taylor*, 332 F.2d 844, 141 U.S.P.Q. 821, 824 (C.C.P.A. 1964).

ω

An application filed on the anniversary date of the issuance of a patent with a claim copied from the patent was held to be filed prior to one year from the date on which the patent was granted within the meaning of 35 U.S.C. § 135. *Switzer and Ward v. Slockman and Brady*, 333 F.2d 935, 142 U.S.P.Q. 226, 230 (C.C.P.A. 1964).

ω

A patentee moved to dissolve an interference on the ground that his patent claims had not been copied by an applicant prior to one year from the date on which his patent was granted. The Examiner's decision to deny the motion was reversed by the Commissioner, on petition. The interference was dissolved, and the applicant subsequently canceled the claims corresponding to the interference counts. The applicant subsequently urged he had timely copied the claims in order to overcome the patent as a reference in ex parte prosecution. The applicant was required to reassert the patent claims, and the interference was reinstated. The Commissioner decided (on petition) that the applicant was bound by the Commissioner's prior decision, from which no appeal was taken. From the applicant's cancellation of claims and failure to appeal, it was concluded that applicant has acquiesced in the prior decision and the applicant was estopped, on the ground of res judicata, from raising the question of whether he had originally copied the patent claims in timely fashion. *Rubenstein v. Schmidt*, 145 U.S.P.Q. 613 (Comm'r Patents 1965).

ω

In evaluating whether a claim under prosecution during the one-year period specified in 35 U.S.C. §135(b) is directed to substantially the same subject matter as that of an interference count, a mere difference in scope may not be a deterrent. *Wetmore v. Miller*, 477 F.2d 960, 177 U.S.P.Q. 699, 701 (C.C.P.A. 1973).

ω

It is well settled that one who abstracts claims from an issued patent must show a clear prior disclosure. Further, when an applicant copies claims from a patent, he must show he is entitled to make the claims. All limitations in the copied claims constituting the count in interference are considered material in determining the question of right to make, and doubts arising as to same must be resolved against the applicant. This is not to say, however, that each limitation in an interference count must be expressly set forth in haec verba in the disclosure relied upon. It is sufficient if the specification is so worded that the necessary and only reasonable construction to be given the disclosure by one skilled in the art is one that will lend clear support for each limitation in the count. The lack of express disclosure is not necessarily fatal, since the right to make may be based upon inherent disclosure. Such inherency cannot be based on theoretical considerations, but must be established by actual evidence. *Natta and Crespi v. Payne*, 165 U.S.P.Q. 466, 470 (PTO Bd. Pat. Int. 1970).

ᛟ

One copying a claim from a patent for the purpose of instituting interference proceedings must show that his application clearly supports the count. There must be no doubt that an application discloses each and every limitation of the claims, and all doubts must be resolved against the copier. Where support must be based on inherent disclosure, it is not sufficient that a person following the disclosure might obtain the results set forth in the count; it must inevitably happen. *Tummers v. Kleimack, Laor, and Theuerer*, 455 F.2d 566, 172 U.S.P.Q. 592, 594 (C.C.P.A. 1972).

ᛟ

One who copies patent claims to invoke an interference in an application filed after the patent issued has a burden of proving beyond a reasonable doubt either conception or reduction to practice of the involved invention prior to the patentee's filing date. *Silvestri and Johnson v. Grant and Alburn*, 496 F.2d 593, 181 U.S.P.Q. 706, 707 (C.C.P.A. 1974).

ᛟ

The PTO, having insisted that applicant should have copied patent claims for interference purposes, must show, in support of that contention, that applicant had support for the claims in his application. One copying claims for the purpose of instituting interference proceedings must show that his application clearly supports the count. There must be no doubt that the application discloses each and every material limitation of the claims, and all doubts must be resolved against the copier. *In re Ogiue*, 517 F.2d 1382, 186 U.S.P.Q. 227, 234 (C.C.P.A. 1975).

ᛟ

Claims canceled during the year subsequent to the issuance of the patent (from which they were copied) could be relied upon to avoid the R.S. 4903 bar in view of the words "for the first time." Thus, regardless of whether the cancellation of claims might have been relevant to the application of the equitable doctrine of *Chapman v. Wintroath*, 252 U.S. 126 (1920), such cancellation is not relevant to the application of its statutory successor. The second paragraph of R.S. 4903, as amended, was codified in its present form in 1952 as the second paragraph of 35 U.S.C. §135, later designated paragraph (b). No substantial change was intended by the changes in language. The words "prior to" in the present code clearly point to a "critical date" prior to which the copier had to be claiming the invention, whether or not the claims were subsequently canceled. No language is found in §135(b), or any of its predecessor statutes, that requires restricting cancellation of claims to cancellation after the patent (from which they are copied) issues. *Corbett v. Chisholm and Schrenk*, 568 F.2d 759, 196 U.S.P.Q. 337 (C.C.P.A. 1977).

ᚹ

The burden of proof on the right to make issue is on the party who has copied claims. This burden is a heavy one regardless of whether the copier is a junior or a senior party, and doubts must be resolved against the copier. Even when the noncopier is placed under an order to show cause, the burden of proof does not shift. Whereas the burden of going forward may shift, the burden of persuasion remains with the copier. *Holmes, Faber, Boykin, and Francis v. Kelly, Hornberger, and Strief,* 586 F.2d 234, 199 U.S.P.Q. 778 (C.C.P.A. 1978).

ᚹ

The appellant refused to copy a patent claim for the purpose of instituting an interference. Both the claims and the disclosure of the patent were treated as prior art with respect to the appellant's claims. The claims of a patent cannot be used as the conceded prior invention of another in this country under 35 U.S.C. §102(g) or as prior art under 35 U.S.C. §103 unless the patentee and applicant are claiming essentially the same invention and it is clearly shown that the applicant in such a case has support for the patented claims in his application. If such conditions are met, the patent disclosure is available only to determine what invention the claims define and, hence, what invention has been claimed. The entire disclosure is not available as conceded prior art. *Ex parte Inoue*, 217 U.S.P.Q. 461 (PTO Bd. App. 1981).

ᚹ

Requiring an applicant to copy a modified claim is improper when the modified claim is not supported by applicant's disclosure. Applicant's refusal to copy the modified claim under such circumstances does not constitute a disclaimer of the involved subject matter. The modified claim thus cannot be treated as a prior-art reference, and a 35 U.S.C. §103 rejection premised thereon fails. *In re Phillips and Crick,* 673 F.2d 1273, 213 U.S.P.Q. 353, 356 (C.C.P.A. 1982).

ᚹ

Claims asserted prior to the issuance of a patent satisfy the requirements of 35 U.S.C. §135(b) with regard to timeliness, notwithstanding the fact that such claims may have been canceled by the applicant either before or after the patent issued. *Tezuka v. Wilson,* 224 U.S.P.Q. 1030 (PTO Bd. Pat. Int. 1984).

ᚹ

One who copies claims from a patent for interference purposes must show by clear and convincing evidence that the disclosure on which he relies supports the copied claims that become the interference counts. *DeGeorge v. Bernier,* 768 F.2d 1318, 226 U.S.P.Q. 758 (Fed. Cir. 1985).

ᚹ

Before an interference was declared, the Examiner rejected (in the Fine application) the newly presented claims that Fine had substantially copied from the Parks patent. One of the grounds of rejection was that, because the earlier Fine claims did not expressly include the absence-of-a-catalyst limitation, the present Fine claims containing that limitation were barred under 35 U.S.C. §135(b) as not having been "made prior to one year from the date" on which the Parks patent was granted. The implication in the specification that catalysts would not or need not be used does not imply that they must not be used. It is not sufficient to compel the inclusion of that limitation into claims not expressly so stating. "The inquiry here is not whether such a step is inherently disclosed, as it might be in a right-to-make case. Rather, the question is whether the step necessarily occurs in the process as claimed." *Parks v. Fine,* 773 F.2d 1577, 227 U.S.P.Q. 432 (Fed. Cir. 1985).

ᙡ

The copier of claims from a patent has the burden of proving, by clear and convincing evidence, that "the disclosure on which he relies supports the copied claims which become the interference counts." This burden requires, as a first step, that the copier go forward and present a prima facie case of support for the copied claim. This prima facie case must itself be established by clear and convincing evidence. If such prima facie case of support for the count is not made, the patentee will prevail without more. It is "not a question of whether one skilled in the art might be able to construct the patentee's device from the teachings of the disclosure . . rather it is a question whether the application necessarily discloses that particular device." *Martin v. Mayer,* 823 F.2d 500, 3 U.S.P.Q.2d 1333 (Fed. Cir. 1987).

ᙡ

When interpretation is required of a claim that is copied for interference purposes, the copied claim is viewed in the context of the patent from which it was copied. A claim copier's specification "must be sufficiently clear that persons of skill in the art will recognize that [he] made the invention having those limitations." *In re Spina,* 975 F.2d 854, 24 U.S.P.Q.2d 1142, 1144 (Fed. Cir. 1992).

ᙡ

A motion under 37 C.F.R. §1.633(a) for judgment on the ground that an opponent's claim corresponding to an interference count lacks written description support in its involved application is a departure from the practice under the old interference rules, wherein the burden as to a party's "right to make" a count was always on the copier of the claims. An interference can be declared under the new rules when an application includes, or is amended to include at least one patentable claim which is drawn to the same patentable invention as a claim of another's unexpired patent. *Behr v. Talbott,* 27 U.S.P.Q.2d 1401, 1405 (B.P.A.I. 1992).

ᙡ

A copied claim is interpreted in light of the originating disclosure. The *Spina* [975 F.2d 854, 24 U.S.P.Q.2d 1142 (Fed. Cir. 1992)] rule sought to ensure that the PTO would only declare an interference if both parties had a right to claim the same subject matter. *Rowe v. Dror,* 112 F.3d 473, 42 U.S.P.Q.2d 1550, 1553 (Fed. Cir. 1997).

Core. *See* **Gist.**

Corporate Officer.

Corporate officers who actively aid and abet their corporation's infringement may be personally liable for inducing infringement under 35 U.S.C. §271(b) regardless of whether the corporation is the alter ego of the corporate officer. *Orthokinetics Inc, v. Safety Travel Chairs Inc.*, 806 F.2d 1565, 1 U.S.P.Q.2d 1081, 1090 (Fed. Cir. 1986).

ϖ

Under 35 U.S.C. §271(b), corporate officers who actively assist with their corporation's patent infringement may be personally liable as an infringer regardless of whether there is evidence to justify piercing the corporate veil. The plaintiff has the burden of showing both that the officer's actions induced infringing acts and that the officer knew or should have known that his or her actions would induce infringements. *Zenith Electronics Corp. v. ExZec Inc.*, 32 U.S.P.Q.2d 1959, 1960 (Ill. 1994).

ϖ

A corporate officer may be personally liable under 35 U.S.C. §271(b) for inducing infringement where he actively aids and abets the corporation's infringement, regardles of whether circumstances justify piercing the corporate veil. The potential for personal liability of a corporate officer, however, is no substitute for a determination of whether the Court may exercise personal jurisdiction over that officer. *Amhil Enterprises Ltd. v. Wawa Inc.*, 34 U.S.P.Q.2d 1640, 1643 (Md. 1994).

ϖ

For a corporate officer to be personally liable for inducing infringement, the officer must act culpably and knowingly assist in the corporation's infringement. The officer must have possessed specific intent to "aid and abet" infringement. It is an insufficient basis for personal liability that the officer had knowledge of the acts alleged to constitute infringement. *Hoover Group Inc. v. Custom Metalcraft Inc.*, 38 U.S.P.Q.2d 1860, 1862 (Fed. Cir. 1996).

Corporate Veil. *See* **Piercing the Corporate Veil.**

Correct.

The disclosure of an application for letters patent need not convince one skilled in the art that assertions therein are correct. The statute merely requires that the disclosure be such as to enable one skilled in the art to practice the invention. *Kaiser Industries Corp. v. Jones & Laughlin Steel Corp.*, 181 U.S.P.Q. 193, 209 (Pa. 1974).

ϖ

There is no requirement in 35 U.S.C. §112 or anywhere else in the patent law that a specification must convince persons skilled in the art that the assertions in the specification are correct. In examining a patent application, the PTO is required to assume that the specification complies with the enablement provisions of §112 unless it has "acceptable evidence or reasoning" to suggest otherwise. The PTO must thus provide reasons supported by the record as a whole why the specification is not enabling. Then and only then does the burden shift to the applicant to show that one of ordinary skill in the art could have practiced the claimed invention without undue experimentation. A patent specification must be enabling as to "the invention" as set forth in the claims. Thus, a disclosure may be insufficient for one claim but sufficient for another. *Gould v. Mossinghoff*, 229 U.S.P.Q. 1 (D.C. 1985).

Correction. *See* Certificate of Correction, Conversion, Reissue.

Correlating.

The inclusion in a patent of a claim to a process that may be performed by a person, but that also is capable of being performed by a machine, is not fatal to patentability. The presence of the steps of correlating and combining, which a machine is capable of doing, does not invalidate a patent. *Alco Standard Corp. v. Tennessee Valley Authority*, 808 F.2d 1490, 1 U.S.P.Q.2d 1337, 1341 (Fed. Cir. 1986).

Corroborate. *See* Authenticate.

Corroboration. *See also* Assistant, Good Cause, Rule of Reason.

In an interference context, testimony of the inventor's assistant showed that she was working under the inventor's supervision and direction. Since the testimony adequately established that her activities were on behalf of the inventor, the presumption is that benefit of her work inured to the benefit of the inventor. It is not material, as a matter of law, that the inventor was not present during all experiments and tests made for him by his assistant. *Damaskus v. Homan and Neutelings*, 141 U.S.P.Q. 923, 925 (P.O. Bd. Pat. Int. 1964).

ʊ

For a witness in an interference to corroborate a process, compounds, and chemical analyses, he must see the operation of the process and have personal knowledge of the product. Corroboration should not be based on facts, the truth of which depends on information received from the inventor. *Anderson and Kaminsky v. Crowther and Young*, 152 U.S.P.Q. 504, 508 (P.O. Bd. Pat. Int. 1965).

ʊ

In antedating a reference, provided evidence need not corroborate the very features of asserted claims that are considered insufficient to distinguish patentably over applied art. *In re Stryker*, 435 F.2d 1340, 168 U.S.P.Q. 372, 373 (C.C.P.A. 1971).

ʊ

A "rule of reason" approach is required in determining the type and amount of evidence necessary for corroboration. *Breuer and Treuner v. DeMarinis*, 558 F.2d 22, 194 U.S.P.Q. 308, 314 (C.C.P.A. 1977).

ʊ

In an interference, even when an inventor's affidavit is complete in and of itself, adequate corroboration, as required by 37 C.F.R. §1.204(c), must be provided. *Amoss,*

Monahan, and Vale v. McKinley and Sarantakis, 195 U.S.P.Q. 452, 454 (PTO Bd. Pat. Int. 1977).

ထ

The statement of an expert's opinion set forth in an affidavit need not be corroborated. However, corroboration may be necessary for other statements. The credibility of an inventor's statements regarding his alleged prior reduction to practice must be established by clear and convincing evidence. The factors bearing on that credibility include: (1) delay between event and trial, (2) interest of witness, (3) contradiction or impeachment, (4) corroboration, (5) witnesses" familiarity with details of alleged prior structure, (6) improbability of prior use considering state of the art, (7) impact of the invention on the industry, and (8) relationship between witness and alleged prior user. *In re Reuter, Vickery, and Everett,* 651 F.2d 751, 210 U.S.P.Q. 249, 255 (C.C.P.A. 1981).

ထ

Derivation is difficult to establish by direct evidence; it can generally be established only by the circumstances of a case. The fact that no one overheard the alleged communication from the junior party to the senior party and the senior party testified that he had no recollection of such a communication is not fatal to the junior party. *Sands v. Bonazoli, Kimball, and Palmer,* 223 U.S.P.Q. 450, 452 (PTO Bd. Pat. Int. 1983).

ထ

Conception must be proved by corroborating evidence that shows that the inventor disclosed to others his "completed thought expressed in such clear terms as to enable those skilled in the art" to make the invention. *Coleman v. Dines,* 754 F.2d 353, 224 U.S.P.Q. 857 (Fed. Cir. 1985).

ထ

Contemporaneously prepared documents alone do not constitute sufficient circumstantial evidence of an independent nature to satisfy the corroboration rule. In order for a contemporaneous document to be accorded any corroborative value, the testimony of a witness other than the inventor, who is shown to have understood the recorded information, is generally necessary to authenticate the document's contents as well as to explain the witness" relationship to the document in question. In the absence of independent testimony, documentary records bearing signatures of persons who have not testified and who have not been shown to be unavailable to testify are inadequate corroborative evidence of the inventor's activities. Exhibits by themselves cannot serve to corroborate the actual performance of work recorded therein, even though they may very well be reproductions of documents from official company records. The so-called Shop-Book Rule does not apply to reports of scientific work in an interference proceeding. Such reports generally cannot be relied upon to prove the facts asserted therein, and therefore cannot be relied on to establish reduction to practice, since they are self-serving and not an independent corroboration of an inventor's testimony. *Horton v. Stevens,* 7 U.S.P.Q.2d 1245, 1248, 1249 (B.P.A.I. 1988).

ထ

Presented affidavits do not establish that the corroborator's activities, i.e., reading and understanding the notebook pages, occurred prior to opponent's effective filing date.

Although exhibits attached to the affidavit do have a stamp indicating such "activity" and include a date, it is well settled in law that exhibits do not ordinarily speak for themselves. It is an essential requirement of interference practice that evidence be offered to show that an exhibit was, in fact, made on the date appearing thereon. *Hahn v. Wong,* 13 U.S.P.Q.2d 1211, 1214, 1215 (B.P.A.I. 1989).

ω

The purpose of the rule requiring corroboration is to prevent fraud. *Hahn v. Wong,* 892 F.2d 1028, 13 U.S.P.Q.2d 1313, 1317 (Fed. Cir. 1989).

ω

To negate the validity of a patent claim on the basis of prior inventorship by another, evidence of such prior inventorship must be corroborated by evidence independent of the alleged prior inventor. *Dentsply Research & Development Corp. v. Cadco Dental Products Inc.,* 14 U.S.P.Q.2d 1039, 1042 (Cal . 1989).

ω

The requirement of corroboration applies only to the testimony of a person claiming to be an inventor. If the inventor was assisted in his work, the assistant's testimony as to what he did need not be corroborated. *De Solms v. Schoenwald,* 15 U.S.P.Q.2d 1507, 1509 (B.P.A.I. 1990).

ω

Prior to the 1984 change in 35 U.S.C. §116 (permitting joint applications to be filed even though each applicant did not make a contribution to the subject matter of every claim of the patent) it was well settled that an opposing party could rely on the rule that conception and reduction to practice must be corroborated by evidence other than that given by joint applicants. Where it was determined that the invention was made by less than all of the joint applicants, they were required to reform the interference diligently by deleting the non-inventors therefrom. In view of the above noted change in the statute, there was some relaxation in the rule prohibiting corroboration of conception and reduction to practice by joint applicants. However, in an interference (where all of the claims of one party have been designated as corresponding to the count) all of the joint applicants must prima facie be deemed to be coinventors of the subject matter of the count. In other words, the burden is on the party asserting that the joint applicant relied upon as a corroborating witness is not a joint inventor of the subject matter of the count to establish that fact through convincing evidence on the record. *Larson v. Joehenning,* 17 U.S.P.Q.2d 1610, 1614 (B.P.A.I. 1990).

ω

Before the BPAI "corroboration" is not necessary to establish what a physical exhibit (in an interference) includes. Only the inventor's testimony requires corroboration before it can be considered. While evidence as to what a drawing would mean to one of skill in the art may assist in evaluating the drawing, the content of an exhibit does not itself require corroboration. *Price v. Symsek,* 988 F.2d 1187, 26 U.S.P.Q.2d 1031, 1037 (Fed. Cir. 1993).

ω

Although oral testimony may be sufficient to establish priority beyond a reasonable doubt, in the absence of any corroborative documentary evidence it must be carefully scrutinized, particularly where it is adduced long after the events. *English v. Ausnit*, 38 U.S.P.Q.2d 1625, 1632 (B.P.A.I. 1993).

ᴡ

While there must generally be corroboration of an inventor's testimony of conception of his or her invention, the utility of the invention need not always be explicitly corroborated. *Kridl v. McCormick*, 41 U.S.P.Q.2d 1686 (Fed. Cir. 1997).

ᴡ

Corroborating evidence may take many forms. Often contemporaneous documents prepared by a putative inventor serve to corroborate an inventor's testimony. Circumstantial evidence about the inventive process may also corroborate. "[S]ufficient circumstantial evidence of an independent nature can satisfy the corroboration rule." Additionally, oral testimony of someone other than the alleged inventor may corroborate. *Ethicon Inc. v. United States Surgical Corp.*, 135 F.3d 1456, 45 U.S.P.Q.2d 1545, 1548 (Fed. Cir. 1998).

ᴡ

"The law does not impose an impossible standard of "independence" on corroborative evidence by requiring that every point of a reduction to practice be corroborated by evidence having a source totally independent of the inventor; indeed, such a standard is the antithesis of the rule of reason." *Knorr v. Pearson*, 671 F.2d 1368, 1374, 213 U.S.P.Q. 196, 201 (C.C.P.A. 1982). "In the final analysis, each corroboration case must be decided on its own facts with a view to deciding whether the evidence as a whole is persuasive." *Cooper v. Goldfarb*, 47 U.S.P.Q.2d 1896, 1904 (Fed. Cir. 1998).

Cost.

A change in shape that results in saving approximately 75 square feet of fabric per hundred shingles was held to warrant patent protection. *Ex parte Mortimer*, 61 F.2d 860, 15 U.S.P.Q. 297, 298 (C.C.P.A. 1932).

Costs.[9] *See also* Attorney's Fees.

Recovery of costs is governed by 28 U.S.C. §1920, which provides that the following costs are recoverable: (1) fees of the clerk and marshalls; (2) fees of the court reporter "for all and any part of the stenographic transcript necessarily obtained for use in the case"; (3) fees and disbursements for printing and witnesses; (4) fees for exemplification and copies of papers "necessarily obtained for use in the case"; (5) docket fees; and (6) compensation of court-appointed experts, compensation of interpreters, and salaries,

---

[9] Federal Rule of Appellate Procedure 39(a) provides that, if a judgment is reversed on appeal, costs shall be taxed against the appellee "unless otherwise ordered." The quoted phrase indicates that the award of costs is within the discretion of the district court. Cf. 6 J. Moore, W. Tagart & J. Wicker, *Moore's Federal Practice* 1154.70 [5] (2d ed. 1990) (the "unless the court otherwise directs" qualification of Fed. R. Civ. P. 54(d) vests in the district court a sound discretion over the allowance, disallowance, or apportionment of costs in civil actions). *See also Bose Corp. v. Consumers Union of the United States, Inc.*, 806 F.2d 304, 305 (1st Cir. 1986) [reviewing district court's taxation of Fed. R. App. P. 39(e) costs for abuse of discretion].

fees, expenses, and costs of special interpretation services under §18.28 of this title. *Sun Studs Inc. v. ATA Equipment Leasing Inc.*, 17 U.S.P.Q.2d 1768, 1769 (Or. 1990).

ᵀ

District courts may only tax costs defined in the "cost statute," 28 U.S.C. §1920: "Section 1920 enumerates expenses that a federal court may tax as cost under the discretionary authority found in [Fed. R. Civ. P. 54(d)]." *Automotive Products plc v. Tilton Engineering Inc.*, 855 F. Supp. 1101, 33 U.S.P.Q.2d 1065, 1093 (Cal. 1994).

Counsel. *See also* Argument, Attorney, Opinion of Counsel.

Reliance on in-house counsel instead of obtaining a timely opinion of outside counsel is an entirely proper consideration as one factor in willfulness. *Minnesota Mining and Manufacturing Co. v. Johnson & Johnson Orthopaedic Inc.*, 22 U.S.P.Q.2d 1401, 1413 (Minn. 1991).

Count. *See also* Interference Count, Lost Count.

When a term, as used in the art, has several possible meanings, it is, to that extent, ambiguous. It is thus necessary to look at the patent in which the count originated in order to determine the intended meaning of the term. *Bethell and Hadley v. Koch, Robinson, and Wiley*, 427 F.2d 1372, 166 U.S.P.Q. 199, 201 (C.C.P.A. 1970).

ᵀ

Section 102(g) of 35 U.S.C. makes the prior invention of another, as established by an adverse award of priority in an interference, a bar to the patentability of the identical subject matter involved in the priority award. The subject matter of a lost interference count, as the prior invention of another, is also prior art under 35 U.S.C. §103. *In re Cormany, Dial, and Pray*, 476 F.2d 998, 177 U.S.P.Q. 450, 453 (C.C.P.A. 1973).

ᵀ

If an ambiguity is apparent from language of an interference count, like a claim that is "indefinite," then it is easy to see that the count is ambiguous, and resort to the specification is clearly permitted to determine the proper construction of the count. Where, however, a latent ambiguity is alleged to exist, a literal application of the rule that "only in the case where a count is ambiguous should resort be had to the patent where it originated" prevents the court from looking to the specification even to determine if there is an ambiguity, let alone to resolve the meaning of the count for purposes of the interference. Notwithstanding the foregoing, the starting point for determining whether the specification of a patent ought to be consulted to determine the gist of the invention there described may be either an apparent ambiguity in the language of a count or the arguments of one or more of the parties that make it clear that the language of the count may have different meanings. *Stansbury v. Bond*, 482 F.2d 968, 179 U.S.P.Q. 88, 92 (C.C.P.A. 1973).

ᵀ

The Board based the rejection under 35 U.S.C. §103 on the theory that an applicant that has lost an interference can never be entitled to claims that are obvious variations of the invention defined in the lost counts. The court found no judicial doctrine that supports this rejection under 35 U.S.C. §103. *In re McKellin, Mageli, and D'Angelo,* 529 F.2d 1324, 188 U.S.P.Q. 428 (C.C.P.A. 1976).

ᘐ

In an interference between a patent and an application, an application claim, a patent claim, and an interference count need not be the same. Each has unique significance in an interference. As a prerequisite to the declaration of an interference, the Commissioner must decide that an application claim, whether or not identical to a patent claim, is both patentable and drawn to substantially the same invention as the patent claim. The count, on the other hand, is merely a vehicle for contesting priority that, in the opinion of the Commissioner, effectively circumscribes the interfering subject matter, thereby determining what evidence will be regarded as relevant on the issue of priority. The count, as distinguished from a party's claim, need not be patentable to either party in the sense of being fully supported by either party's disclosure. *Squires v. Corbett,* 560 F.2d 424, 194 U.S.P.Q. 513, 518, 519 (C.C.P.A. 1977).

ᘐ

Broad language in a count is not rendered ambiguous merely by its readability on more than one embodiment. In construing independent counts, respective dependent counts are appropriately considered. No basis exists for applying a limitation to counts which do not contain such limitation. *Kroekel v. Shah*, 558 F.2d 29, 194 U.S.P.Q. 544, 547 (C.C.P.A. 1977).

ᘐ

When an interference is declared, there is a rebuttable presumption that a claim that is not designated to correspond to the count is not directed to the same patentable invention as the claims designated to correspond to the count. The burden of persuasion and proof to the contrary is on the party that takes such position. *Chiong v. Roland,* 17 U.S.P.Q.2d 1541, 1544 (B.P.A.I. 1990).

ᘐ

Claims are appropriately designated as not corresponding to the count only when there is some basis to conclude that those claims do not define the "same patentable invention" as the count within the context of 37 C.F.R. §1.601(n). If there is doubt as to whether a party's claim does or does not correspond to a count, the claim "should be listed as corresponding to the count". M.P.E.P. §2309.02. There can be no basis for finding that a claim defines a separate patentable invention relative to the count where the scope of that claim is indefinite. *Fritsch v. Lin*, 21 U.S.P.Q.2d 1739, 1742 (B.P.A.I. 1991).

ᘐ

Although claims of one or more of the parties may be identical to the count of an interference, the count is not a claim to an invention; it is merely the vehicle for contesting priority of invention and determining what evidence is relevant to the issue of priority. *In re Van Geuns*, 988 F.2d 1181, 26 U.S.P.Q.2d 1057, 1058 (Fed. Cir. 1993).

Counter. *See* **Teach Away From.**

Counterclaim.

Permissive counterclaims may be entertained in actions under 35 U.S.C. §146. Rule 13(b) confers upon a litigant the right to have his permissive counterclaim heard and determined along with claims of his adversary. The objective of the Federal Rules with respect to counterclaims is to provide complete relief to the parties, to conserve judicial resources, and to avoid proliferation of lawsuits. *Montecatini Edison, S.p.A. v. Ziegler,* 486 F.2d 1279, 179 U.S.P.Q. 458, 459, 460 (D.C. Cir. 1973).

ω

Joinder of additional parties to a counterclaim pursuant to Rule 13(h) does not in itself constitute joinder in the main action. A declaratory judgment, even one involving a claim under federal law, presents no federal jurisdiction where it is sought merely as a defense to an action that itself could not be brought in federal court. *Union Carbide Corp. v. Air Products Chemicals, Inc.,* 202 U.S.P.Q. 43, 52, 54 (N.Y. 1978).

ω

When a defendant's counterclaim has a jurisdictional basis independent of the main action, the provision of Fed. Civ. P. 41(a)(2) relating to counterclaims does not bar dismissal of plaintiff's complaint or require dismissal of defendant's counterclaim. *Farmaceutisk Laboratorium Ferring A/S v. Reid Rowell Inc.,* 20 U.S.P.Q.2d 1476, 1478 (Ga. 1991).

ω

An unnecessary ruling on an affirmative defense is not the same as the necessary resolution of a counterclaim for a declaratory judgment. *Cardinal Chemical Co. v. Morton International Inc.,* 113 S.Ct. 1967, 26 U.S.P.Q.2d 1721, 1726 (S.Ct. 1993).

ω

"[F]iling a counterclaim does not waive an objection to jurisdiction." *College Savings Bank v. Florida Prepaid Postsecondary Education Expense Board,* 42 U.S.P.Q.2d 1487, 1499 (N.J. 1996).

ω

"An unnecessary ruling on an affirmative defense is not the same as the necessary resolution of a counterclaim for a declaratory judgment." *Multiform Desiccants Inc. v. Medzam Ltd.,* 133 F.3d 1473, 45 U.S.P.Q.2d 1429, 1435 (Fed. Cir. 1998).

Counting. *See* Mental Steps.

Court Decision. *See* Precedent.

Court Review of PTO Rulings.

In a concurring opinion, Judge Newman pointed out that a careful study of the legislative history shows that Congress intended, from the beginning of the patent examination system, to provide substantive judicial review of PTO decisions. Over the years there were periodic modifications of these review procedures, but the fundamental principle was reaffirmed that "a party who is refused a patent by the Commissioner will have at the outset a judicial decision as to his right to it or that he has no right to it." *Fregeau v. Mossinghoff,* 776 F.2d 1034, 227 U.S.P.Q. 848 (Fed. Cir. 1985).

Cover. *See* **Construe.**

Creation Test.

There are two types of cases that may be said to "arise under" the patent laws for purposes of 28 U.S.C. §1338. First, a suit arises under the law that creates the cause of action. Although this "creation" test may be helpful in identifying many cases that come within the court's jurisdiction, it has limited value in identifying those that do not. Second, a case arises under the patent laws if the plaintiff seeks to vindicate a right or interest "that would be defeated by one or sustained by an opposite construction" of the patent laws. *Christianson v. Colt Industries Operating Corp.,* 798 F.2d 1051, 230 U.S.P.Q. 840 (7th Cir. 1986).

Credibility. *See also* **Convince.**

Summary judgment is inappropriate where credibility is at issue. Credibility issues are appropriately resolved only after an evidentiary hearing or full trial. *SEC v. Koracorp Indus.,* 575 F.2d 692, 699 (9th Cir.), *cert. denied,* 439 U.S. 953 (1978).

ʊ

The PTO must have adequate support for its challenge to the credibility of applicant's statements as to utility. Only then does the burden shift to appellant to provide rebuttal evidence. *In re Bundy,* 642 F.2d 430, 209 U.S.P.Q. 48, 51 (C.C.P.A. 1981).

ʊ

The credibility of an inventor's statements regarding his alleged prior reduction to practice must be established by clear and convincing evidence. The factors bearing on that credibility include: (1) delay between event and trial, (2) interest of witness, (3) contradiction or impeachment, (4) corroboration, (5) witnesses" familiarity with details of alleged prior structure, (6) improbability of prior use considering state of the art, (7) impact of the invention on the industry, and (8) relationship between witness and alleged prior user. *In re Reuter, Vickery, and Everett,* 651 F.2d 751, 210 U.S.P.Q. 249, 255 (C.C.P.A. 1981).

ʊ

When a credibility determination is involved, Rule 52 demands great deference to the trial court's findings of fact, but a trial judge may not insulate his findings from review by denominating them credibility determinations. When documents or objective evidence contradicts a witness's story, clear error may be found even in a finding purportedly based on a credibility determination. *Hybritech Inc. v. Monoclonal Antibodies, Inc.,* 802 F.2d 1367, 231 U.S.P.Q. 81, 87 (Fed. Cir. 1986).

Crime. *See* **Mismarking.**

Crime-Fraud Exception. *See* **In Camera Review.**

Critical. *See also* **Difference, Gist, Kind.**

One alleging a critical difference (that is, a difference in kind as distinguished from a difference in degree) growing out of claimed proportions of ingredients must establish such criticalness by proof. *In re Waite and Allport,* 168 F.2d 104, 77 U.S.P.Q. 586, 591 (C.C.P.A. 1948).

ω

When other claims do not contain a particular limitation, such limitation cannot be considered to be critical. *In re Ripper,* 171 F.2d 297, 80 U.S.P.Q. 96, 98 (C.C.P.A. 1948).

ω

Under some circumstances, changes in temperature, in concentration, or in both, may impart patentability to a process if the particular ranges claimed produce a new and unexpected result that is different in kind and not merely in degree from the results of the prior art. Such ranges are termed critical ranges, and the applicant has the burden of proving such criticality. Where the general conditions of a claim are disclosed in prior art, it is not inventive merely to discover the optimum or workable ranges by routine experimentation. *In re Aller, Lacey, and Hall,* 220 F.2d 454, 105 U.S.P.Q. 233, 235 (C.C.P.A. 1955).

ω

The mere fact that a limitation does not appear in all claims does not mean that such limitation is not critical in or can be disregarded in those claims in which it does appear. *Ex parte Passino and Wrightson,* 118 U.S.P.Q. 515, 517 (P.O. Bd. App. 1957).

ω

An applicant has a right to submit claims of varying scope. The practice of holding a limitation in a claim as not being critical, merely because it was omitted from other claims, is clearly not proper. *Ex parte Seavey,* 125 U.S.P.Q. 454, 457 (PO Bd. App. 1959).

ω

The critical nature of a difference or of a limitation need not necessarily be pointed out in the specification, and it need not be expressly stated to be critical. It is sufficient if evidence presented at trial shows that the difference is critical and vitally significant. *Jennings v. Brenner,* 255 F. Supp. 410, 150 U.S.P.Q. 167, 169 (D.C. 1966).

ω

Where the chemical identity of a material is not critical, there is no reason why an applicant should not be permitted to define that material partly in terms of its physical properties or in terms of the function that it performs. *In re Metcalfe and Lowe,* 410 F.2d 1378, 161 U.S.P.Q. 789, 793 (C.C.P.A. 1969).

ω

The fact that affidavit evidence shows that products produced by reference techniques do not possess properties asserted by applicant as critical is not necessarily indicative that the claimed process would not have been obvious. The affidavit evidence contains no basis for concluding that the properties asserted as critical are anything other than what one of ordinary skill in the art would have expected from a combination of the teachings of the references relied upon. *In re Lewis,* 443 F.2d 389, 170 U.S.P.Q. 84, 86 (C.C.P.A. 1971).

ᚐ

Evidence may not be disregarded simply because of the manner in which the now-claimed subject matter was denominated in the original application. To rule otherwise would let form triumph over substance, substantially eliminating the right of an applicant to retreat to an otherwise patentable species merely because he erroneously thought he was first with the genus when he filed. *In re Saunders and Gemeinhardt,* 444 F.2d 599, 170 U.S.P.Q. 213, 220 (C.C.P.A. 1971).

ᚐ

To establish criticality of a claimed range does not require showing inoperativeness outside of the range, only a difference in kind, as opposed to a difference in degree, over the range. *In re Waymouth and Koury,* 499 F.2d 1273, 182 U.S.P.Q. 290, 293 (C.C.P.A. 1974).

ᚐ

The criticality of a claimed range can be relied upon for patentability even though the range is not disclosed as critical in the specification. *Scandiamant Aktiebolag v. Commissioner of Patents,* 509 F.2d 463, 184 U.S.P.Q. 201, 206 (D.C. Cir. 1974).

ᚐ

Non-critical features may be supported by a more general disclosure than those at the heart of the invention. *In re Stephens, Benvau, and Benvau,* 529 F.2d 1343, 188 U.S.P.Q. 659, 661 (C.C.P.A. 1976).

ᚐ

In determining whether an unclaimed feature is critical, the entire disclosure must be considered. Broad language in the disclosure (including the abstract) omitting an allegedly critical feature tends to rebut an argument of criticality. Also, features that are merely preferred are not critical. *In re Goffe,* 542 F.2d 564, 191 U.S.P.Q. 429, 432 (C.C.P.A. 1976).

ᚐ

A claim to a new product is not legally required to include critical limitations. *W. L. Gore & Associates, Inc. v. Garlock, Inc.,* 721 F.2d 1540, 220 U.S.P.Q. 303, 315 (Fed. Cir. 1983).

ᚐ

In an action for infringement the burden of proving invalidity is on the alleged infringer. The patentee is under no compulsion either to prove a new and surprising result or to prove criticality of a claimed range. *American Hospital Supply Corp. v. Travenol Laboratories, Inc.,* 745 F.2d 1, 223 U.S.P.Q. 577, 582 (Fed. Cir. 1984).

Criticality. *See also* **Environment.**

There is no reason for requiring a showing of "criticality" of a limitation which finds support in the original disclosure, which is added to claims to advance prosecution of the application, and which is never alleged by applicants to be critical. If an applicant (under such circumstances) narrows the scope of his claims, he should be entitled to do so without being required to prove criticality. *In re Luvisi and Nohejl*, 342 F.2d 102, 144 U.S.P.Q. 646, 651 (C.C.P.A. 1965).

ᴕ

In the absence of convincing evidence of the criticality of limitations that are not in claims, such limitations are not regarded as essential for patentability. *In re Wakefield and Foster*, 422 F.2d 897, 164 U.S.P.Q. 636 (C.C.P.A. 1970).

ᴕ

The criteria provided by 35 U.S.C. §103 do not include "a matter of routine determination capable of being performed by one of ordinary skill in the art" or even absence of any disclosure of criticality for parameters recited in claims. Temperature limitations can render patentable otherwise obvious steps. The proper question is whether it would have been obvious to one of ordinary skill in the art that the particular blends could be subjected to the steps at the claimed temperatures. It is not a matter of the criticality of the recited ranges but of the obviousness of the applicability of said temperatures. *In re Schirmer*, 480 F.2d 1342, 178 U.S.P.Q. 483, 484 (C.C.P.A. 1973).

Cross-Appeal.

A winning interference party is not required to cross-appeal with respect to issues raised by him before the Board of Patent Interferences and decided adversely to him. *Shindelar v. Holderman, Gaeddert, Ratzlaff, Pruitt, and Lohrentz*, 628 F.2d 1337, 207 U.S.P.Q. 112, 115 n.6 (C.C.P.A. 1980).

Cross-Correlating.

Steps, such as "computing," 'determining," "cross-correlating," "comparing," "selecting," "initializing," "testing," "modifying," and "identifying," have implicitly been found to recite the solving of a mathematical algorithm. *In re Warmerdam*, 33 F.3d 1354, 31 U.S.P.Q.2d 1754, 1758 (Fed. Cir. 1994).

Cross-License.

When plural cross-licenses or cross-sublicenses are entered into in connection with or in contemplation of the termination of an interference, a copy of all such agreements must be filed at the PTO to satisfy the requirements of 35 U.S.C. §135(c). *Moog, Inc. v. Pegasus Laboratories, Inc.*, 521 F.2d 501, 187 U.S.P.Q. 279, 282, 283 (6th Cir. 1975).

ᴕ

Both of the parties to an interference signed a royalty-free cross-license agreement, no copy of which was ever filed with the Patent Office. The interference was subsequently dissolved with respect to the claims presently in litigation; plaintiff was awarded priority with respect to a claim that is not in litigation. The interference never went to settlement. Since the interference was decided only with respect to Claim 6, only that claim (if any) was subject to being held unenforceable under 35 U.S.C. §135(c). *Forbro Design Corp. v. Raytheon Co.*, 390 F. Supp. 794, 190 U.S.P.Q. 70, 77, 78 (Mass. 1975).

Cross-Reading. *See also* **Same Invention.**

Cross-reading of claims is not indispensable to a holding of double patenting. *In re Ockert*, 245 F.2d 467, 114 U.S.P.Q. 330, 332 (C.C.P.A. 1957).

Cross-Reference.

Enablement requirements for a pending application can be satisfied by amendment to make a cross-reference to a concurrently or previously filed copending application of the same inventor without involving improper "new matter." *Ex parte Wettstein, Vischer, Meystre, Kahnt, and Neher,* 140 U.S.P.Q. 187, 188 (P.O. Bd. App. 1962).

ᘺ

A division of a parent application, which is a continuation-in-part of a grandparent application, is not accorded the benefit of the filing date of the grandparent application in the absence of direct cross-reference thereto. The fact that the division cross-references the parent application and the parent application cross-references the grandparent application does not satisfy the requirements of 35 U.S.C. §120. *Sticker Industrial Supply Corp. v. Blaw-Knox Co.*, 405 F.2d 90, 160 U.S.P.Q. 177, 178, 179 (7th Cir. 1968).

Cross-Rejection.

It is improper to cross-reject claims of each of two pending applications as unpatentable over claims of the other. *Ex parte Conner and Verplanck,* 119 U.S.P.Q. 182, 184 (PO Bd. App. 1958).

Crowded Art.

In a crowded and comparatively simple art great advances are not to be expected. Patentability will not be denied to an invention that accomplishes a small, but nevertheless genuine, improvement not thought of by others and not obvious. "Small changes in a crowded art may constitute invention." *In re Lange,* 280 F.2d 165, 126 U.S.P.Q. 365, 367 (C.C.P.A. 1960).

ᘺ

The doctrine of equivalents must be narrowly applied in crowded art fields of invention. *Transco Products Inc. v. Performance Contracting Inc.*, 792 F.Supp. 594, 23 U.S.P.Q.2d 1691, 1697 (Ill. 1992).

ᘺ

The "inventor is entitled to a range of equivalents commensurate with the scope of his invention: broad if his invention is broad; narrow if his advance is a small one in a crowded field." *Schneider (USA) Inc. v. Cordis Corp.*, 29 U.S.P.Q.2d 1072, 1074, 1076 (Minn. 1993).

ᘺ

In a crowded art there is a narrow margin of improvement between patents, and patent claims should be read narrowly to avoid prior art wherever possible. The fact that the margin of improvement over the closest available references is as great as, if not greater than, that of previously issued patents demonstrates that the improvement, as claimed, would not have been obvious to one of ordinary skill in the art at the time the invention was made. *Petersen v. Fee International, Ltd.*, 381 F. Supp. 1071, 182 U.S.P.Q. 264, 266, 268 (Okla. 1974).

ω

Prosecution history is especially important when an invention involves a crowded art field, or when there is particular prior art over which an applicant is trying to distinguish. An applicant spent over a decade convincing the PTO that its invention was different from the prior art, the Court placed great weight on the prosecution history in determining the meaning and scope of the patent claims. *Fairfax Dental (Ireland) Ltd. v. Sterling Optical Corp.*, 808 F.Supp. 326, 26 U.S.P.Q.2d 1442, 1449 (N.Y. 1992).

Crux. *See* Gist.

Crystalline. *See also* Form.

The PTO has not challenged the appellants assertion that their 1953 application enabled those skilled in the art in 1953 to make and use "a solid polymer" as described in a claim. The appellants disclosed, as the only then-existing way to make such a polymer, a method of making the crystalline form. To say now that the appellants should have disclosed in 1953 the amorphous form (which did not exist until 1962) would be to impose an impossible burden on inventors and thus on the patent system. There cannot, in an effective patent system, be such a burden placed on the right to broad claims. To restrict the appellants to the crystalline form disclosed, under such circumstances, would be a poor way to stimulate invention, and particularly to encourage its early disclosure. To demand such restriction is merely to state a policy against broad protection for pioneer inventions, a policy both shortsighted and unsound from the standpoint of promoting progress in the useful arts, which is the constitutional purpose of the patent laws. *In re Hogan and Banks*, 559 F.2d 595, 194 U.S.P.Q. 527 (C.C.P.A. 1977).

Culpability. *See also* Fraud.

Attempts to avoid or mitigate infringement, whether or not successful, do not of themselves enlarge the culpability of a continuing activity. *Pall Corp. v. Micron Separations Inc.*, 66 F.3d 1211, 36 U.S.P.Q.2d 1225, 1233 (Fed. Cir. 1995).

ω

Bad faith is used in referring to misconduct in the prosecution of or litigation over a patent. Such conduct includes inequitable conduct during patent prosecution, bringing vexatious or unjustified suits, attorney or client misconduct during litigation, or unnecessarily prolonging litigation. These acts by themselves, however, are not sufficient for an increased damages award under 35 U.S.C. §284 because they are not related to the underlying act of infringement and say nothing about the culpability of the infringer. Only a culpable infringer can be held liable for increased damages, not an innocent one. In an initial determination of culpability, and thus liability for increased damages, "bad faith" properly refers to an infringer's failure to meet his affirmative duty to use due care in avoiding infringement of another's patent rights. *Jurgens v. CBK Ltd.*, 80 F.3d 1566, 38 U.S.P.Q.2d 1397, 1400 (Fed. Cir. 1996).

Culture. *See also* Deposit. *See also* Tissue Culture.

The procedure followed by *Argoudelis* [58 C.C.P.A. 769, 434 F.2d 1390, 168 U.S.P.Q. 99 (1970)] was sufficient to justify the conclusion that the specification satisfied the enablement requirement of 35 U.S.C. §112, first paragraph. The Commissioner's Notice of April 29, 1971, 886 O.G. 638 [now MPEP §608.01(p)] does not purport to set forth the minimum requirements, but only a procedure that will assuredly gain PTO acceptance. *Feldman v. Aunstrup,* 517 F. Supp. 1351, 186 U.S.P.Q. 108, 112 (C.C.P.A. 1975).

Cumulative.

Where the invention is a combination of elements, an undisclosed prior art reference that contains more of the combined elements than the disclosed references is not cumulative simply because various elements of the invention appear in other disclosed references. *Semiconductor Energy Laboratory Co. v. Samsung Electronics Co.*, 46 U.S.P.Q.2d 1874, 1878 (Va. 1998).

Cure of Cancer.

Amelioration of the symptoms or even cure of cancer is no longer considered to be "incredible." Nonetheless, decisional law would seem to indicate that the utility in question is sufficiently unusual to justify an Examiner's requiring substantiating evidence. This may be in the form of animal tests that constitute recognized screening procedures with clear relevance to utility in humans. The specification of the appellant's parent application sets forth several animal tests on numerous types of specific cancers as well as in vitro studies, both of which are asserted to be predictive with regard to utility in humans. The Examiner has not challenged the evidence presented in a single, relevant, material respect. There is only the blanket statement of lack of "patentable utility" per se. In fact, the only specific comments the Examiner has directed toward the appellant's evidence are with regard to the breadth of the types of tumor against which the claimed compounds have been shown to be active. The appealed claims are drawn to compounds and not to a method of treatment. Generally speaking, utility in treating a single disease is an adequate basis for the patentability of a pharmaceutical compound under 35 U.S.C. §101. *Ex parte Krepelka*, 231 U.S.P.Q. 746 (B.P.A.I. 1986).

Customer Suit.

In patent infringement actions, stays are appropriate where a first action is brought against a customer of an offending manufacturer and a subsequent action is brought involving the manufacturer itself. This so-called customer suit exception is based on the manufacturer's presumed greater interest in defending its actions against charges of patent infringement. Stays are warranted where the second action would resolve all charges against the customer in the stayed suit, including liability for damages. *Kahn v. General Motors Corp.*, 889 F.2d 1078, 12 U.S P.Q.2d 1997 (Fed. Cir. 1989).

ῶ

Litigation against or brought by the manufacturer of infringing goods takes precedence over a customer suit by the patent owner against customers of the manufacturer. *Katz v. Lear Siegler Inc.*, 909 F.2d 1459, 15 U.S.P.Q.2d 1554, 1558 (Fed. Cir. 1990).

ῶ

"[W]here a patentee has a separate interest in litigating against the customer, the "real party in interest" rationale for giving priority to the manufacturer's lawsuit is inapplicable." This principle appears particularly relevant in a situation where the patent owner seeks to hold the manufacturer liable solely on a theory of inducement/contributory infringement, claiming direct infringement only against the customer. *American Academy of Science v. Novell Inc.*, 24 U.S.P.Q.2d 1386, 1388 (Cal. 1992).

ῶ

Customer suit cases show that a manufacturer generally can establish jurisdiction based on a threat of suit against its customer only when the manufacturer is itself involved in infringing the patent and the customer is "merely a conduit for the manufacturer." However, a manufacturer's obligation to indemnify customers threatened with suit is a suffi-cient basis for jurisdiction over the manufacturer's declaratory judgment action. *The Dow Chemical Co. v. Viskase Corp.*, 892 F.Supp. 991, 36 U.S.P.Q.2d 1490, 1493, 1494, 1495 (Ill. 1995).

Key Terms and Concepts

Damages. *See also* **Accelerated Reentry Theory, Attorney's Fees, Enhanced Damages, Enhancement of Damages, Entire Market Value Rule, Incremental Income, Interest, Lost Profits, Patent Office License, Prejudgment Interest, Royalty.**

The general rule is that the monopoly of a patent which entitles a patentee to damages for infringement commences only when the patent is granted; but where, in advance of the granting of a patent, an invention is disclosed to one who, in breach of the confidence thus reposed, manufactures and sells articles embodying the invention, such person should be held liable for the profits and damages resulting therefrom, not under the patent statutes, but under the principle that equity will not permit one to unjustly enrich himself at the expense of another. In this case, the complainant offered to disclose his invention to the defendant with a view of selling it to the defendant. The defendant was interested in the proposition and invited the disclosure, otherwise it would not have seen the complainant's specification and drawings until the patent was granted. While there was no express agreement that the defendant was to hold the information so disclosed as a confidential matter and to make no use of it unless it should purchase the invention, we think that in equity and good conscience such an agreement was implied; and having obtained the disclosure under such circumstances, the defendant ought not to be heard to say that there was no obligation to respect the confidence thus reposed in it. *Hoeltke v. C.M. Kemp Manufacturing Co.*, 80 F.2d 912, 26 U.S.P.Q. 114, 126 (4th Cir. 1935), *cert. denied,* 298 U.S. 673 (1936).

ω

Damages in a patent case have been defined as "compensation for the pecuniary loss he [the patentee] has suffered from the infringement, without regard to the question whether the defendant has gained or lost by his unlawful acts." They have been said to constitute "the difference between his pecuniary condition after the infringement, and what his condition would have been if the infringement had not occurred." The question to be asked in determining damages is "how much had the Patent Holder and Licensee suffered by the infringement. And that question [is] primarily: had the Infringer not infringed, what would Patent Holder-Licensee have made?" *Aro Manufacturing Co., Inc. v. Convertible Top Replacement Co., Inc.*, 377 U.S. 476, 141 U.S.P.Q. 681, 694 (1964).

ω

To recover antitrust damages based on an alleged fraud in obtaining a patent, the plaintiff must prove: (1) willful and intentional fraud, (2) injury to business or property caused by the fraudulently procured patent, and (3) the other elements necessary to a section 2 Sherman Act violation. Good faith or an honest mistake is a complete defense to an antitrust action based on fraud on the Patent Office. *Honeywell Inc. v. Sperry Rand Corp.*, 180 U.S.P.Q. 673, 723 (Minn. 1973).

ᘯ

Where a legal injury is of an economic character, "[t]he general rule is, that when a wrong has been done, and the law gives a remedy, the compensation shall be equal to the injury. The latter is the standard by which the former is to be measured. The injured party is to be placed, as near as may be, in the situation he would have occupied if the wrong had not been committed." *Albemarle Paper Co. v. Moody*, 422 U.S. 405, 418-19 (1975).

ᘯ

A patentee has the burden to demonstrate lost profits. If he carries this burden, the burden shifts to the infringer to establish that a portion of those profits is due to unpatented features of the article. If this burden is met, the burden again shifts to the patentee to show the proper apportionment or to prove that an accurate accounting of the properly apportioned damages is impossible. If a patentee is a manufacturer, he may prove his damages by evidence of lost sales and profits. If such proof is inadequate or if he does not himself sell the product, he may nevertheless be injured by the unlicensed practice of his invention. The reasonable royalty that he might lawfully have collected from the infringer (if he had been a licensee) may then be the measure of damages. *Saginaw Products Corp. v. Eastern Airlines, Inc.*, 196 U.S.P.Q. 129, 131 (Mich. 1977).

ᘯ

Damages are not affected by the number of claims infringed. *Square Liner 360°, Inc. v. Chisum*, 215 U.S.P.Q. 1110, 1119 (Minn. 1981).

ᘯ

Where there has been a failure to use reasonable efforts to commercialize, damages are often not susceptible of certain proof. A lesser degree of certainty is required in such cases. *Bailey v. Chattem, Inc.*, 684 F.2d 386, 215 U.S.P.Q. 671, 679 (6th Cir. 1982).

ᘯ

Where the evidence shows that there is an established royalty during the period of patent infringement, the established royalty is the best measure of damages. *Bandag Inc. v. Gerrard Tire Co., Inc. v. Leonard*, 217 U.S.P.Q. 769, 771 (N.C. 1982).

ᘯ

Increased damages are usually based on a finding that the infringer's conduct was willful and in flagrant disregard of the patentee's rights. In this case, the defendant had been on notice of the plaintiff's patent rights and had an affirmative duty to exercise due care to determine whether it was infringing. It was held that the defendant could not avoid a holding of willful infringement because it failed to show that it obtained a competent opinion from counsel and that it had exercised reasonable and good faith adherence to the analysis and advice contained therein. Accordingly, the defendant was found liable to plaintiff for an amount equal to three times the amount of damages actually found or assessed. 35 U.S.C. §285 makes provision for the award of attorney's fees to the prevailing party in exceptional cases. In order to support an award of attorney's fees in a patent case, there must be a showing of conduct that is unfair, in bad faith, inequitable, or unconscionable. In view of the defendant's willful infringement, the case was held to involve those elements set out above and to be an exceptional case, thereby entitling plaintiff to an award of its attorney's fees. The plaintiff was also entitled to prejudgment interest based upon the damages found or assessed in the second phase of the trial. *Great Northern Corp. v. Davis Core & Pad Co.*, 226 U.S.P.Q. 540 (Ga. 1985).

ᚥ

When a party seeks to collect monetary damages from a patentee because of alleged violations of the antitrust law, it is appropriate to require a higher degree of misconduct for that damage award than when a party asserts only a defense against an infringement claim. *Hewlett-Packard Co. v. Bausch & Lomb Inc.*, 882 F.2d 1556, 1563, 11 U.S.P.Q.2d 1750, 1756 (Fed. Cir. 1989), *cert. denied*, 493 U.S. 1076 (1990); *Argus Chemical Corp. v. Fibre Glass-Evercoat Co.*, 812 F.2d 1381, 1384-85, 1 U.S.P.Q.2d 1971, 1973-74 (Fed. Cir. 1987)

ᚥ

The nature of the patent grant weighs against holding that monetary damages will always suffice to make a patentee whole; for the principle value of the patent is its statutory right to exclude. *H. Robertson Co. v. United Steel Deck, Inc.*, 820 F.2d 384, 2 U.S.P.Q.2d 1926 (Fed. Cir. 1987).

ᚥ

When the amount of the damages is not ascertainable with precision, reasonable doubt is appropriately resolved against the infringer. The general rule for determining actual damages to a patentee, that is itself producing the patented item, is to determine the sales and profits lost to the patentee because of the infringement. In order to recover lost profits, a patentee must show a reasonable probability that, but for the infringement, it would have made the sales that were made by the infringer. The patentee is not obliged to negate every possibility that a purchaser might not have bought the patentee's product instead of the infringing one, or might have forgone the purchase altogether. *Del Mar Avionics, Inc. v. Quinton Instrument Co.*, 836 F.2d 1320, 5 U.S.P.Q.2d 1255 (Fed. Cir. 1987).

ᚥ

Regardless of whether the trade secrets were ultimately made public via the issuance of a patent or otherwise, defendant obtained the information by misappropriation and not from public disclosure or any other legitimate business means. There is no distinction between the presence of a disclosure that may destroy secrecy and the head-start concept, for the former is merely an element of the latter. The award for damages compensates the plaintiff for the head start that the defendants obtained through misappropriation. This head start amounted to a preemption of the entire market and prevented the plaintiff from licensing others, as well as making entry into the market by the plaintiff impossible. In fashioning an adequate monetary remedy, the court must consider that the defendants did not merely wrongly obtain and use plaintiff's know-how as a competitor in the marketing, they refused to return the know-how to the plaintiff when ordered to do so, thereby completely precluding the plaintiff from also manufacturing. There is no question that the defendants' conduct was grossly improper and that the plaintiff's monetary recovery should not be limited by a lead time valuation. *The Kilbarr Corp. v. Business Systems, Inc., B.V.*, 679 F. Supp. 422, 6 U.S.P.Q.2d 1698 (N.J. 1988).

ᚥ

Under the entire-market-value rule, a patentee is entitled to lost profits on unpatented components that accompany the sale of patented components where, in all reasonable probability, the patentee would have made the sales that the infringer made. In this case, the record showed that the company that sells the belts also gets the sales of the sprockets, transfer combs, and belt accessories. Under the entire-market-value rule, the Court therefore found that it is reasonably probable that the patentee would have sold the sprockets, transfer combs, and accessories in view of the above findings and the court's prior determination that it is reasonably probable that the patentee would have made the sales but for the infringement. *Rexnord Inc. v. Laitram Corp.*, 6 U.S.P.Q.2d 1817 (Wis. 1988).

ω

A damage award of 25 percent of the infringer's selling price was regarded as adequate to compensate the patentee for infringement. *SmithKline Diagnostics. Inc. v. Helena Laboratories Corp.*, 12 U.S.P.Q.2d 1375. 1381 (Tex. 1989).

ω

Interest on lost profits should be compounded on a daily basis. Daily compounding more accurately reflects modern banking and investment practices, and thereby satisfies more fully the mandate that a patent owner receive full compensation for the infringement of its patent. *Uniroyal Inc. v. Rudkin-Wiley Corp.*, 721 F. Supp. 28, 13 U.S.P.Q.2d 1192, 1203 (Conn. 1989).

ω

To recover lost profits, a patent owner must prove the cause and the amount of the loss as facts, without resorting to speculation. Although the amount of lost profits need not be proven with unerring precision, lost profits cannot be awarded based on speculation. Where lost profits cannot be proved with reasonable certainty, a royalty measure of damages is appropriate. Although the calculation of lost profits is a fact-based analysis, determination of a reasonable royalty, which rests on a legal fiction, occurs in a purely hypothetical setting. The determination of a reasonable royalty, however, like the lost profits calculation, must be based on evidence and not conjecture. *Modine Manufacturing Co. v. Allen Group Inc.*, 14 U.S.P.Q.2d 1210, 1219 (Cal. 1989).

ω

A party to litigation has no absolute right to pursue any and every alternative theory of damages, no matter how complicated or tenuous. A district court has discretion to deny a plaintiff's proposed method of proof of damages that imposes too great a burden on court proceedings. *Micro Motion Inc. v. Kane Steel Co.*, 894 F.2d 1318, 13 U.S.P.Q.2d 1696, 1700 (Fed. Cir. 1990).

ω

One who chooses not to accept a license that is offered may not thereafter rely on the license royalty rate as the measure of damages. *See Beatrice Foods Co. v. New England Printing & Lithographing Co.*, 899 F.2d 1171, 1173, 14 U.S.P.Q.2d 1020, 1022 (Fed. Cir. 1990).

ω

There are two methods by which one may calculate damages. If actual damages cannot be ascertained, a reasonable royalty must be determined. Whether or not a party is entitled to an award of damages on a lost-profits theory is not material if the jury's verdict can also be sustained on the basis of a reasonable royalty. When the amount of damages cannot be ascertained with precision, any doubts regarding the amount must be resolved against the infringer. *ALM Surgical Equipment Inc. v. Kirschner Medical Corp.,* 15 U.S.P.Q.2d 1241, 1250 (S.C. 1990).

ᚹ

In order to prevail on appeal from a damages judgment, an appellant "must convince the court that the district court's decision is based on an erroneous conclusion of law, a clearly erroneous factual finding, or a clear error of judgment amounting to an abuse of discretion." *Kalman v. The Berlyn Corp.,* 914 F.2d 1473, 16 U.S.P.Q.2d 1093, 1100 (Fed. Cir. 1990).

ᚹ

Patentee's after-tax damage award should equal the after-tax sum it would have received had the infringement not taken place. The calculation must include the relevant adjustment for changes in the tax law. *TP Orthodontics Inc. v. Professional Positioners Inc.,* 17 U.S.P.Q.2d 1497, 1510 (Wis. 1990).

ᚹ

Enhanced damages may be awarded only as a penalty for an infringer's increased culpability; namely, willful infringement or bad faith. Damages cannot be enhanced to award a patentee additional compensation to rectify what the district court views as an inadequacy in the actual damages awarded. When the amount of the damages cannot be ascertained with precision, any doubts regarding the amount must be resolved against the infringer. In addition, any adverse consequences must rest on the infringer when the inability to ascertain lost profits is due to the infringer's own failure to keep accurate and complete records. It is the actual damages determined pursuant to the first paragraph of 35 U.S.C. §284, and not the enhanced damages determined pursuant to the second paragraph of that section, that measure the adequacy of the award to compensate the patentee for the infringement. If the patentee believes that the award is inadequate, it may challenge it on appeal. The enhanced damages award cannot be further enhanced, however, on the ground that the award for actual damages is inadequate. *Beatrice Foods Co. v. New England Printing & Lithographing Co.,* 923 F.2d 1576, 17 U.S.P.Q.2d 1553, 1555 (Fed. Cir. 1991).

ᚹ

Damages constitute a finding of fact on which the plaintiff bears the burden of proof by a preponderance of the evidence. Thus, where the amount is fixed by the court, review is in accord with the clearly erroneous standard of Fed. R. Civ. P. 52(a). A finding is clearly erroneous when, although there is evidence to support it, the reviewing court (on the entire evidence) is left with the definite and firm conviction that a mistake has been committed. However, certain subsidiary decisions underlying a damage theory, such as the choice of an accounting method for determining profit margin or the methodology for arriving at a reasonable royalty, are discretionary with the court. Such decisions are reviewed under the abuse-of-discretion standard. *SmithKline Diagnostics Inc. v. Helena Laboratories Corp.*, 926 F.2d 1161, 17 U.S.P.Q.2d 1922, 1924 (Fed. Cir. 1991).

ಠ

Section 289 of 35 U.S.C. contains language precluding a double recovery of profits. This language has been interpreted, however, only to exclude the recovery of certain forms of damages when calculating an infringer's profits, such as royalties, or to permit the reduction of profits through the allocation of costs or fixed expenses. In fact, the treble, or enhanced, damages provision of 35 U.S.C. §284 has been referred to as an independent or permissive provision of that section. Since a trebled award is not provided simply to compensate a plaintiff for his losses, but rather to deter intentional plagiarism, interpreting these sections to permit an enhanced award, irrespective of which base calculation provision is utilized, is consistent with these purposes. A plaintiff who re-covers an infringer's profits under 289 is not precluded from recovering an enhanced award where appropriate. *Braun Inc. v. Dynamics Corp. of America*, 19 U.S.P.Q.2d 1696, 1701 (Conn. 1991).

ಠ

The patent statute's provision for increased damages is permissive, not mandatory: A court *"may* increase the damages up to three times the amount found or assessed." 35 U.S.C. §284 (1988) (emphasis added). A district court's analysis of whether to increase damages, therefore, is a two-step process. First, the court must determine whether willful infringement (or another circumstance justifying an enhanced award) is proven, a finding of fact reviewed by the CAFC only for clear error. Second, if the court finds such a basis proven, it must still determine whether or not, under the totality of the circumstances, increased damages are warranted. This determination is committed to the sound discre-tion of the district court and "will not be overturned absent a clear showing of abuse of discretion." *State Industries Inc. v. Mor-Flo Industries Inc.*, 20 U.S.P.Q.2d 1738, 1740 (Fed. Cir. 1991).

ಠ

In connection with a tort created by a federal statute, the public purpose of the statute and the likely intent of Congress are the overriding considerations respecting the types of injuries for which damages may legally be awarded. *Holmes v. Securities Investor Protec-tion Corp.*, 503 U.S. 258, 274 (1992); *Associated Gen. Contractors, Inc. v. California State Council of Carpenters*, 459 U.S. 519, 538-40 (1983); *see also Brunswick Corp. v. Pueblo Bowl-O-Mat, Inc.*, 429 U.S. 477, 489 (1977).

ಠ

Factors for consideration in determining when an infringer acted in such bad faith as to merit an increase in damages awarded against him include:

1. Whether the infringer deliberately copied the ideas or design of another;
2. Whether the infringer, when he knew of the other's patent protection, investigated the scope of the patent and formed a good faith belief that it was invalid or that it was not infringed;
3. The infringer's behavior as a party to the litigation;
4. Defendant's size (or relative size) and financial condition;

5. Closeness of the case;
6. Duration of defendant's misconduct;
7. Remedial action by defendant;
8. Defendant's motivation for harm; and
9. Whether defendant attempted to conceal its misconduct.

The Read Corp. v. Portec Inc., 970 F.2d 816, 23 U.S.P.Q.2d 1426, 1435 (Fed. Cir. 1992).

ω

Although 35 U.S.C. §284 provides that a patentee may recover "damages adequate to compensate for the infringement" which "the court may increase...up to three times", nothing in 35 U.S.C. §289 authorizes an increase in a patentee's total profit. In fact, 35 U.S.C. §289 explicitly precludes a patentee from "twice recover[ing] the profits made from the infringement." A "design patentee cannot recover both damages under 35 U.S.C. §284 and the profits of the infringer under 35 U.S.C. §289." *Braun Inc. v. Dynamics Corp. of America*, 975 F.2d 815, 24 U.S.P.Q.2d 1121, 1128 (Fed. Cir. 1992).

ω

Enhanced damages are punitive, not compensatory. Therefore, an infringer may generally avoid enhanced damages with meritorious good faith defense and a substantial challenge to infringement. When a court awards damages for infringement, 35 U.S.C. §284's express provision—rather than the general provision of Rule (FRCP) 54(d)—governs the award of costs. *Delta-X Corp. v. Baker Hughes Production Tools Inc.*, 984 F.2d 410, 25 U.S.P.Q.2d 1447, 1449, 1450 (Fed. Cir. 1993).

ω

The Federal Circuit reviews the amount of a court's damage award to determine whether it was based on clearly erroneous factual findings, or whether in other respects it was based on an erroneous conclusion of law or a clear error of judgment amounting to an abuse of discretion. *Transmatic Inc. v. Gulton Industries Inc.*, 53 F.3d 1270, 35 U.S.P.Q.2d 1035, 1039 (Fed. Cir. 1995).

ω

Judicial limitations on damages, either for certain classes of plaintiffs or for certain types of injuries, have been imposed in terms of "proximate cause" or "foreseeability". Such labels have been judicial tools used to limit legal responsibility for the consequences of one's conduct that are too remote to justify compensation. The general principles expressed in the common law tell us that the test of legal compensability is one "to be determined on the facts of each case upon mixed considerations of logic, common sense, justice, policy and precedent. *Rite-Hite Corp. v. Kelley Co. Inc.*, 56 F.3d 1538, 35 U.S.P.Q.2d 1065, 1070 (Fed. Cir. 1995); *but see dissent*.

ω

A patentee can recover damages for infringement, pursuant to 35 U.S.C. §284, under two theories: lost profits and reasonable royalties. Lost profits are available where the record permits an accurate determination of the patentee's loss of sales and profits because of the infringement. Reasonable royalties are always available. An award may be split between lost profits, as actual damages to the extent they are proved, and reasonable royalties for the remainder. Determination of the nature and amount of damages is a question of fact on which the patentee has the burden of proof. *Fonar Corp. v. General Electric Co.*, 41 U.S.P.Q.2d 1088 (N.Y. 1995).

ω

Although a trial court many times has discretion to weigh the closeness of the case and the scope of the infringer's investigation in deciding whether to increase a damages award, it does not have discretion to reweigh this evidence once the matter has been decided by a jury and the court finds evidence sufficient to support the jury determination. *Jurgens v. CBK Ltd.*, 80 F.3d 1566, 38 U.S.P.Q.2d 1397, 1402 (Fed. Cir. 1996).

ω

If actual damages cannot be ascertained with precision because evidence available from the infringer is inadequate, damages may be estimated on the best available evidence, taking cognizance of the reason for the inadequacy of proof and resolving doubt against the infringer. Any adverse consequences rest upon the infringer when inability to ascertain lost profits is due the the infringer's failure to keep accurate or complete records. *Sensonics Inc. v. Aerosonic Corp.*, 81 F.3d 1566, 38 U.S.P.Q.2d 1551, 1555, 1556 (Fed. Cir. 1996).

ω

The use of a willing licensee-willing licensor model for determining damages "risks creation of the perception that blatant, blind appropriation of inventions patented by individual, non-manufacturing inventors is the profitable, can't-lose course." To avoid such a result, the fact finder may consider additional factors to assist in the determination of adequate compensation for infringement. These factors include royalties received by the patentee for licensing the patent in suit, opinion testimony of qualified experts, the patentee's relationship with the infringer, and other factors that might warrant higher damages. *Maxwell v. J. Baker Inc.*, 39 U.S.P.Q.2d 1001, 1008 (Fed. Cir. 1996).

ω

An alleged alternative "must not have a disparately higher price than or possess characteristics significantly different from the patented product." *Clark v. Linzer Products Corp.*, 40 U.S.P.Q.2d 1469, 1472 (Ill. 1996).

ω

The statute that limits recovery in cases where there is no marking refers only to damages. Historically, disgorgement, which is really what the plaintiff seeks in its actions for infringers' profits, was not considered a recovery of damages, but an equitable remedy to restore to the proper owner profits made by an infringer's use of another's property. The limitations imposed by 35 U.S.C. §287(a) are not applicable to an action seeking recovery of an infringer's profits pursuant to 35 U.S.C. §289. *Nike Inc. v. Wal-Mart Stores Inc.*, 138 F.3d 1437, 41 U.S.P.Q.2d 1146 (Va. 1996).

ω

A plaintiff cannot maintain entitlement to damages where it asserts infringement of an apparatus patent and a method patent in which the claimed method is the use of the apparatus. *American Bank Note Holographics Inc. v. The Upper Deck Co.*, 41 U.S.P.Q.2d 2019 (N.Y. 1997).

ω

Where there is a doubt as to the profit margin, the Court must construe the facts in favor of the patentee. *Joy Technologies Inc. v. Flakt Inc.*, 42 U.S.P.Q.2d 1042 (Del. 1996).

ΤΟ

Where a court has found relevant patent claims invalid, a licensor may still recover damages (from the date of an alleged breach until the date that the licensee first challenged validity of the claims) for breach of contract for past royalties due on processes allegedly covered by such claims. *Studiengesellschaft Kohle m.b.H. v. Shell Oil Co.*, 112 F.3d 1561, 42 U.S.P.Q.2d 1674, 1676 (Fed. Cir. 1997).

ΤΟ

The marking statute applies to actions for recovery of the infringer's profits. *Nike Inc. v. Wal-Mart Stores Inc.*, 138 F.3d 1437, 46 U.S.P.Q.2d 1001, 1007 (Fed. Cir. 1998).

ΤΟ

In a matter before the International Trade Commission for violation of a Consent Order "[w]hen calculation of damages is impeded by incomplete records of the infringer, adverse inferences are appropriately drawn." A penalty of about three times the value is well within constitutional limits. *San Huan New Materials High Tech Inc. v. ITC*, 48 U.S.P.Q.2d 1865, 1879 (Fed. Cir. 1998).

Dangling Valence. *See* **Open-Ended Claim.**

Data. *See* **Comparative Test Data.**

Date. *See also* **Effective Date, Filing Date, Same Date, Time.**

Without a showing that prior art devices were unsatisfactory and that workers in the art were looking for a solution to the problem, the mere difference in dates (twenty years) is of little help in determining whether or not the suggested combination of references would have been obvious. *In re Johnson*, 435 F.2d 585, 168 U.S.P.Q. 289, 291 (C.C.P.A. 1971).

ΤΟ

The more remote in time the prior art relied on, the less likely it becomes that the patented invention would be obvious to one of ordinary skill. If there is no rational manner in which the prior art can be modified to result in the patented invention, the patent is valid. *Continuous Curve Contact Lenses, Inc. v. National Patent Development Corporation*, 214 U.S.P.Q. 86, 116 (Cal. 1982).

ΤΟ

The prior art existed for many years, and yet those skilled in the art never created a mechanism comparable to that of the patent. The fact that skilled workers did not create the patented invention despite existence of elements in the prior art is evidence of non-obviousness. *Al-Site Corp. v. Opti-Ray Inc.*, 841 F.Supp. 1318, 28 U.S.P.Q.2d 1915, 1922 (N.Y. 1993).

ΤΟ

"It is an essential requirement that evidence be offered to show that an exhibit . . . was, in fact, made on the date appearing thereon." *English v. Ausnit*, 38 U.S.P.Q.2d 1625, 1629 (B.P.A.I. 1993).

Date of Invention. *See* **Origin.**

Deception. *See also* **35 U.S.C. §116.**

While the lack of joint inventorship is not a favored defense, clear and convincing evidence should be accepted and applied when applicants practiced deception upon the Patent Office with respect to claiming joint inventorship. There is no statutory authorization for correcting inventorship without proof that misjoinder was through error and without any deceptive intention . *Iron Ore Co. of Canada v. The Dow Chemical Company*, 177 U.S.P.Q. 34, 70, 73 (Utah 1972).

ᛟ

While it is generally true that the presumption of validity of a patent may be strengthened where the Patent Office has granted it in the face of certain prior art, this is not so where the Patent Office has been deceived as to the true significance of a reference. *Kahn v. Dynamics Corporation of America*, 367 F.Supp. 63, 180 U.S.P.Q. 247, 252 (N.Y. 1973).

ᛟ

There is nothing improper, illegal or inequitable in filing a patent application for the purpose of obtaining the right to exclude a known competitor's product from the market; nor is it in any manner improper to amend or insert claims intended to cover a competitor's product the applicant's attorney has learned about during the prosecution of a patent application. If any such amendment or insertion complies with all statutes and regulations, its genesis in the marketplace is simply irrelevant and cannot of itself evidence deceitful intent. *Kingsdown Medical Consultants Ltd. v. Hollister Inc.*, 863 F.2d 867, 9 U.S.P.Q.2d 1384, 1390 (Fed. Cir. 1988).

Deceptive Intent. *See also* **"Ambush" Theory, Deception.**

Satisfaction of the traditional two-part test [(1) the declaratory plaintiff has acted, or has made preparations to act, in a way that could constitute infringement, and (2) the patentee has created in the declaratory plaintiff a reasonable apprehension that the patentee will bring suit if the activity in question continues] is not a prerequisite to jurisdiction in every possible patent declaratory judgment action. The two elements merely assure that the declaratory plaintiff has enough interest in the subject matter of the suit and that the disagreement between the parties is real and immediate enough to fulfill the "actual controversy" requirement. *Fina Oil and Chemical Co. V. Ewen*, 123 F.3d 1466, 43 U.S.P.Q.2d 1935, 1939 (Fed. Cir. 1997).

ᛟ

The court declined to create a per se rule that an actual controversy predicated only on inducing infringement may exist only if direct infringement has already occurred. *Fina Research S.A. v. Baroid Ltd.*, 141 F.3d 1479, 46 U.S.P.Q.2d 1461, 1467 (Fed. Cir. 1998).

ᛟ

While a patent holding subsidiary is a legitimate creature and may provide certain business advantages, it cannot fairly be used to insulate patent owners from defending declaratory judgment actions in those fora where its parent company operates under the patent and engages in activities sufficient to create personal jurisdiction and declaratory judgment jurisdiction. *Dainippon Screen Manufacturing Co. v. CFMT Inc.*, 142 F.3d 1266, 46 U.S.P.Q.2d 1616, 1621 (Fed. Cir. 1998).

ω

While lack of deceptive intent, as a negative, may be hard for a patentee to prove when it claims relief under the statute, good faith is presumed in the absence of a persuasive showing of deceptive intent. *Pannu v. Iolab Corp.*, 47 U.S.P.Q.2d 1657, 1662 n.4 (Fed. Cir. 1998).

Decision. *See also* PTO Indices.

Undue liberties should not be taken with court decisions, which should be construed in accord with the precise issue before the court. A fertile source of error in patent law is the misapplication of a sound legal principle established in one case to another case in which the facts are essentially different and the principle has no application whatsoever. *In re Ruscetta and Jenny*, 225 F.2d 687, 118 U.S.P.Q. 101, 103 (C.C.P.A. 1958).

ω

A decision of the CCPA, reversing the Patent Office Board of Appeals in a patent case, does not constitute a holding that the application contains patentable subject matter or is "allowable" and does not direct the Patent Office to issue a patent. All the CCPA does is pass on the propriety of rejections brought before it for review. *In re Citron*, 326 F.2d 418, 140 U.S.P.Q. 220, 221 (C.C.P.A. 1964).

ω

An acceptable "decision", in the jurisdictional sense, refers to an action taken by the Board, in a capacity provided for in the statutes, which has been dispositive of the appeal in that it has adjudicated a legal right. *In re James*, 432 F.2d 473, 167 U.S.P.Q. 403, 405 (C.C.P.A. 1970)

ω

When not all claims are asserted to be invalid for anticipation or obviousness, the patent cannot be held invalid on either ground. Each claim must be presumed valid independently of the validity of any other claim. A court must limit its decision to the claims before it. *Preemption Devices, Inc. v. Minnesota Mining & Manufacturing Co.*, 732 F.2d 903, 221 U.S.P.Q. 841, 843, 844 (Fed. Cir. 1984).

ω

Parties in interference are advised to file petitions under 37 C.F.R. §1.644(a)(2) within 15 days after entry of the Board's final decision and also to include, as part of the petition or in a separate paper, a request for an extension of time to seek judicial review. *Goutzoulis v. Athale*, 15 U.S.P.Q.2d 1461, 1464 (Comm'r Patents & Trademarks 1990).

ω

An Examiner's final rejection, which precipitates the statutory right to appeal to the BPAI, 35 U.S.C. §134 (1988), constitutes the "decision" of the Examiner for the purposes of 35 U.S.C. §1.196(a). *In re Webb,* 916 F.2d 1553, 16 U.S.P.Q.2d 1433, 1435 (Fed. Cir. 1990).

ϖ

A court generally adheres to a decision in a prior appeal in the case unless one of three "exceptional circumstances" exists: the evidence on a subsequent trial is substantially different, controlling authority has since made a contrary decision of the law applicable to such issues, or the decision was clearly erroneous and would work a manifest injustice. *Mendenhall v. Barber-Greene Co.,* 26 F.3d 1573, 31 U.S.P.Q.2d 1001, 1007 (Fed. Cir. 1994).

Decision of the Commissioner.

An action in the district court under 35 U.S.C. §145 is a proceeding de novo and, while it is limited to the invention claimed in the PTO, the court may consider any additional competent evidence that a plaintiff neither intentionally nor negligently failed to submit to the PTO. The presumption of correctness that attaches to the decision of the Commissioner is a rebuttable presumption that may be overcome by the introduction of evidence (at a trial under 35 U.S.C. §145) that is of such character and amount as to carry a thorough conviction of error. At such a trial the plaintiff and defendant may present evidence on any issue properly before the court. This additional evidence may include testimony of expert witnesses and inventors skilled in the art, and evidence of commercial success. In making its determination of non-obviousness, the court in this case recognized the nonanalogous nature of one reference, the lack of teaching or suggestion in the prior art of the useful advantage of a flexible track incapable of self-support, and the commercial success of the highly flexible Hot Wheels trackway toy vehicle combination covered by the plaintiff's Reissue Application. The fact that the claimed invention seemed simple and, when viewed in hind sight, appeared to be obvious was not enough to negate invention. *Lemelson v. Mossinghoff,* 225 U.S.P.Q. 1063 (D.C. 1985).

Declaration. *See also* Affidavit, Citizenship, Comparative Test Data, Evidence, Execution of Patent Application, Oath, Showing, Unsigned Declaration.

As there was nothing in the record to controvert a statement in appellant's affidavit, the statement was accepted as accurate. *In re Nathan, Hogg, and Schneider,* 328 F.2d 1005, 140 U.S.P.Q. 601, 604 (C.C.P.A. 1964).

ϖ

Failure to execute the Declaration (an essential part of a complete application for Letters Patent) amounts to failure to affirm that the applicant is the true inventor of claimed subject matter and should result in deferral of the effective filing date. *Autovox, S.p.A. v. Lenco Italiana [sic], S.p.A.,* 210 U.S.P.Q. 277, 279 (Ill. 1980).

ϖ

A Declaration by a qualified expert in the art stating that questioned elements in the application were well known to those of ordinary skill in the art as of the effective filing date and that such elements were routinely built may not be adequate to overcome a rejection for lack of enablement with regard to the making of such elements. Section 112 of 35 U.S.C. requires that, unless the information is well known in the art, the application itself must contain this information; it is not sufficient to provide it only through an expert's Declaration. An expert's opinion on the ultimate legal issue must be supported by something more than a conclusory statement. A statement by a qualified expert that the elements referred to in the application were well known to those of ordinary skill in the art as of the effective date in that they were routinely built was inadequate because the expert did not provide adequate support for his conclusion. *In re Buchner*, 929 F.2d 660, 18 U.S.P.Q.2d 1331, 1332 (Fed. Cir. 1991).

ω

The filing of the declaration in the amendment of an application from a continuation to a CIP is more of a ministerial act than when the declaration is filed with the initial application. *Molins PLC v. Textron Inc.*, 821 F.Supp. 1551, 26 U.S.P.Q.2d 1889, 1910 (Del. 1992).

ω

An expert's declaration was sufficient to defeat a motion for summary judgment. The expert testified as to both the level of skill in the art and the implication of the specifications and drawings of the patents in suit. He raised a genuine issue as to whether the patent is sufficiently descriptive to allow one skilled in the art to ascertain the best mode symmetrical power/ground configuration. Since the burden lies with MELA and MELCO to prove the inadequacy of best mode disclosure by clear and convincing evidence, even the somewhat conclusory declaration of the expert was sufficient to raise a genuine issue for trial. Even if the declaration were regarded as overly conclusory, summary judgment could not, at least initially, be granted on this basis. The Court would be obliged to allow Wang to provide supporting detail. *Wang Laboratories Inc. v. Mitsubishi Electronics America Inc.*, 32 U.S.P.Q.2d 1641, 1645 (Cal. 1994).

Declaratory Judgment. *See also* Case or Controversy.

Cautioning possible patent infringers is insufficient to create a reasonable apprehension of suit. *Walker Process Equipment, Inc. v. FMC Corp.*, 356 F.2d 449, 452, 148 U.S.P.Q. 308, 309-10 (7th Cir.), *cert. denied*, 385 U.S. 824, 151 U.S.P.Q. 758 (1966).

ω

A letter from a foreign corporation that merely informed plaintiff of a patent in an effort to prevent possible "innocent infringement" is not adequate to provide the court with in personam jurisdiction over the foreign corporation. *Rheem Manufacturing Co. v. Johnson Heater Corp.*, 370 F. Supp. 806, 181 U.S.P.Q. 442 (Minn. 1974).

ω

A declaratory judgment, even one involving a claim under federal law, presents no federal jurisdiction where it is sought merely as a defense to an action that itself could not be brought in federal court. An allegation of "a reasonable apprehension that [plaintiff] may attempt to terminate the License Agreement and commence litigation involving claims of infringement" would appear to constitute a "federal question." Nevertheless, these issues can be addressed in the state courts. *Union Carbide Corp. v. Air Products & Chemicals, Inc.*, 202 U.S.P.Q. 43, 54, 55 (N.Y. 1978).

ᙡ

In patent suits, courts have become more willing to find a controversy between the parties that will warrant their entertaining a suit for a declaratory judgment. The trend has been to recognize the appropriateness of the declaratory judgment action in patent matters as a means of avoiding the multiplicity of actions and endless delays and uncertainties that various suits in different jurisdictions testing different aspects of a broad patent controversy can entail. To meet its burden of demonstrating that a controversy exists, a plaintiff must show that it reasonably apprehended that it was going to be sued by the defendant presently before the court. In determining whether a plaintiff reasonably apprehended a suit for patent infringement, a court looks at the nature and extent of the defendant's acts, the relation between the plaintiff and defendant, the similarity of the two parties' products, and the nature of the art. Defendant's writing a letter suggesting infringement, requesting plaintiff's opinion on whether its product did infringe, asking plaintiff to advise patent owner of all locations of product and for permission for patent owner to inspect those sites has been deemed insufficient to cause a plaintiff to reasonably apprehend a suit for patent infringement. When a licensee has neither actual nor apparent authority to charge others with infringement, a plaintiff's apprehension of suit by that party is unreasonable and unfounded. *DMP Corp. v. Rederiaktiebolaget Nordstjernan*, 223 U.S.P.Q. 560, 561, 562 (D.C. 1983).

ᙡ

The existence of prior infringement suits in foreign forums based on corresponding foreign patents and against the same products is a sufficient basis for reasonable apprehension of identical suits in the United States on such products. *Electro Medical Systems S.A. v. Cooper Laseronics, Inc.*, 617 F. Supp. 1036, 227 U.S.P.Q. 564, 566 (Ill. 1985).

ᙡ

There is an obvious distinction between the alleged injury of a party threatened with a lawsuit for infringement and the alleged injury of a patent holder. In a typical patent case brought under the Declaratory Judgment Act, 28 U.S.C. §2201, the plaintiff asserts his intent and ability to produce a product, which defendant contends is a patent infringement. Courts find a justiciable controversy because to do otherwise would leave the plaintiff no option but to produce the products and be sued for infringement. The patent holder, on the other hand, is injured only if actual infringement occurs. His remedy is provided in 35 U.S.C. §271. *D. G. Rung Industries, Inc. v. Hinnerman*, 626 F. Supp. 1062, 229 U.S.P.Q. 930, 932 (Wash. 1986).

ᙡ

When the declaratory judgment plaintiff is a manufacturer, such plaintiff is obliged to show apprehension on its part that it (no one else) will be sued by defendant for infringement if plaintiff (no one else) commences or continues to manufacture an accused device. The declaratory plaintiff is also obliged to show that it (no one else) has actually produced the accused device or, if not, that it has prepared itself to produce it. In an action by a nonmanufacturer potential licensor seeking a declaratory judgment of patent invalidity, the case or controversy requirement of Article III, section 2, is satisfied:

(1) (a) when a defendant's conduct has created on the part of the declaratory plaintiff a reasonable apprehension that it will face an infringement suit if a potential licensee of plaintiff commences the activity in question; or

(b) when there is an unwillingness on the part of a potential licensee manufacturer to enter into a licensing agreement with a declaratory plaintiff and to manufacture the device, and a substantial factor in that unwillingness is an apprehension on the part of the potential licensee-manufacturer, caused by defendant's conduct, that it will itself face an infringement suit if it commences manufacture; and

(2) (a) when plaintiff's licensee-manufacturer has actually manufactured the accused device; or

(b) it is probable that a potential licensee-manufacturer will commence manufacture, assuming the consumation of a licensng agreement between the licensor and the potential licensee-manufacturer, and assuming judicial elimination of the prospect of an infringement suit by defendant.

Research Institute for Medicine and Chemistry Inc. v. Wisconsin Alumni Research Foundation Inc., 1 U.S.P.Q.2d 1929, 1931, 1933 (Wis. 1986).

ᶲ

Assuming that (a) defendant's attorneys discussed the prospect of suing plaintiff for patent infringement and expressed the expectation of a substantial money judgment based on such patent infringement, (b) defendant's attorneys discussed the need for plaintiff to take a license under defendant's patents, (c) defendants threatened that plaintiff "might be liable for past patent infringement . . . [and] the parties might wind up in federal court on these issues," and (d) defendant is commercially using the allegedly infringing product and its method of application, such does not clearly establish the existence of an actual controversy under the Declaratory Judgment Act, 28 U.S.C. §2201. There has been neither conduct nor a course of action on the part of defendant, but merely discussion indicating the possibility of suit. *The Goodyear Tire & Rubber Company v. Releasomers Inc.,* 3 U.S.P.Q.2d 1233, 1234, 1235 (Ohio 1986).

ᶲ

There is no absolute right to a declaratory judgment. The Declaratory Judgment Act, 28 U.S.C. §2201, says a court "may" grant one. Hence, when there is a clear controversy and thus jurisdiction, a district court's decision on whether to exercise that jurisdiction is discretionary. To support jurisdiction for a declaratory judgment action, the defendant's conduct must have created (on the part of the plaintiff) a reasonable apprehension that the defendant will initiate suit if the plaintiff continues the allegedly infringing activity, and the plaintiff must actually have either produced the device or have prepared to produce that device. Respecting the defendant's conduct, it must be such as to indicate the defendant's intent to enforce its patent. If defendant has expressly charged a current activity of the plaintiff as an infringement, there is clearly an actual controversy, certainty has rendered apprehension irrelevant, and one need say no more. In light of the subtleties in lawyer language, however, the courts have not required an express infringement charge. When the defendant's conduct, including its statements, falls short of an express charge, one must consider the "totality of the circumstances" in determining whether that conduct meets the first prong of the test. If the circumstances warrant, a reasonable apprehension may be found in the absence of any communication from the defendant to the plaintiff. If, on the other hand, the defendant has done nothing but obtain a patent, there can be no basis for the required apprehension, a rule that protects quiescent patent owners against unwarranted litigation. Respecting the plaintiff's conduct, it must be such as to establish that plaintiff has a true interest to be protected by the declaratory judgment. The plaintiff may not, for example, obtain a declaratory judgment merely because it would like an advisory opinion on whether it would be liable for patent infringement if it were to initiate some merely contemplated activity. Basically, the test requires two core elements: (1) acts of the defendant indicating an intent to enforce its patent; and (2) acts of the plaintiff that might subject it or its customers to suit for patent infringement. *Arrowhead Industrial Water Inc. v. Ecolochem Inc.*, 846 F.2d 731, 6 U.S.P.Q.2d 1685, 1869 (Fed. Cir. 1988).

ᴂ

In a case seeking a declaratory judgment of a patent's invalidity or noninfringement, the actual controversy requirement is satisfied when a purported patent owner's conduct has created a "reasonable apprehension" on the part of the plaintiff "that it will face an infringement suit if it commences or continues the activity in question." The right to a declaratory judgment as to the validity of a patent arises when a potential infringer is threatened with litigation and cannot compel the patentee to proceed. When it appears that the Declaratory Judgment Act has been used as a procedural "fencing device" to secure delay or to choose a forum other than that in which the action would normally be heard, it is proper for the court to dismiss or transfer the action to the forum in which the subsequently filed infringement suit is pending. *EMS-American Grilon Inc. v. DSM Resins U.S. Inc.*, 15 U.S.P.Q.2d 1472, 1474, 1475 (N.J. 1989).

ᴂ

To meet the controversy requirement in a declaratory judgment suit by a patentee against an alleged future infringer, two elements must be present: (1) the defendant must be engaged in an activity directed toward making, selling, or using subject to an infringement charge under 35 U.S.C. §271(a)(1982), or be making meaningful preparation for such activity; and (2) acts of the defendant must indicate a refusal to change the course of its actions in the face of acts by the patentee sufficient to create a reasonable apprehension that a suit will be forthcoming. The first prong is identical to one of the requirements in a patent declaratory judgment action where the threatened infringer is the plaintiff. It looks to the accused infringer's conduct and ensures that the controversy is sufficiently real and substantial. The second prong requires conduct by both the accused infringer and the patentee and is similar to the reasonable apprehension prong in the normal action. It ensures that the controversy is definite and concrete between parties having adverse legal interests. Declaratory judgment actions of infringement sought by patentees against parties who will allegedly infringe in the future have been allowed to proceed. If the controversy requirement is met by a sufficient allegation of immediacy and reality, a patentee should be able to seek a declaration of infringement against a future infringer when a future infringer is able to maintain a declaratory judgment action for noninfringement under the same circumstances. *Lang v. Pacific Marine & Supply Co. Ltd.*, 895 F.2d 761, 13 U.S.P.Q.2d 1820, 1822 (Fed. Cir. 1990).

ʊ

At the root of the preference for a manufacturer's declaratory judgment action is the recognition that, in reality, the manufacturer is the true defendant in a customer suit. A manufacturer must protect its customers, either as a matter of contract, or good business, or in order to avoid the damaging impact of an adverse ruling against its products. *Katz v. Lear Siegler Inc.*, 909 F.2d 1459, 15 U.S.P.Q. 1554, 1558, (Fed. Cir. 1990).

ʊ

Under the Declaratory Judgment Act, a live controversy must be present at all stages of review, and not just at the time the complaint is filed. To establish the need for a declaratory judgment, the plaintiff must satisfy a two-part analysis. First, plaintiff must show that defendant's conduct has created a reasonable apprehension that it will be subject to an infringement suit if it commences or continues production. Second, plaintiff must present credible allegations of immediate intent and ability to undertake the business that must bring it into collision with defendant's patent rights. *Bristol Myers Squibb Co. v. Erbamont Inc.*, 734 F. Supp. 661, 16 U.S.P.Q.2d 1887, 1888 (Del. 1990).

ʊ

In promulgating the Declaratory Judgment Act, Congress intended to avoid accrual of avoidable damages to one not certain of his rights and to afford him an early adjudication without waiting until his adversary should see fit to begin suit. An evaluation of the harm to the plaintiff is necessary to determine whether the rendering of a declaratory judgment will serve a useful purpose in settling the legal relations between the parties. It was an abuse of discretion to have dismissed a declaratory judgment action for noninfringement based on a pending interference proceeding when the interference cannot decide (or is not likely to moot) the infringement issues raised and when the declaratory judgment plaintiff is likely to suffer significant ongoing harm during any delay. *Minnesota Mining & Manufacturing Co. v. Norton Co.*, 929 F.2d 670, 18 U.S.P.Q.2d 1302, 1305, 1306 (Fed. Cir. 1991).

ʊ

Litigation against unrelated third parties by the patent owner does not give plaintiff in a declaratory judgment action reason to fear litigation. *West Interactive Corp. v. First Data Resources Inc.*, 972 F.2d 1295, 23 U.S.P.Q.2d 1927, 1930 (Fed. Cir. 1992).

ʊ

A count under the Declaratory Judgment Act should be distinguished from a count under 35 U.S.C. §271 for patent infringement. The latter, "by itself, cannot be interpreted to cover acts other than an actual making, using or selling of the patented invention." *Telectronics Pacing Systems Inc. v. Ventritex Inc.*, 982 F.2d 1520, 25 U.S.P.Q.2d 1196, 1201 n.5 (Fed. Cir. 1992).

ʊ

Requiring an express charge of litigation would destroy the purpose of the Declaratory Judgment Act, which (in patent cases) is to provide the allegedly infringing party relief from uncertainty and delay with regard to its legal rights. It would be unfair to require imminent apprehension of an infringement suit when a defendant could delay such suit until all other enforcement efforts had failed. Resolving the uncertainty and anxiety resulting from a looming lawsuit is the purpose of the Declaratory Judgment Act. It is enough that the defendant's conduct "be such as to indicate defendant's intent to enforce its patent". *Océ-Office Systems Inc. v. Eastman Kodak Co.*, 805 F. Supp. 642, 25 U.S.P.Q.2d 1370, 1373, 1374 (Ill. 1992).

ω

An unnecessary ruling on an affirmative defense is not the same as the necessary resolution of a counterclaim for a declaratory judgment. *Cardinal Chemical Co. v. Morton International Inc.*, 113 S.Ct. 1967, 26 U.S.P.Q.2d 1721, 1726 (S.Ct. 1993).

ω

The exercise of discretion in a declaratory judgment must have a basis in sound reason. *Genentech Inc. v. Eli Lilly and Co.*, 998 F.2d 931, 27 U.S.P.Q.2d 1241, 1243 (Fed. Cir. 1993).

ω

There must be both (1) an explicit threat or other action by the patentee, which creates a reasonable apprehension on the part of the declaratory plaintiff that it will face an infringement suit, and (2) present activity which would constitute infringement or concrete steps taken with the intent to conduct such activity. The element of threat or reasonable apprehension of suit turns on the conduct of the patentee, while the infringement element depends on the conduct of the asserted infringer. The purpose of the two-part test is to determine whether the need for judicial attention is real and immediate or is prospective and uncertain of occurrence. *BP Chemicals Ltd. v. Union Carbide Corp.*, 4 F.3d 975, 28 U.S.P.Q.2d 1124, 1126 (Fed. Cir. 1993).

ω

Permitting a declaratory judgment defendant to engage in "[g]uerilla-like...extra-judicial patent enforcement with scare-the-customer-and-run tactics that infect the competitive environment of the business community with uncertainty and insecurity," and, when those tactics are successful, to avoid proving the validity of its patents and associated claims of infringement in a court of law by claiming that its successful scare-the-customer-and-run tactic somehow mooted the parties' very real controversy would undermine the letter and spirit of the real controversy requirement, and would impermissibly encourage patent owners to engage in "extra-judicial patent enforcement" strategies. *BOC Health Care Inc. v. Nellcor Inc.*, 28 U.S.P.Q.2d 1293, 1298, 1299 (Del. 1993).

ω

An infringement action is preferred over a declaratory judgment action to resolve issues because it is an affirmative action seeking coercive relief, whereas a declaratory judgment action is equitable in nature. *Océ-Office Systems Inc. v. Eastman Kodak Co.*, 828 F.Supp. 37, 29 U.S.P.Q.2d 1157, 1159 (Ill. 1993).

ω

"The court cannot allow a party to secure a more favorable forum by filing an action for declaratory judgment when it has notice that the other party intends to file suit involving the same issues in a different forum." *Serco Services Co. L.P. v. Kelley Co. Inc.*, 31 U.S.P.Q.2d 1795, 1797 n.5 (Tex. 1994).

ϖ

Declaratory judgment actions are, for Seventh Amendment purposes, only as legal or equitable in nature as the controversies on which they are founded. *In re Lockwood*, 50 F.3d 966, 33 U.S.P.Q.2d 1406, 1411 (Fed. Cir. 1995).

ϖ

The CAFC will find subject matter jurisdiction over a declaratory judgment patent action if (1) the declaratory plaintiff has acted, or has made preparations to act, in a way that could constitute infringement, and (2) the patentee has created in the declaratory plaintiff a reasonable apprehension of suit for infringement. *Serco Services Co. L.P. v. Kelley Co. Inc.*, 51 F.3d 1037, 1038, 34 U.S.P.Q.2d 1217, 1218 (Fed. Cir. 1995).

ϖ

The purpose of the Declaratory Judgment Act is to enable those threatened to remove such a cloud on their commercial activity, instead of being obliged to await the convenience of the threatening party. Although the requirement that the declaratory plaintiff be under a reasonable apprehension of suit does not require that the patentee be known to be poised on the courthouse steps, a patentee's attempt to conduct license negotiations is a commercial activity. *Phillips Plastics Corp. v. Kato Hatsujou Kabushiki Kaisha*, 57 F.3d 1051, 35 U.S.P.Q.2d 1222, 1223, 1224 (Fed. Cir. 1995).

ϖ

A district court has discretion to decide a declaratory judgment action. This discretion, although broad, is not unfettered. Courts may not dismiss requests "for declaratory judgment relief 'on the basis of whim or personal disinclination.'" The relevant factors which the district court must consider include, but are not limited to: (1) whether there is a pending state action in which all of the matters in the controversy may be fully litigated; (2) whether the plaintiff filed suit in anticipation of a lawsuit filed by the defendant; (3) whether the plaintiff engaged in forum shopping in bringing the suit; (4) whether possible inequities in allowing the declaratory plaintiff to gain precedence in time or to change forums exists; (5) whether the federal court is a convenient forum for the parties and witnesses; and (6) whether retaining the lawsuit in federal court would serve the purposes of judicial economy. *United National Insurance Co. v. Bradleys' Electric Inc.*, 35 U.S.P.Q.2d 1559, 1561, 1562 (Tex. 1995).

ϖ

An explicit threat or express charge of infringement is sufficient to create reasonable apprehension, but is not necessary; conduct will suffice. *Wright Medical Technology Inc. v. Osteonics Corp.*, 914 F.Supp. 1524, 38 U.S.P.Q.2d 1573, 1576, 1577 (Tenn. 1995).

ϖ

A declaratory judgment action should not be used to force unwanted litigation on "quiescent patent owners." The Declaratory Judgment Act is "an enabling Act" that confers on district courts "unique and substantial discretion is deciding whether to declare the rights of litigants" "because facts bearing on the usefulness of the declaratory judgment remedy, and the fitness of the case for resolution, are peculiarly within their grasp." The Declaratory Judgment Act was not designed to serve as a tactical measure for improving plaintiff's posture in ongoing negotiations for the sale or license of defendant's patents. *EMC Corp. v. Norand Corp.*, 39 U.S.P.Q.2d 1451, 1455, 1456, 1457 (Fed. Cir. 1996).

Dedication.

The effect of disclaiming all claims of a patent is the same as dedication of the patent to the public or abandonment. The court, therefore, no longer has any jurisdiction with respect to the validity or invalidity of the patent. Public dedication terminates all of the patentee's rights to the patent, just as if the patent had expired. *Technimark Inc. v. Crellin Inc.*, 49 U.S.P.Q.2d 1134, 1135 n.3, 1137 (N.C. 1998).

Dedication to the Public. *See also* Abandonment, Disclaimer, Disclosure Without Claiming, Expiration, Late Claiming.

Subject matter disclosed, but not claimed, in a patent application is dedicated to the public. *Edward Miller & Co. v. Bridgeport Brass Co.*, 104 U.S. 350, 352 (1881).

ᗯ

Since the involved application was not filed until several months subsequent to the issuance of appellant's patent, what was disclosed in the patent drawings and not claimed in the patent must be considered dedicated to the public. *In re Phillips*, 148 F.2d 662, 65 U.S.P.Q. 213, 215 (C.C.P.A. 1945).

ᗯ

There is a presumption that subject matter disclosed (but not claimed) in an issued U.S. patent is dedicated to the public. Such dedication may be rebutted when a second application is filed (within one year after the patent issues) for an independent and distinct invention from that claimed in the earlier patent. *In re Bersworth*, 189 F.2d 996, 90 U.S.P.Q. 83 (C.C.P.A. 1951).

ᗯ

There is only an inference of abandonment of disclosed, but unclaimed, subject matter in an issued patent. The inference may be rebutted (1) by an application for reissue of the patent pursuant to statute, 35 U.S.C. §251, last paragraph, which seems to permit a broadening reissue application; (2) by claiming in a copending application before the patent issues and possibly even thereafter; and (3) by the filing of an application within the one-year grace period following the issuance of the patent and before the patent becomes a statutory bar under §102(b). *In re Gibbs and Griffin*, 437 F.2d 486, 168 U.S.P.Q. 578, 584 (C.C.P.A. 1971).

ᗯ

If everything described in the text of a patent, but not literally claimed, is always "dedicated to the public," the requirement to look to the specification for evidence of equivalency is rendered meaningless. *Brunswick Corp. v. U.S.*, 46 U.S.P.Q.2d 1446, 1454 *dissent* (Fed. Cir. 1998—*unpublished*).

Deem. *See also* Allegation, Assertion, Conjecture.

The Examiner should be aware that "deeming" does not discharge him from the burden of providing the requisite factual basis and establishing the requisite motivation to support a conclusion of obviousness. *Ex parte Stern*, 13 U.S.P.Q.2d 1379, 1381 (B.P.A.I. 1987).

Default Judgment.

Abhoring default judgments, the PTO Board of Patent Interferences accepted a de minimis showing as to why newly presented evidence should be considered. *Amoss, Monahan, and Vale v. McKinley and Sarantakis*, 195 U.S.P.Q. 452 (PTO Bd. Pat. Int. 1977).

ϖ

A defaulting party's failure to provide any explanation or any affidavits concerning the default has been held to preclude a finding of "excusable neglect" for purposes of a motion to set aside a default judgment. *Artmatic USA Cosmetics v. Maybelline Co.*, 906 F.Supp. 850, 38 U.S.P.Q.2d 1037, 1040 (N.Y. 1995).

Defect.

Patentability may exist in the discovery of the cause of a defect in an existing machine or process and applying a remedy therefor even though, after the cause is understood, the remedy would be obvious. *In re Wiseman and Kovac*, 596 F.2d 1019, 201 U.S.P.Q. 658, 661 (C.C.P.A. 1979).

ϖ

There are two distinct statutory requirements that a Reissue Oath or Declaration must satisfy. First, it must state that the patent is defective or partly inoperative or invalid because the specification or drawing contains defects or because the patentee has claimed more or less than he is entitled to. Second, the applicant must allege that the defective, inoperative, or invalid patent arose through error without deceptive intent. *In re Wilder*, 736 F.2d 1516, 222 U.S.P.Q. 369, 370 (Fed. Cir. 1984).

"Defense" Prejudice. *See* Evidentiary Prejudice.

Defense Waiver.

The advancing of defenses subsequent to trial raises questions of waiver and res judicata. A defendant's decision not to raise a defense in the trial of a particular action is a waiver of that defense, which waiver is granted res judicata effect. *The Kilbarr Corp. v. Business Systems, Inc., B.V.*, 679 F. Supp. 422, 6 U.S.P.Q.2d 1698 (N.J. 1988).

Defensive Publication.

The effective date of a Defensive Publication as a reference is the date upon which the document was published, and not the filing date of the application from which the publication stemmed. *Ex parte Smolka and Schwuger*, 202 U.S.P.Q. 232, 235 (PTO Bd. App. 1980).

Deference.

To the extent reliance is placed on evidence previously considered by the PTO, there is "the added burden of overcoming the deference that is due to a qualified government agency presumed to have properly done its job, which includes... Examiners who are assumed to have some expertise in interpreting the references and to be familiar from their work with the level of skill in the art and whose duty it is to issue only valid patents." *Sonoco Products Co. v. Mobil Oil Corp.*, 15 U.S.P.Q.2d 1186, 1191 (S.C. 1989).

ω

The rule of deference is limited to the situation where the statutory language has "left a gap" or is ambiguous. In Title 35 (U.S.C.) section 156(f)(2)'s operative terms, individually and as combined in the full definition, have a common and unambiguous meaning, which leaves no gap to be filled in by the administrative agency. Thus, there need be no deference to any reasonable interpretation of the Commissioner. The doctrine that deference is due a contemporaneous construction of the agency charged by Congress with implementing a new statute has been applied when the statutory language is "doubtful and ambiguous" and when the agency's construction is issued soon after the statute's enactment and the circumstances surrounding its enactment are well known. The Commissioner's assertion that his interpretation must be accorded deference because this case involves "highly technical, scientific questions within the agency's special expertise" relates to a rule of jurisprudence that is inapposite to this case. Significant deference is due to an agency's technical expertise when Congress has explicitly or implicitly delegated to the agency the making of scientific determinations, but when "the interpretation rests not on policy considerations but on a narrow dissection of statutory language, the courts are equally skilled in making such an interpretation, and reduced deference is owed." *Glaxo Operations UK Ltd. v. Quigg*, 894 F.2d 392, 13 U.S.P.Q.2d 1628, 1633 (Fed. Cir. 1990).

ω

When prior art that was considered by the PTO is relied upon by an infringer, he has the added burden of overcoming the deference that is due a qualified government agency presumed to have done its job properly. *Stranco Inc. v. Atlantes Chemical Systems Inc.*, 15 U.S.P.Q.2d 1704, 1713 (Tex. 1990).

ω

Where the PTO has considered a piece of prior art, and issued a patent notwithstanding that prior art, a court owes some deference to the PTO's decision. *Minnesota Mining and Manufacturing Co. v. Johnson & Johnson Orthopaedics Inc.*, 976 F.2d 1558, 24 U.S.P.Q.2d 1321, 1332 (Fed. Cir. 1992).

ω

Deference should be given by one court to prior decisions of other tribunals on the same legal issue. Deferential weight on legal conclusions, not evidentiary weight on facts in dispute, must be given to the prior decision. It may be appropriate to admit evidence of prior litigation, but such evidence must pass muster, like any other evidence, as relevant and probative of an issue in the second case. There is no exemption from these requirements for evidence of prior litigation. Further, if relevant, the proffered evidence may, nevertheless, be excluded under Rule (FRCP) 403 if its probative value is substantially outweighed by its prejudice to one's adversary or because of the likelihood of confusion of the jury. *Mendenhall v. Cedarapids Inc.*, 5 F.3d 1557, 28 U.S.P.Q.2d 1081, 1082, 1084, 1085 (Fed. Cir. 1993).

ω

The deference given to a previous Examiner's work is far outweighed by the duty of a subsequent Examiner to issue valid patents. *In re Epstein*, 32 F.3d 1559, 31 U.S.P.Q.2d 1817, 1819 n.2 (Fed. Cir. 1994).

ω

When prior art or other evidence (which was not considered by the PTO) is presented at trial, a court need not accord deference to the PTO's determination of validity when undertaking its own independent review. *The Liposome Co. v. Vestar Inc.*, 36 U.S.P.Q.2d 1295, 1307 (Del. 1994).

ω

Some courts have held that no deference is to be given a plaintiff's choice of forum in cases involving a foreign plaintiff and an American defendant. *Nolan Helmets S.p.A. v. Fulmer Helmets Inc.*, 37 U.S.P.Q.2d 1351, 1352 (Fla. 1995).

Defining Claimed Subject Matter. *See also* **Definiteness, Definition.**

Breadth alone does not constitute indefiniteness when applied to phrases or terms, such as "organic basic nitrogen compound having at least a hydrogen atom attached to the basic nitrogen atom," "aryl," "aralkyl," "alkaryl" and "heterocyclic." Only appellants may determine what constitutes their invention. *Ex parte Scherberich and Pfeifer*, 201 U.S.P.Q. 397, 398, 399 (PTO Bd. App. 1977).

ω

Claims are to be construed in the light of the specification and both are to be read with a view of ascertaining the invention. A patentee can choose his own terms and use them as he wishes so long as he remains consistent in their use and makes their meaning reasonably clear. *Rosemount Inc. v. Beckman Instruments*, Inc., 569 F.Supp. 934, 218 U.S.P.Q. 881, 897, 200 (Cal. 1983).

ω

The court clearly looked to what was defined by the claim and interpreted it in the light of the disclosure upon which the claim was based. The court did not expand the meaning of "comprises" to include further limitations required by the reference. *Ashland Oil, Inc. v. Delta Resins & Refractories, Inc., et al.*, 776 F.2d 281, 227 U.S.P.Q. 657 (Fed. Cir. 1985).

Definiteness. *See also* **Alkyl, Approximately, Aromatic, Aryl, at Least, Bounds, Breadth, Combination, Definition, Indefiniteness, Negative Limitation, Open-Ended Claim, Particularity, Substantially, Substituted, 35 U.S.C. §112.**

The specification is not addressed to lawyers or even to the public generally, but to those of ordinary skill in the art. Any description that is sufficient to apprise them (in the language of the art) of the definite features of the invention, and to serve as a warning to others of that which is claimed, is sufficiently definite. *The Carnegie Steel Company, Ltd. v. The Cambria Iron Company,* 185 U.S. 403 (1866).

ᖙ

Section 112 of 35 U.S.C. does not require that the claims define "the invention," whatever that would mean. The second paragraph of §112 requires that the claims define "the subject matter which the applicant regards as his invention." The meaning of this provision is simply that an applicant is required to set definite boundaries on the patent protection sought. *In re Wakefield and Foster,* 422 F.2d 897, 164 U.S.P.Q. 636 (C.C.P.A. 1970).

ᖙ

Claims that are not limited to disclosed or suggested compositions and would cover "a host of materials produced in any possible manner, including synthetically, which are neither taught nor represented by the specific materials actually formed" in the examples are quite broad. This fact, however, while very important in assessing the sufficiency of the disclosure to see whether it will support such broad coverage, is entirely irrelevant to the issue of definiteness. *In re Fisher,* 427 F.2d 833, 166 U.S.P.Q. 18 (C.C.P.A. 1970).

ᖙ

In determining whether claims do, in fact, set out and circumscribe a particular area with a reasonable degree of precision and particularity, the definiteness of the language employed must be analyzed—not in a vacuum, but always in light of the teachings of the prior art and of the particular application disclosure as it would be interpreted by one possessing the ordinary level of skill in the pertinent art. *In re Moore and Janoski,* 439 F.2d 1232, 169 U.S.P.Q. 236 (C.C.P.A. 1971).

ᖙ

The first sentence of the second paragraph of 35 U.S.C. §112 requires only that claims "set out and circumscribe a particular area with a reasonable degree of precision and particularity." What the claims define is what the applicant regards as his invention. If those skilled in the art can tell whether any particular embodiment is or in not within the scope of a claim, the claim fulfills its purpose as a definition. *In re Miller,* 441 F.2d 689, 169 U.S.P.Q. 597, 599 (C.C.P.A. 1971).

ᖙ

The first sentence of the second paragraph of 35 U.S.C. §112 is essentially a requirement for precision and definiteness of claim language. If the scope of subject matter embraced by a claim is clear, and if the applicant has not otherwise indicated that he intends the claim to be of a different scope, then the claim does particularly point out and distinctly claim the subject matter that the applicant regards as his invention. The requirement is that the language of the claims must make it clear what subject matter they encompass and thus make clear the subject matter from which they would preclude others. *In re Conley, Catherwod, and Lloyd*, 490 F.2d 972, 180 U.S.P.Q. 454, 456 (C.C.P.A. 1974).

ω

While symbols are commonly employed in chemical cases to refer to designated classes of substances and are conventionally defined in the claim itself in order to make clear what are the metes and bounds of the invention, the absence of their definition in the claims may be objectionable rather than subject to rejection under the second paragraph of 35 U.S.C. §112. The reference in the claims to the specification, which is definite in defining and limiting the terms, complies with the requirements of 35 U.S.C. §112. *Ex parte Moon*, 224 U.S.P.Q. 519 (PTO Bd. App. 1984).

ω

The basis of the district court's holding that the claims are indefinite is that "they do not disclose how infringement may be avoided because antibody affinity cannot be estimated with any consistency." Even if the district court's finding and support of this holding—that "there is no standard set of experimental conditions which are used to estimate affinities"—is accurate, under the law pertaining to indefiniteness—"if the claims, read in the light of specification, reasonably apprise those skilled in the art both of the utilization and scope of the invention, and if the language is as precise as the subject matter permits, the courts can demand no more"—the claims clearly are definite. The evidence of record indisputably shows that calculating affinity was known in the art at the time of filing, and notwithstanding the fact that those calculations are not precise, or "standard," the claims, read in the light of the specification, reasonably apprise those skilled in the art and are as precise as the subject matter permits. *Hybritech Inc. v. Monoclonal Antibodies, Inc.*, 802 F.2d 1367, 231 U.S.P.Q. 81 (Fed. Cir. 1986).

ω

The district court employed two measures impermissible in law: (1) it required that Claim I describe the invention, which is the role of the disclosure portion of the specification, not the role of the claims; and (2) it applied the "full, clear, concise, and exact" requirement of the first paragraph of 35 U.S.C. §112 to the claim, when that paragraph only applies to the disclosure portion of the specification, not to the claims. The district court spoke inappropriately of the indefiniteness of the "patent," and it did not review the claim for indefiniteness under the second paragraph of §112. A decision on whether a claim is invalid under §112 requires a determination of whether those skilled in the art would understand what is claimed when the claim is read in the light of the specification. *Orthokinetics Inc. v. Safety Travel Chairs Inc.*, 806 F.2d 1565, 1 U.S.P.Q.2d 1081 (Fed. Cir. 1986).

ω

It is entirely consistent with the claim definiteness requirement of the second paragraph of 35 U.S.C. §112 to present subcombination claims, drawn only to one aspect or combination of elements of an invention that has utility separate and apart from other aspects of the invention. It is not necessary that a claim recite each and every element needed for the practical utilization of the claimed subject matter. *Carl Zeiss Stiftung v. Renishaw plc,* 945 F.2d 1173, 20 U.S.P.Q.2d 1094, 1101 (Fed. Cir. 1991).

ω

Determining whether a patent claim is indefinite requires analysis of whether one skilled in the art would understand the bounds of the claim when read in light of the specification, and if claims read in light of the specification reasonably apprise those skilled in the art of the scope of invention, no more is required. *Altech Controls Corp. v. E.I.L. Instruments Inc.,* 44 U.S.P.Q.2d 1890, 1896 n.12 (Tex. 1997).

Definition. *See also* Approximately, Defining Claimed Subject Matter, Essence, Indefiniteness, Substituted.

An invention must be capable of accurate definition, and it must be accurately defined, to be patentable. *United Carbon Co. v. Binney & Smith Co.,* 317 U.S. 228, 55 U.S.P.Q. 381, 386 (1942).

ω

Section 112 of 35 U.S.C. does not require that the claims define "the invention," whatever that would mean. The second paragraph of that section requires that the claims define "the subject matter which the applicant regards as his invention." The meaning of this provision is simply that an applicant is required to set definite boundaries on the patent protection sought. What the applicant does not regard as an element of his invention need not be specified in claims. *In re Wakefield and Foster,* 422 F.2d 897, 164 U.S.P.Q. 636 (C.C.P.A. 1970).

ω

Claims need not recite limitations that deal with factors that must be presumed to be within the level of ordinary skill in the art, where one of ordinary skill in the art, to whom the specification and claims are directed, would consider such factors obvious. *In re Skrivan,* 427 F.2d 801, 166 U.S.P.Q. 85 (C.C.P.A. 1970).

ω

The first sentence of the second paragraph of 35 U.S.C. §112 requires only that claims "set out and circumscribe a particular area with a reasonable degree of precision and particularity." In the absence of evidence to the contrary, what the claims define is what the applicant regards as his invention. If those skilled in the art can tell whether any particular embodiment is within the scope of a claim, the claim fulfills its purpose as a definition. *In re Miller,* 441 F.2d 689, 169 U.S.P.Q. 597 (C.C.P.A. 1971).

ω

An applicant may invoke the third paragraph of 35 U.S.C. §112 to justify the specification of one or more elements of a claimed compound in "functional" terms, and those "functional" terms may be "negative." The real issue in any such case is not whether the recital is functional or negative, but whether the recital sets definite boundaries on the patent protection sought; that is, whether those skilled in the relevant art can determine what the claim does or does not read on. *In re Barr, Williams, and Whitmore,* 444 F.2d 588, 170 U.S.P.Q. 330, 337 (C.C.P.A. 1971).

ω

In determining the meaning of an expression as used in the context of an application, one must look (not to the dictionary) to the art or technology to which the claimed subject matter pertains. In doing so, due consideration must be given to the interpretation that one of ordinary skill in the art would give the terminology in question. *In re Salem, Butterworth, and Ryan*, 553 F.2d 676, 193 U.S.P.Q. 513, 518 (C.C.P.A. 1977).

ω

If patent claims, read in the light of the specification, reasonably apprise one skilled in the art of the utilization and scope of the invention and if the language is as precise as the subject matter permits, the patent should not be deemed invalid for indefiniteness. A patentee is required to draft the patent specification and claims as precisely as the subject matter permits, and failure to do so may result in invalidation. Absolute specificity and precision, however, are not required. The claims need only go so far as to apprise one reasonably skilled in the area of the true teaching of the invention. Mere breadth of a claim does not in itself cause invalidation. As long as the meaning of the claims is clear in light of the specification and accompanying drawings, breadth merely enhances the risk that the claim will be found invalid. *Andco Environmental Processes, Inc. v. Niagara Environmental Associates, Inc.*, 220 U.S.P.Q. 468 (N.Y. 1983).

ω

A patentee may choose to use terms in a manner other than their ordinary meaning, so long as the special definition of the term is clearly stated in the patent specification or file history. The prosecution history limits the claim's terms to exclude any interpretation disclaimed during the patent's prosecution. *Howes v. Zircon Corp.*, 992 F. Supp. 957, 47 U.S.P.Q.2d 1617, 1619 (Ill. 1998).

ω

"Indiscriminate reliance on definitions found in dictionaries can often produce absurd results.... One need not arbitrarily pick and choose from the various accepted definitions of a word to decide which meaning was intended as the word is used in a given claim. The subject matter, the context, etc., will more often than not lead to the correct conclusion." *Renishaw plc v. Marposs Societa' per Azioni*, 48 U.S.P.Q.2d 1117, 1122 (Fcd. Cir. 1998).

Degree. *See also* **Critical, Difference, Kind, Relative Term.**

The mere carrying forward of an original patented conception involving only change of form, proportions, or degree or the substitution of equivalents doing the same thing as the original invention, by substantially the same means, is not such an invention as will sustain a patent even though the changes are of a kind that produce better results than prior inventions. *In re Paul F. Williams*, 36 F.2d 436, 4 U.S.P.Q. 237, 239 (C.C.P.A. 1930).

ω

Where there is a difference in the structural formulae of the prior art dyes over the dyes defined by the appealed claims and, as a result, the properties imparted to the various dyes are such that those produced according to the present invention possess properties that are important when the dyes are used for their intended purpose, as distinguished from deficiencies noted in the prior art dyes, the claims may well be considered patentable over the references on which they were rejected. The presence of the additional chlorine atom in the claimed dyes is thus of significance, and the results produced amount to more than a mere difference in degree. *Ex parte Carson*, 78 U.S.P.Q. 93, 94 (PO Bd. App. 1948).

ω

When a word of degree is used, the district court must determine whether the patent's specification provides some standard for measuring that degree, that is, whether one of ordinary skill in the art would understand what is claimed when the claim is read in the light of the specification. *Seattle Box Company, Inc. v. Industrial Crating & Packing, Inc.*, 731 F.2d 818, 221 U.S.P.Q. 568, 574 (Fed. Cir. 1984).

ω

A rejection under 35 U.S.C. §103 as obvious over applied art alleged to disclose products that are not seen to differ in kind from those claimed is not sustainable on its face. The statutory inquiry is obviousness and not "differ in kind." The latter is not a proper basis for rejection. *Ex parte Goeddel*, 5 U.S.P.Q.2d 1449 (B.P.A.I. 1985).

ω

When words of degree are used in a claim, the specification must provide some standard for measuring the degree. *Ex parte Donaldson*, 26 U.S.P.Q.2d 1250, 1259 (B.P.A.I. 1992).

ω

"When a word of degree is used, the district court must determine whether the specification provides some standard for measuring that degree." *Allergan Sales Inc. v. Pharmacia & Upjohn Inc.*, 42 U.S.P.Q.2d 1560, 1563 (Cal. 1997).

Delay. *See also* **Continuous Activity, Date, Diligence, Docketing Errors, Estoppel, Funding, General-Verdict-Multiple-Defenses, Inactivity, Inexcusable Delay, Laches, PCT, Rule 82 bis (PCT), Time, Unavoidable Delay, Unreasonable Delay.**

During the critical period in an interference setting, there must be "reasonably continuous activity." *Burns v. Curtis*, 172 F.2d 588, 80 U.S.P.Q. 586 (C.C.P.A. 1949).

ω

Although a long delay in filing (five years in this case) has been held to warrant a presumption that experiments alleged to be a reduction to practice were actually unsuccessful, where there is clearly a reduction to practice, a holding to the contrary will not be rendered because of the delay. *Knowles v. Tibbetts*, 347 F.2d 591, 146 U.S.P.Q. 59, 63 (C.C.P.A. 1965).

ω

The public policy favors early disclosure, and thus the law is reluctant to displace an inventor who was the first to disclose his invention to the public. *Honeywell, Inc. v. Diamond*, 499 F.Supp. 924, 208 U.S.P.Q. 452 (D.C. 1980).

ω

A delay in filing a patent application of more than 17 months after reducing the invention to practice was not regarded as unreasonable (raising an inference of intent to suppress) in view of continued activities to within 6 months of the filing date. *D'Silva v. Drabek,* 214 U.S.P.Q. 556 (PTO Bd. Pat. Int. 1981).

ထ

A delay of 17.5 months between the actual reduction to practice and the filing of a patent application is not so inordinately long as to create an inference of suppression or concealment, particularly when taking the complexity of the involved subject matter into consideration. *Bigham v. Godtfredsen and Von Daehne,* 222 U.S.P.Q. 632, 638 (PTO Bd. Pat. Int. 1984).

ထ

Even if the invention was actually reduced to practice by the junior party in 1977 or 1978, the unexplained hiatus of more than two years between that date and the junior party's filing date was an unreasonably long delay, raising an inference that the junior party suppressed the invention within the meaning of 35 U.S.C. §102(g). Since there is no evidence in the record as to any activity by the junior party during this two-year period, the inference has not been rebutted, and, as a result, the junior party cannot rely on either of the alleged actual reductions to practice. *Latimer v. Wetmore,* 231 U.S.P.Q. 131 (B.P.A.I. 1985).

ထ

A university policy not to fund research projects, but rather to require their research ers to obtain outside support, represents a conscious decision resulting in delay, which is inconsistent with the policy that early public disclosure is the linchpin of the patent system. *Griffith v. Kanamaru,* 231 U.S.P.Q. 892, 893 (B.P.A.I. 1986).

ထ

The board correctly found a delay of approximately 51 months was unreasonably long and sufficient to give rise to an inference of an intent to abandon, suppress, or conceal the invention. An inference of suppression or concealment may be overcome with evidence that the reason for the delay was to perfect the invention. When, however, the delay is caused by working on refinements and improvements that are not elected in the final patent application, the delay will not be excused. Further, when the activities that caused the delay go to commercialization of the invention, the delay will not be excused. *Lutzker v. Plet,* 843 F.2d 1364, 6 U.S.P.Q.2d 1370 (Fed. Cir. 1988).

ထ

Although the plaintiff knew of the defendant's infringing activities as far back as 1983, such activities were not commercially significant until 1988. The plaintiff faced problems in raising sufficient capital and designing an acceptable product of its own, and, thus, from 1983 to 1988 it was unclear to the plaintiff whether it would be economically prudent to take defendant to court. The patent lawyers do not work for free. Patent owners are not expected to incur such large costs to silence commercially insignificant infringers. As the defendant probably did not achieve significant commercial success until mid-1988, the plaintiff's delay in filing suit to mid-1989 probably was not unreasonable. *Illinois Tool Works Inc. v. Grip-Pack Inc.,* 713 F. Supp. 1122, 13 U.S.P.Q.2d 1463, 1465 (Ill. 1989).

ထ

Although no reasonable explanation was given at trial to explain why it took over two and one-half months to spray the test specimens, such a period is not prima facie unreasonable or significant evidence that the inventor did not act diligently in reducing his invention to practice. To impose such temporal restrictions on inventors in their studied approach to experimentation would be not only burdensome but foolhardy and could frustrate and, in many situations, defeat the goals of fostering the inventive spirit. *American Standard Inc. v. Pfizer Inc.*, 722 F. Supp. 86, 14 U.S.P.Q.2d 1673, 1693 (Del. 1989).

ᵚ

Estoppel and the related defense of laches are often asserted together, but there are numerous differences between the law of estoppel and the law of laches. For example, a presumption that, after a six year time period, the burden shifts to plaintiff to show the reasonableness of the delay applies to laches but not to estoppel. Like infringement, laches does not begin until the patent issues. With estoppel, delay is measured from the time of the misrepresentation or the beginning of the misleading silence. In the absence of an express agreement not to sue, the courts have overwhelmingly denied estoppel defenses where the delay was less than six years. *Symbol Technologies Inc. v. Metrologic Instruments Inc.*, 771 F.Supp. 1390, 21 U.S.P.Q.2d 1481, 1484, 1485 (N.J. 1991).

ᵚ

The burden of persuasion does not shift by reason of a patentee's six-year delay. *A.C. Aukerman Co. v. R.L. Chaides Construction Co.*, 960 F.2d 1020, 22 U.S.P.Q.2d 1321, 1333 (Fed. Cir. 1992).

ᵚ

Delay, standing alone, is usually an insufficient basis on which to deny leave to amend. *Ricoh Co. Ltd. v. Nashua Corp.*, 40 U.S.P.Q.2d 1306, 1309 (N.H. 1996).

ᵚ

The *Aukerman* presumption places a burden of production on the patentee. This burden of production relates to both the excusability of the delay and the lack of prejudice resulting from the delay. Where the patentee fails to meet this burden of production by coming forward with *either* affirmative evidence of a lack of prejudice *or* a legally cognizable excuse for its delay in filing suit, the two facts of unreasonable delay and prejudice "*must* be inferred." *Hall v. Aqua Queen Manufacturing Inc.*, 39 U.S.P.Q.2d 1925 (Fed. Cir. 1996).

Deletion. *See* **Cancellation, Omission of Element or Step, Reduction is Scope, Reduction in Steps.**

Deliberate Infringement.

Deliberate infringement coupled with failure to secure the opinion of patent counsel prior to the commencement of litigation constitutes willful infringement warranting the imposition of treble damages as provided by law. *Darda Inc. USA v. Majorette Toys (U.S.) Inc.*, 627 F.Supp. 1121, 229 U.S.P.Q. 103, 117 (Fla. 1986).

Délivré.

In the context of 35 U.S.C. §102(d) under the French procedure délivré is the operative patent date. *The Duplan Corporation v. Deering Milliken Research Corporation*, 487 F.2d 459, 179 U.S.P.Q. 449, 450 (4th Cir. 1973).

ω

The "délivré" date of a French patent is the date upon which the patent was granted, and is the effective date under 35 U.S.C. §102(d). *Ex parte Appeal No. 242-47*, 196 U.S.P.Q. 828, 829 (PTO Bd. App. 1976).

Delta Period.

Under URAA's safe harbor provision, a patent owner may not assert the traditional remedies of 35 U.S.C. §§283, 284, and 285 (1988) for qualifying acts of infringement committed during the period of a patent's extension (the "Delta" period). *Bristol-Myers Squibb Co. v. Royce Laboratories Inc.*, 69 F.3d 1130, 36 U.S.P.Q.2d 1641, 1644 (Fed. Cir. 1995).

De Novo. See also **Trial** *de Novo*, **35 U.S.C. §145, 35 U.S.C. §146.**

Because plaintiffs failed to present and support contentions of commercial success or copying during PTO proceedings and have not set forth any reasons for this omission, they are precluded from presenting such evidence over defendant's objection in an action under 35 U.S.C. §145. *MacKay v. Quigg*, 641 F. Supp. 567, 231 U.S.P.Q. 907, 909 (D.C. 1986).

ω

In reviewing a district court's grant of summary judgment, the CAFC reviews *de novo* the district court's conclusion that there was no genuine issue of material fact and that the moving party was entitled to judgment as a matter of law. *Avia Group Intl., Inc. v. L.A. Gear California, Inc.*, 853 F.2d 1557, 7 U.S.P.Q.2d 1548, 1550 (Fed. Cir. 1988).

ω

Although a 35 U.S.C. §145 action has been characterized as a trial *de novo*, the policy of encouraging full disclosure to administrative tribunals has led courts to limit the admissability of certain kinds of evidence in such actions. Thus, evidence has been excluded if it was available to the plaintiff during the PTO proceeding but was either intentionally or negligently withheld. Furthermore, new evidence may be excluded from trial if it relates to an issue that the plaintiff failed to raise before the PTO, unless the plaintiff can demonstrate that the failure to raise the issue was neither intentional nor negligent. *Holloway v. Quigg*, 9 U.S.P.Q.2d 1751 (D.C. 1988).

ω

In an action under 35 U.S.C. §145, plaintiffs are entitled to a trial *de novo* and may introduce evidence not previously presented to the PTO, though they are precluded from raising new issues, at least absent some reason justifying their failure to present the issue to the agency in the first instance. Although conducted as a trial, a civil action under 145 is in reality a suit to set aside a decision by the Board; however, because obviousness is a legal conclusion, based on underlying facts, the district court need not defer to the PTO's findings on the issue, but is instead free to make an independent determination as to the legal conclusions and inferences to be drawn from the facts. The district court may set aside a finding of fact by the Board if clearly erroneous. *Radix Corp. v. Samuels*, 13 U.S.P.Q.2d 1689, 1691 (D.C. 1989).

ω

The CAFC reviews obviousness determinations of the BPAI *de novo*. *In re Bell*, 991 F.2d 781, 26 U.S.P.Q.2d 1529, 1531 (Fed. Cir. 1993).

ω

The Federal Circuit reviews questions of fact under a clearly erroneous standard; questions of law are subject to full and independent review (sometimes referred to as *"de novo"* or "plenary" review). *In re Asahi/America Inc.*, 68 F.3d 442, 33 U.S.P.Q.2d 1921, 1922 (Fed. Cir. 1995); see 68 F.3d 442, 37 U.S.P.Q.2d 1204 (Fed. Cir. 1995).

Dependent Claim.[1] *See also* Utilize.

A dependent claim should be considered allowable when its parent claim is allowed. *In re McCarn*, 212 F.2d 797, 101 U.S.P.Q. 411, 413 (C.C.P.A. 1954).

ω

A method-of-use claim can be dependent from a product claim. Dependent claims to the use of a new composition in the same application with claims to the composition do not materially increase the scope of protection of an applicant's inchoate patent property under 35 U.S.C. §154, which already includes the right to exclude others from making, using, or selling the composition by allowance of claims thereon, but they do tend to increase the wealth of technical knowledge disclosed in the patent by encouraging description of the use aspects of the applicant's invention in the manner required by 35 U.S.C. §112, paragraph 1. *In re Kuehl*, 475 F.2d 658, 177 U.S.P.Q. 250, 256 (C.C.P.A. 1973).

ω

---

[1] An essential characteristic of a proper dependent claim is that it shall include every limitation of the claim from which it depends (35 U.S.C. §112) or, in other words, that it shall not conceivably be infringed by anything that would not also infringe the basic claim. Thus, for example, if Claim 1 recites the combination of elements a, b, c and d, a claim reciting a structure of Claim 1 in which d was omitted or replaced by e would not be a proper dependent claim, even though it placed further limitations on the remaining elements or added still other elements. The fact that a dependent claim, which is otherwise proper, might require a separate search or be separately classified from the claim on which it depends would not render it an improper dependent claim, although it might result in a requirement for restriction. The fact that a dependent claim and the independent claim from which it depends are in different statutory classes does not, in itself, render the dependent claim improper. Thus, if Claim 1 recites a specific product, a claim for the method of making the product of Claim 1 in a particular manner would be a proper dependent claim since it could not be infringed without infringing Claim 1. Similarly, if Claim 1 recites a method of making a product, a claim for a product made by the method of Claim 1 could be a proper dependent claim. On the other hand, if Claim 1 recites a method of making a specified product, a claim to a product set forth in Claim 1 would not be a proper dependent claim if the product might be made in other ways. [*Commissioner's Notice*, 942 O.G. 15, June 8, 1966 - MPEP 608.01(n).]

One may infringe an independent claim and not infringe a claim dependent on that claim. The reverse is not true. One who does not infringe an independent claim cannot infringe a claim dependent on (and thus containing all the limitations of) that claim. *Wahpeton Canvas Co. v. Frontier Inc.*, 870 F.2d 1546, 10 U.S.P.Q.2d 1201 (Fed. Cir. 1989).

ᛯ

There are exceptions to the axiom that dependent claims cannot be found infringed unless the claims from which they depend have been found to have been infringed. *Wilson Sporting Coods Co. v. David Geoffrey & Associates*, 904 F.2d 676, 14 U.S.P.Q.2d 1942, 1949 (Fed. Cir. 1990).

Deposit.[2] *See also* **Biotechnology, Culture, Hybridoma.**

A pending utility application can be amended by filing a continuing plant application when the parent application contains a written description of the subject matter claimed in the continuing application. The deposit of a culture of the claimed microfungi in a public depository complies with the accepted procedure for meeting the requirements of 35 U.S.C. §112 and 162. *Ex parte Solomons and Scammell*, 201 U.S.P.Q. 42, 43 (PTO Bd . App. 1978).

ᛯ

A description of several newly discovered strains of bacteria (having one particularly desirable metabolic property in terms of the conventionally measured culture characteristics and a number of metabolic and physiological properties) does not enable one of ordinary skill in the relevant art independently to discover additional strains having the same specific, desirable metabolic property (i.e., the production of a particular antibiotic). A verbal description of a new species does not enable one of ordinary skill in the relevant art to obtain strains of that species over and above the specific strains made available through deposit in one of the recognized culture depositories. *Ex parte Jackson, Theriault, Sinclair, Fager, and Karwowski*, 217 U.S.P.Q. 804, 806 (PTO Bd. App 1982).

ᛯ

The appealed claims are directed to a new human cell line and the hybridomas resulting from its fusion with lymphoid cells. The new cell line was developed by mutagenesis and selection from a known cell line by procedures that fill 12 pages of specification. Because of the uncertainties of reproducibility that inhere in such processes, at least in the present state of biotechnology, this invention is of the class covered by the deposit requirement. The inventor filed an application for a patent prior to depositing his new cell line with the American Type Culture Collection (ATCC). 35 U.S.C. §112, first paragraph, does not require the transfer of a sample of the invention to an independent depository prior to the filing date of the patent application. The requirements of PTO access to a sample of the cell line during pendency, and public access after grant, were satisfied by the procedures that were followed. The deposit with the ATCC, which was made after

---

[2]*See generally* Hampar, Patenting of Recombinant DNA Technology: The Deposit Requirement, 67 J. Pat. & Trademark Off. Socy. 569, 607 (1985) ("The deposit requirement is a nonstatutory mechanism for ensuring compliance with the 'enabling provision' under 35 U.S.C. §112.").

filing, but prior to issuance of his patent, and which is referred to in his specification, meets the statutory requirements. *In re Lundak,* 773 F.2d 1216, 227 U.S.P.Q. 90 (Fed. Cir. 1985).

ᴡ

Biological materials need not be deposited when the invention can be practiced without undue experimentation from biological materials available in prior art. *Hybritech Inc. v. Abbott Laboratories,* 4 U.S.P.Q.2d 1001 (Cal. 1987).

ᴡ

In *In re Argoudelis* [434 F.2d 1390, 168 U.S.P.Q. 99 (C.C.P.A. 1970)], it was held that the deposit of a microorganism is necessary to satisfy the enablement requirement of the first paragraph of 35 U.S.C. §112 because of the difficulty involved in satisfying the statutory requirement verbally. [See *Ex parte Jackson,* 217 U.S.P.Q. 804 (PTO Bd. App. 1982).] We do not view *Argoudelis* to establish deposition of a microorganism as the only way to satisfy the enablement requirement of the first paragraph of §112. However, *Argoudelis* does support the proposition that deposition of a new microorganism is required if it is not commonly occurring and not shown to be obtainable from a commonly occurring microorganism by a verbally enabling disclosure. [*See Ex parte Forman,* 230 U.S.P.Q. 546 (B.P.A.I. 1986).] *Ex parte Hata,* 6 U.S.P.Q.2d 1652 (B.P.A.I. 1987).

ᴡ

Even when starting materials are available, a deposit has been necessary where it would require undue experimentation to make the cells of the invention from the starting materials. Although inventions involving microorganisms or other living cells often can be enabled by a deposit, a deposit is not always necessary to satisfy the enablement requirement. No deposit is necessary if the biological organisms can be obtained from readily available sources or derived from readily available starting materials through routine screening that does not require undue experimentation. Whether the specification in an application involving living cells is enabled without a deposit must be decided on the facts of the particular case. *In re Wands,* 858 F.2d 731, 8 U.S.P.Q.2d 1400 (Fed. Cir. 1988).

ᴡ

When a biological sample required for the practice of an invention is an organism obtained from nature, the invention may be incapable of being practiced without access to that organism. A deposit is required in such a case. On the other hand, when the organism is created by insertion of genetic material into a cell obtained from generally available sources, all that is required is description of the best mode and an adequate description of the means for carrying out the invention, not deposit of the cells. If the cells can be prepared without undue experimentation from known materials, based on the description in a patent specification, a deposit is not required. The PTO has prescribed guidelines concerning the deposit of biological materials. See 37 C.F.R. §1.802(b) (1990); biological material need not be deposited "if it is known and readily available to the public or can be made or isolated without undue experimentation." The best mode requirement is a safeguard against the possible selfish desire on the part of some people to obtain patent protection without making a full disclosure. The requirement does not permit an inventor to disclose only what is known to be the second-best embodiment, retaining the best. The fundamental issue that should be addressed is whether there was evidence to show that the quality of an applicant's best-mode disclosure is so poor as to effectively result in concealment. If deposit is the only way to comply with the best-mode requirement, the deposit must be made. 52 Fed. Reg. 34,080, 34,086 (Sept. 8, 1987). *Amgen Inc. v. Chugai Pharmaceutical Co. Ltd.*, 927 F.2d 1200, 18 U.S.P.Q.2d 1016, 1025 (Fed. Cir. 1991).

ω

As the application disclosure failed to provide any information (among the minimum needed by workers in the art to obtain needed enzymes) as to the microbial source of required enzymes, the subsequent (after filing) deposit of microorganisms stated to produce such enzymes did not rectify the omission. Moreover, appellants did not establish that one skilled in the art would be able to isolate the needed enzymes from the deposited materials. *Ex parte DeCastro*, 28 U.S.P.Q.2d 1391, 1394 (B.P.A.I. 1993).

Deposit Account.

Under extenuating circumstances originally unauthorized Deposit Account funds were applied to cover an unsigned check submitted for an application filing fee. *In re Application Papers Filed March 27, 1974*, 186 U.S.P.Q. 363, 364 (Comm'r Patents and Trademarks 1975).

Deposition. *See* Conclusions.

Deposit of Cell Line.

The claimed invention had been reduced to practice prior to the filing date of the subject application, and the appellants had agreed to deposit the hybridoma cell lines at a recognized depository upon the patent grant. In the interim, the cell lines were being maintained at Sloan-Kettering, an institution of renown and integrity. This was regarded as in full compliance with the requirements imposed upon the appellants under *Lundak*, 773 F.2d 1216, [227 U.S.P.Q. 90 (Fed. Cir. 1985)].

Although the technique underlying hybridoma technology is well recognized, the results obtained by its use are clearly unpredictable. Hybridoma technology is an empirical art in which the routineer is unable to foresee what particular antibodies will be produced and which specific surface antigens will be recognized by them. Only by actually carrying out the requisite steps can the nature of the monoclonal antibodies be determined and ascertained; no "expected" results can thus be said to be present. Hence, it may be "obvious to try" the Kohler-Milstein technique as applied to malignant renal cells, but such is not the standard under which obviousness under 35 U.S.C. §103 must be established. *Ex parte Old*, 229 U.S.P.Q. 196 (B.P.A.I. 1985).

Depository.

Assuming that seeds may be deposited in the same manner as microorganisms to comply with 35 U.S.C. §112, there is insufficient evidence in the record as to the availability of the deposited seeds. The depository is not a recognized public depository, and there is no evidence indicating that the depository is under a contractual obligation to maintain the seeds deposited in a permanent collection and to supply samples to anyone seeking them once the patent issues. *Ex parte Hibberd*, 227 U.S.P.Q. 443, 447 (B.P.A.I. 1985).

℧

The fact that a particular culture depository provided for streaking {the preparation of a "streak culture", a culture which is inoculated with an "inoculum implanted (as with a needle drawn across the surface) in a line or stripe upon a solidified culture medium" [Webster's Third New International Dictionary (1971)]; this method gives rise to separate colonies on the culture medium, and may be used to detect contamination if "the contaminating organism has a sufficiently different appearance when growing on [the] medium"} in conjunction with reviving its freeze-dried cultures (but not in conjunction with their subsequent maintenance and transfer) does not indicate that streaking is the only acceptable method to detect contamination in such a culture as it is received from a depository. Depositories are regarded as reliable. *Tabuchi and Abe v. Nubel, Fitts, and Lorenzo*, 559 F.2d 1183, 194 U.S.P.Q. 521, 527 (C.C.P.A. 1977).

Depreciation.

A patent application is an assignable property right, but not a depreciable asset. When a patent is issued, depreciation may be taken over its life. The application, which was sold, constituted a capital asset. *United States Mineral Products Co. v. Commissioner of Internal Revenue*, 52 T.C. 177, 162 U.S.P.Q. 480, 493 (1969).

℧

The patent application was not depreciable property. The proceeds of the sale were entitled to capital gains treatment. *Davis v. Commissioner of Internal Revenue*, 491 F.2d 709, 181 U.S.P.Q. 552 (6th Cir. 1974).

℧

Where payment is made for purchase of a patent on a yearly-percentage-of-production basis, a depreciation deduction of the total annual payment is allowable so that the purchaser will be able to recover the amount of the cost of the patent prorated equitably over its life. This method takes into consideration the fact that, because a patent purchased for percentage payments has no fixed cost, it is impossible to compute the depreciation allowance ratably over its useful life. Thus, permitting the yearly cost payments to be deducted in the year the payments are made provides minimum distortion of income. *Newton Insert Co. v. Commissioner of Internal Revenue*, 181 U.S.P.Q. 765, 775 (U.S.T.C. 1974).

Derivation. *See also* Communication of Conception, Originality.

When a record establishes that an interference party actually derived the invention of a count from his opponent, he cannot prevail on an issue of abandonment, suppression, or concealment; to prevail on such issue, he must be an independent inventor. *Spiner and Hoffman v. Pierce*, 177 U.S.P.Q. 709, 711 (PO Bd. Pat. Int. 1972).

℧

Evidence of activity, knowledge or use concerning an invention in a foreign country is not precluded by 35 U.S.C. §104 in establishing derivation. *Hedgewick v. Akers*, 497 F.2d 905, 182 U.S.P.Q. 167, 168 (C.C.P.A. 1974).

ᛒ

Historically, 35 U.S.C. §102(f) was considered as a section compelling the inventor to be the party applying for a patent and traditionally is applicable in a situation where an applicant has derived an invention from another. In the absence of evidence that the invention, as defined by the claims, has been derived from another, a rejection based on that section of the statute will not be sustained. *Ex parte Billottet and Fechner*, 192 U.S.P.Q. 413 (PTO Bd. App. 1976).

ᛒ

There can be no derivation without prior conception on the part of the one alleging derivation. It must be proved that there was a clear disclosure of the invention by one to the other even though the disclosure need only be sufficient to enable one skilled in the art to practice the invention defined by the interference count without the exercise of anything more than mere mechanical skill. *Marathon Oil Co. v. The Firestone Tire & Rubber Company*, 205 U.S.P.Q. 520, 533 (Ohio 1979).

ᛒ

The site of derivation need not be in this country to bar a deriver from patenting involved subject matter in the United States. *Ex parte Andresen*, 212 U.S.P.Q. 100, 102 (PTO Bd. App. 1981).

ᛒ

Derivation is difficult to establish by direct evidence; it can generally be established only by the circumstances of a case. The fact that no one overheard the alleged communication from the junior party to the senior party and the senior party testified that he had no recollection of such a communication is not fatal to the junior party. *Sands v. Bonazoli, Kimball, and Palmer*, 223 U.S.P.Q. 450, 452 (PTO Bd. Pat. Int. 1983).

ᛒ

An interference party claiming derivation by another party must show prior and complete conception of the claimed subject matter and communication of the complete conception to the other party. Prior conception is an absolute defense to a charge of derivation. *Boyd v. Tamutus*, 1 U.S.P.Q.2d 2080, 2083, 2084 (B.P.A.I. 1986).

ᛒ

By expressly providing that motions thereunder for judgment based on unpatentability may not be based on derivation by an opponent from the moving party, 37 C.F.R. §1.633(a) makes it clear that derivation of that type is not a "patentability" issue under the new interference rules. In contrast, derivation by an opponent from someone who is not a party is a patentability issue. *Behr v. Talbott*, 27 U.S.P.Q.2d 1401, 1411 (B.P.A.I. 1992).

ᛒ

A patented invention is not "derived" from another person unless that other person was in possession of the invention. Invalidity based on derivation requires that the patentee, in the words of the statute, did not invent the subject matter that was patented. *Lamb-Weston Inc. v. McCain Foods Ltd.*, 78 F.3d 540, 37 U.S.P.Q.2d 1856, 1863 (*dissent*) (Fed. Cir. 1996).

ᛟ

The CAFC reviews a finding of derivation as a question of fact. This requires acceptance of the district court's findings unless clearly erroneous or predicated on an improper legal foundation. To show derivation, the party asserting invalidity must prove both prior conception of the invention by another and communication of that conception to the patentee. *Gambro Lundia AB v. Baxter Healthcare Corp.*, 110 F.3d 1573 42 U.S.P.Q.2d 1378, 1381 (Fed. Cir. 1997).

ᛟ

Subject matter derived from another not only is itself unpatentable [under 35 U.S.C. §102(f)] to the party who derived it, but, when combined with other prior art, may make another obvious invention unpatentable to that party under a combination of §§102(f) and 103 of Title 35 (U.S.C.) *OddzOn Products Inc. v. Just Toys Inc.*, 122 F.3d 1396, 43 U.S.P.Q.2d 1641, 1646 (Fed. Cir. 1997).

ᛟ

Claims of prior inventorship and derivation may be established by a preponderance-of-the-evidence for interferences between a patent and a co-pending application, or between interfering patents. *Environ Products Inc. v. Furon Co.*, 47 U.S.P.Q.2d 1040, 1044 (Pa. 1998).

Derivative Application.

A divisional application is entitled to priority rights (based on an earlier foreign filing) properly obtained for a copending parent application even though no claim of priority was made during the prosecution of the divisional application, as long as the earlier foreign filing supports the subject matter claimed in the divisional application. *Deutsche Gold-Und Silber-Scheideanstalt Vormals Roessler v. Commissioner of Patents*, 251 F.Supp. 624, 148 U.S.P.Q. 412, 413 (D.C. 1966).

Describe. *See also* Description, *In Haec Verba, Ipsis Verbis*.

The mere naming of a compound in a reference, without more, cannot constitute a description of the compound, particularly when evidence of record suggests that a method suitable for its preparation was not developed until a date later than that of the reference. *In re Wiggins, James, and Gittos*, 488 F.2d 538, 179 U.S.P.Q. 421, 425 (C.C.P.A. 1973).

ᛟ

Although a specification describes an invention as broadly as it is claimed, thereby eliminating any issue concerning the description requirement, a specification which "describes" does not necessarily also "enable" one skilled in the art to make and use the invention. *In re Armbruster*, 512 F.2d 676, 185 U.S.P.Q. 152, 153 (C.C.P.A. 1975).

ᛟ

There is a description of the invention requirement in 35 U.S.C. §112, first paragraph, which is separate and distinct from the enablement requirement. A specification may contain a disclosure that is sufficient to enable one skilled in the art to make and use the invention and yet fail to comply with the description of the invention requirement. *In re Barker and Pehl*, 559 F.2d 588, 194 U.S.P.Q. 470, 472 (C.C.P.A. 1977).

ϖ

To comply with the description requirement, it is not necessary that the application describe the claimed invention in ipsis verbis; all that is required is that it reasonably convey to persons skilled in the art that, as of the filing date thereof, the inventor had possession of the subject matter later claimed by him. *In re Edwards, Rice, and Soulen*, 568 F.2d 1349, 196 U.S.P.Q. 465, 467 (C.C.P.A. 1978).

Description.[3] *See also* **Antecedent Support, Describe, Disclosure, DNA,** *In Haec Verba***, New Matter, Support.**

Limiting a class, generically disclosed, to a subgenus thereunder, without an original teaching of said subgenus as such, is directed to new matter that is not supported by the original specification. To be claimed, subgenera of lesser scope must be supported as such in the original description. *Ex parte Batchelder and Zimmerman*, 131 U.S.P.Q. 38 (PO Bd. App. 1960).

ϖ

We think the Karrer patent, as a printed publication, describes to one skilled in this art not only the broad class but also this much more limited class within the broad class, and we think it is immaterial that Karrer did not expressly spell out the limited class as we have done here. It is our opinion that one skilled in this art would, on reading the Karrer patent, at once envisage each member of this limited class, even though this skilled person might not at once define in his mind the formal boundaries of the class as we have done here. It is our opinion that Karrer has described to those of ordinary skill in this art each of the various permutations here involved as fully as if he had drawn each structural formula or had written each name. *In re Petering and Fall*, 133 U.S.P.Q. 275, 280 (C.C.P.A. 1962).

ϖ

To obtain the benefit of the filing date of a parent application for subject matter claimed in a cip, the parent application must satisfy the description requirement of the statute with regard to that subject matter. Neither a specific example falling within the scope of (but not commensurate in scope with) nor a disclosure generic to such subject matter will suffice. In either or both cases publication of the applicant's own foreign application more than a year prior to the filing date of the cip serves as a statutory bar. *In re Lukach, Olson, and Spurlin*, 440 F.2d 1263, 169 U.S.P.Q. 795, 796, 797 (C.C.P.A. 1971).

ϖ

Where there is an adequate disclosure of a much broader class of compounds in the main body of the specification, and the only question lies in the delineation of a particular subgenus being claimed, an original claim in itself was regarded as adequate "written description" of the claimed invention. It was equally a "written description" whether

---

[3] *See Vas-Cath v. Mahurkar*, 935 F.2d 1559, 19 U.S.P.Q.2d 1111 (Fed. Cir. 1991).

located among the original claims or in the descriptive part of the specification. Whether the descriptive part of the specification should be amended to include the language of the claim is more of an administrative matter to be settled in the Patent Office. *In re Gardner*, 480 F.2d 879, 178 U.S.P.Q. 149 (C.C.P.A. 1973).

ʊ

In a case where there is no unpredictability and a broader concept than that expressly set forth in the specification would naturally occur to one skilled in the art from reading applicant's description, there is no basis for denying applicant claims that recite the broader concept. The alternative places upon patent applicants, the Patent Office, and the public the undue burden of listing (in the case of applicants), reading and examining (in the case of the Patent Office), and printing and storing (in the case of the public) descriptions of the very many structural or functional equivalents of disclosed elements or steps that are already stored in the minds of those skilled in the arts, ready for instant recall upon reading the descriptions of specific elements or steps. *In re Smythe and Shamos,* 480 F.2d 1376, 178 U.S.P.Q. 279, 285 (C.C.P.A. 1973).

ʊ

The specification as originally filed must convey clearly to those skilled in the art information that the applicant has invented the subject matter later claimed. When the original specification accomplishes that, regardless of how it accomplishes it, the essential goal of the description requirement is realized. *In re Smith,* 481 F.2d 910, 178 U.S.P.Q. 620, 624 (C.C.P.A. 1973).

ʊ

Having been produced by the same process, the product obtained in Example IV of the earlier Sulkowski application is, of necessity, the same product as that obtained in Example III of the Sulkowski interference application. The only difference is in the naming of the product. Based on the process used in the earlier application, Sulkowski is entitled to the benefit of the product of that process with his later application. The fact that an error was made in naming the product in the first application does not deprive Sulkowski of the benefit of that application. *Sulkowski v. Houlihan,* 179 U.S.P.Q. 685, 686 (PTO Bd. Pat. Int. 1973); *see also In re Sulkowski,* 487 F.2d 920, 180 U.S.P.Q. 46 (C.C.P.A. 1973).

ʊ

The so-called "description requirement," which exists in the first paragraph of 35 U.S.C. §112 independent of the enablement (how to make and how to use) portions, serves essentially two functions. In the simple case, where no prior application is relied upon, the description requirement is that the invention claimed be described in the specification as filed. As such, a rejection on the description requirement is tantamount to a new matter rejection under 35 U.S.C. §132. Both are fully defeated by a specification which describes the invention in the same terms as the claims. *In re Bowen,* 492 F.2d 859, 181 U.S.P.Q. 48, 52 (C.C.P.A. 1974).

ʊ

The function of the description requirement is to ensure that the inventor had possession (as of the filing date of the application relied on) of the specific subject matter later claimed by him; how the specification accomplishes this is not material. It is not necessary that the application describe the claim limitations exactly, but only so clearly that persons of ordinary skill in the art will recognize from the disclosure that the appellants invented processes including those limitations. *In re Wertheim,* 541 F.2d 257, 191 U.S.P.Q. 90, 96 (C.C.P.A. 1976).

ω

A parent application stated that it was now feasible to replace a part of the carboxylic acid with water, where the share of the water may be up to 1.6 mol. No lower amount of water was disclosed, except that, of course, some water had to be present. In a continuing application, the share of water was stated to be from 0.6 mol to 1.6 mols, and examples were added to cover that range. The appellants had discovered that "reduction of the amount of water used below 0.6 mol rendered the process unusable in practice owing to greatly prolonged reaction times. It would have been simple for one skilled in the art to run a series of experiments to determine that the reaction time increases greatly when the amount of water decreases below 0.6 mol. The flaw in this argument is that enablement and obviousness are not the issues; description of the invention is. That a person skilled in the art might proceed to run a series of experiments and derive a lower limit of 0.6 mols is not sufficient indication to that person that 0.6 is described as a parameter of the appellants' process. *In re Blaser, Germscheid, and Worms,* 556 F.2d 534, 194 U.S.P.Q. 122 (C.C.P.A. 1977).

ω

The PTO has not challenged the appellants' assertion that their 1953 application enabled those skilled in the art in 1953 to make and use "a solid polymer" as called for by their claim. The appellants disclosed, as the only existing way to make such a polymer, a method of making the crystalline form. To say now that the appellants should have disclosed in 1953 the amorphous form (which did not exist until 1962) would be to impose an impossible burden on the inventors and thus on the patent system. There cannot, in an effective patent system, be such a burden placed on the right to broad claims. To restrict the appellants to the disclosed crystalline form, under such circumstances, would be a poor way to stimulate invention, and particularly to encourage its early disclosure. To demand such restriction is merely to state a policy against broad protection for pioneer inventions, a policy both shortsighted and unsound from the standpoint of promoting progress in the useful arts, which is the constitutional purpose of the patent laws. *In re Hogan and Banks,* 559 F.2d 595, 194 U.S.P.Q. 527 (C.C.P.A. 1977).

ω

The burden of showing that the claimed invention is not described in the application rests on the PTO in the first instance, and it is up to the PTO to give reasons why a description not in ipsis verbis is insufficient. *In re Edwards, Rice, and Soulen,* 568 F.2d 1349, 196 U.S.P.Q. 465, 469 (C.C.P.A. 1978).

ω

The function of the description requirement is to ensure that, as of the filing date of the application relied upon, the inventor had possession of the specific subject matter later claimed by him; how the specification accomplishes this is not material. The claimed subject matter need not be described in haec verba to satisfy the description requirement.

Description

The application need not describe the claim limitations exactly, but only so clearly that one having ordinary skill in the pertinent art would recognize from the disclosure that applicant invented the subject matter including such limitations. *In re Herschler,* 591 F.2d 693, 200 U.S.P.Q. 711, 717 (C.C.P.A. 1979).

ω

The change in a lower limit of a range in a continuing application can be, but is not necessarily, fatal to relying on the filing date of the parent application for the invention claimed in the continuing application. *Synthetic Industries (Texas) Inc. v. Forta Fiber, Inc.,* 590 F. Supp. 1574, 224 U.S.P.Q. 955 (Pa. 1984).

ω

The expressions "free of bleaching agent comprising an alkaline earth metal being capable of releasing hypochlorite or hypobromite in an aqueous solution" and "a non-reducing saccharide" find no support in the specification. They thus do not comply with the description requirement of the first paragraph of 35 U.S.C. §112. The fact that no compounds of this nature are taught to be present in the examples of this case is insufficient basis for the limitations introduced into the claims when (1) quite evidently the presence of a bleaching agent is not intended to be excluded from the claim composition and, in fact, is intended to be present as an ingredient, and (2) nowhere is it indicated that only nonreducing sugars are intended to be within the scope of saccharides as broadly disclosed. That sucrose is a nonreducing sugar does not entitle the appellant to claim a genus of which sucrose is a member. *Ex parte Pearson,* 230 U.S.P.Q. 711 (B.P.A.I. 1985).

ω

Literal infringement requires that an accused device embody every element of a claim as properly interpreted. If the claim describes a combination of functions, and each function is performed by a means described in the specification or an equivalent of such means, then literal infringement holds. When a claimed invention is a novel combination of steps, all possible methods of carrying out each step of the combination are not required to be described in the specification. Correctly construed claims cover "equivalents" of the described embodiments. The purpose is to grant an inventor of a combination invention a fair scope that is not dependent on a catalog of alternative embodiments in the specification. The court has cautioned against limiting the claimed invention to preferred embodiments or specific examples in the specification. The details of performing each step need not be included in the claims unless required to distinguish the claimed invention from the prior art, or otherwise to specifically point out and distinctly claim the invention. Claims should be read in a way that avoids enabling an infringer to "practice a fraud on a patent."

It is not required that those skilled in the art knew, at the time the patent application was filed, of the asserted equivalent means of performing the claimed functions; that equivalence is determined as of the time infringement takes place. Infringement will be found when the material features of a patent have been appropriated, even when those features have been patentably improved. *Texas Instruments, Inc. v. U.S. International Trade Commission,* 805 F.2d 1558, 231 U.S.P.Q. 833 (Fed. Cir. 1986).

ω

The district court employed two measures impermissible in law: (1) it required that Claim 1 describe the invention, which is the role of the disclosure portion of the specification, not the role of the claims; and (2) it applied the "full, clear, concise, and exact" requirement of the first paragraph of 35 U.S.C. §112 to the claim, when that paragraph only applies to the disclosure portion of the specification, not to the claims. The district court spoke inappropriately of the indefiniteness of the "patent," and it did not review the claim for indefiniteness under the second paragraph of §112. A decision on whether a claim is invalid under §112 requires a determination of whether those skilled in the art would understand what is claimed when the claim is read in the light of the specification. *Orthokinetics Inc. v. Safety Travel Chairs Inc.*, 806 F.2d 1565, 1 U.S.P.Q.2d 1081 (Fed. Cir. 1986).

ᅲ

The first paragraph of 35 U.S.C. §112 includes two separate and distinct requirements: (1) that the invention be described and (2) that it be described in such full, clear, concise, and exact terms as to enable any person skilled in the art to make and use it. These two separate and distinct requirements have sometimes been referred to as (1) a description requirement and (2) an enablement requirement. A patent specification may meet the enablement requirement without meeting the description requirement, and thereby fail to comply with §112's mandate. *Kennecott Corp. v. Kyocera International Inc.*, 2 U.S.P.Q.2d 1455 (Cal. 1986).

ᅲ

The test for determining compliance with the written description requirement of 35 U.S.C. §112 is whether the disclosure of the application as originally filed reasonably conveys to the artisan that the inventor had possession of the claimed subject matter, rather than the presence or absence of literal support in the specification for the claim language. *Ex parte Harvey*, 3 U.S.P.Q.2d 1626 (B.P.A.I. 1986).

ᅲ

A party cannot invoke one theory of law based on chemistry (i.e., that bromo and iodo are patentably distinct from chloro in the intended chemical reaction) and, having a bifurcation of Count 1 on that theory, urge a contrary theory (i.e., that halogen, exemplified by chloro, comprises disclosure of the bromo and iodo species) in order to obtain priority as to those species. When the Board held that there was a patentable distinction between chloro, on the one hand, and bromo and iodo on the other, the party's disclosure of halogen and chloro lost the possibility of serving as a "full, clear, concise, and exact" (in the words of 35 U.S.C. §112) written description of the separate invention of the unnamed bromo and iodo compounds. *Bigham v. Godtfredsen*, 857 F.2d 1415, 8 U.S.P.Q.2d 1266, 1268, 1269 (Fed. Cir. 1988).

ᅲ

When scope of a claim has been changed by amendment in such a way as to justify an assertion that it is directed to a different invention than was the original claim, it is proper to inquire whether the newly claimed subject matter was described in the patent application (when filed) as the invention of the applicant. That is the essence of the so-called description requirement of 35 U.S.C. §112, first paragraph. The invention is, necessarily, the subject matter defined in the claim under consideration. The specification as originally filed must convey clearly to those skilled in the art the information that the applicant has invented the specific subject matter later claimed. When the original specification accomplishes that, regardless of how it accomplishes it, the essential goal of the description requirement is realized. The claimed subject matter need not be described in haec verba in the specification in order for that specification to satisfy the description requirement. *In re Wright*, 866 F.2d 422, 9 U.S.P.Q.2d 1649 (Fed. Cir. 1989).

ᴟ

It is not necessary that the claimed subject matter be described identically, but the disclosure originally filed must convey to those skilled in the art that applicant had invented the subject matter later claimed. Precisely how close the original description must come to comply with the description requirement of 35 U.S.C. §112 must be determined on a case-by-case basis. The inquiry into whether the description requirement is met is a question of fact. The subgenus of compounds defined by the claim is not described in the appellant's original disclosure. The claim embraces four species wherein R^1 represents a C_4 alkyl group, and the physiologically acceptable salts of those species. But the original disclosure does not describe any of those species either by way of working example or otherwise. There is no support for any of those species per se. Nor are there guidelines in the original disclosure that would lead a person having ordinary skill in the art toward the subgenus of compounds defined by the claim. On the contrary, the written description in the appellants' specification tends to lead away from the subgenus. In this regard, note the preferred group of compounds described in the specification, wherein the definition of R^1 precludes C_4 alkyl. *Ex parte Winters*, 11 U.S.P.Q.2d 1387 (B.P.A.I. 1989).

ᴟ

The description requirement of 35 U.S.C. §112 is the same for a claim copied for purposes of instituting an interference as for a claim presented during *ex parte* prosecution of a patent application. *In re Spina*, 975 F.2d 854, 24 U.S.P.Q.2d 1142, 1144 (Fed. Cir. 1992).

ᴟ

There is no distinction in law as to the enablement or description requirements of the first paragraph of 35 U.S.C. §112 based on whether the subject matter is chemical or nonchemical. *Ex parte DesOrneaux*, 25 U.S.P.Q.2d 2040, 2043 (B.P.A.I. 1992).

ᴟ

Although [the applicant] does not have to describe exactly the subject matter claimed, . . . the description must clearly allow persons of ordinary skill in the art to recognize that [he or she] invented what is claimed. *In re Hayes Microcomputer Products Inc. Patent Litigation*, 982 F.2d 1527, 25 U.S.P.Q.2d 1241, 1245 (Fed. Cir. 1992).

ᴟ

A motion under 37 C.F.R. §1.633(a) for judgment on the ground that an opponent's claim corresponding to an interference count lacks written description support in its involved application is a departure from the practice under the old interference rules, wherein the burden as to a party's "right to make" a count was always on the copier of the claims. An interference can be declared under the new rules when an application includes, or is amended to include at least one patentable claim which is drawn to the same patentable invention as a claim of another's unexpired patent. *Behr v. Talbott*, 27 U.S.P.Q.2d 1401, 1405 (B.P.A.I. 1992).

ω

When an inventor has not achieved conception of an invention, he cannot adequately describe the invention in a fashion that satisfies paragraph 1 of 35 U.S.C. §112. One cannot describe what one has not conceived. *University of California v. Eli Lilly and Co.*, 119 F.3d 1559, 39 U.S.P.Q.2d 1225, 1240 (Ind. 1995).

ω

Insofar as the written description requirement is concerned, the initial burden of presenting a prima facie case of unpatentability is discharged by "presenting evidence or reasons why persons skilled in the art would not recognize in the disclosure a description of the invention defined by the claims." "If a conception of a DNA requires a precise definition, such as by structure, formula, chemical name, or physical properties, . . . then a description also requires that degree of specificity." *In re Alton*, 76 F.3d 1168, 37 U.S.P.Q.2d 1578, 1582 n.9, 1583 (Fed. Cir. 1996).

ω

Just because a moiety is listed as one possible choice for one position does not mean there is *ipsis verbis* support for every species or subgenus that chooses that moiety. Were this the case, a "laundry list" disclosure of every possible moiety for evey possible position would constitute a written description of every species in the genus. *Fujikawa v. Wattanasin*, 39 U.S.P.Q.2d 1895, 1905 (Fed. Cir. 1996).

ω

Description of one species of a genus is not necessarily a description of the genus. *University of California v. Eli Lilly and Co.*, 119 F.3d 1559, 43 U.S.P.Q.2d 1398, 1405 (Fed. Cir. 1997).

ω

A disclosure in a parent application that merely renders the latter-claimed invention obvious is not sufficient to meet the written description requirement; the disclosure must describe the claimed invention with all its limitations. *Tronzo v. Biomet Inc.*, 950 F. Supp. 1142, 47 U.S.P.Q.2d 1829, 1832 (Fed. Cir. 1998).

Design. *See also* **Design Choice, Designing Around, Design Patent, Infringement, Functionality, Secondary Considerations in Design, Segregable Part, 35 U.S.C. §120, 35 U.S.C. §171.**

The court must determine infringement from the vantage point of an ordinary observer. The patentee must show substantial similarity between the accused and the claimed designs. *Gorham Manufacturing Co. v. White,* 81 U.S. (14 Wall.) 511 (1871).

ω

Where a new and original shape or configuration of an article of manufacture is claimed in a design patent, its utility may also be an element for consideration. *Smith v. Whitman Saddle Company*, 148 U.S. 674, 678 (1893).

ω

In a design patent there must be originality and novelty, as well as beauty. *Goudy v. Hansen*, 247 Fed. 782, 783 (1st Cir. 1917).

ʊ

Appearance is the essential consideration in designs, and such appearance may result from "peculiarity of configuration, or of ornament alone, or of both conjointly". *Whiting Mfg. Co. v. Alvin Silver Co., Inc.*, 283 Fed. 75, 79 (2d Cir. 1922).

ʊ

That the novel element in a necktie design is hidden, if a waistcoat is worn, is immaterial. Neckties are bought, not only because of their utility to the wearer and their attractiveness to others when worn, but also because of the appeal, as novel, ornamental, and pleasing, that the design makes to the aesthetic sense of the purchaser. *Franklin Knitting Mills, Inc. v. Gropper Knitting Mills, Inc.*, 15 F.2d 375 (2d Cir. 1926).

ʊ

More is required for a valid design patent than that the design be new and pleasing enough to catch the trade. Conception of the design must demand some exceptional talent beyond the skill of the ordinary designer. *Neufeld-Furst & Co., Inc. v. Jay-Day Frocks Inc.*, 112 F.2d 715 (2d Cir. 1940).

ʊ

A design patent cannot be used to monopolize functional features which cannot be protected by a mechanical patent. *Rowley v. Tresenberg*, 37 Fed. Supp. 90, 92 (N.Y. 1941).

ʊ

The test of design infringement is whether the two designs have substantially the same effect upon the eye of an ordinary observer who gives the matter such attention as purchasers usually give. *Gold Seal Importers, Inc. v. Morris White Fashions, Inc.*, 124 F.2d 141 (2d Cir. 1941). *See also Gorham v. White*, 81 U.S. 511 (1872).

ʊ

To establish design infringement, the accused device must appropriate the novelty in the patented device that distinguishes it from the prior art. *Sears, Roebuck & Co. v. Talge*, 140 F.2d 395, 60 U.S.P.Q. 434 (8th Cir. 1944).

ʊ

Functional equivalency of portions of reference disclosures are properly considered in evaluating the patentability of a design. *In re Zonenstein*, 172 F.2d 599, 80 U.S.P.Q. 522, 523 (C.C.P.A. 1949).

ʊ

The mere fact that a design may involve some mechanical or utilitarian function will not render it unpatentable, but the patentability of a design may not be predicated on utility. To preclude patentability, the Patent Office tribunals may combine proper references to old forms and shapes, wherever found, to illustrate the fact that an applicant's design may be lacking in novelty, or that the combination of old forms did not require the exercise of the inventive faculty. *In re Jabour*, 182 F.2d 213, 86 U.S.P.Q. 98 (C.C.P.A. 1950).

ʊ

A design patent can anticipate a claim in a utility application. *In re Pio,* 217 F.2d 956, 104 U.S.P.Q. 177 (C.C.P.A. 1954).

ω

No exception was made in the 1952 code for designs from the requirements for invention applicable to other patents. *In re Rousso,* 222 F.2d 729, 106 U.S.P.Q. 99, 101 (C.C.P.A. 1955).

ω

The principle of nonanalogous arts cannot be applied to design cases in exactly the same manner as to mechanical cases. The question in design cases is not whether references sought to be combined are in analogous arts in the mechanical sense, but whether they are so related that the appearance of certain ornamental features in one would suggest the application of those features to the other. When a proposed combination of references involves material modifications of the basic form of one article in view of another, the nature of the articles involved is a definite factor in determining whether the proposed change involves invention. Almost every new design is made up of elements which, individually, are old somewhere in the prior art, but that does not prove want of invention in assembling them. *In re Glavas,* 230 F.2d 447, 109 U.S.P.Q. 50, 52 (C.C.P.A. 1956).

ω

The mere fact that the copyright secured by appellant's assignee will outlive any design patent appellant may secure does not provide a sound basis for rejecting appellant's design patent application. *In re Yardley,* 493 F.2d 1389, 181 U.S.P.Q. 331, 335 (C.C.P.A. 1974).

ω

A design for an article of manufacture may be embodied in less than all of an article of manufacture. Although there are no portions of a design that are immaterial or not important, that does not mean that the design must encompass an entire article. An article may well have portions that are material to a claimed design, and dotted lines are appropriate to indicate portions of an article that are not material to the claimed design. *In re Zahn,* 617 F.2d 261, 204 U.S.P.Q. 988 (C.C.P.A. 1980).

ω

To have double-patenting in a design-utility context, the claims of the respective patents must cross-read. Such double patenting must turn on the presence or absence of design features which produce the novel function claimed in the utility patent. *Wahl v. Rexnord, Inc.,* 624 F.2d 1169, 206 U.S.P.Q. 865, 871 (C.C.P.A. 1980).

ω

A design patent protects a unitary appearance. In other words, every aspect of the design contributes to the overall appearance. A court must not, in comparing a patented design to prior art, break it down into its separate components. *In re Salmon,* 705 F.2d 1579, 1582, 217 U.S.P.Q. 981, 984 (Fed. Cir. 1983).

ω

A claim of priority under 35 U.S.C. §120 may be made in a utility application based upon an earlier-filed design application provided that the design application satisfies the statutory conditions; of particular pertinence is the condition that the disclosure of the design application meet the requirements of the first paragraph of §112 as applied to the claims of the utility application. Similar observations may be made with regard to claiming priority under §120 in a design application based upon an earlier-filed utility application. *Ex parte Duniau*, 1 U.S.P.Q.2d 1652 (B.P.A.I. 1986).

ᚖ

A design patent is invalid if the patented design is "primarily functional," rather than primarily ornamental, or if function dictates the design. If, in the eye of any ordinary observer giving such attention as a purchaser usually gives, two designs are substantially the same and the resemblance is such as to deceive such an observer (inducing him to purchase one supposing it to be the other), the first one patented is infringed by the other. In addition to overall similarity of designs, the accused device must appropriate the novelty in the patented device that distinguishes it from the prior art. *Avia Group International, Inc. v. L.A. Gear California, Inc.*, 853 F.2d 1557, 7 U.S.P.Q.2d 1548 (Fed. Cir. 1988).

ᚖ

Design patents have almost no scope. A design claim is limited to what is shown in the application drawings. We see no way in which an ornamental design for an article of manufacture can be subject to the "experimental use" exception applicable in the case of functioning machines, manufactures, or processes. *In re Mann,* 861 F.2d 1581, 8 U.S.P.Q.2d 2030, 2031 (Fed. Cir. 1988).

ᚖ

That which would be concealed in normal use is not proper subject matter for a design patent. *Ex parte Hansen*, 10 U.S.P.Q.2d 1399 (B.P.A.I. 1988).

ᚖ

In order to determine whether a design is primarily functional, the individual features of the design must be analyzed. In such analysis, every feature of the product in issue need not be considered; analysis must focus on those specific features that constitute or contribute appreciably to the newness, originality, or ornamentation and non-obviousness of the overall design. It is not proper to invalidate a design patent because one or more minor features primarily serve a utilitarian purpose, but invalidation is indicated when the individual features that are found to serve, primarily, a functional purpose may clearly be labeled as dominant, in the sense that they are chiefly relied upon as contributing, to the over-all design, the qualities of newness, originality, ornamentation, and non-obviousness. *Smith v. M&B Sales & Manufacturing*, 13 U.S.P.Q.2d 2002, 2004 (Cal. 1990).

ᚖ

A design patent indicates, presumptively, that the design is not de jure functional. The ownership of a design patent in and of itself, and without more, does not necessarily establish nonfunctionality as to trademark registrability of that same design for particular goods. *In re Witco Corp.*, 14 U.S.P.Q.2d 1557, 1559 (T.T.A.B. 1990).

ᚖ

The fact that isolated elements of a design are functional does not make the design as a whole primarily functional. A showing that a functional aspect could be accomplished in ways other than that adopted by the design at issue is sufficient to rebut a claim that the design is primarily functional. There is no per se prohibition against applying for both a design and a utility patent on the same article. Evidence of other designs that incorporate identical elements may establish that the issuance of a utility patent in connection with the same article does not make the design patent invalid. *Liqui-Box Corp. v. Reid Valve Co. Inc.*, 16 U.S.P.Q.2d 1848, 1853, 1855 (Pa. 1990).

ᗯ

In a field of art, where products are deliberately designed as asymmetrical in order to create distinctive, memorable images, it would have been obvious to one of ordinary skill in the art to create a "normal" or symmetrical orientation for a design. Pleasing symmetry is not nonobvious where it represents no more than ordinary symmetry with convenience in mind. Indeed, knowledge of symmetry is one reason why more complex designs are developed—the *expected* design configuration is one of symmetry. *In re Carlson*, 983 F.2d 1032, 25 U.S.P.Q.2d 1207, 1212 (Fed. Cir. 1992).

ᗯ

The argument that hidden features of articles are not ornamental and cannot be infringed confuses the test for design patent infringement with the standards for patentability. Although generally concealed features are not proper bases for design patent protection because their appearance cannot be a "matter of concern", a design for an article that is hidden in its final use may be patentable because, during some point in its life, its appearance is a "matter of concern". Both overall similarity and appropriation of the point of novelty are required for design patent infringement. *KeyStone Retaining Wall Systems Inc. v. Westrock Inc.*, 997 F.2d 1444, 27 U.S.P.Q.2d 1297, 1302, 1303 (Fed. Cir. 1993).

ᗯ

Unlike an invention in a utility patent, a patented ornamental design has no use other than its visual appearance, and its scope is "limited to what is shown in the application drawings." Therefore, in considering prior art references for purposes of determining patentability of ornamental designs, the focus must be on appearances and not uses. "In determining the patentability of a design, it is the overall appearance, the visual effect as a whole of the design, which must be taken into consideration." The appearance of the design must be viewed as a whole, as shown by the drawing, or drawings, and compared with something in existence—not with something that might be brought into existence by selecting individual features from prior art and combining them, particularly where combining them would require modification of every individual feature. If prior art designs are to be modified in more than one respect to render a claimed design obvious, those modifications must be *de minimis* in nature and unrelated to the overall aesthetic appearance of the design. *In re Harvey*, 12 F.3d 1061, 29 U.S.P.Q.2d 1206, 1208, 1209, 1210 (Fed. Cir. 1993).

ᗯ

As a matter of law, experimentation directed to functional features of a product to which an ornamental design relates may negate what otherwise would be a public use within the meaning of 35 U.S.C. §102(b). *Tone Brothers Inc. v. Sysco Corp.*, 28 F.3d 1192, 31 U.S.P.Q.2d 1321, 1326 (Fed. Cir. 1994).

ϖ

Trade dress protection is not, as a matter of law, unavailable to products for which design patents have expired. *Hubbell Inc. v. Pass & Seymour Inc.*, 94 Civ. 7631, 35 U.S.P.Q.2d 1760, 1762 (N.Y. 1995).

ϖ

If a "particular design is essential to the use of the article, it cannot be the subject of a design patent." Whether or not a design is ornamental is determined by whether or not the design is a matter of concern to the purchaser, that is, whether there is an aesthetic quality to the design which is a matter of concern to a purchaser. *Best Lock Corp. v. Ilco Unican Corp.*, 896 F.Supp. 836, 36 U.S.P.Q.2d 1527, 1533 (Ind. 1995).

ϖ

Although a feature that is "primarily functional" is not protected by a design patent, an overly broad definition of functionality is not supported by case law. Not all features that perform functions are primarily functional; rather, the test is whether the "function dictates the design" and that requires a court to determine whether the function performed by the features in question could be accomplished by other designs. *Herbco International Inc. v. Gemmy Industries Inc.*, 38 U.S.P.Q.2d 1819, 1821 (N.Y. 1996).

ϖ

A finding of obviousness cannot be based on selecting features from the prior art and assembling them to form an article similar in appearance to a claimed design. The claimed design "must be compared with something in existence, not with something that might be brought into existence by selecting individual features from prior art and combining them". *In re Borden*, 90 F.3d 1570, 39 U.S.P.Q.2d 1524, 1526 (Fed. Cir. 1996).

ϖ

To preclude design patentability by combining prior art designs, one must find a single primary reference, "a something in existence, the design characteristics of which are basically the same as the claimed design." Once this primary reference is found, other references may be used to modify it to create a design that has the same overall visual appearance as the claimed design. *Durling v. Spectrum Furniture Co.*, 40 U.S.P.Q.2d 1788, 1790 (Fed. Cir. 1996).

ϖ

The "actual confusion" evidence, like the expert's evidence, was *not* submitted to show that the confusion was caused by ornamental features, but rather to show that the overall designs are similar. *OddzOn Products Inc. v. Just Toys Inc.*, 122 F.3d 1396, 43 U.S.P.Q.2d 1641, 1648 (Fed. Cir. 1997).

ϖ

Consideration of alternative designs, if present, is a useful tool that may allow a court to conclude that a challenged design is not invalid for functionality. As such, alternative designs join a list of other appropriate considerations for assessing whether a patented design as a whole—its overall appearance—was dictated by functional considerations. Other appropriate considerations might include: whether the protected design represents the best design; whether alternative designs would adversely affect the utility of the specified article; whether there are any concomitant utility patents; whether the advertising touts particular features of the design as having specific utility; and whether there are any elements in the design or an overall appearance clearly not dictated by function. *Berry Sterling Corp. V. Pescor Plastics Inc.*, 122 F.3d 1452, 43 U.S.P.Q.2d 1953, 1956 (Fed. Cir. 1997).

ᛞ

The ordinary English meaning of the word "design" is "to plan or have in mind as a purpose; intend." Webster's Third New International Dictionary, at 611. *Regents of the University of California v. Oncor Inc.*, 44 U.S.P.Q.2d 1321, 1326 (Cal. 1997).

ᛞ

"Evidence relating to consumer confusion would not raise a triable issue of fact" because the court may find infringement or noninfringement by merely comparing the designs. *Child Craft Industries Inc. v. Simmons Juvenile Products Co.*, 990 F. Supp. 638, 45 U.S.P.Q.2d 1933, 1938 (Ind. 1998).

ᛞ

"Public use" and "on-sale" bars, while they share the same statutory basis, are grounded on different policy emphases. The primary policy underlying the "public use" case is that of detrimental public reliance, whereas the primary policy underlying an "on-sale" case is that of prohibiting the commercial exploitation of the design beyond the statutorily prescribed time period. *Continental Plastic Containers Inc. v. Owens-Brockway Plastic Products Inc.*, 141 F.3d 1073, 46 U.S.P.Q.2d 1277, 1280 (Fed. Cir. 1998).

ᛞ

The statutory provision governing the effective filing date of the subject matter of continuing applications applies to design patents as well as to utility patents. The common thread, and the criterion to be met, is whether the latter claimed subject matter is described in the earlier application in compliance with 35 U.S.C. §112. *In re Daniels*, 144 F.3d 1452, 46 U.S.P.Q.2d 1788, 1790 (Fed. Cir. 1998).

ᛞ

The merger of the point of novelty test and the ordinary observer test is legal error. *Unidynamics Corp. v. Automatic Products International Ltd.*, 48 U.S.P.Q.2d 1099, 1107 (Fed. Cir. 1998).

Design Application.

An application for a design patent, filed as a division of an earlier-filed application for a utility patent, is entitled to the benefit of the earlier filing date of the utility application under 35 U.S.C. §120 and §121. Section 120 gives to an applicant for a patent complying with its terms the right to have the benefit of the filing date of an earlier application. The language is mandatory: "An application for patent...shall have the same effect...as though filed on the date of the prior application...." Chapter 16 of Title 35 U.S.C., covering design patents, has only three sections. Section 171 provides that "the provisions of this title relating to patents for inventions shall apply to patents for designs, except as otherwise provided." There are no "otherwise provided" statutes to take design patent applications out of the ambit of §120, which makes no distinction between applications for design patents and applications for utility patents, or as the statute calls them, "patents for inventions." However, the statute deems designs to have been invented and to be a kind of invention, subjecting them to all the requirements for patentability pertaining to utility inventions. *Racing Strollers Inc. v. TRI Industries Inc.*, 878 F.2d 1418, 11 U.S.P.Q.2d 1300, 1302 (Fed. Cir. 1989).

Design Choice.

The selection of the ratio for total jaw length to the average jaw height and the narrow range of hardness claimed is not a matter of obvious design choice to one of ordinary skill in the art at the time the invention was made. It is axiomatic that not only must claims be given their broadest reasonable interpretation consistent with the specification, but also all limitations must be considered. Here the characterization of certain specific limitations or parameters as obvious does not make the appellant's invention, considered as a whole, obvious. The fact that the invention may have been the result of experimentation does not negate patentability nor render obvious claimed parameters that were the result of experimentation. *Ex parte Petersen*, 228 U.S.P.Q. 216, 217 (B.P.A.I. 1985).

ᴥ

The BPAI held that appellant had simply made an obvious design choice. However, the different structures of appellant and of the reference achieve different purposes. *In re Gal*, 980 F.2d 717, 25 U.S.P.Q.2d 1076, 1078 (Fed. Cir. 1992).

ᴥ

To require an applicant to include in his specification evidence and arguments regarding whether particular subject matter was a matter of "design choice" would be tantamount to requiring the applicant to devine, before an application is filed, rejections the PTO will proffer. A finding of "obvious design choice" is precluded where claimed structure and the function it performs are different from those of the prior art. *In re Chu*, 66 F.3d 292, 36 U.S.P.Q.2d 1089, 1094, 1095 (Fed. Cir. 1995).

Designing Around.

Bona fide attempts to design a non-infringing product are one of the beneficial results of the incentive-to-disclose system established by the patent statute. Bona fides of such attempts, however, are not governed solely by whether the words of a patent claim can be literally read on the newly designed product. The matter is not one for semantics alone. An infringer appropriates an invention, not words; hence, the doctrine of equivalents. At the same time, the words of a claim may be so limited by the file history or by the prior art as to define an invention that was not appropriated; hence, the doctrine of estoppel. *Caterpillar Tractor Co. v. Berco, S.p.A.*, 714 F.2d 1110, 219 U.S.P.Q. 185 (Fed. Cir. 1983).

ᴥ

Intentionally "designing around" the claims of a patent is not, by itself, a wrong that must be compensated by invocation of the doctrine of equivalents. Designing around a patent is, in fact, one of the ways in which the patent system works to the advantage of the public in promoting progress in the useful arts, its constitutional purpose. Also inherent in our claim based patent system is the principle that the protected invention is what the claims say it is, and thus infringement can be avoided by avoiding the language of the claims. It is only when the changes are so insubstantial as to result in "a fraud on the patent" that application of the equitable doctrine of equivalents becomes desirable. *Slim-fold Manufacturing Co. Inc. v. Kinkead Industries Inc.*, 932 F.2d 1453, 18 U.S.P.Q.2d 1842, 1845 (Fed. Cir. 1991).

ϖ

Designing or inventing around patents to make new inventions is encouraged. Keeping track of a competitor's products and designing new and possibly better or cheaper functional equivalents is the stuff of which competition is made and is supposed to benefit the consumer. One of the benefits of a patent system is its so-called "negative incentive" to "design around" a competitor's products, even when they are patented, thus bringing a steady flow of innovations to the marketplace. It should not be discouraged by punitive damage awards except in cases where conduct is so obnoxious as clearly to call for them. The world of competition is full of "fair fights". *Westvaco Corp. v. International Paper Co.*, 991 F.2d 735, 26 U.S.P.Q.2d 1353, 1361 (Fed. Cir. 1993).

ϖ

Evidence of "designing around" patent claims is relevant to the question of infringement under the doctrine of equivalence. When a competitor becomes aware of a patent, and attempts to design around its claims, the fact-finder may infer that the competitor, presumably one of skill in the art, has designed substantial changes into the new product to avoid infringement. *Evidence of designing around therefore weighs against finding infringement under the doctrine of equivalence.* However, intent to design around is irrelevant to the question of infringement. A defendant may have infringed without intending, or even knowing it; but he is not, on that account, the less an infringer. *ATD Corp. v. Lydall Inc.*, 43 U.S.P.Q.2d 1170, 1178 (Mich. 1997).

Design Patent Infringement.

A test for determining infringement of a design patent requires that "if, in the eye of an ordinary observer, giving such attention as a purchaser usually gives, two designs are substantially the same, if the resemblance is such as to deceive such an observer, inducing him to purchase one supposing it to be the other, the first one patented is infringed by the other." For a design patent to be infringed, however, no matter how similar two items look, "the accused device must appropriate the novelty in the patented device which distinguishes it from the prior art." That is, even though two items are compared through the eyes of an ordinary observer, a court (to find infringement) must nevertheless attribute their similarity to the novelty that distinguishes the patented device from the prior art. This point-of-novelty approach applies only to a determination of infringement. *Litton Systems, Inc. v. Whirlpool Corp.* 728 F.2d 1423, 221 U.S.P.Q. 97 (Fed. Cir. 1984).

ϖ

The purpose of the "point of novelty" approach is to focus on those aspects of a design which render the design different from prior art designs. *Bush Industries Inc. v. O'Sullivan Industries Inc.*, 772 F.Supp. 1442, 21 U.S.P.Q.2d 1561, 1569 (Del. 1991).

ꙍ

If, in the eye of an ordinary observer, giving such attention as a purchaser usually gives, two designs are substantially the same, if the resemblance is such as to deceive such an observer, inducing him to purchase one supposing it to be the other, the first one patented is infringed by the other. The ornamental aspects of the design as a whole (not merely isolated portions of the patented design) must be considered. Patent infringement can be found for a design that is not identical to the patented design. The accused device must appropriate the novelty in the patented device which distinguishes it from the prior art. Where a design is composed of functional, as well as ornamental, features, a patent owner must establish that an ordinary person would be deceived by reason of the common features in the claimed and accused designs which are ornamental. *Braun Inc. v. Dynamics Corp. of America*, 975 F.2d 815, 24 U.S.P.Q.2d 1121, 1125 (Fed. Cir. 1992).

ꙍ

To consider the overall appearance of a design without regard to prior art would eviscerate the purpose of the "point of novelty" approach. (The "point of novelty" test is a supplemental one. In evaluating a claim of design patent infringement, a trier of fact must consider the ornamental aspects of the design as a whole and not merely isolated portions of the patented design.) The overall appearance of a design, however, need not be disregarded. Indeed, the "ordinary observer" test would preclude such a rule. While the point of novelty approach does command an inquiry into specific elements in the prior art as an initial matter, it does not preclude an analysis of how those elements are combined and integrated into an overall design, and of whether that design has been anticipated. Individual design elements, alone or in combination, may well appear again and again in the prior art, but so long as their ultimate integration into the overall design is novel, the patent is valid as to that combination of design elements. *Rubbermaid Commercial Products Inc. v. Contico International Inc.*, 836 F.Supp. 1247, 29 U.S.P.Q.2d 1574, 1582, 1583 (Va. 1993).

ꙍ

Evidence relating to consumer confusion would not raise a triable issue of fact. A finding of infringement or of non-infringement may, as a matter of law, be made relying "exclusively or primarily on a visual comparison of the patented design, as well as the device that embodies the design, and the accused device's design." "Likelihood of confusion as to the source of the goods is not a necessary *or appropriate* factor for determining infringement of a design patent." *Pacific Handy Cutter Inc. v. Quick Point Inc.*, 43 U.S.P.Q.2d 1624, 1628 (Cal. 1997).

Destroy.

References are not properly combined when such combination would destroy that on which the invention of one of the references is based. *Ex parte Hartmann*, 186 U.S.P.Q. 366 (PTO Bd. App. 1974).

Details. *See also* **Derivation, Enablement.**

In claiming a mechanical combination, an applicant is not necessarily limited to the specific composition that he discloses as the material for making up each and every element of the combination. If every element in a mechanical combination claim were required to be so specific as to exclude materials known to be inoperative and that even those not skilled in the art would not try, the claims would fail to comply with 35 U.S.C. §112 because they would be so detailed as to obscure, rather than particularly point out and distinctly claim, the invention. *In re Myers,* 410 F.2d 420, 161 U.S.P.Q. 668, 672 (C.C.P.A. 1969).

ϖ

In cases of inventions for combinations (including chemical compositions), the elements thereof need not be so precisely defined. *Ex parte Dobson, Jacob, and Herschler*, 165 U.S.P.Q. 29, 30 (PO Bd. App. 1969).

ϖ

The claims need not teach in detail how to practice the invention, as this is the function of the specification. *Ex parte Pontius, Endres, and Van Akkeren*, 169 U.S.P.Q. 122, 123 (PO Bd. App. 1970).

Determination of Rights.[4] *See also* **Development, Executive Order No. 10096.**

A government employee-inventor is entitled to a presumption that his invention was made under circumstances that would require that title be left in him subject either (1) to law or (2) to a license for the government when the employee was not hired to invent and the invention was not in his position description or within his official or assigned duties. *Locker v. Department of the Army,* 9 U.S.P.Q.2d 1412, 1414 (Commr. Patents & Trade marks 1988).

Determining. *See also* **Mental Steps.**

Steps, such as "computing," "determining," "cross-correlating," "comparing," "selecting," "initializing," "testing," "modifying," and "identifying," have implicitly been found to recite the solving of a mathematical algorithm. *In re Warmerdam,* 33 F.3d 1354, 31 U.S.P.Q.2d 1754, 1758 (Fed. Cir. 1994).

Development.

Any work done by employees was not the type of "research" contemplated by the Atomic Energy Act of 1946, 42 U.S.C. §1801 et seq. (1952 ed.) Those employees did aid in the development of the invention. However, what they did was only such work as is done in embodying an invention into a commercial device. Their work was not "research". Because the work done by employees was not "federally financed research", the cost to the Government of their work and materials may not be considered in assessing just compensation. *Hobbs v. United States Atomic Energy Commission*, 451 F.2d 849, 171 U.S.P.Q. 713, 728 (5th Cir. 1971).

---

[4]*See Zacharin v. United States*, 38 U.S.P.Q.2d 1826 (U.S. Ct. Fed. Cl. 1996).

Device. *See also* **Apparatus,** FDCA, 25 U.S.C. §271(e)(1).

A combination of a device and the material upon which the device works is not patentable. *In re Hodler*, 73 F.2d 507, 23 U.S.P.Q. 317, 320 (C.C.P.A. 1934).

ᵯ

The rejection of a claim to apparatus comprising a source of material to be acted on was reversed. *Ex parte Deaton and Kirkland*, 146 U.S.P.Q. 549, 551 (PO Bd. App. 1965).

Dictionary. *See also* **Claim Construction, Claim Interpretation, Claim Language, Lexicographer.**

Although the CCPA (in contrast with a court adjudicating an infringement suit on an issued patent) gives "claims yet unpatented...the broadest reasonable interpretation consistent with the specification," it is also settled patent law that the disclosure may serve as a dictionary for terms appearing in the claims and that, in such instances, the disclosure may be used, even by the CCPA, in interpreting the claims and in determining their scope. *In re Barr, Williams, and Whitmore*, 444 F.2d 588, 170 U.S.P.Q. 330, 335 (C.C.P.A. 1971).

ᵯ

Indiscriminate reliance on definitions found in dictionaries can often produce absurd results. One need not arbitrarily pick and choose from the various accepted definitions of a word to decide which meaning was intended as the word is used in a given claim. The subject matter, the context, and so on will more often than not lead to the correct conclusion. Rather than looking to a dictionary, look to the art or technology to which the claimed subject matter pertains. In doing so, give due consideration to the interpretation that one of ordinary skill in the art would give the terminology in question. *In re Salem, Butterworth, and Ryan*, 553 F.2d 676, 193 U.S.P.Q. 513, 518 (C.C.P.A. 1977).

ᵯ

Provision of a dictionary to a jury, although not favored, is not grounds for a new trial. *United States Surgical Corp. v. Ethicon Inc.*, 983 F.Supp. 963, 41 U.S.P.Q.2d 1225 (Fed. Cir. 1997)

ᵯ

While claims actually define the scope of a patent grant, the patent specification acts as a "sort of dictionary, which explains the invention." *Hassel v. Chrysler Corp.*, 982 F. Supp. 515, 43 U.S.P.Q.2d 1554, 1560 n.2 (Ohio 1997).

ᵯ

"Indiscriminate reliance on definitions found in dictionaries can often produce absurd results.... One need not arbitrarily pick and choose from the various accepted definitions of a word to decide which meaning was intended as the word is used in a given claim. The subject matter, the context, etc., will more often than not lead to the correct conclusion." *Renishaw plc v. Marposs Societa' per Azioni*, 48 U.S.P.Q.2d 1117, 1122 (Fed. Cir. 1998).

Dictum.

Dictum consists, *inter alia*, of statements in judicial opinions upon a point or points not necessary to the decision of the case. *In re McGrew*, 43 U.S.P.Q.2d 1633, 1635 (Fed. Cir. 1997).

Difference. *See also* **Change, Degree, Point of Novelty.**

Although the patentee had merely changed the pitch of the Fourdrinier wire of a paper-making machine, the change in pitch was regarded as directed toward a wholly different object from that of the prior art. *Eibel Process Co. v. Minnesota & Ontario Paper Co.*, 261 U.S. 45, 67 (1923).

ᛠ

Where a small structural difference is involved and where there is no apparent reason why that difference should produce a great improvement, the burden is upon the applicant to show, by factual evidence, that he has obtained an unexpectedly good result. *In re Renstrom,* 174 F.2d 140, 81 U.S.P.Q. 390, 391 (C.C.P.A. 1949).

ᛠ

Although it is proper to note the difference in a claimed invention from the prior art, because that difference may serve as one element in determining obviousness, it is improper to consider the differences as the invention. The difference may be slight (as has often been the case with some of history's greatest inventions, e.g., the telephone), but it may also have been the key to success in advancements in the art resulting from the invention. The issue with respect to obviousness is whether a challenger has carried its burden of proving, by clear and convincing evidence, facts from which it must be concluded that one skilled in the art at the time the invention was made would have found it to have been obvious, from the references as a whole, to create the claimed subject matter as a whole. *Jones v. Hardy,* 727 F.2d 1524, 220 U.S.P.Q. 1021, 1024 (Fed. Cir. 1984); *Datascope Corp. v. SMEC, Inc.*, 776 F.2d 320, 227 U.S.P.Q. 838 (Fed. Cir. 1985).

ᛠ

The claimed composition rapidly cures at room temperature, whereas the accused counterpart rapidly cures only at 90°C. It was precisely because of that difference that the district court found that the claimed invention and the accused counterpart do not perform in substantially the same way. That finding, however, would allow the difference itself to dictate a finding of no equivalents; if that were the law, one could never infringe by equivalents. The analysis must go further, and the question the district court should consider on remand is this: Given the difference, would the accused composition at 90°C and the claimed invention at room temperature perform substantially the same function (e.g., filling the pores of the treated material with solid material) in substantially the same way (e.g., by rapidly curing in the absence but not in the presence of oxygen) to give substantially the same results (e.g., a filled material)? There are limitations to the doctrine of equivalents. The doctrine has been judicially devised to do equity in situations where there is no literal infringement but liability is nevertheless appropriate to prevent what is in essence a pirating of the patentee's invention. Concomitently, two policy-oriented limitations, applied as questions of law, have developed. First, the doctrine will not extend to an infringing device within the public domain, i.e., found in the prior art at the time the patent issued; second, prosecution history estoppel will not allow the patentee to recapture through equivalents certain coverage given up during prosecution. *Loctite Corp. v. Ultraseal Ltd.*, 781 F.2d 861, 228 U.S.P.Q. 90 (Fed. Cir. 1985).

ʊ

Focusing on the obviousness of substitutions and differences instead of on the invention as a whole is a legally improper way to simplify the difficult determination of obviousness. *Hybritech Inc. v. Monoclonal Antibodies, Inc.*, 802 F.2d 1367, 231 U.S.P.Q. 81, 93 (Fed. Cir. 1986).

ʊ

While a court must ascertain the differences between a claimed invention and the prior art, it is not proper to focus on the question of whether any particular difference or differences would have been obvious. Rather, 35 U.S.C. §103 requires that the invention be considered "as a whole." Furthermore, a prior-art reference must be considered in its entirety, including portions that teach away from the claimed invention. The fact that a reference teaches away from a claimed invention is highly probative that the reference would not have rendered the claimed invention obvious to one of ordinary skill in the art. *Stranco Inc. v. Atlantes Chemical Systems Inc.*, 15 U.S.P.Q.2d 1704, 1713 (Tex. 1990).

Different. *See* Inconsistent.

Differentiation. *See* Claim Differentiation.

Differ in Kind. *See* Degree.

Dilatory Conduct.

Successors in interest are charged with the knowledge and dilatory conduct of their predecessors. *Valutron N.V. v. NCR Corp.*, 33 U.S.P.Q.2d 1986, 1989 (Ohio 1992), *aff'd* (Fed. Cir. 1993), *cert. denied* (S.Ct. 1994).

Diligence. *See also* Antedating a Reference, Continuous Activity, Conversion, Delay, Hiatus, Revival.

An inventor who assigns his invention, placing it under the control of another, will not be heard to complain when the measure of diligence in an interference proceeding is applied to the assignee as the real party in interest. *Wilson v. Goldmark*, 172 F.2d 575, 80 U.S.P.Q. 508, 514 (C.C.P.A. 1949).

ʊ

A period of over three weeks in which there was no activity by an interference party directed to reducing the invention of the counts to practice precludes a finding that that party was diligent from just prior to his opponent's effective filing date until his alleged reduction to practice, particularly when the record fails to show an adequate excuse for inactivity during that period. *Taub, Wendler, and Slates v. Rausser and Oliveto*, 145 U.S.P.Q. 497, 503 (PO Bd. Pat. Int. 1964).

ʊ

The junior party in an interference was almost continuously active in pursuing the commercialization of the process of the counts. Except for the period from 1959 to 1964, during which no government funds were allocated for the purpose of testing any bactericide, neither the junior party nor his supervisor gave up on the invention of the counts. Neither the pertinent case law nor a rule of reason would dictate that, under these circumstances, there was an abandonment of the invention by the junior party during this period. *Spiner and Hoffman v. Pierce*, 177 U.S.P.Q. 709, 712 (PO Bd. Pat. Int. 1972).

ಐ

Prior conception and simultaneous reduction to practice by an adverse interference party makes diligence irrelevant. *In re Bass, Jenkins, and Horvat*, 474 F.2d 1276, 177 U.S.P.Q. 178, 187 (C.C.P.A. 1973).

ಐ

The activity of those engaged in the preparation of a patent application accrues to the benefit of the inventor for the purpose of showing diligence. Work on related applications can also be relied upon to show reasonable diligence. All of the inventor's activities directed to an actual reduction to practice are considered to determine whether there was diligence. *Rey-Bellet and Spiegelberg v. Engelhardt v. Schindler*, 493 F.2d 1380, 181 U.S.P.Q. 453, 458, 459 (C.C.P.A. 1974).

ಐ

No more than three months elapsed between the approximate date of discovery of the possibility of non-joinder until the date the amendment under 37 C.F.R. §1.45(c) was filed at the PTO. Since the record indicates that applicants were actively engaged in an attempt to determine the facts concerning the non-joinder during this period, the amendment is deemed diligently made. *In re Russell, Jarrett, Bruno, and Remper*, 193 U.S.P.Q. 680, 682 (Comm'r of Patents and Trademarks 1975).

ಐ

An interference party has not shown the necessary diligence during the critical period when, for one month during that period, it is not evident that any relevant activity took place, and there is no explanation for the apparent inactivity. *Bigham v. Godtfredsen and Von Daehne*, 222 U.S.P.Q. 632, 637 (PTO Bd. Pat. Intf. 1984).

ಐ

A showing presented to excuse or justify a belated motion under 37 C.F.R. §1.231(a)(5) goes to the merits of the diligence issue and should be considered in evaluating the showing under 37 C.F.R. §1.45 (now §1.48). *Connin v. Andrews*, 223 U.S.P.Q. 243, 248 (PTO Bd. Pat. Intf. 1984).

ಐ

In an interference contest, "Evidence of diligence during the critical period may be shown either by affirmative acts or acceptable excuses or reasons for failure of action." Sporadic activity in the laboratory cannot be combined with unrelated sporadic activity by and on behalf of the patent attorney to prove reasonable diligence throughout the critical period. *Kondo, Takashima, and Tunemoto v. Martel, Tessier, Demoute, and Jolly*, 223 U.S.P.Q. 528, 532 (PTO Bd. Pat. Intf. 1984).

ಐ

In a priority contest, a party who was second to file was unable to prevail even though he had reduced the invention to practice four years prior to his opponent's filing date. Even if he demonstrated continuous activity from prior to his opponent's effective filing date to his filing date, such should have no bearing on the question of priority. While diligence during the above-noted period may be relied upon by one alleging prior conception and subsequent reduction to practice, it is of no significance in the case of the party who is not last to reduce to practice. Too long a delay may bar the first inventor from reliance on an early reduction to practice. However, the first inventor is not barred from relying on later, resumed activity antedating an opponent's entry into the field merely because the work done before the delay occurred was sufficient to amount to a reduction to practice. *Paulik v. Rizkalla,* 760 F.2d 1270, 226 U.S.P.Q. 224 (Fed. Cir. 1985).

ᚹ

To satisfy the reasonable diligence requirement of 35 U.S.C. §102(g), the work relied on must ordinarily be directly related to reduction to practice of the invention of the interference counts in issue. The policy of the real party in interest not to fund research projects, but rather to require researchers to obtain outside support, represents a conscious decision by the assignee resulting in delay which is inconsistent with the policy underlying that requirement that early public disclosure is the linchpin of the patent system. *Griffith v. Kanamaru,* 231 U.S.P.Q. 892, 893 (B.P.A.I. 1986).

ᚹ

In an interference contest, work on a related case is credited toward reasonable diligence if the work on the related case "contribute[s] substantially to the ultimate preparation of the involved application." *Bey v. Kollonitsch,* 806 F.2d 1024, 231 U.S.P.Q. 967, 970 (Fed. Cir. 1986).

ᚹ

To establish diligence, it is not necessary that an inventor be working on the invention every day. The question of diligence is considered in the light of all the circumstances. For example, people may be sick or even take vacations (thereby creating the absence of activities) while still being diligent. The question is whether they were pursuing their goal in a reasonable fashion. If they were doing the same things reasonably necessary to reduce the idea to practice, then they were diligent even if they did not actually work on the invention every day. *Hybritech Inc. v. Abbott Laboratories,* 4 U.S.P.Q.2d 1001 (Cal. 1987).

ᚹ

Unexplained delays by a patent attorney in preparing an application, and failure by the attorney to take up applications in the order that they are received, forecloses a finding of reasonable diligence. The patent obtained on such an application is not prior art under 35 U.S.C. §102(g), because the invention of that patent was reduced to practice by another before the application was filed, and before diligent preparation of the application began. *Mendenhall v. Astec Industries, Inc.,* 13 U.S.P.Q.2d 1913, 1935 (Tenn. 1988), *aff'd,* 13 U.S.P.Q.2d 1956 (Fed. Cir. 1989).

ᚹ

An inventor may rely on activities directed toward raising capital or funding for a project in order to prove that he acted with due diligence in reducing his invention to practice. *American Standard Inc. v. Pfizer Inc.*, 722 F. Supp. 86, 14 U.S.P.Q.2d 1673, 1694 (Del. 1989).

ᛦ

A practitioner's diligence in seeking to revive an abandoned application or accept a late payment of an issue fee is considered in determining whether any delay was unavoidable. A terminal disclaimer will not be accepted as a substitute for diligent conduct. *In re Application of Takao*, 17 U.S.P.Q.2d 1155, 1160 (Commr. Patents & Trademarks 1990).

ᛦ

The negligence of his attorney does not excuse applicant's duty to exercise due diligence. An applicant has the duty to make sure his application is being prosecuted. Applicant's lack of due diligence over a two and one-half year period overcame and superseded any negligence of his attorney. The delay was not unavoidable because, had applicant exercised the due care of a reasonably prudent person, he would have been able to act to correct the situation in a timely fashion. *Douglas v. Manbeck*, 21 U.S.P.Q.2d 1697, 1700 (Pa. 1991).

Diluent. *See* **Carrier, Composition, Solvent.**

Dimensions.

The claims were intended to cover the use of the invention with various types of automobiles. That a particular chair of the claims may fit within some automobiles and not others is of no moment. The phrase "so dimensioned" is as accurate as the subject matter permits, automobiles being of various sizes. As long as those of ordinary skill in the art realize that the dimensions could be easily obtained, 35 U.S.C. §112, second paragraph, requires nothing more. The patent law does not require that all possible lengths corresponding to the spaces in hundreds of different automobiles be listed in the patent, let alone that they be listed in the claims. *Orthokinetics Inc. v. Safety Travel Chairs Inc.*, 806 F.2d 1565, 1 U.S.P.Q.2d 1081 (Fed. Cir. 1986).

Directed Verdict.

A motion for a directed verdict made at the close of all the evidence is a prerequisite to challenging the sufficiency of the evidence on appeal. *Farley Transp. Co. v. Santa Fe Transp. Co.*, 786 F.2d 1342, 1347 (9th Cir. 1986).

ᛦ

A motion for a directed verdict has to state specific evidentiary deficiencies in order to preserve the right to challenge a jury verdict on appeal. *Lifshitz v. Walter Drake & Sons, Inc.*, 802 F.2d 1426, 1 U.S.P.Q.2d 1254 (9th Cir. 1986).

ᛦ

When a court considers motions for a directed verdict and for judgment notwithstanding the verdict, it must (1) consider all the evidence, (2) in a light most favorable to the non-mover, (3) drawing reasonable inferences favorable to the non-mover, (4) without determining credibility of witnesses, and (5) without substituting its choice for that of the jury between conflicting elements in the evidence. The court should not be guided by its view of which side has the better case or by what it would have done had it been serving on the jury. If, after following those guidelines, the court is convinced upon the record before the jury that reasonable persons could not reach or could not have reached a verdict for the non-mover, it should grant the motion for directed verdict or JNOV. Deference due a jury's fact findings in a civil case is not so great as to require acceptance of findings where those findings are clearly and unquestionably not supported by substantial evidence. *Vieau v. Japax Inc.*, 823 F.2d 1510, 3 U.S.P.Q.2d 1094 (Fed. Cir. 1987).

ᛒ

The view that a jury verdict on non-obviousness is at best advisory would make charades of motions for directed verdict or JNOV under Fed. R. Civ. P. 50 in patent cases. These motions apply only to binding jury verdicts. Moreover, use of an advisory jury is limited to actions not triable of right by a jury. All fact findings of a jury are non-advisory, unless made in an area expressly removed from jury verdict. A jury may decide the questions of anticipation and obviousness, either as separate special verdicts or en route to a verdict on the question of validity, which may also be decided by the jury. No warrant appears for distinguishing the submission of legal questions to a jury in patent cases from such submissions routinely made in other types of cases. So long as the Seventh Amendment stands, the right to a jury trial should not be rationed, nor should particular issues in particular types of cases be treated differently from similar issues in other types of cases. When the judgment arises from a jury verdict, the reviewing court applies the reasonable-jury/substantial-evidence standard, a standard which gives greater deference to the judgment simply because appellate review is more limited, compared with review of a trial judge's decision. The appellate court's function is exhausted when the evidentiary basis of the jury's verdict becomes apparent, it being immaterial that the court might draw a contrary inference or feel that another conclusion is more reasonable. *Richardson v. Suzuki Motor Co., Ltd.*, 868 F.2d 1226, 9 U.S.P.Q.2d 1913, 1915 (Fed. Cir. 1989).

ᛒ

When a motion for directed verdict has been made but not followed by a motion for JNOV, an appellate court that has determined that a jury verdict is not supported by substantial evidence ordinarily has authority only to order a new trial on the issue. *Sun Studs Inc. v. ATA Equipment Leasing Inc.*, 882 F.2d 1583, 11 U.S.P.Q.2d 1479 (Fed. Cir. 1989).

ᛒ

A motion for judgment notwithstanding the verdict (JNOV) will not lie unless it is preceded by a motion for a directed verdict made at the close of all of the evidence. A motion for JNOV cannot be made on a ground that was not raised in the motion for a directed verdict. *ALM Surgical Equipment Inc. v. Kirschner Medical Corp.*, 15 U.S.P.Q.2d 1241, 1245, 1246, 1250 (S.C. 1990).

ᛒ

Although it is true that the standard for summary judgment is virtually the same as that for a directed verdict, this does not mean that a motion for summary judgment is a substitute for a motion for directed verdict. *Wang Laboratories Inc. v. Toshiba Corp.*, 993 F.2d 858, 26 U.S.P.Q.2d 1767, 1777 (Fed. Cir. 1993).

ω

"Directed verdict" has been renamed "judgment as a matter of law." *Markman v. Westview Instruments Inc.*, 52 F.3d 967, 34 U.S.P.Q.2d 1321, 1324 n.2 (Fed. Cir. 1995).

ω

An oral pre-verdict motion requesting a directed verdict on the issue of noninfringement was sufficient to support a post-verdict motion concerning the doctrine of equivalents. *Texas Instruments Inc. v. Cypress Semiconductor Corp.*, 39 U.S.P.Q.2d 1492, 1498 n.6 (Fed. Cir. 1996).

Direction. *See also* **Assistant, Combining References, Destroy, Motivation, Obvious to Try or Experiment, Orientation during Operation, Teach Away From.**

A shotgun type of generic reference disclosure with many variables and no direction toward a restricted class of claimed compounds would not guide one skilled in the art to choose the restricted class from among the host of possible combinations and permutations suggested so as to make that restricted class obvious within the meaning of 35 U.S.C. §103. *Ex parte Strobel and Catino*, 160 U.S.P.Q. 352 (PO Bd. App. 1968). *See also In re Luvisi and Nohejl*, 342 F.2d 102, 144 U.S.P.Q. 646, 650, n.2 (C.C.P.A. 1965).

ω

The mere fact each reference discloses some particular claimed elements is not sufficient for obviousness without some direction from the prior art. *Ex parte Shepard and Gushue*, 188 U.S.P.Q. 536, 538 (PTO Bd. App. 1974).

ω

The non-obviousness of the invention is bolstered by the fact that one skilled in the art would not have searched for a solution to the involved problem in the direction taken by the patentee. *White v. Mar-Bel, Inc.*, 509 F.2d 287, 185 U.S.P.Q. 129, 131 (5th Cir. 1975).

ω

The proposition that the disclosure must provide "guidance which will enable one skilled in the art to determine, with reasonable certainty before performing the reaction, whether the claimed product will be obtained" would render all experimentation undue, since the term "experimentation" implies that the success of the particular activity is uncertain. Such a proposition is contrary to the basic policy of the Patent Act, which is to encourage disclosure of inventions and thereby to promote progress in the useful arts. *In re Angstadt and Griffen*, 537 F.2d 498, 190 U.S.P.Q. 214, 219 (C.C.P.A. 1976).

ω

In determining what constitutes undue experimentation, many factors are taken into account, including the guidance provided by the specification for selecting those embodiments of the invention which achieve the disclosed utility. Such guidance is essential where the invention involves an unpredictable art, such as one which involves physiological activity. *In re Sichert*, 566 F.2d 1154, 196 U.S.P.Q. 209, 215 (C.C.P.A. 1977).

Disadvantage.

Known disadvantages of a drug, which would naturally discourage a search for new uses of that drug, may be taken into account in determining obviousness. *In re Marshall*, 578 F.2d 301, 198 U.S.P.Q. 344, 347 (C.C.P.A. 1978). *See also Ingersoll-Rand Company v. Brunner & Lay, Inc.*, 474 F.2d 491, 177 U.S.P.Q. 112, 116 (5th Cir. 1973).

Disbelief. *See also* **Cancer, Hair Growth, Incredible, Skepticism.**

Expressions of disbelief by experts constitute strong evidence of nonobviousness. *Environmental Designs, Ltd. v. Union Oil Company of California*, 713 F.2d 693, 218 U.S.P.Q. 865, 869 (Fed. Cir. 1983).

Disclaimer.[5] *See also* **Claims Suggested for Interference, Dedication to the Public, File Wrapper Estoppel, Provisional Disclaimer, Recapture, Terminal Disclaimer, Unclaimed Disclosure.**

In patents for combinations of mechanisms, limitations and provisos imposed by the inventor, especially such as were introduced into an application after it had been persistently rejected, must be strictly construed against the inventor and in favor of the public, and looked upon as in the nature of disclaimers. *Sargent v. Hall & Safe Lock Co.*, 114 U.S. 63 (1885).

ᛒ

A claim in a patent (as allowed) must be read and interpreted with reference to claims that have been canceled or rejected, and the claims allowed cannot (by construction) be read to cover what was thus eliminated from the patent. A patentee may not, by resort to the doctrine of equivalents, give to an allowed claim a scope that it might have had without the amendments, the cancellation of which amounts to a disclaimer. *The Schriber-Schroth Company v. The Cleveland Trust Company*, 311 U.S. 211, 47 U.S.P.Q. 345, 349 (1940).

ᛒ

When a party to an interference files an abandonment of the contest, concedes priority, or disclaims the subject matter of an interference count, he stands in the same position as he would had there been an award of priority adverse to him with respect to the interference count. An adverse award of priority bars an applicant from obtaining a claim not patentably distinct from the subject matter awarded his adversary. *In re Fenn*, 315 F.2a 949, 137 U.S.P.Q. 367, 368 (C.C.P.A. 1963).

ᛒ

The disclaimer of the subject matter of a count by one party in an interference, in the absence of fraud, has the effect (between the two interfering parties) of an award of priority to the opposing party. The issue of first inventorship between the two parties, however, is not foreclosed as to third parties. *United States Pipe and Foundry Company v. Woodward Iron Company*, 327 F.2d 242, 140 U.S.P.Q. 208, 212 (4th Cir. 1964).

ᛒ

---

[5] See *Carnegie Mellon University v. Schwartz*, 41 U.S.P.Q.2d 1623 (3d Cir. 1997).

Under the proper circumstances, a concession of priority or disclaimer of an interference count renders that count available with the same effect as a prior-art reference disclosing such subject matter, and the count may be combined with other prior art to show lack of patentable distinction between the count and the appealed claims. The legislative history of 35 U.S.C. §102 and §103 makes it clear that the "prior art," which §103 requires to be compared with "the subject matter sought to be patented" in a given situation, refers to at least the statutory prior-art material named in §102. The subject matter of a count lost in an interference by concession of priority must be regarded as made in this country by another before the losing party's invention thereof. That subject matter is prior art within the meaning of 35 U.S.C. §103, and, in accordance with that provision, the losing party may not obtain any claim that distinguishes over that prior art only in matters that would have been obvious to one having ordinary skill in the art *at the time the losing party's invention was made*. That analysis, however, does not completely dispose of the issue since it requires a finding that the subject matter of the count was invented before the subject matter of the present claims. A concession of priority with regard to the subject matter defined by an interference count does not extend to distinctly different subject matter later claimed by the losing party to an interference in which the count was in issue. *In re Yale, Sowinski, and Bernstein,* 347 F.2d 995, 146 U.S.P.Q. 400, 403 (C.C.P.A. 1965).

ᚦ

The substance of disclaimed patent claims cannot be pursued in a copending application even if a terminal disclaimer is filed in the pending application so that the term of a patent granted thereon would not extend beyond that of the previously-issued patent. *Ex parte Parker,* 152 U.S.P.Q. 627 (PO Bd. App. 1966).

ᚦ

Where there are separate inventions, each of which is considered patentable over the prior art absent a patent on the other, a rejection based upon double patenting can be obviated by the filing of a terminal disclaimer under 35 U.S.C. §253, which may be filed by a common assignee. *In re Bowers and Orr,* 359 F.2d 886, 149 U.S.P.Q. 570, 576 (C.C.P.A. 1966).

ᚦ

Appellant's refusal to copy claims, which he could make, resulted in a concession [termed "disclaimer" in PTO Rule 203(b)] that the subject matter of those claims is the prior invention of another in this country under 35 U.S.C. §102(g) and thus prior art to appellant under 35 U.S.C. §103. *In re Ogiue,* 517 F.2d 1382, 186 U.S.P.Q. 227, 235 (C.C.P.A. 1975).

ᚦ

Disclaimed claims cannot be revived, through reissue or otherwise. Since all of the claims have been disclaimed, the effect of the plaintiff's action is the same as dedication of the patent to the public or abandonment. *W.L. Gore & Associates, Inc. v. Oak Materials Group, Inc.,* 424 F.Supp. 700, 192 U.S.P.Q. 687, 689 (Del. 1976).

ᚦ

"A statutory disclaimer under 35 U.S.C. §253 has the effect of conceling the claims from the patent and the patent is viewed as though the disclaimed claims had never existed in the patent." *Vectra Fitness Inc. v. TNWK Corp.*, 49 U.S.P.Q.2d 1144, 1147 (Fed. Cir. 1998).

Disclose. *See* **Disclosure, Duty to Disclose, Information Disclosure Statement.**

Disclosure. *See also* **Block Diagram, Breadth, Can, Comparative Test Data, Description, Details, Duty to Disclose, Early disclosure, Early Filing, Enabling Disclosure, Encyclopedic Disclosure, Fraud, Information Disclosure Statement, Known, Mixture, Mosita, Privilege, Scope, Specification, Sufficiency of Disclosure, Support, 35 U.S.C. §112.**

An applicant (patentee) may begin at a point where his invention begins and describe what he has made that is new, and what it replaces of the old. That which is common and well known is as if it were written out in the application (patent) and delineated in the drawings. *Webster Loom Co. v. Higgins*, 105 U.S. 580, 586 (1882).

ω

A disclosure in an abandoned application for a patent does not constitute such evidence of prior knowledge as will bar the allowance of a subsequent application. *In re Schlittler and Uffer*, 234 F.2d 882, 110 U.S.P.Q. 304, 306 (C.C.P.A. 1956).

ω

Claims are read in the light of the disclosure of the specification on which they are based, not in a vacuum. *In re Dean*, 291 F.2d 947, 130 U.S.P.Q. 107, 110 (C.C.P.A. 1961).

ω

The key to determining whether a disclosure supports a claim for interference purposes is whether the disclosure teaches the gist of the invention defined by the claim. While all limitations of a claim must be considered in deciding what invention is defined, it is futile merely to compare quantitatively range limits and numbers set out in counts with range limits and numbers disclosed in an allegedly supporting specification. Closer scrutiny is required to get at the essence of what invention the count purports to define. *Hall v. Taylor*, 332 F.2d 844, 141 U.S.P.Q. 821, 824 (C.C.P.A. 1964).

ω

The appellant with the assistance of his assignee prepared and inserted in the application two series of photomicrographs together with extensive descriptions of them for the purpose of showing how the invention differs from the prior filaments in an extensively developed art. The court took the position that this would not have been done unless the photomicrographs in fact showed persons of ordinary skill in the art what the appellant asserted they show and was unwilling to give credence to a contrary opinion expressed by the Board as the basis of the rejection that it originated sua sponte. *In re Ehringer*, 347 F.2d 612, 146 U.S.P.Q. 31, 35 (C.C.P.A. 1965).

ω

It is elementary that claims contained in an application as originally filed may be considered part of the disclosure of the application. *In re Myers,* 410 F.2d 420, 161 U.S.P.Q. 668, 673 (C.C.P.A. 1969).

ထ

A specification disclosure that contains a teaching of the manner and process of making and using the invention in terms that correspond in scope to those used in describing and defining the subject matter sought to be patented must be taken as in compliance with the enabling requirement of the first paragraph of 35 U.S.C. §112 unless there is reason to doubt the objective truth of the statements contained therein that must be relied on for enabling support. Assuming that sufficient reason for such doubt does exist, a rejection for failure to teach how to make and/or use will be proper on that basis. In any event, it is incumbent on the Patent Office, whenever a rejection on this basis is made, to explain why it doubts the truth or accuracy of any statement in a supporting disclosure and to back up assertions of its own with acceptable evidence or reasoning that is inconsistent with the contested statement. Otherwise, there would be no need for the applicant to go to the trouble and expense of supporting his presumptively accurate disclosure. *In re Marzocchi and Horton,* 439 F.2d 220, 169 U.S.P.Q. 367 (C.C.P.A. 1971).

ထ

Although the CCPA (in contrast with a court adjudicating an infringement suit on an issued patent) gives "claims yet unpatented...the broadest reasonable interpretation consistent with the specification," it is also settled patent law that the disclosure may serve as a dictionary for terms appearing in the claims and that, in such instances, the disclosure may be used, even by the CCPA, in interpreting the claims and in determining their scope. *In re Barr, Williams, and Whitmore,* 444 F.2d 588, 170 U.S.P.Q. 330, 335 (C.C.P.A. 1971).

ထ

By disclosing a device that inherently performs a function, operates according to a theory, or has an advantage, a patent applicant necessarily discloses that function, theory, or advantage even though he says nothing concerning it. The application may be later amended to recite the function, theory, or advantage without introducing prohibited new matter. *In re Smythe and Shamos,* 480 F.2d 1376, 178 U.S.P.Q. 279 (C.C.P.A. 1973).

ထ

The statute requires a disclosure that allows one skilled in the art to practice the invention and does not require a patentee to disclose every detail of his commercial operation. It is normal practice to retain commercial details of a manufacturing process in confidence, and such does not constitute patent misuse. *Illinois Tool Works Inc. v. Solo Cup Company,* 179 U.S.P.Q. 322, 366, 371 (Ill. 1973).

ထ

Having been produced by the same process, the product obtained in Example IV of the earlier Sulkowski application is, of necessity, the same product as that obtained in Example III of the Sulkowski interference application. The only difference is in the naming of the product. Based on the process used in the earlier application, Sulkowski is entitled to the benefit of the product of that process with his later application. The fact that error was made in naming the product in the first application does not deprive Sulkowski of the benefit of that application. *Sulkowski v. Houlihan,* 179 U.S.P.Q. 685, 686 (PTO Bd. Pat. Int. 1973); *see also In re Sulkowski,* 487 F.2d 920, 180 U.S.P.Q. 46 (C.C.P.A. 1973).

ω

The enablement requirement of the statute is satisfied when the specification, taken with the prior art, clearly teaches an effective process for making the claimed compounds from corresponding known starting materials and also describes methods of using the claimed compounds. *Ex parte Gastambide, Thal, Rohrbach, and Laroche,* 189 U.S.P.Q. 643, 645 (PTO Bd. App. 1974).

ω

In maintaining that claimed subject matter is not adequately described, the PTO has the initial burden of presenting evidence or reasons why persons skilled in the art would not recognize (in the disclosure) a description of the defined invention. *In re Salem, Butterworth, and Ryan,* 553 F.2d 676, 193 U.S.P.Q. 513, 518 (C.C.P.A. 1977).

ω

The PTO has not challenged the appellants' assertion that their 1953 application enabled those skilled in the art in 1953 to make and use "a solid polymer" as described in Claim 13. The appellants disclosed, as the only then-existing way to make such a polymer, a method of making the crystalline form. To say now that the appellants should have disclosed in 1953 the amorphous form (which did not exist until 1962) would be to impose an impossible burden on the inventors and thus on the patent system. There cannot, in an effective patent system, be such a burden placed on the right to broad claims. To restrict the appellants to the crystalline form disclosed, under such circumstances, would be a poor way to stimulate invention, and particularly to encourage its early disclosure. To demand such restriction is merely to state a policy against broad protection for pioneer inventions, a policy both shortsighted and unsound from the standpoint of promoting progress in the useful arts, which is the constitutional purpose of the patent laws. *In re Hogan and Banks,* 559 F.2d 595, 194 U.S.P.Q. 527 (C.C.P.A. 1977).

ω

Although pharmaceutical compositions were involved, the claimed invention concerned reducing gastro-intestinal-tract incompatibility. Exemplified structures of active components and their uses were previously known. The invention was not in the active component. The specification did not have to teach how to use (pharmacologically) all encompassed active components to satisfy the disclosure requirements of 35 U.S.C. §112, first paragraph. *Ex parte Gleixner, Muller, and Lehrach,* 214 U.S.P.Q. 297, 298 (PTO Bd. App. 1979).

ω

The disclosure of an application embraces not only what is expressly set forth in words or drawings, but what would be understood by persons skilled in the art. Those features that are well known are as if they were written out in the patent. *Ex parte Wolters and Kuypers,* 214 U.S.P.Q. 735, 736 (PTO Bd. App. 1979).

ω

A patentee is not considered the *prima facie* inventor of everything disclosed in his patent. *In re Clemens, Hurwitz, and Walker*, 622 F.2d 1029, 206 U.S.P.Q. 289, 296 (C.C.P.A. 1980).

ω

In exchange for a patent, an applicant must enable others to practice his invention. An inventor need not, however, explain every detail since he is speaking to those skilled in the art. What is conventional knowledge will be read into the disclosure. An applicant's duty to tell all that is necessary to make or use varies greatly depending on the art to which the invention pertains. *In re Howarth*, 654 F.2d 103, 210 U.S.P.Q. 689, 691 (C.C.P.A. 1981).

ω

Early public disclosure is a linchpin of the patent system. As between a prior inventor who benefits from a process by selling its product, but suppresses, conceals, or otherwise keeps the process from the public, and a later inventor who promptly files a patent application from which the public will gain disclosure of the process, the law favors the latter. *W. L. Gore & Associates, Inc. v. Garlock, Inc.*, 721 F.2d 1540, 220 U.S.P.Q. 303 (Fed. Cir. 1983).

ω

Section 112 of 35 U.S.C. requires that the written description of an invention be specific enough to enable one skilled in the art to make and use the invention without undue experimentation. That one skilled in the art must perform some preliminary tests or experiment before he can make or use the invention does not invalidate a patent. A patent does not have to be as detailed as a set of "production specifications" to meet this requirement. *Atlas Powder Co. v. E.I. du Pont de Nemours and Co.*, 588 F. Supp. 1455, 221 U.S.P.Q. 426 (Tex. 1983).

ω

The contention that a claimed configuration would be obvious from a reference claim on which it reads is a non sequitur. According to such reasoning Morse's telegraph patent would have made the Telex obvious. The scope of a patent's claims determines what infringes the patent; it is no measure of what it discloses. A patent discloses only that which it describes, whether specifically or in general terms, so as to convey intelligence to one capable of understanding. *In re Benno*, 768 F.2d 1340, 226 U.S.P.Q. 683 (Fed. Cir. 1985).

ω

There is no requirement in 35 U.S.C. §112 or anywhere else in the patent law that a specification must convince persons skilled in the art that the assertions in the specification are correct. In examining a patent application, the PTO is required to assume that the specification complies with the enablement provisions of §112 unless it has "acceptable evidence or reasoning" to suggest otherwise. The PTO must thus provide reasons supported by the record as a whole why the specification is not enabling. Then and only then does the burden shift to the applicant to show that one of ordinary skill in the art could have practiced the claimed invention without undue experimentation. A patent specification must be enabling as to "the invention" as set forth in the claims. Thus, a disclosure may be insufficient for one claim but sufficient for another. *Gould v. Mossinghoff,* 229 U.S.P.Q. 1 (D.C. 1985).

ω

The ultimate question is whether the specification contains a sufficiently explicit disclosure to enable one having ordinary skill in the relevant field to practice the invention claimed therein without the exercise of undue experimentation. The determination of what constitutes undue experimentation in a given case requires the application of a standard of reasonableness, having due regard for the nature of the invention and the state of the art. The test is not merely quantitative, since a considerable amount of experimentation is permissible if it is merely routine or if the specification in question provides a reasonable amount of guidance with respect to the direction in which the experimentation should proceed to enable the determination of how to practice a desired embodiment of the invention claimed. The factors to be considered have been summarized as the quantity of experimentation necessary, the amount of direction or guidance presented, the presence or absence of working examples, the nature of the invention, the state of the prior art, the relative skill of those in that art, the predictability or unpredictability of the art, and the breadth of the claims. *Ex parte Forman,* 230 U.S.P.Q. 546 (B.P.A.I. 1986).

ω

Enablement is a legal determination of whether a patent enables one skilled in the art to make and use the claimed invention. It is not precluded even if some experimentation is necessary, although the amount of experimentation needed must not be unduly extensive. Enablement is determined as of the filing date of the patent application. Furthermore, a patent need not teach, and preferably omits, what is well known in the art. *Hybri-tech Inc. v. Monoclonal Antibodies, Inc.,* 802 F.2d 1367, 231 U.S.P.Q. 81 (Fed. Cir. 1986).

ω

Amelioration of the symptoms or even cure of cancer is no longer considered to be "incredible." Nonetheless, decisional law would seem to indicate that the utility in question is sufficiently unusual to justify an Examiner's requiring substantiating evidence. Substantiating evidence may be in the form of animal tests that constitute recognized screening procedures with clear relevance to utility in humans. The specification of the appellant's parent application sets forth several animal tests on numerous types of specific cancers as well as in vitro studies, both of which are asserted to be predictive with regard to utility in humans. The Examiner has not challenged the evidence presented in a single, relevant, material respect. There is only the blanket statement of lack of "patentable utility" per se. In fact, the only specific comments the Examiner has directed toward the appellant's evidence are with regard to the breadth of the types of tumor against which the claimed compounds have been shown to be active. The appealed claims are drawn to compounds and not to a method of treatment. Generally speaking, utility in treating a single disease is an adequate basis for the patentability of a pharmaceutical compound under 35 U.S.C. §101. *Ex parte Krepelka,* 231 U.S.P.Q. 746 (B.P.A.I. 1986).

ω

A university policy not to fund research projects, but rather to require their researchers to obtain outside support, represents a conscious decision resulting in delay, which is inconsistent with the policy that early public disclosure is the linchpin of the patent system. *Griffith v. Kanamaru*, 231 U.S.P.Q. 892, 893 (B.P.A.I. 1986).

ᛏ

The district court employed two measures impermissible in law: (1) it required that Claim 1 describe the invention, which is the role of the disclosure portion of the specification, not the role of the claims; and (2) it applied the "full, clear, concise, and exact" requirement of the first paragraph of §112 to the claim, when that paragraph only applies to the disclosure portion of the specification, not to the claims. The district court spoke inappropriately of the indefiniteness of the "patent," and it did not review the claim for indefiniteness under the second paragraph of §112. A decision on whether a claim is invalid under 35 U.S.C. §112 requires a determination of whether those skilled in the art would understand what is claimed when the claim is read in the light of the specification. *Orthokinetics Inc. v. Safety Travel Chairs Inc.*, 806 F.2d 1565, 1 U.S.P.Q.2d 1081 (Fed. Cir. 1986).

ᛏ

By disclosing in a patent application a device that inherently performs a function, operates according to a theory, or has an advantage, a patent applicant necessarily discloses that function, theory, or advantage, even though he says nothing concerning it. The express description of an inherent property, since not "new matter," can be added to a specification with the effect as of the original filing date. The additional description is not that of a new use, but of the existing physical structure of the product. *Kennecott Corp. v. Kyocera International, Inc.*, 835 F.2d 1419, 5 U.S.P.Q.2d 1194 (Fed. Cir. 1987).

ᛏ

A specification that contains a disclosure of utility that corresponds in scope to the subject matter sought to be patented must be taken as sufficient to satisfy the utility requirements of 35 U.S.C. §101 for the entire claimed subject matter unless there is reason for one skilled in the art to question the objective truth of the statement of utility or its scope. *Ex parte Rubin*, 5 U.S.P.Q.2d 1461 (B.P.A.I. 1987).

ᛏ

The argument that a claim to a genus would inherently disclose all species within that genus is wholly meritless whether considered under 35 U.S.C. §102(b) or 103. *Corning Glass Works v. Sumitomo Electric U.S.A. Inc.*, 868 F.2d 1251, 9 U.S.P.Q.2d 1962 (Fed. Cir. 1989).

ᛏ

The test for sufficiency of support in a parent application is whether the disclosure of the application relied upon reasonably conveys to the artisan that the inventor had possession at that time of the later-claimed subject matter. The written description must communicate that which is needed to enable the skilled artisan to make and use the claimed invention. The purpose of the written description requirement is broader than merely to explain how to "make and use"; the applicant must also convey with reasonable clarity to those skilled in the art that, as of the filing date sought, he or she was in possession of the invention. The invention is, for purposes of the written description inquiry, whatever is claimed. Drawings alone may be sufficient to provide the "written description of the invention" required by the first paragraph of 35 U.S.C. §112. *Vas-Cath Inc. v. Mahurkar,* 935 F.2d 1555, 19 U.S.P.Q.2d 1111, 1116, 1117 (Fed. Cir. 1991).

ಠ

The claimed invention need not be described ipsis verbis in order to satisfy the disclosure requirement of 35 U.S.C §112. *Ex parte Holt,* 19 U.S.P.Q.2d 1211, 1213 (B.P.A.I. 1991).

ಠ

The disclosure must adequately guide the art worker to determine, without undue experimentation, which species among those encompassed by a claimed genus possess the disclosed utility. Where the claimed genus represents a diverse and relatively poorly understood group of microorganisms, the required level of disclosure is greater than that for an invention involving a "predictable" factor, such as a mechanical or an electrical element. *In re Vaeck,* 947 F.2d 488, 20 U.S.P.Q.2d 1438, 1445 (Fed. Cir. 1991).

ಠ

The disclosure of a genus and a species of a subgenus within that genus is not sufficient description of the subgenus to comply with the description requirement of 35 U.S.C. §112, unless there are specific facts which lead to a determination that a subgenus is implicitly described. *Ex parte Westphal,* 26 U.S.P.Q.2d 1858, 1860 (B.P.A.I. 1992).

ಠ

There is nothing in 35 U.S.C. §112 which supports a *rejection* on the ground that the specification does not provide enough information for the Examiner to formulate a search and examine the application. However, the disclosure of a patent application must not only be sufficient "to preclude the possibility that a patent could issue without any person skilled in the art being thenceforth enabled to make and use the invention", but also must be sufficient "to permit a thorough examination by the Patent [and Trademark] Office." *Ex parte C,* 27 U.S.P.Q.2d 1492, 1495, 1496 (B.P.A.I. 1992).

ಠ

As the application disclosure failed to provide any information (among the minimum needed by workers in the art to obtain needed enzymes) as to the microbial source of required enzymes, the subsequent (after filing) deposit of microorganisms stated to produce such enzymes did not rectify the omission. Moreover, appellants did not establish that one skilled in the art would be able to isolate the needed enzymes from the deposited materials. *Ex parte DeCastro,* 28 U.S.P.Q.2d 1391, 1394 (B.P.A.I. 1993).

ಠ

"The law does not require the impossible. Hence, it does not require that an applicant describe in his specification every conceivable and possible future embodiment of his invention." *International Rectifier Corp. v. SGS-Thomson Microelectronics Inc.,* 38 U.S.P.Q.2d 1083, 1086 (Cal. 1994).

ಠ

Under the European Patent Convention and the law of most industrialized countries, an unauthorized disclosure of an invention does not immediately destroy its novelty (and thus foreclose the inventor's ability to patent the invention). Instead, such an adverse disclosure bars only patent applications made more than six months after the date of the disclosure [Art. 55 of the *Convention on the Grant of European Patents*, as printed in *European Patent Convention* (4th ed., Munich; European Patent Office, 1987)]. *Russo v. Baxter Healthcare Corp.*, 46 U.S.P.Q.2d 1239, 1241 (1st Cir. 1998).

ʊ

When an explicit limitation in an interference count is not present in the written description whose benefit is sought, it must be shown that a person of ordinary skill would have understood, at the time the patent application was filed, that the description requires that limitation. "It is 'not a question of whether one skilled in the art *might* be able to construct the patentee's device from the teachings of the disclosure ... Rather, it is a question of whether the application necessarily discloses that particular device.'" *Hyatt v. Boone*, 47 U.S.P.Q.2d 1128, 1131 (Fed. Cir. 1998).

Disclosure without Claiming. *See also* **Dedication to the Public, Late Claiming, Unclaimed Disclosure.**

A patentee may claim the whole or only a part of his invention. If he only claims a part, he is presumed to have abandoned the residue to the public. *McLain v. Ortmayer,* 141 U.S. 419 (1891).

ʊ

The mere fact that an appellant's earlier appealed application would have supported claims on appeal in a subsequent case (had they been presented in the former) does not in itself render claims in the latter rejectable on the grounds of res judicata. *In re Gruskin,* 234 F.2d 493, 110 U.S.P.Q. 288, 291 (C.C.P.A. 1956).

ʊ

There is only an inference of abandonment of disclosed but unclaimed subject matter in an issued patent. The inference may be rebutted (a) by an application for reissue of the patent pursuant to statute (35 U.S.C. §251, last paragraph) which seems to permit a broadening reissue application, (b) by claiming in a copending application before the patent issues and possibly even thereafter, and (c) by the filing of an application within the one-year grace period following the issuance of the patent and before the patent becomes a statutory bar under 35 U.S.C. §102(b). *In re Gibbs and Griffen,* 437 F.2d 486, 168 U.S.P.Q. 578, 584 (C.C.P.A. 1971).

ʊ

D and N were joint applicants of an application filed for a combination invention on June 1, 1973 (subsequently issued as U.S.P. 3,842,678 on October 22, 1974). Applicant D was the sole applicant of an application (S.N. 952,695) for reissue of U.S.P. 3,964,519 (issued on an application filed November 18, 1974), claiming a subcombination that was fully disclosed, but not claimed, in U.S.P. 3,842,678. In the prosecution of the reissue application D presented his own Declaration that a drawing of the subcombination invention (dated March 15, 1973) established conception prior to June 1, 1973, and the subcombination was a sole invention originally conceived by D and described to patent counsel prior to June 1, 1973, to enable counsel to satisfy the requirements of 35 U.S.C. §112 in drafting the joint application. The joint patent was used as a reference against the reissue application even though it was silent with regard to who invented the subcombination. There was no basis to presume that the subcombination was the invention of D and N jointly or of either of them. The joint patent of D and N, having issued less than one year before the filing date of D's original patent application, is only available as a reference if the pertinent disclosure is not the sole work of D. An applicant's own work, even though publicly disclosed prior to his application, may not be used against him as a reference, absent a time bar to his application. In spite of the fact that a completed invention requires both conception and reduction to practice, there is no requirement that the inventor be the one to reduce the invention to practice so long as reduction to practice is done on his behalf. *In re DeBaun,* 687 F.2d 459, 214 U.S.P.Q. 933 (C.C.P.A. 1982).

ω

The Court rejected the proposition that subject matter that is disclosed but not claimed is always deemed dedicated to the public. *YBM Magnex Inc. v. International Trade Commission,* 145 F.3d 1317, 46 U.S.P.Q.2d 1843, 1846 (Fed. Cir. 1998).

Discourage. *See* **Disadvantage, Lead Away From.**

Discovery. *See also* **Advice of Counsel, Document Request, Invention, Newly Discovered, Problem, 28 U.S.C. §1782.**

The statute (35 U.S.C. §24) manifests a clear congressional intent to make available to patent interference parties the broad discovery provisions of the Federal Rules of Civil Procedure. *In re Natta,* 388 F.2d 215, 156 U.S.P.Q. 289, 290 (C.C.P.A. 1968).

ω

Because the Patent Office Rules of Practice contain no pre-trial discovery provisions, parties in contested cases in the Patent Office who seek discovery must resort to the United States district courts under 35 U.S.C. §24. The jurisdiction over discovery granted by 35 U.S.C. §24 to the District Court in contested Patent Office matters is exclusive and ancillary to the principal proceeding before the Patent Office. *The Babcock & Wilcox Company v. Foster Wheeler Corporation,* 432 F.2d 385, 167 U.S.P.Q. 65, 66 (3rd Cir. 1970).

ω

Once the Patent Office properly determined that plaintiffs (in an interference) had not shown that discovery was necessary in order to present testimony before the Patent Office, plaintiffs were under an obligation, while they pursued their discovery in an ancillary proceeding, to proceed concurrently before the Patent Office with what evidence they had, or be precluded from presenting any evidence thereafter. *Vogel v. Jones,* 346 F.Supp. 1005, 175 U.S.P.Q. 152, 153 (D.C. 1972).

ω

An order pursuant to 35 U.S.C. §24 (1970), directing a deposition witness to produce certain documents and to testify with respect thereto in connection with a Patent Office interference proceeding, is not appealable. *Shattuck v. Hoegl,* 523 F.2d 509, 187 U.S.P.Q. 1, 2 (2d Cir. 1975).

ω

The discovery of a hitherto unknown property of a known compound does not necessarily constitute basis for claiming a new use. *In re May and Eddy,* 574 F.2d 1082, 197 U.S.P.Q. 601, 607 (C.C.P.A. 1978).

ω

Every discovery is not embraced within the statutory terms of 35 U.S.C. §101. Excluded from such patent protection are laws of nature, physical phenomena, and abstract ideas. A principle, in the abstract, is a fundamental truth, an original cause, a motive; these cannot be patented, and no one can claim in any of them an exclusive right. A new mineral discovered in the earth or a new plant found in the wild is not patentable subject matter. Likewise, Einstein could not patent his celebrated law that $E = mc^2$; nor could Newton have patented the law of gravity. Such discoveries are "manifestations of...nature, free to all men and reserved exclusively to none." *Diamond v. Diehr and Lutton,* 450 U.S. 175, 209 U.S.P.Q. 1, 7 (1981).

ω

An infringer should not be permitted to side step main issues by nit-picking the patent file in every minute respect with the effect of trying the patentee personally, rather than the patent. A patentee's oversights are easily magnified out of proportion by one accused of infringement seeking to escape the reach of the patent by hostilely combing the inventor's files in liberal pretrial discovery proceedings. *Preemption Devices, Inc. v. Minnesota Mining and Manufacturing Co.,* 559 F.Supp. 1250, 218 U.S.P.Q. 245, 257 (Pa. 1983).

ω

There is no absolute privilege for trade secrets and similar confidential information. To resist discovery under Rule 26(c)(7), a person must first establish that the information sought is a trade secret and then demonstrate that its disclosure might be harmful. If these requirements are met, the burden shifts to the party seeking discovery to establish that the disclosure of trade secrets is relevant and necessary to the action. The district court must balance the need for the trade secrets against the claim of injury resulting from disclosure. If proof of relevancy or need is not established, discovery should be denied. On the other hand, if relevancy and need are shown, the trade secrets should be disclosed, unless they are privileged or the subpoenas are unreasonable, oppressive, annoying, or embarrassing. *Heat & Control, Inc. v. Hector Industries, Inc.,* 785 F.2d 1017, 228 U.S.P.Q. 926 (Fed. Cir. 1986).

ω

A trade secret or other confidential research, development, or commercial information may be the subject of a protective order under Fed. R. Civ. P. 26(c)(7). One seeking a protective order under that rule must establish that the information sought is confidential. In support of its motion, Biomet submitted an affidavit explaining why the requested discovery contained "trade secrets and other confidential business information." To be a trade secret under Indiana law, information must be kept secret and must derive economic value from that secrecy. Biomet's affidavit specifies measures Biomet uses to keep secret the information sought and the value thereof as secrets. Having shown the information sought to be confidential, one seeking a protective order must then demonstrate that disclosure might be harmful. Courts have presumed that disclosure to a competitor is more harmful than disclosure to a noncompetitor. Where a party seeking a protective order has shown that the information sought is confidential and that its disclosure might be harmful, the burden shifts to the party seeking discovery to establish that disclosure of trade secrets and confidential information is relevant and necessary to its case. Rule 26(b)(1) allows discovery of any nonprivileged matter that is relevant to the subject matter involved in the pending action. The rule has boundaries, however. Discovery of matter not reasonably calculated to lead to the dlscovery of admissible evidence is outside its scope. *American Standard lnc. v. Pfizer Inc.*, 828 F.2d 734, 3 U.S.P.Q.2d 1817 (Fed. Cir. 1987).

ω

The defendant wanted to depose four former employees of the plaintiff who resided in Germany. The defendant asserted that the four were major participants in the invention of the drug whose patent is at issue in this case. The plaintiff notified the defendant that the four were no longer employed by the plaintiff and thus the plaintiff could not assert control over them to be deposed. The defendant demonstrated its need for deposing the inventors' testimony is logically relevant to the determination of the action. In addition to the relevance of their testimony, the four inventors had entered into a written assignment with the plaintiff that states in pertinent part, "we hereby agree, whenever requested, to . . . testify in any legal proceedings." The court interpreted this clause to mean that the four inventors agreed to testify in any real proceedings, not just those proceedings in which the plaintiff would like them to testify. As the plaintiff has come to a U.S. court, asserting a U.S. patent, the plaintiff must proceed according to the Federal Rules of Civil Procedure and must compel the inventors to testify in an American-style deposition. *In re Nifedipine Capsule Patents Litigation*, 13 U.S.P.Q.2d 1574, 1575 (N.Y. 1989).

ω

Discovery may not be had regarding a matter that is not "relevant to the subject matter involved in the pending action." Even if relevant, discovery is not permitted where no need is shown, or compliance would be unduly burdensome, or the harm to the person from whom discovery is sought outweighs the need of the person seeking discovery of the information. Rule 26(g) specifically requires that a party or attorney seeking discovery must certify that he has made a "reasonable inquiry" that the request is warranted. *Micro Motion Inc. v. Kane Steel Co.*, 894 F.2d 1318, 13 U.S.P.Q.2d 1696, 1699 (Fed. Cir. 1990).

ω

A litigant should not be able to parry a discovery thrust by anticipatory initial, skillful pleading when a counterclaim is filed that legitimately broadens the scope of the case. *Golden Valley Microwave Foods Inc. v. Weaver Popcorn Co.*, 130 F.R.D. 92, 13 U.S.P.Q.2d 2054, 2057 (Ind. 1990).

ω

An order denying or granting discovery is ordinarily not appealable. However, an order denying discovery of a nonparty, issued by a court ancillary to a pending action, is final and appealable. *Katz v. Batavia Marine & Sporting Supplies Inc.*, 984 F.2d 422, 25 U.S.P.Q.2d 1547, 1548 (Fed. Cir. 1993).

ω

A litigant requesting assistance under 28 U.S.C. §1782 has to show that the information sought in the United States would be discoverable under foreign law. *In re Asta Medica S.A.*, 981 F.2d 1, 25 U.S.P.Q.2d 1861, 1866 (1st Cir. 1992).

ω

In discovery disputes sanctions under Rules 26 and 37 are preferable, and sanctions under Rule 11 are no longer allowed. *Tec-Air Inc. v. Nippondenso Manufacturing USA Inc.*, 33 U.S.P.Q.2d 1451, 1457 (Ill. 1994).

ω

"When a party pursues discovery outside the jurisdiction in which its suit is pending, the jurisdiction of the local district court may be invoked to rule on discovery issues in an ancillary proceeding." *Chiron Corp. v. Abbott Laboratories*, 34 U.S.P.Q.2d 1413, 1414 (Pa. 1994).

ω

A patent infringement plaintiff bears a significant pre-filing investigation burden before asserting a patent claim, and such burden cannot be fulfilled by merely filing suit on a suspicion of infringement and then asking for discovery to prove up the suspicions. "To fulfill his duty, an attorney must investigate the fact, examine the law, and then decide whether the Complaint is justified." *Nasatka v. Delta Scientific Corp.*, 34 U.S.P.Q.2d 1649, 1652 (Va. 1994).

ω

Plaintiff is entitled to discovery of documents which pertain to defendant's activities in the state for the purpose of establishing the court's jurisdiction over the defendant. Information regarding defendant's contacts with the state, including its volume of sales and the number of its customers and distributors, is relevant to the issue of personal jurisdiction. *Oregon Precision Industries Inc. v. International Omni-Pac Corp.*, 160 F.R.D. 592, 36 U.S.P.Q.2d 1117, 1119 (Or. 1995).

ω

When there are foreign legal barriers to the production of documents, the courts in the United States must balance the interests and needs of the parties in light of the nature of the foreign laws and the party's efforts to comply in good faith with the demanded production. When two nations have jurisdiction to prescribe and enforce national rules of law that are inconsistent, each nation is required by international law to consider, in good faith, moderating the exercise of its enforcement jurisdiction in light of the law of the other nation. In considering whether to sanction non-production, a court must seek a fair balance of the interests and litigation needs of the parties, without doing violence to constitutional due process. *Cochran Consulting Inc. v. Uwatec USA Inc.*, 41 U.S.P.Q.2d 1161 (Fed. Cir. 1996).

Discredit.

If the Patent Office wishes to discredit expert or lay testimony, the obvious method would be to provide witnesses, rather than merely characterizing the testimony as self-serving. *General Radio Company v. Watson*, 188 F.Supp. 879, 125 U.S.P.Q. 268, 274 (D.C. 1960).

Discretion.

Much of the information passing from client to attorney for purposes of preparation of a patent application is technical material relating to the description of the products and/or processes sought to be patented, explanations of prior art, public use and sale, and samples of the product. So also in connection with the examination, there is no room for game playing or withholding. The attorney exercises no discretion as to what portion of this information must be relayed to the Patent Office. He must turn all such factual information over in full to the Patent Office pursuant to 35 U.S.C. §112; with respect to such material he acts as a conduit between his client and the Patent Office. *Jack Winter, Inc. v. Koratron Company, Inc.*, 50 F.R.D. 225, 166 U.S.P.Q. 295, 297 (Cal. 1970).

Discretionary Ruling.

A discretionary ruling will not be upheld if the trial court's decision is based upon findings of fact that are clearly erroneous, or a misapplication or misinterpretation of law, or if the ruling evidences a clear error of judgment. *Therma-Tru Corp. v. Peachtree Doors Inc.*, 44 F.3d 988, 33 U.S.P.Q.2d 1274, 1279 (Fed. Cir. 1995).

Discriminatory. *See* Discriminatory Licensing.

Discriminatory Licensing.

In order to sustain a finding of patent misuse or a Sherman Act violation based on discriminatory licensing, at least the following must be present: (a) the plaintiff took a license; (b) the royalty rate charged the plaintiff and that charged a competitor were unequal; (c) in all particulars relevant to equality of rates the plaintiff and its licensed competitor were similarly situated; and (d) the royalties were an important expense factor in production costs and the discriminatory rate caused substantial impairment of competition in the relevant market. *Honeywell Inc. v. Sperry Rand Corp.*, 180 U.S.P.Q. 673, 723 (Minn. 1973).

Disgorgement.

The statute that limits recovery in cases where there is no marking refers only to damages. Historically, disgorgement, which is really what the plaintiff seeks in its actions for infringers' profits, was not considered a recovery of damages, but an equitable remedy to restore to the proper owner profits made by an infringer's use of another's property. The limitations imposed by 35 U.S.C. §287(a) are not applicable to an action seeking recovery of an infringer's profits pursuant to 35 U.S.C. §289. *Nike Inc. v. Wal-Mart Stores Inc.*, 41 U.S.P.Q.2d 1146 (Va. 1996).

Dismiss. *See* Motion to Dismiss.

Dismissal. *See also* Rule 12(b)(6).

The authority of a court to dismiss *sua sponte* for lack of prosecution has generally been considered an "inherent power," governed not by rule or statute but by the control necessarily vested in courts to manage their own affairs so as to achieve the orderly and expeditious disposition of cases. *Link v. Wabash R.R.*, 370 U.S. 626, 630, 631 (1962).

ᴥ

[Dismissal with prejudice] must be available to the district court in appropriate cases, not only to penalize those whose conduct may be deemed to warrant such a sanction, but to deter those who might be tempted to such conduct in the absence of such a deterrent. Dismissal review must be for an abuse of discretion. *National Hockey League v. Metropolitan Hockey Club, Inc.*, 427 U.S. 639, 642, 643 (1976).

ᴥ

When a defendant's counterclaim has a jurisdictional basis independent of the main action, the provision of Fed. R. Civ. P. 41(a)(2) relating to counterclaims does not bar dismissing plaintiff's complaint or require dismissal of defendant's counterclaim. *Farmaceutisk Laboratorium Ferring A/S v. Reid Rowell Inc.*, 20 U.S.P.Q.2d 1476, 1478 (Ga. 1991).

ᴥ

Federal Circuit law governs review of decision to dismiss infringement suit based solely on existence of pending interference when justiciability of controversy is not in question. *Cedars-Sinai Medical Center v. Watkins*, 11 F.3d 1573, 29 U.S.P.Q.2d 1188, 1194 (Fed. Cir. 1993).

ᴥ

Dismissal, while a sanction the district court may properly impose, is "draconian" and "must be infrequently resorted to by the district courts." In general, dismissal is such a serious sanction it should not be invoked without first considering the effect the improper conduct had on the course of the litigation. *Tec-Air Inc. v. Nippondenso Manufacturing USA Inc.*, 33 U.S.P.Q.2d 1451, 1452 (Ill. 1994).

ᴥ

"[D]ismissal of a plaintiff's suit with prejudice is tantamount to a judgment on the merits for the defendants, thereby rendering them the prevailing parties." The issue of costs is in the discretion of the trial court, but "as prevailing parties, defendants enjoy a strong presumption that they will be awarded costs." *Super Sack Manufacturing Corp. v. Chase Packaging Corp.*, 37 U.S.P.Q.2d 1394, 1395 (Tex. 1995).

ᴥ

"It is not a bar to dismissal that plaintiff may obtain some tactical advantage thereby." *Carey Crutcher Inc. v. Cameron Equipment Co.*, 37 U.S.P.Q.2d 1479, 1480 (Tex. 1995).

ᴥ

A dismissal by the Court *sua sponte* under Rule 41(b) for failure to prosecute operates as an adjudication on the merits, and such a dismissal is with prejudice. *Hoffman v. Wisner Classic Manufacturing Co. Inc.*, 40 U.S.P.Q.2d 1271, 1274 (N.Y. 1996).

ᴥ

Before the sanction of dismissal can be imposed, the defending party must have notice of the alleged discovery misconduct and be given an opportunity to comply. The sanction of dismissal is ordinarily only "applied in those cases where a party is explicitly ordered by the court to provide discovery but the party fails to respond in a proper or timely manner." *Genentech Inc. v. U.S. International Trade Commission*, 122 F.3d 1409, 43 U.S.P.Q.2d 1722, 1733 (Fed. Cir. 1997).

ω

The dismissal of a claim under Rule 12(b)(6) is proper only when, on the complainant's version of the facts, the premises of a cognizable claim have not been stated. An appellate court, like a district court, tests the sufficiency of a complaint as a matter of law, accepting as true all well-pleaded allegations of fact, construed in the light most favorable to the plaintiff. *Bradley v. Chiron*, 136 F.3d 1317, 45 U.S.P.Q.2d 1819, 1821 (Fed. Cir. 1998).

ω

"The practical importance of the distinction between the two kinds of dismissals is that if the federal claim is substantial enough to invoke federal jurisdiction, the court has power to exercise pendent [now supplemental] jurisdiction over other claims that also may be asserted in the complaint, for which there is no independent jurisdictional basis." *Hunter Douglas Inc. v. Harmonic Design Inc.*, 962 F.Supp 1249, 47 U.S.P.Q.2d 1769, 1775 (Fed. Cir. 1998).

Dispute.

A dispute is genuine for the purposes of summary judgment if a reasonable jury could return a verdict for the non-moving party. *Anderson v. Liberty Lobby, Inc.*, 477 U.S. 242, 248 (1986).

Disqualification.[6] *See also* **Peripheral Representation.**

A motion for disqualification of opponent's counsel because an attorney on such counsel's staff formerly represented the movant can be overcome. The presumption of shared confidences may be rebutted by evidence showing that confidences have not been shared or that timely established institutional screening procedures have been implemented. *Cox v. American Cast Iron Pipe Co.*, 847 F.2d 725, 732 (11th Cir. 1988); *Manning v. Waring, Cox, James, Sklar, and Allen*, 849 F.2d 222, 225-26 (6th Cir. 1988); *Schiessle v. Stephens*, 717 F.2d 417, 420-21 (7th Cir. 1983); *See United States v. Titan Pacific Construction Corp.*, 637 F. Supp. 1556, 1564-55 (Wash. 1986); *Haagen-Dazs Co. v. Perche Nol Gelato, Inc.*, 639 F. Supp. 282, 287 (Cal. 1986).

ω

In enacting 28 U.S.C. §455(a), Congress created an objective standard under which disqualification of a judge is required when a reasonable person, knowing all the facts, would question the judge's impartiality. The test for disqualification under §455(a) is an objective one: whether a reasonable person with knowledge of all the facts would conclude

---

[6] Under New Jersey Rules of Professional Conduct, see *Ciba-Geigy Corp. v. Alza Corp.*, 795 F.Supp. 711, 23 U.S.P.Q.2d 1932 (N.J. 1992).

that the judge's impartiality might reasonably be questioned. *Hewlett-Packard Co. v. Bausch & Lomb Inc.*, 882 F.2d 1556, 11 U.S.P.Q.2d 1750, 1760 (Fed. Cir. 1989).

ʊ

In a case involving disqualification of an expert witness where the parties dispute whether earlier retention and passage of confidential information occurred, a court should undertake a two-step inquiry:

a. Was it objectively reasonable for the first party who claims to have retained the consultant to conclude that a confidential relationship existed?
b. Was any confidential or privileged information disclosed by the first party to the consultant?

Affirmative answers to both inquiries compel disqualification, but disqualification is likely to be inappropriate if either inquiry yields a negative response. *Wang Laboratories Inc. v. Toshiba Corp.*, 762 F. Supp. 1246, 19 U.S.P.Q.2d 1779, 1781 (Va. 1991).

ʊ

A trial attorney's disqualification is in order when he is called upon by opposing counsel to testify in involved litigation and his projected testimony is sufficiently adverse to the factual assertions or account of events offered on behalf of his client. *Summagraphics Corp. v. Sanders Associates Inc.*, 19 U.S.P.Q.2d 1859, 1860, 1861 (Conn. 1991).

ʊ

A court's ultimate objective in weighing disqualification questions is to ensure that the balance of presentations in a litigation will not be tainted by improper disclosures...Courts have been directed to take a "restrained approach that focuses primarily on preserving the integrity of the trial process." A party seeking disqualification must meet a high standard of proof before disqualification will be granted. Although a party seeking disqualification of an attorney on the basis of the substantial relationship test is not required to present evidence that the attorney possesses actual confidences as a result of the prior representation, the Court has discretion to consider evidence proving either that confidences were or were not communicated in the prior representation and to do so in a manner designed to protect confidential evidence from disclosure. "In order for the traditional rule of per se disqualification to be converted from an irrebuttable presumption to a rebuttable one there must be a confluence of three factors: (1) That the involvement of the 'tainted' attorney or law firm in the prior representation giving rise to the conflict must have been miniscule; (2) that the 'tainted' attorney is no longer connected with the law firm seeking to avoid disqualification; and (3) that the configuration of the law firm seeking to avoid disqualification, and the nature of its work, is such that its attorneys are not so intimately acquainted with all the work in the office that they could be expected to share client confidences and ideas about how to handle client problems as a matter of course, but large enough and so segregated into departments that it would be reasonable to assume that the attorneys of the firm as a whole would not necessarily become aware of every client of the firm and share in all of the client confidences and secrets which the firm, as a whole, possessed." *Decora Inc. v. DW Wallcovering Inc.*, 38 U.S.P.Q.2d 1188, 1190, 1193, 1194 (N.Y. 1995).

ʊ

A two-step inquiry in resolving motions to disqualify an expert based on a prior relationship with a party:

1. courts consider whether it was objectively reasonable for the first party to believe that a confidential relationship existed;
2. courts determine whether the first party actually disclosed confidential information to the expert.

In these inquiries, the burden is on the party seeking disqualification to establish the existence of confidentiality and its non-waiver. *Advanced Cardiovascular Systems Inc. v. Medtronic Inc.*, 47 U.S.P.Q.2d 1536, 1537 (Cal. 1998).

Distinct.

Inventions are not "separate" when they differ from each other merely in the scope of claims to the same or equivalent subject matter. *Ex parte Sachs*, 9 U.S.P.Q. 446, 449 (PO Bd. App. 1931).

ϖ

When an Examiner designated an adverse decision as a "withdrawal" of a claim from further consideration, it was "in fact a rejection of that claim on the ground that it encompasses independent and distinct inventions." *Rohm and Haas Company v. Gottschalk*, 504 F.2d 259, 183 U.S.P.Q. 257 (DC 1974).

Distinctly Claim. *See also* Particularity, 35 U.S.C. §112

"The object of the patent law in requiring the patentee [to distinctly claim his invention] is not only to secure to him all to which he is entitled, but to apprise the public as to what is still open to them." *Athletic Alternatives Inc. v. Prince Manufacturing Inc.*, 73 F.3d 1573, 37 U.S.P.Q.2d 1365, 1372 (Fed. Cir. 1996).

Distinctness. *See* Inoperative.

Distributor.

The Federal Circuit has addressed the propriety of an exclusive U.S. distributor joining as a coplaintiff and sharing in damages and injunctive relief with the patent owner. *ALM Surgical Equipment Inc. v. Kirschner Medical Corp.*, 15 U.S.P.Q.2d 1241, 1253 (S.C. 1990).

ϖ

The appointment of a distributor to sell a product covered by a patent is analogous to a grant of a patent license. Such an action conveys an implied license to the distributor, thereby surrendering the patentee's right to exclude the distributor under the patent. *Genetic Implant Systems Inc. v. Core-Vent Corp.*, 123 F.3d 1455, 43 U.S.P.Q.2d 1786, 1789 (Fed. Cir. 1997).

Diverse. *See* **Multiple Utilities.**

Divided. *See* **Separable.**

Dividing Markets. *See also* **Geographical Limitation, Geographic Restriction.**

Foreign licenses, which forbid exportation to the United States by foreign manufacturers of patented products, do not constitute an illegal division of world markets. *The Dunlop Company, Limited v. Kelsey-Hayes Company*, 484 F.2d 407, 179 U.S.P.Q. 129, 136 (6th Cir. 1973).

ω

The division of markets through a "field of use" limitation is perfectly acceptable. An invention may have application in more than one field or industry. A patent owner may limit an assignment or license on lines drawn according to field of use or to sales area, such as industrial area vs. retail area. *In re Reclosable Plastic Bags*, 192 U.S.P.Q. 674, 679 (U.S. ITC 1977).

ω

A patent licensor's use of geographic restrictions in a sublicensing scheme to divide territories to ones of primary or exclusive jurisdiction constitutes a lawful application of the rights derived from a patent grant. 35 U.S.C. §261 immunizes from antitrust analysis an allocation of territories created by a patentee's use of exclusive licenses. *Miller Insituform, Inc. v. Insituform of North America, Inc.*, 605 F.Supp. 1125, 225 U.S.P.Q. 1232, 1235 (Tenn. 1985).

Division. *See also* **Design Application, Restriction.**

A division or divisional application is an application that is filed during the pendency of an application filed earlier by the same inventor (i.e., the parent application) and that discloses and claims only subject matter disclosed in the parent application. A divisional application claims a distinct, separate, and independent invention carved out of its parent application and the invention claimed therein. A claim in a divisional application is entitled to the effective filing date of the parent application that supports such claim. *Rohm & Haas Co. v. Dawson Chemical Co., Inc.*, 557 F. Supp. 739, 217 U.S.P.Q. 515, 535 (Tex. 1983).

Divisional Doctrine.

Where applicant responds to a restriction requirement by canceling claims to a nonelected invention, and then fails to file a divisional application with the canceled claims, the applicant is deemed to have acquiesced to the restriction and is estopped from obtaining the subject matter of the canceled claims by reissue. This "divisional doctrine" has been strictly construed against reissue applicants claiming "error" in failing to file a divisional application after a restriction requirement. *In re Swartzel*, 60 F.3d 843, 36 U.S.P.Q.2d 1510, 1512 (Fed. Cir. 1995).

Division of Markets.

It is well-settled law that the division of markets through a field-of-use limitation is perfectly acceptable. An invention may have applications in more than one field or industry. A patent owner may limit an assignment or license on lines drawn according to field of use. *In re Reclosable Plastic Bags*, 192 U.S.P.Q. 674, 679 (U.S. Intl. Trade Comm'n 1977).

Division of Territory. *See* **Dividing Markets, Geographic Restriction.**

DNA.

Conception of a DNA requires a precise definition, such as by structure, formula, chemical name, or definitive chemical or physical properties. A description also requires that degree of specificity. *Fiers v. Sugano*, 984 F.2d 1164, 25 U.S.P.Q.2d 1601, 1605 (Fed. Cir. 1993).

ω

Complementary DNA ("cDNA") is a complementary copy ("clone") of mRNA, made in the laboratory by reverse transcription of mRNA. The PTO improperly rejected compound claims based on alleged obviousness of a method of making molecules having the claimed DNA sequence. Knowledge of a protein does not give one a conception of a particular DNA encoding it. *In re Deuel*, 51 F.3d 1552, 34 U.S.P.Q.2d 1210, 1211, 1214, 1215 (Fed. Cir. 1995).

ω

Although a close relationship exists between a DNA construct and the protein it encodes, the two are not equal. The count specifically defines a DNA construct, not the protein that is produced by expression from the construct. The specific elements enumerated in the count that necessarily must be included in any DNA construct within the count are a DNA sequence coding for the secretory leader, a processing signal sequence, and a human IGF-I. *Genentech Inc. v. Chiron Corp.*, 112 F.3d 495, 42 U.S.P.Q.2d 1608, 1613 (Fed. Cir. 1997).

ω

An adequate written description of a DNA "requires a precise definition, such as by structure, formula, chemical name, or physical properties," not a mere wish or plan for obtaining the claimed chemical invention. Accordingly, "an adequate written description of a DNA requires more than a mere statement that it is part of the invention and reference to a potential method for isolating it; what is required is a description of the DNA itself." *University of California v. Eli Lilly and Co.*, 119 F.3d 1559, 43 U.S.P.Q.2d 1398, 1404 (Fed. Cir. 1997).

Docketing Errors.

While a reasonable misinterpretation of a regulation may be the basis for a holding of unavoidable delay, misapplication or total ignorance of a rule may not. In order to be entitled to relief under 35 U.S.C. §305 and §133 on the ground of alleged docketing errors, petitioner must show (1) that counsel was justified on relying on the docketing system, i.e., that the docketing system was highly reliable, and (2) that the docketing errors were the cause of the belated response. *In re Egbers,* 6 U.S.P.Q.2d 1869 (Comm'r Patents & Trademarks 1988).

Docket Number. *See also* **Attorney's Docket Number.**

All claims were finally rejected under 35 U.S.C. §132 because of the new matter introduced into the application (filling in the serial number and filing date of the two applications referred to on page 1 of the original specification). The Board's acceptance of the identification of the copending applications as adequate under all the circumstances of the subject appeal is not a suggestion that more definite identification would not be desirable. An attorney would be well advised to utilize such means of identification (as reference in the application as filed) as the attorney's docket number and the fact that the applications have the same filing date, if that is a fact, as it is here. *Ex parte Harvey,* 163 U.S.P.Q. 572, 573 (PTO Bd. App. 1968).

Doctoral Thesis. *See also* **Thesis.**

A doctoral thesis is a printed publication when deposited and catalogued in a public library. *In re Hall,* 781 F.2d 897, 228 U.S.P.Q. 453 (Fed. Cir. 1986).

Doctrine. *See* **Anticipation, Batchelder Doctrine, Blonder Tongue Doctrine, Borcherdt Doctrine, Claim Differentiation, Collateral Order Doctrine, Continuity, Divisional Doctrine, Double Patenting, Equivalents, Exhaustion Doctrine, Experimental Use, File Wrapper Estoppel, Inherency, Interlocutory Order, Intervening Rights, Inverse Doctrine of Equivalents, Issue Preclusion, Judicial Estoppel, Law-of-the-Case Doctrine, Markush, Misuse, Noerr-Pennington Doctrine, Phair Doctrine, Prosecution History Estoppel, Reverse Doctrine of Equivalents, Simultaneous Conception and Reduction to Practice, Thuau Doctrine, Unjust Enrichment, Von Bramer Doctrine, Work Product Doctrine.**

Doctrine of Equivalents. *See also* **Appropriation, Designing Around, Equivalency, Equivalent, Equivalents, File Wrapper Estoppel, Gist, Reliance, Reverse Doctrine of Equivalents, Substantial Equivalency, Unclaimed Disclosure.**

To temper unsparing logic and prevent an infringer from stealing the benefit of an invention, a patentee may invoke the doctrine of equivalents to proceed against the producer of a device if it performs substantially the same function in substantially the same way to obtain the same result. The theory on which this doctrine is founded is that if two devices do the same work in substantially the same way, and accomplish substantially the same result, they are the same, even though they differ in name, form, or shape. *Graver Tank & Manufacturing Co. v. The Linde Air Products Company,* 339 U. S. 605, 85 U.S.P.Q. 328 (1950).

ᴨ

In its early development, the doctrine of equivalents generally was applied in cases involving the equivalence of devices having mechanical components. Today, however, the same principles are applied to compositions of matter where there is equivalence between chemical ingredients. *Ziegler v. Phillips Petroleum Co.*, 483 F.2d 858, 177 U.S.P.Q. 481, 487 (5th Cir. 1973).

ω

The doctrine of equivalents allows a finding of infringement when an accused product and claimed invention perform substantially the same function in substantially the same way to yield substantially the same result. Where defendant has appropriated the material features of the patent in suit, infringement will be found even when those features have been supplemented and modified to such an extent that the defendant may be entitled to a patent for the improvement. It is not a requirement of equivalents that those skilled in the art know of the equivalence when the patent application is filed or the patent issues. *Atlas Powder Co. v. E.I. du Pont de Nemours & Co.*, 750 F.2d 1569, 224 U.S.P.Q. 409 (Fed. Cir. 1984).

ω

Even when an estoppel arises from the file, the doctrine of equivalents is not completely eliminated. Depending on the nature and the purpose of an amendment, it may have a limited effect ranging from great to small to zero. The effect may or may not be fatal to application of a range of equivalents broad enough to encompass a particular accused product. It is not fatal to application of the doctrine of equivalents itself. Whenever the doctrine of file history estoppel is invoked, a close examination must be made as to, not only what was surrendered, but also the reason for such a surrender. The fact that claims were narrowed does not always mean that the doctrine of file history estoppel completely prohibits a patentee from recapturing some of what was originally claimed. *Glaros v. H. H. Robertson Co.*, 615 F. Supp. 186, 227 U.S.P.Q. 448 (Ill. 1985).

ω

The claimed composition rapidly cures at room temperature, whereas the accused counterpart rapidly cures only at 90°C. It was precisely because of that difference that the district court found that the claimed invention and the accused counterpart do not perform in substantially the same way. That finding, however, would allow the difference itself to dictate a finding of no equivalents; if that were the law, one could never infringe by equivalents. The analysis must go further, and the question the district court should consider on remand is this: Given the difference, would the accused composition at 90°C and the claimed invention at room temperature perform substantially the same function (e.g., filling the pores of the treated material with solid material) in substantially the same way (e.g., by rapidly curing in the absence but not in the presence of oxygen) to give substantially the same results (e.g., a filled material). There are limitations to the doctrine of equivalents. The doctrine has been judicially devised to do equity in situations where there is no literal infringement but liability is nevertheless appropriate to prevent what is in essence a pirating of the patentee's invention. Concomitently, two policy-oriented limitations, applied as questions of law, have developed. First, the doctrine will not extend to an infringing device within the public domain, i.e., found in the prior art at the time the patent issued; second, the prosecution history estoppel will not allow the patentee to recapture through equivalents certain coverage given up during prosecution. *Loctite Corp. v. Ultraseal Ltd.*, 781 F.2d 861, 228 U.S.P.Q. 90 (Fed. Cir. 1985).

ω

Under the doctrine of equivalents infringement may be found if an accused device performs substantially the same overall function or work, in substantially the same way, to obtain substantially the same overall result as the claimed invention. *Pennwalt Corp. v. Durand-Weyland Inc.*, 833 F.2d 931, 4 U.S.P.Q.2d 1737 (Fed. Cir. 1987).

᜶

A patentee is not barred by file wrapper estoppel from asserting the doctrine of equivalents because the claims in suit were amended by insertion of the "consisting essentially of" language. The fact that claims are narrowed does not always mean that the doctrine of file history estoppel completely prohibits a patentee from recapturing some of what was originally claimed. *Syntex (U.S.A.) Inc. v. Paragon Optical Inc.*, 7 U.S.P.Q.2d 1001 (Ariz. 1987).

᜶

The purpose of the doctrine of equivalents is to protect a patented invention from circumvention by minor changes or deviations. To restrict protection to devices that literally duplicate would render the patent law a "hollow and useless thing." Its essence being to prevent a fraud on the patent, the scope of the doctrine should be viewed in that spirit. As a wide-angle abstraction, the idea of equivalency could be subject to abuse by either a litigious patentee or a duplicitous infringer. What constitutes equivalence must therefore depend on the contextual setting involved and should not be a prisoner to formula. There is equivalence if the accused device "performs substantially the same function in substantially the same way to obtain the same result." This is the function-means-and-result test. A fact finder cannot properly make a determination of equivalence "absent evidence and argument concerning the doctrine and each of its elements." The patentee has the burden to prove infringement. To do so under the doctrine of equivalence requires a showing that all three components of the equivalency test are met. A jury must be separately directed to the proof of each component. A jury cannot make a factual finding of equivalence without particularized testimony and linking argument. *Malta v. Schulmerich Carillons Inc.*, 13 U.S.P.Q.2d 1900, 1902 (Pa. 1989).

᜶

A patentee should not be able to obtain, under the doctrine of equivalents, coverage that he could not lawfully have obtained from the PTO by literal claims. The doctrine of equivalents exists to prevent a fraud on a patent, not to give a patentee something he could not have lawfully obtained from the PTO had he tried. Since prior art always limits what an inventor could have claimed, it limits the range of permissible equivalents of a claim. *Wilson Sporting Goods Co. v. David Geoffrey & Associates*, 904 F.2d 676, 14 U.S.P.Q.2d 1942, 1948 (Fed. Cir. 1990).

᜶

Only when a substantial change has not been made should an accused infringer be liable for improperly trying to appropriate a claimed invention. *Slimfold Manufacturing v. Kinkead Industries*, 932 F.2d 1453, 18 U.S.P.Q. 1842 (Fed. Cir. 1991).

᜶

In applying the doctrine of equivalents, a district court should also ensure that the range of equivalents sought by the patentee does not "ensnare the prior art." *The Conair*

Group Inc. v. Automatik Apparate-Maschinenbau GmbH, 944 F.2d 862, 20 U.S.P.Q.2d 1067, 1071 (Fed. Cir. 1991).

ᚹ

While comparison of function/way/result is an acceptable way of showing that structure in an accused device is the "substantial equivalent" of a claim limitation, it is not the only way to do so. Under general principles of appellate review a trial court's decision with regard to the doctrine of equivalents should not be disturbed unless clearly erroneous. *Malta v. Schulmerich Carillons Inc.*, 952 F.2d 1320, 21 U.S.P.Q.2d 1161, 1165, 1167 (Fed. Cir. 1991).

ᚹ

Other than the legal conclusion that defendant's product performs the same function as plaintiff's product, performs that function in the same way, and produces substantially the same results, the presented affidavit provides only obvious and undisputed statements of fact, or factual assertions with no explanation of their significance. The statement that defendant's product meets the legal definition of an infringing product under the doctrine of equivalents, offered without underlying factual support, is insufficient to raise a dispute of material fact for summary judgment purposes. *Ciba-Geigy Corp. v. Crompton & Knowles Corp.*, 22 U.S.P.Q.2d 1761, 1766 (Pa. 1991).

ᚹ

The doctrine of equivalents must be narrowly applied in crowded art fields of invention. *Transco Products Inc. v. Performance Contracting Inc.*, 792 F.Supp. 594, 23 U.S.P.Q.2d 1691, 1697 (Ill. 1992).

ᚹ

The doctrine of equivalents "does not mean one can ignore claim limitations." Rather, the doctrine "is designed to do equity...it is not designed...to permit a claim expansion that would encompass more than an insubstantial change." *Valmont Industries Inc. v. Reinke Manufacturing Co. Inc.*, 983 F.2d 1039, 25 U.S.P.Q.2d 1451, 1454 (Fed. Cir. 1993).

ᚹ

Infringement under the doctrine of equivalents has been "judicially devised to do equity" in situations where there is no literal infringement, but liability is nevertheless appropriate to prevent what is in essence a pirating of the patentee's invention. *Texas Instruments Inc. v. International Trade Commission*, 988 F.2d 1165, 26 U.S.P.Q.2d 1018, 1024 (Fed. Cir. 1993).

ᚹ

The doctrine of equivalents "does not mean one can ignore claim limitations." Infringement cannot be established unless every limitation of a claim is satisfied either exactly or by an equivalent in the accused device. *Carroll Touch Inc. v. Electro Mechanical Systems Inc.*, 3 F.3d 404, 27 U.S.P.Q.2d 1836, 1841 (Fed. Cir. 1993).

ᚹ

Prior art and prosecution history estoppel are separate and distinct limitations on the doctrine of equivalents. The limits imposed by prosecution history estoppel can be, and frequently are, broader than those imposed by the prior art. *Haynes International Inc. v. Jessop Steel Co.*, 8 F.3d 1573, 28 U.S.P.Q.2d 1652, 1656, 1657 (Fed. Cir. 1993).

ꟷ

Application of the doctrine of equivalents is the exception . . . not the rule, for if the public comes to believe (or fear) that the language of patent claims can never be relied on, and that the doctrine of equivalents is merely the second prong of every infringement charge, regularly available to extend protection beyond the scope of the claims, then claims will cease to serve their intended purpose. Competitors will never know whether their actions infringe a granted patent. The breadth of the doctrine also varies with the type of invention that has been patented. The "inventor is entitled to a range of equivalents commensurate with the scope of his invention: broad if his invention is broad; narrow if his advance is a small one in a crowded field." The doctrine of equivalents (if applied too broadly) can eviscerate both the claiming system and the goal of providing notice to the public of the scope of a patent. When a new invention is clearly outside of the literal language of a patent's claims, a court should not send the issue of infringement to a fact finder. *Schneider (USA) Inc. v. Cordis Corp.*, 29 U.S.P.Q.2d 1072, 1074, 1076 (Minn. 1993).

ꟷ

There can be a finding of infringement of means-plus-function claims under the doctrine of equivalents even though plaintiff's witnesses failed to testify in terms of the tripartite test. As the case was not tried to a jury, the court (having become familiar with doctrine of equivalents jurisprudence) can base its conclusions on the function/way/result of the claimed invention and the accused devices. *Zygo Corp. v. Wyko Corp.*, 29 U.S.P.Q.2d 1161, 1173 (Ariz. 1993).

ꟷ

A two-prong test for determining whether the Seventh Amendment provides a party the right to a jury trial is: a) a court must examine the case to see if it would have arisen in law or equity in 1791 when the Seventh Amendment was adopted; and b) more importantly, a court must look at the relief requested to see if it is legal or equitable. An action for infringement under the doctrine of equivalents is one that arises in equity. Therefore, no right to a jury attaches. Any reliance placed upon the factual nature of the inquiry in determining infringement by the equivalents as providing a jury trial right is misplaced. *Transmatic Inc. v. Gulton Industries Inc.*, 835 F.Supp. 1026, 29 U.S.P.Q.2d 1541, 1542, 1543, 1545 (Mich. 1993).

ꟷ

Under the doctrine of equivalents, an accused compound can be held to infringe if, *inter alia*, it represents only an insubstantial change from the claimed compound. *Genentech Inc. v. The Wellcome Foundation Ltd.*, 29 F.3d 1555, 31 U.S.P.Q.2d 1161, 1172, *concurring opinion* (Fed. Cir. 1994).

ꟷ

Although the jury found that the function/way/result test was satisfied, that factual finding alone does not require equitable intervention. Nothing in *Graver Tank* states that mere satisfaction of the tripartite test itself establishes infringement by equivalence.

Plaintiff's and defendants' devices were developed through independent research. The accused combination is significantly different than the claimed device, even though a physician might use the two instruments to perform the same function in the same way to obtain the same result. *Beraha v. C.R. Bard Inc.*, 32 U.S.P.Q.2d 1040, 1044 (Ga. 1994).

ᚐ

Paragraph 6 of 35 U.S.C. §112 and the doctrine of equivalents have separate origins and purposes. Section 112, paragraph 6, limits the broad language of means-plus-function limitations in combination claims to equivalents of the structures, materials, or acts in the specification. The doctrine of equivalents equitably expands exclusive patent rights. *Endress + Hauser Inc. v. Hawk Measurement Systems Pty. Ltd.*, 32 U.S.P.Q.2d 1768, 1775 n.3 (Ind. 1994).

ᚐ

The specific issue which a court must address in determining the existence of equivalents is whether the patentee has proved that a hypothetical claim, similar to a claim issued in his behalf, but broad enough to cover the alleged infringer's device literally, would have been patentable. *Ramos v. Boehringer Manheim Corp.*, 861 F.Supp. 1064, 33 U.S.P.Q.2d 1172, 1182 (Fla. 1994).

ᚐ

"Application of the doctrine of equivalents is the exception, ... not the rule." Overzealous application of the doctrine is problematic and must be avoided as, otherwise, "[c]ompetitors will never know whether their actions infringe a granted patent." *Gussin v. Nintendo of America Inc.*, 33 U.S.P.Q.2d 1418, 1419, 1427 (Cal. 1994).

ᚐ

"Application of the doctrine of equivalents is the exception, not the rule; it is not intended to be simply a second prong of every infringement analysis." *Davies v. U.S.*, 31 Fed.Cl. 769, 35 U.S.P.Q.2d 1027, 1035 (U.S. Ct. Fed. Cl. 1994).

ᚐ

The application of the doctrine of equivalents rests on the substantiality of the differences between the claimed and accused products or processes, assessed according to an objective standard. Evidence beyond the triple identity test of function, way, and result is also relevant to the doctrine of equivalents. The test is objective, with proof of the substantiality of the differences resting on objective evidence rather than unexplained subjective conclusions, whether offered by an expert witness or otherwise. Evidence of copying is relevant to infringement under the doctrine of equivalents. Evidence of designing around weighs against finding infringement under the doctrine of equivalents. Evidence of independent development is highly relevant to refute a patent owner's contention that the doctrine of equivalents applies because the accused infringer copied (intentially appropriated) the substance of the claimed invention. Infringement, whether literal or under the doctrine of equivalents, is a question of fact. "Patentees ... are entitled in all cases to invoke to some extent the doctrine of equivalents ...." A finding of infringement under the doctrine of equivalents requires proof of insubstantial differences between the claimed and accused products or processes. A trial judge does not have discretion to choose whether to apply the doctrine of equivalents when the record shows no literal infringement. "Whenever prosecution history estoppel is invoked as a limitation to infringement under the doctrine of equivalents, 'a close examination must be made as to, not only what was surrendered, but also the reason for such a surrender.'" *Hilton Davis Chemical Co. v. Warner-Jenkinson Co. Inc.*, 62 F.3d 1572, 35 U.S.P.Q.2d 1641, 1645-48, 1651 (Fed. Cir. 1995).

ϖ

The doctrine serves to guard against "fraud on a patent" by enabling fair protection of a patentee's contribution. It is not controlling whether the inventor foresaw and described the potential equivalent at the time the patent application was filed. *Pall Corp. v. Micron Separations Inc.*, 66 F.3d 1211, 36 U.S.P.Q.2d 1225, 1231 (Fed. Cir. 1995).

ϖ

The doctrine of equivalents is not a license to ignore or "erase . . . structural and functional limitations of the claim," limitations "on which the public is entitled to rely in avoiding infringement." As a corollary to the "all limitations" rule, "the concept of equivalency cannot embrace a structure that is specifically excluded from the scope of the claims." *Athletic Alternatives Inc. v. Prince Manufacturing Inc.*, 73 F.3d 1573, 37 U.S.P.Q.2d 1365, 1373 (Fed. Cir. 1996).

ϖ

Defendant's patent, during the prosecution of which plaintiff's patent was cited and considered as prior art, is thus presumed nonobvious in view of plaintiff's patent until proven otherwise. The nonobviousness of the accused device, evidenced by the grant of a United States patent, is relevant to the issue of whether the change therein is substantial. *Zygo Corp. v. Wyko Corp.*, 38 U.S.P.Q.2d 1281, 1286 (Fed. Cir. 1996).

ϖ

Other "*objective* evidence rather than unexplained subjective conclusions" may be relevant to the determination whether the differences between the accused product or process and the claimed invention are insubstantial. Such evidence may include evidence of known interchangeability to one of ordinary skill in the art, copying, and designing around. Thus, the doctrine of equivalents is "not the prisoner of a formula" and "the available relevant evidence may vary from case to case." *Texas Instruments Inc. v. Cypress Semiconductor Corp.*, 39 U.S.P.Q.2d 1492, 1499 (Fed. Cir. 1996).

ϖ

Mindful that claims serve both a definitional and a notice function, the better rule is to place the burden on the patent-holder to establish the reason for an amendment required during patent prosecution. The court would then decide whether that reason is sufficient to overcome prosecution history estoppel as a bar to application of the doctrine of equivalents to the element added by that amendment. The determination of equivalence should be applied as an objective inquiry on an element-by-element basis. Prosecution history estoppel continues to be available as a defense to infringement, but if the patent-holder demonstrates that an amendment required during prosecution had a purpose unrelated to patentability, a court must consider that purpose in order to decide whether an estoppel is precluded. Where the patent-holder is unable to establish such a purpose, a court should presume that the purpose behind the required amendment is such that prosecution history estoppel would apply. *Warner-Jenkinson Co. v. Hilton Davis Chemical Co.*, 520 U.S. 17, 41 U.S.P.Q.2d 1865 (S.Ct. 1997).

ω

In evaluating infringement under the doctrine of equivalents, "representation[s] to foreign patent offices should be considered ... when [they] comprise relevant evidence." *Tanabe Seiyaku Co. v. U.S. International Trade Commission*, 41 U.S.P.Q.2d 1976 (Fed. Cir. 1997).

ω

The doctrine of equivalents cannot extend or expand the scope of a claim. *Hassel v. Chrysler Corp.*, 982 F.Supp. 515, 43 U.S.P.Q.2d 1554, 1562 (Ohio 1997).

ω

The panel majority holds that the advantages mentioned in the specification, although not included in the claims, must be possessed by an accused device before there can be a finding of infringement by equivalency. *Vehicular Technologies Corp. v. Titan Wheel International Inc.*, 141 F.3d 1084, 46 U.S.P.Q.2d 1257, 1264 *dissent* (Fed. Cir. 1998).

ω

There is an important difference between the doctrine of equivalents and 35 U.S.C. §112, §6. The doctrine of equivalents is necessary because one cannot predict the future. Due to technological advances, a variant of an invention may be developed after a patent is granted, and that variant may constitute so insubstantial a change from what is claimed in the patent that it should be held to be an infringement. Such a variant, based on after-developed technology, could not have been disclosed in the patent. Even if such element is found not to be a 35 U.S.C. §112, §6, equivalent because it is not equivalent to the structure disclosed in the patent, this analysis should not foreclose it from being an equivalent under the doctrine of equivalents. *Chiuminatta Concrete Concepts Inc. v. Cardinal Industries Inc.*, 145 F.3d 1303, 46 U.S.P.Q.2d 1752, 1758 (Fed. Cir. 1998).

ω

According to the United States, if a claim is amended during prosecution to secure a patent, then the patentee cannot assert the doctrine of equivalents as to the amended claim limitation. In this case, however, a panel of the CAFC has held that the doctrine of equivalents *does* apply to amended claim limitations. *Hughes Aircraft Co. v. U.S.*, 47 U.S.P.Q.2d 1542, 1543 *dissent* (Fed. Cir. 1998).

ω

See *Texas Instruments, Inc. v. Cypress Semiconductor Corp.*, 90 F.3d 1558, 1567, 39 U.S.P.Q.2d 1492, 1499 (Fed. Cir. 1996) ("Generalized testimony as to the overall similarity between the claims and the accused infringer's product or process will not suffice [to show infringement under the doctrine of equivalents].") *Comark Communications Inc. v. Harris Corp.*, 48 U.S.P.Q.2d 1001, 1006 (Fed. Cir. 1998).

Doctrine of Inherency.

Inherency does not mean that a thing might happen. The fact that a procedure might yield an abrasive article is not enough. To rely on the filing date of an earlier application, the desired result must inevitably happen for the doctrine to apply. *Kropa v. Robie and Mahlman,* 187 F.2d 150, 88 U.S.P.Q. 478 (C.C.P.A. 1951).

Documentation.

Validity was denied by a memo that was admittedly not prior art, notwithstanding the fact that the contents of such memo had been concealed by the alleged infringer. *Newell Companies v. Kenney Manufacturing Co.,* 606 F. Supp. 1282, 226 U.S.P.Q. 157 (R.I. 1985).

Document Request.

The plain terms of the Federal Rules of Civil Procedure show that a party served with a document request has four options: (1) respond to the document request by agreeing to produce documents as requested [Rule 34(b)]; (2) respond to the document request by objecting [Rule 34(b)]; (3) move for a protective order [Rule 26(c) and Rule 37(d)]; or (4) ignore the request. If the party chooses the last option, he is subject to sanctions under Rule 37(b). However, if the party responds to the document request, even if he responds by objecting, Rule 37(b) sanctions are not available. *Badalamenti v. Dunham's Inc.,* 896 F.2d 1359, 13 U.S.P.Q.2d 1967, 1970 (Fed. Cir. 1990).

Documents.

Plaintiff's production of certain documents related to the prosecution of his patent constitutes a waiver of the attorney-client privilege with respect to all documents related to prosecution of the patent, even those which constitute "work product." *Bowmar Instrument Corp. v. Texas Instruments Incorporated,* 196 U.S.P.Q. 199, 201 (Ind. 1977).

Doing Business. *See also* Method of Doing Business.

The test of "doing business" is not to be substituted for the test of a "regular and established place of business". *Gould v. The Cornelius Company,* 258 F.Supp. 701, 151 U.S.P.Q. 178, 180 (Okla. 1966).

ω

Defendant's single written communication to Ohio asserting the validity of his patent and expressing a willingness to negotiate for a license is not the sort of purposeful activity that would make it reasonable for the defendant to expect to be haled into court in that state. *Consumer Direct Inc. v. McLaughlin,* 20 U.S.P.Q.2d 1949, 1951 (Ohio 1991).

Dominant or Dominating Claim. *See also* Dominant Patent, Dominating Patent.

Readability of a claim on the subject matter of another (patent) claim (domination) is neither determinative of double patenting nor demonstrative that the claims are directed to the same invention. *In re Sarett,* 327 F.2d 1005, 140 U.S.P.Q. 474, 482 (C.C.P.A. 1964).

Dominant Patent.

An inventor should be allowed to dominate future patentable inventions of others where those inventions are based in some way on his teachings. Such improvements, while unobvious from his teachings, are still within his contribution, since the improvement is made possible by his work. It is equally apparent, however, that he must not be permitted to achieve this dominance by claims that are insufficiently supported and hence not in compliance with the first paragraph of 35 U.S.C. §112. That paragraph requires that the scope of the claims must bear a reasonable correlation to the scope of enablement provided by the specification to persons of ordinary skill in the art. In cases involving predictable factors, such as mechanical or electrical elements, a single embodiment provides broad enablement in the sense that, once imagined, other embodiments can be made without difficulty and their performance characteristics predicted by resort to known scientific laws. In cases involving unpredictable factors, such as most chemical reactions and physiological activity, the scope of enablement obviously varies inversely with the degree of unpredictability of the factors involved. *In re Fisher,* 427 F.2d 833, 166 U.S.P.Q. 18 (C.C.P.A. 1970).

ᴟ

In a true dominant invention/subservient invention situation, the claims of the dominant patent may be of a scope completely encompassing the subservient patent claims, yet both patents may be valid. *In re Frilette and Weisz,* 436 F.2d 496, 168 U.S.P.Q. 368, 371 (C.C.P.A. 1971).

ᴟ

The PTO has not challenged the appellants' assertion that their 1953 application enabled those skilled in the art in 1953 to make and use "a solid polymer" as described in a claim. The appellants disclosed, as the only then-existing way to make such a polymer, a method of making the crystalline form. To say now that the appellants should have disclosed in 1953 the amorphous form (which did not exist until 1962) would be to impose an impossible burden on inventors and thus on the patent system. There cannot, in an effective patent system, be such a burden placed on the right to broad claims. To restrict the appellants to the crystalline form disclosed, under such circumstances, would be a poor way to stimulate invention, and particularly to encourage its early disclosure. To demand such restriction is merely to state a policy against broad protection for pioneer inventions, a policy both shortsighted and unsound from the standpoint of promoting progress in the useful arts, which is the constitutional purpose of the patent laws. *In re Hogan and Banks,* 559 F.2d 595, 194 U.S.P.Q. 527, 537 (C.C.P.A. 1977).

Dominating Patent.

The mere fact that an accused infringer has made a significant improvement over a patented invention does not avoid infringement when making or selling any device that satisfies all of the limitations of a valid patent claim. *Berkeley Park Clothes, Inc. v. Firma Schaffer-Homberg GmbH,* 217 U.S.P.Q. 388 (N.J. 1981).

Domination.

Readability of a claim on the subject matter of another claim (domination) is neither determinative of double patenting nor demonstrative that claims are directed to the same invention. *In re Sarett*, 327 F.2d 1005, 140 U.S.P.Q. 474, 482 (C.C.P.A. 1964); *see also In re Kaplan*, 789 F.2d 1574, 229 U.S.P.Q. 678, 681 (C.C.P.A. 1986).

Dosage. *See also* **Enablement.**

A proper disclosure of utility for a medicinal composition may require at least an indication of dosage and mode of administration. *In re Moureu and Chovin*, 345 F.2d 595, 145 U.S.P.Q. 452 (C.C.P.A. 1965).

ϖ

A disclosure of specific dosage units, ranging all the way from 10 mg. to 150 mg., and a statement about daily dosage of from 10 mg. to 450 mg. provides a range so great as not to be an enabling or how-to-use disclosure as contemplated by the statute. *In re Gardner, Roe, and Willey*, 427 F.2d 786, 166 U.S.P.Q. 138, 140, 141 (C.C.P.A. 1970).

ϖ

Where test methods in the field of the patent are so well known that reference to them in the patent is needless to enable those working in the field to follow the teaching of the patent, even complete silence on dosage and method of administration of the original application suffices to meet the how-to-use requirement of 35 U.S.C. §112. *Carter-Wallace, Inc. v. Davis-Edwards Pharmacal Corp.*, 341 F. Supp. 1303, 173 U.S.P.Q. 65, 104 (N.Y. 1972).

ϖ

The mere absence of dosage and/or host from priority applications directed to compounds having specified pharmacological utilities is not fatal, provided such dosage and host would have been obvious to a person of ordinary skill in the art. *Hester v. Meguro and Kuwada*, 190 U.S.P.Q. 231, 235 (PTO Bd. Pat. Intf. 1975).

ϖ

The sufficiency of disclosure was held to be inadequate to support a claim for applying "sufficient" ultrasonic energy (for rapidly mending fractured animal bones), since the specification failed to disclose what a "sufficient" dosage might be or how those skilled in the art might make an appropriate selection of frequency, intensity and duration. *In re Colianni*, 561 F.2d 220, 195 U.S.P.Q. 150, 152 (C.C.P.A. 1977).

ϖ

Although no specific dosages were disclosed for human use or even for animal tests for novel claimed analogs of known and useful compounds, one of ordinary skill in the art would know how to use the novel analogs to determine specific dosages for various biological purposes. As only compounds were being claimed, the facts were distinguished from a case wherein a therapeutic use was being claimed. *In re Bundy*, 642 F.2d 430, 209 U.S.P.Q. 48, 51, 52 (C.C.P.A. 1981).

ϖ

An application which describes a specific physiological use for claimed compounds, but omits identification of a host or applicable dosages, satisfies the "how to use" requirement of the first paragraph of 35 U.S.C. §112 in view of the fact that a prior art reference discloses a host and dosages for the same use of structurally related compounds. *Bey and Jung v. Kollonitsch and Patchett*, 215 U.S.P.Q. 454, 458 (PTO Bd. Pat. Intf. 1981).

ω

Failure to disclose dosages of novel pharmacologically active compounds was not fatal under 35 U.S.C. §112 in a case involving pharmacological activity or practical utility, not a therapeutic use. One skilled in the art, without the exercise of inventive skill or undue experimentation, could determine dosage level in a microsome environment. *Cross v. Iizuka*, 753 F.2d 1040, 224 U.S.P.Q. 739 (Fed. Cir. 1985).

ω

The specific dosage for a given patient under specific conditions and for a specific disease will routinely vary, but determination of the optimum amount in each case can readily be accomplished by simple routine procedures. *Ex parte Skuballa*, 12 U.S.P.Q.2d 1570, 1571 (B.P.A.I. 1989).

Dotted Lines.

A design for an article of manufacture may be embodied in less than all of an article of manufacture. Although there are no portions of a design that are immaterial or not important, that does not mean that the design must encompass an entire article. An article may well have portions that are material to a claimed design, and dotted lines are appropriate to indicate portions of an article that are not material to the claimed design. *In re Zahn*, 617 F.2d 261, 204 U.S.P.Q. 988 (C.C.P.A. 1980).

Double Inclusion. *See also* Multiple Inclusion.

Double recitation of elements of combination inventions does not necessarily render a claim vague and indefinite, particularly when the claim is drafted in terms of means clauses under 35 U.S.C. §112, or when an element performs more than one function or overlapping functions. The governing consideration is not double inclusion, but rather what is a reasonable construction of the language of the claims. An element that serves dual functions may therefore properly be considered an element of each of two means clauses, which do not render the claim indefinite. A claim having such means clauses complies with 35 U.S.C. §112. *Palmer v. United States*, 423 F.2d 316, 163 U.S.P.Q. 250, 253, 254 (Ct. Cl. 1969).

ω

Multiple inclusion in a claim of a single element may or may not render the claim indefinite. Automatic reliance upon a "rule against double inclusion" leads to as many unreasonable interpretations as does automatic reliance upon a "rule allowing double inclusion." The governing consideration is not double inclusion, but rather what is a reasonable construction of the language of the claim. *Ex parte Ionescu*, 222 U.S.P.Q. 537 (PTO Bd. App. 1984).

Double Patenting. *See also* **Cross-Reading, Dominant or Dominating Claim, Extension of Monopoly, Obviousness-Type Double Patenting, Restriction, Same Invention, Two-Way Test.**

The lower numbered of two patents issued on the same day to the same inventive entity for a related invention was held to be invalidating prior art against the higher numbered of those patents. Unclaimed subject matter in the lower numbered patent was regarded as dedicated to the public. *Underwood v. Gerber*, 149 U.S. 224 (1893).

ᴕ

Since the product in each of the appealed claims is defined essentially in terms of the method by which it is made, the fact that the process claims of appellant's patent and the product claims of the application are, technically, in different statutory classes is not, in itself, enough to avoid a rejection on the ground of double patenting. *In re Freeman,* 166 F.2d 178, 76 U.S.P.Q. 585, 586 (C.C.P.A. 1948).

ᴕ

When a later-filed application to an improvement by a different inventive entity issues as a patent before a copending application (of the same assignee) to the generic invention, claims in the earlier-filed generic application are not properly rejectable over claims of the improvement patent on the ground of double patenting when all the claims of the improvement patent are limited to the improvement and none of the patent claims is readable on the disclosure of the pending application. *In re Stanley and Lowe,* 214 F.2d 151, 102 U.S.P.Q. 234, 239, 240 (C.C.P.A. 1954).

ᴕ

A copending patent to a different inventor is presumed to be owned by the assignee of the subject application, and it is well settled that such an assignee cannot obtain two patents on a single inventive concept, even though applications by different inventors are involved. The copending patent discloses the aqueous emulsions referred to in the appealed claims and states that their use in the sizing of paper is disclosed in the subject application. No other specific use for the emulsions is given, but the claims are directed to the emulsions per se and make no reference to any use. As the use of the emulsions (claimed by the copending patent) for the sizing of paper in the manner set forth in the appealed claims would not be obvious to a skilled worker in the art, the process instantly claimed involves an invention distinct from and patentable over that claimed in the copending patent. Accordingly, a rejection based on double patenting is not in order. *In re Keim and Thompson,* 229 F.2d 466, 108 U.S.P.Q. 330, 332 (C.C.P.A. 1956).

ᴕ

Even though division would have been required by the Patent Office if appellant had included in a single application the disclosures and claims of his patent and of his involved applications, that does not preclude the propriety of a rejection on the ground of double patenting. The fact that the patent claims and the claims of the applications are not cross-readable also fails to preclude a holding of double patenting. If only one inventive concept is present, two patents cannot properly be granted, regardless of the scope or relationship of the claims, or of the order in which the applications were filed or the claims presented. *In re Ockert*, 245 F.2d 467, 114 U.S.P.Q. 330, 332 (C.C.P.A. 1957).

ᴕ

That Congress intended that both process and apparatus for its practice should be patented, and that the allowance of a patent on the one should not be used as an excuse to refuse a patent on the other when a single patent for both is originally sought, is also shown by 35 U.S.C. §121. The fact that Congress did not intend use of one of these two as an excuse for refusing (i.e. rejecting) or invalidating claims to the other (when both are disclosed and urged as patentable in the same case) appears to be clear from 35 U.S.C. §§100(b), 101 and 121. *Ex parte Symons*, 134 U.S.P.Q. 74, 81, 82 (PO Bd. App. 1962).

ᗡ

In a rejection based on double patenting, it is not permissible to dissect and discard portions of claims in a search for or an attempt to isolate "the essential element for patentability," whatever that means, common to two sets of claims. *In re Walles, Tousignant, and Houtman*, 366 F.2d 786, 151 U.S.P.Q. 185, 190 (C.C.P.A. 1966). *Compare with In re Higgins and Le Suer*, 369 F.2d 414, 152 U.S.P.Q. 103 (C.C.P.A. 1966).

ᗡ

A case of "obviousness" double patenting (based on patent claims plus other art) does not present an issue under 35 U.S.C. §103; the issue is not a statutory issue. *In re Land and Rogers*, 368 F.2d 866, 151 U.S.P.Q. 621, 625, n.1 (C.C.P.A. 1966).

ᗡ

Claims to a composition were held unpatentable (based on double patenting) over claims in applicant's copending patent to the essential component of the composition, on which patentability of the composition claims were dependent. The use and advantages (properties) of the essential component disclosed in the patent were relied upon. *In re Higgins and Le Suer,* 369 F.2d 414, 152 U.S.P.Q. 103, 105 (C.C.P.A. 1966).

ᗡ

When claims define overlapping, but different, subject matter, that is enough to warrant giving effect to a terminal disclaimer. A rejection on double-patenting grounds is obviated in view of such terminal disclaimer. *In re Skrivan*, 427 F.2d 801, 166 U.S.P.Q. 85, 87 (C.C.P.A. 1970).

ᗡ

Only one patent may be granted for a single invention. The second patent issued to the same inventor for the same invention is void for double patenting. *Studiengesellschaft Kohle mbH v. Eastman Kodak Co.*, 450 F. Supp. 1211, 197 U.S.P.Q. 164, 175 (Tex. 1977).

ᗡ

"Obviousness-type" double patenting may exist between a design and a utility patent. For the "obviousness-type" double patenting situation the test is whether the subject matter of the claims of the patent sought to be invalidated would have been obvious from the subject mater of the claims of the other patent, and vice versa. Double patenting is rare in the context of utility versus design patents. *Carman Industries, Inc. v. Wahl*, 724 F.2d 932, 220 U.S.P.Q. 481, 487 (Fed. Cir. 1983).

ᗡ

The entire doctrine of double patenting of the obviousness-type applies to commonly owned applications with different inventive entities. A patent may still issue if an applicant faced with such a rejection files a terminal disclaimer under 35 U.S.C. §253 disclaiming any "terminal part of the term...of the patent," thereby guaranteeing that the second patent would expire at the same time as the first patent. It is well established that a common assignee is entitled to proceed with a terminal disclaimer to overcome a rejection based on double patenting of the obviousness-type. *In re Longi,* 759 F.2d 887, 225 U.S.P.Q. 645 (Fed. Cir. 1985).

ω

Patents may be used as evidence of prior inventorship by another or as evidence that the patentee of the reexamination patent has already obtained patent protection for his invention. The second patent would thus be barred by 35 U.S.C. §101 if the inventions are identical or by the judicially created doctrine of double patenting of the obviousness-type, if there are only obvious differences between the claims of the respective patents. Such rejection falls within the ambit of those intended by the statute and is not specifically excluded by *Etter* [756 F.2d 852, 225 U.S.P.Q. I (1985)]. *Ex parte Obiaya,* 227 U.S.P.Q. 58 (B.P.A.I. 1985).

ω

When two patents claim different statutory classes of subject matter, composition, and process, they are not directed to the same invention. This alone is sufficient to avoid same-invention type double patenting. Before two sets of claims may be said to claim the same invention, they must in fact claim the same subject matter. By same invention is meant identical subject matter. Thus, the invention defined by a claim reciting "halogen" is not the same as that defined by a claim reciting "chlorine," because the former is broader than the latter. A good test, and probably the only objective test, for "same invention," is whether one of the claims would be literally infringed without literally infringing the other. If it could be, the claims do not define identically the same invention. *Studiengesellschaft Kohle mbH v. Northern Petrochemical Co.,* 784 F.2d 351, 228 U.S.P.Q. 837 (Fed. Cir. 1986).

ω

The prohibition against double patenting is a judicially created doctrine that precludes one person from obtaining more than one valid patent for the same invention, or for an obvious modification of the same invention. The relevant inquiry is whether the claimed invention in the second patent would have been obvious from the subject matter of the claims in the first patent, in light of the prior art. Obviousness under 103 is a question of law that is to be resolved by consideration of the following four underlying factual issues:

(1) the scope and content of the prior art,
(2) the differences between the prior art, and the claims that issue,
(3) the level of ordinary skill in the art, and
(4) objective evidence of secondary considerations.

Consideration of these four underlying factors necessarily has a slightly different focus in a double patenting analysis, since the ultimate inquiry is not whether the challenged patent is obvious in light of the prior art, but rather whether the challenged patent is obvious from the claims of the earlier patent in light of the prior art material to both patents. With respect to the first factor of the scope and content of the prior art, to be material, the prior art must have existed as of the date of invention of the first patent. *Mirafi Inc. v. Murphy,* 14 U.S.P.Q.2d 1337, 1347 (N.C. 1989).

ω

While a rejection for double patenting of the obviousness-type can be overcome by filing a terminal disclaimer, that does not mean that a 35 U.S.C. §103 rejection for obviousness may be similarly overcome (even if based on the same copending patent with an overlapping, but different, inventive entity). Under §103, a reference patent is available for all it fairly discloses to one of ordinary skill in the art. There is no inquiry as to what is claimed therein. In a rejection for double patenting of the obviousness type, the test is not what would be obvious to one of ordinary skill in the art from reading the specification or claims. Rather, the inquiry is much more limited in nature, and the patent is considered only to compare the invention defined in the patent claims with the invention defined in the application claims. *Ex parte Bartfeld,* 16 U.S.P.Q.2d 1714, 1717 (B.P.A.I. 1990).

ω

With regard to double patenting, 35 U.S.C. §121 (1988) will not apply to remove the parent as a reference where the principle of consonance is violated. Consonance requires that the line of demarcation between the "independent and distinct inventions" that prompted the restriction requirement be maintained. Though the claims may be amended, they may not be so amended as to bring them back over the line imposed in the restriction requirement. Where that line is crossed, the prohibition of the third sentence of 35 U.S.C. §121 does not apply. The judicially created doctrine of double patenting of the obviousness type applies when two applications or patents, not drawn to precisely the same invention, are "drawn to inventions so very much alike as to render one obvious in view of the other and to effectively extend the life of the patent that would have the earlier of the two issue dates." *Symbol Technologies Inc. v. Opticon Inc.,* 935 F.2d 1569, 19 U.S.P.Q.2d 1241, 1249 (Fed. Cir. 1991).

ω

Double patenting of the obviousness type is a judicially created doctrine intended to prevent improper timewise extension of the patent right by prohibiting the issuance of claims in a second patent that are not "patentably distinct" from the claims of a first patent. The difficulty that arises in all cases of double patenting of the obviousness type is determining when a claim is or is not an obvious variation of another claim. A claim often does not describe any particular thing, but instead defines the boundary of patent protection, and it is difficult to try to determine what is a mere obvious variation of a legal boundary. The crux of the subject appeal was whether the Board erred in applying a "one-way" patentability determination instead of a "two-way" determination. When the second-filed (to a combination or improvement) of two related applications is first to issue, criteria for double patenting may be affected. As a matter of law an extension-of-protection objection is not necessarily controlling. *In re Braat,* 937 F.2d 589, 19 U.S.P.Q.2d 1289, 1291-93 (Fed. Cir. 1991).

ω

The notion that a pending claim to a generic invention is necessarily patentably indistinct, in the sense of double patenting of the obviousness type, from a narrower patented claim encompassed by the pending generic claim was scotched by *In re Braat,*

937 F.2d 589 at 594, 19 U.S.P.Q.2d 1289 at 1293 (Fed. Cir. 1991). *See also, In re Kaplan*, 789 F.2d 1574 at 1577, 229 U.S.P.Q. 678 at 681 (Fed. Cir. 1986), wherein the court stated:

> This commonplace situation (domination) is not, per se, double patenting as the board seemed to think. *In re Sarett*, 327 F.2d 1005, 1014, 1015, 140 U.S.P.Q. 474, 482, 483 (C.C.P.A. 1964). [See particularly the quotation from E. Stringham's *Double Patenting* (1933) about terms, such as "covered" and "embraced."]

ω

Only the claims are compared in a rejection for double patenting. Such a rejection by the PTO does not mean that the first-filed patent is a prior art reference under 35 U.S.C. §102 against the later-filed application. Thus, the "obviation" of double patenting of the obviousness type by filing a terminal disclaimer has no effect on a rejection under 35 U.S.C. §103 based on the first-filed patent. Such a rejection cannot be overcome by a terminal disclaimer. A terminal disclaimer is of circumscribed availability and effect. It is not an admission of obviousness of the later-filed claimed invention in light of the earlier-filed disclosure, for that is not the basis of the disclaimer. The filing of a terminal disclaimer simply serves the statutory function of removing the rejection of double patenting and raises neither presumption nor estoppel on the merits of the rejection. It is improper to convert this simple expedient of "obviation" into an admission or acquiescence or estoppel on the merits. *Quad Environmental Technologies Corp. v. Union Sanitary District,* 946 F.2d 870, 20 U.S.P.Q.2d 1392, 1394, 1395 (Fed. Cir. 1991).

ω

The usual inquiry regarding double patenting of the obviousness type is whether the claims of the second patent are obvious from the claims of the first. However, if the second patent to issue was filed first, the test becomes whether the claims of the first-issued patent are obvious from those of the second-issued patent. An exception to this latter rule exists when the delay in issuing the first-filed patent is caused by the applicant, be it with sinister or innocent motives, as opposed to mere administrative delay. If this exception applies, the first test governs. *General Foods Corp. v. Studiengesellschaft Kohle mbH,* 765 F. Supp. 121, 20 U.S.P.Q.2d 1673, 1680 (N.Y. 1991).

ω

Double patenting rejections cannot be based on 35 U.S.C. §103, on disclosures of patents whose claims are relied on to demonstrate double patenting or on the "disclosures" of their claims. While analogous to the non-obviousness requirement of section 103, that section is not itself involved in double patenting rejections because the patent principally underlying the rejection is not prior art. *General Foods Corp. v. Studiengesellschaft Kohle mbH*, 972 F.2d 1272, 23 U.S.P.Q.2d 1839, 1846 (Fed. Cir. 1992).

ω

The "two-way" test revealed in *Braat* [937 F.2d 589, 19 U.S.P.Q.2d 1289 (Fed. Cir. 1991)], or the "one-way" test applied in the right direction in *Borah* [354 F.2d 1009, 148 U.S.P.Q. 213 (C.C.P.A. 1966)], is limited to fact situations where it is not the fault of the applicant that a later-filed application issues while an earlier-filed application is still pending and the claims of the later-filed application are not obvious, considered with or without other prior art, from the claims of the earlier-filed application. The position that the law of obviousness-type double patenting which predates, but was restated in, *Vogel* [422 F.2d 438, 441, 164 U.S.P.Q. 619, 622 (C.C.P.A. 1970)] requires only the determination of whether any claim in an application defines merely an obvious variation of an invention claimed in a prior issued patent, assuming common ownership and/or same inventive entity. This is true notwithstanding the decision in *Braat* even if it is intended to restate the law to require a "two-way" test. *Ex parte Nesbit*, 25 U.S.P.Q.2d 1817, 1821, 1822 (B.P.A.I. 1992).

Double Use.

In a motion for summary judgment, where the plaintiff asserts the "new use" theory (by arguing non-analogous art), the defendant must prove that there are no material questions of fact regarding remoteness, adaptation and value to be entitled to judgment as a matter of law. *Kalkowski v. Ronco, Inc.*, 186 U.S.P.Q. 281, 283 (Ill. 1975).

Doubt.

When a doubt exists whether a claimed process would have been obvious to one skilled in the art who is familiar with the disclosures of the references, such doubt should be resolved in favor of the applicant. *In re Citron*, 251 F.2d 619, 116 U.S.P.Q. 409, 410 (C.C.P.A. 1958).

ᙡ

When there is a doubt as to the factual basis supporting the conclusion of the Board of Appeals that the invention would have been obvious to one of ordinary skill in the art, such doubt should be resolved in favor of the applicant. *In re Sporck*, 301 F.2d 686, 133 U.S.P.Q. 360, 364 (C.C.P.A. 1962).

ᙡ

A specification disclosure that contains a teaching of the manner and process of making and using the invention in terms that correspond in scope to those used in describing and defining the subject matter sought to be patented must be taken as in compliance with the enabling requirement of the first paragraph of 35 U.S.C. §112 unless there is reason to doubt the objective truth of the statements contained therein that must be relied on for enabling support. Assuming that sufficient reason for such doubt does exist, a rejection for failure to teach how to make and/or use will be proper on that basis. In any event, it is incumbent on the Patent Office, whenever a rejection on this basis is made, to explain why it doubts the truth or accuracy of any statement in a supporting disclosure and to back up assertions of its own with acceptable evidence or reasoning that is inconsistent with the contested statement. Otherwise, there would be no need for the applicant to go to the trouble and expense of supporting his presumptively accurate disclosure. *In re Marzocchi and Horton*, 439 F.2d 220, 169 U.S.P.Q. 367 (C.C.P.A. 1971).

ᙡ

Utility, within the meaning of the Patent Laws, means that the object of the patent is capable of performing some beneficial function claimed for it. Doubts relating to utility are resolved against an infringer. *Dart Industries Inc. v. E.I. du Pont de Nemours and Company*, 348 F.Supp. 1338, 175 U.S.P.Q. 540, 553 (Ill. 1972).

ᙡ

The premise that doubts as to patentability should be resolved in favor of a patent applicant is now defunct. *In re The Successor in Interest to Walter Andersen*, 743 F.2d 1578, 223 U.S.P.Q. 378, 379 (Fed. Cir. 1984). *See also In re Naber and Dautzenberg*, 503 F.2d 1059, 183 U.S.P.Q. 245, 246 (C.C.P.A. 1974).

ω

The primary contention of the PTO is that reasonable basis exists for doubting that all of the compounds encompassed by a claim have the asserted utility. Adequate support for the PTO's assertions is an essential requirement for sustaining a rejection on this basis. *In re Gardner*, 475 F.2d 1389, 177 U.S.P.Q. 396, 397 (C.C.P.A. 1973).

ω

Those portions of the MPEP (MPEP §2240 and MPEP §2244), which require the PTO to resolve doubts in the direction of granting a request for reexamination, are contrary to the statutory mandate of 35 U.S.C. §303, and void. *Patlex Corp. v. Mossinghoff*, 771 F.2d 480, 226 U.S.P.Q. 985 (Fed. Cir. 1985).

ω

The 30 percent or greater royalty proposed by the plaintiffs is too high, and the 5 percent proposed by the defendants is too low. The resin involved in this case was a new product, not just an improvement on an old one. As a result, the plaintiffs were not able to present evidence on the royalties or profit margin on comparable products. Nonetheless, we conclude that 20 percent is a reasonable royalty. In determining a reasonable royalty, reasonable doubts are resolved against the infringing party. *Water Technologies Corp. v. Calco Ltd.*, 714 F. Supp. 899, 11 U.S.P.Q.2d 1410 (Ill. 1989).

ω

Unpredictability of a particular art area may, by itself, provide a reasonable doubt as to the accuracy of a broad statement made in support of the enablement of a claim. *Ex parte Singh*, 17 U.S.P.Q.2d 1714, 1715 (B.P.A.I. 1990).

ω

When the amount of the damages cannot be ascertained with precision, any doubts regarding the amount must be resolved against the infringer. *Beatrice Foods Co. v. New England Printing & Lithographing Co.*, 923 F.2d 1576, 17 U.S.P.Q.2d 1553, 1555 (Fed. Cir. 1991).

ω

When the meaning of claims is in doubt, especially when there is close prior art, they are properly declared invalid. *Amgen Inc. v. Chugai Pharmaceutical Co. Ltd.*, 927 F.2d 1200, 18 U.S.P.Q.2d 1016, 1031 (Fed. Cir. 1991).

ω

Only after the PTO provides evidence showing that one of ordinary skill in the art would reasonably doubt the asserted utility does the burden shift to the applicant to provide rebuttal evidence sufficient to convince such a person of the invention's asserted utility. *In re Brana*, 51 F.3d 1560, 34 U.S.P.Q.2d 1436, 1441 (Fed. Cir. 1995).

ω

Where there is a doubt as to the profit margin, the Court must construe the facts in favor of the patentee. *Joy Technologies Inc. v. Flakt Inc.*, 42 U.S.P.Q.2d 1042 (Del. 1996).

Drawings. *See also* **35 U.S.C. §113.**

Matter clearly and conclusively disclosed by the drawings can be described in the specification by amendment without involving improper new matter. Ordinarily, drawings which accompany an application for a patent are merely illustrative of the principles embodied in the alleged invention claimed therein and do not define the precise proportions of elements relied upon to endow the claims with patentability. Patent Office drawings are not normally drawn to scale. *In re Olson*, 212 F.2d 590, 101 U.S.P.Q. 401, 402, 403 (C.C.P.A. 1954).

ᘯ

The Patent Office accepts photoprints of drawings, if clear and definite, as a sufficient compliance with the rules to warrant granting a filing date, subject to the submission of formal drawings within 30 or 60 days. The Application Branch is authorized hereafter to accept photoprints and mounted photographs (presented as drawings) in lieu of drawings for filing only. *In re Application Filed Mar. 7, 1956*, 119 U.S.P.Q. 181, 182 (Comm'r of Patents 1956).

ᘯ

When the claimed invention resides in properties or characteristics incapable of illustration, or in the composition used in making a claimed product, the practice contemplates the acceptance of the application without a drawing. *In re Hacklander*, 122 U.S.P.Q. 278, 279 (Comm'r of Patents 1956).

ᘯ

The Rules of the Patent Office have always contained rigid standards for patent drawings, and strict adherence to the requirements of the rules has been enforced. Only line drawings are considered to be drawings within the terms of the rules. Photographs are not drawings. An application is not complete until the drawing described in the specification is one which meets the requirements of the rule. *In re Myers*, 120 U.S.P.Q. 225, 226 (Comm'r of Patents 1958).

ᘯ

Claims can properly refer to graphically presented data in drawings. The drawings are not referred to for mechanical shapes or combinations, but for data of engineering information for which graphic presentation is well recognized as the efficient manner of expression of the concept. *Ex parte Rinehart and Cocanower,* 141 U.S.P.Q. 303, 304 (PO Bd. App. 1962).

ᘯ

The Oath (or Declaration) is not required by law or the Rules of Practice to refer to drawings. Neither the statute nor the rules require the presence of drawings at the time an application is executed. *In re Youmans*, 142 U.S.P.Q. 447, 450 (Comm'r 1960).

ᘯ

The drawing is not a place to find antecedent basis. *Ex parte Siegmund and Cole*, 156 U.S.P.Q. 477, 478 (PO Bd. App. 1967).

ʊ

A figure of drawing can be referred to in a claim to identify a range of contemplated compositions. *In re Schneider and Stuart*, 481 F.2d 1350, 179 U.S.P.Q. 46, 47 (C.C.P.A. 1973).

ʊ

Absent any written description in the specification of quantitative values, arguments based on measurement of a drawing are of little value. *In re Wright*, 569 F.2d 1124, 193 U.S.P.Q. 332, 335 (C.C.P.A. 1977).

ʊ

A claimed invention may be anticipated or rendered obvious by a drawing in a reference, whether the drawing disclosure be accidental or intentional. When the drawing occurs in a reference which is in no way directed toward the involved problem, it must be viewed in a teaching vacuum so far as the claimed invention is concerned. *In re Meng and Driessen*, 492 F.2d 843, 181 U.S.P.Q. 94, 97 (C.C.P.A. 1974); *but see In re Gordon*, 733 F.2d 900, 221 U.S.P.Q. 1125 (Fed. Cir. 1984).

ʊ

Drawings may be relied upon to satisfy the disclosure requirements of 35 U.S.C. §112. *Ex parte Horton*, 226 U.S.P.Q. 697 (B.P.A.I. 1985).

ʊ

Drawings alone may be sufficient to provide the "written description of the invention" required by the first paragraph of 35 U.S.C. §112. *Vas-Cath Inc. v. Mahurkar*, 935 F.2d 1555, 19 U.S.P.Q.2d 1111, 1116, 1117 (Fed. Cir. 1991).

ʊ

The fact that identical drawings accompany different patent applications is persuasive evidence that only one inventive concept is present. *Jennmar Corp. v. Pattin Manufacturing Co.*, 20 U.S.P.Q.2d 1721, 1730 (Ohio 1991).

ʊ

In a proceeding in the PTO, drawings "may be used like the written specifications to provide evidence relevant to claim interpretation." 1 No. 8 MLRPAT 8 (1993). *Mentor Graphics Corp. v. Quickturn Design Systems Inc.*, 150 F.3d 1374, 44 U.S.P.Q.2d 1621, 1625 (Oreg. 1997).

Drug. *See also* **Bioisosterism, Certainty, Empirical, Kohler-Milstein Technique, Pharmaceutical, Pro-Drug, Relationship, Therapeutic Value.**

Chemical compounds of the involved type, which are intended for human dosage, must be developed empirically. The district court accepted expert opinion:

that minor changes in the substituents of a compound can profoundly affect its analgesic potency; and that reliable prediction of either analgesic potency or addiction liability on the basis of structure cannot be made. Although in hindsight, structure-to-function generalizations can sometimes be made in chemistry, such relationships cannot be predicted in the field of analgesic compounds but can be ascertained only retrospectively after experimentation and testing.

Analogical reasoning is necessarily restricted in many chemical patent cases because of the necessity for physiological experimentation before any use can be determined. In the development of a new drug, the process of chemical synthesis constitutes only a preliminary portion of the invention process, which consists not only of originating the compound but also of establishing, through extensive biological testing, that the newly-synthesized compound is an effective medicine. The fact that no reliable way of predicting utility based on chemical formulas alone had been developed in the field of analgesic research at the time the invention was being made bars the court's use of the more ordinary analysis processes which determine invention in mechanical devices. In fact, such lack of predictability of useful result from the making of even the slightest variation in the atomic structure or spatial arrangement of a complex molecule not only deprives the instant claims of obviousness and anticipation of most of their vitality, but also largely renders impotent the claim that the inventor dealt unfairly with the Patent Office in not noting that the existence of a chemically closely related compound was disclosed in published literature. Therapeutic value, not chemical composition, is the substance of all incentive to invent in the field of drug patents. Except where the state of the medical art and the state of the chemical art have been advanced and coordinated to the point that it is possible for the mind to conceive or predict (with some minimal reliability) a correlation between chemical analogues, homologues or isomers and their therapeutic value, novelty, usefulness and nonobviousness inhere in the true discovery that a chemical compound exhibits a new needed medicinal capability, even though it be closely related in structure to a known or patented drug. *Eli Lilly and Company, Inc. v. Generix Drug Sales, Inc.*, 460 F.2d 1096, 174 U.S.P.Q. 65, 69 (5th Cir. 1972).

ω

When a superior property of a new drug has led to its acceptance in the medical community, the compound's superior property is a "significant enough contribution to be deserving of a patent." *Ortho Pharmaceutical Corp. v. Smith*, 15 U.S.P.Q.2d 1856, 1862 (Pa. 1990).

ω

The policy rationales behind the patent statutes generally apply with even greater strength in the case of drug patents. It is in the public interest to protect the pharmaceutical industry's investment in the discovery of new drugs. The public likewise has an interest in promoting large numbers of drugs that perform the same basic function so that alternatives are available for individual therapy. *Ortho Pharmaceutical Corp. v. Smith*, 18 U.S.P.Q.2d 1977, 1989 (Pa. 1990).

Dry.

Dry is a relative term. *Canaan Products, Inc. v. Edward Don & Company*, 273 F.Supp. 492, 154 U.S.P.Q. 393, 397 (Ill. 1966).

Due Care.

Where a potential infringer has actual notice of another's patent rights, he has an affirmative duty to exercise due care to determine whether he is infringing. Such an affirmative duty includes, inter alia, the duty to seek and obtain competent legal advice from counsel before the initiation of any possible infringing activity. *Underwater Devices Inc. v. Morrison-Knudsen Co.*, 717 F.2d 1380, 219 U.S.P.Q. 569 (Fed. Cir. 1983).

ω

The duty of due care normally requires a party to obtain legal advice before initiating or continuing an operation that might result in infringement. Failure to obtain an opinion of counsel is one of the factors supporting a finding of willfulness. This principle, which addresses the conduct of an accused willful infringer, is part of the substantive law of patents and is not merely a procedural housekeeping rule. A federal court exercising patent jurisdiction is bound by the substantive patent law of the Federal Circuit. When an infringer fails to introduce (at trial) an opinion of counsel pertaining to activity in question, an adverse inference may be drawn against the infringer that any legal advice obtained regarding the activity in question was unfavorable to the infringer. *ALM Surgical Equipment Inc. v. Kirschner Medical Corp.*, 15 U.S.P.Q.2d 1241, 1251 (S.C. 1990).

ω

Willful infringement must be proven by clear and convincing evidence. To question the validity of a patent does not, in and of itself, constitute willful infringement. Where a potential infringer has actual notice of another's patent rights, he has an affirmative duty to exercise due care to determine whether or not he is infringing. Not every failure to seek an opinion of competent counsel will mandate an ultimate finding of willfulness. The court should always look at the totality of the circumstances. That an opinion of counsel was obtained does not always and alone dictate a finding that the infringement was willful. A finding of willful infringement does not require a patentee to prove that defendant's actions were conducted in bad faith. *Stranco Inc. v. Atlantes Chemical Systems Inc.*, 15 U.S.P.Q.2d 1704, 1712 (Tex. 1990).

Due Diligence. *See also* Best Efforts.

The duty to exploit the subject matter of a license is implied on the part of an exclusive licensee where such a covenant is essential as a matter of equity to give meaning to the effect of the contract as a whole. The reason for implying a duty where an agreement grants an exclusive license is that it would be unfair to place the productiveness of a licensed property solely within the control of the licensee. *Willis Bros., Inc. v. Ocean Scallops, Inc.*, 356 F. Supp. 1151, 176 U.S.P.Q. 53 (N.C. 1972).

Due Process. *See also* Applicant's Rights.

Due process requires that an applicant be given notice of the reasons his claims are rejected and why arguments upon which he relies are deemed lacking in merit. This principle is the essence of 35 U.S.C. §132 and should guide the proceedings of the Board of Appeals as well. *Ex parte Hageman*, 179 U.S.P.Q. 747, 751 (PTO Bd. App. 1972).

ω

The forum state does not exceed its power under the Due Process Clause if it asserts personal jurisdiction over a corporation that delivers its products into the stream of commerce with the expectation that they will be purchased by consumers in the forum state. *Wilden Pump & Engineering Co. v. Versa-matic Tool Inc.*, 20 U.S.P.Q.2d 1788, 1790 (Cal. 1991).

ϖ

"[D]ue process requires...that in order to subject a defendant to a judgment *in personam*, if he be not present within the territory of the forum, he have certain *minimum contacts* with it such that the maintenance of the suit not offend 'traditional notions of fair play and substantial justice.'" The minimum contacts must be "purposeful" contacts. The requirement for purposeful minimum contacts helps insure that non-residents have fair warning that a particular activity may subject them to litigation within the forum. "The forum State does not exceed its powers under the Due Process Clause if it asserts personal jurisdiction over a corporation that delivers its products into the stream of commerce with the expectation that they will be purchased by consumers in the forum State. Even if the requisite minimum contacts have been found through an application of the stream of commerce theory or otherwise, if it would be unreasonable for the forum to assert jurisdiction under all the facts and circumstances, then due process requires that jurisdiction be denied. *Beverly Hills Fan Co. v. Royal Sovereign Corp.*, 21 F.3d 1558, 30 U.S.P.Q.2d 1001, 1006, 1007, 1009 (Fed. Cir. 1994).

Duplication.

An accidental or unwitting duplication of an invention cannot constitute an anticipation. *In re Marshall*, 578 F.2d 301, 198 U.S.P.Q. 344, 346 (C.C.P.A. 1978).

Duplication of Parts.

The use of two coil springs instead of one does not avoid infringement. *Jeoffroy Mfg., Inc. v. Graham*, 206 F.2d 772, 98 U.S.P.Q. 424, 429 (5th Cir. 1953).

ϖ

The mere duplication of parts has no patentable significance unless a new and unexpected result is produced. *In re Harza*, 274 F.2d 669, 124 U.S.P.Q. 378, 380 (C.C.P.A. 1960).

Duplicate Claims. *See* Multiplicity.

Duty of Potential Infringers.

Where a potential infringer has actual notice of another's patent rights, he has an affirmative duty to exercise due care to determine whether he is infringing. Such an affirmative duty includes, inter alia, the duty to seek and obtain competent legal advice from counsel before the initiation of any possible infringing activity. *Underwater Devices Inc. v. Morrison-Knudsen Co.*, 717 F.2d 1380, 219 U.S.P.Q. 569 (Fed. Cir. 1983).

Duty to Disclose.[7] *See also* **Failure to Disclose, Fraud, Incorporate by Reference, Inequitable Conduct, Materiality, Test Results.**

Those who have applications pending with the Patent Office or who are parties to Patent Office proceedings have an uncompromising duty to report to it all facts concerning possible fraud or inequitableness underlying applications in issue. Public interest demands that all facts relevant to such matters be submitted formally or informally to the Patent Office, which can then pass upon the sufficiency of the evidence. Only in this way can that agency act to safeguard the public in the first instance against fraudulent patent monopolies. *Precision Instrument Manufacturing Co. v. Automotive Maintenance Machine Co.*, 324 U.S. 806, 65 U.S.P.Q. 133, 139 (1945).

ω

Section 707.05(b) of the MPEP does not mean that, unless citations to prior art are presented in the specified form, they will be ignored or will not be considered by the Examiner. That section also does not mean that mere failure to cite prior art in the specified form will amount to fraud or misrepresentation. To so construe that section would place the full burden of examination on the shoulders of the applicant. *Lundy Electronics & Systems, Inc. v. Optical Recognition Systems, Inc.*, 362 F. Supp. 130, 178 U.S.P.Q. 525, 535 (Va. 1973).

ω

An assignee has a duty to disclose (to both the Patent Office and a prospective licensee) that a person other than named applicant was first inventor of subject matter claimed in patent application. *Ampex Corporation v. Memorex Corporation*, 205 U.S.P.Q. 794, 797 (Cal. 1980).

ω

Establishing that a patent was procured by fraud or with such egregious conduct as to render it unenforceable requires clear, unequivocal, and convincing evidence of an intentional misrepresentation or withholding of a material fact from the PTO. Where a patent has not been issued, the same standard of proof applies with respect to the proceedings before the PTO. In a case involving two interferences, the fact that the counts of either interference may be patentable over the withheld prior art is not relevant. What is relevant is whether a reasonable Examiner would have considered such prior art important in deciding whether to allow the parent application. Where fraud or other egregious conduct is alleged, it cannot be presumed that the PTO considered prior art of particular relevance if it was not cited. *Driscoll v. Cebalo*, 731 F.2d 878, 221 U.S.P.Q. 745 (Fed. Cir. 1984).

ω

A patentee fulfills it's obligation to the PTO where the patent in suit was in the class of patents that was cited. In addition, prior art described in the specification is expected to be considered by the Examiner. Patent Examiners are also presumed to be aware of

---

[7] "It is in the best interest of the Office (PTO) and the public to permit and encourage individuals to cite information to the Office without fear of making an admission against interest." *Cf.* Notice of Final Rulemaking, 57 Fed. Reg. 2021, 2022 (1992).

patents that issued from applications they had earlier examined. *Polaroid Corp. v. Eastman Kodak Co.*, 641 F. Supp. 828, 228 U.S.P.Q. 305 (Mass. 1985).

ᚥ

Failure to satisfy the duty to disclose during the prosecution of an application that matures into a patent cannot be cured by reissue. *In re Jerabek,* 789 F.2d 886, 229 U.S.P.Q. 530 (Fed. Cir. 1986).

ᚥ

Even though the PTO cited and relied upon specific references, the court held the subsequently obtained patent unenforceable because the patentee previously knew of the references and regarded them as material and still did not direct the attention of the Examiner to those references. It is clear from the holding in this case that an applicant cannot merely wait to see whether the PTO will cite a particular reference or group of references during the prosecution of an application. As soon as an applicant is aware of a reference that is regarded as material to the prosecution of a pending application, that applicant has a duty to direct the Examiner's attention to such reference. *A. B. Dick Co. v. Burroughs Corp.*, 798 F.2d 1392, 230 U.S.P.Q. 849 (Fed. Cir. 1986).

ᚥ

A suggestion in the form of a passing mention in an introductory paragraph of the specification, not in the form of a reference to specific prior art likely to catch the eye of a busy Patent Examiner, does not satisfy the duty to disclose. *Zenith Controls Inc. v. Automatic Switch Company*, 648 F.Supp. 1497, 2 U.S.P.Q.2d 1025, 1029 (Ill. 1986).

ᚥ

The issue is not whether patent claims define patentably over the undisclosed subject matter; it is whether the undisclosed subject matter would have been "highly material" to a Patent Examiner's determination. *Gardco Manufacturing Inc. v. Herst Lighting Co.*, 820 F.2d 1209, 2 U.S.P.Q.2d 2015 (Fed. Cir. 1987).

ᚥ

Incorporating by reference a copending application that refers to identified prior art satisfies the duty to disclose at least to the extent of not withholding knowledge of such prior art from the PTO. *Corning Glass Works v. Sumitomo Electric U.S.A. Inc.*, 671 F. Supp. 1369, 5 U.S.P.Q.2d 1545, 1557, 1558 (N.Y. 1987).

ᚥ

In view of the close similarities between the drawings of the applicant's design application and those in his utility application, a reasonable Examiner would have considered the copending design application important in deciding to issue the utility patent. Even though the utility application is still pending, the failure to timely inform the utility Examiner of the design application cannot now be cured. The level of materiality and the level of intent is high, and the applicant is not entitled, in an interference proceeding, to priority for the reason that he, or those representing him, failed to comply with the duty of disclosure required by 37 C.F.R. §1.56(a). *Lutzker v. Plet,* 7 U.S.P.Q.2d 1214 (B.P.A.I. 1987).

ᚥ

An applicant who knew or should have known of prior art or information and of its materiality is not automatically precluded thereby from an effort to convince the fact finder that failure to disclose was nonetheless not due to an intent to mislead the PTO; i.e., that, in light of all the circumstances in the case, an inference of intent to mislead is not warranted. No single factor or combination of factors can be said always to require an inference to mislead. *In re Harita*, 847 F.2d 801, 6 U.S.P.Q.2d 1930 (Fed. Cir. 1988).

ω

The disclosure required of patent claimants applies whether inaccurate evidence is submitted to the PTO willfully or not. The filing of a misleading Rule 131 affidavit makes the resulting patent unenforceable regardless of whether the patent would have been issued "but for" the "fraud." *Greenwood v. Seiko Instruments & Electronics Ltd.*, 711 F. Supp. 30, 13 U.S.P.Q.2d 1245, 1247 (D.C. 1989).

ω

Withholding information from the PTO may so soil a patentee's hands as to render his patent unenforceable. *Consolidated Aluminum Corp. v. Foseco International Ltd.*, 910 F.2d 804, 15 U.S.P.Q.2d 1481, 1487 (Fed. Cir. 1990).

ω

The statute governing reexamination, 35 U.S.C. §301 et seq., nowhere imposes upon the patent owner a duty to identify and disclose to the Examiner all evidence that might arguably invalidate the patent under reexamination; nor does plaintiff cite any case law indicating that courts have imposed such a duty. Indeed, it is precisely the duty of the requestor to cite prior art alleged to have a bearing on the patentability of a challenged claim. *E.I. du Pont de Nemours & Co. v. Cetus Corp.*, 19 U.S.P.Q.2d 1174, 1181 (Cal. 1990).

ω

A patent attorney is not excused from disclosing pre-critical date sales to the Examiner, based solely upon the inventor's representations, in the face of objective evidence that the sales were commercial in nature. Where the decision of whether or not to disclose sales before the critical date is close, the case should be resolved by disclosure, not by the applicant's unilateral decision to the contrary. *Paragon Podiatry Laboratory Inc. v. KLM Laboratories Inc.*, 984 F.2d 1182, 25 U.S.P.Q.2d 1561, 1570 (Fed. Cir. 1993).

ω

Intentionally failing to cite prior art to the PTO or intentionally disregarding one's duty of disclosure to the PTO is not necessarily tantamount to doing those same intentional acts with an intent to deceive the PTO. *Xilinx Inc. v. Altera Corp.*, 33 U.S.P.Q.2d 1149, 1153 (Cal. 1994).

ω

A patent applicant, who has no duty to conduct a prior art search, does not have an obligation to disclose any art of which he "reasonably should be aware." *Nordberg Inc. v. Telsmith Inc.*, 82 F.3d 394, 38 U.S.P.Q.2d 1593, 1595 (Fed. Cir. 1996).

ω

Omission of a reference material to certain claims cannot be cured simply by canceling or amending those claims during prosecution so that they do not issue in the same form in which they were drafted. *Baxter International Inc. v. McGaw Inc.*, 149 F.3d 1321, 47 U.S.P.Q.2d 1225, 1232 (Fed. Cir. 1998).

ω

"[T]here is a duty to disclose or to even go so far as to 'red flag' contradictory information with regard to test results, where the results appear to be in sharp contrast with what the applicant is telling the Patent Office, since the Patent Office is incapable of verifying comparative tests and has to rely on the candor of the parties submitting those test results..." *Bristol-Myers Squibb Co. v. Rhône-Poulenc Rorer Inc.*, 48 U.S.P.Q.2d 1817, 1822 (N.Y. 1998).

Duty to Use. *See also* **Performance.**

The duty to exploit the subject matter of a license is implied on the part of an exclusive licensee where such a covenant is essential as a matter of equity to give meaning to the effect of the contract as a whole. The reason for implying a duty, where an agreement grants an exclusive license, is that it will be unfair to place the productiveness of a licensed property solely within the control of the licensee. *Willis Brothers, Inc. v. Ocean Scallops, Inc.*, 356 F. Supp. 1151, 176 U.S.P.Q. 53 (N.C. 1972).

Dyestuff.

The rejection of a claim to an organic water-soluble dyestuff (of a stated formula wherein A is an organic azo dyestuff residue, a ring carbon of which is bonded in a specified way to defined structure) under 35 U.S.C. §112 (breadth and definiteness) was reversed. *In re Riat, DeMontmollin, and Koller*, 327 F.2d 685, 140 U.S.P.Q. 471 (C.C.P.A. 1964).

ω

The present compounds have many significant properties as dyes in common with the prior art compounds, in addition to a close similarity in chemical structure. Both sets of compounds have the property of being wool dyes and both result in dyeings on wool fabrics which are fast to washing and fulling. The additional ability of the subject compounds to dye cotton is not sufficient to render the subject matter as a whole unobvious. A single variance in the properties of new chemical compounds will not necessarily tip the balance in favor of patentability where otherwise closely related chemical compounds are involved. *In re De Montmollin and Riat*, 344 F.2d 976, 145 U.S.P.Q. 416, 417 (C.C.P.A. 1965); but see *In re Murch*, 464 F.2d 1051, 175 U.S.P.Q. 89, 92 (C.C.P.A. 1972); *In re May and Eddy*, 574 F.2d 1082, 197 U.S.P.Q. 601, 609 (C.C.P.A. 1978).

ω

A rejection under the first paragraph of 35 U.S.C. §112 based on the alleged failure of a specification to support claims containing the terms, "alkyl", "alkoxy", "alkylene" and "a divalent hydrocarbon radical", was reversed. The claims which contained these terms were no broader than the broadest written description of the invention in the specification. Moreover, the Examiner provided no reason why any particular alkyl, alkoxy, alkylene or hydrocarbon group would be expected to be inoperative in the environment of the claimed dyes. *Ex parte Altermatt*, 183 U.S.P.Q. 436, 437, 438 (PO Bd. App. 1974).

Early Disclosure. *See also* **Early Filing.**

In an unpredictable art, does 35 U.S.C. §112 require disclosure of a test with every species covered by a claim? To require such a complete disclosure would apparently necessitate a patent application with thousands of examples or a disclosure with thousands of catalysts along with information as to whether each exhibits catalytic behavior resulting in the production of the desired products. More importantly, such a requirement would force an inventor seeking adequate patent protection to carry out a prohibitive number of actual experiments. This would tend to discourage inventors from filing patent applications in an unpredictable area since the patent claims would have to be limited to those embodiments that are expressly disclosed. A potential infringer could readily avoid "literal" infringement of such claims by merely finding another analogous catalyst complex that could be used in forming the same products. *In re Angstadt and Griffin*, 537 F.2d 498, 190 U.S.P.Q. 214, 218 (C.C.P.A. 1976).

ᛦ

The public policy favors early disclosure, and thus the law is reluctant to displace an inventor who was the first to disclose his invention to the public. *Honeywell, Inc. v. Diamond*, 499 F.Supp. 924, 208 U.S.P.Q. 452 (D.C. 1980).

ᛦ

Early public disclosure is a linchpin of the patent system. As between a prior inventor who benefits from a process by selling its product, but suppresses, conceals, or otherwise keeps the process from the public, and a later inventor who promptly files a patent application from which the public will gain disclosure of the process, the law favors the latter. *W. L. Gore & Associates, Inc. v. Garlock, Inc.*, 721 F.2d 1540, 220 U.S.P.Q. 303 (Fed. Cir. 1983).

Early Filing. *See also* **Early Disclosure.**

Early filing of an application with its disclosure of novel compounds which possess significant therapeutic use is to be encouraged. Requiring specific testing of the thousands of prostaglandin analogs encompassed by the present claim in order to satisfy the how-to-use requirement of 35 U.S.C. §112 would delay disclosure and frustrate, rather than further, the interests of the public. *In re Bundy*, 642 F.2d 430, 209 U.S.P.Q. 48, 52 (C.C.P.A. 1981).

Economic Advantage.

The elements for intentional interference with prospective economic advantage are: (1) an economic relationship between the plaintiff and a third party with probability of ripening into a future economic benefit for the plaintiff; (2) knowledge of the defendant about this relationship; (3) intentional acts by the defendant to disrupt the relationship; (4) actual disruption of the relationship; and (5) damages proximately caused by the defendant's acts. *Litton Systems Inc. v. Honeywell Inc.*, 87 F.3d 1559, 39 U.S.P.Q.2d 1321, 1331 (Fed. Cir. 1996).

Economic Prejudice.

Economic prejudice may arise where a defendant and possibly others will suffer the loss of monetary investments or incur damages which likely would have been prevented by earlier suit. *Wanlass v. General Electric Co.*, 148 E.3d 1334, 46 U.S.P.Q.2d 1915, 1917 (Fed. Cir. 1998).

Economics. *See also* Cost, Funding, Poverty, Saving.

If a new combination and arrangement of known elements produces a new and beneficial result never attained before, such as increased production, this may be evidence of invention. *See Webster Loom Co. v. Elias S. Higgins*, 105 U.S. (15 Otto.) 580, 591, 592 (1882). If the only novelty of a process is greater economy, that may be a sufficient improvement. *See American Wood Paper Co. v. Fiber Disintegrating Co.*, 90 U.S. (23 Wall.) 566 (1874).

ᵿ

Economy of production is as valid a basis for invention as foresight in the disclosure of new means. *Reiner v. The I. Leon Company*, 285 F.2d 501, 128 U.S.P.Q. 25, 27, 28 (2d Cir. 1960).

ᵿ

A new combination of old elements, whereby an old result is obtained in a more facile, economical and efficient way, or whereby a new and useful result is secured, may be protected by a patent. *Elgen Manufacturing Corp. v. Ventfabrics, Inc.*, 207 F.Supp. 240, 134 U.S.P.Q. 5, 14 (Ill. 1962).

ᵿ

If the only novelty of a process is greater economy, that may be a sufficient improvement. *Borden, Inc. v. Occidental Petroleum Corporation*, 381 F.Supp. 1178, 182 U.S.P.Q. 472, 490 (Tex. 1974).

ᵿ

Economics alone would motivate a person of ordinary skill in the art producing a freeze-dried coffee by the reference process to find the highest final moisture content consistent with the excellent properties the reference describes. *In re Clinton, Johnson, Meyer, Pfluger, and Jacobs*, 527 F.2d 1226, 188 U.S.P.Q. 365, 367 (C.C.P.A. 1976).

ᵿ

Eliminating the cost of the preliminary step of wax impregnation would have been sufficient motivation for doing so. *In re Thompson and Ihde*, 545 F.2d 1290, 192 U.S.P.Q. 275, 277 (C.C.P.A. 1976).

ᵿ

An inventor may rely on activities directed toward raising capital or funding for a project in order to prove that he acted with due diligence in reducing his invention to practice. *American Standard Inc. v. Pfizer Inc.*, 722 F. Supp. 86, 14 U.S.P.Q.2d 1673, 1694 (Del. 1989).

ᚹ

The very nature of patent law—the reward to the inventor of a monopoly on the use of his invention—provides an economic incentive to a patent applicant. "[T]here is nothing improper, illegal or inequitable in filing a patent application for the purpose of obtaining a right to exclude a known competitor's product from the market." *Burroughs Wellcome Co. v. Barr Laboratories Inc.*, 828 F.Supp. 1200, 29 U.S.P.Q.2d 1721, 1727 (N.C. 1993).

ᚹ

As a general rule, lack of funds does not excuse a delay in bringing suit. *Valutron N.V. v. NCR Corp.*, 33 U.S.P.Q.2d 1986, 1991 (Ohio 1992), *aff'd* (Fed. Cir. 1993), *cert. denied*, (S.Ct. 1994).

ᚹ

Poverty and personal hardship suffered by a patentee are legitimate factors to be considered when determining the reasonableness of a patentee's delay in bringing suit against an infringer. *Cover v. Hydramatic Packing Co. Inc.*, 34 U.S.P.Q.2d 1128, 1131 (Pa. 1994).

Effect.

If, on final disposition of a writ of error or appeal, the judgment or decree brought under review is not substantially reversed, it is affirmed, and the writ of error or appeal has not been prosecuted to effect. What is meant by prosecuting an appeal to effect? It is an expression substantially equivalent to prosecuting an appeal with success, to make substantial and prevailing one's attempt to reverse the decree or judgment awarded against him. An appeal has been prosecuted to effect when appellee must still prove on remand that he suffered a compensable harm. Conversely, when an appellee has proven that damages are due, and the remand is merely to determine the quantum of injury, it is not unreasonable for a supersedeas bond issued pending appellant's appeal to remain effective during this recalculation period. When an appellant has merely succeeded in having a case remanded for recomputation of damages, it would be a stretch to say that the appeal was "substantially" successful or that the judgment was "substantially" reversed. *Beatrice Foods Co. v. New England Printing & Lithographing Co.*, 930 F.2d 1572, 18 U.S.P.Q.2d 1548, 1550, 1551 (Fed. Cir. 1991).

Effective. *See also* Pharmaceutical, Tumour.

A claim calling for an effective amount is, on its face, indefinite if it fails to state the function that is to be rendered effective. The claim does not point out the invention with the requisite particularity. *In re Frederikksen and Nielsen*, 213 F.2d 547, 102 U.S.P.Q. 35, 36 (C.C.P.A. 1954).

ᚹ

Claims are too broad and indefinite when they call for "an effective amount" of a designated component without specifying what the intended effect is. Claims are also too broad and incomplete when they specify up to about a designated percent by weight of a specified component because they read on compositions totally lacking that component. *Ex parte Dobson, Jacob, and Herschler,* 165 U.S.P.Q. 29, 30 (PO Bd. App. 1969).

ᛒ

A "fungicidally effective" amount was limited to the broadest (exemplary) range disclosed in the specification. *Rhône-Poulenc Agrochime S.A. v. Biagro Western Sales Inc.,* 35 U.S.P.Q.2d 1203, 1205 (Cal. 1994).

Effective Date. *See also* **Foreign, Foreign Patent Application, Patented, 35 U.S.C. §120.**

A reference patent is effective as of the date the application for it was filed in the United States; 35 U.S.C. §119 does not modify the express provision of 35 U.S.C. §102(e) in this regard. *In re Hilmer, Korger, Weyer, and Aumuller,* 359 F.2d 859, 149 U.S.P.Q. 480, 482 (C.C.P.A. 1966).

ᛒ

Evidence of non-obviousness which has developed only after the filing date of an application to a claimed invention cannot be ignored. *In re Tiffin and Erdman,* 443 F.2d 394, 170 U.S.P.Q. 88, 92 (C.C.P.A. 1971).

ᛒ

Specific reference in a patent only to a parent or immediately preceding patent application that, in turn, refers to a grandparent or earlier patent application is not sufficient to provide the issued patent the benefit of the filing date of the grandparent patent application. *Kelley Manufacturing Company v. Lilliston Corporation,* 180 U.S.P.Q. 364, 367 (N.C. 1973).

ᛒ

References are properly cited for the purpose of showing a fact even though their effective date, for prior art purposes, is subsequent to appellant's earliest filing date. *In re Langer,* 503 F.2d 1380, 183 U.S.P.Q. 288, 297 (C.C.P.A. 1974).

ᛒ

35 U.S.C. §102(e) is limited to a United States patent. The effective date, as a reference, of the German document relied upon by the Examiner to defeat another's right to a patent is only the date upon which it was laid open to the public. *Ex parte Smolka and Schwuger,* 207 U.S.P.Q. 232, 235 (PTO Bd. App. 1980).

ᛒ

The effective date of a patent is fixed by 35 U.S.C. §120. An inventor receives the benefit of a parent application's filing date if the second application discloses the same invention as the parent application. Under the statute, therefore, the critical issue becomes whether the parent application discloses the same invention as is claimed by the second application. Where a second application does not disclose the same invention as the parent application, the patent carries two effective dates. Any new subject matter disclosed in the second application carries the effective date of the second application's filing. The filing date of the parent application is the effective date for claims (in the second application) drawn to subject matter that is also disclosed in the parent application, as well as for claims (added through amendment) that define subject matter that is deemed "inherent" in the parent application. *Foseco International Ltd. v. Fireline Inc.*, 607 F. Supp. 1537, 224 U.S.P.Q. 888 (Ohio 1984).

Effective Filing Date. *See also* Effective Date.

The filing date of a copending parent application is the effective date for claims in a second application drawn to subject matter that is also disclosed in the parent application, as well as for claims (added through amendment) that define subject matter that is deemed "inherent" to the parent application. Relying on the MPEP definition of a cip application, the *Litton* Court [*Litton Systems, Inc. v. Whirlpool Corp.*, 728 F.2d 1423, 221 U.S.P.Q. 97 (Fed. Cir. 1984)] held that the filing of a cip application raises an irrebuttable presumption that the cip application adds new subject matter. An applicant's filing of a cip application, therefore, estops the applicant from arguing that the cip application does not disclose new subject matter or that the subject matter was inherent in an earlier application. *Foseco International Ltd. v. Fireline, Inc.*, 607 F. Supp. 1537, 224 U.S.P.Q. 888 (Ohio 1984).

Efficacy.

There is a significant difference between potency and efficacy. Greater potency only means that a smaller pill can be used, whereas greater efficacy refers to clinical superiority. *United States of America v. Ciba-Geigy Corporation*, 508 F.Supp. 1157, 211 U.S.P.Q. 529, 541 (N.J. 1979).

Egg.[1]

EIC (Examiner in Chief).

Election.

In a multi-party interference an assignee of two applications involved in the interference must make an election between them unless the assignee demonstrates an inability to obtain facts upon which to base an election. *Young v. Young, Baker, and Canaday v. Giffard*, 119 U.S.P.Q. 470, 471 (Comm'r of Pat. 1955).

Election of Species. *See also* Species.

After making an election-of-species requirement, repeating same after election and traversal, making the requirement final, and allowing the elected claims, the Examiner withdrew all other claims (including generic claims) from consideration "since they were

---

[1] See claims 1 to 4 of United States Patent No. 5,246,717.

not limited to the elected invention." In withdrawing the so-called generic claims from further prosecution, Rules 141 and 146 (37 C.F.R. §1.141 and §1.146) were violated. *Ex parte Bridgeford, Turbak, and Burke,* 172 U.S.P.Q. 308, 309 (PO Dir. 1971).

Electrical.

The first paragraph of 35 U.S.C. §112 requires that the scope of the claims bear a reasonable correlation to the scope of enablement provided by the specification to persons of ordinary skill in the art. In cases providing predictable factors, such as mechanical or electrical elements, a single embodiment provides broad enablement in the sense that, once imagined, other embodiments can be made without difficulty and their performance characteristics predicted by resort to known scientific laws. In cases involving unpredictable factors, such as most chemical reactions and physiological activity, the scope of enablement obviously varies inversely with the degree of unpredictability of the factors involved. *In re Fisher*, 427 F.2d 833, 166 U.S.P.Q. 18, 24 (C.C.P.A. 1970).

Element. *See also* All Elements Rule, Old Element, Radical, Subcombination.

All "compositions of matter" are "combinations" if they consist of two or more substances in some degree of correlationship. Chemical compounds are clearly included as one kind of "composition of matter." A radical constituting an element of a claimed chemical compound is an "element in a claim for a combination" within the meaning of 35 U.S.C. §112, third paragraph. *In re Barr, Williams, and Whitmore,* 444 F.2d 588, 170 U.S.P.Q. 330, 336 (C.C.P.A. 1971).

ᛦ

The mere fact each reference discloses some particular claimed elements is not sufficient for obviousness without some direction from the prior art. *Ex parte Shepard and Gushue,* 188 U.S.P.Q. 536, 538 (PTO Bd. App. 1974).

ᛦ

Presuming arguendo that the references show the elements or concepts urged, the Examiner presented no line of reasoning as to why the artisan reviewing only the collective teachings of the references would have found it obvious to selectively pick and choose various elements and/or concepts from the several references relied on to arrive at the claimed invention. In the instant application, the Examiner has done little more than cite references to show that one or more elements or some combinations thereof, when each is viewed in a vacuum, are known. The claimed invention, however, is clearly directed to a combination of elements. That is to say, the appellant does not claim that he has invented one or more new elements but has presented claims to a new combination of elements. To support the conclusion that the claimed combination is directed to obvious subject matter, either the references must expressly or impliedly suggest the claimed combination or the Examiner must present a convincing line of reasoning as to why the artisan would have found the claimed invention to have been obvious in light of the teachings of the references. The Board found nothing in the references that would expressly or impliedly teach or suggest the modifications urged by the Examiner. Additionally, the Board found no line of reasoning in the answer as to why the artisan would have found the modifications urged by the Examiner to have been obvious. Based upon the record, the artisan would not have found it obvious to selectively pick and choose elements or concepts from the various references so as to arrive at the claimed invention without using the claims as a guide. *Ex parte Clapp,* 227 U.S.P.Q. 972 (B.P.A.I. 1985).

ᛦ

In situations in which the element or subcombination issues after the combination, the matter should be analyzed as one of a generic claim issued after a later filed specific or improvement claim." *In re Emert,* 124 F.3d 1458 44 U.S.P.Q.2d 1149, 1152 (Fed. Cir. 1997).

Eleventh Amendment. *See also* State, States' Immunity.

The University's charge of patent infringement is the claim that creates the controversy which supports the declaratory judgment action. The Eleventh Amendment does not bar raising defenses to the University's charge of patent infringement, whether these defenses arise under federal or state law. *Genentech Inc. v. Eli Lilly and Co.,* 998 F.2d 931, 27 U.S.P.Q.2d 1241, 1251 (Fed. Cir. 1993).

ᛦ

The Patent Act amendments, which abrogate the States' Eleventh Amendment immunity, are "appropriate legislation" under Section 5 of the Fourteenth Amendment. *College Savings Bank v. Florida Prepaid Postsecondary Education Expense Board,* 42 U.S.P.Q.2d 1487, 1509 (N.J. 1996).

ᛦ

Although the University has the right to refrain from taking actions that implicate federal jurisdiction, and Congress cannot legislate otherwise, when the University chooses to enter the federal arena, when the University's action in creating the controversy is within its sole control and initiative, and when the University invokes the systems of federal law and federal judicial power for enforcement of federal property rights, actionable only in federal court, including property rights extraterritorial to the state, the state is deemed to have waived it immunity from federal authority to resolve that controversy. Although the University argues that it did not consent to the federal declaratory judgment action brought by Genentech, the declaratory action was enabled solely by the University's deliberate acts. *Genentech Inc. v. University of California,* 143 F.3d 1446, 46 U.S.P.Q.2d 1586, 1592 (Fed. Cir. 1998).

Eliminating Elements. *See* Reduction in Elements.

Eliminating Steps. *See* Reduction in Steps.

Embodiment.

A patent is not limited to the embodiment of the invention shown and described in the specification since the claims of the patent measure the invention. An inventor is required only to set forth the best mode contemplated by him for carrying out his invention. Having done so, he is deemed to claim every form in which his invention may be copied.

Dart Industries Inc. v. E.I. du Pont de Nemours and Company, 348 F.Supp. 1338, 175 U.S.P.Q. 540, 544 (Ill. 1972).

Embrace. *See* **Generic Disclosure, Selection.**

Eminent Domain. *See also* **Second Lowest Bidder.**

A patentee takes his patent from the United States subject to the government's eminent domain rights to obtain what it needs for manufacture and to use the same. The government has graciously consented to be sued in the Claims Court for reasonable and entire compensation for what would be infringement if by a private person. The same principles apply to injunctions that are nothing more than giving the aid of the courts to the enforcement of the patentee's right to exclude. Though injunctions may seem to say that making for and selling to the government is forbidden, injunctions based on patent rights cannot in reality do that because of 28 U.S.C. §1498(a). *W.L. Gore & Associates, Inc. v. Garlock, Inc.,* 842 F.2d 1275, 6 U.S.P.Q.2d 1277, 1284 (Fed. Cir. 1988).

Empirical. *See also* **Drug, Predictability, Relationship.**

Although there is a vast amount of knowledge about general relationships in the chemical arts, chemistry is still largely empirical, and there is often great difficulty in predicting precisely how a given compound will behave. While analogy is useful at times, organic [as well as inorganic] chemistry is essentially an experimental science, and results are often uncertain, unpredictable and unexpected. *In re Carleton,* 599 F.2d 1021, 202 U.S.P.Q. 165, 170 (C.C.P.A. 1979).

ω

The law has other tests of invention than subtle conjecture of what might have been seen and yet was not. It regards a change as evidence of novelty and the acceptance and utility of change as further evidence, even as a demonstration. Nor does it detract from its merit that it is the result of experiment and not the instant and perfect product of inventive power. A patentee may be baldly empirical, seeing nothing beyond his experiments and the result; yet, if he has added a new and valuable article to the world's utilities, he is entitled to the rank and protection of an inventor. It is certainly not necessary that he understand or be able to state the scientific principles underlying his invention, and it is immaterial whether he can stand a successful examination as to the speculative ideas involved. *Diamond Rubber Co. v. Consolidated Rubber Tire Co.,* 220 U.S. 428, 435 (1911).

Empirical Formula.

Since the compound can be properly defined by its empirical formula together with its physical and chemical characteristics and infrared absorption spectra, it is improper to include additional claims which define the compound by its method of preparation or only by a coined name. *Ex parte Brian, Radley, Curtis, and Elson,* 118 U.S.P.Q. 242, 244 (PO Bd. App. 1958).

Employee. *See also* **Employment Agreement, Shop Right.**

One employed to make an invention and who succeeds, during his term of service, in accomplishing that task, is bound to assign to his employer any patent obtained. The reason is that he has only produced that which he was employed to invent. His invention is the precise subject of the contract of employment. A term of the agreement necessarily is that what he is paid to produce belongs to his paymaster. On the other hand, if the employment be general, albeit it covers a field of labor and effort in the performance of which the employee conceived the invention for which he obtained a patent, the contract is not so broadly construed as to require an assignment of the patent. *United States v. Dubilier Condensor Corp.*, 289 U.S. 178, 17 U.S.P.Q. 154, 158 (1933).

ʊ

An employee, not specifically hired to invent, who perfects an invention on company time and with company assistance cannot be compelled to assign to his employer a patent obtained on the invention. *Banner Metals, Inc. v. Lockwood*, 125 U.S.P.Q. 29, 35, 178 Cal. App. 2d 643 (Cal. 1960).

ʊ

A prior contribution of another employee of plaintiff was not prior art, but was adequate to qualify the employee as a coinventor and thus justify granting a motion for conversion by the plaintiff in an infringement action. *Norton Co. v. Carborundum Co.*, 397 F. Supp. 639, 186 U.S.P.Q. 189, 196 (Mass. 1975).

ʊ

Employment alone does not require an inventor to assign a patent to his employer. Absent a specific agreement, an employed inventor's rights and duties with respect to an invention or concept arise from the inventor's employment status when he actually designed the invention. Where an employer hires an employee to design a specific invention or solve a specific problem, the employee has a duty to assign the resulting patent. Where the employee is not hired specifically to design or invent, but nevertheless conceives of a device during working hours with the use of the employer's materials and equipment, the employer is granted an irrevocable but non exclusive right to use the invention under the shop-right rule. A shop right is an employer's royalty or fee, a non-exclusive and non-transferable license to use an employee's patented invention. *Ingersoll-Rand Co. v. Ciavatta*, 8 U.S.P.Q.2d 1537, 542 A.2d 879, 110 N.J. 609 (NJ 1988).

ʊ

When an employee has acquired patents on inventions developed by his former employer, the courts will hold the wrongdoer to be a constructive trustee of the property misappropriated and will order a conveyance by the wrongdoer to the former employer. *Richardson v. Suzuki Motor Co., Ltd.*, 868 F.2d 1226, 9 U.S.P.Q.2d 1913 (Fed. Cir. 1989).

ʊ

When a company employee reduces an invention to practice in the course of his employment on behalf of the inventor and does not contest inventorship, such reduction to practice is on the inventor's behalf by a person authorized to do so. *De Solms v. Schoenwald*, 15 U.S.P.Q.2d 1507, 1510 (B.P.A.I. 1990).

ω

An implied-in-fact contract to assign patent rights resulted from employer's assigning employee as chief engineer on project, employee's spending 70% of his time on project, employee's making invention and reducing it to practice using employer's resources, employees, shop tools, materials and time, employee's recognizing employer's role and employer's paying for prosecution of patent application. *Teets v. Chromalloy Gas Turbine Corp.*, 83 F.3d 403, 38 U.S.P.Q.2d 1695, 1698 (Fed. Cir. 1996).

Employer.

A preliminary injunction was granted to an employer to restore claims canceled from a pending application by a former employee and to permit the employer's attorney to prosecute the restored claims. The claims in question covered subject matter which the employer had reason to believe was its property, rights to which would be permanently lost if the subject matter of the canceled claims was not further prosecuted. *Compact Van Equipment Co., Inc. v. Leggett & Platt, Inc.*, 566 F.2d 952, 196 U.S.P.Q. 721, 722 (5th Cir. 1978).

Employment Agreement.[2,3,4]

Contractual provisions requiring assignment of post-employment inventions are commonly referred to as trailer or holdover clauses. Holdover clauses in employment contracts are enforceable only if they constitute a reasonable and justifiable restriction on the right of employees to work in their profession for subsequent employers. Their legitimate purpose is to prevent an employee from appropriating to his own use or to the use of a subsequent employer inventions relating to and stemming from work done for a previous employer. Holdover clauses are simply recognition of the fact of business life that employees sometimes carry with them to new employers inventions or ideas so related to work done for a former employer that, in equity and good conscience, the fruits of that work should belong to the former employer. Holdover clauses must be limited to reasonable times and to subject matter that the employee worked on or had knowledge of during his employment. Unless expressly agreed otherwise, an employer has no right (under a holdover clause) to inventions made outside the scope of the employee's former activities, and made on and with a subsequent employer's time and funds. Regarding the validity of a contractual provision requiring the employee to disclose and assign all ideas and improvements for five years following termination of employment, the court articulated a three part test: (a) Is the restraint reasonable in the sense that it is no greater than necessary to protect the employer in some legitimate interest? (b) Is the restraint reasonable in the sense that it is not unduly harsh or oppressive on the employee? (c) Is the

---

[2] *See Georgia-Pacific Corp. v. Lieberam*, 959 F.2d 901, 22 U.S.P.Q.2d 1383, 1390 (11th Cir. 1992).

[3] *See American Telephone and Telegraph Co. v. Integrated Network Corp.*, 972 F.2d 1321, 23 U.S.P.Q.2d 1918 (Fed. Cir. 1992).

[4] *See Air Products and Chemicals, Inc. v. Johnson*, 442 A.2d 1114, 215 U.S.P.Q. 547, 550 (Pa. 1982).

restraint reasonable in the sense that it is not injurious to the public? *Ingersoll-Rand Co. v. Ciavatta*, 8 U.S.P.Q.2d 1537, 542 A.2d 879, 110 N.J. 609 (NJ 1988).

EMVR. *See* **Entire Market Value Rule.**

Enablement. *See also* **Computer Program, Credibility, Disclosure, Enabling Disclosure, How to Make, How to Use, Objective Enablement, Program.**

When a patent is issued, it constitutes evidence that everything disclosed by it was known by others in this country at least as early as the filing date of the application on which the patent issued. *In re Beck, Siebel, and Bosskuhler*, 155 F.2d 398, 69 U.S.P.Q. 520, 523 (C.C.P.A. 1946).

ω

Enablement requirements for a pending application can be satisfied by amendment to make a cross-reference to a concurrently or previously filed copending application of the same inventor without involving improper "new matter." *Ex parte Wettstein, Vischer, Meystre, Kahnt, and Neher*, 140 U.S.P.Q. 187, 188 (PO Bd. App. 1962).

ω

A specification need not contain a working example if the invention is otherwise disclosed in such a manner that one skilled in the art would be able to practice it without an undue amount of experimentation. *In re Borkowski and Van Venrooy*, 422 F.2d 904, 164 U.S.P.Q. 642 (C.C.P.A. 1970).

ω

An inventor should be allowed to dominate future patentable inventions of others where those inventions are based in some way on his teachings. Such improvements, while unobvious from his teachings, are still within his contribution, since the improvement is made possible by his work. It is equally apparent, however, that he must not be permitted to achieve this dominance by claims that are insufficiently supported and hence not in compliance with the first paragraph of 35 U.S.C. §112. That paragraph requires that the scope of the claims must bear a reasonable correlation to the scope of enablement provided by the specification to persons of ordinary skill in the art. In cases involving predictable factors, such as mechanical or electrical elements, a single embodiment provides broad enablement in the sense that, once imagined, other embodiments can be made without difficulty and their performance characteristics predicted by resort to known scientific laws. In cases involving unpredictable factors, such as most chemical reactions and physiological activity, the scope of enablement obviously varies inversely with the degree of unpredictability of the factors involved. *In re Fisher*, 427 F.2d 833, 166 U.S.P.Q. 18, 24 (C.C.P.A. 1970).

ω

It has never been contended that the appellants, when they included the disputed term in their specification, intended only to indicate a single compound. Accepting, therefore, that the term is a generic one, its recitation must be taken as an assertion by the appellants that all of the "considerable number of compounds" that are included within the generic term would, as a class, be operative to produce the asserted enhancement of adhesion characteristics. The only relevant concern of the Patent Office under these circumstances should be over the truth of any such assertion. The first paragraph of 35 U.S.C. §112 requires nothing more than objective enablement. How such a teaching is set forth, either by the use of illustrative examples or by broad terminology, is of no importance.

A specification disclosure that contains a teaching of the manner and process of making and using the invention in terms that correspond in scope to those used in describing and defining the subject matter sought to be patented must be taken as in compliance with the enabling requirement of the first paragraph of 35 U.S.C. §112 unless there is reason to doubt the objective truth of the statements contained therein that must be relied on for enabling support. Assuming that sufficient reason for such doubt does exist, a rejection for failure to teach how to make and/or use will be proper on that basis. In any event, it is incumbent on the Patent Office, whenever a rejection on this basis is made, to explain why it doubts the truth or accuracy of any statement in a supporting disclosure and to back up assertions of its own with acceptable evidence or reasoning that is inconsistent with the contested statement. Otherwise, there would be no need for the applicant to go to the trouble and expense of supporting his presumptively accurate disclosure. *In re Marzocchi and Horton,* 439 F.2d 220, 169 U.S.P.Q. 367 (C.C.P.A. 1971).

ω

Where test methods in the field of the patent are so well known that reference to them in the patent is needless to enable those working in the field to follow the teaching of the patent, even complete silence on dosage and method of administration of the original application suffices to meet the how-to-use requirement of 35 U.S.C. §112. *Carter-Wallace, Inc. v. Davis-Edwards Pharmacal Corp.,* 341 F. Supp. 1303, 173 U.S.P.Q. 65, 104 (N.Y. 1972).

ω

A method of making starting materials not known in the art must be set forth in order to comply with the enablement requirement. A rejection for failure to enable because of failure to disclose how to obtain starting materials is sustainable only when the method of obtaining them would not be apparent to one of ordinary skill in the art. *In re Brebner,* 455 F.2d 1402, 173 U.S.P.Q. 169 (C.C.P.A. 1972).

ω

If an applicant fails to challenge an Examiner's conclusion regarding enablement or fails to do so in a timely manner, the rejection stands. *In re Eynde, Pollet, and de Cat,* 480 F.2d 1364, 178 U.S.P.Q. 470, 474 (C.C.P.A. 1973).

ω

That experimentation may be involved with the selection of proportions and particle sizes is not determinative of the question of scope of enablement; it is only undue experimentation that is fatal. *In re Geerdes,* 491 F.2d 1260, 180 U.S.P.Q. 789, 793 (C.C.P.A. 1974).

ω

A patent issued after the appellant's filing date cannot be relied upon as evidence that the appellant's specification was enabling. *In re Scarborough,* 500 F.2d 560, 182 U.S.P.Q. 298, 299 (C.C.P.A. 1974).

ω

Enabling requirements of the statute are satisfied when the specification, taken with the prior art, clearly teaches an effective process for making claimed compounds from known starting materials, and the specification describes methods of using the claimed compounds. *Ex parte Gastambide, Thal, Rohrbach, and Laroche,* 189 U.S.P.Q. 643, 645 (PTO Bd. App. 1974).

ω

A specification which "describes" does not necessarily also "enable" one skilled in the art to make or use the claimed invention. *In re Armbruster,* 512 F.2d 676, 185 U.S.P.Q. 152, 153 (C.C.P.A. 1975).

ω

If the appellant's 1953 application provided sufficient enablement, considering all available evidence (whenever that evidence became available) of the 1953 state of the art, i.e., of the condition of knowledge about all art-related facts existing in 1953, then the fact of that enablement was established for all time and a later change in the state of the art cannot change it. The PTO has not challenged the appellants' assertion that their 1953 application enabled those skilled in the art in 1953 to make and use "a solid polymer" as described in a claim. The appellants disclosed, as the only then-existing way to make such a polymer, a method of making the crystalline form. To say now that the appellants should have disclosed in 1953 the amorphous form (which did not exist until 1962) would be to impose an impossible burden on inventors and thus on the patent system. There cannot, in an effective patent system, be such a burden placed on the right to broad claims. To restrict the appellants to the crystalline form disclosed, under such circumstances, would be a poor way to stimulate invention, and particularly to encourage its early disclosure. To demand such restriction is merely to state a policy against broad protection for pioneer inventions, a policy both shortsighted and unsound from the standpoint of promoting progress in the useful arts, which is the constitutional purpose of the patent laws. *In re Hogan and Banks,* 559 F.2d 595, 194 U.S.P.Q. 527 (C.C.P.A. 1977).

ω

A later-existing state of the art cannot be used in determining enablement under 35 U.S.C. §112. *In re Koller, Hartl, and Kirschner,* 613 F.2d 819, 204 U.S.P.Q. 702, 706 (C.C.P.A. 1980); *In re Glass,* 492 F.2d 1228, 181 U.S.P.Q. 31, 34 (C.C.P.A. 1974).

ω

Patents filed prior to, but issued after, the filing date of the applicant's parent application cannot be relied upon as evidence of enablement if applicant wishes to retain the benefit of his parent application's filing date. *In re Strahilevitz,* 668 F.2d 1229, 212 U.S.P.Q. 561 (C.C.P.A. 1982).

ω

An application which describes a specific physiological use for claimed compounds, but omits identification of a host or applicable dosages, satisfies the "how to use" requirement of the first paragraph of 35 U.S.C. §112 in view of the fact that a prior art reference discloses a host and dosages for the same use of structurally related compounds. *Bey and Jung v. Kollonitsch and Patchett,* 215 U.S.P.Q. 454, 458 (PTO Bd. Pat. Intf. 1981).

ω

A description of several newly discovered strains of bacteria (having one particularly desirable metabolic property in terms of the conventionally measured culture characteristics and a number of metabolic and physiological properties) docs not enable one of ordinary skill in the relevant art independently to discover additional strains having the same specific, desirable metabolic property (i.e., the production of a particular antibiotic). A verbal description of a new species does not enable one of ordinary skill in the relevant art to obtain strains of that species over and above the specific strains made available through deposit in one of the recognized culture depositories. *Ex parte Jackson, Theriault, Sinclair, Fager, and Karwowski,* 217 U.S.P.Q. 804, 806 (PTO Bd. App. 1982).

ʊ

A disclosure was regarded as totally inadequate with respect to the manner of using claimed compositions since it lacked any information as to the host, the dosage level, mode or routes of administration, or how to prepare the composition for administration. Experimentation was required to ascertain the parameters of the invention with regard to how to use the claimed materials for inhibiting tissue degradation and treatment of diseases. Determination of effective dose requires pharmaceutical studies. The fact that uses of the claimed products are or may be the subject of later in vivo tests does not render the claimed invention useful at the time of the filing of the involved application. Nowhere in the record did the appellant establish that the doses to be administered were comparable to analogous known compositions nor has the appellant demonstrated that a skilled artisan would know how to use the claimed invention for their intended purposes without undue experimentation. *Ex parte Powers,* 220 U.S.P.Q. 924 (PTO Bd. App. 1982).

ʊ

The PTO argued that a pre-filing deposit with an independent depository, referred to in the specification at the time of filing, was essential to ensure that the disclosure was enabling as of the filing date, which in turn was required so that the filing date might be taken as the date of constructive reduction to practice. The PTO asserted that a post-filing deposit is barred as "new matter," as is the insertion in the specification of reference to such deposit. Constructive reduction to practice, however, does not turn on the question of who has possession of a sample, and thus it does not turn on the inclusion or absence, in the specification as filed, of the name and address of who will have possession of the sample on grant of the patent. The specification, as filed, thus met the requirements of constructive reduction to practice, and the insertion of depository data after filing is not new matter under 35 U.S.C. §132. *In re Lundak,* 773 F.2d 1216, 227 U.S.P.Q. 90 (Fed. Cir. 1985).

ʊ

The test of whether a particular compound described in the prior art may be relied upon to show that claimed subject matter would have been obvious is whether the prior art provides an enabling disclosure with respect to the disclosed prior art compound. No evidence was offered to show an enabling disclosure for the reference structure, while uncontroverted testimony showed the reference structure to be a hypothetical structure. *Ashland Oil, Inc. v. Delta Resins & Refractories, Inc.,* 776 F.2d 281, 227 U.S.P.Q. 657 (Fed. Cir. 1985).

ʊ

There is no requirement in 35 U.S.C. §112 or anywhere else in the patent law that a specification must convince persons skilled in the art that the assertions in the specification are correct. In examining a patent application, the PTO is required to assume that the specification complies with the enablement provisions of §112 unless it has "acceptable evidence or reasoning" to suggest otherwise. The PTO must thus provide reasons supported by the record as a whole why the specification is not enabling. Then and only then does the burden shift to the applicant to show that one of ordinary skill in the art could have practiced the claimed invention without undue experimentation. A patent specification must be enabling as to "the invention" as set forth in the claims. Thus, a disclosure may be insufficient for one claim but sufficient for another. *Gould v. Mossinghoff*, 229 U.S.P.Q. 1 (D.C. 1985).

ϖ

The claimed invention had been reduced to practice prior to the filing date of the subject application, and the appellants had agreed to deposit the hybridoma cell lines at a recognized depository upon the patent grant. In the interim, the cell lines were being maintained at Sloan-Kettering, an institution of renown and integrity. This was regarded as in full compliance with the requirements imposed upon the appellants under *Lundak* [723 F.2d 1216, 227 U.S.P.Q. 90 (Fed. Cir. 1985)]. *Ex parte Old*, 229 U.S.P.Q. 196 (B.P.A.I. 1985).

ϖ

The ultimate question is whether the specification contains a sufficiently explicit disclosure to enable one having ordinary skill in the relevant field to practice the invention claimed therein without the exercise of undue experimentation. The determination of what constitutes undue experimentation in a given case requires the application of a standard of reasonableness, having due regard for the nature of the invention and the state of the art. The test is not merely quantitative, since a considerable amount of experimentation is permissible if it is merely routine or if the specification in question provides a reasonable amount of guidance with respect to the direction in which the experimentation should proceed to enable the determination of how to practice a desired embodiment of the invention claimed. The factors to be considered have been summarized as the quantity of experimentation necessary, the amount of direction or guidance presented, the presence or absence of working examples, the nature of the invention, the state of the prior art, the relative skill of those in that art, the predictability or unpredictability of the art and the breadth of the claims. *Ex parte Forman*, 230 U.S.P.Q. 546 (B.P.A.I. 1986).

ϖ

The fact that the specification is devoid of a working example is without significance. Examples are not necessary. While a full example may have provided additional useful information, one possessed of knowledge of one skilled in this art could practice the invention without the exercise of an undue amount of experimentation. With respect to the best mode rejection, we find no evidence of concealment and are unable to agree with the Examiner that the quality of the appellants' disclosure is so lacking as to effectively result in concealment. *Ex parte Nardi and Simier*, 229 U.S.P.Q. 79 (B.P.A.I. 1986).

ϖ

Enablement is a legal determination of whether a patent enables one skilled in the art to make and use the claimed invention. It is not precluded even if some experimentation is necessary, although the amount of experimentation needed must not be unduly extensive. Enablement is determined as of the filing date of the patent application. Furthermore, a patent need not teach, and preferably omits, what is well known in the art. *Hybritech Inc. v. Monoclonal Antibodies, Inc.*, 802 F.2d 1367, 231 U.S.P.Q. 81 (Fed. Cir. 1986).

ω

Amelioration of the symptoms or even cure of cancer is no longer considered to be "incredible." Nonetheless, decisional law would seem to indicate that the utility in question is sufficiently unusual to justify an Examiner's requiring substantiating evidence. This may be in the form of animal tests that constitute recognized screening procedures with clear relevance to utility in humans. The specification of the appellant's parent application sets forth several animal tests on numerous types of specific cancers as well as in vitro studies, both of which are asserted to be predictive with regard to utility in humans. The Examiner has not challenged the evidence presented in a single, relevant, material respect. There is only the blanket statement of lack of "patentable utility" per se. In fact, the only specific comments the Examiner has directed toward the appellant's evidence are with regard to the breadth of the types of tumor against which the claimed compounds have been shown to be active. The appealed claims are drawn to compounds and not to a method of treatment. Generally speaking, utility in treating a single disease is an adequate basis for the patentability of a pharmaceutical compound under 35 U.S.C. §101. *Ex parte Krepelka*, 231 U.S.P.Q. 746 (B.P.A.I. 1986).

ω

The first paragraph of 35 U.S.C. §112 includes two separate and distinct requirements: (1) that the invention be described and (2) that it be described in such full, clear, concise, and exact terms as to enable any person skilled in the art to make and use it. These two separate and distinct requirements have sometimes been referred to as (1) a description requirement and (2) an enablement requirement. A patent specification may meet the enablement requirement without meeting the description requirement, and thereby fail to comply with §112's mandate. *Kennecott Corp. v. Kyocera International Inc.*, 2 U.S.P.Q.2d 1455 (Cal. 1986).

ω

Claims need not be limited to exemplification or preferred embodiments in order to satisfy enablement requirements. *Ex parte Gould*, 6 U.S.P.Q.2d 1680 (B.P.A.I. 1987).

ω

Enablement is not precluded by the necessity for some experimentation, such as routine screening. However, experimentation needed to practice the invention must not be undue experimentation. The key word is undue, not experimentation. The determination of what constitutes undue experimentation in a case requires the application of a standard of reasonableness, having due regard for the nature of the invention and the state of the art. The test is not merely quantitative since a considerable amount of experimentation is permissible, if it is merely routine, or if the specification in question provides a reasonable amount of guidance with respect to the direction in which the experimentation should proceed. *In re Wands,* 858 F.2d 731, 8 U.S.P.Q.2d 1400, 1404 (Fed. Cir. 1988).

ω

The scope of enablement must be commensurate with the scope of the claims. *Ex parte Sizto,* 9 U.S.P.Q.2d 2081 (B.P.A.I. 1988).

ω

Section 112 of 35 U.S.C. does not require that all of the elements necessary to make the invention work must be described in the specification. Section 112 rather requires that the specification contain a description of a claimed invention in such terms that will enable one skilled in the art to make and use the invention. *Valmont Industries, Inc. v. Reinke Manufacturing Co.,* 14 U.S.P.Q.2d 1374 (Neb. 1990).

ω

Unpredictability of a particular art area may, by itself, provide a reasonable doubt as to the accuracy of a broad statement made in support of the enablement of a claim. *Ex parte Singh,* 17 U.S.P.Q.2d 1714, 1715 (B.P.A.I. 1990).

ω

A Declaration by a qualified expert in the art stating that questioned elements in the application were well known to those of ordinary skill in the art as of the effective filing date and that such elements were routinely built may not be adequate to overcome a rejection for lack of enablement with regard to the making of such elements. Section 112 of 35 U.S.C. requires that, unless the information is well known in the art, the application itself must contain this information; it is not sufficient to provide it only through an expert's Declaration. An expert's opinion on the ultimate legal issue must be supported by something more than a conclusory statement. A statement by a qualified expert that the elements referred to in the application were well known to those of ordinary skill in the art as of the effective date in that they were routinely built was inadequate because the expert did not provide adequate support for his conclusion. *In re Buchner,* 929 F.2d 660, 18 U.S.P.Q.2d 1331, 1332 (Fed. Cir. 1991).

ω

While a reference must enable someone to practice the invention in order to anticipate under 35 U.S.C. §102(b), a non-enabling reference may qualify as prior art for the purpose of determining obviousness under 35 U.S.C. §103, but only for what is disclosed in it. *Symbol Technologies v. Opticon Inc.,* 935 F.2d 1569, 19 U.S.P.Q.2d 1241, 1247 (Fed. Cir. 1991).

ω

The scope of enablement under the first paragraph of 35 U.S.C. §112 varies with the degree of complexity of the subject matter involved. However, there is no distinction in law as to the enablement or description requirements of the first paragraph of 35 U.S.C. §112 based on whether the subject matter is chemical or nonchemical. *Ex parte DesOrneaux,* 25 U.S.P.Q.2d 2040, 2043 (B.P.A.I. 1992).

ω

The test of enablement is whether a person of ordinary skill in the relevant art, using his or her knowledge and the patent disclosure, could make and use the invention without undue experimentation. *Williams Service Group Inc. v. O.B. Cannon & Son Inc.*, 33 U.S.P.Q.2d 1705, 1723 (Pa. 1994).

Enabling Disclosure. *See also* **Enablement, Enabling Prior Art.**

It is not necessary that a reference patent for a device or chemical compound disclose an operative process for producing the article or product. *In re Von Bramer and Ruggles,* 127 F.2d 149, 53 U.S.P.Q. 345, 348 (C.C.P.A. 1942); *overruled.*

ᚹ

A printed publication can constitute an anticipation of a claimed compound even though it fails to disclose how to make or use the compound and it indicates that the compound is "without effect" or "without activity", if (subsequent to the effective date of the reference and prior to the effective date of an application claiming the compound) a further reference teaches how the compound may be made. *In re Samour,* 571 F.2d 559, 197 U.S.P.Q. 1, 3, 4 (C.C.P.A. 1978); *but see In re Stemniski,* 444 F.2d 581, 170 U.S.P.Q. 343 (C.C.P.A. 1971).

ᚹ

The mere naming of a compound in a reference, without more, cannot constitute a description of the compound, particularly when evidence of record suggests that a method suitable for its preparation was not developed until a date later than that of the reference. Compounds listed by name and within the scope of claims in issue were not "described in a printed publication" within the meaning of 35 U.S.C. §102(b). *In re Wiggins, James, and Gittos,* 488 F.2d 538, 179 U.S.P.Q. 421 (C.C.P.A. 1973).

ᚹ

A reference itself must have an enabling disclosure to be used as a proper reference. Section 102(b) of 35 U.S.C. and its predecessor statutes have been interpreted as requiring the description of the invention in a publication to be sufficient to put the public in possession of the invention. *Ex parte Gould,* 231 U.S.P.Q. 943 (B.P.A.I. 1986).

ᚹ

The reexamination statute limits the scope of the reexamination to patents and printed publications. Consequently, the Commissioner may not, on reexamination, consider whether an application contains an enabling disclosure. *Patlex Corp. v. Quigg,* 680 F. Supp. 33, 5 U.S.P.Q.2d 1539 (D.C. 1987).

Enabling Prior Art. *See also* **Enabling Disclosure, Reference.**

The test of whether a particular compound described in the prior art may be relied upon to show that the claimed subject matter would have been obvious is whether the prior art provides an enabling disclosure with respect to the disclosed prior-art compound. No evidence was offered to show an enabling disclosure for the reference structure, while uncontroverted testimony showed the reference structure to be a hypothetical structure. *Ashland Oil, Inc. v. Delta Resins & Refractories, Inc.,* 776 F.2d 281, 227 U.S.P.Q. 657 (Fed. Cir. 1985).

ᚹ

"In order to render a claimed apparatus or method obvious, the prior art must enable one skilled in the art to make and use the apparatus or method." *Rockwell International Corp v. United States*, 147 F.3d 1358, 47 U.S.P.Q.2d 1027, 1032 (Fed. Cir. 1998).

Encompassed. *See also* **Read On.**

If those skilled in the art can tell whether any particular embodiment is or in not within the scope of a claim, the claim fulfills its purpose as a definition. *In re Miller*, 441 F.2d 689, 169 U.S.P.Q. 597, 599 (C.C.P.A. 1971).

Encyclopedia.

Statement in a scientific journal or in an authoritative encyclopedia is not basis for taking judicial notice that controverted phrases are art recognized; the court cannot be certain that the alleged fact is indisputable among reasonable men. However, extra-record references may be used to bolster a weak point that is supported by some evidence in the record even though the court would decline to use them by themselves as a basis for taking judicial notice if there were no evidence at all in the record in support of the point. *In re Barr, Williams, and Whitmore*, 444 F.2d 588, 170 U.S.P.Q. 330, 334 (C.C.P.A. 1971).

ᔭ

Considering the art to which claimed subject matter pertained, the Court of Customs and Patent Appeals took judicial notice of a definition from Kirk-Othmer Encyclopedia of Chemical Technology (2d ed. 1968). *In re Salem, Butterworth, and Ryan*, 553 F.2d 676, 193 U.S.P.Q. 513, 518 (C.C.P.A. 1977).

Encyclopedic Disclosure. *See* **Selection, Shotgun.**

Enforceability.

"Forfeiture [of enforceability] is not favored as a remedy for actions not shown to be culpable." *Molins PLC v. Textron Inc.*, 48 F.3d 1172, 33 U.S.P.Q.2d 1823, 1829 (Fed. Cir. 1995).

Enhanced Damages.

Nine factors that district courts should consider in assessing an infringer's culpability and the appropriate amount of enhanced damages are:

1. whether the infringer deliberately copied the ideas or design of another;
2. whether the infringer investigated the scope of the patent and formed a good-faith belief that it was invalid or that it was not infringed;
3. the infringer's behavior as a party to the litigation;
4. the infringer's size and finacial condition;
5. the closeness of the case;
6. the duration of the infringer's misconduct;
7. remedial action by the infringer;

8. the infringer's motivation for the harm; and
9. the infringer's attempts to conceal its infringement.

Applied Medical Resources Corp. v. United States Surgical Corp., 967 F.Supp. 861 43 U.S.P.Q.2d 1688, 1690 (Va. 1997).

Enhancement of Damages.

When willful infringement or bad faith has been found, the remedy of enhancement of damages not only serves its primary punitive/deterrent role, but in so doing it has the secondary benefit of quantifying the equities as between patentee and infringer. Thus appellate review is conducted on the criteria of abuse of discretion; that is, whether the decision to enhance damages and the amount of any enhancement was grounded on clearly erroneous findings of fact, an incorrect conclusion of law, or a clear error of judgment. *SRI International Inc. v. Advanced Technological Laboratories Inc.*, 127 F.3d 1462, 44 U.S.P.Q.2d 1422, 1427 (Fed. Cir. 1997).

Enlarge. *See* Broaden.

Enlargement.

Enlargement of claims during pendency of a patent application, even if intentionally done to include other inventions, is not sufficient to constitute fraud. *Bolt Associates, Inc. v. Rix Industries*, 178 U.S.P.Q. 171, 173 (Cal. 1973).

Entire-Market-Value Rule. *See also* Convoyed Sale.

In appropriate circumstances the patentee may prove the extent of its lost profits by the entire-market-value rule, based on a showing that the patentee could reasonably anticipate the sale of unpatented components together with the patented components. *Del Mar Avionics, Inc. v. Quinton Instrument Co.*, 836 F.2d 1320, 5 U.S.P.Q.2d 1255 (Fed. Cir. 1987).

ᛒ

Under the entire market value rule, a patentee is entitled to lost profits on unpatented components that accompany the sale of patented components where, in all reasonable probability, the patentee would have made the sales that the infringer made. The record shows that the company that sells the belts also gets the sales of the sprockets, transfer combs, and belt accessories. Under the entire-market-value rule, the court therefore finds that it is reasonably probable that the patentee would have sold the sprockets, transfer combs, and accessories in view of the above findings, and the court's prior determination that it is reasonably probable that the patentee would have made the sales but for the infringement. *Rexnord Inc. v. Laitram Corp.*, 6 U.S.P.Q.2d 1817 (Wis. 1988).

ᛒ

The case law on the entire-market-value rule does not support a holding that a patent holder's licensing agreement determines the parameters of the includable unpatented items. Instead, the law focuses on the patent holder's sales and marketing expectations.

Cases require a court to decide the degree to which the patented items will be extended to include unpatented ones based on a showing by the patent holder of its actual expectations. Licensing agreements are only a factor in determining what categories would be includable. Cases extend inquiry to those unpatented items necessary to make the patented device function, i.e., give it value. Thus, the inquiry attempts to add to an apparatus those elements necessary to the patent's market value that the patent holder had an expectation of selling along with the patented items. An expectation of additional sales must relate back to the patent and not to the unpatented sales. The inquiry should not extend to the universe of every item, no matter how attenuated its relationship to the patented item, simply because a patent holder can establish that it experienced related sales. If unpatented items are to be includable, the patent holder must establish its expectation of compensation for the additional items in marketing the patented ones. *ITT Corp. v. United States,* 17 Cl. Ct. 199, 11 U.S.P.Q.2d 1657, 1669 (1989).

ᴡ

Under the EMVR "[t]he ultimate determining factor (in determining whether the non-patented features should be included in calculating compensation for infringement) is whether the patentee or its licensee can normally anticipate the sale of the unpatented components together with the patented components." Under the entire market value rule, it is not the physical joinder or separation of the contested items that determines their inclusion in or exclusion from the compensation base, so much as their financial and marketing dependence on the patented item under standard marketing procedures for the goods in question. The EMVR involves the extent of compensation rather than a party's entitlement to compensation. *Site Microsurgical Systems Inc. v. The Cooper Companies Inc.,* 797 F.Supp. 333, 24 U.S.P.Q.2d 1463, 1467, 1468, 1469 (Del. 1992).

ᴡ

A patentee has an opportunity, at trial, to establish predicate facts that might entitle him to present evidence of lost sales of unpatented replacement parts as relevant to the calculation of a reasonable royalty for the patented device. *Hilleby v. FMC Corp.,* 25 U.S.P.Q.2d 1423, 1426 (Cal. 1992).

ᴡ

The entire market value rule has typically been applied to include in the compensation base unpatented components of a device when the unpatented and patented components are physically part of the same machine. The rule has been extended to allow inclusion of physically separate unpatented components normally sold with the patented components. However, in such cases, the unpatented and patented components together were considered to be components of a single assembly or parts of a complete machine, or they together constituted a functional unit. *Rite-Hite Corp. v. Kelley Co. Inc.,* 56 F.3d 1538, 35 U.S.P.Q.2d 1065, 1073 (Fed. Cir. 1995).

Entity. *See also* **Another.**

Each of A and B individually is "another" with regard to A&B jointly on a theory of "different legal entities." They are different "entities" in the sense that an invention made jointly by A&B cannot be the sole invention of A or B and vice versa, and certain legal consequences flow from such fact, such as who must apply for patent. However, when A applies for a patent jointly with B, he still has in his head all the information he has as an individual inventor A, the same being true of B. When joint and sole inventions of A and B are related, A commonly discloses the invention of A&B in the course of describing his sole invention. When he so describes the invention of A & B, he is not disclosing "prior art" to the A&B invention, even if he had legal status as "another." *In re Land and Rogers,* 368 F.2d 866, 151 U.S.P.Q. 621, 633 (C.C.P.A. 1966).

Environment.

If an express limitation in a claim does not "pertain to the inventive step but rather to its mere environment," it does not preclude reliance on the doctrine of equivalents to protect against infringement. *Olympic Fastening Systems, Inc. v. Textron Inc.,* 504 F.2d 609, 183 U.S.P.Q. 449, 456 (6th Cir. 1974).

Ephemeral. *See* Transitory.

Equation. *See* Mathematical Equation.

Equipoise.

There is no authority for holding evidence to be in equipoise for the sole reason that a court cannot decide between conflicting experts. The mere fact that experts disagree does not mean that the party with the burden of proof loses. *Andrew Corp. v. Gabriel Electronics, Inc.,* 847 F.2d 819, 6 U.S.P.Q.2d 2010 (Fed. Cir. 1988).

Equitable Defenses. *See also* Clean Hands, Laches, Estoppel.

As with all equitable defenses, a defendant might not be permitted to invoke laches or estoppel if the defendant's own conduct has been inequitable. Although a showing of egregious conduct may persuade a court that the equities do not lie with the defendant, a plaintiff's allegations of "willful infringement" do not automatically bar the alleged infringer from asserting the laches and estoppel defenses; this is a matter for the court to determine in its equitable discretion. *Western Electric Co. Inc. v. Piezo Technology Inc.,* 15 U.S.P.Q.2d 1401, 1409 (Fla. 1990).

Equitable Estoppel.

Equitable estoppel bars claims for patent infringement if Mainland committed itself to act, and acted as a direct consequence of the conduct of Standal's Patents. Estoppel to assert patent rights requires (a) unreasonable and inexcusable delay, (b) prejudice to the defendant, (c) affirmative conduct by patentee's inducing belief of abandonment of claims against the alleged infringer, and (d) detrimental reliance by the infringer. Estoppel by implied license cannot arise out of unilateral expectations or even reasonable hopes of one party. Five years silence alone is not enough to give rise to estoppel. *Mainland Industries, Inc. v. Standal's Patents Ltd.,* 799 F.2d 746, 230 U.S.P.Q. 772 (Fed. Cir. 1986).

As equitable defenses, laches and equitable estoppel are matters committed to the sound discretion of the trial judge, and the trial court's decision is reviewed by the CAFC under the "abuse of discretion" standard.

1. Equitable estoppel is cognizable under 35 U.S.C. §282 as an equitable defense to a claim for patent infringement.
2. Where an alleged infringer establishes the defense of equitable estoppel, the patentee's claim may be entirely barred.
3. Three elements must be established to bar a patentee's suit by reason of equitable estoppel:
   a. The patentee, through misleading conduct, leads the alleged infringer to reasonably infer that the patentee does not intend to enforce its patent against the alleged infringer. "Conduct" may include specific statements, action, inaction, or silence where there was an obligation to speak.
   b. The alleged infringer relies on that conduct.
   c. Due to its reliance, the alleged infringer will be materially prejudiced if the patentee is allowed to proceed with the claim.

A.C. Aukerman Co. v. R.L. Chaides Construction Co., 960 F.2d 1020, 22 U.S.P.Q.2d 1321, 1325 (Fed. Cir. 1992).

ω

By raising the defense of equitable estoppel in a declaratory judgment action, plaintiff has waived the attorney-client privilege as to the patent in suit. *Sig Swiss Industrial Co. v. Fres-Co System USA Inc.*, 22 U.S.P.Q.2d 1601, 1603 (Pa. 1992).

ω

Equitable estoppel does not apply against the Government as it applies against private litigants. The Supreme Court confined the doctrine, as potentially applicable to the Government, to acts of "affirmative misconduct." *MDS Associates v. U.S.*, 31 Fed.Cl. 389, 32 U.S.P.Q.2d 1784, 1787 (U.S. Ct.Fed.Cl. 1994).

ω

Given misleading conduct, there is no reason why equitable estoppel could not arise in three-and-a-half years or even sooner. *Scholle Corp. v. Blackhawk Molding Co.*, 133 F.3d 1469, 45 U.S.P.Q.2d 1468, 1472 (Fed. Cir. 1998).

Equitable Issues. *See* **Special Master.**

Equitable Title.

An equitable title to a patent accrues to a corporation in patents owned by its constituent corporation. A "federal district court has jurisdiction to determine a 'claim for infringement,' asserted by an adjudged equitable title holder, as a prerequisite to awarding equitable relief for that infringement." *Pipe Liners Inc. v. American Pipe & Plastics Inc.*, 893 F.Supp. 704, 36 U.S.P.Q.2d 1798, 1799 (Tex. 1995).

Equity.

Courts are bound to follow express statutory commands under the fundamental principle that equity follows the law. For example, in antitrust cases "whenever some maxim of equity (such as that to get equitable relief you must have 'clean hands') collides with the objectives of antitrust laws, the [equitable] maxim must give way." *Total Containment Inc. v. Environ Products Inc.*, 34 U.S.P.Q.2d 1254, 1256 (Pa. 1995).

Equivalence.

There can be no infringement if the fact of equivalence of the two devices was not known at the date of the patent. *Gould v. Rees*, 82 U.S. 187, 194 (1872); *Gill v. Wells*, 89 U.S. 1, 28-29 (1874).

ᴡ

To rely on an equivalence known only to the applicant to establish obviousness is to assume that this disclosure is a part of the prior art. The mere statement of this proposition reveals its fallaciousness. *In re Ruff and Dukeshire*, 256 F.2d 590, 118 U.S.P.Q. 340, 347 (C.C.P.A. 1958).

ᴡ

Equivalence is determined at the time an alleged infringement occurs. *See Hughes Aircraft Co. v. United States*, 717 F.2d 1351, 1365, 219 U.S.P.Q. 473 (Fed. Cir. 1983); *Atlas Powder Co. v. E.I. du Pont de Nemours & Co.*, 750 F.2d 1569, 1581, 224 U.S.P.Q. 409 (Fed. Cir . 1984); *Texas Instruments, Inc. v. U.S. International Trade Commission*, 805 F.2d 1558, 1563, 231 U.S.P.Q. 833 (Fed. Cir. 1986).

ᴡ

An important factor in a determination of equivalence is whether persons reasonably skilled in the art would have known of the interchangeability of the ingredient not contained in the patent with one that was. A finding can be made that two devices are 35 U.S.C. §112 "equivalents" and, hence, that infringement exists even when the two devices are different in name, form, or shape (i.e., even if there is no equivalence in the physical structures). Limiting §112 "equivalents" to objects that are structurally equivalent to those objects described in a patent specification would undermine Congress's intent in 1952 in adding the third paragraph of §112. *De Graffenried v. United States*, 20 Cl. Ct. 458, 16 U.S.P.Q.2d 1321, 1339 (U.S. Cl. Ct. 1990).

ᴡ

Although an equivalence analysis under 35 U.S.C. §112, §6, and the doctrine of equivalents are not coextensive (for example, 112, §6, requires identical, not equivalent, function) and have different origins and purposes, their tests for equivalence are closely related. Thus, a finding of a lack of literal infringement for lack of equivalent structure under a means-plus-function limitation may preclude a finding of equivalence under the doctrine of equivalents. *Chiuminatta Concrete Concepts Inc. v. Cardinal Industries Inc.*, 145 F.3d 1303, 46 U.S.P.Q.2d 1752, 1757, 1758 (Fed. Cir. 1998).

Equivalency. *See also* **Doctrine of Equivalents, Substantial Equivalency, Unclaimed Disclosure.**

To determine equivalency, the trier of fact must examine: (1) the scope of the prior art, (2) the essence or "heart" of the patented invention or, put another way, "the step forward the invention offers", and (3) the particular circumstances of the case. *Connell v. Sears, Roebuck and Company,* 559 F.Supp. 229, 218 U.S.P.Q. 31, 37, 43 (Ala. 1983).

ω

The "function/way/result" equivalency analysis with respect to a claim limitation resolves the question of equivalency by comparing the function/way/result of the substitution with the function/way/result of a limitation in the context of the invention. *Corning Glass Works v. Sumitomo Electric U.S.A. Inc.,* 868 F.2d 1251, 9 U.S.P.Q.2d 1962 (Fed. Cir. 1989).

ω

As a matter of terminology, the doctrine of equivalents applies only to infringement of a claim and to an equivalent to a limitation of the claim, not "equivalency" between an accused device and a patented invention. To refer to "equivalency" to the invention creates confusion and is technically inaccurate. The statutory requirement for liability is "infringement" of a patent, not "equivalency" between devices or methods. 35 U.S.C. §281. Equivalency to limitations of the claim must be the focus of the inquiry, particularly in jury trials. *The Read Corp. v. Portec Inc.,* 970 F.2d 816, 23 U.S.P.Q.2d 1426, 1431 (Fed. Cir. 1992).

ω

The operative definition for purposes of equivalency analysis is the intended function as seen in the context of the patent, the prosecution history, and the prior art. *Genentech Inc. v. The Wellcome Foundation Ltd.,* 29 F.3d 1555, 31 U.S.P.Q.2d 1161, 1170 (Fed. Cir. 1994).

ω

Interchangeability known to persons reasonably skilled in the art is evidence of equivalency. *Lifescan Inc. v. Home Diagnostics Inc.,* 76 F.3d 358, 37 U.S.P.Q.2d 1595, 1599 (Fed. Cir. 1996).

ω

While equivalency under the doctrine of equivalents and equivalency under paragraph 6 of 35 U.S.C. §112 both relate to insubstantial changes, each has a separate origin, purpose and application. Under §112, the concern is whether the accused device, which performs the claimed function, has the same or an equivalent structure as the structure described in the specification corresponding to the claim's means. Under the doctrine of equivalents, on the other hand, the question is whether the accused device is only insubstantially different than the claimed device. *Alpex Computer Corp. v. Nintendo Co. Ltd.,* 40 U.S.P.Q.2d 1667, 1673 (Fed. Cir. 1996).

ω

"[T]he proper time for evaluating equivalency—and thus knowledge of interchangeability between elements—is at the time of infringement, not at the time the patent was issued." *Semmler v. American Honda Motor Co.*, 990 F. Supp. 967, 44 U.S.P.Q.2d 1553, 1562 (Ohio 1997).

ᢍ

Equivalency is not defeated by using an additional step to achieve what the patentee does in one step. *EMI Group North America Inc. v. Intel Corp.*, 48 U.S.P.Q.2d 1181, 1188 (Fed. Cir. 1998).

Equivalent.

The substantial equivalent of a thing, in the sense of the patent law, is the same as the thing itself; so that if two devices do the same work in substantially the same way, and accomplish substantially the same result, they are the same, even though they differ in name, form, or shape. *Hugh W. Batcheller v. Henry Cole Co.*, 7 F. Supp. 898, 22 U.S.P.Q. 354, 358 (Mass. 1934).

ᢍ

The word "equivalent" in 35 U.S.C. §112 should not be confused with the "doctrine of equivalents." In applying the doctrine of equivalents, the fact finder must determine the range of equivalents to which the claimed invention is entitled, in light of the prosecution history, the pioneer-non-pioneer status of the invention, and the prior art. It must then be determined whether the entirety of the accused device or process is so "substantially the same thing, used in substantially the same way, to achieve substantially the same result" as to fall within that range. In applying the "means plus function" paragraph of §112, however, the sole question is whether the single means in the accused device that performs the function stated in the claim is the same as or an equivalent of the corresponding structure described in the patentee's specification as performing that function. The sixth paragraph of §112 operates to limit a claim from every possible means to those that are "equivalent." Properly understood, that paragraph operates more like the reverse doctrine of equivalents than the doctrine of equivalents because it restricts the scope of the literal claim language. *Intel Corp. v. International Trade Commission*, 946 F.2d 821, 20 U.S.P.Q.2d 1161, 1179 (Fed. Cir. 1991).

ᢍ

The record must establish how close the values for melt index and density of copolymers need be in order for the copolymers to be considered "comparable." If it is intended that comparisons are to be made between resins having the same or equivalent melt index and density, the claims should use such language. The claims cannot leave to surmise and conjecture the specific properties to be compared and how "comparable" their values need be when determining infringement and dominance issues. *Ex parte Anderson*, 21 U.S.P.Q.2d 1241, 1250 (B.P.A.I. 1991).

ᢍ

Claims to DNA by what it does (i.e. encoding either a protein exhibiting certain characteristics, or a biologically functional equivalent thereof) rather than by what it is might be analogized to a single means claim of the type disparaged by *In re Hyatt*, 708 F.2d 712, 218 U.S.P.Q. 195 (Fed. Cir. 1983). The problem with the phrase "biologically functional equivalent thereof" is that it covers any conceivable means, i.e., cell or DNA, which achieves the stated biological result while the specification discloses, at most, only a specific DNA segment known to the inventor. *Ex parte Maizel*, 27 U.S.P.Q.2d 1662, 1665 (B.P.A.I. 1992).

ᵫ

According to a concurring opinion by Rich, J., there is a clear distinction between "*equivalent* structures" and "*structural* equivalents". The statute (35 U.S.C. §112, paragraph 6) requires only that two things be "equivalents" for the purpose at hand, not structural equivalents. Interpretation of that paragraph is not an application of the judge-made *doctrine* of equivalents. The former is a statutory dictate on the interpretation of "means clauses" ; the latter is an equitable doctrine which permits disregard of claim limitations to a degree—quite different things. Precedents involving one are not precedents controlling the other. *Baltimore Therapeutic Equipment Co. v. Loredan Biomedical Inc.*, 26 F.3d 138, 30 U.S.P.Q.2d 1672, 1678 (Fed. Cir. 1994), *(unpublished, not citable as precedent)*.

ᵫ

Decisional law suggests two distinctions between "equivalents" under paragraph 6 of 35 U.S.C. §112 and "equivalents" under the doctrine of equivalents. First, under §112, equivalents are identified by reference to the structure disclosed *in the specification*. By contrast, equivalents under the doctrine of equivalents are measured by the structure disclosed *in the claims*; these equivalents fall outside the literal bounds of the claimed invention, and serve to extend the coverage of the patent beyond the literal claims. The second distinction between §112 and the doctrine of equivalents is that §112 requires an identity of function between the claimed invention and the accused device. Equivalents analysis under the sixth paragraph of §112, therefore, is limited to comparison of the structures at issue. By contrast, the doctrine of equivalence involves an equitable tripartite test, which defines an equivalent as a device that " 'performs substantially the same overall function or work, in substantially the same way, to obtain substantially the same overall result as the claimed invention.'" The doctrine of equivalents is a somewhat broader concept. When literal infringement under §112, paragraph 6, is not present, the doctrine of equivalents may nevertheless apply, and thereby secure to the patentee the fair scope of the patent. *Alpex Computer Corp. v. Nintendo Co. Ltd.*, 86 Civ. 1749, 34 U.S.P.Q.2d 1167, 1177 (N.Y. 1994).

ᵫ

"An 'equivalent' of a claim limitation cannot substantially alter the manner of performing the claimed function." *Zygo Corp v. Wyko Corp.*, 79 F.3d 1563, 38 U.S.P.Q.2d 1281, 1286 (Fed. Cir. 1996).

Equivalents. *See also* **Borcherdt Doctrine, Doctrine of Equivalents, Equivalence, Interchangeable, Paper Patent, Substitution of Equivalents.**

A patent need not be a "pioneer patent" to be entitled to a broad range of equivalents. *Eibel Process Co. v. Minnesota & Ontario Paper Co.*, 261 U.S. 45, 63 (1923).

ᵫ

The substantial equivalent of a thing, in the sense of the patent law, is the same as the thing itself; if two devices do the same work in substantially the same way and accomplish substantially the same result, they are the same even though they differ in name, form, or shape. *Hugh W. Batcheller v. Henry Cole Co.,* 7 F. Supp. 898, 22 U.S.P.Q. 354, 358 (Mass. 1934).

ω

That two things are actually equivalents, in the sense that they will both perform the same function, is not enough to bring into play the rule that when one of them is in the prior art, the use of the other is obvious and cannot give rise to a patentable invention. One need not think very hard to appreciate that the vast majority of patentable inventions perform old functions. Patent applicants more often than not invent and disclose and attempt to claim more than turns out to be novel when the art is searched. They should not be penalized merely because of their own industry and the fullness of their disclosures. *In re Ruff and Dukeshire,* 256 F.2d 590, 118 U.S.P.Q. 340 (C.C.P.A. 1958).

ω

Bona fide attempts to design a non-infringing product are one of the beneficial results of the incentive-to-disclose system established by the patent statute. Bona fides of such attempts, however, are not governed solely by whether the words of a patent claim can be literally read on the newly designed product. The matter is not one for semantics alone. An infringer appropriates an invention, not words; hence, the doctrine of equivalents. At the same time, the words of a claim may be so limited by the file history or by the prior art as to define an invention that was not appropriated; hence, the doctrine of estoppel. *Caterpillar Tractor Co. v. Berco, S.p.A.,* 714 F.2d 1110, 219 U.S.P.Q. 185 (Fed. Cir. 1983).

ω

To interpret means-plus-function claims, one must resort to the last paragraph of 35 U.S.C. §112. The statute expressly states that the patentee is entitled to a claim covering equivalents as well as the specified "structure, material or act." Such a patent claim is construed to cover both the disclosed structure and equivalents thereof. To interpret means-plus-function limitations as limited to a particular means set forth in the specification would be to nullify the provision of §112 requiring that the limitation "shall be construed to cover the structure described in the specification and equivalents thereof." In construing a means-plus-function claim, a number of factors may be considered, including the language of the claim, the patent specification, the prosecution history of the patent, other claims in the patent, and expert testimony. Once such factors are weighed, the scope of the means claim may be determined. *Palumbo v. Don-Joy Co.,* 762 F.2d 969, 226 U.S.P.Q. 5 (Fed. Cir. 1985).

ω

Even when an estoppel arises from the file, the doctrine of equivalents is not completely eliminated. Depending on the nature and the purpose of an amendment, it may have a limited effect ranging from great to small to zero. The effect may or may not be fatal to application of a range of equivalents broad enough to encompass a particular accused product. It is not fatal to application of the doctrine of equivalents itself. Whenever the doctrine of file history estoppel is invoked, a close examination must be made as to not only what was surrendered, but also the reason for such a surrender. The fact that claims were narrowed does not always mean that the doctrine of file history estoppel completely prohibits a patentee from recapturing some of what was originally claimed. *Glaros v. H.H. Robertson Co.*, 615 F. Supp. 186, 227 U.S.P.Q. 448 (Ill. 1985).

ᛠ

The claimed composition rapidly cures at room temperature, whereas the accused counterpart rapidly cures only at 90°C. It was precisely because of that difference that the district court found that the claimed invention and the accused counterpart do not perform in substantially the same way. That finding, however, would allow the difference itself to dictate a finding of no equivalents; if that were the law, one could never infringe by equivalents. The analysis must go further, and the question the district court should consider on remand is this: Given the difference, would the accused composition at 90°C and the claimed invention at room temperature perform substantially the same function (e.g., filling the pores of the treated material with solid material) in substantially the same way (e.g., by rapidly curing in the absence but not in the presence of oxygen) to give substantially the same results (e.g., a filled material)? There are limitations to the doctrine of equivalents. The doctrine has been judicially devised to do equity in situations where there is no literal infringement but liability is nevertheless appropriate to prevent what is in essence a pirating of the patentee's invention. Concommitently, two policy-oriented limitations, applied as questions of law, have developed. First, the doctrine will not extend to an infringing device within the public domain, i.e., found in the prior art at the time the patent issued; second, prosecution history estoppel will not allow the patentee to recapture through equivalents certain coverage given up during prosecution. *Loctite Corp. v. Ultraseal Ltd.*, 781 F.2d 861, 228 U.S.P.Q. 90 (Fed. Cir. 1985).

ᛠ

Literal infringement requires that an accused device embody every element of a claim as properly interpreted. If the claim describes a combination of functions, and each function is performed by a means described in the specification or an equivalent of such means, then literal infringement holds. When a claimed invention is a novel combination of steps, all possible methods of carrying out each step of the combination are not required to be described in the specification. Correctly construed claims cover "equivalents" of the described embodiments. The purpose is to grant an inventor of a combination invention a fair scope that is not dependent on a catalog of alternative embodiments in the specification. The court has cautioned against limiting the claimed invention to preferred embodiments or specific examples in the specification. The details of performing each step need not be included in the claims unless required to distinguish the claimed invention from the prior art, or otherwise to specifically point out and distinctly claim the invention. Claims should be read in a way that avoids enabling an infringer to "practice a fraud on a patent."

It is not required that those skilled in the art knew, at the time the patent application was filed, of the asserted equivalent means of performing the claimed functions; that equivalence is determined as of the time infringement takes place. Infringement will be found when the material features of a patent have been appropriated, even when those features have been patentably improved. *Texas Instruments, Inc. v. U.S. International Trade Commission*, 805 F.2d 1558, 231 U.S.P.Q. 833 (Fed. Cir. 1986).

ᛠ

A charge of infringement is sometimes made out, though the letter of the claims be avoided. The converse is equally true. The patentee may bring the defendant within the letter of his claims, but if the latter has so far changed the principle of the device that the claims of the patent, literally construed, have ceased to represent his actual invention, he is as little subject to be adjudged an infringer as one who has violated the letter of a statute has to be convicted when he has done nothing in conflict with its spirit and intent. "An infringement," says Justice Grier in *Burr v. Duryee* [68 U.S. (1 Wall) 531, 572 (1863)], "involves substantial identity, whether that identity be described by the terms, 'same principle,' same 'modus operandi,' or any other. . . . The argument used to show infringement assumes that every combination of devices in a machine which is used to produce the same effect is necessarily an equivalent for any other combination used for the same purpose. This is a flagrant abuse of the term 'equivalent.'" *Westinghouse v. Boyden Power Brake Co.*, 170 U.S. 537 (1897); *The Gillette Company v. S.C. Johnson & Son, Inc.*, 12 U.S.P.Q.2d 1929, 1942 (Mass. 1989).

ω

Even when a claim literally reads on a device, actual infringement will not exist if the accused device performs in a substantially different way. Thus, irrespective of the existence of literal infringement (i.e., a literal reading of the claim on the accused device), the determination of actual infringement may require that the accused device be examined under the doctrine of equivalents or reverse equivalents. *The Laitram Corp. v. Rexnord Inc.*, 15 U.S.P.Q.2d 1161, 1167 (Wis. 1990).

ω

Consideration of equivalents at the time of prosecution is an unnecessary expenditure of resources and ineffectual because equivalence, and the reverse doctrine in particular, speaks to future advances. *Ex parte Isaksen*, 23 U.S.P.Q.2d 1001, 1013 (B.P.A.I. 1991).

ω

The word "equivalent" in 35 U.S.C. §112 should not be confused with "the doctrine of equivalents". A determination of §112 equivalence does not involve the equitable tripartite test of the doctrine of equivalents. The sole question under §112 involves comparison of the structure in the accused device which performs the claimed function to the structure in the specification. *Valmont Industries Inc. v. Reinke Manufacturing Co. Inc.*, 983 F.2d 1039, 25 U.S.P.Q.2d 1451, 1454, 1455 (Fed. Cir. 1993).

ω

In order to determine whether prior art limits the range of equivalents, the court must visualize a *hypothetical* patent claim, sufficient in scope to *literally* cover the accused product. The pertinent question then becomes whether the hypothetical claim could have been allowed by the PTO over prior art. If not, then it would be improper to permit the patentee to obtain that coverage in an infringement suit under the doctrine of equivalents. If the hypothetical claim could have been allowed, then *prior art* is not a bar to infringement under the doctrine of equivalents. *Gargoyles Inc. v. U.S.*, 32 Fed.Cl. 157, 33 U.S.P.Q.2d 1595, 1599 (U.S Ct. Fed. Cl. 1994).

ω

A patentee may carry his burden of proving a range of equivalents by reference to a hypothgetical claim. *Cameco Industries Inc. v. Louisiana Cane Manufacturing Inc.*, 34 U.S.P.Q.2d 1309, 1312 (La. 1995).

ᙄ

A patented invention is not "derived" from another person unless that other person was in possession of the invention. Invalidity based on derivation requires that the patentee, in the words of the statute, did not invent the subject matter that was patented. *Lamb-Weston Inc. v. McCain Foods Ltd.*, 78 F.3d 540, 37 U.S.P.Q.2d 1856, 1863 (*dissent*)(Fed. Cir. 1996).

ᙄ

An admission of bioequivalence is not an admission of infringement under the doctrine of equivalents. They are two distinct concepts. *Upjohn Co. v. MOVA Pharmaceutical Corp.*, 48 U.S.P.Q.2d 1357, 1360 (PR 1998).

Error. *See also* Certificate of Correction, Clear Error, Conversion, Naming, Recapture Rule, Reissue, 35 U.S.C. §251, 35 U.S.C. §256.

If the appellants wished to object to the Board's statement and to question the correctness of the facts contained therein, they should have requested the Board to cite its authority for the statement. If the cited authority was based upon facts within the personal knowledge of the Board, the appellants should have proceeded under Rules 66 and 76 of the Patent Office and called for an affidavit of the Board. The appellants would then have been in a position to contradict or explain the Board's statement. In the absence of such request, the appellants may not be heard to challenge a statement made in the Board's opinion. The statement of the Board must therefore be accepted as correct. *In re Selmi and Altenburger,* 156 F.2d 96, 70 U.S.P.Q. 197 (C.C.P.A. 1946).

ᙄ

The expression "error...without any deceptive intention" in 35 U.S.C. §116 was intended not only to replace the more cumbersome expression "inadvertence, accident or mistake" previously used, but also to relieve applicants from the narrow application of the old terms as the courts had construed them. *In re Schmidt,* 293 F.2d 274, 130 U.S.P.Q. 404, 409 (C.C.P.A. 1961).

ᙄ

The new reissue statute broadened the term "error" by not limiting it to "error" that had arisen through "inadvertence, accident or mistake." The term, "error", arising as it does in a remedial provision designed to advance both the rights of the public and of the inventor is to be interpreted as "error without any deceptive intention", and in light of Supreme Court decisions favoring the liberal construction of reissue statutes in order to secure to inventors protection for what they have actually invented. *In re Wesseler*, 367 F.2d 838, 151 U.S.P.Q. 339, 347, 348 (C.C.P.A. 1966).

ᙄ

Enforcement of a patent is not denied because of erroneous data in an example, as the error arose from an honest mistake and not because of any fraudulent intent or gross negligence on the part of the patentee. *The Ansul Company v. Uniroyal, Inc.*, 306 F.Supp. 541, 163 U.S.P.Q. 517, 537 (N.Y. 1969).

ω

When the identification of a compound in a reference is in error and would be so recognized by any artisan, it cannot be said that one of ordinary skill in the relevant art would do anything more than mentally disregard it as a misprint. Obvious typographical errors do not convey any teaching whatsoever with regard to an erroneously-depicted compound irrespective of one's ability to produce such a compound. *In re Yale*, 434 F.2d 666, 168 U.S.P.Q. 46, 48, 49 (C.C.P.A. 1970).

ω

Inadvertent errors or honest mistakes, which are caused by neither fraudulent intent nor design, do not constitute fraud within the meaning of *Walker* [382 U.S. 172, 175-17, 179, 147 U.S.P.Q. 404, 406-407, 408 (1965)]. Enlargement of claims during the pendency of a patent application, even when intentionally done to include other inventions, is not sufficient to constitute *Walker* fraud. *Bolt Associates, Inc. v. Rix Industries*, 178 U.S.P.Q. 171, 173 (Cal. 1973).

ω

In drafting combination claims, a patent applicant includes elements at his peril. A court is powerless to relieve him of the mistake of reciting elements which are superfluous to patentability. *Berkey Photo, Inc. v. Klimsch-Repro, Inc.*, 388 F.Supp. 586, 185 U.S.P.Q. 306, 312 (N.Y. 1975).

ω

While 35 U.S.C. §251 is to be construed liberally as a remedial statute, such liberalism does not extend to eradication of a dereliction of a duty by what is, in effect, a reprosecution in which the Examiner is now given an opportunity to pass on patentability in light of a very pertinent reference which the applicant knowingly withheld from him. Such withholding cannot be equated with "error" or with "inadvertence, accident, or mistake". *In re Clark*, 522 F.2d 623, 187 U.S.P.Q. 209, 213 (C.C.P.A. 1975).

ω

Amending a specification by inserting an inherent property or correcting an erroneous structural formula of a compound which is necessarily produced by a disclosed process or example does not involve prohibited "new matter". *Ex parte Marsili, Rossetti, and Pasqualucci*, 214 U.S.P.Q. 904, 906 (PTO Bd. App. 1979).

ω

Though remedial in character, 35 U.S.C. §256 is limited in effect and cannot properly be the vehicle for substituting inventors on a patent in a claim sounding in conspiracy and fraud. The statute remedies only innocent errors in joinder and non-joinder of inventors. *Bemis v. Chevron Research Company*, 599 F.2d 910, 203 U.S.P.Q. 123, 124 (9th Cir. 1979).

ω

While deliberate cancellation of a claim cannot ordinarily be considered error, the CCPA has repeatedly held that the deliberate cancellation of claims may constitute error (in the context of 35 U.S.C. §251), if it occurs without deceptive intent. *Ball Corporation v. United States,* 729 F.2d 1429, 221 U.S.P.Q. 289, 294 (Fed. Cir. 1984).

ω

The attorney who prosecuted the patent declared that his error, misunderstanding the scope of the invention, arose because no prior art search was done and he assumed that limitations were required by the prior art without justification. This is a sufficient explanation of how the error arose to satisfy the requirements of 37 C.F.R. §1.175(a)(5). *In re Wilder,* 736 F.2d 1516, 222 U.S.P.Q. 369, 372 (Fed. Cir. 1984).

ω

An action in the district court under 35 U.S.C. §145 is a proceeding de novo and, while it is limited to the invention claimed in the PTO, the court may consider any additional competent evidence that a plaintiff neither intentionally nor negligently failed to submit to the PTO. The presumption of correctness that attaches to the decision of the Commissioner is a rebuttable presumption that may be overcome by the introduction of evidence (at a trial under §145) that is of such character and amount as to carry a thorough conviction of error. At such a trial the plaintiff and defendant may present evidence on any issue properly before the court. This additional evidence may include testimony of expert witnesses and inventors skilled in the art, and evidence of commercial success. In making its determination of non-obviousness, the court recognized the non-analogous nature of one reference, the lack of teaching or suggestion in the prior art of the useful advantage of a flexible track incapable of self-support, and the commercial success of the highly flexible Hot Wheels trackway-toy vehicle combination covered by the plaintiff's Reissue Application. The fact that the claimed invention seemed simple and, when viewed in hindsight, appeared to be obvious was not enough to negate invention. *Lemelson v. Mossinghoff,* 225 U.S.P.Q. 1063 (D.C. 1985).

ω

The Board's notation that the involved subject matter was "not claimed at all" in the original application, and its finding that nothing in the original patent evidences applicant's "intent to claim" that subject matter, reflect non-statutory language to support and convey the concept that an inventor's failure to claim particular subject matter was not the result of the "error" required by 35 U.S.C. §251. *In re Weiler,* 790 F.2d 1576, 229 U.S.P.Q. 673, 678 (Fed. Cir. 1986).

ω

The showing of "error" under 35 U.S.C. §251 is not identical to the "same invention" showing necessary under that provision. *Sonoco Products Co. v. Durabag Co. Inc.,* 30 U.S.P.Q.2d 1295, 1300 (Cal. 1994).

Essence. *See also* **Gist, Point of Novelty.**

Where a class of materials that does not pertain to the essence of the invention is claimed, the need for the precise definition of that class is not so pressing. *Ex parte Dubbs and Stevens,* 119 U.S.P.Q. 440, 441 (PO Bd. App. 1958).

ω

The key to determining whether a disclosure supports a claim for interference purposes is whether the disclosure teaches the gist of the invention defined by the claim. While all limitations of a claim must be considered in deciding what invention is defined, it is futile merely to compare quantitatively range limits and numbers set out in counts with range limits and numbers disclosed in an allegedly supporting specification. Closer scrutiny is required to get at the essence of what invention the count purports to define. *Hall v. Taylor,* 332 F.2d 844, 141 U.S.P.Q. 821, 824 (C.C.P.A. 1964).

ᗡ

Though consideration of an invention's "gist" is appropriate in some context, e.g., in determining infringement under the doctrine of equivalents, when determining obviousness, there is no legally recognizable or protected "essence," "gist," or "heart" of the invention. Had the district court analyzed the invention in its entirety, it would have had to consider whether it would have been obvious to use the composition defined in the claims in the process defined by those claims. Even when a composition is old, a process using a known composition in a new and unobvious way may be patentable. *Loctite Corp. v. Ultraseal Ltd.,* 781 F.2d 861, 228 U.S.P.Q. 90 (Fed. Cir. 1985).

ᗡ

If alterations which the reissue applicant made were not to correct an "error", they could not be made during reissue. *Nupla Corp. v. IXL Manufacturing Co.,* 42 U.S.P.Q.2d 1711, 1713, 1715 (Fed. Cir. 1997).

ᗡ

Reissue claims fail to meet the "error" requirement when the claims impermissibly recapture surrendered subject matter. *Hester Industries Inc. v. Stein Inc.,* 142 F.3d 1472, 46 U.S.P.Q.2d 1641, 1651 (Fed. Cir. 1998).

ᗡ

An inventor's failure to appreciate the scope of the invention at the time of the original patent grant, and thus an initial intent not to claim the omitted subject matter, is a remediable error. *C.R. Bard Inc. v. M3 Systems Inc.,* 48 U.S.P.Q.2d 1225, 1234 (Fed. Cir. 1998).

Essentially. *See also* About Consisting Substantially.

The word "essentially" opens claims to the inclusion of ingredients that would not materially affect the basic and novel characteristics of appellant's compositions as defined in the balance of the claim. *In re Janakirama Rao,* 317 F.2d 951, 137 U.S.P.Q. 893, 896 (C.C.P.A. 1963).

Ester.

A rejection of claims as failing to define the invention properly and based on the phrases "substituted mononuclear and polynuclear homocyclic compounds," "alkyl," "ester," and "heterocyclic and aromatic compounds being free of substituents containing aliphatic hydroxyl and amino groups," in process claims, was reversed. *Ex parte Westfahl,* 136 U.S.P.Q. 265 (PTO Bd. App. 1962).

ᗡ

All students of organic chemistry know that an ester (R-CO-O-R') cannot be expected to behave like, or have properties like, the "reverse" ester (R-O-CO-R'), unless R and R' are closely similar in structure. As references suggest that esters having the structure of appellant's compounds will possess greater analgesic activity than their "reverse esters", a showing that appellant's compounds are six and nine times more effective than a reference "reverse ester" is not sufficient to establish patentability. *In re Carabateas*, 345 F.2d 1013, 145 U.S.P.Q. 549, 551, 553 (C.C.P.A. 1965).

ᛠ

One of the two compounds, being an ester, is not precisely an adjacent homolog of the reference compound, which is an acid. The difference between the ester and its acid (which would be an adjacent homolog of the reference compound) is not significant because the acid is "trivially obvious" from the ester. This argument is an inference from the statement in *Ex parte Korten* [71 U.S.P.Q. 173 (PTO Bd. App. 1945)] that "an ester is ordinarily unpatentable over the alcohol from which it is derived." *In re Schaub, Vernady, and Weiss*, 537 F.2d 509, 190 U.S.P.Q. 324 (C.C.P.A. 1976).

Estoppel. *See also* **Assignor Estoppel, Collateral Estoppel, Equitable Defenses, Equitable Estoppel, File Wrapper, File Wrapper Estoppel, Inconsistent, Interference Estoppel, Judicial Estoppel, Marking, Mismarking, Promissory Estoppel, Prosecution History, Prosecution History Estoppel, Silence.**

A plea of estoppel by an infringement or royalty suit defendant need not automatically be accepted once the defendant in support of his plea identifies the issue in suit as the identical question finally decided against the patentee or one of his privies in previous litigation. Rather, the patentee plaintiff must be permitted to demonstrate, if he can, that he did not have "a fair opportunity procedurally, substantively and evidentially to pursue his claim the first time." *Blonder-Tongue Laboratories, Inc. v. University of Illinois Foundation*, 402 U.S. 313, 169 U.S.P.Q. 513 (1971).

ᛠ

A Markush group in a claim is a representation that, for the purposes of the claimed invention, the elements of the group are equivalents, and an applicant cannot argue to the contrary. *In re Skoll*, 523 F.2d 1392, 187 U.S.P.Q. 481, 484, 485 (C.C.P.A. 1975).

ᛠ

Bona fide attempts to design a non-infringing product are one of the beneficial results of the incentive-to-disclose system established by the patent statute. Bona fides of such attempts, however, are not governed solely by whether the words of a patent claim can be literally read on the newly designed product. The matter is not one for semantics alone. An infringer appropriates an invention, not words; hence, the doctrine of equivalents. At the same time, the words of a claim may be so limited by the file history or by the prior art as to define an invention that was not appropriated; hence, the doctrine of estoppel. *Caterpillar Tractor Co. v. Berco, S.p.A.*, 714 F.2d 1110, 219 U.S P Q. 185 (Fed. Cir. 1983).

ᛠ

Even when an estoppel arises from the file, the doctrine of equivalents is not completely eliminated. Depending on the nature and the purpose of an amendment, it may have a limited effect ranging from great to small to zero. The effect may or may not be fatal to application of a range of equivalents broad enough to encompass a particular accused product. It is not fatal to application of the doctrine of equivalents itself. Whenever the doctrine of file history estoppel is invoked, a close examination must be made as to, not only what was surrendered, but also the reason for such a surrender. The fact that claims were narrowed does not always mean that the doctrine of file history estoppel completely prohibits a patentee from recapturing some of what was originally claimed. *Glaros v. H. H. Robertson Co.*, 615 F. Supp. 186, 227 U.S.P.Q. 448 (Ill. 1985).

ɯ

That a patent applicant narrows his claim to secure a patent does not always mean that prosecution history estoppel completely prohibits the patentee from recapturing some of what was originally claimed. *Pennwalt Corp. v. Durand-Wayland Inc.*, 833 F.2d 931, 4 U.S.P.Q.2d 1737 (Fed. Cir. 1987).

ɯ

Bad faith on the part of a patentee is not a requirement of an estoppel defense. All that is required is that the patentee conduct itself in such a way as to induce the belief that it has abandoned its claim, regardless of its good or bad faith. *Adelberg Laboratories Inc. v. Miles Inc.*, 921 F.2d 1267, 17 U.S.P.Q.2d 1111, 1116 (Fed. Cir. 1990).

ɯ

Estoppels, when asserted against statutory rights, should never be applied based on conjectural or hypothetical premises. *Ex parte Rohrer*, 20 U.S.P.Q.2d 1460, 1464 (B.P.A.I. 1991).

ɯ

When claims are amended during reexamination (following a rejection based on prior art), the claims are not deemed substantively changed as a matter of law. There is no per se rule. To determine whether a claim change is substantive, it is necessary to analyze the claims of the original and of the reexamined patents in light of the particular facts, including the prior art, the prosecution history, other claims, and any other pertinent information. When the issue is the doctrine of equivalents or substantive change on reexamination, the mere amendment of a claim does not act as a per se estoppel. *The Laitram Corp. v. NEC Corp.*, 952 F.2d 1357, 21 U.S.P.Q.2d 1276, 1280 (Fed. Cir. 1991).

ɯ

An applicant may insert clarifying language in a claim to meet an Examiner's objection without thereby accepting the Examiner's position that the change is substantive. *Tennant Co. v. Hako Minuteman Inc.*, 22 U.S.P.Q.2d 1161, 1168 (Ill. 1991).

ɯ

The previous four-part test for estoppel has been replaced by a three-part test consisting of (1) statements or conduct which communicate something in a misleading way; (2) reliance; and (3) material prejudice as a result of the reliance. However, three aspects of the law of estoppel remain unchanged; first, the requirement that there be some misleading conduct; second, the requirement that action was taken in reliance on that conduct;

and third, that no presumption arises from the passage of time. *Hemstreet v. Computer Entry Systems Corp.*, 972 F.2d 1290, 23 U.S.P.Q.2d 1860, 1864 (Fed. Cir. 1992).

ω

In asserting their affirmative defenses of laches and estoppel, the defendants have waived their attorney-client privilege regarding the opinions of counsel on the validity and enforceability of the patents at issue. *THK America Inc. v. NSK Co. Ltd.*, 157 F.R.D. 637, 33 U.S.P.Q.2d 1248, 1259 (Ill. 1993).

ω

"Although actual reliance by the examiner need not be shown, if an estoppel is to rest upon argument made during the examination process, the circumstances must be such as to permit the inference that such reliance in fact occurred. A showing that the conduct in question played a material role in the issuance of the patent usually suffices." *Zenith Lab., Inc. v. Bristol-Myers Squibb Co.*, 19 F.3d 1418, 1425 n.8, 30 U.S.P.Q.2d 1285, 1292 n.8 (Fed. Cir.), *cert. denied*, 115 S.Ct. 500 (1994).

ω

"Estoppel may arise whether the change is made by amendment of the claims during prosecution, or by refiling the patent application with changed claims." *Pall Corp. v. Micron Separations, Inc.*, 66 F.3d 1211, 1219, 36 U.S.P.Q.2d 1225, 1230 (Fed. Cir. 1995).

ω

"[W]hen claim changes or arguments are made in order to more particularly point out the applicant's invention, the purpose is to impart precision, not to overcome prior art. Such prosecution is not presumed to raise an estoppel..." *Kamyr Inc. v. Clement*, 42 U.S.P.Q.2d 1235, 1239 (D.C. 1997).

ω

With careful consideration of the *Lear* [*Lear v. Atkins*, 395 U.S. 653, 162 U.S.P.Q. 1 (1969)] test and policies, the assignor is estopped from challenging the validity of the patent:

To allow the assignor to make that representation [of the worth of the patent] at the time of the assignment (to his advantage) and later to repudiate it (again to his advantage) could work an injustice against the assignee.... [D]espite the public policy encouraging people to challenge potentially invalid patents, there are still circumstances in which the equities of the contractual relationships between the parties should deprive one party...of the right to bring that challenge.

Lear does not bar enforcement of a) a settlement agreement and consent decree, b) a contract promise to share royalties, or c) a settlement agreement to pay royalties even if the patent is later held invalid. *Studiengesellschaft Kohle m.b.H. v. Shell Oil Co.*, 112 F.3d 1561, 42 U.S.P.Q.2d 1674, 1680 (Fed. Cir. 1997).

ω

"Every statement made by a patentee during a prosecution to distinguish a prior art reference does not create a *separate* estoppel. Arguments must be viewed in context." *Cybor Corp. v. FAS Technologies Inc.*, 138 F.3d 1448, 46 U.S.P.Q.2d 1169, 1178 (Fed. Cir. 1998).

Et al.

The Supreme Court held that the failure of a party to be named in the notice of appeal from a judgment of a district court deprived the appellate court of jurisdiction over that party, and that inclusion of a party in the designation "et al." in the notice of appeal did not serve to identify the party. In an interference, however, Davis and Granger are regarded as a single party and thus appropriately designated as "Davis et al." in the notice of appeal. *Davis v. Loesch,* 998 F.2d 963, 27 U.S.P.Q.2d 1440, 1443 (Fed. Cir. 1993).

Ethylene.

To a pharmaceutical chemist ethylene is obvious from methylene as a link between adamantane and other moieties. *In re Shetty,* 566 F.2d 81, 195 U.S.P.Q. 753, 756 (C.C.P.A. 1977).

Evidence. *See also* **Affidavit, Clear and Convincing, Commensurate in Scope, Comparative Test Data, Declaration, Evidence Commensurate with Claimed Scope, Introduce into Evidence, Newly Discovered Evidence, Opinion Evidence, Showing.**

The appellant with the assistance of his assignee prepared and inserted in the application two series of photomicrographs together with extensive descriptions of them for the purpose of showing how the invention differs from the prior filaments in an extensively developed art. The court took the position that this would not have been done unless the photomicrographs in fact showed persons of ordinary skill in the art what the appellant asserted they show and was unwilling to give credence to a contrary opinion expressed by the Board as the basis of the rejection that it originated sua sponte. *In re Ehringer,* 347 F.2d 612, 146 U.S.P.Q. 31, 35 (C.C.P.A. 1965).

ω

It was not the intent of 35 U.S.C. §103 that the Examiner, the Board, or the CCPA should substitute its speculations for the factual knowledge of those skilled in the art. Where an affidavit states facts that are relevant to the ultimate determination of the legal issue arising under §103, it must be given careful evaluation and properly weighed to determine whether it factually rebuts the bases upon which the Examiner has predicated his finding of obviousness. Thus, an affidavit may well shift the burden of proof to the Examiner to come forward with further support for his conclusion that the invention would have been obvious under the conditions stated in §103. *In re Katzschmann,* 347 F.2d 620, 146 U.S.P.Q. 66, 68 (C.C.P.A. 1965).

ω

The solicitor's reliance on an allegedly standard textbook on chemistry (not previously of record) as further support for the Patent Office position illustrates a growing tendency on the part of appellants and the Patent Office alike to impair the clear and specific language of 35 U.S.C. §144, which requires an appeal to be determined "on the evidence produced before the Patent Office." *In re Cofer,* 354 F.2d 664, 148 U.S.P.Q. 268, 272 (C.C.P.A. 1966).

ω

Despite appellants' specific request for evidence of the factual basis for the Board's decision, the Board has provided no such evidence. *In re Kamal and Rogier*, 398 F.2d 867, 158 U.S.P.Q. 320, 323 (C.C.P.A. 1968).

ᚠ

To reach the Board's conclusion would require that all evidence favorable to the appellant's position be viewed with limitless skepticism and that all evidence unfavorable to the appellant's position be accepted with limitless faith. *In re Petrzilka, Hofmann, Schenk, Troxler, Frey, and Ott*, 424 F.2d 1102, 165 U.S.P.Q. 327 (C.C.P.A. 1970).

ᚠ

The fact that affidavit evidence shows that products produced by reference techniques do not possess properties asserted by applicant as critical is not necessarily indicative that the claimed process would not have been obvious. The affidavit evidence contains no basis for concluding that the properties asserted as critical are anything other than what one of ordinary skill in the art would have expected from a combination of the teachings of the references relied upon. *In re Lewis*, 443 F.2d 389, 170 U.S.P.Q. 84, 86 (C.C.P.A. 1971).

ᚠ

Evidence of non-obviousness which has developed only after the filing date of the application concerned cannot be ignored.

Affidavits are not irrelevant because they compare products of the claimed process to products of prior-art processes seriatim, rather than to products of the composite process fashioned by the Examiner. The Examiner's composite process is appellants' process, and thus cannot be compared with it. *In re Tiffin*, 443 F.2d 394, 170 U.S.P.Q. 88, 92, 93 (C.C.P.A. 1971).

ᚠ

Evidence may not be disregarded simply because of the manner in which the now-claimed subject matter was denominated in the original application. To rule otherwise would let form triumph over substance, substantially eliminating the right of an applicant to retreat to an otherwise patentable species merely because he erroneously thought he was first with the genus when he filed. *In re Saunders and Gemeinhardt*, 444 F.2d 599, 170 U.S.P.Q. 213, 220 (C.C.P.A. 1971).

ᚠ

Favorable correspondence by tradesmen and others working in the technological art area of the invention sheds light on the impressions of those assumed to possess ordinary skill in the art since the invention was made and, accordingly, is considered probative evidence of the level of skill in the art at the time the invention was made. The Board was in error to the extent that it regarded the correspondence of record as legally irrelevant merely because it is of a qualitative, nontechnical character. *In re Palmer*, 451 F.2d 1100, 172 U.S.P.Q. 126, 129 (C.C.P.A. 1971).

ᚠ

What is required as convincing evidence in a given case depends entirely on the proposition sought to be proved by that evidence. *In re Yan*, 463 F.2d 1348, 175 U.S.P.Q. 96, 98 (C.C.P.A. 1972).

ᛡ

For a showing of "unexpected results" to be probative evidence of nonobviousness, it must establish: (1) that there actually is a difference between the results obtained through the claimed invention and those of the prior art, and (2) that the difference actually obtained would not have been expected by one skilled in the art at the time of the invention. *In re Freeman and Burden*, 474 F.2d 1318, 177 U.S.P.Q. 139, 143 (C.C.P.A. 1973).

ᛡ

A patent applicant may offer evidence, such as patents and publications, to show the knowledge possessed by those skilled in the art and thereby establish that a given specification disclosure is enabling. Where the Board advances a position or rationale new to the proceedings, appellant must be afforded an opportunity to respond to that position or rationale by submission of contradicting evidence. If there is evidence to counter a position set forth in an Examiner's Answer, such evidence should be submitted with a reply brief; it need not be considered if presented subsequent to the Board's decision. *In re Eynde, Pollet, and de Cat*, 480 F.2d 1364, 178 U.S.P.Q. 470, 474, 475 (C.C.P.A. 1973).

ᛡ

Where no objection is made to evidence on the ground that it is outside the issues of the case, the issue raised is nevertheless before the trial court for determination, and the pleadings should be regarded as amended in order to conform to the proof. *Technical Development Corp. v. United States*, 202 Ct. Cl. 237, 179 U.S.P.Q. 180, 181 (U.S. Cl. Ct. 1973).

ᛡ

Any assertion by the Patent Office that the enabling disclosure is not commensurate in scope with the protection sought must be supported by evidence or reasoning substantiating the doubts so expressed. *In re Dinh-Nguyen and Stenhagen*, 492 F.2d 856, 181 U.S.P.Q. 46, 47 (C.C.P.A. 1974).

ᛡ

In maintaining that the subject matter claimed in appellants' reissue application is not described in the original patent, the PTO has the initial burden of presenting evidence or reasons why persons skilled in the art would not recognize in the disclosure of the original patent a description of the invention defined by the reissue claims. *In re Salem, Butterworth, and Ryan*, 553 F.2d 676, 193 U.S.P.Q. 513, 518 (C.C.P.A. 1977).

ᛡ

In support of a rejection under 35 U.S.C. §112, later references were cited, not as prior art, but as evidence to prove appellants' disclosure non-enabling for "other species" of the claimed polymer, in an effort to show why the scope of enablement was insufficient to support the claims. As thus implicitly recognized, the references would not have been available in support of a 35 U.S.C. §102 or §103 rejection entered in connection with the

1953 application. To permit use of the same references in support of the §112 rejection herein, however, is to render the "benefit" of 35 U.S.C. §120 illusory. The very purpose of reliance on §120 is to reach back, to avoid the effect of intervening references. Nothing in §120 limits its application to any specific grounds of rejection, or permits the Examiner, denied use of references to reject or to require narrowing of a claim under §102 or 103, to achieve the same result by use of the same references under §112. Just as justice and reason require application of §112 in the same manner to applicants and Examiners, symmetry in the law, and evenness of its application, require that §120 be held applicable to all bases for rejection, that its words "same effect" be given their full meaning and intent. *In re Hogan and Banks,* 559 F.2d 595, 194 U.S.P.Q. 527 (C.C.P.A. 1977).

ω

Appellant requested that an entire article (of record in appellant's parent application and thus in the possession of the PTO) be considered in arriving at a decision on his present application. The entire article is part of "the evidence produced before the Patent and Trademark Office." The statute (35 U.S.C. §144) contains no requirement that such evidence be contained in a single application file. The fact that the Board did not actually consider the article or mention it is immaterial since evidence need not be physically introduced and also considered by a PTO tribunal to be considered "evidence produced before the Patent and Trademark Office." *In re Hutton,* 568 F.2d 1355, 196 U.S.P.Q. 676 (C.C.P.A. 1978).

ω

If an applicant presents rebuttal evidence, the decision-maker must consider all of the evidence of record in determining whether the subject matter as a whole would have been obvious. The question of whether applicant's burden has been successfully carried requires that entire path to decision be retraced. An earlier decision should not be considered as set in concrete, and applicant's rebuttal evidence then evaluated on its knockdown ability. Analytical fixation on earlier decision can tend to provide that decision with an undeservedly broadened umbrella effect. Facts established by rebuttal evidence must be evaluated along with the facts on which the earlier conclusion was reached, not against the conclusion itself. Though the tribunal must begin anew, a final finding of obviousness rests upon evaluation of all facts in evidence, uninfluenced by any earlier conclusion reached by earlier Board upon a different record. *In re Carleton,* 599 F.2d 1021, 202 U.S.P.Q. 165, 168 (C.C.P.A. 1979).

ω

Affidavits regarding the use of a particular reference as prior art were regarded as of limited probative value since they set forth mere conclusions therein without cogent, supporting reasons. None of the affiants states any facts that differentiate the properties of the respective compounds. If, as affiants stated, "no reasonable interpretation" can equate the two, affiants should have submitted factual substantiation of that contention. The affidavits fail to offer the bases upon which their conclusions are built. *In re Grunwell and Petrow,* 609 F.2d 486, 203 U.S.P.Q. 1055, 1059 (C.C.P.A. 1979).

ω

An action in the district court under 35 U.S.C. §145 is a proceeding de novo and, while it is limited to the invention claimed in the PTO, the court may consider any additional competent evidence that a plaintiff neither intentionally nor negligently failed to submit to the PTO. The presumption of correctness that attaches to the decision of the Commissioner is a rebuttable presumption that may be overcome by the introduction of evidence (at a trial under §145) that is of such character and amount as to carry a thorough conviction of error. At such a trial the plaintiff and defendant may present evidence on any issue properly before the court. This additional evidence may include testimony of expert witnesses and inventors skilled in the art, and evidence of commercial success. In making its determination of non-obviousness, the court recognized the non-analogous nature of one reference, the lack of teaching or suggestion in the prior art of the useful advantage of a flexible track incapable of self-support, and the commercial success of the highly flexible Hot Wheels trackway-toy vehicle combination covered by the plaintiff's Reissue Application. The fact that the claimed invention seemed simple and, when viewed in hindsight, appeared to be obvious was not enough to negate invention. *Lemelson v. Mossinghoff,* 225 U.S.P.Q. 1063 (D.C. 1985).

ಶ

Amelioration of the symptoms or even cure of cancer is no longer considered to be "incredible." Nonetheless, decisional law would seem to indicate that the utility in question is sufficiently unusual to justify an Examiner's requiring substantiating evidence. This may be in the form of animal tests that constitute recognized screening procedures with clear relevance to utility in humans. The specification of the appellant's parent application sets forth several animal tests on numerous types of specific cancers as well as in vitro studies, both of which are asserted to be predictive with regard to utility in humans. The Examiner has not challenged the evidence presented in a single, relevant, material respect. There is only the blanket statement of lack of "patentable utility" per se. In fact, the only specific comments the Examiner has directed toward the appellant's evidence are with regard to the breadth of the types of tumor against which the claimed compounds have been shown to be active. The appealed claims are drawn to compounds and not to a method of treatment. Generally speaking, utility in treating a single disease is adequate basis for the patentability of a pharmaceutical compound under 35 U.S.C. §101. *Ex parte Krepelka,* 231 U.S.P.Q. 746 (B.P.A.I. 1986).

ಶ

The commercial success of a patented invention is clearly important. That evidence is "secondary" in time does not mean that it is secondary in importance. Evidence of secondary considerations may often be the most probative and cogent evidence in the record. *Trustwall Systems Corp. v. Hydro-Air Engineering Inc.,* 813 F.2d 1207, 2 U.S.P.Q.2d 1034 (Fed. Cir. 1987).

ಶ

The question is not whether evidence of commercial success is "commensurate in scope with the claims," but rather whether the evidence is relevant to the question of non-obviousness. *E.I. du Pont de Nemours & Co. v. Phillips Petroleum Co.,* 656 F. Supp. 1343, 2 U.S.P.Q.2d 1545 (Del. 1987).

ಶ

The skepticism of an expert, expressed before the inventors proved him wrong, is entitled to fair evidentiary weight, as are the five to six years of research that preceded the claimed invention. *In re Dow Chemical Co.*, 837 F.2d 469, 5 U.S.P.Q.2d 1529 (Fed. Cir. 1988).

ω

Although a 35 U.S.C. §145 action has been characterized as a trial de novo, the policy of encouraging full disclosure to administrative tribunals has led courts to limit the admissability of certain kinds of evidence in such actions. Thus, evidence has been excluded if it was available to the plaintiff during the PTO proceeding but was either intentionally or negligently withheld. Furthermore, new evidence may be excluded from trial if it relates to an issue that the plaintiff failed to raise before the PTO, unless the plaintiff can demonstrate that the failure to raise the issue was neither intentional nor negligent. *Holloway v. Quigg,* 9 U.S.P.Q.2d 1751 (D.C. 1988).

ω

Evidence presented to overcome a prima facie case of obviousness has to be commensurate with the scope of the claims in support of which the evidence is offered. *General Electric Co. v. Hoechst Celanese Corp.*, 683 F. Supp. 305, 16 U.S.P.Q.2d 1977, 1989 (Del. 1990).

ω

"[D]ecisions regarding the admission and exclusion of evidence are peculiarly within the competence of the district court and will not be reversed on appeal unless they constitute a clear abuse of discretion". *National Presto Industries Inc. v. The West Bend Co.,* 76 F.3d 1185, 37 U.S.P.Q.2d 1685, 1694 (Fed. Cir. 1996).

Evidence Commensurate with Claimed Scope. *See also* Comparative Test Data.

Declaration evidence showed greater-than-additive cleaning performance resulting from the combination of zeolites with a variety of auxiliary builders, in the face of diminished (less than additive) depletion of calcium ions for the combination. The Board agreed that the results for some of the combinations tested for cleaning performance are "better than would be expected." A greater-than-expected result is an evidentiary factor pertinent to the legal conclusion of obviousness vel non of the claims at issue. The Board concluded that the evidence demonstrated synergism "to some degree" with respect to cleaning performance, but observed that the appellant's claims were not limited to those specific cobuilders and detergent compositions for which data showing synergism had been submitted. The Board also held that this result, even if unexpected, was not "sufficient to overcome the *prima facie* case of obviousness established by the prior art."

The court could discern no *prima facie* teaching of the prior art with respect to these compositions of components. The PTO failed to point out any reference that suggests combining a known builder with zeolite, or that this combination would produce a greater-than-additive effect in cleaning performance. The PTO failed to establish a *prima facie* case of obviousness with respect to those claims that require the presence of an auxiliary builder. The Board observed that the combination of zeolite and cobuilder were not, in most instances reported in the Declaration, superior in cleaning performance to the auxiliary builder alone. This is not the test. In view of the evidence of a result greater than additive, evidencing some unobvious results in the combination of components where the one component is in itself more active than the other is not controlling. The specification teaches that a broad range of surfactants may be used in combination with zeolite plus auxiliary builders. In the absence of prior art suggesting or otherwise making these compositions obvious to one of ordinary skill in the art, there is inadequate support for the PTO's rejection of these claims. The burden on this point has not shifted to the applicant. *In re Corkill*, 771 F.2d 1496, 226 U.S.P.Q. 1005 (Fed. Cir. 1985).

Evidentiary Prejudice.

Evidentiary, or "defense" prejudice, may arise by reason of a defendant's inability to present a full and fair defense on the merits due to the loss of records, the death of a witness, or the unreliability of memories of long past events, thereby undermining the court's ability to judge the facts. *Wanlass v. General Electric Co.*, 148 F.2d 1334, 46 U.S.P.Q.2d 1915, 1917 (Fed. Cir. 1998).

Examination. *See also* Examiner, Search Record.

The Examiner's search record provides prima facie evidence that he searched all the references in the classes and subclasses noted on the file wrapper as having been searched. References in such subclasses left uncited are presumed to have been regarded by the Examiner as less relevant than those cited. A contrary view would destroy the presumption of administrative regularity on which the presumption of validity rests. *Railroad Dynamics, Inc. v. A. Stucki Co.*, 579 F. Supp. 353, 218 U.S.P.Q. 618 (Pa. 1983).

ω

The rules of the PTO require an Examiner to search the file of a parent application for prior art. Accordingly, because of the PTO's own rule, it must be presumed that the Examiner did know of the existence of references cited in the prosecution of the parent application but chose not to rely on them because they had already been considered and distinguished during the earlier related prosecution. *Creative Industries Inc. v. Mobile Chemical Corp.*, 13 U.S.P.Q.2d 1534, 1538 (Ill. 1989).

ω

An Examiner is required to be clear in his/her rejection and to note specifically in every letter "all requirements outstanding against the case. Every point in the prior action of an examiner which is still applicable must be repeated or referred to, to prevent the implied waiver of the requirement." *Jewish Hospital of St. Louis v. Idexx Laboratories*, 42 U.S.P.Q.2d 1720, 1722 (Me. 1996).

ω

The regulations that prescribe an Examiner's conduct indicate that, in conducting an examination, an Examiner must evaluate each cited reference and then determine which of those references, alone or in combination, provides the most appropriate statutory ground for rejecting the claims. *In re Portola Packaging Inc.*, 42 U.S.P.Q.2d 1295, 1299 (Fed. Cir. 1997), *rhq. denied* 122 F.3d 1473, 44 U.S.P.Q.2d 1060 (Fed. Cir. 1997).

ω

The fact that claims receive their broadest reasonable meaning during the patent examination process does not relieve the PTO of its essential task of examining the entire patent disclosure to discern the meaning of claim words and phrases. *Rowe v. Dror*, 112 F.3d 473, 42 U.S.P.Q.2d 1550, 1555 (Fed. Cir. 1997).

Examiner. *See also* **Administrative Regularity, Cloud, Deference, Field of Search, Search Record, Speculation.**

An Examiner at the PTO can be subpoenaed as a witness to testify as to facts known only to him with respect to material issues of great public interest. *American Cyanamid Co. v. Federal Trade Commission*, 363 F.2d 757, 150 U.S.P.Q. 135, 151 (6th Cir. 1966).

ω

While an Examiner is presumed to be an expert in his field of examination, in making determinations under 35 U.S.C. §103, weight must be given to sworn statements of workers skilled in the art as to the meaning to them of symbols with which they (and not the court) are familiar. This is particularly so when questions of convention and custom come into dispute. *In re Lemin*, 364 F.2d 864, 150 U.S.P.Q. 546, 548 (C.C.P.A. 1966).

ω

No court has found itself bound by the Patent Office's internal policy barring Examiner testimony. Examiners are subject to compulsory testimony only on matters that are factual and that do not invade upon their decision-making mental processes. *Standard Packaging Corporation v. Curwood, Inc.*, 365 F.Supp. 134, 180 U.S.P.Q. 235, 236 (Ill. 1973).

ω

It is presumed that the Examiner considered and discarded uncited patent references that are classified in the class and subclasses in which the patent in suit issued, or in a class and subclass that have otherwise been indicated as having been searched by the Examiner. *Panduit Corp. v. Burndy Corp.*, 378 F. Supp. 775, 180 U.S.P.Q. 498, 505 (Ill. 1973).

ω

When the first of two patents is not a pioneer patent and a patent is subsequently issued over it, there is a presumption that the two patented structures are not equivalents and that there is a substantial difference between the respectively-claimed inventions, especially when the two patents were considered by the same Examiner. *In re Certain Stabilized Hull Units and Components Thereof and Sonar Units Utilizing Said Stabilized Hull Units*, 218 U.S.P.Q. 752, 760, 766 (U.S. Int'l Trade Commission 1982).

ω

To weaken the presumption of validity, there must be some showing that the prior art was not considered by the Examiner, not merely that it was not cited. Since none of the additional prior art references relied upon by the defendant were not considered by the Examiner or disclose any substantial element relating to the patented subject matter that was not considered by the PTO, the statutory presumption of validity is fully effective in this case. *Parkson Corp. v. Proto Circuits, Inc.*, 220 U.S.P.Q. 898 (Md. 1983).

ω

The presumption of validity under 35 U.S.C. §282 carries with it a presumption the Examiner did his duty and knew what claims he was allowing. *Intervet America, Inc. v. Kee-Vet Labs., Inc.*, 887 F.2d 1050, 1054 (Fed. Cir. 1989).

ω

To the extent reliance is placed on evidence previously considered by the PTO, there is "the added burden of overcoming the deference that is due to a qualified government agency presumed to have properly done its job, which includes...Examiners who are assumed to have some expertise in interpreting the references and to be familiar from their work with the level of skill in the art and whose duty it is to issue only valid patents." *Sonoco Products Co. v. Mobil Oil Corp.*, 15 U.S.P.Q.2d 1186, 1191 (S.C. 1989).

ω

Once an application is assigned to a particular Examiner for examination, mandamus is probably not available as a means for forcing the PTO to reassign the application to a different Examiner for examination purposes. *Energy Conservation Devices Inc. v. Manbeck,* 741 F. Supp. 965, 16 U.S.P.Q.2d 1574, 1576 (D.C. 1990).

ω

While Examiners are experts in reviewing patent applications in particular fields, they do not have actual experience in the technology. As a consequence, Examiners would presumably be at a disadvantage when faced with the testimony of true experts. *Sandvik Aktiebolag v. Samuels,* 20 U.S.P.Q.2d 1879 (D.C. 1991).

ω

A former Patent Examiner, now in private practice, may testify both as a fact witness and to give his explanation as to whether he would have granted a patent in issue if certain information were known to him. *Baron v. Bausch & Lomb Inc.*, 25 U.S.P.Q.2d 1641, 1660 (N.Y. 1992).

ω

An assistant Patent Examiner is responsible for examining patent applications and formulating an appropriate Office action with respect to the grant or denial of a patent to a patent applicant. Preparatory to formulating the action, it is necessary that he (i) analyze the disclosure and claims in an application for compliance with requirements of 35 U.S.C. §112, (ii) plan and conduct a search of relevant prior art, and (iii) formulate rejections under 35 U.S.C. §§102 and 103 with supporting rationale, or determine how each claim distinguishes over the prior art. When he formulates a denial of a patent, he is required to draft an Office action containing, where appropriate, objections or rejections for non-compliance with §112, and rejections under §§102 and 103. The thus-drafted action is required to be complete and accurate. *In re Boe*, 26 U.S.P.Q.2d 1809 (PTO Enr-Disc 1993).

ω

The field of search by the Patent Examiner is relevant objective evidence of the scope of the prior art. *Williams Service Group Inc. v. O.B. Cannon & Son Inc.*, 859 F.Supp. 1521, 33 U.S.P.Q.2d 1705, 1725 (Pa. 1994).

ω

If references were in front of the Examiner, it must be assumed that he or she reviewed them. *In re Portola Packaging Inc.*, 42 U.S.P.Q.2d 1295, 1299 (Fed. Cir. 1997), *rhg denied* 122 F.3d 1473, 44 U.S.P.Q.2d 1060 (Fed. Cir. 1997).

ω

Examiners are properly characterized as "quasi-judicial officials trained in the law and presumed to 'have some expertise in interpreting the [prior art] references and to be familiar from their work with the level of skill in the art and whose duty it is to issue only valid patents.'" Thus, Examiners are skilled in the art insofar as they are technically competent to understand information and references in some technical or scientific field, but they are not of ordinary skill in the art to the extent that this might imply that they are aware of all the pertinent prior art. *Semiconductor Energy Laboratory Co. v. Samsung Electronics Co.*, 4 F. Supp.2d 477, 46 U.S.P.Q.2d 1874, 1878 (Va. 1998).

Examiner's Answer. *See* 37 C.F.R. §1.193(a).

Grounds of rejection which are not mentioned by an Examiner in his answer are presumed to have been withdrawn. *Ex parte Kaul*, 125 U.S.P.Q. 70, 73 (PO Bd. App. 1959).

ω

The trial court's findings that plaintiff was dilatory, that he had misled the Patent Office, and that he had failed or refused to meet defendant's specific reasoning and arguments concerning the infringement issue were more than ample to support a finding of conduct "in excess of simple negligence" and a determination of bad faith on plaintiff's part in commencing and litigating this suit. *Kahn v. Dynamics Corporation of America*, 508 F.2d 939, 184 U.S.P.Q. 260, 264 (2d Cir. 1975).

ω

For an Examiner's Answer to cite (for the first time in the prosecution of an application) new references to "show the general state of the art" while expressly stating that "[n]o new prior art has been applied in this Examiner's Answer" is an improper effort to bring these references in the "back door." *Ex parte Raske*, 28 U.S.P.Q.2d 1304, 1305 (B.P.A.I. 1993).

Examiner's Opinion.

A rejection based on 35 U.S.C. §101 on the ground that the specification "does not give reasonable assurance that the scope claimed is operative for the asserted usefulness" was not sustained. The record contained no evidence and the Examiner presented no reasons, other than conclusory statements of opinion, tending to show why the assertion that the compounds are useful as plant growth regulants and fungicides should not be believed. *Ex parte Hageman*, 179 U.S.P.Q. 747, 748, 749 (PTO Bd. App. 1971).

Example. *See also* Prophetic Examples, Specific Example, Working Example.

There is no magical relation between the number of reference examples and the breadth of claims; the number and variety of examples are irrelevant if the disclosure is "enabling" and sets forth the "best mode" contemplated. A specification need not contain a working example if the invention is otherwise disclosed in such a manner that one skilled in the art would be able to practice it without an undue amount of experimentation. *In re Borkowski and Van Venrooy,* 422 F.2d 904, 164 U.S.P.Q. 642 (C.C.P.A. 1970).

ᚥ

Mention of representative compounds encompassed by generic claim language clearly is not required by 35 U.S.C. §112 or any other provision of the statute. But, where no explicit description of a generic invention is to be found in the specification, mention of representative compounds may provide an implicit description upon which to base generic claim language. Similarly, representative examples are not required by the statute and are not an end in themselves. Rather, they are a means by which certain requirements of the statute may be satisfied. Thus, inclusion of a number of representative examples in a specification is one way of demonstrating the operability of a broad chemical invention and, hence, establishing that the utility requirement of 35 U.S.C §101 has been met. It is also one way of teaching how to make and/or how to use the claimed invention, thus satisfying that aspect of §112. *In re Robins,* 429 F.2d 452, 166 U.S.P.Q. 552 (C.C.P.A. 1970).

ᚥ

Examples are merely illustrative and should not be construed as limitations on the scope of claims. *Ziegler v. Phillips Petroleum Co.,* 483 F.2d 858, 177 U.S.P.Q. 481, 493 (5th Cir. 1973).

ᚥ

The Examiner reasoned that, because of the breadth of the invention, a large number of examples (50 to 100) would be required to enable one of ordinary skill in the art to make and use the invention. 35 U.S.C. §112, first paragraph. Although working examples are desirable in complex technology and detailed examples can satisfy the statutory enablement requirement, examples are not required to satisfy §112, first paragraph. The Examiner's statement that "nearly universal applicability" alleged for the invention necessitated numerous examples was erroneous. Although the invention is applicable to a large variety of embodiments, the Examiner offered no reason why these different compounds would require different techniques or process parameters. *In re Strahilevitz,* 668 F.2d 1229, 212 U.S.P.Q. 561, 563 (C.C.P.A. 1982).

ᚥ

The fact that the specification is devoid of a working example is without significance. Examples are not necessary. While a full example may have provided additional useful information, one possessed of the knowledge of one skilled in this art could practice the invention without the exercise of an undue amount of experimentation. With respect to the best mode rejection, we find no evidence of concealment and are unable to agree with the Examiner that the quality of the appellants' disclosure is so lacking as to effectively result in concealment. *Ex parte Nardi and Simier,* 229 U.S.P.Q. 79 (B.P.A.I. 1986).

ᚥ

There is no legal requirement that all of the examples in the patent specification actually be reduced to practice before the filing of an application; it is only required that the specification contain a disclosure that enables those skilled in the art to practice the invention. *Corning Glass Works v. Sumitomo Electric U.S.A. Inc.*, 671 F. Supp. 1369, 5 U.S.P.Q.2d 1545, 1562 (N.Y. 1987).

Exceptional. *See also* **Attorney's Fees, Opinion of Counsel, Spurious.**

Vexatious or harassing litigation, really smelling of bad faith, warrants regarding a case exceptional and subject to an award of reasonable attorney's fees to the prevailing party. Even though the plaintiff's patent claims are manifestly without merit, bad faith has not been established. *Shatterproof Glass Corp. v. Guardian Glass Co.*, 322 F. Supp. 854, 168 U.S.P.Q. 212, 225 (Mich. 1970).

ᾧ

Increased damages are usually based on a finding that the infringer's conduct was willful and in flagrant disregard of the patentee's rights. In this case, the defendant was on notice of the plaintiff's patent rights and had an affirmative duty to exercise due care to determine whether it was infringing. The defendant may not avoid a holding of willful infringement because it failed to show that it obtained a competent opinion from counsel and that it had exercised reasonable and good faith adherence to the analysis and advice contained therein. Accordingly, the defendant is liable to the plaintiff for an amount equal to three times the amount of damages actually found or assessed. Section 285 of 35 U.S.C. makes provision for the award of attorney's fees to the prevailing party in exceptional cases. In order to support an award of attorney's fees in a patent case, there must be a showing of conduct that is unfair, in bad faith, inequitable, or unconscionable. In view of the defendant's willful infringement, this case involves those elements set out above and is an exceptional case, thereby entitling the plaintiff to an award of its attorney's fees. The plaintiff is also entitled to prejudgment interest based upon the damages found or assessed in the second phase of this trial. *Great Northern Corp. v. Davis Core & Pad Co.*, 226 U.S.P.Q. 540 (Ga. 1985).

ᾧ

Only after the prevailing party has established the exceptional nature of the case by clear and convincing evidence should a district court exercise its discretion to award attorney's fees. *Machinery Corp. of America v. Gullfiber AB*, 774 F.2d 467, 227 U.S.P.Q. 368, 371 (Fed. Cir. 1985).

ᾧ

An aggressive strategy may or may not be a factor in a decision to deny or award increased damages. An aggressive strategy, unsupported by any competent advice of counsel, thorough investigation of validity and infringement, discovery of more pertinent uncited prior art, or similar factors, is the type of activity the reference in the patent law to increased damages seeks to prevent. An alleged infringer, who intentionally blinds himself to the facts and law, continues to infringe, and employs the judicial process with no solidly based expectation of success, can hardly be surprised when his infringement is found to have been willful. Willfulness of infringement relates to the accused infringer's conduct in the marketplace. Because that conduct may be seen as producing an unnecessary and outcome-certain lawsuit, it may make the case so exceptional as to warrant attorney's fees under 35 U.S.C. §285. Similarly, bad faith displayed in pretrial and trial stages, by counsel or party, may render the case exceptional under §285. When a court declines to award attorney's fees on the basis of a determination that a case is not exceptional, the fact findings underlying that determination are reviewed under the clearly erroneous standard. When the determination is that a case is exceptional, the election to grant or deny attorney's fees is reviewed under the abuse-of-discretion standard. *Kloster Speedsteel A.B. v. Crucible Inc.*, 793 F.2d 1565, 230 U.S.P.Q. 81 (Fed. Cir. 1986).

ω

Inequitable conduct alone need not compel a finding that a case is exceptional. Not every case deemed "exceptional" must result in an award of attorney's fees. *Consolidated Aluminum Corp. v. Foseco International Ltd.*, 910 F.2d 804, 15 U.S.P.Q.2d 1481, 1489 (Fed. Cir. 1990).

ω

A trial court has the authority to award attorney's fees in patent litigation to the prevailing party "in exceptional cases." An express finding of willful infringement is a sufficient basis for classifying a case as "exceptional," and, indeed, when a trial court denies attorney's fees in spite of a finding of willful infringement, the court must explain why the case is not "exceptional" within the meaning of the statute. Nevertheless, the decision whether or not to award fees is still committed to the discretion of the trial judge, and even an exceptional case does not require (under all circumstances) an award of attorney's fees. *Modine Manufacturing Co. v. The Allen Group Inc.*, 917 F.2d 538, 16 U.S.P.Q.2d 1622, 1626 (Fed. Cir. 1990).

ω

"[T]he exceptional nature of the case must be established by clear and convincing evidence." *Manildra Milling Corp. v. Ogilvie Mills Inc.*, 878 F.Supp. 1417, 30 U.S.P.Q.2d 1020, 1023 (Kan. 1993).

Excipient. *See* **Carrier.**

Exclude. *See also* **Description, Excluding Prior Art, Injunction, Inoperative, Reduction in Scope, Right to Exclude.**

In claiming a mechanical combination, an applicant is not necessarily limited to the specific composition that he discloses as the material for making up each and every element of the combination. If every element in a mechanical combination claim were required to be so specific as to exclude materials known to be inoperative, and that even those not skilled in the art would not try, the claims would fail to comply with 35 U.S.C. §112 because they would be so detailed as to obscure, rather than particularly point out and distinctly claim, the invention. *In re Myers*, 410 F.2d 420, 161 U.S.P.Q. 668, 672 (C.C.P.A. 1969).

ω

It is always possible to put something into a combination to render it inoperative. It is not the function of claims to exclude all such matters, but to point out what the combination is. *In re Anderson,* 471 F.2d 1237, 176 U.S.P.Q. 331, 335 (C.C.P.A. 1973).

ᚥ

The Examiner's notion about the United States granting a contract is inapt. The government grants only a right to exclude. There is no other agreement. While a patent has often been likened to a contract on the theory that it is issued in exchange for the disclosure of the invention (the consideration), the analogy is inexact. A patent is a statutory right. It is granted to whoever fulfills the conditions, 35 U.S.C. §101, unless fraud has been committed. *In re Breslow,* 616 F.2d 516, 205 U.S.P.Q. 221, 224 (C.C.P.A. 1980).

ᚥ

The prosecution history (or file wrapper) limits the interpretation of claims so as to exclude any interpretation that may have been disclaimed or disavowed during prosecution in order to obtain claim allowance. *ZMI Corp. v. Cardiac Resuscitator Corp.,* 844 F.2d 1576, 6 U.S.P.Q.2d 1557 (Fed. Cir. 1988).

ᚥ

The right to exclude recognized in a patent is but the essence of the concept of property. *Richardson v. Suzuki Motor Co., Ltd.,* 868 F.2d 1226, 9 U.S.P.Q.2d 1913 (Fed. Cir. 1989).

ᚥ

In matters involving patent rights, irreparable harm has been presumed when a clear showing is made of patent validity and infringement. This presumption derives in part from the finite form of the patent grant; for patent expiration is not suspended during litigation, and the passage of time can work irremediable harm. The opportunity to practice an invention during the notoriously lengthy course of patent litigation may itself tempt infringers. The nature of the patent grant thus weighs against holding that monetary damages will always suffice to make the patentee whole; for the principal value of a patent is its statutory right to exclude. The patent statute provides injunctive relief to preserve the legal interests of the parties against future infringement, which may have marked effects never fully compensable in money. If monetary relief were the sole relief afforded by the statute, injunctions would be unnecessary, and infringers could become compulsory licensees for as long as the litigation lasts. *Lin v. Fritsch,* 14 U.S.P.Q.2d 1795, 1809 (Comm'r Patents & Trademarks 1989).

ᚥ

A patent effectively enlarges the natural right of an inventor to make, use, and sell his or her invention (absent conflicting patent rights in others) by adding to it the right to exclude others from making, using, or selling the patented invention. *Arachnid Inc. v. Merit Industries Inc.,* 939 F.2d 1574, 19 U.S.P.Q.2d 1513, 1516 (Fed. Cir. 1991).

ᚥ

The right to exclude (35 U.S.C. §154) may be waived in whole or in part. With few exceptions, any conditions which are not in their very nature illegal with regard to this kind of property, imposed by a patentee and agreed to by a licensee for the right to manufacture or use or sell the [patented] article, will be upheld by the courts. *Malinckrodt Inc. v. Medipart Inc.*, 976 F.2d 700, 24 U.S.P.Q.2d 1173, 1176 (Fed. Cir. 1992).

ᅏ

The purpose of the Constitution and Congress in protecting the right to exclude was to promote the progress of the useful arts. If the value of the right to exclude is diminished, the "incentive to engage in the toils of scientific and technological research" is likewise reduced. Therefore, public policy generally favors protection of patent rights. *A & E Products Group v. California Supply Inc.*, 28 U.S.P.Q.2d 1041, 1048 (Cal. 1993).

ᅏ

"[T]here is nothing improper, illegal or inequitable in filing a patent application for the purpose of obtaining a right to exclude a known competitor's product from the market." *Burroughs Wellcome Co. v. Barr Laboratories Inc.*, 828 F.Supp. 1200, 29 U.S.P.Q.2d 1721, 1727 (N.C. 1993).

ᅏ

A rejection of claims (for lack of adequate descriptive support because there was "no literal basis for the" claim limitation "in the absence of a catalyst") was reversed. The observation of lack of literal support does not, in and of itself, establish a *prima facie* case for lack of adequate descriptive support under the first paragraph of 35 U.S.C. §112. It cannot be said that the originally-filed disclosure would not have conveyed to one having ordinary skill in the art that appellants had possession of the *concept* of conducting the decomposition step in the absence of a catalyst. Throughout the discussion which would seem to cry out for a catalyst if one were used, no mention is made of a catalyst. *Ex parte Parks*, 30 U.S.P.Q.2d 1234, 1236 (B.P.A.I. 1993).

ᅏ

"[T]he existence of one's own patent does not constitute a defense to infringement of someone else's patent. A patent grants only the right *to exclude others* and confers no right on its holder to make, use, or sell." *Bio-Technology General Corp. v. Genentech Inc.*, 80 F.3d 1553, 38 U.S.P.Q.2d 1321, 1325 (Fed. Cir. 1996).

Excluded Evidence.

Excluded evidence is viewed in the light most favorable to its proponent, giving the "evidence its maximum reasonable probative force and its minimum reasonable prejudicial value." In order to reverse a decision in this regard made at trial, the reviewing court must be convinced that a prejudicial mistake was made. *Abbott Laboratories v. Brennan*, 952 F.2d 1346, 21 U.S.P.Q.2d 1192, 1197 (Fed. Cir. 1991).

Excluding Prior Art. *See also* Description, Exclude, Narrowing Claim.

The use of a negative limitation (excluding the characteristics of the prior-art products), causing claims to read on a virtually unlimited number of materials, many of which "might be the full equivalents in their effects of those excluded," does not render the claims indefinite. The scope of a claim is still definite when each recited limitation is definite. *In re Wakefield and Foster*, 422 F.2d 897, 164 U.S.P.Q. 636 (C.C.P.A. 1970).

ᅏ

The expressions "free of bleaching agent comprising an alkaline earth metal being capable of releasing hypochlorite or hypobromite in an aqueous solution" and "a non-reducing saccharide" find no support in the specification. They thus do not comply with the description requirement of the first paragraph of 35 U.S.C. §112. The fact that no compounds of this nature are taught to present in the examples of this case is an insufficient basis for the limitations introduced into the claims when (1) quite evidently the presence of a bleaching agent is not intended to be excluded from the claim composition and, in fact, is intended to be present as an ingredient, and (2) nowhere is it indicated that only nonreducing sugars are intended to be within the scope of saccharides as broadly disclosed. That sucrose is a nonreducing sugar does not entitle the appellant to claim a genus of which sucrose is a member. *Ex parte Pearson,* 230 U.S.P.Q. 711 (B.P.A.I. 1985).

Excluding Reference Embodiments. *See also* Narrowing Claim.

The court clearly looked to what was defined by the claim and interpreted it in the light of the disclosure upon which the claim was based. The court did not expand the meaning of "comprises" to include further limitations required by the reference. *Ashland Oil, Inc. v. Delta Resins Refractories, Inc.,* 776 F.2d 281, 227 U.S.P.Q. 657 (Fed. Cir. 1985).

Exclusion. *See* 28 U.S.C. §1581(a).

Exclusion Order.

In a case involving numerous importers and exporters of infringing goods, an exclusion order directed by the Trade Commission can prevent avoidance of an in personam remedy of cease and desist by switching importers and exporters from those active at the time of the remedy finding. *In re Reclosable Plastic Bags,* 192 U.S.P.Q. 674, 681 (U.S. Intl. Trade Comm'n 1977).

ᴛᴅ

In the light of the language and legislative history of 19 U.S.C. §1337, as well as precedent, the appropriate standard is whether the Commission's choice of remedy is arbitrary, capricious, an abuse of discretion, or otherwise not in accordance with law. The Commission's determinations on the public interest, the nature of the domestic market, bonding, and remedy, are subject to a less stringent standard of judicial review than determinations of substantive violations of §337. Of the five other standards of review articulated in 5 U.S.C. §706(2), the Commission's findings on the public health and welfare, competitive conditions in the U.S. economy, the production of like or directly competitive articles in the United States, U.S. consumers, the amount and nature of bond, and the appropriate remedy, are reviewable only for abuse of administrative discretion. *Hyundai Electronics Industries Co. Ltd. v. U.S. International Trade Commission,* 899 F.2d 1204, 14 U.S.P.Q.2d 1396, 1399, 1400 (Fed. Cir. 1990).

Exclusive. *See also* **Exclusive Right.**

An exclusive vendor of a product under a patent can be a coplaintiff in an action for patent infringement. When a sole licensee has been shown to be directly damaged by an infringer in a two-supplier market, and when the nexus between the sole licensee and the patentee is clearly defined, the sole licensee must be recognized as the real party in interest. *Kalman v. The Berlyn Corp.*, 914 F.2d 1473, 16 U.S.P.Q.2d 1093, 1099 (Fed. Cir. 1990).

Exclusive License.

The duty to exploit the subject matter of a license will be implied on the part of an exclusive licensee where such a covenant is essential as a matter of equity to give meaning to the effect of the contract as a whole; it would be unfair to place the productiveness of a licensed property solely within the control of the licensee. *Willis Brothers, Inc. v. Ocean Scallops, Inc.*, 356 F.Supp. 1151, 176 U.S.P.Q. 53, 56 (N.C. 1972).

ω

Where two licenses conflict, the first prevails, even though the taker of the second had no notice of the existence of the first. A purchaser of a patented product abroad from the U.S. patentee can be precluded from selling that product in the United States by an exclusive licensee under the U.S. patent. The purchaser of the product abroad can obtain no greater right from the patentee than was possessed by the patentee at that time. *Sanofi, S.A. v. Med-Tech Veterinarian Products, Inc.*, 565 F. Supp. 931, 220 U.S.P.Q. 416, 423 (N.J. 1983).

ω

A field-of-use license which grants an exclusive license under a patent to use the claimed inventions (DNA sequences and transfected host cells) in the U.S. to make an unpatented product (EPO) for sale abroad exceeds the scope of the patent. Thus, such an exclusive license is merely exclusive against the licensor under contract law, but is not exclusive under patent law against third party infringers. *Amgen Inc. v. Chugai Pharmaceutical Co.*, 808 F.Supp. 894, 27 U.S.P.Q.2d 1578, 1585 (Mass. 1992).

Exclusive Licensee. *See also* **Best Efforts, Release.**

The duty to exploit the subject matter of a license is implied on the part of an exclusive licensee where such a covenant is essential as a matter of equity to give meaning to the effect of the contract as a whole. The reason for implying a duty where an agreement grants an exclusive license is that it will be unfair to place the productiveness of a licensed property solely within the control of the licensee. *Willis Brothers, Inc. v. Ocean Scallops, Inc.*, 356 F. Supp. 1151, 176 U.S.P.Q. 53 (N.C. 1972).

ω

Section 118 of 35 U.S.C. was not intended to permit patent attorneys to sign patent applications on behalf of missing individual clients. The language "sufficient proprietary interest in the matter justifying such action" means that a person filing the application must have such an interest as to be able to participate in the grant of a patent issued on the basis of an application filed pursuant to §118. In order to participate in the grant of the patent, a person must be able to enforce or require enforcement of a patent grant. Examples of such a person are exclusive licensees or trustees in bankruptcy. The PTO will accept a proposed application under 35 U.S.C. §118 and Rule 47(b) signed by a registered patent attorney when the application is owned by an assignee of the inventor when the assignee is a juristic entity, such as a corporation or a government agency. *In re Striker*, 182 U.S.P.Q. 507, 508 (PO Solicitor 1973).

ᖶ

An "exclusive" licensee under a patent, title to which is in the United States may, under some circumstances, maintain a patent infringement action without the United States as a party, when the United States has authorized the licensee to sue for patent infringement in its own name and on its own behalf. *Nutrition 21 v. United States*, 930 F.2d 862, 18 U.S.P.Q.2d 1351, 1352 (Fed. Cir. 1991).

ᖶ

The only way to give meaning to an exclusive license is to allow the licensee to bring suit without the licensor's permission when the licensor refuses to join in the suit. *Brunswick Corp. v. United States*, 22 Cl. Ct. 278, 19 U.S.P.Q.2d 1702, 1705 (U.S. Cl. Ct. 1991).

ᖶ

Where a licensee has been granted the exclusive right to make, use, and sell patented subject matter to the exclusion of all others, and the patentee has not retained a substantial right in the patent, such an exclusive is equivalent of an assignment of the patent. Under these circumstances, there is no substantive difference between the property interests of the exclusive licensee and of an assignee of the patent. In such a situation, the exclusive licensee can bring suit against infringers in its own name without joinder of the patentee. *Arcade Inc. v. Minnesota Mining and Manufacturing Co.*, 43 U.S.P.Q.2d 1511, 1513 (Tenn. 1997).

Exclusive Right. *See also* Exclude.

Congress has not required an author-inventor to elect between several modes provided for securing exclusive rights on particular subject matter. If anything, the concurrent availability of more than one mode of securing exclusive rights aids in achieving the stated purpose of the constitutional provision. *In re Yardley*, 493 F.2d 1389, 181 U.S.P.Q. 331, 336 (C.C.P.A. 1974).

ᖶ

The nature of the patent grant weighs against holding that monetary damages will always suffice to make a patentee whole, for the principle value of the patent is its statutory right to exclude. *H. Robertson Co. v. United Steel Deck, Inc.*, 820 F.2d 384, 2 U.S.P.Q.2d 1926 (Fed. Cir. 1987).

ᖶ

The interest of the public is in protecting patent rights, and the right of a patentee is in the exclusive use of his invention. Without the protection of the patent statute, the incentive to invent and to improve products would be curbed, and the public interest in such inventions would not be served. *The Conair Group Inc. v. Automatik Apparate-Maschinenbau GmbH*, 19 U.S.P.Q.2d 1535, 1540 (Pa. 1990), *decision vacated and case remanded*, 944 F.2d 862, 20 U.S.P.Q.2d 1067 (Fed. Cir. 1991).

Exclusivity.

Section 355(j)(4)(B)(iv) of 21 U.S.C. explicitly provides that a primary generic drug manufacturer may qualify for the 180-day exclusivity in one of two ways: by compliance with subpart I or by compliance with subpart II. One of these methods, set forth in subpart II of Section (IV), by its terms, requires a suit for patent infringement pursuant to §355(j)(4)(B)(iii). The alternative method, set forth in subpart I, does not. Indeed, it makes no mention of a suit for patent infringement, but instead makes the 180-day exclusivity dependent on the first commercial marketing of the product. In light of the clear reference to a Section (iii) lawsuit in subpart II of Section (iv), and the omission of such reference in subpart I of Section (iv), there is no justification whatever for implying such a reference into subpart I notwithstanding Congress' presumably deliberate decision not to incorporate the lawsuit requirement to that subpart. A primary ANDA applicant can qualify for exclusivity beginning either on the date of a court decision invalidating a patent or holding that it is not infringed, or on a date of first commercial marketing of an applicant's product. The trigger for the exclusivity period is the filing of an ANDA containing a IV certification for "a drug for which a previous application has been submitted...." *Inwood Laboratories Inc. v. Young*, 723 F. Supp. 1523, 12 U.S.P.Q.2d 1065, 1066, 1067 (D.C. 1989).

Excusable Neglect.

When analyzing a claim of excusable neglect, court should "tak[e] account of all relevant circumstances surrounding the party's omission," including "the danger of prejudice to the [nonmovant], the length of the delay and its potential impact on judicial proceedings, the reason for the delay, including whether it was within the reasonable control of the movant, and whether the movant acted in good faith." *Advanced Estimating Systems Inc. v. Riney*, 77 F.3d 1322, 38 U.S.P.Q.2d 1208, 1210 (11th Cir. 1996).

Execution. *See* 35 U.S.C. §115.

Execution of Patent Application.

The entire disclosure and claims must be before each applicant at the time the required formal Declaration is executed when such execution is effected prior to filing an application for Letters Patent. Variations from this procedure not only jeopardize the validity or enforceability of any patents subsequently issued on the application, they also subject the attorney effecting the filing to sanctions by the PTO. *Jaskiewicz v. Mossinghoff*, 822 F.2d 1053, 3 U.S.P.Q.2d 1294 (Fed. Cir. 1987).

Executive Order No. 10096. [*See* 37 C.F.R. §501.]. *See also* **Invention Rights, Made, United States Government.**

There was Congressional statutory guidance in the formulation of a policy with respect to government property rights in patents developed by government employees. Executive Order 10096 is constitutional. *Kaplan v. Corcoran*, 545 F.2d 1073, 192 U.S.P.Q. 129, 132 (7th Cir. 1976).

ϖ

An administrative determination by the government agency employing the inventor is reviewable by the Commissioner of Patents and Trademarks. The Commissioner's determination is a final agency action reviewable under the Administrative Procedure Act (APA). 5 U.S.C. §704 (1982). The appropriate standard of review in the U.S. Claims Court of the Commissioner's determination is the "arbitrary or capricious" standard set forth in the APA. The U.S. Claims Court shall "hold unlawful and set aside agency action, findings, and conclusions found to be . . . arbitrary, capricious, an abuse of discretion, or otherwise not in accordance with law." Executive Order No. 10096 and the related regulations have been promulgated pursuant to the authority vested in the president by statute, and the order is constitutional. *Heinemann v. United States*, 796 F.2d 451, 230 U.S.P.Q. 430, 433 (Fed. Cir. 1986).

Exemplification.

Mention of representative compounds encompassed by generic claim language is clearly not required by 35 U.S.C. §112 or any other provision of the statute. But, where no explicit description of a generic invention is to be found in the specification (which is not the case here), mention of representative compounds may provide an implicit description upon which to base generic claim language. Similarly, representative examples are not required by the statute and are not an end in themselves. Rather, they are a means by which certain requirements of the statute may be satisfied. Thus, inclusion of a number of representative examples in a specification is one way of demonstrating the operability of a broad chemical invention and, hence, establishing that the utility requirement of 35 U.S.C. §101 has been met. It is also one way of teaching how to make and/or how to use the claimed invention, thus satisfying that aspect of §112. *In re Robins*, 429 F.2d 452, 166 U.S.P.Q. 552 (C.C.P.A. 1970).

Exhaustion. *See also* **Exclusive License.**

The law of domestic patent exhaustion holds that the first sale of a patented product "exhausts" the patent control by the patentee. Therefore, the patent confers no right upon the patentee to attempt to control the destiny of a product after it has been sold. *In re Reclosable Plastic Bags*, 192 U.S.P.Q. 674, 679 (U.S. Intl. Trade Comm'n 1977).

ϖ

The Patent Exhaustion Doctrine applies as well to the disposition of a product under a license as it does to outright sale. An authorized sale of the patented invention by a licensee to a third party places any resale by the third party beyond the reach of the infringement statute by reason the the third party's "authority to resell the products" derived from the licensee. Where the rights in a claim for a combination are exhausted by the sale of a component of the combination [claim 1 microprocessor], the patentee cannot escape exhaustion by specifying that the combined component [external memory] be performing a specific function when that function is an inherent capability of that component. The purpose of the patent exhaustion doctrine, *e.g.* preventing patentees from extracting double recoveries for an invention, is defeated if the patent owner can "invent" a non-infringing use by licensing systems. *Cyrix Corp. v. Intel Corp.*, 846 F.Supp. 522, 32 U.S.P.Q.2d 1890, 1903, 1904 (Tex. 1994).

Exhaustion Doctrine. *See also* Exhaustion.

It has been held that federal courts may dispense with the exhaustion doctrine in facial challenges to the re-examination procedure. *Allegheny Ludlum Corp. v. Comer*, 24 U.S.P.Q.2d 1771, 1776 (Pa. 1992).

ω

An attempt to collect royalties from two parties for the same product violates the exhaustion doctrine, and impermissibly extends the scope of the patent grant. *PSC Inc. v. Symbol Technologies Inc.*, 48 U.S.P.Q.2d 1838, 1842 (N.Y. 1998).

Exhibits.

An action in the district court under 35 U.S.C. §145 is a proceeding de novo and, while it is limited to the inventioon claimed in the PTO, the court may consider any additional competent evidence that a plaintiff neither intentionally nor negligently failed to submit to the PTO. The presumption of correctness that attaches to the decision of the Commissioner is a rebuttable presumption that may be overcome by the introduction of evidence (at a trial under §145) that is of such character and amount as to carry a thorough conviction of error. At such a trial the plaintiff and defendant may present evidence on any issue properly before the court. This additional evidence may include testimony of expert witnesses and inventors skilled in the art, and evidence of commercial success. In making its determination of non-obviousness, the court recognized the non-analogous nature of one reference, the lack of teaching or suggestion in the prior art of the useful advantage of a flexible track incapable of self-support, and the commercial success of the highly flexible Hot Wheels trackway-toy vehicle combination covered by the plaintiff's Reissue Application. The fact that the claimed invention seemed simple and, when viewed in hindsight, appeared to be obvious was not enough to negate invention. *Lemelson v. Mossinghoff*, 225 U.S.P.Q. 1063 (D.C. 1985).

Expanded Panel.

Legal support for adding additional members to an original panel, without necessity for reargument, can be found in *In re Bose Corp.*, 772 F.2d 866, 227 U.S.P.Q. 1 (Fed. Cir. 1985); *Ex parte Rodgers*, 27 U.S.P.Q.2d 1738 n.1 (B.P.A.I. 1992).

Expectant Interest. *See also* **Future Goods.**

An assignment of an expectant interest (an assignment of rights in an invention made prior to the existence of the invention) can be a valid assignment. In such a situation, the assignee holds at most an equitable title. *Mitchell v. Winslow,* 17 F. Cas. 527, 531, 532 (C.C.D. Me. 1843).

Expectation.

The view that success would have been "inherent" does not necessarily substitute for a showing of reasonable expectation of success. Inherency and obviousness are entirely different concepts. *In re Rinehart,* 531 F.2d 1048, 189 U.S.P.Q. 143, 148 (C.C.P.A. 1976).

ᴡ

Discovery of absence of skin toxicity in the claimed compound does not end the inquiry, because one who claims a compound, per se, which is structurally similar to a prior art compound must rebut the presumed expectation that the structurally similar compounds have similar properties. Because the expectation of similar properties stands unrebutted, it necessarily follows that an expectation of similar uses also stands unrebutted. *In re Wilder,* 563 F.2d 457, 195 U.S.P.Q. 426, 429, 430 (C.C.P.A. 1977).

Expectation of Success. *See also* **Expectation.**

Although the level of skill in the art of producing monoclonal antibodies had progressed to the point where a method had been used to produce numerous monoclonal antibodies specific to a variety of antigens and one may have approached the project with a reasonable expectation of success, it was not established that the claimed products would be "obvious" from prior-art teachings. The mere statement that the method of making the products would be obvious and that there would be a reasonable expectation of success reflects the regularly rejected obvious-to-try standard. *Ex parte Erlich,* 3 U.S.P.Q.2d 1011 (B.P.A.I. 1986).

Experiment. *See also* **Abandoned Experiment, Invitation to Experiment, Test.**

Continued experimentation does not negative a reduction to practice already made. *Breen v. Miller and Stine,* 347 F.2d 623, 146 U.S.P.Q. 127, 131 (C.C.P.A. 1965).

ᴡ

Once a device is actually built satisfactorily for its intended purpose, it is more than an experiment and is a part of the prior art even if it is later abandoned. *Connecticut Valley Enterprises, Incorporated v. United States,* 348 F.2d 949, 146 U.S.P.Q. 404, 406 (U.S. Ct. Cl. 1965).

Experimental Animals. *See also* **Animal Tests, Standard Experimental Animal.**

A demonstration that a compound has desirable or beneficial properties in the prevention, alleviation, or cure of some disease in experimental animals does not necessarily mean that the compound will have the same properties when used with humans. However, this is by no means support for the position that such evidence is not relevant to human utility. Evidence showing substantial activity against experimental tumours in mice in tests customarily used for the screening of anti-cancer agents of potential utility in the treatment of humans is relevant to utility in humans and is not to be disregarded. *In re Jolles*, 628 F.2d 1322, 206 U.S.P.Q. 885, 890 (C.C.P.A. 1980).

Experimental Use. *See also* **Patent Term Restoration, Public Use.**

Uses of a machine that were not made under patentee's surveillance and for the purpose of enabling patentee to test the machine and ascertain whether it would answer the purpose intended and to make such alterations and improvements as experience demonstrates to be necessary, are not excused as experimental uses. *Honeywell Inc. v. Sperry Rand Corp.*, 180 U.S.P.Q. 673, 690 (Minn. 1973).

ω

The so-called "experimental use" defense to liability for infringement has its origins in 1813 in *Whittemore v. Cutter*, 29 F. Cas. 1120 (No. 17,600) (C.C. D. Mass. 1813), when Justice Story, sitting as a circuit judge, commented that it was not the intent of the patent laws to hold liable one who made an infringing device "merely for philosophical experiments, or for the purpose of ascertaining the sufficiency of the machine to produce its described effects." By 1861,[5] it was "well settled that an experiment with a patented article for the sole purpose of gratifying a philosophical taste, or curiosity, or for mere amusement is not an infringement of the rights of the patentee." *Poppenhusen v. Falke*, 19 F. Cas. 1048 (No. 11,279) (C.C. S.D. N.Y. 1861). Many courts have held that the experimental use defense is not available where the use, although of an experimental nature, was in connection with the user's business. The very restricted circumstances under which the defense has been permitted suggests, as at least one court has observed, that the defense is nothing more than an expression of the maxim, de minimus non curit lex. *Radio Corp. of America v. Andrea*, 15 F.Supp. 685, 30 U.S.P.Q. 194 (E.D. N.Y. 1936), modified, 90 F.2d 612, 34 U.S.P.Q. 312 (2d Cir. 1937) (factory testing of units prior to sale). *Douglas v. United States*, 181 U.S.P.Q. 170, 176, 177 (U.S. Ct. Cl. 1974).

ω

Experimental use is not an exception to the bar otherwise created by a public use. If a use is experimental, even though not secret, public use is negated. The starting place for analysis of any case involving experimental use is *City of Elizabeth v. American Nicholson Pavement Co.* [97 U.S. 126, 136 (1877)]. *TP Laboratories Inc. v. Professional Positioners, Inc.*, 724 F.2d 965, 220 U.S.P.Q. 577, 582 (Fed. Cir. 1984).

ω

The experimental exception applies only when commercial exploitation is only incidental to the primary purpose of experimentation to perfect an invention. A challenger of a patent need not initially present evidence negating experimental use as part of its proof of an "on sale" bar. It is incumbent on the patent owner to come forward with evidence

---

[5] For a more complete exposition of the development of the experimental use defense, see Bee, Experimental Use as an Act of Patent Infringement, 39 J. Pat. Off. Soc'y. 357 (1957). See also, 3 Robinson on Patents §§898 (1890).

directed to showing an experimental purpose in order to bring that issue into a case. *Barmag Barmer Maschinenfabrik AG v. Murata Machinery, Ltd.*, 731 F.2d 831, 221 U.S.P.Q. 561, 567 (Fed. Cir. 1984).

ꟷ

The fact that a use or sale occurs under a regulatory testing procedure, such as a FIFRA (Federal Insecticide, Fungicide, and Rodenticide Act, 7 U.S.C. §135) experimental use permit, does not make such uses or sales per se experimental for purposes of 35 U.S.C. §102(b). *Pennwalt Corporation v. Akzona Incorporated*, 740 F.2d 1573, 222 U.S.P.Q. 833, 838 (Fed. Cir. 1984).

ꟷ

Even if the court were to assume that Schulman did conceive of a barbed endocardio lead prior to the critical date and that such a barbed lead was reduced to practice, Pacesetter cannot convince the court that use of such a lead was a public use. Pacesetter makes much of the fact that its experiments were conducted in an area with unusual and frequent public access, that its employees and consultants were not required to maintain any official secrecy obligations with respect to the barbed lead, and that Schulman clearly showed his barbed lead to prospective employees and visitors. But these circumstances do not amount to a meaningful and beneficial disclosure to the public as is inherent in a public use. Pacesetter's use of Schulman's barbed lead was nothing more than experimental and, presumably, subject to alterations and improvements. To the extent the use of Schulman's barbed lead was experimental and within the exclusive control of Pacesetter, the use was not a public use resulting in disclosure of new and useful information. *Medtronic, Inc. v. Daig Corp.*, 611 F. Supp. 1498, 227 U.S.P.Q. 509 (Minn. 1985).

ꟷ

Consideration should be accorded the totality of circumstances relating to the character and extent of commercial activities, along with the character and extent of *bona fide* experimentation. Such considerations historically applied the standard of whether any public use or sale (or offer to sell) was "mainly for the purpose of trade or profit" or "substantially for the purpose of experiment." If a use is experimental, even though not secret, public use is negated. If the challenged use or sales activities were associated with primarily experimental procedures conducted in the course of completing the invention, as the particular invention may require, a 35 U.S.C. §102(b) bar does not vest. Testing by the public in public view is not "public use" if the purpose is primarily experimental. In determining whether a public use or sale was substantially for purposes of experiment, consideration is given to various factors: the necessity for the public testing, the amount of control retained over the operation, the extent of public testing in relation to the nature of the invention, the length of the test period, whether any payment was made, whether there is any secrecy obligation, whether progress records were kept, who conducted the experiments, and the degree of commercial exploitation during the tests in relation to the purpose of the experimentation. *Baker Oil Tools Inc. v. Geo Van Inc.*, 828 F.2d 1558, 4 U.S.P.Q.2d 1210 (Fed. Cir. 1987).

ꟷ

For an assertion of experimental use to have merit, it must be clear that the inventor kept control of his invention in the course of its testing. The experimental-use doctrine operates in the inventor's favor to allow the inventor to refine his invention or to assess its value relative to the time and expense of prosecuting the patent application. If it is not the inventor or someone under his control or "surveillance" who does these things, there appears to be no reason why he should be entitled to rely upon them to avoid the statute. The experimental-use doctrine only lifts the one-year statutory bar where the experimental use is by the inventor or persons under his control. *In re Hamilton,* 882 F.2d 1576, 11 U.S.P.Q.2d 1890, 1893, 1894 (Fed. Cir. 1989).

ಌ

In determining whether an offer or sale occurred, consideration should be given to whether there was a "reduction to practice," although this is not an absolute requirement of the on-sale bar. In addition, consideration should be given to the stage of development of the invention and the nature of the invention. If a sale or offer to sell was made, the on-sale bar does not apply if the offer or sale was "substantially for the purpose of experiment." In determining whether an offer or sale was for experimental purposes, consideration must be given to various factors, including the length of the test period, whether any payment was made for the invention, whether there is any secrecy obligation on the user's part, whether progress records are required, whether persons other than the inventor conducted the experiments, the extent of testing required, length of the test period in relation to test periods for similar devices, and the degree of commercial exploitation during the tests (in relation to the purpose of the experimentation). *Loral Corp. v. The B. F. Goodrich Co.,* 14 U.S.P.Q.2d 1081, 1104 (Ohio 1989).

ಌ

The experimental-use exception to a public use or sale protects an inventor's intellectual property for the period of development and testing prior to patent application. The experimental-use exception to infringing uses, on the other hand, narrows the scope of intellectual property protection. This separate experimental-use exception protects an individual making unauthorized use of a patent (a potential infringer) during tests seeking advancement or commercialization of the patented teaching. Thus, the broader objective standards developed to protect an inventor during experimentation prior to patent application do not apply to experiments by a potential infringer. Acts of infringement must attack the right of the patentee to the emoluments which he does or might receive from the practice of the invention by himself or others. Where an invention is made or used as an experiment, whether for the gratification of scientific tastes, or for curiosity, or for amusement, the interests of the patentee are not antagonized; the sole effect being of an intellectual character in the promotion of the employer's knowledge or the relaxation afforded to his mind. *Deuterium Corp. v. United States,* 19 Cl. Ct. 624, 14 U.S.P.Q.2d 1636, 1643 (1990).

ಌ

The issue is not whether the demonstrations were experiments, but rather whether the demonstrations constituted activities inconsistent with experimentation. *Kearns v. Wood Motors Inc.,* 19 U.S.P.Q.2d 1138, 1142 (Mich. 1990).

ಌ

When sales are made in an ordinary commercial environment and the goods are placed outside the inventor's control, an inventor's secretly held subjective intent to "experiment", even if true, is unavailing without objective evidence to support that contention. For an assertion of experimental use to have merit, it must be clear that the inventor kept control over his invention in the course of its testing. *Paragon Podiatry Laboratory Inc. v. KLM Laboratories Inc.*, 984 F.2d 1182, 25 U.S.P.Q.2d 1561, 1565 (Fed. Cir. 1993).

ᛠ

To defeat summary judgment, patentee "need not prove an experimental purpose, but must submit facts indicating an ability to come forward with evidence that such proof is possible". *McGuire v. Acufex Microsurgical Inc.*, 34 U.S.P.Q.2d 1749, 1754 (Mass. 1994).

ᛠ

"There may be an experimental use following reduction to practice as long as the experiments are...part of an attempt to further refine the device." *Nordberg Inc. v. Telsmith Inc.*, 881 F.Supp. 1252, 36 U.S.P.Q.2d 1577, 1605 (Wis. 1995).

Experimentation. *See also* Routine Experimentation, Undue Experimentation.

To satisfy 35 U.S.C. §112, the specification disclosure must be sufficiently complete to enable one of ordinary skill in the art to make the invention without undue experimentation. The need for a minimum amount of experimentation is not fatal if the skill in the art is such that the disclosure enables one to make the invention. *Martin, Aebi, and Ebner v. Johnson*, 454 F.2d 746, 172 U.S.P.Q. 391, 395 (C.C.P.A. 1972).

ᛠ

That experimentation may be involved with the selection of proportions and particle sizes is not determinative of the question of scope of enablement; it is only undue experimentation that is fatal. *In re Geerdes*, 491 F.2d 1260, 180 U.S.P.Q. 789, 793 (C.C.P.A. 1974).

ᛠ

In determining whether or not experimentation is within the teachings of the art, we "must be ever alert not to read obviousness into an invention on the basis of the [appellants'] own statements; that is, we must view the prior art without reading into that art [appellants'] teachings." *In re Waymouth and Koury*, 499 F.2d 1273, 182 U.S.P.Q. 290, 292 (C.C.P.A. 1974).

ᛠ

The term "experimentation" implies that the success of the particular activity is *uncertain*. The basic policy of the Patent Act is to encourage disclosure of inventions and thereby to promote progress in the useful arts. To require disclosures in patent applications to transcend the level of knowledge of those skilled in the art would stifle the disclosure of inventions in fields we understand imperfectly, like catalytic chemistry. The certainty that the law requires in patents is not greater than is reasonable, having regard for their subject matter. *In re Angstadt and Griffin*, 537 F.2d 498, 190 U.S.P.Q. 214, 219 (C.C.P.A. 1976).

ᛠ

The PTO has the burden of giving reasons, supported by the record as a whole, why the specification is not enabling, and showing that the disclosure entails undue experimentation would be one way of meeting that burden. *In re Morehouse and Bolton,* 545 F.2d 162, 192 U.S.P.Q. 29, 32 (C.C.P.A. 1976).

ω

The plaintiff in an action brought pursuant to 35 U.S.C. §145 has a heavy burden. Because the Patent Office is an expert body preeminently qualified to determine questions of this kind, its conclusions are entitled to a broad presumption of validity. In these circumstances, the court is authorized to reverse the decision only if the Patent Office did not have a rational basis for its conclusions or if the plaintiff presented new evidence that leads to a thorough conviction that the plaintiff should prevail. In trials de novo under §145, great weight attaches to the expertise of the Patent Office, and its findings will not be overturned unless new evidence is introduced that carries thorough conviction that the Patent Office erred. Based upon the opinion testimony of an independent expert, the court was satisfied that the only way one would reach the plaintiff's claimed alloy composition from the reference disclosure was by experimentation. The testimony offered on behalf of a plaintiff at the trial was uncontradicted by the defendant. The court found that testimony to be very persuasive, and the court concluded that the plaintiff demonstrated by clear and convincing evidence that the determination by the Board of Appeals was in error. *Titanium Metals Corp. of America v. Mossinghoff,* 603 F. Supp. 87, 225 U.S.P.Q. 673 (D.C. 1984).

ω

The selection of the ratio of total jaw length to the average jaw height and the narrow range of hardness claimed is not a matter of obvious design choice to one of ordinary skill in the art at the time the invention was made. It is axiomatic that not only must claims be given their broadest reasonable interpretation consistent with the specification, but also all limitations must be considered. Here the characterization of certain specific limitations or parameters as obvious does not make the appellant's invention, considered as a whole, obvious. The fact that the invention may have been the result of experimentation does not negate patentability nor render obvious claimed parameters that were the result of experimentation *Ex parte Petersen,* 228 U.S.P.Q. 216, 217 (B.P.A.I. 1985).

ω

Enablement is a legal determination of whether a patent enables one skilled in the art to make and use the claimed invention. It is not precluded even if some experimentation is necessary, although the amount of experimentation needed must not be unduly extensive. Enablement is determined as of the filing date of the patent application. Furthermore, a patent need not teach, and preferably omits, what is well known in the art. *Hybritech Inc. v. Monoclonal Antibodies, Inc.,* 802 F.2d 1367, 231 U.S.P.Q. 81 (Fed. Cir. 1986).

ω

The mere need for experimentation to determine parameters needed to make a device work is an application of the often-rejected obvious-to-try standard and falls short of the statutory "obviousness" of 35 U.S.C. §103. Inability of an expert to predict the results obtainable with a claimed product suggests non-obviousness, not routine experimentation. *Uniroyal Inc. v. Rudkin-Wiley Corp.*, 837 F.2d 1044, 5 U.S.P.Q.2d 1434 (Fed. Cir. 1988).

ᛒ

Enablement is not precluded by the necessity for some experimentation, such as routine screening. However, experimentation needed to practice the invention must not be undue experimentation. The key word is "undue," not "experimentation." The determination of what constitutes undue experimentation in a case requires the application of a standard of reasonableness, having due regard for the nature of the invention and the state of the art. The test is not merely quantitative, since a considerable amount of experimentation is permissible, if it is merely routine or if the specification in question provides a reasonable amount of guidance with respect to the direction in which the experimentation should proceed. *In re Wands,* 858 F.2d 731, 8 U.S.P.Q.2d 1400, 1404 (Fed. Cir. 1988).

Expert. *See also* **Evidence, Expert Opinion, Expert Testimony, Expert Witness, Independent Expert, Opinion, Opinion Evidence, Witness.**

While the Examiner is presumed to be an expert in his field of examination, in making determinations under 35 U.S.C. §103, weight must be given to sworn statements of workers skilled in the art as to the meaning to them of symbols with which they, and not the court, are familiar, particularly in the absence of any refutation by the Patent Office of the factual statements in provided affidavits. *In re Lemin,* 364 F.2d 864, 150 U.S.P.Q. 546, 548 (C.C.P.A. 1966).

ᛒ

Fees and expenses for experts and consultants are awardable under 35 U.S.C. §285. *Beckman Instruments Inc. v. LKB Produkter A.B.*, 892 F.2d 1547, 13 U.S.P.Q.2d 1301, 1307 (Fed. Cir. 1989).

ᛒ

Although claim interpretation is a question of law, expert testimony is admissible to give an opinion on the ultimate question of infringement. *Symbol Technologies Inc. v. Opticon Inc.*, 935 F.2d 1569, 19 U.S.P.Q.2d 1241, 1245 (Fed. Cir. 1991).

ᛒ

"Under the Federal Rules of Evidence, the only thing a court should be concerned with in determining the qualifications of an expert is whether the expert's knowledge of the subject matter is such that his opinion will likely assist the trier of fact in arriving at the truth." The trial judge has broad discretion in determining whether to admit expert testimony on any subject. The court's ruling may not be disturbed absent clear error. *Abbott Laboratories v. Brennan,* 952 F.2d 1346, 21 U.S.P.Q.2d 1192, 1197 (Fed. Cir. 1991).

ᛒ

An expert's declaration was sufficient to defeat a motion for summary judgment. The expert testified as to both the level of skill in the art and the implication of the specifications and drawings of the patents in suit. He raised a genuine issue as to whether the patent is sufficiently descriptive to allow one skilled in the art to ascertain the best mode symmetrical power/ground configuration. Since the burden lies with MELA and

MELCO to prove the inadequacy of best mode disclosure by clear and convincing evidence, even the somewhat conclusory declaration of the expert was sufficient to raise a genuine issue for trial. Even if the declaration were regarded as overly conclusory, summary judgment could not, at least initially, be granted on this basis. The Court would be obliged to allow Wang to provide supporting detail. *Wang Laboratories Inc. v. Mitsubishi Electronics America Inc.*, 32 U.S.P.Q.2d 1641, 1645 (Cal. 1994).

ᅗ

An expert in the art may provide evidence as to what would be obvious to one of ordinary skill in the art to which his expertise applies, although such evidence is not controlling. Objective factual evidence of non-obviousness is preferable to statement of opinion, but expert's opinion testimony "is entitled to some weight". *Williams Service Group Inc. v. O.B. Cannon & Son Inc.*, 33 U.S.P.Q.2d 1705, 1725 (Pa. 1994).

ᅗ

A two-step inquiry in resolving motions to disqualify an expert based on a prior relationship with a party:

1 courts consider whether it was objectively reasonable for the first party to believe that a confidential relationship existed;
2 courts determine whether the first party actually disclosed confidential information to the expert.

In these inquiries, the burden is on the party seeking disqualification to establish the existence of confidentiality and its non-waiver. *Advanced Cardiovascular Systems Inc. v. Medtronic Inc.*, 47 U.S.P.Q.2d 1536, 1537 (Cal. 1998).

Expertise. *See also* **Administrative Regularity.**

The expertise of a deciding official is not legally relevant to the merits of any decision and is not subject to challenge. There can be no challenge to the authority of the Commissioner to decide a petition in person. *In re Arnott*, 19 U.S.P.Q.2d 1049, 1052 (Commr. Patents & Trademarks 1991).

Expert Opinion. *See also* **Expert, Expert Witness, Opinion, Patent Attorney, Skepticism.**

Evidence from a purported expert, who has expressed an expert opinion, is accorded more weight than an unsupported opinion of the Board on a highly technical subject on which the primary Examiner (presumed to be specializing in the relevant art) expressed no opinion. *In re Ehringer*, 347 F.2d 612, 146 U.S.P.Q. 31 (C.C.P.A. 1965).

ᅗ

Opinions of experts in affidavits must be given consideration and, while not controlling, generally are entitled to some weight unless they amount to an expression of an ultimate legal conclusion. *In re Altenpohl*, 500 F.2d 1151, 183 U.S.P.Q. 38 (C.C.P.A. 1974).

ᅗ

Opinions of experts, based in part on ex parte tests, concerning the ultimate legal issues, are accorded little weight. *Ralston Purina Company v. Far-Mar-Co, Inc.*, 586 F.Supp. 1176, 222 U.S.P.Q. 863, 892 (Kan. 1984).

☼

Affidavits from experts with actual skill in the art may aid the PTO in a patentability determination, but do not substitute for an obviousness determination under the proper standard. Rather, in a 35 U.S.C. §103 analysis, the evidence must be viewed from the position of a person of ordinary skill, not from the position of an expert. *Uniroyal, Inc. v. Rudkin-Wiley Corp.*, 837 F.2d 1044, 1050, 5 U.S.P.Q.2d 1434, 1438 (Fed. Cir.), *cert. denied*, 488 U.S. 825 (1988).

☼

An expert's sworn skepticism is entitled to weight in resolving the ultimate legal conclusion of obviousness under 35 U.S.C. §103. However, a conclusion of nonobviousness is not compelled merely because the magic word "unexpected" appears in a declaration. It is necessary to look at the facts relied upon to support an expert's opinion. *Ex parte George*, 21 U.S.P.Q.2d 1058, 1062 (B.P.A.I. 1991).

☼

Where affidavits are proffered as evidence on a motion for summary judgment, in support of or in opposition to the essential elements of a claim, the Court must be satisfied that such affidavits meet the standards set forth in Rule (Fed.R.Civ.P.) 56(e), as well as relevant evidentiary standards. Although expert witnesses are permitted to offer an opinion on the ultimate issue in the case pursuant to Fed.R. Evid. 704(a), the Court may exclude the expert testimony if such opinions are nothing more than legal conclusions. *Ciba-Geigy Corp. v. Crompton & Knowles Corp.*, 22 U.S.P.Q.2d 1761, 1763 (Pa. 1991).

☼

An affidavit expresses an expert's opinion regarding the insignificance of the differences between two devices, but does not contradict the intrinsic evidence. The testimony is relevant to whether a genuine issue of material fact exists with respect to the alleged infringement. For that reason the motion to strike the expert's affidavit will be denied. With respect to opinions of legal experts, the Federal Circuit has stated:

> [T]he court has complete discretion to adopt the expert legal opinion as its own, to find guidance from it, or to ignore it entirely, or even to exclude it.

Biomedical Polymers Inc. v. Evergreen Industries Inc., 976 F.Supp. 98, 45 U.S.P.Q.2d 1150, 1151 (Mass. 1997).

Expert Testimony. *See also* Discredit, Expert Witness, Opinion, Opinion Evidence.

Experts may be examined to explain terms of art, and the state of the art, at any given time. They may explain to the court and jury the machines, models, or drawings exhibited. They may point out the difference or identity of the mechanical devices involved in their construction. The maxim of "unique in sua arte credendum" permits them to be examined to questions of art or science peculiar to their trade or profession; but professors or mechanics cannot be received to prove to the court or jury what is the proper or legal construction of any instrument of writing. *Winans v. New York and Erie R. Co.*, 62 U.S. (21 How.) 88, 100-01 (1859).

ᛒ

The use of expert testimony about the significance of the similarities and differences between the patented and the prior art processes is of acknowledged value in determining the level of ordinary skill in the art. *Jack Winter, Inc. v. Koratron Company, Inc.*, 375 F.Supp. 1, 181 U.S.P.Q. 353, 378 (Cal. 1974).

ᛒ

Expert testimony may not ordinarily be received for the purpose of explaining the disclosure of an application. Expert testimony as to the scope of the issue is not permitted. However, just as a party may introduce dictionaries and textbooks for the purpose of establishing facts, such as the meaning of various terms to those skilled in the art and the properties of various materials, so may he employ the testimony of an expert for that same purpose. *Philips, Haley, and Clifton v. Matthews*, 197 U.S.P.Q. 776, 777, 778 (PTO Bd. Pat. Intf. 1977).

ᛒ

Although an engineering professor is a person of more than the "ordinary skill" required by the statute, he is in many ways well suited to assist the court in deciding what would be obvious to such a person. He is in contact with students at different levels of developing skill, and is particularly qualified to assess what would be obvious to persons of lesser skill than his own. *Moore v. Wesbar Corporation*, 701 F.2d 1247, 217 U.S.P.Q. 684, 689 (7th Cir. 1983).

ᛒ

While objective factual evidence going toward a 35 U.S.C. §103 determination is preferable to statements of opinion on the issue, the nature of the matter sought to be established, as well as the strength of the opposing evidence, must be taken into consideration in assessing the probative value of expert opinion. Opinion testimony rendered by experts must be given consideration, and, while not controlling, generally is entitled to some weight. Lack of factual support for expert opinion going to a factual determination, however, may render the testimony of little probative value in a validity determination. While the opinion testimony of a party having a direct interest in the pending litigation is less persuasive than opinion testimony by a disinterested party, it cannot be disregarded for that reason alone and may be relied upon when sufficiently convincing. *Ashland Oil, Inc. v. Delta Resins & Refractories, Inc.*, 776 F.2d 281, 227 U.S.P.Q. 657 (Fed. Cir. 1985).

ᛒ

Just as a party may introduce dictionaries and textbooks for the purpose of establishing facts, such as the meaning of various terms to those skilled in the art and the properties of various materials, so may he employ the testimony of an expert for that same purpose, notwithstanding the fact that expert testimony is not ordinarily received for the purpose of explaining a disclosure or for determining the scope of the issue. *Martin v. Mayer*, 823 F.2d 500, 3 U.S.P.Q.2d 1333 (Fed. Cir. 1987).

ᛒ

The trier of fact is not bound to accept expert opinion, even if it is uncontradicted. The court's obligation is to weigh expert and other testimony; it is the court's, not the expert's, responsibility to decide the case. *Del Mar Avionics, Inc. v. Quinton Instrument Co.*, 836 F.2d 1320, 5 U.S.P.Q.2d 1255 (Fed. Cir. 1987).

ᛒ

A technical expert who is not qualified as a legal expert and is not offered as a legal expert is not competent to give testimony on legal issues. *Union Carbide Corp. v. Terancon Corp.*, 682 F. Supp. 535, 6 U.S.P.Q.2d 1847 (Ga. 1988).

ᛒ

There is no authority for holding evidence to be in equipoise for the sole reason that a court cannot decide between conflicting experts. The mere fact that experts disagree does not mean that the party with the burden of proof loses. *Andrew Corp. v. Gabriel Electronics, Inc.*, 847 F.2d 819, 6 U.S.P.Q.2d 2010 (Fed. Cir. 1988).

ᛒ

With regard to the issue of obviousness of applied art, testimony of those who qualified as experts was not acceptable as evidence of what would be obvious to one of ordinary skill in the art. *Dotolo v. Quigg*, 12 U.S.P.Q.2d 1032, 1037 (D.C. 1989).

ᛒ

When expert testimony is needed in support of, or in opposition to, a preliminary motion, a party should:

1. identify the person it expects to call as an expert;
2. state the field in which the person is alleged to be an expert; and
3. state in a Declaration signed by the person: (a) the subject matter on which the person is expected to testify, (b) the facts and opinions to which the person is expected to testify, and (c) a summary of the grounds and basis for each opinion.

When a person is to be called as a fact witness, a Declaration by that person (stating the facts) should be filed. If the other party is to be called, or if evidence in the possession of the other party is necessary, an explanation of the evidence sought, what it will show, and why it is needed must be supplied. When inter partes tests are to be performed, a description of such tests (stating what they will show) must be presented. *Hanagan v. Kimura*, 16 U.S.P.Q.2d 1791, 1794 (Commr. Patents & Trademarks 1990).

ᛒ

In a civil action under 35 U.S.C. §145 in which plaintiff seeks to set aside a BPAI decision affirming an Examiner's final rejection of claims in plaintiff's reissue patent application, the court refused to exclude the testimony of a patent law expert with regard to relevant matters, but did exclude any exposition or opinion as to legal issues in the case or patent law generally. *Ely v. Manbeck,* 17 U.S.P.Q.2d 1252, 1254 (D.C. 1990).

ᵀ

Admission of expert testimony is within the discretion of the trial court. A decision on such a question will not be disturbed unless a court abuses its discretion. *Acoustical Design Inc. v. Control Electronics Co.,* 932 F.2d 939, 18 U.S.P.Q.2d 1707, 1709 (Fed. Cir. 1991).

ᵀ

Under the Federal Rules of Evidence an expert's testimony on infringement, including claim charts, may be sufficient to establish a *prima facie* case of infringement. The full burden of exploration of the facts and assumptions underlying the testimony of an expert witness is squarely on the shoulders of opposing counsel's cross-examination. *Symbol Technologies, Inc. v. Opticon, Inc.,* 935 F.2d 1569, 1574-76, 19 U.S.P.Q.2d 1241, 1245, 1246 (Fed. Cir. 1991).

ᵀ

While an expert may testify to the ultimate issue in a case without giving the basis for that opinion, nothing in the rules requires a fact finder to accept this conclusion. *Rohm and Haas Co. v. Brotech Corp.,* 127 F.3d 1089, 44 U.S.P.Q.2d 1459, 1462 (Fed. Cir. 1997).

ᵀ

In *Daubert v. Merrell Dow Pharmaceuticals, Inc.,* 509 U.S. 579, 27 U.S.P.Q.2d 1200 (1993), the Supreme Court enunciated a protocol for district court judges to use in evaluating the admissibility of expert scientific evidence under Federal Rule of Evidence 702. The approach focuses on assessing the validity of the expert's principles and methodology. The court set forth several factors (593-95):

(1) whether the technique can be tested;
(2) whether the technique has been submitted to peer review and publication;
(3) whether the technique has an acceptable known or potential rate of error;
(4) whether adequate standards control the technique's operation; and
(5) whether the relevant scientific community generally accepts the technique.

Experience alone may provide adequate qualification for expert testimony. The Tenth Circuit concluded that *Daubert* is inapplicable to cases "where expert testimony is based solely upon experience or training." *Daubert* factors and supporting rationale make clear that the test is "applicable only when a proffered expert relies on some principle or methodology." *United States Surgical Corp. v. Orris Inc.,* 45 U.S.P.Q.2d 1125, 1127 (Kan. 1997).

ᵀ

A trial court is quite correct in hearing and relying on expert testimony on an ultimate claim construction question in cases in which the intrinsic evidence (i.e., the patent and its file history—the 'patent record') does not answer the question. "No doubt there will be instances in which intrinsic evidence is insufficient to enable the court to determine the meaning of asserted claims, and in those instances, extrinsic evidence... may...properly be relied upon to understand and construe the claims." What is disapproved of is an attempt to use extrinsic evidence to arrive at a claim construction that is clearly at odds with the claim construction mandated by the claims themselves, the written description, and the prosecution history, in other words, with the written record of the patent. *Key Pharmaceuticals Inc. v. Hercon laboratories Corp.*, 48 U.S.P.Q.2d 1911, 1917 (Fed. Cir. 1998).

Expert Witness. ***See also*** **Expert.**

An action in the district court under 35 U.S.C. §145 is a proceeding de novo and, while it is limited to the invention claimed in the PTO, the court may consider any additional competent evidence that a plaintiff neither intentionally nor negligently failed to submit to the PTO. The presumption of correctness that attaches to the decision of the Commissioner is a rebuttable presumption that may be overcome by the introduction of evidence (at a trial under §145) that is of such character and amount as to carry a thorough conviction of error. At such a trial the plaintiff and defendant may present evidence on any issue properly before the court. This additional evidence may include testimony of expert witnesses and inventors skilled in the art, and evidence of commercial success. In making its determination of non-obviousness, the court recognized the non-analogous nature of one reference, the lack of teaching or suggestion in the prior art of the useful advantage of a flexible track incapable of self-support, and the commercial success of the highly flexible Hot Wheels trackway-toy vehicle combination covered by the plaintiff's Reissue Application. The fact that the claimed invention seemed simple and, when viewed in hindsight, appeared to be obvious was not enough to negate invention. *Lemelson v. Mossinghoff,* 225 U.S.P.Q. 1063 (D.C. 1985).

ϖ

Where affidavits are proffered as evidence on a motion for summary judgment, in support of or in opposition to the essential elements of a claim, the Court must be satisfied that such affidavits meet the standards set forth in Rule (Fed.R.Civ.P.) 56(e), as well as relevant evidentiary standards. Although expert witnesses are permitted to offer an opinion on the ultimate issue in the case pursuant to Fed.R. Evid. 704(a), the Court may exclude the expert testimony if such opinions are nothing more than legal conclusions. *Ciba-Geigy Corp. v. Crompton & Knowles Corp.*, 22 U.S.P.Q.2d 1761, 1763 (Pa. 1991).

ϖ

In a case of willful infringement of the plaintiff's patent wherein the plaintiff expended great time and expense to prove the defendant's infringement, the court let stand an award of expert witness fees in excess of the $30 per day attendance fee specified in 28 U.S.C. §1821. *Dana Corp. v. Nok Inc.*, 9 U.S.P.Q.2d 2004 (Mich. 1988).

ϖ

An award of expert witness fees is not precluded in context of the exceptional case governed by 35 U.S.C. §285. *Trend Products Co. v. Metro Industries, Inc.*, 10 U.S.P.Q.2d 1539, 1541 (Cal. 1989).

ϖ

"[W]hen a prevailing party seeks reimbursement for fees paid to its own expert witnesses, a federal court is bound by the limit of [28 U.S.C.] §1821(b), absent contract or explicit statutory authority to the contrary." Such explicit authority is not provided by 35 U.S.C. §285. A finding of fraud or abuse of the judicial process must be found before a trial court can invoke its inherent sanctioning power to impose expert witness fees in excess of the 28 U.S.C. §1821(b) cap. *Amsted Industries Inc. v. Buckeye Steel Castings Co.*, 23 F.3d 374, 30 U.S.P.Q.2d 1470, 1471, 1474 (Fed. Cir. 1994).

ϖ

The "person of ordinary skill in the art" is a theoretical construct used in determining obviousness under 35 U.S.C. §103. The construct applies to particular individuals and does not disqualify a person of *exceptional* skill from testifying as an expert because such person is not ordinary enough. *Endress + Hauser Inc. v. Hawk Measurement Systems Pty. Ltd.*, 122 F.2d 1040, 43 U.S.P.Q.2d 1849, 1851 (Fed. Cir. 1997).

Expiration.

The public should be able to act on the assumption that, upon expiration of a patent, it will be free to use not only the invention claimed in the patent but also any modifications or variants thereof which would have been obvious to those of ordinary skill in the art at the time the invention was made, taking into account the skill of the art and prior art other than the invention claimed in the issued patent. *In re Zickendraht*, 319 F.2d 225, 138 U.S.P.Q. 22 (C.C.P.A. 1963).

ϖ

Coupled with the sale and delivery during the patent term of a "completed" machine (completed by being ready for assembly after expiration of the patent term and with no useful non-infringing purpose), the amount of required predelivery testing justifies a holding of infringement. To reach a contrary result would emasculate the congressional intent to prevent the making of a patented item during the patent's full term of seventeen years. *Paper Converting Machine Company v. Magna-Graphics Corporation*, 745 F.2d 11, 223 U.S.P.Q. 591, 597 (Fed. Cir. 1984).

Explanation. *See also* Theory.

Where an applicant contends that the discovery of the source of a problem would have been unobvious to one of ordinary skill in the pertinent art at the time the claimed invention was made, it is incumbent upon the PTO to explain its reasons if it disagrees. A mere conclusionary statement that the source of the problem would have been discovered is inadequate. *In re Peehs and Hunner*, 612 F.2d 1287, 204 U.S.P.Q. 835, 837 (C.C.P.A. 1980).

ϖ

When a claim is rejected, the Examiner should explain clearly the reasons for the rejection. *Ex parte Ionescu*, 222 U.S.P.Q. 537, 539 (PTO Bd. App. 1984).

Exploit.

The duty to exploit the subject matter of a license will be implied on the part of an exclusive licensee where such a covenant is essential as a matter of equity to give meaning to the effect of the contract as a whole; it would be unfair to place the productiveness of a licensed property solely within the control of the licensee. An implied obligation to exploit a licensed patent is not binding on an exclusive licensee, however, if its observance would prevent the licensee from meeting market competition with a reasonable chance of success. *Willis Brothers, Inc. v. Ocean Scallops, Inc.*, 356 F.Supp. 1151, 176 U.S.P.Q. 53, 56 (N.C. 1972).

Export.

An export restriction in a license agreement between the parties represents an attempt to control the distribution of products (produced by patented apparatus) not covered by the subject patent, thereby expanding defendant's patent monopoly beyond its lawful scope, and constitutes misuse of the patent. The patentee may not use the courts to enforce its rights under the patent until the misuse is purged. *Robintech, Inc. v. Chemidus Wavin, Ltd.*, 450 F.Supp. 823, 198 U.S.P.Q. 466, 477 (D.C. 1978).

Express Basis. *See Expressis Verbis*, **Support.**

Expressis Verbis. *See also In Haec Verba, Ipsis Verbis.*

While particular words quoted from a claim may not appear as such in the specification, the meaning thereof by other words is clearly present and constitutes adequate antecedent basis for the words in fact used. The drawing is not a place to find antecedent basis. *Ex parte Siegmund and Cole*, 156 U.S.P.Q. 477, 478 (PO Bd. App. 1967).

Extension. *See also* **Patent Term Extension.**

The rule against "double patenting" is to prevent the extension of a patent monopoly beyond the 17 years permitted by the statute. *Spound v. Mohasco Industries, Inc.*, 186 U.S.P.Q. 183, 185 (Mass. 1975).

Extension of Monopoly. *See also* **Double Patenting.**

Appellant may not extend the monopoly incident to his original patent by claiming (in a subsequently filed application) in different phraseology the inventive concept upon which the patent was granted. *In re Weiskopf*, 210 F.2d 287, 100 U.S.P.Q. 383, 385 (C.C.P.A. 1954).

Extraneous Limitation.

The claims of a patent provide the concise formal definition of the invention. One must look to the wording of claims to determine whether there has been infringement. Courts can neither broaden nor narrow the claims to give a patentee something different from what he has set forth. No matter how great the temptation of fairness or policy making, courts do not rework claims; they only interpret them. Courts cannot alter what the patentee has chosen to claim as his invention. Generally, particular limitations or embodiments appearing in the specification are not to be read into the claims. It is entirely proper to use the specification to interpret what a patentee means by a word or phrase in the claims, but this is not to be confused with adding an extraneous limitation appearing in the specification, which is improper. By "extraneous" is meant a limitation read into a claim from the specification wholly apart from any need to interpret what the patentee meant by particular words or phrases in the claim. Where a specification does not require a limitation, that limitation should not be read from the specification to the claims. *E.I. du Pont de Nemours & Co. v. Phillips Petroleum Co.*, 849 F.2d 1430, 7 U.S.P.Q.2d 1129 (Fed. Cir. 1988).

Extraordinary Writ.

Orders whose review is by extraordinary writ may be overturned only where there has been a clear abuse of discretion or usurpation of judicial authority. The petitioner has the burden of establishing that its right to issuance of the writ is "clear and indisputable". *In re University of California*, 964 F.2d 1128, 22 U.S.P.Q.2d 1748, 1754 (Fed. Cir. 1992).

Extrinsic Evidence.

"[E]xtrinsic evidence may be considered when it is used to explain, but not expand, the meaning of a reference." *In re Baxter Travenol Labs.*, 952 F.2d 388, 390, 21 U.S.P.Q.2d 1281, 1284 (Fed. Cir. 1991).

℧

Extrinsic evidence may be considered to explain, but not expand on, the meaning of an anticipatory reference. The Court may look to extrinsic evidence to learn how the person of ordinary skill would interpret an anticipatory reference. Extrinsic evidence may be used "where the common knowledge of technologists is not recorded in the reference; that is, where technological facts are known to those in the field of the invention, albeit not known to judges." *Ciba-Geigy Corp. v. Alza Corp.*, 33 U.S.P.Q.2d 1018, 1023 (N.J. 1994).

℧

Extrinsic evidence is that evidence which is external to the patent and file history, such as expert testimony, inventor testimony, dictionaries, and technical treatises and articles. Extrinsic evidence in general, and expert testimony in particular, may be used only to help the court come to a proper understanding of the claims; it may not be used to vary or contradict the claim language. *Vitronics Corp. v. Conceptronic Inc.*, 90 F.3d 1576, 39 U.S.P.Q.2d 1573, 1578 (Fed. Cir. 1996).

℧

A court may consider extrinsic evidence as an aid in understanding the meaning of the claims' language, though extrinsic evidence may not be used "for the purpose of varying or contradicting the terms of the claims." Extrinsic evidence consists of all evidence external to the patent and prosecution history, including expert and inventor testimony, dictionaries, and learned treatises. This evidence may be helpful to explain scientific principles, the meaning of technical terms, and terms of art that appear in the patent and prosecution history. Extrinsic evidence may demonstrate the state of the prior art at the time of the invention. It is useful to show what was then old, to distinguish what was new, and to aid the court in the construction of the patent. A court may consider extrinsic evidence as an aid in understanding the meaning of the claims' language, though extrinsic evidence may not be used "for the purpose of varying or contradicting the terms of the claims." Extrinsic evidence consists of all evidence external to the patent and prosecution history, including expert and inventor testimony, dictionaries, and learned treatises. This evidence may be helpful to explain scientific principles, the meaning of technical terms, and terms of art that appear in the patent and prosecution history. Extrinsic evidence may demonstrate the state of the prior art at the time of the invention. It is useful to show what was then old, to distinguish what was new, and to aid the court in the construction of the patent. *Caterpillar Inc. v. Detroit Diesel Corp.*, 41 U.S.P.Q.2d 1876 (Ind. 1996).

ω

Expert testimony is to be eschewed and used only as a last resort. The Federal Circuit showed a clear preference for other types of extrinsic evidence, when properly considered, such as dictionaries and prior art documents. *Raleigh v. Tandy Corp.*, 45 U.S.P.Q.2d 1715, 1717 (Cal. 1997).

ω

A trial court is quite correct in hearing and relying on expert testimony on an ultimate claim construction question in cases in which the intrinsic evidence (i.e., the patent and its file history—the 'patent record') does not answer the question. "No doubt there will be instances in which intrinsic evidence is insufficient to enable the court to determine the meaning of asserted claims, and in those instances, extrinsic evidence... may... properly be relied upon to understand and construe the claims." What is disapproved of is an attempt to use extrinsic evidence to arrive at a claim construction that is clearly at odds with the claim construction mandated by the claims themselves, the written description, and the prosecution history, in other words, with the written record of the patent. *Key Pharmaceuticals Inc. v. Hercon Laboratories Corp.*, 48 U.S.P.Q.2d 1911, 1917 (Fed. Cir. 1998).

Key Terms and Concepts

Facsimile.

Service by fax is not sufficient to satisfy Fed. R. Civ. P. 5(b). *Mushroom Associates v. Monterey Mushrooms Inc.*, 25 U.S.P.Q.2d 1304, 1307 (Cal. 1992).

Fact. *See also* **Assertion, Findings of Fact, Knowledge (Later Discovered), Intervening References.**

Facts appearing in the record, rather than prior decisions in and of themselves, must support the legal conclusion of obviousness under 35 U.S.C. §103. Merely stating that a compound or composition is obvious, without actual factual support, is not sufficient. *In re Cofer*, 354 F.2d 664, 148 U.S.P.Q. 268, 271 (C.C.P.A. 1966).

ω

As a matter of law under 35 U.S.C. §103, the Examiner must substantiate his "suspicions" on the basis of facts drawn from proper prior art. The provisions of §103 must be followed realistically to develop the factual background against which the §103 determination must be made. All of the facts must be considered. *In re Lunsford*, 357 F.2d 385, 148 U.S.P.Q. 721, 725 (C.C.P.A. 1966).

ω

In making a rejection, an Examiner may "take notice of facts beyond the record which, while not generally notorious, are capable of such instant and unquestionable demonstration as to defy dispute." *In re Ahlert*, 424 F.2d at 1091, 165 U.S.P.Q. 418, 420 {citing*In re Knapp Monarch Co.*, 296 F.2d 230 [132 U.S.P.Q. 6] (C.C.P.A. 1961)}. Furthermore, although the cases provide that the Examiner should cite prior art references to support assertions of technical fact in esoteric technologies or specific knowledge of the prior art, this is solely to put the applicant on notice so that the correctness of the assertion can be challenged. *Id.*, 165 U.S.P.Q. at 420-21.

ω

A reference having an effective date subsequent to an applicant's earliest filing date is properly cited for the purpose of showing a fact. *In re Langer,* 503 F.2d 1380, 183 U.S.P.Q. 288, 297 (C.C.P.A. 1974).

ω

Prima facie obviousness is a legal conclusion, not a fact. Facts established by rebuttal evidence must be evaluated along with the facts on which the earlier conclusion was reached, not against the conclusion itself. Though the tribunal must begin anew, a final finding of obviousness may be reached, but such finding will rest upon evaluation of all facts in evidence, uninfluenced by any earlier conclusion reached by an earlier Board upon a different record. *In re Rinehart*, 531 F.2d 1048, 189 U.S.P.Q. 143, 147 (C.C.P.A. 1976).

ᵀᵀ

A mere dispute concerning the meaning of a term does not itself create a genuine issue of material fact. *Markman v. Westview Instruments Inc.*, 772 F. Supp. 1535, 20 U.S.P.Q.2d 1955 (Pa. 1991).

ᵀᵀ

A fact, question or right distinctly adjudged in an original action cannot be disputed in a subsequent action even though the determination was rendered upon an erroneous view or an erroneous application of law. *In re Convertible Rowing Exerciser Patent Litigation*, 814 F.Supp. 1197, 26 U.S.P.Q.2d 1677, 1686, 1687 (Del. 1993).

FAFR (First Action Final Rejection) Policy.

The PTO has a First Action Final Rejection (FAFR) policy permitting a final rejection in a first Office Action in those situations where (1) the application is a continuing application of, or a substitute for, an earlier application, and (2) all claims of the continuing or substitute application (a) are drawn to the same invention claimed in the earlier application, and (b) would have been properly finally rejected on the grounds of art of record in the next Office Action if they had been entered in the earlier application. This policy is maintained notwithstanding the provisions of 35 U.S.C. §132: "Whenever, on examination, any claim for a patent is rejected [and] the applicant persists in his claim for a patent, with or without amendment, the application shall be reexamined [by the PTO]." *Molins PLC v. Quigg*, 837 F.2d 1064, 5 U.S.P.Q.2d 1526 (Fed. Cir. 1988).

ᵀᵀ

FAFR practice, which is in accord with the statutory objectives of reducing delay in prosecution, is traceable as far back as 1923 and has existed on a continuous basis until the present date. FAFR practice was crystallized in Office practice in MPEP §706.07(b) at the time the present 35 U.S.C. §120 was enacted in 1952; it must be assumed that legislators were aware of the practice. Section 120 codified the existing law of continuations. Under the circumstances, the practice is entitled to a presumption of correctness. *In re Bogese*, 22 U.S.P.Q.2d 1821, 1827 (Comm'r Patents and Trademarks 1991).

Fail. *See* Inoperative.

Failure of Others. *See also* Problem, Secondary Considerations, Solution.

The differences between the prior art and the invention defined by asserted claims, the availability of that art to all workers in the field, the failure of established competitors in a highly competitive market to make the invention despite the incentive to do so, the admittedly non-obvious performance benefits realized through the claimed invention, the impressive commercial success of the claimed product, the praise of independent commentators and the forbearance of competitors from infringing the patent all go to confirm that the claimed invention was not obvious at the time it was made to a person of ordinary skill in the art. *S. C. Johnson & Son, Inc. v. Carter-Wallace, Inc.*, 614 F. Supp. 1278, 225 U.S.P.Q. 1022 (N.Y. 1985).

ᴍ

Objective evidence of non-obviousness includes commercial success, long felt but unresolved need, failure of others, and copying. When present, such objective evidence must be considered. It can be the most probative evidence of non-obviousness in the record, and enables the district court to avert the trap of hindsight. On the other hand, the absence of objective evidence does not preclude a holding of non-obviousness because such evidence is not a requirement for patentability. *Custom Accessories Inc. v. Jeffrey-Allan Industries Inc.*, 807 F.2d 955, 1 U.S.P.Q.2d 1196 (Fed. Cir. 1986).

ᴍ

It is appropriate to discount evidence of failure of others when a critical portion of the prior art can only be found in an obscure source and their work does not evidence familiarity with either the source or the relevant principles to be learned therefrom. *Tennant Co. v. Hako Minuteman Inc.*, 22 U.S.P.Q.2d 1161, 1180 (Ill. 1991).

Failure to Cite. *See also* **Presumption of Validity.**

The presumption of validity is not destroyed merely by the failure to cite pertinent prior art. *Kearney & Trecker Corporation v. Cincinnati Milacron, Inc.*, 184 U.S.P.Q. 134, 154 (Ohio 1974).

Failure to Commercialize. *See* **Performance.**

Failure to Disclose. *See also* **Duty to Disclose.**

When the Examiner rejected certain claims as being anticipated by prior art, the applicant, instead of accepting suitable limitations on his patent, stubbornly resisted any effort to limit his claims. Claims were proliferated, and, in their excessive zeal and heedless of what applicant knew existed in the prior art, counsel and applicant made arguments the Examiner could not conceivably have accepted had he known what applicant knew. *East Chicago Machine Tool Corporation v. Stone Container Corporation*, 181 U.S.P.Q. 744, 748 (Ill. 1974).

ᴍ

In addition to requiring that a nondisclosed prior art reference be material in a strict but-for sense, the failure to cite the prior art must be done with a "specific intent" to defraud. Without a showing of willful and intentional fraud, no antitrust liability can be sustained. A good faith judgment not to cite the prior art to the PTO, even if erroneous, does not constitute fraud. *Oetiker v. Jurid Werke GmbH*, 556 F.2d 1, 209 U.S.P.Q. 809 (D.C. 1981).

ᴍ

An applicant who knew or should have known of prior art or information and of its materiality is not automatically precluded thereby from an effort to convince the fact finder that failure to disclose was nonetheless not due to an intent to mislead the PTO;

i.e., that, in light of all the circumstances in the case, an inference of intent to mislead is not warranted. No single factor or combination of factors can be said always to require an inference to mislead. *In re Harita,* 847 F.2d 801, 6 U.S.P.Q.2d 1930 (Fed. Cir. 1988).

Fair Notice Function.

"The object of the patent law in requiring the patentee [to distinctly claim his invention] is not only to secure to him all to which he is entitled, but to apprise the public as to what is still open to them." *Athletic Alternatives Inc. v. Prince Manufacturing Inc.*, 73 F.3d 1573, 37 U.S.P.Q.2d 1365, 1372 (Fed. Cir. 1996).

Faith.

To reach the Board's conclusion would require that all evidence favorable to the appellant's position be viewed with limitless skepticism and that all evidence unfavorable to the appellant's position be accepted with limitless faith. *In re Petrzilka, Hofmann, Schenk, Troxler, Frey, and Ott,* 424 F.2d 1102, 165 U.S.P.Q. 327 (C.C.P.A. 1970).

False Marking. *See* Mismarking.

False Oath.

The factual resolutions to be made with regard to an oath of inventorship are whether any incorrect statement was made with a deceptive intent, whether the amendment correcting the statement was diligently made, and whether any advantage was intended or secured by the applicant by the incorrect statement. *SAB Industri AB v. The Bendix Corporation*, 199 U.S.P.Q. 95, 104 (Va. 1978).

False Statement. *See also* Error.

Even if the questioned affidavit were knowingly and willfully false, to establish fraud, it would have to be shown that it was causally related to the allowance of a claim, and that the false statements of the questioned affidavit were essentially material to the issuance of the patent. *Bolt Associates, Inc. v. Rix Industries*, 178 U.S.P.Q. 171, 174 (Cal. 1973).

ϖ

Even a false statement does not destroy the presumption of validity of a patent unless the statement was "essentially material" to its issuance. *In re Certain Slide Fastener Stringers and Machines and Components Thereof for producing Such Slide Fastener Stringers*, 216 U.S.P.Q. 907, 912 (U.S. I.T.C. 1981).

FCIA.

The broad theme of the Federal Courts Improvement Act of 1982 (FCIA)—increasing nationwide uniformity in certain fields of national law—applies to the field of patent law. The availability of a clear, stable, uniform basis for evaluating matters of patent validity/invalidity and infringement/non-infringement renders more predictable the outcome of contemplated litigation, facilitates effective business planning, and adds confidence to investment in innovative new products and technology. Those congressional goals are facilitated when appeals in cases involving non-frivolous claims arising under the patent laws, where they are found in complaints or compulsory counterclaims, are directed to the CAFC. *Aerojet-General Corp. v. Machine Tool Works, Oerlikon-Buehrle Ltd.*, 895 F.2d 736, 13 U.S.P.Q.2d 1670, 1676 (Fed. Cir. 1990).

FDA. *See also* **Abbreviated New Drug Application, Generic Drugs.**

The FDA requires a great of deal of testing concerning the safety and efficacy of a drug before allowing it to be marketed. Section 271(e)(1) of 35 U.S.C. allows scientists to use a patented product or process to gather data and submit them to the FDA in order to obtain regulatory approval to market a drug at a later time, after the patent on the drug expires. The plaintiff in this case alleges that the defendant used the data it gathered, not only to submit it to the FDA in order to gain premarket approval, but also to submit it to regulatory agencies in foreign countries in order to obtain approval to market it there. Since the foreign-related activities fall outside of the limited exception from infringement contained in §271(e)(1), the defendant's position was urged to be insufficient as a matter of law. *Scripps Clinic & Research Foundation v. Baxter Travenol Laboratories, Inc.*, 7 U.S.P.Q.2d 1562 (Del. 1988).

ᛦ

Because plaintiff has already expressed its intent to enforce its patent and because defendant clearly intends to file an NDA and has conducted clinical tests at substantial cost for that purpose, defendant has met the "meaningful preparation" requirement and shown that a real case and controversy exists necessary to permit the court to hear a declaratory judgment action. Those who seriously wish to practice an art facially pre-empted by a (pharmaceutical use) patent are permitted to test the patent's validity before completing the arduous task of obtaining administrative approval without requiring the court to participate in speculation as to the potential infringement of a product whose final formulation has not yet been settled. *Farmaceutisk Laboratorium Ferring A/S v. Solvay Pharmaceuticals Inc.*, 25 U.S.P.Q.2d 1344, 1350, 1352 (Ga. 1992).

ᛦ

A decision to place a protective order on GCP audit reports is not clearly erroneous, since disclosure arguably may result in some chilling effect upon developers of new drugs. The intent of the FDA Compliance Policy is "to encourage firms to conduct quality assurance program audits and inspections that are candid and meaningful." The FDA's decision not to "review or copy reports and records that result from audits and inspections of a written quality assurance program" clearly implies a bar upon a private entity's access to these reports. This FDA policy applies to "any regulated entity which has a written quality assurance program that provides for periodic audits or inspections." *NeoRx Corp. v. Immunomedics Inc.*, 28 U.S.P.Q.2d 1797, 1798 (N.J. 1993).

ᛦ

Declaratory judgment plaintiff's actions in developing Perfluoron and in taking steps to obtain FDA approval sufficiently demonstrate plaintiff's intent to try to bring Perfluoron to market in some form. While plaintiff may not have the present ability to market Perfluoron, it has embarked on a protracted and costly process of obtaining regulatory approval. Plaintiff's conduct thus evinces the kind of "concrete steps" or "meaningful preparation" needed to establish an actual controversy under "all the circumstances." *Infinitech Inc. v. Vitrophage Inc.*, 30 U.S.P.Q.2d 1201, 1205 (Ill. 1994).

ω

Jurisdiction over plaintiff's declaratory judgment action was based on (i) defendant's threat to bring patent infringement suits against generic drug manufacturers who attempt to market their products during the Delta period (creating a reasonable apprehension that plaintiff would face an infringement suit on amending its ANDA to include paragraph IV certification) and (ii) plaintiff's having spent much money in preparation for the potentially infringing activity of submitting ANDA's. *DuPont Merck Pharmaceutical Co. v. Bristol-Myers Squibb Co.*, 62 F.3d 1397, 35 U.S.P.Q.2d 1718, 1721, 1722 (Fed. Cir. 1995).

ω

As the term "substantial investment" is not defined in the statute, the Court has little guidance on this issue. The president of Royce, in a sworn statement, indicated that Royce expended $1 million in preparing to market captopril, including costs for performing in vivo and in vitro tests and other research necessary to obtain FDA approval of its ANDA. Based on the purpose of Congress in creating the "safe harbor", the Court finds that Royce's expenditures satisfy the investment requirement and qualifies it to operate under the "safe harbor" of URAA. *Bristol-Myers Squibb Co. v. Royce Laboratories Inc.*, 69 F.3d 1130, 36 U.S.P.Q.2d 1637, 1640 n.7 (Fla. 1995), *rev'd* 36 U.S.P.Q.2d 1641 (Fed. Cir. 1995).

FDCA[1] (Food, Drug, and Cosmetic Act).

Federal Agency. *See* **Sham Litigation.**

Federal Circuit. *See also* **CAFC.**

The Federal Circuit reviews questions of fact under a clearly erroneous standard; questions of law are subject to full and independent review (sometimes referred to as "*de novo*" or "plenary" review). *In re Asahi/America Inc.*, 68 F.3d 442, 33 U.S.P.Q.2d 1921, 1922 (Fed. Cir. 1995).

---

[1]The Federal Food, Drug, and Cosmetic Act (FDCA), 21 U.S.C. §§301-395 (1994), through the Medical Device Amendments of 1976, classifies medical devices in three categories based on the risk posed by their use. Devices that present no unreasonable risk of illness or injury are designated Class I and are subject only to minimal regulation by "general controls." 21 U.S.C. §360c(a)(1)(A). Devices that are potentially more harmful are designated Class II; although they may be marketed without advance approval, manufacturers of such devices must comply with federal performance regulations known as "special controls." *Id.* §360c(a)(1)(B). Finally, devices that either "present a potential unreasonable risk of illness or injury," or which are "purported or represented to be for a use in supporting or sustaining human life or for a use which is of substantial importance in preventing impairment of human health," are designated Class III. *Id.* §360c(a)(1)(C). *Medtronic, Inc. v. Lohr*, 116 S.Ct. 2240, 2246 (1966).

Federal Court of Claims Action.

The claimant had the burden of establishing the following: that the defendant (PTO) had a duty to him; that the defendant was negligent, i.e., failed to exercise due care in executing the controlling laws and regulations; that the negligence was the proximate cause of the plaintiff's failure to obtain a patent; that the patent would have value (the invention is worth more with a patent than without) and the extent of its value. The claimant had to prove further that the culpable acts of the defendant now foreclosed his obtaining a patent. *Lindsey v. United States,* 222 U.S.P.Q. 507 (Tex. 1983).

Federal Courts Improvement Act. *See* FCIA.

Federal Employee. *See also* Executive Order No. 10096.

Executive Order No. 10096 provides in substance that the United States shall obtain title to any invention made by any Government employee during working hours, or with a contribution by the Government, or which bears a direct relationship to, or is made in consequence of, the inventor's official duties. *Kaplan v. Corcoran,* 545 F.2d 1073, 192 U.S.P.Q. 129 (7th Cir. 1976).

Federal Government.

Section 207(a)(2) of 35 U.S.C. is an exception to 28 U.S.C. §516, which permits the Department of Commerce to delegate enforcement powers to a licensee; the agreement between the Department of Commerce and the licensee grants the licensee the right "to bring suit in its own name, at its own expense, and on its own behalf for infringement of presumably valid claims in a Licensed Patent." By this provision of the License Agreement, the United States has, in effect, consented to its necessary joinder in an infringement action. *Nutrition 21 v. Thorne Research Inc.,* 130 F.R.D. 671, 14 U.S.P.Q.2d 1244, 1245 (Wash. 1990).

Federal Question.

A declaratory judgment action, even one involving a claim under federal law, presents no federal jurisdiction where it is sought merely as a defense to an action which itself could not be brought in federal court. *Union Carbide Corporation v. Air Products & Chemicals,* Inc., 202 U.S.P.Q. 43, 54 (N.Y. 1978).

Federal Register.

The contents of the Federal Register shall be judicially noticed and, without prejudice to any other mode of citation, may be cited by volume and page number. *In re Watson,* 517 F.2d 465, 186 U.S.P.Q. 11, 17 (C.C.P.A. 1975).

Federal Rules of Civil Procedure. *See* Rule.

Federal Shop Book Rule. *See also* **Shop Book Rule.**

The Federal shop book rule of 28 U.S.C. §1732 applies to admissibility of routine documents and records which experience has shown to be trustworthy, but such records must be weighed against all other circumstances. We know of no authority to show that the rule is properly applicable to reports of scientific research and tests, and think such application of the rule would be both improper and unrealistic. *Alpert v. Slatin,* 305 F.2d 891, 134 U.S.P.Q. 296, 300 (C.C.P.A. 1962).

Federal Tort Claims Act. *See* **FTCA.**

Federal Trade Commission.

The Federal Trade Commission Act contains no statutory exemption of PTO proceedings. Section 5 of the Act confers jurisdiction upon the Commission with respect to a violation of the Act growing out of and following proceedings before the PTO. The Federal Trade Commission has jurisdiction to require (as a remedy in antitrust cases) compulsory licensing of patents on a reasonable royalty basis. *American Cyanamid Co. v. Federal Trade Commission,* 363 F.2d 757, 150 U.S.P.Q. 135, 144, 145 (6th Cir. 1966).

Fee. *See also* **Attorney's Fees, Witness.**

In connection with payment of statutory fees there must be strict compliance with the statute involved in order that the policy to expedite patent applications might be effected. Any unjustified deviation from the mandate of the governing statute is a violation which is fatal to the applicant, and the Commissioner of Patents would appear to be powerless to cure such deviation unless the situation qualifies as a rare or unique one to be accommodated by the Patent Office. *BEC Pressure Controls Corporation v. Dwyer Instruments, Inc.,* 380 F.Supp. 1397, 182 U.S.P.Q. 190, 192 (Ind. 1974).

Fiduciary.

The reason for high standards of conduct and candor before the PTO is the ex parte nature of the proceedings there. The PTO and the applicant for a patent are more fiduciaries than antagonists. A duty of candor attaches to an application for a patent and to the extent and nature of the information provided in connection therewith. However, the duty of candor is not without bounds; it does not extend to adversarial proceedings. *United Sweetener U.S.A. Inc. v. The Nutrasweet Company,* 760 F. Supp. 400, 19 U.S.P.Q.2d 1561, 1577 (Del. 1991).

Field of Search. *See also* **Classification.**

Patent Office Examiners are assumed to have considered all references classified in the very subclass in which a patent issues. *Minnesota Mining & Manufacturing Co. v. Berwick Industries, Inc.,* 393 F. Supp. 1230, 185 U.S.P.Q. 536, 540 (Pa. 1975).

ω

The fact that different fields of search are involved does not establish that a Markush group is improper. *Ex parte Brouard, Leroy, and Stiot*, 201 U.S.P.Q. 538, 540 (PTO Bd. App. 1976).

ᛒ

The Examiner's search record provides *prima facie* evidence that he searched all the references in the classes and subclasses noted on the file wrapper as having been searched. References in such subclasses left uncited are presumed to have been regarded by the Examiner as less relevant than those cited. A contrary view would destroy the presumption of administrative regularity on which the presumption of validity rests. *Railroad Dynamics, Inc. v. A. Stucki Co.*, 579 F. Supp. 353, 218 U.S.P.Q. 618 (Pa. 1983).

ᛒ

The field of search by the Patent Examiner is relevant objective evidence of the scope of the prior art. *Williams Service Group Inc. v. O.B. Cannon & Son Inc.*, 33 U.S.P.Q.2d 1705, 1725 (Pa. 1994).

Field of Use.

It is well-settled law that the division of markets through a field-of-use limitation is perfectly acceptable. An invention may have applications in more than one field or industry. A patent owner may limit an assignment or license on lines drawn according to field of use. *In re Reclosable Plastic Bags*, 192 U.S.P.Q. 674, 679 (U.S. Intl. Trade Comm. 1977).

Field Preemption.

Since States may not offer patent-like protection to inventions that otherwise remain unpatented, the "flip-side" must intuitively be true, and state law tort claims may not be able to invalidate a patent where the federal laws have not given the possible infringer the ability to do so. The federal patent law is a "scheme of federal regulation . . . so pervasive as to make reasonable the inference that Congress left no room for the States to supplement it. *Hunter Douglas Inc. v. Harmonic Design Inc.*, 962 F. Supp. 1249, 42 U.S.P.Q.2d 1629, 1631 (Cal. 1997).

File History. *See also* Classification, File Wrapper Estoppel, Prosecution History, Validity Opinion.

An entire article is of record in appellant's parent application, which is in the PTO's possession, and appellant requested that such article be considered in arriving at a decision on his present application. The fact that only the first page of the article was physically inserted into the record as an attachment to appellant's brief to the Board and the Board did not actually consider the article or mention it is immaterial, since evidence need not be physically introduced and also considered by a PTO tribunal to be considered "evidence produced before the Patent and Trademark Office". [There are thus limitations to any requirement that each file wrapper must be complete in itself.] *In re Hutton*, 568 F.2d 1355, 196 U.S.P.Q. 676 (C.C.P.A. 1978).

ᛒ

Ordering a file history is an ordinary and necessary preliminary to a validity or an infringement opinion. *Underwater Devices Incorporated v. Morrison-Knudsen Company, Inc.*, 717 F.2d 1380, 219 U.S.P.Q. 569, 577 (Fed. Cir. 1983).

ω

The significance of the file history is illustrated by the fact that one cannot rely on an attorney opinion of non-infringement as a good faith defense to a charge of willful patent infringement if the attorney did not consult the file history of the patent for which infringement is charged prior to giving his opinion. *Elk Corp. of Dallas v. GAF Building Materials Corp.*, 45 U.S.P.Q.2d 1011, 1014 n.3 (Tex. 1997).

File History Estoppel. *See* **File Wrapper Estoppel.**

File Wrapper. *See* **also File History, File Wrapper Estoppel, Validity Opinion.**

An invention is construed not only in the light of the claims, but also with reference to the file wrapper or prosecution history in the Patent Office. *Graham v. John Deere Co.*, 383 U.S. 1, 33, 148 U.S.P.Q. 459 (1966).

ω

A patentee may be his own lexicographer and grammarian. He "may define his own terms, regardless of common or technical meaning. . . . Fairness to any patentee requires a court to accept his definition of words, phrases and terms." "Claim language is not to be interpreted in a vacuum but is to be read in light of the specification to determine the meaning intended by the inventors." The file wrapper in its entirety, including the definitions and arguments made during the prosecution of the patent in question, can also aid the court in ascertaining the meaning of terminology used in claims. Accordingly, when a patentee argues before a court for a definition that is consistent with the file wrapper, the court will give effect to that definition. *Rohm & Haas Co. v. Dawson Chemical Co., Inc.*, 557 F. Supp. 739, 217 U.S.P.Q. 515, 573 (Tex. 1983).

ω

Claim construction is reviewed as a matter of law. However, interpretation of a claim may depend on evidentiary material about which there is a factual dispute, requiring resolution of factual issues as a basis for interpretation of the claim. The terms of a claim will be given their ordinary meaning, unless it appears that the inventor used them differently. The ordinary meaning of claim language, however, is not dispositive and resort must still be had to the specification and prosecution history to determine whether the inventor used the disputed terms differently than their ordinary accustomed meaning. Patent law allows an inventor to be his own lexicographer. The specification aids in ascertaining the scope and meaning of the language employed in the claims inasmuch as words must be used in the same way in both the claims and the specification. The prosecution history (or file wrapper) limits the interpretation of claims so as to exclude any interpretation that may have been disclaimed or disavowed during prosecution in order to obtain claim allowance. *ZMI Corp. v. Cardiac Resuscitator Corp.*, 844 F.2d 1576, 6 U.S.P.Q.2d 1557 (Fed. Cir. 1988).

File Wrapper Estoppel. *See also* **Claim Construction, File History, File Wrapper, Prosecution History Estoppel.**

A claim in a patent (as allowed) must be read and interpreted with reference to claims that have been canceled or rejected, and the claims allowed cannot (by construction) be read to cover what was thus eliminated from the patent. A patentee may not, by resort to the doctrine of equivalents, give to an allowed claim a scope that it might have had without the amendments, the cancellation of which amounts to a disclaimer. *The Schriber-Schroth Company v. The Cleveland Trust Company*, 311 U.S. 211, 47 U.S.P.Q. 345, 349 (1940).

ᛟ

Since applicants had narrowed the claims in their parent application and restricted all of the original claims in their continuation-in-part application to exclude (in view of prior art applied by the Patent Office) a particular design, it would be improper to permit them to recapture (by way of a later submitted claim) subject matter that they had willingly relinquished. To do so would ignore the well-established doctrine of "file wrapper estoppel", which does not allow recapture of relinquished subject matter under such circumstances. *Jamesbury Corporation v. United States*, 183 U.S.P.Q. 484, 490 (U.S. Ct. Cl. 1974).

ᛟ

The doctrine of file wrapper estoppel does not apply where the claims were not narrowed to overcome a prior art rejection. *Special Metals Corporation v. Teledyne Industries, Inc.*, 215 U.S.P.Q. 698, 708 (N.C. 1982).

ᛟ

When a patentee is aware that the Examiner allowed claims on the basis of a particular interpretation, his acceptance of the patent under such circumstances precludes him from obtaining a claim construction that would resurrect subject matter surrendered during prosecution of his application. An estoppel is created merely by arguments submitted to obtain a patent. *Hughes Aircraft Co. v. United States*, 717 F.2d 1351, 219 U.S.P.Q. 473, 481 (Fed. Cir. 1983).

ᛟ

Even when an estoppel arises from the file, the doctrine of equivalents is not completely eliminated. Depending on the nature and the purpose of an amendment, it may have a limited effect ranging from great to small to zero. The effect may or may not be fatal to application of a range of equivalents broad enough to encompass a particular accused product. It is not fatal to application of the doctrine of equivalents itself. Whenever the doctrine of file history estoppel is invoked, a close examination must be made as to, not only what was surrendered, but also the reason for such a surrender. The fact that claims were narrowed does not always mean that the doctrine of file history estoppel completely prohibits a patentee from recapturing some of what was originally claimed. *Glaros v. H. H. Robertson Co.* 615 F. Supp. 186, 227 U.S.P.Q. 448 (Ill. 1985).

ᛟ

The doctrine of file wrapper estoppel is not restricted to amendments. A patentee having argued a narrow construction for his claims before the PTO should be precluded from arguing a broader construction for the purpose of infringement. This is a sound legal proposition that comports with the rationale underlying the traditional doctrine of file wrapper estoppel, that once a broader scope of interpretation for a claim is disclaimed by an applicant before the PTO, he is not entitled to reinstate the broader scope. *Pero v. General Motors Corp.*, 230 U.S.P.Q. 719 (Mich. 1986).

ω

A patentee is not barred by file wrapper estoppel from asserting the doctrine of equivalents because the claims in suit were amended by insertion of "consisting essentially of" language. The fact that claims are narrowed does not always mean that the doctrine of file history estoppel completely prohibits a patentee from recapturing some of what was originally claimed. *Syntex (U.S.A.) Inc. v. Paragon Optical Inc.*, 7 U.S.P.Q.2d 1001 (Ariz. 1987).

ω

As a matter of law, rejections based upon 35 U. S. C. §112 cannot create a file wrapper estoppel. *ALM Surgical Equipment Inc. v. Kirschner Medical Corp.*, 15 U.S.P.Q.2d 1241, 1248 (S.C. 1990).

ω

An amendment to a claim does not necessarily create prosecution history estoppel precluding all reliance on the doctrine of equivalents. Depending on the nature and purpose of the amendment, it may have a limiting effect within a spectrum ranging from great to small to zero, but it is not fatal to application of the doctrine of equivalents. *Hughes Aircraft Co. v. United States*, 717 F.2d 1351, 219 U.S.P.Q. 473, 481 (Fed. Cir. 1983); *Stranco Inc. v. Atlantes Chemical Systems Inc.*, 15 U.S.P.Q.2d 1704, 1712 (Tex. 1990).

ω

Amendments made merely to define a patentable invention better do not operate as an estoppel, nor do amendments that were made to point out inventions more particularly or those that were unnecessary to issuance of the patent. The doctrine of prosecution history estoppel has no application to a claim that has been literally infringed. *Solomon v. Greco*, 18 U.S.P.Q.2d 1917, 1921 (N.Y. 1990).

ω

"Unmistakable assertions made by the applicant to the Patent and Trademark Office (PTO) in support of patentability, whether or not required to secure allowance of the claim, also may operate to preclude the patentee from asserting equivalency. . . ." *Wang Laboratories Inc. v. Toshiba Corp.*, 993 F.2d 858, 26 U.S.P.Q.2d 1767, 1775 (Fed. Cir. 1993).

ω

Amending process claim 1 by adding the phrase "at a pH from approximately 6.0 to 9.0" during prosecution to distinguish over a reference did not preclude a holding of infringement under the doctrine of equivalents by a corresponding process at a pH of 5. *Hilton Davis Chemical Co. v. Warner-Jenkinson Co. Inc.*, 62 F.3d 1512, 35 U.S.P.Q.2d

1641, 1643, 1654 (Fed. Cir. 1995), *reversed and remanded*, 41 U.S.P.Q.2d 1865 (S.Ct. 1997).

ᚹ

When an applicant makes an amendment to an element to overcome prior art, he has not automatically surrendered all then-known substitutes for the amended element. An applicant cannot surrender that which he does not know. Because the prosecution history is objective evidence of what knowledge the applicant has of the art, prosecution history estoppel should remain limited to the prosecution history. *Litton Systems Inc. v. Honeywell Inc.*, 140 F.3d 1449, 46 U.S.P.Q.2d 1321, 1332, 1333 (Fed. Cir. 1998).

Filing Date. *See also* **Effective Filing Date.**

The doctrine of continuity holds that a second application should be considered a continuation of a first application and entitled to the benefit of the filing date of the first application, where a patent is still sought for the substance of the invention as originally claimed. In order that the doctrine be applicable, it is necessary that the description in both applications be sufficient to support the claims. *Bersworth v. Watson*, 159 F.Supp. 12, 116 U.S.P.Q. 87 (D.C. 1956).

ᚹ

Since the application would not receive a filing date until Monday even if it were ready for filing the preceding Saturday, it is reasonable to compute the year, not from January 8 (Monday), 1962, but from January 6 (Saturday), 1962. In the absence of basis to believe that any of the magazines (mailed in bulk on January 4th) were delivered by January 6th, it cannot be said that the publication was issued more than a year prior to the filing date of the application. *Protein Foundation, Inc. v. Brenner*, 260 F.Supp. 519, 151 U.S.P.Q. 561, 562 (D.C. 1966).

ᚹ

In an interference between two parties who rely on the same date of corresponding foreign filings under the International Convention, neither is entitled to an award of priority. However, prior introduction of conception with regard to one count can be relied upon for priority purposes. *Lassman v. Brossi, Gerecke, and Kyburz*, 159 U.S.P.Q. 182, 184, 185 (PO Bd. Pat. Intf. 1967).

ᚹ

An application mailed to the Patent Office and stolen while in the custody of the United States Postal Service was accorded a filing date prior to that on which a properly-executed application was actually received by the Patent Office. *Sturzinger v. Commissioner of Patents*, 377 F.Supp. 1284, 181 U.S.P.Q. 436, 437 (D.C. 1974).

ᚹ

Entitlement to a filing date does not extend to subject matter which is not disclosed, but would be obvious over what is expressly disclosed. It extends only to that which is disclosed. A prior application itself must describe an invention, and do so in sufficient detail that one skilled in the art can clearly conclude that the inventor invented the claimed invention as of the filing date sought. *Lockwood v. American Airlines Inc.*, 41 U.S.P.Q.2d 1961 (Fed. Cir. 1997).

Filing Fee. *See* **Unsigned Check.**

Final.

When an appeal is certified pursuant to Rule (FRCP) 54(b), an appellate court should review the finality of the judgment *de novo* in order to assure itself that it has jurisdiction. The "District Court *cannot*, in the exercise of its discretion, treat as 'final' that which is not 'final' within the meaning of (28 U.S.C.) §1291." *W.L. Gore & Associates Inc. v. International Medical Prosthetics Research Associates Inc.*, 975 F.2d 858, 24 U.S.P.Q.2d 1195, 1198 (Fed. Cir. 1992).

Final Rejection.[2] *See also* **FAFR Policy.**

A final rejection of amended claims can properly be based on a reference that was only applied as a secondary reference in a prior Office Action. *Ex parte Hoogendam*, 40 U.S.P.Q. 389, 1939 C.D. 3 (Commr. Patents 1939).

ω

When an Examiner fails to mention a rejection in his final action, it has been dropped by the Examiner and needs no further response by the applicant. On appeal, only those grounds of rejection which have been made in the final rejection and commented upon in the Examiner's Answer to brief are considered by the Board. *Ex parte Martin*, 104 U.S.P.Q. 124, 128 (PO Sup. Ex'r 1952).

Financial Inability. *See also* **Economics.**

Even if financial inability were an excuse for delay in filing suit for patent infringement, plaintiff should have communicated such inability to defendants, along with plaintiff's intention to pursue their rights under the patent when able. *B.W.B. Controls, Inc. v. U.S. Industries, Inc.*, 626 F.Supp. 1553, 228 U.S.P.Q. 799, 812 (La. 1985).

ω

As a general rule, lack of funds does not excuse a delay in bringing suit. *Valutron N.V. v. NCR Corp.*, 33 U.S.P.Q.2d 1986, 1991 (Ohio 1992), *aff'd* (Fed. Cir. 1993), *cert. denied* (S.Ct. 1994).

Finding.

Where a trial judge's finding is based on his decision to credit the testimony of one of two or more witnesses, each of whom has told a coherent and facially plausible story that

---

[2] Although it is permissible to withdraw a final rejection for the purpose of entering a new ground of rejection, this practice is to be limited to situations where a new reference fully meets at least one claim or meets it except for differences which are shown to be completely obvious. Normally, the previous rejection should be withdrawn with respect to the claim or claims involved. The practice should not be used for application of subsidiary references, or of references which are merely considered to be better than those of record. Furthermore, the practice should not be used for entring new non-reference or so-called "formal" grounds of rejection, such as those under 35 U.S.C. §112. *Commissioner's Notice*, 817 O.G. 1615 (Asst. Comm'r Richard A. Wahl 1965).

is not contradicted by extrinsic evidence, that finding, if not internally inconsistent, can virtually never be clear error. *State Industries Inc. v. Mor-Flo Industries Inc.*, 948 F.2d 1573, 20 U.S.P.Q.2d 1738, 1741 (Fed. Cir. 1991).

ღ

When equitable claims are joined with legal claims and have factual questions in common, the judge's determination of the equitable claims cannot deprive the litigants of their right to a jury trial on factual questions. When "a party has a right to a jury trial on an issue involved in a legal claim, the judge is . . . bound by the jury's determination of that issue as it affects his disposition of an accompanying equitable claim." *Therma-Tru Corp. v. Peachtree Doors Inc.*, 44 F.3d 988, 33 U.S.P.Q.2d 1274, 1278 (Fed. Cir. 1995).

ღ

A "party desiring more particularized findings at the trial court level must request them from the trial court." *Glaverbel Société Anonyme v. Northlake Marketing & Supply Inc.*, 45 F.3d 1550, 33 U.S.P.Q.2d 1496, 1499 (Fed. Cir. 1995).

Findings of Fact.

The Supreme Court strongly criticized the practice of "verbatim adoption of findings of fact prepared by prevailing parties, particularly when those findings have taken the form of conclusory statements unsupported by citation to the record." A finding is clearly erroneous when, although there is evidence to support it, the reviewing court on the entire evidence is left with the definite and firm conviction that a mistake has been committed. This standard plainly does not entitle a reviewing court to reverse the finding of the trier of fact simply because it is convinced that it would have decided the case differently. Where the district court's account of the evidence is plausible in light of the record viewed in its entirety or where there are two permissible views of the evidence, the fact finder cannot be clearly erroneous. A trial judge may not insulate his findings from review by denominating them credibility determinations; if documents or objective evidence contradict a witness's story, clear error may be found even in a finding purportedly based on a credibility determination. *Hybritech Inc. v. Monoclonal Antibodies, Inc.*, 802 F.2d 1367, 231 U.S.P.Q. 81, 86, 87 (Fed. Cir. 1986).

First Action Final Rejection. *See* FAFR Policy.

First to File.

Early public disclosure is a linchpin of the patent system. As between a prior inventor who benefits from a process by selling its product, but suppresses, conceals, or otherwise keeps the process from the public, and a later inventor who promptly files a patent application from which the public will gain disclosure of the process, the law favors the latter. *W. L. Gore & Associates, Inc. v. Garlock, Inc.*, 721 F.2d 1540, 220 U.S.P.Q. 303 (Fed. Cir. 1983).

ღ

The "first-to-file" rule provides that, when two suits are filed in different forums regarding the same matter, the first suit should generally take priority. Nevertheless, if the first suit is filed as a means of forum-shopping, it should be dismissed. *KPR Inc. v. C&F Packing Co. Inc.*, 30 U.S.P.Q.2d 1320, 1323 (Tex. 1993).

First to File Rule.

In order to avoid duplication and to avoid the possibility of rulings which may impose upon the authority of a sister court, a district court may dismiss an action where the issues presented may be resolved in an earlier-filed action. In the alternative, because "[p]rimary jurisdiction attaches in the forum in which the action is first instituted[,]" a district court may transfer the later-filed action to the district where the earlier-filed action is pending, provided that the transferee district is one where the later-filed action "might have been brought." While the general rule favors the forum of the first-filed case, whether or not it is a declaratory action, the first-to-file principle is not a rigid or inflexible rule to be applied mechanically. The courts are careful to factor into their decisions "considerations of judicial and litigant economy, and the just and effective disposition of disputes. . . . " The first-to-file rule does not compel a final conclusion as to appropriate venue. The rule does, however, compel the court in which the first case was filed to weigh and determine the appropriate venue. *Abbott Laboratories Inc. v. Mead Johnson & Co.*, 47 U.S.P.Q.2d 1305, 1307, 1308, 1310 (Ohio 1998).

Flash of Genius.

A new device, however useful it may be, must reveal the flash of creative genius, not merely the skill of the calling. If it fails, it has not established its right to a private grant on the public domain. *Cuno Engineering Corporation v. Automatic Devices Corporation*, 314 U.S. 84, 51 U.S.P.Q. 272, 275 (1941).

ϖ

A development should not be regarded as obvious merely because it lay somewhere along the general stream of the prior art, although years of labor might be required to achieve it. "[T]he inspiration-perspiration process of the laboratory" is as deserving of reward as the flash of genius, and surely more so than dumb luck. *Carter-Wallace, Inc. v. Otte*, 474 F.2d 529, 176 U.S.P.Q. 2, 12 (2d Cir. 1972).

ϖ

A flash of brilliance which finds a solution, however simple, by departing from the norm has traditionally been rewarded with patent rights. To deny those rights might unjustifiably deter industry members from seeking to invest, innovate and experiment. *U.S. Philips Corp. v. National Micronetics Inc.*, 550 F.2d 716, 193 U.S.P.Q. 65, 71 (2d Cir. 1977).

F.O.B.

The U.S. patent laws do not apply to products manufactured abroad, stored in the United States, and then sold and shipped to entities outside of the United States. As written, those laws apply to manufacture and sale within the United States and do not contain language addressed to products manufactured and sold outside of the United

States, albeit for an American company. Shipment of goods abroad F.O.B. Georgia does not constitute sale within the United States. The primary purpose of the F.O.B. designation is to identify the party that maintains a cause of action against the shipper for damage or loss during transport. As a result, title may pass at the F.O.B. location, but the F.O.B. location does not determine where or when a sale is consummated. It is not appropriate for application of the patent laws to depend on whether goods are designated F.O.B. shipping point or destination. *Fausett v. Pansy Ellen Inc.*, 19 U.S.P.Q.2d 1228, 1230 (Ga. 1991).

ω

Sales of allegedly infringing articles to distributors in the forum could not be said to fall entirely without the forum for purposes of a jurisdictional analysis simply because they were delivered F.O.B. outside the forum. *North American Philips Corp. v. American Vending Sales Inc.*, 35 F.3d 1576, 32 U.S.P.Q.2d 1203, 1205 (Fed. Cir. 1994).

FOIA. *See also* **Abandoned Application.**

In re Gallo [231 U.S.P.Q. 496 (1986)] established an alternative means for obtaining information that has been waived by "incorporation," but it does not undo the holding of *Iron & Sears* [202 U.S.P.Q. 798 (D.C. Cir. 1979)], since the FOIA and administrative roots are separate. Since pending patent applications "are exempt in toto" from FOIA under *Iron & Sears*, and their contents are not subject to "a regime of selective excision" (202 U.S.P.Q. at 803), the plaintiff has no right of access to the information he seeks under FOIA. Although issued patents are subject to FOIA under *Iron & Sears, Gallo* does not establish that all material "incorporated by reference" in an issued patent automatically becomes part of the issued patent, thereby opening up the incorporated material to FOIA. Whether a waiver has occurred remains a matter for case-by-case determination at the PTO. *Leeds v. Quigg,* 720 F. Supp. 193, 11 U.S.P.Q.2d 1574, 1575 (D.C. 1989).

Food and Drug Administration. *See* **FDA.**

Foothold. *See* **Accelerated Reentry Theory.**

Forbearance from Infringement. *See also* **Secondary Considerations.**

The differences between the prior art and the invention defined by asserted claims, the availability of that art to all workers in the field, the failure of established competitors in a highly competitive market to make the invention despite the incentive to do so, the admittedly non-obvious performance benefits realized through the claimed invention, the impressive commercial success of the claimed product, the praise of independent commentators and the forbearance of competitors from infringing the patent all go to confirm that the claimed invention was not obvious at the time it was made to a person of ordinary skill in the art. *S. C. Johnson & Son, Inc. v. Carter-Wallace, Inc.,* 614 F. Supp. 1278, 225 U.S.P.Q. 1022 (N.Y. 1985).

Foreign. *See also* **Auslegeschrift, Boykin Act, Convenience, Discovery, Foreign Patent Application, Foreign Patents and Proceedings, Patented, Reference, 35 U.S.C. §271(g).**

A foreign priority application is prior art with respect to subject matter introduced for the first time in a continuation-in-part application filed more than one year after publication of the foreign priority application. *In re Ruscetta and Jenny*, 255 F.2d 687, 118 U.S.P.Q. 101, 104 (C.C.P.A. 1958).

ᙡ

When patents from two different foreign countries have the same drawings, and one relies on the filing date of the other for priority rights, there is a presumption that both are directed to the same invention. *H. K. Porter Company, Inc. v. The Gates Rubber Company*, 187 U.S.P.Q. 692, 704 (Colo. 1975).

ᙡ

Absent evidence of where an invention was made, conceding priority of the subject matter of an interference count is an admission that such subject matter is the prior invention of another *in this country under section 102(g)* (Title 35) and thus *prior art* under 35 U.S.C. §103. An invention apparently made outside of the United States is not accorded the same effective date as a reference as it would have had had it been made in this country. *In re McKellin, Mageli, and D'Angelo*, 529 F.2d 1324, 188 U.S.P.Q. 428, 434, 435 (C.C.P.A. 1976).

ᙡ

The rights of a licensee under a foreign patent have no bearing on the rights accorded under U.S. patent laws. No foreign license on a product covered by a U.S. patent can interfere with the rights granted the U.S. patentee by U.S. patent laws. The U.S. patent holder's rights in the United States cannot be diminished by the importation of a patented product made by a licensee under a corresponding patent in another country. *In re Reclosable Plastic Bags*, 192 U.S.P.Q. 674, 679 (U.S. Intl. Trade Commn. 1977).

ᙡ

Section 104 of 35 U.S.C. does not preclude using evidence of an inventor's knowledge from a foreign country for all purposes, but only where it is used to "establish a date of invention." *Breuer and Treuner v. DeMarinis*, 558 F.2d 22, 194 U.S.P.Q. 308, 313 (C.C.P.A. 1977).

ᙡ

It may be possible to couple conception in the United States with diligence to a constructive reduction to practice abroad to overcome an intervening reference. *In re Mulder and Wulms*, 716 F.2d 1542, 219 U.S.P.Q. 189, 193 (Fed. Cir. 1983).

ᙡ

Patent attorneys in foreign countries, who are not experts in American patent practice and patent law, are not competent to express an opinion on either validity or infringement of a U.S. patent. Subsequent, willfull, and intentional infringement and the consequences thereof are in no way relieved by reliance on such an opinion. *McDermott v. Omid International Inc.*, 723 F. Supp. 1228, 13 U.S.P.Q.2d 1147, 1150, 1151 (Ohio 1988).

ᙡ

After a patentee prevailed in an infringement action against the same party with regard to the same product based on his Canadian patent, he initiated an infringement action based on his corresponding U.S. patent. Although a court may not say that a U.S. patent is valid and infringed because a corresponding Canadian patent is valid and infringed, it is commonplace for courts in the United States to employ issue preclusion (collateral estoppel) even when claim preclusion is unavailable. When a foreign court renders judgment on a question of fact with significance in each system of law, there is no reason not to take over that decision. *Vas-Cath Inc. v. Mahurkar,* 745 F. Supp. 517, 17 U.S.P.Q.2d 1353, 1359, (Ill. 1990).

ᴥ

The Lanham Act's coverage of foreign activities is governed by the test for extraterritorial application of the antitrust laws, according to which the following three elements must be met: (1) there must be some effect (actual or intended) on American foreign commerce; (2) the effect must be sufficiently great to present a cognizable injury to plaintiffs under the federal statute; and (3) the interests and links to American foreign commerce must be sufficiently strong in relation to those of other nations to justify an assertion of extraterritorial authority. *Baldwin Hardware Corp. v. Franksu Enterprise Corp.,* 24 U.S.P.Q.2d 1700 (Cal. 1992).

ᴥ

Limited discovery of an infringement defendant's foreign sales is significant as to determination of obviousness. *Minnesota Mining and Manufacturing v. Smith and Nephew PLC,* 25 U.S.P.Q.2d 1587, 1591 (Minn. 1992).

ᴥ

The Virginia Long-Arm Statute extends in personam jurisdiction to a foreign company which sells infringing goods to a wholly owned subsidiary doing business in and selling such goods in Virginia. *Loral Fairchild Corp. v. Victor Co. of Japan Ltd.,* 803 F.Supp. 626, 25 U.S.P.Q.2d 1701, 1702 (N.Y. 1992).

ᴥ

The district court lacks original jurisdiction over a foreign patent infringement claim pursuant to 28 U.S.C. §1338(b) because a claim of infringement of a foreign patent is not a claim of unfair competition within the meaning of that provision. In addition, the district court does not have authority to hear the claims under its supplemental jurisdiction pursuant to 28 U.S.C. §1367(a) because the claim is not so related to the claim of infringement of the corresponding U.S. patent that it forms part of the same case or controversy under Article III of the U.S. Constitution. *Mars Inc. v. Kabushiki-Kaisha Nippon Conlux,* 24 F.3d 1368, 30 U.S.P.Q.2d 1621, 1626 (Fed. Cir. 1994).

ᴥ

Some courts have held that no deference is to be given a plaintiff's choice of forum in cases involving a foreign plaintiff and an American defendant. *Nolan Helmets S.p.A. v. Fulmer Helmets Inc.,* 37 U.S.P.Q.2d 1351, 1352 (Fla. 1995).

ᴥ

In all federal actions against aliens, the applicable venue provision is 28 U.S.C. §1391(d), which provides that "[a]n alien may be sued in any district." In federal question cases, due process requires only sufficient contacts with the United States as a whole rather than with any particular state. Section 293 (35 U.S.C.) "authorizes the assertion of [personal] jurisdiction [by the District Court for the District of Columbia] over a non-resident owner of a U.S. patent in cases respecting the patent or rights thereunder." *Miller Pipeline Corp. v. British Gas plc*, 901 F.Supp. 1416, 38 U.S.P.Q.2d 1010, 1012, 1013, 1014 (Ind. 1995).

ω

When there are foreign legal barriers to the production of documents, the courts in the United States must balance the interests and needs of the parties in light of the nature of the foreign laws and the party's efforts to comply in good faith with the demanded production. When two nations have jurisdiction to prescribe and enforce national rules of law that are inconsistent, each nation is required by international law to consider, in good faith, moderating the exercise of its enforcement jurisdiction in light of the law of the other nation. In considering whether to sanction non-production, a court must seek a fair balance of the interests and litigation needs of the parties, without doing violence to constitutional due process. *Cochran Consulting Inc. v. Uwatec USA Inc.*, 41 U.S.P.Q.2d 1161 (Fed. Cir. 1996).

ω

Although 28 U.S.C. §1782 is available to private litigants and foreign courts, its purpose is to facilitate the legitimate gathering of evidence, not to circumvent foreign laws. *In re Jenoptik AG*, 41 U.S.P.Q.2d 1950 (Fed. Cir. 1997—*dissent*).

ω

In evaluating infringement under the doctrine of equivalents, "representation[s] to foreign patent offices should be considered . . . when [they] comprise relevant evidence." *Tanabe Seiyaku Co. v. U.S. International Trade Commission*, 41 U.S.P.Q.2d 1976 (Fed. Cir. 1997).

Foreign Associate.

Documents reflecting communications involving foreign patent agents, if otherwise within the scope of attorney-client privilege, may be regarded as privileged. Documents prepared for one case have the same work-product protection in a second case, at least if the two cases are closely related. *In re Yarn Processing Patent Litigation*, 177 U.S.P.Q. 514 (Fla. 1973).

ω

In order for privilege to apply, the person to whom a communication is made must be a member of a bar of a court or his subordinate. This is so because the general purpose of the attorney-client privilege is to promote freedom of consultation of legal advisors by clients. The attorney-client privilege does not apply to foreign patent agents, for they are not attorneys at law and thus do not satisfy the requirement that the communication be made to a member of the bar. While the attorney-client privilege protects communications to the attorney's clerks and other agents, it does not extend to foreign patent agents for they are not agents of the attorney. Only communications between an attorney or an agent of the attorney and his client are covered by the privilege. Expanding the privilege to treat foreign patent agents as if they are lawyers improperly expands the privilege beyond its proper bounds. *Status Time Corp. v. Sharp Electronics Corp.*, 95 F.R.D. 27, 217 U.S.P.Q. 438 (N.Y. 1982).

ᗡ

When independent foreign associates are not acting strictly as subordinates, communications with them are not privileged. *Quantum Corp. v. Western Digital Corp.*, 15 U.S.P.Q.2d 1062, 1064 (Cal. 1990).

Foreign Corporation. *See also* Long-Arm Statute.

The fact that the defendant, a corporation of a foreign country, gave technical assistance to its U.S. subsidiary within this district in installing and maintaining the machines in question gave jurisdiction over the corporation to the District Court under 28 U.S.C. §1391(d). *Hauni Werke Koerber & Co., KG. v. Molins Limited*, 183 U.S.P.Q. 168, 169 (Va. 1974).

Foreign Deposition.

The defendants were required to submit to pretrial discovery in the United States, including appearing for oral depositions. The defendants were provided with an alternative, under conditions that would not implicate German sovereignty, to voluntarily agree to oral depositions before an American consular official in the embassy at Bonn, Germany, provided such oral depositions were truly voluntary, were of the same scope as if they were occurring here in the United States, and were done only after notice to the government of the Federal Republic of Germany. If the German government objected, the party defendants were required to appear in the United States for the depositions. *Work v. Bier,* 106 F.R.D. 45, 226 U.S.P.Q. 657 (D.C. 1985).

Foreign Filing. *See* Patent Office License.

Foreign Filing License. *See* Patent Office License.

Foreign Judgment.

Principles of international comity, or mutual respect of sovereigns, direct that United States courts, when possible, should recognize and enforce foreign judgments. *Glaverbel Societe Anonyme v. Northlake Marketing & Supply Inc.*, 48 U.S.P.Q.2d 1344, 1346 (Fed. Cir. 1998).

Foreign Knowledge. *See also* Knowledge Abroad.

The prohibitions of 35 U.S.C. §104, the limitations in 35 U.S.C. §§102(a) and 102(g) to "in this country," and the specifying in 35 U.S.C. §102(e) of an application filed "in the United States" clearly demonstrate a policy in our patent statutes to the effect that knowledge and acts in a foreign country are not to defeat the rights of applicants for patents, except as applicants may become involved in priority disputes. *In re Hilmer, Korger, Weyer, and Aumuller*, 359 F.2d 859, 149 U.S.P.Q. 480, 496 (C.C.P.A. 1966).

Foreign Patent.

A foreign patent may be a valid reference only for all that it clearly discloses. *In re Cross*, 62 F.2d 182, 16 U.S.P.Q. 10 (C.C.P.A. 1932).

Foreign Patent Application. *See also* Auslegeschrift, Gebrauchsmuster, Offenlegungsschrift, Printed Publication.

An application for patent filed in a foreign country must contain a disclosure of an invention adequate to satisfy the requirements of 35 U.S.C. §112, first paragraph, if a later-filed United States application claiming that invention is to be accorded the benefit of the filing date of the foreign application under 35 U.S.C. §119. *Kawai, Masuda, and Usui v. Metlesics and Sternbach*, 480 F.2d 880, 178 U.S.P.Q. 158, 159 (C.C.P.A. 1973).

ᛡ

Although the application as filed contained a reference to an identified British application, it contained no cross-reference to any previously filed U.S. application. Introduction of the identity of the U.S. application corresponding to the cited British application was new matter within the meaning of 35 U.S.C. §132. *In re Hawkins*, 486 F.2d 579, 179 U.S.P.Q. 163, 165 (C.C.P.A. 1973).

ᛡ

The laying open to inspection of an applicant's Japanese Utility Model Application 18 months from its filing (or Convention priority) date is not considered to be such patenting as contemplated by 35 U.S.C. §102(d) in view of the very limited rights which may come into existence upon the first publication of such an application. *Ex parte Fujishiro and Ohta*, 199 U.S.P.Q. 36, 38 (PTO Bd. App. 1977).

ᛡ

Material essential to the disclosure of an application for letters patent cannot be incorporated by mere reference to foreign patent applications. *Scheffer v. Shanks*, 207 U.S.P.Q. 211, 213 (Comm'r of Patents and Trademarks 1979).

ᛡ

The contents of appellant's application for an Australian patent (copies of which were classified and laid open to public inspection at the Australian Patent Office and at each of its five "sub-offices" more than one year before appellant filed his application in the United States) were sufficiently accessible to the public and to persons skilled in the pertinent art to qualify as a "printed publication." Even though no fact appears respecting actual viewing or dissemination of any copy of the application, there is no dispute as to whether the records were maintained for this purpose or whether the application was properly classified, indexed, or abstracted. *In re Wyer*, 655 F.2d 221, 210 U.S.P.Q. 790, 794, 795 (C.C.P.A. 1981).

ᛡ

Essential material, improperly incorporated by reference, can be bodily incorporated into an application. *Ernsthausen v. Nakayama*, 1 U.S.P.Q.2d 1539, 1548 (B.P.A.I. 1985).

ᛒ

Foreign patent applications that are made known to and are available to the public without restriction are publications. *Northern Telecom Inc. v. Datapoint Corp.*, 908 F.2d 931, 15 U.S.P.Q.2d 1321, 1325 (Fed. Cir. 1990).

Foreign Patentee.

The bare unasserted statutory power of a foreign patentee to sue for infringement in a particular jurisdiction is not such a significant contact that the one possessing it may be made a defendant therein against its will. By availing itself of the benefits of the patent registration laws of the United States, the foreign patentee did not establish a contact sufficient to subject it to the in personam jurisdiction of this district. *The Gerber Scientific Instrument Company v. Barr and Stroud Ltd.*, 383 F.Supp. 1238, 182 U.S.P.Q. 201, 203 (Conn. 1973).

ᛒ

Section 293 of 35 U.S.C. empowers the District Court for the District of Columbia to assert personal jurisdiction over a foreign holder of U.S. patents in a dispute over the patents' ownership. *National Patent Development Corp. v. T. J. Smith & Nephew Ltd.*, 877 F.2d 1003, 11 U.S.P.Q.2d 1211 (D.C. Cir. 1989).

Foreign Patents and Proceedings. *See also* Foreign Patent Application, Geschmacksmuster, Preclusion.

A foreign patent may be a valid reference only for all that it clearly discloses. *In re Cross*, 62 F.2d 182, 16 U.S.P.Q. 10 (C.C.P.A. 1932).

ᛒ

Patent proceedings in other countries are not controlling, in part because the standards of patentability vary widely from country to country. *Skil Corporation v. Lucerne Products, Inc.*, 684 F.2d 346, 216 U.S.P.Q. 371, 374 (6th Cir. 1982).

ᛒ

Instructions to foreign counsel and a representation to foreign patent offices must be considered when such matters comprise relevant evidence. *Caterpillar Tractor Co. v. Berco, S.P.A.*, 714 F.2d 1110, 219 U.S.P.Q. 185, 188 (Fed. Cir. 1983).

ᛒ

U.S. patent law differs significantly from the patent laws of foreign countries, and foreign determinations as to the patentability of an invention are not controlling in an American court. This does not mean, however, that portions of foreign patent proceedings, foreign patent applications, or the foreign patents themselves may not be relevant evidence on factual issues raised in a U.S. patent action. Foreign patents, patent applications, and patent proceedings may involve information that is relevant to issues presented in litigation. *Max Daetwyler Corp. v. Input Graphics, Inc.*, 583 F. Supp. 446, 222 U.S.P.Q. 150, 159 (Pa. 1984).

ᛒ

While neither a vacated International Trade Commission decision in which the ALJ found the patents valid and infringed nor a Canadian decision in which the corresponding Canadian patent was held to be valid and infringed is binding on the court in this case and the court does not rely on either in reaching its decision as to validity and infringement of the U.S. patents in suit, it is appropriate to consider those decisions in ruling on willfulness of infringement. *Corning Glass Works v. Sumitomo Electric U.S.A. Inc.*, 671 F. Supp. 1369, 5 U.S.P.Q.2d 1545, 1571 (N.Y. 1987).

ω

Where a prior adjudication was by a foreign nation's court applying its patent law to its patents, the barriers to reliance on the foreign judgment for collateral estoppel purposes become almost insurmountable. Differences in the law of the two nations and in the detailed language of the patent are emphasized to avoid issue preclusion in a patent case pending in this country even where the invention, the technological and economic competition between the parties, and the consequences of the judgments are for all practical purposes the same. Even if the court in this country were to apply collateral estoppel to certain factual findings made by a British court as opposed to importing its legal conclusions wholesale, it is not clear that trial time would be significantly shortened. Furthermore, the federal circuit's reluctance to give collateral estoppel effect to foreign judgments would seem to apply to foreign findings of fact insofar as those findings involve mixed questions of fact and foreign law. It is a quiddity of our law that a well and thoroughly reasoned decision reached by a highly skilled and scientifically informed justice of the Patent Court, Chancery Division, in the High Court of Justice of Great Britain after four weeks of trial must be ignored, and essentially the same issues with the same evidence must now be retried by American jurors with no background in science or patents, whose average formal education will be no more than high school. This curious event is the result of the world's chauvinistic view of patents. *Cuno Inc. v. Pall Corp.*, 729 F. Supp. 234, 14 U.S.P.Q.2d 1815, 1819 (N.Y. 1989).

ω

After a patentee prevailed in an infringement action based on his Canadian patent, he initiated an infringement action against the same party with regard to the same product based on his corresponding U.S. patent. Although a court may not say that a U.S. patent is valid and infringed because a corresponding Canadian patent is valid and infringed, it is commonplace for courts in the United States to employ issue preclusion (collateral estoppel) even when claim preclusion is unavailable. When a foreign court renders judgment on a question of fact with significance in each system of law, there is no reason not to take over that decision. *Vas-Cath Inc. v. Mahurkar*, 745 F. Supp. 517, 17 U.S.P.Q.2d 1353, 1359 (Ill. 1990).

ω

Proceedings in a Belgian tribunal are considered "fundamentally fair", and plaintiff has posed no quarrel in that respect. Although the standard of *law* applied by the Belgian tribunal is not the same as ours, the just-recited *factual* findings of the Belgian court conclusively demonstrate that the document is not a "printed *publication*" under the United States patent laws [35 U.S.C. §102(b)] either. *Northlake Marketing & Supply Inc. v. Glaverbel S.A.*, 958 F. Supp. 373, 45 U.S.P.Q.2d 1106, 1111 (Ill. 1997).

Foreign Priority.[3] *See* **35 U.S.C. §119.**

Foreign Sales.

Foreign sales may not be taken into account in any determination of a reasonable royalty. *Enpat Inc. v. Microsoft Corp.*, 6 F.Supp. 537, 47 U.S.P.Q.2d 1218, 1220 (Va. 1998).

Foreseeability. *See also* **Predictability.**

Under 35 U.S.C. §284 of the patent statute the balance between full compensation, which is the meaning that the Supreme Court has attributed to the statute, and the reasonable limits of liability encompassed by general principles of law can best be viewed in terms of reasonable, objective foreseeability. If a particular injury was or should have been reasonabaly foreseeable by an infringing competitor in the relevant market, broadly defined, that injury is generally compensable absent a persuasive reason to the contrary. *Rite-Hite Corp. v. Kelley Co. Inc.*, 56 F.3d 1538, 35 U.S.P.Q.2d 1065, 1070 (Fed. Cir. 1995); *but see dissent* (1090).

Forfeiture.

Justice requires that an issue in legitimate dispute not be held forfeited merely because it would complicate other pending litigation; "forfeitures are never favored. Equity always leans against them, and only decrees in their favor when there is full, clear and strict proof of a legal right thereto." *Advanced Cardiovascular Systems Inc. v. SciMed Life Systems Inc.*, 988 F.2d 1157, 26 U.S.P.Q.2d 1038, 1043 (Fed. Cir. 1993).

Form. *See also* **Change in Form, Crystalline.**

A mere carrying forward of an original patented conception involving only the change of form, proportions, or degree, or the substitution of equivalents doing the same thing as the original invention, by substantially the same means, is not such an invention as will sustain a patent even though the changes produce better results than prior inventions. *In re Paul F. Williams*, 36 F.2d 436, 4 U.S.P.Q. 237, 239 (C.C.P.A. 1930).

ᚦ

One device is an infringement of another if it performs substantially the same function in substantially the same way to obtain the same result. Except where form is the essence of the invention, it has little weight in the decision of such an issue. *Hugh W. Batcheller v. Henry Cole Co.*, 7 F. Supp. 898, 22 U.S.P.Q. 354, 358 (Mass. 1934).

ᚦ

---

[3] A Certificate of Correction under 35 U.S.C. §255 and 37 C.F.R. §1.323 may be requested and issued in order to perfect a claim of foreign priority benefits in a patented continuing application if the requirements of 35 U.S.C. §119 had been satisfied in the parent application prior to issuance of the patent and requirements of 37 C.F.R. §1.55(a) are met. However, a claim of foreign priority benefits cannot be perfected via a Certificate of Correction if the requirements of 35 U.S.C. §119 had not been satisfied in the patented application (or an antecedent application thereof) prior to issuance and the requirements of 37 C.F.R. §1.55(a) are not met. In this latter circumstance, the claim to foreign priority benefits can be perfected only by way of a reissue application. (*Notice*, 1069 T.M.O.G. 4, Aug. 26, 1986.)

Form

A mere change in form over what a reference discloses is not necessarily a patentable difference. *In re Launder and Hosmer,* 222 F.2d 371, 105 U.S.P.Q. 446, 450 (C.C.P.A. 1955).

℧

Noncompliance with Rules of Practice dealing with matters of form (as contrasted with questions of patentability) traditionally results in objection to the specification with review by petition to the Commissioner rather than rejection of the claims and enforcement of the law through appeals to the Board and this court. *In re Newton,* 414 F.2d 1400, 163 U.S.P.Q. 34, 40 (C.C.P.A. 1969).

℧

In *In re Cofer* [354 F.2d 664, 148 U.S.P.Q. 268, 271 (C.C.P.A. 1966)], the court held that a new crystalline form of a compound would not have been obvious absent evidence that "the prior art suggests the particular structure or form of the compound or composition as well as suitable methods of obtaining that structure or form." See also *In re Grose* [592 F.2d 1161, 201 U.S.P.Q. 57, 63 (C.C.P.A. 1979)], wherein the court stated that different crystal forms of zeolites would not have been structurally obvious one from the other, unless there was some chemical theory supporting such a conclusion. *See In re Irani,* 427 F.2d 806, 166 U.S.P.Q. 24, 26 (C.C.P.A. 1970) (holding the crystalline anhydrous form of a known chemical compound not obvious).

Formal Rejection.[4]

Form over Substance.

A problem arises in computer-arts inventions when structure and apparatus claims are defined only as "means for" performing specified functions. If the functionally defined disclosed means and their equivalents are so broad that they encompass any and every means for performing the recited functions, the apparatus claim is an attempt to exalt form over substance, since the claim is really to the method or series of functions itself. In computer-related inventions, the recited means often perform the function of "number crunching" (solving mathematical algorithms and making calculations). In such cases the burden must be placed on the applicant to demonstrate that the claims are truly drawn to specific apparatus distinct from other apparatus capable of performing the identical functions. When this burden is not discharged, the apparatus claims will be treated as if they are drawn to the method or process that encompasses all of the claimed "means." *In re Walter,* 618 F.2d 758, 205 U.S.P.Q. 397 (C.C.P.A. 1980).

℧

A continuing application, based on a parent reissue application, is entitled to the benefit of the filing date of the parent reissue application under 35 U.S.C. §120 even when a different invention is being claimed. To hold that it is impossible to obtain the actual

---

[4]The primary object of the examination of an application is to determine whether or not the claims define a patentable advance over the prior art. This consideration should not be relegated to a secondary position while undue emphasis is given to non-prior art or to "technical" rejections. Effort in examining should be concentrated on truly essentail matters, minimizing or eliminating effort on technical rejections that are not really critical. MPEP √706.03.

filing date of the reissue application because its effective filing date is the patent filing date would exalt form over substance and serve no useful purpose. *In re Bauman,* 683 F.2d 405, 214 U.S.P.Q. 585, 590 (C.C.P.A. 1982).

Formula. *See also* **Mathematical Equation, Mathematical Formula, Name, Recipe, Structure.**

As two claims do not use exactly the same terminology to define the structural formula of the compounds, which is stated to be that of one or the other of the claims, the allowance of both claims is not objectionable since there is no unreasonable multiplicity of claims. *Ex parte Scott,* 54 U.S.P.Q. 148, 149 (PO Bd. App. 1941).

ω

An error in the structural formula of a product in a reference does not void the reference as an enabling disclosure of the involved product. *In re Paquette*, 423 F.2d 1401, 165 U.S.P.Q. 317, 319 (C.C.P.A. 1970).

ω

The disclosure of a structural formula in a reference can be a statutory bar under 35 U.S.C. §102(b) against a claim to a compound of that formula if a method of making such compound was known by, or obvious to, one skilled in the art more than one year prior to applicant's filing date, notwithstanding the fact that there was no known use of the compound prior to applicant's invention. *In re Samour,* 571 F.2d 559, 197 U.S.P.Q. 1, 3, 4, 5 (C.C.P.A. 1978); *compare with In re Stemniski*, 444 F.2d 581, 170 U.S.P.Q. 343, 348 (C.C.P.A. 1971).

ω

Although a new compound was disclosed and named as having an incorrect formula, by which the compound was claimed, the benefit of the filing date was accorded a continuing application in which the compound was properly named and identified by its correct formula. *Sulkowski v. Houlihan*, 179 U.S.P.Q. 685 (PO Bd. Pat. Intf. 1973). *See also In re Sulkowski*, 487 F.2d 920, 180 U.S.P.Q. 46 (C.C.P.A. 1973).

ω

The characterization of a catalyst by defining the atomic ratios of its elements by a formula was held to be subject to more than one interpretation and not to define adequately over art. *Ex parte Grasselli,* 231 U.S.P.Q. 395 (PTO Bd. App. 1983).

ω

The use of mathematical formulae or relationships to describe the electronic structure and operation of an apparatus does not make it nonstatutory. *Arrhythmia Research Technology Inc. v. Corazonix Corp.*, 958 F.2d 1053, 22 U.S.P.Q.2d 1033, 1039 (Fed. Cir. 1992).

Forum. *See also* **Due Process, Stream of Commerce.**

The plaintiff's choice of forum is accorded less respect when that forum is not the plaintiff's "home turf." This is especially true when the chosen forum is merely the statutory home state of the defendant corporation. The home-turf exception does not apply to a plaintiff who has selected a venue that is connected with the subject matter of the lawsuit. When the forum is related to the subject matter of the suit, the home-turf exception is inapplicable, and the plaintiff's forum choice is entitled to the usual degree of deference. *Willemijn Houdstermaatschaapij B.V. v. Apollo Computer Inc.*, 707 F. Supp. 1429, 13 U.S.P.Q.2d 1001, 1005 (Del. 1989).

Forum Shopping.

The "first-to-file" rule provides that, when two suits are filed in different forums regarding the same matter, the first suit should generally take priority. Nevertheless, if the first suit is filed as a means of forum-shopping, it should be dismissed. *KPR Inc. v. C&F Packing Co. Inc.*, 30 U.S.P.Q.2d 1320, 1323 (Tex. 1993).

Four Corners Rule.

A specific embodiment of the invention and the best mode for carrying it out can be established by a search of the four corners of a specification, if not in a specific example which is complete in itself. *Ex parte Butler*, 116 U.S.P.Q. 523, 533 (PO Bd. App. 1957). *See also In re Borkowski and Van Venrooy*, 422 F.2d 904, 164 U.S.P.Q. 642, 645 (C.C.P.A. 1970).

Fragment. *See also* **Subcombination.**

Subcombinations have utility because they are capable of doing useful work in the device of which they are a part. There is no basis in the statute or in case law for distinguishing between a fragment and a subcombination; or any reason why the claimed subject matter involves incoherent fragments or illogical entities. *Ex parte Pritchard*, 162 U.S.P.Q. 384 (PO Bd. App. 1968).

Fraud. *See also* **Duty to Disclose, Inequitable Conduct, Misrepresentation, Sham Litigation, Sherman Act.**

Good faith or an honest mistake is a complete defense to an antitrust action based on fraud on the Patent Office. *Honeywell Inc. v. Sperry Rand Corp.*, 180 U.S.P.Q. 673, 723 (Minn. 1973).

ω

Fraud in obtaining the allowance of any claim renders the entire patent invalid. When several patents stem from an original application that contained fraudulent claims (ultimately allowed), the doctrine of unclean hands bars enforcement of any of the claims of any of the patents. *East Chicago Machine Tool Corp. v. Stone Container Corp.*, 181 U.S.P.Q. 744, 748 (Ill. 1974).

ω

Even though it is not fraud, an applicant or his agent cannot knowingly withhold relevant prior art from the Examiner until he finds out whether such action invalidates his patent, and then apply for reissue only if he loses the gamble on the ground he made an "error". When a holding of invalidity has been decreed by a court of appeals for a flagrant dereliction of duty to disclose, reissue is not available for expiation. *In re Clark*, 522 F.2d 623, 187 U.S.P.Q. 209, 213 (C.C.P.A. 1975).

ᴡ

An argument, premised upon the idea that the mere act of selecting promising experiments (for providing support data to the PTO) can be fraudulent, goes far beyond available precedent which requires no more than the full disclosure of relevant experimental results. *Hercules Incorporated v. Exxon Corporation*, 497 F.Supp. 661, 207 U.S.P.Q. 1088, 1120 (Del. 1980).

ᴡ

Defendant's unsupported assertions that plaintiff and its agents engaged in fraudulent or inequitable conduct in procuring the patent in suit is simply insufficient to establish entitlement to documents through the fraud exception to either the attorney-client privilege or the work product doctrine. *Rohm and Haas Company v. Dawson Chemical Company, Inc.*, 214 U.S.P.Q. 56, 60 (Tex. 1981).

ᴡ

The Department of Justice can sue to cancel a patent procured by fraud. *USM Corporation v. SPS Technologies, Inc.*, 694 F.2d 505, 216 U.S.P.Q. 959, 961 (7th Cir. 1982).

ᴡ

In judging whether misrepresentations made before the PTO rise to the level of fraud or inequitable conduct that would justify invocation of the maxim of unclean hands, false statements or omissions are material so as to constitute fraud before the PTO, when such statements or omissions were a substantial cause of the patent grant or a crucial factor in obtaining the patent. The proper focus in determining materiality of information misrepresented to or withheld from the PTO is on the effect of the misrepresentation or withholding upon the subjective considerations of the patent Examiner. In addition to materiality, a party seeking to invalidate a patent by invocation of the doctrine of unclean hands must establish a sufficiently culpable state of mind on the part of the patent applicant. Only a showing of wrongfulness, willfulness, bad faith, or gross negligence, proved by clear and convincing evidence, will establish sufficient culpability for invocation of the doctrine of unclean hands. *Pfizer Inc. v. International Rectifier Corp.*, 685 F.2d 357, 217 U.S.P.Q. 39 (9th Cir. 1982).

ᴡ

The first requirement to be met by an applicant, aware of misrepresentation in the prosecution of his application and desiring to overcome it, is that he expressly advise the PTO of its existence, stating specifically wherein it resides. The second requirement is that, if the misrepresentation is of one or more facts, the PTO be advised what the actual facts are, the applicant making it clear that further examination in light thereof may be required if the PTO action has been based on the misrepresentation. Finally, on the basis of the new and factually accurate record, the applicant must establish patentability of the claimed subject matter. Considering the overall objectives of the patent system, it is desirable that inventions meeting the statutory requirements for patentability be patented and, therefore, it is desirable to reserve the possibility of expiation of wrongdoing where an applicant chooses to take the necessary action on his own initiative and to take it openly. It does not suffice that one knowing of the misrepresentations in an application or in its prosecution merely supplies the Examiner with accurate facts without calling his attention to the untrue or misleading assertions sought to be overcome, leaving him to formulate his own conclusions. *Rohm & Haas Co. v. Crystal Chemical Co.*, 722 F.2d 1156, 220 U.S.P.Q. 289 (Fed. Cir. 1983).

ᖶ

An applicant for a patent need not "fully disclose all pertinent facts which may affect the decision of the PTO." Nor is an applicant for a patent under any obligation to disclose all pertinent prior art or other pertinent information of which he is aware. It is not enough that the information be simply "relevant" in some general sense to the subject matter of the claimed invention, or even to the invention's patentability. Nor does an applicant for a patent, who has no duty to conduct a prior art search, have an obligation to disclose any art of which he "reasonably should be aware." The PTO "standard" [information is material where there is (1) a substantial likelihood that (2) a reasonable Examiner (3) would consider it important (4) in deciding whether to allow the application to issue as a patent, 37 C.F.R. §1.56(a)] is an appropriate starting point for any discussion of materiality. There is no reason, however, to be bound by any single standard; for the answer to any inquiry into fraud on the PTO does not begin and end with materiality, nor can materiality be said to be unconnected to other considerations. Questions of materiality and culpability are often interrelated and intertwined, so that a lesser showing of the materiality of withheld information may suffice when an intentional scheme to defraud is established, whereas a greater showing of the materiality of withheld information would necessarily create an inference that its nondisclosure was wrongful. Fraud may be determined only by a careful balancing of intent in light of materiality. The result of that balancing is obviously not a fact that may be found to exist or not, nor is it a mere matter of application of the law to the facts, both normal jury functions. It requires that judicial discretion be brought to bear, and the district court shall decide it. *American Hoist & Derrick Co. v. Sowa & Sons, Inc.*, 725 F.2d 1350, 220 U.S.P.Q. 763 (Fed. Cir. 1984).

ᖶ

The Commissioner's October 24, 1991, Notice (1132 O.G. 33, November 19, 1991) authorizes the BPAI to consider allegations of fraud when properly raised in an interference. The two conditions under which such allegations will be considered are described in Chairman Serota's November 14, 1991, notice entitled "Interference Practice: Consideration of Fraud and Inequitable Conduct," published at 1133 O.G. 21 (December 10, 1991). *Gustavsson v. Valentini*, 25 U.S.P.Q.2d 1401, 1413 (B.P.A.I. 1991).

ᖶ

There are issues of great moment to the public in a patent suit. Furthermore, tampering with the administration of justice involves far more than injury to a single litigant. It is a wrong against the institutions set up to protect and safeguard the public, institutions in which fraud cannot complacently be tolerated consistently with the good order of society. Surely it cannot be that preservation of the integrity of the judicial process must always wait upon the diligence of litigants. The public welfare demands that the agencies of public justice be not so impotent that they must always be mute and helpless victims of deception and fraud. *Fraige v. American-National Watermattress Corp.*, 996 F.2d 295, 27 U.S.P.Q.2d 1149, 1152 (Fed. Cir. 1993).

ω

After a year following a consent judgment entered in previous litigation, the only ground for granting a motion under Federal Rule of Civil Procedure 60(b) for the Court to set aside the consent judgment is fraud upon the Court. Fraud upon the court is limited to acts "designed to improperly influence the court in its decision." Plaintiff contended that, in the previous litigation, one of the defendants withheld information that he was not the inventor of the patented product, and he thus failed to disclose the alleged invalidity of the patent. This is not enough to constitute fraud upon the Court. *Auto-Shade Inc. v. Levy*, 28 U.S.P.Q.2d 1310, 1312 (Cal. 1993).

ω

The requirements of common law fraud are in contrast with the broader sweep of "inequitable conduct," an equitable defense that may be satisfied when material information is withheld with the intent to deceive the Examiner, whether or not the Examiner is shown to have relied thereon. *C.R. Bard Inc. v. M3 Systems Inc.*, 48 U.S.P.Q.2d 1225, 1242 (Fed. Cir. 1998).

ω

"[P]roof of scienter required in fraud cases is often a matter of inference from circumstantial evidence." *Bristol-Myers Squibb Co. v. Rhône-Poulenc Rorer Inc.*, 48 U.S.P.Q.2d 1817, 1823 (N.Y. 1998).

Fraud on a Patent.

Literal infringement requires that an accused device embody every element of a claim as properly interpreted. If the claim describes a combination of functions, and each function is performed by a means described in the specification or an equivalent of such means, then literal infringement holds. When a claimed invention is a novel combination of steps, all possible methods of carrying out each step of the combination are not required to be described in the specification. Correctly construed claims cover "equivalents" of the described embodiments. The purpose is to grant an inventor of a combination invention a fair scope of protection that is not dependent on a catalog of alternative embodiments in the specification. The court has cautioned against limiting the claimed invention to preferred embodiments or specific examples in the specification. The details of performing each step need not be included in the claims unless required to distinguish the claimed invention from the prior art, or otherwise to specifically point out and distinctly claim the invention. Claims should be read in a way that avoids enabling an infringer to "practice a fraud on a patent." *Texas Instruments, Inc. v. U.S. International Trade Commission*, 805 F.2d 1367, 231 U.S.P.Q. 833 (Fed. Cir. 1986).

ω

The purpose of the doctrine of equivalents is to protect a patented invention from circumvention by minor changes or deviations. To restrict protection to devices that literally duplicate would render the patent law a "hollow and useless thing." Its essence being to prevent a fraud on the patent, the scope of the doctrine should be viewed in that spirit. As a wide-angle abstraction, the idea of equivalency could be subject to abuse by either a litigious patentee or a duplicitous infringer. What constitutes equivalence must therefore depend on the contextual setting involved and should not be a prisoner to formula. There is equivalence if the accused device "performs substantially the same function in substantially the same way to obtain the same result." This is the function-means-and-result test. A fact finder cannot properly make a determination of equivalence "absent evidence and argument concerning the doctrine and each of its elements." The patentee has the burden to prove infringement. To do so under the doctrine of equivalence requires a showing that all three components of the equivalency test are met. A jury must be separately directed to the proof of each component. A jury cannot make a factual finding of equivalence without particularized testimony and linking argument. *Malta v. Schulmerich Carillons Inc.*, 13 U.S.P.Q.2d 1900, 1902 (Pa. 1989).

ω

A patentee should not be able to obtain, under the doctrine of equivalents, coverage that he could not lawfully have obtained from the PTO by literal claims. The doctrine of equivalents exists to prevent a fraud on a patent, not to give a patentee something he could not have lawfully obtained from the PTO had he tried. Since prior art always limits what an inventor could have claimed, it limits the range of permissible equivalents of a claim. *Wilson Sporting Goods Co. v. David Geoffrey & Associates*, 904 F.2d 676, 14 U.S.P.Q.2d 1942, 1948 (Fed. Cir. 1990).

ω

Intentionally "designing around" the claims of a patent is not, by itself, a wrong that must be compensated by invocation of the doctrine of equivalents. Designing around a patent is, in fact, one of the ways in which the patent system works to the advantage of the public in promoting progress in the useful arts, its constitutional purpose. Also inherent in our claim based patent system is the principle that the protected invention is what the claims say it is, and thus infringement can be avoided by avoiding the language of the claims. It is only when the changes are so insubstantial as to result in "a fraud on the patent" that application of the equitable doctrine of equivalents becomes desirable. *Slim-fold Manufacturing Co. Inc. v. Kinkead Industries Inc.*, 932 F.2d 1453, 18 U.S.P.Q.2d 1842, 1845 (Fed. Cir. 1991).

Fraud on the Patent Office. *See* **Failure to Disclose, Fraud, Inequitable Conduct.**

Fraudulent Concealment

Fraudulent concealment, like inherently unknowable, requires a party to overcome a single threshold question. First, it must be shown that there is sufficient evidence from which a judge or jury can find that facts were fraudulently concealed. Only when that question can be answered in the affirmative does the issue of when the injured party discovered or should have discovered the injury arise so that the time for the statute of limitations to begin running can be set. Fraudulent concealment requires a showing of an affirmative act by the party accused of wrongful behavior. Only when active conceal-mentis shown will the statute of limitations be tolled. *Studiengesellschaft Kohle mbH v. Hercules Inc.*, 748 F. Supp. 247, 18 U.S.P.Q.2d 1773, 1778 (Del. 1990).

FRCP (Federal Rules of Civil Procedure). *See* **Rule.**

Free. *See also* **Excluding Prior Art, Negative Limitation, Pure, Unrecognized.**

The existence of a compound as an ingredient of another substance does not negate novelty in a claim to the pure compound, although it may render the claim unpatentable for lack of invention. The claimed laevorotary compound "substantially free from the dextrorotary form" did not exist in that condition in the reference mixture. *In re Williams*, 171 F.2d 319, 80 U.S.P.Q. 150, 151 (C.C.P.A. 1948).

ϖ

Pure, isomer-free compounds called for by claims are patentable over a brown reference sludge (containing such compounds) because the pure compounds possess new and unobvious properties that are not possessed by the brown sludge. *Ex parte Yale and Bernstein*, 119 U.S.P.Q. 256, 258 (PO Bd. App. 1958).

ϖ

The process claim requirement that the solution be "substantially free from anions other than sulfate" makes the claim sufficiently definite, particularly when it is considered that the limitation narrows the claim. *International Minerals and Chemical Corporation v. Watson*, 186 F.Supp. 712, 126 U.S.P.Q. 98, 99 (D.C. 1960).

ϖ

A method claim containing the expression "heterocyclic and aromatic compounds being free of substituents containing aliphatic hydroxyl groups and amino groups" was considered adequately definitive. *Ex parte Westfahl*, 136 U.S.P.Q. 265, 269, 270 (PO Bd. App. 1962).

ϖ

The expressions "free of bleaching agent comprising an alkaline earth metal being capable of releasing hypochlorite or hypobromite in an aqueous solution" and "a non-reducing saccharide" find no support in the specification. They thus do not comply with the description requirement of the first paragraph of 35 U.S.C. §112. The fact that no compounds of this nature are taught to be present in the examples of this case is insufficient basis for the limitations introduced into the claims when (1) quite evidently the presence of a bleaching agent is not intended to be excluded from the claim composition and, in fact, is intended to be present as an ingredient, and (2) nowhere is it indicated that only nonreducing sugars are intended to be within the scope of saccharides as broadly disclosed. That sucrose is a nonreducing sugar does not entitle the appellant to claim a genus of which sucrose is a member. *Ex parte Pearson*, 230 U.S.P.Q. 711 (B.P.A.I. 1985).

Freedom of Information Act. *See* **FOIA.**

Freeman-Walter-Abele Test. *See* **Algorithm.**

Frivolous. *See also* **Rule 11, Rule 38.**

An assertion that an appeal is frivolous is a serious allegation and should be accompanied by citation to the opposing brief and the record below and by clear argument as to why those citations establish the allegedly frivolous nature of the appeal. An appeal having a small chance for success is not frivolous for that reason alone and thus deserving of sanctions. Even though an appeal is judged "entirely without merit," it may have presented an arguable basis for reversal, and thus not qualify for sanctions. *Biodex Corp. v. Loredan Biomedical Inc.*, 946 F.2d 850, 20 U.S.P.Q.2d 1252, 1263 (Fed. Cir. 1991).

ω

Given the difficulty of showing reversible error in discretionary rulings, counsel should be particularly cautious about filing an appeal that challenges them. There are two distinct (though, in practice, often related) senses in which an appeal may be frivolous. First, where an appeal is taken in a case where "the judgment by the tribunal below was so plainly correct and the legal authority contrary to appellant's position so clear that there really is no appealable issue," the appeal is held to be "frivolous as filed." "Second, even in cases in which genuinely appealable issues may exist, so that the taking of an appeal is not frivolous, the appellant's misconduct in arguing the appeal may be such as to justify holding the appeal to be 'frivolous as argued.'" Sanctionable conduct has been held to include (though is by no means limited to) seeking to relitigate issues already finally adjudicated, failing to explain how the trial court erred or to present clear and cogent arguments for reversal, rearguing frivolous positions for which sanctions had already been imposed in the trial forum, failing to cite authority and ignoring opponent's cited authority, citing irrelevant or inapplicable authority, distorting cited authority by omitting language from quotations, making irrelevant and illogical arguments, and misrepresenting facts or law to the court. *State Industries Inc. v. Mor-Flo Industries Inc.*, 20 U.S.P.Q.2d 1738, 1742, 1743 (Fed. Cir. 1991).

FTC. *See* **Federal Trade Commission.**

FTCA (Federal Tort Claims Act).

Sovereign immunity precludes tort actions against the United States which come within the ambit of the discretionary function exception of the Federal Tort Claims Act. The conduct of an Examiner and of the PTO are well within that sphere. *Lindsey v. United States*, 778 F.2d 1143, 228 U.S.P.Q. 282, 285 (5th Cir. 1985).

ω

Review of a patent Examiner's decision through the medium of tort suits might involve "judicial second guessing" of decisions based on social policy. The Examiner's alleged tortious behavior in this case falls under the discretionary function exception to the FTCA, 28 U.S.C. §2680(a)(1982). The district court properly dismissed the action for lack of subject matter jurisdiction. *Chamberlin v. Isen*, 779 F.2d 522, 228 U.S.P.Q. 369, 372 (9th Cir. 1985).

Full, Clear, Concise, and Exact.

The district court employed two measures impermissible in law: (1) it required that Claim 1 describe the invention, which is the role of the disclosure portion of the specification, not the role of the claims; and (2) it applied the "full, clear, concise, and exact" requirement of the first paragraph of 35 U.S.C. §112 to the claim, when that paragraph only applies to the disclosure portion of the specification, not to the claims. The district court spoke inappropriately of the indefiniteness of the "patent," and it did not review the claim for indefiniteness under the second paragraph of §112. A decision on whether a claim is invalid under §112 requires a determination of whether those skilled in the art would understand what is claimed when the claim is read in the light of the specification. *Orthokinetics Inc. v. Safety Travel Chairs Inc.*, 806 F.2d 1565, 1 U.S.P.Q.2d 1081 (Fed. Cir. 1986).

Function. *See also* Means Plus Function, Negative Function, Property.

A rejection of process claims as being drawn to the function of the appellant's machine is proper unless it appears that the claimed process can be carried out either by some machine having materially different characteristics from the machine disclosed in the application, or by hand. *In re Gartner and Roeber,* 223 F.2d 502, 106 U.S.P.Q. 273, 275 (C.C.P.A. 1955).

ᚳ

The appellant has described his invention as comprehending the use therein of any inorganic salt capable of performing a specific function in a specific combination, and he has specifically disclosed four such salts that are capable of performing his function. The claims are not "unduly broad" merely because one skilled in the art may not know offhand what inorganic salts are capable of so functioning. Nothing is found in patent law that requires the appellant to discover which of all salts have the specified properties and which salts will function properly in his combination. The invention description clearly indicates that any inorganic salt that has such properties is usable in his combination. *In re Fuetterer,* 319 F.2d 259, 138 U.S.P.Q. 217, 223 (C.C.P.A. 1963).

ᚳ

Where the chemical identity of a material is not critical, there is no reason why an applicant should not be permitted to define that material partly in terms of its physical properties or the function that it performs. *In re Metcalfe and Lowe,* 410 F.2d 1378, 161 U.S.P.Q. 789, 793 (C.C.P.A. 1969).

ᚳ

By disclosing a device that inherently performs a function, operates according to a theory, or has an advantage, a patent applicant necessarily discloses that function, theory, or advantage even though he says nothing concerning it. The application may be later amended to recite the function, theory, or advantage without introducing prohibited new matter. *In re Smythe and Shamos,* 480 F.2d 1376, 178 U.S.P.Q. 279 (C.C.P.A. 1973).

ᚳ

Since the claims are the sole measure of the monopoly granted by the patent and the claims are "means-plus-function" claims, it was error to rely on a function of the patented device not mentioned in the claims. *Burgess & Associates, Inc. v. Klingensmith*, 487 F.2d 321, 180 U.S.P.Q. 115, 117 (9th Cir. 1973).

ᰰ

It is not a function of the claims to specifically exclude either possible inoperative substances or ineffective reagent proportions. *In re Dinh-Nguyen and Stenhagen*, 492 F.2d 856, 181 U.S.P.Q. 46 (C.C.P.A. 1974).

ᰰ

Where the Patent Office has reason to believe that a functional limitation asserted to be critical for establishing novelty in the claimed subject matter may, in fact, be an inherent characteristic of the prior art, it possesses the authority to require the applicant to prove that the subject matter shown to be in the prior art does not possess the characteristic relied on. *In re Best, Bolton, and Shaw*, 562 F.2d 1252, 195 U.S.P.Q. 430, 433 (C.C.P.A. 1977).

ᰰ

Most patents are granted on an improvement of a prior device. The improved device inherently achieves the same basic result as that achieved, and performs the same basic function as that performed, by the prior device. To require in every case that a new "function" or new "result" be performed or achieved would be destructive of "the progress of . . . useful arts" goal sought in the constitutional-statutory scheme. *Nickola v. Peterson*, 580 F.2d 898, 198 U.S.P.Q. 385, 397 (6th Cir. 1978).

ᰰ

When the function clause in a claim fails to recite a necessary limitation to render the claim valid, a court may not resort to the specification to make that limitation a part of the claim. *The Toro Company v. L. R. Nelson Corporation*, 524 F.Supp. 586, 213 U.S.P.Q. 207, 210 (Ill. 1981).

ᰰ

Literal infringement requires that an accused device embody every element of a claim as properly interpreted. If the claim describes a combination of functions, and each function is performed by a means described in the specification or an equivalent of such means, then literal infringement holds. When a claimed invention is a novel combination of steps, all possible methods of carrying out each step of the combination are not required to be described in the specification. Correctly construed claims cover "equivalents" of the described embodiments. The purpose is to grant an inventor of a combination invention a fair scope that is not dependent on a catalog of alternative embodiments in the specification. The court has cautioned against limiting the claimed invention to preferred embodiments or specific examples in the specification. The details of performing each step need not be included in the claims unless required to distinguish the claimed invention from the prior art, or otherwise to specifically point out and distinctly claim the invention. Claims should be read in a way that avoids enabling an infringer to "practice a fraud on a patent." *Texas Instruments, Inc. v. United States International Trade Commission*, 805 F.2d 1558, 231 U.S.P.Q. 833 (Fed. Cir. 1986).

ᰰ

The function/way/result equivalency analysis with respect to a claim limitation resolves the question of equivalency by comparing the function/way/result of the substitution with the function/way/result of a limitation in the context of the invention. *Corning Glass Works v. Sumitomo Electric U.S.A., Inc.*, 868 F.2d 1251, 9 U.S.P.Q.2d 1962 (Fed. Cir. 1989).

ᚳ

Although a feature that is "primarily functional" is not protected by a design patent, an overly broad definition of functionality is not supported by case law. Not all features that perform functions are primarily functional; rather, the test is whether the "function dictates the design" and that requires a court to determine whether the function performed by the features in question could be accomplished by other designs. *Herbco International Inc. v. Gemmy Industries Inc.*, 38 U.S.P.Q.2d 1819, 1821 (N.Y. 1996).

Functional. *See also* Computer-Arts Invention, Design, Product by Properties.

The vice of a functional claim exists not only when a claim is "wholly" functional if that is ever true, but also when the inventor is painstaking when he recites what has already been seen, and then uses conveniently functional language at the exact point of novelty. A limited use of terms of effect or result, which accurately define the essential qualities of a product to one skilled in the art, may in some instances be permissible and even desirable, but a characteristic essential to novelty may not be distinguished from the old art solely by its tendency to remedy the problems in the art met by the patent. The difficulty of making adequate description may have some bearing on the sufficiency of the description attempted, but it cannot justify a claim describing nothing new except, perhaps, in functional terms. *General Electric Co. v. Wabash Appliance Corp.*, 304 U.S. 364, 37 U.S.P.Q. 466, 469, 470 (1938).

ᚳ

"Functional" language in claims is not expressly condemned by the patent statutes. On the contrary, the only portion of Title 35 U.S.C. §that makes any reference to the use of statements of function specifically authorizes such use. All elements of a combination can be claimed in terms of what they do as well as in terms of what they are. *In re Fuetterer,* 319 F.2d 259, 138 U.S.P.Q. 217, 222 (C.C.P.A. 1963)..

ᚳ

There is no support, either in the actual holdings of prior cases or in the statute, for the proposition that "functional" language, in and of itself, renders a claim improper. We have found no prior decision of this or any other court that may be said to hold that there is some other ground for objecting to a claim on the basis of any language, "functional" or otherwise, beyond what is already sanctioned by the provisions of 35 U.S.C. §112. *In re Swinehart and Sfiligoj,* 439 F.2d 210, 169 U.S.P.Q. 226 (C.C.P.A. 1971).

ᚳ

The use of "functional" statements in claims to limit a class of chemical compounds used as one element of a composition of matter is specifically sanctioned by the third paragraph of 35 U.S.C. §112. The same rationale is controlling with regard to compound claims. *In re Barr, Williams and Whitmore,* 444 F.2d 588, 170 U.S.P.Q. 330 (C.C.P.A. 1971).

ʊ

Claims to DNA by what it does (i.e. encoding either a protein exhibiting certain characteristics, or a biologically functional equivalent thereof) rather than by what it is might be analogized to a single means claim of the type disparaged by *In re Hyatt,* 708 F.2d 712, 218 U.S.P.Q. 195 (Fed. Cir. 1983). The problem with the phrase "biologically functional equivalent thereof" is that it covers any conceivable means, i.e., cell or DNA, which achieves the stated biological result while the specification discloses, at most, only a specific DNA segment known to the inventor. *Ex parte Maizel,* 27 U.S.P.Q.2d 1662, 1665 (BPAI 1992).

ʊ

An "invention is deemed functional for public use purposes when it can perform the general function for which it has been developed, even though the device may later be refined." *Nordberg Inc. v. Telsmith Inc.,* 881 F.Supp. 1252, 36 U.S.P.Q.2d 1577, 1604 (Wis. 1995).

Functionality

The fact that two alternative reference designs perform the same function as the curved design of the subject design patent illustrates that the particular design patent design may not be essential to the use of the article. *L.A. Gear, Inc. v. Tom McAn Shoe Co.,* 988 F.2d 1117, 1123, 25 U.S.P.Q.2d 1913, 1917 (Fed. Cir.), *cert. denied,* 114 S.Ct. 291 (1993).

Functional Limitation. *See also* Adapted, Intended Use.

Inherency may not be established by probabilities or possibilities. The mere fact that a certain thing may result from a given set of circumstances is not sufficient. Although an applicant may be required to prove that the subject matter shown to be in prior art does not possess characteristics relied upon where an Examiner has reason to believe that a functional limitation asserted to be critical for establishing novelty in the claimed subject matter may, in fact, be an inherent characteristic of the prior art, the Examiner must provide some evidence or scientific reasoning to establish the reasonableness of the Examiner's belief that the functional limitation is an inherent characteristic of the prior art before the applicant can be put through this burdensome task. *Ex parte Skinner,* 2 U.S.P.Q.2d 1788 (B.P.A.I. 1986).

Function of Machine

A rejection that process claims are merely drawn to the function of a claimed machine is proper unless the claimed process can be carried out either by some machine having materially different characteristics from those of the machine disclosed in the application, or by hand. *In re Gartner and Roeber,* 223 F.2d 502, 106 U.S.P.Q. 273 (C.C.P.A. 1955).

Function/Way/Result

The "function/way/result" equivalency analysis with respect to a claim limitation resolves the question of equivalency by comparing the function/way/result of the substitution with the function/way/result of a limitation in the context of the invention. *Corning Glass Works v. Sumitomo Electric U.S.A. Inc.*, 868 F.2d 1251, 9 U.S.P.Q.2d 1962 (Fed. Cir. 1989).

ω

While comparison of function/way/result is an acceptable way of showing that structure in an accused device is the "substantial equivalent" of a claim limitation, it is not the only way to do so. Under general principles of appellate review a trial court's decision with regard to the doctrine of equivalents should not be disturbed unless clearly erroneous. *Malta v. Schulmerich Carillons Inc.*, 952 F.2d 1320, 21 U.S.P.Q.2d 1161, 1165, 1167 (Fed. Cir. 1991).

ω

As the device uses significantly different means to perform the body-attaching function, it cannot be found to perform in "substantially the same way." *Sofamor Danek Group Inc. v. Depuy-Motech Inc.*, 74 F.3d 1216, 37 U.S.P.Q.2d 1529, 1533 (Fed. Cir. 1996).

Fundamental Truth, *See* Principle.

Funding. *See also* Economics.

The junior party in a interference was almost continuously active in pursuing the commercialization of the process of the counts. Except for the period from 1959 to 1964, during which no government funds were allocated for the purpose of testing any bactericide, neither the junior party nor his supervisor gave up on the invention of the counts. Neither the pertinent case law nor a rule of reason would dictate that, under these circumstances, there was an abandonment of the invention by the junior party during this period. *Spiner and Hoffman v. Pierce*, 177 U.S.P.Q. 709, 712 (PO Bd. Pat. Int. 1972).

ω

Financial inability is insufficient to excuse a delay in filing suit. *B.W.B. Controls, Inc. v. U.S. Industries, Inc.*, 626 F.Supp. 1553, 228 U.S.P.Q. 799, 812 (La. 1985)

ω

A university's policy (notwithstanding a large endowment fund) of requiring researchers to obtain outside support for research as a form of a peer review selection process (whereby university research is directed at areas considered justified and appropriate by outsiders) does not constitute an excuse for no action for three months (during a summer period) because of no funds or personnel for use on the invention. *Griffith v. Kanamaru*, 231 U.S.P.Q. 892, 893 (B.P.A.I. 1986).

Fungicide

A disclosure which states that involved compounds may be used to prepare toxic substances, "such as insecticides, fungicides, etc.", is sufficient to meet the requirements of 35 U.S.C. §112. *In re Johnson*, 282 F.2d 370, 127 U.S.P.Q. 216, 218 (C.C.P.A. 1960).

Fusion Proteins[5]

Future Discoveries

It is not required that those skilled in the art knew, at the time the patent application was filed, of the asserted equivalent means of performing the claimed functions; that equivalence is determined as of the time infringement takes place. Infringement will be found when the material features of a patent have been appropriated, even when those features have been patentably improved. *Texas Instruments, Inc. v. United States International Trade Commission*, 805 F.2d 1558, 231 U.S.P.Q. 833 (Fed. Cir. 1986).

Future Goods. *See* Expectant Interest.

Between the time of an invention and the issuance of a patent thereon, rights in the invention may be assigned, and legal title to the ensuing patent will pass to the assignee upon grant of the patent. If an assignment of rights in an invention is made prior to the existence of the invention, this may be viewed as an assignment of an expectant interest (future goods or after acquired property). An assignment of an expectant interest in personal property can be a valid assignment. In such a situation, the assignee holds at most an equitable title. Once the invention is made and an application for patent is filed, however, legal title to the rights accruing thereunder would be in the assignee (subject to the rights of a subsequent purchaser under 35 U.S.C. §261), and the inventor-assignor would have nothing remaining to assign. *FilmTec Corp. v. Allied-Signal Inc.*, 939 F.2d 1568, 19 U.S.P.Q.2d 1508, 1511 (Fed. Cir. 1991).

FWR. *See* Function/Way/Result.

---

[5]For a detailed discussion of fusion proteins, see *Schendel v. Curtis*, 83 F.3d 1399, 1400 & n.3, 38 U.S.P.Q.2d 1743, 1744 & n.3 (Fed. Cir. 1996).

Key Terms and Concepts

Game.

Appeals in patent cases should not be mere games played with pieces of paper called references and the patent in suit. Lawsuits arise out of the affairs of people, real people facing real problems. Litigation grows out of a technical problem solved by a patentee. *Rosemount, Inc. v. Beckman Instruments, Inc.*, 727 F.2d 1540, 221 U.S.P.Q. 1, 5 (Fed. Cir. 1984).

GCP. *See* Good Clinical Practice.

Gebrauchsmuster.

A foreign typewritten application file that has been opened to public inspection in a foreign patent office and a German Gebrauchsmuster, which is typewritten and open to public inspection, are not bars under the printed publication provisions. *In re Tenney, Frank, and Knox,* 254 F.2d 619, 117 U.S.P.Q. 348, 352 (C.C.P.A. 1958).

ᚦ

A Gebrauchsmuster (GM) is a limited type of West German patent. Such a patent only "anticipates" a U.S. patent to the extent of the claims of the GM. Thus, if the claims of the GM do not disclose the invention of the American patent, but the drawing or specification of the GM do disclose the invention, the American patent is not anticipated by the GM. The specifications and drawings in the GM can only be considered under 35 U.S.C. §102(b) to the extent that they help to explain the claims of the GM. *Max Daetwyler Corp. v. Input Graphics, Inc.*, 583 F. Supp. 446, 222 U.S.P.Q. 150 (Pa. 1984).

Gene.

A gene is a chemical compound, albeit a complex one, and conception of a chemical compound requires that the inventor be able to define it so as to distinguish it from other materials and be able to describe how to obtain it. Conception does not occur unless one has a mental picture of the structure of the chemical or is able to define it by its method of preparation, its physical or chemical properties, or whatever characteristics sufficiently distinguish it. It is not sufficient to define it solely by its principal biological property (e.g., encoding human erythropoietin) because an alleged conception having no more specificity than that is simply a wish to know the identity of any material with that biological property. When an inventor is unable to envision the detailed constitution of a gene so as to distinguish it from other materials, as well as a method for obtaining it, conception has not been achieved until reduction to practice has occurred (i.e., until after the gene has been isolated). *Amgen Inc. v. Chugai Pharmaceutical Co. Ltd.*, 927 F.2d 1200, 18 U.S.P.Q.2d 1016, 1020, 1021 (Fed. Cir. 1991).

ϖ

One of ordinary skill in this art, advised of the *existence* and isolation of a functional protein, is also necessarily advised of the *existence* of a gene which codes for the protein, but does not know the gene's structure. There is incentive or motivation to isolate (clone) the gene for any functional and useful protein because it would then enable production of large amounts of the protein for further study and commercial use. A gene, being a chemical compound, could be defined "by its method of preparation, its physical or chemical properties, or whatever characteristics sufficiently distinguished it [from other materials]." *Ex parte Deuel*, 33 U.S.P.Q.2d 1445, 1448 (B.P.A.I. 1993), *rev'd* 51 F.3d 1552, 34 U.S.P.Q.2d 1210 (Fed. Cir. 1995).

ϖ

When an inventor in unable to envision the detailed constitution of a gene so as to distinguish it from other materials, as well as a method for obtaining it, conception has not been achieved until reduction to practice has occurred, *i.e.*, until after the gene has been isolated. *University of California v. Eli Lilly and Co.*, 39 U.S.P.Q.2d 1225, 1240 (Ind. 1995).

Generality.

A determination of obviousness must be based on facts and not on unsupported generalities. *In re Freed*, 425 F.2d 785, 165 U.S.P.Q. 570, 571 (C.C.P.A. 1970).

Generalization.

Generalization should be avoided insofar as specific chemical structures are alleged to be *prima facie* obvious one from the other. There must be adequate prior art support for involved structural changes to complete the PTO's *prima facie* case and shift the burden of going forward to the applicant. The mere fact that it is possible to find two isolated disclosures that might be combined in such a way to produce a new compound does not necessarily render such production obvious unless the art also contains something to suggest the desirability of the proposed combination. In the absence of such a reference suggestion, there is inadequate support for the position that the required modification would *prima facie* have been obvious. *In re Grabiak*, 769 F.2d 729, 226 U.S.P.Q. 870 (Fed. Cir. 1985).

ϖ

References should be applied in accord with their actual teachings. Language should not be extracted out of context for the purpose of making and maintaining an art-based ground of rejection. A generalization from a limited reference disclosure is not a valid basis for precluding patentability. *Ex parte Isshiki, Kijima and Watanabe*, 36 U.S.P.Q.2d 1863 (B.P.A.I. 1993).

General Jurisdiction. *See also* Nonresident Defendant.

If the defendant's contacts with the forum state are not directly related to the plaintiff's cause of action, they will still suffice to establish general jurisdiction if they are sufficiently continuous and systematic to support a reasonable exercise of jurisdiction. *Crystal Semiconductor Corp. v. OPTi Inc.*, 44 U.S.P.Q.2d 1497, 1501 (Tex. 1997).

General-Verdict-Multiple-Defenses.

An undue delay in presenting the argument: even if most of the possible grounds for the invalidity/unenforceability verdict are supported by substantial evidence, a new trial on the invalidity/unenforceability issue must be ordered if any one of the possible grounds is unsupported by substantial evidence, may prove prejudicial. *Arachnid Inc. v. Medalist Marketing Corp.*, 972 F.2d 1300, 23 U.S.P.Q.2d 1946, 1949 (Fed. Cir. 1992).

Generic. *See also* **Breadth, Encyclopedic, Exclusivity, Generic Disclosure, Genus, Shotgun, Species.**

The burden is on an applicant for a patent to prove that he is entitled to a patent. The mere fact that such applicant uses broad or generic terminology in his original disclosure does not necessarily entitle him to claim the subject matter broadly. *Ex parte Dubbs and Stevens,* 119 U.S.P.Q. 440, 442 (PO Bd. App. 1958).

ω

Mention of representative compounds encompassed by generic claim language is not required by 35 U.S.C. §112 or any other provision of the statute. Where no explicit description of a generic invention is to be found in a specification, mention of representative compounds may provide an implicit description upon which to base generic claim language. The inclusion of a number of representative examples in a specification is one way of demonstrating the operability of a broad chemical invention and, hence, establishing that the utility requirement of 35 U.S.C. §101 has been met. *In re Robins,* 429 F.2d 452, 166 U.S.P.Q. 552, 555 (C.C.P.A. 1970).

ω

It has never been contended that the appellants, when they included the disputed term in their specification, intended only to indicate a single compound. Accepting, therefore, that the term is a generic one, its recitation must be taken as an assertion by the appellant that all of the "considerable number of compounds" that are included within the generic term would, as a class, be operative to produce the asserted enhancement of adhesion characteristics. The only relevant concern of the Patent Office under these circumstances should be over the truth of any such assertion. The first paragraph of 35 U.S.C. §112 requires nothing more than objective enablement. How such a teaching is set forth, either by the use of illustrative examples or by broad terminology, is of no importance. *In re Marzocchi and Horton,* 439 F.2d 220, 169 U.S.P.Q. 367 (C.C.P.A. 1971).

ω

To provide effective incentives, claims must adequately protect inventors. To demand that the first to disclose shall limit his claims to what he has found will work or to materials which meet the guidelines specified for "preferred" materials would not serve the constitutional purpose of promoting progress in the useful arts. *In re Johnson and Farnham,* 558 F.2d 1008, 194 U.S.P.Q. 187, 195 (C.C.P.A. 1977).

ω

The contention that a claimed configuration would be obvious from a reference claim on which it reads is a non sequitur. According to such reasoning Morse's telegraph patent would have made the Telex obvious. The scope of a patent's claims determines what infringes the patent; it is no measure of what it discloses. A patent discloses only that which it describes, whether specifically or in general terms, so as to convey intelligence to one capable of understanding. *In re Benno,* 768 F.2d 1340, 226 U.S.P.Q. 683 (Fed. Cir. 1985).

Generic Claim. *See also* **Read On.**

After making an election-of-species requirement, repeating same after election and traversal, making the requirement final, and allowing the elected claims, the Examiner withdrew all other claims (including generic claims) from consideration "since they were not limited to the elected invention." In withdrawing the so-called generic claims from further prosecution, Rules 141 and 146 (37 C.F.R. §1.141 and §1.146) were violated. *Ex parte Bridgeford, Turbak, and Burke,* 172 U.S.P.Q. 308, 309 (PO Dir. 1971).

ʊ

Generic claims covering a species disclosed and claimed in an earlier-filed application can be inserted into a copending application which results in a later-issued patent, provided a terminal disclaimer is filed, so that the later patent expires at the same time as that issued on the earlier-filed application. *Splendor Form Brassiere, Inc. v. Rapid-American Corporation,* 187 U.S.P.Q. 151, 157 (N.Y. 1975).

ʊ

To provide effective incentives, claims must adequately protect inventors. To demand that the first to disclose shall limit his claims to what he has found will work or to materials that meet the guidelines specified for "preferred" materials in a process would not serve the constitutional purpose of promoting progress in the useful arts. *In re Goffe,* 542 F.2d 564, 191 U.S.P.Q. 429, 431 (C.C.P.A. 1976).

ʊ

Claims need not be limited to exemplification or preferred embodiments in order to satisfy enablement requirements. *Ex parte Gould,* 6 U.S.P.Q.2d 1680 (B.P.A.I. 1987).

ʊ

The argument that a claim to a genus would inherently disclose all species within that genus is wholly meritless whether considered under 35 U.S.C. §102(b) or under §103 (1982). *Corning Glass Works v. Sumitomo Electric U.S.A. Inc.,* 868 F.2d 1251, 9 U.S.P.Q.2d 1962 (Fed. Cir. 1989).

Generic Copies of Drugs. *See* **ANDA, Hatch Waxman Amendments.**

Generic Disclosure. *See also* **Encyclopedic Disclosure, Generic, Selection, Shotgun.**

The patentability of an adjacent position isomer of a known compound, which is generically disclosed in a number of references, is not precluded even though the primary utility of the claimed position isomer is a recognized utility of the known compound. *In re Petrzilka, Hofmann, Schenk, Troxler, Frey, and Ott*, 424 F.2d 1102, 165 U.S.P.Q. 327 (C.C.P.A. 1970).

ω

The contention that a claimed configuration would be obvious from a reference claim on which it reads is a non sequitur. According to such reasoning Morse's telegraph patent would have made the Telex obvious. The scope of a patent's claims determines what infringes the patent; it is no measure of what it discloses. A patent discloses only that which it describes, whether specifically or in general terms, so as to convey intelligence to one capable of understanding. *In re Benno*, 768 F.2d 1340, 226 U.S.P.Q. 683 (Fed. Cir. 1985).

ω

The argument that a claim to a genus would inherently disclose all species within that genus is wholly meritless whether considered under 35 U.S.C. §102(b) or under §103 (1982). *Corning Glass Works v. Sumitomo Electric U.S.A. Inc.*, 868 F.2d 1251, 9 U.S.P.Q.2d 1962 (Fed. Cir. 1989).

Generic Drugs.

In order to accelerate the introduction of generic drugs into the market, Congress enacted §202 of the 1984 Act, codified at 35 U.S.C. §271(e)(1). Under that Act the use of a patented invention is exempt so long as that use is only directed at satisfying the reporting requirements of federal drug laws. Furthermore, the uses to which the patented invention is put must be reasonably related to this purpose. *Scripps Clinic & Research Foundation v. Genentech Inc.*, 231 U.S.P.Q. 978 (Cal. 1986).

Generic Invention.

When a later-filed application to an improvement issues as a patent before a copending application (of the same assignee) to the generic invention, claims in the earlier-filed generic application are not properly rejectable over claims of the improvement patent on the ground of double patenting when all the claims of the improvement patent are limited to the improvement. *In re Stanley and Lowe*, 214 F.2d 151, 102 U.S.P.Q. 234, 239, 240 (C.C.P.A. 1954).

Genuine.

A factual dispute is "genuine" when the evidence is such that a reasonable jury could return a verdict for the non-movant. Thus, although the interpretation of claims is a question of law, when it is necessary to resolve disputed issues of fact in the course of interpreting the claims, summary disposition is improper. *The Laitram Corp. v. NEC Corp.*, 952 F.2d 1357, 21 U.S.P.Q.2d 1276, 1281 (Fed. Cir. 1991).

ω

Facts are deemed "material" if a dispute over them "might affect the outcome of the suit under the governing law . . ." A "genuine issue" of material fact exists only when the nonmoving party makes a sufficient showing to establish an essential element to that party's case, and on which that party would bear the burden of proof at trial. *Wang Laboratories Inc. v. Mitsubishi Electronics America Inc.*, 30 U.S.P.Q.2d 1241, 1249 (Cal. 1993).

ᛗ

"In this context (summary judgment), 'genuine' means that the evidence about the fact is such that a reasonable jury could resolve the point in favor of the non-moving party and "material" means that the fact is one that might affect the outcome of the suit under the governing law." *Hoppe v. Baxter Healthcare Corp.*, 878 F.Supp. 303, 34 U.S.P.Q.2d 1619, 1622 (Mass. 1995).

Genus. *See also* Generic, Species.

The naming (in a specification) of one member of a generic or subgeneric group (in the field of chemistry) referred to in a claim is not, in itself, a proper basis for a claim to the entire group. However, it may not be necessary to enumerate a plurality of species if a genus is sufficiently identified in an application by "other appropriate language". In the case of a small and closely related group, such as the halogens, the naming of the group should ordinarily be sufficient since nothing of consequence would be added by also naming each of the well known members of the group. *In re Grimme, Keil, and Schmitz*, 274 F.2d 949, 124 U.S.P.Q. 499, 501 (C.C.P.A. 1960).

ᛗ

A single species reduction to practice may be adequate to overcome a reference showing of a genus when novel properties are attributable to a specific component of the species. *In re DaFano*, 392 F.2d 280, 157 U.S.P.Q. 192, 196 (C.C.P.A. 1968).

ᛗ

Non-critical features may be supported by a more general disclosure than those at the heart of the invention. *In re Stephens, Benvau, and Benvau*, 529 F.2d 1343, 188 U.S.P.Q. 659, 661 (C.C.P.A. 1976).

ᛗ

Early filing of an application with its disclosure of novel compounds which possess significant therapeutic use is to be encouraged. Requiring specific testing of the thousands of prostaglandin analogs encompassed by the present claim in order to satisfy the how-to-use requirement of 35 U.S.C. §112 would delay disclosure and frustrate, rather than further, the interests of the public. *In re Bundy*, 642 F.2d 430, 209 U.S.P.Q. 48, 52 (C.C.P.A. 1981).

ᛗ

The expressions "free of bleaching agent comprising an alkaline earth metal being capable of releasing hypochlorite or hypobromite in an aqueous solution" and "a non-reducing saccharide" find no support in the specification. They thus do not comply with the description requirement of the first paragraph of 35 U.S.C. §112. The fact that no compounds of this nature are taught to be present in the examples of this case is insufficient basis for the limitations introduced into the claims when (1) quite evidently the presence of a bleaching agent is not intended to be excluded from the claim composition and, in fact, is intended to be present as an ingredient, and (2) nowhere is it indicated that only nonreducing sugars are intended to be within the scope of saccharides as broadly disclosed. That sucrose is a nonreducing sugar does not entitle appellant to claim a genus of which sucrose is a member. *Ex parte Pearson*, 230 U.S.P.Q. 711 (B.P.A.I. 1985).

ω

"There is no inconsistency in awarding a generic count to one inventor, while awarding a patentably distinct species count to another [or to the same inventor]. . . ." *International Rectifier Corp. v. SGS-Thomson Microelectronics Inc.*, 38 U.S.P.Q.2d 1083, 1087 (Cal. 1994).

ω

Description of one species of a genus is not necessarily a description of the genus. *University of California v. Eli Lilly and Co.*, 119 F.3d 1559, 43 U.S.P.Q.2d 1398, 1405 (Fed. Cir. 1997).

Geographical Limitation. *See also* Dividing Markets.

Grant-backs of non-exclusive licenses, geographically limited licenses, and quantity limited licenses are not per se unlawful; they do not necessarily constitute patent misuse or violate section 2 of the Sherman Act. *Lightwave Technologies Inc. v. Corning Glass Works*, 19 U.S.P.Q.2d 1838, 1844 (N.Y. 1991).

Geographical Restriction. *See* Dividing Markets.

German Industrial Standard.

Reference in a patent specification to the German Standard is insufficient for compliance with the disclosure requirements of 35 U.S.C. §112, insofar as it is regarded as an essential element of the disclosure. The document is a non-patent publication. It is not available in the United States Patent Office like a United States patent or patent application would be. *Quaker City Gear Works, Inc. v. Skil Corporation*, 223 U.S.P.Q. 533, 534 (Pa. 1983).

Geschmacksmuster.

A design protected by a Geschmacksmuster qualifies under 35 U.S.C. §102(d) as an invention patented in a foreign country for purposes of applying the statutory time bar against an application for a U.S. design patent covering the same subject matter. There is no basis in the Patent Act or in its legislative history for making a distinction between subsections (a) and (d) of 35 U.S.C. §102 when considering whether a Geschmacksmuster is a foreign patent citable as prior art in a 35 U.S.C. §103 analysis. *In re Carlson*, 983 F.2d 1032, 25 U.S.P.Q.2d 1207, 1210 (Fed. Cir. 1992).

Gestalt Factors.

The five "Gestalt" factors are: "(1) the defendant's burden of appearing, (2) the state's interest in adjudicating the dispute, (3) the plaintiff's interest in obtaining convenient and effective relief, (4) the judicial system's interest in obtaining convenient and effective relief, and (5) the common interests of all sovereigns in promoting substantive social policies." *Columbia University v. Boehringer Mannheim GmbH*, 35 U.S.P.Q.2d 1364, 1368 (Mass. 1995).

GIS. *See* German Industrial Standard.

Gist. *See also* Critical, Essence, Point of Novelty.

No single element or group of elements can be deemed to represent the "heart" or "gist" of the invention so that infringement may be found despite the omission of other, insignificant elements from an accused device. *Berkey Photo, Inc. v. Klimsch-Repro, Inc.*, 388 F.Supp. 586, 185 U.S.P.Q. 306, 312 (N.Y. 1975).

℧

Non-critical features may be supported by a more general disclosure than those at the heart of the invention. *In re Stephens, Benvau, and Benvau*, 529 F.2d 1343, 188 U.S.P.Q. 659, 661 (C.C.P.A. 1976).

℧

A court's election to ignore the structural claims, and to substitute a gist drawn from the operation of a disclosed embodiment, cannot convert the fact question raised by the reverse doctrine of equivalents into a legal question of claim construction. That question is simple and direct: Is the accused product so far changed in principle that it performs the function of the claimed invention in a substantially different way? *SRI International v. Matsushita Electric Corp. of America*, 775 F.2d 1107, 227 U.S.P.Q. 577 (Fed. Cir. 1985).

℧

The claimed invention must be viewed as a whole. The district court appeared to distill the invention down to a gist, or core, a superficial mode of analysis that disregards elements of the whole. It disregarded express claim limitations. *Bausch & Lomb, Inc. v. Barnes-Hind/Hydrocurve, Inc.*, 796 F.2d 443, 230 U.S.P.Q. 416 (Fed. Cir. 1986).

GM. *See* Gebrauchsmuster.

Going Forward.

The first sentence of 35 U.S.C. §282 must be read in the context of the remainder of the first paragraph of §282, which provides that a party asserting patent invalidity bears the burden of establishing it. Section 282 thus mandates not only a presumption shifting the burden of going forward in a purely procedural sense, but also places the burden of persuasion on the party who asserts that the patent is invalid. The burden of persuasion is and remains always upon the party asserting invalidity, whether the most pertinent prior art was or was not considered by the Examiner. *Solder Removal Company v. United States International Trade Commission*, 582 F.2d 628, 199 U.S.P.Q. 129, 132, 133 (C.C.P.A. 1978).

Good Cause.

The good-cause showing required by 37 C.F.R. §1.617(b) imposes a stricter standard than was required under the prior rules. Under the good cause standard, ignorance by a party or counsel of the provisions of the rules or substantive requirements of the law do not constitute good cause.

Failure of counsel to provide additional evidence because he did not fully appreciate the kind of corroboration required to demonstrate a *prima facie* case for a complete reduction to practice is not adequate to satisfy the good-cause requirement. Under the good-cause standard, ignorance by a party or counsel of the provisions of the rules or the substance of the requirements of the law does not constitute good cause. *Hahn v. Wong,* 13 U.S.P.Q.2d 1211, 1216 (B.P.A.I. 1989).

ϖ

The good-cause standard in the interference rules was intended to tighten the prior practice. According to the notice accompanying the publication of the new rules, "a major change in practice that was adopted by the new 37 C.F.R. §1.617 was that a stricter standard would be imposed for presenting additional evidence after entry of an order to show cause." The new rules specifically require that "any printed publication or other document which is not self-authenticating shall be authenticated and discussed with particularity in an affidavit." *Hahn v. Wong,* 892 F.2d 1028, 13 U.S.P.Q.2d 1313, 1318, 1319 (Fed. Cir. 1989).

ϖ

The "good cause" requirement of 37 C.F.R. §1.617(b) is not limited to situations where the missing evidence was not previously available. "Good cause" is an equitable term, and must be determined in the light of all the circumstances, with due attention to the interest of justice. A combination of inadequate prosecution and misrepresentation, accompanied by forfeiture on the merits, constitutes "good cause." *Dissent* in *Huston v. Ladner,* 973 F.2d 1564, 23 U.S.P.Q.2d 1910, 1917 (Fed. Cir. 1992).

Good Clinical Practice.

A decision to place a protective order on GCP audit reports is not clearly erroneous, since disclosure arguably may result in some chilling effect upon developers of new drugs. The intent of the FDA Compliance Policy is "to encourage firms to conduct quality assurance program audits and inspections that are candid and meaningful." The FDA's decision not to "review or copy reports and records that result from audits and inspections of a written quality assurance program" clearly implies a bar upon a private entity's access to these reports. This FDA policy applies to "any regulated entity which has a written quality assurance program that provides for periodic audits or inspections." *NeoRx Corp. v. Immunomedics Inc.,* 28 U.S.P.Q.2d 1797, 1798 (N.J. 1993).

Good Faith. *See also* Misleading.

Good faith or an honest mistake is a complete defense to an antitrust action based on fraud on the Patent Office. *Honeywell Inc. v. Sperry Rand Corp.,* 180 U.S.P.Q. 673, 723 (Minn. 1973).

Goodwill.

"Sharing in the goodwill of an article unprotected by patent or trademark is the exercise of a right possessed by all—and in the free exercise of which the consuming public is deeply interested." *Sears, Roebuck & Co. v. Stiffel Company*, 376 U.S. 225, 140 U.S.P.Q. 524, 528 (S. Ct. 1964).

Government. *See also* Determination of Rights, United States Government.

Equitable estoppel does not apply against the Government as it applies against private litigants. The Supreme Court confined the doctrine, as potentially applicable to the Government, to acts of "affirmative misconduct." *MDS Associates v. U.S.*, 31 Fed.Cl. 389, 32 U.S.P.Q.2d 1784, 1787 (U.S. Ct.Fed.Cl. 1994).

ळ

"[A]nyone entering into an arrangement with the Government takes the risk of having accurately ascertained that he who purports to act for the Government stays within the bounds of his authority. The scope of this authority may be explicitly defined by Congress or be limited by delegated legislation, properly exercised through the rule-making power." Thus, while apparent authority cannot serve to bind the government to the acts of its agents, "implied actual authority, like expressed actual authority, will suffice." Implied actual authority exists "when such authority is considered to be an integral part of the duties assigned to a government employee." However, "the Government may not be estopped on the same terms as any other litigant." *Zacharin v. United States*, 38 U.S.P.Q.2d 1826, 1830, 1831, 1832 (U.S. Ct. Fed. Cl. 1996).

Government Contract.

The general burden of persuasion is on the Government to establish that the invention was reduced to practice under the contract. However, the burden of proof is placed on the inventor (contractor) with regard to what happened prior to and outside of the contract (events occurring under the control of the inventor, the facts surrounding which he is in a position to know and the Government is not in a position to know). *In re General Dynamics Corporation*, 177 U.S.P.Q. 773, 788 (Armed Services Bd. Contract Appeals 1973).

ळ

A private party which infringes another's patent by a test demonstration during Government bidding activities may be immune under 28 U.S.C. §1498 from a District Court patent infringement action if it was acting "by and for" the United States and "with its authorization or consent" when it demonstrated the allegedly infringing subject matter for the sole purpose of responding to the Government's demand for a "Product Demonstration", with the objective of acquiring a Government contract. *TVI Energy Corporation v. Blane*, 806 F.2d 1057, 1 U.S.P.Q.2d 1071, 1073 (Fed. Cir. 1986).

Government Employee. *See also* Federal Employee.

Although an invention may not be directly related to the inventor's duties, the government may still be entitled to an assignment if the invention was made in consequence of the inventor's official duties. "In consequence of" in Executive Order 10096, as amended, means that the invention is made as an obvious and direct result of the performance of the inventor's duties. *Menke v. Department of the Army,* 20 U.S.P.Q.2d 1386, 1388 (U.S. Dept. of Commerce 1991).

Grace Period. *See also* **Applicant's Own Work, Origin.**

There is only an inference of abandonment of disclosed but unclaimed subject matter in an issued patent. The inference may be rebutted (a) by an application for reissue of the patent pursuant to statute (35 U.S.C. §251, last paragraph) which seems to permit a broadening reissue application, (b) by claiming in a copending application before the patent issues and possibly even thereafter, and (c) by the filing of an application within the one-year grace period following the issuance of the patent and before the patent becomes a statutory bar under 35 U.S.C. §102(b). *In re Gibbs and Griffen,* 437 F.2d 486, 168 U.S.P.Q. 578, 584 (C.C.P.A. 1971).

ᚠ

Rigid standards are especially unsuited to the on-sale provision where the policies underlying the bar, in effect, define it. The area of law sought to be governed by these rules encompasses an infinite variety of factual situations that, when viewed in terms of the policies underlying 35 U.S.C. §102(b), present an infinite variety of legal problems wholly unsuited to mechanically applied technical rules. Thus, all the circumstances surrounding the sale or offer to sell, including the stage of development of the invention and the nature of the invention, must be considered and weighed against the policies underlying §102(b). The policies underlying the on-sale bar include: (1) discouraging removal of inventions from the public domain that the public justifiably comes to believe are freely available; (2) favoring prompt and widespread disclosure of invention; (3) giving the inventor a reasonable amount of time (following the sales and activity) to determine the value of the patent; and (4) prohibiting an extension of the period for exploiting the invention. Congress provided the one-year grace period to balance these competing interests. *Environtech Corp. v. Westech Engineering, Inc.,* 713 F. Supp. 372, 11 U.S.P.Q.2d 1804, 1807 (Utah 1989).

ᚠ

For an assertion of experimental use to have merit, it must be clear that the inventor kept control of his invention in the course of its testing. The experimental use doctrine operates in the inventor's favor to allow the inventor to refine his invention or to assess its value relative to the time and expense of prosecuting the patent application. If it is not the inventor or someone under his control or "surveillance" who does these things, there appears to be no reason why he should be entitled to rely upon them to avoid the statute. The experimental use doctrine only lifts the one-year statutory bar where the experimental use is by the inventor or persons under his control. *In re Hamilton,* 882 F.2d 1576, 11 U.S.P.Q.2d 1890, 1893, 1894 (Fed. Cir. 1989).

Graham Inquiries.

Obviousness under 35 U.S.C. §103 is a question of law based on the underlying factual inquiries set forth in *Graham v. John Deere Co.* [383 U.S. 1, 17, 148 U.S.P.Q. 459, 467 (1966)]: (1) the scope and content of the prior art; (2) the differences between the prior art and the claims at issue; (3) the level of ordinary skill in the art; and (4) objective evidence of secondary considerations.

The district court improperly determined that the subject matter claimed in the '814 patent was obvious: it failed to make the *Graham* inquiries; it improperly focused on what was obvious to the inventor; it engaged in hindsight analysis; and it considered evidence that was not prior art. *Bausch & Lomb, Inc. v. Barnes-Hind/Hydrocurve, Inc.*, 796 F.2d 443, 230 U.S.P.Q. 416 (Fed. Cir. 1986).

Grammarian. *See also* Lexicographer.

Since a patent applicant is his own lexicographer and his own grammarian, no genuine issue of fact as to the meaning of a term used in a claim will be considered by a court to exist if the meaning is made incontrovertibly clear elsewhere in the patent or in the file wrapper. *The Duplan Corporation v. Deering Milliken, Inc.*, 370 F.Supp. 769, 180 U.S.P.Q. 373, 376 (S.C. 1973).

Grant-Back. *See also* Grant-Forward Clause.

A grant-back (a covenant in a patent license that requires the licensee to assign improvement patents to the licensor) is not "illegal per se and unenforceable." This rule has been applied where there is no evidence that the grant-back provision constitutes an undue restraint or exerts an adverse effect on trade or commerce. Therefore, grant-back provisions are legal even when they cause the licensee to give up complete rights to his improvement invention to his licensor. *In re Reclosable Plastic Bags*, 192 U.S.P.Q. 674, 679 (U.S. Intl. Trade Commn. 1977).

ϖ

Grant-backs of non-exclusive licenses, geographically limited licenses, and quantity limited licenses are not per se unlawful; they do not necessarily constitute patent misuse or violate section 2 of the Sherman Act. *Lightwave Technologies Inc. v. Corning Glass Works*, 19 U.S.P.Q.2d 1838, 1844 (N.Y. 1991).

Grant-Forward Clause.

Provisions of the Patent Transfer Agreement and the Consultant Agreement require Industrial Dynamics Corporation, during the term of the Patent Transfer Agreement, and consultants, during the term of the Consultant Agreement and for a three-year period thereafter, to make available to the defendant, at no further cost to the defendant, all improvements on the two patent applications covered by the agreement. Such provisions are reasonable. These contractual provisions, which the plaintiff described as grant-forward clauses, constitute a reasonable method by which Industrial Dynamics Corporation and consultants could dispose of improvements on the basic bottle inspection machine patents. *San Marino Electronic Corp. v. George J. Meyer Manufacturing Co.*, 155 U.S.P.Q. 617, 624 (Cal. 1967).

Gross Negligence. *See also* **Inequitable Conduct, Spurious.**

A finding that particular conduct amounts to "gross negligence" does not of itself justify an inference of intent to deceive; the involved conduct, viewed in light of all the evidence, including evidence indicative of good faith, must indicate sufficient culpability to require a finding of intent to deceive. *Kingsdown Medical Consultants Ltd. v. Hollister Inc.*, 863 F.2d 867, 876, 9 U.S.P.Q.2d 1384, 1392 (Fed. Cir. 1988).

ᵭ

Gross negligence has been used as a label for various patterns of conduct. A finding that a particular conduct amounts to gross negligence does not of itself justify an inference of intent to deceive; the involved conduct, viewed in light of all the evidence, including evidence indicative of good faith, must indicate sufficient culpability to require a finding of intent to deceive. Intent to deceive should be determined in light of the realities of patent practice, and not as a matter of strict liability whatever the nature of the action before the PTO. A patentee's oversights are easily magnified out of proportion by one accused of infringement. Given a case in which a relatively routine act of patent prosecution can be portrayed as intended to mislead or deceive, clear and convincing evidence of conduct sufficient to support an inference of culpable intent is required. *Northern Telecom Inc. v. Datapoint Corp.*, 908 F.2d 931, 15 U.S.P.Q.2d 1321, 1327 (Fed. Cir. 1990).

Grow Hair. *See* **Hair Growth.**

Guidance. *See also* **Direction.**

The ultimate question is whether the specification contains a sufficiently explicit disclosure to enable one having ordinary skill in the relevant field to practice the invention claimed therein without the exercise of undue experimentation. The determination of what constitutes undue experimentation in a given case requires the application of a standard of reasonableness, having due regard for the nature of the invention and the state of the art. The test is not merely quantitative, since a considerable amount of experimentation is permissible if it is merely routine or if the specification in question provides a reasonable amount of guidance with respect to the direction in which the experimentation should proceed to enable the determination of how to practice a desired embodiment of the invention claimed. The factors to be considered have been summarized as the quantity of experimentation necessary, the amount of direction or guidance presented, the presence or absence of working examples, the nature of the invention, the state of the prior art, the relative skill of those in that art, the predictability or unpredictability of the art, and the breadth of the claims. *Ex parte Forman,* 230 U.S.P.Q. 546 (B.P.A.I. 1986).

GVMD. *See* **General-Verdict-Multiple-Defenses.**

Key Terms and Concepts

Hague Evidence Convention. *See also* **Apostille.**

The defendants were required to submit to pretrial discovery in the United States, including appearing for oral depositions. The defendants were provided with an alternative, under conditions that would not implicate German sovereignty, to voluntarily agree to oral depositions before an American consular official in the embassy at Bonn, Germany, provided such oral depositions were truly voluntary, were of the same scope as if they were occurring here in the United States, and were done only after notice to the government of the Federal Republic of Germany. If the German government objected, the party defendants were required to appear in the United States for the depositions. *Work v. Bier,* 106 F.R.D. 45, 226 U.S.P.Q. 657 (D.C. 1985).

ω

The weight of federal authority indicates that service on a foreign defendant by registered mail (return receipt) is allowed under the Hague Convention. *Meyers v. ASICS Corp.,* 711 F. Supp. 1001, 11 U.S.P.Q.2d 1777, 1783 (Cal. 1989).

ω

Service on a Japanese corporation in a patent infringement action using the substitute service provisions of Virginia's long-arm statute fails for lack of compliance with The Hague Convention, which explicitly sets forth the methods by which service may be made abroad. *Loral Fairchild Corp. v. Matsushita Electric Industrial Co. Ltd.,* 22 U.S.P.Q.2d 1158, 1159 (Va. 1991).

ω

Service pursuant to the Hague Convention need not meet the requirements of Rule (FRCP) 4. Rule 4(j) provides that the 120 day period "shall not apply to service in a foreign country pursuant to subdivision (i) of this rule." *Loral Fairchild Corp. v. Matsushita Electric Industrial Co. Ltd.,* 805 F.Supp. 3, 25 U.S.P.Q.2d 1557, 1558 (N.Y. 1992).

Hair Growth.

An invention concerning growing hair on a bald human scalp requires supporting evidence of utility. *In re Oberweger,* 115 F.2d 826, 47 U.S.P.Q. 455 (C.C.P.A. 1940).

Halogen.

The naming (in a specification) of one member of a generic or subgeneric group (in the field of chemistry) referred to in a claim is not, in itself, a proper basis for a claim to the entire group. However, it may not be necessary to enumerate a plurality of species if a genus is sufficiently identified in an application by "other appropriate language". In the case of a small and closely related group, such as the halogens, the naming of the group should ordinarily be sufficient since nothing of consequence would be added by also naming each of the well known members of the group. *In re Grimme, Keil, and Schmitz*, 274 F.2d 949, 124 U.S.P.Q. 499, 501 (C.C.P.A. 1960).

Hardship. *See also Economics.*

The law does not favor giving a party consideration for a hardship it brings upon itself by undertaking knowing infringement. *Mentor Graphics Corp. v. Quickturn Design Systems Inc.*, 44 U.S.P.Q.2d 1621, 1626 (Oreg. 1997).

Hatch-Waxman Act. *See also* **35 U.S.C. §156.**

Pre-June 8, 1995, patents are entitled to add on the restoration extension to a 20-year from filing term regardless of when such extension is granted except for those patents kept in force on June 8, 1995, only because of a restoration extension. Under this interpretation, all provisions of both URAA and Hatch-Waxman can reasonably be given effect. For pre-June 8, 1995, patents, a patentee would have full exclusionary rights for 17 years, followed by rights only to equitable remuneration (neither lost profits, an injunction, punitive damages, nor attorney fees) with respect to a certain class of infringers for the period from the end of the 17-year term to the end of the new 20-year term (the delta period), followed by entitlement to full exclusionary rights (but only with respect to the approved product) during the period of the restoration extension. *Merck & Co. v. Kessler*, 80 F.3d 1543, 38 U.S.P.Q.2d 1347, 1352, 1353 (Fed. Cir. 1996).

Hatch-Waxman Amendments. *See also* **ANDA, Hatch-Waxman Act.**

The Drug Price Competition and Patent Term Restoration Act [Pub. L. No. 98-417, 98 Stat. 1585 (1984)] is generally known as the Hatch Waxman Amendments to the Federal Food, Drug, and Cosmetic Act, 21 U.S.C. §§301 et seq. The purpose of this legislation was to increase competition in the drug industry by facilitating the approval of generic copies of drugs. Rather than complete the full NDA process, generic copiers could proceed via an Abbreviated New Drug Application (ANDA), which merely required reference to the safety and effectiveness status submitted by the "pioneer" drug manufacturer, along with submission of manufacturing and bioequivalence data for the generic copy. *Mead Johnson Pharmaceutical Group v. Bowen*, 838 F.2d 1332, 6 U.S.P.Q.2d 1565 (D.C. Cir. 1988).

Head Start.

Regardless of whether the trade secrets were ultimately made public via the issuance of a patent or otherwise, the defendant obtained the information by misappropriation and not from public disclosure or any other legitimate business means. There is no distinction between the presence of a disclosure that may destroy secrecy and the head start concept, for the former is merely an element of the latter. The award for damages compensates the plaintiff for the head start that the defendants obtained through its misappropriation. This head start amounted to a preemption of the entire market and prevented the plaintiff from licensing others, as well as making entry into the market by the plaintiff impossible. In fashioning an adequate monetary remedy, the court must consider that the defendants did not merely wrongly obtain and use the plaintiff's know-how as a competitor in the marketing, they refused to return the know-how to the plaintiff when ordered to do so, thereby also completely precluding the plaintiff from manufacturing. There is no question that defendant's conduct was grossly improper and that the plaintiff's monetary recovery should not be limited by a lead-time valuation. *The Kilbarr Corp. v. Business Systems, Inc., B.V.*, 679 F. Supp. 422, 6 U.S.P.Q.2d 1698 (N.J. 1988).

Hearsay.

The inapplicability of hearsay evidence rules in ex parte PTO examination is appropriate in light of the purpose and reason for the hearsay rule. The per se rule that hearsay evidence can never be relied upon to establish facts necessary to support a rejection is unacceptable. *In re Epstein*, 32 F.3d 1559, 31 U.S.P.Q.2d 1817, 1821 (Fed. Cir. 1994).

ῶ

Hearsay "bear[ing] circumstantial indicia of reliability" may be admitted for purposes of determining whether personal jurisdiction obtains. *Akro Corp v. Luker*, 45 F.3d 1541, 33 U.S.P.Q.2d 1505, 1509 (Fed. Cir. 1995).

Heart. *See* Gist.

Herbicide.

The application and the claims affirmatively set up an equivalence between crabgrass and all other "undesired vegetation" insofar as the herbicidal effectiveness of the instant compounds is concerned. The Examiner cited no art, and the Board referred to none, that would show that proof of criticality with respect to crabgrass was insufficient with respect to other undesired vegetation. *In re Lemin*, 332 F.2d 839, 141 U.S.P.Q. 814, 816 (C.C.P.A. 1964).

ῶ

The mere recitation of a new use for an old composition does not render the composition patentable anew. There is nothing in the reference, however, that teaches that the known compound may be combined with a finely divided inert insoluble solid-carrier vehicle. The carriers recited in the claims are those conventionally employed, and the disclosure teaches that compounds having algaecidal and herbicidal properties are usually blended with a solid or liquid carrier vehicle. As the reference does not teach that the known compound has algaecidal and/or herbicidal properties, there is simply no motivation to combine the known compound with conventional herbicidal carriers. There is nothing in the record that establishes the obviousness of mixing the known compound with a finely divided inert insoluble solid-carrier vehicle for any purpose whatsoever. Merely establishing that the particular compound is a known compound and that the carrier vehicles are conventional is not sufficient to render the claimed composition unpatentable. There must be some suggestion in the art to combine these materials for some purpose to support a holding of obviousness. *Ex parte Erdmann, Schneider, and Koch,* 194 U.S.P.Q. 96 (PTO Bd. App. 1975).

ϖ

Providing substitution on a ring of a herbicidally active compound by finding another herbicidally active compound with the same ring and desired optional constituents is not enough to preclude patentability of a claimed herbicide. In the chemical arts the mere fact that it is possible to find two isolated disclosures that might be combined in such a way to produce a new compound does not necessarily render such production obvious unless the art also contains something to suggest the desirability of the proposed combination. In the absence of an express or implied suggestion in at least one of the references that the specifically claimed substitution would be desirable for herbicide compounds other than those of the specific class disclosed in one reference, patentability is not precluded. The mere fact that both references originate from the herbicide art does not provide any teaching or suggestion to combine them. Nor does the fact that both references concern compounds containing a specific ring suggest that substituents suitable in one case would be expected to be suitable in the other. *In re Levitt,* 11 U.S.P.Q.2d 1315, 1316 (Fed. Cir. 1989—unpublished).

Heterocyclic.

A rejection of claims as failing to define the invention properly and based on the phrases "substituted mononuclear and polynuclear homocyclic compounds," "alkyl," "ester," and "heterocyclic and aromatic compounds being free of substituents containing aliphatic hydroxyl and amino groups," in process claims, was reversed. *Ex parte West-fahl,* 136 U.S.P.Q. 265 (PTO Bd. App. 1962).

ϖ

The second paragraph of 35 U.S.C. §112 requires an applicant to "particularly point out and distinctly claim the subject matter sought to be patented." When the scope of the invention sought to be patented is unclear from the language of the claim, a second paragraph rejection lies. *In re Wiggins, James, and Gittos,* 488 F.2d 538, 179 U.S.P.Q. 421, 423 (C.C.P.A. 1973).

ϖ

Although various authorities may place a slightly different interpretation on the meaning of "aryl," when used in conjunction with "aralkyl" and "alkaryl," those in the art readily appreciate the total scope of the subject matter defined. Likewise, "heterocyclic" has an art-recognized meaning. Neither of such terms is indefinite. *Ex parte Scherberich and Pfeifer,* 201 U.S.P.Q. 397 (PTO Bd. App. 1977).

Hiatus.

Even if the invention was actually reduced to practice by the junior party in 1977 or 1978, the unexplained hiatus of more than two years between that date and the junior party's filing date was an unreasonably long delay, raising an inference that the junior party suppressed the invention within the meaning of 35 U.S.C. §102(g). Since there is no evidence in the record as to any activity by the junior party during this two-year period, the inference has not been rebutted, and, as a result, the junior party cannot rely on either of the alleged actual reductions to practice. *Latimer v. Wetmore*, 231 U.S.P.Q. 131 (B.P.A.I. 1985).

Hindsight. *See also* Combining References, Mosaic, Motivation, Reconstruction, Selection, Selective Extraction from Prior Art.

The law has other tests of invention than subtle conjecture of what might have been seen and yet was not. It regards a change as evidence of novelty and the acceptance and utility of change as further evidence, even as a demonstration. Nor does it detract from its merit that it is the result of experiment and not the instant and perfect product of inventive power. A patentee may be baldly empirical, seeing nothing beyond his experiments and the result; yet, if he has added a new and valuable article to the world's utilities, he is entitled to the rank and protection of an inventor. It is certainly not necessary that he understand or be able to state the scientific principles underlying his invention, and it is immaterial whether he can stand a successful examination as to the speculative ideas involved. *Diamond Rubber Co. v. Consolidated Rubber Tire Co.*, 220 U.S. 428, 435 (1911).

ϖ

An art-based ground of rejection of a process claim was considered untenable because the Examiner failed to provide any reason for finding obvious the alteration of the molybdenum-phosphorus ratio in the direction and manner claimed. *Ex parte Parthasarathy and Ciapetta*, 174 U.S.P.Q. 63 (PO Bd. App. 1971).

ϖ

The determination of obviousness is measured not by a subjective standard of quality but by an objective standard of inquiry. Hindsight reconstruction of prior art is not the applicable standard. *Maschinenfabrik Rieter A.G. v. Greenwood Mills*, 340 F. Supp. 1103, 173 U.S.P.Q. 605, 610, 611 (S.C. 1972).

ϖ

The Patent Office has the initial duty of supplying a factual basis for a rejection under 35 U.S.C. §103. It may not, because it may doubt that the invention is patentable, resort to speculation, unfounded assumptions or hindsight reconstruction to supply deficiencies in its factual basis. *In re Rice*, 481 F.2d 1316, 178 U.S.P.Q. 478, 479 (C.C.P.A. 1973).

ϖ

There must be a reason apparent at the time the invention was made to a person of ordinary skill in the art for applying the teaching at hand, or the use of the teaching as evidence of obviousness will entail prohibited hindsight. *In re Nomiya, Kohisa, and Matsumura*, 509 F.2d 566, 184 U.S.P.Q. 607 (C.C.P.A. 1975).

ϖ

To imbue one of ordinary skill in the art with knowledge of the invention in suit, when no prior art reference or references of record convey or suggest that knowledge, is to fall victim to the insidious effect of a hindsight syndrome wherein that which only the inventor taught is used against its teacher. *W. L. Gore & Associates, Inc. v. Garlock, Inc.*, 721 F.2d 1540, 220 U.S.P.Q. 303 (Fed. Cir. 1983).

ϖ

An action in the district court under 35 U.S.C. §145 is a proceeding de novo and, while it is limited to the invention claimed in the PTO, the court may consider any additional competent evidence that a plaintiff neither intentionally nor negligently failed to submit to the PTO. The presumption of correctness that attaches to the decision of the Commissioner is a rebuttable presumption that may be overcome by the introduction of evidence (at a trial under 35 U.S.C. §145) which is of such character and amount as to carry a thorough conviction of error. At such a trial the plaintiff and defendant may present evidence on any issue properly before the court. This additional evidence may include testimony of expert witnesses and inventors skilled in the art, and evidence of commercial success. In making its determination of non-obviousness, the court recognized the non-analogous nature of one reference, the lack of teaching or suggestion in the prior art of the useful advantage of a flexible track incapable of self-support, and the commercial success of the highly flexible Hot Wheels trackway-toy vehicle combination covered by the plaintiff's Reissue Application. The fact that the claimed invention seemed simple and, when viewed in hindsight, appeared to be obvious was not enough to negate invention. *Lemelson v. Mossinghoff,* 225 U.S.P.Q. 1063 (D.C. 1985).

ʊ

There was no suggestion in the prior art to provide the applicant with the motivation to design the valve assembly so that it would be removable as a unit. The Board argued that, if the reference had followed the "common practice" of attaching the valve stem to the valve structure, the valve assembly would be removable as a unit. The only way the Board could have arrived at its conclusion was through hindsight analysis, by reading into the art applicant's own teachings. Hindsight analysis is clearly improper, since the statutory test is whether "the subject matter as a whole would have been obvious at the time the invention was made." *In re Deminski,* 796 F.2d 436, 230 U.S.P.Q. 313 (Fed. Cir. 1986).

ʊ

The district court improperly determined that the subject matter claimed in the '814 patent was obvious: it failed to make the Graham inquiries, it improperly focused on what was obvious to the inventor, it engaged in hindsight analysis, and it considered evidence that was not prior art. *Bausch & Lomb, Inc. v. Barnes-Hind/Hydrocurve, Inc.,* 796 F.2d 443, 230 U.S.P.Q. 416 (Fed. Cir. 1986).

ʊ

Objective evidence of non-obviousness includes commercial success, long felt but unresolved need, failure of others, and copying. When present, such objective evidence must be considered. It can be the most probative evidence of non-obviousness in the record, and enables the district court to avert the trap of hindsight. On the other hand, the absence of objective evidence does not preclude a holding of non-obviousness because such evidence is not a requirement for patentability. *Custom Accessories Inc. v. Jeffrey-Allan Industries Inc.,* 807 F.2d 955, 1 U.S.P.Q.2d 1196 (Fed. Cir. 1986).

ʊ

Selective hindsight is no more applicable to the design of experiments than it is to the combination of prior art teachings. There must be a reason or suggestion in the art for selecting the procedure used, other than the knowledge learned from the applicant's disclosure. *In re Dow Chemical Co.*, 837 F.2d 469, 5 U.S.P.Q.2d 1529 (Fed. Cir. 1988).

ω

Neglect of the hindsight prohibition is reversible error. *Williams Service Group Inc. v. O.B. Cannon & Son Inc.*, 33 U.S.P.Q.2d 1705, 1726 n.11 (Pa. 1994).

Holdover Clause.

Contractual provisions requiring assignment of post-employment inventions are commonly referred to as trailer or holdover clauses. Holdover clauses in employment contracts are enforceable only if they constitute a reasonable and justifiable restriction on the right of employees to work in their profession for subsequent employers. Their legitimate purpose is to prevent an employee from appropriating to his own use or to the use of a subsequent employer inventions relating to and stemming from work done for a previous employer. Holdover clauses are simply recognition of the fact of business life that employees sometimes carry with them to new employers inventions or ideas so related to work done for a former employer that, in equity and good conscience, the fruits of that work should belong to the former employer. Holdover clauses must be limited to reasonable times and to subject matter that the employee worked on or had knowledge of during his employment. Unless expressly agreed otherwise, an employer has no right (under a holdover clause) to inventions made outside the scope of the employee's former activities, and made on and with a subsequent employer's time and funds. Regarding the validity of a contractual provision requiring the employee to disclose and assign all ideas and improvements for five years following termination of employment, the court articulated a three part test: (a) Is the restraint reasonable in the sense that it is no greater than necessary to protect the employer in some legitimate interest? (b) Is the restraint reasonable in the sense that it is not unduly harsh or oppressive on the employee? (c) Is the restraint reasonable in the sense that it is not injurious to the public? *Ingersoll-Rand Co. v. Ciavatta*, 8 U.S.P.Q.2d 1537, 542 A.2d 879, 110 N.J. 609 (NJ 1988).

Home Turf.

The plaintiff's choice of forum is accorded less respect when that forum is not the plaintiff's "home turf." This is especially true when the chosen forum is merely the statutory home state of the defendant corporation. The home-turf exception does not apply to a plaintiff who has selected a venue that is connected with the subject matter of the lawsuit. When the forum is related to the subject matter of the suit, the home-turf exception is inapplicable, and plaintiff's forum choice is entitled to the usual degree of deference. *Willemijn Houdstermaatschaapij B. V. v. Apollo Computer Inc.*, 707 F. Supp. 1429, 13 U.S.P.Q.2d 1001, 1005 (Del. 1989).

ω

"Home turf" has been defined as the forum closest to [plaintiff's] home in which plaintiff could affect personal jurisdiction over the principle defendant. *Tuff Torq Corp. v. Hydro-Gear Limited Partnership*, 882 F.Supp. 359, 33 U.S.P.Q.2d 1846, 1848 (Del. 1994).

Homology. *See also* **Relationship, Structural Obviousness, Structural Similarity.**

Where the invention for which a patent is sought relates to one member of an homologous series and the disclosure of the prior art is of a non-adjacent member of the series, *In re Henze*, 181 F.2d 196, 85 U.S.P.Q. 261, is not authority for a "legal presumption" of obviousness of the claimed invention. *In re Mills*, 281 F.2d 218, 126 U.S.P.Q. 513, 516 (C.C.P.A. 1960).

ω

In *Henze*, [181 F.2d 196, 85 U.S.P.Q.261 (C.C.P.A. 1950)] the application was for claimed compounds, one of which was the next higher homolog of a compound disclosed in a prior publication. This court stated (85 U.S.P.Q. at 264-265):

> The Examiner had held, that the claims in issue were unpatentable, lacking invention over the disclosure of the publication, because the appellant had failed to show that the compounds claimed had an unexpected beneficial property not possessed by the lower adjacent homologue disclosed in the publication. The Examiner held that the affidavit did not aid in conferring patentability upon the rejected claims because there was no showing that the lower homologue would not yield results similar to the claimed compounds under certain dosages.

ω

The burden is on the applicant to rebut that presumption [of unpatentability] by a showing that the claimed compound possesses unobvious and unexpected beneficial properties not actually possessed by the prior art homologue. It is immaterial that the prior art homologue may not be recognized or known to be useful for the same purpose or to possess the same properties as the claimed compound.

Where the prior art does not disclose or suggest any usefulness for the compounds it describes and the applicant does describe a usefulness conforming with statutory requirements for the closely related but novel compounds he discloses, Henze does not state the correct burden of proof to be imposed on an applicant for patent; to the extent it is inconsistent, it is overruled. A disclosure of a particular, significant usefulness for claimed compounds that was not known or obvious in the art is adequate consideration for a patent grant on the compounds, where the prior art previously was unaware of any usefulness for the class of compounds to which the claimed compounds belong. *In re Stemniski,* 444 F.2d 581, 170 U.S.P.Q. 343, 348 (C.C.P.A. 1971).

ω

Homology is not automatically equated with *prima facie* obviousness. *In re Langer and Haynes,* 465 F.2d 896, 175 U.S.P.Q. 169, 171 (C.C.P.A. 1972).

ω

Discovery of absence of skin toxicity in the claimed compound does not end the inquiry, because one who claims a compound, per se, which is structurally similar to a prior art compound must rebut the presumed expectation that the structurally similar compounds have similar properties. Because the expectation of similar properties stands unrebutted, it necessarily follows that an expectation of similar uses also stands unrebutted. *In re Wilder*, 563 F.2d 457, 195 U.S.P.Q. 426, 429, 430 (C.C.P.A. 1977).

ω

Homology

The use of homologues to vary a patented composition establishes a *prima facie* case of obviousness and, therefore, non-patentability. While expert testimony established that hydroxyethylcellulose (HEC) disclosed in one reference patent and hydroxypropylcellulose (HPC) disclosed in another reference patent may be considered homologues if a comparison is made of single links in the chemical combinations making up the chain-like polymer molecules, expert testimony also established that these materials cannot be considered homologues if their entire polymeric chain of chemical combinations is compared. *Forest Laboratories, Inc. v. Lowey*, 218 U.S.P.Q. 646, 655 (N.Y. S.Ct. 1982).

ᴡ

A holding that comparative test data were unpersuasive "because it only compares *one* species and . . . is not commensurate with the scope of the claims" was reversed because provided evidence of unexpected superiority was based on representative compounds which differ only by a methyl versus hydrogen substituent at the very point of structural distinction relied upon. *Ex parte Casagrande, Montanari, and Santangelo*, 36 U.S.P.Q.2d 1860 (B.P.A.I. 1995—*unpublished and nonprecedential*).

Host. *See also* Enablement.

Claims directed to pharmaceutical compositions having a specified pharmacological activity or to producing a specified pharmacological activity which comprises internally administering certain compounds are not indefinite by reason of their failure to name a host. *In re Gardner, Roe, and Willey*, 427 F.2d 786, 166 U.S.P.Q. 138, 140 (C.C.P.A. 1970).

ᴡ

The mere absence of dosage and/or host from priority applications directed to ocompounds having specified pharmacological utilities is not fatal, provided such dosage and host would have been obvious to a person of ordinary skill in the art. *Hester v. Meguro and Kuwada*, 190 U.S.P.Q. 231, 235 (PTO Bd. Pat. Intf. 1975).

ᴡ

An application which describes a specific physiological use for claimed compounds, but omits identification of a host or applicable dosages, satisfies the "how to use" requirement of the first paragraph of 35 U.S.C. §112 in view of the fact that a prior art reference discloses a host and dosages for the same use of structurally related compounds. *Bey and Jung v. Kollonitsch and Patchett*, 215 U.S.P.Q. 454, 458 (PTO Bd. Pat. Intf. 1981).

How to Make. *See also* Starting Material.

An application involved in a interference can comply with the how-to-make requirement of 35 U. S. C. §112 even when it is devoid of a disclosure of how to make the compound of the interference count when the method of synthesis would have been known to one of ordinary skill in the art (without undue experimentation) at the time when the earliest of applications relied upon was filed. *Martin, Aebi, and Ebner v. Johnson*, 454 F.2d 746, 172 U.S.P.Q. 391, 395 (C.C.P.A. 1972).

ᴡ

The relevant inquiry under the how-to-make requirement of paragraph one of 35 U.S.C. §112 is whether the scope of enablement provided to one of ordinary skill in the art by the disclosure is commensurate in scope with the protection sought by the claims. *In re Cescon*, 474 F.2d 1331, 177 U.S.P.Q. 264, 267 (C.C.P.A. 1973).

ᴡ

A patent disclosure may be sufficient "to enable one skilled in the art to practice the" inventions defined by asserted claims without having any explicit teaching of how to make. *Illinois Tool Works Inc. v. Solo Cup Company*, 179 U.S.P.Q. 322, 369 (Ill. 1973).

ᴡ

Enabling requirements of the statute are satisfied when the specification, taken with the prior art, clearly teaches an effective process for making claimed compounds from known starting materials, and the specification describes methods of using the claimed compounds. *Ex parte Gastambide, Thal, Rohrbach, and Laroche*, 189 U.S.P.Q. 643, 645 (PTO Bd. App. 1974).

How to Use.

With regard to the how-to-use requirement of 35 U.S.C. §112, the parent application contains no information whatever concerning methods or manner of administration or dosages, for instance. In short, there is a complete absence of express disclosure of how to use the claimed compounds. Such a lack, however, does not per se render the disclosure inadequate under §112. All the statute requires is that the disclosure be one that will "enable any person skilled in the art to which it pertains, or with which it is most nearly connected," to make and use the invention. Thus, where the manner of using a claimed compound is obvious to one of ordinary skill in the particular art, even though the specification is utterly barren of any express teaching on how to use it, there can be compliance with §112. *In re Hitchings, Elion, and Goodman*, 342 F.2d 80, 144 U.S.P.Q. 637, 642 (C.C.P.A. 1965).

Human.

Where "a human being substitutes for a part of the claimed structure," the infringement standard under 35 U.S.C. §112, §6, that the structure be the same as or equivalent to that disclosed in the specification, is not met. As a matter of law, the exercise of human judgment is not an equivalent of software. *Clintec Nutrition Co. v. Baxa Corp.*, 988 F.Supp. 1109, 44 U.S.P.Q.2d 1719, 1724, 1730 (Ill. 1997).

Human Use.

It is not proper for the Patent Office to require clinical testing in humans to rebut a *prima facie* case for lack of utility when the pertinent references which establish the *prima facie* case show in vitro tests and when they do not show in vivo tests employing standard experimental animals. *In re Langer*, 503 F.2d 1380, 183 U.S.P.Q. 288, 297 (C.C.P.A. 1974).

ᴡ

Even though the ultimate purpose of the claimed compounds was for treatment of human beings, successful testing and use in standard laboratory animals was adequate for a reduction to practice. *Hughes and Smith v. Windholz, Patchett, and Fried*, 184 U.S.P.Q. 753, 757 (PO Bd. Pat. Intf. 1974).

ᵹ

Early filing of an application with its disclosure of novel compounds which possess significant therapeutic use is to be encouraged. Requiring specific testing of the thousands of prostaglandin analogs encompassed by the present claim in order to satisfy the how-to-use requirement of 35 U.S.C. §112 would delay disclosure and frustrate, rather than further, the interests of the public. *In re Bundy*, 642 F.2d 430, 209 U.S.P.Q. 48, 52 (C.C.P.A. 1981).

ᵹ

Amelioration of the symptoms or even cure of cancer is no longer considered to be "incredible." Nonetheless, decisional law would seem to indicate that the utility in question is sufficiently unusual to justify an Examiner's requiring substantiating evidence. Substantiating evidence may be in the form of animal tests that constitute recognized screening procedures with clear relevance to utility in humans. The specification of the appellant's parent application sets forth several animal tests on numerous types of specific cancers as well as in vitro studies, both of which are asserted to be predictive with regard to utility in humans. The Examiner has not challenged the evidence presented in a single, relevant, material respect. There is only the blanket statement of lack of "patentable utility" per se. In fact, the only specific comments the Examiner has directed toward the appellant's evidence are with regard to the breadth of the types of tumor against which the claimed compounds have been shown to be active. The appealed claims are drawn to compounds and not to a method of treatment. Generally speaking, utility in treating a single disease is adequate basis for the patentability of a pharmaceutical compound under 35 U.S.C. §101. *Ex parte Krepelka*, 231 U.S.P.Q. 746 (B.P.A.I. 1986).

Hunch. *See* **Fact.**

Hybrid.[1,2] *See also* **35 U.S.C. §102/§103, Utilize.**

Under *In re Jones* [58 App. D.C. 379, 30 F.2d 1003 (1929)], a product claim cannot properly contain limitations as to the structure and mode of operation of the machine by

---

[1]The fact that a dependent claim is in a different statutory class from the independent claim from which it depends does not, in itself, render the dependent claim improper. Thus, if Claim 1 recites a specific product, a claim for the method of making the product of Claim 1 in a particular manner would be a proper dependent claim, since it could not be infringed without infringing Claim 1. Similarly, if Claim 1 recites a method of making a product, a claim for a product made by the method of Claim 1 could be a proper dependent claim. On the other hand, if Claim 1 recites a method of making a specified product, a claim to the product set forth in Claim 1 would not be a proper dependent claim if the product might be made in other ways. [*Commissioner's Notice*, 942 O.G. 15, June 8, 1966—MPEP §608.01(n)].

A hybrid claim is one that is so drafted that the statutory class to which the claim belongs is not clear from the claim language. An example is Claim 12 of USP 4,626,462 (1073 O.G. 393):

12 The circuit element of claim 11 including the steps of: forming at least one conductive through-hole in said flexible laminate unit in a location outside of said bending region; and forming a circuit pattern in said second conductive layer, a portion of said circuit pattern being formed over said space.

[2]Claims directed to hybrid seeds and to hybrid plants have been allowed because the PVPA and the PPA exclude such subject matter. *Ex parte Hibberd*, 227 U.S.P.Q. 443, 444 n.1 (B.P.A.I. 1985).

which the article sought to be patented is made. There is no proper basis for distinguishing that case merely because the article manufactured in the instant case is the result of a chemical process rather than the result of the operation of a machine. *Levin v. Coe, Commissioner of Patents*, 131 F.2d 589, 55 U.S.P.Q. 224 (D.C. Cir. 1942).

ᛒ

It is improper to include structural limitations in a process claim. *In re Vincent*, 135 F.2d 936, 57 U.S.P.Q. 557, 559 (C.C.P.A. 1943).

ᛒ

A rejection of claims under 35 U.S.C. §102/103 is a hybrid rejection having apparently been made on the theory that, if the claimed subject matter was novel (i.e., not anticipated) in terms of §102, then it would have been obvious under §103. The PTO's practice of basing rejections on §102 or §103 in the alternative has been accepted, provided that appellant is fully apprised of all the grounds of rejection. *In re Spada*, 911 F.2d 705, 15 U.S.P.Q.2d 1655, 1657 (Fed. Cir. 1990).

ᛒ

A combination of two separate and distinct statutory classes of invention is not permitted in a single claim. Patents are authorized by statute, and Congress has indicated that inventions may be patentable only if they fall within one of the statutory classes of subject matter specified in 35 U.S.C. §101 (e.g., "process, machine, manufacture or composition of matter"). *Ex parte Lyell*, 17 U.S.P.Q.2d 1548, 1551 (B.P.A.I. 1990).

ᛒ

A claim that incorporates by reference *all* of the subject matter of another claim (the claim is not broader in any respect) is in compliance with the fourth paragraph of 35 U.S.C. §112. *Ex parte Porter*, 25 U.S.P.Q.2d 1144, 1147 (B.P.A.I. 1992).

ᛒ

Neither the First Circuit nor the Supreme Court has ever addressed the question whether a hybrid agreement in which patents issue can ever survive the expiration or invalidation of the patents where there is a provision for allocation of payments between patent and non-patent rights. Although a hybrid royalty agreement was unenforceable because there was no allocation of the percentage of royalties attributable to trade secrets and know-how, licensor was entitled to compensation for non-patent rights to prevent unjust enrichment. *Baladevon Inc. v. Abbott Laboratories Inc.*, 871 F.Supp. 89, 33 U.S.P.Q.2d 1743, 1747 (Mass. 1994).

Hybridoma.

The claimed invention had been reduced to practice prior to the filing date of the subject application, and the appellants had agreed to deposit the hybridoma cell lines at a recognized depository upon the patent grant. In the interim, the cell lines were being maintained at Sloan-Kettering, an institution of renown and integrity. This was regarded as in full compliance with the requirements imposed upon the appellants under *Lundak* [773 F.2d 1216, 227 U.S.P.Q. 90 (Fed. Cir. 1985)].

Although the technique underlying hybridoma technology is well recognized, the results obtained by its use are clearly unpredictable. Hybridoma technology is an empirical art in which the routineer is unable to foresee what particular antibodies will be produced and which specific surface antigens will be recognized by them. Only by actually carrying out the requisite steps can the nature of the monoclonal antibodies be determined and ascertained; no "expected" results can thus be said to be present. Hence, it may be "obvious to try" the Kohler-Milstein technique as applied to malignant renal cells, but such is not the standard under which obviousness under 35 U.S.C. §103 must be established. *Ex parte Old*, 229 U.S.P.Q. 196 (B.P.A.I. 1985).

Hydrocarbon.

A rejection under the first paragraph of 35 U.S.C. §112 based on the alleged failure of a specification to support claims containing the terms, "alkyl", "alkoxy", "alkylene" and "a divalent hydrocarbon radical", was reversed. The claims which contained these terms were no broader than the broadest written description of the invention in the specification. Moreover, the Examiner provided no reason why any particular alkyl, alkoxy, alkylene or hydrocarbon group would be expected to be inoperative in the environment of the claimed dyes. *Ex parte Altermatt*, 183 U.S.P.Q. 436, 437, 438 (PO Bd. App. 1974).

Hypothetical Claim.

A patentee may carry his burden of proving a range of equivalents by reference to a hypothetical claim. *Cameco Industries Inc. v. Louisiana Cane Manufacturing Inc.*, 34 U.S.P.Q.2d 1309, 1312 (La. 1995).

Hypothetical Claim Analysis.

Hypothetical claim analysis is an optional way of evaluating whether prior art limits the application of the doctrine of equivalents. It is simply a way of expressing the well-established principle "that a patentee should not be able to obtain, under the doctrine of equivalents, coverage which he could not lawfully have obtained from the PTO by literal claims." *International Visual Corp. v. Crown Metal Manufacturing Co. Inc.*, 991 F.2d 768, 26 U.S.P.Q.2d 1588, 1591 (Fed. Cir. 1993).

Hypothetical Person. *See also* Mosita, Skill of the Art.

The issue of obviousness is determined entirely with reference to a hypothetical "person having ordinary skill in the art." It is only that hypothetical person who is presumed to be aware of all the pertinent prior art. The actual inventor's skill is irrelevant to the inquiry, and this is for a very important reason. The statutory emphasis is on a person of ordinary skill. Inventors, as a class, according to the concepts underlying the Constitution and the statutes that have created the patent system, possess something that sets them apart from the workers of ordinary skill, and one should not go about determining obviousness under 35 U.S.C. §103 by inquiring into what patentees (i.e., inventors) would have known or would have been likely to have done faced with the revelation of references. A person of ordinary skill in the art is also presumed to be one who thinks along the line of conventional wisdom in the art and is not one who undertakes to innovate, whether by patient, and often expensive, systematic research or by extraordinary insight; it makes no difference which. *The Standard Oil Company v. American Cyanamid Co.*, 774 F.2d 448, 227 U.S.P.Q. 293 (Fed. Cir. 1985).

ω

That secondary considerations are not considered unless there is evidence that those in the industry knew of the prior art is a non sequitur. Evidence of secondary considerations is considered independently of what any real person knows about the prior art. These considerations are objective criteria of obviousness that help illuminate the subjective determination involved in the hypothesis used to draw the legal conclusion of obviousness based upon the first three factual inquiries delineated in *Graham* [383 U.S. 1, 148 U.S.P.Q. 459 (S. Ct. 1966)]. Thus, to require that actual inventors in the field have the omniscience of the hypothetical person in the art is not only contrary to case law, but eliminates a useful tool for trial judges faced with a non-obviousness determination. *Hodosh v. Block Drug Co.*, 786 F.2d 1136, 229 U.S.P.Q. 182 (Fed. Cir. 1985).

ω

The issue of obviousness is determined entirely with reference to a hypothetical "person having ordinary skill in the art." It is only that person who is presumed to be aware of all the pertinent art. There are six factors relevant to a determination of the level or ordinary skill: educational level of the inventor, type of problems encountered in the art, prior art solutions, rapidity of innovation, sophistication of technology, and educational level of active workers in the field. *Bausch & Lomb, Inc. v. Barnes-Hind/Hydrocurve, Inc.*, 796 F.2d 443, 230 U.S.P.Q. 416 (Fed. Cir. 1986).

ω

Knowledge of all prior art in the field of the inventor's endeavor and of prior-art solutions for a common problem (even if outside that field) is attributed to the hypothetical person of ordinary skill in the art. *In re Nilssen*, 851 F.2d 1401, 7 U.S.P.Q.2d 1500 (Fed. Cir. 1988).

ω

The inquiry into obviousness focuses on what would have been obvious to a hypothetical person having ordinary skill in the art. The actual inventor's skill is irrelevant to the inquiry. One should not go about determining obviousness under 35 U.S.C. §103 by inquiring into what patentees (i.e., inventors) would have known or would likely have done. *E. I. du Pont de Nemours & Co. v. Cetus Corp.*, 19 U.S.P.Q.2d 1174, 1183 (Cal. 1990).

ω

The person of ordinary skill is a hypothetical person who is presumed to be aware of all the pertinent prior art. The actual inventor's skill is not determinative. Factors that may be considered in determining level of skill include: type of problems encountered in art; prior art solutions to those problems; rapidity with which innovations are made; sophistication of the technology; and education level of active workers in the field. Not all such factors may be present in every case, and one or more of them may predominate. *Ex parte GPAC Inc.*, 29 U.S.P.Q.2d 1401, 1413 (B.P.A.I. 1993).

Hypothetical Structure.

The test of whether a particular compound described in the prior art may be relied upon to show that claimed subject matter would have been obvious is whether the prior art provides an enabling disclosure with respect to the disclosed prior art compound. No evidence was offered to show an enabling disclosure for the reference structure, while uncontroverted testimony showed the reference structure to be a hypothetical structure. *Ashland Oil, Inc. v. Delta Resins & Refractories, Inc.*, 776 F.2d 281, 227 U.S.P.Q. 657 (Fed. Cir. 1985).

Key Terms and Concepts

I

Icon.

The word "icon" does not limit a design to use with a display screen of a programmed computer or any other article of manufacture. Mere display of a picture on a screen is not significantly different from the display of a picture on a piece of paper. An integral and active component in the operation of a programmed computer displaying the design, if properly presented and claimed, constitutes statutory subject matter under 35 U.S.C. §171. *Ex parte Strijland*, 26 U.S.P.Q.2d 1259, 1263 (B.P.A.I. 1992).

Idea.

Every discovery is not embraced within the statutory terms of 35 U.S.C. §101. Excluded from such patent protection are laws of nature, physical phenomena, and abstract ideas. A principle, in the abstract, is a fundamental truth, an original cause, a motive; these cannot be patented, and no one can claim in any of them an exclusive right. A new mineral discovered in the earth or a new plant found in the wild is not patentable subject matter. Likewise, Einstein could not patent his celebrated law that $E = mc^2$; nor could Newton have patented the law of gravity. Such discoveries are "manifestations of...nature, free to all men and reserved exclusively to none." *Diamond v. Diehr and Lutton*, 450 U.S. 175, 209 U.S.P.Q. 1, 7 (1981).

Identical.

Because all of the claims of the reexamined patent are now in the category of a "proposed amended or new claim determined to be patentable and incorporated following a reexamination proceeding," those claims have the same effect as that specified in 35 U.S.C. §252 for reissue patents. The first paragraph of §252 makes clear that, if claims in an original and in a reissue patent are "identical", the reissue patent is deemed to have effect from the date of the original patent. If not, then the patentee has no rights to enforce before the date of reissue because the original patent was surrendered and is dead. In context, "identical" means "without substantive change." *Kaufman Co. v. Lantech Inc.*, 807 F.2d 970, 1 U.S.P.Q.2d 1202, 1206, 1207 (Fed. Cir. 1986).

ω

In the reissue statute "identical" means without substantive change. *Slimfold Manufacturing Co. Inc. v. Kinkead Industries Inc.*, 810 F.2d 1113, 1 U.S.P.Q.2d 1563 (Fed. Cir. 1987).

ω

"Identical" does not mean verbatim. No more rigorous standard is intended for reexamined claims than for reissued claims, wherein precedent has established that "identical" in 35 U.S.C. §252 means without substantive change in the scope of the claims. A claim made more definite by adding a term from the specification, without change in scope, is not substantively changed, and the claims are "legally identical." *The Laitram Corp. v. NEC Corp.*, 952 F.2d 1357, 21 U.S.P.Q.2d 1276, 1279 (Fed. Cir. 1991).

Identification.

It is possible to disclose a compound without actually isolating it and identifying it. Even for an actual reduction to practice, a chemical compound may be sufficiently identified by a partial analysis of the compound when considered with other factors. *Hauptschein, Braid, and Lawlor v. McCane and Robinson*, 339 F.2d 460, 144 U.S.P.Q. 16, 19 (C.C.P.A. 1964).

ㅍ

In an interference setting, the identification of new chemical compounds is inadequate when based entirely on the testimony of witnesses who allegedly received their information from the inventor. Inventor's reports cannot be relied upon for establishing the identity of subject compounds on the basis of the Federal shop book rule, 28 U.S.C. §1732. *Rochling, Buchel, and Korte v. Burton, Newbold, Percival, Lambie, Sencial*, 178 U.S.P.Q. 300, 302, 303 (PO Bd. Pat. Intf. 1971).

Identifying.

Steps, such as "computing", "determining", "cross-correlating", "comparing", "selecting", "initializing", "testing", "modifying", and "identifying", have implicitly been found to recite the solving of a mathematical algorithm. *In re Warmerdam*, 33 F.3d 1354, 31 U.S.P.Q.2d 1754, 1758 (Fed. Cir. 1994).

Identity of Invention.

Identity of invention is a question of fact, and one who seeks such a finding must show that each element of the claim in issue is found, either expressly or under principles of inherency, in a single prior art reference, or that the claimed invention was previously known or embodied in a single prior art device or practice. *Minnesota Mining and Manufacturing Co. v. Johnson & Johnson Orthopaedics Inc.*, 976 F.2d 1558, 24 U.S.P.Q.2d 1321, 1326 (Fed. Cir. 1992).

IDS. *See* Information Disclosure Statement.

If Present. *See* Alternative.

Ignorance. *See* Good Cause, Unknowable, Wrongful Intent.

Imagination. *See* Conjecture.

Imitation. *See also* **Copying.**

"Patent infringement, like other imitation, is the sincerest form of flattery." *Classic Corp. v. Charter Oak Fire Insurance Co.*, 35 U.S.P.Q.2d 1726, 1729 (Cal. 1995).

Immunity. *See* **Parker Immunity, States' Immunity.**

Impetus. *See* **Common Properties, Direction, Incentive, Motivation.**

Implicit Decision.

The proposition that issues decided implicitly by courts of appeals may not be reexamined by the district court is actually applicable only to those issues decided by *necessary* implication. *Laitram Corp. v. NEC Corp.*, 42 U.S.P.Q.2d 1897, 1900 (Fed. Cir. 1997).

Implied Cause of Action.

The question of when it is appropriate for the judiciary to recognize an implied cause of action rests upon the application of a four-factor inquiry: (1) whether the plaintiff is "one of the class for whose especial benefit the statute was enacted"; (2) whether there exists "any indication of legislative intent, explicit or implicit, either to create such a remedy or to deny one"; (3) whether it is "consistent with the underlying purposes of the legislative scheme to imply such a remedy"; and (4) whether "the cause of action [is] one traditionally relegated to state law . . . so that it would be inappropriate to infer a cause of action based solely on federal law". *Laerdall Medical Corp. v. Ambu Inc.*, 877 F.Supp. 255, 34 U.S.P.Q.2d 1140, 1144 (Md. 1995).

Implied License.[1]

A patentee, in demanding and receiving full compensation for the wrongful use of his invention in devices made and sold by a manufacturer, adopts the sales as made by himself, and, therefore, necessarily licenses the use of the devices, and frees them from the monopoly of the patent. *Union Tool Co. v. Wilson*, 259 U.S. 107, 113 (1922).

ϖ

No implied license results from circumstances which demonstrate disagreement between the parties, since an implied license can arise only from conduct of the parties which forces the conclusion that they are in accord. *Core Laboratories, Inc. v. Hayward-Wolff Research Corp.*, 136 A.2d 553, 115 U.S.P.Q. 422, 425 (Del. S. Ct. 1957).

ϖ

While an implied license does not require a formal agreement, there must be conduct on the part of the patentee from which the infringer may properly infer that the patentee

---

[1]*See* Gregory M. Luck, "The Implied License: an Evolving Defense to Patent Infringement", *IPL Newsletter*, Vol. 16, No. 1, page 3, Fall 1997.

consents to the use of the patent. *Minnesota Mining and Manufacturing Company v. Berwick Industries, Inc.*, 373 F.Supp. 851, 182 U.S.P.Q. 111, 124 (Pa. 1974).

ω

A patented process cannot be used to "tie" sales of an unpatented staple commodity (having substantial non-infringing use) used in the process. Sales of the staple commodity accompanied by an implied (can label) license to practice the patented process constitutes a non de minimus tying arrangment in violation of §1 of the Sherman Act and constitutes patent misuse, making the patent unenforceable. *Rex Chainbelt Inc. v. Harco Products, Inc.*, 512 F.2d 993, 185 U.S.P.Q. 10 (9th Cir. 1975).

ω

Under the patent law, no formal granting of a license is necessary in order to give it effect. Where the owner of a patent exhibits conduct from which one dealing with him may properly infer that the owner consents to his use of the patent, an implied license will arise. *Sanofi, S.A. v. Med-Tech Veterinarian Products, Inc.*, 565 F.Supp. 931, 220 U.S.P.Q. 416, 422 (N.J. 1983).

ω

A patent owner's unrestricted sales of a machine useful only in performing the claimed process and producing the claimed product "plainly indicate that the grant of a license should be inferred" for the patent owner's customers. *Met-Coil Systems Corp. v. Korners Unlimited, Inc.*, 803 F.2d 684, 231 U.S.P.Q. 474, 476 (Fed. Cir. 1986).

ω

The existence of an implied license is a question of law. There are two requirements for the grant of an implied license by virtue of a sale of nonpatented equipment used to practice a patented invention. First, the equipment involved must have no noninfringing uses. Second, the circumstances of sale must "plainly indicate that the grant of a license should be inferred." *Hoppe v. Baxter Healthcare Corp.*, 878 F.Supp. 303, 34 U.S.P.Q.2d 1619, 1623 (Mass. 1995).

ω

"[N]o license can be implied, where . . . the equipment involved has other noninfringing uses, even if only as replacement parts," and "[a] mere sale does not import a license except where the circumstances clearly indicate that the grant of a license should be inferred." The burden of proving the existence of an implied license is on the accused infringer. *LifeScan Inc. v. Polymer Technology International Corp.*, 35 U.S.P.Q.2d 1225, 1231, 1236 (Wash. 1995).

ω

The sale of nonpatented equipment to practice a patented invention results in an implied license, which, like an express license, is a defense to patent infringement. Unless the circumstances indicate otherwise, an implied license arising from sale of a component to be used in a patented combination extends only for the life of the component whose sale and purchase created the license. *The Carborundum Co. v. Molten Metal Equipment Innovations Inc.*, 72 F.3d 872, 37 U.S.P.Q.2d 1169, 1172, 1173 (Fed. Cir. 1995).

ω

An implied license is a form of implied-in-fact contract. In order to proved [sic] the defense of implied license, defendant must establish by a preponderance of the evidence that (1) there was an existing relationship between plaintiff and defendant; (2) within that relationship, plaintiff transferred a right to use the invention to defendant; (3) the right was transferred for valuable consideration; and (4) plaintiff has now denied the existence of the right it transferred to defendant. *Wang Laboratories Inc. v. Mitsubishi Electronics America Inc.*, 103 F.3d 1571, 41 U.S.P.Q.2d 1263, 1268 (Fed. Cir. 1997).

ϖ

To establish an implied license, the product sold by the patentee or its licensee "must have no noninfringing uses" and the circumstances of sale must "plainly indicate that the grant of an implied license should be inferred." *Elkay Manufacturing Co. v. Abco Manufacturing Co.*, 99 F.3d 1160, 42 U.S.P.Q.2d 1555, 1557 (Fed. Cir. 1996—*unpublished*).

ϖ

When a seller sells a product without restriction, it in effect promises the purchaser that, in exchange for the price paid, it will not interfere with the purchaser's full enjoyment of the product purchased. The buyer has an implied license under any patents of the seller that dominate the product or any uses of the product to which the parties might reasonably contemplate the product will be put. *Hewlett-Packard Co. v. Repeat-O-Type Stencil Manufacturing Corp.*, 123 F.3d 1445, 43 U.S.P.Q.2d 1650, 1655 (Fed. Cir. 1997).

ϖ

The appointment of a distributor to sell a product covered by a patent is analogous to a grant of a patent license. Such an action conveys an implied license to the distributor, thereby surrendering the patentee's right to exclude the distributor under the patent. *Genetic Implant Systems Inc. v. Core-Vent Corp.*, 123 F.3d 1455, 43 U.S.P.Q.2d 1786, 1789 (Fed. Cir. 1997).

ϖ

No formal granting of a license is necessary in order to give it effect. Any language used by the owner of the patent, or any conduct on his part exhibited to another from which that other may properly infer that the owner consents to the use of his patent in making or using it, or selling it, upon which the other acts, constitutes a license and a defense to an action for a tort. *Hewlett-Packard Co. v. Pitney Bowes Corp.*, 46 U.S.P.Q.2d 1595, 1600 (Ore. 1998).

Importation. *See also* Exclusion Order, Industry, Tariff Act, 35 U.S.C. §271(g).

A nonproducing patentee or licensee about to begin production operations, an "embryo industry", can be entitled to a Commission remedy under section 337 of the Tariff Act (19 U.S.C. §1337) if such party can prove it is prevented from being established. Parties seeking Commission remedies under the prevention clause of section 337 must show a readiness to commence production. *In re Certain Ultra-Microtome Freezing Attachments*, 195 U.S.P.Q. 653, 656, 657 (U.S. Int'l Trade Comm'n 1976).

ϖ

The U.S. patent holder's rights in the United States cannot be diminished by the importation of a patented product made by a licensee under a corresponding patent in another country. *In re Reclosable Plastic Bags*, 192 U.S.P.Q. 674, 679 (U.S. Intl. Trade Commn. 1977).

ᚦ

Four factors often considered in 337 (19 U.S.C. §1337) investigations are: (1) significant reduction is sales; (2) idling of production facilities; (3) decrease in employment; and (4) decline in profitability. Two prerequisites to the enforcement to any Commission cease and desist order by use of the Commission's civil fine authority in 19 U.S.C. §1337(f)(2) are: (1) a finding of jurisdiction over the subject matter, that is, a finding that the unfair acts complained of involve the importation of articles into the United States or sale of imported articles, and (2) a finding of in personam jurisdiction over the persons whose acts are sought to be enjoined. *In re Certain Large Video Matrix Display Systems and Components Thereof*, 213 U.S.P.Q. 475, 485, 488 (U.S. Int'l Trade Comm'n 1981).

ᚦ

The use of a process in a foreign country that would infringe the claims of a U.S. process patent (if the process were practiced in the United States) constitutes an unfair practice under 19 U.S.C. §1337(a) when the foreign article manufactured according to the patented process is imported into the United States. [See also 35 U.S.C. §271(g).] *In re Certain Miniature Plug-In Blade Fuses*, 221 U.S.P.Q. 792 (U.S. Intl. Trade Commn. 1983).

ᚦ

Whenever a claim of unfair practice in import trade is premised upon infringement of a United States patent, there is an unavoidable overlap of issues involved in parallel patent proceedings. The ITC is confronted with the necessity of making a "determination" as to the validity, infringement and, if applicable, enforceability of the identical patents which are at issue in the district court. This overlap of issues in the ITC and district court is where the similarity ends. The two proceedings have different jurisdictional foundations, different final adjudications, different purposes, different proof, different time constraints, different remedies, and different issues on appeal. *Diversified Products Corporation v. Weslo Design International*, 228 U.S.P.Q. 726, 729 (Del. 1985).

ᚦ

The terms "importation" and "import" in 35 U.S.C. §271(g) (and the term "imported" in §9006 of the Act) are to have their plain or ordinary meaning of bringing goods into the United States from another country. This term does not depend on or require an analysis of the intent of the person in bringing the goods into the United States. Furthermore, it is not necessary that the goods in issue have passed through U.S. Customs to be imported under §271(g) and §9006 of the Act. *Bristol-Meyers Co. v. Erbamont Inc.*, 723 F. Supp. 1038, 13 U.S.P.Q.2d 1517, 1522 (Del. 1989).

ᚦ

Section 337(a)(1)(B)(ii) of 19 U.S.C. was not intended to prohibit the importation of articles made abroad by a process in which a product claimed in a U.S. patent is used.

Amgen Inc. v. U.S. International Trade Commission, 902 F.2d 1532, 14 U.S.P.Q.2d 1734, 1739 (Fed. Cir. 1990).

ʊ

The PPAA made it an act of patent infringement to import, sell, or use in the United States, without authorization, a product made by a process patented in the United States. 35 U.S.C.A. §271(g). A provision concerning offers to sell was added to 35 U.S.C. §271(g) by the Uruguay Round Agreements Act. *Bio-Technology General Corp. v. Genentech Inc.*, 80 F.3d 1553, 38 U.S.P.Q.2d 1321, 1324 n.4 (Fed. Cir. 1996).

Impossible.

A rejection based on indefiniteness cannot stand simply because the proportions recited in the claims may be read in theory to include compositions that are impossible in fact to formulate. "Subject matter which cannot exist in fact can neither anticipate nor infringe in law." *In re Kroekel and Pfaff,* 504 F.2d 1143, 183 U.S.P.Q. 610, 612 (C.C.P.A. 1974).

Imprimatur.

While the granting of a patent does not legally constitute a certificate that a medicine to which it relates is a good medicine or will cure the disease or successfully make the test which it was intended to do, nevertheless, the granting of such a patent gives a kind of official imprimatur to the medicine in question on which as a moral matter some members of the public are likely to rely. *Isenstead v. Watson*, 157 F.Supp. 7, 115 U.S.P.Q. 408, 410 (D.C. 1957).

Improper Comments. *See* New Trial.

Improper Conduct.

Dismissal, while a sanction the district court may properly impose, is "draconian" and "must be infrequently resorted to by the district courts." In general, dismissal is such a serious sanction it should not be invoked without first considering the effect the improper conduct had on the course of the litigation. *Tec-Air Inc. v. Nippondenso Manufacturing USA Inc.*, 33 U.S.P.Q.2d 1451, 1452 (Ill. 1994).

Improper Markush.[2] *See also* Joinder of Invention, Markush, Misjoinder, Unity of Invention.

An improper Markush claim or group is one in which the members of the group include patentably distinct members. No statute or rule of practice pursuant thereto gives

---

[2]A Markush-type claim can include independent and distinct inventions. This is true when two or more of the members are so unrelated and diverse that a prior art reference anticipating the claim with respect to one of the members would not render the clasim obvious under 35 U.S.C. §103 with respect to the other member(s). MPEP §803.02

a right to an applicant to present this form of claim. Neither 35 U.S.C. §131 nor Patent Office Rule 104(a) [37 C.F.R. §1.104(a)] compels the Commissioner to examine improper Markush-type claims, and certainly not those that are directed to multiple inventions. *Rohm and Haas Company v. Commissioner of Patents*, 387 F.Supp. 673, 177 U.S.P.Q. 625, 626, 627 (D.C. 1973).

ᛒ

Claims had been withdrawn from further consideration on the ground that they included multiple "patentably distinct" inventions. The claims were withdrawn from consideration not only in the subject application but prospectively in a subsequent application because of their content. In effect there had been a denial of patentability of the claims. The absolute "withdrawal" cannot properly be categorized as merely a "requirement" or "objection" to restrict review to petition. An Examiner's action of this nature is a rejection, a denial of substantive rights. *In re Haas*, 486 F.2d 1053, 179 U.S.P.Q. 623 (C.C.P.A. 1973).

ᛒ

An applicant has a right to define what he regards as his invention as he chooses, so long as his definition is distinct, as required by the second paragraph of 35 U.S.C. §112, and supported by enabling disclosure, as required by the first paragraph of 35 U.S.C. §112. *In re Harnisch*, 631 F.2d 716, 206 U.S.P.Q. 300, 305 (C.C.P.A. 1980).

Improper Practices.

Improper practices in connection with patents include use of invalid patents in price fixing, cross-licensing of patents, attempts to extend the scope of patent monopoly, illegal price fixing activities in connection with patents, tying patents to unpatented devices or processes, and seeking to extend the effect of an expired patent. *BEAL Corp. Liquidating Trust v. Valleylab Inc.*, 40 U.S.P.Q.2d 1072, 1077 (Col. 1996).

Improvement. *See also* Advance the Art, Advantage, Avoiding Infringement, Crowded Art.

When a later-filed application to an improvement by a different inventive entity issues as a patent before a copending application (of the same assignee) to the generic invention, claims in the earlier-filed generic application are not properly rejectable over claims of the improvement patent on the ground of double patenting when all the claims of the improvement patent are limited to the improvement and none of the patent claims is readable on the disclosure of the pending application. *In re Stanley and Lowe*, 214 F.2d 151, 102 U.S.P.Q. 234, 239, 240 (C.C.P.A. 1954).

ᛒ

If those skilled in the mechanical arts are working in a given field and have failed to discover a new and useful improvement, the one who first makes the discovery frequently has done more than make an obvious improvement which would have suggested itself to a mechanic skilled in the art, and such an invention is entitled to the grant of a patent thereon. *In re Sporck*, 301 F.2d 686, 133 U.S.P.Q. 360, 363 (C.C.P.A. 1962).

ᛒ

An inventor should be allowed to dominate future patentable inventions of others where those inventions are based in some way on his teachings. Such improvements, while non-obvious from his teachings, are still within his contribution, since the improvement is made possible by his work. It is equally apparent, however, that he must not be permitted to achieve this dominance by claims that are insufficiently supported and hence not in compliance with the first paragraph of 35 U.S.C. §112. That paragraph requires that the scope of the claims must bear a reasonable correlation to the scope of enablement provided by the specification to persons of ordinary skill in the art. In cases involving predictable factors, such as mechanical or electrical elements, a single embodiment provides broad enablement in the sense that, once imagined, other embodiments can be made without difficulty and their performance characteristics predicted by resort to known scientific laws. In cases involving unpredictable factors, such as most chemical reactions and physiological activity, the scope of enablement obviously varies inversely with the degree of unpredictability of the factors involved. *In re Fisher,* 427 F.2d 833, 166 U.S.P.Q. 18 (C.C.P.A. 1970).

ᚖ

The standard of patentability does not depend upon a showing of advantages or improvements, but rather upon obviousness. The Examiner's failure to indicate any reason for finding obvious the alteration of the ratio employed in the prior art in the direction and manner claimed renders the rejection untenable. *Ex parte Parthasarathy and Ciapetta,* 174 U.S.P.Q. 63 (PTO Bd. App. 1971).

ᚖ

To be patentable, an invention need not advance the art in the sense that it be shown to be better than that which came before. *Ex parte Maxey and Harrington,* 177 U.S.P.Q. 468 (PTO Bd. App. 1972).

ᚖ

Work done on improvements which were not required to reduce to practice the subject matter of an interference count cannot be relied upon to establish required diligence during a critical period. *Fleming v. Bosch and Pollmann,* 181 U.S.P.Q. 761, 765 (PO Bd. Pat. Intf. 1973).

ᚖ

The presence of an improved result is persuasive of patentability, but the absence of such a showing is not conclusive of unpatentability. *Ex parte Kaiser,* 194 U.S.P.Q. 47, 48 (PTO Bd. App. 1975).

ᚖ

Most patents are granted on an improvement of a prior device. The improved device inherently achieves the same basic result as that achieved, and performs the same basic function as that performed, by the prior device. To require in every case that a new "function" or new "result" be performed or achieved would be destructive of "the progress of . . . useful arts" goal sought in the constitutional-statutory scheme. *Nickola v. Peterson,* 580 F.2d 898, 198 U.S.P.Q. 385, 397 (6th Cir. 1978).

ᚖ

The reference in Jepson-type claims to the "improvement" clearly says that the defined invention was subsequent in time to the subject matter defined in the Jepson preamble. *Margolis, Rushmore, Liu, and Anderson v. Banner,* 599 F.2d 435, 202 U.S.P.Q. 365, 368 n.3 (C.C.P.A. 1979).

ಹ

Nothing in the patent statute requires that an invention be superior to prior art in order to be patentable. Any superiority or lack of it is irrelevant to the question of obviousness. *Ryco Inc. v. Ag-Bag Corp.,* 857 F.2d 1418, 8 U.S.P.Q.2d 1323 (Fed. Cir. 1988).

Impure. *See* **Advance the Art.**

Imputation.

Imputation creates burdens both for clients and lawyers. Imputation means that a client who wishes to be represented by a trusted or highly recommended lawyer may not retain that lawyer as counsel. Imputation may prohibit literally hundreds of lawyers in several cities from acting even though only one of their number is personally prohibited from acting. Concern about prospective imputed prohibition may inhibit mobility of lawyers from one firm or employer to another. It therefore is important that imputation not inappropriately inhibit the mobility of lawyers. The burden of prohibition should end when material risks to confidentiality and loyalty resulting from shared income and access to information have been avoided by appropriate measures." *Decora Inc. v. DW Wallcovering Inc.,* 38 U.S.P.Q.2d 1188, 1190 1194 (N.Y. 1995).

Inactivity. *See also* **Delay.**

Passage of a long period between reduction to practice and filing can raise an inference that the purported reduction to practice was an abandoned experiment. This inference only arises where there is doubt that the activities relied upon constitute a reduction to practice. Corporate inactivity subsequent to the inventor's filing his invention disclosure does not raise an inference that the inventor later thought his work incomplete or unsuccessful. *Peeler, Godfrey, and Forby v. Miller,* 535 F.2d 647, 190 U.S.P.Q. 117, 122 (C.C.P.A. 1976).

Inadvertence. *See* **Error.**

Inadvertent. *See* **Error.**

In Camera Review. *See also* **Seal Record.**

A lesser evidentiary showing is needed to trigger in camera review than is required ultimately to overcome attorney-client privilege. Before engaging in in camera review to determine the applicability of the crime-fraud exception, the judge should require a showing of a factual basis, adequate to support a good faith belief by a reasonable person, that in camera review of the material may reveal evidence to establish a claim that the crime-fraud exception applies. *General Electric Co. v. Hoechst Celanese Corp.*, 740 F. Supp. 305, 15 U.S.P.Q.2d 1673, 1677 (Del. 1990).

Incentive. *See also* Modification, Motivation, Protection.

A novel chemical compound can be non-obvious to one having ordinary skill in the art notwithstanding that it may possess a known property in common with a known structurally similar compound. Where it is disclosed that the prior-art compound "cannot be regarded as useful" for the sole use disclosed, a person having ordinary skill in the art would lack the "necessary impetus" to make the claimed compound. *In re Albrecht*, 514 F.2d 1389, 185 U.S.P.Q. 585, 590 (C.C.P.A. 1975).

ω

To provide effective incentives, claims must adequately protect inventors. To demand that the first to disclose shall limit his claims to what he has found will work or to materials that meet the guidelines specified for "preferred" materials in a process would not serve the constitutional purpose of promoting progress in the useful arts. *In re Goffe*, 542 F.2d 564, 191 U.S.P.Q. 429, 431 (C.C.P.A. 1976).

ω

The differences between the prior art and the invention defined by the asserted claims, the availability of that art to all workers in the field, the failure of established competitors in a highly competitive market to make the invention despite the incentive to do so, the admittedly nonobvious performance benefits realized through the claimed invention, the impressive commercial success of the claimed product, the praise of independent commentators and the forbearance of competitors from infringing the patent all go to confirm that the claimed invention was not obvious at the time it was made to a person of ordinary skill in the art. *S. C. Johnson & Son, Inc. v. Carter-Wallace, Inc.*, 614 F. Supp. 1278, 225 U.S.P.Q. 1022 (N.Y. 1985).

ω

The interest of the public is in protecting patent rights, and the right of a patentee is in the exclusive use of his invention. Without the protection of the patent statute, the incentive to invent and to improve products would be curbed, and the public interest in such inventions would not be served. *The Conair Group Inc. v. Automatik Apparate-Maschinenbau GmbH*, 19 U.S.P.Q.2d 1535, 1540 (Pa. 1990).

ω

A general incentive does not make obvious a particular result, nor does existence of techniques by which those efforts can be carried out. *In re Deuel*, 51 F.3d 1552, 34 U.S.P.Q.2d 1210, 1216 (Fed. Cir. 1995).

Incentive to Disclose.

Bona fide attempts to design a non-infringing product are one of the beneficial results of the incentive-to-disclose system established by the patent statute. Bona fide of such attempts, however, are not governed solely by whether the words of a patent claim can be literally read on the newly designed product. The matter is not one for semantics alone.

An infringer appropriates an invention, not words; hence, the doctrine of equivalents. At the same time, the words of a claim may be so limited by the file history or by the prior art as to define an invention that was not appropriated; hence, the doctrine of estoppel. *Caterpillar Tractor Co. v. Berco, S.p.A.*, 714 F.2d 1110, 219 U.S.P.Q. 185 (Fed. Cir. 1983).

Including. *See also* Comprising.

The claim term "including" is synonymous with "comprising", thereby permitting the inclusion of unnamed components. *Hewlett-Packard Co. v. Repeat-O-Type Stencil Manufacturing Corp.*, 43 U.S.P.Q.2d 1650, 1655 (Fed. Cir. 1997).

Inclusio Unis Est Exclusio Alterius.

The doctrine *inclusio unis est exclusio alterius* instructs that where law expressly describes a particular situation to which it shall apply, an irrefutable inference must be drawn that what was omitted or excluded was intended to be omitted or excluded. *In re Lueders*, 42 U.S.P.Q.2d 1481, 1486 n.12 (Fed. Cir. 1997)

Incomplete. *See also* Fragment, Subcombination, Open-Ended Claim.

A rejection on the ground of indefiniteness because it is not apparent how elements recited in the claim cooperate to produce a unitary result will not be sustained when each of the elements of the claim appears to be sufficiently defined in its relation to other recited elements even though additional elements would be necessary to produce a complete operative machine. It is not a fatal defect where the recited elements define a proper subcombination. *In re Gartner and Roeber*, 223 F.2d 502, 106 U.S.P.Q. 273, 276 (C.C.P.A. 1955).

ω

It is entirely consistent with the claim definiteness requirement of the second paragraph of 35 U.S.C. §112 to present subcombination claims, drawn only to one aspect or combination of elements of an invention that has utility separate and apart from other aspects of the invention. It is not necessary that a claim recite each and every element needed for the practical utilization of the claimed subject matter. *Carl Zeiss Stiftung v. Renishaw plc*, 945 F.2d 1173, 20 U.S.P.Q.2d 1094, 1101 (Fed. Cir. 1991).

Inconceivable. *See also* Unbelievable.

Even though it may not be inconceivable to substitute sulfur for oxygen to obtain compounds having the same expected properties, that is not the standard; the standard is whether it would have been obvious in terms of 35 U.S.C. §103. *In re Grabiak*, 769 F.2d 729, 226 U.S.P.Q. 870 (Fed. Cir. 1985).

Inconsistent. *See also* Judicial Estoppel.

For the same counsel to take inconsistent positions in different litigation does not necessarily reflect bad faith. *Orthopedic Equipment Company, Inc. v. All Orthopedic Appliances, Inc.*, 707 F.2d 1376, 217 U.S.P.Q. 1281, 1287 (Fed. Cir. 1983).

ω

A patent owner will not be precluded from taking inconsistent positions in litigation unless the party opposing the subsequent position demonstrates either personal reliance on a decision granted in the prior suit, prejudice in the current litigation by reason of the prior decision, or the patent holder's apparent misuse of the court. *The Liposome Co. v. Vestar Inc.*, 36 U.S.P.Q.2d 1295, 1306 (Del. 1994).

Incorporate by Reference. *See also* **Access, Foreign Patent Application, New Matter.**

Already-abandoned applications less than twenty years old can be incorporated by reference to the same extent as copending applications. Both types are open to the public upon the referencing application issuing as a patent. *In re Fouche*, 439 F.2d 1237, 169 U.S.P.Q. 429, 431 n.1 (C.C.P.A. 1971).

ᛦ

A pending application, incorporated by reference in a subsequently-issued patent, is made an actual part of the patent disclosure. The specific legal incorporation by reference of such application must be construed as a waiver of the confidentiality requirement of 35 U.S.C. §122 insofar as it relates to the disclosure of the application. *In re Yang and Olsen*, 177 U.S.P.Q. 88, 89 (PO Solicitor 1973).

ᛦ

Because the Patent Commissioner has authority to and did issue a patent upon an application wherein the disclosure incorporates by reference a portion of a disclosure [which was "essential material" as defined by MPEP §608.01(p)] of a then existing patent that was available to the public, because there appears to be no abuse of discretion in doing so, and because the Examiner did not question the adequacy of the disclosure of the involved apparatus, the incorporation by reference was effective, and the claim was not held to be invalid as being without support in the disclosure. *Lundy Electronics & Systems, Inc. v. Optical Recognition Systems, Inc.*, 362 F. Supp. 130, 178 U.S.P.Q. 525, 539 (Va. 1973).

ᛦ

With respect to matters necessary for an enabling disclosure and which are not common and well known, an applicant may incorporate certain types of documents by specific reference in his application to such source materials. With regard to the doctrine of incorporation by reference "any reference to a disclosure which is available to the public is permissible." *In re Howarth*, 654 F.2d 103, 210 U.S.P.Q. 689, 692 (C.C.P.A. 1981).

ᛦ

Essential material, improperly incorporated by reference, can be bodily incorporated into an application. *Ernsthausen v. Nakayama*, 1 U.S.P.Q.2d 1539, 1548 (B.P.A.I. 1985).

ᛦ

Incorporating by reference a copending application that refers to identified prior art satisfies the duty to disclose at least to the extent of not withholding knowledge of such prior art from the PTO. *Corning Glass Works v. Sumitomo Electric U.S.A. Inc.*, 671 F. Supp. 1369, 5 U.S.P.Q.2d 1545, 1557, 1558 (N.Y. 1987).

ᛦ

In re Gallo [231 U.S.P.Q. 496 (1986)] established an alternative means for obtaining information that has been waived by incorporation, but it does not undo the holding of *Iron & Sears* [202 U.S.P.Q. 798 (D.C. Cir. 1979)], since the FOIA and administrative roots are separate. Since pending patent applications "are exempt in toto" from FOIA under *Iron & Sears*, and their contents are not subject to "a regime of selective excision" (202 U.S.P.Q. at 803), the plaintiff has no right of access to the information he seeks under FOIA. Although issued patents are subject to FOIA under *Iron & Sears*, *Gallo* does not establish that all material incorporated by reference in an issued patent automatically becomes part of the issued patent, thereby opening up the incorporated material to FOIA. Whether a waiver has occurred remains a matter for case-by-case determination at the PTO. *Leeds v. Quigg*, 720 F. Supp. 193, 11 U.S.P.Q.2d 1574, 1575 (D.C. 1989).

ω

MPEP §608.01(p) merely indicates that "particular attention should" be directed, not that such "must" be directed, to the specific portions of the referenced document, in order to obtain a proper incorporation by reference. *In re Goodwin*, 43 U.S.P.Q.2d 1856, 1859 (Comm'r Patents and Trademarks 1997—*unpublished*).

Incredible. *See* Unbelievable.

Incremental Income.

The incremental-income approach recognizes that, once fixed costs have been paid, it does not cost as much to produce additional units. *King Instrument Corp. v. Perego*, 737 F. Supp. 1227, 16 U.S.P.Q.2d 1994, 2006 (Mass. 1990).

Indefinite. *See* Indefiniteness.

Indefinite Article. *See also* A.

The claimed use of a solvent may be regarded as in the nature of a manipulative expedient. A number of solvents of widely different chemical structure and solvent action are disclosed. With knowledge that what is desired is a solvent that dissolves the starting materials but has little solvent action on the adduct, the average chemist can readily select many solvents other than those specifically named. Under these particular circumstances, the claims are not rejectable for undue breadth in use of the term "an organic solvent." *Ex parte Dubbs and Stevens*, 119 U.S.P.Q. 440, 441 (PO Bd. App. 1958).

ω

A rejection under 35 U.S.C. §112, second paragraph, of a claim defining a variable Y as "an unsubstituted or substituted alkyl, alkenyl, or alkynyl group of 1 to 18 carbon atoms, an unsubstituted or substituted cycloalkyl group having a 3 to 6 carbon atom ring and up to 12 carbon atoms, an unsubstituted or substituted aralkyl group of up to 10 carbon atoms, or an unsubstituted or substituted aryl group of up to 10 carbon atoms" was reversed. The claim was regarded as circumscribing a group of N-substituted isothiazolones with a reasonable degree of precision and particularity. *Ex parte Lewis, Miller, and Law*, 197 U.S.P.Q. 543, 544 (PTO Bd. App. 1977).

Indefiniteness. *See also* **Alternative, Aromatic, Aryl, Breadth, Conditions, Definiteness, Definition, Double Inclusion, Hybrid, Intelligible, Relative Terms, Test Method, 35 U.S.C. §112, Vague.**

A rejection of claims as failing to define the invention properly and based on the phrases "substituted mononuclear and polynuclear homocyclic compounds," "alkyl," "ester," and "heterocyclic and aromatic compounds being free of substituents containing aliphatic hydroxyl and amino groups," in process claims, was reversed. *Ex parte West-fahl,* 136 U.S.P.Q. 265 (PTO Bd. App. 1962).

ഌ

The ability of the Examiner to enumerate radicals encompassed by the claim language points up the weakness of the indefiniteness argument. Giving the language its broadest possible meaning, the breadth of the claim is indeed immense. However, breadth is not indefiniteness. *In re Robins,* 429 F.2d 452, 166 U.S.P.Q. 552 (C.C.P.A. 1970).

ഌ

A rejection based on indefiniteness cannot stand simply because the proportions recited in the claims may be read in theory to include compositions that are impossible in fact to formulate. "Subject matter which cannot exist in fact can neither anticipate nor infringe in law." *In re Kroekel* and Pfaff, 504 F.2d 1143, 183 U.S.P.Q. 610, 612 (C.C.P.A. 1974).

ഌ

Although there are undoubtedly a large number of acids that come within the scope of "organic and inorganic acids," the expression is not for that reason indefinite. There is no reason to believe that the public would be confused as to what subject matter is circumscribed by that expression in the claim. *In re Skoll,* 523 F.2d 1392, 187 U.S.P.Q. 481 (C.C.P.A. 1975).

ഌ

The first sentence of the second paragraph of 35 U.S.C. §112 is essentially a requirement for precision and definiteness of claim language. If the scope of subject matter embraced by a claim is clear, and if the applicant has not otherwise indicated that he intends the claim to be of a different scope, then the claim does particularly point out and distinctly claim the subject matter which the applicant regards as his invention. If the "enabling" disclosure of a specification is not commensurate in scope with the subject matter encompassed by a claim, that fact does not render the claim imprecise or indefinite or otherwise not in compliance with the second paragraph of §112. *In re Ehrreich and Avery,* 590 F.2d 902, 200 U.S.P.Q. 504, 508 (C.C.P.A. 1979).

ഌ

A term is only indefinite if one skilled in the relevant art would not understand what is claimed even when the claim is read in light of the specification. "A decision on whether a claim is invalid [for indefiniteness] requires a determination of whether those skilled in the art would understand what is claimed when the claim is read in light of the specification." *Rhône-Poulenc Agrochime S.A. v. Biagro Western Sales Inc.,* 35 U.S.P.Q.2d 1203, 1205 (Cal. 1994).

ഌ

Whether a claim is invalid for indefiniteness depends on whether those skilled in the art would understand the scope of the claim when the claim is read in the light of the specification. *Breuer Electric Mfg. Co. v. Tennant Co.*, 44 U.S.P.Q.2d 1259, 1266 (Ill. 1997).

ω

If it is shown by clear and convincing evidence that claims are indefinite (those skilled in the art cannot understand what is claimed when the claims are read in the light of the specifications), they may be held invalid as a matter of law. *Semmler v. American Honda Motor Co.*, 44 U.S.P.Q.2d 1553, 1559 (Ohio 1997).

Indemnification Agreement.

The mere act of entering into an indemnification agreement, without more, does not amount to inducement of infringement. *Hewlett Packard Co. v. Bausch & Lomb Inc.*, 722 F. Supp. 595, 13 U.S.P.Q.2d 1105, 1115 (Cal. 1989).

Independent. *See* Distinct.

Independent Development.

Evidence of independent development is highly relevant to refute a patent owner's contention that the doctrine of equivalents applies because the accused infringer copied (intentially appropriated) the substance of the claimed invention. *Hilton Davis Chemical Co. v. Warner-Jenkinson Co. Inc.*, 62 F.3d 1512, 35 U.S.P.Q.2d 1641, 1647 (Fed. Cir. 1995), *reversed and remanded*, 41 U.S.P.Q.2d 1865 (S.Ct. 1997).

Independent Expert.

The plaintiff in an action brought pursuant to 35 U.S.C. §145 has a heavy burden. Because the Patent Office is an expert body preeminently qualified to determine questions of this kind, its conclusions are entitled to a broad presumption of validity. In these circumstances, the court is authorized to reverse the decision only if the Patent Office did not have a rational basis for its conclusions or if the plaintiff presented new evidence that led to a thorough conviction that the plaintiff should prevail. In trials de novo under §145, great weight attaches to the expertise of the Patent Office, and its findings will not be overtuned unless new evidence is introduced that carries the thorough conviction that the Patent Office erred. Based upon the opinion testimony of an independent expert, the court was satisfied that the only way one would reach the plaintiff's claimed alloy composition from the reference disclosure was by experimentation. The testimony offered on behalf of the plaintiff at the trial was uncontradicted by the defendant. The court found that testimony to be very persuasive, and the court concluded that the plaintiff demonstrated by clear and convincing evidence that the determination by the Board of Appeals was in error. *Titanium Metals Corp. of America v. Mossinghoff*, 603 F. Supp. 87, 225 U.S.P.Q. 673 (D.C. 1984).

Indicia. *See* **Objective Indicia.**

Indifference. *See* **Wrongful Intent.**

Indirect Evidence.

Indirect circumstantial evidence established that a claimed composition, more likely than not, does possess properties different from those possessed by a composition containing a reference isomer, and that such differences would have been unexpected to one having ordinary skill in the art. *In re Wilder*, 429 F.2d 447, 166 U.S.P.Q. 545, 549 (C.C.P.A. 1970).

ω

Comparative test data which provide only an indirect comparison between claimed and prior art subject matter can be effective to establish unexpected results and nonobviousness. *In re Blondel, Fouche, and Gueremy*, 499 F.2d 1311, 182 U.S.P.Q. 294, 298 (C.C.P.A. 1974).

ω

A direct comparison with the closest prior art may not be necessary; an indirect comparison may be persuasive of unobviousness. *In re Merchant*, 575 F.2d 865, 197 U.S.P.Q. 785, 788 (C.C.P.A. 1978).

Indirect Infringement.

Indirect infringement occurs when someone *"actively induces* infringement of a patent [by another]."* 35 U.S.C. §271(b)(emphasis added). Although Section 271(b) does not specifically define the level of knowledge or intent required for liability, "proof of actual intent to cause the acts which constitute the infringement is a necessary prerequisite to finding active inducement." In this regard, knowledge that the direct infringer was performing the acts that are later alleged to constitute infringement is not enough; there must also be a specific intent to encourage infringement of the patent. *L.A. Gear Inc. v. E.S. Originals Inc.*, 859 F.Supp. 1294, 32 U.S.P.Q.2d 1613, 1617 (Cal. 1994).

Indispensable. *See* **Indispensable Party, Party.**

Indispensable Party.

The monopoly granted by the patent laws cannot be divided into parts, except as authorized by those laws, and a patentee may assign (1) the whole patent, (2) an undivided part or share of that patent, or (3) the exclusive right under the patent "to the whole or any specified part of the United States". "Any assignment or transfer, short of one of these, is a mere license, giving the licensee no title in the patent, and no right to sue at law in his own name for an infringement". An exclusive license to make, use and vend is in the same category as an assignment on the theory that the licensor holds title to the patent in trust for such licenses. Even though an exclusive license is restricted to a specified territory or covers less than the full life of the patent, this still remains true. *Channel*

Master Corporation v. JFD Electronics Corporation, 260 F.Supp. 568, 151 U.S.P.Q. 498, 500 (N.Y. 1966).

ᖜ

Traditionally, an owner of an undivided share of a patent can sue for infringement only when he sues jointly with his co-owner. However, the adoption of amended Rule 19 (FRCP) in 1966 makes inappropriate any contention that patent co-owners are per se indispensable in infringement suits. *Catanzaro v. International Telephone & Telegraph Corporation*, 378 F.Supp. 203, 183 U.S.P.Q. 273, 274 (Del. 1974).

ᖜ

One does not waive the defense of failure to join an indispensable party by filing a responsive pleading. The failure to join an indispensable party can be raised at any time. *International Business Machines Corp. v. Conner Periferaals Inc.*, 30 U.S.P.Q.2d 1315, 1318 (Cal. 1994).

ᖜ

Prejudice to an absent party is mitigated when the interests of that party are "adequately protected by those who are present." If so, the "person is not indispensable." *Dainippon Screen Manufacturing Co. v. CFMT Inc.*, 142 F.3d 1266, 46 U.S.P.Q.2d 1616, 1622 (Fed. Cir. 1998).

Induce. *See also* Contributory Infringement, Corporate Officer, Inducement of Infringement.

To establish liability under 35 U.S.C. §271(b) does not require the acts of inducement, themselves, to have been committed within the territorial confines of this country. Also, an inducement under §271(b), like a direct infringement under §271(a), does not require a specific intent. *Hauni Werke Koerber & Co., KG. v. Molins Limited*, 183 U.S.P.Q. 168, 170, 171 (Va. 1974).

ᖜ

A person may be liable under 35 U.S.C. §271(b) or §271(c) for actions constituting patent infringement but that occurred prior to the date of patent issuance. To establish such liability, the patent holder or his successor in interest must make three showings. First, it must be demonstrated that the challenged party acted knowingly to induce infringement under §271(b) or to contribute to infringement under §271(c) by selling either a material component of the patented product or a material apparatus for use in practicing a patented process. Second, it must be shown that the party's act culminated in a direct infringement of the patent. Third, it must be demonstrated that the eventual direct infringement occurred within the statutory 17-year life of the patent. If these three showings are made, a complaint in infringement will not be dismissed solely because the challenged actions occurred prior to the date the patent was issued. *Mixing Equipment Co. v. Innova-Tech, Inc.*, 2 U.S.P.Q.2d 1212 (Pa. 1986).

ᖜ

Rather than a limiting factor for liability under 35 U.S.C. §271(f)(1), the legislative history suggests the phrase "actively induced" was intended to broaden the basis for liability, extending it to cover both those who actually supply the components as well as those "contributory infringers" who cause others to supply components. *T. D. Williamson Inc. v. Laymon,* 723 F. Supp. 587, 13 U.S.P.Q.2d 1417, 1419 (Okla. 1989).

ᚣ

Active inducement to infringe is a separate action from contributory infringement, although the two may overlap. Contributory infringement is limited to selling nonstaple articles, while one can induce infringement by a variety of conduct, including by selling staple or nonstaple products. As a matter of law, liability for inducement is only contingent on a finding of active solicitation. *Oak Industries, Inc. v. Zenith Electronics Corp.,* 726 F. Supp. 1525, 14 U.S.P.Q.2d 1417, 1430 (Ill. 1989).

ᚣ

Liability for inducement under 35 U.S.C. §271(b) can be based on preissuance activities. As long as a viable claim for direct infringement exists, there can be liability for inducement, regardless of the timing of the inducing acts. *The Upjohn Company v. Syntro Corp.,* 14 U.S.P.Q.2d 1469, 1473 (Del. 1990).

ᚣ

Proof of actual intent to cause the acts that constitute infringement is a necessary prerequisite to finding active inducement. *Hewlett-Packard Co. v. Bausch & Lomb Inc.,* 909 F.2d 1464, 15 U.S.P.Q.2d 1525, 1529 (Fed. Cir. 1990).

ᚣ

Although the defendant no longer directly makes, uses or sells patent infringing devices, it has provided sufficient technology, drawings, and know-how to its licensee to enable the licensee to infringe the patent directly. On the basis of defendant's inducement of direct infringement, defendant is liable for any infringement by its licensee. *Baldwin Technology Corp. v. Dahlgren International Inc.,* 819 F.Supp. 568, 27 U.S.P.Q.2d 1096, 1102 (Tex. 1992).

ᚣ

Indirect infringement occurs when someone "*actively induces* infringement of a patent [by another]." 35 U.S.C. §271(b)(emphasis added). Although Section 271(b) does not specifically define the level of knowledge or intent required for liability, "proof of actual intent to cause the acts which constitute the infringement is a necessary prerequisite to finding active inducement." In this regard, knowledge that the direct infringer was performing the acts that are later alleged to constitute infringement is not enough; there must also be a specific intent to encourage infringement of the patent. *L.A. Gear Inc. v. E.S. Originals Inc.,* 859 F.Supp. 1294, 32 U.S.P.Q.2d 1613, 1617 (Cal. 1994).

ᚣ

Under 35 U.S.C. §271(b), corporate officers who actively assist with their corporation's patent infringement may be personally liable as an infringer regardless of whether there is evidence to justify piercing the corporate veil. The plaintiff has the burden of showing both that the officer's actions induced infringing acts and that the officer knew or should have known that his or her actions would induce infringements. *Zenith Electronics Corp. v. ExZec Inc.,* 32 U.S.P.Q.2d 1959, 1960 (Ill. 1994).

ᚣ

If a product does not directly infringe, it may infringe due to the inducement of a party. *Total Containment Inc. v. Buffalo Environmental Products Corp.*, 35 U.S.P.Q.2d 1385, 1389 (Va. 1995).

ᚥ

Where a manufacturer's product does not infringe a patent in question, but its customers use the product to make an infringing device, courts typically hold that the manufacturer lacks any reasonable apprehension of suit for direct infringement, even if the customers are being threatened with legal action. *The Dow Chemical Co. v. Viskase Corp.*, 892 F.Supp. 991, 36 U.S.P.Q.2d 1490, 1493 (Ill. 1995).

ᚥ

Inducement of infringement under 35 U.S.C. §271(b) does not lie when the acts of inducement occurred before there existed a patent to be infringed. *National Presto Industries Inc. v. The West Bend Co.*, 76 F.3d 1185, 37 U.S.P.Q.2d 1685, 1693 (Fed. Cir. 1996). But see *The Upjohn Company v. Syntro Corp.*, 14 U.S.P.Q. 2d 1469, 1473 (Del. 1990).

Inducement. *See also* Induce.

Failure to act when there is a duty to act might amount to inducement. "[T]he principle of liability for 'aiding and abetting'...is not imposed retrospectively, to make illegal an act that was not illegal when done." This does not mean that pre-notice actions are never relevant to inducement. Such actions may be relevant in certain circumstances where, for instance, they create a post-notice duty to act. *Black & Decker (US) Inc. v. Catalina Lighting Inc.*, 42 U.S.P.Q.2d 1254, n.3 1255, 1256 (Va. 1997).

Inducement of Infringement. *See also* Induce.

Direct infringement must be pleaded in the complaint in order to state a claim for inducement of infringement and contributory infringement. *Fuji Machine Manufacturing Co. v. Hover-Davis Inc.*, 40 U.S.P.Q.2d 1313, 1315 (N.Y. 1996).

Industry.

In cases under 19 U.S.C. §1337 involving United States article patents, the relevant domestic "industry" extends only to articles which come within the claims of the patent relied upon. In proper cases, "industry" may include more than the manufacturing of the patented item. *Schaper Manufacturing Co. v. U.S. International Trade Commission*, 717 F.2d 1368, 219 U.S.P.Q. 665, 667, 669 (Fed. Cir. 1983).

Industry Acceptance.

In evaluating a patent claiming a combination of known mechanical elements, a pertinent question is whether, considering the invention as a whole, it would have been obvious to combine the elements in the claimed relationship. In this regard a court may look to such evidence of unobviousness as new and advantageous results achieved by the claimed invention, industry acceptance, commercial success, and copying by others.

Saturn Manufacturing, Inc. v. Williams Patent Crusher & Pulverizer Co., 713 F.2d 1347, 219 U.S.P.Q. 533, 537 (Fed. Cir. 1983).

Ineffective.

It is not a function of the claims to specifically exclude either possible inoperative conditions or ineffective reactant proportions. *Ex parte Vollheim, Troger, and Lippert*, 191 U.S.P.Q. 407, 408 (PTO Bd. App. 1975).

Inequitable Conduct. *See also* Conduct, Duty to Disclose, Fraud, Intent, Materiality, Misconduct.

Patentee's failure to inform the Examiner of acts alleged to constitute a possible onsale bar under 35 U.S.C. §102(b) to other interrelated patents in suit does not constitute inequitable conduct or unclean hands with respect to a patent to which the onsale bar does not apply. *SSIH Equipment, S.A. v. United States International Trade Commission*, 713 F.2d 746, 218 U.S.P.Q. 678, 689 (Fed. Cir. 1983).

ω

Inequitable conduct may be sufficient to render a patent unenforceable, but that standard is not a test for piercing the attorney-client privilege. *Research Corp. v. Gourmet's Delight Mushroom Co.*, 560 F. Supp. 811, 219 U.S.P.Q. 1023 (Pa. 1983).

ω

Inequitable conduct requires proof by clear and convincing evidence of a threshold degree of materiality of the nondisclosed or false information. That threshold can be established by any of four tests: (1) objective "but for"; (2) subjective "but for"; (3) "but it may have been"; and (4) 37 C.F.R. §1.56(a), i.e., whether there is a substantial likelihood that a reasonable Examiner would have considered the omitted or false information important in deciding whether to allow the application to issue as a patent. The PTO standard is the appropriate starting point because it is the broadest and most closely aligned with how one ought to conduct business with the PTO. Inequitable conduct also requires proof of a threshold intent. Proof of deliberate scheming is not needed; gross negligence is sufficient. *J. P. Stevens & Co. v. Lex Tex, Ltd., Inc.*, 747 F.2d 1553, 223 U.S.P.Q. 1089, 1092 (Fed. Cir. 1984).

ω

Increased damages are usually based on a finding that the infringer's conduct was willful and in flagrant disregard of the patentee's rights. In this case, the defendant was on notice of the plaintiff's patent rights and had an affirmative duty to exercise due care to determine whether it was infringing. The defendant may not avoid a holding of willful infringement because it failed to show that it obtained a competent opinion from counsel and that it had exercised reasonable and good faith adherence to the analysis and advice contained therein. Accordingly, defendant is liable to the plaintiff for an amount equal to three times the amount of damages actually found or assessed. Section 285 of 35 U.S.C. §makes provision for the award of attorney's fees to the prevailing party in exceptional cases. In order to support an award of attorney's fees in a patent case, there must be a showing of conduct that is unfair, in bad faith, inequitable, or unconscionable. In view of defendant's willful infringement, this case involved those elements set out above and was considered an exceptional case, thereby entitling the plaintiff to an award of its attorney's fees. The plaintiff was also entitled to prejudgment interest based upon the damages found or assessed in the second phase of the trial. *Great Northern Corp. v. Davis Core & Pad Co.*, 226 U.S.P.Q. 540 (Ga. 1985).

ɯ

Questions of good faith, intent to deceive, scienter, and honest mistake are all questions of fact. A summary judgment of fraud or inequitable conduct, reached while denying the person accused of the fraud or inequitable conduct the opportunity to be heard on the issue, is a draconian result. *KangaROOS U.S.A., Inc. v. Caldor, Inc.*, 778 F.2d 1571, 228 U.S.P.Q. 32 (Fed. Cir. 1985).

ɯ

The defense of inequitable conduct requires proof of (1) an act of misrepresentation (2) that was material, (3) involving information that was known or should have been known to the patentee and (4) that was committed with requisite intent. The elements of materiality and intent must be determined separately and then weighted together to ascertain whether the patentee engaged in inequitable conduct. The tribunal must then carefully balance the materiality and intent; the less material the proffered or withheld information, the greater the degree of intent that must be proven. In contrast, a lesser degree of intent must be proven when the information has a great degree of materiality. Indeed, gross negligence can be the intended level of intent when the misrepresentation has a high degree of materiality. Simple negligence, however, or an error in judgment is never sufficient for holding of inequitable conduct. *Akzo M. V. Aramide Maatschappij V.O.F. v. E. I. du Pont de Nemours*, 810 F.2d 1148, 1 U.S.P.Q.2d 1704 (Fed. Cir. 1987).

ɯ

The party seeking to establish inequitable conduct must establish by clear and convincing evidence (1) the materiality of the claimed and undisclosed or false information—that there is a substantial likelihood that a reasonable Examiner would consider the omission or misrepresentation important in deciding whether to issue the patent, and (2) that the applicant's omission or misrepresentation was grossly negligent or intentional. *Beckman Instruments, Inc. v. LKB Produkter A.B.*, 5 U.S.P.Q.2d 1462 (Md. 1987).

ɯ

The habit of charging inequitable conduct in almost every major patent case has become an absolute plague. Reputable lawyers seem to feel compelled to make the charge against other reputable lawyers on the slenderest grounds—to represent their clients' interests adequately, perhaps. Even though they get anywhere with the accusation in but a small percentage of the cases, such charges are not inconsequential on that account. They destroy the respect for one another's integrity; for being fellow members of an honorable profession used to make the bar a valuable help to the courts in making a sound disposition of cases, and sustain the good name of the bar itself. A patent litigant should be made to feel, therefore, that an unsupported charge of "inequitable conduct in the Patent Office" is a negative contribution to the rightful administration of justice. The charge was formerly known as "fraud on the Patent Office," a more pejorative term, but the change of name does not make the thing itself smell any sweeter. Even after complete testimony the court should find inequitable conduct only if shown clear and convincing evidence. A summary judgment that a reputable attorney has been guilty of inequitable conduct, over his denials, ought to be, and can properly be, rare indeed. *Burlington Industries Inc. v. Dayco Corp.*, 849 F.2d 1418, 7 U.S.P.Q.2d 1158 (Fed. Cir. 1988).

ᴡ

Evidence of intent is not only material but is a requirement for a holding of inequitable conduct. Such evidence need not be direct; it may be inferred from the patentee's conduct. Nevertheless, evidence on the issue must exist. *SmithKline Diagnostics, Inc. v. Helena Laboratories Corp.*, 859 F.2d 878, 8 U.S.P.Q.2d 1468 (Fed. Cir. 1988).

ᴡ

(a) A finding that particular conduct amounts to gross negligence does not of itself justify an inference of intent to deceive. The involved conduct, viewed in light of all the evidence must indicate sufficient culpability to require a finding of intent to deceive.
(b) The inequitable conduct question is equitable in nature, and is not a "question of law."
(c) As an equitable issue, inequitable conduct is committed to the discretion of the trial court and is reviewable on appeal under an abuse of discretion standard.
(d) When inequitable conduct occurs in relation to one or more claims during prosecution of a patent application, the entire patent is rendered unenforceable.

Kingsdown Medical Consultants Ltd. v. Hollister Inc., 863 F.2d 867, 9 U.S.P.Q.2d 1384, 1392 (Fed. Cir. 1988), *cert. denied*, 490 U.S. 1067 (1989).

ᴡ

A finding of gross negligence is insufficient to afford a holding of inequitable conduct. Inequitable conduct requires a finding of an intent to mislead or deceive the PTO. Such intent usually can only be found as a matter of inference from circumstantial evidence. Although proof of gross negligence may be circumstantial evidence that gives rise to an inference of intent to mislead in some instances, the label "gross negligence" covers too wide a range of culpable conduct to create such an inference in all cases. Thus, gross negligent conduct may or may not compel an inference of an intent to mislead. Such an inference depends upon the totality of the circumstances, including the nature and level of culpability of the conduct and the absence or presence of good faith. *Hewlett-Packard Co. v. Bausch & Lomb Inc.*, 882 F.2d 1556, 11 U.S.P.Q.2d 1750, 1755-1757 (Fed. Cir. 1989).

ᴡ

A patent application requires the "highest duty of candor." Accordingly, when the plaintiff presented its applications for improvement patents on its prior patent, it should have disclosed to the PTO that the best mode for the prior patent was concealed in the patent application for that patent. Such an admission would not have negated the plaintiff's inequitable conduct but might have reduced the effect of such conduct on its subsequent patent applications. It would have given the Examiner a sufficient opportunity to compare its patent applications with the prior art and would have evidenced an intent to deal with the PTO in good faith. It certainly is information that the patent Examiner would have deemed material. Thus, the failure to disclose prior inequitable conduct during later patent applications was itself inequitable conduct. Failure in a later application to correct erroneous statements previously made to the PTO has been held to be inequitable conduct. *Consolidated Aluminum Corp. v. Foseco International Ltd.*, 716 F. Supp. 316, 11 U.S.P.Q.2d 1817, 1828 (Ill. 1989).

ᚥ

For there to be inequitable conduct, the involved conduct must indicate sufficient culpability to require a finding of intent to deceive. Absent a finding of an intent to deceive, the district court abused its discretion in holding that the conduct involved rendered the patent unenforceable. *Greenwood v. Hattori Seiko Co. Ltd.*, 900 F.2d 238, 14 U.S.P.Q.2d 1474, 1476 (Fed. Cir. 1990).

ᚥ

Because disclosure of the best mode is statutorily required, failure to disclose the best mode is inherently material and reaches the minimal level of materiality necessary for a finding of inequitable conduct. Inequitable conduct is no more than the unclean hands doctrine applied to particular conduct before the PTO. Inequitable conduct alone need not compel a finding that a case is exceptional. *Consolidated Aluminum Corp. v. Foseco International Ltd.*, 910 F.2d 804, 15 U.S.P.Q.2d 1481, 1484, 1487, 1489 (Fed. Cir. 1990).

ᚥ

Inequitable conduct requires proof by clear and convincing evidence of a threshold degree of materiality of nondisclosed or false information. Since materiality is required, it is clear that an applicant is under no obligation to disclose all pertinent prior art or other pertinent information of which he is aware. Gross negligence does not of itself support a finding of inequitable conduct to defeat the validity of a patent, although it may be considered in determining whether there was an intent to deceive. *Saes Getters S.P.A. v. Ergenics Inc.*, 17 U.S.P.Q.2d 1581, 1588 (N.J. 1990).

ᚥ

The plaintiff's burden (as the non-moving party) to come forward with evidence to prevent summary judgment on the issue of inequitable conduct is less stringent than that normally placed on a non-moving party. *Schneider (USA) Inc. v. C. R. Bard Inc.*, 18 U.S.P.Q.2d 1076, 1080 (Mass. 1990).

ᚥ

Under Fed. R. Civ. P. 9(b), "[t]he circumstances constituting fraud . . . shall be stated with particularity." In order to comply with this pleading requirement, defendants must specify the time, place, and content of any alleged misrepresentations that plaintiffs made to the PTO. *Sun-Flex Co. Inc. v. Softview Computer Products Corp.*, 750 F. Supp. 962, 18 U.S.P.Q.2d 1171, 1172 (Ill. 1990).

ᚥ

Inequitable conduct is a much-abused and too often last-resort allegation. The issue of inequitable conduct deflects the court's attention from the issues of validity and infringement. An infringement defendant in complex litigation should not be permitted to side-step these main issues by nit picking the patent file in every minute respect with the effect of trying the patentee personally, rather than the patent. *Ortho Pharmaceutical Corp. v. Smith,* 18 U.S.P.Q.2d 1977, 1991 (Pa. 1990).

ʊ

Conduct that requires forfeiture of all patent rights must be deliberate and proved by clear and convincing evidence. While absence of reference by the court to intent does not mean that the court did not find intent, the court's remark that it acted "without implying improper motives [to the inventors]" contravenes this argument. Even were the inventors' statements in error, a finding of disputed fact that is not appropriate on summary judgment, the absence of a finding of intent to deceive or mislead the Examiner precludes summary judgment of inequitable conduct. A disputed question of intent to deceive is not appropriate for summary resolution. A reference that is material only to withdrawn claims cannot be the basis of a holding of inequitable conduct. *Scripps Clinic & Research Foundation v. Genentech Inc.,* 927 F.2d 1565, 18 U.S.P.Q.2d 1001, 1008 (Fed. Cir. 1991).

ʊ

Inequitable conduct carries the consequence of permanent unenforceability of the patent claims. Forfeiture is not favored as a remedy for actions not shown to be culpable. Thus, the requirement of clear and convincing proof of the factual predicates of inequitable conduct is an essential safeguard. "Given the ease with which a relatively routine act of patent prosecution can be portrayed as intended to mislead or deceive, clear and convincing evidence of conduct sufficient to support an inference of culpable intent is required." *Tol-O-Matic Inc. v. Proma Produkt-Und Marketing Gesellschaft m.b.H.,* 945 F.2d 1546, 20 U.S.P.Q.2d 1332, 1339 (Fed. Cir. 1991).

ʊ

The duty of candor extends to withholding unfavorable test data even when such data may be incomplete and even when it is subsequently shown to be irrelevant. *Imperial Chemical Industries PLC v. Barr Laboratories,* 87 Civ. 7833, 22 U.S.P.Q.2d 1906, 1910 (N.Y. 1992).

ʊ

A decision respecting inequitable conduct is a discretionary decision to be made by a judge on his or her own factual findings. Thus, a disputed finding of intent to mislead or to deceive is one for the judge to resolve, not the jury, albeit not on summary judgment if there is a genuine dispute. A patentee has no right to a jury trial respecting the factual element of culpable intent as part of the defense of inequitable conduct. *Paragon Podiatry Laboratory Inc. v. KLM Laboratories Inc.,* 984 F.2d 1182, 25 U.S.P.Q.2d 1561, 1568 (Fed. Cir. 1993).

ʊ

Given the Federal Circuit's frustration with unsupported allegations of inequitable conduct, the weight of authority is in favor of applying Rule 9(b) [FRCP] to the defense of inequitable conduct, and the more persuasive argument that inequitable conduct is a broader form of common law fraud. *IPPV Enterprises v. Cable/Home Communications,* 25 U.S.P.Q. 2d 1894, 1896 (Cal. 1992).

ʊ

There is no Seventh Amendment right to a jury trial on the defense of inequitable conduct. Rather, "the decision respecting inequitable conduct is a discretionary decision to be made by the judge on his or her own factual findings". *The Quikrete Companies Inc. v. Nomix Corp.*, 874 F.Supp. 1362, 33 U.S.P.Q.2d 1032, 1037, 1038 (Ga. 1993).

ᚭ

Defendant's allegations of inequitable conduct must satisfy the particularity requirements of Rule (FRCP) 9(b). As a guide, amended pleadings should identitfy: (1) the particular statements, misrepresentations, or omissions made; (2) when the complained of acts or omissions occurred; (3) the reasons why those acts or omissions were inequitable; and (4) the basis for the belief. *The Laitram Corp. v. OKI Electric Industry Co. Ltd.*, 30 U.S.P.Q.2d 1527, 1533 (La. 1994).

ᚭ

If a party alleging fraud "offers no specific facts demonstrating wrongdoing which [the other party] could deny or otherwise contravert", then it fails to plead the allegation with sufficient particularity under (FRCP) Rule 9(b). *Chiron Corp. v. Abbott Laboratories*, 156 F.R.D. 219, 31 U.S.P.Q.2d 1848, 1851 (Cal. 1994).

ᚭ

Invalidity for inequitable conduct requires a showing, by clear and convincing evidence, of intent to deceive or mislead the patent Examiner into granting the patent. *Therma-Tru Corp. v. Peachtree Doors Inc.*, 44 F.3d 988, 33 U.S.P.Q.2d 1274, 1279 (Fed. Cir. 1995).

ᚭ

There is no legal basis for a holding that inequitable conduct, or the assertion of a patent procured through inequitable conduct, constitutes unfair competition. *Pro-Mold and Tool Co. v. Great Lakes Plastics Inc.*, 75 F.3d 1568, 37 U.S.P.Q.2d 1626, 1631 (Fed. Cir. 1996).

ᚭ

Inequitable conduct cannot be based on an applicant's non-disclosure of a prior art reference if the Examiner independently discovers that reference. *Litton Systems Inc. v. Honeywell Inc.*, 87 F.3d 1559, 39 U.S.P.Q.2d 1321, 1334 (Fed. Cir. 1996).

ᚭ

When an alleged misconduct relates to the submission of test results and data, a higher standard is demanded of an applicant than the mere avoidance of intentional fraud. Submission of a misleading affidavit will usually support a conclusion that the affidavit was a chosen instrument of an intent to deceive the PTO. *Ott v. Goodpasture Inc.*, 40 U.S.P.Q.2d 1831 (Tex 1996).

ᚭ

To establish inequitable conduct, clear and convincing proof of each of the following is required: (1) that the applicant or one substantially involved with the prosecution of a patent omitted or misrepresented material prior art or information; (2) that such person knew of the materiality of the prior art; and (3) intended to deceive the Patent Office by deliberately withholding the prior art or information. *Heidelberg Harris Inc. v. Mitsubishi Heavy Industries Inc.*, 42 U.S.P.Q.2d 1369, 1373 (Ill. 1996).

ᙍ

"Those who have applications pending with the Patent Office...have an uncompromising duty to report to it all facts concerning possible fraud or inequitableness underlying the applications in issue." The inequitable conduct allegation contained in Plaintiff's affirmative defense requires Defendant to comply with Rule 9(b) Fed. R. Civ. P. *Emerson Electric Co. v. Encon Industries L.P.*, 42 U.S.P.Q.2d 1575, 1576 (Miss. 1997).

ᙍ

"[A]ny assertion that is made by a litigant...during litigation, which is contradictory to the assertions made...to the patent examiner, comprises material information...." *Environ Products Inc. v. Total Containment Inc.*, 43 U.S.P.Q.2d 1288, 1291 (Pa. 1997).

ᙍ

Intent may be inferred where a patent applicant knew, or should have known, that withheld information would be material to the PTO's consideration of the patent application. *Critikon Inc. v. Becton Dickinson Vascular Access Inc.*, 43 U.S.P.Q.2d 1666, 1668 (Fed. Cir. 1997).

ᙍ

Courts rarely grant summary judgment on inequitable conduct, and the issue is not amenable to summary judgment if the facts of materiality or intent are reasonably disputed. *Regents of the University of California v. Oncor Inc.*, 44 U.S.P.Q.2d 1321, 1329 (Cal. 1997).

ᙍ

An inequitable conduct defense and a Walker Process counterclaim are not identical in scope or consequence for "[t]he patent fraud proscribed by *Walker* is extremely circumscribed" in comparison with inequitable conduct. Nevertheless, we are satisfied that the facts underlying Cabnetware's inequitable conduct defense and its Walker Process counterclaim possess "substantial commonality" so that, because the jury answered question 7, the Seventh Amendment constrains the court's equitable determination. *Cabinet Vision v. Cabnetware*, 129 F.2d 595, 44 U.S.P.Q.2d 1683, 1687 (Fed. Cir. 1997).

ᙍ

Inequitable conduct that will render a patent unenforceable is a broader more inclusive concept than the "fraud" needed to support a *Walker Process* counterclaim. *Nobelpharma AB v. Implant Innovations Inc.*, 129 F.3d 1463, 44 U.S.P.Q.2d 1705, 1713 (Fed. Cir. 1997).

ᙍ

Defendant never waived (by failing to put on additional evidence, as allowed by the court, after the jury had retired to consider the validity and infringement issues; neither did it move for judgment as a matter of law) its inequitable conduct defense or abandoned it in any other way; it simply chose not to put on additional evidence, relying instead on evidence already presented at trial. Additionally, its current motion is not one for JMOL, just one properly directed to the court to resolve an issue arising in equity. *Nursery Supplies Inc. v. Lerio Corp.*, 45 U.S.P.Q.2d 1332, 1338 (Pa. 1997).

ᙍ

Inequitable conduct in original application which gave rise to multiple divisional applications resulted in all three resulting patents being held unenforceable, even when inequitable conduct did not affect the claims of one of the resulting patents. *Semiconductor Energy Laboratory Co. v. Samsung Electronics Co.*, 4 F. Supp.2d 477, 46 U.S.P.Q.2d 1874, 1882 (Va. 1998).

ʊ

Where claims are subsequently separated from those tainted by inequitable conduct through a divisional application, and where the issued claims have no relation to the omitted prior art, the patent issued from the divisional application will not also be unenforceable due to inequitable conduct committed in the parent application. *Baxter International Inc. v. McGaw Inc.*, 149 F.3d 1321, 47 U.S.P.Q.2d 1225, 1233 (Fed. Cir. 1998).

Inexcusable Delay.

In order to assert the defense of laches successfully, one must prove (1) unreasonable and inexcusable delay in the assertion of the claim and (2) material prejudice resulting from the delay. Laches, however, bars only the right to recover prefiling damages.

Equitable estoppel bars claims for patent infringement if Mainland committed itself to act, and acted as a direct consequence of the conduct of Standal's Patents. Estoppel to assert patent rights requires (1) unreasonable and inexcusable delay, (2) prejudice to the defendant, (3) affirmative conduct by patentee's inducing belief of abandonment of claims against the alleged infringer, and (4) detrimental reliance by the infringer. Estoppel by implied license cannot arise out of unilateral expectations or even reasonable hopes of one party. Five years silence alone is not enough to give rise to estoppel. *Mainland Industries, Inc. v. Standals Patents Ltd.*, 799 F.2d 746, 230 U.S.P.Q. 772 (Fed. Cir. 1986).

Inference.

To combine references (A) and (B) properly to reach the conclusion that the subject matter of a patent would have been obvious, case law requires that there must be some teaching, suggestion, or inference in either reference (A) or (B), or both, or knowledge generally available to one of ordinary skill in the relevant art, that would lead one skilled in the art to combine the relevant teachings of references (A) and (B). Consideration must be given to teachings in the references that would have led one skilled in the art away from the claimed invention. A claim cannot properly be used as a blueprint for extracting individual teachings from references. *Ashland Oil, Inc. v. Delta Resins & Refractories, Inc.*, 776 F.2d 281, 227 U.S.P.Q. 657 (Fed. Cir. 1985).

Information Disclosure Statement (IDS). *See also* Duty to Disclose.

When an applicant cites references and fails to provide the PTO with copies of such references and fails to explain the pertinency of the references, there is no assurance that references were considered by the Examiner. Since there is no assurance that the Examiner considered the cited references or that such references are more relevant than art cited by the Examiner, an infringement defendant has met its burden of proving that such prior art references were not considered in the examination of the patent application. *Consolidated Aluminum Corp. v. Foseco International Ltd.*, 10 U.S.P.Q. 2d 1143 (Ill. 1988).

ʊ

An IDS is part of the prosecution history on which the Examiner, the courts, and the public are entitled to rely. An argument contained in an IDS which purports to distinguish an invention from prior art may thus affect the scope of the patent ultimately granted. Accordingly, statements made in an IDS can be the basis for a court to interpret the scope of claims of a granted patent. *Ekchian v. Home Depot Inc.*, 41 U.S.P.Q.2d 1364, 1368 (Fed. Cir. 1997).

Infra-Red.

Since the compound can be properly defined by its empirical formula together with its physical and chemical characteristics and infra-red absorption spectra, it is improper to include additional claims which define the compound by its method of preparation or only by a coined name. *Ex parte Brian, Radley, Curtis, and Elson*, 118 U.S.P.Q. 242, 244 (PO Bd. App. 1958).

Infringement.[3] *See also* **Accelerated Reentry Theory, Advice of Counsel, All-Elements Rule, Appropriation, Deliberate Infringement, Doctrine of Equivalents, Equivalents, Nit Picking, Patent Notice Letter, Presumption of Infringement, 35 U.S.C. §271(e)(2).**

A patentee, in demanding and receiving full compensation for the wrongful use of his invention in devices made and sold by a manufacturer, adopts the sales as made by himself, and, therefore, necessarily licenses the use of the devices, and frees them from the monopoly of the patent. *Union Tool Co. v. Wilson*, 259 U.S. 107, 113 (1922).

ʊ

One device is an infringement of another if it performs substantially the same function in substantially the same way to obtain the same result. Except where form is the essence of the invention, it has little weight in the decision of such an issue. *Hugh W. Batcheller v. Henry Cole Co.*, 7 F. Supp. 898, 22 U.S.P.Q. 354, 358 (Mass. 1934).

ʊ

The general rule is that the monopoly of patent that entitles a patentee to damages for infringement commences only when the patent is granted; but where, in advance of the granting of a patent, an invention is disclosed to one who, in breach of the confidence thus

---

[3]The Federal Circuit [*Heidelberg Harris, Inc. v. Loebach*, 46 U.S.P.Q.2d 1948 (Fed. Cir. 1998)] "held that a patent owner cannot sue for patent infringement occurring prior to the time the patent owner actually obtained legal title to the asserted patent. Therefore, the declaratory Defendant was not able to assert claims for infringement arising before the date he acquired title under court order even though the original assignment of the invention was void *ab initio*. Further, the Court held that a licensee is immune from infringement liability if the licensee purchased the license for value before receiving notice of the plaintiff's claim to the patent. The relevant date for notice is the date that the licensee's right to the license vests, i.e., before the licensee has paid the consideration or before the licensee has performed his purchase obligations." *Federal Circuit Case Digest*, Vol. 1, No. 7, page 4, 1998.

reposed, manufactures, and sells articles embodying the invention, such persons should be held liable for the profits and damages resulting therefrom, not under the patent statutes, but under the principle that equity will not permit one to unjustly enrich himself at the expense of another.

The complainant offered to disclose his invention to the defendant with a view of selling it to defendant. The defendant was interested in the proposition and invited the disclosure, otherwise it would not have seen the complainant's specification and drawings until the patent was granted. While there was no express agreement that the defendant was to hold the information so disclosed as a confidential matter and to make no use of it unless it should purchase the invention, we think that in equity and good conscience such an agreement was implied; and having obtained the disclosure under such circumstances, the defendant ought not to be heard to say that there was no obligation to respect the confidence thus reposed in it. *Hoeltke v. C. M. Kemp Manufacturing Co.*, 80 F.2d 912, 26 U.S.P.Q. 114 (4th Cir. 1935), cert. denied, 298 U.S. 673 (1936).

ᴡ

The fact that a device may be used in a manner so as not to infringe the patent is not a defense to a claim of infringement against a manufacturer of the device if it is also reasonably capable of a use that infringes the patent. In this respect a distinction is drawn between an alleged manufacturing infringer on the one hand and an alleged using infringer on the other hand. For a person who uses a device, infringement is determined by the use to which the invention is actually put. For a manufacturer, infringement is determined by the use to which the device may reasonably be put or of which it is reasonably capable. *Huck Manufacturing Company*, 187 U.S.P.Q. 388, 408 (Mich. 1975).

ᴡ

A product, even if encompassed by a literal reading of claims, does not necessarily constitute infringement. *Westwood Chemical, Inc. v. Dow Corning Corporation*, 189 U.S.P.Q. 649, 679 (Mich. 1975).

ᴡ

An infringer should not be permitted to sidestep main issues by nit-picking the patent file in every minute respect with the effect of trying the patentee personally, rather than the patent. A patentee's oversights are easily magnified out of proportion by one accused of infringement seeking to escape the reach of the patent by hostilely combing the inventor's files in liberal pretrial discovery proceedings. *Preemption Devices, Inc. v. Minnesota Mining and Manufacturing Co.*, 559 F.Supp. 1250, 218 U.S.P.Q. 245, 257 (Pa. 1983).

ᴡ

There is an obvious distinction between the alleged injury of a party threatened with a lawsuit for infringement and the alleged injury of a patent holder. In a typical patent case brought under the Declaratory Judgment Act, 28 U.S.C. §2201, the plaintiff asserts his intent and ability to produce a product, which defendant contends is a patent infringement. Courts find a justiciable controversy because to do otherwise would leave the plaintiff no option but to produce the products and be sued for infringement. The patent holder, on the other hand, is injured only if actual infringement occurs. His remedy is provided in 35 U.S.C. §271. *D. G. Rung Industries, Inc. v. Tinnerman*, 626 F. Supp. 1062, 229 U.S.P.Q. 930, 932 (Wash. 1986).

ɷ

Literal infringement requires that an accused device embody every element of a claim as properly interpreted. If the claim describes a combination of functions, and each function is performed by a means described in the specification or an equivalent of such means, then literal infringement holds. When a claimed invention is a novel combination of steps, all possible methods of carrying out each step of the combination are not required to be described in the specification. Correctly construed claims cover "equivalents" of the described embodiments. The purpose is to grant an inventor of a combination invention a fair scope that is not dependent on a catalog of alternative embodiments in the specification. The court has cautioned against limiting the claimed invention to preferred embodiments or specific examples in the specification. The details of performing each step need not be included in the claims unless required to distinguish the claimed invention from the prior art, or otherwise to specifically point out and distinctly claim the invention. Claims should be read in a way that avoids enabling an infringer to "practice a fraud on a patent."

It is not required that those skilled in the art knew, at the time the patent application was filed, of the asserted equivalent means of performing the claimed functions; that equivalence is determined as of the time infringement takes place. Infringement will be found when the material features of a patent have been appropriated, even when those features have been patentably improved. *Texas Instruments, Inc. v. United States International Trade Commission*, 805 F.2d 1558, 231 U.S.P.Q. 833 (Fed. Cir. 1986).

ɷ

Use or manufacture for the United States is immune from suit for patent infringement in the district courts against the user or manufacturer. If and when such making and/or using takes place, a patentee's only recourse is to sue the United States in the Claims Court for its entire compensation. The patentee takes his patent from the United States subject to the government's eminent domain rights to obtain what it needs from manufacturers and to use the same. The government has graciously consented to be sued in the Claims Court for reasonable and entire compensation for what would be infringement if by a private person. *W. L. Gore & Associates, Inc. v. Garlock, Inc.*, 842 F.2d 1275, 6 U.S.P.Q.2d 1277 (Fed. Cir. 1988).

ɷ

Under the entire-market-value rule, a patentee is entitled to lost profits on unpatented components that accompany the sale of patented components where, in all reasonable probability, the patentee would have made the sales that the infringer made. The record shows that the company that sells the belts also gets the sales of the sprockets, transfer combs, and belt accessories. Under the entire-market-value rule, the court therefore finds that it is reasonably probable that the patentee would have sold the sprockets, transfer combs, and accessories in view of the above findings and the court's prior determination that it is reasonably probable that the patentee would have made the sales but for the infringement. *Rexnord Inc. v. Laitram Corp.*, 6 U.S.P.Q.2d 1817 (Wis. 1988).

ɷ

Each one of the States of the United States has sovereign immunity under the Eleventh Amendment and thus cannot be sued by an individual of another state for patent infringement in a federal district court. *Chew v. California*, 893 F.2d 331, 13 U.S.P.Q.2d 1393, 1395, 1396 (Fed. Cir. 1990).

ᚹ

There are exceptions to the axiom that dependent claims cannot be found infringed unless the claims from which they depend have been found to have been infringed. *Wilson Sporting Goods Co. v. David Geoffrey & Associates*, 904 F.2d 676, 14 U.S.P.Q.2d 1942, 1949 (Fed. Cir. 1990).

ᚹ

Even when a claim literally reads on a device, actual infringement will not exist if the accused device performs in a substantially different way. Thus, irrespective of the existence of literal infringement (i.e., a literal reading of the claim on the accused device), the determination of actual infringement may require that the accused device be examined under the doctrine of equivalents or reverse equivalents. *The Laitram Corp. v. Rexnord Inc.*, 15 U.S.P.Q.2d 1161, 1167 (Wis. 1990).

ᚹ

The duty of due care normally requires a party to obtain legal advice before initiating or continuing an operation that might result in infringement. Failure to obtain an opinion of counsel is one of the factors supporting a finding of willfulness. This principle, which addresses the conduct of an accused willful infringer, is part of the substantive law of patents and is not merely a procedural housekeeping rule. A federal court exercising patent jurisdiction is bound by the substantive patent law of the Federal Circuit. When an infringer fails to introduce (at trial) an opinion of counsel pertaining to the activity in question, an adverse inference may be drawn against the infringer that any legal advice obtained regarding the activity in question was unfavorable to the infringer. *ALM Surgical Equipment Inc. v. Kirschner Medical Corp.*, 15 U.S.P.Q.2d 1241, 1251 (S.C. 1990).

ᚹ

One who does not infringe an independent claim cannot infringe a claim dependent on (and thus containing all the limitations of) that claim. *Becton Dickinson & Co. v. C. R. Bard Inc.*, 922 F.2d 792, 17 U.S.P.Q.2d 1097, 1101 (Fed. Cir. 1990).

ᚹ

In an infringement action, the court found that defendant's entire prosecution of its inequitable conduct counterclaim constituted misconduct for which plaintiff was entitled to compensation under 35 U.S.C. §285. *Beckman Instruments Inc. v. LKB Produkter AB*, 17 U.S.P.Q.2d 1190 (Md. 1990).

ᚹ

Uses of a patented invention not "solely for uses reasonably related to the development and submission of information under Federal law which regulates the manufacture, use, or sale of drugs" is an act of infringement. The statute does not permit other uses, such as obtaining foreign pre-marketing approval and any promotional or commercial use in the United States or abroad. The intent of this statute was narrowly limited by Congress to permitting generic manufacturers to establish the bioequivalency of a generic substitute drug. *Ortho Pharmaceutical Corp. v. Smith*, 18 U.S.P.Q.2d 1977, 1992 (Pa. 1990).

ω

Although claim interpretation is a question of law, expert testimony is admissible to give an opinion on the ultimate question of infringement. *Symbol Technologies Inc. v. Opticon Inc.*, 935 F.2d 1569, 19 U.S.P.Q.2d 1241, 1245 (Fed. Cir. 1991).

ω

As stated by the Supreme Court in *Crown Die & Tool Co. v. Nye Tool Mach. Works*, 261 U.S. 24 (1923):

> The law as to who should bring a suit at law for damages by infringement of a patent is clearly and correctly stated in *III Robinson on Patents*, 937 [1890], as follows:
>
> With a single exception the plaintiff in an action at law must be the person or persons in whom the legal title to the patent resided at the time of the infringement. An infringement is an invasion of the monopoly created by the patent, and the law which defines and authorizes this monopoly confers only upon its legal owners the right to institute proceedings for its violation. These owners are the patentee, his assignee, his grantee, or his personal representatives; and none but these are able to maintain an action for infringement in a court of law....

261 U.S. at 40-41 (emphasis added). The exception referred to by Robinson is where the assignment of a patent is coupled with an assignment of a right of action for past infringements. *Arachnid Inc. v. Merit Industries Inc.*, 939 F.2d 1574, 19 U.S.P.Q.2d 1513, 1517 (Fed. Cir. 1991).

ω

The question of infringement can be dealt with as a matter of law. *Intellicall Inc. v. Phonometrics Inc.*, 952 F.2d 1384, 21 U.S.P.Q.2d 1383 (Fed. Cir. 1992).

ω

A court (in a patent action) may grant summary judgment on the question of infringement, yet reserve other issues, such as validity of the patent or damages, for trial. "Though an invalid [patent] claim cannot give rise to liability for infringement, whether it is infringed is an entirely separate question capable of determination without regard to its validity." Nonetheless, "[b]ecause both validity and infringement involve construction of a claim, and the construction must be the same in determining both, it is desirable to decide both questions at the same time." *Al-Site Corp. v. Opti-Ray Inc.*, 23 U.S.P.Q.2d 1235, 1237 (N.Y. 1992).

ω

As a matter of terminology, the doctrine of equivalents applies only to infringement of a claim and to an equivalent to a limitation of the claim, not "equivalency" between an accused device and a patented invention. To refer to "equivalency" to the invention creates confusion and is technically inaccurate. The statutory requirement for liability is "infringement" of a patent, not "equivalency" between devices or methods. 35 U.S.C. §281. Equivalency to limitations of the claim must be the focus of the inquiry, particularly in jury trials. *The Read Corp. v. Portec Inc.*, 970 F.2d 816, 23 U.S.P.Q.2d 1426, 1431 (Fed. Cir. 1992).

ᴡ

The Federal Circuit's affirmance of a finding that a patent has not been infringed is not *per se* a sufficient reason for vacating a declaratory judgment holding the patent invalid. *Cardinal Chemical Co. v. Morton International Inc.*, 113 S.Ct. 1967, 26 U.S.P.Q.2d 1721, 1722 (S.Ct. 1993).

ᴡ

Infringement of a process patent can be based on unbuilt plants for which contracts exist when the plants are for a system which will practice the patented process. *Joy Technologies Inc. v. Flakt Inc.*, 820 F.Supp. 802, 27 U.S.P.Q.2d 1766, 1771 (Del. 1993).

ᴡ

There are significant differences between the reexamination procedure and patent litigation in the federal courts. The two forms of proceedings are distinct, with different records and different standards of proof. When considering validity, the PTO gives claims their broadest reasonable interpretation consistent with the specification of the patent. In contrast, courts may construe claims liberally to uphold a patent's validity, rather than to destroy an inventor's right to protect the substance of his or her invention. *Whistler Corp. v. Dynascan Corp.*, 29 U.S.P.Q.2d 1866, 1871 (Ill. 1993).

ᴡ

While it is true that the issues of ownership and infringement are unrelated in terms of the legal issues and matters of proof, they are yet inextricably intertwined in that proof of one is necessary for actions on the other. ("Status as an assignee or patentee is a crucial prerequisite to bringing suit on infringement.") *Loral Fairchild Corp. v. Matsushita Electric Industrial Co. Ltd.*, 840 F.Supp. 211, 31 U.S.P.Q.2d 1499, 1503 (N.Y. 1994).

ᴡ

"Neither intent to infringe nor knowledge that a subsisting patent covers what one is making, using, or selling is an element of a direct patent infringement action under 35 U.S.C. §271(a)." Further, " '[w]here the (corporate) officer or director has directed or ordered the infringing method of manufacture or has controlled the sale of the infringing goods, he is jointly liable with the corporation for patent infringement without regard to his specific intent or knowledge.' " Many courts "have recognized and imposed personal liability on corporate officers for participating in, inducing, and approving acts of patent infringement." *Flowdata Inc. v. Cotton*, 871 F.Supp. 925, 32 U.S.P.Q.2d 1743, 1746 (Tex. 1994).

ᴡ

"In deciding whether to conduct contempt proceedings, a trial court must act expeditiously to protect litigants from continuing infringements after an adjudication. Further, a trial court may act expeditiously to enforce its orders in the face of conduct ignoring judicial authority. "Infringement is the *sine qua non* of violation of an injunction against infringements." *Additive Controls and Measurement Systems Inc. v. Flowdata Inc.*, 32 U.S.P.Q.2d 1747, 1753 (Tex. 1994).

ᴡ

If the allegedly infringing device fails to meet even a single patent claim limitation, no infringement exists. If one claim limitation is missing, there is no infringement as a matter of law. A dependent claim is infringed where all of the express limitations of the dependent claim are satisfied and where all of the limitations of the claim to which the dependent claim refers are satisfied. *Endress + Hauser Inc. v. Hawk Measurement Systems Pty. Ltd.*, 32 U.S.P.Q.2d 1768, 1774, 1775 (Ind. 1994).

ᚖ

Patent infringement is a tort. Its injury occurs in the state where the patentee resides if an infringing article is sold there. *Hupp v. Siroflex of America Inc.*, 848 F.Supp. 744, 32 U.S.P.Q.2d 1842 (Tex. 1994).

ᚖ

The issue of infringement is a factual determination. *Ramos v. Boehringer Manheim Corp.*, 861 F.Supp. 1064, 33 U.S.P.Q.2d 1172, 1180 (Fla. 1994).

ᚖ

An assignment by the patent owner of the whole of the patent right, or of an undivided part of the right, or of all rights in a specified geographical region, gives an assignee the right to bring an action for infringement in his own name. Any less complete transfer of rights is a license rather than an assignment. If the patent owner grants only a license, the title remains in the owner of the patent; and suit must be brought in his name, and never in the name of the licensee alone, unless that is necessary to prevent an absolute failure of justice, as where the patentee is the infringer, and cannot sue himself. Any rights of the licensee must be enforced through or in the name of the owner of the patent, and perhaps, if necessay to protect the rights of all parties, joining the licensee with him as a plaintiff. *Abbott Laboratories v. Ortho Diagnostic Systems Inc.*, 47 F.3d 1128, 33 U.S.P.Q.2d 1771, 1773 (Fed. Cir. 1995).

ᚖ

A patentee is "under an obligation to make a diligent inquiry into any factual circumstances that might reasonably suggest the possibility of infringement." *Valutron N.V. v. NCR Corp.*, 33 U.S.P.Q.2d 1986, 1989 (Ohio 1992), *aff'd* (Fed. Cir. 1993), *cert. denied,* (S.Ct. 1994).

ᚖ

A patent infringement plaintiff bears a significant pre-filing investigation burden before asserting a patent claim, and such burden cannot be fulfilled by merely filing suit on a suspicion of infringement and then asking for discovery to prove up the suspicions. "To fulfill his duty, an attorney must investigate the fact, examine the law, and then decide whether the Complaint is justified." *Nasatka v. Delta Scientific Corp.*, 34 U.S.P.Q.2d 1649, 1652 (Va. 1994).

ᚖ

Claim interpretation in view of the prosecution history is a preliminary step in determining literal infringement, while prosecution history estoppel applies as a limitation on the range of equivalents if, after the claims have been properly interpreted, no literal infringement has been found. *Southwall Technologies Inc. v. Cardinal IG Co.*, 54 F.3d 1570, 34 U.S.P.Q.2d 1673, 1679 (Fed. Cir. 1995).

ᚖ

If a patentee's failure to practice a patented invention frustrates an important public need for the invention, a court need not enjoin infringement of the patent. *Rite-Hite Corp. v. Kelley Co. Inc.*, 56 F.3d 1538, 35 U.S.P.Q.2d 1065, 1071 (Fed. Cir. 1995).

ʊ

When plaintiff alleges that defendant has sold an infringing product, "a patent infringement occurs where allegedly infringing sales are made." When no sales of an accused product have occurred, promotion and advertising of the product in Massachusetts is an "infringing activity" or "offending act". *Hologic Inc. v. Lunar Corp.*, 36 U.S.P.Q.2d 1182, 1187 (Mass. 1995).

ʊ

Infringement is a strict liability offense, and a court must award "damages adequate to compensate for the infringement," regardless of the intent, culpability or motivation of the infringer. *Jurgens v. CBK Ltd.*, 80 F.3d 1566, 38 U.S.P.Q.2d 1397, 1400 n.2 (Fed. Cir. 1996).

ʊ

Modern patent infringement actions derive "from the infringement actions tried at law in the 18th century, and there is no dispute that infringement cases today must be tried to a jury." *Markman v. Westview Instruments, Inc.*, 116 S.Ct. 1384, 1389, 38 U.S.P.Q.2d 1461 (1996).

ʊ

A patent on an alleged infringing article is irrelevant to the issue of infringement. *Enforcer Products Inc. v. Birdsong*, 40 U.S.P.Q.2d 1958 (Fed. Cir.—unpublished).

ʊ

In evaluating infringement under the doctrine of equivalents, "representation[s] to foreign patent offices should be considered...when [they] comprise relevant evidence." *Tanabe Seiyaku Co. v. U.S. International Trade Commission*, 41 U.S.P.Q.2d 1976 (Fed. Cir. 1997).

ʊ

The common law bona fide purchaser for value rule provides an affirmative defense to patent infringement and conversion claims. *Heidelberg Harris Inc. v. Loebach*, 145 F.3d 1454, 43 U.S.P.Q.2d 1049, 1052 (N.H. 1997).

ʊ

The grant of a patent on an accused device does not conclusively avoid infringement. The fact, however, that an accused infringer's patent overcame a prior art reference to plaintiff's patent is a factor indicating that plaintiff's device is substantially different. *Aeroquip Corp. v. U.S.*, 43 U.S.P.Q.2d 1503, 1509 (U.S. Ct. Fed. Cl. 1997).

ʊ

Although a claim need not be limited to a preferred embodiment, in a given case, the scope of the right to exclude may be limited by a narrow disclosure. *The Gentry Gallery Inc. v. The Berkline Corp.*, 134 F.3d 1473, 45 U.S.P.Q.2d 1498, 1503 (Fed. Cir. 1998).

ʊ

If a device is designed to be altered or assembled before operation, manufacturer may be liable for infringement if the device, as altered or assembled, infringes a valid patent. A device which is programmable, as made and sold, to perform a patented function, is deemed presently capable and therefore infringing. *Stryker Corp. v. Davol Inc.*, 47 U.S.P.Q.2d 1740, 1743 (Mich. 1998).

ʊ

The fact of separate patentability presents no legal or evidentiary presumption of noninfringement. *Hoechst Celanese Corp. v. BP Chemicals Ltd.*, 78 F.3d 1575, 1582, 38 U.S.P.Q.2d 1126, 1132 (Fed. Cir. 1996); *Victus Ltd. v. Collezione Europa U.S.A. Inc.*, 48 U.S.P.Q.2d 1145, 1147 (N.C. 1998).

Infringement Charge.

A mere verbal charge of infringement, if made, followed by silence is not sufficient affirmative conduct to induce a belief that a patentee has abandoned an infringement claim. *Meyers v. Brooks Shoe Inc.*, 912 F.2d 1459, 16 U.S.P.Q.2d 1055, 1057 (Fed. Cir. 1990).

Infringement Notice.

Infringement notices have been enjoined when the patentee acted in bad faith, for example by making threats without intending to file suit, or when the patentee had no good faith belief in the validity of its patent. *Elkhart Brass Manufacturing Co. Inc. v. Task Force Tips Inc.*, 867 F.Supp. 782, 34 U.S.P.Q.2d 1402, 1406 (Ind. 1994).

Infringement of Title.

No reasonable layperson would read "infringement of title" in the context of "advertising injury" in an insurance policy and conclude that it refers to direct patent infringement, contributory patent infringement, or inducement of patent infringement. *Classic Corp. v. Charter Oak Fire Insurance Co.*, 35 U.S.P.Q.2d 1726, 1728 (Cal. 1995).

Infringement Opinion.

Ordering file histories is a normal and necessary preliminary to a validity or infringement opinion. *Underwater Devices Inc. v. Morrison-Knudsen Co.*, 717 F.2d 1380, 219 U.S.P.Q. 569 (Fed. Cir. 1983).

Infringer.

An infringer should not be permitted to side-step main issues by nit-picking the patent file in every minute respect with the effect of trying the patentee personally, rather than the patent. A patentee's oversights are easily magnified out of proportion by one accused of infringement seeking to escape the reach of the patent by hostilely combing the inventor's files in liberal pretrial discovery proceedings. *Preemption Devices, Inc. v. Minnesota Mining and Manufacturing Co.*, 559 F.Supp. 1250, 218 U.S.P.Q. 245, 257 (Pa. 1983).

Ingenuity.

In judging what requires uncommon ingenuity, the best standard is what common ingenuity has failed to contrive. Once a problem has been solved, it may be easy to see how prior art references can be modified and manipulated to reconstruct the solution. The change may be simple and, by hindsight, seem obvious. However, the simplicity of new inventions is oftentimes the very thing that is not obvious before they are made. *In re Sporck,* 301 F.2d 686, 133 U.S.P.Q. 360, 363 (C.C.P.A. 1962).

Ingredient.

The active ingredient of Ceftin Tablets is cefuroxime axetil. Unique properties of this distinct pharmaceutical compound make it therapeutically active and effective when administered orally. Cefuroxime axetil is an ester of cefuroxime, an organic acid. This acid and its salts are antibiotics that are therapeutically active only when administered intramuscularly or intravenously. Neither is effective if administered orally. Since two sodium salts of cefuroxime had been previously marketed, the Commissioner denied approval of a request for patent term extension, asserting that cefuroxime axetil was not eligible for patent term extension because FDA approval of Ceftin Tablets was not the first permitted commercial marketing or use of the product. Cefuroxime axetil, active on oral administration, is absorbed from the gastrointestinal tract and then hydrologized in the blood and intestinal tract to release cefuroxime into the circulation. It is cefuroxime that is the effective antibacterial agent. Because the therapeutic of cefuroxime axetil is ultimately related to the cefuroxime released in the digestive tract, the Commissioner argued that cefuroxime is "the active moiety" of Ceftin Tablets and therefore falls within 35 U.S.C. §156 (a)(5)(A). This rationale is untenable, its form manifest. The statute says "ingredient" not "moiety," and ingredient must be present in the drug product when administered. This is an insurmountable obstacle for the Commissioner's proposed rationale; he concedes that "cefuroxime itself is not an ingredient of Ceftin Tablets." Even if a moiety in pharmaceutical parlance, is something that results from chemical changes occurring after the drug is administered and need not itself be present in the drug product at the time of administration, this is not the plain meaning of ingredient. *GLAXO Operations U.K. Ltd. v. Quigg,* 706 F. Supp. 1224, 10 U.S.P.Q.2d 1100 (Va. 1989).

In Haec Verba. See also **Describe**, *Expressis Verbis*, *Ipsis Verbis*.

Claimed subject matter need not be described in the specification in haec verba to satisfy the description requirement. It is not necessary that the application describe the claim limitations exactly, but only so clearly that one having ordinary skill in the pertinent art would recognize from the disclosure that appellants invented processes including those limitations. *In re Herschler*, 591 F.2d 693, 200 U.S.P.Q. 711, 717 (C.C.P.A. 1979).

Inherency. *See also* **Doctrine of Inherency, Inherent.**

By disclosing a device that inherently performs a function, operates according to a theory, or has an advantage, a patent applicant necessarily discloses that function, theory, or advantage even though he says nothing concerning it. The application may be later amended to recite the function, theory, or advantage without introducing prohibited new matter. *In re Smythe and Shamos*, 480 F.2d 1376, 178 U.S.P.Q. 279 (C.C.P.A. 1973).

ω

Nothing in the record would lead one of ordinary skill to anticipate successful production on a commercial scale from a combination of elements of reference processes, without increase in glycol-acid ratio. The record in fact reflects the contrary. The view that success would have been inherent cannot substitute for a showing of reasonable expectation of success. Inherency and obviousness are entirely different concepts. *In re Rinehart*, 531 F.2d 1048, 189 U.S.P.Q. 143 (C.C.P.A. 1976).

ω

Where claimed and prior-art products are identical or substantially identical, or are produced by identical or substantially identical processes, the PTO can require an applicant to prove that the prior-art products do not necessarily or inherently possess the characteristics of the claimed product. Whether the rejection is based on "inherency" under 35 U.S.C. §102 and/or on "*prima facie* obviousness" under 35 U.S.C. §103, jointly or alternatively, the burden of proof is the same. *In re Best*, 562 F.2d 1252, 195 U.S.P.Q. 430 (C.C.P.A. 1977).

ω

The inherency of an advantage and its obviousness are entirely different questions. That which may be inherent is not necessarily known. Obviousness cannot be predicated on what is unknown. *In re Shetty*, 566 F.2d 81, 195 U.S.P.Q. 753, 757 (C.C.P.A. 1977).

ω

Inherency may not be established by probabilities or possibilities. The mere fact that a certain thing may result from a given set of circumstances is not sufficient. *Hansgirg v. Kemmer*, 102 F.2d 212, 40 U.S.P.Q. 665, 667 (C.C.P.A. 1939); *In re Oelrich and Divigard*, 666 F.2d 578, 212 U.S.P.Q. 323, 326 (C.C.P.A. 1981).

ω

Patentability of a new use (of an old material) based on an inherent, but previously unrecognized, property is not precluded. A contrary conclusion confuses anticipation by inherency, i.e., lack of novelty, with obviousness. *Jones v. Hardy*, 727 F.2d 1524, 220 U.S.P.Q. 1021, 1025 (Fed. Cir. 1984).

ω

Before an interference was declared, the Examiner rejected (in the Fine application) the newly presented claims that Fine had substantially copied from the Parks patent. One of the grounds of rejection was that, because the earlier Fine claims did not expressly include the absence-of-a-catalyst limitation, the present Fine claims containing that limitation were barred under 35 U.S.C. §135(b) as not having been "made prior to one year from the date" on which the Parks patent was granted. The implication in the specification that catalysts would not or need not be used does not imply that they must not be used. It is not sufficient to compel the inclusion of that limitation into claims not expressly so stating. "The inquiry here is not whether such a step is inherently disclosed, as it might be in a right-to-make case. Rather, the question is whether the step necessarily occurs in the process as claimed." *Parks v. Fine*, 773 F.2d 1577, 227 U.S.P.Q. 432 (Fed. Cir. 1985).

ω

There is no presumptive correlation that two similar processes form substantially the same product where the processes differ by a materially limiting step. When prior art fails to disclose a method for making a claimed compound, at the time the invention was made, it cannot be legally concluded that the compound itself is in the possession of the public. *Ashland Oil, Inc. v. Delta Resins & Refractories, Inc.*, 776 F.2d 281, 227 U.S.P.Q. 657 (Fed. Cir. 1985).

ω

Inherency may not be established by probabilities or possibilities. The mere fact that a certain thing may result from a given set of circumstances is not sufficient. An applicant may be required to prove that the subject matter shown to be in prior art does not possess characteristics relied upon, where an Examiner has reason to believe that a functional limitation asserted to be critical for establishing novelty in the claimed subject matter may, in fact, be an inherent characteristic of the prior art. However, the Examiner must provide some evidence or scientific reasoning to establish the reasonableness of the Examiner's belief that the functional limitation is an inherent characteristic of the prior art before the applicant can be put through this burdensome task. *Ex parte Skinner*, 2 U.S.P.Q. 2d 1788 (B.P.A.I. 1986).

ω

A reference that discloses the same process does not have to recognize a particular inherent property of any aspect of that process to negate validity of a claim to the process. *Verdegaal Brothers Inc. v. Union Oil Co. of California*, 814 F.2d 628, 2 U.S.P.Q. 2d 1051 (Fed. Cir. 1987).

ω

A retrospective view of inherency is not a substitute for some teaching or suggestion that supports the selection and use of the elements in the particular claimed combination. In deciding that a novel combination would have been obvious, there must be supporting teaching in the prior art; for that which may be inherent is not necessarily known, and obviousness cannot be predicated on what is unknown. *In re Newell*, 891 F.2d 899, 13 U.S.P.Q.2d 1248, 1250 (Fed. Cir. 1989).

ω

Inherency and obviousness are distinct concepts. The inherency of an advantage and obviousness are entirely different questions. That which may be inherent was not necessarily known; obviousness cannot be predicated on what is unknown. When the PTO asserts that there is an explicit or implicit teaching or suggestion in the prior art, the PTO must produce supporting references. *In re Dillon*, 892 F.2d 1554, 13 U.S.P.Q.2d 1337, 1348 (Fed. Cir. 1989); *opinion withdrawn*, 919 F.2d 688, 16 U.S.P.Q.2d 1897, 1899 (Fed. Cir. 1990).

ω

Anticipation is not avoided where a prior achievement was deliberate or a necessary consequence of what was intended even though the achiever did not fully appreciate the uses, purposes, or properties of the product or process. This concept is known as "inherency." *General Electric Co. v. Hoechst Celanese Corp.*, 683 F. Supp. 305, 16 U.S.P.Q.2d 1977, 1982 (Del. 1990).

ᴛ

Anticipation by inherency requires that 1) the missing descriptive matter be "necessarily present" in the prior art reference and that 2) it would be so recognized by persons of ordinary skill in the art. *Continental Can Co. v. Monsanto Co.*, 948 F.2d 1264, 1268, 20 U.S.P.Q.2d 1746, 1749 (Fed. Cir. 1991).

Inherency Doctrine.

This doctrine infers a lack of novelty in a product under 35 U.S.C. §101 when a comparable process for making a product is found to exist in prior art. In this case the claimed product (if produced by the reference process) was produced in such minuscule amounts and under such conditions that its presence was undetectable. Under the circumstances, the reference is not an anticipation. *In re Seaborg*, 328 F.2d 996, 140 U.S.P.Q. 662 (C.C.P.A. 1964).

ᴛ

For the doctrine of inherency to apply, it must be inevitable that the application of the winning party in a prior interference uses an undenatured soybean meal. Since the PTO has failed to show that the use of undenatured starting material is inherent in that application, it has failed to demonstrate that the claimed subject matter is clearly common to both appellant's application and that of the adverse interference party. *In re Wilding*, 535 F.2d 631, 190 U.S.P.Q. 59, 63 (C.C.P.A. 1976).

Inherent. *See also* Inherency, Result.

Even when a specific inherent property is not disclosed, it can be relied upon for patentability if it is manifest in the disclosed use of a claimed product. *In re Zenitz*, 333 F.2d 924, 142 U.S.P.Q. 158, 161 (C.C.P.A. 1964).

ᴛ

Having been produced by the same process, the product obtained in Example IV of the earlier Sulkowski application is, of necessity, the same product as that obtained in Example III of the Sulkowski interference application. The only difference is in the naming of the product. Based on the process used in the earlier application, Sulkowski is entitled to the benefit of the product of that process with his later application. The fact that error was made in naming the product in the first application does not deprive Sulkowski of the benefit of that application. *Sulkowski v. Houlihan*, 179 U.S.P.Q. 685, 686 (PTO Bd. Pat. Int. 1973). *See also In re Sulkowski*, 487 F.2d 920, 180 U.S.P.Q. 46 (C.C.P.A. 1973).

ᴛ

To preclude patentability under 35 U.S.C. §103, there must be some predictability of success in any attempt to combine elements of reference processes. The view that success would have been "inherent" cannot substitute for a showing of reasonable expectation of success. *In re Rinehart*, 531 F.2d 1048, 189 U.S.P.Q. 143, 148 (C.C.P.A. 1976).

ᢍ

A newly-discovered function or property, inherently possessed by things in the prior art, does not cause a claim drawn to those things to distinguish over the prior art. Where claimed and prior-art products are identical or substantially identical, or are produced by identical or substantially identical processes, the PTO can require an applicant to prove that the prior-art products do not necessarily or inherently possess the characteristics of the claimed product. Whether the rejection is based on "inherency" under 35 U.S.C. §102 and/or on "*prima facie* obviousness" under 35 U.S.C. §103, jointly or alternatively, the burden of proof is the same, and its fairness is evidenced by the PTO's inability to manufacture products or to obtain and compare prior-art products. *In re Best*, 562 F.2d 1252, 195 U.S.P.Q. 430, 433 (C.C.P.A. 1977).

ᢍ

The filing of a cip application to overcome a PTO rejection does not give rise to an irrebuttable presumption of acquiescence in the rejection. Whether claims are entitled to a cip application's filing date or that of a parent application becomes important when an intervening event occurs that will invalidate the claims under 35 U.S.C. §102 if they are only accorded the later filing date. When a cip is filed subsequent to receipt of a "new matter" rejection, the applicant may be estopped from arguing that the cip application only added subject matter that was inherent in the parent application. *Foseco International Ltd. v. Fireline, Inc.*, 607 F. Supp. 1537, 226 U.S.P.Q. 33 (Ohio 1984).

ᢍ

Declaration evidence of unexpected results is not negated by an Examiner's assertion that such results are inherent. *Ex parte Ohsaka*, 2 U.S.P.Q.2d 1461 (B.P.A.I. 1987).

ᢍ

By disclosing in a patent application a device that inherently performs a function, operates according to a theory, or has an advantage, a patent applicant necessarily discloses that function, theory, or advantage, even though he says nothing concerning it. The express description of an inherent property, since not "new matter," can be added to a specification with effect as of the original filing date. The additional description is not that of a new use, but of the existing physical structure of the product. *Kennecott Corp. v. Kyocera International, Inc.*, 835 F.2d 1419, 5 U.S.P.Q.2d 1194 (Fed. Cir. 1987); *see also In re Smythe and Shamos*, 480 F.2d 1376, 178 U.S.P.Q. 279 (C.C.P.A. 1973).

ᢍ

Inherent properties of known compositions are not patentable. *General Electric Co. v. Hoechst Celanese Corp.*, 683 F. Supp. 305, 16 U.S.P.Q.2d 1977, 1985 (Del. 1990).

ᢍ

"That which may be inherent is not necessarily known. Obviousness cannot be predicated on what is unknown." A retrospective view of inherency is not a substitute for some teaching or suggestion supporting an obviousness rejection. *In re Rijckaert*, 9 F.3d 1531, 28 U.S.P.Q.2d 1955, 1957 (Fed. Cir. 1993).

Inherent Characteristic or Property.

Amendatory material concerned with an inherent characteristic of an illustrative product (already sufficiently identified in an original disclosure as filed) is not prohibited by statute. In *Ex parte Davisson and Finlay* [133 U.S.P.Q. 400, 402 (PO Bd. App. 1958)] for example, the Board noted that the Examiner had entered an amendment reciting the optical rotation data and elemental analysis of the sulfate of a claimed substance as well as the spectroscopic characteristics of the claimed substance "apparently regarding them as a statement of inherent properties of the material adequately disclosed" in an original disclosure and stated that it saw no reason for "taking a different view of the matter." *In re Nathan, Hogg, and Schneider*, 328 F.2d 1005, 140 U.S.P.Q. 601 (C.C.P.A. 1964).

In-House Counsel.

A party may recover in-house counsel fees only when sufficient documentation is provided; contemporaneous time records are not necessary, as long as the records are reasonably accurate and substantially reconstruct the time spent. Fees for in-house counsel are appropriate only when counsel is performing legal work that would otherwise be performed by outside counsel; time spent by in-house counsel in the role of a client, such as time spent keeping abreast of the progress of the litigation and advising outside counsel of the client's views as to litigation strategy, is not compensable in a fee award. *Scripps Clinic & Research Foundation v. Baxter Travenol Laboratories, Inc.*, 17 U.S.P.Q.2d 1046, 1047 (Del. 1990).

In-House Documentation.

Validity was denied by a memo that was admittedly not prior art, notwithstanding the fact that the contents of such memo had been concealed by the alleged infringer. *Newell Companies, Inc. v. Kenney Manufacturing Co.*, 606 F. Supp. 1282, 226 U.S.P.Q. 157 (R.I. 1985).

Initializing.

Steps, such as "computing", "determining", "cross-correlating", "comparing", "selecting", "initializing", "testing", "modifying", and "identifying", have implicitly been found to recite the solving of a mathematical algorithm. *In re Warmerdam*, 33 F.3d 1354, 31 U.S.P.Q.2d 1754, 1758 (Fed. Cir. 1994).

Injunction. *See also* Injunctive Relief, Irreparabale Harm, Lanham Act, Permanent Injunction, Preliminary Injunction, Public Interest, Right to Exclude.

A patentee takes his patent from the United States subject to the government's eminent domain rights to obtain what it needs for manufacture and to use the same. The government has graciously consented to be sued in the Claims Court for reasonable and entire compensation for what would be infringement if by a private person. The same principles apply to injunctions that are nothing more than giving the aid of the courts to the enforcement of the patentee's right to exclude. Though injunctions may seem to say that making for and selling to the government is forbidden, injunctions based on patent rights cannot in reality do that because of 28 U.S.C. §1498(a). *W. L. Gore & Associates, Inc. v. Garlock, Inc.*, 842 F.2d 1275, 6 U.S.P.Q.2d 1277, 1284 (Fed. Cir. 1988).

ᚠ

One who elects to build a business on a product found to infringe cannot be heard to complain when an injunction against continuing infringement destroys the business so elected. An injunction after trial on the merits prohibits infringement by any product, not just those involved in the original suit. The burden of avoiding infringement at the risk of contempt falls upon the one enjoined. *ALM Surgical Equipment Inc. v. Kirschner Medical Corp.*, 15 U.S.P.Q.2d 1241, 1255 (S.C. 1990).

ᚠ

Without the right to obtain an injunction, a patentee's right to exclude others would be worth only a fraction of its intended value, which would sharply diminish the incentive to create and innovate created by the patent statute. *Ortho Pharmaceutical Corp. v. Smith*, 18 U.S.P.Q.2d 1977, 1992 (Pa. 1990).

ᚠ

For one federal court to issue an injunction forbidding litigation in another is extraordinary; for a bankruptcy judge to issue an injunction with the effect of preempting resolution of a pending motion in a district court is without authority. Because of the collateral bar doctrine, even legally erroneous injunctions must be obeyed until vacated or stayed. *In re Mahurkar Double Lumen Hemodialysis Catheter Patent Litigation*, 140 BRW 969, 23 U.S.P.Q.2d 1903, 1906, 1907 (Ill. 1992).

ᚠ

An injunction for infringement may not be punitive. *Joy Technologies, Inc. v. Flakt, Inc.*, 6 F.3d 770, 774, 28 U.S.P.Q.2d 1378 (Fed. Cir. 1993).

ᚠ

Injunctions typically "carry a prohibition against further infringement...as to the particular device found to be infringement and as to all other devices which are merely 'colorable' changes of the infringing one." *Valmet Paper Machinery Inc. v. Beloit Corp.*, 39 U.S.P.Q.2d 1878, 1890 (Wis. 1995).

Injunctive Relief. *See also* Injunction.

In matters involving patent rights, irreparable harm has been presumed when a clear showing has been made of patent validity and infringement. *Smith International, Inc. v. Hughes Tool Co.*, 718 F.2d 1573, 1581, 219 U.S.P.Q. 686, 692 (Fed. Cir.), *cert. denied*, 464 U.S. 996, 220 U.S.P.Q. 385 (1983).

ᚠ

The patent statute provides injunctive relief to preserve the legal interests of the parties against future infringement that may have marked effects never fully compensable in money. If monetary relief were the sole relief afforded by the patent statute, then injunctions would be unnecessary, and infringers could become compulsory licensees for as long as the litigation lasts. *We Care Inc. v. Ultra-Mark International Corp.*, 14 U.S.P.Q.2d 1804, 1809 (Minn. 1989).

Injury.

Among indications of possible injury four factors are often considered in 19 U.S.C. §1337 investigations: (1) significant reduction in sales, (2) idling of production facilities, (3) decrease in employment, and (4) decline in profitability. *In re Certain Large Video Matrix Display Systems and Components Thereof*, 213 U.S.P.Q. 475, 485 (U.S. ITC 1981).

Inoperable. *See also* **Inoperative.**

An inoperable invention or one that fails to achieve its intended result does not negative novelty. *United States v. Adams*, 383 U.S. 39, 148 U.S.P.Q. 479, 483 (1966).

ω

Inoperable prior-art references do not negate novelty. *Kaiser Industries Corp. v. Jones & Laughlin Steel Corp.*, 181 U.S.P.Q. 193 (Pa. 1974).

ω

A reference relied upon by the PTO appears to disclose all of the structure defined by the claims and with respective elements in the same general relationship to each other as required by such claims. Notwithstanding the foregoing, the reference apparatus is operated (for its intended purpose) only when positioned in a particular orientation that is the complete opposite from that required for the claimed apparatus (in operation). The question is not whether a patentable distinction is created by viewing a prior art apparatus from one direction and a claimed apparatus from another, but, rather, whether it would have been obvious from a fair reading of the prior art reference as a whole to turn the prior-art apparatus upside down. The reference teaches a liquid strainer that relies, at least in part, upon the assistance of gravity to separate undesired dirt and water from gasoline and other oils. Therefore, it is not seen that such reference would have provided any motivation to one of ordinary skill in the art to employ the involved apparatus in an upside-down orientation. The mere fact that the prior art could be so modified would not have made the modification obvious unless the prior art suggested the desirability of the modification. If the reference apparatus were turned upside down, it would be rendered inoperable for its intended purpose. In effect, therefore, the reference actually teaches away from the claimed invention. *In re Gordon*, 733 F.2d 900, 221 U.S.P.Q. 1125 (Fed. Cir. 1984).

Inoperative. *See also* **Inoperable, Limiting.**

When a composition is found to be inoperative for the purpose disclosed, it would be unobvious to one skilled in the art to expect that a particular composition having (as the essential component) a different chemical compound (but from the same general class) would possess the necessary properties and therefore be operative for the same purpose. *Douglas Aircraft Company, Inc. v. Mueller*, 194 F.Supp. 268, 130 U.S.P.Q. 426, 430 (D.C. 1961).

ω

In claiming a mechanical combination, an applicant is not necessarily limited to the specific composition that he discloses as the material for making up each and every element of the combination. If every element in a mechanical combination claim were required to be so specific as to exclude materials known to be inoperative and that even those not skilled in the art would not try, the claims would fail to comply with 35 U.S.C. §112 because they would be so detailed as to obscure, rather than particularly point out and distinctly claim, the invention. *In re Myers,* 410 F.2d 420, 161 U.S.P.Q. 668, 672 (C.C.P.A. 1969).

ᙡ

The mere possibility of inclusion of inoperative subject matter does not prevent allowance of broad claims. When an Examiner sets forth reasonable grounds in support of his conclusion that an applicant's claims may read on inoperative subject matter, it becomes incumbent upon the applicant either to reasonably limit his claims to the approximate area where operativeness has not been challenged or to rebut the Examiner's challenge either by the submission of representative evidence or by persuasive arguments based on known laws of physics and chemistry. *In re Cook and Merigold,* 439 F.2d 730, 169 U.S.P.Q. 298 (C.C.P.A. 1971).

ᙡ

It is almost always possible to so construe a claim as to have it read on inoperative embodiments, but the alternative of requiring an applicant to be so specific in his claims "as to exclude materials known to be inoperative and which even those not skilled in the art would not try" would result in claims that would fail to comply with 35 U.S.C. §112, second paragraph, because they would be so detailed eas to obscure, rather than to particularly point out and distinctly claim, the invention. *In re Smythe and Shamos,* 480 F.2d 1376, 178 U.S.P.Q. 279, 286 (C.C.P.A. 1973).

ᙡ

An inoperable prior art reference does not negate novelty. *Kaiser Industries Corporation v. Jones & Laughlin Steel Corporation,* 181 U.S.P.Q. 193, 197 (Pa. 1974).

ᙡ

When claims state an objective together with process steps, use of materials which might prevent achievement of the objective (by rendering the process inoperative) can hardly be said to be within the scope of the claims. Arguing that process claims encompass inoperative embodiments on the premise of unrealistic or vague assumptions is not a valid basis for rejection. *In re Geerdes,* 491 F.2d 1260, 180 U.S.P.Q. 789, 793 (C.C.P.A. 1974).

ᙡ

It is not a function of the claims to specifically exclude either possible inoperative substances or ineffective reactant proportions. *In re Dinh-Nguyen and Stenhagen,* 492 F.2d 856, 181 U.S.P.Q. 46 (C.C.P.A. 1974).

ᙡ

To prove the legal inadequacy of a disclosure of an application for letters patent based on inoperativeness, one must show (1) that it described an inoperative device, and (2) that the device so described could not be made operative by changes obvious to one of ordinary skill in the art. *Hughes Aircraft Company v. General Instrument Corporation*, 374 F.Supp. 1166, 182 U.S.P.Q. 11, 17 (Del. 1974).

ᚎ

Evidence as a whole, including both inoperative and operative examples, can negate the position that persons of ordinary skill in the relevant art, given its unpredictability, must engage in undue experimentation to determine which embodiments (complexes) work. *In re Angstadt and Griffin*, 537 F.2d 498, 190 U.S.P.Q. 214, 219 (C.C.P.A. 1976).

ᚎ

In an interference context patent claims are not read to include inoperative embodiments. *Tsuchiya v. Woods*, 220 U.S.P.Q. 984, 988 (PTO Bd. Pat. Int. 1983).

ᚎ

Even if a reference discloses an inoperative device, it is prior art for all that it teaches. *Beckman Instruments Inc. v. LKB Produkter A.B.*, 892 F.2d 1547, 13 U.S.P.Q.2d 1301, 1304 (Fed. Cir. 1989).

Inoperative Embodiments. *See also* Overclaiming.

Many patented claims read on vast numbers of inoperative embodiments in the trivial sense that they can and do omit "factors which must be presumed to be within the level of ordinary skill in the art," and therefore read on embodiments in which such factors may be included in such a manner as to make the embodiments inoperative. There is nothing wrong with this so long as it would be obvious to one of ordinary skill in the relevant art how to include those factors in such manner as to make the embodiment operative rather than inoperative. *In re Cook and Merigold*, 439 F.2d 730, 169 U.S.P.Q. 298 (C.C.P.A. 1971).

ᚎ

It is not the function of claims to specifically exclude either possible inoperative substances or ineffective reactant proportions. *Ex parte Hradcovsky*, 214 U.S.P.Q. 554 (PTO Bd. App. 1982).

ᚎ

The mere listing of emulsifiers that do not work does not necessarily invalidate a patent. Where there are a myriad of operative combinations, the inclusion of a few that are not operative need not invalidate the patent. The patent's claims can be construed to exclude those inoperative combinations. Including such inoperative combinations within the scope of a claim does not constitute invalidating "overclaiming." *Atlas Powder Co. v. E. I. du Pont de Nemours & Co.*, 588 F. Supp. 1455, 221 U.S.P.Q. 426 (Tex. 1983).

ᚎ

It is not the function of a claim to exclude possible inoperative substances. *Atlas Powder Co. v. E. I. du Pont de Nemours & Co.*, 750 F.2d 1569, 224 U.S.P.Q. 409 (Fed. Cir. 1984).

ᚎ

The claims were intended to cover the use of the invention with various types of automobiles. That a particular chair on which the claims read may fit within some automobiles and not others is of no moment. The phrase "so dimensioned" is as accurate as the subject matter permits, automobiles being of various sizes. As long as those of ordinary skill in the art realize that the dimensions could be easily obtained, 35 U.S.C. §112, second paragraph, requires nothing more. The patent law does not require that all possible lengths corresponding to the spaces in hundreds of different automobiles be listed in the patent, let alone that they be listed in the claims. *Orthokinetics Inc. v. Safety Travel Chairs Inc.*, 806 F.2d 1565, 1 U.S.P.Q.2d 1081 (Fed. Cir. 1986).

ϖ

The term "substituted alkyl" is precise and definite. The issue is not whether the Examiner can conjure a substituent group that does not exist; a person having ordinary skill in the art would readily appreciate that compounds containing such substituent group do not exist. Nobody will use inoperative embodiments, and the claims do not cover them. The skilled artisan could and would readily ascertain an embodiment or embodiments that cannot be made. *Ex parte Breuer,* 1 U.S.P.Q.2d 1906 (B.P.A.I. 1986).

Inoperativeness.

It is not a function of the claims to specifically exclude either possible inoperative substances or ineffective reactant proportions. *In re Dinh-Nguyen and Stenhagen,* 492 F.2d 856, 181 U.S.P.Q. 46 (C.C.P.A. 1974).

ϖ

Claims that include a substantial measure of inoperatives are fairly rejected under 35 U.S.C. §112. *In re Corkill,* 771 F.2d 1496, 226 U.S.P.Q. 1005 (Fed. Cir. 1985).

Inorganic.

Although there are undoubtedly a large number of acids that come within the scope of "organic and inorganic acids," the expression is not for that reason indefinite. There is no reason to believe that the public would be confused as to what subject matter is circumscribed by that expression in the claim. *In re Skoll,* 523 F.2d 1392, 187 U.S.P.Q. 481 (C.C.P.A. 1975).

In Rem.

The law does not provide for an in rem determination of patent validity in a class action. *Technitrol, Incorporated v. Control Data Corporation,* 164 U.S.P.Q. 552 (Md. 1970).

Insecticide.

In view of a considerable degree of unpredictability in the insecticide field, wherein homologs, isomers and analogs of known insecticides have been found to be ineffective as insecticides, a rejection of a claim (including homologs and isomers of reference compounds) was reversed. *In re Schechter and LaForge,* 205 F.2d 185, 98 U.S.P.Q. 144, 150 (C.C.P.A. 1953).

ϖ

The statement in a specification: "The products...are valuable as chemical intermediates for organic synthesis, for solvent uses and for the preparation of toxic substances such as insecticides, fungicides, etc." is a sufficient statement of utility under 35 U.S.C. §§101 and 112 (first paragraph). *In re Johnson*, 282 F.2d 370, 127 U.S.P.Q. 216, 217, 218 (C.C.P.A. 1960).

Inspection.

Where an application for reissue of a patent is filed while the patent is involved in interference, the PTO opens the reissue application to inspection by the opposing interference party. The purpose for opening the reissue application to inspection is to afford the opposing party an opportunity to assert claims to any common invention disclosed or claimed in the reissue application so that "the entire controversy between the parties may be terminated in one proceeding". *Bandel v. Samfield, Brock, and Locklair*, 168 U.S.P.Q. 725, 728 (PO Bd. Pat. Intf. 1961).

Inspiration.

Neither inspiration nor spur is a "teaching, suggestion, or motivation" to combine selected references in a specific way to make a specifically detailed new product. *Lamb-Weston Inc. v. McCain Foods Ltd.*, 78 F.3d 540, 37 U.S.P.Q.2d 1856, 1862 *(dissent)*(Fed. Cir. 1996).

Inspiration-Perspiration.

A development should not be regarded as obvious merely because it lay somewhere along the general stream of the prior art, although years of labor may be required to achieve it. "[T]he inspiration-perspiration process of the laboratory" is as deserving of reward as the flash of genius, and surely more so than dumb luck. *Carter-Wallace, Inc. v. Otte*, 474 F.2d 529, 176 U.S.P.Q. 2, 12 (2d Cir. 1972).

Insurance.[4]

Integral. *See also* Making Integral.

Where different parts of an integrally-connected structure have different purposes and effects, such parts may be separately recited as individual components. *Ex parte Vibber*, 144 U.S.P.Q. 278, 280 (PO Bd. App. 1959).

ω

The term, "integral", is not limited to "one piece"; it is sufficiently broad to embrace constructions united by such means as fastening and welding. *In re Hotte*, 475 F.2d 644, 177 U.S.P.Q. 326, 328 (C.C.P.A. 1973).

ω

The term "integral" is a relatively broad term inclusive of means for maintaining parts in a fixed relationship as a single unit. It is distinguished from unitary or one-piece

---

[4]*See Intex Plastics Sales Co. v. United National Insurance Co.*, 18 U.S.P.Q.2d 1567 (Cal. 1990).

construction or "fused together...to form a single part". *In re Morris*, 127 F.3d 1048, 44 U.S.P.Q.2d 1023, 1027, 1029 (Fed. Cir. 1997).

ᙡ

Although the term "integrally formed in" is not defined in the written description portion of the specification, the word "integral" means "complete" or "entire," and the word "in," as used in this context, means "indicating a point or place thought of as spatially surrounded or bounded." *See Webster's New International Dictionary* 1253, 1290 (2d ed. 1939). *Hazani v. U.S. International Trade Commission*, 126 F.3d 1473, 44 U.S.P.Q.2d 1358, 1363, 1364 (Fed. Cir. 1997).

Integration. *See* Integral, Integration Clause, Making Integral.

Integration Clause.

An integration clause is one that states, for example, that the written contract "constitutes the entire agreement between the parties,...supersedes all previous agreements, whether written or oral," and can be modified only "in writing...signed by the party against whom such modification or waiver is sought." As a general rule, covenants may only be implied into an integrated agreement "when the implied term is not inconsistent with some express term of the contract and where there arises from the language of the contract itself, and the circumstances under which it was entered into, an inference that it is absolutely necessary to introduce the term to effectuate the intention of the parties." *Eli Lilly & Co. v. Genentech Inc.*, 17 U.S.P.Q.2d 1531, 1534, 1535 (Ind. 1990).

Intelligible.

Claims which are intelligible are not indefinite. *In re Farrow, Kimber, Cole, Miles, and Griffiths*, 554 F.2d 468, 193 U.S.P.Q. 689, 693 (C.C.P.A. 1977).

Intended Meaning

During patent examination the pending claims must be interpreted as broadly as their terms reasonably allow. When the applicant states the meaning that the claimed terms are intended to have, the claims are examined with that meaning, in order to achieve complete exploration of the applicant's invention and its relation to the prior art. Before an application is granted, there is no reason to read into the claim the limitations of the specification. The reason is simply that, during patent prosecution when claims can be amended, ambiguity should be recognized, scope and breadth of language explored, and clarification imposed. The issued claims are the measure of the protected right. An essential purpose of patent examination is to fashion claims that are precise, clear, correct, and unambiguous. Only in this way can uncertainties of claimed scope be removed, as much as possible, during the administrative process. Thus, the inquiry during examination is patentability of the invention as "the applicant regards" it; and, if the claims do not particularly point out and distinctly claim, in the words of 35 U.S.C. §112, that which examination shows the applicant is entitled to claim as his invention, the appropriate PTO action is to reject the claims for that reason. A claim that reads on subject matter beyond the applicant's invention fails to comply with §112. *In re Zletz,* 893 F.2d 319, 13 U.S.P.Q.2d 1320, 1322 (Fed. Cir. 1989).

Intended Use. *See also* Preamble.

The introductory words: "A composition for setting hair", give life and meaning to the claims. An examination of the patent specification, including the objects of the invention, the discussion of the prior art, and the examples set forth, reveals that it is directed solely to compositions for setting hair. *In re Walles, Tousignant, and Houtman,* 366 F.2d 786, 151 U.S.P.Q. 185, 190 (C.C.P.A. 1966).

ω

Terms that merely set forth an intended use for, or a property inherent in, an otherwise old composition do not differentiate a claimed composition from those known to the prior art. *In re Pearson,* 494 F.2d 1399, 181 U.S.P.Q. 641 (C.C.P.A. 1974).

ω

The preamble characterization of a claimed compound as a reactive dyestuff is regarded as specifying a functional property or limitation, rather than merely an intended use. *Ex parte Schundehutte and Trautner,* 184 U.S.P.Q. 697, 698, 699 (PO Bd. App. 1974).

ω

Terms appearing in a preamble may be deemed limitations of a claim when they "give meaning to the claim and properly define the invention." *In re Paulsen,* 30 F.3d 1475, 31 U.S.P.Q.2d 1671, 1673 (Fed. Cir. 1994).

Intent. *See also* Fraud, Induce Infringement, Inequitable Conduct, Intended Use, Intent to Deceive, Intent to Mislead, 35 U.S.C. §271(b), Wrongful Intent.

Privilege, when challenged by a misrepresentation or omission before the PTO, should be pierced when and only when a *prima facie* case of fraud has been shown. In order to pierce the privilege, it is not enough to show merely inequitable conduct before the PTO. Rather, it is necessary to establish a case of fraudulent procurement: i.e., one must show (1) a knowing, willful and intentional act of misrepresentation or omission before the PTO; (2) the misrepresentation or omission must be material; and (3) the PTO must have relied upon the misrepresentation or omission. While a fraudulent intent is usually a necessary element to prove in a common law action of deceit, this intent can be presumed where there is a knowing misrepresentation of a material fact before the PTO. Of course, this presumption can be rebutted at trial by a showing of good faith on the part of applicants. *American Optical Corp. v. United States,* 179 U.S.P.Q. 682 (Ct. Cl. 1973).

ω

Although contributory infringement under 35 U.S.C. §271(c) requires a specific intent, direct infringement under §271(a) does not. *Hauni Werke Koerber & Co., KG. v. Molins Limited,* 183 U.S.P.Q. 168, 171 (Va. 1974).

ω

Intent need not, and rarely can, be proven by direct evidence. It is most often proven by a showing of acts the natural consequences of which are presumably intended by the actor. *Merck & Co. v. Danbury Pharmacal, Inc.,* 873 F.2d 1418, 10 U.S.P.Q.2d 1682, 1686 (Fed. Cir. 1989).

ʊ

Neither intent nor preparation constitutes infringement under 35 U.S.C. §271. *The Laitram Corp. v. The Cambridge Wire Cloth Co.,* 919 F.2d 1579, 16 U.S.P.Q.2d 1929, 1932 (Fed. Cir. 1990).

ʊ

Inequitable conduct requires an intent to act inequitably. Materiality of an undisclosed reference does not presume an intent to deceive. Further, a mere showing that references having some degree of materiality were not disclosed does not establish inequitable conduct. Gross negligence does not of itself justify an inference of intent to deceive. Negligent conduct can support an inference of intent only when, "viewed in light of all the evidence, including evidence of good faith," the conduct is culpable enough "to require a finding of intent to deceive." *Halliburton Co. v. Schlumberger Technology Corp.,* 925 F.2d 1435, 17 U.S.P.Q.2d 1834, 1841 (Fed. Cir. 1991).

ʊ

Actual abandonment under 35 U.S.C. §102(c) requires that the inventor intend to abandon the invention, and intent can be implied from the inventor's conduct with respect to the invention. Such intent to abandon an invention will not be imputed, and every reasonable doubt should be resolved in favor of the inventor. *Ex parte Dunne,* 20 U.S.P.Q.2d 1479, 1480 (B.P.A.I. 1991).

ʊ

The objective intent of a patentee cannot, alone, form the basis for a denial of reissue claims. There are two distinct statutory requirements that a reissue oath or declaration must satisfy. First, it must state that the patent is defective or partly inoperative or invalid either because of defects in the specification or drawing or because the patentee has claimed more or less than he is entitled to. Second, the applicant must allege that the defective, inoperative, or invalid patent arose through error without deceptive intent. "Intent to claim" is not the criterion for reissue and has little to do with "intent" per se, but rather is analogous to the requirement of 35 U.S.C. §112, first paragraph, that the specification contain a "written description of the invention, and of the manner and process of making and using it." It is synonymous with "right to claim." *In re Amos,* 953 F.2d 613, 21 U.S.P.Q.2d 1271, 1273, 1274 (Fed. Cir. 1991).

ʊ

Invalidity for inequitable conduct requires a showing, by clear and convincing evidence, of intent to deceive or mislead the patent Examiner into granting the patent. *Therma-Tru Corp. v. Peachtree Doors Inc.,* 44 F.3d 988, 33 U.S.P.Q.2d 1274, 1279 (Fed. Cir. 1995).

ʊ

No inquiry as to the subjective intent of the applicant or of the PTO is appropriate or even possible in the context of a patent infringement suit. The subjective intent of the inventor when he used a particular term is of little or no probative weight in determining the scope of a claim (except as documented in the prosecution history). *Markman v. Westview Instruments Inc.*, 52 F.3d 967, 34 U.S.P.Q.2d 1321, 1334 (Fed. Cir. 1995).

ᛦ

"The law governing interpretation of written instruments establishes that the *subjective intent* of a party is of no moment in ascertaining the meaning of the words used in the instruments.... Although Civil Code §1636 provides that a contract must be interpreted to give effect to the 'mutual intention' of the parties as it existed at the time of contracting, it is well settled that the correct approach is to avoid the terminology of 'intention' and look for the *expressed intent* under an *objective standard*." *International Rectifier Corp. v. SGS-Thomson Microelectronics Inc.*, 38 U.S.P.Q.2d 1083, 1101 (Cal. 1994).

ᛦ

A defendant may have infringed without intending, or even knowing it; but he is not, on that account, the less an infringer. *ATD Corp. v. Lydall Inc.*, 43 U.S.P.Q.2d 1170, 1178 (Mich. 1997).

ᛦ

An inventor need not have the subjective intent to claim a broadened invention for a reissue (claiming the broadened invention) to be appropriate. *Hester Industries Inc. v. Stein Inc.*, 43 U.S.P.Q.2d 1236, 1244 (Va. 1997).

ᛦ

Infringement under the doctrine of equivalents requires no proof of intent, just as with literal infringement. However, proof of intent may be relevant to whether the equivalency was apparent. "[W]hile proof of independent experimentation" would not always reflect upon the objective question whether a person skilled in the art would have known of the interchangeability between two elements,... in many cases it would likely be probative of such knowledge." *James River Corp. of Virginia v. Hallmark Cards Inc.*, 43 U.S.P.Q.2d 1422, 1427 (Wis. 1997).

ᛦ

A seller's intent, unless embodied in an enforceable contract, does not create a limitation on the right of a purchaser to use, sell, or modify a patented product as long as a reconstruction of the patented combination is avoided. *Hewlett-Packard Co. v. Repeat-O-Type Stencil Manufacturing Corp.*, 123 F.3d 1445, 43 U.S.P.Q.2d 1650, 1658 (Fed. Cir. 1997).

ᛦ

Intent may be inferred where a patent applicant knew, or should have known, that withheld information would be material to the PTO's consideration of the patent application. *Critikon Inc. v. Becton Dickinson Vascular Access Inc.*, 43 U.S.P.Q.2d 1666, 1668 (Fed. Cir. 1997).

Intent of Congress.

In assessing the validity of an agency's interpretation of a statute, we begin by asking whether "Congress has directly spoken to the precise question at issue"; if so, "the court, as well as the agency, must give effect to the unambiguously expressed intent of Congress". If we find that the statute is silent or ambiguous with respect to the specific issue, the question for the court is whether the agency's answer is based on a permissible construction of the statute." *Mova Pharmaceutical Corp. v. Shalala*, 140 F.3d 1060, 46 U.S.P.Q.2d 1385, 1390 (D.C. Cir. 1998).

Intent to Abandon.

The Board correctly found a delay of approximately 51 months was unreasonably long and sufficient to give rise to an inference of an intent to abandon, suppress, or conceal the invention. An inference of suppression or concealment may be overcome with evidence that the reason for the delay was to perfect the invention. When, however, the delay is caused by working on refinements and improvements that are not reflected in the final patent application, the delay will not be excused. Further, when the activities that caused the delay go to commercialization of the invention, the delay will not be excused. *Lutzker v. Plet*, 843 F.2d 1364, 6 U.S.P.Q.2d 1370 (Fed. Cir. 1988).

Intent to Claim.

"Intent to claim" has little to do with "intent" per se, but rather is analogous to the requirement of 35 U.S.C. §112, first paragraph, that the specification contain "a written description of the invention, and of the manner and process of making and using it". It is synonymous with "right to claim." *In re Mead*, 581 F.2d 251, 256; 198 U.S.P.Q. 412, 417 (C.C.P.A. 1978).

ᚦ

Lack of "intent to claim" is not an independent basis for denying a reissue application under 35 U.S.C. §251. *In re Hounsfield*, 669 F.2d 1320, 1323; 216 U.S.P.Q. 1045, 1048 (C.C.P.A. 1983).

ᚦ

That the subject matter of reissue claims was "not claimed at all" in the original application and nothing in the original patent evidences an "intent to claim" that subject matter supports a conclusion that such failure to claim particular subject matter was not the result of the "error" required by 35 U.S.C. §251. *In re Weiler*, 790 F.2d 1576, 229 U.S.P.Q. 673, 678 (Fed. Cir. 1986).

ᚦ

An inventor's failure to appreciate the scope of the invention at the time of the original patent grant, and thus an initial intent not to claim the omitted subject matter, is a remediable error. *C.R. Bard Inc. v. M3 Systems Inc.*, 48 U.S.P.Q.2d 1225, 1234 (Fed. Cir. 1998).

Intent to Deceive. *See also* Gross Negligence, Intent to Mislead.

A finding that particular conduct amounts to "gross negligence" does not of itself justify an inference of intent to deceive; the involved conduct, viewed in light of all the evidence, including evidence indicative of good faith, must indicate sufficient culpability to require a finding of intent to deceive. *Hoffmann-La Roche Inc. v, Lemmon Co.*, 906 F.2d 684, 15 U.S.P.Q.2d 1363, 1367 (Fed. Cir. 1990). *See also Symbol Technologies Inc. v. Opticon Inc.*, 935 F.2d 1569, 19 U.S.P.Q.2d 1241, 1251 (Fed. Cir. 1991).

ϖ

To determine whether a patent applicant acted with the necessary intent to deceive, a court must evaluate all of the facts and circumstances in the case, including those indicative of good faith. Because the issue of inequitable conduct is so closely tied to the underlying facts, summary judgment is rarely appropriate. *Burroughs Wellcome Co. v. Barr Laboratories Inc.*, 828 F.Supp. 1200, 29 U.S.P.Q.2d 1721, 1727 (N.C. 1993).

ϖ

Intentionally failing to cite prior art to the PTO or intentionally disregarding one's duty of disclosure to the PTO is not necessarily tantamount to doing those same intentional acts with an intent to deceive the PTO. *Xilinx Inc. v. Altera Corp.*, 33 U.S.P.Q.2d 1149, 1153 (Cal. 1994).

ϖ

"Given the ease with which a relatively routine act of patent prosecution can be portrayed as intended to mislead of deceive, clear and convincing evidence of misconduct sufficient to support an inference of culpable intent is required." *Molins PLC v. Textron Inc.*, 48 F.3d 1172, 33 U.S.P.Q.2d 1823, 1829 (Fed. Cir. 1995).

Intent to Mislead. *See also* Inequitable Conduct, Intent to Deceive.

An applicant who knew or should have known of prior art or information and of its materiality is not automatically precluded thereby from an effort to convince the fact finder that failure to disclose was nonetheless not due to an intent to mislead the PTO; i.e., that, in light of all the circumstances in the case, an inference of intent to mislead is not warranted. No single factor or combination of factors can be said always to require an inference to mislead. *In re Harita*, 847 F.2d 801, 6 U.S.P.Q.2d 1930 (Fed. Cir. 1988).

Interchangeability.

"[T]he proper time for evaluating equivalency—and thus knowledge of interchangeability between elements—is at the time of infringement, not at the time the patent was issued." *Semmler v. American Honda Motor Co.*, 99 F. Supp. 967, 44 U.S.P.Q.2d 1553, 1562 (Ohio 1997).

Interchangeable.

Patentability of a product claim is not precluded merely because the claim recites alternatively used or interchangeable parts. *In re Worrest*, 201 F.2d 930, 96 U.S.P.Q. 381 (C.C.P.A. 1953).

ϖ

Although "interchangeability" to those skilled in the art is *one factor* to be considered in a doctrine of equivalents analysis, *Graver Tank & Manufacturing Co. v. The Linde*

Air Products Company, 339 U.S. 605, 609, 85 U.S.P.Q. 328, 331 (1950), "an interchangeable device is not necessarily an equivalent device." *Key Manufacturing Group, Inc. v. Microdot, Inc.,* 925 F.2d 1444, 1449, 17 U.S.P.Q.2d 1806, 1810 (Fed. Cir. 1991).

ᘐ

Interchangeability known to persons reasonably skilled in the art is evidence of equivalency. *Lifescan Inc. v. Home Diagnostics Inc.,* 76 F.3d 358, 37 U.S.P.Q.2d 1595, 1599 (Fed. Cir. 1996).

ᘐ

A finding of known interchangeability, while an important factor in determining equivalence, is certainly not dispositive. *Chiuminatta Concrete Concepts Inc. v. Cardinal Industries Inc.,* 145 F.3d 1303, 46 U.S.P.Q.2d 1752, 1757 (Fed. Cir. 1998).

Interest. *See also* **Damages, Postjudgment Interest, Prejudgment Interest, Royalty, 28 U.S.C. §1961(a) (1988).**

Postjudgment interest is calculated from the date of a judgment establishing the right to an award. *Fox Industries, Inc. v. Structural Preservation Systems Inc.,* 922 F.2d 801, 17 U.S.P.Q.2d 1579, 1581 (Fed. Cir. 1990).

ᘐ

The commercial paper rate should serve as the rate for calculation of prejudgment interest in this case. "Interest is not a 'penalty' of any kind; it simply represents the time value of money and is an element of complete compensation putting the victim in the position it would have occupied had there been no wrong." *Alpex Computer Corp. v. Nintendo Co. Ltd.,* 34 U.S.P.Q.2d 1167, 1209 n.29 (N.Y. 1994).

ᘐ

The court is prepared to take judicial notice that compound interest is a market or commercial reality for any corporation that does business in the United States. *Hughes Aircraft Co. v. U.S.,* 31 Fed.Cl. 481, 35 U.S.P.Q.2d 1243, 1253 n.15 (U.S. Ct. Fed. Cl. 1994).

Interference. *See also* **37 C.F.R. §1.671(e), Conception, Contractual Relations, Copying Claims, Count, Cross-Appeal, Economic Advantage, Interference Count, Interference Estoppel, Interrogatories, Judicial Review, Losing Interference Party, Lost Count, Motion, Patent Interference, Phantom Count, Preliminary Statement, Proof, Reduction to Practice, 35 U.S.C. §291.**

Where an application for reissue of a patent is filed while the patent is involved in interference, the PTO opens the reissue application to inspection by the opposing interference party. The purpose for opening the reissue application to inspection is to afford the opposing party an opportunity to assert claims to any common invention disclosed or claimed in the reissue application so that "the entire controversy between the parties may be terminated in one proceeding". *Bandel v. Samfield, Brock, and Locklair,* 168 U.S.P.Q. 725, 728 (PO Bd. Pat. Intf. 1961).

ᘐ

The key to determining whether a disclosure supports a claim for interference purposes is whether the disclosure teaches the gist of the invention defined by the claim. While all limitations of a claim must be considered in deciding what invention is defined, it is futile merely to compare quantitatively range limits and numbers set out in counts with range limits and numbers disclosed in an allegedly supporting specification. Closer scrutiny is required to get at the essence of what invention the count purports to define. *Hall v. Taylor*, 332 F.2d 844, 141 U.S.P.Q. 821, 824 (C.C.P.A. 1964).

ʊ

Two interfering parties, relying for priority on corresponding foreign applications filed on the same day in Convention countries, have identical effective filing dates. Neither party carries a greater burden of proving priority than the other, and neither party may be entitled to judgment of priority. *Lassman v. Brossi, Gerecke, and Kyburz*, 159 U.S.P.Q. 182, 184, 185 (PO Bd. Pat. Int. 1967).

ʊ

In an interference between a patentee and a reissue applicant, the junior party patentee had the burden of proving priority by a preponderance of the evidence. *Poage v. Dyer*, 184 U.S.P.Q. 223, 225 (PO Bd. Pat. Int. 1974).

ʊ

There is an estoppel against a junior party from claiming subject matter of the interference counts when that party failed to contest priority with respect to the same subject matter in a prior interference. A party to an interference has a duty to present all claims involving common subject matter with any of the other parties in the proceeding. Failure to timely present such claims estops him from presenting them at a later time. Also, a senior party does not have to move for the benefit of his parent application with regard to counts added to the interference since the parent application was specified in the notice of interference. If the junior party questioned whether such reliance extended to added counts, it was for the junior party to raise the issue after the testimony period was set. *Meitzner and Oline v. Mindick and Svarz*, 549 F.2d 775, 193 U.S.P.Q. 17, 21 (C.C.P.A. 1977).

ʊ

A party who is first to reduce to practice an embodiment of a species falling within a generic count is entitled to prevail in an interference. *Weil v. Fritz*, 572 F.2d 856, 196 U.S.P.Q. 600, 608 n.16 (C.C.P.A. 1978).

ʊ

Printed publications may properly be introduced into evidence (in an interference proceeding) during the taking of testimony relative thereto only if they are listed and served in accordance with the requirements of 37 C.F.R. §1.287(a) or a proper motion is filed under 37 C.F.R. §1.287(d)(1). *Bey and Jung v. Kollonitsch and Patchett*, 215 U.S.P.Q. 454, 456 (PTO Bd. Pat. Intf. 1981).

ʊ

In a priority contest a party who was second to file was unable to prevail even though he had reduced the invention to practice four years prior to his opponent's filing date.

Even if he demonstrated continuous activity from prior to his opponent's effective filing date to his filing date, such should have no bearing on the question of priority. While diligence during the above-noted period may be relied upon by one alleging prior conception and subsequent reduction to practice, it is of no significance in the case of the party who is not last to reduce to practice. Too long a delay may bar the first inventor from reliance on an early reduction to practice. However, the first inventor is not barred from relying on a later, resumed activity antedating an opponent's entry into the field merely because the work done before the delay occurred was sufficient to amount to a reduction to practice. *Paulik v. Rizkalla,* 760 F.2d 1270, 226 U.S.P.Q. 224 (Fed. Cir. 1985).

ω

The defendants were required to submit to pretrial discovery in the United States, including appearing for oral depositions. The defendants were provided with an alternative, under conditions that would not implicate German sovereignty, to voluntarily agree to oral depositions before an American consular official in the embassy at Bonn, Germany, provided such oral depositions were truly voluntary, were of the same scope as if they were occurring here in the United States, and were done only after notice to the government of the Federal Republic of Germany. If the German government objected, the party defendants were required to appear in the United States for the depositions. *Work v. Bier,* 106 F.R.D. 45, 226 U.S.P.Q. 657 (D.C. 1985).

ω

Reissue is not available for the sole purpose of invoking an interference that was overlooked by the PTO. *In re Keil,* 808 F.2d 830, 1 U.S.P.Q.2d 1427 (Fed. Cir. 1987).

ω

The PTO has the discretion to issue a patent to a winning party in an interference involving only applications where judicial review has been sought under 35 U.S.C. §146. However, the "normal" practice is not to issue a patent when judicial review is sought under §146. There are two situations where the PTO will not issue a patent to a winning party in an interference. First, if the interference involves a patent and an application, the Board holds that the applicant is entitled to prevail, and the patentee seeks judicial review by civil action under 35 U.S.C. §146, a patent is not issued to the winning party. Second, if judicial review is sought in the U.S. Court of Appeals for the Federal Circuit under 35 U.S.C. §141, a patent is not issued to the winning party. *Martin v. Clevenger,* 11 U.S.P.Q.2d 1399 (Comm'r Patents & Trademarks 1989).

ω

In order to establish priority in an interference, the party who files later is "required to establish reduction to practice before the filing date of the party who filed first, or conception before that date coupled with reasonable diligence from before that date to the filing date of the party who files later." To establish a *prima facie* case entitling them to proceed with the interference, however, the party who filed later was required only to prove (by way of affidavits setting forth facts) at least so much of his case as would entitle him to an award of priority if the senior party were to rely only on his filing date and were not to rebut any of the junior party's case. To establish reduction to practice of a chemical composition, it is sufficient to prove "that the inventor actually prepared the composition and knew it would work." The inventor, however, must provide independent corroborating evidence in addition to his own statements and documents. Such evidence "may consist of testimony of a witness, other than an inventor, to the actual reduction to practice or it may consist of evidence of surrounding facts and circumstances independent of information received from the inventor." The purpose of the rule requiring corroboration is to prevent fraud. *Hahn v. Wong,* 892 F.2d 1028, 13 U.S.P.Q.2d 1313, 1317 (Fed. Cir. 1989).

ϖ

The rules specifically note that the press of other business is not normally a reason for extending times set in interference cases. *Voisin v. Collier,* 18 U.S.P.Q.2d 1169, 1171 (Comm'r Patents & Trademarks 1989).

ϖ

After an Examiner-in-Chief (EIC) has ruled on a preliminary motion brought under 37 C.F.R. §1.633 (1989), further consideration of the matter raised in the motion may be pursued in different ways, depending on the procedural circumstances. If a show-cause order has issued, an interference party may request a final hearing that may address all issues specified in 37 C.F.R. §1.655(b) that were previously decided by the EIC. Such issues include §1.633 preliminary motions, whether denied or granted. A party can also request reconsideration of any §1.633 motion that did not result in a show-cause order. However, such a request must be made within 14 days from the date of the decision. *Chester v. Miller,* 906 F.2d 1574, 15 U.S.P.Q.2d 1333, 1338 (Fed. Cir. 1990).

ϖ

Parties in interference are advised to file petitions under 37 C.F.R. §1.644(a)(2) within 15 days after entry of the Board's final decision and also to include, as part of the petition or in a separate paper, a request for an extension of time to seek judicial review. *Goutzoulis v. Athale,* 15 U.S.P.Q.2d 1461, 1464 (Comm'r Patents & Trademarks 1990).

ϖ

Pursuant to 37 C.F.R. §1.607(a) an applicant may request an interference by presenting a proposed count, presenting at least one claim corresponding to the proposed count, and, where the claim does not correspond exactly to the proposed count, explaining why such claim corresponds to the proposed count.

One purpose of the 1994 amendment to 35 U S.C. §135 and the new rules of practice (37 C.F.R. §1.601 et seq.) was to permit the Board to decide all patentability issues in an interference, if properly raised by the parties. As set forth in MPEP §2300.02, the object of an interference is to resolve all controversies as to all interfering subject matter defined by one or more counts. *Brooks v. Street,* 16 U.S.P.Q.2d 1374, 1377 (B.P.A.I. 1990).

ϖ

The fact that defendant filed an interference against the patent-in-suit is evidence of non-obviousness. That a major competitor of the patentee felt the invention worthy of patent has some weight. That all those in the art recognized a need to draw upon a different art is evidence of non-obviousness. *CSS International Corp. v. Maul Technology Co.,* 16 U.S.P.Q.2d 1657, 1666 (Ind. 1989).

ϖ

Decisions of a Primary Examiner during ex parte prosecution are not binding on the BPAI in inter partes proceedings. *Okada v. Hitotsumachi,* 16 U.S.P.Q.2d 1789, 1790 (Comm'r Patents & Trademarks 1990).

ᚖ

When expert testimony is needed in support of, or in opposition to, a preliminary motion, a party should:

1. identify the person it expects to call as an expert;
2. state the field in which the person is alleged to be an expert; and
3. state in a Declaration signed by the person (a) the subject matter on which the person is expected to testify, (b) the facts and opinions to which the person is expected to testify, and (c) a summary of the grounds and basis for each opinion.

When a person is to be called as a fact witness, a Declaration by that person (stating the facts) should be filed. If the other party is to be called, or if evidence in the possession of the other party is necessary, an explanation of the evidence sought, what it will show, and why it is needed must be supplied. When inter partes tests are to be performed, a description of such tests (stating what they will show) must be presented. *Hanagan v. Kimura,* 16 U.S.P.Q.2d 1791, 1794 (Comm'r Patents & Trademarks 1990).

ᚖ

The interference rules do not specifically prohibit a party patentee (dissatisfied with the EIC's decision on preliminary motions) from filing a request for reexamination. Nonetheless, filing such a request subverts the purpose of the interference rules, which is to resolve all controversies between the parties in an inter partes forum. *Shaked v. Taniguchi,* 21 U.S.P.Q.2d 1285, 1287 (B.P.A.I. 1990).

ᚖ

No statute precludes addition of a reexamination to an interference involving the patent sought to be reexamined. PTO practice permits adding an application to reissue a patent to an interference involving the patent. Both the reexamination and the interference must be carried out with "special dispatch" within the PTO to comply with the mandate of 35 U.S.C. §305. *Shaked v. Taniguchi,* 21 U.S.P.Q.2d 1288, 1289 (Comm'r Patents & Trademarks 1990).

ᚖ

An involved application claim can be amended during an interference proceeding only if the resulting claim corresponds to the count, and, conversely, a motion under 37 C.F.R. §1.633(c)(4) can only be brought with respect to an already existing claim as originally designated as corresponding to the count. *L'Esperance v. Nishimoto,* 18 U.S.P.Q.2d 1534, 1537 (B.P.A.I. 1991).

ᚖ

From a decision in an interference by the BPAI that the counts of the interference are unpatentable, an ex parte appeal to the CAFC by one party on the issue of patentability is independent of a district court action under 35 U.S.C. §146 by a different party, and both actions can be processed independently. *In re Van Geuns,* 946 F.2d 845, 20 U.S.P.Q.2d 1291, 1295 (Fed. Cir. 1991).

ᚖ

An interference may be declared when the scope of the claims in two applications or an application and a patent is identical, different and overlapping in scope or different and mutually exclusive in scope. *Ex parte Deckler*, 21 U.S.P.Q.2d 1872, 1875 (B.P.A.I. 1991).

ω

The opening brief of the junior party must contain a statement of the issues presented for decision, a statement of the facts relevant to the issues and an argument which shall contain the contentions of the party with respect to the issues and the reasons therefor. *Suh v. Hoefle*, 23 U.S.P.Q.2d 1321, 1323 (B.P.A.I. 1991).

ω

Once an interference has been declared, the parties are entitled to remain in the interference and to be heard on *all* of the issues in the interference, including unpatentability issues pertaining to their opponent(s), even if they themselves have no basis for obtaining a favorable judgment as to any claim corresponding to a count. The BPAI, by resolving both priority and patentability when these questions are fully presented, settles not only the rights between the parties but also rights of concern to the public. The public interest in the benefits of a patent system is best met by procedures which resolve administratively questions affecting patent validity that arise before the PTO. To do otherwise is contrary to the PTO's mission to grant presumptively valid patents, and this disserves the public interest. *Gustavsson v. Valentini*, 25 U.S.P.Q.2d 1401, 1403, 1404 (B.P.A.I. 1991).

ω

A motion under 37 C.F.R. §1.633(a) for judgment on the ground that an opponent's claim corresponding to an interference count lacks written description support in its involved application is a departure from the practice under the old interference rules, wherein the burden as to a party's "right to make" a count was always on the copier of the claims. An interference can be declared under the new rules when an application includes, or is amended to include at least one patentable claim which is drawn to the same patentable invention as a claim of another's unexpired patent. *Behr v. Talbott*, 27 U.S.P.Q.2d 1401, 1405 (B.P.A.I. 1992).

ω

Once an interference has been declared and a party seeks to change the status of the parties by motion, the burden is then on the movant under the new rules. *Kubota v. Shibuya*, 999 F.2d 517, 27 U.S.P.Q.2d 1418, 1422 (Fed. Cir. 1993).

ω

Where the parties' applications were not copending, the junior party has the burden of proving priority and/or derivation by clear and convincing evidence, evidence that produces in the mind of the trier of fact an abiding conviction that the truth of the factual contention is "highly probable". Once an interference has been declared, it never reverts to the summary judgment stage. The interference "rules are designed to provide an orderly procedure and the parties are entitled to rely on their being followed in the absence of such circumstances as might justify waiving them under Rule 183 (37 CFR §1.183). To hold that they may be ignored, in the absence of such circumstances, merely because no special damage has been shown would defeat the purpose of the rules and substantially confuse interference practice." *English v. Ausnit*, 38 U.S.P.Q.2d 1625, 1630, 1636, 1637 (B.P.A.I. 1993).

ʊ

The language of the statute itself militates against the interpretation that disclaiming all claims relating to a single count in an interference divests the Board of jurisdiction over an interference. *Guinn v. Kopf*, 40 U.S.P.Q.2d 1157, 1159 (Fed. Cir. 1996).

ʊ

In an interference setting, where testing is required to establish utility, there must be some recognition of successful testing prior to the critical date for an invention to be reduced to practice. *Estee Lauder Inc. v. L'Oreal S.A.*, 129 F.3d 588, 44 U.S.P.Q.2d 1610, 1614 (Fed. Cir. 1997).

ʊ

In an interference proceeding wherein the only issue on appeal from a BPAI decision is the patentability of claims of the winning party, the losing party (which properly challenged that patentability during the *inter partes* proceedings below) is an "adverse" party in light of the Board's final judgment. *Wu v. Wang*, 129 F.3d 1237, 44 U.S.P.Q.2d 1641, 1644 (Fed. Cir. 1997).

ʊ

Because Title 35 provides for interference proceedings, it implicitly recognizes that contemporaneous independent invention may not alone show obviousness. *Monarch Knitting Machinery Corp. v. Sulzer Morat GmbH*, 139 F.3d 877, 45 U.S.P.Q.2d 1977, 1983 (Fed. Cir. 1998).

ʊ

Claims of prior inventorship and derivation may be established by a preponderance-of-the-evidence for interferences between a patent and a co-pending application, or between interfering patents. *Environ Products Inc. v. Furon Co.*, 47 U.S.P.Q.2d 1040, 1044 (Pa. 1998).

Interference Count.

The purpose of 35 U.S.C. §135(a) was, in part, to provide a procedure to economize time and work in the further prosecution of a losing party's application. The final refusal of claims by the PTO may be based, inter alia, on statutory prior art or loss of right to a patent or an estoppel. The inference that the counts (i.e., the subject matter of the counts) must be statutory prior art to the losing party merely because §135(a), as a matter of PTO procedure, provides for automatic "final refusal" of claims corresponding to the counts by virtue of the adverse award of priority, is unwarranted. Neither the counts nor the subject matter of the counts is statutory prior art by virtue of 135(a). *In re McKellin, Mageli, and D'Angelo*, 529 F.2d 1324, 188 U.S.P.Q. 428 (C.C.P.A. 1976).

ʊ

The appellant was initially the senior party and subsequently the losing party in an interference in which the winning party prevailed on the basis of a Convention filing in a foreign country. The Board held that the appellant's claims were not patentably distinct from the subject matter defined by the counts lost in the interference. The issue here was not obviousness under 35 U.S.C. §103 or so-called interference estoppel. Rather, the Board relied on the more general principle of res judicata and collateral estoppel wherein a judgment previously rendered bars consideration of questions of fact or mixed questions of fact and law that were, or should have been, resolved in earlier litigation. An interference should settle all issues that are decided or that could have been decided. When an applicant loses an interference, the applicant is not entitled to a patent containing claims corresponding to the count or claims that are not patentably distinct from the count. *Ex parte Tytgat, Clerbois, and Noel*, 225 U.S.P.Q. 907 (PTO Bd. App. 1985).

ᵱ

Interference counts are given the broadest reasonable interpretation possible, and resort to the specification is necessary only when there are ambiguities inherent in the claim language or obvious from arguments of counsel. If there is such ambiguity, resort must be had to the specification of the patent from which the copied claim came. *DeGeorge v. Bernier*, 768 F.2d 1318, 226 U.S.P.Q. 758 (Fed. Cir. 1985).

Interference Estoppel. *See also* Interference Count.

A well-established principle of estoppel is that an interference not only settles the rights of the parties under the issues or counts of the interference, but also settles every question of the rights to any claim that might have been presented and determined in the interference proceeding. The doctrine of estoppel has been applied where a party has neglected or refused to contest priority of patentable subject matter that is clearly common to his application and the application of his opponent in interference. Under the judicial doctrine of interference estoppel not all of the disclosure of the winning interference party's application can be used against the losing party's claims. Only those disclosures that are clearly common to both applications in interference can be so used. Interference estoppel and prior art are separate and distinct matters that should not be confused. With regard to interference estoppel the losing party is only estopped to obtain claims that read directly on disclosures of subject matter clearly common to both the winning party's application and that of the losing party; with regard to prior art (including prior invention) the losing party cannot obtain claims to subject matter that is either barred under 35 U.S.C. §102(g) or rendered obvious under 35 U.S.C. §103 by the invention defined in the interference counts. *In re Risse, Horlein, and Wirth*, 378 F.2d 948, 154 U.S.P.Q. 1, 7, 8 (C.C.P.A. 1967).

ᵱ

Although a prior interference was dissolved because the senior party lacked support for the interference count, claims now rejected on the ground of interference estoppel in the junior party's application are fully supported by the application of the senior party in the interference. *Ex parte Keith and Lavanchy*, 167 U.S.P.Q. 409, 410 (PO Bd. App. 1970).

ᵱ

The claims of a losing interference party cannot be rejected under 35 U.S.C. §103 on the entire disclosure of the winning interference party since the sole basis for using the disclosure of the winning interference party to reject the losing party's claims is interference estoppel. The entire disclosure cannot be used as "prior art" in a rejection under 35 U.S.C. §102 or §103, only that portion thereof corresponding to the claimed subject matter which is clearly common to both the losing party's and the winning party's applications. However, the lost count alone is available as prior art under section 102(g) and thus 103 to the extent that it represents the prior invention of another in this country. For the doctrine of interference estoppel to apply, the PTO must show that appellant's claims read on disclosures which are clearly common to both the winning party's application and that of the losing party. As proponent of the rejection the PTO has the burden of showing that the application of the winning interference party had support for the invention defined by claims so rejected. *In re Wilding*, 535 F.2d 631, 190 U.S.P.Q. 59, 61, 63 (C.C.P.A. 1976).

ω

Because one party may not be able to support a generic invention does not preclude having the subject adjudicated in an interference. Since the losing party failed to attempt to broaden the count to include subject matter subsequently claimed in ex parte prosecution, he was estopped from claiming subject matter lost in the interference. If the losing party had attempted to broaden the count and the PTO had prevented him from doing so, he would not be estopped from later claiming the broader subject matter. Also, if the subject matter subsequently claimed in ex parte prosecution were patentably distinct from the lost count, it could not be denied to the losing party on the sole ground of interference estoppel. *In re Kroekel*, 803 F.2d 705, 231 U.S.P.Q. 640 (Fed. Cir. 1986).

Interference in Fact.

In determining the issue of whether or not there is an interference-in-fact, the test is whether there is any patentable distinction between the counts and said claims of [the] patent, whether the counts of the interference and the claims of the patent call for the same invention. A further inquiry is whether, the substance of the count makes obvious the substance of the patent claim, or vice versa. *Mezrich v. Lee*, 201 U.S.P.Q. 922, 926 (PTO Bd. Pat. Intf. 1978).

ω

A moving party in an interference has the burden of showing no interference in fact, i.e., of showing that the parties' corresponding claims are drawn to different inventions. This may be done by showing that the parties' corresponding claims are patentably distinct. *Logan v. Neuzil*, 206 U.S.P.Q. 668, 669 (Comm'r of Patents and Trademarks 1979).

ω

The issue, "no interference in fact," is not the same as and must not be confused with the issue of "no right to make". The phrase "no interference in fact" simply means that the parties are each claiming (in their involved claims) different (i.e. patentably distinct) inventions; such an interference must be dissolved, and two patents must issue as to their respective involved claims. *Kalnoki-Kis v. Land*, 214 U.S.P.Q. 636, 638 (PTO Bd. Pat. Intf. 1982).

ω

The Examiner should not deny a motion to add counts solely on the ground that there is no interference in fact if there is any reasonable doubt on that issue. *Brandon v. Murphy*, 231 U.S.P.Q. 490, 491 (Comm'r of Patents and Trademarks 1986).

ω

The burden of establishing that there was no interference in fact clearly rests with the party raising such issue. *Okada v. Hitotsumachi,* 16 U.S.P.Q.2d 1789, 1791 (Comm'r Patents & Trademarks 1990).

Interfering Patents. *See* **35 U.S.C. §291.**

Interlocutory Appeal.

It is within the Court's discretion whether to certify an order, but "the rule of interlocutory appeals is to be applied 'sparingly and only in exceptional cases' in furtherance of the longstanding federal policy against piecemeal appeals." The party seeking certification bears the burden to show the presence of "exceptional circumstances where consideration of judicial economy and fairness demand interlocutory review of an order." *Mont-Bell Co. Ltd. v. Mountain Hardwear Inc.,* 44 U.S.P.Q.2d 1568, 1577 (Cal. 1997).

Interlocutory Order.

The Supreme Court has articulated a three-pronged test to determine whether an interlocutory order is appealable pursuant to the *Cohen* [*Cohen v. Beneficial Industrial Loan Corp.,* 337 U.S. 541 (1949)] collateral order doctrine. The order must (1) conclusively determine the disputed question, (2) resolve an important issue completely separate from the merits of the action, and (3) be effectively unreviewable on appeal from a final judgment. *Gulfstream Aerospace Corp. v. Mayacamas Corp.,* 485 U.S. 271, 276 (1988).

ω

The EIC's decision on preliminary motions dismissing a junior party patentee's preliminary motion constitutes an interlocutory order. Pursuant to 37 C.F.R. §1.655(a), all interlocutory orders are presumed to have been correct, and the burden of showing manifest error or an abuse of discretion is upon the party attacking the order. *Brown v. Bravet,* 25 U.S.P.Q.2d 1147, 1149 (B.P.A.I. 1992).

ω

"[S]o long as [a] district court has jurisdiction over [a] case, it possesses inherent power over interlocutory orders, and can reconsider them when it is consonant with justice to do so." *Total Containment Inc. v. Environ Products Inc.,* 33 U.S.P.Q.2d 1316 (Pa. 1994).

Intermediate. *See also* **Intermediate as Reference, Pro-Drug.**

The best evidence of unexpected beneficial properties of a claimed intermediate is evidence of unexpected advantageous properties of the final product derived from the claimed intermediate. *Deutsche Gold-Und Silber Scheideanstalt vormals Roessler v. Commissioner of Patents,* 251 F. Supp. 624, 148 U.S.P.Q. 412 (D.C. 1966).

ω

Just as the practical utility of a compound produced by a chemical process "is an essential element" in establishing patentability of the process, so the practical utility of the compound, or the compounds, produced from a chemical intermediate, the "starting material" in such a process, is an essential element in establishing patentability of that intermediate. If a process for producing a product of only conjectural use is not itself "useful" within 35 U.S.C. §101, it cannot be said that the starting material for such a process, i.e., claimed intermediates, are useful. It is not enough that the specification disclose that the intermediate exists and that it "works," reacts, or can be used to produce some intended product of no known use. Nor is it enough that the product disclosed to be obtained from the intermediate belongs to some class of compounds that now is, or in the future might be, the subject of research to determine some specific use. *In re Kirk and Petrow*, 376 F.2d 936, 153 U.S.P.Q. 48, 56 (C.C.P.A. 1967).

ω

No common properties presumption rises from the mere occurrence of a claimed compound at an intermediate point in a conventional reaction yielding a specifically named prior-art compound. That an intermediate/end-product relationship exists between a claimed compound and a prior art compound does not alone create a common-properties presumption. The mere ability of a compound to act as an intermediate toward the production of other compounds does not alone constitute the sort of "property" that the cases on obviousness of chemical compounds contemplate. *In re Gyurik and Kingsbury*, 596 F.2d 1012, 201 U.S.P.Q. 552, 557, 558 (C.C.P.A. 1979).

ω

A reference intermediate is of limited value for precluding patentability of claimed compounds having self utility. *In re Lalu and Foulletier*, 747 F.2d 703, 223 U.S.P.Q. 1257, 1260 (Fed. Cir. 1984).

ω

The capacity of an intermediate to contribute to an end product that feature that causes the end product to possess an activity or property that is unexpectedly superior to that of a prior-art end product is a "property" that inures to the benefit of the intermediate and that can be considered as part of the "subject matter as a whole" in determining the non-obviousness of the intermediate. In other words the contributing-cause test is met when one of ordinary skill in the art would reasonably ascribe to a claimed intermediate the contributing cause for such an unexpectedly superior activity or property. That the unexpectedly superior activity or property of an end product has to do with a pharmaceutical utility is an insufficient justification for precluding a determination that the claimed intermediate is the contributing cause of the end product's unexpectedly superior activity or property. Although the action of many pharmaceuticals, as well as many chemical compounds, is "unpredictable" and "generally highly specific," such factors will be reflected in the evidence required to meet the contributing-cause test. In order to establish that the claimed intermediate is the contributing cause of the unexpectedly superior activity or property of the end product, an applicant must identify the cause of the unexpectedly superior activity or property (compared to the prior art) in the end product and establish a nexus for that cause between the intermediate and the end product. *In re Magerlein*, 602 F.2d 366, 202 U.S.P.Q. 473, 479 (C.C.P.A. 1979); somewhat limited by *Ex parte Heymes*, 30 U.S.P.Q.2d 1237, 1239, 1240 (B.P.A.I. 1993).

ω

A rejection of a claim for containing an improper Markush group was reversed. The encompassed compounds were sequential intermediates in a process for synthesizing a patented compound. The criteria for evaluating the propriety of a Markush group are (1) structural similarity and (2) "unity of invention." When these two criteria are met, the Markush group is proper even when it involves and embraces intermediates of each other. Unity of invention encompasses both structural similarity and communality of properties and/or utility. Here, the Markush group members are structurally similar. The fact that the group members are used seriately to make a patented product is indicative of the same invention being involved, each member being a precursor of the other and leading to the making of a novel and useful material. Each of the individual members of the Markush group has no utility except in the chain of reaction leading to the patented product. As such, common utility is present within the meaning of the unity-of-invention requirement, the claimed intermediates being the cause and effect of the property and usefulness of the final patented product. *Ex parte Della Bella and Chiarino*, 7 U.S.P.Q.2d 1669 (B.P.A.I. 1984).

ɯ

With regard to a claims of patents to a chemical process of hydration of acrylonitrile to acrylamide in the presence of a reduced copper oxide catalyst, it is apparent that the original BASF catalyst and the alleged revised catalyst utilized in Cyanamid's process are obtained by the reduction of a copper compound, particularly malachite, with hydrogen. The presence of malachite in the non-reduced catalyst does not allow Cyanamid to avoid infringement of the patents, especially since the malachite in the BASF catalyst, when reduced, proceeds through an intermediate copper oxide phase. *Dow Chemical Co. v. American Cyanamid Company*, 229 U.S.P.Q. 171, 181 (La. 1985).

Intermediate as Reference.

The Examiner appears to recognize that it is not structural similarity alone that gives rise to obviousness, but the concomitant assumption that the structurally similar compounds will have like properties. This is what provides the motivation to modify the prior-art compound. In the present case, however, the only utility disclosed for the relevant compound in the reference is as an intermediate for the production of another compound. The Examiner has not suggested that the compound claimed here would have been useful in the same manner and, from the disclosure of the reference itself, it appears that it wouldn't have been. Thus, on the record before us, no *prima facie* case of obviousness has been made out against the appellant's claims. *Ex parte Chwang*, 231 U.S.P.Q. 751 (B.P.A.I. 1986).

International Convention. *See* Claim of Priority, Priority.

International Trade Commission. *See* ITC

Internet.

Even if the defendant's website could be construed as a prohibited offer to sell, its accessibility to New Yorkers did not vest the district court with personal jurisdiction. *Agar Corp. Inc. v. Multi-Fluid Inc.*, 45 U.S.P.Q.2d 1444, 1448 (Tex. 1997).

Interpretation. *See also* **Claim Construction, Claim Interpretation, Remedial Statute, Statutory Interpretation.**

The PTO's expanded interpretation of conditions covered by the disclosure of pharmacological utility was not accepted by the Court. *In re Sichert*, 566 F.2d 1154, 196 U.S.P.Q. 209, 212 (C.C.P.A. 1977).

ω

"The law governing interpretation of written instruments establishes that the *subjective intent* of a party is of no moment in ascertaining the meaning of the words used in the instruments.... Although Civil Code §1636 provides that a contract must be interpreted to give effect to the 'mutual intention' of the parties as it existed at the time of contracting, it is well settled that the correct approach is to avoid the terminology of 'intention' and look for the *expressed intent* under an *objective standard*." *International Rectifier Corp. v. SGS-Thomson Microelectronics Inc.*, 38 U.S.P.Q.2d 1083, 1101 (Cal. 1994).

Interrogatories.

Under interference rules, a party seeking discovery via interrogatories must file a motion for additional discovery under 37 C.F.R. §1.287(c) therefor (unless the opponent will answer voluntarily). If the opponent wishes to object to particular proposed interrogatories, he must raise his objections in opposition to the motion. He cannot oppose the motion only in general terms and then, after the Board grants the motion, object to specific interrogatories or other items. *Asari v. Zilges*, 8 U.S.P.Q.2d 1117 (B.P.A.I. 1987).

Intervening References.

In support of a rejection under 35 U.S.C. §112, later references were cited, not as prior art, but as evidence to prove the appellants' disclosure non-enabling for "other species" of the claimed polymer, in an effort to show why the scope of enablement was insufficient to support the claims. As thus implicitly recognized, the references would not have been available in support of a 35 U.S.C. §102 or §103 rejection entered in connection with the 1953 application. To permit use of the same references in support of the §112 rejection herein, however, is to render the "benefit" of 35 U.S.C. §120 illusory. The very purpose of reliance on §120 is to reach back, to avoid the effect of intervening references. Nothing in §120 limits its application to any specific grounds of rejection, or permits the Examiner, denied use of references to reject or to require narrowing of a claim under §102 or §103, to achieve the same result by use of the same references under §112. Just as justice and reason require application of §112 in the same manner to applicants and Examiners, symmetry in the law, and evenness of its application, require that §120 be held applicable to all bases for rejection, that its words "same effect" be given their full meaning and intent. *In re Hogan and Banks*, 559 F.2d 595, 194 U.S.P.Q. 527 (C.C.P.A. 1977).

Intervening Rights.[5]

The second paragraph of 35 U.S.C. §252 applies to narrowed reissues as well as to broadened reissues. *Wayne-Gossard Corp. v. Moretz Hosiery, Inc.,* 539 F.2d 986, 191 U.S.P.Q. 543, 546 (4th Cir. 1976).

ᙍ

When the doctrine of intervening rights is properly raised, the court must consider whether to use its broad equity powers to fashion an appropriate remedy. The court is given the discretion to fashion a remedy from a wide range of options available to it. The court may, for example, (1) confine the intervenor to the use of infringing products already in existence; (2) permit the intervenor to continue in business under conditions that limit the amount, type, or geographical location of its activities; or (3) permit the intervenor to continue in business unconditionally. *Seattle Box Co., Inc. v. Industrial Crating & Packing, Inc.,* 731 F.2d 818, 221 U.S.P.Q. 568, 576, 577 (Fed. Cir. 1984).

ᙍ

An assignor is entitled to intervene as of right as of Fed. R. Civ. P. 24(a)(2) after a decision of the district court granting summary judgment (on the ground of patent invalidity) in favor of a putative infringer, from which the plaintiff assignee decided not to appeal. The inventor-assignor both knew of, and was actively involved in, the litigation prior to the granting of summary judgment. As of the time the assignee decided not to appeal, its representation of the assignor's interest became inadequate; even prior to that time the assignor satisfied the other requirements for intervention as of right. *The Triax Company v. TRW, Inc.,* 724 F.2d 1224, 221 U.S.P.Q. 1133, 1135 (6th Cir. 1984).

ᙍ

The doctrine of intervening rights arises in certain circumstances when a reissue patent is asserted against someone who has been manufacturing the patented device prior to the date of the reissue. If the defendant is found to be entitled to intervening rights, then no damages would be owing to the plaintiff for sales prior to the date of reissue, and the defendant would have an equitable license to continue manufacturing its machines following reissue for a length of time sufficient to allow it to recoup its investment made prior to the reissue. *Valmont Industries Inc. v. Reinke Manufacturing Co.,* 14 U.S.P.Q.2d 1374, 1383 (Nev. 1990).

ᙍ

Under 35 U.S.C. §252, a court's discretion to fashion the terms of future dealings is extremely broad, including, for example, the power to limit use of infringing goods to specific items already in existence; to limit the amount, type, or geographical location for exercise of intervening rights; or to permit the unconditional enjoyment of those rights. The imposition of royalty payments has been found to be equitable under §252, provided the infringer has recouped initial investments. *Mine Safety Appliances Co. v. Becton Dickinson & Co.,* 744 F. Supp. 578, 17 U.S.P.Q.2d 1642, 1644 (N.Y. 1990).

ᙍ

---

[5]See *Carnegie Mellon University v. Schwartz*, 41 U.S.P.Q.2d 1623 (3d Cir. 1997).

There are at least three factors that weigh against permitting defendant to continue infringement. First, the majority of defendant's capital expenditures were made after plaintiff filed for reissue; defendant participated in the reissue proceedings and knew (at all stages of the proceedings) that the reissue patent might issue; and the continued investment in the infringing products was thus at defendant's risk and was not made with the good faith required under 35 U.S.C. §252. Second, in 1987, defendant admitted that it had manufactured and sold and presently sells non-infringing cleaning compositions to some of its customers; although defendant avers that the non-infringing compositions are somewhat more expensive, such a price difference does not excuse infringement where defendant has an admitted alternative; permitting defendant to continue its blatant infringement would not be equitable. Third, the reissue is a "narrowed reissue"; any activity that would infringe the narrowed claims of the reissue patent would also have infringed the broad claims of the original patent if committed previously; any investments made by defendant in products accused of infringing the reissue patent after reissue was imminent are not the types of investments equitable intervening rights are intended to protect. *Henkel Corp. v. Coral Inc.*, 754 F. Supp. 1280, 21 U.S.P.Q.2d 1081, 1100, 1101 (Ill. 1990).

ϖ

When a reissue patent has a claim having the same scope as an original claim, an accused infringer cannot assert intervening rights under 35 U.S.C. §252 as an affirmative defense; if there is no such claim, then the accused infringer can. *In re Arnott,* 19 U.S.P.Q.2d 1049, 1054 (Comm'r Patents & Trademarks 1991).

ϖ

New or amended claims in a reissue patent are enforceable only from the date of reissue, and, as stated by Pasquale J. Federico, "[t]he specific things made before the date of the reissue, which infringe the new reissue claims, are absolutely free of the reissued patent and may be used or sold after the date of reissue without regard to the patent." P.J. Federico, Commentary on the New Patent Act, 35 U.S.C.A. 1, 46 (1954). *Spectronics Corp. v. H. B. Fuller Co. Inc.*, 940 F.2d 631, 19 U.S.P.Q.2d 1545, 1550 (Fed. Cir. 1991).

ϖ

A binding commitment (as of the reissue date) to purchase ordered products constituted a purchase of those products within the meaning of 35 U.S.C. §252. *Bic Leisure Products Inc. v. Windsurfing International Inc.*, 774 F.Supp. 832, 21 U.S.P.Q.2d 1548, 1551 (N.Y. 1991).

ϖ

The language of the first sentence of 35 U.S.C. 41(c)(2) and several courts' interpretations of the corresponding provision in 35 U.S.C. §252 entitle defendants to "absolute" intervening rights is a case wherein they constructed the "specific thing" patented after the six-month grace period but before the late maintenance fee was accepted. *Haden Schweitzer Corp. v. Arthur B. Myr Industries Inc.*, 901 F.Supp. 1235, 36 U.S.P.Q.2d 1020, 1026 (Mich. 1995).

Intervenor.

Pursuant to Fed. R. Civ. P. 24(b), an intervenor is authorized to intervene as a party defendant (in a civil action under 35 U.S.C. §145 in which plaintiff seeks to set aside a BPAI decision affirming an Examiner's final rejection of claims in plaintiff's reissue patent application) and is permitted to participate fully in the civil action subject to the following:

1. Intervenor's affirmative defenses are limited to the affirmative defenses advanced by the Commissioner; and
2. Intervenor shall bear all of its costs and expenses.

Ely v. Manbeck, 17 U.S.P.Q.2d 1252, 1253 (D.C. 1990).

ॼ

An intervenor may move to dismiss a proceeding. The intervenor is to be treated as if it were an original party to the claim once intervention has been allowed. *Hallmark Cards Inc. v. Lehman*, 959 F.Supp. 539, 42 U.S.P.Q.2d 1134 (D.C. 1997).

Intervention.

To intervene as a matter of right, the proposed intervenor must demonstrate (a) that he has an interest in the property or transaction that is the subject matter of the litigation; (b) that the disposition of the action as a practical matter may impair or impede his ability to protect that interest; and (c) that parties already in the litigation cannot adequately protect that interest. A non-party inventor (patentee), who knew of and was actively involved in patent infringement litigation prior to a grant of summary judgment in favor of defendants, was entitled to intervene as of right to prosecute an appeal after the plaintiff (patent assignee) decided not to appeal. *The Triax Company v. TRW, Inc.*, 724 F.2d 1224, 221 U.S.P.Q. 1133, 1135 (6th Cir. 1984).

ॼ

A third party has no right to intervene in the prosecution of a particular patent application to prevent issuance of an allegedly invalid patent. *Animal Legal Defense Fund v. Quigg*, 932 F.2d 920, 18 U.S.P.Q.2d 1677, 1685 (Fed. Cir. 1991).

ॼ

A motion to intervene as of right turns on four factors: (1) the timeliness of the motion; (2) whether the applicant "claims an interest relating to the property or transaction which is the subject of the action," Fed. R. Civ. P. 24(a); (3) whether "the applicant is so situated that the disposition of the action may as a practical matter impair or impede the applicant's ability to protect that interest"; and (4) whether "the applicant's interest is adequately represented by existing parties." *Mova Pharmaceutical Corp. v. Shalala*, 140 F.3d 1060, 46 U.S.P.Q.2d 1385, 1396 (D.C. Cir. 1998).

Interview.

What transpired during an interview between an Examiner and patentee's counsel prior to allowance of the application which matured into the patent on which infringement litigation is based may not be readily ascertainable by deposing patentee's counsel. Before an attorney involved in patent litigation can be deposed in reference thereto, the party seeking discovery must show that he has substantial need of the materials in the preparation of his case and that he is unable, without undue hardship, to obtain the substantial equivalent of the materials by other means. *MacLaren v. B-I-W Group Inc.*, 180 U.S.P.Q. 387, 388 (Va. 1973).

ᘐ

Multiple interviews are not illegal, and persistence in patent prosecution is not grist for patent invalidity. *Magnivision Inc. v. The Bonneau Co.*, 42 U.S.P.Q.2d 1925, 1929 (Fed. Cir. 1997).

Intrinsic Evidence.

A trial court is quite correct in hearing and relying on expert testimony on an ultimate claim construction question in cases in which the intrinsic evidence (i.e., the patent and its file history—the 'patent record') does not answer the question. "No doubt there will be instances in which intrinsic evidence is insufficient to enable the court to determine the meaning of asserted claims, and in those instances, extrinsic evidence...may...properly be relied upon to understand and construe the claims." What is disapproved of is an attempt to use extrinsic evidence to arrive at a claim construction that is clearly at odds with the claim construction mandated by the claims themselves, the written description, and the prosecution history, in other words, with the written record of the patent. *Key Pharmaceuticals Inc. v. Hercon Laboratories Corp.*, 48 U.S.P.Q.2d 1911, 1917 (Fed. Cor. 1998).

Introduce into Evidence.

Failure of an interference party to state explicitly on the record that exhibits are "offered into evidence" is not so defective as to warrant exclusion from consideration of exhibits marked for identification and intended to be included in the record as evidence to be considered in support of the party's position. *Gunn v. Bosch and Pollmann*, 181 U.S.P.Q. 758, 759 (PO Bd. Pat. Intf. 1973).

ᘐ

After they have ruled on the evidence, the Court is reluctant to nullify that ruling because they received too much evidence, when all of the evidence was relevant, competent and indisputably admissible but for the lack of proper notice of defendant's intention to introduce it, an omission unremarked at the trial. *Ortho Diagnostic Systems Inc. v. Miles Inc.*, 865 F.Supp. 1073, 35 U.S.P.Q.2d 1263, 1268 (N.Y. 1994).

Introduction.

Introduction into the United States of a disclosure (in Dutch) is adequate to establish conception in this country even if the disclosure is not translated into English or even read. *Clevenger v. Kooi*, 190 U.S.P.Q. 188, 192 (PTO Bd. Pat. Int. 1974).

ᘐ

When an interference count is directed to a method of making a product, a person's bringing into the United States an explanation of the method and a product made by the method does not, in and of itself, constitute such an introduction of the invention into this country as would support a finding of conception and reduction to practice, since it appears that the person who brought the explanation and product into this country had only a general understanding of the invention, and was not aware of all the subject matter as set forth in the count. Knowledge of the invention in this country by an agent of the inventor is not equivalent to an introduction of the invention into this country "in the absence of a disclosure to others or reduction of the invention to practice by [the agent] within a reasonable time." The question of whether there was introduction of the invention into this country on behalf of the inventor must be judged by what knowledge thereof was imparted to others by items brought into this country. *Tapia v. Micheletti v. Wignall, Shelton, and Klee*, 202 U.S.P.Q. 123, 124, 125 (PTO Bd. App. 1976).

ᴂ

The prior invention of one of two coapplicants is available as "prior art" to an application of the coapplicants under 35 U.S.C. §102(g) by virtue of its admitted introduction into this country prior to the effective filing date of the coapplicants' application. *Ex parte Hachiken and Ogino*, 223 U.S.P.Q. 879, 880 (PTO Bd. App. 1984).

Introductory Phrase. *See* **Preamble.**

Inurement.

Inurement involves a claim by an inventor that, as a matter of law, the acts of another person should accrue to the benefit of the inventor. In particular, experiments conducted at the request of an inventor by another party may inure to the benefit of the inventor for purposes of establishing a reduction to practice. In order to establish inurement, an inventor must show, among other things, that the other person was working either explicitly or implicitly at the inventor's request. *Cooper v. Goldfarb*, 47 U.S.P.Q.2d 1896, 1904, 1905 (Fed. Cir. 1998).

In Vacuo.

The words of patent claims are never considered in vacuo, but are interpreted in light of the patent specification. *Chisholm-Ryder Company, Inc. v. Mecca Bros., Inc.*, 217 U.S.P.Q. 1322, 1336 (N.Y. 1983).

Invalidation. *See* **Revocation.**

Invalid Claim.

The presence of an invalid (not disclaimed) claim in a patent does not render the entire patent invalid or preclude an infringement action based on a different claim of the same patent. *National Business Systems, Inc. v. AM International, Inc.*, 546 F. Supp. 340, 217 U.S.P.Q. 235 (Ill. 1982).

ᴂ

Where a court has found relevant patent claims invalid, a licensor may still recover damages (from the date of an alleged breach until the date that the licensee first challenged validity of the claims) for breach of contract for past royalties due on processes allegedly covered by such claims. *Studiengesellschaft Kohle m.b.H. v. Shell Oil Co.*, 112 F.3d 1561, 42 U.S.P.Q.2d 1674, 1676 (Fed. Cir. 1997).

Invalidity. *See also* **Blonder-Tongue Doctrine, Relitigating Invalidity, Validity.**

The conclusion as to invalidity is reinforced by the fact that this patent was involved in at least eleven interferences with other patents or patent applications. The fact that so many inventors in the field came forward at about the same time with similar solutions for the problems involved suggests strongly that these solutions involved not invention but only the skill of persons competent in the art. *Pierce v. American Communications Company, Inc.*, 169 F.Supp. 351, 119 U.S.P.Q. 456, 459 (Mass. 1958).

ω

Defendants' alleged sale and manufacture of products in violation of terms of an agreement arises under general principles of contract law. The fact that the manufacture and sale of the products may also be an infringement of plaintiff's patent does not alter this conclusion, for the defendants have agreed that the involved patent is valid and infringed by the manufacture and sale of the products in question. A determination of the merits, in the first instance, requires an analysis of the agreement, not an analysis of the validity and infringement of the patent. The defendants cannot turn the matter into one arising under the patent laws by asserting the invalidity defense. *Wham-O Mfg. Co. v. All-American Yo-Yo Corporation*, 377 F.Supp. 993, 181 U.S.P.Q. 320, 321 (N.Y. 1973).

ω

A party which attacks the validity of a patent has the burden of proving invalidity and must overcome, by clear and convincing proof, the presumption of validity established by 35 U.S.C. §282. *National Business Systems, Inc. v. AM International, Inc.*, 546 F.Supp. 340, 217 U.S.P.Q. 235, 240 (Ill. 1982).

ω

To support a counterclaim for a declaratory judgment of the "invalidity, unenforceability and non-infringement" of a patent, defendant was required to plead, specifically, the time, place, and content of any alleged misrepresentation to the PTO and also to plead the requisite intent. *Energy Absorption Systems Inc. v. Roadway Safety Service Inc.*, 28 U.S.P.Q.2d 1079, 1080 (Ill. 1993).

Invalid Patent.

The mere bringing of a single infringement suit by the holder of a patent that is invalid for lack of enablement in and of itself cannot establish a violation of §2 of the Sherman Act. *Technicon Instruments Corp. v. Alpkem Corp.*, 866 F.2d 417, 9 U.S.P.Q.2d 1540 (Fed. Cir. 1989).

Inventing Around. *See* **Designing Around.**

Invention. *See also* **Algorithm, Claim, Crowded Art, Definition, Improvement, Multiple Inventions, Same Invention, Simple, Whole.**

If a new combination and arrangement of known elements produces a new and beneficial result never attained before, such as increased production, this may be evidence of invention. *See Webster Loom Co. v. Elias S. Higgins*, 105 U.S. (15 Otto.) 580, 591, 592 (1882).

ω

Patentability is gauged not only by the extent or simplicity of physical changes, but also by the perception of the necessity or desirability of making such changes to produce a new result. When viewed after disclosure, the changes may seem simple and such as should have been obvious to those in the field. However, this does not necessarily negative invention or patentability. The conception of a new and useful improvement must be considered along with the actual means of achieving it in determining the presence or absence of invention. The discovery of a problem calling for an improvement is often a very essential element in an invention correcting such a problem. Though the problem, once realized, may be solved by use of old and known elements, this does not necessarily negative patentability. *In re Bisley*, 197 F.2d 355, 94 U.S.P.Q. 80, 86 (C.C.P.A. 1952).

ω

On the authority of *Hotchkiss v. Greenwood*, 11 How. 248, 52 U.S. 248 (1850), "if an improvement is to obtain the privileged position of a patent more ingenuity must be involved than the work of a mechanic skilled in the art." *Lyon v. Bausch & Lomb*, 224 F.2d 530, 106 U.S.P.Q. 1, 6 (2d Cir. 1955).

ω

The test for the presence or absence of "invention", and along with it the subsidiary question of whether a device or process is or is not an "aggregation", or a "combination", or an "unpatentable combination" for want of "invention", was replaced by the statutory test of 35 U.S.C. §103. *In re Gustafson*, 331 F.2d 905, 141 U.S.P.Q. 585, 588, 589 (C.C.P.A. 1964).

ω

The basic principle of the patent system is to protect inventions which meet the statutory requirements. Valuable inventions should be given protection of value in the real world of business and the courts. *In re Ruschig, Aumüller, Korger, Wagner, Scholz, and Bänder*, 343 F.2d 965, 145 U.S.P.Q. 274, 286 (C.C.P.A. 1965).

ω

The term "invention" now means the *subject matter* which the applicant claims and regards as his "invention". *In re Walles, Tousignant, and Houtman*, 366 F.2d 786, 151 U.S.P.Q. 185, 188 (C.C.P.A. 1966).

ω

A claim that reads on subject matter for which appellants do not seek coverage, and therefore tacitly admit to be beyond that which "applicant regards as his invention," fails to comply with 35 U.S.C. §112. *In re Prater and Wei*, 415 F.2d 1393, 162 U.S.P.Q. 541, 550 (C.C.P.A. 1969).

ω

The subject matter set out in a claim must be presumed, in the absence of evidence to the contrary, to be that "which the applicant regards as his invention." *In re Moore and Janoski*, 439 F.2d 1232, 169 U.S.P.Q. 236 (C.C.P.A. 1971).

ω

The purpose of 35 U.S.C. §101 is to define patentable subject matter, not to limit a patent to one invention. *In re Haas*, 486 F.2d 1053, 179 U.S.P.Q. 623, 625 (C.C.P.A. 1973).

ω

Each claim of a patent is considered as setting forth a complete and independent invention. *Westwood Chemical, Inc. v. United States*, 525 F.2d 1367, 186 U.S.P.Q. 383, 387 (Ct. Cl. 1975).

ω

Section 112 of 35 U.S.C. does not permit an Examiner to determine whether claims satisfy the requirements of §112 by studying the disclosure, formulating a conclusion as to what he (the Examiner) regards as the broadest invention supported by the disclosure, and then determining whether the claims are broader than the Examiner's concept of what "the invention" is. *In re Ehrreich and Avery*, 590 F.2d 902, 200 U.S.P.Q. 504, 508 (C.C.P.A. 1979).

ω

There has not been a requirement for "invention" in the patentability sense in the laws since 1952; the requirement was replaced by the 35 U.S.C. §103 requirement for non-obviousness. *In re Berry, Coats, and Malik*, 596 F.2d 952, 201 U.S.P.Q. 352, 362 (C.C.P.A. 1979).

ω

A fundamental principle of patent law is "that claims are to be construed in the light of the specifications and both are to be read with a view to ascertaining the invention." *In re Clemens, Hurwitz, and Walker*, 622 F.2d 1029, 206 U.S.P.Q. 289, 297 (C.C.P.A. 1980).

ω

The defense that making a support structure in one piece "does not rise to the standard of invention" is passé in view of the establishment of nonobviousness as the standard. *Carl Schenk, A.G. v. Nortron Corporation*, 713 F.2d 782, 218 U.S.P.Q. 698, 699 (Fed. Cir. 1983).

ω

Treating an advantage as the invention disregards the statutory requirement that the invention be viewed "as a whole", ignores the problem-recognition element, and injects an improper "obvious to try" consideration. *Jones v. Hardy*, 727 F.2d 1524, 220 U.S.P.Q. 1021, 1026 (Fed. Cir. 1984).

ω

The differences between the prior art and the invention defined by the asserted claims, the availability of that art to all workers in the field, the failure of established competitors in a highly competitive market to make the invention despite the incentive to do so, the admittedly non-obvious performance benefits realized through the claimed invention, the impressive commercial success of the claimed product, the praise of independent commentators, and the forbearance of competitors from infringing the patent all go to confirm that the claimed invention was not obvious at the time it was made to a person of ordinary skill in the art. *S. C. Johnson & Son, Inc. v. Carter-Wallace, Inc.*, 614 F. Supp. 1278, 225 U.S.P.Q. 1022 (N.Y. 1985).

ϖ

An action in the district court under 35 U.S.C. §145 is a proceeding de novo and, while it is limited to the invention claimed in the PTO, the court may consider any additional competent evidence that a plaintiff neither intentionally nor negligently failed to submit to the PTO. The presumption of correctness that attaches to the decision of the Commissioner is a rebuttable presumption that may be overcome by the introduction of evidence (at a trial under §145) that is of such character and amount as to carry a thorough conviction of error. At such a trial the plaintiff and defendant may present evidence on any issue properly before the court. This additional evidence may include testimony of expert witnesses and inventors skilled in the art, and evidence of commercial success. In making its determination of non-obviousness, the court recognized the non-analogous nature of one reference, the lack of teaching or suggestion in the prior art of the useful advantage of a flexible track incapable of self-support, and the commercial success of the highly flexible Hot Wheels trackway-toy vehicle combination covered by the plaintiff's Reissue Application. The fact that the claimed invention seemed simple and, when viewed in hindsight, appeared to be obvious was not enough to negate invention. *Lemelson v. Mossinghoff*, 225 U.S.P.Q. 1063 (D.C. 1985).

ϖ

Although the formal written assignment occurred after the critical date, the district court held that, even if there were an earlier oral agreement, an assignment or sale of the rights in the invention and potential patent rights is not a sale of the invention within the meaning of 35 U.S.C. §102(b). *Moleculon Research Corp. v. CBS, Inc.*, 793 F.2d 1261, 229 U.S.P.Q. 805 (Fed. Cir. 1986).

ϖ

It is a claim that defines the "actual" invention, not the other way around. *See E. I. du Pont de Nemours & Co. v. Phillips Petroleum Co.*, 849 F.2d 1430, 7 U.S.P.Q.2d 1129, 1131 (Fed. Cir.), *cert. denied*, 488 U.S. 986 (1988).

ϖ

Reference to the "invention" in 35 U.S.C. §119 clearly refers to what the claims define, not what is disclosed in the foreign application. *In re Gosteli*, 872 F.2d 1008, 10 U.S.P.Q.2d 1614, 1616 (Fed. Cir. 1989).

ϖ

The act of invention itself vests an inventor with a common law or "natural" right to make, use, and sell his or her invention absent conflicting patent rights in others (and, in certain circumstances, may similarly vest such rights in an employer of the inventor). *Arachnid Inc. v. Merit Industries Inc.*, 939 F.2d 1574, 19 U.S.P.Q.2d 1513, 1516 (Fed. Cir. 1991).

℧

Each claim of a patent constitutes a separate invention and gives rise to separate rights. *Cyrix Corp. v. Intel Corp.*, 846 F.Supp. 522, 32 U.S.P.Q.2d 1890, 1901 (Tex. 1994).

℧

In most patent law contexts, a date an invention is made is the date the invention was reduced to practice. For purposes of the second paragraph of 35 U.S.C. §103, however, the PTO has taken the position that the date of invention is the date the invention was conceived. 50 Fed. Reg. 9373 (1985); Donald S. Chisum, *Patents* §5.05[3], at 5-174 (1978 & Supp. 1995). The court believes that the usual rule should be applied in both situations for two compelling reasons. First, the court agrees with the authoritative treatise on patents that "[i]t can be assumed that Congress intended that the date of invention be determined in a consistent fashion for all purposes of patent law unless there are clear reasons for a variation." Chisum, *supra*, §5.03[3], at 5-174 n.57.38e. Second, from a perspective of proof, reduction to practice usually will be easier for a factfinder to determine because the evidence often involves tangible evidence, such as models and tests. Conception, on the other hand, is entirely a mental notion and, for that reason, is much more difficult for a factfinder to resolve with certainty. *Graco Children's Products Inc. v. Century Products Co. Inc.*, 38 U.S.P.Q.2d 1331, 1344 n.21 (Pa. 1996).

℧

Invention itself is the process of combining prior art in a nonobvious manner. *In re Rouffet*, 149 F.3d 1350, 47 U.S.P.Q.2d 1453, 1459 (Fed. Cir. 1998).

Invention as a Whole.

Disregard for the unobviousness of the results of "obvious to try" experiments disregards the "invention as a whole" concept of 35 U.S.C. §103. Overemphasis on the routine nature of the data gathering required to arrive at appellant's discovery, after its existence became expected, overlooks the last sentence of §103. *In re Antonie*, 559 F.2d 618, 195 U.S.P.Q. 6, 8 (C.C.P.A. 1977).

℧

The claimed invention must be viewed as a whole. The district court appeared to distill the invention down to a "gist," or "core," a superficial mode of analysis that disregards elements of the whole. It disregarded express claim limitations. *Bausch & Lomb, Inc. v. Barnes-Hind/Hydrocurve, Inc.*, 796 F.2d 443, 230 U.S.P.Q. 416 (Fed. Cir. 1986).

Invention Rights. *See also* Executive Order No. 10096.

An invention rights questionnaire, signed by a government employee inventor, reveals the following:

a. Twenty-eight hours were spent making the invention; eight of those hours were on government time.

    b. A drawing board, drafting machine, and drafting room supplies, all owned by the government, were used to prepare a drawing of the invention.

    c. The making of the invention was prompted when a problem was offered to the drafting department as a design challenge, the solution for which came from the inventor's experience as an auto mobile mechanic.

    d. The inventor was neither employed nor assigned to do any of the following: invent, improve, or perfect any process; conduct or perform research or development; act in a liaison capacity for research and development.

The design proposed by the inventor "was accomplished over and above his assigned duties." On the basis of his position as an engineering draftsman, the inventor is entitled to a presumption that the invention was made under circumstances that would require that title be left in him subject either (1) to law or (2) to a license for the government. *Locker v. Department of the Army,* 9 U.S.P.Q.2d 1412, 1413, 1414 (Comm'r Patents & Trademarks 1988).

ʊ

Although an invention may not be directly related to the inventor's duties, the government may still be entitled to an assignment if the invention was made in consequence of the inventor's official duties. "In consequence of" in Executive Order 10096 means that the invention is made as an obvious and direct result of the performance of the inventor's duties. *Menke v. Department of the Army,* 20 U.S.P.Q.2d 1386, 1388 (U.S. Dept. of Commerce 1991).

Inventive Entity. *See also* Another, Conversion, Inventorship.

While the lack of joint inventorship is not a favored defense, clear and convincing evidence should be accepted and applied when applicants practiced deception upon the Patent Office with respect to claiming joint inventorship. There is no statutory authorization for correcting inventorship without proof that misjoinder was through error and without any deceptive intention. *Iron Ore Co. of Canada v. The Dow Chemical Company,* 177 U.S.P.Q. 34, 70, 73 (Utah 1972).

ʊ

Congress having provided for the correction of innocent error in stating inventive entity when an application is filed, there is no reason to discriminate against the correction of the same innocent error involving sole inventors and their assignees. *A. F. Stoddard & Co. Ltd. v. Dann, Commissioner of Patents,* 564 F.2d 556, 195 U.S.P.Q. 97 (D.C. Cir. 1977).

ʊ

Authorship of an article by itself does not raise a presumption of inventorship with respect to the subject matter disclosed in the article. Thus, co-authors may not be presumed to be coinventors merely from the fact of co-authorship. On the other hand, when the PTO is aware of a printed publication, which describes the subject matter of the claimed invention and is published before an application is filed (the only date of invention on which it must act in the absence of other proof), the article may or may not raise a substantial question whether the applicant is the inventor. *In re Katz,* 687 F.2d 450, 215 U.S.P.Q. 14, 18 (C.C.P.A. 1982).

ʊ

The fact that an application has named a different (even overlapping) inventive entity than a patent does not necessarily make that patent prior art. *Applied Materials Inc. v. Gemini Research Corp.*, 835 F.2d 279, 5 U.S.P.Q.2d 1127, 1129 (Fed. Cir. 1987).

ω

The proposition that the inventive entity must be the same in both the foreign and the corresponding U.S. application in order to obtain benefit can no longer be accepted as a hard and fast rule in view of the liberalization of the requirements for filing a U.S. application as joint inventors wrought by the 1984 amendment of 35 U.S.C. §116. *Reitz v. Inoue*, 39 U.S.P.Q.2d 1838, 1840 (B.P.A.I. 1995).

Inventor. *See also* Applicant, Hypothetical Person.

The PTO, in discharging its duties to the public, has commendably required applicants for patents to provide an adequate quid pro quo in exchange for the monopoly sought. It should be equally alert in protecting the rights of applicants who have legally and properly established such a right. To do otherwise would be to enrich the public unjustly at the expense of the inventor, a result Congress could not have intended. *In re Herr*, 377 F.2d 610, 153 U.S.P.Q. 548, 549 (C.C.P.A. 1967).

ω

The Solicitor relies on *In re Winslow*, 365 F.2d 1017, 151 U.S.P.Q. 48 (C.C.P.A. 1966), for the proposition that a combination of features shown by references is legally obvious if it would have been obvious to "the inventor . . . working in his shop with the prior art references—which he is presumed to know—hanging on the wall around him," 151 U.S.P.Q. at 51, a statement limited by reference to "a case like this." In *Winslow*, the principal secondary reference was "in the very same art" as appellant's invention; all of the references were characterized as "very pertinent art." The language relied on by the Solicitor does not apply in cases where the very point in issue is whether one of ordinary skill in the art would have *selected*, without the advantage of hindsight and knowledge of the applicant's disclosure, the particular references that the Examiner applied. The inventor is presumed (under 35 U.S.C. §103) to have full knowledge of the prior art *in the field of his endeavor*, but not full knowledge of prior art *outside the field of his endeavor* (i.e., of "non-analogous" art). The inventor is only presumed to have that ability to select and utilize knowledge from other arts reasonably pertinent to his particular problem that would be expected of a person of ordinary skill in the art to which the subject matter pertains. *In re Antle*, 444 F.2d 1168, 170 U.S.P.Q. 285, 287, 288 (C.C.P.A. 1971).

ω

Plaintiff-inventor is "bound by the acts" of his lawyer-agent since he voluntarily chose him as his representative and cannot avoid the consequences of his acts or omissions. *Smith v. Diamond*, 209 U.S.P.Q. 1091, 1093 (D.C. 1981).

ω

Inventors, as a class, according to the concepts underlying the Constitution and the statutes that have created the patent system, possess something that sets them apart from the workers of ordinary skill, and one should not go about determining obviousness under 35 U.S.C. §103 by inquiring into what patentees (i.e., inventors) would have known or would have been likely to have done faced with the revelation of references. *The Standard Oil Company v. American Cyanamid Co.*, 774 F.2d 448, 227 U.S.P.Q. 293 (Fed. Cir. 1985).

ω

This statute (35 U.S.C. §115) creates no duty between the patent applicant and the purported inventor. Instead, because the Patent and Trademark Office's interest is in rewarding the true inventor with the issuance of a letter patent, the sole duty created is between the applicant and the Office. Breach of this duty results in the patent being "unauthorized by law and void...." *The University of Colorado Foundation v. American Cyanamid*, 880 F.Supp. 1387, 35 U.S.P.Q.2d 1737, 1745 (Colo. 1995).

ω

In order to be considered an inventor, a person must contribute to the conception of the invention. Corroborating evidence must show that the alleged inventor disclosed to others his "completed thought expressed in such clear terms as to enable those skilled in the art to make the invention." *Sturtevant v. Van Remortel*, 38 U.S.P.Q.2d 1134, 1137, 1138 (N.Y. 1995).

ω

To qualify as an "inventor", a person must have conceived of every feature of the invention at one point in time. *Graco Children's Products Inc. v. Century Products Co. Inc.*, 38 U.S.P.Q.2d 1331, 1341 (Pa. 1996).

Inventor's Contribution.

Evaluation of the worth of an inventor's contribution is left to the public, not to the judiciary, in determining patentability. A judge is nowhere authorized to declare a patent invalid on his or her personal evaluation. Emphasis on non-obviousness is one of inquiry, not quality. *Panduit Corp. v. Dennison Manufacturing Co.*, 810 F.2d 1561, 1 U.S.P.Q.2d 1593 (Fed. Cir. 1987).

Inventorship. *See also* Coauthors of Publication, Conversion, Derivation.

Courts have been reluctant to hold a patent invalid merely for incorrect inventorship. An allegation of invalidity, much less fraud, for incorrect inventorship has always been regarded as "technical". Although the patent laws require the naming of the correct inventor, the misjoinder or nonjoinder of inventors is not fatal and can be corrected by a court provided that the error was without deceptive intention. The burden of showing incorrect inventorship is a heavy one and must be proven by clear and convincing evidence. *Oetiker v. Jurid Werke GmbH*, 209 U.S.P.Q. 809, 822, 823 (D.C. 1981).

ω

Willful naming of an incorrect inventive entity constitutes grounds for invalidation of a patent. Failure to use diligence in seeking to correct the inventive entity cannot be corrected. A patent was held to be invalid for failure to name the correct inventive entity and because it was filed with a false oath. *Ashlow Limited v. Morgan Construction Co.*, 213 U.S.P.Q. 671 (S.C. 1982).

ω

The patent laws clearly distinguish between ownership and inventorship. Compare 35 U.S.C. §111 with 35 U.S.C. §261; the former requires that a patent be issued in the name of the inventor. The statute (35 U.S.C. §116) also provides for a joint application to be filed by joint inventors. *Shelcore, Inc. v. CBS, Inc.*, 220 U.S.P.Q. 459, 461 (N.J. 1983).

ᙡ

Inventorship is not ancillary to priority. *DeGeorge v. Bernier,* 768 F.2d 1318, 226 U.S.P.Q. 758 (Fed. Cir. 1985).

ᙡ

Plaintiff filed a complaint seeking declaratory, injunctive and other relief for defendant's failure to name plaintiff as a joint inventor in an issued patent. Plaintiff was required to file a statement setting forth precisely the specific facts relevant to her claim. Only if her claim is one of erroneous omission does the court have jurisdiction to proceed further. *Dee v. Aukerman*, 625 F.Supp. 427, 228 U.S.P.Q. 600, 603 (Ohio 1986).

ᙡ

The all-claims rule (that a patent is invalid for failure to name proper inventors unless the inventorship entity named is that of the true original inventors of every claim in a patent containing more than one claim) was not uniformly accepted as "the substantive law" before the 1984 Act. *SmithKline Diagnostics, Inc. v. Helena Laboratories Corp.*, 859 F.2d 878, 8 U.S.P.Q.2d 1468 (Fed. Cir. 1988).

ᙡ

Section 1.633(a) of 37 C.F.R. authorizes a junior party in an interference to move for judgment on the ground that the claims of the senior party are unpatentable under 35 U.S.C. §102(f) because the invention defined by the senior party's claims corresponding to the count is the joint invention of the junior and senior party. *Kramer v. Ballard,* 11 U.S.P.Q.2d 1148, 1150 (Comm'r Patents & Trademarks 1989).

ᙡ

The issuance of a patent constitutes notice to the world of its existence. Patent indexes are published weekly, and patent records are readily available to the public. A coinventor is put on constructive notice when a patent issues without listing him as an inventor. A belated inventorship contest can be barred by laches. *Advanced Cardiovascular Systems Inc. v. SciMed Life Systems Inc.*, 20 U.S.P.Q.2d 1870, 1872 (Minn. 1991).

ᙡ

A knew-or-should-have-known criterion is appropriate to actions to correct inventorship. It is in harmony with the patent statute, for in accordance with 35 U.S.C. §256 inventorship may be corrected at any time, whether by direct application to the Commissioner or by the court. Since the defense of patent invalidity based on incorrect inventorship can be raised at any time, correction of inventorship should be similarly available at any time. Were laches measured constructively from the date of patent issuance, an erroneously omitted inventor could be barred from remedy before learning of the existence of the patent. Such a stricture does not accord with either §256 or the practice which allows challenges to patent validity throughout the patent life. However, a delay of more than six years after an omitted inventor knew or should have known of the issuance of the patent will produce a rebuttable presumption of laches. *Advanced Cardiovascular Systems Inc. v. SciMed Life Systems Inc.*, 988 F.2d 1157, 26 U.S.P.Q.2d 1038, 1042, 1043 (Fed. Cir. 1993).

ᚠ

After a year following a consent judgment entered in previous litigation, the only grounds for granting a motion under Federal Rule of Civil Procedure 60(b) for the Court to set aside the consent judgment is fraud upon the Court. Fraud upon the court is limited to acts "designed to improperly influence the court in its decision." Plaintiff contended that, in the previous litigation, one of the defendants withheld information that he was not the inventor of the patented product, and he thus failed to disclose the alleged invalidity of the patent. This is not enough to constitute fraud upon the Court. *Auto-Shade Inc. v. Levy*, 28 U.S.P.Q.2d 1310, 1312 (Cal. 1993).

ᚠ

The inventorship issue falls within the exclusive jurisdiction of the federal court. *Roach v. Crouch*, 524 NW2d 400, 33 U.S.P.Q.2d 1361, 1362 (Iowa 1994).

ᚠ

An error in determining inventorship is not, by itself, inequitable conduct. *Pro-Mold and Tool Co. v. Great Lakes Plastics Inc.*, 75 F.3d 1568, 37 U.S.P.Q.2d 1626, 1632 (Fed. Cir. 1996).

ᚠ

A patent claim was held invalid because the patentee deliberately failed to name all the proper inventors thereof in violation of 35 U.S.C. §§116 and 256. *Haworth Inc. v. Steelcase Inc.*, 43 U.S.P.Q.2d 1223, 1224 (Mich. 1996).

ᚠ

Improper inventorship is not presumed simply because a large number of individuals are listed on the patent as joint inventors. On the contrary, the 'inventors as named in an issued patent are presumed to be correct." Incorrect inventorship is a technical defect in a patent that may be easily curable. *See* 35 U.S.C. §256 (1994). *Canon Computer Systems Inc. v. Nu-Kote International Inc.*, 134 F.3d 1085, 45 U.S.P.Q.2d 1355, 1358, 1359 (Fed. Cir. 1998).

ᚠ

A patent with improper inventorship does not avoid invalidation simply because it *might* be corrected under 35 U.S.C. §256. Rather, the patentee must claim entitlement to relief under the statute, and the court must give the patentee an opportunity to correct the inventorship. If the inventorship is successfully corrected, 35 U.S.C. §102(f) will not render the patent invalid. When the patentee does not claim relief under the statute and a party asserting invalidity proves incorrect inventorship, the court should hold the patent invalid for failure to comply with section 102(f). *Pannu v. Iolab Corp.*, 47 U.S.P.Q.2d 1657, 1662, 1663 (Fed. Cir. 1998).

Inventor's Signature.

This appeal is from a decision of the PTO Board of Appeals rejecting claims of a reissue application on the ground that a broadening reissue application that was filed within two years of the patent issue date (but was erroneously filed by the assignee) could not be corrected by a Declaration of the inventor filed more than two years after the patent issue date. The CAFC reversed. Recognizing that all of the provisions of a unified statute must be read in harmony, the portion of 35 U.S.C. §251 that requires that a broadening reissue application must be signed by the inventor does not mean that an error in compliance with §251 is insulated from the remedial ruling of *Stoddard* [564 F.2d 556, 195 U.S.P.Q. 97 (D.C. Cir. 1977)] or the statutory provision for the correction of error. The purpose of the reissue statute is to remedy errors. Reissue is remedial in nature and is based on fundamental principles of equity and fairness. These fundamental principles must not be forgotten in implementation of the statute. *In re Bennett,* 766 F.2d 524, 226 U.S.P.Q. 413 (Fed. Cir. 1985).

Inverse Doctrine of Equivalents. *See* **Reverse Doctrine of Equivalents.**

Inverted Lawsuit.

"The right to a jury trial in a declaratory judgment action depends . . . on whether the action is simply the counterpart of a suit in equity—that is, whether an action in equity could be maintained if declaratory judgment were unavailable—or whether the action is merely an inverted lawsuit." *In re Lockwood*, 50 F.3d 966, 33 U.S.P.Q.2d 1406, 1414 (Fed. Cir. 1995).

Invitation to Experiment. *See also* **Obvious to Try or Experiment.**

By claiming pharmaceutical compositions "having antidepressant activity" and methods "of producing antidepressant activity" that consist of administering identified compounds, appellants are claiming in terms of use. It behooves them, therefore, to disclose how to use, as 35 U.S.C. §112 ordains, "in such full, clear, concise, and exact terms as to enable any person skilled in the art . . . to . . . use" their invention. Appellants have in effect said to those skilled in the art: Here is a new group of compounds in which we have discovered antidepressant activity; you can put them up in convenient dosage units, and you can try them out on human patients or animal subjects, as you wish, and somewhere along the line, from daily doses of from 10 mg. to 450 mg., you will probably get the effect you are after. Such a great range is not an enabling or how-to-use disclosure as contemplated by the statute. There is not a single specific example or embodiment by way of an illustration of how the invention is to be practiced on any kind of host. It comprises an invitation to experiment in order to determine how to make use of appellants' alleged discovery of the antidepressant activity. *In re Gardner, Roe, and Willey,* 427 F.2d 786, 166 U.S.P.Q. 138, 140, 141 (C.C.P.A. 1970).

In Vitro. See In Vitro **Testing.**

Use of *in vitro* experiments to establish *in vivo* events is, in principle, a valid methodology. *Cross v. Iizuka,* 753 F.2d 1040, 1050, 224 U.S.P.Q. 739 (Fed. Cir. 1985); *Nelson v. Bowler*, 626 F.2d 853, 856, 206 U.S.P.Q. 881 (C.C.P.A. 1980).

ᴥ

In vitro studies and animal tests may be adequate to overcome rejections under 35 U.S.C. §§101 and 112 "as being based on an insufficient disclosure of the utility required" even when claims encompass treating humans for cancer. *Ex parte Chwang*, 231 U.S.P.Q. 751, 752 (B.P.A.I. 1986).

In Vitro **Testing.** *See also In Vitro*, **Screening.**

Simply because a drug gives positive results in vitro, it does not necessarily follow that there is a reasonable probability of success for therapeutic use of that drug in vivo. *In re Carroll,* 601 F.2d 1184, 202 U.S.P.Q. 571 (C. C. P.A. 1979).

ω

Successful in vitro testing marshalls resources and directs the expenditure of effort to further in vivo testing of the most potent compounds, thereby providing an immediate benefit to the public, analogous to the benefit provided by the showing of an in vivo utility. *Cross v. Iizuka,* 753 F.2d 1040, 224 U.S.P.Q. 739 (Fed. Cir. 1985).

In Vivo.

It is not proper for the Patent Office to require clinical testing in humans to rebut a *prima facie* case for lack of utility when the pertinent references which establish the *prima facie* case show *in vivo* tests employing standard experimental animals. *In re Langer,* 379 F.2d 278, 183 U.S.P.Q. 288, 297 (C.C.P.A. 1974).

ω

Use of *in vitro* experiments to establish *in vivo* events is, in principle, a valid methodology. *Cross v. Iizuka,* 753 F.2d 1040, 1050, 224 U.S.P.Q. 739 (Fed. Cir. 1985); *Nelson v. Bowler,* 626 F.2d 853, 856, 206 U.S.P.Q. 881 (C.C.P.A. 1980).

ω

The P388 and L1210 cell lines, though technically labeled tumor models, were originally derived from lymphocytic leukemias in mice. Therefore, these cell lines represent actual specific lymphocytic tumors; these models will produce this particular disease once implanted in mice. If applicants were required to wait until an animal actually developed this specific tumor before testing the effectiveness of a compound against the tumor *in vivo*, as would be implied from the Commissioner's argument, there would be no effective way to test compounds *in vivo* on a large scale. These tumor models represent a specific disease against which the claimed compounds are alleged to be effective. In asserting that *in vivo* tests in animals are only preclinical tests to determine whether a compound is suitable for processing in the second stage of testing, which apparently means *in vivo* testing in humans, and therefore are not reasonably predictive of the success of the claimed compounds for treating cancer in humans, the Commissioner, as did the BPAI, confuses the requirements under the law for obtaining a patent with the requirements for obtaining government approval to market a particular drug for human consumption. *In re Brana,* 51 F.3d 1560, 34 U.S.P.Q.2d 1436, 1440, 1442 (Fed. Cir. 1995).

Involuntary Plaintiff.

Rule (FRCP) 19(a) does not authorize making a co-owner (not under the court's jurisdiction) of a patent an involuntary plaintiff in infringement litigation. *Catanzaro v.*

International Telephone and Telegraph Corporation, 378 F.Supp. 203, 183 U.S.P.Q. 273, 277 (Del. 1974).

Ion Exchange.

The *Skogseid* decision [195 F.2d 924, 93 U.S.P.Q. 308 (C.C.P.A. 1952)] does not bar all patents on the treatment of particular substances with particular ion exchange materials under particular conditions. *Ex parte Perlman*, 123 U.S.P.Q. 447, 449 (PO Bd. App. 1958).

Ipsis Verbis. *See also* **Describe, Description,** *In Haec Verba.*

A term in a claim lacks an antecedent, in violation of proper practice, when the term does not appear in the specification. *In re Menough*, 324 F.2d 1011, 139 U.S.P.Q. 278 (C.C.P.A. 1963).

ᢍ

While the particular words quoted may not appear as such in the specification, the meaning thereof by other words is clearly present and constitutes adequate antecedent basis for the words in fact used. *Ex parte Siegmund and Cole*, 156 U.S.P.Q. 477 (PTO Bd. App. 1967).

ᢍ

For an application to be entitled to the benefit of the date of a previously filed copending application, such application must contain a written description of the invention claimed in the second application that complies with the first requirement of the first paragraph of 35 U.S.C. §112. However, the invention claimed in the later application does not have to be described (in the parent application) in ipsis verbis in order to satisfy the description requirement of §112. The question in cases in which the parent application does not contain language contained in the claims of the later application is whether the language that is contained in the parent application is the legal equivalent of the claim language, in the sense that the "necessary and only reasonable construction to be given the disclosure [in the parent application] by one skilled in the art" is the same as the construction that such person would give the language in the claims of the later application (emphasis in original). *Wagoner and Protzman v. Barger and Haggerty*, 463 F.2d 1377, 175 U.S.P.Q. 85, 86 (C.C.P.A. 1972).

ᢍ

The invention does not have to be described in ipsis verbis to satisfy the description requirement of 35 U.S.C. §112. If the grandfather application plus knowledge in the art equals the ultimate range recited, then the grandfather application adequately disclosed the invention. *Electronic Memories & Magnetics Corporation v. Control Data Corporation*, 188 U.S.P.Q. 448, 449 (Ill. 1975).

ᢍ

The claimed invention does not have to be described in ipsis verbis in order to satisfy the description requirement of 35 U.S.C. §112. The burden of showing that the claimed invention is not described in the specification rests on the PTO in the first instance, and it is up to the PTO to give reasons why a description not in ipsis verbis is insufficient. *In re Wertheim*, 541 F.2d 257, 191 U.S.P.Q. 90 (C.C.P.A. 1976).

ω

The burden of showing that the claimed invention is not described in the application rests on the PTO in the first instance, and it is up to the PTO to give reasons why a description not in ipsis verbis is insufficient. *In re Edwards, Rice, and Soulen*, 568 F.2d 1349, 196 U.S.P.Q. 465, 469 (C.C.P.A. 1978).

ω

A claimed invention need not be described ipsis verbis in order to satisfy the disclosure requirement of 35 U.S.C. §112. *Ex parte Holt*, 19 U.S.P.Q.2d 1211, 1213 (B.P.A.I. 1991).

Irreparable Harm. *See also* Injunction, Right to Exclude.

A delay of sixteen months in bringing suit is fatal to a contention or irreparable harm. *Rexnord, Inc. v. The Laitram Corporation*, 229 U.S.P.Q. 370, 376 (Wis. 1986).

ω

In matters involving patent rights, irreparable harm has been presumed when a clear showing has been made of patent validity and infringement. This presumption derives in part from the finite term of the patent grant; for patent expiration is not suspended during litigation, and the passage of time can work irremediable harm. The opportunity to practice an invention during the notoriously lengthy course of patent litigation may itself tempt infringers. *H. Robertson Co. v. United Steel Deck, Inc.*, 820 F.2d 384, 2 U.S.P.Q.2d 1926 (Fed. Cir. 1987).

ω

Where validity and continuing infringement have been clearly established, immediate irreparable harm is presumed. To hold otherwise would be contrary to the public policy underlying the patent laws. *The Laitram Corp. v. Rexnord Inc.*, 15 U.S.P.Q.2d 1161, 1175 (Wis. 1990).

ω

Loss of market share constitutes irreparable injury "because market share is so difficult to recover." *Ortho Pharmaceutical Corp. v. Smith*, 15 U.S.P.Q.2d 1856, 1863 (Pa. 1990).

ω

Harm to patentee who licenses all willing competitors and divests itself of manufacturing business is distinct from irreparable harm to a patentee who is practicing its invention and fully excluding others. *Wang Laboratories Inc. v. Mitsubishi Electronics America Inc.*, 29 U.S.P.Q.2d 1481, 1500 (Cal. 1993).

ω

If, in adjudicating irreparable harm, the district court has declined to make findings on likelihood of success, the CAFC must give the movant the benefit of the presumption before denying a motion requesting a preliminary injunction. *Reebok International Ltd. v. J. Baker Inc.*, 31 U.S.P.Q.2d 1781, 1784 (Fed. Cir. 1994).

ᚖ

Loss of market share has itself been recognized as an irreparable injury because it is so difficult to recover. *Maitland Co. Inc. v. Terra First Inc.*, 33 U.S.P.Q.2d 1882, 1892 (S.C. 1994).

ᚖ

Although a patentee's failure to practice an invention does not necessarily defeat the patentee's claim of irreparable harm, the lack of commercial activity by the patentee is a significant factor in the calculus. *High Tech Medical Instrumentation Inc. v. New Image Industries Inc.*, 49 F.3d 1551, 33 U.S.P.Q.2d 2005, 2009 (Fed. Cir. 1995).

ᚖ

If the right to exclude during the litigation period alone established irreparable harm. the presumption of irreparable harm stemming from a finding of likely success could never be rebutted, for every patentee whose motion for a preliminary injunction is denied loses the right to exclude an accused infringer from the market place pending the trial. *Eli Lilly and Co. v. American Cyanamid Co.*, 896 F.Supp. 851, 36 U.S.P.Q.2d 1011, 1019 (Ind. 1995).

ᚖ

"Irreparable harm" includes a situation where there exists an "impossibility of ascertaining, with any accuracy, the extent of the loss." *Dynamic Manufacturing Inc. v. Craze*, 46 U.S.P.Q.2d 1548, 1550 (Va. 1998).

Irreparable Injury. *See* **Irreparable Harm.**

Irreparable Loss. *See* **Irreparable Harm.**

Isolated. *See also* **Free, Pure, Transitory.**

The existence of a compound as an ingredient of another substance does not negative novelty in a claim to the pure compound. In the so-called aspirin case it was held that a pure compound may be patentable over the same compound in an impure form. This principle was approved in the case of *In re Merz*, 97 F.2d 599, 38 U.S.P.Q. 143. *In re Williams*, 171 F.2d 319, 80 U.S.P.Q. 150, 151 (C.C.P.A. 1948).

ᚖ

The argument that l-arterenol exists in the human body in certain glands in combination with other compounds and, therefore, is not patentable ignores the fact that it has no therapeutic value unless isolated and available in its pure form, and no compound of this kind has been derived from natural sources, except as it was accomplished by the seeding with crystal from the compound here claimed. *Sterling Drug Inc. v. Watson*, 135 F.Supp. 173, 108 U.S.P.Q. 37, 39 (D.C. 1955).

ᚖ

Whether or not a compound, which previously existed in fermentation broth, was known or recognized, claims which are not limited to a pure compound or to a compound freed from the fermentation broth do not satisfy the novelty requirements of 35 U.S.C. §101. *Ex parte Frohardt, Dion, and Ehrlich*, 139 U.S.P.Q. 377, 378 (PO Bd. App 1962).

ᛠ

It is possible to disclose a compound without actually isolating it and identifying it. Even for an actual reduction to practice, a chemical compound may be sufficiently identified by a partial analysis of the compound when considered with other factors. *Hauptschein, Braid, and Lawlor v. McCane and Robinson*, 339 F.2d 460, 144 U.S.P.Q. 16, 19 (C.C.P.A. 1964).

ᛠ

Obviousness at the time the invention was made is determined in view of the sum of all the relevant teachings in the art, not in view of first one and then another of isolated teachings in the art. *In re Kuderna and Phillips*, 426 F.2d 385, 165 U.S.P.Q. 575, 578, 579 (C.C.P.A. 1970).

ᛠ

The fact that compounds may be unstable and cannot be isolated does not preclude their being statutory subject matter. They are still compositions of matter if they exist, if they can be produced at will, and if they are useful for their intended purpose. *In re Breslow*, 616 F.2d 516, 205 U.S.P.Q. 221, 226 (C.C.P.A. 1980).

Isomer. *See also* **Optical Isomer, Relationship, Separation, Stereoisomer, Structural Obviousness, Structural Similarity, Substituents.**

The patentability of an adjacent position isomer of a known compound, which is generically disclosed in a number of references, is not precluded even though the primary utility of the claimed position isomer is a recognized utility of the known compound. *In re Petrzilka, Hofmann, Schenk, Troxler, Frey, and Ott*, 424 F.2d 1102, 165 U.S.P.Q. 327 (C.C.P.A. 1970).

ᛠ

Discovery of absence of skin toxicity in the claimed compound does not end the inquiry, because one who claims a compound, per se, which is structurally similar to a prior art compound must rebut the presumed expectation that the structurally similar compounds have similar properties. Because the expectation of similar properties stands unrebutted, it necessarily follows that an expectation of similar uses also stands unrebutted. *In re Wilder*, 563 F.2d 457, 195 U.S.P.Q. 426, 429, 430 (C.C.P.A. 1977).

ᛠ

The novelty of an optical isomer is not negated by the prior art disclosure of its racemate. *In re May and Eddy*, 574 F.2d 1082, 197 U.S.P.Q. 601, 607 (C.C.P.A. 1978).

Issue. *See also* **Issues, Waiver, Withdraw from Issue.**

Where no objection is made to evidence on the ground that it is outside the issues of the case, the issue raised is nevertheless before the trial court for determination, and the pleadings should be regarded as amended in order to conform to the proof. *Technical Development Corp. v. United States*, 202 Ct. Cl. 237, 179 U.S.P.Q. 180, 181 (1973).

ᛠ

Although the Patent Office refrains from issuing a patent containing a count in interference when that count is the subject of a 35 U.S.C. §141 appeal to the CCPA, in contests between applicants when appeal is to a district court pursuant to 35 U.S.C. §146, the Patent Office cannot withhold issuance pending the outcome of the appeal. When an interference is declared between an applicant and a patentee, the Patent Office can withhold issuance of a patent to a prevailing applicant pending the outcome of a 146 review. The only issues properly triable in a §§146 action are those issues that were first presented to the Patent Office Board. *Standard Oil Company of Indiana v. Montedison S.p.A.*, 398 F.Supp. 420, 187 U.S.P.Q. 549, 550, 551 (Del. 1975).

ᛒ

The proper issue before the court was whether the Board erred, as a matter of law, in holding that the claims were properly rejected under 35 U.S.C. §103. In deciding this issue, the court makes "an independent determination as to the legal conclusions and inferences which should be drawn from...[the findings of fact]." When an applicant presents rebuttal evidence, the decision-maker must consider all of the evidence of record (both that supporting and that rebutting the *prima facie* case) in determining whether the subject matter as a whole would have been obvious. An earlier decision should not be considered as set in concrete, and applicant's rebuttal evidence then be evaluated only on its knockdown ability. *Prima facie* obviousness is a legal conclusion, not a fact. Facts established by rebuttal evidence must be evaluated along with the facts on which the earlier conclusion was reached, not against the conclusion itself. A final finding regarding obviousness must rest upon evaluation of all facts in evidence, uninfluenced by any earlier conclusion reached by an earlier Board upon a different record. *In re Carleton,* 599 F.2d 1021, 202 U.S.P.Q. 165, 168, 169 (C.C.P.A. 1979).

ᛒ

A mere dispute concerning the meaning of a term does not itself create a genuine issue of material fact. *Markman v. Westview Instruments Inc.,* 772 F. Supp. 1535, 20 U.S.P.Q.2d 1955 (Pa. 1991).

ᛒ

An appellate court will consider an issue not presented below only if: (i) the issue involves a pure question of law and refusal to consider it would result in a miscarriage of justice; (ii) the proper resolution is beyond any doubt, (iii) the appellant had no opportunity to raise the objection at the district court level; (iv) the issue presents "significant questions of general impact or of great public concern[;]" or (v) the interest of substantial justice is at stake. *L.E.A. Dynatech Inc v. Allina*, 49 F.3d 1527, 33 U.S.P.Q.2d 1839, 1843 (Fed. Cir. 1995).

Issue Fee. *See also* Fee.

In an infringement action (based on a revived application) defendant's motion for summary judgment of patent invalidity was granted on the basis that the Commissioner lacked authority to revive an application which became abandoned for failure to pay the issue fee on time. *BEC Pressure Controls Corporation v. Dwyer Instruments, Inc.*, 380 F.Supp. 1397, 182 U.S.P.Q. 190 (Ind. 1974).

Issue of Law. *See also* Issues.

Classic issues of claim construction (i.e., what do the claims mean) are issues of law. They are for the court to decide and explicate on the record. Prosecution history estoppel is a question of law, which the court is free to analyze on appeal without deference to any implied finding of the jury on this issue. *Genentech Inc. v. The Wellcome Foundation Ltd.*, 29 F.3d 1555, 31 U.S.P.Q.2d 1161, 1170 n.35 (Fed. Cir. 1994).

Issue Preclusion. *See also* Collateral Estoppel, Preclusion.

Issue preclusion in patent litigation may arise under the same conditions as in any litigation, the principle requirements being that the issue must have actually been litigated in a prior proceeding, the parties must have been given a full and fair opportunity to do so, and the issue must provide the basis for the final judgment entered therein. Issue preclusion may also arise, apart from the above requirements or by reason of a stipulated judgment or consent decree. Under the latter, the primary consideration is the intent of the parties. Where the rulings made after a full and fair opportunity to litigate are firm and consistent with a subsequent settlement agreement by the parties and judgment is actually entered in the case, issue preclusion has been applied as to those issues when raised in a subsequent suit. Moreover, a stipulated final judgment may rest in part on a court's rulings during the course of a trial and in part on the agreement of the parties. Thus, that a judgment is entered by stipulation does not in and of itself remove a court's prior determination of specific issues in the litigation. A stipulated or consent judgment, like a contract, must be construed to determine its effect in light of all the circumstances. Issues that could not be appealed are never precluded. An application of that premise would be where a party wins on its claim, but loses on an issue. No issue preclusion attaches to the lost issue that could not by itself be appealed. However, voluntary relinquishment of one's right to appeal, where one stands as overall loser, does not fall within that rationale. *Hartley v. Mentor Corp.*, 869 F.2d 1469, 10 U.S.P.Q.2d 1138, 1140, 1141 (Fed. Cir. 1989).

ᅲ

Where a prior adjudication was by a foreign nation's court, applying its patent law to its patents, the barriers to reliance on the foreign judgment for collateral estoppel purposes become almost insurmountable. Differences in the law of the two nations and in the detailed language of the patent are emphasized to avoid issue preclusion in a patent case pending in this country even where the invention, the technological and economic competition between the parties, and the consequences of the judgments are for all practical purposes the same. Even if the court in this country were to apply collateral estoppel to certain factual findings made by a British court as opposed to importing its legal conclusions wholesale, it is not clear that the trial time would be significantly shortened. Furthermore, the federal circuit's reluctance to give collateral estoppel effect to foreign judgments would seem to apply here to foreign findings of fact insofar as those findings involve mixed questions of fact and foreign law. It is a quiddity of our law that a well and thoroughly reasoned decision reached by a highly skilled and scientifically informed justice of the Patent Court, Chancery Division, in the High Court of Justice of Great Britain after four weeks of trial must be ignored, and essentially the same issues with the same evidence must now be retried by American jurors with no background in science or patents, whose average formal education will be no more than high school. This curious event is the result of the world's chauvinistic view of patents. *Cuno Inc. v. Pall Corp.*, 729 F. Supp. 234, 14 U.S.P.Q.2d 1815, 1819 (N.Y. 1989).

ᛟ

A rationale for the rule of issue preclusion is that once a legal or factual issue has been settled by the court after a trial in which it was fully and fairly litigated, that issue should enjoy repose. Such litigated issues may not be relitigated even in an action on a different claim between the parties. *Foster v. Hallco Manufacturing Co. Inc.*, 947 F.2d 469, 20 U.S.P.Q.2d 1241, 1249 (Fed. Cir. 1991).

ᛟ

It is sound policy to apply principles of issue preclusion to the factfinding of administrative bodies acting in a judicial capacity. Giving preclusive effect to administrative factfinding serves the values underlying general principles of collateral estoppel. *In re Convertible Rowing Exerciser Patent Litigation*, 814 F.Supp. 1197, 26 U.S.P.Q.2d 1677, 1681 (Del. 1993).

ᛟ

The doctrine of issue preclusion is premised on principles of fairness. Thus, a court is not without some discretion to decide whether a particular case is appropriate for aplication of the doctrine. Accordingly, under certain circumstances, where all of the requirements of issue preclusion have been met, the doctrine will not be applied. Preclusion will not be effected when the quality or effectiveness of the procedures followed in the two suits differ. For instance, issue preclusion will not be applied if the scope of review of the first action is very narrow. Issue preclusion may be inappropriate in subsequent litigation with others when:

> (2) The forum in the second action affords the party against whom preclusion is asserted procedural opportunities in the presentation and determination of the issues that were not available in the first action and could likely result in the issue being differently determined.

> (8) Other compelling circumstances make it appropriate that the party be permitted to relitigate the issue.

Restatement (Second) of Judgments 29 (1980). *In re Freeman*, 30 F.3d 1459, 31 U.S.P.Q.2d 1444, 1450 (Fed. Cir. 1994).

ᛟ

A dismissal with prejudice before an issue or claim has been decided in an adversarial setting constitutes a final judgment barring relitigation for the purposes of claim preclusion but not for issue preclusion. *InterDigital Technology Corp. v. OKI America Inc.*, 866 F.Supp. 212, 32 U.S.P.Q.2d 1850, 1852 (Pa. 1994).

ᛟ

"In the case of a judgment entered by confession, consent, or default, none of the issues is actually litigated" and issue preclusion does not apply. *Kearns v. General Motors Corp.*, 94 F.3d 1553, 39 U.S.P.Q.2d 1949, 1952 (Fed. Cir. 1996).

ᛟ

A consent judgment should be "narrowly construed", and intention to give rise to issue preclusion "should not be readily inferred". *Scosche Industries Inc. v. Visor Gear Inc.*, 121 F.3d 675, 43 U.S.P.Q.2d 1659, 1663 (Fed. Cir. 1997).

ω

"No issue preclusion attaches to the lost issue which could not by itself be appealed." *Genentech Inc. v. U.S. International Trade Commission*, 122 F.3d 1409, 43 U.S.P.Q.2d 1722, 1728 (Fed. Cir. 1997).

Issues. *See also* Reasons for Appeal.

No one can doubt that a court has the power to revisit issues resolved earlier in a case. *Grain Processing Corp. v. American Maize-Products Co.*, 893 F.Supp. 1386, 37 U.S.P.Q.2d 1299, 1305 (Ind. 1995).

ITC.

While determinations of the ITC are given preclusive effect in cases not involving patent validity or invalidity, they have no such effect in patent cases. *Bio-Technology General Corp. v. Genentech Inc.*, 886 F.Supp. 377, 36 U.S.P.Q.2d 1169, 1175 (N.Y. 1995).

ω

The legislative history of the Trade Reform Act of 1974 supports the view that ITC decisions with respect to patent issues should have no claim preclusive effect in later district court litigation. "[T]he ITC takes the position that its decisions have no *res judicata* effect in [district court] litigation." *Bio-Technology General Corp. v. Genentech Inc.*, 80 F.3d 1553, 38 U.S.P.Q.2d 1321, 1329 (Fed. Cir. 1996).

ω

Any disposition of an International Trade Commission action by a Federal Court should not have res judicata or collateral estoppel effect on cases before such courts. ITC decisions are not binding on district courts in subsequent cases brought before them; accused infringers can raise whatever defenses they believe are justified, regardless whether they previously raised them and lost in the ITC. *Texas Instruments Inc. v. Cypress Semiconductor Corp.*, 90 F.3d 1558, 39 U.S.P.Q.2d 1492, 1501, 1502 (Fed. Cir. 1996).

J

Jepson. *See also* **Preamble.**

The preamble elements in a Jepson-type claim are impliedly admitted to be old in the art, but it is only an implied admission. The fact that none of the art cited by the Examiner shows the combination recited in the claim preamble gives credence to the appellants' explanation for drafting the claims in Jepson format, which was not intended as an admission, but was to avoid a double patenting rejection in a copending case unavailable to the public. A finding of obviousness should not be based on an implied admission erroneously creating imaginary prior art. That is not the intent of 35 U.S.C. §103. *In re Ehrreich and Avery,* 590 F.2d 902, 200 U.S.P.Q. 504 (C.C.P.A. 1979).

ᙡ

The reference in Jepson-type claims to the "improvement" clearly says that the defined invention was subsequent in time to the subject matter defined in the Jepson preamble. *Margolis, Rushmore, Liu, and Anderson v. Banner,* 599 F.2d 435, 202 U.S.P.Q. 365, 368 n.3 (C.C.P.A. 1979).

ᙡ

The appellants' admission that they had actual knowledge of a prior invention described in the preamble constitutes an admission that the preamble is prior art to them. The subject matter defined by the preamble is the acknowledged point of departure, and the implied admission that the Jepson format preamble describes prior art is not overcome. It is not unfair or contrary to the policy of the patent system that the appellants' invention be judged on obviousness against their actual contribution to the art. *In re Fout, Mishkin, and Roychoudhury,* 675 F.2d 297, 213 U.S.P.Q. 532 (C.C.P.A. 1982).

ᙡ

"Jepson" claims begin with a (frequently lengthy) preamble setting forth the environment of the claimed improvement. The preamble begins with a phrase, such as "In a machine [or other device] for performing [a specified operation] including..." and proceeds to describe a known type of machine or other device in which the improvement is incorporated. The claim then concludes with a description of the improvement, usually beginning with a phrase, such as "the improvement which comprises..." Such claims are favored because they clearly separate the elements of the overall combination which are admittedly old from those which are claimed as new. *Naso v. Park,* 856 F.Supp. 201, 34 U.S.P.Q.2d 1463, 1465 (N.Y. 1994).

ᙡ

When this form is employed, the claim preamble defines not only the context of the claimed invention, but also its scope. ("Although a preamble is impliedly admitted to be prior art when a Jepson claim is used, . . . the claimed invention consists of the preamble in combination with the improvement.") *Rowe v. Dror*, 112 F.3d 473, 42 U.S.P.Q.2d 1550, 1553 (Fed. Cir. 1997)

JMOL (Judgment as a Matter of Law). *See also* **JNOV, Judgment After Trial, Judgment as a Matter of Law.**

When an appellant contests the denial of a renewed motion for JMOL, the CAFC presumes that, on issues of law with underlying issues of fact, the jury made the proper findings necessary to support its verdict. *Shearing v. Iolab Corp.* 975 F.2d 1541, 1544, 24 U.S.P.Q.2d 1133, 1136 (Fed. Cir. 1992).

ϖ

Unobjected to jury instructions are not law of the case for purposes of JMOL. *Markman v. Westview Instruments Inc.*, 52 F.3d 967, 34 U.S.P.Q.2d 1321, 1326 n.5 (Fed. Cir. 1995).

ϖ

A failure to request or object to a jury instruction on a particular issue does not bar a motion for a judgment as a matter of law on that same issue. *Texas Instruments Inc. v. Cypress Semiconductor Corp.*, 39 U.S.P.Q.2d 1481, 1484 (Tex. 1995), *aff'd*, 39 U.S.P.Q.2d 1492 (Fed. Cir. 1996).

ϖ

When a court does not grant a motion for judgment as a matter of law made at the close of all the evidence, the court is considered to have "submitted the action to the jury subject to the court's later deciding the legal questions raised by the motion." Under Rule 50, a motion is appropriate when either: (1) a party raises a pure legal issue for determination based upon undisputed facts or (2) a party is unable to produce *substantial* evidence to support a jury verdict in its favor on an issue. When addressing the second type of motion, the court need not require that there be "a complete absence of facts to support a jury verdict" for the non-moving party before granting a judgment as a matter of law. To the contrary, "there must be a substantial conflict in evidence to support a jury question." The standard is "[i]f the facts and inferences point overwhelmingly in favor of one party, such that reasonable people could not arrive at a contrary verdict, then the motion [is] properly granted." *Tronzo v. Biomet Inc.*, 41 U.S.P.Q.2d 1403 (Fla. 1996).

ϖ

Appellant's failure to move (in the district court proceeding) for JMOL precludes the CAFC (on appeal) from reviewing the jury's findings in order to determine whether they are supported by substantial evidence. *Ameritek Inc. v. Carolina Lasercut Corp.*, 42 U.S.P.Q.2d 1411, 1412 (Fed. Cir. 1996–*unpublished*).

ϖ

In unusual cases an admission made by a plaintiff's witness can be sufficient to support entry of a JMOL in favor of a defendant after the close of the plaintiff's case-in-chief, even when the defendant bears the burden of proof on the decided issue. *Nobelpharma AB v. Implant Innovations Inc.*, 149 F.3d 1463, 44 U.S.P.Q.2d 1705, 1709 (Fed. Cir. 1997).

JNOV (Judgment Notwithstanding the Verdict). *See also* **Directed Verdict, JMOL, Judgment After Trial.**

On judicial review following a duly made motion for judgment n.o.v., the evidence must be viewed and reasonable inferences drawn in the light most favorable to the party with the jury verdict. *Continental Ore Co. v. Union Carbide & Carbon Corp.*, 370 U.S. 696 (1962).

ᚳ

To establish that a trial judge erred in granting a motion for JNOV, an appellant need only show that there was substantial evidence to support the jury's findings and that those findings can support the jury's legal conclusion. *Orthokinetics, Inc. v. Safety Travel Chairs, Inc.*, 806 F.2d 1565, 1571, 1 U.S.P.Q.2d 1081, 1085 (Fed. Cir. 1986).

ᚳ

When a court considers motions for directed verdict and for judgment notwithstanding the verdict, it must (1) consider all the evidence (2) in a light most favorable to the non-mover, (3) drawing reasonable inferences favorable to the non-mover (4) without determining credibility of witnesses and (5) without substituting its choice for that of the jury between conflicting elements in the evidence. The court should not be guided by its view of which side has the better case or by what it would have done had it been serving on the jury. If, after following those guidelines, the court is convinced upon the record before the jury that reasonable persons could not reach or could not have reached a verdict for the non-mover, it should grant the motion for directed verdict or JNOV.

Deference due a jury's fact findings in a civil case is not so great as to require acceptance of findings where those findings are clearly and unquestionably not supported by substantial evidence.

The burden on one who appeals the grant of a motion for JNOV is to show that the jury's factual findings were supported by at least substantial evidence and the legal conclusions made by the jury can be supported by those findings. Substantial evidence is such relevant evidence from the record taken as a whole as might be accepted by a reasonable mind as adequate to support the finding under review. *Vieau v. Japax Inc.*, 823 F.2d 1510, 3 U.S.P.Q.2d 1094 (Fed. Cir. 1987).

ᚳ

The view that a jury verdict on non-obviousness is at best advisory would make charades of motions for directed verdict or JNOV under Fed. R. Civ. P. 50 in patent cases. These motions apply only to binding jury verdicts. Moreover, use of an advisory jury is limited to actions not triable of right by a jury. All fact findings of a jury are non-advisory, unless made in an area expressly removed from jury verdict. A jury may decide the questions of anticipation and obviousness, either as separate special verdicts or en route to a verdict on the question of validity, which may also be decided by the jury. No warrant appears for distinguishing the submission of legal questions to a jury in patent cases from such submissions routinely made in other types of cases. So long as the Seventh Amendment stands, the right to a jury trial should not be rationed, nor should particular issues in particular types of cases be treated differently from similar issues in other types of cases.

When the judgment arises from a jury verdict, the reviewing court applies the reasonable-jury/substantial-evidence standard, a standard that gives greater deference to the judgment simply because appellate review is more limited, compared with review of a trial judge's decision. The appellate court's function is exhausted when evidentiary basis of the jury's verdict becomes apparent, it being immaterial that the court might draw a contrary inference or feel that another conclusion is more reasonable.

When there are sufficient established facts of record, an appellate court has jurisdiction to determine the merits of a JNOV motion. *Richardson v. Suzuki Motor Co., Ltd.,* 868 F.2d 1226, 9 U.S.P.Q.2d 1913 (Fed. Cir. 1989).

ʊ

The law presumes the existence of findings necessary to support a verdict reached by the jury. Whether there is trial evidence favorable to both sides is not the question. The question is whether there is substantial evidence to support the verdict. Even where evidence may be contradictory, the resolution of that conflict is a role assigned to the jury, and inferences are to be drawn in favor of the non-movant. Where there are alleged conflicts in the evidence, the trial court, on motion for JNOV, should not substitute its judgment for that of the jury. When, without question, reasonable jurors could have concluded that the patent claims in issue were infringed, denial of a motion for JNOV is required.

A motion for judgment notwithstanding the verdict will not lie unless it is preceded by a motion for a directed verdict made at the close of all of the evidence. A motion for JNOV cannot be made on a ground that was not raised in the motion for a directed verdict. *ALM Surgical Equipment Inc. v. Kirschner Medical Corp.,* 15 U.S.P.Q.2d 1241, 1245, 1246, 1250 (S.C. 1990).

ʊ

In ruling on a motion for JNOV, judges must accept the factual findings, presumed from a favorable jury verdict, that are supported under the substantial evidence/reasonable juror standard. *Modine Manufacturing Co. v. The Allen Group Inc.,* 917 F.2d 538, 16 U.S.P.Q.2d 1622, 1624 (Fed. Cir. 1990).

ʊ

JNOV should not be granted unless:

1. there is such a complete absence of evidence supporting the verdict that the jury's findings could only have been the result of sheer surmise and conjecture, or
2. there is such an overwhelming amount of evidence in favor of the movant that reasonable and fair-minded persons could not arrive at a verdict against him.

Defendants carry a particularly heavy burden on the issue of patent validity because, on that issue, a patentee need submit no evidence in support of a conclusion of validity by a jury. *In re Hayes Microcomputer Products Inc. Patent Litigation,* 766 F. Supp 818, 20 U.S.P.Q.2d 1836, 1838 (Cal. 1991).

Joinder. *See* **Conversion.**

Joinder of Invention. *See also* **Improper Markush, Unity of Invention.**

The purpose of 35 U.S.C. §101 is to define patentable subject matter, not to limit a patent to one invention. *In re Haas,* 486 F.2d 1053, 179 U.S.P.Q. 623, 625 n.4 (C.C.P.A. 1973).

ᵈ

If a single claim is required to be divided up and presented in several applications, that claim would never be considered on its merits. The totality of the resulting fragmentary claims would not necessarily be the equivalent of the original claim. Further, since the subgenera would be defined by the Examiner rather than by the applicant, it is not inconceivable that a number of the fragments would not be described in the specification. *In re Weber, Soder, and Boksay,* 580 F.2d 455, 198 U.S.P.Q. 328, 331 (C.C.P.A. 1978).

Joinder Rule

Co-owners may avoid "the inconvenience or undesirability of the joinder rule by structuring their interests so that one party is no longer (in law) an "owner". Chisum, *Patents*, 21.03[3], 21-296, n. 23. *International Business Machines Corp. v. Conner Peripherals Inc.,* 30 U.S.P.Q.2d 1315, 1319 (Cal. 1994).

Joined.

To be joined or connected does not necessitate a *direct* joining or connection. Therefore, the count encompasses DNA constructs that have intevening nucleotide sequences between the alpha-factor processing sequences and the human IGF-I sequence, as long as the proper reading frame is maintained between the two joined sequences. *Genentech Inc. v. Chiron Corp.,* 112 F.3d 495, 42 U.S.P.Q.2d 1608, 1613 (Fed. Cir. 1997).

Joint-Defense Doctrine.

The joint-defense doctrine is an extension of the attorney-client privilege. The doctrine clarifies the protection of attorney-client privilege in certain situations:

> If two or more clients with a common interest in a litigated or non-litigated matter are represented by separate lawyers and they agree to exchange information concerning the matter, a communication of any such client *that otherwise qualifies as privileged...* that relates to the matter is privileged as against third persons. Any such client may invoke the privilege, unless it has been waived by the client who made the communication.

Restatement (Third of the Law Governing Lawyers §126(1) (Proposed Final Draft 1996)(emphasis added). *B.E. Meyers & Co. v. United States,* 48 U.S.P.Q.2d 1679, 1681, 1682 (U.S. Ct. Fed. Cl. 1998).

Joint Invention. *See also* **Collaboration.**

To constitute a joint invention, it is necessary that each of the inventors work on the same subject matter and make some contribution to the inventive thought and to the final result. Each needs to perform but a part of the task if an invention emerges from all of the steps taken together. It is not necessary that the entire inventive concept should occur to each of the joint inventors, or that they should physically work on the project together.... One may do more of the experimental work while the other makes suggestions from time to time. The fact that each of the inventors plays a different role and that the contribution of one may not be as great as that of another does not detract from the fact that the invention is joint, if each makes some original contribution, though partial, to the final solution of the problem. *The Boots Co. plc v. Analgesic Associates*, 91 Civ. 2739, 26 U.S.P.Q.2d 1144, 1145 (N.Y. 1993).

Joint Inventors. *See also* Coinventor.

Persons are joint inventors when they work together to solve a particular problem. *Graco Children's Products Inc. v. Century Products Co. Inc.*, 38 U.S.P.Q.2d 1331, 1341 (Pa. 1996).

ϖ

A joint inventor must contribute in some significant manner to the conception of the invention. As such, "each inventor must contribute to the joint arrival at a definite and permanent idea of the invention as it will be used in practice." *Fina Oil and Chemical Co. V. Ewen*, 123 F.3d 1466, 43 U.S.P.Q.2d 1935, 1941 (Fed. Cir. 1997).

ϖ

Improper inventorship is not presumed simply because a large number of individuals are listed on the patent as joint inventors. On the contrary, the 'inventors as named in an issued patent are presumed to be correct." Incorrect inventorship is a technical defect in a patent that may be easily curable. *See* 35 U.S.C. §256 (1994). *Canon Computer Systems Inc. v. Nu-Kote International Inc.*, 134 F.3d 1085, 45 U.S.P.Q.2d 1355, 1358, 1359 (Fed. Cir. 1998).

ϖ

In the context of joint inventorship, each co-inventor presumptively owns a pro rata undivided interest in the entire patent, no matter what their respective contributions. A joint inventor as to even one claim enjoys a presumption of ownership in the entire patent. *Ethicon Inc. v. United States Surgical Corp*, 135 F.3d 1456, 45 U.S.P.Q.2d 1545, 1552 (Fed. Cir. 1998).

ϖ

All that is required of a joint inventor is that he or she (1) contribute in some significant manner to the conception or reduction to practice of the invention, (2) make a contribution to the claimed invention that is not insignificant in quality, when that contribution is measured against the dimension of the full invention, and (3) do more than merely explain to the real inventors well-known concepts and/or the current state of the art. *Pannu v. Iolab Corp.*, 47 U.S.P.Q.2d 1657, 1663 (Fed. Cir. 1998).

Joint Inventorship.

In an interference setting, uncorroborated testimony of the junior p
to establish joint inventorship. *Linkow v. Linkow and Edelman*, 51
U.S.P.Q. 223, 225 (C.C.P.A. 1975).

ϖ

Although "the exact parameters of what constitutes joint inventorship...is one of the muddiest concepts in the muddy metaphysics of the patent law", certain guidelines are available. Plaintiff must, at a minimum, have contributed to the conception of the invention. The Federal Circuit has adopted the following definition of "conception" from the Court of Customs and Patent Appeals: "[Conception is] the formation, in the mind of the inventor of *a definite* and permanent idea of the complete and operative invention as it is thereafter to be applied in practice...." One district court held that an individual must have played an "inventive" role in making an "original contribution" to the "final solution" of a problem to qualify as a joint inventor. *Brown v. University of California*, 866 F.Supp. 439, 31 U.S.P.Q.2d 1463, 1465 (Cal. 1994).

Joint Licensing.

Communications between partners in a joint licensing program may be privileged even when one of the partners is not a party to involved patent infringement litigation. *The Stanley Works v. Haeger Potteries, Inc.*, 35 F.R.D. 551, 142 U.S.P.Q. 256, 258, 259 (Ill. 1964).

Judge's Impartiality.

In enacting 28 U.S.C. §455(a), Congress created an objective standard under which disqualification of a judge is required when a reasonable person, knowing all the facts, would question the judge's impartiality. The test for disqualification under 455(a) is an objective one: whether a reasonable person with knowledge of all the facts would conclude that the judge's impartiality might reasonably be questioned. *Hewlett-Packard Co. v. Bausch & Lomb Inc.*, 882 F.2d 1556, 11 U.S.P.Q.2d 1750, 1760 (Fed. Cir. 1989).

Judgment. *See also* Consent Judgment, Default Judgment.

The Court of Appeals, Federal Circuit, reviews judgments, not opinions. *Milliken Research Corporation v. Dan River, Inc.*, 739 F.2d 587, 222 U.S.P.Q. 571, 576 (Fed. Cir. 1984).

ᛒ

When the judgment arises from a jury verdict, the reviewing court applies the reasonable jury/substantial evidence standard: A standard gives greater deference to the judgment simply because appellate review is more limited, compared with review of a trial judge's decision. The appellate court's function is exhausted when the evidentiary basis of the jury's verdict becomes apparent, it being immaterial that the court might draw a contrary inference or feel that another conclusion is more reasonable. *Richardson v. Suzuki Motor Co., Ltd.*, 868 F.2d 1226, 9 U.S.P.Q .2d 1913 (Fed. Cir. 1989).

ᛒ

The Commissioner lacks authority to reopen the reexamination proceeding after receipt of the Federal Circuit's mandate affirming the Examiner's rejection of all claims since the case is no longer considered pending. See MPEP 1216.06 (5th ed., rev. 12, July 1989) under "Office Procedure Following Decision by the Federal Circuit," subheading "1. All claims rejected"; *Morganroth v. Quigg*, 885 F.2d 843, 12 U.S.P.Q.2d 1125, 1128 (Fed.

Cir. 1989) (Commissioner does not have authority to revive application abandoned by termination of proceedings resulting from a failure to appeal a final district court judgment); *In re Jones*, 542 F.2d 65, 191 U.S.P.Q. 249, 252 (C.C.P.A. 1976) ("receipt of the mandate by the PTO terminated proceedings in the case"); *In re Willis*, 537 F.2d 513, 190 U.S.P.Q. 327, 329 (C.C.P.A. 1976) ("When, on January 12, 1976, our mandate was received in the PTO, no claims having been allowed, the appealed application suffered its demise."); *Continental Can Co. v. Schuyler*, 326 F. Supp. 283, 168 U.S.P.Q. 625 (D.C. 1970), ("where rejection of all claims is affirmed by the Court of Customs and Patent Appeals, the responsibility is upon the plaintiff to stay the Court's judgment if the pendency of the application is to be preserved"). Petitioner's relief, if any, lies in a motion for the Federal Circuit to withdraw its mandate, not with the Commissioner. *See Jones*, 542 F.2d at 68, 191 U.S.P.Q. at 252 (CCPA "has the power, in the interest of justice, to recall its mandate in an appropriate case, and this power should be exercised sparingly and only upon a showing of good cause"). *In re Eckerle*, 1115 O.G. 6 (Commr. Patents & Trademarks 1990).

ळ

"[A] judgment should be altered 'because of a mistake in jury instructions only if the error was prejudicial....' *Automotive Products plc v. Tilton Engineering Inc.*, 855 F.Supp. 1101, 33 U.S.P.Q.2d 1065, 1089 (Cal. 1994).

ळ

A final judgment is not voided if the precedent on which it was based is later modified or overruled. *U.S. Philips Corp. v. Sears Roebuck & Co.*, 55 F.3d 592, 34 U.S.P.Q.2d 1699, 1704 (Fed. Cir. 1995).

ळ

An appeal court judgment that does not specifically provide for a remand is not necessarily incompatible with further proceedings to be undertaken in the district court. *Exxon Chemical Patents Inc. v. Lubrizol Corp.*, 137 F.3d 1475, 45 U.S.P.Q.2d 1865, 1872 (Fed. Cir. 1998).

Judgment After Trial. *See also* **JNOV, Judgment as a Matter of Law.**

Effective December 1, 1991, Fed. R. Civ. P. 50(b) was amended to eliminate the term "Motion for Judgment Notwithstanding the Verdict" and to substitute it with "Renewal of Motion for Judgment After Trial." In all substantive respects the amended version has the same effect as the former rule. *Braun Inc. v. Dynamics Corp. of America*, 915 F.2d 815, 24 U.S.P.Q.2d 1121, 1123 n.3 (Fed. Cir. 1992).

ळ

[A] party may only base a motion for judgment notwithstanding the verdict on a ground that he included in a prior motion for directed verdict at the close of all the evidence." *Hoechst Celanese Corp. v. BP Chemicals Ltd.*, 78 F.3d 1575, 38 U.S.P.Q.2d 1126, 1131 (Fed. Cir. 1996).

Judgment as a Matter of Law (JMOL). *See also* **JMOL.**

The CAFC reviews a trial court's denial of a renewed motion for JNOV (JMOL) under Rule 50(b) of the Federal Rules of Civil Procedure and must decide for itself whether reasonable jurors, viewing the evidence as a whole, could have found the facts needed to support the verdict in the light of the applicable law. If it is concluded that no reasonable findings of fact, supported by substantial evidence, could support the verdict that was incorporated into the trial court's judgment, the CAFC must conclude that the trial court erred in not granting the motion for JNOV [JMOL]. *Lemelson v. General Mills Inc.*, 968 F.2d 1202, 1207, 23 U.S.P.Q.2d 1284, 1288 (Fed. Cir. 1992), *cert. denied*, 113 S. Ct. 976 (1993).

ω

"Directed verdict" has been renamed "judgment as a matter of law." *Markman v. Westview Instruments Inc.*, 52 F.3d 967, 34 U.S.P.Q.2d 1321, 1324 n.2 (Fed. Cir. 1995).

Judgment Notwithstanding the Verdict. *See* JNOV.

Judicial Economy.

When the rest of the industry is not impeded by involved patents, it seems manifestly unjust to rely merely on "judicial economy" as *justification* for holding appellants liable and impairing their ability to compete. *Mendenhall v. Barber-Greene Co.*, 26 F.3d 1573, 31 U.S.P.Q.2d 1001, 1008 (Fed. Cir. 1994).

Judicial Estoppel. *See also* Inconsistent.

The doctrine of judicial estoppel "applies to preclude a party from assuming a position in a legal proceeding inconsistent with one previously asserted." The doctrine prevents the use of inconsistent statements "that would result in an 'affront to judicial dignity' and 'a means of obtaining unfair advantage.'" *Saes Getters S.P.A. v. Ergenics Inc.*, 17 U.S.P.Q.2d 1581, 1586 (N.J. 1990).

ω

Judicial estoppel is a procedural matter, reviewd under the law of the regional circuit in which the trial court sits. *Water Technologies Corp. v. Calco, Ltd.*, 850 F.2d 660, 665 & n.4, 7 U.S.P.Q.2d 1097, 1101 & n.4 (Fed. Cir.), *cert. denied*, 488 U.S. 968 (1988).

ω

The doctrine of judicial estoppel is the general proposition that, where a party assumes a certain position in a legal proceeding, and succeeds in maintaining that position, he may not thereafter, simply because his interests have changed, assume a contrary position. In order to be subject to judicial estoppel, a party, having obtained a litigation benefit, must have attempted to invoke the authority of one tribunal to override a bargain made with another. *Wang Laboratories Inc. v. Applied Computer Sciences Inc.*, 958 F.2d 355, 22 U.S.P.Q.2d 1055, 1058 (Fed. Cir. 1992).

ω

Judicial estoppel, which is not recognized by some circuits, is a rarely used doctrine and exists to protect the court, not a party, from a party's chicanery. "The principle is that if you prevail in Suit /1 by representing that A is true, you are stuck with A in all later litigation growing out of the same events." "The offense is not taking inconsistent positions so much as it is *winning, twice*, on the basis of incompatible positions." *Loral Fairchild Corp. v. Matsushita Electric Industrial Co. Ltd.*, 840 F.Supp. 211, 31 U.S.P.Q.2d 1499, 1505 (N.Y. 1994).

ω

Judicial estoppel is an equitable principle that holds a party to a position on which it prevailed, as against later litigation arising from the same events. Because the doctrine of judicial estoppel "is intended to protect the courts rather than the litigants", it is proper for an appellate court to raise the estoppel "in an appropriate case". *U.S. Philips Corp. v. Sears Roebuck & Co.*, 55 F.3d 592, 34 U.S.P.Q.2d 1699, 1703 (Fed. Cir. 1995).

ω

To permit a party to assume a position inconsistent with a position it had successfully relied upon in a past proceeding "would most flagrantly exemplify...playing 'fast and loose with the courts' which has been emphasized as an evil the courts should not tolerate." *College Savings Bank v. Florida Prepaid Postsecondary Education Expense Board*, 42 U.S.P.Q.2d 1487, 1494 (N.J. 1996).

Judicial Notice.

The CCPA was reluctant to take judicial notice of a monograph (not of record) in a highly technical area of biochemistry. *In re Petering and Fall*, 301 F.2d 676, 133 U.S.P.Q. 275, 279 (C.C.P.A. 1962).

ω

With regard to the nature of safety in the field of drugs and medicaments, the court took judicial notice that many valued therapeutic substances or materials with desirable physiological properties, when administered to lower animals or humans, entailed certain risks or may have undesirable side effects. It is true that such substances would be more useful if they were not dangerous or did not have undesirable side effects, but the fact remains that they are useful, useful to doctors, veterinarians and research workers, useful to patients, both human and lower animal, and therefore useful in the meaning of of 35 U.S.C. §101. *In re Hartop and Brandes*, 311 F.2d 249, 135 U.S.P.Q. 419, 424, 425 (C.C.P.A. 1962).

ω

The CCPA refused to take judicial notice of the issuance of a design patent (not of record) directed to similar subject matter and granted over the same references relied upon by the Patent Office. *In re Phillips*, 315 F.2d 943, 137 U.S.P.Q. 369, 370 (C.C.P.A. 1963).

ω

The solicitor's reliance on an allegedly standard textbook on chemistry (not previously of record) as further support for the Patent Office position illustrates a growing tendency on the part of appellants and the Patent Office alike to impair the clear and specific language of 35 U.S.C. §144, which requires an appeal to be determined "on the evidence produced before the Patent Office." *In re Cofer*, 354 F.2d 664, 148 U.S.P.Q. 268, 272 (C.C.P.A. 1966).

ω

It is improper for the Board to, in effect, judicially notice the "inoperability" of species of compounds within the bounds of an asserted claim. *In re Kamal and Rogier*, 398 F.2d 867, 158 U.S.P.Q. 320, 323 (C.C.P.A. 1968).

ᘃ

With regard to an attack of "judicial notice" by the Board the court agreed with the solicitor's assertion that there is no real dispute as to the facts of which the Board took notice. As to the propriety of the Board's taking such notice at all, the court has previously determined that the Patent Office appellate tribunals, where it is found necessary, may take notice of facts beyond the record which, while not generally notorious, are capable of such instant and unquestionable demonstration as to defy dispute. This rule is not, however, as broad as it first might appear, and the court will always construe it narrowly and will regard facts found in such manner with an eye toward narrowing the scope of any conclusions to be drawn therefrom. Where an appellant fails to challenge a judicially noticed fact and it is clear that he has been amply apprised of such finding so as to have the opportunity to make such challenge, the Board's finding will be considered conclusive by the CCPA. *In re Ahlert and Kruger*, 424 F.2d 1088, 165 U.S.P.Q. 418, 420, 421 (C.C.P.A. 1970).

ᘃ

Ordinarily, citation by the Board of a new reference and reliance thereon to support a rejection will be considered as tantamount to assertion of a new ground of rejection. This will not be the case, however, where such a reference is a standard work, cited only to support a fact judicially noticed and the fact so noticed plays a minor role, serving only "to 'fill in the gaps' which might exist in the evidentiary showing made by the Examiner to support a particular ground for rejection." Under such circumstances an applicant must be given the opportunity to challenge either the correctness of the fact asserted or the notoriety or repute of the reference cited in support of the assertion. A challenge to the Board's judicial notice must contain adequate information or argument so that on its face it creates a reasonable doubt regarding the circumstances justifying the judicial notice. *In re Boon*, 439 F.2d 724, 169 U.S.P.Q. 231, 234 (C.C.P.A. 1971).

ᘃ

Statement in a scientific journal or in an authoritative encyclopedia is not basis for taking judicial notice that controverted phrases are art recognized; the court cannot be certain that the alleged fact is indisputable among reasonable men. However, extra-record references may be used to bolster a weak point that is supported by some evidence in the record even though the court would decline to use them by themselves as a basis for taking judicial notice if there were no evidence at all in the record in support of the point. *In re Barr, Williams, and Whitmore*, 444 F.2d 588, 170 U.S.P.Q. 330, 334 (C.C.P.A. 1971).

ᘃ

Facts constituting the state of the art are normally subject to the possibility of rational disagreement among reasonable persons and are not amenable to the taking of judicial or administrative notice. If evidence of the knowledge possessed by those skilled in the art is to be properly considered, it must be timely injected into the proceedings. *In re Eynde, Pollet, and de Cat*, 480 F.2d 1364, 178 U.S.P.Q. 470, 474 (C.C.P.A. 1973).

ᘃ

The contents of the Federal Register shall be judicially noticed and, without prejudice to any other mode of citation, may be cited by volume and page number. *In re Watson*, 517 F.2d 465, 186 U.S.P.Q. 11, 17 (C.C.P.A. 1975).

ʊ

Considering the art to which claimed subject matter pertained, the Court of Customs and Patent Appeals took judicial notice of a definition from Kirk-Othmer Encyclopedia of Chemical Technology (2d ed. 1968). *In re Salem, Butterworth, and Ryan,* 553 F.2d 676, 193 U.S.P.Q. 513, 518 (C.C.P.A. 1977).

ʊ

Judicial notice is appropriately taken of a publicly accessible patent (not part of the record on appeal) referred to at the argument) and PTO correspondence which is part of the public record. *Hoganas AB v. Dresser Industries Inc.*, 9 F.3d 948, 28 U.S.P.Q.2d 1936, 1941 n.27 (Fed. Cir. 1993).

Judicial Precedent.

The CAFC does not accept the PTO's statement that it can "administratively set aside the judicially created rule of *In re Spina*" [975 F.2d 854, 24 U.S.P.Q.2d 1142 (Fed. Cir. 1992)]. Judicial precedent is as binding on administrative agencies as are statutes. *Rowe v. Dror*, 112 F.3d 473, 42 U.S.P.Q.2d 1550, 1554 n.2 (Fed. Cir. 1997).

Judicial Redrafting.

Nothing in any precedent permits judicial redrafting of claims. At most there are admonitions to construe words in claims narrowly, if possible, so as to sustain their validity. *Becton Dickinson & Co. v. C. R. Bard Inc.*, 922 F.2d 792, 17 U.S.P.Q.2d 1097, 1102 (Fed. Cir. 1990).

Judicial Review.

Parties in interference are advised to file petitions under 37 C.F.R. §1.644(a)(2) within 15 days after entry of the Board's final decision and also to include, as part of the petition or in a separate paper, a request for an extension of time to seek judicial review. *Goutzoulis v. Athale*, 15 U.S.P.Q.2d 1461, 1464 (Commr. Patents & Trademarks 1990).

Jurisdiction. *See also* **Appeal, Jurisdiction of the CAFC, Long-Arm Statute, Moot, Motion to Dismiss, Nonresident Defendant, Personal Jurisdiction, Ripeness, Stream of Commerce, Subject Matter Jurisdiction, Summary Judgment, Venue.**

Jurisdiction is not defeated by the possibility that averments might fail to state a cause of action on which petitioners could actually recover. The failure to state a proper cause of action calls for a judgment on the merits and not for a dismissal for want of jurisdiction. Whether the complaint states a cause of action on which relief can be granted is a question of law and, just as issues of fact, it must be decided after and not before the court has assumed jurisdiction over the controversy. If the court does later exercise its jurisdiction to determine that the allegations in the complaint do not state a ground for relief, then dismissal of the case would be on the merits, not for want of jurisdiction. *Bell v. Hood*, 327 U.S. 678, 682 (1946).

ω

A request for reconsideration filed at the Board of Appeals on the same day as a Notice of Appeal to the CCPA was considered for the purpose of correcting the decision appealed from and certifying reversal of the rejection of two claims. The Board did nothing more than exercise a purely ministerial function in its administrative capacity. It made no new or different determination of an issue. It exercised no judicial function. It was well within its province to certify the fact of an unrecorded determination made when the matter was within the full competence of its jurisdiction. *In re Grier*, 342 F.2d 120, 144 U.S.P.Q. 654, 656, 657 (C.C.P.A. 1965).

ω

The CCPA has an inherent power to review any action of the Board which affects the CCPA's appellate jurisdiction. Both 28 U.S.C. §1542 and 35 U.S.C. §141 limit the CCPA's jurisdiction to appeals of "decisions" of the Board. The Board's authority to make such "decisions" is set forth in 35 U.S.C. §7, but the CCPA has the right to determine whether the Board properly refused to make such "decisions" in its statutory capacity. In order to confer subject matter jurisdiction upon the CCPA, the Board must have reviewed an adverse decision of an Examiner relating at least indirectly to a rejection of claims. *In re Haas*, 486 F.2d 1053, 179 U.S.P.Q. 623, 624, 625 (C.C.P.A. 1973).

ω

The State Courts have jurisdiction to determine questions arising under the patent laws, when merely incidental to cases which do not arise under that law. *In re Lefkowitz*, 362 F.Supp. 922, 179 U.S.P.Q. 282, 284 (N.Y. 1973).

ω

Asserting a defense of patent invalidity does not convert an action for breach of contract to one arising under the patent laws. *Wham-O Manufacturing Co. v. All-American Yo-Yo Corp.*, 377 F. Supp. 993, 181 U.S.P.Q. 320, 321 (N.Y. 1973).

ω

State courts have jurisdiction to pass upon questions or issues involving patent laws. In an action in a state court to recover patent royalties required to be paid pursuant to contract, the state court has jurisdiction to consider the issue of patent validity as a defense to the action. State courts have passed upon the defense of patent validity in breach of contract cases. *Consolidated Kinetics Corp. v. Marshall, Neil, and Pauley*, 521 P.2d 1209, 182 U.S.P.Q. 434, 435, 436 (Wash. 1974).

ω

The CCPA has no jurisdiction over a claim that was allowed by the Examiner and was not the subject of the Board's decision. *In re Hayashibara and Sugimoto*, 525 F.2d 1062, 188 U.S.P.Q. 4 (C.C.P.A. 1975).

ω

Substantial business activity, beyond mere solicitation, by a distributor of an alien corporation on that corporation's behalf can be sufficient to provide in personam jurisdiction over the alien coporation. Such activities were sufficiently important to the alien corporation that, if the distributor were not performing them, the alien corporation would have to do so itself, as it in fact did on two occasions. *Nippon Electric Co. Ltd. v. American Broadcasting Companies, Inc.*, 204 U.S.P.Q. 496, 497 (N.Y. 1978).

ω

Once a patent of invention has been granted, the Patent Office has no authority to invalidate the claims of the original patent in subsequent reissue proceedings. The PTO does not regain power over the original patent's validity when a reissue patent is applied for. When a patent has received the signature of the Secretary of the Interior, countersigned by the Commissioner of Patents, and has had affixed to it the seal of the Patent Office, it has passed beyond the control and jurisdiction of that office, and is not subject to be revoked or canceled by the President, or any other officer of the Government. *National Business Systems, Inc. v. AM International, Inc.*, 546 F.Supp. 340, 217 U.S.P.Q. 235, 241 (Ill. 1982).

ω

That resolution of a question of state law (holding a license valid) may render federal questions moot does not deprive a federal court of subject matter jurisdiction where the plaintiff bases his claim upon, and seeks remedies under, the patent laws, even where the complaint anticipates a defense of license. *Air Products & Chemicals, Inc. v. Reichhold Chemicals Inc.*, 755 F.2d 1559, 225 U.S.P.Q. 121, 124 (Fed. Cir.), *cert. dismissed*, 473 U.S. 929 (1985).

ω

Where it appears on appeal that the controversy has become entirely moot, it is the duty of the appellate court to set aside the decree below and to remand the cause with directions to dismiss. This case did not become moot on appeal; rather a consent judgment was entered pursuant to a settlement agreement entered into by the parties. The agreed settlement and entry of consent judgment mooted any possiblity of pursuing an appeal and foreclosed the appellate court from obtaining jurisdiction. *Gould v. Control Laser Corp.*, 866 F.2d 1391, 9 U.S.P.Q.2d 1718 (Fed. Cir. 1989).

ω

Section 293 of 35 U.S.C. §empowers the District Court for the District of Columbia to assert personal jurisdiction over a foreign holder of U.S. patents in a dispute over the patents' ownership. *National Patent Development Corp. v. T. J. Smith & Nephew Ltd.*, 877 F.2d 1003, 11 U.S.P.Q.2d 1211 (D.C. Cir. 1989).

ω

After a district court determines that federal jurisdiction exists, it is precluded from remanding the federal claims to a state court on the basis of expediency. *Stanford Telecommunications Inc. v. U.S. District Court for the Northern District of California*, 11 U.S.P.Q.2d 1480 (9th Cir. 1989).

ω

Jurisdiction is not defeated by the possibility that an averment might fail to state a cause of action on which petitioners could actually recover. Failure to state a proper cause of action calls for a judgment on the merits and not for a dismissal for want of jurisdiction. Whether a complaint states a cause of action on which relief can be granted is a question of law, and, just like issues of fact, it must be decided after and not before the court has assumed jurisdiction over a controversy. If the court later exercises its jurisdiction to determine that the allegations in the complaint do not state a ground for relief, then dismissal of the case would be on the merits, not for want of jurisdiction. *Amgen Inc. v. U.S. International Trade Commission,* 902 F.2d 1532, 14 U.S.P.Q.2d 1734, 1738 (Fed. Cir. 1990).

ᚺ

A federal court exercising patent jurisdiction is bound by the substantive patent law of the Federal Circuit. *ALM Surgical Equipment Inc. v. Kirschner Medical Corp.,* 15 U.S.P.Q.2d 1241, 1251 (S.C. 1990).

ᚺ

One letter from a patent owner threatening suit is sufficient to satisfy due process requirements for the exercise of "limited" personal jurisdiction. *Burbank Aeronautical Corp. II v. Aeronautical Development Corp.,* 16 U.S.P.Q.2d 1069, 1071 (Cal. 1990).

ᚺ

Where the questions of jurisdiction and the merits of the case are intertwined, a plaintiff's allegations supporting jurisdiction are accepted as true when being reviewed on a motion to dismiss. Defendant's argument that plaintiff has no cognizable right under U.S. patent law does not go to the court's subject matter jurisdiction over the plaintiff's claims, but rather to the merits of those claims. *Quantum Corp. v. Sony Corp.,* 16 U.S.P.Q.2d 1447, 1449 (Cal. 1990).

ᚺ

Two requirements must be met before the exercise of jurisdiction over a nonresident defendant will satisfy due process concerns: First, the non-resident must have some minimum contacts with the forum that result in an affirmative act on its part; and second, it must not be unreasonable or unfair to require the nonresident to defend the suit in the forum state. Two types of in personam jurisdiction are recognized, specific and general. When a state exercises personal jurisdiction over a defendant in a suit arising out of or related to the defendant's contact with the forum, the state is exercising specific jurisdiction over the defendant. If the contact resulted from the defendant's conduct and created a substantial connection with the forum state, even a single act can support specific jurisdiction. When a state exercises personal jurisdiction over a defendant in a suit not arising out of or related to the defendant's contact with the forum, the state is said to be exercising general jurisdiction over the defendant. For general jurisdiction to exist, there must be a continuous and systematic contact between the state and the nonresident. *Gesco International Inc. v. Luther Medical Products Inc.,* 17 U.S.P.Q.2d 1168, 1170 (Tex. 1990).

ᚺ

Under the Federal Rules, an untimely postjudgment motion "[can]not toll the running of the time to appeal." Therefore, the appellate court "lacks jurisdiction to review the subsequent order." Moreover, parties may not waive a defect in jurisdiction by consent.

Registration Control Systems Inc. v. Compusystems Inc., 922 F.2d 805, 17 U.S.P.Q.2d 1212, 1213 (Fed. Cir. 1990).

ϖ

When a district court's jurisdiction depends in part on 28 U.S.C. §1338, an appeal lies to the Federal Circuit even when the relief sought depends entirely on state law. *Unique Concepts Inc. v. Manuel*, 930 F.2d 573, 18 U.S.P.Q.2d 1654, 1655 (7th Cir. 1991).

ϖ

The forum state does not exceed its power under the Due Process Clause if it asserts personal jurisdiction over a corporation that delivers its products into the stream of commerce with the expectation that they will be purchased by consumers in the forum state. *Wilden Pump & Engineering Co. v. Versa-matic Tool Inc.*, 20 U.S.P.Q.2d 1788, 1790 (Cal. 1991).

ϖ

Defendant's single written communication to Ohio asserting the validity of his patent and expressing a willingness to negotiate for a license is not the sort of purposeful activity that would make it reasonable for the defendant to expect to be haled into court in that state. *Consumer Direct Inc. v. McLaughlin*, 20 U.S.P.Q.2d 1949, 1951 (Ohio 1991).

ϖ

Three separate statutory provisions together operate to confer jurisdiction on the federal district court with regard to a motion for a temporary restraining order to enjoin the Commissioner of Patents and Trademarks from continuing a reexamination proceeding. First, the question in this suit "arises under" a law or laws of the United States. Second, Congress has waived, in 5 U.S.C. §702, the bar of sovereign immunity which would otherwise deprive the federal district court of jurisdiction under 28 U.S.C. §1331. Third, by enactment of 28 U.S.C. §1361, Congress specifically and irrefutably vested jurisdiction in all district courts to entertain suits in the nature of mandamus. *Standard Havens Inc. v. Manbeck*, 762 F.Supp. 1349, 21 U.S.P.Q.2d 1635, 1636 (Mo. 1991).

ϖ

In those cases in which the CAFC, and only the CAFC, has jurisdiction over any appeal from a final decision, the CAFC has jurisdiction to hear and decide a mandamus petition. Issues properly before the Federal Circuit on appeal are no less within its jurisdiction when raised by extraordinary writ. *In re University of California*, 964 F.2d 1128, 22 U.S.P.Q.2d 1748, 1750 (Fed. Cir. 1992).

ϖ

A claim supported by alternative theories in the complaint may not form the basis for 28 U.S.C. §1338(a) jurisdiction unless patent law is essential to each of those theories. *American Telephone and Telegraph Co. v. Integrated Network Corp.*, 972 F.2d 1321, 23 U.S.P.Q.2d 1918, 1919 (Fed. Cir. 1992).

ϖ

That part of the "objection" which relates to the Examiner's desire for information concerning (a) an explanation of the "gist" of the invention, (b) the phenotypic characteristics of the parent plants and the inheritability thereof, and (c) the goals sought to be achieved by the inventors relates solely to the ease and accuracy of the examination process and the ability of the Examiner to obtain sufficient information therefrom to examine the application effectively. It concerns either the rules of practice or established customs and practices. It is outside the jurisdiction of the BPAI. *Ex parte C*, 27 U.S.P.Q.2d 1492, 1494 (B.P.A.I. 1992).

ω

The district court lacks original jurisdiction over a foreign patent infringement claim pursuant to 28 U.S.C. §1338(b) because a claim of infringement of a foreign patent is not a claim of unfair competition within the meaning of that provision. In addition, the district court does not have authority to hear the claims under its supplemental jurisdiction pursuant to 28 U.S.C. §1367(a) because the claim is not so related to the claim of infringement of the corresponding U.S. patent that it forms part of the same case or controversy under Article III of the U.S. Constitution. *Mars Inc. v. Kabushiki-Kaisha Nippon Conlux*, 24 F.3d 1368, 30 U.S.P.Q.2d 1621, 1626 (Fed. Cir. 1994).

ω

Refusal of a federal court to exercise its jurisdiction by either dismissing the claims or staying the action in favor of another court is a rare occurrence and is only done in limited circumstances that "would clearly serve an important countervailing interest". Such action in a federal court is only available in limited, narrowly circumscribed instances. Abstention from exercising jurisdiction is appropriate where a federal constitutional issue might be avoided by a state court decision; where difficult questions of state law are presented that would have substantial impact on important public policy; or where federal jurisdiction has been invoked to restrain state criminal proceedings. However, "in exceptional circumstances, there are other compelling reasons for declining jurisdiction." 28 U.S.C. §1367(c)(4). Present in such cases are "consideration of '[w]ise judicial administration giving regard to conservation of judicial resources and comprehensive disposition of litigation.'" *Loral Fairchild Corp. v. Matsushita Electric Industrial Co. Ltd.*, 840 F.Supp. 211, 31 U.S.P.Q.2d 1499, 1503 (N.Y. 1994).

ω

Sales of allegedly infringing articles to distributors in the forum could not be said to fall entirely without the forum for purposes of a jurisdictional analysis simply because they were delivered f.o.b. outside the forum. *North American Philips Corp. v. American Vending Sales Inc.*, 35 F.3d 1576, 32 U.S.P.Q.2d 1203, 1205 (Fed. Cir. 1994).

ω

If the Court relies on the pleading and affidavits alone when considering a motion to dismiss for lack of jurisdiction, the plaintiff need only make a *prima facie* showing of jurisdiction in order to defeat the motion. In that event, the pleading and affidavits are construed in the light most favorable to the plaintiff, and all doubts are resolved in his or her favor. If the jurisdictional issue requires an evidentiary hearing, the plaintiff must establish jurisdiction by a preponderance of evidence. *Modern Computer Corp. v. Ma*, 862 F.Supp. 938, 32 U.S.P.Q.2d 1586, 1589 (N.Y. 1994).

ω

"The district court has the authority to consider matters outside the pleadings on a motion challenging subject matter jurisdiction under Federal Rule of Civil Procedure 12(b)(1)." *Sealrite Windows Inc. v. Amesbury Group Inc.*, 33 U.S.P.Q.2d 1688, 1689 (Neb. 1994).

ᙍ

The Federal Circuit need not defer to the regional circuits regarding the exercise of personal jurisdiction in the interests of developing and applying a uniform body of law in the field of patent law. A corporate officer may be personally liable under 35 U.S.C. §271(b) for inducing infringement where he actively aids and abets the corporation's infringement, regardles of whether circumstances justify piercing the corporate veil. The potential for personal liability of a corporate officer, however, is no substitute for a determination of whether the Court may exercise personal jurisdiction over that officer. Personal jurisdiction depends on the state's long-arm statute and the requirements of due process. "If grounds exist for 'piercing the corporate veil' generally, the corporate veil can be pierced for jurisdictional purposes." *Amhil Enterprises Ltd. v. Wawa Inc.*, 34 U.S.P.Q.2d 1640, 1642, 1643, 1644 (Md. 1994).

ᙍ

"Whether a case is one arising under the Constitution or a law or treaty of the United States, in the sense of the jurisdictional statute, . . . must be determined from what necessarily appears in the plaintiff's statement of his own claim in the bill or declaration . . . " If a claim has both federal and state law components, the district court must determine whether the claim as a whole "arises under" the laws of the United States. The general rule is that a suit arises under the law that creates the cause of action. *United National Insurance Co. v. Bradleys' Electric Inc.*, 35 U.S.P.Q.2d 1559, 1561 (Tex. 1995).

ᙍ

Plaintiff is entitled to discovery of documents which pertain to defendant's activities in the state for the purpose of establishing the court's jurisdiction over the defendant. Information regarding defendant's contacts with the state, including its volume of sales and the number of its customers and distributors, is relevant to the issue of personal jurisdiction. *Oregon Precision Industries Inc. v. International Omni-Pac Corp.*, 160 F.R.D. 592, 36 U.S.P.Q.2d 1117, 1119 (Or. 1995).

ᙍ

The Federal circuit uses a three-part test for determining whether the exercise of limited jurisdiction is consistent with due process: (1) the non-resident defendant must have purposefully directed activities at residents of the forum by some affirmative act or conduct; (2) the plaintiff's claim must arise out of or relate to the forum-related activities of the defendant; and (3) the exercise of jurisdiction must not be constitutionally unreasonable. The following factors are relevant to a determination of the reasonableness of a court which exercises limited jurisdiction over a non-resident defendant: (1) the extent of the defendant's purposeful interjection into the forum state's affairs; (2) the burden on the defendant; (3) conflicts of law between the forum and defendant's home jurisdiction; (4) the forum's interest in adjudicating the dispute; (5) the most efficient judicial resolution of the dispute; (6) the plaintiff's interest in convenient and effective relief; and (7) the existence of an alternative forum. *Oregon Precision Industries Inc. v. International Omni-Pac Corp.*, 889 F.Supp. 412, 36 U.S.P.Q.2d 1708, 1711, 1713 (Or. 1995).

ʊ

Section 293 (35 U.S.C.) "authorizes the assertion of [personal] jurisdiction [by the District Court for the District of Columbia] over a non-resident owner of a U.S. patent in cases respecting the patent or rights thereunder." *Miller Pipeline Corp. v. British Gas plc*, 901 F.Supp. 1416, 38 U.S.P.Q.2d 1010, 1013 (Ind. 1995).

ʊ

Entering into an exclusive distributorship agreement authorizing the distribution of its trademarked and patented products in Washington is sufficiently analogous to entering into a patent licensing agreement, which the CAFC has previously concluded is a sufficient contact, in combination with cease-and-desist letters, to comply with the requirements of due process. *Genetic Implant Systems Inc. v. Core-Vent Corp.*, 123 F.3d 1455, 43 U.S.P.Q.2d 1786, 1790 (Fed. Cir. 1997).

ʊ

The statute (35 U.S.C. §146) gives the U.S. District Court for the District of Columbia a special long-arm jurisdiction beyond that conferred by the D.C. Code. *Eastman Kodak Co. v. Duracell Inc.*, 48 U.S.P.Q.2d 1061, 1063 (D.C. 1998).

Jurisdiction of the CAFC (28 U.S.C. §1295). *See also* Arise under Patent Laws, Dismissal, 28 U.S.C. §1338(a).

The United States Court of Customs and Patent Appeals (CCPA) had an inherent power to review any action of the Board that affected its appellate jurisdiction. Both 28 U.S.C. §1542 and 35 U.S.C. §141 limit the jurisdiction of the CCPA to appeals of "decisions" of the Board. The Board's authority to make such decisions is set forth in 35 U.S.C. §7. The CCPA, however, had the right to determine whether the Board properly refused to make such decisions in its statutory capacity. To hold otherwise would be to confer upon the Board the power to control the subject matter jurisdiction of the CCPA. *In re Haas,* 486 F.2d 1053, 179 U.S.P.Q. 623 (C.C.P.A. 1973).

ʊ

The jurisdiction of the Court of Appeals for the Federal Circuit (CAFC) is predicated on whether the district court's jurisdiction was based in whole or in part on 28 U.S.C. §1338. When it is, patent issues will be present; but the reverse is not true, for the mere presence of patent issues has no power to create jurisdiction in the district court. Congress said cases are within the court's patent jurisdiction "in the same sense that cases are said to 'arise under' federal law for purposes of federal question jurisdiction." Whether an action arises under federal law "must be determined from what necessarily appears in the plaintiff's statement of his own claim in the bill or declaration, unaided by anything alleged in anticipation or avoidance of defenses which it is thought the defendant may interpose." *Christianson v. Colt Industries Operating Corp.*, 822 F.2d 1544, 3 U.S.P.Q.2d 1241 (Fed. Cir. 1987).

ʊ

When an applicant files a notice of appeal *after* filing a Rule (37 C.F.R. §) 197(b) request and *before* the Board has rendered its decision in response to that request, *and* when no appealable decision exists when the applicant files the notice of appeal, the mere filing of the notice does not deprive the Board of jurisdiction to render its reconsideration decision, and the applicant has filed the notice "within the time prescribed by law." The CAFC, however, cannot exercise jurisdiction over the appeal before the Board enters its reconsideration decision on the Rule 197(b) request. *In re Graves*, 69 F.3d 1147, 36 U.S.P.Q.2d 1697, 1699 (Fed. Cir. 1995).

ʊ

If the district court's jurisdiction rests on a patent claim, then an appeal from an entirely non-patent disposition goes to the federal circuit. Because mandamus is designed to aid or anticipate jurisdiction, a court that lacks jurisdiction over the final decision lacks power to issue a writ of mandamus. *In re BBC International Ltd.*, 99 F.3d 811, 40 U.S.P.Q.2d 1381, 1382 (7th Cir. 1996).

ʊ

The application of a state law tort is preempted if, in holding a defendant liable for the conduct alleged and proved by the plaintiff, there would be conflict with federal patent law. Otherwise, if the state law tort, as applied, does not conflict with federal patent law, then the tort is not preempted. The combined result of these rulings is to divest state courts of jurisdiction over state law torts that are subject to [28 USC] 1338(a) jurisdiction, and to allow only those that survive the preemption analysis to proceed. State judiciaries will thus lose the opportunity to interpret state law in those limited circumstances when a state law cause of action pleads a substantial question of federal patent law as a necessary element. *Hunter Douglas Inc. v. Harmonic Design Inc.*, 47 U.S.P.Q.2d 1769, 1770, 1783 (Fed. Cir. 1998).

ʊ

Because of supplemental jurisdiction under 28 U.S.C. §1367, the propriety of jurisdiction in light of federal due process for both the state law claims and the federal patent law claims is to be analyzed using Federal Circuit law. *3D Systems Inc. v. Aarotech Laboratories Inc.*, 48 U.S.P.Q.2d 1773, 1776 (Fed. Cir. 1998).

Jury. *See also* **Untimely Jury Demand.**

An order denying a claimed right to a jury trial is reviewable by mandamus. *Beacon Theatres, Inc. v. Westover*, 359 U.S. 500, 511 (1959).

ʊ

"The right to a jury trial on issues of patent validity that may arise in a suit for patent infringement is protected by the Seventh Amendment." *Patlex Corp. v. Mossinghoff*, 759 F.2d 594, 603, 225 U.S.P.Q. 543 (Fed. Cir. 1985).

ʊ

The view that a jury verdict on non-obviousness is at best advisory would make charades of motions for directed verdict or JNOV under Fed. R. Civ. P. 50 in patent cases. These motions apply only to binding jury verdicts. Moreover, use of an advisory jury is limited to actions not triable of right by a jury. All fact findings of a jury are non-advisory, unless made in an area expressly removed from jury verdict. A jury may decide the questions of anticipation and obviousness, either as separate special verdicts or en route to a verdict on the question of validity, which may also be decided by the jury. No warrant appears for distinguishing the submission of legal questions to a jury in patent cases from such submissions routinely made in other types of cases. So long as the Seventh Amendment stands, the right to a jury trial should not be rationed, nor should particular issues in particular types of cases be treated differently from similar issues in other types of cases. When the judgment arises from a jury verdict, the reviewing court applies the reasonable-jury/substantial-evidence standard: a standard that gives greater deference to the judgment simply because appellate review is more limited, compared with review of a trial judge's decision. The appellate court's function is exhausted when an evidentiary basis of the jury's verdict becomes apparent, it being immaterial that the court might draw a contrary inference or feel that another conclusion is more reasonable. *Richardson v. Suzuki Motor Co., Ltd.*, 868 F.2d 1226, 9 U.S.P.Q.2d 1913 (Fed. Cir. 1989).

ω

The law presumes the existence of findings necessary to support a verdict reached by the jury. Whether there is trial evidence favorable to both sides is not the question. The question is whether there is substantial evidence to support the verdict. Even where evidence may be contradictory, the resolution of that conflict is a role assigned to the jury, and inferences are to be drawn in favor of the non-movant. Where there are alleged conflicts in the evidence, the trial court, on motion for JNOV, should not substitute its judgment for that of the jury. When, without question, reasonable jurors could have concluded that the patent claims in issue were infringed, denial of a motion for JNOV is required. *ALM Surgical Equipment Inc. v. Kirschner Medical Corp.* 15 U.S.P.Q.2d 1241, 1245, 1246 (S.C. 1990).

ω

The right to a jury trial "includes more than the common-law forms of action recognized in 1791; the phrase 'Suits at common law' refers to 'suits in which legal rights [are] to be ascertained and determined, in contradistinction to those where equitable rights alone [are] recognized, and equitable remedies [are] administered." A two-step inquiry to resolve legal rights involves a) comparing the statutory action to 18th-century actions brought in the courts of England prior to the merger of the courts of law and equity, and b) examining the remedy sought and determining whether it is legal or equitable in nature. The second inquiry is the more important. *Chauffeurs, Teamsters and Helpers Local No. 391 v. Terry*, 494 U.S. 558, 564, 565 (1990).

ω

("[N]o case is inherently too complex for juries to decide. If juries find issues and facts too complex, it is because lawyers have failed to present their cases clearly or judges have failed to structure the proceedings in a way that would simplify matters for the jury to understand them.") The essential constitutional right to a jury trial is founded on the trust reposed in the jury to weigh the evidence and reach just conclusions. To assume that there is a significant danger that the jury will abdicate its responsibility by placing undue reliance on another court's opinion is impermissible. For the court to conclude further that the danger of the jury's attaching undue weight to the evidence *substantially out-weighs* its clear probative value and need only compounds the error. *Mendenhall v. Cedarapids Inc.*, 5 F.3d 1557, 28 U.S.P.Q.2d 1081, 1102 (Fed. Cir. 1993), *dissent*.

ᖡ

When equitable claims are joined with legal claims and have factual questions in common, the judge's determination of the equitable claims cannot deprive the litigants of their right to a jury trial on factual questions. When "a party has a right to a jury trial on an issue involved in a legal claim, the judge is...bound by the jury's determination of that issue as it affects his disposition of an accompanying equitable claim." *Therma-Tru Corp. v. Peachtree Doors Inc.*, 44 F.3d 988, 33 U.S.P.Q.2d 1274, 1278 (Fed. Cir. 1995).

ᖡ

In the fiscal years 1992-1994, 163 of 274 patent trials were tried to a jury. In fiscal year 1994, 70% of patent trials were tried to juries. *In re Lockwood*, 50 F.3d 966, 980, 33 U.S.P.Q.2d 1907, 1908 n.1 (Fed. Cir. 1995), *dissent*.

Jury Demand.

If a particular action entails either the adjudication of legal rights or the implementation of legal remedies, the district court must honor a jury demand to the extent that disputed issues of fact concerning those rights and remedies require a trial. *Hoechst Marion Roussel Inc. v. Par Pharmaceutical Inc.*, 39 U.S.P.Q.2d 1363, 1364 (N.J. 1996—unpublished).

Jury Instruction.

To support a contention that failure to give a requested jury instruction was prejudicial error, a party must prove that the jury instructions, read in their entirety, were incorrect or incomplete as given and must also demonstrate that the suggested instruction could have cured the error. *Biodex Corp. v. Loredan Biomedical Inc.*, 946 F.2d 850, 20 U.S.P.Q.2d 1252, 1255 (Fed. Cir. 1991).

ᖡ

To prevail on a challenge to jury instructions, a party must show both fatal flaws in the jury instructions and a request for alternative instructions which could have corrected the flaws. *Delta-X Corp. v. Baker Hughes Production Tools Inc.*, 984 F.2d 410, 25 U.S.P.Q.2d 1447, 1451 (Fed. Cir. 1993).

ᖡ

"[A] judgment should be altered 'because of a mistake in jury instructions only if the error was prejudicial...'" *Automotive Products plc v. Tilton Engineering Inc.*, 855 F.Supp. 1101, 33 U.S.P.Q.2d 1065, 1089 (Cal. 1994).

ᖡ

"Jury instructions must be confined to the issues as presented by the pleadings and evidence." *Hilton Davis Chemical Co. v. Warner-Jenkinson Co. Inc.*, 62 F.3d 1512, 35 U.S.P.Q.2d 1641, 1648 (Fed. Cir. 1995), *rev'd and remanded*, 41 U.S.P.Q.2d 1865 (S.Ct. 1997).

Jury Trial.[1] *See also* **Jury.**

When the relief sought is limited to an award of compensatory money damages, which may be trebled in appropriate circumstances, then the case may be designated as a civil jury action in the nature of an action at law, and the parties are entitled to a trial by jury as a matter of constitutional right. On the other hand, when the relief sought is primarily equitable, such as preliminary and final injunctions and an accounting of profits, with a prayer for incidental legal relief in the form of an award of money damages, then the case is a civil nonjury action in the nature of a suit in equity, and the parties are not entitled to demand trial by jury as a matter of right either under the Seventh Amendment or the Patent Act of 1952, Title 35 U.S.C. §*Railex Corp. v. Joseph Guss & Sons, Inc.*, 40 F.R.D. 119, 148 U.S.P.Q. 640, 643 (D.C. 1966).

ᙁ

So long as the Seventh Amendment stands, the right to a jury trial should not be rationed, nor should particular issues in particular types of cases be treated differently from similar issues in other types of cases. *Connell v. Sears, Roebuck & Co.*, 722 F.2d 1542, 1547, 220 U.S.P.Q. 193, 197 (Fed. Cir. 1983).

ᙁ

In an appeal from a decision of the PTO Board of Patent Appeals and Interferences the defendant's motion to strike the plaintiff's demand for a jury trial was granted. The Seventh Amendment right to a trial by jury does not apply in actions against the federal government. As sovereign, the United States is immune from suit "save as it consents to be sued...and the terms of its consent to be sued in any court define that court's jurisdiction to entertain the suit." The accepted principles of sovereign immunity require that a jury trial right be clearly provided for in the legislation creating the cause of action. It cannot be said that 35 U.S.C. §145 contains a clear and unequivocal waiver of the United States immunity from trial by jury. The statute makes no mention whatever of a jury trial for a dissatisfied applicant on appeal from the Board of Patent Appeals. *Tompkins v. Quigg*, 6 U.S.P.Q.2d 1400 (D.C. 1987).

ᙁ

A two-prong test for determining whether the Seventh Amendment provides a party the right to a jury trial is: a) a court must examine the case to see if it would have arisen in law or equity in 1791 when the Seventh Amendment was adopted; and b) more importantly, a court must look at the relief requested to see if it is legal or equitable. An action for infringement under the doctrine of equivalents is one that arises in equity. Therefore, no right to a jury attaches. Any reliance placed upon the factual nature of the inquiry in determining infringement by the equivalents as providing a jury trial right is misplaced. *Transmatic Inc. v. Gulton Industries Inc.*, 835 F.Supp. 1026, 29 U.S.P.Q.2d 1541, 1542, 1543, 1545 (Mich. 1993).

ᙁ

---

[1]There is no reason for considering patent cases as somehow out of the mainstream of the law and rules of procedure applicable to jury trials for centuries under our jurisprudence. *Railroad Dynamics, Inc. v. A. Stucki Co.*, 727 F.2d 1506, 1515, 220 U.S.P.Q. 929, 937 (Fed. Cir.) *cert. denied*, 469 U.S. 871 (1984); *see* Manak, "Confusion In The Law Of Patent Infringement: The Federal Circuit's Decisions In Markman and Hilton Davis", *BIOTECH Patent News*, Vol. 9, No. 10, October 1995.

"The right of jury trial in civil cases at common law is a basic and fundamental feature of our system of federal jurisprudence which is protected by the Seventh Amendment. A right so fundamental and sacred to the citizen, whether guaranteed by the Constitution or provided by statute, should be jealously guarded by the courts." Accordingly, "the right to grant mandamus to require jury trial where it has been improperly denied is settled." It is "the responsibility of the Federal Courts of Appeals to grant mandamus where necessary to protect the constitutional right to trial by jury." A right to a jury trial on the factual questions relating to patent validity is protected by the Seventh Amendment when those questions arise in a paradigmatic patent infringement suit. *In re Lockwood*, 50 F.3d 966, 33 U.S.P.Q.2d 1406, 1409 (Fed. Cir. 1995).

ω

In a patent infringement suit seeking only injunctive relief, the defendant is entitled to a jury trial on its counterclaims for declaratory judgments of invalidity and non-infringement. *In re SGS-Thomson Microelectronics Inc.*, 60 F.3d 839, 35 U.S.P.Q.2d 1572, 1573 (Fed. Cir. 1995—*unpublished and not citable as precedent*).

ω

An accused infringer has a right to a jury trial on its declaratory judgment counterclaim for invalidity, even when the complaint sought only equitable relief. *Hoechst Marion Roussel Inc. v. Par Pharmaceutical Inc.*, 39 U.S.P.Q.2d 1363, 1366 (N.J. 1996—*unpublished*).

ω

The Supreme Court [*Beacon Theatres, Inc. v. Westover*, 359 U.S. 500, 79 S.Ct. 948 (1959)] reemphasized the jury's preeminent role in making factual determinations when simultaneously trying legal and equitable claims that are based on common factual elements "In the Federal Courts this [jury] right cannot be dispensed with, except by the assent of the parties entitled to it, nor can it be impaired by any blending with a claim, properly cognizable by law, of a demand for equitable relief in aid of the legal action or during its pendency." This longstanding principle of equity dictates that only under the most imperative circumstances...can the right to a jury trial of legal issues be lost through prior determination of equitable claims. *Cabinet Vision v. Cabnetware*, 129 F.3d 595, 44 U.S.P.Q.2d 1683, 1686 (Fed. Cir. 1997).

Jury Verdict. *See also* Verdict.

The view that a jury verdict on non-obviousness is at best advisory would make charades of motions for directed verdict or JNOV under Fed. R. Civ. P. 50 in patent cases. These motions apply only to binding jury verdicts. Moreover, use of an advisory jury is limited to actions not triable of right by a jury. All fact findings of a jury are non-advisory, unless made in an area expressly removed from jury verdict. A jury may decide the questions of anticipation and obviousness, either as separate special verdicts or en route to a verdict on the question of validity, which may also be decided by the jury. No warrant appears for distinguishing the submission of legal questions to a jury in patent cases from such submissions routinely made in other types of cases. So long as the Seventh Amendment stands, the right to a jury trial should not be rationed, nor should particular issues in particular types of cases be treated differently from similar issues in other types of cases.

Jury Verdict

When the judgment arises from a jury verdict, the reviewing court applies the reasonable-jury/substantial-evidence standard, a standard that gives greater deference to the judgment simply because appellate review is more limited, compared with review of a trial judge's decision. The appellate court's function is exhausted when evidentiary basis of the jury's verdict becomes apparent, it being immaterial that the court might draw a contrary inference or feel that another conclusion is more reasonable. *Richardson v. Suzuki Motor Co., Ltd.*, 868 F.2d 1226, 9 U.S.P.Q.2d 1913 (Fed. Cir. 1989).

Key Terms and Concepts

K

Key. *See* **Difference, Gist.**

Kind. *See* **Critical, Degree.**

Nothing is found in 35 U.S.C. §103 which warrants the Board's attempted dismissal of the differences between appellant's claimed compound and the prior art as not being "differences in kind", whatever this may mean. This phrase as here encountered is used by the Board to infer that unless a "difference in kind" is found, the invention is obvious under section 103. Section 103 simply requires a determination as to whether the invention as a whole would have been obvious to one of ordinary skill in the art at the time of appellant's invention. *In re Wagner and Folkers*, 371 F.2d 877, 152 U.S.P.Q. 552, 560 (C.C.P.A. 1967).

ϖ

As unexpected results follow from the selection of appellants' critical range, which is within and narrower than the extremely broad range inherently disclosed in a reference, it is not necessary to establish inoperability outside of the claimed critical range. It is enough to have a difference in kind, rather than a difference in degree, over the critical range. *In re Waymouth and Koury*, 499 F.2d 1273, 182 U.S.P.Q. 290, 293 (C.C.P.A. 1974).

Kit.

A claim to an assembly of elements in the form of a kit, which is clear and precise and which would be clearly understandable to those skilled in the art, is not subject to rejection under 35 U.S.C. §112 because no physical cooperation is recited between the various components or because the assembly is not an integral structural unit. *Ex parte Wolters and Kuypers*, 214 U.S.P.Q. 735, 736 (PTO Bd. App. 1979).

Knockdown.

If an applicant presents rebuttal evidence, the decision-maker must consider all of the evidence of record in determining whether the subject matter as a whole would have been obvious. The question of whether applicant's burden has been successfully carried requires that the entire path to decision be retraced. An earlier decision should not be considered as set in concrete, and applicant's rebuttal evidence then evaluated on its knockdown ability. Analytical fixation on an earlier decision can tend to provide that decision with an undeservedly broadened umbrella effect. Facts established by rebuttal evidence must be evaluated along with the facts on which the earlier conclusion was reached, not against the conclusion itself. Though the tribunal must begin anew, a final finding of obviousness rests upon evaluation of all facts in evidence, uninfluenced by any earlier conclusion reached by an earlier Board upon a different record. *In re Carleton*, 599 F.2d 1021, 202 U.S.P.Q. 165, 168 (C.C.P.A. 1979).

Know How. *See* **Trade Secrets.**

Knowledge. *See also* **Abandoned Application, Contributory Infringement, Enablement, Knowledge Abroad, Knowledge (Later Discovered), Known, Prior Knowledge.**

The specification is not addressed to lawyers or even to the public generally, but to those of ordinary skill in the art. Any description that is sufficient to apprise them (in the language of the art) of the definite features of the invention, and to serve as a warning to others of that which is claimed, is sufficiently definite. *The Carnegie Steel Company, Ltd. v. The Cambria Iron Co.*, 185 U.S. 403, 437 (1902).

℧

When a patent is issued, it constitutes evidence that everything disclosed by it was known by others in this country at least as early as the filing date of the application on which the patent issued. *In re Beck, Siebel, and Bosskuhler,* 155 F.2d 398, 69 U.S.P.Q. 520, 523 (C.C.P.A. 1946).

℧

A patentee is presumed to have known and is chargeable with knowledge of everything disclosed by the prior art in the involved field and of all devices in that field which have been in prior public use. *DeBurgh v. Kindel Furniture Company*, 125 F.Supp. 468, 103 U.S.P.Q. 203, 208 (Mich. 1954).

℧

Before enactment of the Patent Act of 1952, prior knowledge (in order to defeat a claim for a patent) had to be knowledge of a complete and operative device, as distinguished from knowledge of a conception only. When individuals in this country have full knowledge of a device being successfully used abroad before its invention by a patentee, there is no such prior knowledge in this country as would invalidate the patent. Knowledge of a conception that has not been reduced to practice can be no more effective than knowledge in this country of a conception that has been reduced to practice abroad. A disclosure in an abandoned application for a patent does not constitute such evidence of prior knowledge as will bar the allowance of a subsequent application. Knowledge of a prior conception of an invention in this country is not enough to defeat claims of a subsequent inventor. An invention is "known," as that word is used in the statute, when it is "reduced to practice." *In re Schlittler and Uffer,* 234 F.2d 882, 110 U.S.P.Q. 304, 306, 307 (C.C.P.A. 1956).

℧

There seems to be no logical reason why the granting of a secret patent abroad should be a bar to patenting in this country. Such a foreign patent is of no value to persons in this country unless and until it is made available to the public. Even widespread public knowledge of an invention abroad does not alone bar the grant of a patent in this country, and it is not reasonable to suppose that Congress intended to give greater effect to secret patenting abroad than to public knowledge there. *In re Ekenstam*, 256 F.2d 321, 118 U.S.P.Q. 349, 351 (C.C.P.A. 1958).

ᴡ

Although the patentee may not have had actual knowledge of prior art suggesting the use of PVP as a hair fixative, he is presumed to have had such knowledge. *La Maur, Inc. v. DeMert & Dougherty, Inc.*, 265 F.Supp. 961, 148 U.S.P.Q. 59, 73 (Ill. 1965).

ᴡ

An applicant need not expressly set forth in his specification that which would be understood by persons skilled in the art. *In re Honn and Sims*, 364 F.2d 454, 150 U.S.P.Q. 652 (C.C.P.A. 1966).

ᴡ

Section 102 of 35 U.S.C. lists items that can be considered as prior art against an applicant either for the purpose of anticipation or for the purpose of considering obviousness under 35 U.S.C. §103. Paragraphs (b), (c), and (d) of §102 are obviously not applicable to subject matter initially disclosed in, but subsequently canceled from, the specification (prior to issuance) of a copending patent of another. Such subject matter can be considered as part of the stock of public knowledge on the date of issuance of the copending patent. Paragraph (a) includes "known or used by others in this country." However, this section has been interpreted as meaning publicly known. Prior private or secret information is made available as prior art, as of a date when it was private or secret, by paragraphs (e), (f), and (g) of §102. Paragraph (e) makes the contents of the specification of an issued patent available as prior art as of the filing date of the application resulting in the patent. This paragraph specifically refers to the description "in a patent." What is meant by a patent and the specification of a patent is indicated by 35 U.S.C. §154; canceled portions of the application are not part of the patent. Under paragraph (f) of §102 (and presumably also under 35 U.S.C. §101) prior private or secret knowledge of which an applicant had actual knowledge would be available against him. Also prior private or secret knowledge is available under and in accordance with the provisions of paragraph (g) of §102. *Ex parte Thelin*, 152 U.S.P.Q. 624, 625 (PO Bd. App. 1966).

ᴡ

In legal contemplation, one of ordinary skill in the art is chargeable with comprehensive knowledge of the prior art. *Continental Can Co., Inc. v. Crown Cork & Seal Co., Inc.*, 415 F.2d 601, 163 U.S.P.Q. 1, 3 (3d Cir. 1969), *cert. denied*, 397 U.S. 914, 164 U.S.P.Q. 481 (1970).

ᴡ

Facts constituting the state of the art are normally subject to the possibility of rational disagreement among reasonable men and are not amenable to the taking of judicial or administrative notice. If evidence of the knowledge possessed by those skilled in the art is to be properly considered, it must be timely injected into the proceedings. *In re Eynde, Pollet, and de Cat*, 480 F.2d 1364, 178 U.S.P.Q. 470, 474 (C.C.P.A. 1973).

ᴡ

Unpublished documents or private discussions (not of common knowledge) do not fall within the scope of limitations contained in 35 U.S.C. §102 and hence are not prior art within the meaning of 35 U.S.C. §103. Prior knowledge and use must have been accessible to the general public. *Layne-New York Co., Inc. v. Allied Asphalt Co., Inc.*, 363 F. Supp. 299, 180 U.S.P.Q. 81, 85 (Pa. 1973).

ʊ

Matters that are well within the knowledge of those skilled in the art and are generally understood by such persons need not be expressly set forth in a specification. *Ex parte Richter*, 185 U.S.P.Q. 380, 381, 382 (PO Bd. App. 1974).

ʊ

The invention does not have to be described in ipsis verbis to satisfy the description requirement of 35 U.S.C. §112. If the grandfather application plus knowledge in the art equals the ultimate range recited, then the grandfather application adequately disclosed the invention. *Electronic Memories & Magnetics Corporation v. Control Data Corporation*, 188 U.S.P.Q. 448, 449 (Ill. 1975).

ʊ

Knowledge in this country of the invention by an agent of the inventor is not equivalent to an introduction of the invention into this country "in the absence of a disclosure to others or reduction of the invention to practice by [the agent] within a reasonable time." The question of whether there was introduction of the invention into this country on behalf of the inventor must be judged by what knowledge thereof was imparted to others by items brought into this country. *Tapia v. Micheletti v. Wignall, Shelton, and Klee*, 202 U.S.P.Q. 123, 125 (PTO Bd. Pat. Intf. 1976).

ʊ

Affidavit evidence is competent to the extent that it refers to matters known to or observed by the affiant prior to or contemporaneous with the actual reduction to practice of another in an interference, where it was offered as evidence of the level of knowledge in the art at the time the invention was made. *In re Farrenkopf and Usategui-Gomez, and Travenol Laboratories, Inc., Intervenor*, 713 F.2d 714, 219 U.S.P.Q. 1, 6 (Fed. Cir. 1983)

ʊ

The inventor, for the purposes of legal reasoning, has been replaced by the statutory hypothetical "person having ordinary skill in the art" who has been provided by 35 U.S.C. §103. Since the effective date of the 1952 Patent Act, there has been no need to presume that the inventor knows anything about the prior art. We hereby declare the presumption that the inventor has knowledge of all material prior art to be dead. *Kimberly-Clark Corporation v. Johnson & Johnson and Personal Products Company*, 745 F.2d 1437, 223 U.S.P.Q. 603, 614 (Fed. Cir. 1984).

ʊ

To combine references (A) and (B) properly to reach the conclusion that the subject matter of a patent would have been obvious, case law requires that there must be some teaching, suggestion, or inference in either reference (A) or (B), or both, or knowledge generally available to one of ordinary skill in the relevant art, that would lead one skilled in the art to combine the relevant teachings of references (A) and (B). Consideration must be given to teachings in the references that would have led one skilled in the art away from the claimed invention. A claim cannot properly be used as a blueprint for extracting individual teachings from references. *Ashland Oil, Inc. v. Delta Resins & Refractories, Inc.*, 776 F.2d 281, 227 U.S.P.Q. 657 (Fed. Cir. 1985).

ω

Knowledge of all prior art in the field of the inventor's endeavor and of prior-art solutions for a common problem (even if outside that field) is attributed to the hypothetical person of ordinary skill in the art. *In re Nilssen*, 851 F.2d 1401, 7 U.S.P.Q.2d 1500 (Fed. Cir. 1988).

Knowledge Abroad. *See also* **Foreign Knowledge.**

A previous foreign invention does not invalidate a patent granted here if it has not been patented or described in a printed publication. *Alexander Milburn Company v. Davis-Bournonville Company*, 270 U.S. 390, 400 (1926)

ω

Mishimura was a published Japanese patent application, the publication date of which was subsequent to the appellants' established Convention date. The appellants' description of Mishimura was no more than an admission that the appellants did not invent the subject matter of Mishimura. Mishimura is thus prior art to appellants under 35 U.S.C. §102(f). Since the appellants had not made a showing under 35 U.S.C. §103 that disqualifies this as prior art, it is available as evidence of obviousness and can be combined with other prior art under §103. *Ex parte Yoshino and Takasu*, 227 U.S.P.Q. 52 (B.P.A.I. 1985).

Knowledge (Later Discovered). *See also* **Symmetry in the Law.**

A later state of the art is that state coming into existence after the filing date of an application. Later publications are useful as evidence of the state of the art existing on the filing date of an application. That does not mean, however, that a later publication disclosing a later existing state of the art can be used in testing an earlier application for compliance with 35 U.S.C. §112, first paragraph. The difference may be described as that between the permissible application of later knowledge about art-related facts existing on the filing date and the impermissible application of later knowledge about later art-related facts that did not exist on the filing date. Thus, if the appellant's 1953 application provided sufficient enablement, considering all available evidence (whenever that evidence became available) of the 1953 state of the art, i.e., of the condition of knowledge about all art-related facts existing in 1953, then the fact of that enablement was established for all time and a later change in the state of the art cannot change it. *In re Hogan and Banks*, 559 F.2d 595, 194 U.S.P.Q. 527 (C.C.P.A. 1977).

Known. *See also* **Knowledge.**

An applicant (patentee) may begin at a point where his invention begins and describe what he has made that is new, and what it replaces of the old. That which is common and well known is as if it were written out in the application (patent) and delineated in the drawings. *Webster Loom Co. v. Higgins,* 105 U.S. 580, 586 (1882).

ᴡ

Under 35 U.S.C. §112, a specification need not teach that which is obvious to those in the art. *In re Sureau, Kremer, and Dupre*, 373 F.2d 1002, 153 U.S.P.Q. 66, 70 (C.C.P.A. 1967).

ᴡ

The contents of a patent application which may be available as "prior art" under 35 U.S.C. §102(e) to show that another was the first inventor may not have been known to anyone other than the inventor, his attorney, the Patent Office Examiner and, perhaps, the assignee (if there was one) until it issued as a patent. As of its filing date it does not show what is known generally to "any person skilled in the art", to quote from §112. On the other hand, 35 U.S.C. §112 requires an applicant to so describe his invention as to enable any person skilled in the art to practice it, the purpose being to make the invention understandable to all such persons as soon as the patent issues. *In re Glass*, 492 F.2d 1228, 181 U.S.P.Q. 31, 34 (C.C.P.A. 1974).

ᴡ

Presuming arguendo that the references show the elements or concepts urged, the Examiner presented no line of reasoning as to why the artisan reviewing only the collective teachings of the references would have found it obvious to selectively pick and choose various elements and/or concepts from the several references relied on to arrive at the claimed invention. In the instant application, the Examiner has done little more than cite references to show that one or more elements or some combinations thereof, when each is viewed in a vacuum, is known. The claimed invention, however, is clearly directed to a combination of elements. That is to say, the appellant does not claim that he has invented one or more new elements but has presented claims to a new combination of elements. To support the conclusion that the claimed combination is directed to obvious subject matter, either the references must expressly or impliedly suggest the claimed combination or the Examiner must present a convincing line of reasoning as to why the artisan would have found the claimed invention to have been obvious in light of the teachings of the references. The Board found nothing in the references that would expressly or impliedly teach or suggest the modifications urged by the Examiner. Additionally, the Board found no line of reasoning in the answer as to why the artisan would have found the modifications urged by the Examiner to have been obvious. Based upon the record, the artisan would not have found it obvious to selectively pick and choose elements or concepts from the various references so as to arrive at the claimed invention without using the claims as a guide. *Ex parte Clapp,* 227 U.S.P.Q. 972 (B.P.A.I. 1985).

ᴡ

A patent need not teach, and preferably omits, what is well known in the art. *Spectra-Physics Inc. v. Coherent Inc.*, 827 F.2d 1524, 3 U.S.P.Q.2d 1737, 1743 (Fed. Cir. 1987).

ᴡ

A Declaration by a qualified expert in the art stating that questioned elements in the application were well known to those of ordinary skill in the art as of the effective filing date and that such elements were routinely built may not be adequate to overcome a rejection for lack of enablement with regard to the making of such elements. Section 112 of 35 U.S.C. requires that, unless the information is well known in the art, the application itself must contain this information; it is not sufficient to provide it only through an expert's Declaration. An expert's opinion on the ultimate legal issue must be supported by something more than a conclusory statement. A statement by a qualified expert that the elements referred to in the application were well known to those of ordinary skill in the art as of the effective date in that they were routinely built was inadequate because the expert did not provide adequate support for his conclusion. *In re Buchner*, 929 F.2d 660, 18 U.S.P.Q.2d 1331, 1332 (Fed. Cir. 1991).

ϖ

"That which may be inherent is not necessarily known. Obviousness cannot be predicated on what is unknown." A retrospective view of inherency is not a substitute for some teaching or suggestion supporting an obviousness rejection. *In re Rijckaert*, 9 F.3d 1531, 28 U.S.P.Q.2d 1955, 1957 (Fed. Cir. 1993).

Known Principles.

"That the claimed invention may employ known principles does not itself establish that the invention would have been obvious. Most inventions do." *Maitland Co. Inc. v. Terra First Inc.*, 33 U.S.P.Q.2d 1882, 1890 (S.C. 1994).

Kohler-Milstein Technique.

Although the technique underlying hybridoma technology is well recognized, the results obtained by its use are clearly unpredictable. Hybridoma technology is an empirical art in which the routineer is unable to foresee what particular antibodies will be produced and which specific surface antigens will be recognized by them. Only by actually carrying out the requisite steps can the nature of the monoclonal antibodies be determined and ascertained; no "expected" results can thus be said to be present. Hence, it may be "obvious to try" the Kohler-Milstein technique as applied to malignant renal cells, but such is not the standard under which obviousness under 35 U.S.C. §103 must be established. *Ex parte Old,* 229 U.S.P.Q. 196 (B.P.A.I. 1985).

Kokai.

A Kokai is not a patent within the meaning of 35 U.S.C. §102(d). While a Kokai may result in certain legal consequences similar to an inventor's certificate, it is not in fact an inventor's certificate. Because Congress saw fit to include inventor's certificates along with patents in §102(d), documents that may have similar legal consequences, as inventor's certificates in the country in which they are issued, do not per se rise to the level of inventor's certificates as to their legal consequences under §102(d). Congress has not seen fit to include Kokai in §102(d); it defies acceptable principles of statutory interpretation to include Kokai because of its (alleged) analogy to inventor's certificates. *Ex parte Fujii,* 13 U.S.P.Q.2d 1073, 1074, 1075 (B.P.A.I. 1989).

Key Terms and Concepts

Label.[1]

Label License. *See also* **Reuse.**

A purchaser of a patented product having actual notice of a limited patent license in the form of a written label notice (attached to the product) restricting the use to which the purchaser may put the product, and who uses and sells such product in violation of the limited patent license is an infringer of the patent for such product. *Chemagro Corporation v. Universal Chemical Company*, 244 F.Supp. 486, 146 U.S.P.Q. 466, 468 (Tex. 1965).

ღ

A patented process cannot be used to "tie" sales of an unpatented staple commodity (having substantial non-infringing use) used in the proess. Sales of the staple commodity accompanied by an implied (can label) license to practice the patented process constitutes a non de minimus tying arrangment in violation of §1 of the Sherman Act and constitutes patent misuse, making the patent unenforceable. *Rex Chainbelt Inc. v. Harco Products, Inc.*, 512 F.2d 993, 185 U.S.P.Q. 10 (9th Cir. 1975).

Labelling.

Labelling infringing goods serves the purposes of deterring future infringement and is not an unreasonable requirement when a foreign manufacturer has been found to violate U.S. law. *Automotive Products plc v. Tilton Engineering Inc.*, 855 F.Supp. 1101, 33 U.S.P.Q.2d 1065, 1084 (Cal. 1993).

Laboratory Animal. *See* **Standard Experimental Animal.**

Laboratory Notebook. *See also* **Notebook.**

Entries in a laboratory notebook are seldom self-explanatory. Therefore, a witness relying on laboratory notebook entries to explain acts performed by him must generally

---

[1] *See* Kelly, Patrick D., "Old Drug, New Use: Article Of Manufacture Claims", BIO/TECHNOLOGY, Vol. 11, pp 839 and 840, July 1993, which refers directly to claim 18 of USP 5,011,853 and to claim 7 of USP 5,208,031, as well as to claim 7 of USP 4,988,710, which reads (in part): "An article of manufacture comprising packaging material and a pharmaceutical agent contained within the packaging material, wherein the pharmaceutical agent . . . , and wherein the packaging material comprises a label which indicates that the pharmaceutical agent can be used for reducing neurotoxic brain damage that might otherwise be caused by at least one cholinesterase inhibitor. . . ."

explain the specific entries. *Amoss, Monahan, and Vale v. McKinley and Sarantakis*, 195 U.S.P.Q. 452, 454 (PTO Bd. Pat. Intf. 1977).

Laches. *See also* **Delay, Diligence, Equitable Defenses, Funding, Prejudice, Unavoidable Delay, 35 U.S.C. §286.**

In order to assert the defense of laches successfully, one must prove (1) unreasonable and inexcusable delay in the assertion of the claim and (2) material prejudice resulting from the delay. Laches, however, bars only the right to recover prefiling damages. *Mainland Industries Inc. v. Standal's Patents Ltd.*, 799 F.2d 746, 230 U.S.P.Q. 772 (Fed. Cir. 1986).

ᛠ

A showing of laches alone is insufficient to bar a patentee's request for prospective injunctive relief or damages arising after the filing of suit. The defendant must also prove estoppel by demonstrating actions on the part of the patentee that justify a belief by the alleged infringer that the patent would not be enforced against him. Additionally, the defendant must show that it actually relied on the misleading conduct to its detriment. Although silence alone (even for a period of five years) is not sufficient affirmative conduct to give rise to estoppel, there is precedence for applying estoppel where there has been intentionally misleading silence. *Stambler v. Diebold Inc.*, 11 U.S.P.Q.2d 1709, 1714 (N.Y. 1988), *aff'd*, 11 U.S.P.Q.2d 1715 (Fed. Cir. 1989).

ᛠ

The general rule is that license negotiations do not necessarily push back the running of time in a laches defense. For such tolling, the negotiations must ordinarily be continuous and bilaterally progressing, with a fair chance of success, so as to justify significant delays. *Western Electric Co. Inc. v. Piezo Technology Inc.*, 15 U.S.P.Q.2d 1401, 1410 (Fla. 1990).

ᛠ

In determining laches, the court must consider whether the patent owner knew or should have known of the defendant's alleged infringement. But, like infringement, laches does not begin until the patent issues. Where a plaintiff alleges infringement of more than one patent, laches must be determined separately for each. *Meyers v. Brooks Shoe Inc.*, 912 F.2d 1459, 16 U.S.P.Q.2d 1055, 1057 (Fed. Cir. 1990).

ᛠ

The period from which delay is measured begins at the time the patentee knew, or in the exercise of reasonable diligence should have known, of the allegedly infringing activity. When a patentee delays more than six years before filing suit, the delay is presumed to be both unreasonable and prejudicial to the defendant. A potential legal impediment to an infringement action, such as the defense of having a sublicense, is not an excuse for not pursuing the infringement action. Moreover, an obligation exists on the part of a patentee to communicate to an accused infringer, whom it has contacted and failed to sue because of other litigation, that it was not acquiescing in the infringement. *Adelberg Laboratories Inc. v. Miles Inc.*, 921 F.2d 1267, 17 U.S.P.Q.2d 1111, 1113, 1115 (Fed. Cir. 1990).

ᛠ

A patent owner may avoid the consequences of what would otherwise be an unreasonable delay in filing suit by establishing that he or she was engaged in "other litigation." For other litigation to excuse a delay in bringing suit, there must be adequate notice of the proceedings to the accused infringer. The notice must also inform the alleged infringer of the patentee's intention to enforce its patent upon completion of that proceeding. Where there is explicit notice of a reissue proceeding in which an alleged infringer actively participated, and the evidence as a whole shows that the accused infringer was in fear of suit, there is no further requirement to notify the alleged infringer of an intent to sue after the reissue proceeding has been concluded in order to avoid a holding of laches. Such a notification would be superfluous, telling the accused infringer what he already knew. Patentees shouuld be encouraged to avoid litigation when their patents are being reevaluated in the PTO, rather than being forced into premature litigation on penalty of being held to have been guilty of laches. *Vaupel Textimaschinen KG v. Meccanica Euro Italia s.p.a.*, 944 F.2d 870, 20 U.S.P.Q.2d 1045, 1050, 1051, 1052 (Fed. Cir. 1991).

ω

Laches may be defined as the neglect or delay in bringing suit to remedy an alleged wrong, which (taken together with lapse of time and other circumstances) causes prejudice to the adverse party and operates as an equitable bar.

1. Laches is cognizable under 35 U.S.C. §282 (1988) as an equitable defense to a claim for patent infringement.
2. Where the defense of laches is established, the patentee's claim for damages prior to suit may be barred.
3. Two elements underlie the defense of laches: a) the patentee's delay in bringing suit was unreasonable and inexcusable, and b) the alleged infringer suffered material prejudice attributable to the delay. The district court should consider these factors and all of the evidence and other circumstances to determine whether equity should intercede to bar pre-filing damages.
4. A presumption of laches arises where a patentee delays bringing suit for more than six years after the date the patentee knew or should have known of the alleged infringer's activity.
5. A presumption has the effect of shifting the burden of going forward with evidence, not the burden of persuasion.

As equitable defenses, laches and equitable estoppel are matters committed to the sound discretion of the trial judge, and the trial judge's decision is reviewed by the CAFC under the abuse of discretion standard. To invoke the laches defense, a defendant has the burden to prove two factors:

a) the plaintiff delayed filing suit for an unreasonable and inexcusable length of time from the time the plaintiff knew or reasonably should have known of its claim against the defendant, and
b) the delay operated to the prejudice or injury of the defendant.

The establishment of the factors of undue delay and prejudice, whether by actual proof or by presumption, does not *mandate* recognition of a laches defense in every case.

Laches remains an equitable judgment of the trial court in light of all the circumstances. Laches is not *established* by undue delay and prejudice. Those factors merely lie the foundation for the trial court's exercise of discretion. Where there is evidence of other factors which would make it inequitable to recognize the defense despite undue delay and prejudice, the defense may be denied. For laches, the length of delay, the seriousness of prejudice, the reasonableness of excuses, and the defendant's conduct or culpability must be weighed to determine whether the patentee dealt unfairly with the alleged infringer by not bringing suit promptly. Courts faced with patent infringement actions "borrowed" the six-year damage limitation period in the patent statute, set out in 35 U.S.C. §286, as the time period for giving rise to a rebuttable presumption of laches. The six years in the statute begins with the date of suit and counts backward. The six years for laches begins with a patentee's knowledge of infringement and counts forward. Thus, the two periods in real time may be completely unrelated. The "borrowing" of section 286's time period for the use of laches defense was, thus, an extension or modification of the "borrowing" concept. Nevertheless, the section 286 time period has been embraced by virtually all circuits as a reasonable period for creation of a presumption of laches in patent cases. The appropriate evidentiary standard to establish the facts relating to the laches issue is "preponderance of the evidence". Laches bars relief on a patentee's claim only with respect to damages accrued prior to suit. *A.C. Aukerman Co. v. R.L. Chaides Construction Co.*, 960 F.2d 1020, 22 U.S.P.Q.2d 1321, 1324, 1325, 1328-31, 1335, 1339 (Fed. Cir. 1992).

ᛒ

The presumption of laches, which arises after a defendant proves a six-year delay, is a "double bursting bubble" which the plaintiff punctures with introduction of evidence sufficient to raise a genuine dispute as to either delay or prejudice. With the presumption burst, a defendant (who invokes laches as a defense) must affirmatively prove (1) unreasonable and inexcusable delay and (2) prejudice resulting from that delay. *Hemstreet v. Computer Entry Systems Corp.*, 972 F.2d 1290, 23 U.S.P.Q.2d 1860, 1863 (Fed. Cir. 1992).

ᛒ

When an infringement action is brought on a series of patents, the delay period for all of the patents is not based on the issue date of the first patent to issue. A patentee may wait until a subsequent patent in the series issues so that reliance can be placed on all previously-issued patents. *Meyers v. Asics Corp.*, 974 F.2d 1304, 24 U.S.P.Q.2d 1036, 1038 (Fed. Cir. 1992).

ᛒ

A knew-or-should-have-known criterion is appropriate to actions to correct inventorship. It is in harmony with the patent statute, for in accordance with 35 U.S.C. §256 inventorship may be corrected at any time, whether by direct application to the Commissioner or by the court. Since the defense of patent invalidity based on incorrect inventorship can be raised at any time, correction of inventorship should be similarly available at any time. Were laches measured constructively from the date of patent issuance, an erroneously omitted inventor could be barred from remedy before learning of the existence of the patent. Such a stricture does not accord with either §256 or the practice which allows challenges to patent validity throughout the patent life. However, a delay of more than six years after an omitted inventor knew or should have known of the issuance of the patent will produce a rebuttable presumption of laches. *Advanced Cardiovascular Systems Inc. v. SciMed Life Systems Inc.*, 988 F.2d 1157, 26 U.S.P.Q.2d 1038, 1042, 1043 (Fed. Cir. 1993).

ω

In order to establish laches on summary judgment, defendant must demonstrate that plaintiff's delay in waiting between six and eight years to file its pending patent infringement claims was unreasonable, *and* it was unexcused, *and* it caused defendant to suffer material prejudice. *Haworth Inc. v. Herman Miller Inc.*, 30 U.S.P.Q.2d 1555, 1557 (Mich. 1994).

ω

In asserting their affirmative defenses of laches and estoppel, the defendants have waived their attorney-client privilege regarding the opinions of counsel on the validity and enforceability of the patents at issue. *THK America Inc. v. NSK Co. Ltd.*, 157 F.R.D. 637, 33 U.S.P.Q.2d 1248, 1259 (Ill. 1993).

ω

As a general rule, license negotiations may toll the running of a laches period. However, "the negotiations must ordinarily be continuous and bilaterally progressing, with a fair chance of success, so as to justify significant delays." *Valutron N.V. v. NCR Corp.*, 33 U.S.P.Q.2d 1986, 1990 (Ohio 1992), *affirmed* (Fed. Cir. 1993), *cert. denied*, (S.Ct. 1994).

ω

The applicability of laches is flexible and does not follow "mechanical rules." Consequently, the application of laches must be determined by the particular facts and circumstances of each case. *Cover v. Hydramatic Packing Co. Inc.*, 34 U.S.P.Q.2d 1128, 1130 (Pa. 1994).

ω

If successful, the laches defense bars relief only for damages accrued prior to suit. Even if the elements of laches are established, however, a court need not bar a plaintiff's suit. The application of the laches defense is discretionary, and as an equitable matter, the district court is to look at all of the facts and circumstances of the case and weight the equities of the parties. "It is not enough that the alleged infringer changed his position— i.e., invested in production of the allegedly infringing device. The change must be because of and as a result of the delay, not simply a business decision to capitalize on a market opportunity." On a motion for summary judgment of laches a court must consider "all pertinent factors." One such factor is whether the infringer "has engaged in particularly egregious conduct which would change the equities significantly in plaintiff's favor." Intentional copying of the plaintiff's product may so qualify. *Gasser Chair Co. Inc. v. Infanti Chair Manufacturing Corp.*, 60 F.3d 770, 34 U.S.P.Q.2d 1822, 1824, 1825, 1826 (Fed. Cir. 1995).

ω

While the proper focus of a laches inquiry should be "on the dilatory conduct of the patentee and the prejudice which the patentee's delay has caused," the trial judge was correct in considering the effect of defendant's secrecy policy on plaintiff's efforts to protect it rights. *Eastman Kodak Co. v. The Goodyear Tire & Rubber Co.*, 42 U.S.P.Q.2d 1737, 1745, 1746 (Fed. Cir. 1997).

ᛟ

Laches remains an equitable judgment of the trial court in light of all the circumstances. Laches is not established by undue delay and prejudice. Those factors merely lay the foundation for the trial court's exercise of discretion. Where there is evidence of other factors where it would make it inequitable to recognize the defense despite undue delay and prejudice, the defense may be denied. Prejudice must result from the patent holder's delay in bringing suit, not from a business decision of the purported infringer. *Nursery Supplies Inc. v. Lerio Corp.*, 45 U.S.P.Q.2d 1332, 1340, 1341 (Pa. 1997).

ᛟ

Where the question of laches is in issue, "the plaintiff is chargeable with such knowledge as he might have obtained upon inquiry, provided the facts already known by him were such as to put upon a man or ordinary intelligence the duty of inquiry." *Wanlass v. General Electric Co.*, 148 F.3d 1334, 46 U.S.P.Q.2d 1915, 1917 (Fed. Cir. 1998).

ᛟ

Once a presumption of laches is applied, a *prima facie* defense of laches is made. With the presumption, the facts of unreasonable and inexcusable delay and of prejudice are inferred, absent rebuttal evidence. The standard of review of the conclusion of laches is abuse of discretion. An appellate court, however, may set aside a discretionary decision if the decision rests on an erroneous interpretation of the law or on clearly erroneous underpinnings. If such error is absent, the determination can be overturned only if the trial court's decision represents an unreasonable judgment in weighing relevant factors. *Wanlass v. Fedders Corp.*, 145 F.3d 1461, 47 U.S.P.Q.2d 1097 (Fed. Cir. 1998).

ᛟ

A finding of laches precludes a patentee from obtaining an injunction prohibiting the use of any infringing product that was manufactured and sold during the laches period. A defendant who is found to have infringed a patent wilfully may be foreclosed from invoking the laches defense. *Odetics Inc. v. Storage Technology Corp.*, 47 U.S.P.Q.2d 1573, 1578, 1580 (Va. 1998).

Lack of Funds. *See* Economics.

Laid Open to Public Inspection. *See* Foreign Patent Application.

Landmark. *See* Pioneer.

Language. *See also* Claim Language, Lexicographer.

There is no support, either in the actual holdings of prior cases or in the statute, for the proposition that "functional" language, in and of itself, renders a claim improper. We have found no prior decision of this or any other court that may be said to hold that there is some other ground for objecting to a claim on the basis of any language, functional or otherwise, beyond what is already sanctioned by the provisions of 35 U.S.C. §112. No merit is seen in any proposition that would require the denial of a claim solely because of the type of language used to define the subject matter for which patent protection is sought. *In re Swinehart and Sfiligoj,* 439 F.2d 210, 169 U.S.P.Q. 226, 228, n.4 (C.C.P.A. 1971).

ʊ

The language used in a patent must be measured and interpreted in relation to the disclosure of the patent as a whole. *Scandiamant Aktiebolag v. Commissioner of Patents,* 509 F.2d 463, 184 U.S.P.Q. 201, 205 (CA D.C. 1974).

ʊ

A judge is not usually a person conversant in the particular technical art involved and is not the hypothetical person skilled in the art to whom a patent is addressed. Extrinsic evidence, therefore, may be necessary to inform the court about the language in which the patent is written. But this evidence is not for the purpose of clarifying ambiguity in claim terminology. It is not ambiguity in the document that creates the need for extrinsic evidence but rather unfamiliarity of the court with the terminology of the art to which the patent is addressed. *Markman v. Westview Instruments Inc.,* 52 F.3d 967, 34 U.S.P.Q.2d 1321, 1335 (Fed. Cir. 1995).

Lanham Act.

The Lanham Act's coverage of foreign activities is governed by the test for extraterritorial application of the antitrust laws, according to which the following three elements must be met: (1) there must be some effect (actual or intended) on American foreign commerce; (2) the effect must be sufficiently great to present a cognizable injury to plaintiffs under the federal statute; and (3) the interests and links to American foreign commerce must be sufficiently strong in relation to those of other nations to justify an assertion of extraterritorial authority. *Baldwin Hardware Corp. v. Franksu Enterprise Corp.,* 24 U.S.P.Q.2d 1700 (Cal. 1992).

ʊ

The safeguard against an impermissible extension of a patent monopoly by a trademark is the functionality doctrine: a configuration of an article cannot receive trademark registration if its purpose is to contribute functional advantages to the article or if the configuration results from functional considerations. *Thomas & Betts Corp. v. Panduit Corp.,* 138 F.3d 277, 46 U.S.P.Q.2d 1026, 1033 (7th Cir. 1998).

Lapsed Patent. *See* Reinstatement.

Late Claiming. *See also* Broaden, Disclosure without Claiming.

A decision granted a petition to the Commissioner from an Examiner's refusal to examine an application because the claims "cover subject-matter shown but not claimed in an earlier patent granted to the same inventors seven days prior to the present application." The Examiner contended that the applicants' only remedy lay in applying for a reissue. The

Commissioner disagreed about the possibility of reissue, found the Examiner in error, and ordered him to examine. Matter disclosed, but not claimed, in a patent is not necessarily dedicated to the public or legally abandoned under the statute where there is a hiatus between the issuance of the patent and the filing of a subsequent application. *Ex parte Mullen and Mullen,* 1890 C.D. 9, 50 O.G. 837 (Comm'r Patents 1890).

ℬ

Generally speaking, the filing of an application for a patent, which application discloses novel features without making accompanying claims to all of the novel features disclosed, and the acceptance of a patent thereon give rise to the legitimate inference that the applicant intended to dedicate to the public the unclaimed novel features of his invention. There is, however, a limitation to the inference of dedication, which arises when the inventor, within the time fixed by statute, files another application for the unclaimed novel features referred to. The statute fixes the time within which an applicant may make application for a patent, and, so long as he acts within the time fixed, he is strictly within his legal rights. *Shipp v. Scott School Township,* 54 F.2d 1019, 12 U.S.P.Q. 5, 7, 8 (7th Cir. 1931).

ℬ

What was disclosed and not claimed in appellant's issued patent was dedicated to the public and could not be claimed in an application filed several months after the patent issued. *In re Phillips,* 148 F.2d 662, 65 U.S.P.Q. 213, 215 (C.C.P.A. 1945).

ℬ

Although one might infer that subject matter disclosed, but not claimed, in an issued patent has been dedicated to the public, such inference can be rebutted by the subsequent filing (within the statutory period) of an application claiming such subject matter. *Ex parte Spence,* 82 U.S.P.Q. 449, 450 (PO Bd. App. 1946).

ℬ

Where an invention has been continuously disclosed in an application, an intervening public use or sale prior to the claiming of the invention will not constitute a bar. *Azoplate Corp. v. Silverlith, Inc.,* 367 F. Supp. 711, 180 U.S.P.Q. 616, 631 (Del. 1973).

ℬ

Claims were invalidated because they were not presented in either an original or a continuation application until more than one year after equipment substantially the same as that charged to infringe had been on sale and delivered to customers. *Kahn v. Dynamics Corp. of America,* 508 F.2d 939, 184 U.S.P.Q. 260, 263 (2d Cir. 1975), *cert. denied,* 421 U.S. 930, 185 U.S.P.Q. 505 (1975).

ℬ

A public use of an invention more than one year prior to the time the invention is specifically claimed renders the claim for the invention invalid, regardless of the fact that the invention may have been disclosed (but not formally claimed) in the application as originally filed less than one year after the public use. *Maclaren v. B-I-W Group, Inc.,* 401 F. Supp. 283, 187 U.S.P.Q. 345, 357, 358 (N.Y. 1975).

ℬ

Where an invention has been continuously disclosed in an application, an intervening public use or sale prior to the claiming of the invention will not constitute a bar. The late-claiming doctrine does not apply. *In re Goldman*, 205 U.S.P.Q. 1086, 1089 (Comm'r Patents & Trademarks 1980).

ᚊ

It is immaterial to the defense of late claiming whether or not the claims in suit were supported by the application as originally filed. The dispositive question is whether or not they are directed to essentially the same subject matter as claims originally presented. If they are not, but rather are directed to more specific subject matter which has been in public use or on sale more than one year prior to the presentation of these or substantially similar claims in the patent application, then it is immaterial that broad, unpatentable claims were presented in the application as originally filed. The applicability of the late-claiming defense is not dependent on whether the claims in issue are based on new matter added to the disclosure subsequent to the filing of the application, and is not rendered inapplicable because broader claims were present in the application as originally filed. Rather, this defense relies on the fact that the claims are directed to subject matter not essentially the same as that originally claimed in the application, and which indeed may be more specific and limited than those originally presented. *Kahn v. Dynamics Corporation of America*, 367 F.Supp. 63, 180 U.S.P.Q. 247, 253 (N.Y. 1973); but *see also Brown v. Trion Industries, Inc.*, 575 F.Supp. 511, 223 U.S.P.Q. 1106, 1108 (N.Y. 1983).

ᚊ

The clear and unambiguous language of 35 U.S.C. §120 states that "[a]n application*** for an invention disclosed in the manner provided by the first paragraph of section 112*** in an application previously filed in the United States*** shall have the same effect, as to such invention, as though filed on the date of the prior application***." (Emphasis added.) This applies even to claims which cover inventions made subsequent to the filing date of a parent or other antecedent application relied upon. *In re Hogan and Banks*, 559 F.2d 595, 194 U.S.P.Q. 527, 536 (C.C.P.A. 1977).

ᚊ

Cardinal of Adrian, Inc. v. Peerless Wood Prod. Inc., 515 F.2d 534, 538, 185 U.S.P.Q. 712, 715-716 (6th Cir. 1975), restates the two-pronged test that is necessary to determine whether a patent is invalid for late claiming. The first prong is to determine whether amendments to the patent application contain new matter or merely a clarification or refinement of the original claim. The second prong of the test is whether the amendments constituted the first disclosure of the devices if they had been on sale for more than a year. *Interlake, Inc. v. Weld-Loc Systems, Inc.*, 213 U.S.P.Q. 154, 169 (Ohio 1981).

ᚊ

A patentee can avoid the restrictions applicable to reissue applications by filing a regular application directed to subject matter disclosed (but not claimed) in his patent within one year of the patent's issue date. *In re Bauman*, 683 F.2d 405, 214 U.S.P.Q. 585, 589 (C.C.P.A. 1982).

ᚊ

There is nothing improper, illegal or inequitable in filing a patent application for the purpose of obtaining the right to exclude a known competitor's product from the market; nor is it in any manner improper to amend or insert claims intended to cover a competitor's product the applicant's attorney has learned about during the prosecution of a patent application. If any such amendment or insertion complies with all statutes and regulations, its genesis in the marketplace is simply irrelevant and cannot of itself evidence deceitful intent. *Kingsdown Medical Consultants Ltd. v. Hollister Inc.*, 863 F.2d 867, 9 U.S.P.Q.2d 1384, 1390 (Fed. Cir. 1988).

ϖ

In a case wherein the first asserted method claim was added by amendment during reexamination and in which there is no indication in the file record that the applicant ever objectively intended or considered his invention to include the method, the method claim was not directed to "the invention as claimed" in the patent, as required by 35 U.S.C. §305. Moreover, addition of such a claim (drawn to a method) enlarges the scope of the claims in the patent in violation of 305. *Ex parte Wikdahl*, 10 U.S.P.Q.2d 1546, 1549 (B.P.A.I. 1989).

Later Discoveries.

The clear and unambiguous language of 35 U.S.C. §120 states that "[a]n application*** for an invention disclosed in the manner provided by the first paragraph of section 112*** in an application previously filed in the United States*** *shall have the same effect, as to such invention, as though filed on the date of the prior application*** .*" (Emphasis added.) This applies even to claims which cover inventions made subsequent to the filing date of a parent or other antecedent application relied upon. *In re Hogan and Banks*, 559 F.2d 595, 194 U.S.P.Q. 527, 536 (C.C.P.A. 1977).

Later Reference. *See* Knowledge (Later Discovered), Skill of the Art, Symmetry in the Law.

Law of the Case.

The doctrine of the law of the case dictates that "when a court decides upon a rule of law, that rule should continue to govern the same issues in subsequent stages in the litigation." Law of the case rules apply "both to issues expressly decided by a court in prior rulings and to issues decided by necessary implication." *College Savings Bank v. Florida Prepaid Postsecondary Education Expense Board*, 42 U.S.P.Q.2d 1487, 1494 (N.J. 1996)

Law-of-the-Case Doctrine.

As a matter of sound judicial practice, a court generally adheres to a decision in a prior appeal in the case unless one of three exceptional circumstances exists: the evidence on a subsequent trial was substantially different, controlling authority has since made a contrary decision of the law applicable to such issues, or the decision was clearly erroneous and would work a manifest injustice. The law-of-the-case doctrine is designed to provide finality to judicial decisions. Although the doctrine applies only to issues that were decided in the former proceeding, not the questions that might have been decided but were not, it comprehends things decided by necessary implication as well as those decided explicitly. *Smith International, Inc. v. Hughes Tool Co.*, 759 F.2d 1572, 225 U.S.P.Q. 889 (Fed. Cir. 1985).

ω

This doctrine was judicially created to ensure judicial efficiency and to prevent the possibility of endless litigation. The doctrine applies not only to issues discussed and decided but also to those decided by necessary implication. In an earlier decision, this court held that the patent claims were not invalid under 35 U.S.C. §112 for indefiniteness. There was uncontradicted evidence with regard to the meaning of "stretch rate" at the time the application was filed. The holding of anticipation was predicated on the noted meaning of the cited expression. The district court was bound by this court's interpretation of said expression as the law of the case in deciding on remand. *W. L. Gore & Associates, Inc. v. Garlock, Inc.*, 842 F.2d 1275, 6 U.S.P.Q.2d 1277 (Fed. Cir. 1988).

ω

Law of the case "is a judicially created doctrine, the purposes of which are to prevent the relitigation of issues that have been decided and to ensure that trial courts follow the decisions of appellate courts." Under this doctrine, findings of fact reviewed in and relied upon in an appellate court's decision become the law of the case and, absent certain exceptional circumstances, may not be disturbed by a trial court on remand. *State Industries Inc. v. Mor-Flo Industries Inc.*, 948 F.2d 1573, 20 U.S.P.Q.2d 1738, 1740 (Fed. Cir. 1991).

ω

"[L]aw of the case phrases are occasionally used to describe the consequences of failure to appeal an issue or to preserve it for appeal." *See 18* Charles A. Wright et al., *Federal Practice and Procedure*, §4478, at 788 (1981). But "The general rule is that, without taking a cross-appeal, the prevailing party may present any argument that supports the judgment in its favor." *Genentech Inc. v. The Wellcome Foundation Ltd.*, 29 F.3d 1555, 31 U.S.P.Q.2d 1161, 1165 (Fed. Cir. 1994).

ω

A "decision on an issue of law made at one stage of a case becomes a binding precedent to be followed in successive stages of the same litigation." James W. Moore et al., Moore's Federal Practice, §0.404 [1] (2d ed. 1995). An exception may be made when new evidence is available. *The F.B. Leopold Co. v. Roberts Filter Manufacturing Co.*, 36 U.S.P.Q.2d 1439, 1442 (Pa. 1995).

ω

The law of the case should not lightly be discarded. *Grain Processing Corp. v. American Maize-Products Co.*, 893 F.Supp. 1386, 37 U.S.P.Q.2d 1299, 1305 (Ind. 1995).

Law of Nature.

Every discovery is not embraced within the statutory terms of 35 U.S.C. §101. Excluded from such patent protection are laws of nature, physical phenomena, and abstract ideas. A principle, in the abstract, is a fundamental truth, an original cause, a motive; these cannot be patented, and no one can claim in any of them an exclusive right. A new mineral discovered in the earth or a new plant found in the wild is not patentable subject matter. Likewise, Einstein could not patent his celebrated law that $E = mc^2$; nor could Newton have patented the law of gravity. Such discoveries are "manifestations of...nature, free to all men and reserved exclusively to none." *Diamond v. Diehr and Lutton,* 450 U.S. 175, 209 U.S.P.Q. 1, 7 (1981).

Lawyer. *See* **Argument, Attorney.**

Laying Open to Inspection. *See* **Foreign Patent Application.**

Lead Away From. *See also* **Teach Away From.**

As the hypothetical person of ordinary skill in the art defined by 35 U.S.C. §103 is presumed to know of all pertinent prior art, consideration must be given to prior art that would lead one away from the invention as well as that which is argued to lead toward it. *Mendenhall v. Astec Industries, Inc.,* 13 U.S.P.Q.2d 1913, 1939 (Tenn. 1988), *aff'd,* 13 U.S.P.Q.2d 1956 (Fed. Cir. 1989).

Lead-Time Valuation.

Regardless of whether the trade secrets were ultimately made public via the issuance of a patent or otherwise, defendant obtained the information by misappropriation and not from public disclosure or any other legitimate business means. There is no distinction between the presence of a disclosure that may destroy secrecy and the head start concept, for the former is merely an element of the latter. The award for damages compensates the plaintiff for the head start that the defendants obtained through its misappropriation. This head start amounted to a preemption of the entire market and prevented the plaintiff from licensing others, as well as making entry into the market by the plaintiff impossible. In fashioning an adequate monetary remedy, the court must consider that the defendants did not merely wrongly obtain and use the plaintiff's know-how as a competitor in the marketing, they refused to return the know-how to the plaintiff when ordered to do so, thereby completely precluding the plaintiff also from manufacturing. There is no question that the defendant's conduct was grossly improper and that the plaintiff's monetary recovery should not be limited by a lead-time valuation. *The Kilbarr Corp. v. Business Systems, Inc.,* B.V., 679 F. Supp. 422, 6 U.S.P.Q.2d 1698 (N.J. 1988).

Lear Test.

With careful consideration of the *Lear* [*Lear v. Atkins,* 395 U.S. 653, 162 U.S.P.Q. 1 (1969)] test and policies, the assignor is estopped from challenging the validity of the patent:

> To allow the assignor to make that representation [of the worth of the patent] at the time of the assignment (to his advantage) and later to repudiate it (again to his

advantage) could work an injustice against the assignee.... [D]espite the public policy encouraging people to challenge potentially invalid patents, there are still circumstances in which the equities of the contractual relationships between the parties should deprive one party... of the right to bring that challenge.

Lear does not bar enforcement of a) a settlement agreement and consent decree, b) a contract promise to share royalties, or c) a settlement agreement to pay royalties even if the patent is later held invalid. *Studiengesellschaft Kohle m.b.H. v. Shell Oil Co.*, 112 F.3d 1561, 42 U.S.P.Q.2d 1674, 1680 (Fed. Cir. 1997).

Leave to Amend.

Leave to amend may be denied on the basis of undue delay, bad faith, or prejudice to the opposing party. *PreVent Inc. v. WNCK Inc.*, 33 U.S.P.Q.2d 1701, 1702 (Penn. 1994).

ω

Delay, standing alone, is usually an insufficient basis on which to deny leave to amend. *Ricoh Co. Ltd. v. Nashua Corp.*, 40 U.S.P.Q.2d 1306, 1309 (N.H. 1996).

ω

If the complaint fails to state a claim, the court should grant leave to amend unless it appears beyond a doubt the plaintiff would not be entitled to relief under any set of facts proved. *Amylin Pharmaceuticals Inc. v. University of Minnesota*, 45 U.S.P.Q.2d 1949, 1952 (Cal. 1998).

Legal Fees. *See also* Attorney's Fees.

The identity of the party which pays legal fees for the patent in issue is a significant factor in deciding ownership of the patent. *National Texture Corporation v. Hymes*, 200 U.S.P.Q. 59, 63 (Minn. 1977).

Legal Issues. *See* Special Master.

Legalization for Foreign Public Documents. *See* Apostille.

Legal Question.

The view that a jury verdict on non-obviousness is at best advisory would make charades of motions for directed verdict or JNOV under Fed. R. Civ. P. 50 in patent cases. These motions apply only to binding jury verdicts. Moreover, use of an advisory jury is limited to actions not triable of right by a jury. All fact findings of a jury are non-advisory, unless made in an area expressly removed from jury verdict. A jury may decide the questions of anticipation and obviousness, either as separate special verdicts or en route to a verdict on the question of validity, which may also be decided by the jury. No warrant appears for distinguishing the submission of legal questions to a jury in patent cases from such submissions routinely made in other types of cases. So long as the Seventh Amendment stands, the right to a jury trial should not be rationed, nor should particular issues in particular types of cases be treated differently from similar issues in other types of cases. When the judgment arises from a jury verdict, the reviewing court applies the reasonable-jury/substantial-evidence standard: a standard that gives greater deference to the judgment simply because appellate review is more limited, compared with review of a trial judge's decision. The appellate court's function is exhausted when the evidentiary basis of the jury's verdict becomes apparent, it being immaterial that the court might draw a contrary inference or feel that another conclusion is more reasonable. *Richardson v. Suzuki Motor Co., Ltd.*, 868 F.2d 1226, 9 U.S.P.Q.2d 1913 (Fed. Cir. 1989).

Legal Theory.

Although an attorney may be deposed and required to disclose what he knows about the subject matter, he cannot be required to disclose his mental impressions, conclusions, opinions, or legal theories concerning the litigation. He may be required to refer to his file to refresh his recollection, but he cannot be compelled to state why he amended the claims or what he meant by this or that word or phrase; that would require him to express an opinion, one of the exceptions provided for in Fed. R. Civ. P. 26(b)(3). *MacLaren v. B-I-W Group Inc.*, 180 U.S.P.Q. 387 (Va. 1973).

Legislative History.

No requirement of or authority for any duty of candor is found in requiring a patentee (who requests administrative action from the PTO under the provisions of a statute) to provide a legislative history of that statute to the PTO. It is up to the legal advisors of the PTO to provide any appropriate statutory interpretation, including legislative history, of laws under consideration by the PTO. This is so even if the applicant before the PTO participated in that legislative history. *United Sweetener U.S.A. Inc. v. The Nutrasweet Company,* 760 F. Supp. 400, 19 U.S.P.Q.2d 1561, 1578 (Del. 1991).

Legislative Intent.

The best evidence of legislative intent is the language of the statute itself. If it is clear and unambiguous, resort cannot properly be had to legislative history to give it another meaning. *Rubenstein v. Schmidt*, 133 U.S.P.Q. 91, 92 (Comm'r of Patents 1962).

Lengthy Prosecution. *See also* Crowded Art.

The fact that fourteen years were required to persuade the Patent Office to allow the claims might indicate doubt as to their validity. *The Hoover Company v. Mitchell Manufacturing Company*, 269 F.2d 795, 122 U.S.P.Q. 314, 317 (7th Cir, 1959).

ᅜ

The presumption in this case is strengthened because of the intensive controversy for eight years in the Patent Office and the CCPA over the issuance of the patent. *Union Carbide Corporation v. The Dow Chemical Company*, 213 U.S.P.Q. 128, 144, 145 (Tex. 1981).

Less Than. *See also* **Zero.**

Claims are also too broad and incomplete when they specify up to about a designated percent by weight of a specified component because they read on compositions totally lacking that component. *Ex parte Dobson, Jacob, and Herschler,* 165 U.S.P.Q. 29, 30 (PO Bd. App. 1969).

Lexicographer. *See also* **Dictionary, Grammarian.**

A patentee may be his own lexicographer and grammarian. He "may define his own terms, regardless of common or technical meaning. . . . Fairness to any patentee requires a court to accept his definition of words, phrases and terms." "Claim language is not to be interpreted in a vacuum but is to be read in light of the specification to determine the meaning intended by the inventors." The file wrapper in its entirety, including the definitions and arguments made during the prosecution of the patent in question, can also aid the court in ascertaining the meaning of terminology used in claims. Accordingly, when a patentee argues before a court for a definition that is consistent with the file wrapper, the court will give effect to that definition. *Rohm & Haas Co. v. Dawson Chemical Co., Inc.,* 557 F. Supp 739, 217 U.S.P.Q. 515, 573 (Tex. 1983).

ᗉ

The patent law allows an inventor to be his own lexicographer. To ascertain the true meaning of disputed claim language, resort should be made to the claims at issue, the specification, and the prosecution history. Moreover, claims are construed as they would be by those skilled in the art. That the specific examples set forth in the patents occur at room temperature does not mean that the claims are imbued with a room temperature limitation. Generally, particular limitations or embodiments appearing in the specification will not be read into the claims. *Loctite Corp. v. Ultraseal Ltd.,* 781 F.2d 861, 228 U.S.P.Q. 90 (Fed. Cir. 1985).

ᗉ

Though inventors may be their own lexicographers, they must use words in the same way in the claims and in the specification. *Fonar Corp. v. Johnson & Johnson,* 821 F.2d 627, 3 U.S.P.Q.2d 1109 (Fed. Cir. 1987).

ᗉ

Claim construction is reviewed as a matter of law. However, interpretation of a claim may depend on evidentiary material about which there is a factual dispute, requiring resolution of factual issues as a basis for interpretation of the claim. The terms of a claim will be given their ordinary meaning, unless it appears that the inventor used them differently. The ordinary meaning of claim language, however, is not dispositive and resort must still be had to the specification and prosecution history to determine whether the inventor used the disputed terms differently than their ordinary accustomed meaning. Patent law allows an inventor to be his own lexicographer. The specification aids in ascertaining the scope and meaning of the language employed in the claims inasmuch as words must be used in the same way in both the claims and the specification. The prosecution history (or file wrapper) limits the interpretation of claims so as to exclude any interpretation that may have been disclaimed or disavowed during prosecution in order to obtain claim allowance. *ZMI Corp. v. Cardiac Resuscitator Corp.*, 844 F.2d 1576, 6 U.S.P.Q.2d 1557 (Fed. Cir. 1988).

ϖ

Where an inventor chooses to be his own lexicographer and to give terms uncommon meanings, he must set out his uncommon definition in some manner within the patent disclosure. *Intellicall Inc. v. Phonometrics Inc.*, 952 F.2d 1384, 21 U.S.P.Q.2d 1383, 1386 (Fed. Cir. 1992).

Lexicography.

It would be unfair to allow a patentee to exercise his "lexicographic license" retroactively once litigation alleging infringement has commenced to define patent terms so as to support a claim of literal infringement. *Hilleby v. FMC Corp.*, 25 U.S.P.Q.2d 1423, 1426 (Cal. 1992).

License. *See also* **Compulsory Licensing, Conditions, Discriminatory, Exclusive License, Implied License, Label License, Limited Patent License, Package License, Patent Office License, Record, Royalty, Tying Arrangement.**

Royalty payments under a license were based only on sales of an unpatented element of a patented combination. The license was an attempt to prevent the sale or use of the unpatented element in the patented combination unless such element was purchased from or through the licensor. The owner of a patent may not employ it to secure a limited monopoly of an unpatented material used in applying the invention. *The Mercoid Corporation v. Mid-Continent Investment Company*, 320 U.S. 661, 60 U.S.P.Q. 21, 23, 24 (S. Ct. 1944).

ϖ

The monopoly granted by the patent laws cannot be divided into parts, except as authorized by those laws. The patentee may assign (1) the whole patent, (2) an undivided part or share of that patent, or (3) the exclusive right under the patent "to the whole or any specified part of the United States. Any assignment or transfer, short of these, is a mere license, giving the licensee no title in the patent, and no right to sue at law in his own name for an infringement." In accordance with these principles an exclusive license to make, use, and vend is in the same category as an assignment on the theory that the licensor holds title to the patent in trust for such licensee. Even though the exclusive license is restricted to a specified territory or covers less than the full life of the patent, this still remains true. *Channel Master Corp. v. JFD Electronics Corp.*, 260 F. Supp. 568, 151 U.S.P.Q. 498, 500 (N.Y. 1966).

ϖ

A patent confers upon the owner the right to exclude others from making, using, or selling the invention during the life of the patent; in order that a transfer constitute a sale, there must be a grant of all substantial rights of value in the patent. The transfer of anything less is a license that conveys no proprietary interest to the licensee. Whether a transfer constitutes a sale or license is determined by the substance of the transaction, and a transfer will suffice as a sale if it appears from the agreement and surrounding circumstances that the parties intended that the patentee surrender all his substantial rights to the invention. The question does not depend upon the labels or the terminology used in the agreement; hence, the fact that an agreement is termed a license and that the parties are referred to as licensor and licensee is not decisive. Nor is the question governed by the method of payment; it is, therefore, immaterial that payment is based on a percentage of sales or profits, or on an amount per unit manufactured. Moreover, clauses in an agreement permitting termination by the grantor upon the occurrence of stated conditions or events will not preclude the transaction from being considered a sale; such clauses are uniformly treated as conditions subsequent. The fact that the grantee has the right to terminate the agreement at will does not defeat a sale. *Bell Intercontinental Corp. v. United States*, 381 F.2d 1004, 152 U.S.P.Q. 182, 184 (Ct. Cl. 1966).

ω

Considering that the defendant paid a considerable sum of money at the time that the Patent Transfer Agreement was executed, it was reasonable for him to provide against competition by Industrial Dynamics Corporation and the manufacturer of machines (for which the patent applications were filed) during the period between the execution of the agreement and the issuance of the patents. Provisions of the Patent Transfer Agreement and the Consultant Agreement require Industrial Dynamics Corporation, during the term of the Patent Transfer Agreement, and consultants during the Consultant Agreement and for a three-year period thereafter, to make available to the defendant, at no extra cost to the defendant, all improvements to the two patent applications covered by the agreement. Such provisions are reasonable. These contractual provisions, which the plaintiff described as grant forward clauses, constitute a reasonable method by which Industrial Dynamics Corporation and consultants could dispose of improvements on the basic bottle machine patents. They could not license or assign these improvements to a third party because no third party would be able to manufacture and sell bottle inspection machines coming within the claims of the basic patents owned by the defendant and so would have no interest in the improvements that build upon or add to the basic machines and that cannot be used apart from the basic machines. It was to the advantage of Industrial Dynamics Corporation and consultants to make the improvements available to the defendant, rather than to others, so that the bottle inspection machines marketed by the defendant might be as good as they could be made and sales and royalties were thereby maximized. *San Marion Electronic Corp. v. George J. Meyer Manufacturing Co.*, 155 U.S.P.Q. 617, 622, 624 (Cal. 1967).

ω

Different uses of a patented invention can be separately licensed. *The Barr Rubber Products Company v. The Sun Rubber Company*, 277 F.Supp. 484, 156 U.S.P.Q. 374, 391 (N.Y. 1967).

ω

A license agreement that promises not to challenge the validity of a patent is void and unenforceable because it contravenes the strong federal policy in favor of the full and free use of ideas in the public domain. *Lear, Inc. v. Adkins*, 395 U.S. 653, 673, 674, 162 U.S.P.Q. 1 (1969).

ω

The law treats a license under a patent as personal to the licensee, and non-assignable and non-transferable, as if it contained these restrictions, in the absence of express provisions to the contrary. *PPG Industries, Inc. v. Guardian Industries Corporation*, 597 F.2d 1090, 202 U.S.P.Q. 95, 98 (6th Cir. 1979).

ᛒ

In any commercial agreement in which the compensation promised by one to the other is a percentage of profits or receipts, or is a royalty on goods sold, manufactured, or mined, there will nearly always be found an implied promise of diligent and careful performance in good faith and of forbearance to make performance impossible by going out of business or otherwise. 3 A. Corbin, *Corbin on Contracts* §568 (1960). This rule of law has been applied with full force to patent license agreements. *Bailey v. Chattem, Inc.*, 684 F.2d 386, 215 U.S.P.Q. 671, 679 (6th Cir. 1982).

ᛒ

There are two types of licenses. A non-exclusive license confers on the licensee a mere privilege that protects him from a claim of infringement by the owner of the patent. The non-exclusive licensee has no property interest in the patent monopoly, nor any contract with the patent owner that others shall not practice the invention. The patent owner who grants a non-exclusive license to another is not precluded from further licensing the product, and may freely tolerate infringement without violating the rights of the patent licensees. An exclusive license, on the other hand, has the promise of the patent owner that others shall be excluded from practicing the patent within the field of use for which the license has been given. Exclusive licensees have the right to enjoin acts of infringement, and, because the presence of the patentee is usually necessary to pursue such relief, may compel the patentee to become a party to the lawsuit. The patentee has no more right to practice his patent (in a field of use where an exclusive license has been given) than does a stranger. Therefore, if the exclusive license has been violated by the patentee, the patentee may be sued for infringement. *Sanofi, S.A. v. Med-Tech Veterinarian Products, Inc.*, 565 F. Supp. 931, 220 U.S.P.Q. 416, 419, 420 (N.J. 1983).

ᛒ

A basic distinction between the transfer of a license and the transfer of a patent is whether the transferee has received the right to sue for infringement. If such a right to sue for infringement is transferred, the transferee has received an assignment. If no such right to sue is transferred, the transferee has received a license. In co-owner situations the right to sue independently for infringement cannot be inferred; all co-owners must join in a patent infringement suit. Thus, one co-owner cannot sue independently for infringement or compel other co-owners to join in such a suit absent an agreement among all co-owners permitting him to do so. *Eickmeyer v. United States*, 10 Cl. Ct. 598, 231 U.S.P.Q. 820, 821, 822 (1986).

ᛒ

Grantbacks of non-exclusive licenses, geographically limited licenses, and quantity limited licenses are not per se unlawful; they do not necessarily constitute patent misuse or violate §2 of the Sherman Act. *Lightwave Technologies Inc. v. Corning Glass Works*, 19 U.S.P.Q.2d 1838, 1844 (N.Y. 1991).

ᛒ

License

A patentee may grant a license "upon any condition the performance of which is reasonably within the reward which the patentee by the grant of the patent is entitled to secure". The right to exclude (35 U.S.C. §154) may be waived in whole or in part. With few exceptions, any conditions which are not in their very nature illegal with regard to this kind of property, imposed by a patentee and agreed to by a licensee for the right to manufacture or use or sell the [patented] article, will be upheld by the courts. *Mallinckrodt Inc. v. Medipart Inc.*, 976 F.2d 700, 24 U.S.P.Q.2d 1173, 1176 (Fed. Cir. 1992).

ᚥ

Patent licensing agreements which show commercial success, long-felt need, and copying by others are objective evidence that the patented inventions were non-obvious. Licenses taken by large and strong companies are evidence of a reasonable royalty rate obtained after negotiation between a willing licensor and a willing licensee. *B&H Manufacturing Inc. v. Foster-Forbes Glass Co.*, 26 U.S.P.Q.2d 1066 (Ind. 1993).

ᚥ

Under patent and copyright law, a party cannot be compelled to license its proprietary software to anyone. *Tricom Inc. v. Electronic Data Systems Corp.*, 902 F.Supp. 741, 36 U.S.P.Q.2d 1778, 1780 (Mich. 1995).

ᚥ

"Whether express or implied, a license is a contract 'governed by ordinary principles of state contract law.'" Federal law governs the assignability of patent licenses because of the conflict between federal patent policy and state laws that would allow assignability. "It is well settled that a nonexclusive licensee of a patent has only a personal and not a property interest in the patent and that this personal right cannot be assigned unless the patent owner authorizes the assignment or the license itself permits assignment." *Everex Systems Inc. v. Cadtrak Corp.*, 89 F.3d 673, 39 U.S.P.Q.2d 1518, 1522, 1523 (9th Cir. 1996)

ᚥ

If an agreement is ambiguous, extrinsic evidence to aid in interpretation or construction of the agreement is admissible. *Mid-West Conveyor Co. v. Jervis B. Webb Co.*, 92 F.3d 992, 39 U.S.P.Q.2d 1754, 1756 (10th Cir. 1996)

Licensee.[2] *See also* **Agreement, Exclusive Licensee.**

A court's finding of patent invalidity does not relieve a licensee of its obligation to pay royalties for the period during which it was enjoying the benefit of its license and representing to the public that its product was licensed under the patent. So long as licensee sought the protection of the patent, it is only equitable that it should discharge its royalty obligation under the license agreement. *Kraly v. National Distillers and Chemical Corporation*, 177 U.S.P.Q. 364, 370 (Ill. 1973).

ᚥ

---

[2]The Federal Circuit [*Heidelberg Harris, Inc. v. Loebach*, 46 U.S.P.Q.2d 1948 (Fed. Cir. 1998)] "held that a licensee is immune from infringement liability if the licensee purchased the license for value before receiving notice of the plaintiff's claim to the patent. The relevant date for notice is the date that the licensee's right to the license vests, i.e., before the licensee has paid the consideration or before the licensee has performed his purchase obligations." *Federal Circuit Case Digest*, Vol. 1, No. 7, page 4, 1998.

An assignee of the legal patent holder granted a licensee two principal rights: the nonexclusive right to make, have made, use and sell the claimed invention and the right to grant further sublicenses within the United States on such terms as the licensee "in its sole discretion may determine". That bundle of rights was a property interest in the patent and gave the licensee the right to sue and recover damages as co-plaintiff (with the assignee) in an infringement action. *Schneider (Europe) AG v. SciMed Life Systems Inc.*, 28 U.S.P.Q.2d 1225, 1230, 1231 (Minn. 1993).

Licensee Estoppel.

Licensees may avoid further royalty payments, regardless of the provisions of their contract, once a third party proves that the patent is invalid. *Lear, Inc. v. Adkins,* 395 U.S. 653, 162 U.S.P.Q. 1 (1969).

ᵚ

The U.S. Supreme Court abrogated licensee estoppel, thus permitting challenges to validity to proceed not only in the typical situation involving the grant of a license after a patent issues, but also in the case of a preissuance licensee. Principles of res judicata, however, bar a licensee's challenge to the validity of a patent when prior litigation was terminated by a consent decree that, by its terms, acknowledged the patent's validity. *Foster v. Hallco Manufacturing Co. Inc.*, 947 F.2d 469, 20 U.S.P.Q.2d 1241, 1245, 1247 (Fed. Cir. 1991).

License Recordation.

No license is required to be recorded, and no record of a license affects the rights of any person; for a license is good against the world, whether it is recorded or not. A purchaser of a patent takes it subject to all outstanding licenses. *Sanofi, S.A. v. Med-Tech Veterinarian Products, Inc.*, 565 F. Supp. 931, 220 U.S.P.Q. 416 (N.J. 1983).

Life Form.[3] *See also* **Mammal, Microorganism, Mouse, Oyster, Plant, Product of Nature.**

Man-made life forms are patentable under 35 U.S.C. §101, which includes non-naturally occurring manufactures or compositions of matter. *Ex parte Allen,* 2 U.S.P.Q.2d 1425 (B.P.A.I. 1987).

ᵚ

The PTO is now examining claims directed to multicellular living organisms, including animals. To the extent that claimed subject matter is directed to a nonhuman "non-naturally occurring manufacture or composition of matter—a product of human ingenuity," such claims will not be rejected under 35 U.S.C. §101 as being directed to nonstatutory subject matter. *Animal Legal Defense Fund v. Quigg,* 932 F.2d 920, 18 U.S.P.Q.2d 1677, 1680 (Fed. Cir. 1991).

---

[3] (Refer to Rosenstock, "The Law of Chemical and Pharmaceutical Invention," §5.4, Little, Brown and Company, 1993.)

Like.

It was not necessary for the specification, having stated that the mixture should be "paint-like" or "paste-like," to go further and give specific illustrative examples of appropriate compositions. *In re Franck and Schettini*, 255 F.2d 931, 118 U.S.P.Q. 284, 287 (C.C.P.A. 1958).

ᛦ

The phrase "and the like" is vague and uncertain and renders a claim indefinite when it is not clear from the specification what is intended to be covered by that recitation. *Ex parte Remark*, 15 U.S.P.Q.2d 1498, 1500 (B.P.A.I. 1990).

ᛦ

The phrase "or the like" renders a claim indefinite when it is not apparent from the record what icons are "like" a softkey display. The specification does not provide any standards for determining the other icons which would fall within the scope of the claim. *Ex parte Donaldson*, 26 U.S.P.Q.2d 1250, 1259 (B.P.A.I. 1992).

Likelihood of Success.

Most technological advance is the fruit of methodical, persistent investigation, as is recognized in 35 U.S.C. §103 ("Patentability shall not be negatived by the manner in which the invention was made"). The consistent criterion for determination of obviousness is whether the prior art would have suggested to one of ordinary skill in the art that this process should be carried out and would have a reasonable likelihood of success, viewed in the light of the prior art. Both the suggestion and the expectation of success must be founded in the prior art, not in the applicant's disclosure. *In re Dow Chemical Co.*, 837 F.2d 469, 5 U.S.P.Q.2d 1529 (Fed. Cir. 1988).

Limit. *See also* Narrowing Claim.

The public purpose on which the patent law rests requires the granting of claims commensurate in scope with the invention disclosed. This requires as much the granting of broad claims on broad inventions as it does granting of specific claims on more specific inventions. It is neither contemplated by the public purpose of the patent laws nor required by the statute that an inventor shall be forced to accept claims narrower than his invention in order to secure allowance of his patent. *In re Sus and Schaefer*, 306 F.2d 494, 134 U.S.P.Q. 301, 304 (C.C.P.A. 1962).

ᛦ

The Commissioner is granted authority to restrict the specification so that it is not overbroad. However, to preclude a limiting amendment under the guise of inappropriate "new matter" was excessive, and cancellation of selected subject matter by the Patent Office was arbitrary and capricious. *Rhone-Poulenc S.A. v. Dann*, 507 F.2d 261, 184 U.S.P.Q. 196 (4th Cir. 1974).

ᛦ

To provide effective incentives, claims must adequately protect inventors. To demand that the first to disclose shall limit his claims to what he has found will work or to materials that meet the guidelines specified for "preferred" materials in a process would not serve the constitutional purpose of promoting progress in the useful arts. *In re Goffe*, 542 F.2d 564, 191 U.S.P.Q. 429, 431 (C.C.P.A. 1976).

ᛒ

Claims need not be limited to exemplification or preferred embodiments in order to satisfy enablement requirements. *Ex parte Gould*, 6 U.S.P.Q.2d 1680 (B.P.A.I. 1987).

Limitation. *See also* **Claim Limitation, Narrowing Claims, Quantity Limitation, Restriction.**

There is no need to state in a claim a result or advantage, which will inherently occur through a recited limitation, in order to rely on such result or advantage. *In re Estes*, 420 F.2d 1397, 164 U.S.P.Q. 519, 521 (C.C.P.A. 1970).

ᛒ

Not only must claims be given their broadest reasonable interpretation consistent with the specification (when evaluating their patentability), but all limitations therein must also be considered. *In re Saether*, 492 F.2d 849, 181 U.S.P.Q. 36, 39 (C.C.P.A. 1974).

ᛒ

No "applicant should have limitations of the specification read into a claim where no express statement of the limitation is included in the claim." *In re Priest*, 582 F.2d 33, 199 U.S.P.Q. 11, 15 (C.C.P.A. 1978).

ᛒ

The selection of the ratio of the total jaw length to the average jaw height and the narrow range of hardness claimed is not a matter of obvious design choice to one of ordinary skill in the art at the time the invention was made. It is axiomatic that not only must claims be given their broadest reasonable interpretation consistent with the specification, but also all limitations must be considered. Here the characterization of certain specific limitations or parameters as obvious does not make the appellant's invention, considered as a whole, obvious. The fact that the invention may have been the result of experimentation does not negate patentability nor render obvious claimed parameters that were the result of experimentation. *Ex parte Petersen*, 228 U.S.P.Q. 216, 217 (B.P.A.I. 1985).

ᛒ

The reason a particular claim limitation is added during prosecution is a question of fact, not law. *See Mannesmann Demag Corp. v. Engineered Metal Products Co.*, 793 F.2d 1279, 1285, 230 U.S.P.Q. 45, 48 (Fed. Cir. 1986).

ᛒ

Where a claim of a patent is clearly broader in scope than one which was rejected during prosecution of the application on which the patent issued, a court "is not permitted to read [those removed limitations] back into the claims." *United States v. Telectronics, Inc.*, 857 F.2d 778, 783, 8 U.S.P.Q.2d 1217, 1221 (Fed. Cir. 1988), *cert. denied*, 490 U.S. 1046 (1989).

ᛒ

Where a specification does not require a limitation, that limitation should not be read from the specification into the claims. *Electro Medical Systems S.A. v. Cooper Life Sciences Inc.*, 34 F.3d 1048, 32 U.S.P.Q.2d 1017, 1021 (Fed. Cir. 1994).

ω

The PTO must consider all claim limitations when determining patentability of an invention over the prior art. *In re Lowry*, 32 F.3d 1579, 32 U.S.P.Q.2d 1031, 1034 (Fed. Cir. 1994).

ω

"All limitations of a claim must be considered meaningful." *D.O.C.C. Inc. v. Spin-tech Inc.*, 93 Civ. 4679, 36 U.S.P.Q.2d 1145, 1151 (N.Y. 1994).

ω

It is usually incorrect to read numerical precision into a claim from which it is absent, particularly when other claims contain the numerical limitation. However, when the preferred embodiment is described in the specification as the invention itself, the claims are not necessarily entitled to a scope broader than that embodiment. *Modine Manufacturing Co. v. U.S. International Trade Commission*, 75 F.3d 1545, 37 U.S.P.Q.2d 1609, 1612 (Fed. Cir. 1996).

Limited Patent License.

Limited patent licenses are waivers of the right to sue, so that violation of a license restriction gives rise to a patent infringement suit. Violation of the license restriction does not give rise to an action for breach of contract. *Eli Lilly & Co. v. Genentech Inc.*, 17 U.S.P.Q.2d 1531, 1534 (Ind. 1990).

Limiting. *See also* Reduction in Scope.

Claims are not defective because they fail to include all the subject matter which may exhibit the purported improvement. Underclaiming is not evidence of empiricism and does not suggest that compounds within the scope of the claims are "inoperative." *Ex parte Maxey and Harrington*, 177 U.S.P.Q. 468, 472 (PO Bd. App. 1972).

Limits.

A rejection under the second paragraph of 35 U.S.C. §112 was reversed notwithstanding the Examiner's conclusion that one skilled in the art would not know the limits of the patent protection sought. *Ex parte Altermatt*, 183 U.S.P.Q. 436, 437 (PO Bd. App. 1974).

List.

The presentation of lists from which reagents may be selected is not a sufficient disclosure to support subsequently-asserted claims to a particular class of reaction product which might be produced by a proper selection of reagents and determining reaction conditions. *In re Prutton*, 200 F.2d 706, 96 U.S.P.Q. 147, 151 (C.C.P.A. 1952).

ω

When an applicant recites two or more lists of ingredients and indicates that any one in one list may be combined with any one in another, he is not necessarily entitled to claim any specific combination of elements which may fall within the scope of such disclosure. *Prutton v. Fuller and Johnson*, 230 F.2d 459, 109 U.S.P.Q. 59, 61 (C.C.P.A. 1956).

ᴡ

The mere naming of a compound in a reference, without more, cannot constitute a description of the compound, particularly when the evidence of record suggests that a method suitable for its preparation was not developed until a date later than that of the reference. Otherwise, lists of thousands of theoretically possible compounds could be generated and published which, assuming it would be within the level of skill in the art to make them, would bar a patent to the actual discoverer of a named compound no matter how beneficial to mankind it might be. Such a result would be repugnant to the statute. *In re Wiggins, James, and Gitton*, 483 F.2d 538, 179 U.S.P.Q. 421, 425 (C.C.P.A. 1973).

ᴡ

Just because a moiety is listed as one possible choice for one position does not mean there is *ipsis verbis* support for every species or subgenus that chooses that moiety. Were this the case, a "laundry list" disclosure of every possible moiety for evey possible position would constitute a written description of every species in the genus. *Fujikawa v. Wattanasin*, 93 F.3d 1559, 39 U.S.P.Q.2d 1895, 1905 (Fed. Cir. 1996).

Listing. *See* **Enabling Disclosure.**

Literal Infringement.

Where a device serves the same or a similar purpose to the patented invention, but functions in a substantially different way, the fact that it falls within the literal language of the claim does not warrant a finding of infringement. The patent law is designed to protect the originality and technical merit of the device, not to reward the literary skills of the those drafting patent claims. *Mechanical Plastics Corp. v. Unifast Industries, Inc.*, 657 F. Supp. 502, 4 U.S.P.Q.2d 1734 (N.Y. 1987).

Litigation.

There are significant differences between the reexamination procedure and patent litigation in the federal courts. The two forms of proceedings are distinct, with different records and different standards of proof. When considering validity, the PTO gives claims their broadest reasonable interpretation consistent with the specification of the patent. In contrast, courts may construe claims liberally to uphold a patent's validity, rather than to destroy an inventor's right to protect the substance of his or her invention. *Whistler Corp. v. Dynascan Corp.*, 29 U.S.P.Q.2d 1866, 1871 (Ill. 1993).

Living Matter. *See* **Life Form.**

Living Organism. *See* **Life Form.**

Lodestar. *See* **Billing. Long-Arm Statute.**

A state long-arm statute was held to be inadequate to obtain personal jurisdiction over a non-U.S. corporation through activity of its U.S. subsidiary. *Hollister Inc. v. Coloplast AIS,* 16 U.S.P.Q.2d 1718, 1721, 1722 (Ill. 1990).

ᚳ

In order to arrive at the amount of an award, a court must multiply the number of hours spent on the litigation by the reasonable hourly rate. This product, known as the lodestar, "provides an objective basis on which to make an initial estimate of the value of a lawyer's services." The lodestar method is the proper method to use under 35 U.S.C. §285 and is presumed to be the reasonable fee. *Comark Communications Inc. v. Harris Corp.,* 47 U.S.P.Q.2d 1469, 1471 (Pa. 1998).

Long-Arm Statute.

Among the factors that courts may consider in making a determination of personal jurisdiction are (1) the burden on the defendant, (2) the forum State's interest in adjudicating the dispute, (3) the plaintiff's interest in obtaining convenient and effective relief, (4) the interstate judicial system's interest in obtaining the most efficient resolution of controversies, and (5) the shared interests of the several States in furthering fundamental substantive social policies. *Worldtronics International Inc. v. Ever Splendor Enterprise Co.,* 969 F.Supp. 1136, 44 U.S.P.Q.2d 1447, 1451 (Ill. 1997).

Long-Felt Need. *See also* **Secondary Considerations.**

In view of the apparent need which so long had persisted, the obvious benefits to be gained by both the inventor and the industry from meeting the need, and the failure of anyone to meet it, the finding of patentable invention can be sustained even without considering the statutory presumption of validity. *Marvel Specialty Company, Inc. v. Bell Hosiery Mills, Inc.,* 330 F.2d 164, 141 U.S.P.Q. 269, 275 (4th Cir. 1964).

ᚳ

Objective evidence of non-obviousness includes commercial success, long-felt but unresolved need, failure of others, and copying. When present, such objective evidence must be considered. It can be the most probative evidence of non-obviousness in the record, and enables the district court to avert the trap of hindsight. On the other hand, the absence of objective evidence does not preclude a holding of non-obviousness because such evidence is not a requirement for patentability. *Custom Accessories Inc. v. Jeffrey-Allan Industries Inc.,* 807 F.2d 955, 1 U.S.P.Q.2d 1196 (Fed. Cir. 1986).

ᚳ

Long-felt need is analyzed as of the date of an articulated problem and evidence of efforts to solve that problem. *Texas Instruments Inc. v. International Trade Commission,* 988 F.2d 1165, 26 U.S.P.Q.2d 1018, 1027 (Fed. Cir. 1993).

Losing Interference Party. *See also* **Interference Estoppel.**

The Board based the rejection under 35 U.S.C. §103 on the theory that an applicant that has lost an interference can never be entitled to claims that are obvious variations of the invention defined in the lost counts. The court found no judicial doctrine that supports this rejection under §103. *In re McKellin, Mageli, and D'Angelo*, 529 F.2d 1324, 188 U.S.P.Q. 428 (C.C.P.A. 1976).

ᴡ

Appellant was initially the senior party and subsequently the losing party in an interference in which the winning party prevailed on the basis of a Convention filing in a foreign country. The Board held that the appellant's claims were not patentably distinct from the subject matter defined by the counts lost in the interference. The issue here was not obviousness under 35 U.S.C. §103 or so-called interference estoppel. Rather, the Board relied on the more general principle of res judicata and collateral estoppel wherein a judgment previously rendered bars consideration of questions of fact or mixed questions of fact and law that were, or should have been, resolved in earlier litigation. An interference should settle all issues that are decided or that could have been decided. When an applicant loses an interference, the applicant is not entitled to a patent containing claims corresponding to the count or claims that are not patentably distinct from the count. *Ex parte Tytgat, Clerbois, and Noel*, 225 U.S.P.Q. 907 (PTO Bd. App. 1985).

Loss of Right.

An applicant cannot, under 37 C.F.R. §1.131, swear back of obviousness-establishing references published more than one year prior to the applicant's filing date. *In re Foster*, 343 F.2d 980, 145 U.S.P.Q. 166, 173 (C.C.P.A. 1965).

Lost Art.

An abandoned invention will not defeat the patentability of the rediscovery of "lost art." *Dunlop Holdings Limited v. Ram Golf Corporation*, 524 F.2d 33, 188 U.S.P.Q. 481, 483 (7th Cir. 1975).

Lost Count.

When a party to an interference files an abandonment of the contest, concedes priority, or disclaims the subject matter of an interference count, he stands in the same position as he would had there been an award of priority adverse to him with respect to the interference count. An adverse award of priority bars an applicant from obtaining a claim not patentably distinct from the subject matter awarded his adversary. *In re Fenn*, 315 F.2d 949, 137 U.S.P.Q. 367, 368 (C.C.P.A. 1963).

ᴡ

When a party who has contested and lost priority with respect to a count in an interference presents claims ex parte that define subject matter obvious in view of the subject matter of the lost count, as shown by prior art references or by reference to the ordinary skill of the art, rejection of those claims under 35 U.S.C. §103 may be proper if the subject matter of the count falls within any of the paragraphs of 35 U.S.C. §102. The same result obtains where the party concedes priority of invention of the count. Such a rejection is based not on interference estoppel, but on a determination that the subject matter of the count is the prior invention of another under §102(g), or falls within another paragraph of §102, and may be used as "prior art" in combination with other references under §103. *In re Ogiue,* 517 F.2d 1382, 186 U.S.P.Q. 227, 234 (C.C.P.A. 1975)

ᴡ

No judicial doctrine supports a rejection under 35 U.S.C. §103 on the theory that an applicant who has lost an interference can never be entitled to claims which are obvious variations of the invention defined in lost counts. An invention (defined in lost counts) apparently made outside the United States is not accorded the same effective date as a reference as it would have had, had it been made in this country. *In re McKellin, Mageli, and D'Angelo,* 529 F.2d 1324, 188 U.S.P.Q. 428, 435 (C.C.P.A. 1976).

ᴡ

A losing party to an interference, on showing that the invention now claimed is not "substantially the same" as that of the lost count, may employ the procedures of Rule 131 in order to antedate the filing date of the interfering application. The lost count of the interference is not prior art against a different invention, for prior art in the sense of 35 U.S.C. §102(g) cannot be the basis of a 35 U.S.C. §102(a) rejection, the invention not being publicly known or used. The law developed in our Rule 131 cases has little bearing on the law relating to interference practice. *In re Zletz,* 893 F.2d 319, 13 U.S.P.Q.2d 1320, 1323 (Fed. Cir. 1989).

Lost Profits. *See also* **Damages, Prejudgment Interest, Royalty, Substitute.**

The general rule for determining the actual damages to a patentee, that is itself producing the patented item, is to determine the sale and profits lost to the patentee because of the infringement. In order to recover lost profits, a patentee must show a reasonable probability that, but for the infringement, it would have made the sales that were made by the infringer. The patentee is not obliged to negate every possibility that a purchaser might not have bought the patentee's product instead of the infringing one, or might have foregone the purchase altogether. *Del Mar Avionics, Inc. v. Quinton Instrument Co.,* 836 F.2d 1320, 5 U.S.P.Q.2d 1255 (Fed. Cir. 1987).

ᴡ

Under the entire-market-value rule, a patentee is entitled to lost profits on unpatented components that accompany the sale of patented components where, in all reasonable probability, the patentee would have made the sales that the infringer made. The record shows that the company that sells the belts also gets the sales of the sprockets, transfer combs, and belt accessories. Under the entire-market-value rule, the court therefore finds that it is reasonably probable that the patentee would have sold the sprockets, transfer combs, and accessories in view of the above findings and the court's prior determination that it is reasonably probable that the patentee would have made the sales but for the infringement. *Rexnord Inc. v. Laitram Corp.,* 6 U.S.P.Q.2d 1817 (Wis. 1988).

ᴡ

To obtain lost profits, a patent owner must prove: (1) a demand for the patented product during the period of infringing sales; (2) an absence of acceptable non-infringing substitutes; (3) the patent owner had the ability to meet the demand for the products covered by the patent; and (4) the amount of profit the patent owner would have made. The amount of lost profits awarded cannot be speculative, but the amount need not be proven with unerring precision. When the amount of damages cannot be ascertained with precision, any doubts regarding the amount must be resolved against the infringer. *Ryco Inc. v. Ag-Bag Corp.*, 857 F.2d 1418, 8 U.S.P.Q.2d 1323 (Fed. Cir. 1988).

ω

To recover damages on the theory of lost profits, a patentee must show that, but for the infringement, it would have made the infringer's sales. This requirement of causation implicates the patentee's manufacturing capacity and marketing capability, the desires of customers for the claimed invention, the relationship of the claimed invention to the product sold and other factors pertinent to the particular market or parties. Causation is most easily found where only two companies, the patentee and the infringer, are in the market. Where there is evidence of a third party competitor, the lost profits theory would appear to be nonviable inasmuch as the third party could have made the sale rather than the patentee. Under such circumstances, there appears to be no possible causation. However, such is not the law. The patentees have successfully urged modifications to the basic damages theory so as to cover situations other than the simple two-supplier market. There is basis for finding causation despite an alternative source of supply if that source is an infringer or puts out a non-infringing product that is an unacceptable alternative, or has insignificant sales. Other litigants have been held entitled to lost-profits damages calculated on a portion of an infringer's sales based on the patentee's market share. *Micro Motion Inc. v. Kane Steel Co. Inc.*, 894 F.2d 1318, 13 U.S.P.Q.2d 1696, 1698 (Fed. Cir. 1990).

ω

In determining whether infringing sales caused a patentee to lose profits, the district court must have concluded: (1) that the patent owner would have made the sale but for the infringement—such as, causation existed—and (2) that proper evidence supporting the computation of lost profits was presented at trial. To obtain damages for lost profits, the patentee must prove: (1) a demand for the patented product, (2) the marketing and manufacturing capability to exploit demand, (3) an absence of acceptable noninfringing substitutes, and (4) the amount of profit the patentee would have made. *Kaufman Co. Inc. v. Lantech Inc.*, 926 F.2d 1136, 17 U.S.P.Q.2d 1828, 1831 (Fed. Cir. 1991).

ω

Lost profits (as a result of price erosion) are compensable damages that stand on the same ground as damages caused by lost sales. In most price erosion cases a patent owner has reduced the actual price of its patented product in response to an infringer's competition. A patent holder who proves that he would have increased his prices had the infringer not been in competition with him can also sustain a price erosion claim. *Micro Motion Inc. v. Exac Corp.*, 761 F. Supp. 1420, 19 U.S.P.Q.2d 1001, 1010 (Cal. 1991).

ω

Courts will not award contract damages that are too remote, too uncertain, or based wholly upon speculative expectations. A claim of lost profits on future sales, however, is possible if made "reasonably certain by proof of actual facts which present data for a rational estimate of such profits." *Standard Havens Products Inc. v. Gencor Industries Inc.*, 953 F.2d 1360, 21 U.S.P.Q.2d 1321, 1333 (Fed. Cir. 1991).

ω

Where an alleged infringer competed directly with the patent owner's product in a two-supplier market, there is no reason to deny the patentee an opportunity to prove damages he claims to have suffered as a result of the infringement and to recover lost profits even though the patent owner's product was distinctly different (covered by a different patent) and did not infringe the patent in issue. *Scripto-Tokai Corp. v. The Gillette Co.*, 788 F.Supp. 439, 22 U.S.P.Q.2d 1678, 1681 (Cal. 1992).

ω

A patent owner who has suffered lost profits is entitled to lost profits damages regardless of whether the patent owner has made, used, or sold the patented device. *King Instrument Corp. v. Perego*, 65 F.3d 941, 36 U.S.P.Q.2d 1129, 1133 (Fed. Cir. 1995).

ω

There is precedent for finding causation for lost profits damages if the alternative source of supply is an infringer. *Pall Corp. v. Micron Separations Inc.*, 66 F.3d 1211, 36 U.S.P.Q.2d 1225, 1233 (Fed. Cir. 1995).

ω

When a two-supplier market exists, it is reasonable to assume that the patentee would have made the infringer's sales. This conclusion comports with the rationale that in a two-supplier market, one being the patentee and the other being an infringer, there is necessarily an absence of acceptable noninfringing substitutes. *The Read Corp. v. Freiday*, 38 U.S.P.Q.2d 1220, 1222 (Fed. Cir. 1995—*unpublished, not citable as precedent*).

ω

Where there is a doubt as to the profit margin, the Court must construe the facts in favor of the patentee. *Joy Technologies Inc. v. Flakt Inc.*, 42 U.S.P.Q.2d 1042 (Del. 1996).

Lost Profits Damages.

If defendant, unlike the infringer in *Rite-Hite Corp. v. Kelley Co.*, 1995, U.S. App. Lexis 14681, 56 F.3d 1538, 35 U.S.P.Q.2d 1065 (Fed. Cir. 1995) (en banc), was able to offer perfectly lawful competition, then plaintiff cannot show lost-profits damages. *Grain Processing Corp. v. American Maize-Products Co.*, 893 F.Supp. 1386, 37 U.S.P.Q.2d 1299, 1303 (Ind. 1995).

Lower.[4]

Luck.

"[T]he inspiration-perspiration process of the laboratory" is as deserving of reward as the flash of genius, and surely more so than dumb luck. *Carter-Wallace, Inc. v. Otte*, 474 F.2d 529, 176 U.S.P.Q. 2, 12 (2d Cir. 1972).

---

[4]The term "lower" is a term of chemical art which (when applied to an aliphatic radical, such as alkyl, alkoxy, alkenyl, alkynyl, alkylthio, haloalkyl, alkanoyl, alkylamino and hydroxyalkyl) normally refers to a radical having up to six to eight carbon atoms unless expressly limited otherwise. The term is also applied to compounds, such as lower alkanes, lower alkenes and lower olefins. Examples of patent claims containing this term are found in the following patents issued over a period of twenty years in the United States: 3,840,598; 3,849,412; 4,255,431; 4,470,980; 5,641,859; 5,652,237; 5,652,241; 5,652,247.

Key Terms and Concepts

M

Machine. *See also* **Apparatus.**

The fact that a claim reads on a general purpose computer program used to carry out a claimed invention does not, by itself, justify holding that the claim is unpatentable as directed to nonstatutory subject matter. Such programming creates a new machine, because a general purpose computer in effect becomes a special purpose computer once it is programmed to perform particular functions pursuant to instructions from program software. *In re Alappat*, 33 F.3d 1526, 1544, 31 U.S.P.Q.2d 1545, 1558 (Fed. Cir. 1994).

Made.

The meaning of "made" in Executive Order No. 10096 is interpreted in the same way as the meaning of "made" in laws passed by Congress also dealing with rights to inventions made with government resources. Some statutes specifically define "made" as being conception or the first actual reduction to practice. These statutes provide that the government shall have rights in inventions that are conceived or first actually reduced to practice using government resources. In other statutes the word "made" would not necessarily include "conceived." The word "made" in Executive Order No. 10096 will be construed to mean conceived or first actually reduced to practice. Thus, if government resources are used by or on behalf of a government employee to either conceive or first actually reduce to practice an invention, then the invention can be deemed to have been "made" within the meaning of paragraph l(a) of the Executive Order. *In re King*, 3 U.S.P.Q.2d 1747, 1750, 1751 (Comm'r Patents & Trademarks 1987).

Magistrate Judge.

When a matter has been referred to a magistrate judge, acting as a special master or 28 U.S.C. §636(b)(2) jurist, a party waives his right to appeal if he has not preserved the issues for appeal by first presenting them to the District Judge as objections to the magistrate judge's order. Pursuant to Rule (FRCP) 72(a), parties are given ten days following entry of the Order to file exceptions thereto. *THK America Inc. v. Nippon Seiko K.K.*, 141 F.R.D. 463, 21 U.S.P.Q.2d 1705, 1707 (Ill. 1991).

Magistrate's Order.

Motions on nondispositive matters, which are ordinarily referred to a magistrate to "hear and determine" pursuant to 28 U.S.C. §636(b)(1)(A), may be reconsidered only where the magistrate's order is "clearly erroneous or contrary to law." *General Electric Co. v. Hoechst Celanese Corp.*, 740 F. Supp. 305, 15 U.S.P.Q.2d 1673, 1676 (Del. 1990).

Maintenance Fee. *See also* **Reinstatement.**

In determining whether a delay in paying a maintenance fee was unavoidable, one looks to whether the party responsible for payment of the maintenance fee exercised the due care of a reasonably prudent person. *Ray v. Lehman*, 55 F.3d 606, 34 U.S.P.Q.2d 1786, 1787 (Fed. Cir. 1995).

ω

The language of the first sentence of 35 U.S.C. 41(c)(2) and several courts' interpretations of the corresponding provision in 35 U.S.C. §252 entitle defendants to "absolute" intervening rights in a case wherein they constructed the "specific thing" patented after the six-month grace period but before the late maintenance fee was accepted. *Haden Schweitzer Corp. v. Arthur B. Myr Industries Inc.*, 901 F.Supp. 1235, 36 U.S.P.Q.2d 1020, 1026 (Mich. 1995).

Make.

The absence of a known or obvious process for making the claimed compounds overcomes a presumption that the compounds are obvious, based on close relationships between their structures and those of prior art compounds. *In re Hoeksema*, 399 F.2d 269, 158 U.S.P.Q. 596, 601 (C.C.P.A. 1968).

ω

"[M]akes" [in the context of 35 U.S.C. §271(a)] means what it ordinarily connotes— the substantial manufacture of the constituent parts of a machine. *The Laitram Corporation v. Deepsouth Packing Co., Inc.*, 443 F.2d 269, 170 U.S.P.Q. 196, 198 (5th Cir. 1971).

ω

The rejection of a compound claim for anticipation under 35 U.S.C. §102(b) does not preclude reliance on additional evidence to show that one of ordinary skill in the art would have known how to prepare the claimed compound(s) at the time appellants' invention was made. *In re Wiggins, James, and Gittos*, 488 F.2d 538, 179 U.S.P.Q. 421, 424 (C.C.P.A. 1973).

Making. *See* **Method of Making, Starting Material.**

Making Adjustable. *See* **Adjustability.**

Making Integral.

The mere integration of elements that were previously in two or more parts is not generally of patentable significance. *In re Fridolph*, 309 F.2d 509, 135 U.S.P.Q. 319, 321 (C.C.P.A. 1962). See also *In re Larson, Russler, and Meldahl*, 340 F.2d 965, 144 U.S.P.Q. 347, 349 (C.C.P.A. 1965).

ω

The defense that making a support structure in one piece "does not rise to the standard of invention" is passé in view of the establishment of nonobviousness as the standard. *Carl Schenk, A.G. v. Nortron Corporation*, 713 F.2d 782, 218 U.S.P.Q. 698, 699 (Fed. Cir. 1983).

Making Portable. *See* **Portable.**

Making Separate. *See* **Separable.**

Mammal.[1] *See* **Life Form.**

Mandamus. *See also* **Extraordinary Writ.**

A party seeking a writ bears the burden of proving that it has no other means of attaining the relief desired and the right to issuance of the writ is "clear and indisputable." *Allied Chemical Corp. v. Daiflon, Inc.*, 449 U.S. 33, 35 (1980).

ω

Mandamus is available only in extraordinary situations to correct a clear abuse of discretion or usurpation of judicial power. *In re Calmar, Inc*, 854 F.2d 461, 464, 7 U.S.P.Q.2d 1713 (Fed. Cir. 1988).

ω

Three separate statutory provisions together operate to confer jurisdiction on the federal district court with regard to a motion for a temporary restraining order to enjoin the Commissioner of Patents and Trademarks from continuing a reexamination proceeding. First, the question in this suit "arises under" a law or laws of the United States. Second, Congress has waived, in 5 U.S.C. §702, the bar of sovereign immunity which would otherwise deprive the federal district court of jurisdiction under 28 U.S.C. §1331. Third, by enactment of 28 U.S.C. §1361, Congress specifically and irrefutably vested jurisdiction in all district courts to entertain suits in the nature of mandamus. *Standard Havens Inc. v. Manbeck*, 762 F.Supp. 1349, 21 U.S.P.Q.2d 1635, 1636 (Mo. 1991).

ω

In those cases in which the CAFC, and only the CAFC, has jurisdiction over any appeal from a final decision, the CAFC has jurisdiction to hear and decide a mandamus petition. Issues properly before the Federal Circuit on appeal are no less within its jurisdiction when raised by extraordinary writ. *In re University of California*, 964 F.2d 1128, 22 U.S.P.Q.2d 1748, 1750 (Fed. Cir. 1992).

ω

If the district court's jurisdiction rests on a patent claim, then an appeal from an entirely non-patent disposition goes to the federal circuit. Because mandamus is designed to aid or anticipate jurisdiction, a court that lacks jurisdiction over the final decision lacks power to issue a writ of mandamus. *In re BBC International Ltd.*, 40 U.S.P.Q.2d 1381, 1382 (7th Cir. 1996).

ω

---

[1](Refer to U.S. Patent No. 4,736,866.)

Mandamus review may be granted of discovery orders that turn on claims of privilege when (1) there is raised an important issue of first impression, (2) the privilege would be lost if review were denied until final judgment, and (3) immediate resolution would avoid the development of doctrine that would undermine the privilege. *In re University of California*, 40 U.S.P.Q.2d 1784, 1785 (Fed. Cir. 1996).

ω

"A writ of mandamus may be sought to prevent the wrongful exposure of privileged communications." *In re Rhône-Poulenc Rorer Inc.*, 48 U.S.P.Q.2d 1823, 1825 (Fed. Cir. 1998 - *unpublished*).

Mandate.

The Commissioner lacks authority to reopen the reexamination proceeding after receipt of the Federal Circuit's mandate affirming the Examiner's rejection of all claims since the case is no longer considered pending. See MPEP §1216.06 (5th ed., rev. 12, July 1989) under "Office Procedure Following Decision by the Federal Circuit," subheading "1. All claims rejected"; *Morganroth v. Quigg*, 885 F.2d 843, 12 U.S.P.Q.2d 1125, 1128 (Fed. Cir. 1989) (Commissioner does not have authority to revive application abandoned by termination of proceedings resulting from a failure to appeal a final district court judgment); Petitioner's relief, if any, lies in a motion for the Federal Circuit to withdraw its mandate, not with the Commissioner. *See Jones*, 542 F.2d at 68, 191 U.S.P.Q. at 252 (CCPA "has the power, in the interest of justice, to recall its mandate in an appropriate case, and this power should be exercised sparingly and only upon a showing of good cause"). *In re Eckerle*, 1115 O.G. 6 (Commr. Patents & Trademarks 1990). *In re Jones*, 542 F.2d 65, 191 U.S.P.Q. 249, 252 (C.C.P.A. 1976) ("receipt of the mandate by the PTO terminated proceedings in the case"); *In re Willis*, 537 F.2d 513, 190 U.S.P.Q. 327, 329 (C.C.P.A. 1976) ("When, on January 12, 1976, our mandate was received in the PTO, no claims having been allowed, the appealed application suffered its demise."); *Continental Can Co. v. Schuyler*, 326 F. Supp. 283, 168 U.S.P.Q. 625 (D.C. 1970) ("where rejection of all claims is affirmed by the Court of Customs and Patent Appeals, the responsibility is upon the plaintiff to stay the Court's judgment if the pendency of the application is to be preserved").

ω

The interpretation by an appellate court of its own mandate is properly considered a question of law, reviewable de novo. *Laitram Corp. v. NEC Corp.*, 42 U.S.P.Q.2d 1897, 1899 (Fed. Cir. 1997).

Mandate Rule.

The mandate rule, a specific application of the law of the case doctrine, requires this (District) Court to comply with the command of an appellate court on remand. The mandate rule is subject to "a modicum of residual flexibility"; in the absence of any change in controlling legal authority, new evidence, or blatant error in the decision that will result in manifest injustice, this (District) Court declines to depart from the Federal Circuit's mandate. *Stark v. Advanced Magnetics Inc.*, 894 F.Supp. 555, 36 U.S.P.Q.2d 1764, 1766, 1767 n.2 (Mass. 1995).

Man of Ordinary Skill in the Art. *See* MOSITA.

Manual of Patent Examining Procedure. *See* MPEP.

Manufacture. *See also* **Apparatus, Article, Product, Statutory Subject Matter.**

Neither mere material without form nor highly fugitive articles, such as a gob of molten glass, are included by the term "manufacture." However, an article of commerce is included even when it is material in an intermediate stage of manufacture. *Ex parte Howard*, 328 O.G. 251, 1924 C.D. 75 (Asst. Comm'r 1922). *But see* Transitory.

ω

An article is prepared "for use from raw or prepared materials by giving to these materials new forms, qualities, properties, or combinations, whether by hand labor or by machinery." Addition of borax to the rind of natural fruit does not produce from the raw material an article for use that possesses a new or distinctive form, quality, or property. The added substance only protects the natural article against deterioration by inhibiting development of extraneous spores upon the rind. There is no change in the name, appearance, or general character of the fruit. To be a manufacture, there must be a transformation; a new and different article must emerge having a distinctive name, characteristic, or use. *American Fruit Growers, Inc. v. Brogdex Co.*, 283 U.S. 1, 8 U.S.P.Q. 131 (1931).

ω

The method of manufacture may be relevant to the patentability of claims drawn to articles. *In re Epple and Kaiser*, 477 F.2d 582, 177 U.S.P.Q. 696, 699 (C.C.P.A. 1973).

ω

Under 35 U.S.C. §101 a person may have invented a machine or manufacture, which may include anything under the sun that is made by humans. A microorganism that is not a hitherto unknown natural phenomenon, but a non-naturally occurring manufacture or composition of matter, a product of human ingenuity having a distinctive name, character, and use, plainly qualifies as patentable subject matter. *Diamond, Commissioner of Patents and Trademarks v. Chakrabarty*, 447 U.S. 303, 206 U.S.P.Q. 193, 197 (1980).

ω

A memory containing a stored data structure is distinguishable from printed matter by requiring that contained information be processed not by the mind but by a machine, a computer. Claims directed to a memory containing stored information recite an article of manufacture, statutory subject matter. *In re Lowry*, 32 F.3d 1579, 1583, 32 U.S.P.Q.2d 1031, 1033, 1034 (Fed. Cir. 1994).

Manufacturer.

Where a manufacturer's product does not infringe a patent in question, but its customers use the product to make an infringing device, courts typically hold that the manufacturer lacks any reasonable apprehension of suit for direct infringement, even if the customers are being threatened with legal action. Customer suit cases show that a manufacturer generally can establish jurisdiction based on a threat of suit against its customer only when the manufacturer is itself involved in infringing the patent and the customer is "merely a conduit for the manufacturer." *The Dow Chemical Co. v. Viskase Corp.*, 892 F. Supp. 991, 36 U.S.P.Q.2d 1490, 1493, 1494 (Ill. 1995).

Manuscript.

A printed publication does not constitute a reduction to practice; it is evidence of conception only. The same would certainly be true of the manuscript on which a publication is based. *In re Schlittler and Uffer*, 234 F.2d 882, 110 U.S.P.Q. 304, 305, 306 (C.C.P.A. 1956).

Manuscript Decisions.[2]

Market.

The contention that, since in excess of 110 customer-licensees of plaintiff have been and are forced, by contract, to purchase unpatented connector plates from plaintiff, they are compelled at the same time not to purchase them from defendant is not supported by the record because the defendant has not shown (with reasonable certainty and probability) that its prospective market for sales of unpatented connector plates has been effectively reduced and restricted by the customers who have assumedly been removed from the arena of competition and brought under compulsion to purchase from plaintiff. *Automated Building Components, Inc. v. Hydro-Air Engineering, Inc.*, 237 F.Supp. 247, 144 U.S.P.Q. 631, 636 (Mo. 1964).

ω

An implied obligation to exploit a licensed patent is not binding on an exclusive licensee if its observance would prevent the licensee from meeting market competition with a reasonable chance of success. *William Hodges & Co., Inc. v. Sterwood Corp.*, 348 F.Supp. 383, 176 U.S.P.Q. 49, 57 (N.Y. 1972).

ω

The boundaries of a relevant market "may be determined by examining such practical indicia as industry or public recognition of the submarket as a separate economic entity, the product's peculiar characteristics or uses, unique production facilities, distinct customers, distinct prices, sensitivity to price changes, and specialized vendors." *Image Technical Services Inc. v. Eastman Kodak Co.*, 125 F.3d 1195, 44 U.S.P.Q.2d 1065, 1069 (9th Cir. 1997).

Marketability.

A display of a claimed invention to a limited number of buyers at a trade show (at which no purchase orders were solicited or accepted) in order to assess its marketability is not a public use. *Maclaren v. B-I-W Group Inc.*, 401 F.Supp. 283, 187 U.S.P.Q. 345, 358 (N.Y. 1975).

ω

---

[2] *See Irons v. Gottschalk*, 369 F.Supp. 403, 180 U.S.P.Q. 492 (D.C. 1974).

The testing of the marketability of a product may constitute an experimental use under appropriate circumstances. *Interlego A. G. v. F.A.O. Schwartz, Inc.*, 191 U.S.P.Q. 129, 133 (Ga. 1976).

Market Participant.

The Supreme Court suggested in dicta that there may be a market participant exception to state immunity. *See City of Columbia and Columbia Outdoor Advertising v. Omni Outdoor Advertising*, 499 U.S. 365, 111 S.Ct. 1344, 113 L.Ed.2d 382 (1991). As yet, however, the market participant exception is merely a suggestion and is not a rule of law. *Paragould Cablevision v. City of Paragould, Ark.*, 930 F.2d 1310 (8th Cir.), *cert. denied*, 112 S.Ct. 430, 116 L.Ed.2d 450 (1991).

Market Power.

Maintenance and enforcement of a patent procured by knowing and willful fraud may meet the intent and conduct elements of violation of the Sherman Act, provided that the ability to lessen or destroy competition, including market power in the relevant market, can also be shown. A patent does not of itself establish a presumption of market power in the antitrust sense. Determination of whether a patentee meets the Sherman Act elements of monopolization or attempt to monopolize is governed by the rules of application of the antitrust laws to market participants, with due consideration to the exclusivity that inheres in the patent grant. *Abbott Laboratories v. Brennan*, 952 F.2d 1346, 21 U.S.P.Q.2d 1192, 1199 (Fed. Cir. 1991).

ᖶ

"Any effort to enlarge the scope of a patent monopoly by using the market power it confers to restrain competition in the market for a second product will undermine competition on the merits in that second market." (The ability to compel a purchaser to do something he would not do in a competitive market is usually called "market power.") *DiscoVision Associates v. Disc Manufacturing Inc.*, 42 U.S.P.Q.2d 1749, 1758, 1759 (Del. 1997).

ᖶ

To demonstrate market power by circumstantial evidence, a plaintiff must: "(1) define the relevant market, (2) show that the defendant owns a dominant share of that market, and (3) show that there are significant barriers to entry and show that existing competitors lack the capacity to increase their output in the short run." *Image Technical Services Inc. v. Eastman Kodak Co.*, 125 F.3d 1195, 44 U.S.P.Q.2d 1065, 1068 (9th Cir. 1997).

Market Share.

Loss of market share constitutes irreparable injury "because market share is so difficult to recover." *Ortho Pharmaceutical Corp. v. Smith*, 15 U.S.P.Q.2d 1856, 1863 (Pa. 1990).

ᖶ

Neither the difficulty in calculating losses in market share nor speculation that such losses may occur amount to proof of special circumstances justifying the extraordinary relief of an injunction prior to trial. *Nutrition 21 v. United States*, 930 F.2d 867, 18 U.S.P.Q.2d 1347, 1351 (Fed. Cir. 1991).

ᛒ

Proof of loss in market share is not sufficient to support a finding of irreparable harm if it is speculative. The fact that any sale of a product infringing on the patent is potentially one less sale for the patent owner (because the patent gives its owner an exclusive license) is not speculative but rather lends support to provided testimony. *Motorola Inc. v. Alexander Manufacturing Co.*, 786 F.Supp. 808, 21 U.S.P.Q.2d 1573, 1578 (Iowa 1991).

ᛒ

Loss of market share has itself been recognized as an irreparable injury because it is so difficult to recover. *Maitland Co. Inc. v. Terra First Inc.*, 33 U.S.P.Q.2d 1882, 1892 (S.C. 1994).

ᛒ

"[M]arket share percentages may give rise to presumptions, but will rarely conclusively establish or eliminate market or monopoly power." *Ultradent Products Inc. v. Life-Like Cosmetics Inc.*, 39 U.S.P.Q.2d 1969, 1980 (Utah 1996)

Market Value Rule.

Under the entire-market-value rule, a patentee is entitled to lost profits on unpatented components that accompany the sale of patented components where, in all reasonable probability, the patentee would have made the sales that the infringer made. The record shows that the company that sells the belts also gets the sales of the sprockets, transfer combs, and belt accessories. Under the entire-market-value rule, the court therefore finds that it is reasonably probable that the patentee would have sold the sprockets, transfer combs, and accessories in view of the above findings and the court's prior determination that it is reasonably probable that the patentee would have made the sales but for the infringement. *Rexnord Inc. v. Laitram Corp.*, 6 U.S.P.Q.2d 1817 (Wis. 1988).

Marking. *See also* False Marking, Marking Estoppel, Mismarking.

When products are covered by one of several patents listed on an attached label, they are not "unpatented products", and the statute (35 U.S.C. §292), by its terms, is not applicable. The plain language of the statute, being penal in nature, must be strictly construed. *The Ansul Company v. Uniroyal, Inc.*, 306 F.Supp. 541, 163 U.S.P.Q. 517, 536 (N.Y. 1969).

ᛒ

The controlling standard regarding false marking is not whether the patent incontravertably covers the product, but whether it reads on the product so that a person could hold an honest belief that it applied. *United States on relation of Scharmer v. Carrollton Manufacturing Company*, 377 F.Supp. 218, 181 U.S.P.Q. 451, 453 (Ohio 1974).

ᛒ

The fact that a nonlicensee purchaser of a patented bulk product (appropriately marked with the patent number) repackaged and sold the product without marking it with the patent number does not bar the patentee's right to recover damages despite the lack of actual notice to the defendant. *Analytical Controls v. American Hospital Supply Corp.*, 518 F. Supp. 896, 217 U.S.P.Q. 1004 (Ind. 1981).

ω

The notice requirements of 35 U.S.C. §287 do not apply to a patent directed to a process or method. *Bandag Inc. v. Gerrard Tire Co., Inc. v. Leonard*, 217 U.S.P.Q. 769, 771 (N.C. 1982).

ω

Since the Government does not consider the question whether the device it takes by eminent domain is protected by patents or not, requiring a patent owner to mark his device or to give notice pursuant to 35 U.S.C. §287 would be meaningless in this context. Accordingly, §287 is not incorporated into 28 U.S.C. §1498 by Government procurement policy. *Motorola, Inc. v. United States*, 729 F.2d 765, 221 U.S.P.Q. 297, 302 (Fed. Cir. 1984).

ω

According to a line of "marking estoppel" cases, a party that marked its product with a patent number is, under some circumstances, estopped from asserting that the product is not covered by the patent. An admittedly non-infringing product cannot be converted by estoppel to an infringing product. *SmithKline Diagnostics, Inc. v. Helena Laboratories Corp.*, 859 F.2d 878, 8 U.S.P.Q.2d 1468 (Fed. Cir. 1988).

ω

The notice provision of 35 U.S.C. §287 is liberally construed. It is satisfied whenever the infringer is notified of the same information which the statute requires for patent marking, which need only include the word "patent", or its abbreviation, and the patent number. It does not appear that the notice must be accompanied by a threat of litigation, as an offer of a license of a patented article has been held to constitute actual notice under 35 U.S.C. §287. *Konstant Products Inc. v. Frazier Industrial Co. Inc.*, 25 U.S.P.Q.2d 1223, 1226 (Ill. 1992).

ω

Alternative marking of a package may sufficiently comply with the statute when there is some reasonable consideration presented for not marking the article due to physical constraints or other limitations, or, for reasons that go to the very purpose of the statute, marking the article itself would not provide sufficient notice to the public. *In re Asta Medica S.A.*, 981 F.2d 1, 25 U.S.P.Q.2d 1861, 1869 (1st Cir. 1992).

ω

A patentee's shipping unmarked (patented) products misleads the public into thinking that the product is freely available. *American Medical Systems Inc. v. Medical Engineering Corp.*, 6 F.3d 1523, 28 U.S.P.Q.2d 1321, 1332 (Fed. Cir. 1993).

ω

Patentee's customers, to whom patentee sold one element of the patented combination with the expectation that they would use that element to make and sell the patented invention, were implied licensees who were "making or selling [the] patented article for or under [patentee]" within the meaning of 35 U.S.C. §287. "The distribution or manufacturing arrangement of a patentee, unilaterally chosen by the patentee, cannot be allowed to relieve the patentee of its duty to mark under Section 287." A licensee who makes or sells a patented article does so "for or under" the patentee, thereby limiting the patentee's damage recovery when the patented article is not marked. *Amsted Industries Inc. v. Buckeye Steel Castings Co.*, 24 F.3d 178, 30 U.S.P.Q.2d 1462, 1467 (Fed. Cir. 1994).

ᙡ

With third parties unrelated to a patentee, it is often more difficult for the patentee to assure compliance with the marking provisions. A "rule of reason" approach is justified in such a case, and substantial compliance may be found to satisfy the statute. *Maxwell v. J. Baker Inc.*, 86 F.3d 1098, 39 U.S.P.Q.2d 1001, 1010 (Fed. Cir. 1996).

ᙡ

The statute that limits recovery in cases where there is no marking refers only to damages. Historically, disgorgement, which is really what the plaintiff seeks in its actions for infringers' profits, was not considered a recovery of damages, but an equitable remedy to restore to the proper owner profits made by an infringer's use of another's property. The limitations imposed by 35 U.S.C. §287(a) are not applicable to an action seeking recovery of an infringer's profits pursuant to 35 U.S.C. §289. *Nike Inc. v. Wal-Mart Stores Inc.*, 41 U.S.P.Q.2d 1146, 1149 (Va. 1996).

ᙡ

Where a patent contains both apparatus and method claims, to the extent to which there is a tangible item to mark by which notice of the asserted method claims can be given, a party is obliged to do so if it intends to avail itself of the constructive notice provisions of 35 U.S.C. §287(a). *American Bank Note Holographics Inc. v. The Upper Deck Co.*, 41 U.S.P.Q.2d 2019, 2020 (N.Y. 1997).

ᙡ

"When failure to mark is caused by someone other than the patentee, the court may consider whether the patentee made reasonable efforts to ensure compliance with the marking requirements." The Federal Circuit has stated, in dicta, that "once marking has begun, it must be substantially consistent and continuous in order for the party to avail itself of the constructive notice provisions of the statute." *Clancy Systems International Inc. v. Symbol Technologies Inc.*, 42 U.S.P.Q.2d 1290, 1292, 1293 (Col. 1997).

ᙡ

When patent claims are directed to a product which is sold as a bulk liquid, storage tanks are the "packages" (subject to marking) in which the patented article is found. *Western Emulsions Inc. v. Copperstate Emulsions Inc.*, 42 U.S.P.Q.2d 1856, 1861 (Ariz. 1997).

ᙡ

The marking statute applies to actions for recovery of the infringer's profits. *Nike Inc. v. Wal-Mart Stores Inc.*, 138 F.3d 1437, 46 U.S.P.Q.2d 1001, 1007 (Fed. Cir. 1998).

Marking Estoppel.

Marking a product with a patent number estops the marking party from either avoiding royalty liability or asserting non-infringement in an action by the patentee. Discontinuance of marking will not obviate or cure the estoppel. While wrongful intent has been held to be a necessary element of proof in patent "mismarking" cases under 35 U.S.C. §292, no similar requirement is found in "marking estoppel" cases. *Crane Co. v. Aeroquip Corporation*, 364 F.Supp. 547, 179 U.S.P.Q. 596, 606 (Ill. 1973).

Markman Trial.

The exact character of a *Markman* trial is currently unsettled in the federal courts. What is clear is that prior to the jury trial portion of a patent case, the court must hear arguments, take evidence as it deems necessary in its discretion, and make a determination, as to the meaning and scope of the patent claims in question. *Huang v. Auto-Shade Inc.*, 41 U.S.P.Q.2d 1053 (Cal. 1996).

Markush.[3] *See also* **Borcherdt Doctrine, Improper Markush, Nucleus, Restriction, Unity of Invention.**

Markush groups—so-called from the title of the case in which they were first permitted (*Ex parte Markush*, 1925 C.D. 126)—were originally regarded as an exception to the previously acceptable claim terminology and were rigidly restricted to groups of substances belonging to some recognized class. However, the original rigid, emergency-engendered restrictions have been progressively relaxed through the years to the point where it is no longer possible to indulge in a presumption that the members of a Markush group are recognized by anyone to be equivalents except as they "possess at least one property in common which is mainly responsible for their function in the claimed relationship." Actual equivalence is not enough to justify refusal of a patent on one member of a group when another member is in the prior art. The equivalence must be disclosed in the prior art or be obvious within the terms of 35 U.S.C. §103. *In re Ruff and Dukeshire*, 256 F.2d 590, 118 U.S.P.Q. 340, 348 (C.C.P.A. 1958).

ᚥ

An applicant is not entitled to examination of more than one invention under 35 U.S.C. §131, even when they are included in a single Markush-type claim. *Rohm and Haas Company v. Commissioner of Patents*, 387 F.Supp. 673, 177 U.S.P.Q. 625, 626, 627 (D.C. 1973).

ᚥ

A Markush group in a claim is a representation that, for the purposes of the claimed invention, the elements of the group are equivalents, and an applicant cannot argue to the contrary. *In re Skoll*, 523 F.2d 1392, 187 U.S.P.Q. 481, 484, 485 (C.C.P.A. 1975).

ᚥ

The fact that different fields of search are involved does not establish that a Markush

---

[3]*See* MPEP §803.02.

group is improper. *Ex parte Brouard, Leroy, and Stiot*, 201 U.S.P.Q. 538, 540 (PTO Bd. App. 1976).

ω

As all of the claimed compounds are dyes and are coumarin compounds (i.e., have a single structural similarity), the claimed compounds all belong to a subgenus that is not repugnant to scientific classification. Under these circumstances, the claimed compounds are part of a single invention; the requisite "unity of invention" is thus satisfied. *In re Harnisch*, 631 F.2d 716, 206 U.S.P.Q. 300, 305 (C.C.P.A. 1980).

ω

The determinative factor for establishing whether a Markush group is proper is whether "unity of invention" exists or whether the claims are drawn to a collection of "unrelated inventions." When all of the claimed subject matter has in common a functional utility related to a substantial, structural feature disclosed as being essential to that utility, adequate unity of invention is present. *Ex parte Hozumi*, 3 U.S.P.Q.2d 1059 (B.P.A.I. 1984).

ω

A rejection of a claim for containing an improper Markush group was reversed. The encompassed compounds were sequential intermediates in a process for synthesizing a patented compound. The criteria for evaluating the propriety of a Markush group are (1) structural similarity and (2) "unity of invention." When these two criteria are met, the Markush group is proper even when it involves and embraces intermediates of each other. Unity of invention encompasses both structural similarity and communality of properties and/or utility. Here, the Markush group members are structurally similar. The fact that the group members are used seriately to make a patented product is indicative of the same invention being involved, each member being a precursor of the other and leading to the making of a novel and useful material. Each of the individual members of the Markush group has no utility except in the chain of reaction leading to the patented product. As such, common utility is present within the meaning of the unity-of-invention requirement, the claimed intermediates being the cause and effect of the property and usefulness of the final patented product. *Ex parte Della Bella and Chiarino*, 7 U.S.P.Q.2d 1669 (B.P.A.I. 1984).

ω

It is never proper for an Examiner to reject a Markush claim under 35 U.S.C. §121. Section 121 simply does not authorize such a rejection. *In re Watkinson*, 900 F.2d 230, 14 U.S.P.Q.2d 1407, 1409 (Fed. Cir. 1990).

Maskwork.[4] *See* **Maskwork Act.**

---

[4] Maskworks are defined in 17 U.S.C. §901(a)(2) as:
A series of related images, however fixed or encoded—

> a) having or representing the predetermined, three dimensional pattern of metallic, insulating or semiconductor material present or removed from the layers of a semiconductor chip product; and

> b) in which series the relation of the images to one another is that each image has the pattern of the surface of one form of the semiconductor chip product.

Maskwork Act. *See also* **Reverse Engineering.**

The Maskwork Act protects against the literal copying of a maskwork and against the misappropriation of a material portion of a maskwork. However, the Maskwork Act does not prohibit independent development of a maskwork; an identical but original second maskwork is not an infringement of the first. In addition, the Maskwork Act specifically allows for reverse engineering. *Brooktree Corp. v. Advanced Micro Devices, Inc.*, 705 F. Supp. 491, 10 U.S.P.Q.2d 1374, 1376 (Cal. 1988).

ω

If the copied portion is qualitatively important, the finder of fact may properly find substantial similarity under the Semiconductor Chip Protection Act. No hard and fast percentages govern what constitutes a "substantial" copying because substantial similarity may exist where an important part of a maskwork is copied even though the percentage copied may be relatively small. *Brooktree Corp. v. Advanced Micro Devices Inc.*, 977 F.2d 1555, 24 U.S.P.Q.2d 1401, 1406, 1407 (Fed. Cir. 1992).

Master.

A master's findings of fact are reviewed by a District Judge as an appellate tribunal under the typical restraints imposed by the "clearly erroneous" rule. A decision by the CAFC that the district court erred in setting aside a finding of the master will necessarily make a contrary finding by the district court ineffectual. The CAFC evaluates the district court's decision on an objection to the master's report, not the district court's substitute finding. Upholding the district court ruling that the master's finding was clearly erroneous does not ipso facto uphold a substitute finding by the district court. The latter is subject to review in accordance with Rule 52(a). The CAFC must review, as a matter of law, the correctness of the district court's setting aside any factual finding by the master and, if that is upheld, review any substitute or additional findings of the district court under the "clearly erroneous" standard of Rule 52(a). *Milliken Research Corporation v. Dan River, Inc.*, 739 F.2d 587, 222 U.S.P.Q. 571, 575, 576 (Fed. Cir. 1984).

Material. *See also* **Materiality, Material Prejudice, Method, Saving.**

Where a machine has acquired new functions and useful properties, it may be patentable, though the only change made in the machine has been supplanting one of its materials by another. The use of hard rubber for a set of artificial teeth was held to be patentable; the artificial teeth were light and elastic, easily adapted to the contour of the mouth, and flexible, yet firm and strong. *Smith v. Goodyear Dental Vulcanite Co.*, 93 U.S. 486, 493 (1877).

ω

Substitution of a celluloid cap for a metal or glass top for a saltcellar (dredge) yields a new function by insulating salt in the cellar from the humidity of external air, a function

---

Chapter 9 provides for a ten-year term of protection for original maskworks, measured from the earlier of their date of registration in the U.S. Copyright Office, or their first commercial exploitation anywhere in the world. Maskworks must be registered within two years of their first commercial exploitation to maintain protection.

performed by neither glass nor metal. Even though the patentee did not know of this peculiar function (which keeps salt in a salt shaker from caking) at the time the patent was applied for, such is not fatal to the validity of the issued patent. *Westmoreland Specialty Co. v. Hogan*, 167 F. 327, 328 (3d Cir. 1909).

ω

Substitution of a nickel-chromium alloy for ineffective and practically discarded prior-art electrical resistance elements was such a remarkable advance that it turned failure into unquestioned success and involved patentable invention. *General Electric Co. v. Hoskins Manufacturing Co.*, 224 F. 464, 468 (7th Cir. 1915).

ω

A mere change in proportion involves only mechanical skill and does not amount to invention, nor is it invention to adopt different materials in the construction of a device. *Hugh W. Batcheller v. Henry Cole Co.*, 7 F. Supp. 898, 22 U.S.P.Q. 354, 358 (Mass. 1934).

ω

A combination of a device and the material upon which the device works is not patentable. *In re Hodler*, 73 F.2d 507, 23 U.S.P.Q. 317, 320 (C.C.P.A. 1934).

ω

Merely substituting superior for inferior materials, in making one or more or all of the parts of a machine or manufacture, is not invention, although the substitution may be of materials that are both new and useful in high degree. As exceptions to this general rule, when the substitution involves a new mode of construction, when it develops new properties and uses of the article made, when it produces a new mode of operation or results in a new function, when it is the first practical success in the art in which the substitution is made, or when the practice shows its superiority to consist not only in greater cheapness and greater utility, but also in more efficient action, it may amount to invention. *Gasoline Products Co., Inc. v. Conway P. Coe*, 87 F.2d 550, 31 U.S.P.Q. 407, 413 (D.C. Cir. 1936).

ω

The substitution of one material for another does not involve invention, regardless of any improvement growing out of the substitution, if the prior art reasonably taught or suggested the expediency thereof to the worker ordinarily skilled in the art. *In re Krogman*, 223 F.2d 497, 106 U.S.P.Q. 276, 279 (C.C.P.A. 1955).

ω

The mere selection of a different known material from which a claimed product is made on the basis of suitability for intended use is entirely obvious under 35 U.S.C. §103. *In re Leshin*, 277 F.2d 197, 125 U.S.P.Q. 416, 418 (C.C.P.A. 1960).

ω

The Patent Act of 1952, 35 U.S.C. §100(b), specifies that "process . . . includes a new use of a known process, machine, manufacture, composition of matter, or material." Therefore, the material employed in carrying out a claimed process cannot be ignored in resolving the question of patentability of process claims. *Ex parte Macy*, 132 U.S.P.Q. 545, 546 (PO Bd. App. 1960).

ω

Materials on which a process is carried out must be accorded weight in determining the obviousness of that process. *Ex parte Leonard and Brandes*, 187 U.S.P.Q. 122 (PTO Bd. App. 1974).

ω

The "before and after" actions and judgments of those in the field are the most persuasive evidence that the claimed subject matter was an unobvious development. After Teflon-bonded electrodes became known, virtually the entire industry shifted to it, even though no one understood why the electrode was so superior to the prior art. *Leesona Corporation v. United States*, 185 U.S.P.Q. 156, 161 (U.S. Ct. Cl. 1975).

ω

The substitution of one material for another is not patentable. *Becton, Dickenson and Co. v. Sherwood Medical Industries, Inc.*, 516 F.2d 514, 187 U.S.P.Q. 200, 206 (5th Cir. 1975).

ω

Facts are deemed "material" if a dispute over them "might affect the outcome of the suit under the governing law...." A "genuine issue" of material fact exists only when the nonmoving party makes a sufficient showing to establish an essential element to that party's case, and on which that party would bear the burden of proof at trial. *Wang Laboratories Inc. v. Mitsubishi Electronics America Inc.*, 30 U.S.P.Q.2d 1241, 1249 (Cal. 1993).

ω

Undisclosed prior art items are material to patentability when they disclose more relevant features than cited items. *Molins PLC v. Textron Inc.*, 48 F.3d 1172, 33 U.S.P.Q.2d 1823, 1828 (Fed. Cir. 1995).

ω

"In this context (summary judgment), 'genuine' means that the evidence about the fact is such that a reasonable jury could resolve the point in favor of the non-moving party and 'material' means that the fact is one that might affect the outcome of the suit under the governing law." *Hoppe v. Baxter Healthcare Corp.*, 878 F. Supp. 303, 34 U.S.P.Q.2d 1619, 1622 (Mass. 1995).

Material Information.

There is no policy reason which would support the unprecedented expansion of the interpretation of "material information" to include legal arguments. *Environ Products Inc. v. Total Containment Inc.*, 41 U.S.P.Q.2d 1942 (Pa. 1997).

Materiality. *See also* **But-for Rule or Test, Fraud, Intent, Material.**

If an applicant copies claims from a patent omitting patent claim limitations which are material, an interference should not be declared. A claim limitation added during the prosecution of an application to avoid pertinent prior art is a material limitation. The question of patentability per se is not considered in determining the materiality of a limitation in a patent claim omitted from an interference count. Omission of material limitations from a patent claim copied for interference purposes results in a count drawn to a different invention. *Johnson, Nadeau, Nieuweboer, and Truett v. Bednar, Reid, and Yahiro*, 201 U.S.P.Q. 919, 921, 922 (Comm'r of Patents and Trademarks 1976).

ᙍ

The fact that reduction to practice of the coating step was accomplished with a previously used aromatic coating of undetermined viscosity substantiates the conclusion that the specific viscosity limitation in the coating step is not a material limitation. *Marathon Oil Company v. The Firestone Tire and Rubber Company*, 205 U.S.P.Q. 520, 537 (Ohio 1979).

ᙍ

An Examiner's independent discovery of undisclosed prior art does not preclude a finding of materiality. *A. B. Dick Co. v. Burroughs Corp.*, 798 F.2d 1392, 230 U.S.P.Q. 849, 853 (Fed. Cir. 1986).

ᙍ

Failure to disclose material prior art during the prosecution of a patent cannot be cured by reissue. *Ex parte Harita*, 1 U.S.P.Q.2d 1887 (B.P.A.I. 1986).

ᙍ

The defense of inequitable conduct requires proof of (1) an act of misrepresentation (2) that was material (3) involving information that was known or should have been known to the patentee and (4) that was committed with requisite intent. The elements of materiality and intent must be determined separately and then weighed together to ascertain whether the patentee engaged in inequitable conduct. The tribunal must then carefully balance the materiality and intent; the less material the proffered or withheld information, the greater the degree of intent that must be proven. In contrast, a lesser degree of intent must be proven when the information has a great degree of materiality. Indeed, gross negligence can be the intended level of intent when the misrepresentation has a high degree of materiality. Simple negligence, however, or an error in judgment is never sufficient for holding of inequitable conduct. *Akzo M. V. Aramide Maatschappij V.O.F. v. E.I. du Pont de Nemours*, 810 F.2d 1148, 1 U.S.P.Q.2d 1704 (Fed. Cir. 1987).

ᙍ

The issue is not whether patent claims define patentably over the undisclosed subject matter; it is whether the undisclosed subject matter would have been "highly material" to a patent Examiner's determination. *Gardco Manufacturing Inc. v. Herst Lighting Co.*, 820 F.2d 1209, 2 U.S.P.Q.2d 2015 (Fed. Cir. 1987).

ᙍ

In view of the close similarities between the drawings of the applicant's design application and those in his utility application, a reasonable Examiner would have considered the copending design application important in deciding to issue the utility patent. Even though the utility application is still pending, the failure to timely inform the utility Examiner of the design application cannot now be cured. The level of materiality and the level of intent is high and the applicant is not entitled, in an interference proceeding, to priority for the reason that he, or those representing him, failed to comply with the duty of disclosure required by 37 C.F.R. §1.56(a). *Lutzker v. Plet*, 7 U.S.P.Q.2d 1214 (B.P.A.I. 1987).

☒

An applicant who knew or should have known of prior art or information and of its materiality is not automatically precluded thereby from an effort to convince the fact finder that failure to disclose was nonetheless not due to an intent to mislead the PTO; i.e., that, in light of all the circumstances in the case, an inference of intent to mislead is not warranted. No single factor or combination of factors can be said always to require an inference to mislead. *In re Harita*, 847 F.2d 801, 6 U.S.P.Q.2d 1930 (Fed. Cir. 1988).

☒

The legal standard for materiality is "whether there is a substantial likelihood that a reasonable Examiner would have considered the omitted reference or false information important in deciding whether to allow the application to issue as a patent." Since the inquiry is directed to what a reasonable Examiner would have considered important, the fact that a particular thesis is not a prior art reference is insignificant if a reasonable Examiner would have regarded the thesis "important information" in his decision to allow the application to issue as a patent. *American Standard Inc. v. Pfizer Inc.*, 722 F. Supp. 86, 14 U.S.P.Q.2d 1673, 1720 (Del. 1989).

☒

"[A]ny assertion that is made by a litigant . . . during litigation, which is contradictory to the assertions made . . . to the patent examiner, comprises material information. . . ." *Environ Products Inc. v. Total Containment Inc.*, 43 U.S.P.Q.2d 1288, 1291 (Pa. 1997).

Material Prejudice.

In order to assert the defense of laches successfully, one must prove (1) unreasonable and inexcusable delay in the assertion of the claim and (2) material prejudice resulting from the delay. Laches, however, bars only the right to recover prefiling damages. *Mainland Industries Inc. v. Standal's Patents Ltd.*, 799 F.2d 746, 230 U.S.P.Q. 772 (Fed. Cir. 1986).

Mathematical Equation. *See also* Algorithm.

Patent property rights may not be secured on mathematical equations. A method claim in which the point of novelty is a mathematical equation to be solved as the final step of the method is not directed to a statutory method. *In re Christensen*, 478 F.2d 1392, 178 U.S.P.Q. 35, 37 (C.C.P.A. 1973).

☒

Patentability of a process is not precluded under 35 U.S.C. §101 just because it includes, in several of its steps, the use of a mathematical formula and a programmed digital computer. *Diamond v. Diehr and Lutton*, 450 U.S. 175, 209 U.S.P.Q. 1, 4, 7 (S.Ct. 1981).

Mathematical Formula. *See also* Algorithm.

The mere presence of a mathematical equation or formula in a claim is not a *prima facie* ground for holding that claim to be nonstatutory, but, for the claim to be statutory, there must be some substance to it other than the recitation and solution of the equation or formula. The formula, as an embodiment of a scientific principle, must be applied in some useful manner in a method or process, or be embodied in the design of some useful structure, machine or apparatus. *In re Diehr and Lutton*, 602 F.2d 982, 203 U.S.P.Q. 44, 51 (C.C.P.A. 1979).

ᴦ

Every discovery is not embraced within the statutory terms of 35 U.S.C. §101. Excluded from such patent protection are laws of nature, physical phenomena, and abstract ideas. A principle, in the abstract, is a fundamental truth, an original cause, a motive; these cannot be patented, and no one can claim in any of them an exclusive right. A new mineral discovered in the earth or a new plant found in the wild is not patentable subject matter. Likewise, Einstein could not patent his celebrated law that $E = mc^2$; nor could Newton have patented the law of gravity. Such discoveries are "manifestations of... nature, free to all men and reserved exclusively to none." *Diamond v. Diehr and Lutton*, 450 U.S. 175, 209 U.S.P.Q. 1, 7 (1981).

Maximum.

The imposition of a maximum limit on the quantity of one of several reactants without specifying a minimum (thus allegedly being inclusive of none of that reactant) does not warrant distorting the overall meaning of the claim in a manner which would preclude performing the claimed process. *In re Kirsch, Barmby, and Potts*, 498 F.2d 1389, 182 U.S.P.Q. 286, 290 (C.C.P.A. 1974).

Maximum Recovery Rule.

The "maximum recovery rule" requires that the determination be based on the highest amount of damages that the jury could properly have awarded based on the relevant evidence. *Unisplay S.A. v. American Electronic Sign Co.*, 69 F.3d 512, 36 U.S.P.Q.2d 1540, 1546 (Fed. Cir. 1995).

May. *See also* Alternative, Can, Circumstances, Shall.

In this patent specification "may" should be interpreted as illustrative and not as limiting the description of diamines to aliphatic and aromatic diamines. *In re DiLeone and Lucas*, 436 F.2d 1404, 168 U.S.P.Q. 592, 594 (C.C.P.A. 1971).

Meaning. *See also* Claim Construction, Definition, Intended Meaning, Lexicographer.

A patentee can choose his own terms and use them as he wishes as long as he remains consistent in their use and makes their meaning reasonably clear. *Rosemount Inc. v. Beckman Instruments, Inc.*, 569 F.Supp. 934, 218 U.S.P.Q. 881, 900 (Cal. 1983).

ᴦ

Disputed issues, such as the meaning of a term, should be construed by resort to extrinsic evidence, such as the specification, other claims, and the prosecution history.

Bausch & Lomb, Inc. v. Barnes-Hind/Hydrocurve, Inc., 796 F.2d 443, 230 U.S.P.Q. 416 (Fed. Cir. 1986).

ᚠ

"When the applicant states the meaning that the claim terms are intended to have, the claims are examined with that meaning, in order to achieve a complete exploration of the applicant's invention and its relation to the prior art." *In re Zletz*, 893 F.2d 319, 321, 13 U.S.P.Q.2d 1320, 1322 (Fed. Cir. 1989).

ᚠ

A mere dispute concerning the meaning of a term does not itself create a genuine issue of material fact. *Markman v. Westview Instruments Inc.*, 772 F. Supp. 1535, 20 U.S.P.Q.2d 1955 (Pa. 1991).

ᚠ

The meaning of a term used in a patent claim is a question of law for the court, not a question of fact for the jury, and on appeal is decided de novo when there is a disputed question requiring interpretation of claim terms. *National Presto Industries Inc. v. The West Bend Co.*, 76 F.3d 1185, 37 U.S.P.Q.2d 1685, 1687 (Fed. Cir. 1996).

ᚠ

A patentee may choose to use terms in a manner other than their ordinary meaning, so long as the special definition of the term is clearly stated in the patent specification or file history. The prosecution history limits the claim's terms to exclude any interpretation disclaimed during the patent's prosecution. *Howes v. Zircon Corp.*, 992 F.Supp. 957, 47 U.S.P.Q.2d 1617, 1619 (Ill. 1998).

Means. *See also* **Equivalents, Form over Substance, Means Plus Function, Single Means.**

Though a claim expressed in "means for" (functional) terms is said to be an apparatus claim, the subject matter as a whole of that claim may be indistinguishable from that of a method claim drawn to the steps performed by the "means." *In re Freeman*, 573 F.2d 1237, 197 U.S.P.Q. 464, 472 (C.C.P.A. 1978).

ᚠ

Literal infringement requires that an accused device embody every element of a claim as properly interpreted. If the claim describes a combination of functions, and each function is performed by a means described in the specification or an equivalent of such means, then literal infringement holds. When a claimed invention is a novel combination of steps, all possible methods of carrying out each step of the combination are not required to be described in the specification. Correctly construed claims cover "equivalents" of the described embodiments. The purpose is to grant an inventor of a combination invention a fair scope of protection that is not dependent on a catalog of alternative embodiments in the specification. The court has cautioned against limiting the claimed invention to preferred embodiments or specific examples in the specification. The details of performing each step need not be included in the claims unless required to distinguish the claimed invention from the prior art, or otherwise to specifically point out and distinctly claim the invention. Claims should be read in a way that avoids enabling an infringer to "practice a fraud on a patent."

It is not required that those skilled in the art knew, at the time the patent application was filed, of the asserted equivalent means of performing the claimed functions; that equivalence is determined as of the time infringement takes place. Infringement will be found when the material features of a patent have been appropriated, even when those features have been patentably improved. *Texas Instruments, Inc. v. United States International Trade Commission*, 805 F.2d 1558, 231 U.S.P.Q. 833 (Fed. Cir. 1986).

ω

Where a claim sets forth a means for performing a specific function, without reciting any specific structure for performing that function, the structure disclosed in the specification must be considered and the patent claim construed to cover both the disclosed structure and equivalents thereof. *Jonsson v. The Stanley Works*, 903 F.2d 812, 14 U.S.P.Q.2d 1863, 1869 (Fed. Cir. 1990).

ω

As paragraph six of 35 U.S.C. §112 states: "An element in a claim for a combination may be expressed as a means or step for performing a specified function without the recital of structure, material, or acts in support thereof…"; that paragraph is inapplicable to means-plus-function language, which includes a recital of structure. *The Laitram Corp. v. Rexnord Inc.*, 15 U.S.P.Q.2d 1161, 1170 (Wis. 1990).

ω

In prosecution of claims before the PTO, a recitation of "means" for performing a function is interpreted broadly to cover all means capable of performing the stated function and is not limited to the particular structure which the application may disclose. Limitations from the specification will not, during examination before the PTO, be imputed to the claims in order to avoid prior art; such limitations must be specifically stated in the claims. The last clause of 35 U.S.C. §112's last paragraph has no place in prosecution of pending claims before the PTO under 35 U.S.C. §§102 and 103. *Ex parte Isaksen*, 23 U.S.P.Q.2d 1001, 1009, 1010, 1012 (B.P.A.I. 1991).

ω

35 U.S.C. §112 does not authorize the claiming of apparatus entirely in terms of "means for" performing a *non-statutory* process. When a "means for" claim differs from a method claim only in "means for" terms before the steps, the claim is indistinguishable from a method claim, and whether the method is statutory subject matter is controlling unless the applicant demonstrates that the claims are truly drawn to specific apparatus distinct from other apparatus capable of performing the identical functions. If this burden is not discharged, the apparatus claim will be treated as though it were drawn to the method or process which encompasses all of the claimed "means". The statutory nature of the apparatus "means for" claim under 35 U.S.C. §101 will then depend on whether the corresponding method is statutory. Nevertheless, nothing stops applicants from defining statutory subject matter using only "means" limitations. *Ex parte Alappat*, 23 U.S.P.Q.2d 1340, 1342, 1343 (B.P.A.I. 1992).

ω

The use of the word "means" in a claim does not (as a matter of law) refer to an element expressed in means-plus-function form. Whether the bare use of the term "means" renders a claim indefinite depends on the interpretation of that claim. *Waterloo Furniture Components Ltd. v. Haworth Inc.*, 798 F.Supp. 489, 25 U.S.P.Q.2d 1138, 1142 (Ill. 1992).

ᴡ

"[T]here is no objection to having one or more specific elements of structure included as part of two different means clauses, as long as the entire train of parts to perform each function is not identical." Robert C. Faber, Landis on Mechanics of Patent Claim Drafting §34 at 87 (3d ed. 1990). *Davies v. U.S.*, 31 Fed.Cl. 769, 35 U.S.P.Q.2d 1027, 1032 n.3 (U.S. Ct. Fed. Cl. 1994).

ᴡ

The fact that a particular mechanism is defined in functional terms is not sufficient to convert a claim element containing that term into a "means for performing a specified function" within the meaning of paragraph 6 of 35 U.S.C. §112, but the CAFC confirms the PTO's rejection of the argument that only the term "means" will invoke §112(6), *see* 1162 O.G. 59 n.2 (May 17, 1994). Nonetheless, the use of the term "means" has come to be so closely associated with "means-plus-function" claiming that it is fair to say that the use of the term "means" (particularly as used in the phrase "means for") generally invokes §112(6) and that the use of a different formulation generally does not. *Greenberg v. Ethicon Endo-Surgery Inc.*, 39 U.S.P.Q.2d 1783, 1786, 1787 (Fed. Cir. 1996)

ᴡ

"In determining whether to apply the statutory procedures of [35 U.S.C. §112, ¶6], the use of the word 'means' triggers a presumption that the inventor used the term advisedly to invoke the statutory mandates of means-plus-function clauses", and that the failure to use the word "means" creates a presumption that §112, ¶6, does not apply. "[W]here a claim recites a function, but then goes on to elaborate sufficient structure, material, or acts within the claim itself to perform entirely the recited function, the claim is not in means-plus-function format" even if the claim uses the term "means". *Personalized Media Communications LLC v. ITC*, 48 U.S.P.Q.2d 1880, 1886, 1887 (Fed. Cir. 1998).

Means Plus Function. *See also* Computer Arts, Means.

A problem arises in computer-arts inventions when structure and apparatus claims are defined only as "means for" performing specified functions. If the functionally defined disclosed means and their equivalents are so broad that they encompass any and every means for performing the recited functions, the apparatus claim is an attempt to exalt form over substance since the claim is really to the method or series of functions itself. In computer-related inventions, the recited means often perform the function of "number crunching" (solving mathematical algorithms and making calculations). In such cases the burden must be placed on the applicant to demonstrate that the claims are truly drawn to specific apparatus distinct from other apparatus capable of performing the identical functions. When this burden is not discharged, the apparatus claims will be treated as if they are drawn to the method or process that encompasses all of the claimed "means." *In re Walter*, 618 F.2d 758, 205 U.S.P.Q. 397 (C.C.P.A. 1980).

ᴡ

Given the basic validity of a claim as drawn by the patentee, reference may be had to the specification to ascertain the structure of certain means asserted in the claim. However, the means-plus-function language does not create any exception to the rigid descriptive and definitive requirements of 35 U.S.C. §112. An otherwise unpatentable claim cannot be rendered patentable merely by stating the results obtained from using the recited structure. The particular feature or fact upon which patentability is predicated not only must be disclosed in the specification, but also must be clearly stated in the claim. A deficient claim cannot be aided by reading into it parts of other claims or the specification. When the function clause in a claim fails to recite a necessary limitation to render the claim valid, a court cannot resort to the specification to make that limitation part of the claim. *The Toro Company v. L. R. Nelson Corp.*, 524 F. Supp. 586, 213 U.S.P.Q. 207, 210 (Ill. 1981).

ᴡ

To interpret means-plus-function claims, one must resort to the last paragraph of 35 U.S.C. §112. The statute expressly states that the patentee is entitled to a claim covering equivalents as well as the specified "structure, material or act." Such a patent claim is construed to cover both the disclosed structure and equivalents thereof. To interpret means-plus-function limitations as limited to a particular means set forth in the specification would be to nullify the provision of §112 requiring that the limitation "shall be construed to cover the structure described in the specification and equivalents thereof." In construing a means-plus-function claim, a number of factors may be considered, including the language of the claim, the patent specification, the prosecution history of the patent, other claims in the patent, and expert testimony. Once such factors are weighed, the scope of the "means" claim may be determined. *Palumbo v. Don-Joy Co.*, 762 F.2d 969, 226 U.S.P.Q. 5 (Fed. Cir. 1985).

ᴡ

To determine whether a claim limitation is meant literally where expressed as a means for performing a stated function, a court must compare the accused structure with the disclosed structure and must find equivalent structure as well as identity of claimed function for that structure. Where the issue is raised, it is part of the ultimate burden of proof of the patent owner to establish, with respect to a claim limitation in means-plus-function form, that the structure in the accused device that performs that function is the same as or an equivalent of the structure disclosed in the specification. *Pennwalt Corp. v. Durand-Wayland Inc.*, 833 F.2d 931, 4 U.S.P.Q.2d 1737 (Fed. Cir. 1987).

ᴡ

Paragraph six of 35 U.S.C. §112 does not expand the scope of the claim. An element of a claim described as a means for performing a function, if read literally, would encompass any means for performing the function. But §112 (paragraph six) operates to cut back on the types of means that could literally satisfy the claim language. The section has no effect on the function specified; it does not extend the element to equivalent functions. Properly understood §112 (paragraph six) operates more like the reverse doctrine of equivalents than the doctrine of equivalents because it restricts the scope of the literal claim language. For a means-plus-function limitation to read on an accused device, the accused device must incorporate the means for the function disclosed in the specification or a structure equivalent to that means, plus it must perform the identical function. Paragraph six of 35 U.S.C. §112 can never provide a basis for finding that a means-plus-function claim element is met literally where the function part of the element is not literally met in an accused device. *Johnston v. IVAC Corp.*, 885 F.2d 1574, 12 U.S.P.Q.2d 1382, 1386, 1387 (Fed. Cir. 1989).

ʊ

Paragraph 6 of 35 U.S.C. §112 cannot be ignored when a claim is before the PTO any more than when it is before the courts in an issued patent. *In re Iwahashi*, 888 F.2d 1370, 1375 n.1, 12 U.S.P.Q.2d 1908, 1912 n.1 (Fed. Cir. 1989).

ʊ

While a means-plus-function limitation may appear to include all means capable of achieving the desired function, the statute requires that it be "construed to cover the corresponding structure, material, or acts described in the specification and equivalents thereof." *In re Bond*, 910 F.2d 831, 15 U.S.P.Q.2d 1566, 1567, 1568 (Fed. Cir. 1990).

ʊ

Limiting literal infringement of means-plus-function claims to objects that have physical structures equivalent to those objects specifically described in the patent specification could seriously undermine the usefulness of such claims. *De Graffenried v. United States*, 20 Cl. Ct. 458, 16 U.S.P.Q.2d 1321 (1990).

ʊ

By its express terms, paragraph six of 35 U.S.C. §112 permits an element in a claim to be expressed as a means or as a step for performing a specified function. However, the scope of such a claim is not limitless, but is confined to structures expressly disclosed in the specification and to corresponding equivalents. *Symbol Technologies Inc. v. Opticon Inc.*, 935 F.2d 1569, 19 U.S.P.Q.2d 1241, 1245 (Fed. Cir. 1991).

ʊ

The recitation of some structure in a means-plus-function element does not preclude the applicability of 35 U.S.C. §112, sixth paragraph. Paragraph six "rules out the possibility that any and every means which performs the function specified in the claim *literally* satisfies that limitation. While encompassing equivalents of those means disclosed in the specification, the provision, nevertheless, acts as a restriction on the literal satisfaction of a claim limitation" (emphasis in original). Not only must the means-plus-function language read on the accused device, but also, if the accused structure is different from that described in the patent, the patentee must prove, for literal infringement, that the means in the accused device is structurally equivalent to the means described in the specification. The *Laitram Corp. v. Rexnord Inc.*, 939 F.2d 1533, 19 U.S.P.Q.2d 1367, 1369, 1370 (Fed. Cir. 1991).

ʊ

Because no distinction is made between prosecution in the PTO and enforcement in the courts, or between validity and infringement, 35 U.S.C. §112, paragraph 6, applies regardless of the context in which the interpretation of means-plus-function language arises, i.e., whether as part of a patentability determination in the PTO or as part of a validity or infringement determination in a court. Any precedent of the Federal Circuit to the contrary is expressly overruled. The "broadest reasonable interpretation" that and Examiner may give means-plus-function language is that statutorily mandated in paragraph six. Accordingly, the PTO may not disregard the structure disclosed in the specification corresponding to such language when rendering a patentability determination. *In re Donaldson Co. Inc.*, 16 F.3d 1189, 29 U.S.P.Q.2d 1845, 1849, 1850 (Fed. Cir. 1994).

ω

"To determine whether a claim limitation is met literally, where expressed as a means for performing a stated function, the court must compare the accused structure *with the disclosed structure*, and must find equivalent *structure* as well as *identity* of claimed *function* for that structure." "The means-plus-function language must not only read on the accused device, but also, if the accused structure is different from that described in the patent, the patentee must prove, for literal infringement, that the means in the accused device is structurally equivalent to the means described in the specification." *Endress + Hauser Inc. v. Hawk Measurement Systems Pty. Ltd.*, 32 U.S.P.Q.2d 1768, 1975 n.4 (Ind. 1994).

ω

The rule of construction that claims with means-plus-function language "cover the corresponding structure, material, or acts described in the specification and equivalents thereof" applies whether the claimed language is being construed in the context of an infringement or invalidity determination. *Fonar Corp. v. General Electric Co.*, 41 U.S.P.Q.2d 1088, 1095 (N.Y. 1995).

ω

The "perforation means . . . for tearing" element of the claims fails to satisfy the statute because it describes the structure supporting the tearing function (i.e., perforations). The claim describes not only the structure that supports the tearing function, but also its location and extent. An element with such a detailed recitation of its structure, as opposed to its function, cannot meet the requirements of 35 U.S.C. §112, paragraph 6. *Cole v. Kimberly-Clark Corp.*, 41 U.S.P.Q.2d 1001 (Fed. Cir. 1996)

ω

[I]f one employs means-plus-function language in a claim, one must set forth in the specification an adequate disclosure showing what is meant by that language. If an applicant fails to set forth an adequate disclosure, the applicant has, in effect, failed to particularly point out and distinctly claim the invention as required by the second paragraph of 35 U.S.C. §112. *B. Braun Medical Inc. v. Abbott Laboratories*, 124 F.3d 1419, 43 U.S.P.Q.2d 1896, 1900 (Fed. Cir. 1997).

ω

Neither the Supreme Court nor the Federal Circuit have determined whether the construction of a means-plus-function claim is a question of law or fact. *Contempo Tobacco Products Inc. v. McKinnie*, 45 U.S.P.Q.2d 1969, 1974 (Ill. 1997).

ω

The scope of a means-plus-function claim is such that unless the accused structure reads very closely on the disclosed structure, the two will not be deemed equivalent under 35 U.S.C. §112, ¶6. In such a case, doctrine of equivalents infringement is also absent, unless the technology used in the accused structure was developed after the patent issued. *Odetics Inc. v. Storage Technology Corp.*, 47 U.S.P.Q.2d 1923, 1926 (Va. 1998).

ΰ

Paragraph 6 of 35 U.S.C. §112 is triggered [not] only when a claim uses the word "means." The PTO has rejected the argument that only the term "means" will invoke section 112(6), *see* 1162 O.G. 59 N. 2 (May 17, 1994). While traditional "means" language does not automatically make an element a means-plus-function element, conversely, lack of such language does not *prevent* a limitaion from being construed as a means-plus-function limitation. *Mas-Hamilton Group Inc. v. LaGard Inc.*, 48 U.S.P.Q.2d 1010, 1016 (Fed. Cir. 1998).

ΰ

A "means-plus-function limitation is not made open-ended by the presence of another claim specifically claiming the disclosed structure which underlies the means clause or an equivalent of that structure." *C.R. Bard Inc. v. M3 Systems Inc.*, 48 U.S.P.Q.2d 1225, 1242 (Fed. Cir. 1998).

Measuring. *See* **Mental Steps.**

Mechanical.

The first paragraph of 35 U.S.C. §112 requires that the scope of the claims bear a reasonable correlation to the scope of enablement provided by the specification to persons of ordinary skill in the art. In cases providing predictable factors, such as mechanical or electrical elements, a single embodiment provides broad enablement in the sense that, once imagined, other embodiments can be made without difficulty and their performance characteristics predicted by resort to known scientific laws. In cases involving unpredictable factors, such as most chemical reactions and physiological activity, the scope of enablement obviously varies inversely with the degree of unpredictability of the factors involved. *In re Fisher*, 427 F.2d 833, 166 U.S.P.Q. 18, 24 (C.C.P.A. 1970).

Mechanize.

It is not "invention" broadly to provide a mechanical or automatic means to replace manual activity that has accomplished the same result. *In re Venner and Bowser*, 262 F.2d 91, 120 U.S.P.Q. 192, 194 (C.C.P.A. 1958).

Medical Device Amendments of 1976. *See* **FDCA.**

Medical Devices.[5] *See* **FDCA.**

Medicament. *See* **Pharmaceutical.**

---

[5] *See* 35 U.S.C. §271(e)(1).

Medicine. *See* **Pharmaceutical.**

Memorandum. *See also* **Self-Serving.**

Validity was denied by a memo that was admittedly not prior art, notwithstanding the fact that the contents of such memo had been concealed by the alleged infringer. *Newell Companies v. Kenney Manufacturing Co.*, 606 F. Supp. 1282, 226 U.S.P.Q. 157 (R.I. 1985).

ϖ

A particular memorandum was held not to be a printed publication. The memorandum was filed in a special vault in the Stanford Research Institute (SRI) library with classified government documents. The library personnel maintained the memorandum as confidential, and only members of the SRI library staff had access to it. In order to ensure that the proprietary information was not compromised, the SRI personnel only prepared a limited number of copies of the memorandum, and each copy was identified to control its distribution. The SRI memorandum was never loaned to another library and was not made available to the public. The SRI memorandum was listed on a project card in the library; however, the library personnel were required to advise members of the public that the memorandum was "not available" from the SRI library. The memorandum was kept in a part of the library where the general public did not have access to it. *RCA Corp. v. Data General Corp.*, 701 F. Supp. 456, 8 U.S.P.Q.2d 1305 (Del. 1988).

Mental Impressions.

Although an attorney may be deposed and required to disclose what he knows about the subject matter, he cannot be required to disclose his mental impressions, conclusions, opinions, or legal theories concerning the litigation. He may be required to refer to his file to refresh his recollection, but he cannot be compelled to state why he amended the claims or what he meant by this or that word or phrase; that would require him to express an opinion, one of the exceptions provided for in Fed. R. Civ. P. 26(b)(3). *MacLaren v. B-l-W Group Inc.*, 180 U.S.P.Q. 387 (Va. 1973).

Mental Steps. *See also* **Algorithm, By Hand, Combining.**

A patent was held invalid for want of invention because novelty was found only in certain mental steps, described in the claims by the following descriptive words: "determining," "registering," "counting," "observing," "measuring," "comparing," "recording," and "computing." A patent may be obtained only on an invention of a "new and useful art, machine, manufacture, or composition of matter. A process is a mode of treatment of certain materials to produce a given result. It is an act, or a series of acts, performed upon the subject matter to be transformed and reduced to a different state or thing. If the claimed method were patentable, the patentee would have a monopoly much broader than would the patentee of a particular apparatus. *Halliburton Oil Well Cementing Co. v. Walker*, 146 F.2d 817, 64 U.S.P.Q. 278, 282, 283 (9th Cir. 1944).

ϖ

Purely mental steps do not form a process which falls within the scope of patentability as defined by statute. To be patentable, "the steps of an art or method must be performed upon physical materials and produce some change in their character or condition." *In re Yuan*, 188 F.2d 377, 89 U.S.P.Q. 324, 327 (C.C.P.A. 1951).

ᛒ

Patent protection for a process disclosed as being a sequence or combination of steps capable of performance without human intervention and directed to an industrial technology (a "useful art" within the intendment of the Constitution) is not precluded by the mere fact that the process could alternatively be carried out by mental steps. *In re Prater and Wei*, 415 F.2d 1378, 159 U.S.P.Q. 583, 593 (C.C.P.A. 1968).

ᛒ

The statutory language [35 U.S.C. §101(b)] contains nothing whatever which would either include or exclude claims containing "mental steps". The law does not require all steps of a statutory "process" to be physical acts applied to physical things. All that is necessary to make a sequence of operational steps a statutory "process" within 35 U.S.C. §101 is that it be in the technological arts so as to be in consonance with the Constitutional purpose to promote the progress of "useful arts." *In re Musgrave*, 431 F.2d 882, 167 U.S.P.Q. 280, 287, 289, 290 (C.C.P.A. 1970).

ᛒ

The inclusion in a patent of a process that may be performed by a person, but that also is capable of being performed by a machine, is not fatal to patentability. The presence in claims of the steps of correlating and combining, which a machine is capable of doing, does not invalidate a patent. *Alco Standard Corporation v. Tennessee Valley Authority*, 808 F.2d 1490, 1 U.S.P.Q.2d 1337, 1341 (Fed. Cir. 1986).

Merit.

For commercial success to be a significant factor with regard to patentability, a nexus must be established between the commercial success and the merits of the invention. *In re Noznick, Tatter, and Obenauf*, 478 F.2d 1260, 178 U.S.P.Q. 43, 44 (C.C.P.A. 1973).

ᛒ

Due process requires that an applicant be given notice of the reasons his claims are rejected and why arguments upon which he relies are deemed lacking in merit. This principle is the essence of 35 U.S.C. §132 and should guide the proceedings of the Board of Appeals as well. *Ex parte Hageman*, 179 U.S.P.Q. 747, 751 (PTO Bd. App. 1972).

Metabolic Property.

A description of several newly-discovered strains of bacteria having one particularly desirable metabolic property in terms of the conventionally-measured culture characteristics and a number of metabolic and physical properties would not enable one of ordinary skill in the relevant art to discover, independently, additional strains having the same specific, desirable metabolic property. *Ex parte Jackson*, 217 U.S.P.Q. 804, 806 (PTO Bd. App. 1982).

Metabolite.[6] *See also* **Conversion (*in situ* or *in vivo*), Pro-Drug.**

Infringement may result from the *in vivo* conversion of one product or compound into another. The proper inquiry requires comparison of the claimed (patent) [compound] with the alleged infringing compound *after ingestion*. Infringement may apply in situations involving *in vivo* conversions if the infringer uses an equivalent element to perform the same function as the claimed compound. *Marion Merrell Dow Inc. v. Geneva Pharmaceuticals Inc.*, 877 F.Supp. 531, 33 U.S.P.Q.2d 1673, 1676 (Colo. 1994).

Metallurgy.

Metallurgy is but the chemistry of metals. *Eutectic Corporation v. Metco, Inc.*, 418 F.Supp. 1186, 191 U.S.P.Q. 505, 521 (N.Y. 1976).

Metes. *See* **Bounds.**

Method. *See also* **Analogy Process, Chemical Reaction, Function of Machine, Method of Doing Business, Method of Making, Method of Use, Mode of Administration, Process, Single-Step Method Claim, Steps.**

As neither the power to hear nor the power to repeat what is heard is patentable, combining these faculties in a reporting method which included recording and transcribing was held to be outside the purview of the patent statute. *In re Holmes*, 37 F.2d 440, 4 U.S.P.Q. 179 (C.C.P.A. 1930).

ϖ

Claims to a method were held to be patentably indistinct from claims to apparatus for performing the method. *In re Abernathy*, 118 F.2d 358, 49 U.S.P.Q. 82 (C.C.P.A. 1941).

ϖ

In evaluating the patentability of process claims, the "material acted upon" must be given weight. *Ex parte Zbornik and Peterson*, 109 U.S.P.Q. 508, 509 (PO Bd. App. 1956).

ϖ

A material used in a claimed method is part of the invention as a whole and must be considered in evaluating patentability. *In re Kuehl*, 475 F.2d 658, 177 U.S.P.Q. 250, 255 (C.C.P.A. 1973).

ϖ

Method and process claims are equivalents. *In re Bergy, Coats, and Malik*, 596 F.2d 952, 201 U.S.P.Q. 352, 364 (C.C.P.A. 1979).

ϖ

Durden [763 F.2d 1406, 226 U.S.P.Q. 359 (Fed. Cir. 1985)] did not hold that all methods involving old process steps are obvious; the court in that case concluded that the particularly claimed process was obvious; it refused to adopt an unvarying rule that the

---

[6]See Rollins, "Novelty of Metabolic Product", 65 JPOS 403 (1983), commentary on *Ex parte Biel* (file of USP 3,454,554, Paper No. 22) (PTOBA 1964).

fact that non-obvious starting materials and non-obvious products are involved ipso facto makes the process non-obvious. Such an invariant rule, always leading to the opposite conclusion, is also not the law. *In re Dillon*, 919 F.2d 688, 16 U.S.P.Q.2d 1897, 1903 (Fed. Cir. 1990).

Method of Doing Business. *See also* Algorithm, Transacting Business.

A system of transacting business, apart from the means for carrying out such system, is not within the purview of R.S. §4886, nor is an abstract idea or theory, regardless of its importance or the ingenuity with which it was conceived, apart from the means for carrying such idea or theory into effect, patentable subject matter. *In re Patton*, 127 F.2d 324, 53 U.S.P.Q. 376, 379 (C.C.P.A. 1942).

ω

The claimed method does not merely facilitate business dealings. That translation of business data into mathematical language intelligible to computers is employed in carrying them out does not make a method of automatically controlling a system of manufacturing plants a method of "doing business." *In re Deutsch*, 553 F.2d 689, 193 U.S.P.Q. 645 (C.C.P.A. 1977).

ω

Since its inception, the "business method" exception to statutory subject matter has merely represented the application of some general, but no longer applicable legal principle, perhaps arising out of the "requirement for invention" — which was eliminated by 35 U.S.C. §103. Since the 1952 Patent Act, business methods have been, and should have been, subject to the same legal requirements for patentability as applied to any other process or method. *State Street Bank & Trust Co. v. Signature Financial Group Inc.*, 149 F.3d 1368, 47 U.S.P.Q.2d 1596, 1602 (Fed. Cir. 1998).

Method of Making.[7] *See also* Analogy Process, How to Make, Starting Material, Synthesis.

A determination that a claim to a new compound is patentable does not impart patentability to a method of making the new compound. *In re Larsen*, 292 F.2d 531, 130 U.S.P.Q. 209, 210 (C.C.P.A. 1961).

ω

The patentability of a new chemical structure is independent of how it is made. See, e.g, *In re Hoeksema*, 332 F.2d 374, 141 U.S.P.Q. 733, 736 (C.C.P.A. 1964) (product patentable, although the process was unpatentable for obviousness).

ω

---

[7]In a Notice issued on February 28, 1996, the PTO announced that henceforth it would analyze process claims in accordance with the *Ochiai* [37 U.S.P.Q.2d 1127 (Fed. Cir. 1995)] and *Brouwer* [37 U.S.P.Q.2d 1663 (Fed. Cir. 1995)] decisions of the Federal Circuit and treat as material limitations any recitations in process claims of the use of nonobvious starting materials or the making of nonobvious products. *AIPLA BULLETIN*, 36, 1997 Annual Meeting Issue.

The issue is whether it was obvious to make the relevant compounds, not whether it was obvious how to make them once their desirability was ascertained. *In re Cescon*, 474 F.2d 1331, 177 U.S.P.Q. 264, 266 (C.C.P.A. 1973).

ᛡ

The method of manufacture may be relevant to the patentability of claims drawn to articles. *In re Epple and Kaiser*, 477 F.2d 582, 177 U.S.P.Q. 696 (C.C.P.A. 1973).

ᛡ

The PTO has improperly rejected product claims to molecules on the alleged obviousness of a method of making the molecules. As the claims define new chemical entities in structural terms, a *prima facie* case of unpatentability requires that the teachings of the prior art suggest *the claimed compounds* to a person of ordinary skill in the art. *In re Deuel*, 51 F.3d 1552, 34 U.S.P.Q.2d 1210, 1214 (Fed. Cir. 1995).

Method of Use.[8] *See also* Analogy Process, New Use, Use, Utility, Utilize.

It is in the public interest to permit claiming a method of use as well as the novel product being used in the method of use. The constitutional purpose of the patent system is promoted by encouraging applicants to claim, and therefore to describe in the manner required by 35 U.S.C. §112, all aspects of what they regard as their inventions, regardless of the number of statutory classes involved. Dependent use claims in the same application with composition claims do not materially increase the scope of protection of an inchoate patent property under 35 U.S.C. §154, which already includes the right to exclude others from making, using, or selling the composition by allowance of claims thereon, but they do tend to increase the wealth of technical knowledge disclosed in the patent by encouraging description of the use aspects of the invention in the manner required by paragraph one of 35 U.S.C. §112. *In re Kuehl*, 475 F.2d 658, 177 U.S.P.Q. 250, 256 (C.C.P.A. 1973).

ᛡ

Under 35 U.S.C. §103 neither a novel product made by nor a novel starting material used in a claimed process can be treated as prior art. In method-of-use cases the novelty of the starting material may lend unobviousness to the process. In cases where the invention is a method for making a new product, however novel the product may be, the claimed process steps and starting materials may themselves still be old and the process therefore obvious. Process claims may not be rejected simply because they recite the use

---

[8] Method-of-use claims (without specifying steps) appear in United States Patent No. 5,677,150 (issued October 14, 1997):

13. A method of producing an antibody, which inhibits intercellular adhesion of monocyte/macrophage cells stimulated by a differentiation factor which comprises using a lipopolysaccharide-stimulated monocyte/macrophage cell line as the antigen, wherein said lipopolysaccharide is obtained from a gram-negative strain of microorganism.

15. A method of producing an antibody which induces intercellular aggregation of monocyte/macrophage cells in the process of differentiation under stimulation by a differentiation factor, which comprises using a lipopolysaccharide-stimulated monocyte/macrophage cell line as the antigen, wherein said lipopolysaccharide is obtained from a gram-negative strain of microorganism.

of new materials in an old process, which process is otherwise proper. It is not required for unobviousness of a method-of-use claim that a new starting material employed therein be patentable. *In re Mancy, Florent, and Preud'Homme*, 499 F.2d 1289, 182 U.S.P.Q. 303, 306 (C.C.P.A. 1974).

ʊ

When a claimed process is considered to be one of "using" a novel material, patentability of the process is linked to the patentability of the material used. However, when a claimed process is considered to be directed to a "method of making" a novel material, patentability of the process is based on the inventiveness of the process steps themselves. Linkage between product and use thereof is logical because the obviousness of a process of using a novel product must be ascertained without knowledge of the thing used and its properties. In chemical cases, a compound and its properties are inseparable. Logic dictates that one cannot use a novel material without prior knowledge of the *specific* material and its properties. *Ex parte Ochiai*, 24 U.S.P.Q.2d 1265, 1268 (B.P.A.I. 1992); *see also In re Pleuddemann*, 910 F.2d 823, 15 U.S.P.Q.2d 1738, 1740, 1741 (Fed. Cir. 1990).

Method of Using.[9]

Methylene. *See* **Ethylene.**

Microfilm. *See also* **Printed Publication.**

A microfilm, which allegedly was made available to the public only by virtue of the publication of a bibliography, there being no evidence of record that any copies of said microfilm had been made or seen by any member of the public, was held not to be a "printed publication" within the meaning of that term as used in 35 U.S.C. §102(b). While microfilming furnishes a means of multiplying copies, there is no probability, from a mere showing that a microfilm copy of a disclosure has been produced, that the disclosure has achieved wide circulation and that, therefore, the public has knowledge of it. The nature of present-day microfilm reproduction differs from that of normal printing methods. Though one would be more likely than not to produce a number of copies of printed material, one producing an item by microfilming would be as apt to make one copy as many. In the case of printing, unless a number of copies were produced, a waste of time, labor, and materials would result; present-day microfilming methods, on the other hand, are designed to produce one microfilm as well as many without waste. *In re Tenney, Frank, and Knox*, 254 F.2d 619, 117 U.S.P.Q. 348, 350, 354 (C.C.P.A. 1958).

ʊ

A microfilm is not printed and is not prior art. *The General Tire & Rubber Company v. The Firestone Tire & Rubber Company*, 349 F.Supp. 333, 349 F.Supp. 345, 174 U.S.P.Q. 427, 441 (Ohio 1972).

---

[9]In a Notice issued on February 28, 1996, the PTO announced that henceforth it would analyze process claims in accordance with the *Ochiai* [37 U.S.P.Q.2d 1127 (Fed. Cir. 1995)] and *Brouwer* [37 U.S.P.Q.2d 1663 (Fed. Cir. 1995)] decisions of the Federal Circuit and treat as material limitations any recitations in process claims of the use of nonobvious starting materials or the making of nonobvious products. *AIPLA BULLETIN*, 36, 1997 Annual Meeting Issue.

Microorganism. *See also* **Culture, Deposit, Strain.**

Microorganisms have long been important tools in the chemical industry, and when such a useful, industrial tool (which is new and unobvious, so that it complies with those conditions for patentability) is invented, there is no reason to deprive it or its creator or owner of the protection and advantages of the patent system by arbitrarily excluding it at the outset from the 35 U.S.C. §101 categories of patentable invention on the sole ground that it is alive. *In re Bergy, Coats, and Malik; In re Chakrabarty*, 596 F.2d 952, 201 U.S.P.Q. 352, 373 (C.C.P.A. 1979).

ϖ

A microorganism that is not a hitherto unknown natural phenomenon, but a non-naturally occurring manufacture or composition of matter, a product of human ingenuity having a distinctive name, character, and use, plainly qualifies as patentable subject matter. *Diamond, Commissioner of Patents and Trademarks v. Chakrabarty*, 447 U.S. 303, 206 U.S.P.Q. 193, 197 (1980).

Mineral.

Every discovery is not embraced within the statutory terms of 35 U.S.C. §101. Excluded from such patent protection are laws of nature, physical phenomena, and abstract ideas. A principle, in the abstract, is a fundamental truth, an original cause, a motive; these cannot be patented, and no one can claim in any of them an exclusive right. A new mineral discovered in the earth or a new plant found in the wild is not patentable subject matter. Likewise, Einstein could not patent his celebrated law that $E = mc^2$; nor could Newton have patented the law of gravity. Such discoveries are "manifestations of...nature, free to all men and reserved exclusively to none." *Diamond v. Diehr and Lutton*, 450 U.S. 175, 209 U.S.P.Q. 1, 7 (1981).

Minimum. *See also* **At Least.**

The imposition of a maximum limit on the quantity of one of several reactants without specifying a minimum (thus allegedly being inclusive of none of that reactant) does not warrant distorting the overall meaning of the claim in a manner which would preclude performing the claimed process. *In re Kirsch, Barmby, and Potts*, 498 F.2d 1389, 182 U.S.P.Q. 286, 290 (C.C.P.A. 1974).

Misappropriation. *See also* **Trade Secret.**

Regardless of whether the trade secrets were ultimately made public via the issuance of a patent or otherwise, defendant obtained the information by misappropriation and not from public disclosure or any other legitimate business means. There is no distinction between the presence of a disclosure that may destroy secrecy and the head-start concept, for the former is merely an element of the latter. The award for damages compensates the plaintiff for the head start that the defendants obtained through its misappropriation. This head start amounted to a preemption of the entire market and prevented the plaintiff from licensing others, as well as making entry into the market by the plaintiff impossible. In fashioning an adequate monetary remedy, the court must consider that defendants did not merely wrongly obtain and use the plaintiff's know-how as a competitor in the marketing, they refused to return the know-how to the plaintiff when ordered to do so, thereby completely precluding the plaintiff also from manufacturing. There is no question that the defendant's conduct was grossly improper and that the plaintiff's monetary recovery should not be limited by a lead-time valuation. *The Kilbarr Corp. v. Business Systems, Inc.*, B. V., 679 F. Supp. 422, 6 U.S.P.Q.2d 1698 (N.J. 1988).

ω

When an employee has acquired patents on inventions developed by his former employer, the courts will hold the wrongdoer to be a constructive trustee of the property misappropriated and will order a conveyance by the wrongdoer to the former employer. *Richardson v. Suzuki Motor Co., Ltd.*, 868 F.2d 1226, 9 U.S.P.Q.2d 1913 (Fed. Cir. 1989).

Misconduct. *See also* **Misdeed, New Trial.**

When a party seeks to collect monetary damages from a patentee because of alleged violations of the antitrust law, it is appropriate to require a higher degree of misconduct for that damage award than when a party asserts only a defense against an infringement claim. *Hewlett-Packard Co. v. Bausch & Lomb Inc.*, 882 F.2d 1556, 1563, 11 U.S.P.Q.2d 1750, 1756 (Fed. Cir. 1989), *cert. denied*, 493 U.S. 1076 (1990); *Argus Chemical Corp. v. Fibre Glass-Evercoat Co.*, 812 F.2d 1381, 1384-85, 1 U.S.P.Q.2d 1971, 1973-74 (Fed. Cir. 1987).

ω

In an infringement action, the court found that defendant's entire prosecution of its inequitable conduct counterclaim constituted misconduct for which plaintiff was entitled to compensation under 35 U.S.C. §285. *Beckman Instruments Inc. v. LKB Produkter AB*, 17 U.S.P.Q.2d 1190, 1194 (Md. 1990).

ω

A letter terrorizing the trade by threatening retailers and competitors is not grounds for an affirmative defense of unclean hands in an action where the issues are infringement and priority of invention. The defense of unclean hands does not close the courthouse door to plaintiffs simply because they have behaved improperly, or even unlawfully. For the maxim that equity helps only those with clean hands to apply, a plaintiff's misconduct must be "unconscionable" and have some immediate and necessary relationship to the equity he seeks. In a patent case, the misconduct should "bear upon the validity of the patent or defendant's infringement of the patent for the unclean hands defense to be available." *National Presto Industries Inc. v. Black & Decker (U.S.) Inc.*, 760 F. Supp. 699, 19 U.S.P.Q.2d 1457, 1459 (Ill. 1991).

ω

CAFC cases reflect three standards for judging the misconduct by a patentee, dependent upon the nature of the relief which the opposing litigant seeks: (1) misconduct which makes a patent unenforceable ("inequitable conduct"); (2) misconduct which makes a case "exceptional" so as to warrant an award of attorney fees [*see* 35 U.S.C. §285 (1994)]; and (3) misconduct which rises to the level of fraud and which will support an antitrust claim. *Nobelpharma AB v. Implant Innovations Inc.*, 129 F.3d 1463, 44 U.S.P.Q.2d 1705, 1718 (Fed. Cir. 1997—*dissent*).

Misdeed.

Taking human frailty and all of the objectives of the patent system into account, misdeeds may be overcome under certain limited circumstances. *Rohm & Haas Co. v. Crystal Chemical Co.*, 722 F.2d 1156, 220 U.S.P.Q. 289, 301 (Fed. Cir. 1983).

Misjoinder. *See also* Conversion, One Invention, Unity of Invention.

An applicant has a right to have each claim examined on the merits and in a form which he considers to define his invention best. In drawing priorities between the Commissioner (as administrator) and the applicant (as beneficiary of his statutory rights), the statutory rights are paramount. A rejection under 35 U.S.C. §121 violates the basic right of the applicant to claim his invention as he chooses. *In re Weber, Soder, and Boksay*, 580 F.2d 455, 198 U.S.P.Q. 328, 331, 332 (C.C.P.A. 1978).

ω

Misjoinder of inventors is a technical defense and is not looked upon with favor by the courts. Clear and convincing proof is required to sustain the defense. The good faith misjoinder of a joint inventor shall not invalidate a patent where such error can be corrected as provided in 35 U.S.C. §256. *Rosemount Inc. v. Beckman Instruments, Inc.*, 569 F.Supp. 934, 218 U.S.P.Q. 881, 902 (Cal. 1983).

Misleading. *See also* Duty to Disclose.

When the Examiner rejected certain claims as being anticipated by prior art, the applicant, instead of accepting suitable limitations on his patent, stubbornly resisted any effort to limit his claims. Claims were proliferated, and, in their excessive zeal and heedless of what applicant knew existed in the prior art, counsel and applicant made arguments the Examiner could not conceivably have accepted had he known what applicant knew. *East Chicago Machine Tool Corporation v. Stone Container Corporation*, 181 U.S.P.Q. 744, 748 (Ill. 1974).

ω

The trial court's findings that plaintiff was dilatory, that he had misled the Patent Office, and that he had failed or refused to meet defendant's specific reasoning and arguments concerning the infringement issue were more than ample to support a finding of conduct "in excess of simple negligence" and a determination of bad faith on plaintiff's part in commencing and litigating this suit. *Kahn v. Dynamics Corporation of America*, 508 F.2d 939, 184 U.S.P.Q. 260, 264 (2d Cir. 1975).

Mismarking.

Marking a product with a patent number estops the marking party from either avoiding royalty liability or asserting non-infringement in an action by the patentee. Discontinuance of marking will not obviate or cure the estoppel. While wrongful intent has been held to be a necessary element of proof in patent "mismarking" cases under 35

U.S.C. §292, no similar requirement is found in "marking estoppel" cases. *Crane Co. v. Aeroquip Corporation*, 364 F.Supp. 547, 179 U.S.P.Q. 596, 606 (Ill. 1973).

ω

As a general proposition, there can be no violation of 35 U.S.C. §292 absent an evidentiary showing that the false marking or mismarking was "for the purpose of deceiving the public." Furthermore, the omission of "applicable patents" from a label listing patents purporting to cover the contents of a box cannot, in itself, be a violation of the false marking statute. *Arcadia Machine & Tool, Inc. v. Sturm, Ruger & Co., Inc.*, 786 F.2d 1124, 229 U.S.P.Q. 124, 125 (Fed. Cir. 1986).

ω

Federal law makes patent mismarking a criminal offense. 35 U.S.C. §292 (1988). The act of impermissibly placing a patent number on a product, if limited in time and quantity, does not inevitably have such adverse effects for the patentee or for the consuming public as to bar the mismarker from establishing that his product does not use the patent. Though a patentee or licensor normally will understandably have evidence only of sporadic instances of mismarking and need not identify widespread mismarking to raise a claim of estoppel, an accused mismarker should be able to defeat the claim by showing how inadvertent and limited the mismarking was. Of course, deliberate mismarking of even a limited nature or inadvertent mismarking over a prolonged period would justify an estoppel. *Boyd v. Schieldkraut Giftsware Corp.*, 936 F.2d 76, 19 U.S.P.Q.2d 1223, 1224, 1225 (2d Cir. 1991).

ω

The defendant's invoices bearing the legend:

THIS PRODUCT IS PRODUCED UNDER US PATENT #4,566,294

constitute a "use in advertising" within the meaning of 35 U.S.C. §292. When competing manufacturers share customers, invoices serve the function of advertising by targeting a specific market, trade, or class of customers. This reading of §292 is consistent with its purpose of protecting not only patentees but also other members of the public who trade in unpatented goods from false representations regarding the status of a product and to prevent false markings from improperly discouraging competition in the marketplace. *Accent Designs Inc. v. Jan Jewelry Designs*, 92 Civ. 0482, 30 U.S.P.Q.2d 1734, 1741 (N.Y. 1993).

Misprint.

When the identification of a compound in a reference is in error and would be so recognized by any artisan, it cannot be said that one of ordinary skill in the relevant art would do anything more than mentally disregard it as a misprint. Obvious typographical errors do not convey any teaching whatsoever with regard to an erroneously-depicted compound irrespective of one's ability to produce such a compound. *In re Yale*, 434 F.2d 666, 168 U.S.P.Q. 46, 48, 49 (C.C.P.A. 1970).

Misrepresentation. *See also* **Collateral Attack, False Statement, Fraud.**

Appellants' collateral attack on a reference patent, by alleging that the patentee's misrepresentation of a material fact led to the issuance of the reference patent, raises issues that are not properly considered in an ex parte proceeding in which the patentee is not a party. *In re Ludovici and Megla*, 482 F.2d 958, 179 U.S.P.Q. 84, 88 (C.C.P.A. 1973).

ᚣ

Misrepresentation in an application oath, even though applicable only to a product described in a subsequently canceled claim, was held to be material to and to taint the entire application and patent claims in suit. *St. Regis Paper Company v. Royal Industries*, 186 U.S.P.Q. 83, 87, 88 (Cal. 1974).

ᚣ

Voluntary efforts during prosecution (by or on behalf of an applicant), knowing that misrepresentations have been made to the Examiner, can alleviate the effect of such misrepresentations. Taking human frailty and all of the objectives of the patent system into account, misdeeds may be overcome under certain limited circumstances. *Rohm & Haas Co. v. Crystal Chemical Co.*, 722 F.2d 1156, 220 U.S.P.Q. 289, 301 (Fed. Cir. 1983).

Mistake. *See* **Error.**

Misuse. *See also* **Control of Unpatented Goods, Patent Misuse.**

A process patent can be used to restrict the use of a claimed process but cannot be used to control the sale of unpatented articles produced by the process. *Ethyl Corp. v. Hercules Powder Co.*, 232 F. Supp. 453, 139 U.S.P.Q. 471, 474 (Del. 1963).

ᚣ

General Electric [272 U.S. 476 (1926)] stands for the proposition that a patent holder does not violate the antitrust laws by seeking to dispose of his products directly to a consumer and fixing the price by which his agents transfer the title from him directly to the consumer. *General Electric* does not allow the patent holder to sell his product to a person and then control the resale price. Assuming that the subject contract was a contract of agency, whatever protection *General Electric* afforded such contract ended when the patent expired. Since the contract was in effect continuously since 1950, the jury could have correctly concluded that the contract extended the life of the patent beyond its expiration date and thus constituted a contract in restraint of trade.

In *Walker Process Equipment, Inc. v. Food Machinery & Chemical Corp.*, 382 U.S. 172, 147 U.S.P.Q. 404 (1965), the Supreme Court held that enforcement of a fraudulently procured patent may violate section 2 of the Sherman Act provided all other elements are established. It is not enough to argue that one has used a patent in a predatory manner, thereby enlarging the scope or life of the patent. One must look to economic data to determine the impact of the purported illegal activity on the market which is the subject of the attempt to monopolize. *Agrashell, Inc. v. Hammons Products Company*, 479 F.2d 269, 177 U.S.P.Q. 501, 507, 512 (8th Cir. 1973).

ᚣ

To recover antitrust damages based on an alleged fraud in obtaining a patent, the plaintiff must prove (1) willful and intentional fraud, (2) injury to business or property caused by the fraudulently procured patent, and (3) the other elements necessary to a section 2 Sherman Act violation. Good faith or an honest mistake is a complete defense to an antitrust action based on fraud on the Patent Office.

In order to sustain a finding of patent misuse or a Sherman Act violation based in discriminatory licensing, at least the following must be present: (1) the plaintiff took a license; (2) the royalty rate charged plaintiff and that charged a competitor were unequal; (3) in all particulars relevant to equality of rates plaintiff and its licensed competitor were similarly situated; and (4) the royalties were an important expense factor in production costs, and the discriminatory rate caused substantial impairment of competition in the relevant market. *Honeywell Inc. v. Sperry Rand Corp.*, 180 U.S.P.Q. 673, 723 (Minn. 1973).

ᛒ

The misuse of a patent does not depend on a showing that an improper tying provision of a license may have a substantial effect on competition as is required to establish liability under section 3 of The Clayton Act, 15 U.S.C. §14. As a matter of patent law the inclusion of tying provisions in a mandatory package patent license constitutes a misuse of patents absent some showing justifying the practice, such as business convenience or necessity. Even then, when the business necessity terminates, the licensee's rights are reactivated. Tie-ins are noncoercive and, therefore, legal only if the components are separately available to the customer on a basis as favorable as the tie-in arrangement. A patentee who sells a patented item only in conjunction with some other item "raises serious suspicions of tying behavior and misuse" and bears a heavy burden in overcoming this suspicion and in bringing himself within one of the recognized justifications. In addition to constituting coercion to accept unlawful tying arrangements incorporated in package licenses, the requirement that the royalty rate remain at a constant level also raises the question of the legality of collecting royalties attributable to patents that expire while the license agreement is in effect. *The Duplan Corp. v. Deering Milliken, Inc.*, 444 F. Supp. 648, 197 U.S.P.Q. 342, 385, 386 (S.C. 1977).

ᛒ

The owner of a patent on a chemical process is not guilty of patent misuse and therefore barred from seeking relief against contributory infringement of its patent rights if it exploits the patent only in conjunction with the sale of an unpatented article that constitutes a material part of the invention and is not suited for commercial use outside the scope of the patent claims. *Dawson Chemical Co. v. Rohm & Haas Co.*, 448 U.S. 176, 206 U.S.P.Q. 385, 389, 407 (1980).

ᛒ

A patentee of a method of using a composition, which is not a staple article of manufacture but comprises, as an essential component thereof, a staple article of manufacture, can sell the composition for the intended use (thus licensing under the patent all those who buy the composition from him) and refuse to license others under the patent without being guilty of patent misuse. Control exerted by the patentee over the composition (specifically designed for infringing use) is not the same as control over sale of the essential component alone. *Milton Hodosh v. Block Drug Co. Inc.*, 833 F.2d 1575, 4 U.S.P.Q.2d 1935, 1939 (Fed. Cir. 1987).

ᴆ

The doctrine of patent misuse is an equitable concept designed to prevent a patent owner from improperly extending or enhancing the "fiscal or temporal scope" of a patent grant with the effect of restraining competition. However, in application, a finding of patent misuse has been confined to a few specific practices by patent holders, such as fixing the price at which a purchaser of a patented item could resell it, requiring a licensee to pay royalties beyond the expiration of the patent grant, and requiring a licensee to refrain from manufacturing items that would compete with the patented item. The most common application of the doctrine occurs when the sale of an unpatented staple item is "tied" to the sale of a patented device. Every use of a patent as a means of obtaining a limited monopoly of unpatented material is prohibited. *NL Chemicals Inc. v. United Catalysts Inc.*, 11 U.S.P.Q.2d 1239, 1240 (Ky. 1989).

ᴆ

To the extent plaintiff seeks a declaration that defendants' patents are invalid, federal patent law preempts their misuse claim based on tortious interference with contract. When state law touches upon the area of federal patent law, the federal policy may not be set at naught, or its benefits denied, by state law. Federal patent law expressly prescribes the circumstances under which a patent may be declared invalid based on allegations of misuse. 35 U.S.C.A. §271(d) (Supp. 1989). Proof of the elements of interference with contract is less difficult than the proof required to entitle a defendant in a patent infringement action to a declaration invalidating the patent. If plaintiff were permitted to invalidate defendants' patents using state interference with contract principles, the federal patent laws and state law would be in direct conflict. *Medtronic Inc. v. Eli Lilly & Co.*, 15 U.S.P.Q.2d 1465, 1468 (Minn. 1990).

ᴆ

"Misuse" and "unclean hands" are not interchangeable. The doctrine of misuse requires a showing "that the patentee has impermissibly broadened the 'physical or temporal scope' of the patent grant with anticompetitive effect." Generally speaking, claims of patent misuse have been tested by conventional antitrust principles, and application of the doctrine has been confined to a small number of specific anti-competitive practices. Misuse has not traditionally been treated as a broad equitable defense akin to dirty hands. Misuse has been applied and limited to practices, such as tying arrangements coupled with market power (requiring the purchase of unpatented goods for use with a patented apparatus or process), covenants not to deal (requiring a licensee not to deal in products that compete with the licensor's patent), and mandatory package licensing (insisting that a licensee pay license fees on two patents to get a license on either one). *National Presto Industries Inc. v. Black & Decker (U.S.) Inc.*, 760 F. Supp. 699, 19 U.S.P.Q.2d 1457, 1459 (Ill. 1991).

ᴆ

Conditioning the grant of a patent license upon payment of royalties on products that do not use the teaching of the patent or upon payment of royalties on products that use the teaching of patents that have expired amounts to patent misuse. When direct or indirect conditioning, as opposed to sound business judgment, good faith bargaining, and mutual convenience, governs the grant of a license, the patent holder engages in patent misuse. Coercion, or attempted coercion, is an essential element of patent misuse by improper patent packaging. *Lightwave Technologies Inc. v. Corning Glass Works*, 19 U.S.P.Q.2d 1838, 1840, 1841 (N.Y. 1991).

ω

Collection of two royalties on the same product under the same patents constitutes patent misuse. *PSC Inc. v. Symbol Technologies Inc.*, 48 U.S.P.Q.2d 1838, 1843 (N.Y. 1998).

Mixture. *See also* Combination, Transitory.

A claim calling for a mixture of components (which will react together on standing) is patentable. Since the ingredients of the composition do not instantaneously react and the application discloses examples of compositions containing the recited ingredients, the compositions are fully disclosed and supported by the application. *Ex parte Dubsky and Stark*, 162 U.S.P.Q. 567, 568 (PO Bd. App. 1968).

ω

An application having claims calling for a mixture of compounds does not have to specify just where all the substituents are positioned on each ring in each compound in each mixture of each working example. *In re Steinhauer and Valenta*, 410 F.2d 411, 161 U.S.P.Q. 595, 599 (C.C.P.A. 1969).

Model. *See* 35 U.S.C. §114.

Mode of Administration. *See also* Enablement.

A proper disclosure of utility for a medicinal composition may require at least an indication of dosage and mode of administration. *In re Moureu and Chovin*, 345 F.2d 595, 145 U.S.P.Q. 452 (C.C.P.A. 1965).

ω

Where test methods in the field of the patent are so well known that reference to them in the patent is needless to enable those working in the field to follow the teaching of the patent, even complete silence on dosage and method of administration of the original application suffices to meet the how-to-use requirement of §112. *Carter-Wallace, Inc. v. Davis-Edwards Pharmacal Corp.*, 341 F. Supp. 1303, 173 U.S.P.Q. 65, 104 (N.Y. 1972).

Mode of Operation.

To copy the principle or mode of operation described is an infringement, although such copy is totally unlike the original in form or proportions. *Blumenthal v. Barber-Colman Holdings Corp.*, 62 F.3d 1433, 38 U.S.P.Q.2d 1031, 1036 (Fed. Cir. 1995).

Modification. *See also* **Change, Destroy, Incentive, Motivation, Optimize.**

An art-based ground of rejection of a process claim was considered untenable because the Examiner failed to provide any reason for finding obvious the alteration of the molybdenum-phosphorus ratio in the direction and manner claimed. *Ex parte Parthasarathy and Ciapetta*, 174 U.S.P.Q. 63 (PO Bd. App. 1971).

ᚦ

Prior patents are references only for what they clearly disclose or suggest. It is not proper use of a patent as a reference to modify its structure to one which prior art references do not suggest. *In re Randol and Redford*, 425 F.2d 1268, 165 U.S.P.Q. 586, 588 (C.C.P.A. 1970). *See also In re Taborsky*, 502 F.2d 775, 183 U.S.P.Q. 50, 55 (C.C.P.A. 1974).

ᚦ

The Examiner's failure to indicate anywhere in the record any reason for his finding alteration of the reference obvious militates against the rejection based thereon. *Ex parte Kaiser*, 194 U.S.P.Q. 47, 48 (PTO Bd. App. 1975).

ᚦ

The more remote in time the prior art relied on, the less likely it becomes that the patented invention would be obvious to one of ordinary skill. If there is no rational manner in which the prior art can be modified to result in the patented invention, the patent is valid. *Continuous Curve Contact Lenses, Inc. v. National Patent Development Corporation*, 214 U.S.P.Q. 86, 116 (Cal. 1982).

ᚦ

Modification unwarranted by the disclosure of a reference is unwarranted. *Carl Schenck, A.G. v. Nortron Corporation*, 713 F.2d 782, 218 U.S.P.Q. 698, 702 (Fed. Cir. 1983).

ᚦ

Modification by a mere addition of elements or functions, whenever made, cannot negate infringement. *Stranco Inc. v. Atlantes Chemical Systems Inc.*, 15 U.S.P.Q.2d 1704, 1711 (Tex. 1990).

ᚦ

The prior art must provide one of ordinary skill in the art the motivation to make the proposed molecular modifications needed to arrive at the claimed compound. *In re Jones*, 958 F.2d 347, 21 U.S.P.Q.2d 1941, 1944 (Fed. Cir. 1992).

ᚦ

Obviousness cannot be established by combining teachings of prior art to produce a claimed invention, absent some teaching or suggestion supporting the combination. Under 35 U.S.C. §103, teachings of references may be combined only if there is some suggestion or incentive to do so. Although couched in terms of combining teachings found in the prior art, the same inquiry must be carried out in the context of a purported obvious "modification" of the prior art. The mere fact that the prior art may be modified in the manner suggested by the Examiner does not make the modification obvious unless the prior art suggested the desirability of the modification. *In re Fritch*, 972 F.2d 1260, 23 U.S.P.Q.2d 1780, 1783 (Fed. Cir. 1992).

Modified Count.

It is incumbent on any party who desires to continue an interference on a modified basis (in the event that a motion to dissolve is granted) to bring a timely motion seeking such action. *Moore v. Hignett*, 152 U.S.P.Q. 337, 338 (Comm'r 1966).

Modifying.

Steps, such as "computing", "determining", "cross-correlating", "comparing", "selecting", "initializing", "testing", "modifying", and "identifying", have implicitly been found to recite the solving of a mathematical algorithm. *In re Warmerdam*, 33 F.3d 1354, 31 U.S.P.Q.2d 1754, 1758 (Fed. Cir. 1994).

Moiety. *See* Ingredient, Radical.

Monetary Damages. *See also* Right to Exclude.

The nature of the patent grant weighs against holding that monetary damages will always suffice to make a patentee whole; for the principle value of the patent is its statutory right to exclude. *H. Robertson Co. v. United Steel Deck, Inc.*, 820 F.2d 384, 2 U.S.P.Q.2d 1926 (Fed. Cir. 1987).

Monetary Relief.

The patent statute provides injunctive relief to preserve the legal interests of the parties against future infringement that may have marked effects never fully compensable in money. If monetary relief were the sole relief afforded by the patent statute, then injunctions would be unnecessary, and infringers could become compulsory licensees for as long as the litigation lasts. *Lin v Fritsch*, 14 U.S.P.Q.2d 1795, 1809 (Comm'r Patents & Trademarks 1989).

Monoclonal Antibodies.

The claimed invention had been reduced to practice prior to the filing date of the subject application, and the appellants had agreed to deposit the hybridoma cell lines at a recognized depository upon the patent grant. In the interim, the cell lines were being maintained at Sloan-Kettering, an institution of renown and integrity. This was regarded as in full compliance with the requirements imposed upon the appellants under *Lundak* [773 F.2d 1216, 227 U.S.P.Q. 90 (Fed. Cir. 1985)].

Although the technique underlying hybridoma technology is well recognized, the results obtained by its use are clearly unpredictable. Hybridoma technology is an empirical art in which the routineer is unable to foresee what particular antibodies will be produced and which specific surface antigens will be recognized by them. Only by actually carrying out the requisite steps can the nature of the monoclonal antibodies be determined and ascertained; no "expected" results can thus be said to be present. Hence, it may be "obvious to try" the Kohler-Milstein technique as applied to malignant renal cells, but such is not the standard under which obviousness under 35 U.S.C. §103 must be established. *Ex parte Old*, 229 U.S.P.Q. 196 (B.P.A.I. 1985).

Monopolize.

To establish an attempt to monopolize in violation of Section 2 of the Sherman Act, defendant must have proven: (1) a specific intent by plaintiff to control prices or to exclude competition; (2) that plaintiff engaged in predatory or anticompetitive conduct to accomplish the monopolization; (3) that plaintiff had a dangerous probability of success in its venture; and (4) that plaintiff's actions caused defendant to suffer an antitrust injury. *Automotive Products plc v. Tilton Engineering Inc.*, 855 F.Supp. 1101, 33 U.S.P.Q.2d 1065, 1090, 1091 (Cal. 1994).

Monopoly. *See also* Extension of Monopoly.

A patent is not, accurately speaking, a monopoly, for it is not created by the executive authority at the expense and to the prejudice of all the community except the grantee of the patent. The term "monopoly" connotes the giving of an exclusive privilege for buying, selling, working, or using a thing that the public freely enjoyed prior to the grant. Thus, a monopoly takes something from the people. An inventor deprives the public of nothing that it enjoyed before his discovery, but gives something of value to the community by adding to the sum of human knowledge. He may keep his invention secret and reap its fruits indefinitely. In consideration of its disclosure and the consequent benefit to the community, the patent is granted. *United States v. Dubilier Condenser Corp.*, 289 U.S. 178, 17 U.S.P.Q. 154, 157 (1933).

ᙡ

A patent, under the statute, is property. 35 U.S.C. §261. Nowhere in any statute is a patent described as a monopoly. It is but an obfuscation to refer to a patent as "the patent monopoly" or to describe a patent as an "exception to the general rule against monopolies." *Carl Schenck, A.G. v. Nortron Corporation*, 713 F.2d 782, 218 U.S.P.Q. 698, 701 n.3 (Fed. Cir. 1983).

ᙡ

The patent system, which antedated the Sherman Act by a century, is not an "exception" to the antitrust laws, and patent rights are not legal monopolies in the antitrust sense of that word. Accordingly, if a patent is held to have been obtained illegally, it is not properly said, ipso facto, that it was all along an illegal monopoly and, thus, that its procurement and attempted enforcement were per se violations of the antitrust laws. A holding that monopoly analysis should end in favor of liability on a determination of fraud, without more, would signal a fundamental misunderstanding of the substance and purposes of both the patent and the antitrust laws. *American Hoist & Derrick Company v. Sowa & Sons, Inc.*, 725 F.2d 1350, 220 U.S.P.Q. 763, 776 (Fed. Cir. 1984).

ᙡ

A process patent in a chemical field that has not been developed creates a monopoly of knowledge that should be granted only if clearly commanded by the statute. This is because such patents may engross unknown and perhaps unknowable areas and may confer power "to block off whole areas of scientific development, without compensating benefit to the public." *Ex parte Kranz*, 19 U.S.P.Q.2d 1216, 1219 (B.P.A.I. 1990).

ϖ

Monopoly power may be shown by evidence of a company's reducing or restricting the share of the market held by competitors by means other than through the unilateral and lawful exercise of rights granted by a lawful patent, and a court's instruction to a jury to that effect is both proper and fair. *Lightwave Technologies Inc. v. Corning Glass Works*, 19 U.S.P.Q.2d 1838, 1845 (N.Y. 1991).

ϖ

"[E]very use of a patent as a means of obtaining a limited monopoly on unpatented material is prohibited...whatever the nature of the device by which the owner of the patent seeks to effect unauthorized extension of the monopoly." *Rite-Hite Corp. v. Kelley Co. Inc.*, 56 F.3d 1538, 35 U.S.P.Q.2d 1065, 1070 (Fed. Cir. 1995).

ϖ

The elements of the offense of monopolization are: "(1) the possession of monopoly power in the relevant market and (2) the willful acquisition or maintenance of that power as distinguished from growth or development as a consequence of a superior product, business acumen, or historic accident." The elements of attempted monopolozation are: (1) exclusionary or anticompetitive conduct; (2) a specific intent to monopolize; and (3) a dangerous probability of achieving monopoly power. *DiscoVision Associates v. Disc Manufacturing Inc.*, 42 U.S.P.Q.2d 1749, 1755 (Del. 1997).

Moot.

"Mootness" is jurisdictional when the dispute between the parties, or at least an issue in the case, no longer exists. That is, the issue no longer presents an actual case or controversy. If an issue is moot in this sense, a court has no discretion, but *must* dismiss for lack of jurisdiction. *Powell v. McCormack*, 395 U.S. 486, 496 n.7 (1969).

ϖ

Where it appears on appeal that the controversy has become entirely moot, it is the duty of the appellate court to set aside the decree below and to remand the cause with directions to dismiss. This case did not become moot on appeal; rather, a consent judgment was entered pursuant to a settlement agreement entered into by the parties. The agreed settlement and entry of the consent judgment mooted any possibility of pursuing an appeal and foreclosed the appellate court from obtaining jurisdiction. *Gould v. Control Laser Corp.*, 866 F.2d 1391, 9 U.S.P.Q.2d 1718 (Fed. Cir. 1989).

ϖ

Patents may be declared invalid at the district court level for a variety of reasons, at least some of which should not be permitted to be swept under a concealing settlement rug. After finding that a settlement moots the parties' controversy, the Federal Circuit vacates the lower court's finding of invalidity without reviewing the merits. The result of such a scenario may be that an invalid patent, even one fraudulently obtained, is foisted off on the public and left to distort the market. *Wang Laboratories Inc. v. Toshiba Corp.*, 793 F.Supp. 676, 23 U.S.P.Q.2d 1953, 1954 (Va. 1992).

ω

The issue of validity is not mooted when a finding of noninfringement is affirmed by the CAFC because "the Federal Circuit is not a court of last resort." *Morton International Inc. v. Cardinal Chemical Co.*, 5 F.3d 1464, 28 U.S.P.Q.2d 1190, 1192 (Fed. Cir. 1993).

Mootness.

"[M]ootness by reason of settlement does not [except under exceptional circumstances, which do not include the mere fact that the settlement agreement provides for vacatur] justify vacatur of a judgment under review." *Zeneca Limited v. Novopharm Limited*, 38 U.S.P.Q.2d 1585, 1586 (Md. 1996).

Mortgaged Patent.

A patentee, who mortgaged his patent to secure a debt and paid off the debt prior to the mortgage maturity date, regained equitable title to the patent and was entitled to invoke the jurisdiction of a court of equity in a case for patent infringement without joining the mortgagee (holder of bare legal title to the patent), who was neither an indispensable nor a necessary party to the proceedings. *Railex Corporation v. Joseph Guss & Sons, Inc.*, 40 F.R.D. 119, 148 U.S.P.Q. 640, 642, 643, 645 (D.C. 1966).

Mosaic.

In determining "obviousness" over prior art, and having learned the details of the patentee's invention, the district court found it within the skill of the art to stretch other material rapidly, to stretch PTFE to increase porosity, and to stretch at high temperatures. The result is that the patent claims were used as a frame, and individual, naked parts of separate prior art references were employed as a mosaic to recreate a facsimile of the claimed invention. No explanation was given as to why that mosaic would have been obvious to one skilled in the art at the time of the patentee's invention, or what there was in the prior art that would have caused those skilled in the art to disregard the teachings there found against making just such a mosaic. To imbue one of ordinary skill in the art with knowledge of the invention in suit, where no prior-art reference or references of record convey or suggest that knowledge, is to fall victim to the insidious effect of a hindsight syndrome wherein that which only the inventor taught is used against its teacher. *W. L. Gore & Associates, Inc. v. Garlock, Inc.*, 721 F.2d 1540, 220 U.S.P.Q. 303 (Fed. Cir. 1983).

ω

When prior-art references require a selective combination to render obvious a subsequent invention, there must be some reason for the combination other than the hindsight gleaned from the invention itself. Something in the prior art as a whole must suggest the desirability, and thus the obviousness, of making the combination. It is impermissible to use the claims as a frame and the prior-art references as a mosaic to piece together a facsimile of the claimed invention. *Uniroyal Inc. v. Rudkin-Wiley Corp.*, 837 F.2d 1044, 5 U.S.P.Q.2d 1434 (Fed. Cir. 1988).

ω

It is impermissible to use a claimed invention as an instruction manual or "template" to piece together the teachings of the prior art so that the claimed invention is rendered obvious. "[O]ne cannot use hindsight reconstruction to pick and choose among isolated disclosures in the prior art to deprecate the claimed invention." *In re Fritch*, 972 F.2d 1260, 23 U.S.P.Q.2d 1780, 1784 (Fed. Cir. 1992).

MOSITA (Man of Ordinary Skill in the Art). *See also* Hypothetical Person, Ordinary Skill.

The specification is not addressed to lawyers or even to the public generally, but to those of ordinary skill in the art. Any description that is sufficient to apprise them (in the language of the art) of the definite features of the invention, and to serve as a warning to others of that which is claimed, is sufficiently definite. *The Carnegie Steel Company, Ltd. v. The Cambria Iron Company*, 185 U.S. 403, 437 (1902).

ω

What would be obvious to the "ordinary farmer" (clearly one of less than ordinary skill in the herbicide art) has no bearing on the determination of obviousness with respect to a person of a particular skill, namely: a person of ordinary skill in the art to which the subject matter pertains as of the time the invention was made. *In re Luvisi and Nohejl*, 342 F.2d 102, 144 U.S.P.Q. 646, 650 (C.C.P.A. 1965).

ω

In legal contemplation, one of ordinary skill in the art is chargeable with comprehensive knowledge of the prior art. *Continental Can Co., Inc. v. Crown Cork & Seal Co., Inc.*, 415 F.2d 601, 163 U.S.P.Q. 1, 3 (3d Cir. 1969), *cert. denied*, 397 U.S. 914, 164 U.S.P.Q. 481 (1970).

ω

To prove the legal inadequacy of a disclosure of an application for letters patent based on inoperativeness, one must show (1) that it described an inoperative device, and (2) that the device so described could not be made operative by changes obvious to one of ordinary skill in the art. *Hughes Aircraft Company v. General Instrument Corporation*, 374 F.Supp. 1166, 182 U.S.P.Q. 11, 17 (Del. 1974).

ω

The hypothetical person of ordinary skill is not deemed to be omniscient, but he must be assumed to share the knowledge available in his art (to persons of ordinary skill) wherever it may originate. *Steelcase, Inc. v. Delwood Furniture Co., Inc.*, 578 F.2d 74, 199 U.S.P.Q. 69, 73 (5th Cir. 1978).

ω

The hypothetical person of ordinary skill in the art is one "who is attempting to solve the problems the inventor addressed," although he is not required to match the expertise of the inventor himself. *Micro Motion Inc. v. Exac Corp.*, 741 F. Supp. 1426, 16 U.S.P.Q.2d 1001, 1008 (Cal. 1990).

ῶ

The "person of ordinary skill in the art" is a theoretical construct used in determining obviousness under 35 U.S.C. §103. The construct applies to particular individuals and does not disqualify a person of *exceptional* skill from testifying as an expert because such person is not ordinary enough. *Endress + Hauser Inc. v. Hawk Measurement Systems Pty. Ltd.*, 122 F.3d 1040, 43 U.S.P.Q.2d 1849, 1851 (Fed. Cir. 1997).

Most Favored Licensee.

A licensor's grant of immunity from suit in settlement of a dispute under a prior license agreement is "the equivalent of a license" and may trigger another licensee's most-favored-licensee clause. *Willemijn Houdstermaatschappij BV v. Standard Microsystems Corp.*, 39 U.S.P.Q.2d 1528, 1530 (N.Y. 1996).

Motion. *See also* Directed Verdict, Magistrate's Order, Post Judgment Motion, Reconsideration, Transfer.

Efficient administration of interference cases in the PTO dictates that a party make out its case when it first presents a motion. If additional evidence routinely can be presented with requests for reconsideration, a party could, in effect, indefinitely renew its motion and present additional showings until relief is granted or the other party gives up. The proscription against filing an additional showing with a request for reconsideration under the "new" interference rules is firmly established. The same proscription also governs any interference still being conducted under the "old" interference rules unless a party can show "sufficient cause" why the additional showing could not have been presented with the original motion. *Clevenger v. Martin*, 230 U.S.P.Q. 374 (Commr. Patents & Trademarks 1986).

ῶ

The grant or denial of either a motion for a new trial or a motion to amend the judgment must be reviewed on the basis of a determination of whether the district court abused its discretion. Abuse of discretion may be established by showing that the district court either made an error of law, or a clear error of judgment, or made findings that were really erroneous. *Richardson v. Suzuki Motor Co., Ltd.*, 868 F.2d 1226, 9 U.S.P.Q.2d 1913 (Fed. Cir. 1989).

ῶ

Parties to an interference do not, in general, know [when they submit a preliminary motion under 37 C.F.R. §1.633(a)] whether the other party's allegations in a preliminary statement will antedate a reference under 35 U.S.C. §102(a) or §102(e). Thus, these motions are proper when the reference has been authored by one of the parties. However, since unpatentability under §102(a) or §102(e) involves issues of priority as to a date, albeit not to the date of invention, the Board should consider the allegations of the preliminary statements and only enter an order to show cause based on unpatentability under §102(a) or §102(e) where there is no alleged "prior invention." This practice should be followed regardless of whether the prior art is §102(a) prior art of one of the parties in the interference, or §102(a) or §102(e) prior art by a third party. The practice should also be followed regardless of whether the §102(a) or §102(e) prior art is applicable to one or all parties, and regardless of whether the prior art is cited by the junior or the senior party. *Goutzoulis v. Athale*, 15 U.S.P.Q.2d 1461, 1465 (Commr. Patents & Trademarks 1990).

ω

When expert testimony is needed in support of, or in opposition to, a preliminary motion, a party should:

1. identify the person it expects to call as an expert;
2. state the field in which the person is alleged to be an expert; and
3. state in a Declaration signed by the person (a) the subject matter on which the person is expected to testify, (b) the facts and opinions to which the person is expected to testify, and (c) a summary of the grounds and basis for each opinion.

When a person is to be called as a fact witness, a Declaration by that person (stating the facts) should be filed. If the other party is to be called, or if evidence in the possession of the other party is necessary, an explanation of the evidence sought, what it will show, and why it is needed must be supplied. When inter partes tests are to be performed, a description of such tests (stating what they will show) must be presented. *Hanagan v. Kimura*, 16 U.S.P.Q.2d 1791, 1794 (Comm'r Patents & Trademarks 1990).

ω

If the requirements of 37 C.F.R. §1.633 could be avoided via a miscellaneous motion under §1.635 or the EIC's discretion under §1.610(e), then §1.633 would be rendered a nullity. *Gerk v. Cottringer*, 17 U.S.P.Q.2d 1615, 1616 (B.P.A.I. 1990).

ω

"[I]f a post-judgment motion is filed within ten days of the entry of judgment and calls into question the correctness of such judgment, it should be treated as a motion under Rule (FRCP) 59(e), however it may be formally styled." The text of Rule 59(e) contains no requirement that the grounds must be based on newly-discovered evidence. *Beverly Hills Fan Co. v. Royal Sovereign Corp.*, 21 F.3d 1558, 30 U.S.P.Q.2d 1001, 1004 (Fed. Cir. 1994).

Motion by Examiner.

While it may be proper under special circumstances for an Examiner to suggest a new claim for the purpose of prolonging an interference which has been dissolved and in which neither party has proposed a proper substitute claim, such action should not ordinarily be resorted to. This is especially true where the proposed basis for prolonging the interference is a claim differing materially from any claim previously asserted by either party. *Garty and Gibb v. Price*, 158 U.S.P.Q. 559, 560 (Comm'r 1964).

ω

It is incumbent on any party who desires to continue an interference on a modified basis (in the event that a motion to dissolve is granted) to bring a timely motion seeking such action. In the absence of any such motion it is to be assumed that all parties are willing to stand or fall on the original issue, and it is not the duty of the Examiner to supply such a lack by sua sponte action. This is particularly true with regard to an interference involving a patentee. *Moore v. Hignett*, 152 U.S.P.Q. 337, 338 (Comm'r 1966).

Motion for a New Trial. *See also* **New Trial.**

The grant or denial of either a motion for a new trial or a motion to amend the judgment must be reviewed on the basis of a determination of whether the district court abused its discretion. Abuse or discretion may be established by showing that the district court either made an error of law or a clear error of judgment, or made findings that were clearly erroneous. *Richardson v. Suzuki Motor Co., Ltd.*, 868 F.2d 1226, 9 U.S.P.Q.2d 1913 (Fed. Cir. 1989).

ω

The grant or denial of a motion for a new trial is a matter "confided almost entirely to the exercise of discretion on the part of the trial court." *ATD Corp. v. Lydall Inc.*, 43 U.S.P.Q.2d 1170, 1173 (Mich. 1997).

Motion for Directed Verdict. *See* **Directed Verdict.**

Motion to Add Count.

A motion to add counts should not be denied solely on the ground that there is no interference in fact if there is any reasonable doubt on that issue. *Brandon v. Murphy*, 231 U.S.P.Q. 490, 491 (Comm'r 1986).

Motion to Add or Substitute.

A patentee's motion to add or substitute a copending application to an interference does not fall within any of the provisions of 37 C.F.R. §1.633, since the rule does not provide for any such motion by a party patentee. Moreover, such motion is not a "miscellaneous motion" of the type contemplated by 37 C.F.R. §1.635, but is a motion which would fall into the "preliminary motion" category. *Theeuwes v. Bogentoft*, 2 U.S.P.Q.2d 1378, 1379 (Comm'r 1986).

Motion to Amend. *See* **Abuse of Discretion, Amending Answer.**

Motion to Compel.

Neither Congress nor the Commissioner of Patents has authorized initiation of reissue proceedings by anyone other than the inventor or his assignee. A motion by an infringement defendant to compel patentee to apply for a reissue patent was thus denied. *Cooper Industries, Inc. v. J. & J. Fabrics, Inc.*, 211 U.S.P.Q. 226 (Ga. 1981).

ω

When a defendant in a patent infringement suit requests reexamination by the PTO of the patent in suit, the plaintiff has a right to compel the defendant to disclose all prior art the defendant intends to rely upon at trial so that such prior art can be addressed in the reexamination proceeding. *Output Technology Corp. v. Dataproducts Corp.*, 22 U.S.P.Q.2d 1639, 1640 (Wash. 1992).

Motion to Dismiss. *See also* **Rule 12(b)(6).**

If the Court relies on the pleading and affidavits alone when considering a motion to dismiss for lack of jurisdiction, the plaintiff need only make a *prima facie* showing of jurisdiction in order to defeat the motion. In that event, the pleading and affidavits are construed in the light most favorable to the plaintiff, and all doubts are resolved in his or her favor. If the jurisdictional issue requires an evidentiary hearing, the plaintiff must establish jurisdiction by a preponderance of evidence. *Modern Computer Corp. v. Ma*, 862 F.Supp. 938, 32 U.S.P.Q.2d 1586, 1589 (N.Y. 1994).

ᛒ

"[A] motion to dismiss after the pleadings have been closed may be treated as a motion for a judgment on the pleadings". *Eldridge v. Springs Industries Inc.*, 882 F.Supp. 356, 35 U.S.P.Q.2d 1378 (N.Y. 1995).

ᛒ

A motion to dismiss for failure to state a claim may only be granted if it appears, beyond doubt, that the plaintiff can prove no facts in support of its claim that entitle him to relief. *Sturtevant v. Van Remortel*, 38 U.S.P.Q.2d 1134, 1137, 1139 (N.Y. 1995).

ᛒ

On a motion to dismiss for failure to state a claim, "the court should not dismiss the complaint pursuant to Rule 12(b)(6) unless it appears 'beyond doubt that the plaintiff can prove no set of facts in support of his claim which would entitle him to relief'". *Hoffman v. Wisner Classic Manufacturing Co. Inc.*, 40 U.S.P.Q.2d 1271, 1273 (N.Y. 1996).

ᛒ

"If a Rule 12(b)(1) motion denies or controverts the pleader's allegations of jurisdiction...the movant is deemed to be challenging the factual basis for the court's subject matter jurisdiction." *Biogen Inc. v. Schering AG*, 42 U.S.P.Q.2d 1681, 1684 (Mass. 1996)

ᛒ

A motion to dismiss is appropriate "only if 'it is clear that no relief could be granted under any set of facts that could be proven consistent with the allegations.'" *Eastman Kodak Co. v. Duracell Inc.*, 48 U.S.P.Q.2d 1061, 1062 (D.C. 1998).

Motion to Dissolve.

A party making a motion (based on no interference in fact) to dissolve an interference has the burden of showing that the parties' corresponding claims are drawn to different inventions. If a Primary Examiner desires to dissolve an interference for a reason not raised by the parties, he should do so by way of a motion under 37 C.F.R. §1.237, which does not authorize a motion based on no interference in fact. *Logan v. Neuzil*, 206 U.S.P.Q. 668, 670 (Comm'r 1979).

Motion to Intervene. *See* **Intervention.**

Motion to Stay. *See* **Stay Motion.**

Motion to Strike. *See also* **Motion to Suppress.**

Motions to strike a defense are not favored by the courts, and will only be granted "when the defense is insufficient as a matter of law." *Laser Diode Array Inc. v. Paradigm Lasers Inc.*, 44 U.S.P.Q.2d 1677, 1679 (N.Y. 1997).

Motion to Suppress.

When a party intends to rely on objections to an opponent's testimony, he must file a motion to suppress or strike the alleged improper testimony. The mere listing of objections in an appendix does not provide an adequate briefing of the issues as is contemplated by the requirement for a motion to suppress. *Fisher v. Bouzard*, 3 U.S.P.Q.2d 1677, 1680 (B.P.A.I. 1987).

Motivation. *See also* **Combination, Combining References, Common Properties, Deem, Direction, Economics, Incentive, Inoperable, Orientation During Operation, Purpose, Reason, Structural Similarity, Suggestion.**

The mere fact that a worker in the art could rearrange the parts of the reference device to meet the terms of the claims on appeal is not, by itself, sufficient to support a finding of obviousness. The prior art must provide a motivation or reason for the worker in the art, without the benefit of the appellant's specification, to make the necessary changes in the reference device. The Examiner has not presented any evidence to support the conclusion that a worker in this art would have had any motivation to make the necessary changes in the reference device to render the here-claimed device unpatentable. *Ex parte Chicago Rawhide Manufacturing Co.*, 226 U.S.P.Q. 438 (PTO Bd. App. 1984).

ϖ

There was no suggestion in the prior art to provide the applicant with the motivation to design the valve assembly so that it would be removable as a unit. The Board argued that, if the reference had followed the "common practice" of attaching the valve stem to the valve structure, the valve assembly would be removable as a unit. The only way the Board could have arrived at its conclusion was through hindsight analysis by reading into the art applicant's own teachings. Hindsight analysis is clearly improper, since the statutory test is whether "the subject matter as a whole would have been obvious at the time the invention was made." *In re Deminski*, 796 F.2d 436, 230 U.S.P.Q. 313 (Fed. Cir. 1986).

ϖ

The Examiner appears to recognize that it is not structural similarity alone that gives rise to obviousness, but the concomitant assumption that the structurally similar compounds will have like properties. This is what provides the motivation to modify the prior-art compound. In the present case, however, the only utility disclosed for the relevant compound in the reference is as an intermediate for the production of another compound. The Examiner has not suggested that the compound claimed here would have been useful in the same manner and, from the disclosure of the reference itself, it appears that it would not have been. Thus, on the record before us, no prima facie case of obviousness has been made out against the appellant's claims. *Ex parte Chwang*, 231 U.S.P.Q. 751 (B.P.A.I. 1986).

ᙡ

The motivation to make a specific structure is not abstract, but practical, and is always related to the properties or uses one skilled in the art would expect the structure to have, if made. The critical inquiry is whether there is something in the prior art as a whole to suggest the desirability, and thus the obviousness, of making the combination. *In re Newell*, 891 F.2d 899, 13 U.S.P.Q.2d 1248, 1250 (Fed. Cir. 1989).

ᙡ

Before obviousness may be established, the Examiner must show that there is either a suggestion in the art to produce the claimed invention or a compelling motivation based on sound scientific principles. Logic compels that the suggestion or motivation be accompanied by a general knowledge of the existence of art-recognized techniques for carrying out the proposed invention. *Ex parte Kranz*, 19 U.S.P.Q.2d 1216, 1218 (B.P.A. I. 1990).

ᙡ

The prior art must provide one of ordinary skill in the art the motivation to make the proposed molecular modifications needed to arrive at the claimed compound. *In re Jones*, 958 F.2d 347, 21 U.S.P.Q.2d 1941, 1944 (Fed. Cir. 1992).

ᙡ

A commercial motivation is not a technologic suggestion to combine reference teachings. The concept of a new product is not the "motivation" that negates patentability. That the inventors hope to profit from their invention is irrelevant to the determination of obviousness. The motivation to which precedent is directed is that which would make obvious the technologic advance, not the motivation to achieve a competitive advantage. *Lamb-Weston Inc. v. McCain Foods Ltd.*, 78 F.3d 540, 37 U.S.P.Q.2d 1856 (dissent— 1863, 1864)(Fed. Cir. 1996).

ᙡ

The motivation in the prior art to combine references does not have to be identical to that of the applicant to establish obviousness. *In re Kemps*, 97 F.3d 1427, 40 U.S.P.Q.2d 1309, 1311 (Fed. Cir. 1996).

ᙡ

A "trend" might very well constitute a suggestion or teaching to one of ordinary skill in the art to make "minor" changes from the prior art in accordance with that trend to produce a claimed invention. Whether the prior art discloses a "trend" is a question of fact. The existence of a trend depends on the content of the prior art, i.e., what the prior art would have taught one of ordinary skill in the art at the time of the invention. By defining the inventor's problem in terms of its solution, the district court missed the necessary ancillary question, namely: whether the prior art contains a suggestion or motivation to combine references *to form a trend. Monarch Knitting Machinery Corp. v. Sulzer Morat GmbH*, 139 F.3d 877, 45 U.S.P.Q.2d 1977, 1981, 1982 (Fed. Cir. 1998).

ᙡ

The PTO must explain the reasons one of ordinary skill in the art would have been motivated to select the references and to combine them to render the claimed invention obvious. The Examiner must show reasons that the skilled artisan, confronted with the same problems as the inventor and with no knowledge of the claimed invention, would select the elements from the cited prior art references for combination in the manner claimed. While skill level is a component of the inquiry for a suggestion to combine, a lofty level of skill alone does not suffice to supply a motivation to combine. Otherwise a high level of ordinary skill in an art field would almost always preclude patentable inventions. *In re Rouffet*, 149 F.3d 1350, 47 U.S.P.Q.2d 1453, 1458, 1459 (Fed. Cir. 1998).

Motive. *See also* **Motivation, Principle.**

The motive or purpose of a patent assignment is irrelevant to the assignee's standing to enforce the assigned patent. Even a motive solely and expressly to facilitate litigation "is of no concern to the defendant and does not bear on the effectiveness of the assignment." *Discovery Rights, Inc. v. Avon Prods., Inc.*, 182 U.S.P.Q. 396, 398 (N.D. Ill. 1974).

Mouse.[10]

MPEP (Manual of Patent Examining Procedure). *See also* **Formal Rejection.**

The PTO is constrained to follow a ruling of its reviewing court (CCPA) when such is in variance with the MPEP. *Ex parte Hartmann*, 186 U.S.P.Q. 366, 367 (PTO Bd. App. 1974).

ᛦ

The MPEP "is primarily a set of instructions to the examining corps of the PTO from the Commissioner." It governs the details of the PTO examination, is made available to the public and describes procedures on which the public can rely. *Patlex Corp. v. Mossinghoff*, 771 F.2d 480, 226 U.S.P.Q. 985, 989 (Fed. Cir. 1985).

ᛦ

The MPEP contains some mandatory language. For the most part, however, the MPEP only suggests or authorizes procedures for patent Examiners to follow. For example, MPEP §707.03(d) provides that Examiners "should allow claims which define the patentable novelty with a reasonable degree of particularity and distinctness." The section further provides, "the Examiner's action should be constructive in nature...." The decision as to what is "reasonable" and "constructive" under the circumstances is necessarily a matter of the Examiner's discretion and judgment. The Foreword to the Fifth Edition of the MPEP, dated August 1983, states that the MPEP "contains instructions to examiners," but "does not have the force of law or the force of the Patent Rules of Practice in Title 37, Code of Federal Regulations." The MPEP does not eliminate a patent Examiner's discretion when examining patent applications. Rather, the MPEP is merely

---

[10]Refer to U.S. Patent No. 5,175,383; U.S. Patent No. 5,175,384; and U.S. Patent No. 5,175,385.

part of the overall scheme providing for discretionary examination of patent applications. *Chamberlin v. Isen*, 779 F.2d 522, 228 U.S.P.Q. 369, 372 (9th Cir. 1985).

ᵹ

While the MPEP may not have the force of law, or wield as much authority as the rules of practice, its interpretation of the statutes and rules is nevertheless entitled to considerable deference with respect to issues not specifically addressed by the courts. *Reitz v. Inoue*, 39 U.S.P.Q.2d 1838, 1840 (B.P.A.I. 1995).

ᵹ

The MPEP does not have the force and effect of law; however, it is entitled to judicial notice as the agency's official interpretation of statutes or regulations, provided it is not in conflict with the statutes or regulations. *Refac International Ltd. v. Lotus Development Corp.*, 81 F.3d 1576, 38 U.S.P.Q.2d 1665, 1671 n.2 (Fed. Cir. 1996).

MPEP §804.03

The Examiner improperly required, under threat of abandonment per MPEP §804.03, that petitioner's assignee limit the claims of one of two copending applications owned by that assignee. Although 37 C.F.R. §1.78(b) provides for "elimination" of conflicting claims from all but one application of the same applicant, 37 C.F.R. §1.78(c) provides no such authority when the applications are from different inventors and are owned by a common assignee. *Margolis, Rushmore, Liu, and Anderson v. Banner*, 599 F.2d 435, 202 U.S.P.Q. 365, 372 (C.C.P.A. 1979).

MPEP §2258

To the extent that M.P.E.P. §2258 enlarges the statutory authorization (no grounds of reexamination were to be permitted other than based on new prior art and sections 102 and 103), it is void. *In re Recreative Technologies Corp.*, 83 F.3d 1394, 38 U.S.P.Q.2d 1776, 1778, 1779 (Fed. Cir. 1996).

Multiple Inclusion.

When a submechanism really performs two independent functions, there is no objection to including it twice in a claim, once under each separate function. *Ex parte Olsson*, 65 U.S.P.Q. 52, 54 (PO Bd. App. 1944).

ᵹ

Double inclusion of an element in a claim (including overlapping members of a Markush group) is objectionable since it makes the claims vague and indefinite and fails to point out and distinctly claim the invention as required by 35 U.S.C. §112. *Ex parte White and Cates*, 127 U.S.P.Q. 261 (PO Bd. App. 1958).

ᵹ

A single structural element, such as a piston, that performs two separate functions supports a claim broadly reciting the separate functions. Such an interpretation of the claims is reasonable because, even though the piston is contained in a unitary housing during both its functions, the piston does in fact perform two distinct and separate functions, reducing the pressure and engaging the clutch or other friction means. An arbitrary application of the "rule against double inclusion" to the facts of this appeal leads to a result that is contrary to a reasonable interpretation of the claims. *In re Kelley*, 305 F.2d 909, 134 U.S.P.Q. 397, 401 (C.C.P.A. 1962).

ᢍ

Multiple inclusion in a claim of a single element may or may not render the claim indefinite. Automatic reliance upon a "rule against double inclusion" leads to as many unreasonable interpretations as does automatic reliance upon a "rule allowing double inclusion." The governing consideration is not double inclusion, but rather what is a reasonable construction of the language of the claim. *Ex parte Ionescu*, 222 U.S.P.Q. 537 (PTO Bd. App. 1984).

Multiple Inventions.

Claims had been withdrawn from further consideration on the ground that they included multiple "patentably distinct" inventions. The claims were withdrawn from consideration not only in the subject application but prospectively in any subsequent application because of their content. In effect there had been a denial of patentability of the claims. The absolute "withdrawal" cannot properly be categorized as merely a "requirement" or "objection" to restrict review to petition. An Examiner's action of this nature is a rejection, a denial of substantive rights. *In re Haas*, 486 F.2d 1053, 179 U.S.P.Q. 623 (C.C.P.A. 1973).

Multiple Rejections.

The use of multiple rejections should be avoided where they confuse the issue. The rejection of claims as fully met by selected references considered individually, and the rejection of the same claims on a combination of references (including one or more of the selected references) confuses the record as to the real pertinence of the several references. *In re Leflar*, 85 U.S.P.Q. 377 (PO Supervisory Examiner 1947).

ᢍ

A rejection of one or more claims based on combinations or permutations of nine or more enumerated references defeats the intent or purpose of 35 U.S.C. §132. The Court declined to substitute speculation as to the rejection for the greater certainty which should come from the Patent Office in a more definite statement of the grounds of rejection. *In re Herrick and Bock*, 344 F.2d 713, 145 U.S.P.Q. 400, 401, 402 (C.C.P.A. 1965).

Multiple Utilities.

A method-of-use claim is not rendered indefinite because it recites diverse utilities. *Ex parte Skuballa*, 12 U.S.P.Q.2d 1570, 1571 (B.P.A.I. 1989).

Multiplication of Parts. *See* Separable.

Multiplicity.

When two claims do not use exactly the same terminology to define the structural formula of the compounds, which is stated to be that of one or the other of the claims, the allowance of both claims is not objectionable since there is no unreasonable multiplicity of claims. *Ex parte Scott*, 54 U.S.P.Q. 148, 149 (PO Bd. App. 1941).

ω

While forty pages of claims may seem to be unnecessarily prolix, the mere psychological reaction to this amount of material does not, in and of itself, constitute a legal basis for rejection. The Examiner must show either that the claims are so unduly multiplied that they are difficult to understand, making examination almost impossible, or that the claims are for the most part duplicates. *Ex parte Birnbaum*, 161 U.S.P.Q. 635, 637 (PO Bd. App. 1968).

ω

Applicants should be allowed reasonable latitude in stating their claims in regard to number and phraseology employed. The right of applicants to freedom of choice in selecting phraseology which truly points out and defines their inventions should not be abridged. Such latitude, however, should not be extended to sanction that degree of repetition and multiplicity which beclouds definition in a maze of confusion. *In re Flint*, 411 F.2d 1353, 162 U.S.P.Q. 228, 230 (C.C.P.A. 1969).

ω

It is rarely possible to determine any necessity for narrower claims at the time of prosecution. An applicant often does not know the prior art that may be asserted against his broader claims when he litigates his patent. Further, he is never sure that the broader claims will not be successfully attacked on other grounds when litigated in the courts. Moreover, there is no statutory authority for rejecting claims as being "unnecessary." An applicant should be allowed to determine the necessary number and scope of his claims, provided he pays the required fees and otherwise complies with the statute. We disagree with the Board's view that the number of claims was so large as to obscure the invention, thereby failing to comply with the second paragraph of 35 U.S.C. §112. Each appealed claim is relatively brief and clear in its meaning. Examination of 40 claims in a single application may be tedious work, but this is no reason for saying that the invention is obscured by the large number of claims. *In re Wakefield and Foster*, 422 F.2d 897, 164 U.S.P.Q. 636 (C.C.P.A. 1970).

ω

There is no statutory support for a rejection (allegedly under 35 U.S.C. §112) based on undue multiplicity of claims in an application when considered in combination with the claims of a U.S. patent. *Ex parte Shelton*, 172 U.S.P.Q. 319, 320 (PO Bd. App. 1971).

ω

Practice has long recognized that "claims may be multiplied . . . to define the metes and bounds of the invention in a variety of different ways." Thus, two claims that read differently can cover the same subject matter. *Tandon Corp. v. United States International Trade Commission*, 831 F.2d 1017, 4 U.S.P.Q.2d 1283 (Fed. Cir. 1987).

Mutual Interest.

Where attorneys for parties having a mutual interest in litigation exchange their work product, it remains protected by a qualified privilege. *The Stanley Works v. Haeger Potteries, Inc.*, 35 F.R.D. 551, 142 U.S.P.Q. 256, 258 (Ill. 1964).

Key Terms and Concepts

N

Name. *See also* **Enabling Disclosure, Formula, Naming.**

The substantial equivalent of a thing, in the sense of the patent law, is the same as the thing itself; if two devices do the same work in substantially the same way and accomplish substantially the same result, they are the same even though they differ in name, form, or shape. *Hugh W. Batcheller v. Henry Cole Co.*, 7 F. Supp. 898, 22 U.S.P.Q. 354, 358 (Mass. 1934).

ᛦ

It is irrelevant that appellant (a party to an interference) never referred to or appreciated the support material to be eta-alumina or to contain eta alumina *by that name*. However, it is fatal to appellant's case that he did not recognize (until after his interference opponent's filing date) that his "ammonia-aged" catalyst *contained any different form of alumina at all!*" (Emphasis in original.) The count calls for a *particular* form of alumina. Appellant's failure to recognize that he had produced a new form, regardless of what he called it, is indicative that he never conceived the invention prior to his opponent's filing date. *Heard v. Burton, Kaufman, Lefrancois, and Riblett*, 333 F.2d 239, 142 U.S.P.Q. 97, 100 (C.C.P.A. 1964).

ᛦ

Names and structural formulae are not chemical compounds, but mere designations therefor. When a claimed invention is a group of compounds, the obviousness or unobviousness of the compounds is in issue. Certainly, the structure and/or name of a compound might well be suggested when the compound itself is not. *In re Krazinski, Shepherd, and Taft,* 347 F.2d 656, 146 U.S.P.Q. 25, 28 (C.C.P.A. 1965).

Naming. *See also* **Enabling Disclosure.**

The mere naming of a compound in a reference, without more, cannot constitute a description of the compound, particularly when the evidence of record suggests that a method suitable for its preparation was not developed until a date later than that of the reference. Otherwise, lists of thousands of theoretically possible compounds could be generated and published which, assuming it would be within the level of skill in the art to make them, would bar a patent to the actual discoverer of a named compound no matter how beneficial to mankind it might be. Such a result would be repugnant to the statute. *In re Wiggins, James, and Gitton*, 483 F.2d 538, 179 U.S.P.Q. 421, 425 (C.C.P.A. 1973).

ᛦ

Having been produced by the same process, the product obtained in Example IV of the earlier Sulkowski application is, of necessity, the same product as that obtained in Example III of the Sulkowski interference application. The only difference is in the naming of the product. Based on the process used in the earlier application, Sulkowski is entitled to the benefit of the product of that process with his later application. The fact that error was made in naming the product in the first application does not deprive Sulkowski of the benefit of that application. *Sulkowski v. Houlihan*, 179 U.S.P.Q. 685, 686 (PTO Bd. Pat. Int. 1973). *See also In re Sulkowski*, 487 F.2d 920, 180 U.S.P.Q. 46 (C.C.P.A. 1973).

Naphthyl. *See* **Benzyl, Phenyl vs. Naphthyl.**

Narrowing Claim. *See also* **Claim Limitation, Description, Limiting, Limitation, File Wrapper Estoppel, Recapture, Reduction in Scope, Retreat.**

When the narrowing of claims creates a new subgenus for which there is no express basis or exemplification in the original disclosure, such narrowing can involve prohibited "new matter" and can also subject involved claims to rejection on the basis of lack of description. *In re Welstead*, 463 F.2d 1110, 174 U.S.P.Q. 449 (C.C.P.A. 1972).

ω

The notion that one who fully discloses (and teaches those skilled in the art how to make and use) a genus and numerous species therewithin has somehow failed to disclose (and teach those skilled in the art how to make and use) a genus minus two of those species, and thus has failed to satisfy the requirements of 35 U.S.C. §112, first paragraph, appears to result from a hypertechnical application of legalistic prose relating to that provision of the statute. All that happened here is that the appellants narrowed their claims to avoid having them read on a lost interference count. Though it is true that insufficiency under §112 cannot be cured by citing the causes for such insufficiency, it is not true that the factual context out of which a question under §112 arose was immaterial. Quite the contrary. The "written description" in the 1963 specification supported the claims in the absence of the limitation, and the parent specification having described the whole, necessarily described the part remaining. The facts of the prosecution are properly presented and relied on, under these circumstances, to indicate that the appellants are merely excising the invention of another, to which they are not entitled, and are not creating an "artificial subgenus" or claiming "new matter." *In re Johnson and Farnham*, 558 F.2d 1008, 194 U.S.P.Q. 187 (C.C.P.A. 1977).

ω

Even when an estoppel arises from the file, the doctrine of equivalents is not completely eliminated. Depending on the nature and the purpose of an amendment, it may have a limited effect ranging from great to small to zero. The effect may or may not be fatal to application of a range of equivalents broad enough to encompass a particular accused product. It is not fatal to application of the doctrine of equivalents itself. Whenever the doctrine of file history estoppel is invoked, a close examination must be made as to not only what was surrendered, but also the reason for such a surrender. The fact that claims were narrowed does not always mean that the doctrine of file history estoppel completely prohibits a patentee from recapturing some of what was originally claimed. *Glaros v. H.H. Robertson Co.*, 615 F. Supp. 186, 227 U.S.P.Q. 448 (Ill. 1985).

ω

That a patent applicant narrows his claim to secure a patent does not always mean that prosecution history estoppel completely prohibits the patentee from recapturing some of what was originally claimed. *Pennwalt Corp. v. Durand-Wayland Inc.*, 833 F.2d 931, 4 U.S.P.Q.2d 1737 (Fed. Cir. 1987).

Natural Law. *See* **Law of Nature.**

Natural Product. *See also* **Life Form.**

Merely because there is evidence that a product exists in nature with other substances is not invariably sufficient reason for denying claims to such product. Appellants have not merely obtained a pure product of the same utility as the substance from which it was isolated. The product does not differ from its source only in purity, but has a new utility on which invention may rest. *Ex parte Reed and Gunsalus*, 135 U.S.P.Q. 105, 106 (PO Bd. App. 1961).

ω

Since the prior art Aureomycin fermentation broths and antibiotics contained insufficient tetracycline to be of any benefit to mankind, they do not, as a matter of law, negate the validity of tetracycline patent claims. The prior existence of tetracycline and Aureomycin in trace amounts, unrecognized and of no use, does not invalidate the patent. *Chas. Pfizer & Co., Inc. v. Barry-Martin Pharmaceuticals, Inc.*, 241 F.Supp. 191, 145 U.S.P.Q. 29, 32 (Fla. 1965).

ω

A claim to a "synthetically produced" or a "substantially pure" substance may well have the requisite novelty to distinguish over a counterpart which occurs in nature only in impure form. *In re Kratz and Strasburger*, 592 F.2d 1169, 201 U.S.P.Q. 71, 75 (C.C.P.A. 1979).

NDA (New Drug Application). *See also* **ANDA.**

An approved NDA simply signifies that a drug has met federal safety and efficacy requirements and therefore can be introduced into interstate commerce. It is not equivalent to the product it addresses; it does not authorize anyone to make, use, or sell cephalexin, and certainly not in derogation of another's patent. In short, the NDA is a separate property that was not involved in the *Eli Lilly-Premo* injunction action and was not mentioned in the dismissal order. At least insofar as the settlement agreement was concerned, Premo's wrong was its infringement of Eli Lilly's patents, not its acquisition of the NDA. It cannot be said that, by acquiring the NDA, Vitarine "succeeded in interest to the subject matter of the prior decree." Because Vitarine did not succeed to Premo's interest in the subject of the dismissal order, the injunction does not apply, and it cannot be held in contempt. The courts may not grant an enforcement order or injunction so broad as to make punishable the conduct of persons who act independently and whose rights have not been adjudged according to law. *Eli Lilly & Co. v. Premo Pharmaceutical Laboratories Inc.*, 843 F.2d 1378, 6 U.S.P.Q.2d 1367 (Fed. Cir. 1988).

ω

The Drug Price Competition and Patent Term Restoration Act [Pub. L. No. 98-417, 98 Stat. 1585 (1984)] is generally known as the Hatch Waxman Amendments to the

Federal Food, Drug, and Cosmetic Act (21 U.S.C. §§301 et seq.). The purpose of this legislation was to increase competition in the drug industry by facilitating the approval of generic copies of drugs. Rather than complete the full NDA process, generic copiers could proceed via an Abbreviated New Drug Application (ANDA), which required merely reference to the safety and effectiveness status submitted by the "pioneer" drug manufacturer, along with submission of manufacturing and bioequivalence data for the generic copy. *Mead Johnson Pharmaceutical Group v. Bowen,* 838 F.2d 1332, 6 U.S.P.Q.2d 1565 (D.C. Cir. 1988).

ω

As the subparagraphs of 21 U.S.C. §355(j) must be read as a whole and in context with the other paragraphs of §355, namely: §355(b), and as 35 U.S.C. §271(e)(2)(A) expressly incorporates §355(j), an action for patent infringement brought pursuant to §271(e)(2)(A) cannot be premised on a patent not included in an NDA filed pursuant to §355(b)(1), and thus not connected with a drug listed by the Secretary pursuant to §355(j)(6). *Abbott Laboratories v. Zenith Laboratories Inc.,* 35 U.S.P.Q.2d 1161, 1168 (Ill. 1995).

Nearly.

The descriptive word "about" is not indefinite, and its meaning is not broad and arbitrary. The term is clear, but flexible, and is deemed to be similar in meaning to terms such as approximately or nearly. *Ex parte Eastwood, Brindle, and Kolb,* 163 U.S.P.Q. 316 (PTO Bd. App. 1968).

Necessary. *See* Party.

Need. *See* Secondary Considerations.

Negative Function.

A negative definition of a valve in terms of a condition to which it is not subject presents nothing of patentable significance. The characterization of an element in terms of an operation or result with which it is not concerned does not particularly point out the subject matter which appellants regard as their invention. *Ex parte Ball and Hair,* 99 U.S.P.Q. 146, 150 (PO Bd. App. 1953).

Negative Limitation. *See also* Free, Narrowing Claim.

The use of a negative limitation (excluding characteristics of prior-art products), causing claims to read on a virtually unlimited number of materials, many of which "might be the full equivalents in their effects of those excluded," does not render the claims indefinite. The scope of a claim is still definite when each recited limitation is definite. *In re Wakefield and Foster,* 422 F.2d 897, 164 U.S.P.Q. 636 (C.C.P.A. 1970).

ω

There is no preclusion of negative limitations, notwithstanding the breadth of asserted claims. There is no problem under the second paragraph of 35 U.S.C. §112, so long as the scope of the claim is definite. *In re Barr, Williams, and Whitmore,* 444 F.2d 588, 170 U.S.P.Q. 330 (C.C.P.A. 1971).

ᴛᴏ

Negative limitations do not, per se, subject a claim to rejection based on alleged indefiniteness. *Ex parte Hradcovsky,* 214 U.S.P.Q. 554 (PTO Bd. App. 1982).

ᴛᴏ

A rejection of claims (for lack of adequate descriptive support because there was "no literal basis for the" claim limitation "in the absence of a catalyst") was reversed. The observation of lack of literal support does not, in and of itself, establish a *prima facie* case for lack of adequate descriptive support under the first paragraph of 35 U.S.C. §112. It cannot be said that the originally-filed disclosure would not have conveyed to one having ordinary skill in the art that appellants had possession of the *concept* of conducting the decomposition step in the absence of a catalyst. Throughout the discussion, which would seem to cry out for a catalyst if one were used, no mention is made of a catalyst. *Ex parte Parks,* 30 U.S.P.Q.2d 1234, 1236 (B.P.A.I. 1993).

Negative Rules of Invention. *See also* Change.

The negative rules of invention are to the effect that, ordinarily, it does not require anything more than mechanical skill to increase or decrease the size of a device or of any of its parts, or to increase the strength of one or more of its parts, but this rule (like the other negative rules) finds exceptions in special instances where it can be shown that the change in size or strength produces an unexpected or disproportionate result. *Ex parte McLean and Ives,* 86 U.S.P.Q. 517, 519 (PO Bd. App. 1950).

ᴛᴏ

Partially in response to the judicially created "negative rules of invention," Congress amended the patent laws in 1952, retaining the requirements of novelty and utility, but adding for the first time a requirement of invention. Congress decided, moreover, to "start fresh semantically and to promote uniformity" by imparting to the invention requirement a new rubric—non-obviousness. The Supreme Court in *Graham* [383 U.S. 1, 148 U.S.P.Q. 459 (1966)] seemed to regard 35 U.S.C. §103 as abolishing the judicially fashioned "negative rules of inference" and replacing them with a unitary inquiry into obviousness. *Rengo Co. Ltd. v. Molins Machine Co., Inc.,* 657 F.2d 535, 211 U.S.P.Q. 303, 312, 313 (3d Cir. 1981).

Negligence. *See also* Excusable Neglect.

The defense of inequitable conduct requires proof of (1) an act of misrepresentation (2) that was material, (3) involving information that was known or should have been known to the patentee and (4) that was committed with requisite intent. The elements of materiality and intent must be determined separately and then weighted together to ascertain whether the patentee engaged in inequitable conduct. The tribunal must then carefully balance the materiality and intent; the less material the proffered or withheld information, the greater the degree of intent that must be proven. In contrast, a lesser degree of intent must be proven when the information has a great degree of materiality.

Indeed, gross negligence can be the intended level of intent when the misrepresentation has a high degree of materiality. Simple negligence, however, or an error in judgment is never sufficient for holding of inequitable conduct. *Akzo M. V. Aramide Maatschappij V.O.F. v. E. I. du Pont de Nemours*, 810 F.2d 1148, 1 U.S.P.Q.2d 1704 (Fed. Cir. 1987).

ω

Even a finding of gross negligence does not of itself justify an inference of intent to deceive; the involved conduct, viewed in the light of all the evidence, including evidence indicative of good faith, must indicate culpability sufficient to require a finding of intent to deceive. *Symbol Technologies Inc. v. Opticon Inc.*, 935 F.2d 1569, 19 U.S.P.Q.2d 1241, 1251 (Fed. Cir. 1991).

ω

The negligence of his attorney does not excuse applicant's duty to exercise due diligence. An applicant has the duty to make sure his application is being prosecuted. Applicant's lack of due diligence over a two and one-half year period overcame and superseded any negligence of his attorney. The delay was not unavoidable because, had applicant exercised the due care of a reasonably prudent person, he would have been able to act to correct the situation in a timely fashion. *Douglas v. Manbeck*, 21 U.S.P.Q.2d 1697, 1700 (Pa. 1991).

Negotiations.

As a general rule, license negotiations may toll the running of a laches period. However, "the negotiations must ordinarily be continuous and bilaterally progressing, with a fair chance of success, so as to justify significant delays." *Valutron N.V. v. NCR Corp.*, 33 U.S.P.Q.2d 1986, 1990 (Ohio 1992), *affirmed* (Fed. Cir. 1993), *cert. denied*, (S.Ct. 1994).

New. *See* Novelty.

New Argument.

In an appeal before the CCPA the Solicitor cannot raise a new ground of rejection or apply a new rationale to support the rejection affirmed by the Board. *In re Strahilevitz*, 668 F.2d 1229, 212 U.S.P.Q. 561, 565 (C.C.P.A. 1982).

New Combination.

A new combination of old elements, whereby an old result is obtained in a more facile, economical and efficient way, or whereby a new and useful result is secured, may be protected by a patent. *Elgen Manufacturing Corp. v. Ventfabrics, Inc.*, 207 F.Supp. 240, 134 U.S.P.Q. 5, 14 (Ill. 1962).

ω

One element of a combination claim, though an old element, may serve to distinguish from the art by making a new combination, and the same is true of the recitation of this old feature when taken in conjunction with the other recited features. *In re Civitello,* 339 F.2d 243, 144 U.S.P.Q. 10, 13 (C.C.P.A. 1964).

ω

The character of a new composition of individually old substances cannot be determined from an examination of its component elements alone. It must be judged rather by the intrinsic attributes of the composition as a new combination. See *Robinson on Patents* §194 (1890). *In re Henderson,* 348 F.2d 550, 146 U.S.P.Q. 372, 373 (C.C.P.A. 1965).

New Facts.

An action in the district court under 35 U.S.C. §145 is a proceeding de novo and, while it is limited to the invention claimed in the PTO, the court may consider any additional competent evidence that a plaintiff neither intentionally nor negligently failed to submit to the PTO. The presumption of correctness that attaches to the decision of the Commissioner is a rebuttable presumption that may be overcome by the introduction of evidence (at a trial under §145) that is of such character and amount as to carry a thorough conviction of error. At such a trial the plaintiff and defendant may present evidence on any issue properly before the court. This additional evidence may include testimony of expert witnesses and inventors skilled in the art, and evidence of commercial success. In making its determination of non-obviousness, the court recognized the non-analogous nature of one reference, the lack of teaching or suggestion in the prior art of the useful advantage of a flexible track incapable of self-support, and the commercial success of the highly flexible Hot Wheels trackway-toy vehicle combination covered by the plaintiff's Reissue Application. The fact that the claimed invention seemed simple and, when viewed in hindsight, appeared to be obvious was not enough to negate invention. *Lemelson v. Mossinghoff,* 225 U.S.P.Q. 1063 (D.C. 1985).

New Ground of Rejection.[1] *See also* **37 C.F.R. §1.193(a) and 37 C.F.R. §1.193(b).**

The authority of the BPAI is limited by 35 U.S.C. §7(b) to "review adverse decisions of Examiners upon applications for patents...." No authority is granted to that body to review favorable decisions. To the extent that Rule 196(b) is inconsistent with the statute, it must fall. *Watson, Commissioner of Patents v. Bruns,* 239 F.2d 948, 111 U.S.P.Q. 325 (D.C. Cir. 1956).

ω

New reliance by the Board on a specific reference alone is, in effect, a new ground of rejection. New portions of the reference are relied upon to support an entirely new theory,

---

[1] Although it is permissible to withdraw a final rejection for the purpose of entering a new ground of rejection, this practice is to be limited to situations where a new reference fully meets at least one claim or meets it except for differences which are shown to be completely obvious. Normally, the previous rejection should be withdrawn with respect to the claim or claims involved. The practice should not be used for application of subsidiary references, or of references which are merely considered to be better than those of record. Furthermore, the practice should not be used for entering new non-reference or so-called "formal" grounds of rejection, such as those under 35 U.S.C. §112. Commissioner's Notice, 817 O.G. 1615 (Asst. Comm'r Richard A. Wahl 1965).

and the statutory basis for the rejection appears to have been shifted to 35 U.S.C. §102. *In re Echerd and Watters*, 471 F.2d 632, 176 U.S.P.Q. 321, 323 (C.C.P.A. 1973).

ᚹ

The fact that both parties have joined in requesting the court to rule on the merits of a new rejection does not preclude the court from remanding the case for further proceedings before the Patent Office. *In re Waymouth and Koury*, 489 F.2d 1297, 180 U.S.P.Q. 453, 454 (C.C.P.A. 1974).

ᚹ

Upon appeal from a decision by the Board of Appeals, the practice of raising a new ground of rejection (by the solicitor) is unfair to the other party, adds to the burden of the court, and serves to obscure the raising party's position on the issues that actually were raised below. Similarly, the solicitor's attempt to apply a new rationale to support the rejection based on a patent of record that was not relied on below cannot be condoned. New grounds of rejection, if valid, may be applied in further proceedings (referred to in 35 U.S.C. §144) before the PTO. *In re Armbruster*, 512 F.2d 676, 185 U.S.P.Q. 152 (C.C.P.A. 1975).

ᚹ

The criterion of whether a rejection is considered "new" in a decision by the BPAI is whether the appellants have had a fair opportunity to react to the thrust of the rejection. *Ex parte Maas*, 14 U.S.P.Q.2d 1762, 1764 (B.P.A.I. 1987).

ᚹ

The fact that the Examiner's conclusion of obviousness can be seen to be proper when based upon fewer references than relied upon in the rejection does not necessarily amount to a new ground of rejection. *Ex parte Raychem Corp.*, 25 U.S.P.Q.2d 1265, 1272 (B.P.A.I. 1992).

New Issues.

The court cannot consider new issues or new grounds of rejection on appeal. This does not preclude the court from considering each nuance or shift in approach urged by a party simply because it was not similarly urged below. *In re Osweiler*, 346 F.2d 617, 145 U.S.P.Q. 691, 694 (C.C.P.A. 1965).

ᚹ

In a patent interference case before the court parties are not permitted to raise new issues or to submit evidence omitted at the agency level out of negligent disregard for the administrative process. *Cody v. Aktiebolaget Flymo*, 452 F.2d 1274, 171 U.S.P.Q. 206, 210 (CA D.C. 1971).

ᚹ

A counterclaim (beyond the jurisdiction of a Patent Office tribunal) which pleads a common law cause of action sounding in tort and seeks variable equitable and legal relief can properly be presented in an action under 35 U.S.C. §146 even though not presented before the Board of Patent Interferences (because it could not be presented there). *Montecatini Edison, S.P.A. v. Ziegler*, 486 F.2d 1279, 179 U.S.P.Q. 458, 460 (CA D.C. 1973).

ᾧ

Consideration of an issue, raised in a interference for the first time at final hearing, is contrary to the PTO Rules of Practice. *Becker, Mitchell, and Pierson v. Ishibashi*, 201 U.S.P.Q. 319, 320 (PTO Bd. Pat. Intf. 1977).

ᾧ

An action in the district court under 35 U.S.C. §145 is a proceeding de novo and, while it is limited to the invention claimed in the PTO, the court may consider any additional competent evidence that a plaintiff neither intentionally nor negligently failed to submit to the PTO. The presumption of correctness that attaches to the decision of the Commissioner is a rebuttable presumption that may be overcome by the introduction of evidence (at a trial under §145) that is of such character and amount as to carry a thorough conviction of error. At such a trial the plaintiff and defendant may present evidence on any issue properly before the court. This additional evidence may include testimony of expert witnesses and inventors skilled in the art, and evidence of commercial success. In making its determination of non-obviousness, the court recognized the non-analogous nature of one reference, the lack of teaching or suggestion in the prior art of the useful advantage of a flexible track incapable of self-support, and the commercial success of the highly flexible Hot Wheels trackway-toy vehicle combination covered by the plaintiff's Reissue Application. The fact that the claimed invention seemed simple and, when viewed in hindsight, appeared to be obvious was not enough to negate invention. *Lemelson v. Mossinghoff*, 225 U.S.P.Q. 1063 (D.C. 1985).

Newly Discovered.

A newly-discovered function or property, inherently possessed by things in the prior art, does not cause a claim drawn to those things to distinguish over the prior art. *In re Best, Bolton, and Shaw*, 562 F.2d 1252, 195 U.S.P.Q. 430, 433 (C.C.P.A. 1977).

Newly Discovered Evidence.

The spirit of finality which is implicit in all judgments commands that courts be cautious in exercising the discretion vested in them to reopen proceedings for a new trial based on newly discovered evidence. While the sound discretion of a district judge in granting such a motion is not to be reversed except for clear abuse of discretion, that exercise is not free from review. *Ag Pro, Inc. v. Sakraida*, 512 F.2d 141, 185 U.S.P.Q. 642, 643 (5th Cir. 1975).

New Matter. *See also* cip, Error, *Ipsis Verbis*, Limit, Naming, Narrowing Claim, Support, Tumor.

A proposed amendment (including a new specification and drawing corresponding to those later filed as parts of a copending, but later-filed, application) was refused entry because the substance thereof had not been required and it contained new matter not supported by the original disclosure. While the proposed substitute specification and drawing (which were identical to those of a subsequently filed application) were physically part of the record of the previously filed application, they never formed part of the official disclosure of that application. The added subject matter has an effective date only as of the filing date of the subsequently filed application. *In re McIntosh*, 230 F.2d 615, 109 U.S.P.Q. 101, 103 (C.C.P.A. 1956).

ω

Enablement requirements for a pending application can be satisfied by amendment to make a cross-reference to a concurrently or previously filed copending application of the same inventor without involving improper "new matter." *Ex parte Wettstein, Vischer, Meystre, Kahnt, and Neher*, 140 U.S.P.Q. 187, 188 (PO Bd. App. 1962).

ω

Amendatory material concerned with an inherent characteristic of an illustrative product (already sufficiently identified in an original disclosure as filed) is not prohibited by statute. In *Ex parte Davisson and Finlay* [133 U.S.P.Q. 400, 402 (PO Bd. App. 1958)] for example, the Board noted that the Examiner had entered an amendment reciting optical rotation data and elemental analysis of the sulfate of a claimed substance as well as the spectroscopic characteristics of the claimed substance "apparently regarding them as a statement of inherent properties of the material adequately disclosed" in an original disclosure. The Board stated that it saw no reason for "taking a different view of the matter." *In re Nathan, Hogg, and Schneider*, 328 F.2d 1005, 140 U.S.P.Q. 601 (C.C.P.A. 1964).

ω

All claims were finally rejected under 35 U.S.C. §132 because of the new matter introduced into the application (i.e., filling in the serial number and filing date of the two applications referred to on page 1 of the original specification). The Board's acceptance of the identification of the copending applications as adequate under all the circumstances of the subject appeal is not a suggestion that more definite identification would not be desirable. An attorney would be well advised to utilize such means of identification as reference in the application as filed to the attorney's docket number and to the fact that the applications have the same filing date, if that is a fact, as it is here. *Ex parte Harvey*, 163 U.S.P.Q. 572, 573 (PTO Bd. App. 1968).

ω

In a sense, anything inserted in a specification that was not there before is new to the specification, but that does not necessarily mean that it is prohibited as "new matter." Prohibited new matter is that which is not found in the specification, drawings, or model, as first filed, and that involves a departure from the original invention [*Robinson on Patents* §561 (1890)]. The rule against new matter is intended to prevent an applicant (under the guise of an amendment) from introducing into his application a wholly different invention, or changing the construction of a fully disclosed invention, or presenting a different or preferred form of the invention. The applicant must stand or fall on his original disclosure, and all amendments must conform thereto. [Rivise and Caesar, *Patentability and Validity* §248 (1936).] *In re Oda, Fujii, Moriga, and Higaki*, 443 F.2d 1200, 170 U.S.P.Q. 268 (C.C.P.A. 1971).

ω

Limiting a class, generically disclosed, to a subgenus thereunder, without an original teaching of said subgenus as such, is directed to new matter that is not supported by the original specification. To be claimed, subgenera of lesser scope must be supported as such in the original description. *Ex parte Batchelder and Zimmerman*, 131 U.S.P.Q. 38 (PTO Bd. App. 1960); *In re Welstead*, 463 F.2d 1110, 174 U.S.P.Q. 449 (C.C.P.A. 1972).

ѡ

By disclosing a device that inherently performs a function, operates according to a theory, or has an advantage, a patent applicant necessarily discloses the function, theory, or advantage even though he says nothing concerning it. The application may be later amended to recite the function, theory, or advantage without introducing prohibited new matter. In a case where there is no unpredictability and where a broader concept than that expressly set forth in the specification would naturally occur to one skilled in the art from reading applicant's description, there is no basis for denying applicant claims that recite the broader concept. The alternative places upon patent applicants, the Patent Office, and the public the undue burden of listing (in the case of applicants), reading and examining (in the case of the Patent Office), and printing and storing (in the case of the public) descriptions of the very many structural or functional equivalents of disclosed elements or steps that are already stored in the minds of those skilled in the art, ready for instant recall upon reading the descriptions of specific elements or steps. *In re Smythe and Shamos*, 480 F.2d 1376, 178 U.S.P.Q. 279, 285 (C.C.P.A. 1973).

ѡ

Although an application, as filed, expressly referred to an identified copending British application, an attempt to insert the serial number of the corresponding U.S. application was met with a "new matter" rejection, which was sustained. *In re Hawkins*, 486 F.2d 579, 179 U.S.P.Q. 163, 165 (C.C.P.A. 1973).

ѡ

Although a new compound was disclosed and named as having an incorrect formula, by which the compound was claimed, the benefit of the filing date was accorded a continuing application in which the compound was properly named and identified by its correct formula. Having been produced by the same process, the product obtained in Example IV of the earlier Sulkowski application is, of necessity, the same product as that obtained in Example III of the Sulkowski interference application. The only difference is in the naming of the product. Based on the process used in the earlier application, Sulkowski is entitled to the benefit of the product of that process with his later application. The fact that error was made in naming the product in the first application does not deprive Sulkowski of the benefit of that application. *Sulkowski v. Houlihan*, 179 U.S.P.Q. 685, 686 (PTO Bd. Pat. Int. 1973). *See also In re Sulkowski*, 487 F.2d 920, 180 U.S.P.Q. 46 (C.C.P.A. 1973).

ѡ

Where a late-filed amendment of the patent specification is important enough to constitute the basis for alleged patentability, the amendment constitutes new matter and cannot in fact be a basis for patentability. *Honeywell Inc. v. Sperry Rand Corp.*, 180 U.S.P.Q. 673, 704 (Minn. 1973).

ѡ

The Primary Examiner objected to the words "and anti-tumour" and required either "cancellation of said term or proof that the instant compound is safe, reliable and effective for the utility set forth...." Considerable evidence was adduced, which the Commissioner concedes is sufficient to support a conclusion that the compound has anti-tumour effect in treating certain tumours. The Primary Examiner adhered to his requirement that the phrase be stricken because it was broader than the proof offered in support. The Commissioner went beyond his interpretation of the disputed words to reject amending language that would restrict the assertion to those uses supported by the proof. Such amendment would not be objectionable "new matter." "Amendments to specifications for the purpose of clarity and definiteness are permissible." *Helms Products, Inc. v. Lake Shore Manufacturing Co.*, 227 F.2d 677, 107 U.S.P.Q. 313, 314 (7th Cir. 1955). *See also Aerosol Research Co. v. Scovill Manufacturing Co.*, 334 F.2d 751, 141 U.S.P.Q. 758 (7th Cir. 1964). Cancellation of the words "and anti-tumour" by the Patent Office was arbitrary and capricious. The cancellation requirement is set aside with leave to the Commissioner to allow an amendment restricting the specification to assertions that are supported by applicants' proof. *Rhone Poulenc S.A. v. Dann*, 507 F.2d 261, 184 U.S.P.Q. 196 (4th Cir. 1974).

ϖ

Although the opinion of the Examiner is to be given great weight on the question of what constitutes new matter in an amendment to an application for patent, an amendment made more than one year after the invention went on sale does not disqualify applicant where the amendment was clarifying in its form and effect, rather than new matter. *Milgo Electronics Corp. v. United Telecommunications, Inc*, 189 U.S.P.Q. 160, 169 (Kan. 1976).

ϖ

The function of the description requirement is to ensure that, as of the filing date of the application relied upon, the inventor had possession of the specific subject matter later claimed by him; how the specification accomplishes this is not material. The claimed subject matter need not be described in haec verba to satisfy the description requirement. The application need not describe the claim limitations exactly, but only so clearly that one having ordinary skill in the pertinent art would recognize from the disclosure that applicant invented the subject matter including such limitations. *In re Herschler*, 591 F.2d 693, 200 U.S.P.Q. 711, 717 (C.C.P.A. 1979).

ϖ

Amending a specification by inserting an inherent property or correcting an erroneous structural formula of a compound which is necessarily produced by a disclosed process or example does not involve prohibited "new matter." *Ex parte Marsili, Rossetti, and Pasqualucci*, 214 U.S.P.Q. 904, 906 (PTO Bd. App. 1979).

ϖ

A patent application which discloses a device that inherently performs a function, operates according to a theory, or has an advantage, necessarily discloses that function, theory or advantage even though it says nothing concerning it. *In re Lange*, 644 F.2d 856, 209 U.S.P.Q. 288, 295 (C.C.P.A. 1981).

ϖ

The filing of a cip application to overcome a PTO rejection does not give rise to an irrebuttable presumption of acquiescence in the rejection. Whether claims are entitled to a cip application's filing date or that of a parent application becomes important when an intervening event occurs that will invalidate the claims under 35 U.S.C. §102 if they are only accorded the later filing date. When a cip is filed subsequent to receipt of a "new matter" rejection, the applicant may be estopped from arguing that the cip application only added subject matter that was inherent in the parent application. *Foseco International Ltd. v. Fireline, Inc.*, 607 F. Supp. 1537, 226 U.S.P.Q. 33 (Ohio 1984).

ω

After the PTO holds that an amendment to the specification involves new matter, the filing of a continuing application that includes the amendatory material and designating the application as a continuation-in-part (cip) application constitutes an acquiesence in the PTO's conclusion that the amendment contained new matter. *Max Daetwyler Corp. v. Input Graphics, Inc.*, 608 F. Supp. 1549, 226 U.S.P.Q. 393 (Pa. 1985).

ω

The PTO argued that a prefiling deposit with an independent depository, referred to in the specification at the time of filing, was essential to ensure that the disclosure was enabling as of the filing date, which in turn was required so that the filing date might be taken as the date of constructive reduction to practice. The PTO asserted that a post-filing deposit is barred as "new matter," as is the insertion in the specification of reference to such deposit. Constructive reduction to practice, however, does not turn on the question of who has possession of a sample, and thus it does not turn on the inclusion or absence, in the specification as filed, of the name and address of who will have possession of the sample on grant of the patent. The specification, as filed, thus met the requirements of constructive reduction to practice, and the insertion of depository data after filing is not "new matter" under 35 U.S.C. §132. *In re Lundak*, 773 F.2d 1216, 227 U.S.P.Q. 90 (Fed. Cir. 1985).

ω

The expressions "free of bleaching agent comprising an alkaline earth metal being capable of releasing hypochlorite or hypobromite in an aqueous solution" and "a non-reducing saccharide" find no support in the specification. They thus do not comply with the description requirement of the first paragraph of 35 U.S.C. §112. The fact that no compounds of this nature are taught to be present in the examples of this case is an insufficient basis for the limitations introduced into the claims when (1) quite evidently the presence of a bleaching agent is not intended to be excluded from the claim composition and, in fact, is intended be present as an ingredient, and (2) nowhere is it indicated that only nonreducing sugars are intended to be within the scope of saccharides as broadly disclosed. That sucrose is a nonreducing sugar does not entitle the appellant to claim a genus of which sucrose is a member. *Ex parte Pearson*, 230 U.S.P.Q. 711 (B.P.A.I. 1985).

ω

By disclosing in a patent application a device that inherently performs a function, operates according to a theory, or has an advantage, a patent applicant necessarily discloses that function, theory, or advantage, even though he says nothing concerning it. The express description of an inherent property, since not "new matter," can be added to a specification with effect as of the original filing date. The additional description is not that of a new use, but of the existing physical structure of the product. *Kennecott Corp. v. Kyocera International, Inc.*, 835 F.2d 1419, 5 U.S.P.Q.2d 1194 (Fed. Cir. 1987).

ᚹ

Including the term "polyvinyl chloride" in the specification is not an addition of new matter. The term is simply referred to in the amendment of the specification as an example of the type of vinyl that would be appropriate as a material in the grommet. As a more specific form of the generic vinyl term, it merely clarifies and makes more definite that which was already disclosed in the specification. *Chemcast Corp. v. Arco Industries Corp.*, 5 U.S.P.Q.2d 1225 (Mich. 1987).

ᚹ

The question of whether new matter has been added to a specification is petitionable, rather than appealable. *Ex parte Logan*, 20 U.S.P.Q.2d 1465, 1469 (B.P.A.I. 1991).

ᚹ

Section 120 (35 U.S.C.) neither establishes nor implies a requirement that a continuation application must be identical to the original application in all respects. As long ago explained in *Godfrey v. Eames*, 68 U.S. (1 Wall.) 317, 324-25 (1863):

> A change in the specification as filed in the first instance, or the subsequent filing of a new one, whereby a patent is still sought for the substance of the invention as originally claimed, or a part of it, cannot in any wise affect the sufficiency of the original application or the legal consequences flowing from it. To produce that result the new or amended application must be intended to serve as the basis of the patent for a distinct and different invention, and one not contemplated by the specification, as submitted at the outset.

Transco Products Inc. v. Performance Contracting Inc., 821 F.Supp 537, 28 U.S.P.Q.2d 1739, 1748 (Ill. 1993).

ᚹ

Since "routine experimentation" may involve rather extensive studies without straying from "undue" experimentation, and since appellants have provided no countervailing evidence, changes made during the prosecution of the reference patent are regarded to be of a type condoned by prior decisions. A change, per se, in an application disclosure does not constitute proscribed new matter. The question that first must be answered is whether the initial application provided by the patentee adequately enabled a person skilled in the subject art to practice the invention as claimed. *Ex parte D*, 27 U.S.P.Q.2d 1067, 1069, 1070 (B.P.A.I. 1993).

New Rationale.

Although the Board presented "amplified reasons in support" of affirmance, which reasons rely on additional facts not previously of record (of which the Board took notice), no new ground of rejection was involved, as the "evidentiary scheme" supporting the

Board's position did not differ in substance from that of the Examiner. *In re Boon*, 439 F.2d 724, 169 U.S.P.Q. 231, 234 (C.C.P.A. 1971).

ʊ

In an appeal before the CCPA the Solicitor cannot raise a new ground of rejection or apply a new rationale to support the rejection affirmed by the Board. *In re Strahilevitz*, 668 F.2d 1229, 212 U.S.P.Q. 561, 565 (C.C.P.A. 1982).

New Reference.

Ordinarily, citation by the Board of a new reference and reliance thereon to support a rejection will be considered as tantamount to the assertion of a new ground of rejection. This will not be the case, however, where such a reference is a standard work, cited only to support a fact judicially noticed and the fact so noticed plays a minor role, serving only "to 'fill in the gaps' which might exist in the evidentiary showing made by the examiner to support a particular ground for rejection." *In re Boon*, 439 F.2d 724, 169 U.S.P.Q. 231, 234 (C.C.P.A. 1971).

New Specification.

A proposed amendment (including a new specification and drawing corresponding to those later filed as parts of a copending, but later-filed, application) was refused entry because the substance thereof had not been required, and it contained new matter not supported by the original disclosure. While the proposed substitute specification and drawing (which were identical to those of a subsequently filed application) were physically part of the record of the previously filed application, they never formed part of the official disclosure of that application. The added subject matter has an effective date only as of the filing date of the subsequently filed application. *In re McIntosh*, 230 F.2d 615, 109 U.S.P.Q. 101, 103 (C.C.P.A. 1956).

New Starting Material. *See also* New Use.

Although an otherwise old process becomes a new process when a previously unknown starting material is used in it and is subjected to a conventional manipulation or reaction to produce a product that may also be new, albeit the expected result of what is done, it does not necessarily mean that the whole process has become non-obvious in the sense of 35 U.S.C. §103. In short, a new process may still be obvious, even when considered "as a whole," notwithstanding the fact that the specific starting material or resulting product, or both, are not to be found in the prior art. *In re Durden*, 763 F.2d 1406, 226 U.S.P.Q. 359 (Fed. Cir. 1985).

New Strain.

Without knowledge (supplied by applicant's disclosure) of a new Streptomyces strain, one skilled in the art would not find it obvious to produce a particular antibiotic by aerobically cultivating that strain even if all previously-known Streptomyces strains produce the same antibiotic under the conditions called for by applicant's claims. *In re Mancy, Florent, and Preud'Homme*, 499 F.2d 1289, 182 U.S.P.Q. 303, 305 (C.C.P.A. 1974).

New Theory. *See also* Theory.

New reliance by the Board on a particular reference, alone, is, in effect, a new ground of rejection. New portions of the reference are relied upon to support an entirely new theory, and the statutory basis for rejection appears to have been shifted to 35 U.S.C. §102. Under such circumstances, appellants should have been accorded an opportunity to present rebuttal evidence as to the new assumptions of inherent characteristics made by the Board. *In re Echerd and Watters*, 471 F.2d 632, 176 U.S.P.Q. 321, 323 (C.C.P.A. 1973).

New Trial. *See also* Motion for a New Trial, Newly Discovered Evidence.

A motion for a new trial under FRCP 60(b)(2) is an extraordinary motion and the requirements of the rule must be strictly met. The motion may not be granted unless (1) the evidence was discovered following the trial; (2) due diligence on the part of the movant to discover the new evidence is shown or may be inferred; (3) the evidence is not merely cumulative or impeaching; (4) the evidence is material; and (5) the evidence is such that a new trial would probably produce a new result. *Ag Pro, Inc. v. Sakraida*, 512 F.2d 141, 185 U.S.P.Q. 642, 643 (5th Cir. 1975).

ϖ

The right to a new trial requires that the movant is diligent, that the newly discovered prior art is not merely cumulative, that the prior art is material, and that the prior art will probably produce a different result. *Underwater Devices Inc. v. Morrison-Knudsen Co.*, 717 F.2d 1380, 219 U.S.P.Q. 569 (Fed. Cir. 1983).

ϖ

Even when comments or an attorney's conduct is clearly improper, unless the "misconduct so permeates the trial that the jury is necessarily prejudiced," no new trial is warranted. When allegedly improper comments occur in isolated and brief instances during the course of an otherwise fairly litigated trial, it cannot be said that a new trial is required. The conduct must be such as to impair gravely the calm and dispassionate consideration of the case by the jury.

A trial judge should not denigrate the jury system by granting a new trial on grounds of insufficient evidence and substituting his own judgment of the facts and witness credibility. *ALM Surgical Equipment Inc. v. Kirschner Medical Corp.*, 15 U.S.P.Q.2d 1241, 1252, 1253 (S.C. 1990).

ϖ

In ruling on a motion for a new trial, a trial judge has a duty to set aside a verdict and grant a new trial, even though the verdict is supported by substantial evidence, if he is of the opinion that the verdict is against the clear weight of the evidence or is based upon evidence that is false or will result in a miscarriage of justice. The granting or denial of a motion for a new trial is a ruling committed to the sound discretion of the trial court. The burden of showing error rests on the party seeking a rehearing on the merits. *Tenax Corp. v. Tensar Corp.*, 19 U.S.P.Q.2d 1881, 1884 (Md. 1991).

ᛦ

When a motion for new trial is based on the verdict being against the weight of the evidence, the trial court determines whether the jury's verdict is against the clear or great weight of the evidence. As a district court has discretion in granting a new trial, the abuse of discretion standard applies in reviewing a denial of a motion for new trial. *Standard Havens Products Inc. v. Gencor Industries Inc.*, 953 F.2d 1360, 21 U.S.P.Q.2d 1321, 1326 (Fed. Cir. 1991).

ᛦ

The standard for obtaining the grant of a new trial is a far less demanding one than the standard for an award for a judgment as a matter of law, but it does require a finding that the jury's verdict is against the clear weight of the evidence. A motion for a new trial is one directed to the discretion of the court, which has authority to set aside a verdict even though there is substantial evidence to support it, if left with the firm conviction that a mistake has been committed. *Valmet Paper Machinery Inc. v. Beloit Corp.*, 39 U.S.P.Q.2d 1878, 1884 (Wis. 1995).

ᛦ

Denial of a rehearing petition does not constitute a decision on the merits of whether the losing party may obtain a new trial on remand. *Exxon Chemical Patents Inc. v. Lubrizol Corp.*, 137 F.3d 1475, 45 U.S.P.Q.2d 1865, 1868 (Fed. Cir. 1998).

New Use.[2] *See also* **Analogy Processes, Double Use, Method of Use, New Starting Material, Starting Material, Use, Utilize.**

Each statutory class of claims should be considered independently on its own merits. The fact that the starting materials and the final product are the subject matter of allowed claims does not necessarily indicate that the process employed is patentable. *In re Albertson*, 332 F.2d 379, 141 U.S.P.Q. 730, 732 (C.C.P.A. 1964).

ᛦ

A new use of a known composition of matter can be properly claimed only by claiming the invention as a process or method. *Clinical Products Limited v. Brenner*, 255 F. Supp. 131, 149 U.S.P.Q. 475, 477 (D.C. 1966).

ᛦ

---

[2]*See* Kelly, Patrick D., "Old Drug, New Use: Article Of Manufacture Claims", BIO/TECHNOLOGY, Vol. 11, pp 839 and 840, July 1993, which refers directly to claim 18 of USP 5,011,853 and to claim 7 of USP 5,208,031, as well as to claim 7 of USP 4,988,710, which reads (in part): "An article of manufacture comprising packaging material and a pharmaceutical agent contained within the packaging material, wherein the pharmaceutical agent . . . , and wherein the packaging material comprises a label which indicates that the pharmaceutical agent can be used for reducing neurotoxic brain damage that might otherwise be caused by at least one cholinesterase inhibitor. . . ."

Where the invention resides in the use of a particular material in a particular article, a properly expressed article claim is an appropriate definition of the invention. *Ex parte Dunki*, 153 U.S.P.Q. 678, 679 (PO Bd. App. 1967).

ᄑ

The discovery of a hitherto unknown property of a known compound does not necessarily constitute basis for claiming a new use. *In re May and Eddy*, 574 F.2d 1082, 197 U.S.P.Q. 601, 607 (C.C.P.A. 1978).

ᄑ

Patentability of a new use (of an old material) based on an inherent, but previously unrecognized, property is not precluded. A contrary conclusion confuses anticipation by inherency, i.e., lack of novelty, with obviousness. *Jones v. Hardy*, 727 F.2d 1524, 220 U.S.P.Q. 1021, 1025 (Fed. Cir. 1984).

ᄑ

Though consideration of an invention's "gist" is appropriate in some context, e.g., in determining infringement under the doctrine of equivalents, when determining obviousness, there is no legally recognizable or protected "essence," "gist," or "heart" of the invention. Had the district court analyzed the invention in its entirety, it would have had to consider whether it would have been obvious to use the composition defined in the claims in the process defined by those claims. Even when a composition is old, a process using a known composition in a new and non-obvious way may be patentable. *Loctite Corp. v. Ultraseal Ltd.*, 781 F.2d 861, 228 U.S.P.Q. 90 (Fed. Cir. 1985).

ᄑ

A new *process* may still be obvious, even when considered "as a whole," notwithstanding the specific starting material or resulting product, or both, is not to be found in the prior art. (From the text of the decision it appears that patents had already issued on a parent and on a division of the parent application for products and for starting materials for producing the products, respectively. The decision was rendered in another divisional application in which, apparently, a single claim was directed to an analogy method of preparing products from the starting materials. The decision does not reflect that a "new use" argument was made.) *In re Durden, Jr.*, 763 F.2d 1406, 226 U.S.P.Q. 359, 362 (Fed. Cir. 1985). *But see In re Pleuddemann*, 910 F.2d 823, 15 U.S.P.Q.2d 1738, 1740, 1741 (Fed. Cir. 1990).

Nexus.

For commercial success to be a significant factor with regard to patentability, a nexus must be established between the commercial success and the merits of the invention. *In re Noznick, Tatter, and Obenauf*, 478 F.2d 1260, 178 U.S.P.Q. 43, 44 (C.C.P.A. 1973).

ᄑ

In order to establish that the claimed intermediate is the contributing cause of the unexpectedly superior activity or property of the end product, an applicant must identify the cause of the unexpectedly superior activity or property (compared to the prior art) in the end product and establish a nexus for that cause between the intermediate and the end product. *In re Magerlein*, 602 F.2d 366, 202 U.S.P.Q. 473, 479 (C.C.P.A. 1979).

ϖ

With respect to the objective indicia of non-obviousness, while there is evidence that marketing and financing played a role in the success of Hybritech's kits, as they do with any product, it is clear to us on the entire record that the commercial success here was due to the merits of the claimed invention. It cannot be argued on this record that Hybritech's success would have been as great and as prolonged, as admittedly it has been, if that success were not due to the merits of the invention. The evidence is that these kits compete successfully with numerous others for the trust of persons who have to make fast, accurate, and safe diagnoses. This is not the kind of merchandise that can be sold by advertising hyperbole. H*ybritech Inc. v. Monoclonal Antibodies, Inc.*, 802 F.2d 1367, 231 U.S.P.Q. 81 (Fed. Cir. 1986).

ϖ

Prima facie evidence of nexus is established when there is commercial success and when the invention disclosed in the patent was that which was commercially successful. *Ryko Manufacturing Co. v. Nu-Star Inc.*, 950 F.2d 714, 21 U.S.P.Q.2d 1053, 1058 (Fed. Cir. 1991).

ϖ

When a patented device is a commercial product, there is an inference that its commercial success is due to the patented device itself, absent a showing to the contrary. *See, e.g., Hughes Tool Co. v. Dresser Indus., Inc.*, 816 F.2d 1549, 1556, 2 U.S.P.Q.2d 1396, 1402 (Fed. Cir.), *cert denied*, 484 U.S. 914 (1987), as interpreted in the opinion for *Comair Rotron Inc. v. Matsushita Electric Corp. of America*, 33 U.S.P.Q.2d 1785, 1788 (Fed. Cir. 1994—unpublished).

ϖ

Congress could have chosen to protect U.S. process patents by defining an act of infringement to include every foreign-made product that is manufactured by a patented process. It chose, however, to restrict the scope of 35 U.S.C. §271(g) to exclude down-stream products that, due to intervening processing, cease to have a strong nexus to the patented process. *Eli Lilly and Co. v. American Cyanamid Co.*, 896 F.Supp. 851, 36 U.S.P.Q.2d 1011, 1018 (Ind. 1995).

ϖ

The burden of establishing a *prima facie* case of nexus is on the patent owner. *Indian Head Industries Inc. v. Ted Smith Equipment Co.*, 859 F.Supp. 1095, 36 U.S.P.Q.2d 1316, 1327 (Mich. 1994).

Nit Picking.

An infringer should not be permitted to side-step main issues by nit-picking the patent file in every minute respect with the effect of trying the patentee personally, rather than the patent. A patentee's oversights are easily magnified out of proportion by one accused of infringement and seeking to escape the reach of the patent by hostilely combing the inventor's files in liberal pretrial discovery proceedings. *Preemption De-*

vices, Inc. v. Minnesota Mining and Manufacturing Co., 559 F.Supp. 1250, 218 U.S.P.Q. 245, 257 (Pa. 1983).

Noerr-Pennington Doctrine.

The Noerr-Pennington doctrine holds that genuine attempts to influence the government are protected from Sherman Act liability by the overriding protections of the First Amendment. If the plaintiff can prove that the defendants fraudulently misrepresented their challenge to the patent to injure the competitive rights of the plaintiff, the Noerr-Pennington doctrine will not immunize the defendants from liability for those injuries. Actively misleading a federal agency is an abuse of administrative proceedings for which liability can be imposed under the sham-litigation exception. The First Amendment does not protect fraudulent misrepresentations to the PTO made to injure a competitor. *Ball Corp. v. Xidex Corp.*, 705 F. Supp. 1470, 9 U.S.P.Q.2d 1491 (Colo. 1988).

ω

A long line of Supreme Court cases has secured in our jurisprudence the notion that legitimate efforts to influence the government and courts to take anticompetitive actions cannot be the basis for antitrust liability. This immunity from antitrust liability is generally called the Noerr-Pennington doctrine. This name derives from the two leading cases that established the right to use governmental process despite the prohibitions of the Sherman Act. In 1972, the Supreme Court specifically extended this antritrust immunity to court actions having an anticompetitive result. Therefore, though a suit brought to protect patents or enforce exclusive license agreements may have anticompetitive consequences, such action is often protected against antitrust liability. The Noerr-Pennington doctrine rests upon a party's First Amendment right to petition the government. Access to the courts is one form of the right to petition. This right cannot be abridged despite a party's intent or anticompetitive purpose. The intention to harm a competitor is not, alone, sufficient grounds to find that a suit is a sham. Supreme Court cases are replete with references that anticompetitive motives do not per se eliminate Noerr-Pennington immunity. The requisite motive for establishing a sham exception is the intent to harm one's competitor not by the result of the litigation but "by the simple fact of the institution of litigation." Thus, the touchstone of the sham exception is whether "the desire for relief was a significant factor underlying the actual bringing and prosecution of the suit." *Collins & Aikman Corp. v. Stratton Industries Inc.*, 728 F. Supp. 1570, 14 U.S.P.Q.2d 1001, 1009 (Ga. 1989).

ω

A two-part definition of "sham" litigation for purposes of determining whether or not an antitrust defendant is entitled to immunity from antitrust litigation under the Noerr-Pennington doctrine is:

> First, the lawsuit must be objectively baseless in the sense that no reasonable litigant would realistically expect success on the merits. If an objective litigant could conclude that the suit is reasonably calculated to elicit a favorable outcome, the suit is immunized under Noerr, and an antitrust claim premised on the sham exception must fail.
>
> Second, the court should focus on whether the baseless lawsuit conceals an

attempt to interfere directly with the business relationships of a competitor through the use of the governmental process—as opposed to the outcome of that process—as an anticompetitive weapon.

This two-tiered process requires the plaintiff to disprove the challenged lawsuit's legal viability before the court will entertain evidence of the suit's economic viability. *Novo Nordisk of North America Inc. v. Genentech Inc.*, 885 F.Supp. 522, 35 U.S.P.Q.2d 1058, 1059, 1060, 1061 (N.Y. 1995).

ω

Litigation cannot be deprived of its antitrust immunity as a sham unless it is objectively baseless, regardless of whether the subjective intent of the litigation is to interfere with competition. *Hydranautics v. FilmTec Corp.*, 70 F.3d 533, 36 U.S.P.Q.2d 1773, 1777 (9th Cir. 1995).

ω

"*Noerr* immunity bars any claim, federal or state, common law or statutory, that has as its gravamen constitutionally-protected petitioning activity." *Raines v. Switch Manufacturing*, 44 U.S.P.Q.2d 1195, 1200 (Cal. 1997).

ω

Under the *Noerr-Pennington* doctrine, "[t]hose who petition government for redress are generally immune from antitrust liability". Given this broad immunity, a litigant may only proceed with antitrust counterclaims which are based upon the filing of a lawsuit if it "pierces" the presumption that a patent infringement suit is brought in good faith. *Mitek Surgical Products Inc. v. Arthrex Inc.*, 49 U.S.P.Q.2d 1275, 1282 (Utah 1998).

Non-Analogous. *See* Analogous Art.

Non-Critical.

Non-critical features of an invention may be supported by a more general disclosure than those at the heart of the invention. *In re Stephens, Benvau, and Benvau*, 529 F.2d 1343, 188 U.S.P.Q. 659, 661 (C.C.P.A. 1976).

Non-elected Species.

A rejection of a claim solely on the ground that it is drawn to a non-elected species was reversed because there was no ruling by either the Examiner or the Board as to whether claims (held allowable by the court) are generic. *In re Kelley*, 230 F.2d 435, 109 U.S.P.Q. 42, 45 (C.C.P.A. 1956).

Nonenabling.

Even though the claimed invention was disclosed as useful with a product of commerce, identified only by trademark, it is somewhat unrealistic to suggest that the specification would become nonenabling in the future by change of the manufacturer's requirements for the thus-identified product. *In re Comstock and Gilmer*, 481 F.2d 905, 178 U.S.P.Q. 616, 620 (C.C.P.A. 1973).

Nonexclusive.

An assignee of the legal patent holder granted a licensee two principal rights: the nonexclusive right to make, have made, use and sell the claimed invention and the right to grant further sublicenses within the United States on such terms as the licensee "in its sole discretion may determine". That bundle of rights was a property interest in the patent and gave the licensee the right to sue and recover damages as co-plaintiff (with the assignee) in an infringement action. *Schneider (Europe) AG v. SciMed Life Systems Inc.*, 28 U.S.P.Q.2d 1225, 1230, 1231 (Minn. 1993).

Nonjoinder. *See* Conversion.

Non-obvious. *See* Obviousness.

Nonresident Defendant.

Personal jurisdiction is acquired when parties file interfering applications at the Patent Office. The resulting "interference" in the Patent Office is the primary proceeding. A motion for discovery of documents under FRCP 35, being necessarily limited to a party in the action already commenced in the Patent Office, requires no new or independent assertion of personal jurisdiction or issuance of summons for a federal district court to order discovery in patent interference proceedings pursuant to 35 U.S.C. §24, even when the motion relates to a subject and resident of a foreign country. *Vogel v. Jones*, 443 F.2d 257, 170 U.S.P.Q. 188, 189 (3rd Cir. 1971).

ω

Two requirements must be met before the exercise of jurisdiction over a nonresident defendant will satisfy due process concerns: First, the nonresident must have some minimum contacts with the forum resulting in an affirmative act on its part; and second, it must not be unreasonable or unfair to require the nonresident to defend the suit in the forum state. Two types of in personam jurisdiction are recognized, specific and general. When a state exercises personal jurisdiction over a defendant in a suit arising out of or related to the defendant's contact with the forum, the state is exercising specific jurisdiction. When a state exercises personal jurisdiction over a defendant in a suit not arising out of or related to the defendant's contact with the forum, the state is said to be exercising general jurisdiction over the defendant. For general jurisdiction to exist, there must be a continuous and systematic contact between the state and the nonresident. *Gesco International Inc. v. Luther Medical Products Inc.*, 17 U.S.P.Q.2d 1168, 1170 (Tex. 1990).

ω

In *Akro Corp. v. Luker*, 45 F.3d 1541, 1545-46, 33 U.S.P.Q.2d 1505, 1508-09 (Fed. Cir. 1995), the CAFC outlined a three-prong minimum contacts test for determining whether specific jurisdiction exists: (1) whether the defendant purposefully directed its activities at residents of the forum, (2) whether the claim arises out of or relates to those activities, and (3) whether assertion of personal jurisdiction is reasonable and fair. *3D Systems Inc. v. Aarotech Laboratories Inc.*, 48 U.S.P.Q.2d 1773, 1776 (Fed. Cir. 1998).

Nonstaple. *See* **Staple Article of Commerce.**

Nonstatutory.

Efforts to explain nonstatutory subject matter in other terms has bred such phrases as "method of doing business", "transformation of subject matter", and "reactions of an individual". *In re Warmerdam*, 33 F.3d 1354, 31 U.S.P.Q.2d 1754, 1758 n.2 (Fed. Cir. 1994).

Norm. *See* **Flash of Genius.**

Notebook. *See also* **Laboratory Notebook.**

Applying a "rule of reason" and recognizing that (1) a deceased laboratory assistant's notebook was offered to prove a material fact, (2) the notebook was more probative on the point for which it was offered than any other evidence the interference party could produce, and (3) the interests of justice were best served by admitting the notebook, the notebook was admitted in evidence. *Flynn v. Arkley, Eardley, and Long*, 187 U.S.P.Q. 513, 520 (PTO Bd. Pat. Intf. 1975).

ω

Averments in an interference party's affidavits, which do not sufficiently correlate attached copies of various (rather cryptic in nature) laboratory notebook pages to explain or establish the conclusion that the product of the interference count was prepared, and recognized as such, prior to the interference opponent's filing date, are inadequate. Documentary exhibits are not self proving. *Amoss, Monahan, and Vale v. McKinley and Sarantakis*, 195 U.S.P.Q. 452, 453 (PTO Bd. Pat. Intf. 1977).

Notice.[3] *See also* **Judicial Notice, Marking.**

In making a rejection, an Examiner may "take notice of facts beyond the record which, while not generally notorious, are capable of such instant and unquestionable demonstration as to defy dispute." *In re Ahlert*, 424 F.2d at 1091, 165 U.S.P.Q. at 420 {citing *In re Knapp Monarch Co.*, 296 F.2d 230 [132 U.S.P.Q. 6] (C.C.P.A. 1961)}. Furthermore, although the cases provide that the Examiner should cite prior art references to support assertions of technical fact in esoteric technologies or specific knowledge of the prior art, this is solely to put the applicant on notice so that the correctness of the assertion can be challenged. *Id.*, 165 U.S.P.Q. at 420-21.

ω

Due process requires that an applicant be given notice of the reasons his claims are rejected and why arguments upon which he relies are deemed lacking in merit. This

---

[3] See *Wokas v. Dresser Industries Inc.*, 45 U.S.P.Q.2d 1600, 1604 (Ind. 1997).

principle is the essence of 35 U.S.C. §132 and should guide the proceedings of the Board of Appeals as well. *Ex parte Hageman*, 179 U.S.P.Q. 747, 751 (PTO Bd. App. 1972).

ω

Printed publications may properly be introduced into evidence (in an interference proceeding) during the taking of testimony relative thereto only if they are listed and served in accordance with the requirements of 37 C.F.R. §1.287(a) or a proper motion is filed under 37 C.F.R. §1.287(d)(1). *Bey and Jung v. Kollonitsch and Patchett*, 215 U.S.P.Q. 454, 456 (PTO Bd. Pat. Intf. 1981).

ω

See CMS Indus., Inc. v. L.P.S. Int'l, Ltd., 643 F.2d 289, 294, 217 U.S.P.Q. 20, 23 (5th Cir. 1981) (Markey, C.J., sitting by designation)("years of manufacturing and selling products embodying the invention" may indicate an ownership interest). "A person must use ordinary thoughtfulness and make accessible inquiries. If he does not, and avoids the inquiry, he is chargeable with the knowledge that ordinary diligence would have elicited, and cannot be considered a *bona fide* purchaser." *United States v. Orozco-Prada*, 636 F.Supp. 1537, 1543 (S.D.N.Y. 1986), *aff'd*, 847 F.2d 836 (2d Cir. 1988)(table).

ω

The issuance of a patent constitutes notice to the world of its existence. Patent indexes are published weekly, and patent records are readily available to the public. A coinventor is put on constructive notice when a patent issues without listing him as an inventor. A belated inventorship contest can be barred by laches. *Advanced Cardiovascular Systems Inc. v. SciMed Life Systems Inc.*, 20 U.S.P.Q.2d 1870, 1872 (Minn. 1991).

ω

A patentee that has a good faith belief that its patents are being infringed violates no protected right when it so notifies infringers. Patents would be of little value if infringers could not be notified of the consequences of infringement or proceeded against in the courts. *Mallinckrodt Inc. v. Medipart Inc.*, 976 F.2d 700, 24 U.S.P.Q.2d 1173, 1180 (Fed. Cir. 1992).

ω

Any requirement that notice to a patent infringer include the patent number has been engrafted onto the statute by the courts, and is not part of its plain language. The fact that the patent number is specifically required by statute for a marking, but is not mentioned with respect to actual notice, suggests that the actual number is only required for the former. *Ceeco Machinery Manufacturing Ltd. v. Intercole Inc.*, 817 F.Supp. 979, 25 U.S.P.Q.2d 1774, 1780 (Mass. 1992).

ω

For purposes of 35 U.S.C. §287(a), notice must be of "the infringement," not merely notice of the patent's existence or ownership. Actual notice requires the affirmative communication of a specific charge of infringement by a specific accused product or device. *Amsted Industries Inc. v. Buckeye Steel Castings Co.*, 24 F.3d 178, 30 U.S.P.Q.2d 1462, 1469 (Fed. Cir. 1994).

ω

The proper focus when determining the adequacy of notice is on the actions of the patentee, not the knowledge or intent of the infringer. *Cover v. Hydramatic Packing Co.*, 36 U.S.P.Q.2d 1199, 1200 (Pa. 1995).

ᴡ

Although there are numerous possible variations in form and content, the purpose of the actual notice requirement is met when the recipient is notified, with sufficient specificity, that the patent holder believes that the recipient of the notice may be an infringer. Thus, the actual notice requirement of 35 U.S.C. §287(a) is satisfied when the recipient is informed of the identity of the patent and the activity that is believed to be an infringement, accompanied by a proposal to abate the infringement, whether by license or otherwise. *SRI International Inc. v. Advanced Technological Laboratories Inc.*, 127 F.3d 1462, 44 U.S.P.Q.2d 1422, 1428 (Fed. Cir. 1997).

ᴡ

"For purposes of [35 U.S.C.] section 287(a), notice must be of the 'infringement,' not merely notice of the patent's existence or ownership." "Actual notice requires the affirmative communication of a specific charge of infringement by a specific accused product or devices." However, the notice need not necessarily include the word "infringement"; phrases such as "covered in" may be enough to suffice. *Wokas v. Dresser Industries Inc.*, 978 F.Supp.839, 45 U.S.P.Q.2d 1600, 1604 (Ind. 1997).

ᴡ

Determination of the propriety of actions in giving notice of patent rights is governed by federal statute and precedent and is not a matter of state tort law. "[F]ederal patent law bars the imposition of liability for publicizing a patent in the marketplace unless the plaintiff can show that the patent holder acted in bad faith." *Mikohn Gaming Corp. v. Acres Gaming Inc.*, 49 U.S.P.Q.2d 1308, 1311, (Fed. Cir. 1998).

Notice of Appeal.

The Supreme Court held that the failure of a party to be named in the notice of appeal from a judgment of a district court deprived the appellate court of jurisdiction over that party, and that inclusion of a party in the designation "et al." in the notice of appeal did not serve to identify the party. In an interference, however, Davis and Granger are regarded as a single party and thus appropriately designated as "Davis et al." in the notice of appeal. *Davis v. Loesch*, 998 F.2d 963, 27 U.S.P.Q.2d 1440, 1443 (Fed. Cir. 1993).

Novelty.[4] *See also* Anticipation, Change, Point of Novelty, 35 U.S.C. §101, 35 U.S.C. §102.

It is irrelevant that appellant (a party to an interference) never referred to or appreciated the support material to be *eta*-alumina or to contain *eta*-alumina *by that name*. However, it is fatal to appellant's case that he did not recognize (until after his interference

---

[4] See A. José Cortina, "When is Absolute Novelty Not Absolute Novelty?", *Intellectual Property Today*™, Vol. 4, No. 11, page 30, Nov., 1997.

opponent's filing date) that his "ammonia-aged" catalyst *"contained any different form of alumina at all!"* (Emphasis in original.) The count calls for a particular form of alumina. Appellant's failure to recognize that he had produced a new form, regardless of what he called it, is indicative that he never conceived the invention prior to his opponent's filing date. *Heard v. Burton, Kaufman, Lefrancois, and Riblett,* 333 F.2d 239, 142 U.S.P.Q. 97, 100 (C.C.P.A. 1964).

ω

An inoperable invention or one that fails to achieve its intended result does not negative novelty. *United States v. Adams,* 383 U.S. 39, 148 U.S.P.Q. 479, 483 (1966).

ω

The criteria for determining whether given subject matter is "new" within the meaning of 35 U.S.C. §101 are no different from the criteria for determining whether that subject matter possesses the "novelty" expressed in the title of 35 U.S.C. §102. The word "new" in §101 is defined and is to be construed in accordance with the provisions of §102. That which possesses statutory novelty under the provisions of §102 is also new within the intendment of 101. *In re Bergstrom and Sjovall,* 427 F.2d 256, 166 U.S.P.Q. 256, 262 (C.C.P.A. 1970).

ω

There is no conception or reduction to practice of a new form of an otherwise old composition of matter where there has been no recognition or appreciation of the existence of the new form. *Silvestri and Johnson v. Grant and Alburn,* 496 F.2d 593, 181 U.S.P.Q. 706, 708 (C.C.P.A. 1974).

ω

A claim to a "synthetically produced" or a "substantially pure" substance may well have the requisite novelty to distinguish over a counterpart which occurs in nature only in impure form. *In re Kratz and Strasburger,* 592 F.2d 1169, 201 U.S.P.Q. 71, 75 (C.C.P.A. 1979).

ω

Under the European Patent Convention and the law of most industrialized countries, an unauthorized disclosure of an invention does not immediately destroy its novelty (and thus foreclose the inventor's ability to patent the invention). Instead, such an adverse disclosure bars only patent applications made more than six months after the date of the disclosure [Art. 55 of the *Convention on the Grant of European Patents,* as printed in *European Patent Convention* (4th ed., Munich; European Patent Office, 1987)]. *Russo v. Baxter Healthcare Corp.,* 140 F.3d 6, 46 U.S.P.Q.2d 1239, 1241 (1st Cir. 1998).

Nucleus.

As all of the claimed compounds have a common nucleus which would exhibit certain characteristics irrespective of the single variant Y, claim 1 meets the standard for Markush claims and cannot properly be regarded as objectionably alternative, i.e., as covering several distinct inventions. *Ex parte Taylor,* 167 U.S.P.Q. 637 (PO Bd. App. 1970).

ω

Compounds of a claim which have a common utility and "a single structural sim-ilarity" (belong to a subgenus which is not repugnant to scientific classification) are part of a single invention so that there is unity of invention. *In re Harnisch*, 631 F.2d 716, 206 U.S.P.Q. 300, 305 (C.C.P.A. 1980).

Number.

The couching in patent claims of components of a chemical mixture in terms of numerical values of ratios placed a heavy burden on a busy Examiner and further weak-ened the presumption of patent validity. *Borden, Inc. v. Occidental Petroleum Corpora-tion*, 381 F.Supp. 1178, 182 U.S.P.Q. 472, 482 (Tex. 1974).

ᛒ

A numerical limitation in a claim cannot be availed of as a distinction over prior art unless the recited boundary "corresponds with physical phenomena, and the patentee has discovered the point at which such physical phenomena occur." *Fansteel, Inc. v. Carmet Company*, 210 U.S.P.Q. 413, 420 (Ill. 1981).

ᛒ

Damages are not affected by the number of claims infringed. *Square Liner 360°, Inc. v. Chisum*, 215 U.S.P.Q. 1110, 1119 (Minn. 1981).

Number Crunching.

A problem arises in computer-arts inventions when structure and apparatus claims are defined only as "means for" performing specified functions. If the functionally defined disclosed means and their equivalents are so broad that they encompass any and every means for performing the recited functions, the apparatus claim is an attempt to exalt form over substance, since the claim is really to the method or series of functions itself. In computer-related inventions, the recited means often perform the function of "number crunching" (solving mathematical algorithms and making calculations). In such cases the burden must be placed on the applicant to demonstrate that the claims are truly drawn to specific apparatus distinct from other apparatus capable of performing the identical functions. When this burden is not discharged, the apparatus claims will be treated as if they are drawn to the method or process that encompasses all of the claimed means. *In re Walter*, 618 F.2d 758, 205 U.S.P.Q. 397 (C.C.P.A. 1980).

Number of References.

Citation of many references almost always means either that none of them is in point and that the patentee has brought together (for the purpose of his invention) devices to be found in prior patents of different character, or that there have been prior attempts to solve the problem with which he was confronted which have not met with success. *Berry Brothers Corporation v. Sigmon*, 206 F.Supp. 653, 134 U.S.P.Q. 283, 291 (N.C. 1962).

ᛒ

The volume of the prior art points to the novelty of the invention. Voluminous prior art indicates that none of the prior art is in point or that prior attempts to solve the problem have not met with success. *Adams v. United States,* 330 F.2d 622, 141 U.S.P.Q. 361, 362 (U.S. Ct. Cl. 1964).

ω

Reliance upon a large number of references as prior art, in addition to the numerous references considered by the Patent Office, is indicative of invention as well as the futility of prior attempts to solve the problem. *Corometrics Medical Systems, Inc. v. Berkeley Bio-Engineering, Inc.,* 193 U.S.P.Q. 467, 477 (Cal. 1977).

ω

Reliance by a putative infringer on a large number of references as prior art, in addition to the references relied upon by the Patent Office, is indicative of invention, as well as the clear failure of the prior art to accomplish what the patentee accomplished. *Racal-Vadic, Inc. v. Universal Data Systems,* 207 U.S.P.Q. 902, 927 (Ala. 1980).

ω

The criterion with regard to the strength of the presumption of validity is "not the number of references but what they would have meant to a person of ordinary skill in the field of invention". *In re Gorman,* 933 F.2d 982, 986, 18 U.S.P.Q.2d 1885, 1888 (Fed. Cir. 1991).

ω

When a large number of prior art references come from the same field or industry as the claims-in-suit and where they, taken as a whole, use all of the elements of the patented invention in substantially the same manner for the same result, they actually strengthen the obviousness conclusion. *Nordberg Inc. v. Telsmith Inc.,* 881 F.Supp. 1252, 36 U.S.P.Q.2d 1577, 1614 (Wis. 1995).

Nunc Pro Tunc.

Neither conception nor reduction to practice can be established nunc pro tunc. *Langer and Tornqvist v. Kaufman and McMullen,* 465 F.2d 915, 175 U.S.P.Q. 172, 174 (C.C.P.A. 1972).

ω

Nunc pro tunc assignments are not sufficient to confer retroactive standing. As a general matter, parties should possess patent rights before seeking to have them vindicated in court. *Enzo APA & Son Inc. v. Geapag A.G.,* 134 F.3d 1090, 45 U.S.P.Q.2d 1368, 1371 (Fed. Cir. 1998).

Key Terms and Concepts

Oath. *See also* **Declaration, False Oath.**

Patentee's oath (accompanying his patent application) falsely stated that the product described and claimed in the application had not been in public use or on sale in the United States for more than one year prior to the filing date. This misrepresentation regarding the product described in original claim 1 was considered material to and tainted the entire application and patent claims even though the subject matter of claim 1 was canceled from the application before the patent issued. *St. Regis Paper Company v. Royal Industries*, 186 U.S.P.Q. 83, 87, 88 (Cal. 1974).

ʊ

An applicant's oath is not a requirement of 35 U.S.C. §112, first paragraph, but of 35 U.S.C. §115. Therefore, the sufficiency of an oath is not material under 35 U.S.C. §120, which incorporates only the requirements of §112, first paragraph. *Weil v. Fritz, Evans, and Cooke*, 572 F.2d 856, 196 U.S.P.Q. 600, 606 (C.C.P.A. 1978).

ʊ

The provisional acceptance of a Declaration and Power of Attorney in which the applicant fails to state his citizenship is not beyond the scope of discretion conferred on the PTO under 35 U.S.C. §26. *Autovox S.p.A. v. Lenco Italiana [sic], S.p.A.*, 210 U.S.P.Q. 277, 278 (Ill. 1980).

Objection.

When a party intends to rely on objections to an opponent's testimony, he must file a motion to suppress or strike the alleged improper testimony. The mere listing of objections in an appendix does not provide an adequate briefing of the issues as is contemplated by the requirement for a motion to suppress. *Fisher v. Bouzard*, 3 U.S.P.Q.2d 1677, 1680 (B.P.A.I. 1987).

ʊ

That part of the Examiner's "objection" which centers on description, enablement and best mode concerns the correspondence of the specification to the statutory requirements set forth in 35 U.S.C. §112 and is within the jurisdiction of the BPAI. However, that part of the "objection" which relates to the Examiner's desire for information concerning (a) an explanation of the "gist" of the invention, (b) the phenotypic characteristics of the parent plants and the inheritability thereof, and (c) the goals sought to be achieved by the inventors relates solely to the ease and accuracy of the examination process and the ability of the Examiner to obtain sufficient information therefrom to examine the application effectively. It concerns either the rules of practice or established customs and practices. It is outside the jurisdiction of the BPAI. *Ex parte C*, 27 U.S.P.Q.2d 1492, 1494 (B.P.A.I. 1992).

Objective Criteria. *See* **Secondary Considerations.**

Objective Enablement.

The first paragraph of 35 U.S.C. §112 requires nothing more than objective enablement. How such a teaching is set forth, either by the use of illustrative examples or by broad terminology, is of no importance. *In re Marzocchi and Horton,* 439 F.2d 220, 169 U.S.P.Q. 367 (C.C.P.A. 1971).

ᚶ

Affidavit evidence (reciting experiments and results), showing that the teaching in the specification is truly enabling, can be considered in demonstrating objective enablement. *In re Armbruster,* 512 F.2d 676, 185 U.S.P.Q. 152, 155 (C.C.P.A. 1975).

ᚶ

Claims were rejected because the term "comprising" permits the use of additional steps and/or additional treating agents that could yield results other than those desired; limiting the claims to "consist essentially of" the recited steps was recommended since the claimed subject matter related to the highly unpredictable and empirical art of catalysis. The rejection under 35 U.S.C. §112, first paragraph, was not sustained. The rejection is improper in the absence of any prior art that necessitates restriction of the claims to the suggested terminology and in the absence of some cogent reason to question the objective enablement provided by the disclosure in the application. *Ex parte Vollheim, Troger, and Lippert,* 191 U.S.P.Q. 407 (PTO Bd. App. 1975).

Objective Evidence. *See also* **Secondary Considerations.**

Mere conclusory statements in the specification, unsupported by objective evidence, are entitled to little weight when the PTO questions the efficacy of those statements. *In re Greenfield and DuPont,* 571 F.2d 1185, 197 U.S.P.Q. 227, 229 (C.C.P.A. 1978).

ᚶ

At the time of the invention the art taught away from the invention. Those skilled in the art were looking to higher mass and denser materials to block sound. Mr. Gardner went in a direction different from that of others in the art, and his invention thus produced unexpected results. Unexpected results provide objective evidence of non-obviousness. *Specialty Composites v. Cabot Corp.,* 845 F.2d 981, 6 U.S.P.Q.2d 1601 (Fed. Cir. 1988).

Objective Indicia. *See* **Secondary Considerations.**

Objective Truth. *See also* **Accuracy.**

A specification that contains a disclosure of utility that corresponds in scope to the subject matter sought to be patented must be taken as sufficient to satisfy the utility requirements of 35 U.S.C. §101 for the entire claimed subject matter unless there is reason for one skilled in the art to question the objective truth of the statement of utility or its scope. *Ex parte Rubin,* 5 U.S.P.Q.2d 1461 (B.P.A.I. 1987).

Obscure. *See also* **Inoperative.**

It is rarely possible to determine any necessity for narrower claims at the time of prosecution. An applicant often does not know the prior art that may be asserted against his broader claims when he litigates his patent. Further, he is never sure that the broader claims will not be successfully attacked on other grounds when litigated in the courts. Moreover, there is no statutory authority for rejecting claims as being "unnecessary." An applicant should be allowed to determine the necessary number and scope of his claims, provided he pays the required fees and otherwise complies with the statute. We disagree with the Board's view that the number of claims was so large as to obscure the invention, thereby failing to comply with the second paragraph of 35 U.S.C. §112. Each appealed claim is relatively brief and clear in its meaning. Examination of forty claims in a single application may be tedious work, but this is no reason for saying that the invention is obscured by the large number of claims. *In re Wakefield and Foster,* 422 F.2d 897, 164 U.S.P.Q. 636 (C.C.P.A. 1970).

Observing. *See* **Mental Steps.**

Obviousness. *See also* **Advance the Art, Analogy Process, Bioisosterism, Change, Characteristic, Chemical Obviousness, Color, Combining References, Compound, Contemplate, Crowded Art, Difference, Disadvantage, Enabling Prior Art, Generality, Gist, Improvement, Incentive, Inspiration-Perspiration, Knockdown, Modification, Motivation, Obvious to Try or Experiment, Paper Patent, Predictability,** *Prima Facie*, **Prior Art, Problem, Properties, Purpose, Secondary Considerations, Showing, Structural Obviousness, Suggestion, Teach Away From, Unexpected Results, 35 U.S.C. §103, Use.**

Patentability is gauged not only by the extent or simplicity of physical changes, but also by the perception of the necessity or desirability of making such changes to produce a new result. When viewed after disclosure, the changes may seem simple and such as should have been obvious to those in the field. However, this does not necessarily negative invention or patentability. The conception of a new and useful improvement must be considered along with the actual means of achieving it in determining the presence or absence of invention. The discovery of a problem calling for an improvement is often a very essential element in an invention correcting such a problem. Though the problem, once realized, may be solved by use of old and known elements, this does not necessarily negative patentability. *In re Bisley,* 197 F.2d 355, 94 U.S.P.Q. 80, 86 (C.C.P.A. 1952).

ᛒ

The conclusion as to invalidity is reinforced by the fact that this patent was involved in at least eleven interferences with other patents or patent applications. The fact that so many inventors in the field came forward at about the same time with similar solutions for the problems involved suggests strongly that these solutions involved not invention but only the skill of persons competent in the art. *Pierce v. American Communications Company, Inc.,* 169 F.Supp. 351, 119 U.S.P.Q. 456, 459 (Mass. 1958).

ᛒ

Signposts of obviousness include: How many tried to find the way? How long did the surrounding and accessory arts disclose the means? How immediately was the invention recognized as an answer by those who used the new variant? Economy of production is as valid a basis for invention as foresight in the disclosure of new means. *Reiner v. The I. Leon Company,* 285 F.2d 501, 128 U.S.P.Q. 25, 27, 28 (2d Cir. 1960).

ω

The 35 U.S.C. §103 requirement of non-obviousness is no different in chemical cases than with respect to other categories of patentable inventions. The problem of obviousness under 103 in determining the patentability of new and useful chemical compounds (or, as it is sometimes called, the problem of "chemical obviousness") is not really a problem in chemistry or pharmacology or in any other related field of science, such as biology, biochemistry, pharmacodynamics, ecology, or others yet to be conceived; it is a problem of patent law. *In re Papesch,* 315 F.2d 381, 137 U.S.P.Q. 43 (C.C.P.A. 1963).

ω

Facts appearing in the record, rather than prior decisions in and of themselves, must support the legal conclusion of obviousness under 35 U.S.C. §103. Merely stating that a compound or composition is obvious, without actual factual support, is not sufficient. *In re Cofer,* 354 F.2d 664, 148 U.S.P.Q. 268, 271 (C.C.P.A. 1966).

ω

Obviousness under 35 U.S.C. §103 is a question of law based on the following factual inquiries: (1) the scope and the content of the prior art; (2) the differences between the prior art and the claims at issue; (3) the level of ordinary skill in the art; and (4) objective evidence of secondary considerations. *Graham v. John Deere Co.,* 383 U.S. 1, 17, 148 U.S.P.Q. 459, 567 (1966).

ω

Evidence of non-obviousness which has developed only after the filing date of an application to a claimed invention cannot be ignored. *In re Tiffin and Erdman,* 443 F.2d 394, 170 U.S.P.Q. 88, 92 (C.C.P.A. 1971).

ω

A finding of a *prima facie* case of obviousness, which is predicated on obviousness of the compounds' structure "to a chemist", is not necessarily conclusive as to obviousness of the subject matter as a whole under 35 U.S.C. §103. Progress in the useful arts is illserved by denying patents to inventors in situations where the prior art does not disclose or suggest any usefulness for the compounds it describes and the applicant does describe a usefulness conforming with statutory requirements for the closely related, but novel, compounds he discloses. *In re Stemniski,* 444 F.2d 581, 170 U.S.P.Q. 343, 347, 348 (C.C.P.A. 1971).

ω

The standard of patentability does not depend upon a showing of advantages or improvements, but rather upon obviousness. The Examiner's failure to indicate any reason for finding obvious the alteration of the ratio employed in the prior art in the direction and manner claimed renders the rejection untenable. *Ex parte Parthasarathy and Ciapetta,* 174 U. S. P. Q. 63 (PTO Bd. App. 1971).

ω

The determination of obviousness is measured not by a subjective standard of quality but by an objective standard of inquiry. Hindsight reconstruction of prior art is not the applicable standard. *Maschinenfabrik Rieter A.G. v. Greenwood Mills,* 340 F. Supp. 1103, 173 U.S.P.Q. 605, 610, 611 (S.C. 1972).

ω

As elementary as it may be to patent law under the 1952 Act, 35 U.S.C. §103 requires having to show obviousness of the invention "as a whole." To evaluate obviousness, a comparison must be made between the prior art as a whole and the claimed subject matter as a whole. *In re Langer and Haynes,* 465 F.2d 896, 175 U.S.P.Q. 169, 171 (C.C.P.A. 1972).

ω

Since the inventions of the patents in suit were not obvious to persons having more than ordinary skill in the art, they were not obvious to persons having ordinary skill in the art. *Mobil Oil Corp. v. W. R. Grace & Co.,* 367 F. Supp. 207, 180 U.S.P.Q. 418, 452 (Conn. 1973).

ω

A novel chemical compound can be non-obvious to one having ordinary skill in the art notwithstanding that it may possess a known property in common with a known structurally similar compound. Where it is disclosed that the prior-art compound "cannot be regarded as useful" for the sole use disclosed, a person having ordinary skill in the art would lack the "necessary impetus" to make the claimed compound. *In re Albrecht,* 514 F.2d 1389, 185 U.S.P.Q. 585 (C.C.P.A. 1975).

ω

The Board based the rejection under 35 U.S.C. §103 on the theory that an applicant that has lost an interference can never be entitled to claims that are obvious variations of the invention defined in the lost counts. The court found no judicial doctrine that supports this rejection under 35 U.S.C. §103. *In re McKellin, Mageli, and D'Angelo,* 529 F.2d 1324, 188 U.S.P.Q. 428 (C.C.P.A. 1976).

ω

Contemporaneous and independent development of the same subject matter by others is evidence of obviousness. *Norris Industries, Inc. v. The Tappan Company,* 193 U.S.P.Q. 521, 530 (Cal. 1976).

ω

The inherency of an advantage and its obviousness are entirely different questions. That which may be inherent is not necessarily known. Obviousness cannot be predicated on what is unknown. *In re Shetty,* 566 F.2d 81, 195 U.S.P.Q. 753, 757 (C.C.P.A. 1977).

ω

The Patent Office has a high level of expertise in the area of obviousness, and its decision cannot be overturned without clear and convincing evidence. *Sarkisian v. Winn-Proof Corporation,* 203 U.S.P.Q. 60, 66 (Or. 1978).

ω

The proper issue before the court was whether the Board erred, as a matter of law, in holding that the claims were properly rejected under 35 U.S.C. §103. In deciding this issue, the court makes "an independent determination as to the legal conclusions and inferences which should be drawn from...[the findings of fact]." When an applicant presents rebuttal evidence, the decision-maker must consider all of the evidence of record (both that supporting and that rebutting the *prima facie* case) in determining whether the subject matter as a whole would have been obvious. An earlier decision should not be considered as set in concrete, and applicant's rebuttal evidence then be evaluated only on its knockdown ability. *Prima facie* obviousness is a legal conclusion, not a fact. Facts established by rebuttal evidence must be evaluated along with the facts on which the earlier conclusion was reached, not against the conclusion itself. A final finding regarding obviousness must rest upon evaluation of all facts in evidence, uninfluenced by any earlier conclusion reached by an earlier Board upon a different record. *In re Carleton*, 599 F.2d 1021, 202 U.S.P.Q. 165, 168, 169 (C.C.P.A. 1979).

ω

The burden of establishing a *prima facie* case of obviousness falls upon the Examiner. Therefore, the evidence upon which the Examiner relies must clearly indicate that a worker of routine skill in the art would view the claimed invention as being obvious, as meant by 35 U.S.C. §103. *Ex parte Wolters and Kuypers*, 214 U.S.P.Q. 735 (PTO Bd. App. 1979).

ω

There is nothing in the statutes or the case law which makes "that which is within the capabilities of one skilled in the art" synonymous with obviousness. *Ex parte Gerlach and Woerner*, 212 U.S.P.Q. 471 (PTO Bd. App. 1980).

ω

Obviousness is measured by considering whether a hypothetical person having all the art at hand would have found the same solution when addressing himself to the same problem. *Stratoflex, Inc. v. Aeroquip Corporation*, 561 F.Supp. 618, 218 U.S.P.Q. 231, 239 (Mich. 1982).

ω

The statement that "obviousness of the invention is measured by the knowledge of a hypothetical person skilled in the art who has thought about the subject matter of the patented invention in light of the art", taken literally, is an improper statement of a test for obviousness, insofar as it rests on the notion that it is possible for those skilled in the art to think about an actual invention before the inventor makes it. *Medtronic, Inc. v. Cardiac Pacemakers, Inc.*, 721 F.2d 1563, 220 U.S.P.Q. 97, 100 (Fed. Cir. 1983).

ω

Though anticipation is the epitome of obviousness, they are separate and distinct concepts. *Jones v. Hardy*, 727 F.2d 1524, 220 U.S.P.Q. 1021, 1025 (Fed. Cir. 1984).

ω

If the teachings of a prior-art reference would lead one skilled in the art to make a modification that would render another prior-art device inoperable, such a modification would generally not be obvious. *See In re Gordon,* 733 F.2d 900, 221 U.S.P.Q. 1125, 1127 (Fed. Cir. 1984).

ᛡ

The inventor, for the purposes of legal reasoning, has been replaced by the statutory hypothetical "person having ordinary skill in the art" who has been provided by 35 U.S.C. §103. Since the effective date of the 1952 Patent Act, there has been no need to presume that the inventor knows anything about the prior art. We hereby declare the presumption that the inventor has knowledge of all material prior art to be dead. *Kimberly-Clark Corporation v. Johnson & Johnson and Personal Products Company,* 745 F.2d 1437, 223 U.S.P.Q. 603, 614 (Fed. Cir. 1984).

ᛡ

The mere fact that a worker in the art could rearrange the parts of the reference device to meet the terms of the claims on appeal is not, by itself, sufficient to support a finding of obviousness. The prior art must provide a motivation or reason for the worker in the art, without the benefit of the appellant's specification, to make the necessary changes in the reference device. The Examiner has not presented any evidence to support the conclusion that a worker in this art would have had any motivation to make the necessary changes in the reference device to render the here-claimed device unpatentable. *Ex parte Chicago Rawhide Manufacturing Co.,* 226 U.S.P.Q. 438 (PTO Bd. App. 1984).

ᛡ

The fact that a patent specifically discloses and claims a combination of features previously used in two separate devices is not fatal to patentability. A basic issue is whether applied references, alone or in any combination, suggest the claimed invention as a solution to the specific problem solved. The claimed invention achieved new and unexpected results nowhere suggested in the prior art, and that achievement was overlooked. The district court erroneously focused its inquiry "solely on the product created, rather than on the obviousness or non-obviousness of its creation." The initial inquiry should be directed to the vantage point of attacking the problem solved by the invention at the time the invention was made. When prior art itself does not suggest or render obvious the claimed solution to that problem, the art involved does not satisfy the criteria of 35 U.S.C. §103 for precluding patentability. *Lindemann Maschinenfabrik GmbH v. American Hoist and Derrick Co.,* 730 F.2d 1452, 221 U.S.P.Q. 481 (Fed. Cir. 1984).

ᛡ

The appellant was initially the senior party and subsequently the losing party in an interference in which the winning party prevailed on the basis of a Convention filing in a foreign country. The Board held that the appellant's claims were not patentably distinct from the subject matter defined by the counts lost in the interference. The issue here was not obviousness under 35 U.S.C. §103 or so-called interference estoppel. Rather, the Board relied on the more general principle of res judicata and collateral estoppel wherein a judgment, previously rendered, bars consideration of questions of fact or mixed questions of fact and law that were, or should have been, resolved in earlier litigation. An interference should settle all issues that are decided or that could have been decided. When an applicant loses an interference, the applicant is not entitled to a patent containing claims corresponding to the count or claims that are not patentably distinct from the count. *Ex parte Tytgat, Clerbois, and Noel*, 225 U.S.P.Q. 907 (PTO Bd. App. 1985).

ᛒ

A reference is not available under 35 U.S.C. §103 if it is not within the field of the inventor's endeavor and was not directly pertinent to the particular problem with which the inventor was involved. *King Instrument Corp. v. Otari Corp.*, 767 F.2d 853, 226 U.S.P.Q. 402 (Fed. Cir. 1985).

ᛒ

When chemical compounds have "very close" structural similarities and similar utilities, without more, a prima facie case may be made. When such "close" structural similarity to prior art compounds is shown, in accordance with established precedents, the burden of coming forward shifts to the applicant, and evidence affirmatively supporting non-obviousness is required. Generalization should be avoided insofar as specific chemical structures are alleged to be prima facie obvious one from the other. There must be adequate prior-art support for involved structural changes in order to complete the PTO's *prima facie* case and shift the burden of going forward to the applicant. The mere fact that it is possible to find two isolated disclosures that might be combined in such a way to produce a new compound does not necessarily render such production obvious unless the art also contains something to suggest the desirability of the proposed combination. In the absence of such a reference suggestion, there is inadequate support for the position that the required modification would *prima facie* have been obvious.

Even though it may not be inconceivable to substitute sulfur for oxygen to obtain compounds having the same expected properties, that is not the standard; the standard is whether it would have been obvious in terms of 35 U.S.C. §103. *In re Grabiak*, 769 F.2d 729, 226 U.S.P.Q. 870 (Fed. Cir. 1985).

ᛒ

The issue of obviousness is determined entirely with reference to a hypothetical "person having ordinary skill in the art." It is only that hypothetical person who is presumed to be aware of all the pertinent prior art. The actual inventor's skill is irrelevant to the inquiry, and this is for a very important reason. The statutory emphasis is on a person of ordinary skill. Inventors, as a class, according to the concepts underlying the Constitution and the statutes that have created the patent system, possess something that sets them apart from the workers of ordinary skill, and one should not go about determining obviousness under 35 U.S.C. §103 by inquiring into what patentees (i.e., inventors) would have known or would likely have done, faced with the revelation of references. A person of ordinary skill in the art is also presumed to be one who thinks along the line of conventional wisdom in the art and is not one who undertakes to innovate, whether by patient, and often expensive, systematic research or by extraordinary insight; it makes no difference which. *The Standard Oil Company v. American Cyanamid Co.*, 774 F.2d 448, 227 U.S.P.Q. 293 (Fed. Cir. 1985).

ᛒ

The question is never whether claims are obvious, but whether claimed inventions would have been obvious. Although it is proper to note the difference in a claimed invention from the prior art, because that difference may serve as one element in determining the obviousness/non-obviousness issue, it is improper to consider the difference as the invention. The difference may be slight (as has often been the case with some of history's greatest inventions, e.g., the telephone), but it may also have been the key to success in advancement in the art resulting from the invention. The issue with respect to obviousness is whether a challenger has carried its burden of proving, by clear and convincing evidence, facts from which it must be concluded that one skilled in the art at the time the invention was made would have found it to have been obvious, from the references as a whole, to create the claimed subject matter as a whole. *Datascope Corp. v. SMEC, Inc.,* 776 F.2d 320, 227 U.S.P.Q. 838 (Fed. Cir. 1985).

ω

Presuming arguendo that the references show the elements or concepts urged, the Examiner presented no line of reasoning as to why the artisan reviewing only the collective teachings of the references would have found it obvious to selectively pick and choose various elements and/or concepts from the several references relied on to arrive at the claimed invention. In the instant application, the Examiner has done little more than cite references to show that one or more elements or some combinations thereof, when each is viewed in a vacuum, is known. The claimed invention, however, is clearly directed to a combination of elements. That is to say, the appellant does not claim that he has invented one or more new elements but has presented claims to a new combination of elements. To support the conclusion that the claimed combination is directed to obvious subject matter, either the references must expressly or impliedly suggest the claimed combination or the Examiner must present a convincing line of reasoning as to why the artisan would have found the claimed invention to have been obvious in light of the teachings of the references. The Board found nothing in the references that would expressly or impliedly teach or suggest the modifications urged by the Examiner. Additionally, the Board found no line of reasoning in the answer as to why the artisan would have found the modifications urged by the Examiner to have been obvious. Based on the record, the artisan would not have found it obvious to selectively pick and choose elements or concepts from the various references so as to arrive at the claimed invention without using the claims as a guide. *Ex parte Clapp,* 227 U.S.P.Q. 972 (B.P.A.I. 1985).

ω

Although the technique underlying hybridoma technology is well recognized, the results obtained by its use are clearly unpredictable. Hybridoma technology is an empirical art in which the routineer is unable to foresee what particular antibodies will be produced and which specific surface antigens will be recognized by them. Only by actually carrying out the requisite steps can the nature of the monoclonal antibodies be determined and ascertained; no "expected" results can thus be said to be present. Hence, it may be "obvious to try" the Kohler-Milstein technique as applied to malignant renal cells, but such is not the standard under which obviousness under 35 U.S.C. §103 must be established. *Ex parte Old,* 229 U.S.P.Q. 196 (B.P.A.I. 1985).

ω

A rejection of product claims under 35 U.S.C. §103 based on references that disclose products "which are not seen to differ in kind" from the products claimed is not sustainable on its face. The statutory inquiry is obviousness and not "different in kind." *Ex parte Goeddel*, 5 U.S.P.Q.2d 1449 (B.P.A.I. 1985).

ω

The issue of obviousness is determined entirely with reference to a hypothetical "person having ordinary skill in the art." It is only that person who is presumed to be aware of all the pertinent art. There are six factors relevant to a determination of the level of ordinary skill: educational level of the inventor, type of problems encountered in the art, prior art solutions, rapidity of innovation, sophistication of technology, and educational level of active workers in the field. *Bausch & Lomb, Inc. v. Barnes-Hind/Hydrocurve, Inc.*, 796 F.2d 443, 230 U.S.P.Q. 416 (Fed. Cir. 1986).

ω

Focusing on the obviousness of substitutions and differences instead of on the invention as a whole is a legally improper way to simplify the difficult determination of obviousness. Arguing that "it would be obvious," rather than that "it would have been obvious," shifts the court's focus to the wrong period of time; namely, to a time long after the invention was made, in which, more likely than not, the prior art and the level of ordinary skill in the art are more advanced. *Hybritech Inc. v. Monoclonal Antibodies, Inc.*, 802 F.2d 1367, 231 U.S.P.Q. 81, 93 (Fed. Cir. 1986).

ω

In attempting to predict the biological activities of a drug, a skilled medicinal chemist would not proceed randomly but would base his attempts on the available knowledge of prior research techniques, and literature used in his field. One such technique is "bioisosteric replacement," or the theory of bioisosterism—where the substitution of one atom or group of atoms for another atom or group of atoms having similar size, shape, and electron density provides molecules having the same type of biological activity. Application of this technique led to a holding of obviousness with a new use of a known compound. *In re Merck & Co.*, 800 F.2d 1091, 231 U.S.P.Q. 375 (Fed. Cir. 1986).

ω

The "evidence" showed that use of vertical heights for range finding, use of multiple elements on a site, and use of circular apertures were each known in the art, but the prior art lacked any teaching or suggestion to combine the separate features in a manner permitting use of circular apertures for simultaneous range finding and aiming. Obviousness cannot be established by combining the teachings of the prior art to produce the claimed invention, absent some teaching, suggestion, or incentive supporting the combination. *Carela v. Starlight Archery*, 804 F.2d 135, 231 U.S.P.Q. 644 (Fed. Cir. 1986).

ω

The Examiner appears to recognize that it is not structural similarity alone that gives rise to obviousness, but the concomitant assumption that the structurally similar compounds will have like properties. This is what provides the motivation to modify the prior art compound. In the present case, however, the only utility disclosed for the relevant compound in the reference is as an intermediate for the production of another compound. The Examiner has not suggested that the compound claimed here would have been useful in the same manner and, from the disclosure of the reference itself, it appears that it would not have been. Thus, on the record before us, no *prima facie* case of obviousness has been made out against the appellant's claims. *Ex parte Chwang,* 231 U.S.P.Q. 751 (B.P.A.I. 1986).

ᘯ

Evaluation of the worth of an inventor's contribution is left to the public, not to the judiciary, in determining patentability. A judge is nowhere authorized to declare a patent invalid on his or her personal evaluation. Emphasis on non-obviousness is one of inquiry, not quality. *Panduit Corp. v. Dennison Manufacturing Co.,* 810 F.2d 1561, 1 U.S.P.Q.2d 1593 (Fed. Cir. 1987).

ᘯ

Although each of the references relied upon under 35 U.S.C. §103 generally teaches what the Examiner asserts it teaches, the rejection fails because there is no concept in any of the art relied on, either express or implied, of providing a composition including both interferon and a tyrosinase inhibitor. None of the art teaches increasing the effectiveness of interferon. None of the art teaches inhibiting the patient's serum tyrosinase as it increases concomitantly with interferon treatment. *Ex parte Rubin,* 5 U.S.P.Q.2d 1461 (B.P.A.I. 1987).

ᘯ

Only a reasonable expectation of success, not absolute predictability, is necessary for a conclusion of obviousness. *Ex parte Beck,* 9 U.S.P.Q.2d 2000 (B.P.A.I. 1987).

ᘯ

When prior-art references require a selective combination to render obvious a subsequent invention, there must be some reason for the combination other than the hindsight gleaned from the invention itself. Something in the prior art as a whole must suggest the desirability, and thus the obviousness, of making the combination. *Uniroyal Inc. v. Rudkin-Wiley Corp.,* 837 F.2d 1044, 5 U.S.P.Q.2d 1434 (Fed. Cir. 1988).

ᘯ

Most technological advance is the fruit of methodical, persistent investigation, as is recognized in 35 U.S.C. §103 ("Patentability shall not be negatived by the manner in which the invention was made"). The consistent criterion for determination of obviousness is whether the prior art would have suggested to one of ordinary skill in the art that this process should be carried out and would have reasonable likelihood of success, viewed in the light of the prior art. Both the suggestion and the expectation of success must be founded in the prior art, not in the applicant's disclosure. *In re Dow Chemical Co.,* 837 F.2d 469, 5 U.S.P.Q.2d 1529 (Fed. Cir. 1988).

ᘯ

It is the invention as a whole that must be considered in obviousness determinations. The invention as a whole embraces the structure, its properties, and the problem it solves. In evaluating obviousness, the hypothetical person of ordinary skill in the pertinent art is presumed to have the ability to select and utilize knowledge from other arts reasonably pertinent to the particular problem to which the invention is directed. In delineating the invention as a whole, one must look not only to the subject matter that is literally cited in a claim in question, but also to those properties of the subject matter that are inherent in the subject matter and are disclosed in the specification. The determination of whether a novel structure is or is not "obvious" requires cognizance of the properties of that structure and the problem that it solves, viewed in the light of the teachings of the prior art. The particular problem facing the inventor must be considered in determining obviousness. It is error to focus solely on the product created, rather than on the obviousness or non-obviousness of its creation. Thus, the question is whether what the inventor did would have been obvious to one of ordinary skill in the art attempting to solve the problem upon which the inventor was working. The problem solved by the invention is always relevant. The entirety of a claimed invention, including the combination viewed as a whole, the elements thereof, and the properties and purpose of the invention, must be considered. Factors, including unexpected results, new features, solution of a different problem, and novel properties, are all considerations in the determination of obviousness in terms of 35 U.S.C. §103. When such factors are described in the specification, they are weighed in determining, in the first instance, whether the prior art presents a *prima facie* case of obviousness. Comparative data in the specification must be considered in a PTO determination of unexpected results, as part of the entire body of evidence that must be weighed in the first instance by the PTO. When such factors are brought out in prosecution before the PTO, they are considered in determining whether a *prima facie* case, if based on the prior art, has been rebutted. Rebuttal evidence is considered along with all other evidence of record. The requisite view of the whole invention mandates consideration of not only its structure but also its properties and the problem solved. Notwithstanding the fact that only old elements are used, the patentability of a new combination of old elements, that produces a result that is not suggested in the references, is of ancient authority. Virtually all inventions are combinations, and every invention is formed of old elements. *In re Wright,* 848 F.2d 1216, 6 U.S.P.Q.2d 1959, 1961, 1962 (Fed. Cir. 1988).

ω

Whether phenomena just outside of claim limits are qualitatively different from that which is claimed is immaterial. A patentee is not required to show that some technological discontinuity exists between a claimed invention and subject matter just outside of the claims, but only that the claimed subject matter would have been non-obvious in view of the prior art. *Andrew Corp. v. Gabriel Electronics, Inc.,* 847 F.2d 819, 6 U.S.P.Q.2d 2010 (Fed. Cir. 1988).

ω

Obviousness does not require absolute predictability of success. Indeed, for many inventions that seem quite obvious, there is no absolute predictability of success until the invention is reduced to practice. There is always at least a possibility of unexpected results, that would then provide an objective basis for showing that the invention, although apparently obvious, was in law non-obvious. To constitute obviousness under 35 U.S.C. §103, all that is required is a reasonable expectation of success. *In re O'Farrell,* 853 F.2d 894, 7 U.S.P.Q.2d 1673, 1681 (Fed. Cir. 1988).

ω

Nothing in the patent statute requires that an invention be superior to prior art to be patentable. Any superiority or lack of it is irrelevant to the question of obviousness. *Ryco Inc. v. Ag-Bag Corp.*, 857 F.2d 1418, 8 U.S.P.Q.2d 1323 (Fed. Cir. 1988).

ω

A jury may decide the questions of anticipation and obviousness, either as separate special verdicts or en route to a verdict on the question of validity, which may also be decided by the jury. No warrant appears for distinguishing the submission of legal questions to a jury in patent cases from such submissions routinely made in other types of cases. So long as the Seventh Amendment stands, the right to a jury trial should not be rationed, nor should particular issues in particular types of cases be treated differently from similar issues in other types of cases. When the judgment arises from a jury verdict, the reviewing court applies the reasonable-jury/substantial-evidence standard: a standard that gives greater deference to the judgment simply because appellate review is more limited, compared with review of a trial judge's decision. The appellate court's function is exhausted when the evidentiary basis of the jury's verdict becomes apparent, it being immaterial that the court might draw a contrary inference or feel that another conclusion is more reasonable. *Richardson v. Suzuki Motor Co., Ltd.*, 868 F.2d 1226, 9 U.S.P.Q.2d 1913, 1919 (Fed. Cir. 1989).

ω

With regard to the issue of obviousness of applied art, testimony of those who qualified as experts was not acceptable as evidence of what would be obvious to one of ordinary skill in the art. *Dotolo v. Quigg*, 12 U.S.P.Q.2d 1032, 1037 (D.C. 1989).

ω

The weight of precedent is to the effect that when the claimed subject matter is a new chemical compound or composition, a *prima facie* case of obviousness is not deemed made unless both (1) the new compound or composition is structurally similar to the reference compound or composition, and (2) there is some suggestion or expectation in the prior art that the new compound or composition will have the same or a similar utility as that discovered by the applicant.

There must be some reason, arising in the prior art, to expect that the claimed compounds or compositions will have the properties found by the applicant. This rule finds pragmatic support in today's state of chemical science, wherein few new compounds are of such imaginative structure that "structurally similar" compounds are not to be found in the prior art. *In re Dillon*, 892 F.2d 1554, 13 U.S.P.Q.2d 1337, 1341, 1345 (Fed. Cir. 1989), *opinion withdrawn*, 919 F.2d 688, 16 U.S.P.Q.2d 1897, 1899 (Fed. Cir. 1990).

ω

It is proper to require that a prior-art reference (cited as anticipating a claimed invention) be shown to lack the characteristics of the claimed invention. However, it is not pertinent to a rejection based on obviousness whether the prior-art device possesses the functional characteristics of the claimed invention if the reference does not describe or suggest its structure. *In re Mills*, 916 F.2d 680, 16 U.S.P.Q.2d 1430, 1432, 1433 (Fed. Cir. 1990).

ω

The fact that defendant filed an interference against the patent-in-suit is evidence of non-obviousness. That a major competitor of the patentee felt the invention worthy of patent has some weight. That all in the art recognized a need to draw upon a different art is evidence of non-obviousness. *CSS International Corp. v. Maul Technology Co.*, 16 U.S.P.Q.2d 1657, 1666 (Ind. 1989).

ᚄ

Evidence presented to overcome a prima facie case of obviousness has to be commensurate with the scope of the claims in support of which the evidence is offered. *General Electric Co. v. Hoechst Celanese Corp.*, 683 F. Supp. 305, 16 U.S.P.Q.2d 1977, 1989 (Del. 1990).

ᚄ

The inquiry into obviousness focuses on what would have been obvious to a hypothetical person having ordinary skill in the art. The actual inventor's skill is irrelevant to the inquiry. One should not go about determining obviousness under 35 U.S.C. §103 by inquiring into what patentees (i.e., inventors) would have known or would likely have done. *E. I. du Pont de Nemours & Co. v. Cetus Corp.*, 19 U.S.P.Q.2d 1174, 1183 (Cal. 1990).

ᚄ

Before obviousness may be established, the Examiner must show that there is either a suggestion in the art to produce the claimed invention or a compelling motivation based on sound scientific principles. Logic compels that the suggestion or motivation be accompanied by a general knowledge of the existence of art-recognized techniques for carrying out the proposed invention. *Ex parte Kranz*, 19 U.S.P.Q.2d 1216, 1218 (B.P.A.I. 1990).

ᚄ

Obviousness under 35 U.S.C. §103 is a question of law. Both the suggestion and the expectation of success must be founded in the prior art, not in applicant's disclosure. *Amgen Inc. v. Chugai Pharmaceutical Co. Ltd.*, 927 F.2d 1200, 18 U.S.P.Q.2d 1016, 1022 (Fed. Cir. 1991).

ᚄ

What is obvious to the inventor would not necessarily have been obvious to one of ordinary skill in the art. *Suh v. Hoefle*, 23 U.S.P.Q.2d 1321, 1325 (B.P.A.I. 1991).

ᚄ

In proceedings before the PTO, the Examiner bears the burden of establishing a prima facie case of obviousness based upon prior art. The Examiner can satisfy this burden only by showing some objective teaching in the prior art or that knowledge generally available to one of ordinary skill in the art would lead that individual to combine the relevant teachings of the references. The patent applicant may then attack the Examiner's *prima facie* determination as improperly made out, or the applicant may present objective evidence tending to support a conclusion of nonobviousness. *In re Fritch*, 972 F.2d 1260, 23 U.S.P.Q.2d 1780, 1783 (Fed. Cir. 1992).

ᚄ

Prima facie obviousness is a procedural tool employed in ex parte proceedings before the PTO. *In re Oetiker*, 977 F.2d 1443, 1445, 24 U.S.P.Q.2d 1443, 1444 (Fed. Cir. 1992).

ᖶ

Limited discovery of an infringement defendant's foreign sales is significant as to determination of obviousness. *Minnesota Mining and Manufacturing v. Smith and Nephew PLC*, 25 U.S.P.Q.2d 1587, 1591 (Minn. 1992).

ᖶ

"A *prima facie* case of obviousness is established when the teachings from the prior art itself would appear to have suggested the claimed subject matter to a person of ordinary skill in the art." If the Examiner fails to establish a *prima facie* case, the rejection is improper and will be overturned. *In re Rijckaert*, 9 F.3d 1531, 28 U.S.P.Q.2d 1955, 1956 (Fed. Cir. 1993).

ᖶ

The consistent criterion for determination of obviousness is whether the prior art would have suggested to one of ordinary skill in the art that a claimed process should be carried out and would have a reasonable likelihood of success, viewed in the light of the prior art. Both the suggestion and the expectation of success must be founded in the prior art, not in the applicant's disclosure. *University of California v. Synbiotics Corp.*, 29 U.S.P.Q.2d 1463, 1466 (Cal. 1993).

ᖶ

The test is not subjective obviousness to the inventor, but objective obviousness to an artisan. *Hoechst Celanese Corp. v. BP Chemicals Ltd.*, 846 F.Supp. 542, 31 U.S.P.Q.2d 1825, 1829 (Tex. 1994).

ᖶ

As a general rule, the Examiner's decision is "evidence the court must consider in determining whether the party asserting invalidity has met its statutory burden by clear and convincing evidence." *Indian Head Industries Inc. v. Ted Smith Equipment Co.*, 859 F.Supp. 1095, 36 U.S.P.Q.2d 1316, 1319 (Mich. 1994).

ᖶ

Knowledge of a protein does not give one a conception of a particular DNA encoding it. What cannot be contemplated or conceived cannot be obvious. The PTO has improperly rejected product claims to molecules on the alleged obviousness of a method of making the molecules. As the claims define new chemical entities in structural terms, a *prima facie* case of unpatentability requires that the teachings of the prior art suggest *the claimed compounds* to a person of ordinary skill in the art. The existence of a general method of isolating cDNA or DNA molecules is essentially irrelevant to the question of whether specific molecules themselves would have been obvious, in the absence of other prior art that suggests the claimed DNAs. A prior art disclosure of a process *reciting a particular compound* or obvious variant thereof as a product of the process is, of course, another matter, raising issues of anticipation under 35 U.S.C. §102 as well as obviousness under §103. *In re Deuel*, 51 F.3d 1552, 34 U.S.P.Q.2d 1210, 1214, 1215 (Fed. Cir. 1995).

ᖶ

The ultimate determination of obviousness is a question of law, which the CAFC reviews without deference to the BPAI's judgment. *In re Napier*, 55 F.3d 610, 34 U.S.P.Q.2d 1782, 1784 (Fed. Cir. 1995).

ω

There is no logical support for a proposition that a patent applicant's evidence and/or arguments traversing a rejection under 35 U.S.C. §103 must be contained within the specification. Obviousness is determined by the totality of the record, including, in some instances most significantly, evidence and arguments proffered during the give-and-take of ex parte patent prosecution. *In re Chu*, 66 F.3d 292, 36 U.S.P.Q.2d 1089, 1095 (Fed. Cir. 1995).

ω

"That which may be made clear and thus 'obvious' to a court, with the invention fully diagrammed and aided...by experts in the field, may have been a breakthrough of substantial dimension when first unveiled." However, contemporaneous and independent development of the [invention defined by the] claims-in-suit by another inventor strongly suggests that the invention of the patent was obvious [if the other was merely one of ordinary skill in the art]. *Nordberg Inc. v. Telsmith Inc.*, 881 F.Supp. 1252, 36 U.S.P.Q.2d 1577, 1611, 1613 (Wis. 1995).

ω

If the invention is different from what is disclosed in one reference, but the differences are such that combination with another reference would lead to what is claimed, the obviousness question then requires inquiry as to whether there is reason, suggestion, or motivation to make that combination. Such a suggestion may come expressly from the references themselves. It may come from knowledge of those skilled in the art that certain references, or disclosures in the references, are known to be of special interest or importance in the particular field. It may also come from the nature of a problem to be solved, leading inventors to look to references relating to possible solutions to that problem. *Pro-Mold and Tool Co. v. Great Lakes Plastics Inc.*, 75 F.3d 1568, 37 U.S.P.Q.2d 1626, 1630 (Fed. Cir. 1996).

ω

The prior art must contain a teaching to modify the prior art food warmer to include all of the features of the claimed invention. *Stein Industries Inc. v. Jarco Industries Inc.*, 40 U.S.P.Q.2d 1955 (N.Y. 1996).

ω

It is perfectly acceptable to consider the method by which a compound is made in evaluating the obviousness of the compound. *Ex parte Goldgaber*, 41 U.S.P.Q.2d 1172 (B.P.A.I. 1995).

Obviousness-Type Double Patenting.

The CAFC has set forth two tests for obviousness-type double patenting rejections. A two-way patentability test is applicable when the second of two applications filed by an applicant issues first due to the PTO's unjustified delays in the prosecution of the earlier-filed application. Under the two-way analysis, each claim is examined to determine whether it is an obvious variant of the other, rather than just examining the application claim for patentable distinctness from the patent claim. *In re Emert*, 124 F.3d 1458, 44 U.S.P.Q.2d 1149, 1152 (Fed. Cir. 1997).

Obvious to Try or Experiment. *See also* **Optimize.**

Treating an advantage as the invention disregards the statutory requirement that the invention be viewed "as a whole," ignores the problem recognition element, and injects an improper obvious-to-try consideration. *Jones v. Hardy,* 727 F.2d 1524, 220 U.S.P.Q. 1021, 1026 (Fed. Cir. 1984).

ᴡ

The Examiner is of the view that here "obvious to try" becomes "obvious to try with a reasonably good chance for success," whatever "success" means inasmuch as he himself does not urge that the character of the monoclonal antibodies or of the renal antigenic systems could be predicted, and that, consequently, the rationale of *Tomlinson* [363 F.2d 928, 150 U.S.P.Q. 623 (C.C.P.A. 1966)] becomes inapplicable. This attempted distinction is one of semantics, not of substance, and cannot be the basis for vitiating the well established axiom that "obvious to try" is not the same as "obviousness" under 35 U.S.C. §103 of the statute. *Ex parte Old,* 229 U.S.P.Q. 196 (B.P.A.I. 1985).

ᴡ

Even though the issue was one of reforming an interference, it appears from the wording of the opinion that unwarranted weight may have inadvertently been accorded to testimony that only established obviousness to try. An expert testified that it would be obvious for someone testing or making the phenyl-substituted compounds also to make and test the benzyl substituted compounds. Nothing in the opinion appears to address the issue as to whether either the benzyl- or phenyl-subgenus would have been obvious (as a whole) prior to testing that particular subgenus. *Winter v. Banno,* 229 U.S.P.Q. 212 (B.P.A.I. 1985).

ᴡ

The mere statement that the method of making claimed products would be obvious and that there would be a reasonable expectation of success without determining that the claimed products would be "obvious" from prior-art teachings reflects application of the regularly rejected obvious-to-try standard. *Ex parte Erlich,* 3 U.S.P.Q.2d 1011 (B.P.A.I. 1986).

ᴡ

Although the fact that each of the three components of the composition used in the claimed method was conventionally employed in the art for treating cooling water systems, to employ these components in combination for their known functions and to optimize the amount of each additive were not regarded as obvious. Obviousness cannot be established by combining the teachings of the prior art to produce a claimed invention, absent some teaching, suggestion or incentive supporting the combination. At best, in view of the prior art, one skilled in the art might find it obvious to try various combinations of these known scale and corrosion prevention agents. This is not the standard of 35 U.S.C. §103. *In re Geiger,* 815 F.2d 686, 2 U.S.P.Q.2d 1276 (Fed. Cir. 1987).

ω

The mere need for experimentation to determine parameters needed to make a device work is an application of the often rejected obvious-to-try standard and falls short of the statutory obviousness of 35 U.S.C. §103. Inability of an expert to predict the results obtainable with a claimed product suggests non-obviousness, not routine experimentation. *Uniroyal Inc. v. Rudkin-Wiley Corp.,* 837 F.2d 1044, 5 U.S.P.Q.2d 1434 (Fed. Cir. 1988).

ω

An obvious-to-experiment standard is not an acceptable alternative for obviousness. Selective hindsight is no more applicable to the design of experiments than it is to the combination of prior-art teachings. There must be a reason or suggestion in the art for selecting the procedure used, other than the knowledge learned from the applicant's disclosure. *In re Dow Chemical Co.,* 837 F.2d 469, 5 U.S.P.Q.2d 1529 (Fed. Cir. 1988).

ω

The admonition that "obvious to try" is not the standard under 35 U.S.C. §103 has been directed mainly to two kinds of error. In some cases, what would have been obvious to try would have been to vary all parameters or to try each of numerous possible choices until one possibly arrived at a successful result, where the prior art gave either no indication of which parameters where critical or no direction as to which of many possible choices is likely to be successful. In others, what was obvious to try was to explore a new technology or approach that seemed to be a promising field of experimentation, where the prior art gave only general guidance as to the particular form of the claimed invention or how to achieve it. For obviousness under 103, all that is required is a reasonable expectation of success. *In re O'Farrell,* 853 F.2d 894, 7 U.S.P.Q.2d 1673 (Fed. Cir. 1988).

ω

An "obvious-to-try" situation exists when a general disclosure may pique the scientist's curiosity, such that further investigation might be done as a result of the disclosure, but the disclosure itself does not contain a sufficient teaching of how to obtain the desired result or indicate that the claimed result would be obtained if certain directions were pursued. *In re Eli Lilly & Co.,* 902 F.2d 943, 14 U.S.P.Q.2d 1741, 1743 (Fed. Cir. 1990).

Offenlegungsschrift.

No bar under 35 U.S.C. §102(d) arises from publication of appellant's Offenlegungsschrift. *Ex parte Links,* 184 U.S.P.Q. 429, 432 (PO Bd. App. 1974).

Offer in Evidence. *See* **Introduce into Evidence.**

O.G. *(Official Gazette).*

Oil.

A claim to a lubricating oil composition comprising stated amounts of specified components is not merely a "recipe" for making the composition. *Exxon Chemical Patents Inc. v. Lubrizol Corp.*, 64 F.3d 1553, 35 U.S.P.Q.2d 1801, 1804 (Fed. Cir. 1995).

Old Combination.

The improvement of one part of an old combination gives no right to claim that improvement in combination with other old parts which perform no new function in the combination. *Lincoln Engineering Company of Illinois v. Stewart-Warner Corporation*, 303 U.S. 545, 37 U.S.P.Q. 1, 3 (1938).

ᜂ

A claim to an old composition is not imparted with novelty by recitation therein of a new use of the composition. *In re Thuau*, 135 F.2d 344, 57 U.S.P.Q. 324, 325 (C.C.P.A. 1943).

ᜂ

The rejection of claims as being directed to an "old combination" has no basis under the patent statute. *Ex parte Barber, Brandenburg, and Frost*, 187 U.S.P.Q. 244, 246 (PTO Bd. App. 1974).

ᜂ

Casting an invention as "a combination of old elements" leads improperly to an analysis of the claimed invention by the parts, not by the whole. The critical inquiry is whether there is something in the prior art as a whole to suggest the desirability, and thus the obviousness, of making the combination. A traditional problem with focusing on a patent as a combination of old elements is the attendant notion that patentability is undeserving without some "synergistic" or "different" effect. Here, the district court spoke of the need for "a new and useful result." Such tests for patentability have been soundly rejected by this court. Though synergism is relevant when present, its "absence has no place in evaluating the evidence on obviousness." *Custom Accessories Inc. v. Jeffrey-Allan Industries, Inc.*, 807 F.2d 955, 1 U.S.P.Q.2d 1196 (Fed. Cir. 1986).

Old Element.

Presuming arguendo that the references show the elements or concepts urged, the Examiner presented no line of reasoning as to why the artisan reviewing only the collective teachings of the references would have found it obvious to selectively pick and choose various elements and/or concepts from the several references relied on to arrive at the claimed invention. In the instant application, the Examiner has done little more than cite references to show that one or more elements or some combinations thereof, when each is viewed in a vacuum, is known. The claimed invention, however, is clearly directed to a combination of elements. That is to say, the appellant does not claim that he has invented one or more new elements but has presented claims to a new combination of elements. To support the conclusion that the claimed combination is directed to obvious subject matter, either the references must expressly or impliedly suggest the claimed combination or the

Examiner must present a convincing line of reasoning as to why the artisan would have found the claimed invention to have been obvious in light of the teachings of the references. The Board found nothing in the references that would expressly or impliedly teach or suggest the modifications urged by the Examiner. Additionally, the Board found no line of reasoning in the answer as to why the artisan would have found the modifications urged by the Examiner to have been obvious. Based on the record, the artisan would not have found it obvious to selectively pick and choose elements or concepts from the various references so as to arrive at the claimed invention without using the claims as a guide. *Ex parte Clapp*, 227 U.S.P.Q. 972 (B.P.A.I. 1985).

Omission.

An omission from the specification is not fatal where the disclosure is sufficient to enable those skilled in the art to practice the invention. *In re Myers*, 410 F.2d 420, 161 U.S.P.Q. 668, 671 (C.C.P.A. 1969).

Omission of Element or Step. *See also* Description, Limiting, Reduction in Elements, Reduction in Steps.

If the omission of an element is attended by a corresponding omission of the function performed by that element, there is no invention if the elements retained perform the same functions as before. *In re Porter*, 68 F.2d 971, 20 U.S.P.Q. 298, 301 (C.C.P.A. 1934).

ω

Dispensing of an element, along with its function, leads to an arrangement which is not suggested by a reference. *Ex parte Bellsnyder, Sr., and Ritchie*, 73 U.S.P.Q. 269 (PO Bd. App. 1947).

ω

The dropping out of any element essential to the success of a patented device calls into play entirely new principles. *Myers v. Beall Pipe & Tank Corp.*, 80 F.Supp. 265, 79 U.S.P.Q. 173, 176 (Or. 1948).

ω

Omission of some of the elements of the device makes the claim broad, but not vague, indefinite or misdescriptive. *Ex parte Schaefer*, 171 U.S.P.Q. 110 (PO Bd. App. 1970).

ω

The mere omission of claim limitations does not suggest omission of steps or parts. *In re Smythe and Shamos*, 480 F.2d 1376, 178 U.S.P.Q. 279, 283 (C.C.P.A. 1973).

Omitted Element Test.

Patent claims are invalid under 35 U.S.C. §112 if they omit an element that someone skilled in the art would understand to be essential to the invention as originally disclosed. Under the omitted element test a court can limit the claims of a patent on the basis of the disclosure in the application. *Reiffin v. Microsoft Corp.*, 48 U.S.P.Q.2d 1274, 1277 (Cal. 1998).

One. *See also* **A.**

A claim calling for "means responsive to flow through one of said inlet orifices" reads on means responsive to flow through two orifices because flow through two includes flow through one. As the claim does not say "only one," it must be construed as meaning "at least one." *In re Teague,* 254 F.2d 145, 117 U.S.P.Q. 284, 289 (C.C.P.A. 1958).

One Invention. *See also* **Unity of Invention.**

The purpose of 35 U.S.C. §101 is to define patentable subject matter, not to limit a patent to one invention. *In re Haas,* 486 F.2d 1053, 179 U.S.P.Q. 623, 625 (C.C.P.A. 1973).

ᛟ

A rejection of claims under 35 U.S.C. §121 for containing "improper Markush groups and [for] misjoinder of invention" because they are viewed as being directed to independent and distinct inventions was reversed. Section 121 of 35 U.S.C. does not provide the basis for rejecting a claim. *In re Haas,* 580 F.2d 461, 198 U.S.P.Q. 334, 336 (C.C.P.A. 1978).

One of Ordinary Skill in the Art. *See* **MOSITA.**

One or More. *See* **At Least.**

One-Step Claim. *See* **Single-Step Method Claim.**

On Hand.

The "on hand" test requires that "a device incorporating the invention must have existed in its ordinary or contemplated usable form, and must have been on hand and ready for delivery more than one year prior to the application filing date". This rule produced results contrary to the basic underlying principles relating to the "on sale" bar of 35 U.S.C. §102(b). *American Sunroof Corp. v. Cars & Concepts, Inc.,* 224 U.S.P.Q. 144, 146 (Mich. 1984).

On Sale. *See also* **F.O.B., On Hand, Prior Sale.**

A sale or offer to sell made prior to the time when the experimental stage has been passed, the invention reduced to practice and manufactured in its perfected form, is not a "prior use" or placing the invention "on sale" within the meaning of 35 U.S.C. §102(b). *Dart Industries Inc. v. E.I. du Pont de Nemours and Company,* 348 F.Supp. 1338, 175 U.S.P.Q. 540, 554 (Ill. 1972).

ᛟ

Whether or not a sale is consummated in a foreign country, a product is "on sale" in the United States, within the proscription of the statute, if substantial activity prefatory to the sale occurs in the United States. An offer for sale, made in this country, is sufficient prefatory activity occurring here to bring the matter within the statute. *The Robbins Company v. Lawrence Manufacturing Company*, 482 F.2d 426, 178 U.S.P.Q. 577, 583 (9th Cir. 1973).

ᚹ

While the accused products were displayed at a show in Chicago and orders were solicited there for acceptance in Connecticut, this would not amount to acts of infringement within Illinois for venue purposes. *Scovill Manufacturing Company v. Sunbeam Corporation*, 179 U.S.P.Q. 833, 834 (Del. 1973).

ᚹ

The controlling date for purposes of 35 U.S.C. §102(b), where an item had not yet been manufactured at the time of the order, is the date on which the order is filled, and not the date on which the order is first placed. *Forbro Design Corp. v. Raytheon Co.*, 390 F.Supp. 794, 190 U.S.P.Q. 70, 77 (Mass. 1975).

ᚹ

An invention claimed in a cip, which is not patentably distinct from that claimed in a patent issued on the parent application, may not be salvageable with a terminal disclaimer if the invention claimed in the issued patent was on sale more than one year prior to the filing date of the cip. The on-sale bar cannot be overcome by a terminal disclaimer. *Gemveto Jewelry Co. v. Jeff Cooper Inc.*, 368 F. Supp. 319, 219 U.S.P.Q. 806 (N.Y. 1983).

ᚹ

In soliciting orders during an early period, samples were shown to potential customers; it was explained at trial that the samples were made using a prior-art technique. No evidence was adduced that any samples were produced following claims of the Method or Apparatus patents, or that the claimed method or apparatus was disclosed to potential customers. A few weeks before the critical date, the patentee started testing the apparatus. Although the resulting product was unacceptable, the putative infringer argued that these tests closed the on-sale circle that was opened with the solicitation and acceptance of orders, since most of the segments of the plant worked as intended; and that because the plant did work as intended, albeit after the critical date, the earlier tests were merely routine adjustments and therefore adequate to trigger the on-sale bar. The patentee countered with the testimony that the tests were not routine; that the technology was unproven; and that it was unknown, at the time, how long it would take for the plant to start up and operate. At the critical date there was not a completed invention that had been shown to be commercially useful for the intended purpose. Therefore, there was no on-sale bar. *Locotte v. Thomas*, 758 F.2d 611, 225 U.S.P.Q. 633 (Fed. Cir. 1985).

ᚹ

When an executory sales contract is entered into (or offered), before a critical date, the purchaser must know how the invention embodied in the offer will perform. The policies underlying the on-sale bar, however, concentrate on the attempt by an inventor to exploit his invention, not whether the potential purchaser was cognizant of the invention. Accordingly, the purchaser need not have actual knowledge of the invention for it to be on sale. *King Instrument Corp. v. Otari Corp.*, 767 F.2d 853, 226 U.S.P.Q. 402, 407 (Fed. Cir. 1985).

ᚹ

A patent may be invalid if the subject matter of that patent was on sale or in public use more than one year before the date that the patent application was filed. A three-part test applicable to this portion of the statute requires (1) the complete invention claimed must have been embodied in or obvious in view of the things offered for sale, (2) the invention must have been tested sufficiently to verify that it was operable and commercially marketable, and (3) the same must be primarily for profit rather than for experimental purposes. A less stringent standard might be appropriate in some circumstances where the underlying statutory policies might otherwise be frustrated. *R. E. Phelon Co. v. Wabash Inc.*, 640 F. Supp. 1383, 1 U.S.P.Q.2d 1680 (Ind. 1986).

ω

The challenger has the burden of proving that there was a definite sale or offer to sell more than one year before the application for the subject patent, and that the subject matter of the sale or offer to sell fully anticipated the claimed invention or would have rendered the claimed invention obvious by its addition to the prior art. If these facts are established, the patent owner is called upon to come forward with an explanation of the circumstances that would otherwise appear to be commercialization outside the grace period. *UMC Electronics Co. v. United States*, 816 F.2d 647, 2 U.S.P.Q.2d 1465 (Fed. Cir. 1987).

ω

There is a three-prong test for ascertaining whether patented subject matter is on sale in cases "where the offer to sell concerns articles which have not been produced at the time the purchase is solicited": (1) the invention has been "reduced to practice"; (2) the invention was embodied in the proposed products for sale; and (3) the proposed products were on sale for profit rather than primarily for experimental purposes. *Modine Manufacturing Co. v. The Allen Group Inc.*, 8 U.S.P.Q.2d 1622 (Cal. 1988).

ω

Reduction to practice is not an absolute requirement of the on-sale bar. The absence of reduction to practice may not itself prevent application of the on-sale bar, but there is nothing to prevent its being considered with other factors in determining whether the invention is operable and commercially marketable, i.e., whether the invention as ultimately claimed will work for its intended purpose. *Construction Technology Inc. v. Lockformer Co.*, 713 F. Supp. 100, 11 U.S.P.Q.2d 1716, 1719 (N.Y. 1989).

ω

Rigid standards are especially unsuited to the on-sale provision where the policies underlying the bar, in effect, define it. The area of law sought to be governed by these rules encompasses an infinite variety of factual situations that, when viewed in terms of the policies underlying 35 U.S.C. §102(b), present an infinite variety of legal problems wholly unsuited to mechanically applied technical rules. Thus, all the circumstances surrounding the sale or offer to sell, including the stage of development of the invention and the nature of the invention, must be considered and weighed against the policies underlying §102(b). The policies underlying the on-sale bar include: (1) discouraging removal of inventions from the public domain that the public justifiably comes to believe are freely available; (2) favoring prompt and widespread disclosure of invention; (3) giving the inventor a reasonable amount of time (following the sales and activity) to determine the value of the patent; and (4) prohibiting an extension of the period for exploiting the invention. Congress provided the one-year grace period to balance these competing interests. *Environtech Corp. v. Westech Engineering, Inc.,* 713 F. Supp. 372, 11 U.S.P.Q.2d 1804, 1807 (Utah 1989).

ᛟ

An invention is on sale within the meaning of 35 U.S.C. §102(b) when: (1) there was a definite sale or offer to sell more than one year before the patent application was filed, and (2) "the subject matter of the sale or offer to sell fully anticipated the claimed invention or would have rendered the claimed invention obvious by its addition to the prior art." The sale need not be consummated, nor accepted. All of the circumstances surrounding the alleged offer or sale must be considered. In determining whether an offer or sale occurred, consideration should be given to whether there was a "reduction to practice," although this is not an absolute requirement of the on-sale bar. In addition, consideration should be given to the stage of development of the invention and the nature of the invention. If a sale or offer to sell was made, the on-sale bar does not apply if the offer or sale was "substantially for the purpose of experiment." In determining whether an offer or sale was for experimental purposes, consideration must be given to various factors, including the length of the test period, whether any payment was made for the invention, whether there is any secrecy obligation on the user's part, whether progress records are required, whether persons other than the inventor conducted the experiments, the extent of testing required, length of the test period in relation to test periods for similar devices, and the degree of commercial exploitation during the tests (in relation to the purpose of the experimentation). *Loral Corp. v. The B. F. Goodrich Company,* 14 U.S.P.Q.2d 1081, 1104 (Ohio 1989).

ᛟ

Whether an invention is on sale is a question of law, and no single finding or conclusion is a sine qua non to its resolution. The totality of the circumstances must always be considered in order to ascertain whether an offer of the new invention was in fact made. The totality-of-the-circumstances approach is necessary because the policies or purposes underlying the on-sale bar, in effect, define it. These policies include discouraging removal of inventions from the public domain that the public reasonably has come to believe are freely available; favoring the prompt and widespread disclosure of inventions; allowing the inventor a reasonable amount of time following sales activity to determine the potential economic value of a patent; and prohibiting an inventor from commercially exploiting his invention beyond the statutorily prescribed time. While policies underlying the on-sale bar concentrate on the inventor's attempt to exploit his invention, rather than on the potential purchaser's cognizance of it, the inventor's attempted exploitation must be objectively manifested as a definite sale or offer to sell the invention. The subjective, uncommunicated, and ultimate intention of the offeror, however clear, is not alone sufficient. *Envirotech Corp. v. Westech Engineering Inc.,* 904 F.2d 1571, 15 U.S.P.Q.2d 1230, 1232 (Fed. Cir. 1990).

ᛟ

As applied to an offer for sale, the most stringent requirements for determining whether an invention was "on sale" for purposes of 35 U.S.C. §102(b) are:

a. the invention was embodied in or obvious in view of the thing offered for sale;
b. the invention offered for sale had been tested sufficiently to verify that it is operable and commercially marketable;
c. the product was on sale for profit rather than for experimental purposes.

The on-sale bar is not limited to sales or offers by the inventor or assignees, but may result from the commercial activities of a third party. *American Home Products Corp. v. California Biological Vaccine Laboratories,* 21 U.S.P.Q.2d 1230, 1231 (Cal. 1991).

ω

To invoke the on-sale bar, a defendant must prove that a complete claimed invention is embodied in or obvious in view of the thing sold or offered for sale before the critical date. The on-sale bar invalidates a patent for an invention offered for sale, even though not ready for satisfactory commercial marketing. If a patent owner seeks to avoid the on-sale bar on the basis that a sale or offer was experimental, a trial court must determine whether the patent owner sought the sale primarily for profit rather than as part of a testing program. To determine whether profit motivated a transaction, a court must examine the claimed features, the offeror's objective intent, and the totality of the circumstances. *Atlantic Thermoplastics Co. Inc. v. Faytex Corp.*, 970 F.2d 834, 23 U.S.P.Q.2d 1481, 1483 (Fed. Cir. 1992).

ω

Reduction to practice of a claimed invention is not an absolute requirement of the on-sale bar. *B.F. Goodrich Co. v. Aircraft Braking Systems Corp.*, 825 F.Supp. 65, 27 U.S.P.Q.2d 1209, 1212 (Del. 1993).

ω

For on-sale purposes, experimentation ends with reduction to practice. Where there is no sale, a definite offer to sell is an essential requirement of the on-sale bar. *Atlantic Thermoplastics Co. Inc. v. Faytex Corp.*, 5 F.3d 1477, 28 U.S.P.Q.2d 1343, 1350 (Fed. Cir. 1993).

ω

Beyond finding that the products, including the features upon which the Examiner relied in rejecting the claims, were in public use or on sale, there is no requirement for an enablement-type inquiry. ("[O]ur precedent holds that the question is not whether the sale, even a third party sale, 'discloses' the invention at the time of the sale, but whether the sale relates to a device that embodies the invention.") *In re Epstein*, 32 F.3d 1559, 31 U.S.P.Q.2d 1817, 1823 (Fed. Cir. 1994).

ω

"While there is no requirement that the purchaser have actual knowledge of the invention to invoke the on sale bar, what the purchaser reasonably believes the inventor to be offering is relevant to whether, on balance, the offer objectively may be said to be of the patented invention." *Ferag AG v. Quipp Inc.*, 45 F.3d 1562, 33 U.S.P.Q.2d 1512, 1516 (Fed. Cir. 1995).

ω

Whether an invention was "on-sale" or in "public use" under 35 U.S.C. §102(b) must be determined in light of the policies underlying §102(b). These policies include requiring prompt disclosure, discouraging the removal of devices from the public domain once they are there, prohibiting the extension of the inventor's monopoly period for exploiting the invention, and giving the inventor a reasonable amount of time after his initial sales activity (i.e., one year) to determine whether the patent is a worthwhile investment. *Nordberg Inc. v. Telsmith Inc.*, 881 F.Supp. 1252, 36 U.S.P.Q.2d 1577, 1602 (Wis. 1995).

ᴛ

"[E]ven free distribution of a prototype may raise the on-sale bar if it is done to solicit a sale." *Monon Corp. v. Stoughton Trailers Inc.*, 38 U.S.P.Q.2d 1503, 1505 (Ill. 1996).

ᴛ

The on-sale bar starts to accrue when a completed invention is offered for sale. Facts underlying the on-sale bar must be proved by clear and convincing evidence. *Seal-Flex Inc. v. Athletic Track and Court Construction*, 98 F.3d 1318, 40 U.S.P.Q.2d 1450, 1454 (Fed. Cir. 1996).

ᴛ

Even though the technical requirements of a reduction to practice have not been met, a sale or a definite offer to sell a substantially completed invention, with reason to expect that it would work for its intended purpose upon completion, suffices to generate a statutory bar. However, an alleged offer to sell a device is not an on-sale bar to the patentability of a method of using the device unless the activities involving the device meet the criteria for the on-sale bar. An offer of sale, to be a bar within the meaning of 35 U.S.C. §102(b), must be of an invention which is substantially complete at the time of the offer. The development of software was essential to the substantial completion of the device to be provided for use in practicing the claimed method, even if it was not part of the claims. Without a substantially completed invention, there could be no on-sale bar. If the software was completed before the critical date, then it validates the offer to sell the machine to be used in the method of the patent, and the patent is invalid because of the on-sale bar. If it occurred after the critical date, then the earlier offer was not an on-sale bar. The alleged offer by itself before the critical date could not have triggered the on-sale bar, as the invention was not substantially completed at that time. *Robotic Vision Systems Inc. v. View Engineering Inc.*, 42 U.S.P.Q.2d 1619, 1623, 1624 (Fed. Cir. 1997).

ᴛ

An inventor's request for aid and advice in developing and patenting an invention is not an on-sale event as contemplated by 35 U.S.C. §102(b). *Hupp v. Siroflex of America Inc.*, 122 F.3d 1456, 43 U.S.P.Q.2d 1887, 1891 (Fed. Cir. 1997).

ᴛ

The existence of a sales contract or the signing of a purchase order is sufficient to demonstrate "on-sale" status. The thrust of the on-sale inquiry is whether the inventor thought he had a product which could be and was offered to customers, not whether he could prevail under the technicalities of reduction to practice. Accordingly, the appropriate question is whether the invention was substantially complete at the time of sale such that there was "reason to expect that it would work for its intended purpose upon completion." *Pfaff v. Wells Electronics Inc.*, 43 U.S.P.Q.2d 1928, 1931, 1932 (Fed. Cir. 1997).

ω

"Public use" and "on-sale" bars, while they share the same statutory basis, are grounded on different policy emphases. The primary policy underlying the "public use" case is that of detrimental public reliance, whereas the primary policy underlying an "on-sale" case is that of prohibiting the commercial exploitation of the design beyond the statutorily prescribed time period. *Continental Plastic Containers Inc. v. Owens-Brockway Plastic Products Inc.*, 141 F.3d 1073, 46 U.S.P.Q.2d 1277, 1280 (Fed. Cir. 1998).

ω

An offer of sale originating in a foreign country, directed to a consumer in the United States, can establish an on-sale bar as to what was offered. *C.R. Bard Inc. v. M3 Systems Inc.*, 48 U.S.P.Q.2d 1225, 1237 (Fed. Cir. 1998).

ω

The on-sale bar applies when two conditions are satisfied before the critical date. First, the product must be the subject of a commercial offer for sale. Second, the invention must be ready for patenting. The second condition may be satisfied in at least two ways: by proof of reduction to practice before the critical date; or by proof that prior to the critical date the inventor had prepared drawings or other descriptions of the invention that were sufficiently specific to enable a person skilled in the art to practice the invention. *Pfaff v. Wells Electronics Inc.*, 48 U.S.P.Q.2d 1641, 1646, 1647 (S.Ct. 1998).

Open-Ended Claim. *See also* **At Least, Incomplete, Subcombination, Substituted.**

Claims employing "dangling valences" to indicate undefined substituents are improper because they are indeterminate in scope and generally broader than any possible supporting disclosure. *Ex parte Diamond*, 123 U.S.P.Q. 167 (PO Bd. App. 1959).

ω

The rejection of a claim to a water-soluble organic dyestuff (of a stated formula wherein A is an organic azo dyestuff residue, a ring carbon of which is bonded in a specified way to defined structure) under 35 U.S.C. §112 (based on breadth and definiteness) was reversed. *In re Riat, DeMontmollin, and Koller*, 327 F.2d 685, 140 U.S.P.Q. 471 (C.C.P.A. 1964).

ω

The fact that a claim defines only a portion of a molecule referred to therein, namely: at least 24 amino acids in a certain sequence, and the absence of a limitation as to amino acids beyond the 24th position obviously broaden the claim do not support a rejection based on undue breadth or indefiniteness under the second paragraph of 35 U.S.C. §112. However, they may well support a rejection for lack of support under the first paragraph of 35 U.S.C. §112, which requires that the scope of the claims must bear a reasonable correlation to the scope of enablement provided by the specification to persons of ordinary skill in the art. The first paragraph of 35 U.S.C. §112 requires that the scope of the claims must bear a reasonable correlation to the scope of enablement provided by the specification to persons of ordinary skill in the art. *In re Fisher*, 427 F.2d 833, 166 U.S.P.Q. 18, 23, 24 (C.C.P.A. 1970).

ω

The rejection of claims, calling for a photographic color coupler of the formula COUP-S-R [wherein COUP is a photographic color coupler radical (a five-pyrazolone color coupler radical or an open-chain ketomethylene color coupler radical) and R is an organic radical incapable of forming a dye with an oxidized developing agent], for lack of support and definition under 35 U.S.C. §112 was reversed. *In re Barr, Williams, and Whitmore*, 444 F.2d 588, 170 U.S.P.Q. 330 (C.C.P.A. 1971).

ω

Open-ended claims are not inherently improper; as for all claims their appropriateness depends on the particular facts of the invention, the disclosure, and the prior art. They may be supported if there is an inherent, albeit not previously known, upper limit and if the specification enables one of skill in the art to approach that limit. *Scripps Clinic & Research Foundation v. Genentech Inc.*, 927 F.2d 1565, 18 U.S.P.Q.2d 1001, 1006 (Fed. Cir. 1991).

Operability. *See* **Utility.**

Operative. *See* **Inoperative.**

Opinion. *See also* **Authoritative Opinion, Examiner's Opinion, Expert Opinion, Expert Testimony, Infringement Opinion, Opinion Evidence, Opinion Letter, Opinion of Counsel, Rule 702.**

If the appellants wished to object to the Board's statement and to question the correctness of the facts contained therein, they should have requested the Board to cite its authority for the statement. If the cited authority was based upon facts within the personal knowledge of the Board, the appellants should have proceeded under Rule 66 and 76 of the Patent Office and called for an affidavit of the Board. The appellants would then have been in a position to contradict or explain the Board's statement. In the absence of such request, the appellants may not be heard to challenge a statement made in the Board's opinion. The statement of the Board must therefore be accepted as correct. *In re Selmi and Altenburger*, 156 F.2d 96, 70 U.S.P.Q. 197 (C.C.P.A. 1946).

ω

As there was nothing in the record to controvert a statement in appellant's affidavit, the statement was accepted as accurate. *In re Nathan, Hogg, and Schneider*, 328 F.2d 1005, 140 U.S.P.Q. 601, 604 (C.C.P.A. 1964).

ω

An affidavit, which is the opinion of one having broader expertise than that of ordinary skill and is directed to the ultimate legal issue, is not evidence. Nonetheless, statements of fact in such an affidavit, however commingled with inadmissible assertions, ought to be considered. A sworn statement, made of the affiant's own knowledge, must be accepted as fact in the absence of a challenge to the affiant's qualifications or, at the very least, a contrary inference from other record evidence. *In re Naquin,* 398 F.2d 863, 158 U.S.P.Q. 317, 319 (C.C.P.A. 1968).

ᵿ

A finding of a new fact, supporting an alternative ground for sustaining an Examiner's rejection, and based on apparently nothing more than a bare allegation of scientific fact, does everything but cry out for an opportunity to respond. Appellant challenged the Board's assertion with an allegation of his own to the contrary and supported his assertion with an affidavit opinion of an acknowledged expert in the art. Appellant's response was more than mere "argument"; it was a direct challenge to a finding of fact made for the first time by the Board and included with it some evidence in the nature of rebuttal. It was thus entitled to more serious consideration. *In re Moore,* 444 F.2d 572, 170 U.S.P.Q. 260, 263 (C.C.P.A. 1971).

ᵿ

Expert opinion is entitled to be given consideration along with other evidence on the issue of obviousness. *In re Mochel,* 470 F.2d 638, 176 U.S.P.Q. 194, 196 (C.C.P.A. 1972).

ᵿ

While the Board is not inclined to substitute for its judgment the affidavit opinion of an expert as to obviousness, the Board does recognize opinions of experts in the field and considers them persuasive as to non-obviousness in the absence of valid reason by the Examiner to the contrary. *Ex parte Copping,* 180 U.S.P.Q. 475, 476 (PTO Bd. App. 1972).

ᵿ

Although an attorney may be deposed and required to disclose what he knows about the subject matter, he cannot be required to disclose his mental impressions, conclusions, opinions, or legal theories concerning the litigation. He may be required to refer to his file to refresh his recollection, but he cannot be compelled to state why he amended the claims or what he meant by this or that word or phrase; that would require him to express an opinion, one of the exceptions provided for in Fed. R. Civ. P. 26(b)(3). *MacLaren v. B-l-W Group Inc.,* 180 U.S.P.Q. 387 (Va. 1973).

ᵿ

Mere conclusions set forth in an affidavit without cogent supporting reasons are of limited probative value. If, as affiants stated, "no reasonable interpretation" can equate the respective products involved, affiants should have submitted factual substantiation of that contention. *In re Grunwell and Petrow,* 609 F.2d 486, 203 U.S.P.Q. 1055, 1059 (C.C.P.A. 1979).

ᵿ

The Court should pay deference to the opinions of experts and to the opinions of lay jurors who brought their intelligence to bear upon the matter at hand and should not substitute its judgment for the opinions of those experts and jurors who have spoken unless there is a good reason for doing so. *The Celotex Corporation v. United States Gypsum Company,* 204 U.S.P.Q. 745, 747 (Ill. 1979).

ᵿ

Opinion

An affidavit opinion of an expert on the ultimate legal issue is entitled to no weight. However, his factual statement regarding the state of the art, known to him in his capacity as an expert, absent any contrary evidence, is entitled to full consideration. *In re Reuter, Vickery, and Everett*, 651 F.2d 751, 210 U.S.P.Q. 249, 256 (C.C.P.A. 1981).

ω

Even if a finding of infringement had been upheld, the fact that the defendants requested an opinion from their patent attorney and did not manufacture and sell the lamps (accused of infringement) until after receiving that attorney's opinion that they did not infringe the patent negates an inference of willful infringement. *Moore v. Wesbar Corp.*, 701 F.2d 1247, 217 U.S.P.Q. 684, 691 (7th Cir. 1983).

ω

Ordering a file history is an ordinary and necessary preliminary to a validity or an infringement opinion. *Underwater Devices Incorporated v. Morrison-Knudsen Company, Inc.*, 717 F.2d 1380, 219 U.S.P.Q. 569, 577 (Fed. Cir. 1983).

ω

The plaintiff in an action brought pursuant to 35 U.S.C. §145 has a heavy burden. Because the Patent Office is an expert body preeminently qualified to determine questions of this kind, its conclusions are entitled to a broad presumption of validity. In these circumstances, the court is authorized to reverse the decision only if the Patent Office did not have a rational basis for its conclusions or if the plaintiff presented new evidence that leads to a thorough conviction that the plaintiff should prevail. In trials de novo under 35 U.S.C. §145, great weight attaches to the expertise of the Patent Office, and its findings will not be overturned unless new evidence is introduced that carries thorough conviction that the Patent Office erred. Based upon the opinion testimony of an independent expert, the court was satisfied that the only way one would reach the plaintiff's claimed alloy composition from the reference disclosure was by experimentation. The testimony offered on behalf of the plaintiff at the trial was uncontradicted by the defendant. The court found that testimony to be very persuasive, and the court concluded that the plaintiff demonstrated by clear and convincing evidence that the determination by the Board of Appeals was in error. *Titanium Metals Corp. of America v. Mossinghoff*, 603 F. Supp. 87, 225 U.S.P.Q. 673 (D.C. 1984).

ω

Opinions of the contemporaneous beliefs of those skilled in the field as to the nonobviousness of an invention merit fair weight. *In re Corkill*, 771 F.2d 1496, 226 U.S.P.Q. 1005 (Fed. Cir. 1985).

ω

While objective factual evidence going toward a 35 U.S.C. §103 determination is preferable to statements of opinion on the issue, the nature of the matter sought to be established, as well as the strength of the opposing evidence, must be taken into consideration in assessing the probative value of expert opinion. Opinion testimony rendered by experts must be given consideration, and while not controlling, generally is entitled to some weight. Lack of factual support for expert opinion going to a factual determination, however, may render the testimony of little probative value in a validity determination.

While the opinion testimony of a party having a direct interest in the pending litigation is less persuasive than opinion testimony by a disinterested party, it cannot be disregarded for that reason alone and may be relied upon when sufficiently convincing. *Ashland Oil, Inc. v. Delta Resins & Refractories, Inc.*, 776 F.2d 281, 227 U.S.P.Q. 657 (Fed. Cir. 1985).

ᚳ

An "aggressive strategy" may or may not be a factor in a decision to deny or award increased damages. An aggressive strategy unsupported by any competent advice of counsel, thorough investigation of validity and infringement, discovery of more pertinent uncited prior art, or similar factors, is the type of activity the reference in the patent law to increased damages seeks to prevent. An alleged infringer, who intentionally blinds himself to the facts and law, continues to infringe, and employs the judicial process with no solidly based expectation of success, can hardly be surprised when his infringement is found to have been willful. Willfulness of infringement relates to the accused infringer's conduct in the marketplace. Because that conduct may be seen as producing an unnecessary and outcome-certain lawsuit, it may make the case so exceptional as to warrant attorney's fees under 35 U.S.C. §285. Similarly, bad faith displayed in pretrial and trial stages, by counsel or party, may render the case exceptional under §285. When a court declines to award attorney's fees on the basis of a determination that a case is not exceptional, the fact findings underlying that determination are reviewed under the clearly erroneous standard. When the determination is that a case is exceptional, the election to grant or deny attorney's fees is reviewed under the abuse-of-discretion standard. *Kloster Speedsteel A.B. v. Crucible Inc.*, 793 F.2d 1565, 230 U.S.P.Q. 81 (Fed. Cir. 1986).

ᚳ

The trier of fact is not bound to accept expert opinion, even if it is uncontradicted. The court's obligation is to weigh expert and other testimony; it is the court's, not the expert's, responsibility to decide the case. *Del Mar Avionics, Inc. v. Quinton Instrument Co.*, 836 F.2d 1320, 5 U.S.P.Q.2d 1255 (Fed. Cir. 1987).

ᚳ

Where the evidence of infringement consists merely of one expert's opinion without support in tests or data, the district court is under no obligation to accept it. *W. L. Gore & Associates, Inc. v. Garlock, Inc.*, 842 F.2d 1275, 6 U.S.P.Q.2d 1277 (Fed. Cir. 1988).

ᚳ

Although a letter opinion from outside counsel postdates some infringing conduct, it is nevertheless an indicia of good faith. *Polysius Corp. v. Fuller Co.*, 709 F. Supp. 560, 10 U.S.P.Q.2d 1417 (Pa. 1989).

ᚳ

Disregard for the opinion of a sales engineer with neither an aerodynamic nor a legalbackground and who was thus not qualified to make either a technical or legal determination of infringement does not justify an award of treble damages or attorney's fees. *Uniroyal Inc. v. Rudkin-Wiley Corp.*, 721 F. Supp. 28, 13 U.S.P.Q.2d 1192, 1201 (Conn. 1989).

ᚳ

Good-faith reliance by a party on counsel's opinion is a question of the party's state of mind, not counsel's state of mind. To establish a defense of nondeliberate infringement on the basis of counsel's opinion, a party must show not only that it received an opinion from competent counsel, but also that it exercised reasonable and good-faith adherence to the analysis and advice therein. This defense does not require an inquiry into counsel's state of mind. Matters held to be relevant inquiries into the competence of counsel's opinion of non-infringement include whether counsel examined the file history of the patents, whether the opinion came from in-house or outside counsel, whether there was a pattern of attorney shopping by the alleged infringer, and whether the opinion came from a patent attorney. *Liqui-Box Corp. v. Reid Valve Co. Inc.*, 16 U.S.P.Q.2d 1074, 1075 (Pa. 1989).

ω

Defendant's attorney may proffer his opinion on such questions as whether the claims of the patent are vague or indefinite, whether they are anticipated by a single reference in the prior art, and whether the invention set forth in the patent was obvious. To some degree, testimony on these subjects necessarily requires the attorney to speak of the manner in which the claims were drafted and, by way of illustration, the way in which they might have been drafted differently to embrace elements or processes that, in his opinion, are outside the scope of the claims as they were actually written. However, it would not be appropriate for defendant's attorney to speculate on how he would have drafted the patent application in question, to discuss the law governing patent validity, or to predict how a judge or jury would or should rule on the question of whether the patent is valid. Such testimony would simply not be relevant and would stray into matters of law as to which it is the court's responsibility to instruct the jury. *Amsted Industries Inc. v. National Castings Inc.*, 16 U.S.P.Q.2d 1737, 1761 (Ill. 1990).

ω

Although claim interpretation is a question of law, expert testimony is admissible to give an opinion on the ultimate question of infringement. *Symbol Technologies Inc. v. Opticon Inc.*, 935 F.2d 1569, 19 U.S.P.Q.2d 1241, 1245 (Fed. Cir. 1991).

Opinion Evidence.

Affidavit evidence admitted in a protested reissue proceeding is treated in the same manner as if it had been submitted in ex parte proceedings before the PTO. Such evidence has been held to be competent to the extent that it refers to matters known to or observed by the affiant prior to or contemporaneous with the actual reduction to practice by another in an interference, where it was offered as evidence of the level of knowledge in the art at the time the invention was made. *In re Farrenkopf and Usategui Gomez, and Travenol Laboratories, Inc., Intervenor,* 713 F.2d 714, 219 U.S.P.Q. 1, 6 (Fed. Cir. 1983).

ω

The CAFC stated that it was aware of no reason why opinion evidence relating to a fact issue should not be considered by an Examiner. *In re Alton*, 76 F.3d 1168, 37 U.S.P.Q.2d 1578, 1583 n.10 (Fed. Cir. 1996).

ω

Opinion evidence must be considered in the determination of obviousness. *United States Surgical Corp. v. Ethicon Inc.*, 41 U.S.P.Q.2d 1225 (Fed. Cir. 1997).

Opinion Letter.

An opinion letter was criticized for not giving a reasonable basis for believing in good faith that the subject patent was invalid. The letter treated the claims of the patent superficially, failed to set out a standard for one of ordinary skill in the art, failed to consider secondary considerations in determining obviousness, mischaracterized prior art, and failed to perform a proper best mode analysis. Additionally, the letter only addressed invalidity and did not discuss infringement. It makes broad and conclusory statements with little, if any, support and discusses concepts rather than analyzing patent claims. Evidence shows that the advice of counsel was more of a protective device than a genuine effort to determine (before infringing) whether the patent was invalid. *In re Hayes Microcomputer Products Inc. Patent Litigation*, 982 F.2d 1527, 25 U.S.P.Q.2d 1241, 1253 (Fed. Cir. 1992).

Opinion of Counsel. *See also* Authoritative Opinion.

Increased damages are usually based on a finding that the infringer's conduct was willful and in flagrant disregard of the patentee's rights. In this case, the defendant was on notice of the plaintiff's patent rights and had an affirmative duty to exercise due care to determine whether it was infringing. The defendant may not avoid a holding of willful infringement because it failed to show that it obtained a competent opinion from counsel and that it had exercised reasonable and good-faith adherence to the analysis and advice contained therein. Accordingly, the defendant is liable to the plaintiff for an amount equal to three times the amount of damages actually found or assessed. Section 285 of 35 U.S.C. makes provision for the award of attorney's fees to the prevailing party in exceptional cases. In order to support an award of attorney's fees in a patent case, there must be a showing of conduct that is unfair, in bad faith, inequitable, or unconscionable. In view of defendant's willful infringement, this case involves those elements set out above and is an exceptional case, thereby entitling the plaintiff to an award of its attorney's fees. The plaintiff is also entitled to prejudgment interest based upon the damages found or assessed in the second phase of this trial. *Great Northern Corp. v. Davis Core & Pad Co.*, 226 U.S.P.Q. 540 (Ga. 1985).

ϖ

Not every failure to seek an opinion of competent counsel will mandate an ultimate finding of willfulness. *Spindelfabrik Suesson-Schurr Stahlecker & Grill GmbH v. Schubert & Salzer Maschinenfabrik Aktiengesellschaft*, 829 F.2d 1075, 4 U.S.P.Q.2d 1044, 1051, n.13 (Fed. Cir. 1987), *cert. denied*, 108 S. Ct. 1022 (1988).

ϖ

When an infringer fails to introduce an exculpatory opinion of counsel at trial, a court must be free to infer that either no opinion was obtained or, if an opinion were obtained, it was contrary to the infringer's desire to initiate or continue its use of the patentee's invention. *Fromson v. Western Litho Plate & Supply Co.*, 853 F.2d 1568, 7 U.S.P.Q.2d 1606 (Fed. Cir. 1988).

ᅲ

Patent attorneys in foreign countries, who are not experts in American patent practice and patent law, are not competent to express an opinion on either validity or infringement of a U.S. patent. Subsequent, willfull, and intentional infringement and the consequences thereof are in no way relieved by reliance on such an opinion. *McDermott v. Omid International Inc.*, 723 F. Supp. 1228, 13 U.S.P.Q.2d 1147, 1150, 1151 (Ohio 1988).

ᅲ

The duty of due care normally requires a party to obtain legal advice before initiating or continuing an operation that might result in infringement. Failure to obtain an opinion of counsel is one of the factors supporting a finding of willfulness. This principle, which addresses the conduct of an accused willful infringer, is part of the substantive law of patents and is not merely a procedural housekeeping rule. A federal court exercising patent jurisdiction is bound by the substantive patent law of the Federal Circuit. When an infringer fails to introduce (at trial) an opinion of counsel pertaining to the activity in question, an adverse inference may be drawn against the infringer that any legal advice obtained regarding the activity in question was unfavorable to the infringer. *ALM Surgical Equipment Inc. v. Kirschner Medical Corp.*, 15 U.S.P.Q.2d 1241, 1251 (S.C. 1990).

ᅲ

A party does not avoid willful infringement merely by asserting that it acted on the advice of counsel. Rather, a potential infringer must secure and rely upon timely advice from counsel and must supply all pertinent facts to counsel as a basis for a reliable opinion. The defendant's contention that it had relied upon two outside opinions before engaging in infringement was unavailing as a good-faith defense because, inter alia, there is nothing in the record to suggest that the outside firms were supplied with all relevant facts. *Amsted Industries Inc. v. National Castings Inc.*, 16 U.S.P.Q.2d 1737, 1741, 1742 (Ill. 1990).

ᅲ

Counsel's opinion must be thorough enough, as combined with other factors, to instil a belief in the infringer that a court might reasonably hold the patent is invalid, not infringed, or unenforceable. In considering the reasonableness of the accused infringer's reliance on an opinion of counsel, the opinion letter should be reviewed for its "overall tone, its discussion of case law, its analysis of the particular facts and its reference to inequitable conduct. *Westvaco Corp. v. International Paper Co.*, 991 F.2d 735, 26 U.S.P.Q.2d 1353, 1360 (Fed. Cir. 1993).

ᅲ

Opinions of counsel received subsequent to the decision to produce an infringing product, although relevant as part of the totality of the circumstances, do not dictate a conclusion that the infringement was not willful. *Alpex Computer Corp. v. Nintendo Co. Ltd.*, 86 Civ. 1749, 34 U.S.P.Q.2d 1167, 1205 (N.Y. 1994).

ᅲ

To serve as exculpatory legal advice, the opinion of counsel is viewed objectively to determine whether it was obtained in a timely manner, whether counsel analyzed the relevant facts and explained the conclusions in light of the applicable law, and whether the opinion warranted a reasonable degree of certainty that the infringer had a reasonable right to conduct the infringing activity. *SRI International Inc. v. Advanced Technological Laboratories Inc.*, 127 F.3d 1462, 44 U.S.P.Q.2d 1422, 1426 (Fed. Cir. 1997).

ω

The significance of the file history is illustrated by the fact that one cannot rely on an attorney opinion of non-infringement as a good faith defense to a charge of willful patent infringement if the attorney did not consult the file history of the patent for which infringement is charged prior to giving his opinion. *Elk Corp. of Dallas v. GAF Building Materials Corp.*, 45 U.S.P.Q.2d 1011, 1014 n.3 (Tex. 1997).

Opposite Direction. *See* **Orientation, Teach Away From.**

Optical Isomer. *See also* **Stereoisomer.**

In the absence of unexpected or unobvious beneficial properties, an optically active isomer is unpatentable over either the isomer of opposite rotation or the racemic compound itself. *Brenner v. Ladd*, 247 F.Supp. 51, 147 U.S.P.Q. 87, 91 (D.C. 1965).

ω

The novelty of an optical isomer is not negated by the prior art disclosure of its racemate. *In re May and Eddy*, 574 F.2d 1082, 197 U.S.P.Q. 601, 607 (C.C.P.A. 1978).

Optimize. *See also* **Design Choice, Dosage, Experimentation, Parameters.**

Under some circumstances, changes in temperature, in concentration, or in both, may impart patentability to a process if the particular ranges claimed produce a new and unexpected result that is different in kind and not merely in degree from the results of the prior art. Such ranges are termed "critical" ranges, and the applicant has the burden of proving such criticality. Where the general conditions of a claim are disclosed in prior art, it is not inventive merely to discover the optimum or workable ranges by routine experimentation. *In re Aller, Lacey, and Hall*, 220 F.2d 454, 105 U.S.P.Q. 233, 235 (C.C.P.A. 1955).

ω

The standard of patentability does not depend upon a showing of advantages or improvements, but rather upon obviousness. The Examiner's failure to indicate any reason for finding obvious the alteration of the ratio employed in the prior art in the direction and manner claimed renders the rejection untenable. *Ex parte Parthasarathy and Ciapetta*, 174 U.S.P.Q. 63 (PTO Bd. App. 1971).

ω

While, ordinarily, the determination of optimum values for parameters of a prior-art process would be at least *prima facie* obvious, that conclusion depends upon what the prior art discloses with respect to those parameters. Where prior art suggests the outer limits of a range of suitable values, and that the optimum resides within that range, and where there are indications elsewhere that the optimum should, in fact, be sought within that range, a determination of optimum values outside that range may not be obvious. In an area of technology shown to be highly unpredictable in process values, the discovery of optimum values not in any way suggested by the prior art is more likely to be unobvious than obvious within the meaning of 35 U.S.C. §103. *In re Sebek*, 465 F.2d 904, 175 U.S.P.Q. 93, 95 (C.C.P.A. 1972).

ᵹ

Exceptions to the rule that the discovery of an optimum value of a variable in a known process is normally obvious include:

a) cases where the results of optimizing a variable, which was known to be result effective, are unexpectedly good; and

b) cases in which the parameter optimized was not recognized to be a result-effective variable.

In re Antonie, 559 F.2d 618, 195 U.S.P.Q. 6, 8, 9 (C.C.P.A. 1977).

ᵹ

Although the discovery of an optimum value of a result-effective variable in a known process is ordinarily within the skill of the art, a *prima facie* case of obviousness may be rebutted where the results of optimizing a variable, which was known to be result effective, are unexpectedly good. *In re Boesch and Slaney*, 617 F.2d 272, 205 U.S.P.Q. 215, 219 (C.C.P.A. 1980).

ᵹ

In many instances it is "not unobvious to discover optimum or workable ranges by routine experimentation." The problem, however, with such "rules of patentability" (and the ever-lengthening list of exceptions which they engender) is that they tend to becloud the ultimate legal issue—obviousness—and exalt the formal exercise of squeezing new factual situations into preestablished pigeonholes. Additionally, the emphasis upon routine experimentation is contrary to the last sentence of 35 U.S.C. §103. *In re Yates*, 663 F.2d 1054, 211 U.S.P.Q. 1149, 1151 n.4 (C.C.P.A. 1981).

ᵹ

Although the fact that each of the three components of the composition used in the claimed method was conventionally employed in the art for treating cooling water systems, to employ these components in combination for their known functions and to optimize the amount of each additive were not regarded as "obvious." Obviousness cannot be established by combining the teachings of the prior art to produce a claimed invention, absent some teaching, suggestion, or incentive supporting the combination. At best, in view of the prior art, one skilled in the art might find it obvious to try various combinations of these known scale-and-corrosion prevention agents. This is not the standard of 35 U.S.C. §103. *In re Geiger*, 815 F.2d 686, 2 U.S.P.Q.2d 1276 (Fed. Cir. 1987).

ᵹ

The mere need for experimentation to determine parameters required to make a device work is an application of the often-rejected obvious-to-try standard and falls short of statutory "obviousness" of 35 U.S.C. §103. Inability of an expert to predict the results obtainable with a claimed product suggests non-obviousness, not routine experimentation. *Uniroyal Inc. v. Rudkin-Wiley Corp.*, 837 F.2d 1044, 5 U.S.P.Q.2d 1434 (Fed. Cir. 1988).

Optionally. *See* **Alternative.**

The recitation "optionally" denotes that the specified material may or may not be employed. It is not apparent why the use of such alternative language fails to particularly point out and distinctly claim the subject matter that appellants regard as their invention. The use of the alternative expression, "optionally," in the rejected claims does not obfuscate the subject matter appellants regard as their invention. Such alternative language does not normally render claims indefinite under the second paragraph of 35 U.S.C. §112. *Ex parte Cordova,* 10 U.S.P.Q.2d 1949, 1950, 1952 (B.P.A.I. 1988).

ᗧ

The term "optionally" clearly indicates that identified material may or may not be present as a fourth component in an otherwise three-component composition. Claims often include the accepted expressions: "up to," "0 to... %," "not more than," which are recognized to indicate the possible, but not required, presence of a component. Whatever confusion exists in this matter is not attributable to the words of the claim. It seems that the argument is premised on the fact that the claim might mean one thing when the "optionally..." phrase is ignored and might mean something else when the phrase is considered. The BPAI knew of no basis for interpreting the claim by ignoring the specific words used in the claim. It therefore saw no rational basis for the Examiner's finding that confusion would result should such an unwarranted method of claim interpretation be followed. *Ex parte Wu,* 10 U.S.P.Q.2d 2031, 2033, 2034 (B.P.A.I. 1988).

Oral Testimony.

Unsupported oral testimony can be sufficient, but must be regarded with suspicion and subjected to close scrutiny. *E.I. duPont de Nemours & Company v. Berkley & Company, Inc.*, 620 F.2d 1247, 205 U.S.P.Q. 1, 11 (8th Cir. 1980).

ᗧ

A party claiming anticipation under 35 U.S.C. §102 because of prior use is put to "the strictest of proofs." Because of the unsatisfactory character of mere oral testimony to prove an anticipation, a party attempting to establish an anticipation has the burden of doing so by "clear and satisfactory evidence." *Trend Products Co. v. Metro Industries, Inc.*, 10 U.S.P.Q.2d 1531, 1538 (Cal. 1989).

ᗧ

An alleged prior use must be established by clear and convincing evidence. Oral testimony as to such purported prior use must normally be corroborated by other evidence. Oral testimony of alleged prior use, unsupported by contemporaneous documents, must be subject to appropriate scrutiny under the clear and convincing standard of proof. *Henkel Corp. v. Coral Inc.*, 754 F. Supp. 1280, 21 U.S.P.Q.2d 1081, 1103 (Ill. 1990).

Order.

There is no necessary relationship between the order of making inventions and the order of filing applications on them. However, there may be evidentiary significance in the fact that appellant's filing date was almost a year after that of another. *In re Bass, Jenkins, and Horvat*, 474 F.2d 1276, 177 U.S.P.Q. 178, 187 (C.C.P.A. 1973).

ᅲ

The controlling date for purposes of 35 U.S.C. §102(b), where an item had not yet been manufactured at the time of the order, is the date on which the order is filled, and not the date on which the order is first placed. *Forbro Design Corp. v. Raytheon Co.*, 390 F.Supp. 794, 190 U.S.P.Q. 70, 77 (Mass. 1975).

Order to Show Cause.

The good-cause standard in the interference rules was intended to tighten the prior practice. According to the notice accompanying the publication of the new rules, "a major change in practice that was adopted by the new 37 C.F.R. §1.617 was that a stricter standard would be imposed for presenting additional evidence after entry of an order to show cause." The new rules specifically require that "any printed publication or other document which is not self-authenticating shall be authenticated and discussed with particularity in an affidavit." *Hahn v. Wong*, 892 F.2d 1028, 13 U.S.P.Q.2d 1313, 1318, 1319 (Fed. Cir. 1989).

Ordinary Income.

The patent and patent application, which were the subject of the transfer of CAF-CAN, did not constitute petitioner's stock in trade or inventory, nor were they "property held by [petitioner] primarily for sale by customers in the ordinary course of [its] trade or business." The determinative issue is whether the transfer in question constituted a "sale" or a "license." If it was in the nature of a license, the consideration paid for it constituted a royalty and is taxable as ordinary income. Whether the payment is made in a lump sum or over a period of time in amounts based upon the use of the invention by the grantee is immaterial to this determination. *United States Mineral Products Co. v. Commissioner of Internal Revenue*, 52 T.C. 177, 162 U.S.P.Q. 480, 492 (U.S.T.C. 1969).

Ordinary Skill. *See also* **MOSITA, Skilled in the Art, Skill of the Art, Specification.**

The specification is not addressed to lawyers or even to the public generally, but to those of ordinary skill in the art. Any description that is sufficient to apprise them (in the language of the art) of the definite features of the invention, and to serve as a warning to others of that which is claimed, is sufficiently definite. *The Carnegie Steel Company, Ltd. v. The Cambria Iron Co.*, 185 U.S. 403, 437 (1902).

ᅲ

The issue is whether or not it can fairly and reasonably be said that one of ordinary skill in the art, through a reading of the entire reference, has possession of the thing itself, as opposed to possession of mere language which embraces the name of that thing. *In re Luvisi and Nohejl*, 342 F.2d 102, 144 U.S.P.Q. 646, 650 (C.C.P.A. 1965).

ⱳ

Patent specifications and claims are addressed to men of ordinary skill in the art. The question under 35 U.S.C. §112 is whether the specification and claims are sufficiently detailed to enable a man of ordinary skill in the art to construct the claimed invention and to determine from the claim language the scope of protection encompassed thereby. *Maschinenfabrik Rieter A.G. v. Greenwood Mills*, 340 F. Supp. 1103, 173 U.S.P.Q. 605, 610 (S.C. 1972).

ⱳ

Reference to the subjective reaction of a person who was familiar with and practiced the art at the time the invention was made is the usual way of determining the level of ordinary skill in the art. *In re Meng and Driessen*, 492 F.2d 843, 181 U.S.P.Q. 94, 98 (C.C.P.A. 1974).

ⱳ

Indiscriminate reliance on definitions found in dictionaries can often produce absurd results. One need not arbitrarily pick and choose from the various accepted definitions of a word to decide which meaning was intended as the word is used in a given claim. The subject matter, the context, and so on will more often than not lead to the correct conclusion. Rather than looking to a dictionary, look to the art or technology to which the claimed subject matter pertains. In doing so, give due consideration to the interpretation that one of ordinary skill in the art would give the terminology in question. *In re Salem, Butterworth, and Ryan*, 553 F.2d 676, 193 U.S.P.Q. 513, 518 (C.C.P.A. 1977).

ⱳ

The issue of obviousness is determined entirely with reference to a hypothetical "person having ordinary skill in the art." It is only that hypothetical person who is presumed to be aware of all the pertinent prior art. The actual inventor's skill is irrelevant to the inquiry, and this is for a very important reason. The statutory emphasis is on a person of ordinary skill. Inventors, as a class, according to the concepts underlying the Constitution and the statutes that have created the patent system, possess something that sets them apart from the workers of ordinary skill, and one should not go about determining obviousness under 35 U.S.C. §103 by inquiring into what patentees (i.e., inventors) would have known or would likely have done, faced with the revelation of references. A person of ordinary skill in the art is also presumed to be one who thinks along the line of conventional wisdom in the art and is not one who undertakes to innovate, whether by patient, and often expensive, systematic research or by extraordinary insight; it makes no difference which. *The Standard Oil Company v. American Cyanamid Co.*, 774 F.2d 448, 227 U.S.P.Q. 293 (Fed. Cir. 1985).

ⱳ

The issue of obviousness is determined entirely with reference to a hypothetical "person having ordinary skill in the art." It is only that person who is presumed to be aware of all the pertinent art. There are six factors relevant to a determination of the level of ordinary skill: educational level of the inventor, type of problems encountered in the art, prior-art solutions, rapidity of innovation, sophistication of technology, and educational level of active workers in the field. B*ausch & Lomb, Inc. v. Barnes-Hind/Hydro-curve, Inc.*, 796 F.2d 443, 230 U.S.P.Q. 416 (Fed. Cir. 1986).

ᴂ

Affidavits from experts with actual skill in the art may aid the PTO in a patentability determination, but do not substitute for an obviousness determination under the proper standard. Rather, in a 35 U.S.C. §103 analysis, the evidence must be viewed from the position of a person of ordinary skill, not from the position of an expert. *Uniroyal, Inc. v. Rudkin-Wiley Corp.*, 837 F.2d 1044, 1050, 5 U.S.P.Q.2d 1434, 1438 (Fed. Cir. 1988), *cert. denied*, 488 U.S. 825 (1988).

ᴂ

In evaluating the level of ordinary skill in the art, the following factors are considered:

(a) the various prior-art approaches employed;
(b) the types of problems encountered in the art;
(c) the rapidity with which innovations are made;
(d) the sophistication of the technology involved;
(e) the education background of those actively working in the field;
(f) commercial success; and
(g) the failure of others.

California Irrigation Services, Inc. v. Bartron Corp., 9 U.S.P.Q.2d 1859 (Cal. 1988).

ᴂ

With regard to the issue of obviousness of applied art, testimony of those who qualified as experts was not acceptable as evidence of what would be obvious to one of ordinary skill in the art. *Dotolo v. Quigg*, 12 U.S.P.Q.2d 1032, 1037 (D.C. 1989).

ᴂ

The usual way of determining the level of ordinary skill in a particular art is by referring to the subjective reaction of a person thoroughly familiar with the particular art, and if possible, one who has practiced the art at the crucial time in question. The opinion of a patent attorney on what would have been obvious to a person skilled in the art is not sufficient to overcome the presumption of the validity of a patent if he is not skilled in the art. *Henkin v. Letro Products, Inc.*, 12 U.S.P.Q.2d 1397, 1398 (Ca. 1989).

ᴂ

Factors to consider in determining the level of ordinary skill in the art include:

a. the educational level of the inventor,
b. the types of problems encountered in the art,
c. prior-art solutions to those problems,
d. the rapidity with which innovations are made in the art,
e. the sophistication of the technology, and
f. the educational level of workers active in the field.

Micro Motion Inc. v. Exac Corp., 741 F. Supp. 1426, 16 U.S.P.Q.2d 1001, 1008 (Cal. 1990).

ᴂ

To the extent that a publication (which is not prior art) establishes the level of ordinary skill in relevant art at and around the time of the subject invention, it is properly relied upon as a basis for rejecting claims under 35 U.S.C. §103. *Ex parte Erlich*, 22 U.S.P.Q.2d 1463, 1465 (B.P.A.I. 1992).

ᡠ

The level of ordinary skill in the pertinent art may be determined by inquiring into the types of problems encountered in the art, prior art solutions to those problems, the rapidity with which innovations are made, the sophistication of the technology, and the education level of active workers in the field. The experience level of active workers in the field is also relevant. *Gargoyles Inc. v. U.S.*, 32 Fed.Cl. 157, 33 U.S.P.Q.2d 1595, 1601 (U.S Ct. Fed. Cl. 1994).

ᡠ

"A person of ordinary skill in the art is . . . presumed to be one who thinks along the line of conventional wisdom in the art and is not one who undertakes to innovate, whether by patient, and often expensive, systematic research or by extraordinary insights." The test is whether the invention is obvious "to one of *ordinary skill* in the art," not to a genius or an expert in the art, or to a judge or other layperson after learning all about the invention. *Williams Service Group Inc. v. O.B. Cannon & Son Inc.*, 33 U.S.P.Q.2d 1705, 1725 (Pa. 1994).

ᡠ

In determining the level of ordinary skill in the art, consideration is accorded various factors, including "type of problems encountered in the art; prior art solutions to those problems; rapidity with which innovations are made; sophistication of the technology; and educational level of active workers in the field." *In re GPAC Inc.*, 57 F.3d 1573, 35 U.S.P.Q.2d 1116, 1121 (Fed. Cir. 1995).

ᡠ

The PTO must explain the reasons one of ordinary skill in the art would have been motivated to select the references and to combine them to render the claimed invention obvious. The Examiner must show reasons that the skilled artisan, confronted with the same problems as the inventor and with no knowledge of the claimed invention, would select the elements from the prior art references for combination in the manner claimed. While skill level is a component of the inquiry for a suggestion to combine, a lofty level of skill alone does not suffice to supply a motivation to combine. Otherwise a high level of ordinary skill in the art field would almost always preclude patentable inventions. *In re Rouffet*, 47 U.S.P.Q.2d 1453, 1458 (Fed. Cir. 1998).

Organic. *See also* **Solvent.**

Although there are undoubtedly a large number of acids that come within the scope of "organic and inorganic acids," the expression is not for that reason indefinite. There is no reason to believe that the public would be confused as to what subject matter is circumscribed by that expression in the claim. *In re Skoll*, 523 F.2d 1392, 187 U.S.P.Q. 481 (C.C.P.A. 1975).

Orientation. *See also* **Orientation during Operation.**

The fact that the orientation of the patented electrode was contrary to accepted practice in the art is evidence of nonobviousness. *Leesona Corporation v. United States*, 185 U.S.P.Q. 156, 162 (U.S. Ct. Cl. 1975).

Orientation during Operation.

A reference relied on by the PTO appears to disclose all of the structure defined by the claims and with respective elements in the same general relationship to each other as required by such claims. Notwithstanding the foregoing, the reference apparatus is operated (for its intended purpose) only when positioned in a particular orientation that is the complete opposite from that required for the claimed apparatus (in operation). The question is not whether a patentable distinction is created by viewing a prior art apparatus from one direction and a claimed apparatus from another, but, rather, whether it would have been obvious from a fair reading of the prior art reference as a whole to turn the prior art apparatus upside down. The reference teaches a liquid strainer that relies, at least in part, upon the assistance of gravity to separate undesired dirt and water from gasoline and other oils. Therefore, it is not seen that such reference would have provided any motivation to one of ordinary skill in the art to employ the involved apparatus in an upside-down orientation. The mere fact that the prior art could be so modified would not have made the modification obvious unless the prior art suggested the desirability of the modification. If the reference apparatus were turned upside down, it would be rendered inoperable for its intended purpose. In effect, therefore, the reference actually teaches away from the claimed invention. *In re Gordon*, 733 F.2d 900, 221 U.S.P.Q. 1125 (Fed. Cir. 1984).

Origin. *See also* **Derivation.**

One's own invention, whatever the form of disclosure to the public, may not be prior art against oneself, absent a statutory bar. *In re Facius*, 408 F.2d 1396, 161 U.S.P.Q. 294, 302 (C.C.P.A. 1969).

℧

Section 104 of 35 U.S.C. is applicable only when an applicant is trying to establish a "date of invention" in order to, for example, antedate a date of invention "of another." Establishing origin of invention is completely different from "date of invention" and is not precluded by 35 U.S.C. §104. (Emphasis in original.) *Oetiker v. Jurid Werke GmbH*, 556 F.2d 1, 209 U.S.P.Q. 809, 823 (D.C. 1981).

Original Cause. *See* **Principle.**

Original Claims.

It is elementary that claims contained in an application as originally filed may be considered part of the disclosure of the application. *In re Myers*, 410 F.2d 420, 161 U.S.P.Q. 668, 673 (C.C.P.A. 1969).

℧

When there is an adequate disclosure of a much broader class of compounds in the main body of the specification and the only question lies in the delineation of the particular subgenus being claimed, an original claim is, by itself, adequate "written description" of the claimed invention. It was equally a "written description" whether located among the original claims or in the descriptive part of the specification. *In re Gardner*, 480 F.2d 879, 178 U.S.P.Q. 149 (C.C.P.A. 1973).

Original Expiration Date.

For a pre-URAA patent the "original expiration date" need not be fixed at 17 years from issuance under 35 U.S.C. §156(a). The statute, as amended, requires a more flexible interpretation of the phrase "original expiration date." Accordingly, we see no impediment to applying the restoration extension to a 20-year from filing term by reason of this statutory language. *Merck & Co. v. Kessler*, 80 F.3d 1543, 38 U.S.P.Q.2d 1347, 1352 (Fed. Cir. 1996).

Originality. *See also* **Derivation.**

The jumping off point for determining obviousness is the point at which appellant was after he received the basic information from Rasmussen. Since the appellant has agreed that his contribution thereafter would have been obvious, the rejection must be affirmed. The fact that the events concerning the invention occurred abroad is not fatal to the rejection. *Ex parte Andresen*, 212 U.S.P.Q. 100, 102 (PTO Bd. App. 1981).

"Original Patent" Clause.

"[T]he essential inquiry under the 'original patent' clause of [35 U.S.C] §251...is whether one skilled in the art, reading the specification, would identify the subject matter of the new claims as invented and disclosed by the patentees." *Hester Industries Inc. v. Stein Inc.*, 142 F.3d 1472, 46 U.S.P.Q.2d 1641, 1651 (Fed. Cir. 1998).

Ornamental Design. *See* **Design.**

OTCA (Omnibus Trade and Competitiveness Act of 1988). *See* **Exclusion Order.**

Out of Context. *See* **Teaching Away From.**

Overclaiming. *See also* **Breadth, Inoperative Embodiments, Supplemental Declaration, Support.**

The improvement of one part of an old combination gives no right to claim that improvement in combination with other old parts which perform no new function in the combination. *Lincoln Engineering Company of Illinois v. Stewart-Warner Corporation*, 303 U.S. 545, 37 U.S.P.Q. 1, 3 (1938).

Overclaiming

Claims fail to perform their function as a measure of the grant when they overclaim the invention. When they do so to the point of invalidity and are free from ambiguity that might justify resort to the specification, they are not to be saved because the latter is less inclusive. *Graver Tank Manufacturing Co. v. The Linde Air Products Company*, 336 U.S. 271, 80 U.S.P.Q. 451, 453 (1949).

☼

In claiming a mechanical combination, an applicant is not necessarily limited to the specific composition that he discloses as the material for making up each and every element of the combination. If every element in a mechanical combination claim were required to be so specific as to exclude materials known to be inoperative and that even though those not skilled in the art would not try, the claims would fail to comply with 35 U.S.C. §112 because they would be so detailed as to obscure, rather than particularly point out and distinctly claim, the invention. *In re Myers*, 410 F.2d 420, 161 U.S.P.Q. 668, 672 (C.C.P.A. 1969).

☼

The decisions which support the judicial doctrine of "overclaiming" are as applicable to claims which describe manufactures as they are to claims covering other types of inventions. *In re Hobbs*, 165 U.S.P.Q. 99, 123 (Atomic Energy Commission 1970).

☼

Overclaiming is properly asserted as a defense when the claims include by their breadth "that which is conceded to have been known in the prior art—that which the prior art anticipated or made obvious." It has also been recognized as a defense where the claims were not limited to a structure essential to accomplish the advantage claimed for the invention. Claims are almost always broader than the inventor's own conception as revealed in the specification and drawings, since he is only required to set forth the "best mode" of carrying out the invention. The breadth of the claim does not itself cause their invalidity—it merely enhances the risk that the claims will be anticipated or made obvious by prior art. *Dennison Manufacturing Co. v. Ben Clements & Sons, Inc.*, 467 F. Supp. 391, 203 U.S.P.Q. 895, 906, 907 (N.Y. 1979).

☼

The mere listing of emulsifiers that do not work does not necessarily invalidate a patent. Where there are a myriad of operative combinations, the inclusion of a few that are not operative need not invalidate the patent. The patent's claims can be construed to exclude those inoperative combinations. The inclusion of such inoperative combinations within the scope of the claims does not constitute overclaiming that would invalidate the patent. *Atlas Powder Co. v. E,. I. du Pont de Nemours & Co.*, 588 F. Supp. 1455, 221 U.S.P.Q. 426 (Tex. 1983).

Ownership.

An uncontroverted statement by the PTO to an applicant that his application is presumed to be owned by the assignee of a specified patent will be accepted as correct. *In re Keim and Thompson*, 229 F.2d 466, 108 U.S.P.Q. 330, 331 (C.C.P.A. 1956).

☼

The requirement that a patent granted on the basis of an application under 35 U.S.C. §118 issue to the inventor pretermits any determination by the Patent Office of the ownership of such a patent. *In re Schuyler*, 119 U.S.P.Q. 97, 98 (Comm'r 1957).

ʊ

The identity of the party which pays legal fees for a patent is a significant factor in deciding ownership of the patent. *National Texture Corp. v. Hymes*, 200 U.S.P.Q. 59, 63 (Minn. 1977).

ʊ

While it is true that the issues of ownership and infringement are unrelated in terms of the legal issues and matters of proof, they are yet inextricably intertwined in that proof of one is necessary for actions on the other. ("Status as an assignee or patentee is a crucial prerequisite to bringing suit on infringement.") *Loral Fairchild Corp. v. Matsushita Electric Industrial Co. Ltd.*, 840 F.Supp. 211, 31 U.S.P.Q.2d 1499, 1503 (N.Y. 1994).

ʊ

In "patent litigation between private parties the equitable rights of ownership of strangers to the suit cannot be raised as defenses against the legal titleholder of the patent." *Kahn v. General Motors Corp.*, 88 Civ. 2982, 33 U.S.P.Q.2d 2011, 2014 (N.Y. 1995).

Oxygen.

Sulfur and oxygen in starting materials for respectively claimed processes in applications of two interfering parties did not impart patentable distinctness to such processes. *Moore v. McGrew*, 170 U.S.P.Q. 149, 153 (PO Bd. Pat. Intf. 1971).

ʊ

Even though it may not be inconceivable to substitute sulfur for oxygen to obtain compounds having the same expected properties, that is not the standard; the standard is whether it would have been obvious in terms of 35 U.S.C. §103. *In re Grabiak*, 769 F.2d 729, 226 U.S.P.Q. 870 (Fed. Cir. 1985).

Oyster.

That the claimed polyploid oysters are "held to be living entities" is not controlling on the question of whether the claims are drawn to patentable subject matter under 35 U.S.C. §101. *Ex parte Allen*, 2 U.S.P.Q.2d 1425, 1426 (B.P.A.I. 1987).

Package License.

A license agreement covering a package of patents, voluntarily entered into by the parties, is not unlawful by reason of the fact that the royalties payable thereunder are based upon the licensee's overall operations and upon a package of patents, some of which have expired or will expire during the effective period of the agreement. *McCullough Tool Co. v. Well Surveys, Inc.*, 343 F.2d 381, 145 U.S.P.Q. 6, 28 (10th Cir. 1965).

ᚦ

In addition to constituting coercion to accept unlawful tying arrangements incorporated in package licenses, the requirement that the royalty rate remain at a constant level raises the question of the legality of collecting royalties attributable to patents that expire while the license agreement is in effect. *The Duplan Corp. v. Deering Milliken, Inc.*, 444 F. Supp. 648, 197 U.S.P.Q. 342, 385, 386 (S.C. 1977).

Packaging Material.[1]

Panduit Test.[2]

The *Panduit* test appears to require actual use of the substitute product and not merely its "availability"; the court there identified an "acceptable substitute" as one which customers in general were "willing to buy in place of the infringing product" and stated that "[a] product lacking the advantages of that patent can hardly be termed a substitute "acceptable" to the customer who wants these advantages." *T.D. Williamson Inc. v. Laymon*, 723 F.Supp. 587, 13 U.S.P.Q.2d 1417, 1423 (Okla. 1989).

Paper. *See* Paper Patent, Printed Publication, Professional Paper, Thesis.

---

[1] *See* Kelly, Patrick D., "Old Drug, New Use: Article Of Manufacture Claims", BIO/TECHNOLOGY, Vol. 11, pp 839 and 840, July 1993, which refers directly to claim 18 of USP 5,011,853 and to claim 7 of USP 5,208,031, as well as to claim 7 of USP 4,988,710, which reads (in part): "An article of manufacture comprising packaging material and a pharmaceutical agent contained within the packaging material, wherein the pharmaceutical agent..., and wherein the packaging material comprises a label which indicates that the pharmaceutical agent can be used for reducing neurotoxic brain damage that might otherwise be caused by at least one cholinesterase inhibitor...."

[2] In *Panduit Corp. v. Stahlin Bros. Fibre Works, Inc.*, 575 F.2d 1152, 197 U.S.P.Q. T26 (6th Cir. 1978), under the test for damages in the form of lost profits, a plaintiff must show, among other elements, detailed computations as to the loss of profits.

Paper Patent.

Everyone is charged with knowledge of the prior patents, and the failure of a patentee to properly exploit his invention does not furnish grounds for the subsequent granting of another patent on substantially the same invention. *In re Coey and Petersen,* 190 F.2d 347, 90 U.S.P.Q. 216 (C.C.P.A. 1951).

ʊ

Prior paper patents have little, if any, weight on the question of non-obviousness as distinguished from anticipation. *Dart Industries Inc. v. E. I. du Pont de Nemours & Co.,* 348 F. Supp. 1338, 175 U.S.P.Q. 540, 553 (Ill. 1972).

ʊ

In determining obviousness, prior paper patents should be given little weight. *Columbia Broadcasting System, Inc. v. Zenith Radio Corp.,* 391 F. Supp. 780, 185 U.S.P.Q. 662, 668 (Ill. 1975).

ʊ

Patents describing inventions that have never been built—"paper patents"—are entitled to a limited range or to no range of equivalents. *Gardner v. Ford Motor Co.,* 17 U.S.P.Q.2d 1177, 1190 (Wash. 1990).

Parameters. *See also* **Optimize.**

While it may ordinarily be the case that the determination of optimum values for the parameters of a prior art process would be at least *prima facie* obvious, that conclusion depends upon what the prior art discloses with respect to those parameters. *In re Sebek,* 465 F.2d 904, 175 U.S.P.Q. 93, 95 (C.C.P.A. 1972).

ʊ

The proper question is whether it would have been obvious to one of ordinary skill in the art that these particular blends could be subjected to these steps at the claimed temperatures. It is not a matter of criticality of the recited ranges but of the obviousness of the applicability of said temperatures. *In re Schirmer,* 480 F.2d 1342, 178 U.S.P.Q. 483, 484 (C.C.P.A. 1973).

ʊ

The mere need for experimentation to determine parameters required to make a device work is an application of the often-rejected obvious-to-try standard and falls short of statutory "obviousness" of 35 U.S.C. §103. Inability of an expert to predict the results obtainable with a claimed product suggests non-obviousness, not routine experimentation. *Uniroyal Inc. v. Rudkin-Wiley Corp.,* 837 F.2d 1044, 5 U.S.P.Q.2d 1434 (Fed. Cir. 1988).

Parent Application.

Specific reference in a patent only to a parent or immediately preceding patent application that, in turn, refers to a grandparent or earlier patent application is not sufficient to provide the issued patent the benefit of the filing date of the grandparent patent application. *Kelley Manufacturing Company v. Lilliston Corporation*, 180 U.S.P.Q. 364, 367 (N.C. 1973).

ω

A Board decision in the prosecution of a parent application is not controlling with regard to even substantially similar claims in a continuation-in-part application when the prosecution of the latter includes affidavit evidence not presented in the prosecution of the parent application. When *prima facie* obviousness is established and evidence is submitted in rebuttal, the decision-maker must start over. An earlier decision should not be considered as set in concrete, and applicant's rebuttal evidence then be evaluated only on its knockdown ability. The question of whether the burden of going forward has been successfully carried requires that the entire path to decision be retraced. Facts established by rebuttal evidence must be evaluated along with the facts on which the earlier conclusion was reached, not against the conclusion itself. *In re Rinehart*, 531 F.2d 1048, 189 U.S.P.Q. 143, 147 (C.C.P.A. 1976).

Parker Immunity.

In *Community Communications Co., Inc. v. City of Boulder, Colo.*, 455 U.S. 40, 51, 70 L.Ed.2d 810, 818-19 (1982), the Supreme Court described two circumstances in which *Parker* immunity was available: first, when a challenged act constitutes the action of the State itself in its sovereign capacity, and second, when the challenged act constitutes action "in furtherance or implementation of clearly articulated and afirmatively expressed state policy." *In re Recombinant DNA Technology Patent and Contract Litigation*, 874 F.Supp. 904, 34 U.S.P.Q.2d 1097, 1100 (Ind. 1994).

Part. *See* Incomplete, Radical, Subcombination.

Particle Size.

That experimentation may be involved with the selection of proportions and particle sizes is not determinative of the question of scope of enablement; it is only undue experimentation that is fatal. *In re Geerdes*, 491 F.2d 1260, 180 U.S.P.Q. 789, 793 (C.C.P.A. 1974).

Particularity. *See also* Accuracy, Approximately, Definiteness, Definition, Inoperative, Rule 7(b)(1), Rule 9, 35 U.S.C. §112.

Where the validity of a patent claim is questioned, it frequently becomes proper to interpret the claim by looking to the specification, but where one seeks a patent, the statute very definitely requires that applicant shall particularly point out and distinctly claim that which he claims to be his invention or discovery. Method claims calling "for a time sufficient to produce a substantially homogeneous product but insufficient to cause the formation of a substantial proportion of oil-soluble reaction products" were held to lack the requisite particularity. *In re Jolly*, 172 F.2d 566, 80 U.S.P.Q. 504, 506 (C.C.P.A. 1949).

ω

A claim calling for "an effective amount" is, on its face, indefinite if it fails to state the function that is to be rendered effective. The claim does not point out the invention with the requisite particularity. *In re Frederikksen and Nielsen*, 213 F.2d 547, 102 U.S.P.Q. 35, 36 (C.C.P.A. 1954). But see *Ex parte Skiballa*, 12 U.S.P.Q.2d 1570 (B.P.A.I. 1989).

ထ

In claiming a mechanical combination, an applicant is not necessarily limited to the specific composition that he discloses as the material for making up each and every element of the combination. If every element in a mechanical combination claim were required to be so specific as to exclude materials known to be inoperative and that even though those not skilled in the art would not try, the claims would fail to comply with 35 U.S.C. §112 because they would be so detailed as to obscure, rather than particularly point out and distinctly claim, the invention. *In re Myers*, 410 F.2d 420, 161 U.S.P.Q. 668, 672 (C.C.P.A. 1969).

ထ

The definiteness of claim language must be analyzed not in a vacuum, but always in light of the teachings of the prior art and of the particular application disclosure as it would be interpreted by one possessing the ordinary level of skill in the pertinent art. *In re Moore*, 439 F.2d 1232, 169 U.S.P.Q. 236 (C.C.P.A. 1971).

ထ

The second paragraph of 35 U.S.C. §112 requires an applicant to "particularly point out and distinctly claim the subject matter sought to be patented." When the scope of the invention sought to be patented is unclear from the language of the claim, a second paragraph rejection lies. *In re Wiggins, James, and Gittos*, 488 F.2d 538, 179 U.S.P.Q. 421, 423 (C.C.P.A. 1973).

ထ

The PTO has not challenged appellants' assertion that their 1953 application enabled those skilled in the art in 1953 to make and use "a solid polymer" as described in Claim 13. The appellants disclosed, as the only then-existing way to make such a polymer, a method of making the crystalline form. To say now that the appellants should have disclosed in 1953 the amorphous form (which did not exist until 1962) would be to impose an impossible burden on inventors and thus on the patent system. There cannot, in an effective patent system, be such a burden placed on the right to broad claims. To restrict the appellants to the crystalline form disclosed, under such circumstances, would be a poor way to stimulate invention, and particularly to encourage its early disclosure. To demand such restriction is merely to state a policy against broad protection for pioneer inventions, a policy both shortsighted and unsound from the standpoint of promoting progress in the useful arts, which is the constitutional purpose of the patent laws. *In re Hogan and Banks*, 559 F.2d 595, 194 U.S.P.Q. 527, 537 (C.C.P.A. 1977).

ထ

The MPEP contains some mandatory language. For the most part, the MPEP only suggests or authorizes procedures for patent Examiners to follow. For example, MPEP §707.03(d) provides that Examiners "should allow claims which define the patentable novelty with a reasonable degree of particularity and distinctness." The section further provides, "the Examiner's action should be constructive in nature." The decision as to what is "reasonable" and "constructive" under the circumstances is necessarily a matter of the Examiner's discretion and judgment. The Foreword to the Fifth Edition of the MPEP, dated August 1983, states that the MPEP "contains instructions to examiners," but "does not have the force of law or the force of the Patent Rules of Practice in Title 37, Code of Federal Regulations." The MPEP does not eliminate a patent Examiner's discretion when examining patent applications. Rather, the MPEP is merely part of the overall scheme providing for discretionary examination of patent applications. *Chamberlin v. Isen*, 779 F.2d 522, 228 U.S.P.Q. 369, 372 (9th Cir. 1985).

ω

The claims were intended to cover the use of the invention with various types of automobiles. That a particular chair of the claims may fit within some automobiles and not others is of no moment. The phrase "so dimensioned" is as accurate as the subject matter permits, automobiles being of various sizes. As long as those of ordinary skill in the art realize that the dimensions could be easily obtained, 35 U.S.C. §112, second paragraph, requires nothing more. The patent law does not require that all possible lengths corresponding to the spaces in hundreds of different automobiles be listed in the patent, let alone that they be listed in the claims. *Orthokinetics Inc. v. Safety Travel Chairs Inc.*, 806 F.2d 1565, 1 U.S.P.Q.2d 1081 (Fed. Cir. 1986).

ω

An amendment is best characterized as a clarification, not an avoidance of the prior art.

> [W]hen claim changes or arguments are made in order to more particularly point out the applicant's invention, the purpose is to impart precision, not to overcome prior art. . . . Such prosecution is not presumed to raise and estoppel, but is reviewed on its facts, with the guidance of precedent.

Pall Corp. v. Micron Separations, Inc., 66 F.3d 1211, 1220 , 36 U.S.P.Q.2d 1050 (Fed. Cir. 1995); *James River Corp. of Virginia v. Hallmark Cards Inc.*, 43 U.S.P.Q.2d 1422, 1430, 1431 (Wis. 1997).

Parts.

Although the specification fails to disclose whether the parts referred to in claims are parts by weight or parts by volume, the omission is too inconsequential to justify a rejection on that basis, since it is common practice in the involved art to use parts by weight and the obtained products are identical whether parts by weight or parts by volume are used. *Ex parte Snook*, 119 U.S.P.Q. 255, 256 (PO Bd. App. 1954).

Party.

A patentee may assign (1) a whole patent, (2) an undivided part or share of that patent, or (3) the exclusive right under the patent "to the whole or any specified part of the United States." Any assignment or transfer, short of one of these, is a mere license, giving the licensee no title in the patent, and no right to sue at law in his own name for an infringement." An exclusive license to make, use and vend is in the same category as an assignment on the theory that the licensor holds title to the patent in trust for such licensee. Even when an exclusive license is restricted to a specified territory or covers less than the full life of the patent, this still remains true, but it does not apply when an exclusive license is restricted to a particular field. *Channel Master Corporation v. LFD Electronics Corporation*, 260 F.Supp. 568, 151 U.S.P.Q. 498, 500 (N.Y. 1966).

ω

Traditionally, courts have declared that an owner of an undivided share of a patent can sue for infringement only when he sues jointly with his co-owner. However, the adoption of amended Rule 19 (FRCP) in 1966 makes inappropriate any contention that patent co-owners are per se indispensable in infringement suits. Whether or not a party is indispensable is the conclusion, not the starting point, of legal analysis. *Catanzaro v. International Telephone & Telegraph Corporation*, 378 F.Supp. 203, 183 U.S.P.Q. 273, 274 (Del. 1974).

Patent. *See also* Accumulation, Contract, Dominant Patent, Dominating Patent, Foreign Patent Application, Monopoly, Paper Patent, Pioneer Patent, Secret Patent.

The specification is not addressed to lawyers or even to the public generally, but to those of ordinary skill in the art. Any description that is sufficient to apprise them (in the language of the art) of the definite features of the invention, and to serve as a warning to others of that which is claimed, is sufficiently definite. *The Carnegie Steel Company, Ltd. v. The Cambria Iron Company,* 185 U.S. 403 (1902).

ω

While the granting of a patent does not legally constitute a certificate that a medicine to which it relates is a good medicine or will cure the disease or successfully make the test which it was intended to do, nevertheless, the granting of such a patent gives a kind of official imprimatur to the medicine in question on which as a moral matter some members of the public are likely to rely. *Isenstead v. Watson*, 157 F.Supp. 7, 115 U.S.P.Q. 408, 410 (D.C. 1957).

ω

The word "patent" is derived from the Latin "patere," meaning, "to be opened," and the significance of "opened" is still commonly attached to that word. For example, *Funk & Wagnalls' Standard Dictionary* defines "letters patent" as "an open document, under seal of the Government, granting some special right, authority, privilege or property, or conferring some title; especially a document giving to the person named the exclusive right to use, make, or sell some invention." Similarly, the *Century Dictionary and Cyclopedia*, after stating that "letters patent" means an open letter, explains that " 'Letters patent' are so called because they were commonly addressed by the sovereign to all subjects at large and were not sealed up like a secret commission, but open, ready to be shown to whom it might concern." The *Encyclopedia Britannica* says of letters patent that "they are not sealed up, but are left open (hence the term 'patent')...." The word "patented" as used in 35 U.S.C. §102(a) and (b) is limited to patents that are available to the public. *In re Ekenstam*, 256 F.2d 321, 118 U.S.P.Q. 349, 351, 353 (C.C.P.A. 1958).

ω

The Examiner's notion about the United States granting a contract is inapt. The government grants only a right to exclude. There is no other agreement. While a patent has often been likened to a contract on the theory that it is issued in exchange for the disclosure of the invention (the consideration), the analogy is inexact. A patent is a statutory right. It is granted to whoever fulfills the conditions, 35 U.S.C. §101, unless fraud has been committed. *In re Breslow,* 616 F.2d 516, 205 U.S.P.Q. 221, 224 (C.C.P.A. 1980).

ᛒ

Not every foreign document labelled a "patent" is a patent within the meaning of 35 U.S.C. §102(a) or (b). Foreign "patents" and foreign "printed publications" preclude the grant of a patent whether or not the information therein is commonly known. Under 35 U.S.C. §102 a conclusive presumption of knowledge of such prior art is, in effect, a statutorily required fiction. Such a presumption cannot be found in 35 U.S.C. §112. *In re Howarth,* 654 F.2d 103, 210 U.S.P.Q. 689, 691, 692 (C.C.P.A. 1981).

ᛒ

Once a patent of invention has been granted, the Patent Office has no authority to invalidate the claims of the original patent in subsequent reissue proceedings. The PTO does not regain power over the original patent's validity when a reissue patent is applied for. When a patent has received the signature of the Secretary of the Interior, counter-signed by the Commissioner of Patents, and has had affixed to it the seal of the Patent Office, it has passed beyond the control and jurisdiction of that office, and is not subject to be revoked or canceled by the President, or any other officer of the Government. *National Business Systems, Inc. v. AM International, Inc.,* 546 F.Supp. 340, 217 U.S.P.Q. 235, 241 (Ill. 1982).

ᛒ

A patent is a written contract between an inventor and the government. The consideration given on the part of the inventor to the government is the disclosure of his invention. The consideration on the part of the government given to the patentee for such disclosure is a monopoly for 17 years of the invention disclosed to the extent of the claims allowed in the patent. The interpretation of patent claims is conducted according to the same general rules of construction as other contracts. *Amgen Inc. v. Chugai Pharmaceutical Co.,* 706 F. Supp. 94, 9 U.S.P.Q.2d 1833 (Mass. 1989).

ᛒ

Patent, trademark, and copyright rights all exist independent one of another, and the presence or absence of one does not automatically preclude protection under another. A thing may be in the public domain for one area of law, but not for the others. The presence or absence of any patent protection for a particular product does not affect any independent rights under trademark law. *Nabisco Brands Inc. v. Conusa Corp.,* 722 F. Supp. 1287, 11 U.S.P.Q.2d 1788, 1792 (N.C. 1989).

ᛒ

A federal patent claim can be related to a state law trade-secret or contract claim if they share a common nucleus of operative fact. *Beech Aircraft Corp. v. EDO Corp.,* 18 U.S.P.Q.2d 1881, 1884 (D.C. 1991).

ᛒ

The September 19, 1989, issue of the Official Gazette listed USP 4,867,890 among the patents issued on that date. The Official Gazette entry stated the title of the patent, gave the names and addresses of the inventors, listed the filing and priority dates, printed the text of patent Claim 1, and stated that there were 32 claims. The federal district court, at which an infringement suit (based on that patent) was filed on that very date, had subject matter jurisdiction even though neither copies of the patent nor access to the official file was available until some time later, and Commissioner Quigg's facsimile signature (on the formal patent grant) was affixed and attested to subsequent to the effective date of his resignation as Commissioner of Patents and Trademarks. *Exxon Chemical Patents Inc. v. The Lubrizol Corp.*, 935 F.2d 1263, 19 U.S.P.Q.2d 1061, 1062 (Fed. Cir. 1991).

ϖ

Advertising that one's product is covered by a patent or pending application when in fact it is not, or not yet, may be tortious and may be grounds for a counterclaim in a suit for infringement, but it is not a legally sufficient affirmative defense. *National Presto Industries Inc. v. Black & Decker (U.S.) Inc.*, 760 F. Supp. 699, 19 U.S.P.Q.2d 1457, 1459 (Ill. 1991).

ϖ

A patent effectively enlarges the natural right of an inventor to make, use, and sell his or her invention (absent conflicting patent rights in others) by adding to it the right to exclude others from making, using, or selling the patented invention. *Arachnid Inc. v. Merit Industries Inc.*, 939 F.2d 1574, 19 U.S.P.Q.2d 1513, 1516 (Fed. Cir. 1991).

ϖ

The interest of the public is in protecting patent rights, and the right of a patentee is in the exclusive use of his invention. Without the protection of the patent statute, the incentive to invent and to improve products would be curbed, and the public interest in such inventions would not be served. *The Conair Group Inc. v. Automatik Apparate-Maschinenbau GmbH*, 19 U.S.P.Q.2d 1535, 1540 (Pa. 1990), *decision vacated and case remanded*, 944 F.2d 862, 20 U.S.P.Q.2d 1067 (Fed. Cir. 1991).

ϖ

A patent grants only the right to exclude others and confers no right on its holder to make, use, or sell. *Vaupel Textilmaschinen KG v. Meccanica Euro Italia s.p.a.*, 944 F.2d 870, 20 U.S.P.Q.2d 1045, 1052 (Fed. Cir. 1991).

ϖ

Under the supremacy clause of the U.S. Constitution, federal patent law preempts state awards of patentlike protection. "[S]tate regulation of intellectual property must yield to the extent that it clashes with the balance struck by Congress in our patent laws." *Bonito Boats, Inc. v. Thunder Craft Boats, Inc.*, 489 U.S. 141, 152, 9 U.S.P.Q.2d 1847 (1989). However, federal patent law does not necessarily prohibit states from enforcing valid contracts under state contract law when such contracts provide protection for unpatented products. *Darling v. Standard Alaska Production Co.*, 20 U.S.P.Q.2d 1688, 1691 (Alaska S. Ct. 1991).

ϖ

The commercial advantage gained by new technology and its statutory protection by patent does not convert the possessor thereof into a prohibited monopolist. *Abbott Laboratories v. Brennan*, 952 F.2d 1346, 21 U.S.P.Q.2d 1192, 1199 (Fed. Cir. 1991).

ω

Under United States patent law, a patent owner has no enforceable rights under a patent until the patent issues. Congress has determined that "it is necessary to grant temporary monopolies on inventions in order to induce those skilled in the 'useful arts' to expend the time and money necessary to research and develop new products." *LifeScan Inc. v. Polymer Technology International Corp.*, 35 U.S.P.Q.2d 1225, 1237, 1241 (Wash. 1995).

ω

Where a disputed product configuration is part of a claim in a utility patent, and the configuration is a described, significant inventive aspect of the invention, *see* 35 U.S.C. §112, so that without it the invention could not fairly be said to be the same invention, patent law prevents its protection as trade dress, even if the configuration is nonfunctional. *Vornado Air Circulation Systems Inc. v. Duracraft Corp.*, 58 F.3d 1498, 35 U.S.P.Q.2d 1332, 1342 (10th Cir. 1995).

ω

"[T]he existence of one's own patent does not constitute a defense to infringement of someone else's patent. A patent grants only the right *to exclude others* and confers no right on its holder to make, use, or sell." *Bio-Technology General Corp. v. Genentech Inc.*, 80 F.3d 1553, 38 U.S.P.Q.2d 1321, 1325 (Fed. Cir. 1996).

ω

Improper practices in connection with patents include use of invalid patents in price fixing, cross-licensing of patents, attempts to extend the scope of patent monopoly, illegal price fixing activities in connection with patents, tying patents to unpatented devices or processes, and seeking to extend the effect of an expired patent. *BEAL Corp. Liquidating Trust v. Valleylab Inc.*, 40 U.S.P.Q.2d 1072, 1077 (Col. 1996).

ω

A patent for an invention is as much property as a patent for land. The right rests on the same foundation and is surrounded and protected by the same sanctions. *College Savings Bank v. Florida Prepaid Postsecondary Education Expense Board*, 42 U.S.P.Q.2d 1487, 1507 (N.J. 1996).

ω

"Within the limits of the patentee's rights under his patent, monopoly of the product or process by him is authorized by the patent statutes."... Indeed, "[t]he very object of [the patent] laws is monopoly."... Therefore, ownership of a valid patent precludes antitrust liability for monopolization of a product or process within the scope of the patent. *Baxa Corp. v. McGaw Inc.*, 996 F.Supp. 1044, 45 U.S.P.Q.2d 1504, 1507 (Colo. 1997).

Patentability. *See also* Claim, Rejected Claim.

Patentability may not be predicated on a result which would flow naturally from the teaching of the prior art, even though the art does not suggest that particular result or its desirability. *In re Wynne and Cousen*, 255 F.2d 956, 118 U.S.P.Q. 306, 307, 308 (C.C.P.A. 1958).

ᚹ

The validity of a patent is determined under the applicable criteria of patentability. *Carman Industries, Inc. v. Wahl*, 724 F.2d 932, 220 U.S.P.Q. 481, 485 n.5 (Fed. Cir. 1983).

ᚹ

Since appellants failed to argue the separate patentability of claims 1 to 3 and 20 or that of other claims which depend, explicitly or effectively, from independent claim 20, all contested claims stand or fall together. *In re Van Geuns*, 988 F.2d 1181, 1186, 26 U.S.P.Q.2d 1057, 1060 (Fed. Cir. 1993); *In re King*, 801 F.2d 1324, 1325, 231 U.S.P.Q. 136, 137 (Fed. Cir. 1986).

ᚹ

Defendant's patent, during the prosecution of which plaintiff's patent was cited and considered as prior art, is thus presumed nonobvious in view of plaintiff's patent until proven otherwise. The nonobviousness of the accused device, evidenced by the grant of a United States patent, is relevant to the issue of whether the change therein is substantial. *Zygo Corp. v. Wyko Corp.*, 38 U.S.P.Q.2d 1281, 1286 (Fed. Cir. 1996).

Patentability Standard.

The standard for determining unpatentability in the PTO is a preponderance of the evidence. *Total Containment Inc. v. Buffalo Environmental Products Corp.*, 35 U.S.P.Q.2d 1385, 1393 (Va. 1995).

Patentable Distinctness. *See also* Plural Claims.

Claims to a method were held to be patentably indistinct from claims to apparatus for performing the method. *In re Abernathy*, 118 F.2d 358, 49 U.S.P.Q. 82 (C.C.P.A. 1941).

ᚹ

Claims in an application do not have to distinguish patentably over other claims or over an allowed claim. *Ex parte Gieseler*, 92 U.S.P.Q. 41, 43 (PO Bd. App. 1951).

ᚹ

Whether phenomena just outside of claim limits are qualitatively different from that which is claimed is immaterial. A patentee is not required to show that some technological discontinuity exists between a claimed invention and subject matter just outside of the claims, but only that the claimed subject matter would have been non-obvious in view of the prior art. *Andrew Corp. v. Gabriel Electronics, Inc.*, 847 F.2d 819, 6 U.S.P.Q.2d 2010 (Fed. Cir. 1988).

Patentably Distinct Inventions. *See also* Improper Markush, Unity of Invention.

In an interference, a claim is patentably distinct from the interference count, in the sense of 35 U.S.C. §103, if the apparatus claimed by the count does not render obvious what is being claimed by the claim at issue. *Davis v. Loesch*, 998 F.2d 963, 27 U.S.P.Q.2d 1440, 1442 (Fed. Cir. 1993).

ᚌ

The fact of separate patentability presents no legal or evidentiary presumption of noninfringement. *Hoechst Celanese Corp. v. BP Chemicals Ltd.*, 78 F.3d 1575, 1582, 38 U.S.P.Q.2d 1126, 1132 (Fed. Cir. 1996); *Victus Ltd. v. Collezione Europa U.S.A. Inc.*, 48 U.S.P.Q.2d 1145, 1147 (N.C. 1998).

Patent Act.

The safeguard against an impermissible extension of a patent monopoly by a trademark is the functionality doctrine: a configuration of an article cannot receive trademark registration if its purpose is to contribute functional advantages to the article or if the configuration results from functional considerations. *Thomas & Betts Corp. v. Panduit Corp.*, 138 F.3d 277, 46 U.S.P.Q.2d 1026, 1033 (7th Cir. 1998).

Patent Agent.

A "patent agent" acts as the inventor's attorney before the PTO. The label "patent agent" does not mean that there is an agency relationship, rather than an attorney-client relationship, between the inventor and such individual for all purposes. An agency relationship may exist during prosecution before the PTO where the patent attorney is acting on the inventor's behalf. An agency relationship does not exist, however, with respect to what an inventor must disclose in order to obtain a patent on his invention. *Glaxo Inc. v. Novopharm Ltd.*, 52 F.3d 1043, 34 U.S.P.Q.2d 1565, 1571 (Fed. Cir. 1995).

Patent and Trademark Office. *See* PTO.

Patentanwaltzskandidat.

A Patentanwaltzskandidat, studying to become a Patentassessor, qualified to render advice and opinions on patent issues to a company by which he is employed, and under the supervision of and reporting directly to a Patentassessor, shares a relationship similar to that which exists between an American attorney and a paralegal or law clerk. Legal communications emanating from or received by him are subject to attorney-client privilege. *Heidelberg Harris, Inc. v. Mitsubishi Heavy Industries, Ltd. and MLP U.S.A., Inc.*, 1996 U.S. Dist. LEXIS 19274 1, 26, 27 (Ill. 1996).

Patent Application. *See also* Disclosure, Specification.

A patent application, which requires a specification and claims, 35 U.S.C. §112, "constitute[s] one of the most difficult legal instruments to draw with accuracy." *Sperry v. State of Florida*, 378 U.S. 378, 383, 137 U.S.P.Q. 578, 580 (1965).

ᚌ

The appellant with the assistance of his assignee prepared and inserted in the application two series of photomicrographs together with extensive descriptions of them for the purpose of showing how the invention differs from the prior filaments in an extensively developed art. The court took the position that this would not have been done unless the photomicrographs in fact showed persons of ordinary skill in the art what the appellant asserted they show and was unwilling to give credence to a contrary opinion expressed by the Board as the basis of the rejection that it originated sua sponte. *In re Ehringer,* 347 F.2d 612, 146 U.S.P.Q. 31, 35 (C.C.P.A. 1965).

ω

A patent application is not depreciable property or property subject to allowance of depreciation. Proceeds from the sale of a patent application are entitled to capital gains treatment. *Davis v. Comm'r. Internal Revenue*, 491 F.2d 709, 181 U.S.P.Q. 552 (6th Cir. 1974).

ω

The language in 35 U.S.C. §122 creating confidentiality speaks of "applications for patents." The language is broad enough to include all categories of applications (pending, abandoned, and granted) and that would appear to be the legislative intent of Congress. *Sears v. Gottschalk, Commissioner of Patents,* 502 F.2d 122, 183 U.S.P.Q. 134, 137 (4th Cir. 1974).

Patentassessor.

A Patentassessor is an in-house patent attorney who is qualified to practice before the German Patent Office and may also provide legal advice to a client on such issues as patentability, patent infringement and validity. He is the functional equivalent of an attorney. The attorney-client privilege therefore applies to legal communications with which he is involved. *Heidelberg Harris, Inc. v. Mitsubishi Heavy Industries, Ltd. and MLP U.S.A., Inc.*, 1996 U.S. Dist. LEXIS 19274 1, 24, 26 (Ill. 1996).

Patent Attorney.

What transpired during an interview between an Examiner and patentee's counsel prior to allowance of the application which matured into the patent on which infringement litigation is based may not be readily ascertainable by deposing patentee's counsel. Before an attorney involved in patent litigation can be deposed in reference thereto, the party seeking discovery must show that he has substantial need of the materials in the preparation of his case and that he is unable, without undue hardship, to obtain the substantial equivalent of the materials by other means. *MacLaren v. B-I-W Group Inc.*, 180 U.S.P.Q. 387, 388 (Va. 1973).

ω

Defendant's attorney may proffer his opinion on such questions as whether the claims of the patent are vague or indefinite, whether they are anticipated by a single reference in the prior art, and whether the invention set forth in the patent was obvious. To some degree, testimony on these subjects necessarily requires the attorney to speak of the manner in which the claims were drafted and, by way of illustration, the way in which they might have been drafted differently to embrace elements or processes that, in his opinion, are outside the scope of the claims as they were actually written. However, it would not be appropriate for defendant's attorney to speculate on how he would have drafted the patent application in question, to discuss the law governing patent validity, or to predict how a judge or jury would or should rule on the question of whether the patent is valid. Such testimony would simply not be relevant and would stray into matters of law as to which it is the court's responsibility to instruct the jury. *Amsted Industries Inc. v. National Castings Inc.*, 16 U.S.P.Q.2d 1737, 1761 (Ill. 1990).

ᴡ

A patent attorney does not enter into an agency relationship with an inventor for purposes of what is disclosed in the inventor's patent application. The inventor never authorizes his patent attorney to "act on his behalf" with respect to disclosing the invention. The patent attorney's authority does not include inventing, i.e., either supplementing or supplanting the inventor's knowledge of his own invention. The information disclosed in the inventor's patent application must be that which is actually known to him. *Glaxo Inc. v. Novopharm Ltd.*, 52 F.3d 1043, 34 U.S.P.Q.2d 1565, 1571 (Fed. Cir. 1995).

Patent Cooperation Treaty. *See* **PCT.**

Patented. *See also* **35 U.S.C. §102(b).**

The word "patented" as used in 35 U.S.C. §102(a) and (b) is limited to patents that are available to the public. *In re Ekenstam*, 256 F.2d 321, 118 U.S.P.Q. 349, 353 (C.C.P.A. 1958).

ᴡ

The mere issuance of the specification of a patent in printed form is unessential to the question of whether an invention has been patented in a foreign country. *Ex parte Gruschwitz and Fritz*, 138 U.S.P.Q. 505 (PTO Bd. App. 1961).

ᴡ.

With regard to construing "patented . . . in a foreign country" under 35 U.S.C. §102(d), Federico concluded that the rights and privileges attaching to the protection granted by foreign governments need not be coextensive with the exclusive rights granted under U.S. law, so long as the foreign rights granted are both substantial and exclusive in nature. "Not every foreign document labelled a 'patent' is a patent within the meaning of 35 U.S.C. §102(a) or (b)." *In re Carlson*, 983 F.2d 1032, 25 U.S.P.Q.2d 1207, 1210 (Fed. Cir. 1992).

ᴡ

A foreign patent need not be publicly available to be "patented" under 35 U.S.C §102(d). An invention is "patented" in a foreign country under section 102(d) when the patentee's rights under the patent become fixed. When an applicant files a foreign application fully disclosing his invention and having the potential to claim his invention in a number of different ways, the reference in section 102(d) to "invention . . . patented" necessarily includes all disclosed aspects of the invention. Thus, the section 102(d) bar applies regardless whether the foreign patent contains claims to less than all aspects of the invention. *In re Kathawala*, 9 F.3d 942, 28 U.S.P.Q.2d 1785, 1787, 1788, 1789 (Fed. Cir. 1993).

ᴡ

A patent on an alleged infringing article is irrelevant to the issue of infringement. *Enforcer Products Inc. v. Birdsong*, 40 U.S.P.Q.2d 1958 (Fed. Cir.—*unpublished*).

Patentee.

A patentee must be allowed to test the validity or enforceability of its patent, even if it fears that the patent may be invalid or unenforceable. *Nobelpharma AB v. Implant Innovations Inc.*, 129 F.3d 1463, 44 U.S.P.Q.2d 1705, 1714 (Fed. Cir. 1997).

Patent Exhaustion Doctrine. *See* Exhaustion.

Patent Holding Subsidiary.

While a patent holding subsidiary is a legitimate creature and may provide certain business advantages, it cannot fairly be used to insulate patent owners from defending declaratory judgment actions in those fora where its parent company operates under the patent and engages in activities sufficient to create personal jurisdiction and declaratory judgment jurisdiction. *Dainippon Screen Manufacturing Co. v. CFMT Inc.*, 142 F.3d 1266, 46 U.S.P.Q.2d 1616, 1621 (Fed. Cir. 1998).

Patent Interference. *See* Interference, 35 U.S.C 291.

Patent Laws.

The public purpose on which the patent law rests requires the granting of claims commensurate in scope with the invention disclosed. This requires as much the granting of broad claims on broad inventions as it does granting of specific claims on more specific inventions. It is neither contemplated by the public purpose of the patent laws nor required by the statute that an inventor shall be forced to accept claims narrower than his invention in order to secure allowance of his patent. *In re Sus and Schaefer*, 306 F.2d 494, 134 U.S.P.Q. 301, 304 (C.C.P.A. 1962).

ᴡ

There are two types of cases that may be said to "arise under" the patent laws for purposes of 28 U.S.C. §1338. First, a suit arises under the law that creates the cause of action. Although this "creation" test may be helpful in identifying many cases that come within the court's jurisdiction, it has limited value in identifying those that do not. Second, a case arises under the patent laws if the plaintiff seeks to vindicate a right or interest "that would be defeated by one or sustained by an opposite construction" of the patent laws. *Christianson v. Colt Industries Operating Corp.*, 798 F.2d 1051, 230 U.S.P.Q. 840 (7th Cir. 1986).

ᴡ

Through the years courts have found *per se* patent misuse in varying forms of tying arrangements. In some cases, the patentee is conditioning the license of his patent on the licensee's agreeing to use some specific unpatented product. In other cases, the patentee is conditioning the license of his patent on the licensee's agreeing not to use the products or devices of a competitor. The two situations involve slightly different factual arrangements, but, generally, both are referred to as tying arrangements. Some commentators have referred to the former situations as "tie-ins" and the latter as "tie-outs". The language of the 1988 Patent Misuse Reform Act is meant to encompass both types of tying arrangements. *In re Recombinant DNA Technology Patent and Contract Litigation*, 850 F.Supp. 769, 30 U.S.P.Q.2d 1881, 1897, 1898 (Ind. 1993).

Patent Misuse. *See also* Misuse.

Patent misuse is an affirmative defense to an accusation of patent infringement, the successful assertion of which "requires that the alleged infringer show that the patentee has impermissibly broadened the 'physical or temporal scope' of the patent grant with anticompetitive effect." *Virginia Panel Corp. v. MAC Panel Co.*, 133 F.3d 860, 45 U.S.P.Q.2d 1225, 1232 (Fed. Cir. 1997).

Patent Misuse Reform Act.

Through the years courts have found *per se* patent misuse in varying forms of tying arrangements. In some cases, the patentee is conditioning the license of his patent on the licensee's agreeing to use some specific unpatented product. In other cases, the patentee is conditioning the license of his patent on the licensee's agreeing not to use the products or devices of a competitor. The two situations involve slightly different factual arrangements, but, generally, both are referred to as tying arrangements. Some commentators have referred to the former situations as "tie-ins" and the latter as "tie-outs". The language of the 1988 Patent Misuse Reform Act is meant to encompass both types of tying arrangements. *In re Recombinant DNA Technology Patent and Contract Litigation*, 850 F.Supp. 769, 30 U.S.P.Q.2d 1881, 1897, 1898 (Ind. 1993).

Patent Notice Letter.[3]

Patent Office License. *See also* Retroactive License.

When one fails to comply with 35 U.S.C. §§184 and 185, a resulting patent must be declared invalid. *Kelley Manufacturing Company v. Lilliston Corp.*, 180 U.S.P.Q. 364, 371 (N.C. 1973).

ʊ

The policy of 35 U.S.C. §§181 to 185 is not best served by limiting damages to the period after the date of a retroactive license. Nothing in the statute, in the license, or in the case law supports such a position. *Spound v. Mohasco Industries, Inc.*, 186 U.S.P.Q. 183, 188 (Mass. 1975).

ʊ

---

[3] Enclosed for your information is a copy of one of our recently issued patents, U.S. Patent No. 5,527,521 entitled "Low Density Microspheres and Suspensions and Their use as Contrast Agents for Computed Tomography and In Other Applications." This patent is directed to, among other things, perfluorocarbon gas-filled microspheres useful in diagnostics imaging (see, for example, claim 20), and represents the latest of a number of patents issued to ImaRx in the diagnostic field. *Mallinckrodt Medical Inc. v. Sonus Pharmaceuticals Inc.*, 45 U.S.P.Q.2d 1811, 1815 (D.C. 1998).

The purpose of 35 U.S.C. §§184 and 185 is to prevent exportation of information potentially detrimental to the security of our country. Congress intended that strict compliance be paramount to the interests of an individual inventor. Failure to secure a license for filing foreign applications containing technical information or "subject matter" not previously disclosed in a U.S. application renders later-filed CIP rejectable under 35 U.S.C. §§184 and 185. *In re Gaertner*, 604 F.2d 1348, 202 U.S.P.Q. 714, 719, 721 (C.C.P.A. 1979).

ᅗ

In challenging the validity of the issuance of a foreign filing license, a party need not be restricted to bringing an independent direct action against the Commissioner. Inequitable conduct in obtaining a foreign filing license renders a corresponding U.S. patent unenforceable. *Stauffer Chemical Company v. Monsanto Company*, 623 F. Supp. 148, 227 U.S.P.Q. 401, 402 (Mo. 1985).

Patent Pending. *See also* Pending Application.

To infringe a patent willfully, the patent must exist and one must have knowledge of it. A "patent pending" notice gives one no knowledge whatsoever. It is not even a guarantee that an application has been filed. *State Industries, Inc. v. A.O. Smith Corporation*, 751 F.2d 1226, 224 U.S.P.Q. 418, 425 (Fed. Cir. 1985).

Patent Pooling. *See* Pooling.

Patent Protection.

Kodak had sold more than 16 million instant cameras. Kodak pointed out that enjoining production and sale of its instant film would render its cameras useless since neither Polaroid nor any other company had film on the market that could be substituted for Kodak's. Such an outcome was particularly damaging to a company whose reputation and goodwill were based in part on the fact that Kodak does not desert its customers. Kodak further pointed out that, when forced to shut down its instant camera production, 800 full-time and 3700 part-time employees would lose their jobs, and the company would lose its $200-million investment in plant and equipment. When the stakes are this high and patents are held to be valid and infringed, the patent system gains much credibility. *Polaroid Corp. v. Eastman-Kodak Co.*, 641 F. Supp. 828, 228 U.S.P.Q. 305 (Mass. 1985).

Patent Remedy Act.

Protecting a privately-held patent from infringement by a state is certainly a legitimate congressional objective under the Fourteenth Amendment, which empowers Congress to prevent state-sponsored deprivation of private property. *College Savings Bank v. Florida Prepaid Postsecondary Education Expense Board*, 148 F.3d 1343, 47 U.S.P.Q.2d 1161, 1165 (Fed. Cir. 1998).

Patent Rights.

The patent system is one in which uniform federal standards are carefully used to promote invention while, at the same time, preserving free competition. A State cannot, consistently with the Supremacy Clause of the Constitution, extend the life of a patent beyond its expiration date or give a patent on an article which lacks the level of invention required for federal patents. To do either would run contrary to the policy of Congress of granting patents only to true inventions, and then only for a limited time. Just as a State cannot encroach on the federal patent laws directly, it cannot, under some other law, such as that forbidding unfair competition, give protection of a kind that clashes with the objectives of the federal patent laws. "Sharing in the goodwill of an article unprotected by patent or trademark is the exercise of a right possessed by all—and in the free exercise of which the consuming public is deeply interested." *Sears, Roebuck & Co. v. Stiffel Company*, 376 U.S. 225, 140 U.S.P.Q. 524, 528 (S. Ct. 1964).

ϖ

Emphasis on an individual inventor's lack of money and manufacturing capacity can lend to distinguish the respect due the patent rights of impecunious inventors from that due the patent rights of well-funded, well lawyered, large manufacturing corporations. Any such distinction should be rejected as the disservice it is to the public and technological advancement. That "survival of the fittest," jungle mentality was intended to be replaced, not served, by the law. *Fromson v. Western Litho Plate & Supply Co.*, 853 F.2d 1568, 7 U.S.P.Q.2d 1606 (Fed. Cir. 1988).

ϖ

Opinions of counsel received subsequent to the decision to produce an infringing product, although relevant as part of the totality of the circumstances, do not dictate a conclusion that the infringement was not willful. *Alpex Computer Corp. v. Nintendo Co. Ltd.*, 86 Civ. 1749, 34 U.S.P.Q.2d 1167, 1205 (N.Y. 1994).

Patent Rights Clause.

While there does not appear to be any ambiguity in the language used by the drafters, the test is whether the contractor, who realistically had to acquiesce in the government's proffered form, could reasonably construe it that way. This rule places the risk of ambiguity, lack of clarity, and absence of proper warning on the drafting party, which could have forestalled the controversy; it pushes the drafters toward improving contractual forms; and it saves contractors from hidden traps not of their own making. *Lockheed Aircraft Corp. v. United States*, 190 U.S.P.Q. 134, 154 (Ct. Cl. 1976).

ϖ

The patent rights clause is not self-enforcing. It does not effect a transfer of title in an invention from the University (or inventor) to the government. Instead, it insures that the government is given notice of actions taken by the University, and it describes a mechanism by which the government, under certain circumstances, can obtain title. *Mead Corporation v. United States of America*, 652 F.2d 1050, 211 U.S.P.Q. 491, 492 (C.A. D.C. 1981).

Patent Term.

Coupled with the sale and delivery during the patent term of a "completed" machine (completed by being ready for assembly after expiration of the patent term and with no useful non-infringing purpose), the amount of required predelivery testing justifies a holding of infringement. To reach a contrary result would emasculate the congressional intent to prevent the making of a patented item during the patent's full term of seventeen years. *Paper Converting Machine Company v. Magna-Graphics Corporation*, 745 F.2d 11, 223 U.S.P.Q. 591, 597 (Fed. Cir. 1984).

Patent Term Extension. *See also* **Patent Term Restoration.**

The issue is whether the permission for commercial marketing or use of Opticrom 4% on October 3, 1984, or Intal Nebulizer Solution on January 19, 1985, represents the first permitted commercial marketing or use of the product within the meaning of 35 U.S.C. §156(a)(5)(A).

By the explicit terms of the statute, the term "product" as it relates to a human drug product means the active ingredient of a new drug. The active ingredient in both the approved products is cromolyn sodium. As noted in the FDA letters, the active ingredient had been approved for commercial marketing in 1973 and 1983, both prior to the approval of Opticrom 4% and Intal Nebulizer Solution for commercial marketing under 21 U.S.C. §355. Applying the explicit language of this statute to the facts: The permission for commercial marketing or use of the product after such regulatory review period was not the first permitted commercial marketing or use of the product under the provision of law under which the regulatory review occurred.

There is no basis in the statutory language for making a distinction between the content of a "product" vis-a-vis an "approved product." An approved product is a product that has been approved by the FDA for commercial marketing or use. The statute is explicit in defining the meaning of product in §156(f). The statute does not state that the product referred to in paragraphs (4) and (5) is the approved product. Thus, the statute itself clearly dictates that the product referred to in paragraphs (4) and (5) be defined in the manner required in §156(f). *In re Fisons Pharmaceuticals Ltd.*, 231 U.S.P.Q. 305 (Comm'r Patents & Trademarks 1986).

ᛟ

The term "product" is defined as a "human drug product." 35 U.S.C. §156(f)(1)(a). This term is further defined in the next paragraph as "the active ingredient of a new drug, antibiotic drug, or human biological product...including any salt or ester of the active ingredient, as a single entity or in combination with another active ingredient." 35 U.S.C. §156(f)(2). Substituting this definition directly back into 156(a)(5)(A) yields the statement that a patent is ineligible for patent term extension if it is not the first permitted commercial marketing or use of the active ingredient contained in that approved patented product. *Fisons Plc v. Quigg*, 8 U.S.P.Q.2d 1491 (D.C. 1988), *aff'd*, 876 F.2d 99, 10 U.S.P.Q.2d 1869 (Fed. Cir. 1989).

ᛟ

The active ingredient of Ceftin Tablets is cefuroxime axetil. Unique properties of this distinct pharmaceutical compound make it therapeutically active and effective when administered orally. Cefuroxime axetil is an ester of cefuroxime, an organic acid. This acid and its salts are antibiotics that are therapeutically active only when administered intramuscularly or intravenously. Neither is effective if administered orally. Since two sodium salts of cefuroxime had been previously marketed, the Commissioner denied approval of a request for patent term extension, asserting that cefuroxime axetil was not eligible for patent term extension because FDA approval of Ceftin Tablets was not the first permitted commercial marketing or use of the product. Cefuroxime axetil, active on oral administration, is absorbed from the gastrointestinal tract and then hydrologized in the blood and intestinal tract to release cefuroxime into the circulation. It is cefuroxime that is the effective antibacterial agent. Because the therapeutic of cefuroxime axetil is ultimately related to the cefuroxime released in the digestive tract, the Commissioner argued that cefuroxime is "the active moiety" of Ceftin Tablets and therefore falls within (a)(5)(A). This rationale is untenable, its form manifest. The statute says "ingredient" not "moiety," and the "ingredient" must be present in the drug product when administered. This is an insurmountable obstacle for the Commissioner's proposed rationale; he concedes that "cefuroxime itself is not an ingredient of Ceftin Tablets." Even if a moiety, in pharmaceutical parlance, is something that results from chemical changes occurring after the drug is administered and need not itself be present in the drug product at the time of administration, this is not the plain meaning of "ingredient." *GLAXO Operations U.K. Ltd. v. Quigg*, 706 F. Supp. 1224, 10 U.S.P.Q.2d 1100 (Va. 1989).

ω

Section 1.765(d) states that there is no third-party participation in a patent term extension. However, 37 C.F.R. §1.183 allows for the suspension or waiver of the rules in an extraordinary situation, when justice requires. The circumstances do not rise to the level of extraordinary when they fall clearly within the scope of the determination made based on the face of the application in conjunction with the duty of disclosure. *In re Dubno*, 12 U.S.P.Q.2d 1153, 1154, 1155 (Comm'r Patents & Trademarks 1989).

ω

Section 156 of 35 U.S.C. does not provide for patent term extension of a drug that was both patented and approved by the FDA prior to the enactment of that statutory provision. *Hoechst Aktiengesellschaft v. Quigg*, 724 F. Supp. 398, 13 U.S.P.Q.2d 1543, 1547 (Va. 1989), *reversed and remanded*, 917 F.2d 522, 16 U.S.P.Q.2d 1549 (Fed. Cir. 1990).

ω

Section 156 of 35 U.S.C. has two general purposes: (1) to increase the availability of low-cost drugs by expanding a generic drug approval procedure, and (2) to encourage new drug research by restoring some of the patent term lost while drug products undergo testing and await FDA pre-market approval. The plain meaning of the Act can be said to provide exactly how the general objectives of the Act are to be sought. Commerce clearly articulated policy reasons for making more types of patents eligible for extension including to encourage research. *Glaxo Operations U.K. Ltd. v. Quigg*, 894 F.2d 392, 13 U.S.P.Q.2d 1628, 1631 (Fed. Cir. 1990).

ω

The granting of an extension under 35 U.S.C. §155 does not exonerate a patentee of any inequitable conduct committed before the PTO in obtaining the initial award of the patent. However, a patent does carry with it a presumption of validity, which persists until the patent is determined to be void or unenforceable. In light of the presumption of validity, a patentee does not have to challenge the validity of its own patent in seeking an extension under §155. *United Sweetener U.S.A. Inc. v. The Nutrasweet Company,* 760 F. Supp. 400, 19 U.S.P.Q.2d 1561, 1577 (Del. 1991).

ᚹ

Pre-June 8, 1995, patents are entitled to add on the restoration extension to a 20-year from filing term regardless of when such extension is granted except for those patents kept in force on June 8, 1995, only because of a restoration extension. Under this interpretation, all provisions of both URAA and Hatch-Waxman can reasonably be given effect. For pre-June 8, 1995, patents, a patentee would have full exclusionary rights for 17 years, followed by rights only to equitable remuneration (neither lost profits, an injunction, punitive damages, nor attorney fees) with respect to a certain class of infringers for the period from the end of the 17-year term to the end of the new 20-year term (the delta period), followed by entitlement to full exclusionary rights (but only with respect to the approved product) during the period of the restoration extension. *Merck & Co. v. Kessler,* 80 F.3d 1543, 38 U.S.P.Q.2d 1347, 1352, 1353 (Fed. Cir. 1996).

ᚹ

Class II devices are not eligible for patent term extensions. *AbTox Inc. v. Exitron Corp.,* 122 F.3d 1019, 43 U.S.P.Q.2d 1545, 1553 (Fed. Cir. 1997).

Patent Term Restoration. *See also* **Patent Term Extension.**

The Drug Price Competition and Patent Term Restoration Act [Pub. L. No. 98-417, 98 Stat. 1585 (1984)] is generally known as the Hatch Waxman Amendments to the Federal Food, Drug, and Cosmetic Act (21 U.S.C. §§301 et seq). The purpose of this legislation was to increase competition in the drug industry by facilitating the approval of generic copies of drugs. Rather than complete the full NDA process, generic copiers could proceed via an Abbreviated New Drug Application (ANDA), which required merely reference to the safety and effectiveness status submitted by the "pioneer" drug manufacturer, along with submission of manufacturing and bioequivalence data for the generic copy. *Mead Johnson Pharmaceutical Group v. Bowen,* 838 F.2d 1332, 6 U.S.P.Q.2d 1565 (D.C. Cir. 1988).

ᚹ

Section 271(e)(1) of 35 U.S.C. §now permits individuals to "make, use, or sell, a patented invention (other than a new animal drug or veterinary biological product...) solely for use reasonably related to the development and submission of information under a Federal law which regulates the manufacture, use, or sale of drugs." Congress excluded new animal drugs and veterinary products because the rest of the complex patent term restoration law excluded these drugs. Although it changed the narrow application of the doctrine affecting reporting requirements for federal drug laws, Congress did not disturb the federal circuit's enunciation of the parameters of the experimental use exception. *Deuterium Corp. v. United States*, 19 Cl. Ct. 624, 14 U.S.P.Q.2d 1636, 1642, n.14 (U.S. Cl. Ct. 1990).

ᵭ

The parenthetical phrase ("including any ester or salt of the active ingredient") can refer either to the active ingredient in the original approved drug or to the active ingredient in the new drug, depending upon how "the" in the parenthetical and the words surrounding the parenthetical—"no active ingredient . . . of which has been approved"—are interpreted. The ambiguity of reference in the phrase reflects the possibility that it can refer to the latest subsection (b) application as well as to all prior subsection (b) applications. *Abbott Laboratories v. Young*, 920 F.2d 984, 17 U.S.P.Q.2d 1027, 1029 (D.C. Cir. 1990).

Payment of PTO Fee. *See* Unsigned Check.

PCT (Patent Cooperation Treaty).

The scope of the Commissioner's authority to excuse an international applicant's delay in meeting time limits is set out at 35 U.S.C. §364(b). Congress intended an international application to be strictly bound by the requirements of the PCT Rules and the PCT itself, along with any additional regulations the Commissioner might promulgate. The implementing regulation established by the Commissioner on the question of delays in international applications is found at 37 C.F.R. §1.468, which does not expand the Commissioner's authority to excuse delays beyond what the PCT and the PCT Rules authorize. The PCT, the PCT Rules, the Commissioner's own Regulations, and 35 U.S.C. §364(b) limit the Commissioner's authority to excuse a delay in meeting time limits to those situations in which the delay is related to a mail disruption or disfunction. *Farnum v. Manbeck*, 21 U.S.P.Q.2d 1691, 1694, 1695 (D.C. 1991).

Pendency. *See also* Continuing Application.

Where rejection of all claims is affirmed by the Court of Customs and Patent Appeals, the responsibility is upon the plaintiff to stay the court's judgment if the pendency of the application is to be preserved (for filing a continuing application), even though that is not necessary for Supreme Court review. *Continental Can Co., Inc. v. Schuyler, Commissioner of Patents*, 326 F. Supp. 283, 168 U.S.P.Q. 625 (D.C. 1970).

Pending. *See also* Unpatented Claim.

Advertising that one's product is covered by a patent or pending application when in fact it is not, or not yet, may be tortious and may be grounds for a counterclaim in a suit for infringement, but it is not a legally sufficient affirmative defense. *National Presto Industries Inc. v. Black & Decker (U.S.) Inc.*, 760 F. Supp. 699, 19 U.S.P.Q.2d 1457, 1459 (Ill. 1991).

Pending Application. *See also* **FOIA.**

An intentional announcement that a device is covered by an unissued patent may be held to constitute unfair competition. *Mixing Equipment Co., Inc. v. Innova-Tech, Inc.*, 228 U.S.P.Q. 221 (Pa. 1985).

Percentage. *See* **Proportions.**

Performance. *See also* **Commercialize.**

In any commercial agreement in which the compensation promised by one to the other is a percentage of profits or receipts, or is a royalty on goods sold, manufactured, or mined, there will nearly always be found an implied promise of diligent and careful performance in good faith and of forbearance to make performance impossible by going out of business or otherwise. 3 A. Corbin, *Corbin on Contracts* §568 (1960). This rule of law has been applied with full force to patent license agreements. *Bailey v. Chattem, Inc.*, 684 F.2d 386, 215 U.S.P.Q. 671, 679 (6th Cir. 1982).

ω

The differences between the prior art and the invention defined by the asserted claims, the availability of that art to all workers in the field, the failure of established competitors in a highly competitive market to make the invention despite the incentive to do so, the admittedly unobvious performance benefits realized through the claimed invention, the impressive commercial success of the claimed product, the praise of independent commentators and the forbearance of competitors from infringing the patent all go to confirm that the claimed invention was not obvious at the time it was made to a person of ordinary skill in the art. *S. C. Johnson & Son., Inc. v. Carter-Wallace, Inc.*, 614 F. Supp. 1278, 225 U.S.P.Q. 1022 (N.Y. 1985).

Peripheral Representation.

Under the peripheral-representation standard an attorney previously associated with a firm that handled matter substantially related to those in which the attorney's disqualification is sought may avoid disqualification by showing he had no personal involvement in the matters. *Atasi Corp. v. Seagate Technology*, 847 F.2d 826, 6 U.S.P.Q.2d 1955 (Fed. Cir. 1988).

Perjured Testimony.

In cases in which a court or jury is presented with perjured testimony which is relevant and material to the issue decided, and relief from judgment is sought pursuant to newly discovered evidence, the court should not attempt to weigh the effect of the perjured testimony on the trier of fact and should instead order a new trial. *Viskase Corp. v. American National Can Co.*, 979 F.Supp. 697, 45 U.S.P.Q.2d 1675, 1678 (Ill. 1997).

Permanent Injunction.

In a patent infringement case, where the infringing products will continue to infringe and thus damage a plaintiff in the future, monetary damages are not generally considered adequate. *E. I. du Pont de Nemours & Co. v. Phillips Petroleum Co.*, 659 F. Supp. 92, 3 U.S.P.Q.2d 1034 (Del. 1987).

Perpetual Motion.

An Examiner will not reject a claim as being directed to a so-called "perpetual motion" structure without giving the same careful consideration. When he has reached such conclusion, it disposes of the whole case unless his views are found to be untenable. When an application is made for a patent on an alleged invention based on principles which run counter to such a well-recognized law as that of the conservation of energy, the Office is justified in holding that the applicant has not complied with the statutory requirement of showing that his invention is "sufficiently useful and important" to warrant the grant of a patent therefor until he has shown that the invention is capable of operation. *Ex parte Payne*, 1904 C.D. 42, 43, 108 O.G. 1049 (Comm'r 1903).

Persistence.

Multiple interviews are not illegal, and persistence in patent prosecution is not grist for patent invalidity. *Magnivision Inc. v. The Bonneau Co.*, 42 U.S.P.Q.2d 1925, 1929 (Fed. Cir. 1997).

Person Aggrieved.

That test limits appellate standing to "those persons who are directly and adversely affected pecuniarily by an order of the bankruptcy court." *Everex Systems Inc. v. Cadtrak Corp.*, 89 F.3d 673, 39 U.S.P.Q.2d 1518, 1520 (9th Cir. 1996).

Personal Jurisdiction. *See also* Stream of Commerce.

In the context of an action for non-infringement in copyright or patent cases, the sending of a cease and desist letter to the alleged infringer is alone insufficient to establish the minimum contacts necessary for personal jurisdiction. Certain factors should be considered in determining whether asserting personal jurisdiction comports with "fair play and substantial justice." These factors include the burden on the defendant, the forum state's interest in adjudicating the dispute, the plaintiff's interest in obtaining convenient and effective relief, and the interstate judicial system's interest in obtaining the most efficient resolution of the controversies. *Modern Computer Corp. v. Ma*, 862 F.Supp. 938, 32 U.S.P.Q.2d 1586, 1590, 1591 (N.Y. 1994).

ᴥ

When a defendant moves to dismiss for lack of personal jurisdiction, the burden shifts to the plaintiff to make a *prima facie* showing of jurisdiction. The Supreme Court has developed an extensive body of case law describing the limitations that the 14th Amendment's Due Process Clause places on a state's exercise of personal jurisdiction over non-residents. *Columbia University v. Boehringer Mannheim GmbH*, 35 U.S.P.Q.2d 1364, 1366, 1367 n.4 (Mass. 1995).

ᛒ

A court must consider the bottom-line reasonableness and fairness of the exercise of personal jurisdiction over a nonresident defendant, using what the First Circuit has termed the "Gestalt factors:" (1) the defendant's burden of appearing, (2) the forum state's interest in adjudicating the dispute, (3) the plaintiff's interest in obtaining the most effective resolution of the controversy, (4) the judicial system's interest in obtaining the most effective resolution of the controversy, and (5) the common interest of all sovereigns in promoting substantive social policies. *Hologic Inc. v. Lunar Corp.*, 36 U.S.P.Q.2d 1182, 1184 (Mass. 1995).

ᛒ

The choice of law regarding the applicable rule governing personal jurisdiction is the Federal Circuit rule, not the regional circuit rule. (The Supreme Court's International Shoe jurisprudence is set in the context of state and diversity cases, which turn on 14th Amendment due process. In patent cases the CAFC applies the same test to personal jurisdiction questions arising under the 5th Amendment.) *Viam Corp. v. Iowa Export-Import Trading Co.*, 38 U.S.P.Q.2d 1833, 1835 (Fed. Cir. 1996).

ᛒ

In deciding whether the plaintiff has proved a prima facie case of personal jurisdiction, the district court must draw all reasonable inferences arising from the proof, and resolve all factual disputes in the plaintiff's favor. In addressing any appeal of the district court's jurisdictional holding based on defendant's activities, the Federal Circuit would rely on Federal Circuit precedent. Specific jurisdiction over a defendant may only be maintained if "the litigation results from alleged injuries that arise out of or relate to those activities." *Zeneca Ltd. v. Pharmachemie B.V.*, 42 U.S.P.Q.2d 1212, 1213, 1217 (Md. 1996).

ᛒ

Although issues of personal jurisdiction are generally procedural in nature, they are sufficiently related to substantive patent law, and thus the law of the Federal Circuit controls. A non-resident defendant is subject to federal jurisdiction in a federal district court if (1) the defendant is within the reach of the forum state's long arm statute, and (2) due process is satisfied. Jurisdiction is proper...where the contacts proximately result from actions by the defendant *himself* that create a "substantial connection" with the forum state. Thus where the defendant has "deliberately" engaged is significant activities within a State, or has created "continuing obligations" between himself and residents of the forum, he manifestly has availed himself of the privilege of conducting business there, and because his activities are shielded by the "benefits and protections" of the forum's laws, it is presumptively not unreasonable to require him to submit to the burdens of litigation in that forum as well. *Crystal Semiconductor Corp. v. OPTi Inc.*, 44 U.S.P.Q.2d 1497, 1499, 1501 (Tex. 1997).

ᛒ

Even if the defendant's website could be construed as a prohibited offer to sell, its accessibility to New Yorkers did not vest the district court with personal jurisdiction. *Agar Corp. Inc. v. Multi-Fluid Inc.*, 45 U.S.P.Q.2d 1444, 1448 (Tex. 1997).

Person of Ordinary Skill in the Art. *See* MOSITA.

Perspiration.

"[T]he inspiration-perspiration process of the laboratory" is as deserving of reward as the flash of genius, and surely more so than dumb luck. *Carter-Wallace, Inc. v. Otte*, 474 F.2d 529, 176 U.S.P.Q. 2, 12 (2d Cir. 1972).

Persuasion.

The junior party, patentee, responded to an order to show cause with a motion to dissolve that, if granted, would have been good and sufficient cause for judgment not to be rendered against him. In view thereof, the senior party, who copied claims from the junior party, patentee, had at least the burden of persuasion before the board to show clear and unambiguous support for each limitation of the counts. *Holmes, Faber, Boykin, and Francis v. Kelly, Hornberger, and Strief,* 586 F.2d 234, 199 U.S.P.Q. 778, 781 (C.C.P.A. 1978).

ᴥ

The statutory presumption of validity provided in 35 U.S.C. §282 places the burden of proof upon the party attacking the validity of a patent, and that burden of persuasion does not shift at any time to the patent owner. It is constant and remains throughout suit on the challenger. *TP Laboratories Inc. v. Professional Positioners, Inc.*, 724 F.2d 965, 220 U.S.P.Q. 577, 582 (Fed. Cir. 1984).

ᴥ

The burden of persuasion does not shift by reason of a patentee's six-year delay. *A.C. Aukerman Co. v. R.L. Chaides Construction Co.*, 960 F.2d 1020, 22 U.S.P.Q.2d 1321, 1333 (Fed. Cir. 1992).

Petition to Revive. *See* Revival.

Phair Doctrine.

Patentability may exist in the discovery of the cause of a defect in an existing machine or process and applying a remedy therefor even though, after the cause is understood, the remedy would be obvious. *In re Wiseman and Kovac*, 596 F.2d 1019, 201 U.S.P.Q. 658, 661 (C.C.P.A. 1979).

Phantom Count.

Section 1.231(a)(2) of 37 C.F.R. requires that a motion to add or substitute new counts "demonstrate patentability of the count[s] to all parties." Where proposed counts are phantom counts, they are by definition not patentable to either party under 35 U.S.C. §112, i.e., they are not fully supported by the disclosure of either party. Therefore, when a party poses new phantom counts, the requisite demonstration of patentability (as far as §112 is concerned) must be made with respect to the claims of the other party that correspond to the proposed counts, or, if there are no such claims already in the other party's application, such claims should be proposed in the motion. The vagaries of phantom and modified count practice are such that parties should be liberally permitted to correct errors and deficiencies in 37 C.F.R. §1.231 motions and related papers that result from failure to comply with requirements unique to that practice, particularly when the motion or other paper in question is not opposed. *Foulkes v. Isa,* 214 U.S.P.Q. 466 (Comm'r Patents & Trademarks 1981).

ω

Phantom counts were invented for the sole purpose of adjudicating first inventorship when more than one party claims substantially the same invention. There is a significant difference between supporting a claim for patentability purposes and supporting a phantom count in an interference. The "count," as distinguished from a party's "claim," need not be patentable to either party in the sense of being fully supported by either party's disclosure. In fact, where the interference is conducted on a "phantom count" or on the basis of a modified patent claim, at least one party, by definition, will not have full support for all the limitations of the count. The purpose of the count is to determine what evidence is relevant to the issue of priority. A phantom count merely represents the inventive concept that may in some cases portray two mutually exclusive, but patentably indistinct, sets of claims. *In re Kroekel,* 803 F.2d 705, 231 U.S.P.Q. 640 (Fed. Cir. 1986).

Pharmaceutical. *See also* Certainty, Dosage, Drug, Mode of Administration, Packaging Material, Patent Term Extension, Pharmaceutical Obviousness, Physiological, Potency, Product, Safety, Therapeutic Value.

While the granting of a patent does not legally constitute a certificate that a medicine to which it relates is a good medicine or will cure the disease or successfully make the test which it was intended to do, nevertheless, the granting of such a patent gives a kind of official imprimatur to the medicine in question on which as a moral matter some members of the public are likely to rely. *Isenstead v. Watson,* 157 F.Supp. 7, 115 U.S.P.Q. 408, 410 (D.C. 1957).

ω

Even though the application made no mention of the separation of hypotensive and tranquilizing activity, the advantage of minimized hypotensive activity would inherently flow from the indicated use of the compounds as tranquilizers. When claimed compounds are used for their disclosed tranquilizer activity, they are better insofar as they minimize the side effects of hypotensive activity. The latter undisclosed property must thus be considered in determining patentability of the claimed compounds. *In re Zenitz,* 333 F.2d 924, 142 U.S.P.Q. 158, 161 (C.C.P.A. 1964).

ω

Unpredictability is particularly notorious with regard to pharmaceutical compounds. *In re Kamal and Rogier,* 398 F.2d 867, 158 U.S.P.Q. 320, 323 (C.C.P.A. 1968).

ω

To reach the Board's conclusion, i.e., that the properties of 10-MD do not differ strikingly from those of reserpine, would require that all evidence favorable to appellants' position be viewed with limitless skepticism and that all evidence unfavorable to appellants' position be accepted with limitless faith. *In re Petrzilka, Hofmann, Schenk, Trexler, Frey, and Ott*, 424 F.2d 1102, 165 U.S.P.Q. 327, 329 (C.C.P.A. 1970).

ω

An indirect comparison to establish unexpected activity may be adequate to overcome a prior art rejection. *In re Blondel, Fouche, and Gueremy*, 499 F.2d 1311, 182 U.S.P.Q. 294, 298 (C.C.P.A. 1974).

ω

Even if proof of utility of the claimed invention as an anti-arthritic agent for humans is lacking, there remains the proven utility as an anti-arthritic agent for lower animals. Having found that the claimed composition has utility as contemplated in the specification, 35 U.S.C. §101 is satisfied, and it is unnecessary to decide whether it is in fact useful for the other purposes indicated in the specification as possibilities. *In re Malachowski*, 530 F.2d 1402, 189 U.S.P.Q. 432, 435 (C.C.P.A. 1976).

ω

That the unexpectedly superior activity or property of an end product has to do with a pharmaceutical utility is an insufficient justification for precluding a determination that the claimed intermediate is the "contributing cause" of the end product's unexpectedly superior activity or property. *In re Magerlein*, 602 F.2d 366, 202 U.S.P.Q. 473, 478 (C.C.P.A. 1979).

ω

Although pharmaceutical compositions were involved, the claimed invention concerned reducing gastro-intestinal-tract incompatibility. Exemplified structures of active components and their uses were previously known. The invention was not in the active component. The specification did not have to teach how to use (pharmacologically) all encompassed active components to satisfy the disclosure requirements of 35 U.S.C. §112, first paragraph. The utility of the invention was distinguished from the utility of specific compositions embodying the invention. *Ex parte Gleixner, Muller, and Lehrach*, 214 U.S.P.Q. 297, 298 (PTO Bd. App. 1979).

ω

Since it is crucial to provide researchers with an incentive to disclose pharmacological activities in as many compounds as possible, adequate proof of any such activity constitutes a showing of practical utility. *Thomas, Draber, Schmidt, and Eue v. Eiken, Rohr, Zech, and Wuerzer*, 219 U.S.P.Q. 900, 907 (PTO Bd. Pat. Intf. 1983).

ω

The issue is whether permission for commercial marketing or use of Opticrom 4% on October 3, 1984, or Intal Nebulizer Solution on January 19, 1985, represents the first permitted commercial marketing or use of the product within the meaning of §156(a)(5)(A).

By the explicit terms of the statute, the term product, as it relates to a human drug product, means the active ingredient of a new drug. The active ingredient in both of the approved products is cromolyn sodium. As noted in the FDA letters, the active ingredient had been approved for commercial marketing in 1973 and 1983, both prior to the approval of Opticrom 4% and Intal Nebulizer Solution for commercial marketing under 21 U.S.C. 355. Applying the explicit language of this statute to the facts: The permission for commercial marketing or use of the product after such regulatory review period was not the first permitted commercial marketing or use of the product under the provision of law under which the regulatory review occurred.

There is no basis in the statutory language for making a distinction between the content of a "product" vis-a-vis an "approved product." An approved product is a product that has been approved by the FDA for commercial marketing or use. The statute is explicit in defining the meaning of product in §156(f); the statute does not state that the product referred to in paragraphs (4) and (5) is the approved product. Thus, the statute itself clearly dictates that the product referred to in paragraphs (4) and (5) be defined in the manner required in §156(f). *In re Fisons Pharmaceuticals Ltd.,* 231 U.S.P.Q. 305 (Comm'r Patents & Trademarks 1986).

ω

Amelioration of the symptoms or even cure of cancer is no longer considered to be "incredible." Nonetheless, decisional law would seem to indicate that the utility in question is sufficiently unusual to justify an Examiner's requiring substantiating evidence, which may be in the form of animal tests that constitute recognized screening procedures with clear relevance to utility in humans. The specification of the appellant's parent application sets forth several animal tests on numerous types of specific cancers as well as in vitro studies, both of which are asserted to be predictive with regard to utility in humans. The Examiner has not challenged the evidence presented in a single, relevant, material respect. There is only the blanket statement of lack of "patentable utility" per se. In fact, the only specific comments the Examiner has directed toward the appellant's evidence are with regard to the breadth of the types of tumor against which the claimed compounds have been shown to be active. The appealed claims are drawn to compounds and not to a method of treatment. Generally speaking, utility in treating a single disease is an adequate basis for the patentability of a pharmaceutical compound under 35 U.S.C. §101. *Ex parte Krepelka,* 231 U.S.P.Q. 746 (B.P.A.I. 1986).

ω

Pharmaceutical utility of a compound for patent purposes is established when recognized screening procedures employing such compound produce results which are interpreted by those skilled in the art as showing such utility. *Ex parte Busse*, 1 U.S.P.Q.2d 1908, 1909 (B.P.A.I. 1986).

ω

A claim to a pharmaceutical composition comprising an effective amount of a specified compound and suitable carrier adequately sets forth the use to comply with requirements of 35 U.S.C. §112. The recitation of a more specific use in composition claims calling for "an effective amount" is not necessary; claims are read in the light of the specification on which they are based, and the specification must provide essential particulars. *Ex parte Skuballa,* 12 U.S.P.Q.2d 1570, 1571 (B.P.A.I. 1989).

ω

In the pharmaceutical arts, the CAFC has long held that practical utility may be shown by adequate evidence of any pharmacological activity. *Fujikawa v. Wattanasin,* 93 F.3d 1559, 39 U.S.P.Q.2d 1895, 1899 (Fed. Cir. 1996)

ω

One who has taught the public that a compound exhibits some desirable pharmaceutical property in a standard experimental animal has made a significant and useful contribution to the art, even though it may eventually appear that the compound is without value in the treatment of humans. *In re Brana,* 51 F.3d 1560, 34 U.S.P.Q.2d 1436, 1442 (Fed. Cir. 1995).

Pharmaceutical Obviousness.

In attempting to predict the biological activities of a drug, a skilled medicinal chemist would not proceed randomly but would base his attempts on the available knowledge of prior research techniques, and literature used in his field. One such technique is "bio-isosteric replacement" or the theory of bioisosterism—where the substitution of one atom or group of atoms for another atom or group of atoms having similar size, shape, and electron density provides molecules having the same type of biological activity. Application of this technique led to a holding of obviousness with a new use of a known compound. *In re Merck & Co.,* 800 F.2d 1091, 231 U.S.P.Q. 375 (Fed. Cir. 1986).

Pharmacological. *See* Pharmaceutical.

Phenomenon of Nature. *See also* Physical Phenomenon.

Phenomena of nature, though just discovered, mental processes, and abstract intellectual concepts are not patentable, as they are the basic tools of scientific and technological work. *Gottschalk, Comm'r. Pats. v. Benson,* 409 U.S. 63, 175 U.S.P.Q. 673, 675 (S.Ct. 1972).

Phenyl vs. Benzyl.

Even though the issue was one of reforming an interference, it appears from the wording of the opinion that unwarranted weight may have inadvertently been accorded to testimony that only established obviousness to try. An expert testified that it would be obvious for someone testing or making the phenyl-substituted compounds also to make and test the benzyl substituted compounds. Nothing in the opinion appears to address the issue as to whether either the benzyl- or phenyl-subgenus would have been obvious (as a whole) prior to testing that particular subgenus. *Winter v. Banno,* 229 U.S.P.Q. 212 (B.P.A.I. 1985).

Phenyl vs. Naphthyl.

The general relationship between naphthyl (in compounds of prior art compositions) and phenyl (in compounds of claimed compositions) is insufficient basis for rejecting the claims in the absence of prior art indication that the phenyl derivative would be expected to be effective as a fungicide once the effectiveness of the naphthyl derivative as a fungicide had been determined. *Ex parte Ligett, Wolf, and Closson*, 121 U.S.P.Q. 324, 326 (PO Bd. App. 1958).

Photograph.

Photographs are "printed publications" under the statute. *J.A. LaPorte, Inc. v. Norfolk Dredging Company*, 625 F. Supp. 36, 227 U.S.P.Q. 382, 385 (Va. 1985).

Photographic Color Coupler.

The rejection of claims, calling for a photographic color coupler of the formula COUP-S-R [wherein COUP is a photographic color coupler radical (a 5-pyrazolone color coupler radical or an open-chain ketomethylene color coupler radical) and R is an organic radical incapable of forming a dye with an oxidized developing agent], for lack of support and definition under 35 U.S.C. §112 was reversed. *In re Barr, Williams, and Whitmore*, 444 F.2d 588, 170 U.S.P.Q. 330 (C.C.P.A. 1971).

Physical Phenomenon.

Every discovery is not embraced within the statutory terms of 35 U.S.C. §101. Excluded from such patent protection are laws of nature, physical phenomena, and abstract ideas. A principle, in the abstract, is a fundamental truth, an original cause, a motive; these cannot be patented, and no one can claim in any of them an exclusive right. A new mineral discovered in the earth or a new plant found in the wild is not patentable subject matter. Likewise, Einstein could not patent his celebrated law that $E = mc^2$; nor could Newton have patented the law of gravity. Such discoveries are "manifestations of . . . nature, free to all men and reserved exclusively to none." *Diamond v. Diehr and Lutton*, 450 U.S. 175, 209 U.S.P.Q. 1, 7 (1981).

Physical Structure.

By disclosing in a patent application a device that inherently performs a function, operates according to a theory, or has an advantage, a patent applicant necessarily discloses that function, theory, or advantage, even though he says nothing concerning it. The express description of an inherent property, since not "new matter," can be added to a specification with the effect as of the original filing date. The additional description is not that of a new use, but of the existing physical structure of the product. *Kennecott Corp. v. Kyocera International, Inc.*, 835 F.2d 1419, 5 U.S.P.Q.2d 1194 (Fed. Cir. 1987).

Physiological. *See also* **Pharmaceutical.**

An inventor should be allowed to dominate future patentable inventions of others where those inventions are based in some way on his teachings. Such improvements, while non-obvious from his teachings, are still within his contribution, since the improvement is made possible by his work. It is equally apparent, however, that he must not be permitted to achieve this dominance by claims that are insufficiently supported and hence not in compliance with the first paragraph of 35 U.S.C. §112. That paragraph requires that the scope of the claims must bear a reasonable correlation to the scope of enablement provided by the specification to persons of ordinary skill in the art. In cases involving predictable factors, such as mechanical or electrical elements, a single embodiment provides broad enablement in the sense that, once imagined, other embodiments can be made without difficulty and their performance characteristics predicted by resort to known scientific laws. In cases involving unpredictable factors, such as most chemical reactions and physiological activity, the scope of enablement obviously varies inversely with the degree of unpredictability of the factors involved. *In re Fisher,* 427 F.2d 833, 166 U.S.P.Q. 18 (C.C.P.A. 1970).

Pick and Choose. *See also* **Blueprint, Mosaic, Retrospective Reconstruction, Selection, Selective Extraction from Prior Art, Teach Away From.**

Indiscriminate reliance on definitions found in dictionaries can often produce absurd results. One need not arbitrarily pick and choose from the various accepted definitions of a word to decide which meaning was intended as the word is used in a given claim. The subject matter, the context, and so on will more often than not lead to the correct conclusion. Rather than looking to a dictionary, look to the art or technology to which the claimed subject matter pertains. In doing so, give due consideration to the interpretation that one of ordinary skill in the art would give the terminology in question. *In re Salem, Butterworth, and Ryan,* 553 F.2d 676, 193 U.S.P.Q. 513, 518 (C.C.P.A. 1977).

ʊ

Presuming arguendo that the references show the elements or concepts urged, the Examiner presented no line of reasoning as to why the artisan reviewing only the collective teachings of the references would have found it obvious to selectively pick and choose various elements and/or concepts from the several references relied on to arrive at the claimed invention. In the instant application, the Examiner has done little more than cite references to show that one or more elements or some combinations thereof, when each is viewed in a vacuum, is known. The claimed invention, however, is clearly directed to a combination of elements. That is to say, the appellant does not claim that he has invented one or more new elements but has presented claims to a new combination of elements. To support the conclusion that the claimed combination is directed to obvious subject matter, either the references must expressly or impliedly suggest the claimed combination or the Examiner must present a convincing line of reasoning as to why the artisan would have found the claimed invention to have been obvious in light of the teachings of the references. The Board found nothing in the references that would expressly or impliedly teach or suggest the modifications urged by the Examiner. Additionally, the Board found no line of reasoning in the answer as to why the artisan would have found the modifications urged by the Examiner to have been obvious. Based upon the record, the artisan would not have found it obvious to selectively pick and choose elements or concepts from the various references so as to arrive at the claimed invention without using the claims as a guide. *Ex parte Clapp*, 227 U.S.P.Q. 972 (B.P.A.I. 1985).

ω

When a claimed invention is not identically disclosed in a reference, and instead requires picking and choosing among a number of different options disclosed by the reference, then the reference does not anticipate. *Mendenhall v. Astec Industries, Inc.*, 13 U.S.P.Q.2d 1913, 1928 (Tenn. 1988), *aff'd*, 13 U.S.P.Q.2d 1956 (Fed. Cir. 1989).

Picture. *See* **Icon.**

Piecemeal. *See also* **Retrospective Reconstruction.**

Piecemeal reconstruction of prior art patents in the light of an applicant's disclosure is not a basis for a holding of obviousness under 35 U.S.C. §103. *In re Kamm and Young*, 452 F.2d 1052, 172 U.S.P.Q. 298, 301 (C.C.P.A. 1972).

Piercing the Corporate Veil.

Piercing the corporate veil is a power for the Court to exercise "reluctantly" and "cautiously", with the burden of proof resting on the party asserting such a claim. *Amhil Enterprises Ltd. v. Wawa Inc.*, 34 U.S.P.Q.2d 1640, 1644 (Md. 1994).

Pioneer Invention.

An inventor should be allowed to dominate future patentable inventions of others where those inventions are based in some way on his teachings. Such improvements, while non-obvious from his teachings, are still within his contribution, since the improvement is made possible by his work. It is equally apparent, however, that he must not be permitted to achieve this dominance by claims that are insufficiently supported and hence not in compliance with the first paragraph of 35 U.S.C. §112. That paragraph requires that the scope of the claims must bear a reasonable correlation to the scope of enablement provided by the specification to persons of ordinary skill in the art. In cases involving predictable factors, such as mechanical or electrical elements, a single embodiment provides broad enablement in the sense that, once imagined, other embodiments can be made without difficulty and their performance characteristics predicted by resort to known scientific laws. In cases involving unpredictable factors, such as most chemical reactions and physiological activity, the scope of enablement obviously varies inversely with the degree of unpredictability of the factors involved. *In re Fisher*, 427 F.2d 833, 166 U.S.P.Q. 18 (C.C.P.A. 1970).

ω

A claim relating to a landmark and pioneer invention is entitled to the widest possible range of equivalents. *Eli Lilly and Company, Inc. v. Generix Drug Sales, Inc.*, 324 F.Supp. 715, 169 U.S.P.Q. 13, 20 (Fla. 1971).

ω

The PTO has not challenged the appellants' assertion that their 1953 application enabled those skilled in the art in 1953 to make and use "a solid polymer" as described in a claim. The appellants disclosed, as the only then-existing way to make such a polymer, a method of making the crystalline form. To say now that the appellants should have disclosed in 1953 the amorphous form (which did not exist until 1962) would be to impose an impossible burden on inventors and thus on the patent system. There cannot, in an effective patent system, be such a burden placed on the right to broad claims. To restrict the appellants to the crystalline form disclosed, under such circumstances, would be a poor way to stimulate invention, and particularly to encourage its early disclosure. To demand such restriction is merely to state a policy against broad protection for pioneer inventions, a policy both shortsighted and unsound from the standpoint of promoting progress in the useful arts, which is the constitutional purpose of the patent laws. *In re Hogan and Banks,* 559 F.2d 595, 194 U.S.P.Q. 527, 537 (C.C.P.A. 1977).

ϖ

The judically "liberal" view of both claim interpretation and equivalency accorded a pioneer invention is not a manifestation of a different legal standard based on an abstract legal concept denominated "pioneer." Rather, the liberal view flows directly from the relative sparseness of prior art in nascent fields of technology. Even pioneer status does not change the way infringement is determined. The patentee's disclosure, the prosecution history, and the prior art still provide the background against which the scope of claims is determined. *Texas Instruments, Inc. v. U.S. International Trade Commission,* 846 F.2d 1369, 6 U.S.P.Q.2d 1886 (Fed. Cir. 1988).

Pioneer Patent.

A pioneer patent is a distinct step in the progress of the art, distinguished from a mere improvement or pefection of what has gone before. *Breuer Electric Mfg. Co. v. Tennant Co.,* 44 U.S.P.Q.2d 1259, 1267 (Ill. 1997).

Piracy.

The term "piracy", in an insurance contract's definition of "advertising injury", encompasses patent infringement. *Aqua Queen Manufacturing Inc. v. Charter Oak Fire Insurance,* 830 F.Supp. 536, 26 U.S.P.Q.2d 1940, 1942 (Cal. 1993).

ϖ

While patent infringement can be piracy of an advertised product, generally it is not piracy of the elements of an advertisement itself. In the context of insurance policies written to protect against claims of advertising injury, "piracy" means misappropriation or plagiarism found in the elements *of the advertisement itself*—in its text form, logo, or pictures—rather than in the product being advertised. *Iolab Corp. v. Seaboard Surety Co.,* 15 F.3d 1500, 29 U.S.P.Q.2d 1610, 1614 (9th Cir. 1994).

ϖ

Reference in an insurance policy to "advertising injury caused by piracy" is limited to those cases in which there is a causal connection between the injury arising out of piracy and the advertising activities. *New Hampshire Insurance Co. v. R.L. Chaides Construction Co. Inc.*, 847 F.Supp. 1452, 30 U.S.P.Q.2d 1474, 1478 (Cal. 1994).

ω

"Piracy", as used in the advertising injury provision of an insurance contract, does not include direct patent infringement, contributory patent infringement, or inducement of patent infringement. *Classic Corp. v. Charter Oak Fire Insurance Co.*, 35 U.S.P.Q.2d 1726, 1728 (Cal. 1995).

Pirating. *See also* Appropriation.

The claimed composition rapidly cures at room temperature, whereas the accused counterpart rapidly cures only at 90°C. It was precisely because of that difference that the district court found that the claimed invention and the accused counterpart do not perform in substantially the same way. That finding, however, would allow the difference itself to dictate a finding of no equivalents; if that were the law, one could never infringe by equivalents. The analysis must go further, and the question the district court should consider on remand is this: given the difference, would the accused composition at $90ffC$ and the claimed invention at room temperature perform substantially the same function (e.g., filling the pores of the treated material with solid material) in substantially the same way (e.g., by rapidly curing in the absence but not in the presence of oxygen) to give substantially the same results (e.g., a filled material). There are limitations to the doctrine of equivalents. The doctrine has been judicially devised to do equity in situations where there is no literal infringement but liability is nevertheless appropriate to prevent what is in essence a pirating of the patentee's invention. Concommitently, two policy-oriented limitations, applied as questions of law, have developed. First, the doctrine will not extend to an infringing device within the public domain and found in the prior art at the time the patent issued; second, prosecution history estoppel will not allow the patentee to recapture through equivalents certain coverage given up during prosecution. *Loctite Corp. v. Ultraseal Ltd.*, 781 F.2d 861, 228 U.S.P.Q. 90 (Fed. Cir. 1985).

Plant.[4]

Congress intended that the provisions of 35 U.S.C. §102(b), as applied to plant patents, should not be interpreted otherwise than they had been with respect to other inventions, i.e., that only an "enabling" publication is effective as a bar to a subsequent patent. *In re LeGrice*, 301 F.2d 929, 133 U.S.P.Q. 365, 374 (C.C.P.A. 1962).

ω

A pending utility application can be amended by filing a continuing plant application when the parent application contains a written description of the subject matter claimed in the continuing application. The deposit of a culture of the claimed microfungi in a public depository complies with the accepted procedure for meeting the requirements of 35 U.S.C. §112 and §162. *Ex parte Solomons and Scammell*, 201 U.S.P.Q. 42, 43 (PTO Bd. App. 1978).

ω

---

[4]Claims directed to hybrid seeds and to hybrid plants have been allowed because the PVPA and the PPA exclude such subject matter. *Ex parte Hibberd*, 227 U.S.P.Q. 443, 444 n.1 (B.P.A.I. 1985).

Every discovery is not embraced within the statutory terms of 35 U.S.C. §101. Excluded from such patent protection are laws of nature, physical phenomena, and abstract ideas. A principle, in the abstract, is a fundamental truth, an original cause, a motive; these cannot be patented, and no one can claim in any of them an exclusive right. A new mineral discovered in the earth or a new plant found in the wild is not patentable subject matter. Likewise, Einstein could not patent his celebrated law that $E = c^2$; nor could Newton have patented the law of gravity. Such discoveries are "manifestations of... nature, free to all men and reserved exclusively to none." *Diamond v. Diehr and Lutton*, 450 U.S. 175, 209 U.S.P.Q. 1, 7 (1981).

ϖ

The scope of patentable subject matter under 35 U.S.C. §101 has not been narrowed or restricted by the passage of the PPA (Plant Patent Act) and the PVPA (Plant Variety Protection Act). Those plant-specific Acts do not represent the exclusive forms of protection for plant life covered by those acts. The term "plant" in the PPA (35 U.S.C. §161) has its common, ordinary meaning which is limited to those things having roots, stems, leaves and flowers or fruits. *Ex parte Hibberd*, 227 U.S.P.Q. 443, 444, 447 (B.P.A.I. 1985).

ϖ

"It is generally assumed that one infringes [a plant patent] only if the accused plant is a direct or indirect asexual reproduction of the patentee's original parent plant." 1 Donald S. Chisum, *Patents* §1.05[1][d](1944). It is necessarily a defense to plant patent infringement that the alleged infringing plant is not an asexual reproduction of the patented plant. *Imazio Nursery Inc. v. Dania Greenhouses*, 69 F.3d 1560, 36 U.S.P.Q.2d 1673, 1681 (Fed. Cir. 1995).

Plant Variety Protection Act.[5] *See also* PVPA.

The Plant Variety Protection Act (PVPA) supplements the Plant Patent Act and grants patent-like protection for sexually reproduced plants. In effect, the PVPA awards the equivalent of patent protection to sexually reproduced plants that meet the Act's certification requirements. Because of the similarity in purpose and construction between the PVPA and the patent laws, cases construing the patent statutes supply compelling analogies to aid the court in interpreting the PVPA. A party must be an assignee before he is entitled to bring suit in his own name under the PVPA, and a mere licensee cannot bring suit, except with the owner or through the name of the owner. *Public Varieties of Mis-*

---

[5] "On October 6, 1994, President Clinton signed the Plant Variety Protection Act (PVPA)(S.1406, P.L. 103-349) into law. The PVPA extends the term of plant variety protection to 20 years for non-woody plants, including potatoes and other tubers, and to 25 years for woody plants and extends the act's protection to first generation hybrids and harvested plant parts. The bill also brings U.S. law into conformity with 1991 revisions agreed to by the International Union for the Protection of New Plant Varieties. Finally, the bill modifies the farmer's exemption to bar the sale of saved seed for reproductive purposes. House amendments to the corresponding House bill, H.R. 2927, further permitted seed producers to sell seed which the owner of the plant variety refuses to buy under contract. The House amendments were adopted by the Senate before passage of S. 1406 on September 21, 1994." Intellectual Property Law Section, The District of Columbia Bar, *Newsletter*, Vol. 2, No. 1, page 11, October 1994.

sissippi Inc. v. Sun Valley Seed Co. Inc., 734 F. Supp. 250, 14 U.S.P.Q.2d 2055, 2056 (Mich. 1990).

ಠ

In 7 U.S.C. §2543 Congress specifically protected the historical and traditional right of small farmers to make seed sales to fellow farmers. However, the intent of Congress in enacting the PVPA was not to give a farmer an unrestricted right to sell seed. *The Asgrow Seed Co. v. Winterboer*, 795 F.Supp. 915, 22 U.S.P.Q.2d 1937, 1939 (Iowa 1991).

ಠ

The PVPA, 7 U.S.C. §§2321-2582 (1988), protects novel varieties of sexually re-produced seed, transplants, and plants. This protection extends to distinct, uniform, and stable new seed varieties. 7 U.S.C. §2401. The developer of a novel variety obtains protection by acquiring a certificate of protection from the Plant Variety Protection Office. 7 U.S.C. §§2421, 2422, 2481-2483. A PVPA certificate grants the breeder the right to exclude others from "selling the variety, or offering it for sale, or reproducing it, or importing it, or exporting it, or using it in producing . . . a hybrid or different variety therefrom." 7 U.S.C. §2483(a). PVPA protection lasts for 18 years. 7 U.S.C. §2483(b). The PVPA provides remedies for infringement of exclusive rights under the Act. 7 U.S.C. §§2541, 2561. *Asgrow Seed Co. v. Winterboer*, 982 F.2d 486, 25 U.S.P.Q.2d 1202, 1203 (Fed. Cir. 1992), *petition for rehearing denied*, 989 F.2d 1227, 26 U.S.P.Q.2d 1227 (Fed. Cir. 1993).[6]

Pleadings.

Pleadings do not suffice to support a judgment when the subject matter was not litigated, or fairly placed in issue, during the trial. There must be sufficient and explicit notice of the claims at risk; patent claims not at issue are not properly declared invalid. When the pleadings are not in complete harmony with the issues that were litigated and adjudicated, it is the pleadings that may be conformed to the judgment, not vice versa. *Tol-O-Matic Inc. v. Proma Produkt-Und Marketing Gesellschaft m.b.H.*, 945 F.2d 1546, 20 U.S.P.Q.2d 1332, 1339 (Fed. Cir. 1991).

Plenary Review.

The Federal Circuit reviews questions of fact under a clearly erroneous standard; questions of law are subject to full and independent review (sometimes referred to as '*de novo*" or "plenary" review). *In re Asahi/America Inc.*, 68 F.3d 442, 33 U.S.P.Q.2d 1921, 1922 (Fed. Cir. 1995).

Plural. *See also* Utility.

The granting of a motion for partial summary judgment of noninfringement of claims (requiring the processing of a plurality of components simultaneously) by a product which processes only a single component at a time was refused because a triable issue of material fact remained as to whether the product infringed under the Doctrine of Equiv-

---

[6]See dissent.

alents. *Applied Materials Inc. v. Advanced Semiconductor Materials America Inc.*, 26 U.S.P.Q.2d 1153, 1154, 1155 (Cal. 1992).

Plural Claims. *See also* **Multiplicity, Patentable Distinctness.**

Claims in the same application, unlike those in separate applications, need not distinguish patentably from each other, in the sense of being capable of supporting different patents. They need only distinguish in scope. *Ex parte Siebach*, 151 U.S.P.Q. 62, 63 (PO Bd. App. 1966).

Plural Inventions. *See* **Unity of Invention.**

A determination by the Patent Office that earlier, separate claims encompass a "plurality of different inventions" cannot serve, under 35 U.S.C. §112, as the basis for a rejection of a later combined claim. An applicant is free under that provision to set the metes and bounds of "his invention" as he sees them. Subsequent compliance with an Office restriction requirement with traverse cannot be considered a voluntary realignment of the claim boundaries or a concession that more than one invention was originally claimed. Whether a plurality of inventions had been claimed was not "settled" by the restriction requirement and the denial of a petition therefrom, the present appeal having in effect kept that issue alive. Appellant remained free to regard the claimed subject matter as his invention. *In re Wolfrum and Gold*, 486 F.2d 588, 179 U.S.P.Q. 620, 622 (C.C.P.A. 1973).

Point of Novelty. *See also* **Design Patent Infringement, Difference, Gist.**

The vice of a functional claim exists not only when a claim is "wholly" functional, if that is ever true, but also when the inventor is painstaking when he recites what has already been seen, and then uses conveniently functional language at the exact point of novelty. A limited use of terms of effect or result, which accurately define the essential qualities of a product to one skilled in the art, may in some instances be permissible and even desirable, but a characteristic essential to novelty may not be distinguished from the old art solely by its tendency to remedy the problems in the art met by the patent. *General Electric Co. v. Wabash Appliance Corp.*, 304 U.S. 364, 37 U.S.P.Q. 466, 469 (1938).

ᙡ

When a claimed invention lies in a combination, the point of novelty is the combination and not the individual components thereof. Under such circumstances the components need not be so precisely defined. *Ex parte Dobson, Jacob, and Herschler*, 165 U.S.P.Q. 29, 30 (PO Bd. App. 1969).

ᙡ

Any concern over the use of functional language at the so-called "point of novelty" stems largely from the fear that an applicant will attempt to distinguish over a reference disclosure by emphasizing a property or function which may not be mentioned by the reference and thereby assert that his claimed subject matter is novel. Such a concern is not only irrelevant, it is misplaced. *In re Swinehart and Sfiligoj*, 439 F.2d 210, 169 U.S.P.Q. 226, 228 (C.C.P.A. 1971).

ᙡ

The "point of novelty" approach in determining whether a claimed invention is statutory subject matter under 35 U.S.C. §101 is inappropriate. *In re Freeman,* 573 F.2d 1237, 197 U.S.P.Q. 464, 469, 470 (C.C.P.A. 1978).

ᚳ

If a "point of novelty" approach to 35 U.S.C. §101 were adopted, it would immeasurably debilitate the patent system. *In re Walter,* 618 F.2d 758, 205 U.S.P.Q. 397, 406 (C.C.P.A. 1980).

"Point of Novelty" Test.

In the "points of novelty" test, the court must determine whether an allegedly infringing design "appropriate[s] the novelty in the patented device which distinguishes [the patented device] from the prior art." *Motorola Inc. v. Qualcomm Inc.,* 45 U.S.P.Q.2d 1558, 1563 (Cal. 1997).

Polymer.

In this patent specification "may" should be interpreted as illustrative and not as limiting the description of diamines to aliphatic and aromatic diamines. *In re DiLeone and Lucas,* 436 F.2d 1404, 168 U.S.P.Q. 592, 594 (C.C.P.A. 1971).

ᚳ

The expression "copolymer" has a generic meaning defining polymers containing two or more monomers. *Price v. Vandenberg v. Bailey,* 174 U.S.P.Q. 42, 43 (PO Bd. Pat. Intf. 1971).

ᚳ

Neither the Examiner nor the Board articulated any reason for doubting that all polymers falling within the scope of the claims can be used in the same manner as those specifically disclosed in the specification. *In re Smith and Hubin,* 481 F.2d 910, 178 U.S.P.Q. 620, 625 (C.C.P.A. 1973).

ᚳ

Issues concerning patents in polymer chemistry are not too complex for a trial by jury. *American Can Company v. Dart Industries, Inc.,* 205 U.S.P.Q. 1006, 1008 (Ill. 1979).

ᚳ

The record must establish how close the values for melt index and density of copolymers need to be in order for the copolymers to be considered "comparable." If it is intended that comparisons are to be made between resins having the same or equivalent melt index and density, the claims should use such language. The claims cannot leave to surmise and conjecture the specific properties to be compared and how "comparable" their values need to be when determining infringement and dominance issues. *Ex parte Anderson,* 21 U.S.P.Q.2d 1241, 1250 (B.P.A.I. 1991).

ᚳ

Molecular weight limitation resulted in significantly improved physical and electrical properties. *In re Soni,* 54 F.3d 746, 34 U.S.P.Q.2d 1684, 1685 (Fed. Cir. 1995).

Polynuclear.

A rejection of claims as failing to define the invention properly and based on the phrases "substituted mononuclear and polynuclear homocyclic compounds," "alkyl," "ester," and "heterocyclic and aromatic compounds being free of substituents containing aliphatic hydroxyl and amino groups," in process claims, was reversed. *Ex parte West-fahl*, 136 U.S.P.Q. 265 (PTO Bd. App. 1962).

Pooling.[7]

The combination represented by the patent pools in Canada, England and Australia had as their express purpose the prevention of importation into those markets of radio and television apparatus made in the United States and other countries. Plaintiff, knowing of the restrictions against imports imposed by those Pools, nevertheless chose to permit its patents to be used in furtherance of the scheme and thereby obtained a substantial share of the Pool's income. It thereby became a co-conspirator and legally liable for all the acts of the Pools and its members performed in furtherance of their patent licensing plan to divide markets and prevent competition from imported sets. *Hazeltine Research, Inc. v. Zenith Radio Corporation*, 239 F.Supp. 51, 144 U.S.P.Q. 381, 402 (Ill. 1965).

ω

Although an arrangement under which patents are pooled is not per se illegal, "[i]f combining patent owners effectively dominate an industry, the power to fix and maintain royalties is tantamount to the power to fix prices Where domination exists, a pooling of competing process patents, or an exchange of licenses for the purpose of curtailing the manufacture and supply of an unpatented product, is beyond the privileges conferred by the patents and constitutes a violation of the Sherman Act. The lawful individual monopolies granted by the patent statutes cannot be unitedly exercised to restrain competition." *The Duplan Corporation v. Deering Milliken, Inc.*, 444 F.Supp. 648, 197 U.S.P.Q. 342, 375 (S.C. 1977).

Portable.

Merely making an old device portable without producing any new or unexpected result is not patentably significant. *In re Lindberg*, 194 F.2d 732, 93 U.S.P.Q. 23, 26 (C.C.P.A. 1952).

Position. *See also* **Orientation, Orientation during Operation, Ring, Substituents.**

The involved structural similarity was not concerned solely with homology; it was predicated on alkyl substitution in one or both of two specific places in the reference Compound B. There were, however, eleven places to make such substitution, the prior art Compound C being one such possible combination of two substituents. Neither the Examiner nor the Board pointed to facts demonstrating that it would have been obvious to one of ordinary skill in this art to make the substitution at those particular positions at which appellants placed the substituents so as to enhance the biological or pharmaceutical

---

[7] *See Lightwave Technologies Inc. v. Corning Glass Works*, 19 U.S.P.Q.2d 1838, 1841 (N.Y. 1991).

activity of the compound instead of diminishing it as in Compound C. *In re Wagner and Folkers*, 371 F.2d 877, 152 U.S.P.Q. 552, 559 (C.C.P.A. 1967).

ᵀᵀ

The failure of an application to disclose and the failure of claims to specify ring positions of contemplated substituents does not subject such claims to rejection based on insufficiency of disclosure or undue breadth when the claims are to mixtures of compounds and the ring positions are unimportant to the disclosed utility of such mixtures. *In re Steinhauer and Valenta*, 410 F.2d 411, 161 U.S.P.Q. 595, 599 (C.C.P.A. 1969).

Possession. *See also* Support.

The function of the description requirement is to ensure that the inventor had possession (as of the filing date of the application relied on) of the specific subject matter later claimed by him; how the specification accomplishes this is not material. It is not necessary that the application describe the claim limitations exactly, but only so clearly that persons of ordinary skill in the art will recognize from the disclosure that the appellants invented processes including those limitations. *In re Wertheim*, 541 F.2d 257, 191 U.S.P.Q. 90 (C.C.P.A. 1976).

ᵀᵀ

There is no presumptive correlation that two similar processes form substantially the same product where the processes differ by a materially limiting step. When prior art fails to disclose a method for making a claimed compound, at the time the invention was made, it cannot be legally concluded that the compound itself is in the possession of the public. *Ashland Oil, Inc. v. Delta Resins & Refractories, Inc.*, 776 F.2d 281, 227 U.S.P.Q. 657 (Fed. Cir. 1985).

ᵀᵀ

The test for determining compliance with the written description requirement of 35 U.S.C. §112 is whether the disclosure of the application, as originally filed, reasonably conveys to the artisan that the inventor had possession of the claimed subject matter, rather than the presence or absence of literal support in the specification for the claim language. *Ex parte Harvey*, 3 U.S.P.Q.2d 1626 (B.P.A.I. 1986).

Possibility. *See* Circumstances.

Inherency may not be established by probabilities or possibilities. The mere fact that a certain thing may result from a given set of circumstances is not sufficient. *Hansgirg v. Kemmer*, 102 F.2d 212, 40 U.S.P.Q. 665, 667 (C.C.P.A. 1939); *In re Oelrich and Divigard*, 666 F.2d 578, 212 U.S.P.Q. 323, 326 (C.C.P.A. 1981).

ᵀᵀ

Inherency may not be established by probabilities or possibilities. The mere fact that a certain thing may result from a given set of circumstances is not sufficient. Although an applicant may be required to prove that subject matter shown to be in prior art does not possess characteristics relied upon, where an Examiner has reason to believe that a functional limitation asserted to be critical for establishing novelty in the claimed subject matter may, in fact, be an inherent characteristic of the prior art, the Examiner must provide some evidence or scientific reasoning to establish the reasonableness of the Examiner's belief that the functional limitation is an inherent characteristic of the prior art before the applicant can be put through this burdensome task. *Ex parte Skinner,* 2 U.S.P.Q.2d 1788 (B.P.A.I. 1986).

Post-Employment Invention.

Contractual provisions requiring assignment of post-employment inventions are commonly referred to as "trailer" or "holdover" clauses. Holdover clauses in employment contracts are enforceable only if they constitute a reasonable and justifiable restriction on the right of employees to work in their profession for subsequent employers. Their legitimate purpose is to prevent an employee from appropriating to his own use or to the use of a subsequent employer inventions relating to and stemming from work done for a previous employer. Holdover clauses are simply recognition of the fact of business life that employees sometimes carry with them to new employers inventions or ideas so related to work done for a former employer that, in equity and good conscience, the fruits of that work should belong to the former employer. Holdover clauses must be limited to reasonable times and to subject matter that the employee worked on or had knowledge of during his employment. Unless expressly agreed otherwise, an employer has no right (under a holdover clause) to inventions made outside the scope of the employee's former activities, and made on and with a subsequent employer's time and funds. Regarding the validity of a contractual provision requiring the employee to disclose and assign all ideas and improvements for five years following termination of employment, the court articulated a three part test: (a) Is the restraint reasonable in the sense that it is no greater than necessary to protect the employer in some legitimate interest? (b) Is the restraint reasonable in the sense that it is not unduly harsh or oppressive on the employee? (c) Is the restraint reasonable in the sense that it is not injurious to the public? *Ingersoll-Rand Co. v. Ciavatta,* 8 U.S.P.Q.2d 1537, 542 A.2d 879, 110 N.J. 609 (N.J. 1988).

Post-Judgment Interest.

According to 28 U.S.C. §1961(a)(1988) interest shall be calculated from the date of the entry of the judgment, at a rate equal to the coupon issue yield equivalent (as determined by the Secretary of the Treasury) of the average accepted auction price for the last auction of fifty-two week United States Treasury bills settled immediately prior to the date of the judgment. *Goodwall Construction Co. v. Beers Construction Co.,* 991 F.2d 751, 26 U.S.P.Q.2d 1420, 1427 (Fed. Cir. 1993).

Post-Judgment Motion.

Under the Federal Rules, an untimely postjudgment motion "[can]not toll the running of the time to appeal." Therefore, the appellate court "lacks jurisdiction to review the subsequent order." Moreover, parties may not waive a defect in jurisdiction by consent. *Registration Control Systems Inc. v. Compusystems Inc.,* 922 F.2d 805, 17 U.S.P.Q.2d 1212, 1213 (Fed. Cir. 1990).

Potency.

There is a significant difference between potency and efficacy. Greater potency only means that a smaller pill can be used, whereas greater efficacy refers to clinical superiority. *United States of America v. Ciba-Geigy Corporation*, 508 F.Supp. 1157, 211 U.S.P.Q. 529, 541 (N.J. 1979).

Poverty. *See also* **Economics, Financial Inability.**

Poverty and personal hardship suffered by a patentee are legitimate factors to be considered when determining the reasonableness of a patentee's delay in bringing suit against an infringer. *Cover v. Hydramatic Packing Co. Inc.*, 34 U.S.P.Q.2d 1128, 1131 (Pa. 1994).

ω

Poverty, by itself, is never an excuse for laches purposes. *Hall v. Aqua Queen Manufacturing Inc.*, 93 F.3d 1548, 39 U.S.P.Q.2d 1925, 1929 (Fed. Cir. 1996).

PPAA (Process Patent Amendments Act).

The PPAA made it an act of patent infringement to import, sell, or use in the United States, without authorization, a product made by a process patented in the United States. 35 U.S.C.A. §271(g). A provision concerning offers to sell was added to 35 U.S.C. §271(g) by the Uruguay Round Agreements Act. *Bio-Technology General Corp. v. Genentech Inc.*, 80 F.3d 1553, 38 U.S.P.Q.2d 1321, 1324 n.4 (Fed. Cir. 1996).

ω

Act does not apply when the product made by the patented process is "materially changed by subsequent processes" before it is imported. In the chemical context, a "material" change in a compound is a significant change in the compound's structure and properties. However, when an intermediate (that is the product of a patented process) undergoes significant changes in the course of conversion into an end product, the end product will be deemed to be made by the patented process if (and only if) it would not be commercially feasible to make the end product other than by using the patented process. *Eli Lilly and Company v. American Cyanamid Company*, 81 F.3d 1568, 38 U.S.P.Q.2d 1705, 1709 (Fed. Cir. 1996).

Praise. *See* **Secondary Considerations.**

Praiseworthiness. *See* **Secondary Considerations.**

Preamble. *See also* **Jepson.**

The preamble of a claim (or count) is not a limitation where the claim is drawn to a structure and the portion of the claim following the preamble is a self-contained description of the structure not depending for completeness upon the introductory clause; or where the claim is drawn to a product and the introductory clause merely recites a property inherent in the old composition defined by the remaining part of the claim. In those cases, the claim apart from the introductory clause completely defines the subject matter, and the preamble merely states a purpose or intended use of that subject matter. On the other hand, in those cases where the preamble to a claim is expressly or by necessary implication given the effect of a limitation, the introductory phrase is deemed essential to point out the invention defined by the claim. In the latter class of cases, the preamble is considered necessary to give life, meaning, and vitality to the claims. Usually, in those cases, there inheres in the article specified in the preamble a problem that transcends that before prior artisans and the solution of which is not conceived by or known to them. The nature of the problem characterizes the elements comprising the article, and recited in the body of the claim following the introductory clause, so as to distinguish the claim over the prior art. *Kropa v. Robie and Mahlman*, 187 F.2d 150, 88 U.S.P.Q. 478 (C.C.P.A. 1951).

ᴡ

A limitation that is only in the preamble of a claim cannot be relied upon to distinguish the claim patentably over applied art. When the portion of the claim following the preamble is a self-contained description of structure not depending for completeness upon the introductory clause, the introductory clause is not regarded as a patentable limitation. *In re Harmon*, 222 F.2d 743, 106 U.S.P.Q. 101, 103 (C.C.P.A. 1955).

ᴡ

The introductory words: "A composition for setting hair", give life and meaning to the claims. An examination of the patent specification, including the objects of the invention, the discussion of the prior art, and the examples set forth, reveals that it is directed solely to compositions for setting hair. *In re Walles, Tousignant, and Houtman*, 366 F.2d 786, 151 U.S.P.Q. 185, 190 (C.C.P.A. 1966).

ᴡ

The introductory claim language "stable color developer concentrate" of a composition claim was held to be more than a mere statement of purpose; it was regarded as essential to point out the invention defined by the claims with the requisite particularity. *In re Bulloch and Kim*, 604 F.2d 1362, 203 U.S.P.Q. 171, 174 (C.C.P.A. 1979).

ᴡ

The terms in the preamble to a claim are deemed limitations in the claims only where necessary to give meaning to the claim and properly define the invention. *Slimmery International Inc. v. Stauffer-Meiji Inc.*, 6 U.S.P.Q.2d 1671 (Mo. 1987).

ᴡ

A claim preamble cannot be disregarded simply because it is directed to an intended field of use. A preamble that must necessarily be relied upon to give life and meaning to the remainder of the claim limitations is, itself, a proper claim limitation. The fact that a preamble is necessary to provide antecedent basis for subsequent language in the claim is significant in determining that the preamble is a claim limitation. *Stranco Inc. v. Atlantes Chemical Systems Inc.*, 15 U.S.P.Q.2d 1704, 1713 (Tex. 1990).

ᴡ

When patent claims comprise a preamble, the claimed invention consists of the preamble in combination with the improvement. Although a preamble is impliedly admitted to be prior art, where an inventor is improving on his own work product, his foundational work product should not be treated as prior art solely because he admits knowledge of his own work. *Dyson v. Amway Corp.,* 19 U.S.P.Q.2d 1557, 1560 (Mich. 1991).

ᚹ

Although no "litmus test" exists as to what effect should be accorded to words contained in a preamble, review of a patent in its entirety should be made to determine whether the inventors intended such language to represent an additional structural limitation or mere introductory language. *In re Paulsen*, 30 F.3d 1475, 31 U.S.P.Q.2d 1671, 1673 (Fed. Cir. 1994).

ᚹ

A claim preamble has the import that the claim as a whole suggests for it. When the claim drafter chooses to use both the preamble and the body to define the subject matter of the claimed invention, the invention so defined, and not some other, is the one the patent protects. A claim preamble "may entirely fail to supply a necessary element in a combination, yet it may so affect the enumerated elements as to give life and meaning and vitality to them, as they appear in the combination." *Bell Communications Research Inc. v. Vitalink Communications Corp.*, 55 F.3d 615, 34 U.S.P.Q.2d 1816, 1820 (Fed. Cir. 1995).

ᚹ

When the body of a claim (having a preamble) references and/or further limits an element set forth in the preamble, the preamble imposes a limitation on the scope of the claim. *Derman v. PC Guardian*, 37 U.S.P.Q.2d 1733, 1734 (Fed. Cir. 1995—*unpublished, not citable as precedent*).

ᚹ

Where a patentee uses a claim preamble to recite structural limitations of his claimed invention, the PTO and courts give effect to that usage. Conversely, where a patentee defines a structurally complete invention in the claim body and uses the preamble only to state a purpose or intended use for the invention, the preamble is not a claim limitation. *Rowe v. Dror*, 112 F.3d 473, 42 U.S.P.Q.2d 1550, 1553 (Fed. Cir. 1997).

Precedent.[8] *See also Stare Decisis.*

Undue liberties should not be taken with a court decision, which should be construed in accord with the precise issue before the court. A fertile source of error in patent law is the misapplication of a sound legal principle (established in one case) to another case in which the facts are essentially different and the principle has no application whatsoever. *In re Ruscetta and Jenny,* 255 F.2d 687, 118 U.S.P.Q. 101, 103 (C.C.P.A. 1958).

ᚹ

---

[8]*See* Tramposch, The Dilemma of Conflicting Precedent: Three Options in the Federal Circuit, 17 AIPLA Q.J. 323 (No. 4, 1989).

A court need not overrule a prior case in order to clarify that case by stating a requirement that was met but not discussed. A court may refine holdings in its precedent that were stated or have been interpreted too broadly. *Woodard v. Sage Products, Inc.*, 818 F.2d 841, 2 U.S.P.Q.2d 1649, 1656 (Fed. Cir. 1987).

Precision. *See also* Accuracy, Claim Language, Definiteness.

If patent claims, read in the light of the specification, reasonably apprise one skilled in the art of the utilization and scope of the invention, and if the language is as precise as the subject matter permits, the patent should not be deemed invalid for indefiniteness. A patentee is required to draft the patent specification and claims as precisely as the subject matter permits, and failure to do so may result in invalidation. Absolute specificity and precision, however, are not required. The claims need only go so far as to apprise one reasonably skilled in the area of the true teaching of the invention. Mere breadth of a claim does not in itself cause invalidation. As long as the meaning of the claims is clear in light of the specification and accompanying drawings, breadth merely enhances the risk that the claim will be found invalid. *Andco Environmental Processes, Inc. v. Niagara Environmental Associates, Inc.*, 220 U.S.P.Q. 468 (N.Y. 1983).

ϖ

An amendment is best characterized as a clarification, not an avoidance of the prior art.

[W]hen claim changes or arguments are made in order to more particularly point out the applicant's invention, the purpose is to impart precision, not to overcome prior art. . . . Such prosecution is not presumed to raise and estoppel, but is reviewed on its facts, with the guidance of precedent.

Pall Corp. v. Micron Separations, Inc., 66 F.3d 1211, 1220 , 36 U.S.P.Q.2d 1050 (Fed. Cir. 1995); *James River Corp. of Virginia v. Hallmark Cards Inc.*, 43 U.S.P.Q.2d 1422, 1430, 1431 (Wis. 1997).

Preclusion. *See also* Claim Preclusion, Issue Preclusion.

A claim need not preclude inclusion of materials which would not apparently be operative in a claimed process. Having stated the objective (foamed product) together with the process steps, use of materials which might prevent achievement of the objective (by rendering the process inoperative) can hardly be said to be within the scope of the claims. *In re Geerdes*, 491 F.2d 1260, 180 U.S.P.Q. 789, 793 (C.C.P.A. 1974).

ϖ

It is not important that Canada does not afford parties the same discovery rights as the Federal Rules of Civil Procedure do. Preclusion survives substantial differences in the rules of procedure (provided the differences are not so great that the original judgment was obtained without due process of law, as we understand that phrase). Even within the United States, some states are more stingy with discovery than are federal courts, yet their judgments are honored. *Vas-Cath Inc. v. Mahurkar,* 745 F. Supp. 517, 17 U.S.P.Q.2d 1353, 1360 (Ill. 1990).

ϖ

Congress' failure to adopt any proposals or include specific language in 19 U.S.C. §1337 clearly manifesting an intention to have ITC findings non-binding is extremely indicative of its intent *not* to disturb the common-law presumption of preclusion. *In re Convertible Rowing Exerciser Patent Litigation*, 814 F.Supp. 1197, 26 U.S.P.Q.2d 1677, 1683 (Del. 1993).

ᴡ

Res judicata, or *claim* preclusion, deals with the effect of a prior judgment on the identical claim or cause of action between the same parties. Collateral estoppel, or *issue* preclusion, deals with the relitigation of issues previously decided, when such issues arise in a subsequent litigation on a claim not barred by res judicata. 1B James W. Moore et al., Moore's Federal Practice §0.401 (2d ed. 1992). *Pfaff v. Wells Electronics Inc.*, 5 F.3d 514, 28 U.S.P.Q.2d 1119, 1122 (Fed. Cir. 1993).

Precursor. *See* **Intermediate.**

Predictability. *See also* **Bioisosterism, Empirical, Kohler-Milstein Technique.**

The law has other tests of invention than subtle conjecture of what might have been seen and yet was not. It regards a change as evidence of novelty, and the acceptance and utility of change as further evidence, even as demonstration. Nor does it detract from its merit that it is the result of experiment and not the instant and perfect product of inventive power. A patentee may be baldly empirical, seeing nothing beyond his experiments and the result; yet, if he has added a new and valuable article to the world's utilities, he is entitled to the rank and protection of an inventor. It is certainly not necessary that he understand or be able to state the scientific principles underlying his invention, and it is immaterial whether he can stand a successful examination as to the speculative ideas involved. *Diamond Rubber Co. v. Consolidated Rubber Tire Co.*, 220 U.S. 428, 435 (1911).

ᴡ

Although the exact color or shade of the claimed isomer was unpredictable, it was not unexpected; it was a shade somewhere in the family of reddish tints encompassed by a reference disclosure. Absolute predictability is not the law. *In re Crounse*, 363 F.2d 881, 150 U.S.P.Q. 554, 557 (C.C.P.A. 1966).

ᴡ

Unpredictability is particularly notorious with regard to pharmaceutical compounds. *In re Kamal and Rogier*, 398 F.2d 867, 158 U.S.P.Q. 320, 323 (C.C.P.A. 1968).

ᴡ

An inventor should be allowed to dominate future patentable inventions of others where those inventions are based in some way on his teachings. Such improvements, while non-obvious from his teachings, are still within his contribution, since the improvement is made possible by his work. It is equally apparent, however, that he must not be permitted to achieve this dominance by claims that are insufficiently supported and hence not in compliance with the first paragraph of 35 U.S.C. §112. That paragraph requires that the scope of the claims must bear a reasonable correlation to the scope of enablement provided by the specification to persons of ordinary skill in the art. In cases involving predictable factors, such as mechanical or electrical elements, a single embodiment provides broad enablement in the sense that, once imagined, other embodiments can be made without difficulty and their performance characteristics predicted by resort to known scientific laws. In cases involving unpredictable factors, such as most chemical reactions and physiological activity, the scope of enablement obviously varies inversely with the degree of unpredictability of the factors involved. *In re Fisher,* 427 F.2d 833, 166 U.S.P.Q. 18 (C.C.P.A. 1970).

ω

In an area of technology shown to be highly unpredictable in process values, the discovery of optimum values not in any way suggested by the prior art is more likely to be unobvious than obvious within the meaning of 35 U.S.C. §103. *In re Sebek*, 465 F.2d 904, 175 U.S.P.Q. 93, 95 (C.C.P.A. 1972).

ω

The unpredictability noted in the decision of the Board was in the admittedly chemical fact that the "properties of 'polymerizable materials' can vary over a wide range," but no reasons were given to appellant by the Patent Office for the alleged failure—or at least uncertainty—of the class of "polymerizable materials" to work in the claimed process to controvert the statement in appellant's application that his invention, in its broader aspects, is applicable to other polymers. Even in cases involving the unpredictable world of chemistry, such reasons are required. *In re Bowen,* 492 F.2d 859, 181 U.S.P.Q. 48, 50, 51 (C.C.P.A. 1974).

ω

The evidence as a whole, including the inoperative as well as the operative examples, negates the PTO position that persons of ordinary skill in this art, given its unpredictability, must engage in undue experimentation to determine which complexes work. *In re Angstadt and Griffin*, 537 F.2d 498, 190 U.S.P.Q. 214, 219 (C.C.P.A. 1976).

ω

One who claims a compound, per se, which is structurally similar to a prior art compound must rebut the presumed expectation that the structurally similar compounds have similar properties. *In re Wilder*, 563 F.2d 457, 195 U.S.P.Q. 426, 429 (C.C.P.A. 1977).

ω

In determining what constitutes undue experimentation, many factors are taken into account, including the guidance provided by the specification for selecting those embodiments of the invention which achieve the disclosed utility. Such guidance is essential where the invention involves an unpredictable art, such as one which involves physiological activity. *In re Sichert,* 566 F.2d 1154, 196 U.S.P.Q. 209, 215 (C.C.P.A. 1977).

ω

Considering the entire record, including the fact that not a single reference relied upon by the PTO suggests that any compound with a closely-related structure exhibits the combined properties of claimed compounds, it was totally unexpected that the claimed compounds would have exhibited such a combination of properties. *In re May and Eddy*, 574 F.2d 1082, 197 U.S.P.Q. 601, 609 (C.C.P.A. 1978); *but compare In re de Montmollin and Riat*, 344 F.2d 976, 145 U.S.P.Q. 416, 417 (C.C.P.A. 1965), and *In re Murch*, 464 F.2d 1051, 175 U.S.P.Q. 89, 90 (C.C.P.A. 1972).

ळ

The written description of a class of compounds must provide a measure of predictability for the utility described for that class. *In re Herschler*, 591 F.2d 693, 200 U.S.P.Q. 711, 717 (C.C.P.A. 1979).

ळ

While recognizing that obviousness does not require complete predictability, the prior art itself must provide some foreseeability or predictability that the compound (found in strawberries) involved in a claimed flavor-imparting process or flavor-modifying composition is a significant strawberry flavor ingredient. *In re Kratz and Strasburger*, 592 F.2d 1169, 201 U.S.P.Q. 71, 76 (C.C.P.A. 1979).

ळ

Although there is a vast amount of knowledge about general relationships in the chemical arts, chemistry is still largely empirical, and there is often great difficulty in predicting precisely how a given compound will behave. *In re Carleton*, 599 F.2d 1021, 202 U.S.P.Q. 165, 170 (C.C.P.A. 1979).

ळ

The district court erred (in its consideration of the prior art) in not taking into account the import of the markedly different behavior of PTFE from that of conventional thermoplastic polymers, and in thus disregarding the unpredictability and unique nature of the unsintered PTFE to which the claimed inventions relate. *W.L. Gore & Associates, Inc. v. Garlock, Inc.*, 721 F.2d 1540, 220 U.S.P.Q. 303, 311 (Fed. Cir. 1983).

ळ

The application stood in condition for allowance and ready for the issuance of a patent grant except for the presence in the specification disclosure of certain asserted utilities that the Examiner believed to be too speculative—i.e., not believable on their face to those of ordinary skill in the art in view of the contemporary knowledge of the art. While it may be clear that workers in this art had shown that some cancers can be treated successfully in some patients, the effective treatment of various forms of malignant tumors remains a highly unpredictable art. Under these circumstances, the Examiner does not need to provide reasons why this speculative assertion should not be believed. The mere fact that the art of cancer chemotherapy is highly unpredictable places the burden on applicants to provide a basis for believing the speculative statements that they chose to place in the specification in the form of a positive assertion. *In re Application of Hozumi*, 226 U.S.P.Q. 353 (Comm'r Patents & Trademarks 1985).

ळ

Although the technique underlying hybridoma technology is well recognized, the results obtained by its use are clearly unpredictable. Hybridoma technology is an empirical art in which the routineer is unable to foresee what particular antibodies will be produced and which specific surface antigens will be recognized by them. Only by actually carrying out the requisite steps can the nature of the monoclonal antibodies be determined and ascertained; no "expected" results can thus be said to be present. Hence, it may be "obvious to try" the Kohler-Milstein technique as applied to malignant renal cells, but such is not the standard under which obviousness under 35 U.S.C. §103 must be established. *Ex parte Old,* 229 U.S.P.Q. 196 (B.P.A.I. 1985).

ω

The ultimate question is whether the specification contains a sufficiently explicit disclosure to enable one having ordinary skill in the relevant field to practice the invention claimed therein without the exercise of undue experimentation. The determination of what constitutes undue experimentation in a given case requires the application of a standard of reasonableness, having due regard for the nature of the invention and the state of the art. The test is not merely quantitative, since a considerable amount of experimentation is permissible if it is merely routine or if the specification in question provides a reasonable amount of guidance with respect to the direction in which the experimentation should proceed to enable the determination of how to practice a desired embodiment of the invention claimed. The factors to be considered have been summarized as the quantity of experimentation necessary, the amount of direction or guidance presented, the presence or absence of working examples, the nature of the invention, the state of the prior art, the relative skill of those in that art, the predictability or unpredictability of the art, and the breadth of the claims. *Ex parte Forman,* 230 U.S.P.Q. 546 (B.P.A.I. 1986).

ω

Only a reasonable expectation of success, not absolute predictability, is necessary for a conclusion of obviousness. *Ex parte Beck,* 9 U.S.P.Q.2d 2000 (B.P.A.I. 1987).

ω

Most technological advance is the fruit of methodical, persistent investigation, as is recognized in 35 U.S.C. §103 ("Patentability shall not be negatived by the manner in which the invention was made"). The consistent criterion for determination of obviousness is whether the prior art would have suggested to one of ordinary skill in the art that this process should be carried out and would have reasonable likelihood of success, viewed in the light of the prior art. Both the suggestion and the expectation of success must be found in the prior art, not in the applicant's disclosure. *In re Dow Chemical Co.,* 837 F.2d 469, 5 U.S.P.Q.2d 1529 (Fed. Cir. 1988).

ω

The mere need for experimentation to determine parameters required to make a device work is an application of the often rejected obvious-to-try standard and falls short of the statutory "obviousness" of 35 U.S.C. §103. Inability of an expert to predict the results obtainable with a claimed product suggests non-obviousness, not routine experimentation. *Uniroyal Inc. v. Rudkin-Wiley Corp.,* 837 F.2d 1044, 5 U.S.P.Q.2d 1434 (Fed. Cir. 1988).

ω

Obviousness does not require absolute predictability of success. Indeed, for many inventions that seem quite obvious, there is no absolute predictability of success until the invention is reduced to practice. There is always at least a possibility of unexpected results, that would then provide an objective basis for showing that the invention, although apparently obvious, was in law non-obvious. For obviousness under 35 U.S.C. §103, all that is required is a reasonable expectation of success. *In re O'Farrell,* 853 F.2d 894, 7 U.S.P.Q.2d 1673, 1681 (Fed. Cir. 1988).

ᴕ

The scope of patent claims must be narrowly construed in fields of technology where the outcome of substitutions are unpredictable. What constitutes equivalence must be determined against the context of the patent, prior art, and the particular circumstances of the case. Consideration must be given to the purpose for which an ingredient is used in the patent, the qualities it has when combined with other ingredients, and the function that it is intended to perform. *Genentech Inc. v. The Wellcome Foundation Ltd.,* 14 U.S.P.Q.2d 1363, 1371 (Del. 1990).

ᴕ

Unpredictability of a particular art area may, by itself, provide a reasonable doubt as to the accuracy of a broad statement made in support of the enablement of a claim. *Ex parte Singh,* 17 U.S.P.Q.2d 1714, 1715 (B.P.A.I. 1990).

Predictable. *See* **Electrical, Mechanical.**

Preemption. *See also* **Conflict Preemption, Field Preemption.**

Congress can preempt portions of a field of law without preempting the field of law in its entirety, thereby leaving a state free to act when, in so doing, the state does not impede the objectives of Congress. Preemption thus does not preclude *all* relief, but merely limits relief available to the extent that Congress intended to preclude the application of state law. *Jacobs Wind Electric Co. Inc. v. Florida Department of Transportation,* 626 So.2d 1333, 29 U.S.P.Q.2d 1763, 1764 (Fla. S.Ct. 1993).

ᴕ

With regard to preemption of a state statute, the Supreme Court has set forth three grounds: (1) Explicit pre-emption, whereby Congress explicitly provided for pre-emption of state law in the federal statute; (2) Field pre-emption, wherein "the field of federal regulation is so pervasive as to make reasonable the inference that Congress left no room for the States to supplement it"; and (3) Conflict pre-emption, "where 'compliance with both federal and state regulations is a physical impossibility,'...or where state law 'stands as an obstacle to the accomplishment and execution of the full purposes and objectives of Congress.'" *Cover v. Hydramatic Packing Co.,* 83 F.3d 1390, 38 U.S.P.Q.2d 1783, 1786 (Fed. Cir. 1996).

ᴕ

Under the CAFC's preemption jurisprudence, the presumption against preemption has greater force because of the states' long-standing governance of such affairs. That reinforced presumption instructs against field preemption. *Hunter Douglas Inc. v. Harmonic Design Inc.,* 47 U.S.P.Q.2d 1769, 1770, 1780, 1781 (Fed. Cir. 1998).

Preferred Embodiment.

To provide effective incentives, claims must adequately protect inventors. To demand that the first to disclose shall limit his claims to what he has found will work or to materials that meet the guidelines specified for "preferred" materials in a process would not serve the constitutional purpose of promoting progress in the useful arts. *In re Goffe*, 542 F.2d 564, 191 U.S.P.Q. 429, 431 (C.C.P.A. 1976).

Preissuance Activity. *See* Contributory Infringement.

Prejudice.

There is a difference between prejudice that results from delay and prejudice that is due to reliance upon delay. Conclusory statements that there are missing witnesses, that witnesses' memories have lessened, and that there is missing documentary evidence are not sufficient to establish prejudice. *Meyers v. Asics Corp.*, 974 F.2d 1304, 24 U.S.P.Q.2d 1036, 1038, 1039 (Fed. Cir. 1992).

Prejudgment Interest. *See also* Interest.

Ordinarily, prejudgment interest should be awarded on both the lost profits and the royalty portions of the damages awarded for patent infringement. (The court upheld a district court's award of 6 percent in one case and at the prime rate in another.) *The Gyromat Corporation v. Champion Spark Plug Company*, 222 U.S.P.Q. 4, 9 (Fed. Cir. 1984).

ᛩ

Increased damages are usually based on a finding that the infringer's conduct was willful and in flagrant disregard of the patentee's rights. In this case, the defendant was on notice of the plaintiff's patent rights and had an affirmative duty to exercise due care to determine whether it was infringing. The defendant may not avoid a holding of willful infringement because it failed to show that it obtained a competent opinion from counsel and that it had exercised reasonable and good-faith adherence to the analysis and advice contained therein. Accordingly, the defendant is liable to the plaintiff for an amount equal to three times the amount of damages actually found or assessed. Section 285 of 35 U.S.C. makes provision for the award of attorney's fees to the prevailing party in exceptional cases. In order to support an award of attorney's fees in a patent case, there must be a showing of conduct that is unfair, in bad faith, inequitable, or unconscionable. In view of defendant's willful infringement, this case involves those elements set out above and is an exceptional case, thereby entitling the plaintiff to an award of its attorney's fees. The plaintiff is also entitled to prejudgment interest based upon the damages found or assessed in the second phase of this trial. *Great Northern Corp. v. Davis Core & Pad Co.*, 226 U.S.P.Q. 540 (Ga. 1985).

ᛩ

Prejudgment interest is ordinarily awarded absent some justification for withholding such an award. *Fromson v. Western Litho Plate & Supply Co.*, 853 F.2d 1568, 7 U.S.P.Q.2d 1606 (Fed. Cir. 1988).

ᛩ

Prejudgment interest is the rule governing both patent infringement and trade secret damage awards. *Richardson v. Suzuki Motor Co., Ltd.*, 868 F.2d 1226, 9 U.S.P.Q.2d 1913 (Fed. Cir. 1989).

ᛟ

The district court's inherent equitable power and informed discretion remain available in determining the level of exceptionality arising out of an offender's particular conduct, and in then determining, in light of that conduct, the compensatory question of the award under 35 U.S.C. §285, including the amount of attorney's fees and the rate of prejudgment interest, if any, on the award. Since the defendant's willful infringement made it necessary for the plaintiffs to bring this suit, an award of prejudgment interest is proper to fully compensate the plaintiffs for the expenses they incurred during litigation. *Water Technologies Corp. v. Calco Ltd.*, 714 F. Supp. 899, 11 U.S.P.Q.2d 1410, 1415 (Ill. 1989).

ᛟ

Prejudgment interest should be awarded as a general rule in patent cases. Such interest should be computed "from the time that the royalty payment would have been received" because prejudgment interest is awarded to compensate for the delay in payment of damages, and not to punish the infringer. Annual compounding, rather than simple interest, is proper. The plaintiff is entitled to interest on the running royalty at 12 percent compounded annually "from the time that the royalty payments would have been received." In addition, the plaintiff shall receive interest on the up-front payment at a 12 percent rate compounded annually from the date on which the complaint was filed. *Johns-Manville Corp. v. Guardian Industries Inc.*, 718 F. Supp. 1310, 13 U.S.P.Q.2d 1684, 1686, 1689 (Mich. 1989).

ᛟ

Prejudgment interest should run from the date of liquidation of damages to the date of judgment. Prejudgment interest was granted at the 52 week T-bill rate compounded annually. *Fromson v. Western Litho Plate Supply Co.*, 13 U.S.P.Q.2d 1856, 1862, 1863 (Mo. 1989).

ᛟ

Prejudgment interest should be awarded under 35 U.S.C. §284 absent some justification for withholding such award. The purpose of the award is to afford patent owners complete compensation for the delay experienced in payment of damages by the infringer. Prejudgment interest applies both to lost profits and to a reasonable royalty. Calculating prejudgment interest on the average prime rate has been approved by the Federal Circuit. Interest has been denied on increased damages. *ALM Surgical Equipment Inc. v. Kirschner Medical Corp.*, 15 U.S.P.Q.2d 1241, 1256, 1257 (S.C. 1990).

ᛟ

Prejudgment interest should be awarded from the date of infringement to the date of judgment. *Stranco Inc. v. Atlantes Chemical Systems Inc.*, 15 U.S.P.Q.2d 1704, 1715 (Tex. 1990).

ᛟ

Setting the rate of prejudgment interest and whether it should be simple or compounded are matters well within the discretion of the court. The key to exercising this discretion is to
ensure that the awardee is placed in as good a position as he would have been had the events giving rise to the award not occurred. *Beckman Instruments Inc. v. LKB Produkter AB,* 17 U.S.P.Q.2d 1190, 1199 (Md. 1990).

ω

Prejudgment interest is designed to compensate for the delay a patentee experiences in obtaining money he would have received sooner if no infringement occurred, while damages are trebled as punishment. Prejudgment interest can only be applied to the primary or actual damage portion and not to the punitive or enhanced portion of a damage award. *Beatrice Foods Co. v. New England Printing & Lithographing Co.,* 923 F.2d 1576, 17 U.S.P.Q.2d 1553, 1556 (Fed. Cir. 1991).

ω

The rate of prejudgment interest and whether it should be compounded or not are matters left largely to the discretion of the trial court. Prejudgment interest is awarded to compensate the patentee for its foregone use of the money between the time of the infringement and the date of the judgment. In order that the patentee may be compensated adequately, either the prime rate or the rate that the patentee paid on its corporate borrowings during the infringing period is used. *Tenax Corp. v. Tensar Corp.,* 19 U.S.P.Q.2d 1881, 1895 (Md. 1991).

ω

As an interest rate higher than the treasury bill rate has not been demonstrated to be necessary to compensate the patentee for economic loss caused by infringement, the patentee is entitled to prejudgment interest at that rate. *Bic Leisure Products Inc. v. Windsurfing International Inc.,* 761 F. Supp. 1032, 19 U.S.P.Q.2d 1922, 1929 (N.Y. 1991).

ω

Prejudgment interest should be analyzed as if the patentee had lent funds to the infringer during the pendency of the litigation. *Alpex Computer Corp. v. Nintendo Co. Ltd.,* 86 Civ. 1749, 34 U.S.P.Q.2d 1167, 1208 (N.Y. 1994).

ω

The right rate of prejudgment interest in principle is the rate the infringer paid for money during the years in question. In default of this figure, courts regularly use the prime rate. The function of prejudgment interest is to give patent holders damages adequate to compensate for the infringement— "to ensure that the patent owner is placed in as good a position as he would have been had the infringer entered into a reasonable royalty agreement." *Grain Processing Corp. v. American Maize-Products Co.,* 893 F.Supp. 1386, 37 U.S.P.Q.2d 1299, 1307 (Ind. 1995).

ω

In setting the rate for prejudgment interest, courts have used: the prime rate, the prime rate plus a percentage, the U.S. Treasury bill rate, the state statutory rate, corporate bond rates, a set consumer credit rate, a set percentage rate, the rate the patentee actually paid for borrowed funds and others. *Joy Technologies Inc. v. Flakt Inc.*, 42 U.S.P.Q.2d 1042 (Del. 1996).

Prejudice. *See also* **Economic Prejudice, Evidentiary Prejudice.**

Preliminary Injunction. *See also* **Injunctive Relief, Market Share, TRO.**

Long-continued public acquiescence in the monopoly created by a patent claim furnishes a valid basis of reinforcement for the statutory presumption of the patent's validity for purposes of a preliminary injunction. *Eli Lilly & Co., Inc. v. Generix Drug Sales, Inc.*, 460 F.2d 1096, 174 U.S.P.Q. 65, 69 (5th Cir. 1972).

ᠶ

An alleged infringer's ability to compensate need not end a court's inquiry regarding a preliminary injunction. To hold otherwise would encourage infringement by the rich, to cause frequent devastation of a less affluent patentee's business, and to suggest the ready grant of injunctions against the less affluent among alleged infringers. That result would be unsupported by statute and manifestly inequitable. *Roper Corp. v. Litton Systems, Inc.*, 757 F.2d 1266, 225 U.S.P.Q. 345 (Fed. Cir. 1985).

ᠶ

A preliminary injunction is a remedy against future infringement. *Atlas Powder Co. v. Ireco Chemicals*, 773 F.2d 1230, 227 U. S. P. Q. 289 (Fed . Cir. 1985).

ᠶ

A delay of sixteen months in bringing suit is fatal to a contention or irreparable harm. *Rexnord, Inc. v. The Laitram Corporation*, 229 U.S.P.Q. 370, 376 (Wis. 1986).

ᠶ

An applicant for a preliminary injunction against patent infringement must show:

(1) a reasonable probability of eventual success in the litigation, and
(2) that the movant will be irreparably injured pendente lite if relief is not granted. Moreover, while the burden rests upon the moving party to make these two requisite showings, the district court should take into account (when they are relevant):
(3) the possibility of harm to other interested persons from the grant or denial of the injunction; and
(4) the public interest.

The movant for preliminary injunction must show not only a reasonable likelihood of success on the merits, but also the lack of adequate remedy at law or other irreparable harm. In matters involving patent rights, irreparable harm has been presumed when a clear showing has been made of patent validity and infringement. This presumption derives in part from the finite term of the patent grant, for patent expiration is not suspended during litigation, and the passage of time can work irremediable harm. The opportunity to practice an invention during the notoriously lengthy course of patent litigation may itself tempt infringers. *H. Robertson Co. v. United Steel Deck, Inc.*, 820 F.2d 384, 2 U.S.P.Q.2d 1926 (Fed. Cir. 1987).

ᠶ

To obtain a preliminary injunction in a patent infringement action pursuant to 35 U.S.C. §283, a party must establish a right thereto in light of four factors: (a) reasonable likelihood of success on the merits; (b) irreparable harm; (c) a balance of hardships tipping in its favor; and (d) that the issuance of the injunction is in the public interest. *T. J. Smith v. Consolidated Medical Equipment, Inc.*, 821 F.2d 646, 3 U.S.P.Q.2d 1316 (Fed. Cir. 1987).

ᖡ

Generally, appellate review of a motion to dissolve a preliminary injunction is limited to the propriety of the denial of the motion and does not extend to the propriety of the grant of the underlying injunction. *Sierra On Line, Inc. v. Phoenix Software, Inc.*, 739 F.2d 1415, 1418 n.4 (9th Cir. 1984); *Township of Franklin Sewerage Authority v. Middlesex County Utilities Authority*, 787 F.2d 117, 120-121 (3d Cir.), *cert. denied*, 479 U.S. 828 (1986); *Illinois v. Peters*, 871 F.2d 1336, 1339 (7th Cir. 1989).

ᖡ

Rule 52(a) requires that the court, in denying a preliminary injunction, shall "set forth the findings of fact and conclusions of law which constitute the grounds of its action." *See Mayo v. Lakeland Highlands Canning Co.*, 309 U.S. 310, 316-17 (1940); *Pretty Punch Shoppettes, Inc. v. Hauk*, 844 F.2d 782, 784, 6 U.S.P.Q.2d 1563, 1565 (Fed. Cir. 1988)

ᖡ

To obtain a preliminary injunction, the plaintiff must establish (a) irreparable harm, and (b) either likelihood of success on the merits or sufficiently serious questions going to the merits to make them fair ground for litigation and a balance of hardships tipping decidedly in its favor. In copyright cases where validity of the copyright and infringement have been established, irreparable injury is presumed. Similarly, in patent cases, irreparable harm is presumed when the moving party makes a strong showing of validity of the patent and infringement. When the plaintiff was aware of possible infringement by the defendant two years before the motion and when the suit is more than a year old, the plaintiff's ability to withstand the alleged infringement for this amount of time undercuts the plaintiff's request for speedy relief. The plaintiff's delay is not due to a resolution attempt, fraud by the defendant, or inability to determine infringement. In contrast, it was only when the defendant exercised certain rights during the course of the action that the plaintiff saw the need for a preliminary injunction. The plaintiff's dissatisfaction with the progress of the case certainly is not the type of reason contemplated as an excusable delay. *Russell William Ltd. v. ABC Display & Supply Inc.*, 11 U.S.P.Q.2d 1812, 1813 (N.Y. 1989).

ᖡ

The standard for preliminary injunctive relief in patent cases differs somewhat from the standard applied in other areas of the law. According to the federal circuit, the applicable inquiries are as follows:

  (a) whether the plaintiff will have an adequate remedy at law or will be irreparably harmed if the injunction does not issue;
  (b) whether the threatened injury to the plaintiff outweighs the threatened harm the injunction may inflict on the defendant;

(c) whether the plaintiff has at least a reasonable likelihood of success on the merits; and

(d) whether the granting of a preliminary injunction will disserve the public interest.

An injunction is appropriate where the patentee "clearly shows that his patent is valid and is infringed..." Where validity and infringement have been clearly established, immediate irreparable harm is presumed. The presumption of irreparable injury is not dispositive of whether an injunction should issue. *J. Star Industries Inc. v. Oakley,* 720 F. Supp. 1291, 13 U.S.P.Q.2d 1993, 1995 (Miss. 1989).

ᛟ

Because the burden on the issue of patent validity is ultimately on the party challenging the patent to demonstrate by clear and convincing evidence that the patent is invalid, the burden on the patentee at the preliminary injunction stage is to demonstrate a reasonable likelihood that the putative infringer is not likely to prove, by clear and convincing evidence, that the patent is invalid. *Moore Business Forms, Inc. v. Wallace Computer Services, Inc.,* 14 U.S.P.Q.2d 1849, 1861 (Ind. 1989).

ᛟ

The granting of a preliminary injunction is an extraordinary remedy. The court must examine carefully extraordinary relief that precludes the filing of civil lawsuits for an indeterminate period of time. A preliminary injunction must be supported by sufficient factual evidence, and a sufficient basis must be articulated by the court in the order granting the injunction. *Atari Games Corp. v. Nintendo of America Inc.,* 897 F.2d 1572, 14 U.S.P.Q.2d 1034, 1038 (Fed. Cir. 1990).

ᛟ

A grant of a preliminary injunction does not require proof of infringement beyond all question. The corollary proposition is that a denial of a preliminary injunction does not require that non-infringement be clear beyond all question. A preliminary injunction is a drastic remedy. The hardship on a preliminarily enjoined manufacturer who must withdraw its product from the market before trial can be devastating. On the other hand, the hardship on a patentee denied an injunction after showing a strong likelihood of success on validity and infringement lies in a frequently and equally serious delay in the exercise of his limited-in-time property right to exclude. Neither hardship can be controlling in all cases. Because the court must balance the hardships, at least in part in light of its estimate of what is likely to happen at trial, it must consider the movant's showing of likelihood of success. Yet, a court must remain free to deny a preliminary injunction, whatever be the showing of likelihood of success, when equity in the light of all the factors so requires. *Illinois Tool Works Inc. v. Grip-Pak Inc.,* 906 F.2d 679, 15 U.S.P.Q.2d 1307, 1309, 1310 (Fed. Cir. 1990).

ᛟ

The issuance of a preliminary injunction is within the discretion of the trial court. However, this discretion is not absolute. To reverse a preliminary injunction on appeal, the aggrieved party must show that the trial court abused its discretion, committed an error of law, or seriously misjudged the evidence. *Lund Industries Inc. v. GO Industries Inc.,* 938 F.2d 1273, 19 U.S.P.Q.2d 1383, 1385 (Fed. Cir. 1991).

ᛟ

If, in adjudicating irreparable harm, the district court has declined to make findings on likelihood of success, the CAFC must give the movant the benefit of the presumption before denying a motion requesting a preliminary injunction. *Reebok International Ltd. v. J. Baker Inc.*, 32 F.3d 1552, 31 U.S.P.Q.2d 1781, 1784 (Fed. Cir. 1994).

ω

On a motion for preliminary injunction, the alleged infringer must come forward with clear and convincing evidence of defenses to the patent. However, as Defendant has made no showing to overcome the presumption of validity, which is strengthened by the PTO's consideration of all prior art, the presumption is sufficient at this stage to find that the patent is likely to be found valid. *Atari Corp. v. Sega of America Inc.*, 161 F.R.D. 417, 32 U.S.P.Q.2d 1237, 1240 (Cal. 1994).

ω

The standards set by the Court of Appeals for the Federal Circuit are the standards to be used in considering a preliminary injunction in a patent case. *Maitland Co. Inc. v. Terra First Inc.*, 33 U.S.P.Q.2d 1882, 1886 (S.C. 1994).

ω

Absent a good explanation, 17 months is a substantial period of delay that militates against the issuance of a preliminary injunction by demonstrating that there is no apparent urgency to the request for injunctive relief. *High Tech Medical Instrumentation Inc. v. New Image Industries Inc.*, 49 F.3d 1551, 33 U.S.P.Q.2d 2005, 2010 (Fed. Cir. 1995).

ω

At the preliminary injunction stage a patentee bears the burden of showing a likelihood of success on the merits of the substantive issues relating to validity and enforceability of patents. The patentee must either clearly show that his patent is valid or that the alleged infringer's invalidity defense lacks substantial merit. Neither the difficulty of calculating losses in market share, nor speculation that such losses might occur, amount to proof of special circumstances justifying the extraordinary relief of an injunction prior to trial. *Eli Lilly and Co. v. American Cyanamid Co.*, 896 F.Supp. 851, 36 U.S.P.Q.2d 1011, 1014, 1019 (Ind. 1995).

ω

The law does not favor giving a party consideration for a hardship it brings upon itself by undertaking knowing infringement. *Mentor Graphics Corp. v. Quickturn Design Systems Inc.*, 44 U.S.P.Q.2d 1621, 1626 (Oreg. 1997).

ω

The statutory presumption of validity does not apply for a preliminary injunction. *Dippin' Dots v. Mosey*, 44 U.S.P.Q.2d 1812, 1816 (Tex. 1997).

ω

The district court did not abuse its discretion in denying preliminary injunction, in part based on public interest, because the infringing product involved was a catheter preferred by many physicians in the treatment of heart patients. *Odetics Inc. v. Storage Technology Corp.*, 47 U.S.P.Q.2d 1573, 1583 (Va. 1998).

Preliminary Motion. *See also* **37 C.F.R. §1.633, Motion.**

A preliminary motion to designate that specified claims do not correspond to the interference count was granted. *Shaked v. Taniguchi*, 21 U.S.P.Q.2d 1285, 1286 (B.P.A.I. 1990).

ᚖ

In any interference preliminary motion, including a motion attacking the benefit of a priority date under 37 C.F.R. §1.633(g), the new interference rules place the burden of proof on the moving party, which has an opportunity during the preliminary motion period either to present testimony or to request that the EIC set a time for taking testimony under 37 C.F.R. §1.639(c). *Kubota v. Shibuya*, 999 F.2d 517, 27 U.S.P.Q.2d 1418, 1420 (Fed. Cir. 1993).

ᚖ

In an interference, a preliminary motion for judgment of unpatentability is only proper as to the claims *then* corresponding to the count of the interference. *Wm. T. Burnett & Co. Inc. v. Cumulus Fibres Inc.*, 825 F.Supp. 734, 27 U.S.P.Q.2d 1953, 1955 (N.C. 1993).

Preliminary Statement. *See* **Supplemental Preliminary Satement.**

While a party to an interference cannot get the benefit of a date (even if proved) prior to the earliest date asserted in his preliminary statement, it is certainly not error to accept and consider evidence of activity prior to that date. *Biel v. Chessin*, 347 F.2d 898, 146 U.S.P.Q. 293, 297 (C.C.P.A. 1965).

ᚖ

Although proper interpretation of the law does not ordinarily provide an excuse for amending a preliminary statement, a contingent motion to amend a preliminary statement (made subsequent to decision on priority) was granted pursuant to the "essential ends of justice" requirement of the rule. *Chan v. Kunz*, 231 U.S.P.Q. 462 (B.P.A.I. 1984).

ᚖ

Where an interference has been declared, a preliminary statement alleging invention prior to the date of a reference can be accepted as a substitute for an affidavit under Rule 131, making out a *prima facie* case of prior invention justifying the setting of a testimony period to take proofs. The test for sufficiency of a Rule 131 (37 C.F.R. §1.131) affidavit parallels (albeit is not identical to) that for determining priority under 35 U.S.C. §102(g). *Goutzoulis v. Athale*, 15 U.S.P.Q.2d 1461, 1464 (Comm'r Patents & Trademarks 1990).

Presumption. *See also Aukerman* **Presumption, Bursting Bubble, Irreparable Harm, Presumption of Validity.**

A patentee is presumed to have known and is chargeable with knowledge of everything disclosed by the prior art in the involved field and of all devices in that field which have been in prior public use. *DeBurgh v. Kindel Furniture Company*, 125 F.Supp. 468, 103 U.S.P.Q. 203, 208 (Mich. 1954).

ᚖ

Presumption

A specification disclosure that contains a teaching of the manner and process of making and using the invention in terms that correspond in scope to those used in describing and defining the subject matter sought to be patented must be taken as in compliance with the enabling requirement of the first paragraph of 35 U.S.C. §112 unless there is reason to doubt the objective truth of the statements contained therein that must be relied on for enabling support. Assuming that sufficient reason for such doubt does exist, a rejection for failure to teach how to make and/or use will be proper on that basis. In any event, it is incumbent on the Patent Office, whenever a rejection on this basis is made, to explain why it doubts the truth or accuracy of any statement in a supporting disclosure and to back up assertions of its own with acceptable evidence or reasoning that is inconsistent with the contested statement. Otherwise, there would be no need for the applicant to go to the trouble and expense of supporting his presumptively accurate disclosure. *In re Marzocchi and Horton,* 439 F.2d 220, 169 U.S.P.Q. 367 (C.C.P.A. 1971).

ω

Even though not cited as a reference by the Examiner, there is no presumption in a patent infringement proceeding that uncited patents were overlooked since they may have been considered and cast aside as not pertinent. It is as reasonable to conclude that an uncited prior-art patent was considered and cast aside as not pertinent as it is to conclude that it was inadvertently overlooked. The question of whether the failure of the Examiner to cite certain art is consistent with his examination and rejection depends on the pertinency of the uncited art. The fact that the Examiner searched the specific subclass in which an uncited reference appears prevents finding affirmatively that the reference was not brought to the Examiner's attention. *Lundy Electronics & Systems, Inc. v. Optical Recognition Systems, Inc.,* 362 F. Supp. 130, 178 U.S.P.Q. 525, 534, 535 (Va. 1972).

ω

It is presumed that the Examiner considered and discarded uncited patent references that are classified in the class and subclasses in which the patent in suit issued, or in a class and subclass that have otherwise been indicated as having been searched by the Examiner. *Panduit Corp. v. Burndy Corp.,* 378 F. Supp. 775, 180 U.S.P.Q. 498, 505 (Ill. 1973).

ω

One who claims a compound, per se, which is structurally similar to a prior-art compound must rebut the presumed expectation that the structurally similar compounds have similar properties. *In re Wilder,* 563 F.2d 457, 195 U.S.P.Q. 426, 429 (C.C.P.A. 1977).

ω

We hereby declare the presumption that the inventor has knowledge of all material prior art to be dead. *Kimberly-Clark Corporation v. Johnson & Johnson and Personal Products Company,* 745 F.2d 1437, 223 U.S.P.Q. 603, 614 (Fed. Cir. 1984).

ω

An action in the district court under 35 U.S.C. §145 is a proceeding de novo and, while it is limited to the invention claimed in the PTO, the court may consider any additional competent evidence that a plaintiff neither intentionally nor negligently failed to submit to the PTO. The presumption of correctness that attaches to the decision of the Commissioner is a rebuttable presumption that may be overcome by the introduction of evidence (at a trial under §145) that is of such character and amount as to carry a thorough conviction of error. At such a trial the plaintiff and defendant may present evidence on any issue properly before the court. This additional evidence may include testimony of expert witnesses and inventors skilled in the art, and evidence of commercial success. In making its determination of non-obviousness, the court recognized the non-analogous nature of one reference, the lack of teaching or suggestion in the prior art of the useful advantage of a flexible track incapable of self-support, and the commercial success of the highly flexible Hot Wheels trackway-toy vehicle combination covered by the plaintiff's Reissue Application. The fact that the claimed invention seemed simple and, when viewed in hindsight, appeared to be obvious was not enough to negate invention. *Lemelson v. Mossinghoff,* 225 U.S.P.Q. 1063 (D.C. 1985).

ω

There is no presumptive correlation that two similar processes form substantially the same product where the processes differ by a materially limiting step. When prior art fails to disclose a method for making a claimed compound, at the time the invention was made, it cannot be legally concluded that the compound itself is in the possession of the public. *Ashland Oil, Inc. v. Delta Resins & Refractories, Inc.,* 776 F.2d 281, 227 U.S.P.Q. 657 (Fed. Cir. 1985).

ω

In matters involving patent rights, irreparable harm has been presumed when a clear showing has been made of patent validity and infringement. This presumption derives in part because the patent grant has a finite form, patent expiration is not suspended during litigation, and the passage of time can work irremediable harm. The opportunity to practice an invention during the notoriously lengthy course of patent litigation may itself tempt infringers. The nature of the patent grant thus weighs against holding that monetary damages will always suffice to make the patentee whole, for the principal value of a patent is its statutory right to exclude. The patent statute provides injunctive relief to preserve the legal interests of the parties against future infringement, which may have marked effects never fully compensable in money. If monetary relief were the sole relief afforded by the statute, injunctions would be unnecessary, and infringers could become compulsory licensees for as long as the litigation lasts. *Lin v. Fritsch,* 14 U.S.P.Q.2d 1795, 1809 (Comm'r Patents & Trademarks 1989).

ω

The law presumes the existence of findings necessary to support a verdict reached by the jury. Whether there is trial evidence favorable to both sides is not the question. The question is whether there is substantial evidence to support the verdict. Even where evidence may be contradictory, the resolution of that conflict is a role assigned to the jury, and inferences are to be drawn in favor of the non-movant. Where there are alleged conflicts in the evidence, the trial court, on motion for JNOV, should not substitute its judgment for that of the jury. When, without question, reasonable jurors could have concluded that the patent claims in issue were infringed, denial of a motion for JNOV is required. *ALM Surgical Equipment Inc. v. Kirschner Medical Corp.*, 15 U.S.P.Q.2d 1241, 1245, 1246 (S.C. 1990).

ω

A presumption of a fact is nothing more than a process of reasoning from one fact to another, an argument that infers a fact otherwise doubtful from a fact that is proved. Rules of evidence as to inferences from facts are to aid reason, not to override it. *Rosemount Inc. v. U.S. International Trade Commission*, 910 F.2d 819, 15 U.S.P.Q.2d 1569, 1572 (Fed. Cir. 1990).

ω

There is no presumption of the inventor's knowledge of material prior art in connection with the duty of candor. *Code Alarm Inc. v. Electromotive Technologies Corp.*, 26 U.S.P.Q.2d 1561, 1563 (Mich. 1992).

ω

The presumption of validity is based on the presumption of administrative correctness of actions of the agency charged with examination of patentability. The government agency is presumed to have done its job. *Applied Materials Inc. v. Advanced Semiconductor Materials*, 98 F.3d 1563, 40 U.S.P.Q.2d 1481, 1485 (Fed. Cir. 1996).

ω

When a claim is amended, but the prosecution history does not reveal the reason for the change, it should be presumed that there was "a substantial reason related to patentability for including the limiting element added by amendment." *Hilton Davis Chemical Co. v. Warner-Jenkinson Co.*, 43 U.S.P.Q.2d 1152, 1153 (Fed. Cir. 1997).

Presumption of Administrative Regularity. *See also* Administrative Regularity.

The Examiner's search record provides prima facie evidence that he searched all the references in the classes and subclasses noted on the file wrapper as having been searched. References in such subclasses left uncited are presumed to have been regarded by the Examiner as less relevant than those cited. A contrary view would destroy the presumption of administrative regularity on which the presumption of validity rests. *Railroad Dynamics, Inc. v. A. Stucki Co.*, 579 F. Supp. 353, 218 U.S.P.Q. 618 (Pa. 1983).

Presumption of Enablement.

While numerous courts have stated that prior art references are entitled to a presumption of enablement, these courts have each relied incorrectly upon *In re Sasse*, 629 F.2d 675, 681 (C.C.P.A. 1980), for the proposition that the patent holder bears the burden of proving that prior art references are not enabling. Since the burden is always on one who challenges validity to show invalidity by clear and convincing evidence, the patent holder only has the burden of producing some material evidence which places the enablement of the reference in question. Once it has done so, the challenger must show by clear and convincing evidence that the reference was, in fact, enabling. *Abbott Laboratories v. Diamedix Corp.*, 969 F.Supp. 1064, 43 U.S.P.Q.2d 1448, 1451 (Ill. 1997).

Presumption of Infringement.

Although a patent is presumptively valid, no similar presumption attaches to an allegation of infringement. *Machinery Corp. of America v. Gullfiber A.B.*, 774 F.2d 467, 227 U.S.P.Q. 368, 372 (Fed. Cir. 1985).

ᛒ

Ultraseal argues that *Handgards* [601 F.2d 986, 202 U.S.P.Q. 342 (9th Cir. 1979), *cert. denied*, 444 U.S. 1025, 204 U.S.P.Q. 880 (1980)] should apply only to suits where the plaintiff knew that the patent was invalid, not to those where the plaintiff knew there was no infringement. The alleged basis for that argument is a statement in *Handgards* that the presumption of good faith attached to a patentee's infringement suit "accords the patentee a presumption commensurate with the statutory presumption of patent validity." Ultraseal argues that, though the presumption of validity warrants a presumption that the patentee has a good-faith belief in validity, there is no similar presumption of infringement warranting a presumption that the patentee has a good-faith belief in infringement. Ultraseal's argument is unpersuasive. The cited statement was not the sole, nor even the primary, reason for Handgards' establishing the presumption of a good-faith infringement suit. The primary, if not sole, reason was the public policy of erecting a barrier against thwarting patentees from asserting legitimate patent rights. Because that policy applies to a good-faith belief in infringement as well as validity, there is no persuasive reason to apply the presumption to one but not the other. *Loctite Corp. v. Ultraseal Ltd.*, 781 F.2d 861, 228 U.S.P.Q. 90, 101 (Fed. Cir. 1985).

Presumption of Irreparable Harm.

The movant for preliminary injunction must show not only a reasonable likelihood of success on the merits, but also the lack of adequate remedy at law or other irreparable harm. In matters involving patent rights, irreparable harm has been presumed when a clear showing has been made of patent validity and infringement. This presumption derives in part from the finite term of the patent grant, for patent expiration is not suspended during litigation, and the passage of time can work irremediable harm. The opportunity to practice an invention during the notoriously lengthy course of patent litigation may itself tempt infringers. *H. Robertson Co. v. United Steel Deck, Inc.*, 820 F.2d 384, 2 U.S.P.Q.2d 1926 (Fed. Cir. 1987).

Presumption of Validity. *See also* Failure to Cite, Lengthy Prosecution, Validity.

Long-continued public acquiescence in the monopoly created by a patent claim furnishes a valid basis of reinforcement for the statutory presumption of the patent's validity for purposes of a preliminary injunction. *Eli Lilly & Co., Inc. v. Generix Drug Sales, Inc.*, 460 F.2d 1096, 174 U.S.P.Q. 65, 69 (5th Cir. 1972).

ᛒ

While it is generally true that the presumption of validity of a patent may be strengthened where the Patent Office has granted it in the face of certain prior art, this is not so where the Patent Office has been deceived as to the true significance of a reference. *Kahn v. Dynamics Corporation of America*, 367 F.Supp. 63, 180 U.S.P.Q. 247, 252 (N.Y. 1973).

ᛒ

The most pertinent prior art was considered by the Patent Office before granting each of the patents in suit; the normal presumption of validity accorded the patents in suit is therefore strengthened. The normal presumption of validity accorded a patent is reinforced after the patent has been adjudicated valid. *Mobil Oil Corp. v. W. R. Grace & Co.*, 367 F. Supp. 207, 180 U.S.P.Q. 418, 452 (Conn. 1973).

ထ

Application of 35 U.S.C. §282 in its entirety has suffered from analogy of the presumption itself to the deference due administrative agencies. "This presumption is based upon (a) the acknowledged experience and expertise of the Patent Office personnel, and (b) recognition that patent approval is a species of administrative determination supported by evidence." The rationale of assumed administrative correctness finds its genesis in *Morgan v. Daniels* [153 U.S. 120 (1894)]. *Solder Removal Co. v. United States International Trade Commission*, 582 F.2d 628, 199 U.S.P.Q. 129, 133, n.10 (C.C.P.A. 1978).

ထ

The presumption of validity can be rebutted only by a showing that prior art that was not before the Examiner was more pertinent to the subject matter of the invention than the art that was considered by the Examiner. *In re Certain Headboxes and Papermaking Machine Forming Sections for the Continuous Production of Paper, and Components Thereof*, 213 U.S.P.Q. 291, 298 (U.S. Int'l Trade Comm'r 1981).

ထ

The statutory presumption of validity is lessened by the difference in standards applied by the Patent Office and the courts, the volume of applications processed through the Patent Office and the ex parte nature of the proceedings therein. *Colt Industries Operating Corp. v. Index Werke, K.G.*, 217 U.S.P.Q. 1176, 1179 (D.C. 1982).

ထ

The presumption of validity that is normally accorded a patent is strengthened "where the [patent was] given extended scrutiny by the PTO and its tribunals on matters within their specific field of expertise, including the interpretation and pertinency of the prior art." *Rohm & Haas Co. v. Dawson Chemical Co., Inc.*, 557 F. Supp. 739, 217 U.S.P.Q. 515, 562 (Tex. 1983).

ထ

The Examiner's search record provides *prima facie* evidence that he searched all the references in the classes and subclasses noted on the file wrapper as having been searched. References in such subclasses left uncited are presumed to have been regarded by the Examiner as less relevant than those cited. A contrary view would destroy the presumption of administrative regularity on which the presumption of validity rests. *Railroad Dynamics, Inc. v. A. Stucki Co.*, 579 F. Supp. 353, 218 U.S.P.Q. 618 (Pa. 1983).

ထ

To weaken the presumption of validity, there must be some showing that the prior art was not considered by the Examiner, not merely that it was not cited. Since none of the additional prior art references relied upon by the defendant were not considered by the Examiner or disclose any substantial element relating to the patented subject matter that was not considered by the PTO, the statutory presumption of validity is fully effective in this case. *Parkson Corp. v. Proto Circuits, Inc.*, 220 U.S.P.Q. 898 (Md. 1983).

ᛟ

A patent shall be presumed valid. The burden of establishing invalidity of a patent rests on the party asserting it. That burden never shifts. When no prior art other than that which was considered by the Examiner is relied on by an attacker, he has the added burden of overcoming the deference that is due to a qualified government agency presumed to have properly done its job, which involves one or more Examiners who are assumed to have expertise in interpreting the references and to be familiar from their work with the level of skill in the art and whose duty it is to issue only valid patents. When an attacker produces prior art or other evidence not considered in the PTO, there is no reason to defer to the PTO so far as its effect on validity is concerned. New prior art not before the PTO may so clearly invalidate a patent that the burden is fully sustained merely by proving its existence and applying the proper law, but that has no effect on the presumption or on who has burden of proof. They are static and in reality different expressions of the same thing. Neither does the standard of proof change; it must be by clear and convincing evidence or its equivalent, by whatever form of words may be expressed. When new evidence touching validity of the patent not considered by the PTO is relied on, the tribunal considering it is not faced with having to disagree with the PTO or with deferring to its judgment or with taking its expertise into account. The evidence may, therefore, carry more weight and go further toward sustaining the attacker's unchanging burden. *American Hoist & Derrick Co. v. Sowa & Sons, Inc.*, 725 F.2d 1350, 220 U.S.P.Q. 763 (Fed. Cir. 1984).

ᛟ

Section 282 (Presumption of Validity) of 35 U.S.C. has no application in reexamination proceedings. Injection of the presumption into the examination process could add nothing but legalistic confusion. In reexamination, claims can be amended and new claims added; there is no litigating adversary present. *In re Etter*, 756 F.2d 852, 225 U.S.P.Q. 1 (Fed. Cir. 1985).

ᛟ

Patents are born valid. The presumption that a patent is valid, 35 U.S.C. §282, continues until the validity-challenger has "so carried his burden as to have persuaded the decision maker that the patent can no longer be accepted as valid." *Datascope Corp. v. SMEC, Inc.*, 776 F.2d 320, 227 U.S.P.Q. 838 (Fed. Cir. 1985).

ᛟ

Under 35 U.S.C. §282, a patent is presumed valid, and the one attacking validity has the burden of proving invalidity by clear and convincing evidence. Notwithstanding that the introduction of prior art not before the Examiner may facilitate the challenger's meeting the burden of proof on invalidity, the presumption remains intact and on the challenger throughout the litigation, and the clear and convincing standard does not change. The only indication that the district court recognized the presumption of validity and its proper application was its statement that "the key issue in this case is whether the defendant has overcome the presumption of nonobviousness." That statement, however, speaks only part of the truth; the presumption of validity goes to validity of the patent in relation to the patent statute as a whole, not just to the non-obviousness under 103. *Hybritech Inc. v. Monoclonal Antibodies, Inc.*, 802 F.2d 1367, 231 U.S.P.Q. 81 (Fed. Cir. 1986).

ω

The statutory presumption of validity under 35 U.S.C. §282 does not apply to patent claims undergoing reexamination. *Ex parte Gould*, 231 U.S.P.Q. 943 (B.P.A.I. 1986).

ω

As the burden of proving invalidity is with the party attacking validity, evidence educed in connection with a motion for preliminary relief must be considered in this light. A patentee retains the burden of showing a reasonable likelihood that an attack on its patent's validity would fail. This does not change the immutable allocation to the challenger of the burden of proving invalidity, but rather reflects the rule that the burden is always on the movant to demonstrate entitlement to preliminary relief. Such entitlement, however, is determined in the context of the presumptions and burdens that would inhere at trial on the merits. *H. Robertson Co. v. United Steel Deck, Inc.*, 820 F.2d 384, 2 U.S.P.Q.2d 1926 (Fed. Cir. 1987).

ω

The presumption of validity under 35 U.S.C. §282 carries with it a presumption the Examiner did his duty and knew what claims he was allowing. *Intervet America, Inc. v. Kee-Vet Labs., Inc.*, 887 F.2d 1050, 1054, 12 U.S.P.Q.2d 1474 (Fed. Cir. 1989).

ω

The presumption of validity is not strengthened by reissue or by reexamination. At most, reexamination would have the effect of making a putative infringer's ultimate burden of proving invalidity more difficult to satisfy to the extent that the challenge is concerned with matters (such as prior art) that were considered by the PTO in the reexamination proceeding. *Moore Business Forms, Inc. v. Wallace Computer Services, Inc.*, 14 U. S. P. Q.2d 1849, 1861 (Ind. 1989).

ω

The presumption of validity may be rebutted by clear and convincing evidence of invalidity. The burden of proof in overcoming this presumption rests on the party challenging the validity of a patent. The presumption is never diminished, but rather the presumption operates to place the burden of production of evidence and the burden of persuasion on the party who attacks the patent. The standard of evidence by which the burden must be carried is clear and convincing evidence. Each patent claim is presumed to be valid independently of other claims. The burden of persuasion in overcoming the presumption of patent validity is less easily carried when the evidence relied upon consists only of prior art considered by the Examiner or merely cumulative thereto. This is because deference is due to the Patent Office decision to issue the patent with respect to evidence bearing on validity that it considered. *Stranco Inc. v. Atlantes Chemical Systems Inc.*, 15 U.S.P.Q.2d 1704, 1712 (Tex. 1990).

ω

The presumption of validity of 35 U.S.C. §282 is not applicable in interferences. *Okada v. Hitotsumachi*, 16 U.S.P.Q.2d 1789, 1790 (Comm'r Patents & Trademarks 1990).

ᙏ

The criterion with regard to the strength of the presumption of validity is "not the number of references but what they would have meant to a person of ordinary skill in the field of invention". *In re Gorman*, 933 F.2d 982, 986, 18 U.S.P.Q.2d 1885, 1888 (Fed. Cir. 1991).

ᙏ

On a motion for preliminary injunction, the alleged infringer must come forward with clear and convincing evidence of defenses to the patent. However, as Defendant has made no showing to overcome the presumption of validity, which is strengthened by the PTO's consideration of all prior art, the presumption is sufficient at this stage to find that the patent is likely to be found valid. *Atari Corp. v. Sega of America Inc.*, 869 F.Supp. 783, 161 F.R.D. 417, 32 U.S.P.Q.2d 1237, 1240 (Cal. 1994).

ᙏ

The presumption of validity is based on the presumption of administrative correctness of actions of the agency charged with examination of patentability. The government agency ir presumed to have done its job. *Applied Materials Inc. v. Advanced Semiconductor Materials*, 98 F.3d 1563, 40 U.S.P.Q.2d 1481, 1485 (Fed. Cir. 1996).

ᙏ

The statutory presumption of validity does not apply for a preliminary injunction. *Dippin' Dots v. Mosey*, 44 U.S.P.Q.2d 1812, 1816 (Tex. 1997).

Prevailing Party.

If an appellate court reverses and vacates a judgment, the party which prevails on appeal is generally not bound by adverse trial court rulings on other issues. *Hydranautics v. FilmTec Corp.*, 70 F.3d 533, 36 U.S.P.Q.2d 1773, 1776 (9th Cir. 1995).

ᙏ

A party who has a competitor's patent declared invalid meets the definition of "prevailing party". *Manildra Milling Corp. v. Ogilvie Mills Inc.*, 76 F.3d 1178, 37 U.S.P.Q.2d 1707, 1711 (Fed. Cir. 1996).

ᙏ

A party prevails "when actual relief on the merits of his claim materially alters the legal relationship between the parties by modifying the defendant's behavior in a way that directly benefits the plaintiff." *E.I. du Pont de Nemours and Co. v. Monsanto Corp.*, 42 U.S.P.Q.2d 1152 (Del. 1997).

ᙏ

Plaintiffs may be considered "prevailing parties" for attorney's fees purposes if they succeed on any significant issue in litigation which achieves some of the benefit the parties sought in bringing suit. In short, a plaintiff "prevails" when actual relief on the merits of his claim materially alters the relationship between the parties by modifying the defendants' behavior in a way that directly benefits the plaintiff. As a matter of law, a party who has a competitor's patent declared invalid meets the definition of "the prevailing party". *The Gentry Gallery Inc. v. The Berkline Corp.*, 134 F.3d 1473, 45 U.S.P.Q.2d 1498, 1504 (Fed. Cir. 1998).

Price Descrimination.

There is no antitrust prohibition against a patent owner's using price discrimination to maximize his income from the patent. *USM Corporation v. SPS Technologies, Inc.*, 694 F.2d 505, 216 U.S.P.Q. 959, 965 (7th Cir. 1982).

Price Erosion.

Lost profits (as a result of price erosion) are compensable damages that stand on the same ground as damages caused by lost sales. In most price erosion cases a patent owner has reduced the actual price of its patented product in response to an infringer's competition. A patent holder who proves that he would have increased his prices had the infringer not been in competition with him can also sustain a price erosion claim. *Micro Motion Inc. v. Exac Corp.*, 761 F. Supp. 1420, 19 U.S.P.Q.2d 1001, 1010 (Cal. 1991).

Price Fixing.

Where a conspiracy to restrain trade or an effort to monopolize is not involved, a patentee may license another to make and vend a patented device with a provision that the licensee's sale price shall be fixed by the patentee. *United States v. Line Material Company*, 333 U.S. 287, 76 U.S.P.Q. 399, 407 (S.Ct. 1948).

ᵥ

The doctrine of patent misuse is an equitable concept designed to prevent a patent owner from improperly extending or enhancing the "physical or temporal scope" of a patent grant with the effect of restraining competition. However, in application, a finding of patent misuse has been confined to a few specific practices by patent holders, such as fixing the price at which a purchaser of a patented item could resell it, requiring a licensee to pay royalties beyond the expiration of the patent grant, and requiring a licensee to refrain from manufacturing items that would compete with the patented item. The most common application of the doctrine occurs when the sale of an unpatented staple item is "tied" to the sale of a patented device. Every use of a patent as a means of obtaining a limited monopoly of unpatented material is prohibited. *N.L. Chemicals Inc. v. United Catalysts Inc.*, 11 U.S.P.Q.2d 1239, 1240 (Ky. 1989).

Prima Facie. See also Chemical Theory, Obviousness.

The concept of rebuttable *prima facie* obviousness is well established. It is not, however, a segmented concept. When *prima facie* obviousness is established and evidence is submitted in rebuttal, the decision maker must start over. Though the burden of going forward to rebut the *prima facie* case remains with the applicant, the question of whether that burden has been successfully carried requires that the entire path to decision be retraced. An earlier decision should not be considered as set in concrete, with applicant's rebuttal evidence then evaluated only on its knockdown ability. Analytical fixation on an earlier decision can tend to provide that decision with an undeservedly broadened umbrella effect. *Prima facie* obviousness is a legal conclusion, not a fact. Facts established by rebuttal evidence must be evaluated along with the facts on which the earlier conclusion was reached, not judged against the conclusion itself. Though the tribunal must begin anew, a final finding of obviousness may of course be reached, but such finding will rest upon evaluation of all facts in evidence, uninfluenced by any earlier conclusion reached by an earlier Board upon a different record. *In re Rinehart*, 531 F.2d 1048, 189 U.S.P.Q. 143, 147 (C.C.P.A. 1976). *See also In re Carleton*, 599 F.2d 1021, 202 U.S.P.Q. 165, 168 (C.C.P.A. 1979).

ω

Claims to new compositions can be regarded as *prima facie* obvious under 35 U.S.C. §103 when the additives in the new compositions are structurally similar to additives in known compositions, having a different use, even though the method of using the compositions is neither taught nor suggested by the prior art. Structural similarity between claimed and prior-art subject matter, proved by combining references or otherwise, where the prior art gives reason or motivation to make the claimed compositions, creates a *prima facie* case of obviousness, and the burden (and opportunity) then falls on an applicant to rebut the prima facie case. The discovery that a claimed composition possesses a property not disclosed for the prior-art subject matter does not itself defeat a *prima facie* case. *In re Dillon*, 919 F.2d 688, 16 U.S.P.Q.2d 1897, 1901 (Fed. Cir. 1990).

ω

In order to complete the PTO's *prima facie* case and shift the burden of going forward to applicant, there must be evidence (other than speculation by the PTO) that one of ordinary skill in the subject art would have been motivated to make the modifications of the prior art necessary to arrive at the claimed subject matter. *In re Jones*, 958 F.2d 347, 21 U.S.P.Q.2d 1941, 1944 (Fed. Cir. 1992).

ω

In proceedings before the PTO, the Examiner bears the burden of establishing a *prima facie* case of obviousness based upon prior art. The Examiner can satisfy this burden only by showing some objective teaching in the prior art or that knowledge generally available to one of ordinary skill in the art would lead that individual to combine the relevant teachings of the references. The patent applicant may then attack the Examiner's *prima facie* determination as improperly made out, or the applicant may present objective evidence tending to support a conclusion of nonobviousness. *In re Fritch*, 972 F.2d 1260, 23 U.S.P.Q.2d 1780, 1783 (Fed. Cir. 1992).

ω

The *prima facie* case is a procedural tool of patent examination, allocating the burdens of going forward, as between Examiner and applicant. The term "*prima facie* case" refers only to the initial examination step. The Examiner bears the initial burden, on review of the prior art or on any other ground, of presenting a *prima facie* case of unpatentability. If that burden is met, the burden of coming forward with evidence or argument shifts to the applicant. After evidence or argument is submitted by the applicant in response, patentability is determined on the totality of the record, by a preponderance of the evidence with due consideration to persuasiveness of argument. If examination at the initial stage does not produce a *prima facie* case of unpatentability, then without more the applicant is entitled to grant of the patent. In reviewing the Examiner's position on appeal, the Board must necessarily weigh all of the evidence and argument. An observation by the Board that the Examiner made a *prima facie* case is not improper, as long as the ultimate determination of patentability is made on the entire record. *In re Oetiker*, 977 F.2d 1443, 24 U.S.P.Q.2d 1443, 1444 (Fed. Cir. 1992).

ω

When the difference between the claimed invention and the prior art is the range or value of a particular variable, then a *prima facie* rejection is properly established when the difference in range or value is minor. *Haynes International Inc. v. Jessop Steel Co.*, 8 F.3d 1573, 28 U.S.P.Q.2d 1652, 1655 n.3 (Fed. Cir. 1993).

Principle. *See also* Scientific Principle.

Every discovery is not embraced within the statutory terms of 35 U.S.C. §101. Excluded from such patent protection are laws of nature, physical phenomena, and abstract ideas. A principle, in the abstract, is a fundamental truth, an original cause, a motive; these cannot be patented, and no one can claim in any of them an exclusive right. A new mineral discovered in the earth or a new plant found in the wild is not patentable subject matter. Likewise, Einstein could not patent his celebrated law that $E = mc^2$; nor could Newton have patented the law of gravity. Such discoveries are "manifestations of . . . nature, free to all men and reserved exclusively to none." *Diamond v. Diehr and Lutton*, 450 U.S. 175, 209 U.S.P.Q. 1, 7 (1981).

ω

To copy the principle or mode of operation described is an infringement, although such copy is totally unlike the original in form or proportions. *Blumenthal v. Barber-Colman Holdings Corp.*, 62 F.3d 1433, 38 U.S.P.Q.2d 1031, 1036 (Fed. Cir. 1995—unpublished).

Printed Matter.[9] *See also* Packaging Material.

Printed matter, in an article of manufacture claim, can be given "patentable weight." The fact that printed matter by itself is not patentable subject matter, because non-statutory, is no reason for ignoring it when a claim is directed to a combination. *In re Miller*, 418 F.2d 1392, 164 U.S.P.Q. 46, 49 (C.C.P.A. 1969).

ω

Differences between an invention and the prior art cited against it cannot be ignored merely because those differences reside in the content of printed matter. A "printed

---

[9]See Kelly, Patrick D., "Old Drug, New Use: Article Of Manufacture Claims", BIO/TECHNOLOGY, Vol. 11, pp 839 and 840, July 1993, which refers directly to claim 18 of USP 5,011,853 and to claim 7 of USP 5,208,031, as well as to claim 7 of USP 4,988,710, which reads (in part): "An article of manufacture comprising packaging material and a pharmaceutical agent contained within the packaging material, wherein the pharmaceutical agent . . . , and wherein the packaging material comprises a label which indicates that the pharmaceutical agent can be used for reducing neurotoxic brain damage that might otherwise be caused by at least one cholinesterase inhibitor. . . . "

matter rejection" under 35 U.S.C. §103 stands on questionable legal and logical footing. Standing alone, the description of an element of the invention as printed matter tells nothing about the differences between the invention and the prior art or about whether that invention was suggested by the prior art. A printed matter rejection is based on case law antedating the 1952 Patent Act, employing a point of novelty approach. The 1952 Act legislatively revised that approach through its requirement that the claim be viewed as a whole in determining obviousness. Printed matter may well constitute structural limitations upon which patentability can be predicated. Under §103, the Board cannot dissect a claim, excise the printed matter from it, and declare the remaining portion of the mutilated claim to be unpatentable. The claim must be read as a whole. *In re Gulack,* 703 F.2d 1381, 217 U.S.P.Q. 401 (Fed. Cir. 1983).

ᚹ

The printed matter cases have no practical relevance where "the invention as defined by the claims *requires* that the information be processed not by the mind but by a machine, the computer." *In re Lowry*, 32 F.3d 1579, 1583, 32 U.S.P.Q.2d 1031, 1034 (Fed. Cir. 1994).

ᚹ

The Commissioner now states "that computer programs embodied in a tangible medium, such as floppy diskettes, are patentable subject matter under 35 U.S.C. §101 and must be examined under 35 U.S.C. §§102 and 103." The printed matter doctrine is not applicable. *In re Beauregard*, 53 F.3d 1583, 35 U.S.P.Q.2d 1383, 1384 (Fed. Cir. 1995).

Printed Publication. *See also* **Coauthors, Foreign Patent Application, Microfilm, Photograph, Publication, Research Paper, Thesis, 35 U.S.C. §21.**

A foreign typewritten application file that has been opened to public inspection in a foreign patent office and a German Gebrauchsmuster, which is typewritten and open to public inspection, are not bars under the printed publication provisions. The reason the foreign patent applications are not applied as bars by the courts is found in the requirement that a publication, to be a bar, must be "printed." However, typewritten college theses, placed on library shelves, have been held to be "printed publications." Once it has been established that an item has been both printed and published, it is not necessary to show further that any given number of people actually saw it or that any specific number of copies have been circulated. The law sets up a *conclusive presumption* to the effect that the public has knowledge of the publication when a single printed copy is proved to have been so published. *In re Tenney, Frank, and Knox*, 254 F.2d 619, 117 U.S.P.Q. 348, 352, 354 (C.C.P.A. 1958).

ᚹ

Filing a copy of plans that had been abandoned and that were never in public use or on sale in this country with the Pennsylvania Department of Mines does not amount to a description of the device in a printed publication in this or a foreign country, as required by 35 U.S.C. §102(a). *Layne-New York Co., Inc. v. Allied Asphalt Co., Inc.,* 363 F. Supp. 299, 180 U.S.P.Q. 81, 86 (Pa. 1973).

ᚹ

A printed document may qualify as a "publication" under 35 U.S.C. §102(b), notwithstanding that accessibility thereto is restricted to a "part of the public," so long as accessibility is sufficient "to raise a presumption that the public concerned with the art would know of [the invention]." Accessibility to appellant's thesis by the three members of the graduate committee and appellant's thesis defense before the graduate committee in its official capacity as arbiter of appellant's entitlement to a master's degree were not transmuted into a patent-defeating publication merely by depositing the thesis in the university library where it remained uncatalogued and unshelved as of the critical date in question. *In re Bayer,* 568 F.2d 1357, 196 U.S.P.Q. 670, 674, 675 (C.C.P.A. 1978).

ᛟ

"Printed publication" should be approached as a unitary concept. The traditional dichotomy between "printing" and "publication" is no longer valid. Given the state of technology in document duplication, data storage, and data-retrieval systems, the "probability of dissemination" of an item very often has little to do with whether or not it is "printed" in the sense of that word when it was introduced into the patent statutes in 1836. Interpretation of the words "printed" and "publication" to mean "probability of dissemination" and "public accessibility," respectively, now seems to render their use in the phrase "printed publication" somewhat redundant. *In re Wyer,* 655 F.2d 221, 210 U.S.P.Q. 790, 794 (C.C.P.A. 1981).

ᛟ

The effective date of a printed publication is the date that it is received by the public and not the date that it is printed or even the date that it is mailed. The burden is clearly upon appellants to disprove the *prima facie* publication date established by the Examiner, and unsworn third-hand information is clearly inadequate to meet that burden. *Ex parte Albert,* 18 U.S.P.Q.2d 1325, 1326 (B.P.A.I. 1984).

ᛟ

Between 50 to 500 persons interested and of ordinary skill in the subject matter were actually told of the existence of a paper and informed of its contents by an oral presentation at a professional conference, and the document itself was actually disseminated without restriction to at least six persons. A document may be deemed a printed publication upon a satisfactory showing that it has been disseminated or otherwise made available to the extent that persons interested and of ordinary skill in the subject matter or art, exercising reasonable diligence, can locate it and recognize and comprehend therefrom the essentials of the claimed invention without need of further research or experimentation. *Massachusetts Institute of Technology v. A.B. Fortia,* 774 F.2d 1104, 227 U.S.P.Q. 428 (Fed. Cir. 1985).

ᛟ

A doctoral thesis is a printed publication when deposited and catalogued in a public library. *In re Hall,* 781 F.2d 897, 228 U.S.P.Q. 453 (Fed. Cir. 1986).

ᛟ

One who wishes to characterize information, in whatever form it may be, as a printed publication should produce sufficient proof of its dissemination or that it has otherwise been available and accessible to persons concerned with the art to which the document relates and thus most likely to avail themselves of its contents. A magazine is effective as a publication under 35 U.S.C. §102 on the date it reaches the addressee, not on the day of mailing. *Carela v. Starlight Archery,* 804 F.2d 135, 231 U.S.P.Q. 644 (Fed. Cir. 1986).

ᛡ

In the absence of direct evidence from the publisher of the journal attesting to the mailing date and from the Italian post office establishing at least an estimated delivery period for mail of the class used, appellants have not carried their burden of proving that the journal was not received by any significant number of subscribers before the critical date. *Ex parte Albert,* 18 U.S.P.Q.2d 1326, 1327 (B.P.A.I. 1988).

ᛡ

The following documents are regarded as printed publications:

(a) a report, filed in the engineering library of Oxford University, which was indexed by year and student's names, but not by subject matter;
(b) documents, which are in a library on a military base with security and subject to approval of the librarian, but were distributed to commercial companies and private individuals without restriction;
(c) the grandparent application in Sweden, which was not published in a journal, but was available to the public upon request after February 3, 1969, which is more than a year before the application for the patent in suit was filed.

The difficulty in locating these documents does not diminish the public's right of access once they are found. *Siemens-Elema A.B. v. Puriton Bennett Corp.*, 13 U.S.P.Q.2d 1804, 1806 (Cal. 1989).

ᛡ

The Third Progress Letter was not regarded as a printed publication under 35 U.S.C. §102(b). The "touchstone" of a printed publication is "public accessibility," and information is publicly accessible if "interested members of the relevant public could obtain [it] if they wanted to." Thirty three copies of the Third Progress Letter were made and distributed, and not just to government groups. Thirteen non-governmental companies and individuals received copies too, including big commercial competitors. Though there was no evidence of any express limit on public access, other than an export stamp, the court found no logic in requiring that a limit should necessarily have to be expressed in order to protect a progress report, distributed pursuant to a government defense contract, from being deemed a publication. *Aluminum Co. of America v. Reynolds Metals Co.,* 14 U.S.P.Q.2d 1170, 1172 (Ill. 1989).

ᛡ

The requirements of public disclosure are greater for 35 U.S.C. §102(a) prior art than for 35 U.S.C. §102(g) prior art. *Oak Industries, Inc. v. Zenith Electronics Corp.,* 726 F. Supp. 1525, 14 U.S.P.Q.2d 1417, 1426 (Ill. 1989).

ᛡ

A document, to serve as a "printed publication," must be generally available. While distribution to government agencies and personnel alone may not constitute publication, distribution to commercial companies without restriction on use clearly does. A paper orally presented at a scientific meeting open to all persons interested in the subject matter, with written copies distributed without restriction to all who request it, is a printed publication. Foreign patent applications that are made known to and are available to the public without restriction are publications. *Northern Telecom Inc. v. Datapoint Corp.*, 908 F.2d 931, 15 U.S.P.Q.2d 1321, 1325 (Fed. Cir. 1990).

ᚥ

One who wishes to characterize information, in whatever form it may be, as a "printed publication" should produce sufficient proof that it has been disseminated or that it has otherwise been made available and accessible to persons concerned with the art to which the document relates and thus most likely to avail themselves of its contents. *De Graffenried v. United States,* 20 Cl. Ct. 458, 16 U.S.P.Q.2d 1321, 1330 (Cl. Ct. 1990).

ᚥ

The fact that the author of a publication did not attempt to make his disclosed invention does not indicate (one way or the other) whether the publication would have been enabling. *General Electric Co. v. Hoechst Celanese Corp.*, 683 F. Supp. 305, 16 U.S.P.Q.2d 1977, 1985 (Del. 1990).

ᚥ

It is an open question, which must be determined on the specific facts of each case, whether a foreign patent application that is available to the public is a "printed publication" under 35 U.S.C. §102(b). *See, e.g., In re Wyer*, 655 F.2d 221, 210 U.S.P.Q. 790, (C.C.P.A. 1981); *see also* Donald S. Chisum, Chisum On Patents 3.04[2] n.17 (Rel. 37 Feb. 1991); *Abbott Laboratories v. Diamedix Corp.*, 969 F.Supp. 1064, 43 U.S.P.Q.2d 1448, 1450 n.2 (Ill. 1997).

Prior Adjudication. *See also* Blonder-Tongue Doctrine.

The fact that two different forums had held the patent invalid was not controlling. The United States International Trade Commission's investigation under 19 U.S.C. §1337, regarding unfair competition, is not determinative in a different proceeding in the District Court, and the Fourth Circuit Court of Appeals expressly stated that the other finding of invalidity was not so clearly correct that it could support a motion for summary judgment. *Antonious v. Kamata-Ri & Company, Limited*, 204 U.S.P.Q. 294, 295 (Md. 1979).

ᚥ

A patent is not held valid for all purposes, but, rather, not invalid on the record before the court. The weight given a prior holding of validity varies, depending on the additional prior art or other evidence on patentability that is produced in a subsequent suit. If, however, the record produced in the second suit is substantially identical to the record produced in the first suit, it is extremely likely that the court will give its prior holding stare decisis effect. The rule appears to be that a prior holding of validity should be given weight in a subsequent suit on the issue of validity, but the prior holding does not necessarily have stare decisis effect. *Fromson v. RVP Chemical Corp.*, 15 U.S.P.Q.2d 1689, 1693 (Wis. 1990).

Prior Application.

To obtain the benefit of the filing date of a prior application, an issued patent must make specific reference to that application. It is not enough for a patent to make specific reference to a parent copending application that makes specific reference to a grandparent application; the patent must make direct reference to the grandparent application in order to obtain the benefit of its filing date. *Sampson v. Ampex Corporation*, 463 F.2d 1042, 174 U.S.P.Q. 417, 419 (2d Cir. 1972).

Prior Art. *See also* **Analogous Art, Anticipation, Canceled Subject Matter, Classified, Deference, Difference, Disclaimer, Enabling Disclosure, Failure to Disclose, Knowledge, Number of References, Obviousness, On Sale, Origin, Paper Patent, Prior Invention, Prior Knowledge, Prior Use, Reference, Relevant Art, Search Record, Selective Extraction from Prior Art, 35 U.S.C. §102(g)/103, 35 U.S.C. §103.**

A patent issued on an application pending in the Patent Office at the time another application is filed constitutes part of the prior art available in the prosecution of the other application. *Hazeltine Research, Inc. v. Brenner*, 382 U.S. 252, 147 U.S.P.Q. 429, 430, 431 (1965).

ᘯ

Prior unappreciated and unrecognized results are insufficient in law to invalidate an otherwise valid patent. This is especially true where the patented result was not necessary for the prior-art purposes, but purely a matter of chance and not the inherent or inevitable result of the prior method. *Dart Industries Inc. v. E. I. du Pont de Nemours & Co.*, 348 F. Supp. 1338, 175 U.S.P.Q. 540, 553 (Ill. 1972).

ᘯ

A reference patent issued on an application filed the same day as appellant's application was regarded as prior art with respect to subject matter therein admitted by appellant to be prior art. *In re Hellsund*, 474 F.2d 1307, 177 U.S.P.Q. 170, 173 (C.C.P.A. 1973).

ᘰ

A statement by an applicant, whether in the application or in other papers submitted during prosecution, that certain matter is "prior art" to him is an admission that the matter is prior art for all purposes, whether or not a basis in 35 U.S.C. §102 can be found for its use as prior art. *In re Nomiya, Kohisa, and Matsumura*, 509 F.2d 566, 184 U.S.P.Q. 607, 611 n.4 (C.C.P.A. 1975).

ᘯ

When a party who has contested and lost priority with respect to a count in an interference presents claims ex parte that define subject matter obvious in view of the subject matter of the lost count, as shown by prior art references or by reference to the ordinary skill of the art, rejection of those claims under 35 U.S.C. §103 may be proper if the subject matter of the count falls within any of the paragraphs of 35 U.S.C. §102. The same result obtains where the party concedes priority of invention of the count. Such a rejection is based not on interference estoppel, but on a determination that the subject matter of the count is the prior invention of another under §102(g), or falls within another paragraph of §102, and may be used as prior art in combination with other references under §103. *In re Ogiue,* 517 F.2d 1382, 186 U.S.P.Q. 227, 234 (C.C.P.A. 1975).

ϖ

In an interference in which the winning party relied upon a Convention filing in a foreign country, the subject matter of the counts lost in the interference does not fall within any "prior art" paragraph of 35 U.S.C. §102 other than §102(g), as to claims subsequently prosecuted by the losing party. The subject matter of the lost counts is not prior art under §102(a) because it was neither known nor used by others in this country before the appellants' effective filing date. Further, there is no evidence that the invention disclosed in the winning party's foreign application was either patented or published before the appellants' effective filing date. With respect to §102(b), the noted foreign application was not even filed more than one year before the appellants' effective filing date. With respect to §102(e), the effective date of the disclosure of the winning party's patent is the U.S. filing date, which is subsequent to the appellants' effective date; therefore, the disclosure of the winning party's patent cannot be prior art under §102(e). There is no other statutory basis for finding that either the subject matter of the lost counts or the disclosure of the winning party's patent is prior art, in the sense of 35 U.S.C. §103, to the appellants.

A prior invention made in the United States is prior art under 102(g). An invention apparently made outside the United States, however, does not have the same effective date as a reference as it would have had, had it been made in this country. This is confirmed by the express desire of Congress and statutory limitations to events that take place in the United States.

The Board based the rejection under 35 U.S.C. §103 on the theory that an applicant that has lost an interference can never be entitled to claims that are obvious variations of the invention defined in the lost counts. The court found no judicial doctrine that supports this rejection under 35 U.S.C. §103.

The purpose of 35 U.S.C. §135(a) was, in part, to provide a procedure to economize time and work in the further prosecution of a losing party's application. The final refusal of claims by the PTO may be based, inter alia, on statutory prior art or loss of right to a patent or an estoppel. The inference that the counts (i.e., the subject matter of the counts) must be statutory prior art to the losing party merely because §135(a), as a matter of PTO procedure, provides for automatic "final refusal" of claims corresponding to the counts by virtue of the adverse award of priority, is unwarranted. Neither the counts nor the subject matter of the counts is statutory prior art by virtue of 35 U.S.C. §135(a). *In re McKellin, Mageli, and D'Angelo,* 529 F.2d 1324, 188 U.S.P.Q. 428 (C.C.P.A. 1976).

ϖ

Valid prior art may be created by the admission of the parties. Certain art may be prior art as to one inventive entity, but not to the public in general. Absent a statutory bar under 35 U.S.C. §102(b), (c), or (d), an applicant's own invention cannot be prior art to him. *In re Fout, Mishkin, and Roychoudhury,* 675 F.2d 297, 213 U.S.P.Q. 532 (C.C.P.A. 1982).

ϖ

To weaken the presumption of validity, there must be some showing that the prior art was not considered by the Examiner, not merely that it was not cited. Since none of the additional prior art references relied upon by the defendant were not considered by the Examiner or disclose any substantial element relating to the patented subject matter that was not considered by the PTO, the statutory presumption of validity is fully effective in this case. *Parkson Corp. v. Proto Circuits, Inc.*, 220 U.S.P.Q. 898 (Md. 1983).

ᛠ

The Examiner's search record provides prima facie evidence that he searched all the references in the classes and subclasses noted on the file wrapper as having been searched. References in such subclasses left uncited are presumed to have been regarded by the Examiner as less relevant than those cited. A contrary view would destroy the presumption of administrative regularity on which the presumption of validity rests. *Railroad Dynamics, Inc. v. A. Stucki Co.*, 579 F. Supp. 353, 218 U.S.P.Q. 618 (Pa. 1983).

ᛠ

The scope of prior art is limited to that which would have been considered by those endeavoring to solve the problem that the patent solves. *Atlas Powder Co. v. E. I. du Pont de Nemours & Co.*, 588 F. Supp. 1455, 221 U.S.P.Q. 426 (Tex. 1983).

ᛠ

The differences between the prior art and the invention defined by the asserted claims, the availability of that art to all workers in the field, the failure of established competitors in a highly competitive market to make the invention despite the incentive to do so, the admittedly nonobvious performance benefits realized through the claimed invention, the impressive commercial success of the claimed product, the praise of independent commentators and the forbearance of competitors from infringing the patent all go to confirm that the claimed invention was not obvious at the time it was made to a person of ordinary skill in the art. *S. C. Johnson & Son, Inc. v. Carter-Wallace, Inc.*, 614 F. Supp. 1278, 225 U.S.P.Q. 1022 (N.Y. 1985)

ᛠ

Validity was denied by a memo that was admittedly not prior art, notwithstanding the fact that the contents of such memo had been concealed by the alleged infringer. *Newell Companies v. Kenney Manufacturing Co.*, 606 F. Supp. 1282, 226 U.S.P.Q. 157 (R.I. 1985).

ᛠ

The contention that a claimed configuration would be obvious from a reference claim on which it reads is a non sequitur. According to such reasoning Morse's telegraph patent would have made the Telex obvious. The scope of a patent's claims determines what infringes the patent; it is no measure of what it discloses. A patent discloses only that which it describes, whether specifically or in general terms, so as to convey intelligence to one capable of understanding. *In re Benno*, 768 F.2d 1340, 226 U.S.P.Q. 683 (Fed. Cir. 1985).

ᛠ

Mishimura was a published Japanese patent application, the publication date of which was subsequent to the appellant's established Convention date. The appellant's description of Mishimura was no more than an admission that the appellant did not invent the subject matter of Mishimura. Mishimura is thus prior art to appellant under 35 U.S.C. §102(f). Since the appellant had not made a showing under 35 U.S.C. §103 that disqualifies this as prior art, it is available as evidence of obviousness and can be combined with other prior art under §103. *Ex parte Yoshino and Takasu*, 227 U.S.P.Q. 52 (B.P.A.I. 1985).

ᛟ

Although it is proper to note the difference in a claimed invention from the prior art, because that difference may serve as one element in determining the obviousness/non-obviousness issue, it is improper to consider the difference as the invention. The "difference" may be slight (as has often been the case with some of history's greatest inventions, e.g., the telephone), but it may also have been the key to success in advancements in the art resulting from the invention. The issue with respect to obviousness is whether a challenger has carried its burden of proving, by clear and convincing evidence, facts from which it must be concluded that one skilled in the art at the time the invention was made would have found it to have been obvious, from the references as a whole, to create the claimed subject matter as a whole. *Datascope Corp. v. SMEC, Inc.*, 776 F.2d 320, 227 U.S.P.Q. 838 (Fed. Cir. 1985).

ᛟ

Enablement is a legal determination of whether a patent enables one skilled in the art to make and use the claimed invention. It is not precluded even if some experimentation is necessary, although the amount of experimentation needed must not be unduly extensive. Enablement is determined as of the filing date of the patent application. Furthermore, a patent need not teach, and preferably omits, what is well known in the art. *Hybritech Inc. v. Monoclonal Antibodies, Inc.*, 802 F.2d 1367, 231 U.S.P.Q. 81 (Fed. Cir. 1986).

ᛟ

Even when a claimed invention is disclosed in a printed publication, such disclosure does not suffice as prior art if it is not enabling. The disclosure must be such as will give possession of the invention to a person of ordinary skill. *Paperless Accounting, Inc. v. Bay Area Rapid Transit System*, 804 F.2d 659, 231 U.S.P.Q. 649, 653 (Fed. Cir. 1986).

ᛟ

A prior patent must be considered in its entirety (i.e., as a whole), including portions that would lead away from the invention in issue. *Panduit Corp. v. Dennison Manufacturing Co.*, 810 F.2d 1561, 1 U.S.P.Q.2d 1593 (Fed. Cir. 1987).

ᛟ

In determining whether a patented device would have been obvious to a person of ordinary skill in the art, a court must assume that the hypothetical person had knowledge of all prior art disclosed at the time of his invention, regardless of how obscure the source. The starting place for determining the issue of obviousness is to picture the hypothetical person working in his workshop with all the prior-art references hanging on the walls around him. Prior art is knowledge that is available, including what would be obvious from it, at a given time, to a person of ordinary skill in the art. The scope of the prior art is that which is reasonably pertinent to the particular problem with which the inventor was involved. References are within the scope of the prior art if the problem presented and overcome by them is basically the same problem presented and overcome by the invention in question. If the inventor consults a reference in his search for a solution to the problem, this act constitutes an acknowledgment by the problem solver of what he considered relevant prior art. The content of the prior art includes everything a reference teaches. A reference's teachings cannot be disregarded because of differences between the inventions. A reference should be considered for what it and all references collectively suggest to one of ordinary skill in the art. If the teachings relied upon are repeated in a number of references, obviousness is strenghtened. *Consolidated Aluminum Corp. v. Foseco International Ltd.*, 10 U.S.P.Q.2d 1143, 1165 (Ill. 1988).

ω

A patent is not prior art under 35 U.S.C. §102(g) when the invention thereof was reduced to practice by another before the application for the patent was filed and before diligent preparation of the application began. *Mendenhall v. Astec Industries, Inc.*, 13 U.S.P.Q.2d 1913, 1935 (Tenn. 1988), *aff'd*, 13 U.S.P.Q.2d 1956 (Fed. Cir. 1989).

ω

The requirements of public disclosure are greater for 35 U.S.C. §102(a) prior art than for 35 U.S.C. §102(g) prior art. *Oak Industries, Inc. v. Zenith Electronics Corp.*, 726 F. Supp. 1525, 14 U.S.P.Q.2d 1417, 1426 (Ill. 1989).

ω

Simply because a patent is issued to joint inventors does not mean that everything disclosed in that patent is necessarily joint work that would constitute prior art against a subsequent patent application by one of the two joint inventors. *De Graffenried v. United States,* 20 Cl. Ct. 458, 16 U.S.P.Q.2d 1321, 1328 (Cl. Ct. 1990).

ω

Only the claims are compared in a rejection for double patenting. Such a rejection by the PTO does not mean that the first-filed patent is a prior art reference under 35 U.S.C. §102 against the later-filed application. Thus, the "obviation" of double patenting of the obviousness-type by filing a terminal disclaimer has no effect on a rejection under 35 U.S.C. §103 based on the first-filed patent. Such a rejection cannot be overcome by a terminal disclaimer. A terminal disclaimer is of circumscribed availability and effect. It is not an admission of obviousness of the later-filed claimed invention in light of the earlier-filed disclosure, for that is not the basis of the disclaimer. The filing of a terminal disclaimer simply serves the statutory function of removing the rejection of double patenting and raises neither presumption nor estoppel on the merits of the rejection. It is improper to convert this simple expedient of "obviation" into an admission or acquiescence or estoppel on the merits. *Quad Environmental Technologies Corp. v. Union Sanitary District,* 946 F.2d 870, 20 U.S.P.Q.2d 1392, 1394, 1395 (Fed. Cir. 1991).

ω

"Prior art is knowledge that is available, including what would be obvious from it, at a given time, to a person of ordinary skill in the art." Robert L. Harmon, Patents in the Federal Circuit 52 (2d ed. 1991). *Wang Laboratories Inc. v. Mitsubishi Electronics America Inc.*, 860 F.Supp. 1448, 30 U.S.P.Q.2d 1241, 1245 (Cal. 1993).

ω

In determining the scope and content of the prior art, an inventor is presumed knowledgeable only of prior art in the field of his endeavor that is reasonably related to the particular problem the invention solved. Prior art references must be evaluated on what they taught or suggested in their entireties when the invention was made. The field of search by the Patent Examiner is relevant objective evidence of the scope of the prior art. *Williams Service Group Inc. v. O.B. Cannon & Son Inc.*, 33 U.S.P.Q.2d 1705, 1725 (Pa. 1994).

ᛩ

It is an abuse of discretion for a trial court to refuse to allow a party to introduce prior art produced within thirty days of the trial, if the opposing party had an opportunity to review the documents and to produce rebuttal evidence. *Donelly Corp. v. Gentex Corp.*, 37 U.S.P.Q.2d 1146, 1149 (Mich. 1995).

ᛩ

Any suggestion that a document is prior art because it appears before the filing date of a patent ignores the requirements of 35 U.S.C. §102(a). Section 102(a) explicitly refers to invention dates, not filing dates. Thus, under section 102(a), a document is prior art only when published before the invention date. *Mahurkar v. C.R. Bard Inc.*, 79 F.3d 1572, 38 U.S.P.Q.2d 1288, 1290 (Fed. Cir. 1996).

ᛩ

The prior art relied upon by the applicant "gives clues as to what the claims do not cover." *Mitek Surgical Products Inc. v. Arthrex Inc.*, 49 U.S.P.Q.2d 1275, 1278 (Utah 1998).

Prior-Art Anagrams. *See* **Combining References.**

Prior Art as a Whole. *See also* **References as a Whole, Teach Away From.**

It is impermissible within the framework of 35 U.S.C. §103 to pick and choose from any one reference only so much of it as will support a given position to the exclusion of other parts necessary to the full appreciation of what such reference fairly suggests to one skilled in the art. *Bausch & Lomb, Inc. v. Barnes-Hind/Hydrocurve, Inc.*, 796 F.2d 443, 230 U.S.P.Q. 416 (Fed. Cir. 1986).

Prior Invention.

An award of priority based on a prior invention in this country is prior art under 35 U.S.C. §§102(g) and 103, as opposed to an award based on a prior invention in a foreign country, which is not prior art under 35 U.S.C. §103. *In re McKellin, Mageli, and D'Angelo*, 529 F.2d 1324, 188 U.S.P.Q. 428, 433 (C.C.P.A. 1976).

ᛩ

To find anticipation of claims, the prior-art embodiments must possess the properties expressly recited in the claims. Property limitations can serve to distinguish claimed subject matter from other products. Identity of invention is a question of fact, and a challenger must show that each element of a claim is found in a prior patent or publication, either expressly or under principles of inherency. To establish anticipation, however, it is not necessary to prove that prior artisans were aware that their products possessed the recited properties. *E. I. du Pont de Nemours & Co. v. Phillips Petroleum Co.*, 849 F.2d 1430, 7 U.S.P.Q.2d 1129 (Fed. Cir. 1988).

Prior Inventorship.

Claims of prior inventorship and derivation may be established by a preponderance-of-the-evidence for interferences between a patent and a co-pending application, or between interfering patents. *Environ Products Inc. v. Furon Co.*, 47 U.S.P.Q.2d 1040, 1044 (Pa. 1998).

Priority.[10] *See also* **Combining Priority Applications, Derivative Application, 35 U.S.C. §119, 35 U.S.C. §120, 35 U.S.C. §146.**

Where the question decided 1in the Patent Office is one between contesting parties as to priority of invention, the decision there must be accepted as controlling upon that question of fact in any subsequent suit between the same parties unless the contrary is established by testimony that, in character and amount, carries thorough conviction. *United States v. Szuecs*, 240 F.2d 886, 112 U.S.P.Q. 86, 87 (D.C. Cir. 1957).

ᴡ

Section 119 of 35 U.S.C. sets the time limit for claiming priority as being "before the patent is granted or at such time during the pendency of the application as required by the Commissioner..." Under this provision the terminal date beyond which priority may not be claimed is "before the patent is granted." When this fact occurs, the right of priority is lost insofar as §119 is concerned. *Ex parte Arkless*, 116 U.S.P.Q. 214, 215 (PO Bd. App. 1955).

ᴡ

During prosecution of the parent application, priority under 35 U.S.C. §119 (based on a previously filed German application) was claimed. Although priority of the original German application was not claimed for the divisional application, such divisional application is nevertheless entitled (under 35 U.S.C. §§120 and 121) "to the benefit of the filing date of the original application," which, according to §119, is the original German filing date, which is also the date of invention for the invention of the divisional case under 35 U.S.C. §104. *Deutsche Gold-Und Silber-Scheideanstalt vormals Roessler v. Commissioner of Patents*, 251 F. Supp. 624, 148 U.S.P.Q. 412 (D.C. 1966).

ᴡ

It is first filing in a foreign convention country that creates the priority right, not the nationality of the applicant. It often happens that American inventors domiciled in the

---

[10] A Certificate of Correction under 35 U.S.C. §255 and 37 C.F.R. §1.323 may be requested and issued in order to perfect a claim of foreign priority benefits in a patented continuing application if the requirements of 35 U.S.C. §119 had been satisfied in the parent application, prior to issuance of the patent, and requirements of 37 C.F.R. §1.55(a) are met. However, a claim of foreign priority benefits cannot be perfected via a Certificate of Correction if the requirements of 35 U.S.C. §119 had not been satisfied in the patented application (or an antecedent application thereof), prior to issuance, and the requirements of 37 C.F.R. §1.55(a) are not met. In this latter circumstance, the claim to foreign priority benefits can be perfected only by way of a reissue application. (*Notice*, 1069 T.M.O.G. 4, Aug. 26, 1986.)

United States file abroad before filing here and claim priority rights in their own country as a result. *In re Hilmer, Korger, Weyer, and Aumuller*, 359 F.2d 859, 149 U.S.P.Q. 480, 496 (C.C.P.A. 1966).

ᚳ

Where the inventive entity differs in the foreign and in the U.S. applications, the Examiner should refuse to recognize the priority date "until the inconsistency or disagreement is eliminated." The requirements of 35 U.S.C. §116 and Rule 45 are inapplicable to foreign applications where the claim to the benefit of an earlier filing date is made under 35 U.S.C. §119. *Schmitt and Panouse v. Babcock and Herr*, 377 F.2d 994, 153 U.S.P.Q. 719, 725 (C.C.P.A. 1967).

ᚳ

In an interference between two parties who rely on the same date of corresponding foreign filings under the International Convention, neither is entitled to an award of priority. However, prior introduction of conception with regard to one count can be relied upon for priority purposes. *Lassman v. Brossi, Gerecke, and Kyburz*, 159 U.S.P.Q. 182, 184, 185 (PO Bd. Pat. Intf. 1967).

ᚳ

Section 251 (35 U.S.C.), which provides for the reissue of defective patents, is sufficiently broad in application to overcome the literal language of 35 U.S.C. §119, and to entitle appellee to a reissued patent to include the priority rights which Section 119 gives to applicants who have previously obtained certain foreign patents. *Brenner v. The State of Israel, Ministry of Defence*, 400 F.2d 789, 158 U.S.P.Q. 584, 585 (CA D.C. 1968)

ᚳ

In a case involving a first-filed foreign application at the head of a chain of later-filed properly copending U.S. applications, there must be compliance, in the first instance, with the provisions of the second paragraph of 35 U.S.C. §119 during the pendency of that first U.S. application that, as is mandated in §119, was actually "filed" within the 12-month period in order to secure the benefit of the date that the application "was first filed" in the foreign country as an effective filing date. In addition, there must be compliance with the provisions of 35 U.S.C. §120 to provide a basis for according the last-filed U.S. application in the chain the benefit of the actual filing of the first U.S. application and with it the benefit of the foreign filing date that has been accorded to it. *Justus v. Appenzeller*, 177 U.S.P.Q. 332, 339 (PO Bd. Pat. Int. 1971).

ᚳ

A party dissatisfied with a decision of the Board of Patent Interference on a question of priority of invention between conflicting patent applications may pursue a civil action against the other parties to the interference proceeding. This action is not a standard civil action; it is more in the nature of a review of an administrative proceeding with inherent limitations on the issues that may be raised in the original claim or by counterclaim. Cases under 35 U.S.C. §146 are limited to a review of the administrative proceedings in the Patent Office supplemented by additional evidence and testimony only insofar as it relates to contentions advanced below. *Montecatini Edison, S.p.A. v. Ziegler*, 172 U.S.P.Q. 519, 520 (D.C. 1972).

ᚳ

The reference to "application for patent" in 35 U.S.C. §119 is not limited to the first-filed application in a chain of copending applications. The purpose of having the record of the United States patent complete in this country would not be best served by filing the claim for priority and the priority document in an abandoned application. *In re Tangsrud*, 184 U.S.P.Q. 746 (Comm'r 1973)

ᴡ

In a priority contest a party who was second to file was unable to prevail even though he had reduced the invention to practice four years prior to his opponent's filing date. Even if he demonstrated continuous activity from prior to his opponent's effective filing date to his filing date, such should have no bearing on the question of priority. While diligence during the above-noted period may be relied upon by one alleging prior conception and subsequent reduction to practice, it is of no significance in the case of the party who is not last to reduce to practice. Too long a delay may bar the first inventor from reliance on an early reduction to practice. However, the first inventor is not barred from relying on later resumed activity antedating an opponent's entry into the field merely because the work done before the delay occurred was sufficient to amount to a reduction to practice. *Paulik v. Rizkalla*, 760 F.2d 1270, 226 U.S.P.Q. 224 (Fed. Cir. 1985).

ᴡ

A claim of priority under 35 U.S.C. §120 may be made in a utility application based upon an earlier-filed design application provided that the design application satisfies the statutory conditions; of particular pertinence is the condition that the disclosure of the design application must meet the requirements of the first paragraph of 35 U.S.C. §112 as applied to the claims of the utility application. Similar observations may be made with regard to claiming priority under §120 in a design application based upon an earlier-filed utility application. *Ex parte Duniau*, 1 U.S.P.Q.2d 1652 (B.P.A.I. 1986).

ᴡ

Reference to the "invention" in 35 U.S.C. §119 clearly refers to what the claims define, not what is disclosed in the foreign application. Section 119 provides that a foreign application "shall have the same effect" as if it had been filed in the United States. Accordingly, if the effective date of what is claimed in a U.S. application is at issue, to preserve symmetry of treatment between §120 and §119, the foreign priority application must be examined to ascertain whether it supports, within the meaning of 35 U.S.C. §112, paragraph 1, what is claimed in the U.S. application. *In re Gosteli*, 872 F.2d 1008, 10 U.S.P.Q.2d 1614, 1616 (Fed. Cir. 1989).

ᴡ

In order to establish priority in an interference, the party who files later is required to establish reduction to practice before the filing date of the party who filed first, or conception before that date coupled with reasonable diligence from before that date to the filing date of the party who files later. To establish a *prima facie* case entitling them to proceed with the interference, however, the party who filed later was required only to prove (by way of affidavits setting forth facts) at least so much of his case as would entitle him to an award of priority if the senior party were to rely only on his filing date and were not to rebut any of the junior party's case. To establish reduction to practice of a chemical composition, it is sufficient to prove that the inventor actually prepared the composition and knew it would work. The inventor, however, must provide independent corroborating evidence in addition to his own statements and documents. Such evidence may consist of testimony of a witness, other than the inventor, to the actual reduction to practice or it may consist of evidence of surrounding facts and circumstances independent of information received from the inventor. The purpose of the rule requiring corroboration is to prevent fraud. *Hahn v. Wong,* 892 F.2d 1028, 13 U.S.P.Q.2d 1313, 1317 (Fed. Cir. 1989).

ω

Priority depends on a demonstration that a party has "possession of every feature" of the invention. When a design patent is relied upon for priority in a utility application, the design drawings must show which of the attributes of the invention are "the features" upon which patentability is predicated. When such cannot be ascertained from the design drawings alone, design patents may not satisfy the first paragraph of 35 U.S.C. §112. *Vas-Cath Inc. v. Mahurkar,* 745 F. Supp. 517, 17 U.S.P.Q.2d 1353, 1358 (Ill. 1990).

ω

The proposition that the inventive entity must be the same in both the foreign and the corresponding U.S. application in order to obtain benefit can no longer be accepted as a hard and fast rule in view of the liberalization of the requirements for filing a U.S. application as joint inventors wrought by the 1984 amendment of 35 U.S.C. §116. Since 35 U.S.C. §§116 and 120 now accommodate situations where different claims in an application may have different inventive entities, 35 U.S.C. §119 can and should be construed to accommodate those situations as well to preserve symmetry of treatment between §§119 and 120. *Reitz v. Inoue,* 39 U.S.P.Q.2d 1838, 1840, 1841 (B.P.A.I. 1995)

Prior Knowledge. *See also* Known.

Enablement is a legal determination of whether a patent enables one skilled in the art to make and use the claimed invention. It is not precluded even if some experimentation is necessary, although the amount of experimentation needed must not be unduly extensive. Enablement is determined as of the filing date of the patent application. Furthermore, a patent need not teach, and preferably omits, what is well known in the art. *Hybritech Inc. v. Monoclonal Antibodies, Inc.,* 802 F.2d 1367, 231 U.S.P.Q. 81 (Fed. Cir. 1986).

Prior Sale.

A defendant's argument and evidence that the claimed subject matter was in use and on sale five years prior to the patentee's filing date were not adequate to overcome a partial summary judgment motion because the defendant was unable to present documentary evidence regarding written production standards for the commercialized product and also failed to produce any research and development papers that record the production of the product in the same manner as defined by the patent claims. Furthermore, defendant could point to only one customer of the product and one location where it was purchased. After the customer lost interest in the product, defendant abandoned manufacturing it. An absence of contemporaneous documentation and a conflict in the testimony of defendant's witnesses bode ill for defendant's case at the summary judgment state. *Fromson v. RVP Chemical Corp.,* 15 U.S.P.Q.2d 1689, 1694 (Wis. 1990).

Prior Use. *See also* **Experimental Use.**

A party claiming anticipation under 35 U.S.C. §102 because of prior use is put to "the strictest of proofs." Because of the unsatisfactory character of mere oral testimony to prove an anticipation, a party attempting to establish an anticipation has the burden of doing so by "clear and satisfactory evidence." *Trend Products Co. v. Metro Industries, Inc.*, 10 U.S.P.Q.2d 1531, 1538 (Cal. 1989). .

ᚥ

An alleged prior use must be established by clear and convincing evidence. Oral testimony as to such purported prior use must normally be corroborated by other evidence. Oral testimony of alleged prior use, unsupported by contemporaneous documents, must be subject to appropriate scrutiny under the clear and convincing standard of proof. *Henkel Corp. v. Coral Inc.*, 754 F. Supp. 1280, 21 U.S.P.Q.2d 1081, 1103 (Ill. 1990).

Prior Work. *See also* **35 U.S.C. §102(g)/103.**

Under the Clemens test {*see In re Clemens*, 622 F.2d 1029, 1040, 206 U.S.P.Q. 289 (C.C.P.A. 1980)}, prior work is considered prior art only when the work is well known to the art or to the patentee before the patentee made the invention at issue; prior work not known to the patentee or to the art cannot be considered prior art. *CSS International Corp. v. Maul Technology Co.*, 16 U.S.P.Q.2d 1657, 1662 (Ind. 1989).

Privilege. *See also* **Attorney-Client Privilege, Foreign Associate, Self-Evaluative Privilege, Work-Product Privilege.**

Generally, when factual information is communicated so that an attorney can disclose it in a patent or trademark application, the communication is viewed as nonprivileged. On the other hand, documents containing considerable technical factual information, but that are nevertheless primarily concerned with giving legal guidance to the client, are classified as privileged. Doubts are resolved in favor of privilege. *Jack Winter Inc. v. Koratron Co.*, 54 F.R.D. 44, 172 U.S.P.Q. 201 (Cal. 1971).

ᚥ

By instituting a Declaratory Action proceeding in which validity of a patent and its infringement are placed in issue, the plaintiff may have waived the attorney-client and work-product privilege with regard to identification and content of all documents in its possession that relate to the patent in suit and its foreign counterparts. *U.S. Industries, Inc. v. Norton Co.*, 174 U.S.P.Q. 513 (N.Y. 1972).

ᚥ

Documents reflecting communications involving foreign patent agents, if otherwise within the scope of attorney-client privilege, may be regarded as privileged. Documents prepared for one case have the same work-product protection in a second case, at least if the two cases are closely related. *In re Yarn Processing Patent Litigation*, 177 U.S.P.Q. 514 (Fla. 1973).

ᚥ

Privilege, when challenged by a misrepresentation or omission before the PTO, should be pierced when and only when a *prima facie* case of fraud has been shown. In order to pierce the privilege, it is not enough to show merely inequitable conduct before the PTO. Rather, it is necessary to establish a case of fraudulent procurement; that is, one must show (1) a knowing, willful and intentional act of misrepresentation or omission before the PTO; (2) the misrepresentation or omission must be material; and (3) the PTO must have relied upon the misrepresentation or omission. While a fraudulent intent is usually a necessary element to prove in a common law action of deceit, this intent can be presumed where there is a knowing misrepresentation of a material fact before the PTO. Of course, this presumption can be rebutted at trial by a showing of good faith on the part of applicants. *American Optical Corp. v. United States*, 179 U.S.P.Q. 682 (Ct. Cl. 1973).

ω

The defendant's unsupported assertions that the plaintiff and its agents engaged in fraudulent or inequitable conduct in procuring the patent in suit is simply insufficient to establish entitlement to privileged documents through the fraud exception. Accordingly, as the documents sought by the defendants are protected by the attorney-client privilege or work-product doctrine, the defendant's motion to compel production is denied. *Rohm & Haas Co. v. Dawson Chemical Co.*, 214 U.S.P.Q. 56, 60 (Tex. 1981).

ω

In order for privilege to apply, the person to whom a communication is made must be a member of a bar of a court or his subordinate. This is so because the general purpose of the attorney-client privilege is to promote freedom of consultation of legal advisors by clients. The attorney-client privilege does not apply to foreign patent agents, for they are not attorneys at law and thus do not satisfy the requirement that the communication be made to a member of the bar. While the attorney-client privilege protects communications to the attorney's clerks and other agents, it does not extend to foreign patent agents for they are not agents of the attorney. Only communications between an attorney or an agent of the attorney and his client are covered by the privilege. Expanding the privilege to treat foreign patent agents as if they are lawyers improperly expands the privilege beyond its proper bounds. *Status Time Corp. v. Sharp Electronics Corp.*, 95 F.R.D. 27, 217 U.S.P.Q. 438 (N.Y. 1982).

ω

In order to negate the attorney-client privilege, a party seeking to obtain information that may arguably be privileged must establish that the client seeking to invoke the privilege consulted and obtained the advice of counsel for the purpose of conducting fraudulent activities. The person seeking to negate the privilege must make out a *prima facie* case of fraud. The alleged fraudulent activities must be of such a serious nature as to warrant the obviation of the privilege.

The work-product privilege protects (from discovery) materials prepared in anticipation of litigation. The mere likelihood of litigation in the future is insufficient for invoking the privilege. Rather, the probability of litigation must be substantial and the commencement of the litigation imminent. Materials that are prepared in the ordinary course of business do not fall within the work-product exception. While all documents generated in the patent application process may not be protected from discovery, in any given situation there can be documents that do in fact fall within the work product privilege. *Stauffer Chemical Co. v. Monsanto Co.*, 623 F. Supp. 148, 227 U.S.P.Q. 401 (Mo. 1985).

ᚥ

There is no absolute privilege for trade secrets and similar confidential information. To resist discovery under Rule 26(c)(7), a person must first establish that the information sought is a trade secret and then demonstrate that its disclosure might be harmful. If these requirements are met, the burden shifts to the party seeking discovery to establish that the disclosure of trade secrets is relevant and necessary to the action. The district court must balance the need for the trade secrets against the claim of injury resulting from disclosure. If proof of relevancy or need is not established, discovery should be denied. On the other hand, if relevancy and need are shown, the trade secrets should be disclosed, unless they are privileged or the subpoenas are unreasonable, oppressive, annoying, or embarrassing. *Heat & Control, Inc. v. Hector Industries, Inc.*, 785 F.2d 1017, 228 U.S.P.Q. 926 (Fed. Cir. 1986).

ᚥ

The law seems to be split three ways on the question whether an inadvertent disclosure of privileged documents can be a waiver. At one extreme are cases that say that an inadvertent disclosure never constitutes a waiver. The view of such cases is that waiver must be an intentional relinquishment of a known right; if the disclosure is truly inadvertent, whether by negligence or oversight, the privilege is not waived. At the other end there is the rule that says disclosure is disclosure, period, regardless of the intent of the disclosing party. Under those cases, an objective test is applied. The only issue is whether there has been a disclosure. If there has been a disclosure, there has been a waiver. The courts do not look to the intent of the disclosing party. A middle ground rule is that an inadvertent disclosure does not necessarily constitute a waiver. This line of cases looks to a number of factors, including the reasonableness of precautions, the time taken to rectify the disclosure, and other factors. *Dyson v. Amway Corp.*, 17 U.S.P.Q.2d 1965, 1966, 1967 (Mich. 1990).

ᚥ

Disclosure of privileged information during settlement conferences constitutes a waiver of the privilege. *Bausch & Lomb Inc. v. Alcon Laboratories Inc.*, 38 U.S.P.Q.2d 1761, 1765 (N.Y. 1996).

Privilege Log.

The Second Circuit has made clear that a privilege log should contain specific explanations of why each particular document is privileged. *Bristol-Meyers Squibb Co. v. Rhône-Poulenc Rorer Inc.*, 44 U.S.P.Q.2d 1463, 1466 (N.Y. 1997).

Privity.

What constitutes "privity" varies, depending on the purposes for which privity is asserted. Privity, like the doctrine of assignor estoppel, itself, is determined upon a balance of the equities. If an inventor assigns his invention to his employer company A and leaves to join company B, whether company B is in privity and thus bound by the doctrine will depend on the equities dictated by the relationship between the inventor and company B in light of the act of infringement. The closer that relationship, the more the equities will favor applying the doctrine to company B. *Intel Corp. v. International Trade Commission,* 946 F.2d 821, 20 U.S.P.Q.2d 1161, 1176 (Fed. Cir. 1991); *Shamrock Technologies, Inc. v. Medical Sterilization Inc.,* 903 F.2d 789, 14 U.S.P.Q.2d 1728, 1732 (Fed. Cir. 1990).

Privy.

Defendants (alleged to have acquired title to and to have sold products, knowing the same to be falsely marked, for the purpose of deceiving the public) were not privy to the Patent Office proceedings and are not bound by the patentee's admissions against interest. *United States v. Carrollton Manufacturing Company,* 377 F.Supp. 218, 181 U.S.P.Q. 451, 453 (Ohio 1974).

Probability.

In order to recover lost profits rather than merely a reasonable royalty in a patent infringement action, the patent holder must demonstrate that "but for" the infringement, he would have made sales that the infringer made. No presumption operates in the patent holder's favor that he would have made the sales in question. The patent holder must advance affirmative proof of the demand for his patented product in the marketplace, the absence of acceptable non-infringing substitutes, and his production and marketing capacity to meet the demand. Yet, the but-for rule necessarily expresses a hypothesis. Neither the trial court nor the appellate court can demand absolute proof that purchasers of the infringing product would have bought the patent holder's product instead. It is impossible and therefor unnecessary for the patent holder to negate every possibility that the purchasers might not have bought another product. The plaintiff's burden of proof is not absolute, but rather one of reasonable probability. *Milgo Electronic Corp. v. United Business Communications, Inc.,* 623 F.2d 645, 206 U.S.P.Q. 481 (10th Cir. 1980).

ω

Inherency may not be established by probabilities or possibilities. The mere fact that a certain thing may result from a given set of circumstances is not sufficient. *In re Oelrich and Divigard,* 666 F.2d 578, 212 U.S.P.Q. 323, 326 (C.C.P.A. 1981); *Hansgirg v. Kemmer,* 102 F.2d 212, 40 U.S.P.Q. 665, 667 (C.C.P.A. 1939).

ω

Inherency may not be established by probabilities or possibilities. The mere fact that a certain thing may result from a given set of circumstances is not sufficient. Although an applicant may be required to prove that the subject matter shown to be in prior art does not possess characteristics relied upon, where an Examiner has reason to believe that a functional limitation asserted to be critical for establishing novelty in the claimed subject matter may, in fact, be an inherent characteristic of the prior art, the Examiner must provide some evidence or scientific reasoning to establish the reasonableness of the Examiner's belief that the functional limitation is an inherent characteristic of the prior art before the applicant can be put through this burdensome task. *Ex parte Skinner,* 2 U.S.P.Q.2d 1788 (B.P.A.I. 1986).

ω

A patentee need not negative every possibility that a purchaser might have bought a product other than his, absent the infringement. Indeed, the patentee need only show that there was a reasonable probability that the sales would have been made "but for" the infringement. Therefore, the issue of whether a patentee deserves lost-profit damages is based not on a subjective, individualized inquiry, but on an objective standard of "reasonable probability." When the patentee and the infringer are the only suppliers present in the market, it is reasonable to infer that the infringement probably caused the loss of profits. Any doubts regarding the calculatory precision of the damage amount must be resolved against the infringer. *Kaufman Co. Inc. v. Lantech Inc.*, 926 F.2d 1136, 17 U.S.P.Q.2d 1828, 1831, 1832 (Fed. Cir. 1991).

Problem. *See also* **Analogous Art, Cause, Purpose, Solution, Source, Time.**

Although the patentee had merely changed the pitch of the Fourdrinier wire of a paper-making machine, the change in pitch was regarded as directed toward a wholly different object from that of the prior art. *Eibel Process Co. v. Minnesota & Ontario Paper Co.*, 261 U.S. 45, 67 (1923).

ᵫ

Patentability is gauged not only by the extent or simplicity of physical changes, but also by the perception of the necessity or desirability of making such changes to produce a new result. When viewed after disclosure, the changes may seem simple and such as should have been obvious to those in the field. However, this does not necessarily negative invention or patentability. The conception of a new and useful improvement must be considered—along with the actual means of achieving it in determining the presence or absence of invention. The discovery of a problem calling for an improvement is often a very essential element in an invention correcting such a problem. Though the problem, once realized, may be solved by use of old and known elements, this does not necessarily negative patentability.

Although the physical means of accomplishing the appellant's improvement and its new and useful results are simple, the conception of so improving on the prior art devices would not be obvious to those skilled in the art. *In re Bisley,* 197 F.2d 355, 94 U.S.P.Q. 80, 86, 87 (C.C.P.A. 1952).

ᵫ

When a person, having the references before him and not cognizant of applicant's disclosure, would not be informed that a problem (solved by applicant's claimed invention) ever existed, such references (which never recognized the problem) could not have suggested its solution. The references were thus improperly combined since there is no suggestion in either of them that they can be combined to produce the result obtained by the claimed invention. *In re Shaffer,* 229 F.2d 476, 108 U.S.P.Q. 326, 329 (C.C.P.A. 1956).

ᵫ

The 35 U.S.C. §103 requirement of non-obviousness is no different in chemical cases than with respect to other categories of patentable inventions. The problem of obviousness under §103 in determining the patentability of new and useful chemical compounds—or, as it is sometimes called, the problem of "chemical obviousness"—is not really a problem in chemistry or pharmacology or in any other related field of science, such as biology, biochemistry, pharmacodynamics, ecology, or others yet to be conceived; it is a problem of patent law. *In re Papesch,* 315 F.2d 381, 137 U.S.P.Q. 43 (C.C.P.A. 1963).

ᴡ

Because the problem affects the definition of the prior art, it therefore affects each of the first three *Graham* factors: the prior art's scope and content, the art's level of ordinary skill, and the prior art's differences from the claimed invention. *See Graham v. John Deere Co.,* 383 U.S. 1, 17-18, 148 U.S.P.Q. 459 (1966).

ᴡ

A novel chemical compound can be non-obvious to one having ordinary skill in the art notwithstanding that it may possess a known property in common with a known structurally similar compound. Where it is disclosed that the prior-art compound "cannot be regarded as useful" for the sole use disclosed, a person having ordinary skill in the art would lack the "necessary impetus" to make the claimed compound. *In re Albrecht,* 514 F.2d 1389, 185 U.S.P.Q. 585 (C.C.P.A. 1975).

ᴡ

Patentability may exist in the discovery of the cause of a defect in an existing machine or process and applying a remedy therefor even though, after the cause is understood, the remedy would be obvious. *In re Wiseman and Kovac,* 596 F.2d 1019, 201 U.S.P.Q. 658, 661 (C.C.P.A. 1979).

ᴡ

For the teachings of a reference to be prior art under 35 U.S.C. §103, there must be some basis for concluding that the reference would have been considered by one skilled in the particular art working on the pertinent problem to which the invention pertains; for no matter what a reference teaches, it could not have rendered obvious anything (at the time the invention was made) to a person having ordinary skill in the art to which the subject matter pertains unless that hypothetical person would have considered it. *In re Horn, Horn, Horn, and Horn,* 203 U.S.P.Q. 969 (C.C.P.A. 1979).

ᴡ

Where an applicant contends that the discovery of the source of a problem would have been unobvious to one of ordinary skill in the pertinent art at the time the claimed invention was made, it is incumbent upon the PTO to explain its reasons if it disagrees. A mere conclusory statement that the source of a problem would have been discovered is inadequate. A "patentable invention may lie in the discovery of the source of the problem even though the remedy may be obvious once the source of the problem is identified." *In re Peehs and Hunner,* 612 F.2d 1287, 204 U.S.P.Q. 835, 837 (C.C.P.A. 1980).

ᴡ

The scope of prior art is limited to that which would have been considered by those endeavoring to solve the problem that the patent solves. *Atlas Powder Co. v. E. I. du Pont de Nemours & Co.,* 588 F. Supp. 1455, 221 U.S.P.Q. 426 (Tex. 1983).

ᴡ

Treating an advantage as the invention disregards the statutory requirement that the invention be viewed "as a whole," ignores the problem recognition element, and injects an improper obvious-to-try consideration. *Jones v. Hardy,* 727 F.2d 1524, 220 U.S.P.Q. 1021, 1026 (Fed. Cir. 1984).

ᛒ

The fact that a patent specifically discloses and claims a combination of features previously used in two separate devices is not fatal to patentability. A basic issue is whether applied references, alone or in any combination, suggest the claimed invention as a solution to the specific problem solved. The claimed invention achieved new and unexpected results nowhere suggested in the prior art, and that achievement was overlooked. The district court erroneously focused its inquiry "solely on the product created, rather than on the obviousness or non-obviousness of its creation." The initial inquiry should be directed to the vantage point of attacking the problem solved by the invention at the time the invention was made. When prior art itself does not suggest or render "obvious" the claimed solution to that problem, the art involved does not satisfy the criteria of 35 U.S.C. §103 for precluding patentability. *Lindemann Maschinenfabrik GmbH v. American Hoist & Derrick Co.,* 730 F.2d 1452, 221 U.S.P.Q. 481 (Fed. Cir. 1984).

ᛒ

A reference is not available under 35 U.S.C. §103 if it is not within the field of the inventor's endeavor and was not directly pertinent to the particular problem with which the inventor was involved. *King Instrument Corp. v. Otari Corp.* 767 F.2d 853, 226 U.S.P.Q. 402 (Fed. Cir. 1985).

ᛒ

In dismissing Dante as a reference, the court pointed out that Dante did not even hint at the problem the appellants sought to solve. Dante would not even have encountered the problem because it would not have appeared in what he was doing. *In re Benno,* 768 F.2d 1340, 226 U.S.P.Q. 683 (Fed. Cir. 1985).

ᛒ

To determine whether a reference is within the scope and contect of the prior art, first determine if the reference is within the field of the inventor's endeavor. If it is not, then next consider whether the reference is reasonably pertinent to the particular problem with which the inventor was involved. *Bausch & Lomb, Inc. v. Barnes-Hind/Hydrocurve, Inc.,* 796 F.2d 443, 230 U.S.P.Q. 416 (Fed. Cir. 1986).

ᛒ

Although each of the references does teach in general what the Examiner asserts it teaches, the rejection under 35 U.S.C. §103 fails because there is no concept in any of the art relied upon, either express or implied, ov providing a composition that includes both interferon and a tryosinase inhibitor. None of the art teaches increasing the effectiveness of interferon. None of the art teaches inhibiting the patient's serum tyrosinase as it increases concomitantly with interferon treatment. *Ex parte Rubin,* 5 U.S.P.Q.2d 1461 (B.P.A.I. 1987).

ᛒ

The PTO erred in holding that the non-obviousness (for the intended purpose) of the claimed structure was not relevant. The problem solved by the invention is always relevant. The entirety of a claimed invention, including the combination viewed as a whole, the elements thereof, and the properties and purpose of the invention, must be considered. Factors, including unexpected results, new features, solution of a different problem, and novel properties, are all considerations in the determination of obviousness in terms of 35 U.S.C. §103. When such factors are described in a specification, they are weighted in determining whether the prior art represents a *prima facie* case of obviousness.

A determination of whether a structure is or is not obvious requires cognizance of the properties of that structure and the problem that it solves, viewed in light of the teaching of the prior art. *In re Wright*, 848 F.2d 1216, 6 U.S.P.Q.2d 1959, 1962 (Fed. Cir. 1988).

ω

In comparing the differences between the structure and the properties taught in the prior art and those of the applicant's invention, there is a need to include consideration of the problem solved by the inventor. The determination of whether a novel structure is or is not obvious requires cognizance of the properties of that structure and the problem that it solves, viewed in the light of the teachings of the prior art. Where the invention for which a patent is sought solves a problem that persisted in the art, one must look to the problem as well as to its solution if he is to appraise properly what was done and to evaluate it against what would be obvious to one having the ordinary skills in the art. *In re Newell*, 891 F.2d 899, 13 U.S.P.Q.2d 1248, 1250 (Fed. Cir. 1989).

ω

Claims to new compositions can be regarded as *prima facie* obvious under 35 U.S.C. §103 when the additives in the new compositions are structurally similar to additives in known compositions, having a different use, even though the method of using the compositions is neither taught nor suggested by the prior art. Structural similarity between claimed and prior-art subject matter, proved by combining references or otherwise, where the prior art gives reason or motivation to make the claimed compositions, creates a *prima facie* case of obviousness, and the burden (and opportunity) then falls on an applicant to rebut the *prima facie* case. The discovery that a claimed composition possesses a property not disclosed for the prior-art subject matter does not itself defeat a *prima facie* case. The fact that the prior art is not directed to and does not concern the problem faced and solved by the claimed invention is not controlling. *In re Dillon*, 919 F.2d 688, 16 U.S.P.Q.2d 1897, 1901, 1902 (Fed. Cir. 1990).

ω

The relevant art is defined as that "reasonably pertinent to the particular problem with which the inventor was involved." *Gargoyles Inc. v. U.S.*, 32 Fed.Cl. 157, 33 U.S.P.Q.2d 1595, 1600 (U.S. Ct. Fed. Cl. 1994).

ω

The nature of the problem solved affects all of the four factual inquiries underlying obviousness. Prior art is relevant to the obviousness inquiry if it is analogous, i.e., if it is drawn from the inventor's field of endeavor or if it is "reasonably pertinent to the *particular problem* with which the inventor is involved." *In re Paulsen*, 30 F.3d 1475, 1481, 31 U.S.P.Q.2d 1671, 1676 (Fed. Cir. 1994).

ω

The problem the inventors (in their application) claim to have solved is relevant to the obviousness inquiry. *Oscar Mayer Foods Corp. v. ConAgra Inc.*, 35 U.S.P.Q.2d 1278, 1281 (Fed. Cir. 1994—*unpublished, not citable as precedent*).

ळ

The district court's formulation of the problem confronting the . . . inventors presumes the solution to the problem—modification of the stem segment. Defining the problem in terms of its solution reveals improper hindsight in the selection of the prior art relevant to obviousness. . . . By importing the ultimate solution into the problem facing the inventor, the district court adopted an overly narrow view of the scope of the prior art. It also infected the district court's determinations about the content of the prior art. *Monarch Knitting Machinery Corp. v. Sulzer Morat GmbH*, 139 F.3d 877, 45 U.S.P.Q.2d 1977, 1981 (Fed. Cir. 1998).

Procedural Matters.

The Federal Circuit clearly stated that, where procedural matters pertain to patent issues, a district court must conform to Federal Circuit law. *ALM Surgical Equipment Inc. v. Kirschner Medical Corp.*, 15 U.S.P.Q.2d 1241, 1251 (S.C. 1990).

ळ

In reviewing procedural matters that are not unique to patent law, the CAFC applies the law of the regional circuit where appeals from the particular district court would normally lie. *Beech Aircraft Corp. v. EDO Corp.*, 990 F.2d 1237, 26 U.S.P.Q.2d 1572, 1580 (Fed. Cir. 1993)

Proceeding *de Novo.* **See De Novo.**

Process.[11] *See also* **Analogy Processes, Control of Unpatented Goods, Mental Steps, Method, Method of Making, Method of Use, Process Parameter, Reduction in Steps, Starting Material.**

A process is a mode of treatment of certain materials to produce a given result. It is an act, or a series of acts, performed upon the subject matter to be transformed and reduced to a different state or thing. If new and useful, it is just as patentable as a piece of machinery. In the language of the patent law, it is an art. The machinery pointed out as being suitable to perform the process may or may not be new or patentable, while the process itself may be altogether new and produce an entirely new result. The process requires that certain things be done with certain substances, and in a certain order; but

---

[11] "[T]here are not '*Durden* [226 U.S.P.Q. 359 (Fed. Cir. 1985)] obviousness rejections' or '*Albertson* [141 U.S.P.Q. 730 (CCPA 1964)] obviousness rejections,' but rather only [35 U.S.C.] 103 obviousness rejections." *In re Brouwer*, 77 F.3d 422, 37 U.S.P.Q.2d 1663, 1666 (Fed. Cir. 1996). In a Notice issued on February 28, 1996, the PTO announced that henceforth it would analyze process claims in accordance with *Ochiai* [37 U.S.P.Q.2d 1127 (Fed. Cir. 1995)] and *Brouwer* decisions of the Federal Circuit, and treat as material limitations any recitations in process claims of the use of nonobvious starting materials or the making of nonobvious products. *AIPLA BULLETIN*, 36, 1997 Annual Meeting Issue.

the tools to be used in doing this may be of secondary consequence. *Cochrane v. Deener,* 94 U.S. 780 (1876).

ᚐ

A process is not uninventive merely because it requires one more step than a reference process. *Ex parte Quattlebaum and Noffsinger,* 84 U.S.P.Q. 377, 379 (PO Bd. App. 1948).

ᚐ

A rejection of process claims as being drawn to the function of the appellant's machine is proper unless it appears that the claimed process can be carried out either by some machine having materially different characteristics from the machine disclosed in the application, or by hand. *In re Gartner and Roeber,* 223 F.2d 502, 106 U.S.P.Q. 273, 275 (C.C.P.A. 1955).

ᚐ

Single-step method claims are patentable in the same manner as multiple-step method claims if they satisfy the statutory prerequisites to patentability. *Ex parte Macy,* 132 U.S.P.Q. 545, 546 (PO Bd. App. 1960).

ᚐ

A process patent can be used to restrict the use of a claimed process but cannot be used to control the sale of unpatented articles produced by the process. *Ethyl Corp. v. Hercules Powder Co.,* 232 F. Supp. 453, 139 U.S.P.Q. 471, 474 (Del. 1963).

ᚐ

A process is not limited to the means used in performing it. The law does not require that a machine, to be patentable, must act on physical substances—for example, an electric meter. It is not consistent to impose such a requirement on the other category of 35 U.S.C. §101—a "process"—without clearly evident and distinguishing reasons. The use of materials in a particular manner to secure the performance of a function by a means that had never occurred in nature and was not anticipated by prior art is a patentable method or process. Patent protection for a process disclosed as being a sequence or combination of steps capable of performance without human intervention and directed to an industrial technology (a "useful art" within the intendment of the Constitution) is not precluded by the mere fact that the process could alternatively be carried out by mental steps. *In re Prater and Wei,* 415 F.2d 1378, 159 U.S.P.Q. 583, 592, 593 (C.C.P.A. 1968).

ᚐ

A process is not unpatentable [in the sense of not being subject matter within the categories named in 35 U.S.C. §101] simply because it contains a law of nature or a mathematical algorithm. A claim for an improved method of calculation, even when tied to a specific end use, is unpatentable subject matter under 35 U.S.C. §101. *In re Walter,* 618 F.2d 758, 205 U.S.P.Q. 397, 405 (C.C.P.A. 1980).

ᚐ

Arrhenius' equation is not patentable in isolation, but when a process for curing rubber is devised which incorporates in it a more efficient solution of the equation, that process is at the very least not barred at the threshold by 35 U.S.C. §101. *Diamond v. Diehr and Lutton*, 450 U.S. 175, 209 U.S.P.Q. 1, 9 (S.Ct. 1981).

ꙍ

It is the function of the descriptive portion of the specification and not that of the claims to set forth operable proportions and similar process parameters. Claims are not rendered indefinite by the absence of the recitation of such limitations. *Ex parte Jackson, Theriault, Sinclair, Fager, and Karwowski*, 217 U.S.P.Q. 804, 806 (PTO Bd. App. 1982).

ꙍ

The use of a novel and patentable reactant may impart patentability to an analogy process. *Ex parte Klioze and Ehrgott*, 220 U.S.P.Q. 91, 92 (PTO Bd. App. 1983).

ꙍ

The inclusion in a patent of a claim to a process that may be performed by a person, but that also is capable of being performed by a machine, is not fatal to patentability. The presence of the steps of correlating and combining, which a machine is capable of doing, does not invalidate a patent. *Alco Standard Corp. v. Tennessee Valley Authority*, 808 F.2d 1490, 1 U.S.P.Q.2d 1337, 1341 (Fed. Cir. 1986).

ꙍ

A process patent in a chemical field that has not been developed creates a monopoly of knowledge that should be granted only if clearly commanded by the statute. This is because such patents may engross unknown and perhaps unknowable areas and may confer power "to block off whole areas of scientific development, without compensating benefit to the public." *Ex parte Kranz*, 19 U.S.P.Q.2d 1216, 1219 (B.P.A.I. 1990).

ꙍ

The Process Patent Act, 35 U.S.C. §271(g), allows U.S. patent holders to sue foreign companies who manufacture products using a process claimed in a U.S. patent and then ship the goods for sale into the United States. The Act also contains a grandfather clause, which was only to be used to protect domestic companies and interests during the transition from enactment of the law to the time that these companies were able to obtain new sources of the product. *Allegheny Ludlum Corp. v. Nippon Steel Corp.*, 20 U.S.P.Q.2d 1553, 1554 (Pa. 1991).

ꙍ

The sale of equipment to perform a process is not a sale of a patented process within the meaning of 35 U.S.C. §271(a). An injunction cannot be sustained on the ground that sales of equipment without use of the method within the patent term constitute contributory infringement of the method claim. *Joy Technologies Inc. v. Flakt Inc.*, 6 F.3d 770, 28 U.S.P.Q.2d 1378, 1381, 1383 (Fed. Cir. 1993).

ꙍ

Changes to *intangible* subject matter representative of or constituting physical activity or objects are included in the definition of "process". *In re Schrader*, 22 F.3d 290, 295, 30 U.S.P.Q.2d 1455, 1459 n.12 (Fed. Cir. 1994).

Process Claims.

Where a patent contains both apparatus and method claims, to the extent to which there is a tangible item to mark by which notice of the asserted method claims can be given, a party is obliged to do so if it intends to avail itself of the constructive notice provisions of 35 U.S.C. §287(a). *American Bank Note Holographics Inc. v. The Upper Deck Co.*, 41 U.S.P.Q.2d 2019 (N.Y. 1997).

Process Parameter.

Under normal rules of syntax "at" and "under" imply a controlled value (such as a process parameter), whereas "to" implies a measured or intended goal or condition (such as a polymer temperature). This context suggests that a step performed "at" a temperature indicates a process condition, not the condition of the matter under process. *Eastman Kodak Co. v. The Goodyear Tire & Rubber Co.*, 42 U.S.P.Q.2d 1737, 1740 (Fed. Cir. 1997)

Process Patent Act. *See* PPAA.

Process Patent Amendments Act. *See* PPAA.

Pro-Drug. *See also* Conversion (in situ or in vivo).

A drug which makes an inner body transformation to an active drug is often referred to as a "pro-drug". *Ortho Pharmaceutical Corp. v. Smith*, 959 F.2d 936, 22 U.S.P.Q.2d 1119, 1122 n.4 (Fed. Cir. 1992).

ϖ

When an ingested drug is converted in the body into a patented compound, the sale of the ingested drug is an "inducement" of infringement. *Zenith Labs. Inc. v. Bristol-Myers Squibb Co.*, 24 U.S.P.Q.2d 1652, 1671, 1672 (D.N.J. 1992), *aff'd in pertinent part*, 19 F.3d 1418, 1421, 1422 & n.4, 30 U.S.P.Q.2d 1285 (Fed. Cir. 1994), *cert. denied*, 115 S.Ct. 500 (1994). But see *Marion Merrell Dow Inc. v. Baker Norton Pharmaceuticals Inc.*, 41 U.S.P.Q.2d 1127 (Fla. 1996).

Product. *See also* Apparatus, Article, Chemical, Composition, Compound, Control of Unpatented Goods, Device, Intermediate, Isolated, Manufacture, Product by Process, Product by Properties, Product Claim, Product of a Commercialized Process, Product of Nature, Product of Prior-Art Process, Pure, Purity, Structural Similarity, Synthetic, Transitory, Work Product.

From a standpoint of patent law, a product and all of its properties are inseparable; they are one and the same thing. The patentability of the product does not depend on the similarity of its structure to that of another product but of the similarity of the former product to the latter. There is no basis in law for ignoring any property in making such a comparison. *In re Papesch*, 315 F.2d 381, 137 U.S.P.Q. 43 (C.C.P.A. 1963).

ϖ

Product claims have practical advantages over method-of-use claims from the standpoint of protection. Where we are concerned with new compounds in which non-obvious properties have been found, the properties being inherent in the compounds, it is "somewhat irrational" to say the "invention" is not in the compounds. The basic principle of the patent system is to protect inventions that meet the statutory requirements. Valuable inventions should be given protection of value in the real world of business and the courts. *In re Ruschig, Aümuller, Korger, Wagner, Scholz, and Bänder*, 343 F.2d 965, 145 U.S.P.Q. 274 (C.C.P.A. 1965).

ᴡ

Having been produced by the same process, the product obtained in Example IV of the earlier Sulkowski application is, of necessity, the same product as that obtained in Example III of the Sulkowski interference application. The only difference is in the naming of the product. Based on the process used in the earlier application, Sulkowski is entitled to the benefit of the product of that process with his later application. The fact that error was made in naming the product in the first application does not deprive Sulkowski of the benefit of that application. *Sulkowski v. Houlihan*, 179 U.S.P.Q. 685, 686 (PTO Bd. Pat. Int. 1973). *See also In re Sulkowski*, 487 F.2d 920, 180 U.S.P.Q. 46 (C.C.P.A. 1973).

ᴡ

The issue is whether the permission for commercial marketing or use of Opticrom 4% on October 3, 1984, or Intal Nebulizer Solution on January 19, 1985, represents the first permitted commercial marketing or use of the product within the meaning of 35 U.S.C. §156(a)(5)(A).

By the explicit terms of the statute, the term "product" as it relates to a human drug product means the active ingredient of a new drug. The active ingredient in both the approved products is cromolyn sodium. As noted in the FDA letters, the active ingredient had been approved for commercial marketing in 1973 and 1983, both prior to the approval of Opticrom 4% and Intal Nebulizer Solution for commercial marketing under 21 U.S.C. §355. Applying the explicit language of this statute to the facts: The permission for commercial marketing or use of the product after such regulatory review period was not the first permitted commercial marketing or use of the product under the provision of law under which the regulatory review occurred.

There is no basis in the statutory language for making a distinction between the content of a "product" vis-a-vis an "approved product." An approved product is a product that has been approved by the FDA for commercial marketing or use. The statute is explicit in defining the meaning of product in §156(f). The statute does not state that the product referred to in paragraphs (4) and (5) is the approved product. Thus, the statute itself clearly dictates that the product referred to in paragraphs (4) and (5) be defined in the manner required in §156(f). *In re Fisons Pharmaceuticals Ltd.*, 231 U.S.P.Q. 305 (Comm'r Patents & Trademarks 1986).

ᴡ

The term "product" is defined as a "human drug product." 35 U.S.C. §156(f)(1)(a). This term is further defined in the next paragraph as "the active ingredient of a new drug, antibiotic drug, or human biological product... including any salt or ester of the active ingredient, as a single entity or in combination with another active ingredient." 35 U.S.C. §156(f)(2). Substituting this definition directly back into §156(a)(5)(A) yields the statement that a patent is ineligible for patent term extension if it is not the first permitted commercial marketing or use of the active ingredient contained in that approved patented product. *Fisons Plc v. Quigg,* 8 U.S.P.Q.2d 1491 (D.C. 1988), *aff'd,* 876 F.2d 99, 10 U.S.P.Q.2d 1869 (Fed. Cir. 1989).

ᛒ

For a patent to be eligible for a patent term extension, the claimed product must have been "subject to a regulatory review period" and "the permission for the commercial marketing or use of the product after such regulatory review period [must have been] the first permitted commercial marketing or use of the product under the provision of law under which such regulatory review period occurred." (Emphasis in original.) Moreover, the Act explicitly defines "product" as "the active ingredient of a new drug, ... including any salt or ester of the active ingredient ... " Congress qualified its express authorization to the Commissioner to determine whether patents are eligible for extension by providing an explicit and precise definition of "product" in 35 U.S.C. §156(f)(2), using well-established scientific terms. Although the definition does involve technical subject matter, Congress specifically selected terms with narrow meanings that it chose from among many alternatives. Congress could have selected broad terms with a range of possible meanings, but did not. If it had, Congress could be said to have implicitly delegated discretion to the Commissioner to use his scientific expertise to determine what further definition would best carry out the purpose of the Act. All Congress left to the Commissioner's technical expertise was determining whether any patented chemical compound named in a patent term extension application fell within the statutory definition of "product," but not what "product" was to mean. Great deference is due to the Commissioner's determinations as to which patented chemical compounds fall within Congress's definition of "products," but little or no deference is due to the Commissioner's surmise of Congress's intent in framing its definition. *Glaxo Operations UK Ltd. v. Quigg,* 894 F.2d 392, 13 U.S.P.Q.2d 1628, 1629, 1633 (Fed. Cir. 1990).

ᛒ

Normally a *prima facie* case of obviousness is based upon structural similarity, *i.e.,* an established structural relationship between a prior art compound and a claimed compound. Structural relationships may provide the requisite motivation or suggestion to modify known compounds to obtain new compounds. For example, a prior art compound may suggest its homologs because homologs often have similar properties, and therefore chemists of ordinary skill would ordinarily contemplate making them to try to obtain compounds with improved properties. Similarly, a known compound may suggest its analogs or isomers, either geometric isomers (cis v. trans) or position isomers (*e.g.,* ortho v. para). Knowledge of a protein does not give one a conception of a particular DNA encoding it. What cannot be contemplated or conceived cannot be obvious. The PTO has improperly rejected product claims to molecules on the alleged obviousness of a method of making the molecules. As the claims define new chemical entities in structural terms, a *prima facie* case of unpatentability requires that the teachings of the prior art suggest *the claimed compounds* to a person of ordinary skill in the art. The existence of a general method of isolating cDNA or DNA molecules is essentially irrelevant to the question of whether specific molecules themselves would have been obvious, in the absence of other prior art that suggests the claimed DNAs. A prior art disclosure of a process *reciting a particular compound* or obvious variant thereof as a product of the process is, of course, another matter, raising issues of anticipation under 35 U.S.C. §102 as well as obviousness under §103. *In re Deuel*, 51 F.3d 1552, 34 U.S.P.Q.2d 1210, 1214, 1215 (Fed. Cir. 1995).

Product by Process. *See also* **Condensate.**

A patentee who does not distinguish his product from what is old except by reference, express or constructive, to the process by which he produced it cannot secure a monopoly on the product by whatever means produced. Every patent for a product or composition of matter must identify it so that it can be recognized aside from the description of the process for making it, or else nothing can be held to infringe the patent that is not made by that process. *General Electric Co. v. Wabash Appliance Corp.*, 304 U.S. 364, 37 U.S.P.Q. 466, 470 (S.Ct. 1938).

ω

A product-by-process claim is not subject to rejection as improper under 35 U.S.C. §112 merely because the product can be adequately described other than by reference to the process of making it. *Ex parte Hartmann*, 186 U.S.P.Q. 366, 367 (PTO Bd. App. 1974).

ω

A product-by-process claim is infringed only by a product produced by following the same process described in the claim. Unless it is shown that the process of the patent was followed to produce the defendant's article, or unless it is shown that the article could not be produced by any other process, the defendant's article cannot be identified as a product of the process of the patent. A patent granted on a product-by-process claim grants no monopoly as to identical products manufactured by a different process. *Scripps Clinic & Research Foundation v. Genentech Inc.*, 666 F. Supp. 1379, 3 U.S.P.Q.2d 1481 (Cal. 1987).

ω

The patentability of a product-by-process claim is based upon the product formed and not upon the method by which it was produced. *Ex parte Jungfer*, 18 U.S.P.Q.2d 1796, 1799 (B.P.A.I. 1990).

ω

Since claims must be construed the same way for validity and for infringement, the correct reading of product-by-process claims is that they are not limited to products prepared by the process set forth in the claims. *Scripps Clinic & Research Foundation v. Genentech Inc.*, 927 F.2d 1565, 18 U.S.P.Q.2d 1001, 1016 (Fed. Cir. 1991).

ω

Process terms in product-by-process claims serve as limitations in determining infringement. *Atlantic Thermoplastics Co. Inc. v. Faytex Corp.*, 970 F.2d 834, 23 U.S.P.Q.2d 1481, 1491 (Fed. Cir. 1992); see also *Atlantic Thermoplastics Co. Inc. v. Faytex Corp.*, 974 F.2d 1279, 23 U.S.P.Q.2d 1801 (Fed. Cir. 1992); *Tropix Inc. v. Lumigen Inc.*, 825 F.Supp. 7, 27 U.S.P.Q.2d 1475, 1477 (Mass. 1993).

Product by Properties.

A product may be defined in a claim by any of three methods: (1) a formula that is adequate to show complete and correct structure of the compound, (2) a detailed description of its preparation where the structure is not known, and (3) its empirical formula and physical and chemical characteristics coupled with its infra-red absorption spectra. *Ex parte Brian, Radley, Curtis, and Elson*, 118 U.S.P.Q. 242, 245 (PO Bd. App. 1958).

ᴥ

Where the chemical identity of a material is not critical, an applicant should be permitted to define that material partly in terms of its physical properties or the function that it performs. *In re Metcalfe and Lowe*, 410 F.2d 1378, 161 U.S.P.Q. 789, 793 (C.C.P.A. 1969). See the claims under consideration in *In re Goffe*, 526 F.2d 1393, 188 U.S.P.Q. 131 (1975); *In re Luck and Gainer*, 476 F.2d 650, 177 U.S.P.Q. 523 (C.C.P.A. 1973); *In re Saether*, 492 F.2d 849, 181 U.S.P.Q. 36 (C.C.P.A. 1974); *In re Miller*, 441 F.2d 689, 169 U.S.P.Q. 597 (C.C.P.A. 1971); *Ex parte Brockmann and Bohne*, 127 U.S.P.Q. 57 (PO Bd. App. 1959).

ᴥ

A rejection under the first paragraph of 35 U.S.C. §112, based on an allegedly insufficient disclosure, was not sustained. Appellants' invention did not reside in the use of any particular pharmaceutical, as long as it evidenced gastro-intestinal-tract incompatibility unsafe for oral administration in unit-dosage form. *Ex parte Gleixner, Muller, and Lehrach*, 214 U.S.P.Q. 297, 298 (PTO Bd. App. 1979).

ᴥ

To find anticipation of claims, the prior-art embodiments must possess the properties expressly recited in the claims. Property limitations can serve to distinguish claimed subject matter from other products. Identity of invention is a question of fact, and a challenger must show that each element of a claim is found in a prior patent or publication, either expressly or under principles of inherency. To establish anticipation, however, it is not necessary to prove that prior artisans were aware that their products possessed the recited properties. *E. I. du Pont de Nemours & Co. v. Phillips Petroleum Co.*, 849 F.2d 1430, 7 U.S.P.Q.2d 1129 (Fed. Cir. 1988).

Product Claim. *See also* Product.

Product claims have practical advantages from the standpoint of protection. When new compounds have non-obvious inherent properties, it is "somewhat irrational" to say that the "invention" is not in the compounds. The basic principle of the patent system is to protect inventions that meet statutory requirements. Valuable inventions should be given protection of value in the real world of business and the courts. Product claims are more valuable than method-of-use claims. *In re Ruschig, Aümuller, Korger, Wagner, Scholz, and Bänder*, 343 F.2d 965, 145 U.S.P.Q. 274 (C.C.P.A. 1965).

ᴥ

The mere statement that the method of making claimed products would be obvious and that there would be a reasonable expectation of success without determining that the claimed products would be obvious from prior art teachings reflects application of the regularly rejected obvious-to-try standard. *Ex parte Erlich,* 3 U.S.P.Q.2d 1011 (B.P.A.I. 1986).

Production Detail.

The expression is used to refer to commercial considerations, such as the equipment on hand, or prior relationships with suppliers that were satisfactory. Such commercial considerations do not constitute a best mode of practicing the claimed invention because they do not relate to the quality or nature of the invention. "Production details" is also used to refer to details which do relate to the quality or nature of the invention but which need not be disclosed because they are routine—i.e., details of production about which those of ordinary skill in the art would already know. In this latter scenario, the omitted detail constitutes a best mode but the disclosure is deemed adequate because the detail is routine. *Great Northern Corp. v. Henry Molded Products Inc.*, 94 F.3d 1569, 39 U.S.P.Q.2d 1997, 1999 (Fed. Cir. 1996)

Production of Documents.

"Control" with respect to the production of documents is defined "not only as possession, but as the legal right to obtain the documents requested upon demand." *Cochran Consulting Inc. v. Uwatec USA Inc.*, 41 U.S.P.Q.2d 1161 (Fed. Cir. 1996)

Product of a Commercialized Process.

Early public disclosure is a linchpin of the patent system. As between a prior inventor who benefits from a process by selling its product, but suppresses, conceals, or otherwise keeps the process from the public, and a later inventor who promptly files a patent application from which the public will gain disclosure of the process, the law favors the latter. In determining obviousness over prior art, and having learned the details of the patentee's invention, the district court found it within the skill of the art to stretch other material rapidly, to stretch PTFE to increase porosity and to stretch at high temperatures. The result is that the patent claims were used as a frame, and individual, naked parts of separate prior art references were employed as a mosaic to recreate a facsimile of the claimed invention. No explanation was given as to why that mosaic would have been obvious to one skilled in the art at the time of the patentee's invention, or what there was in the prior art that would have caused those skilled in the art to disregard the teachings there found against making just such a mosaic. To imbue one of ordinary skill in the art with knowledge of the invention in suit, where no prior art reference or references of record convey or suggest that knowledge, is to fall victim to the insidious effect of a hindsight syndrome wherein that which only the inventor taught is used against its teacher. *W. L. Gore & Associates, Inc. v. Garlock, Inc.*, 721 F.2d 1540, 220 U.S.P.Q. 303 (Fed. Cir. 1983).

Product of Nature. *See also* Life Form, Natural Product, Oyster, Plant.

Pure vanadium is not new in the inventive sense. As it is a product of nature, no one is entitled to a monopoly of the same. *In re Marden and Rich*, 47 F.2d 958, 8 U.S.P.Q. 347, 348 (C.C.P.A. 1931).

Product of Prior-Art Process.

There is no presumptive correlation that two similar processes form substantially the same product where the processes differ by a materially limiting step. When prior art fails to disclose a method for making a claimed compound, at the time the invention was made, it cannot be legally concluded that the compound itself is in the possession of the public. *Ashland Oil, Inc. v. Delta Resins & Refractories, Inc.*, 776 F.2d 281, 227 U.S.P.Q. 657 (Fed. Cir. 1985).

Professional Paper.

A document may be deemed a printed publication upon a satisfactory showing that it has been disseminated or otherwise made available to the extent that persons interested and of ordinary skill in the subject matter or art, exercising reasonable diligence, can locate it and recognize and comprehend therefrom the essentials of the claimed invention without need of further research or experimentation. *Massachusetts Institute of Technology v. A.B. Fortia*, 774 F.2d 1104, 227 U.S.P.Q. 428 (Fed. Cir. 1985).

Profits.

The statute that limits recovery in cases where there is no marking refers only to damages. Historically, disgorgement, which is really what the plaintiff seeks in its actions for infringers' profits, was not considered a recovery of damages, but an equitable remedy to restore to the proper owner profits made by an infringer's use of another's property. The limitations imposed by 35 U.S.C. §287(a) are not applicable to an action seeking recovery of an infringer's profits pursuant to 35 U.S.C. §289. *Nike Inc. v. Wal-Mart Stores Inc.*, 41 U.S.P.Q.2d 1146 (Va. 1996).

Program.[12] *See also* **Algorithm, Computer Program.**

In such arts as computer programming, where one or more skilled programmers may be able to produce a program required to practice a claimed invention only after working for "many months and years," it is not unreasonable for an Examiner to require an applicant (who has prepared such a program) to give at least an appraisal of the amount of time involved in its production or to disclose at least a bare bones flow chart of that program to the Patent Office so that the Examiner may determine whether one skilled in the art could produce it without unreasonable experimentation and delays. *In re Brandstadter, Kienzle, and Sykes*, 484 F.2d 1395, 179 U.S.P.Q. 286, 294, 295 (C.C.P.A. 1973).

ω

Arrhenius' equation is not patentable in isolation, but when a process for curing rubber is devised which incorporates in it a more efficient solution of the equation, that

---

[12] See *In re Alappat*, 33 F.3d 1526, 31 U.S.P.Q.2d 1545 (Fed. Cir. 1994), which has been interpreted as confirming patentability of software (*The Law Works*™, Vol. 1, No. 9, page 20, September, 1994). *See also* Rogitz, John, "And You Thought You Understood Alappat", *The Law Works*™, Vol. 2, No. 2, page 19, February 1995.

process is at the very least not barred at the threshold by 35 U.S.C. §101. *Diamond v. Diehr and Lutton*, 450 U.S. 175, 209 U.S.P.Q. 1, 9 (S.Ct. 1981).

ω

Changes to *intangible* subject matter representative of or constituting physical activity or objects are included in the definition of "process." *In re Schrader*, 22 F.3d 290, 295, 30 U.S.P.Q.2d 1455, 1459 n.12 (Fed. Cir. 1994).

ω

A memory containing a stored data structure is distinguishable from printed matter by requiring that contained information be processed not by the mind but by a machine, a computer. Claims directed to a memory containing stored information recite an article of manufacture, statutory subject matter. *In re Lowry*, 32 F.3d 1579, 1583, 32 U.S.P.Q.2d 1031, 1033, 1034 (Fed. Cir. 1994).

ω

The fact that a claim reads on a general purpose computer program used to carry out a claimed invention does not, by itself, justify holding that the claim is unpatentable as directed to nonstatutory subject matter. Such programming creates a new machine, because a general purpose computer in effect becomes a special purpose computer once it is programmed to perform particular functions pursuant to instructions from program software. *In re Alappat*, 33 F.3d 1526, 1544, 31 U.S.P.Q.2d 1545, 1558 (Fed. Cir. 1994).

Progress. *See also* **Advance the Art, Promote Progress.**

Congress has not seen fit to include in the statutes a requirement that each and every patentable *invention* shall involve "progress" in the sense that each new invention must also be shown to possess some definite advantage over the prior art. *In re Ratti*, 270 F.2d 810, 123 U.S.P.Q. 349, 353 n.1 (C.C.P.A. 1959).

Prolix.

While forty pages of claims may seem to be unnecessarily prolix, the mere psychological reaction to this amount of material does not, in and of itself, constitute a legal basis for rejection. The Examiner must either show that the claims are so unduly multiplied that they are difficult to understand, making examination almost impossible, or that the claims are for the most part duplicates. *Ex parte Birnbaum*, 161 U.S.P.Q. 635, 637 (PO Bd. App. 1968).

Promissory Estoppel.

A finding of promissory estoppel bars all relief for a patentee. *Digital Systems International Inc. v. Davox Corp.*, 30 U.S.P.Q.2d 1170, 1172 (Wash. 1993).

Promote Progress.

The basic policy of the Patent Act is to encourage disclosure of inventions and thereby to promote progress in the useful arts. To require disclosures in patent applications to transcend the level of knowledge of those skilled in the art would stifle the disclosure of inventions in fields we understand imperfectly, like catalytic chemistry. The certainty that the law requires in patents is not greater than is reasonable, having regard for their subject matter. *In re Angstadt and Griffin,* 537 F.2d 498, 190 U.S.P.Q. 214, 219 (C.C.P.A. 1976).

ᛜ

To provide effective incentives, claims must adequately protect inventors. To demand that the first to disclose shall limit his claims to what he has found will work or to materials that meet the guidelines specified for "preferred" materials in a process would not serve the constitutional purpose of promoting progress in the useful arts. *In re Goffe,* 542 F.2d 564, 191 U.S.P.Q. 429, 431 (C.C.P.A. 1976); *In re Johnson and Farnham,* 558 F.2d 1008, 194 U.S.P.Q. 187, 195 (C.C.P.A. 1977).

ᛜ

The PTO has not challenged the appellants' assertion that their 1953 application enabled those skilled in the art in 1953 to make and use "a solid polymer" as described in a claim. The appellants disclosed, as the only then-existing way to make such a polymer, a method of making the crystalline form. To say now that the appellants should have disclosed in 1953 the amorphous form (which did not exist until 1962) would be to impose an impossible burden on inventors and thus on the patent system. There cannot, in an effective patent system, be such a burden placed on the right to broad claims. To restrict the appellants to the crystalline form disclosed, under such circumstances, would be a poor way to stimulate invention, and particularly to encourage its early disclosure. To demand such restriction is merely to state a policy against broad protection for pioneer inventions, a policy both shortsighted and unsound from the standpoint of promoting progress in the useful arts, which is the constitutional purpose of the patent laws. *In re Hogan and Banks,* 559 F.2d 595, 194 U.S.P.Q. 527, 537 (C.C.P.A. 1977).

ᛜ

Most patents are granted on an improvement of a prior device. The improved device inherently achieves the same basic result as that achieved, and performs the same basic function as that performed, by the prior device. To require in every case that a new "function" or new "result" be performed or achieved would be destructive of "the progress of...useful arts" goal sought in the constitutional-statutory scheme. *Nickola v. Peterson,* 580 F.2d 898, 198 U.S.P.Q. 385, 397 (6th Cir. 1978).

ᛜ

Where claims to a compound or group of compounds (the product claims) are allowable, it is in the public interest to permit claiming a process of use as well as the product. The result is to encourage a more detailed disclosure of the specific methods of using the novel composition invented in order to provide support for the process claims. The constitutional purpose of the patent system is promoted by encouraging an applicant to claim, and therefore to describe in the manner required by 35 U.S.C. §112, all aspects of what he regards as his invention, regardless of the number of statutory classes involved. *In re Pleuddemann,* 910 F.2d 823, 15 U.S.P.Q.2d 1738, 1740, 1741 (Fed. Cir. 1990).

Promotion.

When plaintiff alleges that defendant has sold an infringing product, "a patent infringement occurs where allegedly infringing sales are made." When no sales of an accused product have occurred, promotion and advertising of the product in Massachusetts is an "infringing activity" or "offending act." *Hologic Inc. v. Lunar Corp.*, 36 U.S.P.Q.2d 1182, 1187 (Mass. 1995).

Proof. *See also* **Burden, Statement in the Specification.**

Notwithstanding the fact that the senior party to an interference failed to present any testimony and was thus restricted to his filing date for inventive acts, that party is still presumed to be the first inventor. The burden of proof (by a preponderence of the evidence) rests upon the junior party to overcome this presumption. *Fitch v. Cooper*, 139 U.S.P.Q. 382 (PO Bd. Pat. Int. 1962).

ᛒ

The burden rests upon the junior party in an inteference to prove his priority over that of the senior party by a preponderance of the evidence. *Carusi and Kolec v. Looker*, 342 F.2d 112, 144 U.S.P.Q. 670, 672 (C.C.P.A. 1965).

ᛒ

As the respective priority applications of both parties to an interference were filed on the same day, both parties have identical effective filing dates, and neither party carries a greater burden of proving priority than the other. The fact that one of the interference parties filed his application in the United States before the other was not accorded any weight in determining burden of proof. *Lassman v. Brossi, Gerecke, and Kyburz*, 159 U.S.P.Q. 182 (PO Bd. Pat. Int. 1967).

ᛒ

The burden of proof generally lies on the party asserting the affirmative of a proposition or the party seeking to change the present state of affairs. Where a party is in a position to have peculiar knowledge of the facts with regard to an issue, the burden of proof as to that issue lies upon that party. The burden of going forward with the evidence on an issue generally rests upon the party having the burden of proof on that issue. Section 305 of the National Aeronautics and Space Act of 1958 (42 U.S.C. §2457) clearly treats an invention as property, the right to which is in the inventor or his assignee unless the invention was made (conception or first actual reduction to practice) in the performance of work under a NASA contract. As the Board ruled here, title to the application remains in the applicant (or assignee) at the time of declaration of the §305(d) proceeding. The Administrator should bear the general burden of proving that he is entitled to receive the patent on the involved application, i.e., he should bear the general burden of proof as to the acts that he alleges took place under the contract and that would entitle the United States to the patent. *Williams v. The Administrator of the National Aeronautics and Space Administration*, 463 F.2d 1391, 175 U.S.P.Q. 5, 12 (C.C.P.A. 1972).

ᛒ

The burden of proof, which is by a fair preponderance of the evidence, of any exemption from the public use bar, such as by reason of experimentation essential to the completion of the making or perfecting of "the invention," rests with the patentee. *Honeywell Inc. v. Sperry Rand Corp.*, 180 U.S.P.Q. 673, 689, 690 (Minn. 1973).

ᴟ

The burden of proof on the right to make issue (in an interference) is on the party who has copied the claims. This burden is a heavy one, regardless of whether the copier is a junior or senior party, and doubts must be resolved against the copier. *Holmes, Faber, Boykin, and Francis v. Kelly, Hornberger, and Strief,* 586 F.2d 234, 199 U.S.P.Q. 778, 781 (C.C.P.A. 1978).

ᴟ

A party asserting patent invalidity bears the burden of proof even if prior-art references relied upon were not before the PTO. *Underwater Devices Inc. v. Morrison-Knudsen Co.*, 717 F.2d 1380, 219 U.S.P.Q. 569, 574 (Fed. Cir. 1983).

ᴟ

The burden of proving patent invalidity is on the party asserting such invalidity. *American Hospital Supply Corp. v. Travenol Laboratories, Inc.*, 745 F.2d 1, 223 U.S.P.Q. 577, 582 (Fed. Cir. 1984).

ᴟ

In an interference setting, the standard for burden of proof required to establish conception, communication (issue of derivation), and diligent reduction to practice is the "clear and convincing evidence" standard, not beyond a reasonable doubt. A party who copies claims from a patent to provoke an interference "is required to establish a prior date of invention by *clear and convincing evidence.*" The "clear and convincing evidence" standard has uniformly been invoked in resolving the issues of priority and derivation in infringement suits between private parties. The imposition of an erroneous burden of proof, which is more difficult to overcome than the proper burden of proof, cannot ordinarily be classified as "harmless." *Price v. Symsek*, 988 F.2d 1187, 26 U.S.P.Q.2d 1031, 1033, 1035, 1036 (Fed. Cir. 1993).

Proof of Utility.[13] *See also* Experimental Animals.

Where a claimed discovery does not appear to be of such a "speculative", abstruse or esoteric nature that it must inherently be considered unbelievable, "incredible", or " factually misleading"; where its operativeness does not appear "unlikely" or an assertion thereof appear to run counter "to what would be believed would happen by the ordinary person" in the art; where the field of endeavor does not appear to be one where "little of a successful nature has been developed" or one which "from common knowledge has long been the subject matter of much humbuggery and fraud"; and where the Examiner has not presented evidence inconsistent with the assertions and evidence of operativeness presented by appellant, the Patent Office is in effect seeking to require too much proof of the asserted usefulness. *In re Gazave*, 379 F.2d 973, 154 U.S.P.Q. 92, 96 (C.C.P.A. 1967).

ᴟ

---

[13] Refer to GUIDELINES FOR CONSIDERING DISCLOSURES OF UTILITY IN DRUG CASES, MPEP §608.01(p).

It is not proper for the Patent Office to require clinical testing in humans to rebut a prima facie case for lack of utility when the pertinent references which establish the prima facie case show in vitro tests and when they do not show in vivo tests employing standard experimental animals. *In re Langer*, 503 F.2d 1380, 183 U.S.P.Q. 288, 297 (C.C.P.A. 1974).

ω

Even if proof of utility of the claimed invention as an anti-arthritic agent for humans is lacking, there remains the proven utility as an anti-arthritic agent for lower animals. Having found that the claimed composition has utility as contemplated in the specification, 35 U.S.C. §101 is satisfied, and it is unnecessary to decide whether it is in fact useful for the other purposes indicated in the specification as possibilities. *In re Malachowski*, 530 F.2d 1402, 189 U.S.P.Q. 432, 435 (C.C.P.A. 1976).

Properties. *See also* **Characteristic, Comparative Test Data, Intended Use, Obviousness, Predictability, Product by Properties, Property, Relationship, Structural Similarity.**

From a standpoint of patent law, a product and all of its properties are inseparable; they are one and the same thing. The patentability of the product does not depend on the similarity of its structure to that of another product but of the similarity of the former product to the latter. There is no basis in law for ignoring any property in making such a comparison. *In re Papesch*, 315 F.2d 381, 137 U.S.P.Q. 43 (C.C.P.A. 1963).

ω

The appellant described his invention as comprehending the use therein of any inorganic salt capable of performing a specific function in a specific combination, and he specifically disclosed four such salts that are capable of performing his function. The claims are not "unduly broad" merely because one skilled in the art may not know offhand which inorganic salts are capable of so functioning. Nothing is found in patent law that requires the appellant to discover which of all salts have the specified properties and which will function properly in his combination. The invention description clearly indicates that any inorganic salt that has such properties is usable in his combination. *In re Fuetterer*, 319 F.2d 259, 138 U.S.P.Q. 217, 223 (C.C.P.A. 1963).

ω

Product claims have practical advantages over method-of-use claims from the standpoint of protection. Where we are concerned with new compounds in which non-obvious properties have been found, the properties being inherent in the compounds, it is "somewhat irrational" to say the "invention" is not in the compounds. The basic principle of the patent system is to protect inventions that meet the statutory requirements. Valuable inventions should be given protection of value in the real world of business and the courts. *In re Ruschig, Aümuller, Korger, Wagner, Scholz, and Bänder*, 343 F.2d 965, 145 U.S.P.Q. 274 (C.C.P.A. 1965).

ω

When a new compound so closely related to a prior art compound as to be structurally obvious is sought to be patented based on the alleged greater effectiveness of the new compound for the same purpose as the old compound, clear and convincing evidence of substantially greater effectiveness is needed. *In re Wiechert*, 370 F.2d 927, 152 U.S.P.Q. 247, 250 (C.C.P.A. 1967).

ʊ

Where the chemical identity of a material is not critical, there is no reason why an applicant should not be permitted to define that material partly in terms of its physical properties or the function that it performs. *In re Metcalfe and Lowe*, 410 F.2d 1378, 161 U.S.P.Q. 789, 793 (C.C.P.A. 1969).

ʊ

Unexpected results relied upon for patentability need not be recited in the claims. *In re Merchant*, 575 F.2d 865, 197 U.S.P.Q. 785, 788 (C.C.P.A. 1978).

ʊ

The differences between the prior art and the invention defined by the asserted claims, the availability of that art to all workers in the field, the failure of established competitors in a highly competitive market to make the invention despite the incentive to do so, the admittedly non-obvious performance benefits realized through the claimed invention, the impressive commercial success of the claimed product, the praise of independent commentators and the forbearance of competitors from infringing the patent all go to confirm that the claimed invention was not obvious at the time it was made to a person of ordinary skill in the art. *S. C. Johnson & Son, Inc. v. Carter-Wallace, Inc.*, 614 F. Supp. 1278, 225 U.S.P.Q. 1022 (N.Y. 1985).

ʊ

The Examiner appears to recognize that it is not structural similarity alone that gives rise to obviousness, but the concomitant assumption that the structurally similar compounds will have like properties. This is what provides the motivation to modify the prior-art compound. In the present case, however, the only utility disclosed for the relevant compound in the reference is as an intermediate for the production of another compound. The Examiner has not suggested that the compound claimed here would have been useful in the same manner and, from the disclosure of the reference itself, it appears that it would not have been. Thus, on the record before us, no *prima facie* case of obviousness has been made out against the appellant's claims. *Ex parte Chwang*, 231 U.S.P.Q. 751 (B.P.A.I. 1986).

ʊ

The presented comparative test data established that the claimed compound yielded superior results, exhibiting selectivity factors at least five times greater than those of the closest prior-art compounds. The claimed compound is novel. That its superior activity in corn and soybeans is a new and unexpected property was confirmed by the allowance of the method claims to its use on corn and soybeans. The grant of method claims is persuasive of the compound's non-obviousness. *Papesch* [137 U.S.P.Q. 43 (1963)] held that a compound can be patented on the basis of its properties; it did not hold that those properties must produce superior results in every environment in which the compound may be used. To be patentable, a compound need not excel over prior art compounds in all common properties. Evidence that a compound is unexpectedly superior in one of a spectrum of common properties can be enough to rebut a *prima facie* case of obviousness. *In re Chupp*, 816 F.2d 643, 2 U.S.P.Q.2d 1437 (Fed. Cir. 1987).

ᛦ

The PTO erred in holding that the non-obviousness (for the intended purpose) of the claimed structure was not relevant. The problem solved by the invention is always relevant. The entirety of a claimed invention, including the combination viewed as a whole, the elements thereof, and the properties and purpose of the invention, must be considered. Factors, including unexpected results, new features, solution of a different problem, and novel properties, are all considerations in the determination of obviousness in terms of 35 U.S.C. §103. When such factors are described in a specification, they are weighted in determining whether the prior art represents a *prima facie* case of obviousness. *In re Wright*, 848 F.2d 1216, 6 U.S.P.Q.2d 1959 (Fed. Cir. 1988).

ᛦ

To find anticipation of claims, the prior-art embodiments must possess the properties expressly recited in the claims. Property limitations can serve to distinguish claimed subject matter from other products. Identity of invention is a question of fact, and a challenger must show that each element of a claim is found in a prior patent or publication, either expressly or under principles of inherency. To establish anticipation, however, it is not necessary to prove that prior artisans were aware that their products possessed the recited properties. *E. I. du Pont de Nemours & Co. v. Phillips Petroleum Co.*, 849 F.2d 1430, 7 U.S.P.Q.2d 1129 (Fed. Cir. 1988).

ᛦ

In comparing the differences between the structure and the properties taught in the prior art and those of the applicant's invention, there is a need to include consideration of the problem solved by the inventor. The determination of whether a novel structure is obvious requires cognizance of the properties of that structure and the problem that it solves, viewed in the light of the teachings of the prior art. Where the invention for which a patent is sought solves a problem that persisted in the art, one must look to the problem as well as to its solution if he is to appraise properly what was done and to evaluate it against what would be obvious to one having the ordinary skills in the art. *In re Newell*, 891 F.2d 899, 13 U.S.P.Q.2d 1248, 1250 (Fed. Cir. 1989).

ᛦ

When a superior property of a new drug has led to its acceptance in the medical community, the compound's superior property is a "significant enough contribution to be deserving of a patent." *Ortho Pharmaceutical Corp. v. Smith*, 15 U.S.P.Q.2d 1856, 1862 (Pa. 1990).

ᛦ

Inherent properties of known compositions are not patentable. *General Electric Co. v. Hoechst Celanese Corp.*, 683 F. Supp. 305, 16 U.S.P.Q.2d 1977, 1985 (Del. 1990).

Property. *See also* **Intended Use, Advantage, Properties.**

Where the balance of a claim fully identifies a compound, a statement in the claim of an inherent property does not add anything to the claim definition. *In re Ruschig,*

Aümuller, Korger, Wagner, Scholz, and Bänder, 343 F.2d 965, 145 U.S.P.Q. 274, 281 (C.C.P.A. 1965).

ω

Terms that merely set forth an intended use for, or a property inherent in, an otherwise old composition do not differentiate a claimed composition from those known to the prior art. *In re Pearson,* 494 F.2d 1399, 181 U.S.P.Q. 641 (C.C.P.A. 1974).

ω

A newly discovered activity of a claimed novel compound that bears no material relationship to the activity disclosed for prior art analogs is clear evidence, not to be ignored, of the non-obviousness of the claimed invention. *In re Albrecht,* 514 F.2d 1389, 185 U.S.P.Q. 585, 590 (C.C.P.A. 1975).

ω

The mere recitation of a newly-discovered function or property, inherently possessed by things in the prior art, does not cause a claim drawn to those things to distinguish over the prior art. *In re Best, Bolton, and Shaw,* 562 F.2d 1252, 195 U.S.P.Q. 430, 433 (C.C.P.A. 1977).

ω

A single variance in the properties of new chemical compounds will not necessarily tip the balance in favor of patentability where otherwise closely related chemical compounds are involved. *In re De Montmollin and Riat,* 344 F.2d 976, 145 U.S.P.Q. 416, 417 (C.C.P.A. 1965); but see *In re May and Eddy,* 574 F.2d 1082, 197 U.S.P.Q. 601, 609 (C.C.P.A. 1978).

ω

Patentability of a new use (of an old material) based on an inherent but previously unrecognized property is not precluded. A contrary conclusion confuses anticipation by inherency, i.e., lack of novelty, with obviousness. *Jones v. Hardy,* 727 F.2d 1524, 220 U.S.P.Q. 1021, 1025 (Fed. Cir. 1984).

ω

A determination of whether a structure is or is not obvious requires cognizance of the properties of that structure and the problem that it solves, viewed in light of the teachings of the prior art. *In re Wright,* 848 F.2d 1216, 6 U.S.P.Q.2d 1959 (Fed. Cir. 1988).

ω

The right to exclude, which is recognized in a patent, is but the essence of the concept of property. *Richardson v. Suzuki Motor Co., Ltd.,* 868 F.2d 1226, 9 U.S.P.Q.2d 1913 (Fed. Cir. 1989).

ω

A patent for an invention is as much property as a patent for land. The right rests on the same foundation and is surrounded and protected by the same sanctions. *College Savings Bank v. Florida Prepaid Postsecondary Education Expense Board,* 42 U.S.P.Q.2d 1487, 1507 (N.J. 1996).

Prophetic Examples.

Although applicant's disclosure provided details as to how some 150 specifically named compounds "were prepared" or "can be prepared," a rejection based on undue breadth and speculation was affirmed because the only compounds actually tested that demonstrated the particular disclosed pharmacological properties were far more limited in structure than those claimed. *In re Surrey,* 370 F.2d 349, 151 U.S.P.Q. 724 (C.C.P.A. 1966).

ᐓ

Use of prophetic examples does not automatically make a patent nonenabling. *Atlas Powder Co. v. E. I. du Pont de Nemours & Co.,* 750 F.2d 1569, 224 U.S.P.Q. 409 (Fed. Cir. 1984).

Proportions. *See also* **Dimensions, Number.**

A mere carrying forward of an original patented conception involving only the change of form, proportions, or degree, or the substitution of equivalents doing the same thing as the original invention, by substantially the same means, is not such an invention as will sustain a patent even though the changes are of a kind that produces better results than prior inventions. *In re Paul F. Williams,* 36 F.2d 436, 4 U.S.P.Q. 237, 239 (C.C.P.A. 1930).

ᐓ

A mere change in proportion involves only mechanical skill and does not amount to invention, nor is it invention to adopt different materials in the construction of a device. *Hugh W. Batcheller v. Henry Cole Co.,* 7 F. Supp. 898, 22 U.S.P.Q. 354, 358 (Mass. 1934).

ᐓ

One alleging a critical difference (that is, a difference in kind as distinguished from a difference in degree) growing out of claimed proportions of ingredients must establish such criticalness by proof. *In re Waite and Allport,* 168 F.2d 104, 77 U.S.P.Q. 586, 591 (C.C.P.A. 1948).

ᐓ

While the ingredients in the reference and in the claimed compositions are the same, the proportioning thereof is so different that the resulting compositions exhibit distinct and unrelated functions. It is not enough that the ingredients be identical. They must be similarly proportioned or substantially similarly proportioned so that the functions thereof are inherently the same. *Ex parte Ritchie,* 92 U.S.P.Q. 381, 382 (PO Bd. App. 1950).

ᐓ

Where percentages or proportions are given, they are normally considered as weight percentages or proportions by weight unless otherwise stated. *Ex parte Kronenthal and Rich,* 163 U.S.P.Q. 571 (PO Bd. App. 1969).

ᐓ

Proportions need not be recited in composition claims when they are not critical to the disclosed and claimed invention. Failure to recite proportions in such claims does not subject them to rejection for indefiniteness. *In re Conley, Catherwood, and Lloyd*, 490 F.2d 972, 180 U.S.P.Q. 454, 456 (C.C.P.A. 1974).

ᴥ

That experimentation may be involved with the selection of proportions and particle sizes is not determinative of the question of scope of enablement; it is only undue experimentation that is fatal. *In re Geerdes*, 491 F.2d 1260, 180 U.S.P.Q. 789, 793 (C.C.P.A. 1974).

ᴥ

It is not a function of the claims to specifically exclude either possible inoperative substances or ineffective reactant proportions. *In re Dinh-Nguyen and Stenhagen*, 492 F.2d 856, 181 U.S.P.Q. 46 (C.C.P.A. 1974).

ᴥ

A rejection based on indefiniteness cannot stand simply because the proportions recited in the claims may be read in theory to include compositions that are impossible in fact to formulate. "Subject matter which cannot exist in fact can neither anticipate nor infringe in law." *In re Kroekel and Pfaff*, 504 F.2d 1143, 183 U.S.P.Q. 610, 612 (C.C.P.A. 1974).

ᴥ

It is the function of the descriptive portion of the specification and not that of the claims to set forth operable proportions and similar process parameters. Claims are not rendered indefinite by the absence of the recitation of such limitations. *Ex parte Jackson, Theriault, Sinclair, Fager, and Karwowski*, 217 U.S.P.Q. 804, 806 (PTO Bd. App. 1982).

Proprietary. *See also* 35 U.S.C. §118.

The language "sufficient proprietary interest in the matter justifying such action" means that the person filing the application must have such an interest as to be able to participate in the grant of a patent issued on the basis of an application filed pursuant to 35 U.S.C. §118. In order to participate in the grant of a patent, a person must be able to enforce, or require enforcement of, a patent grant. *In re Striker*, 182 U.S.P.Q. 507 (PO Solicitor 1973).

Prosecution History. *See also* File Wrapper, Lengthy Prosecution.

The prosecution history (or file wrapper) limits the interpretation of claims so as to exclude any interpretation that may have been disclaimed or disavowed during prosecution in order to obtain claim allowance. *ZMI Corp. v. Cardiac Resuscitator Corp.*, 844 F.2d 1576, 6 U.S.P.Q.2d 1557 (Fed. Cir. 1988).

ᴥ

Arguments made during the prosecution history are relevant in determining the meaning of terms in claims. Those arguments, and other aspects of the prosecution history, as well as the specification and other claims, must be examined to ascertain the true meaning of what the inventor intended to convey in the claims. Using the prosecution history in that manner is different from prosecution history estoppel, which is applied as a limitation upon the doctrine of equivalents after the claims have been properly interpreted. The use of prosecution history is not limited to the available scope of equivalents. *E. I. du Pont de Nemours & Co. v. Phillips Petroleum Co.*, 849 F.2d 1430, 7 U.S.P.Q.2d 1129 (Fed. Cir. 1988).

ᚁ

Prosecution history is especially important when an invention involves a crowded art field, or when there is particular prior art over which an applicant is trying to distinguish. As applicant spent over a decade convincing the PTO that its invention was different from the prior art, the Court placed great weight on the prosecution history in determining the meaning and scope of the patent claims. *Fairfax Dental (Ireland) Ltd. v. Sterling Optical Corp.*, 808 F.Supp. 326, 26 U.S.P.Q.2d 1442, 1449 (N.Y. 1992).

ᚁ

The analysis of prosecution history essentially applies to both literal infringement and infringement under the doctrine of equivalents. For purposes of literal infringement, the prosecution history is used to interpret the claims in a manner consistent with [the patentee's] representations during prosecution. In the context of the doctrine of equivalents, the prosecution history acts as formal estoppel to prevent the patent owner from obtaining a scope of equivalency that would resurrect subject matter surrendered during prosecution. *Gussin v. Nintendo of America Inc.*, 33 U.S.P.Q.2d 1418, 1419, 1422 (Cal. 1994).

ᚁ

Using the prosecution history to interpret claim language is different from application of the doctrine of prosecution history estoppel. *Magnesystems Inc. v. Nikken Inc.*, 34 U.S.P.Q.2d 1112, 1116 (Cal. 1994).

Prosecution History Estoppel. *See also* File Wrapper Estoppel.

That a patent applicant narrows his claim to secure a patent does not always mean that prosecution history estoppel completely prohibits the patentee from recapturing some of what was originally claimed. *Pennwalt Corp. v. Durand-Wayland Inc.*, 833 F.2d 931, 4 U.S.P.Q.2d 1737 (Fed. Cir. 1987).

ᚁ

Whenever prosecution history estoppel is invoked as a limitation to infringement under the doctrine of equivalents, "a close examination must be made as to, not only what was surrendered, but also the reason for such a surrender." *Insta-Foam Products, Inc. v. Universal Foam Systems, Inc.*, 906 F.2d 698, 703, 15 U.S.P.Q.2d 1295, 1298 (Fed. Cir. 1990).

ᚁ

Amendment of a claim in light of a prior art reference is not the *sine qua non* to establish prosecution history estoppel. Unmistakable assertions made by the applicant to the PTO in support of patentability, whether or not required to secure allowance of a claim, also may operate to preclude the patentee from asserting equivalency between a limitation of a claim and a substituted structure or process step. *Texas Instruments Inc. v. International Trade Commission*, 988 F.2d 1165, 26 U.S.P.Q.2d 1018, 1025 (Fed. Cir. 1993).

ᛒ

The essence of prosecution history estoppel is that a patentee should not be able to obtain, through litigation, coverage of subject matter relinquished during prosecution. The legal standard for determining what subject matter was relinquished is an objective one, measured from the vantage point of what a competitor was reasonably entitled to conclude, from the prosecution history, that the applicant gave up to procure issuance of the patent. A classic example of prosecution history estoppel is an amendment in response to a prior art rejection, but other conduct is also included: statements contained in a disclosure document placed in the PTO file as well as representations made during prosecution of a parent application, remarks made during prosecution of a claim not in suit as well as statements made after the Examiner indicated the claims in suit were allowable, and arguments submitted to obtain the patent. Thus, an estoppel can be created even when the claim, which is the basis for the assertion of infringement under the doctrine of equivalents, was not amended during prosecution. *Haynes International Inc. v. Jessop Steel Co.*, 8 F.3d 1573, 28 U.S.P.Q.2d 1652, 1655, 1656, 1657 (Fed. Cir. 1993).

ᛒ

The limits imposed by prosecution history estoppel on the permissible range of equivalents can be broader than those imposed by the prior art. Once an argument is made regarding a claim term so as to create an estoppel, the estoppel will apply to that term in other claims. *Southwall Technologies Inc. v. Cardinal IG Co.*, 54 F.3d 1570, 34 U.S.P.Q.2d 1673, 1681, 1683 (Fed. Cir. 1995).

ᛒ

Prosecution history estoppel is not limited to the claims with respect to which the applicant's statements were made. Rather, clear assertions made during prosecution in support of patentability, whether or not actually required to secure allowance, may create an estoppel. *American Permahedge Inc. v. Barcana Inc.*, 41 U.S.P.Q.2d 1614 (Fed. Cir. 1997).

ᛒ

The standard for determining whether particular subject matter was relinquished is an objective one. It depends on what a competitor would reasonably conclude from the patent's prosecution history. *Semmler v. American Honda Motor Co.*, 990 F.Supp. 967, 44 U.S.P.Q.2d 1553, 1562 (Ohio 1997).

ᛒ

Although the doctrine of prosecution history estoppel technically applies only to the doctrine of equivalents, a particular interpretation of claim language can be disclaimed during prosecution. *Baxa Corp. v. McGaw Inc.*, 981 F.Supp. 1348, 44 U.S.P.Q.2d 1801, 1805 (Col. 1997).

ᛒ

Applicants often submit lengthy lists of references in compliance with Rule 56 (37 CFR §1.56), lest they be charged with inequitable conduct for whatever they leave out. The filing of a list of references in accordance with Rule 97, and their description under Rule 98(a)(2), does not create an estoppel as to the full technical content of every reference on the list. Estoppel arises from an Examiner's rejection based on a specific reference and an applicant's position taken to avoid that specific reference. *Litton Systems Inc. v. Honeywell Inc.*, 140 F.3d 1449, 46 U.S.P.Q.2d 1321, 1332, 1336 *dissent* (Fed. Cir. 1998).

Prosecution Irregularities.

Imperfection in patent examination, whether by an Examiner or by an applicant, does not create a new defense called "prosecution irregularities" and does not displace the experience-based criteria of *Kingsdown Medical Consultants, Ltd. v. Hollister, Inc.*, 863 F.2d 867, 9 U.S.P.Q.2d 1384 (Fed. Cir. 1988)(*en banc*), *cert. denied*, 490 U.S. 1067 (1989). *Magnivision Inc. v. The Bonneau Co.*, 42 U.S.P.Q.2d 1925, 1929 (Fed. Cir. 1997).

Prospective. *See* Economic Advantage.

Protection. *See also* Applicant's Rights.

The public purpose on which the patent law rests requires the granting of claims commensurate in scope with the invention disclosed. This requires as much the granting of broad claims on broad inventions as it does granting of specific claims on more specific inventions. It is neither contemplated by the public purpose of the patent laws nor required by the statute that an inventor shall be forced to accept claims narrower than his invention in order to secure allowance of his patent. *In re Sus and Schaefer*, 306 F.2d 494, 134 U.S.P.Q. 301, 304 (C.C.P.A. 1962).

ᛒ

Product claims have practical advantages over method-of-use claims from the standpoint of protection. Where we are concerned with new compounds in which non-obvious properties have been found, the properties being inherent in the compounds, one could even say it is "somewhat irrational" to say the "invention" is not in the compounds. The basic principle of the patent system is to protect inventions that meet the statutory requirements. Valuable inventions should be given protection of value in the real world of business and the courts. *In re Ruschig, Aümuller, Korger, Wagner, Scholz, and Bänder*, 343 F.2d 965, 145 U.S.P.Q. 274 (C.C.P.A. 1965).

ᛒ

To provide effective incentives, claims must adequately protect inventors. To demand that the first to disclose shall limit his claims to what he has found will work or to materials which meet the guidelines specified for "preferred" materials would not serve the constitutional purpose of promoting progress in the useful arts. *In re Johnson and Farnham*, 558 F.2d 1008, 194 U.S.P.Q. 187, 195 (C.C.P.A. 1977).

ᛒ

Unless a patentee can demonstrate that it has a specific need for evidence available only from third-party customers, an infringement action defendant and its customers are entitled to protection. *Joy Technologies Inc. v. Flakt Inc.*, 772 F. Supp. 842, 20 U.S.P.Q.2d 1934, 1940 (Del. 1991).

Protective Order.[14] *See also* **Document Request.**

A trade secret or other confidential research, development, or commercial informa- tion may be the subject of a protective order under Fed. R. Civ. P. 26(c)(7). One seeking a protective order under that rule must establish that the information sought is confidential. In support of its motion, Biomet submitted an affidavit explaining why the requested discovery contained "trade secrets and other confidential business information." To be a trade secret under Indiana law, information must be kept secret and must derive economic value from that secrecy. Biomet's affidavit specifies measures Biomet uses to keep secret the information sought and the value thereof as secrets. Having shown the information sought to be confidential, one seeking a protective order must then demonstrate that disclosure might be harmful. Courts have presumed that disclosure to a competitor is more harmful than disclosure to a non-competitor. Where a party seeking a protective order has shown that the information sought is confidential and that its disclosure might be harmful, the burden shifts to the party seeking discovery to establish that disclosure of trade secrets and confidential information is relevant and necessary to its case. Rule 26(b)(1) allows discovery of any non-privileged matter that is relevant to the subject matter involved in the pending action. The rule has boundaries, however. Discovery of matter not reasonably calculated to lead to the discovery of admissible evidence is outside its scope. *American Standard Inc. v. Pfizer Inc.*, 828 F.2d 734, 3 U.S.P.Q.2d 1817 (Fed. Cir. 1987).

ω

A protective order in a prior lawsuit, the purpose of which was to prevent commercial injury to the parties through disclosure of confidential information and trade secrets, was not intended to protect any party from further litigation. As the plaintiff's attorney has not disclosed to his client the information that serves as a partial basis for a second lawsuit, there are no grounds for finding a violation of the protective order. *Sumitomo Electric Industries Ltd. v. Corning Glass Works*, 8 U.S.P.Q.2d 1453 (N.Y. 1988).

ω

In order to determine whether a court should modify a protective order so that an intervenor can have access to the discovery conducted by the litigants, the court must ask:

1) Can access to the discovery be granted without harm to legitimate secrecy interests?
2) If the answer to the first question is no, then the burden shifts to the movant, who must show why the secrecy interest now deserves less protection than when the protective order was granted, and why its need for the information outweighs existing privacy concerns.

Haworth Inc. v. Steelcase Inc., 26 U.S.P.Q.2d 1152, 1153 (Mich. 1993).

ω

---

[14]*See Advanced Nuclear Fuels Corp. v. General Electric Co.*, 15 U.S.P.Q.2d 1304 (Wash. 1990).

The standard in determining the scope of in-house counsel's access to confidential information is set forth in *Brown Bag Software v. Symantec Corp.*, 960 F.2d 1465 [22 U.S.P.Q.2d 1429] (9th Cir. 1992); and *U.S. Steel Corp. v. United States*, 730 F.2d 1465 (Fed. Cir. 1984). *Fluke Corp. v. Fine Instruments Corp.*, 32 U.S.P.Q.2d 1789, 1792 (Wash. 1994).

ᛖ

Although courts have discretionary authority to modify a stipulated protective order, the burden of demonstrating that an agreed protective order should be modified is on the moving party. *Phillips Petroleum Co. v. Rexene Products Co.*, 158 F.R.D. 43, 32 U.S.P.Q.2d 1839, 1841 (Del. 1994).

ᛖ

Plaintiff's motion for a protective order was denied. The court permitted defendant's discovery of plaintiff's research activities "unless the parties advise the court, within five days of the filing of this opinion, that the present confidentiality order is insufficient" for protecting plaintiff's research activities from improper use by defendant. *Bristol-Meyers Squibb Co. v. Rhone-Poulenc Rorer Inc.*, 40 U.S.P.Q.2d 1863 (N.Y. 1996).

Protest. *See* **28 U.S.C. §1581(a).**

Protestor.

A reissue proceeding may be initiated only by the holder of a patent, and a party desiring to contest the validity of the patent is assured of only limited participation as a "protestor". A protestor may initially file with the Examiner any papers or documents which rebut the assertions made by the patentee, in the reissue application, including citations of prior art and information relating thereto. The protestor may also continue to monitor the reissue proceeding and file such additional papers as it deems appropriate. *Rohm and Haas Company v. Mobil Oil Corporation*, 525 F.Supp. 1298, 212 U.S.P.Q. 354, 360 (Del. 1981).

Provisional Disclaimer.

Although there was no indication either in the terminal disclaimer itself or in the simultaneously filed amendment that the terminal disclaimer was being filed "provisionally," contingent on any finding by the Board of Appeals or higher authority with respect to the Examiner's rejections under 35 U.S.C. §103, the reference in this opinion to a provisional terminal disclaimer is a clear indication by the PTO that such a document is a viable option. *Ex parte Anthony*, 230 U.S.P.Q. 467, 469 (PTO Bd. App. 1982).

PTO (U.S. Patent and Trademark Office). *See also* **Revocation.**

The Patent Office follows the U.S. Court of Customs and Patent Appeals in its interpretation of the patent laws in the event of apparent conflict in the decisions of that court and any of the circuit courts of appeal. *Ex parte Mohr*, 77 U.S.P.Q. 510, 512 (PO Bd. App. 1948).

ᛖ

The law as applied in the Patent Office must be uniform with the law as applied in the courts in passing on patent validity. *In re Bass, Jenkins, and Horvat*, 474 F.2d 1276, 177 U.S.P.Q. 178, 185 (C.C.P.A. 1973).

ω

The PTO cannot appeal from a decision of the BPAI reversing an Examiner's ground of rejection. *Holmes, Faber, Boykin, and Francis v. Kelley, Hornberger, and Strief*, 586 F.2d 234, 199 U.S.P.Q. 778 (C.C.P.A. 1978).

ω

Once a patent of invention has been granted, the Patent Office has no authority to invalidate the claims of the original patent in subsequent reissue proceedings. The PTO does not regain power over the original patent's validity when a reissue patent is applied for. When a patent has received the signature of the Secretary of the Interior, counter-signed by the Commissioner of Patents, and has had affixed to it the seal of the Patent Office, it has passed beyond the control and jurisdiction of that office, and is not subject to be revoked or canceled by the President, or any other officer of the Government. *National Business Systems, Inc. v. AM International, Inc.*, 546 F.Supp. 340, 217 U.S.P.Q. 235, 241 (Ill. 1982).

ω

The plaintiff in an action brought pursuant to 35 U.S.C. §145 has a heavy burden. Because the Patent Office is an expert body preeminently qualified to determine questions of this kind, its conclusions are entitled to a broad presumption of validity. In these circumstances, the court is authorized to reverse the decision only if the Patent Office did not have a rational basis for its conclusions or if the plaintiff presented new evidence that leads to a thorough conviction that the plaintiff should prevail. In trials de novo under 35 U.S.C. §145, great weight attaches to the expertise of the Patent Office, and its findings will not be overturned unless new evidence is introduced that carries thorough conviction that the Patent Office erred. Based upon the opinion testimony of an independent expert, the court was satisfied that the only way one would reach the plaintiff's claimed alloy composition from the reference disclosure was by experimentation. The testimony offered on behalf of the plaintiff at the trial was uncontradicted by the defendant. The court found that testimony to be very persuasive, and the court concluded that the plaintiff demonstrated by clear and convincing evidence that the determination by the Board of Appeals was in error. *Titanium Metals Corp. of America v. Mossinghoff*, 603 F. Supp. 87, 225 U.S.P.Q. 673 (D.C. 1984).

ω

To the extent reliance is placed on evidence previously considered by the PTO, there is "the added burden of overcoming the deference that is due to a qualified government agency presumed to have properly done its job, which includes...Examiners who are assumed to have some expertise in interpreting the references and to be familiar from their work with the level of skill in the art and whose duty it is to issue only valid patents." *Sonoco Products Co. v. Mobil Oil Corp.*, 15 U.S.P.Q.2d 1186, 1191 (S.C. 1989).

ω

"[Agencies] are in reality miniature independent governments. . . . They constitute a headless "fourth branch" of the Government, a haphazard deposit of irresponsible agencies and uncoordinated powers. . . . Furthermore, the same men are obliged to serve both as prosecutors and as judges. This not only undermines judicial fairness; it weakens public confidence in that fairness." *In re Zurko*, 142 F.3d 1447, 46 U.S.P.Q.2d 1691, 1694 (Fed. Cir. 1998—*in banc*).

PTO History.[15]

PTO Indices.

There are 14 specific types of decisions, which fall under four categories [(1) whether patent rights are to be granted, maintained, extended, or reexamined; (2) whether a trademark is entitled to the benefits of federal registration; (3) whether penalties are to be imposed on an individual for violation of regulations relating to the use of PTO records or search facilities; and (4) whether individuals are entitled to practice before the PTO] and for which the PTO maintains indices:

1. Decisions denying delayed payment of maintenance fees under 37 C.F.R. §1.378(e);
2. Decisions denying relief from provisions related to reexamination under 37 C.F.R. §1.181-1.183;
3. Decisions upholding the denial of reexamination requests under 37 C.F.R. §1.515(c);
4. Decisions denying extensions of time in a reexamination under 37 C.F.R. §1.550(c);
5. Commissioner's decisions in disciplinary matters;
6. Commissioner's decisions concerning practice before the PTO;
7. Commissioner's decisions in regard to the PTO registration examination;
8. Commissioner's decisions concerning scientific and technical training;
9. Eligibility for extension of patent term under 37 C.F.R. §1.750;
10. Ex parte decisions of the Board of Patent Appeals and Interferences;
11. Inter partes decisions of the Board of Patent Appeals and Interferences;
12. Decisions of the Trademark Trial and Appeal Board;
13. Commissioner's decisions in trademark matters; and
14. The Index of Patents.

Leeds v. Quigg, 745 F. Supp. 1, 15 U.S.P.Q.2d 1821, 1822 (D.C. 1990).

Public. *See also* 35 U.S.C. §102(a).

The public has an interest in upholding and preserving patent rights. *Solarex Corp. v. Advanced Photovoltaic Systems Inc.*, 34 U.S.P.Q.2d 1234, 1241 (Del. 1995).

---

[15] See *In re Zurko*, 142 F.3d 1447, 46 U.S.P.Q.2d 1691, 1696 (Fed. Cir. 1998—in banc).

Publication. *See also* **Applicant's Publication, Coauthors, Foreign Patent Application, Microfilm, Photograph, Printed Publication, Research Paper, Thesis, 35 U.S.C. §21.**

A printed publication does not constitute a reduction to practice, but is evidence of conception only. The same is true of the manuscript on which a publication is based. The mere placing of a manuscript in the hands of a publisher does not necessarily make it available to the public and does not constitute either prima facie or conclusive evidence of use by others in this country of the invention disclosed by the article, within the meaning of 35 U.S.C. §102(a), since the knowledge involved is of a conception only and not of a reduction to practice. *In re Schlittler and Uffer*, 234 F.2d 882, 110 U.S.P.Q. 304, 305, 308 (C.C.P.A. 1956).

ᚠ

Descriptions in printed publications of new plant varieties, before they may be used as statutory bars under 35 U.S.C. §102(b), must meet the same standards which must be met before a description in a printed publication becomes a bar in non-plant patent cases. *In re LeGrice*, 301 F.2d 929, 133 U.S.P.Q. 365, 378 (C.C.P.A. 1962).

ᚠ

Internal government reports are not publications. A report distributed to a limited group with an injunction to secrecy is not a publication within the meaning of 35 U.S.C. §102. The statutory language "printed publication" implies that numerous copies were printed and made accessible to the general public. *The General Tire & Rubber Company v. The Firestone Tire & Rubber Company*, 349 F.Supp. 333, 349 F.Supp. 345, 174 U.S.P.Q. 427, 441 (Ohio 1972).

ᚠ

As long as those persons "in the class of people to whom [the document] is directed" could have a copy "merely for the asking", the document is deemed to be publicly available. *In re Certain Caulking Guns*, 223 U.S.P.Q. 388, 397 (U.S. Int'l Trade Comm'n 1984).

ᚠ

A doctoral thesis is a printed publication when deposited and cataloged in a public library. *In re Hall*, 781 F.2d 897, 228 U.S.P.Q. 453 (Fed. Cir. 1986).

ᚠ

An association's internal confidential research report is not a printed publication as specified in 35 U.S.C. §102(b). *In re George*, 2 U.S.P.Q.2d 1880, 1882 (B.P.A.I. 1987).

ᚠ

A particular memorandum was held not to be a printed publication. The memorandum was filed in a special vault in the Stanford Research Institute (SRI) library with classified government documents. The library personnel maintained the memorandum as confidential, and only members of the SRI library staff had access to it. In order to ensure that the proprietary information was not compromised, the SRI personnel only prepared a limited number of copies of the memorandum, and each copy was identified to control its distribution. The SRI memorandum was never loaned to another library and was not made available to the public. The SRI memorandum was listed on a project card in the library; however, the library personnel were required to advise members of the public that the memorandum was "not available" from the SRI library. The memorandum was kept in a part of the library where the general public did not have access to it. *RCA Corp. v. Data General Corp.*, 701 F. Supp. 456, 8 U.S.P.Q.2d 1305 (Del. 1988).

ϖ

A paper submitted for peer review and considered by nine or ten experts for that purpose is not a printed publication even if the experts make the paper available to others. Even though the experts are from competing companies, they do not constitute the public or interested persons in their field, as contemplated by 35 U.S.C. §102(b). *National Semiconductor Corp. v. Lenier Technology Corp.*, 703 F. Supp. 845, 8 U.S.P.Q.2d 1359 (Cal. 1988).

ϖ

A Belgian court determined that the document at issue was found "in a private library" and that it could not qualify as having been printed or published because, under Belgian law, those terms refer to documents "available to the public." The just-recited *factual* findings of the Belgian court conclusively demonstrate that the document is not a "printed *publication*" under the United States patent laws [35 U.S.C. §102(b)] either. *Northlake Marketing & Supply Inc. v. Glaverbel S.A.*, 958 F.Supp. 373, 45 U.S.P.Q.2d 1106, 1111 (Ill. 1997).

Public Interest.

Congress has made the legislative determination that it is not in the public interest to permit the infringement of those temporary monopolies (patents), as it undermines inventor incentive. *LifeScan Inc. v. Polymer Technology International Corp.*, 35 U.S.P.Q.2d 1225, 1241 (Wash. 1995).

ϖ

The district court did not abuse its discretion in denying preliminary injunction, in part based on public interest, because the infringing product involved was a catheter preferred by many physicians in the treatment of heart patients *Odetics Inc. v. Storage Technology Corp.*, 47 U.S.P.Q.2d 1573, 1583 (Va. 1998).

Public Use. *See also* Experimental Use, Marketability.

The use of an invention in secret for commercial purposes is considered public use. *Kewanee Oil Company v. Bicron Corporation*, 478 F.2d 1074, 178 U.S.P.Q. 3, 6 (6th Cir. 1973).

ϖ

Private laboratory research use, occurring after a laboratory "reduction to practice," does not become a public use under 35 U.S.C. §102(b). *Cf. W.L. Gore & Assoc., Inc. v. Garlock Inc.*, 721 F.2d 1540, 1550, 220 U.S.P.Q. 303, 310 (Fed. Cir. 1983) [a third person's secret commercial activity, more than one year before the patent application of another, is not a 35 U.S.C. §102(b) bar to the patent of another], *cert. denied*, 469 U.S. 851 (1984).

ϖ

Demonstration of the operation of a prototype at a convention booth was held to be public use within the meaning of 35 U.S.C. §102(b), even though the involved machine, which still had a number of bugs, was not on sale. *Electro-Nucleonics, Inc. v. Mossinghoff*, 593 F.Supp. 125, 224 U.S.P.Q. 435, 436 (D.C. 1984).

ω

Although there may not have been a confidentiality agreement in place between the patent owner and non-company people involved in testing more than a year prior to filing the patent application, three test analysts testified that it was their practice to inform the non-company people at the test site that the patent owner's equipment was experimental and confidential. Each of them also made clear by his testimony that his work with the equipment during the critical period was directed toward working the bugs out of an experimental machine that had not been refined to the point where it was ready for commercial use. *Schrag v. Strosser*, 21 U.S.P.Q.2d 1025, 1029 (B.P.A.I. 1991).

ω

Equipment including the structural features of the subject invention had been on public display before visitors for years prior to filing an application for letters patent. Telling tour groups that the equipment "may be operating" is adequate to draw an inference of public use. Once a *prima facie* case of public use has been established, the burden is on appellants to come forward with evidence that will counter such a case. *Ex parte Kuklo*, 25 U.S.P.Q.2d 1387, 1389, 1390 (B.P.A.I. 1992).

ω

"If an inventor . . . gives or sells [his invention] to another, to be used by the donee or vendee, without limitation or restriction, or injunction of secrecy and it is so used, such use is public, even though the use and knowledge of the use may be confined to one person." *The National Research Development Corp. v. Varian Associates Inc.*, 17 F.3d 1444, 30 U.S.P.Q.2d 1537, 1539 (Fed. Cir. 1994).

ω

Beyond finding that the products, including the features upon which the Examiner relied in rejecting the claims, were in public use or on sale, there is no requirement for an enablement-type inquiry. ("[O]ur precedent holds that the question is not whether the sale, even a third party sale, 'discloses' the invention at the time of the sale, but whether the sale relates to a device that embodies the invention."). *In re Epstein*, 32 F.3d 1559, 31 U.S.P.Q.2d 1817, 1823 (Fed. Cir. 1994).

ω

To be a "public" use, the use must be by a person other than the inventor who is under no limitation, restriction or obligation to secrecy. *Automotive Products plc v. Tilton Engineering Inc.*, 855 F.Supp. 1101, 33 U.S.P.Q.2d 1065, 1085 (Cal. 1994).

ω

"The essence of 'public use' is the free and unrestricted giving over of an invention to a member of the public or the public in general." *Gargoyles Inc. v. U.S.*, 32 Fed.Cl. 157, 33 U.S.P.Q.2d 1595, 1603 (U.S Ct. Fed. Cl. 1994).

ω

Whether an invention was "on-sale" or in "public use" under 35 U.S.C. §102(b) must be determined in light of the policies underlying §102(b). These policies include requiring prompt disclosure, discouraging the removal of devices from the public domain once they are there, prohibiting the extension of the inventor's monopoly period for exploiting the invention, and giving the inventor a reasonable amount of time after his initial sales activity (i.e., one year) to determine whether the patent is a worthwhile investment. *Nordberg Inc. v. Telsmith Inc.*, 881 F.Supp. 1252, 36 U.S.P.Q.2d 1577, 1602 (Wis. 1995).

ω

A commercial use of a machine or process is a public use, even if the machine or process is kept secret. *Lockwood v. American Airlines Inc.*, 37 U.S.P.Q.2d 1534, 1535 (Cal. 1995).

ω

Public use includes "any use of [the claimed] invention by a person other than the inventor who is under no limitation, restriction or obligation of secrecy to the inventor." *Petrolite Corp. v. Baker Hughes Inc.*, 96 F.3d 1423, 40 U.S.P.Q.2d 1201, 1203 (Fed. Cir. 1996).

ω

The question of public use under 35 U.S.C. §102(b) is a question of law. *Lough v. Brunswick Corp.*, 41 U.S.P.Q.2d 1385 (Fed. Cir. 1997).

ω

"Public use" and "on-sale" bars, while they share the same statutory basis, are grounded on different policy emphases. The primary policy underlying the "public use" case is that of detrimental public reliance, whereas the primary policy underlying an "on-sale" case is that of prohibiting the commercial exploitation of the design beyond the statutorily prescribed time period. *Continental Plastic Containers Inc. v. Owens-Brock-way Plastic Products Inc.*, 141 F.3d 1073, 46 U.S.P.Q.2d 1277, 1280 (Fed. Cir. 1998).

Public Use Proceeding.

An Examiner properly granted a motion by a senior party patentee to suspend proceedings in an interference pending action by the Commissioner on a petition for institution of public use proceedings against the junior party in the interference. *Rapata v. Hershberger and Rickey*, 140 U.S.P.Q. 66 (Comm'r 1961).

ω

Under *Heckler v. Chaney*, 470 U.S. 821, 838 (1985), the final decision of the PTO is not reviewable as it is action "committed to agency discretion." Thus, while the court has jurisdiction to review whether the Commissioner followed the correct procedure, it does not have jurisdiction to review the propriety of the final decision to grant or deny the request for a public use proceeding. "The general exception to reviewability provided by [the Administrative Procedure Act, 5 U.S.C.] §701(a)(2) for action 'committed to agency discretion' remains a narrow one ... but within that exception are included *agency refusals to instigate investigative of enforcement proceedings. . . .*" (Emphasis added.) *Intel Corp. v. Lehman*, 47 U.S.P.Q.2d 1221, 1222 n.2 (Cal. 1997).

Purchaser.

When a seller sells a product without restriction, it in effect promises the purchaser that, in exchange for the price paid, it will not interfere with the purchaser's full enjoyment of the product purchased. The buyer has an implied license under any patents of the seller that dominate the product or any uses of the product to which the parties might reasonably contemplate the product will be put. *Hewlett-Packard Co. v. Repeat-O-Type Stencil Manufacturing Corp.*, 123 F.3d 1445, 43 U.S.P.Q.2d 1650, 1655 (Fed. Cir. 1997).

Purchaser for Value.

When a legal title holder of a patent transfers title to a third-party purchaser for value without notice of an outstanding equitable claim or title, the purchaser takes the entire ownership of the patent, free of any prior equitable encumbrance. This is an application of the common law bona fide-purchaser-for-value rule. Going a step further, 35 U.S.C. §261 adopts the principle of the real property recording acts and provides that the bona fide purchaser for value cuts off the rights of a prior assignee who has failed to record the prior assignment in the PTO by the dates specified in the statute. The statute is intended to cut off prior legal interests, which the common law rule did not. Both the common law rule and the statute contemplate that the subsequent purchaser is exactly that—a transferee who pays valuable consideration and is without notice of the prior transfer. *FilmTek Corp. v. Allied-Signal Inc.*, 939 F.2d 1568, 19 U.S.P.Q.2d 1508, 1512 (Fed. Cir. 1991).

Pure. *See also* Free, Isolated.

Pure, isomer-free compounds called for by claims are patentable over a brown reference sludge (containing such compounds) because they possess new and unobvious properties that are not possessed by the brown sludge. *Ex parte Yale and Bernstein*, 119 U.S.P.Q. 256, 258 (PO Bd. App. 1958).

ω

A pure compound has the requisite novelty over prior art which refers only to an impure form of the compound. *In re Bergstrom and Sjovall*, 427 F.2d 1394, 166 U.S.P.Q. 256, 262 (C.C.P.A. 1970).

ω

A claim to a "synthetically produced" or a "substantially pure" substance may well have the requisite novelty to distinguish over a counterpart which occurs in nature only in impure form. *In re Kratz and Strasburger*, 592 F.2d 1169, 201 U.S.P.Q. 71, 75 (C.C.P.A. 1979).

Purity.

Where a claimed product and that of a reference have the same utility, any change in the form, purity, color, or any of the other characteristics of the claimed product does not render the product patentable. Not only do the asserted color and stability changes in appellant's product appear as inherent properties in the pure crystalline form but also, because these differences do not change the utility of the product, patentability is not conferred thereon. *Ex parte Hartop,* 139 U.S.P.Q. 525, 527 (PO Bd. App. 1963).

ᖡ

The novel purity of a reactant which is instrumental in making a commercially acceptable process is sufficient to impart patentability to the reactant of such purity even though the involved compound of lesser purity was known. *In re Doyle, Nayler, and Robinson,* 327 F.2d 513, 140 U.S.P.Q. 421, 425 (C.C.P.A. 1964).

Purpose. *See also* **Direction, Incentive, Motivation.**

Although the Board described one of appellant's key discoveries as merely an "obviously desirable" characteristic, this would not make appellant's invention, considered as a whole, obvious. Obviousness is not to be determined on the basis of purpose alone. *In re Saether,* 492 F.2d 849, 181 U.S.P.Q. 36, 39 (C.C.P.A. 1974).

ᖡ

The BPAI held that appellant had simply made an obvious design choice. However, the different structures of appellant and of the reference achieve different purposes. *In re Gal,* 980 F.2d 717, 25 U.S.P.Q.2d 1076, 1078 (Fed. Cir. 1992)

PVPA. *See* **Plant Variety Protection Act.**

By reason of its proviso the first sentence of 7 U.S.C. §2543 allows seed that has been preserved for reproductive purposes ("saved seed") to be sold for such purposes. The structure of the sentence is such, however, that this authorization does *not* extend to saved seed that was *grown for the very purpose* of sale ("marketing") for replanting—because in that case, §2541(3) would be violated, and the above-discussed exception would apply. *Asgrow Seed Co. v. Winterboer,* 115 S.Ct. 788, 33 U.S.P.Q.2d 1430, 1435 (S.Ct. 1995).

Pyridyl.

Even though pyridine and benzene are similar in many respects, the effect of their interchange in the instant complex nucleus could hardly be foretold, considering that there is little predictability in the subject art. *Ex parte Koo,* 150 U.S.P.Q. 131, 132 (PO Bd. App. 1965).

Key Terms and Concepts

Quantity Limitation.

Grant-backs of non-exclusive licenses, geographically limited licenses, and quantity limited licenses are not per se unlawful; they do not necessarily constitute patent misuse or violate section 2 of the Sherman Act. *Lightwave Technologies Inc. v. Corning Glass Works*, 19 U.S.P.Q.2d 1838, 1844 (N.Y. 1991).

Quayle.

When all claims in a pending application are allowed, prosecution on the merits can be closed and the applicant can be accorded a fixed period of time within which to complete previously unsatisfied formal requirements. *Ex parte Quayle,* 25 U.S.P.Q. 74 (Comm'r Patents 1935).

Question.

A fact, question or right distinctly adjudged in an original action cannot be disputed in a subsequent action even though the determination was rendered upon an erroneous view or an erroneous application of law. *In re Convertible Rowing Exerciser Patent Litigation*, 814 F.Supp. 1197, 26 U.S.P.Q.2d 1677, 1686, 1687 (Del. 1993).

Quid Pro Quo.

The PTO, in discharging its duties to the public, has commendably required applicants for patents to provide an adequate quid pro quo in exchange for the monopoly sought. It should be equally alert in protecting the rights of applicants who have legally and properly established such a right. To do otherwise would be to enrich the public unjustly at the expense of the inventor, a result Congress could not have intended. *In re Herr,* 377 F.2d 610, 153 U.S.P.Q. 548, 549 (C.C.P.A. 1967).

Key Terms and Concepts

Racemate.

A particular stereoisomer is not patentable over a reference to the racemic mixture from which it is derived. *In re Adamson and Duffin*, 275 F.2d 952, 125 U.S.P.Q. 233, 235 (C.C.P.A. 1960).

ᵀ

The novelty of an optical isomer is not negated by the prior art disclosure of its racemate. *In re May and Eddy,* 574 F.2d 1082, 197 U.S.P.Q. 601, 607 (C.C.P.A. 1978).

Radical. *See also* Substituted.

All compositions of matter are combinations if they consist of two or more substances in some degree of correlationship. Chemical compounds are clearly included as one kind of composition of matter. A radical constituting an element of a claimed chemical compound is an element in a claim for a combination within the meaning of 35 U.S.C. §112, third paragraph. *In re Barr, Williams, and Whitmore,* 444 F.2d 588, 170 U.S.P.Q. 330, 336 (C.C.P.A. 1971).

Range. *See also* Proportion.

The ranges set forth in the claim are based on all of the examples in the application in which all elements recited in the claims are present. These ranges are, therefore, not arbitrary. It is ordinarily not improper to use all of the examples to set up a range of established operativeness. *Ex parte Jackson*, 110 U.S.P.Q. 561, 562 (PTO Bd. App. 1956).

ᵀ

Although the reference range of possible ratios envelops the claimed range, unexpected results follow from the selected and critical claimed range. In order to show a required unexpected result, there must be a difference in kind, rather than one in degree, over the critical range. *In re Waymouth and Koury*, 499 F.2d 1273, 182 U.S.P.Q. 290, 293 (C.C.P.A. 1974).

ᵀ

The criticality of a claimed range can be relied upon for patentability even though the range is not disclosed as critical in the specification. *Scandiamant Aktiebolag v. Commissioner of Patents*, 509 F.2d 463, 184 U.S.P.Q. 201, 206 (D.C. Cir. 1974).

ᵀ

The change in a lower limit of a range in a continuing application can be, but is not necessarily, fatal to relying on the filing date of the parent application for the invention claimed in the continuing application. *Synthetic Industries (Texas) Inc. v. Forta Fiber, Inc.*, 590 F. Supp. 1574, 224 U.S.P.Q. 955 (Pa. 1984).

ω

A reference disclosure of a polyolefin resin having a "preferred" range of "melt index of 0.1 to 40" was regarded as an anticipation of a claim limitation to a polyolefin resin having "a melt index of less than about 5 grams/10 minutes." The lower limit of the reference range was relied on as a disclosure of the noted resin having that melt index. *Ex parte Lee*, 31 U.S.P.Q.2d 1105, 1106 (B.P.A.I. 1993).

Range of Equivalents.

An appropriate range of equivalents may extend to post invention advances in the art. *American Hospital Supply Corporation v. Travenol Laboratories, Inc.*, 745 F.2d 1, 223 U.S.P.Q. 577, 583 (Fed. Cir. 1984).

Ratio.

The standard of patentability does not depend upon a showing of advantages or improvements, but rather upon obviousness. The Examiner's failure to indicate any reason for finding obvious the alteration of the ratio employed in the prior art in the direction and manner claimed renders the rejection untenable. *Ex parte Parthasarathy and Ciapetta,* 174 U.S.P.Q. 63 (PTO Bd. App. 1971).

ω

The couching in patent claims of components of a chemical mixture in terms of numerical values of ratios placed a heavy burden on a busy Examiner and further weakened the presumption of patent validity. *Borden, Inc. v. Occidental Petroleum Corporation*, 381 F.Supp. 1178, 182 U.S.P.Q. 472, 482 (Tex. 1974).

Rationale.

Where the Board advances a position or rationale new to the proceedings, as it is empowered to do and quite capable of doing, the appellant must be afforded an opportunity to respond to that position or rationale by submission of contradicting evidence. The Board's refusal to consider evidence which responds to such a new rationale is error. *In re Eynde, Pollet, and de Cat*, 480 F.2d 1364, 178 U.S.P.Q. 470, 474 (C.C.P.A. 1973).

Reacting.

When the claimed invention does not lie in particular conditions of a reaction and those conditions would be obvious to a skilled chemist, the patentability of the claim is not precluded as being functional in the recitation of reacting. *Ex parte Biel,* 137 U.S.P.Q. 315, 317 (PO Bd. App. 1962).

Reaction. *See* Reduction in Steps.

Reaction Product.

The patentability of a claim to a reaction product of A with B is not precluded. *Ex parte Simons*, 86 U.S.P.Q. 336 (PO Bd. App. 1949).

ω

Congress has placed no limitations on how an applicant claims his invention, so long as the specification concludes with claims that particularly point out and distinctly claim that invention. Defining a claimed product as the acid phosphate of the condensation product of formaldehyde and a salt of a certain compound does not make the claim a product-by-process claim. *In re Steppan, Rebenstock, and Neugebauer*, 394 F.2d 1013, 156 U.S.P.Q. 143 (C.C.P.A. 1967).

Readability.

Readability of a claim on the subject matter of another (patent) claim (domination) is neither determinative of double patenting nor demonstrative that the claims are directed to the same invention. *In re Sarett*, 327 F.2d 1005, 140 U.S.P.Q. 474, 482 (C.C.P.A. 1964).

***Read* Factors. *See* Enhanced Damages.**

Reading Frame—The term "reading frame" relates to the way in which a protein is expressed from a DNA construct. DNA is made up of a series of nucleotides. To express the DNA construct to yield a protein, the cell machinery reads nucleotides in sets of three, which are called triplets or codons, to incorporate specific amino acids into the protein. If an extra nucleotide is inserted or deleted from a DNS sequence, the series of triplets is changed and different amino acids are incorporated into the protein. The term "reading frame" describes this phenomenon. To maintain "proper reading frame," the triplets in the DNA sequence must be read so that the proper amino acids are incorporated into the resulting protein. *Genentech Inc. v. Chiron Corp.*, 112 F.3d 495, 42 U.S.P.Q.2d 1608, 1613 (Fed. Cir. 1997).

Read On. *See also* Generic Disclosure.

The contention that a claimed configuration would be obvious from a reference claim on which it reads is a non sequitur. According to such reasoning Morse's telegraph patent would have made the Telex obvious. The scope of a patent's claims determines what infringes the patent; it is no measure of what it discloses. A patent discloses only that which it describes, whether specifically or in general terms, so as to convey intelligence to one capable of understanding. *In re Benno*, 768 F.2d 1340, 226 U.S.P.Q. 683 (Fed. Cir. 1985).

Real World. *See* Value.

Rearranging Parts. *See also* Reversal of Parts.

There is no invention in shifting a component to a different position when the operation of a claimed device is not modified thereby. *In re Japikse*, 181 F.2d 1019, 86 U.S.P.Q. 70, 73 (C.C.P.A. 1950).

Reason. *See also* **Explanation, Incentive, Motivation, Truth.**

An art-based ground or rejection of a process claim was considered untenable because the Examiner failed to provide any reason for finding obvious the alteration of the molybdenum-phosphorus ratio in the direction and manner claimed. *Ex parte Parthasarathy and Ciapetta,* 174 U.S.P.Q. 63 (PO Bd. App. 1971).

ᙂ

Due process requires that an applicant be given notice of the reasons his claims are rejected and why arguments upon which he relies are deemed lacking in merit. This principle is the essence of 35 U.S.C. §132 and should guide the proceedings of the Board of Appeals as well. *Ex parte Hageman,* 179 U.S.P.Q. 747, 751 (PTO Bd. App. 1972).

ᙂ

In the absence of appellant's own teachings, one skilled in the art would have no reason to go from a simple system, in which only the toner particles need be accelerated, to a more complicated one, in which the carrier particles have to be accelerated up to the screen with sufficient force to dislodge the toner particles they carry, which must then continue to travel until they reach the printing surface. *In re Rarey and Kennedy,* 480 F.2d 1345, 178 U.S.P.Q. 463, 467 (C.C.P.A. 1973).

ᙂ

The unpredictability noted in the decision of the Board was in the admittedly chemical fact that the "properties of 'polymerizable materials' can vary over a wide range," but no reasons were given to appellant by the Patent Office for the alleged failure—or at least uncertainty—of the class of "polymerizable materials" to work in the claimed process to controvert the statement in appellant's application that his invention, in its broader aspects, is applicable to other polymers. Even in cases involving the unpredictable world of chemistry, such reasons are required. *In re Bowen,* 492 F.2d 859, 181 U.S.P.Q. 48, 50, 51 (C.C.P.A. 1974).

ᙂ

There must be a reason apparent at the time the invention was made to a person of ordinary skill in the art for applying the teaching at hand, or the use of the teaching as evidence of obviousness will entail prohibited hindsight. *In re Nomiya, Kohisa, and Matsumura,* 509 F.2d 566, 184 U.S.P.Q. 607 (C.C.P.A. 1975).

ᙂ

The purpose of the reasons of appeal is to alert the parties to the issues before the court. With regard to a rejection under 35 U.S.C. §101, the PTO must do more than merely question operability—it must set forth factual reasons which would lead one skilled in the art to question the objective truth of the statement of operability. *In re Gaubert,* 524 F.2d 1222, 187 U.S.P.Q. 664, 665, 666 (C.C.P.A. 1975).

ᙂ

The PTO has the initial burden of presenting evidence or reasons why persons of ordinary skill in the art would not recognize (in the disclosure of the original patent) a description of the invention defined by the reissue claims. *In re Salem, Butterworth, and Ryan,* 553 F.2d 676, 193 U.S.P.Q. 513, 518 (C.C.P.A. 1977).

ᙂ

The burden of showing that the claimed invention is not described in the application rests on the PTO in the first instance, and it is up to the PTO to give reasons why a description not in ipsis verbis is insufficient. *In re Edwards, Rice, and Soulen,* 568 F.2d 1349, 196 U.S.P.Q. 465, 469 (C.C.P.A. 1978).

ᚹ

Presuming arguendo that the references show the elements or concepts urged, the Examiner presented no line of reasoning as to why the artisan reviewing only the collective teachings of the references would have found it obvious to selectively pick and choose various elements and/or concepts from the several references relied on to arrive at the claimed invention. In the instant application, the Examiner has done little more than cite references to show that one or more elements, or some combinations thereof, when each is viewed in a vacuum, is known. The claimed invention, however, is clearly directed to a combination of elements. That is to say, the appellant does not claim that he has invented one or more new elements but has presented claims to a new combination of elements. To support the conclusion that the claimed combination is directed to obvious subject matter, either the references must expressly or impliedly suggest the claimed combination or the Examiner must present a convincing line of reasoning as to why the artisan would have found the claimed invention to have been obvious in light of the teachings of the references. The Board found nothing in the references that would expressly or impliedly teach or suggest the modifications urged by the Examiner. Additionally, the Board found no line of reasoning in the answer as to why the artisan would have found the modifications urged by the Examiner to have been obvious. Based upon the record, the artisan would not have found it obvious to selectively pick and choose elements or concepts from the various references so as to arrive at the claimed invention without using the claims as a guide. *Ex parte Clapp,* 227 U.S.P.Q. 972 (B.P.A.I. 1985).

ᚹ

The reason a particular claim limitation is added during prosecution is a question of fact, not law. *See Mannesmann Demag Corp. v. Engineered Metal Products Co.,* 793 F.2d 1279, 1285, 230 U.S.P.Q. 45, 48 (Fed. Cir. 1986).

ᚹ

To combine references to reach a conclusion that claimed subject matter would have been obvious, case law requires that there must be some teaching, suggestion, or inference in either reference, or both, or knowledge generally available that would have led one of ordinary skill in the art to combine the relevant teachings of the references. When the incentive to combine the teachings of the references is not readily apparent, it is the duty of the Examiner to explain why a combination of the reference teachings is proper. Absent such reasons or incentives, the teachings of the references are not combinable. *Ex parte Skinner,* 2 U.S.P.Q.2d 1788 (B.P.A.I. 1986).

ᚹ

When prior-art references require a selective combination to render obvious a subsequent invention, there must be some reason for the combination other than the hindsight gleaned from the invention itself. Something in the prior art as a whole must suggest the desirability, and thus the obviousness, of making the combination. It is impermissible to use the claims as a frame and the prior-art references as a mosaic to piece together a facsimile of the claimed invention. *Uniroyal Inc. v. Rudkin-Wiley Corp.*, 837 F.2d 1044, 5 U.S.P.Q.2d 1434 (Fed. Cir. 1988).

ᚣ

An obvious-to-experiment standard is not an acceptable substitute for obviousness. Selective hindsight is no more applicable to the design of experiments than it is to the combination of prior-art teachings. There must be a reason or suggestion in the art for selecting the procedure used, other than the knowledge learned from the applicant's disclosure. *In re Dow Chemical Co.*, 837 F.2d 469, 5 U.S.P.Q.2d 1529 (Fed. Cir. 1988).

ᚣ

A presumption of a fact is nothing more than a process of reasoning from one fact to another, an argument that infers a fact otherwise doubtful from a fact that is proved. Rules of evidence as to inferences from facts are to aid reason, not to override it. *Rosemount Inc. v. U.S. International Trade Commission*, 910 F.2d 819, 15 U.S.P.Q.2d 1569, 1572 (Fed. Cir. 1990).

ᚣ

It is important to understand "the *reasoning* behind the Patent Office's insistence upon a change in the claims." The critical fact is "the reason for an *amendment* required during patent prosecution," not the reason for the PTO's objection. The burden on the patent-holder to establish the reason for the amendment suggests that any evidence that may assist it in carrying this burden is relevant. *James River Corp. of Virginia v. Hallmark Cards Inc.*, 43 U.S.P.Q.2d 1422, 1427 (Wis. 1997).

Reasonable. *See also* Doubt, Probability, Royalty.

The MPEP contains some mandatory language. For the most part, however, the MPEP only suggests or authorizes procedures for patent Examiners to follow. For example, MPEP §707.03(d) provides that Examiners "should allow claims which define the patentable novelty with a reasonable degree of particularlity and distinctness". The section further provides, "the Examiner's action should be constructive in nature...." The decision as to what is "reasonable" and "constructive" under the circumstances is necessarily a matter of the Examiner's discretion and judgment. The Foreword to the Fifth Edition of the MPEP, dated August 1983, states that the MPEP "contains instructions to examiners," but "does not have the force of law or the force of the Patent Rules of Practice in Title 37, Code of Federal Regulations." The MPEP does not eliminate a patent Examiner's discretion when examining patent applications. Rather, the MPEP is merely part of the overall scheme providing for discretionary examination of patent applications. *Chamberlin v. Isen*, 779 F.2d 522, 228 U.S.P.Q. 369, 372 (9th Cir. 1985).

ᚣ

According to the Examiner, the definition comes full circle and raises the specter that the claims embrace compounds containing a never-ending substituent group. This claim construction, though literal, is not reasonable and is not how a person having ordinary skill would view the claims. The only reasonable construction precludes never-ending substituent groups. The Examiner's claim construction, though possible, is not reasonable and is incorrect. *Ex parte Breuer,* 1 U.S.P.Q.2d 1906, 1907 (B.P.A.I. 1986).

ϖ

Inherency may not be established by probabilities or possibilities. The mere fact that a certain thing may result from a given set of circumstances is not sufficient. Although an applicant may be required to prove that the subject matter shown to be in prior art does not possess characteristics relied upon, where an Examiner has reason to believe that a functional limitation asserted to be critical for establishing novelty in the claimed subject matter may, in fact, be an inherent characteristic of the prior art, the Examiner must provide some evidence or scientific reasoning to establish the reasonableness of the Examiner's belief that the functional limitation is an inherent characteristic of the prior art before the applicant can be put through this burdensome task. *Ex parte Skinner,* 2 U.S.P.Q.2d 1788 (B.P.A.I. 1986).

ϖ

For obviousness under 35 U.S.C. §103, all that is required is a reasonable expectation of success. *In re O'Farrell,* 853 F.2d 894, 7 U.S.P.Q.2d 1673, 1681 (Fed. Cir. 1988).

Reasonable and Entire Compensation.

"Reasonable and entire" compensation necessarily includes delay damages, i.e., recompense tantamount to interest for loss of use of royalties which a prevailing patentee would have enjoyed had payment of such royalties been timely. There is a strong judicial policy in favor of uniform rates to apply to all those entitled to delay damages for a given period. The series of specific rates set forth in *Pitcairn,* 212 Ct. Cl. at 191, 547 F.2d at 1121, based on long-term corporate bond yields, was adopted as the interest rates to be paid "from now on" in just compensation cases "without need of proof in the individual instance." *Hughes Aircraft Co. v. U.S.,* 31 Fed.Cl. 481, 35 U.S.P.Q.2d 1243, 1251, 1252 (U.S. Ct. Fed. Cl. 1994).

Reasonable Apprehension.

The "reasonable apprehension of suit" test requires more than the nervous state of mind of a possible infringer; it requires that the objective circumstances support such an apprehension. *Phillips Plastics Corp. v. Kato Hatsujou Kabushiki Kaisha,* 57 F.3d 1051, 35 U.S.P.Q.2d 1222, 1223, 1224 (Fed. Cir. 1995).

Reasonable Correlation.

The first paragraph of 35 U.S.C. §112 requires that the scope of the claims bear a reasonable correlation to the scope of enablement provided by the specification to persons of ordinary skill in the art. In cases involving predictable factors, such as mechanical or electrical elements, a single embodiment provides broad enablement in the sense that, once imagined, other embodiments can be made without difficulty and their performance characteristics predicted by resort to known scientific laws. In cases involving unpredictable factors, such as most chemical reactions and physiological activity, the scope of enablement obviously varies inversely with the degree of unpredictability of the factors involved. *In re Fisher,* 427 F.2d 833, 166 U.S.P.Q. 18, 24 (C.C.P.A. 1970).

Reasonable Effort. *See also* Duty to Use.

Where there has been a failure to use reasonable efforts to commercialize, damages are often not susceptible of certain proof. A lesser degree of certainty is required in such cases. *Bailey v. Chattem, Inc.,* 684 F.2d 386, 215 U.S.P.Q. 671, 679 (6th Cir. 1982).

Reasonable Royalty. *See also* Prejudgment Interest.

A reasonable royalty (a twenty-five percent royalty rate was regarded as credible and reasonable under the circumstances) is determined by ascertaining the royalties that would have eminated from ficticious hypothetical negotiations between the patentee and infringer. The following factors are germane when determining a reasonable royalty for an infringed product:

1. The royalties received by the patentee for the licensing for the patent in suit, proving or tending to prove an established royalty.
2. The rates paid by the licensee for the use of other patents comparable to the patent in suit.
3. The nature and scope of the license, as exclusive or non-exclusive; or as restricted or non-restricted in terms of territory or with respect to whom the manufactured product may be sold.
4. The licensor's established policy and marketing program to maintain his patent monopoly by not licensing others to use the invention or by granting licenses under special conditions designed to preserve that monopoly.
5. The commercial relationship between the licensor and licensee, such as, whether they are competitors in the same territory in the same line of business; or whether they are inventor and promoter.
6. The effect of selling the patented specialty in promoting sales of other products of the licensee; that existing value of the invention to the licensor as a generator of sales of his non-patented items; and the extent of such derivative or convoyed sales.
7. The duration of the patent and the term of the license.
8. The established profitability of the product made under the patent; its commercial success; and its current popularity.
9. The utility and advantages of the patent property over the old modes or devices, if any, that had been used for working out similar results.
10. The nature of the patented invention; the character of the commercial embodiment of it as owned and produced by the licensor; and the benefits to those who have used the invention.
11. The extent to which the infringer has made use of the invention; and any evidence probative of the value of that use.
12. The portion of the profit or of the selling price that may be customary in the

particular business or in comparable businesses to allow for the use of the invention or analogous inventions.

13. The portion of the realization profit that should be credited to the invention as distinguished from non-patented elements, the manufacturing process, business risks, or significant features or improvements added by the infringer.

14. The opinion testimony of qualified experts.

15. The amount that a licensor (such as the patentee) and a licensee (such as the infringer) would have agreed upon (at the time the infringement began) if both had been reasonably and voluntarily trying to reach an agreement; that is, the amount which a prudent licensee—who desired, as a business proposition, to obtain a license to manufacture and sell a particular article embodying the patented invention would have been willing to pay as a royalty and yet be able to make a reasonable profit and which amount would have been acceptable by a prudent patentee who was willing to grant a license.

The issue of the amount of a "reasonable royalty" is to be determined, not on the basis of a hindsight evaluation of what actually happened, but on the basis of what the parties to the hypothetical license negotiations would have considered at the time of the negotiations. *Additive Controls & Measurement Systems Inc. v. Flowdata Inc.*, 29 U.S.P.Q.2d 1890, 1896, 1899, 1900 (Tex. 1993).

ω

In calculating a reasonable royalty, the criteria followed by the court are those of the willing buyer-willing seller rule: "[t]he royalties received by the patentee for the licensing of the patent in suit . . . [.] [t]he rates paid by the licensee for the use of other patents comparable to the patent in suit[.] [t]he nature and scope of the license, as exclusive or non-exclusive; or as restricted or non-restricted in terms of territory or with respect to whom the manufactured product may be sold[,] [t]he licensor's established policy and, marketing program to maintain his patent monopoly . . . [t]he commercial relationship between the licensor and licensee . . . [,] [t]he effect of selling the patented specialty in promoting sales of other products of the licensee . . . [,] [t]he duration of the patent and the term of the license[,] [t]he established profitability of the product made under the patent; its commercial success; and its current popularity[,] [t]he utility and advantages of the patent property over the old modes or devices, if any, that had been used for working out similar results[,] [t]he nature of the patented invention; the character of the commercial embodiment of it as owned and produced by the licensor; and the benefits to those who have used the invention[,] [t]he extent to which the infringer has made use of the invention; and any evidence probative of the value of that use[,] [t]he portion of the profit or of the selling price that may be customary in the particular business or in comparable businesses to allow for the use of the invention or analogous inventions[,] [t]he portion of the realizable profit that should be credited to the invention . . . [,] [t]he opinion testimony of qualified experts[,] [t]he amount that a licensor (such as the patentee) and a licensee (such as the infringer) would have agreed upon (at the time the infringement began) if both had been reasonably and voluntarily trying to reach an agreement[.]" *Avco Corp. v. PPG Industries Inc.*, 867 F.Supp. 84, 34 U.S.P.Q.2d 1026, 1038 n.13 (Mass. 1994).

ω

"License offers made to the trade and rejected by all can fix the ceiling below which the reasonable royalty must fall. . . ." *Hughes Aircraft Co. v. U.S.*, 31 Fed.Cl. 481, 35 U.S.P.Q.2d 1243, 1248 (U.S. Ct. Fed. Cl. 1994).

ᚳ

"A court is not restricted in finding a reasonable royalty to a specific figure put forth by one of the parties." Rather, a jury's choice simply must be within the range encompassed by the record as a whole. *Unisplay S.A. v. American Electronic Sign Co.*, 69 F.3d 512, 36 U.S.P.Q.2d 1540, 1546 (Fed. Cir. 1995).

ᚳ

A post litigation reasonable royalty should be higher than a negotiated reasonable royalty because otherwise "the infringer would have nothing to lose, and everything to gain if he could count on paying only the normal, routine royalty non-infringers might have paid." *Ramp Research and Development Inc. v. Structural Panels Inc.*, 977 F.Supp. 1169, 43 U.S.P.Q.2d 1432, 1439 (Fla. 1997).

ᚳ

Foreign sales may not be taken into account in any determination of a reasonable royalty. *Enpat Inc. v. Microsoft Corp.*, 6 F.Supp. 587, 47 U.S.P.Q.2d 1218, 1220 (Va. 1998).

Reasoning. *See* Summary Judgment Motion.

Reasons for Appeal.

In an appeal to the court from an adverse holding from the Board of Appeals, issues that are not included in the reasons of appeal are not before the court. *In re DeLancey*, 177 F.2d 377, 83 U.S.P.Q. 388, 393 (C.C.P.A. 1949).

Reassert Cancelled Subject Matter. *See also* Recapture.

Cancellation of certain subject matter to obtain a patent as to other claimed subject matter does not justify application of the doctrine of estoppel or a conclusion that the subject matter had been abandoned where it appears that claims were asserted to the cancelled subject matter in a copending application and at a time when the applicant still had the right to claim the same in a divisional application, even though no divisional requirement had been made. *Harnsberger v. Youker*, 109 F.2d 806, 44 U.S.P.Q. 534, 538 (C.C.P.A. 1940).

ᚳ

A preliminary injunction was granted to an employer to restore claims canceled from a pending application by a former employee and to permit the employer's attorney to prosecute the restored claims. The claims in question covered subject matter which the employer had reason to believe was its property, rights to which would be permanently lost if the subject matter of the canceled claims was not further prosecuted. *Compact Van Equipment Co., Inc. v. Leggett & Platt, Inc.*, 566 F.2d 952, 196 U.S.P.Q. 721, 722 (5th Cir. 1978).

Rebuilding. *See* **Reconstruction.**

Rebuttal. *See* **Due Process.**

Rebuttal Evidence.

In view of the PTO's failure to challenge the sufficiency of the appellants' rebuttal evidence prior to appeal (when the appellants could no longer offer evidence), the Board's decision was vacated and the case remanded to afford the appellants the opportunity to submit objective evidence of unexpected results. *In re De Blauwe,* 736 F.2d 699, 222 U.S.P.Q. 191 (Fed. Cir. 1984).

Recapture. *See also* **Reassert Cancelled Subject Matter.**

An applicant for a patent is not barred from restoring to his application (before a patent issues thereon) any claim which he might theretofore have cancelled, even if the cancellation was made because of prior art citations. *General Electric Company v. Hygrade Sylvania Corporation,* 61 F.Supp. 539, 67 U.S.P.Q. 72, 75 (N.Y. 1944).

ʊ

An agreement entitled "Exclusive License Agreement" granted licensee an exclusive right to make, to sell, and to use a patented invention in return for a specified royalty of the licensee's gross income. The licensor reserved to itself a lien upon the licenses granted and could terminate the agreement upon default by the licensee. The licensor retained legal title to the patents and retained a right to recapture the patents in the event of default of payment. An agreement that grants an exclusive license to make, to sell, and to use is a sale of the patent even if it is called a license. The fact that compensation is to be paid by a percentage of the gross licensed income or the existence of a term for recapture of the patents in default of payment does not convert an otherwise valid assignment into a license. *Transducer Patents Co. v. Renegotiation Board,* 485 F.2d 26, 179 U.S.P.Q. 398, 399 (9th Cir. 1973).

ʊ

Since applicants had narrowed the claims in their parent application and restricted all of the original claims in their continuation-in-part application to exclude (in view of prior art applied by the Patent Office) a particular design, it would be improper to permit them to recapture (by way of a later submitted claim) subject matter that they had willingly relinquished. To do so would ignore the well-established doctrine of "file wrapper estoppel", which does not allow recapture of relinquished subject matter under such circumstances. *Jamesbury Corporation v. United States,* 183 U.S.P.Q. 484, 490 (U.S. Ct. Cl. 1974).

ʊ

Subject matter once abandoned may not lawfully be resurrected and recaptured in a later-filed patent application. *USM Corp. v. SPS Technologies, Inc.,* 514 F.Supp. 213, 211 U.S.P.Q. 112, 134 (Ill. 1981).

ʊ

When an application satisfies the requirements for continuing application status, the parent and continuing applications "are to be considered as parts of the same transaction, and both as constituting one continuous application, within the meaning of the law." Thus, canceling generic claims from a parent application and (before issuance of a patent on the parent application and as part of what was, as a matter of law, the same transaction) adding the generic claims to a continuation-in-part application cannot properly be considered relinquishment, disclaimer, or acquiescence in abandonment of the subject matter of the generic claims. *Square Liner 360Á, Inc. v. Chisum*, 691 F.2d 362, 216 U.S.P.Q. 666, 673 (8th Cir. 1982).

ᴡ

A patentee is not barred by file wrapper estoppel from asserting the doctrine of equivalents because the claims in suit were amended by insertion of the "consisting essentially of" language. The fact that claims are narrowed does not always mean that the doctrine of file history estoppel completely prohibits a patentee from recapturing some of what was originally claimed. *Syntex (U.S.A.) Inc. v. Paragon Optical Inc.*, 7 U.S.P.Q.2d 1001 (Ariz. 1987).

ᴡ

Once a patentee has canceled patented claims, he cannot, as a matter of law, recapture that which he has voluntarily disclaimed. *Ex parte Morimoto*, 18 U.S.P.Q.2d 1540, 1543 (B.P.A.I. 1990).

ᴡ

The recapture rule does not apply where there is no evidence that amendment of an originally filed claim was in any sense an admission that the scope of that claim was not in fact patentable. If a reissue claim is broader in a way that does not attempt to reclaim what was surrendered earlier, the recapture rule may not apply. *Mentor Corp. v. Coloplast Inc.*, 998 F.2d 992, 27 U.S.P.Q.2d 1521, 1524, 1525 (Fed. Cir. 1993).

ᴡ

Amending process claim 1 by adding the phrase "at a pH from approximately 6.0 to 9.0" during prosecution to distinguish over a reference did not preclude a holding of infringement under the doctrine of equivalents by a corresponding process at a pH of 5. *Hilton Davis Chemical Co. v. Warner-Jenkinson Co. Inc.*, 62 F.3d 1512, 35 U.S.P.Q.2d 1641, 1643, 1654 (Fed. Cir. 1995).

ᴡ

Reissue claims fail to meet the "error" requirement when the claims impermissibly recapture surrendered subject matter. *Hester Industries Inc. v. Stein Inc.*, 142 F.3d 1472, 46 U.S.P.Q.2d 1641, 1651 (Fed. Cir. 1998).

Recapture Rule.

The principle that a claim is broadened if it is broader in any respect than the original claim serves to effect the bar of 35 U.S.C. §251 against a reissue filed later than 2 years after issuance of the original patent. The rigidity of the broader-in-any-respect rule makes it inappropriate in an estoppel situation. The CAFC declined to apply that rule where the broader feature relates to an aspect of the invention that is not material to the alleged error supporting reissue. *Ball Corporation v. United States*, 729 F.2d 1429, 221 U.S.P.Q. 289, 296 (Fed. Cir. 1984).

ᴡ

The recapture rule does not apply when there is no evidence that amendment of an originally filed claim was in any sense an admission that the scope of that claim was not in fact patentable. *Seattle Box Company, Inc. v. Industrial Crating & Packing, Inc.*, 731 F.2d 818, 826, 221 U.S.P.Q. 568, 574 (Fed. Cir. 1984).

ω

Under the recapture rule, a patentee ordinarily is barred from securing through reissue a claim that is the same or of broader scope than those claims that were canceled or narrowed by amendment during prosecution of the original patent. The recapture rule should not bar a patentee from securing a reissue that is broader in a material respect than a canceled claim when the reissue claim is also narrower than the canceled claim in a way that is material to the "error." *Patecell v. United States,* 16 Cl. Ct. 644, 12 U.S.P.Q.2d 1440, 1445, 1447 (Cl. Ct. 1989).

ω

The recapture rule bars a patentee from acquiring, through reissue, claims that are the same or of broader scope than those claims that were canceled from the original application. The deliberate cancellation of claims in order to obtain a patent constitutes a bar to obtaining the same claims by inclusion in a reissue patent. *In re Watkinson,* 900 F.2d 230, 14 U.S.P.Q.2d 1407, 1409 (Fed. Cir. 1990).

ω

Reissue claims that are broader in some respects and narrower in others may avoid the effect of the recapture rule. If a reissue claim is broader in a way that does not attempt to reclaim what was surrendered earlier, the recapture rule may not apply. *Sonoco Products Co. v. Durabag Co. Inc.*, 30 U.S.P.Q.2d 1295, 1301 (Cal. 1994).

ω

Although the recapture rule does not apply in the absence of evidence that the applicant's amendment was "an admission that the scope of that claim was not in fact patentable," "the court may draw inferences from changes in claim scope when other reliable evidence of the patentee's intent is not available." Deliberately canceling or amending a claim in an effort to overcome a reference strongly suggests that the applicant admits that the scope of the claim before the cancellation or amendment is unpatentable, but it is not dispositive because other evidence in the prosecution history may indicate the contrary. *In re Clement*, 131 F.3d 1464, 45 U.S.P.Q.2d 1161, 1164 (Fed. Cir. 1997).

Recipe.

New recipes or formulas for cooking food which involve the addition or elimination of common ingredients, or for treating them in ways which differ from the former practice, do not amount to invention merely because it is not disclosed that, in the constantly developing art of preparing food, no one else ever did the particular thing upon which the applicant asserts his right to a patent. There is nothing patentable unless the applicant further establishes (by a proper showing) a coaction or cooperative relationship between the selected ingredients which produces a new, unexpected, and useful function. *In re Levin*, 178 F.2d 945, 84 U.S.P.Q. 232, 234 (C.C.P.A. 1949).

ω

A claim to a lubricating oil composition comprising stated amounts of specified components is not merely a "recipe" for making the composition. *Exxon Chemical Patents Inc. v. Lubrizol Corp.*, 64 F.3d 1553, 35 U.S.P.Q.2d 1801, 1804 (Fed. Cir. 1995).

Recklessness. *See* **Spurious.**

Recognition.

It is irrelevant that appellant (a party to an interference) never referred to or appreciated the support material to be *eta*-alumina or to contain *eta*-alumina *by that name*. However, it is fatal to appellant's case that he did not recognize (until after his interference opponent's filing date) that his "ammonia-aged" catalyst "*contained any different form of alumina at all!*" (Emphasis in original.) The count calls for a particular form of alumina. Appellant's failure to recognize that he had produced a new form, regardless of what he called it, is indicative that he never conceived the invention prior to his opponent's filing date. *Heard v. Burton, Kaufman, Lefrancois, and Riblett*, 333 F.2d 239, 142 U.S.P.Q. 97, 100 (C.C.P.A. 1964).

ᚸ

Having been produced by the same process, the product obtained in Example IV of the earlier Sulkowski application is, of necessity, the same product as that obtained in Example III of the Sulkowski interference application. The only difference is in the naming of the product. Based on the process used in the earlier application, Sulkowski is entitled to the benefit of the product of that process with his later application. The fact that error was made in naming the product in the first application does not deprive Sulkowski of the benefit of that application. *Sulkowski v. Houlihan*, 179 U.S.P.Q. 685, 686 (PTO Bd. Pat. Int. 1973); *see also In re Sulkowski*, 487 F.2d 920, 180 U.S.P.Q. 46 (C.C.P.A. 1973).

ᚸ

There is no conception or reduction to practice of a new form of an otherwise old composition of matter where there has been no recognition or appreciation of the existence of the new form. *Silvestri and Johnson v. Crant and Alburn*, 496 F.2d 593, 181 U.S.P.Q. 706, 708 (C.C.P.A. 1974).

ᚸ

A party to an interference must show an appreciation or recognition by the inventor of the invention of the counts to establish a prior actual reduction to practice. *In re Farrenkopf and Usategui-Gomez*, 713 F.2d 714, 219 U.S.P.Q. 1, 6 (Fed. Cir. 1983).

ᚸ

The fact that the claimed invention has an asserted advantage that went unrecognized for years by those working in the relevant art argues for, not against, nonobviousness. Further, treating the advantage as the invention disregards the statutory requirement that the invention be viewed "as a whole," ignores the problem-recognition element, and injects an improper "obvious to try" consideration. *Jones v. Hardy*, 727 F.2d 1524, 220 U.S.P.Q. 1021, 1026 (Fed. Cir. 1984).

Recollection.

Testimony, based merely on recollection and given more than four years after the events to which it relates, must be closely scrutinized. *Jacobs v. Sohl*, 280 F.2d 140, 126 U.S.P.Q. 399, 402 (C.C.P.A. 1960).

Recombinant DNA Technology.[1,2]

Reconsideration.

The "No reconsideration" sentence in a decision on motions is reserved for use in the general procedure in interferences where the Primary Examiner decides motions filed by the parties and was never intended to be used in a decision where the Primary Examiner moves sua sponte. *Hester v. Allgeier*, 193 U.S.P.Q. 54, 56 (Comm'r 1976).

ϖ

Efficient administration of interference cases in the PTO dictates that a party make out its case when it first presents a motion. If additional evidence routinely can be presented with requests for reconsideration, a party could, in effect, indefinitely renew its motion and present additional showings until relief is granted or the other party gives up. The proscription against filing an additional showing with a request for reconsideration under the "new" interference rules is firmly established. The same proscription also governs any interference still being conducted under the "old" interference rules unless a party can show "sufficient cause" why the additional showing could not have been presented with the original motion. *Clevenger v. Martin*, 230 U.S.P.Q. 374 (Comm'r Patents & Trademarks 1986).

ϖ

A motion for reconsideration will only be granted "where the Court has overlooked matters or controlling decisions which might have materially influenced the earlier decision." *Lon Tai Shing Co. Ltd. v. Koch + Lowy*, 90 Civ. 4464, 25 U.S.P.Q.2d 1375 (N.Y. 1992).

ϖ

When a three-member panel of the BPAI has rendered its decision, the Commissioner has authority to constitute a new panel for the purposes of reconsideration. Although a distinction is made between "rehearing" and "reconsideration" in some contexts, the two terms are often used interchangeably. It would not be unreasonable to construe "rehearings" under 35 U.S.C. §7(b) broadly as also encompassing reconsideration by the Board wherein the Board allows an applicnt to supplement the existing record or wherein the Board allows both the applicant and the Examiner to brief the issues anew. *In re Alappat*, 33 F.3d 1526, 31 U.S.P.Q.2d 1545, 1546, 1548 n.6 and 7 (Fed. Cir. 1994).

ϖ

---

[1] For information concerning the science underlying recombinant DNA technology, *see In re O'Farrell*, 853 F.2d 894, 7 U.S.P.Q.2d 1673 (Fed. Cir. 1988).

[2] For a detailed discussion of recombinant DNA technology, see *Amgen, Inc. v. Chugai Pharm. Co.*, 927 F.2d 1200, 1207-08 n.4, 18 U.S.P.Q.2d 1016, 1022 n.4 (Fed. Cir. 1991), and *In re O'Farrell*, 853 F.2d 894, 895-99, 7 U.S.P.Q.2d 1673, 1674-77 (Fed. Cir. 1988) and references therein.

A motion for reconsideration that challenges the merits of a district court's decision falls under Rule (FRCP) 59(e) or Rule (FRCP) 60(b). *Paradigm Sales Inc. v. Weber Marking Systems Inc.*, 880 F.Supp. 1237, 1242, 34 U.S.P.Q.2d 1039, 1044 (Ind. 1994).

ထ

"A motion for reconsideration is proper when the court has 'made a mistake not of reasoning but of apprehension... [or] if there has been a significant change or development in the law or facts since submission.'" *University of Colorado Foundation Inc. v. American Cyanamid*, 902 F.Supp. 221, 37 U.S.P.Q.2d 1406, 1407 (Colo. 1995).

Reconstruction. *See also* **Claim Reconstruction, Combining References, Contributory Infringement, Hindsight, Modification, Mosaic, Piecemeal, Repair, Replacement, Restoration.**

In judging what requires uncommon ingenuity, the best standard is what common ingenuity has failed to contrive. Once a problem has been solved, it may be easy to see how prior-art references can be modified and manipulated to reconstruct the solution. The change may be simple and, by hindsight, seem obvious. However, the simplicity of new inventions is oftentimes the very thing that is not obvious before they are made. *In re Sporck*, 301 F.2d 686, 133 U.S.P.Q. 360, 363 (C.C.P.A. 1962).

ထ

It is inappropriate to attempt to reconstruct the prior art or otherwise modify it in an attempt to anticipate structure which is not shown in the prior art. *Harris-Hub Company, Inc. v. Lear Siegler, Inc.*, 179 U.S.P.Q. 469, 476 (Ill. 1973).

ထ

A license to use a patented combination includes the right "to preserve its fitness for use so far as it may be affected by wear and breakage." A licensed user may replace any element no matter "how essential it may be to the patented combination" as long as the replaced element is not itself separately claimed. Replacement of a worn part in a patented combination is repair rather than reconstruction. *Porter v. Farmers Supply Service*, 790 F.2d 882, 229 U.S.P.Q. 814 (Fed. Cir. 1986).

ထ

The replacement of a worn part in a patented combination constitutes a repair rather than a reconstruction. Any other sales of spare parts (i.e., for reconstruction or, possibly at the onset of the sale, as mere extra parts or as spare parts connected with new machine sales) do not fall into an implied license under past machine sales for which the plaintiff has already been compensated. *King Instrument Corp. v. Otari Corp.*, 814 F.2d 1560, 2 U.S.P.Q.2d 1201 (Fed. Cir. 1987).

ထ

The Supreme Court has "eschewed the suggestion that the legal distinction between 'reconstruction' and 'repair' should be affected by whether the element of the combination that has been replaced is an 'essential' or 'distinguishing' part of the invention". The policy behind requiring any component, itself, to be the subject of a separate patent before entitling it to patent monopoly applies with as much force to a unique disposable component as it does to longer-lived components. The courts are "not to distinguish between a repair and a reconstruction merely because of the significance of the costs of the replaced or the repaired item or because of the duration of its lifespan". Unless a replacement constitutes "reconstruction" to create a new product, replacement parts are permissible repair. *Surgical Laser Technologies Inc. v. Surgical Laser Products Inc.*, 25 U.S.P.Q.2d 1806, 1808 (Pa. 1992).

ᚥ

The "maintenance of the 'use of the whole' of the patented combination through replacement of a spent, unpatented element does not constitute reconstruction." Reconstruction of a patented entity (comprised of unpatented elements) is limited to such a true reconstruction of the entity as to "in fact make a whole new article," after the entity, viewed as a whole, has become spent. In order to call the monopoly, conferred by the patent grant, into play for a second time, it must be a second creation of the patented device. *Mere replacement of individual unpatented parts, one at a time, whether of the same part repeatedly or of different parts successively, is no more than the lawful right of the owner to repair his property. FMC Corp. v. Up-Right Inc.*, 21 F.3d 1073, 30 U.S.P.Q.2d 1361, 1363 (Fed. Cir. 1994).

ᚥ

Plaintiff did not manufacture or sell replacement drill tips. It did not publish instructions on how to retip its patented drills or suggest that the drills could or should be retipped. Plaintiff was aware that the drill tip would need occasional resharpening and instructed its customer on how to resharpen the tip. There is, therefore, no objective evidence that plaintiff's drill tip was intended to be a replaceable part. Although the repair or reconstruction issue does not turn on the intention of the patentee alone, the fact that no replacement drill tips have ever been made or sold by the patentee is consistent with the conclusion that replacement of the carbide tip is not a permissible repair. *Sandvik Aktiebolag v. E.J. Co.*, 121 F.3d 669, 43 U.S.P.Q.2d 1620, 1624 (Fed. Cir. 1997).

Record. *See* Mental Steps.

An entire article is of record in appellant's parent application, which is in the PTO's possession, and appellant requested that such article be considered in arriving at a decision on his present application. The fact that only the first page of the article was physically inserted into the record as an attachment to appellant's brief to the Board and the Board did not actually consider the article or mention it is immaterial, since evidence need not be physically introduced and also considered by a PTO tribunal to be considered "evidence produced before the Patent and Trademark Office." [There are thus limitations to any requirement that each file wrapper must be complete in itself.] *In re Hutton*, 568 F.2d 1355, 196 U.S.P.Q. 676 (C.C.P.A. 1978).

ᚥ

Although assignments are required to be recorded in order for an assignee to prevail against one who has acquired rights in a patent without notice, there is no obligation to record a license. The purchaser of a patent takes subject to outstanding licenses. *Sanofi, S.A. v. Med-Tech Veterinarian Products, Inc.*, 565 F.Supp. 931, 220 U.S.P.Q. 416, 422 (N.J. 1983).

Recording. *See* **Mental Steps.**

Rediscovery.

An abandoned invention will not defeat the patentability of the rediscovery of "lost art." Moreover, an inventor who had merely made a secret use of his discovery should not be regarded as the first inventor. *Dunlop Holdings Limited v. Ram Golf Corporation*, 524 F.2d 33, 188 U.S.P.Q. 481, 483 (7th Cir. 1975).

Redrafting Claims. *See also* **Lexicographer.**

The general proposition that a court may not redraft a claim for purposes of avoiding a defense of anticipation does not apply where "extraneous" limitations from the specification are not being read into the claim wholly apart from any need to interpret what the patentee meant by particular words or phrases in the claim. When the question is what effect to give to words in a claim, it is entirely proper to use the specification to interpret what the patentee meant by a word or phrase in the claim. *Corning Glass Works v. Sumitomo Electric U.S.A. Inc.*, 868 F.2d 1251, 9 U.S.P.Q.2d 1962 (Fed. Cir. 1989).

Reduction in Elements. *See also* **Omission of Element or Step.**

A machine or article that is made with fewer parts or fewer components than the prior art, but which accomplishes all of the functions of the prior art, is the type of improvement which merits a patent. *Deering Milliken Research Corporation v. Beaunit Corporation*, 382 F.Supp. 403, 182 U.S.P.Q. 421, 425 (N.C. 1974).

Reduction in References.

The fact that the Examiner's conclusion of obviousness can be seen to be proper when based upon fewer references than relied upon in the rejection does not necessarily amount to a new ground of rejection. *Ex parte Raychem Corp.*, 25 U.S.P.Q.2d 1265, 1272 (B.P.A.I. 1992).

Reduction in Scope.[3] *See also* **Description, Exclude, Excluding Prior Art, Limit, Narrowing Claim, New Matter.**

That two things are actually equivalents, in the sense that they will both perform the same function, is not enough to bring into play the rule that when one of them is in the prior art, the use of the other is obvious and cannot give rise to a patentable invention. One need not think very hard to appreciate that the vast majority of patentable inventions perform old functions. Patent applicants more often than not invent and disclose and attempt to claim more than turns out to be novel when the art is searched. They should not

---

[3]In a case in which there was actually an increase (rather than a reduction) in scope (by deleting an element) in a continuation design application, the CAFC reversed the denial of the benefit of the parent application, and stated that test for sufficiency of the written description is the same, whether for a design or a utility patent. The inquiry is simply to determine whether the inventor had possession at the earlier date of what was claimed at the later date. *In re Daniels*, 46 U.S.P.Q.2d 1788, 1790 (Fed. Cir. 1998).

be penalized merely because of their own industry and the fullness of their disclosures. *In re Ruff and Dukeshire,* 256 F.2d 590, 118 U.S.P.Q. 340 (C.C.P.A. 1958).

ω

Limiting a class, generically disclosed, to a subgenus thereunder, without an original teaching of said subgenus as such, is directed to new matter that is not supported by the original specification. To be claimed, subgenera of lesser scope must be supported as such in the original description. *Ex parte Batchelder and Zimmerman,* 131 U.S.P.Q. 38 (Bd. App. 1960).

ω

Evidence may not be disregarded simply because of the manner in which the now-claimed subject matter was denominated in the original application. To rule otherwise would let form triumph over substance, substantially eliminating the right of an applicant to retreat to an otherwise patentable species merely because he erroneously thought he was first with the genus when he filed. *In re Saunders and Gemeinhardt,* 444 F.2d 599, 170 U.S.P.Q. 213, 220 (C.C.P.A. 1971).

ω

The limitation of a claim to a subgeneric group that was not delineated or supported as such in the original application involves objectionable new matter. *In re Welstead,* 463 F.2d 1110, 174 U.S.P.Q. 449, 450, 451 (C.C.P.A. 1972).

ω

It is for the inventor to decide what bounds of protection he will seek. Applicant's right to retreat to an otherwise patentable species is not precluded merely because he erroneously thought he was first with the genus when he filed. *In re Johnson and Farnham,* 558 F.2d 1008, 194 U.S.P.Q. 187, 196 (C.C.P.A. 1977).

ω

The disclosure of a genus and a species of a subgenus within that genus is not sufficient description of the subgenus to comply with the description requirement of 35 U.S.C. §112, unless there are specific facts which lead to a determination that a subgenus is implicitly described. *Ex parte Westphal,* 26 U.S.P.Q.2d 1858, 1860 (B.P.A.I. 1992).

Reduction in Steps.

Since a reference disclosure is clear and specific in teaching a separate two-stage reaction, the Patent Office position has to be based at least in part on the assumption that, looking at the disclosure as a whole, there would be no reason not to conclude that the process could be performed in a single stage. This is, in effect, a conclusion that must have some support, either in logic or in cold, hard facts. No evidence has been submitted to support it, and it seems more logical and reasonable to infer that one teaching a chemical reaction process would set out the least number of reactions thought necessary to accomplish the desired objective. Thus, one skilled in the art who reads the teaching would have to presume that, if the reactants were not combined in the manner shown, some adverse side reaction or no reaction at all would occur. *In re Freed,* 425 F.2d 785, 165 U.S.P.Q. 570, 572 (C.C.P.A. 1970).

ω

When omitting steps would run counter to the teaching of the reference patent relied upon, the patentability of a process with fewer steps is not precluded by 35 U.S.C. §103. *Ex parte Kaiser,* 189 U.S.P.Q. 816 (PTO Bd. App. 1974).

Reduction of Elements or Steps. *See* **Omission of Element or Step, Reduction in Steps.**

Reduction to Practice. *See also* **Compound, Constructive Reduction to Practice, Corroboration, Simultaneous Conception and Reduction to Practice, Standard Laboratory Animal, Test.**

In rare cases, where a device is so extraordinarily simple that its mere construction is sufficient demonstration of its operability, testing is unnecessary. *Mason v. Hepburn,* 13 App. D.C. 86, 89 (1898); *Sachs v. Wadsworth,* 48 F.2d 928, 9 U.S.P.Q. 252, 254 (C.C.P.A. 1931).

ᛟ

It was incumbent upon the junior party to prove by a preponderance of evidence that he was first to conceive the invention defined by the interference counts and first to reduce it to actual practice prior to the date on which the senior party filed his application, or that he was first to conceive and was actively engaged in reducing the invention to practice at and immediately prior to the time the senior party filed his application and entered the field, and that he continued such activity to the time of his own filing date. *Land v. Dreyer,* 155 F.2d 383, 69 U.S.P.Q. 602, 603 (C.C.P.A. 1946).

ᛟ

A test under service conditions is necessary in those cases, and in those cases only, in which those qualified in the art would require such a test before they would be willing to manufacture and sell the invention as it stands. *Sinko Tool & Manufacturing Co. v. Automatic Devices Corp.,* 157 F.2d 974, 71 U.S.P.Q. 199 (2d Cir. 1946).

ᛟ

A printed publication does not constitute a reduction to practice; it is evidence of conception only. The same would certainly be true of the manuscript on which a publication is based. *In re Schlittler and Uffer,* 234 F.2d 882, 110 U.S.P.Q. 304, 305, 306 (C.C.P.A. 1956).

ᛟ

Only testing under commercial or actual conditions of intended use is adequate to establish actual reduction to practice. *Gaiser v. Linder,* 253 F.2d 433, 117 U.S.P.Q. 209 (C.C.P.A. 1958); *Elmore v. Schmitt,* 278 F.2d 510, 125 U.S.P.Q. 653 (C.C.P.A. 1960).

ᛟ

The testing required to establish actual reduction to practice necessitates examining the prior art to determine what advance is relied upon for the claimed invention. *Farrand Optical Co. v. United States,* 325 F.2d 328, 139 U.S.P.Q. 249 (2d Cir. 1963).

ᛟ

When testing is necessary to demonstrate workability and, therefore, necessary for an actual reduction to practice, laboratory testing of the invention so as to demonstrate its workability for its intended purpose or use is sufficient. *Schnick v. Fenn,* 277 F.2d 935, 125 U.S.P.Q. 567 (C.C.P.A. 1960); *Paivinen v. Sands,* 339 F.2d 217, 144 U.S.P.Q. 1, 9 (C.C.P.A. 1964).

ω

To establish reduction to practice, test data must be such as to indicate that the invention worked as intended in practical use. This may be done in several ways. The invention may be tested under actual conditions of use. The invention may be given "bench tests" that fully duplicate each and every condition of actual use. Finally, in some cases, bench tests may be performed that do not duplicate all of the conditions of actual use. In order to show reduction to practice based on such tests, the evidence must establish such a relationship between the test conditions and the intended functional setting of the invention. *White v. Lemmerman,* 341 F.2d 110, 144 U.S.P.Q. 409, 411 (C.C.P.A. 1965).

ω

Although tests under actual conditions of use are not necessarily a requirement for reduction to practice, the tests must prove that the invention will perform satisfactorily in the intended functional setting. Although a long delay in filing (five years in this case) has been held to warrant a presumption that experiments alleged to be a reduction to practice were actually unsuccessful, where there is clearly a reduction to practice, a holding to the contrary will not be rendered because of the delay. *Knowles v. Tibbetts,* 347 F.2d 591, 146 U.S.P.Q. 59, 61, 63 (C.C.P.A. 1965).

ω

Neither conception nor reduction to practice can be established nunc pro tunc. *Langer and Tornqvist v. Kaufman and McMullen,* 465 F.2d 915, 175 U.S.P.Q. 172, 174 (C.C.P.A. 1972).

ω

In an interference setting, a significant, and often controlling, consideration in determining the sufficiency of tests for reduction to practice lies in whether the tests show that the invention will serve the purpose for which it is intended so conclusively that practical men, men skilled in the art, would take the risk of putting it into commercial use. *Williams v. The Administrator of the National Aeronautics and Space Administration,* 463 F.2d 1391, 175 U.S.P.Q. 5, 11 (C.C.P.A. 1972).

ω

A fortuitous reduction to practice is inconsistent with the exercise of diligence toward reduction to practice. *Gunn v. Bosch and Pollmann,* 181 U.S.P.Q. 758, 761 (PO Bd. Pat. Intf. 1973).

ω

Since the interference count contains no limitation related to any utility of the defined chemical compound, evidence that would establish a substantial utility of that compound for any purpose is sufficient to show its reduction to practice. *Rey-Bellet and Spiegelberg v. Engelhardt v. Schindler*, 493 F.2d 1380, 181 U.S.P.Q. 453, 454 (C.C.P.A. 1974).

ϖ

There is no conception or reduction to practice of a new form of an otherwise old composition of matter where there has been no recognition or appreciation of the existence of the new form. *Silvestri and Johnson v. Grant and Alburn*, 496 F.2d 593, 181 U.S.P.Q. 706, 708 (C.C.P.A. 1974).

ϖ

It is not necessary to describe in the specification all possible forms in which a claimed limitation may be reduced to practice. *Stevenson v. International Trade Commission*, 612 F.2d 546, 204 U.S.P.Q. 276, 283 (C.C.P.A. 1979).

ϖ

In an interference setting, a reduction to practice by one who derived the invention of the count from another inures to the benefit of the other. As coating particles of the character of those involved is an art-recognized expedient, it does not constitute part of the "essence" of the invention, and thus need not have been communicated. *Marathon Oil Company v. The Firestone Tire and Rubber Company*, 205 U.S.P.Q. 520, 534, 537 (Ohio 1979).

ϖ

A practical utility must be established for a novel compound before it can be said to have been reduced to practice. *Bindra v. Kelly*, 206 U.S.P.Q. 570, 575 (PTO Bd. Pat. Int. 1979).

ϖ

D and N were joint applicants of an application filed for a combination invention on June 1, 1973 (subsequently issued as U.S.P. 3,842,678 on October 22, 1974). Applicant D was the sole applicant of an application (S.N. 952,695) for reissue of U.S.P. 3,964,519 (issued on an application filed November 18, 1974), claiming a subcombination that was fully disclosed, but not claimed, in U.S.P. 3,842,678. In the prosecution of the reissue application D presented his own Declaration that a drawing of the subcombination invention (dated March 15, 1973) established conception prior to June 1, 1973, and the subcombination was a sole invention originally conceived by D and described to patent counsel prior to June 1, 1973, to enable counsel to satisfy the requirements of 35 U.S.C. §112 in drafting the joint application. The joint patent was used as a reference against the reissue application even though it was silent with regard to who invented the subcombination. There was no basis to presume that the subcombination was the invention of D and N jointly or of either of them. The joint patent of D and N, having issued less than one year before the filing date of D's original patent application, is only available as a reference if the pertinent disclosure is not the sole work of D. An applicant's own work, even though publicly disclosed prior to his application, may not be used against him as a reference, absent a time bar to his application. In spite of the fact that a completed invention requires both conception and reduction to practice, there is no requirement that the inventor be the one to reduce the invention to practice so long as reduction to practice is done on his behalf. *In re DeBaun*, 687 F.2d 459, 214 U.S.P.Q. 933 (C.C.P.A. 1982).

ϖ

Even if the invention was actually reduced to practice by the junior party in 1977 or 1978, the unexplained hiatus of more than two years between that date and the junior party's filing date was an unreasonably long delay, raising an inference that the junior party suppressed the invention within the meaning of 35 U.S.C. §102(g). Since there is no evidence in the record as to any activity by the junior party during this two-year period, the inference has not been rebutted, and, as a result, the junior party cannot rely on either of the alleged actual reductions to practice. *Latimer v. Wetmore*, 231 U.S.P.Q. 131 (B.P.A.I. 1985).

ᛒ

Actual reduction to practice requires that the claimed invention work for its intended purpose, and, as has long been the law, constructive reduction to practice occurs when a patent application on the claimed invention is filed. *Hybritech Inc. v. Monoclonal Antibodies, Inc.*, 802 F.2d 1367, 231 U.S.P.Q. 81 (Fed. Cir. 1986).

ᛒ

An invention is reduced to practice when a prototype has been developed. Although "there is no requirement that the invention, when tested, be in a commercially satisfactory phase of development," the prototype "might have been sufficiently tested to demonstrate that it will work for its intended purpose." *Modine Manufacturing Co. v. The Allen Group Inc.*, 8 U.S.P.Q.2d 1622 (Cal. 1988).

ᛒ

A reduction to practice of a particular product is generally not considered to be complete until that product is successfully tested to establish its utility. In an interference setting, there must be adequate corroboration or supporting documentation. *Chai v. Frame*, 10 U.S.P.Q.2d 1460 (B.P.A.I. 1988).

ᛒ

As the product is rather straightforward, and its function can be readily calculated by persons with some engineering background, and the inventors themselves indicated on their Invention Record that there was no need for testing it to predict how it would function, the invention had been sufficiently reduced to practice when detailed drawings of it were made. *Environtech Corp. v. Westech Engineering, Inc.*, 713 F. Supp. 372, 11 U.S.P.Q.2d 1804, 1807 (Utah 1989).

ᛒ

When a company employee reduces an invention to practice in the course of his employment on behalf of the inventor and does not contest inventorship, such reduction to practice is on the inventor's behalf by a person authorized to do so. *De Solms v. Schoenwald*, 15 U.S.P.Q.2d 1507, 1510 (B.P.A.I. 1990).

ᛒ

Tests performed outside of the intended environment can be sufficient to show reduction to practice if the testing conditions are sufficiently similar to those of the intended environment. There is certainly no requirement that an invention, when tested, be in a commercially satisfactory stage of development in order to reduce the invention to practice. *DSL Dynamic Sciences Ltd. v. Union Switch & Signal Inc.*, 928 F.2d 1122, 18 U.S.P.Q.2d 1152, 1154, 1155 (Fed. Cir. 1991).

ᛒ

As to proving reduction to practice, tests on a claimed invention, though conducted subsequent to a claimed reduction to practice, might either confirm or call into question the reliability of earlier tests of utility and thus be highly relevant in determining the actual date of reduction to practice. An essential requirement for actual reduction to practice is a contemporaneous recognition and conviction on the part of the inventor that he has successfully completed and tested his invention. *The Heil Company v. Snyder Industries Inc.*, 763 F. Supp. 422, 18 U.S.P.Q.2d 2022, 2026 (Neb. 1991).

ω

An actual reduction to practice in another country is irrelevant in an interference proceeding concerning priority of invention. Some evidence of activity in the United States establishing utility for a product introduced and identified is required to establish an actual reduction to practice in this country. *Staehelin v. Secher*, 24 U.S.P.Q.2d 1513, 1522, 1523 (B.P.A.I. 1992).

ω

A certain amount of "common sense" must be applied in determining the extent of testing required. Depending on its nature, the invention may be tested under actual conditions of use, or may be tested under "bench" or laboratory conditions which fully duplicate each and every condition of actual use, or, in some cases, may be tested under laboratory conditions which do not duplicate all of the conditions of actual use. In instances where the invention is sufficiently simple, mere construction or synthesis of the subject matter may be sufficient to show that it will operate satisfactorily. An essential inquiry is whether the advance in the art represented by the invention was embodied in a workable device that demonstrated that it could do what it was claimed to be capable of doing. *Scott v. Finney*, 34 F.3d 1058, 32 U.S.P.Q.2d 1115, 1118, 1119 (Fed. Cir. 1994).

ω

The court discerned no distinction in its precedents between interference cases and "on sale" cases with respect to the meaning of "reduction to practice." *Nordberg Inc. v. Telsmith Inc.*, 881 F.Supp. 1252, 36 U.S.P.Q.2d 1577, 1604 (Wis. 1995).

ω

Reduction to practice can be shown through preparation of a composition meeting the elements of the count, recognition of the contents of the composition, and submission of the composition for appropriate testing, the results of which demonstrate that the invention actually works for its intended purpose. The patent law is more concerned with whether the results of tests submitted by the inventor in fact show success than whether this success was recognized by the inventor prior to the critical date. *Estee Lauder Inc. v. L'Oreal S.A.*, 40 U.S.P.Q.2d 1425, 1436 (D.C. 1996).

ω

A reduction to practice does not occur until the inventor has determined that the invention will work for its intended purpose. *Estee Lauder Inc. v. L'Oreal S.A.*, 129 F.3d 588, 44 U.S.P.Q.2d 1610, 1614 (Fed. Cir. 1997).

Redundant.

As a general rule, claims should not be interpreted in a manner that renders two claims redundant. *Atari Games Corp. v. Nintendo of America Inc.*, 30 U.S.P.Q.2d 1401, 1414 n.25 (Cal. 1993).

Reexamination. *See also* **Claim Construction, Reissue, Review.**

In deciding appeals and reversing the Board in patent cases, the CCPA merely passes on the propriety of rejections brought before it for review; it does not hold that an application contains "patentable subject matter", it does not hold that the application is "allowable", and it does not direct the Patent Office to issue a patent. Subsequent to its decision the Patent Office has the right and the duty to reopen prosecution on finding more pertinent prior art so that such art may be applied to the claims. *In re Citron*, 326 F.2d 418, 140 U.S.P.Q. 220, 221 (C.C.P.A. 1964).

ᚧ

Sections 132 and 134 (Title 35) do not require that each and every claim presented during the prosecution of an application must be twice examined and twice rejected on the same ground. Section 134 appears to imply the contrary since it permits an appeal to be taken when any claim has been twice rejected. *In re Szajna and Lump*, 422 F.2d 443, 164 U.S.P.Q. 632, 635 (C.C.P.A. 1970).

ᚧ

Prevailing practice represents a reasonable attempt by the PTO to accommodate potential conflicts between trial schedules and patent reexamination proceedings for the agency. Challenge provisions of reexamination procedures were found to be constitutional. *Patlex Corp. v. Mossinghoff*, 585 F. Supp. 713, 220 U.S.P.Q. 342 (Pa. 1983).

ᚧ

Reexamination should not be allowed to be used as a tool to circumvent the burden of proof placed on an alleged infringer during litigation. *In re The Successor in Interest to Walter Andersen*, 743 F.2d 1578, 223 U.S.P.Q. 378, 380 (Fed. Cir. 1984).

ᚧ

The propriety of the entire reexamination proceeding was questioned on the ground that the patent was subjected to a reexamination procedure based upon a reference that was considered by the PTO prior to the granting of the patent. The public interest may demand a finding that "a substantial new question of patentability affecting" a patent claim has been raised where a reference cited during prosecution of the patent is presented and viewed in a different light than it was considered during the prosecution of the application that issued as a patent. The public interest in valid patents intended to be served by the patent reexamination sections of the patent laws cannot be disregarded where a reasonable new interpretation of a reference disclosure is presented for the first time via a request for reexamination. *Ex parte Chicago Rawhide Manufacturing Co.*, 226 U.S.P.Q. 438 (PTO Bd. App. 1984).

ᚧ

The PTO will act in harmony with the courts and will not "relitigate" in a reexamination proceeding an issue of patentability which has been resolved by a federal court on the merits. *In re Johnson*, 230 U.S.P.Q. 240, 241 (Comm'r 1984).

ᚳ

Section 282 (Presumption of Validity) of 35 U.S.C. has no application in reexamination proceedings. Injection of the presumption into the examination process could add nothing but legalistic confusion. In reexamination, claims can be amended and new claims added; there is no litigating adversary present. *In re Etter*, 756 F.2d 852, 225 U.S.P.Q. 1 (Fed. Cir. 1985).

ᚳ

The limitation to consideration of patents and printed publications in reexamination proceedings is not limited to new art submitted at the time of the request for reexamination. *Ex parte Horton*, 226 U.S.P.Q. 697 (B.P.A.I. 1985).

ᚳ

In accordance with 37 C.F.R. §1.530(a), a patentee is barred from communication with the PTO during the three-month statutory period during which the PTO is required to decide whether any substantial new question of patentability is raised by a reexamination request. The PTO must rely solely on the representations of the person who requested reexamination, without opportunity for any explanation or correction by the patentee. The reexamination statute does not prohibit such participation. The provision of 37 C.F.R. §1.530(a) that bars threshold participation by the patent holder is within tolerable limits of the authority delegated to the PTO by Congress in enacting the reexamination statute, and does not violate the due process clause. *Patlex Corp. v. Mossinghoff*, 771 F.2d 480, 226 U.S.P.Q. 985 (Fed. Cir. 1985).

ᚳ

Patents may be used as evidence of prior inventorship by another or as evidence that the patentee of the reexamination patent has already obtained patent protection for his invention. The second patent would thus be barred by 35 U.S.C. §101 if the inventions are identical or by the judicially created doctrine of double patenting of the obviousness type, if there are only obvious differences between the claims of the respective patents. Such rejection falls within the ambit of those intended by the statute and is not specifically excluded by the *Etter* case [756 F.2d 852, 225 U.S.P.Q. 1 (1985)]. *Ex parte Obiaya*, 227 U.S.P.Q. 58 (B.P.A.I. 1985).

ᚳ

The statutory presumption of validity under 35 U.S.C. §282 does not apply to patent claims undergoing reexamination. *Ex parte Gould*, 231 U.S.P.Q. 943 (B.P.A.I. 1986).

ᚳ

Because all of the claims of the reexamined patent are now in the category of a "proposed amended or new claim determined to be patentable and incorporated following a reexamination proceeding," those claims "have the same effect as that specified in Section 252 of Title 35 for reissued patents. . . ." The first paragraph of §252 makes clear that, if claims in an original and in a reissued patent are identical, the reissued patent is deemed to have effect from the date of the original patent. If not, then the patentee has no rights to enforce before the date of reissue because the original patent was surrendered and is dead. In context, "identical" means at most "without substantive change." *Kaufman Co. v. Lantech Inc.*, 807 F.2d 970, 1 U.S.P.Q.2d 1202 (Fed. Cir. 1986).

ᚖ

It is in the public interest for the PTO to accept a request for reexamination (based on issues not resolved by a federal court) from "any person," including parties to a prior adjudication who have not otherwise acquiesced in the validity of the claims in question. *In re Eis,* 1 U.S.P.Q.2d 1418 (Commr. Patents & Trademarks 1986).

ᚖ

By limiting reexamination to a consideration of prior patents and printed publications, the PTO is given a task that can be performed effectively at a reasonable cost to the requestor. *In re Lanham,* 1 U.S.P.Q.2d 1877 (Commr. Patents & Trademarks 1986).

ᚖ

A settlement agreement wherein a litigant agrees not to bring suit in any U.S. court challenging the validity of a patent does not bar filing a request for reexamination in the PTO. *Joy Manufacturing Co. v. National Mine Service Co.*, 810 F.2d 1127, 1 U.S.P.Q.2d 1627 (Fed. Cir. 1987).

ᚖ

The statutory provisions regarding the reexamination of a patent and the rules promulgated in support thereof do not provide for opposition to the grant of a Reexamination Certificate by an interested third party, nor do they provide for judiciary review of a decision rendered in a reexamination proceeding for any party other than the patent owner. *Yuasa Battery Co. v. Commissioner of Patents and Trademarks,* 3 U.S.P.Q.2d 1143 (D.C. 1987).

ᚖ

Reexamination claims have "continuous effect" from the date of the original patent, and damages can be recovered for infringing activities performed before the date of the reexamination certificate when the reexamination claims are without substantive change from the original claims and therefore are legally identical thereto within the meaning of 35 U.S.C. §252. Recovery of damages for infringing activities performed before the date of the Reexamination Certificate is not available with respect to any claim that is substantively different from an original claim of the patent. *Fortel Corp. v. Phone-Mate, Inc.,* 825 F.2d 1577, 3 U.S.P.Q.2d 1771 (Fed. Cir. 1987).

ᚖ

The reexamination statute limits the scope of the reexamination to patents and printed publications. Consequently, the Commissioner may not, on reexamination, consider whether the specification of a patent being reexamined contains an enabling disclosure for the issued patent claims. *Patlex Corp. v. Quigg,* 680 F. Supp. 33, 6 U.S.P.Q.2d 1296 (D.C. 1988).

ᚖ

While a petition to revive a terminated reexamination proceeding on the ground of unavoidable delay is appropriately filed under 35 U.S.C. §133, filing such a petition under 37 C.F.R. §1.137(a) is inappropriate, because §1.137(a) is limited to revival of an "application" and a reexamination proceeding does not involve an application. Inasmuch as the unavoidable-delay standard is statutory rather than merely regulatory and because 37 C.F.R. §1.183 does not empower the Commissioner to waive statutory requirements, petitions under §1.183 concerning untimely responses in reexamination proceedings will be dismissed as inappropriate. *In re Katrapat A.G.*, 6 U.S.P.Q.2d 1863 (Comm'r Patents & Trademarks 1988).

ω

Congress did not give the Commissioner authority to stay reexaminations; it told him to conduct them with special dispatch. The suspension of PTO proceedings does not prevent duplication; it precludes access to the forum where there is no presumption of validity. That one challenging validity in court bears the burden assigned by 35 U.S.C. §282, that the same party may request reexamination on submission of art not previously cited, and that, if that art raises a substantial new question of patentability, the PTO may during reexamination consider the same and new and amended claims in light of that art free of any presumption or concepts not in conflict. On the contrary, those concepts are but further indication that litigation and reexamination are distinct proceedings, with distinct parties, purposes, procedures, and outcomes. *Ethicon Inc. v. Quigg,* 849 F.2d 1422, 7 U.S.P.Q.2d 1152 (Fed. Cir. 1988).

ω

In a case wherein the first asserted method claim was added by amendment during reexamination and in which there is no indication in the file record that the applicant ever objectively intended or considered his invention to include the method, the method claim was not directed to "the invention as claimed" in the patent, as required by §305. Moreover, addition of such a claim (drawn to a method) enlarges the scope of the claims in the patent in violation of 35 U.S.C. §305. *Ex parte Wikdahl,* 10 U.S.P.Q.2d 1546, 1549 (B.P.A.I. 1989).

ω

The statute (35 U.S.C. §306) expressly grants patent owners the right to review of the Examiner's final reexamination decision, but not directly by a court. The decision appealed to a court is that of the Board, which may review an Examiner's decision unfavorable to the patent owner. The government has no right to review of an Examiner or Board decision favorable to the patent owner. Also under 35 U.S.C. §303(c)(1982), no one, not even the patent owner, may appeal a PTO decision denying a request for reexamination. In view of such a clear, comprehensive statutory scheme, it follows, at least tentatively, that Congress intended to limit appeals from final reexamination decisions to those initiated by patent owners seeking to reverse an unfavorable decision. Although a third-party requestor has some rights, vis-a-vis the PTO, such a requestor has no right to question the validity of the Reexamination Certificate by suit against the PTO. *Syntex (U.S.A.) Inc. v. United States Patent and Trademark Office,* 882 F.2d 1570, 11 U.S.P.Q.2d 1866, 1869, 1871 (Fed. Cir. 1989).

ω

The Commissioner's determination that a substantial new question of patentability was raised in connection with a request for reexamination is a matter committed to discretion by law and is not reviewable. *Joy Technologies v. Quigg,* 12 U.S.P.Q.2d 1112, 1114 (D.C. 1989).

ᙡ

The purpose of reexamination is to permit the government to start over and determine whether it should have granted the right it did in the first place to a patentee. Moreover, anyone can request reexamination of a patent at any time. In this case the defendant requested reexamination four years after being sued for infringement. Unless and until the PTO decides that it originally erred, the patent's validity is presumed and the patentee is entitled to the remedy for its infringement. A decision by the PTO would be of limited utility to the court at this point in time, since the liability issue (including the validity of the patent) has been completely litigated. Where there has been no decree by the government that it erred, initially, in issuing the patent, and where the liability issues have been completely decided by the court, the fact that the government may subsequently decide that the issuing of the patent was, to some extent, error, is not a just reason to delay an otherwise provident certification for appeal. *E.I. du Pont de Nemours & Co. v. Phillips Petroleum Co.,* 720 F. Supp. 373, 12 U.S.P.Q.2d 1401, 1411 (Del. 1989).

ᙡ

The identity of the requestor in a reexamination proceeding is subject to protection under 35 U.S.C. §301 and §302. *Parker Hanifin Corp. v. Davco Manufacturing Corp.,* 128 F.R.D. 91, 13 U.S.P.Q.2d 1412, 1413 (Ohio 1989).

ᙡ

The Commissioner lacks authority to reopen the reexamination proceeding after receipt of the Federal Circuit's mandate affirming the Examiner's rejection of all claims since the case is no longer considered pending. See MPEP §1216.06 (5th ed., rev. 12, July 1989) under "Office Procedure Following Decision by the Federal Circuit," subheading "1. All claims rejected"; *Morganroth v. Quigg,* 885 F.2d 843, 12 U.S.P.Q.2d 1125, 1128 (Fed. Cir. 1989) (Commissioner does not have authority to revive application abandoned by termination of proceedings resulting from a failure to appeal a final district court judgment); *In re Jones,* 542 F.2d 65, 191 U.S.P.Q. 249, 252 (C.C.P.A. 1976) ("receipt of the mandate by the PTO terminated proceedings in the case"); *In re Willis,* 537 F.2d 513, 190 U.S.P.Q. 327, 329 (C.C.P.A. 1976) ("When, on January 12, 1976, our mandate was received in the PTO, no claims having been allowed, the appealed application suffered its demise."); *Continental Can Co. v. Schuyler,* 326 F. Supp. 283, 168 U.S.P.Q. 625 (D.C. 1970) ("where rejection of all claims is affirmed by the Court of Customs and Patent Appeals, the responsibility is upon the plaintiff to stay the Court's judgment if the pendency of the application is to be preserved"). Petitioner's relief, if any, lies in a motion for the Federal Circuit to withdraw its mandate, not with the Commissioner. *See Jones,* 542 F.2d at 68, 191 U.S.P.Q. at 252 (CCPA "has the power, in the interest of justice, to recall its mandate in an appropriate case, and this power should be exercised sparingly and only upon a showing of good cause"). *In re Eckerle,* 1115 O.G. 6 (Comm'r Patents & Trademarks 1990).

ᙡ

In an infringement suit before a district court, the invalidity of a patent under 35 U.S.C. §103 must be decided on the basis of prior art adduced in the proceeding before the court. The issue cannot be decided merely by accepting or rejecting the adequacy of the positions taken by the patentee in order to obtain a Certificate of Reexamination for the patent. Once issued by the PTO, a patent is presumed valid, and the burden of proving otherwise rests solely on the challenger. Whether or not a Reexamination Certificate should have issued is not an issue before the district court. *Greenwood v. Hattori Seiko Co. Ltd.*, 900 F.2d 238, 14 U.S.P.Q.2d 1474, 1476 (Fed. Cir. 1990).

ᙡ

Claims amended during reexamination in order to overcome prior-art based grounds of rejection are effective only (for infringement purposes) as of the date of the reexamination certificate. *The Laitram Corp. v. NEC Corp.*, 17 U.S.P.Q.2d 1407, 1409 (La. 1990).

ᙡ

Whereas a challenged patent in litigation enjoys a presumption of validity that the challenger must overcome by clear and convincing evidence, in a reexamination proceeding the posture is essentially that of an initial PTO examination, and the patent enjoys no presumption of validity. It is therefore highly significant that the patents were upheld by the PTO against a higher standard than that to be applied by the district court. In addition, one function of the reexamination finding is "to facilitate trial of that issue by providing the district court with the expert view of the PTO (when a claim survives the reexamination proceeding)." Secondly, litigation before a district court and PTO reexamination differ in their approach to claim construction in a way that favors a patent owner in a proceeding before the district court. Whereas claims in reexamination "will be given their broadest reasonable interpretation," thus increasing the likelihood of a finding of anticipation and therefore of invalidity, claims in litigation are to be "so construed, if possible, as to sustain their validity." District courts follow the approach of the Federal Circuit in giving deference to PTO findings with respect to evidence considered by the PTO. When an attacker simply goes over the same ground traveled by the PTO, part of the burden is to show that the PTO was wrong in its decision to grant the patent. A reexamination by the PTO is not an adversary proceeding of the sort that occurs in litigation; although a third party may bring a request for reexamination, that party is heard only on the question of whether "a substantial question" of validity exists, justifying the reexamination procedure. The reexamination per se of the claims is entirely ex parte. *E. I. du Pont de Nemours & Co. v. Cetus Corp.*, 19 U.S.P.Q.2d 1174, 1179, 1181 (Cal. 1990).

ᙡ

The interference rules do not specifically prohibit a party patentee (dissatisfied with the EIC's decision on preliminary motions) from filing a request for reexamination. Nonetheless, filing such a request subverts the purpose of the interference rules, which is to resolve all controversies between the parties in an inter partes forum. *Shaked v. Taniguchi*, 21 U.S.P.Q.2d 1285, 1287 (B.P.A.I. 1990).

ᙡ

No statute precludes addition of a reexamination to an interference involving the patent sought to be reexamined. PTO practice permits adding an application to reissue a patent to an interference involving the patent. Both the reexamination and the interference must be carried out with "special dispatch" within the PTO to comply with the mandate of 35 U.S.C. §305. *Shaked v. Taniguchi*, 21 U.S.P.Q.2d 1288, 1289 (Comm'r Patents & Trademarks 1990).

ᛣ

Defendant's motion for a stay of the patent infringement litigation pending the PTO's consideration of defendant's request for reexamination was granted. *Brown v. Shimano American Corp.*, 18 U.S.P.Q.2d 1496 (Cal. 1991).

ᛣ

Although a rejection of a claim in a reexamination proceeding must be based upon patents and/or printed publications, it would be contrary to 35 U.S.C. §305 and §132 to preclude consideration of other "information" (e.g., affidavits, Declarations, and transcripts) to help define the scope and content of the prior art or to establish that a claimed invention is not anticipated under 35 U.S.C. §102 or unpatentable under 35 U.S.C. §103 based on obviousness. *In re Chambers*, 20 U.S.P.Q.2d 1470, 1474 (Comm'r Patents & Trademarks 1991).

ᛣ

Reexamination provides a mechanism for enabling the PTO to review and correct an initial examination. The purposes of reexamination include to "permit efficient resolution of questions about the validity of issued patents without recourse to expensive and lengthy infringement litigation [and to]...promote industrial innovation by assuring the kind of certainty about patent validity which is a necessary ingredient of sound investment decisions." H.R. Rep. No. 1307, 96th Cong., 2d Sess. 4. Reexamination is conducted afresh, without the burdens and presumptions that accompany litigation of an issued patent. *The Laitram Corp. v. NEC Corp.*, 952 F.2d 1357, 21 U.S.P.Q.2d 1276, 1278 (Fed. Cir. 1991).

ᛣ

When a defendant in a patent infringement suit requests reexamination by the PTO of the patent in suit, the plaintiff has a right to compel the defendant to disclose all prior art the defendant intends to rely upon at trial so that such prior art can be addressed in the reexamination proceeding. *Output Technology Corp. v. Dataproducts Corp.*, 22 U.S.P.Q.2d 1639, 1640 (Wash. 1992).

ᛣ

It has been held that federal courts may dispense with the exhaustion doctrine in facial challenges to the re-examination procedure. *Allegheny Ludlum Corp. v. Comer*, 24 U.S.P.Q.2d 1771, 1776 (Pa. 1992).

ᛣ

Conduct of reexamination proceedings under 35 U.S.C. §305 differs from the granting of requests under 35 U.S.C. §302. *Ex parte Raychem Corp.*, 25 U.S.P.Q.2d 1265, 1270 (B.P.A.I. 1992).

ᛣ

Claims added during a reexamination proceeding and determined to be patentable therein nevertheless remain "[a]mended or new claims presented during a reexamination proceeding...[which] will be examined...for compliance with the requirements of 35 USC 112", as required by 37 C.F.R. §1.552(b), in any later reexamination proceeding. Indeed, there appears to be nothing in the statutory scheme which would prevent reexamination of even original patent claims for compliance with 35 U.S.C. §112. *Ex parte Rodgers*, 27 U.S.P.Q.2d 1738, 1742 (B.P.A.I. 1992).

ϖ

A jury determination of patent validity and wilfull infringement (confirmed by the CAFC) is not affected in any way by a subsequent determination (on reexamination by the PTO) that the patent is invalid. *Standard Havens Products Inc. v. Gencor Industries Inc.*, 810 F.Supp. 1072, 25 U.S.P.Q.2d 1949, 1951 (Mo. 1993).

ϖ

A stay of a declaratory judgment action pending resolution of patentee's reexamination was denied, as the reexamination was not likely to settle the controversy over the patent any time in the near future. *American Ceramicraft Inc. v. Eisenbraun Reiss Inc.*, 28 U.S.P.Q.2d 1241, 1249 (N.J. 1993—*unpublished*).

ϖ

There are significant differences between the reexamination procedure and patent litigation in the federal courts. The two forms of proceedings are distinct, with different records and different standards of proof. When considering validity, the PTO gives claims their broadest reasonable interpretation consistent with the specification of the patent. In contrast, courts may construe claims liberally to uphold a patent's validity, rather than to destroy an inventor's right to protect the substance of his or her invention. *Whistler Corp. v. Dynascan Corp.*, 29 U.S.P.Q.2d 1866, 1871 (Ill. 1993).

ϖ

The Court properly excluded evidence of preliminary reexamination findings by the Patent Office as having little or no probative value, and as being overly prejudicial. The Patent Office grants 86% of all requests for reexamination, but only 12% of these grants result in refusals to find patentable claims. *Hoechst Celanese Corp. v. BP Chemicals Ltd.*, 846 F.Supp. 542, 31 U.S.P.Q.2d 1825, 1829 (Tex. 1994).

ϖ

The functions of the courts and the Patent Office are very different and " 'are concepts not in conflict.' " The awkwardness presumed to result if the PTO and court reached different conclusions is more apparent than real. The two forums take different approaches in determining invalidity and on the same evidence could quite correctly come to different conclusions. Furthermore, we see nothing untoward about the PTO upholding the validity of a reexamined patent which the district court later finds invalid. This is essentially what occurs when a court finds a patent invalid after the PTO has granted it. Once again, it is important that the district court and the PTO can consider different evidence. Accordingly, different results between the two forums may be entirely reasonaable. *Accent Designs Inc. v. Jan Jewelry Designs Inc.*, 92 Civ. 0482, 32 U.S.P.Q.2d 1036, 1039, 1040 (N.Y. 1994).

ϖ

A federal district court is not bound by a PTO's Reexamination decision upholding the validity of a patent. *L.A. Gear Inc. v. E.S. Originals Inc.*, 35 U.S.P.Q.2d 1497, 1498 (Cal. 1995).

ᚳ

Improperly broadening claims during reexamination is a violation of 35 U.S.C. §305 and thus supports summary judgment of invalidity. *Quantum Corp. v. Rodime PLC*, 65 F.3d 1577, 36 U.S.P.Q.2d 1162, 1168 (Fed. Cir. 1995).

ᚳ

The Annual Report of the Patent and Trademark Office for 1994 states that 89% of the reexamination requests were granted for that year, but only 5.6% of the reexamined patents were completely rejected with no claims remaining after reexamination. *Hoechst Celanese Corp. v. BP Chemicals Ltd.*, 78 F.3d 1575, 38 U.S.P.Q.2d 1126, 1133 n.2 (Fed. Cir. 1996).

ᚳ

A district court may not compel a party to seek reexamination. *In re Continental General Tire Inc.*, 81 F.3d 1089, 38 U.S.P.Q.2d 1365, 1369 (Fed. Cir. 1996).

ᚳ

Section 305 (35 U.S.C.) contains no provision for introduction of amendments and/or claims which are directed to an invention other than the invention defined by any claim of a patent undergoing reexamination. *Ex parte Logan*, 38 U.S.P.Q.2d 1852, 1854 (B.P.A.I. 1994—*unpublished, not binding precedent*).

ᚳ

The test to determine whether a claim has been impermissibly broadened during reexamination is the same as that used to determine whether a claim has been impermissibly broadened during reissue. "An amended or new claim is enlarged if it includes within its scope any subject matter that would not have infringed the original patent." *Thermalloy Inc. v. Aavid Engineering Inc.*, 39 U.S.P.Q.2d 1457, 1460 (N.H. 1996).

ᚳ

An infringement plaintiff's choice of what, if anything, to file with the PTO, in a reexamination proceeding initiated by a third party, should remain undisturbed by the courts. *Emerson Electric Co. v. Daviol Inc.*, 88 F.3d 1051, 39 U.S.P.Q.2d 1474, 1477 (Fed. Cir. 1996).

ᚳ

Claims, though amended during reexamination, retain their original effective date unless changed in scope from the original patent. *Minco Inc. v. Combustion Engineering Inc.*, 95 F.3d 1109, 40 U.S.P.Q.2d 1001, 1005 (Fed. Cir. 1996).

ᚳ

Reexamination was only intended for those instances at which the Examiner did not have all of the relevant prior art at his disposal when he originally considered the patentability of an invention. The narrow mandate of the reexamination statute requires that reexamination proceedings be considered in light of the presumption that earlier examinations complied with the applicable statutes and regulations, and that earlier Examiners did their work correctly with respect to the prior art references at their disposal. Whether the earlier examination was correct or not, reexamination of the same claims in light of the same references does not raise a substantially new question of patentability, which is the statutory criterion for reexamination. A rejection made during reexamination does not raise a substantial new question of patentability if it is supported only by prior art previously considered by the PTO in relation to the same or broader claims. *In re Portola Packaging Inc.*, 42 U.S.P.Q.2d 1295, 1299, 1300 (Fed. Cir. 1997), *rhg denied* 122 F.3d 1473, 44 U.S.P.Q.2d 1060 (Fed. Cir. 1997).

ω

Double patenting is an issue that can properly be raised during reexamination. *In re Lonardo*, 119 F.3d 960, 43 U.S.P.Q.2d 1262, 1267 (Fed. Cir. 1997), *but see dissent.*

ω

The court, faced with the issue of whether the doctrine of assignor estoppel bars a party from seeking reexamination of a patent, reasoned that, because the doctrine of assignor estoppel is an equitable doctrine and the reexamination provisions are statutory mandates, the conflict between the two should be resolved in favor of the statute, and the motion to stay pending the reexamination outcome should be granted. *Vitronics Corp. v. Conceptronic Inc.*, 44 U.S.P.Q.2d 1536, 1538 (N.H. 1977).

ω

An affidavit may not be used in a reexamination proceeding to swear behind a United States patent claiming the same invention. MPEP §706.02(b)(4) (6th ed.. 1997). *Slip Track Systems Inc. v. Metal Lite Inc.*, 48 U.S.P.Q.2d 1055, 1056 (Fed. Cir. 1998).

ω

A claim amendment made during reexamination following a prior art rejection is not automatically to be regarded as a substantive change. *Laitram Corp. v. NEC Corp.*, 49 U.S.P.Q.2d 1199, 1201 (Fed. Cir. 1998).

Reexamination Certificate.

The public must be able to rely upon the published findings in a reexamination certificate as representing a final disposition of the patentability of such subject matter by the PTO. The public has a right to rely upon the reexamination certificate and assume that the canceled subject matter and the limitations held unpatentable represent matter within the public domain. *Ex parte Morimoto*, 18 U.S.P.Q.2d 1540, 1544 (B.P.A.I. 1990).

Reexamination Requestor's Standing on Appeal. *See also* Review.

Although neither the patent owner nor the Commissioner objected to intervention by the requestor in the appeal proceeding at the district court, the requestor has no independent right to appeal to the CAFC from the decision of the district court. To maintain its appeal in the CAFC, an intervenor in the district court proceeding is required to establish its own standing independently and cannot rely on its intervenor status where the parties to the district court action have not appealed. *The Boeing Company v. Commissioner of Patents and Trademarks*, 853 F.2d 878, 7 U.S.P.Q.2d 1487 (Fed. Cir. 1988).

Reference. *See also* **Analogous Art, Applicant's Own Work, Circumstances, Collateral Attack, Copending Patent, Defensive Publication, Enabling Disclosure, Encyclopedic Disclosure, Fact, Generic Disclosure, Information Disclosure Statement, Number of References, Paper Patent, Printed Publication, Prior Art, Problem, Same Effect, Search Record, Teach Away From.**

A foreign patent may be a valid reference only for all that it clearly discloses. *In re Cross*, 62 F.2d 182, 16 U.S.P.Q. 10 (C.C.P.A. 1932).

ᚱ

The inoperativeness of patented machines (as a whole) could hardly serve to render each and every portion of the machines (as described in reference patents) worthless as a disclosure of a new and useful application of an art. *Gilbert v. Marzall*, 182 F.2d 389, 85 U.S.P.Q. 288, 293 (D.C. Cir. 1950).

ᚱ

Since the disclosure in an abandoned application was referred to in an issued patent, it became part of the patent disclosure. Any reference to a disclosure which is available to the public is permissible. *In re Heritage*, 182 F.2d 639, 86 U.S.P.Q. 160, 164 (C.C.P.A. 1950).

ᚱ

A reference may be valid even though it states that its disclosure is not practical. *In re Aller, Lacey, and Hall*, 220 F.2d 454, 105 U.S.P.Q. 233, 237 (C.C.P.A. 1955).

ᚱ

The validity or invalidity of a patent has nothing to do with its effectiveness as a reference if the patent discloses and claims the invention claimed by appellant. *In re McIntosh*, 230 F.2d 615, 109 U.S.P.Q. 101, 104 (C.C.P.A. 1956).

ᚱ

A reference is valid only for what it discloses. If an applicant establishes priority with respect to that disclosure, and there is no statutory bar, the reference is of no effect at all. A reference is nothing more than a patent or publication cited to show that all or part of the invention for which a patent is sought was in the prior art, either more than a year before the filing date to which the applicant is entitled, in which case it is a "statutory bar", and cannot be sworn back of, or before the applicant's date of invention. When a reference is not a statutory bar, Rule 131 (37 C.F.R. §1.131) provides a procedure by which the applicant is permitted to show, if he can, that his date of invention was earlier than the date of reference. The rule must be construed in accordance with the rights given to inventors by statute and this excludes a construction permitting the further use of a reference as a ground of rejection after all pertinent subject matter in it has been ante-dated to the satisfaction of the Patent Office. *In re Stempel*, 241 F.2d 755, 113 U.S.P.Q. 77, 81 (C.C.P.A. 1957).

ᚱ

Appellant's own British priority application, published more than one year prior to the filing date of the subject continuation-in-part (cip) application, is a statutory bar against subject matter added to the cip and which is not patentably distinct from what is disclosed in the published application. The fact that appellant's copending parent application contained the entire subject matter disclosed in the British publication does not overcome the statutory bar. *In re Ruscetta and Jenny,* 255 F.2d 687, 118 U.S.P.Q. 101, 104 (C.C.P.A. 1958).

ᚼ

Any reference, patent or otherwise, foreign or domestic, is good "for only what it clearly and definitely discloses". There is no basis in the statute (35 U.S.C. §102 or 35 U.S.C. §103) for discriminating either in favor of or against prior art references on the basis of nationality. *In re Boling and Tigges,* 292 F.2d 306, 130 U.S.P.Q. 161, 164 (C.C.P.A. 1961).

ᚼ

A reference article, published two and one half years after appellants' filing date was properly used to show that appellants' claims were unduly broad. *In re Rainer, Redding, Hitov, Sloan, and Stewart,* 305 F.2d 505, 134 U.S.P.Q. 343, 345 n.1 (C.C.P.A. 1962).

ᚼ

While a species may be patentably distinct from a genus, when an earlier disclosed species is broadly the same invention as the genus, the requirement of 35 U.S.C. §119 that only "the same invention" (in the later application as is shown in the earlier) will obtain the benefit of the earlier filing date is satisfied for the purpose of overcoming references. *In re Ziegler, Breil, Holzkamp, and Martin,* 347 F.2d 642, 146 U.S.P.Q. 76, 82 (C.C.P.A. 1966).

ᚼ

Subject matter canceled from the specification of an application that subsequently issues as a patent and thus does not appear in the issued patent is not prior art with regard to an application that has an effective filing date prior to the issuance of the patent. Whether that subject matter is prior art as of the date on which the patent issued was not determined. *Ex parte Stalego,* 839 O.G. 828, 829, 830 (PO Bd. App. 1966).

ᚼ

An inoperable invention or one that fails to achieve its intended result does not negative novelty. *United States v. Adams,* 383 U.S. 39, 148 U.S.P.Q. 479, 483 (1966).

ᚼ

A reference which does not disclose or suggest any usefulness for the compounds it describes does not negate the patentability of related, but novel, compounds, the usefulness (conforming with statutory requirements) of which is properly disclosed. *In re Stemniski,* 444 F.2d 581, 170 U.S.P.Q. 343, 348 (C.C.P.A. 1971).

ᚼ

The mere naming of a compound in a reference, without more, cannot constitute a description of the compound, particularly when evidence of record suggests that a method suitable for its preparation was not developed until a date later than that of the reference. Compounds listed by name and within the scope of claims in issue were not "described in a printed publication" within the meaning of 35 U.S.C. §102(b). *In re Wiggins, James, and Gittos,* 488 F.2d 538, 179 U.S.P.Q. 421 (C.C.P.A. 1973).

ᚼ

A patent that is obscure and ambiguous in its teaching is too ambiguous to be used as a reference. *Mobil Oil Corp., v. W. R. Grace & Co.*, 367 F. Supp. 207, 180 U.S.P.Q. 418, 452 (Conn. 1973).

ᖫ

Disclosures in foreign publications and patents are strictly construed and are restricted in their teaching to exactly what they clearly and fully disclose without alteration. *Corometrics Medical Systems, Inc. v. Berkeley Bio-Engineering, Inc.*, 193 U.S.P.Q. 467, 475 (Cal. 1977).

ᖫ

A printed publication can constitute an anticipation of a claimed compound even though it fails to disclose how to make the compound and it indicates that the compound is "without effect" or "without activity", if (subsequent to the effective date of the reference and prior to the effective date of an application claiming the compound) a further reference teaches how the compound may be made. *In re Samour*, 571 F.2d 559, 197 U.S.P.Q. 1, 3, 4 (C.C.P.A. 1978).

ᖫ

For the teachings of a reference to be prior art under 35 U.S.C. §103, there must be some basis for concluding that the reference would have been considered by one skilled in the particular art working on the pertinent problem to which the invention pertains; for no matter what a reference teaches, it could not have rendered obvious anything (at the time the invention was made) to a person having ordinary skill in the art to which the subject matter pertains unless that hypothetical person would have considered it. *In re Horn, Horn, Horn, and Horn*, 203 U.S.P.Q. 969 (C.C.P.A. 1979).

ᖫ

An abandoned U.S.A. application (by a different and unrelated inventive entity) is not made available as a reference as of its filing date when a subsequently-filed counterpart foreign application is published. *Ex parte Smolka and Schwuger*, 207 U.S.P.Q. 232, 234 (PTO Bd. App. 1980).

ᖫ

With respect to matters necessary for an enabling disclosure and which are not common and well known, an applicant may incorporate certain types of documents by specific reference in his application to such source materials. In this regard "any reference to a disclosure which is available to the public is permissible". *In re Howarth*, 654 F.2d 103, 210 U.S.P.Q. 689, 692 (C.C.P.A. 1981).

ᖫ

D and N were joint applicants of an application filed for a combination invention on June 1, 1973 (subsequently issued as U.S.P. 3,842,678 on October 22, 1974). Applicant D was the sole applicant of an application (S.N. 952,695) for reissue of U.S.P. 3,964,519 (issued on an application filed November 18, 1974), claiming a subcombination that was fully disclosed, but not claimed, in U.S.P. 3,842,678. In the prosecution of the reissue application D presented his own Declaration that a drawing of the subcombination invention (dated March 15, 1973) established conception prior to June 1, 1973, and the subcombination was a sole invention originally conceived by D and described to patent counsel prior to June 1, 1973, to enable counsel to satisfy the requirements of 35 U.S.C. §112 in drafting the joint application. The joint patent was used as a reference against the reissue application even though it was silent with regard to who invented the subcombination. There was no basis to presume that the subcombination was the invention of D and N jointly or of either of them. The joint patent of D and N, having issued less than one year before the filing date of D's original patent application, is only available as a reference if the pertinent disclosure is not the sole work of D. An applicant's own work, even though publicly disclosed prior to his application, may not be used against him as a reference, absent a time bar to his application. In spite of the fact that a completed invention requires both conception and reduction to practice, there is no requirement that the inventor be the one to reduce the invention to practice so long as reduction to practice is done on his behalf. *In re DeBaun,* 687 F.2d 459, 214 U.S.P.Q. 933 (C.C.P.A. 1982).

ᛡ

The appellant filed (with his application) a Declaration in which he acknowledged his coauthorship of a paper (published less than a year earlier) and further stated unequivocally that he was the sole inventor of the subject matter that is disclosed in that publication. Unlike the filing of a patent application, the publication of an article is not a constructive reduction to practice of the subject matter described therein. Therefore, disclosure in a publication does not prove that any "invention" within the meaning of 35 U.S.C. §102(g) has ever been made by anyone. Since §102(g) is predicated on the invention having been made in this country by another, nothing short of an actual or constructive reduction to practice could provide a valid basis for the rejection. Even though a printed publication, which describes the subject matter of a claimed invention and is published before an application is filed, may raise a substantial question whether the applicant is the inventor, coauthors of the publication may not be presumed to be coinventors merely from the fact of coauthorship. The appellant's Declaration that he was the sole inventor and that the coauthors "were students working under the direction and supervision of the inventor" was accepted as a sufficient showing to establish that the subject disclosure was his original work, and his alone. *In re Katz,* 687 F.2d 450, 215 U.S.P.Q. 14 (C.C.P.A. 1982).

ᛡ

A reference is not available under 35 U.S.C. §103 if it is not within the field of the inventor's endeavor and was not directly pertinent to the particular problem with which the inventor was involved. *King Instrument Corp. v. Otari Corp.,* 767 F.2d 853, 226 U.S.P.Q. 402 (Fed. Cir. 1985).

ᛡ

In dismissing *Dante* as a reference, the court pointed out that *Dante* didn't even hint at the problem the appellants sought to solve. *Dante* would not even have encountered the problem because it would not have appeared in what he was doing. *In re Benno,* 768 F.2d 1340, 226 U.S.P.Q. 683 (Fed. Cir. 1985).

ᛡ

The test of whether a particular compound described in the prior art may be relied upon to show that claimed subject matter would have been obvious is whether the prior art provides an enabling disclosure with respect to the disclosed prior art compound. No evidence was offered to show an enabling disclosure for the reference structure, while uncontroverted testimony showed the reference structure to be a hypothetical structure. *Ashland Oil, Inc. v. Delta Resins & Refractories, Inc.*, 776 F.2d 281, 227 U.S.P.Q. 657 (Fed. Cir. 1985).

ʊ

To determine whether a reference is within the scope and content of the prior art, first determine if the reference is within the field of the inventor's endeavor. If it is not, then next consider whether the reference is reasonably pertinent to the particular problem with which the inventor was involved. *Bausch & Lomb, Inc. v. Barnes-Hind/Hydrocurve, Inc.*, 796 F.2d 443, 230 U.S.P.Q. 416 (Fed. Cir. 1986).

ʊ

A reference itself must have an enabling disclosure to be used as a proper reference. Section 102(b) of 35 U.S.C. and its predecessor statutes have been interpreted as requiring the description of the invention in a publication to be sufficient to put the public in possession of the invention. *Ex parte Gould*, 231 U.S.P.Q. 943 (B.P.A.I. 1986).

ʊ

If any claim of a patent issued on a cip is determined to be limited to the filing date of the cip on the basis that the disclosure of the parent was insufficient to support such claim, a corresponding foreign publication that is substantially the same as the parent is also insufficient to anticipate such claim under 35 U.S.C. §102(b). The correct role of the foreign publication in such case is as a reference under 35 U.S.C. §103. *Paperless Accounting, Inc. v. Bay Area Rapid Transit System*, 804 F.2d 659, 231 U.S.P.Q. 649, 653 (Fed. Cir. 1986).

ʊ

When a reference was before the Examiner, whether through the Examiner's search or the applicant's disclosure, it cannot be deemed to have been withheld from the Examiner. A reference that is material only to withdrawn claims cannot be the basis of a holding of inequitable conduct. *Scripps Clinic & Research Foundation v. Genentech Inc.*, 927 F.2d 1565, 18 U.S.P.Q.2d 1001, 1015 (Fed. Cir. 1991).

ʊ

While a reference must enable someone to practice the invention in order to anticipate under 35 U.S.C. §102(b), a non-enabling reference may qualify as prior art for the purpose of determining obviousness under 35 U.S.C. §103, but only for what is disclosed in it. *Symbol Technologies v. Opticon Inc.*, 935 F.2d 1569, 19 U.S.P.Q.2d 1241, 1247 (Fed. Cir. 1991).

Reference Dissection.

It is impermissible within the framework of 35 U.S.C. §103 to pick and choose from any one reference only so much of it as will support a given position to the exclusion of other parts necessary to the full appreciation of what such reference fairly suggests to one skilled in the art. *Bausch & Lomb, Inc. v. Barnes-Hind/Hydrocurve, Inc.*, 796 F.2d 443, 230 U.S.P.Q. 416 (Fed. Cir. 1986).

Reference Generic to Claimed Invention. *See also* **Encyclopedic Disclosure, Shotgun.**

The contention that a claimed configuration would be obvious from a reference claim on which it reads is a non sequitur. According to such reasoning Morse's telegraph patent would have made the telex obvious. The scope of a patent's claims determines what infringes the patent; it is no measure of what it discloses. A patent discloses only that which it describes, whether specifically or in general terms, so as to convey intelligence to one capable of understanding. *In re Benno*, 768 F.2d 1340, 226 U.S.P.Q. 683 (Fed. Cir. 1985).

References as a Whole. *See also* **Prior Art as a Whole.**

Although it is proper to note the difference in a claimed invention from the prior art, because that difference may serve as one element in determining the obviousness/non-obviousness issue, it is improper to consider the difference as the invention. The difference may be slight (as has often been the case with some of history's greatest inventions, e.g., the telephone), but it may also have been the key to success in advancements in the art resulting from the invention. The issue with respect to obviousness is whether a challenger has carried its burden of proving, by clear and convincing evidence, facts from which it must be concluded that one skilled in the art at the time the invention was made would have found it to have been obvious, from the references as a whole, to create the claimed subject matter as a whole. *Datascope Corp. v. SMEC, Inc.*, 776 F.2d 320, 227 U.S.P.Q. 838 (Fed. Cir. 1985).

Refiling. *See* **Continuing Application.**

Refusing to Copy Claims.

The appellant refused to copy a patent claim for the purpose of instituting an interference; both the claims and the disclosure of the patent were treated as "prior art" with respect to the appellant's claims. The claims of a patent cannot be used as the conceded prior invention of another in this country under 35 U.S.C. §102(g) or as prior art under 35 U.S.C. §103 unless the patentee and applicant are claiming essentially the same invention and it is clearly shown that the applicant in such a case has support for the patented claims in his application. If such conditions are met, the patent disclosure is available only to determine what invention the claims define and, hence, what invention has been claimed. The entire disclosure is not available as conceded prior art. *Ex parte Inoue*, 217 U.S.P.Q. 461 (PTO Bd. App. 1981).

ω

Since the requirement to copy the modified claim was improper because it lacks support in their disclosure, appellants have not disclaimed its subject matter. The modified claim thus cannot be treated as a prior art reference, and the 35 U.S.C. §103 rejection premised upon it fails. *In re Phillips and Crick*, 673 F.2d 1273, 213 U.S.P.Q. 353, 356 (C.C.P.A. 1982).

"Regards" Test.[4]

The second paragraph of 35 U.S.C. §112 does not prohibit an applicant from changing what he "regards as his invention" during the pendency of his application. *In re Saunders and Gemeinhardt*, 444 F.2d 599, 170 U.S.P.Q. 213, 220 (C.C.P.A. 1971).

Registering. *See* Mental Steps.

Regulatory Review Period.

Congress intended 35 U.S.C. §156(g) (1)-(3) to define the "regulatory review period" and for §156(g)(6) to be a limitation on the extension term. Whether a drug has undergone a regulatory review period and the related patent is eligible for a term extension, and how that extension should be limited are two completely different issues. *Hoechst Aktiengesellschaft v. Quigg*, 917 F.2d 522, 16 U.S.P.Q.2d 1549, 1553 (Fed. Cir. 1990).

Rehearing.

When a three-member panel of the BPAI has rendered its decision, the Commissioner has authority to constitute a new panel for the purposes of reconsideration. Although a distinction is made between "rehearing" and "reconsideration" in some contexts, the two terms are often used interchangeably. It would not be unreasonable to construe "rehearings" under 35 U.S.C. §7(b) broadly as also encompassing reconsideration by the Board wherein the Board allows an applicant to supplement the existing record or wherein the Board allows both the applicant and the Examiner to brief the issues anew. *In re Alappat*, 33 F.3d 1526, 31 U.S.P.Q.2d 1545, 1546, 1548 n.6 and 7 (Fed. Cir. 1994).

ᛡ

A summary denial of rehearing en banc is insufficient to confer any implication or inference regarding the court's opinion relative to the merits of the case." *Exxon Chemical Patents Inc. v. Lubrizol Corp.*, 137 F.3d 1475, 45 U.S.P.Q.2d 1865, 1868 (Fed. Cir. 1998).

Reinstatement.[5]

Reissue. *See also* Broadened Reissue, Claim Construction, Inspection, Intent to Claim, Protestor, Remedial Statute, 35 U.S.C. §251.

When a patent owner applies for reissue of the patent, and includes among the claims in the reissue application the same claims as those which were included in the original patent, and the Examiner rejects some such claims for want of patentable novelty (by reference to prior patents) and allows others (both old and new), by failing to take an appeal and by abandoning the reissue application, the patent owner does not hold the original patent (the return of which he procures from the Patent Office) invalidated as to those of its claims which were disallowed for want of patentable novelty by the Primary

---

[4] See Jones, Eric T., The "Regards" Test of 35 U.S.C. §112 ¶2, *The Law Works*, Vol. 2, No. 4, page 16, April 1995.

[5] *See Chapman v. Manbeck*, 931 F.2d 46, 18 U.S.P.Q.2d 1565 (Fed. Cir. 1991).

Examiner in the reissue proceeding. *McCormick Harvesting Machine Co. v. Aultman*, 169 U.S. 606, 612 (1898).

ᴡ

Section 251 (35 U.S.C.) demonstrates that it was not intended that an assignee of a patent be permitted to make and swear to an application for reissue when the application seeks to enlarge the scope of the claims of the original patent. *In re Schuyler*, 119 U.S.P.Q. 97, 99 (Comm'r 1957).

ᴡ

The invention disclosed in the patent (not that to which patent claims are directed) is that which the patentee intended and attempted to gain protection for. Supreme Court decisions favor liberal construction of reissue statutes in order to secure to inventors protection for what they have actually invented. *In re Wesseler*, 367 F.2d 838, 151 U.S.P.Q. 339, 346, 348 (C.C.P.A. 1966).

ᴡ

A limitation added to a claim in obtaining its allowance can be broadened by reissue if the limitation turns out to be more restrictive than the prior art required. One might err without deceptive intention in adding a particular limitation where a less specific limitation regarding the same feature, or an added limitation relative to another element, would have been sufficient to render the claims patentable over the prior art. *In re Richman*, 409 F.2d 269, 161 U.S.P.Q. 359, 363 (C.C.P.A. 1969).

ᴡ

The reissue statute is based on fundamental principles of equity and fairness. As a remedial provision it should be liberally construed so as to carry out its purpose to the end that justice may be done to both patentees and the public. *In re Oda, Fujii, Moriga, and Higaki*, 443 F.2d 1200, 170 U.S.P.Q. 268, 270 (C.C.P.A. 1971).

ᴡ

The fact that a patent was allowed on applicant's original application does not mean that the question of sufficiency of disclosure has been determined in applicant's favor by the Patent Office and that a policy of res judicata bars a contrary holding during the prosecution of a reissue application. The statutory provision for reissue of patents, 35 U.S.C. §251, by its third paragraph, dictates that the provisions applicable to applications for patents, including 35 U.S.C. §112, are applicable to reissue applications as well. *In re Doyle*, 482 F.2d 1385, 179 U.S.P.Q. 227, 232 (C.C.P.A. 1973).

ᴡ

The statement in a reissue oath that the original patent was "inoperative to protect his invention fully and properly" is a far cry from an admission that the patent was inoperative per se. *Tee-Pak, Inc. v. St. Regis Paper Company*, 491 F.2d 1193, 181 U.S.P.Q. 75, 81 (6th Cir. 1974).

ᴡ

A reissue applicant is, at most, prevented from obtaining claims which are of the same scope as the claims previously cancelled in the original application. *In re Wadlinger, Kerr, and Rosinski*, 496 F.2d 1200, 181 U.S.P.Q. 826, 832 (C.C.P.A. 1974).

ᴡ

Lack of antecedent basis in a claim could render it invalid under 35 U.S.C. §112, second paragraph, and correction of such a defect by reissue should not have to depend on difference in scope of the claim. Inasmuch as 35 U.S.C. §251 is a remedial provision, which should be liberally construed, a patentee should be allowed to correct an error or ambiguity in a claim without having to rely on the implication of litigation. Lack of antecedent basis in a claim is a proper ground for reissue under §251. *In re Altenpohl,* 500 F.2d 1151, 183 U.S.P.Q. 38 (C.C.P.A. 1974).

ω

Even though it is not fraud, an applicant or his agent cannot knowingly withhold relevant prior art from the Examiner until he finds out whether such action invalidates his patent, and then apply for reissue only if he loses the gamble on the ground he made an "error". When a holding of invalidity has been decreed by a court of appeals for a flagrant dereliction of duty to disclose, reissue is not available for expiation. *In re Clark,* 522 F.2d 623, 187 U.S.P.Q. 209, 213 (C.C.P.A. 1975).

ω

Broadened claims added in a reissue application (not made through "inadvertence, accident or mistake, by reason of which the specification as originally drawn is defective or insufficient...") to enlarge the claimed subject matter in order to embrace another's non-infringing device (known to applicant, but not brought to the attention of the PTO), which had or was about to come into legitimate use, were held to be invalid. *SAB Industri AB v. The Bendix Corporation,* 199 U.S.P.Q. 95, 106 (Va. 1978).

ω

Neither Congress nor the Commissioner of Patents has authorized initiation of reissue proceedings by anyone other than the inventor or his assignee. A motion by an infringement defendant to compel patentee to apply for a reissue patent was thus denied. *Cooper Industries, Inc. v. J. & J. Fabrics, Inc.,* 211 U.S.P.Q. 226 (Ga. 1981).

ω

A patentee can avoid the restrictions applicable to reissue applications by filing a regular application directed to subject matter disclosed (but not claimed) in his patent within one year of the patent's issue date. A continuing application, based on a parent reissue application, is entitled to the benefit of the filing date of the parent reissue application under 35 U.S.C. §120, even when a different invention is being claimed. To hold that it is impossible to obtain the actual filing date of the reissue application because its effective filing date is the patent filing date would exalt form over substance and serve no useful purpose. *In re Bauman,* 683 F.2d 405, 214 U.S.P.Q. 585, 589, 590 (C.C.P.A. 1982).

ω

This appeal is from a decision of the PTO Board of Appeals rejecting claims of a Reissue Application on the ground that a broadening Reissue Application that was filed within two years of the patent issue date (but was erroneously filed by the assignee) could not be corrected by a Declaration of the inventor filed more than two years after the patent issue date. The CAFC reversed. Recognizing that all of the provisions of a unified statute must be read in harmony, the portion of 35 U.S.C. §251 that requires that a broadening reissue application must be signed by the inventor does not mean that an error in compliance with §251 is insulated from the remedial ruling of *Stoddard* [564 F.2d 556, 195 U.S.P.Q. 97 (D.C. Cir. 1977)] or the statutory provision for the correction of error. The purpose of the reissue statute is to remedy errors. Reissue is remedial in nature and is based on fundamental principles of equity and fairness. These fundamental principles must not be forgotten in implementation of the statute. *In re Bennett,* 766 F.2d 524, 226 U.S.P.Q. 413 (Fed. Cir. 1985).

ᚤ

Failure to satisfy the duty to disclose during the prosecution of an application that matures into a patent cannot be cured by reissue. *In re Jerabek,* 789 F.2d 886, 229 U.S.P.Q. 530 (Fed. Cir. 1986).

ᚤ

Failure to disclose material prior art during the prosecution of a patent cannot be cured by reissue. *Ex parte Harita,* 1 U.S.P.Q.2d 1887 (B.P.A.I. 1986).

ᚤ

Reissue is not available for the sole purpose of invoking an interference that was overlooked by the PTO. *In re Keil,* 808 F.2d 830, 1 U.S.P.Q.2d 1427 (Fed. Cir. 1987).

ᚤ

In the reissue statute "identical" means without substantive change. *Slimfold Manufacturing Co. v. Kinkead Industries Inc.,* 810 F.2d 1113, 1 U.S.P.Q.2d 1563 (Fed. Cir. 1987).

ᚤ

In addition to case law, the patent statutes and regulations support the conclusion that carry-over claims not amended in a Reissue Application ought not be extinguished with the rejection of reissue claims. Under the relevant regulations, even the denial of a Reissue Application does not affect the original patent claims. Hence, under 37 C.F.R. §1.178 if a Reissue Application is refused, "the original patent will be returned to [the] applicant upon his request." By analogy, when a district court strikes a reissue patent after the Reissue Application has been granted, those claims carried over from the original patent (which were not implicated in the Reissue Application) should remain valid despite the surrender and extinction of the original patent. While, analytically, it may appear odd to retain claims without a valid patent, the anomaly is merely one of semantics that Congress itself adopted. In 35 U.S.C. §253, Congress provides that whenever, without any deceptive intention, a claim of a patent is invalid, the remaining claims shall not thereby be rendered invalid. A similar provision allows for the maintenance of infringement suits based on such remaining claims. *Hewlett Packard Co. v. Bausch & Lomb, Inc.,* 8 U.S.P.Q.2d 1177, 1178 (Cal. 1988).

ᚤ

It is appropriate to give the same extent of unenforceability to a reissue patent as to an original patent. The same level of misconduct is required in both instances. Established inequitable conduct renders all claims unenforceable.

Although neither "more" nor "less" in the sense of scope of the claims, the practice of allowing reissue for the purpose of narrower claims as a hedge against the possible invalidation of a broad claim has been tacitly approved. The lack of error warranting reissue invalidates only new claims and not original claims. *Hewlett-Packard Co. v. Bausch & Lomb, Inc.*, 882 F.2d 1556, 11 U.S.P.Q.2d 1750, 1759 (Fed. Cir. 1989).

ᗡ

Applicants are "estopped from obtaining by reissue claims which, because of a requirement for restriction in which they had acquiesced, they could not claim in their patent." The failure to file a divisional application, regardless of the propriety of the underlying restriction requirement, is not an error correctable by reissue under 35 U.S.C. §251. *In re Watkinson*, 900 F.2d 230, 14 U.S.P.Q.2d 1407, 1409 (Fed. Cir. 1990).

ᗡ

Pursuant to Fed. R. Civ. P. 24(b), an intervenor is authorized to intervene as a party defendant (in a civil action under 35 U.S.C. §145 in which plaintiff seeks to set aside a BPAI decision affirming an Examiner's final rejection of claims in plaintiff's reissue patent application) and is permitted to participate fully in the civil action subject to the following:

1. Intervenor's affirmative defenses are limited to the affirmative defense advanced by the Commissioner; and
2. Intervenor shall bear all of its costs and expenses.

Ely v. Manbeck, 17 U.S.P.Q.2d 1252, 1253 (D.C. 1990).

ᗡ

A Reissue Declaration must provide an explanation particularly specifying the errors and how they arose. The mere conclusion that the error was made through oversight in drafting by the patent attorney, without more, falls short of what the regulation requires. Because the affidavit is insufficient evidence of reissuable error, the Examiner was wrong in reissuing the patent. *Alcon Laboratories Inc. v. Allergan Inc.*, 17 U.S.P.Q.2d 1365, 1375 (Tex. 1990).

ᗡ

An error of law is not excluded from the class of error subject to correction in accord with the reissue statute. Although attorney error is not an open invitation to reissue in every case in which it may appear, the purpose of the reissue statute is to avoid forfeiture of substantive rights due to error made without intent to deceive. Not every event or circumstance that may be labeled "error" is correctable by reissue. When the statutory requirements are met, reissuance of a patent is not discretionary with the Commissioner; it is mandatory. The whole purpose of the statute, so far as claims are concerned, is to permit limitations to be added to claims that are too broad or to be taken from claims that are too narrow. The district court holding (that there was insufficient reason for reissue) appeared to interpret 35 U.S.C. §251 as requiring a showing that the error in claiming the product could not have been avoided in order to be eligible for cure. This is not the framework of the reissue statute. *Scripps Clinic & Research Foundation v. Genentech Inc.*, 927 F.2d 1565, 18 U.S.P.Q.2d 1001, 1009 (Fed. Cir. 1991).

ᗡ

In the prosecution of a Reissue Application, a supplemental reissue oath (SRO) stated that the error of underestimating the scope of the invention arose because prior art, of which applicant subsequently became aware, was not known or accounted for in drafting the original claims. Applicant provided specific evidence as it became aware of the prior-art references only during the discovery phase of an infringement action initiated subsequent to issuance of the original patent. *Quantum Corp. v. Tandon Corp.*, 18 U.S.P.Q.2d 1597, 1601 (Cal. 1991).

ω

Proceedings on Reissue Applications are open to the public. 37 C.F.R. §1.11(b). Hence, counsel for defendants may attend the hearing before the BPAI and listen to applicant's argument, even though he cannot otherwise participate in the hearing. Although a court ordered that "plaintiff allow defendants to participate in all phases of the reissue proceedings before the Patent Office," the order is not directed to the PTO. Indeed, the doctrine of separation of powers precludes applying the order against the PTO. Rule 291 (37 C.F.R. §1.291) has the force and effect of law and does not permit defendants in an infringement litigation proceeding to participate in plaintiff's oral argument (in the prosecution of his Reissue Application) before the BPAI. *In re Blaese*, 19 U.S.P.Q.2d 1232, 1235 (Comm'r Patents & Trademarks 1991).

ω

Congress has not vested district courts with the power to initiate reissue proceedings, nor do courts possess inherent power that extends to compulsion upon patentees to seek reissue. *Green v. The Rich Iron Company Inc.*, 944 F.2d 852, 20 U.S.P.Q.2d 1075, 1077 (Fed. Cir. 1991).

ω

Congress provided only for administrative and judicial review of reissue decisions at the behest of reissue applicants. Although PTO rules authorize third parties to file protests against reissue applications, the rules explicitly confine the participation of third parties in reissue proceedings to the filing of protests. The PTO regulation implementing the patent statute's intent to limit third-party involvement in the patent examination process is entitled to judicial deference. *Hitachi Metals Ltd. v. Quigg*, 20 U.S.P.Q.2d 1920, 1924, 1925 (D.C. 1991).

ω

The objective intent of a patentee cannot, alone, form the basis for a denial of reissue claims. There are two distinct statutory requirements that a reissue oath or Declaration must satisfy. First, it must state that the patent is defective or partly inoperative or invalid because of defects in the specification or drawing, or because the patentee has claimed more or less than he is entitled to. Second, the applicant must allege that the defective, inoperative, or invalid patent arose through error without deceptive intent. "Intent to claim" is not the criterion for reissue and has little to do with "intent" per se, but rather is analogous to the requirement of 35 U.S.C. §112, first paragraph, that the specification contain a "written description of the invention, and of the manner and process of making and using it." It is synonymous with "right to claim." *In re Amos*, 953 F.2d 613, 21 U.S.P.Q.2d 1271, 1273, 1274 (Fed. Cir. 1991).

ω

Broadening claims may be presented in a reissue application filed within two years after a patent grant even though such claims were not presented until more than two years after the patent grant and were broader than the original patent claims and the broadened reissue claims originally submitted. *Buell v. Beckestrom*, 22 U.S.P.Q.2d 1128, 1131 (B.P.A.I. 1992).

ᛠ

Neither 35 U.S.C. §251 nor the reexamination statutes, 35 U.S.C. §301, et seq., permit a reissue application to present claims broader in scope subsequent to two years from the grant of the original patent. *Ex parte Alpha Industries Inc.*, 22 U.S.P.Q.2d 1851, 1855 (B.P.A.I. 1992).

ᛠ

Upon reissue, the "burden of proving invalidity was made heavier." *Boyett v. St. Martin's Press Inc.*, 884 F.Supp. 479, 34 U.S.P.Q.2d 1828, 1830 (Fla. 1995).

ᛠ

The test to determine whether a claim has been impermissibly broadened during reexamination is the same as that used to determine whether a claim has been impermissibly broadened during reissue. "An amended or new claim is enlarged if it includes within its scope any subject matter that would not have infringed the original patent." *Thermalloy Inc. v. Aavid Engineering Inc.*, 39 U.S.P.Q.2d 1457, 1460 (N.H. 1996).

ᛠ

The reissue statute requires that proposals to broaden a patented invention must be brought to public notice within two years of patent issuance. *In re Graff*, 42 U.S.P.Q.2d 1471, 1474 (Fed. Cir. 1997).

ᛠ

"Every departure from the original patent...must be particularly and distinctly specified and supported in the original, or a supplemental, reissue oath or declaration under 37 C.F.R. §1.175." The reissue regulations require full explanation of each "excess" in the original claims. Section 1.175(a)(3) concerns "the patentee claiming more...than he [or she] had the right to claim in the patent", and the subsection then expressly requires that the declaration meet the test of "distinctly specifying the excess...in the claims." *Nupla Corp. v. IXL Manufacturing Co.*, 42 U.S.P.Q.2d 1711, 1713, 1715 (Fed. Cir. 1997)

ᛠ

The PTO's issuance of two reissue patents for the same invention is a curiosity. Federal Circuit precedent suggests that the burden of proving invalidity is "made heavier" by reissue. *Hester Industries Inc. v. Stein Inc.*, 43 U.S.P.Q.2d 1236, 1237 n.2, 1240 n.9 (Va. 1997)

ᛠ

An inventor's failure to appreciate the scope of the invention at the time of the original patent grant, and thus an initial intent not to claim the omitted subject matter, is a remediable error. *C.R. Bard Inc. v. M3 Systems Inc.*, 48 U.S.P.Q.2d 1225, 1234 (Fed. Cir. 1998).

Rejected Claim.

Rejected claims may not properly be measured by allowed claims in order to determine patentability of the former, but must be considered in the light of their own limitations. *In re Eitzen,* 86 F.2d 759, 32 U.S.P.Q. 72, 73 (C.C.P.A. 1936).

ᵫ

"Reissue claims that are broader in certain respects and narrower in others may avoid the effect of the recapture rule." However, in *Mentor Corp. v. Colorplast*, Inc., 998 F.2d 992, 996, 27 U.S.P.Q.2d 1521, 1525 (Fed. Cir. 1993), the court explained that, if the patentee is seeking to recover subject matter that had been surrendered during the initial prosecution, this flexibility of analysis is eliminated, for the prosecution history establishes the substantiality of the change and estops its recapture. Thus, although the circumstances of presentation in the specification may temper the general rule that broadening of any term of a claim is fatal, even when other terms are narrowed, it is appropriate to consider other factors, including whether the applicant intended to have originally covered the challenged subject matter. *Anderson v. International Engineering and Manufacturing Inc.*, 48 U.S.P.Q.2d 1631, 1634 (Fed. Cir. 1998).

ᵫ

A reissue application filed more than two years after the grant of the original patent is bounded by the claims remaining in the patent after a disclaimer is filed rather than by the claims originally contained in the patent. *Vectra Fitness Inc. v. TNWK Corp.*, 49 U.S.P.Q.2d 1144, 1145, 1146 (Fed. Cir. 1998).

Rejection. *See* **Rejection of Claims.**

Rejection of Claims. *See also* **Cross-Rejection, Knockdown, Multiple Rejection, 35 U.S.C. §112, 35 U.S.C. §132.**

A new rejection by the Board of Appeals (replacing a rejection by the Examiner) is an action within the meaning of the statute. Accordingly, the applicant is entitled to the statutory period for requesting reconsideration by the Primary Examiner unless a shorter period is specified by the Board in its action. *In re Application filed July 13, 1950*, 105 U.S.P.Q. 154 (Comm'r 1955).

ᵫ

The cross-rejection of claims of each of two applications (of the same inventor or assignee) over the claims of the other is unwarranted. *Ex parte Conner and Verplanck*, 119 U.S.P.Q. 182, 184 (PO Bd. App. 1958).

ᵫ

Appellant's proper avenue for review of the dismissal of an appeal by the Board (because appellant failed to file a reply brief in response to a new ground of rejection presented in the Examiner's Answer) is by recourse to 37 C.F.R. §181 and 5 U.S.C. §§701-6. *In re James*, 432 F.2d 473, 167 U.S.P.Q. 403, 405 (C.C.P.A. 1970).

ᵫ

It is incumbent upon the Patent Office in the first instance to set forth clearly why it regards a claim to be anticipated, obvious or otherwise defective. The pertinence of each reference, if not apparent, must be clearly explained. *In re Mullin, Wetherby, and Chevalier*, 481 F.2d 1333, 179 U.S.P.Q. 97, 100 (C.C.P.A. 1973).

ᚤ

Claims had been withdrawn from further consideration on the ground that they included multiple "patentably distinct" inventions. The claims were withdrawn from consideration not only in the subject application but prospectively in any subsequent application, because of their content. Presumably only by dividing the subject matter into separate, and thus different, claims in plural applications could an examination of the patentability of their subject matter be obtained. In effect there had been a denial of patentability of the claims. The absolute "withdrawal" cannot properly be categorized as merely a "requirement" or "objection" to restrict review to petition. An Examiner's action of this nature is a rejection, a denial of substantive rights. *In re Haas,* 486 F.2d 1053, 179 U.S.P.Q. 623, 624, 625 (C.C.P.A. 1973).

ᚤ

The Examiner's demands, under threat of abandonment, that petitioners do more than they did amounted to a de facto rejection of petitioners' claims. *Margolis, Rushmore, Liu, and Anderson v. Banner*, 599 F.2d 435, 202 U.S.P.Q. 365, 372 (C.C.P.A. 1979).

ᚤ

Preponderance of the evidence is the standard that must be met by the PTO in making rejections (other than for "fraud" or "violation of the duty of disclosure" which requires clear and convincing evidence). In appeals from PTO rejections, the Federal Circuit reviews PTO findings under the clearly erroneous standard, under which PTO findings are overturned only if the court is left with the definite and firm conviction that a mistake has been made. *In re Caveney and Moody*, 761 F.2d 671, 226 U.S.P.Q. 1, 3 (Fed. Cir. 1985).

ᚤ

A question of the correctness of an Examiner's rejection is "properly addressed on direct appeal from the denial of the patent, and will not be revisited in a infringement action." *University of California v. Eli Lilly and Co.*, 119 F.3d 1559, 43 U.S.P.Q.2d 1398, 1409 n.6 (Fed. Cir. 1997).

ᚤ

When an applicant disagrees with an Examiner's prior art rejection and fails to prevail by argument, he has two choices: either to amend the claim or to appeal the rejection. He may not both make the amendment and then challenge its necessity in a subsequent infringement action on the allowed claim. *Bai v. L&L Wings Inc.*, 48 U.S.P.Q.2d 1674, 1678 (Fed. Cir. 1998)

Relationship. *See also* **Analog, Drug, Empirical, Homology, Isomer, Optical Isomer, Structural Obviousness, Structural Similarity, Substituents.**

In view of a considerable degree of unpredictability in the insecticide field, wherein homologs, isomers and analogs of known insecticides have been found to be ineffective as insecticides, a rejection of a claim (including homologs and isomers of reference compounds) was reversed. *In re Schechter and LaForge*, 205 F.2d 185, 98 U.S.P.Q. 144, 150 (C.C.P.A. 1953).

ᚳ

A single variance in the properties of new chemical compounds does not necessarily tip the balance in favor of patentability where otherwise closely related chemical compounds are involved. [The claimed invention provided a single dyestuff that would dye either wool or cellulose. There was no teaching of such a dye in anything of record except appellants' own disclosure.—*dissent*] *In re de Montmollin and Riat*, 344 F.2d 976, 145 U.S.P.Q. 416, 417, 418 (C.C.P.A. 1965).

ᚳ

Inasmuch as the claimed and reference compounds possess a close structural relationship and have a specific, significant property in common, the additional antimicrobial activity (discovered by appellants for the claimed compounds) was not regarded as sufficient ground to hold that the subject matter as a whole was unobvious. *In re Mod, Skau, Fore, Magne, Novak, Dupuy, Ortego, and Fisher*, 408 F.2d 1055, 161 U.S.P.Q. 281, 283 (C.C.P.A. 1969).

ᚳ

A terminal disclaimer obviates a double-patenting rejection of generic claims (based on a commonly-assigned patent claiming a species within that genus), notwithstanding wholly different inventive entities. *In re Frilette and Weise*, 412 F.2d 269, 162 U.S.P.Q. 163, 169 (C.C.P.A. 1969).

ᚳ

To give meaning to the language of 35 U.S.C. §103, which speaks to the subject matter "as a whole," weight must be given to the properties of a compound or composition of matter. There is one very crucial distinction between *Mod* and *De Montmollin* on the one hand and the present case on the other. The fact here is that the prior art is not only silent on the matter of weld line toughness, but appellant has proved that the closest blends disclosed in the prior art possess inferior weld line toughness. *In re Murch*, 464 F.2d 1051, 175 U.S.P.Q. 89, 92 (C.C.P.A. 1972).

ᚳ

As distinguished from a disclosure of equivalents, the disclosure of a known relationship does nothing more than teach that it would have been obvious to try, which is insufficient under 35 U.S.C. §103. *In re Mercier*, 515 F.2d 1161, 185 U.S.P.Q. 774 (C.C.P.A. 1975).

ᚳ

Preponderance of the evidence is the standard that must be met by the PTO in making rejections (other than for "fraud" or "violation of the duty of disclosure" which requires clear and convincing evidence). In appeals from PTO rejections, the Federal Circuit reviews PTO findings under the clearly erroneous standard, under which PTO findings are overturned only if the court is left with the definite and firm conviction that a mistake has been made. *In re Caveney and Moody*, 761 F.2d 671, 226 U.S.P.Q. 1, 3 (Fed. Cir. 1985).

Relatively.

The use of the term "relatively" does not automatically render the patent claim invalid. The issue in this case is whether the question "relative to what" can be answered. *Allergan Sales Inc. v. Pharmacia & Upjohn Inc.*, 42 U.S.P.Q.2d 1560, 1563 (Cal. 1997).

Relative Term. *See also* Degree, Small, Substantial, Superior.

The dependence of the claims on the indefinite and indeterminate difference between the coarse and fine particles (purely relative terms) renders the claims indefinite in the absence of a clear explanation in the specification of such difference. *In re Eiane*, 189 F.2d 1004, 90 U.S.P.Q. 87, 88 (C.C.P.A. 1951).

ω

The terms, "slightly soluble" and "practically insoluble," are used in literature to connote totally different degrees of solubility. The court found no generally accepted or textbook use of the term, "partially soluble." *Standard Oil Company v. American Cyanamid Company*, 585 F.Supp. 1481, 224 U.S.P.Q. 210, 217 (La. 1984).

Release.

A release by a patentee for past infringement by a stranger generally operates to discharge any claims by an exclusive licensee as to such infringement. *Biosyntec Inc. v. Baxter Health Care Corp.*, 746 F. Supp. 5, 17 U.S.P.Q.2d 1221, 1225 (Or. 1990).

Relevant Art. *See also* Analogous Art.

The relevant art "is defined by the nature of the problem confronting the would-be inventor." *Ryko Manufacturing Co. v. Nu-Star Inc.*, 950 F.2d 714, 21 U.S.P.Q.2d 1053, 1055 (Fed. Cir. 1991).

ω

In deciding whether a reference is from a relevant art, the CAFC must first determine whether the reference is within the inventor's field of endeavor, and if it is not it next must determine whether the reference is reasonably pertinent to the particular problem confronting the inventor. "A reference is reasonably pertinent if, even though it may be in a different field of endeavor, it is one which, because of the matter with which it deals, logically would have commended itself to an inventor's attention in considering his problem." *In re GPAC Inc.*, 57 F.3d 1573, 35 U.S.P.Q.2d 1116, 1120 (Fed. Cir. 1995).

Reliance.

Equitable estoppel bars claims for patent infringement if Mainland committed itself to act, and acted as a direct consequence of the conduct of Standal's Patents. Estoppel to assert patent rights requires (a) unreasonable and inexcusable delay, (b) prejudice to the defendant, (c) affirmative conduct by patentee's inducing belief of abandonment of claims against the alleged infringer, and (d) detrimental reliance by the infringer. Estoppel by implied license cannot arise out of unilateral expectations or even reasonable hopes of one party. Five years silence alone is not enough to give rise to estoppel. *Mainland Industries, Inc. v. Standal's Patents Ltd.*, 799 F.2d 746, 230 U.S.P.Q. 772 (Fed. Cir. 1986).

ᛟ

A Court may not, under the guise of applying the doctrine of equivalence, erase a plethora of meaningful structural and functional limitations of a patent claim on which the public is entitled to rely in avoiding infringements. *Perkin-Elmer v. Westinghouse*, 822 F.2d 1528, 3 U.S.P.Q.2d 1321 (Fed. Cir. 1987).

Relief. *See* **Remedial Statute.**

Relitigating Invalidity. *See also* **Blonder-Tongue Doctrine.**

The appellate treatment by the federal circuit of ITC determinations as to patent validity or as to patent invalidity does not estop other tribunals from considering anew the question of patent validity. *In re Convertible Rowing Exerciser Patent Litigation*, 721 F. Supp. 596, 12 U.S.P.Q.2d 1275, 1280 (Del. 1989).

Remainder.

"Adverbs of time—as where, there, after, from, &c.—in a devise of a remainder, are construed to relate merely to the time of the enjoyment of the estate, and not the time of the vesting in interest." *Heidelberg Harris Inc. v. Loebach*, 145 F.3d 1454, 46 U.S.P.Q.2d 1948, 1951 (Fed. Cir. 1998).

Remand (Grounds for).

Appellant became aware of a patent issued to a third party after his appeal to the CCPA. His motion to remand (for the purpose of initiating an interference with the patent) was filed at the Court within a month after his appeal was formally docketed. *In re Fischer*, 360 F.2d 230, 149 U.S.P.Q. 631, 633 (C.C.P.A. 1966).

ᛟ

The Board of Patent Interferences refused to consider a motion by the winning party to "cancel" from the interference the counts (now regarded as unpatentable over a reference) on which priority was awarded and to substitute a new count because the losing party had, in the meantime, appealed to the CCPA, thus taking the matter out of the Board's jurisdiction. The Court granted the losing interference party's motion to remand. *Loshbough v. Allen*, 359 F.2d 910, 149 U.S.P.Q. 633, 635 (C.C.P.A. 1966).

ᛟ

A motion to remand to the Patent Office Board of Interferences by a plaintiff in an action under 35 U.S.C. §146 was granted for reconsideration in the light of a subsequent and contrary decision in another interference. *Hercules Incorporated v. Union Carbide Corporation*, 168 U.S.P.Q. 394, 395 (D.C. 1971).

ᛟ

After the appellant's brief was filed at the CCPA, the Commissioner's motion to remand was granted for the purpose of adding a further ground of rejection to a rejected claim and applying a new ground of rejection to a previously allowed claim. The CCPA passes only on rejections actually made and does not decree the issuance of patents. After a decision in an ex parte patent case, the PTO can always reopen prosecution and cite new references. By granting the motion to remand, judicial economy was preserved. *In re Gould*, 673 F.2d 1385, 213 U.S.P.Q. 628 (C.C.P.A. 1982).

ϖ

The district court improperly determined that the subject matter claimed in the '814 patent was obvious: it failed to make the Graham inquiries, it improperly focused on what was obvious to the inventor, it engaged in hindsight analysis, and it considered evidence that was not prior art. *Bausch & Lomb, Inc. v. Barnes-Hind/Hydrocurve, Inc.*, 796 F.2d 443, 230 U.S.P.Q. 416 (Fed. Cir. 1986).

ϖ

A remand, with its accompanying expenditure of additional judicial resources in a case thought to be completed, is a step not lightly taken and one that should be limited to cases in which further action must be taken by the district court [and] in which the appellate court has no way open to it to affirm or reverse the district court's action under review. *Molins PLC v. Textron Inc.*, 48 F.3d 1172, 33 U.S.P.Q.2d 1823, 1838 (Fed. Cir. 1995).

ϖ

An appeal court judgment that does not specifically provide for a remand is not necessarily incompatible with further proceedings to be undertaken in the district court. *Exxon Chemical Patents Inc. v. Lubrizol Corp.*, 137 F.3d 1475, 45 U.S.P.Q.2d 1865, 1872 (Fed. Cir. 1998).

Remedial Statute.

The reissue statute is based on fundamental principles of equity and fairness and, as a remedial provision, is intended to bail applicants out of difficult situations into which they get "without any deceptive intention." It should be liberally construed so as to carry out its purpose to the end that justice may be done to both patentees and the public. *In re Oda, Fujii, Moriga, and Higaki*, 443 F.2d 1200, 170 U.S.P.Q. 268, 270 (C.C.P.A. 1971).

ϖ

Lack of antecedent basis in a claim could render it invalid under 35 U.S.C. §112, second paragraph, and correction of such a defect by reissue should not have to depend on difference in scope of the claim. Inasmuch as 35 U.S.C. §251 is a remedial provision, which should be liberally construed, a patentee should be allowed to correct an error or ambiguity in a claim without having to rely on the implication of litigation. Lack of antecedent basis in a claim is a proper ground for reissue under §251. *In re Altenpohl*, 500 F.2d 1151, 183 U.S.P.Q. 38 (C.C.P.A. 1974).

ϖ

This appeal is from a decision of the PTO Board of Appeals rejecting claims of a Reissue Application on the ground that a broadening Reissue Application that was filed within two years of the patent issue date (but was erroneously filed by the assignee) could not be corrected by a Declaration of the inventor filed more than two years after the patent issue date. The CAFC reversed. Recognizing that all of the provisions of a unified statute must be read in harmony, the portion of 35 U.S.C. §251 that requires that a broadening Reissue Application must be signed by the inventor does not mean that an error in compliance with §251 is insulated from the remedial ruling of *Stoddard* [564 F.2d 556, 195 U.S.P.Q. 97 (D.C. Cir. 1977)] or the statutory provision for the correction of error. The purpose of the reissue statute is to remedy errors. Reissue is remedial in nature and is based on fundamental principles of equity and fairness. These fundamental principles must not be forgotten in implementation of the statute. *In re Bennett*, 766 F.2d 524, 226 U.S.P.Q. 413 (Fed. Cir. 1985).

ᚳ

The statute governing conversion (35 U.S.C. §116, third paragraph) is remedial in nature and must be liberally construed. This is especially true in view of the intervening statutory expansion in the definition of joint inventorship. Furthermore, for a party to convert, the fact of joint inventorship need not be conclusively proved. Conversely, it stands to reason, that a party (opposing conversion) in an interference bears the burden of going forward with the evidence once a *prima facie* case of joint inventorship has been established. *Chai v. Frame,* 10 U.S.P.Q.2d 1460 (B.P.A.I. 1988).

Reopen Prosecution.

A challenge to a Board's judicial notice of a fact must contain adequate information or argument (so that on its face it creates a reasonable doubt regarding the circumstances justifying the judicial notice) to warrant reopening of the prosecution so that the applicant can respond. *In re Boon*, 439 F.2d 724, 169 U.S.P.Q. 231, 234 (C.C.P.A. 1971).

Repair. *See also* Reconstruction, Replacement.

Generally, the purchaser of a patented invention, lawfully sold, enjoys the right to have it repaired to prolong its useful life, so long as the "repair" is not tantamount to a full "reconstruction" of the invention. *Aro Manufacturing Co. v. Convertible Top Replacement Co.,* 365 U.S. 336, 346, 128 U.S.P.Q. 354 (1961).

ᚳ

When a patented structure is unlicensed, the traditional rule is that even repair constitutes infringement. *Malinckrodt Inc. v. Medipart Inc.*, 976 F.2d 700, 24 U.S.P.Q.2d 1173, 1180 (Fed. Cir. 1992).

ᚳ

Once a patentee has been compensated for infringement by money damages, the infringer has the right to repair, but not reconstruct, the infringing device. *FMC Corp. v. Up-Right, Inc.*, 21 F.3d 1073, 1076-77, 30 U.S.P.Q.2d 1361, 1363-64 (Fed. Cir. 1994).

ᚳ

In many instances, it is rather difficult to draw a line of distinction between *permissible repair* and *non-permissible reconstruction*. The distinction between repair and reconstruction, while clearly defined at the extreme ends, presents a problem of factual determination at the boundary where legitimate repair ends and illegitimate repair begins. Repair may be said to be the restoration to a sound, good or complete state after decay, injury, dilapidation, deterioration, wear or partial destruction. Reconstruction is the act of rebuilding. While absolute definitions serve to point out that, on the one hand, *repair implies correction* which may be due to the temporary nature of a machine, article or the like, and *reconstruction implies a creation* of a new life or capacity, in the final analysis each case must be decided on its own factual situation. It is impractical, as well as unwise, to attempt to lay down any rigid rule on this subject owing to the number and infinite variety of patented inventions. Each case, as it arises, must be decided in light of all the facts and circumstances as presented and with an intelligent comprehension of the scope, nature, and purpose of the patented invention and the fair and reasonable intention of the parties. Having clearly in mind the specification and claims of the patent, together with the condition of decay, destruction, etc., of the patented machine, article, or the like, the question whether its restoration to a sound state was legitimate repair, or substantial reproduction of the patented invention, should be determined less by technical definitions and technical rules than by the exercise of sound common sense and intelligent judgment. 6 Ernest B. Lipscomb III, *Lipscomb's Walker on Patents* 22.9, 438-39 (3d ed. 1984). *Wahpeton Canvas Co. South Dakota Inc. v. Bremer*, 893 F.Supp. 863, 35 U.S.P.Q.2d 1001, 1005 n.8 (Iowa 1995).

ℼ

"Where use infringes, repair does also, for it perpetuates the infringing use." "[A] patented article may be repaired without making the repairer an infringer[]...where the device in patented form has come lawfully into the hands of the person for whom it is repaired." *Fonar Corp. v. General Electric Co.*, 41 U.S.P.Q.2d 1088 (N.Y. 1995).

Replacement. *See also* Reconstruction, Repair.

When replacement of essential parts of a patented device is designed to change and in fact does change the capacity or effectiveness of the patented entity, the result is not only a new, but a different, article, embodying the unique patented combination, but not made by the patentee to whom, alone, is reserved the right to make articles embodying the patented combination. *Kuther v. Leuschner*, 200 F.Supp. 841, 131 U.S.P.Q. 463, 465 (Cal. 1961).

ℼ

Where a patentee has explicitly authorized purchasers of a patented product to use the product, he cannot thereafter restrict that use by imposing a condition that replacement parts may be purchased only from a licensed supplier. *Aro Manufacturing Co., Inc. v. Convertible Top Replacement Co., Inc.*, 377 U.S. 476, 141 U.S.P.Q. 681, 690 (1964).

ℼ

As an authorized user of a product who purchases one of defendant's replacement parts would not directly infringe the patent, defendant's manufacture and sale does not constitute contributory or induced infringement. *Biuro Projektow Zaklodow Przerobki Mechanicznej Wegla "Separator" v. UOP, Inc.*, 203 U.S.P.Q. 175, 179 (Ill. 1979).

ℼ

A license to use a patented combination includes the right "to preserve its fitness for use so far as it may be affected by wear and breakage." A licensed user may replace any element no matter "how essential it may be to the patented combination" as long as the replaced element is not itself separately claimed. Replacement of a worn part in a patented combination is repair rather than reconstruction. *Porter v. Farmers Supply Service*, 790 F.2d 882, 229 U.S.P.Q. 814 (Fed. Cir. 1986).

Reporting.

As neither the power to hear nor the power to repeat what is heard is patentable, combining these faculties in a reporting method which included recording and transcribing was held to be outside the purview of the patent statute. *In re Holmes*, 37 F.2d 440, 4 U.S.P.Q. 179 (C.C.P.A. 1930).

Repose.

The decision of a transferor court should not be reviewed again by the transferee court. Such an independent review would implicate those concerns which underlie the rule of repose and decisional order we term the law of the case. "If the motion to transfer is granted and the case is transferred to another district, the transferee-district should acccept the ruling on the transfer as the law of the case and should not re-transfer 'except under the most compelling and unusual circumstances' or if the transfer order is 'manifestly erroneous.'" *KPR Inc. v. C&F Packing Co. Inc.*, 30 U.S.P.Q.2d 1320, 1324 (Tex. 1993).

Representation. *See also* Misrepresentation.

Where the plaintiff was induced to accept the terms of a compromise settlement offer by representations that the litigation and its consequential legal expenses would be at an end, defendant's almost immediate collateral attack upon the subsequent consent judgment was sufficient bad faith conduct to warrant treatment as an "exceptional case" under the statute. *Research Corporation v. Pfister Associated Growers, Inc.*, 318 F.Supp. 1405, 168 U.S.P.Q. 206, 207, 208 (Ill. 1970).

ω

A patentee's inability to find willing counsel is widely rejected as a legally cognizable reason to excuse an unreasonable delay in filing suit. *Hall v. Aqua Queen Manufacturing Inc.*, 93 F.3d 1548, 39 U.S.P.Q.2d 1925, 1929 (Fed. Cir. 1996).

Representative Claim. *See also* 37 C.F.R. §1.192(c)(5).

Where parties to patent infringement litigation stipulate to "representative" claims, a validity resolution for the representative claims applies to other claims as well. *Miles Laboratories Inc. v. Shandon Inc.*, 997 F.2d 870, 27 U.S.P.Q.2d 1123, 1129 (Fed. Cir. 1993).

Repudiation.

A finding of patent invalidity does not relieve a licensee of its obligation to pay royalties for the period during which it was enjoying the benefit of its license and representing to the public that its product was licensed under the patent. Once it ceased to represent that its product was licensed under the patent, defendant had repudiated the license agreement and assumed the risk of being found liable for infringing without receiving the concomitant commercial benefit of being a licensee. *Kraly v. National Distillers and Chemical Corporation*, 177 U.S.P.Q. 364, 370 (Ill. 1973).

ᗡ

A licensee is relieved of his obligation to pay royalties the moment he effectively repudiates the license agreement. *Bahamas Paper Company, Limited v. Imperial Packaging Corporation*, 58 F.R.D. 355, 177 U.S.P.Q. 440, 442 (N.Y. 1973).

Repugnant.

The fact that all of the claimed compounds share a common cinnamonitrile group and have the capability to dye polyester fibers suggests that it would not be repugnant to scientific classification to associate them together as a genus. *Ex parte Brouard, Leroy, and Stiot*, 201 U.S.P.Q. 538, 540 (PTO Bd. App. 1976).

ᗡ

As all of the claimed compounds are dyes and are coumarin ("a single structural similarity") compounds, they all belong to a subgenus which is not repugnant to scientific classification. There is the requisite unity of invention. *In re Harnisch*, 631 F.2d 716, 206 U.S.P.Q. 300, 305 (C.C.P.A. 1980).

Repugnant to Scientific Classification. *See* Classification, Repugnant.

Request for Reexamination.

MPEP §2240 and §2244, which require the PTO to resolve doubts in the direction of granting a request for reexamination, are contrary to the statutory mandate of 35 U.S.C. §303, and void. *Patlex Corp. v. Mossinghoff*, 771 F.2d 480, 226 U.S.P.Q. 985 (Fed. Cir. 1985).

Request to Admit.

Any ambiguity in a request to admit is construed against the drafter. *Ortho Diagnostic Systems Inc. v. Miles Inc.*, 865 F.Supp. 1073, 35 U.S.P.Q.2d 1263, 1267 (N.Y. 1994).

Requestor. *See also* Reexamination Requestor's Standing on Appeal.

The identity of the requestor in a reexamination proceeding is subject to protection under 35 U.S.C. §301 and §302. *Parker Hanifin Corp. v. Davco Manufacturing Corp.*, 128 F.R.D. 91, 13 U.S.P.Q.2d 1412, 1413 (Ohio 1989).

Research.

Work done by a contractor's employees in embodying an invention into a commercial device is not the type of "research" contemplated by section 11(a)(3) of the Atomic

Energy Act of 1946. *Hobbs v. United States*, 451 F.2d 849, 171 U.S.P.Q. 713, 728 (5th Cir. 1971).

Research Paper.

Copies of a paper, orally presented at a congress, were distributed on request, without any restrictions, to as many as six persons more than one year before the filing date of the application which matured into the subject patent. The paper was regarded as a printed publication. *Massachusetts Institute of Technology v. AB Fortia*, 774 F.2d 1104, 227 U.S.P.Q. 428, 432 (Fed. Cir. 1985).

Reside. *See also* Venue.

Change of language in 28 U.S.C. §1391(c) apparently modifies significantly 28 U.S.C. §1400(b). The revised §1391(c) plainly indicates that the definition of "reside" contained therein is to be applied across the board to all the venue provisions found in Chapter 87 of Title 28, United States Code. Accordingly, for the purposes of §1400(b), "resides" is defined as "any judicial district in which [a defendant or corporation in a patent infringement suit] is subject to personal jurisdiction at the time the action is commenced." *Century Wrecker Corp. v. Vulcan Equipment Co. Ltd.*, 733 F. Supp. 1170, 13 U.S.P.Q.2d 1715, 1717 (Tenn. 1989).

ω

Under 28 U.S.C. §1400(b), venue in a patent case is proper where the defendant "resides". Under 28 U.S.C. §139(c), a corporate defendant resides where it is subject to personal jurisdiction. *VE Holding Corp. v. Johnson Gas Appliance Co.*, 917 F.2d 1574, 1578, 1584, 16 U.S.P.Q.2d 1614, 1617, 1621 (Fed. Cir. 1990), *cert. denied*, 111 S.Ct. 1315 (1991).

Residue

As azo dyes are well known, the expression "an organic azo dyestuff residue" is not unduly broad in the definition of a claimed dyestuff when the structure of the azo component is not critical. *In re Riat, DeMontmollin, and Koller*, 327 F.2d 685, 140 U.S.P.Q. 471, 472, 473 (C.C.P.A. 1964).

Res Judicata. *See also* Preclusion.

After the CCPA reverses a rejection of a patent application, the PTO may still deny the application on the basis of additional prior art not previously relied upon. The decision of the CCPA does not operate as a mandate to issue a patent. Its effect is simply to remand the case for further proceedings by the PTO not inconsistent with the court's decision. The court's decision is not a judgment; it carries no mandate to issue the patent. It is simply an instruction, which the Commissioner must follow, regarding the particular points involved in the appeal. The fact that the public has a substantial interest in the granting of every patent is a further reason why *res judicata* should not apply to the subject circumstances. *The Jeffrey Manufacturing Company v. Kingsland, Commissioner of Patents,* 179 F.2d 35, 83 U.S.P.Q. 494, 495 (D.C. Cir. 1949).

ω

A patentee moved to dissolve an interference on the ground that his patent claims had not been copied by applicant prior to one year from the date on which his patent was granted. The Examiner's decision to deny the motion was reversed by the Commissioner, on petition. The interference was dissolved, and the applicant subsequently canceled the claims corresponding to the interference counts. The applicant subsequently urged that he had timely copied the claims in order to overcome the patent as a reference in ex parte prosecution. The applicant was required to reassert the patent claims, and the interference was reinstated. The Commissioner decided (on petition) that the applicant was bound by the Commissioner's prior decision, from which no appeal was taken. From the applicant's cancellation of claims and failure to appeal, it was concluded that applicant had acquiesced in the prior decision, and applicant was estopped, on the ground of *res judicata*, from raising the question of whether he had originally copied the patent claims in timely fashion. *Rubenstein v. Schmidt,* 145 U.S.P.Q. 613 (Comm'r Patents 1965).

ω

Even though the CCPA had previously affirmed the holding of the Board of Appeals with respect to the identical claims, the issues of patentability are different when the record before the PTO is different for a cip application, and *res judicata* thus does not apply. *In re Herr,* 377 F.2d 610, 153 U.S.P.Q. 548, 549 (C.C.P.A. 1967).

ω

An applicant has a right to file a continuation application (following an adverse Board of Appeals decision) within the time allowed for further appeal. He has the further right to have such continuation application examined. A holding of *res judicata* without reliance on any other ground of rejection is not an examination on the merits of the application and may not be used in such a situation. *In re Kaghan, Schmitt, and Kay,* 387 F.2d 398, 156 U.S.P.Q. 130, 132 (C.C.P.A. 1967).

ω

While *res judicata* has its proper place in the law as a reflection of a policy invoked to settle disputes and to put an end to litigation, prosecution of patent applications is not exactly either a dispute or litigation in the usual sense of these terms. There are additional public policy considerations that have a bearing: namely, furtherance of a policy inherent in the patent laws to grant patents when the PTO finds that patentable inventions have been disclosed and properly claimed so that such inventions are made public through the grant. The granting of such patents is also in the public interest in that it may stimulate the commercialization of the patented inventions, thus bringing them into actual use for the benefit of the public. Society stands to lose (if there is any validity at all to the theories underlying the patent system) when a patent is refused on an invention that is patentable under the statute. MPEP §706.03(w), MPEP §201.07, 35 U.S.C. §120 and Rule 197(c) establish the right of an applicant to file a continuation application following an adverse Board of Appeals decision within the time allowed for further appeal, and as to establishing his right to have that application examined. A holding of *res judicata* without reliance on any other ground of rejection is not an examination on the merits of the application and so may not be used in such a situation. *In re Craig and Street,* 411 F.2d 1333, 162 U.S.P.Q. 157, 159, 160 (C.C.P.A. 1969).

ω

The fact that a patent was allowed on applicant's original application does not mean that the question of sufficiency of disclosure has been determined in applicant's favor by the Patent Office and that a policy of res judicata bars a contrary holding during the prosecution of a Reissue Application. The statutory provision for reissue of patents, 35 U.S.C. §251, by its third paragraph, dictates that the provisions applicable to applications for patents, including 35 U.S.C. §112, are applicable to reissue applications as well. *In re Doyle,* 482 F.2d 1385, 179 U.S.P.Q. 227, 232 (C.C.P.A. 1973).

ω

In *In re Kaghan,* 387 F.2d 398, 156 U.S.P.Q. 130 (C.C.P.A. 1967), the Court of Customs and Patent Appeals concluded that the continuation procedure, as it then existed, estopped the Patent Office from asserting an unappealed Board of Appeals rejection of a parent application as having *res judicata* effect in proceedings on a duly filed continuation application. *The Plastic Contact Lense Company v. Gottschalk,* 484 F.2d 837, 179 U.S.P.Q. 262, 263 (D.C. Cir. 1973).

ω

Although consent judgments may, in rare cases, be denied *res judicata* effect, "judicial decrees disposing of issues cannot be treated as idle ceremonies without denigrating the judicial process." *Wallace Clarke & Co. v. Acheson Industries, Inc.,* 532 F.2d 846, 190 U.S.P.Q. 321 (2d Cir. 1976).

ω

In patent cases consent decrees entered in settlement of an infringement action are entitled to *res judicata* effect. *American Equipment Corp. v. Wikomi Manufacturing Co.,* 630 F.2d 544, 208 U.S.P.Q. 465 (7th Cir. 1980).

ω

Res judicata does not have its usual impact when considering ex parte patent appeals; the public interest in granting valid patents outweighs the public interest underlying collateral estoppel and res judicata, particularly where the issue presented is not substantially identical to that previously decided. *In re Oelrich and Divigard,* 666 F.2d 578, 212 U.S.P.Q. 323, 325, n.2 (C.C.P.A. 1981).

ω

The doctrines of *res judicata* and collateral estoppel have been developed to protect litigants from the expense and vexation attending multiple law suits and to conserve judicial resources. They are fully applicable to the patent area. *Shelcore, Inc. v. CBS, Inc.,* 220 U.S.P.Q. 459, 463 (N.J. 1983).

ω

The appellant was initially the senior party and subsequently the losing party in an interference in which the winning party prevailed on the basis of a Convention filing in a foreign country. The Board held that the appellant's claims were not patentably distinct from the subject matter defined by the counts lost in the interference. The issue here was not obviousness under 35 U.S.C. §103 or so-called interference estoppel. Rather, the Board relied on the more general principle of *res judicata* and collateral estoppel wherein a judgment previously rendered bars consideration of questions of fact or mixed questions of fact and law that were, or should have been, resolved in earlier litigation. An interference should settle all issues that are decided or that could have been decided. When an applicant loses an interference, the applicant is not entitled to a patent containing claims corresponding to the count or claims that are not patentably distinct from the count. *Ex parte Tytgat, Clerbois, and Noel,* 225 U.S.P.Q. 907 (PTO Bd. App. 1985).

ᚦ

The advancing of defenses subsequent to trial raises questions of waiver and *res judicata.* A defendant's decision not to raise a defense in the trial of a particular action is a waiver of that defense, which waiver is granted res judicata effect. *The Kilbarr Corp. v. Business Systems, Inc., B.V.,* 679 F. Supp. 422, 6 U.S.P.Q.2d 1698 (N.J. 1988).

ᚦ

A fundamental principle of common-law adjudication embodied in the related doctrines of *res judicata* and collateral estoppel is that a right, question or fact distinctly put in issue and directly determined by a court of competent jurisdiction cannot be disputed in a subsequent suit between the same parties. *In re Convertible Rowing Exerciser Patent Litigation,* 814 F.Supp. 1147, 26 U.S.P.Q.2d 1677, 1680 (Del. 1993).

ᚦ

An adverse holding by the CCPA with regard to claims in a parent application does not preclude the validity of similar claims of a patent issued on a continuation application. *Applied Materials Inc. v. Gemini Research Corp.,* 835 F.2d 279, 5 U.S.P.Q.2d 1127, 1129 (Fed. Cir. 1987).

ᚦ

While determinations of the ITC are given preclusive effect in cases not involving patent validity or invalidity, they have no such effect in patent cases. *Bio-Technology General Corp. v. Genentech Inc.,* 886 F.Supp. 377, 36 U.S.P.Q.2d 1169, 1175 (N.Y. 1995).

ᚦ

A district court must follow Federal Circuit precedent in a case arising under patent laws. However, the application of general res judicata principles is not a matter committed to the exclusive jurisdiction of the Federal Circuit. Therefore, the court followed Seventh Circuit precedent on the general law of res judicata, and concluded that the *res judicata* holding in *Foster v. Hallco Mfg. Co.* {947 F.2D 469, 475, 20 U.S.P.Q.2D 1241 (Fed. Cir. 1991)} is inapplicable to this case. *Williams v. The Gillette Co.,* 887 F.Supp. 181, 36 U.S.P.Q.2d 1374, 1375 n.2 (Ill. 1995).

ᚦ

A "point not in litigation in one action cannot be received as conclusively settled in any subsequent action upon a different cause, because it might have been determined in the first action." When applying *res judicata* to bar causes of action that were not before the court in the prior action, due process of law and the interest of justice require cautious restraint. Restraint is particularly warranted when the prior action was dismissed on procedural grounds. *Kearns v. General Motors Corp.*, 94 F.3d 1553, 39 U.S.P.Q.2d 1949, 1951 (Fed. Cir. 1996).

ᛜ

Res judicata does not bar claims that could not have been asserted in a prior action. *Turbocare Division of Demag Delaval Turbomachinery Corp. v. General Electric Co.*, 40 U.S.P.Q.2d 1795, 1797 (Mass. 1996).

Resolution of Doubt.

MPEP §2240 and §2244, which require the PTO to resolve doubts in the direction of granting a request for reexamination, are contrary to the statutory mandate of 35 U.S.C. §303, and void. *Patlex Corp. v. Mossinghoff,* 771 F.2d 480, 226 U.S.P.Q. 985 (Fed. Cir. 1985).

Restitution. *See also* Unjust Enrichment.

In general, civil law organizes and conceptualizes wrongs in terms of the harms they cause for the plaintiff rather than the benefits they generate for the defendant, seeking to remedy wrongs by compensating for injuries rather than requiring the wrongdoer to give up the benefits of his misdeed. The law of restitution, and in particular the principle of unjust enrichment, is an exception to this general rule. *University of Colorado Foundation Inc. v. American Cyanamid Co.*, 974 F.Supp. 1339, 44 U.S.P.Q.2d 1231, 1248 (Col. 1997).

Restoration. *See also* Reconstruction, Repair, Replacement.

"When the wearing or injury is partial, then repair is restoration, and not reconstruction. . . . [R]epairing partial injuries, whether they occur from accident or from wear and tear, is only refitting a machine for use. And it is no more than that, though it shall be a replacement of an essential part of a combination." *FMC Corp. v. Up-Right Inc.*, 21 F.3d 1073, 30 U.S.P.Q.2d 1361, 1364 (Fed. Cir. 1994).

ᛜ

Pre-June 8, 1995, patents are entitled to add on the restoration extension to a 20-year from filing term regardless of when such extension is granted except for those patents kept in force on June 8, 1995, only because of a restoration extension. Under this interpretation, all provisions of both URAA and Hatch-Waxman can reasonably be given effect. For pre-June 8, 1995, patents, a patentee would have full exclusionary rights for 17 years, followed by rights only to equitable remuneration (neither lost profits, an injunction, punitive damages, nor attorney fees) with respect to a certain class of infringers for the period from the end of the 17-year term to the end of the new 20-year term (the delta period), followed by entitlement to full exclusionary rights (but only with respect to the approved product) during the period of the restoration extension. *Merck & Co. v. Kessler*, 80 F.3d 1543, 38 U.S.P.Q.2d 1347, 1352, 1353 (Fed. Cir. 1996).

Restraint of Trade.

General Electric [272 U.S. 476, 488 (1926)] stands for the proposition that a patent holder does not violate the antitrust laws by seeking to dispose of his products directly to the consumer and fixing the price by which his agents transfer the title from him directly to the consumer. On the other hand, *General Electric* does not allow the patent holder to sell his product to a person and then control the resale price. Assuming that the contract in dispute was a contract of agency, whatever protection *General Electric* afforded, the contract ended when the patent expired. Since the contract was in effect subsequent to the expiration of the patent, the contract extended the life of the patent beyond the expiration date and constituted a contract in restraint of trade. *Agrashell, Inc. v. Hammons Products Co.*, 479 F.2d 269, 177 U.S.P.Q. 501, 507 (8th Cir. 1973).

ᙡ

Defendant's collection of a double royalty from plaintiff and from a customer constitutes an unreasonable restraint on competition. *PSC Inc. v. Symbol Technologies Inc.*, 48 U.S.P.Q.2d 1838, 1843 (N.Y. 1998).

Restraint on Use.

Patent licensee's "attempt to continue to exercise control over [the fill's] use or resale after the initial sale by Munters [was] a restraint outside the scope of the patent monopoly protection" afforded to Munters (licensee) on the fill. *Munters Corporation v. Burgess Industries Incorporated*, 201 U.S.P.Q. 756 (N.Y. 1978).

Restrict. *See* **Exclude, Limit, Restriction.**

Restriction.[6] *See also* **Classification, Consonance, Double Patenting, Election of Species, Field of Use, Geographic Limitation, Joinder of Invention, Narrowing Claim, One Invention, Quantity Limitation, Reduction in Scope, Reuse, Species, Statutory Class, Unity of Invention.**

The constitutional purpose of the patent system is promoted by encouraging applicants to claim, and therefore to describe in the manner required by 35 U.S.C. §112, all aspects of what they regard as their inventions, regardless of the number of statutory classes involved. Dependent claims to the use of a new composition in the same application with claims to the composition do not materially increase the scope of protection of an applicant's inchoate patent property under 35 U.S.C. §154, which already includes the right to exclude others from making, using, or selling the composition by allowance of claims thereon, but they do tend to increase the wealth of technical knowledge disclosed in the patent by encouraging description of the use aspects of the applicant's invention in the manner required by 35 U.S.C. §112, paragraph one. *In re Kuehl*, 475 F.2d 658, 177 U.S.P.Q. 250, 256 (C.C.P.A. 1973).

ᙡ

Whether a plurality of inventions had been claimed was not "settled" by a restriction requirement and the Commissioner's denial of a petition therefrom, the present appeal having in effect kept that issue alive. *In re Wolfrum and Gold*, 486 F.2d 588, 179 U.S.P.Q. 620, 622 (C.C.P.A. 1973).

ᙡ

---

[6] For applications prosecuted under the Patent Cooperation Treaty national phase, *see* C.F.R. §499.

Claims were withdrawn from consideration not only in the subject application, but also prospectively in any subsequent application. Because of their content, they were held to include multiple "patentably distinct" inventions. In effect, there had been a denial of patentability of the claims. Presumably, only by dividing the subject matter into separate, and thus different, claims in plural applications could an examination of the patentability of their subject matter be obtained. An Examiner's adverse action of this nature is a rejection, a denial of substantive rights. *In re Haas*, 486 F.2d 1053, 179 U.S.P.Q. 623, 624, 625 (C.C.P.A. 1973).

ᚥ

Section 121 [35 U.S.C.] provides the Commissioner with the authority to promulgate rules designed to restrict an application to one of several claimed inventions when those inventions are found to be "independent and distinct." It does not, however, provide a basis for an Examiner (acting under the authority of the Commissioner) to reject a particular claim on that same basis. *In re Weber, Soder, and Boksay*, 580 F.2d 455, 198 U.S.P.Q. 328, 331 (C.C.P.A. 1978).

ᚥ

The law treats a license under a patent as personal to the licensee, and non-assignable and non-transferable, as if it contained these restrictions, in the absence of express provisions to the contrary. *PPG Industries, Inc. v. Guardian Industries Corporation*, 597 F.2d 1090, 202 U.S.P.Q. 95, 98 (6th Cir. 1979).

ᚥ

Patent Cooperation Treaty Rule 13.1(ii) permits, in addition to an independent claim for a given process, the inclusion in the same international application of one independent claim for one apparatus or means specifically designed for carrying out the said process. The expression "specifically designed" clearly does not mean that the apparatus or means *"cannot be used to practice another materially different process,"* as indicated in 37 C.F.R. §1.141(b)(2). The emphasized portion of the PTO rule and its interpretation are contrary to the PCT and thus contrary to law. *Caterpillar Tractor Co. v. Commissioner of Patents and Trademarks*, 650 F. Supp. 218, 231 U.S.P.Q. 590 (Va. 1986).

ᚥ

With regard to double patenting, 35 U.S.C. §121 (1988) will not apply to remove the parent as a reference where the principle of consonance is violated. Consonance requires that the line of demarcation between the "independent and distinct inventions" that prompted the restriction requirement be maintained. Though the claims may be amended, they may not be so amended as to bring them back over the line imposed in the restriction requirement. Where that line is crossed, the prohibition of the third sentence of 35 U.S.C. §121 does not apply. The judicially created doctrine of double patenting of the obviousness-type applies when two applications or patents, not drawn to precisely the same invention, are "drawn to inventions so very much alike as to render one obvious in view of the other and to effectively extend the life of the patent that would have the earlier of the two issue dates." *Symbol Technologies Inc. v. Opticon Inc.*, 935 F.2d 1569, 19 U.S.P.Q.2d 1241, 1249 (Fed. Cir. 1991).

ᚥ

According to PTO policy, it is important from the standpoint of public interest that no restriction requirements be made which might result in the issuance of two patents for the same invention. The nullification of double patenting as a ground of rejection provided for in the third sentence of 35 U.S.C. 121 imposes a heavy burden on the Office to guard against erroneous requirements for restriction where the claims define essentially the same invention and which, if acquiesced in, might result in more than one patent for essentially the same invention with attendant prolongation of patent monopoly. *In re Gold*, 42 U.S.P.Q.2d 1095 (Comm'r of Patents 1996—*unpublished*).

Restriction (Compound/Composition).

Even though the MPEP provides some very specific requirements for restriction between claims to compounds and claims to compositions wherein the compounds comprise the essential component upon which patentability of the composition claims is predicated, the PTO was previously sustaining restriction requirements when the broadest composition claim was not of the same scope as the broadest claim to compounds. Such differences in scope were often brought about by having to limit a generic claim to compounds in view of the lack of novelty of several members, even though a broader composition claim had the requisite novelty. A Decision on Petition (dated October 11, 1985) directed the Examiner to withdraw a restriction requirement and to examine the respective claims on the merits after the applicant presented a composition claim of the same scope as that to which the generic compound claim was limited. The applicant pointed out that the compound defined by Claim 7 was of identical scope with that defined in composition Claim 20 and argued that restriction is not proper between a combination and an essential subcombination thereof unless two way distinctness is shown. (File of U.S.P. 4,616,020, Paper No. 18.)

Restrictive Amendment. *See* Description, Excluding Prior Art, Reduction in Scope.

Result. *See also* Circumstances, Inherency, Properties, Purpose, Summary Judgment Motion, Whole.

A patent may not properly be granted on the basis of a result which would flow naturally from the teachings of the prior art. *In re Hotchkin*, 223 F.2d 490, 106 U.S.P.Q. 267, 270 (C.C.P.A. 1955).

ϖ

There is no need for a claim to recite a result that inherently occurs through other claim limitations. The Board refused to consider the clarity of film and the degree of substitution obtained by appellant's process because the claims were not directed to a process yielding a film and did not recite the degree of substitution. There can be no doubt from the record that these advantages accrue from the claimed process, and they are not required to be recited in the claims. *In re Estes,* 420 F.2d 1397, 164 U.S.P.Q. 519, 521 (C.C.P.A. 1970).

ϖ

Result

Most patents are granted on an improvement of a prior device. The improved device inherently achieves the same basic result as that achieved, and performs the same basic function as that performed, by the prior device. To require in every case that a new "function" or new "result" be performed or achieved would be destructive of "the progress of...useful arts" goal sought in the constitutional-statutory scheme. *Nickola v. Peterson*, 580 F.2d 898, 198 U.S.P.Q. 385, 397 (6th Cir. 1978).

ϖ

The claims of the patent in suit define patentable, and unobvious inventions in that they accomplish a result which the prior art and defendants themselves said could not be done. *Reynolds Metals Company v. Aluminum Company of America*, 457 F.Supp. 482, 198 U.S.P.Q. 529, 553 (Ind. 1978).

ϖ

Casting an invention as "a combination of old elements" leads improperly to an analysis of the claimed invention by the parts, not by the whole. The critical inquiry is whether there is something in the prior art as a whole to suggest the desirability, and thus the obviousness, of making the combination. A traditional problem with focusing on a patent as a combination of old elements is the attendant notion that patentability is undeserving without some "synergistic" or "different" effect. Here, the district court spoke of the need for "a new and useful result." Such tests for patentability have been soundly rejected by this court. Though synergism is relevant when present, its "absence has no place in evaluating the evidence on obviousness." *Custom Accessories Inc. v. Jeffrey-Allan Industries, Inc.*, 807 F.2d 955, 1 U.S.P.Q.2d 1196 (Fed. Cir. 1986).

Results. *See also* Advantages.

Unexpected results relied upon for patentability need not be recited in the claims. *In re Merchant*, 575 F.2d 865, 197 U.S.P.Q. 785, 788 (C.C.P.A. 1978).

Resumed Activity.

In a priority contest, a party who was second to file was unable to prevail even though he had reduced the invention to practice four years prior to his opponent's filing date. Even if he demonstrated continuous activity from prior to his opponent's effective filing date to his filing date, such should have no bearing on the question of priority. While diligence during the above-noted period may be relied upon by one alleging prior conception and subsequent reduction to practice, it is of no significance in the case of the party who is not last to reduce to practice. Too long a delay may bar the first inventor from reliance on an early reduction to practice. However, the first inventor is not barred from relying on later resumed activity antedating an opponent's entry into the field merely because the work done before the delay occurred was sufficient to amount to a reduction to practice. *Paulik v. Rizkalla*, 760 F.2d 1270, 226 U.S.P.Q. 224 (Fed. Cir. 1985).

Retaining Lien.

Since a retaining lien never affects the rights of ownership (but only the right of possession), a retaining lien is an insufficient interest in a patent or application to warrant recordation. The retaining lien exists regardless of recordation and stays in place until discharged. An attorney's retaining lien cannot affect the title of the patent or invention to which it relates. Moreover, notice is not required to protect an attorney's retaining lien against assignment by the client or attachment by the client's creditors. *In re Refusal of Assignment Branch to Record Attorney's Lien*, 8 U.S.P.Q.2d 1446 (Comm'r Patents & Trademarks 1988).

Retreat. *See also* **Narrowing Claim.**

Appellants' evidence may not be disregarded simply because of the manner in which the now-claimed processes were denominated in the original application. To rule otherwise would substantially eliminate the right of an applicant to retreat to an otherwise patentable species merely because he erroneously thought he was first with the genus when he filed. The second paragraph of 35 U.S.C. §112 does not prohibit an applicant from changing what he "regards as his invention" during the pendency of his application. *In re Saunders and Gemeinhardt*, 444 F.2d 599, 170 U.S.P.Q. 213, 220 (C.C.P.A. 1971).

Retroactive License.

The uniform practice of the Patent Office has been to issue retroactive licenses (after the granting of patents) under 35 U.S.C. §184 where it has been satisfactorily shown that the filing abroad resulted from inadvertence and that diligence was exercised in discovering such inadvertence and applying for a retroactive license. *In re Rinker and Duva*, 145 U.S.P.Q. 156 (Comm'r 1964); *Engelhard Industries, Inc. v. Sel-Rex Corporation*, 145 U.S.P.Q. 319, 324 (N.J. 1965).

ω

The Patent Office does not have the power to issue a retroactive license to cure patents which were invalid upon issuance because of violations of 35 U.S.C. §184. *Minnesota Mining and Manufacturing Company v. Norton Company*, 240 F.Supp. 150, 145 U.S.P.Q. 81, 84 (Ohio 1965).

ω

The invention disclosed in the '695 patent being within the scope of 35 U.S.C. §181, the Commissioner of Patents was without authority, in view of the limitations specified in 35 U.S.C. §184, to grant a valid retroactive license. No valid retroactive license was or can be obtained, and the '695 patent is subject to the penalty of invalidity specified in 35 U.S.C. §185. *Iron Ore Company of Canada v. The Dow Chemical Company*, 177 U.S.P.Q. 34, 55 (Utah 1972).

ω

Having attempted to comply with the statutes by seeking a retroactive license, having been informed by the Patent Office that all the subject matter included in the application (on which the patent issued) had been properly licensed under the provisions of 35 U.S.C. §184 and there was no need for a retroactive license to issue, and having a petition for a retroactive license dismissed by the Patent Office, nothing further was required of defendant for compliance with 35 U.S.C. §§184 and 185. *Kelley Manufacturing Company v. Lilliston Corporation*, 180 U.S.P.Q. 364, 371 (N.C. 1973).

ω

USP 2,884,992 was granted on May 5, 1959, on an application filed on January 17, 1958. Through inadvertence a corresponding application was filed abroad prior to six months after the filing date without first obtaining a Patent Office license. A subsequent petition for a retroactive license was granted on December 19, 1973, retroactive to July 5, 1958. The foreign licensing requirement was complied with. The retroactive license was valid. The court refused to limit damages to the period after the date of the retroactive license. *Spound v. Mohasco Industries, Inc.*, 186 U.S.P.Q. 183, 187 (Mass. 1975).

ω

Because *In re Gaertner* [604 F.2d 1348, 1351, 1352, 202 U.S.P.Q. 714, 718, 719 (C.C.P.A. 1979)] holds that 35 U.S.C. §§184 and 185 must be strictly construed, pursuant to legislative history; because patentee's 14 year subsequent request for a retroactive license circumvents and frustrates the purpose of the law; and because the PTO did not grant a retroactive license nor determine that patentee's foreign filing was made through inadvertence; and because patentee's broader claims and broader specification filed prematurely abroad did contain new matter; 184 and 185 were violated. *Twin Disc, Inc. v. U.S.*, 10 Cl. Ct. 713, 231 U.S.P.Q. 417, 446 (U.S. Cl. Ct. 1986).

Retrospective Reconstruction. *See also* Claim Reconstruction, Combining References, Hindsight, Reconstruction.

To combine references (A) and (B) properly to reach the conclusion that the subject matter of a patent would have been obvious, case law requires that there must be some teaching, suggestion, or inference in either reference (A) or (B), or both, or knowledge generally available to one of ordinary skill in the relevant art, that would lead one skilled in the art to combine the relevant teachings of references (A) and (B). Consideration must be given to teachings in the references that would have led one skilled in the art away from the claimed invention. A claim cannot properly be used as a blueprint for extracting individual teachings from references. *Ashland Oil, Inc. v. Delta Resins & Refractories, Inc.*, 776 F.2d 281, 227 U.S.P.Q. 657 (Fed. Cir. 1985).

ω

Presuming arguendo that the references show the elements or concepts urged, the Examiner presented no line of reasoning as to why an artisan reviewing only the collective teachings of the references would have found it obvious to selectively pick and choose various elements and/or concepts from the several references relied on to arrive at the claimed invention. In the instant application, the Examiner has done little more than cite references to show that one or more elements or some combinations thereof, when each is viewed in a vacuum, is known. The claimed invention, however, is clearly directed to a combination of elements. That is to say, the appellant does not claim that he has invented one or more new elements but has presented claims to a new combination of elements. To support the conclusion that the claimed combination is directed to obvious subject matter, either the references must expressly or impliedly suggest the claimed combination or the Examiner must present a convincing line of reasoning as to why the artisan would have found the claimed invention to have been obvious in light of the teachings of the references. The Board found nothing in the references that would expressly or impliedly teach or suggest the modifications urged by the Examiner. Additionally, the Board found no line of reasoning in the answer as to why the artisan would have found the modifications urged by the Examiner to have been obvious. Based upon the record, the artisan would not have found it obvious to selectively pick and choose elements or concepts from the various references so as to arrive at the claimed invention without using the claims as a guide. *Ex parte Clapp,* 227 U.S.P.Q. 972 (B.P.A.I. 1985).

ϖ

When prior-art references require a selective combination to render obvious a subsequent invention, there must be some reason for the combination other than the hindsight gleaned from the invention itself. Something in the prior art as a whole must suggest the desirability, and thus the obviousness, of making the combination. It is impermissible to use the claims as a frame and the prior-art references as a mosaic to piece together a facsimile of the claimed invention. *Uniroyal Inc. v. Rudkin-Wiley Corp.,* 837 F.2d 1044, 5 U.S.P.Q.2d 1434 (Fed. Cir. 1988).

Return of Royalties.

Both parties bargained in good faith with the benefit of counsel in the well-founded belief that the invention was patentable and that the pending application would be granted in normal course. Both parties reasonably believed that the licensing agreement was valid under the then-existing state of the law. The applicant pursued his patent application with diligence, in good faith and at considerable expense. The licensee began manufacturing the claimed invention and continued to do so for more than five years, and paid royalties to the inventor (applicant) as provided in the agreement until May 31, 1965. Licensee was not bound to manufacture and sell the claimed product for any particular period of time, and could have terminated at any time without further obligation. It must therefore be assumed that the operation was profitable and that the licensee not only suffered no damages but received substantial benefits from its contract. If a patent issued, the licensee would receive even further benefits in the form of a valid license for the life of the patent. Under these circumstances, it would seem unconscionable to require the applicant to return the royalties to the licensee, thus permitting the licensee to "have its cake and eat it too." *Pollack v. Angelus Block Co.,* Inc., 171 U.S.P.Q. 182, 185 (Cal. S. Ct. 1971).

Reuse.

A restriction on reuse is not, as a matter of law, unenforceable under the patent law. If sale of a patented product is validly conditioned under applicable law, such as the law governing sales and licenses, and if the restriction on reuse is within the scope of the patent grant or otherwise justified, violation of the restriction may be remedied by action for patent infringement. *Mallinckrodt Inc. v. Medipart Inc.,* 976 F.2d 700, 24 U.S.P.Q.2d 1173, 1180 (Fed. Cir. 1992).

Revenue Act. *See* **Taxation.**

Reversal.

Absent changed circumstances or unforeseen issues not previously litigated, this Court cannot reverse itself unless the prior decision was clearly wrong. *Haworth Inc. v. Herman Miller Inc.*, 37 U.S.P.Q.2d 1094, 1095 (Mich. 1995).

Reversal of Parts. *See also* **Rearranging Parts.**

Mere reversal of parts or the relative movement of parts is an obvious expedient and not of patentable significance. *In re Gazda,* 219 F.2d 449, 104 U.S.P.Q. 400, 402 (C.C.P.A. 1955).

ω

Infringement is not avoided by a mere reversal or transposition of parts or components, or a mere change in form without a change in function. *Corning Glass Works v. Sumitomo Electric U.S.A. Inc.,* 671 F. Supp. 1369, 5 U.S.P.Q.2d 1545 (N.Y. 1987).

Reverse and Vacate.

If an appellate court reverses and vacates a judgment, the party which prevails on appeal is generally not bound by adverse trial court rulings on other issues. *Hydranautics v. FilmTec Corp.*, 70 F.3d 533, 36 U.S.P.Q.2d 1773, 1776 (9th Cir. 1995).

Reverse Doctrine of Equivalents.

Even where an "unambiguous" claim may literally read on an accused machine, there may nevertheless be no infringement if there is not real identity of means, operation and result. An incidental infringement is no infringement at all. *The Duplan Corporation v. Deering Milliken, Inc.,* 444 F.Supp. 648, 197 U.S.P.Q. 342, 410 (S.C. 1977).

ω

A court's election to ignore the structural claims, and to substitute a "gist" drawn from the operation of a disclosed embodiment, cannot convert the fact question raised by the reverse doctrine of equivalents into a legal question of claim construction. That question is simple and direct: Is the accused product so far changed in principle that it performs the function of the claimed invention in a substantially different way?

The law acknowledges that one may appropriate another's patented contribution not only with a product precisely described in a patent claim (literal infringement), but also with a product that is not quite so described but is in fact "substantially the same thing used in substantially the same way, to achieve substantially the same result" (doctrine of equivalents). The law also acknowledges that one may only appear to have appropriated the patented contribution when a product precisely described in a patent claim is in fact "so far changed in principle" that it performs in a "substantially different way" and is not therefore an appropriation (reverse doctrine of equivalents). One who takes a claim structure and merely uses it in a way that differs from that in which a specification-described embodiment uses it, does not thereby escape infringement. *SRI International v. Matsushita Electric Corp. of America,* 775 F.2d 1107, 227 U.S.P.Q. 577 (Fed. Cir. 1985).

ω

The so-called "reverse doctrine of equivalents" is an equitable doctrine invoked in applying properly construed claims to an accused device. Just as the purpose of the doctrine of equivalents is to prevent "pirating" of a patentee's invention, the purpose of the reverse doctrine is to prevent unwarranted extension of the claims beyond a fair scope of the patentee's invention. *Scripps Clinic & Research Foundation v. Genentech Inc.*, 927 F.2d 1565, 18 U.S.P.Q.2d 1001, 1013 (Fed. Cir. 1991).

Reverse Engineering.

Reverse engineering is that activity which "spurs innovation and technological progress, as competitors seek to develop even faster or more efficient chips, to perform similar or related functions". The statute does not reflect an intent to excuse copying, as a matter of law, if the copier had first tried and failed to do the job without copying. *Brooktree Corp. v. Advanced Micro Devices Inc.*, 977 F.2d 1555, 24 U.S.P.Q.2d 1401, 1411 (Fed. Cir. 1992).

Review. *See also* Plenary Review, Standard, Standard of Review.

The statute governing reexamination provides that a patent owner may appeal an adverse reexamination finding to the CAFC. 35 U.S.C. §306. However, the district court has no power to review a PTO finding favorable to the patent owner at the behest of a patent challenger. *E. I du Pont de Nemours & Co. v. Cetus Corp.*, 19 U.S.P.Q.2d 1174, 1181 (Cal. 1990).

Revival.

The discretionary action of the Commissioner in reviving an abandoned patent application is not subject to collateral attack in an interference proceeding. *Fryer v. Tachikawa*, 179 U.S.P.Q. 381, 382 (PO Bd. Pat. Intf. 1972).

ᵦ

The Commissioner of Patents has a large measure of discretion in determining whether to permit the revival of an abandoned patent application. Such discretion, however, is not wholly uncontrolled, plenary, or unreviewable by the courts. Moreover, such discretion appears to have been limited by the 1965 amendments to 35 U.S.C. §151, particularly with regard to the payment of issue fees to the Patent Office. *BEC Pressure Controls Corporation v. Dwyer Instruments, Inc.*, 380 F.Supp. 1397, 182 U.S.P.Q. 190, 191 (Ind. 1974).

ᵦ

Plaintiff-inventor is "bound by the acts" of his lawyer-agent since he voluntarily chose him as his representative and cannot avoid the consequences of his acts or omissions. *Smith v. Diamond*, 209 U.S.P.Q. 1091, 1093 (D.C. 1981).

ᵦ

The PTO has jurisdiction to revive most applications that become abandoned. However, that jurisdiction does not properly extend to all abandoned applications. Thus, where (1) there was an action that an applicant could have taken in connection with the application that became abandoned and that would have maintained pendency of that application, (2) that action could be taken in the PTO, and (3) the applicant failed to take that action in the PTO in a timely fashion, the Commissioner generally has jurisdiction to entertain a petition to revive under 35 U.S.C. §133 (unavoidable delay) and/or §41(a)7 (unintentional abandonment). However, where an application becomes abandoned or the "termination of proceedings" occurs because (A) of an action taken by another tribunal or (B) an applicant fails to take a required action in another tribunal to keep an application pending, it generally is not appropriate to consider a petition to revive under either 35 U.S.C. §133 or §41(a)7 based on the action or inaction. *In re Morganroth*, 6 U.S.P.Q.2d 1802 (Comm'r Patents & Trademarks 1988).

ᴡ

While a petition to revive a terminated reexamination proceeding on the ground of unavoidable delay is appropriately filed under 35 U.S.C. §133, filing such a petition under 37 C.F.R. §1.137(a) is inappropriate, because §1.137(a) is limited to revival of an "application" and a reexamination proceeding does not involve an application. Inasmuch as the unavoidable-delay standard is statutory rather than merely regulatory and because 37 C.F.R. §1.183 does not empower the Commissioner to waive statutory requirements, petitions under §1.183 concerning untimely responses in reexamination proceedings will be dismissed as inappropriate. *In re Katrapat, A.G.*, 6 U.S.P.Q.2d 1863 (Comm'r Patents & Trademarks 1988).

ᴡ

While a reasonable misinterpretation of a regulation may be the basis for a holding of unavoidable delay, misapplication or total ignorance of a rule may not. In order to be entitled to relief under 35 U.S.C. §305 and §133 on the ground of alleged docketing errors, petitioner must show (1) that counsel was justified in relying on the docketing system, i.e., that the docketing system was highly reliable, and (2) that the docketing errors were the cause of the belated response. *In re Egbers*, 6 U.S.P.Q.2d 1869 (Comm'r Patents & Trademarks 1988).

ᴡ

The Commissioner's denial of a petition to revive a patent application is subject to review in the district court. Whatever may be the scope of the Commissioner's discretion to deny a petition to revive a patent application, the existence of that discretion does not bar judicial review of the Commissioner's decision. The statutory provision and the Commissioner's regulations governing abandonment and revival deal with the abandonment of applications during the prosecution of those applications before the PTO. They do extend to an alleged abandonment resulting from a failure to appeal from a final district court judgment upholding the denial of a patent application. *Morganroth v. Quigg*, 885 F.2d 843, 12 U.S.P.Q.2d 1125, 1127, 1128 (Fed. Cir. 1989).

ᴡ

The Commissioner lacks authority to reopen the reexamination proceeding after receipt of the Federal Circuit's mandate affirming the Examiner's rejection of all claims since the case is no longer considered pending. See MPEP 1216.06 (5th ed., rev. 12, July 1989) under "Office Procedure Following Decision by the Federal Circuit," subheading "1. All claims rejected"; *Morganroth v. Quigg*, 885 F.2d 843, 12 U.S.P.Q.2d 1125, 1128

(Fed. Cir. 1989) (Commissioner does not have authority to revive application abandoned by termination of proceedings resulting from a failure to appeal a final district court judgment); *In re Jones,* 542 F.2d 65, 191 U.S.P.Q. 249, 252 (C.C.P.A. 1976) ("receipt of the mandate by the PTO terminated proceedings in the case"); *In re Willis,* 537 F.2d 513, 190 U.S.P.Q. 327, 329 (C.C.P.A. 1976) ("When, on January 12, 1976, our mandate was received in the PTO, no claims having been allowed, the appealed application suffered its demise."); *Continental Can Co. v. Schuyler,* 326 F. Supp. 283, 168 U.S.P.Q. 625 (D.C. 1970) ("where rejection of all claims is affirmed by the Court of Customs and Patent Appeals, the responsibility is upon the plaintiff to stay the Court's judgment if the pendency of the application is to be preserved"). Petitioner's relief, if any, lies in a motion for the Federal Circuit to withdraw its mandate, not with the Commissioner. *See Jones,* 542 F.2d at 68, 191 U.S.P.Q. at 252 (C.C.P.A. "has the power, in the interest of justice, to recall its mandate in an appropriate case, and this power should be exercised sparingly and only upon a showing of good cause"). *In re Eckerle,* 1115 O.G. 6 (Comm'r Patents & Trademarks 1990).

ω

A showing of unavoidable delay must embrace the period from the time of the action by the PTO (requiring a response by applicant) to the time both the response and a showing of unavoidable delay (acceptable to the Commissioner) are filed. The test that is most often applied in determining whether the delay of an attorney in seeking to revive an application from its abandoned status has been unavoidable (within the meaning of the patent statute) is whether the attorney has used such care and diligence as a prudent and careful person would have used under the circumstances. While the PTO does have a policy of requiring a terminal disclaimer in those situations where there has been a delay of more than six months in filing a petition to revive an application that has become abandoned [37 C.F.R. §1.316(d)], the terminal disclaimer has never been authorized or set forth in the rules as a substitute for a showing of unavoidable delay. Section 1.316(b) of 37 C.F.R. requires that a petition to accept late payment be filed promptly. *In re Application of Takao,* 17 U.S.P.Q.2d 1155, 1158, 1159, 1160 (Comm'r Patents & Trademarks 1990).

ω

The negligence of his attorney does not excuse applicant's duty to exercise due diligence. An applicant has the duty to make sure his application is being prosecuted. Applicant's lack of due diligence over a two and one-half year period overcame and superseded any negligence of his attorney. The delay was not unavoidable because, had applicant exercised the due care of a reasonably prudent person, he would have been able to act to correct the situation in a timely fashion. *Douglas v. Manbeck,* 21 U.S.P.Q.2d 1697, 1700 (Pa. 1991), *aff'd* 975 F.2d 869, 24 U.S.P.Q.2d 1318 (Fed. Cir. 1992).

Revocation.

The Patent Office has no power to revoke, cancel or annul a patent, because, once issued, the Patent Office loses jurisdiction over the patent. The United States may, in appropriate circumstances, bring a civil action to cancel a patent. *United States v. General Electric Co.,* 183 U.S.P.Q. 551, 552, 553 n.11 (Comm'r 1974).

ω

Revocation

Once a patent of invention has been granted, the Patent Office has no authority to invalidate the claims of the original patent in subsequent reissue proceedings. The PTO does not regain power over the original patent's validity when a reissue patent is applied for. When a patent has received the signature of the Secretary of the Interior, counter-signed by the Commissioner of Patents, and has had affixed to it the seal of the Patent Office, it has passed beyond the control and jurisdiction of that office, and is not subject to be revoked or canceled by the President, or any other officer of the Government. *National Business Systems, Inc. v. AM International, Inc.*, 546 F.Supp. 340, 217 U.S.P.Q. 235, 241 (Ill. 1982).

Ridicule.

The ridicule and skepticism (encountered by swimmers when they began wearing the Hart suit) are hallmarks of invention. *Hart v. Baarcke*, 396 F.Supp. 408, 186 U.S.P.Q. 275, 279 (Fla. 1975).

Right. *See also* Right to Exclude, Right to Refuse to Deal.

A fact, question or right distinctly adjudged in an original action cannot be disputed in a subsequent action even though the determination was rendered upon an erroneous view or an erroneous application of law. *In re Convertible Rowing Exerciser Patent Litigation*, 814 F.Supp. 497, 26 U.S.P.Q.2d 1677, 1686, 1687 (Del. 1993).

ω

Under United States patent law, a patent owner has no enforceable rights under a patent until the patent issues. *LifeScan Inc. v. Polymer Technology International Corp.*, 35 U.S.P.Q.2d 1225, 1227 (Wash. 1995).

Rights. *See also* Applicant's Rights, Assignment, Determination of Rights, Exclusive Rights, Intervening Rights, License, Patent Rights, *Quid Pro Quo*.

The interest of the public is in protecting patent rights, and the right of a patentee is in the exclusive use of his invention. Without the protection of the patent statute, the incentive to invent and to improve products would be curbed, and the public interest in such inventions would not be served. *The Conair Group Inc. v. Automatik Apparate-Maschinenbau GmbH*, 19 U.S.P.Q.2d 1535, 1540 (Pa. 1990).

ω

The act of invention itself vests an inventor with a common law or "natural" right to make, use, and sell his or her invention absent conflicting patent rights in others (and, in certain circumstances, may similarly vest such rights in an employer of the inventor). *Arachnid Inc. v. Merit Industries Inc.*, 939 F.2d 1574, 19 U.S.P.Q.2d 1513, 1516 (Fed. Cir. 1991).

ω

The law pertaining to trade dress infringement differs from that pertaining to patent infringement. Patent, trademark, and copyright rights all exist independently of one another, and the presence or absence of one does not automatically compel or preclude protection under another. *Tenax Corp. v. Tensar Corp.*, 19 U.S.P.Q.2d 1881, 1889 (Md. 1991).

ᙡ

The word "right" is one of the most deceptive pitfalls: it is so easy to slip from a qualified meaning in the premise to an unqualified one in the conclusion. Most rights are qualified. *DiscoVision Associates v. Disc Manufacturing Inc.*, 42 U.S.P.Q.2d 1749, 1756 (Del. 1997).

Right to Claim. *See* **Intent to Claim.**

Right to Exclude (35 U.S.C. §154). *See also* **Exclude, Exclusive Right.**

Only an owner of a patent may bring a civil action to enforce the exclusionary right that the patent grants. *Waterman v. Mackenzie*, 138 U.S. 252 (1891).

ᙡ

The nature of the patent grant weighs against holding that monetary damages will always suffice to make a patentee whole, for the principle value of the patent is its statutory right to exclude. *H. Robertson Co. v. United Steel Deck, Inc.*, 820 F.2d 384, 2 U.S.P.Q.2d 1926 (Fed. Cir. 1987).

ᙡ

In matters involving patent rights, irreparable harm is presumed when a clear showing is made of patent validity and infringement. This presumption derives in part from the finite form of the patent grant; for patent expiration is not suspended during litigation, and the passage of time can work irremediable harm. The opportunity to practice an invention during the notoriously lengthy course of patent litigation may itself tempt infringers. The nature of the patent grant thus weighs against holding that monetary damages will always suffice to make the patentee whole, for a principal value of a patent is its statutory right to exclude. The patent statute provides injunctive relief to preserve the legal interests of the parties against future infringement, which may have marked effects never fully compensable in money. If monetary relief were the sole relief afforded by the statute, injunctions would be unnecessary, and infringers could become compulsory licensees for as long as the litigation lasts. *We Care Inc. v. Ultra-Mark International Corp.* 14 U.S.P.Q.2d 1804, 1809 (Minn. 1989).

ᙡ

"[W]hile exclusionary conduct can include a monopolist's unilateral refusal to license a [patent or] copyright," or to sell its patented or copyrighted work, a monopolist's "desire to exclude others from its [protected] work is a presumptively valid business justification for any immediate harm to consumers." *Image Technical Services Inc. v. Eastman Kodak Co.*, 125 F.3d 1195, 44 U.S.P.Q.2d 1065, 1081 (9th Cir. 1997).

ᙡ

A compulsory license, which may arise from a refusal to enjoin, is fundamentally at odds with the right of exclusion built into our patent system. *Odetics Inc. v. Storage Technology Corp.*, 47 U.S.P.Q.2d 1573, 1585 (Va. 1998).

Right to Make.

It is at best confusing, and perhaps erroneous, to speak of a party's right to make the "count". The semantically appropriate statement of the inquiry is whether the party has the right to make that claim presently pending in his application which the Commissioner has determined to be both patentable and drawn to substantially the same invention as the patent claim. For an applicant to have a right to copy a patent claim, he must have support for the full scope of the claim. *Squires v. Corbett*, 560 F.2d 424, 194 U.S.P.Q. 513, 519, 520 (C.C.P.A. 1977).

ᗡ

The burden of proof on the right to make issue is on the party who had copied the claims. This burden is a heavy one regardless of whether the copier is a junior or senior party, and doubts must be resolved against the copier. *Holmes, Faber, Boykin, and Francis v. Kelly, Hornberger, and Strief*, 586 F.2d 234, 199 U.S.P.Q. 778, 781 (C.C.P.A. 1978).

ᗡ

A motion under 37 C.F.R. §1.633(a) for judgment on the ground that an opponent's claim corresponding to an interference count lacks written description support in its involved application is a departure from the practice under the old interference rules, wherein the burden as to a party's "right to make" a count was always on the copier of the claims. An interference can be declared under the new rules when an application includes, or is amended to include at least one patentable claim which is drawn to the same patentable invention as a claim of another's unexpired patent. *Behr v. Talbott*, 27 U.S.P.Q.2d 1401, 1405 (B.P.A.I. 1992).

Right to Refuse to Deal.

The right to refuse to deal is "neither absolute nor exempt from regulation" and when used "as a purposeful means of monopolizing interstate commerce", the exercise of that right violates the Sherman Act. *Image Technical Services Inc. v. Eastman Kodak Co.*, 125 F.3d 1195, 44 U.S.P.Q.2d 1065, 1075 (9th Cir. 1997).

Right to Sue.

A patentee may not give a right to sue to a party who has no proprietary interest in the patent. *Ortho Pharmaceutical Corp. v. Genetics Institute Inc.*, 52 F.3d 1026, 34 U.S.P.Q.2d 1444, 1450 (Fed. Cir. 1995).

Ring. *See also* **Benzyl.**

Failure of claims to specify the ring positions of substituents does not warrant a rejection on undue breadth when the disclosure shows that position is unimportant to the utility of claimed mixtures. A rejection on undue breadth must be based on a discrepancy between scope of disclosure and scope of claim. *In re Steinhauer and Valenta*, 410 F.2d 411, 161 U.S.P.Q. 595, 599 (C.C.P.A. 1969).

ᗡ

Rearranging substitution on a ring of a herbicidally-active compound by finding another herbicidally-active compound with the same ring and desired optional substituents is not enough to preclude patentability of a claimed herbicide. In the chemical arts the mere fact that it is possible to find two isolated disclosures that might be combined in such a way to produce a new compound does not necessarily render such production obvious unless the art also contains something to suggest the desirability of the proposed combination. In the absence of express or implied suggestion in at least one of the references that the specifically claimed substitution would be desirable for herbicide compounds other than those of the specific class disclosed in one reference, patentability is not precluded. The mere fact that both references originate from the herbicide art does not provide any teaching or suggestion to combine them. Nor does the fact that both references concern compounds containing a specific ring suggest that substituents suitable in one case would be expected to be suitable in the other. *In re Levitt,* 11 U.S.P.Q.2d 1315, 1316 (Fed. Cir. 1989).

Ripeness.

When reviewing a district court's conclusion that causes of action in a case are not ripe for adjudication, and therefore are beyond the Article III jurisdiction of the federal courts, the CAFC applies the law of the regional circuit in which the district court sits. However, in the context of a ripeness determination, "[t]he district court's factual findings on jurisdictional issues must be accepted unless clearly erroneous." A two-part test to determine whether a case is ripe for judicial action requires: First, whether the issues are fit for judicial action—that is, whether there is a present case or controversy between the parties; and second, whether there is sufficient risk of suffering immediate hardship to warrant prompt adjudication—that is, whether withholding judicial decision would work undue hardship on the parties. *Cedars-Sinai Medical Center v. Watkins*, 11 F.3d 1573, 29 U.S.P.Q.2d 1188, 1194 (Fed. Cir. 1993).

ω

Standing tells us who may bring an action, while ripeness determines when a proper party may bring an action. *Procter & Gamble Co. v. Paragon Trade Brands Inc.*, 917 F.Supp. 305, 38 U.S.P.Q.2d 1678, 1682 (Del. 1995).

Routine.

The criteria provided by 35 U.S.C. §103 do not include "a matter of routine determination capable of being performed by one of ordinary skill in the art" or even absence of any disclosure of criticality for parameters recited in claims. *In re Schirmer*, 480 F.2d 1342, 178 U.S.P.Q. 483, 484 (C.C.P.A. 1973).

ω

That which determines whether the mental formulation of an invention rises to the level of conception is whether or not the inventor has also conceived the means of putting that formulation in the hands of the public where no more than routine skill would be required to do so. The extent of testing or other research done after the mental formulation of an invention is not a reliable indicator of the adequacy of that which preceded it. *Rey-Bellet and Spiegelberg v. Engelhardt v. Schindler*, 493 F.2d 1380, 181 U.S.P.Q. 453, 457 (C.C.P.A. 1974).

Routine Experimentation. *See also* **Optimize, Undue Experimentation.**

Under some circumstances, changes in temperature, in concentration, or in both, may impart patentability to a process if the particular ranges claimed produce a new and unexpected result that is different in kind and not merely in degree from the results of the prior art. Such ranges are termed "critical" ranges, and the applicant has the burden of proving such criticality. Where the general conditions of a claim are disclosed in prior art, it is not inventive merely to discover the optimum or workable ranges by routine experimentation. *In re Aller, Lacey, and Hall,* 220 F.2d 454, 105 U.S.P.Q. 233, 235 (C.C.P.A. 1955).

ω

Although it is "not unobvious to discover operable or workable ranges by routine experimentation" in many instances, the problem with such "rules of patentability" (and the ever-lengthening list of exceptions which they engender) is that they tend to becloud the ultimate legal issue—obviousness—and exalt the formal exercise of squeezing new factual situations into preestablished pigeonholes. Additionally, the emphasis upon routine experimentation is contrary to the last sentence of 35 U.S.C. §103. *In re Yates,* 663 F.2d 1054, 211 U.S.P.Q. 1149, 1151 n.4 (C.C.P.A. 1981).

ω

The ultimate question is whether the specification contains a sufficiently explicit disclosure to enable one having ordinary skill in the relevant field to practice the invention claimed therein without the exercise of undue experimentation. The determination of what constitutes undue experimentation in a given case requires the application of a standard of reasonableness, having due regard for the nature of the invention and the state of the art. The test is not merely quantitative, since a considerable amount of experimentation is permissible if it is merely routine or if the specification in question provides a reasonable amount of guidance with respect to the direction in which the experimentation should proceed to enable the determination of how to practice a desired embodiment of the invention claimed. The factors to be considered have been summarized as the quantity of experimentation necessary, the amount of direction or guidance presented, the presence or absence of working examples, the nature of the invention, the state of the prior art, the relative skill of those in that art, the predictability or unpredictability of the art, and the breadth of the claims. *Ex parte Forman,* 230 U.S.P.Q. 546 (B.P.A.I. 1986).

ω

The mere need for experimentation to determine parameters needed to make a device work is an application of the often rejected obvious-to-try standard and falls short of statutory "obviousness" of 35 U.S.C. §103. Inability of an expert to predict the results obtainable with a claimed product suggests non-obviousness, not routine experimentation. *Uniroyal Inc. v. Rudkin-Wiley Corp.,* 837 F.2d 1044, 5 U.S.P.Q.2d 1434 (Fed. Cir. 1988).

ω

Since "routine experimentation" may involve rather extensive studies without straying from "undue" experimentation, and since appellants have provided no countervailing evidence to persuade us otherwise, we are satisfied that the changes in the application of the reference patent were of the type condoned by prior decisions. *Ex parte D*, 27 U.S.P.Q.2d 1067, 1069, 1070 (B.P.A.I. 1993).

Royalty. *See also* Hybrid, Reasonable Royalty, Return of Royalties.

In determining a reasonable royalty, it is improper to give substantial evidentiary weight to existing license agreements having a royalty rate that was arrived at under conditions of open, industrywide infringement and lack of respect for the patent. This is true even if application of the reasonable royalty thus determined would not allow defendant a reasonable profit from the infringing activity. A patentee who has attempted to avoid costly and time-consuming litigation by settling for less than a reasonable royalty should not be penalized when an infringer forces full litigation. A rule to the contrary would allow the giants of a given industry to use threats of costly and protracted litigation to extort an unreasonably low royalty from an impecunious patentee and then to force the patentee into the litigation while maintaining the hedge that the unreasonably low royalty rate would put a ceiling on damages. *Tights, Inc. v. Kayser-Roth Corp.* 442 F. Supp. 159, 196 U.S.P.Q. 750, 755 (N.C. 1977).

ϖ

Although the patent law states that the damage award shall not be "less than a reasonable royalty," the purpose of this alternative is not to provide a simple accounting method, but to set a floor below which the courts are not authorized to go. *Del Mar Avionics, Inc. v. Quinton Instrument Co.*, 836 F.2d 1320, 5 U.S.P.Q.2d 1255 (Fed. Cir. 1987).

ϖ

A royalty that is "reasonable" under 35 U.S.C. §284 may be greater than an established royalty. A higher figure may be awarded when the evidence clearly shows that widespread infringement makes the established royalty artificially low. *Nickson Industries, Inc. v. Rol Manufacturing Co. Ltd.*, 847 F.2d 795, 6 U.S.P.Q.2d 1878 (Fed. Cir. 1988).

ϖ

The methodology for determining a fair and reasonable royalty has been problematic as a mechanism for doing justice to individual nonmanufacturing patentees. Because courts routinely deny injunctions to such patentees, infringers could perceive nothing to fear but the possibility of a compulsory license at a reasonable royalty, resulting in some quarters in a lowered respect for the rights of patentees and a failure to recognize the innovation-encouraging social purpose of the patent system. Thus a cold "bottom line" logic would dictate to some a total disregard of the individual's patent because: (1) ill-financed, he probably would not sue; (2) cost of counsel's opinion could await suit; (3) the patent may well be held invalid on one of many possible bases; (4) infringement may not be proven; (5) if the case be lost, a license can be compelled, probably at the same royalty that would have been paid if the patentee's rights had been respected at the outset. Though the methodology must on occasion be used for want of a better, it must be carefully applied to achieve a truly reasonable royalty; for the methodology risks creation of the perception that blatant, blind appropriation of inventions patented by the individual non-manufacturing inventors is the profitable, "can't lose" course. In applying the methodology, the emphasis on an individual inventor's lack of money and manufacturing capacity can lend to distinguish the respect due the patent rights of impecunious inventors from that due the patent rights of well-funded, well lawyered, large manufacturing corporations. Any such distinction should be rejected as the disservice it is to the public and technological advancement. That "survival of the fittest," jungle mentality was intended to be replaced, not served, by the law. *Fromson v. Western Litho Plate & Supply Co.*, 853 F.2d 1568, 7 U.S.P.Q.2d 1606 (Fed. Cir. 1988).

ᴡ

A jury's assessment of a 25 percent royalty as damages was supported by substantial evidence. *Gavin v. Starbrite Corp.*, 10 U.S.P.Q.2d 1253 (Fed. Cir. 1988). See also *TWM Manufacturing v. Dura*, 789 F.2d 897, 228 U.S.P.Q. 453 (Fed. Cir. 1986).

ᴡ

The 30 percent or greater royalty proposed by the plaintiffs is too high, and the 5 percent proposed by the defendants is too low. The resin involved in this case was a new product, not just an improvement on an old one. As a result, the plaintiffs were not able to present evidence on the royalties or profit margin on comparable products. Nonetheless, we conclude that 20 percent is a reasonable royalty. In determining a reasonable royalty, reasonable doubts are resolved against the infringing party. *Water Technologies Corp. v. Calco Ltd.*, 714 F. Supp. 899, 11 U.S.P.Q.2d 1410 (Ill. 1989).

ᴡ

In determining the royalty rate to be applied to the compensation base in a 28 U.S.C. §1498 setting, an attempt is made to establish a royalty that will adequately compensate the patentee for his loss. The focus of this inquiry is on the date when the infringement began. A court should look to existing licensing agreements. Where an established royalty rate for the patented invention is shown to exist, that rate will usually be adopted as the best measure of reasonable and entire compensation. However, where no such royalty is shown, alternative methods must be employed. The royalty comparison approach is the preferred methodology. To accomplish this task, a hypothetical negotiation between a "willing buyer and a willing seller" may be used. However, this analysis permits and often requires a court to look to events and facts that occurred thereafter and that could not have been known or predicted by the hypothesized negotiators. Although a licensing agreement reached after a finding of validity may be highly probative of a reasonable royalty, other circumstances may discount its probative value. *ITT Corp. v. United States*, 17 Cl. Ct. 199, 11 U.S.P.Q.2d 1657, 1676 (Cl. Ct. 1989).

ᴡ

The so-called analytical approach starts with the infringer's selling price, deducts its costs in order to find its gross profit, then allocates to the infringer its normal profit, and ends up with the share of the gross profit that can be assigned to the patentee as its royalty. The analytical approach is not well-suited to process patent (as opposed to product patent) infringement wherein practicing the patent simply results in production of a fungible item at a decreased expense, thus merely reducing variable costs.

Prejudgment interest should be awarded as a general rule in patent cases. Such interest should be computed "from the time that the royalty payment would have been received" because prejudgment interest is awarded to compensate for the delay in payment of damages, and not to punish the infringer. Annual compounding, rather than simple interest, is proper. The plaintiff is entitled to interest on the running royalty at 12 percent compounded annually "from the time that the royalty payments would have been received." In addition, the plaintiff shall receive interest on the up-front payment at a 12 percent rate compounded annually from the date on which the complaint was filed. *Johns-Manville Corp. v. Guardian Industries Inc.*, 718 F. Supp. 1310, 13 U.S.P.Q.2d 1684, 1686, 1689 (Mich. 1989).

ᗯ

Patentee is at least entitled to a royalty that prohibits the defendants from profiting from their infringement by retaining the difference between a reasonable royalty and their net profit. *DNIC Brokerage Co. v. Morrison Dempsey Communications Inc.*, 14 U.S.P.Q.2d 1043, 1047 (Cal. 1989).

ᗯ

There are two methods by which one may calculate damages. If actual damages cannot be ascertained, a reasonable royalty must be determined. Whether or not a party is entitled to an award of damages on a lost-profit theory is not material if the jury's verdict can also be sustained on the basis of a reasonable royalty. When the amount of damages cannot be ascertained with precision, any doubts regarding the amount must be resolved against the infringer. *ALM Surgical Equipment Inc. v. Kirschner Medical Corp.*, 15 U.S.P.Q.2d 1241, 1250 (S.C. 1990).

ᗯ

As a general rule of thumb, a royalty of 25 percent of net profits is used in license negotiations. *W. L. Gore & Associates Inc. v. International Medical Prosthetics Research Associates Inc.*, 16 U.S.P.Q.2d 1241, 1257 (Ariz. 1990).

ᗯ

A factual determination of a reasonable royalty need not be supported and, indeed, frequently is not supported by the specific figures advanced by either party. The determination of a reasonable royalty must be based upon the entirety of the evidence, and the court is free to, and indeed must, reject the royalty figures proffered by the litigants where the record as a whole leads the court to a different figure. *SmithKline Diagnostics Inc. v. Helena Laboratories Corp.*, 926 F.2d 1161, 17 U.S.P.Q.2d 1922, 1927, 1928 (Fed. Cir. 1991).

ᗯ

"A reasonable royalty is the amount that 'a person, desiring to manufacture [, use, or] sell a patented article, as a business proposition, would be willing to pay as a royalty and yet be able to make [, use, or] sell the patented article, in the market, at a reasonable profit.'" When an established royalty does not exist, a court may determine a reasonable royalty based on "hypothetical negotiations between willing licensor and willing licensee." "The key element in setting a reasonable royalty . . . is the necessity for return to the date when the infringement began." *Wang Laboratories Inc. v. Toshiba Corp.*, 993 F.2d 858, 26 U.S.P.Q.2d 1767, 1777, 1778 (Fed. Cir. 1993).

ᗯ

A contract requiring a licensee to pay royalties after a patent expired was per se unlawful because the patent owner had abused the leverage of the monopoly to project royalties into the period after expiration. However, federal patent law is not a barrier to enforcement of "contractual obligations, freely undertaken in arm's-length negotiation and with no fixed reliance on a patent or a probable patent grant." *Baladevon Inc. v. Abbott Laboratories Inc.*, 871 F.Supp. 89, 33 U.S.P.Q.2d 1743, 1746 (Mass. 1994).

Royalty-Free License.

Merely because plaintiff later used aspects of technology (it had previously conceived and reduced to practice) in the performance of a government contract does not give the government (defendant) any rights under the patent. Defendant received the benefit of that technology without paying for its development; it does not also get a royalty-free license. *Leesona Corp. v. United States*, 185 U.S.P.Q. 156, 165 (U.S. Ct. Cl. 1975).

Royalty Rate.

A reasonable royalty rate to redress an infringement must be based on the time period during which the infringement occurred. A contracted royalty rate of some 12 years prior thereto is of little probative value. *Chisum v. Brewco Sales and Manufacturing Inc.*, 726 F. Supp. 1499, 13 U.S.P.Q.2d 1657, 1668 (Ky. 1989).

Rule. *See* All-Claims Rule, All-Elements Rule, But-For Rule, 37 C.F.R., Entire-Market-Value Rule, Federal Shop Book Rule, First-to-File, Four Corners Rule, Hearsay, Joinder Rule, Mandate Rule, Maximum Recovery Rule, Multiple Inclusion, Recapture Rule, Shop Right, Stockholder Rule, Visibility Rule, Well-Pleaded Complaint, Willing Buyer-Willing Seller Rule.

Rule 4(a)(5) [Federal Rules of Appellate Procedure].

When analyzing a claim of excusable neglect, court should "tak[e] account of all relevant circumstances surrounding the party's omission," including "the danger of prejudice to the [nonmovant], the length of the delay and its potential impact on judicial proceedings, the reason for the delay, including whether it was within the reasonable control of the movant, and whether the movant acted in good faith." *Advanced Estimating Systems Inc. v. Riney*, 77 F.3d 1322, 38 U.S.P.Q.2d 1208, 1210 (11th Cir. 1996).

Rule 5(b)

Service by facsimile is not sufficient to satisfy Fed. R. Civ. P. 5(b). *Mushroom Associates v. Monterey Mushrooms Inc.*, 25 U.S.P.Q.2d 1304, 1307 (Cal. 1992).

Rule 7(b)(1)

The particularity requirement of Rule 7 (FRCP) "is flexible . . . , and non-particularized motions have been allowed where the opposing party knew or had notice of the particular grounds being relied upon." 2A J. Moore & J. Lucas, *Moore's Federal Practice* §7.05, at 7-16 (2d ed. 1990). *Registration Control Systems Inc. v. Compusystems Inc.*, 922 F.2d 805, 17 U.S.P.Q.2d 1212, 1214 (Fed. Cir. 1990).

Rule 8

The Federal Rules of Civil Procedure require "a short and plain statement of the claim showing the pleader is entitled to relief." The Seventh Circuit has stated that Rule (FRCP) 8 mandates only "a generalized statement of the facts from which the defendant can craft a responsive pleading." Further, the district court has a duty to consider whether a plaintiff's allegations could provide relief under *any* available legal theory. The complaint need not support a viable claim only under the particular legal theory intended by the plaintiff. *In re Recombinant DNA Technology Patent and Contract Litigation*, 874 F.Supp. 904, 34 U.S.P.Q.2d 1097, 1104 (Ind. 1994).

Rule 8(c)

Generally, a failure to plead an affirmative defense, as required by Rule (FRCP) 8(c), results in the forced waiver of that defense and its exclusion from the case. Waiver need not result, however, if the defendant "raised the issue at a pragmatically sufficient time, and the [opposing party] was not prejudiced in its ability to respond." *Surgical Laser Technologies Inc. v. Heraeus Laseronics Inc.*, 34 U.S.P.Q.2d 1226, 1228 (Pa. 1995).

Rule 9

Defendant's allegations of inequitable conduct must satisfy the particularity requirements of Rule (FRCP) 9(b). As a guide, amended pleadings should identitfy: (1) the particular statements, misrepresentations, or omissions made; (2) when the complained of acts or omissions occurred; (3) the reasons why those acts or omissions were inequitable; and (4) the basis for the belief. *The Laitram Corp. v. OKI Electric Industry Co. Ltd.*, 30 U.S.P.Q.2d 1527, 1533 (La. 1994).

Rule 9(b)

(FRCP) Rule 9(b)'s particularity requirements apply to the affirmative defense of inequitable conduct. The pleading requirements of Rule 9(b) also apply to the defense of unclean hands if the allegation of unclean hands involves the elements of fraud. As such, "allegations of fraud must be pleaded with specificity as to time, place and content of any misrepresentations or else be stricken." *Xilinx Inc. v. Altera Corp.*, 33 U.S.P.Q.2d 1149, 1151, 1152 (Cal. 1994).

ω

One of the rule's purposes in requiring particularity in the pleadings is "to deter the filing of charges of fraud as a pretext for discovery of unknown wrongs." Claims of fraud, including claims of inequitable conduct, should be supported by specific allegations as mandated by Rule (FRCP) 9(b). Such a requirement prevents claims of fraud from being used to impugn the integrity of attorneys involved in patent prosecution without sufficient evidence that wrongdoing has in fact occurred, and constrains the utilization of such claims to redressing wrongs committed, rather than to uncovering wrongs merely suspected. *Heidelberg Harris Inc. v. Mitsubishi Heavy Industries Inc.*, 42 U.S.P.Q.2d 1369, 1372 (Ill. 1996).

Rule 11

Rule 11 (FRCP) sanctions shall be imposed if plaintiff and/or his attorney "could not form a reasonable belief that the pleading is well-grounded in fact." *Eastway Construction Corp. v. City of New York*, 762 F.2d 243, 254 (2d Cir. 1985).

℧

When the filing of a complaint is alleged to be in violation of Rule 11 (FRCP), the test under the rule is what the plaintiff knew when the complaint was filed, not what was learned later. A complaint filed in sheer ignorance of the facts violates Rule 11, notwithstanding that its allegations may later be learned to be completely true. A shot in the dark is a sanctionable event, even if it somehow hits the mark. Accordingly, what the plaintiff may have learned later in discovery is immaterial to whether there has been a Rule 11 violation (although it might be quite pertinent as to the choice of sanctions), even if later events confirm what was alleged, on insufficient inquiry, in the complaint. An attorney takes a frivolous position if he fails to make a reasonable inquiry into alleged facts that later prove to be false. *Vista Manufacturing Inc. v. Trac-Four Inc.*, 131 F.R.D. 134, 15 U.S.P.Q.2d 1345, 1347 (Ind. 1990).

℧

All aspects of Rule 11 (FRCP) determinations are reviewed under an abuse of discretion standard. Rule 11 is aimed at curbing baseless filings, which put the machinery of justice in motion and burden courts and individuals alike with needless expense and delay. While the choice of "appropriate sanction" is discretionary, the imposition of sanctions (once a violation has been found) is mandatory. Rule 11 is intended to be applied vigorously to curb widely acknowledged abuse. *Refac International Ltd. v. Hitachi Ltd.*, 921 F.2d 1247, 16 U.S.P.Q.2d 1347, 1354, 1355 (Fed. Cir. 1990).

℧

Under Rule (FRCP) 11, attorneys have a firm duty to conduct a reasonable investigation of the facts and law prior to submitting any pleading, motion, or paper. By signing a pleading, an attorney "represents that, after appropriate investigation and inquiry, he reasonably believes that a proper legal claim or defense is stated." Whether the requirements of Rule 11 have been satisfied must be decided using an objective standard of reasonableness. To determine whether Rule 11 sanctions are appropriate in a given case, the Court must consider three factors: (1) whether the signing attorney made a reasonable inquiry; (2) to determine that the motion is well grounded in fact and is warranted by existing law or a good faith extension, modification, or reversal of existing law; and (3) that it is not interposed for any improper purpose, such as to harass or to cause unnecessary delay or needless increase in the cost of litigation. *Nasatka v. Delta Scientific Corp.*, 34 U.S.P.Q.2d 1649, 1651 (Va. 1994).

℧

A district court decision imposing Rule 11 (FRCP) sanctions is not final, and hence not appealable, until the amount of the sanction has been decided by the district court.

View Engineering Inc. v. Robotic Vision Systems Inc., 42 U.S.P.Q.2d 1956, 1958 (Fed. Cir. 1997).

Rule 12(b)(1). *See also* Motion to Dismiss.

"The district court has the authority to consider matters outside the pleadings on a motion challenging subject matter jurisdiction under Federal Rule of Civil Procedure 12(b)(1)." *Sealrite Windows Inc. v. Amesbury Group Inc.*, 33 U.S.P.Q.2d 1688, 1689 (Neb. 1994).

Rule 12(b)(6)

A motion made under Rule (FRCP) 12(b)(6) challenges the legal theory of the complaint, not the sufficiency of any evidence that might be adduced. The purpose of the rule is to allow the court to eliminate actions that are fatally flawed in their legal premises and destined to fail, and thus to spare litigants the burdens of unnecessary pretrial and trial activity. Such a motion, which cuts off a claimant at the threshold, must be denied "unless it appears beyond doubt that the plaintiff can prove no set of facts in support of his claim which would entitle him to relief." *Advanced Cardiovascular Systems Inc. v. SciMed Life Systems Inc.*, 988 F.2d 1157, 26 U.S.P.Q.2d 1038, 1041 (Fed. Cir. 1993).

ᖚ ·

A motion to dismiss pursuant to (FRCP) Rule 12(b)(6) should be granted only if it appears beyond doubt that plaintiffs can prove no set of facts in support of their claims which would entitle them to relief. Therefore, on a motion to dismiss, all factual allegations of the complaint must be accepted as true, and all reasonable inferences must be made in plaintiff's favor. "The court's function on a Rule 12(b)(6) motion is not to weigh the evidence that might be presented at a trial but merely to determine whether the complaint itself is legally sufficient." *Novo Nordisk of North America Inc. v. Genentech Inc.*, 885 F.Supp. 522, 35 U.S.P.Q.2d 1058, 1059, 1060 (N.Y. 1995).

ᖚ

A (FRCP) Rule 12(b)(6) dismissal is proper only where there is either a "lack of cognizable legal theory" or "the absence of sufficient facts alleged under a cognizable legal theory." Furthermore, unless a court converts a Rule 12(b)(6) motion into a motion for summary judgment, a court cannot consider material outside of the complaint (e.g., facts presented in briefs, affidavits, or discovery materials). A court may, however, consider exhibits submitted with the complaint and matters that may be judicially noticed pursuant to Federal Rule of Evidence 201. *K-Lath v. Davis Wire Corp.*, 49 U.S.P.Q.2d 1161, 1169 (Cal. 1998).

Rule 13 (FRCP)

Whether a claim arises out of the same transaction or occurrence is determined by analyzing "whether the essential facts of the various claims are so logically connected that considerations of judicial economy and fairness dictate that all the issues be resolved in one lawsuit." *Hydranautics v. FilmTec Corp.*, 70 F.3d 533, 36 U.S.P.Q.2d 1773, 1776 (9th Cir. 1995).

RULE 13(a).

There is an exception to Rule 13(a) for antitrust counterclaims in which the gravamen is a patent infringement lawsuit initiated by the counterclaim defendant. *Tank Insulation International Inc. v. Insultherm Inc.*, 41 2d 1545 (5th Cir. 1997)

Rule 13(f).

As with other motions for leave to amend, "the district court has discretion, pursuant to Fed. R. Civ. P. 13(f), to deny leave to amend based upon a balancing of the equities, including whether the non-moving party will be prejudiced, whether additional discovery will be required, and whether the court's docket will be strained." "Although the standard is 'oversight, inadvertence or excusable neglect,' Rule 13(f) does not give a party the privilege of totally neglecting its case and ignoring time limits imposed by the Federal Rules of Civil Procedure even absent bad faith or dilatory motive on its part. *Agar Corp. v. Multi-Fluid Inc.*, 47 U.S.P.Q.2d 1375, 1376, 1377 (Tex. 1998).

Rule 15(a)

Under Fed.R.Civ.P. 15(a), pleadings may be amended once as a matter of course before a responsive pleading is served, and thereafter by leave of court. The rule provides that such leave "shall be freely given when justice so requires," id., but "it is by no means automatic." In deciding whether to grant leave to file an amended pleading, the district court may consider such factors as undue delay, bad faith or dilatory motive on the part of the movant, repeated failure to cure deficiencies by amendments previously allowed, undue prejudice to the opposing party, and futility of amendment. However, "if the district court lacks a 'substantial reason' to deny leave, its discretion 'is not broad enough to permit denial'." *United National Insurance Co. v. Bradleys' Electric Inc.*, 35 U.S.P.Q.2d 1559, 1560 (Tex. 1995).

Rule 19(a)

The present Rule 19(a) (FRCP), where reference to joining an involuntary plaintiff is found, is concerned only with "a person who is subject to service of process and whose joinder will not deprive the court of jurisdiction over the subject matter". In a patent infringement action Rule 19(a) does not authorize a court to make an owner of an undivided share of the patent, who is outside the jurisdiction of the court, an involuntary plaintiff. *Catanzaro v. International Telephone & Telegraph Corporation*, 378 F. Supp. 203, 183 U.S.P.Q. 273, 277 (Del. 1974).

Rule 23 (FRCP). *See* **Class Action.**

Rule 26(b)(1)

Rule 26(b)(1) allows discovery of any nonprivileged matter that is relevant to the subject matter involved in the pending action. The rule has boundaries, however. Discovery of matter not reasonably calculated to lead to the discovery of admissible evidence is outside its scope. *American Standard lnc. v. Pfizer Inc.*, 828 F.2d 734, 3 U.S.P.Q.2d 1817 (Fed. Cir. 1987).

Rule 26(c)(7)

There is no absolute privilege for trade secrets and similar confidential information. To resist discovery under Rule 26(c)(7), a person must first establish that the information sought is a trade secret and then demonstrate that its disclosure might be harmful. If these requirements are met, the burden shifts to the party seeking discovery to establish that the disclosure of trade secrets is relevant and necessary to the action. The district court must balance the need for the trade secrets against the claim of injury resulting from disclosure. If proof of relevancy or need is not established, discovery should be denied. On the other hand, if relevancy and need are shown, the trade secrets should be disclosed, unless they are privileged or the subpoenas are unreasonable, oppressive, annoying, or embarrassing. *Heat & Control, Inc. v. Hector Industries, Inc.*, 785 F.2d 1017, 228 U.S.P.Q. 926 (Fed. Cir. 1986).

A trade secret or other confidential research, development, or commercial information may be the subject of a protective order under Fed. R. Civ. P. 26(c)(7). One seeking a protective order under that rule must establish that the information sought is confidential. In support of its motion, Biomet submitted an affidavit explaining why the requested discovery contained "trade secrets and other confidential business information." To be a trade secret under Indiana law, information must be kept secret and must derive economic value from that secrecy. Biomet's affidavit specifies measures Biomet uses to keep secret the information sought and the value thereof as secrets. Having shown the information sought to be confidential, one seeking a protective order must then demonstrate that disclosure might be harmful. Courts have presumed that disclosure to a competitor is more harmful than disclosure to a noncompetitor. Where a party seeking a protective order has shown that the information sought is confidential and that its disclosure might be harmful, the burden shifts to the party seeking discovery to establish that disclosure of trade secrets and confidential information is relevant and necessary to its case. Rule 26(b)(1) allows discovery of any nonprivileged matter that is relevant to the subject matter involved in the pending action. The rule has boundaries, however. Discovery of matter not reasonably calculated to lead to the discovery of admissible evidence is outside its scope. *American Standard lnc. v. Pfizer Inc.*, 828 F.2d 734, 3 U.S.P.Q.2d 1817 (Fed. Cir. 1987).

Rule 26(e)(2).

"The purpose of [Rule (FRCP) 26(e)(2)] is to prevent trial by ambush." *Heidelberg Harris Inc. v. Mitsubishi Heavy Industries Inc.*, 42 U.S.P.Q.2d 1369, 1377 (Ill. 1996).

Rule 34

If the requirements of personal jurisdiction over a party to a pending interference are met by a filing in the Patent Office, notice to defendants' attorney of record in the Patent Office and also to the defendants directly by mail is both reasonable and adequate to satisfy due process service requirements of a Rule 34 (FRCP) motion (in connection with the interference) before a court. *Vogel v. Jones*, 443 F.2d 257, 170 U.S.P.Q. 188, 189 (3rd Cir. 1971).

Rule 35

Personal jurisdiction is acquired when the parties file interfering applications in the Patent Office. The resulting "interference" in the Patent Office is the primary proceeding. A motion for discovery of documents under Fed. R. Civ. P. 35, being necessarily limited to a party in the action already commenced in the Patent Office, requires no new or independent assertion of personal jurisdiction or issuance of summons. *Vogel v. Jones*, 443 F.2d 257, 170 U.S.P.Q. 188, 189 (3d Cir. 1971).

Rule 37

Plaintiff applied for sanctions against defendant under Rule 37 (FRCP). Defendant was ordered to produce documents and to answer interrogatories relating to the issues in the case. Defendant pled inability to comply with this order and to produce required documents because the responsive information and the documents were in the possession of a foreign corporation (not a party to the litigation) which refused to cooperate. The foreign corporation had an intimate connection with the litigation; it was financing defendant's litigation costs, had agreed to hold defendant harmless, and was exercising an apparent and substantial control over the course of the litigation. After the foreign corporation refused to provide the requested information, defendant was precluded from offering at trial evidence which would have been responsive to pending notices to produce. *Elox, Inc. v. Astral Precision Equipment Company*, 178 U.S.P.Q. 607, 608 (Ill. 1971).

Rule 38

A frivolous appeal filed or proceeded with in the CAFC will result in imposition of damages and costs upon appellant and counsel in accordance with Rule 38 (Federal Rules of Appellate Procedure). *Asberry v. United States Postal Service*, 686 F.2d 1040, 215 U.S.P.Q. 921 (Fed. Cir. 1982).

Rule 39(b)

FRCP 39(b) clearly allows that "the court in its discretion upon motion may order a trial by jury of any or all issues." The factors which bear on the decision to exercise the discretion authorized by Rule 39(b) and grant a jury trial include: (1) whether the issues are more appropriate for determination by a jury or by a judge...(2) any prejudice that granting a jury trial would cause the opposing party...(3) the timing of the motion...(4) any effect a jury trial would have had on the court's docket and the orderly administration of justice....*B. Braun Medical Inc. v. Abbott Laboratories*, 892 F.Supp.112, 36 U.S.P.Q.2d 1846, 1849 (Pa. 1995).

Rule 41(a)(2)

When a defendant's counterclaim has a jurisdictional basis independent of the main action, the provision of Rule 41(a)(2) (of the Federal Rules of Civil Procedure) relating to counterclaims does not bar dismissal of plaintiff's complaint or require dismissal of defendant's counterclaim. *Farmaceuutisk Laboratorium Ferring A/S v. Reid Rowell Inc.*, 20 U.S.P.Q.2d 1476, 1478 (Ga. 1991).

Rule 42(a)

Fed. R. Civ. P. 42(a) allows a court to consolidate actions involving common questions of law or fact and to order joint hearings of any or all matters at issue. The decision is left to the sound discretion of the trial judge and may be appropriate in patent infringement actions involving the same patents and multiple defendants. Cases can be consolidated solely for pretrial matters. *Sage Products Inc. v. Devon Industries Inc.*, 148 F.R.D. 213, 28 U.S.P.Q.2d 1149, 1150 (Ill. 1993).

Rule 45

The limitations of the first sentence of 35 U.S.C. §24 would appear to apply if an interference party seeks to compel the attendance of a witness through the use of a subpoena under Fed. R. Civ. P. 45. *Vogel v. Jones*, 443 F.2d 257, 170 U.S.P.Q. 188, 189 (3rd Cir. 1971).

Rule 49

The label "verdict" in Rule (FRCP) 49(a) is an unfortunate choice. Special verdicts are jury answers to factual interrogatories. "Verdict" is apparently employed because returning verdicts is what juries do. Doubtless the drafters expected courts and counsel to distinugish between a general verdict, naked or accompanied by answers to interrogatories under Rule 49(b) (in returning of either of which a jury finds the facts, applies the law as instructed, and designates the winning side), and a special verdict (in returning of which a jury supplies only written answers to fact questions). *Wahpeton Canvas Co. v. Frontier Inc.*, 870 F.2d 1546, 10 U.S.P.Q.2d 1201 (Fed. Cir. 1989).

Rule 50.

When a court does not grant a motion for judgment as a matter of law made at the close of all the evidence, the court is considered to have "submitted the action to the jury subject to the court's later deciding the legal questions raised by the motion." Under Rule 50, a motion is appropriate when either: (1) a party raises a pure legal issue for determination based upon undisputed facts or (2) a party is unable to produce *substantial* evidence to support a jury verdict in its favor on an issue. When addressing the second type of motion, the court need not require that there be "a complete absence of facts to support a jury verdict" for the non-moving party before granting a judgment as a matter of law. To the contrary, "there must be a substantial conflict in evidence to support a jury question." The standard is "[i]f the facts and inferences point overwhelmingly in favor of one party, such that reasonable people could not arrive at a contrary verdict, then the motion [is] properly granted." *Tronzo v. Biomet Inc.*, 41 U.S.P.Q.2d 1403 (Fla. 1996).

Rule 52(a)

Rule (FRCP) 52(a) requires that the court, in denying a preliminary injunction, shall "set forth the findings of fact and conclusions of law which constitute the grounds of its action." *See Mayo v. Lakeland Highlands Canning Co.*, 309 U.S. 310, 316-17 (1940); *Pretty Punch Shoppettes, Inc. v. Hauk*, 844 F.2d 782, 784, 6 U.S.P.Q.2d 1563, 1565 (Fed. Cir. 1988).

Rule 54(b)

Rule 54(b) {FRCP} allows a district court to sever an individual claim that has been finally resolved. In order for Rule 54(b) to apply to a judgment, the judgment must be final with respect to one or more claims. A judgment is not final for Rule 54(b) purposes unless it is "an *ultimate* disposition of an *individual* claim entered in the course of a multiple claims action." Courts analyzing whether Rule 54(b) applies must focus on both the finality of the judgment and the separateness of the claims for relief. *W.L. Gore & Associates Inc. v. International Medical Prosthetics Research Associates Inc.*, 975 F.2d 858, 24 U.S.P.Q.2d 1195, 1198 (Fed. Cir. 1992).

Rule 56 (FRCP). *See also* Summary Judgment.

Rule (FRCP) 56 places a substantial burden upon the non-movant to place in dispute the material facts of the case. *Advanced Cardiovascular Systems Inc. v. SciMed Life Systems Inc.*, 988 F.2d 1157, 26 U.S.P.Q.2d 1038, 1044 (Fed. Cir. 1993).

Rule 59

The ten-day period provided in Rule 59 (FRCP) is mandatory and jurisdictional and cannot be extended in the discretion of the district court. *See Fiester v. Turner,* 783 F.2d 1474, 1476 (9th Cir. 1986); *Scott v. Younger,* 739 F.2d 1464, 1467 (9th Cir. 1984).

Rule 60(a)

Rule 60(a) (FRCP) finds application where the record makes apparent that the court intended one thing, but, by mere clerical mistake or oversight, did another. Such a mistake may not be one of judgment or even misidentification, but merely a recitation of the sort that a clerk or an amanuensis might commit, mechanical in nature. In such instances the judgment can be corrected to speak the truth. *Polaroid Corp. v. Eastman Kodak Co.*, 17 U.S.P.Q.2d 1711 (Mass. 1991).

Rule 60(b). *See also* New Trial.

Relief under this FRCP is an extraordinary remedy and is granted only in exceptional circumstances. "Motions for reconsideration serve a limited function: to correct manifest errors of law or fact or to present newly discovered evidence. *Such motions cannot in any case be employed as a vehicle to introduce new evidence that could have been adduced during pendency of the summary judgment motion.* The nonmovant has an affirmative duty to come forward to meet a properly supported motion for summary judgment...*Nor should a motion for reconsideration serve as the occasion to tender new legal theories for the first time." Paradigm Sales Inc. v. Weber Marking Systems Inc.*, 880 F.Supp. 1237, 1242, 34 U.S.P.Q.2d 1039, 1044 (Ind. 1994).

ᙡ

"[A] change in decisional law is not grounds for relief under Rule 60(b)(6)." *Concept Design Electronics and Manufacturing Inc. v. Duplitronics Inc.*, 79 F.3d 1167, 43 U.S.P.Q.2d 1114, 1118 (Fed. Cir. 1996—*unpublished*).

ᙡ

In cases in which a court or jury is presented with perjured testimony which is relevant and material to the issue decided, and relief from judgment is sought pursuant to newly discovered evidence, the court should not attempt to weigh the effect of the perjured testimony on the trier of fact and should instead order a new trial. *Viskase Corp. v. American National Can Co.*, 979 F.Supp. 697, 45 U.S.P.Q.2d 1675, 1678 (Ill. 1997).

ᙡ

A decision on a Rule 60(b) motion, when the motion does not toll the time for filing an appeal from the final judgment, is a separate final action by the district court and, as such, must be appealed separately from the underlying action. *Phonometrics Inc. v. Northern Telecom Inc.*, 133 F.3d 1459, 45 U.S.P.Q.2d 1421, 1428 (Fed. Cir. 1998).

Rule 65(d).

The reference in (FRCP) Rule 65(d) to "officers" means only *current* officers. *Saga International Inc. v. John D. Brush & Co.*, 984 F.Supp. 1283, 44 U.S.P.Q.2d 1947, 1949 (Cal. 1997).

Rule 68.

Through a Rule 68 (FRCP) judgment the parties to a patent dispute could explicitly agree to resolve the issue of past infringement by the payment of money, but to leave open the broader issue of patent invalidity for resolution at a later stage of the same case or in a subsequent lawsuit. *Scosche Industries Inc. v. Visor Gear Inc.*, 43 U.S.P.Q.2d 1659, 1662 (Fed. Cir. 1997).

Rule 82 bis (PCT)

Rule 82 bis (PCT) refers to the power of any designated State in an international application to excuse a delay, involving that application, in accordance with its own laws. *Farnum v. Manbeck*, 21 U.S.P.Q.2d 1691, 1695 (D.C. 1991).

Rule 408

Rule 408 (of the Federal Rules of Evidence) is designed to promote "the public policy favoring the compromise and settlement of disputes." Fed. R. Evid. 408 advisory committee's note. It is true that complete confidentiality of settlements may promote this goal. But Rule 408 is merely a rule of evidence, which promotes compromise in one limited way—it provides that evidence of compromise is not admissible to show invalidity of a claim or its amount. "Although the intent of FRE 408 is to foster settlement negotiations, the sole means used to effectuate that end is a limitation on the admission of evidence produced during settlement negotiations for the purpose of proving liability at trial." *Alpex Computer Corp. v. Nintendo Co. Ltd.*, 20 U.S.P.Q.2d 1782, 1787 (N.Y. 1991).

Rule 702 (Fed. R. Evid.)

Rule 702, governing expert testimony, provides:

"If scientific, technical, or other specialized knowledge will assist the trier of fact to understand the evidence or to determine a fact in issue, a witness qualified as an expert by knowledge, skill, experience, training, or education, may testify thereto in the form of an opinion or otherwise."

Nothing in the text of this Rule establishes "general acceptance" as an absolute prerequisite to admissibility. *Daubert v. Merrell Dow Pharmaceuticals Inc.*, 113 S.Ct. 2786, 27 U.S.P.Q.2d 1200, 1204 (S.Ct. 1993).

Rule Making.

Under 5 U.S.C. §553 of the Administrative Procedure Act, certain agency actions require prior public notice and comment. Courts interpreting §553 generally speak in terms of "substantive" or legislative rules requiring notice and comment in contrast to the exempt "interpretive" rules of §553(b), which do not. A rule is substantive when it "effects a change in existing law or policy" that "affect[s] individual rights and obligations." To be substantive, a rule must also be promulgated pursuant "to statutory authority . . . and implement the statute." In contrast, a rule that merely clarifies or explains existing law or regulations is interpretive. *Animal League Defense Fund v. Quigg*, 932 F.2d 920, 18 U.S.P.Q.2d 1677, 1683 (Fed. Cir. 1991).

ω

Courts presented with challenges to the lawfulness of a regulation must engage in a two-step analysis. First, courts must decide whether Congress has "directly spoken to the precise question at issue." If so, the judicial task is ended. Courts must give effect to Congress' clearly expressed intention, and if such intention is manifest in the statute's language, there is no need to proceed to the second step of the analysis. But, if the answer to the first inquiry is negative, that is, where Congress has been silent regarding the "precise question at issue," or if the statutory language is ambiguous, then courts must then ask whether the agency's regulation stems from "a permissible construction of the statute." In this regard, courts may not substitute their own interpretation of the statute for that of the agency, provided the agency's construction is "permissible." Finally, in determining whether an agency's construction is permissible, courts must give "considerable weight" to an agency's interpretation of the statutes it has been directed to administer. *Centigram Communications Corp. v. Lehman*, 862 F.Supp. 113, 32 U.S.P.Q.2d 1346, 1350 (Va. 1994).

ω

The broadest of the PTO's rulemaking powers—35 U.S.C. §6(a)—authorizes the Commissioner to promulgate regulations directed only to "the conduct of proceedings in the [PTO]"; it does *not* grant the Commissioner the authority to issue substantive rules. *Merck & Co. v. Kessler*, 80 F.3d 1543, 38 U.S.P.Q.2d 1347, 1351 (Fed. Cir. 1996),

Rule of Deference. *See* Deference.

Rule of Reason.

A "rule of reason" approach is required in determining the type and amount of evidence necessary for corroboration. *Breuer and Treuner v. DeMarinis*, 558 F.2d 22, 194 U.S.P.Q. 308, 314 (C.C.P.A. 1977).

ㅠ

The adoption of the rule of reason, which has eased the requirement of corroboration with respect to evidence necessary to establish the credibility of the inventor, has not altered the requirement that evidence of corroboration must not depend solely on the inventor himself. Independent corroboration may consist of testimony of a witness, other than the inventor, to the actual reduction to practice or it may consist of evidence of surrounding facts and circumstances independent of information received from the inventor. *Reese and Katz v. Hurst and Krouse v. Wiewiorowski and Miller*, 661 F.2d 1222, 211 U.S.P.Q. 936, 940 (C.C.P.A. 1981).

ㅠ

This rule was developed over the years in order to ease the requirement of corroboration. It is usually applied when establishing actual reduction to practice. The rule suggests a reasoned examination, analysis, and evaluation of all pertinent evidence so that a sound determination of the credibility of the inventor's story may be reached. The rule of reason, however, does not dispense with the requirement for some evidence of independent corroboration. *Coleman v. Dines*, 754 F.2d 224 U.S.P.Q. 857 (Fed. Cir. 1985).

ㅠ

Under a rule of reason analysis, "[a]n evaluation of all pertinent evidence must be made so that a sound determination of the credibility of the inventor's story may be reached." *Mahurkar v. C.R. Bard Inc.*, 79 F.3d 1572, 38 U.S.P.Q.2d 1288, 1291 (Fed. Cir. 1996).

ㅠ

Under the "rule of reason" standard, "the Patent and Trademark Office [must] examine, analyze, and evaluate reasonably all [the] pertinent evidence." But a rule of reason analysis cannot overcome a lack of meaningful evidence that a claimed substance was obtained. *Schendel v. Curtis*, 83 F.3d 1399, 38 U.S.P.Q.2d 1743, 1747 n.7 (Fed. Cir. 1996).

ㅠ

With third parties unrelated to a patentee, it is often more difficult for the patentee to assure compliance with the marking provisions. A "rule of reason" approach is justified in such a case, and substantial compliance may be found to satisfy the statute. *Maxwell v. J. Baker Inc.*, 86 F.3d 1098, 39 U.S.P.Q.2d 1001, 1010 (Fed. Cir. 1996).

ʊ

"The law does not impose an impossible standard of 'independence' on corroborative evidence by requiring that every point of a reduction to practice be corroborated by evidence having a source totally independent of the inventor; indeed, such a standard is the antithesis of the rule of reason." *Knorr v. Pearson*, 671 F.2d 1368, 1374, 213 U.S.P.Q. 196, 201 (C.C.P.A. 1982). "In the final analysis, each corroboration case must be decided on its own facts with a view to deciding whether the evidence as a whole is persuasive." Although subsequent testing or later recognition may not be used to show that a party had contemporaneous appreciation of the invention, evidence of subsequent testing may be admitted for the purpose of showing that an embodiment was produced and that it met the limitations of the count. *Cooper v. Goldfarb*, 47 U.S.P.Q.2d 1896, 1904 (Fed. Cir. 1998).

Key Terms and Concepts

Safe Harbor. *See also* **35 U.S.C. §271(e)(2).**

As the term "substantial investment" is not defined in the statute, the Court has little guidance on this issue. Based on the purpose of Congress in creating the "safe harbor", the Court finds that expenditures of $1 million in preparing to market captopril, including costs for performing in vivo and in vitro tests and other research necessary to obtain FDA approval of its ANDA, satisfy the investment requirement and qualifies for operation under the "safe harbor" of URAA. *Bristol-Myers Squibb Co. v. Royce Laboratories Inc.*, 36 U.S.P.Q.2d 1637, 1640 n.7 (Fla. 1995), *rev'd* 69 F.3d 1130, 36 U.S.P.Q.2d 1641 (Fed. Cir. 1995).

ω

Under URAA's safe harbor provision, a patent owner may not assert the traditional remedies of 35 U.S.C. §283, 284, and 285 (1988) for qualifying acts of infringement committed during the period of a patent's extension (the "Delta" period). *Bristol-Myers Squibb Co. v. Royce Laboratories Inc.*, 69 F.3d 1130, 36 U.S.P.Q.2d 1641, 1644 (Fed. Cir. 1995).

Safety.

There is nothing in the patent statute which gives the Patent Office the right or the duty to require an applicant to prove that compounds or other materials which he is claiming, and which he has stated are useful for "pharmaceutical applications," are safe, effective, and reliable for use with humans. *In re Krimmel*, 292 F.2d 948, 130 U.S.P.Q. 215, 220 (C.C.P.A. 1961).

ω

With regard to the nature of safety in the field of drugs and medicaments, the court took judicial notice that many valued therapeutic substances or materials with desirable physiological properties, when administered to lower animals or humans, entailed certain risks or may have undesirable side effects. It is true that such substances would be more useful if they were not dangerous or did not have undesirable side effects, but the fact remains that they are useful, useful to doctors, veterinarians and research workers, useful to patients, both human and lower animal, and therefore useful in the meaning of of 35 U.S.C. §101. *In re Hartop and Brandes*, 311 F.2d 249, 135 U.S.P.Q. 419, 424, 425 (C.C.P.A. 1962).

ω

Having disclosed that claimed compounds are useful as tranquilizers, proof that hypotensive activity side effect is minimized (as compared to that of closest prior art counterpart) when so used is sufficient to establish unobviousness even though specific property of minimizing side effect was not disclosed in specification. *In re Zenitz*, 333 F.2d 924, 142 U.S.P.Q. 158, 161 (C.C.P.A. 1964).

ω

Congress has given the responsibility to the FDA, not to the Patent Office, to determine in the first instance whether drugs are sufficiently safe for use that they can be introduced in the commercial market. The FDA need not necessarily determine that a drug is commercially useful or usable before it may be "useful" in the patent law sense. *In re Anthony*, 414 F.2d 1383, 162 U.S.P.Q. 594, 604 (C.C.P.A. 1969).

ω

Although the patent statutes do not establish "safety" as a criterion for patentability of any of the statutory classes of patentable subject matter mentioned in 35 U.S.C. §101, it is undoubtedly true that the Patent Office and the courts over the years have considered "safety" as an aspect of the broader question of whether certain inventions (pharmaceuticals in particular) are "useful" within the meaning of 101 and its predecessors. At the same time it must be recognized that safety is a relative matter, and that absolute proof of complete safety is realistically impossible. *In re Watson*, 517 F.2d 465, 186 U.S.P.Q. 11, 19 (C.C.P.A. 1975).

Said.

The claim repeatedly refers to "said chamber" as it describes various portions of the apparatus. This term itself, "said chamber," reinforces the singular nature of the chamber. The claim does not place the sterilization zone vaguely within "a chamber," but within "said chamber." This language clarifies that only one chamber is in question. *AbTox Inc. v. Exitron Corp.*, 122 F.3d 1019, 43 U.S.P.Q.2d 1545, 1548 (Fed. Cir. 1997).

Sale. *See also* Agreement to Assign, Assignment, Capital Gains, Exhaustion, On Sale, Prior Sale.

For income tax purposes it is not significant (in determining whether an agreement constitutes a sale of a patent) that a patent has not been issued or even applied for at the time that all substantial rights are transferred. The 1966 letter amendment (to the 1961 agreement), which provided that the granted license would become non-exclusive if minimum stated royalties were not paid, does not preclude the 1961 agreement from being a sale of a patent. Assuming the retroactive effectiveness of the amendment, this clause merely established a condition subsequent, which does not negate a sale. *Newton Insert Co. v. Commissioner of Internal Revenue*, 181 U.S.P.Q. 765, 771, 772 (U.S.T.C. 1974).

ω

Where a method is kept secret, and remains secret after a sale of the product of the method, that sale will not bar another inventor from the grant of a patent on that method. The situation is different where that sale is made by the applicant for patent or his assignee. *The D.L. Auld Company v. Chroma Graphics Corp.*, 714 F.2d 1144, 219 U.S.P.Q. 13, 16 (Fed. Cir. 1983).

ω

When an executory sales contract is entered into (or offered), before a critical date, the purchaser must know how the invention embodied in the product will perform. The policies underlying the on-sale bar concentrate on the attempt by an inventor to exploit his invention, not whether the potential purchaser was cognizant of the invention. Accordingly, the purchaser need not have actual knowledge of the invention for it to be on sale. *King Instrument Corp. v. Otari Corp.*, 767 F.2d 853, 226 U.S.P.Q. 402 (Fed. Cir. 1985).

ω

Although the formal written assignment occurred after the critical date, the district court held that, even if there were an earlier oral agreement, an assignment or sale of the rights in the invention and potential patent rights is not a sale of "the invention" within the meaning of 35 U.S.C. §102(b). *Moleculon Research Corp. v. CBS, Inc.*, 793 F.2d 1261, 229 U.S.P.Q. 805 (Fed. Cir. 1986).

ω

A binding commitment (as of the reissue date) to purchase ordered products constituted a purchase of those products within the meaning of 35 U.S.C. §252. *Bic Leisure Products Inc. v. Windsurfing International Inc.*, 774 F.Supp. 832, 21 U.S.P.Q.2d 1548, 1551 (N.Y. 1991).

ω

A manufacturer's sales representative's solicitation of orders does not constitute the sale or use of infringing devices. *Ardco Inc. v. Page, Ricker, Felson Marketing Inc.*, 25 U.S.P.Q.2d 1382, 1384 (Ill. 1992).

Salt.

A claim directed to defined compounds "and the salts thereof" was rejected as being unduly broad insofar as it includes toxic as well as nontoxic materials and as being unsupported by the specification. Only simple salts were disclosed as yielding the desired result, and that was held to afford insufficient basis for assuming that all metals of the periodic system would be suitable for the intended purpose. *Ex parte Reed and Gunsalus*, 135 U.S.P.Q. 34, 36, 37 (PO Bd. App. 1961).

Same.

The substantial equivalent of a thing, in the sense of the patent law, is the same as the thing itself; so that if two devices do the same work in substantially the same way, and accomplish substantially the same result, they are the same, even though they differ in name, form, or shape. *Hugh W. Batcheller v. Henry Cole Co.*, 7 F. Supp. 898, 22 U.S.P.Q. 354, 358 (Mass. 1934).

Same Art.

The mere fact that both references originate from the herbicide art does not provide any teaching or suggestion to combine them. Nor does the fact that both references concern compounds containing a specific ring suggest that substituents suitable in one case would be expected to be suitable in the other. *In re Levitt,* 11 U.S.P.Q.2d 1315, 1316 (Fed. Cir. 1989—*unpublished*).

Same Date. *See also* **Simultaneous, Tie.**

The lower numbered of two patents issued on the same day to the same inventive entity for a related invention was held to be invalidating prior art against the higher numbered of those patents. Unclaimed subject matter in the lower numbered patent was regarded as dedicated to the public. *Underwood v. Gerber,* 149 U.S. 224 (1893).

ᚹ

A copending reference patent was issued to a different inventor on an application filed on the same date and refers to the subject application. The Patent Office tribunals stated that the subject application is presumed to be owned by the assignee of the copending reference patent. Since that statement was not controverted, it was accepted as correct. *In re Keim and Thompson,* 229 F.2d 466, 108 U.S.P.Q. 330, 331 (C.C.P.A. 1956).

ᚹ

In an interference between two parties who rely on the same date of corresponding foreign filings under the International Convention, neither is entitled to an award of priority. However, prior introduction of conception with regard to one count can be relied upon for priority purposes. *Lassman v. Brossi, Gerecke, and Kyburz,* 159 U.S.P.Q. 182, 184, 185 (PO Bd. Pat. Intf. 1967).

ᚹ

Having determined that each of two interference parties was entitled to the same effective filing date, the Board of Patent Interferences held that there was no first inventor of the subject matter of the count. Priority was "awarded against" each party. One of the parties was denied that filing date on appeal. *Anderson and Stamatoff v. Natta, Pino, and Mazzanti v. Ziegler, Martin, Breil, and Holzkamp,* 480 F.2d 1392, 178 U.S.P.Q. 458, 459, 463 (C.C.P.A. 1973).

Same Effect.

In support of a rejection under §112, later references were cited, not as prior art, but as evidence to prove the appellant's disclosure non-enabling for "other species" of the claimed polymer, in an effort to show why the scope of enablement was insufficient to support the claims. As thus implicitly recognized, the references would not have been available in support of a 35 U.S.C. §102 or §103 rejection entered in connection with the 1953 application. To permit use of the same references in support of the 35 U.S.C. §112 rejection herein, however, is to render the "benefit" of 35 U.S.C. §120 illusory. The very purpose of reliance on 120 is to reach back, to avoid the effect of intervening references. Nothing in §120 limits its application to any specific grounds of rejection, or permits the Examiner, denied use of references to reject or to require narrowing of a claim under §102 or §103, to achieve the same result by use of the same references under §112. Just as justice and reason require application of §112 in the same manner to applicants and Examiners, symmetry in the law, and evenness of its application, require that §120 be held applicable to all bases for rejection, that its words "same effect" be given their full meaning and intent. *In re Hogan and Banks,* 559 F.2d 595, 194 U.S.P.Q. 527 (C.C.P.A. 1977).

Same Invention. *See also* **Contemporaneous Independent Invention, Unity of Invention.**

Readability of a claim on the subject matter of another (patent) claim (domination) is neither determinative of double patenting nor demonstrative that the claims are directed to the same invention. *In re Sarett,* 327 F.2d 1005, 140 U.S.P.Q. 474, 482 (C.C.P.A. 1964).

ᗢ

While a species may be patentably distinct from a genus, when an earlier disclosed species is broadly the same invention as the genus, the requirement of 35 U.S.C. §119 that only "the same invention" (in the later application as is shown in the earlier) will obtain the benefit of the earlier filing date is satisfied for the purpose of overcoming references. *In re Ziegler, Breil, Holzkamp, and Martin,* 347 F.2d 642, 146 U.S.P.Q. 76, 82 (C.C.P.A. 1966).

ᗢ

Before two sets of claims may be said to claim the "same invention", they must *in fact* claim the *same subject matter.* Claims to a resin per se are not directed to the same invention as patent claims to a hair-setting composition comprising the resin dispersed in a solvent. *In re Walles, Tousignant, and Houtman,* 366 F.2d 786, 151 U.S.P.Q. 185, 188, 189 (C.C.P.A. 1966).

ᗢ

Section 101 of 35 U.S.C. prevents two patents from issuing on the same invention. "Invention" here means what is defined by the claims, whether new or old, obvious or unobvious; it must not be used in the ancient sense of "patentable invention," or hopeless confusion will ensue. A good test, and probably the only objective test, for "same invention" is whether one of the claims could be literally infringed without literally infringing the other. If it could be, the claims do not define identically the same invention. *In re Vogel and Vogel,* 422 F.2d 438, 164 U.S.P.Q. 619, 621, 622 (C.C.P.A. 1970).

ᗢ

When two patents claim different statutory classes of subject matter, composition and process, they are not directed to the same invention. This alone is sufficient to avoid same-invention-type double patenting. Before two sets of claims may be said to claim the same invention, they must in fact claim the same subject matter. By same invention is meant identical subject matter. Thus, the invention defined by a claim reciting "halogen" is not the same as that defined by a claim reciting "chlorine," because the former is broader than the latter. A good test, and probably the only objective test, for "same invention," is whether one of the claims would be literally infringed without literally infringing the other. If it could be, the claims do not define identically the same invention. *Studiengesellschaft Kohle mbH v. Northern Petrochemical Co.,* 784 F.2d 351, 228 U.S.P.Q. 837 (Fed. Cir. 1986).

ᗢ

The showing of "error" under 35 U.S.C. §251 is not identical to the "same invention" showing necessary under that provision. *Sonoco Products Co. v. Durabag Co. Inc.*, 30 U.S.P.Q.2d 1295, 1300 (Cal. 1994).

Same Inventor.

The term "the same inventor," as used in 35 U.S.C. §120, does not have a literal, narrow technical meaning. It must be construed with all other relevant sections of the statute, including §116 and §256; it thus embraces the possibility permitted by §116 and §256 that the earlier application may be corrected thereunder by changes in the name or names of the applicants under the conditions stated in §116. *In re Schmidt*, 293 F.2d 274, 130 U.S.P.Q. 404, 409 (C.C.P.A. 1961).

Same Patentable Invention.

In determining whether it is proper to designate a claim as corresponding to the Count, the pertinent inquiry is whether that claim and the Count define the same patentable invention, i.e., whether they are patentably distinct. If they are patentably distinct, then they do not define "the same patentable invention" under 37 C.F.R. §1.637 (c)(3)(ii). If they are not patentably distinct, then they do define the "the same patentable invention". The "same patentable invention" requirement of 37 C.F.R. §1.637(c)(3)(ii) concerns only the relationship between the Count and the claims sought to be additionally designated. It does not concern general patentability over the prior art. In that regard, what constitutes "the same patentable invention" in the context of an interference is defined by 37 C.F.R. §1.601(n). *Maier v. Hanawa*, 26 U.S.P.Q.2d 1606, 1609 (PTO Comm'r 1992).

Same Subject Matter.

When an applicant files two applications containing the same subject matter and makes a full assignment of one of the applications, the applicant conclusively elects to give preference to the assigned application and to assert in the unassigned application only such portion, if any, of the invention as is special thereto. *Ex parte Ferla*, 65 U.S.P.Q. 285, 286 (PO Bd. App. 1944).

Sanction.

A sanction against an attorney is not reviewable until final judgment is entered on the underlying action, even though the amount of that sanction has already been determined. *View Engineering Inc. v. Robotic Vision Systems Inc.*, 42 U.S.P.Q.2d 1956, 1958 (Fed. Cir. 1997).

Sanctions.

A court may impose sanctions where "a party 'shows bad faith by delaying or disrupting the litigation or by hampering enforcement of a court order.'" Without a finding of fraud or bad faith whereby the "very temple of justice has been defiled", a court enjoys no discretion to employ inherent powers to impose sanctions. *Amsted Industries Inc. v. Buckeye Steel Castings Co.*, 23 F.3d 374, 30 U.S.P.Q.2d 1470, 1473 (Fed. Cir. 1994).

ω

In discovery disputes sanctions under Rules 26 and 37 are preferable, and sanctions under Rule 11 are no longer allowed. *Tec-Air Inc. v. Nippondenso Manufacturing USA Inc.*, 33 U.S.P.Q.2d 1451, 1457 (Ill. 1994).

Saved Seed.

By reason of its proviso the first sentence of 7 U.S.C. §2543 allows seed that has been preserved for reproductive purposes ("saved seed") to be sold for such purposes. The structure of the sentence is such, however, that this authorization does *not* extend to saved seed that was *grown for the very purpose* of sale ("marketing") for replanting—because in that case, 2541(3) would be violated, and the above-discussed exception would apply. *Asgrow Seed Co. v. Winterboer*, 115 S.Ct. 788, 33 U.S.P.Q.2d 1430, 1435 (S.Ct. 1995).

Saving. *See also* Economics.

A change in shape that results in saving approximately 75 square feet of fabric per hundred shingles was held to warrant patent protection. *Ex parte Mortimer,* 61 F.2d 860, 15 U.S.P.Q. 297, 298 (C.C.P.A. 1932).

ω

The commercial use of these developments has already resulted in estimated savings of approximately 2 billion dollars in the United States alone. Such worthwhile inventions are worthy of patent protection. *Mobil Oil Corporation v. W.R. Grace & Company,* 367 F.Supp. 207, 180 U.S.P.Q. 418, 437 (Conn. 1973).

Scare Tactics.

Permitting a declaratory judgment defendant to engage in "[g]uerilla-like ... extra-judicial patent enforcement with scare-the-customer-and-run tactics that infect the competitive environment of the business community with uncertainty and insecurity," and, when those tactics are successful, to avoid proving the validity of its patents and associated claims of infringement in a court of law by claiming that its successful scare-the-customer-and-run tactic somehow mooted the parties' very real controversy would undermine the letter and spirit of the real controversy requirement, and would impermissibly encourage patent owners to engage in "extra-judicial patent enforcement" strategies. *BOC Health Care Inc. v. Nellcor Inc.*, 28 U.S.P.Q.2d 1293, 1298, 1299 (Del. 1993).

Scientific Classification. *See* Repugnant.

Scientific Evidence. *See* Rule 702.

Scientific Principle.

The law has other tests of invention than subtle conjecture of what might have been seen and yet was not. It regards a change as evidence of novelty, and the acceptance and utility of change as further evidence, even as demonstration. Nor does it detract from its merit that it is the result of experiment and not the instant and perfect product of inventive power. A patentee may be baldly empirical, seeing nothing beyond his experiments and the result; yet, if he has added a new and valuable article to the world's utilities, he is entitled to the rank and protection of an inventor. It is certainly not necessary that he understand or be able to state the scientific principles underlying his invention, and it is immaterial whether he can stand a successful examination as to the speculative ideas involved. *Diamond Rubber Co. v. Consolidated Rubber Tire Co.*, 220 U.S. 428, 435 (1911).

ᴡ

Where statements in a disclosure concerning utility are not contrary to generally accepted scientific principles and the Examiner has not presented reasons to doubt their objective truth, the Examiner's unsupported skepticism as to the utility of the claimed invention does not provide a legally acceptable basis for rejecting the claims. *Ex parte Krenzer,* 199 U.S.P.Q. 227, 229 (PTO Bd. App. 1978).

ᴡ

Claims which attempt to patent the scientific truth itself, rather than an application of the truth or a structure created by its use, are nonstatutory. *In re Diehr and Lutton*, 602 F.2d 982, 203 U.S.P.Q. 44, 49, 50 (C.C.P.A. 1979).

ᴡ

That the patented inventions were discoveries in disregard of scientific principles accepted by experts in the field indicates that the inventions were not obvious. *Continuous Curve Contact Lenses, Inc. v. National Patent Development Corporation*, 214 U.S.P.Q. 86, 115 (Cal. 1982).

ᴡ

A proper combination of references requires the presence of a teaching or suggestion in any of the references, or in the prior art as a whole, that would lead one of ordinary skill in the art to make the combination. The mere fact that a device or process utilizes a known scientific principle does not alone make that device or process obvious. *Uniroyal Inc. v. Rudkin-Wiley Corp.*, 837 F.2d 1044, 5 U.S.P.Q.2d 1434 (Fed. Cir. 1988).

Scientific Reasoning.

Inherency may not be established by probabilities or possibilities. The mere fact that a certain thing may result from a given set of circumstances is not sufficient. An applicant may be required to prove that the subject matter shown to be in prior art does not possess characteristics relied upon where an Examiner has reason to believe that a functional limitation asserted to be critical for establishing novelty in the claimed subject matter may, in fact, be an inherent characteristic of the prior art. However, the Examiner must provide some evidence or scientific reasoning to establish the reasonableness of the Examiner's belief that the functional limitation is an inherent characteristic of the prior art before the applicant can be put through this burdensome task. *Ex parte Skinner*, 2 U.S.P.Q.2d 1788 (B.P.A.I. 1986).

Scoffing.

A suit design which met with scorn and scoffing when first worn at the Nationals indicates that the design was novel and startling to persons at the National A.A.U. Tournament in 1965. *Hart v. Baarcke*, 396 F.Supp. 408, 186 U.S.P.Q. 275, 277 (Fla. 1975).

Scope. *See also* **Breadth, Commensurate in Scope, Limits, 35 U.S.C. §112.**

An applicant has a right to submit claims of varying scope. The practice of holding a limitation in a claim as not being critical, merely because it was omitted from other claims, is clearly not proper. *Ex parte Seavey*, 125 U.S.P.Q. 454, 457 (PO Bd. App. 1959).

ᙢ

A claim is a group of words defining only the boundary of the patent monopoly. It may not describe any physical thing, and indeed may encompass physical things not yet dreamed of. *In re Vogel and Vogel*, 422 F.2d 438, 164 U.S.P.Q. 619, 622 (C.C.P.A. 1970).

ᙢ

Significant evidence, if not the best evidence, of the scope of any one claim is the language employed in other claims. *Bethell and Hadley v. Koch, Robinson, and Wiley*, 427 F.2d 1372, 166 U.S.P.Q. 199, 201 (C.C.P.A. 1970).

ᙢ

If those skilled in the art can tell whether any particular embodiment is or in not within the scope of a claim, the claim fulfills its purpose as a definition. *In re Miller*, 441 F.2d 689, 169 U.S.P.Q. 597, 599 (C.C.P.A. 1971).

ᙢ

Although the CCPA (in contrast with a court adjudicating an infringement suit on an issued patent) gives "claims yet unpatented...the broadest reasonable interpretation consistent with the specification," it is also settled patent law that the disclosure may serve as a dictionary for terms appearing in the claims and that, in such instances, the disclosure may be used, even by the CCPA, in interpreting the claims and in determining their scope. *In re Barr, Williams, and Whitmore*, 444 F.2d 588, 170 U.S.P.Q. 330, 335 (C.C.P.A. 1971).

ᙢ

The first sentence of the second paragraph of 35 U.S.C. §112 is essentially a requirement for precision and definiteness of claim language. If the scope of subject matter embraced by a claim is clear, and if the applicant has not otherwise indicated that he intends the claim to be of a different scope, then the claim does particularly point out and distinctly claim the subject matter that the applicant regards as his invention. The requirement is that the language of the claims must make it clear what subject matter they encompass, and thus make clear the subject matter from which they would preclude others. *In re Conley, Catherwood, and Lloyd,* 490 F.2d 972, 180 U.S.P.Q. 454, 456 (C.C.P.A. 1974).

ω

That experimentation may be involved with the selection of proportions and particle sizes is not determinative of the question of scope of enablement; it is only undue experimentation that is fatal. *In re Geerdes,* 491 F.2d 1260, 180 U.S.P.Q. 789, 793 (C.C.P.A. 1974).

ω

In determining obviousness, three factual inquiries must be made: (1) the scope and content of the prior art, (2) differences between the prior art and the claims at issue, and (3) the level of ordinary skill in the art. To determine equivalency, the trier of fact must examine (1) the scope of the prior art, (2) the essence or "heart" of the patented invention or, put another way, "the step forward the invention offers", and (3) the particular circumstances of the case. *Connell v. Sears, Roebuck and Company,* 559 F.Supp. 229, 218 U.S.P.Q. 31, 37, 43 (Ala. 1983).

ω

The scope of the prior art is that art that would have been considered by those endeavoring to solve the problem that the patent in-suit allegedly solves. *Atlas Powder Company v. E.I. duPont de Nemours and Company,* 588 F.Supp. 1455, 221 U.S.P.Q. 426, 431 (Tex. 1983).

ω

The claims were intended to cover the use of the invention with various types of automobiles. That a particular chair of the claims may fit within some automobiles and not others is of no moment. The phrase "so dimensioned" is as accurate as the subject matter permits, automobiles being of various sizes. As long as those of ordinary skill in the art realize that the dimensions could be easily obtained, 35 U.S.C. §112, second paragraph, requires nothing more. The patent law does not require that all possible lengths corresponding to the spaces in hundreds of different automobiles be listed in the patent, let alone that they be listed in the claims. *Orthokinetics Inc. v. Safety Travel Chairs Inc.,* 806 F.2d 1565, 1 U.S.P.Q.2d 1081 (Fed. Cir. 1986).

ω

Where a claim of a patent is clearly broader in scope than one which was rejected during prosecution of the application on which the patent issued, a court "is not permitted to read [those removed limitations] back into the claims." *United States v. Telectronics, Inc.,* 857 F.2d 778, 783, 8 U.S.P.Q.2d 1217, 1221 (Fed. Cir. 1988), *cert. denied,* 490 U.S. 1046 (1989).

ω

[J]udicial statements regarding the scope of patent claims are hypothetical insofar as they purport to resolve the question of whether prior art or products not before the court would, respectively, anticipate or infringe the patent claims." *A.B. Dick Co. v. Burroughs Corp.,* 713 F.2d 700, 704, 218 U.S.P.Q. 965, 968 (Fed. Cir. 1983). "A device not previously before the court, and shown to differ from those structures previously litigated, requires determination on its own facts." *Del Mar Avionics, Inc. v. Quinton Instrument Co.*, 836 F.2d 1320, 1324, 5 U.S.P.Q.2d 1255, 1258 (Fed. Cir. 1987). *Young Engineers, Inc. v. United States Int'l Trade Commn*, 721 F.2d 1305, 1316, 219 U.S.P.Q. 1142, 1152 (Fed. Cir. 1983) ("With respect to patent litigation, we are unpersuaded that an "infringement claim," for purposes of claim preclusion, embraces more than the specific devices before the court in the first suit." However, "where a determination of the scope of patent claims was made in a prior case, and the determination was essential to the judgment there on the issue of infringement, there is collateral estoppel in a later case on the scope of such claims." *Molinaro v. Fanon/Couerier Corp.*, 745 F.2d 651, 655, 233 U.S.P.Q. 706, 708 (Fed. Cir. 1984). *Pfaff v. Wells Electronics Inc.*, 5 F.3d 514, 28 U.S.P.Q.2d 1119, 1122 (Fed. Cir. 1993).

ω

The field of search by the Patent Examiner is relevant objective evidence of the scope of the prior art. *Williams Service Group Inc. v. O.B. Cannon & Son Inc.*, 33 U.S.P.Q.2d 1705, 1725 (Pa. 1994).

ω

The rule against enlargement of claim scope during claim construction is well settled. *Hilton Davis Chemical Co. v. Warner-Jenkinson Co. Inc.*, 62 F.3d 1512, 35 U.S.P.Q.2d 1641, 1653 (Fed. Cir. 1995).

ω

The law does not require the impossible. Hence, it does not require that an applicant describe in his specification every conceivable and possible future embodiment of his invention." *International Rectifier Corp. v. SGS-Thomson Microelectronics Inc.*, 38 U.S.P.Q.2d 1083, 1086 (Cal. 1994).

ω

A patent's scope refers not to the geographical area within which the patent provides protection, but to the nature of the products covered by the patent's claims. *Mid-West Conveyor Co. v. Jervis B. Webb Co.*, 92 F.3d 992, 39 U.S.P.Q.2d 1754, 1757 (10th Cir. 1996).

ω

The scope of a claim and the number of compounds included within the scope are not irrelevant to a 35 U.S.C. §101 and/or a 35 U.S.C §112, first paragraph, analysis. However, no evidence was cited by the Examiner that any different reactivities would make some compounds useful and others not useful. *Ex parte Bhide*, 42 U.S.P.Q.2d 1441, 1447 (B.P.A.I. 1996).

ω

The presumption that separate claims have different scope "is a guide, not a rigid rule." *ATD Corp. v. Lydall Inc.*, 48 U.S.P.Q.2d 1321, 1325 (Fed. Cir. 1998).

Scope of Enablement.

In support of a rejection under 35 U.S.C. §112, later references were cited, not as prior art, but as evidence to prove the appellant's disclosure non-enabling for "other species" of the claimed polymer, in an effort to show why the scope of enablement was insufficient to support the claims. As thus implicitly recognized, the references would not have been available in support of a 35 U.S.C. §102 or §103 rejection entered in connection with the 1953 application. To permit use of the same references in support of the 35 U.S.C. §112 rejection herein, however, is to render the "benefit" of 35 U.S.C. §120 illusory. The very purpose of reliance on §120 is to reach back, to avoid the effect of intervening references. Nothing in §120 limits its application to any specific grounds of rejection, or permits the Examiner, denied use of references, to reject or to require narrowing of a claim under §102 or §103, to achieve the same result by use of the same references under §112. Just as justice and reason require application of §112 in the same manner to applicants and Examiners, symmetry in the law, and evenness of its application, require that §120 be held applicable to all bases for rejection, that its words "same effect" be given their full meaning and intent. *In re Hogan and Banks*, 559 F.2d 595, 194 U.S.P.Q. 527 (C.C.P.A. 1977).

Scope of Patent Protection.

The scope of claims of a patent can be read to cover subsequent advances. *American Hospital Supply Corp. v. Travenol Laboratories, Inc.*, 745 F.2d 1, 223 U.S.P.Q. 577 (Fed. Cir. 1984).

Scorn. *See* Scoffing.

Screening. *See also* Animal Tests.

A selection of various strains of a species identified in a Japanese application and screening (requiring at most 15 calendar days) those strains for efficacy in producing citric acid by following a provided example is not regarded as undue experimentation. *Tabuchi and Abe v. Nubel, Fitts, and Lorenzo*, 559 F.2d 1183, 194 U.S.P.Q. 521, 525 (C.C.P.A. 1977).

ω

A demonstration that a compound has desirable or beneficial properties in the prevention, alleviation, or cure of some disease in experimental animals does not necessarily mean that the compound will have the same properties when used with humans. However, this is by no means support for the position that such evidence is not relevant to human utility. Evidence showing substantial activity against experimental tumors in mice in tests customarily used for the screening of anti-cancer agents of potential utility in the treatment of humans is relevant to utility in humans and is not to be disregarded. *In re Jolles*, 628 F.2d 1322, 206 U.S.P.Q. 885, 890 (C.C.P.A. 1980).

ω

Amelioration of the symptoms or even cure of cancer is no longer considered to be "incredible." Nonetheless, decisional law would seem to indicate that the utility in question is sufficiently unusual to justify an Examiner's requiring substantiating evidence. Substantiating evidence may be in the form of animal tests that constitute recognized screening procedures with clear relevance to utility in humans. The specification of the appellant's parent application sets forth several animal tests on numerous types of specific cancers as well as in vitro studies, both of which are asserted to be predictive with regard to utility in humans. The Examiner has not challenged the evidence presented in a single, relevant, material respect. There is only the blanket statement of lack of "patentable utility" per se. In fact, the only specific comments the Examiner has directed toward the appellant's evidence are with regard to the breadth of the types of tumor against which the claimed compounds have been shown to be active. The appealed claims are drawn to compounds and not to a method of treatment. Generally speaking, utility in treating a single disease is an adequate basis for the patentability of a pharmaceutical compound under 35 U.S.C. §101. *Ex parte Krepelka*, 231 U.S.P.Q. 746 (B.P.A.I. 1986).

℧

Pharmaceutical utility of a compound (for patent purposes) is established when recognized screening procedures employing such compound produce results which are interpreted by those skilled in the art as showing such utility. *Ex parte Busse*, 1 U.S.P.Q.2d 1908, 1909 (B.P.A.I. 1986).

℧

Enablement is not precluded by the necessity for some experimentation, such as routine screening. However. experimentation needed to practice the invention must not be undue experimentation. The key word is "undue," not "experimentation." The determination of what constitutes undue experimentation in a case requires the application of a standard of reasonableness, having due regard for the nature of the invention and the state of the art. The test is not merely quantitative since a considerable amount of experimentation is permissible, if it is merely routine, or if the specification in question provides a reasonable amount of guidance with respect to the direction in which the experimentation should proceed. *In re Wands*, 858 F.2d 731, 8 U.S.P.Q.2d 1400, 1404 (Fed. Cir. 1988).

℧

Although rigorous correlation is not necessary, a test for pharmacological activity must be reasonably indicative of the desired response for screening tests to qualify as a "practical utility." There should be some evidence that one skilled in the art at the time the tests were performed would have been reasonably certain from the test data that the substance involved had practical utility. There must be some evidence of correlation between the tests and the treatment for some useful purpose. Mere activity in an in vitro test is inadequate in the absence of establishing appropriate correlation. *Hoffman v. Klaus*, 9 U.S.P.Q.2d 1657 (B.P.A.I. 1988).

Seal Record.

The determination of what constitutes a "proper case" in which to seal our record requires balancing the triangular interests of a trade secret owner, the court as an institution, and the public. Wherever possible, trade secret law and patent law should be administered in such manner that the former will not deter an inventor from seeking the benefit of the latter, because the public is most benefitted by the early disclosure of the invention in consideration of the patent grant. *In re Sarkar*, 575 F.2d 870, 197 U.S.P.Q. 788, 790, 791 (C.C.P.A. 1978).

Search.[1]

A patent applicant is entitled to a reasonable degree of latitude in complying with the second paragraph of 35 U.S.C. §112, and the Examiner may not dictate the literal terms of the claims for the stated purpose of facilitating a search of the prior art. Just how an applicant must comply with the second paragraph of 35 U.S.C. §112, within reason, is within applicant's discretion. *Ex parte Tanksley*, 37 U.S.P.Q.2d 1382, 1386 (B.P.A.I. 1994).

ʊ

The Federal Circuit has defined a "careful and thorough prior art search" in this context as normally "going beyond one's internal sources." *Graco Children's Products Inc. v. Century Products Co. Inc.*, 38 U.S.P.Q.2d 1331, 1342 (Pa. 1996).

Search Record. *See also* **Classification, Examiner, Field of Search.**

Even though not cited as a reference by the Examiner, there is no presumption in a patent infringement proceeding that uncited patents were overlooked since they may have been considered and cast aside as not pertinent. It is as reasonable to conclude that an uncited prior-art patent was considered and cast aside as not pertinent as it is to conclude that it was inadvertently overlooked. The question of whether the failure of the Examiner to cite certain art is consistent with its examination and rejection depends on the pertinency of the uncited art. The fact that the Examiner searched the specific subclass in which an uncited reference appears prevents finding affirmatively that the reference was not brought to the Examiner's attention. *Lundy Electronics & Systems, Inc. v. Optical Recognition Systems, Inc.*, 362 F. Supp. 130, 178 U.S.P.Q. 525, 534, 535 (Va. 1972).

ʊ

It is presumed that the Examiner considered and discarded uncited patent references that are classified in the class and subclasses in which the patent in suit issued, or in a class and subclass that have otherwise been indicated as having been searched by the Examiner. *Panduit Corp. v. Burndy Corp.*, 378 F. Supp. 775, 180 U.S.P.Q. 498, 505 (Ill. 1973).

ʊ

The Examiner's search record provides prima facie evidence that he searched all the references in the classes and subclasses noted on the file wrapper as having been searched. References in such subclasses left uncited are presumed to have been regarded by the Examiner as less relevant than those cited. A contrary view would destroy the presumption of administrative regularity on which the presumption of validity rests. *Railroad Dynamics, Inc. v. A. Stucki Co.*, 579 F. Supp. 353, 218 U.S.P.Q. 618 (Pa. 1983);

---

[1]It is a prerequisite to a speedy and just determination of the issues involved in the examination of an application that a careful and comprehensive search, commensurate with the limitations appearing in the most detailed claims in the case, be made in preparing the first action on the merits so that the second action on the merits can be made final or the application allowed with no further searching other than to update the original search. It is normally not enough that references be selected to meet only the terms of the claims alone, especially if only broad claims are presented; but the search should, insofar as possible, also cover all subject matter which the Examiner reasonably anticipates might be incorporated into applicant's amendment. MPEP 904.02 .

E.I. du Pont de Nemours & Co. v. Berkley & Company, Inc., 620 F.2d 1247, 205 U.S.P.Q. 1, 16 (8th Cir. 1980).

ϖ

It cannot be presumed, where fraud or other egregious conduct is alleged, that the PTO considered uncited prior art (among references included within the scope of the PTO's search) of particular relevance. *Driscoll v. Cebalo*, 731 F.2d 878, 221 U.S.P.Q. 745, 751 (Fed. Cir. 1984).

ϖ

The field of search by the Patent Examiner is relevant objective evidence of the scope of the prior art. *Williams Service Group Inc. v. O.B. Cannon & Son Inc.*, 33 U.S.P.Q.2d 1705, 1725 (Pa. 1994).

Secondary Characteristics. *See* **Secondary Considerations.**

Secondary Considerations. *See also* **Commercial Success, Copying, Disbelief, Failure of Others, Graham Inquiries, Industry Acceptance, Long-Felt Need, Objective Evidence, Skepticism, Widespread Use.**

The most pertinent prior art was considered by the Patent Office before granting each of the patents in suit; the normal presumption of validity accorded the patents in suit is therefore strengthened. The normal presumption of validity accorded a patent is reinforced after the patent has been adjudicated valid. The claimed catalysts have been remarkably commercially successful; while commercial success is not a substitute for invention, it is evidence thereof. The fact that defendant copied the inventions of the patents in suit rather than the prior art is further evidence of invention. The fact that the catalysts of the patents in suit promptly displaced the best prior-art commercial catalyst (in use for more than 20 years) is persuasive evidence of the validity of said patents. The fact that defendant hailed the catalysts of the patents in suit as a "breakthrough of major proportions" and as "the most...significant catalyst advance in...27 years" is persuasive evidence that the inventions of the patents in suit were not obvious. The facts that the individual elements of the catalysts of the patents in suit were available to the art, that industrywide research was conducted over a period of years in an effort to improve the catalysts then in use, that all such efforts were unsuccessful, and that, when the catalysts of the patents in suit appeared, they displaced the best prior-art commercial catalysts (which had been used for 20 years) are persuasive evidence of non-obviousness. When news of the patented catalysts first reached scientific experts in the art, they were skeptical of the feasibility of the patented catalysts; after reviewing results of tests conducted using the patented catalysts, at least one of those experts subsequently hailed the inventions as being "revolutionary;" this is persuasive evidence of non-obviousness. *Mobil Oil Corp. v. W. R. Grace & Co.*, 367 F. Supp. 207, 180 U.S.P.Q. 418, 452 (Conn. 1973).

ϖ

The longstanding need for an innovation like appellants" claimed invention, the attempt and failure of others to satisfy that need, and the outstanding commercial success of the device, once marketed, strongly suggest that the patented combination was not obvious to others working in the same field. *Shackelton v. J. Kaufman Iron Works, Inc.*, 689 F.2d 334, 217 U.S.P.Q. 98, 103 (2d Cir. 1982).

ᛖ

The so-called "secondary" indicia of non-obviousness, such as the commercial success of the device, long-felt but unsolved needs, and prior unsuccessful attempts to solve the problem ultimately addressed by the new invention, are valid and relevant criteria in determining the level of ordinary skill in the relevant art and, therefore, in determining obviousness. *Sarkisian v. Winn-Proof Corp.*, 696 F.2d 1313, 217 U.S.P.Q. 702, 709 (9th Cir. 1983).

ᛖ

[E]vidence of secondary considerations may often be the most probative and cogent evidence in the record. It may often establish that an invention appearing to have been obvious in light of the prior art was not. It is to be considered as part of all the evidence, not just when the decisionmaker remains in doubt after reviewing the art. *In re Piasecki and Meyers*, 745 F.2d 1468, 223 U.S.P.Q. 785, 790 (Fed. Cir. 1984).

ᛖ

The differences between the prior art and the invention defined by the asserted claims, the availability of that art to all workers in the field, the failure of established competitors in a highly competitive market to make the invention despite the incentive to do so, the admittedly non-unobvious performance benefits realized through the claimed invention, the impressive commercial success of the claimed product, the praise of independent commentators and the forbearance of competitors from infringing the patent all go to confirm that the claimed invention was not obvious at the time it was made to a person of ordinary skill in the art. *S.C. Johnson & Son, Inc. v. Carter-Wallace, Inc.*, 614 F. Supp. 1278, 225 U.S.P.Q. 1022 (N.Y. 1985).

ᛖ

Evidence of secondary considerations is to be taken into account always, not just when the decision maker remains in doubt after reviewing the art. Nevertheless, a nexus between the merits of the claimed invention and the evidence of secondary considerations is required in order for the evidence to be given substantial significance in an obviousness decision. Thus, the weight to be accorded evidence on secondary considerations is to be carefully appraised in relation to the facts of the actual case in which it is offered. For commercial success of a product embodying a claimed invention to have true relevance to the issue of non-obviousness, that success must be shown to have been due in some way to the nature of the claimed invention, as opposed to other economic and commercial factors unrelated to the technical quality of the patented subject matter. Thus, a nexus is required between the merits of the claimed invention and the evidence offered, if that evidence is to be given substantial weight en route to a conclusion on the obviousness issue. *Cable Electric Products, Inc. v. Genmark, Inc.*, 770 F.2d 1015, 226 U.S.P.Q. 881 (Fed. Cir. 1985).

ᛖ

The objective evidence of secondary considerations may be entitled to more or less weight, depending on its nature and its relationship to the merits of the invention. Secondary considerations may be the most important, probative, and revealing evidence available to the decision maker in reaching a conclusion on the obviousness/non-obviousness issue. While it is incumbent upon the decision maker to recognize that evidence of secondary considerations need not be necessarily conclusive on the obviousness/non-obviousness issue, the decision maker must also bear in mind that, under certain circumstances, the evidence on secondary considerations may be particularly strong and entitled to such weight that it may be decisive. *Ashland Oil, Inc. v. Delta Resins & Refractories, Inc.*, 776 F.2d 281, 227 U.S.P.Q. 657 (Fed. Cir. 1985).

ω

That secondary considerations are not considered unless there is evidence that those in the industry knew of the prior art is a non sequitur. Evidence of secondary considerations is considered independently of what any real person knows about the prior art. These considerations are objective criteria of obviousness that help illuminate the subjective determination involved in the hypothesis used to draw the legal conclusion of obviousness based upon the first three factual inquiries delineated in *Graham* [383 U.S. 1, 148 U.S.P.Q. 459 (1966)]. Thus, to require that actual inventors in the field have the omniscience of the hypothetical person in the art is not only contrary to case law, but eliminates a useful tool for trial judges faced with a non-obviousness determination. *Hodosh v. Block Drug Co.*, 786 F.2d 1136, 229 U.S.P.Q. 182 (Fed. Cir. 1985).

ω

The court found that "the commercial success of the kits may well be attributed to the business expertise and acumen of the plaintiff's personnel, together with its capital base and marketing abilities" and later that "where commercial success is based on the sudden availability of starting materials, in this instance, the availability of monoclonal antibodies as a result of the Kohler and Milstein discovery, business acumen, marketing ability, and capital sources, no causal relationship is proven."

The undisputed evidence is that Hybritech's diagnostic kits had a substantial market impact. The first diagnostic kit sales occurring in mid 1981, sales increased $7 million in just over one year, sales in 1980 were nonexistent. Competing with products from industry giants, Hybritech's HCG kit became the market leader with roughly 25 percent of the market at the expense of market shares of the other companies. Hybritech's other kits, indisputably embodying the invention claimed in the '110 patent, obtained similar substantial market positions.

With respect to the objective indicia of non-obviousness, while there is evidence that marketing and financing played a role in the success of Hybritech's kits, as they do with any product, it is clear to us on the entire record that the commercial success here was due to the merits of the claimed invention. It cannot be argued on this record that Hybritech's success would have been as great and as prolonged as admittedly it has been if that success were not due to the merits of the invention. The evidence is that these kits compete successfully with numerous others for the trust of persons who have to make fast, accurate, and safe diagnoses. This is not the kind of merchandise that can be sold by advertising hyperbole. *Hybritech Inc. v. Monoclonal Antibodies, Inc.*, 802 F.2d 1367, 231 U.S.P.Q. 81, 92, 93 (Fed. Cir. 1986).

ω

Objective evidence of non-obviousness includes commercial success, long-felt but unresolved need, failure of others, and copying. When present, such objective evidence must be considered. It can be the most probative evidence of non-obviousness in the record, and enables the district court to avert the trap of hindsight. On the other hand, the absence of objective evidence does not preclude a holding of non-obviousness because such evidence is not a requirement for patentability. *Custom Accessories Inc. v. Jeffrey-Allan Industries Inc.*, 807 F.2d 955, 1 U.S.P.Q.2d 1196 (Fed. Cir. 1986).

ω

The commercial success of a patented invention is clearly important. That evidence is "secondary" in time does not mean that it is secondary in importance. Evidence of secondary considerations may often be the most probative and cogent evidence in the record. *Trustwall Systems Corp. v. Hydro-Air Engineering Inc.*, 813 F.2d 1207, 2 U.S.P.Q.2d 1034 (Fed. Cir. 1987).

ω

Satisfaction of a long-felt, but unfilled, need for a device is evidence that the device is a significant advance in the art. Other factors that demonstrate the significance of an invention include unsuccessful attempts by others to accomplish the results of the patented invention, commercial success of the patented invention, and praise or awards for the patented device. *Micro Motion Inc. v. Exac Corp.*, 741 F. Supp. 1426, 16 U.S.P.Q.2d 1001, 1008 (Cal. 1990).

ω

Considerations, such as commercial success, long-felt but unsolved needs, and the failure of others to invent, are relevant to the obviousness inquiry. In reviewing the grant of summary judgment, the CAFC accepts appellant's evidence on secondary considerations as true. *Ryko Manufacturing Co. v. Nu-Star Inc.*, 950 F.2d 714, 21 U.S.P.Q.2d 1053, 1057 (Fed. Cir. 1991).

ω

"[T]he weight to be accorded evidence of secondary considerations is to be carefully appraised in relation to the facts of the actual case in which it is offered." *Alpex Computer Corp. v. Nintendo Co. Ltd.*, 88 Civ. 1749, 34 U.S.P.Q.2d 1167, 1189 (N.Y. 1994).

Secondary Considerations in Design.

No evidence of long-felt need or failure of others was adduced at trial to show either the efforts or the failure of others who have employed similar designs in their furniture to correct any "problem" that the patented design solved. Since a design patent covers only the optional aesthetic features, there is never a long-felt need or any unsuccessful search, and it is rarely possible to allocate the specific portions of the profits on a commercial product that are respectively attributable to its utilitarian advantages and to its visual appeal. Thus, in the final analysis, the court's evaluation of a design is essentially subjective, and personal artistic tastes are unpredictable and inapplicable—one viewer's mural is another's graffiti. *Benchcraft Inc. v. Broyhill Furniture Industries, Inc.*, 681 F. Supp. 1190, 7 U.S.P.Q.2d 1257, 1278 (Miss. 1988).

Secondary Reference.

A final rejection of amended claims can properly be based on a reference that was only applied as a secondary reference in a prior Office Action. *Ex parte Hoogendam,* 1939 C.D. 3, 40 U.S.P.Q. 389 (Commr. Patents 1939).

Secondary Tests. *See* **Secondary Considerations.**

Second Lowest Bidder.

The theory for recovery against the government for patent infringement is not analogous to that in litigation between private parties; the government's infringement is deemed a "taking" of a patent license under an eminent domain theory, rather than under a patent-infringement damages statute. The federal government and contract bid procedures also cannot be compared to the contract dealings between private companies. The patentee need not be the second lowest bidder in order to recover lost profits on survey jobs lost to defendant. *T. D. Williamson Inc. v. Laymon,* 723 F. Supp. 587, 13 U.S.P.Q.2d 1417, 1432 (Okla. 1989).

Secrecy. *See* **Access, Confidentiality, FOIA.**

Secret. *See also* **Classified.**

The use of an invention in secret for commercial purposes is considered public use. *Kewanee Oil Company v. Bicron Corporation,* 478 F.2d 1074, 178 U.S.P.Q. 3, 6 (6th Cir. 1973).

ϖ

An inventor who had merely made a secret use of his discovery should not be regarded as the first inventor. *Dunlop Holdings Limited v. Ram Golf Corporation,* 524 F.2d 33, 188 U.S.P.Q. 481, 483 (7th Cir. 1975).

ϖ

Where a method is kept secret, and remains secret after a sale of the product of the method, that sale will not bar another inventor from the grant of a patent on that method. The situation is different where that sale is made by the applicant for patent or his assignee. *The D.L. Auld Company v. Chroma Graphics Corp.,* 714 F.2d 1144, 219 U.S.P.Q. 13, 16 (Fed. Cir. 1983).

ϖ

Early public disclosure is a linchpin of the patent system. As between a prior inventor who benefits from a process by selling its product, but suppresses, conceals, or otherwise keeps the process from the public, and a later inventor who promptly files a patent application from which the public will gain disclosure of the process, the law favors the latter. *W. L. Gore & Associates, Inc. v. Garlock, Inc.,* 721 F.2d 1540, 220 U.S.P.Q. 303 (Fed. Cir. 1983).

ϖ

Private laboratory research use, occurring after a laboratory "reduction to practice," does not become a public use under 35 U.S.C. 102(b). *Cf. W.L. Gore & Assoc., Inc. v.*

Garlock Inc., 721 F.2d 1540, 1550, 220 U.S.P.Q. 303, 310 (Fed. Cir. 1983) [a third person's secret commercial activity, more than one year before the patent application of another, is not a 35 U.S.C. 102(b) bar to the patent of another], *cert. denied*, 469 U.S. 851 (1984). The term "secret prior art" is used for prior art under 35 U.S.C. §102(e). This law reflects a careful balancing of public policies, for it is an exception to the rule that "prior art" is that which is available to the public. *Hazeltine Research v. Brenner*, 382 U.S. 252, 254-55, 147 U.S.P.Q. 429, 431 (1965).

Secret Patent.

There seems to be no logical reason why the granting of a secret patent abroad should be a bar to patenting in this country. Such a foreign patent is of no value to persons in this country unless and until it is made available to the public. Even widespread public knowledge of an invention abroad does not alone bar the grant of a patent in this country, and it is not reasonable to suppose that Congress intended to give greater effect to secret patenting abroad than to public knowledge there. *In re Ekenstam*, 256 F.2d 321, 118 U.S.P.Q. 349, 351 (C.C.P.A. 1958).

Security. *See* Classified.

Seed.[2]

Assuming that seeds may be deposited in the same manner as microorganisms to comply with 35 U.S.C. §112, there is insufficient evidence in the record as to the availability of the deposited seeds. The depository is not a recognized public depository, and there is no evidence indicating that the depository is under a contractual obligation to maintain the seeds deposited in a permanent collection and to supply samples to anyone seeking them once the patent issues. *Ex parte Hibberd*, 227 U.S.P.Q. 443, 447 (B.P.A.I. 1985).

Segregable Part.

If a thing is a "segregable part" of a combination design, the thing is "patentably distinct" from the combination. Otherwise, design patent rights for the combination would extend to the part as well. *Blumcraft of Pittsburgh v. Ladd*, 238 F.Supp. 648, 144 U.S.P.Q. 562, 564 (D.C. 1965).

Selecting.

Steps, such as "computing," "determining," "cross-correlating," "comparing," "selecting," "initializing," "testing," "modifying," and "identifying," have implicitly been found to recite the solving of a mathematical algorithm. *In re Warmerdam*, 33 F.3d 1354, 31 U.S.P.Q.2d 1754, 1758 (Fed. Cir. 1994).

---

[2]Claims directed to hybrid seeds and to hybrid plants have been allowed because the PVPA and the PPA exclude such subject matter. *Ex parte Hibberd*, 227 U.S.P.Q. 443, 444 n.1 (B.P.A.I. 1985).

Selection.[3] *See also* **Encyclopedic Disclosure, Generic, Generic Disclosure, Limitation, Mosaic, Selective Extraction from Prior Art, Shotgun.**

The mere selection of a different known material from which a claimed product is made on the basis of suitability for intended use is entirely obvious under 35 U.S.C. §103. *In re Leshin*, 277 F.2d 197, 125 U.S.P.Q. 416, 418 (C.C.P.A. 1960).

ω

There is nothing unobvious in choosing "some" among "many" indiscriminately. However, obviousness is overcome by showing that the choice is based on a discovery that some compounds, falling within a prior-art genus, have a special significance, particularly where there is nothing in the prior art to suggest the established criticality of the "some." *In re Lemin*, 332 F.2d 839, 141 U.S.P.Q. 814, 815, 816 (C.C.P.A. 1964).

ω

The Solicitor relies on *In re Winslow*, 365 F.2d 1017, 151 U.S.P.Q. 48 (1966), for the proposition that a combination of features shown by references is legally obvious if it would have been obvious to "the inventor...working in his shop with the prior art references—which he is presumed to know—hanging on the wall around him," 151 U.S.P.Q. at 51, a statement limited by reference to "a case like this." In Winslow, the principal secondary reference was "in the very same art" as appellant's invention; all of the references were characterized as "very pertinent art." The language relied on by the Solicitor does not apply in cases where the very point in issue is whether one of ordinary skill in the art would have *selected*, without the advantage of hindsight and knowledge of the applicant's disclosure, the particular references that the Examiner applied. The inventor is presumed (under 35 U.S.C. §103) to have full knowledge of the prior art *in the field of his endeavor*, but not full knowledge of prior art *outside the field of his endeavor* (i.e., of "non-analogous" art). The inventor is only presumed to have that ability to select and utilize knowledge from other arts reasonably pertinent to his particular problem that

---

[3]The Commissioner of Patents and Trademarks contends that *Baird* [29 U.S.P.Q.2d 1550 (Fed. Cir. 1994)] was wrongly decided "because an improper standard of patentability under 35 U.S.C. §103 was applied in assessing the obviousness question before the Court." The PTO (in a Notice distributed to Examiners) stated:

The Court's decision in *Baird* is inconsistent with applicable binding precedent. The Board of Patent Appeals and Interferences (Board), in correctly deciding the case, applied and cited the proper binding precedent, which includes *In re Susi*, 440 F.2d 442, 169 USPQ 423 (CCPA 1971), followed by the Federal Circuit in *Merck & Co. v. Biocraft Laboratories, Inc.*, 74 F.2d 804, 10 USPQ2d 1843 (Fed. Cir.), *cert. denied*, 493 U.S. 975 (1989).

To maintain uniform standards in the examination of patent applications, patent Examiners were directed to follow the *Susi* and *Merck* decisions rather than the *Baird* decision and to cite the Notice as a full response to any applicant who may rely on the *Baird* decision in responding to rejections. Bruce A. Lehman, March 22, 1994, 1161 OG 314, April 19, 1994. This Commissioner's Notice was criticized as creating significant confusion because the cases relied upon by the Commissioner are not incompatible with the *Baird* decision. In *Merck & Co. v. Biocraft Laboratories, Inc.*, "the prior art clearly led in very specific ways to the claimed invention." In the *Baird* Case, "the prior art fell significantly short of leading toward the claimed invention. So in one case the Court found the claims obvious, in the second case, found them nonobvious." We now have an incomprehensible "order issued by the Patent Office basically saying they will follow one case; they will not follow the other case." American Bar Association, Section of Intellectual Property Law, "Annual Report 1993-1994", page 459.

would be expected of a person of ordinary skill in the art to which the subject matter pertains. *In re Antle*, 444 F.2d 1168, 170 U.S.P.Q. 285, 287, 288 (C.C.P.A. 1971).

ᗡ

That experimentation may be involved with the selection of proportions and particle sizes is not determinative of the question of scope of enablement; it is only undue experimentation that is fatal. *In re Geerdes*, 491 F.2d 1260, 180 U.S.P.Q. 789, 793 (C.C.P.A. 1974).

ᗡ

The claimed combination of physical characteristics is not suggested by the references, alone or combined; no showing has been made that one skilled in the art would select the four specifically claimed physical characteristics, much less the ranges specified for them; the claimed ranges are critical and produce unexpected results in an improved elastomeric platform; and the relationship of the claimed physical characteristics is one of random, rather than mathematical, correlation. *In re Saether*, 492 F.2d 849, 181 U.S.P.Q. 36, 41 (C.C.P.A. 1974).

ᗡ

A reference disclosure that is generic to or suggestive of a claimed product does not preclude patentability of the product if the product possesses one or more significant properties that are not shared by its closest counterpart(s) within the disclosed or suggested genus, or if the claimed product is significantly better (with regard to a material property) than its closest counterpart(s) within the disclosed or suggested genus. *In re Ruschig, Aümuller, Korger, Wagner, Scholz, and Bänder*, 343 F.2d 965, 145 U.S.P.Q. 274, 281, 283 (C.C.P.A. 1965); *In re Krazinski, Shepherd, and Taft*, 347 F.2d 656, 146 U.S.P.Q. 25, 29, 30 (C.C.P.A. 1965); *In re Fay and Fox*, 347 F.2d 597, 146 U.S.P.Q. 47, 50 (C.C.P.A. 1965); *In re Petrzilka, Hofmann, Schenk, Troxler, Frey, and Ott*, 424 F.2d 1102, 165 U.S.P.Q. 327, 328, 329 (C.C.P.A. 1970); *In re Waymouth and Koury*, 499 F.2d 1273, 182 U.S.P.Q. 290, 292, 293 (C.C.P.A. 1974).

ᗡ

Validity is dependent upon whether the inventor's selection of particular elements to produce the results achieved was obvious prior to the time the invention was made. *Rosemount Inc. v. Beckman Instruments, Inc.*, 569 F.Supp. 934, 218 U.S.P.Q. 881, 899 (Cal. 1983).

ᗡ

The selection of the ratio of total jaw length to the average jaw height and the narrow range of hardness claimed is not a matter of obvious design choice to one of ordinary skill in the art at the time the invention was made. It is axiomatic that not only must claims be given their broadest reasonable interpretation consistent with the specification, but also all limitations must be considered. Here the characterization of certain specific limitations or parameters as obvious does not make the appellant's invention, considered as a whole, obvious. The fact that the invention may have been the result of experimentation does not negate patentability nor render obvious claimed parameters that were the result of experimentation. *Ex parte Petersen*, 228 U.S.P.Q. 216, 217 (B.P.A.I. 1985).

ᗡ

When a claimed invention is not identically disclosed in a reference, and instead requires picking and choosing among a number of different options disclosed by the reference, then the reference does not anticipate. *Mendenhall v. Astec Industries, Inc.*, 13 U.S.P.Q.2d 1913, 1928 (Tenn. 1988), *aff'd*, 13 U.S.P.Q.2d 1956 (Fed. Cir. 1989).

ϖ

That a reference patent discloses a multitude of effective combinations does not render any particular formulation less obvious. This is especially true when the claimed composition is used for the identical purpose taught by the prior art. {Decision relied uopn an *ex parte* affirmation of an obviousness rejection where the disclosure of the prior art was "huge, but it undeniably include[d] at least some of the compounds recited in appellant's generic claims and it is of a class of chemicals to be used for the same purpose as appellant's additives".} *Merck & Co. Inc. v. Biocraft Laboratories Inc.*, 874 F.2d 804, 10 U.S.P.Q.2d 1843, 1846 (Fed. Cir. 1989), *cert. denied*, 493 U.S. 975 (1989).

ϖ

The generic diphenol formula disclosed in the reference relied upon contains a large number of variables (including, perhaps, more than 100 million different diphenols, only one of which is that called for by appellant's claim). While the reference formula unquestionably encompasses bisphenol A when specific variables are chosen, there is nothing in the reference disclosure suggesting that one should select such variables. Indeed, the reference appears to teach away from the selection of bisphenol A by focusing on more complex diphenols. The Board clearly erred in finding that the reference would have provided the requisite motivation for the selection of bisphenol A in the preparation of the claimed compounds. *In re Baird*, 16 F.3d 380, 29 U.S.P.Q.2d 1550, 1552 (Fed. Cir. 1994).

ϖ

When an appropriate selection is made for a number of different variables provided by a reference generic formula, a subclass of compounds (not separately set forth in the reference) results. The subclass of compounds differs from claimed compounds in only one respect—a hydrogen is attached to a nitrogen of the reference subclass, whereas a methyl is attached to the corresponding nitrogen of the claimed compounds. A rejection based on structural similarity was overcome by pointing out that, with regard to another variable, the reference distinguished between -NH- and $-NCH_3-$. *Ex parte Casagrande, Montanari, and Santangelo*, 36 U.S.P.Q.2d 1860 (B.P.A.I. 1995—*unpublished*).

Selective Extraction from Prior Art. *See also* **Combination Invention, Reason, Retrospective Reconstruction, Selection.**

Presuming arguendo that the references show the elements or concepts urged, the Examiner presented no line of reasoning as to why the artisan reviewing only the collective teachings of the references would have found it obvious to selectively pick and choose various elements and/or concepts from the several references relied on to arrive at the claimed invention. In the instant application, the Examiner has done little more than cite references to show that one or more elements or some combinations thereof, when each is viewed in a vacuum, is known. The claimed invention, however, is clearly directed to a combination of elements. That is to say, the appellant does not claim that he has invented one or more new elements but has presented claims to a new combination of elements. To support the conclusion that the claimed combination is directed to obvious subject matter, either the references must expressly or impliedly suggest the claimed combination or the Examiner must present a convincing line of reasoning as to why the artisan would have found the claimed invention to have been obvious in light of the teachings of the references. The Board found nothing in the references that would expressly or impliedly teach or suggest the modifications urged by the Examiner. Additionally, the Board found no line of reasoning in the answer as to why the artisan would have found the modifications urged by the Examiner to have been obvious. Based upon the record, the artisan would not have found it obvious to selectively pick and choose elements or concepts from the various references so as to arrive at the claimed invention without using the claims as a guide. *Ex parte Clapp*, 227 U.S.P.Q. 972 (B.P.A.I. 1985).

ϖ

It is impermissible within the framework of 35 U.S.C. §103 to pick and choose from any one reference only so much of it as will support a given position to the exclusion of other parts necessary to the full appreciation of what such reference fairly suggests to one skilled in the art. *Bausch & Lomb, Inc. v. Barnes-Hind/Hydrocurve, Inc.*, 796 F.2d 443, 230 U.S.P.Q. 416 (Fed. Cir. 1986).

Self-Evaluative Privilege.

The three-pronged self-evaluative privilege test is:

a) the information which is the subject of a production request must be the criticisms or evaluations or the product of an evaluation or critique conducted by the party opposing the production request;

b) the "public need for confidentiality" of such analysis must be such that the unfettered internal availability of such information should be encouraged as a matter of public policy; and

c) the analysis or evaluation or opinion must be of the character that would uresult in the termination of such self-evaluative inquiries or critical input in future situations if this information is subject to disclosure.

NeoRx Corp. v. Immunomedics Inc., 28 U.S.P.Q.2d 1797, 1798 (N.J. 1993).

Self-Serving.

If the Patent Office wishes to discredit expert or lay testimony, the obvious method would be to provide witnesses, rather than merely characterizing the testimony as self-serving. *General Radio Company v. Watson*, 188 F.Supp. 879, 125 U.S.P.Q. 268, 274 (D.C. 1960).

ϖ

An intercompany memorandum of what took place during a meeting was a self-serving document presented in an interference proceeding and the only contemporaneous evidence close enough in point of time to the subject meeting. The author of the memorandum averred that the unrebutted statements therein are true, and there is thus a strong presumption that such statements are accurate. *Beyard and Horai v. Conte*, 179 U.S.P.Q. 499, 502 (PO Bd. Pat. Intf. 1972).

ϖ

The so-called "shop-book rule" does not apply to reports of scientific work in an interference proceeding. Such reports generally cannot be relied upon to prove the facts asserted therein and, therefore, cannot be relied on to establish reduction to practice since they are self-serving and not an independent corroboration of an inventor's testimony. *Horton v. Stevens*, 7 U.S.P.Q.2d 1245, 1249 (B.P.A.I. 1988).

Sell. *See* **Sale.**

Semiconductor Chip Protection Act. *See* **Maskwork Act.**

Separable. *See also* **Making Integral.**

A structure having a removable cap was held to be unpatentable over a similar structure with a "press fitted" cap. *In re Dulberg*, 283 F.2d 522, 129 U.S.P.Q. 348, 349 (C.C.P.A. 1961).

Separate. *See also* **Distinct.**

Where different parts of an integrally-connected structure have different purpose and effect, such parts may be separately recited as individual components. *Ex parte Vibber*, 144 U.S.P.Q. 278, 280 (PO Bd. App. 1959).

Separation.

Since separation and identification of the individual isomers involved are operations within the skill of the art and are not essential to the disclosed uses, they need not be set forth in a patent application to render it a constructive reduction to practice. *Hauptschein, Braid, and Lawlor v. McCane and Robinson*, 339 F.2d 460, 144 U.S.P.Q. 16, 19 (C.C.P.A. 1964).

Service. *See also* **Hague Evidence Convention.**

Service by facsimile is not sufficient to satisfy Fed. R. Civ. P. 5(b). *Mushroom Associates v. Monterey Mushrooms Inc.*, 25 U.S.P.Q.2d 1304, 1307 (Cal. 1992).

Service on Foreign National. *See* **Hague Convention.**

Settlement.

The plaintiff was induced to accept the terms of a compromise settlement offer by representations that this litigation and its consequential legal expenses would be at an end.

The promised bargain was not realized by the plaintiff because of the Asgrow Companies'' almost immediate collateral attack upon the consent judgment once it was approved and entered by this court. As a direct result, the plaintiff sustained unforeseen legal expenses in seeking to preserve and enforce the settlement agreement to which the Asgrow Companies had silently acquiesced during negotiations and hearings prior to entry of the final order. The conduct of the Asgrow Companies demonstrates sufficient bad faith to warrant an award of attorney's fees to the plaintiff. *Research Corp. v. Pfister Associates Growers, Inc.*, 318 F. Supp. 1405, 168 U.S.P.Q. 206, 208 (Ill. 1970).

ᛒ

Patents may be declared invalid at the district court level for a variety of reasons, at least some of which should not be permitted to be swept under a concealing settlement rug. After finding that a settlement moots the parties'' controversy, the Federal Circuit vacates the lower court's finding of invalidity without reviewing the merits. The result of such a scenario may be that an invalid patent, even one fraudulently obtained, is foisted off on the public and left to distort the market. *Wang Laboratories Inc. v. Toshiba Corp.*, 793 F.Supp. 676, 23 U.S.P.Q.2d 1953, 1954 (Va. 1992).

ᛒ

A voluntary settlement of litigation does not retrospectively transform an accused infringing product into a "noninfringing substitute". *Pall Corp. v. Micron Separations Inc.*, 66 F.3d 1211, 36 U.S.P.Q.2d 1225, 1233 (Fed. Cir. 1995).

ᛒ

"Questions regarding settlements are governed by state law applicable to contracts in general." *International Rectifier Corp. v. SGS-Thomson Microelectronics Inc.*, 38 U.S.P.Q.2d 1083, 1101 (Cal. 1994).

ᛒ

"[M]ootness by reason of settlement does not [except under exceptional circumstances, which do not include the mere fact that the settlement agreement provides for vacatur] justify vacatur of a judgment under review." *Zeneca Limited v. Novopharm Limited*, 38 U.S.P.Q.2d 1585, 1586 (Md. 1996).

Settlement Agreement.

The court limited the effect of failure to file a copy of an agreement (reached by interfering parties in connection with the substance of the interference) to claims in issue in infringement litigation. Since the interference was dissolved with respect to those claims, the enforceability of the patent (priority with regard to another claim of which had been determined in the interference) was held to be unaffected. *Forbro Design Corp. v. Raytheon Co.*, 390 F.Supp. 794, 190 U.S.P.Q. 70, 78 (Mass. 1975).

ᛒ

Settlement agreements with others are secondary evidence, which cannot be used as a substitute for invention or to offset a conclusion of obviousness based on analysis of primary factual inquiries. *The Allen Group, Inc. v. Nu-Star, Inc.*, 213 U.S.P.Q. 513, 522, 524 (Ill. 1977).

ᛒ

Failure to heed the requirements of 35 U.S.C. §135(c) by filing at the Patent Office a copy of an agreement or understanding between parties to an interference made "in connection with or in contemplation of" the termination of the interference results in the permanent unenforceability of the patent issued. In order for there to be a violation of 35 U.S.C. §135(c), the unfiled agreements must have the effect of rendering the decision of the Patent Office meaningless to the parties or affect the parties" motivation to litigate the interference. *United States of America v. FMC Corporation*, 215 U.S.P.Q. 43, 49, 52 (Pa. 1982).

ω

A defendant in a patent infringement action entered into a settlement agreement, agreeing not to bring suit in any United States court challenging the validity of the patent. Filing a request for reexamination in the PTO is not such a suit and is thus not in violation of the agreement. *Joy Manufacturing Co. v. National Mine Service Company Inc.*, 810 F.2d 1127, 1 U.S.P.Q.2d 1627, 1629 (Fed. Cir. 1987).

ω

After a previous infringement suit had been on trial for a week, the parties settled it. A settlement was memorialized in a Settlement Order, which both the district court and counsel for the parties signed. According to the terms of the settlement, the putative infringer agreed to make specified payments as they became due, notwithstanding that patents in suit may subsequently be held invalid and/or unenforceable in any other proceeding at a later date. After the involved patents were held to be unenforceable in another proceeding, the putative infringer petitioned seeking an order relieving it from making any further payments under the Settlement Order. The requested relief was refused. To permit the putative infringer to escape its obligation under the settlement would seriously decrease the willingness of parties to settle litigation on mutually agreeable terms and thus weaken the efficacy of settlements generally. Settlement is of particular value in patent litigation, the nature of which is often inordinately complex and time consuming. Settlement agreements should be upheld whenever equitable and policy considerations so permit. *Hemstreet v. Spiegel Inc.*, 851 F.2d 348, 7 U.S.P.Q.2d 1502 (Fed. Cir. 1988).

ω

Where it appears on appeal that the controversy has become entirely moot, it is the duty of the appellate court to set aside the decree below and to remand the cause with directions to dismiss. This case did not become moot on appeal; rather, a consent judgment was entered pursuant to a settlement agreement entered into by the parties. The agreed settlement and entry of the consent judgment mooted any possibility of pursuing an appeal and foreclosed the appellate court from obtaining jurisdiction. *Gould v. Control Laser Corp.*, 866 F.2d 1391, 9 U.S.P.Q.2d 1718 (Fed. Cir. 1989).

ω

Prior acquiescence (in a settlement agreement) in the validity of a patent by one previously sued for infringement of the patent constitutes a strong showing of validity of such patent. *Moore Business Forms, Inc. v. Wallace Computer Services, Inc.*, 14 U.S.P.Q.2d 1849, 1861 (Ind. 1989).

ω

A prior action was dismissed with prejudice pursuant to a settlement agreement (whereby defendant waived its right to challenge the validity and enforceability of the subject patent with respect to products covered by the agreement) entered into by the parties. As the product is covered by the agreement, evidence relating to invalidity and unenforceability defenses was properly excluded. *Interspiro USA Inc. v. Figgie International Inc.*, 18 F.3d 927, 30 U.S.P.Q.2d 1070, 1071, 1073 (Fed. Cir. 1994).

ᙡ

A federal district court may excercise ancillary jurisdiction over a non-federal matter (such as a settlement agreement) (1) if the issues presented are "factually interdependent" with a federal matter before the court (federal courts have jurisdiction to consider ancillary non-federal claims when the non-federal and federal matters "derive from a common nucleus of operative fact") and (2) as needed to manage its proceedings, vindicate its authority, and effectuate its decrees. To bring a settlement agreement under this inherent court power, an order or judgment of the court must incorporate the settlement agreement such that a breach of the agreement also violates the court's decree. *National Presto Industries Inc. v. Dazey Corp.*, 107 F.3d 1576, 42 U.S.P.Q.2d 1070 (Fed. Cir. 1997).

ᙡ

Ancillary jurisdiction to enforce a settlement agreement exists only when the parties' obligation to comply with the terms of the agreement is made part of the order of dismissal. *Gjerlov v. Schuyler Laboratories Inc.*, 131 F.3d 1016, 44 U.S.P.Q.2d 1881, 1885 n.1 (Fed. Cir. 1997).

ᙡ

Oral settlement agreements reached during a mediation or pretrial conference are fully enforceable by the court presiding over the underlying litigation. "[A] contract can be formed before there is an official document memorializing the deal." Furthermore, the fact that a settlement agreement calls for the parties to reach another agreement in the future—in other words, an "agreement to agree"—will not prevent the settlement from being enforced. In fact, a party cannot avoid its performance of such an agreement to agree by withholding its consent, in bad faith, to the unresolved term. A party may not arbitrarily avoid performance based on "a condition peculiarly within the power of that party". *Thermos Co. v. Starbucks Corp.*, 48 U.S.P.Q.2d 1310, 1313 (Ill. 1998).

Seventh Amendment. *See also* Jury Trial.

The Seventh Amendment...requires that questions of fact in common law actions shall be settled by a jury, and that the court shall not assume directly or indirectly to take from the jury or to itself such prerogative. *Walker v. New Mexico & So. Pac. R. Co.*, 165 U.S. 593, 596 (1897).

ᙡ

Declaratory judgment actions are, for Seventh Amendment purposes, only as legal or equitable in nature as the controversies on which they are founded. *In re Lockwood*, 50 F.3d 966, 33 U.S.P.Q.2d 1406, 1411 (Fed. Cir. 1995).

Shade.

Although the exact color or shade of the claimed isomer was unpredictable, it was not unexpected; it was a shade somewhere in the family of reddish tints encompassed by a reference disclosure. Absolute predictability is not the law. *In re Crounse*, 363 F.2d 881, 150 U.S.P.Q. 554, 557 (C.C.P.A. 1966).

Shall.

"Shall" may sometimes be directory only, just as "may" may be mandatory. The interpretation of these words depends upon the background, circumstance, and context in which they are used and the intention of the legislative body or administrative agency that used them. *In re Certain Crystalline Cefadroxil Monohydrate*, 15 U.S.P.Q.2d 1263, 1273 (U.S. Intl. Trade Comm. 1990).

Sham Litigation. *See also* **Rule 38.**

The Noerr-Pennington doctrine holds that genuine attempts to influence the government are protected from Sherman Act liability by the overriding protections of the First Amendment. If the plaintiff can prove that the defendants fraudulently misrepresented their challenge to the patent to injure the competitive rights of the plaintiff, the Noerr-Pennington doctrine will not immunize the defendants from liability for those injuries. Actively misleading a federal agency is an abuse of administrative proceedings for which liability can be imposed under the sham-litigation exception. The First Amendment does not protect fraudulent misrepresentations to the PTO made to injure a competitor. *Ball Corp. v. Xidex Corp.*, 705 F. Supp. 1470, 9 U.S.P.Q.2d 1491 (Colo. 1988).

ϖ

A two-part definition of "sham" litigation:

First, the lawsuit must be objectively baseless in the sense that no reasonable litigant could realistically expect success on the merits. If an objective litigant could conclude that the suit is reasonably calculated to elicit a favorable outcome, the suit is immunized under *Noerr*,[4] and an antitrust claim premised on the sham exception must fail.

Only if challenged litigation is objectively meritless, may a court examine the litigant's subjective motivation. Under this second part of our definition of sham, the court should focus on whether the baseless lawsuit conceals "an attempt to interfere directly with the business relationships of a competitor," *Noerr*, [365 U.S.] at 144 (emphasis added), through the "use [of] the government process—as opposed to the outcome of that processas an anticompetitive weapon," *Omni*,[5] [111 S.Ct. 1354].

Carroll Touch Inc. v. Electro Mechanical Systems Inc., 3 F.3d 404, 27 U.S.P.Q.2d 1836, 1844 (Fed. Cir. 1993).

---

[4]*Eastern Railroad Presidents Conference v. Noerr Motor Freight, Inc.*, 365 U.S. 127 (1961).

[5]*City of Columbia and Columbia Outdoor Advertising, Inc. v. Omni Outdoor Advertising, Inc.*, 499 U.S. 365, 111 S.Ct. 1344 (1991).

Shape. *See also* Form.

By using the change in shape from preexisting art made by appellant, he has produced a new and useful result, not previously known to the art, and no reason is apparent why he should not have the protection that the law gives in such cases. *Ex parte Charles W. Mortimer,* 61 F.2d 860, 15 U.S.P.Q. 297, 298 (C.C.P.A. 1932).

ᗡ

The substantial equivalent of a thing, in the sense of the patent law, is the same as the thing itself; so that if two devices do the same work in substantially the same way, and accomplish substantially the same result, they are the same, even though they differ in name, form, or shape. *Hugh W. Batcheller v. Henry Cole Co.,* 7 F. Supp. 898, 22 U.S.P.Q. 354, 358 (Mass. 1934).

ᗡ

When a shape is novel and serves a purpose in a manner not "obvious" from prior art, it can lend patentability to a claimed product. *In re Hofmann*, 95 F.2d 257, 37 U.S.P.Q. 222, 224 (C.C.P.A. 1938).

Sherman Act. *See also* Antitrust, Discriminatory, Grant Back, Market Power, Tying Arrangement.

In *Walker Process Equipment Inc. v. Food Machinery & Chemical Corp.* [382 U.S. 172, 147 U.S.P.Q. 404 (1965)], the Supreme Court held that enforcement of a fraudulently procured patent may violate §2 of the Sherman Act [15 U.S.C. §2 (1964 ed.)] provided all other elements are established. Even though one possesses a fraudulently procured patent or a patent that is allegedly used in a way to enlarge scope or life, an analysis of market factors is still necessary. It is not enough to argue that one has used a patent in a predatory manner, thereby enlarging the scope or life of the patent; one must look to economic data to determine the impact of the purported illegal activity on the market that is the subject of the attempt to monopolize. *Agrashell, Inc. v. Hammons Products Co.,* 479 F.2d 269, 177 U.S.P.Q. 501, 512 (8th Cir. 1973).

ᗡ

To recover antitrust damages based on an alleged fraud in obtaining a patent, the plaintiff must prove: (1) willful and intentional fraud, (2) injury to business or property caused by the fraudulently procured patent, and (3) the other elements necessary to a §2 Sherman Act violation. Good faith or an honest mistake is a complete defense to an antitrust action based on fraud on the Patent Office.

In order to sustain a finding of patent misuse or a Sherman Act violation based in discriminatory licensing, at least the following must be present: (1) the plaintiff took a license; (2) the royalty rate charged plaintiff and that charged a competitor were unequal; (3) in all particulars relevant to equality of rates plaintiff and its licensed competitor were similarly situated; and (4) the royalties were an important expense factor in production costs, and the discriminatory rate caused substantial impairment of competition in the relevant market. *Honeywell Inc. v. Sperry Rand Corp.*, 180 U.S.P.Q. 673, 723 (Minn. 1973).

ᗡ

A patented process cannot be used to "tie" sales of an unpatented staple commodity (having substantial non-infringing use) used in the process. Sales of the staple commodity accompanied by an implied (can label) license to practice the patented process constitutes a non de minimus tying arrangment in violation of §1 of the Sherman Act and constitutes patent misuse, making the patent unenforceable. *Rex Chainbelt Inc. v. Harco Products, Inc.*, 512 F.2d 993, 185 U.S.P.Q. 10 (9th Cir. 1975).

ω

An exclusive license agreement for sale in the United States of a product made pursuant to a patented process and to limit all other licensees to production of the product for captive use only was entered into for the purpose of restraining and controlling the sale of the product in the United States and with the specific intent of conferring upon the licensee a monopoly over the sale of the product in the United States. It is a violation of Section 2 of the Sherman Act, 15 U.S.C. §2. *United States v. Studiengesellschaft Kohle, m.b.H.*, 200 U.S.P.Q. 389, 404 (D.C. 1978).

ω

Perpetrating a fraud on the PTO during prosecution of a patent constitutes one element of a Sherman Act cause of action. Enforcement of a patent procured by fraud on the PTO may be violative of §2 of the Sherman Act, provided the other elements necessary to a §2 case are present. Only "intentional fraud", consisting of knowing and willful misrepresentation of material facts, is actionable. Mere "technical fraud," or honest mistake in judgment, does not support a Sherman Act claim. Intentional fraud involves affirmative dishonesty. Although inequitable conduct amounting to gross negligence may support a finding that the patentee breached its duty of candor to the PTO, such a finding does not support a Sherman Act claim. A patentee's breach of duty of frank disclosure does not answer the question of whether applicant engaged in willful and knowing misrepresentation of material facts. A Sherman Act cause of action is not established when an applicant obtains a patent on an "obvious" invention or when a patentee fails to disclose nonrelevant prior art. *Jackson Jordan, Inc. v. Plasser American Corp.*, 219 U.S.P.Q. 922, 933 (Va. 1983).

ω

The Noerr-Pennington doctrine holds that genuine attempts to influence the government are protected from Sherman Act liability by the overriding protections of the First Amendment. If the plaintiff can prove that the defendants fraudulently misrepresented their challenge to the patent to injure the competitive rights of the plaintiff, the Noerr-Pennington doctrine will not immunize the defendants from liability for those injuries. Actively misleading a federal agency is an abuse of administrative proceedings for which liability can be imposed under the sham-litigation exception. The First Amendment does not protect fraudulent misrepresentations to the PTO made to injure a competitor. *Ball Corp. v. Xidex Corp.*, 705 F. Supp. 1470, 9 U.S.P.Q.2d 1491 (Colo. 1988).

ω

The mere bringing of a single infringement suit by the holder of a patent that is invalid for lack of enablement in and of itself cannot establish a violation of §2 of the Sherman

Act. *Technicon Instruments Corp. v. Alpkem Corp.*, 866 F.2d 417, 9 U.S.P.Q.2d 1540 (Fed. Cir. 1989).

ⲱ

The maintenance and enforcement of a patent obtained by fraud on the Patent Office may be the basis of an action under §2 of the Sherman Act. Maintaining monopoly power by prosecuting patent infringement actions in bad faith may give rise to a violation of §2. A scheme in violation of §1, involving the tying of patent licenses, can establish the "willful" and "predatory" misconduct necessary for a violation of §2. *Grid Systems Corp. v. Texas Instruments Inc.*, 771 F. Supp. 1033, 20 U.S.P.Q.2d 1207, 1211 (Cal. 1991).

ⲱ

Maintenance and enforcement of a patent procured by knowing and willful fraud may meet the intent and conduct elements of violation of the Sherman Act, provided that the ability to lessen or destroy competition, including market power in the relevant market, can also be shown. A patent does not of itself establish a presumption of market power in the antitrust sense. Determination of whether a patentee meets the Sherman Act elements of monopolization or attempt to monopolize is governed by the rules of application of the antitrust laws to market participants, with due consideration given to the exclusivity that inheres in the patent grant. *Abbott Laboratories v. Brennan*, 952 F.2d 1346, 21 U.S.P.Q.2d 1192, 1199 (Fed. Cir. 1991).

ⲱ

To establish an attempt to monopolize in violation of Section 2 of the Sherman Act, defendant must have proven: (1) a specific intent by plaintiff to control prices or to exclude competition; (2) that plaintiff engaged in predatory or anticompetitive conduct to accomplish the monopolization; (3) that plaintiff had a dangerous probability of success in its venture; and (4) that plaintiff's actions caused defendant to suffer an antitrust injury. *Automotive Products plc v. Tilton Engineering Inc.*, 855 F.Supp. 1101, 33 U.S.P.Q.2d 1065, 1090, 1091 (Cal. 1994).

ⲱ

Actions of the state are protected from Sherman Act liability through *Parker* immunity. *See Parker v. Brown*, 317 U.S. 341, 350-51, 87 L.Ed. 315 (1943) (holding that "[w]e find nothing in the language of the Sherman Act or in its history which suggests that its purpose was to restrain a state or its officers or agents from activities directed by its legislature."). *In re Recombinant DNA Technology Patent and Contract Litigation*, 874 F.Supp. 904, 34 U.S.P.Q.2d 1097, 1100 (Ind. 1994).

ⲱ

To form the basis of a 15 U.S.C. §2 violation, conduct must be the type that "actually monopolizes or dangerously threatens to do so." This is consistent with the overall purpose of the Sherman Act, which "directs itself not against conduct which is competitive, even severely so, but against conduct which unfairly tends to destroy competition itself." *DiscoVision Associates v. Disc Manufacturing Inc.*, 42 U.S.P.Q.2d 1749, 1755 (Del. 1997).

ⲱ

The right to refuse to deal is "neither absolute nor exempt from regulation" and when used "as a purposeful means of monopolizing interstate commerce", the exercise of that right violates the Sherman Act. *Image Technical Services Inc. v. Eastman Kodak Co.*, 125 F.35 1195, 44 U.S.P.Q.2d 1065, 1075 (9th Cir. 1997).

Shop-Book Rule. ***See also*** **Federal Shop-Book Rule, 28 U.S.C. §1732.**

In an interference setting, the identification of new chemical compounds is inadequate when based entirely on the testimony of witnesses who allegedly received their information from the inventor. Inventor's reports cannot be relied upon for establishing the identity of subject compounds on the basis of the Federal shop book rule, 28 U.S.C. 1732. *Rochling, Buchel, and Korte v. Burton, Newbold, Percival, Lambie, Sencial*, 178 U.S.P.Q. 300, 302, 303 (PO Bd. Pat. Intf. 1971).

ϖ

The so-called "shop-book rule" does not apply to reports of scientific work in an interference proceeding. Such reports generally cannot be relied upon to prove the facts asserted therein and, therefore, cannot be relied on to establish reduction to practice since they are self-serving and not an independent corroboration of an inventor's testimony. *Horton v. Stevens,* 7 U.S.P.Q.2d 1245, 1249 (B.P.A.I. 1988).

Shop Right.

Where a servant, during his hours of employment, working with his master's materials and appliances, conceives and perfects an invention for which he obtains a patent, he must accord his master a non-exclusive right to practice the invention. The employer in such case, however, has no equity to demand a conveyance of the invention, which is the original conception of the employee alone, in which the employer had no part. The invention remains the property of he who conceived it, together with the right conferred by the patent, to exclude all others than the employer from the accruing benefits. *United States v. Dubilier Condensor Corp.*, 289 U.S. 178, 17 U.S.P.Q. 154, 158 (1933).

ϖ

An employer's assistance in reducing an idea to practice is not necessary to his obtaining a shop right in an invention. An employee may reduce his idea to practice on his own time before showing his invention to his employer, and nevertheless subsequent employer-employee cooperation on the invention may be sufficient to confer a shop right on the employer. The principal consideration in the shop right determination is not the employer's assistance, but the employee's consent. *Wommack v. Durham Pecan Company*, 715 F.2d 962, 219 U.S.P.Q. 1153, 1157 (5th Cir. 1983).

ϖ

Where an employer hires an employee to design a specific invention or solve a specific problem, the employee has a duty to assign the resulting patent. Where the employee is not hired specifically to design or invent, but nevertheless conceives of a device during working hours with the use of the employer's materials and equipment, the employer is granted an irrevocable but non-exclusive right to use the invention under the shop right rule. Shop right is an employer's royalty or fee, a non-exclusive and nontransferrable license to use an employee's patented invention. *Ingersoll Rand Co. v. Ciavatta*, 8 U.S.P.Q.2d 1537, 542 A.2d 879, 110 N.J. 609 (N.J. 1988).

ᔕ

A shop right is a non-exclusive right to practice an invention made by an employee who, during his hours of employment, working with his employer's materials and appliances, conceives and perfects an invention for which he obtains a patent. *Moore v. American Barmag Corp.*, 693 F. Supp. 399, 9 U.S.P.Q.2d 1904 (N.C. 1988).

Shotgun. *See also* **Encyclopedic, Generic, Selection.**

A shotgun type of generic reference disclosure with many variables and no direction toward a restricted class of claimed compounds would not guide one skilled in the art to choose the restricted class from among the host of possible combinations and permutations suggested so as to make that restricted class obvious within the meaning of 35 U.S.C. §103. *Ex parte Strobel and Catino*, 160 U.S.P.Q. 352 (PO Bd. App. 1968). *See also In re Luvisi and Nohejl*, 342 F.2d 102, 144 U.S.P.Q. 646, 650 n.2 (C.C.P.A. 1965).

Showing. *See also* **Comparative Test Data, Declaration, Evidence, Statistically Significant, Unexpected Results.**

A showing of superiority over prior art requires evidence of comparative testing in the record and not mere assertions by counsel in briefs. *In re Swentzel*, 219 F.2d 216, 104 U.S.P.Q. 343 (C.C.P.A. 1955).

ᔕ

Indirect circumstantial evidence established that a claimed composition, more likely than not, does possess properties different from those possessed by a composition containing a reference isomer, and that such differences would have been unexpected to one having ordinary skill in the art. *In re Wilder*, 429 F.2d 447, 166 U.S.P.Q. 545, 549 (C.C.P.A. 1970).

ᔕ

Since the PTO made no objection to the form of an affidavit, it waived any requirement that the statements therein be made under oath before they are accorded evidentiary status. *In re Way*, 514 F.2d 1057, 185 U.S.P.Q. 580, 582 n.1 (C.C.P.A. 1975).

ᔕ

A comparative showing to rebut a *prima facie* case must compare the claimed invention with the closest prior art. A direct comparison with the closest prior art may not be necessary; an indirect comparison may be persuasive of unobviousness. *In re Merchant*, 575 F.2d 865, 197 U.S.P.Q. 785, 788 (C.C.P.A. 1978).

ᔕ

Whether phenomena just outside of claim limits are qualitatively different from that which is claimed is immaterial. A patentee is not required to show that some technological discontinuity exists between a claimed invention and subject matter just outside of the claims, but only that the claimed subject matter would have been non-obvious in view of the prior art. *Andrew Corp. v. Gabriel Electronics, Inc.*, 847 F.2d 819, 6 U.S.P.Q.2d 2010 (Fed. Cir. 1988).

Side Effects. *See* **Safety.**

Side Reaction.

A claimed process without side reactions is not obvious over a prior art related process with side reactions. *In re Mercier*, 515 F.2d 1161, 185 U.S.P.Q. 774, 779 (C.C.P.A. 1975).

Signature.

This appeal is from a decision of the PTO Board of Appeals rejecting claims of a Reissue Application on the ground that a broadening Reissue Application that was filed within two years of the patent issue date (but was erroneously filed by the assignee) could not be corrected by a Declaration of the inventor filed more than two years after the patent issue date. The CAFC reversed. Recognizing that all of the provisions of a unified statute must be read in harmony, the portion of 35 U.S.C. §251 that requires that a broadening Reissue Application must be signed by the inventor does not mean that an error in compliance with §251 is insulated from the remedial ruling of *Stoddard* [564 F.2d 556, 195 U.S.P.Q. 97 (D.C. Cir. 1977)] or the statutory provision for the correction of error. The purpose of the reissue statute is to remedy errors. Reissue is remedial in nature and is based on fundamental principles of equity and fairness. These fundamental principles must not be forgotten in implementation of the statute. *In re Bennett,* 766 F.2d 524, 226 U.S.P.Q. 413 (Fed. Cir. 1985).

Significance.

Other than the legal conclusion that defendant's product performs the same function as plaintiff's product, performs that function in the same way, and produces substantially the same results, the presented affidavit provides only obvious and undisputed statements of fact, or factual assertions with no explanation of their significance. The statement that defendant's product meets the legal definition of an infringing product under the doctrine of equivalents, offered without underlying factual support, is insufficient to raise a dispute of material fact for summary judgment purposes. *Ciba-Geigy Corp. v. Crompton & Knowles Corp.*, 22 U.S.P.Q.2d 1761, 1766 (Pa. 1991).

Silence. *See also* **Infringement Charge.**

Equitable estoppel bars claims for patent infringement when a party commits itself to act and then acts as a direct consequence of the conduct of a patentee. Estoppel by implied license cannot arise out of unilateral expectations or even reasonable hopes of one party. Five years of silence alone is not enough to give rise to estoppel. *Mainland Industries, Inc. v. Standal's Patents Ltd.*, 799 F.2d 746, 230 U.S.P.Q. 772 (Fed. Cir. 1986).

ᵀᵁ

A showing of laches alone is insufficient to bar a patentee's request for prospective injunctive relief or damages arising after the filing of suit. The defendant must also prove estoppel by demonstrating actions on the part of the patentee that justify a belief by the alleged infringer that the patent would not be enforced against him. Additionally, the defendant must show that it actually relied on the misleading conduct to its detriment. Although silence alone (even for a period of five years) is not sufficient affirmative conduct to give rise to estoppel, there is precedence for applying estoppel where there has been intentionally misleading silence. *Stambler v. Diebold Inc.*, 11 U.S.P.Q.2d 1709, 1714 (N.Y. 1988), *aff'd*, 11 U.S.P.Q.2d 1715 (Fed. Cir. 1989).

ω

Silence alone, unless it is intentionally misleading, is not sufficient affirmative conduct to support an estoppel. *C. R. Bard Inc. v. Cordis Corp.*, 17 U.S.P.Q.2d 1391, 1394 (Mass. 1990).

ω

Nowhere is it said that there must be a threat of enforcement or an assertion of rights followed by silence before there can be an estoppel. Indeed, where nothing has happened other than silence so misleading that the infringer believes the patentee has abandoned its claims, more reason exists for finding an estoppel than where a threat or an assertion of rights has, in fact, been explicated. A patentee who asserts its rights and then does nothing has at least initially put an alleged infringer on notice that something might be amiss, which "something" it may, for whatever reason, not choose to pursue expeditiously. A patentee who, with knowledge of the alleged infringing activity, does nothing over a period of years other than mislead a purported infringer and those who have gone before to believe that there was and is no problem, lying in wait until it becomes "commercially and economically worthwhile" to do something has engaged in affirmatively misleading silence of the worst order and should not be insulated merely because, for whatever reason, it did not articulate a threat or assert a right, but, rather, chose to mislead from day one. It is impermissible to lie low for four years and then invoke a claim against the patent when the matter could have been resolved from the start. *Stryker Corp. v. Zimmer Inc.*, 741 F. Supp. 509, 17 U.S.P.Q.2d 1945, 1948, 1949 (N.J. 1990).

Similarity. *See also* Relationship.

The fact that a reference process produces results similar to those of the patented process does not justify a conclusion that the specific steps of the two processes are "substantially the same" or that the differences between the processes are "obvious". The use of expert testimony about the significance of the similarities and differences between the patented and the prior art processes is of acknowledged value in determining the level of ordinary skill in the art. *Jack Winter, Inc. v. Koratron Company, Inc.*, 375 F. Supp. 1, 181 U.S.P.Q. 353, 374, 378 (Cal. 1974).

Simple. *See also* Advance the Art.

Patentability is gauged not only by the extent or simplicity of physical changes, but also by the perception of the necessity or desirability of making such changes to produce a new result. When viewed after disclosure, the changes may seem simple and such as should have been obvious to those in the field. However, this does not necessarily negative invention or patentability. The conception of a new and useful improvement must be considered along with the actual means of achieving it in determining the presence or absence of invention. The discovery of a problem calling for an improvement is often a very essential element in an invention correcting such a problem. Though the problem, once realized, may be solved by use of old and known elements, this does not necessarily negative patentability.

Although the physical means of accomplishing the appellant's improvement, and its new and useful results, are simple, the conception of so improving on the prior-art devices would not be obvious to those skilled in the art. *In re Bisley,* 197 F.2d 355, 94 U.S.P.Q. 80, 86, 87 (C.C.P.A. 1952).

Simplicity.

Although the patentee had merely changed the pitch of the Fourdrinier wire of a paper-making machine, the change in pitch was regarded as directed toward a wholly different object from that of the prior art. *Eibel Process Co. v. Minnesota & Ontario Paper Co.,* 261 U.S. 45, 67 (1923).

ω

Patentability is not gauged solely by the extent or simplicity of the physical changes made, but also by the perception of the necessity or desirability of making the desired changes to produce a new result. When viewed after disclosure, changes may seem simple and ones that should have been obvious to those in the field, but such does not necessarily negative patentability. *In re Bisley,* 197 F.2d 355, 94 U.S.P.Q. 80, 86 (C.C.P.A. 1952).

ω

In judging what requires uncommon ingenuity, the best standard is what common ingenuity has failed to contrive. Once a problem has been solved, it may be easy to see how prior-art references can be modified and manipulated to reconstruct the solution. The change may be simple and, by hindsight, seem obvious. However, the simplicity of new inventions is oftentimes the very thing that is not obvious before they are made. *In re Sporck,* 301 F.2d 686, 133 U.S.P.Q. 360, 363 (C.C.P.A. 1962).

ω

Simplicity itself has, on occasion, been held to be an indicia of non-obviousness. *In re Mixon and Wahl,* 470 F.2d 1374, 176 U.S.P.Q. 296, 299 (C.C.P.A. 1973).

ω

Simplicity, particularly in an old and crowded art, may argue for rather than against patentability. *In re Meng and Driessen,* 492 F.2d 843, 181 U.S.P.Q. 94, 97 (C.C.P.A. 1974).

ω

Simplicity and hindsight are not proper criteria for resolving the issue of obviousness. *In re Horn, Horn, Horn, and Horn,* 203 U.S.P.Q. 969, 971 (C.C.P.A. 1979).

ω

The very simplicity of a new idea is the truest and most reliable indication of novelty and invention. *AMI Industries, Inc. v. EA Industries, Incorporated,* 204 U.S.P.Q. 568, 587 (N.C. 1979).

ω

In making its determination of non-obviousness, the court recognized the non-analogous nature of one reference, the lack of teaching or suggestion in the prior art of the useful advantage of a flexible track incapable of self-support, and the commercial success of the highly flexible Hot Wheels trackway-toy vehicle combination covered by the plaintiff's Reissue Application. The fact that the claimed invention seemed simple and, when viewed in hindsight, appeared to be obvious was not enough to negate invention. *Lemelson v. Mossinghoff,* 225 U.S.P.Q. 1063 (D.C. 1985).

Simultaneous. *See also* **Reduction in Steps, Same Date.**

As a general rule, no invention is involved in the broad concept of performing simultaneously operations which have previously been performed in sequence. *In re Tatincloux and Guy,* 228 F.2d 238, 108 U.S.P.Q. 125, 128 (C.C.P.A. 1955).

ᴦ

Simultaneous invention is "some evidence, cumulative to be sure" of the impact of the prior art on those of ordinary skill in the art. However, it is not conclusive on the issue of obviousness. *United States of America v. Ciba-Geigy Corporation,* 508 F.Supp. 1157, 211 U.S.P.Q. 529, 540 (N.J. 1979).

Simultaneous Conception and Reduction to Practice.

Under the doctrine of simultaneous conception and reduction to practice, the Federal Circuit has held that complex chemical compounds are not conceived until they have been reduced to practice. The rationale behind the doctrine is that "[c]onception requires both the idea of the invention's structure and possession of an operative method of making it" and that, in the case of chemical compounds, an inventor cannot acquire the latter until she has reduced the idea to practice through a successful experiment. *Brown v. University of California,* 866 F.Supp. 439, 31 U.S.P.Q.2d 1463, 1466 (Cal. 1994).

Single Element. *See also* **Double Inclusion.**

When a patent disclosure shows two elements which perform two different functions and the patent claim is drawn to define both as separate elements, a disclosure which has only one element, performing both functions, will not be regarded as supporting an interference count. *Big Four Automotive Equipment Corporation v. Jordan,* 184 U.S.P.Q. 80, 99 (Ohio 1974).

Single Invention. *See also* **Unity of Invention.**

Where an invention can be claimed with equal facility in terms either of method or of structure and it is doubtful whether the invention resides in the process or in the structure, both types of claims may properly be allowed to issue in a single patent where they are but alternative expressions for defining a single invention. *In re Conover,* 304 F.2d 680, 134 U.S.P.Q. 238, 241 (C.C.P.A. 1962).

Single Means.

Claims to DNA by what it does (i.e. encoding either a protein exhibiting certain characteristics, or a biologically functional equivalent thereof) rather than by what it is might be analogized to a single means claim of the type disparaged by *In re Hyatt*, 708 F.2d 712, 218 U.S.P.Q. 195 (Fed. Cir. 1983). The problem with the phrase "biologically functional equivalent thereof" is that it covers any conceivable means, i.e., cell or DNA, which achieves the stated biological result while the specification discloses, at most, only a specific DNA segment known to the inventor. *Ex parte Maizel*, 27 U.S.P.Q.2d 1662, 1665 (B.P.A.I. 1992).

Single Property.

A single variance in the properties of new chemical compounds does not necessarily tip the balance in favor of patentability where otherwise closely related chemical compounds are involved. *In re DeMontmollin and Riat*, 344 F.2d 976, 145 U.S.P.Q. 416, 417 (C.C.P.A. 1965); *but see In re Murch*, 464 F.2d 1051, 175 U.S.P.Q. 89, 92 (C.C.P.A. 1972).

ω

An unexpected improvement in a single property may be adequate to establish patentability. *In re Ackermann, Duennenberger, and Siegrist*, 444 F.2d 1172, 170 U.S.P.Q. 340, 343 (C.C.P.A. 1971).

Single-Step Method Claim.

There is no statutory prohibition against single-step method claims. *Ex parte Macy*, 132 U.S.P.Q. 545, 546 (PO Bd. App. 1960).

ω

The step of "utilizing" was approved in a single-step method claim:

> 6. A method of unloading . . . catalyst and bead material . . . which comprises utilizing the nozzle of claim 7.

by an expanded panel of the BPAI which confirmed that the manner in which that claim is drafted has been an acceptable format for years. The claim is neither ambiguous nor unstatutory. Rejections under the second and fourth paragraphs of 35 U.S.C. §112 were reversed; a claim that incorporates by reference *all* of the subject matter of another claim (the claim is not broader in any respect) is in compliance with the fourth paragraph of 35 U.S.C. §112. *Ex parte Porter*, 25 U.S.P.Q.2d 1144, 1147 (B.P.A.I. 1992).

Singular. *See also* **A, One.**

The claim repeatedly refers to "said chamber" as it describes various portions of the apparatus. This term itself, "said chamber," reinforces the singular nature of the chamber. The claim does not place the sterilization zone vaguely within "a chamber," but within "said chamber." This language clarifies that only one chamber is in question. *AbTox Inc. v. Exitron Corp.*, 122 F.3d 1019, 43 U.S.P.Q.2d 1545, 1548 (Fed. Cir. 1997).

Situs.

Some courts consider the legal situs of an injury to intellectual property rights to be the residence of the owner of the interest. Among the most important rights in the bundle of rights owned by a patent holder is the right to exclude others. This right is not limited to a particular situs, but exists anywhere the patent is recognized. It seems questionable to attribute to a patent right a single situs. A patent is a federally created property right, valid throughout the United States. Its legal situs would seem to be anywhere it is called into play. This point is illustrated by the fact that, when an infringement occurs by a sale of an infringing product, the right to exclude is violated at the situs where the sale occurs. Although economic harm to the interests of the patent holder is conceptually different from the tortious injury to a patent holder's right to exclude others, recognizing the relationship between these concepts permits a court to assess realistically the legal situs of injury for purposes of determining jurisdiction over the patent holder's infringement claim. *Beverly Hills Fan Co. v. Royal Sovereign Corp.*, 21 F.3d 1558, 30 U.S.P.Q.2d 1001, 1011 (Fed. Cir. 1994).

Size. *See also* Proportion.

There is no invention in changing the size or proportion of a device or machine so long as the construction and mode of operation remain the same. *In re Paul F. Williams*, 36 F.2d 436, 4 U.S.P.Q. 237, 239 (C.C.P.A. 1930).

ᅲ

Limitations relating to the size of an article are not ordinarily patentably significant. *In re Rose*, 220 F.2d 459, 105 U.S.P.Q. 237, 240 (C.C.P.A. 1955).

ᅲ

That experimentation may be involved with the selection of proportions and particle sizes is not determinative of the question of scope of enablement; it is only undue experimentation that is fatal. *In re Geerdes*, 491 F.2d 1260, 180 U.S.P.Q. 789, 793 (C.C.P.A. 1974).

Skepticism. *See also* Disbelief.

The appellant with the assistance of his assignee prepared and inserted in the application two series of photomicrographs together with extensive descriptions of them for the purpose of showing how the invention differs from the prior filaments in an extensively developed art. The court took the position that this would not have been done unless the photomicrographs in fact showed persons of ordinary skill in the art what the appellant asserted they show and was unwilling to give credence to a contrary opinion expressed by the Board as the basis of the rejection that it orginated sua sponte. *In re Ehringer*, 347 F.2d 612, 146 U.S.P.Q. 31, 35 (C.C.P.A. 1965).

ᅲ

To reach the Board's conclusion would require that all evidence favorable to the appellant's position be viewed with limitless skepticism and that all evidence unfavorable to the appellant's position be accepted with limitless faith. *In re Petrzilka, Hofmann, Schenk, Troxler, Frey, and Ott,* 424 F.2d 1102, 165 U.S.P.Q. 327 (C.C.P.A. 1970).

ω

The correctness of an assertion in the specification may always be challenged, but only if there is sound basis therefor. Mere surmise, speculation, and conjecture are insufficient to refute an explicit teaching about operability. An appellant's assertion must be accepted in the absence of factual evidence (not merely unsupported skepticism) to the contrary. *Ex parte Dunn and Mathis,* 181 U.S.P.Q. 652, 653 (PO Bd. App. 1973).

ω

Initial encounters of ridicule and skepticism by others are hallmarks of invention. *Hart v. Baarke,* 396 F.Supp. 408, 186 U.S.P.Q. 275, 279 (Fla. 1975).

ω

Unsupported skepticism as to the utility of a claimed invention does not provide a legally acceptable basis for rejecting claims. *Ex parte Krenzer,* 199 U.S.P.Q. 227, 229 (PTO Bd. App. 1978).

ω

The fact that an invention is met with skepticism may be of assistance in determining whether combining elements to achieve the accomplished result was "obvious" to those of ordinary skill in the relevant art. Such skepticism suggests that achieving a certain result by combining particular elements in the manner done was so far removed from the typical practitioner's perception of the state of the art that the achievement seemed not only not obvious, but highly improbable. This "requirement of skepticism", however, is not a sine qua non for the patentability of combination devices. *Sarkisian v. Winn-Proof Corp.,* 662 F.2d 596, 213 U.S.P.Q. 912, 922 (9th Cir. 1981).

ω

Skepticism of experts, commercial success, long felt but unsolved needs, and the failure of others are relevant secondary considerations. *Ebeling v. Pak-Mor Manufacturing Company,* 683 F.2d 909, 216 U.S.P.Q. 563, 566 (5th Cir. 1982).

ω

No matter how much skepticism an invention is met with and no matter how much acclaim it eventually receives as an innovation, if the elements comprising the invention are disclosed by an examination of prior art, it is irrelevant that no one previously availed himself of the knowledge. *Connell v. Sears, Roebuck and Company,* 559 F.Supp. 229, 218 U.S.P.Q. 31, 37 (Ala. 1983).

ω

The skepticism of an expert, expressed before the inventors proved him wrong, is entitled to fair evidentiary weight, as are the five to six years of research that preceded the claimed invention. *In re Dow Chemical Co.,* 837 F.2d 469, 5 U.S.P.Q.2d 1529 (Fed. Cir. 1988).

ω

Skepticism

An expert's sworn skepticism is entitled to weight in resolving the ultimate legal conclusion of obviousness under 35 U.S.C. §103. However, a conclusion of non-obviousness is not compelled merely because the magic word "unexpected" appears in a declaration. It is necessary to look at the facts relied upon to support an expert's opinion. *Ex parte George*, 21 U.S.P.Q.2d 1058, 1062 (B.P.A.I. 1991).

Skilled in the Art. *See also* MOSITA, Ordinary Skill.

The specification need describe the invention only in such detail as to enable a person skilled in the most relevant art to make and use it. When an invention, in its different aspects, involves distinct arts, that specification is adequate that enables adepts of each art, those who have the best chance of being enabled, to carry out the aspect proper to their specialty. *In re Naquin*, 398 F.2d 863, 158 U.S.P.Q. 317, 319 (C.C.P.A. 1968).

ᛒ

The limitation, "a bonded hard metal carbide rim," is not unduly broad, as it defines an article which is old and well-known to one skilled in the metal slitting wheel art. *In re Myers*, 410 F.2d 420, 161 U.S.P.Q. 668, 672 (C.C.P.A. 1969).

ᛒ

A claimed invention is "illustrated," in the sense of 35 U.S.C. §103, by a drawing which, independently of an applicant's disclosure, would lead those skilled in the art to recognize the claimed invention as the solution to the problem it solved, i.e., by a drawing which renders the invention "obvious". A drawing is available as a reference for all that it teaches a person of ordinary skill in the art. *In re Meng and Driessen*, 492 F.2d 843, 181 U.S.P.Q. 94, 97 (C.C.P.A. 1974).

ᛒ

A person of ordinary skill in the art is presumed to be aware of references directed to the same technological field as the claimed subject matter. *In re Skoll*, 523 F.2d 1392, 187 U.S.P.Q. 481, 484 (C.C.P.A. 1975).

ᛒ

The law does not require that an applicant describe in his specification every conceivable and possible future embodiment of his invention. The law recognizes that patent specifications are written for those skilled in the art, and requires only that the inventor describe the "best mode" of making and using the invention known to him at the time. *SRI International v. Matsushita Electric Corp. of America*, 775 F.2d 1107, 227 U.S.P.Q. 577 (Fed. Cir. 1985).

ᛒ

The patent law allows an inventor to be his own lexicographer. To ascertain the true meaning of disputed claim language, resort should be made to the claims at issue, the specification, and the prosecution history. Moreover, claims are construed as they would be by those skilled in the art. That the specific examples set forth in the patent occur at room temperature does not mean that the claims are imbued with a room temperature limitation. Generally, particular limitations or embodiments appearing in the specification will not be read into the claims. *Loctite Corp. v. Ultraseal Ltd.*, 781 F.2d 861, 228 U.S.P.Q. 90 (Fed. Cir. 1985).

ᛡ

Proximity of application filing dates of patents (not prior art) related to the patent in suit permit the inference that the work underlying those patents was done at about the same time as the work on the patent in suit. These patents thereby indicate the level of skill in the art at the relevant time. *Polaroid Corp. v. Eastman Kodak Co.*, 641 F. Supp. 828, 228 U.S.P.Q. 305, 332 (Mass. 1985), *aff'd*, 789 F.2d 1556, 229 U.S.P.Q. 561 (Fed. Cir.), *cert. denied*, 107 S.Ct 178 (1986).

ᛡ

It is not required that those skilled in the art knew, at the time the patent application was filed, of the asserted equivalent means of performing the claimed functions; that equivalence is determined as of the time infringement takes place. Infringement will be found when the material features of a patent have been appropriated, even when those features have been patentably improved. *Texas Instruments, Inc. v. United States International Trade Commission*, 805 F.2d 1558, 231 U.S.P.Q. 833 (Fed. Cir. 1986).

ᛡ

The court framed its analysis of the level of skill in the art in terms of someone with a very high degree of skill in the art. If the invention here would not have been obvious to one of extraordinary skill, it follows that, in this case, it would not be obvious to one with lesser skills. Any error in choosing too high a level of skill would not be prejudicial to Specialty, and would not be grounds for reversal. *Specialty Composites v. Cabot Corp.*, 845 F.2d 981, 6 U.S.P.Q.2d 1601 (Fed. Cir. 1988).

Skill of the Art. *See also* **Knowledge, Ordinary Skill, Skilled in the Art, State of the art.**

The law has other tests of invention than subtle conjecture of what might have been seen and yet was not. It regards a change as evidence of novelty, and the acceptance and utility of change as further evidence, even as demonstration. Nor does it detract from its merit that it is the result of experiment and not the instant and perfect product of inventive power. A patentee may be baldly empirical, seeing nothing beyond his experiments and the result; yet, if he has added a new and valuable article to the world's utilities, he is entitled to the rank and protection of an inventor. It is certainly not necessary that he understand or be able to state the scientific principles underlying his invention, and it is immaterial whether he can stand a successful examination as to the speculative ideas involved. *Diamond Rubber Co. v. Consolidated Rubber Tire Co.*, 220 U.S. 428, 435 (1911).

ᛡ

Claims need not recite factors that must be presumed to be within the level of ordinary skill in the art where one of ordinary skill in the art, to whom the specification and claims are directed, would consider them obvious. *In re Skrivan*, 427 F.2d 801, 166 U.S.P.Q. 85, 88 (C.C.P.A. 1970).

ᛡ

A patent does not show, as of its filing date, what is known generally to "any person skilled in the art." *In re Glass*, 492 F.2d 1228, 181 U.S.P.Q. 31, 34 (C.C.P.A. 1974).

ᴡ

There is nothing in the statutes or the case law which makes "that which is within the capabilities of one skilled in the art" synonymous with obviousness. *Ex parte Gerlach and Woerner*, 212 U.S.P.Q. 471 (PTO Bd. App. 1980).

ᴡ

Patents (issued after the filing date of the applicant's parent application) cited to show the level of ordinary skill in the art cannot be relied upon as evidence of enablement if the applicant wishes to retain the benefit of his parent application's filing date. *In re Strahilevitz*, 668 F.2d 1229, 212 U.S.P.Q. 561 (C.C.P.A. 1982).

ᴡ

The patent law allows an inventor to be his own lexicographer. To ascertain the true meaning of disputed claim language, resort should be made to the claims at issue, the specification, and the prosecution history. Moreover, claims are construed as they would be by those skilled in the art. That the specific examples set forth in the patent occur at room temperature does not mean that the claims are imbued with a room temperature limitation. Generally, particular limitations or embodiments appearing in the specification will not be read into the claims. *Loctite Corp. v. Ultraseal Ltd.*, 781 F.2d 861, 228 U.S.P.Q. 90 (Fed. Cir. 1985).

ᴡ

The proximity of the application filing dates of patents (not prior art) to that of the patent in suit permits an inference that the work underlying those patents was done at about the same time as was the work on the patent in suit. The non-prior-art patents thereby indicate the level of skill in the art at the relevant time. *Polaroid Corporation v. Eastman Kodak Company*, 641 F.Supp. 828, 228 U.S.P.Q. 305, 332 (Mass. 1985), *aff'd*, 789 F.2d 1556, 229 U.S.P.Q. 561 (Fed. Cir.), *cert. denied*, 107 S.Ct. 178 (1986).

ᴡ

An inventor's testimony as to how he developed an invention is not relevant to an obviousness analysis because the inventor may be of a higher level of skill than someone of ordinary skill in the art, and what is obvious to the inventor would not necessarily have been obvious to one of ordinary skill in the art. *Suh v. Hoefle*, 23 U.S.P.Q.2d 1321, 1325 (B.P.A.I. 1991).

ᴡ

"Probative of the required level of skill in the art are factors, such as the educational level of the inventor, educational level of those who work in the industry . . . , and the sophistication of technology involved. . . ." *Liberty Leather Products Co. v. VT International Ltd.*, 894 F.Supp. 136, 37 U.S.P.Q.2d 1342, 1346 (N.Y. 1995).

Small.

A rejection of claims as failing to particularly point out the invention as required by 35 U.S.C. §112 was reversed. The Examiner regarded the claims as too broad in the absence of definite proportions for each ingredient; he maintained that the phrase "small percentage" was indefinite. *Ex parte Mosher and Moore*, 136 U.S.P.Q. 662 (PTO Bd. App. 1962).

ᗡ

Technical terms are not per se indefinite when expressed in qualitative terms ("relatively small") without numerical limits. *Modine Manufacturing Co. v. U.S. International Trade Commission*, 75 F.3d 1545, 37 U.S.P.Q.2d 1609, 1617 (Fed. Cir. 1996).

Small Entity.[6]

While 37 C.F.R. §1.28(c) governs the correction of an erroneous payment of the small entity issue fee and does not limit the time during which such error may be corrected, the regulation does provide meaningful limits on the circumstances in which correction is permissible. A patentee may correct the erroneous payment of the small entity issue fee "[i]f status as a small entity is established in good faith" and the small entity issue fee was "paid in good faith." *DH Technology Inc. v. Synergystex International Inc.*, 47 U.S.P.Q.2d 1865, 1873 (Fed. Cir. 1998).

Small Entity Status.

Rule 28(c) [37 C.F.R. §1.28(c)] must be read in conjunction with the deadlines set forth in 37 C.F.R. §1.317 for correcting the payment of an insufficient issue fee. Pursuant to §1.317(c), a good-faith error in claiming small-entity status, and in paying a small-entity issue fee, must be corrected no later than one year and three months after the date of the notice of allowance, or within three months of the PTO's denial of a timely petition to accept late payment due to unavoidable delay. *DH Technology Inc. v. Synergystex International Inc.*, 40 U.S.P.Q.2d 1754, 1761 (Cal. 1996).

ᗡ

The court could find no intimation in the statutory language that a patent lapses because improper claiming of "small-entity" status led to inadequate payment of all fees. When "small entity" status is claimed fraudulently or with intent to deceive, that is treated by the PTO as a fraud practiced or attempted fraud on the PTO. *Jewish Hospital of St. Louis v. Idexx Laboratories*, 42 U.S.P.Q.2d 1720, 1721 (Mc. 1996).

Software[7] *See also* Program.

Under patent and copyright law, a party cannot be compelled to license its proprietary software to anyone. *Tricom Inc. v. Electronic Data Systems Corp.*, 902 F.Supp. 741, 36 U.S.P.Q.2d 1778, 1780 (Mich. 1995).

ᗡ

---

[6] A party qualifying for reduced fees is referred to as a "small entity". The regulations define a small business concern "as one whose number of employees, including those of its affiliates, does not exceed 500 persons." To establish small entity status, "[t]he number of employees of a business concern is determined by averaging the number of persons of the concern and its affiliates employed on a full-time, part-time, or temporary basis during each of the pay periods for the preceding completed twelve (12) calendar months." §MPEP 509.02. *DH Technology Inc. v. Synergystex International Inc.*, 47 U.S.P.Q.2d 1865, 1870 (Fed. Cir. 1998).

[7] See Alter, Scott M., "The Rest Of The Wall Comes Down: Federal Circuit Holds Software Is Freely Patentable", *Intellectual Property Today*, Vol. 5, No. 9, pp 32 to 35, September 1998.

Transformation of data, representing discrete dollar amounts, by a machine through a series of mathematical calculations into a final share price, constitutes a practical application of a mathematical algorithm, formula, or calculation, because it produces "a useful concrete and tangible result"—a final share price momentarily fixed for recording and reporting purposes and even accepted and relied upon by regulatory authorities and in subsequent trades. *State Street Bank & Trust Co. v. Signature Financial Group Inc.*, 149 F.3d 1368, 47 U.S.P.Q.2d 1596, 1601 (Fed. Cir. 1998).

Sole. *See also* **Exclusive.**

Congress having provided for the correction of innocent error in stating the inventive entity when an application is filed, whether that entity be singular or plural, there is no rational reason to preclude sole-to-sole conversion and thus discriminate against the correction of the same innocent error involving sole inventors and their assignees, or to impute that intent to Congress. *A.F. Stoddard & Company, Ltd. v. Dann*, 564 F.2d 556, 195 U.S.P.Q. 97, 106 (D.C. Cir. 1977).

Sole Proprietorship.

A sole proprietorship, unlike a partnership, is not an "association". Rather, it is an individual doing business under a trade name. The rationales for applying 28 U.S.C. §1391(c) to partnerships do not apply to sole proprietorships. Accordingly, 28 U.S.C. §1400(b) controls the venue issue. *Kabb Inc. v. Sutera*, 25 U.S.P.Q.2d 1554, 1555 (La. 1992).

Soluble.

The terms, "slightly soluble" and "practically insoluble", are used in literature to connote totally different degrees of solubility. The court found no generally accepted or textbook use of the term, "partially soluble". *Standard Oil Company v. American Cyanamid Company*, 585 F.Supp. 1481, 224 U.S.P.Q. 210, 217 (La. 1984).

Solution. *See also* **Problem.**

An allegation that there may have been an unsolved problem in the art is not evidence of unobviousness unless it is shown that widespread efforts of skilled workers (having knowledge of the prior art) had failed to find a solution to the problem. *In re Allen*, 324 F.2d 993, 139 U.S.P.Q. 492, 495 (C.C.P.A. 1963).

ω

Patentability of an invention under 35 U.S.C. §103 must be evaluated against the background of the highly developed and specific art to which it relates, and this background includes an understanding of those unsolved problems persisting in the art which appellant asserts to have been solved by his invention. *In re Cable*, 347 F.2d 872, 146 U.S.P.Q. 175, 177 (C.C.P.A. 1965).

ω

Without a showing that prior art devices were unsatisfactory and that workers in the art were looking for a solution to the problem, the mere difference in dates (twenty years) is of little help in determining whether or not the suggested combination of references would have been obvious. *In re Johnson*, 435 F.2d 585, 168 U.S.P.Q. 289, 291 (C.C.P.A. 1971).

ᛒ

The fact that the solution to the problem had baffled workers of extraordinary skill in the art for many years, but, when revealed, was immediately and extensively adopted, establishes the existence of patentable invention worthy of protection by the courts under the patent laws. *Mobil Oil Corporation v. W.R. Grace & Company*, 367 F.Supp. 207, 180 U.S.P.Q. 418, 437 (Conn. 1973).

ᛒ

Evidence that others skilled in the field had been unable to find a satisfactory solution to the problem is a weighty indication that, at the then level of skill, the patented discovery was not obvious. *Cool-Fin Electronics Corporation v. International Electronic Research Corporation*, 491 F.2d 660, 180 U.S.P.Q. 481, 483 (9th Cir. 1974).

ᛒ

When there is no evidence that a person of ordinary skill in the art (at the time of the invention) would have expected a problem to exist, it is not proper to conclude that an invention which solves the problem would have been obvious to the hypothetical person of ordinary skill in the art. *In re Nomiya, Kohisa, and Matsumura*, 509 F.2d 566, 184 U.S.P.Q. 607, 612 (C.C.P.A. 1975).

ᛒ

Nonobviousness is supported by the fact that one skilled in the art would not have searched for the solution to the problem in the direction which the inventors took. *Berghauser v. Dann*, 204 U.S.P.Q. 393, 396 (D.C. 1979).

ᛒ

The art of record clearly fails to recognize the specific problem addressed by appellant, and just as clearly fails to suggest the claimed solution. *Ex parte Keyes*, 214 U.S.P.Q. 579, 581 (PTO Bd App 1982).

ᛒ

The focus of the inquiry as to what constitutes "pertinent" prior art against which obviousness of a patent claim is to be measured is on the problem solver and not on the user of the solution; i.e., it is the subject matter of the invention and not the field or industry which might thereafter have a use for the invention which must be looked to. *May v. American Southwest Waterbed Distributors, Inc.*, 715 F.2d 876, 219 U.S.P.Q. 862, 865 (5th Cir. 1983).

ᛒ

The district court's formulation of the problem confronting the . . . inventors presumes the solution to the problem—modification of the stem segment. Defining the problem in terms of its solution reveals improper hindsight in the selection of the prior art relevant to obviousness. . . . By importing the ultimate solution into the problem facing the inventor, the district court adopted an overly narrow view of the scope of the prior art. It also infected the district court's determinations about the content of the prior art. *Monarch*

Knitting Machinery Corp. v. Sulzer Morat GmbH, 139 F.3d 877, 45 U.S.P.Q.2d 1977, 1981 (Fed. Cir. 1998).

Solvent. *See also* Carrier.

The claimed use of a solvent may be regarded as in the nature of a manipulative expedient. A number of solvents of widely different chemical structure and solvent action are disclosed. With knowledge that what is desired is a solvent that dissolves the starting materials but has little solvent action on the adduct, the average chemist can readily select many solvents other than those specifically named. Under these particular circumstances, the claims are not rejectable for undue breadth in use of the term "an organic solvent." *Ex parte Dubbs and Stevens,* 119 U.S.P.Q. 440, 441 (PO Bd. App. 1958).

ᙙ

Although choice of a particular solvent from a known class of solvents is not inventive, a selection from compounds which are not known as solvents is not subject to the same conclusion. *Ex parte Taras and Randall*, 126 U.S.P.Q. 418, 419 (PO Bd. App. 1959).

ᙙ

Claims to a hair setting composition comprising a resin dispersed in a solvent do not define the "same invention" as claims directed to the resin per se. *In re Walles, Tousignant, and Houtman*, 366 F.2d 786, 151 U.S.P.Q. 185, 189 (C.C.P.A. 1966).

Some.

The fact that some catalysts do not or may not work in a claimed process is not adequate basis for precluding patentability for an inadequate disclosure under the first paragraph of 35 U.S.C. §112 under the guise of requiring undue experimentation. *In re Angstadt and Griffin*, 537 F.2d 498, 190 U.S.P.Q. 214, 218 (C.C.P.A. 1976).

Source. *See also* Cause, Problem.

When the unobvious aspect of a claimed invention resides in recognition of the source of a problem, the inquiries in the Patent Office should be directed, in part at least, to the question of whether or not such a recognition would have been obvious to one of ordinary skill in the art. *In re Roberts and Burch,* 470 F.2d 1399, 176 U.S.P.Q. 313, 314 (C.C.P.A. 1973).

ᙙ

Where an applicant contends that the discovery of the source of a problem would have been unobvious to one of ordinary skill in the pertinent art at the time the claimed invention was made, it is incumbent upon the PTO to explain its reasons if it disagrees. A mere conclusionary statement that the source of a problem would have been discovered is inadequate. A patentable invention may lie in the discovery of the source of a problem, even though the remedy may be obvious once the source of the problem is identified. This is part of the "subject matter as a whole," which should always be considered in determining the obviousness of an invention under 35 U.S.C. §103. *In re Peehs and Hunner,* 612 F.2d 128, 204 U.S.P.Q. 835, 837 (C.C.P.A. 1980).

Sovereign. *See also* **Sovereign Immunity, State, State's Immunity.**

One of the States of the United States has sovereign immunity under the Eleventh Amendment and thus cannot be sued by an individual of another state for patent infringement in a federal district court. *Chew v. California*, 893 F.2d 331, 13 U.S.P.Q.2d 1393, 1395, 1396 (Fed. Cir. 1990).

Sovereign Immunity. *See also* **Sovereign, State's Immunity.**

In an action in federal court, sovereign immunity does not bar the federal court from enforcing a federal subpoena against the federal government. Applying the doctrine of sovereign immunity to shield government agencies from federal subpoenas would, in effect, "authorize the executive branch to make conclusive determinations on whether federal employees may comply with a valid federal court subpoena. Because this effect would "raise serious separation of powers questions," the court "decline[d] to hold that federal courts cannot compel federal officers to give factual testimony." *Connaught Laboratories Inc. v. SmithKline Beecham P.L.C.*, 7 F.Supp.2d 477, 47 U.S.P.Q.2d 1699, 1700, 1701 (Del. 1998).

Space.

The word "space" cannot be considered as anything tangible. It is something without limits, or might be aptly described as "nothing." *In re Hall*, 168 F.2d 92, 77 U.S.P.Q. 618, 623 (C.C.P.A. 1948).

ᛒ

Launching a spacecraft containing a patented attitude control system constitutes use of that system even though the latter cannot be activated until the spacecraft separates from its launch vehicle in space. The availability of the attitude control system on the spacecraft at a time when the spacecraft is being operated constitutes a use thereof. *Hughes Aircraft Co. v. U.S.*, 29 Fed.Cl. 197, 29 U.S.P.Q.2d 1974, 1996 (U.S. Ct. Fed. Cl. 1993).

Spare Parts.

The replacement of a worn part in a patented combination constitutes a repair rather than a reconstruction. Any other sales of spare parts (i.e., for reconstruction or, possibly at the onset of the sale, as mere extra parts or as spare parts connected with new machine sales) do not fall into an implied license under past machine sales for which the plaintiff has already been compensated. *King Instrument Corp. v. Otari Corp.*, 814 F.2d 1560, 2 U.S.P.Q.2d 1201 (Fed. Cir. 1987).

Special Interrogatories.

When a jury, which is charged with returning special interrogatories pursuant to FRCP 49(a), fails to agree unanimously on some of the answers, a trial judge has several procedural actions available prior to dismissing the jury:

a) simply resubmitting the issues to the jury for further deliberations in hope of obtaining a unanimous verdict,

b) asking the parties whether they would be willing to forego the requirement of unanimity and accept a majority verdict,

c) entering judgment on the basis of the unanimous verdicts if they are dispositive of the case,

d) declaring the entire case a mistrial and ordering the case reheard in its entirety with a different jury, or

e) in certain situations, ordering a partial retrial only as to those issues which were not unanimously agreed upon by the jury.

Baxter Healthcare Corp. v. Spectramed Inc., 49 F.3d 1575, 34 U.S.P.Q.2d 1120, 1124, 1125 (Fed. Cir. 1995).

Special Master.

There is no impermissible factual overlap between the equitable issues of inequitable conduct, champerty, laches, and double patenting of the obviousness-type and the legal issues. A Special Master may try these issues prior to a jury trial on the legal issues. If a patent claim cannot be construed as a matter of law, there is an impermissible overlap between the factual determination made for literal infringement, a legal issue, and the equitable issues encompassed by the doctrine of equivalents. Therefore, the Special Master may try the claim of infringement by reason of equivalents and the defense of lack of infringement by the reverse doctrine of equivalents only if the patent claim can be construed as a matter of law. *Refac International Ltd. v. Matsushita Electric Corp. of America*, 17 U.S.P.Q.2d 1293, 1299 (N.J. 1990).

Special Verdict.

One noted scholar long ago described the benefits as follows:

The special verdict compels detailed consideration. But above all it enables the public, the parties and the court to see what the jury has done. The general verdict is either all wrong or all right, because it is inseparable and inscrutable. A single error completely destroys it. But the special verdict enables errors to be localized so that the sound portions of the verdict may be saved and only the unsound portions be subject to redeterminations through a new trial.

Sunderland, *Verdicts, General and Special*, 29 Yale L.J. 253, 259 (1920). "[I]n cases that reach the jury, a special verdict and/or interrogatories on each claim element could be very useful in facilitating review, uniformity, and possibly post-verdict judgments as a matter of law." *Richardson-Vicks Inc. v. The Upjohn Co.*, 122 F.3d 1476, 44 U.S.P.Q.2d 1181, 1188 (Fed. Cir. 1997).

Special Verdict Interrogatories.

The use of special verdict interrogatories drawn to each claim element has been endorsed and indeed encouraged by the Supreme Court as "very useful in facilitating review, uniformity, and possibly post-verdict judgments as a matter of law." *Warner-*

Jenkinson Co., Inc. v. Hilton Davis Chem. Co., 117 S. Ct. 1040, 1053 n.8, 520 U.S. 17, 41 U.S.P.Q.2d 1865, 1875 n.8 (1997); *Comark Communications Inc. v. Harris Corp.*, 48 U.S.P.Q.2d 1001, 1006 n.1 (Fed. Cir. 1998).

Species. *See also* **37 C.F.R. §1.312, Reduction in Scope.**

If an Examiner makes a requirement for restriction with respect to species, and applicant files a divisional application in consonance with the requirement, the species claimed in the divisional application cannot be rejected as unpatentable over any of the species claimed in the parent application. *In re Joyce*, 115 U.S.P.Q. 412 (Commr. Patents 1957).

ω

A decision on petition from a requirement (made final) to restrict the number of claimed species to five instructed the Examiner to withdraw the requirement completely if the non-elected species are obviously unpatentable over the other species claimed in the case, but to insist on the requirement for restriction if he is prepared to allow a divisional application (claiming the non-elected species) over the species claimed in the subject case. *In re Herrick, Conger, and Savio*, 115 U.S.P.Q. 412 (Comm'r Patents 1957).

ω

Disclosure of a species in a reference is sufficient to prevent a later applicant from obtaining generic claims unless the reference can be overcome. *In re Ruscetta and Jenny*, 255 F.2d 687, 118 U.S.P.Q. 101, 104 (C.C.P.A. 1958).

ω

In the context of double patenting, a claim to a genus is not directed to the same subject matter as a claim to a species within that genus. *In re Sarett*, 327 F.2d 1005, 140 U.S.P.Q. 474, 481 (C.C.P.A. 1964).

ω

While a species may be patentably distinct from a genus, in this case the earlier disclosed species is broadly the same invention as the genus. Thus the requirement of 35 U.S.C. §119 that only "the same invention" in the later application as is shown in the earlier will obtain the benefit of the earlier filing date is satisfied here. *In re Ziegler, Breil, Holzkamp, and Martin*, 347 F.2d 642, 146 U.S.P.Q. 76, 82 (C.C.P.A. 1965).

ω

A single species reduction to practice is adequate to overcome a reference showing of a genus when applicant's inference that other species would behave similarly is reasonable and subsequent developments appear to indicate that it was well founded. *In re DaFano*, 392 F.2d 280, 157 U.S.P.Q. 192, 196 (C.C.P.A. 1968).

ω

A terminal disclaimer obviates a double-patenting rejection in genus-species situations. *In re Plank and Rosinski*, 399 F.2d 241, 158 U.S.P.Q. 328, 330 (C.C.P.A. 1968).

ω

Prior reduction to practice (either constructive or actual) of a species within the scope of a generic count is sufficient to support an award of priority as to the generic count. *Miller v. Walker*, 214 U.S.P.Q. 845, 847 (PTO Bd. Pat. Intf. 1982).

ᛟ

A description of several newly discovered strains of bacteria (having one particularly desirable metabolic property) in terms of conventionally measured culture characteristics and a number of metabolic and physiological properties would not enable one of ordinary skill in the relevant art to discover, independently, additional strains having the same specific, desirable metabolic property. *Ex parte Jackson, Theriault, Sinclair, Fager, and Karwowski*, 217 U.S.P.Q. 804, 806 (PTO Bd. App. 1982).

ᛟ

"There is no inconsistency in awarding a generic count to one inventor, while awarding a patentably distinct species count to another [or to the same inventor]...." *International Rectifier Corp. v. SGS-Thomson Microelectronics Inc.*, 38 U.S.P.Q.2d 1083, 1087 (Cal. 1994).

Specifically Designed.

Patent Cooperation Treaty Rule 13.1(ii) permits, in addition to an independent claim for a given process, the inclusion in the same international application of one independent claim for one apparatus or means specifically designed for carrying out the said process. The expression "specifically designed" clearly does not mean that the apparatus or means cannot be used to practice another materially different process, as indicated in 37 C.F.R. §1.141(b)(2). The emphasized portion of the PTO rule and its interpretation are contrary to the Patent Cooperation Treaty and thus contrary to law. *Caterpillar Tractor Co. v. Commissioner of Patents and Trademarks*, 650 F. Supp. 218, 231 U.S.P.Q. 590 (Va. 1986).

Specification. *See also* **Abstract, Claim, Disclosure, Patent Application, Specific Mode, Statement in Disclosure, Statement in Specification, Symbols, Truthfulness of Specification.**

The specification is not addressed to lawyers or even to the public generally, but to those of ordinary skill in the art. Any description that is sufficient to apprise them (in the language of the art) of the definite features of the invention, and to serve as a warning to others of that which is claimed, is sufficiently definite. *The Carnegie Steel Company, Ltd. v. The Cambria Iron Co.*, 185 U.S. 403, 437 (1902).

ᛟ

While the claims of a patent limit the invention, and the specifications cannot be utilized to expand the patent monopoly, the claims are to be construed in the light of the specifications and both are to be read with a view to ascertaining the invention. *United States v. Adams*, 383 U.S. 39, 148 U.S.P.Q. 479, 482 (S.Ct. 1966).

ᛟ

The claims define limits of the claimed invention. It is the function of the specification to detail how the invention is to be practiced. *In re Roberts and Burch*, 470 F.2d 1399, 176 U.S.P.Q. 313, 315 (C.C.P.A. 1973).

ᛟ

A specification which "describes" an invention as broadly as it is claimed does not necessarily also "enable" one skilled in the art to make and use the claimed invention. *In re Armbruster*, 512 F.2d 676, 185 U.S.P.Q. 152, 153 (C.C.P.A. 1975).

ω

It is the function of the specification, not the claims, to set forth the "practical limits of operation" of an invention. One does not look to claims to find out how to practice the invention they define, but to the specification. The specification as a whole must be considered in determining whether the scope of enablement provided by the specification is commensurate with the scope of the claims. *In re Johnson and Farnham*, 558 F.2d 1008, 194 U.S.P.Q. 187, 195 (C.C.P.A. 1977).

ω

No "applicant should have limitations of the specification read into a claim where no express statement of the limitation is included in the claim." *In re Priest*, 582 F.2d 33, 199 U.S.P.Q. 11, 15 (C.C.P.A. 1978).

ω

Mere lawyer's arguments and conclusory statements in the specification, unsupported by objective evidence, are insufficient to establish unexpected results. *In re Wood, Whittaker, Stirling, and Ohta*, 582 F.2d 638, 199 U.S.P.Q. 137, 140 (C.C.P.A. 1978).

ω

While symbols are commonly employed in chemical cases to refer to designated classes of substances and are conventionally defined in the claim itself in order to make clear what are the metes and bounds of the invention, the absence of their definition in the claims may be objectionable rather than subject to rejection under the second paragraph of 35 U.S.C. §112. The reference in the claims to the specification, which is definite in defining and limiting the terms, complies with the requirements of 35 U.S.C. §112. *Ex parte Moon*, 224 U.S.P.Q. 519 (PTO Bd. App. 1984).

ω

The law does not require that an applicant describe in his specification every conceivable and possible future embodiment of his invention. The law recognizes that patent specifications are written for those skilled in the art, and requires only that the inventor describe the "best mode" of making and using the invention known to him at the time. *SRI International v. Matsushita Electric Corp. of America*, 775 F.2d 1107, 227 U.S.P.Q. 577 (Fed. Cir. 1985).

ω

Data presented in the specification must be considered in reaching a conclusion as to whether the claimed invention as a whole would have been obvious. *In re Margolis*, 785 F.2d 1029, 228 U.S.P.Q. 940, 942 (Fed. Cir. 1986).

ω

The basis of the district court's holding that the claims are indefinite is that "they do not disclose how infringement may be avoided because antibody affinity cannot be estimated with any consistency." Even if the district court's finding and support of this holding—that "there is no standard set of experimental conditions which are used to estimate affinities"— is accurate, under the law pertaining to indefiniteness—"if the claims, read in the light of specification, reasonably apprise those skilled in the art both of the utilization and scope of the invention, and if the language is as precise as the subject matter permits, the courts can demand no more"—the claims clearly are definite. The evidence of record indisputably shows that calculating affinity was known in the art at the time of filing, and notwithstanding the fact that those calculations are not precise, or "standard," the claims, read in the light of the specification, reasonably apprise those skilled in the art and are as precise as the subject matter permits. *Hybritech Inc. v. Monoclonal Antibodies, Inc.*, 802 F.2d 1367, 231 U.S.P.Q. 81 (Fed. Cir. 1986).

ω

While a failure to draft specifications "as precisely as the subject matter permits" may, in some cases, result in judicial invalidation of a patent, mechanical errors should not necessarily warrant such an extreme result. Immaterial errors in and omissions from the specification, resulting from copying errors or from the ignorance of the patentee's attorney concerning chemical processes, are insufficient to void a patent where "one skilled in the art would [not] be misled." Errors that would be detected at once by one skilled in the art, as demonstrated by successful application of the patent in commercial use, would not result in invalidation of the patent. *Pentech International Inc. v. Hayduchok*, 18 U.S.P.Q.2d 1337 (N.Y. 1990).

Specific Embodiment.

There is no statutory antecedent basis for the "specific embodiment" requirement of 37 C.F.R §1.71(b) except insofar as it implements the first paragraph of 35 U.S.C. §112. The terms "specific embodiment" of 37 C.F.R. §1.71(b) and the "best mode contemplated" of 35 U.S.C. §112 are not equated. If by "specific embodiment" is meant a working example, then the same is not required where sufficient working procedure has been set forth showing that one skilled in the art may prepare the claimed subject matter without undue experimentation. *In re Long*, 368 F.2d 842, 151 U.S.P.Q. 640, 641, 642 (C.C.P.A. 1966).

ω

Mention of representative compounds encompassed by generic claim language is not required by 35 U.S.C. §112 or any other provision of the statute. Where no explicit description of a generic invention is to be found in a specification, mention of representative compounds may provide an implicit description upon which to base generic claim language. The inclusion of a number of representative examples in a specification is one way of demonstrating the operability of a broad chemical invention and, hence, establishing that the utility requirement of 35 U.S.C. §101 has been met. *In re Robins*, 429 F.2d 452, 166 U.S.P.Q. 552, 555 (C.C.P.A. 1970).

Specific Example. *See also* **Example, Range.**

Literal infringement requires that an accused device embody every element of a claim as properly interpreted. If the claim describes a combination of functions, and each function is performed by a means described in the specification or an equivalent of such means, then literal infringement holds. When a claimed invention is a novel combination of steps, all possible methods of carrying out each step of the combination are not required to be described in the specification. Correctly construed claims cover "equivalents" of the described embodiments. The purpose is to grant an inventor of a combination invention a fair scope that is not dependent on a catalog of alternative embodiments in the specification. The court has cautioned against limiting the claimed invention to preferred embodiments or specific examples in the specification. The details of performing each step need not be included in the claims unless required to distinguish the claimed invention from the prior art, or otherwise to specifically point out and distinctly claim the invention. Claims should be read in a way that avoids enabling an infringer to "practice a fraud on a patent." *Texas Instruments, Inc. v. United States International Trade Commission*, 805 F.2d 1558, 231 U.S.P.Q. 833 (Fed. Cir. 1986).

Specificity. *See also* **Claim Language, Particularity.**

The claims were intended to cover the use of the invention with various types of automobiles. That a particular chair of the claims may fit within some automobiles and not others is of no moment. The phrase "so dimensioned" is as accurate as the subject matter permits, automobiles being of various sizes. As long as those of ordinary skill in the art realize that the dimensions could be easily obtained, 35 U.S.C. §112, second paragraph, requires nothing more. The patent law does not require that all possible lengths corresponding to the spaces in hundreds of different automobiles be listed in the patent, let alone that they be listed in the claims. *Orthokinetics Inc. v. Safety Travel Chairs Inc.*, 806 F.2d 1565, 1 U.S.P.Q.2d 1081 (Fed. Cir. 1986).

Specific Jurisdiction. *See* **Nonresident Defendant.**

Specific Mode.

All that is required by statute is that the specification set forth an illustrative method to teach one skilled in the art how the test can be carried out. The claims of the patent are not, however, then restricted to the specific mode described in the specification. *Rohm and Haas Company v. Owens-Corning Fiberglas Corporation*, 196 U.S.P.Q. 726, 744 (Ala. 1977).

Specimen. *See* **35 U.S.C. § 114.**

Speculation. *See also* **Assertion, Assumption, Cancer.**

It was not the intent of 35 U.S.C. §103 that the Examiner, the Board, or the CCPA should substitute its speculations for the factual knowledge of those skilled in the art. Where an affidavit states facts that are relevant to the ultimate determination of the legal issue arising under §103, it must be given careful evaluation and properly weighed to determine whether it factually rebuts the bases upon which the Examiner has predicated his finding of obviousness. Thus, an affidavit may well shift the burden of proof to the Examiner to come forward with further support for his conclusion that the invention would have been obvious under the conditions stated in §103. *In re Katzschmann,* 347 F.2d 620, 146 U.S.P.Q. 66, 68 (C.C.P.A. 1965).

ʊ

Although applicant's disclosure provided details as to how some 150 specifically named compounds "were prepared" or "can be prepared," a rejection based on undue breadth and speculation was affirmed because the only compounds actually tested that demonstrated the particular disclosed pharmacological properties were far more limited in structure than those claimed. *In re Surrey,* 370 F.2d 349, 151 U.S.P.Q. 724 (C.C.P.A. 1966).

ʊ

The correctness of an assertion in the specification may always be challenged, but only if there is sound basis therefor. Mere surmise, speculation, and conjecture are insufficient to refute an explicit teaching about operability. An appellant's assertion must be accepted in the absence of factual evidence (not merely unsupported skepticism) to the contrary. *Ex parte Dunn and Mathis,* 181 U.S.P.Q. 652, 653 (PO Bd. App. 1973).

ʊ

The application stood in condition for allowance and ready for the issuance of a patent grant except for the presence in the specification disclosure of certain asserted utilities that the Examiner believed to be too speculative—i.e., not believable on their face to those of ordinary skill in the art in view of the contemporary knowledge of the art. While it may be clear that workers in this art had shown that some cancers can be treated successfully in some patients, the effective treatment of various forms of malignant tumors remains a highly unpredictable art. Under these circumstances, the Examiner does not need to provide reasons why this speculative assertion should not be believed. The mere fact that the art of cancer chemotherapy is highly unpredictable places the burden on applicants to provide a basis for believing the speculative statements that they chose to place in the specification in the form of a positive assertion. *In re Application of Hozumi,* 226 U.S.P.Q. 353 (Comm'r Patents & Trademarks 1985).

ʊ

We note the Examiner's speculation that the declaration evidence may reflect only an anomalous "interaction" between the 2-methylpropyl group and the 2-methylphenyl group that causes an unexpected and surprising increase in potency for the claimed species. This speculation, however, is not supported by any facts of record or by sound scientific reasoning. *Ex parte Winters,* 11 U.S.P.Q.2d 1387, 1388 (B.P.A.I. 1989).

ʊ

"[The Board] may not...resort to speculation, unfounded assumptions or hindsight reconstruction to supply deficiencies in its factual basis." *In re GPAC Inc.,* 57 F.3d 1573, 35 U.S.P.Q.2d 1116, 1123 (Fed. Cir. 1995).

Spur.

Neither inspiration nor spur is a "teaching, suggestion, or motivation" to combine selected references in a specific way to make a specifically detailed new product. *Lamb-*

Weston Inc. v. McCain Foods Ltd., 78 F.3d 540, 37 U.S.P.Q.2d 1856, 1862 (dissent) (Fed. Cir. 1996).

Spurious. *See also* Exceptional.

Where a patentee is manifestly unreasonable in assessing infringement, while continuing to assert infringement in court, an inference of bad faith is proper, whether grounded in or denominated wrongful intent, recklessness, or gross negligence. *Eltech Systems Corp. v. PPG Industries, Inc.*, 903 F.2d 805, 14 U.S.P.Q.2d 1965, 1970 (Fed. Cir. 1990).

Spurring. *See also* Concealment.

Spurring is not an essential element of suppression. Proof of specific intent to suppress is not necessary where the time between actual reduction to practice and filing is unreasonable. An unreasonable delay may raise an inference of intent to suppress. *Peeler, Godfrey, and Forby v. Miller*, 535 F.2d 647, 190 U.S.P.Q. 117, 122 (C.C.P.A. 1976).

Stability. *See also* Isolated, Transitory.

Where a claimed product and that of a reference have the same utility, any change in the form, purity, color, or any of the other characteristics of the claimed product does not render the product patentable. Not only do the asserted color and stability changes in appellant's product appear as inherent properties in the pure crystalline form, but also, as these differences do not change the utility of the product, patentability is not conferred thereon. *Ex parte Hartop*, 139 U.S.P.Q. 525, 527 (PO Bd. App. 1963).

ᴦ

The fact that compounds may be unstable and cannot be isolated does not preclude their being statutory subject matter. They are still compositions of matter if they exist, if they can be produced at will, and if they are useful for their intended purpose. *In re Breslow*, 616 F.2d 516, 205 U.S.P.Q. 221, 226 (C.C.P.A. 1980).

Standard. *See also* Exclusion Order, German Industrial Standard (GIS), Standard Experimental Animal, Standard for Reversal, Standard of Proof, Standard of Review, Standard Text, Standard Work, Substantial Evidence.

The defense that making a support structure in one piece "does not rise to the standard of invention" is passé in view of the establishment of nonobviousness as the standard. *Carl Schenk, A.G. v. Nortron Corporation*, 713 F.2d 782, 218 U.S.P.Q. 698, 699 (Fed. Cir. 1983).

ᴦ

When a word of degree is used, the district court must determine whether the patent's specification provides some standard for measuring that degree, that is, whether one of ordinary skill in the art would understand what is claimed when the claim is read in the light of the specification. *Seattle Box Company, Inc. v. Industrial Crating & Packing, Inc.*, 731 F.2d 818, 221 U.S.P.Q. 568, 574 (Fed. Cir. 1984).

ᴦ

Standard

The CAFC does not review findings of the U.S. International Trade Commission under the clearly erroneous standard applicable to the findings of a district court as provided in Fed. R. Civ. P. 52(a). The CAFC reviews the factual findings of the Commission to determine whether they are unsupported by substantial evidence. The CAFC is not bound by the Commission's legal conclusions. *American Hospital Supply Corp. v. Travenol Laboratories, Inc.*, 745 F.2d 1, 223 U.S.P.Q. 577, 581 (Fed. Cir. 1984).

ω

Preponderance of the evidence is the standard that must be met by the PTO in making rejections (other than for "fraud" or "violation of the duty of disclosure" which requires clear and convincing evidence). In appeals from PTO rejections, the Federal Circuit reviews PTO findings under the clearly erroneous standard, under which PTO findings are overturned only if the court is left with the definite and firm conviction that a mistake has been made. *In re Caveney and Moody*, 761 F.2d 671, 226 U.S.P.Q. 1, 3 (Fed. Cir. 1985).

ω

There are two decision makers in a jury trial, the judge and the jury. In general, the judge decides issues of law and issues committed to his discretion, and the jury decides issues of fact that are material to the case and in genuine dispute. On proper appeal from a judgment in a jury case, the CAFC reviews the decisions made by the judge for prejudicial legal error (e.g., jury instructions) or abuse of discretion (e.g., increasing damages), with the standard depending upon the particular issue. In contrast, the CAFC reviews the sufficiency of the evidence underlying a jury verdict on an issue of fact to determine whether the jury's decision was supported by substantial evidence. Between these simple extremes of issues decided by the judge and issues decided by the jury are issues of law submitted to the jury upon disputed facts. When an issue of law has been submitted to the jury upon disputed facts (e.g., a jury's special verdict on patent claim obviousness where the underlying facts have been disputed), the standard of review has two parts. The CAFC first presumes that the jury resolved the underlying factual disputes in favor of the verdict winner and leaves those presumed findings undisturbed if they are supported by substantial evidence. The CAFC examines the legal conclusion de novo to see whether it is correct in light of the presumed jury fact findings. *Jurgens v. McKasy*, 927 F.2d 1552, 18 U.S.P.Q.2d 1031, 1035 (Fed. Cir. 1991).

ω

PTO factual determinations are reviewed by the CAFC under the "clearly erroneous" standard [not the "arbitrary and capricious" standard of review provided by the Administrative Procedure Act (APA) for use in informal adjudicative proceedings]. *In re Kemps*, 97 F.3d 1427, 40 U.S.P.Q.2d 1309, 1312 (Fed. Cir. 1996)

ω

During an interference involving a patent issued from an application that was copending with the interfering application, the appropriate standard of proof for validity challenges is the preponderance of the evidence standard. *Bruning v. Hirose*, 48 U.S.P.Q.2d 1934, 1938 (Fed. Cir. 1998).

Standard Experimental Animal. *See also* **Animal Tests, Screening, Standard Laboratory Animal.**

A utility (limited at the time an application is filed to a therapeutic effect on test animals) is not insufficient at least where usefulness in human therapy is adumbrated. *Carter-Wallace, Inc. v. Davis-Edwards Pharmacal Corp.*, 341 F. Supp. 303, 173 U.S.P.Q. 65, 104 (N.Y. 1972).

ᛒ

For reduction to practice it is sufficient that the compounds, when administered to a standard experimental animal, possessed the significant property of preventing pregnancy—the intended purpose—and were tolerated by the animals during the test periods. *Campbell and Babcock v. Wettstein, Anner, Wieland, and Heusler*, 476 F.2d 642, 177 U.S.P.Q. 376, 379 (C.C.P.A. 1973).

ᛒ

A "standard experimental animal" is "whatever animal is usually used by those skilled in the art to establish the particular pharmaceutical application in question." *In re Langer*, 503 F.2d 1380, 183 U.S.P.Q. 288, 297 (C.C.P.A. 1974).

ᛒ

One who has taught the public that a compound exhibits some desirable pharmaceutical property in a standard experimental animal has made a significant and useful contribution to the art, even though it may eventually appear that the compound is without value in the treatment of humans. *In re Brana*, 51 F.3d 1560, 34 U.S.P.Q.2d 1436, 1442 (Fed. Cir. 1995).

Standard Laboratory Animal. *See also* **Standard Experimental Animal.**

Even though applicants' ultimate purpose was treatment of human beings, their successful testing and use in standard laboratory animals was adequate for a reduction to practice. *Hughes and Smith v. Windholz, Patchett, and Fried*, 184 U.S.P.Q. 753, 757 (PO Bd. Pat. Intf. 1974).

Standard for Reversal.

The plaintiff in an action brought pursuant to 35 U.S.C. §145 has a heavy burden. Because the Patent Office is an expert body preeminently qualified to determine questions of this kind, its conclusions are entitled to a broad presumption of validity. In these circumstances, the court is authorized to reverse the decision only if the Patent Office did not have a rational basis for its conclusions or if the plaintiff presented new evidence that led to a thorough conviction that the plaintiff should prevail. In trials de novo under 35 U.S.C. §145, great weight attaches to the expertise of the Patent Office, and its findings will not be overturned unless new evidence is introduced that carries the thorough conviction that the Patent Office erred. Based upon the opinion testimony of an independent expert, the court was satisfied that the only way one would reach the plaintiff's claimed alloy composition from the reference disclosure was by experimentation. The testimony offered on behalf of a plaintiff at the trial was uncontradicted by the defendant. The court found that testimony to be very persuasive, and the court concluded that the plaintiff demonstrated by clear and convincing evidence that the determination by the Board of Appeals was in error. *Titanium Metals Corp. of America v. Mossinghoff,* 603 F. Supp. 87, 225 U.S.P.Q. 673 (D.C. 1984).

Standard of Conduct. *See* **Duty to Disclose.**

Standard of Proof. *See also* **Administrative Regularity.**

When the Patent Office has decided a question of priority of invention, followed by an action under 35 U.S.C. §146 contesting the decision, the question of priority is tried de novo in the district court, but the standard of proof that must be applied by the district court to reach a conclusion contrary to that of the Patent Office is one that, in character and amount, carries through conviction. *United States v. Szuecs,* 240 F.2d 886, 112 U.S.P.Q. 86, 87 (D.C. Cir. 1957).

Standard of Review. *See also* **Plenary Review.**

All the CCPA does is pass on the propriety of rejections brought before it for review. *In re Citron,* 326 F.2d 418, 140 U.S.P.Q. 220, 221 (C.C.P.A. 1964).

ω

In an appeal before the CCPA the Solicitor cannot raise a new ground of rejection or apply a new rationale to support the rejection affirmed by the Board. *In re Strahilevitz,* 668 F.2d 1229, 212 U.S.P.Q. 561, 565 (C.C.P.A. 1982).

ω

"We review the court's ruling [of inequitable conduct] on the standard of abuse of discretion; that is, was the conclusion contrary to law, in clear error, unsupported by the evidence, or otherwise in excess of the court's discretionary power." *Tol-O-Matic, Inc. v. Proma Produkt-Und Mktg. Gesellschaft m.b.H.,* 945 F.2d 1546, 1553, 20 U.S.P.Q.2d 1332, 1338 (Fed. Cir. 1991).

ω

The Federal Circuit reviews questions of fact under a clearly erroneous standard; questions of law are subject to full and independent review (sometimes referred to as "*de novo*" or "plenary" review). *In re Asahi/America Inc.,* 68 F.3d 442, 33 U.S.P.Q.2d 1921, 1922 (Fed. Cir. 1995).

ω

The CAFC's standard of review when deciding cases on appeal from the PTO is:

a) with regard to questions of law, that review is without deference to the views of the Agency;
b) with regard to questions of fact, the court defers to the Agency unless its findings are "clearly erroneous;
c) with regard to judgment calls, those questions that fall "[s]omewhere near the middle of the fact-law spectrum", the court has recognized "the falseness of the fact-law dichotomy, since the determination at issue, involving as it does the

application of a general legal standard to particular facts, is probably most realistically described as neither of fact nor law, but mixed; when these questions of judgment are before the court, whether it defers, and the extent to which it defers, turns on the nature of the case and the nature of the judgment.

In re Brana, 51 F.3d 1560, 34 U.S.P.Q.2d 1436, 1443 (Fed. Cir. 1995).

ϖ

The CAFC reviews a district court's grant of summary judgment de novo, resolving all doubt respecting the presence or absence of genuine factual issues in the nonmovant's favor. The disposition of an appeal, turning largely on whether the trial court properly construed a claim (a question of law), is reviewed de novo. *Bell Communications Research Inc. v. Vitalink Communications Corp.*, 55 F.3d 615, 34 U.S.P.Q.2d 1816, 1819 (Fed. Cir. 1995).

ϖ

The Federal Circuit reviews the amount of a court's damage award to determine whether it was based on clearly erroneous factual findings, or whether in other respects it was based on an erroneous conclusion of law or a clear error of judgment amounting to an abuse of discretion. *Transmatic Inc. v. Gulton Industries Inc.*, 53 F.3d 1270, 35 U.S.P.Q.2d 1035, 1039 (Fed. Cir. 1995).

ϖ

This court reviews factual findings of the ITC under the "substantial evidence" standard. Under this standard, we will not disturb the ITC's factual findings if they are supported by "such relevant evidence as a reasonable mind might accept as adequate to support a conclusion". This court will not review an issue that has not been properly raised before the ITC in a petition for review of an Initial Determination. *Checkpoint Systems Inc. v. U.S. International Trade Commission*, 54 F.3d 756, 35 U.S.P.Q.2d 1042, 1045 (Fed. Cir. 1995).

ϖ

Whether a reference or a combination of references renders a claimed invention obvious under 35 U.S.C. §103 is a question of law subject to full and independent review in the Federal Circuit Court of Appeals (CAFC), which reviews for clear error the underlying factual findings leading to an obviousness conclusion. Furthermore, under this standard of review that court disturbs a factual finding of the BPAI only if definitely and firmly convinced that the Board has erred. These factual findings include: (1) the scope and content of the prior art; (2) the level of ordinary skill in the art at the time of the invention; (3) objective evidence of nonobviousness; and (4) the differences between the prior art and the claimed subject matter. In determining the scope and content of the prior art, "[w]hether a reference . . . is "analogous" is a fact question" that is reviewed for clear error. *In re GPAC Inc.*, 57 F.3d 1573, 35 U.S.P.Q.2d 1116, 1119 (Fed. Cir. 1995).

ϖ

Absent decision of an issue at trial, it is not before the CAFC for appellate review. Issues of patent validity that were decided at trial require appellate review, even when patents are found not infringed upon appeal. *Hoover Group Inc. v. Custom Metalcraft Inc.*, 66 F.3d 299, 36 U.S.P.Q.2d 1101, 1104 (Fed. Cir. 1995).

ϖ

If we were reviewing whether properly construed claims encompass the accused structure after a full trial, our standard of review would be *de novo*. If this were an appeal after a bench trial, we would review the district court's determination of whether properly construed claims encompass the accused structure for clear error. If this were an appeal after a jury trial, we would review the jury's determination of whether properly construed claims encompass the accused structure and decide whether the determination is supported by substantial evidence. *Cole v. Kimberly-Clark Corp.*, 41 U.S.P.Q.2d 1001 (Fed. Cir. 1996).

ϖ

A precondition that must be met before the CAFC can decide the standard of review issue is that the resolution of the review standard not be "irrelevant to the determination of the case." *In re Mac Dermid Inc.*, 42 U.S.P.Q.2d 1479, 1480 (Fed. Cir. 1997).

ϖ

Throughout the history of the CAFC, of the CAFC's predecessor court, the CCPA, and of that court's predecessor, the Court of Appeals of the District of Columbia, the decisions of the PTO boards have been reviewed on the record, by the same standards as applied to a decision from a district court, without enhanced deference. ("Findings of fact, whether based on oral or documentary evidence, shall not be set aside unless clearly erroneous.") *Stare decisis* argues against a change in the Court's standard of review. A long-standing practice should not be set aside absent substantial reason to do so. *In re Lueders*, 42 U.S.P.Q.2d 1481, 1485, 1487 (Fed. Cir. 1997).

ϖ

The Administrative Procedure Act, in 5 U.S.C. § 559, permits, and *stare decisis* warrants continued application of the clearly erroneous standard in review of PTO fact findings by the CAFC. *In re Zurko*, 142 F.3d 1447, 46 U.S.P.Q.2d 1691, 1693 (Fed. Cir. 1998 — *in banc*).

Standard Text.

Reliance (for the first time) before the court on an allegedly standard textbook on chemistry as further support for the Patent Office position illustrates a growing tendency on the part of appellants and the Patent Office to impair the clear and specific language of 35 U.S.C. §144, which requires the court to determine an appeal "on the evidence produced before the Patent Office." *In re Cofer*, 354 F.2d 664, 148 U.S.P.Q. 268, 271 (C.C.P.A. 1966).

Standard Work.

Ordinarily, citation by the Board of a new reference and reliance thereon to support a rejection will be considered as tantamount to assertion of a new ground of rejection. This will not be the case, however, where such a reference is a standard work, cited only to support a fact judicially noticed and the fact so noticed plays a minor role, serving only "to 'fill in the gaps' which might exist in the evidentiary showing made by the Examiner to support a particular ground for rejection." Under such circumstances an applicant must be given the opportunity to challenge either the correctness of the fact asserted or the notoriety or repute of the reference cited in support of the assertion. A challenge to the Board's judicial notice must contain adequate information or argument so that on its face it creates a reasonable doubt regarding the circumstances justifying the judicial notice. *In re Boon,* 439 F.2d 724, 169 U.S.P.Q. 231, 234 (C.C.P.A. 1971).

Standing.

To bring a suit for infringement, a plaintiff must have standing to sue under the patent laws at the time the complaint is filed. *Cf. Jones v. Sullivan,* 938 F.2d 801, 805 (7th Cir. 1991) (the "case or controversy" requirement of Article III of the Constitution, of which standing is a part, must be satisfied when the suit is brought as well as at all times during its pendency). "The requisite personal interest that must exist at the commencement of the litigation (standing) must continue throughout its existence (mootness)." *United States Parole Commission v. Geraghty,* 445 U.S. 388, 397 (1980), quoting Monaghan, *Constitutional Adjudication: The Who and When,* 82 Yale L.J. 1363, 1384 (1973).

ᴥ

Similar to section 337(c) of the Tariff Act [19 U.S.C. §1337(c)], section 10(a) of the Administrative Procedure Act (5 U.S.C. §702) states, inter alia, that any person adversely affected or aggrieved by agency action within the meaning of a relevant statute is entitled to judicial review. Adversely affected or aggrieved requires a showing of injury in fact as a sine qua non for standing. *Rohm and Haas Company v. International Trade Commission,* 554 F.2d 462, 193 U.S.P.Q. 693, 694 (C.C.P.A. 1977).

ᴥ

Defendant, insofar as it sues as a stockholder, lacks standing in its antitrust counterclaim (based on patent's being obtained by fraud on the Patent Office, the enforcement of such a patent may be violative of the Sherman Act and, even absent fraud on the Patent Office, plaintiff is liable for bringing an infringement action on a patent known to be invalid) since it "was neither a consumer nor a competitor in the market in which trade was restrained" and the decreased value in its holdings in its independently-operated and wholly-owned subsidiary is "only an indirect result" of the antitrust violation alleged. *D.L. Auld Company v. Park Electrochemical Corp.,* 651 F.Supp. 582, 1 U.S.P.Q.2d 2071, 2073 (N.Y. 1986).

ᴥ

The statute governing reexamination provides that a patent owner may appeal an adverse reexamination finding to the CAFC. 35 U.S.C. §306. However, the district court has no power to review a PTO finding favorable to the patent owner at the behest of a patent challenger. *E. I. du Pont de Nemours & Co. v. Cetus Corp.,* 19 U.S.P.Q.2d 1174, 1181 (Cal. 1990).

ᴥ

To establish standing to sue, a party must, at an irreducible minimum, show (1) that he has personally suffered some actual or threatened injury as a result of the putatively illegal conduct (personal injury), (2) that the injury can be fairly traced to the challenged action (causation), and (3) that the injury is likely to be redressed by a favorable decision. In addition to these requirements for standing, the Supreme Court has further limited standing to those parties "within the zone of interests addressed by the substantive provisions of the law they seek to invoke." *Animal Legal Defense Fund v. Quigg*, 932 F.2d 920, 18 U.S.P.Q.2d 1677, 1681, 1691 (Fed. Cir. 1991).

ᚹ

A patent is a creature of statute, as is the right of a patentee to have a remedy for infringement of his patent (35 U.S.C. §281). Suit must be brought on the patent, as ownership only of the invention gives no right to exclude, which is obtained only from the patent grant. In order to exercise that right, a plaintiff must necessarily have standing as comprehended by the patent statute. *Arachnid Inc. v. Merit Industries Inc.*, 939 F.2d 1574, 19 U.S.P.Q.2d 1513, 1516 (Fed. Cir. 1991).

ᚹ

Courts have disagreed on the ability of a post-filing assignment to confer standing upon a party that lacked standing on the day it filed its patent infringement action. *Valmet Paper Machinery Inc. v. Beloit Corp.*, 868 F.Supp. 1085, 32 U.S.P.Q.2d 1794, 1796 (Wis. 1994).

ᚹ

Courts have not recognized standing to appeal where a party does not seek reversal of a judgment but asks only for a review of unfavorable findings. "An indirect financial stake in another party's claims is insufficient to create standing on appeal." A person named as a defendant in an action is not bound by the judgment therein if the subject matter of the action involves an obligation other than his own and that fact is known to the plaintiff. *Penda Corp. v. U.S.*, 44 F.3d 967, 33 U.S.P.Q.2d 1200, 1203, 1204 (Fed. Cir. 1994).

ᚹ

Standing cannot be inferred from the averments of the pleadings. Standing tells us who may bring an action, while ripeness determines when a proper party may bring an action. *Procter & Gamble Co. v. Paragon Trade Brands Inc.*, 917 F. Supp. 305, 38 U.S.P.Q.2d 1678, 1680, 1682 (Del. 1995).

ᚹ

A firm has constitutional standing to challenge a competitor's entry into its market. *Mova Pharmaceutical Corp. v. Shalala*, 140 F.3d 1060, 46 U.S.P.Q.2d 1385, 1397 (D.C. Cir. 1998).

ᚹ

Even where there is a clear oral agreement to assign a patent, to establish standing in a case under the Patent Act, the party must have and actual assignment in writing. *Dynamic Manufacturing Inc. v. Craze*, 46 U.S.P.Q.2d 1548, 1555 (Va. 1998).

ᚹ

LaGard was the owner of the subject patent when the declaratory judgment action was filed. Title to the patent was not transferred (in writing) to Masco until after the present appeal was filed. LaGard is not a separate entity from Masco because (after the trial) LaGard merged with Masco and is now a division of Masco. Hence, standing was not, and is not, lacking on the part of either LaGard or Masco in this appeal. *Mas-Hamilton Group Inc. v. LaGard Inc.*, 48 U.S.P.Q.2d 1010, 1014 (Fed. Cir. 1998).

Stand or Fall Together.

Section 1.192(c)(5) of 37 C.F.R. requires appellant to perform two affirmative acts in his brief in order to have the separate patentability of a plurality of claims subject to the same rejection considered. The appellant must (1) state that the claims do not stand or fall together and (2) present arguments why the claims subject to the same rejection are separately patentable. Where the appellant does neither, it is appropriate for the Examiner and the Board to rely upon the presumption created by the words of the rule and to treat all claims as standing or falling together. Where, however, the appellant (1) omits the statement required by 37 C.F.R. §1.192(c)(5), yet presents arguments in the argument section of his brief, or (2) includes the statement required by 37 C.F.R. §1.192(c)(5) to the effect that one or more claims do not stand or fall with the rejection of the other claims, yet does not offer arguments in support in the argument section of the brief, it is imperative that the inconsistency apparent on the face of the brief be resolved. A brief evidencing either form of inconsistency is not in compliance with 37 C.F.R. §1.192. When appellant presents a brief having either form of inconsistency, the Examiner invokes the presumption of 37 C.F.R. §1.192(c)(5), and appellant allows the Examiner's invocation of the presumption to go unchallenged by petition under 37 C.F.R. §1.181, the BPAI will simply decide the appeal and will decline to consider the patentability of the claims separately in reaching its decision. *Ex parte Schier,* 21 U.S.P.Q.2d 1016, 1018, 1019 (B.P.A.I. 1991).

ᴤ

When a brief on appeal to the BPAI omits the statement required by 37 C.F.R. §1.192(c)(5), yet presents arguments in the argument section, it is not in compliance with 37 C.F.R. §1.192(c). Appellant will be notified of the reasons for noncompliance and provided with a period of one month within which to file an amended brief. If appellant does not file an amended brief within the one-month period, or files an amended brief that does not overcome all the reasons for noncompliance stated in the notification, the appeal will be dismissed. In any instance where an Examiner and appellant engage in an interchange over such compliance, the BPAI will treat the matter as one within the jurisdiction of the Examiner, requiring an appellant dissatisfied with the Examiner's holding to seek relief by way of petition under 37 C.F.R. §1.181, rather than by way of appeal under 37 C.F.R. §1.191. *Ex parte Ohsumi,* 21 U.S.P.Q.2d 1020, 1023 (B.P.A.I. 1991).

Staple.

The manufacture and sale of an unpatented part of a patented combination does not constitute infringement under 35 U.S.C. §271(a), (b) or (c). This is true where the part is a replacement part and is not a staple article or commodity of commerce suitable for substantial use other than as part of plaintiff's patented invention. *Biuro Projektow Zaklodow Przerobki Mechanicznej Wegla "Separator" v. UOP, Inc.,* 203 U.S.P.Q. 175, 179 (Ill. 1979).

ᴤ

A supplier is not liable if it merely makes a staple available, even though it knows that some purchasers will use it to infringe, and 35 U.S.C. §271(c) makes that distinction. *Oak Industries, Inc. v. Zenith Electronics Corp.,* 697 F. Supp. 988, 994, 9 U.S.P.Q.2d 1138, 1144 (Ill. 1988).

Staple Article of Commerce.

"Staple" products are commodities or products with substantial uses apart from a patented invention. "Nonstaple" denotes a product or material lacking substantial uses other than infringing uses. *Robintech, Inc. v. Chemidus Wavin Ltd.*, 628 F.2d 142, 205 U.S.P.Q. 873, 878 (D.C. Cir. 1980).

ʊ

The term "nonstaple" refers to a component, as defined in 35 U.S.C. §271(c), the unlicensed sale of which would constitute contributory infringement. A "staple" component is one that does not fit this definition. *Dawson Chemical Company v. Rohm and Haas Company*, 65 L.Ed. 696, 206 U.S.P.Q. 385, 392 (S.Ct. 1980).

ʊ

In order to establish that a product is a staple component under 35 U.S.C. §271, it must be shown that it has an actual and substantial non-infringing use; a theoretical capability does not suffice. Additionally, the "quality, quantity and efficiency of the suggested uses are to be considered." *Rohm & Haas Co. v. Dawson Chemical Co. Inc.*, 557 F. Supp. 739, 217 U.S.P.Q. 515, 575 (Tex. 1983).

Staple Commodity. *See* **Tying Arrangement.**

Stare Decisis. *See also* **Precedent, Prior Adjudication.**

The CCPA's latest decision controls because that court always sat en banc. *In re Gosteli*, 872 F.2d 1008, 10 U.S.P.Q.2d 1614, 1617 (Fed. Cir. 1989).

ʊ

Where conflicting statements appear in the court's precedent, the panel is obligated to review the cases and reconcile or explain the statements, if possible. If not reconcilable and if not merely conflicting dicta, the panel is obligated to follow the earlier case law, which is the binding precedent. Alternatively, a panel may seek en banc consideration if it believes a later decision correctly states the law. *Johnston v. IVAC Corp.*, 885 F.2d 1574, 12 U.S.P.Q.2d 1382, 1386 (Fed. Cir. 1989).

ʊ

The principle of *stare decisis* is integral to our jurisprudence "because it promotes the evenhanded, predictable, and consistent development of legal principles, fosters reliance on judicial decisions, and contributes to the actual and perceived integrity of the judicial process." *In re Zurko*, 142 F.3d 1447, 46 U.S.P.Q.2d 1691, 1700 (Fed. Cir. 1998—*in banc*).

Starting Material.

A method of making starting materials not known in the art must be set forth in order to comply with the enablement requirement. A rejection for failure to enable because of failure to disclose how to obtain starting materials is sustainable only when the method of obtaining them would not be apparent to one of ordinary skill in the art. *In re Brebner*, 455 F.2d 1402, 173 U.S.P.Q. 169 (C.C.P.A. 1972).

ʊ

The use of a previously-unknown microorganism strain to produce an antibiotic previously produced by other strains of the same microorganism is not obvious because the process as a whole could not be obvious to anyone in the absence of the new strain. *In re Mancy, Florent, and PreudHomme*, 499 F.2d 1289, 182 U.S.P.Q. 303, 305 (C.C.P.A. 1974).

ℳ

Although an otherwise old process becomes a new process when a previously unknown starting material is used in it and is subjected to a conventional manipulation or reaction to produce a product that may also be new, albeit the expected result of what is done, it does not necessarily mean that the whole process has become non-obvious in the sense of 35 U.S.C. §103. In short, a new process may still be obvious, even when considered "as a whole," notwithstanding the fact that the specific starting material or resulting product, or both, are not to be found in the prior art. *In re Durden*, 763 F.2d 1406, 226 U.S.P.Q. 359 (Fed. Cir. 1985).

State. *See also* Parker Immunity, Preemption, States' Immunity, Supremacy Clause.

The patent system is one in which uniform federal standards are carefully used to promote invention while, at the same time, preserving free competition. A State cannot, consistently with the Supremacy Clause of the Constitution, extend the life of a patent beyond its expiration date or give a patent on an article which lacks the level of invention required for federal patents. To do either would run contrary to the policy of Congress of granting patents only to true inventions, and then only for a limited time. Just as a State cannot encroach on the federal patent laws directly, it cannot, under some other law, such as that forbidding unfair competition, give protection of a kind that clashes with the objectives of the federal patent laws. "Sharing in the goodwill of an article unprotected by patent or trademark is the exercise of a right possessed by alland in the free exercise of which the consuming public is deeply interested." *Sears, Roebuck & Co. v. Stiffel Company*, 376 U.S. 225, 140 U.S.P.Q. 524, 528 (S. Ct. 1964).

ℳ

State governmental units have no authority to violate the patent laws. When they do so, they act outside the scope of their authority. *Lemelson v. Ampex Corporation*, 372 F.Supp. 708, 181 U.S.P.Q. 313, 314 (Ill. 1974).

ℳ

The most important factor in determining whether a particular agency is the "alter ego" of the State for Eleventh Amendment purposes is whether payment of a judgment will have to be made out of the state treasury (i.e., whether the fund in question has both the independent power and the resources to pay the judgment without further action by the state legislature or other governmental officer). *Hutchison v. Lake Oswego School District No. 7*, 519 F.2d 1961, 1966 (9th Cir. 1975), *vacated on other grounds*, 429 U.S. 1033 (1977).

ℳ

One of the States of the United States has sovereign immunity under the Eleventh Amendment and thus cannot be sued by an individual of another state for patent infringement in a federal district court. *Chew v. California*, 893 F.2d 331, 13 U.S.P.Q.2d 1393, 1395, 1396 (Fed. Cir. 1990).

ᚬ

Eleventh Amendment immunity bars suit by a resident or nonresident, absent waiver of Congress's legitimate exercise of the power to abrogate that immunity. A state resident could have sought relief in the Florida legislature through a claims bill, but chose instead to file a patent infringement suit in the U.S. district court. Plaintiff also may assert a "takings" claim against the state under the Fifth and Fourteenth Amendments. Further, although a state court is without power to invalidate an issued patent, there is no limitation on the ability of a state court to decide the question of validity when properly raised in a state court proceeding. *Jacobs Wind Electric Co. Inc. v. Florida Department of Transportation*, 919 F.2d 726, 16 U.S.P.Q.2d 1972, 1973, 1974 (Fed. Cir. 1990).

ᚬ

The University of California (U.C.) and the Board of Regents are considered to be instrumentalities of the state. As agents of the state they are immune from a 35 U.S.C. §291 counterclaim under the doctrine of sovereign immunity under the Eleventh Amendment. A state plaintiff does not waive its sovereign immunity with respect to all plausible counterclaims. In order to be a cognizable counterclaim, the counterclaim must "arise from the same event underlying the state's action" and "be asserted defensively, by way of recoupment, for the purpose of defeating or diminishing the State's recovery, but not for the purpose of obtaining an affirmative judgment against the State." Affirmative relief would result if the court were to grant defendant's prayer for a counterclaim of interference and declare U.C.'s patent invalid. Such relief goes beyond more recoupment or set-off from U.C.'s infringement action against defendant and, therefore, is barred by the Eleventh Amendment. *University of California v. Eli Lilly & Co.*, 19 U.S.P.Q.2d 1668, 1673, 1674 (Cal. 1991).

ᚬ

Under the supremacy clause of the U.S. Constitution, federal patent law preempts state awards of patentlike protection. "[S]tate regulation of intellectual property must yield to the extent that it clashes with the balance struck by Congress in our patent laws." *Bonito Boats, Inc. v. Thunder Craft Boats, Inc.*, 489 U.S. 141, 152, 9 U.S.P.Q.2d 1847 (1989). However, federal patent law does not necessarily prohibit states from enforcing valid contracts under state contract law when such contracts provide protection for unpatented products. *Darling v. Standard Alaska Production Co.*, 20 U.S.P.Q.2d 1688, 1691 (Alaska S. Ct. 1991).

ᚬ

Congress can preempt portions of a field of law without preempting the field of law in its entirety, thereby leaving a state free to act when, in so doing, the state does not impede the objectives of Congress. Preemption thus does not preclude *all* relief, but merely limits relief available to the extent that Congress intended to preclude the application of state law. *Jacobs Wind Electric Co. Inc. v. Florida Department of Transportation*, 626 So.2d 1333, 29 U.S.P.Q.2d 1763, 1764 (Fla. S.Ct. 1993).

ᚬ

"[W]ith the possible market participant exception, *any* action that qualifies as state action is "ipso facto...exempt from the operation of antitrust laws." *In re Recombinant DNA Technology Patent and Contract Litigation*, 874 F.Supp. 904, 34 U.S.P.Q.2d 1097, 1100 (Ind. 1994).

State Action.

Federal patent law issues housed in a state law cause of action are capable of being adjudicated, even if there is no accompanying federal claim. To determine whether a state law tort is in conflict with federal patent law and accordingly preempted, a defendant's allegedly tortious conduct is assessed. If a plaintiff bases its tort action on conduct that is protected or governed by federal patent law, then the plaintiff may not invoke the state law remedy, which must be preempted for conflict with federal patent law. Conversely, if the conflict is not so protected or governed, then the remedy is not preempted. *Hunter Douglas Inc. v. Harmonic Design Inc.*, 47 U.S.P.Q.2d 1769, 1770, 1781 (Fed. Cir. 1998).

State Court.

State courts do have jurisdiction to determine questions arising under the patent laws, when merely incidental to cases which do not arise under that law. 7 Deller's Walker on Patents (2d ed.) §471 at 19. *In re Lefkowitz*, 362 F.Supp. 922, 179 U.S.P.Q. 282, 284 (N.Y. 1973).

ω

Whether or not a device (manufactured and marketed by defendants) is in conflict with plaintiff's patent cannot be determined under state unfair competition laws without encroaching on the federal patent laws. *Chapman Performance Products, Inc. v. Producers Sales, Inc.*, 306 NE2d 615, 181 U.S.P.Q. 101, 102 (Ill. 1973).

ω

Defendants" alleged sale and manufacture of products (protected by plaintiff's valid patent) in violation of terms of an agreement arises under general principles of contract law. A determination of the merits, in the first instance, requires an analysis of the agreement and not an analysis of the validity and infringement of the patent. Defendants cannot turn the matter into one arising under the patent laws of the United States by asserting an invalidity defense. *Wham-O Mfg. Co. v. All-American Yo-Yo Corporation*, 377 F.Supp. 993, 181 U.S.P.Q. 320, 321 (N.Y. 1973).

ω

State courts have jurisdiction to pass upon questions or issues involving patent laws. In an action in a state court to recover patent royalties required to be paid pursuant to contract, the state court has jurisdiction to consider the issue of patent validity as a defense to the action. State courts have passed upon the defense of patent validity in breach of contract cases. *Consolidated Kinetics Corp. v. Marshall, Neil, and Pauley*, 521 P.2d 1209, 182 U.S.P.Q. 434, 435, 436 (Wash. 1974).

ω

A declaratory judgment, even one involving a claim under federal law, presents no federal jurisdiction where it is sought merely as a defense to an action which itself could not be brought in federal court. *Union Carbide Corporation v. Air Products & Chemicals, Inc.*, 202 U.S.P.Q. 43, 54 (N.Y. 1978).

State Law.

A patentee must be able to engage in legitimate enforcement efforts to protect its rights in the face of potential infringement. An entity cannot be liable under state law for conduct that is permitted by federal law. *Loctite Corp. v. Ultraseal Ltd.*, 781 F.2d at 877, 228 U.S.P.Q. at 100-01 {following *Handgards, Inc. v. Ethicon, Inc.*, 601 F.2d 986, 202 U.S.P.Q. 342 (9th Cir. 1979), *cert. denied*, 444 U.S. 1025 [204 U.S.P.Q. 880] (1980)}.

ϖ

To the extent plaintiff seeks a declaration that defendants'' patents are invalid, federal patent law preempts their misuse claim based on tortious interference with contract. When state law touches upon the area of federal patent law, the federal policy may not be set at naught, or its benefits denied, by state law. Federal patent law expressly prescribes the circumstances under which a patent may be declared invalid based on allegations of misuse. 35 U.S.C.A. §271(d) (West Supp. 1989). Proof of the elements of interference with contract is less difficult than the proof required to entitle a defendant in a patent infringement action to a Declaration invalidating the patent. If plaintiff were permitted to invalidate defendants'' patents using state interference with contract principles, the federal patent laws and state law would be in direct conflict. *Medtronic Inc. v. Eli Lilly & Co.*, 15 U.S.P.Q.2d 1465, 1468 (Mich. 1990).

State Law Tort.

The application of a state law tort is preempted if, in holding a defendant liable for the conduct alleged and proved by the plaintiff, there would be conflict with federal patent law. Otherwise, if the state law tort, as applied, does not conflict with federal patent law, then the tort is not preempted. The combined result of these rulings is to divest state courts of jurisdiction over state law torts that are subject to [28 USC] § 1338(a) jurisdiction, and to allow only those that survive the preemption analysis to proceed. *Hunter Douglas Inc. v. Harmonic Design Inc.*, 47 U.S.P.Q.2d 1769, 1770 (Fed. Cir. 1998).

Statement. ***See also*** **Assertion, Speculation, Statement by the Board, Statement in Disclosure, Statement in the Specification.**

A copending reference patent issued to a different inventor on an application filed on the same date and refers to the subject application. The Patent Office tribunals stated that the subject application is presumed to be owned by the assignee of the copending reference patent. Since that statement was not controverted, it was accepted as correct. *In re Keim and Thompson*, 229 F.2d 466, 108 U.S.P.Q. 330, 331 (C.C.P.A. 1956).

ϖ

As there was nothing in the record to controvert a statement in appellant's affidavit, the statement was accepted as accurate. *In re Nathan, Hogg, and Schneider*, 328 F.2d 1005, 140 U.S.P.Q. 601, 604 (C.C.P.A. 1964).

ϖ

Section 112 of 35 U.S.C. does not require that a specification convince persons skilled in the art that the assertions therein are correct. *In re Robins,* 429 F.2d 452, 166 U.S.P.Q. 552 (C.C.P.A. 1970).

ᵹ

A mere conclusory statement of expectancy (without evidence or reasoning) does not provide adequate basis for upholding a Board decision. *In re Nolan,* 553 F.2d 1261, 193 U.S.P.Q. 641, 644, 645 (C.C.P.A. 1977).

ᵹ

Mere lawyers' arguments and conclusory statements in the specification, unsupported by objective evidence, are insufficient to establish unexpected results. *In re Wood, Whittaker, Stirling, and Ohta,* 582 F.2d 638, 199 U.S.P.Q. 137, 140 (C.C.P.A. 1978).

ᵹ

Where an applicant contends that the discovery of the source of a problem would have been unobvious to one of ordinary skill in the pertinent art at the time the claimed invention was made, it is incumbent upon the PTO to explain its reasons if it disagrees. A mere conclusionary statement that the source of a problem would have been discovered is inadequate. A patentable invention may lie in the discovery of the source of a problem, even though the remedy may be obvious once the source of the problem is identified. This is part of the "subject matter as a whole," which should always be considered in determining the obviousness of an invention under 35 U.S.C. §103. *In re Peehs and Hunner,* 612 F.2d 128, 204 U.S.P.Q. 835, 837 (C.C.P.A. 1980).

ᵹ

The PTO must have adequate support for its challenge to the credibility of applicant's statements as to utility. Only then does the burden shift to appellant to provide rebuttal evidence. *In re Bundy,* 642 F.2d 430, 209 U.S.P.Q. 48, 51 (C.C.P.A. 1981).

ᵹ

Conclusory statements in the specification cannot establish patentability. *In re De Blauwe,* 736 F.2d 699, 222 U.S.P.Q. 191 (Fed. Cir. 1984).

ᵹ

A petition was filed in response to a requirement to cancel from the specification all assertions pertaining to cancer utility. The Examiner took the position that the recitation in the specification of a broad genus (e.g., malignant tumors) without specific examples of human and animal in vivo and additional in vitro data does not meet minimum standards. Reference to utility as an antitumor agent in a warm-blooded animal afflicted by malignant tumors was not regarded by the Examiner as believable on its face to those of ordinary skill in the art in view of contemporary knowledge in the art. The Examiner does not need to provide reasons why this speculative assertion should not be believed. The mere fact that the art of cancer chemotherapy is highly unpredictable places the burden on applicants to provide a basis for believing the speculative statements that they chose to place in the specification in the form of a positive assertion. The ignorance of the PTO and applicants in not being able to provide a scientific reason why the assertion is not sound is not a sound reason or justification for permitting such an assertion to be made in a patent document where those of ordinary skill in this art would not accept it as believable on its face without some data or other evidence to support it. The PTO does not want to spend the time or resources that may be necessary to provide a scientifically reasoned opinion as to why the speculative statements would not be believed by a person skilled in the art. *In re Application of Hozumi,* 226 U.S.P.Q. 353 (Commr. Patents & Trademarks 1985).

ᙡ

Unpredictability of a particular art area may, by itself, provide a reasonable doubt as to the accuracy of a broad statement made in support of the enablement of a claim. *Ex parte Singh,* 17 U.S.P.Q.2d 1714, 1715 (B.P.A.I. 1990).

Statement by the Board.

If the appellants wished to object to the Board's statement and to question the correctness of the facts contained therein, they should have requested the Board to cite its authority for the statement. If the cited authority was based upon facts within the personal knowledge of the Board, the appellants should have proceeded under Rules 66 and 76 of the Patent Office and called for an affidavit of the Board. The appellants would then have been in a position to contradict or explain the Board's statement. In the absence of such request, the appellants may not be heard to challenge a statement made in the Board's opinion. The statement of the Board must therefore be accepted as correct. *In re Selmi and Altenburger,* 156 F.2d 96, 70 U.S.P.Q. 197 (C.C.P.A. 1946).

ᙡ

A finding of a new fact, supporting an alternative ground for sustaining an Examiner's rejection, and based on apparently nothing more than a bare allegation of scientific fact, does everything but cry out for an opportunity to respond. Appellant challenged the Board's assertion with an allegation of his own to the contrary and supported his assertion with an affidavit opinion of an acknowledged expert in the art. Appellant's response was more than mere "argument"; it was a direct challenge to a finding of fact made for the first time by the Board and included with it some evidence in the nature of rebuttal. It was thus entitled to more serious consideration. *In re Moore,* 444 F.2d 572, 170 U.S.P.Q. 260, 263 (C.C.P.A. 1971).

Statement in Disclosure. *See also* **Assertion, Cancer, Statement, Truth.**

The application stood in condition for allowance and ready for the issuance of a patent grant except for the presence in the specification disclosure of certain asserted utilities that the Examiner believed to be too speculative—i.e., not believable on their face to those of ordinary skill in the art in view of the contemporary knowledge of the art. While it may be clear that workers in this art had shown that some cancers can be treated successfully in some patients, the effective treatment of various forms of malignant tumors remains a highly unpredictable art. Under these circumstances, the Examiner does not need to provide reasons why this speculative assertion should not be believed. The mere fact that the art of cancer chemotherapy is highly unpredictable places the burden on applicants to provide a basis for believing the speculative statements that they chose to place in the specification in the form of a positive assertion. *In re Application of Hozumi,* 226 U.S.P.Q. 353 (Commr. Patents & Trademarks 1985).

Statement in the Specification. ***See also*** **Assertion, Statement, Truth.**

The discovery does not appear to be of such a "speculative," abstruse, or esoteric nature that it must inherently be considered unbelievable, "incredible," or "factually misleading." Nor does operativeness appear "unlikely" or an assertion thereof appear to run counter "to what would be believed would happen by the ordinary person" in the art. Nor does the field of endeavor appear to be one where "little of a successful nature has been developed" or one that "from common knowledge has long been the subject matter of much humbuggery and fraud." Nor has the Examiner provided evidence inconsistent with the assertions and evidence of operativeness presented by the appellant. To the contrary, the appellant's assertions of usefulness in his specification appear to be believable on their face and straightforward, at least in the absence of reason or authority in variance. The Examiner and Board have simply provided inadequate reason to disbelieve the statements and evidence of usefulness provided in appellant's specification. *In re Gazave,* 379 F.2d 973, 154 U.S.P.Q. 92, 96, 97 (C.C.P.A. 1967).

ϖ

The positive statements at the beginning of the specification that variances in the substituents will not qualitatively affect the asserted activity cannot be ignored. *In re Gardner,* 475 F.2d 1389, 177 U.S.P.Q. 396, 398 (C.C.P.A. 1973).

ϖ

The accuracy of an unchallenged statement in the specification is presumed. *In re De La Chevreliere,* 485 F.2d 1403, 179 U.S.P.Q. 492, 495 (C.C.P.A. 1973).

ϖ

The correctness of an assertion in the specification may always be challenged, but only if there is sound basis therefor. Mere surmise, speculation, and conjecture are insufficient to refute an explicit teaching about operability. An appellant's assertion must be accepted in the absence of factual evidence (not merely unsupported skepticism) to the contrary. *Ex parte Dunn and Mathis,* 181 U.S.P.Q. 652, 653 (PO Bd. App. 1973).

ϖ

The unpredictability noted in the decision of the Board was in the admittedly chemical fact that the "properties of "polymerizable materials" can vary over a wide range," but no reasons were given to appellant by the Patent Office for the alleged failureor at least uncertainty—of the class of "polymerizable materials" to work in the claimed process to controvert the statement in appellant's application that his invention, in its broader aspects, is applicable to other polymers. Even in cases involving the unpredictable world of chemistry, such reasons are required. *In re Bowen,* 492 F.2d 859, 181 U.S.P.Q. 48, 50, 51 (C.C.P.A. 1974).

ϖ

Appellants point to certain statements in the disclosure of their application, which, they allege, establish that the claimed moisture content is critical. Absent any evidence to the contrary, these statements are accepted as proof that the claimed final moisture content is critical. *In re Clinton, Johnson, Meyer, Pfluger, and Jacobs,* 527 F.2d 1226, 188 U.S.P.Q. 365, 367 (C.C.P.A. 1976).

ϖ

Mere conclusory statements in the specification, unsupported by objective evidence, are entitled to little weight when the PTO questions the efficacy of those statements. *In re Greenfield and DuPont*, 571 F.2d 1185, 197 U.S.P.Q. 227, 229 (C.C.P.A. 1978).

ᛦ

Mere lawyer's arguments and conclusory statements in the specification, unsupported by objective evidence, are insufficient to establish unexpected results. *In re Wood, Whittaker, Stirling, and Ohta*, 582 F.2d 638, 199 U.S.P.Q. 137, 140 (C.C.P.A. 1978).

ᛦ

Conclusory statements in the specification cannot establish patentability. *In re De Blauwe*, 736 F.2d 699, 222 U.S.P.Q. 191 (Fed. Cir. 1984).

ᛦ

A specification that contains a disclosure of utility that corresponds in scope to the subject matter sought to be patented must be taken as sufficient to satisfy the utility requirements of 35 U.S.C. §101 for the entire claimed subject matter unless there is reason for one skilled in the art to question the objective truth of the statement of utility or its scope. *Ex parte Rubin*, 5 U.S.P.Q.2d 1461 (B.P.A.I. 1987).

ᛦ

When an applicant demonstrates *substantially* improved results and *states* that the results were *unexpected*, this should suffice to establish unexpected results *in the absence of* evidence to the contrary. *In re Soni*, 54 F.3d 746, 34 U.S.P.Q.2d 1684, 1688 (Fed. Cir. 1995).

Statement of Invention.

An Examiner may require that the statement of the invention in the specification be made to conform to what has been found to be allowable. *In re Dinwiddie*, 347 F.2d 1016, 146 U.S.P.Q. 497, 502 n.3 (C.C.P.A. 1965).

State of Mind.

Good-faith reliance by a party on counsel's opinion is a question of the party's state of mind, not the counsel's state of mind. To establish a defense of nondeliberate infringement on the basis of counsel's opinion, a party must show not only that it received an opinion from competent counsel, but also that it exercised reasonable and good-faith adherence to the analysis and advice therein. This defense does not require an inquiry into counsel's state of mind. Matters held to be relevant inquiries into the competence of counsel's opinion of noninfringement include whether counsel examined the file history of the patents, whether the opinion came from in-house or outside counsel, whether there was a pattern of attorney shopping by the alleged infringer, and whether the opinion came from a patent attorney. *Liqui-Box Corp. v. Reid Valve Co. Inc.*, 16 U.S.P.Q.2d 1074, 1075 (Pa. 1989).

State of the Art. *See also* **Skill of the Art.**

Facts constituting the state of the art are normally subject to the possibility of rational disagreement among reasonable persons and are not amenable to the taking of judicial or administrative notice. If evidence of the knowledge possessed by those skilled in the art is to be properly considered, it must be timely injected into the proceedings. *In re Eynde, Pollet, and de Cat,* 480 F.2d 1364, 178 U.S.P.Q. 470, 474 (C.C.P.A. 1973).

ᛟ

The disclosure of an earlier-filed, but copending, patent cannot be relied on to establish the state of the art at the time of an applicant's filing date. *In re Glass,* 492 F.2d 1228, 181 U.S.P.Q. 31, 34 (C.C.P.A. 1974); *In re Budnick,* 537 F.2d 535, 190 U.S.P.Q. 422, 424 (C.C.P.A. 1976).

ᛟ

A later state of the art is that state coming into existence after the filing date of an application. Later publications can be used as evidence of the state of the art existing on the filing date of an application. A later publication (disclosing a later existing state of the art) cannot, however, be used in testing an earlier application for compliance with 35 U.S.C. §112, first paragraph. The difference may be that described as between the permissible application of later knowledge about art-related facts existing on the filing date and the impermissible application of later knowledge about later art related facts that did exist on the filing date. If an earlier-filed application provided sufficient enablement, considering all available evidence (whenever that evidence became available) of the state of the art at the time of the filing date, the fact of that enablement was established for all time, and a later change in the state of the art cannot change it. *In re Hogan and Banks,* 559 F.2d 595, 194 U.S.P.Q. 527, 537 (C.C.P.A. 1977).

ᛟ

Under certain narrow circumstances, later-issued patents and publications may be used to show the state of the art existing on the filing date of an application in question. A later publication might be used as evidence that, as of applicant's filing date, undue experimentation would have been required; that a parameter, absent from the claims, was or was not critical; that a statement in the specification was inaccurate; that an invention was inoperative or lacked utility; that a claim was indefinite; or that characteristics of prior art products were known. A later-existing state of the art cannot be used in determining enablement under 35 U.S.C. §112. *In re Koller, Hartl, and Kirschner,* 613 F.2d 819, 204 U.S.P.Q. 702, 706 (C.C.P.A. 1980).

ᛟ

Affidavit evidence admitted in a protested reissue proceeding is treated in the same manner as if it had been submitted in ex parte proceedings before the PTO. Such evidence has been held to be competent to the extent that it refers to matters known to or observed by the affiant prior to or contemporaneous with the actual reduction to practice by another in an interference, where it was offered as evidence of the level of knowledge in the art at the time the invention was made. *In re Farrenkopf and Usategui-Gomez, and Travenol Laboratories, Inc., Intervenor,* 713 F.2d 714, 219 U.S.P.Q. 1, 6 (Fed. Cir. 1983).

ᛟ

For an Examiner's Answer to cite (for the first time in the prosecution of an application) new references to "show the general state of the art" while expressly stating that "[n]o new prior art has been applied in this examiner's Answer" is an improper effort to bring these references in the "back door." *Ex parte Raske*, 28 U.S.P.Q.2d 1304, 1305 (B.P.A.I. 1993).

ᙡ

In seeking to establish noninfringement (rather than invalidity), the assignor may use "the state of the art . . . to construe and narrow the claims of the patent, conceding [its] validity." *Total Containment Inc. v. Environ Products Inc.*, 33 U.S.P.Q.2d 1316, 1317 (Pa. 1994).

States' Immunity. *See also* **Market Participant, Parker Immunity, Sovereign, State.**

Neither §271 nor §281 of Title 35 contains "unmistakable language" indicating congressional intent to abrogate the states" immunity under the Eleventh Amendment from suit in a federal court. *Chew v. California,* 11 U.S.P.Q.2d 1159, 1160 (Cal. 1988).

ᙡ

In legislation enacted October 28, 1992, Congress abrogated state immunity from suit for violation of patent law. *Genentech Inc. v. Eli Lilly and Co.*, 998 F.2d 931, 27 U.S.P.Q.2d 1241, 1247 (Fed. Cir. 1993).

ᙡ

Were a patentee suing UC for patent infringement, the Fourteenth Amendment would provide Congress with the power necessary to abrogate UC's Eleventh Amendment immunity. Although a State can waive its immunity, the sovereign's intention to do so must be unmistakably clear. In this case UC is a patent owner who has accused Genentech of patent infringement and threatened suit. Notwithstanding that, UC's sovereign immunity protects it from a declaratory Judgment action by Genentech without UC's consent. *Genentech Inc. v. University of California*, 40 U.S.P.Q.2d 1768, 1772 (Ind. 1996).

ᙡ

The Patent Act amendments, which abrogate the States' Eleventh Amendment immunity, are "appropriate legislation" under Section 5 of the Fourteenth Amendment. *College Savings Bank v. Florida Prepaid Postsecondary Education Expense Board*, 42 U.S.P.Q.2d 1487, 1509 (N.J. 1996).

ᙡ

Article I of the Constitution does not empower Congress to abrogate a state's Eleventh Amendment immunity. The contrary holding of *Pennsylvania v. Union Gas Co.*, 491 U.S. 1 (1989), was expressly overruled. *Seminole Tribe of Florida v. Florida*, 517 U.S. 44 (1996).

Statistically Significant.

There is no reason to question the statistical significance of data without some indication (either from the data or from the prior art) that the types of tests employed give unreliable results. *In re Kollman and Irwin*, 595 F.2d 48, 201 U.S.P.Q. 193, 199 n.8 (C.C.P.A. 1979).

Statute.

Lack of antecedent basis in a claim could render it invalid under 35 U.S.C. §112, second paragraph, and correction of such a defect by reissue should not have to depend on difference in scope of the claim. Inasmuch as 35 U.S.C. §251 is a remedial provision, which should be liberally construed, a patentee should be allowed to correct an error or ambiguity in a claim without having to rely on the implication of litigation. Lack of antecedent basis in a claim is a proper ground for reissue under §251. *In re Altenpohl,* 500 F.2d 1151, 183 U.S.P.Q. 38 (C.C.P.A. 1974).

Statute of Limitations. *See also* **Unknowable, 35 U.S.C. §286.**

Section 102(b) (35 U.S.C.) presents a sort of statute of limitations within which an inventor (even though he has made a patentable invention) must act on penalty of loss of his right to patent. What starts the period running is clearly the availability of the invention to the public through the categories of disclosure enumerated in §102(b). *In re Foster,* 343 F.2d 980, 145 U.S.P.Q. 166, 173 (C.C.P.A. 1965).

ω

Section 135(b) of 35 U.S.C. is a statute of limitations on interferences so that a patentee might be more secure in his property right. *Corbett v. Chisholm and Schrenk,* 568 F.2d 759, 196 U.S.P.Q. 337, 342 (C.C.P.A. 1977).

ω

There is a distinction between the class of devices that infringes claims and the discreet individual devices which, together, constitute the class of infringing devices. The class is not foreclosed from infringing merely because one of its members was manufactured or used by the government more than six years prior to the filing of the suit. Each device, i.e., each individual member of the universe of infringing devices, can be taken only once in its lifetime, and if that taking occurs prior to the six-year period which immediately precedes the filing of the lawsuit in the Court of Claims, then recovery as to that particular device is barred forever by 28 U.S.C. §2501. *Starobin v. United States,* 662 F.2d 747, 213 U.S.P.Q. 449, 452 (U.S. Cl. Ct. 1981).

ω

Section 135(b) of 35 U.S.C. acts as a statute of limitations on copying claims for the purpose of instigating interferences and thus operates as a procedural statutory bar proscribing the instigation of an interference after a specified interval. *Gustavsson v. Valentini,* 25 U.S.P.Q.2d 1401, 1410 (B.P.A.I. 1991).

ω

Historically, a statute of limitations applied only to claims at law, not to a companion equitable claim. Laches was the only basis for time-barring an equitable claim. However, where the reasons for repose of the claim were equally applicable to remedies at law and equity, the equity courts became inclined to "borrow" the time period from the statute of limitations and apply it presumptively against the equitable claim. This practice of creating rebuttable presumptions (using a statute of limitations as a guide) was extended to situations where the legal and equitable claims were not the same, but only analogous. *A.C. Aukerman Co. v. R.L. Chaides Construction Co.,* 960 F.2d 1020, 22 U.S.P.Q.2d 1321, 1330 (Fed. Cir. 1992).

Statutory.

The fact that a claim reads on both statutory and nonstatutory subject matter does not preclude its being in compliance with the second paragraph of 35 U.S.C. §112. To inject any question of statutory subject matter into that paragraph is to depart from its wording and to complicate the law unnecessarily. *In re Mahony*, 421 F.2d 742, 164 U.S.P.Q. 572, 575 (C.C.P.A. 1970).

Statutory Bar.

The patentability of subject matter disclosed and claimed for the first time in a cip more than one year after publication of subject matter in the parent application is subject to statutory bar preclusions even when the publication is that of applicant's own foreign counterpart application. The parent application cannot be used to antedate the publication. *In re Ruscetta and Jenny,* 255 F.2d 687, 118 U.S.P.Q. 101, 104 (C.C.P.A. 1958).

ϖ

Congress intended that the provisions of 35 U.S.C. §102(b), as applied to plant patents, should not be interpreted otherwise than they had been with respect to other inventions, i.e., that only an "enabling" publication is effective as a bar to a subsequent patent. *In re LeGrice*, 301 F.2d 929, 133 U.S.P.Q. 365, 374 (C.C.P.A. 1962).

ϖ

A Rule 131 (37 C.F.R. §1.131) affidavit cannot be used to overcome a statutory bar. *Ex parte Naito and Nakagawa*, 168 U.S.P.Q. 437, 439 (PO Bd. App. 1969).

ϖ

To obtain the benefit of the filing date of a parent application for subject matter claimed in a cip, the parent application must satisfy the description requirement of the statute with regard to that subject matter. Neither a specific example falling within the scope of (but not commensurate in scope with) nor a disclosure generic to such subject matter will suffice. In either or both cases publication of the applicant's own foreign application more than a year prior to the filing date of the cip serves as a statutory bar. *In re Lukach, Olson, and Spurlin,* 440 F.2d 1263, 169 U.S.P.Q. 795, 796, 797 (C.C.P.A. 1971).

Statutory Class. *See also* **Class, Hybrid, Same Invention, Unity of Invention.**

Since the product in each of the appealed claims is defined essentially in terms of the method by which it is made, the fact that the process claims of appellant's patent and the product claims of the application are, technically, in different statutory classes is not, in itself, enough to avoid a rejection on the ground of double patenting. *In re Freeman,* 166 F.2d 178, 76 U.S.P.Q. 585, 586 (C.C.P.A. 1948).

ϖ

Each statutory class of claims should be considered independently on its own merits. The fact that the starting materials and the final product are the subject matter of allowed claims does not necessarily indicate that the process employed is patentable. *In re Albertson*, 332 F.2d 379, 141 U.S.P.Q. 730, 732 (C.C.P.A. 1964).

ϖ

The mere presence of a method limitation in an otherwise allowable article claim does not so poison the claim as to render it unpatentable. *In re Garnero*, 412 F.2d 276, 162 U.S.P.Q. 221, 223 (C.C.P.A. 1969).

ᚹ

The constitutional purpose of the patent system is promoted by encouraging applicants to claim, and therefore to describe in the manner required by 35 U.S.C. §112, all aspects of what they regard as their inventions, regardless of the number of statutory classes involved. Dependent claims to the use of a new composition in the same application with claims to the composition do not materially increase the scope of protection of an applicant's inchoate patent property under 35 U.S.C. §154, which already includes the right to exclude others from making, using, or selling the composition by allowance of claims thereon. But they do tend to increase the wealth of technical knowledge disclosed in the patent by encouraging description of the use aspects of an applicant's invention in the manner required by 35 U.S.C. §112, paragraph one. *In re Kuehl*, 475 F.2d 658, 177 U.S.P.Q. 250, 256 (C.C.P.A. 1973). *See also In re Pleuddemann*, 910 F.2d 823, 15 U.S.P.Q.2d 1738, 1740, 1741 (Fed. Cir. 1990).

ᚹ

When two patents claim different statutory classes of subject matter, composition, and process, they are not directed to the same invention. This alone is sufficient to avoid same invention-type double patenting. Before two sets of claims may be said to claim the same invention, they must in fact claim the same subject matter. By "same invention" is meant identical subject matter. Thus, the invention defined by a claim reciting "halogen" is not the same as that defined by a claim reciting "chlorine," because the former is broader than the latter. A good test, and probably the only objective test, for "same invention," is whether one of the claims would be literally infringed without literally infringing the other. If it could be, the claims do not define identically the same invention. *Studiengesellschaft Kohle mbH v. Northern Petrochemical Co.*, 784 F.2d 351, 228 U.S.P.Q. 837 (Fed. Cir. 1986).

Statutory Construction. *See also* **Remedial Statute, Shall, Statutory Interpretation.**

Supreme Court decisions favor liberal construction of reissue statutes in order to secure to inventors protection for what they have actually invented. *In re Wesseler*, 367 F.2d 838, 151 U.S.P.Q. 339, 348 (C.C.P.A. 1966).

ᚹ

When products are covered by one of several patents listed on an attached label, they are not "unpatented products", and the statute (35 U.S.C. §292), by its terms, is not applicable. The plain language of the statute, being penal in nature, must be strictly construed. *The Ansul Company v. Uniroyal, Inc.*, 306 F.Supp. 541, 163 U.S.P.Q. 517, 536 (N.Y. 1969).

ᚹ

This appeal is from a decision of the PTO Board of Appeals rejecting claims of a Reissue Application on the ground that a broadening Reissue Application that was filed within two years of the patent issue date (but was erroneously filed by the assignee) could not be corrected by a Declaration of the inventor filed more than two years after the patent issue date. The CAFC reversed. Recognizing that all of the provisions of a unified statute must be read in harmony, the portion of 35 U.S.C. §251 that requires that a broadening Reissue Application must be signed by the inventor does not mean that an error in compliance with §251 is insulated from the remedial ruling of *Stoddard* [564 F.2d 556, 195 U.S.P.Q. 97 (D.C. Cir. 1977)] or the statutory provision for the correction of error. The purpose of the reissue statute is to remedy errors. Reissue is remedial in nature and is based on fundamental principles of equity and fairness. These fundamental principles must not be forgotten in implementation of the statute. *In re Bennett,* 766 F.2d 524, 226 U.S.P.Q. 413 (Fed. Cir. 1985).

ω

The construction of a statute by those charged with its execution should be followed unless there are compelling indications that it is wrong. Because the Commissioner's decision is consistent with the statutory language and it is not arbitrary or capricious nor contrary to law, it will not be disturbed. *Westwood Pharmaceuticals Inc. v. Quigg,* 13 U.S.P.Q.2d 2067, 2069 (D.C. 1989).

ω

While an agency's interpretation of a statute it administers is entitled to deference, the courts are the final authority on issues of statutory construction. They must reject administrative constructions, whether reached by adjudication or administrative rule making, that are inconsistent with the statutory mandate or that frustrate the policy Congress sought to implement. If a court, employing the traditional tool of statutory construction, ascertains that the Congress had an intention on the precise question at issue, the intention is the law and must be given effect. The plain and unambiguous meaning of the words used by Congress prevails in the absence of a clearly expressed legislative intent to the contrary. When there is an ambiguity, it is incumbent upon the court to examine the legislative history to discern Congress's intent. The fact that Congress might have acted with greater clarity or foresight does not give courts carte blanche to redraft statutes in an effort to achieve that which Congress is perceived to have failed to do. It is not for the courts to distort the statute to "fix" what Congress either intentionally or inadvertently failed to anticipate. Laws enacted with good intention, when put to the test, frequently turn out to be mischievous, absurd, or otherwise objectionable. In such case the remedy lies with the law-making authority, and not with the courts. *Hoechst Aktiengesellschaft v. Quigg,* 917 F.2d 522, 16 U.S.P.Q.2d 1549, 1552, 1554 (Fed. Cir. 1990).

ω

A statute should be construed in departure from its plain language only when "the literal application of a statute will produce a result demonstrably at odds with the intention of its drafters". *Genentech Inc. v. Eli Lilly and Co.*, 998 F.2d 931, 27 U.S.P.Q.2d 1241, 1248 (Fed. Cir. 1993).

ω

As "an agency's construction of a statute it is charged with enforcing is entitled to deference if it is reasonable and not in conflict with the expressed intent of Congress," the FDA's decision provides further support for the Court's determination that an ANDA applicant need provide certification, pursuant to 21 U.S.C. §355(j)(2)(A)(vii), only for patents listed by an NDA applicant in its application and, subsequently, by the FDA in the Orange Book. *Abbott Laboratories v. Zenith Laboratories Inc.*, 36 U.S.P.Q.2d 1801, 1808 (Ill. 1995).

ᴡ

Under *Chevron, U.S.A., Inc. v. Natural Resources Defense Council, Inc.*, 467 U.S. 837, 842-45 (1984), where Congress has authorized an agency to promulgate substantive rules under a statute it is charged with administering, we must uphold the agency's interpretation of an ambiguity or omission in that statute if the interpretation is a reasonable one. However, "only statutory interpretations by agencies *with rulemaking powers* deserve substantial deference." *Merck & Co. v. Kessler*, 80 F.3d 1543, 38 U.S.P.Q.2d 1347, 1351 (Fed. Cir. 1996).

ᴡ

"[T]he courts are the final authorities on statutory construction. They must reject administrative constructions of the statute, whether reached by adjudication or by rulemaking, that are inconsistent with the statutory mandate or that frustrate the policy that Congress sought to implement. "*In re Portola Packaging Inc.*, 42 U.S.P.Q.2d 1295, 1298 (Fed. Cir. 1997), *rhg. denied* 122 F.3d 1473, U.S.P.Q.2d 1060 (Fed. Cir. 1997).

Statutory Implementation.

Courts presented with challenges to the lawfulness of a regulation must engage in a two-step analysis. First, courts must decide whether Congress has "directly spoken to the precise question at issue." If so, the judicial task is ended. Courts must give effect to Congress" clearly expressed intention, and if such intention is manifest in the statute's language, there is no need to proceed to the second step of the analysis. But, if the answer to the first inquiry is negative, that is, where Congress has been silent regarding the "precise question at issue," or if the statutory language is ambiguous, then courts must ask whether the agency's regulation stems from "a permissible construction of the statute." In this regard, courts may not substitute their own interpretation of the statute for that of the agency, provided the agency's construction is "permissible." Finally, in determining whether an agency's construction is permissible, courts must give "considerable weight" to an agency's interpretation of the statutes it has been directed to administer. *Centigram Communications Corp. v. Lehman*, 862 F.Supp. 113, 32 U.S.P.Q.2d 1346, 1350 (Va. 1994).

Statutory Interpretation. *See also* Intent of Congress, Statutory Construction.

The reissue statute is based on fundamental principles of equity and fairness and, as a remedial provision, it should be liberally construed so as to carry out its purpose to the end that justice may be done to both patentees and the public. *In re Oda, Fujii, Moriga, and Higaki*, 443 F.2d 1200, 170 U.S.P.Q. 268, 270 (C.C.P.A. 1971).

ᴡ

When statutory interpretation is at issue, the plain and unambiguous meaning of a statute prevails in the absence of clearly expressed legislative intent to the contrary. *In re Donaldson Co. Inc.*, 16 F.3d 1189, 29 U.S.P.Q.2d 1845, 1848 (Fed. Cir. 1994).

Statutory Limitations.

While, technically, 35 U.S.C. §286 is not a statute of limitations barring suit, there is no viable or remediable case or controversy between the parties for either monetary or injunctive relief when the only possibly infringing acts occurred more than six years before suit. *Lang & Swath Ocean Systems, Inc. v. Pacific Marine & Supply Co.*, 895 F.2d 761, 13 U.S.P.Q.2d 1820 (Fed. Cir. 1990).

Statutory Period.

The filing of a timely response to a paper issued by the Patent Office suggesting a claim for interference purposes satisfies a statutory period for responding to a previously-issued Patent Office action if the paper was mailed during the statutory period. *Bain and Hampton v. Hasselstrom and Brennan*, 165 F.2d 436, 76 U.S.P.Q. 302, 304 (C.C.P.A. 1948).

Statutory Subject Matter.

Consideration of novelty or obviousness is of no effect whatever in determining whether particular claims define statutory subject matter under 35 U.S.C. §101. The "point of novelty" approach in determining whether a claimed invention is statutory subject matter under 35 U.S.C. §101 is inappropriate. Analysis of specific facts in a 35 U.S.C. §103 case cannot serve as an "example" to be followed in determining whether claimed subject matter is within a statutory class of §101. *In re Freeman*, 573 F.2d 1237, 197 U.S.P.Q. 464, 469, 470 (C.C.P.A. 1978).

ω

A "transitory intermediate" which would not and could not be readily isolated was a manufacture or composition of matter within the meaning of 35 U.S.C. §101. *In re Breslow*, 616 F.2d 516, 205 U.S.P.Q. 221, 226 (C.C.P.A. 1980).

Stay. *See also* Customer Suit.

Where rejection of all claims is affirmed by the Court of Customs and Patent Appeals, the responsibility is upon the plaintiff to stay the court's judgment if the pendency of the application is to be preserved, even though that is not necessary for Supreme Court review. *Continental Can Co., Inc. v. Schuyler, Commissioner of Patents*, 326 F. Supp. 283, 168 U.S.P.Q. 625 (D.C. 1970).

ω

There are four guiding factors relating to the issuance of a stay of execution of a judgment pending appeal:

(1) whether the stay applicant has made a strong showing that he is likely to succeed on the merits;
(2) whether the applicant will be irreparably injured absent a stay;
(3) whether issuance of the stay will substantially injure the other parties interested in the proceedings; and

(4) where the public interest lies.

Each factor, however, need not be given equal weight. Also, likelihood of success in the appeal is not a rigid concept. *Standard Havens Products Inc. v. Gencor Industries, Inc.*, 897 F.2d 511, 13 U.S.P.Q.2d 2029 (Fed. Cir. 1990).

ᙡ

A stay of a declaratory judgment action pending resolution of patentee's reexamination was denied, as the reexamination was not likely to settle the controversy over the patent any time in the near future. *American Ceramicraft Inc. v. Eisenbraun Reiss Inc.*, 28 U.S.P.Q.2d 1241, 1249 (N.J. 1993—*unpublished*).

ᙡ

The functions of the courts and the Patent Office are very different and " 'are concepts not in conflict.' " The awkwardness presumed to result if the PTO and court reached different conclusions is more apparent than real. The two forums take different approaches in determining invalidity and on the same evidence could quite correctly come to different conclusions. Furthermore, we see nothing untoward about the PTO upholding the validity of a reexamined patent which the district court later finds invalid. This is essentially what occurs when a court finds a patent invalid after the PTO has granted it. Once again, it is important that the district court and the PTO can consider different evidence. Accordingly, different results between the two forums may be entirely reasonable. *Accent Designs Inc. v. Jan Jewelry Designs Inc.*, 92 Civ. 0482, 32 U.S.P.Q.2d 1036, 1039, 1040 (N.Y. 1994).

ᙡ

In deciding whether to grant a stay pending appeal, this court "assesses the movant's chances of success on the merits and weighs the equities as they affect the parties and the public." To prevail, a movant must establish a strong likelihood of success on the merits or, failing that, nonetheless demonstrate a susbstantial case on the merits provided that the other factors militate in its favor. The other factors include whether the movant will be irreparably injured absent a stay, whether issuance of a stay would substantially injure the other parties, and considering where the public interest lies. *L.E.A. Dynatech Inc. v. Allina*, 32 U.S.P.Q.2d 1701, 1702, 1703 (Fed. Cir. 1994—*unpublished*).

ᙡ

Federal courts have often found jurisdiction to review stays in favor of state court suits when the state court judgment would have fully preclusive effect on the federal action or moot the federal action entirely. Stays in favor of administrative proceedings are similarly reviewed on an "effectively out of court" standard. *Slip Track Systems Inc. v. Metal Lite Inc.*, 48 U.S.P.Q.2d 1055, 1057 (Fed. Cir. 1998).

Stay Motion.

A stay motion in a patent infringement suit could not be decided solely by a race to the courthouse. A proceeding against a supplier or manufacturer as a primary defendant should be accorded precedence over proceeding with an action against that manufacturer's customers. *Gassaway v. Business Machine Security*, 9 U.S.P.Q.2d 1572 (Cal. 1988).

ᙡ

Defendant's motion for a stay of the patent infringement litigation pending the PTO's consideration of defendant's request for reexamination was granted. *Brown v. Shimano American Corp.*, 18 U.S.P.Q.2d 1496 (Cal. 1991).

ω

The court, faced with the issue of whether the doctrine of assignor estoppel bars a party from seeking reexamination of a patent, reasoned that, because the doctrine of assignor estoppel is an equitable doctrine and the reexamination provisions are statutory mandates, the conflict between the two should be resolved in favor of the statute, and the motion to stay pending the reexamination outcome should be granted. *Vitronics Corp. v. Conceptronic Inc.*, 44 U.S.P.Q.2d 1536, 1538 (N.H. 1977).

Steps. *See also* Combining Steps, Mental Steps, Method, Reduction in Steps.

The appellant seeks to obtain process (not product) claims because of alleged differences between the proposed ingredients used by him and those used in the reference patent together with alleged differences in their respective final products. It is proper to compare steps with steps, not products with products, in evaluating process claims. *In re Fahrni*, 210 F.2d 362, 100 U.S.P.Q. 388, 390 (C.C.P.A. 1954). But see *Ex parte Macy*, 132 U.S.P.Q. 545, 546 (PO Bd. App. 1960).

ω

Temperature limitations can render patentable otherwise obvious steps. The proper question is whether it would have been obvious to one of ordinary skill in the art that the particular blends could be subjected to the steps at the claimed temperatures. It is not a matter of the criticality of the recited ranges but of the obviousness of the applicability of said temperatures. *In re Schirmer*, 480 F.2d 1342, 178 U.S.P.Q. 483, 484 (C.C.P.A. 1973).

ω

It is not proper to determine patentability of a process solely on the lack of novelty of physical manipulative steps. The specific nature of the material employed in the process has a bearing on the patentability of the process and, if its use therein is not obvious from the art or is responsible for unexpected results, the method "as a whole" must be considered unobvious. Process claims cannot be rejected simply because they recite use of new materials in an old process. *Ex parte MacAdams, Wu, and Joyner*, 206 U.S.P.Q. 445, 447 (PTO Bd. App. 1978).

Stereoisomer. *See also* Optical Isomer.

Notwithstanding a showing that the claimed laevo-enantiomer was significantly more active than the reference racemate and that the corresponding dextro-enantiomer was virtually without activity, patentability was denied. *In re Adamson and Duffin*, 275 F.2d 952, 125 U.S.P.Q. 233, 235 (C.C.P.A. 1960).

Steroid.

The enablement requirement of the statute is satisfied when the specification, taken with the prior art, clearly teaches an effective process for making the claimed compounds from corresponding known starting materials and also describes methods of using the claimed compounds. *Ex parte Gastambide, Thal, Rohrbach, and Laroche*, 189 U.S.P.Q. 643, 645 (PTO Bd. App. 1974).

Stipulation.

Bearing in mind that the record is stipulated and not attacked by cross-examination nor refuted by rebuttal evidence, the statement by an affiant that he "supervised" the testing procedures, which procedures were standard, is sufficient without the testimony of the persons who actually conducted the work. *Olin v. Duerr, Aebi and Ebner*, 175 U.S.P.Q. 707, 710 (PO Bd. Pat. Intf. 1972).

ω

When an agreed statement of facts is actually a tabulation of stipulated facts and a record of what a particular witness would testify to if called, the latter does not constitute stipulated facts. *Spiner and Hoffman v. Pierce*, 177 U.S.P.Q. 709, 710 (PO Bd. Pat. Int. 1972).

ω

If a stipulation is to be treated as an agreement concerning the legal effect of admitted fact, it is inoperative, since a court cannot be controlled by agreement of counsel on a subsidiary question of law. A court is not bound to accept, as controlling, stipulations as to questions of law. *Technicon Instruments Corp. v. Alpkem Corp.*, 866 F.2d 417, 9 U.S.P.Q.2d 1540 (Fed. Cir. 1989).

Stockholder Rule.

A stockholder has no cause of action for the loss of the value of stock caused by injuries sustained by the corporation as a result of violation of anti-trust laws. *D.L. Auld Company v. Park Electrochemical Corp.*, 651 F.Supp. 582, 1 U.S.P.Q.2d 2071, 2073 (N.Y. 1986).

Stolen.

An application mailed to the Patent Office and stolen while in the custody of the United States Postal Service was accorded a filing date prior to that on which a properly-executed application was actually received by the Patent Office. *Sturzinger v. Commissioner of Patents*, 377 F.Supp. 1284, 181 U.S.P.Q. 436, 437 (D.C. 1974).

Strain.

Without knowledge (supplied by applicant's disclosure) of a new Streptomyces strain, one skilled in the art would not find it obvious to produce a particular antibiotic by aerobically cultivating that strain even if all previously-known Streptomyces strains produce the same antibiotic under the conditions called for by applicant's claims. *In re Mancy, Florent, and PreudHomme*, 499 F.2d 1289, 182 U.S.P.Q. 303, 305 (C.C.P.A. 1974).

ω

A selection of various strains of a species identified in a Japanese application and screening (requiring at most 15 calendar days) those strains for efficacy in producing citric acid by following a provided example is not regarded as undue experimentation. *Tabuchi and Abe v. Nubel, Fitts, and Lorenzo*, 559 F.2d 1183, 194 U.S.P.Q. 521, 525 (C.C.P.A. 1977).

ᚳ

A verbal description of a new species is inadequate to enable one of ordinary skill in the relevant art to obtain strains of that species over and above the specific strains made available through deposit in one of the recognized culture depositories. *Ex parte Jackson, Theriault, Sinclair, Fager, and Karwowski*, 217 U.S.P.Q. 804, 806 (PTO Bd. App. 1982).

Streamlined Continuation.

A streamlined continuation filed with claims directed only to a non-elected (pursuant to a restriction requirement) invention originally claimed in the parent application was treated as a divisional application under 37 C.F.R. §1.147. [See 37 C.F.R. §1.62.] *In re Paddington*, 164 U.S.P.Q. 312, 214 (Comm'r of Pat. 1969).

Stream of Commerce.

If the sale of a product of a manufacturer or distributor...is not simply an isolated occurrence, but arises from the efforts of the [defendants] to serve, directly or indirectly, the market for its product..., it is not unreasonable to subject it to suit....The forum state does not exceed its powers under the Due Process Clause if it asserts personal jurisdiction over a corporation that delivers its products into the stream of commerce with the expectation that they will be purchased by consumers in the forum state. *World-Wide Volkswagen Corp. v. Woodson*, 444 U.S. 286, 297-8 (1980).

ᚳ

Under this doctrine courts have sustained jurisdiction over non-resident manufacturers whose products pass through a protracted chain of distribution prior to reaching the ultimate consumer in the forum state. *Allen Organ Company v. Kawai Musical Instruments Manufacturing Co., Ltd.*, 593 F.Supp. 107, 224 U.S.P.Q. 907, 909 (Pa. 1984)

ᚳ

"The foreseeability that is critical to due process analysis is not the mere likelihood that a product will find its way into the forum state. Rather, it is that the defendant's connections with the forum state are such that he should reasonably anticipate being haled into court there." A defendant must have "purposefully availed" itself of the privilege of conducting activities in the forum. *Narco Avionics Inc. v. Sportsman's Market Inc.*, 792 F.Supp. 398, 24 U.S.P.Q.2d 1283, 1287 (Pa. 1992)

ᚳ

"The forum State does not exceed its powers under the Due Process Clause if it asserts personal jurisdiction over a corporation that delivers its products into the stream of commerce with the expectation that they will be purchased by consumers in the forum

State." Even if the requisite minimum contacts have been found through an application of the stream of commerce theory or otherwise, if it would be unreasonable for the forum to assert jurisdiction under all the facts and circumstances, then due process requires that jurisdiction be denied. *Beverly Hills Fan Co. v. Royal Sovereign Corp.*, 21 F.3d 1558, 30 U.S.P.Q.2d 1001, 1007, 1009 (Fed. Cir. 1994)

ळ

In *Asahi Metal Industry Co. v. Superior Court of California, Solano County*, 480 U.S. 102, 112 (1987), four Justices held that an exercise of personal jurisdiction requires more than the mere act of placing a product in the stream of commerce. As Justice O'Connor expressed it:

> [T]he placement of a product into the stream of commerce, without more, is not an act of the defendant purposely directed toward the forum State. Additional conduct of the defendant may indicate an intent or purpose to serve the market in the forum State, for example, designing the product for the market in the forum State, advertising in the forum State, establishing channels for providing regular advice to customers in the forum State, or marketing the product through a distributor who has agreed to serve as a sales agent in the forum State. But a defendant's awareness that the stream of commerce may or will sweep the product into the forum State does not convert the mere act of placing the product in the stream into an act purposefully directed toward the forum State.

But four of the Justices considered the showing of 'additional conduct' unneeded:

> The stream of commerce refers not to unpredictable currents or eddies, but to the regular and anticipated flow of products from manufacture to distribution to retail sale. . . . A defendant who has placed goods in the stream of commerce benefits economically from the retail sale of the final product in the forum State, and indirectly benefits from the State's laws that regulate and facilitate commercial activity.

Id. at 117, 107 S.Ct. at 1034-35 (Brennan, White, Marshall, & Blackmun JJ., concurring in part and concurring in the judgment). *Agridyne Technologies Inc. v. W.R. Grace & Co - Conn.*, 863 F.Supp. 1522, 32 U.S.P.Q.2d 1777, 1790, 1791 (Utah 1994)

Strength.

The negative rules of invention are to the effect that, ordinarily, it does not require anything more than mechanical skill to increase or decrease the size of a device or of any of its parts, or to increase the strength of one or more of its parts, but this rule (like the other negative rules) finds exceptions in special instances where it can be shown that the change in size or strength produces an unexpected or disproportionate result. *Ex parte McLean and Ives*, 86 U.S.P.Q. 517, 519 (PO Bd. App. 1950).

Structural Difference. *See also* **Structural Obviousness.**

Where a small structural difference is involved and where there is no apparent reason why that difference should produce a great improvement, the burden is upon the applicant to show, by factual evidence, that he has obtained an unexpectedly good result. *In re Renstrom*, 174 F.2d 140, 81 U.S.P.Q. 390, 391 (C.C.P.A. 1949).

Structural Formula. *See* Formula.

Structural Limitation.

The term, "preassembled", in the context in which it was used in the specification and claims was a structural limitation, not a process limitation. *Petersen v. Fee International, Ltd.*, 381 F.Supp. 1071, 182 U.S.P.Q. 264, 268 (Okla. 1974).

Structural Obviousness. *See also* Drug, Relationship, Substituents.

A disclosure of a particular, significant usefulness for claimed novel compounds that was not known or obvious to those in the art is relevant evidence of unobviousness and is adequate consideration for a patent grant on the compounds where the prior art was previously unaware of any usefulness for the class of compounds to which the claimed compounds belong. Progress in the useful arts is ill-served by denying patents to inventors under such circumstances. *In re Stemniski*, 444 F.2d 581, 170 U.S.P.Q. 343, 348 (C.C.P.A. 1971).

ω

The ability of the Board to originate a method, not suggested by the prior art, to make a structure derived from appellant's own disclosure does not demonstrate that the structure would have been obvious. *In re Corth*, 478 F.2d 1248, 178 U.S.P.Q. 39, 42 (C.C.P.A. 1973).

Structural Similarity. *See also* Analog, Drug, Homology, Isomer, Properties, Relationship, Structural Obviousness, Structure.

In *Adams* [*In re Adams, Kirk, and Petrow*, 316 F.2d 476, 137 U.S.P.Q. 333 (C.C.P.A. 1963)] we held that because the claimed compound was similar to other known compounds, it would be apparent that the claimed compound could be used in the same manner as the known compounds. *In re Moureu and Chovin*, 345 F.2d 595, 145 U.S.P.Q. 452, 454 (C.C.P.A. 1965).

ω

The involved structural similarity was not concerned solely with homology; it was predicated on alkyl substitution in one or both of two specific places in the reference Compound B. There were, however, eleven places to make such substitution, the prior art Compound C being one such possible combination of two substituents. Neither the Examiner nor the Board pointed to facts demonstrating that it would have been obvious to one of ordinary skill in this art to make the substitution at those particular positions at which appellants placed the substituents so as to enhance the biological or pharmaceutical activity of the compound instead of diminishing it as in Compound C. *In re Wagner and Folkers*, 371 F.2d 877, 152 U.S.P.Q. 552, 559 (C.C.P.A. 1967).

ω

Discovery of absence of skin toxicity in the claimed compound does not end the inquiry, because one who claims a compound, per se, which is structurally similar to a prior art compound must rebut the presumed expectation that the structurally similar compounds have similar properties. Because the expectation of similar properties stands unrebutted, it necessarily follows that an expectation of similar uses also stands unrebutted. *In re Wilder,* 563 F.2d 457, 195 U.S.P.Q. 426, 429 (C.C.P.A. 1977).

ω

An application which describes a specific physiological use for claimed compounds, but omits identification of a host or applicable dosages, satisfies the "how to use" requirement of the first paragraph of 35 U.S.C. §112 in view of the fact that a prior art reference discloses a host and dosages for the same use of structurally related compounds. *Bey and Jung v. Kollonitsch and Patchett,* 215 U.S.P.Q. 454, 458 (PTO Bd. Pat. Intf. 1981).

ω

There is no disclosure that the reference compounds would have any properties in common with those of appellants'' claimed compounds. The mere fact that the reference compounds can be used as intermediates in the production of the corresponding sulfonic acids does not provide adequate motivation for one of ordinary skill in the art to stop the reference synthesis and investigate the intermediates with an expectation of arriving at appellants'' claimed sulfonyl halides for use as corrosion inhibiting agents, surface active agents, or leveling agents. *In re Lalu and Foulletier,* 747 F.2d 703, 223 U.S.P.Q. 1257, 1260 (C.C.P.A. 1984).

ω

"Unity of invention", as discussed by the court in *Harnisch* [631 F.2d 716, 206 U.S.P.Q. 300 (C.C.P.A. 1980)], encompasses both structural similarity and communality of properties and/or utility. *Ex parte Bella and Chiaino,* 224 U.S.P.Q. 293, 294 (PTO Bd. App. 1984).

ω

Where the foreign priority application discloses an in vitro utility and where the disclosed in vitro utility is supplemented by the similar in vitro and in vivo pharmacological activity of structurally similar compounds, i.e., the parent imidazole and 1-methylimidazole compounds, this in vitro utility is sufficient to comply with the practical utility requirement of 35 U.S.C. §101. *Cross v. Iizuka,* 753 F.2d 1040, 224 U.S.P.Q. 739, 748 (Fed. Cir. 1985).

ω

When chemical compounds have "very close" structural similarities and similar utilities, without more, a *prima facie* case may be made. When such "close" structural similarity to prior art compounds is shown, in accordance with established precedents, the burden of coming forward shifts to the applicant, and evidence affirmatively supporting obviousness is required. Generalization should be avoided insofar as specific chemical structures are alleged to be *prima facie* obvious one from the other. There must be adequate prior art support for involved structural changes to complete the PTO's *prima facie* case and shift the burden of going forward to the applicant. The mere fact that it is possible to find two isolated disclosures that might be combined in such a way to produce a new compound does not necessarily render such production obvious unless the art also contains something to suggest the desirability of the proposed combination. In the absence of such a reference suggestion, there is inadequate support for the position that the required modification would *prima facie* have been obvious. *In re Grabiak*, 769 F.2d 729, 226 U.S.P.Q. 870 (Fed. Cir. 1985).

ω

The Examiner appears to recognize that it is not structural similarity alone that gives rise to obviousness, but the concomitant assumption that the structurally similar compounds will have like properties. This is what provides the motivation to modify a prior-art compound. In the present case, however, the only utility disclosed for the relevant compound in the reference is as an intermediate for the production of another compound. The Examiner has not suggested that the compound claimed here would have been useful in the same manner and, from the disclosure of the reference itself, it appears that it would not have been. Thus, on the record before us, no *prima facie* case of obviousness has been made out against the appellant's claims. *Ex parte Chwang*, 231 U.S.P.Q. 751 (B.P.A.I. 1986).

ω

Claims to new compositions can be regarded as prima facie obvious under 35 U.S.C. §103 when the additives in the new compositions are structurally similar to additives in known compositions, having a different use, even though the method of using the compositions is neither taught nor suggested by the prior art. Structural similarity between claimed and prior-art subject matter, proved by combining references or otherwise, where the prior art gives reason or motivation to make the claimed compositions, creates a *prima facie* case of obviousness, and the burden (and opportunity) then falls on an applicant to rebut the prima facie case. The discovery that a claimed composition possesses a property not disclosed for the prior-art subject matter does not itself defeat a *prima facie* case. *In re Dillon*, 919 F.2d 688, 16 U.S.P.Q.2d 1897, 1901 (Fed. Cir. 1990).

ω

The instant case is not a situation in which the claimed compound is a "branched isomer" of a corresponding prior-art compound. The R groups are attached to the base molecules via different atoms, carbon in one case and nitrogen in the other; the R groups are substantially different, acetamido in one case and carbamoylmethyl in the other. These distinctions negate an inference of close structural similarity, particularly where the prior art does not teach or suggest an equivalency or interchangeability between acetamido and carbamoylmethyl. *Imperial Chemical Industries PLC v. Danbury Pharmacal Inc.*, 745 F. Supp. 998, 18 U.S.P.Q.2d 1497, 1504 (Del. 1990).

ω

Normally a *prima facie* case of obviousness is based upon structural similarity, *i.e.*, an established structural relationship between a prior art compound and a claimed compound. Structural relationships may provide the requisite motivation or suggestion to modify known compounds to obtain new compounds. For example, a prior art compound may suggest its homologs because homologs often have similar properties, and therefore chemists of ordinary skill would ordinarily contemplate making them to try to obtain compounds with improved properties. Similarly, a known compound may suggest its analogs or isomers, either geometric isomers (cis v. trans) or position isomers (*e.g.*, ortho v. para). *In re Deuel*, 51 F.3d 1552, 34 U.S.P.Q.2d 1210, 1214 (Fed. Cir. 1995).

ω

When an appropriate selection is made for a number of different variables provided by a reference generic formula, a subclass of compounds (not separately set forth in the reference) results. The subclass of compounds differs from claimed compounds in only one respect—a hydrogen is attached to a nitrogen of the reference subclass, whereas a methyl is attached to the corresponding nitrogen of the claimed compounds. A rejection based on structural similarity was overcome by pointing out that, with regard to another variable, the reference distinguished between -NH- and -NCH3-. *Ex parte Casagrande, Montanari, and Santangelo*, 36 U.S.P.Q.2d 1860 (B.P.A.I. 1995—*unpublished*).

Structure. *See also* **Apparatus, Formula.**

Names and structural formulae are not chemical compounds, but mere designations therefor. When a claimed invention is a group of compounds, the obviousness or unobviousness of the compounds is in issue. Certainly, the structure and/or name of a compound might well be suggested when the compound itself is not. *In re Krazinski, Shepherd, and Taft*, 347 F.2d 656, 146 U.S.P.Q. 25, 28 (C.C.P.A. 1965).

ω

Patentability of a method claim must rest on the method steps recited, not on the structure used, unless that structure affects the method steps. *Leesona Corporation v. United States*, 185 U.S.P.Q. 156, 165 (U.S. Ct. Cl. 1975).

ω

Normally a *prima facie* case of obviousness is based upon structural similarity, *i.e.*, an established structural relationship between a prior art compound and a claimed compound. Structural relationships may provide the requisite motivation or suggestion to modify known compounds to obtain new compounds. For example, a prior art compound may suggest its homologs because homologs often have similar properties, and therefore chemists of ordinary skill would ordinarily contemplate making them to try to obtain compounds with improved properties. Similarly, a known compound may suggest its analogs or isomers, either geometric isomers (cis v. trans) or position isomers (*e.g.*, ortho v. para). *In re Deuel*, 51 F.3d 1552, 34 U.S.P.Q.2d 1210, 1214 (Fed. Cir. 1995).

Subclass. *See also* **Classification.**

It is presumed that the Patent Examiner examined prior patents that were in the class and subclass in which the patent in question was officially classified and had discarded them. *Amerace Esna Corporation v. Highway Safety Devices, Incorporated*, 330 F.Supp. 313, 171 U.S.P.Q. 186, 190 (Tex. 1971); *Minnesota Mining and Manufacturing Company v. Berwick Industries, Inc.*, 393 F.Supp. 1230, 185 U.S.P.Q. 536, 540 (Pa. 1975).

Subcombination. *See also* **Fragment, Incomplete, Open-Ended Claim.**

A rejection on the ground of indefiniteness because it is not apparent how elements recited in the claim cooperate to produce a unitary result will not be sustained when each of the elements of the claim appears to be sufficiently defined in its relation to other recited elements even though additional elements would be necessary to produce a complete operative machine. It is not a fatal defect where the recited elements define a proper subcombination. *In re Gartner and Roeber*, 223 F.2d 502, 106 U.S.P.Q. 273, 276 (C.C.P.A. 1955).

ω

A disclosure which adequately supports a combination also supports an essential subcombination thereof even when claims to the subcombination are presented for the first time in an application for reissue. *In re Farrow, Kimber, Cole, Miles, and Griffiths*, 554 F.2d 468, 193 U.S.P.Q. 689, 692 (C.C.P.A. 1977).

ω

"It has long been recognized that claims for combinations and also subcombinations may be validly allowed by the Patent Office and that a claim need not include all the elements necessary to make up a complete operative device. Admitting that additional elements are necessary to render the device operative, it does not necessarily follow that the omission of these elements invalidates the claim, or that the precise elements described in the patent as rendering it operative must be read into the claim." (emphasis added). *Velo-Bind, Incorporated v. Minnesota Mining & Manufacturing Company*, 647 F.2d 965, 211 U.S.P.Q. 926, 931 (9th Cir. 1981).

ω

An invention need not be the best or the only way to accomplish a certain result, and it need only be useful to some extent and in certain applications. The fact that an invention has only limited utility and is only operable in certain applications is not grounds for finding lack of utility. *Carl Zeiss Stiftung v. Renishaw plc*, 945 F.2d 1173, 20 U.S.P.Q.2d 1094, 1100 (Fed. Cir. 1991).

ω

In situations in which the element or subcombination issues after the combination, the matter should be analyzed as one of a generic claim issued after a later filed specific or improvement claim." *In re Emert*, 124 F.3d 1458, 44 U.S.P.Q.2d 1149, 1152 (Fed. Cir. 1997).

Subgenus. *See* **Reduction in Scope, Selection.**

Subjective. *See* **Ordinary Skill.**

Subject Matter as a Whole. *See also* **Retrospective Reconstruction.**

Where an applicant contends that the discovery of the source of a problem would have been unobvious to one of ordinary skill in the pertinent art at the time the claimed invention was made, it is incumbent upon the PTO to explain its reasons if it disagrees. A mere conclusionary statement that the source of a problem would have been discovered is inadequate. A patentable invention may lie in the discovery of the source of a problem, even though the remedy may be obvious once the source of the problem is identified. This is part of the "subject matter as a whole," which should always be considered in determining the obviousness of an invention under 35 U.S.C. §103. *In re Peehs and Hunner,* 612 F.2d 128, 204 U.S.P.Q. 835, 837 (C.C.P.A. 1980).

ʊ

Although it is proper to note the difference in a claimed invention from the prior art, because that difference may serve as one element in determining the obviousness/non-obviousness issue, it is improper to consider the difference as the invention. The "difference" may be slight (as has often been the case with some of history's greatest inventions, e.g., the telephone), but it may also have been the key to success in advancements in the art resulting from the invention. The issue with respect to obviousness is whether a challenger has carried its burden of proving, by clear and convincing evidence, facts from which it must be concluded that one skilled in the art at the time the invention was made would have found it to have been obvious, from the references as a whole, to create the claimed subject matter as a whole. *Datascope Corp. v. SMEC, Inc.,* 776 F.2d 320, 227 U.S.P.Q. 838 (Fed. Cir. 1985).

Subject Matter Jurisdiction.

When a district court's subject matter jurisdiction is founded on a federal question, it is the Due Process Clause of the Fifth Amendment, not the Fourteenth Amendment, that fixes the constitutional limits of the court's personal jurisdiction. *Hologic Inc. v. Lunar Corp.,* 36 U.S.P.Q.2d 1182, 1184 (Mass. 1995).

Subpoena.

An order quashing a subpoena and an ancillary proceeding not only terminates that proceeding but also is unreviewable on appeal of the final judgment in the principal action. Thus, such order is deemed a final order and is immediately appealable as of right. *Micro Motion Inc. v. Kane Steel Co.,* 894 F.2d 1318, 13 U.S.P.Q.2d 1696, 1697 (Fed. Cir. 1990).

ʊ

In an action in federal court, sovereign immunity does not bar the federal court from enforcing a federal subpoena against the federal government. Applying the doctrine of sovereign immunity to shield government agencies from federal subpoenas would, in effect, "authorize the executive branch to make conclusive determinations on whether federal employees may comply with a valid federal court subpoena. Because this effect would "raise serious separation of powers questions," the court "decline[d] to hold that federal courts cannot compel federal officers to give factual testimony." *Connaught Laboratories Inc. v. SmithKline Beecham P.L.C.,* 7 F.Supp.2d 477, 47 U.S.P.Q.2d 1699, 1700, 1701 (Del. 1998).

Subsidiary.

A foreign parent company may be insulated from an action (for patent infringement) against its dependent subsidiary if sufficient formal procedures have been taken to require recognition of the two corporations as separate entities. *Kearney & Trecker Corp. v. The Cincinnati Milling Machine Co.,* 254 F.Supp. 130, 149 U.S.P.Q. 551, 553 (Ill. 1966).

Substance. *See* **Form over Substance.**

Substantial.[8,9] *See also* **Maskwork Act, Substantially.**

Where the validity of a patent claim is questioned, it frequently becomes proper to interpret the claim by looking to the specification, but where one seeks a patent, the statute very definitely requires that applicant particularly point out and distinctly claim that which he claims to be his invention or discovery. Method claims calling "for a time sufficient to produce a substantially homogeneous product but insufficient to cause the formation of a substantial proportion of oil-soluble reaction products" were held to lack the requisite particularity. *In re Jolly,* 172 F.2d 566, 80 U.S.P.Q. 504, 506 (C.C.P.A. 1949).

ᛟ

Only when a substantial change has not been made should an accused infringer be liable for improperly trying to appropriate a claimed invention. *Slimfold Manufacturing v. Kinkead Industries,* 932 F.2d 1453, 18 U.S.P.Q. 1842 (Fed. Cir. 1991).

ᛟ

While comparison of function/way/result is an acceptable way of showing that structure in an accused device is the "substantial equivalent" of a claim limitation, it is not the only way to do so. Under general principles of appellate review a trial court's decision with regard to the doctrine of equivalents should not be disturbed unless clearly erroneous. *Malta v. Schulmerich Carillons Inc.,* 952 F.2d 1320, 21 U.S.P.Q.2d 1161, 1165, 1167 (Fed. Cir. 1991).

ᛟ

From the free and frequent use of the terms "substantial" and "substantially" in court opinions, it is clear that courts are fully familiar with and completely understand what is meant thereby. The following are quotations from *Dentsply International Inc. v. Kerr Manufacturing Co.,* 25 U.S.P.Q.2d 1870 (Del. 1992), at 1873:

> ...Dentsply presented substantial evidence showing the substantially similar function, way, and result of the component of both versions of Kerr's product....

ᛟ

"To be a 'substantial equivalent,' the element substituted in the accused device for the element set forth in the claim must not be such as would substantially change the way in which the function of the claimed invention is performed." The specification and prosecution history help interpret the meaning of "substantially" and the literal coverage of the claim. *Amhil Enterprises Ltd. v. Wawa Inc.,* 34 U.S.P.Q.2d 1645, 1648 (Md. 1995).

ᛟ

---

[8] *See Gargoyles Inc. v. U.S.,* 32 Fed.Cl. 157, 33 U.S.P.Q.2d 1595, 1598 (U.S. Ct. Fed. Cl. 1994).

[9] In a series of cases, the Supreme Court described successorship liability as turning on whether there is a "substantial continuity of identity" between the two organizations. *Additive Controls & Measurement Systems Inc. v. Flowdata Inc.,* 47 U.S.P.Q.2d 1906, 1913 (Fed. Cir. 1998).

The non-obviousness of the accused device, evidenced by the grant of a United States patent, is relevant to the issue of whether the change therein is substantial. *Zygo Corp v. Wyko Corp.*, 79 F.3d 1563, 38 U.S.P.Q.2d 1281, 1286 (Fed. Cir. 1996).

ω

Substantial evidence is "such relevant evidence from the record taken as a whole as might be accepted by a reasonable mind as adequate to support the finding under review." Even if an accused device or process does not literally infringe, it may infringe under the doctrine of equivalents if the differences between the claimed invention and the accused device or process are "insubstantial." To find process infringement under the doctrine of equivalents, the process must perform substantially the same function, in substantially the same way, to produce substantially the same results as the elements recited in the corresponding patent claim. *Texas Instruments Inc. v. Cypress Semiconductor Corp.*, 90 F.3d 1558, 39 U.S.P.Q.2d 1492, 1496, 1497, 1500 n.8 (Fed. Cir. 1996).

ω

Defendant's patent, during the prosecution of which plaintiff's patent was cited and considered as prior art, is thus presumed nonobvious in view of plaintiff's patent until proven otherwise. The nonobviousness of the accused device, evidenced by the grant of a United States patent, is relevant to the issue of whether the change therein is substantial. *Zygo Corp. v. Wyko Corp.*, 38 U.S.P.Q.2d 1281, 1286 (Fed. Cir. 1996).

ω

To determine equivalence under the doctrine of equivalents, this court applies the "insubstantial differences" test, recognizing the admitted short-comings of that test. Under the function-way-result test, one considers whether the element of the accused device at issue performs substantially the same function, in substantially the same way, to achieve substantially the same result, as the limitation at issue in the claim. *Dawn Equipment Co. v. Kentucky Farms Inc.*, 140 F.3d 1009, 46 U.S.P.Q.2d 1109, 1113 (Fed. Cir. 1998).

Substantial Equivalency.

Not only must plaintiff produce particularized testimony establishing substantial similarity in terms of all three elements of equivalence, but plaintiff must also produce "linking argument" explaining precisely why the allegedly infringing device is substantially similar. Although the issue of "substantial equivalency" generally involves a fact-specific analysis, several clear principles have emerged. First, in cases where a patent arises in a crowded field, the scope of protection afforded to plaintiff is limited. Second, where the allegedly infringing product poses an improvement over the patent claim, it should not be found infringing under the Doctrine of Equivalents. Finally, plaintiff may not obtain, through the Doctrine of Equivalents, protection over designs which plaintiff could not have patented directly. *Powell v. Iolab Corp.*, 32 U.S.P.Q.2d 1579, 1584 (Cal. 1994).

Substantial Equivalent.

To be a "substantial equivalent", the element substituted in the accused device for the element set forth in the claim must not substantially change the way in which the function of the claimed invention is performed. *L.A. Gear Inc. v. E.S. Originals Inc.*, 35 U.S.P.Q.2d 1497, 1501 (Cal. 1995).

Substantial Evidence.

The substantial evidence standard is particularly inapplicable to judicial review of patent validity issues under §337 of the Tariff Act (19 U.S.C. §1337). Some prior art is citable against virtually every issued patent. With what, in most cases, would constitute "substantial evidence" thus present, effective judicial review of Commission invalidity holdings would be nullified if the standard were that of 5 U.S.C. §706(2)(e). *Solder Removal Co. v. U.S. International Trade Commission*, 582 F.2d 628, 199 U.S.P.Q. 129, 132 (C.C.P.A. 1978).

ᙡ

Substantial evidence is such relevant evidence, considering the record as a whole, on which a reasonable jury might base the verdict under review. *Perkin-Elmer Corp. v. Computervision Corp.*, 732 F.2d 888, 893, 221 U.S.P.Q. 669, 673 (Fed. Cir.), *cert. denied*, 469 U.S. 857 (1984).

ᙡ

The burden on one who appeals the grant of a motion for JNOV is to show that the jury's factual findings were supported by at least substantial evidence and the legal conclusions made by the jury can be supported by those findings. Substantial evidence is such relevant evidence from the record, taken as a whole, as might be accepted by a reasonable mind as adequate to support the finding under review. *Vieau v. Japax Inc.*, 823 F.2d 1510, 3 U.S.P.Q.2d 1094 (Fed. Cir. 1987).

ᙡ

Substantial evidence is more than a mere scintilla. It means such relevant evidence as a reasonable mind might accept as adequate to support a conclusion. *Braun Inc. v. Dynamics Corp. of America*, 975 F.2d 815, 24 U.S.P.Q.2d 1121, 1124 (Fed. Cir. 1992).

ᙡ

"Substantial evidence" is relevant evidence from the record which, when reviewed as a whole, would reasonably support the jury's finding under review. The substantial evidence standard means that the jury's finding must stand unless it is demonstrated that no reasonable juror could have made it. *ATD Corp. v. Lydall Inc.*, 43 U.S.P.Q.2d 1170, 1172, 1173 (Mich. 1997).

Substantial Investment.

As the term "substantial investment" is not defined in the statute, the Court has little guidance on this issue. Based on the purpose of Congress in creating the "safe harbor", the Court finds that expenditures of $1 million in preparing to market captopril, including costs for performing in vivo and in vitro tests and other research necessary to obtain FDA approval of its ANDA, satisfy the investment requirement and qualifies for operation under the "safe harbor" of URAA. *Bristol-Myers Squibb Co. v. Royce Laboratories Inc.*, 36 U.S.P.Q.2d 1637, 1640 n.7 (Fla. 1995), *reversed* 69 F.3d 1130, 36 U.S.P.Q.2d 1641 (Fed. Cir. 1995).

Substantially.[10,11] *See also* **Approximately, Description, Substantial, Support, Three-Pronged Analysis, Tripartite Test.**

When claims particularly and distinctly point out the novel features of the invention described, there is no objection to defining a product as one that is "substantially identical with" one made by a stated process. *Ex parte Smith*, 43 U.S.P.Q. 157, 158 (PTO Bd. App. 1937).

ᛡ

A product that is claimed as being substantially identical with that obtainable by a specified process is indefinite. *Ex parte Lichty*, 64 U.S.P.Q. 430, 431 (PTO Bd. App. 1944).

ᛡ

Where the validity of a patent claim is questioned, it frequently becomes proper to interpret the claim by looking to the specification, but where one seeks a patent, the statute very definitely requires that applicant shall particularly point out and distinctly claim that which he claims to be his invention or discovery. Method claims calling "for a time sufficient to produce a substantially homogeneous product but insufficient to cause the formation of a substantial proportion of oil-soluble reaction products" were held to lack the requisite particularity. *In re Jolly*, 172 F.2d 566, 80 U.S.P.Q. 504, 506 (C.C.P.A. 1949).

ᛡ

A patentee may invoke the doctrine of equivalents to proceed against the producer of a device "if it performs substantially the same function in substantially the same way to obtain the same result". *Graver Tank & Mfg. Co. v. The Linde Air Products Company*, 339 U.S. 605, 85 U.S.P.Q. 328, 330 (S.Ct. 1950).

ᛡ

Since the patent claim requires that the blind head be "substantially," rather than absolutely, uniform throughout its length, unless the second flare on the alleged infringing device performs some function not performed by the claimed fastener, this feature alone will not avoid infringement. *Olympic Fastening Systems, Inc. v. Textron Inc.*, 504 F.2d 609, 183 U.S.P.Q. 449, 455 (6th Cir. 1974).

ᛡ

The use of the words "substantially" and "approximately" in a claim does not necessarily render it vague and therefore invalid under 35 U.S.C. §112. *H. M. Chase Corp. v. Idaho Potato Processors, Inc.*, 529 P.2d 1270, 185 U.S.P.Q. 106, 116 (Idaho 1974).

ᛡ

The rejection of a claim to a compound under the first and second paragraphs of 35 U.S.C. §112 (because of the term, "substantially", in the expression: "being so selected and positioned on the aromatic ring to substantially increase the efficiency of the com-

---

[10]The court was able to determine the meaning of "substantially" (in context) without having such meaning set forth in the specification, and the involved claim was not invalidated for indefiniteness. *The John Hopkins University v. Cellpro Inc.*, 47 U.S.P.Q.2d 1705 (Fed. Cir. 1998).

[11]Claim 29 of USP 4,773,750, count of Interference No. 102,567 ("said assembly to exhibit substantially no chromatic aberrations.") *Bruning v. Hirose*, 48 U.S.P.Q.2d 1934, 1936 (Fed. Cir. 1998).

pound as a copper extractant") was reversed. *In re Mattison and Swanson*, 509 F.2d 563, 184 U.S.P.Q. 484, 486 (C.C.P.A. 1975).

ᛟ

Words such as "substantially," "approximately," and "about," are often used in claims to prevent a potential infringer from avoiding literal infringement simply by making a minor modification. While the modifier certainly does broaden the term that it modifies to some degree, it cannot be allowed to negate the meaning of the word it modifies. *Arvin Industries, Inc. v. Berns Air King Corp.*, 525 F.2d 182, 188 U.S.P.Q. 49, 51 (7th Cir. 1975); *Borg-Warner Corp. v. Paragon Gear Works, Inc.*, 355 F.2d 400, 148 U.S.P.Q. 1, 4 (1st Cir. 1965), *cert. dismissed*, 384 U.S. 935, 149 U.S.P.Q. 905 (1966).

ᛟ

In an interference contest, work on a related case is credited toward reasonable diligence if the work on the related case contribute[s] substantially to the ultimate preparation of the involved application." *Bey v. Kollonitsch*, 806 F.2d 1024, 231 U.S.P.Q. 967, 970 (Fed. Cir. 1986).

ᛟ

The word "substantially" in patent claims gives rise to some definitional leeway. Thus, the word "substantially" may prevent avoidance of infringement by minor changes that do not affect the results sought to be accomplished. *C. E. Equipment Co. v. United States*, 17 Cl. Ct. 293, 13 U.S.P.Q.2d 1363, 1368 (Cl. Ct. 1989).

ᛟ

Even when a claim literally reads on a device, actual infringement will not exist if the accused device performs in a substantially different way. *The Laitram Corp. v. Rexnord Inc.*, 15 U.S.P.Q.2d 1161, 1167 (Wis. 1990).

ᛟ

Phrases in claims referring back to the description and drawing, such as "substantially as described" or "as herein shown and described" were once customary in claims in the days of the central definition. *Ex parte Fressola*, 27 U.S.P.Q.2d 1608, 1610 (B.P.A.I. 1993).

ᛟ

Ordinarily, "substantially" means "considerable in...extent." American Heritage Dictionary Second College Edition, 1213 (2d ed. 1982), or "largely but not wholly that which is specified." Webster's Ninth New Collegiate Dictionary, 1176 (9th ed. 1983). *York Products Inc. v. Central Tractor Farm & Family Center*, 99 F.3d 1568, 40 U.S.P.Q.2d 1619, 1622 (Fed. Cir. 1996).

Substantial Right. *See* **Assignment, Capital Gains.**

Substantiating Evidence.

Amelioration of the symptoms or even cure of cancer is no longer considered to be "incredible." Nonetheless, decisional law would seem to indicate that the utility in question is sufficiently unusual to justify an Examiner's requiring substantiating evidence. This may be in the form of animal tests that constitute recognized screening procedures with clear relevance to utility in humans. The specification of the appellant's parent application sets forth several animal tests on numerous types of specific cancers as well as in vitro studies, both of which are asserted to be predictive with regard to utility in humans. The Examiner has not challenged the evidence presented in a single, relevant, material respect. There is only the blanket statement of lack of "patentable utility" per se. In fact, the only specific comments the Examiner has directed toward the appellant's evidence are with regard to the breadth of the types of tumor against which the claimed compounds have been shown to be active. The appealed claims are drawn to compounds and not to a method of treatment. Generally speaking, utility in treating a single disease is an adequate basis for the patentability of a pharmaceutical compound under 35 U.S.C. §101. *Ex parte Krepelka*, 231 U.S.P.Q. 746 (B.P.A.I. 1986).

Substantive. *See also* 5 U.S.C. §553.

When claims are amended during reexamination (following a rejection based on prior art), the claims are not deemed substantively changed as a matter of law. There is no per se rule. To determine whether a claim change is substantive, it is necessary to analyze the claims of the original and of the reexamined patents in light of the particular facts, including the prior art, the prosecution history, other claims, and any other pertinent information. When the issue is the doctrine of equivalents or substantive change on reexamination, the mere amendment of a claim does not act as a per se estoppel. *The Laitram Corp. v. NEC Corp.*, 952 F.2d 1357, 21 U.S.P.Q.2d 1276, 1280 (Fed. Cir. 1991).

Substantive Change.

A claim amendment made during reexamination following a prior art rejection is not automatically to be regarded as a substantive change. *Laitram Corp. v. NEC Corp.*, 49 U.S.P.Q.2d 1199, 1201 (Fed. Cir. 1998).

Substituents. See also *Structural Obviousness*.

Rearranging substitution on a ring of a herbicidally-active compound by finding another herbicidally-active compound with the same ring and desired optional substituents is not enough to preclude patentability of a claimed herbicide. In the chemical arts the mere fact that it is possible to find two isolated disclosures that might be combined in such a way to produce a new compound does not necessarily render such production obvious unless the art also contains something to suggest the desirability of the proposed combination. In the absence of express or implied suggestion in at least one of the references that the specifically claimed substitution would be desirable for herbicide compounds other than those of the specific class disclosed in one reference, patentability is not precluded. The mere fact that both references originate from the herbicide art does not provide any teaching or suggestion to combine them. Nor does the fact that both references concern compounds containing a specific ring suggest that substituents suitable in one case would be expected to be suitable in the other. *In re Levitt*, 11 U.S.P.Q.2d 1315, 1316 (Fed. Cir. 1989—*unpublished*).

Substitute. *See also* **Availability.**

The fact that the processing details of the claimed invention are substantially identical to those set forth in a reference lends nothing to a rejection over the reference unless it can be shown that it would have been obvious to substitute acetals or hemi-acetals as reactants for the reference esters. The adequacy of any such showing of equivalency must be scrutinized especially carefully where it is alleged to have been obvious to substitute one starting material for another in a catalytic process. *In re Mercier,* 515 F.2d 1161, 185 U.S.P.Q. 774, 780 (C.C.P.A. 1975).

ᙡ

Even though it may not be inconceivable to substitute sulfur for oxygen to obtain compounds having the same expected properties, that is not the standard; the standard is whether it would have been obvious in terms of 35 U.S.C. §103. *In re Grabiak,* 769 F.2d 729, 226 U.S.P.Q. 870 (Fed. Cir. 1985).

ᙡ

The *Panduit* test appears to require actual use of the substitute product and not merely its "availability; the court there identified an "acceptable substitute" as one which customers in general were "willing to buy in place of the infringing product" and stated that "[a] product lacking the advantages of that patent can hardly be termed a substitute "acceptable" to the customer who wants these advantages." The patentee's burden in demonstrating an absence of acceptable substitutes is not stringent. The patent holder does not need to negate all possibilities that a purchaser might have bought a different product or might have foregone the purchase altogether. The but-for rule only requires the patentee to provide proof to a reasonable probability that the sale would have been made but for the infringement. *T.D. Williamson Inc. v. Laymon,* 723 F. Supp. 587, 13 U.S.P.Q.2d 1417, 1423, 1427 (Okla. 1989).

ᙡ

To be deemed acceptable (in a lost-profit determination), an alleged acceptable non-infringing substitute must not have a disparately higher price than or possess characteristics significantly different from the patented product. *Kaufman Co. Inc. v. Lantech Inc.,* 926 F.2d 1136, 17 U.S.P.Q.2d 1828, 1832 (Fed. Cir. 1991).

Substituted.

While the term "aryl and substituted aryl radicals" is a broad term, it is not objectionable for this reason alone if the term (1) is supported by the specification, and it (2) properly defines the novel subject matter described in the specificaiton. *In re Sus and Schaefer,* 306 F.2d 494, 134 U.S.P.Q. 301, 304 (C.C.P.A. 1962).

ᙡ

A rejection of claims as failing to define the invention properly and based on the phrases "substituted mononuclear and polynuclear homocyclic compounds," "alkyl," "ester," and "heterocyclic and aromatic compounds being free of substituents containing aliphatic hydroxyl and amino groups," in process claims, was reversed. *Ex parte Westfahl,* 136 U.S.P.Q. 265 (PTO Bd. App. 1962).

ᙡ

Expressions, such as "substituted alkylene" and "substituted phenylene", are not indefinite under the second paragraph or 35 U.S.C. §112, notwithstanding the Examiner's conclusion that one skilled in the art would not know the limits of the patent protection sought. *Ex parte Altermatt*, 183 U.S.P.Q. 436, 437 (PO Bd. App. 1974).

ᛒ

A rejection under 35 U.S.C. §112, second paragraph, of a claim defining a variable Y as "an unsubstituted or substituted alkyl, alkenyl, or alkynyl group of 1 to 18 carbon atoms, an unsubstituted or substituted cycloalkyl group having a 3 to 6 carbon atom ring and up to 12 carbon atoms, an unsubstituted or substituted aralkyl group of up to 10 carbon atoms, or an unsubstituted or substituted aryl group of up to 10 carbon atoms" was reversed. The claim was regarded as circumscribing a group of N-substituted iso-thiazolones with a reasonable degree of precision and particularity. *Ex parte Lewis, Miller, and Law*, 197 U.S.P.Q. 543, 544 (PTO Bd. App. 1977).

ᛒ

The term "substituted alkyl" is precise and definite. The issue is not whether the Examiner can conjure a substituent group that does not exist; a person having ordinary skill in the art would readily appreciate that compounds containing such substituent group do not exist. Nobody will use inoperative embodiments, and the claims do not cover them. The skilled artisan could and would readily ascertain an embodiment or embodiments that cannot be made. *Ex parte Breuer*, 1 U.S.P.Q.2d 1906 (B.P.A.I. 1986).

Substituted Count.

Where a Primary Examiner substitutes a count (in an interference) for an existing count, his act consists of dissolving the interference as to the existing count and adding his own count. *Sulkowski v. Metlesics and Sternbach v. Houlihan*, 179 U.S.P.Q. 687, 690 (PO Bd. Pat. Intf. 1973).

Substitution. *See also* Borcherdt Doctrine, Change, Material, Position, Starting Material.

The substitution of one old element for another will not sustain a patent when the substituted element performs the same function in the same way and with the same result. *Hugh W. Batcheller v. Henry Cole Co.*, 7 F. Supp. 898, 22 U.S.P.Q. 354, 357 (Mass. 1934).

ᛒ

Where the substitution made by appellants is shown to be possible in a large number of positions, and one example of such substitution is shown in the prior art to be detrimental, and where there is no teaching in the art that the specific position of substitution here claimed would be beneficial, the comparison between all elements of the prior art and the claimed compound demonstrates no reasonable factual basis for the Board's decision. Where the art teaching is that having two methyl substituents on the basic ring structure is detrimental for the contemplated utility, and where there is no teaching that substitution on certain other spots is beneficial, one who teaches otherwise has made an unobvious contribution to the art. *In re Wagner and Folkers*, 371 F.2d 877, 152 U.S.P.Q. 552, 560 (C.C.P.A. 1967).

ᘓ

Focusing on the obviousness of substitutions and differences instead of on the invention as a whole is a legally improper way to simplify the difficult determination of obviousness. *Hybritech Inc. v. Monoclonal Antibodies, Inc.*, 802 F.2d 1367, 231 U.S.P.Q. 81, 93 (Fed. Cir. 1986).

Substitution of Equivalents. *See also* **Substitution.**

A mere carrying forward of an original patented conception involving only the change of form, proportions, or degree, or the substitution of equivalents doing the same thing as the original invention, by substantially the same means, is not such an invention as will sustain a patent even though the changes are of a kind that produces better results than prior inventions. *In re Paul F. Williams*, 36 F.2d 436, 4 U.S.P.Q. 237, 239 (C.C.P.A. 1930).

ᘓ

To rely on an equivalence known only to the applicant to establish obviousness is to assume that his disclosure is a part of the prior art. The mere statement of this proposition reveals its fallaciousness. *In re Ruff and Dukeshire*, 256 F.2d 590, 118 U.S.P.Q. 340, 347 (C.C.P.A. 1958).

ᘓ

Even though it may not be inconceivable to substitute sulfur for oxygen to obtain compounds having the same expected properties, that is not the standard; the standard is whether it would have been obvious in terms of 35 U.S.C. §103. *In re Grabiak*, 769 F.2d 729, 226 U.S.P.Q. 870 (Fed. Cir. 1985).

Subtracting Components, Elements, Parts or Steps. *See* **Omission of Element or Step, Reduction in Elements, Reduction in Steps, Subcombination.**

Success.

For failure of the record to establish, prior to the record date of Moller, the production of a satisfactory foam by purportedly employing the process of the count, Castro cannot prevail. *Castro and Marsh v. Moller, Muhlhausen, and Hauptmann*, 182 U.S.P.Q. 502, 505 (PO Bd. Pat. Int. 1973).

ᘓ

To preclude patentability under 35 U.S.C. §103, there must be some predictability of success in any attempt to combine elements of reference processes. The view that success would have been "inherent" cannot substitute for a showing of reasonable expectation of success. *In re Rinehart*, 531 F.2d 1048, 189 U.S.P.Q. 143, 148 (C.C.P.A. 1976).

ᘓ

The mere statement that the method of making claimed products would be obvious and that there would be a reasonable expectation of success without determining that the claimed products would be obvious from prior art teachings reflects application of the regularly rejected obvious-to-try standard. *Ex parte Erlich,* 3 U.S.P.Q.2d 1011 (B.P.A.I. 1986).

ᚌ

Only a reasonable expectation of success, not absolute predictability, is necessary for a conclusion of obviousness. *Ex parte Beck,* 9 U.S.P.Q.2d 2000 (B.P.A.I. 1987).

ᚌ

Most technological advance is the fruit of methodical, persistent investigation, as is recognized in 35 U.S.C. §103 ("Patentability shall not be negatived by the manner in which the invention was made"). The consistent criterion for determination of obviousness is whether the prior art would have suggested to one of ordinary skill in the art that this process should be carried out and would have a reasonable likelihood of success, viewed in the light of the prior art. Both the suggestion and the expectation of success must be found in the prior art, not in the applicant's disclosure. *In re Dow Chemical Co.,* 837 F.2d 469, 5 U.S.P.Q.2d 1529 (Fed. Cir. 1988).

ᚌ

Obviousness does not require absolute predictability of success. Indeed, for many inventions that seem quite obvious, there is no absolute predictability of success until the invention is reduced to practice. There is always at least a possibility of unexpected results, that would then provide an objective basis for showing that the invention, although apparently obvious, was in law non-obvious. For obviousness under 35 U.S.C. §103, all that is required is a reasonable expectation of success. *In re OFarrell,* 853 F.2d 894, 7 U.S.P.Q.2d 1673, 1681 (Fed. Cir. 1988).

ᚌ

Where claimed subject matter has been rejected as obvious in view of a combination of prior-art references, a proper analysis under 35 U.S.C. §103 requires, inter alia, consideration of two factors: (1) whether the prior art would have suggested to those of ordinary skill in the art that they should make the claimed composition or device, or carry out the claimed process; and (2) whether the prior art would also have revealed that, in so making or carrying out, those of ordinary skill would have a reasonable expectation of success. Both the suggestion and the reasonable expectation of success must be founded in the prior art, not in the applicant's disclosure. *In re Vaeck,* 947 F.2d 488, 20 U.S.P.Q.2d 1438, 1442 (Fed. Cir. 1991).

Successful Defense.

The FDA's successful-defense requirement is inconsistent with the unambiguously expressed intent of Congress. The rule is gravely inconsistent with the text and structure of the statute. Nor can the FDA show that the successful-defense requirement is needed to avoid "a result demonstrably at odds with the intentions of [section 355(j)(5)(B)(iv)'s] drafters." *Mova Pharmaceutical Corp. v. Shalala,* 140 F.3d 1060, 46 U.S.P.Q.2d 1385, 1392 (D.C. Cir. 1998).

Successor Entity.

The general rule is that the sale or transfer of a business' assets to a successor entity does not automatically include the liabilities of the predecessor. This general rule of successor non-liability does not apply if, inter alia, the successor corporation is "merely a continuation of the selling corporation." *Chiuminatta Concrete Concepts Inc. v. Cardinal Industries Inc.*, 48 U.S.P.Q.2d 1421, 1428 (Cal. 1998).

Successor in Interest.

Successors in interest are charged with the knowledge and dilatory conduct of their predecessors. *Valutron N.V. v. NCR Corp.*, 33 U.S.P.Q.2d 1986, 1989 (Ohio 1992), *aff'd* (Fed. Cir. 1993), *cert. denied,* (S.Ct. 1994).

Successor Liability.

A corporation that succeeds to a prior corporation's assets can be held accountable on the seller's liabilities: (1) where there is an express or implied agreement of assumption; (2) where the transaction amounts to a consolidation or merger of two corporations; (3) where the purchasing corporation is a "mere continuation" of the seller; and (4) where the transfer of assets to the purchaser is for the fraudulent purpose of escaping lia-bility for the seller's debts. *Hemstreet v. Compuscan Inc.*, 16 U.S.P.Q.2d 1208, 1211 (Ill. 1990).

Such As.

In the prior decisions: *Ex parte Steigerwald*, 131 U.S.P.Q. 73 (Bd. App. 1961), and *Ex parte Grundy*, 63 Ms. D. 219 (Bd. App.), the term "such as" was found to render claims indefinite. *Ex parte Wu*, 10 U.S.P.Q.2d 2031, 2033 (B.P.A.I. 1988). See also *Ex parte Hall*, 83 U.S.P.Q. 38, 39 (Bd. App. 1948), and *Ex parte Hasche*, 86 U.S.P.Q. 481, 482 (Bd. App. 1949).

Sufficiency.

If any claim of the '300 patent is limited to the filing date of the '529 c-i-p on the basis that the disclosure of the '196 parent is insufficient to support such claim, a corresponding foreign publication that is substantially the same as the parent is also insufficient to anticipate such claim under 35 U.S.C. §102(b). *Paperless Accounting, Inc. v. Bay Area Rapid Transit System*, 804 F.2d 659, 231 U.S.P.Q. 649, 653 (Fed. Cir. 1986).

Sufficiency of Disclosure. *See also* **Breadth, Challenge, Disclosure, Enablement, Incorporate by Reference, Invitation to Experiment, Reissue, Specification, Support.**

The naming (in a specification) of one member of a generic or subgeneric group (in the field of chemistry) referred to in a claim is not, in itself, a proper basis for a claim to the entire group. However, it may not be necessary to enumerate a plurality of species if a genus is sufficiently identified in an application by "other appropriate language". In the case of a small and closely related group, such as the halogens, the naming of the group should ordinarily be sufficient since nothing of consequence would be added by also naming each of the well known members of the group. *In re Grimme, Keil, and Schmitz*, 274 F.2d 949, 124 U.S.P.Q. 499, 501 (C.C.P.A. 1960).

ᚹ

A specification need not contain a working example if the invention is otherwise disclosed in such a manner that one skilled in the art would be able to practice it without an undue amount of experimentation. *In re Borkowski and Van Venrooy*, 422 F.2d 904, 164 U.S.P.Q. 642 (C.C.P.A. 1970).

ᚹ

A rejection under the first paragraph of 35 U.S.C. §112 must be reversed inasmuch as the specification contains a statement of the invention that is as broad as the broadest claims, and inasmuch as the sufficiency of the specification to satisfy the "best mode" requirement of §112 and to enable one skilled in the art to practice the process as broadly as it is claimed has not been questioned. *In re Robins*, 429 F.2d 452, 166 U.S.P.Q. 552 (C.C.P.A. 1970).

ᚹ

The patentability of a claim is not precluded as based on an insufficient disclosure merely because it encompasses embodiments or classes of embodiments that are not cited in the specification. *In re DiLeone and Lucas*, 436 F.2d 1404, 168 U.S.P.Q. 592 (C.C.P.A. 1971).

ᚹ

The fact that a patent was allowed on applicant's original application does not mean that the question of sufficiency of disclosure has been determined in applicant's favor by the Patent Office and that a policy of res judicata bars a contrary holding during the prosecution of a Reissue Application. The statutory provision for reissue of patents, 35 U.S.C. §251, by its third paragraph, dictates that the provisions applicable to applications for patents, including 35 U.S.C. §112, are applicable to reissue applications as well. *In re Doyle*, 482 F.2d 1385, 179 U.S.P.Q. 227, 232 (C.C.P.A. 1973).

ᚹ

In an unpredictable art, does 35 U.S.C. §112 require disclosure of a test with every species covered by a claim? To require such a complete disclosure would apparently necessitate a patent application with thousands of examples or a disclosure with thousands of catalysts along with information as to whether each exhibits catalytic behavior resulting in the production of the desired products. More importantly, such a requirement would force an inventor seeking adequate patent protection to carry out a prohibitive number of actual experiments. This would tend to discourage inventors from filing patent applications in an unpredictable area since the patent claims would have to be limited to those embodiments that are expressly disclosed. A potential infringer could readily avoid "literal" infringement of such claims by merely finding another analogous catalyst complex that could be used in forming the same products. *In re Angstadt and Griffin*, 537 F.2d 498, 190 U.S.P.Q. 214, 218 (C.C.P.A. 1976).

ᚹ

Mere lack of literal support in the specification is not enough to carry the PTO's initial burden. For compliance with the first paragraph of 35 U.S.C. §112, it is only necessary for the specification to describe the invention sufficiently for those of ordinary skill in the art to recognize that applicant invented the subject matter he claims. *In re Voss*, 557 F.2d 812, 194 U.S.P.Q. 267, 271 (C.C.P.A. 1977).

ᵡ

A specification may contain a disclosure that is sufficient to enable one skilled in the art to make and use the invention and yet fail to comply with the description of the invention requirement. *In re Barker and Pehl*, 559 F.2d 588, 194 U.S.P.Q. 470, 472 (C.C.P.A. 1977).

ᵡ

Early filing of an application with its disclosure of novel compounds which possess significant therapeutic use is to be encouraged. Requiring specific testing of the thousands of prostaglandin analogs encompassed by the present claim in order to satisfy the how-to-use requirement of 35 U.S.C. §112 would delay disclosure and frustrate, rather than further, the interests of the public. *In re Bundy*, 642 F.2d 430, 209 U.S.P.Q. 48, 52 (C.C.P.A. 1981).

ᵡ

To supplement a specification which on its face appears deficient under 35 U.S.C. §112, evidence must establish that the information which must be read into the specification to make it complete is known to those having ordinary skill in the art. *In re Howarth*, 654 F.2d 103, 210 U.S.P.Q. 689, 692 (C.C.P.A. 1981).

ᵡ

The specification must be complete enough to enable one of ordinary skill in the art to make and use the invention without undue experimentation. The specification need not describe the conventional nor disclose what the skilled already possess. *White Consolidated Industries, Inc. v. Vega Servo-Control, Inc.*, 214 U.S.P.Q. 796, 823 (Mich. 1982).

ᵡ

Failure to disclose details of the best mode which can be provided by routine skill and which does not constitute concealment does not render a patent invalid under 35 U.S.C. §112 for failure to disclose the best mode for practicing the invention. *H.H. Robertson Company v. Barger Metal Fabricating Co.*, 225 U.S.P.Q. 1191, 1205 (Ohio 1984).

Sufficient.

Method claims calling "for a time sufficient to produce a substantially homogeneous product but insufficient to cause the formation of a substantial proportion of oil-soluble reaction products" were held to lack the requisite particularity. *In re Jolly*, 172 F.2d 566, 80 U.S.P.Q. 504, 506 (C.C.P.A. 1949).

ᵡ

A claim calling for applying electrical energy at different potentials sufficient to achieve a specified result was adequate to define over applied art. *In re Michlin*, 256 F.2d 317, 118 U.S.P.Q. 353, 355 (C.C.P.A. 1958).

ᵡ

The expression "sufficient to render said condensation product substantially insoluble in aromatic hydrocarbon solvents but insufficient to render it thermosetting" defines the limits of the invention more precisely than would have been practically possible by wholly mathematical expressions. *Locklin v. Switzer Brothers, Inc.*, 125 U.S.P.Q. 515, 519 (Cal. 1959).

ᚹ

The application of "sufficient" ultrasonic energy is essential to the claimed method, but the specification does not disclose what a "sufficient" dosage of ultrasonic energy might be or how those skilled in the art might make an appropriate selection of frequency, intensity, and duration. *In re Colianni*, 561 F.2d 220, 195 U.S.P.Q. 150, 152 (C.C.P.A. 1977).

ᚹ

The claims were intended to cover the use of the invention with various types of automobiles. That a particular chair of the claims may fit within some automobiles and not others is of no moment. The phrase "so dimensioned" is as accurate as the subject matter permits, automobiles being of various sizes. As long as those of ordinary skill in the art realize that the dimensions could be easily obtained, 35 U.S.C. §112, second paragraph, requires nothing more. The patent law does not require that all possible lengths corresponding to the spaces in hundreds of different automobiles be listed in the patent, let alone that they be listed in the claims. *Orthokinetics Inc. v. Safety Travel Chairs Inc.*, 806 F.2d 1565, 1 U.S.P.Q.2d 1081 (Fed. Cir. 1986).

Sufficiency of Evidence.

The sufficiency of the evidence cannot be reviewed on appeal after a jury verdict absent some post-verdict disposition, either by a deferred ruling or upon a post-verdict motion. *Biodex Corp. v. Loredan Biomedical Inc.*, 946 F.2d 850, 20 U.S.P.Q.2d 1252, 1261 (Fed. Cir. 1991).

Suggestion. *See also* Incentive, Motivation.

The law does not require an express suggestion in a prior-art reference to make a claimed combination obvious. The proper test is whether the references, taken as a whole, would suggest the invention to one of ordinary skill in the art. *Milliken Research Corp. v. Dan River, Inc.*, 739 F.2d 587, 222 U.S.P.Q. 571, 583 (Fed. Cir. 1984).

ᚹ

To combine references (A) and (B) properly to reach the conclusion that the subject matter of a patent would have been obvious, case law requires that there must be some teaching, suggestion, or inference in either reference (A) or (B), or both, or knowledge generally available to one of ordinary skill in the relevant art, that would lead one skilled in the art to combine the relevant teachings of references (A) and (B). Consideration must be given to teachings in the references that would have led one skilled in the art away from the claimed invention. A claim cannot properly be used as a blueprint for extracting individual teachings from references. *Ashland Oil, Inc. v. Delta Resins & Refractories, Inc.*, 776 F.2d 281, 227 U.S.P.Q. 657 (Fed. Cir. 1985).

ω

The "evidence" showed that use of vertical heights for range finding, use of multiple elements on a site, and use of circular apertures were each known in the art, but the prior art lacked any teaching or suggestion to combine the separate features in a manner permitting use of circular apertures for simultaneous range finding and aiming. Obviousness cannot be established by combining the teachings of the prior art to produce the claimed invention, absent some teaching, suggestion, or incentive supporting the combination. *Carela v. Starlight Archery*, 804 F.2d 135, 231 U.S.P.Q. 644 (Fed. Cir. 1986).

ω

To combine references to reach a conclusion that claimed subject matter would have been obvious, case law requires that there must be some teaching, suggestion, or inference in either reference, or both, or knowledge generally available that would have led one of ordinary skill in the art to combine the relevant teachings of the references. When the incentive to combine the teachings of the references is not readily apparent, it is the duty of the Examiner to explain why a combination of the reference teachings is proper. Absent such reasons or incentives, the teachings of the references are not combinable. *Ex parte Skinner*, 2 U.S.P.Q.2d 1788 (B.P.A.I. 1986).

ω

When prior-art references require a selective combination to render obvious a subsequent invention, there must be some reason for the combination other than the hindsight gleaned from the invention itself. Something in the prior art as a whole must suggest the desirability, and thus the obviousness, of making the combination. It is impermissible to use the claims as a frame and the prior-art references as a mosaic to piece together a facsimile of the claimed invention. *Uniroyal Inc. v. Rudkin-Wiley Corp.*, 837 F.2d 1044, 5 U.S.P.Q.2d 1434 (Fed. Cir. 1988).

ω

The consistent criterion for determination of obviousness is whether the prior art would have suggested to one of ordinary skill in the art that a claimed process should be carried out and would have reasonable likelihood of success, viewed in the light of the prior art. Both the suggestion and the expectation of success must be found in the prior art, not in the applicant's disclosure. *In re Dow Chemical Co.*, 837 F.2d 469, 5 U.S.P.Q.2d 1529 (Fed. Cir. 1988).

ω

Obviousness cannot be established by combining teachings of prior art to produce a claimed invention, absent some teaching or suggestion supporting the combination. Under section 103 (35 U.S.C.), teachings of references may be combined only if there is some suggestion or incentive to do so. Although couched in terms of combining teachings found in the prior art, the same inquiry must be carried out in the context of a purported obvious "modification" of the prior art. The mere fact that the prior art may be modified in the manner suggested by the Examiner does not make the modification obvious unless the prior art suggested the desirability of the modification. *In re Fritch*, 972 F.2d 1260, 23 U.S.P.Q.2d 1780, 1783 (Fed. Cir. 1992).

Suitable.

The claims were intended to cover the use of the invention with various types of automobiles. That a particular chair of the claims may fit within some automobiles and not others is of no moment. The phrase "so dimensioned" is as accurate as the subject matter permits, automobiles being of various sizes. As long as those of ordinary skill in the art realize that the dimensions could be easily obtained, 35 U.S.C. §112, second paragraph, requires nothing more. The patent law does not require that all possible lengths corresponding to the spaces in hundreds of different automobiles be listed in the patent, let alone that they be listed in the claims. *Orthokinetics Inc. v. Safety Travel Chairs Inc.*, 806 F.2d 1565, 1 U.S.P.Q.2d 1081 (Fed. Cir. 1986).

Sulfur.

Sulfur and oxygen in starting materials for respectively claimed processes in applications of two interfering parties did not impart patentable distinctness to such processes. *Moore v. McGrew*, 170 U.S.P.Q. 149, 153 (PO Bd. Pat. Intf. 1971).

ᴦ

Even though it may not be inconceivable to substitute sulfur for oxygen to obtain compounds having the same expected properties, that is not the standard; the standard is whether it would have been obvious in terms of 35 U.S.C. §103. *In re Grabiak*, 769 F.2d 729, 226 U.S.P.Q. 870 (Fed. Cir. 1985).

Summary Judgment. *See also* Prior Sale.

Summary Judgment is inappropriate where credibility is at issue. Credibility issues are appropriately resolved only after an evidentiary hearing or full trial. *SEC v. Koracorp Indus.*, 575 F.2d 692, 699 (9th Cir.), *cert. denied*, 439 U.S. 953 (1978).

ᴦ

A denial of summary judgment is not properly reviewable on an appeal from the final judgment entered after trial. *Glaros v. H. H. Robertson Co.*, 797 F.2d 1564, 230 U.S.P.Q. 393, 399 (Fed. Cir. 1986).

ᴦ

A dispute is genuine for the purposes of summary judgment if a reasonable jury could return a verdict for the non-moving party. *Anderson v. Liberty Lobby, Inc.*, 477 U.S. 242, 248 (1986).

ᴦ

Summary judgment is as appropriate in a patent case as in any other. A non-movant must do more than merely raise some doubt as to the existence of a fact; evidence must be forthcoming from the non-movant that would be sufficient to require for submission to the jury the dispute over the fact. Such evidence must be viewed in a light most favorable to the non-movant, and all reasonable inferences must be drawn in the non-movant's favor.

The movant bears the burden of demonstrating the absence of all genuine issues of material fact. Such burden is not as heavy as some decisions have held. The moving party need not produce evidence showing the absence of a genuine issue of material fact; rather, the burden on the moving party may be discharged by showing or pointing out that there is an absence of evidence to support the non-moving party's case. In reviewing a district court's grant of summary judgment, the CAFC reviews de novo the district court's conclusion that there was no genuine issue of material fact and that the moving party was entitled to judgment as a matter of law. *Avia Group International Inc. v. L.A. Gear California Inc.*, 853 F.2d 1557, 7 U.S.P.Q.2d 1548 (Fed. Cir. 1988).

ᚥ

Summary judgment may be granted in favor of a defendant on an ultimate issue of a fact where the defendant carries the burden of "pointing out to the District Court that there is an absence of evidence to support the non-moving party's case." Summary judgments can only lie where no dispute with respect to a material fact is "genuine." A dispute is genuine if the evidence is such that a reasonable jury could return a verdict for the non-moving party. *Johnston v. IVAC Corp.*, 885 F.2d 1574, 12 U.S.P.Q.2d 1382, 1383, 1384 (Fed. Cir. 1989).

ᚥ

Although all inferences must be drawn in favor of the non-movant on a motion for summary judgment, the non-movant must do more than merely present some evidence on an issue it asserts is disputed. Sufficient evidence for a jury to return a verdict in favor of the non-movant must be forthcoming. *Shamrock Technologies Inc. v. Medical Sterilization Inc.*, 903 F.2d 789, 14 U.S.P.Q.2d 1728, 1731 (Fed. Cir. 1990).

ᚥ

In a ruling on a motion for summary judgment, the district court must view the evidence in the light most favorable to the non-moving party, and any doubt as to the existence of issues of material fact must be resolved in favor of the party opposing the motion. Nevertheless, to create a genuine issue of fact, the non-movant must do more than present some evidence on an issue it asserts is disputed. The non-movant's evidence must present a question of material fact, which requires submission to a jury. On appeal, a grant of summary judgment will be upheld where there is no literal infringement, and a prosecution history estoppel makes clear that no actual infringement under the doctrine of equivalents can be found. *Jonsson v. The Stanley Works*, 903 F.2d 812, 14 U.S.P.Q.2d 1863, 1867 (Fed. Cir. 1990).

ᚥ

The jurisdiction of the CAFC over appeals from interlocutory orders, such as one that constitutes a partial summary judgment and a denial of a motion for summary judgment, neither of which is appealable, is governed by 28 U.S.C. §1292. Thus, there must be either an order certified, 28 U.S.C. §1292(c)(1), or a judgment otherwise appealable and final except for an accounting, 28 U.S.C. §1292(c)(2). *Syntex Pharmaceuticals International Ltd. v. K-Line Pharmaceuticals Ltd.*, 905 F.2d 1525, 15 U.S.P.Q.2d 1239 (Fed. Cir. 1990).

ᚥ

The purpose of Fed. R. Civ. P. 56 is to avoid an unnecessary trial, but it must be used carefully because an improper grant of summary judgment "may deny a party a chance to prove a worthy case." The district court cannot engage in fact finding on a motion for summary judgment. If there is a real dispute about a material fact or factual inference, summary judgment is inappropriate; the factual dispute should be reserved for trial. The moving party has the burden to demonstrate the absence of any genuine issue over all the material facts; and, where the moving party has the burden of proof on a claim or defense raised in a summary judgment motion, it must show that the undisputed facts establish every element of the claim or defense. *Meyers v. Brooks Shoe Inc.*, 912 F.2d 14, 16 U.S.P.Q.2d 1055, 1056 (Fed. Cir. 1990).

ᛡ

A mere dispute concerning the meaning of a term does not itself create a genuine issue of material fact. *Becton Dickinson & Co. v. C. R. Bard Inc.*, 922 F.2d 792, 17 U.S.P.Q.2d 1097, 1100 (Fed. Cir. 1990).

ᛡ

Normally, a motion for summary judgment is made by the party that does not bear the burden of proof. Thus, in the usual case, a defendant who moves for summary judgment argues that the plaintiff has failed to introduce competent evidence—the plaintiff bearing the burden of proof by a preponderance of the evidence—that would allow the jury to find in the plaintiff's favor. When a defendant in a patent infringement suit moves for summary judgment on an affirmative defense, the elements of which the defendant must show by clear and convincing evidence, the plaintiff, as the non-moving party, must simply produce enough evidence to allow a rational trier of fact to find that there is not clear and convincing evidence. As a result of this unusual procedural posture, the plaintiff's burden (as the non-moving party) to come forward with evidence to prevent summary judgment on the issue of inequitable conduct is less stringent than that normally placed on a non-moving party. *Schneider (USA) Inc. v. C. R. Bard Inc.*, 18 U.S.P.Q.2d 1076, 1080 (Mass. 1990).

ᛡ

The fact that both sides moved for summary judgment does not establish that there is no issue of fact and does not require that judgment be granted for one side or the other. Trial by document is an inadequate substitute for a trial with witnesses, who are subject to examination and cross-examination in the presence of the decision maker. *Scripps Clinic Research Foundation v. Genentech Inc.*, 927 F.2d 1565, 18 U.S.P.Q.2d 1001, 1008, 1011 (Fed. Cir. 1991).

ᛡ

Opposing a summary judgment motion based on anticipation by or obviousness over a reference does not, for purposes of reserving a right of appeal, require more than that the opposing party assert, with substantiation, that the prior-art references cited by the movant do not disclose or render obvious the invention of the patent. The court can determine what the prior-art references disclose without the aid of extrinsic facts. *Stoller v. Ford Motor Co.*, 18 U.S.P.Q.2d 1545, 1546 (Fed. Cir. 1991—*unpublished*).

ᛡ

Though not expressly authorized by Fed. R. Civ. P. 56, a district court's independently raising and granting a summary judgment motion in favor of a non-moving party has become an acceptable method of expediting litigation. The prevailing view in the Second Circuit is that a court need not give notice of its intention to enter summary judgment against a moving party. *Coach Leatherware Co. Inc. v. Ann Taylor Inc.*, 933 F.2d 162, 18 U.S.P.Q.2d 1907, 1911 (2d Cir. 1991).

ᗡ

In reviewing a district court's grant of summary judgment, the CAFC is not bound by the district court's holding that no material facts are in dispute and must make an independent determination as to whether the standards for summary judgment have been met. *Vas-Cath Inc. v. Mahurkar,* 935 F.2d 1555, 19 U.S.P.Q.2d 1111, 1114 (Fed. Cir. 1991).

ᗡ

In determining whether an invention would have been obvious at the time it was made, 35 U.S.C. §103 requires a court (1) to determine the scope and content of the prior art; (2) to ascertain the differences between the prior art and the claims at issue; and (3) to resolve the issue of ordinary skill in the pertinent art. "Such secondary considerations as commercial success, long felt but unsolved needs, [and] failure of others [to invent]" are also relevant to the obviousness inquiry. Since the facts to support a conclusion of invalidity of an issued patent must be proved by clear and convincing evidence, this standard must be applied by the court in deciding whether requirements have been met for summary determination of obviousness. *Ryko Manufacturing Co. v. Nu-Star Inc.*, 950 F.2d 714, 21 U.S.P.Q.2d 1053, 1055 (Fed. Cir. 1991).

ᗡ

A factual dispute is "genuine" when the evidence is such that a reasonable jury could return a verdict for the non-movant. Thus, although the interpretation of claims is a question of law, when it is necessary to resolve disputed issues of fact in the course of interpreting the claims, summary disposition is improper. *The Laitram Corp. v. NEC Corp.*, 952 F.2d 1357, 21 U.S.P.Q.2d 1276, 1281 (Fed. Cir. 1991).

ᗡ

Where affidavits are proffered as evidence on a motion for summary judgment, in support of or in opposition to the essential elements of a claim, the Court must be satisfied that such affidavits meet the standards set forth in Rule (Fed.R.Civ.P.) 56(e), as well as relevant evidentiary standards. Although expert witnesses are permitted to offer an opinion on the ultimate issue in the case pursuant to Fed.R. Evid. 704(a), the Court may exclude the expert testimony if such opinions are nothing more than legal conclusions. *Ciba-Geigy Corp. v. Crompton & Knowles Corp.*, 22 U.S.P.Q.2d 1761, 1763 (Pa. 1991).

ᗡ

The plain language of Fed. R. Civ. P. 56(c) mandates the entry of summary judgment against a party who fails to make a showing to establish the existence of an element (i.e., a factor) essential to that party's case, and on which that party will bear the burden of proof at trial. *Intellicall Inc. v. Phonometrics Inc.*, 952 F.2d 1384, 21 U.S.P.Q.2d 1383, 1388 (Fed. Cir. 1992).

ᗡ

A court (in a patent action) may grant summary judgment on the question of infringement, yet reserve other issues, such as validity of the patent or damages, for trial. "Though an invalid [patent] claim cannot give rise to liability for infringement, whether it is infringed is an entirely separate question capable of determination without regard to its validity." Nonetheless, "[b]ecause both validity and infringement involve construction of a claim, and the construction must be the same in determining both, it is desirable to decide both questions at the same time." *Al-Site Corp. v. Opti-Ray Inc.*, 23 U.S.P.Q.2d 1235, 1237 (N.Y. 1992); see also *Nobell Inc. v. Sharper Image Corp.*, 24 U.S.P.Q.2d 1919, 1921 (Cal. 1992).

ᛒ

Once a patent owner presents sufficient evidence on a motion for summary judgment to make a *prima facie* case of infringement, a challenge to the weight of an expert's declaration does not create a genuine issue of material fact. *Blandford v. Masco Industries Inc.*, 799 F.Supp. 666, 25 U.S.P.Q.2d 1074, 1076 (Tex. 1992).

ᛒ

A trial court does not have to set forth findings and conclusions explicitly to support its decision on summary judgment. However, if the "district court's 'underlying holdings would otherwise be ambiguous or inascertainable,' the reasons for entering summary judgment must be stated somewhere in the record....Federal Rule of Civil Procedure 52(a) does not relieve the trial court of this burden." *Telectronics Pacing Systems Inc. v. Ventritex Inc.*, 982 F.2d 1520, 25 U.S.P.Q.2d 1196, 1201 (Fed. Cir. 1992).

ᛒ

Claim interpretation is a question of law amenable to summary judgment, and disagreement over the meaning of a term in a claim does not necessarily give rise to a *genuine* issue of material fact. Moreover, where a disputed word in a claim would be understood by one of ordinary skill in the art to have its ordinary meaning on the basis of the patent specification and its prosecution history, extrinsic evidence that the inventor may have intended a different meaning does not preclude summary judgment. *Alcon Laboratories Inc. v. Entravision Inc.*, 976 F.2d 748, 26 U.S.P.Q.2d 1137, 1139, 1140 (Fed. Cir. 1992).

ᛒ

Summary judgment for noninfringement for defendant is not precluded merely because defendant did not move for summary judgment on that ground. *International Visual Corp. v. Crown Metal Manufacturing Co. Inc.*, 991 F.2d 768, 26 U.S.P.Q.2d 1588, 1590 (Fed. Cir. 1993).

ᛒ

Once an interference has been declared, it never reverts to the summary judgment stage. *English v. Ausnit*, 38 U.S.P.Q.2d 1625, 1636 (B.P.A.I. 1993).

ᛒ

In a trilogy of 1986 cases, the Supreme Court clarified the standard for summary judgment. *See Celotex Corporation v. Catrett*, 477 U.S. 317 (1986); *Anderson v. Liberty Lobby, Inc.*, 477 U.S. 242 (1986); *Matsushita Electrical Industry Co. v. Zenith Radio*

Corp., 475 U.S. 574 (1986). The moving party bears the initial burden of demonstrating the absence of a genuine issue of material fact for trial. Whether a fact is material is determined by looking to the governing substantive law; if the fact may affect the outcome, it is material. If the moving party seeks summary adjudication with respect to a claim or defense upon which it bears the burden of proof at trial, its burden must be satisfied by affirmative admissible evidence. By contrast, when the non-moving party bears the burden of proving the claim or defense, the moving party can meet its burden by pointing out the absence of evidence from the non-moving party. The moving party need not disprove the other party's case. When the moving party meets its burden, the "adverse party may not rest upon the mere allegations or denials of the adverse party's pleadings, but the adverse party's response, by affidavits or as otherwise provided in this rule, must set forth specific facts showing that there is a genuine issue for trial." In assessing whether the non-moving party has raised a genuine issue, its evidence is to be believed, and all justifiable inferences are to be drawn in its favor. Nonetheless, "the mere existence of a scintilla of evidence" is insufficient. *Wang Laboratories Inc. v. Mitsubishi Electronics America Inc.*, 32 U.S.P.Q.2d 1641, 1643 (Cal. 1994).

ᚥ

The moving party does not have the burden to produce any evidence showing the absence of a genuine issue of material fact. "Instead, . . . the burden on the moving party may be discharged by 'showing—that is, pointing out to the district court—that there is an absence of evidence to support the nonmoving party's case." "[T]he adverse party's response . . . must set forth specific facts showing that there is a genuine issue for trial." The evidence of the nonmovant is to be believed, and all justifiable inferences are to be drawn in its favor. "To create a genuine issue of fact, the nonmovant must do more than present some evidence of an issue it asserts to be disputed." "Instead, the nonmovant's evidence must present a question of material fact, which requires submission to a jury." *Gussin v. Nintendo of America Inc.*, 33 U.S.P.Q.2d 1418, 1419, 1422 (Cal. 1994).

ᚥ

Summary judgment is a drastic remedy and should not be granted when the parties have not had an opportunity to conduct pretrial discovery. *Cobe Laboratories Inc. v. Baxter Healthcare Corp.*, 34 U.S.P.Q.2d 1472, 1473 (Colo. 1994).

ᚥ

One principal goal of summary judgment under Federal Rule 56 is "to isolate and dispose of factually unsupported claims or defenses." However, "district courts are not obligated to scour the record to determine which facts are disputed." *Recycling Sciences International Inc. v. Canonie Environmental Services Corp.*, 34 U.S.P.Q.2d 1532, 1535, 1536 (Ill. 1994).

ᚥ

Although some courts have expressed reservations about granting summary judgment of non-infringement under the doctrine of equivalents, summary judgment is appropriate when no reasonable jury could conclude that the accused device infringes. *Sage Products Inc. v. Devon Industries Inc.*, 880 F.Supp. 718, 35 U.S.P.Q.2d 1321, 1325 (Cal. 1994).

ᚥ

"[T]he inquiry involved in a ruling on a motion for summary judgment ... necessarily implicates the substantive evidentiary standard of proof that would apply at the trial on the merits." *Surgical Laser Technologies Inc. v. Heraeus Laseronics Inc.*, 34 U.S.P.Q.2d 1226, 1232 (Pa. 1995).

ω

"The moving party bears the initial burden of averring an absence of evidence to support the nonmoving party's case." Once this burden has been met, "the non-moving party must demonstrate the existence of a genuine issue of material fact pertaining to those issues on which it would have the burden of proof on trial. "In this context, 'genuine' means that the evidence about the fact is such that a reasonable jury could resolve the point in favor of the non-moving party and "material" means that the fact is one that might affect the outcome of the suit under the governing law." *Hoppe v. Baxter Healthcare Corp.*, 878 F.Supp. 303, 34 U.S.P.Q.2d 1619, 1622 (Mass. 1995).

ω

"To create a genuine issue of fact, the nonmovant must do more than present *some* evidence it asserts is disputed." There must be sufficient evidence presented "favoring the nonmoving party for a jury to return a verdict for that party. If the evidence [of the nonmovant] is merely colorable, or is not significantly probative, summary judgment may be granted." *LifeScan Inc. v. Polymer Technology International Corp.*, 35 U.S.P.Q.2d 1225, 1227 (Wash. 1995).

ω

"[D]istrict courts are widely acknowledged to possess the power to enter summary judgment sua sponte, so long as the losing party was on notice that she had to come forward with all of her evidence." A sua sponte summary judgment should not be granted when it takes the affected party by surprise. *National Presto Industries Inc. v. The West Bend Co.*, 76 F.3d 1185, 37 U.S.P.Q.2d 1685, 1686 (Fed. Cir. 1996).

ω

Patent actions are often fraught with factual issues which make summary judgment inappropriate. *Ford Motor Co. v. Lemelson*, 40 U.S.P.Q.2d 1349, 1351 (Nev. 1996).

ω

Even when material facts are in dispute, summary adjudication may be appropriate if, with all factual inferences drawn in favor of the nonmovant, the movant would nonetheless be entitled to judgment as a matter of law. *Oiestad v. Ag-Industrial Equipment Co. Inc.*, 44 U.S.P.Q.2d 1526 (Fed. Cir. 1997—*unpublished*).

ω

A party seeking summary judgment bears the initial responsibility of informing the district court of the basis for its motion, and identifying those portions of the pleadings, depositions, interrogatories, and admissions on file together with affidavits, if any, that it believes demonstrate the absence of genuine issues for trial. Once a properly supported summary judgment motion is made, the opposing party may not rest on the allegations contained in his complaint, but must respond with specific facts showing the existence of a genuine factual issue to be tried. The substantive burden of proof that the plaintiff must meet at trial also applies at the summary judgment stage. *Baxa Corp. v. McGaw Inc.*, 996 F.Supp. 1044, 45 U.S.P.Q.2d 1504, 1506 (Colo. 1997).

ω

"[S]ummary judgment may be affirmed, regardless of the correctness of the district court's rulings, when [the CAFC] finds in the record an adequate, independent basis for that result." *Glaxo Inc. v. TorPharm Inc.*, 47 U.S.P.Q.2d 1836, 1840 (Fed. Cir. 1997).

Summary Judgment Motion.

Since the CAFC reviews issues of obviousness as one of law on which it must exercise independent judgment, the CAFC must be convinced not only that the decision maker engaged in a faulty analysis in applying the law to the facts, but also that a correct application of the law to those facts would bring a different result. If the district court failed to place the burden of proof properly, the CAFC would do so. If the district court improperly focused on a particular feature, the CAFC would consider the invention as a whole. If the district court wholly disregarded submitted evidence of secondary considerations supporting patentability, the evidence would become part of the CAFC equation and, on a motion for summary judgment, would be construed most favorably to the nonmovant. If the district court required synergistic results in a combination, the CAFC could not reverse unless, under the 35 U.S.C. §103 standard, the result, as opposed to the reasoning, was erroneous as a matter of law. This is not to say that reasoning is to be ignored, since faulty reasoning is likely to lead to a wrong result. Nevertheless, the appellant must not only show error in reasoning, but error in results. *Union Carbide Corp. v. American Can Co.*, 724 F.2d 1567, 220 U.S.P.Q. 584 (Fed. Cir. 1984).

Superior.

In the absence of any definition in the specification, the meaning and scope of "superior" are not clear from the mere presence of this term in claims. *Ex parte Anderson*, 21 U.S.P.Q.2d 1241, 1250 (B.P.A.I. 1991).

Superiority.

Nothing in the patent statute requires that an invention be superior to prior art to be patentable. Any superiority or lack of it is irrelevant to the question of obviousness. *Ryco Inc. v. Ag-Bag Corp.*, 857 F.2d 1418, 8 U.S.P.Q.2d 1323 (Fed. Cir. 1988).

Supersedeas Bond. *See* **Effect.**

Supervision. *See* **Assistant.**

Supplemental Declaration or Oath.

A patent is not invalid for failure to file a separate oath or declaration in support of claims inserted by amendment when the claims are fully supported in the original disclosure. Under the same circumstances, a patent is not invalid for lack of a supplemental oath or declaration. *Railroad Dynamics, Inc. v. A. Stucki Co.*, 727 F.2d 1506, 220 U.S.P.Q. 929 (Fed. Cir. 1984).

ω

When amendments correcting an overclaiming are made during reissue prosecution in response to a rejection, a patentee is obligated to file a supplementary declaration explaining the source of the overclaiming error, that it was non-deceptive and otherwise excusable, and how the amendment corrects the overclaiming. *Nupla Corp. v. IXL Manufacturing Co.*, 42 U.S.P.Q.2d 1711, 1715 (Fed. Cir. 1997).

Supplemental Preliminary Statement.

The determination of whether to request supplemental preliminary statements *before* the redeclaration of an interference is left to the discretion of the Examiner-in-chief. *Unisys Corp. v. Commissioner of Patents and Trademarks*, 39 U.S.P.Q.2d 1842, 1845 (D.C. 1993).

Supplier.

[S]upplier/trade name information must be provided only when a skilled artisan could not practice the best mode of the claimed invention absent this information." Because the composition of Sil-42 perlite was not defined in the literature (it was a trade secret) or disclosed in the specification, supplier/trade name information alone may not have satisfied the PTO's guidelines. *United States Gypsum Co. v. National Gypsum Co.*, 74 F.3d 1209, 37 U.S.P.Q.2d 1388, 1392 (Fed. Cir. 1996).

Support. *See also* Alkyl, Antecedent Basis, Antecedent Support, Aromatic, Aryl, At Least, Breadth, Commensurate in Scope, Copying Claims, Crystalline, Deem, Describe, Description, Disclosure, Explanation, *Expressis Verbis*, *Ipsis Verbis*, Objective Enablement, Possession, Reduction in Scope, Substituted, Sufficiency of Disclosure.

When it is clear from the disclosure that the principle of the claimed process is of a physical, rather than of a chemical, nature and that the specific nature of the employed polymers in the blend is not the significant aspect of the invention, there is no reason for restricting the claims to the specific polymers disclosed in the application, particularly in view of the fact that no basis is found for assuming that polymers coming within the recited scope would be inoperative. *Ex parte White and Cates*, 127 U.S.P.Q. 261, 262 (PO Bd. App. 1958).

ω

The key to determining whether a disclosure supports a claim for interference purposes is whether the disclosure teaches the gist of the invention defined by the claim. While all limitations of a claim must be considered in deciding what invention is defined, it is futile merely to compare quantitatively range limits and numbers set out in counts with range limits and numbers disclosed in an allegedly supporting specification. Closer scrutiny is required to get at the essence of what invention the count purports to define. *Hall v. Taylor*, 332 F.2d 844, 141 U.S.P.Q. 821, 824 (C.C.P.A. 1964).

ω

A priority showing for the purpose of overcoming a reference is distinguished from the amount of disclosure which an application must provide to support a generic claim. *In re Ziegler, Breil, Holzkamp, and Martin*, 347 F.2d 642, 146 U.S.P.Q. 76, 82 (C.C.P.A. 1965).

ᙡ

It is manifestly impracticable for an applicant who discloses a generic invention to give an example of every species falling within it, or even to name every such species. It is sufficient if the disclosure teaches those skilled in the art what the invention is and how to practice it. *In re Kamal and Rogier*, 398 F.2d 867, 158 U.S.P.Q. 320, 323 (C.C.P.A. 1968).

ᙡ

A claim is a group of words defining only the boundary of the patent monopoly. It may not describe any physical thing, and indeed may encompass physical things not yet dreamed of. *In re Vogel and Vogel*, 422 F.2d 438, 164 U.S.P.Q. 619, 622 (C.C.P.A. 1970).

ᙡ

An original claim constituted a description in the original disclosure equivalent in scope and identical in language to the total subject matter being claimed. Nothing more is necessary for compliance with the description requirement of the first paragraph of 35 U.S.C. §112. *In re Gardner*, 475 F.2d 1389, 177 U.S.P.Q. 396, 397 (C.C.P.A. 1973).

ᙡ

In a case where there is no unpredictability and a broader concept than that expressly set forth in the specification would naturally occur to one skilled in the art from reading applicant's description, there is no basis for denying applicant claims that recite the broader concept. The alternative places upon patent applicants, the Patent Office, and the public the undue burden of listing (in the case of applicants), reading and examining (in the case of the Patent Office), and printing and storing (in the case of the public) descriptions of the very many structural or functional equivalents of disclosed elements or steps that are already stored in the minds of those skilled in the arts, ready for instant recall upon reading the descriptions of specific elements or steps. *In re Smythe and Shamos*, 480 F.2d 1376, 178 U.S.P.Q. 279, 285 (C.C.P.A. 1973).

ᙡ

An application for Letters Patent must contain support for the broadest reasonable interpretation of a disputed claim recitation. *In re Sabatino and Orlando*, 480 F.2d 911, 178 U.S.P.Q. 357, 358 (C.C.P.A. 1973).

ᙡ

Because the Patent Commissioner has authority to and did issue a patent upon an application wherein the disclosure incorporates by reference a portion of a disclosure [which was "essential material" as defined by MPEP §608.01(p)] of a then existing patent that was available to the public, because there appears to be no abuse of discretion in doing so, and because the Examiner did not question the adequacy of the disclosure of the involved apparatus, the incorporation by reference was effective, and the claim was not held to be invalid as being without support in the disclosure. *Lundy Electronics &*

Systems, Inc. v. Optical Recognition Systems, Inc., 362 F. Supp. 130, 178 U.S.P.Q. 525, 539 (Va. 1973).

ᅲ

Compliance with the first paragraph of 35 U.S.C. §112 is adjudged from the perspective of the person skilled in the relevant art. Claimed subject matter need not be described in haec verba in the specification in order for that specification to satisfy the description requirement, although where there is exact correspondence between the claim language and original specification disclosure, the description requirement would normally be satisfied. The specification as originally filed must convey clearly to those skilled in the art the information that the applicant has invented the specific subject matter later claimed. When the original specification accomplishes that, regardless of how it accomplishes it, the essential goal of the description requirement is realized. *In re Smith and Hubin*, 481 F.2d 910, 178 U.S.P.Q. 620, 624 (C.C.P.A. 1973).

ᅲ

Having been produced by the same process, the product obtained in Example IV of the earlier Sulkowski application is, of necessity, the same product as that obtained in Example III of the Sulkowski interference application. The only difference is in the naming of the product. Based on the process used in the earlier application, Sulkowski is entitled to the benefit of the product of that process with his later application. The fact that error was made in naming the product in the first application does not deprive Sulkowski of the benefit of that application. *Sulkowski v. Houlihan*, 179 U.S.P.Q. 685, 686 (PTO Bd. Pat. Int. 1973). *See also In re Sulkowski*, 487 F.2d 920, 180 U.S.P.Q. 46 (C.C.P.A. 1973).

ᅲ

Non-critical features may be supported by a more general disclosure than those at the heart of the invention. *In re Stephens, Benvau, and Benvau*, 529 F.2d 1343, 188 U.S.P.Q. 659, 661 (C.C.P.A. 1976).

ᅲ

In an unpredictable art, does 35 U.S.C. §112 require disclosure of a test with every species covered by a claim? To require such a complete disclosure would apparently necessitate a patent application with thousands of examples or a disclosure with thousands of catalysts along with information as to whether each exhibits catalytic behavior resulting in the production of the desired products. More importantly, such a requirement would force an inventor seeking adequate patent protection to carry out a prohibitive number of actual experiments. This would tend to discourage inventors from filing patent applications in an unpredictable area since the patent claims would have to be limited to those embodiments that are expressly disclosed. A potential infringer could readily avoid "literal" infringement of such claims by merely finding another analogous catalyst complex that could be used in forming the same products. *In re Angstadt and Griffin*, 537 F.2d 498, 190 U.S.P.Q. 214, 218 (C.C.P.A. 1976).

ᅲ

To provide effective incentives, claims must adequately protect inventors. To demand that the first to disclose shall limit his claims to what he has found will work or to materials which meet the guidelines specified for "preferred" materials would not serve the constitutional purpose of promoting progress in the useful arts. *In re Johnson and Farnham*, 558 F.2d 1008, 194 U.S.P.Q. 187, 195 (C.C.P.A. 1977).

ᛰ

The burden of showing that the claimed invention is not described in the application rests on the PTO in the first instance, and it is up to the PTO to give reasons why a description not in ipsis verbis is insufficient. *In re Edwards, Rice, and Soulen*, 568 F.2d 1349, 196 U.S.P.Q. 465, 469 (C.C.P.A. 1978).

ᛰ

A continuation-in-part of two parent applications is entitled to the benefit of the filing dates of the respective parent applications even though support for the subject matter of one claim is dependent upon the combined disclosures of both parent applications. *Ex parte Janin*, 209 U.S.P.Q. 761, 764 (PTO Bd. App. 1979).

ᛰ

In order to establish unexpected results for a claimed invention, objective evidence of non-obviousness must be commensurate in scope with the claims which the evidence is offered to support. *In re Clemens, Hurwitz, and Walker*, 622 F.2d 1029, 206 U.S.P.Q. 289, 296 (C.C.P.A. 1980).

ᛰ

A description of several newly discovered strains of bacteria (having one particularly desirable metabolic property in terms of the conventionally measured culture characteristics and a number of metabolic and physiological properties) does not enable one of ordinary skill in the relevant art independently to discover additional strains having the same specific, desirable metabolic property (i.e., the production of a particular antibiotic). A verbal description of a new species does not enable one of ordinary skill in the relevant art to obtain strains of that species over and above the specific strains made available through deposit in one of the recognized culture depositories. *Ex parte Jackson, Theriault, Sinclair, Fager, and Karwowski*, 217 U.S.P.Q. 804, 806 (PTO Bd. App. 1982).

ᛰ

The test for determining compliance with the written description requirement of 35 U.S.C. §112 is whether the disclosure of the application as originally filed reasonably conveys to the artisan that the inventor had possession of the claimed subject matter, rather than the presence or absence of literal support in the specification for the claim language. *Ex parte Harvey*, 3 U.S.P.Q.2d 1626 (B.P.A.I. 1986).

ᛰ

The test for sufficiency of support in a parent application is whether the disclosure of the application relied upon "reasonably conveys to the artisan that the inventor had possession at that time of the later claimed subject matter." *In re Hayes Microcomputer Products Inc. Patent Litigation*, 982 F.2d 1527, 25 U.S.P.Q.2d 1241, 1245 (Fed. Cir. 1992).

ᛰ

A rejection of claims (for lack of adequate descriptive support because there was "no literal basis for the" claim limitation "in the absence of a catalyst") was reversed. The observation of lack of literal support does not, in and of itself, establish a *prima facie* case for lack of adequate descriptive support under the first paragraph of 35 U.S.C. §112. It cannot be said that the originally-filed disclosure would not have conveyed to one having ordinary skill in the art that appellants had possession of the *concept* of conducting the decomposition step in the absence of a catalyst. Throughout the discussion, which would seem to cry out for a catalyst if one were used, no mention is made of a catalyst. *Ex parte Parks*, 30 U.S.P.Q.2d 1234, 1236 (B.P.A.I. 1993).

Suppress.

A court may find that an invention was abandoned, suppressed, or concealed if, within a reasonable time after the invention was reduced to practice, the inventor took no steps to make the invention publicly known. Factors supporting a finding of abandonment, concealment, or suppression include not filing a patent application, not publicly disseminating documents describing the invention, and not publicly using the invention. Although not filing a patent application within a reasonable time after reduction to practice may negate a 35 U.S.C. §102(g) defense, it is only one factor. It appears that not filing or delaying the filing of a patent application may support a conclusion of suppression or concealment. However, it is not clear that failure to file a patent application would show abandonment. In fact, there simply is no requirement to file a patent application if a party is not seeking protection of the patent laws. *Oak Industries, Inc. v. Zenith Electronics Corp.*, 726 F. Supp. 1525, 14 U.S.P.Q.2d 1417, 1422, 1423 (Ill. 1989).

Suppression. ***See also*** **Conceal, Concealment, Spurring, Suppress, 35 U.S.C. §102(g).**

The question whether suppression or concealment under 35 U.S.C. §102(g) is negated ought to be determined by asking whether the public has gained knowledge of the invention that will ensure its preservation in the public domain. When commercial use does not convey knowledge of the invention to the public, it does not negate a legal conclusion of concealing the invention within the meaning of §102(g). *Palmer and Taylor v. Dudzik,* 481 F.2d 1377, 178 U.S.P.Q. 608, 616 (C.C.P.A. 1973).

ϖ

A delay in filing a patent application of more than 17 months after reducing the invention to practice was not regarded as unreasonable (raising an inference of intent to suppress) in view of continued activities to within six months of the filing date. *DSilva v. Drabek,* 214 U.S.P.Q. 556 (PTO Bd. Pat. Int. 1981).

ϖ

Early public disclosure is a linchpin of the patent system. As between a prior inventor who benefits from a process by selling its product, but suppresses, conceals, or otherwise keeps the process from the public, and a later inventor who promptly files a patent application from which the public will gain disclosure of the process, the law favors the latter. In determining "obviousness" over prior art, and having learned the details of the patentee's invention, the district court found it within the skill of the art to stretch other material rapidly, to stretch PTFE to increase porosity, and to stretch at high temperatures. The result is that the patent claims were used as a frame, and individual, naked parts of separate prior-art references were employed as a mosaic to recreate a facsimile of the claimed invention. No explanation was given as to why that mosaic would have been obvious to one skilled in the art at the time of the patentee's invention, or what there was in the prior art that would have caused those skilled in the art to disregard the teachings there found against making just such a mosaic. To imbue one of ordinary skill in the art with knowledge of the invention in suit, where no prior art reference or references of record convey or suggest that knowledge, is to fall victim to the insidious effect of a hindsight syndrome wherein that which only the inventor taught is used against its teacher. *W. L. Gore & Associates, Inc. v. Garlock, Inc.*, 721 F.2d 1540, 220 U.S.P.Q. 303 (Fed. Cir. 1983).

ω

Even if the invention was actually reduced to practice by the junior party in 1977 or 1978, the unexplained hiatus of more than two years between that date and the junior party's filing date was an unreasonably long delay, raising an inference that the junior party suppressed the invention within the meaning of 35 U.S.C. §102(g). Since there is no evidence in the record as to any activity by the junior party during this two-year period, the inference has not been rebutted, and, as a result, the junior party cannot rely on either of the alleged actual reductions to practice. *Latimer v. Wetmore*, 231 U.S.P.Q. 131 (B.P.A.I. 1985).

ω

The Board correctly found a delay of approximately 51 months was unreasonably long and sufficient to give rise to an inference of an intent to abandon, suppress, or conceal the invention. An inference of suppression or concealment may be overcome with evidence that the reason for the delay was to perfect the invention. When, however, the delay is caused by working on refinements and improvements that are not reflected in the final patent application, the delay will not be excused. Further, when the activities that caused the delay go to commercialization of the invention, the delay will not be excused. *Lutzker v. Plet*, 843 F.2d 1364, 6 U.S.P.Q.2d 1370 (Fed. Cir. 1988).

Supremacy Clause. *See also* State.

The patent system is one in which uniform federal standards are carefully used to promote invention while, at the same time, preserving free competition. A State cannot, consistently with the Supremacy Clause of the Constitution, extend the life of a patent beyond its expiration date or give a patent on an article which lacks the level of invention required for federal patents. To do either would run contrary to the policy of Congress of granting patents only to true inventions, and then only for a limited time. Just as a State cannot encroach on the federal patent laws directly, it cannot, under some other law, such as that forbidding unfair competition, give protection of a kind that clashes with the objectives of the federal patent laws. "Sharing in the goodwill of an article unprotected by patent or trademark is the exercise of a right possessed by alland in the free exercise of which the consuming public is deeply interested." *Sears, Roebuck & Co. v. Stiffel Company*, 376 U.S. 225, 140 U.S.P.Q. 524, 528 (S. Ct. 1964).

ω

Under the supremacy clause of the U.S. Constitution, federal patent law preempts state awards of patentlike protection. "[S]tate regulation of intellectual property must yield to the extent that it clashes with the balance struck by Congress in our patent laws." *Bonito Boats, Inc. v. Thunder Craft Boats, Inc.*, 489 U.S. 141, 152, 9 U.S.P.Q.2d 1847 (1989). However, federal patent law does not necessarily prohibit states from enforcing valid contracts under state contract law when such contracts provide protection for unpatented products. *Darling v. Standard Alaska Production Co.*, 20 U.S.P.Q.2d 1688, 1691 (Alaska S. Ct. 1991).

Supreme Court. *See* **Pendency.**

Surmise. *See also* **Assertion.**

The correctness of an assertion in the specification may always be challenged, but only if there is sound basis therefor. Mere surmise, speculation, and conjecture are insufficient to refute an explicit teaching about operability. An appellant's assertion must be accepted in the absence of factual evidence (not merely unsupported skepticism) to the contrary. *Ex parte Dunn and Mathis*, 181 U.S.P.Q. 652, 653 (PO Bd. App. 1973).

Surprising Results. *See* **Unexpected Results.**

Suspicion. *See* **Fact.**

Swear Back Of. *See* **Antedating a Reference.**

Symbols.

The rejection of a claim to a chemical compound (of a specified structure "where R_1, R_2, R_4, R_6, R_7, R_8, R_9, R_{10}, R_{11}, n and q are defined in the specification") under the second paragraph of 35 U.S.C. §112 was reversed. The absence of the definitions of the symbols in the claim itself may be objectionable. *Ex parte Moon*, 224 U.S.P.Q. 519 (PTO Bd. App. 1984).

Symmetry in the Law. *See also* **Fact.**

In support of a rejection under 35 U.S.C. §112, later references were cited, not as prior art, but as evidence to prove the appellants" disclosure as non-enabling for "other species" of the claimed polymer, in an effort to show why the scope of enablement was insufficient to support the claims. As thus implicitly recognized, the references would not have been available in support of a rejection under 35 U.S.C. §102 or §103 entered in connection with the 1953 application. To permit use of the same references in support of the §112 rejection herein, however, is to render the "benefit" of 35 U.S.C. §120 illusory. The very purpose of reliance on §120 is to reach back, to avoid the effect of intervening references. Nothing in §120 limits its application to any specific grounds of rejection, or permits the Examiner, denied use of references to reject or to require narrowing of a claim under §102 or §103, to achieve the same result by use of the same references under §112. Just as justice and reason require application of §112 in the same manner to applicants and

Examiners, symmetry in the law, and evenness of its application, require that §120 be held applicable to all bases for rejection, that its words "same effect" be given their full meaning and intent. *In re Hogan and Banks*, 559 F.2d 595, 194 U.S.P.Q. 527 (C.C.P.A. 1977).

☼

Reference to the "invention" in 35 U.S.C. §119 clearly refers to what the claims define, not what is disclosed in the foreign application. Section 119 provides that a foreign application "shall have the same effect" as if it had been filed in the U.S. Accordingly, if the effective date of what is claimed in a U.S. application is at issue, to preserve symmetry of treatment between §120 and §119, the foreign priority application must be examined to ascertain whether it supports, within the meaning of §112, paragraph one, what is claimed in the U.S. application. *In re Gosteli*, 872 F.2d 1008, 10 U.S.P.Q.2d 1614, 1616 (Fed. Cir. 1989).

Synergism.

The remarkable performance achievements and synergisms of the patented catalysts are persuasive evidence that these catalysts embody patentable combinations. *Mobil Oil Corp. v. W. R. Grace & Co.*, 367 F. Supp. 207, 180 U.S.P.Q. 418, 452 (Conn. 1973).

☼

"Any definition of synergism necessarily varies depending upon whether the particular claim in issue is for a process, a formula, or a utility patent. Courts have roughly defined synergism as when the 'whole in some way exceeds the sum of its parts,' when the combination produces a 'new or different function,' or 'unusual or surprising consequences.' *Foseco International Limited v. Chemincon, Inc.*, 507 F.Supp. 1253, 210 U.S.P.Q. 697, 708 (Mich. 1981).

☼

Declaration evidence showed greater-than-additive cleaning performance resulting from the combination of zeolites with a variety of auxiliary builders, in the face of diminished (less than additive) depletion of calcium ions for the combination. The Board agreed that the results for some of the combinations tested for cleaning performance are "better than would be expected." A greater-than-expected result is an evidentiary factor pertinent to the legal conclusion of obviousness vel non of the claims at issue. The Board concluded that the evidence demonstrated synergism "to some degree" with respect to cleaning performance, but observed that the appellant's claims were not limited to those specific cobuilders and detergent compositions for which data showing synergism had been submitted. The Board also held that this result, even if unexpected, was not "sufficient to overcome the prima facie case of obviousness established by the prior art.

The court could discern no *prima facie* teaching of the prior art with respect to these compositions of components. The PTO failed to point out any reference that suggests combining a known builder with zeolite, or that this combination would produce a greater-than-additive effect in cleaning performance. The PTO failed to establish a *prima facie* case of obviousness with respect to those claims that require the presence of an auxiliary builder. The Board observed that the combination of zeolite and cobuilder were not, in most instances reported in the Declaration, superior in cleaning performance to the auxiliary builder alone. This is not the test. In view of the evidence of a result greater than additive, evidencing some non-obvious results in the combination of components where the one component is in itself more active than the other is not controlling. The specification teaches that a broad range of surfactants may be used in combination with zeolite plus auxiliary builders. In the absence of prior art suggesting or otherwise making these compositions obvious to one of ordinary skill in the art, there is inadequate support for the PTO's rejection of these claims. The burden on this point has not shifted to the applicant. *In re Corkill,* 771 F.2d 1496, 226 U.S.P.Q. 1005 (Fed. Cir. 1985).

ω

Casting an invention as "a combination of old elements" leads improperly to an analysis of the claimed invention by the parts, not by the whole. The critical inquiry is whether there is something in the prior art as a whole to suggest the desirability, and thus the obviousness, of making the combination. A traditional problem with focusing on a patent as a "combination of old elements" is the attendant notion that patentability is undeserving without some "synergistic" or "different" effect. Here, the district court spoke of the need for "a new and useful result." Such tests for patentability have been soundly rejected by this court. Though synergism is relevant when present, its "absence has no place in evaluating the evidence on obviousness." *Custom Accessories Inc. v. Jeffrey-Allan Industries, Inc.,* 807 F.2d 955, 1 U.S.P.Q.2d 1196 (Fed. Cir. 1986).

ω

The absence of synergism is irrelevant to the issue of obviousness. Synergism is probative only of non-obviousness. *Ryko Manufacturing Co. v. Nu-Star Inc.,* 950 F.2d 714, 21 U.S.P.Q.2d 1053, 1056 (Fed. Cir. 1991).

Synthesis. *See also* **Method of Making.**

When, given the conception of a compound, processes by which it may be prepared are obvious, the invention resides in the compound per se and is not properly defined as a process. Even though a product is patentable, a claim to a process for producing such product need not necessarily be patentable. *In re Larsen,* 292 F.2d 531, 130 U.S.P.Q. 209, 210 (C.C.P.A. 1961).

ω

Although an otherwise old process becomes a new process when a previously un-known starting material is used in it and is subjected to a conventional manipulation or reaction to produce a product that may also be new, albeit the expected result of what is done, it does not necessarily mean that the whole process has become non-obvious in the sense of 35 U.S.C. §103. In short, a new process may still be obvious, even when considered "as a whole," notwithstanding the fact that the specific starting material or resulting product, or both, are not to be found in the prior art. *In re Durden,* 763 F.2d 1406, 226 U.S.P.Q. 359 (Fed. Cir. 1985).

Synthetic.

New synthesized intermediates are affirmatively recited in a claim, and exclusion of known prior compounds results merely from claiming a subgroup of lesser scope (having a common quality that is distinctive from the characteristics of the major group). This common distinctive quality is that the recited compounds are novel synthesized intermediates produced by a novel process from a novel synthesized starting material for use in a novel method of providing, by synthesis, the novel desired insecticides. *In re Schechter and LaForge*, 205 F.2d 185, 98 U.S.P.Q. 144, 149 (C.C.P.A. 1953).

ᘓ

To persons skilled in the rubber art, the word "synthetic" (defined as "man-made") does not include a purified natural product. *In re Wakefield and Foster*, 422 F.2d 897, 164 U.S.P.Q. 636, 640, 641 (C.C.P.A. 1970).

ᘓ

A claim to a "synthetically produced" or a "substantially pure" substance may well have the requisite novelty to distinguish over a counterpart which occurs in nature only in impure form. *In re Kratz and Strasburger*, 592 F.2d 1169, 201 U.S.P.Q. 71, 75 (C.C.P.A. 1979).

ᘓ

A microorganism that is not a hitherto unknown natural phenomenon, but a non-naturally occurring manufacture or composition of matter, a product of human ingenuity having a distinctive name, character, and use, plainly qualifies as patentable subject matter. *Diamond, Commissioner of Patents & Trademarks v. Chakrabarty*, 447 U.S. 303, 206 U.S.P.Q. 193, 197 (1980).

Key Terms and Concepts

$\mathcal{T}$

Tariff Act. *See also* **Importation, Industry, Injury, 19 U.S.C. §1337.**

Membership in the domestic industry does not operate to shield an importer from the purview of section 337 (19 U.S.C. §1337). *Texas Instruments Inc. v. International Trade Commission*, 988 F.2d 1165, 26 U.S.P.Q.2d 1018, 1030 (Fed. Cir. 1993).

Taxation. *See also* **Capital Asset, Capital Gains, Depreciation, Ordinary Income.**

The transfer of all substantial rights to a patent by a holder is considered the sale or exchange of a capital asset held for more than six months, even though the payment therefor is not made at the time of the transfer, but is made periodically later over a period of time. *Puschelberg v. United States,* 330 F.2d 56, 141 U.S.P.Q. 323 (6th Cir. 1964).

ᴔ

A patent application is not depreciable property or property subject to the allowance of depreciation. Proceeds of the sale of a patent application are entitled to capital gains treatment. A patent application for which a notice of allowance has been received has sufficiently matured so as to be property subject to depreciation and taxable as ordinary income. *Davis v. Commissioner of Internal Revenue,* 491 F.2d 709, 181 U.S.P.Q. 552 (6th Cir. 1974).

ᴔ

For income tax purposes it is not significant (in determining whether an agreement constitutes a sale of a patent) that a patent has not been issued or even applied for at the time that all substantial rights are transferred. The 1966 letter amendment (to the 1961 agreement), which provided that the granted license would become non-exclusive if minimum stated royalties were not paid, does not preclude the 1961 agreement from being a sale of the patent. Assuming the retroactive effectiveness of the amendment, this clause merely established a condition subsequent, which does not negate a sale. *Newton Insert Co. v. Commissioner of Internal Revenue,* 181 U.S.P.Q. 765, 771, 772 (U.S.T.C. 1974).

ᴔ

It is the policy of the Internal Revenue Service to tax damage awards when they are received and to diminish the actual damages by the amount of the taxes it would have been paid had plaintiff received greater profits in the years it was damaged. This would apply a double deduction for taxation, leaving plaintiff with less income than it would have had if the defendant had not injured it. *Kalman v. The Berlyn Corp.,* 914 F.2d 1473, 16 U.S.P.Q.2d 1093, 1100 (Fed. Cir. 1990).

Teach Away From.[1] *See also* **Avoid, Destroy, Disadvantage, Lead Away From.**

Inventing a method for producing an effective product, in the face of art which strongly suggests that such a method would produce unacceptable results, is the very antithesis of obviousness. *In re Rosenberger and Brandt*, 386 F.2d 1015, 156 U.S.P.Q. 24, 26 (C.C.P.A. 1967).

ϖ

The fact that the prior art contains numerous negative teachings, which would have discouraged and deterred a person having ordinary skill in the art from making the inventions of the patents in suit, is further evidence of non-obviousness. *Mobil Oil Corp. v. W. R. Grace & Co.*, 367 F. Supp. 207, 180 U.S.P.Q. 418, 452 (Conn. 1973).

ϖ

A novel chemical compound can be non-obvious to one having ordinary skill in the art notwithstanding that it may possess a known property in common with a known structurally similar compound. Where it is disclosed that the prior-art compound "cannot be regarded as useful" for the sole use disclosed, a person having ordinary skill in the art would lack the "necessary impetus" to make the claimed compound. *In re Albrecht,* 514 F.2d 1389, 185 U.S.P.Q. 585 (C.C.P.A. 1975).

ϖ

The claimed method involves doing what the reference tries to avoid. The prior art strongly suggests that such a method would produce unacceptable results. This is the very antithesis of obviousness. *In re Buehler,* 515 F.2d 1134, 185 U.S.P.Q. 781, 786, 787 (C.C.P.A. 1975).

ϖ

Where all elements of an invention were known in the prior art, but not utilized together, if the combination produces unexpected results different from the prior art, the invention may be patentable, particularly where the prior art indicates that the procedure utilized by the patent will be unproductive. *Milgo Electronics Corp. v. United Telecommunications, Inc.*, 189 U.S.P.Q. 160, 168 (Kan. 1976).

ϖ

An invention's contradicting the teachings and express expectations of the prior art has long been a criterion of patentability. *Racal-Vadic, Inc. v. Universal Data Systems*, 207 U.S.P.Q. 902, 927 (Ala. 1980).

ϖ

Proceeding contrary to the accepted wisdom of the prior art is strong evidence of nonobviousness. *W.L. Gore & Associates, Inc. v. Garlock, Inc.*, 721 F.2d 1540, 220 U.S.P.Q. 303, 312 (Fed. Cir. 1983); *In re Hedges,* 783 F.2d 1038, 228 U.S.P.Q. 685, 687 (Fed. Cir. 1986).

ϖ

---

[1] See *Arkie Lures Inc. v. Gene Larew Tackle Inc.*, 119 F.3d 953, 43 U.S.P.Q.2d 1294 (Fed. Cir. 1997).

It is impermissible within the framework of 35 U.S.C. §103 to pick and choose from any one reference only so much of it as will support a given position to the exclusion of other parts necessary to the full appreciation of what such reference fairly suggests to one skilled in the art. *Bausch & Lomb, Inc. v. Barnes-Hind/Hydrocurve, Inc.*, 796 F.2d 443, 230 U.S.P.Q. 416 (Fed. Cir. 1986).

ᵹ

At the time of the invention the art taught away from the invention. Those skilled in the art were looking to higher mass and denser materials to block sound. Mr. Gardner went in a direction different from that of others in the art, and his invention thus produced unexpected results. Unexpected results provide objective evidence of non-obviousness. *Specialty Composites v. Cabot Corp.*, 845 F.2d 981, 6 U.S.P.Q.2d 1601 (Fed. Cir. 1988).

ᵹ

As the hypothetical person of ordinary skill in the art defined by 35 U.S.C. §103 is presumed to know of all pertinent prior art, consideration must be given to prior art that would lead one away from the invention as well as that which is argued to lead toward it. *Mendenhall v. Astec Industries, Inc.*, 13 U.S.P.Q.2d 1913, 1939 (Tenn. 1988), *aff'd*, 13 U.S.P.Q.2d 1956 (Fed. Cir. 1989).

Teaching(s). *See also* **State of the Art.**

All relevant teachings of cited references must be considered in determining what they fairly teach to one having ordinary skill in the art. The relevant portions of a reference include not only those teachings which would suggest particular aspects of an invention to one having ordinary skill in the art, but also those teachings which would lead such a person away from the claimed invention. *In re Mercier*, 515 F.2d 1161, 185 U.S.P.Q. 774, 778 (C.C.P.A. 1975).

ᵹ

To combine references (A) and (B) properly to reach the conclusion that the subject matter of a patent would have been obvious, case law requires that there must be some teaching, suggestion, or inference in either reference (A) or (B), or both, or knowledge generally available that would lead one skilled in the art to combine the relevant teachings of references (A) and (B). Consideration must be given to teachings in the references that would have led one skilled in the art away from the claimed invention. A claim cannot properly be used as a blueprint for extracting individual teachings from references. *Ashland Oil, Inc. v. Delta Resins & Refractories, Inc.*, 776 F.2d 281, 227 U.S.P.Q. 657 (Fed. Cir. 1985).

ᵹ

The "evidence" showed that use of vertical heights for range finding, use of multiple elements on a site, and use of circular apertures were each known in the art, but the prior art lacked any teaching or suggestion to combine the separate features in a manner permitting use of circular apertures for simultaneous range finding and aiming. Obviousness cannot be established by combining the teachings of the prior art to produce the claimed invention, absent some teaching, suggestion, or incentive supporting the combination. *Carela v. Starlight Archery*, 804 F.2d 135, 231 U.S.P.Q. 644 (Fed. Cir. 1986).

ʊ

To combine references to reach a conclusion that claimed subject matter would have been obvious, case law requires that there must be some teaching, suggestion, or inference in either reference, or both, or knowledge generally available that would have led one of ordinary skill in the art to combine the relevant teachings of the references. When the incentive to combine the teachings of the references is not readily apparent, it is the duty of the Examiner to explain why a combination of the reference teachings is proper. Absent such reasons or incentives, the teachings of the references are not combinable. *Ex parte Skinner*, 2 U.S.P.Q.2d 1788 (B.P.A.I. 1986).

ʊ

Although each of the references does teach in general what the Examiner asserts it teaches, the rejection under 35 U.S.C. §103 fails because there is no concept in any of the art relied upon, either express or implied, of providing a composition that includes both interferon and a tyrosinase inhibitor. None of the art teaches increasing the effectiveness of interferon. None of the art teaches inhibiting the patient's serum tyrosinase as it increases concomitantly with interferon treatment. *Ex parte Rubin*, 5 U.S.P.Q.2d 1461 (B.P.A.I. 1987).

ʊ

A proper combination of references requires the presence of a teaching or suggestion in any of the references, or in the prior art as a whole, that would lead one of ordinary skill in the art to make the combination. The mere fact that a device or process utilizes a known scientific principle does not alone make that device or process obvious. *Uniroyal Inc. v. Rudkin-Wiley Corp.*, 837 F.2d 1044, 5 U.S.P.Q.2d 1434 (Fed. Cir. 1988).

ʊ

When the PTO asserts that there is an explicit or implicit teaching or suggestion in the prior art, it must indicate where such a teaching or suggestion appears in a reference. *In re Rijckaert*, 9 F.3d 1531, 28 U.S.P.Q.2d 1955, 1957 (Fed. Cir. 1993).

Technical Block. *See* **Block.**

Technical Rejection. *See* **Formal Rejection.**

Technological Block.

The fact that there was a technological block in the practical implementation of a concept that those skilled in the art had failed to eliminate is strongly supportive of the concept of lack of obviousness. *Kaiser Industries Corp. v. Jones & Laughlin Steel Corp.*, 181 U.S.P.Q. 193 (Pa. 1974).

Temperature.

Under some circumstances, changes in temperature, in concentration, or in both, may impart patentability to a process if the particular ranges claimed produce a new and unexpected result that is different in kind and not merely in degree from the results of the prior art. Such ranges are termed "critical" ranges, and the applicant has the burden of proving such criticality. Where the general conditions of a claim are disclosed in prior art, it is not inventive merely to discover the optimum or workable ranges by routine experimentation. *In re Aller, Lacey, and Hall*, 220 F.2d 454, 105 U.S.P.Q. 233, 235 (C.C.P.A. 1955).

ω

Temperature limitations can render patentable otherwise obvious steps. The proper question is whether it would have been obvious to one of ordinary skill in the art that the particular blends could be subjected to the steps at the claimed temperatures. It is not a matter of the criticality of the recited ranges but of the obviousness of the applicability of said temperatures. *In re Schirmer*, 480 F.2d 1342, 178 U.S.P.Q. 483, 484 (C.C.P.A. 1973).

Template. *See* **Mosaic.**

Temporary Restraining Order. *See* **TRO.**

Term. *See also* **Lexicographer.**

All words in a claim must be considered in judging the patentability of that claim against the prior art. If no reasonably definite meaning can be ascribed to certain terms in a claim, the subject matter does not become obvious; the claim becomes indefinite. *In re Wilson*, 424 F.2d 1382, 165 U.S.P.Q. 494, 496 (C.C.P.A. 1970).

ω

Whether a term used in a claim is conventional is not necessarily controlling on the question of indefiniteness. *In re Mercier*, 515 F.2d 1161, 185 U.S.P.Q. 774, 780 (C.C.P.A. 1975).

ω

Each patentee may define his own terms, regardless of common or technical meaning. Fairness to any patentee requires the court to accept his definition of words, phrases, and terms. *The Magnavox Company v. Mattell, Inc.*, 216 U.S.P.Q. 28, 56 (Ill. 1982).

Terminal Disclaimer. *See also* **Provisional Disclaimer, Revival.**

When a terminal disclaimer is filed in response to a "double patenting" ground of rejection, the only concern need be a determination of whether any substantive difference exists between the subject matter of the claims on appeal and that claimed in appellant's patent or whether the only difference is in the language of the claims—whether the differences "are sham or real, semantic or actual." *In re Skrivan*, 427 F.2d 801, 166 U.S.P.Q. 85, 87 (C.C.P.A. 1970).

ω

The PTO can refuse entry of a terminal disclaimer filed subsequent to oral hearing, but before decision by the Board of Appeals. *In re Deters*, 515 F.2d 1152, 185 U.S.P.Q. 644, 648 (C.C.P.A. 1975).

ω

Refusal to accord due weight to a terminal disclaimer in a cip because a similar terminal disclaimer was not filed in the copending parent application was unwarranted. *In re Driscoll*, 562 F.2d 1245, 195 U.S.P.Q. 434, 439 (C.C.P.A. 1977).

ω

Although there was no indication either in the terminal disclaimer itself or in the simultaneously filed amendment that the terminal disclaimer was being filed "provisionally," contingent on any finding by the Board of Appeals or higher authority with respect to the Examiner's rejections under 35 U.S.C. §103, the reference in this opinion to a provisional terminal disclaimer is a clear indication by the PTO that such a document is a viable option. *Ex parte Anthony*, 230 U.S.P.Q. 467, 469 (PTO Bd. App. 1982).

ω

The entire doctrine of double patenting of the obviousness type applies to commonly owned applications with different inventive entities. A patent may still issue if an applicant faced with such a rejection files a terminal disclaimer under 35 U.S.C. §253, disclaiming any "terminal part of the term . . . of the patent," thereby guaranteeing that the second patent would expire at the same time as the first patent. It is well established that a common assignee is entitled to proceed with a terminal disclaimer to overcome a rejection based on double patenting of the obviousness type. *In re Longi*, 759 F.2d 887, 225 U.S.P.Q. 645 (Fed. Cir. 1985).

ω

After receiving a Notice of Allowance, the applicant filed a terminal disclaimer with respect to the allowed application and four other pending applications. According to the terminal disclaimer, applicant agreed that the patent issuing on the application "shall expire immediately if it ceases to be commonly owned with the patent issuing on each of the other applications." After the patent issued, Merck obtained a non-exclusive right under the patent and subsequently obtained an assignment of the patent. Merck filed a complaint with the International Trade Commission with regard to importation into the United States of a product manufactured abroad by a process that allegedly violated the assigned patent covering the process. Subsequently, the patentee assigned to Merck each of the patents issuing on the other four copending applications; the latter assignment was made on September 4, 1984, effective December 27, 1983 (the date on which the first patent was assigned to Merck). Considering the preceding circumstances, the court concluded that the Commission should not summarily have terminated the investigation. It should have permitted Merck to introduce whatever evidence it had to show the actual intent of the parties to the December 1983 Assignment Agreement in determining what interests the patentee conveyed to Merck under that agreement. *Merck & Co. v. United States International Trade Commission*, 774 F.2d 483, 227 U.S.P.Q. 779 (Fed. Cir. 1985).

ω

While a rejection for double patenting of the obviousness-type can be overcome by filing a terminal disclaimer, that does not mean that a 35 U.S.C. §103 rejection for obviousness may be similarly overcome (even if based on the same copending patent with an overlapping, but different, inventive entity). Under §103, a reference patent is available for all it fairly discloses to one of ordinary skill in the art. There is no inquiry as to what is claimed therein. In a rejection for double patenting of the obviousness type, the test is not what would be obvious to one of ordinary skill in the art from reading the specification or claims. Rather, the inquiry is much more limited in nature, and the patent is considered only to compare the invention defined in the patent claims with the invention defined in the application claims. *Ex parte Bartfeld,* 16 U.S.P.Q.2d 1714, 1717 (B.P.A.I. 1990).

ω

While the PTO does have a policy of requiring a terminal disclaimer in those situations where there has been a delay of more than six months in filing a petition to revive an application that has become abandoned [37 C.F.R. §1.316(d)], the terminal disclaimer has never been authorized or set forth in the rules as a substitute for a showing of unavoidable delay. Section 1.316(b) of 37 C.F.R. requires that a petition to accept late payment be filed promptly. A practitioner's diligence in seeking to revive an abandoned application or accept a late payment of an issue fee is considered in determining whether any delay was unavoidable. A terminal disclaimer will not be accepted as a substitute for diligent conduct. *In re Application of Takao,* 17 U.S.P.Q.2d 1155, 1159, 1160 (Comm'r Patents & Trademarks 1990).

ω

Only the claims are compared in a rejection for double patenting. Such a rejection by the PTO does not mean that the first-filed patent is a prior art reference under 35 U.S.C. §102 against the later-filed application. Thus, the "obviation" of double patenting of the obviousness-type by filing a terminal disclaimer has no effect on a rejection under 35 U.S.C. §103 based on the first-filed patent. Such a rejection cannot be overcome by a terminal disclaimer. A terminal disclaimer is of circumscribed availability and effect. It is not an admission of obviousness of the later-filed claimed invention in light of the earlier-filed disclosure, for that is not the basis of the disclaimer. The filing of a terminal disclaimer simply serves the statutory function of removing the rejection of double patenting and raises neither presumption nor estoppel on the merits of the rejection. It is improper to convert this simple expedient of "obviation" into an admission or acquiescence or estoppel on the merits. *Quad Environmental Technologies Corp. v. Union Sanitary District,* 946 F.2d 870, 20 U.S.P.Q.2d 1392, 1394, 1395 (Fed. Cir. 1991).

ω

The filing of a terminal disclaimer simply serves the statutory function of removing the rejection of double patenting, and raises neither presumption nor estoppel on the merits of the rejection. It is improper to convert this simple expedient of "obviation" into an admission or acquiescence or estoppel on the merits. *Ortho Pharmaceutical Corp. v. Smith,* 959 F.2d 936, 22 U.S.P.Q.2d 1119, 1124 (Fed. Cir. 1992).

ω

Neither delay nor intent preclude filing a terminal disclaimer to preclude or overcome obviousness-type double patenting. *Bayer AG v. Barr Laboratories Inc.,* 798 F.Supp. 196, 24 U.S.P.Q.2d 1864, 1867 (N.Y. 1992).

Termination of Proceedings.

Where rejection of all claims is affirmed by the Court of Customs and Patent Appeals, the responsibility is upon the plaintiff to stay the court's judgment if the pendency of the application is to be preserved, even though that is not necessary for Supreme Court review. *Continental Can Co. Inc. v. Schuyler, Commissioner of Patents,* 326 F. Supp. 283, 168 U.S.P.Q. 625 (D.C. 1970).

ϖ

The Commissioner lacks authority to reopen the reexamination proceeding after receipt of the Federal Circuit's mandate affirming the Examiner's rejection of all claims since the case is no longer considered pending. See MPEP §1216.06 (5th ed., rev. 12, July 1989) under "Office Procedure Following Decision by the Federal Circuit," subheading "1. All claims rejected;" *Morganroth v. Quigg,* 885 F.2d 843, 12 U.S.P.Q.2d 1125, 1128 (Fed. Cir. 1989) (Commissioner does not have authority to revive application abandoned by termination of proceedings resulting from a failure to appeal a final district court judgment); *In re Jones,* 542 F.2d 65, 191 U.S.P.Q. 249, 252 (C.C.P.A. 1976) ("receipt of the mandate by the PTO terminated proceedings in the case"); *In re Willis,* 537 F.2d 513, 190 U.S.P.Q. 327, 329 (C.C.P.A. 1976) ("When, on January 12, 1976, our mandate was received in the PTO, no claims having been allowed, the appealed application suffered its demise."); *Continental Can Co. v. Schuyler,* 326 F. Supp. 283, 168 U.S.P.Q. 625 (D.C. 1970) ("where rejection of all claims is affirmed by the Court of Customs and Patent Appeals, the responsibility is upon the plaintiff to stay the Court's judgment if the pendency of the application is to be preserved"). Petitioner's relief, if any, lies in a motion for the Federal Circuit to withdraw its mandate, not with the Commissioner. *See Jones,* 542 F.2d at 68, 191 U.S.P.Q. at 252 (C.C.P.A. "has the power, in the interest of justice, to recall its mandate in an appropriate case, and this power should be exercised sparingly and only upon a showing of good cause"). *In re Eckerle,* 1115 O.G. 6 (Comm'r Patents & Trademarks 1990).

ϖ

With regard to ex parte proceedings, "[a] civil action [under 35 U.S.C. §145] is terminated when the time to appeal the judgment expires." Consistent with 37 C.F.R. §1.197(c) as amended, if a civil action under 35 U.S.C. §146 is filed and the district court's decision is not appealed, the interference will be considered terminated as of the date that the time to appeal the decision expires. *Hunter v. Beissbarth,* 15 U.S.P.Q.2d 1343, 1344 (Comm'r Patents & Trademarks 1990).

Territory. *See* **Dividing Markets.**

Test. *See also* **Animal Tests, Bench Test, Comparative Test Data, Control, Contributing Cause, Experiment, Experimental Animals, Experimental Use, FDA, Freeman-Walter-Abele Test, Panduit Test, "Regards" Test, Testing, Test Method, Test Results, Tripartite Test.**

The "signposts" of non-obviousness include the long felt need for such a device which was not theretofore available, its fairly instant commercial success, copying by the defendants, and a new, useful and unique permutation of various prior art combined into a subject matter as a whole which was previously unobvious. When a competitor suddenly gives up his way of doing things and switches to the invention or, after poo-pooing the invention and reporting that it won't work, the defendant adopts it and uses it successfully on a large scale, the evidence thereof may be more convincing than what he says. *Maclaren v. B-I-W Group Inc.*, 401 F.Supp. 283, 187 U.S.P.Q. 345, 356 (N.Y. 1975).

ΤΩ

To satisfy the statute, there must have been a test available (to determine whether claim limitations are met) at the time of filing a patent application which could have been employed by a person skilled in the art to which a patent issuing thereon applies. While some preliminary tests may be required to apprise those skilled in the art of how to practice or avoid practicing the claimed process, a requirement for costly independent experimentation amounting to a separate research effort would not meet the statutory standard. Testing which is not necessary for determining what the patent discloses but merely to adopt a process to particular materials will not invalidate the patent. *National Research Development Corporation v. Great Lakes Carbon Corporation*, 410 F.Supp. 1108, 188 U.S.P.Q. 327, 339 (Del. 1975).

ΤΩ

Patent applicants are held to a high standard of conduct before the PTO due in part to the Office's inability to verify independently many of the representations made to it. This is particularly true when the representations pertain to the results of tests or experiments conducted by applicants. Since patent Examiners are not equipped to perform their own tests and experiments, they must rely upon the candor and good faith of the applicants in reporting such results. Some courts have been particularly vigilant in requiring patent applicants to disclose all pertinent test results, including the unfavorable as well as the favorable results. *Grefco Inc. v. Kewanee Industries, Inc.*, 499 F. Supp. 844, 208 U.S.P.Q. 218 (Del. 1980).

ΤΩ

Appellants were fully justified in testing the closest compounds actually taught (exemplified) in the reference. *Ex parte Westphal, Meiser, Eue, and Hack*, 223 U.S.P.Q. 630, 633 (PTO Bd. App. 1983).

ΤΩ

Physical samples as well as analytical tests performed thereon do not provide independent corroboration unless an independent party can testify that he observed those actual samples being made by the claimed process. Ex parte tests have little probative value in patent litigation. Opinions of experts, based in part on ex parte tests, concerning the ultimate legal issues, are accorded little weight. *Ralston Purina Company v. Far-Mar-Co, Inc.*, 586 F.Supp. 1176, 222 U.S.P.Q. 863, 892 (Kan. 1984).

ΤΩ

When expert testimony is needed in support of, or in opposition to, a preliminary motion, a party should:

1. identify the person it expects to call as an expert;
2. state the field in which the person is alleged to be an expert; and
3. state in a Declaration signed by the person: (a) the subject matter on which the person is expected to testify, (b) the facts and opinions to which the person is expected to testify, and (c) a summary of the grounds and basis for each opinion.

When a person is to be called as a fact witness, a Declaration by that person (stating the facts) should be filed. If the other party is to be called, or if evidence in the possession of the other party is necessary, an explanation of the evidence sought, what it will show, and why it is needed must be supplied. When inter partes tests are to be performed, a description of such tests (stating what they will show) must be presented. *Hanagan v. Kimura,* 16 U.S.P.Q.2d 1791, 1794 (Comm'r Patents & Trademarks 1990).

Test Animal. *See* **Experimental Animals, Standard Experimental Animal.**

Test Data.

The duty of candor extends to withholding unfavorable test data even when such data may be incomplete and even when it is subsequently shown to be irrelevant. *Imperial Chemical Industries PLC v. Barr Laboratories,* 87 Civ. 7833, 22 U.S.P.Q.2d 1906, 1910 (N.Y. 1992).

Testimony. *See also* **Discredit, Expert Testimony, Objection, Patent Attorney.**

Printed publications may properly be introduced into evidence (in an interference proceeding) during the taking of testimony relative thereto only if they are listed and served in accordance with the requirements of 37 C.F.R. §1.287(a) or a proper motion is filed under 37 C.F.R. §1.287(d)(1). *Bey and Jung v. Kollonitsch and Patchett,* 215 U.S.P.Q. 454, 456 (PTO Bd. Pat. Intf. 1981).

ϖ

An action in the district court under 35 U.S.C. §145 is a proceeding de novo and, while it is limited to the invention claimed in the PTO, the court may consider any additional competent evidence that a plaintiff neither intentionally nor negligently failed to submit to the PTO. The presumption of correctness that attaches to the decision of the Commissioner is a rebuttable presumption that may be overcome by the introduction of evidence (at a trial under §145) that is of such character and amount as to carry a thorough conviction of error. At such a trial the plaintiff and defendant may present evidence on any issue properly before the court. This additional evidence may include testimony of expert witnesses and inventors skilled in the art, and evidence of commercial success. In making its determination of non-obviousness, the court recognized the non-analogous nature of one reference, the lack of teaching or suggestion in the prior art of the useful advantage of a flexible track incapable of self-support, and the commercial success of the highly flexible Hot Wheels trackway-toy vehicle combination covered by the plaintiff's Reissue Application. The fact that the claimed invention seemed simple and, when viewed in hindsight, appeared to be obvious was not enough to negate invention. *Lemelson v. Mossinghoff,* 225 U.S.P.Q. 1063 (D.C. 1985).

ϖ

Although claim interpretation is a question of law, expert testimony is admissible to give an opinion on the ultimate question of infringement. *Symbol Technologies Inc. v. Opticon Inc.,* 935 F.2d 1569, 19 U.S.P.Q.2d 1241, 1245 (Fed. Cir. 1991).

Testing. *See also* **Experimentation, Screening, Reduction to Practice, Test Data, Test Results.**

Claims to a method of testing beverages through human sensory reactions were held not to constitute a "new and useful art, machine, manufacture, composition of matter, or any new and useful improvements thereof", within the meaning of section 4886 of the Revised Statutes. *Joseph E. Seagram & Sons, Inc. v. Marzall*, 180 F.2d 26, 84 U.S.P.Q. 180, 181 (CA D.C. 1950).

ω

Although tests under actual conditions of use are not necessarily a requirement for reduction to practice, the tests must prove that the invention will perform satisfactorily in the intended functional setting. *Knowles v. Tibbetts*, 347 F.2d 591, 146 U.S.P.Q. 59, 61 (C.C.P.A. 1965).

ω

That which determines whether a mental formulation of an invention rises to the level of conception is whether or not the inventor has also conceived means of putting that formulation in the hands of the public (where no more than routine skill would be required to do so). Conception of NTL as an antidepressant is sufficient to complete the conception of utility because nothing beyond the exercise of routine skill would have been required to demonstrate that it had this activity. Although the testing done was not sufficient to establish an actual reduction to practice, the policy of conducting such testing is to be applauded rather than penalized. *Rey-Bellet and Spiegelberg v. Engelhardt v. Schindler,* 493 F.2d 1380, 181 U.S.P.Q. 453, 457, 458 (C.C.P.A. 1974).

ω

Even though the ultimate purpose of the subject compounds is the treatment of human beings, successful testing and use in standard laboratory animals is adequate for a reduction to practice. *Hughes and Smith v. Windholz, Patchett, and Fried*, 184 U.S.P.Q. 753, 757 (PO Bd. Pat. Intf. 1974).

ω

The testing of the marketability of a product may constitute an experimental use under appropriate circumstances. *Interlego A. G. v. F.A.O. Schwartz, Inc.*, 191 U.S.P.Q. 129, 133 (Ga. 1976).

ω

Although comparative test data showing an unexpected result will rebut a *prima facie* case of obviousness, the comparative testing must be between the claimed invention and the closest prior art. An "indirect showing of unexpected superiority" will also rebut a *prima facie* case of obviousness. *In re Fenn, Pless, Harris, and O'Leary*, 639 F.2d 762, 208 U.S.P.Q. 470, 472, 473 (C.C.P.A. 1981).

ω

Early filing of an application with its disclosure of novel compounds that possess significant therapeutic use is to be encouraged. Requiring specific testing of the thousands of analogs encompassed by the claims in order to satisfy the how-to-use requirement of 35 U.S.C. §112 would delay disclosure and frustrate, rather than further, the interests of the public. *In re Bundy,* 642 F.2d 430, 209 U.S.P.Q. 48, 52 (C.C.P.A. 1981).

ᚖ

A party cannot use later testing to prove an actual reduction to practice nunc pro tunc where, at the time of the use of a process to produce a product, the manufacturer either does not appreciate the product, does not realize the usefulness of the process or product, or is not satisfied that he has successfully completed the process so as to produce a product that performs its alleged function. *Ralston Purina Company v. Far-Mar-Co, Inc.,* 586 F.Supp. 1176, 222 U.S.P.Q. 863, 893 (Kan. 1984).

ᚖ

Steps, such as "computing," "determining," "cross-correlating," "comparing," "selecting," "initializing," "testing," "modifying," and "identifying," have implicitly been found to recite the solving of a mathematical algorithm. *In re Warmerdam,* 33 F.3d 1354, 31 U.S.P.Q.2d 1754, 1758 (Fed. Cir. 1994).

ᚖ

The P388 and L1210 cell lines, though technically labeled tumor models, were originally derived from lymphocytic leukemias in mice. Therefore, these cell lines represent actual specific lymphocytic tumors; these models will produce this particular disease once implanted in mice. If applicants were required to wait until an animal actually developed this specific tumor before testing the effectiveness of a compound against the tumor *in vivo*, as would be implied from the Commissioner's argument, there would be no effective way to test compounds *in vivo* on a large scale. These tumor models represent a specific disease against which the claimed compounds are alleged to be effective. *In re Brana,* 51 F.3d 1560, 34 U.S.P.Q.2d 1436, 1440 (Fed. Cir. 1995).

Test Method.

In 1970, persons of ordinary skill in the art of fabricating PTFE materials were as likely to follow the test method of ASTM D-638 or D-1708 as to follow the test method of ASTM D-882. The patent does not teach how any product produced in accordance with one of the claims should be tested to determine its matrix tensile strength. Consequently, it must be concluded that the relevant claims of the patent are too indefinite to establish that IMPRA infringed them. *W. L. Gore & Associates Inc. v. International Medical Prosthetics Research Associates Inc.,* 16 U.S.P.Q.2d 1241, 1256 (Ariz. 1990).

Test Results. *See also* Test Data.

Some courts have been particularly vigilant in requiring patent applicants to disclose all pertinent test results, including those that are unfavorable. *Grefco Inc. v. Kewanee Industries, Inc.,* 499 F. Supp. 844, 208 U.S.P.Q. 218 (Del. 1980).

ᚖ

One who submits test results to the PTO tending to show that a prior art suggestion is not universally valid has no duty to undertake testing to explore all possible applications of the prior art suggestion. *Imperial Chemical Industries, PLC v. Henkel Corporation,* 545 F.Supp. 635, 215 U.S.P.Q. 314, 330 (Del. 1982).

ᚖ

Patent applicants are entitled, and are expected, to make good-faith judgment as to what test results are pertinent and require disclosure. Applicants are obliged to present to the PTO only those test results that fairly and accurately represent the true scientific facts. *Air Products & Chemicals Inc. v. Chas. S. Tanner Co.*, 219 U.S.P.Q. 223 (S.C. 1983).

Theory. *See also* **Bursting Bubble, Chemical Theory, Legal Theory, New Theory, Scientific Principle.**

An inventor need not know the why of the scientific and technologic principles underlying an invention. *Diamond Rubber Co. v. Consolidated Rubber Tire Co.*, 220 U.S. 428, 435-36 (1911).

ϖ

An applicant need not understand the theory or scientific principle underlying his invention. *In re Isaacs and Lindenmann*, 347 F.2d 887, 146 U.S.P.Q. 193, 197 (C.C.P.A. 1965).

ϖ

The statute does not require an inventor to understand and to disclose the theory of his invention. *Tapco Products Co. v. Van Mark Products Corp.*, 446 F.2d 420, 170 U.S.P.Q. 550 (6th Cir. 1971).

ϖ

By disclosing a device that inherently performs a function, operates according to a theory, or has an advantage, a patent applicant necessarily discloses that function, theory, or advantage even though he says nothing concerning it. The application may be later amended to recite the function, theory, or advantage without introducing prohibited new matter. *In re Smythe and Shamos*, 480 F.2d 1376, 178 U.S.P.Q. 279 (C.C.P.A. 1973).

ϖ

There is no requirement that a patentee know the specific chemical explanations for how his invention works. *Armstrong Cork Company v. Congoleum Industries, Inc.*, 399 F.Supp. 1141, 188 U.S.P.Q. 679, 688 (Pa. 1975)

ϖ

"But where a patent discloses means by which a novel and successful result is secured, it is immaterial whether the patentee understands or correctly states the theory or philosophical principles of the mechanism which produces the new result." *CTS Corporation v. Electro Materials Corp. of America*, 469 F.Supp. 801, 202 U.S.P.Q. 22, 41 (N.Y. 1979).

ϖ

A patent application which discloses a device that inherently performs a function, operates according to a theory, or has an advantage, necessarily discloses that function, theory or advantage even though it says nothing concerning it. *In re Lange*, 644 F.2d 856, 209 U.S.P.Q. 288, 295 (C.C.P.A. 1981).

ϖ

Theory

An inventor is not required to understand the theory of how his invention works, so long as his patent adequately discloses to a person of ordinary skill in the art how to make and use the invention. A patentee is not responsible for the correctness of his theories and explanations when their correctness is not related to the validity of claims under consideration. In other words, an inventor is entitled to the merits of his invention, even when they surpass his expectations or go beyond what was known or commercially available at the time of the invention. *Micro Motion Inc. v. Exac Corp.*, 741 F. Supp. 1426, 16 U.S.P.Q.2d 1001, 1013, 1014 (Cal. 1990).

Therapeutic. *See* **Pharmaceutical.**

Therapeutic Value.

Therapeutic value, not chemical composition, is the substance of all incentive to invent in the field of drug patents. Except where the state of the medical art and the state of the chemical art have been advanced and coordinated to the point that it is possible for the mind to conceive or predict (with some minimal reliability) a correlation between chemical analogues, homologues or isomers and their therapeutic value, novelty, usefulness and nonobviousness inhere in the true discovery that a chemical compound exhibits a new needed medicinal capability, even though it be closely related in structure to a known or patented drug. *Eli Lilly and Company, Inc. v. Generix Drug Sales, Inc.*, 460 F.2d 1096, 174 U.S.P.Q. 65, 69 (5th Cir. 1972).

Thesis. *See also* **Doctoral Thesis.**

A typewritten thesis, lodged in a college library, is a printed publication within the meaning of 35 U.S.C. §102(b). *Indiana General Corporation v. Lockheed Aircraft Corporation*, 249 F.Supp. 809, 148 U.S.P.Q. 312, 316 (Cal. 1966).

ʊ

Accessibility to appellant's thesis by the three members of the graduate committee and appellant's thesis defense before the graduate committee in its official capacity as arbiter of appellant's entitlement to a master's degree were not transmuted into a patent-defeating publication merely by depositing the thesis in the university library where it remained uncatalogued and unshelved as of the critical date in question. *In re Bayer*, 568 F.2d 1357, 196 U.S.P.Q. 670, 674, 675 (C.C.P.A. 1978).

ʊ

Student theses, which were not accessible to the public because they had not been either cataloged or indexed in a meaningful way, do not qualify as printed publications. Although the titles of these theses were listed on three out of 450 cards filed alphabetically by author in a shoebox in the chemistry department library, such "availability" was not sufficient to make them reasonably accessible to the public. Here, the only research aid was the student's name, which, of course, has no relationship to the subject of the student's thesis. *In re Cronyn*, 890 F.2d 1158, 13 U.S.P.Q.2d 1070, 1071 (Fed. Cir. 1989).

ʊ

The legal standard for materiality is "whether there is a substantial likelihood that a reasonable Examiner would have considered the omitted reference or false information important in deciding whether to allow the application to issue as a patent." Since the inquiry is directed to what a reasonable Examiner would have considered important, the fact that a particular thesis is not a prior-art reference is insignificant if a reasonable Examiner would have considered the thesis "important information" in his decision to allow the application to issue as a patent. *American Standard Inc. v. Pfizer Inc.*, 722 F. Supp. 86, 14 U.S.P.Q.2d 1673, 1720 (Del. 1989).

Third Party.

The equitable rights of a third party (the United States) cannot be raised as a defense to a claim of patent infringement. *The Narda Microwave Corporation v. General Microwave Corporation*, 201 U.S.P.Q. 231, 232 (N.Y. 1978).

Third Party Inventorship. *See* Derivation.

Thorough Conviction of Error.

An action in the district court under 35 U.S.C. §145 is a proceeding de novo and, while it is limited to the invention claimed in the PTO, the court may consider any additional competent evidence that a plaintiff neither intentionally nor negligently failed to submit to the PTO. The presumption of correctness that attaches to the decision of the Commissioner is a rebuttable presumption that may be overcome by the introduction of evidence (at a trial under §145) that is of such character and amount as to carry a thorough conviction of error. At such a trial the plaintiff and defendant may present evidence on any issue properly before the court. This additional evidence may include testimony of expert witnesses and inventors skilled in the art, and evidence of commercial success. In making its determination of non-obviousness, the court recognized the non-analogous nature of one reference, the lack of teaching or suggestion in the prior art of the useful advantage of a flexible track incapable of self-support, and the commercial success of the highly flexible Hot Wheels trackway-toy vehicle combination covered by the plaintiff's Reissue Application. The fact that the claimed invention seemed simple and, when viewed in hindsight, appeared to be obvious was not enough to negate invention. *Lemelson v. Mossinghoff*, 225 U.S.P.Q. 1063 (D.C. 1985).

Threat. *See* Declaratory Judgment.

Threatened Infringement.

It is well settled that threatened [patent] infringement affords ground for relief. *Smeeth v. Fox Copper & Bronze Co.*, 130 F. 455 (3d Cir. 1904).

ϖ

A completed act of infringement is not necessary to afford ground of relief in an action for contributory infringement; threatened infringement is sufficient. *Graham Paper*

Company v. International Paper Company, 46 F.2d 881, 8 U.S.P.Q. 463, 468 (8th Cir. 1931).

ω

It is well settled that a court will enjoin a threatened infringement. *Leavitt v. The McBee Company*, 124 F.2d 938, 52 U.S.P.Q. 193, 196 (1st Cir. 1942).

ω

Section 271 (35 U.S.C.) provides no relief for threatened patent infringement. [But see 35 U.S.C. §283.] *Eli Lilly and Co. v. Medtronic Inc.*, 915 F.2d 670, 16 U.S.P.Q.2d 2020, 2024 (Fed. Cir. 1990).

Three-Pronged Analysis. *See also* Tripartite Test.

Under the three-pronged analysis infringement under the doctrine of equivalents depends on whether the accused device performs substantially the same function in substantially the same way to achieve the same result. *ZMI Corp. v. Cardiac Resuscitator Corp.*, 844 F.2d 1576, 6 U.S.P.Q.2d 1557, 1563 (Fed. Cir. 1988).

Thuau Doctrine.

A claim to an old composition is not imparted with novelty by recitation therein of a new use of the composition. *In re Thuau*, 135 F.2d 344, 57 U.S.P.Q. 324, 325 (C.C.P.A. 1943).

Tie. *See also* Date, Same Date, Tying Arrangement.

In an interference between two parties who rely on the same date of corresponding foreign filings under the International Convention, neither is entitled to an award of priority. However, prior introduction of conception with regard to one count can be relied upon for priority purposes. *Lassman v. Brossi, Gerecke, and Kyburz*, 159 U.S.P.Q. 182, 184, 185 (PO Bd. Pat. Intf. 1967); see also *Wood v. Eames*, 1880 C.D. 106, 17 O.G. 512 (Comm'r Pat. 1880).

ω

Simultaneous invention is "some evidence, cumulative to be sure" of the impact of the prior art on those of ordinary skill in the art. However, it is not conclusive on the issue of obviousness. *United States of America v. Ciba-Geigy Corporation*, 508 F. Supp. 1157, 211 U.S.P.Q. 529, 540 (N.J. 1979).

ω

In the event of a tie in an interference proceeding, priority must be awarded to the senior party. *Oka v. Youssefyeh*, 849 F.2d 581, 7 U.S.P.Q.2d 1169 (Fed. Cir. 1988).

Tie-in. *See* Tying Arrangement.

Time. *See also* Date, Delay, Diligence, Laches.

A reference article, published two and one half years after appellants' filing date was properly used to show that appellants' claims were unduly broad. *In re Rainer, Redding,*

Hitov, Sloan, and Stewart, 305 F.2d 505, 134 U.S.P.Q. 343, 345 n.1 (C.C.P.A. 1962). *But see* Symmetry in the Law.

ω

The length of time a problem has existed is relevant to whether a solution to it is obvious. *Goodyear Tire and Rubber Company v. Ladd*, 349 F.2d 710, 146 U.S.P.Q. 93, 95 n.2 (CA D.C. 1965).

ω

If the experts knew of the prior art and of the problem for some 20 years and yet the method of the subject patent was not used or thought of, it is difficult to say as a matter of law that such method was no invention, but "obvious." *Associated Pipe & Fitting Company, Inc. v. Belgian Line, Inc.*, 247 F.Supp. 757, 147 U.S.P.Q. 307, 309 (N.Y. 1965).

ω

As 72 years elapsed between issuance of the Harmel patent in 1885 and the Varga invention in 1957, and no one prior to Varga had actually applied the Harmel burr crushers to the fine cotton processing system, the long lapse of time is itself indicative that it was unobvious to transplant these Harmel burr crushers, or the principle of their operation, from one fiber system to another. *Abington Textile Machinery Works v. Carding Specialists (Canada) Limited*, 249 F.Supp. 823, 148 U.S.P.Q. 33, 39, 40 (D.C. 1965).

ω

Relevant aerator nozzles were available for 13 years before the primary reference cooler, a very commonplace consumer item, was patented. Under the circumstances it was significant that Adams was the first to suggest the use of aerated streams in a water spray cooler for cans or other rounded objects. *In re Adams*, 356 F.2d 998, 148 U.S.P.Q. 742, 745 (C.C.P.A. 1966).

ω

The lapse of 45 years between the publication of one reference patent in 1906 and the making of the subject invention further indicates that it was not obvious to one skilled in the art to combine that reference with a patent issued in 1899. *Eastern Rotorcraft Corp. v. United States*, 150 U.S.P.Q. 124, 127 (U.S. Ct. Cl. 1966).

ω

Prosecution history is especially important when an invention involves a crowded art field, or when there is particular prior art over which an applicant is trying to distinguish. As applicant spent over a decade convincing the PTO that its invention was different from the prior art, the Court placed great weight on the prosecution history in determining the meaning and scope of the patent claims. *Fairfax Dental (Ireland) Ltd. v. Sterling Optical Corp.*, 808 F.Supp. 326, 26 U.S.P.Q.2d 1442, 1449 (N.Y. 1992).

ω

"Adverbs of time—as where, there, after, from, &c.—in a devise of a remainder, are construed to relate merely to the time of the enjoyment of the estate, and not the time of the vesting in interest." *Heidelberg Harris Inc. v. Loebach*, 145 F.3d 1454, 46 U.S.P.Q.2d 1948, 1951 (Fed. Cir. 1998).

Time Bar. *See* **Statute of Limitations.**

Tissue Culture.

Tissue cultures are not "plants" within the purview of 35 U.S.C. §161. *Ex parte Hibberd*, 227 U.S.P.Q. 443, 447 (B.P.A.I. 1985).

Title.

A patent's title is an interpretative aid. *Exxon Chemical Patents Inc. v. Lubrizol Corp.*, 64 F.3d 1553, 35 U.S.P.Q.2d 1801, 1804 (Fed. Cir. 1995).

Together.

Since appellants failed to argue the separate patentability of claims 1 to 3 and 20 or that of other claims which depend, explicitly or effectively, from independent claim 20, all contested claims stand or fall together. *In re Van Geuns*, 988 F.2d 1181, 1186, 26 U.S.P.Q.2d 1057, 1060 (Fed. Cir. 1993); *In re King*, 801 F.2d 1324, 1325, 231 U.S.P.Q. 136, 137 (Fed. Cir. 1986).

Tort. *See also* **Corporate Officer, Pending.**

Even though the Japanese corporation defendant has no business contacts with Virginia, personal service may be effected under the tortious conduct provisions of the long-arm statute, since patent infringement is a tort and tortious injury occurred in this state, if the act of infringing also occurred within Virginia. *Marston v. L.E. Gant, Ltd.*, 351 F.Supp. 1122, 176 U.S.P.Q. 180, 182 (Va. 1972).

ᴡ

Infringement is a tort, and officers of a corporation are personally liable for tortious conduct of the corporation if they personally took part in the commission of the tort or specifically directed other officers, agents, or employees of the corporation to commit the tortious act. *Symbol Technologies Inc. v. Metrologic Instruments Inc.*, 771 F.Supp. 1390, 21 U.S.P.Q.2d 1481, 1491 (N.J. 1991).

ᴡ

Patent infringement is a tort. Its injury occurs in the state where the patentee resides if an infringing article is sold there. *Hupp v. Siroflex of America Inc.*, 848 F.Supp. 744, 32 U.S.P.Q.2d 1842 (Tex. 1994).

Tortious Interference.

To prove a claim of tortious interference, plaintiffs must show that defendant, "by fraud or intimidation, procur[ed] the breach of a contract that would have continued but for such wrongful interference." Interference with contract and interference with prospective economic advantage are state causes of action. When the subject matter of the contract interfered with is a patent or the prospective economic advantage relates to a patent, questions of patent law will often arise in the controversy. But that fact does not make the action one arising under the patent laws. *McArdle v. Bornhofft*, 980 F.Supp. 68, 44 U.S.P.Q.2d 1470, 1472 (Maine 1997).

ᴚ

Determination of the propriety of actions in giving notice of patent rights is governed by federal statute and precedent and is not a matter of state tort law. "[F]ederal patent law bars the imposition of liability for publicizing a patent in the marketplace unless the plaintiff can show that the patent holder acted in bad faith." *Mikohn Gaming Corp. v. Acres Gaming Inc.*, U.S.P.Q.2d 1308, 1311, (Fed. Cir. 1998).

Totality of Circumstances.

Willfulness of infringement is a question of fact to be determined by looking at the "totality of the circumstances." Such may include proceedings in foreign courts with regard to corresponding patents for the same invention. *Corning Glass Works v. Sumitomo Electric U.S.A. Inc.*, 671 F. Supp. 1369, 5 U.S.P.Q.2d 1545 (N.Y. 1987).

Trade Dress.

Trade dress protection is not, as a matter of law, unavailable to products for which design patents have expired. *Hubbell Inc. v. Pass & Seymour Inc.*, 883 F.Supp. 955, 35 U.S.P.Q.2d 1760, 1762 (N.Y. 1995).

ᴚ

Granting trade dress protection to an item for which a patent has expired creates tension because the product may have obtained secondary meaning or inherent distinctiveness precisely because the product was patented. If so, the trade dress protection does not have an independent basis and effectively extends the monopoly granted by the patent. This partially thwarts the patent laws' goals. Although the designer has been encouraged to disclose his or her design, the public's access remains restricted even though the patent inspired monopoly period has expired. *Winning Ways Inc. v. Holloway Sportswear Inc.*, 37 U.S.P.Q.2d 1462, 1464 (Kan. 1995).

ᴚ

Because the wall mount assembly's configuration is a significant inventive component of the '060 patent, patentee may not also seek to protect this configuration through an unfair competition claim as well as a patent claim. Product configurations which are patented as inventions may be freely marketed when the patent expires, rather than protected under two different doctrines. This is so even when the configuration is non-functional. *Mid-America Building Products Corp. v. Richwood Building Products Inc.*, 970 F.Supp. 612, 44 U.S.P.Q.2d 1207, 1210 (Mich. 1997).

Trademark. *See also* **Nonenabling, Supplier.**

A petition for a Certificate of Correction under Rule 322 (37 C.F.R. §1.322) to delete specific trademarks from an issued patent was filed by the owner of the trademarks, not the patentee. The petitioner asserted that MPEP §608.01(v) places upon the Examiner the affirmative duty of ensuring the proper use of trademarks; that prior practice has been to regard the misuse of a trademark in a patent as a mistake on the part of the Patent Office; and that a literal reading of Rule 322 and of the corresponding section of the statute would indicate that petitioner is entitled to the requested relief. The petition was granted. *In re Johnson*, 146 U.S.P.Q. 547 (Comm. Patents 1965).

ᴡ

It is no doubt true that a manufacturer may change a product under a given trademark and may even discontinue the product altogether. It is also no doubt true that in some instances, where either of these occurs, the worker skilled in the art to which a given invention pertains may not be able by himself to duplicate (or have duplicated) that precise product or prepare (or have prepared) a substitute therefor. But carrying this rationale to the extreme, it is always possible that practice of a given patented invention may become impossible because an essential material (or even apparatus) becomes unavailable due to a lack of raw materials, public disaster, or other occurrence not within the control of the patentees; and this possibility exists whether or not the "essential material" was identified in the patent only by trademark. *In re Metcalfe and Lowe*, 410 F.2d 1378, 161 U.S.P.Q. 789, 792, 793 (C.C.P.A. 1969).

ᴡ

The fact that the sole exemplification of the employed anion permeable membrane was by trademark did not preclude the patentability of process claims since anion permeable membranes in general were well known prior to applicants' effective filing date, and the selection of an appropriate membrane would have been within the ordinary skill in the art at that time. *In re Barrett, Sanchez, and Vanik*, 440 F.2d 1391, 169 U.S.P.Q. 560, 561, 562 (C.C.P.A. 1971).

ᴡ

Where an unpredictable chemical reaction is not a factor and there is no real likelihood of all, or even most, of either the specific materials disclosed being removed from the market, or the trademarks or trade names being applied to significantly different products, such as to render the disclosure nonenabling, any risk that may be present is small, and occurrence of the event of nonenablement is too remote and speculative to support a rejection under the first paragraph of 35 U.S.C. §112. *In re Coleman*, 472 F.2d 1062, 176 U.S.P.Q. 522, 524 (C.C.P.A. 1973).

ᴡ

Even though the claimed invention was disclosed as useful with a product of commerce, identified only by trademark, it is somewhat unrealistic to suggest that the specification would become nonenabling in the future by change of the manufacturer's requirements for the thus-identified product. *In re Comstock and Gilmer*, 481 F.2d 905, 178 U.S.P.Q. 616, 620 (C.C.P.A. 1973).

ᴡ

Although a trade name alone may be inappropriate in a best-mode disclosure when suitable substitutes are unavailable, here commercial substitutes were readily available in the prior art and the trade name is mere surplusage, in addition to the generic description. Contrary to the district court's conclusion, the patentee's disclosure was not an attempt to conceal its cleaning fluid formula; it disclosed the contents of the fluid as "a non-residue detergent solution," the same solution as the surgical detergent solution used in the prior art. *Randomex Inc. v. Scopus Corp.*, 849 F.2d 585, 7 U.S.P.Q.2d 1050 (Fed. Cir. 1988).

ω

A design patent indicates, presumptively, that the design is not de jure functional. The ownership of a design patent in and of itself, and without more, does not necessarily establish nonfunctionality as to trademark registrability of that same design for particular goods. *In re Witco Corp.*, 14 U.S.P.Q.2d 1557, 1559 (T.T.A.B. 1990).

ω

Particular materials (for a specific embodiment) disclosed in the specification by trademark and supplier are not necessarily insufficient to satisfy the best mode of that embodiment at the time the application was filed. There is no per se requirement to provide names for sources of materials absent evidence that the name of the source would not be known or easily available. *Wahl Instruments Inc. v. Acvious Inc.*, 950 F.2d 1575, 21 U.S.P.Q.2d 1123, 1130 (Fed. Cir. 1991).

ω

The safeguard against an impermissible extension of a patent monopoly by a trademark is the functionality doctrine: a configuration of an article cannot receive trademark registration if its purpose is to contribute functional advantages to the article or if the configuration results from functional considerations. *Thomas & Betts Corp. v. Panduit Corp.*, 138 F.3d 277, 46 U.S.P.Q.2d 1026, 1033 (7th Cir. 1998).

Trade Name. *See also* Trademark.

When an inventor makes a claimed product from a material that he can identify only by trade name, as he does not know the formula, composition, or method of manufacture, 35 U.S.C. §112 obligates him to disclose the specific supplier and trade name of this preferred material. *Chemcast Corp. v. Arco Industries Corp.*, 913 F.2d 923, 16 U.S.P.Q.2d 1033, 1038 (Fed. Cir. 1990).

Trade Reform Act.

The legislative history of the Trade Reform Act of 1974 supports the view that ITC decisions with respect to patent issues should have no claim preclusive effect in later district court litigation. "[T]he ITC takes the position that its decisions have no *res judicata* effect in [district court] litigation." *Bio-Technology General Corp. v. Genentech Inc.*, 80 F.3d 1553, 38 U.S.P.Q.2d 1321, 1329 (Fed. Cir. 1996).

Trade Secret.

To safeguard trade secrets, the Court granted a motion for In Camera Proceedings and To Seal the Record under the Court's Rule 5.13(g). *In re Sarkar*, 588 F.2d 1330, 200 U.S.P.Q. 132, 135 n.1 (C.C.P.A. 1978).

ω

When a computer program (held proprietary by maintaining its processor as a trade secret) is the only known way of practicing a patented invention of which it is an integral part, there has been a failure to disclose the best mode of practicing the invention, as well as a failure to satisfy the enablement requirements of 35 U.S.C. §112. *White Consolidated Industries, Inc. v. Vega Servo-Control, Inc.*, 214 U.S.P.Q. 796, 825 (Mich. 1982).

ʊ

There is no absolute privilege for trade secrets and similar confidential information. To resist discovery under Fed. R. Civ. P. 26(c)(7), a person must first establish that the information sought is a trade secret and then demonstrate that its disclosure might be harmful. If these requirements are met, the burden shifts to the party seeking discovery to establish that the disclosure of trade secrets is relevant and necessary to the action. The district court must balance the need for the trade secrets against the claim of injury resulting from disclosure. If proof of relevancy or need is not established, discovery should be denied. On the other hand, if relevancy and need are shown, the trade secrets should be disclosed, unless they are privileged or the subpoenas are unreasonable, oppressive, annoying, or embarrassing. *Heat & Control, Inc. v. Hector Industries, Inc.*, 785 F.2d 1017, 228 U.S.P.Q. 926 (Fed. Cir. 1986).

ʊ

A trade secret or other confidential research, development, or commercial information may be the subject of a protective order under Fed. R. Civ. P. 26(c)(7). One seeking a protective order under that rule must establish that the information sought is confidential. In support of its motion, Biomet submitted an affidavit explaining why the requested discovery contained "trade secrets and other confidential business information." To be a trade secret under Indiana law, information must be kept secret and must derive economic value from that secrecy. Biomet's affidavit specifies measures Biomet uses to keep secret the information sought and the value thereof as secrets. Having shown the information sought to be confidential, one seeking a protective order must then demonstrate that disclosure might be harmful. Courts have presumed that disclosure to a competitor is more harmful than disclosure to a noncompetitor. Where a party seeking a protective order has shown that the information sought is confidential and that its disclosure might be harmful, the burden shifts to the party seeking discovery to establish that disclosure of trade secrets and confidential information is relevant and necessary to its case. Rule 26(b)(1) allows discovery of any nonprivileged matter that is relevant to the subject matter involved in the pending action. The rule has boundaries, however. Discovery of matter not reasonably calculated to lead to the discovery of admissible evidence is outside its scope. *American Standard Inc. v. Pfizer Inc.*, 828 F.2d 734, 3 U.S.P.Q.2d 1817 (Fed. Cir. 1987).

ʊ

Regardless of whether the trade secrets were ultimately made public via the issuance of a patent or otherwise, defendant obtained the information by misappropriation and not from public disclosure or any other legitimate business means. There is no distinction between the presence of a disclosure that may destroy secrecy and the head start concept, for the former is merely an element of the latter. The award for damages compensates the plaintiff for the head start that the defendants obtained through its misappropriation. This head start amounted to a preemption of the entire market and prevented the plaintiff from licensing others, as well as making entry into the market by the plaintiff impossible. In fashioning an adequate monetary remedy, the court must consider that the defendants did not merely wrongly obtain and use plaintiff's know-how as a competitor in the marketing, they refused to return the know-how to the plaintiff when ordered to do so, thereby also completely precluding the plaintiff from manufacturing. There is no question that the defendant's conduct was grossly improper and that the plaintiff's monetary recovery should not be limited by a lead-time valuation. *The Kilbarr Corp. v. Business Systems, Inc., B.V.*, 679 F. Supp. 422, 6 U.S.P.Q.2d 1698 (N.J. 1988).

ᚹ

A corporate assignee of a patent application may be ordered to assign to the original holder of trade secrets all rights to the patent application based thereon. The courts are not powerless to redress wrongful appropriation of intellectual property by those subject to the court's jurisdiction. *Richardson v. Suzuki Motor Co., Ltd.*, 868 F.2d 1226, 9 U.S.P.Q.2d 1913 (Fed. Cir. 1989).

ᚹ

As the invention claimed in defendant's patent claim 1 constitutes a misappropriation of plaintiff's trade secret, plaintiff is entitled to have defendant's patent assigned to it. *Union Carbide Corp. v. Tarancon Corp.*, 742 F. Supp. 565, 15 U.S.P.Q.2d 1833, 1846 (Ga. 1990).

ᚹ

A trade secret may consist of any formula, pattern, device, or compilation of information that is used in one's business and that gives one an opportunity to obtain an advantage over competitors who do not know or use it. However, to constitute a trade secret, a "substantial element of secrecy must exist, to the extent that there would be difficulty in acquiring the information except by the use of improper means." "Some of the factors to be considered in determining whether given information is a trade secret are: (1) the extent to which the information is known outside the business; (2) the extent to which it is known by employees and others involved in the business; (3) the extent of measures taken by the employer to guard the secrecy of the information; (4) the value of the information to the employer and to his competitor; (5) the amount of effort and money expended by the employer in developing the information; (6) the ease or difficulty with which the information could be properly acquired or duplicated by others. Restatement, 4 Torts & 767; comment b." *Otis Elevator Co. v. Intelligence Systems Inc.*, 17 U.S.P.Q.2d 1773, 1779 (Conn. 1990).

Trade Show.

A display of a claimed invention to a limited number of buyers at a trade show (at which no purchase orders were solicited or accepted) in order to assess its marketability is not a public use. *Maclaren v. B-I-W Group Inc.*, 401 F.Supp. 283, 187 U.S.P.Q. 345, 358 (N.Y. 1975).

Trailer Clause.

Contractual provisions requiring assignment of post-employment inventions are commonly referred to as trailer or holdover clauses. Holdover clauses in employment contracts are enforceable only if they constitute a reasonable and justifiable restriction on the right of employees to work in their profession for subsequent employers. Their legitimate purpose is to prevent an employee from appropriating to his own use or to the use of a subsequent employer inventions relating to and stemming from work done for a previous employer. Holdover clauses are simply recognition of the fact of business life that employees sometimes carry with them to new employers inventions or ideas so related to work done for a former employer that, in equity and good conscience, the fruits of that work should belong to the former employer. Holdover clauses must be limited to reasonable times and to subject matter that the employee worked on or had knowledge of during his employment. Unless expressly agreed otherwise, an employer has no right (under a holdover clause) to inventions made outside the scope of the employee's former activities, and made on and with a subsequent employer's time and funds. Regarding the validity of a contractual provision requiring the employee to disclose and assign all ideas and improvements for five years following termination of employment, the court articulated a three part test: (a) Is the restraint reasonable in the sense that it is no greater than necessary to protect the employer in some legitimate interest? (b) Is the restraint reasonable in the sense that it is not unduly harsh or oppressive on the employee? (c) Is the restraint reasonable in the sense that it is not injurious to the public? *Ingersoll-Rand Co. v. Ciavatta*, 8 U.S.P.Q.2d 1537, 542 A.2d 879, 110 N.J. 609 (N.J. 1988).

Transacting Business. *See also* Business Activity.

Under a state long-arm statute, sending a letter threatening suit was held to constitute transacting business within the state. *FMC Corp. v. Hunter Engineering Co.*, 20 U.S.P.Q.2d 1077, 1078 (Ark. 1991).

ʊ

"Both federal and state courts have regularly construed the 'transacting any business' language of the statute in a generous manner." *Columbia University v. Boehringer Mannheim GmbH*, 35 U.S.P.Q.2d 1364, 1366 (Mass. 1995).

Transfer.

An attempt to transfer (by way of amendment) from a prior copending application subject matter which constitutes a species of the originally disclosed and claimed invention (including claims to that species) in order to consolidate the two disclosures into one application was precluded as involving the introduction of improper new matter. *In re Application Filed April 1, 1957*, 119 U.S.P.Q. 329 (Comm'r 1958); *but see Ex parte Janin*, 209 U.S.P.Q. 761, 764 (PTO Bd. App. 1979).

ʊ

Transfer motions in large patent cases depend far more heavily on the interest of justice than on considerations of party or witness convenience. One important consideration in determining which venue is favored by the interest of justice is the "economic and efficient utilization of judicial resources...." A second consideration in determining whether the interest of justice warrants a transfer is the effect transfer would have on the cost of litigation on the parties. Access to proof and the availability of compulsory process are the third and fourth considerations in the interest of justice calculus. *Willemijn*

Houdstermaatschaapij B. V. v. Apollo Computer Inc., 707 F. Supp. 1429, 13 U.S.P.Q.2d 1001, 1007 (Del. 1989).

ᆱ

When the first of two related actions is for a declaratory judgment and appears triggered by a notice of patent infringement letter, courts have concluded that special circumstances warrant an exception to the first-to file rule. The decision whether to transfer is left to the discretion of the court, to be exercised to secure "wise judicial administration, giving regard to conservation of judicial resources and comprehensive disposition of litigation. . . ." Particularly where an affirmative suit is about to begin, the right to a declaratory suit is weak. *Cobe Laboratories Inc. v. Baxter International Inc.*, 17 U.S.P.Q.2d 1973, 1974 (Colo. 1990).

ᆱ

The decision of a transferor court should not be reviewed again by the transferee court. Such an independent review would implicate those concerns which underlie the rule of repose and decisional order we term the law of the case. "If the motion to transfer is granted and the case is transferred to another district, the transferee-district should acccept the ruling on the transfer as the law of the case and should not re-transfer 'except under the most compelling and unusual circumstances' or if the transfer order is 'manifestly erroneous.'" *KPR Inc. v. C&F Packing Co. Inc.*, 30 U.S.P.Q.2d 1320, 1324 (Tex. 1993).

ᆱ

Transfer is appropriate under 28 U.S.C. §1404(a) where the moving party demonstrates (1) venue is proper in the transferor district, (2) venue and jurisdiction are proper in the transferee district, and (3) the transfer is for the convenience of the parties and witnesses and in the interest of justice. Though §1404(a) derives from the common law doctrine of *forum non conveniens*, the moving party under §1404(a) has a lesser burden of showing inconvenience than is required under the common law doctrine. The weight to be afforded each factor considered under §1404(a) is left to the discretion of the court. *Abbott Laboratories v. Zenith Laboratories Inc.*, 35 U.S.P.Q.2d 1161, 1162 (Ill. 1995).

ᆱ

In examining a motion to transfer venue under 28 U.S.C. §1404(a), the Court must consider the following factors: plaintiff's choice of venue, which is entitled to substantial weight; convenience of the parties and witnesses; and the interests of justice, which is intended to encompass all those factors unrelated to witness and party convenience. The interest of justice factors include such circumstances as "the pendency of a related action, the court's familiarity with applicable law, docket conditions, access to premises that might have to be viewed, the possibility of an unfair trial, the ability to join other parties, [and] the possibility of harassment." *Hester Industries Inc. v. Stein Inc.*, 40 U.S.P.Q.2d 1844 (Va. 1996).

ᆱ

Rulings under 28 U.S.C. §1404(a) generally turn on the courts evaluation of the following, relevant considerations: (1) convenience of witnesses; (2) judicial economy; (3)

relative ease of access to proof; (4) availability of compulsory process; and (5) relative docket congestion. The convenience of counsel and claims of local prejudice are usually not weighed in the balance. *Steelcase Inc. v. Haworth Inc.*, 41 U.S.P.Q.2d 1468 (Cal. 1996).

ᴛ

Consideration of the interest of justice, which includes judicial economy, "may be determinative to a particular transfer motion, even if the convenience of the parties and witnesses might call for a different result." *University of California v. Eli Lilly and Co.*, 119 F.3d 1559, 43 U.S.P.Q.2d 1398, 1403 (Fed. Cir. 1997).

ᴛ

"For the convenience of parties and witnesses, in the interest of justice, a district court may transfer any civil action to any other district or division where it might have been brought." [28 U.S.C. §1404(a)] The decision rests within the sound discretion of the transferor court. *Dunhall Pharmaceuticals Inc. v. Discus Dental Inc.*, 45 U.S.P.Q.2d 1061, 1062 (Colo. 1997).

Transitory. *See also* Stability.

Neither mere material without form nor highly fugitive articles, such as a gob of molten glass, are included by the term "manufacture." However, an article of commerce is included even when it is material in an intermediate stage of manufacture. *Ex parte Howard*, 328 O.G. 251, 1924 C.D. 75 (Asst. Comm'r 1922).

ᴛ

Claims to a product including partly cured concrete were regarded as improper because they are drawn to a product in its transitory stage instead of in its final form. *Ex parte Stubbs*, 58 F.2d 447, 13 U.S.P.Q. 358 (C.C.P.A. 1932).

ᴛ

The patentability of claims to a composition (comprising a mixture of components which, on standing or upon being heated, results in the formation of a polymer) is not precluded by 35 U.S.C. §112. *Ex parte Dubsky and Stark*, 162 U.S.P.Q. 567, 568 (PO Bd. App. 1968).

ᴛ

A "transitory intermediate" which would not and could not be readily isolated was a manufacture or composition of matter within the meaning of 35 U.S.C. §101. *In re Breslow*, 616 F.2d 516, 205 U.S.P.Q. 221, 226 (C.C.P.A. 1980).

Translation.

An error in the translator's affidavit filed with the translation of the certified German application and an error in the translation of the German Patent Office certificate noted by an interference party for the first time on appeal do not comprise the extraordinary circumstances in which the CCPA will consider issues not raised below. *Stevens v. Schmid and Kirbach*, 406 F.2d 776, 160 U.S.P.Q. 623, 624 n.2 (C.C.P.A. 1969).

ᴛ

Receipt in this country of an initial translation of an application of one of two coinventors is evidence of conception of the invention disclosed therein and (coupled with the subsequent diligent filing of an application to the sole invention) is available as prior art against another application (having an effective filing date subsequent to the noted conception, but prior to the actual filing of the sole application) of the coinventors. *Ex parte Hachiken and Ogino*, 223 U.S.P.Q. 879, 880 (PTO Bd. App. 1984).

Transposition of Parts. *See* **Reversal of Parts.**

Treble Damages.

It is not unfair or unjust to claim treble damages for infringement and other classes of money damages when, in its earlier stages, the case was directed only to a declaratory judgment and injunction. *Hoffmann-La Roche, Inc. v. Premo Pharmaceutical Laboratories, Inc.*, 210 U.S.P.Q. 374, 378 (N.J. 1980).

Trend.

A "trend" might very well constitute a suggestion or teaching to one of ordinary skill in the art to make "minor" changes from the prior art in accordance with that trend to produce a claimed invention. Whether the prior art discloses a "trend" is a question of fact. The existence of a trend depends on the content of the prior art, i.e., what the prior art would have taught one of ordinary skill in the art at the time of the invention. By defining the inventor's problem in terms of its solution, the district court missed the necessary ancillary question, namely: whether the prior art contains a suggestion or motivation to combine references *to form a trend. Monarch Knitting Machinery Corp. v. Sulzer Morat GmbH*, 139 F.3d 877, 45 U.S.P.Q.2d 1977, 1981, 1982 (Fed. Cir. 1998).

Trial. *See De Novo*, **New Trial.**

Trial by Jury. *See also* **Jury Trial.**

The Seventh Amendment provides that "[i]n Suits at common law, where the value in controvery shall exceed twenty dollars, the right of trial by jury shall be preserved..." Since Justice Story's day, we have understood that "[t]he right of trial by jury thus preserved is the right that existed under the English common law when the Amendment was adopted." In keeping with our long-standing adherence to this "historical text," we ask, first, whether we are dealing with a cause of action that either was tried at law at the time of the Founding or is at least analogous to one that was. If the action in question belongs in the law category, we then ask whether the particular trial decision must fall to the jury in order to preserve the substance of the common-law right as it existed in 1791. *Markman v. Westview Instruments Inc.*, 116 S.Ct. 1384, 38 U.S.P.Q.2d 1461, 1464, 1465 (S.Ct. 1996).

Trial *de Novo. See also De Novo*, **35 U.S.C. §145, 35 U.S.C. §146.**

The provision for further testimony in 35 U.S.C. §146 must not be read in a vacuum. The remedy provided by that section is not a full trial de novo; rather, allowance of evidence in addition to the Patent Office record must be tempered and circumscribed to some degree to effectuate the policy favoring full disclosure to administrative tribunals. *Kirschke v. Lamar*, 426 F.2d 870, 165 U.S.P.Q. 679, 682 (8th Cir. 1970).

ᛦ

A 35 U.S.C. §146 proceeding, although nominated a "trial de novo", is in reality a review of a patent proceeding by the unsuccessful party, in which courts will allow certain supplementary evidence. A presumption of regularity attaches to the decisions of the Patent Office; and evidence can only be introduced with regard to issues previously raised before the Patent Office, supported by testimony before the Patent Office, and on which the Patent Office has ruled on the merits. *Vogel v. Jones*, 346 F.Supp. 1005, 175 U.S.P.Q. 152, 153 (D.C. 1972).

ᛦ

An action in the district court under 35 U.S.C. §145 is a proceeding de novo and, while it is limited to the invention claimed in the PTO, the court may consider any additional competent evidence that a plaintiff neither intentionally nor negligently failed to submit to the PTO. The presumption of correctness that attaches to the decision of the Commissioner is a rebuttable presumption that may be overcome by the introduction of evidence (at a trial under §145) that is of such character and amount as to carry a thorough conviction of error. At such a trial the plaintiff and defendant may present evidence on any issue properly before the court. This additional evidence may include testimony of expert witnesses and inventors skilled in the art, and evidence of commercial success. In making its determination of non-obviousness, the court recognized the non-analogous nature of one reference, the lack of teaching or suggestion in the prior art of the useful advantage of a flexible track incapable of self-support, and the commercial success of the highly flexible Hot Wheels trackway-toy vehicle combination covered by the plaintiff's Reissue Application. The fact that the claimed invention seemed simple and, when viewed in hindsight, appeared to be obvious was not enough to negate invention. *Lemelson v. Mossinghoff,* 225 U.S.P.Q. 1063 (D.C. 1985).

ᛦ

Although a 35 U.S.C. §145 action has been characterized as a trial *de novo*, the policy of encouraging full disclosure to administrative tribunals has led courts to limit the admissibility of certain kinds of evidence in such actions. Thus, evidence has been excluded if it was available to the plaintiff during the PTO proceeding but was either intentionally or negligently withheld. Furthermore, new evidence may be excluded from trial if it relates to an issue that the plaintiff failed to raise before the PTO, unless the plaintiff can demonstrate that the failure to raise the issue was neither intentional nor negligent. *Holloway v. Quigg,* 9 U.S.P.Q.2d 1751 (D.C. 1988).

Tripartite Test. *See also* **Three-Pronged Analysis.**

The district court's opinion clearly delineates the Graver Tank tripartite test of substantially the same function, way, and result. *Atlas Powder Company v. E.I. Du Pont De Nemours & Company*, 750 F.2d 1569, 224 U.S.P.Q. 409, 416 (Fed. Cir. 1984).

TRO.

The movant must show that the patent is valid and infringed and that irreparable harm will result if relief is not granted. Long acquiescence in the patent's validity by the industry will satisfy that showing. *Premo Pharmaceutical Laboratories, Inc. v. USV Laboratories, Inc.*, 481 F.Supp. 193, 203 U.S.P.Q. 852 (N.Y. 1979).

ω

The substantive law of the Federal Circuit governs the issuance of a preliminary injunction, and since the issuance of a TRO is governed by the same standards, Federal Circuit law also applies to a motion for a TRO. *Cobraco Manufacturing Co. v. Valley View Specialties Co. Inc.*, 727 F. Supp. 282, 15 U.S.P.Q.2d 1072, 1073 (Ill. 1990).

Truth. *See also* **Assertion, Principle, Statement in the Specification.**

A petition was filed in response to a requirement to cancel from the specification all assertions pertaining to cancer utility. The Examiner took the position that the recitation in the specification of a broad genus (e.g., malignant tumors) without specific examples of human and animal in vivo and additional in vitro data does not meet minimum standards. Reference to utility as an antitumor agent in a warm-blooded animal afflicted by malignant tumors was not regarded by the Examiner as believable on its face to those of ordinary skill in the art in view of contemporary knowledge in the art. The Examiner does not need to provide reasons why this speculative assertion should not be believed. The mere fact that the art of cancer chemotherapy is highly unpredictable places the burden on applicants to provide a basis for believing the speculative statements that they choose to place in the specification in the form of a positive assertion. The ignorance of the PTO and the applicants in not being able to provide a scientific reason why the assertion is not sound is not a sufficient reason or justification for permitting such an assertion to be made in a patent document where those of ordinary skill in this art would not accept it as believable on its face without some data or other evidence to support it. The PTO does not want to spend the time or resources that may be necessary to provide a scientifically reasoned opinion as to why the speculative statements would not be believed by a person skilled in the art. *In re Application of Hozumi*, 226 U.S.P.Q. 353 (Comm'r Patents & Trademarks 1985).

ω

A specification that contains a disclosure of utility that corresponds in scope to the subject matter sought to be patented must be taken as sufficient to satisfy the utility requirements of 35 U.S.C. §101 for the entire claimed subject matter unless there is reason for one skilled in the art to question the objective truth of the statement of utility or its scope. *Ex parte Rubin*, 5 U.S.P.Q.2d 1461 (B.P.A.I. 1987).

Truthfulness of Specification.

There is no requirement in 35 U.S.C. §112 or anywhere else in the patent law that a specification must convince persons skilled in the art that the assertions in the specification are correct. In examining a patent application, the PTO is required to assume that the specification complies with the enablement provisions of §112 unless it has "acceptable evidence or reasoning" to suggest otherwise. The PTO must thus provide reasons supported by the record as a whole why the specification is not enabling. Then and only then does the burden shift to the applicant to show that one of ordinary skill in the art could have practiced the claimed invention without undue experimentation. A patent specification must be enabling as to "the invention" as set forth in the claims. Thus, a disclosure may be insufficient for one claim but sufficient for another. *Gould v. Mossinghoff,* 229 U.S.P.Q. 1 (D.C. 1985).

Try. *See* **Obvious to Try or Experiment.**

Tumor. *See also* **Cancer.**

The Primary Examiner objected to the words "and anti-tumour" and required either "cancellation of said term or proof that the instant compound is safe, reliable and effective for the utility set forth. . . ." Considerable evidence was adduced, which the Commissioner concedes is sufficient to support a conclusion that the compound has an anti-tumor effect in treating certain tumors. The Primary Examiner adhered to his requirement that the phrase be stricken because it was broader than the proof offered in support. The Commissioner went beyond his interpretation of the disputed words to reject amending language that would restrict the assertion to those uses supported by the proof. Such amendment would not be objectionable "new matter." "Amendments to specifications for the purpose of clarity and definiteness are permissible." *Helms Products, Inc. v. Lake Shore Manufacturing Co.,* 227 F.2d 677, 107 U.S.P.Q. 313, 314 (7th Cir. 1955). *See also Aerosol Research Co. v. Scovill Manufacturing Co.,* 334 F.2d 751, 141 U.S.P.Q. 758 (7th Cir. 1964). Cancellation of the words "and anti-tumour" by the Patent Office was arbitrary and capricious. The cancellation requirement is set aside with leave to the Commissioner to allow an amendment restricting the specification to assertions that are supported by applicants' proof. *Rhone Poulenc S.A. v. Dann,* 507 F.2d 261, 184 U.S.P.Q. 196 (4th Cir. 1974).

Tumor Models.

The P388 and L1210 cell lines, though technically labeled tumor models, were originally derived from lymphocytic leukemias in mice. Therefore, these cell lines represent actual specific lymphocytic tumors; these models will produce this particular disease once implanted in mice. If applicants were required to wait until an animal actually developed this specific tumor before testing the effectiveness of a compound against the tumor *in vivo,* as would be implied from the Commissioner's argument, there would be no effective way to test compounds *in vivo* on a large scale. These tumor models represent a specific disease against which the claimed compounds are alleged to be effective. *In re Brana,* 51 F.3d 1560, 34 U.S.P.Q.2d 1436, 1440 (Fed. Cir. 1995).

Two-Supplier Market.

While there may be competing devices available in the marketplace, the mere existence of a competing device does not make that device an acceptable substitute. A product lacking the advantages of a patented device can hardly be termed a substitute acceptable to the customer who wants those advantages. *Kalman v. The Berlyn Corp.*, 914 F.2d 1473, 16 U.S.P.Q.2d 1093, 1102 (Fed. Cir. 1990).

Two-Way Test.

The court in *Braat* [937 F.2d 589, 594, 19 U.S.P.Q.2d 1289, 1292 (Fed. Cir. 1991)] emphasized the more typical scenario in which, despite common inventive entities, the two-way test applied: "when a *later-filed improvement* patent issues before an *earlier filed basic* invention"; *accord Borah*, 345 F.2d 1009, 148 U.S.P.Q. 213, 214 (CCPA 1966) (allowing the earlier filed but later allowed basic patent application to issue without a terminal disclaimer because the two applications could not have been filed as one since the improvements were not made until after the application on the basic invention was filed). The two-way exception can only apply when the applicant could not avoid separate filings, and even then, only if the PTO controlled the rates of prosecution to cause the later filed species claims to issue before the claims for a genus in an earlier application. *In re Berg*, 140 F.3d 1428, 46 U.S.P.Q.2d 1226, 1230, 1232 (Fed. Cir. 1998).

Tying Arrangement. *See also* **Misuse, 35 U.S.C. §271(d).**

Although defendant was coerced into taking a license under a patent and the license covered unpatented, as well as patented, goods, there was no patent misuse in view of the fact that plaintiff had a policy of making available to manufacturers licenses under the patent which covered only patented goods, albeit at a higher rate. *The Plastic Contact Lens Company v. Young Contact Lens Laboratories, Inc.*, 175 U.S.P.Q. 573, 574 (Mass. 1972).

ᛟ

A patented process cannot be used to "tie" sales of an unpatented staple commodity (having substantial non-infringing use) used in the process. Sales of the staple commodity accompanied by an implied (can label) license to practice the patented process constitutes a non de minimus tying arrangement in violation of 1 of the Sherman Act and constitutes patent misuse, making the patent unenforceable. *Rex Chainbelt Inc. v. Harco Products, Inc.*, 512 F.2d 993, 185 U.S.P.Q. 10 (9th Cir. 1975).

ᛟ

The doctrine of patent misuse is an equitable concept designed to prevent a patent owner from improperly extending or enhancing the "physical or temporal scope" of a patent grant with the effect of restraining competition. However, in application, a finding of patent misuse has been confined to a few specific practices by patent holders, such as fixing the price at which a purchaser of a patented item could resell it, requiring a licensee to pay royalties beyond the expiration of the patent grant, and requiring a licensee to refrain from manufacturing items that would compete with the patented item. The most common application of the doctrine occurs when the sale of an unpatented staple item is "tied" to the sale of a patented device. Every use of a patent as a means of obtaining a limited monopoly of unpatented material is prohibited. *N.L. Chemicals Inc. v. United Catalysts Inc.*, 11 U.S.P.Q.2d 1239, 1240 (Ky. 1989).

ᛟ

Tying Arrangement

Three elements constitute a tying claim: (1) purchases of the tying product must be conditioned on purchases of a distinct tied product; (2) the actor must possess sufficient power in the tying market to compel acceptance of the tied product; and (3) the arrangement must foreclose to competitors of the tied product a substantial volume of commerce. *BEAL Corp. Liquidating Trust v. Valleylab Inc.*, 40 U.S.P.Q.2d 1072, 1082 (Colo. 1996)

Type.

The term, "type," in "ZSM-5-type aluminosilicate zeolites" was held to be indefinite under 35 U.S.C. §112, second paragraph, notwithstanding the fact that the zeolites have been defined in various patents and claimed with the terminology "ZSM...type." *Ex parte Attig*, 7 U.S.P.Q.2d 1092, 1093 (B.P.A.I. 1986).

Typographical Error.

When the identification of a compound in a reference is in error and would be so recognized by any artisan, it cannot be said that one of ordinary skill in the relevant art would do anything more than mentally disregard it as a misprint. Obvious typographical errors do not convey any teaching whatsoever with regard to an erroneously-depicted compound irrespective of one's ability to produce such a compound. *In re Yale*, 434 F.2d 666, 168 U.S.P.Q. 46, 48, 49 (C.C.P.A. 1970).

Key Terms and Concepts

U

Unavoidable.

In terms of applying 35 U.S.C. §41(c)(1) and determining whether or not a failure has been "unavoidable", determinations by the PTO must be accorded a large degree of discretion. The principle purpose behind 35 U.S.C. §41(b) and (c)(1) was that Congress desired that patent holders help to finance the operation of the PTO by paying maintenance fees. The only indication of third party rights with regard to determinations made under 35 U.S.C. §41(c)(1) is explicitly contained in §41(c)(2), which section allows a court to fashion terms equitably to protect any investments made or business commenced by a third party after the six-month grace period expires, but before reinstatement of a patent under §41(c)(1). *Laerdall Medical Corp. v. Ambu Inc.*, 877 F.Supp. 255, 34 U.S.P.Q.2d 1140, 1143, 1144 (Md. 1995).

Unavoidable Delay. *See also* **Revival.**

The preoccupation of plaintiff's attorney with other legal matters or with moving his residence does not relieve him of the burden of complying with Patent Office regulations. Plaintiff's delay due to inadvertence or mistake does not constitute "unavoidable" delay under 35 U.S.C. §133. Further, plaintiff-inventor is "bound by the acts" of his lawyer-agent since he voluntarily chose him as his representative and cannot avoid the consequences of his acts or omissions. *Smith v. Diamond*, 209 U.S.P.Q. 1091, 1093 (D.C. 1981).

Unbelievable. *See also* **Inconceivable.**

The application stood in condition for allowance and ready for the issuance of a patent grant except for the presence in the specification disclosure of certain asserted utilities that the Examiner believed to be too speculative—i.e., not believable on their face to those of ordinary skill in the art in view of the contemporary knowledge of the art. While it may be clear that workers in this art had shown that some cancers can be treated successfully in some patients, the effective treatment of various forms of malignant tumors remains a highly unpredictable art. Under these circumstances, the Examiner does not need to provide reasons why this speculative assertion should not be believed. The mere fact that the art of cancer chemotherapy is highly unpredictable places the burden on applicants to provide a basis for believing the speculative statements that they chose to place in the specification in the form of a positive assertion. *In re Application of Hozumi*, 226 U.S.P.Q. 353 (Comm'r Patents & Trademarks 1985).

ত

Amelioration of the symptoms or even cure of cancer is no longer considered to be "incredible." Nonetheless, decisional law would seem to indicate that the utility in question is sufficiently unusual to justify an Examiner's requiring substantiating evidence. Substantiating evidence may be in the form of animal tests that constitute recognized screening procedures with clear relevance to utility in humans. The specification of the appellant's parent application sets forth several animal tests on numerous types of specific cancers as well as in vitro studies, both of which are asserted to be predictive with regard to utility in humans. The Examiner has not challenged the evidence presented in any relevant material respect. There is only the blanket statement of lack of "patentable utility" per se. In fact, the only specific comments the Examiner has directed toward the appellant's evidence are with regard to the breadth of the types of tumor against which the claimed compounds have been shown to be active. The appealed claims are drawn to compounds and not to a method of treatment. Generally speaking, utility in treating a single disease is adequate basis for the patentability of a pharmaceutical compound under 35 U.S.C. §101. *Ex parte Krepelka,* 231 U.S.P.Q. 746 (B.P.A.I. 1986).

ω

The "contemporary knowledge in the art" has far advanced since the days when any statement of utility in treating cancer was per se "incredible." The medical treatment of a specific cancer is not such an inherently unbelievable undertaking and does not involve such implausible scientific principles as to be considered incredible. *Ex parte Rubin,* 5 U.S.P.Q.2d 1461 (B.P.A.I. 1987).

ω

Only after the PTO provides evidence showing that one of ordinary skill in the art would reasonably doubt the asserted utility does the burden shift to the applicant to provide rebuttal evidence sufficient to convince such a person of the invention's asserted utility. The purpose of treating cancer with chemical compounds does not suggest an inherently unbelievable undertaking or involve implausible scientific principles. *In re Brana,* 51 F.3d 1560, 34 U.S.P.Q.2d 1436, 1441 (Fed. Cir. 1995).

Unchallenged. *See* **Challenge.**

Uncited References. *See* **Search Record.**

Unclaimed Disclosure. *See also* **Disclosure without Claiming.**

A patentee may so state his claims (which measure the scope of his monopoly) as to include only a portion of his disclosed invention and abandon the remainder to the public. *Helene Curtis Industries, Inc. v. Sales Affiliates, Inc.,* 233 F.2d 148, 109 U.S.P.Q. 159, 163 (2d Cir. 1956).

ω

The holding in *Maxwell v. J. Baker Inc.,* 86 F.3d 1098, 39 U.S.P.Q.2d 1001 (Fed. Cir. 1996), does not foreclose, as a matter of law, application of the doctrine of equivalents to encompass disclosed, but unclaimed, subject matter. *YBM Magnex Inc. v. International Trade Commission,* 145 F.3d 1317, 46 U.S.P.Q.2d 1843, 1845, 1847 (Fed. Cir. 1998).

Unclean Hands. *See also* **Fraud.**

Courts of equity do not make quality of suitors a test; they apply the maxim requiring clean hands only where some unconscionable act of one coming for relief has immediate and necessary relation to the equity that he seeks in respect of the matter in litigation. *Consolidated Aluminum Corp. v. Foseco International Ltd.*, 910 F.2d 804, 15 U.S.P.Q.2d 1481, 1485 (Fed. Cir. 1990).

ω

A letter terrorizing the trade by threatening retailers and competitors is not grounds for an affirmative defense of unclean hands in an action where the issues are infringement and priority of invention. The defense of unclean hands does not close the courthouse door to plaintiffs simply because they have behaved improperly, or even unlawfully. For the maxim that equity helps only those with clean hands to apply, a plaintiff's misconduct must be "unconscionable" and have some immediate necessary relationship to the equity he seeks. In a patent case, the misconduct should "bear upon the validity of the patent or defendant's infringement of the patent for the unclean hands defense to be available." *National Presto Industries Inc. v. Black & Decker (U.S.) Inc.*, 760 F. Supp. 699, 19 U.S.P.Q.2d 1457, 1459 (Ill. 1991).

ω

A defendant with unclean hands cannot raise a misuse defense against plaintiff's infringement claims. *A.C. Aukerman Co. v. R.L. Chaides Construction Co.*, 29 U.S.P.Q.2d 1054, 1059 (Cal. 1993).

Unconscionable. *See* **Willful Infringement.**

Uncontradicted. *See* **Challenge**

Under. *See* **Up To.**

Underclaiming. *See* **Limiting.**

Undisclosed Patent. *See also* **Classification.**

The fact that an Examiner does not cite certain prior patents does not establish that he did not consider them. When there is no evidence that the Examiner was aware of the most pertinent prior art, his failure to cite relevant undisclosed patents leads to an inference that he was unaware of them. *CMI Corporation v. Barber-Greene Company*, 683 F.2d 1061, 217 U.S.P.Q. 456, 458 n.2 (7th Cir. 1982).

Undisclosed Property.

When patentability is predicated on an unexpected result, such result must be disclosed in the specification. *In re Stewart*, 222 F.2d 747, 106 U.S.P.Q. 115, 121 (C.C.P.A. 1955); but *see In re Zenitz*, 333 F.2d 924, 142 U.S.P.Q. 158, 161 (C.C.P.A. 1964).

Undisclosed Subject Matter. *See* **Best Mode, Scope of Patent Protection.**

Undue. *See* **Breadth, Undue Experimentation, Multiplicity.**

Undue Breadth. *See also* **Breadth.**

A claim to a novel compound is not subject to rejection on "undue breadth" merely because unexpected results achieved with the compound involve a very limited use or environment. *In re Chupp,* 816 F.2d 643, 2 U.S.P.Q.2d 1437 (Fed. Cir. 1987).

Undue Experimentation. *See also* **Experimentation.**

The fact that some catalysts do not or may not work in a claimed process is not adequate basis for precluding patentability for an inadequate disclosure under the first paragraph of 35 U.S.C. §112 under the guise of requiring undue experimentation. The evidence as a whole, including the inoperative as well as the operative examples, negates the PTO position that persons of ordinary skill in this art, given its unpredictability, must engage in undue experimentation to determine which complexes work. *In re Angstadt and Griffin,* 537 F.2d 498, 190 U.S.P.Q. 214, 218, 219 (C.C.P.A. 1976).

ᴕ

A selection of various strains of a species identified in a Japanese application and screening (requiring at most 15 calendar days) those strains for efficacy in producing citric acid by following a provided example is not regarded as undue experimentation. *Tabuchi and Abe v. Nubel, Fitts, and Lorenzo,* 559 F.2d 1183, 194 U.S.P.Q. 521, 525 (C.C.P.A. 1977).

ᴕ

In determining what constitutes undue experimentation, many factors are taken into account, including the guidance provided by the specification for selecting those embodiments of the invention that achieve the disclosed utility. *In re Sichert,* 566 F.2d 1154, 196 U.S.P.Q. 209, 215 (C.C.P.A. 1977).

ᴕ

A disclosure was regarded as totally inadequate with respect to the manner of using claimed compositions since it lacked any information as to the host, the dosage level, mode or routes of administration, or how to prepare the composition for administration. Experimentation was required to ascertain the parameters of the invention with regard to how to use the claimed materials for inhibiting tissue degradation and treatment of diseases. Determination of effective dose requires pharmaceutical studies. The fact that uses of the claimed products are or may be the subject of later in vivo tests does not render the claimed invention useful at the time of the filing of the involved application. Nowhere in the record did the appellant establish that the doses to be administered were comparable to analogous known compositions nor has the appellant demonstrated that a skilled artisan would know how to use the claimed invention for their intended purposes without undue experimentation. *Ex parte Powers,* 220 U.S.P.Q. 924 (PTO Bd. App. 1982).

ᴕ

The key to analyzing an "undue experimentation" attack on the enablement of a patent, and therefore of an anticipatory reference, is in determining what is "undue," because some trial and error is permissible. *W.L. Gore & Assocs. v. Garlock, Inc.*, 721 F.2d 1540, 1557, 220 U.S.P.Q. 303, 316 (Fed. Cir. 1983).

ω

The ultimate question is whether the specification contains a sufficiently explicit disclosure to enable one having ordinary skill in the relevant field to practice the invention claimed therein without the exercise of undue experimentation. *Ex parte Forman*, 230 U.S.P.Q. 546 (B.P.A.I. 1986).

ω

The determination of what constitutes undue experimentation in a given case requires the application of a standard of reasonableness, having due regard for the nature of the invention and the state of the art. The test is not merely quantitative, since a considerable amount of experimentation is permissible, if it is merely routine, or if the specification in question provides a reasonable amount of guidance with respect to the direction in which the experimentation should proceed. Factors to be considered in determining whether a disclosure would require undue experimentation include: (1) the quantity of experimentation necessary, (2) the amount of direction or guidance presented, (3) the presence or absence of working examples, (4) the nature of the invention, (5) the state of the prior art, (6) the relative skill of the those in the art, (7) the predictability or unpredictability of the art, and (8) the breadth of the claims. *In re Wands*, 858 F.2d 731, 8 U.S.P.Q.2d 1400 (Fed. Cir. 1988).

ω

Since "routine experimentation" may involve rather extensive studies without straying from "undue experimentation", and since appellants have provided no countervailing evidence, changes made during the prosecution of the reference patent are regarded to be of a type condoned by prior decisions. *Ex parte D*, 27 U.S.P.Q.2d 1067, 1069, 1070 (B.P.A.I. 1993).

ω

A requirement of from 18 months to two years' work to practice the patented invention is "undue experimentation." *PPG Industries Inc. v. Guardian Industries Corp.*, 75 F.3d 1558, 37 U.S.P.Q.2d 1618, 1624 (Fed. Cir. 1996).

Unexpected.

Although the exact color or shade of the claimed isomer was unpredictable, it was not unexpected; it was a shade somewhere in the family of reddish tints encompassed by a reference disclosure. Absolute predictability is not the law. *In re Crounse*, 363 F.2d 881, 150 U.S.P.Q. 554, 557 (C.C.P.A. 1966).

ω

An expert's sworn skepticism is entitled to weight in resolving the ultimate legal conclusion of obviousness under 35 U.S.C. §103. However, a conclusion of non-obviousness is not compelled merely because the magic word "unexpected" appears in a Declaration. It is necessary to look at the facts relied upon to support an expert's opinion. *Ex parte George*, 21 U.S.P.Q.2d 1058, 1062 (B.P.A.I. 1991).

Unexpected Properties. *See also* **Properties.**

After a rejection is based on a portion of a reference and a showing of unexpected properties is based thereon, the PTO must afford applicant an opportunity to present a further showing if a different portion of the same reference is subsequently relied on. *In re Wiechert*, 370 F.2d 927, 152 U.S.P.Q. 247, 251, 252 (C.C.P.A. 1967).

ᴦ

The existence of novel or superior unexpected properties, undisclosed by the prior art, weighs heavily in favor of a conclusion that the claimed composition is not obvious. *Air Products and Chemicals, Inc. v. Chas. S. Tanner Co.*, 219 U.S.P.Q. 223, 231 (S.C. 1983).

ᴦ

The differences between the prior art and the invention defined by the asserted claims, the availability of that art to all workers in the field, the failure of established competitors in a highly competitive market to make the invention despite the incentive to do so, the admittedly nonobvious performance benefits realized through the claimed invention, the impressive commercial success of the claimed product, the praise of independent commentators, and the forbearance of competitors from infringing the patent all go to confirm that the claimed invention was not obvious at the time it was made to a person of ordinary skill in the art. *S. C. Johnson & Son, Inc. v. Carter-Wallace, Inc.*, 614 F. Supp. 1278, 225 U.S.P.Q. 1022 (N.Y. 1985).

Unexpected Results. *See also* **Advantage, Results, Showing, Skepticism.**

Where a small structural difference is involved and where there is no apparent reason why that difference should produce a great improvement, the burden is upon the applicant to show, by factual evidence, that he has obtained an unexpectedly good result. *In re Renstrom,* 174 F.2d 140, 81 U.S.P.Q. 390, 391 (C.C.P.A. 1949).

ᴦ

When patentability is predicated on an unexpected result, such result must be disclosed in the specification. *In re Stewart*, 222 F.2d 747, 106 U.S.P.Q. 115, 121 (C.C.P.A. 1955); but *see In re Zenitz*, 333 F.2d 924, 142 U.S.P.Q. 158, 161 (C.C.P.A. 1964).

ᴦ

To show an unexpected result for a selected range (within the scope of a reference range), it is not necessary to establish inoperativeness over other ranges, only that there is a difference in kind (not merely in degree) over the claimed critical range. *In re Waymouth and Koury*, 499 F.2d 1273, 182 U.S.P.Q. 290, 293 (C.C.P.A. 1974).

ᴦ

Unexpected results must be taken fully into account, pursuant to the congressional mandate for consideration of the invention as a whole. *Ex parte Leonard and Brandes*, 187 U.S.P.Q. 122, 123 (PTO Bd. App. 1974).

ᴦ

In order to establish unexpected results for a claimed invention, objective evidence of non-obviousness must be commensurate in scope with the claims which the evidence is offered to support. *In re Clemens, Hurwitz, and Walker*, 622 F.2d 1029, 206 U.S.P.Q. 289, 296 (C.C.P.A. 1980).

ω

In the absence of any prior art, claims need not restrict ingredients to encompass only those that produce unexpected results. *Ex parte Hradcovsky,* 214 U.S.P.Q. 554 (PTO Bd. App. 1982).

ω

When an article is said to achieve unexpected (i.e., superior) results, those results must logically be shown as superior compared to the results achieved with other articles. Moreover, an applicant relying on comparative tests to rebut a prima facie case of obviousness must compare his claimed invention to the closest prior art. In the absence of comparative test data, assertions of unexpected results constitute mere argument; conclusory statements in the specification cannot establish patentability. *In re De Blauwe,* 736 F.2d 699, 222 U.S.P.Q. 191 (Fed. Cir. 1984).

ω

The burden is on the party challenging validity to establish lack of new and surprising results or lack of criticality. *American Hospital Supply Corporation v. Travenol Laboratories, Inc.*, 745 F.2d 1, 223 U.S.P.Q. 577, 582 (Fed. Cir. 1984).

ω

Declaration evidence showed greater-than-additive cleaning performance resulting from the combination of zeolites with a variety of auxiliary builders, in the face of diminished (less than additive) depletion of calcium ions for the combination. The Board agreed that the results for some of the combinations tested for cleaning performance are "better than would be expected." A greater-than-expected result is an evidentiary factor pertinent to the legal conclusion of obviousness vel non of the claims at issue. The Board concluded that the evidence demonstrated synergism "to some degree" with respect to cleaning performance, but observed that the appellant's claims were not limited to those specific cobuilders and detergent compositions for which data showing synergism had been submitted. The Board also held that this result, even if unexpected, was not "sufficient to overcome the *prima facie* case of obviousness established by the prior art."

The court could discern no *prima facie* teaching of the prior art with respect to these compositions of components. The PTO failed to point out any reference that suggests combining a known builder with zeolite, or that this combination would produce a greater-than-additive effect in cleaning performance. The PTO failed to establish a *prima facie* case of obviousness with respect to those claims that require the presence of an auxiliary builder. The Board observed that the combination of zeolite and cobuilder were not, in most instances reported in the Declaration, superior in cleaning performance to the auxiliary builder alone. This is not the test. In view of the evidence of a result greater than additive, evidencing some non-obvious results in the combination of components where the one component is in itself more active than the other is not controlling. The specification teaches that a broad range of surfactants may be used in combination with zeolite plus auxiliary builders. In the absence of prior art suggesting or otherwise making these compositions obvious to one of ordinary skill in the art, there is inadequate support for the PTO's rejection of these claims. The burden on this point has not shifted to the applicant. *In re Corkill,* 771 F.2d 1496, 226 U.S.P.Q. 1005 (Fed. Cir. 1985).

ω

As evidence of unexpected results, data presented in the specification must be evaluated in a patentability determination. *In re Margolis,* 785 F.2d 1029, 228 U.S.P.Q. 940, 941 (Fed. Cir. 1986).

ω

At the time of the invention the art taught away from the invention. Those skilled in the art were looking to higher mass and denser materials to block sound. Mr. Gardner went in a direction different from that of others in the art, and his invention thus produced unexpected results. Unexpected results provide objective evidence of non-obviousness. *Specialty Composites v. Cabot Corp.,* 845 F.2d 981, 6 U.S.P.Q.2d 1601 (Fed. Cir. 1988).

ω

When an applicant demonstrates *substantially* improved results and *states* that the results were *unexpected*, this should suffice to establish unexpected results *in the absence of* evidence to the contrary. *In re Soni,* 54 F.3d 746, 34 U.S.P.Q.2d 1684, 1688 (Fed. Cir. 1995).

ω

Evidence of secondary considerations, including evidence of unexpected results and commercial success, are but a part of the "totality of the evidence" that is used to reach the ultimate conclusion of obviousness. The existence of such evidence, however, does not control the obviousness determination. *Richardson-Vicks Inc. v. The Upjohn Co.,* 122 F.3d 1476, 44 U.S.P.Q.2d 1181, 1187 (Fed. Cir. 1997).

Unfair Competition.

Direct patent infringement, contributory patent infringement and inducement of patent infringement have no connection with "passing off", and do not fall within "unfair competition", as used in the advertising injury provision of an insurance policy. *Classic Corp. v. Charter Oak Fire Insurance Co.,* 35 U.S.P.Q.2d 1726, 1728 (Cal. 1995).

ω

There is no legal basis for a holding that inequitable conduct, or the assertion of a patent procured through inequitable conduct, constitutes unfair competition. *Pro-Mold and Tool Co. v. Great Lakes Plastics Inc.,* 75 F.3d 1568, 37 U.S.P.Q.2d 1626, 1631 (Fed. Cir. 1996).

Unification of Parts. *See* Making Integral.

Unintentional Abandonment.

Petitioner has not carried his burden of proof to establish that the abandonment was intentional as required by 35 U.S.C. §41(a)7 and 37 C.F.R. §1.137(b). The record clearly establishes that the applicants and their assignee through their representatives deliberately allowed this application to become abandoned. A deliberate act is not rendered unintentional when an applicant or assignee reviews the same facts (e.g., patentability of the claims) a second time, which changes their minds as to the appropriate course of action to pursue. An application abandoned as a result of a deliberate, intentional course of action, after comparing the claimed invention with the prior art, does not amount to an unintentional abandonment within the meaning of 35 U.S.C. §41(a)7 and 37 C.F.R. §1.137(b). *In re Application of G,* 11 U.S.P.Q.2d 1378 (Comm'r Patents & Trademarks 1989).

Unitary. *See* **Integral.**

United States.

In infringement litigation in a federal district court, the United States can be joined as a third party defendant when there is an issue as to legal title of a patent relied upon in a counterclaim. *The Narda Microwave Corporation v. General Microwave Corporation,* 201 U.S.P.Q. 231, 232 (N.Y. 1978).

ϖ

An "exclusive" licensee under a patent, title to which is in the United States (U.S.), may, under some circumstances, maintain a patent infringement action without the U.S. as a party, when the U.S. has authorized the licensee to sue for patent infringement in its own name and on its own behalf. *Nutrition 21 v. United States,* 930 F.2d 862, 19 U.S.P.Q.2d 1351, 1352 (Fed. Cir. 1991).

ϖ

United States involvement in a joint international spacecraft program is sufficient to make any use of a resulting spacecraft a use "by" or "for" the government within the meaning of 28 U.S.C. §1498 if the project is a cooperative one with the potential of substantial benefits to the United States. *Hughes Aircraft Co. v. U.S.,* 29 Fed.Cl. 197, 29 U.S.P.Q.2d 1974, 1998 (U.S. Ct. Fed. Cl. 1993).

United States Government. *See also* **Eminent Domain, Executive Order No. 10096, Federal Government, Made, Sham Litigation.**

The envelope cathode and mechanical-recharge concept were conceived and reduced to practice by plaintiff prior to its entering into a contract with the government. Merely because plaintiff later used aspects of that technology in the performance of the contract does not give defendant any rights under plaintiff's patent therefor. Defendant received the benefit of that technology without paying for its development; it does not also get a royalty-free license. *Leesona Corp. v. United States,* 185 U.S.P.Q. 156, 165 (Ct. Cl. 1975).

ϖ

Use or manufacture for the United States is immune from suit for patent infringement in the district courts against the user or manufacturer. If and when such making and/or using takes place, a patentee's only recourse is to sue the United States in the U.S. Claims Court for its entire compensation. The patentee takes his patent from the United States, subject to the government's eminent domain rights, to obtain what it needs for manufacture and to use the same. The government has graciously consented to be sued in the Claims Court for reasonable and entire compensation for what would be infringement if by a private person. *W. L. Gore & Associates, Inc. v. Garlock, Inc.*, 842 F.2d 1275, 6 U.S.P.Q.2d 1277 (Fed. Cir. 1988).

ʊ

A contract that expressly grants the government rights in any future invention (not merely obligating a contractor to grant future rights) ordinarily requires no further act once an invention comes into being; transfer of title occurs by operation of law. *FilmTek Corp. v. Allied-Signal Inc.*, 939 F.2d 1568, 19 U.S.P.Q.2d 1508, 1512 (Fed. Cir. 1991).

ʊ

"Because section 1498 (28 U.S.C.) authorizes the Government to take a license in any ... patent, the Government is never 'guilty' of 'direct infringement' of a patent insofar as ... [this] connotes tortious or wrongful conduct." *Hughes Aircraft Co. v. U.S.*, 31 Fed.Cl. 481, 35 U.S.P.Q.2d 1243, 1250 (U.S. Ct. Fed. Cl. 1994).

Unity of Invention.[1] *See also* **Improper Markush, Joinder of Invention, Patentable Distinctness, Repugnant, Restriction, Single Invention, Withdrawal.**

An applicant is not entitled to examination of more than one invention under 35 U.S.C. §131, even when they are included in a single Markush-type claim. *Rohm and Haas Company v. Commissioner of Patents*, 387 F.Supp. 673, 177 U.S.P.Q. 625, 626, 627 (D.C. 1973).

ʊ

A determination by the Patent Office that earlier, separate claims encompass a "plurality of different inventions" cannot serve, under 35 U.S.C. §112, as the basis for a rejection of a later combined claim. An applicant is free under that provision to set the metes and bounds of "his invention" as he sees them. *In re Wolfrum and Gold*, 486 F.2d 588, 179 U.S.P.Q. 620, 622 (C.C.P.A. 1973).

ʊ

Claims had been withdrawn from further consideration on the ground that they included multiple "patentably distinct" inventions. The claims were withdrawn from consideration not only in the subject application but prospectively in any subsequent application because of their content. In effect, there had been a denial of patentability of the claims. The absolute "withdrawal" cannot properly be categorized as merely a "requirement" or "objection" to restrict review to the petition. An Examiner's action of this nature is a rejection, a denial of substantive rights. *In re Haas*, 486 F.2d 1053, 179 U.S.P.Q. 623 (C.C.P.A. 1973).

ʊ

Two patents directed to the same combination cannot be sustained where patentability of the claims in both is predicated on the same feature. *Leesona Corporation v. United States*, 185 U.S.P.Q. 156, 166 (U.S. Ct.Cl. 1975).

ʊ

---

[1] See 37 C.F.R. §1.499 for PCT (Patent Cooperation Treaty) National Phase. See MPEP §803.02 for Markush.

The second paragraph of 35 U.S.C. §112 allows an inventor to claim his invention as he contemplates it. An applicant has a right to have each of his claims examined, on the merits, in the form he considers to define his invention best. *In re Weber, Soder, and Boksay*, 580 F.2d 455, 198 U.S.P.Q. 328, 331 (C.C.P.A. 1978).

ω

As all of the claimed compounds are dyes and are coumarin compounds (i.e., have a single structural similarity), the claimed compounds all belong to a subgenus that is not repugnant to scientific classification. Under these circumstances, the claimed compounds are part of a single invention; the requisite "unity of invention" is thus satisfied. The "unity of Invention" concept is not to be confused with a "misjoinder under 35 U.S.C. §121" rejection, which deals only with restriction requirements, to support the rejection of a single claim. The concept of "unity of invention" is not satisfied where *unrelated* inventions are involved—inventions which are truly independent *and* distinct. *In re Harnisch*, 631 F.2d 716, 206 U.S.P.Q. 300, 305, 306 (C.C.P.A. 1980).

ω

Only a very few compounds need be discussed when it is shown that they and the large group of compounds they represent share a key structural feature from which a common utility derives. *Hercules Incorporated v. Exxon Corporation*, 497 F.Supp. 661, 207 U.S.P.Q. 1088, 1106 (Del. 1980).

ω

"Unity of invention" encompasses both structural similarity and communality of properties and/or utility. *Ex parte Bella and Chiaino*, 224 U.S.P.Q. 293, 294 (PTO Bd. App. 1984).

ω

The determinative factor in deciding if a Markush group is proper is whether unity of invention exists or whether the claims are drawn to a collection of "unrelated inventions." When all of the claimed subject matter has in common a functional utility related to a substantial, structural feature disclosed as being essential to that utility, adequate unity of invention is present. *Ex parte Hozumi*, 3 U.S.P.Q.2d 1059 (B.P.A.I. 1984).

ω

A rejection of a claim for containing an improper Markush group was reversed. The encompassed compounds were sequential intermediates in a process for synthesizing a patented compound. The criteria for evaluating the propriety of a Markush group are (1) structural similarity and (2) unity of invention. When these two criteria are met, the Markush group is proper even when it involves and embraces intermediates of each other. Unity of invention encompasses both structural similarity and communality of properties and/or utility. Here, the Markush group members are structurally similar. The fact that the group members are used seriately to make a patented product is indicative of the same invention being involved, each member being a precursor of the other and leading to the making of a novel and useful material. Each of the individual members of the Markush group has no utility except in the chain of reaction leading to the patented product. As such, common utility is present within the meaning of the unity-of-invention requirement, the claimed intermediates being the cause and effect of the property and usefulness of the final patented product. *Ex parte Della Bella and Chiarino,* 7 U.S.P.Q.2d 1669 (B.P.A.I. 1984).

ᵺ

Patent Cooperation Treaty Rule 13.1(ii) permits, in addition to an independent claim for a given process, the inclusion in the same international application of one independent claim for one apparatus or means specifically designed for carrying out the said process. The expression "specifically designed" clearly does not mean that the apparatus or means cannot be used to practice another materially different process, as indicated in 37 C.F.R. §1.141(b)(2). The emphasized portion of the PTO rule and its interpretation are contrary to the Patent Cooperation Treaty and thus contrary to law. *Caterpillar Tractor Co. v. Commissioner of Patents and Trademarks,* 650 F. Supp. 218, 231 U.S.P.Q. 590 (Va. 1986).

ᵺ

When a new and useful compound or group of compounds (having a particular use) is invented or discovered, it is often the case that what is really a single invention may be viewed legally as having three or more different aspects (permitting it to be claimed in different ways); for example:

    a. the compounds themselves,
    b. the method or process of making the compounds, and
    c. the method or process of using the compounds for their intended purpose.

Where claims to a compound or group of compounds (the product claims) are allowable, it is in the public interest to permit claiming a process of use as well as the product. The result is to encourage a more detailed disclosure of the specific methods of using the novel composition invented in order to provide support for the process claims. The constitutional purpose of the patent system is promoted by encouraging an applicant to claim, and therefore to describe in the manner required by 35 U.S.C. §112, all aspects of what he regards as his invention, regardless of the number of statutory classes involved. *In re Pleuddemann,* 910 F.2d 823, 15 U.S.P.Q.2d 1738, 1740, 1741 (Fed. Cir. 1990).

ᵺ

Apparatus claims may be directed to the same inventions as method claims. *Symbol Technologies, Inc. v. Opticon, Inc.,* 935 F.2d 1569, 19 U.S.P.Q.2d 1241 (Fed. Cir. 1991).

ᵺ

The fact that identical drawings accompany different patent applications is persuasive evidence that only one inventive concept is present. *Jennmar Corp. v. Pattin Manufacturing Co.,* 20 U.S.P.Q.2d 1721, 1730 (Ohio 1991).

ᵺ

When a "means for" claim differs from a method claim only in "means for" terms before the steps, the claim is indistinguishable from a method claim. *Ex parte Akamatsu,* 22 U.S.P.Q.2d 1915, 1920 (B.P.A.I. 1992).

Unjust Enrichment. *See also* **Restitution.**

The general rule is that the monopoly of patent that entitles a patentee to damages for infringement commences only when the patent is granted; but where, in advance of the granting of a patent, an invention is disclosed to one who, in breach of the confidence thus reposed, manufactures, and sells articles embodying the invention, such persons should be held liable for the profits and damages resulting therefrom, not under the patent statutes, but under the principle that equity will not permit one to unjustly enrich himself at the expense of another.

The complainant offered to disclose his invention to the defendant with a view of selling it to defendant. The defendant was interested in the proposition and invited the disclosure, otherwise it would not have seen the complainant's specification and drawings until the patent was granted. While there was no express agreement that the defendant was to hold the information so disclosed as a confidential matter and to make no use of it unless it should purchase the invention, we think that in equity and good conscience such an agreement was implied; and having obtained the disclosure under such circumstances, the defendant ought not to be heard to say that there was no obligation to respect the confidence thus reposed in it. *Hoeltke v. C. M. Kemp Manufacturing Co.,* 80 F.2d 912, 26 U.S.P.Q. 114 (4th Cir. 1935), *cert. denied,* 298 U.S. 673 (1936).

ω

Unjust enrichment is an equitable doctrine that permits recovery when a plaintiff shows " '(1) that a benefit was conferred on the defendant by the plaintiff, (2) that the benefit was appreciated by the defendant, and (3) that the benefit was accepted by the defendant under such circumstances that it would be inequitable for it to be retained without payment.' " *University of Colorado Foundation Inc. v. American Cyanamid Co.,* 974 F.Supp. 1339, 44 U.S.P.Q.2d 1231, 1244 (Col. 1997).

Unknowable.

Only by showing his own "blameless ignorance" may a person (alleging that an injury was inherently unknowable) use the time the injury manifests itself as the time the injury occurred for statute of limitations purposes. Upon finding that facts supporting a cause of action were inherently unknowable, a determination must be made as to when a person of ordinary intelligence and prudence would have facts sufficient to put him on "inquiry which, if pursued, would lead to the discovery" of the injury. *Studiengesellschaft Kohle mbH v. Hercules Inc.,* 748 F. Supp. 247, 18 U.S.P.Q.2d 1773, 1777 (Del. 1990).

Unknown.

That which may be inherent is not necessarily known, and obviousness cannot be predicated on what is unknown. *In re Newell,* 891 F.2d 899, 13 U.S.P.Q.2d 1248, 1250 (Fed. Cir. 1989).

Unnecessary.

It is rarely possible to determine any necessity for narrower claims at the time of prosecution. An applicant often does not know the prior art that may be asserted against his broader claims when he litigates his patent. Further, he is never sure that the broader claims will not be successfully attacked on other grounds when litigated in the courts. Moreover, there is no statutory authority for rejecting claims as being "unnecessary." An applicant should be allowed to determine the necessary number and scope of his claims, provided he pays the required fees and otherwise complies with the statute. We disagree with the Board's view that the number of claims was so large as to obscure the invention, thereby failing to comply with the second paragraph of 35 U.S.C. §112. Each appealed claim is relatively brief and clear in its meaning. Examination of 40 claims in a single application may be tedious work, but this is no reason for saying that the invention is obscured by the large number of claims. *In re Wakefield and Foster,* 422 F.2d 897, 164 U.S.P.Q. 636 (C.C.P.A. 1970).

ᚥ

A separate claim embodying a figure of the drawings was treated as unnecessary because it was merely descriptive of the use to be made of the patented device. Under these circumstances cancellation of the claim should not be considered an abandonment of the embodiment of the invention that it had described. *Olympic Fastening Systems, Inc. v. Textron Inc.,* 504 F.2d 609, 183 U..S.P.Q. 449, 452 (6th Cir. 1974).

ᚥ

An unnecessary ruling on an affirmative defense is not the same as the necessary resolution of a counterclaim for a declaratory judgment. *Cardinal Chemical Co. v. Morton International Inc.,* 113 S.Ct. 1967, 26 U.S.P.Q.2d 1721, 1726 (S.Ct. 1993).

Unobvious. *See* Obviousness.

Unpatented Claim.

Unpatented claims are given the broadest reasonable interpretation consistent with the specification during the examination of a patent application, since the applicant may then amend his claims, the thought being to reduce the possibility that, after the patent is granted, the claims may be interpreted as giving broader coverage than is justified. Prior to the grant of a patent, an applicant should not have limitations of the specification read into a claim where no express statement of the limitation is included in the claim. *In re Prater and Wei,* 415 F.2d 1393, 162 U.S.P.Q. 541, 550, 551 (C.C.P.A. 1969).

ᚥ

Claims subject to examination are given their broadest reasonable interpretation consistent with the specification, and limitations appearing in the specification are not to be read into the claims. When an application is pending in the PTO, the applicant has the ability to correct errors in claim language and adjust the scope of claim protection as needed. This opportunity is not available in an infringement action in a district court. A district court may find it necessary to interpret claims to protect only that which constitutes patentable subject matter in order to do justice between the parties. The same policies warranting the PTO's approach to claim interpretation when an original application is involved have been held applicable to reissue proceedings because the reissue provision, 35 U.S.C. §251, permits amendment to the claims to avoid prior art. The reasons underlying the PTO's interpretation of the claims in reissue proceedings justify using the same approach in reexamination proceedings. *In re Yamamoto,* 740 F.2d 1569, 222 U.S.P.Q. 934, 936, 937 (C.C.P.A. 1984).

ω

During patent examination the pending claims must be interpreted as broadly as their terms reasonably allow. When the applicant states the meaning that the claimed terms are intended to have, the claims are examined with that meaning, in order to achieve complete exploration of the applicant's invention and its relation to the prior art. Before an application is granted, there is no reason to read into the claim the limitations of the specification. The reason is simply that, during patent prosecution when claims can be amended, ambiguity should be recognized, scope and breadth of language explored, and clarification imposed. The issued claims are the measure of the protected right. An essential purpose of patent examination is to fashion claims that are precise, clear, correct, and unambiguous. Only in this way can uncertainties of claimed scope be removed, as much as possible, during the adminstrative process. Thus, the inquiry during examination is patentability of the invention as "the applicant regards" it; and, if the claims do not particularly point out and distinctly claim, in the words of 35 U.S.C. §112, that which examination shows the applicant is entitled to claim as his invention, the appropriate PTO action is to reject the claims for that reason. A claim that reads on subject matter beyond the applicant's invention fails to comply with §112. *In re Zletz,* 893 F.2d 319, 13 U.S.P.Q.2d 1320, 1322 (Fed. Cir. 1989).

Unpatented Components. *See also* Entire-Market-Value Rule.

Under the entire-market-value rule, a patentee is entitled to lost profits on unpatented components that accompany the sale of patented components where, in all reasonable probability, the patentee would have made the sales that the infringer made. The record shows that the company that sells the belts also gets the sales of the sprockets, transfer combs, and belt accessories. Under the entire-market-value rule, the court therefore finds that it is reasonably probable that the patentee would have sold the sprockets, transfer combs, and accessories in view of the above findings and the court's prior determination that it is reasonably probable that the patentee would have made the sales but for the infringement. *Rexnord Inc. v. Laitram Corp.,* 6 U.S.P.Q.2d 1817 (Wis. 1988).

Unpatented Goods.

Although defendant was coerced into taking a license under a patent and the license covered unpatented, as well as patented, goods, there was no patent misuse in view of the fact that plaintiff had a policy of making available to manufacturers licenses under the patent which covered only patented goods, albeit at a higher rate. *The Plastic Contact Lens Company v. Young Contact Lens Laboratories, Inc.,* 175 U.S.P.Q. 573, 574 (Mass. 1972).

Unpredictability. *See* **Catalysis, Chemical, Predictability.**

Unpredictable Art. *See also* **Cancer.**

In an unpredictable art, does 35 U.S.C. §112 require disclosure of a test with every species covered by a claim? To require such a complete disclosure would apparently necessitate a patent application with thousands of examples or a disclosure with thousands of catalysts along with information as to whether each exhibits catalytic behavior resulting in the production of the desired products. More importantly, such a requirement would force an inventor seeking adequate patent protection to carry out a prohibitive number of actual experiments. This would tend to discourage inventors from filing patent applications in an unpredictable area since the patent claims would have to be limited to those embodiments that are expressly disclosed. A potential infringer could readily avoid "literal" infringement of such claims by merely finding another analogous catalyst complex that could be used in forming the same products. *In re Angstadt and Griffin*, 537 F.2d 498, 190 U.S.P.Q. 214, 218 (C.C.P.A. 1976).

ω

The application stood in condition for allowance and ready for the issuance of a patent grant except for the presence in the specification disclosure of certain asserted utilities that the Examiner believed to be too speculative—i.e., not believable on their face to those of ordinary skill in the art in view of the contemporary knowledge of the art. While it may be clear that workers in this art had shown that some cancers can be treated successfully in some patients, the effective treatment of various forms of malignant tumors remains a highly unpredictable art. Under these circumstances, the Examiner does not need to provide reasons why this speculative assertion should not be believed. The mere fact that the art of cancer chemotherapy is highly unpredictable places the burden on applicants to provide a basis for believing the speculative statements that they chose to place in the specification in the form of a positive assertion. *In re Application of Hozumi*, 226 U.S.P.Q. 353 (Comm'r Patents & Trademarks 1985).

Unreasonable. *See* **Spurious.**

Unreasonable Delay.

In order to assert the defense of laches successfully, one must prove: (1) unreasonable and inexcusable delay in the assertion of the claim and (2) material prejudice resulting from the delay. Laches, however, bars only the right to recover prefiling damages.

Equitable estoppel bars claims for patent infringement if Mainland committed itself to act, and acted as a direct consequence of the conduct of Standal's Patents. Estoppel to assert patent rights requires: (1) unreasonable and inexcusable delay, (2) prejudice to the defendant, (3) affirmative conduct by patentee's inducing belief of abandonment of claims against the alleged infringer, and (4) detrimental reliance by the infringer. Estoppel by implied license cannot arise out of unilateral expectations or even reasonable hopes of one party. Five years silence alone is not enough to give rise to estoppel. *Mainland Industries, Inc. v. Standals Patents Ltd.*, 799 F.2d 746, 230 U.S.P.Q. 772 (Fed. Cir. 1986).

Unrecognized.

Compounds that previously existed unrecognized only in undesirable polymeric by-products of no recognized utility are patentable to one who discovers the compounds and how to make and use them for a wide variety of purposes. *Ex parte Hillyer and Nicewander,* 102 U.S.P.Q. 126, 128 (PO Bd. App. 1953).

Unsigned Check.

As funds necessary to cover the filing fee were present in Counsel's Office deposit account on the required date, the Commissioner decided that justice dictates that otherwise undesignated deposit account funds be used or considered to satisfy the statutory requirements for a filing fee. I*n re Application Papers Filed March 27, 1974*, 186 U.S.P.Q. 363, 364 (Comm'r of Patents and Trademarks 1975).

ϖ

Prior to the amendment of 35 U.S.C. §111, the PTO had consistently taken the position that the Commissioner had no discretion to accord an application a filing date where the application, as deposited, was accompanied by an unsigned check as payment of the fee required by the statute. The underlying basis of those previous decisions was that an unsigned check did not constitute payment. The Federal Circuit has now determined that an unsigned check may be accepted as "conditional" payment at the discretion of the Commissioner. *In re Dubost,* 231 U.S.P.Q. 887, 888 (Comm'r Patents & Trademarks 1986).

Unsigned Declaration.

The application did not become abandoned for failure to provide a signed Declaration since, during the pendency of the application, the PTO never notified applicant of the defect. The application would only become abandoned if the PTO informed applicant of the defect and applicant failed to correct the defect in a timely manner. *In re Rosenberg,* 15 U.S.P.Q.2d 1751, 1752 (Comm'r Patents & Trademarks 1990).

Unsolved Need. *See* Long-Felt Need.

Unstable. *See* Stability.

Unsuccessful Attempts by Others. *See* Secondary Considerations.

Unsupported. *See* Assertion.

Untimely Jury Demand.

In the absence of strong and compelling reasons to the contrary, untimely jury demands should be granted. This liberal rule in favor of jury trials, even when untimely demanded, stems from the esteem that our legal system holds for the right of a litigant to have his fellow citizens weigh the evidence. Yet the burden of proving the propriety of a decision to grant a jury trial under Rule 38(b) is still on the demanding party. The factors courts consider in their exercise of discretion under Rule 39(b) include:

1. whether the case involves issues best tried by a jury;
2. whether granting the motion would result in a disruption of the court's schedule or that of the adverse party;
3. the degree of prejudice to the non-movant;
4. the length of the delay in having requested a jury trial; and
5. the reason for the movant's tardiness in requesting a jury trial.

Complexity is not a basis for distinguishing the right to a jury trial of patent litigants. *Fromson v. RVP Chemical Corp.*, 15 U.S.P.Q.2d 1689, 1703 (Wis. 1990).

Upside-Down. *See* **Orientation.**

Up To. *See also* **Zero.**

Claims are also too broad and incomplete when they specify up to about a designated percent by weight of a specified component because they read on compositions totally lacking that component. *Ex parte Dobson, Jacob, and Herschler,* 165 U.S.P.Q. 29, 30 (PO Bd. App. 1969).

URAA.

The Uraguay Round Agreements Act (URAA) works no change on the definition of infringement under 35 U.S.C. §271(e)(2) and has no effect on the statutory provisions relating to FDA approval of ANDAs that are triggered by that act of infringement. *DuPont Merck Pharmaceutical Co. v. Bristol-Myers Squibb Co.*, 62 F.3d 1397, 35 U.S.P.Q.2d 1718, 1722 (Fed. Cir. 1995).

ᵿ

The URAA creates a limited safe harbor for persons who commenced particular acts, or made substantial investment toward commission of those acts before June 8, 1995 (the date six months after the URAA was enacted), which acts became infringing because of the extension of the patent period by the URAA. *Bristol-Myers Squibb Co. v. Royce Laboratories Inc.*, 69 F.3d 1130, 36 U.S.P.Q.2d 1641, 1644 (Fed. Cir. 1995).

ᵿ

Pre-June 8, 1995, patents are entitled to add on the restoration extension to a 20-year from filing term regardless of when such extension is granted except for those patents kept in force on June 8, 1995, only because of a restoration extension. Under this interpretation, all provisions of both URAA and Hatch-Waxman can reasonably be given effect. For pre-June 8, 1995, patents, a patentee would have full exclusionary rights for 17 years, followed by rights only to equitable remuneration (neither lost profits, an injunction, punitive damages, nor attorney fees) with respect to a certain class of infringers for the period from the end of the 17-year term to the end of the new 20-year term (the delta period), followed by entitlement to full exclusionary rights (but only with respect to the approved product) during the period of the restoration extension. *Merck & Co. v. Kessler*, 80 F.3d 1543, 38 U.S.P.Q.2d 1347, 1352, 1353 (Fed. Cir. 1996).

5 U.S.C. §552.

The Patent Office was required [under 5 U.S.C. §552(a)(2)] to create and maintain a current index of unpublished manuscript decisions. *Irons v. Gottschalk*, 369 F.Supp. 403, 180 U.S.P.Q. 492, 493 (D.C. 1974).

ʊ

Abandoned patent applications are statutorily exempt from the necessity of disclosure under FOIA [5 U.S.C. 552(b)(3)]. *Sears v. Gottschalk*, 502 F.2d 122, 183 U.S.P.Q. 134 (4th Cir. 1974).

5 U.S.C. §553.

Under 5 U.S.C. §553 of the Administrative Procedure Act, certain agency actions require prior public notice and comment. Courts interpreting §553 generally speak in terms of "substantive" or legislative rules requiring notice and comment in contrast to the exempt "interpretive" rules of §553(b), which do not. A rule is substantive when it "effects a change in existing law or policy" that "affect[s] individual rights and obligations." To be substantive, a rule must also be promulgated pursuant "to statutory authority . . . and implement the statute." In contrast, a rule that merely clarifies or explains existing law or regulations is interpretive. *Animal League Defense Fund v. Quigg*, 932 F.2d 920, 18 U.S.P.Q.2d 1677, 1683 (Fed. Cir. 1991).

7 U.S.C. §2543. *See* Plant Variety Protection Act (PVPA).

11 U.S.C. §362. *See* Bankruptcy.

15 U.S.C. §2.

Defendants contend that the plaintiffs (by bringing a patent infringement action on invalid patents) have violated Section 2 of the Sherman Act (15 U.S.C. §2) and that they are entitled to damages under Section 4 of the Clayton Act (15 U.S.C. §15). The burden of proof, which is a heavy one, rests upon the defendants. *Fishburne Equipment Co., Inc. v. Lee Machine-Hydraulic, Inc.*, 203 U.S.P.Q. 601, 619 (N.C. 1978).

17 U.S.C. §901. *See* Maskwork.

19 U.S.C. §1337. *See also* Importation, Standing.

A patent infringing design of imported articles is an unfair act, unremediable except by exclusion. *In re Certain Thermometer Sheath Packages*, 205 U.S.P.Q. 932, 946 (U.S. Int'l Trade Comm'l 1979).

ʊ

Four indications of possible injury that have been considered in section 337 investigations are: (1) significant reduction in sales; (2) idling of production facilities; (3) decrease in employment; and (4) decline in profitability. *In re Certain Large Video Matrix Display Systems and Components Thereof*, 213 U.S.P.Q. 475, 485 (U.S. Int'l Trade Comm'l 1981).

ᚥ

Where a complainant agrees as part of a settlement agreement to the return of a bond, the bond itself purports not to apply to sales authorized by the complainant, and the purpose of the bond is to protect the complainant as well as the public interest, the Commission abuses its discretion by declining to release the bond merely because of sales by a respondent of goods known to the complainant at the time of the agreement. *Biocraft Laboratories Inc. v. International Trade Commission*, 947 F.2d 483, 20 U.S.P.Q.2d 1446, 1449 (Fed. Cir. 1991).

19 U.S.C. §1337(a).

The exercise by the ITC of its temporary relief authority should generally parallel that of the district courts. *Rosemount Inc. v. U.S. International Trade Commission*, 910 F.2d 819, 15 U.S.P.Q.2d 1569, 1571 (Fed. Cir. 1990).

19 U.S.C. §1337(c). *See also* Importation.

The Commission's premature termination of an ongoing investigation in light of an arbitration agreement was contrary to law because the governing statutory section, 19 U.S.C. §1337(c), does not authorize such termination except in certain specified nonpresent circumstances. Section 337(c) requires that the Commission determine whether there is a violation of this section in each investigation it conducts. The "all defenses" provision was not intended to deprive the Commission of its jurisdiction to conclude §337 investigations, but rather to afford the accused party a "full due process hearing" before the Commission, which "determine[s] whether there is a violation...*in each investigation it conducts*" (emphasis in original). The "all defenses" provision was enacted to protect the public interest "in cases where there is any evidence of price gouging or monopolistic practices in the domestic industry" by the complainant. *Farrel Corp. v. International Trade Commission*, 949 F.2d 1147, 20 U.S.P.Q.2d 19

21 U.S.C. §355.

Section 355(j)(4)(B)(iv) of 21 U.S.C. explicitly provides that a primary generic drug manufacturer may qualify for the 180-day exclusivity in one of two ways—by compliance with subpart I or by compliance with subpart II. One of these methods, set forth in subpart II of Section (iv), by its terms, requires a suit for patent infringement pursuant to §355(j)(4)(b)(iii). The alternative method, set forth in subpart I, does not. Indeed, it makes no mention of a suit for patent infringement, but instead makes the 180-day exclusivity dependent on the first commercial marketing of the product. In light of the clear reference to a Section (iii) lawsuit in subpart II of Section (iv), and the omission of such reference in subpart I of Section (iv), there is no justification whatever for implying such a reference into subpart I, notwithstanding Congress" presumably deliberate decision not to incorporate the lawsuit requirement to that subpart. A primary ANDA applicant can qualify for exclusivity beginning either on the date of a court decision invalidating a patent or holding that it is not infringed, or on a date of first commercial marketing of an applicant's product. The trigger for the exclusivity period is the filing of an ANDA containing a Section (iv) certification for "drug for which a previous application has been submitted. . . ." *Inwood Laboratories Inc. v. Young,* 723 F. Supp. 1523, 12 U.S.P.Q.2d 1065, 1066, 1067 (D.C. 1989).

ϖ

As the subparagraphs of 21 U.S.C. §355(j) must be read as a whole and in context with the other paragraphs of §355, namely: §355(b), and as 35 U.S.C. §271(e)(2)(A) expressly incorporates §355(j), an action for patent infringement brought pursuant to §271(e)(2)(A) cannot be premised on a patent not included in an NDA filed pursuant to §355(b)(1), and thus not connected with a drug listed by the Secretary pursuant to §355(j)(6). *Abbott Laboratories v. Zenith Laboratories Inc.*, 35 U.S.P.Q.2d 1161, 1168 (Ill. 1995).

21 U.S.C. §355(j)(4)(B)(iii).

Once a patent infringement suit is filed against the first ANDA applicant, the [FDA] approval [of the generic drug] shall be made effective upon the expiration of the 30-month period beginning on the date of the receipt [of the required notice to patent owners] or such shorter or longer period as the court may order because either party to the action failed to reasonably cooperate in expediting the action [with certain enumerated exceptions]. . . ." *Mova Pharmaceutical Corp. v. Shalala*, 41 U.S.P.Q.2d 2012, (D.C. 1997).

21 U.S.C. §372(d).

The PTO's requesting information or research on compositions (claimed in an application for letters patent) from the Secretary of Health, Education, and Welfare is specifically provided for. *In re Sichert*, 566 F.2d 1154, 196 U.S.P.Q. 209, 213 (C.C.P.A. 1977).

28 U.S.C. §139(c).

Under 28 U.S.C. §1400(b), venue in a patent case is proper where the defendant "resides". Under 28 U.S.C. §139(c), a corporate defendant resides where it is subject to personal jurisdiction. *VE Holding Corp. v. Johnson Gas Appliance Co.*, 917 F.2d 1574, 1578, 1584, 16 U.S.P.Q.2d 1614, 1617, 1621 (Fed. Cir. 1990), *cert. denied*, 111 S.Ct. 1315 (1991).

28 U.S.C. §516.

Section 207(a)(2) of 35 U.S.C. is an exception to 28 U.S.C. §516, which permits the Department of Commerce to delegate enforcement powers to a licensee; the agreement between the Department of Commerce and the licensee grants the licensee the right "to bring suit in its own name, at its own expense, and on its own behalf for infringement of presumably valid claims in a Licensed Patent." By this provision of the License Agreement, the United States has, in effect, consented to its necessary joinder in an infringement action. *Nutrition 21 v. Thorne Research Inc.*, 130 F.R.D. 671, 14 U.S.P.Q.2d 1244, 1245 (Wash. 1990).

28 U.S.C. §636.

When a matter has been referred to a magistrate judge, acting as a special master or 28 U.S.C. §636(b)(2) jurist, a party waives his right to appeal if he has not preserved the issues for appeal by first presenting them to the District Judge as objections to the magistrate judge's order. Pursuant to Rule (FRCP) 72(a), parties are given ten days following entry of the Order to file exceptions thereto. *THK America Inc. v. Nippon Seiko K.K.*, 141 F.R.D. 461, 463, 21 U.S.P.Q.2d 1705, 1707 (Ill. 1991).

28 U.S.C. §636(b)(1)(A). *See* Magistrate's Order.

28 U.S.C. §1292(b).

It is within the Court's discretion whether to certify an order, but "the rule of interlocutory appeals is to be applied "sparingly and only in exceptional cases" in furtherance of the longstanding federal policy against piecemeal appeals." The party seeking certification bears the burden to show the presence of "exceptional circumstances where consideration of judicial economy and fairness demand interlocutory review of an order." *Mont-Bell Co. Ltd. v. Mountain Hardwear Inc.*, 44 U.S.P.Q.2d 1568, 1577 (Cal. 1997).

28 U.S.C. §1338.

Congress has not expressed an intent that the factual findings made by the ITC in the context of making an unfair trade practices determination are not binding on federal District Courts in the context of determining the validity of a patent pursuant to 28 U.S.C. §1338. *In re Convertible Rowing Exerciser Patent Litigation*, 814 F.Supp. 1197, 26 U.S.P.Q.2d 1677, 1682 (Del. 1993).

ᛦ

Although the claims asserted in the plaintiffs" complaint are not created by federal law, their well-pleaded complaint necessarily depends on the resolution of a substantial federal question. The court refused to allow the plaintiffs to deny the defendants "a federal forum when the plaintiff[s'] complaint contains a federal claim "artfully pled" as a state law claim." *RustEvader Corp. v. Cowatch*, 842 F.Supp. 171, 29 U.S.P.Q.2d 1076, 1079 (Penn. 1993).

28 U.S.C. §1338(a). *See also* Civil Action.

Every case involving patent issues is not a "civil action arising under any Act of Congress relating to patents," as set forth in 28 U.S.C. §1338(a). Actions to enforce patent license agreements are not within exclusive federal jurisdiction notwithstanding the availability of the invalidity defense. *Kysor Industrial Corp. v. Pet*, 459 F.2d 1010, 173

U.S.P.Q. 642, 643 (6th Cir. 1972).

ᛏ

Neither the language of 35 U.S.C. §146, its legislative history nor the cases decided under it indicate that it confers exclusive subject matter jurisdiction upon the District of Columbia Court or restricts another district court's subject matter jurisdiction granted by 28 U.S.C. §1338(a). *Standard Oil Company (Indiana) v. Montecatini Edison S.p.A.; Phillips Petroleum Company v. E.I. du Pont de Nemours & Co.; E.I. du Pont de Nemours & Co. v. Montecatini Edison S.p.A.*, 342 F.Supp. 125, 174 U.S.P.Q. 7, 9 (Del. 1972).

ᛏ

The application of a state law tort is preempted if, in holding a defendant liable for the conduct alleged and proved by the plaintiff, there would be conflict with federal patent law. Otherwise, if the state law tort, as applied, does not conflict with federal patent law, then the tort is not preempted. The combined result of these rulings is to divest state courts of jurisdiction over state law torts that are subject to [28 USC] § 1338(a) jurisdiction, and to allow only those that survive the preemption analysis to proceed. For purposes of §1338(a) jurisdiction, at least four issues of federal patent law are substantial enough to satisfy the jurisdictional test. They are infringement (validity and enforceability are treated the same as infringement); inventorship issues under 35 U.S.C. §§ 116 and 256; attorney fees under 35 U.S.C. §285; and the revival and an allegedly unintentionally abandoned patent application under 35 U.S.C. §§41 and 133, or, in the alternative, the right to file a continuation application under 35 U.S.C. § 120. *Hunter Douglas Inc. v. Harmonic Design Inc.*, 47 U.S.P.Q.2d 1769, 1770, 1777 (Fed. Cir. 1998).

28 U.S.C. §1391.

For purposes of venue under Chapter 87 of Title 28 of the U.S. Code, a defendant that is a corporation shall be deemed to reside in any judicial district in which it is subject to personal jurisdiction at the time an action is commenced (28 U.S.C. §1391). Section 1400(b) of 28 U.S.C. is contained within that chapter. The language of the statute controls in the absence of a clearly expressed legislative intention to the contrary. An inspection of the legislative history does not reveal any intent to exempt §1400 from the operation of §1391. If Congress intended that §1391(c) only modify the general venue rules contained in §1391, Congress would presumably have stated that §1391(c) only "applied for the purposes of this section." The statute does not contain such language. The courts must enforce statutes as they are written. *Diamond-Chase Co. v. Stretch Devices Inc.*, 16 U.S.P.Q.2d 1568, 1570 (Cal. 1990).

28 U.S.C. §1391(c).

The amendment to 28 U.S.C. §1391(c) in no way indicates that an alteration was intended in the operation of 28 U.S.C. §1400(b). Not only is the language of the statute itself silent in this respect, the legislative history behind the amendment of §1391(c) is devoid of any indication that an amendment to §1400(b) was intended or even contemplated. Absent clear indication in the language of the statute or unmistakable intent expressed in the legislative history, elementary principles of statutory construction preclude finding that venue in patent actions shall hereafter be governed by amended

28 U.S.C. §1391(c)

§1391(c). *Doelcher Products v. Hydrofoil International Inc.*, 735 F. Supp. 666, 14 U.S.P.Q.2d 1067, 1069 (Md. 1989).

᭏

A sole proprietorship, unlike a partnership, is not an "association". Rather, it is an individual doing business under a trade name. The rationales for applying 28 U.S.C. §1391(c) to partnerships do not apply to sole proprietorships. Accordingly, 28 U.S.C. §1400(b) controls the venue issue. *Kabb Inc. v. Sutera*, 25 U.S.P.Q.2d 1554, 1555 (La. 1992).

28 U.S.C. §1391(d).

To establish jurisdiction in a district court, it is sufficient that a foreign defendant gave technical assistance to its subsidiary in installing and maintaining machines [acts arguably constituting acts of "inducement" within the meaning of 35 U.S.C. §271(b)] in question in the district. In addition, the acts of direct infringement charged are themselves alleged to have occurred within the district, albeit through the acts of the subsidiary. *Hauni Werke Koerber & Co., KG. v. Molins Limited*, 183 U.S.P.Q. 168, 169 (Va. 1974).

᭏

An alien corporation may be sued in any district. Section 1391(d) applies to all federal actions against aliens, including patent infringement suits. *Brunswick Corporation v. Suzuki Motor Company, Ltd.*, 575 F.Supp. 14

28 U.S.C. §1391(e).

When a non-resident alien is a party to a patent interference, the other party may seek discovery of documents from him in any district. *Vogel v. Jones*, 443 F.2d 257, 170 U.S.P.Q. 188, 190 (3rd Cir. 1971).

28 U.S.C. §1400(b). *See also* Reside.

Where the defendant "resides" is one of the bases for establishing venue in patent infringement actions set forth in 28 U.S.C. §1400(b). The first test for venue under that section with respect to a defendant that is a corporation, in light of the 1988 amendment to 28 U.S.C. §1391(c), is whether the defendant was subject to personal jurisdiction in the district of suit at the time the action was commenced. The amendment to §1391(c) adopts a new definition of "reside" as it applies to venue for corporate defendants, and the new definition applies to the term as it is used in §1400(b). *VE Holding Corp. v. Johnson Gas Appliance Co.*, 917 F.2d 1574, 16 U.S.P.Q.2d 1614, 1641 (Fed. Cir. 1990), *cert. denied*, 111 S.Ct. 1315 (1991).

28 U.S.C. §1404(a).

The power of transfer under 28 U.S.C. §1404(a) does not depend upon the wish or waiver of the defendants. Defendants may not establish venue in a tranferee district by merely waiving possible objections to venue. *Tuff Torq Corp. v. Hydro-Gear Limited*

Partnership, 882 F.Supp. 359, 33 U.S.P.Q.2d 1846, 1848 (Del. 1994).

ᛒ

Rulings under 28 U.S.C. §1404(a) generally turn on the courts evaluation of the following, relevant considerations: (1) convenience of witnesses; (2) judicial economy; (3) relative ease of access to proof; (4) availability of compulsory process; and (5) relative docket congestion. The convenience of counsel and claims of local prejudice are usually not weighed in the balance. *Steelcase Inc. v. Haworth Inc.*, 41 U.S.P.Q.2d 1468 (Cal. 1996).

ᛒ

"For the convenience of parties and witnesses, in the interest of justice, a district court may transfer any civil action to any other district or division where it might have been brought." [28 U.S.C. §1404(a)] The decision rests within the sound discretion of the transferor court. *Dunhall Pharmaceuticals Inc. v. Discus Dental Inc.*, 45 U.S.P.Q.2d 1061, 1062 (Colo. 1997).

28 U.S.C. §1447(d).

The "no review" restriction of §1447(d) precludes the CAFC from reviewing the matter. The Ninth Circuit construed the language of §1447(d) as barring "not only appellate review but also reconsideration by the district court." *In re Foster*, 36 U.S.P.Q.2d 1503, 1506 (Fed. Cir. 1995—unpublished, not citable as precedent).

28 U.S.C. §1491.

The legislative history of §1491 makes clear that Congress intended to confer jurisdiction to the Claims Court to award injunctive relief against the government in a pre-award stage of the procurement process. Such authority was meant to prevent "arbitrary or capricious action by the contracting officials which would deny qualified firms the opportunity to compete fairly for the procurement award." The type of equitable power granted by §1491(a)(3) has no applicability to patent infringement litigation. A supplier or potential supplier of an infringing product for the government is "immune" from injunctive relief barring manufacture, sale, or bidding to supply such a product. Because §1498 "is paramount," injunctive relief is always subject to the condition that a patent owner's only recourse, when an infringer is dealing with the government, is to "sue the United States in the United States Claims Court for its entire compensation." Section 1498(a) would be emasculated if a patent holder could enjoin bidding to supply infringing products. Section 1498(a) precludes an injunction against an infringer's bidding to supply the government with infringing devices. *Trojan Inc. v. Shat-R-Shield Inc.*, 885 F.2d 854, 12 U.S.P.Q.2d 1132, 1134, 1135 (Fed. Cir. 1989).

28 U.S.C. §1498.

A patent owner whose patented invention is used or manufactured by or for the United States without a license may bring a suit in the Claims Court and recover from the United States "reasonable and entire compensation", which has two components. The first is the value of the license that, in effect, was taken by the government; the value is "determined ordinarily as of the time the Government takes the license." The second component involves compensation for the government's delay in paying for that license. *de Graffenried v. U.S.*, 25 Cl.Ct. 209, 24 U.S.P.Q.2d 1594, 1599 (U.S. Cl. Ct. 1992).

28 U.S.C. §1581(a).

In order for jurisdiction to attach under 28 U.S.C. §1581(a), there need be a written document sent to the District Director of Customs that contains the essential elements of a protest. Of relevance here, the protest must evidence a claim against prior Customs Service Action, the reasons for the claim, the entries involved, and the importer. The entry dates and importer number are also required. *Atmel Corp. v. United States*, 719 F. Supp. 1101, 13 U.S.P.Q.2d 1547, 1548 (U.S. Ct. Intl. Trade 1989).

28 U.S.C. §1732. *See* Federal Shop Book Rule, Shop Book Rule.

28 U.S.C. §1782.

28 U.S.C. §1782(a) provides that a United States District Court may, upon the application of any interested person, order a person residing in the district to give testimony or a statement or to produce documents for use in a foreign proceeding. The broadened power of the district courts under amended §1782 was expressly designed to make the federal judicial system more generous in its assistance to foreign litigation. The authority of district court judges is wholly discretionary. Under the statute, a district court "may" order testimony or documents; the statute does not direct the court to do so. It is enough to determine that the subject matter is generally pertinent, and that improper goals or effects, such as harassment and unnecessary expense and delay, are minimized. *In re Asta Medica S.A.*, 794 F.Supp. 442, 23 U.S.P.Q.2d 1756, 1757, 1759, 1760 (Me. 1992).

ϖ

Imposing a requirement that the materials sought be discoverable in the foreign jurisdiction would be inconsistent with both the letter and spirit of the statute. When "a foreign or international tribunal has ruled that production of the evidence pursuant to Section 1782 would not be appropriate, an American court should heed that ruling and deny the application". *In re Bayer A.G.*, 47 U.S.P.Q.2d 1001, 1005, 1007 (3d Cir. 1998).

28 U.S.C. §1920. *See* Costs.

28 U.S.C. §2201 (Declaratory Judgment Act)

28 U.S.C. §2501.

There is a distinction between the class of devices that infringes claims and the discreet individual devices which, together, constitute the class of infringing devices. The class is not foreclosed from infringing merely because one of its members was manufactured or used by the government more than six years prior to the filing of the suit. Each device, i.e., each individual member of the universe of infringing devices, can be taken only once in its lifetime, and if that taking occurs prior to the six-year period which immediately precedes the filing of the lawsuit in the Court of Claims, then recovery as to that particular device is barred forever by 28 U.S.C. §2501. *Starobin v. United States*, 662 F.2d 747, 213 U.S.P.Q. 449, 452 (U.S. Cl. Ct. 1981).

35 U.S.C. §21.

Since the application would not receive a filing date until Monday even if it were ready for filing the preceding Saturday, it is reasonable to compute the year, not from January 8 (Monday), 1962, but from January 6 (Saturday), 1962. In the absence of basis to believe that any of the magazines (mailed in bulk on January 4th) were delivered by January 6th, it cannot be said that the publication was issued more than a year prior to the filing date of the application. *Protein Foundation, Inc. v. Brenner*, 260 F.Supp. 519, 151 U.S.P.Q. 561, 562 (D.C. 1966).

35 U.S.C. §24. *See also* Discovery.

The limitations of the first sentence of 35 U.S.C. §24 would appear to apply if an interference party seeks to compel the attendance of a witness through the use of a subpoena under Fed. R. Civ. P. 45. *Vogel v. Jones*, 443 F.2d 257, 170 U.S.P.Q. 188, 189 (3d Cir. 1971).

ω

The statute does not grant broad discovery authorization to the district courts in patent interference cases, but limits ancillary jurisdiction to the issuance of subpoenas as permitted by prior practice. In referring to "provisions of the Federal Rules of Civil Procedure relating to the attendance of witnesses and to the production of documents", 35 U.S.C. §24 refers to the matters encompassed by Fed. R. Civ. P. 45(a), (b), (c), (d)(2), (e) and (f). *Frilette v. Kimberlin*, 500 F.2d 205, 184 U.S.P.Q. 266, 271 (3rd Cir. 1974).

ω

The prevailing interpretation of 35 U.S.C. §24 has been that it authorizes district courts to grant discovery beyond that permitted by the Board of Patent Interference's discovery rules and rules of admissibility. *Brown v. Braddick*, 595 F.2d 961, 203 U.S.P.Q. 95, 100 (5th Cir. 1979).

35 U.S.C. §26. *See* Citizenship.

35 U.S.C. §33.

The purpose of section 33 is to protect patent applicants against predation by unauthorized practitioners during the patent application process. There is a substantial difference between statutes directly relating to patents and those concerning merely collateral aspects of practice before the Patent Office. Section 33 does not relate to patents, but is merely connected with patents. *Enders v. American Patent Search Company*, 535 F.2d 1085, 189 U.S.P.Q. 569, 573 (9th Cir. 1976).

35 U.S.C. §41.

In terms of applying 35 U.S.C. §41(c)(1) and determining whether or not a failure has been "unavoidable", determinations by the PTO must be accorded a large degree of discretion. The principle purpose behind 35 U.S.C. §41(b) and (c)(1) was that Congress desired that patent holders help to finance the operation of the PTO by paying maintenance fees. The only indication of third party rights with regard to determinations made under 35 U.S.C. §41(c)(1) is explicitly contained in §41(c)(2), which section allows a court to fashion terms equitably to protect any investments made or business commenced by a third party after the six-month grace period expires, but before reinstatement of a patent under §41(c)(1). *Laerdall Medical Corp. v. Ambu Inc.*, 877 F.Supp. 255, 34 U.S.P.Q.2d 1140, 1143, 1144 (Md. 1995).

35 U.S.C. §100(b).

That Congress intended that both process and apparatus for its practice should be patented, and that the allowance of a patent on the one should not be used as an excuse to refuse a patent on the other, when a single patent for both is originally sought, is also shown by 35 U.S.C. §121. The fact that Congress did not intend use of one of these two as an excuse for refusing (i.e. rejecting) or invalidating claims to the other (when both are disclosed and urged as patentable in the same case) appears to be clear from 35 U.S.C. §§100(b), 101 and 121. *Ex parte Symons*, 134 U.S.P.Q. 74, 81, 82 (PO Bd. App. 1962).

35 U.S.C. §101. *See also* **Anticipation, Composition, Computer, Examiner's Opinion, Inoperative, Life Forms, Machine, Manufacture, Mental Steps, Method of Doing Business, New Use, Novelty, Process, Safety, Same Invention, Statutory Subject Matter, Transitory, Utility.**

The statement that claimed compounds inhibit the growth of a transplanted cancer strain is sufficient to satisfy the express language of 35 U.S.C. §101, and is in harmony with the basic constitutional concept of promoting the progress of science and the useful arts. *In re Bergel and Stock,* 292 F.2d 955, 130 U.S.P.Q. 206, 209 (C.C.P.A. 1961).

ω

Machine implementation vs. mental implementation is not a determinative dichotomy in deciding whether a method is statutory under 35 U.S.C. §101. "[A] process having no practical value other than enhancing the internal operation of [digital computers]" is in the technological or useful arts and hence is statutory under §101. *In re McIlroy,* 422 F.2d 1397, 170 U.S.P.Q. 31 (C.C.P.A. 1971).

ω

The purpose of 35 U.S.C. §101 is to define patentable subject matter, not to limit a patent to one invention. *In re Haas*, 486 F.2d 1053, 179 U.S.P.Q. 623 (C.C.P.A. 1973).

ω

Even if proof of utility of the claimed invention as an anti-arthritic agent for humans is lacking, there remains the proven utility as an anti-arthritic agent for lower animals. Having found that the claimed composition has utility as contemplated in the specification, 35 U.S.C. §101 is satisfied, and it is unnecessary to decide whether it is in fact useful for other purposes indicated in the specification as possibilities. *In re Malachowski,* 530 F.2d 1402, 189 U.S.P.Q. 432, 435 (C.C.P.A. 1976).

ω

Microorganisms have long been important tools in the chemical industry, and when such a useful, industrial tool (which is new and unobvious, so that it complies with those conditions for patentability) is invented, there is no reason to deprive it or its creator or owner of the protection and advantages of the patent system by arbitrarily excluding it at the outset from the §101 categories of patentable invention on the sole ground that it is alive. *In re Bergy, Coats, and Malik; In re Chakrabarty*, 596 F.2d 952, 201 U.S.P.Q. 352, 373 (C.C.P.A. 1979).

ω

Claims may be rejected under §101 because they attempt to embrace only a mathematical formula, mathematical algorithm, or method of calculation, but not merely because they define inventions having something to do with a computer. I*n re Diehr and Lutton*, 602 F.2d 982, 203 U.S.P.Q. 44, 50 (C.C.P.A. 1979); *aff'd* 209 U.S.P.Q. 1 (S.Ct. 1981).

ω

Every discovery is not embraced within the statutory terms of 35 U.S.C. §101. Excluded from such patent protection are laws of nature, physical phenomena, and abstract ideas. A principle, in the abstract, is a fundamental truth, an original cause, a motive; these cannot be patented, and no one can claim in any of them an exclusive right. A new mineral discovered in the earth or a new plant found in the wild is not patentable subject matter. Likewise, Einstein could not patent his celebrated law that $E = mc2$; nor could Newton have patented the law of gravity. Such discoveries are "manifestations of . . . nature, free to all men and reserved exclusively to none." When a claim recites a mathematical formula (or scientific principle or phenomenon of nature), an inquiry must be made into whether the claim is seeking patent protection for that formula in the abstract. A mathematical formula as such is not accorded the protection of our patent laws, and this principle cannot be circumvented by attempting to limit the use of the formula to a particular technological environment. Similarly, insignificant post-solution activity will not transform an unpatentable principle into a patentable process. On the other hand, when a claim containing a mathematical formula implements or applies that formula in a structure or process that, when considered as a whole, is performing a function that the patent laws were designed to protect, then the claim satisfies the requirements of 35 U.S.C. §101. *Diamond v. Diehr and Lutton,* 450 U.S. 175, 209 U.S.P.Q. 1, 7, 10 (1981).

ω

A specification that contains a disclosure of utility that corresponds in scope to the subject matter sought to be patented must be taken as sufficient to satisfy the utility requirements of §101 for the entire claimed subject matter unless there is reason for one skilled in the art to question the objective truth of the statement of utility or its scope. *Ex parte Rubin*, 5 U.S.P.Q.2d 1461 (B.P.A.I. 1987).

ଫ

In considering a claim for compliance with 35 U.S.C. §101, it must be determined whether a scientific principle, law of nature, idea, or mental process, which may be represented by a mathematical algorithm, is included in the subject matter of the claim. If it is, it must then be determined whether such principle, law, idea, or mental process is applied in an invention of the type set forth in 35 U.S.C. §101. Although the line separating statutory processes from nonstatutory processes is unclear, the mere presence of a calculation or the computer implementation of the method does not mandate a holding that the claimed procedure is not a "process" within the meaning of 35 U.S.C. §101. But, where the claims solely recite a method whereby a set of numbers is computed from a different set of numbers by merely performing a series of mathematical computations, the claims do not set forth a statutory process. *Ex parte Logan*, 20 U.S.P.Q.2d 1465, 1467 (B.P.A.I. 1991).

ଫ

The Supreme Court has acknowledged that Congress intended 35 U.S.C. §101 to extend to "anything under the sun that is made by man." Thus, it is improper to read into §101 limitations as to the subject matter that may be patented where the legislative history does not indicate that Congress clearly intended such limitations. *In re Alappat*, 33 F.3d 1526, 31 U.S.P.Q.2d 1545, 1556 (Fed. Cir. 1994).

ଫ

The scope of a claim and the number of compounds included within the scope are not irrelevant to a 35 U.S.C. §101 and/or a 35 U.S.C §112, first paragraph, analysis. However, no evidence was cited by the Examiner that any different reactivities would make some compounds useful and others not useful. *Ex parte Bhide*, 42 U.S.P.Q.2d 1441, 1447 (B.P.A.I. 1996)

35 U.S.C. §102. *See* **Abandonment, Anticipation, Concealment, Dedication to the Public, Derivation, Inventorship, Known, Name, Naming, Novelty, On Sale, Prior Knowledge, Prior Use, Publication, Read On, Reference, Sale.**

35 U.S.C. §102/§103.

A rejection of claims under 35 U.S.C. §102/§103 is a hybrid rejection having apparently been made on the theory that, if the claimed subject matter was novel (i.e., not anticipated), in terms of §102, then it would have been obvious under §103. The PTO's practice of basing rejections on §102 or §103 in the alternative has been accepted, provided that appellant is fully apprised of all the grounds of rejection. *In re Spada*, 911 F.2d 705, 15 U.S.P.Q.2d 1655, 1657 (Fed. Cir. 1990).

35 U.S.C. §102(a). *See also* **Another.**

Classified documents, whose security classification was not removed until after the invention of the patent in suit, are not prior publications or evidence of prior knowledge, as they are not "public" within the meaning of §102(a). *Del Mar Engineering Laboratories v. United States*, 524 F.2d 1178, 186 U.S.P.Q. 42, 45 (U.S. Ct. Cl. 1975).

ᚹ

To negate validity, the claimed inventions must be shown to have been publicly known prior to the patentee's claimed invention. *Reynolds Metals Company v. Aluminum Company of America*, 457 F.Supp. 482, 198 U.S.P.Q. 529, 543 (Ind. 1978).

ᚹ

One's own invention, whatever the form of disclosure to the public, may not be prior art against oneself, absent a statutory bar under 35 U.S.C. §102(b). *In re Katz*, 687 F.2d 450, 215 U.S.P.Q. 14, 17 (C.C.P.A. 1982).

35 U.S.C. §102(b)[2].

The express language "described in a printed publication" does not preclude the use of more than one reference; "a printed publication" can include two or more printed publications. *In re Foster*, 343 F.2d 980, 145 U.S.P.Q. 166, 173 (C.C.P.A. 1965).

ᚹ

The disclosure of a structural formula in a reference can be a statutory bar under §102(b) against a claim to a compound of that formula if a method of making such compound was known by, or obvious to, one skilled in the art more than one year prior to applicant's filing date, notwithstanding the fact that there was no known use of the compound prior to applicant's invention. *In re Samour*, 571 F.2d 559, 197 U.S.P.Q. 1, 3, 4, 5 (C.C.P.A. 1978); *compare with In re Stemniski*, 444 F.2d 581, 170 U.S.P.Q. 343, 348 (C.C.P.A. 1971).

ᚹ

A contract to construct from plans and to deliver in the future a machine not proven to be previously completed is not proof that the product was "on sale" under §102(b). *Orton v. Robicon Corporation*, 378 F.Supp. 930, 183 U.S.P.Q. 477, 482 (Pa. 1974).

ᚹ

The "délivré" date of a French patent is not the patent date for §102(b) purposes. *In re Voss*, 557 F.2d 812, 194 U.S.P.Q. 267, 269 n.3 (C.C.P.A. 1977).

ᚹ

A printed document may qualify as a "publication" under 35 U.S.C. §102(b), notwithstanding that accessibility thereto is restricted to a "part of the public", so long as accessibility is sufficient "to raise a presumption that the public concerned with the art would know of [the invention]". *In re Bayer*, 568 F.2d 1357, 196 U.S.P.Q. 670, 674 (C.C.P.A. 1978).

ᚹ

A mere offer for sale is sufficient to constitute a patentability bar under 35 U.S.C. §102(b). If a buyer has authority to use an invention commercially, there is a sale under 35 U.S.C. §102(b). *Kahl v. Scoville*, 219 U.S.P.Q. 725, 732 (PTO Bd. Pat. Intf. 1982).

ᚹ

---

[2]*See in re Petering and Fall*, 301 F.2d 676, 133 U.S.P.Q. 275, 280 (C.C.P.A. 1962).

35 U.S.C. §102(b)

As long as those persons "in the class of people to whom [the document] is directed" could have a copy "merely for the asking," the document is deemed to be publicly available. *In re Certain Caulking Guns*, 223 U.S.P.Q. 388, 397 (U.S. Int'l Trade Comm'l 1984).

ᵹ

A §102(b) reference "must sufficiently describe the claimed invention to have placed the public in possession of it." If any claim of a patent issued on a cip is limited to the filing date of the cip based on the insufficiency of the disclosure of its parent application for support, a corresponding foreign patent (having substantially the same disclosure as the parent application) is also insufficient to anticipate such claim under §102(b). *Paperless Accounting, Inc. v. Bay Area Rapid Transit System*, 804 F.2d 659, 231 U.S.P.Q. 649, 653 (Fed. Cir. 1986).

ᵹ

The policy embodied in 35 U.S.C. §102(b) does not require that the one-year period start to accrue on an invention that is not yet known to work satisfactorily for its intended purpose. *Seal-Flex Inc. v. Athletic Track and Court Construction*, 98 F.3d 1318, 40 U.S.P.Q.2d 1450, 1453 (Fed. Cir. 1996).

ᵹ

A third party's secret commercial activity, more than one year before the patent application of another, is not a §102(b) bar. *Woodland Trust v. Flowertree Nursery Inc.*, 148 F.3d 1368, 47 U.S.P.Q.2d 1363, 1366 (Fed. Cir. 1998).

35 U.S.C. §102(c).

To the extent that an assignor (appellant) has divested himself of all right, title and interest in his prior application, he has abandoned any interest which he may have had in the invention, in favor of the assignee, and therefore comes under 35 U.S.C. §102(c). Appellant's prior patent is thus treated as prior art for all that it discloses. *Ex parte Ohmart*, 143 U.S.P.Q. 119, 120 (PO Bd. App. 1962).

ᵹ

Actual abandonment under 35 U.S.C. §102(c) requires that the inventor intend to abandon the invention, and intent can be implied from the inventor's conduct with respect to the invention. Such intent to abandon an invention will not be imputed, and every reasonable doubt should be resolved in favor of the inventor. *Ex parte Dunne*, 20 U.S.P.Q.2d 1479, 1480 (B.P.A.I. 1991).

35 U.S.C. §102(d).

The mere issuance of the specification of a patent in printed form is unessential to the question of whether an invention has been patented in a foreign country. Section 102(d) does not refer to "granting" or "issuing" a patent in a foreign country, nor does it refer to any particular paper or procedure, but merely uses the language "the invention was patented in a foreign country", and is not concerned with the particular procedure whereby an invention becomes patented in the foreign country. *Ex parte Gruschwitz and Fritz*, 138 U.S.P.Q. 505, 506, 511 (PO Bd. App. 1961).

ᵹ

The registration of an industrial design (Geschmacksmuster) under the laws of Germany (even when the subject matter of the German grant is maintained in secrecy, i.e., not available for public inspection, until after a corresponding application is filed in the United States) may be considered for purposes of applying the statutory time bar of §102(d) against the application for a United States design patent on the same subject matter. *In re Talbott*, 443 F.2d 1397, 170 U.S.P.Q. 281 (C.C.P.A. 1971).

ω

In order for a foreign patent to constitute a bar under 35 U.S.C. §102(d), the foreign patent must be for the same invention as the United States application. *Ex parte Razavi*, 194 U.S.P.Q. 175, 176 (PTO Bd. App. 1973).

ω

In the context of §102(d) under the French procedure the délivré date is the operative patent date. *The Duplan Corporation v. Deering Milliken Research Corporation*, 487 F.2d 459, 179 U.S.P.Q. 449 (4th Cir. 1973), cert. denied, 181 U.S.P.Q. 129 (1974).

ω

A foreign patent which is a bar under 35 U.S.C. §102(d) can be combined with other patents or with literature references to bar a patent on subject matter which would have been obvious from the barred subject matter in the light of other references. *Ex parte Appeal No. 242a-47*, 196 U.S.P.Q. 828, 829 (PTO Bd. App. 1976).

ω

Patenting, within the meaning of §102(d), does not occur upon laying open of a Japanese utility model application (18 months from either the actual Japanese filing date or the date of the "home country" application under the Paris Convention, whichever is first). *Ex parte Fujishiro and Ohta*, 199 U.S.P.Q. 36, 38 (PTO Bd. App. 1977).

35 U.S.C. §102(e). *See also* **Another.**

A description that is canceled from the text of a pending application before the application results in a patent or comes to the public notice is not such a published description of an invention as is within the inhibition of the statute. *Fessenden v. Wilson*, 48 F.2d 422, 9 U.S.P.Q. 274, 277 (C.C.P.A.), *cert. denied*, 284 U.S. 640 (1931).

ω

A United States patent is available as a reference under §102(e), even when issued on a copending application. *In re Gregg*, 244 F.2d 316, 113 U.S.P.Q. 526, 529 (C.C.P.A. 1957); *In re Rosicky*, 276 F.2d 656, 125 U.S.P.Q. 341, 344 (C.C.P.A. 1960).

ω

Sections 119 and 102(e) (35 U.S.C) deal with unrelated concepts. The historical origins of the two sections show that neither was intended to affect the other, wherefore they should not be read together in violation of the most basic rule of statutory construction, the "master rule", of carrying out the legislative intent. A United States patent is not effective as a reference as of its foreign priority date. Section 102(e) was a codification of the Milburn doctrine. The *Milburn* case [*Alexander Milburn Co. v. Davis-Bournonville Co.*, 270 U.S. 390 (1926)] accorded a U.S. patent effect as a reference as of its U.S. filing date and stated that the policy of the statute on domestic inventions "cannot be applied to foreign affairs". *In re Hilmer, Korger, Weyer, and Aumuller*, 359 F.2d 859, 149 U.S.P.Q. 480, 491, 499 (C.C.P.A. 1966).

ω

A rejection under §102(e) may be overcome by a Rule 132 (37 C.F.R. §1.132) affidavit of the reference patentee averring that the relevant unclaimed subject matter disclosed in his patent was not invented by the patentee, but was first disclosed to him by the appellant. *In re Mathews,* 408 F.2d 1393, 161 U.S.P.Q. 276, 277 (C.C.P.A. 1969).

ω

An abandoned U.S.A. application (by a different and unrelated inventive entity) is not made available as a reference as of its filing date when a subsequently-filed counterpart foreign application is published. 35 U.S.C. §102(e) is limited to a United States patent. The effective date (as a reference) of the German document relied upon (to defeat another's right to a patent) is only the date upon which it was laid open to the public. *Ex parte Smolka and Schwuger*, 207 U.S.P.Q. 232, 235 (PTO Bd. App. 1980).

35 U.S.C. §102(f). *See* Derivation.

This section applies to an applicant who has acquired particular subject matter or information from another (either in this or in another country), and thereafter seeks to patent either the same or obvious variants of that acquired subject matter or information. A rejection can be based on 35 U.S.C. 102(f)/103. *Ex parte Andresen*, 212 U.S.P.Q. 100, 102 (PTO Bd. App. 1981).

ω

That which is prior art under §102(f) can be used alone or in combination with other prior art to support a rejection under 35 U.S.C. §103. *Ex parte Yoshino and Takasu*, 227 U.S.P.Q. 52, 54 (B.P.A.I. 1985).

ω

"Subject matter which is developed by another person which qualifies as prior art only under 35 U.S.C. §102(f) or (g) may be used as prior art under 35 U.S.C. §103 against a claimed invention...." As summarized, however, in 2 Donald S. Chisum, *Patents* §5.03[3][c][vi][B] (Rel.55 1995):

A few decisions by lower courts and the Board of Appeals view specific derived knowledge as prior art under [§102(f)], but neither the Federal Circuit nor its two predecessor...has so held.

Lamb-Weston Inc. v. McCain Foods Ltd., 78 F.3d 540, 37 U.S.P.Q.2d 1856, 1859 n., 1863 (dissent)(Fed. Cir. 1996).

ω

Subject matter derived from another not only is itself unpatentable [under 35 U.S.C. §102(f)] to the party who derived it, but, when combined with other prior art, may make another obvious invention unpatentable to that party under a combination of §§102(f) and 103 of Title 35 (U.S.C.) *OddzOn Products Inc. v. Just Toys Inc.*, 122 F.3d 1396, 43 U.S.P.Q.2d 1641, 1646 (Fed. Cir. 1997).

35 U.S.C. §102(g). *See also* **Abandoned, Abandoned Application, Claims Suggested for Interference, Conceal, Concealment, Conception, Contemplate, Deem, Delay, Diligence, Obviousness, Reduction to Practice, Suppression.**

When a record establishes that an interference party actually derived the invention of a count from his opponent, he cannot prevail on an issue of abandonment, suppression, or concealment; to prevail on such issue, he must be an independent inventor. *Spiner and Hoffman v. Pierce,* 177 U.S.P.Q. 709, 711 (PO Bd. Pat. Int. 1972).

ឃ

To satisfy the reasonable diligence requirement in an interference setting, work relied on must ordinarily be directly related to reduction to practice of the invention of the counts in issue. *Naber v. Cricchi,* 567 F.2d 382, 196 U.S.P.Q. 294 (C.C.P.A. 1977), *cert. denied,* 439 U.S. 826, 200 U.S.P.Q. 64 (1978).

ឃ

Unlike the filing of a patent application, the publication of an article is not deemed a constructive reduction to practice of the subject matter described therein. Therefore, disclosure in a publication does not prove that any "invention" within the meaning of §102(g) has ever been made by anyone. *In re Katz,* 687 F.2d 450, 215 U.S.P.Q. 14, 17 (C.C.P.A. 1982).

ឃ

In a priority contest a party who was second to file was unable to prevail even though he had reduced the invention to practice four years prior to his opponent's filing date. Even if he demonstrated continuous activity from prior to his opponent's effective filing date to his filing date, such should have no bearing on the question of priority. While diligence during the above-noted period may be relied upon by one alleging prior conception and subsequent reduction to practice, it is of no significance in the case of the party who is not last to reduce to practice. Too long a delay may bar the first inventor from reliance on an early reduction to practice. However, the first inventor is not barred from relying on later, resumed activity antedating an opponent's entry into the field merely because the work done before the delay occurred was sufficient to amount to a reduction to practice. *Paulik v. Rizkalla,* 760 F.2d 1270, 226 U.S.P.Q. 224 (Fed. Cir. 1985).

ឃ

Unexplained delays by a patent attorney in preparing an application, and failure by the attorney to take up applications in the order that they are received, forecloses a finding of reasonable diligence. The patent obtained on such an application is not prior art under 35 U.S.C. §102(g), because the invention of that patent was reduced to practice by another before the application was filed, and before diligent preparation of the application began.

35 U.S.C. §102(g)

Mendenhall v. Astec Industries, Inc., 13 U.S.P.Q.2d 1913, 1935 (Tenn. 1988), *aff'd*, 13 U.S.P.Q.2d 1956 (Fed. Cir. 1989).

ω

While more commonly applied to interferences, §102(g) is indeed applicable to prior-invention situations other than in the context of an interference. When the claimed invention was made in this country by another (who had not abandoned, suppressed, or concealed it) before the invention by the patentee, the patent claims are invalid under 35 U.S.C. §102(g). *New Ideal Farm Equipment Corp. v. Sperry Corp. & New Holland Inc.*, 916 F.2d 1561, 16 U.S.P.Q.2d 1424, 1428 (Fed. Cir. 1990).

ω

The issue of abandonment, suppression or concealment, within the meaning of 35 U.S.C. §102(g) "cannot arise unless and until a prior actual reduction to practice has been established." *Buell v. Beckestrom*, 22 U.S.P.Q.2d 1128, 1130 (B.P.A.I. 1992).

ω

A purpose of the 1984 amendment to 35 U.S.C. §103 was to overturn a line of cases under which a prior invention which was not public could be treated under 35 U.S.C. §102(g) as prior art for purposes of Section 103 with respect to a later invention made by another employee of the same organization. *Kimberly-Clark Corp. v. The Procter & Gamble Distributing Co. Inc.*, 972 F.2d 911, 23 U.S.P.Q.2d 1921, 1926 (Fed. Cir. 1992).

35 U.S.C. §102(g)/§103.

A prior invention by another who had not abandoned, suppressed, or concealed it, including the disclosure of such invention in an issued patent, is available as "prior art" within the meaning of that term in 35 U.S.C. §103 by virtue of 35 U.S.C. §102(g). *In re Bass, Jenkins, and Horvat*, 474 F.2d 1276, 177 U.S.P.Q. 178, 186 (C.C.P.A. 1973).

ω

The priority finding of an interference does not totally control the §102(g)/§103 determination of prior work as prior art. The safeguards of 35 U.S.C. §103 serve to protect both the public domain and the simultaneous inventors. The burden of proof on the §102(g)/§103 issue is on the defendant, the party urging the obviousness. *CSS International Corp. v. Maul Technology Co.*, 16 U.S.P.Q.2d 1657, 1662 (Ind. 1989).

35 U.S.C. §103. *See also* Analogous Art, Antedating a Reference, Circumstances, Combining References, Contemplate, Deem, Description, Difference, Disclosure, Equivalence, Graham Inquiries, Hindsight, MOSITA, Motivation, Obviousness, Obvious to Try or Experiment, Old Combination, Optimize, Ordinary Skill, Prior Art, Prior-Art Anagrams, Problem, Product, Reference, Secondary Considerations, Selection, Skill of the Art, Steps, Subject Matter as a Whole, Teach Away From, Teaching, Unexpected Properties, Unexpected Results, Whole.

A Rule 131 (37 C.F.R. §1.131) affidavit was permitted to overcome a rejection under §103 based on a reference published more than one year prior to appellants'' filing date. *In re Palmquist and Erwin*, 319 F.2d 547, 138 U.S.P.Q. 234, 238 (C.C.P.A. 1963).

ω

Patentability of the appellant's invention under 35 U.S.C. §103 must be evaluated against the background of the highly developed and specific art to which it relates, and this background improves an understanding of those unsolved problems persisting in the art that the appellant asserts have been solved by his invention. *In re Cable,* 347 F.2d 872, 146 U.S.P.Q. 175, 177 (C.C.P.A. 1965).

ᴕ

The Solicitor relies on *In re Winslow,* 365 F.2d 1017, 151 U.S.P.Q. 48 (C.C.P.A. 1966), for the proposition that a combination of features shown by references is legally obvious if it would have been obvious to "the inventor...working in his shop with the prior-art references—which he is presumed to know—hanging on the wall around him," 151 U.S.P.Q. at 51, a statement limited by reference to "a case like this." In *Winslow*, the principal secondary reference was "in the very same art" as appellant's invention; all of the references were characterized as "very pertinent art." The language relied on by the Solicitor does not apply in cases where the very point in issue is whether one of ordinary skill in the art would have selected, without the advantage of hindsight and knowledge of the applicant's disclosure, the particular references that the Examiner applied. The inventor is presumed (under 35 U.S.C. §103) to have full knowledge of the prior art in the field of his endeavor, but not full knowledge of prior art outside the field of his endeavor (i.e., of "non-analogous" art). The inventor is only presumed to have that ability to select and utilize knowledge from other arts reasonably pertinent to his particular problem that would be expected of a person of ordinary skill in the art to which the subject matter pertains. *In re Antle,* 444 F.2d 1168, 170 U.S.P.Q. 285, 287, 288 (C.C.P.A. 1971).

ᴕ

The Board based the rejection under 35 U.S.C. §103 on the theory that an applicant that has lost an interference can never be entitled to claims that are obvious variations of the invention defined in the lost counts. The court found no judicial doctrine that supports this rejection under 35 U.S.C. §103. An invention (defined in lost counts) apparently made outside the United States is not accorded the same effective date as a reference as it would have had, had it been made in this country. *In re McKellin, Mageli, and D'Angelo,* 529 F.2d 1324, 188 U.S.P.Q. 428, 435 (C.C.P.A. 1976).

ᴕ

The issue of patentability must be approached in terms of what would have been obvious to one of ordinary skill in the art at the time the invention was made in view of the sum of all of the relevant teachings in the art, not in view of first one and then another of isolated teachings in the art. The entirety of the disclosure made by references must be considered to avoid combining them indiscriminately. *In re Ehrreich and Avery*, 590 F.2d 902, 200 U.S.P.Q. 504, 510 (C.C.P.A. 1979).

ᴕ

Though it is proper to note the difference in a claimed invention from the prior art because that difference may serve as one element in determining the obviousness/non-obviousness issue, it is improper (even if erroneously suggested by a party) to consider the difference as the invention. The "difference" may have seemed slight (as has often been the case with some of history's great inventions, for example, the telephone), but it may also have been the key to success and advancement in the art resulting from the invention. Further, it is irrelevant in determining obviousness that all or other aspects of the claim may have been well known in the art. The statute requires that the invention as claimed be considered "as a whole" when considering whether that invention would have been obvious when it was made. A conclusion that "the discovery of a use of an inherent quality of a product well known in the art is not patentable because of obviousness" confuses anticipation by inherency (i.e., lack of novelty with obviousness); though anticipation is the epitome of obviousness, they are separate and distinct concepts. A conclusion that "the discovery does not involve that degree of inventiveness which the courts have required" would engraft on 35 U.S.C. §103 a nonstatutory requirement for a "degree of inventiveness." *Jones v. Hardy,* 727 F.2d 1524, 220 U.S.P.Q. 1021, 1024, 1025, 1026 (C.C.P.A. 1984).

ᗡ

Most technological advance is the fruit of methodical, persistent investigation, as is recognized in 35 U.S.C. §103 ("Patentability shall not be negatived by the manner in which the invention was made"). The consistent criterion for determination of obviousness is whether the prior art would have suggested to one of ordinary skill in the art that this process should be carried out and would have a reasonable likelihood of success, viewed in the light of the prior art. Both the suggestion and the expectation of success must be found in the prior art, not in the applicant's disclosure. *In re Dow Chemical Co.,* 837 F.2d 469, 5 U.S.P.Q.2d 1529 (Fed. Cir. 1988).

ᗡ

The test under 35 U.S.C. §103 is whether, in view of the prior art, the invention as a whole would have been obvious at the time it was made. The prior art does not include applicant's claimed products, claims to which are regarded as allowable. The obviousness of the process of use must be determined without reference to knowledge of the claimed products and their properties. The claimed products constitute an essential limitation of the claimed method of use thereof. That being so, the Board's hindsight comparison of the functioning of the new compounds with the functioning of the compounds of the prior art was legal error. It uses appellant's specification teaching as though it were prior art in order to make claims to methods of using his admittedly novel compounds appear to be obvious. *In re Pleuddemann,* 910 F.2d 823, 15 U.S.P.Q.2d 1738, 1742 (Fed. Cir. 1990).

ᗡ

While a rejection for double patenting of the obviousness-type can be overcome by filing a terminal disclaimer, that does not mean that a 35 U.S.C. §103 rejection for obviousness may be similarly overcome (even if based on the same copending patent with an overlapping, but different, inventive entity). Under §103, a reference patent is available for all it fairly discloses to one of ordinary skill in the art. There is no inquiry as to what is claimed therein. In a rejection for double patenting of the obviousness type, the test is not what would be obvious to one of ordinary skill in the art from reading the specification or claims. Rather, the inquiry is much more limited in nature, and the patent is considered only to compare the invention defined in the patent claims with the invention defined in the application claims. *Ex parte Bartfeld,* 16 U.S.P.Q.2d 1714, 1717 (B.P.A.I. 1990).

ᗡ

The criterion of 35 U.S.C. §103 is not whether the differences from the prior art are "simple enhancements," but whether it would have been obvious to make the claimed structure. *Continental Can Co. USA Inc. v. Monsanto Co.*, 948 F.2d 1264, 20 U.S.P.Q.2d 1746, 1752 (Fed. Cir. 1991).

ω

A purpose of the 1984 amendment to 35 U.S.C. §103 was to overturn a line of cases under which a prior invention which was not public could be treated under 35 U.S.C. §102(g) as prior art for purposes of Section 103 with respect to a later invention made by another employee of the same organization. *Kimberly-Clark Corp. v. The Procter & Gamble Distributing Co. Inc.*, 972 F.2d 911, 23 U.S.P.Q.2d 1921, 1926 (Fed. Cir. 1992).

ω

A reference acknowledged as not being prior art was held to be properly considered in determining the patentability under 35 U.S.C. §103 of claims on appeal as relevant evidence with regard to (1) characteristics of prior art products, and (2) the knowledge possessed by and the level of skill of the ordinary person in the art. *Ex parte Raychem Corp.*, 25 U.S.P.Q.2d 1265, 1268 (B.P.A.I. 1992).

ω

References should be applied in accord with their actual teachings. Language should not be extracted out of context for the purpose of making and maintaining an art-based ground of rejection. A generalization from a limited reference disclosure is not a valid basis for precluding patentability. *Ex parte Isshiki, Kijima and Watanabe*, 36 U.S.P.Q.2d 1863 (B.P.A.I. 1993—*unpublished*).

35 U.S.C. §104. *See also* Origin.

This section relates only to what an applicant or patentee may and may not do to protect himself against patent-defeating events occurring between his invention date and his U.S. filing date. *In re Hilmer, Korger, Weyer and Aumuller*, 424 F.2d 1108, 165 U.S.P.Q. 255, 258 (C.C.P.A. 1970).

ω

This section does not preclude using evidence of an inventor's knowledge from a foreign country for all purposes, but only where it is used to "establish a date of invention." Knowledge of the inventors, embodied in the Transmission Record, is admissible evidence to prove the chemical structure of the compound introduced into this country. *Breuer and Treuner v. DeMarinis*, 558 F.2d 22, 194 U.S.P.Q. 308, 313 (C.C.P.A. 1977).

35 U.S.C. §111.

Since 35 U.S.C. §111 requires that the application be signed by the applicant, the waiver of signature and execution authorized by 35 U.S.C. §121 is warranted only in those situations in which the proposed divisional application is (1) directed to a single non-elected invention, one not elected after a requirement for restriction in the original application, and (2) a copy of the original application as filed, accompanied by a proposed amendment cancelling the irrelevant claims or other matter. *In re Application Papers Filed December 22, 1958*, 123 U.S.P.Q. 71, 72 (Comm'r 1959).

ʊ

Though not expressly authorizing sole-to-sole conversion of an application, the statute is equally devoid of any express prohibition thereagainst. 35 U.S.C. 111 (1970) does require an oath "by the applicant" and that the application be signed "by the applicant". As the parent application was filed by an assignee of the true inventor and thus by a true party in interest in the application, it was filed by an applicant capable of recognition by the PTO and was not, under any statutory provision, a nullity. *A.F. Stoddard & Company, Ltd. v. Dann*, 564 F.2d 556, 195 U.S.P.Q. 97, 104, 105 (D.C. Cir. 1977).

35 U.S.C. §112. *See also* **Accuracy, Alternative, Antecedent Support, Art, Best Mode, Breadth, Claim, Combination, Construe, Definiteness, Definition, Dependent Claim, Description, Disclosure, Distinctly Claim, Element, Enablement, Enabling Disclosure, Exclude, Exemplification, Formal Rejection, Function, Functional, Generic, Genus, How to Make, How to Use, Hybrid, Incentive, Incomplete, Indefiniteness, Inoperative, Invention, Invitation to Experiment, Lexicographer, Limits, Means, Means Plus Function, Mode of Administration, Multiplicity, Negative Limitation, Objective Enablement, Particularity, Possession, Precision, Presumption, Process, Product by Properties, Properties, Scope, Skilled in the Art, Skill of the Art, Specification, Specific Example, Starting Material, State of the Art, Steps, Sufficiency of Disclosure, Support, Synergism, Truth, Unbelievable, Undue Breadth, Undue Experimentation, Unpredictable Art, Use, Utility, Unity of Invention, Vague, Working Example.**

A patent application, which requires a specification and claims, 35 U.S.C. §112, "constitute[s] one of the most difficult legal instruments to draw with accuracy." *Sperry v. State of Florida*, 378 U.S. 378, 383, 137 U.S.P.Q. 578, 580 (1965).

ʊ

Under 35 U.S.C. §112, a specification need not teach that which is obvious to those in the art. *In re Sureau, Kremer, and Dupre*, 373 F.2d 1002, 153 U.S.P.Q. 66, 70 (C.C.P.A. 1967).

ʊ

A claim that reads on subject matter for which appellants do not seek coverage, and therefore tacitly admit to be beyond that which "applicant regards as his invention," fails to comply with 35 U.S.C. §112. *In re Prater and Wei*, 415 F.2d 1393, 162 U.S.P.Q. 541, 550 (C.C.P.A. 1969).

ʊ

The fact that a claim reads on both statutory and nonstatutory subject matter does not preclude its being in compliance with the second paragraph of 35 U.S.C. §112. To inject any question of statutory subject matter into that paragraph is to depart from its wording and to complicate the law unnecessarily. *In re Mahony*, 421 F.2d 742, 164 U.S.P.Q. 572, 575 (C.C.P.A. 1970).

ʊ

Section 112 does not require that the claims define "the invention," whatever that would mean. The second paragraph of that section requires that the claims define "the subject matter which the applicant regards as his invention." The meaning of this provision is simply that an applicant is required to set definite boundaries on the patent protection sought. What the applicant does not regard as an element of his invention need not be specified in claims. *In re Wakefield and Foster,* 422 F.2d 897, 164 U.S.P.Q. 636 (C.C.P.A. 1970).

ᚹ

The purpose of the second paragraph of 35 U.S.C. §112 is to provide those who would endeavor, in future enterprise, to approach the area circumscribed by the claims of a patent, with the adequate notice demanded by due process of law, with the ability to determine, readily and accurately, the boundaries of protection involved and to evaluate the possibility of infringement and dominance. *In re Hammack,* 427 F.2d 1378, 166 U.S.P.Q. 204 (C.C.P.A. 1970).

ᚹ

Perhaps more so with respect to 35 U.S.C. §112 than with any other section of the statute, it is essential for the orderly resolution of issues that the specific requirement on which a rejection is based be clearly identified. *In re Robins,* 429 F.2d 452, 166 U.S.P.Q. 552 (C.C.P.A. 1970).

ᚹ

Assuming that an applicant is claiming what he regards as his invention, there are in reality only two basic grounds for rejecting a claim under §112. The first is that the language used is not precise and definite enough to provide a clear-cut indication of the scope of subject matter embraced by the claim. This ground finds its basis in the second paragraph of §112. The second is that the language is so broad that it causes the claim to have a potential scope of protection beyond that which is justified by the specification disclosure. This ground of rejection is now recognized as stemming from the requirements of the first paragraph of 35 U.S.C. §112. *In re Swinehart and Sfiligoj,* 439 F.2d 210, 169 U.S.P.Q. 226, 229 (C.C.P.A. 1971).

ᚹ

If those skilled in the art can tell whether any particular embodiment is or in not within the scope of a claim, the claim fulfills its purpose as a definition. *In re Miller,* 441 F.2d 689, 169 U.S.P.Q. 597, 599 (C.C.P.A. 1971).

ᚹ

The second paragraph of 35 U.S.C. §112 provides no authority for rejecting a claim on the basis of an "arbitrary" Patent Office determination that the claim contains a plurality of inventions. *In re Wolfrum and Gold,* 486 F.2d 588, 179 U.S.P.Q. 620, 622 (C.C.P.A. 1973).

ᚹ

The three requirements of 35 U.S.C. §112 are: (1) the written description requirement, paragraph 1, (2) the requirement for an adequate enabling disclosure to support the scope of the claims, paragraph 1, and (3) the requirement that the claims be precise and definite enough to provide a clear-cut indication of the scope of subject matter embraced therein, paragraph 2. The PTO has the burden of giving reasons, supported by the record as a whole, why the specification is not enabling, and showing that the disclosure entails undue experimentation would be one way of meeting that burden. *In re Morehouse and Bolton*, 545 F.2d 162, 192 U.S.P.Q. 29, 31, 32 (C.C.P.A. 1976).

ω

How a parent application achieves compliance with 35 U.S.C. §112, first paragraph, is immaterial. The only requirement is that the specification describe the claimed invention sufficiently for those of ordinary skill in the art to recognize that the applicant invented the subject matter he now claims. *In re Voss*, 557 F.2d 8, 194 U.S.P.Q. 267, 271 (C.C.P.A. 1977).

ω

In support of a rejection under 35 U.S.C. §112, later references were cited, not as prior art, but as evidence to prove the appellants' disclosure non-enabling for "other species" of the claimed polymer, in an effort to show why the scope of enablement was insufficient to support the claims. As thus implicitly recognized, the references would not have been available in support of a rejection under 35 U.S.C. §102 or §103 entered in connection with the 1953 application. To permit use of the same references in support of the §112 rejection herein, however, is to render the "benefit" of 35 U.S.C. §120 illusory. The very purpose of reliance on §120 is to reach back, to avoid the effect of intervening references. Nothing in §120 limits its application to any specific grounds of rejection, or permits the Examiner, denied use of references to reject or to require narrowing of a claim under §102 or §103, to achieve the same result by use of the same references under §112. Just as justice and reason require application of §112 in the same manner to applicants and Examiners, symmetry in the law, and evenness of its application, require that §120 be held applicable to all bases for rejection, that its words "same effect" be given their full meaning and intent. *In re Hogan and Banks*, 559 F.2d 595, 194 U.S.P.Q. 527 (C.C.P.A. 1977).

ω

Product claims meet the requirements of the first paragraph of 35 U.S.C. §112 when the specification contains a description of the products, the claims are of a similar scope, and the disclosure does not fail to teach one of ordinary skill in the art how to make and use any of the claimed products. *In re Priest*, 582 F.2d 33, 199 U.S.P.Q. 11, 15 (C.C.P.A. 1978).

ω

When a rejection is based on 35 U.S.C. §112, the Examiner should indicate whether the rejection is based on the first or second paragraph of §112. If the rejection is based on the first paragraph of §112, the Examiner should further explain whether the rejection is based on lack of a written description, enablement, or best mode. If the rejection is based on the second paragraph of §112, the Examiner should further explain whether the rejection is based on indefiniteness or failure to claim what the inventor regards as the invention. *Ex parte Ionescu*, 222 U.S.P.Q. 537 (PTO Bd. App. 1984).

ω

While symbols are commonly employed in chemical cases to refer to designated classes of substances and are conventionally defined in the claim itself in order to make clear what are the metes and bounds of the invention, the absence of their definition in the claims may be objectionable rather than subject to rejection under the second paragraph of

35 U.S.C. §112. The reference in the claims to the specification, which is definite in defining and limiting the terms, complies with the requirements of 35 U.S.C. §112. *Ex parte Moon*, 224 U.S.P.Q. 519 (PTO Bd. App. 1984).

ᴡ

The claims were intended to cover the use of the invention with various types of automobiles. That a particular chair on which the claims read may fit within some automobiles and not others is of no moment. The phrase "so dimensioned" is as accurate as the subject matter permits, automobiles being of various sizes. As long as those of ordinary skill in the art realize that the dimensions could be easily obtained, 35 U.S.C. §112, second paragraph, requires nothing more. The patent law does not require that all possible lengths corresponding to the spaces in hundreds of different automobiles be listed in the patent, let alone that they be listed in the claims. *Orthokinetics Inc. v. Safety Travel Chairs Inc.*, 806 F.2d 1565, 1 U.S.P.Q.2d 1081 (Fed. Cir. 1986).

ᴡ

The first paragraph of 35 U.S.C. §112 includes two separate and distinct requirements: (1) that the invention be described and (2) that it be described in such full, clear, concise, and exact terms as to enable any person skilled in the art to make and use it. These two separate and distinct requirements have sometimes been referred to as (1) a description requirement and (2) an enablement requirement. A patent specification may meet the enablement requirement without meeting the description requirement, and thereby fail to comply with §112's mandate. *Kennecott Corp. v. Kyocera International Inc.*, 2 U.S.P.Q.2d 1455 (Cal. 1986).

ᴡ

In rejecting a claim under the second paragraph of 35 U.S.C. §112, it is incumbent on the Examiner to establish that one of ordinary skill in the pertinent art, when reading the claims in the light of the supporting specification, would not have been able to ascertain with a reasonable degree of precision and particularity the particular area set out and circumscribed by the claims. *Ex parte Wu*, 10 U.S.P.Q.2d 2031, 2033 (B.P.A.I. 1988).

ᴡ

A claim that incorporates by reference *all* of the subject matter of another claim (the claim is not broader in any respect) is in compliance with the fourth paragraph of 35 U.S.C. §112. *Ex parte Porter*, 25 U.S.P.Q.2d 1144, 1147 (B.P.A.I. 1992).

ᴡ

The scope of a claim and the number of compounds included within the scope are not irrelevant to a 35 U.S.C. §101 and/or a 35 U.S.C §112, first paragraph, analysis. However, no evidence was cited by the Examiner that any different reactivities would make some compounds useful and others not useful. *Ex parte Bhide*, 42 U.S.P.Q.2d 1441, 1447 (B.P.A.I. 1996).

35 U.S.C. §113.

When a drawing is described in an application, the application is not complete unless the described drawing, prepared in accordance with the standards and requirements of

Rule 84 (37 C.F.R. §1.84), accompanies the papers. Photolithographs of photographs are not the drawings required by the rules. *In re Ihrig*, 124 U.S.P.Q. 418, 419 (Comm'r 1959).

35 U.S.C. §114.

Even though 35 U.S.C. §114 authorizes the Commissioner, if he so desires, to require models, specimens, and ingredients, such was not intended to impose any limitations on the scope of 35 U.S.C. §101. *In re Breslow*, 616 F.2d 516, 205 U.S.P.Q. 221, 227 (C.C.P.A. 1980).

35 U.S.C. §115.

The absence of the requisite finding of deliberate misrepresentation is fatal to reliance on the oath of inventorship required of patent applicants to support a contention that plaintiff was guilty of fraud and unclean hands in its application before the Patent Office. *Scott Paper Company v. Fort Howard Paper Company*, 432 F.2d 1198, 167 U.S.P.Q. 4, 9 (7th Cir. 1970).

ᙡ

The requirements of Section 115 and of the implementing rules are concerned with substance and not with form. Everything that at the time the patentees supposed that they had invented and intended to claim was before them when the oath was made. The application as filed faithfully presented to the Patent Office, although partly in re-typewritten form, all that the applicants had sworn to and only what they had taken oath was comprised in their invention. Claim 10 was apparently added by the attorney at an applicant's suggestion. No defect in the execution of the original application was found to exist. *Carter-Wallace, Inc. v. Davis-Edwards Pharmacal Corp.*, 341 F.Supp. 1303, 173 U.S.P.Q. 65, 91 (N.Y. 1972).

35 U.S.C. §116. *See also* Conversion, Deception, Error, Inventorship.

Even if it is not mandatory that an application filed under Section 116, paragraph 2, by a single joint inventor include the exact words, "on behalf of", somewhere therein, such an application (as filed) must use that expression or language from which it is implicit that the application was in fact being filed on behalf of said inventor and of the omitted joint inventor or, in case of the death of the omitted joint inventor, on behalf of his legal representative. *In re Schwartz and Paul*, 147 U.S.P.Q. 394, 395 (Comm'r 1960).

ᙡ

Sections 116 and 256 of 35 U.S.C. should be given a liberal construction in favor of applicants. *In re Schmidt*, 293 F.2d 274, 130 U.S.P.Q. 404 (C.C.P.A. 1961).

ᙡ

The third paragraph of 35 U.S.C. §116 contains no provision requiring that joint inventorship be conclusively proved before conversion of an application will be permitted. The requirements of the statute and of Rule 45(c) [37 C.F.R. §1.45(c)] will ordinarily be satisfied if an allegation of joint inventorship is made, coupled with sufficient evidence to enable a determination regarding the facts of error in not including one or more inventors in the application, and the lack of deceptive intent. *In re Searles*, 422 F.2d 431, 164 U.S.P.Q. 623, 627 (C.C.P.A. 1970).

ω

The expression, "deceptive intention," means an evil motive to conceal, mislead or trick. *Azoplate Corporation v. Silverlith, Inc.*, 367 F.Supp. 711, 180 U.S.P.Q. 616, 628 (Del. 1973).

ω

The 1984 amendment to 35 U.S.C. §103 does not indicate that the collaboration requirement of 35 U.S.C. §116 was eliminated. For persons to be joint inventors under 36 U.S.C. §116, there must be some element of joint behavior, such as collaboration or working under common direction, one inventor seeing a relevant report and building upon it or hearing another's suggestion at a meeting. *Kimberly-Clark Corp. v. The Procter & Gamble Distributing Co. Inc.*, 972 F.2d 911, 23 U.S.P.Q.2d 1921, 1926 (Fed. Cir. 1992).

ω

The proposition that the inventive entity must be the same in both the foreign and the corresponding U.S. application in order to obtain benefit can no longer be accepted as a hard and fast rule in view of the liberalization of the requirements for filing a U.S. application as joint inventors wrought by the 1984 amendment of 35 U.S.C. §116. *Reitz v. Inoue*, 39 U.S.P.Q.2d 1838, 1840 (B.P.A.I. 1995).

35 U.S.C. §117.

The statutes, 35 U.S.C. §§117 and 118 (1970), expressly provide for acceptance of applications and issuance of patents where the application is filed in the name of an inventive entity not represented by any signature. The clear thrust of §§116, 117 and 118 is to encourage disclosure of inventions, in accord with the constitutional objective, even though the signature or signatures of the true inventive entity may be either incorrect or entirely absent. *A.F. Stoddard & Company, Ltd. v. Dann*, 564 F.2d 556, 195 U.S.P.Q. 97, 104 (D.C. Cir. 1977).

35 U.S.C. §118. *See also* Attorney, Proprietary.

The requirement that a patent granted on the basis of an application under 35 U.S.C. §118 issue to the inventor pretermits any determination by the Patent Office of the ownership of such a patent. *In re Schuyler*, 119 U.S.P.Q. 97, 98 (Comm'r 1957).

ω

A "proprietary" interest at the very least suggests some element of ownership or dominion, and since its passage in 1952 the Commissioner has consistently adhered to that interpretation of the statute, and the interpretation so made has been left untouched by the Courts. *Staeger v. Commissioner of Patents and Trademarks*, 189 U.S.P.Q. 272, 274 (D.C. 1976).

35 U.S.C. §119. *See also* Foreign Priority, Priority, Same Invention.

The statutory provision (35 U.S.C. §251) for the reissue of defective patents is sufficiently broad in application to overcome the literal language of 35 U.S.C. §119 and to make it possible for a reissued patent to include the priority rights (not claimed and perfected during the prosecution of the basic patent) for which §119 provides. *Brenner v. The State of Israel, Ministry of Defence*, 400 F.2d 789, 158 U.S.P.Q. 584, 585 (CA D.C. 1968).

ᴡ

A claim of priority based on a corresponding foreign-filed application is untimely when perfected for the first time in the prosecution of a cip application filed more than one year after the filing of the foreign-filed application. *Justus v. Appenzeller*, 177 U.S.P.Q. 332, 339 (PO Bd. Pat. Int. 1971).

ᴡ

The language, "application for patent," does not mean only the first-filed application in a chain of copending applications. A claim of priority (based on a prior foreign filing) can be perfected in a continuation application filed more than one year after the foreign filing if the first-filed antecedent application in the chain was filed within one year from the foreign filing relied upon. *In re Tangsrud*, 184 U.S.P.Q. 746 (Comm'r 1973).

ᴡ

A foreign application need not claim the same invention as that being claimed in the U.S. application in order for the applicant to be able to rely upon the foreign application for benefit under 35 U.S.C. §119. In order for an earlier-filed foreign application to defeat priority rights under 35 U.S.C. §119, that application should be in compliance with the requirements of the first paragraph of 35 U.S.C. §112. *Olson v. Julia*, 209 U.S.P.Q. 159, 163 (PTO Bd. Pat. Intf. 1979).

ᴡ

Section 119 (35 U.S.C.) is a patent-saving provision for the benefit of applicants, and an applicant is entitled to rely on it as a constructive reduction to practice to overcome the date of a reference under 37 C.F.R. §1.131. As entitlement to a foreign filing date can completely overcome a reference, it can provide the constructive reduction to practice element of proof required by 37 C.F.R. §1.131. It is a statutory priority right which cannot be interfered with by a construction placed on a PTO rule. *In re Mulder and Wulms*, 716 F.2d 1542, 219 U.S.P.Q. 189, 193 (Fed. Cir. 1983).

35 U.S.C. §120.

Where a claim to a compound contains no "use" limitation, a parent case need not disclose the same utility as a later application to entitle the latter to the benefit of the filing date of the parent. *In re Kirchner*, 305 F.2d 897, 134 U.S.P.Q. 324, 330 (C.C.P.A. 1962).

ᴡ

Appellant is entitled to rely on the filing date of an earlier-filed application under 35 U.S.C. §120 for his claimed invention only if that invention is disclosed in the earlier-filed application. The invention disclosed in the earlier-filed application is a composition containing at least three essential ingredients, while the subject invention is directed to a composition consisting essentially of two ingredients. The appealed claims are thus not entitled to the filing date of the earlier-filed application. (The facts are distinguished over those wherein an affidavit is presented to swear back of a reference, which is not a statutory bar.) *In re Moreton*, 312 F.2d 954, 136 U.S.P.Q. 479, 482 (C.C.P.A. 1963).

ω

The right to have the benefit of an earlier application under this section of the statute is not to be confused with incorporation by reference in an application of matter written down elsewhere. *In re Voss*, 557 F.2d 812, 194 U.S.P.Q. 267, 270 (C.C.P.A. 1977).

ω

In support of a rejection under 35 U.S.C. §112, later references were cited, not as prior art, but as evidence to prove the appellants' disclosure non-enabling for "other species" of the claimed polymer, in an effort to show why the scope of enablement was insufficient to support the claims. As thus implicitly recognized, the references would not have been available in support of a rejection under 35 U.S.C. §102 or §103 entered in connection with the 1953 application. To permit use of the same references in support of the 35 U.S.C. §112 rejection herein, however, is to render the "benefit" of §120 illusory. The very purpose of reliance on §120 is to reach back, to avoid the effect of intervening references. Nothing in §120 limits its application to any specific grounds of rejection, or permits the Examiner, denied use of references to reject or to require narrowing of a claim under §102 or §103, to achieve the same result by use of the same references under §112. Just as justice and reason require application of §112 in the same manner to applicants and Examiners, symmetry in the law, and evenness of its application, require that §120 be held applicable to all bases for rejection, that its words "same effect" be given their full meaning and intent. *In re Hogan and Banks*, 559 F.2d 595, 194 U.S.P.Q. 527 (C.C.P.A. 1977).

ω

A claim of priority under 35 U.S.C. §120 may be made in a utility application based upon an earlier-filed design application provided that the design application satisfies the statutory conditions; of particular pertinence is the condition that the disclosure of the design application meet the requirements of the first paragraph of 35 U.S.C. §112 as applied to the claims of the utility application. Similar observations may be made with regard to claiming priority under §120 in a design application based upon an earlier-filed utility application. *Ex parte Duniau*, 1 U.S.P.Q.2d 1652 (B.P.A.I. 1986). .

ω

An application for a design patent, filed as a division of an earlier-filed application for a utility patent, is entitled to the benefit of the earlier filing date of the utility application under 35 U.S.C. §120 and §121. Section 120 gives to any application for a patent complying with its terms the right to have the benefit of the filing date of an earlier application. The language is mandatory: "application for patent...shall have the same effect...as though filed on the date of the prior application...." Chapter 16 of Title 35 U.S.C., covering design patents, has only three sections. Section 171 provides that "the provisions of this title relating to patents for inventions shall apply to patents for designs, except as otherwise provided." There are no "otherwise provided" statutes to take design patent applications out of the ambit of §120, which makes no distinction between applications for design patents and applications for utility patents, or as a statute calls them, "patents for inventions." However, the statute deems designs to have been invented and to be a kind of invention, subjecting them to all of the requirements for patentability pertaining to utility inventions. *Racing Strollers Inc. v. TRI Industries Inc.*, 878 F.2d 1418, 11 U.S.P.Q.2d 1300, 1302 (Fed. Cir. 1989).

ᗡ

Section 120 (35 U.S.C.) plainly allows continuation, divisional, and continuation-in-part applications to be filed and afforded the filing date of the parent application even though there is not complete identity of inventorship between the parent and subsequent applications. D. Chisum, *Patents* §13.07 (1955). *In re Chu*, 66 F.3d 292, 36 U.S.P.Q.2d 1089, 1093 (Fed. Cir. 1995).

ᗡ

Section 120 does not permit the combination of two earlier disclosures to acquire an earlier filing date, because "an earlier application must comply with the requirements of [35 U.S.C.] §112 for each claim that seeks the benefit of the filing date of that earlier application." *Studiengesellschaft Kohle m.b.H. v. Shell Oil Co.*, 112 F.3d 1561, 42 U.S.P.Q.2d 1674, 1677 (Fed. Cir. 1997).

ᗡ

The statutory provision governing the effective filing date of the subject matter of continuing applications applies to design patents as well as to utility patents. The common thread, and the criterion to be met, is whether the latter claimed subject matter is described in the earlier application in compliance with 35 U.S.C. §112. *In re Daniels*, 144 F.3d 1452, 46 U.S.P.Q.2d 1788, 1790 (Fed. Cir. 1998).

35 U.S.C. §121. *See also* Restriction.

A rejection of claims under 35 U.S.C. §121 for containing "improper Markush groups and [for] misjoinder of invention" because they are viewed as being directed to independent and distinct inventions was reversed. Section 121 of 35 U.S.C. does not provide a basis for rejecting a claim. *In re Haas*, 580 F.2d 461, 198 U.S.P.Q. 334, 336 (C.C.P.A. 1978).

35 U.S.C. §122. *See also* 37 C.F.R. §1.108, Confidentiality.

Section 122 of Title 35 U.S.C. requires the Patent Office to keep applications in confidence and not to give information concerning the same without the consent of the applicant or owner except under certain special circumstances. Rule 14(b) [37 C.F.R. §1.14(b)] implements the statute with respect to abandoned applications and spells out the exception that an abandoned application is open to the public if it is referred to in a United States patent and is available, i.e., it has not been destroyed. The exception of Rule 14(b) does not apply to an abandoned application referred to in a Canadian patent. *In re Campbell and McCune*, 170 U.S.P.Q. 354 (Comm'r 1971).

ᗡ

A mere gratuitous reference in a patent to a pending application, e.g., one not claiming the benefit of the application's filing date, does not give rise to a right of access by the public to that application. The situation is quite different, however, where the application is formally and positively incorporated by reference into the patent. *In re Yang and Olsen*, 177 U.S.P.Q. 88, 89 (PO Solicitor 1973).

ᛒ

Where the concept of an abandoned application has been published or practiced so as to become "prior art", 35 U.S.C. §122 would not prevent a litigant in a suit over the validity of a patent from discovering any relevant and material abandoned patent applications. *Sears v. Gottschalk*, 502 F.2d 122, 183 U.S.P.Q. 134, 140 (4th Cir. 1974).

ᛒ

Although 35 U.S.C. §122 provides that the Patent Office shall maintain the confidentiality of a patent application, that prohibition is not binding on a district court. *Paper Converting Machine Company v. Magna-Graphics Corporation*, 207 U.S.P.Q. 1136 (Wis. 1980).

35 U.S.C. §131.

An applicant is not entitled to examination of more than one invention under 35 U.S.C. §131, even when they are included in a single Markush-type claim. *Rohm and Haas Company v. Commissioner of Patents*, 387 F.Supp. 673, 177 U.S.P.Q. 625, 626, 627 (D.C. 1973).

35 U.S.C. §132. *See also* New Matter, Reason.

Due process requires that an applicant be given notice of the reasons his claims are rejected and why arguments upon which he is relying are deemed lacking in merit. This principle is the essence of 35 U.S.C. §132. *Ex parte Hageman,* 179 U.S.P.Q. 747, 751 (PO Bd. App. 1972).

ᛒ

The PTO has a FAFR policy permitting a final rejection in a first Office Action in those situations where (1) the application is a continuing application of, or a substitute for, an earlier application, and (2) all claims of the continuing or substitute application (a) are drawn to the same invention claimed in the earlier application, and (b) would have been properly finally rejected on the grounds of art of record in the next Office Action if they had been entered in the earlier application. This policy is maintained notwithstanding the provisions of 35 U.S.C. §132: "Whenever, on examination, any claim for a patent is rejected [and] the applicant persists in his claim for a patent, with or without amendment, the application shall be reexamined [by the PTO]." *Molins PLC v. Quigg,* 837 F.2d 1064, 5 U.S.P.Q.2d 1526 (Fed. Cir. 1988).

ᛒ

Section 132 of 35 U.S.C. merely ensures that an applicant is at least informed of the broad statutory basis for the rejection of his claims so that he may determine what the issues are on which he can or should produce evidence. Section 132 is violated when a rejection is so uninformative that it prevents the applicant from recognizing and seeking to counter the grounds of rejection. *Chester v. Miller,* 906 F.2d 1574, 15 U.S.P.Q.2d 1333, 1337 (Fed. Cir. 1990).

35 U.S.C. §134.

The "claims" as used in (35 U.S.C.) §134 is a reference to the repeated "claim for a patent" as used in (35 U.S.C.) §132 rather than a reference to a particular claim "of an application." So long as the applicant has twice been denied a patent, an appeal may be filed. *Ex parte Lemoine*, 46 U.S.P.Q.2d 1420, 1423 (B.P.A.I. 1994).

35 U.S.C. §135. *See also* Copying Claims, Interference.

The language of the statute itself militates against the interpretation that disclaiming all claims relating to a single count in an interference divests the Board of jurisdiction over an interference. *Guinn v. Kopf*, 40 U.S.P.Q.2d 1157, 1159 (Fed. Cir. 1996).

35 U.S.C. §135(a).

The purpose of 35 U.S.C. §135(a) was, in part, to provide a procedure to economize time and work in the further prosecution of a losing party's application. The final refusal of claims by the PTO may be based, inter alia, on statutory prior art or loss of right to a patent or an estoppel. The inference that the counts (i.e., the subject matter of the counts) must be statutory prior art to the losing party merely because §135(a), as a matter of PTO procedure, provides for automatic "final refusal" of claims corresponding to the counts by virtue of the adverse award of priority, is unwarranted. Neither the counts nor the subject matter of the counts is statutory prior art by virtue of 35 U.S.C. §135(a). *In re McKellin, Mageli, and D'Angelo*, 529 F.2d 1324, 188 U.S.P.Q. 428 (C.C.P.A. 1976).

ʊ

The legislative history shows that Congress intended that, if patentability is fairly placed at issue in an interference proceeding, it will be determined. The word "may" in §135(a) accommodates the situation when patentability is not placed at issue during the priority contest, but it would contradict the remedial purpose of the legislation if the BPAI could refuse to decide questions of patentability for which there had been adduced an appropriate record. *Gustavsson v. Valentini*, 25 U.S.P.Q.2d 1401, 1410 (B.P.A.I. 1991).

35 U.S.C. §135(b). *See also* Copying Claims.

Party is not estopped from contesting the interference since claims directed to substantially the same invention of the counts in issue were present in his parent application prior to one year from the date on which his opponent's patent was granted. The claims were also present in his involved copending application, as filed. *Olin v. Duerr, Aebi, and Ebner*, 175 U.S.P.Q. 707, 708, 709 (PO Bd. Pat. Intf. 1972).

ʊ

The requirements of 35 U.S.C. §135(b) are satisfied if what is claimed by the patentee would necessarily occur in the subject matter claimed by the applicant within the one-year period. *Connin v. Andrews*, 223 U.S.P.Q. 243, 247 (PTO Bd. Pat. Intf. 1984).

ʊ

Section 135(b) acts as a statute of limitations on copying claims for the purpose of instigating interferences and thus operates as a procedural statutory bar proscribing the instigation of an interference after a specified interval. *Gustavsson v. Valentini*, 25 U.S.P.Q.2d 1401, 1410 (B.P.A.I. 1991).

ʊ

This section is not limited to *inter partes* interference proceedings but may be used, in accordance with its literal terms, as a basis for *ex parte* rejections. *In re McGrew*, 43 U.S.P.Q.2d 1633, 1635 (Fed. Cir. 1997).

35 U.S.C. §135(c). *See also* Cross-License.

An understanding is not exempted from the requirements of section 135(c) merely because it is tentative or informal or because certain details are to be filled in at a later date. *Moog, Inc. v. Pegasus Laboratories, Inc.*, 376 F.Supp. 445, 183 U.S.P.Q. 225, 228 (Mich. 1974).

ʊ

Whether an interference is terminated by a settlement or by the Board of Patent Interferences is unimportant if the effect of an agreement is to remove the adversary character of the proceedings. The harm to the public from such an agreement is present in either situation. *Forbro Design Corp. v. Raytheon Co.*, 390 F. Supp. 794, 190 U.S.P.Q. 70, 78 (Mass. 1975).

ʊ

The statute requires only the filing of agreements made in settlement of interferences or those which totally destroy the incentives of the parties to an interference to litigate in an adverse manner. *PPG Industries, Inc. v. Bausch & Lomb, Inc.*, 205 U.S.P.Q. 914, 919 (N.Y. 1979).

35 U.S.C. §141.

Rejecting claims as indefinite would compel the CCPA to raise a ground of rejection not of record, and thus to act beyond its statutory authority. *In re Fleissner*, 264 F.2d 897, 121 U.S.P.Q. 270, 272 (C.C.P.A. 1959).

ʊ

A party (whether a "winner" or a "loser") to an interference dissatisfied with the board's decision "on the question of priority" has a right to appeal to the CCPA. *Nenzell v. Hutson, Imboden, and Englis*, 299 F.2d 864, 132 U.S.P.Q. 635, 636 (C.C.P.A. 1962).

35 U.S.C. §144.

The CCPA is precluded from considering an issued United States patent (not a matter of which judicial notice can be taken) which was not part of the record in the case before the Patent Office. *In re Phillips*, 315 F.2d 943, 137 U.S.P.Q. 369, 370 (C.C.P.A. 1963).

35 U.S.C. §145. *See also De Novo*.

To overturn an adverse holding below, the evidence must be clear and convincing and carry thorough conviction that the Patent Office erred in refusing to grant a patent. *Harpman v. Watson*, 181 F.Supp. 919, 124 U.S.P.Q. 169, 173 (D.C. 1959).

ʊ

The plaintiff in an action brought pursuant to 35 U.S.C. §145 has a heavy burden. Because the Patent Office is an expert body preeminently qualified to determine questions of this kind, its conclusions are entitled to a broad presumption of validity. In these circumstances, the court is authorized to reverse the decision only if the Patent Office did not have a rational basis for its conclusions or if the plaintiff presented new evidence that led to a thorough conviction that the plaintiff should prevail. In trials de novo under 35 U.S.C. §145, great weight attaches to the expertise of the Patent Office, and its findings will not be overturned unless new evidence is introduced that carries a thorough conviction that the Patent Office erred. Based on the opinion testimony of an independent expert, the court was satisfied that the only way one would reach the plaintiff's claimed alloy composition from the reference disclosure was by experimentation. The testimony offered on behalf of a plaintiff at the trial was uncontradicted by the defendant. The court found that testimony to be very persuasive, and the court concluded that the plaintiff demonstrated by clear and convincing evidence that the determination by the Board of Appeals was in error. *Titanium Metals Corp. of America v. Mossinghoff,* 603 F. Supp. 87, 225 U.S.P.Q. 673 (D.C. 1984).

ω

The facts found by the board "must be accepted as controlling" unless the court has a "thorough conviction" that the contrary is established. *Fregeau v. Mossinghoff,* 776 F.2d 1034, 227 U.S.P.Q. 848, 851 (Fed. Cir. 1985).

35 U.S.C. §146. *See also* **Trial *de Novo*.**

When the Patent Office has decided a question of priority of invention, followed by an action under 35 U.S.C. §146 contesting the decision, the question of priority is tried de novo in the district court, but the standard of proof that must be applied by the district court to reach a conclusion contrary to that of the Patent Office is one that, in character and amount, carries thorough conviction. *United States v. Szuecs,* 240 F.2d 886, 112 U.S.P.Q. 86, 87 (D.C. Cir. 1957).

ω

A party dissatisfied with a decision of the Board of Patent Interferences on a question of priority of invention between conflicting patent applications may pursue a civil action against the other parties to the interference proceeding. This action is not a standard civil action; it is more in the nature of a review of an administrative proceeding with inherent limitations on the issues that may be raised in the original claim or by counterclaim. Cases under 35 U.S.C. §146 are limited to a review of the administrative proceedings in the Patent Office supplemented by additional evidence and testimony only insofar as it relates to contentions advanced below. *Montecatini Edison, s.p.a. v. Ziegler,* 172 U.S.P.Q. 519, 520 (D.C. 1972).

ω

Unless and until the rule of *Hill v. Wooster,* 132 U.S. 693 (1890), is modified, a court that overrules the Board of Patent Interferences and decides in favor of an appealing plaintiff must consider all questions of patentability to that plaintiff, whether or not the parties to the 35 U.S.C. §146 proceeding actually raise those questions. *Standard Oil*

Company (Indiana) v. Montedison, S.p.A.; Phillips Petroleum Company v. Montedison, S.p.A.; E.I. du Pont de Nemours & Company v. Montedison, S.p.A., 494 F.Supp. 370, 207 U.S.P.Q. 298, 300 (Del. 1980).

ᛟ

Evidence going to issues of priority (i.e., issues of conception, reduction to practice, and diligence) is admissible in a §146 proceeding. A party to such proceeding, however, may not challenge patentability before the issue of priority is resolved. *Allied Signal Inc. v. Allegheny Ludlum Corp.*, 132 F.R.D. 134, 17 U.S.P.Q.2d 1638, 1640, 1641 (Conn. 1990).

ᛟ

A proceeding pursuant to 35 U.S.C. §146 has the hybrid nature of an appeal and of a trial de novo. The statute authorizes the district court to accept all proffered testimony on issues raised by the parties during the proceedings below or by the Board's decision. Far from standing for the broad proposition that estoppel precludes discovery of all issues not specifically raised before or by the Board, the case-law rule precludes consideration only of those issues not raised before the Board that are ancillary to priority. *Allied-Signal Inc. v. Allegheny Ludlum Corp.*, 132 F.R.D. 134, 18 U.S.P.Q.2d 1080, 1082 (Conn. 1990).

ᛟ

District court review of an interference proceeding under section 146 is an equitable remedy of long standing, in which the district court may exercise its discretion and admit testimony on issues which were not raised before the Board. A party's abject failure properly to raise an issue (it had an opportunity to and should have raised) in the interference proceeding warranted the court's discretionary decision to deny admission of testimony on the issue at trial. *General Instrument Corp. Inc. v. Scientific-Atlanta Inc.*, 995 F.2d 209, 27 U.S.P.Q.2d 1145, 1149 (Fed. Cir. 1993).

ᛟ

A decision of a federal district court is binding on the PTO pursuant to 35 U.S.C. §146. *Wm. T. Burnett & Co. Inc. v. Cumulus Fibres Inc.*, 825 F.Supp. 734, 27 U.S.P.Q.2d 1953, 1955 (N.C. 1993).

ᛟ

In actions in the district court to set aside decisions of the PTO, the court serves as a finder of fact. The following principles apply to a Section 146 action:

(1) Issues of fact that were resolved by the BPAI are reviewed according to a "clearly erroneous" standard, even where the parties have presented new evidence with respect to these issues during the Section 146 proceeding.

(2) Issues of fact that were not resolved by the BPAI are reviewed *de novo*, even where the evidence being considered by the court was also contained in the record before the BPAI.

(3) Conclusions of law are reviewed *de novo*, even where they are closely connected to findings of fact that are reviewed according to a "clearly erroneous" standard. Specifically, the BPAI's decisions on issues of conception, reduction to practice, and diligence are conclusions of law and must therefore be reviewed *de novo*.

Allied-Signal Inc. v. Allegheny Ludlum Corp., 29 U.S.P.Q.2d 1039, 1042 n.9, 1043 (Conn. 1993).

ω

New evidence is permitted so long as it pertains to an issue raised by the parties or the Patent Board during the proceedings below, even though it was known (to the party presenting it) and deliberately not presented during the interference proceeding before the Patent Board. *Estee Lauder Inc. v. L'Oreal S.A.*, 40 U.S.P.Q.2d 1425, 1432 (D.C. 1996).

35 U.S.C. §151.

Where the payment of fees to the Patent Office is involved, the discretion of the Commissioner of Patents is significantly curtailed. Any unjustified deviation from the mandate of the governing statute is a violation which is fatal to the applicant, and the Commissioner of Patents would appear to be powerless to cure such deviation unless the situation qualifies as a rare or unique one to be accommodated by the Patent Office. *BEC Pressure Controls Corporation v. Dwyer Instruments, Inc.*, 380 F.Supp. 1397, 182 U.S.P.Q. 190, 192 (Ind. 1974).

35 U.S.C. §154. *See also* Exclusive Right, Patent Rights, Right to Exclude, URAA.

Cancelled portions of an application are not part of a patent issued on the application. The most that the cancelled portions could be used for would be as evidence of conception, and nothing more. *Ex parte Thelin*, 152 U.S.P.Q. 624, 625, 626 (PO Bd. App. 1966).

35 U.S.C.§155. *See* Patent Term Extension.

35 U.S.C.§156. *See also* Hatch-Waxman Act, Patent Term Extension.

The URAA in effect extended the original expiration date to twenty years from the date of application. It effected a change in the "term" as used in §156(a) *and* §156(c). *Merck & Co. v. Kessler*, 903 F.Supp. 964, 36 U.S.P.Q.2d 1727, 1729 (Va. 1995).

35 U.S.C. §161.

Both the Plant Patent Act and the PVPA use the term "variety" and grant some form of intellectual property protection. However, the two statutes differ significantly in their purposes. The Plant Patent Act grants a plant patent to one who "invents or discovers and asexually reproduces any distinct and new variety of plant." Conversely, one is entitled to plant variety protection under the PVPA if he has sexually reproduced the variety and has otherwise met the requirements of 7 U.S.C. §2402(a). The term "variety" in both statutes cannot be read divorced from the very different circumstances in which that term is used. *Imazio Nursery Inc. v. Dania Greenhouses*, 69 F.3d 1560, 36 U.S.P.Q.2d 1673, 1679 (Fed. Cir. 1995).

35 U.S.C.§171.

This section authorizes patents on ornamental designs for articles of manufacture. While the design must be embodied in some article, the statute is not limited to designs for complete articles, or "discrete" articles, and certainly not to articles separately sold. *In re Zahn*, 617 F.2d 261, 204 U.S.P.Q. 988, 995 (C.C.P.A. 1980).

ω

Articles that are concealed or obscure are not proper subjects for design patents since their appearance cannot be a matter of concern. Almost every article is visible when it is made and while it is being applied to the position in which it is to be used. Those special circumstances, however, do not justify the granting of design patent on an article that is always concealed in its normal and intended uses. Although "normal and intended use" excludes the time during which the article is manufactured or assembled, it does not follow that evidence that an article is visible at other times is legally irrelevant to ascertaining whether the article is ornamental for purposes of §171. Articles are designed for sale and display, and such occasions are normal uses of an article for purposes of §171. The likelihood that articles would be observed during occasions of display or sale could have a substantial influence on the design or ornamentality of the article. The law manifestly contemplates that giving certain new and original appearances to a manufactured article may enhance its salable value. *In re Webb*, 916 F.2d 1553, 16 U.S.P.Q.2d 1433, 1435, 1436 (Fed. Cir. 1990).

35 U.S.C. §172.

The registration of an industrial design (Geschmacksmuster) under the laws of Germany (even when the subject matter of the German grant is maintained in secrecy, i.e., not available for public inspection, until after a corresponding application is filed in the United States) may be considered for purposes of applying the statutory time bar of §172 against the application for a United States design patent on the same subject matter. *In re Talbott*, 443 F.2d 1397, 170 U.S.P.Q. 281 (C.C.P.A. 1971).

35 U.S.C. §184. *See also* **Patent Office License, 35 U.S.C. §185.**

When an invention disclosed in an application for letters patent is within the scope of 35 U.S.C. §181, the Commissioner of Patents is without authority to grant a valid retroactive license. *Iron Ore Company of Canada v. The Dow Chemical Company*, 177 U.S.P.Q. 34, 55 (Utah 1972).

35 U.S.C. §185.

Express Congressional authorization in 35 U.S.C. §184 gives the right to grant retroactive licenses, and §185 refers to the license prescribed in §184. One such license prescribed in §184 is the retroactive license. A retroactive license is effective in preserving the validity of a patent even when it issues subsequent to the issuance of the patent. *Blake v. The Bassick Company*, 245 F.Supp. 635, 146 U.S.P.Q. 160, 162 (Ill. 1965).

35 U.S.C. §196(b).

The appellant with the assistance of his assignee prepared and inserted in the application two series of photomicrographs together with extensive descriptions of them for the purpose of showing how the invention differs from the prior filaments in an extensively developed art. The court took the position that this would not have been done unless the photomicrographs in fact showed persons of ordinary skill in the art what the appellant asserted they show and was unwilling to give credence to a contrary opinion expressed by the Board as the basis of the rejection that it originated sua sponte. *In re Ehringer*, 347 F.2d 612, 146 U.S.P.Q. 31, 35 (C.C.P.A. 1965).

35 U.S.C. §202(c)(7)(B).

No private cause of action exists under 35 U.S.C. §202(c)(7)(B) of the Bayh-Dole Act. *Platzer v. Sloan-Kettering Institute for Cancer Research*, 787 F.Supp. 360, 22 U.S.P.Q.2d 1845, 1849 (N.Y. 1992).

35 U.S.C. §207[3].

An "exclusive" licensee under a patent, title to which is in the United States (U.S.), may, under some circumstances, maintain a patent infringement action without the U.S. as a party, when the U.S. has authorized the licensee to sue for patent infringement in its own name and on its own behalf. *Nutrition 21 v. United States*, 930 F.2d 862, 18 U.S.P.Q.2d 1351, 1352 (Fed. Cir. 1991).

35 U.S.C. §207(a)(2).

Section 207(a)(2) of 35 U.S.C. is an exception to 28 U.S.C. §516, which permits the Department of Commerce to delegate enforcement powers to a licensee; the agreement between the Department of Commerce and the licensee grants the licensee the right "to bring suit in its own name, at its own expense, and on its own behalf for infringement of presumably valid claims in a License Patent." By this provision of the License Agreement, the United States has, in effect, consented to its necessary joinder in an infringement action. *Nutrition 21 v. Thorne Research Inc.*, 130 F.R.D. 671, 14 U.S.P.Q.2d 1244, 1245 (Wash. 1990).

35 U.S.C. §209[4].

35 U.S.C. §251. *See also* **Intent to Claim, Reissue.**

The error provision of 35 U.S.C. §251 is to be liberally construed to permit correction of defects. An attorney's failure to appreciate the full scope of the invention is one of the most common sources of defects in patents. *In re Wilder*, 736 F.2d 1516, 222 U.S.P.Q. 369, 371 (Fed. Cir. 1984).

---

[3] *See Southern Research Institute v. Griffin Corp.*, 938 F.2d 1761, 19 U.S.P.Q.2d 1761, 1764 (11th Cir. 1991).

[4] *See Southern Research Institute v. Griffen Corp.*, 938 F.2d 1761, 19 U.S.P.Q.2d 1761, 1764 (11th Cir. 1991).

35 U.S.C. §252. *See* **Intervening Rights.**

35 U.S.C. §253. *See also* **Disclaimer.**

This section preserves valid claims, despite the invalidity of other claims, if the invalid claims were made without "deceptive intention" (more than mere technical fraud, as might be revealed by a finding of obviousness, and requires actual fraud or other inequitable conduct). *Chisholm-Ryder Company, Inc. v. Lewis Manufacturing Company, Inc.*, 398 F.Supp. 1287, 187 U.S.P.Q. 93, 103 (Pa. 1975).

35 U.S.C. §254. *See* **Certificate of Correction.**

35 U.S.C. §255. *See* **Certificate of Correction.**

35 U.S.C. §256. *See also* **Conversion, Inventorship.**

Sections 116 and 256 of 35 U.S.C. should be given a liberal construction in favor of applicants. *In re Schmidt*, 293 F.2d 274, 130 U.S.P.Q. 404 (C.C.P.A. 1961).

ω

The legislative history of the 1982 amendments to 35 U.S.C. §§116 and 256 strongly suggests that Congress intended to permit correction of inventorship, without regard to the conduct of the named inventor, as long as there was not deceptive intention on the part of the true inventor. *Stark v. Advanced Magnetics Inc.*, 894 F.Supp. 555, 36 U.S.P.Q.2d 1764, 1768 (Mass. 1995).

ω

This section allows deletion of a misjoined inventor whether error occurred by deception or by innocent mistake. The section also allows addition of an unnamed actual inventor, but this error of nonjoinder cannot betray any deceptive intent by that inventor. In other words, the statute allows correction in all misjoinder cases featuring an error and in those nonjoinder cases where the unnamed inventor is free of deceptive intent. *Stark v. Advanced Magnetics Inc.*, 43 U.S.P.Q.2d 1321, 1324 (Fed. Cir. 1997).

ω

If Plaintiff J&J acted without deceptive intent and Defendant Logan acted with deceptive intent, then there is little justification for refusing Plaintiff recovery for infringement of a patent saved from invalidity by the proper invocation of section 256. Pursuant to the holding in *Stark v. Advanced Magnetics, Inc.*, 119 F.3d 1551, 43 U.S.P.Q.2d 1321 (Fed. Cir. 1997), that complete substitution of inventors is possible under section 256 so long as the true inventors acted without deceptive intent, Defendant inventors, found to have acted with deceptive intent, can no longer seek shelter in the oft cried "but he didn't have *legal* title to the patent" in order to avoid paying damages for infringement. Otherwise, named inventors acting with deceptive intent would avoid damages for patent infringement simply because their deceptive intent prevented the patent from being valid and protecting the innocent inventor. The *Stark* decision prevents such an inequitable result. *J&J Manufacturing Inc. v. Logan*, 48 U.S.P.Q.2d 1412 (Texas 1998).

35 U.S.C. §261[5].

When a legal title holder of a patent transfers title to a third-party purchaser for value without notice of an outstanding equitable claim or title, the purchaser takes the entire ownership of the patent, free of any prior equitable encumbrance. This is an application of the common law bona-fide-purchaser-for-value rule. Going a step further, 35 U.S.C. §261 adopts the principle of the real property recording acts and provides that the bona fide purchaser for value cuts off the rights of a prior assignee who has failed to record the prior assignment in the PTO by the dates specified in the statue. The statute is intended to cut off prior legal interests, which the common law rule did not. Both the common law rule and the statute contemplate that the subsequent purchaser be exactly that—a transferee who pays valuable consideration and is without notice of the prior transfer. *FilmTek Corp. v. Allied-Signal Inc.*, 939 F.2d 1568, 19 U.S.P.Q.2d 1508, 1512 (Fed. Cir. 1991).

35 U.S.C. §271. *See also* Contributory Infringement, Induce, Infringement, Staple Article of Commerce.

Subsections 271(c) and (d) of 35 U.S.C. appear to permit the owner of a patented method to monopolize and reserve to himself sale of unpatented nonstaple products that are, materially, component parts of his patented process. *Robintech, Inc. v. Chemidus Wavin Ltd.*, 628 F.2d 142, 205 U.S.P.Q. 873, 877 (D.C. Cir. 1980).

ω

Under 35 U.S.C. §271(f)(1), the components may be staple articles or commodities of commerce that are also suitable for substantial non-infringing use, but under §271(f)(2) the components must be especially made or adapted for use in the invention. The passage in §271(f)(2) reading "especially made or especially adapted for use in an infringement of such patent, and not a staple article or commodity of commerce suitable for substantial non-infringing use" comes from existing §271(c) of the patent law, which governs contributory infringement. Section 271(f)(2), like existing subsection §271(c), requires the infringer to have knowledge that the component is especially made or adopted. Section 271(f)(2) also contains a further requirement that infringers must have an intent that the components will be combined outside of the United States in a manner that would infringe if the combination occurred within the United States. *T. D. Williamson Inc. v. Laymon*, 723 F. Supp. 587, 13 U.S.P.Q.2d 1417, 1419 (Okla. 1989).

ω

The "use" requirement of 35 U.S.C. §271 does not include the mere displaying of a device for promotional purposes. Marketing activities, including publishing promotional

---

[5]The "notice" of 35 U.S.C. §261, which derives from common law and equity principles, is broader than actual notice, and includes constructive and inquiry notice. *See FilmTec Corp. v. Allied-Signal Inc.*, 939 F.2d 1568, 1574, 19 U.S.P.Q.2d 1508, 1512-13 (Fed. Cir. 1991); *see also Taylor Engines, Inc. v. All Steel Engines, Inc.*, 192 F.2d 171, 174, 92 U.S.P.Q. 35, 37 (9th Cir. 1951)(the "same notice" which prevents cutting off equitable rights precludes reliance on the recordation statute); W. Rogers, *Rogers on Patents* 190 (1914).

materials and offering a product for sale, are not sufficient to satisfy the requirements of §271, which requires an actual completed sale. *Quantum Corp. v. Sony Corp.*, 16 U.S.P.Q.2d 1447, 1450 (Cal. 1990).

ʊ

Neither intent nor preparation constitutes infringement under 35 U.S.C. §271. *The Laitram Corp. v. The Cambridge Wire Cloth Co.*, 919 F.2d 1579, 16 U.S.P.Q.2d 1929, 1932 (Fed. Cir. 1990).

ʊ

This section of the statute provides no relief for threatened patent infringement. *Eli Lilly and Co. v. Medtronic Inc.*, 915 F.2d 670, 16 U.S.P.Q.2d 2020, 2024 (Fed. Cir. 1990—*unpublished*).

ʊ

Defendant's activities in using clinical data (gathered to be sent to the Food and Drug Administration for analysis because FDA approval is required before defendant is permitted to market its device) for fund-raising and marketing purposes in demonstrations to physicians and nonphysicians do not preclude defendant's exemption from claims of infringement under 35 U.S.C. §271(e). *Telectronics Pacing Systems Inc. v. Ventritex Inc.*, 19 U.S.P.Q.2d 1960 (Cal. 1991).

ʊ

By enacting §§271(c) and (d), Congress granted to patent holders a statutory right to control *nonstaple goods that are capable only of infringing use in a patented invention*, and that are essential to that invention's advance over prior art. *BEAL Corp. Liquidating Trust v. Valleylab Inc.*, 40 U.S.P.Q.2d 1072, 1077 (Col. 1996)

35 U.S.C. §271(a).

"[M]akes" means what it ordinarily connotes—the substantial manufacture of the constituent parts of a machine. *The Laitram Corporation v. Deepsouth Packing Co., Inc.*, 443 F.2d 936, 170 U.S.P.Q. 196, 198 (5th Cir. 1971).

ʊ

This section of the statute might properly be invoked [despite apparent independence of domestic distributors from defendants (foreign manufacturers)] upon the ground that the distributors generate domestic business which benefits the defendants and which establishes a quasi-agency relationship, thus tying the domestic sales to the defendants. *Engineered Sports Products v. Brunswick Corporation*, 362 F.Supp. 722, 179 U.S.P.Q. 486, 489 (Utah 1973).

35 U.S.C. §271(b).

Liability under this section is dependent upon a showing that (1) the conduct being induced constitutes direct infringement of a patent, and (2) the person inducing the infringement "actively" and knowingly aided and abetted another's direct infringement of the patent. *In re Certain Headboxes and Papermaking Machine Forming Sections for the*

Continuous Production of Paper, and Components Thereof, 213 U.S.P.Q. 291, 300 (U.S. Int'l Trade Comm'l 1981).

☞

If a party lacks knowledge that his activity involves the infringement of a valid patent, this supports a finding that he lacked actual intent to induce infringement. *Ardco Inc. v. Page, Ricker, Felson Marketing Inc.*, 25 U.S.P.Q.2d 1382, 1385 (Ill. 1992).

☞

Under 35 U.S.C. §271(b), corporate officers who actively assist with their corporation's patent infringement may be personally liable as an infringer regardless of whether there is evidence to justify piercing the corporate veil. The plaintiff has the burden of showing both that the officer's actions induced infringing acts and that the officer knew or should have known that his or her actions would induce infringements. *Zenith Electronics Corp. v. ExZec Inc.*, 32 U.S.P.Q.2d 1959, 1960 (Ill. 1994).

☞

Inducement of infringement under 35 U.S.C. §271(b) does not lie when the acts of inducement occurred before there existed a patent to be infringed. *National Presto Industries Inc. v. The West Bend Co.*, 76 F.3d 1185, 37 U.S.P.Q.2d 1685, 1693 (Fed. Cir. 1996).

35 U.S.C. §271(c).

This section identifies the basic dividing line between contributory infringement and patent misuse. It adopts a restrictive definition of contributory infringement that distinguishes between staple and nonstaple articles of commerce. It also defines the class of nonstaple articles narrowly. The limitations on contributory infringement written into §271(c) are counterbalanced by limitations on patent misuse in §271(d). *Dawson Chemical Company v. Rohm and Haas Company*, 65 L.Ed. 696, 206 U.S.P.Q. 385, 398 (S.Ct. 1980).

35 U.S.C. §271(d).

This section effectively confers upon a patentee a limited power to exclude others from competition in nonstaple goods. A patentee may sell a nonstaple article himself, while enjoining others from marketing that same good without his authorization. *Dawson Chemical Company v. Rohm and Haas Company*, 65 L.Ed. 696, 206 U.S.P.Q. 385, 399 (S.Ct. 1980).

☞

Through the years courts have found *per se* patent misuse in varying forms of tying arrangements. In some cases, the patentee is conditioning the license of his patent on the licensee's agreeing to use some specific unpatented product. In other cases, the patentee is conditioning the license of his patent on the licensee's agreeing not to use the products or devices of a competitor. The two situations involve slightly different factual arrangements, but, generally, both are referred to as tying arrangements. Some commentators have referred to the former situations as "tie-ins" and the latter as "tie-outs". The language of the 1988 Patent Misuse Reform Act is meant to encompass both types of tying arrangements. *In re Recombinant DNA Technology Patent and Contract Litigation*, 850 F.Supp. 769, 30 U.S.P.Q.2d 1881, 1897, 1898 (Ind. 1993).

ʊ

"[T]he provisions of Sec. 271(d) effectively confer upon the patentee, as a lawful adjunct to his patent rights, a limited power to exclude others from competition in nonstaple goods. A patentee may sell a nonstaple article himself while enjoining others from marketing the same good without his authorization." It is clear from the legislative history of the Patent Misuse Reform act of 1988, codified at 35 U.S.C. §271(d)(4)(5), that Congress intended to extend, not limit, the protection provided by *Dawson v. Rohm & Haas Co*, 448 U.S. 176, 206 U.S.P.Q. 385 (1980). *LifeScan Inc. v. Polymer Technology International Corp.*, 35 U.S.P.Q.2d 1225, 1237, 1238 (Wash. 1995).

35 U.S.C. §271(e)(1).

Section 271(e)(1) of 35 U.S.C. exempts from infringement the use of patented inventions reasonably related to the development and submission of information needed to obtain marketing approval of medical devices under the Food, Drug, and Cosmetic Act. *Eli Lilly & Co. v. Medtronic Inc.*, 110 S. Ct. 2683, 15 U.S.P.Q.2d 1121, 1123 (1990).

ʊ

The statutory exemption provided by 35 U.S.C. §271(e)(1) is available not only for drug and veterinary products, but also for medical devices that cannot be marketed without FDA approval under §515 of the Federal Food, Drug, and Cosmetic Act, 21 U.S.C. §360e. Through §271(e)(1), Congress changed the status in law only of acts that, but for this exemption, would constitute acts of infringement. Thus, the only kinds of acts to which this legislation applies are acts that would constitute acts of infringement. When trying to determine whether a party is protected by this exemption, the *target of a court's inquiry* is *those acts of manufacture, use, or sale* of a patented invention *that would constitute acts of infringement*, but for this exemption. It is these kinds of acts, only, that must be "solely for uses reasonably related" to generating data for submission to the FDA. It is these kinds of acts whose uses are in issue, and the exemption is lost only if the court concludes that acts of these kinds have been undertaken for uses that are outside those permitted under the statute. In other words, by enacting this exemption, Congress has said to the public: "You may commit acts of *infringement* only so long as *those* acts are solely for uses reasonably related to gaining FDA approval to market your product. If you engage in infringing activities for other uses, the exemption will not protect you. But, if you engage in *non-infringing* acts for other uses, you do not lose the benefits of this statutory amendment." *Intermedics Inc. v. Ventritex Inc.*, 20 U.S.P.Q.2d 1422, 1427 (Cal. 1991).

ʊ

Since only Class III medical devices must endure the requisite "regulatory review period", Congress only intended to provide a patent-term extension for Class III medical devices. Accordingly, infringing use related to the development of regulatory data for a Class I or II medical device is not protected by 35 U.S.C. §271(e)(1). *Baxter Diagnostics Inc. v. AVL Scientific Corp.*, 798 F.Supp. 612, 25 U.S.P.Q.2d 1428, 1434 (Cal. 1992).

ʊ

Although the decisional law contains little guidance as to how closely and directly an applicant's activities must relate or refer to the FDA approval process in order to be entitled to the protection of 35 U.S.C. §271(e)(1) (that is, what the precise meaning of "reasonably related" is in this conext), the consensus among the few courts that have considered the issue is that Congress intended that "the courts give parties some latitude in making judgments about the nature and extent of the otherwise infringing activities they would engage in as they sought to develop information to satisfy the FDA." *Abtox Inc. v. Exitron Corp.*, 888 F.Supp. 6, 35 U.S.P.Q.2d 1508, 1510 (Mass. 1995).

ᚳ

This section applies to any use reasonably related to regulation under the FDCA, which certainly includes Class II devices. The statute does not look to the underlying purpose or attendant consequences of the activity (*e.g.*, tests led to the sale of the patent), as long as the use is reasonably related to FDA approval. In other words, the statutory language allows defendant to use its data from the tests for more than FDA approval. *AbTox Inc. v. Exitron Corp.*, 122 F.3d 1019, 43 U.S.P.Q.2d 1545, 1552, 1553 (Fed. Cir. 1997); *Amgen Inc. v. Hoechst Marion Roussel Inc.*, 3 F.Supp. 104, 46 U.S.P.Q.2d 1906, 1910 (Mass. 1998).

35 U.S.C. §271(e)(2).

"What is achieved by §271(e)(2) [is] the creation of a highly artificial act of infringement that consists of submitting an ANDA ... containing a [paragraph IV] certification [that the patent on a drug "is invalid or that it will not be infringed by the manufacture, use, or sale of the new drug" for which an ANDA is submitted] that is in error as to whether commercial manufacture, use, or sale of the new drug (none of which ... has actually occurred) violates the relevant patent." *Bristol-Myers Squibb Co. v. Royce Laboratories Inc.*, 69 F.3d 1130, 36 U.S.P.Q.2d 1641, 1646 (Fed. Cir. 1995).

35 U.S.C. §271(e)(2)(A).

As the subparagraphs of 21 U.S.C. §355(j) must be read as a whole and in context with the other paragraphs of §355, namely: §355(b), and as 35 U.S.C. §271(e)(2)(A) expressly incorporates §355(j), an action for patent infringement brought pursuant to §271(e)(2)(A) cannot be premised on a patent not included in an NDA filed pursuant to §355(b)(1), and thus not connected with a drug listed by the Secretary pursuant to §355(j)(6). *Abbott Laboratories v. Zenith Laboratories Inc.*, 35 U.S.P.Q.2d 1161, 1168 (Ill. 1995).

ᚳ

An action for patent infringement brought pursuant to §271(e)(2)(A) cannot be premised on a patent not included in an NDA filed pursuant to 21 U.S.C. §355(b)(1) or amended pursuant to 21 U.S.C. §355(c)(2), and thus not connected with a drug listed by the Secretary pursuant to 21 U.S.C. §355(j)(6). *Abbott Laboratories v. Zenith Laboratories Inc.*, 36 U.S.P.Q.2d 1801, 1807 (Ill. 1995).

35 U.S.C. §271(f).

The legislative history states that §271(f) "will prevent copiers from avoiding U.S. patents by supplying components of a patented *product* in this country so that the assembly of the components may be completed abroad." (Emphasis added.) *Enpat Inc. v. Microsoft Corp.*, 47 U.S.P.Q.2d 1218, 1219 (Va. 1998).

35 U.S.C. §271(g). *See also* **Importation, PPAA.**

The legislative history actually supports the application of 35 U.S.C. §271(g) to domestic sellers of infringing goods as well as to manufacturers and importers of such goods. The purpose of §271(g) is to provide "meaningful protection to owners of patented processes" because (prior to its enactment) there was "no remedy against parties who use or sell the product, regardless of where it is made." Section 271(g) "was crafted to apply equally to the use or sale of a product made by a process patented in this country whether the product was made (and the process used) in this country or in a foreign country." *Shamrock Technologies Inc. v. Precision Micron Powders Inc.*, 20 U.S.P.Q.2d 1797, 1798 n.4 (N.Y. 1991).

ω

Congress could have chosen to protect U.S. process patents by defining an act of infringement to include every foreign-made product that is manufactured by a patented process. It chose, however, to restrict the scope of 35 U.S.C. §271(g) to exclude downstream products that, due to intervening processing, cease to have a strong nexus to the patented process. *Eli Lilly and Co. v. American Cyanamid Co.*, 896 F.Supp. 851, 36 U.S.P.Q.2d 1011, 1018 (Ind. 1995).

ω

Act does not apply when the product made by the patented process is "materially changed by subsequent processes" before it is imported. In the chemical context, a "material" change in a compound is a significant change in the compound's structure and properties. However, when an intermediate (that is the product of a patented process) undergoes significant changes in the course of conversion into an end product, the end product will be deemed to be made by the patented process if (and only if) it would not be commercially feasible to make the end product other than by using the patented process. *Eli Lilly and Company v. American Cyanamid Company*, 83 F.3d 1568, 38 U.S.P.Q.2d 1705, 1709 (Fed. Cir. 1996).

35 U.S.C. §282. *See also* **Presumption of Validity.**

The first sentence of 35 U.S.C. §282, that "[a] patent shall be presumed valid", must be read in the context of the remainder of the first paragraph of that section, which provides that the party asserting invalidity bears the burden of establishing it. Section 282 thus mandates not only a presumption shifting the burden of going forward in a purely procedural sense, but also places the burden of persuasion on the party who asserts that a patent is invalid. The burden of persuasion is and always remains upon the party asserting invalidity. *Solder Removal Company v. United States International Trade Commission*, 582 F.2d 628, 199 U.S.P.Q. 129, 132, 133 (C.C.P.A. 1978).

ω

The presumption of validity is not weakened or destroyed where more pertinent non-considered prior art is introduced, but the offering party is more likely to carry the burden of persuasion imposed by 35 U.S.C. §282 when art more pertinent than that considered is introduced. This section of the statute requires that claims be considered independently of each other. *Medtronic, Inc. v. Cardiac Pacemakers, Inc.*, 421 F.2d 1563, 220 U.S.P.Q. 97, 100, 111 (Fed. Cir. 1983).

ᴥ

The presumption of validity of 35 U.S.C. §282 is not applicable in interferences. *Okada v. Hitotsumachi*, 16 U.S.P.Q.2d 1789, 1790 (Comm'r Patents & Trademarks 1990).

35 U.S.C. §284. *See also* **Prejudgment Interest.**

The patent statute's provision for increased damages is permissive, not mandatory: A court "*may* increase the damages up to three times the amount found or assessed." 35 U.S.C. §284 (1988) (emphasis added). A district court's analysis of whether to increase damages, therefore, is a two-step process. First, the court must determine whether willful infringement (or another circumstance justifying an enhanced award) is proven, a finding of fact reviewed by the CAFC only for clear error. Second, if the court finds such a basis proven, it must still determine whether or not, under the totality of the circumstances, increased damages are warranted. This determination is committed to the sound discretion of the district court and "will not be overturned absent a clear showing of abuse of discretion." *State Industries Inc. v. Mor-Flo Industries Inc.*, 948 F.2d 1573, 20 U.S.P.Q.2d 1738, 1740 (Fed. Cir. 1991).

ᴥ

The primary difference between 35 U.S.C. §284 and Rule (FRCP) 54(d) is that §284 requires the district court to refer to precedent of the CAFC to determine the bounds of its discretion. *Delta-X Corp. v. Baker Hughes Production Tools Inc.*, 984 F.2d 410, 25 U.S.P.Q.2d 1447, 1449, 1450 (Fed. Cir. 1993).

ᴥ

The "test" for compensability of damages under 35 U.S.C. §284 is not merely a "but for" test in the sense that an infringer must compensate a patentee for any and all damages that proceed from the act of patent infringement. Notwithstanding the broad language of §284, judicial relief cannot redress every conceivabale harm that can be traced to an alleged wrongdoing. Under §284 of the patent statute the balance between full compensation, which is the meaning that the Supreme Court has attributed to the statute, and the reasonable limits of liability encompassed by general principles of law can best be viewed in terms of reasonable, objective foreseeability. If a particular injury was or should have been reasonably foreseeable by an infringing competitor in the relevant market, broadly defined, that injury is generally compensable absent a persuasive reason to the contrary. *Rite-Hite Corp. v. Kelley Co. Inc.*, 56 F.3d 1538, 35 U.S.P.Q.2d 1065, 1069, 1070 (Fed. Cir. 1995); *but see dissent* (1090).

35 U.S.C.§285. *See also* **Attorney's Fees, Lodestar, Misconduct.**

Findings that evidence of a course of conduct that, if not properly characterized as actually fraudulent, reveals a calculated recklessness about the truth and that constitutes a serious breach of duty to the PTO support a conclusion that the case is exceptional. *Monolith Portland Midwest Co. v. Kaiser Aluminum & Chemical Corp.*, 407 F.2d 288, 160 U.S.P.Q. 577, 583 (9th Cir. 1969).

ᚧ

The purpose of 35 U.S.C. §285 when applied to accused infringers is generally said to be two-fold: (1) it discourages infringements by penalizing the infringer, and (2) it prevents "gross injustice" when the accused infringer has litigated in bad faith. *Beckman Instruments Inc. v. LKB Produkter A.B.*, 892 F.2d 1547, 13 U.S.P.Q.2d 1301, 1305 (Fed. Cir. 1989).

ᚧ

Section 285 of 35 U.S.C. provides an alternative mechanism for sanctioning frivolous appeals in patent cases where bad faith is also shown, in addition to the more general sanctions provisions of Fed. R. App. P. 38, which do not require a showing of bad faith. *State Industries Inc. v. Mor-Flo Industries Inc.*, 948 F.2d 1573, 20 U.S.P.Q.2d 1738, 1741 (Fed. Cir. 1991).

ᚧ

The purpose of this section is to provide for an award of attorney's fees "where it would be *grossly unjust* that the winner be left to bear the burden of his own counsel fees which prevailing litigants normally bear." *Molins PLC v. Textron Inc.*, 840 F.Supp. 306, 30 U.S.P.Q.2d 1054, 1055 (Del. 1993).

ᚧ

"[W]hen an action embraces both patent and non-patent claims, no fees under [35 U.S.C.] §285 can be awarded for time incurred in the litigation of the non-patent issues." *Automotive Products plc v. Tilton Engineering Inc.*, 855 F.Supp. 1101, 33 U.S.P.Q.2d 1065, 1074 (Cal. 1993).

ᚧ

In deciding the applicability of attorney's fees under 35 U.S.C. §285, the CAFC looks to the rights at issue and whether they properly invoke the patent laws. It matters not whether those rights arise in a patent suit or in an action to enforce an agreement settling that litigation. *Interspiro USA Inc. v. Figgie International Inc.*, 18 F.3d 927, 30 U.S.P.Q.2d 1070, 1074 (Fed. Cir. 1994).

35 U.S.C. §286. *See also* Laches.

While, technically, 35 U.S.C. §286 is not a statute of limitations barring suit, there is no viable or remediable case or controversy between the parties for either monetary or injunctive relief when the only possibly infringing acts occurred more than six years before suit. *Lang & Swath Ocean Systems, Inc. v. Pacific Marine & Supply Co.*, 895 F.2d 761, 13 U.S.P.Q.2d 1820 (Fed. Cir. 1990).

ᚧ

As explained in *Standard Oil Co. v. Nippon Shokubai Kagaku Kogyo*, 754 F.2d 345, 347-48, 224 U.S.P.Q. 863, 865-66 (Fed. Cir. 1985), section 286 is not a statute of limitations in the sense of barring a suit for infringement. Assuming a finding of liability, the effect of section 286 is to limit recovery to damages for infringing acts committed within six years of the date of the filing of the infringement action. One counts backwards from the date of the complaint to limit pre-filing damages arbitrarily. *Northlake Marketing & Supply Inc. v. Glaverbel S.A.*, 958 F.Supp. 373, 45 U.S.P.Q.2d 1106, 1108 (Ill. 1997).

35 U.S.C. §287. *See* Marking.

35 U.S.C. §287(a). *See also* Notice.

Section 287(a) does not limit recovery in a patent infringement action when an unmarked article, which has been made or sold, contains one of the inventions disclosed in the patent but does not contain the invention of the predicate suit. Since 35 U.S.C. §287(a) refers to a "patented article" which has not been properly marked, the logical reading of the statute indicates that the infringement action under which damages are limited is an infringement action based upon that same unmarked "patented article." *The Toro Co. v. McCulloch Corp.*, 898 F.Supp. 679, 35 U.S.P.Q.2d 1622, 1626 (Minn. 1995).

35 U.S.C. §288.

Sections 253 and 288 (35 U.S.C.) preserve valid claims, despite the invalidity of other claims, if the invalid claims were made without "deceptive intention". *Chisholm-Ryder Company, Inc. v. Lewis Manufacturing Company, Inc.*, 398 F.Supp. 1287, 187 U.S.P.Q. 93, 103 (Pa. 1975).

35 U.S.C.§291. *See also* Interpleader.

Absent interference, a court has no power *under* §291 to adjudicate the validity of any patent. The court has no jurisdiction under §291 unless interference is established. *Albert v. Kevex Corporation*, 727 F.2d 757, 221 U.S.P.Q. 202, 205 (Fed. Cir. 1984).

ϖ

Generally, interference claims are resolved while patent applications claiming the same subject matter are pending in the PTO. Nevertheless, once two or more patents are issued to different owners, and thereafter are found to contain interfering claims (i.e., both owners" claims are directed to the same invention), the only way to solve priority of inventorship is under 35 U.S.C. §291. The purpose of an interference action is to "destroy" patents, and, therefore, all owners of the patents must be before the court. *University of California v. Eli Lilly & Co.*, 19 U.S.P.Q.2d 1668, 1671, 1672 (Cal. 1991).

ϖ

A cause of action under 35 U.S.C. §291 does not require that "the owner of an interfering patent" accuse "the owner of another" of infringement. Section 291 gives patent owners a separate and distinct basis of jurisdiction if two patents interfere. *Kimberly-Clark Corp. v. The Procter & Gamble Distributing Co. Inc.*, 972 F.2d 911, 23 U.S.P.Q.2d 1921, 1924 (Fed. Cir. 1992).

35 U.S.C.§292. *See* Mismarking.

35 U.S.C. §293.

The bare unasserted statutory power of a foreign national to sue in a particular state is not such a significant contact that one possessing it may be made a defendant in the state against its will. By availing themselves of the benefits of the patent registration laws of the United States, foreign defendants did not establish a contact sufficient to subject them to the in personam jurisdiction of a district within such state. *The Gerber Scientific Instrument Company v. Barr and Stroud Ltd.*, 383 F.Supp. 1238, 182 U.S.P.Q. 201, 203 (Conn. 1973).

35 U.S.C. §296(a).

Protecting a privately-held patent from infringement by a state is certainly a legitimate congressional objective under the Fourteenth Amendment, which empowers Congress to prevent state-sponsored deprivation of private property. *College Savings Bank v. Florida Prepaid Postsecondary Education Expense Board*, 148 F.3d 1343, 47 U.S.P.Q.2d 1161, 1165 (Fed. Cir. 1998).

35 U.S.C. §305.

Improperly broadening claims during reexamination is a violation of 35 U.S.C. §305 and thus supports summary judgment of invalidity. *Quantum Corp. v. Rodime PLC*, 65 F.3d 1577, 36 U.S.P.Q.2d 1162, 1168 (Fed. Cir. 1995).

ω

Section 305 (35 U.S.C.) contains no provision for introduction of amendments and/or claims which are directed to an invention other than the invention defined by any claim of a patent undergoing reexamination. *Ex parte Logan*, 38 U.S.P.Q.2d 1852, 1854 (B.P.A.I. 1994—*unpublished, not binding precedent*).

42 U.S.C. §2182.

Decisions of the Board of Patent Interferences made pursuant to 42 U.S.C. §2182 are reviewable only in the Court of Customs and Patent Appeals and not in the district courts. *UMC Industries, Inc. v. Seaborg*, 439 F.2d 953, 169 U.S.P.Q. 325, 327 (9th Cir. 1971).

42 U.S.C. §2185.

Section 2185 (Title 42 of the United States Code) is not an acceptable statutory basis for rejecting claims. It is merely a statutory exception to the provisions of 35 U.S.C. §102. *Ex parte Kuklo*, 25 U.S.P.Q.2d 1387, 1389 n.2 (B.P.A.I. 1992).

U.S. Claims Court.

The U.S. Claims Court does not have jurisdiction under 28 U.S.C. §1491 to grant a declaratory judgment for prospective infringement by the United States. Section 1498 is the sole remedy available to a patentee for the unauthorized use of a patent by the United States. Under 28 U.S.C. §1498, when the government makes unauthorized use of a patent, it is deemed to have taken a license in that patent. The license taken at a given instant covers only what the government is using or has manufactured as of that instant. Thus, the United States has not waived its sovereign immunity with respect to prospective patent infringement. *NPD Research Inc. v. United States,* 15 Cl. Ct. 113, 8 U.S.P.Q.2d 1125 (Cl. Ct. 1988).

Use. *See also* **Commercial Use, Experimental Use, How to Use, Intended Use, Method of Use, New Use, Orientation during Operation, Pharmaceutical, Prior Use, Public Use, Reuse, Utilize, Utility.**

A claim to an old composition is not imparted with novelty by recitation therein of a new use of the composition. *In re Thuau,* 135 F.2d 344, 57 U.S.P.Q. 324, 325 (C.C.P.A. 1943).

ᗡ

A limitation reciting only manner of operation or use will not suffice to sustain the patentability of an apparatus claim. *In re Arbeit, DuBois, and Lambert,* 201 F.2d 923, 96 U.S.P.Q. 397, 402 (C.C.P.A. 1953).

ᗡ

A patentee is entitled to every use of which his invention is susceptible. *In re Spears,* 223 F.2d 956, 106 U.S.P.Q. 290, 292 (C.C.P.A. 1955).

ᗡ

The discovery was simply a new soil-suspending agent; a new use for a known compound. Because the law does not permit the claiming of such an invention in terms of use, the claims are directed to a process, a washing solution, or a composition for making the latter; these are conventional and recognized ways of claiming inventions predicated on the discovery of a new use. *In re Fong, Ward, and Lundgren,* 288 F.2d 932, 129 U.S.P.Q. 264, 266 (C.C.P.A. 1961).

ᗡ

Different uses of a patented invention can be separately licensed. *The Barr Rubber Products Company v. The Sun Rubber Company,* 277 F.Supp. 484, 156 U.S.P.Q. 374, 391 (N.Y. 1967).

ᗡ

A disclosure of a particular, significant usefulness for claimed compounds that was not known or obvious in the art is adequate consideration for a patent grant on the compounds, where the prior art previously was unaware of any usefulness for the class of compounds to which the claimed compounds belong. *In re Stemniski,* 444 F.2d 581, 170 U.S.P.Q. 343, 348 (C.C.P.A. 1971).

ᗡ

Dependent claims to the use of a new composition in the same application with claims to the composition do not materially increase the scope of protection of an applicant's inchoate patent property under 35 U.S.C. §154, which already includes the right to exclude others from making, using, or selling the composition by allowance of claims thereon. But they do tend to increase the wealth of technical knowledge disclosed in the patent by encouraging description of the use aspects of the applicant's invention in the manner required by 35 U.S.C. §112, paragraph one. *In re Kuehl,* 475 F.2d 658, 177 U.S.P.Q. 250, 256 (C.C.P.A. 1973).

ᴡ

The use of an invention in secret for commercial purposes is considered public use. *Kewanee Oil Company v. Bicron Corporation,* 478 F.2d 1074, 178 U.S.P.Q. 3, 6 (6th Cir. 1973).

ᴡ

Unpublished documents or private discussions (not of common knowledge) do not fall within the scope of limitations contained in 35 U.S.C. §102 and hence are not prior art within the meaning of 35 U.S.C. §103. Prior knowledge and use must have been accessible to the general public. *Layne-New York Co., Inc. v. Allied Asphalt Co., Inc.,* 363 F. Supp. 299, 180 U.S.P.Q. 81, 85 (Pa. 1973).

ᴡ

Terms that merely set forth an intended use for, or a property inherent in, an otherwise old composition do not differentiate a claimed composition from those known to the prior art. *In re Pearson,* 494 F.2d 1399, 181 U.S.P.Q. 641 (C.C.P.A. 1974).

ᴡ

A sufficient disclosure with respect to one use is all that is required for compliance with the statutory requirements. Though specific details with respect to the use of the compounds against mites and ticks have not been set forth, such are well within the knowledge of those skilled in the art. *In re Johnson,* 282 F.2d 370, 127 U.S.P.Q. 216 (C.C.P.A. 1960); *Ex parte Richter,* 185 U.S.P.Q. 380, 381 (PO Bd. App. 1974).

ᴡ

Claims drawn to the use of known chemical compounds in a manner auxiliary to the invention must have a corresponding written description only so specific as to lead one having ordinary skill in the art to that class of compounds. Occasionally, a functional recitation of those compounds in the specification may be sufficient as that description. *In re Herschler,* 591 F.2d 693, 200 U.S.P.Q. 711, 718 (C.C.P.A. 1979).

ᴡ

A new method of use may be manifested as a composition and so claimed. *In re Bulloch and Kim,* 604 F.2d 1362, 203 U.S.P.Q. 171, 172, 173, 174 (C.C.P.A. 1979).

ᴡ

There is no requirement that all claimed compounds have the same degree of activity for each use. What is necessary to satisfy the how-to-use requirement of 35 U.S.C. §112 is the disclosure of some activity coupled with knowledge as to the use of this activity. *In re Bundy,* 642 F.2d 430, 209 U.S.P.Q. 48, 51 (C.C.P.A. 1981).

ᴡ

The fact that a sale or use occurs under a regulatory testing procedure, such as a FIFRA experimental use permit, does not make such uses or sales experimental for purposes of 35 U.S.C. §102(b). *Pennwalt Corporation v. Akzona Incorporated*, 740 F.2d 1573, 222 U.S.P.Q. 833, 838 (Fed. Cir. 1984).

ᙡ

The statutory language, "known and used by others in this country", means publicly known so as to be available to and of benefit to the public. "Public use" under 35 U.S.C. §102(b) is antithetical to keeping the information confidential. *Ralston Purina Company v. Far-Mar-Co, Inc.*, 586 F.Supp. 1176, 222 U.S.P.Q. 863, 894 (Kan. 1984).

ᙡ

Display of a new product at a trade show constitutes public use, even where the product does not go on sale for two years thereafter. *Electro-Nucleonics, Inc. v. Mossinghoff*, 593 F.Supp. 1252, 224 U.S.P.Q. 435, 437 (D.C. 1984).

ᙡ

Even if the court were to assume that Schulman did conceive of a barbed endocardio lead prior to the critical date and that such a barbed lead was reduced to practice, Pacesettter cannot convince the court that use of such a lead was a public use. Pacesetter makes much of the fact that its experiments were conducted in an area with unusual and frequent public access, that its employees and consultants were not required to maintain any official secrecy obligations with respect to the barbed lead, and that Schulman clearly showed his barbed lead to prospective employees and visitors. But these circumstances do not amount to a meaningful and beneficial disclosure to the public as is inherent in a public use. Pacesetter's use of Schulman's barbed lead was nothing more than experimental and, presumably, subject to alterations and improvements. To the extent the use of Schulman's barbed lead was experimental and within the exclusive control of Pacesetter, the use was not a public use resulting in the disclosure of new and useful information. *Medtronic, Inc. v. Daig Corp.*, 611 F. Supp. 1498, 227 U.S.P.Q. 509 (Minn. 1985).

ᙡ

Design patents were not intended to provide protection for designs glimpsed in isolated circumstances. "Almost every article is visible when it is made and while it is being applied to the position in which it is to be used. Those special circumstances, however, do not justify the granting of a design patent on an article...which is always concealed in its normal and intended use." *Norco Products, Inc. v. Mecca Development, Inc.*, 617 F.Supp. 1079, 227 U.S.P.Q. 724, 726 (Conn. 1985).

ᙡ

Displaying models to other persons, such as colleagues at school, without any mention of secrecy is not public use. The essence of "public use" is the free and unrestricted giving over of an invention to a member of the public or the public in general. Private use of one's own invention is permissible. *Moleculon Research Corporation v. CBS, Inc.*, 793 F.2d 1261, 229 U.S.P.Q. 805, 807 (Fed. Cir. 1986).

ᙡ

A claim to a pharmaceutical composition comprising an effective amount of a specified compound and suitable carrier adequately sets forth the use to comply with requirements of 35 U.S.C. §112. The recitation of a more specific use in composition claims calling for "an effective amount" is not necessary; claims are read in the light of the specification on which they are based, and the specification must provide essential particulars. *Ex parte Skuballa,* 12 U.S.P.Q.2d 1570, 1571 (B.P.A.I. 1989).

ω

The test under 35 U.S.C. §103 is whether, in view of the prior art, the invention as a whole would have been obvious at the time it was made. The prior art does not include applicant's claimed products, claims to which are regarded as allowable. The obviousness of the process of use must be determined without reference to knowledge of the claimed products and their properties. The claimed products constitute an essential limitation of the claimed method of use thereof. That being so, the Board's hindsight comparison of the functioning of the new compounds with the functioning of the compounds of the prior art was legal error. It uses appellant's specification teaching as though it were prior art in order to make claims to methods of using his admittedly novel compounds appear to be obvious. *In re Pleuddemann,* 910 F.2d 823, 15 U.S.P.Q.2d 1738, 1742 (Fed. Cir. 1990).

ω

The "use" requirement of 35 U.S.C. §271 does not include the mere displaying of a device for promotional purposes. *Quantum Corp. v. Sony Corp.,* 16 U.S.P.Q.2d 1447, 1450 (Cal. 1990).

ω

While secrecy is a factor to be considered in determining whether a use is public or experimental, it is not necessarily the controlling factor. *Kearns v. Wood Motors Inc.,* 19 U.S.P.Q.2d 1138, 1141 (Mich. 1990).

ω

A manufacturer's sales representative's solicitation of orders does not constitute the sale or use of infringing devices. *Ardco Inc. v. Page, Ricker, Felson Marketing Inc.,* 25 U.S.P.Q.2d 1382, 1384 (Ill. 1992).

ω

Launching a spacecraft containing a patented attitude control system constitutes use of that system even though the latter cannot be activated until the spacecraft separates from its launch vehicle in space. The availability of the attitude control system on the spacecraft at a time when the spacecraft is being operated constitutes a use thereof. *Hughes Aircraft Co. v. U.S.,* 29 Fed.Cl. 197, 29 U.S.P.Q.2d 1974, 1996 (U.S. Ct. Fed. Cl. 1993).

ω

The defendant's invoices bearing the legend:
THIS PRODUCT IS PRODUCED UNDER US PATENT #4,566,294
constitute a "use in advertising" within the meaning of 35 U.S.C. §292. When competing manufacturers share customers, invoices serve the function of advertising by targeting a specific market, trade, or class of customers. This reading of §292 is consistent with its purpose of protecting not only patentees but also other members of the public who trade in unpatented goods from false representations regarding the status of a product and to prevent false markings from improperly discouraging competition in the marketplace.

Accent Designs Inc. v. Jan Jewelry Designs, 92 Civ. 0482, 30 U.S.P.Q.2d 1734, 1741 (N.Y. 1993).

Used.

The term "known or used" in 35 U.S.C. §102(a) means knowledge or use available to the public. *Carboline Company v. Mobil Oil Corporation*, 301 F.Supp. 141, 163 U.S.P.Q. 273, 279 (Ill. 1969).

Useful. *See* Utility.

Using. *See* Method of Use.

Utility.[6] ***See also* Beauty, Cancellation from Disclosure, Challenge, Hair Growth, How to Use, Proof of Utility, Safety, Screening, Structural Similarity, Tumor, Use.**

A disclosure which states that involved compounds may be used to prepare toxic substances, "such as insecticides, fungicides, etc.," is sufficient to meet the requirements of 35 U.S.C. §112. *In re Johnson*, 282 F.2d 370, 127 U.S.P.Q. 216, 218 (C.C.P.A. 1960).

ω

The statement that claimed compounds inhibit the growth of a transplanted cancer strain is sufficient to satisfy the express language of 35 U.S.C. §101, and is in harmony with the basic constitutional concept of promoting the progress of science and the useful arts. *In re Bergel and Stock*, 292 F.2d 955, 130 U.S.P.Q. 206, 209 (C.C.P.A. 1961).

ω

A proper disclosure of utility for a medicinal composition may require at least an indication of dosage and mode of administration. *In re Moureu and Chovin*, 345 F.2d 595, 145 U.S.P.Q. 452 (C.C.P.A. 1965).

ω

Neither a chemical process nor a product produced thereby is useful within the meaning of 35 U.S.C. §101 merely (1) because the process works—i.e., produces the intended product, or (2) because the compound yielded belongs to a class of compounds currently the subject of serious scientific investigation. Unless and until a process is refined to a point where it produces a product shown to be useful—where specific benefit exists in currently available form—there is insufficient justification for permitting an applicant to engross what may prove to be a broad field. *Brenner v. Manson*, 383 U.S. 519, 148 U.S.P.Q. 689, 695 (1966).

ω

Applicant must provide those of ordinary skill in the art with reasonable assurance, as by adequate representative examples, that the compounds falling within the scope of the

---

[6]Refer to GUIDELINES FOR CONSIDERING DISCLOSURES OF UTILITY IN DRUG CASES, MPEP §608.01(p).

claim will possess the asserted usefulness. *In re Surrey*, 370 F.2d 349, 151 U.S.P.Q. 724, 730 (C.C.P.A. 1966).

ᴚ

Just as the practical utility of a compound produced by a chemical process "is an essential element" in establishing patentability of the process, so the practical utility of the compound, or the compounds, produced from a chemical "intermediate," the "starting material" in such a process, is an essential element in establishing patentability of that intermediate. If a process for producing a product of only conjectural use is not itself "useful" within 35 U.S.C. §101, it cannot be said that the starting material for such a process (i.e., claimed intermediates) are "useful." It is not enough that the specification disclose that the intermediate exists and that it "works," reacts, or can be used to produce some intended product of no known use. Nor is it enough that the product disclosed to be obtained from the intermediate belongs to some class of compounds that now is, or in the future might be, the subject of research to determine some specific use. *In re Kirk and Petrow,* 376 F.2d 936, 153 U.S.P.Q. 48, 56 (C.C.P.A. 1967).

ᴚ

The discovery does not appear to be of such a "speculative," abstruse, or esoteric nature that it must inherently be considered unbelievable, "incredible," or "factually misleading." Nor does operativeness appear "unlikely" or an assertion thereof appear to run counter "to what would be believed would happen by the ordinary person" in the art. Nor does the field of endeavor appear to be one where "little of a successful nature has been developed" or one that "from common knowledge has long been the subject matter of much humbuggery and fraud." Nor has the Examiner provided evidence inconsistent with the assertions and evidence of operativeness presented by the appellant. To the contrary, the appellant's assertions of usefulness in his specification appear to be believable on their face and straightforward, at least in the absence of reason or authority in variance. *In re Gazave,* 379 F.2d 973, 154 U.S.P.Q. 92, 96 (C.C.P.A. 1967).

ᴚ

Utility under 35 U.S.C. §103 can reside in beauty and/or increasing visual appeal. *Ex parte Contrael, Stahlhut, and Trippeer,* 174 U.S.P.Q. 61 (PTO Bd. App. 1971).

ᴚ

Utility, within the meaning of the Patent Laws, means that the object of the patent is capable of performing some beneficial function claimed for it. Doubts relating to utility are resolved against an infringer. *Dart Industries Inc. v. E.I. du Pont de Nemours and Company,* 348 F.Supp. 1338, 175 U.S.P.Q. 540, 553 (Ill. 1972).

ᴚ

Development of a product to the extent that it is presently commercially salable in the market place is not required to establish "usefulness" within the meaning of 35 U.S.C. §101. *In re Langer*, 503 F.2d 1380, 183 U.S.P.Q. 288, 298 (C.C.P.A. 1974).

ᴚ

Where statements in a disclosure concerning utility are not contrary to generally accepted scientific principles and the Examiner has not presented reasons to doubt their objective truth, the Examiner's unsupported skepticism as to the utility of the claimed invention does not provide a legally acceptable basis for rejecting the claims. *Ex parte Krenzer*, 199 U.S.P.Q. 227, 229 (PTO Bd. App. 1978).

ω

A practical utility can be established other than by actual testing if sufficient properties of a novel compound are determined so that the sought for utility is readily apparent, as by demonstrating a similarity of properties of the new compound to established properties of a known class of compounds having a known utility. Probable utility does not establish practical utility. Practical utility can be established only by testing therefor or by establishing such facts as would be convincing that such utility could be "foretold with certainty." *Bindra v. Kelly*, 206 U.S.P.Q. 570, 575 (PTO Bd. Pat. Int. 1979).

ω

The utility of the invention was distinguished from the utility of specific compositions embodying the invention. *Ex parte Gleixner, Muller, and Lehrach*, 214 U.S.P.Q. 297, 298 (PTO Bd. App. 1979).

ω

A disclosure of utility of claimed compounds as being useful and used in the same manner as defined known compounds is sufficient to satisfy the how-to-use requirement of the first paragraph of 35 U.S.C. §112. *In re Bundy*, 642 F.2d 430, 209 U.S.P.Q. 48, 51 (C.C.P.A. 1981).

ω

A disclosure of in vitro utility supplemented by similar in vitro and in vivo pharmacological activity of structurally similar compounds is sufficient to comply with the practical utility requirement of 35 U.S.C. §101. *Cross v. Iizuka*, 753 F.2d 1040, 224 U.S.P.Q. 739 (Fed. Cir. 1985).

ω

The Examiner appears to recognize that it is not structural similarity alone that gives rise to obviousness, but the concomitant assumption that the structurally similar compounds will have like properties. This is what provides the motivation to modify the prior-art compound. In the present case, however, the only utility disclosed for the relevant compound in the reference is as an intermediate for the production of another compound. The Examiner has not suggested that the compound claimed here would have been useful in the same manner, and, from the disclosure of the reference itself, it appears that it wouldn't have been. Thus, on the record before us, no *prima facie* case of obviousness has been made out against the appellant's claims. *Ex parte Chwang*, 231 U.S.P.Q. 751 (B.P.A.I. 1986).

ω

The "contemporary knowledge in the art" has far advanced since the days when any statement of utility in treating cancer was per se "incredible." The medical treatment of a specific cancer is not such an inherently unbelievable undertaking and does not involve such implausible scientific principles as to be considered incredible.

A specification that contains a disclosure of utility that corresponds in scope to the subject matter sought to be patented must be taken as sufficient to satisfy the utility requirements of 35 U.S.C. §101 for the entire claimed subject matter unless there is reason for one skilled in the art to question the objective truth of the statement of utility or its scope. *Ex parte Rubin,* 5 U.S.P.Q.2d 1461 (B.P.A.I. 1987).

ᛒ

A method-of-use claim is not rendered indefinite because it recites diverse utilities. *Ex parte Skuballa,* 12 U.S.P.Q.2d 1570, 1571 (B.P.A.I. 1989).

ᛒ

Unless utility could have been foretold with certainty, sufficient testing to establish practical utility of a claimed compound is required to establish an actual reduction to practice. *DeSolms v. Schoenwald,* 15 U.S.P.Q.2d 1507, 1511 (B.P.A.I. 1990).

ᛒ

When a properly claimed invention meets at least one stated objective, utility is clearly shown. The defense of non-utility or non-operability cannot be sustained without proof of total incapacity. If a party has made, sold, or used a properly claimed device, and has thus infringed, proof of that device's utility is thereby established. The commercial success of a claimed invention is evidence of its operability. *Stranco Inc. v. Atlantes Chemical Systems Inc.,* 15 U.S.P.Q.2d 1704, 1714 (Tex. 1990).

ᛒ

An invention need not be the best or the only way to accomplish a certain result, and it need only be useful to some extent and in certain applications. The fact that an invention has only limited utility and is only operable in certain applications is not grounds for finding lack of utility. *Carl Zeiss Stiftung v. Renishaw plc,* 945 F.2d 1173, 20 U.S.P.Q.2d 1094, 1100 (Fed. Cir. 1991).

ᛒ

The P388 and L1210 cell lines, though technically labeled tumor models, were originally derived from lymphocytic leukemias in mice. Therefore, these cell lines represent actual specific lymphocytic tumors; these models will produce this particular disease once implanted in mice. If applicants were required to wait until an animal actually developed this specific tumor before testing the effectiveness of a compound against the tumor *in vivo*, as would be implied from the Commissioner's argument, there would be no effective way to test compounds *in vivo* on a large scale. These tumor models represent a specific disease against which the claimed compounds are alleged to be effective. Were Phase II testing required in order to prove utility, the associated costs would prevent many companies from obtaining patent protection on promising new inventions, thereby eliminating an incentive to pursue, through research and development, potential cures in many crucial areas, such as the treatment of cancer. Only after the PTO provides evidence showing that one of ordinary skill in the art would reasonably doubt the asserted utility does the burden shift to the applicant to provide rebuttal evidence sufficient to convince such a person of the invention's asserted utility. *In re Brana,* 51 F.3d 1560, 34 U.S.P.Q.2d 1436, 1440, 1441, 1442, 1443 (Fed. Cir. 1995).

ᛒ

In the pharmaceutical arts, the CAFC has long held that practical utility may be shown by adequate evidence of any pharmacological activity. *Fujikawa v. Wattanasin*, 93 F.3d 1559, 39 U.S.P.Q.2d 1895, 1899 (Fed. Cir. 1996).

While there must generally be corroboration of an inventor's testimony of conception of his or her invention, the utility of the invention need not always be explicitly corroborated. *Kridl v. McCormick*, 41 U.S.P.Q.2d 1686 (Fed. Cir. 1997)

Utilize.

The step of "utilizing" was approved in a single-step method claim:

6. A method of unloading . . . catalyst and bead material . . . which comprises utilizing the nozzle of claim 7.

by an expanded panel of the BPAI which confirmed that the manner in which that claim is drafted has been an acceptable format for years. The claim is neither ambiguous nor nonstatutory. Rejections under the second and fourth paragraphs of 35 U.S.C. §112 were reversed; a claim that incorporates by reference *all* of the subject matter of another claim (the claim is not broader in any respect) is in compliance with the fourth paragraph of 35 U.S.C. §112. *Ex parte Porter*, 25 U.S.P.Q.2d 1144, 1147 (B.P.A.I. 1992).

Vacatur.

Although vacatur is the general rule in the Federal Circuit, it need not always be granted. When settlement includes all of the parties to an appeal and all of the claims of the appealed judgments have become entirely moot, vacatur of the judgments on appeal is appropriate. *U.S. Phillips Corp. v. Windmere Corp.*, 971 F.2d 728, 23 U.S.P.Q.2d 1709, 1711 (Fed. Cir. 1992).

ᖚ

"[M]ootness by reason of settlement does not [except under exceptional circumstances, which do not include the mere fact that the settlement agreement provides for vacatur] justify vacatur of a judgment under review." *Zeneca Limited v. Novopharm Limited*, 38 U.S.P.Q.2d 1585, 1586 (Md. 1996).

Vacuum. *See also* **In Vacuo, Retrospective Reconstruction.**

Claims are read in the light of the disclosure of the specification on which they are based, not in a vacuum. *In re Dean*, 291 F.2d 947, 130 U.S.P.Q. 107, 110 (C.C.P.A. 1961).

ᖚ

In determining whether claims do, in fact, set out and circumscribe a particular area with a reasonable degree of precision and particularity, the definiteness of the language employed must be analyzed—not in a vacuum, but always in light of the teachings of the prior art and of the particular application disclosure as it would be interpreted by one possessing the ordinary level of skill in the pertinent art. *In re Moore and Janoski*, 439 F.2d 1232, 169 U.S.P.Q. 236 (C.C.P.A. 1971).

ᖚ

We must not here consider a reference in a vacuum, but against the background of the other references of record that may disprove theories and speculations in a reference, or reveal previously undiscovered or unappreciated problems. The question in a 35 U.S.C. §103 case is what the references would collectively suggest to one of ordinary skill in the art. It is only by proceeding in this manner that we may fairly determine the scope and content of the prior art according to the mandate of *Graham v. John Deere Co.* [383 U.S. 1, 17, 148 U.S.P.Q. 459, 467 (1966)]. Therefore, combining the references would not have rendered obvious the particle size limitation or the particular volume-percent limitation, and certainly not the subject matter as a whole that encompasses these limitations. *In re Ehrreich and Avery*, 590 F.2d 902, 200 U.S.P.Q. 504 (C.C.P.A. 1979).

ᖚ

Presuming arguendo that the references show the elements or concepts urged, the Examiner presented no line of reasoning as to why the artisan reviewing only the collective teachings of the references would have found it obvious to selectively pick and choose various elements and/or concepts from the several references relied on to arrive at the claimed invention. In the instant application, the Examiner has done little more than cite references to show that one or more elements or some combinations thereof, when each is viewed in a vacuum, is known. The claimed invention, however, is clearly directed to a combination of elements. That is to say, the appellant does not claim that he has invented one or more new elements but has presented claims to a new combination of elements. To support the conclusion that the claimed combination is directed to obvious subject matter, either the references must expressly or impliedly suggest the claimed combination or the Examiner must present a convincing line of reasoning as to why the artisan would have found the claimed invention to have been obvious in light of the teachings of the references. The Board found nothing in the references that would expressly or impliedly teach or suggest the modifications urged by the Examiner. Additionally, the Board found no line of reasoning in the answer as to why the artisan would have found the modifications urged by the Examiner to have been obvious. Based upon the record, the artisan would not have found it obvious to selectively pick and choose elements or concepts from the various references so as to arrive at the claimed invention without using the claims as a guide. *Ex parte Clapp,* 227 U.S.P.Q. 972 (B.P.A.I. 1985).

Vague. *See also* **Confusing, Indefiniteness, 35 U.S.C. §112.**

The use of the words "substantially" and "approximately" in a claim does not necessarily render it vague and therefore invalid under 35 U.S.C. §112. *H. M. Chase Corp. v. Idaho Potato Processors, Inc.,* 529 P.2d 1270, 185 U.S.P.Q. 106, 116, (Idaho S. Ct. 1974).

Validity. *See also* **Administrative Regularity, Blonder-Tongue Doctrine, Jury, Preliminary Injunction, Presumption of Validity, Prior Adjudication, Settlement Agreement.**

The district court, on a bill and answer, held the patent in suit "valid", but not infringed. The patentee did not appeal. However, the victorious defendant sought to appeal the judgment to the extent it ruled the patent "valid." The circuit court dismissed the appeal on the theory that a winning party could not take an appeal. The Supreme Court reversed, holding that the winner/defendant could appeal to obtain, not a ruling on the merits, but reformation of the decree. The court appeared concerned that the defendant may otherwise be precluded by the judgment from attacking the patent in another suit. *Electrical Fittings Corp. v. Thomas & Betts Co.,* 307 U.S. 241, 41 U.S.P.Q. 556 (1939).

ω

A judgment entered by a district court on a declaratory claim for invalidity must be reviewed on the merits (on appeal) by the appellate court so long as a case or controversy exists at that time to support the assertion of the declaratory claim. *Altvater v. Freeman,* 319 U.S. 359, 57 U.S.P.Q. 285 (1943). [See *Morton International Inc. v. Cardinal Chemical Co.,* 967 F.2d 1571, 23 U.S.P.Q.2d 1362, 1363, *dissent* (Fed. Cir. 1992)].

ω

A district court's conclusion (based on findings of fact which are not regarded as clearly erroneous) that patent claims are valid will not be disturbed on appeal. *Pacific Contact Laboratories, Inc. v. Solex Laboratories, Inc.*, 209 F.2d 529, 100 U.S.P.Q. 12, 13 (9th Cir. 1953).

ᴥ

The use of an invention by another who has been trying to develop a similar product is evidence of the validity of a patent. *Neff Instrument Corporation v. Cohu Electronics, Inc.*, 298 F.2d 82, 132 U.S.P.Q. 98, 101 n.11 (9th Cir. 1961).

ᴥ

A license agreement that promises not to challenge the validity of a patent is void and unenforceable because it contravenes the strong federal policy in favor of the full and free use of ideas in the public domain. *Lear, Inc. v. Adkins,* 395 U.S. 653, 162 U.S.P.Q. 1 (1969).

ᴥ

A prior finding of patent ·validity against a different defendant is entitled to comity. Therefore, the usual presumption of validity attaching to a patent is, in such instances, increased. Without violating due process, a court can require a defendant to prove that a factual or legal error occurred in the previous adjudication of validity or that the previous litigation was incomplete in some material aspect. If defendant cannot come forward with appropriate supporting evidence, summary judgment under F. R. Civ. P. 56 might well be appropriate. *Columbia Broadcasting System, Inc. v. Zenith Radio Corporation*, 391 F.Supp. 780, 185 U.S.P.Q. 662, 666 (Ill. 1975).

ᴥ

Validity and infringement are separate issues. The validity of a patent is determined under the applicable criteria of patentability. *Carman Industries, Inc. v. Wahl*, 724 F.2d 932, 220 U.S.P.Q. 481, 485 n.5 (Fed. Cir. 1983).

ᴥ

When not all claims are asserted to be invalid for anticipation or obviousness, the patent cannot be held invalid on either ground. Each claim must be presumed valid independently of the validity of any other claim. A court must limit its decision to the claims before it. *Preemption Devices, Inc. v. Minnesota Mining & Manufacturing Co.*, 732 F.2d 903, 221 U.S.P.Q. 841, 843 (Fed. Cir. 1984).

ᴥ

Patents are born valid. The presumption that a patent is valid, 35 U.S.C. §282, continues until the validity-challenger has "so carried his burden as to have persuaded the decision maker that the patent can no longer be accepted as valid." *Datascope Corp. v. SMEC, Inc.,* 776 F.2d 320, 227 U.S.P.Q. 838 (Fed. Cir. 1985).

ᴥ

The CAFC does not review the validity of asserted patent claims when affirmation can be based on noninfringement. *Vieau v. Japax, Inc.,* 823 F.2d 1510, 3 U.S.P.Q.2d 1094, 1100 (Fed. Cir. 1987).

ᴥ

To the extent reliance is placed on evidence previously considered by the PTO, there is "the added burden of overcoming the deference that is due to a qualified government agency presumed to have properly done its job, which includes...Examiners who are assumed to have some expertise in interpreting the references and to be familiar from their work with the level of skill in the art and whose duty it is to issue only valid patents." *Sonoco Products Co. v. Mobil Oil Corp.*, 15 U.S.P.Q.2d 1186, 1191 (S.C. 1989).

ᙡ

In an infringement suit before a district court, the invalidity of a patent under 35 U.S.C. §103 must be decided on the basis of prior art adduced in the proceeding before the court. The issue cannot be decided merely by accepting or rejecting the adequacy of the positions taken by the patentee in order to obtain a Certificate of Reexamination for the patent. Once issued by the PTO, a patent is presumed valid, and the burden of proving otherwise rests solely on the challenger. Whether or not a reexamination certificate should have issued is not an issue before the district court. *Greenwood v. Hattori Seiko Co. Ltd.*, 900 F.2d 238, 14 U.S.P.Q.2d 1474, 1476 (Fed. Cir. 1990).

ᙡ

The Supreme Court held that a license agreement that promised not to challenge the validity of a patent was void and unenforceable because it contravened the strong federal policy in favor of the full and free use of ideas in the public domain. Six circuits have ruled that a consent judgment of validity and infringement is enforceable despite the Supreme Court's holding in *Lear* [395 U.S. 653, 162 U.S.P.Q. 1 (1969)]. *Foster v. Hallco Manufacturing Co.*, 14 U.S.P.Q.2d 1746, 1747 (Or. 1990).

ᙡ

There is strong public interest in upholding and enforcing valid patents. If a patent holder cannot rely on its patent to exclude others, then "research and development budgets in the science and technology based industries would shrink, resulting in the public no longer benefitting from the labors of these talented people." *Ortho Pharmaceutical Corp. v. Smith*, 15 U.S.P.Q.2d 1856, 1864 (Pa. 1990).

ᙡ

Only either a Reissue or a Reexamination Application is the proper vehicle for having the validity of patent claims determined by the PTO. In the present case, by the transfer of the appealed claim subject matter to an application not filed under 35 U.S.C. §251 or 35 U.S.C. §§301 et seq., appellants are attempting to circumvent the provisions of the specific statute under which they originally filed the Reexamination Application. *Ex parte Morimoto*, 18 U.S.P.Q.2d 1540, 1543 (B.P.A.I. 1990).

ᙡ

When presented with both the issue of a patent's validity and the issue of infringement, the "better practice" is to determine the validity of the patent first. This is so because, of the two questions, validity is of greater public importance. *Flow-Rite of Tennessee Inc. v. Sears Roebuck & Co. Inc.*, 20 U.S.P.Q.2d 1361, 1363 (Ill. 1991).

ᙡ

The issue of validity of a patent, presented in a counterclaim for a declaratory judgment, becomes "moot," in the sense of no longer presenting a case or controversy, upon the CAFC's finding that: (1) the patent in issue is not infringed and (2) the dispute raised by the counterclaim does not extend beyond the patentee's infringement claim. *Vieau v. Japax, Inc.*, 823 F.2d 1510, 3 U.S.P.Q.2d 1094 (Fed. Cir. 1987). [*Vieau* is somewhat unusual in that the issue of validity was raised on "cross-appeal" by the *winner* of a declaratory judgment of a patent's invalidity. However, the cross-appeal was taken because of the district court's failure to hold the patent invalid under 35 U.S.C. §103, as well as under 35 U.S.C. §112. *Morton International Inc. v. Cardinal Chemical Co.*, 967 F.2d 1571, 23 U.S.P.Q.2d 1362, 1365 n.2 dissent (Fed. Cir. 1992).]

ω

The Federal Circuit's affirmance of a finding that a patent has not been infringed is not *per se* a sufficient reason for vacating a declaratory judgment holding the patent invalid. *Cardinal Chemical Co. v. Morton International Inc.*, 113 S.Ct. 1967, 26 U.S.P.Q.2d 1721, 1722 (S. Ct. 1993).

ω

Issues of patent validity that were decided at trial require appellate review, even when patents are found not infringed upon appeal. *Roton Barrier Inc. v. The Stanley Works*, 79 F.3d 1112, 37 U.S.P.Q.2d 1816, 1827 (Fed. Cir. 1996).

ω

A finding by a district court that a patent is not invalid does not bind the PTO, because each forum applies a different standard of proof and can consider different evidence. Similarly, a PTO determination of patent validity is not binding on a district court. Thus, it is possible that a district court and the PTO could reach inconsistent conclusions regarding the same patent. *Bausch & Lomb Inc. v. Alcon Laboratories Inc.*, 914 F.Supp. 951, 38 U.S.P.Q.2d 1377, 1378 (N.Y. 1996).

ω

With careful consideration of the *Lear* [*Lear v. Atkins*, 395 U.S. 653, 162 U.S.P.Q. 1 (1969)] test and policies, the assignor is estopped from challenging the validity of the patent:

> To allow the assignor to make that representation [of the worth of the patent] at the time of the assignment (to his advantage) and later to repudiate it (again to his advantage) could work an injustice against the assignee.... [D]espite the public policy encouraging people to challenge potentially invalid patents, there are still circumstances in which the equities of the contractual relationships between the parties should deprive one party...of the right to bring that challenge.

Lear does not bar enforcement of a) a settlement agreement and consent decree, b) a contract promise to share royalties, or c) a settlement agreement to pay royalties even if the patent is later held invalid. *Studiengesellschaft Kohle m.b.H. v. Shell Oil Co.*, 112 F.3d 1561, 42 U.S.P.Q.2d 1674, 1680 (Fed. Cir. 1997).

ω

Multiple interviews are not illegal, and persistence in patent prosecution is not grist for patent invalidity. "Prosecution irregularities" by an Examiner or by an applicant are not relevant to patent validity. *Magnivision Inc. v. The Bonneau Co.*, 42 U.S.P.Q.2d 1925, 1929 (Fed. Cir. 1997).

ထ

The court is obligated to interpret claims to uphold their validity when a fairly possible reading will permit it. *Baxa Corp. v. McGaw Inc.*, 981 F.Supp. 1348, 44 U.S.P.Q.2d 1801, 1808 (Col. 1997).

Validity Opinion.

Ordering file histories is a normal and necessary preliminary to a validity or infringement opinion. *Underwater Devices Inc. v. Morrison-Knudsen Co.*, 717 F.2d 1380, 219 U.S.P.Q. 569 (Fed. Cir. 1983).

Value. *See also* Applicant's Rights, Entire-Market-Value Rule, Promote Progress.

Product claims have practical advantages over method-of-use claims from the standpoint of protection. Where we are concerned with new compounds in which non-obvious properties have been found, the properties being inherent in the compounds, one could even say it is "somewhat irrational" to say the "invention" is not in the compounds. The basic principle of the patent system is to protect inventions that meet the statutory requirements. Valuable inventions should be given protection of value in the real world of business and the courts. *In re Ruschig, Aümuller, Korger, Wagner, Scholz, and Bänder,* 343 F.2d 965, 145 U.S.P.Q. 274 (C.C.P.A. 1965).

ထ

To provide effective incentives, claims must adequately protect inventors. To demand that the first to disclose shall limit his claims to what he has found will work or to materials that meet the guidelines specified for "preferred" materials in a process would not serve the constitutional purpose of promoting progress in the useful arts. *In re Goffe,* 542 F.2d 564, 191 U.S.P.Q. 429, 431 (C.C.P.A. 1976).

ထ

The interest of the public is in protecting patent rights, and the right of a patentee is in the exclusive use of his invention. Without the protection of the patent statute, the incentive to invent and to improve products would be curbed, and the public interest in such inventions would not be served. *The Conair Group Inc. v. Automatik Apparate-Maschinenbau GmbH,* 19 U.S.P.Q.2d 1535, 1540 (Pa. 1990).

Variety.

Both the Plant Patent Act and the PVPA use the term "variety" and grant some form of intellectual property protection. However, the two statutes differ significantly in their purposes. The Plant Patent Act grants a plant patent to one who "invents or discovers and asexually reproduces any distinct and new variety of plant." Conversely, one is entitled to plant variety protection under the PVPA if he has sexually reproduced the variety and has otherwise met the requirements of 7 U.S.C. §2402(a). The term "variety" in both statutes cannot be read divorced from the very different circumstances in which that term is used. Due to the asexual reproduction prerequisite, plant patents cover a single plant and its asexually reproduced progeny. Thus, the term "variety" in 35 U.S.C. §161 must be interpreted consistently with this requirement. Accordingly, "variety" in section 161 cannot be read as affording plant patent protection to a range of plants. *Imazio Nursery Inc. v. Dania Greenhouses*, 69 F.3d 1560, 36 U.S.P.Q.2d 1673, 1678, 1679 (Fed. Cir. 1995).

Vehicle. *See* **Carrier.**

Vendee. *See* **Purchaser.**

Vendor. *See* **Exclusive.**

Venue.[1] *See also* **Forum, Transfer, 28 U.S.C. §1391, 28 U.S.C. §1400(b).**

In determining whether a corporate defendant has a regular and established place of business in a district, the appropriate inquiry is whether the corporate defendant does its business in that district through a permanent and continuous presence there and not whether it has a fixed physical presence in the same sense of a formal office or store. *In re Cordis Corp.*, 769 F.2d 733, 226 U.S.P.Q. 784 (Fed. Cir. 1985).

ϖ

Unlike jurisdiction, which pertains to the court's power over defendants, venue instead pertains to the "convenience of litigants." Since unnamed members of a class need not appear in court, there is little reason to consider their convenience. *Webcraft Technologies, Inc. v. Alden Press,* Inc., 228 U.S.P.Q. 182, 183 (Ill. 1985).

ϖ

The amendment to 28 U.S.C. §1391(c) in no way indicates that an alteration was intended in the operation of 28 U.S.C. §1400(b). Not only is the language of the statute

---

[1]In *Commercial Casualty Insurance Co. v. Consolidated Stone Co.*, 278 U.S. 177 (1929), the Supreme Court held that a defendant cannot seek to vacate a default judgment on the ground that venue was improper because venue, merely a personal privilege of the defendant, is waived upon default. Per the Court, the privilege of venue "must be 'seasonably' asserted; else it is waived." *Id.* at 179. The Court continued:

> [Venue] must be asserted at latest before the expiration of the period allotted for entering a general appearance and challenging the merits.... To hold that such a privilege may be retained until after the suit has reached the stage for dealing with the merits and then be asserted would be in our opinion subversive of orderly procedure and make for harmful delay and confusion.

Id. at 179-80. Although this decision antedated the current Federal Rules of Civil Procedure, the Court has reiterated more recently that a "defendant, properly served with process by a court having subject matter jurisdiction, waives venue by failing seasonably to assert it, or even simply by making default." *Hoffman v. Blaski*, 363 U.S. 336, 343 (1960) (citing *Commercial Ins. Co.*, 278 U.S. 179-80); *see also Industrial Addition Assoc. v. Commissioner of Internal Revenue*, 323 U.S. 310, 313-314 (1945); *Freeman v. Bee Machine Co.*, 319 U.S. 448, 453 (1943); *Neirbo Co. v. Bethlehem Shipbuilding Corp.*, 308 U.S. 165, 167-68 (1939). Thus it is well established that "[v]enue is waived by a defendant who defaults." 15 Wright, Miller & Cooper, *Federal Practice and Procedure; Jurisdiction §3829 (2d ed. 1986).*

itself silent in this respect, the legislative history behind the amendment of §1391(c) is devoid of any indication that an amendment to §1400(b) was intended or even contemplated. Absent a clear indication in the language of the statute or unmistakable intent expressed in the legislative history, elementary principles of statutory construction preclude finding that venue in patent actions shall hereafter be governed by amended §1391(c). *Doelcher Products v. Hydrofoil International Inc.*, 735 F. Supp. 666, 14 U.S.P.Q.2d 1067, 1069 (Md. 1989).

ω

The change to 28 U.S.C. §1391(c) was to restrict venue in multidistrict states to the district where a corporation is subject to personal jurisdiction. Previously, venue was proper in any district in a multidistrict state, even if a defendant corporation confined its activities to one district. Because the congressional history shows no clear intent to change settled law, the 1988 amendment of §1391(c) has no effect on the exclusivity of §1400(b). Although a completed sale is not necessary to establish venue, demonstrations of an accused apparatus, coupled with continuous and systematic solicitation of orders within a district, will establish venue. *Joslyn Manufacturing Co. v. Amerace Corp.*, 729 F. Supp. 1219, 14 U.S.P.Q.2d 1223, 1225, 1227 (Ill. 1990).

ω

For purposes of venue under Chapter 87 of Title 28 of the U.S. Code, a defendant that is a corporation shall be deemed to reside in any judicial district in which it is subject to personal jurisdiction at the time an action is commenced (28 U.S.C. §1391). Section §1400(b) of 28 U.S.C. is contained within that chapter. The language of the statute controls in the absence of a clearly expressed legislative intention to the contrary. An inspection of the legislative history does not reveal any intent to exempt §1400 from the operation of §1391. If Congress intended that §1391(c) only modify the general venue rules contained in §1391, Congress would presumably have stated that 1391(c) only "applied for the purposes of this section." The statute does not contain such language. The courts must enforce statutes as they are written. *Diamond-Chase Co. v. Stretch Devices Inc.*, 16 U.S.P.Q.2d 1568, 1570 (Cal. 1990).

ω

Considerations pertinent to a change of venue under 28 U.S.C. §1404(a) are not the same as those pertinent to coordination of pretrial proceedings in multiple cases involving common parties. *In re University of California*, 964 F.2d 1128, 22 U.S.P.Q.2d 1748, 1752 (Fed. Cir. 1992).

ω

Courts must examine the defendant's contacts with the forum at the time of the events underlying the dispute when determining whether they have jurisdiction. *Tomar Electronics Inc. v. Whelen Technologies Inc.*, 819 F.Supp. 871, 25 U.S.P.Q.2d 1464, 1467 (Ariz. 1992).

ω

A sole proprietorship, unlike a partnership, is not an "association". Rather, it is an individual doing business under a trade name. The rationales for applying 28 U.S.C. §1391(c) to partnerships do not apply to sole proprietorships. Accordingly, 28 U.S.C.

§1400(b) controls the venue issue. *Kabb Inc. v. Sutera*, 25 U.S.P.Q.2d 1554, 1555 (La. 1992).

ω

In all federal actions against aliens, the applicable venue provision is 28 U.S.C. §1391(d), which provides that "[a]n alien may be sued in any district." In federal question cases, due process requires only sufficient contacts with the United States as a whole rather than with any particular state. *Miller Pipeline Corp. v. British Gas plc*, 901 F.Supp. 1416, 38 U.S.P.Q.2d 1010, 1012, 1014 (Ind. 1995).

Verdict. *See also* **Directed Verdict, Special Verdict.**

The label "verdict" in Rule (FRCP) 49(a) is an unfortunate choice. Special verdicts are jury answers to factual interrogatories. "Verdict" is apparently employed because returning verdicts is what juries do. Doubtless the drafters expected courts and counsel to distinugish between a general verdict, naked or accompanied by answers to interrogatories under Rule 49(b) (in returning of either of which a jury finds the facts, applies the law as instructed, and designates the winning side), and a special verdict (in returning of which a jury supplies only written answers to fact questions). *Wahpeton Canvas Co. v. Frontier Inc.*, 870 F.2d 1546, 10 U.S.P.Q.2d 1201 (Fed. Cir. 1989).

ω

The law presumes the existence of findings necessary to support a verdict reached by the jury. Whether there is trial evidence favorable to both sides is not the question. The question is whether there is substantial evidence to support the verdict. Where there are alleged conflicts in the evidence, the trial court, on motion for JNOV, should not substitute its judgment for that of the jury. Even where evidence may be contradictory, the resolution of that conflict is a role assigned to the jury, and inferences are to be drawn in favor of the non-movant. When, without question, reasonable jurors could have concluded that the patent claims in issue were infringed, denial of a motion for JNOV is required. *ALM Surgical Equipment Inc. v. Kirschner Medical Corp.*, 15 U.S.P.Q.2d 1241, 1245, 1246 (S.C. 1990).

Verified. *See* **Declaration.**

Visibility Rule.

Design patents were not intended to provide protection for designs glimpsed in isolated circumstances. "Almost every article is visible when it is made and while it is being applied to the position in which it is to be used. Those special circumstances, however, do not justify the granting of a design patent on an article...which is always concealed in its normal and intended use." *Norco Products, Inc. v. Mecca Development, Inc.*, 617 F.Supp. 1079, 227 U.S.P.Q. 724, 726 (Conn. 1985).

Visual Appeal.

Utility under 35 U.S.C. §103 can reside in beauty and/or increasing visual appeal. *Ex parte Contrael, Stahlhut, and Trippeer,* 174 U.S.P.Q. 61 (PTO Bd. App. 1971).

Vitamin.

The propriety of defendant's filing and obtaining a patent on a reformulated prescription prenatal vitamin was contested. *The University of Colorado Foundation Inc. v. American Cyanamid*, 35 U.S.P.Q.2d 1737, 1738 (Colo. 1995).

Von Bramer Doctrine. *See* **Enabling Disclosure.**

Key Terms and Concepts

W – Z

Waiver. *See also* **Appellee, Late Claiming, Privilege.**

The advancing of defenses subsequent to trial raises questions of waiver and res judicata. A defendant's decision not to raise a defense in the trial of a particular action is a waiver of that defense, which waiver is granted res judicata effect. *The Kilbarr Corp. v. Business Systems, Inc., B.V.,* 679 F. Supp. 422, 6 U.S.P.Q.2d 1698 (N.J. 1988).

ω

The practice of waiving an issue not raised by an appellant in its opening brief is not governed by a rigid rule. As a matter of discretion, it may not be adhered to where circumstances indicate that it would result in basically unfair procedure. *Becton Dickinson & Co. v. C. R. Bard Inc.,* 922 F.2d 792, 17 U.S.P.Q.2d 1097, 1103 (Fed. Cir. 1990).

ω

Generally, a failure to plead an affirmative defense, as required by Rule (FRCP) 8(c), results in the forced waiver of that defense and its exclusion from the case. Waiver need not result, however, if the defendant "raised the issue at a pragmatically sufficient time, and the [opposing party] was not prejudiced in its ability to respond." *Surgical Laser Technologies Inc. v. Heraeus Laseronics Inc.,* 34 U.S.P.Q.2d 1226, 1228 (Pa. 1995).

ω

Given that a court must indulge every reasonable presumption against a finding of waiver, ambiguity should be resolved against interfering waiver. *Cabinet Vision v. Cabnetware,* 129 F.3d 595, 44 U.S.P.Q.2d 1683, 1687 (Fed. Cir. 1997).

Walker Process Claim.

A Walker Process claim arises when a patentee baselessly institutes litigation to enforce a patent known to be unenforceable because the patent was procured by fraud. *Novo Nordisk of North America Inc. v. Genentech Inc.,* 885 F.Supp. 522, 35 U.S.P.Q.2d 1058, 1061 (N.Y. 1995).

ω

An inequitable conduct defense and a Walker Process counterclaim are not identical in scope or consequence for "[t]he patent fraud proscribed by *Walker* is extremely circumscribed" in comparison with inequitable conduct. Nevertheless, we are satisfied that the facts underlying Cabnetware's inequitable conduct defense and its Walker Process counterclaim possess "substantial commonality" so that, because the jury answered question 7, the Seventh Amendment constrains the court's equitable determination. *Cabinet Vision v. Cabnetware,* 129 F.3d 595, 44 U.S.P.Q.2d 1683, 1687 (Fed. Cir. 1997).

ω

Walker Process requires a showing that the patent was obtained through deliberate, affirmative misrepresentations, *i.e.*, knowingly false statements, not mere omissions. *Nobelpharma AB v. Implant Innovations Inc.*, 129 F.3d 1463, 44 U.S.P.Q.2d 1705, 1712 (Fed. Cir. 1997).

Walker Process Fraud.

A finding of *Walker Process* (147 USPQ 404) fraud requires higher threshold showings of both intent and materiality than does a finding of inequitable conduct. Moreover, unlike a finding of inequitable conduct...a finding of *Walker Process* fraud may not be based in an equitable balancing of lesser degrees of materiality and intent. Rather, *it must be based on independent and clear evidence of deceptive intent together with a clear showing of reliance, i.e., that the patent would not have been issued but for the misrepresentation or omission.*" A patent procured by fraud "by definition would not have issued but for the misrepresentation or non-disclosure". *In re Rhône-Poulenc Rorer Inc.*, 48 U.S.P.Q.2d 1823, 1825 (Fed. Cir. 1998 - *unpublished*).

Wanton. *See* Willful.

Weight. *See also* Standard.

A limitation to the relative size or weight of an article is not regarded as patentably significant since it at most relates to the size of the article under consideration, which is not ordinarily a matter of invention. *In re Rose*, 220 F.2d 459, 105 U.S.P.Q. 237, 240 (C.C.P.A. 1955).

Well Known. *See also* Known.

An applicant (patentee) may begin at a point where his invention begins and describe what he has made that is new, and what it replaces of the old. That which is common and well known is as if it were written out in the application (patent) and delineated in the drawings. *Webster Loom Co. v. Higgins*, 105 U.S. 580, 586 (1882).

ᛦ

The disclosure of an application embraces not only what is expressly set forth in words and drawings, but what would be understood by persons skilled in the art. Those features that are well known are as if they were written out in the patent. *Ex parte Wolters and Kuypers*, 214 U.S.P.Q. 735 (PTO Bd. App. 1979).

ᛦ

Enablement is a legal determination of whether a patent enables one skilled in the art to make and use the claimed invention. It is not precluded even if some experimentation is necessary, although the amount of experimentation needed must not be unduly extensive. Enablement is determined as of the filing date of the patent application. Furthermore, a patent need not teach, and preferably omits, what is well known in the art. *Hybritech Inc. v. Monoclonal Antibodies, Inc.*, 802 F.2d 1367, 231 U.S.P.Q. 81 (Fed. Cir. 1986).

Well-Pleaded Complaint.

The phrase "well-pleaded complaint" is merely the name of the rule, not a statement of a principle of law. Thus, its application to the complaint cannot be read as overruling the many cases in which counterclaims arising under 28 U.S.C. §1338 and other federal statutes have been held to support the jurisdiction of a court. Though designed to answer the different state/federal jurisdiction questions, the ramifications of the well-pleaded-complaint rule are useful and statutorily mandated analytical tools in determining the appellate jurisdiction of the CAFC when the relevant pleadings are only a complaint and answer. The rule can also be useful in testing whether a counterclaim passes muster as the equivalent of a well-pleaded complaint. However, using the ramifications of a well-pleaded-complaint rule to limit the appellate jurisdiction of the CAFC in every case by an exclusive focus on the complaint and a compelled disregard of compulsory counterclaims for patent infringement would disserve the intent of Congress in creating the CAFC. *AeroJet-General Corp. v. Machine Tool Works, Oerlikon-Buehrle Ltd.*, 895 F.2d 736, 13 U.S.P.Q.2d 1670, 1676 (Fed. Cir. 1990).

ᛋ

The well-pleaded complaint rule focuses on claims, not theories of recovery. *United National Insurance Co. v. Bradleys' Electric Inc.*, 35 U.S.P.Q.2d 1559, 1561 (Tex. 1995).

Whereby Clause.

A "whereby" clause, which is a statement of result, cannot, by itself, impart patentability to an apparatus claim. *In re Boileau,* 163 F.2d 562, 75 U.S.P.Q. 88, 90, 91 (C.C.P.A. 1947).

ᛋ

When terms appearing in a whereby clause of a claim are emphasized as being effective for distinguishing over prior art and in securing the allowance of the claim during prosecution of an application for letters patent, those terms must be deemed as an essential feature necessary to the establishment of infringement. If an accused product or process lacks the essential feature, it does not infringe. *Eltech Systems Corp. v. PPG Industries,* Inc., 710 F. Supp. 622, 11 U.S.P.Q.2d 1174, 1183 (La. 1988).

ᛋ

A "whereby" clause that merely states the results of the limitations in a claim adds nothing to the patentability or the substance of the claim. *Texas Instruments Inc. v. International Trade Commission*, 988 F.2d 1165, 26 U.S.P.Q.2d 1018, 1023 (Fed. Cir. 1993).

Whip-Saw Problem.

An infringer avoids paying lost profits damages altogether by developing a device using a first patented technology to compete with a device that uses a second patented technology and developing a device using the second patented technology to compete with a device that uses the first patented technology. *Rite-Hite Corp. v. Kelley Co. Inc.*, 56 F.3d 1538, 35 U.S.P.Q.2d 1065, 1068 (Fed. Cir. 1995); *but see dissent* (1090).

Whole. *See also* **Difference, Incomplete, Invention as a Whole, Printed Matter, Prior Art as a Whole, References as a Whole, Retrospective Reconstruction, Subject Matter as a Whole, 35 U.S.C. §103.**

As elementary as it may be to patent law under the 1952 Act, 35 U.S.C. §103 requires having to show obviousness of the invention "as a whole." To evaluate obviousness, a comparison must be made between the prior art as a whole and the claimed subject matter as a whole. *In re Langer and Haynes,* 465 F.2d 896, 175 U.S.P.Q. 169, 171 (C.C.P.A. 1972).

ᛦ

Unexpected results must be taken fully into account, pursuant to the congressional mandate for consideration of the invention as a whole. *Ex parte Leonard and Brandes,* 187 U.S.P.Q. 122, 123 (PTO Bd. App. 1974).

ᛦ

Treating an advantage as the invention disregards the statutory requirement that the invention be viewed as a whole, ignores the problem-recognition element, and injects an improper "obvious to try" consideration. *Jones v. Hardy,* 727 F.2d 1524, 220 U.S.P.Q. 1021, 1026 (Fed. Cir. 1984).

ᛦ

Although it is proper to note the difference in a claimed invention from the prior art, because that difference may serve as one element in determining the obviousness/non-obviousness issue, it is improper to consider the difference as the invention. The "difference" may be slight (as has often been the case with some of history's greatest inventions, e.g., the telephone), but it may also have been the key to success in advancements in the art resulting from the invention. The issue with respect to obviousness is whether a challenger has carried its burden of proving, by clear and convincing evidence, facts from which it must be concluded that one skilled in the art at the time the invention was made would have found it to have been obvious, from the references as a whole, to create the claimed subject matter as a whole. *Datascope Corp. v. SMEC, Inc.,* 776 F.2d 320, 227 U.S.P.Q. 838 (Fed. Cir. 1985).

ᛦ

The claimed invention must be viewed as a whole. The district court appeared to distill the invention down to a "gist" or "core," a superficial mode of analysis that disregards elements of the whole. It disregarded express claim limitations. *Bausch & Lomb, Inc. v. Barnes-Hind/Hydrocurve, Inc.,* 796 F.2d 443, 230 U.S.P.Q. 416 (Fed. Cir. 1986).

ᛦ

Focusing on the obviousness of substitutions and differences instead of on the invention as a whole is a legally improper way to simplify the difficult determination of obviousness. *Hybritech Inc. v. Monoclonal Antibodies, Inc.,* 802 F.2d 1367, 231 U.S.P.Q. 81, 93 (Fed. Cir. 1986).

ᛦ

Casting an invention as "a combination of old elements" leads improperly to an analysis of the claimed invention by the parts, not by the whole. The critical inquiry is whether there is something in the prior art as a whole to suggest the desirability, and thus the obviousness, of making the combination. A traditional problem with focusing on a patent as a combination of old elements is the attendant notion that patentability is undeserving without some "synergistic" or "different" effect. Here, the district court spoke of the need for "a new and useful result." Such tests for patentability have been soundly rejected by this court. Though synergism is relevant when present, its "absence has no place in evaluating the evidence on obviousness." *Custom Accessories Inc. v. Jeffrey-Allan Industries, Inc.*, 807 F.2d 955, 1 U.S.P.Q.2d 1196 (Fed. Cir. 1986).

Widespread Use.

Resolution of a thorny problem and the device's subsequent widespread use buttress the conclusion of nonobviousness. *Austin v. Marco Dental Products, Inc.*, 560 F.2d 966, 195 U.S.P.Q. 529, 533, 534 (9th Cir. 1977).

Willful. *See also* Willful Infringement.

An aggressive strategy may or may not be a factor in a decision to deny or award increased damages. Such a strategy unsupported by any competent advice of counsel, thorough investigation of validity and infringement, discovery of more pertinent uncited prior art, or similar factors, is the type of activity the reference in the patent law to increased damages seeks to prevent. An alleged infringer who intentionally blinds himself to the facts and law, continues to infringe, and employs the judicial process with no solidly based expectation of success can hardly be surprised when his infringement is found to have been willful. Willfulness of infringement relates to the accused infringer's conduct in the marketplace. Because that conduct may be seen as producing an unnecessary and outcome-certain lawsuit, it may make the case so exceptional as to warrant attorney's fees under 35 U.S.C. §285. Similarly, bad faith displayed in pretrial and trial stages, by counsel or party, may render the case exceptional under §285. When a court declines to award attorney's fees on the basis of a determination that a case is not exceptional, the fact findings underlying that determination are reviewed under the clearly erroneous standard. When the determination is that a case is exceptional, the election to grant or deny attorney's fees is reviewed under the abuse-of-discretion standard. *Kloster Speedsteel A.B. v. Crucible Inc.*, 793 F.2d 1565, 230 U.S.P.Q. 81 (Fed. Cir. 1986).

ω

Neither a vacated decision of the International Trade Commission in which the ALJ found the patents valid and infringed nor a Canadian decision in which the corresponding Canadian patent was held to be valid and infringed is binding on the court in this case. Further, the court does not rely on either in reaching its decision as to validity and infringement of the U.S. patents in suit. It is appropriate, however, to consider those decisions in ruling on willfulness of infringement. *Corning Glass Works v. Sumitomo Electric U.S.A. Inc.*, 671 F. Supp. 1369, 5 U.S.P.Q.2d 1545, 1571 (N.Y. 1987).

ω

Not every failure to seek an opinion of competent counsel will mandate an ultimate finding of willfulness. *Spindelfabrik Suesson-Schurr Stahlecker Grill GmbH v. Schubert & Salzer Maschsnenfabrik Aktiengesellschaft,* 829 F.2d 1075, 4 U.S.P.Q.2d 1044, 1051, n.13 (Fed. Cir. 1987), *cert. denied,* 108 S. Ct. 1022 (1988).

ꙮ

Where a potential infringer has actual notice of another's patent rights, he has an affirmative duty of due care. The test is whether, under all the circumstances, a reasonable person would prudently conduct himself with any confidence that a court might hold the patent invalid or not infringed. The duty of due care normally requires that a potential infringer obtain competent legal advice before infringing or continuing to infringe. Although the failure to obtain legal advice is not determinative, it is one of the factors supporting a finding of willfulness. If the infringement is willful, increased damages may be awarded at the discretion of the district court, and the amount of the increase, up to three times, may be set in the exercise of that same discretion. Willful infringement may also be a sufficient basis for finding a case "exceptional" for purposes of awarding attorney's fees under 35 U.S.C. §285. A finding that a case is exceptional is one of fact and must be made in the first instance by the district court. *Ryco Inc. v. Ag-Bag Corp.,* 857 F.2d 1418, 8 U.S.P.Q.2d 1323 (Fed. Cir. 1988).

ꙮ

Disregard for the opinion of a sales engineer with neither an aerodynamic nor a legal background and who was thus not qualified to make either a technical or legal determination of infringement does not justify an award of treble damages or attorney's fees. *Uniroyal Inc. v. Rudkin-Wiley Corp.,* 721 F. Supp. 28, 13 U.S.P.Q.2d 1192, 1201 (Conn. 1989).

ꙮ

The disclosure required of patent claimants applies whether inaccurate evidence is submitted to the PTO willfully or not. The filing of a misleading Rule 131 affidavit makes the resulting patent unenforceable regardless of whether the patent would have been issued "but for" the "fraud." *Greenwood v. Seiko Instruments & Electronics Ltd.,* 711 F. Supp. 30, 13 U.S.P.Q.2d 1245, 1247 (D.C. 1989).

Willful Infringement.[1] *See also* **Due Care, Enhancement of Damages, Exceptional, Willful.**

Increased damages are usually based on a finding that the infringer's conduct was willful and in flagrant disregard of the patentee's rights. In this case, the defendant was on notice of the plaintiff's patent rights and had an affirmative duty to exercise due care to determine whether it was infringing. The defendant may not avoid a holding of willful infringement because it failed to show that it obtained a competent opinion from counsel and that it had exercised reasonable and good-faith adherence to the analysis and advice contained therein. Accordingly, the defendant is liable to the plaintiff for an amount equal to three times the amount of damages actually found or assessed. Section 285 of 35 U.S.C. provides for the award of attorney's fees to the prevailing party in exceptional

---

[1] See Racine, Richard B., and Bosch, Michele C., "Willful Infringement: A Real Concern," *The Federal Circuit Bar Journal,* Vol. 3, No. 4, pp. 409-424, Winter 1993.

cases. In order to support an award of attorney's fees in a patent case, there must be a showing of conduct that is unfair, in bad faith, inequitable, or unconscionable. In view of the defendant's willful infringement, this case involves those elements set out above and is an exceptional case, thereby entitling plaintiff to an award of its attorney's fees. The plaintiff is also entitled to prejudgment interest based upon the damages found or assessed in the second phase of this trial. *Great Northern Corp. v. Davis Core & Pad Co.*, 226 U. S. P. Q. 540 (Ga. 1985).

ʊ

Where a potential infringer has actual notice of another's patent rights, he has an affirmative duty of due care. The duty of due care normally requires a potential infringer to obtain competent legal advice of counsel before infringing or continuing to infringe. Willful infringement may be sufficient basis in a particular case for finding the case "exceptional" for purposes of awarding attorney's fees to the prevailing patent owner. *Avia Group International, Inc. v. L.A. Gear California, Inc.*, 853 F.2d 1557, 7 U.S.P.Q.2d 1548 (Fed. Cir. 1988).

ʊ

Not all infringement is willful infringement. "Willful infringement" is a term of art applied in appropriate cases in order to support an enhancement of the damage award. In determining whether an infringer engaged in willful infringement, a court should consider the totality of the circumstances, including (1) whether the infringer deliberately copied the ideas or design of another; (2) whether the infringer, when he knew of the other's patent protection, investigated the scope of the patent and formed a good-faith belief that it was invalid or that it was not infringed; and (3) the infringer's behavior as a party to the litigation. *Western Electric Co. v. Piezo Technology Inc.*, 15 U.S.P.Q.2d 1401, 1409 (Fla. 1990).

ʊ

A finding of willful infringement is a factual question based on the totality of the circumstances. It is the patent owner's burden to prove willful infringement by clear and convincing evidence. The factors to be weighed in assessing whether an infringer's conduct is willful are:

1. whether the infringer deliberately copied the ideas of another;
2. whether the infringer knew of the patent and formed a good-faith belief as to non-infringement and/or invalidity; and
3. the infringer's behavior as party to the litigation.

The law is settled that one with knowledge of another's patent rights has the affirmative duty to determine whether or not his conduct could result in an infringement of rights of the patent owner. This obligation usually includes the duty to seek and obtain competent legal advice before engaging in activity that may result in infringement. While courts have recognized that good-faith reliance on an "authoritative" opinion of counsel may be a defense to a charge of willful infringement, conclusory statements (without supporting reasons) do not constitute an "authoritative opinion" upon which good-faith reliance may be founded. Willfulness is suggested by facts that, as a matter of law, indicate that an infringer has no reasonable basis to believe it has a right to do the acts. *Fromson v. RVP Chemical Corp.*, 15 U.S.P.Q.2d 1689, 1699 (Wis. 1990).

ᚐ

Willful infringement must be proven by clear and convincing evidence. To question the validity of a patent does not, in and of itself, constitute willful infringement. Where a potential infringer has actual notice of another's patent rights, he has an affirmative duty to exercise due care to determine whether or not he is infringing. Not every failure to seek an opinion of competent counsel will mandate an ultimate finding of willfulness. The court should always look at the totality of the circumstances. That an opinion of counsel was obtained does not always and alone dictate a finding that the infringement was willful. A finding of willful infringement does not require a patentee to prove that defendant's actions were conducted in bad faith. *Stranco Inc. v. Atlantes Chemical Systems Inc.*, 15 U.S.P.Q.2d 1704, 1712 (Tex. 1990).

ᚐ

A finding of willful infringement is a finding of fact, not a conclusion of law. When a potential infringer has actual notice of another's patent rights, he has the duty to exercise due care to determine whether or not he is infringing, including the duty to seek and obtain competent legal advice before engaging in activity that may result in infringement. Obtaining an opinion of counsel after manufacture of the infringing device and after receipt of a notice of infringement has been held to indicate that the infringer was not acting in good faith. Willfulness is to be determined from the totality of the circumstances presented in the case. *Tenax Corp. v. Tensar Corp.*, 19 U.S.P.Q.2d 1881, 1885 (Md. 1991).

ᚐ

It is possible to have willful infringement before a patent issues. The patent in issue was in the Patent Office for some nine years before it was granted, and the patentee had previously obtained a very similar patent in the European Patent Office. *Exxon Chemical Patents Inc. v. Lubrizol Corp.*, 26 U.S.P.Q.2d 1871, 1872, 1873 (Tex. 1993).

ᚐ

Where a jury has found willful infringement, a district court must find reasons for refusing to enhance damages. And in so doing, the district court must take care to avoid second guessing the jury or contradicting its findings. *Applied Medical Resources Corp. v. United States Surgical Corp.*, 967 F. Supp. 861, 43 U.S.P.Q.2d 1688, 1689 (Va. 1997).

ᚐ

Willful infringement is a question if fact, and must be established by clear and convincing evidence, for "the boundary between unintentional and culpable acts is not always bright." Thus a finding of willful infringement will be sustained unless the reviewing court has a definite and firm conviction that the trier of fact erred. *SRI International Inc. v. Advanced Technological Laboratories Inc.*, 127 F.3d 1462, 44 U.S.P.Q.2d 1422, 1424 (Fed. Cir. 1997).

ᚐ

Defendant's ANDA filing constituted a willful infringement since it was not made on a reasonable basis, causing the case to be an "exceptional" one and making it appropriate for an award of attorney's fees to plaintiffs. In filing its paragraph IV certification along with its ANDA, defendant represented that "in the opinion of the applicant and to the best of its knowledge" the famotidine patent was invalid. However, the patent law imposes an affirmative duty of due care on one making such an assertion, and this standard is applied in determining whether one, such as the defendant, had an objective good faith basis for such action. *Yamanouchi Pharmaceutical Co. v. Danbury Pharmacal Inc.*, 48 U.S.P.Q.2d 1741, 1748 (N.Y. 1998).

Willfulness.

Reliance on in-house counsel instead of obtaining a timely opinion of outside counsel is an entirely proper consideration as one factor in willfulness. *Minnesota Mining and Manufacturing Co. v. Johnson & Johnson Orthopaedic Inc.*, 22 U.S.P.Q.2d 1401, 1413 (Minn. 1991).

ᗡ

Once a defendant asserts that he is faced with a dilemma of choosing between waiving attorney-client privilege in order to protect itself from a willfulness finding (in which case it may risk prejudicing itself on the question of liability) and maintaining the privilege (in which case it may risk being found to be a willful infringer if liability is found), a trial court should inspect the defendant's attorney-client documents *in camera* to ascertain that the dilemma is legitimate. If the dilemma is real, bifurcation of the willfulness issue is an appropriate way to proceed. *Neorx Corp. v. Immunomedics Inc.*, 28 U.S.P.Q.2d 1395, 1396 (N.J. 1993).

ᗡ

A willfulness finding is generally inappropriate when the infringer mounts a good faith and substantial challenge to the existence of infringement. *Electro Medical Systems S.A. v. Cooper Life Sciences Inc.*, 34 F.3d 1048, 32 U.S.P.Q.2d 1017, 1024 (Fed. Cir. 1994).

Willing Buyer—Willing Seller Rule.

A comprehensive list of evidentiary facts relevant, in general, to the determination of the amount of a reasonable royalty for a patent license may be drawn from a conspectus of the leading cases. The following are some of the more pertinent factors:

1. The royalties received by the patentee for the licensing of the patent in suit, proving or tending to prove an established royalty.
2. The rates paid by the licensee for the use of other patents comparable to the patent in suit.
3. The nature and scope of the license, as exclusive or non-exclusive; or as restricted or non-restricted in terms of territory or with respect to whom the manufactured product may be sold.
4. The licensor's established policy and marketing program to maintain his patent monopoly by not licensing others to use the invention or by granting licenses under special conditions designed to preserve that monopoly.
5. The commercial relationship between the licensor and licensee, such as, whether

they are competitors in the same terrritory in the same line of business, or whether they are inventor and promotor.

6. The effect of selling the patented specialty in promoting sales of other products of the licensee; the existing value of the invention to the licensor as a generator of sales of his non-patented items; and the extent of such derivative or convoyed sales.

7. The duration of the patent and the term of the license.

8. The established profitability of the product made under the patent; its commercial success; and its current popularity.

9. The utility and advantages of the patent property over the old modes or devices, if any, that had been used for working out similar results.

10. The nature of the patented invention; the character of the commercial rembodiment of it as owned and produced by the licensor, and the benefits to those who have used the invention.

11. The extent to which the infringer has made use of the invention, and any evidence probative of the value of that use.

12. The portion of the profit or of the selling price that may be customary in the particular business or in comparable businesses to allow for the use of the invention or analogous inventions.

13. The portion of the realizable profit that should be credited to the invention as distinguished from non-patented elements, the manufacturing process, business risks, or significant features or improvements added by the infringer.

14. The opinion testimony of qualified experts.

15. The amount that a licensor (such as the patentee) and a licensee (such as the infringer) would have agreed upon (at the time the infringement began) if both had been reasonably and voluntarily trying to reach an agreement; that is, the amount that a prudent licensee—who desired, as a business proposition, to obtain a license to manufacture and sell a particular article embodying the patented invention—would have been willing to pay as a royalty and yet be able to make a reasonable profit and which amount would have been acceptable by a prudent patentee who was willing to grant a license.

Georgia-Pacific Corporation v. U.S. Plywood-Champion Papers Inc., 318 F.Supp. 116, 166 U.S.P.Q. 235, 238 (N.Y. 1970).

ᛒ

The use of a willing licensee-willing licensor model for determining damages "risks creation of the perception that blatant, blind appropriation of inventions patented by individual, non-manufacturing inventors is the profitable, can't-lose course." To avoid such a result, the fact finder may consider additional factors to assist in the determination of adequate compensation for infringement. These factors include royalties received by the patentee for licensing the patent in suit, opinion testimony of qualified experts, the patentee's relationship with the infringer, and other factors that might warrant higher damages. *Maxwell v. J. Baker Inc.*, 39 U.S.P.Q.2d 1001, 1008 (Fed. Cir. 1996).

Wishful Thinking. *See* **Conjecture.**

Withdrawal. *See also* **Unity of Invention.**

After making an election-of-species requirement, repeating same after election and traversal, making the requirement final, and allowing the elected claims, the Examiner withdrew all other claims (including generic claims) from consideration "since they were not limited to the elected invention." In withdrawing the so-called generic claims from further prosecution, Rules 141 and 146 were violated. *Ex parte Bridgeford, Turbak, and Burke,* 172 U.S.P.Q. 308, 309 (PO Dir. 1971).

ω

Claims were withdrawn from consideration not only in the subject application, but also prospectively in any subsequent application. Because of their content, they were held to include multiple "patentably distinct" inventions. In effect, there had been a denial of patentability of the claims. Presumably, only by dividing the subject matter into separate, and thus different, claims in plural applications could an examination of the patentability of their subject matter be obtained. An Examiner's adverse action of this nature is a rejection, a denial of substantive rights. *In re Haas,* 486 F.2d 1053, 179 U.S.P.Q. 623, 624, 625 (C.C.P.A. 1973).

ω

When an Examiner designated an adverse decision as a "withdrawal" of a claim from further consideration, it was "in fact a rejection of that claim on the ground that it encompasses independent and distinct inventions." *Rohm and Haas Company v. Gottschalk,* 504 F.2d 259, 183 U.S.P.Q. 257 (DC 1974).

Withdraw Final Rejection.[2]

Withdraw from Issue.

Abandonment of an allowed application by an assignee after the application is allowed, the final fee is paid, and a number has been assigned to the patent is contrary to 37 C.F.R §1.313 in the absence of a showing of an extraordinary situation justifying waiver of that rule under the provisions of 37 C.F.R. §1.183. *Schmidt v. Reynolds,* 1964 C.D. 1, 140 U.S.P.Q. 118 (D.C. 1963).

Withheld Evidence.

Section 146 (Title 35 U.S.C.) does not contemplate the withholding of pertinent evidence that was within the knowledge of and readily available to the parties at the time of the patent proceeding. A party should not be allowed to withhold part of the available

---

[2] Although it is permissible to withdraw a final rejection for the purpose of entering a new ground of rejection, this practice is to be limited to situations where a new reference fully meets at least one claim or meets it except for differences which are shown to be completely obvious. Normally, the previous rejection should be withdrawn with respect to the claim or claims involved. The practice should not be used for application of subsidiary references, or of references which are merely considered to be better than those of record. Furthermore, the practice should not be used for entering new non-reference or so-called "formal" grounds of rejection, such as those under 35 U.S.C. §112. Commissioner's Notice, 817 O.G. 1615 (Asst. Comm'r Richard A. Wahl 1965).

and highly pertinent evidence from the patent board on its belief or conclusion that it is not needed to prevail, and then on losing at the administrative level, seek to prevail in a subsequent trial by means of the withheld evidence. *Kirschke v. Lamar*, 300 F.Supp. 146, 163 U.S.P.Q. 99, 105 (Mo. 1969).

ᚥ

While 35 U.S.C. §251 is to be liberally construed as a remedial statute, such liberalism does not extend to eradication of a dereliction of a duty by what is, in effect, a re-prosecution in which the Examiner is now given an opportunity to pass on patentability in light of a very pertinent reference which the applicant previously knowingly withheld from him. *In re Clark*, 522 F.2d 623, 187 U.S.P.Q. 209, 213 (C.C.P.A. 1975).

Withholding Information. *See* Duty to Disclose.

Witness. *See also* Disqualification, Examiner, Expert Witness.

There is nothing wrong with a qualified expert testifying at the behest of one party or the other to a lawsuit and being paid reasonable compensation in return for that testimony, or any other assistance that he may render. To become a very highly paid employee of one of the parties is an altogether different matter. *Bally Manufacturing Corporation v. D. Gottlieb & Co.*, 222 U.S.P.Q. 681, 686 (Ill. 1984).

ᚥ

An action in the district court under 35 U.S.C. §145 is a proceeding de novo and, while it is limited to the invention claimed in the PTO, the court may consider any additional competent evidence that a plaintiff neither intentionally nor negligently failed to submit to the PTO. The presumption of correctness that attaches to the decision of the Commissioner is a rebuttable presumption that may be overcome by the introduction of evidence (at a trial under §145) that is of such character and amount as to carry a thorough conviction of error. At such a trial the plaintiff and defendant may present evidence on any issue properly before the court. This additional evidence may include testimony of expert witnesses and inventors skilled in the art, and evidence of commercial success. In making its determination of non-obviousness, the court recognized the non-analogous nature of one reference, the lack of teaching or suggestion in the prior art of the useful advantage of a flexible track incapable of self-support, and the commercial success of the highly flexible Hot Wheels trackway-toy vehicle combination covered by the plaintiff's Reissue Application. The fact that the claimed invention seemed simple and, when viewed in hindsight, appeared to be obvious was not enough to negate invention. *Lemelson v. Mossinghoff*, 225 U.S.P.Q. 1063 (D.C. 1985).

ᚥ

Absent extraordinary circumstances or compelling reasons, an attorney who participates in a case should not be called as a witness. *Liqui-Box Corp. v. Reid Valve Co. Inc.*, 16 U.S.P.Q.2d 1074, 1075 (Pa. 1989).

ᚥ

In 35 U.S.C. §284 Congress has allowed the court to include "costs as fixed by the Court" in its assessment of damages. Furthermore, the section's mandate is to "award [the prevailing] claimant damages adequate to compensate for the infringement." Part of the damages of the infringement are the expenses incurred in litigation necessary to protect the patent rights. Expert witnesses are practically a requirement in patent litigation. Since there is no reference to the allowed amounts of 28 U.S.C. §1821(b), it would appear that Congress has provided for expert fees as costs to not be bound by the $30-per-day limitation. The court may therefore assess expert fees in excess of $30 per day. *Eldon Industries Inc. v. Vanier Manufacturing Inc.*, 14 U.S.P.Q.2d 1075, 1076 (Cal. 1990).

ϖ

When expert testimony is needed in support of, or in opposition to, a preliminary motion, a party should:

1. identify the person it expects to call as an expert;
2. state the field in which the person is alleged to be an expert; and
3. state in a Declaration signed by the person (a) the subject matter on which the person is expected to testify, (b) the facts and opinions to which the person is expected to testify, and (c) a summary of the grounds and basis for each opinion.

When a person is to be called as a fact witness, a Declaration by that person (stating the facts) should be filed. If the other party is to be called, or if evidence in the possession of the other party is necessary, an explanation of the evidence sought, what it will show, and why it is needed must be supplied. When inter partes tests are to be performed, a description of such tests (stating what they will show) must be presented. *Hanagan v. Kimura,* 16 U.S.P.Q.2d 1791, 1794 (Commr. Patents & Trademarks 1990).

Witness Fee.

A magistrate judge's ruling: a refusal to pay a highly experienced patent attorney more than the statutory fact-witness fee of $40 per day for his deposition testimony in a civil suit would not impose an undue burden on the attorney, was not regarded as unreasonable; loss of earnings did not constitute an undue burden. *Irons v. Karceski,* 74 F.3d 1262, 37 U.S.P.Q.2d 1599, 1600, 1601 (D.C. Cir. 1996).

Word. *See also* Term.

The jury are to judge of the meaning of words of art, and technical phrases, in commerce and manufactures, and of the surrounding circumstances, which may materially affect, enlarge or control the meaning of the words of the patent and specification. *Washburn v. Gould,* 29 F. Cas. 312, 325 (C.C.D. Mass. 1844).

ϖ

A word is not a crystal, transparent and unchanged; it is the skin of a living thought and may vary greatly in color and content according to the circumstances and the time in which it is used. *Towne v. Eisner,* 245 U.S. 418, 425 (1918).

ϖ

"The very nature of words would make a clear and unambiguous [patent] claim a rare occurrence." *Autogiro Co. of *America v. United States*, 384 F.2d 391, 397, 155 U.S.P.Q. 697, 702 (Ct. Cl. 1967).

Workable Range. *See* **Optimize.**

Working Example. *See also* **Example.**

A specification need not contain a working example if the invention is otherwise disclosed in such a manner that one skilled in the art would be able to practice it without an undue amount of experimentation. *In re Borkowski and Van Venrooy,* 422 F.2d 904, 164 U.S.P.Q. 642 (C.C.P.A. 1970).

ᛒ

A working example is not always necessary. A specification need be no more specific under Rule 71(b) [37 C.F.R. §1.71(b)] than is required by the enablement provision of 35 U.S.C. §112. The test is whether there is sufficient working procedure for one skilled in the art to practice the claimed invention without undue experimentation. *In re Stephens, Benvau, and Benvau,* 529 F.2d 1343, 188 U.S.P.Q. 659, 661 (C.C.P.A. 1976).

ᛒ

The fact that the specification is devoid of a working example is without significance. Examples are not necessary. While a full example may have provided additional useful information, one possessed of knowledge of one skilled in this art could practice the invention without the exercise of an undue amount of experimentation. With respect to the best-mode rejection, we find no evidence of concealment and are unable to agree with the Examiner that the quality of the appellants' disclosure is so lacking as to effectively result in concealment. *Ex parte Nardi and Simier,* 229 U.S.P.Q. 79 (B.P.A.I. 1986).

ᛒ

Though not controlling, the lack of working examples is, nevertheless, a factor to be considered in a case involving both physiological activity and an undeveloped art. When a patent applicant chooses to forego exemplification and bases utility on broad terminology and general allegations, he runs the risk that, unless one with ordinary skill in the art would accept the allegations as obviously valid and correct, the Examiner may, properly, ask for evidence to substantiate them. *Ex parte Sudilovsky,* 21 U.S.P.Q.2d 1702, 1705 (B.P.A.I. 1991).

Work Product.

One of the realities of litigation is that the work product doctrine furnishes no shield against discovery, by interrogatories or by deposition, of facts that the adverse party's lawyer has learned. To the extent that work product reveals the opinions, judgments, and thought process of counsel, it receives some higher level of protection, and a party seeking discovery must show extraordinary justification. An attorney's opinion work product is discoverable where such information is directly at issue and the need for production is compelling. *Bio-Rad Laboratories Inc. v. Pharmacia Inc.,* 130 F.R.D. 116, 14 U.S.P.Q.2d 1924, 1927 (Cal. 1990).

ᛒ

Absent an extraordinary showing of unfairness that goes well beyond the interests generally protected by the work product doctrine, written and oral communications from a lawyer to an expert that are related to matters about which the expert will offer testimony are discoverable, even when those communications would otherwise be deemed opinion work product. *Intermedics Inc. v. Ventritex Inc.*, 139 F.R.D. 384, 22 U.S.P.Q.2d 1481, 1483 (Cal. 1991).

Work-Product Doctrine.

In light of the protracted history of the patent in suit (which includes the ex parte prosecution of the patent before the PTO), the interference proceedings before the PTO, and prior litigation, documents involving communications between the attorneys employed by the firm representing the plaintiff during prosecution of the patent in suit and a telex between an attorney employed by a wholly owned affiliate of the plaintiff and an attorney and Chief Patent Counsel for the plaintiff must be regarded as having been "prepared in anticipation of litigation." Accordingly, as the subject documents contain legal strategies, opinions, conclusions, and proposals concerning issues in the litigation presently before the court, the documents fall within the scope of the work-product doctrine. As these documents are entitled to qualified immunity from discovery, the defendants bear the burden of establishing (1) a substantial need for the documents in order to prepare their case, and (2) virtual unavailability of obtaining information contained in the documents without undergoing undue hardship. *Rohm & Haas Co. v. Dawson Chemical Co.*, 214 U.S.P.Q. 56, 59 (Tex. 1981).

ᛒ

Impressions protected by the work-product doctrine may be discovered when directly relevant to the litigation and when the need for production is compelling. *Environ Products Inc. v. Total Containment Inc.*, 41 U.S.P.Q.2d 1302 (Pa. 1996).

ᛒ

The work-product doctrine protects only documents "prepared in anticipation of litigation..." *Bristol-Meyers Squibb Co. v. Rhône-Poulenc Rorer Inc.*, 44 U.S.P.Q.2d 1463, 1465, 1466 (N.Y. 1997).

Work-Product Immunity. *See also* Privilege.

In order to claim this type of immunity, involved documents must be prepared in anticipation of litigation or in preparation for trial. Although the work-product immunity applies to materials prepared when litigation is merely a contingency, more than a mere possibility of litigation must be evident. In patent cases, work-product immunity does not extend to preparation for ex parte proceedings, such as patent proceedings. Work-product immunity can be negated by committing fraud during the prosecution of an application before the PTO. A prima facie showing that the lawyer's advice was designed to serve his client in the furtherance of its wrongful conduct is necessary to vitiate work-product immunity. *Detection Systems, Inc. v. Pittway Corp.*, 96 F.R.D. 152, 220 U.S.P.Q. 716 (N.Y. 1982).

ᛒ

Some courts have found that the invocation of the advice of counsel defense waives both the attorney-client privilege and work product immunity. *Mushroom Associates v. Monterey Mushrooms Inc.*, 24 U.S.P.Q.2d 1767, 1770 (Cal. 1992).

ᛒ

Patent prosecution documents and related materials may be classified as work product if the primary purpose for their creation was for use in pending or anticipated litigation. *Burroughs Welcome Co. v. Barr Laboratories Inc.*, 143 F.R.D. 611, 25 U.S.P.Q.2d 1274, 1278 (N.C. 1992).

ω

In patent cases, the work product immunity applies to documents prepared in anticipation of proceedings before the Board of Patent Interferences. In addition, the work product immunity has been held applicable in the following specific instances: preliminary drafts of legal documents, license agreements and/or assignments, opinion letters and background memoranda with respect to the scope and validity of patents and patent applications, attorney's analysis or assessments of a party's position with respect to other parties in an ongoing interference, and intra-office or file notes and memoranda containing summaries of conferences, legal research and comments on technical information prepared by outside patent counsel or patent department attorneys in connection with an interference. With respect to documents prepared during nonadversarial *ex parte* applications, the work product immunity applies if the primary concern of the attorney is with future litigation rather than the ongoing patent application prosecution. *Conner Peripherals Inc. v. Western Digital Corp.*, 31 U.S.P.Q.2d 1042, 1045 (Cal. 1993).

Work-Product Privilege. *See also* Mutual Interest, Privilege.

Plaintiff's production of certain documents related to the prosecution of a patent constitutes a waiver of the attorney-client privilege with respect to all documents related to prosecution of the patent. This renders all of the attorney's files with respect to the prosecution of the patent discoverable, despite the fact that they may constitute "work product". *Bowmar Instrument Corp. v. Texas Instruments Incorporated*, 196 U.S.P.Q. 199, 201 (Ind. 1977).

ω

A responsible patent attorney always anticipates the possibility of future litigation involving the patent. It is possible that, during ex parte prosecution, certain memoranda or recordings prepared by the attorney may reflect concerns more relevant to future litigation than to the ongoing prosecution. If the primary concern of the attorney is with claims which would potentially arise in future litigation, the work-product immunity applies. *Hercules Incorporated v. Exxon Corporation*, 434 F.Supp. 136, 196 U.S.P.Q. 401, 412 (Del. 1977).

ω

The work-product doctrine does not apply to patent agent communications. *The Dow Chemical Company v. Atlantic Richfield Company*, 227 U.S.P.Q. 129, 135 (Mich. 1985).

ω

The work-product privilege protects from discovery materials prepared in anticipation of litigation. The mere likelihood of litigation in the future is insufficient for invoking the privilege. Rather, the probability of litigation must be substantial and the commencement of the litigation imminent. Materials that are prepared in the ordinary course of business do not fall within the work-product exception. While all documents generated in the patent application process may not be protected from discovery, in any given situation there can be documents that do in fact fall within the work product privilege. *Stauffer Chemical Co. v. Monsanto Co.*, 623 F. Supp. 148, 227 U.S.P.Q. 401 (Mo. 1985).

Written Description.

An original claim may provide adequate "written description" of the claimed invention. It is equally a "written description" whether located among the original claims or in the descriptive part of the specification. *In re Gardner*, 480 F.2d 879, 178 U.S.P.Q. 149 (C.C.P.A. 1973).

ω

A description which renders obvious a claimed invention need not be sufficient to satisfy the written description requirement of that invention. A written description of an invention involving a chemical genus, like a description of a chemical species, "requires a precise definition, such as by structure, formula, [or] chemical name," of the claimed subject matter sufficient to distinguish it from other materials. *University of California v. Eli Lilly and Co.*, 119 F.3d 1559, 43 U.S.P.Q.2d 1398, 1405 (Fed. Cir. 1997).

Wrongful Intent. *See also* **Spurious.**

A studied ignorance of the facts, a reckless indifference to the truth, and a complete absence of evidence of good faith are circumstances that may give rise to an inference of wrongful intent. *Hewlett-Packard Co. v. Bausch & Lomb Inc.*, 746 F. Supp. 1413, 14 U.S.P.Q.2d 1906, 1907 (Cal. 1990).

Zeolite.

A zeolite is not a compound which is a homolog or an isomer of another, but is a mixture of various compounds related to each other by a particular crystal structure. No reason exists for applying the law relating to structural obviousness of those compounds which are homologs or isomers of each other to zeolites. No other chemical theory has been cited as a basis for considering claimed zeolite as *prima facie* obvious in view of a reference zeolite. *In re Grose and Flanigen*, 592 F.2d 1161, 201 U.S.P.Q. 57, 63 (C.C.P.A. 1979).

Zero.

The phrase "up to" includes zero as the lower limit. *In re Mochel*, 470 F.2d 638, 176 U.S.P.Q. 194, 195 (C.C.P.A. 1972).

Table of Cases

-A-

Accent Designs Inc. v. Jan Jewelry Designs Inc., 92 Civ. 0482, 32 U.S.P.Q.2d 1036 (N.Y. 1994) - REEXAMINATION, STAY

In re Ackermann, Duennenberger, and Siegrist, 444 F.2d 1172, 170 U.S.P.Q. 340 (C.C.P.A. 1971) - SINGLE PROPERTY

Acme Resin Corp. v. Ashland Oil Inc., 20 U.S.P.Q.2d 1305 (Ohio 1991) - CONSIST

Acoustical Design Inc. v. Control Electronics Co., 932 F.2d 939, 18 U.S.P.Q.2d 1707 (Fed. Cir. 1991) - ASSIGNOR ESTOPPEL, CAFC, EXPERT TESTIMONY

In re Adams, 356 F.2d 998, 148 U.S.P.Q. 742 (C.C.P.A. 1966) - TIME

Adams v. United States, 330 F.2d 622, 141 U.S.P.Q. 361 (U.S. Ct. Cl. 1964) - NUMBER OF REFERENCES

In re Adamson and Duffin, 275 F.2d 952, 125 U.S.P.Q. 233 (C.C.P.A. 1960) - RACE-MATE, STEREOISOMER

Additive Controls & Measurement Systems Inc. v. Flowdata Inc., 29 U.S.P.Q.2d 1890 (Tex. 1993) - ROYALTY

Additive Controls and Measurement Systems Inc. v. Flowdata Inc., 32 U.S.P.Q.2d 1747 (Tex. 1994) - CONTEMPT, INFRINGEMENT

Additive Controls & Measurement Systems Inc. v. Flowdata Inc., 47 U.S.P.Q.2d 1906 (Fed. Cir. 1998) - CONTEMPT, SUBSTANTIAL

Adelberg Laboratories Inc. v. Miles Inc., 921 F.2d 1267, 17 U.S.P.Q.2d 1111 (Fed. Cir. 1990) - ABUSE OF DISCRETION, BAD FAITH, ESTOPPEL, LACHES

Advanced Cardiovascular Systems Inc. v. C.R. Bard Inc., 144 F.R.D. 372, 25 U.S.P.Q.2d 1354 (Cal. 1992) - ATTORNEY-CLIENT PRIVILEGE

Advanced Cardiovascular Systems Inc. v. Medtronic Inc., 47 U.S.P.Q.2d 1536 (Cal. 1998) - DISQUALIFICATION, EXPERT

Advanced Cardiovascular Systems Inc. v. SciMed Life Systems Inc., 20 U.S.P.Q.2d 1870 (Minn. 1991) - COINVENTOR, NOTICE

Advanced Cardiovascular Systems Inc. v. SciMed Life Systems Inc., 988 F.2d 1157, 26 U.S.P.Q.2d 1038 (Fed. Cir. 1993) - FORFEITURE, INVENTORSHIP, LACHES, RULE 12(b)(6), RULE 56

Advanced Estimating Systems Inc. v. Riney, 77 F.3d 1322, 38 U.S.P.Q.2d 1208 (11th Cir. 1996) - EXCUSABLE NEGLECT, RULE 4(a)(5)

Aerojet-General Corp. v. Machine Tool Works, Oerlikon-Buehrle Ltd., 895 F.2d 736, 13 U.S.P.Q.2d 1670 (Fed. Cir. 1990) - FCIA, WELL-PLEADED COMPLAINT

Aeroquip Corp. v. U.S., 43 U.S.P.Q.2d 1503 (U.S. Ct. Fed. Cl. 1997) - INFRINGEMENT

Aerosol Research Co. v. Scovill Manufacturing Co., 334 F.2d 751, 141 U.S.P.Q. 758 (7th Cir. 1964) - CANCELLATION, NEW MATTER

A.F. Stoddard & Company, Ltd. v. Dann, 564 F.2d 556, 195 U.S.P.Q. 97 (D.C. Cir. 1977) - APPLICANT, BROADENED REISSUE, CONVERSION, INVENTIVE ENTITY, INVENTOR'S SIGNATURE, REISSUE, REMEDIAL STATUTE, SIGNATURE, SOLE, STATUTORY CONSTRUCTION, 35 U.S.C. §111, 35 U.S.C. §117

Agar Corp. Inc. v. Multi-Fluid Inc., 45 U.S.P.Q.2d 1444 (Tex. 1997) - INTERNET, PERSONAL JURISDICTION

Agar Corp. v. Multi-Fluid Inc., 47 U.S.P.Q.2d 1375 (Tex. 1998) - RULE 13(f)

Ag Pro, Inc. v. Sakraida, 512 F.2d 141, 185 U.S.P.Q. 642 (5th Cir. 1975) -NEWLY DISCOVERED EVIDENCE, NEW TRIAL

Agrashell, Inc. v. Hammons Products Company, 479 F.2d 269, 177 U.S.P.Q. 501 (8th Cir. 1973) - MISUSE, RESTRAINT OF TRADE, SHERMAN ACT

Agridyne Technologies Inc. v. W.R. Grace & Co.-Conn., 863 F. Supp. 1522, 32 U.S.P.Q.2d 1777 (Utah 1994) - STREAM OF COMMERCE

In re Ahlert and Kruger, 424 F.2d 1088, 165 U.S.P.Q. 418 (C.C.P.A. 1970) - FACT, JUDICIAL NOTICE, NOTICE

Air Products and Chemicals, Inc. v. Johnson, 442 A.2d 1114, 215 U.S.P.Q. 547 (Pa. 1982) - EMPLOYMENT AGREEMENT

Air Products and Chemicals, Inc. v. Chas. S. Tanner Co., 219 U.S.P.Q. 223 (S.C. 1983) - TEST RESULTS, UNEXPECTED PROPERTIES

Air-Shields Inc. v. The BOC Group, 23 U.S.P.Q.2d 1955, 1956 (Md. 1992) - BIFURCATION

Ex parte Akamatsu, 22 U.S.P.Q.2d 1915 (B.P.A.I. 1992) - MEANS, UNITY OF INVENTION

Akiebolag v. Waukesha Cutting Tools Inc., 640 F. Supp. 1139, 1 U.S.P.Q.2d 2002 (Wis. 1986) - CONVERSION

Akro Corp v. Luker, 45 F.3d 1541, 33 U.S.P.Q.2d 1505 (Fed. Cir. 1995) - HEARSAY, NON-RESIDENT DEFENDANT

Akzo M.V. Aramide Maatschappij V.O.F. v. E.I. du Pont de Nemours, 810 F.2d 1148, 1 U.S.P.Q.2d 1704 (Fed. Cir. 1987) - INEQUITABLE CONDUCT, MATERIALITY, NEGLIGENCE

Ex parte Alappat, 23 U.S.P.Q.2d 1340, 1342 (B.P.A.I. 1992) - MEANS

In re Alappat, 33 F.3d 1526, 31 U.S.P.Q.2d 1545 (Fed. Cir. 1994) - COMMISSIONER, COMMISSIONER'S AUTHORITY, COMPUTER, MACHINE, PROGRAM, RECONSIDERATION, REHEARING, 35 U.S.C. §101

Albemarle Paper Co. v. Moody, 422 U.S. 405 (1975) - DAMAGES

Ex parte Albert, 18 U.S.P.Q.2d 1325 (B.P.A.I. 1984) - PRINTED PUBLICATION

Ex parte Albert, 18 U.S.P.Q.2d 1326 (B.P.A.I. 1988) - PRINTED PUBLICATION

Albert v. Kevex Corporation, 727 F.2d 757, 221 U.S.P.Q. 202 (Fed. Cir. 1984) - 35 U.S.C. §291

In re Albertson, 332 F.2d 379, 141 U.S.P.Q. 730 (C.C.P.A. 1964) - NEW ANALOGY PROCESS, PROCESS, USE, STATUTORY CLASS

In re Albrecht, 514 F.2d 1389, 185 U.S.P.Q. 585 (C.C.P.A. 1975) - ANALOG, INCENTIVE, OBVIOUSNESS, PROBLEM, PROPERTY, TEACH AWAY FROM

Alcon Laboratories Inc. v. Allergan Inc., 17 U.S.P.Q.2d 1365 (Tex. 1990) - REISSUE

Alcon Laboratories Inc. v. Entravision Inc., 976 F.2d 748, 26 U.S.P.Q.2d 1137 (Fed. Cir. 1992) - SUMMARY JUDGMNENT

Alco Standard Corporation v. Tennessee Valley Authority, 808 F.2d 1490, 1 U.S.P.Q.2d 1337 (Fed. Cir. 1986) - BY HAND, CLAIM, COMBINING, CORRELATING, MENTAL STEPS, PROCESS

Alexander Milburn Co. v. Davis-Bournonville Co., 270 U.S. 390 (1926) - COPENDING PATENT, KNOWLEDGE ABROAD, 35 U.S.C. §102(e)

Allan Archery Inc. v. Precision Shooting Equipment Inc., 865 F.2d 896, 9 U.S.P.Q.2d 1728 (7th Cir. 1989) - ACCESSORY

Allegheny Ludlum Corp. v. Comer, 24 U.S.P.Q.2d 1771 (Pa. 1992) - EXHAUSTION DOCTRINE, REEXAMINATION

Allegheny Ludlum Corp. v. Nippon Steel Corp., 20 U.S.P.Q.2d 1553 (Pa. 1991) - PROCESS

Ex parte Allen, 2 U.S.P.Q.2d 1425 (B.P.A.I. 1987) - LIFE FORM, OYSTER

In re Allen, 324 F.2d 993, 139 U.S.P.Q. 492 (C.C.P.A. 1963) - SOLUTION

The Allen Group, Inc. v. Nu-Star, Inc., 213 U.S.P.Q. 513 (Ill. 1977) - SETTLEMENT AGREEMENT

Allen Organ Company v. Kawai Musical Instruments Manufacturing Co., Ltd., 593 F. Supp. 107, 224 U.S.P.Q. 907 (Pa. 1984) - STREAM OF COMMERCE

Allergan Sales Inc. v. Pharmacia & Upjohn Inc., 42 U.S.P.Q.2d 1560, 1563 (Cal. 1997) - DEGREE, RELATIVELY

In re Aller, Lacey, and Hall, 220 F.2d 454, 105 U.S.P.Q. 233 (C.C.P.A. 1955) - CHANGE, CONCENTRATION, CRITICAL, OPTTIMIZE, REFERENCE, ROUTINE EXPERIMENTATION, TEMPERATURE

Allied Chemical Corp. v. Daiflon, Inc., 449 U.S. 33 (1980) -MANDAMUS

Allied Signal Inc. v. Allegheny Ludlum Corp., 132 F.R.D. 134, 17 U.S.P.Q.2d 1638 (Conn. 1990) - 35 U.S.C. §146

Allied-Signal Inc. v. Allegheny Ludlum Corp., 132 F.R.D. 134, 18 U.S.P.Q.2d 1080 (Conn. 1990) - 35 U.S.C. §146

Allied-Signal Inc. v. Allegheny Ludlum Corp., 29 U.S.P.Q.2d 1039 (Conn. 1993) - 35 U.S.C. §146

Allied-Signal Inc. v. Field Tec Corp., 17 U.S.P.Q.2d 1692 (Cal. 1990) - BEST MODE

ALM Surgical Equipment Inc. v. Kirschner Medical Corp., 15 U.S.P.Q.2d 1241 (S.C. 1990) - CAFC, CONDUCT, DAMAGES, DIRECTED VERDICT, DISTRIBUTOR, DUE CARE, FILE WRAPPER ESTOPPEL, INFRINGEMENT, INJUNCTION, JURISDICTION, JURY, NEW TRIAL, OPINION OF COUNSEL, PREJUDGMENT INTEREST, PRESUMPTION, PROCEDURAL MATTERS, ROYALTY, VERDICT

Alpert v. Slatin, 305 F.2d 891, 134 U.S.P.Q. 296 (C.C.P.A. 1962) - FEDERAL SHOP BOOK RULE

Alpex Computer Corp. v. Nintendo Co. Ltd., 20 U.S.P.Q.2d 1782 (N.Y. 1991) - RULE 408

Alpex Computer Corp. v. Nintendo Co. Ltd., 86 Civ. 1749, 34 U.S.P.Q.2d 1167 (N.Y. 1994) - COMMERCIAL SUCCESS, EQUIVALENT, INTEREST, OPINION OF COUNSEL, PATENT RIGHTS, PREJUDGMENT INTEREST, SECONDARY CONSIDERATIONS

Alpex Computer Corp. v. Nintendo Co. Ltd., 40 U.S.P.Q.2d 1667 (Fed. Cir. 1996) - EQUIVALENCY

Ex parte Alpha Industries Inc., 22 U.S.P.Q.2d 1851 (B.P.A.I. 1992) - BPAI, REISSUE

Al-Site Corp. v. Opti-Ray Inc., 23 U.S.P.Q.2d 1235 (N.Y. 1992) -INFRINGEMENT, SUMMARY JUDGMENT

Al-Site Corp. v. Opti-Ray Inc., 841 F. Supp. 1318, 28 U.S.P.Q.2d 1915 (N.Y. 1993) - DATE

Al-Site Corp. v. VSI International Inc., 36 U.S.P.Q.2d 1054 (Fla. 1995) - COLLATERAL ESTOPPEL

Altech Controls Corp. v. E.I.L. Instruments Inc., 44 U.S.P.Q.2d 1890 (Tex. 1997) - DEFINITENESS

In re Altenpohl, 500 F.2d 1151, 183 U.S.P.Q. 38 (C.C.P.A. 1974) - ADVANTAGE,

AMBIGUITY, ANTECEDENT BASIS, COMMENSURATE IN SCOPE, EX-
PERT OPINION, REISSUE, REMEDIAL STATUTE

Ex parte Altermatt, 183 U.S.P.Q. 436 (PO Bd. App. 1974) - DYESTUFF, HYDROCAR-
BON, LIMITS, SUBSTITUTED

In re Alton, 76 F.3d 1168, 37 U.S.P.Q.2d 1578 (Fed. Cir. 1996) - DESCRIPTION,
OPINION EVIDENCE

Altvater v. Freeman, 319 U.S. 359, 57 U.S.P.Q. 285 (1943) - VALIDITY

In re Alul and McEwan, 468 F.2d 939, 175 U.S.P.Q. 700 (C.C.P.A. 1972) -
CONDITIONS

Aluminum Co. of America v. Reynolds Metals Co., 14 U.S.P.Q.2d 1170 (Ill. 1989) -
PRINTED PUBLICATION

Amerace Esna Corporation v. Highway Safety Devices, Incorporated, 330 F. Supp. 313,
171 U.S.P.Q. 186 (Tex. 1971) - SUBCLASS

American Academy of Science v. Novell Inc., 24 U.S.P.Q.2d 1386 (Cal. 1992) - CUS-
TOMER SUIT

American Bank Note Holographics Inc. v. The Upper Deck Co., 41 U.S.P.Q.2d 2019 (N.Y.
1997) - DAMAGES, MARKING, PROCESS CLAIMS

American Can Company v. Dart Industries, Inc., 205 U.S.P.Q. 1006 (Ill. 1979)
-POLYMER

American Ceramicraft Inc. v. Eisenbraun Reiss Inc., 28 U.S.P.Q.2d 1241 (N.J. 1993 -
unpublished) - REEXAMINATION, STAY

American Cyanamid Co. v. Federal Trade Commission, 363 F.2d 757, 150 U.S.P.Q. 135
(6th Cir. 1966) - COMPULSORY LICENSING, EXAMINER, FEDERAL TRADE
COMMISSION

American Dental Association Health Foundation v. Bisco Inc., 24 U.S.P.Q.2d 1524 (Ill.
1992) - CLAIM LANGUAGE

American Equipment Corp. v. Wikomi Manufacturing Co., 630 F.2d 544, 208 U.S.P.Q.
465 (7th Cir. 1980) - CONSENT DECREE, RES JUDICATA

American Fruit Growers, Inc. v. Brogdex Co., 283 U.S. 1, 8 U.S.P.Q. 131 (1931) -
MANUFACTURE

American Hoist & Derrick Company v. Sowa & Sons, Inc., 725 F.2d 1350, 220 U.S.P.Q.
763 (Fed. Cir. 1984) - ADMINISTRATIVE REGULARITY, FRAUD, MONOP-
OLY, PRESUMPTION OF VALIDITY

American Home Products Corp. v. California Biological Vaccine Laboratories, 21
U.S.P.Q.2d 1230 (Cal. 1991) - ON SALE

American Hospital Supply Corporation v. Travenol Laboratories, Inc., 745 F.2d 1, 223
U.S.P.Q. 577 (Fed. Cir. 1984) - CAFC, CRITICAL, PROOF, RANGE OF EQUIV-
ALENTS, UNEXPECTED RESULTS, SCOPE OF PATENT PROTECTION,
STANDARD

American Medical Systems Inc. v. Medical Engineering Corp., 6 F.3d 1523, 28
U.S.P.Q.2d 1321 (Fed. Cir. 1993) - MARKING

American Optical Corp. v. United States, 179 U.S.P.Q. 682 (Ct. Cl. 1973) - INTENT,
PRIVILEGE

American Permahedge Inc. v. Barcana Inc., 41 U.S.P.Q.2d 1614 (Fed. Cir. 1997) -
PROSECUTION HISTORY ESTOPPEL

American Standard Inc. v. Pfizer Inc., 828 F.2d 734, 3 U.S.P.Q.2d 1817 (Fed. Cir. 1987) - DISCOVERY, PROTECTIVE ORDER, RULE 26(b)(1), RULE 26(c)(7), TRADE SECRET

American Standard Inc. v. Pfizer Inc., 722 F. Supp. 86, 14 U.S.P.Q.2d 1673 (Del. 1989) - COMMERCIAL SUCCESS, DELAY, DILIGENCE, ECONOMICS, MATERIALITY, THESIS

American Sunroof Corp. v. Cars & Concepts, Inc., 224 U.S.P.Q. 144 (Mich. 1984) - ON HAND

American Telephone and Telegraph Co. v. Integrated Network Corp., 972 F.2d 1321, 23 U.S.P.Q.2d 1918 (Fed. Cir. 1992) - EMPLOYMENT AGREEMENT, JURISDICTION

American Wood Paper Co. v. Fiber Disintegrating Co., 90 U.S. (23 Wall.) 566 (1874) - ECONOMICS

Ameritek Inc. v. Carolina Lasercut Corp., 42 U.S.P.Q.2d 1411 (Fed. Cir. 1996 - *unpublished*) - JMOL

Amgen Inc. v. Chugai Pharmaceutical Co., 706 F. Supp. 94, 9 U.S.P.Q.2d 1833 (Mass. 1989) - CONTRACT, PATENT

Amgen Inc. v. Chugai Pharmaceutical Co., Ltd., 13 U.S.P.Q.2d 1737 (Mass. 1989) - CONCEPTION

Amgen Inc. v. Chugai Pharmaceutical Co. Ltd., 927 F.2d 1200, 18 U.S.P.Q.2d 1016 (Fed. Cir. 1991) - ABOUT, BEST MODE, CONCEPTION, DEPOSIT, DOUBT, GENE, OBVIOUSNESS

Amgen Inc. v. Chugai Pharmaceutical Co., 808 F. Supp. 894, 27 U.S.P.Q.2d 1578 (Mass. 1992) - EXCLUSIVE LICENSE

Amgen Inc. v. Hoechst Marion Roussel Inc., 3 F. Supp. 104, 46 U.S.P.Q.2d 1906 (Mass. 1998) - 35 U.S.C 271 (e)(1)

Amgen Inc. v. U.S. International Trade Commission, 902 F.2d 1532, 14 U.S.P.Q.2d 1734 (Fed. Cir. 1990) - IMPORTATION, JURISDICTION

Amhil Enterprises Ltd. v. Wawa Inc., 34 U.S.P.Q.2d 1640 (Md. 1994) - CORPORATE OFFICER, JURISDICTION, PIERCING THE CORPORATE VEIL

Amhil Enterprises Ltd. v. Wawa Inc., 34 U.S.P.Q.2d 1645 (Md. 1995) - SUBSTANTIAL

Amhil Enterprises Ltd. v. Wawa Inc., 81 F.3d 1554, 38 U.S.P.Q.2d 1471 (Fed. Cir. 1996) - CLEARLY ERRONEOUS

AMI Industries, Inc. v. EA Industries, Incorporated, 204 U.S.P.Q. 568 (N.C. 1979) - SIMPLICITY

Ami/Rec-Pro Inc. v. Illinois Tool Works Inc., 46 U.S.P.Q.2d 1369 (Ill. 1998) - *CONDUIT THEORY*

In re Amos, 953 F.2d 613, 21 U.S.P.Q.2d 1271 (Fed. Cir. 1991) - INTENT, REISSUE

Amoss, Monahan, and Vale v. McKinley and Sarantakis, 195 U.S.P.Q. 452 (PTO Bd. Pat. Intf. 1977) - CORROBORATION, DEFAULT JUDGMENT, LABORATORY NOTEBOOK, NOTEBOOK

Ampex Corporation v. Memorex Corporation, 205 U.S.P.Q. 794 (Cal. 1980) - ABANDONED EXPERIMENT, ASSIGNEE, CONSTRUCTIVE REDUCTION TO PRACTICE, DUTY TO DISCLOSE

Amsted Industries Inc. v. Buckeye Steel Castings Co., 24 F.3d 178, 30 U.S.P.Q.2d 1462 (Fed. Cir. 1994) - MARKING, NOTICE

Amsted Industries Inc. v. Buckeye Steel Castings Co., 23 F.3d 374, 30 U.S.P.Q.2d 1470 (Fed. Cir. 1994) - EXPERT WITNESS FEE, SANCTIONS

Amsted Industries Inc. v. National Castings Inc., 16 U.S.P.Q.2d 1737 (Ill. 1990) - ACCELERATED REENTRY THEORY, ATTORNEY-CLIENT PRIVILEGE, OPINION, OPINION OF COUNSEL, PATENT ATTORNEY

Amylin Pharmaceuticals Inc. v. University of Minnesota, 45 U.S.P.Q.2d 1949 (Cal. 1998) - COMPLAINT, LEAVE TO AMEND

Analytical Controls v. American Hospital Supply Corp., 518 F. Supp. 896, 217 U.S.P.Q. 1004 (Ind. 1981) - MARKING

Andco Environmental Processes, Inc. v. Niagara Environmental Associates, Inc., 220 U.S.P.Q. 468 (N.Y. 1983) - CLAIM LANGUAGE, DEFINITION, PRECISION

Ex parte Anderson, 21 U.S.P.Q.2d 1241 (B.P.A.I. 1991) - COMPARABLE, COPYING, EQUIVALENT, POLYMER, SUPERIOR

In re Anderson, 471 F.2d 1237, 176 U.S.P.Q. 331 (C.C.P.A. 1973) - COMBINATION, EXCLUDE

Anderson v. Liberty Lobby, Inc., 477 U.S. 242 (1986) - DISPUTE, SUMMARY JUDGMENT

Anderson and Kaminsky v. Crowther and Young, 152 U.S.P.Q. 504 (P.O. Bd. Pat. Int. 1965) - CORROBORATION

Anderson and Stamatoff v. Natta, Pino, and Mazzanti v. Ziegler, Martin, Breil, and Holzkamp, 480 F.2d 1392, 178 U.S.P.Q. 458 (C.C.P.A. 1973) - SAME DATE

Ex parte Andresen, 212 U.S.P.Q. 100 (PTO Bd. App. 1981) - DERIVATION, ORIGINALITY, 35 U.S.C. §102(f)

Andrew Corp. v. Gabriel Electronics, Inc., 847 F.2d 819, 6 U.S.P.Q.2d 2010 (Fed. Cir. 1988) - COMPARATIVE TEST DATA, EQUIPOISE, EXPERT TESTIMONY, OBVIOUSNESS, PATENTABLE DISTINCTNESS, SHOWING

In re Angstadt and Griffen, 537 F.2d 498, 190 U.S.P.Q. 214 (C.C.P.A. 1976) - CATALYST, CERTAINTY, COMMENSURATE IN SCOPE, DIRECTION, EARLY DISCLOSURE, EXPERIMENTATION, INOPERATIVE, PREDICTABILITY, PROMOTE PROGRESS, SOME, SUFFICIENCY OF DISCLOSURE, UNDUE EXPERIMENTATION, UNPREDICTABLE ART

Animal Legal Defense Fund v. Quigg, 932 F.2d 920, 18 U.S.P.Q.2d 1677 (Fed. Cir. 1991) - INTERVENTION, LIFE FORM, RULE MAKING, STANDING, 5 U.S.C. §553

The Ansul Company v. Uniroyal, Inc., 306 F. Supp. 541, 163 U.S.P.Q. 517 (N.Y. 1969) - ERROR, MARKING, STATUTORY CONSTRUCTION

Ex parte Anthony, 230 U.S.P.Q. 467 (PTO Bd. App. 1982) - PROVISIONAL DISCLAIMER, TERMINAL DISCLAIMER

In re Anthony, 414 F.2d 1383, 162 U.S.P.Q. 594 (C.C.P.A. 1969) - SAFETY

In re Antle, 444 F.2d 1168, 170 U.S.P.Q. 285 (C.C.P.A. 1971) - SELECTION, 35 U.S.C. §103

In re Antonie, 559 F.2d 618, 195 U.S.P.Q. 6 (C.C.P.A. 1977) - INVENTION AS A WHOLE, OPTIMIZE

Antonious v. Kamata-Ri & Company, Limited, 204 U.S.P.Q. 294 (Md. 1979) - PRIOR ADJUDICATION

Ex parte Appeal No. 242-47, 196 U.S.P.Q. 828 (PTO Bd. App. 1976) - DÉLIVRÉ, 35 U.S.C. §102(d)

In re Application Filed July 13, 1950, 105 U.S.P.Q. 154 (Comm'r 1955) - REJECTION

In re Application Filed Mar. 7, 1956, 119 U.S.P.Q. 181 (Comm'r of Patents 1956) - DRAWING

In re Application Filed April 1, 1957, 119 U.S.P.Q. 329 (Comm'r 1958) - TRANSFER

In re Application for an Order for Judicial Assistance in a Foreign Proceeding in the High Court of Justice, Chancery Division, England, 147 F.R.D. 223 (C.D. Cal. 1993) - OREIGN

In re Application Papers Filed Mar. 27, 1963, 138 U.S.P.Q. 393 (Comm'r 1963) - 37 C.F.R. §1.52

In re Application Papers Filed March 27, 1974, 186 U.S.P.Q. 363 (Comm'r Patents and Trademarks 1975) - DEPOSIT ACCOUNT, UNSIGNED CHECK

In re Application Papers Filed December 22, 1958, 123 U.S.P.Q. 71 (Comm'r 1959) - 35 U.S.C. §111

Applied Materials Inc. v. Advanced Semiconductor Materials America Inc., 26 U.S.P.Q.2d 1153 (Cal. 1992) - PLURAL

Applied Materials Inc. v. Advanced Semiconductor Materials America Inc., 32 U.S.P.Q.2d 1865 (Cal. 1994) - BEST MODE

Applied Materials Inc. v. Advanced Semiconductor Materials, 98 F.3d 1563, 40 U.S.P.Q.2d 1481 (Fed. Cir. 1996) - ADMINISTRATIVE CORRECTNESS, COMMERCIAL SUCCESS, PRESUMPTION

Applied Materials Inc. v. Gemini Research Corp., 835 F.2d 279, 5 U.S.P.Q.2d 1127 (Fed. Cir. 1987) - COLLATERAL ESTOPPEL, INVENTIVE ENTITY, RES JUDICATA

Applied Materials Inc. v. Gemini Research Corp., 835 F.2d 279, 15 U.S.P.Q.2d 1816 (Fed. Cir. 1988) - ANOTHER

Applied Medical Resources Corp. v. United States Surgical Corp., 967 F. Supp. 861, 43 U.S.P.Q.2d 1688 (Va. 1997) - ENHANCED DAMAGES, WILLFUL INFRINGEMENT

Applied Medical Resources Corp. v. United States Surgical Corp., 147 F.3d 1374, 47 U.S.P.Q.2d 1289 (Fed. Cir. 1998) - BEST MODE

Aqua Queen Manufacturing Inc. v. Charter Oak Fire Insurance, 830 F. Supp. 536, 26 U.S.P.Q.2d 1940 (Cal. 1993) - PIRACY

Arachnid Inc. v. Medalist Marketing Corp., 972 F.2d 1300, 23 U.S.P.Q.2d 1946 (Fed. Cir. 1992) - GENERAL-VERDICT-MULTIPLE-DEFENSES

Arachnid Inc. v. Merit Industries Inc., 939 F.2d 1574, 19 U.S.P.Q.2d 1513 (Fed. Cir. 1991) - APPLICANT'S RIGHTS, ASSIGNMENT, EXCLUDE, INFRINGEMENT, INVENTION, PATENT, RIGHTS, STANDING

In re Arbeit, DuBois, and Lambert, 201 F.2d 923, 96 U.S.P.Q. 397 (C.C.P.A. 1953) - USE

Arbek Manufacturing Inc. v. Moazzam, 55 F.3d 1567, 34 U.S.P.Q.2d 1670 (Fed. Cir. 1995) - CONTEMPT

Arcade Inc. v. Minnesota Mining and Manufacturing Co., 43 U.S.P.Q.2d 1511 (Tenn. 1997) - EXCLUSIVE LICENSEE

Arcadia Machine & Tool, Inc. v. Sturm, Ruger & Co., Inc., 786 F.2d 1124, 229 U.S.P.Q. 124 (Fed. Cir. 1986) - MISMARKING

Ardco Inc. v. Page, Ricker, Felson Marketing Inc., 25 U.S.P.Q.2d 1382 (Ill. 1992) - SALE, 35 U.S.C. §271(b), USE

Ex parte Argabright and Hall, 161 U.S.P.Q. 703 (PO Bd. App. 1967) - BREADTH

In re Argoudelis, 58 C.C.P.A. 769, 434 F.2d 1390, 168 U.S.P.Q. 99 (1970) - CULTURE, DEPOSIT, MICROORGANISM

Argus Chemical Corp. v. Fibre Glass-Evercoat Co., 812 F.2d 1381, 1 U.S.P.Q.2d 1971 (Fed. Cir. 1987) - DAMAGES, MISCONDUCT

Arkie Lures Inc. v. Gene Larew Tackle Inc., 119 F.3d 953, 43 U.S.P.Q.2d 1294 (Fed. Cir. 1997) - TEACH AWAY FROM

Ex parte Arkless, 116 U.S.P.Q. 214 (PO Bd. App. 1955)- PRIORITY

In re Armbruster, 512 F.2d 676, 185 U.S.P.Q. 152 (C.C.P.A. 1975) - ABSTRACT, ASSERTION, CONVINCE, DESCRIBE, ENABLEMENT, OBJECTIVE ENABLEMENT, NEW GROUND OF REJECTION, SPECIFICATION

Armstrong Cork Company v. Congoleum Industries, Inc., 399 F. Supp. 1141, 188 U.S.P.Q. 679 (Pa. 1975) - TEST RESULTS

In re Arnott, 19 U.S.P.Q.2d 1049 (Commr. Patents & Trademarks 1991) - CERTIFICATE OF CORRECTION, CHALLENGE, EXPERTISE, INTERVENING RIGHTS

Aro Manufacturing Co. v. Convertible Top Replacement Co., 365 U.S. 336, 128 U.S.P.Q. 354 (1961) - REPAIR

Aro Mfg. Co. v. Convertible Top Replacement Co., 377 U.S. 476, 141 U.S.P.Q. 681 (1964) - CONTRIBUTORY INFRINGEMENT, DAMAGES, REPLACEMENT

Arrhythmia Research Technology Inc. v. Corazonix Corp., 958 F.2d 1053, 22 U.S.P.Q.2d 1033 (Fed. Cir. 1992) - ALGORITHM, FORMULA

Arrowhead Industrial Water Inc. v. Ecolochem Inc., 846 F.2d 731, 6 U.S.P.Q.2d 1685 (Fed. Cir. 1988) - DECLARATORY JUDGMENT

Artmatic USA Cosmetics v. Maybelline Co., 906 F. Supp. 850, 38 U.S.P.Q.2d 1037 (N.Y. 1995) - COLLATERAL ESTOPPEL, DEFAULT JUDGMENT

In re Asahi/America Inc., 68 F.3d 442, 33 U.S.P.Q.2d 1921 (Fed. Cir. 1995) - DE NOVO, FEDERAL CIRCUIT, PLENARY REVIEW, STANDARD OF REVIEW

In re Asahi/America Inc., 68 F.3d 442, 37 U.S.P.Q.2d 1204 (Fed. Cir. 1995) - DE NOVO

Asahi Metal Industry Co. v. Superior Court of California, Solano County, 480 U.S. 102 (1987) - STREAM OF COMMERCE

Asari v. Zilges, 8 U.S.P.Q.2d 1117 (B.P.A.I. 1987) - INTERROGATORIES

Asberry v. United States Postal Service, 686 F.2d 1040, 215 U.S.P.Q. 921 (Fed. Cir. 1982) - RULE 38

The Asgrow Seed Co. v. Winterboer, 795 F. Supp. 915, 22 U.S.P.Q.2d 1937 (Iowa 1991) - PLANT VARIETY PROTECTION ACT

Asgrow Seed Co. v. Winterboer, 982 F.2d 486, 25 U.S.P.Q.2d 1202 (Fed. Cir. 1992) - BROWN BAG SALES, PLANT VARIETY PROTECTION ACT

Asgrow Seed Co. v. Winterboer, 115 S.Ct. 788, 33 U.S.P.Q.2d 1430 (S.Ct. 1995) - PVPA, SAVED SEED

Ashland Oil, Inc. v. Delta Resins & Refractories, Inc., 776 F.2d 281, 227 U.S.P.Q. 657 (Fed. Cir. 1985) - BLUEPRINT, CLAIM CONSTRUCTION, COMBINING REFERENCES, COMPOUND, COMPRISE, DEFINING CLAIMED SUBJECT MATTER, ENABLEMENT, ENABLING PRIOR ART, EXCLUDING REFERENCE EMBODIMENTS, EXPERT TESTIMONY, HYPOTHETICAL STRUCTURE, INFERENCE, INHERENCY, KNOWLEDGE, OPINION, POSSESSION, PRE-

SUMPTION, PRODUCT OF PRIOR-ART PROCESS, REFERENCE, RETRO-
SPECTIVE RECONSTRUCTION, SECONDARY CONSIDERATIONS, SUG-
GESTION, TEACHING(S)

Associated Gen. Contractors, Inc. v. California State Council of Carpenters, 459 U.S.
519, 103 S. Ct. 897 (1983) - DAMAGES

Associated Pipe & Fitting Company, Inc. v. Belgian Line, Inc., 247 F. Supp. 757, 147
U.S.P.Q. 307 (N.Y. 1965) - TIME

In re Asta Medica S.A., 794 F. Supp. 442, 23 U.S.P.Q.2d 1756 (Me. 1992) - 28 U.S.C.
§1782

In re Asta Medica S.A., 981 F.2d 1, 25 U.S.P.Q.2d 1861 (1st Cir. 1992) - DISCOVERY,
MARKING

Atari Corp. v. Sega of America Inc., 161 F.R.D. 417, 32 U.S.P.Q.2d 1237 (Cal. 1994) -
PRELIMINARY INJUNCTION, PRESUMPTION OF VALIDITY

Atari Games Corp. v. Nintendo of America Inc., 897 F.2d 1572, 14 U.S.P.Q.2d 1034 (Fed.
Cir. 1990) - ANTITRUST, PRELIMINARY INJUNCTION

Atari Games Corp. v. Nintendo of America Inc., 30 U.S.P.Q.2d 1401 (Cal. 1993) -
REDUNDANT

Atasi Corp. v. Seagate Technology, 847 F.2d 826, 6 U.S.P.Q.2d 1955 (Fed. Cir. 1988) -
ATTORNEY DISQUALIFICATION, PERIPHERAL REPRESENTATION

ATD Corp. v. Lydall Inc., 43 U.S.P.Q.2d 1170 (Mich. 1997) - DESIGNING AROUND,
INTENT, MOTION FOR A NEW TRIAL, SUBSTANTIAL EVIDENCE

ATD Corp. v. Lydall Inc., 48 U.S.P.Q.2d 1321 (Fed. Cir. 1998) - CLAIM DIFFEREN-
TIATION, SCOPE

Athletic Alternatives Inc. v. Prince Manufacturing Inc., 73 F.3d 1573, 37 U.S.P.Q.2d 1365
(Fed. Cir. 1996) - AFFIRM, ALL LIMITATIONS RULE, DISTINCTLY CLAIM,
DOCTRINE OF EQUIVALENTS, EQUIVALENCY, FAIR NOTICE FUNCTION,
35 U.S.C. §112

Atlantic Thermoplastics Co. Inc. v. Faytex Corp., 970 F.2d 834, 23 U.S.P.Q.2d 1481 (Fed.
Cir. 1992) - ON SALE, PRODUCT BY PROCESS

Atlantic Thermoplastics Co. Inc. v. Faytex Corp., 974 F.2d 1279, 23 U.S.P.Q.2d 1801
(Fed. Cir. 1992) - PRODUCT BY PROCESS

Atlas Powder Company v. E.I. duPont de Nemours and Company, 588 F. Supp. 1455, 221
U.S.P.Q. 426 (N.D. Tex. 1983), *aff'd* 750 F.2d 1569, 224 U.S.P.Q. 409 (Fed. Cir.
1984) - ANALOGOUS ART, CONVERSION (*IN SITU* OR *IN VIVO*), DIS-
CLOSURE, INOPERATIVE EMBODIMENTS, OVERCLAIMING, PRIOR
ART, PROBLEM, SCOPE

Atlas Powder Co. v. E.I. DuPont De Nemours & Co., 750 F.2d 1569, 224 U.S.P.Q. 409
(Fed. Cir. 1984) - APPROPRIATION, CONSISTING ESSENTIALLY OF, DOC-
TRINE OF EQUIVALENTS, EQUIVALENCE, INOPERATIVE EMBODI-
MENTS, PROPHETIC EXAMPLES, TRIPARTITE TEST

Atlas Powder Co. v. Ireco Chemicals, 773 F.2d 1230, 227 U. S. P. Q. 289 (Fed . Cir. 1985)
- PRELIMINARY INJUNCTION

Atmel Corp. v. United States, 719 F. Supp. 1101, 13 U.S.P.Q.2d 1547 (U.S. Ct. Intl. Trade
1989) - 28 U.S.C. §1581(a)

Ex parte Attig, 7 U.S.P.Q.2d 1092 (B.P.A.I. 1986) - TYPE

-*B*-

Ex parte Ball and Hair, 99 U.S.P.Q. 146 (PO Bd. App. 1953) - NEGATIVE FUNCTION

Ball Corp. v. American National Can Co., 27 U.S.P.Q.2d 1958 (Ind. 1993) - ATTORNEY-CLIENT PRIVILEGE

Ball Corporation v. United States, 729 F.2d 1429, 221 U.S.P.Q. 289 (Fed. Cir. 1984) - ERROR, RECAPTURE RULE

Ball Corp. v. Xidex Corp., 705 F. Supp. 1470, 9 U.S.P.Q.2d 1491 (Colo. 1988) - ABUSE OF ADMINISTRATIVE PROCEEDINGS, NOERR-PENNINGTON DOCTRINE, SHAM LITIGATION, SHERMAN ACT

Bally Manufacturing Corporation v. D. Gottlieb & Co., 222 U.S.P.Q. 681 (Ill. 1984) - WITNESS

Baltimore Therapeutic Equipment Co. v. Loredan Biomedical Inc., 26 F.3d 138, 30 U.S.P.Q.2d 1672 (Fed. Cir. 1994 - *unpublished*) - EQUIVALENT

Bandag Incorporated v. Gerrard Tire Company, Inc. v. Leonard, 217 U.S.P.Q. 769 (N.C. 1982) - DAMAGES, MARKING

Bandel v. Samfield, Brock, and Locklair, 168 U.S.P.Q. 725 (PO Bd. Pat. Intf. 1961) - INSPECTION, INTERFERENCE

Banner Metals, Inc. v. Lockwood, 125 U.S.P.Q. 29, 178 Cal. App. 2d 643, (Cal. 1960) - ASSIGNMENT, EMPLOYEE

Ex parte Barber, Brandenburg, and Frost, 187 U.S.P.Q. 244 (PTO Bd. App. 1974) - OLD COMBINATION

In re Barker and Pehl, 559 F.2d 588, 194 U.S.P.Q. 470 (C.C.P.A. 1977) - DESCRIBE, SUFFICIENCY OF DISCLOSURE

Barmag Barmer Maschinenfabrik AG v. Murata Machinery, Ltd., 731 F.2d 831, 221 U.S.P.Q. 561 (Fed. Cir. 1984) - EXPERIMENTAL USE

Baron v. Bausch & Lomb Inc., 25 U.S.P.Q.2d 1641 (N.Y. 1992) - EXAMINER

In re Barr, Williams, and Whitmore, 444 F.2d 588, 170 U.S.P.Q. 330 (C.C.P.A. 1971) - BREADTH, CLAIM INTERPRETATION, COMBINATION, COMPOSITION, COMPOUND, DEFINITION, DICTIONARY, DISCLOSURE, ELEMENT, ENCYCLOPEDIA, FUNCTIONAL, NEGATIVE LIMITATION, OPEN-ENDED CLAIM, PHOTOGRAPHIC COLOR COUPLER, RADICAL, SCOPE

The Barr Rubber Products Company v. The Sun Rubber Company, 277 F. Supp. 484, 156 U.S.P.Q. 374 (N.Y. 1967) - LICENSE, USE

In re Barrett, Sanchez, and Vanik, 440 F.2d 1391, 169 U.S.P.Q. 560 (C.C.P.A. 1971) - TRADEMARK

Ex parte Bartfeld, 16 U.S.P.Q.2d 1714 (B.P.A.I. 1990) - DOUBLE PATENTING, TERMINAL DISCLAIMER, 35 U.S.C. §103

In re Bartholome, Lehrer, and Schierwater, 386 F.2d 1019, 156 U.S.P.Q. 20 (C.C.P.A. 1967) - 37 C.F.R. §1.71(b)

In re Bass, Jenkins, and Horvat, 474 F.2d 1276, 177 U.S.P.Q. 178 (C.C.P.A. 1973) - DILIGENCE, ORDER, PTO, 35 U.S.C. §102(g)/103

Ex parte Batchelder and Zimmerman, 131 U.S.P.Q. 38 (PO Bd. App. 1960) - DESCRIPTION, NEW MATTER, REDUCTION IN SCOPE

The Battelle Development Corp. v. Angevine-Funke, Inc., 165 U.S.P.Q. 776 (Ohio 1970) - CONTRACT

In re Bauman, 683 F.2d 405, 214 U.S.P.Q. 585 (C.C.P.A. 1982) - CONTINUATION

Beatrice Foods Co. v. New England Printing & Lithographing Co., 930 F.2d 1572, 18 U.S.P.Q.2d 1548 (Fed. Cir. 1991) - EFFECT

In re Beauregard, 53 F.3d 1583, 35 U.S.P.Q.2d 1383 (Fed. Cir. 1995) - COMPUTER PROGRAM, PRINTED MATTER

In re Beaver, 893 F.2d 329, 13 U.S.P.Q.2d 1409 (Fed. Cir. 1989) - APPEAL, APPLICANT'S RIGHTS

Ex parte Beck, 9 U.S.P.Q.2d 2000 (B.P.A.I. 1987) - OBVIOUSNESS, PREDICTABILITY, SUCCESS

In re Beck, Siebel, and Bosskuhler, 155 F.2d 398, 69 U.S.P.Q. 520 (C.C.P.A. 1946) - COPENDING PATENT, ENABLEMENT, KNOWLEDGE

Becker, Mitchell, and Pierson v. Ishibashi, 201 U.S.P.Q. 319 (PTO Bd. Pat. Intf. 1977) - NEW ISSUES

Becket v. Coe, 98 F.2d 332, 38 U.S.P.Q. 26 (App DC 1938) - ALLOY

Beckman Instruments, Inc. v. LKB Produkter A.B., 5 U.S.P.Q.2d 1462 (Md. 1987) - CONTINUATION APPLICATION, INQUITABLE CONDUCT

Beckman Instruments Inc. v. LKB Produkter A.B., 892 F.2d 1547, 13 U.S.P.Q.2d 1301 (Fed. Cir. 1989) - ATTORNEY'S FEES, EXPERT, INOPERATIVE, 35 U.S.C.285

Beckman Instruments Inc. v. LKB Produkter AB, 17 U.S.P.Q.2d 1190 (Md. 1990) - INFRINGEMENT, MISCONDUCT, PREJUDGMENT INTEREST

BEC Pressure Controls Corporation v. Dwyer Instruments, Inc., 380 F. Supp. 1397, 182 U.S.P.Q. 190 (Ind. 1974) - FEE, ISSUE FEE, REVIVAL, 35 U.S.C. §151

Becton Dickinson & Co. v. C.R. Bard Inc., 922 F.3d 792, 17 U.S.P.Q.2d 1097 (Fed. Cir. 1990) - INFRINGEMENT, SUMMARY JUDGMENT, WAIVER

Becton, Dickenson and Co. v. Sherwood Medical Industries, Inc., 516 F.2d 514, 187 U.S.P.Q. 200 (5th Cir. 1975) - MATERIAL

Beech Aircraft Corp. v. EDO Corp., 18 U.S.P.Q.2d 1881 (D.C. 1991) - PATENT

Beech Aircraft Corp. v. EDO Corp., 990 F.2d 1237, 26 U.S.P.Q.2d 1572 (Fed. Cir. 1993) - CAFC, CONTRACT, PROCEDURAL MATTERS

Behr v. Talbott, 27 U.S.P.Q.2d 1401 (B.P.A.I. 1992) - COPYING CLAIMS, DERIVATION, DESCRIPTION, INTERFERENCE, RIGHT TO MAKE

In re Bell, 991 F.2d 781, 26 U.S.P.Q.2d 1529 (Fed. Cir. 1993) - DE NOVO

Ex parte Bella and Chiaino, 224 U.S.P.Q. 293 (PTO Bd. App. 1984) - STRUCTURAL SIMILARITY, UNITY OF INVENTION

Bell Communications Research Inc. v. Vitalink Communications Corp., 55 F.3d 615, 34 U.S.P.Q.2d 1816 (Fed. Cir. 1995) - PREAMBLE, STANDARD OF REVIEW

Bell & Howell Document Management Products Co. v. Altek Systems, 132 F.3d 701, 45 U.S.P.Q.2d 1033 (Fed. Cir. 1997) - CLAIM CONSTRUCTION

Bell Intercontinental Corp. v. United States, 381 F.2d 1004, 152 U.S.P.Q. 182 (Ct. Cl. 1966) - AGREEMENT TO ASSIGN, ASSIGNMENT, CAPITAL GAINS, LICENSE

Ex parte Bellsnyder, Sr., and Ritchie, 73 U.S.P.Q. 269 (PO Bd. App. 1947) - OMISSION OF ELEMENT OR STEP

Bemis v. Chevron Research Company, 599 F.2d 910, 203 U.S.P.Q. 123 (9th Cir. 1979) - ERROR

Benchcraft Inc. v. Broyhill Furniture Industries, Inc., 681 F. Supp. 1190, 7 U.S.P.Q.2d 1257 (Miss. 1988) - COPYING, SECONDARY CONSIDERATIONS IN DESIGN

In re Bennett, 766 F.2d 524, 226 U.S.P.Q. 413 (Fed. Cir. 1985) - BROADENED RE-ISSUE, REMEDIAL STATUTE, SIGNATURE, STATUTORY CONSTRUCTION

In re Benno, 768 F.2d 1340, 226 U.S.P.Q. 683 (Fed. Cir. 1985) - BREADTH, CLAIM, DISCLOSURE, GENERIC, GENERIC DISCLOSURE, PRIOR ART, PROBLEM, READ ON, REFERENCE, REFERENCE GENERIC TO CLAIMED INVENTION

Benson [see *Gottschalk, Comm'r. Pats. v. Benson*, 409 U.S. 63, 175 U.S.P.Q. 548 (1972)]

Beraha v. Baxter Health Care Corp., 956 F.2d 1436, 22 U.S.P.Q.2d 1100 (7th Cir. 1992) - BEST EFFORTS CLAUSE

Beraha v. C.R. Bard Inc., 32 U.S.P.Q.2d 1040 (Ga. 1994) - DOCTRINE OF EQUIVALENTS

Berenter v. Quigg, 737 F. Supp. 5, 14 U.S.P.Q.2d 1175 (D.C. 1988) - COMPRISE, CONSISTING

In re Berg, 43 U.S.P.Q.2d 1703 (Fed. Cir. 1997 - *unpublished*) - CD-ROM

In re Berg, 140 F.3d 1428, 46 U.S.P.Q.2d 1226 (Fed. Cir. 1998) - TWO-WAY TEST

In re Bergel and Stock, 292 F.2d 955, 130 U.S.P.Q. 206 (C.C.P.A. 1961) - CANCER, CHLORINE ANALOG, COMBINATION, COMBINING REFERENCES, COMPOUND, 35 U.S.C. §101, UTILITY

Berg Electronics Inc. v. Molex Inc., 875 F. Supp. 261, 34 U.S.P.Q.2d 1315 (Del. 1995) - ATTORNEY-CLIENT PRIVILEGE

Berghauser v. Dann, 204 U.S.P.Q. 393 (D.C. 1979) - SOLUTION

In re Bergstrom and Sjovall, 427 F.2d 1394, 166 U.S.P.Q. 256 (C.C.P.A. 1970) - NOVELTY, PURE

In re Bergy, Coats, and Malik, 596 F.2d 952, 201 U.S.P.Q. 352 (C.C.P.A. 1979) - CAUSE, INVENTION, METHOD, MICROORGANISM, 35 U.S.C. §101

Berkeley Park Clothes, Inc. v. Firma Schaeffer-Homberg GmbH, 217 U.S.P.Q. 388 (N.J. 1981) - ATTORNEY'S FEES, AVOIDING INFRINGEMENT, DOMINATING PATENT

Berkey Photo, Inc. v. Klimsch-Repro, Inc., 388 F. Supp. 586, 185 U.S.P.Q. 306 (N.Y. 1975) - ERROR, GIST

Berry Brothers Corporation v. Sigmon, 206 F. Supp. 653, 134 U.S.P.Q. 283 (N.C. 1962) - NUMBER OF REFERENCES

Berry Sterling Corp. v. Pescor Plastics Inc., 122 F.3d 1452, 43 U.S.P.Q.2d 1953 (Fed. Cir. 1997) - DESIGN

In re Bersworth, 189 F.2d 996, 90 U.S.P.Q. 83 (C.C.P.A. 1951) - DEDICATION TO THE PUBLIC

Bersworth v. Watson, 159 F. Supp. 12, 116 U.S.P.Q. 87 (D.C. 1956) - CONTINUITY, FILING DATE

In re Best, Bolton, and Shaw, 562 F.2d 1252, 195 U.S.P.Q. 430 (C.C.P.A. 1977) - CHARACTERISTIC, FUNCTION, INHERENCY, INHERENT, NEWLY DISCOVERED, PROPERTY

Best Lock Corp. v. Ilco Unican Corp., 896 F. Supp. 836, 36 U.S.P.Q.2d 1527 (Ind. 1995) - DESIGN

Bethell and Hadley v. Koch, Robinson, and Wiley, 427 F.2d 1372, 166 U.S.P.Q. 199 (C.C.P.A. 1970) - AMBIGUITY, CLAIM, COUNT, SCOPE

Beverly Hills Fan Co. v. Royal Sovereign Corp., 21 F.3d 1558, 30 U.S.P.Q.2d 1001 (Fed. Cir. 1994) - DUE PROCESS, MOTION, SITUS, STREAM OF COMMERCE

Bey v. Kollonitsch, 806 F.2d 1024, 231 U.S.P.Q. 967 (Fed. Cir. 1986) - DILIGENCE, SUBSTANTIALLY

Bey and Jung v. Kollonitsch and Patchett, 215 U.S.P.Q. 454 (PTO Bd. Pat. Intf. 1981) - DOSAGE, ENABLEMENT, HOST, INTERFERENCE, NOTICE, STRUCTURAL SIMILARITY, TESTIMONY

Beyard and Horai v. Conte, 179 U.S.P.Q. 499 (PO Bd. Pat. Intf. 1972) - SELF-SERVING

B.F. Goodrich Co. v. Aircraft Braking Systems Corp., 825 F. Supp. 65, 27 U.S.P.Q.2d 1209 (Del. 1993) - ON SALE

Ex parte Bhide, 42 U.S.P.Q.2d 1441 (B.P.A.I. 1996) - CANCER, SCOPE, 35 U.S.C. §101, 35 U.S.C. §112

Bic Leisure Products Inc. v. Windsurfing International Inc., 761 F. Supp. 1032, 19 U.S.P.Q.2d 1922 (N.Y. 1991) - PREJUDGMENT INTEREST

Bic Leisure Products Inc. v. Windsurfing International Inc., 774 F. Supp. 832, 21 U.S.P.Q.2d 1548 (N.Y. 1991) - INTERVENING RIGHTS, SALE

Ex parte Biel, 137 U.S.P.Q. 315 (PO Bd. App. 1962) - BREADTH, REACTING

Ex parte Biel (file of USP 3,454,554, Paper No. 22) (PTOBA 1964) - METABOLITE

Biel v. Chessin, 347 F.2d 898, 146 U.S.P.Q. 293 (C.C.P.A. 1965) - CONCEPTION, PRELIMINARY STATEMENT

Biel v. Coan, 130 U.S.P.Q. 241 (PO Bd. Pat. Int. 1959) - CONSTRUCTIVE REDUCTION TO PRACTICE

Ex parte Bielstein, 135 U.S.P.Q. 402 (PO Bd. App. 1962) - ATTORNEY, COMMENSURATE

Big Four Automotive Equipment Corporation v. Jordan, 184 U.S.P.Q. 80 (Ohio 1974) - SINGLE ELEMENT

Bigham v. Godtfredsen and Von Daehne, 222 U.S.P.Q. 632 (PTO Bd. Pat. Intf. 1984) - DELAY, DILIGENCE

Bigham v. Godtfredsen, 857 F.2d 1415, 8 U.S.P.Q.2d 1266 (Fed. Cir. 1988) - DESCRIPTION

Ex parte Billman, 71 U.S.P.Q. 253 (PO Bd. App. 1946) - CARRIER, COMPOSITION

Ex parte Billottet and Fechner, 192 U.S.P.Q. 413 (PTO Bd. App. 1976) - BLOCK DIAGRAM, DERIVATION

Bindra v. Kelly, 206 U.S.P.Q. 570 (PTO Bd. Pat. Int. 1979) - REDUCTION TO PRACTICE, UTILITY

Biocraft Laboratories Inc. v. International Trade Commission, 947 F.2d 483, 20 U.S.P.Q.2d 1446 (Fed. Cir. 1991) - 19 U.S.C. §1337

Biodex Corp. v. Loredan Biomedical Inc., 946 F.2d 850, 20 U.S.P.Q.2d 1252 (Fed. Cir. 1991) - CAFC, FRIVOLOUS, JURY INSTRUCTION, SUFFICIENCY OF EVIDENCE

Biogen Inc. v. Schering AG, 42 U.S.P.Q.2d 1681 (Mass. 1996) - MOTION TO DISMISS

Biomedical Polymers Inc. v. Evergreen Industries Inc., 976 F. Supp. 98, 45 U.S.P.Q.2d 1150 (Mass. 1997) - EXPERT OPINION

Bio-Rad Laboratories Inc. v. Pharmacia Inc., 130 F.R.D. 116, 14 U.S.P.Q.2d 1924 (Cal. 1990) - WORK PRODUCT

Biosyntec Inc. v. Baxter Health Care Corp., 746 F. Supp. 5, 17 U.S.P.Q.2d 1221 (Or. 1990) - RELEASE

Bio-Technology General Corp. v. Genentech Inc., 886 F. Supp. 377, 36 U.S.P.Q.2d 1169 (N.Y. 1995) - ITC, RES JUDICATA

Bio-Technology General Corp. v. Genentech Inc., 80 F.3d 1553, 38 U.S.P.Q.2d 1321 (Fed. Cir. 1996) - EXCLUDE, IMPORTATION, ITC, PATENT, PPAA, TRADE REFORM ACT

Ex parte Birnbaum, 161 U.S.P.Q. 635 (PO Bd. App. 1968) - MULTIPLICITY, PROLIX

In re Bisley, 197 F.2d 355, 94 U.S.P.Q. 80 (C.C.P.A. 1952) - CHANGE, CONCEPTION, INVENTION, OBVIOUSNESS, PROBLEM, SIMPLE, SIMPLICITY

Biuro Projektow Zaklodow Przerobki Mechanicznej Wegla "Separator" v. UOP, Inc., 203 U.S.P.Q. 175 (Ill. 1979) - COMBINATION, CONTRIBUTORY INFRINGEMENT, REPLACEMENT, STAPLE

Black & Decker (US) Inc. v. Catalina Lighting Inc., 42 U.S.P.Q.2d 1254, n.3 1255 (Va. 1997) - INDUCEMENT

Black & Decker Inc. v. Greenfield Industries Inc., 22 U.S.P.Q.2d 1637 (Md. 1991) - AMENDING ANSWER

In re Blaese, 19 U.S.P.Q.2d 1232 (Commr. Patents & Trademarks 1991) - 37 C.F.R. §1.291, REISSUE

Blake v. The Bassick Company, 245 F. Supp. 635, 146 U.S.P.Q. 160 (Ill. 1965) - 35 U.S.C. §185

Blandford v. Masco Industries Inc., 799 F. Supp. 666, 25 U.S.P.Q.2d 1074 (Tex. 1992) - SUMMARY JUDGMENT

In re Blaser, Germscheid, and Worms, 556 F.2d 534, 194 U.S.P.Q. 122 (C.C.P.A. 1977) - DESCRIPTION

Bliss & Laughlin Industries, Inc. v. Bil-Jax, Inc., 356 F. Supp. 577, 176 U.S.P.Q. 119 (Ohio 1972) - COMPONENT

In re Blondel, Fouche, and Gueremy, 499 F.2d 1311, 182 U.S.P.Q. 294 (C.C.P.A. 1974) - INDIRECT EVIDENCE, PHARMACEUTICAL

Blonder-Tongue v. University Foundation, 402 U.S. 313, 169 U.S.P.Q. 513 (1971) - BLONDER-TONGUE DOCTRINE, COLLATERAL ESTOPPEL, ESTOPPEL

Blumcraft of Pittsburgh v. Kawneer Company, Inc., 174 U.S.P.Q. 14 (Ga. 1972) - BLONDER-TONGUE DOCTRINE

Blumcraft of Pittsburgh v. Ladd, 238 F. Supp. 648, 144 U.S.P.Q. 562 (D.C. 1965) - SEGREGABLE PART

Blumenthal v. Barber-Colman Holdings Corp., 62 F.3d 1433, 38 U.S.P.Q.2d 1031 (Fed. Cir. 1995 - unpublished) - COPY, MODE OF OPERATION, PRINCIPLE

BOC Health Care Inc. v. Nellcor Inc., 28 U.S.P.Q.2d 1293 (Del. 1993) - DECLARATORY JUDGMENT, SCARE TACTICS

In re Boe, 26 U.S.P.Q.2d 1809 (PTO Enr-Disc 1993) - EXAMINER

The Boeing Company v. Commissioner of Patents and Trademarks, 853 F.2d 878, 7 U.S.P.Q.2d 1487 (Fed. Cir. 1988) - REEXAMINATION REQUESTOR'S STANDING ON APPEAL

In re Boesch and Slaney, 617 F.2d 272, 205 U.S.P.Q. 215 (C.C.P.A. 1980) - OPTIMIZE

In re Bogese, 22 U.S.P.Q.2d 1821 (Comm'r Patents and Trademarks 1991) - FAFR

In re Boileau, 163 F.2d 562, 75 U.S.P.Q. 88 (C.C.P.A. 1947) - WHEREBY CLAUSE

In re Boileau, 168 F.2d 753, 78 U.S.P.Q. 146 (C.C.P.A. 1948) - ALLOWED CLAIM

In re Boling and Tigges, 292 F.2d 306, 130 U.S.P.Q. 161 (C.C.P.A. 1961) -REFERENCE

Bolt Associates, Inc. v. Rix Industries, 178 U.S.P.Q. 171 (Cal. 1973) - ENLARGEMENT, ERROR, FALSE STATEMENT

In re Bond, 910 F.2d 831, 15 U.S.P.Q.2d 1566 (Fed. Cir. 1990) - ANTICIPATION, MEANS PLUS FUNCTION

Bonito Boats, Inc. v. Thunder Craft Boats, Inc., 489 U.S. 141, 9 U.S.P.Q.2d 1847 (1989) - SUPREMACY CLAUSE

Ex parte Bonnefoy, 156 U.S.P.Q. 423 (PO Bd. App. 1967) - 37 C.F.R. §1.75(d)

In re Boon, 439 F.2d 724, 169 U.S.P.Q. 231 (C.C.P.A. 1971) - CHALLENGE, NEW RATIONALE, NEW REFERENCE, REOPEN PROSECUTION, STANDARD WORK

The Boots Co. plc v. Analgesic Associates, 91 Civ. 2739, 26 U.S.P.Q.2d 1144 (N.Y. 1993) - CONVERSION, JOINT INVENTION

In re Borah, 345 F.2d 1009, 148 U.S.P.Q. 213 (CCPA 1966) - TWO-WAY TEST

In re Borden, 90 F.3d 1570, 39 U.S.P.Q.2d 1524 (Fed. Cir. 1996) - DESIGN

Borden, Inc. v. Occidental Petroleum Corporation, 381 F. Supp. 1178, 182 U.S.P.Q. 472 (Tex. 1974) - CERTIFICATE OF CORRECTION, CONVERSION, ECONOMIC, NUMBER, RATIO

Borg-Warner Corp. v. Paragon Gear Works, Inc., 355 F.2d 400, 148 U.S.P.Q. 1 (1st Cir. 1965), *cert. dismissed*, 384 U.S. 935, 149 U.S.P.Q. 905 (1966) - SUBSTANTIALLY

In re Borkowski and Van Venrooy, 422 F.2d 904, 164 U.S.P.Q. 642 (C.C.P.A. 1970) - BREADTH, ENABLEMENT, EXAMPLE, FOUR CORNERS RULE, SUFFICIENCY OF DISCLOSURE, WORKING EXAMPLE

In re Bose Corp., 772 F.2d 866, 227 U.S.P.Q. 1 (Fed. Cir. 1985) - EXPANDED PANEL

Bose Corp. v. Consumers Union of the United States, Inc., 806 F.2d 304 (1st Cir. 1986) - COSTS

In re Bosy, 360 F.2d 972, 149 U.S.P.Q. 789 (C.C.P.A. 1966) - BEST MODE

In re Bowen, 492 F.2d 859, 181 U.S.P.Q. 48 (C.C.P.A. 1974) - CHEMICAL, DESCRIPTION, PREDICTABILITY, REASON, STATEMENT IN THE SPECIFICATION

In re Bowers and Orr, 359 F.2d 886, 149 U.S.P.Q. 570 (C.C.P.A. 1966) - DISCLAIMER

Bowmar Instrument Corp. v. Texas Instruments Incorporated, 196 U.S.P.Q. 199 (Ind. 1977) - ATTORNEY-CLIENT PRIVILEGE, DOCUMENTS, WORK-PRODUCT PRIVILEGE

Boyd v. Schieldkraut Giftsware Corp., 936 F.2d 76, 19 U.S.P.Q.2d 1223 (2d Cir. 1991) - MISMARKING

Boyd v. Tamutus, 1 U.S.P.Q.2d 2080 (B.P.A.I. 1986) - DERIVATION

Boyett v. St. Martin's Press Inc., 884 F. Supp. 479, 34 U.S.P.Q.2d 1828 (Fla. 1995) - REISSUE

BP Chemicals Ltd. v. Union Carbide Corp., 4 F.3d 975, 28 U.S.P.Q.2d 1124 (Fed. Cir. 1993) - CONTROVERSY, DECLARATORY JUDGMENT

In re Braat, 937 F.2d 589, 19 U.S.P.Q.2d 1289 (Fed. Cir. 1991) - DOUBLE PATENTING, TWO-WAY TEST

Bradley v. Chiron, 136 F.3d 1317, 45 U.S.P.Q.2d 1819 (Fed. Cir. 1998) - CONTRACT, DISMISSAL

In re Brana, 51 F.3d 1560, 34 U.S.P.Q.2d 1436 (Fed. Cir. 1995) - CANCER, CELL LINE, DOUBT, IN VIVO, PHARMACEUTICAL, STANDARD EXPERIMENTAL ANIMAL, STANDARD OF REVIEW, TESTING, TUMOR MODELS, UNBELIEVABLE, UTILITY

Brandon v. Murphy, 231 U.S.P.Q. 490 (Comm'r of Patents and Trademarks 1986) - INTERFERENCE IN FACT, MOTION TO ADD COUNT

In re Brandstadter, Kienzle, and Sykes, 484 F.2d 1395, 179 U.S.P.Q. 286 (C.C.P.A. 1973) - PROGRAM

Braun Inc. v. Dynamics Corp. of America, 19 U.S.P.Q.2d 1696 (Conn. 1991) - DAMAGES

Braun Inc. v. Dynamics Corp. of America, 975 F.2d 815, 24 U.S.P.Q.2d 1121 (Fed. Cir. 1992) - DAMAGES, DESIGN PATENT INFRINGEMENT, JUDGMENT AFTER TRIAL, SUBSTANTIAL EVIDENCE

In re Brebner, 455 F.2d 1402, 173 U.S.P.Q. 169 (C.C.P.A. 1972) - ENABLEMENT, STARTING MATERIAL

Breen v. Miller and Stine, 347 F.2d 623, 146 U.S.P.Q. 127 (C.C.P.A. 1965) -EXPERIMENT

Brenner v. Ladd, 247 F. Supp. 51, 147 U.S.P.Q. 87 (D.C. 1965) - OPTICAL ISOMER

Brenner v. Manson, 383 U.S. 519, 148 U.S.P.Q. 689 (1966) - UTILITY

Brenner v. The State of Israel, Ministry of Defence, 400 F.2d 789, 158 U.S.P.Q. 584 (CA D.C. 1968) - PRIORITY, 35 U.S.C. §119

In re Breslow, 616 F.2d 516, 205 U.S.P.Q. 221 (C.C.P.A. 1980) - CONTRACT, EXCLUDE, PATENT, STABILITY, STATUTORY SUBJECT MATTER, TRANSITORY,35 U.S.C. §114

Ex parte Breuer, 1 U.S.P.Q.2d 1906 (B.P.A.I. 1986) - CLAIM CONSTRUCTION, INOPERATIVE EMBODIMENTS, REASONABLE, SUBSTITUTED

Breuer Electric Mfg. Co. v. Tennant Co., 44 U.S.P.Q.2d 1259 (Ill. 1997) - INDEFINITENESS, PIONEER PATENT

Breuer and Treuner v. DeMarinis, 558 F.2d 22, 194 U.S.P.Q. 308 (C.C.P.A. 1977) - CORROBORATION, FOREIGN, RULE OF REASON, 35 U.S.C. §104

Ex parte Brian, Radley, Curtis, and Elson, 118 U.S.P.Q. 242 (PO Bd. App. 1958) - COINED NAME, EMPIRICAL FORMULA, INFRA-RED, PRODUCT BY PROPERTIES

Ex parte Bridgeford, Turbak, and Burke, 172 U.S.P.Q. 308 (PO Dir. 1971) - ELECTION OF SPECIES, GENERIC CLAIM, WITHDRAWAL

Bristol-Meyers Co. v. Erbamont Inc., 723 F. Supp. 1038, 13 U.S.P.Q.2d 1517 (Del. 1989) - IMPORTATION

Bristol Myers Squibb Co. v. Erbamont Inc., 734 F. Supp. 661, 16 U.S.P.Q.2d 1887 (Del. 1990) - DECLARATORY JUDGMENT

Bristol-Meyers Squibb Co. v. Rhone-Poulenc Rorer Inc., 40 U.S.P.Q.2d 1863 (N.Y. 1996) - PROTECTIVE ORDER, RULE 26(c)

Bristol-Meyers Squibb Co. v. Rhône-Poulenc Rorer Inc., 44 U.S.P.Q.2d 1463 (N.Y. 1997) - ATTORNEY-CLIENT PRIVILEGE, PRIVILEGE LOG, WORK PRODUCT DOCTRINE

Bristol-Myers Squibb Co. v. Rhône-Poulenc Rorer Inc., 45 U.S.P.Q.2d 1775 (N.Y. 1998) - ATTORNEY-CLIENT PRIVILEGE

Bristol-Myers Squibb Co. v. Royce Laboratories Inc., 36 U.S.P.Q.2d 1637 (Fla. 1995), *reversed* 69 F.3d 1397, 36 U.S.P.Q.2d 1641 (Fed. Cir. 1995) - CASE OR CONTROVERSY, DELTA PERIOD, SAFE HARBOR, SUBSTANTIAL INVESTMENT

Bristol-Myers Squibb Co. v. Royce Laboratories Inc., 69 F.3d 1130, 36 U.S.P.Q.2d 1641 (Fed. Cir. 1995) - ANDA, FDA, SAFE HARBOR, URAA, 35 U.S.C. §271(e)(2)

Ex parte Brockmann and Bohne, 127 U.S.P.Q. 57 (PO Bd. App. 1959) - COINED NAME, PRODUCT BY PROPERTIES

Brooks v. Street, 16 U.S.P.Q.2d 1374 (B.P.A.I. 1990) - 37 C.F.R. §1.607(a), INTERFERENCE

Brooktree Corp. v. Advanced Micro Devices, Inc., 705 F. Supp. 491, 10 U.S.P.Q.2d 1374, 1376 (Cal. 1988) - MASKWORK ACT

Brooktree Corp. v. Advanced Micro Devices Inc., 977 F.2d 1555, 24 U.S.P.Q.2d 1401 (Fed. Cir. 1992) - MASKWORK, REVERSE ENGINEERING

Ex parte Brouard, Leroy, and Stiot, 201 U.S.P.Q. 538 (PTO Bd. App. 1976) - CLASSIFICATION, FIELD OF SEARCH, MARKUSH, REPUGNANT

In re Brouwer, 77 F.3d 422, 37 U.S.P.Q.2d 1663, 1666 (Fed. Cir. 1996) - ANALOGY PROCESS, METHOD OF MAKING, METHOD OF USING, PROCESS

Brown v. Braddick, 595 F.2d 961, 203 U.S.P.Q. 95 (5th Cir. 1979) - 35 U.S.C. §24

Brown v. Bravet, 25 U.S.P.Q.2d 1147 (B.P.A.I. 1992) - INTERLOCUTORY ORDER

Brown v. Shimano American Corp., 18 U.S.P.Q.2d 1496 (Cal. 1991) - REEXAMINATION, STAY MOTION

Brown v. Trion Industries, Inc., 575 F. Supp. 511, 223 U.S.P.Q. 1106 (N.Y. 1983) - LATE CLAIMING

Brown v. University of California, 866 F. Supp. 439, 31 U.S.P.Q.2d 1463 (Cal. 1994) - JOINT INVENTORSHIP, SIMULTANEOUS CONCEPTION AND REDUCTION TO PRACTICE

Brown Bag Software v. Symantec Corp., 960 F.2d 1465, 22 U.S.P.Q.2d 1429 (9th Cir. 1992) - PROTECTIVE ORDER

Bruning v. Hirose, 48 U.S.P.Q.2d 1934 (Fed. Cir. 1998) - STANDARD, SUBSTANTIALLY

Brunswick Corp. v. Pueblo Bowl-O-Mat, Inc., 429 U.S. 477 (1977) - DAMAGES

Brunswick Corporation v. Suzuki Motor Company, Ltd., 575 F. Supp. 1412, 220 U.S.P.Q. 822 (Wis. 1983) - ALIEN, 28 U.S.C. §1391(d)

Brunswick Corp. v. United States, 22 Cl. Ct. 278, 19 U.S.P.Q.2d 1702 (U.S. Cl. Ct. 1991) - EXCLUSIVE LICENSEE

Brunswick Corp. v. U.S., 46 U.S.P.Q.2d 1446 (Fed. Cir. 1998 - *unpublished*) - DEDICATION TO THE PUBLIC

In re Buchner, 929 F.2d 660, 18 U.S.P.Q.2d 1331 (Fed. Cir. 1991) - DECLARATION, ENABLEMENT, KNOWN

In re Budnick, 537 F.2d 535, 190 U.S.P.Q. 422 (C.C.P.A. 1976) - STATE OF THE ART

In re Buehler, 515 F.2d 1134, 185 U.S.P.Q. 781 (C.C.P.A. 1975) - AVOID, TEACH AWAY FROM

Buell v. Beckestrom, 22 U.S.P.Q.2d 1128 (BPAI 1992) - REISSUE, 35 U.S.C. §102(g)

Buildex Inc. v Kason Indus., Inc., 849 F.2d 1461 7 U.S.P.Q.2d 1325 (Fed. Cir. 1988) - CLEAR AND CONVINCING

-C-

California Irrigation Services, Inc. v. Bartron Corp., 9 U.S.P.Q.2d 1859 (Cal. 1988) - ORDINARY SKILL

California Medical Products Inc. v. Emergency Medical Products Inc., 796 F. Supp. 640, 24 U.S.P.Q.2d 1205 (R.I. 1992) - CONSENT JUDGMENT

In re Calmar, Inc, 854 F.2d 461, 7 U.S.P.Q.2d 1713 (Fed. Cir. 1988) - MANDAMUS

Cameco Industries Inc. v. Louisiana Cane Manufacturing Inc., 34 U.S.P.Q.2d 1309 (La. 1995) - EQUIVALENTS, HYPOTHETICAL CLAIM

In re Campbell and McCune, 170 U.S.P.Q. 354 (Comm'r 1971) - 35 U.S.C. §122

Campbell and Babcock v. Wettstein, Anner, Wieland, and Heusler, 476 F.2d 642, 177 U.S.P.Q. 376 (C.C.P.A. 1973) - ANIMAL TESTS, CONTROL, STANDARD EXPERIMENTAL ANIMAL

Canaan Products, Inc. v. Edward Don & Company, 273 F. Supp. 492, 154 U.S.P.Q. 393 (Ill. 1966) - DRY

Canon Computer Systems Inc. v. Nu-Kote International Inc., 134 F.3d 1085, 45 U.S.P.Q.2d 1355 (Fed. Cir. 1998) - INVENTORSHIP, JOINT INVENTORS

In re Carabateas, 345 F.2d 1013, 145 U.S.P.Q. 549 (C.C.P.A. 1965) - ESTER

Carboline Company v. Mobil Oil Corporation, 301 F. Supp. 141, 163 U.S.P.Q. 273 (Ill. 1969) - USED

The Carborundum Co. v. Molten Metal Equipment Innovations Inc., 72 F.3d 872, 37 U.S.P.Q.2d 1169 (Fed. Cir. 1995) - IMPLIED LICENSE

Cardinal Chemical Co. v. Morton International Inc., 113 S.Ct. 1967, 26 U.S.P.Q.2d 1721 (S.Ct. 1993) - AFFIRMATIVE DEFENSE, COUNTERCLAIM, DECLARATORY JUDGMENT, INFRINGEMENT, UNNECESSARY, VALIDITY

Cardinal of Adrian, Inc. v. Peerless Wood Prod. Inc., 515 F.2d 534, 185 U.S.P.Q. 712 (6th Cir. 1975) - LATE CLAIMING

Carela v. Starlight Archery, 804 F.2d 135, 231 U.S.P.Q. 644 (Fed. Cir. 1986) - COMBINATION, COMBINING REFERENCES, OBVIOUSNESS, PRINTED PUBLICATION, SUGGESTION, TEACHING

Carey Crutcher Inc. v. Cameron Equipment Co., 37 U.S.P.Q.2d 1479 (Tex. 1995) - DISMISSAL

In re Carleton, 599 F.2d 1021, 202 U.S.P.Q. 165 (C.C.P.A. 1979) - CHEMICAL, EMPIRICAL, EVIDENCE, ISSUE, KNOCKDOWN, OBVIOUSNESS, PREDICTABILITY, PRIMA FACIE

Carl Schenk, A.G. v. Nortron Corporation, 713 F.2d 782, 218 U.S.P.Q. 698 (Fed. Cir. 1983) - INVENTION, MAKING INTEGRAL, MODIFICATION, MONOPOLY, STANDARD

In re Carlson, 983 F.2d 1032, 25 U.S.P.Q.2d 1207 (Fed. Cir. 1992) -DESIGN, GESCHMACKSMUSTER, PATENTED

Carl Zeiss Stiftung v. Renishaw plc, 945 F.2d 1173, 20 U.S.P.Q.2d 1094 (Fed. Cir. 1991) - DEFINITENESS, INCOMPLETE, SUBCOMBINATION, UTILITY

Carman Industries, Inc. v. Wahl, 724 F.2d 932, 220 U.S.P.Q. 481 (Fed. Cir. 1983) - DOUBLE PATENTING, PATENTABILITY, VALIDITY

The Carnegie Steel Company, Ltd. v. The Cambria Iron Company, 185 U.S. 403 (1866) - DEFINITENESS, KNOWLEDGE, MOSITA, ORDINARY SKILL, PATENT, SPECIFICATION

Carroll Touch Inc. v. Electro Mechanical Systems Inc., 3 F.3d 404, 27 U.S.P.Q.2d 1836

Chapman v. Wintroath, 252 U.S. 126 (1920) - CANCELLATION, COPYING CLAIMS

Chapman Performance Products, Inc. v. Producers Sales, Inc., 306 NE2d 615, 181 U.S.P.Q. 101 (Ill. 1973) - STATE COURT

Charles Pfizer Co., Inc. v. Davis-Edwards Pharmacal Corp., 267 F. Supp. 42, 152 U.S.P.Q. 803 (N.Y. 1967) - CONTEMPT

Ex parte Charles W. Mortimer, 61 F.2d 860, 15 U.S.P.Q. 297 (C.C.P.A. 1932) - SHAPE

Charvat v. Commissioner of Patents, 503 F.2d 138, 182 U.S.P.Q. 577 (D.C. Cir. 1974) - BREADTH

Chas. Pfizer & Co., Inc. v. Barry-Martin Pharmaceuticals, Inc., 241 F. Supp. 191, 145 U.S.P.Q. 29 (Fla. 1965) - ACCIDENTAL, NATURAL PRODUCT

In re Chatfield, 545 F.2d 152, 191 U.S.P.Q. 730 (C.C.P.A. 1976), *cert. denied,* 434 U.S. 875, 195 U.S.P.Q. 465 (1977) - ALGORITHM, COMPUTER-ARTS INVENTION

Chauffeurs, Teamsters and Helpers Local No. 391 v. Terry, 494 U.S. 558 (1990) - JURY

Checkpoint Systems Inc. v. U.S. International Trade Commission, 54 F.3d 756, 35 U.S.P.Q.2d 1042 (Fed. Cir. 1995) - STANDARD OF REVIEW

Chemagro Corporation v. Universal Chemical Company, 244 F. Supp. 486, 146 U.S.P.Q. 466 (Tex. 1965) - LABEL LICENSE

Chemcast Corp. v. Arco Industries Corp., 5 U.S.P.Q.2d 1225 (Mich. 1987) - NEW MATTER

Chemcast Corp. v. Arco Industries Corp., 913 F.2d 923, 16 U.S.P.Q.2d 1033 (Fed. Cir. 1990) - BEST MODE, TRADE NAME

Chemical Cleaning Corp. v. Dow Chemical Co., 379 F.2d 294, 155 U.S.P.Q. 49 (5th Cir. 1967), *cert. denied,* 389 U.S. 1040, 156 U.S.P.Q. 719 (1968) - CONVERSION (*IN SITU* OR *IN VIVO*)

Chemical Construction Corp. v. Jones & Laughlin Steel Corp., 311 F.2d 367, 136 U.S.P.Q. 150 (3d Cir. 1962) - ALLOWED CLAIM, AGGREGATION, CANCELED CLAIMS, CLAIM CONSTRUCTION

Chester v. Miller, 906 F.2d 1574, 15 U.S.P.Q.2d 1333 (Fed. Cir. 1990) - APPLICANT'S OWN WORK, INTERFERENCE, 37 C.F.R. §1.633, 35 U.S.C. §132

Chevron, U.S.A., Inc. v. Natural Resources Defense Council, Inc., 467 U.S. 837 (1984) - STATUTORY CONSTRUCTION

Chew v. California, 11 U.S.P.Q.2d 1159 (Cal. 1988) - STATES' IMMUNITY

Chew v. California, 893 F.2d 331, 13 U.S.P.Q.2d 1393 (Fed. Cir. 1990) - INFRINGEMENT, STATE

Ex parte Chicago Rawhide Manufacturing Co., 226 U.S.P.Q. 438 (PTO Bd. App. 1984) - MOTIVATION, OBVIOUSNESS, REEXAMINATION

Child Craft Industries Inc. v. Simmons Juvenile Products Co., 990 F. Supp. 638, 45 U.S.P.Q.2d 1933 (Ind. 1998) - DESIGN

Chiong v. Roland, 17 U.S.P.Q.2d 1541 (B.P.A.I. 1990) - COUNT

Chiron Corp. v. Abbott Laboratories, 156 F.R.D. 219, 31 U.S.P.Q.2d 1848 (Cal. 1994) - INEQUITABLE CONDUCT

Chiron Corp. v. Abbott Laboratories, 34 U.S.P.Q.2d 1413 (Pa. 1994) - DISCOVERY

Chisholm-Ryder Company, Inc. v. Lewis Manufacturing Company, Inc., 398 F. Supp. 1287, 187 U.S.P.Q. 93 (Pa. 1975) - 35 U.S.C. §253, 35 U.S.C. §288

Chisholm-Ryder Company, Inc. v. Mecca Bros., Inc., 217 U.S.P.Q. 1322 (N.Y. 1983) - IN VACUO

Chisum v. Brewco Sales and Manufacturing Inc., 726 F. Supp. 1499, 13 U.S.P.Q.2d 1657 (Ky. 1989) - ROYALTY RATE

Chiuminatta Concrete Concepts Inc. v. Cardinal Industries Inc., 145 F.3d 1303, 46 U.S.P.Q.2d 1752 (Fed. Cir. 1998) - DOCTRINE OF EQUIVALENTS, EQUIVALENCE, INTERCHANGEABLE

Chiuminatta Concrete Concepts Inc. v. Cardinal Industries Inc., 48 U.S.P.Q.2d 1421 (Cal. 1998) - SUCCESSOR ENTITY

In re Christensen, 478 F.2d 1392, 178 U.S.P.Q. 35 (C.C.P.A. 1973) -COMPUTER-ARTS INVENTION, COMPUTER PROGRAM, MATHEMATICAL EQUATION

Christianson v. Colt Industries Operating Corp., 798 F.2d 1051, 230 U.S.P.Q. 840 (7th Cir. 1986) - ARISE UNDER PATENT LAWS, CASE, CREATION TEST, PATENT LAWS

Christianson v. Colt Industries Operating Corp., 822 F.2d 1544, 3 U.S.P.Q.2d 1241 (Fed. Cir. 1987) - JURISDICTION OF THE CAFC

Christianson v. Colt Indus. Operating Corp, 486 U.S. 800, 7 U.S.P.Q.2d 1109 (1988) -ARISE UNDER PATENT LAWS

Chromalloy American Corp. v. Alloy Surfaces Co., Inc., 353 F. Supp. 429, 176 U.S.P.Q. 508 (Del. 1973) - ATTORNEY'S FEES, BILLING RATE

In re Chu, 66 F.3d 292, 36 U.S.P.Q.2d 1089 (Fed. Cir. 1995) - CONTINUING APPLICATION, DESIGN CHOICE, OBVIOUSNESS, 35 U.S.C. §120

In re Chupp, 816 F.2d 643, 2 U.S.P.Q.2d 1437 (Fed. Cir. 1987) - COMPARATIVE TEST DATA, PROPERTIES, UNDUE BREADTH

Ex parte Chwang, 231 U.S.P.Q. 751 (B.P.A.I. 1986) - CANCER, CHALLENGE, INTERMEDIATE, INTERMEDIATE AS REFERENCE, IN VITRO, MOTIVATION, OBVIOUSNESS, PROPERTIES, STRUCTURAL SIMILARITY, UTILITY

Ciba-Geigy Corp. v. Alza Corp., 795 F. Supp. 711, 23 U.S.P.Q.2d 1932 (N.J. 1992) - DISQUALIFICATION

Ciba-Geigy Corp. v. Alza Corp., 864 F. Supp. 429, 33 U.S.P.Q.2d 1018 (N.J. 1994) - ANTICIPATION, EXTRINSIC EVIDENCE

Ciba-Geigy Corp. v. Crompton & Knowles Corp., 22 U.S.P.Q.2d 1761 (Pa. 1991) - AFFIDAVIT, DOCTRINE OF EQUIVALENTS, EXPERT OPINION, EXPERT WITNESS, SIGNIFICANCE, SUMMARY JUDGMENT

Ex parte Cillario, 14 U.S.P.Q.2d 1079 (B.P.A.I. 1989) - BPAI

In re Citron, 251 F.2d 619, 116 U.S.P.Q. 409 (C.C.P.A. 1958) - DOUBT

In re Citron, 326 F.2d 418, 140 U.S.P.Q. 220 (C.C.P.A. 1964) - CCPA, DECISION, REEXAMINATION, STANDARD OF REVIEW

City of Elizabeth v. American Nicholson Pavement Co., 97 U.S. 126 (1877) - EXPERIMENTAL USE

In re Civitello, 339 F.2d 243, 144 U.S.P.Q. 10 (C.C.P.A. 1964) - COMBINATION, NEW COMBINATION

Clancy Systems International Inc. v. Symbol Technologies Inc., 42 U.S.P.Q.2d 1290 (Col. 1997) - MARKING

Ex parte Clapp, 227 U.S.P.Q. 972 (B.P.A.I. 1985) - BLUEPRINT, COMBINATION INVENTION, COMBINING REFERENCES, ELEMENT, KNOWN, OBVIOUS-

In re Coey and Petersen, 190 F.2d 347, 90 U.S.P.Q. 216 (C.C.P.A. 1951) - ANTICIPA-
TION, PAPER PATENT

In re Cofer, 354 F.2d 664, 148 U.S.P.Q. 268 (C.C.P.A. 1966) - APPEAL, EVIDENCE,
FACT, FORM, JUDICIAL NOTICE, OBVIOUSNESS, STANDARD TEXT

Cohen v. Beneficial Industrial Loan Corp., 337 U.S. 541 (1949) - INTERLOCUTORY
ORDER

In re Coker, Phillips, and Miller, 463 F.2d 1344, 175 U.S.P.Q. 26, 28 (C.C.P.A. 1972) -
CONJECTURE

Colbert v. Lofdahl, 21 U.S.P.Q.2d 1068 (B.P.A.I. 1991) - CONCEPTION

Cole v. Kimberly-Clark Corp., 41 U.S.P.Q.2d 1001 (Fed. Cir. 1996) - MEANS PLUS
FUNCTION, STANDARD OF REVIEW

In re Coleman, 472 F.2d 1062, 176 U.S.P.Q. 522 (C.C.P.A. 1973) - TRADEMARK

Coleman v. Dines, 754 F.2d 353, 224 U.S.P.Q. 857 (Fed. Cir. 1985) -CONCEPTION,
CORROBORATION, RULE OF REASON

In re Colianni, 561 F.2d 220, 195 U.S.P.Q. 150 (C.C.P.A. 1977) - DOSAGE,
SUFFICIENT

College Savings Bank v. Florida Prepaid Postsecondary Education Expense Board, 42
U.S.P.Q.2d 1487 (N.J. 1996) - COUNTERCLAIM, ELEVENTH AMENDMENT,
JUDICIAL ESTOPPEL, LAW OF THE CASE, PATENT, PROPERTY, STATES'
IMMUNITY

College Savings Bank v. Florida Prepaid Postsecondary Education Expense Board, 148
F.3d 1343, 47 U.S.P.Q.2d 1161 (Fed. Cir. 1998) - PATENT REMEDY ACT, 35
U.S.C. §296(a)

Collins & Aikman Corp. v. Stratton Industries Inc., 728 F. Supp. 1570, 14 U.S.P.Q.2d
1001 (Ga. 1989) - NOERR-PENNINGTON DOCTRINE

Colortronic Reinhard & Co., K.G. v. Plastic Controls, Inc., 668 F.2d 1, 213 U.S.P.Q. 801
(1st Cir. 1981) - COMMERCIAL SUCCESS

Colt Industries Operating Corp. v. Index Werke, K.G., 217 U.S.P.Q. 1176 (D.C. 1982) -
PRESUMPTION OF VALIDITY

Columbia Broadcasting System, Inc. v. Zenith Radio Corporation, 391 F. Supp. 780, 185
U.S.P.Q. 662 (Ill. 1975) - BEST MODE, PAPER PATENT, VALIDITY

Columbia Cascade Co. v. Interplay Design Ltd., 17 U.S.P.Q.2d 1882 (Or. 1990) - AD-
VICE OF COUNSEL

Columbia University v. Boehringer Mannheim GmbH, 35 U.S.P.Q.2d 1364 (Mass. 1995) -
GESTALT FACTORS, PERSONAL JURISDICTION, TRANSACTING
BUSINESS

Comair Rotron Inc. v. Matsushita Electric Corp. of America, 33 U.S.P.Q.2d 1785 (Fed.
Cir. 1994 - unpublished) - COMMERCIAL SUCCESS, NEXUS

Comair Rotron Inc. v. Nippon Densan Corp., 49 F.3d 1535, 33 U.S.P.Q.2d 1929 (Fed. Cir.
1995) - COLLATERAL ESTOPPEL

Comark Communications Inc. v. Harris Corp., 48 U.S.P.Q.2d 1001 (Fed. Cir. 1998) -
CLAIM CONSTRUCTION, DOCTRINE OF EQUIVALENTS, SPECIAL VER-
DICT INTERROGATORIES

Commercial Casualty Insurance Co. v. Consolidated Stone Co., 278 U.S. 177 (1929) -
VENUE

Core Laboratories, Inc. v. Hayward-Wolff Research Corp., 136 A.2d 553, 115 U.S.P.Q. 422 (Del. S. Ct. 1957) - IMPLIED LICENSE

In re Corkill, 771 F.2d 1496, 226 U.S.P.Q. 1005 (Fed. Cir. 1985) - CLEANING COMPOSITION, COMBINATION INVENTION, EVIDENCE COMMENSURATE WITH CLAIMED SCOPE, INOPERATIVENESS, OPINION, SYNERGISM, UNEXPECTED RESULTS

In re Cormany, Dial, and Pray, 476 F.2d 998, 177 U.S.P.Q. 450 (C.C.P.A. 1973) - COUNT

Corning Class Works v. Sumitomo Electric USA Inc., 671 F. Supp. 1369, 5 U.S.P.Q.2d 1545 (N.Y. 1987) - CHANGE IN FORM, DUTY TO DISCLOSE, EXAMPLE, FOREIGN PATENTS AND PROCEEDINGS, INCORPORATE BY REFERENCE, REVERSAL OF PARTS, TOTALITY OF CIRCUMSTANCES, WILLFUL

Corning Glass Works v. Sumitomo Electric U.S.A. Inc., 868 F.2d 1251, 9 U.S.P.Q.2d 1962 (Fed. Cir. 1989) - ALL-ELEMENTS RULE, CLAIM INTERPRETATION, DISCLOSURE, EQUIVALENCY, FUNCTION, FUNCTION/WAY/RESULT, GENERIC CLAIM, GENERIC DISCLOSURE, REDRAFTING CLAIMS

Corometrics Medical Systems, Inc. v. Berkeley Bio-Engineering, Inc., 193 U.S.P.Q. 467 (Cal. 1977) - NUMBER OF REFERENCES, REFERENCE

Corona Cord Tire Co. v. Dovan Chemical Corp., 276 U.S. 358, 1928 C.D. 253 (1928) - ABANDONMENT, CATALYST

In re Corth, 478 F.2d 1248, 178 U.S.P.Q. 39 (C.C.P.A. 1973) - STRUCTURAL OBVIOUSNESS

In re Costello and McClean, 717 F.2d 1346, 219 U.S.P.Q. 389 (Fed. Cir. 1983) - ABANDONED APPLICATION, CONSTRUCTIVE REDUCTION TO PRACTICE

In re Cother, 437 F.2d 1399, 168 U.S.P.Q. 773 (C.C.P.A. 1971) - CHALLENGE

Cover v. Hydramatic Packing Co. Inc., 34 U.S.P.Q.2d 1128 (Pa. 1994) - ECONOMICS, LACHES, POVERTY

Cover v. Hydramatic Packing Co., 36 U.S.P.Q.2d 1199 (Pa. 1995) - NOTICE

Cover v. Hydramatic Packing Co., 83 F.3d 1390, 38 U.S.P.Q.2d 1783 (Fed. Cir. 1996) - PREEMPTION

Cox v. American Cast Iron Pipe Co., 847 F.2d 725 (11th Cir. 1988) -DISQUALIFICATION

CPC International Inc. v. Archer Daniels Midland Co., 831 F. Supp. 1091, 30 U.S.P.Q.2d 1427 (Del 1993) - BEST MODE

In re Craig and Street, 411 F.2d 1333, 162 U.S.P.Q. 157 (C.C.P.A. 1969) - RES JUDICATA

Crane Co. v. Aeroquip Corporation, 364 F. Supp. 547, 179 U.S.P.Q. 596 (Ill. 1973) - MARKING ESTOPPEL, MISMARKING

Crane Co. v. The Goodyear Tire & Rubber Company, 204 U.S.P.Q. 502 (Ohio 1979) - ATTORNEY-CLIENT PRIVILEGE

C.R. Bard Inc. v. Cordis Corp., 17 U.S.P.Q.2d 1391 (Mass. 1990) - SILENCE

C.R. Bard Inc. v. M3 Systems Inc., 48 U.S.P.Q.2d 1225 (Fed. Cir. 1998) - ERROR, FRAUD, INTENT TO CLAIM, MEANS PLUS FUNCTION, ON SALE, REISSUE

Creative Industries Inc. v. Mobile Chemical Corp., 13 U.S.P.Q.2d 1534 (Ill. 1989) - EXAMINATION

Ex parte Crigler, 125 U.S.P.Q. 448 (PO Bd. App. 1959) - 37 C.F.R. §1.141, 37 C.F.R. §1.146

In re Cronyn, 890 F.2d 1158, 13 U.S.P.Q.2d 1070 (Fed. Cir. 1989) - THESIS

In re Cross, 62 F.2d 182, 16 U.S.P.Q. 10 (C.C.P.A. 1932) - FOREIGN PATENT, FOREIGN PATENTS AND PROCEEDINGS, REFERENCE

Cross v. Iizuka, 753 F.2d 1040, 224 U.S.P.Q. 739 (Fed. Cir. 1985) -ANIMAL TESTS, DOSAGE, IN VITRO, IN VIVO, STRUCTURAL SIMILARITY, UTILITY

In re Crounse, 363 F.2d 881, 150 U.S.P.Q. 554 (C.C.P.A. 1966) - COLOR, PREDICTABILITY, SHADE, UNEXPECTED

Crown Die & Tool Co. v. Nye Tool Mach. Works, 261 U.S. 24 (1923) - INFRINGEMENT

Crystal Semiconductor Corp. v. OPTi Inc., 44 U.S.P.Q.2d 1497 (Tex. 1997) - GENERAL JURISDICTION, PERSONAL JURISDICTION

CSS International Corp. v. Maul Technology Co., 16 U.S.P.Q.2d 1657 (Ind. 1989) - INTERFERENCE, OBVIOUSNESS, PRIOR WORK, 35 U.S.C. §102(g)/103

CTS Corporation v. Electro Materials Corp. of America, 469 F. Supp. 801, 202 U.S.P.Q. 22 (N.Y. 1979) - TEST RESULTS

Ex parte Cullis, 11 U.S.P.Q.2d 1876 (B.P.A.I. 1989) - CLAIMS SUGGESTED FOR INTERFERENCE

Cuno Engineering Corporation v. Automatic Devices Corporation, 314 U.S. 84, 51 U.S.P.Q. 272 (1941) - FLASH OF GENIUS

Cuno Inc. v. Pall Corp., 729 F. Supp. 234, 14 U.S.P.Q.2d 1815 (N.Y. 1989) - COLLATERAL ESTOPPEL, FOREIGN PATENTS AND PROCEEDINGS

Custom Accessories Inc. v. Jeffrey-Allan Industries, Inc., 807 F.2d 955, 1 U.S.P.Q.2d 1196 (Fed. Cir. 1986) - COMBINATION OF ELEMENTS, COMMERCIAL SUCCESS, COPYING, FAILURE OF OTHERS, HINDSIGHT, LONG-FELT NEED, OLD COMBINATION, RESULT, SECONDARY CONSIDERATIONS, SYNERGISM, WHOLE

Cybor Corp. v. FAS Technologies Inc., 138 F.3d 1448, 46 U.S.P.Q.2d 1169 (Fed. Cir. 1998) - CLAIM CONSTRUCTION, ESTOPPEL

Cyrix Corp. v. Intel Corp., 846 F. Supp. 522, 32 U.S.P.Q.2d 1890 (Tex. 1994) - CLAIM, EXHAUSTION, INVENTION

-*D*-

Ex parte D, 27 U.S.P.Q.2d 1067 (B.P.A.I. 1993) - NEW MATTER, ROUTINE EXPERIMENTATION, UNDUE EXPERIMENTATION

In re DaFano, 392 F.2d 280, 157 U.S.P.Q. 192 (C.C.P.A. 1968) - COMMENSURATE IN SCOPE, GENUS, SPECIES

Dainippon Screen Manufacturing Co. v. CFMT Inc., 142 F.3d 1266, 46 U.S.P.Q.2d 1616 (Fed. Cir. 1998) - DECLARATORY JUDGMENT, INDISPENSABLE PARTY, PATENT HOLDING SUBSIDIARY

Dale Electronics, Inc. v. R. C. L. Electronics, Inc., 178 U.S.P.Q. 525 (N.H. 1972) - CONSTRUCTION

Damaskus v. Homon and Neutlings, 141 U.S.P.Q. 923 (PO Bd. Pat. Int. 1964) - ASSISTANT, CORROBORATION

Dana Corp. v. Nok Inc., 9 U.S.P.Q.2d 2004 (Mich. 1988) - EXPERT WITNESS FEES

Dana Corp. v. NOK Inc., 882 F.2d 505, 11 U.S.P.Q.2d 1883 (Fed. Cir. 1989) - COLLATERAL ESTOPPEL

In re D'Ancicco, Collings, and Shine, 439 F.2d 1244, 169 U.S.P.Q. 303 (C.C.P.A. 1971) - ADVANTAGE

In re Daniels, 144 F.3d 1452, 46 U.S.P.Q.2d 1788 (Fed. Cir. 1998) - DESIGN, REDUCTION IN SCOPE, 35 U.S.C. §120

Darda Inc. USA v. Majorette Toys (U.S.) Inc., 627 F. Supp. 1121, 229 U.S.P.Q. 103 (Fla. 1986) - DELIBERATE INFRINGEMENT

In re Dardick, 496 F.2d 1234, 181 U.S.P.Q. 834 (C.C.P.A. 1974) - 37 C.F.R. §1.131

Darling v. Standard Alaska Production Co., 20 U.S.P.Q.2d 1688 (Alaska S. Ct. 1991) - PATENT, STATE, SUPREMACY CLAUSE

Dart Industries Inc. v. E.I. du Pont de Nemours and Company, 348 F. Supp. 1338, 175 U.S.P.Q. 540 (Ill. 1972) - DOUBT, EMBODIMENT, ON SALE, PAPER PATENT, PRIOR ART, UTILITY

Datascope Corp. v. SMEC, Inc., 776 F.2d 320, 227 U.S.P.Q. 838 (Fed. Cir. 1985) - DIFFERENCE, OBVIOUSNESS, PRESUMPTION OF VALIDITY, PRIOR ART, REFERENCES AS A WHOLE, SUBJECT MATTER AS A WHOLE, VALIDITY, WHOLE

Daubert v. Merrell Dow Pharmaceuticals Inc., 509 U.S. 579, 113 S.Ct. 2786, 27 U.S.P.Q.2d 1200 (S.Ct. 1993) - EXPERT TESTIMONY, RULE 702

Davies v. U.S., 31 Fed.Cl. 769, 35 U.S.P.Q.2d 1027 (U.S. Ct. Fed. Cl. 1994) - DOCTRINE OF EQUIVALENTS, MEANS

In re Davies and Hopkins, 475 F.2d 667, 177 U.S.P.Q. 381 (C.C.P.A. 1973) - COMPARATIVE TEST DATA

Ex parte Davis and Tuukkanen, 80 U.S.P.Q. 448 (PO Bd. App. 1949) - COMPRISING, CONSISTING, CONSISTING ESSENTIALLY OF

Davis v. Comm'r. Internal Revenue, 491 F.2d 709, 181 U.S.P.Q. 552 (6th Cir. 1974) - PATENT APPLICATION, CAPITAL GAINS, DEPRECIATION, TAXATION

Davis v. Loesch, 998 F.2d 963, 27 U.S.P.Q.2d 1440 (Fed. Cir. 1993) - ET AL., NOTICE OF APPEAL, PATENTABLY DISTINCT

Davis v. Uke, 27 U.S.P.Q.2d 1180 (PTO Comm'r 1993) - CONVERSION

Ex parte Davisson and Finlay, 133 U.S.P.Q. 400 (PO Bd. App. 1958) -INHERENT CHARACTERISTIC OR PROPERTY, NEW MATTER

Dawn Equipment Co. v. Kentucky Farms Inc., 140 F.3d 1009, 46 U.S.P.Q.2d 1109 (Fed. Cir. 1998) - SUBSTANTIAL

Dawson Chemical Company v. Rohm and Haas Company, 65 L.Ed. 696, 206 U.S.P.Q. 385 (S.Ct. 1980) - CONTRIBUTORY INFRINGEMENT, MISUSE, STAPLE ARTICLE OF COMMERCE, 35 U.S.C. §271(c), 35 U.S.C. §271(d)

In re Dean, 291 F.2d 947, 130 U.S.P.Q. 107 (C.C.P.A. 1961) - CLAIM, CLAIM CONSTRUCTION, DISCLOSURE, VACUUM

Ex parte Deaton and Kirkland, 146 U.S.P.Q. 549 (PO Bd. App. 1965) - DEVICE

In re DeBaun, 687 F.2d 459, 214 U.S.P.Q. 933 (C.C.P.A. 1982) - APPLICANT'S OWN WORK, DISCLOSURE WITHOUT CLAIMING, REDUCTION TO PRACTICE, REFERENCE

In re De Blauwe, 736 F.2d 699, 222 U.S.P.Q. 191 (Fed. Cir. 1984) - APPEAL, ARGU-
MENT, CHALLENGE, REBUTTAL EVIDENCE, STATEMENT, STATEMENT
IN THE SPECIFICATION, UNEXPECTED RESULTS

DeBurgh v. Kindel Furniture Company, 125 F. Supp. 468, 103 U.S.P.Q. 203 (Mich. 1954)
- KNOWLEDGE, PRESUMPTION

Ex parte DeCastro, 28 U.S.P.Q.2d 1391 (B.P.A.I. 1993) - DEPOSIT, DISCLOSURE

Ex parte Deckler, 21 U.S.P.Q.2d 1872 (B.P.A.I. 1991) - INTERFERENCE

Decora Inc. v. DW Wallcovering Inc., 38 U.S.P.Q.2d 1188 (N.Y. 1995) - DIS-
QUALIFICATION, IMPUTATION

Dee v. Aukerman, 625 F. Supp. 1427, 228 U.S.P.Q. 600 (Ohio 1986) - CONVERSION,
INVENTORSHIP

Deering Milliken Research Corporation v. Beaunit Corporation, 382 F. Supp. 403, 182
U.S.P.Q. 421 (N.C. 1974) - REDUCTION IN ELEMENTS

DeGeorge v. Bernier, 768 F.2d 1318, 226 U.S.P.Q. 758 (Fed. Cir. 1985) - AMBIGUITY,
BEST MODE, COPYING CLAIMS, INTERFERENCE COUNT

De Graffenried v. U.S., 20 Cl. Ct. 458, 16 U.S.P.Q.2d 1321 (Cl. Ct. 1990) - ANOTHER,
EQUIVALENCE, MEANS PLUS FUNCTION, PRINTED PUBLICATION,
PRIOR ART

de Graffenried v. U.S., 25 Cl.Ct. 209, 24 U.S.P.Q.2d 1594 (U.S. Cl. Ct. 1992) - 28
U.S.C. §1498

In re De La Chevreliere, 485 F.2d 1403, 179 U.S.P.Q. 492 (C.C.P.A. 1973) - STATE-
MENT IN THE SPECIFICATION

In re DeLancey, 177 F.2d 377, 83 U.S.P.Q. 388 (C.C.P.A. 1949) - REASONS FOR
APPEAL

Ex parte Della, Bella and Chiarino, 7 U.S.P.Q.2d 1669 (B.P.A.I. 1984) - INTERMEDI-
ATE, MARKUSH, UNITY OF INVENTION

Del Mar Avionics, Inc. v. Quinton Instrument Co., 836 F.2d 1320, 5 U.S.P.Q.2d 1255
(Fed. Cir. 1987) - DAMAGES, ENTIRE-MARKET-VALUE RULE, EXPERT
TESTIMONY, LOST PROFITS, OPINION, ROYALTY, SCOPE

Del Mar Engineering Laboratories v. United States, 524 F.2d 1178, 186 U.S.P.Q. 42 (U.S.
Ct. Cl. 1975) - CLASSIFIED, CONCEALMENT, 35 U.S.C. §102(a)

Delta-X Corp. v. Baker Hughes Production Tools Inc., 984 F.2d 410, 25 U.S.P.Q.2d 1447
(Fed. Cir. 1993) - DAMAGES, JURY INSTRUCTIONS, 35 U.S.C. §284

Demaco Corp. v. Von Langsdorff Licensing Ltd., 851 F.2d 1387, 7 U.S.P.Q.2d 1222 (Fed.
Cir.), *cert. denied,* 488 U.S. 956 (1988) - ADVANCE THE ART

In re Deminski, 796 F.2d 436, 230 U.S.P.Q. 313 (Fed. Cir. 1986) - HINDSIGHT,
MOTIVATION

In re De Montmollin and Riat, 344 F.2d 976, 145 U.S.P.Q. 416 (C.C.P.A. 1965) -
COMMON PROPERTIES, DYESTUFF, PREDICTABILITY, RELATIONSHIP,
SINGLE PROPERTY

Dennison Manufacturing Co. v. Ben Clements & Sons, Inc., 467 F. Supp. 391, 203
U.S.P.Q. 895 (N.Y. 1979) - OVERCLAIMING

Dentsply Research & Development Corp. v. Cadco Dental Products Inc., 14 U.S.P.Q.2d
1039 (Cal. 1989) - CORROBORATION

Dentsply International Inc. v. Kerr Manufacturing Co., 25 U.S.P.Q.2d 1870 (Del. 1992) -
SUBSTANTIAL

Digital Biometrics Inc. v. Identix Inc., 149 F.3d 1335, 47 U.S.P.Q.2d 1418 (Fed. Cir. 1998) - ARGUMENT, CLAIM INTERPRETATION

Digital Equipment Corporation v. Parker v. Computer Operations, Inc., 487 F. Supp. 1104, 206 U.S.P.Q. 428 (Mass. 1980) - 37 C.F.R. §1.56

Digital Systems International Inc. v. Davox Corp., 30 U.S.P.Q.2d 1170 (Wash. 1993) - PROMISSORY ESTOPPEL

In re DiLeone and Lucas, 436 F.2d 1404, 168 U.S.P.Q. 592 (C.C.P.A. 1971) - CAN, MAY, POLYMER, SUFFICIENCY OF DISCLOSURE

In re Dillon, 892 F.2d 1554, 13 U.S.P.Q.2d 1337 (Fed. Cir. 1989); *opinion withdrawn*, 919 F.2d 688, 16 U.S.P.Q.2d 1897 (Fed. Cir. 1990) - INHERENCY, OBVIOUSNESS

In re Dillon, 919 F.2d 688, 16 U.S.P.Q.2d 1897 (Fed. Cir. 1990) - METHOD, PRIMA FACIE, PROBLEM, STRUCTURAL SIMILARITY

In re Dinh-Nguyen and Stenhagen, 492 F.2d 856, 181 U.S.P.Q. 46 (C.C.P.A. 1974) - ASSERTION, CLAIM, COMMENSURATE IN SCOPE, EVIDENCE, FUNCTION, INOPERATIVE, INOPERATIVENESS, PROPORTIONS

In re Dinwiddie, 347 F.2d 1016, 146 U.S.P.Q. 497 (C.C.P.A. 1965) - STATEMENT OF INVENTION

Dippin' Dots v. Mosey, 44 U.S.P.Q.2d 1812 (Tex. 1997) - PRELIMINARY iNJUNCTION, PRESUMPTION OF VALIDITY

Discovery Rights, Inc. v. Avon Prods., Inc., 182 U.S.P.Q. 396 (N.D. Ill. 1974) - ASSIGNMENT, CHAMPERTY, MOTIVE

DiscoVision Associates v. Disc Manufacturing Inc., 42 U.S.P.Q.2d 1749 (Del. 1997) - MARKET POWER, MONOPOLY, RIGHTS, SHERMAN ACT

Diversified Products Corporation v. Weslo Design International, 228 U.S.P.Q. 726 (Del. 1985) - IMPORTATION

The D.L. Auld Company v. Chroma Graphics Corp., 714 F.2d 1144, 219 U.S.P.Q. 13 (Fed. Cir. 1983) - SALE, SECRET

D.L. Auld Company v. Park Electrochemical Corp., 651 F. Supp. 582, 1 U.S.P.Q.2d 2071 (N.Y. 1986) - STANDING, STOCKHOLDER RULE

DMP Corporation v. Rederiaktiebolaget Nordstjernan, 223 U.S.P.Q. 560 (D.C. 1983) - DECLARATORY JUDGMENT

DNIC Brokerage Co. v. Morrison Dempsey Communications Inc., 14 U.S.P.Q.2d 1043 (Cal. 1989) - ROYALTY

Ex parte Dobson, Jacob, and Herschler, 165 U.S.P.Q. 29 (PO Bd. App. 1969) - BREADTH, DETAILS, COMBINATION, EFFECTIVE, LESS THAN, POINT OF NOVELTY, UP TO

D.O.C.C. Inc. v. Spintech Inc., 93 Civ. 4679, 36 U.S.P.Q.2d 1145 (N.Y. 1994) - CONTRIBUTORY INFRINGEMENT, LIMITATION

Doelcher Products v. Hydrofoil International Inc., 735 F. Supp. 666, 14 U.S.P.Q.2d 1067 (Md. 1989) - 28 U.S.C. §1391(c), VENUE

Ex parte Donaldson, 26 U.S.P.Q.2d 1250 (B.P.A.I. 1992) - DEGREE, LIKE

In re Donaldson Co. Inc., 16 F.3d 1189, 29 U.S.P.Q.2d 1845 (Fed. Cir. 1994) - MEANS PLUS FUNCTION, STATUTORY INTERPRETATION

Donelly Corp. v. Gentex Corp., 913 F. Supp. 1014, 37 U.S.P.Q.2d 1146 (Mich. 1995) - ABUSE OF DISCRETION, PRIOR ART

In re Donohue, 766 F.2d 531, 226 U.S.P.Q. 619 (Fed. Cir. 1985) - ANTICIPATION

Dunhall Pharmaceuticals Inc. v. Discus Dental.Inc., 45 U.S.P.Q.2d 1061 (Colo. 1997) - TRANSFER, 28 U.S.C. §1404(a)

Dunhall Pharmaceuticals Inc. v. Discus Dental Inc., 994 F. Supp. 1202,46 U.S.P.Q.2d 1365 (Cal. 1998) - ADVICE OF COUNSEL

Ex parte Duniau, 1 U.S.P.Q.2d 1652 (B.P.A.I. 1986) - DESIGN, PRIORITY, 35 U.S.C. §120

Ex parte Dunki, 153 U.S.P.Q. 678 (PO Bd. App. 1967) - NEW USE

The Dunlop Company, Limited v. Kelsey-Hayes Company, 484 F.2d 407, 179 U.S.P.Q. 129 (6th Cir. 1973) - DIVIDING MARKETS

Dunlop Holdings Limited v. Ram Golf Corporation, 524 F.2d 33, 188 U.S.P.Q. 481 (7th Cir. 1975) - LOST ART, REDISCOVERY, SECRET

Ex parte Dunn and Mathis, 181 U.S.P.Q. 652 (PO Bd. App. 1973) - ASSERTION, SKEPTICISM, SPECULATION, STATEMENT IN THE SPECIFICATION, SURMISE

Ex parte Dunne, 20 U.S.P.Q.2d 1479 (B.P.A.I. 1991) - ABANDONMENT, INTENT, 35 U.S.C. §102(c)

The Duplan Corporation v. Deering Milliken Research Corporation, 487 F.2d 459, 179 U.S.P.Q. 449 (4th Cir. 1973) - DÉLIVRÉ, 35 U.S.C. §102(d)

The Duplan Corporation v. Deering Milliken, Inc., 370 F. Supp. 769, 180 U.S.P.Q. 373 (S.C. 1973) - GRAMMARIAN

The Duplan Corporation v. Deering Milliken, Inc., 444 F. Supp. 648, 197 U.S.P.Q. 342 (S.C. 1977) - CLAYTON ACT, MISUSE, POOLING, REVERSE DOCTRINE OF EQUIVALENTS, PACKAGE LICENSE

DuPont Merck Pharmaceutical Co. v. Bristol-Myers Squibb Co., 62 F.3d 1397, 35 U.S.P.Q.2d 1718 (Fed. Cir. 1995) - ANDA, CASE OR CONTROVERSY, FDA, URAA

Durango Associates Inc. v. Reflange Inc., 912 F.2d 1423, 15 U.S.P.Q.2d 1910 (Fed. Cir. 1990) - APPEAL

In re Durden, Jr., 763 F.2d 1406, 226 U.S.P.Q. 359 (Fed. Cir. 1985) - ANALOGY PROCESSES, METHOD, NEW STARTING MATERIAL, NEW USE, STARTING MATERIAL, PROCESS, SYNTHESIS

Durling v. Spectrum Furniture Co., 101 F.3d 100, 40 U.S.P.Q.2d 1788 (Fed. Cir. 1996) - DESIGN

Dynamic Manufacturing Inc. v. Craze, 46 U.S.P.Q.2d 1548 (Va. 1998) - AGREEMENT TO ASSIGN, IRREPARABLE HARM, STANDING

Dyson v. Amway Corp., 19 U.S.P.Q.2d 1557 (Mich. 1991) - PREAMBLE, PRIVILEGE

-ε-

East Chicago Machine Tool Corporation v. Stone Container Corporation, 181 U.S.P.Q. 744 (Ill. 1974) - FAILURE TO DISCLOSE, FRAUD, MISLEADING

Eastern Rotorcraft Corp. v. United States, 150 U.S.P.Q. 124 (U.S. Ct. Cl. 1966) - TIME

Eastman Kodak Co. v. Duracell Inc., 48 U.S.P.Q.2d 1061 (D.C. 1998) - JURISDICTION, MOTION TO DISMISS

Eastman Kodak Co. v. The Goodyear Tire & Rubber Co., 42 U.S.P.Q.2d 1737 (Fed. Cir. 1997) - LACHES, PROCESS PARAMETER

CLAIM INTERPRETATION, EXTRANEOUS LIMITATION, INVENTION, PRIOR INVENTION, PRODUCT BY PROCESS, PRODUCT BY PROPERTIES, PROPERTIES, PROSECUTION HISTORY

E.I. du Pont de Nemours & Co. v. Phillips Petroleum Co., 720 F. Supp. 373, 12 U.S.P.Q.2d 1401 (Del. 1989) - REEXAMINATION

E.I. du Pont de Nemours & Co. v. United States, 432 F.2d 1052, 167 U.S.P.Q. 321 (3d Cir. 1970) - CAPITAL GAINS

In re Eis, 1 U.S.P.Q.2d 1418 (Commr. Patents & Trademarks 1986) - REEXAMINATION

Eiselstein v. Frank, 52 F.3d 1035, 34 U.S.P.Q.2d 1467 (Fed. Cir. 1995) - ABOUT, ALLOY

In re Eitzen, 86 F.2d 759, 32 U.S.P.Q. 72 (C.C.P.A. 1936) - REJECTED CLAIM

Ekchian v. Home Depot Inc., 41 U.S.P.Q.2d 1364 (Fed. Cir. 1997) - INFORMATION DISCLOSURE STATEMENT

In re Ekenstam, 256 F.2d 321, 118 U.S.P.Q. 349 (C.C.P.A. 1958) - BREVET OCTROYÉ, KNOWLEDGE, PATENT, PATENTED, SECRET PATENT

Eldon Industries Inc. v. Vanier Manufacturing Inc., 14 U.S.P.Q.2d 1075 (Cal. 1990) - WITNESS

Eldridge v. Springs Industries Inc., 882 F. Supp. 356, 35 U.S.P.Q.2d 1378 (N.Y. 1995) - MOTION TO DISMISS

Electrical Fittings Corp. v. Thomas & Betts Co., 307 U.S. 241, 41 U.S.P.Q. 556 (1939) - VALIDITY

Electro Medical Systems S.A. v. Cooper Laseronics, Inc., 617 F. Supp. 1036, 227 U.S.P.Q. 564 (Ill. 1985) - DECLARATORY JUDGMENT

Electro Medical Systems S.A. v. Cooper Life Sciences Inc., 34 F.3d 1048, 32 U.S.P.Q.2d 1017 (Fed. Cir. 1994) - LIMITATION, WILLFULNESS

Electronic Memories & Magnetics Corporation v. Control Data Corporation, 188 U.S.P.Q. 448 (Ill. 1975) - IPSIS VERBIS, KNOWLEDGE

Electro-Nucleonics, Inc. v. Mossinghoff, 593 F. Supp. 125, 224 U.S.P.Q. 435 (D.C. 1984) - PUBLIC USE, USE

Elgen Manufacturing Corp. v. Ventfabrics, Inc., 207 F. Supp. 240, 134 U.S.P.Q. 5 (Ill. 1962) - ECONOMICS, NEW COMBINATION

In re Eli Lilly & Co., 902 F.2d 943, 14 U.S.P.Q.2d 1741 (Fed. Cir. 1990) - OBVIOUS TO TRY OR EXPERIMENT

Eli Lilly and Co. v. American Cyanamid Co., 896 F. Supp. 851, 36 U.S.P.Q.2d 1011 (Ind. 1995) - IRREPARABLE HARM, NEXUS, PRELIMINARY INJUNCTION, 35 U.S.C. §271(g)

Eli Lilly and Company v. American Cyanamid Company, 81 F.3d 1568, 38 U.S.P.Q.2d 1705 (Fed. Cir. 1996) - PPAA, 35 U.S.C. §271(g)

Eli Lilly & Co. v. Genentech Inc., 17 U.S.P.Q.2d 1531 (Ind. 1990) - INTEGRATION CLAUSE, LIMITED PATENT LICENSE

Eli Lilly and Company, Inc. v. Generix Drug Sales, Inc., 324 F. Supp. 715, 169 U.S.P.Q. 13 (Fla. 1971) - PIONEER

Eli Lilly and Company, Inc. v. Generix Drug Sales, Inc., 460 F.2d 1096, 174 U.S.P.Q. 65 (5th Cir. 1972) - ACQUIESCENCE, DRUG, PRELIMINARY INJUNCTION, PRESUMPTION OF VALIDITY, THERAPEUTIC VALUE

Eli Lilly & Co. v. Medtronic Inc., 110 S. Ct. 2683, 15 U.S.P.Q.2d 1121 (1990) - 35 U.S.C. §271(e)(1)

Eli Lilly and Co. v. Medtronic Inc., 915 F.2d 670, 16 U.S.P.Q.2d 2020 (Fed. Cir. 1990 - unpublished) - THREATENED INFRINGEMENT, 35 U.S.C. §271

Eli Lilly & Co. v. Premo Pharmaceutical Laboratories Inc., 843 F.2d 1378, 6 U.S.P.Q.2d 1367 (Fed. Cir. 1988) - NDA

Elkay Manufacturing Co. v. Abco Manufacturing Co., 99 F.3d 1160, 42 U.S.P.Q.2d 1555 (Fed. Cir. 1996 - *unpublished*) - IMPLIED LICENSE

Elk Corp. of Dallas v. GAF Building Materials Corp., 45 U.S.P.Q.2d 1011 (Tex. 1997) - FILE HISTORY, OPINION OF COUNSEL

Elkhart Brass Manufacturing Co. Inc. v. Task Force Tips Inc., 867 F. Supp. 782, 34 U.S.P.Q.2d 1402 (Ind. 1994) - INFRINGEMENT NOTICE

Elmore v. Schmitt, 278 F.2d 510, 125 U.S.P.Q. 653 (C.C.P.A. 1960) - REDUCTION TO PRACTICE

Elox, Inc. v. Astral Precision Equipment Company, 178 U.S.P.Q. 607 (Ill. 1971) - RULE 37

Eltech Systems Corp. v. PPG Industries, Inc., 710 F. Supp. 622, 11 U.S.P.Q.2d 1174 (La. 1988) - WHEREBY CLAUSE

Eltech Systems Corp. v. PPG Industries, Inc., 903 F.2d 805, 14 U.S.P.Q.2d 1965 (Fed. Cir. 1990) - SPURIOUS

Ely v. Manbeck, 17 U.S.P.Q.2d 1252 (D.C. 1990) - ATTORNE, EXPERT TESTIMONY, INTERVENOR, REISSUE

EMC Corp. v. Norand Corp., 39 U.S.P.Q.2d 1451 (Fed. Cir. 1996) - CONTROVERSY, DECLARATORY JUDGMENT

Emerson Electric Co. v. Daviol Inc., 88 F.3d 1051, 39 U.S.P.Q.2d 1474 (Fed. Cir. 1996) - COLLATERAL ORDER DOCTRINE, REEXAMINATION

Emerson Electric Co. v. Encon Industries L.P., 42 U.S.P.Q.2d 1575 (Miss. 1997) - INEQUITABLE CONDUCT

In re Emert, 124 F.3d 1458, 44 U.S.P.Q.2d 1149 (Fed. Cir. 1997) - ELEMENT, OBVIOUSNESS-TYPE DOUBLE PATENTING, SUBCOMBINATION

EMS-American Grilon Inc. v. DSM Resins U.S. Inc., 15 U.S.P.Q.2d 1472 (N.J. 1989) - DECLARATORY JUDGMENT

Enders v. American Patent Search Company, 535 F.2d 1085, 189 U.S.P.Q. 569 (9th Cir. 1976) - 35 U.S.C. §33

Endress + Hauser Inc. v. Hawk Measurement Systems Pty. Ltd., 32 U.S.P.Q.2d 1768 (Ind. 1994) - DOCTRINE OF EQUIVALENTS, INFRINGEMENT, MEANS PLUS FUNCTION

Endress + Hauser Inc. v. Hawk Measurement Systems Pty. Ltd., 122 F.3d 1040, 43 U.S.P.Q.2d 1849 (Fed. Cir. 1997) - EXPERT WITNESS, MOSITA

Enercon GmbH v. International Trade Commission, 47 U.S.P.Q.2d 1725 (Fed. Cir. 1998) - SALE

Energy Absorption Systems Inc. v. Roadway Safety Service Inc., 28 U.S.P.Q.2d 1079 (Ill. 1993) - INVALIDITY

Energy Conservation Devices Inc. v. Manbeck, 741 F. Supp. 965, 16 U.S.P.Q.2d 1574 (D.C. 1990) - EXAMINER

Enforcer Products Inc. v. Birdsong, 40 U.S.P.Q.2d 1958 (Fed. Cir. 1996 - *unpublished*) - INFRINGEMENT

Engelhard Industries, Inc. v. Sel-Rex Corporation, 145 U.S.P.Q. 319 (N.J. 1965) - RETROACTIVE LICENSE

Engelhard Industries, Inc. v. Sel-Rex Corp., 253 F. Supp. 832, 149 U.S.P.Q. 607 (N.J. 1966) - BEST MODE

Engineered Sports Products v. Brunswick Corporation, 362 F. Supp. 722, 179 U.S.P.Q. 486 (Utah 1973) - CONTRIBUTORY INFRONGEMENT, 35 U.S.C. §271(a)

English v. Ausnit, 38 U.S.P.Q.2d 1625 (B.P.A.I. 1993) - BURDEN, CORROBORATION, DATE, INTERFERENCE, SUMMARY JUDGMENT

English v. Heredero, 200 U.S.P.Q. 597 (PTO Bd. Pat. Int. 1978) - CONCEALMENT

Enpat Inc. v. Microsoft Corp., 6 F. Supp. 537, 47 U.S.P.Q.2d 1218 (Va. 1998) - FOREIGN SALES, REASONABLE ROYALTY, 35 U.S.C. §271(f)

Environmental Designs, Ltd. v. Union Oil Company of California, 713 F.2d 693, 218 U.S.P.Q. 865 (Fed. Cir. 1983) - DISBELIEF

Environ Products Inc. v. Furon Co., 47 U.S.P.Q.2d 1040 (Pa. 1998) - DERIVATION, INTERFERENCE, PRIOR INVENTORSHIP

Environ Products Inc. v. Total Containment Inc., 41 U.S.P.Q.2d 1302 (Pa. 1996) - WORK PRODUCT DOCTRINE

Environ Products Inc. v. Total Containment Inc., 41 U.S.P.Q.2d 1942 (Pa. 1997) - MATERIAL INFORMATION *Environ Products Inc. v. Total Containment Inc.*, 43 U.S.P.Q.2d 1288 (Pa. 1997) - INEQUITABLE CONDUCT, MATERIALITY

Envirotech Corp. v. Westech Engineering, Inc., 713 F. Supp. 372, 11 U.S.P.Q.2d 1804 (Utah 1989) - GRACE PERIOD, ON SALE, REDUCTION TO PRACTICE

Envirotech Corp. v. Westech Engineering Inc., 904 F.2d 1571, 15 U.S.P.Q.2d 1230 (Fed. Cir. 1990) - ON SALE

Enzo APA & Son Inc. v. Geapag A.G., 134 F.3d 1090, 45 U.S.P.Q.2d 1368 (Fed. Cir. 1998) - ASSIGNMENT, NUNC PRO TUNC

In re Epple and Kaiser, 477 F.2d 582, 177 U.S.P.Q. 696 (C.C.P.A. 1973) - ARTICLE, MANUFACTURE, METHOD OF MAKING

In re Epstein, 32 F.3d 1559, 31 U.S.P.Q.2d 1817 (Fed. Cir. 1994) - DEFERENCE, HEARSAY, ON SALE, PUBLIC USE, RULES OF EVIDENCE

Ex parte Erdmann, Schneider, and Koch, 194 U.S.P.Q. 96 (PTO Bd. App. 1975) - CARRIER, COMPOSITION, CONVENTIONAL, HERBICIDE

Ex parte Erlich, 3 U.S.P.Q.2d 1011 (B.P.A.I. 1986) - BIOTECHNOLOGY, EXPECTATION OF SUCCESS, OBVIOUS TO TRY OR EXPERIMENT, PRODUCT CLAIM, SUCCESS

Ex parte Erlich, 22 U.S.P.Q.2d 1463 (BPAI 1992) - ORDINARY SKILL

Ernster v. Ralston Purina Co., 740 F. Supp. 724, 16 U.S.P.Q.2d 1222 (Mo. 1990) - CONSPIRACY TO INFRINGE

Ernsthausen v. Nakayama, 1 U.S.P.Q.2d 1539 (B.P.A.I. 1985) - FOREIGN PATENT APPLICATION, INCORPORATE BY REFERENCE

In re Eskild and Houghton, 387 F.2d 987, 156 U.S.P.Q. 208 (C.C.P.A. 1968) - CHALLENGE, COMMON PRACTICE

Estee Lauder Inc. v. L'Oreal S.A., 40 U.S.P.Q.2d 1425 (D.C. 1996) - REDUCTION TO PRACTICE, 35 U.S.C. §146

Estee Lauder Inc. v. L'Oreal S.A., 129 F.3d 588, 44 U.S.P.Q.2d 1610 (Fed. Cir. 1997) - INTERFERENCE, REDUCTION TO PRACTICE

In re Estes, 420 F.2d 1397, 164 U.S.P.Q. 519 (C.C.P.A. 1970) - ADVANTAGE, LIMITATION, RESULT

Ethicon Endo-Surgery v. United States Surgical Corp., 900 F. Supp. 172, 38 U.S.P.Q.2d 1385 (Ohio 1995) - CLAIM CONSTRUCTION

Ethicon Endo-Surgery Inc. v. United States Surgical Corp., 40 U.S.P.Q.2d 1019 (Fed. Cir. 1996) - AMBIGUOUS, CLAIM INTERPRETATION

Ethicon Inc. v. Quigg, 849 F.2d 1422, 7 U.S.P.Q.2d 1152 (Fed. Cir. 1988) - REEXAMINATION

Ethicon Inc. v. United States Surgical Corp., 135 F.3d 1456, 45 U.S.P.Q.2d 1545 (Fed. Cir. 1998) - COINVENTOR, CO-OWNER, CORROBORATION, JOINT INVENTORS

Ethyl Corp. v. Hercules Powder Co., 232 F. Supp. 453, 139 U.S.P.Q. 471 (Del. 1963) - CONTROL OF UNPATENTED GOODS, MISUSE, PROCESS

In re Etter, 756 F.2d 852, 225 U.S.P.Q. 1 (Fed. Cir. 1985) - DOUBLE PATENTING, PRESUMPTION OF VALIDITY, REEXAMINATION

Eutectic Corporation v. Metco, Inc., 418 F. Supp. 1186, 191 U.S.P.Q. 505 (N.Y. 1976) - METALLURGY

Evans Cooling Systems Inc. v. General Motors Corp., 125 F.3d 1448, 44 U.S.P.Q.2d 1037 (Fed. Cir. 1997) - ON SALE

Everex Systems Inc. v. Cadtrak Corp., 89 F.3d 673, 39 U.S.P.Q.2d 1518 (9th Cir. 1996) - BANKRUPTCY, LICENSE, PERSON AGGRIEVED

Exxon Chemical Patents Inc. v. The Lubrizol Corp., 935 F.2d 1263, 19 U.S.P.Q.2d 1061 (Fed. Cir. 1991) - PATENT

Exxon Chemical Patents Inc. v. Lubrizol Corp., 26 U.S.P.Q.2d 1871 (Tex. 1993) - WILLFUL INFRINGEMENT

Exxon Chemical Patents Inc. v. Lubrizol Corp., 64 F.3d 1553, 35 U.S.P.Q.2d 1801 (Fed. Cir. 1995) - CLAIM INTERPRETATION, COMPOSITION, OIL, RECIPE, TITLE

Exxon Chemical Patents Inc. v. Lubrizol Corp., 137 F.3d 1475, 45 U.S.P.Q.2d 1865 (Fed. Cir. 1998) - JUDGMENT, NEW TRIAL, REHEARING, REMAND

In re Eynde, Pollet, and de Cat, 480 F.2d 1364, 178 U.S.P.Q. 470 (C.C.P.A. 1973) - CHALLENGE, ENABLEMENT, EVIDENCE, KNOWLEDGE, RATIONALE, STATE OF THE ART

-F-

In re Facius, 408 F.2d 1396, 161 U.S.P.Q. 294 (C.C.P.A. 1969) - ORIGIN

In re Fahrni, 210 F.2d 362, 100 U.S.P.Q. 388 (C.C.P.A. 1954) - STEPS

Fairfax Dental (Ireland) Ltd. v. Sterling Optical Corp., 808 F. Supp. 326, 26 U.S.P.Q.2d 1442 (N.Y. 1992) - CROWDED ART, PROSECUTION HISTORY, TIME

Fansteel, Inc. v. Carmet Company, 210 U.S.P.Q. 413 (Ill. 1981) - NUMBER

Farley Transp. Co. v. Santa Fe Transp. Co., 786 F.2d 1342 (9th Cir. 1986) - DIRECTED VERDICT

Farmaceutisk Laboratorium Ferring A/S v. Reid Rowell Inc., 20 U.S.P.Q.2d 1476 (Ga. 1991) - COUNTERCLAIM, DISMISSAL, RULE 41(a)(2)

In re Fischer, 360 F.2d 230, 149 U.S.P.Q. 631 (C.C.P.A. 1966) - REMAND (GROUNDS FOR)

Fishburne Equipment Co., Inc. v. Lee Machine-Hydraulic, Inc., 203 U.S.P.Q. 601 (N.C. 1978) - 15 U.S.C. §2

In re Fisher, 427 F.2d 833, 166 U.S.P.Q. 18 (C.C.P.A. 1970) - AT LEAST, BREADTH, CHEMICAL, CHEMICAL REACTION, COMMENSURATE IN SCOPE, DEFINITENESS, DOMINANT PATENT, ELECTRICAL, ENABLEMENT, IMPROVEMENT, MECHANICAL, OPEN-ENDED CLAIM, PHYSIOLOGICAL, PIONEER INVENTION, PREDICTABILITY, REASONABLE CORRELATION

Fisher v. Bouzard, 3 U.S.P.Q.2d 1677 (B.P.A.I. 1987) - OBJECTION, MOTION TO SUPPRESS

Fisher and Speer v. Gardiner and Aymami, 215 U.S.P.Q. 620 (PTO Bd. Pat. Int. 1981) - CONVERSION

In re Fisons Pharmaceuticals Ltd., 231 U.S.P.Q. 305 (Commr. Patents & Trademarks 1986) - COMMERCIAL MARKETING, PATENT TERM EXTENSION, PHARMACEUTICAL, PRODUCT

Fisons Plc v. Quigg, 8 U.S.P.Q.2d 1491 (D.C. 1988), *aff'd*, 876 F.2d 99, 10 U.S.P.Q.2d 1869 (Fed. Cir. 1989) - PATENT TERM EXTENSION, PRODUCT

Fitch v. Cooper, 139 U.S.P.Q. 382 (PO Bd. Pat. Int. 1962) - PROOF

In re Fleissner, 264 F.2d 897, 121 U.S.P.Q. 270 (C.C.P.A. 1959) - 35 U.S.C. §141

Fleming v. Bosch and Pollmann, 181 U.S.P.Q. 761 (PO Bd. Pat. Intf. 1973) - IMPROVEMENT

In re Flint, 411 F.2d 1353, 162 U.S.P.Q. 228 (C.C.P.A. 1969) - CONVENTIONAL, MULTIPLICITY

Flowdata Inc. v. Cotton, 871 F. Supp. 925, 32 U.S.P.Q.2d 1743 (Tex. 1994) - INFRINGEMENT

Flow-Rite of Tennessee Inc. v. Sears Roebuck & Co. Inc., 20 U.S.P.Q.2d 1361 (Ill. 1991) - VALIDITY

Fluke Corp. v. Fine Instruments Corp., 32 U.S.P.Q.2d 1789 (Wash. 1994) - PROTECTIVE ORDER

Flynn v. Arkley, Eardley, and Long, 187 U.S.P.Q. 513 (PTO Bd. Pat. Intf. 1975) - NOTEBOOK

FMC Corp. v. Hunter Engineering Co., 20 U.S.P.Q.2d 1077 (Ark. 1991) - TRANSACTING BUSINESS

FMC Corp. v. Up-Right Inc., 21 F.3d 1073, 30 U.S.P.Q.2d 1361 (Fed. Cir. 1994) - RECONSTRUCTION, REPAIR, RESTORATION

Fonar Corp. v. General Electric Co., 41 U.S.P.Q.2d 1088 (N.Y. 1995) - DAMAGES, MEANS PLUS FUNCTION, REPAIR

Fonar Corp. v. Johnson & Johnson, 821 F.2d 627, 3 U.S.P.Q.2d 1109 (Fed. Cir. 1987) - LEXICOGRAPHER

In re Fong, Ward, and Lundgren, 288 F.2d 932, 129 U.S.P.Q. 264 (C.C.P.A. 1961) - USE

Forbro Design Corp. v. Raytheon Co., 390 F. Supp. 794, 190 U.S.P.Q. 70 (Mass. 1975) - CROSS-LICENSE, ON SALE, ORDER, SETTLEMENT AGREEMENT, 35 U.S.C. §135(c)

Ford Motor Co. v. Lemelson, 40 U.S.P.Q.2d 1349 (Nev. 1996) - CLAIM, CONTINUING APPLICATION, SUMMARY JUDGMENT

In re Freeman, 30 F.3d 1459, 31 U.S.P.Q.2d 1444 (Fed. Cir. 1994) - ISSUE PRECLUSION

In re Freeman and Burden, 474 F.2d 1318, 177 U.S.P.Q. 139 (C.C.P.A. 1973) - EVIDENCE

Freeman v. Bee Machine Co., 319 U.S. 448 (1943) - VENUE

Fregeau v. Mossinghoff, 776 F.2d 1034, 227 U.S.P.Q. 848 (Fed. Cir. 1985) - COURT REVIEW OF PTO RULINGS, 35 U.S.C. §145

In re Fressola, 22 U.S.P.Q.2d 1828 (Comm'r Patents and Trademarks 1992) - CLAIM FORMAT

Ex parte Fressola, 27 U.S.P.Q.2d 1608 (B.P.A.I. 1993) - BACKFIRING, CENTRAL DEFINITION, CLAIM, SUBSTANTIALLY

Ex parte Frey, Hepp, and Morey, 69 U.S.P.Q. 623 (PO Bd. App. 1946) - CLOUD

In re Fridolph, 309 F.2d 509, 135 U.S.P.Q. 319 (C.C.P.A. 1962) - MAKING INTEGRAL

Frilette v. Kimberlin, 500 F.2d 205, 184 U.S.P.Q. 266 (3rd Cir. 1974) - 35 U.S.C. §24

In re Frilette and Weisz, 412 F.2d 269, 162 U.S.P.Q. 163 (C.C.P.A. 1969) - RELATIONSHIP

In re Frilette and Weisz, 423 F.2d 1397, 165 U.S.P.Q. 259 (C.C.P.A. 1970) - BREADTH

In re Frilette and Weisz, 436 F.2d 496, 168 U.S.P.Q. 368 (C.C.P.A. 1971) - DOMINANT PATENT

In re Fritch, 972 F.2d 1260, 23 U.S.P.Q.2d 1780 (Fed. Cir. 1992) - MODIFICATION, MOSAIC, OBVIOUSNESS, PRIMA FACIE, SUGGESTION

Fritsch v. Lin, 21 U.S.P.Q.2d 1739 (B.P.A.I. 1991) - COUNT

Ex parte Frohardt, Dion, and Ehrlich, 139 U.S.P.Q. 377 (PO Bd. App 1962) - ISOLATED

Fromberg, Inc. v. Thornhill, 315 F.2d 407, 137 U.S.P.Q. 84 (5th Cir. 1963) - CONTRIBUTORY INFRINGEMENT

Fromson v. RVP Chemical Corp., 15 U.S.P.Q.2d 1689 (Wis. 1990) - AUTHORITATIVE OPINION, PRIOR ADJUDICATION, PRIOR SALE, UNTIMELY JURY DEMAND, WILLFUL INFRINGEMENT

Fromson v. Western Litho Plate Supply Co., 853 F.2d 1568, 7 U.S.P.Q.2d 1606 (Fed. Cir. 1988) - APPEAL, OPINION OF COUNSEL, PATENT RIGHTS, PREJUDGMENT INTEREST, ROYALTY

Fromson v. Western Litho Plate Supply Co., 13 U.S.P.Q.2d 1856 (Mo. 1989) - PREJUDGMENT INTEREST

Fryer v. Tachikawa, 179 U.S.P.Q. 381 (PO Bd. Pat. Intf. 1972) - 37 C.F.R. §1.47, REVIVAL

In re Fuetterer, 319 F.2d 259, 138 U.S.P.Q. 217 (C.C.P.A. 1963) - BREADTH, COMBINATION, FUNCTION, FUNCTIONAL, PROPERTIES

Ex parte Fujii, 13 U.S.P.Q.2d 1073, 1074 (B.P.A.I. 1989) - KOKAI

Fujikawa v. Wattanasin, 39 U.S.P.Q.2d 1895 (Fed. Cir. 1996) - DESCRIPTION, LIST, PHARMACEUTICAL, UTILITY

Fuji Machine Manufacturing Co. v. Hover-Davis Inc., 40 U.S.P.Q.2d 1313 (N.Y. 1996) - CONTRIBUTORY INFRINGEMENT, INDUCEMENT OF INFRINGEMENT

Fuji Machine Manufacturing v. Hover-Davis Inc., 982 F. Supp. 923, 45 U.S.P.Q.2d 1158 (N.Y. 1997) - BIFURCATION DESCRIPTION, LIST, PHARMACEUTICAL, UTILITY

Ex parte Fujishiro and Ohta, 199 U.S.P.Q. 36 (PTO Bd. App. 1977) - FOREIGN PATENT APPLICATION, 35 U.S.C. §102(d)

-*G*-

In re Application of G, 11 U.S.P.Q.2d 1378 (Commr. Patents & Trademarks 1989) - UNINTENTIONAL ABANDONMENT

In re Gaertner, 604 F.2d 1348, 202 U.S.P.Q. 714 (C.C.P.A. 1979) - PATENT OFFICE LICENSE

Gaiser v. Linder, 253 F.2d 433, 117 U.S.P.Q. 209 (C.C.P.A. 1958) - REDUCTION TO PRACTICE

In re Gal, 980 F.2d 717, 25 U.S.P.Q.2d 1076 (Fed. Cir. 1992) - DESIGN CHOICE, PURPOSE

In re Gallo, 231 U.S.P.Q. 496 (1986) - INCORPORATE BY REFERENCE

Gambro Lundia AB v. Baxter Healthcare Corp., 110 F.3d 1573, 42 U.S.P.Q.2d 1378 (Fed. Cir. 1997) - COMMUNICATION OF CONCEPTION, DERIVATION

Gardco Manufacturing Inc. v. Herst Lighting Co., 820 F.2d 1209, 2 U.S.P.Q.2d 2015 (Fed. Cir. 1987) - DUTY TO DISCLOSE, MATERIALITY

In re Gardner, 475 F.2d 1389, 177 U.S.P.Q. 396 (C.C.P.A. 1973) - ASSERTION, DOUBT, STATEMENT IN THE SPECIFICATION, SUPPORT

In re Gardner, 480 F.2d 879, 178 U.S.P.Q. 149 (C.C.P.A. 1973) - DESCRIPTION, ORIGINAL CLAIMS, WRITTEN DESCRIPTION

In re Gardner, Roe, and Willey, 427 F.2d 786, 166 U.S.P.Q. 138 (C.C.P.A. 1970) - DOSAGE, HOST

Gardner v. Ford Motor Co., 17 U.S.P.Q.2d 1177 (Wash. 1990) - PAPER PATENT

Gargoyles Inc. v. U.S., 32 Fed.Cl. 157, 33 U.S.P.Q.2d 1595 (U.S Ct. Fed. Cl. 1994) - EQUIVALENTS, ORDINARY SKILL, PROBLEM, PUBLIC USE, SUBSTANTIAL

In re Garnero, 412 F.2d 276, 162 U.S.P.Q. 221 (C.C.P.A. 1969) - CONSISTING ESSENTIALLY OF, STATUTORY CLASS

In re Gartner and Roeber, 223 F.2d 502, 106 U.S.P.Q. 273 (C.C.P.A. 1955) - APPARATUS, FUNCTION, FUNCTION OF MACHINE, INCOMPLETE, PROCESS, SUBCOMBINATION

Garty and Gibb v. Price, 158 U.S.P.Q. 559 (Comm'r 1964) - MOTION BY EXAMINER

Gasoline Products Co., Inc. v. Conway P. Coe, 87 F.2d 550, 31 U.S.P.Q. 407 (D.C. Cir. 1936) - MATERIAL

Gassaway v. Business Machine Security, 9 U.S.P.Q.2d 1572 (Cal. 1988) - STAY MOTION

Gasser Chair Co. Inc. v. Infanti Chair Manufacturing Corp., 60 F.3d 770, 34 U.S.P.Q.2d 1822 (Fed. Cir. 1995) - LACHES

Ex parte Gastambide, Thal, Rohrbach, and Laroche, 189 U.S.P.Q. 643 (PTO Bd. App. 1974) - DISCLOSURE, ENABLEMENT, HOW TO MAKE, STEROID

In re Gaubert, 524 F.2d 1222, 187 U.S.P.Q. 664 (C.C.P.A. 1975) - ALTERNATIVE, ANY OTHER, AT LEAST, REASON

Gavin v. Starbrite Corp., 10 U.S.P.Q.2d 1253 (Fed. Cir. 1988) - ROYALTY

In re Gay, 309 F.2d 769, 135 U.S.P.Q. 311 (C.C.P.A. 1962) - BEST MODE

General Electric Co. v. Wabash Appliance Corp., 304 U.S. 364, 37 U.S.P.Q. 466 (1938) - FUNCTIONAL, POINT OF NOVELTY, PRODUCT BY PROCESS

General Foods Corp. v. Studiengesellschaft Kohle mbH, 765 F. Supp. 121, 20 U.S.P.Q.2d 1673 (N.Y. 1991) - DOUBLE PATENTING

General Foods Corp. v. Studiengesellschaft Kohle mbH, 972 F.2d 1272, 23 U.S.P.Q.2d 1839 (Fed. Cir. 1992) - CLAIM CONSTRUCTION, DOUBLE PATENTING

General Instrument Corp. Inc. v. Scientific-Atlanta Inc., 995 F.2d 209, 27 U.S.P.Q.2d 1145 (Fed. Cir. 1993) - 35 U.S.C. §146

General Radio Company v. Watson, 188 F. Supp. 879, 125 U.S.P.Q. 268 (D.C. 1960) - DISCREDIT, SELF-SERVING

The General Tire & Rubber Company v. The Firestone Tire & Rubber Company, 349 F. Supp. 333, 349 F. Supp. 345, 174 U.S.P.Q. 427 (Ohio 1972) - MICROFILM, PUBLICATION

Genetic Implant Systems Inc. v. Core-Vent Corp., 123 F.3d 1455, 43 U.S.P.Q.2d 1786 (Fed. Cir. 1997) - DISTRIBUTOR, IMPLIED LICENSE, JURISDICTION

The Gentry Gallery Inc. v. The Berkline Corp., 134 F.3d 1473, 45 U.S.P.Q.2d 1498 (Fed. Cir. 1998) - COMBINING REFERENCES, INFRINGEMENT, PREVAILING PARTY

Ex parte George, 230 U.S.P.Q. 575 (B.P.A.I. 1984) - CONTINUATION APPLICATION

Ex parte George, 21 U.S.P.Q.2d 1058 (B.P.A.I. 1991) - COMMENSURATE, EXPERT OPINION, SKEPTICISM, UNEXPECTED

In re George, 2 U.S.P.Q.2d 1880 (B.P.A.I. 1987) - PUBLICATION

Georgia-Pacific Corp. v. Lieberam, 959 F.2d 901, 22 U.S.P.Q.2d 1383 (11th Cir. 1992) - EMPLOYMENT AGREEMENT

Georgia-Pacific Corporation v. U.S. Plywood-Champion Papers Inc., 318 F. Supp. 116, 166 U.S.P.Q. 235 (N.Y. 1970) - WILLING BUYER - WILLING SELLER RULE

The Gerber Scientific Instrument Company v. Barr and Stroud Ltd., 383 F. Supp. 1238, 182 U.S.P.Q. 201 (Conn. 1973) - FOREIGN PATENTEE, 35 U.S.C. §293

Gerk v. Cottringer, 17 U.S.P.Q.2d 1615 (B.P.A.I. 1990) - MOTION

Ex parte Gerlach and Woerner, 212 U.S.P.Q. 471 (PTO Bd. App. 1980) - CAPABILITY, CLAIM, OBVIOUSNESS, SKILL OF THE ART

Gerritsen v. Shirai, 24 U.S.P.Q.2d 1912 (Fed. Cir. 1992) - ABUSE OF DISCRETION

Gesco International Inc. v. Luther Medical Products Inc., 17 U.S.P.Q.2d 1168 (Tex. 1990) - JURISDICTION, NON-RESIDENT DEFENDANT

In re Gibbs and Griffin, 437 F.2d 486, 168 U.S.P.Q. 578 (C.C.P.A. 1971) - ABANDONMENT, DEDICATION TO THE PUBLIC, DISCLOSURE WITHOUT CLAIMING, GRACE PERIOD

Ex parte Gieseler, 92 U.S.P.Q. 41 (PO Bd. App. 1951) - PATENTABLE DISTINCTNESS

Gilbert v. Marzall, 182 F.2d 389, 85 U.S.P.Q. 288 (D.C. Cir. 1950) - REFERENCE

Gill v. Wells, 89 U.S. 1 (1874) - EQUIVALENCE

The Gillette Company v. S.C. Johnson & Son, Inc., 12 U.S.P.Q.2d 1929 (Mass. 1989) - EQUIVALENTS

Ginos and Cotzias v. Nedelec, Frechet, and Dumont, 220 U.S.P.Q. 831 (PTO Bd. Pat. Int. 1983) - CONCEALMENT

Gold Seal Importers, Inc. v. Morris White Fashions, Inc., 124 F.2d 141 (2d Cir. 1941) -
DESIGN

Goodwall Construction Co. v. Beers Construction Co., 991 F.2d 751, 26 U.S.P.Q.2d 1420
(Fed. Cir. 1993) - POST-JUDGMENT INTEREST

In re Goodwin, 43 U.S.P.Q.2d 1856 (Comm'r Patents and Trademarks 1997 - *unpublished*) - INCORPORATE BY REFERENCE

Goodyear v. Brush, 104 U.S.P.Q. 346 (Comm'r 1954) - 37 C.F.R. §1.292

Goodyear Tire and Rubber Company v. Ladd, 349 F.2d 710, 146 U.S.P.Q. 93 (CA D.C.
1965) - TIME

The Goodyear Tire & Rubber Company v. Releasomers Inc., 3 U.S.P.Q.2d 1233 (Ohio
1986) - DECLARATORY JUDGMENT

In re Gordon, 733 F.2d 900, 221 U.S.P.Q. 1125 (Fed. Cir. 1984) - DRAWING, INOPER-
ABLE, OBVIOUSNESS, ORIENTATION DURING OPERATION

The Gorham Manufacturing Co. v. George C. White, 81 U.S. (14 Wall.) 511 (1872) -
DESIGN

In re Gorman, 933 F.2d 982, 18 U.S.P.Q.2d 1885 (Fed. Cir. 1991) - NUMBER OF
REFERENCES, PRESUMPTION OF VALIDITY

In re Gosteli, 872 F.2d 1008, 10 U.S.P.Q.2d 1614 (Fed. Cir. 1989) - ANTEDATING A
REFERENCE, INVENTION, PRIORITY, *STARE DECISIS, SYMMETRY IN THE
LAW*

In re Gottlieb, 328 F.2d 1016, 140 U.S.P.Q. 665 (C.C.P.A. 1964) - CANCELLATION

Gottschalk, Comm'r. Pats. v. Benson, 409 U.S. 63, 175 U.S.P.Q. 673 (S.Ct. 1972) -
ALGORITHM, COMPUTER-ARTS INVENTION, PHENOMENA OF NATURE

Goudy v. Hansen, 247 Fed. 782 (1st Cir. 1917) - DESIGN

Ex parte Gould, 231 U.S.P.Q. 943 (B.P.A.I. 1986) - ENABLING DISCLOSURE, RE-
EXAMINATION, REFERENCE

Ex parte Gould, 6 U.S.P.Q.2d 1680 (B.P.A.I. 1987) - CLAIM, ENABLEMENT, LIMIT,
PRESUMPTION OF VALIDITY

In re Gould, 673 F.2d 1385, 213 U.S.P.Q. 628 (C.C.P.A. 1982) - REMAND (GROUNDS
FOR)

Gould v. Control Laser Corp., 866 F.2d 1391, 9 U.S.P.Q.2d 1718 (Fed. Cir. 1989) -
CONSENT JUDGMENT, MOOT, SETTLEMENT AGREEMENT

Gould v. The Cornelius Company, 258 F. Supp. 701, 151 U.S.P.Q. 178 (Okla. 1966) -
DOING BUSINESS

Gould v. Mossinghoff, 215 U.S.P.Q. 310 (D.C. 1982) - COMPRISING

Gould v. Mossinghoff, 229 U.S.P.Q. 1 (D.C. 1985) - ASSERTION, CONVINCE, COR-
RECT, DISCLOSURE, ENABLEMENT, TRUTHFULNESS OF SPECIFICATION

Gould v. Rees, 82 U.S. 187, 194 (1872) - EQUIVALENCE

Goutzoulis v. Athale, 15 U.S.P.Q.2d 1461 (Commr. Patents & Trademarks 1990) - 37
C.F.R. §1.131, 37 C.F.R. §1.644(a)(2), DECISION, INTERFERENCE, MOTION,
PRELIMINARY STATEMENT

Ex parte GPAC Inc., 29 U.S.P.Q.2d 1401 (B.P.A.I. 1993) - 37 C.F.R. §1.132, COPYING,
HYPOTHETICAL PERSON

In re GPAC Inc., 57 F.3d 1573, 35 U.S.P.Q.2d 1116 (Fed. Cir. 1995) - ANALOGOUS
ART, COMMERCIAL SUCCESS, ORDINARY SKILL, RELEVANT ART, SPEC-
ULATION, STANDARD OF REVIEW

In re Grabiak, 769 F.2d 729, 226 U.S.P.Q. 870 (Fed. Cir. 1985) - ANALOG, COMPOUND, GENERALIZATION, INCONCEIVABLE, OBVIOUSNESS, OXYGEN, STRUCTURAL SIMILARITY, SUBSTITUTE, SUBSTITUTION OF EQUIVALENTS, SULFUR

Graco Children's Products Inc. v. Century Products Co. Inc., 38 U.S.P.Q.2d 1331 (Pa. 1996) - INVENTION, INVENTOR, JOINT INVENTORS, SEARCH

In re Graff, 42 U.S.P.Q.2d 1471 (Fed. Cir. 1997) - REISSUE

Graham v. John Deere Co., 383 U.S. 1, 148 U.S.P.Q. 459 (1966) - COMBINING REFERENCES, FILE WRAPPER, GRAHAM INQUIRIES, OBVIOUSNESS, PROBLEM, VACUUM

Graham Paper Company v. International Paper Company, 46 F.2d 881, 8 U.S.P.Q. 463 (8th Cir. 1931) - CONTRIBUTORY INFRINGEMENT, THREATENED INFRINGEMENT

Grain Processing Corp. v. American Maize-Products Co., 893 F. Supp. 1386, 37 U.S.P.Q.2d 1299 (Ind. 1995) - ISSUES, LAW OF THE CASE, LOST-PROFITS, DAMAGES, PREJUDGMENT INTEREST

Ex parte Grasselli, 231 U.S.P.Q. 395 (PTO Bd. App. 1983) - FORMULA

Graver Tank Manufacturing Co. v. The Linde Air Products Company, 336 U.S. 271, 80 U.S.P.Q. 451 (1949) - OVERCLAIMING

Graver Tank & Mfg. Co. v. The Linde Air Products Company, 339 U.S. 605, 85 U.S.P.Q. 328 (S.Ct. 1950) - SUBSTANTIALLY, DOCTRINE OF EQUIVALENTS

In re Graves, 69 F.3d 1147, 36 U.S.P.Q.2d 1697 (Fed. Cir. 1995) - ANTICIPATION, BPAI, JURISDICTION OF THE CAFC

Great Northern Corp. v. Davis Core & Pad Co., 226 U.S.P.Q. 540 (Ga. 1985) - ATTORNEY'S FEES, DAMAGES, EXCEPTIONAL, INEQUITABLE CONDUCT, OPINION OF COUNSEL, PREJUDGMENT INTEREST, WILLFUL INFRINGEMENT

Great Northern Corp. v. Henry Molded Products Inc., 39 U.S.P.Q.2d 1997 (Fed. Cir. 1996) - BEST MODE, PRODUCTION DETAIL

Green v. The Rich Iron Company Inc., 944 F.2d 852, 20 U.S.P.Q.2d 1075 (Fed. Cir. 1991) - REISSUE

Greenberg v. Ethicon Endo-Surgery Inc., 39 U.S.P.Q.2d 1783 (Fed. Cir. 1996) - MEANS

In re Greenfield and DuPont, 571 F.2d 1185, 197 U.S.P.Q. 227 (C.C.P.A. 1978) - COMMENSURATE IN SCOPE, OBJECTIVE EVIDENCE, STATEMENT IN THE SPECIFICATION

Greenwood v. Hattori Seiko Co. Ltd., 900 F.2d 238, 14 U.S.P.Q.2d 1474 (Fed. Cir. 1990) - INEQUITABLE CONDUCT, REEXAMINATION, VALIDITY

Greenwood v. Seiko Instruments & Electronics Ltd., 711 F. Supp. 30, 13 U.S.P.Q.2d 1245 (D.C. 1989) - DUTY TO DISCLOSE, WILLFUL

Grefco Inc. v. Kewanee Industries, Inc., 499 F. Supp. 844, 208 U.S.P.Q. 218 (Del. 1980) - CANDOR, CONDUCT, TEST, TEST RESULTS

In re Gregg, 244 F.2d 316, 113 U.S.P.Q. 526 (C.C.P.A. 1957) - 35 U.S.C. §102(e)

Grid Systems Corp. v. Texas Instruments Inc., 771 F. Supp. 1033, 20 U.S.P.Q.2d 1207 (Cal. 1991) - SHERMAN ACT

In re Grier, 342 F.2d 120, 144 U.S.P.Q. 654 (C.C.P.A. 1965) - JURISDICTION

-*H*-

Ex parte Hageman, 179 U.S.P.Q. 747 (PTO Bd. App. 1972) - ARGUMENT, DUE PROCESS, EXAMINER'S OPINION, MERIT, NOTICE, REASON, 35 U.S.C. §132

Hahn v. Wong, 13 U.S.P.Q.2d 1211 (B.P.A.I. 1989) - CORROBORATION, GOOD CAUSE

Hahn v. Wong, 892 F.2d 1028, 13 U.S.P.Q.2d 1313 (Fed. Cir. 1989) - CORROBORATION, GOOD CAUSE, INTERFERENCE, ORDER TO SHOW CAUSE, PRIORITY

Ex parte Hall, 83 U.S.P.Q. 38 (Bd. App. 1948) - SUCH AS

In re Hall, 168 F.2d 92, 77 U.S.P.Q. 618 (C.C.P.A. 1948) - SPACE

In re Hall, 781 F.2d 897, 228 U.S.P.Q. 453 (Fed. Cir. 1986) - DOCTORAL THESIS, PRINTED PUBLICATION, PUBLICATION

Hall v. Aqua Queen Manufacturing Inc., 93 F.3d 1548, 39 U.S.P.Q.2d 1925 (Fed. Cir. 1996) - POVERTY, REPRESENTATION

Hall v. Taylor, 332 F.2d 844, 141 U.S.P.Q. 821 (C.C.P.A. 1964) - COPYING CLAIMS, DISCLOSURE, ESSENCE, INTERFERENCE, SUPPORT

Halliburton Co. v. Schlumberger Technology Corp., 925 F.2d 1435, 17 U.S.P.Q.2d 1834 (Fed. Cir. 1991) - INTENT

Halliburton Oil Well Cementing Co. v. Walker, 146 F.2d 817, 64 U.S.P.Q. 278 (9th Cir. 1944) - MENTAL STEPS

Hallmark Cards Inc. v. Lehman, 959 F. Supp. 539, 42 U.S.P.Q.2d 1134 (D.C. 1997) - CERTIFICATE OF CORRECTION, INTERVENOR

In re Hamilton, 882 F.2d 1576, 11 U.S.P.Q.2d 1890 (Fed. Cir. 1989) - EXPERIMENTAL USE, GRACE PERIOD

In re Hammack, 427 F.2d 1378, 166 U.S.P.Q. 204 (C.C.P.A. 1970) - 35 U.S.C. §112

Hanagan v. Kimura, 16 U.S.P.Q.2d 1791 (Commr. Patents & Trademarks 1990) - EXPERT TESTIMONY, INTERFERENCE, MOTION, TEST, WITNESS

Handgards, Inc. v. Ethicon, Inc., 601 F.2d 986, 202 U.S.P.Q. 342 (9th Cir. 1979), *cert. denied*, 444 U.S. 1025, 204 U.S.P.Q. 880 (1980) - PRESUMPTION OF INFRINGEMENT, STATE LAW

Ex parte Hansen, 10 U.S.P.Q.2d 1399 (B.P.A.I. 1988) - DESIGN

Hansgirg v. Kemmer, 102 F.2d 212, 40 U.S.P.Q. 665 (C.C.P.A. 1939) - INHERENCY, POSSIBILITY, PROBABILITY

Ex parte Harita, 1 U.S.P.Q.2d 1887 (B.P.A.I. 1986) - MATERIALITY, REISSUE

In re Harita, 847 F.2d 801, 6 U.S.P.Q.2d 1930 (Fed. Cir. 1988) - DUTY TO DISCLOSE, FAILURE TO DISCLOSE, INTENT TO MISLEAD, MATERIALITY

In re Harmon, 222 F.2d 743, 106 U.S.P.Q. 101 (C.C.P.A. 1955) - PREAMBLE

In re Harnisch, 631 F.2d 716, 206 U.S.P.Q. 300 (C.C.P.A. 1980) - CLASSIFICATION, IMPROPER MARKUSH, MARKUSH, NUCLEUS, REPUGNANT, STRUCTURAL SIMILARITY, UNITY OF INVENTION

Harnsberger v. Youker, 109 F.2d 806, 44 U.S.P.Q. 534 (C.C.P.A. 1940) - REASSERT CANCELLED SUBJECT MATTER

Harpman v. Watson, 181 F. Supp. 919, 124 U.S.P.Q. 169 (D.C. 1959) - 35 U.S.C. §145

Harris-Hub Company, Inc. v. Lear Siegler, Inc., 179 U.S.P.Q. 469 (Ill. 1973) - RECONSTRUCTION

Ex parte Harrison, 1925 C.D. 122 (Commr. Patents 1924) - ASSIGNEE

Hart v. Baarcke, 396 F. Supp. 408, 186 U.S.P.Q. 275 (Fla. 1975) - RIDICULE, SCOFF-ING, SKEPTICISM

Ex parte Hartmann, 186 U.S.P.Q. 366 (PTO Bd. App. 1974) - CCPA, COMBINING REFERENCES, DESTROY, MPEP, PRODUCT BY PROCESS

Ex parte Hartop, 139 U.S.P.Q. 525 (PO Bd. App. 1962) - CHANGE IN FORM, COLOR, PURITY, STABILITY

In re Hartop and Brandes, 311 F.2d 249, 135 U.S.P.Q. 419 (C.C.P.A. 1962) - SAFETY

Ex parte Harvey, 163 U.S.P.Q. 572 (PTO Bd. App. 1968) - DOCKET NUMBER, NEW MATTER

Ex parte Harvey, 3 U.S.P.Q.2d 1626 (B.P.A.I. 1986) - DESCRIPTION, POSSESSION, SUPPORT

In re Harvey, 12 F.3d 1061, 29 U.S.P.Q.2d 1206 (Fed. Cir. 1993) - DESIGN

In re Harza, 274 F.2d 669, 124 U.S.P.Q. 378 (C.C.P.A. 1960) - DUPLICATION OF PARTS

Ex parte Hasche, 86 U.S.P.Q. 481 (Bd. App. 1949) - SUCH AS

Haskell, Hench, and Yates v. Colebourne, Rolfe, McAloon, and Orton, 671 F.2d 1362, 213 U.S.P.Q. 192 (C.C.P.A. 1982) - CONCEPTION

Hassel v. Chrysler Corp., 982 F. Supp. 515, 43 U.S.P.Q.2d 1554 (Ohio 1997) - DICTION-ARY, DOCTRINE OF EQUIVALENTS

Ex parte Hata, 6 U.S.P.Q.2d 1652 (B.P.A.I. 1987) - DEPOSIT

Hauni Werke Koerber & Co., KG. v. Molins Limited, 183 U.S.P.Q. 168 (Va. 1974) - CONTRIBUTORY INFRINGEMENT, FOREIGN CORPORATION, INDUCE, INTENT, 28 U.S.C. §1391(d)

Hauptschein, Braid, and Lawlor v. McCane and Robinson, 339 F.2d 460, 144 U.S.P.Q. 16 (C.C.P.A. 1964) - IDENTIFICATION, ISOLATED, SEPARATION

In re Hawkins, 486 F.2d 579, 179 U.S.P.Q. 163 (C.C.P.A. 1973) - FOREIGN PATENT APPLICATION, NEW MATTER

Haworth Inc. v. Herman Miller Inc., 30 U.S.P.Q.2d 1555 (Mich. 1994) - LACHES

Haworth Inc. v. Herman Miller Inc., 37 U.S.P.Q.2d 1094 (Mich. 1995) - REVERSAL

Haworth Inc. v. Steelcase Inc., 26 U.S.P.Q.2d 1152 (Mich. 1993) - ALTERNATIVE DISPUTE RESOLUTION, PROTECTIVE ORDER

Haworth Inc. v. Steelcase Inc., 43 U.S.P.Q.2d 1223 (Mich. 1996) - INVENTORSHIP

In re Hayes Microcomputer Products Inc. Patent Litigation, 982 F.2d 1527, 25 U.S.P.Q.2d 1241 (Fed. Cir. 1992) - ADVICE OF COUNSEL, BEST MODE, DESCRIPTION, OPINION LETTER, SUPPORT

In re Hayashibara and Sugimoto, 525 F.2d 1062, 188 U.S.P.Q. 4 (C.C.P.A. 1975) - ASSERTION

Haynes International Inc. v. Jessop Steel Co., 8 F.3d 1573, 28 U.S.P.Q.2d 1652 (Fed. Cir. 1993) - DOCTRINE OF EQUIVALENTS, PRIMA FACIE, PROSECUTION HIS-TORY ESTOPPEL

Hazani v. U.S. International Trade Commission, 126 F.3d 1473, 44 U.S.P.Q.2d 1358 (Fed. Cir. 1997) - INTEGRAL

Hazeltine Research v. Brenner, 382 U.S. 252, 147 U.S.P.Q. 429 (1965) - COPENDING REFERENCE, SECRET

Hazeltine Research, Inc. v. Zenith Radio Corporation, 239 F. Supp. 51, 144 U.S.P.Q. 381 (Ill. 1965) - POOLING, PRIOR ART

Hercules Incorporated v. Exxon Corporation, 434 F. Supp. 136, 196 U.S.P.Q. 401 (Del. 1977) - WORK-PRODUCT PRIVILEGE

Hercules Incorporated v. Exxon Corporation, 497 F. Supp. 661, 207 U.S.P.Q. 1088 (Del. 1980) - FRAUD, UNITY OF INVENTION

Hercules Incorporated v. Union Carbide Corporation, 168 U.S.P.Q. 394 (D.C. 1971) - REMAND (GROUNDS FOR)

In re Heritage, 182 F.2d 639, 86 U.S.P.Q. 160 (C.C.P.A. 1950) - ABANDONED APPLICATION, ACCESS, REFERENCE

In re Herr, 377 F.2d 610, 153 U.S.P.Q. 548 (C.C.P.A. 1967) - APPLICANT'S RIGHTS, *QUID PRO QUO, RES JUDICATA*

In re Herrick, Conger, and Savio, 115 U.S.P.Q. 412 (Commr. Patents 1957) - SPECIES

In re Herrick and Bock, 344 F.2d 713, 145 U.S.P.Q. 400 (C.C.P.A. 1965) - MULTIPLE REJECTIONS

In re Herschler, 591 F.2d 693, 200 U.S.P.Q. 711 (C.C.P.A. 1979) - CONVERSION, DESCRIPTION, *IN HAEC VERBA*, NEW MATTER, PREDICTABILITY, USE

In re Herz, 537 F.2d 549, 190 U.S.P.Q. 461 (C.C.P.A. 1976) - CONSISTING ESSENTIALLY OF

Hester v. Allgeier, 193 U.S.P.Q. 54 (Comm'r 1976) - RECONSIDERATION

Hester v. Meguro and Kuwada, 190 U.S.P.Q. 231 (PTO Bd. Pat. Intf. 1975) - DOSAGE, HOST

Hester Industries Inc. v. Stein Inc., 40 U.S.P.Q.2d 1844 (Va. 1996) - TRANSFER, 28 U.S.C. 1404(a)

Hester Industries Inc. v. Stein Inc., 43 U.S.P.Q.2d 1236 (Va. 1997) - INTENT, REISSUE

Hester Industries Inc. v. Stein Inc., 142 F.3d 1472, 46 U.S.P.Q.2d 1641 (Fed. Cir. 1998) - ERROR, "ORIGINAL PATENT" CLAUSE, RECAPTURE

Hewlett Packard Co. v. Bausch & Lomb, Inc., 8 U.S.P.Q.2d 1177 (Cal. 1988) - REISSUE

Hewlett-Packard Co. v. Bausch & Lomb Inc., 882 F.2d 1556, 11 U.S.P.Q.2d 1750 (Fed. Cir. 1989), *cert. denied*, 493 U.S. 1076 (1990) - DAMAGES, DISQUALIFICATION, INEQUITABLE CONDUCT, MISCONDUCT, REISSUE

Hewlett Packard Co. v. Bausch & Lomb Inc., 722 F. Supp. 595, 13 U.S.P.Q.2d 1105 (Cal. 1989) - INDEMNIFICATION AGREEMENT

Hewlett-Packard Co. v. Bausch & Lomb Inc., 746 F. Supp. 1413, 14 U.S.P.Q.2d 1906 (Cal. 1990) - WRONGFUL INTENT

Hewlett-Packard Co. v. Bausch & Lomb Inc., 909 F.2d 1464, 15 U.S.P.Q.2d 1525 (Fed. Cir. 1990) - APPARATUS, INDUCE

Hewlett-Packard Co. v. Pitney Bowes Corp., 46 U.S.P.Q.2d 1595 (Ore. 1998) - IMPLIED LICENSE

Hewlett-Packard Co. v. Repeat-O-Type Stencil Manufacturing Corp., 123 F.3d 1445, 43 U.S.P.Q.2d 1650 (Fed. Cir. 1997) - IMPLIED LICENSE, INCLUDING, INTENT, PURCHASER

Hexcel Corp. v. Advanced Textiles Inc., 716 F. Supp. 974, 12 U.S.P.Q.2d 1390 (Tex. 1989) - ASSIGNOR ESTOPPEL

Ex parte Heymes, 30 U.S.P.Q.2d 1237 (B.P.A.I. 1993) - INTERMEDIATE

H.H. Robertson Company v. Barger Metal Fabricating Co., 225 U.S.P.Q. 1191 (Ohio 1984) - BEST MODE, SUFFICIENCY OF DISCLOSURE

Ex parte Hibberd, 227 U.S.P.Q. 443 (B.P.A.I. 1985) - DEPOSITORY, PLANT, SEED, TISSUE CULTURE

In re Higgins and Le Suer, 369 F.2d 414, 152 U.S.P.Q. 103 (C.C.P.A. 1966) - COPENDING PATENT, DOUBLE PATENTING

High Tech Medical Instrumentation Inc. v. New Image Industries Inc., 49 F.3d 1551, 33 U.S.P.Q.2d 2005 (Fed. Cir. 1995) - IRREPARABLE HARM, PRELIMINARY INJUNCTION

Ex parte Hildebrand, 15 U.S.P.Q.2d 1662 (B.P.A.I. 1990) - BUDAPEST TREATY

Hilleby v. FMC Corp., 25 U.S.P.Q.2d 1423 (Cal. 1992) - ENTIRE MARKET VALUE RULE, LEXICOGRAPHY

Ex parte Hillyer and Nicewander, 102 U.S.P.Q. 126 (PO Bd. App. 1953) - UNRECOGNIZED

In re Hilmer, Korger, Weyer, and Aumuller, 359 F.2d 859, 149 U.S.P.Q. 480 (C.C.P.A. 1966) - EFFECTIVE DATE, FOREIGN KNOWLEDGE, PRIORITY, 35 U.S.C. §102(e)

In re Hilmer, Korger, Weyer and Aumuller, 424 F.2d 1108, 165 U.S.P.Q. 255 (C.C.P.A. 1970) - 35 U.S.C. §104

Hilton Davis Chemical Co. v. Warner-Jenkinson Co. Inc., 62 F.3d 1512, 35 U.S.P.Q.2d 1641 (Fed. Cir. 1995), *cert. granted*, 116 S.Ct. 1014 (1996) - APPROPRIATE, CLAIM CONSTRUCTION, DOCTRINE OF EQUIVALENTS, FILE WRAPPER ESTOPPEL, INDEPENDENT DEVELOPMENT, JURY INSTRUCTIONS, RE-CAPTURE, SCOPE

Hilton Davis Chemical Co. v. Warner-Jenkinson Co., 43 U.S.P.Q.2d 1152 (Fed. Cir. 1997) - AMENDMENT, PRESUMPTION

Hirschfeld v. Banner, 462 F. Supp. 135, 200 U.S.P.Q. 276 (D.C. 1978) - BLOCK DIAGRAM, CONVENTIONAL

Hitachi Metals Ltd. v. Quigg, 20 U.S.P.Q.2d 1920 (D.C. 1991) - REISSUE

In re Hitchings, Elion, and Goodman, 342 F.2d 80, 144 U.S.P.Q. 637 (C.C.P.A. 1965) - HOW TO USE

H.K. Porter Company, Inc. v. The Gates Rubber Company, 187 U.S.P.Q. 692 (Colo. 1975) - FOREIGN, SAME INVENTION

H.M. Chase Corp. v. Idaho Potato Processors, Inc., 185 U.S.P.Q. 106, 529 P.2d 1270 (Idaho 1974) - APPROXIMATELY, VAGUE

In re Hobbs, 165 U.S.P.Q. 99 (Atomic Energy Commission 1970) - OVERCLAIMING

Hobbs v. United States Atomic Energy Commission, 451 F.2d 849, 171 U.S.P.Q. 713 (5th Cir. 1971) - DEVELOPMENT, RESEARCH

In re Hodler, 73 F.2d 507, 23 U.S.P.Q. 317 (C.C.P.A. 1934) - COMBINATION, DEVICE, MATERIAL

Hodosh v. Block Drug Co., 786 F.2d 1136, 229 U.S.P.Q. 182 (Fed. Cir. 1985) - HYPOTHETICAL PERSON, SECONDARY CONSIDERATIONS

Hoechst Aktiengesellschaft v. Quigg, 724 F. Supp. 398, 13 U.S.P.Q.2d 1543 (Va. 1989); *reversed and remanded*, 16 U.S.P.Q.2d 1549 (Fed. Cir. 1990) - PATENT TERM EXTENSION

Hoechst Aktiengesellschaft v. Quigg, 917 F.2d 522, 16 U.S.P.Q.2d 1549 (Fed. Cir. 1990) - REGULATORY REVIEW PERIOD, STATUTORY CONSTRUCTION

Hoechst Celanese Corp. v. BP Chemicals Ltd., 846 F. Supp. 542, 31 U.S.P.Q.2d 1825 (Tex. 1994) - OBVIOUSNESS, REEXAMINATION

Hoechst Celanese Corp. v. BP Chemicals Ltd., 78 F.3d 1575, 38 U.S.P.Q.2d 1126 (Fed. Cir. 1996) - INFRINGEMENT, JUDGMENT AFTER TRIAL, PATENTABLY DISTINCT INVENTIONS, REEXAMINATION

Hoechst Marion Roussel Inc. v. Par Pharmaceutical Inc., 39 U.S.P.Q.2d 1363 (N.J. 1996 - unpublished) - JURY DEMAND, JURY TRIAL

Hoechst-Roussel Pharmaceuticals Inc. v. Lehman, 42 U.S.P.Q.2d 1220, *concurring opinion* 1227 (Fed. Cir. 1997) - CONVERSION (*in situ* or *in vivo*)

In re Hoeksema, 332 F.2d 374, 141 U.S.P.Q. 733 (C.C.P.A. 1964) - CHEMICAL, METHOD OF MAKING

In re Hoeksema, 399 F.2d 269, 158 U.S.P.Q. 596 (C.C.P.A. 1968) - MAKE

Hoeltke v. C.M. Kemp Manufacturing Co., 80 F.2d 912, 26 U.S.P.Q. 114 (4th Cir. 1935), *cert. denied*, 298 U.S. 673 (1936) - DAMAGES, INFRINGEMENT, UNJUST ENRICHMENT

Ex parte Hoffman, 12 U.S.P.Q.2d 1061 (B.P.A.I. 1989) - CONSISTING ESSENTIALLY OF

Hoffman v. Blaski, 363 U.S. 336 (1960) - VENUE

Hoffman v. Klaus, 9 U.S.P.Q.2d 1657 (B.P.A.I. 1988) - SCREENING

Hoffman v. Wisner Classic Manufacturing Co. Inc., 40 U.S.P.Q.2d 1271 (N.Y. 1996) - DISMISSAL, MOTION TO DISMISS

Hoffmann-La Roche Inc. v. Lemmon Co., 13 U.S.P.Q.2d 1224 (Pa. 1989), *vacated and remanded*, 906 F.2d 684, 15 U.S.P.Q.2d 1363 (Fed. Cir. 1990) - ATTORNEY'S FEES

Hoffmann-La Roche Inc. v. Lemmon Co., 906 F.2d 684, 15 U.S.P.Q.2d 1363 (Fed. Cir. 1990) - INTENT TO DECEIVE

Hoffmann-La Roche, Inc. v. Premo Pharmaceutical Laboratories, Inc., 210 U.S.P.Q. 374 (N.J. 1980) - TREBLE DAMAGES

In re Hofmann, 95 F.2d 257, 37 U.S.P.Q. 222 (C.C.P.A. 1938) - SHAPE

In re Hogan and Banks, 559 F.2d 595, 194 U.S.P.Q. 527 (C.C.P.A. 1977) - ASSERTION, BASIC INVENTION OR PATENT, BREADTH, BURDEN, CONTINUING APPLICATION, CRYSTALLINE, DESCRIPTION, DISCLOSURE, DOMINANT PATENT, ENABLEMENT, EVIDENCE, INTERVENING REFERENCES, KNOWLEDGE (LATER DISCOVERED), LATE CLAIMING, LATER DISCOVERIES, PARTICULARITY, PIONEER INVENTION, PROMOTE PROGRESS, SAME EFFECT, SCOPE OF ENABLEMENT, STATE OF THE ART, SYMMETRY IN THE LAW, 35 U.S.C. §112, 35 U.S.C. §120

Hoganas AB v. Dresser Industries Inc., 9 F.3d 948, 28 U.S.P.Q.2d 1936 (Fed. Cir. 1993) - JUDICIAL NOTICE

In re Holladay, 584 F.2d 384, 199 U.S.P.Q. 516 (C.C.P.A. 1978) - ASSERTION, COMPARATIVE TEST DATA

Hollister Inc. v. Coloplast AIS, 16 U.S.P.Q.2d 1718 (Ill. 1990) - LONG-ARM STATUTE

Holloway v. Quigg, 9 U.S.P.Q.2d 1751 (D.C. 1988) - DE NOVO, EVIDENCE, TRIAL DE NOVO

In re Holmes, 37 F.2d 440, 4 U.S.P.Q. 179 (C.C.P.A. 1930) - METHOD, REPORTING

Holmes v. Securities Investor Protection Corp., 503 U.S. 258 (1992) - DAMAGES

Holmes v. The Thew Shovel Company, 162 U.S.P.Q. 559 (Ohio 1969) - ATTORNEY'S FEES, CONFIDENTIAL RELATIONSHIP

Holmes, Faber, Boykin, and Francis v. Kelly, Hornberger, and Strief, 586 F.2d 234, 199 U.S.P.Q. 778 (C.C.P.A. 1978) - APPEAL, BPAI, COPYING CLAIMS, PERSUASION, PROOF, PTO, RIGHT TO MAKE

Holmwood v. Cherpeck, 2 U.S.P.Q.2d 1942 (B.P.A.I. 1986) - 37 C.F.R. §1.608(b), CONCEALMENT

Hologic Inc. v. Lunar Corp., 36 U.S.P.Q.2d 1182 (Mass. 1995) - ADVERTISING, INFRINGEMENT, PERSONAL JURISDICTION, PROMOTION, SUBJECT MATTER JURISDICTION

Ex parte Holt, 19 U.S.P.Q.2d 1211 (B.P.A.I. 1991) - ALTERNATIVE, BPAI, DISCLOSURE, *IPSIS VERBIS*

Honeywell, Inc. v. Diamond, 499 F. Supp. 924, 208 U.S.P.Q. 452 (D.C. 1980) - DELAY, EARLY DISCLOSURE, NEW MATTER

Honeywell Inc. v. Sperry Rand Corporation, 180 U.S.P.Q. 673 (Minn. 1973) - BROADEN, DAMAGES, DISCRIMINATORY, DISCRIMINATORY LICENSING, EXPERIMENTAL USE, FRAUD, GOOD FAITH, MISUSE, PROOF, SHERMAN ACT

In re Honn and Sims, 364 F.2d 454, 150 U.S.P.Q. 652 (C.C.P.A. 1966) - BEST MODE, KNOWLEDGE

Ex parte Hoogendam, 40 U.S.P.Q. 389, 1939 C.D. 3 (Commr. Patents 1939) - FINAL REJECTION, SECONDARY REFERENCE

The Hoover Company v. Mitchell Manufacturing Company, 269 F.2d 795, 122 U.S.P.Q. 314 (7th Cir, 1959) - LENGTHY PROSECUTION

Hoover Group Inc. v. Custom Metalcraft Inc., 66 F.3d 299, 36 U.S.P.Q.2d 1101 (Fed. Cir. 1995) - STANDARD OF REVIEW

Hoover Group Inc. v. Custom Metalcraft Inc., 38 U.S.P.Q.2d 1860 (Fed. Cir. 1996) - CORPORATE OFFICER

Hoppe v. Baxter Healthcare Corp., 878 F. Supp. 303, 34 U.S.P.Q.2d 1619 (Mass. 1995) - GENUINE, IMPLIED LICENSE, MATERIAL, SUMMARY JUDGMENT

In re Horn, Horn, Horn, and Horn, 203 U.S.P.Q. 969 (C.C.P.A. 1979) - PROBLEM, REFERENCE, SIMPLICITY

Horphag Research Ltd. v. Consac Industries Inc., 42 U.S.P.Q.2d 1567 (Fed. Cir. 1997) - ASSIGNMENT

Ex parte Horton, 226 U.S.P.Q. 697 (B.P.A.I. 1985) - ADMISSION, DRAWINGS, REEXAMINATION

Horton v. Stevens, 7 U.S.P.Q.2d 1245 (B.P.A.I. 1988) - CORROBORATION, SELF-SERVING, SHOP-BOOK RULE

In re Hotchkin, 223 F.2d 490, 106 U.S.P.Q. 267 (C.C.P.A. 1955) - RESULT

Hotchkiss v. Greenwood, 11 How. 248, 52 U.S. 248 (1850) - INVENTION

In re Hotte, 475 F.2d 644, 177 U.S.P.Q. 326 (C.C.P.A. 1973) - INTEGRAL

In re Hounsfield, 669 F.2d 1320, 216 U.S.P.Q. 1045 (C.C.P.A. 1983) - INTENT TO CLAIM

Ex parte Howard, 1924 C.D. 75, 328 O.G. 251 (Asst. Comm'r 1922) - MANUFACTURE, TRANSITORY

In re Howarth, 654 F.2d 103, 210 U.S.P.Q. 689 (C.C.P.A. 1981) - DISCLOSURE,

INCORPORATE BY REFRENCE, PATENT, REFERENCE, SUFFICIENCY OF DISCLOSURE

Howes v. Medical Components Inc., 741 F. Supp. 528, 17 U.S.P.Q.2d 1591 (Pa. 1990) - ATTORNEY'S FEES

Howes v. Medical Components Inc., 741 F. Supp. 528, 16 U.S.P.Q.2d 1671 (Pa. 1990) - CLAIM CONSTRUCTION

Howes v. Zircon Corp., 992 F. Supp. 957, 47 U.S.P.Q.2d 1617 (Ill. 1998) - DEFINITION, MEANING

Ex parte Hozumi, 3 U.S.P.Q.2d 1059 (B.P.A.I. 1984) - MARKUSH, UNITY OF INVENTION

In re Application of Hozumi, 226 U.S.P.Q. 353 (Commr. Patents & Trademarks 1985) - CANCELLATION, CANCELLATION FROM DISCLOSURE, CANCER, PREDICTABILITY, SPECULATION, STATEMENT, STATEMENT IN DISCLOSURE, TRUTH, UNBELIEVABLE, UNPREDICTABLE ART

Ex parte Hradcovsky, 214 U.S.P.Q. 554 (PTO Bd. App. 1982) - INOPERATIVE EMBODIMENTS, NEGATIVE LIMITATION, UNEXPECTED RESULTS

H. Robertson Co. v. United Steel Deck, Inc., 820 F.2d 384, 2 U.S.P.Q.2d 1926 (Fed. Cir. 1987) - BURDEN, DAMAGES, EXCLUSIVE RIGHT, MONETARY DAMAGES, PRELIMINARY INJUNCTION, PRESUMPTION OF IRREPARABLE HARM, PRESUMPTION OF VALIDITY, RIGHT TO EXCLUDE

In re Huang, 40 U.S.P.Q.2d 1685 (Fed. Cir. 1996) - COMMERCIAL SUCCESS

Huang v. Auto-Shade Inc., 41 U.S.P.Q.2d 1053 (Cal. 1966) - *MARKMAN* TRIAL

Hubbell Inc. v. Pass & Seymour Inc., 94 Civ. 7631, 35 U.S.P.Q.2d 1760 (N.Y. 1995) - DESIGN, TRADE DRESS

Huck Manufacturing Company v. Textron, Inc., 187 U.S.P.Q. 388 (Mich. 1975) - INFRINGEMENT

Hughes and Smith v. Windholz, Patchett, and Fried, 184 U.S.P.Q. 753 (PO Bd. Pat. Intf. 1974) - HUMAN USE, STANDARD LABORATORY ANIMAL, TESTING

Hughes Aircraft Company v. General Instrument Corporation, 374 F. Supp. 1166, 182 U.S.P.Q. 11 (Del. 1974) - INOPERATIVE, MOSITA

Hughes Aircraft Co. v. United States, 717 F.2d 1351, 219 U.S.P.Q. 473 (Fed. Cir. 1983) - CLAIM INTERPRETATION, EQUIVALENCE, FILE WRAPPER ESTOPPEL

Hughes Aircraft Co. v. U.S., 29 Fed.Cl. 197, 29 U.S.P.Q.2d 1974 (U.S. Ct. Fed. Cl. 1993) - SPACE, UNITED STATES, USE

Hughes Aircraft Co. v. U.S., 31 Fed.Cl. 481, 35 U.S.P.Q.2d 1243 (U.S. Ct. Fed. Cl. 1994) - INTEREST, REASONABLE AND ENTIRE COMPENSATION, REASONABLE ROYALTY, UNITED STATES GOVERNMENT

Hughes Aircraft Co. v. U.S., 47 U.S.P.Q.2d 1542 (Fed. Cir. 1998) - DOCTRINE OF EQUIVALENTS

Hughes Tool Co. v. Dresser Indus., Inc., 816 F.2d 1549, 2 U.S.P.Q.2d 1396 (Fed. Cir.), *cert denied*, 484 U.S. 914 (1987) - COMMERCIAL SUCCESS

Hugh W. Batcheller v. Henry Cole Co., 7 F. Supp. 898, 22 U.S.P.Q. 354 (Mass. 1934) - COMBINATION, EQUIVALENT, EQUIVALENTS, FORM, INFRINGEMENT, MATERIAL, NAME, PROPORTIONS, SAME, SHAPE, SUBSTITUTION

Hunter v. Beissbarth, 15 U.S.P.Q.2d 1343 (Commr. Patents & Trademarks 1990) - TERMINATION OF PROCEEDINGS

-J-

Imagineering Inc. v. Van Klassens Inc., 53 F.3d 1260, 34 U.S.P.Q.2d 1526 (Fed. Cir. 1995) - ABUSE OF DISCRETION

Imazio Nursery Inc. v. Dania Greenhouse, 29 U.S.P.Q.2d 1217 (Cal. 1992) - CLASSIFICATION, PLANT

Imazio Nursery Inc. v. Dania Greenhouses, 69 F.3d 1560, 36 U.S.P.Q.2d 1673 (Fed. Cir. 1995) - PLANT, 35 U.S.C. §161, VARIETY

Imperial Chemical Industries PLC v. Barr Laboratories, 87 Civ. 7833, 22 U.S.P.Q.2d 1906 (N.Y. 1992) - CANDOR, INEQUITABLE CONDUCT, TEST DATA

Imperial Chemical Industries PLC v. Danbury Pharmacal Inc., 745 F. Supp. 998, 18 U.S.P.Q.2d 1497 (Del. 1990) - STRUCTURAL SIMILARITY

Imperial Chemical Industries, PLC v. Henkel Corporation, 545 F. Supp. 635, 215 U.S.P.Q. 314 (Del. 1982) - TEST RESULTS

In re Incomplete Application filed November 28, 1958, 123 U.S.P.Q. 70 (Comm'r 1959) - 37 C.F.R. §1.84

Indiana General Corp. v. Krystinel Corp., 297 F. Supp. 427, 161 U.S.P.Q. 82 (N.Y. 1968) - BEST MODE

Indiana General Corporation v. Lockheed Aircraft Corporation, 249 F. Supp. 809, 148 U.S.P.Q. 312 (Cal. 1966) - THESIS

Indian Head Industries Inc. v. Ted Smith Equipment Co., 859 F. Supp. 1095, 36 U.S.P.Q.2d 1316 (Mich. 1994) - NEXUS, OBVIOUSNESS

Industrial Addition Assoc. v. Commissioner of Internal Revenue, 323 U.S. 310 (1945) - VENUE

Infinitech Inc. v. Vitrophage Inc., 30 U.S.P.Q.2d 1201 (Ill. 1994) - CASE OR CONTROVERSY, CONTROVERSY, FDA

Ingersoll-Rand Company v. Brunner & Lay, Inc., 474 F.2d 491, 177 U.S.P.Q. 112 (5th Cir. 1973) - DISADVANTAGE

Ingersoll-Rand Co. v. Ciavatta, 8 U.S.P.Q.2d 1537, 542 A.2d 879, 110 N.J. 609 (N.J. S.Ct.1988) - EMPLOYEE, EMPLOYMENT AGREEMENT, HOLDOVER CLAUSE, POST-EMPLOYMENT INVENTION, SHOP RIGHT, TRAILER CLAUSE

Ingersoll-Rand Co. v. Joy Manufacturing Co., 185 U.S.P.Q. 21 (Ga. 1975) - COMPLAINT

Ex parte Inoue, 217 U.S.P.Q. 461 (PTO Bd. App. 1981) - COPYING CLAIMS, REFUSING TO COPY CLAIMS

Insta-Foam Products, Inc. v. Universal Foam Systems, Inc., 906 F.2d 698, 15 U.S.P.Q.2d 1295 (Fed. Cir. 1990) - PROSECUTION HISTORY ESTOPPEL

Intel Corp. v. International Trade Commission, 946 F.2d 821, 20 U.S.P.Q.2d 1161 (Fed. Cir. 1991) - ASSIGNOR ESTOPPEL, CLAIM, EQUIVALENT, PRIVITY

Intel Corp. v. Lehman, 47 U.S.P.Q.2d 1221 (Cal. 1997) - PUBLIC USE PROCEEDING

Intellicall Inc. v. Phonometrics Inc., 952 F.2d 1384, 21 U.S.P.Q.2d 1383 (Fed. Cir. 1992) - CLAIM INTERPRETATION, INFRINGEMENT, LEXICOGRAPHER, SUMMARY JUDGMENT

Interconnect Planning Corp. v. Feil, 774 F.2d 1132, 227 U.S.P.Q. 543 (Fed. Cir. 1985) - BLUEPRINT, COMBINING REFERENCES

InterDigital Technology Corp. v. OKI America Inc., 866 F. Supp. 212, 32 U.S.P.Q.2d 1850 (Pa. 1994) - CLAIM PRECLUSION, ISSUE PRECLUSION

Ex parte Isshiki, Kijima and Watanabe, 36 U.S.P.Q.2d 1863 (B.P.A.I. 1993 - unpublished) - GENERALIZATION, 35 U.S.C.103

ITT Corp. v. United States, 17 Cl. Ct. 199, 11 U.S.P.Q.2d 1657 (U.S.Cl.Ct. 1989) - ENTIRE-MARKET-VALUE RULE, ROYALTY

In re Iwahashi, 888 F.2d 1370, 12 U.S.P.Q.2d 1908 (Fed. Cir. 1989) - CONSTRUE, MEANS PLUS FUNCTION

-J-

J&J Manufacturing Inc. v. Logan, 48 U.S.P.Q.2d 1412 (Texas 1998) - 35 U.S.C. §256

In re Jabour, 182 F.2d 213, 86 U.S.P.Q. 98 (C.C.P.A. 1950) - DESIGN

Ex parte Jackson, 110 U.S.P.Q. 561 (PTO Bd. App. 1956) - RANGE

Ex parte Jackson, Theriault, Sinclair, Fager, and Karwowski, 217 U.S.P.Q. 804 (PTO Bd. App. 1982) - BACTERIA, DEPOSIT, ENABLEMENT, METABOLIC PROPERTY, MICROORGANISM, PROCESS, PROPORTIONS, SPECIES, STRAIN, SUPPORT

Jackson v. Washington Monthly Co., 569 F.2d 119 (D.C. Cir. 1977) - ATTORNEY

Jackson Jordan, Inc. v. Plasser American Corp., 219 U.S.P.Q. 922 (Va. 1983) - CANDOR, SHERMAN ACT

Jack Winter, Inc. v. Koratron Company, Inc., 50 F.R.D. 225, 166 U.S.P.Q. 295 (Cal. 1970) - DISCRETION

Jack Winter Inc. v. Koratron Co., 54 F.R.D. 44, 172 U.S.P.Q. 201 (Cal. 1971) - PRIVILEGE

Jack Winter, Inc. v. Koratron Company, Inc., 375 F. Supp. 1, 181 U.S.P.Q. 353 (Cal. 1974) - EXPERT TESTIMONY, SIMILARITY

Jacobs v. Sohl, 280 F.2d 140, 126 U.S.P.Q. 399 (C.C.P.A. 1960) - CONCEPTION, RECOLLECTION

Jacobs Wind Electric Co. Inc. v. Florida Department of Transportation, 919 F.2d 726, 16 U.S.P.Q.2d 1972 (Fed. Cir. 1990) - STATE

Jacobs Wind Electric Co. Inc. v. Florida Department of Transportation, 626 So.2d 1333, 29 U.S.P.Q.2d 1763, 1764 (Fla. S.Ct. 1993) - PREEMPTION, STATE

J.A. LaPorte, Inc. v. Norfolk Dredging Company, 625 F. Supp. 36, 227 U.S.P.Q. 382 (Va. 1985) - PHOTOGRAPH

In re James, 432 F.2d 473, 167 U.S.P.Q. 403 (C.C.P.A. 1970) - DECISION, REJECTION

Jamesbury Corporation v. United States, 183 U.S.P.Q. 484 (U.S. Ct. Cl. 1974) - FILE WRAPPER ESTOPPEL, RECAPTURE

James River Corp. of Virginia v. Hallmark Cards Inc., 43 U.S.P.Q.2d 1422 (Wis. 1997) - CLAIM CONSTRUCTION, CLARIFICATION, DOCTRINE OF EQUIVALENTS, EQUIVALENCY, INTENT, PARTICULARITY, PRECISION, REASON

In re Janakirama Rao, 317 F.2d 951, 137 U.S.P.Q. 893 (C.C.P.A. 1963) - ESSENTIALLY

Ex parte Janin, 209 U.S.P.Q. 761 (PTO Bd. App. 1979) - COMBINATION, CONTINUATION-IN-PART APPLICATION, CONTINUING APPLICATION, SUPPORT, TRANSFER

In re Japikse, 181 F.2d 1019, 86 U.S.P.Q. 70 (C.C.P.A. 1950) - REARRANGING PARTS

Jaskiewicz v. Mossinghoff, 822 F.2d 1053, 3 U.S.P.Q.2d 1294 (Fed. Cir. 1987) - EXECUTION OF PATENT APPLICATION

The Jeffrey Manufacturing Company v. Kingsland, Commissioner of Patents, 179 F.2d 35, 83 U.S.P.Q. 494 (D.C. Cir. 1949) - RES JUDICATA

Jennings v. Brenner, 255 F. Supp. 410, 150 U.S.P.Q. 167 (D.C. 1966) - CRITICAL

Jennmar Corp. v. Pattin Manufacturing Co., 20 U.S.P.Q.2d 1721 (Ohio 1991) - DRAWINGS, UNITY OF INVENTION

In re Jenoptik AG, 41 U.S.P.Q.2d 1950 (Fed. Cir. 1997 - *dissent*) - FOREIGN, 28 U.S.C. §1782 *Jeoffroy Mfg., Inc. v. Graham*, 206 F.2d 772, 98 U.S.P.Q. 424 (5th Cir. 1953) - DUPLICATION OF PARTS

In re Jerabek, 789 F.2d 886, 229 U.S.P.Q. 530 (Fed. Cir. 1986) - DUTY TO DISCLOSE, REISSUE

Jewish Hospital of St. Louis v. Idexx Laboratories, 42 U.S.P.Q.2d 1720 (Me. 1996) - EXAMINATION, SMALL ENTITY STATUS

The Johns Hopkins University v. CellPro, 160 F.R.D. 30, 34 U.S.P.Q.2d 1276 (Del. 1995) - BIFURCATION

The John Hopkins University v. Cellpro Inc., 47 U.S.P.Q.2d 1705 (Fed. Cir. 1998) - SUBSTANTIALLY

Johns-Manville Corp. v. Guardian Industries Inc., 718 F. Supp. 1310, 13 U.S.P.Q.2d 1684 (Mich. 1989) - PREJUDGMENT INTEREST, ROYALTY

In re Johnson, 282 F.2d 370, 127 U.S.P.Q. 216 (C.C.P.A. 1960) - FUNGICIDE, INSECTICIDE, USE, UTILITY

In re Johnson, 146 U.S.P.Q. 547 (Commr. Patents 1965) - CERTIFICATE OF CORRECTION, 37 C.F.R. §1.322, TRADEMARK

In re Johnson, 435 F.2d 585, 168 U.S.P.Q. 289 (C.C.P.A. 1971) - DATE, SOLUTION

In re Johnson, 230 U.S.P.Q. 240 (Comm'r 1984) - CONSENT DECREE, REEXAMINATION

In re Johnson and Farnham, 558 F.2d 1008, 194 U.S.P.Q. 187 (C.C.P.A. 1977) - APPLICANT'S RIGHTS, GENERIC, NARROWING CLAIM, PROMOTE PROGRESS, PROTECTION, REDUCTION IN SCOPE, SPECIFICATION, SUPPORT

Johnson, Nadeau, Nieuweboer, and Truett v. Bednar, Reid, and Yahiro, 201 U.S.P.Q. 919 (Comm'r of Patents and Trademarks 1976) - MATERIALITY

In re Johnston, 502 F.2d 765, 183 U.S.P.Q. 172, 183 (C.C.P.A. 1974) - COMPUTER

Johnston v. IVAC Corp., 885 F.2d 1574, 12 U.S.P.Q.2d 1382 (Fed. Cir. 1989) - ALL-ELEMENTS RULE, CLAIM INTERPRETATION, MEANS PLUS FUNCTION, *STARE DECISIS*, SUMMARY JUDGMENT

In re Jolles, 628 F.2d 1322, 206 U.S.P.Q. 885 (C.C.P.A. 1980) - CANCER, EXPERIMENTAL ANIMALS, SCREENING

In re Jolly, 172 F.2d 566, 80 U.S.P.Q. 504 (C.C.P.A. 1949) - PARTICULARITY, SUBSTANTIAL, SUBSTANTIALLY, SUFFICIENT

In re Jones, 58 App. D.C. 379, 30 F.2d 1003 (1929) - HYBRID

In re Jones, 149 F.2d 501, 65 U.S.P.Q. 480 (C.C.P.A. 1945) - BENZYL

In re Jones, 542 F.2d 65, 191 U.S.P.Q. 249 (C.C.P.A. 1976) - MANDATE, REEXAMINATION, REVIVAL, TERMINATION OF PROCEEDINGS

In re Jones, 958 F.2d 347, 21 U.S.P.Q.2d 1941 (Fed. Cir. 1992) - COMBINING REFERENCES, MODIFICATION, MOTIVATION, PRIMA FACIE

Jones v. Hardy, 727 F.2d 1524, 220 U.S.P.Q. 1021 (Fed. Cir. 1984) - ADVANTAGE, ANTICIPATION, DIFFERENCE, INHERENCY, INVENTION, NEW USE, OBVIOUSNESS, OBVIOUS TO TRY OR EXPERIMENT, PROBLEM, PROPERTY, RECOGNITION, 35 U.S.C. §103, WHOLE

Jones v. Sullivan, 938 F.2d 801 (7th Cir. 1991) - STANDING

Jonsson v. The Stanley Works, 903 F.2d 812, 14 U.S.P.Q.2d 1863 (Fed. Cir. 1990) - CONTINUATION-IN-PART APPLICATION, MEANS, SUMMARY JUDGMENT

Joseph E. Seagram & Sons, Inc. v. Marzall, 180 F.2d 26, 84 U.S.P.Q. 180 (CA D.C. 1950) - TESTING

Joslyn Manufacturing Co. v. Amerace Corp., 729 F. Supp. 1219, 14 U.S.P.Q.2d 1223 (Ill. 1990) - VENUE

In re Joyce, 115 U.S.P.Q. 412 (Commr. Patents 1957) - SPECIES

Joy Manufacturing Co. v. National Mine Service Company Inc., 810 F.2d 1127, 1 U.S.P.Q.2d 1627 (Fed. Cir. 1987) - REEXAMINATION, SETTLEMENT AGREEMENT

Joy Technologies Inc. v. Flakt Inc., 772 F. Supp. 842, 20 U.S.P.Q.2d 1934 (Del. 1991) - PROTECTION

Joy Technologies Inc. v. Flakt Inc., 820 F. Supp. 802, 27 U.S.P.Q.2d 1766 (Del. 1993) - INFRINGEMENT

Joy Technologies, Inc. v. Flakt, Inc., 6 F.3d 770, 28 U.S.P.Q.2d 1378 (Fed. Cir. 1993) - INJUNCTION, PROCESS

Joy Technologies Inc. v. Flakt Inc., 42 U.S.P.Q.2d 1042 (Del. 1996) - DAMAGES, DOUBT, LOST PROFITS, PREJUDGMENT INTEREST

Joy Technologies v. Quigg, 12 U.S.P.Q.2d 1112 (D.C. 1989) - COMMON LAW RIGHT, REEXAMINATION

J.P. Stevens & Co., Inc. v. Lex Tex, Ltd., Inc., 747 F.2d 1553, 223 U.S.P.Q. 1089 (Fed. Cir. 1984) - BUT-FOR RULE OR TEST, INEQUITABLE CONDUCT

J. Star Industries Inc. v. Oakley, 720 F. Supp. 1291, 13 U.S.P.Q.2d 1993 (Miss. 1989) - PRELIMINARY INJUNCTION

J.T. Eaton & Co. v. Atlantic Paste & Glue Co., 106 F.3d 1563, 41 U.S.P.Q.2d 1641 (Fed. Cir. 1997) - COMMERCIAL SUCCESS

Ex parte Jungfer, 18 U.S.P.Q.2d 1796 (B.P.A.I. 1990) - PRODUCT BY PROCESS

Juno Lighting Inc. v. Cooper Industries Inc., 17 U.S.P.Q.2d 1802 (Ill. 1990) - BEST MODE

Jurgens v. CBK Ltd., 80 F.3d 1566, 38 U.S.P.Q.2d 1397 (Fed. Cir. 1996) - BAD FAITH, CULPABILITY, DAMAGES, INFRINGEMENT,

Jurgens v. McKasy, 927 F.2d 1552, 18 U.S.P.Q.2d 1031 (Fed. Cir. 1991) - CAFC, STANDARD

Justus v. Appenzeller, 177 U.S.P.Q. 332 (PO Bd. Pat. Int. 1971) - PRIORITY, 35 U.S.C. §119

-K-

Kabb Inc. v. Sutera, 25 U.S.P.Q.2d 1554 (La. 1992) - SOLE PROPRIETORSHIP, 28 U.S.C. §1391(c), VENUE

In re Kaghan, Schmitt, and Kay, 387 F.2d 398, 156 U.S.P.Q. 130 (C.C.P.A. 1967) - CONTINUATION APPLICATION, RES JUDICATA

Kahl v. Scoville, 219 U.S.P.Q. 725 (PTO Bd. Pat. Intf. 1982) - CONVERSION, 35 U.S.C. §102(b)

Kahn v. Dynamics Corporation of America, 367 F. Supp. 63, 180 U.S.P.Q. 247 (N.Y. 1973) - DECEPTION, LATE CLAIMING, PRESUMPTION OF VALIDITY

Kahn v. Dynamics Corporation of America, 508 F.2d 939, 184 U.S.P.Q. 260 (2d Cir. 1975), *cert. denied,* 421 U.S. 930, 185 U.S.P.Q. 505 (1975) - EXCEPTIONAL, MISLEADING, LATE CLAIMING

Kahn v. General Motors Corp., 889 F.2d 1078, 12 U.S P.Q.2d 1997 (Fed. Cir. 1989) - CUSTOMER SUIT

Kahn v. General Motors Corp., 88 Civ. 2982, 33 U.S.P.Q.2d 2011 (N.Y. 1995) - OWNERSHIP

Ex parte Kaiser, 189 U.S.P.Q. 816 (PTO Bd. App. 1974) - REDUCTION IN STEPS

Ex parte Kaiser, 194 U.S.P.Q. 47 (PTO Bd. App. 1975) - IMPROVEMENT, MODIFICATION

Kaiser Industries Corporation v. Jones & Laughlin Steel Corporation, 181 U.S.P.Q. 193 (Pa. 1974) - BLOCK, CONVINCE, CORRECT, INOPERABLE, INOPERATIVE, TECHNOLOGICAL BLOCK

Kaiser Industries Corp. v. Jones & Laughlin Steel Corp., 515 F.2d 964, 185 U.S.P.Q. 343 (3d Cir. 1975) - BLONDER-TONGUE DOCTRINE

Kalkowski v. Ronco, Inc., 186 U.S.P.Q. 281 (Ill. 1975) - DOUBLE USE

Kalman v. The Berlyn Corp., 914 F.2d 1473, 16 U.S.P.Q.2d 1093 (Fed. Cir. 1990) - DAMAGES, EXCLUSIVE, TAXATION, TWO-SUPPLIER MARKET

Kalman v. Kimberly-Clark Corp., 713 F.2d 760, 218 U.S.P.Q. 781 (Fed. Cir. 1983) - ANTICIPATION

Kalnoki-Kis v. Land, 214 U.S.P.Q. 636 (PTO Bd. Pat. Intf. 1982) - INTERFERENCE IN FACT

In re Kamal and Rogier, 398 F.2d 867, 158 U.S.P.Q. 320 (C.C.P.A. 1968) - CHALLENGE, EVIDENCE, PHARMACEUTICAL, PREDICTABILITY, SUPPORT

In re Kamm and Young, 452 F.2d 1052, 172 U.S.P.Q. 298 (C.C.P.A. 1972) - COMBINING REFERENCES, PIECEMEAL

Kamyr Inc. v. Clement, 42 U.S.P.Q.2d 1235 (D.C. 1997) - ESTOPPEL

KangaROOS U.S.A., Inc. v. Caldor, Inc., 778 F.2d 1571, 228 U.S.P.Q. 32 (Fed. Cir. 1985) - INEQUITABLE CONDUCT

Kansas Jack, Inc. Appliance v. Kuhn, 719 F.2d 1144, 219 U.S.P.Q. 857 (Fed. Cir. 1983) - COMMERCIAL SUCCESS

In re Kaplan, 789 F.2d 1574, 229 U.S.P.Q. 678 (C.C.P.A. 1986) - DOMINATION, DOUBLE PATENTING

Kaplan v. Corcoran, 545 F.2d 1073, 192 U.S.P.Q. 129 (7th Cir. 1976) - EXECUTIVE ORDER NO. 10096, FEDERAL EMPLOYEE

In re Kathawala, 9 F.3d 942, 28 U.S.P.Q.2d 1785 (Fed. Cir. 1993) - PATENTED

In re Katrapat A.G., 6 U.S.P.Q.2d 1863 (Commr. Patents & Trademarks 1988) - REEXAMINATION, REVIVAL

Katrapat A.G. v. Advanced Machine and Engineering Co., 28 U.S.P.Q.2d 1270 (Ill. 1993) - BEST MODE

In re Katz, 687 F.2d 450, 215 U.S.P.Q. 14 (C.C.P.A. 1982) - APPLICANT'S OWN WORK, 37 C.F.R. §1.132, COAUTHOR, INVENTIVE ENTITY, REFERENCE, 35 U.S.C. §102(a), 35 U.S.C. §102(g)

Katz v. Batavia Marine & Sporting Supplies Inc., 984 F.2d 422, 25 U.S.P.Q.2d 1547 (Fed. Cir. 1993) - DISCOVERY

Katz v. Lear Siegler Inc., 909 F.2d 1459, 15 U.S.P.Q.2d 1554 (Fed. Cir. 1990) - CONCURRENT LITIGATION, CUSTOMER SUIT, DECLARATORY JUDGMENT

In re Katzschmann, 347 F.2d 620, 146 U.S.P.Q. 66 (C.C.P.A. 1965) - EVIDENCE, SPECULATION

Kaufman Co. v. Lantech Inc., 807 F.2d 970, 1 U.S.P.Q.2d 1202 (Fed. Cir. 1986) - IDENTICAL, REEXAMINATION

Kaufman Co. Inc. v. Lantech Inc., 926 F.2d 1136, 17 U.S.P.Q.2d 1828 (Fed. Cir. 1991) - LOST PROFITS, PROBABILITY, SUBSTITUTE

Kaufman Malchman & Kirby P.C. v. Hasbro Inc., 897 F. Supp. 719, 37 U.S.P.Q.2d 1458 (N.Y. 1995) - ARISE UNDER PATENT LAWS

Ex parte Kaul, 125 U.S.P.Q. 70 (PO Bd. App. 1959) - EXAMINER'S ANSWER

Kawai, Masuda, and Usui v. Metlesics and Sternbach, 480 F.2d 880, 178 U.S.P.Q. 158 (C.C.P.A. 1973) - FOREIGN PATENT APPLICATION

Kearney & Trecker Corp. v. The Cincinnati Milling Machine Co., 254 F. Supp. 130, 149 U.S.P.Q. 551 (Ill. 1966) - SUBSIDIARY

Kearney & Trecker Corporation v. Cincinnati Milacron, Inc., 184 U.S.P.Q. 134 (Ohio 1974) - FAILURE TO CITE

Kearns v. General Motors Corp., 94 F.3d 1553, 39 U.S.P.Q.2d 1949 (Fed. Cir. 1996) - CLAIM PRECLUSION, ISSUE PRECLUSION, RES JUDICATA

Kearns v. Wood Motors Inc., 19 U.S.P.Q.2d 1138 (Mich. 1990) - EXPERIMENTAL USE, USE

In re Keil, 808 F.2d 830, 1 U.S.P.Q.2d 1427 (Fed. Cir. 1987) - INTERFERENCE, REISSUE

In re Keim and Thompson, 229 F.2d 466, 108 U.S.P.Q. 330 (C.C.P.A. 1956) - ASSIGNMENT, CHALLENGE, COPENDING PATENT, DOUBLE PATENTING, OWNERSHIP, SAME DATE, STATEMENT

Ex parte Keith and Lavanchy, 167 U.S.P.Q. 409 (PO Bd. App. 1970) - INTERFERENCE ESTOPPEL

In re Kelley, 230 F.2d 435, 109 U.S.P.Q. 42 (C.C.P.A. 1956) - NON-ELECTED SPECIES

In re Kelley, 305 F.2d 909, 134 U.S.P.Q. 397 (C.C.P.A. 1962) - MULTIPLE INCLUSION

Kelley Manufacturing Company v. Lilliston Corporation, 180 U.S.P.Q. 364 (N.C. 1973) - EFFECTIVE DATE, PARENT APPLICATION, PATENT OFFICE LICENSE, RETROACTIVE LICENSE

In re Kemps, 97 F.3d 1427, 40 U.S.P.Q.2d 1309 (Fed. Cir. 1996) - MOTIVATION, STANDARD

Ex parte Kenaga, 190 U.S.P.Q. 346 (PTO Bd. App. 1974) - CONSTRUCTION

Kennecott Corp. v. Kyocera International Inc., 2 U.S.P.Q.2d 1455 (Cal. 1986) - DESCRIPTION, ENABLEMENT, 35 U.S.C. §112

Kennecott Corp. v. Kyocera International, Inc., 835 F.2d 1419, 5 U.S.P.Q.2d 1194 (Fed.

K-Lath v. Davis Wire Corp., 49 U..S.P.Q.2d 1161 (Cal. 1998) - RULE 12(b)(6)

In re Klein, 5 U.S.P.Q. 259 (Commr. Patents 1930) - CONTINUATION-IN-PART APPLICATION

Ex parte Klioze and Ehrgott, 220 U.S.P.Q. 91 (PTO Bd. App. 1983) - ANALOGY PROCESSES, PROCESS

Klipsch Inc. v. WWR Technology Inc., 127 F.3d 729, 44 U.S.P.Q.2d 1588 (8ᵗʰ Cir. 1997) - CLAIM SPLITTING

Kloster Speedsteel AB v. Crucible Inc., 793 F.2d 1565, 230 U.S.P.Q. 81 (Fed. Cir. 1986), *cert. denied*, 479 U.S. 1034 (1987) - ADVICE OF COUNSEL, AGGRESSIVE, ATTORNEY'S FEES, BIFURCATION, EXCEPTIONAL, OPINION, WILLFUL

In re Knapp Monarch Co., 296 F.2d 230, 132 U.S.P.Q. 6 (C.C.P.A. 1961) - FACT, NOTICE

Knorr v. Pearson, 671 F.2d 1368, 1374, 213 U.S.P.Q. 196, 201 (C.C.P.A. 1982) - CORROBORATION

Knowles v. Tibbetts, 347 F.2d 591, 146 U.S.P.Q. 59 (C.C.P.A. 1965) - DELAY, REDUCTION TO PRACTICE, TESTING

In re Knowlton, 481 F.2d 1357, 178 U.S.P.Q. 486 (C.C.P.A. 1973) - COMPUTER-ARTS INVENTION

In re Koller, Hartl, and Kirschner, 613 F.2d 819, 204 U.S.P.Q. 702 (C.C.P.A. 1980) - ENABLEMENT, STATE OF THE ART

In re Kollman and Irwin, 595 F.2d 48, 201 U.S.P.Q. 193 (C.C.P.A. 1979) - STATISTICALLY SIGNIFICANT

Kondo, Takashima, and Tunemoto v. Martel, Tessier, Demoute, and Jolly, 223 U.S.P.Q. 528 (PTO Bd. Pat. Intf. 1984) - DILIGENCE

Konstant Products Inc. v. Frazier Industrial Co. Inc., 25 U.S.P.Q.2d 1223 (Ill. 1992) - MARKING

Ex parte Koo, 150 U.S.P.Q. 131 (PO Bd. App. 1965) - BENZENE, PYRIDYL

Ex parte Korten, 71 U.S.P.Q. 173 (PTO Bd. App. 1945) - ESTER

KPR Inc. v. C&F Packing Co. Inc., 30 U.S.P.Q.2d 1320 (Tex. 1993) - FIRST-TO-FILE, FORUM SHOPPING, REPOSE, TRANSFER

Kraly v. National Distillers and Chemical Corporation, 177 U.S.P.Q. 364 (Ill. 1973) - LICENSEE, REPUDIATION

Ex parte Kranz, 19 U.S.P.Q.2d 1216 (B.P.A.I. 1990) - 37 C.F.R. §1.196(b), CHEMICAL, MONOPOLY, MOTIVATION, OBVIOUSNESS, PROCESS

In re Kratz and Strasburger, 592 F.2d 1169, 201 U.S.P.Q. 71 (C.C.P.A. 1979) - NATURAL PRODUCT, NOVELTY, PREDICTABILITY, PURE, SYNTHETIC

In re Krazinski, Shepherd, and Taft, 347 F.2d 656, 146 U.S.P.Q. 25 (C.C.P.A. 1965) - COMPOUND, NAME, SELECTION, STRUCTURE

Ex parte Krenzer, 199 U.S.P.Q. 227 (PTO Bd. App. 1978) - BEST MODE, SCIENTIFIC PRINCIPLE, SKEPTICISM, UTILITY

Ex parte Krepelka, 231 U.S.P.Q. 746 (B.P.A.I. 1986) - AMELIORATION, ANIMAL TESTS, CANCER, CHALLENGE, COMPOUND, CURE OF CANCER, DISCLOSURE, ENABLEMENT, EVIDENCE, HUMAN USE, PHARMACEUTICAL, SCREENING, SUBSTANTIATING EVIDENCE, UNBELIEVABLE

Kridl v. McCormick, 41 U.S.P.Q.2d 1686 (Fed. Cir. 1997) - CORROBORATION, UTILITY

In re Krimmel, 292 F.2d 948, 130 U.S.P.Q. 215 (C.C.P.A. 1961) - SAFETY

In re Kroekel and Pfaff, 504 F.2d 1143, 183 U.S.P.Q. 610 (C.C.P.A. 1974) - IMPOSS-IBLE, INDEFINITENESS, PROPORTIONS

In re Kroekel, 803 F.2d 705, 231 U.S.P.Q. 640 (Fed. Cir. 1986) - INTERFERENCE ESTOPPEL, - PHANTOM COUNT

Kroekel v. Shah, 558 F.2d 29, 194 U.S.P.Q. 544 (C.C.P.A. 1977) - AMBIGUITY, COUNT

In re Krogman, 223 F.2d 497, 106 U.S.P.Q. 276 (C.C.P.A. 1955) - MATERIAL

Ex parte Kronenthal and Rich, 163 U.S.P.Q. 571 (PO Bd. App. 1969) - PROPORTIONS

Kropa v. Robie and Mahlman, 187 F.2d 150, 88 U.S.P.Q. 478 (C.C.P.A. 1951) - DOC-TRINE OF INHERENCY, PREAMBLE

KSM Fastening Systems, Inc. v. H. A. Jones Co., Inc., 776 F.2d 1522, 227 U.S.P.Q. 676 (Fed. Cir. 1985) - CONTEMPT

Kubota v. Shibuya, 999 F.2d 517, 27 U.S.P.Q.2d 1418 (Fed. Cir. 1993) - INTER-FERENCE, PRELIMINARY MOTION

In re Kuderna and Phillips, 426 F.2d 385, 165 U.S.P.Q. 575 (C.C.P.A. 1970) - ISOLATED

In re Kuehl, 475 F.2d 658, 177 U.S.P.Q. 250 (C.C.P.A. 1973) - DEPENDENT CLAIM, METHOD, METHOD OF USE, RESTRICTION, STATUTORY CLASS, USE

Ex parte Kuklo, 25 U.S.P.Q.2d 1387 (B.P.A.I. 1992) - PUBLIC USE, 42 U.S.C. §2185

In re Kulling, 897 F.2d 1147, 14 U.S.P.Q.2d 1056 (Fed. Cir. 1990) - CAFC

Kuther v. Leuschner, 200 F. Supp. 841, 131 U.S.P.Q. 463 (Cal. 1961) - REPLACEMENT

Kysor Industrial Corp. v. Pet, 459 F.2d 1010, 173 U.S.P.Q. 642 (6th Cir. 1972) - ARISE UNDER PATENT LAWS, CIVIL ACTION, 28 U.S.C. §1338(a)

-*L*-

Lacotte v. Thomas, 758 F.2d 611, 225 U.S.P.Q. 633 (Fed. Cir. 1985) - ANALOGOUS ART

Laerdall Medical Corp. v. Ambu Inc., 877 F. Supp. 255, 34 U.S.P.Q.2d 1140 (Md. 1995) - IMPLIED CAUSE OF ACTION, UNAVOIDABLE, 35 U.S.C. §41

L.A. Gear Inc. v. E.S. Originals Inc., 859 F. Supp. 1294, 32 U.S.P.Q.2d 1613 (Cal. 1994) - INDIRECT INFRINGEMENT, INDUCEMENT

L.A. Gear Inc. v. E.S. Originals Inc., 35 U.S.P.Q.2d 1497 (Cal. 1995) - REEXAMINA-TION, SUBSTANTIAL EQUIVALENT

L.A. Gear, Inc. v. Tom McAn Shoe Co., 988 F.2d 1117, 25 U.S.P.Q.2d 1913 (Fed. Cir.), *cert. denied*, 114 S.Ct. 291 (1993) - FUNCTIONALITY

The Laitram Corp. v. The Cambridge Wire Cloth Co., 919 F.2d 1579, 16 U.S.P.Q.2d 1929 (Fed. Cir. 1990) - INTENT, 35 U.S.C. §271

The Laitram Corporation v. Deepsouth Packing Co., Inc., 443 F.2d 936, 170 U.S.P.Q. 196 (5th Cir. 1971) - APPARATUS, MAKE, 35 U.S.C. §271(a)

The Laitram Corp. v. NEC Corp., 17 U.S.P.Q.2d 1407 (La. 1990) - REEXAMINATION

The Laitram Corp. v. NEC Corp., 952 F.2d 1357, 21 U.S.P.Q.2d 1276 (Fed. Cir. 1991) - AMENDMENT, CLAIM INTERPRETATION, ESTOPPEL, GENUINE, IDEN-TICAL, REEXAMINATION, SUBSTANTIVE, SUMMARY JUDGMENT

Laitram Corp. v. NEC Corp., 42 U.S.P.Q.2d 1897 (Fed. Cir. 1997) - APPELLEE, IMPLIED DECISION, MANDATE

The Laitram Corp. v. NEC Corp., 49 U.S.P.Q.2d 1199 (Fed. Cir. 1998) - REEXAMINA-
TION, SUBSTANTIVE CHANGE

The Laitram Corp. v. OKI Electric Industry Co. Ltd., 30 U.S.P.Q.2d 1527 (La. 1994) -
INEQUITABLE CONDUCT, RULE 9

The Laitram Corp. v. Rexnord Inc., 15 U.S.P.Q.2d 1161 (Wis. 1990) - EQUIVALENTS,
INFRINGEMENT, MEANS, SUBSTANTIALLY

The Laitram Corp. v. Rexnord Inc., 939 F.2d 1533, 19 U.S.P.Q.2d 1367 (Fed. Cir. 1991) -
CLAIM DIFFERENTIATION, MEAANS PLUS FUNCTION

In re Lalu and Foulletier, 747 F.2d 703, 223 U.S.P.Q. 1257 (Fed. Cir. 1984) - INTER-
MEDIATE, STRUCTURAL SIMILARITY

La Maur, Inc. v. DeMert & Dougherty, Inc., 265 F. Supp. 961, 148 U.S.P.Q. 59 (Ill. 1965)
- KNOWLEDGE

In re Lambrech, 202 U.S.P.Q. 620 (Commr. Patents & Trademarks 1976) - CERTIFI-
CATE OF CORRECTION

Lamb-Weston Inc. v. McCain Foods Ltd., 78 F.3d 540, 37 U.S.P.Q.2d 1856 (Fed. Cir.
1996) - DERIVATION, EQUIVALENTS, INSPIRATION, MOTIVATION, SPUR,
35 U.S.C.102(f)

Land v. Dreyer, 155 F.2d 383, 69 U.S.P.Q. 602 (C.C.P.A. 1946) - REDUCTION TO
PRACTICE

In re Land and Rogers, 368 F.2d 866, 151 U.S.P.Q. 621 (C.C.P.A. 1966) - ANOTHER,
DOUBLE PATENTING, ENTITY

Lang v. Pacific Marine and Supply Co. Ltd., 895 F.2d 761, 13 U.S.P.Q.2d 1820 (Fed. Cir.
1990) - DECLARATORY JUDGMENT

Lang & Swath Ocean Systems, Inc. v. Pacific Marine & Supply Co., 895 F.2d 761, 13
U.S.P.Q.2d 1820 (Fed. Cir. 1990) - STATUTORY LIMITATIONS, 35 U.S.C. §286

In re Lange, 280 F.2d 165, 126 U.S.P.Q. 365 (C.C.P.A. 1960) - CROWDED ART

In re Lange, 644 F.2d 856, 209 U.S.P.Q. 288 (C.C.P.A. 1981) - NEW MATTER, TEST
RESULTS

In re Langer, 503 F.2d 1380, 183 U.S.P.Q. 288 (C.C.P.A. 1974) - CLINICAL TESTING,
EFFECTIVE DATE, FACT, HUMAN USE, IN VIVO, PROOF OF UTILITY,
STANDARD EXPERIMENTAL ANIMAL, UTILITY

In re Langer and Haynes, 465 F.2d 896, 175 U.S.P.Q. 169 (C.C.P.A. 1972) - HOMOL-
OGY, OBVIOUSNESS, WHOLE

Langer and Tornqvist v. Kaufman and McMullen, 465 F.2d 915, 175 U.S.P.Q. 172
(C.C.P.A. 1972) - CONCEPTION, CONTINUATION APPLICATION, *NUNC PRO
TUNC*, REDUCTION TO PRACTICE

In re Lanham, 1 U.S.P.Q.2d 1877 (Commr. Patents & Trademarks 1986) -
REEXAMINATION

In re Larsen, 292 F.2d 531, 130 U.S.P.Q. 209 (C.C.P.A. 1961) - METHOD OF MAK-
ING, SYNTHESIS

In re Larson, Russler, and Meldahl, 340 F.2d 965, 144 U.S.P.Q. 347 (C.C.P.A. 1965) -
MAKING INTEGRAL

Larson v. Joehenning, 17 U.S.P.Q.2d 1610 (B.P.A.I. 1990) - CORROBORATION

Laser Diode Array Inc. v. Paradigm Lasers Inc., 44 U.S.P.Q.2d 1677 (N.Y. 1997) -
MOTION TO STRIKE

Lemelson v. TRW, Inc., 760 F.2d 1254, 225 U.S.P.Q. 697 (Fed. Cir. 1985) - CONTINUITY

Lemelson v. U.S., 6 U.S.P.Q.2d 1657 (U.S. Cl. Ct. 1988) - CLAIM LIMITATION

In re Lemin, 332 F.2d 839, 141 U.S.P.Q. 814 (C.C.P.A. 1964) - COMMENSURATE, HERBICIDE, SELECTION

In re Lemin, 364 F.2d 864, 150 U.S.P.Q. 546 (C.C.P.A. 1966) - EXAMINER, EXPERT

Ex parte Lemoine, 46 U.S.P.Q.2d 1420 (B.P.A.I. 1994) - CLAIM, 35 U.S.C. §134

Ex parte Lemoine, 46 U.S.P.Q.2d 1432 (B.P.A.I. 1995 - *unpublished*) - 37 C.F.R. §1.191(c)

Lenzing Aktiengesellschaft v. Courtaulds Fibers Inc., 119 F.3d 16, 44 U.S.P.Q.2d 1832 (Fed. Cir. 1997 - *unpublished*) - BEST MODE

Ex parte Leonard and Brandes, 187 U.S.P.Q. 122 (PTO Bd. App. 1974) - ADHESIVE, MATERIAL, UNEXPECTED RESULTS, WHOLE

In re Leshin, 277 F.2d 197, 125 U.S.P.Q. 416 (C.C.P.A. 1960) - MATERIAL, SELECTION

L'Esperance v. Nishimoto, 18 U.S.P.Q.2d 1534 (B.P.A.I. 1991) - INTERFERENCE

Ex parte Levengood, 28 U.S.P.Q.2d 1300 (B.P.A.I. 1993) - COMBINING REFERENCES

In re Levin, 178 F.2d 945, 84 U.S.P.Q. 232 (C.C.P.A. 1949) - RECIPE

Levin v. Coe, Commissioner of Patents, 131 F.2d 589, 55 U.S.P.Q. 224 (D.C. Cir. 1942) - HYBRID

In re Levitt, 11 U.S.P.Q.2d 1315 (Fed. Cir. 1989 - *unpublished*) - COMBINING REFERENCES, HERBICIDE, RING, SAME ART, SUBSTITUENTS

In re Lewis, 443 F.2d 389, 170 U.S.P.Q. 84 (C.C.P.A. 1971) - CRITICAL, EVIDENCE

Ex parte Lewis, Miller, and Law, 197 U.S.P.Q. 543 (PTO Bd. App. 1977) - INDEFINITE ARTICLE, SUBSTITUTED

Lewmar Marine Inc. v. Barient Inc., 827 F.2d 744, 3 U.S.P.Q.2d 1766 (Fed. Cir. 1987) - ANTICIPATION

Liberty Leather Products Co. v. VT International Ltd., 894 F. Supp. 136, 37 U.S.P.Q.2d 1342 (N.Y. 1995) - SKILL OF THE ART

Ex parte Lichty, 64 U.S.P.Q. 430 (PTO Bd. App. 1944) - SUBSTANTIALLY

Lifescan Inc. v. Home Diagnostics Inc., 76 F.3d 358, 37 U.S.P.Q.2d 1595 (Fed. Cir. 1996) - EQUIVALENCY, INTERCHANGEABLE

LifeScan Inc. v. Polymer Technology International Corp., 35 U.S.P.Q.2d 1225 (Wash. 1995) - IMPLIED LICENSE, PATENT, PUBLIC INTEREST, RIGHT, SUMMARY JUDGMENT, 35 U.S.C. §271(d)

Lifshitz v. Walter Drake & Sons, Inc., 802 F.2d 1426, 1 U.S.P.Q.2d 1254 (9th Cir. 1986) - DIRECTED VERDICT

Ex parte Ligett, Wolf, and Closson, 121 U.S.P.Q. 324 (PO Bd. App. 1958) - PHENYL VS. NAPHTHYL

Lightwave Technologies Inc. v. Corning Glass Works, 19 U.S.P.Q.2d 1838 (N.Y. 1991) - ANTITRUST, GEOGRAPHICAL LIMITATION, GRANT-BACK, LICENSE, MISUSE, MONOPOLY, POOLING, QUANTITY LIMITATION

Lin v. Fritsch, 14 U.S.P.Q.2d 1795 (Commr. Patents & Trademarks 1989) - EXCLUDE, MONETARY RELIEF, PRESUMPTION

Ex parte Logan, 20 U.S.P.Q.2d 1465 (B.P.A.I. 1991) - NEW MATTER, 35 U.S.C. §101

Ex parte Logan, 38 U.S.P.Q.2d 1852 (B.P.A.I. 1994 - *unpublished*) - REEXAMINATION, 35 U.S.C. §305

Logan v. Neuzil, 206 U.S.P.Q. 668 (Comm'r of Patents and Trademarks 1979) - INTERFERENCE IN FACT, MOTION TO DISSOLVE

In re Lonardo, 119 F.3d 960, 43 U.S.P.Q.2d 1262 (Fed. Cir. 1997), *but see dissent* - REEXAMINATION

In re Long, 368 F.2d 892, 151 U.S.P.Q. 640 (C.C.P.A. 1966) - 37 C.F.R. §1.71(b), SPECIFIC EMBODIMENT

In re Longi, 759 F.2d 887, 225 U.S.P.Q. 645 (Fed. Cir. 1985) - DOUBLE PATENTING, TERMINAL DISCLAIMER

Longwood Manufacturing Corp. v. Wheelabrator Clean Water Systems Inc., 40 U.S.P.Q.2d 1638 (Me. 1996) - ANTITRUST

Lon Tai Shing Co. Ltd. v. Koch ¢ Lowy, 90 Civ. 4464, 25 U.S.P.Q.2d 1375 (N.Y. 1992) - RECONSIDERATION

Loral Corp. v. The B. F. Goodrich Co., 14 U.S.P.Q.2d 1081 (Ohio 1989) - EXPERIMENTAL USE, ON SALE

Loral Fairchild Corp. v. Matsushita Electric Industrial Co. Ltd., 22 U.S.P.Q.2d 1158 (Va. 1991) - HAGUE CONVENTION

Loral Fairchild Corp. v. Matsushita Electric Industrial Co. Ltd., 805 F. Supp. 3, 25 U.S.P.Q.2d 1557 (N.Y. 1992) - HAGUE CONVENTION

Loral Fairchild Corp. v. Matsushita Electric Industrial Co. Ltd., 840 F. Supp. 211, 31 U.S.P.Q.2d 1499 (Cal. 1994) - COMITY, INFRINGEMENT, JUDICIAL ESTOPPEL, JURISDICTION, OWNERSHIP

Loral Fairchild Corp. v. Victor Co. of Japan Ltd., 803 F. Supp. 626, 25 U.S.P.Q.2d 1701 (N.Y. 1992) - FOREIGN

Loshbough v. Allen, 359 F.2d 910, 149 U.S.P.Q. 633 (C.C.P.A. 1966) - REMAND (GROUNDS FOR)

Lough v. Brunswick Corp., 41 U.S.P.Q.2d 1385 (Fed. Cir. 1997) - PUBLIC USE

In re Lowry, 32 F.3d 1579, 32 U.S.P.Q.2d 1031 (Fed. Cir. 1994) - LIMITATION, MANUFACTURE, PRINTED MATTER, PROGRAM

In re Luck and Gainer, 476 F.2d 650, 177 U.S.P.Q. 523 (C.C.P.A. 1973) - PRODUCT BY PROPERTIES

In re Ludovici and Megla, 482 F.2d 958, 179 U.S.P.Q. 84 (C.C.P.A. 1973) - COLLATERAL ATTACK, MISREPRESENTATION

In re Lueders, 42 U.S.P.Q.2d 1481 (Fed. Cir. 1997) - *INCLUSIO UNIS EST*

In re Lukach, Olson, and Spurlin, 440 F.2d 1263, 169 U.S.P.Q. 795 (C.C.P.A. 1971) - CONTINUATION-IN-PART APPLICATION, DESCRIPTION, STATUTORY BAR

Lund Industries Inc. v. GO Industries Inc., 938 F.2d 1273, 19 U.S.P.Q.2d 1383 (Fed. Cir. 1991) - CONTEMPT, PRELIMINARY INJUNCTION

In re Lundak, 773 F.2d 1216, 227 U.S.P.Q. 90 (Fed. Cir. 1985) - BIOTECHNOLOGY, CELL LINE, CONSTRUCTIVE REDUCTION TO PRACTICE, DEPOSIT, DEPOSIT OF CELL LINE, ENABLEMENT, HYBRIDOMA, MONOCLONAL ANTIBODIES, NEW MATTER

Lundy Electronics & Systems, Inc. v. Optical Recognition Systems, Inc., 362 F. Supp. 130, 178 U.S.P.Q. 525 (Va. 1973) - DUTY TO DISCLOSE, INCORPORATE BY REFERENCE, PRESUMPTION, SEARCH RECORD, SUPPORT

In re Lunsford, 357 F.2d 385, 148 U.S.P.Q. 721 (C.C.P.A. 1966) - FACT

Lutzker v. Plet, 843 F.2d 1364, 6 U.S.P.Q.2d 1370 (Fed. Cir. 1988) - ABANDONMENT, DELAY, INTENT TO ABANDON, SUPPRESSION

Lutzker v. Plet, 7 U.S.P.Q.2d 1214 (B.P.A.I. 1987) - DUTY TO DISCLOSE, MATERIALITY

In re Luvisi and Nohejl, 342 F.2d 102, 144 U.S.P.Q. 646 (C.C.P.A. 1965) - CRITICALITY, DIRECTION, MOSITA, ORDINARY SKILL, SHOTGUN

Ex parte Lyell, 17 U.S.P.Q.2d 1548 (B.P.A.I. 1990) - HYBRID

Lyon v. Bausch & Lomb, 224 F.2d 530, 106 U.S.P.Q. 1 (2d Cir. 1955) - ANTICIPATION, INVENTION

-M-

Ex parte Maas, 14 U.S.P.Q.2d 1762 (B.P.A.I. 1987) - NEW GROUND OF REJECTION

Ex parte MacAdams, Wu, and Joyner, 206 U.S.P.Q. 445 (PTO Bd. App. 1978) - ANALOGY PROCESSES, STEPS

In re Mac Dermid Inc., 42 U.S.P.Q.2d 1479 (Fed. Cir. 1997) - STANDARD OF REVIEW

Machinery Corporation of America v. Gullfiber A.B., 225 U.S.P.Q. 743 (Pa. 1984) - ATTORNEY'S FEES

Machinery Corp. of America v. Gullfiber AB, 774 F.2d 467, 227 U.S.P.Q. 368 (Fed. Cir. 1985) - ATTORNEY'S FEES, EXCEPTIONAL, PRESUMPTION OF INFRINGEMENT

MacKay v. Quigg, 641 F. Supp. 567, 231 U.S.P.Q. 907 (D.C. 1986) - COMMERCIAL SUCCESS, *DE NOVO*

MacLaren v. B-I-W Group Inc., 180 U.S.P.Q. 387 (Va. 1973) - ATTORNEY, ATTORNEY'S FILE, CONCLUSION, INTERVIEW, LEGAL THEORY, MENTAL IMPRESSIONS, OPINION, PATENT ATTORNEY

Maclaren v. B-I-W Group Inc., 401 F. Supp. 283, 187 U.S.P.Q. 345 (N.Y. 1975) - LATE CLAIMING, MARKETABILITY, TEST, TRADE SHOW

Ex parte Macy, 132 U.S.P.Q. 545 (PO Bd. App. 1960) - MATERIAL, PROCESS, SINGLE-STEP METHOD CLAIM, STEPS

In re Magerlein, 602 F.2d 366, 202 U.S.P.Q. 473 (C.C.P.A. 1979) - CONTRIBUTING CAUSE, INTERMEDIATE, NEXUS, PHARMACEUTICAL

The Magnavox Company v. Mattell, Inc., 216 U.S.P.Q. 28 (Ill. 1982) - BREADTH, TERM

Magnesystems Inc. v. Nikken Inc., 34 U.S.P.Q.2d 1112 (Cal. 1994) - CLAIM CONSTRUCTION, PROSECUTION HISTORY

Magnivision Inc. v. The Bonneau Co., 42 U.S.P.Q.2d 1925 (Fed. Cir. 1997) - INTERVIEW, PERSISTENCE, PROSECUTION IRREGULARITIES, VALIDITY

In re Mahony, 421 F.2d 742, 164 U.S.P.Q. 572 (C.C.P.A. 1970) - STATUTORY, 35 U.S.C. §112

In re Mahurkar Double Lumen Hemodialysis Catheter Patent Litigation, 23 U.S.P.Q.2d 1903 (Ill. 1992) - BANKRUPTCY, INJUNCTION

Mahurkar v. C.R. Bard Inc., 79 F.3d 1572, 38 U.S.P.Q.2d 1288 (Fed. Cir. 1996) - PRIOR ART, RULE OF REASON

Maier v. Hanawa, 26 U.S.P.Q.2d 1606 (PTO Comm'r 1992) - SAME PATENTABLE INVENTION

Mainland Industries, Inc. v. Standal's Patents Ltd., 799 F.2d 746, 230 U.S.P.Q. 772 (Fed. Cir. 1986) - EQUITABLE ESTOPPEL, INEXCUSABLE DELAY, LACHES, MATERIAL PREJUDICE, RELIANCE, SILENCE, UNREASONABLE DELAY

Ex parte Maino Des Granges, 862 O.G. 657 (PTO Bd. App. 1968) - AUSLEGESCHRIFT

Maitland Co. Inc. v. Terra First Inc., 33 U.S.P.Q.2d 1882 (S.C. 1994) - AFFIDAVIT, IRREPARABLE INJURY, KNOWN PRINCIPLES, MARKET SHARE, PRELIMINARY INJUNCTION

Ex parte Maizel, 27 U.S.P.Q.2d 1662 (B.P.A.I. 1992) - COMMENSURATE IN SCOPE, EQUIVALENT, FUNCTIONAL, SINGLE MEANS

In re Malachowski, 530 F.2d 1402, 189 U.S.P.Q. 432 (C.C.P.A. 1976) - COMMENSURATE, PHARMACEUTICAL, PROOF OF UTILITY, 35 U.S.C. §101

In re Malagari, 499 F.2d 1297, 182 U.S.P.Q. 549 (C.C.P.A. 1974) - ANTICIPATION

Mallinckrodt Inc. v. Medipart Inc., 976 F.2d 700, 24 U.S.P.Q.2d 1173 (Fed. Cir. 1992) - CONDITIONS, EXCLUDE, LICENSE, NOTICE, REPAIR, REUSE

Mallinckrodt Medical Inc. v. Sonus Pharmaceuticals Inc., 989 F. Supp. 265, 45 U.S.P.Q.2d 1811 (D.C. 1998) - INTERPLEADER

Malta v. Schulmerich Carillons Inc., 13 U.S.P.Q.2d 1900 (Pa. 1989) - DOCTRINE OF EQUIVALENTS, FRAUD ON A PATENT

Malta v. Schulmerich Carillons Inc., 952 F.2d 1320, 21 U.S.P.Q.2d 1161 (Fed. Cir. 1991) - DOCTRINE OF EQUIVALENTS, FUNCTION/WAY/RESULT, SUBSTANTIAL

In re Mancy, Florent, and Preud'Homme, 499 F.2d 1289, 182 U.S.P.Q. 303 (C.C.P.A. 1974) - ANALOGY PROCESSES, NEW STRAIN, STARTING MATERIAL, METHOD OF USE, STRAIN

Manildra Milling Corp. v. Ogilvie Mills Inc., 878 F. Supp. 1417, 30 U.S.P.Q.2d 1020 (Kan. 1993) - BAD FAITH, EXCEPTIONAL

Manildra Milling Corp. v. Ogilvie Mills Inc., 76 F.3d 1178, 37 U.S.P.Q.2d 1707 (Fed. Cir. 1996) - PREVAILING PARTY

In re Mann, 861 F.2d 1581, 8 U.S.P.Q.2d 2030 (Fed. Cir. 1988) - DESIGN

Mannesmann Demag Corp. v. Engineered Metal Products Co., 793 F.2d 1279, 230 U.S.P.Q. 45 (Fed. Cir. 1986) - LIMITATION, REASON

Manning v. Waring, Cox, James, Sklar, and Allen, 849 F.2d 222 (6th Cir. 1988) - DISQUALIFICATION

Manufacturing Research Corp. v. Graybar Electric Co., Inc., 679 F.2d 1355, 215 U.S.P.Q. 29 (11th Cir. 1982) - CLASSIFICATION

Marathon Oil Company v. The Firestone Tire and Rubber Company, 205 U.S.P.Q. 520 (Ohio 1979) - DERIVATION, MATERIALITY, REDUCTION TO PRACTICE

In re Marden and Rich, 47 F.2d 958, 8 U.S.P.Q. 347 (C.C.P.A. 1931) - PRODUCT OF NATURE

In re Margolis, 785 F.2d 1029, 228 U.S.P.Q. 940 (Fed. Cir. 1986) - SPECIFICATION, UNEXPECTED RESULTS

Margolis, Rushmore, Liu, and Anderson v. Banner, 599 F.2d 435, 202 U.S.P.Q. 365 (C.C.P.A. 1979) - CONFLICTING CLAIMS, IMPROVEMENT, MPEP 804.03, REJECTION

Marion Merrell Dow Inc. v. Baker Norton Pharmaceuticals Inc., 41 U.S.P.Q.2d 1127 (Fla. 1996) - METABOLITE, PRODRUG

Marion Merrell Dow Inc. v. Geneva Pharmaceuticals Inc., 877 F. Supp. 531, 33 U.S.P.Q.2d 1673 (Colo. 1994) - METABOLITE

Markman v. Westview Instruments Inc., 772 F. Supp. 1535, 20 U.S.P.Q.2d 1955 (Pa. 1991) - FACT, MEANING OF TERMS

Markman v. Westview Instruments Inc., 52 F.3d 967, 34 U.S.P.Q.2d 1321 (Fed. Cir. 1995); *confirmed*, 38 U.S.P.Q.2d 1461 (S.Ct. 1996) - CLAIM CONSTRUCTION, CLAIM INTERPRETATION, DIRECTED VERDICT, INTENT, JMOL, JUDGMENT AS A MATTER OF LAW (JMOL), LANGUAGE

Markman v. Westview Instruments Inc., 116 S.Ct. 1384, 38 U.S.P.Q.2d 1461 (S.Ct. 1996) - CAFC, CLAIM CONSTRUCTION, INFRINGEMENT, TRIAL BY JURY

Ex parte Markush, 1925 C.D. 126 - MARKUSH

Mars Inc. v. Kabushiki-Kaisha Nippon Conlux, 24 F.3d 1368, 30 U.S.P.Q.2d 1621 (Fed. Cir. 1994) - FOREIGN, JURISDICTION

Mars Inc. v. Nippon Conlux Kabushiki-Kaisha, 58 F.3d 616, 35 U.S.P.Q.2d 1311 (Fed. Cir. 1995) - CLAIM PRECLUSION, CLAIM SPLITTING

In re Marshall, 578 F.2d 301, 198 U.S.P.Q. 344 (C.C.P.A. 1978) - ACCIDENTAL, ANTICIPATION, DISADVANTAGE, DUPLICATION

Ex parte Marsili, Rossetti, and Pasqualucci, 214 U.S.P.Q. 904 (PTO Bd. App. 1979) - ERROR, NEW MATTER

Marston v. L.E. Gant, Ltd., 351 F. Supp. 1122, 176 U.S.P.Q. 180 (Va. 1972) - TORT

Ex parte Martin, 104 U.S.P.Q. 124 (PO Sup. Ex'r 1952) - FINAL REJECTION

Martin v. Clevenger, 11 U.S.P.Q.2d 1399 (Commr. Patents & Trademarks 1989) - INTERFERENCE

Martin v. Mayer, 823 F.2d 500, 3 U.S.P.Q.2d 1333 (Fed. Cir. 1987) - COPYING CLAIMS, EXPERT TESTIMONY

Martin, Aebi, and Ebner v. Johnson, 454 F.2d 746, 172 U.S.P.Q. 391 (C.C.P.A. 1972) - EXPERIMENTATION, HOW TO MAKE

Marvel Specialty Company, Inc. v. Bell Hosiery Mills, Inc., 330 F.2d 164, 141 U.S.P.Q. 269 (4th Cir. 1964) - LONG-FELT NEED

In re Marzocchi and Horton, 439 F.2d 220, 169 U.S.P.Q. 367 (C.C.P.A. 1971) - ASSERTION, ACCURACY, BREADTH, DISCLOSURE, DOUBT, ENABALEMENT, GENERIC, OBJECTIVE ENABLEMENT, PRESUMPTION

Maschinenfabrik Rieter A.G. v. Greenwood Mills, 340 F. Supp. 1103, 173 U.S.P.Q. 605 (S.C. 1972) - HINDSIGHT, OBVIOUSNESS, ORDINARY SKILL

Mas-Hamilton Group Inc. v. LaGard Inc., 48 U.S.P.Q.2d 1010 (Fed. Cir. 1998) - MEANS PLUS FUNCTION, STANDING

Mason v. Hepburn, 13 App. D.C. 86 (1898) - REDUCTION TO PRACTICE

Massachusetts Institute of Technology v. AB Fortia, 774 F.2d 1104, 227 U.S.P.Q. 428 (Fed. Cir. 1985) - PRINTED PUBLICATION, PROFESSIONAL PAPER, RESEARCH PAPER

In re Mathews, 408 F.2d 1393, 161 U.S.P.Q. 276 (C.C.P.A. 1969) - 35 U.S.C. §102(e)

Matsushita Electrical Industry Co. v. Zenith Radio Corp., 475 U.S. 574 (1986) - SUMMARY JUDGMENT

In re Mattison and Swanson, 509 F.2d 563, 184 U.S.P.Q. 484 (C.C.P.A. 1975) - SUBSTANTIALLY

Max Daetwyler Corp. v. Input Graphics, Inc., 583 F. Supp. 446, 222 U.S.P.Q. 150 (Pa. 1984) - ANTICIPATION, FOREIGN PATENTS AND PROCEEDINGS, GEBRAUCHSMUSTER

Max Daetwyler Corp. v. Input Graphics, Inc., 608 F. Supp. 1549, 226 U.S.P.Q. 393 (Pa. 1985) - ACQUIESCENCE, CONTINUATION-IN-PART APPLICATION, NEW MATTER

Ex parte Maxey and Harrington, 177 U.S.P.Q. 468 (PO Bd. App. 1972) - BETTER, IMPROVEMENT, LIMITING

Maxwell v. J. Baker Inc., 86 F.3d 1098, 39 U.S.P.Q.2d 1001 (Fed. Cir. 1996) - DAMAGES, MARKING, RULE OF REASON, WILLING BUYER-WILLING SELLER RULE

May v. American Southwest Waterbed Distributors, Inc., 715 F.2d 876, 219 U.S.P.Q. 862 (5th Cir. 1983) - SOLUTION

In re May and Eddy, 574 F.2d 1082, 197 U.S.P.Q. 601 (C.C.P.A. 1978) - DISCOVERY, DYESTUFF, ISOMER, NEW USE, OPTICAL ISOMER, PREDICTABILITY, PROPERTY, RACEMATE

Mayo v. Lakeland Highlands Canning Co., 309 U.S. 310 (1940) - PRELIMINARY INJUNCTION, RULE 52(a)

Maxwell v. J. Baker Inc., 86 F.3d 1098, 39 U.S.P.Q.2d 1001 (Fed. Cir. 1996) - UNCLAIMED DISCLOSURE, WILLING BUYER - WILLING SELLER RULE

McArdle v. Bornhofft, 980 F. Supp. 68, 44 U.S.P.Q.2d 1470 (Maine 1997) - TORTIOUS INTERFERENCE

In re McCarn, 212 F.2d 797, 101 U.S.P.Q. 411 (C.C.P.A. 1954) - DEPENDENT CLAIM

McCormick Harvesting Machine Co. v. Aultman, 169 U.S. 606 (1898) - REISSUE

McCormick-Morgan Inc. v. Teledyne Industries Inc., 765 F. Supp. 611, 21 U.S.P.Q.2d 1412 (Cal. 1991) - ATTORNEY-CLIENT PRIVILEGE

McCullough Tool Co. v. Well Surveys, Inc., 343 F.2d 381, 145 U.S.P.Q. 6 (10th Cir. 1965) - PACKAGE LICENSE

McDermott v. Omid International Inc., 723 F. Supp. 1228, 13 U.S.P.Q.2d 1147 (Ohio 1988) - FOREIGN, OPINION OF COUNSEL

In re McGrew, 43 U.S.P.Q.2d 1633 (Fed. Cir. 1997) - DICTUM, 35 U.S.C. §135(b)
McGuire v. Acufex Microsurgical Inc., 34 U.S.P.Q.2d 1749 (Mass. 1994) - EXPERIMENTAL USE

In re McIlroy, 422 F.2d 1397, 170 U.S.P.Q. 31 (C.C.P.A. 1971) - 35 U.S.C. §101

In re McIntosh, 230 F.2d 615, 109 U.S.P.Q. 101 (C.C.P.A. 1956) - BOYKIN ACT, REFERENCE, CONSTRUCTIVE REDUCTION TO PRACTICE, NEW MATTER, NEW SPECIFICATION

In re McKellin, Mageli, and D'Angelo, 529 F.2d 1324, 188 U.S.P.Q. 428 (C.C.P.A. 1976) - CONCESSION, COUNT, FOREIGN, INTERFERENCE COUNT, LOSING INTERFERENCE PARTY, LOST COUNT, OBVIOUSNESS, PRIOR ART, PRIOR INVENTION, 35 U.S.C. §103, 35 U.S.C. §135(a)

Mentor Graphics Corp. v. Quickturn Design Systems Inc., 150 F.3d 1374, 47 U.S.P.Q.2d 1683 (Fed. Cir. 1998) - ASSIGNOR ESTOPPEL

In re Merchant, 575 F.2d 865, 197 U.S.P.Q. 785 (C.C.P.A. 1978) - COMPARATIVE TEST DATA, INDIRECT EVIDENCE, PROPERTIES, RESULTS, SHOWING

In re Mercier, 515 F.2d 780, 185 U.S.P.Q. 774 (C.C.P.A. 1975) - CATALYSIS, CONVENTIONAL, RELATIONSHIP, SIDE REACTION, SUBSTITUTE, TEACHING(S), TERM

In re Merck & Co., 800 F.2d 1091, 231 U.S.P.Q. 375 (Fed. Cir. 1986) - BIOISOSTERISM, OBVIOUSNESS, PHARMACEUTICAL OBVIOUSNESS

Merck & Co. Inc. v. Biocraft Laboratories Inc., 874 F.2d 804, 10 U.S.P.Q.2d 1843 (Fed. Cir. 1989), *cert. denied*, 493 U.S. 975 (1989) - SELECTION

Merck & Co. v. Danbury Pharmacal, Inc., 873 F.2d 1418, 10 U.S.P.Q.2d 1682 (Fed. Cir. 1989) - INTENT

Merck & Co. v. Kessler, 903 F. Supp. 964, 36 U.S.P.Q.2d 1727 (Va. 1995) - 35 U.S.C. §156

Merck & Co. v. Kessler, 80 F.3d 1543, 38 U.S.P.Q.2d 1347 (Fed. Cir. 1996) - HATCH-WAXMAN ACT, ORIGINAL EXPIRATION DATE, PATENT TERM EXTENSION, RESTORATION, RULEMAKING, STATUTORY CONSTRUCTION, STATUTORY INTERPRETATION, URAA

Merck & Co. v. United States International Trade Commission, 774 F.2d 483, 227 U.S.P.Q. 779 (Fed. Cir. 1985) - TERMINAL DISCLAIMER

The Mercoid Corporation v. Mid-Continent Investment Company, 320 U.S. 661, 60 U.S.P.Q. 21 (S.Ct. 1944) - LICENSE

In re Merz, 97 F.2d 599, 38 U.S.P.Q. 143 (C.C.P.A. 1938) - ISOLATED

In re Metcalfe and Lowe, 410 F.2d 1378, 161 U.S.P.Q. 789 (C.C.P.A. 1969) - AVAILABILITY, BREADTH, CONVENIENCE, CRITICAL, FUNCTION, PRODUCT BY PROPERTIES, PROPERTIES, TRADEMARK

Met-Coil Systems Corp. v. Korners Unlimited, Inc., 803 F.2d 684, 231 U.S.P.Q. 474 (Fed. Cir. 1986) - CONTRIBUTORY INFRINGEMENT, IMPLIED LICENSE

Meyers v. ASICS Corp., 711 F. Supp. 1001, 11 U.S.P.Q.2d 1777 (Cal. 1989) - HAGUE EVIDENCE CONVENTION

Meyers v. Asics Corp., 974 F.2d 1304, 24 U.S.P.Q.2d 1036 (Fed. Cir. 1992) - LACHES, PREJUDICE

Meyers v. Brooks Shoe Inc., 912 F.2d 1459, 16 U.S.P.Q.2d 1055 (Fed. Cir. 1990) - INFRINGEMENT CHARGE, LACHES, SUMMARY JUDGMENT

Mezrich v. Lee, 201 U.S.P.Q. 922 (PTO Bd. Pat. Intf. 1978) - INTERFERENCE IN FACT

In re Michlin, 256 F.2d 317, 118 U.S.P.Q. 353 (C.C.P.A. 1958) - SUFFICIENT

Micro-Acoustics Corp. v. Bose Corp., 493 F. Supp. 356, 207 U.S.P.Q. 378 (N.Y. 1980) - BROADEN

Micro Motion Inc. v. Exac Corp., 741 F. Supp. 1426, 16 U.S.P.Q.2d 1001 (Cal. 1990) - MOSITA, ORDINARY SKILL, SECONDARY CONSIDERATIONS, THEORY

Micro Motion Inc. v. Exac Corp., 761 F. Supp. 1420, 19 U.S.P.Q.2d 1001 (Cal. 1991) - ADVICE OF COUNSEL, LOST PROFITS, PRICE EROSION

Micro Motion Inc. v. Kane Steel Co., 894 F.2d 1318, 13 U.S.P.Q.2d 1696 (Fed. Cir. 1990) - DAMAGES, DISCOVERY, LOST PROFITS, SUBPOENA

Mid-America Building Products Corp. v. Richwood Building Products Inc., 970 F. Supp. 612, 44 U.S.P.Q.2d 1207 (Mich. 1997) - TRADE DRESS

Mid-West Conveyor Co. v. Jervis B. Webb Co., 92 F.3d 992, 39 U.S.P.Q.2d 1754 (10th Cir. 1996) - LICENSE, SCOPE

Mikohn Gaming Corp. v. Acres Gaming Inc., 49 U.S.P.Q.2d 1308 (Fed. Cir. 1998) - NOTICE, TORTIOUS INTERFERENCE WITH BUSINESS RELATIONSHIP

Milburn [see *Alexander Milburn Co. v. Davis-Bournonville Co.*, 270 U.S. 390 (1926)]

Miles Laboratories Inc. v. Shandon Inc., 997 F.2d 870, 27 U.S.P.Q.2d 1123 (Fed. Cir. 1993) - REPRESENTATIVE CLAIM

Milgo Electronic Corp. v. United Business Communications, Inc., 623 F.2d 645, 206 U.S.P.Q. 481 (10th Cir. 1980) - BUT-FOR RULE OR TEST, PROBABILITY

Milgo Electronics Corp. v. United Telecommunications, Inc, 189 U.S.P.Q. 160 (Kan. 1976) - AMENDMENT, NEW MATTER, TEACH AWAY FROM

In re Miller, 418 F.2d 1392, 164 U.S.P.Q. 46 (C.C.P.A. 1969) - PRINTED MATTER

In re Miller, 441 F.2d 689, 169 U.S.P.Q. 597 (C.C.P.A. 1971) - BREADTH, DEFINITE-NESS, DEFINITION, ENCOMPASSED, PRODUCT BY PROPERTIES, SCOPE, 35 U.S.C. §112

Miller v. Walker, 214 U.S.P.Q. 845 (PTO Bd. Pat. Intf. 1982) SPECIES

Miller Insituform, Inc. v. Insituform of North America, Inc., 605 F. Supp. 1125, 225 U.S.P.Q. 1232 (Tenn. 1985) - DIVIDING MARKETS

Miller Pipeline Corp. v. British Gas plc, 901 F. Supp. 1416, 38 U.S.P.Q.2d 1010 (Ind. 1995) - ALIEN, FOREIGN, JURISDICTION, VENUE

Milliken Research Corporation v. Dan River, Inc., 739 F.2d 587, 222 U.S.P.Q. 571 (Fed. Cir. 1984) - CAFC, CLAIM, COMBINING REFERENCES, JUDGMENT, MAS-TER, SUGGESTION

In re Mills, 281 F.2d 218, 126 U.S.P.Q. 513 (C.C.P.A. 1960) - HOMOLOGY

In re Mills, 916 F.2d 680, 16 U.S.P.Q.2d 1430 (Fed. Cir. 1990) - OBVIOUSNESS

Milton Hodosh v. Block Drug Co. Inc., 833 F.2d 1575, 4 U.S.P.Q.2d 1935 (Fed. Cir. 1987) - MISUSE

Minco Inc. v. Combustion Engineering Inc., 95 F.3d 1109, 40 U.S.P.Q.2d 1001 (Fed. Cir. 1996) - ASSIGNMENT, REEXAMINATION

Mine Safety Appliances Co. v. Becton Dickinson & Co., 744 F. Supp. 578, 17 U.S.P.Q.2d 1642 (N.Y. 1990) - INTERVENING RIGHTS

Minnesota Mining and Manufacturing Company v. Berwick Industries, Inc., 373 F. Supp. 851, 182 U.S.P.Q. 111 (Pa. 1974) - IMPLIED LICENSE

Minnesota Mining and Manufacturing Company v. Berwick Industries, Inc., 393 F. Supp. 1230, 185 U.S.P.Q. 536 (Pa. 1975) - FIELD OF SEARCH, SUBCLASS

Minnesota Mining and Manufacturing Co. v. Johnson & Johnson Orthopaedic Inc., 22 U.S.P.Q.2d 1401 (Minn. 1991) - COUNSEL, WILLFULNESS

Minnesota Mining and Manufacturing Co. v. Johnson & Johnson Orthopaedics Inc., 976 F.2d 1558, 24 U.S.P.Q.2d 1321 (Fed. Cir. 1992) - ANTICIPATION, DEFERENCE, IDENTITY OF INVENTION

Minnesota Mining and Manufacturing Company v. Neisner Brothers, Inc., 101 F. Supp. 926, 92 U.S.P.Q. 272 (Ill. 1951) - ADHESIVE

Minnesota Mining and Manufacturing Company v. Norton Company, 240 F. Supp. 150, 145 U.S.P.Q. 81 (Ohio 1965) - RETROACTIVE LICENSE

Minnesota Mining & Manufacturing Co. v. Norton Co., 929 F.2d 670, 18 U.S.P.Q.2d 1302 (Fed. Cir. 1991) - DECLARATORY JUDGMENT

Minnesota Mining and Manufacturing v. Smith and Nephew PLC, 25 U.S.P.Q.2d 1587 (Minn. 1992) - FOREIGN, OBVIOUSNESS

Mirafi Inc. v. Murphy, 14 U.S.P.Q.2d 1337 (N.C. 1989) - DOUBLE PATENTING

Mitchell v. Winslow, 17 F. Cas. 527 (C.C.D. Me. 1843) - EXPECTANT INTEREST

Mitek Surgical Products Inc. v. Arthrex Inc., 49 U.S.P.Q.2d 1275 (Fed. Cir. 1998) - ANTITRUST, NOERR-PENNINGTON DOCTRINE, PRIOR ART

Mixing Equipment Co., Inc. v. Innova-Tech, Inc., 228 U.S.P.Q. 221 (Pa. 1985) - PENDING APPLICATION

Mixing Equipment Co., Inc. v. Innova-Tech, Inc., 2 U.S.P.Q.2d 1212 (Pa. 1986) - CONTRIBUTORY INFRINGEMENT, INDUCE

In re Mixon and Wahl, 470 F.2d 1374, 176 U.S.P.Q. 296 (C.C.P.A. 1973) - SIMPLICITY

In re Mlot-Fijalkowski, 676 F.2d 666, 213 U.S.P.Q. 713 (C.C.P.A. 1982) - ANALOGOUS ART, CLASSIFICATION

Mobil Oil Corporation v. Dann, 421 F. Supp. 995, 197 U.S.P.Q. 59 (D.C. 1976) - 37 C.F.R. §1.183

Mobil Oil Corporation v. W.R. Grace & Company, 367 F. Supp. 207, 180 U.S.P.Q. 418 (Conn. 1973) - CATALYSIS, CATALYST, CHEMICAL, OBVIOUSNESS, PRESUMPTION OF VALIDITY, REFERENCE, SAVING, SECONDARY CONSIDERATIONS, SOLUTION, SYNERGISM, TEACH AWAY FROM

In re Mochel, 470 F.2d 638, 176 U.S.P.Q. 194 (C.C.P.A. 1972) - ALLEGATION, CHALLENGE, OPINION, ZERO

In re Mod, Skau, Fore, Magne, Novak, Dupuy, Ortego, and Fisher, 408 F.2d 1055, 161 U.S.P.Q. 281 (C.C.P.A. 1969) - RELATIONSHIP

Modern Computer Corp. v. Ma, 862 F. Supp. 938, 32 U.S.P.Q.2d 1586 (N.Y. 1994) - CEASE AND DESIST LETTER, JURISDICTION, MOTION TO DISMISS, PERSONAL JURISDICTION

Modine Manufacturing Co. v. The Allen Group Inc., 8 U.S.P.Q.2d 1622 (Cal. 1988) - ON SALE, REDUCTION TO PRACTICE

Modine Manufacturing Co. v. Allen Group Inc., 14 U.S.P.Q.2d 1210 (Cal. 1989) - DAMAGES

Modine Manufacturing Co. v. The Allen Group Inc., 917 F.2d 538, 16 U.S.P.Q.2d 1622 (Fed. Cir. 1990) - EXCEPTIONAL

Modine Manufacturing Co. v. U.S. International Trade Commission, 75 F.3d 1545, 37 U.S.P.Q.2d 1609 (Fed. Cir. 1996) - ABOUT, LIMITATION, SMALL

Ex parte Mohr, 77 U.S.P.Q. 510 (PO Bd. App. 1948) - PTO

Moleculon Research Corporation v. CBS, Inc., 793 F.2d 1261, 229 U.S.P.Q. 805 (Fed. Cir. 1986) - ASSIGNMENT, INVENTION, SALE, USE

Molinaro v. Burnbaum, 201 U.S.P.Q. 150 (Mass. 1978) - ATTORNEY'S FEES

Molinaro v. Fanon/Courier Corp., 745 F.2d 651, 223 U.S.P.Q. 706 (Fed. Cir. 1984) - SCOPE

Molins PLC v. Quigg, 837 F.2d 1064, 5 U.S.P.Q.2d 1526 (Fed. Cir. 1988) - FAFR POLICY, 35 U.S.C. §132

Molins PLC v. Textron Inc., 821 F. Supp. 1551, 26 U.S.P.Q.2d 1889 (Del. 1992) - DECLARATION

Molins PLC v. Textron Inc., 840 F. Supp. 306, 30 U.S.P.Q.2d 1054 (Del. 1993) - 35 U.S.C. §285

Molins PLC v. Textron Inc., 48 F.3d 1172, 33 U.S.P.Q.2d 1823 (Fed. Cir. 1995) - ENFORCEABILITY, INTENT TO DECEIVE, MATERIAL, REMAND

Moll v. Northern Telecom Inc., 37 U.S.P.Q.2d 1839 (Pa. 1995) - CLAIM CONSTRUCTION

Monarch Knitting Machinery Corp. v. Sulzer Morat GmbH, 139 F.3d 877, 45 U.S.P.Q.2d 1977 (Fed. Cir. 1998) - CONTEMPORANEOUS INDEPENDENT INVENTION, INTERFERENCE, MOTIVATION, PROBLEM, SOLUTION, TREND

Monolith Portland Midwest Co. v. Kaiser Aluminum & Chemical Corp., 407 F.2d 288, 160 U.S.P.Q. 577 (9th Cir. 1969) - ATTORNEY'S FEES, 35 U.S.C.285

Monon Corp. v. Stoughton Trailers Inc., 38 U.S.P.Q.2d 1503 (Ill. 1996) - ON SALE

Mont-Bell Co. Ltd. v. Mountain Hardwear Inc., 44 U.S.P.Q.2d 1568 (Cal. 1997) - CERTIFICATION, INTERLOCUTORY APPEAL, 28 U.S.C. §1292(b)

Montecatini Edison, S.p.A. v. Ziegler, 172 U.S.P.Q. 519 (D.C. 1972) - CIVIL ACTION, PRIORITY, 35 U.S.C. §146

Montecatini Edison, S.P.A. v. Ziegler, 486 F.2d 1279, 179 U.S.P.Q. 458 (CA D.C. 1973) - COUNTERCLAIM, NEW ISSUES

Moog, Inc. v. Pegasus Laboratories, Inc., 376 F. Supp. 445, 183 U.S.P.Q. 225 (Mich. 1974) - 35 U.S.C. §135(c)

Moog, Inc. v. Pegasus Laboratories, Inc., 521 F.2d 501, 187 U.S.P.Q. 279 (6th Cir. 1975) - CROSS-LICENSE

Ex parte Moon, 224 U.S.P.Q. 519 (PTO Bd. App. 1984) - CLAIM, DEFINITENESS, SPECIFICATION, SYMBOLS, 35 U.S.C. §112

In re Moore, 439 F.2d 1232, 169 U.S.P.Q. 236 (C.C.P.A. 1971) - PARTICULARITY, VACUUM

In re Moore, 444 F.2d 572, 170 U.S.P.Q. 260 (C.C.P.A. 1971) - ALLEGATION, CHALLENGE, OPINION, STATEMENT BY THE BOARD

In re Moore and Janoski, 439 F.2d 1232, 169 U.S.P.Q. 236 (C.C.P.A. 1971) - DEFINITENESS, INVENTION

Moore v. American Barmag Corp., 693 F. Supp. 399, 9 U.S.P.Q.2d 1904 (N.C. 1988) - SHOP RIGHT

Moore v. Hignett, 152 U.S.P.Q. 337 (Comm'r 1966) - MODIFIED COUNT, MOTION BY EXAMINER

Moore v. McGrew, 170 U.S.P.Q. 149 (PO Bd. Pat. Intf. 1971) - OXYGEN, SULFUR

Moore v. Wesbar Corporation, 701 F.2d 1247, 217 U.S.P.Q. 684 (7th Cir. 1983) - EXPERT TESTIMONY, OPINION

Moore Business Forms, Inc. v. Wallace Computer Services, Inc., 14 U.S.P.Q.2d 1849 (Ind. 1989) - PRELIMINARY INJUNCTION, PRESUMPTION OF VALIDITY, SETTLEMENT AGREEMENT

In re Morehouse and Bolton, 545 F.2d 162, 192 U.S.P.Q. 29 (C.C.P.A. 1976) - EXPERIMENTATION, 35 U.S.C. §112

In re Moreton, 312 F.2d 954, 136 U.S.P.Q. 479 (C.C.P.A. 1963) - 35 U.S.C. §120

Morgan v. Daniels, 153 U.S. 120 (1894) - PRESUMPTION OF VALIDITY

In re Morganroth, 6 U.S.P.Q.2d 1802 (Commr. Patents & Trademarks 1988) - REVIVAL

Morganroth v. Quigg, 885 F.2d 843, 12 U.S.P.Q.2d 1125 (Fed. Cir. 1989) - MANDATE, REEXAMINATION, REVIVAL, TERMINATION OF PROCEEDINGS

Ex parte Morimoto, 18 U.S.P.Q.2d 1540 (B.P.A.I. 1991) - CANCELED CLAIMS, RE-CAPTURE, REEXAMINATION CERTIFICATE, VALIDITY

In re Morris, 127 F.3d 1048, 44 U.S.P.Q.2d 1023 (Fed. Cir. 1997) - CLAIM CON-STRUCTION, INTEGRAL

Ex parte Mortimer, 61 F.2d 860, 15 U.S.P.Q. 297 (C.C.P.A. 1932) - COST, SAVING

Morton International Inc. v. Cardinal Chemical Co., 967 F.2d 1571, 23 U.S.P.Q.2d 1362 dissent (Fed. Cir. 1992) - VALIDITY

Morton International Inc. v. Cardinal Chemical Co., 5 F.3d 1464, 28 U.S.P.Q.2d 1190 (Fed. Cir. 1993) - MOOT

Ex parte Mosher and Moore, 136 U.S.P.Q. 662 (PTO Bd. App. 1962) - SMALL

Mother's Restaurant, Inc. v. Mama's Pizza, Inc, 723 F.2d 1566, 221 U.S.P.Q. 394 (Fed. Cir. 1983) - COLLATERAL ESTOPPEL

Motorola Inc. v. Alexander Manufacturing Co., 786 F. Supp. 808, 21 U.S.P.Q.2d 1573 (Iowa 1991) - MARKET SHARE

Motorola Inc. v. Qualcomm Inc., 45 U.S.P.Q.2d 1558 (Cal. 1997) - "POINT OF NOV-ELTY" TEST

Motorola, Inc. v. United States, 729 F.2d 765, 221 U.S.P.Q. 297 (Fed. Cir. 1984) - MARKING

In re Moureu and Chovin, 345 F.2d 595, 145 U.S.P.Q. 452 (C.C.P.A. 1965) - DOSAGE, MODE OF ADMINISTRATION, STRUCTURAL SIMILARITY, UTILITY

Mova Pharmaceutical Corp. v. Shalala, 41 U.S.P.Q.2d 2012, (D.C. 1997) - AGENCY INTERPRETATION, ANDA, 21 U.S.C. §355(j)(4)(B)(iii)

Mova Pharmaceutical Corp. v. Shalala, 140 F.3d 1060, 46 U.S.P.Q.2d 1385 (D.C. Cir. 1998) - 21 C.F.R. §314.107(c)(1), INTENT OF CONGRESS, INTERVENTION, STANDING, SUCCESSFUL DEFENSE

In re Mulder and Wulms, 716 F.2d 1542, 219 U.S.P.Q. 189 (Fed. Cir. 1983) - ANTEDAT-ING A REFERENCE, 37 C.F.R. §1.131, CONCEPTION, FOREIGN, 35 U.S.C. §119

Ex parte Mullen and Mullen, 1890 C.D. 9, 50 O.G. 837 (Commr. Patents 1890) - LATE CLAIMING

In re Mullin, Wetherby, and Chevalier, 481 F.2d 1333, 179 U.S.P.Q. 97 (C.C.P.A. 1973) - 37 C.F.R. §1.106, REJECTION

Multiform Desiccants Inc. v. Medzam Ltd., 133 F.3d 1473, 45 U.S.P.Q.2d 1429 (Fed. Cir. 1998) - AFFIRMATIVE DEFENSE, CLAIM CONSTRUCTION, COUNTERCLAIM

Munters Corporation v. Burgess Industries Incorporated, 201 U.S.P.Q. 756 (N.Y. 1978) - RESTRAINT ON USE

In re Murch, 464 F.2d 1051, 175 U.S.P.Q. 89 (C.C.P.A. 1972) - COMMON PROPER-TIES, DYESTUFF, PREDICTABILITY, RELATIONSHIP, SINGLE PROPERTY

Murton v. Ladd, 352 F.2d 942, 146 U.S.P.Q. 699 (D.C. Cir. 1965) - BREADTH

In re Musgrave, 431 F.2d 882, 167 U.S.P.Q. 280 (C.C.P.A. 1970) - MENTAL STEPS

Mushroom Associates v. Monterey Mushrooms Inc., 24 U.S.P.Q.2d 1767 (Cal. 1992) - ADVICE OF COUNSEL, ATTORNEY-CLIENT PRIVILEGE, WORK PRODUCT IMMUNITY

Mushroom Associates v. Monterey Mushrooms Inc., 25 U.S.P.Q.2d 1304 (Cal. 1992) - FACSIMILE, RULE 5(b), SERVICE

Ex parte Musselman, 94 U.S.P.Q. 212 (PO Bd. App. 1949) - CLASSIFICATION

In re Myers, 104 F.2d 391, 42 U.S.P.Q. 32 (C.C.P.A. 1939) - COMPACTNESS

In re Myers, 120 U.S.P.Q. 225 (Comm'r of Patents 1958) - DRAWING

In re Myers, 410 F.2d 420, 161 U.S.P.Q. 668 (C.C.P.A. 1969) - DETAILS, DISCLOSURE, EXCLUDE, INOPERATIVE, OMISSION, ORIGINAL CLAIMS, OVERCLAIMING, PARTICULARITY, SKILLED IN THE ART

Myers v. Beall Pipe & Tank Corp., 80 F. Supp. 265, 79 U.S.P.Q. 173 (Or. 1948) - OMISSION OF ELEMENT OR STEP

-n-

Naber v. Cricchi, 567 F.2d 382, 196 U.S.P.Q. 294 (C.C.P.A. 1977), *cert. denied*, 439 U.S. 826, 200 U.S.P.Q. 64 (1978) - 35 U.S.C. §102(g)

In re Naber and Dautzenberg, 503 F.2d 1059, 183 U.S.P.Q. 245 (C.C.P.A. 1974) - DOUBT

Nabisco Brands Inc. v. Conusa Corp., 722 F. Supp. 1287, 11 U.S.P.Q.2d 1788 (N.C. 1989) - PATENT

Ex parte Naito and Nakagawa, 168 U.S.P.Q. 437 (PO Bd. App. 1969) - STATUTORY BAR

In re Napier, 55 F.3d 610, 34 U.S.P.Q.2d 1782 (Fed. Cir. 1995) - OBVIOUSNESS

In re Naquin, 398 F.2d 863, 158 U.S.P.Q. 317 (C.C.P.A. 1968) - OPINION, SKILLED IN THE ART

Narco Avionics Inc. v. Sportsman's Market Inc., 792 F. Supp. 398, 24 U.S.P.Q.2d 1283 (Pa. 1992) - STREAM OF COMMERCE

The Narda Microwave Corporation v. General Microwave Corporation, 201 U.S.P.Q. 231 (N.Y. 1978) - THIRD PARTY, UNITED STATES

Ex parte Nardi and Simier, 229 U.S.P.Q. 79 (B.P.A.I. 1986) - BEST MODE, CONCEALMENT, ENABLEMENT, EXAMPLE, WORKING EXAMPLE

Nasatka v. Delta Scientific Corp., 34 U.S.P.Q.2d 1649 (Va. 1994) - BURDEN, DISCOVERY, INFRINGEMENT, RULE 11

Naso v. Park, 856 F. Supp. 201, 34 U.S.P.Q.2d 1463 (N.Y. 1994) - JEPSON

Ex parte Natale, 11 U.S.P.Q.2d 1222 (B.P.A.I. 1989) - CHALLENGE

In re Nathan, Hogg, and Schneider, 328 F.2d 1005, 140 U.S.P.Q. 601 (C.C.P.A. 1964) - CHALLENGE, DECLARATION, INHERENT CHARACTERISTIC OR PROPERTY, NEW MATTER, OPINION, STATEMENT

National Business Systems, Inc. v. AM International, Inc., 546 F. Supp. 340, 217 U.S.P.Q. 235 (Ill. 1982) - INVALID CLAIM, INVALIDITY, JURISDICTION, PATENT, PTO, REVOCATION

National Hockey League v. Metropolitan Hockey Club, Inc., 427 U.S. 639 (1976) - DISMISSAL

National Patent Development Corp. v. T. J. Smith & Nephew Ltd., 877 F.2d 1003, 11 U.S.P.Q.2d 1211 (D.C. Cir. 1989) - FOREIGN PATENTEE

National Presto Industries Inc. v. Black & Decker (U.S.) Inc., 760 F. Supp. 699, 19 U.S.P.Q.2d 1457 (Ill. 1991) - ADVERTISING, CONCEALMENT, MISCONDUCT, MISUSE, PATENT, PENDING, UNCLEAN HANDS

National Presto Industries Inc. v. Dazey Corp., 107 F.3d 1576, 42 U.S.P.Q.2d 1070 (Fed. Cir. 1997) - ANCILLARY JURISDICTION, SETTLEMENT AGREEMENT

National Presto Industries Inc. v. The West Bend Co., 76 F.3d 1185, 37 U.S.P.Q.2d 1685 (Fed. Cir. 1996) - CLAIM, INDUCEMENT, EVIDENCE, MEANING, SUMMARY JUDGMENT, 35 U.S.C. §271(b)

National Research Development Corporation v. Great Lakes Carbon Corporation, 410 F. Supp. 1108, 188 U.S.P.Q. 327 (Del. 1975) - TEST

The National Research Development Corp. v. Varian Associates Inc., 17 F.3d 1444, 30 U.S.P.Q.2d 1537 (Fed. Cir. 1994) - PUBLIC USE

National Semiconductor Corp. v. Lenier Technology Corp., 703 F. Supp. 845, 8 U.S.P.Q.2d 1359 (Cal. 1988) - PUBLICATION

National Texture Corporation v. Hymes, 200 U.S.P.Q. 59 (Minn. 1977) - LEGAL FEES, OWNERSHIP

In re Natta, 388 F.2d 215, 156 U.S.P.Q. 289 (C.C.P.A. 1968) - DISCOVERY

Natta and Crespi v. Payne, 165 U.S.P.Q. 466 (PTO Bd. Pat. Int. 1970) - COPYING CLAIMS

Neff Instrument Corporation v. Cohu Electronics, Inc., 298 F.2d 82, 132 U.S.P.Q. 98 (9th Cir. 1961) - COPYING, VALIDITY

Neirbo Co. v. Bethlehem Shipbuilding Corp., 308 U.S. 165 (1939) - VENUE

Nelson v. Bowler, 626 F.2d 853, 206 U.S.P.Q. 881 (C.C.P.A. 1980) - *IN VITRO, IN VIVO*

Nenzell v. Hutson, Imboden, and Englis, 299 F.2d 864, 132 U.S.P.Q. 635 (C.C.P.A. 1962) - 35 U.S.C. §141

Neorx Corp. v. Immunomedics Inc., 28 U.S.P.Q.2d 1395 (N.J. 1993) - ATTORNEY-CLIENT PRIVILEGE, BIFURCATION, WILLFULNESS

NeoRx Corp. v. Immunomedics Inc., 28 U.S.P.Q.2d 1797 (N.J. 1993) - FDA, GOOD CLINICAL PRACTICE, SELF-EVALUATIVE PRIVILEGE

Ex parte Nesbit, 25 U.S.P.Q.2d 1817 (B.P.A.I. 1992) - DOUBLE PATENTING

Neufeld-Furst & Co., Inc. v. Jay-Day Frocks Inc., 112 F.2d 715 (2d Cir. 1940) - DESIGN

In re Newell, 891 F.2d 899, 13 U.S.P.Q.2d 1248 (Fed. Cir. 1989) - COMBINATION, INHERENCY, MOTIVATION, PROBLEM, PROPERTIES, UNKNOWN

Newell Companies v. Kenney Manufacturing Co., 606 F. Supp. 1282, 226 U.S.P.Q. 157 (R.I. 1985) - CONCEALED DISCLOSURE, DOCUMENTATION, IN-HOUSE DOCUMENTATION, MEMORANDUM, PRIOR ART

New Hampshire Insurance Co. v. R.L. Chaides Construction Co. Inc., 847 F. Supp. 1452, 30 U.S.P.Q.2d 1474 (Cal. 1994) - PIRACY

New Ideal Farm Equipment Corp. v. Sperry Corp. & New Holland Inc., 916 F.2d 1561, 16 U.S.P.Q.2d 1424 (Fed. Cir. 1990) - 35 U.S.C. §102(g)

In re Newton, 414 F.2d 1400, 163 U.S.P.Q. 34 (C.C.P.A. 1969) - 37 C.F.R. §1.71(b), FORM, RULES OF PRACTICE

Newton Insert Co. v. Commissioner of Internal Revenue, 181 U.S.P.Q. 765 (U.S.T.C. 1974) - ASSIGNMENT, CAPITAL ASSET, CAPITAL GAINS, DEPRECIATION, SALE, TAXATION

Nickola v. Peterson, 580 F.2d 898, 198 U.S.P.Q. 385 (6th Cir. 1978) - FUNCTION, IMPROVEMENT, PROMOTE PROGRESS, RESULT

Nickson Industries, Inc. v. Rol Manufacturing Co. Ltd., 847 F.2d 795, 6 U.S.P.Q.2d 1878 (Fed. Cir. 1988) - ROYALTY

-O-

In re Ockert, 245 F.2d 467, 114 U.S.P.Q. 330 (C.C.P.A. 1957) - CROSS-READING, DOUBLE PATENTING

In re Oda, Fujii, Moriga, and Higaki, 443 F.2d 1200, 170 U.S.P.Q. 268 (C.C.P.A. 1971) - NEW MATTER, REISSUE, STATUTORY INTERPRETATION, REMEDIAL STATUTE

OddzOn Products Inc. v. Just Toys Inc., 122 F.3d 1396, 43 U.S.P.Q.2d 1641 (Fed. Cir. 1997) - CONFUSION, DERIVATION, DESIGN, 35 U.S.C. §102(f)

Odetics Inc. v. Storage Technology Corp., 47 U.S.P.Q.2d 1573 (Va. 1998) - COMPULSORY LICENSE, LACHES, PRELIMINARY INJUNCTION, PUBLIC INTEREST, RIGHT TO EXCLUDE

Odetics Inc. v. Storage Technology Corp., 47 U.S.P.Q.2d 1923 (Va. 1998) - MEANS PLUS FUNCTION

In re Oelrich and Divigard, 666 F.2d 578, 212 U.S.P.Q. 323 (C.C.P.A. 1981) - COLLATERAL ESTOPPEL, INHERENCY, POSSIBILITY, PROBABILITY, *RES JUDICATA*

In re Oetiker, 977 F.2d 1443, 1445, 24 U.S.P.Q.2d 1443 (Fed. Cir. 1992) - OBVIOUSNESS, PRIMA FACIE

Oetiker v. Jurid Werke GmbH, 209 U.S.P.Q. 809 (D.C. 1981) - BUT-FOR RULE OR TEST, FAILURE TO DISCLOSE, INVENTORSHIP, ORIGIN

In re O'Farrell, 853 F.2d 894, 7 U.S.P.Q.2d 1673 (Fed. Cir. 1988) - OBVIOUSNESS, OBVIOUS TO TRY OR EXPERIMENT, PREDICTABILITY, REASONABLE, RECOMBINANT DNA TECHNOLOGY, SUCCESS

In re Ogiue, 517 F.2d 382, 186 U.S.P.Q. 227 (C.C.P.A. 1975) - CLAIMS SUGGESTED FOR INTERFERENCE, CONCESSION, COPYING CLAIMS, DISCLAIMER, LOST COUNT, PRIOR ART

Ex parte Ohmart, 143 U.S.P.Q. 119 (PO Bd. App. 1962) - 35 U.S.C. §102(c)

Ex parte Ohsaka, 2 U.S.P.Q.2d 1461 (B.P.A.I. 1987) - COMPARATIVE TEST DATA, INHERENT

Ex parte Ohsumi, 21 U.S.P.Q.2d 1020 (B.P.A.I. 1991) - 37 C.F.R. §1.192(c)(5), CLAIMS, STAND OR FALL TOGETHER

O.I. Corp. v. Tekmar Co., 42 U.S.P.Q.2d 1777 (Fed. Cir. 1997) - CLAIM DIFFERENTIATION

Oiestad v. Ag-Industrial Equipment Co. Inc., 44 U.S.P.Q.2d 1526 (Fed. Cir. 1997 - *unpublished*) - SUMMARY JUDGMENT

Oka v. Youssefyeh, 849 F.2d 581, 7 U.S.P.Q.2d 1169 (Fed. Cir. 1988) - TIE

Okada v. Hitotsumachi, 16 U.S.P.Q.2d 1789 (Commr. Patents & Trademarks 1990) - INTERFERENCE, INTERFERENCE IN FACT, PRESUMPTION OF VALIDITY, 35 U.S.C. §282

Ex parte Old, 229 U.S.P.Q. 196 (B.P.A.I. 1985) - ANTIBODY, ANTIGEN, DEPOSIT OF CELL LINE, ENABLEMENT, HYBRIDOMA, KOHLER-MILSTEIN TECHNIQUE, MONOCLONAL ANTIBODIES, OBVIOUSNESS, OBVIOUS TO TRY OR EXPERIMENT, PREDICTABILITY

Olin v. Duerr, Aebi and Ebner, 175 U.S.P.Q. 707 (PO Bd. Pat. Intf. 1972) - STIPULATION, 35 U.S.C. §135(b)

In re Olson, 212 F.2d 590, 101 U.S.P.Q. 401 (C.C.P.A. 1954) - DRAWING

Olson v. Julia, 209 U.S.P.Q. 159 (PTO Bd. Pat. Intf. 1979) - 35 U.S.C. §119

Ex parte Olsson, 65 U.S.P.Q. 52 (PO Bd. App. 1944) - MULTIPLE INCLUSION

Olympic Fastening Systems, Inc. v. Textron Inc., 504 F.2d 609, 183 U.S.P.Q. 449 (6th Cir. 1974) - ABANDONMENT, CANCELLATION, ENVIRONMENT, SUBSTAN-TIALLY, UNNECESSARY

In re Application for an Order for Judicial Assistance in a Foreign Proceeding in the High Court of Justice, Chancery Division, England, 147 F.R.D. 223 (C.D. Cal. 1993) - FOREIGN

Oregon Precision Industries Inc. v. International Omni-Pac Corp., 160 F.R.D. 592, 36 U.S.P.Q.2d 1117 (Or. 1995) - DISCOVERY, JURISDICTION

Oregon Precision Industries Inc. v. International Omni-Pac Corp., 889 F. Supp. 412, 36 U.S.P.Q.2d 1708 (Or. 1995) - JURISDICTION

Ortho Diagnostic Systems Inc. v. Miles Inc., 865 F. Supp. 1073, 35 U.S.P.Q.2d 1263 (N.Y. 1994) - INTRODUCE INTO EVIDENCE, REQUEST TO ADMIT

Orthokinetics Inc. v. Safety Travel Chairs Inc., 806 F.2d 1565, 1 U.S.P.Q.2d 1081 (Fed. Cir. 1986) - BREADTH, CLAIM, CLAIM LANGUAGE, CONTRIBUTORY IN-FRINGEMENT, CORPORATE OFFICER, DEFINITENESS, DESCRIPTION, DIMENSIONS, DISCLOSURE, (FULL, CLEAR, CONCISE, AND EXACT), IN-OPERATIVE EMBODIMENTS, PARTICULARITY, SCOPE, SPECIFICITY, SUFFICIENT, SUITABLE, 35 U.S.C. §112

Orthopaedic Equipment Co. v. United States, 702 F.2d 1005, 217 U.S.P.Q. 193 (Fed. Cir. 1983) - COMBINING REFERENCES

Orthopedic Equipment Company, Inc. v. All Orthopedic Appliances, Inc., 707 F.2d 1376, 217 U.S.P.Q. 1281 (Fed. Cir. 1983) - INCONSISTENT

Ortho Pharmaceutical Corp. v. Genetics Institute Inc., 52 F.3d 1026, 34 U.S.P.Q.2d 1444 (Fed. Cir. 1995) - RIGHT TO SUE

Ortho Parmaceutical Corp. v. Smith, 15 U.S.P.Q.2d 1856 (Pa. 1990) - COMPOUND, DRUG, MARKET SHARE, PROPERTIES, VALIDITY

Ortho Pharmaceutical Corp. v. Smith, 18 U.S.P.Q.2d 1977 (Pa. 1990) - CONVERSION (*IN SITU* OR *IN VIVO*), DRUG, INEQUITABLE CONDUCT, INFRINGEMENT, INJUNCTION

Ortho Pharmaceutical Corp. v. Smith, 959 F.2d 936, 22 U.S.P.Q.2d 1119 (Fed. Cir. 1992) - PRO-DRUG, TERMINAL DISCLAIMER

Orton v. Robicon Corporation, 378 F. Supp. 930, 183 U.S.P.Q. 477 (Pa. 1974) - 35 U.S.C. §102(b)

Oscar Mayer Foods Corp. v. ConAgra Inc., 35 U.S.P.Q.2d 1278 (Fed. Cir. 1994 - *un-published*) - PROBLEM

In re Osweiler, 346 F.2d 617, 145 U.S.P.Q. 691 (C.C.P.A. 1965) - NEW ISSUES

Otis Elevator Co. v. Intelligence Systems Inc., 17 U.S.P.Q.2d 1773 (Conn. 1990) - TRADE SECRET

Ott v. Goodpasture Inc., 40 U.S.P.Q.2d 1831 (Tex. 1996) - INEQUITABLE CONDUCT

Output Technology Corp. v. Dataproducts Corp., 22 U.S.P.Q.2d 1639 (Wash. 1992) - MOTION TO COMPEL, REEXAMINATION

Ex parte Ovshinsky, 10 U.S.P.Q.2d 1075 (B.P.A.I. 1989) - 37 C.F.R. §1.131

-*P*-

649 (Fed. Cir. 1986) - CONTINUATION-IN-PART APPLICATION, PRIOR ART, REFERENCE, SUFFICIENCY, 35 U.S.C. §102(b)

In re Papesch, 315 F.2d 381, 137 U.S.P.Q. 43 (C.C.P.A. 1963) - CHEMICAL OBVIOUS-NESS, COMPARATIVE TEST DATA, OBVIOUSNESS, PROBLEM, PRODUCT, PROPERTIES

Ex parte Pappas, 23 U.S.P.Q.2d 1636 (B.P.A.I. 1992) - COMBINING REFERENCES

Ex parte Papst-Motoren, 1 U.S.P.Q.2d 1655 (B.P.A.I. 1986) - CONSTRUCTION OF CLAIMS

In re Paquette, 423 F.2d 1401, 165 U.S.P.Q. 317 (C.C.P.A. 1970) - FORMULA

Paradigm Sales Inc. v. Weber Marking Systems Inc., 880 F. Supp. 1237, 34 U.S.P.Q.2d 1039 (Ind. 1994) - RECONSIDERATION, RULE 60(b)

Paragon Podiatry Laboratory Inc. v. KLM Laboratories Inc., 984 F.2d 1182, 25 U.S.P.Q.2d 1561 (Fed. Cir. 1993) - DUTY TO DISCLOSE, EXPERIMENTAL USE, INEQUITABLE CONDUCT

Paragould Cablevision v. City of Paragould, Ark., 930 F.2d 1310 (8th Cir.), *cert. denied,* 112 S.Ct. 430, 116 L.Ed.2d 450 (1991) - MARKET PARTICIPANT

Ex parte Parker, 152 U.S.P.Q. 627 (PO Bd. App. 1966) - DISCLAIMER

Parker v. Brown, 317 U.S. 341, 87 L.Ed. 315 (1943) - SHERMAN ACT

Parker Hanifin Corp. v. Davco Manufacturing Corp., 128 F.R.D. 91, 13 U.S.P.Q.2d 1412 (Ohio 1989) - REEXAMINATION, REQUESTOR

Ex parte Parks, 30 U.S.P.Q.2d 1234 (B.P.A.I. 1993) - EXCLUDE, NEGATIVE LIM-ITATION, SUPPORT

Parks v. Fine, 773 F.2d 1577, 227 U.S.P.Q. 432 (Fed. Cir. 1985) - COPYING CLAIMS, INHERENCY

Parkson Corp. v. Proto Circuits, Inc., 220 U.S.P.Q. 898 (Md. 1983) - EXAMINER, PRESUMPTION OF VALIDITY, PRIOR ART

Ex parte Parthasarathy and Ciapetta, 174 U.S.P.Q. 63 (PO Bd. App. 1971) - HINDSIGHT, IMPROVEMENT, MODIFICATION, OBVIOUSNESS, OPTI-MIZE, RATIO, REASON

Ex parte Passino and Wrightson, 118 U.S.P.Q. 515 (P.O. Bd. App. 1957) - CRITICAL

Patecell v. United States, 16 Cl. Ct. 644, 12 U.S.P.Q.2d 1440 (Cl. Ct. 1989) - RECAP-TURE RULE

Patlex Corp. v. Mossinghoff, 585 F. Supp. 713, 220 U.S.P.Q. 342 (Pa. 1983) - CHAL-LENGE, REEXAMINATION

Patlex Corp. v. Mossinghoff, 759 F.2d 594, 225 U.S.P.Q. 543 (Fed. Cir. 1985) - JURY

Patlex Corp. v. Mossinghoff, 771 F.2d 480, 226 U.S.P.Q. 985 (Fed. Cir. 1985) - 37 C.F.R. §1.530(a), DOUBT, MPEP, REEXAMINATION, REQUEST FOR REEXAMINA-TION, RESOLUTION OF DOUBT

Patlex Corp. v. Quigg, 680 F. Supp. 33, 5 U.S.P.Q.2d 1539 (D.C. 1987) - ENABLING DISCLOSURE, REEXAMINATION

Patlex Corp. v. Quigg, 680 F. Supp. 33, 6 U.S.P.Q.2d 1296 (D.C. 1988) - REEXAMINATION

In re Patton, 127 F.2d 324, 53 U.S.P.Q. 376 (C.C.P.A. 1942) - METHOD OF DOING BUSINESS

In re Paul F. Williams, 36 F.2d 436, 4 U.S.P.Q. 237 (C.C.P.A. 1930) - DEGREE, FORM, PROPORTIONS, SIZE, SUBSTITUTION OF EQUIVALENTS

Paulik v. Rizkalla, 760 F.2d 1270, 226 U.S.P.Q. 224 (Fed. Cir. 1985) - DILIGENCE, INTERFERENCE, PRIORITY, RESUMED ACTIVITY, 35 U.S.C. §102(g)

In re Paulsen, 30 F.3d 1475, 31 U.S.P.Q.2d 1671 (Fed. Cir. 1994) - INTENDED USE, PREAMBLE, PROBLEM

Ex parte Payne, 1904 C.D. 42, 108 O.G. 1049 (Comm'r 1903) - PERPETUAL MOTION

Ex parte Pearson, 230 U.S.P.Q. 711 (B.P.A.I. 1985) - ANTECEDENT SUPPORT, DESCRIPTION, EXCLUDING PRIOR ART, FREE, GENUS, NEW MATTER

In re Pearson, 494 F.2d 1399, 181 U.S.P.Q. 641 (C.C.P.A. 1974) - COMPOSITION, INTENDED USE, PROPERTY, USE

In re Peehs and Hunner, 612 F.2d 1287, 204 U.S.P.Q. 835 (C.C.P.A. 1980) - EXPLANATION, PROBLEM, SOURCE, STATEMENT, SUBJECT MATTER AS A WHOLE

Peeler, Godfrey, and Forby v. Miller, 535 F.2d 647, 190 U.S.P.Q. 117 (C.C.P.A. 1976) - INACTIVITY, SPURRING

Penda Corp. v. U.S., 44 F.3d 967, 33 U.S.P.Q.2d 1200 (Fed. Cir. 1994) - COPARTY, STANDING

Pennsylvania v. Union Gas Co., 491 U.S. 1 (1989) - STATES' IMMUNITY

Pennwalt Corporation v. Akzona Incorporated, 740 F.2d 1573, 222 U.S.P.Q. 833 (Fed. Cir. 1984) - CONTINUATION-IN-PART APPLICATION, EXPERIMENTAL USE, USE

Pennwalt Corp. v. Durand-Weyland Inc., 833 F.2d 931, 4 U.S.P.Q.2d 1737 (Fed. Cir. 1987) - DOCTRINE OF EQUIVALENTS, ESTOPPEL, MEANS PLUS FUNCTION, NARROWING CLAIM, PROSECUTION HISTORY ESTOPPEL

Pentech International Inc. v. Hayduchok, 18 U.S.P.Q.2d 1337 (N.Y. 1990) - SPECIFICATION

Perkin-Elmer Corp. v. Computervision Corp., 732 F.2d 888, 221 U.S.P.Q. 669 (Fed. Cir.), *cert. denied*, 469 U.S. 857 (1984) - SUBSTANTIAL EVIDENCE

Perkin-Elmer v. Westinghouse, 822 F.2d 1528, 3 U.S.P.Q.2d 1321 (Fed. Cir. 1987) - RELIANCE

Ex parte Perlman, 123 U.S.P.Q. 447 (PO Bd. App. 1958) - ION EXCHANGE

Permanence Corp. v. Kennametal Inc., 908 F.2d 98, 15 U.S.P.Q.2d 1550 (6th Cir. 1990) - BEST EFFORTS

Pero v. General Motors Corp., 230 U.S.P.Q. 719 (Mich. 1986) - FILE WRAPPER ESTOPPEL

Personalized Media Communications LLC v. ITC, 48 U.S.P.Q.2d 1880 (Fed. Cir. 1998) - MEANS

In re Petering and Fall, 301 F.2d 676, 133 U.S.P.Q. 275 (C.C.P.A. 1962) - DESCRIPTION, JUDICIAL NOTICE, 35 U.S.C. §102(b) Ex parte Petersen, 228 U.S.P.Q. 216 (B.P.A.I. 1985) - DESIGN CHOICE, EXPERIMENTATION, LIMITATION, SELECTION

In re Petersen, 223 F.2d 508, 106 U.S.P.Q. 281 (C.C.P.A. 1955) - COMBINING STEPS

Petersen v. Fee International, Ltd., 381 F. Supp. 1071, 182 U.S.P.Q. 264 (Okla. 1974) - CROWDED ART, STRUCTURAL LIMITATION

Petersen Manufacturing Co. Inc. v. Adjustable Clamp Co. Inc., 30 U.S.P.Q 2d 1193 (Ill. 1993) - CASE OR CONTROVERSY

Petersen Manufacturing Co., Inc. v. Central Purchasing, Inc., 740 F.2d 1541, 222 U.S.P.Q. 562 (Fed. Cir. 1984) - CAFC

Petrolite Corp. v. Baker Hughes Inc., 96 F.3d 1423, 40 U.S.P.Q.2d 1201 (Fed. Cir. 1996) - PUBLIC USE

In re Petrzilka, Hofmann, Schenk, Trexler, Frey, and Ott, 424 F.2d 1102, 165 U.S.P.Q. 327 (C.C.P.A. 1970) - EVIDENCE, FAITH, PHARMACEUTICAL, GENERIC DISCLOSURE, SELECTION, SKEPTICISM

Pfaff v. Wells Electronics Inc., 5 F.3d 514, 28 U.S.P.Q.2d 1119 (Fed. Cir. 1993) - PRECLUSION, SCOPE

Pfaff v. Wells Electronics Inc., 43 U.S.P.Q.2d 1928 (Fed. Cir. 1997) - ON SALE

Pfizer Inc. v. International Rectifier Corp., 685 F.2d 357, 217 U.S.P.Q. 39 (9th Cir. 1982) - FRAUD

Philips, Haley, and Clifton v. Matthews, 197 U.S.P.Q. 776 (PTO Bd. Pat. Intf. 1977) - EXPERT TESTIMONY

In re Phillips, 148 F.2d 662, 65 U.S.P.Q. 213 (C.C.P.A. 1945) - DEDICATION TO THE PUBLIC, LATE CLAIMING

In re Phillips, 315 F.2d 943, 137 U.S.P.Q. 369 (C.C.P.A. 1963) - JUDICIAL NOTICE, 35 U.S.C. §144

In re Phillips and Crick, 673 F.2d 1273, 213 U.S.P.Q. 353 (C.C.P.A. 1982) - COPYING CLAIMS, REFUSING TO COPY CLAIMS

Phillips Petroleum Company v. E.I. du Pont de Nemours & Co.; E.I. du Pont de Nemours & Co. v. Montecatini Edison S.p.A., 342 F. Supp. 125, 174 U.S.P.Q. 7 (Del. 1972) - 28 U.S.C. §1338(a)

Phillips Petroleum Company v. Montedison, S.p.A.; E.I. du Pont de Nemours & Company v. Montedison, S.p.A., 494 F. Supp. 370, 207 U.S.P.Q. 298 (Del. 1980) - 35 U.S.C. §146

Phillips Petroleum Co. v. Rexene Products Co., 158 F.R.D. 43, 32 U.S.P.Q.2d 1839 (Del. 1994) - PROTECTIVE ORDER

Phillips Plastics Corp. v. Kato Hatsujou Kabushiki Kaisha, 57 F.3d 1051, 35 U.S.P.Q.2d 1222 (Fed. Cir. 1995) - DECLARATORY JUDGMENT, REASONABLE APPREHENSION

Phonometrics Inc. v. Northern Telecom Inc., 133 F.3d 1459, 45 U.S.P.Q.2d 1421 (Fed. Cir. 1998 - RULE 60(b)

In re Piasecki and Meyers, 745 F.2d 1468, 223 U.S.P.Q. 785 (Fed. Cir. 1984) - SECONDARY CONSIDERATIONS

Picard v. United Aircraft Corp., 128 F.2d 632, 53 U.S.P.Q. 563 (2d Cir.), *cert. denied*, 317 U.S. 651, 55 U.S.P.Q. 493 (1942) - BEST MODE

Pickering v. McCullough, 104 U.S. (14 Otto) 310 (1881) - COMBINATION

Pierce v. American Communications Company, Inc., 169 F. Supp. 351, 119 U.S.P.Q. 456 (Mass. 1958) - INVALIDITY, OBVIOUSNESS

Pierce v. Watson, Commissioner of Patents, 275 F.2d 890, 124 U.S.P.Q. 356 (D.C. Cir. 1960) - ASSIGNEE

In re Pio, 217 F.2d 956, 104 U.S.P.Q. 177 (C.C.P.A. 1954) - ANTICIPATION, DESIGN

Pipe Liners Inc. v. American Pipe & Plastics Inc., 893 F. Supp. 704, 36 U.S.P.Q.2d 1798 (Tex. 1995) - EQUITABLE TITLE

Pirkle v. Ogontz Controls Co., 39 U.S.P.Q.2d 1317 (Pa. 1996) - CONTEMPT

Ex parte Powers, 220 U.S.P.Q. 924 (PTO Bd. App. 1982) - ENABLEMENT, UNDUE EXPERIMENTATION

PPG Industries, Inc. v. Bausch & Lomb, Inc., 205 U.S.P.Q. 914 (N.Y. 1979) - 35 U.S.C. §135(c)

PPG Industries, Inc. v. Guardian Industries Corporation, 597 F.2d 1090, 202 U.S.P.Q. 95 (6th Cir. 1979) - LICENSE, RESTRICTION

PPG Industries Inc. v. Guardian Industries Corp., 75 F.3d 1558, 37 U.S.P.Q.2d 1618 (Fed. Cir. 1996) - UNDUE EXPERIMENTATION

PPG Industries Inc. v. Guardian Industries Corp., 48 U.S.P.Q.2d 1351 (Fed. Cir. 1998) - CONSISTING ESSENTIALLY OF

In re Prater and Wei, 415 F.2d 1378, 159 U.S.P.Q. 583 (C.C.P.A. 1968) - APPARATUS, ART, MENTAL STEPS, PROCESS

In re Prater and Wei, 415 F.2d 1393, 162 U.S.P.Q. 541 (C.C.P.A. 1969) - CLAIM CONSTRUCTION, INVENTION, UNPATENTED CLAIM, 35 U.S.C. §112

Precision Instrument Manufacturing Co. v. Automotive Maintenance Machine Co., 324 U.S. 806, 65 U.S.P.Q. 133 (1945) - DUTY TO DISCLOSE

Preemption Devices, Inc. v. Minnesota Mining and Manufacturing Co., 559 F. Supp. 1250, 218 U.S.P.Q. 245 (Pa. 1983) - DISCOVERY, INFRINGEMENT, INFRINGER, NIT-PICKING

Preemption Devices, Inc. v. Minnesota Mining & Manufacturing Co., 732 F.2d 903, 221 U.S.P.Q. 841 (Fed. Cir. 1984) - ADVANTAGE, CLAIM, DECISION, VALIDITY

Premo Pharmaceutical Laboratories, Inc. v. USV Laboratories, Inc., 481 F. Supp. 193, 203 U.S.P.Q. 852 (N.Y. 1979) - TRO

Premysler v. Lehman, 33 U.S.P.Q.2d 1859 (D.C. 1994) - ADMISSION TO PRACTICE BEFORE THE PTO

Pretty Punch Shoppettes, Inc. v. Hauk, 844 F.2d 782, 784, 6 U.S.P.Q.2d 1563 (Fed. Cir. 1988) - PRELIMINARY INJUNCTION, RULE 52(a)

PreVent Inc. v. WNCK Inc., 33 U.S.P.Q.2d 1701 (Penn. 1994) - AFFIRMATIVE DEFENSE, LEAVE TO AMEND

Price v. Symsek, 988 F.2d 1187, 26 U.S.P.Q.2d 1031 (Fed. Cir. 1993) - CORROBORATION, PROOF

Price v. Vandenberg v. Bailey, 174 U.S.P.Q. 42 (PO Bd. Pat. Intf. 1971) - CONTAIN, POLYMER

In re Priest, 582 F.2d 33, 199 U.S.P.Q. 11 (C.C.P.A. 1978) - CLAIM, LIMITATION, SPECIFICATION, 35 U.S.C. §112

Princeton Biochemicals Inc. v. Beckman Instruments Inc., 180 F.R.D. 254, 45 U.S.P.Q.2d 1757 (N.J. 1997) - BIFURCATION

Ex parte Pritchard, 162 U.S.P.Q. 384 (PO Bd. App. 1968) - FRAGMENT

The Procter & Gamble Company v. Nabisco Brands, Inc., 604 F. Supp. 1485, 225 U.S.P.Q. 929 (Del. 1985) - CONTRIBUTORY INFRINGEMENT

Procter & Gamble Co. v. Paragon Trade Brands Inc., 917 F. Supp. 305, 38 U.S.P.Q.2d 1678 (Del. 1995) - ASSIGNMENT, RIPENESS, STANDING

Progressive Technology in Lighting Inc. v. Lumatech Corp., 45 U.S.P.Q.2d 1928 (Mich. 1998) - APPREHENSION

Pro-Mold and Tool Co. v. Great Lakes Plastics Inc., 75 F.3d 1568, 37 U.S.P.Q.2d 1626

(Fed. Cir. 1996) - COMBINING REFERENCES, INEQUITABLE CONDUCT, INVENTORSHIP, OBVIOUSNESS, UNFAIR COMPETITION

Protein Foundation, Inc. v. Brenner, 260 F. Supp. 519, 151 U.S.P.Q. 561 (D.C. 1966) - FILING DATE, 35 U.S.C. §21

In re Prutton, 200 F.2d 706, 96 U.S.P.Q. 147 (C.C.P.A. 1952) - LIST

Prutton v. Fuller and Johnson, 230 F.2d 459, 109 U.S.P.Q. 59 (C.C.P.A. 1956) - LIST

Public Varieties of Mississippi Inc. v. Sun Valley Seed Co. Inc., 734 F. Supp. 250, 14 U.S.P.Q.2d 2055 (Mich. 1990) - PLANT VARIETY PROTECTION ACT

Puschelberg v. United States, 330 F.2d 56, 141 U.S.P.Q. 323 (6th Cir. 1964) - CAPITAL GAINS, TAXATION

-Q-

Q.G. Products Inc. v. Shorty Inc., 992 F.2d 1211, 26 U.S.P.Q.2d 1778 (Fed. Cir. 1993) - ASSIGNOR ESTOPPEL

Quad Environmental Technologies Corp. v. Union Sanitary District, 946 F.2d 870, 20 U.S.P.Q.2d 1392 (Fed. Cir. 1991) - DOUBLE PATENTING, PRIOR ART, TERMINAL DISCLAIMER

Quaker City Gear Works, Inc. v. Skil Corporation, 223 U.S.P.Q. 533 (Pa. 1983)- GERMAN INDUSTRIAL STANDARD

Qualcomm Inc. v. Motorola Inc., 989 F. Supp. 1048, 45 U.S.P.Q.2d 1472 (Cal. 1997) - AMEND PLEADINGS, CASE OR CONTROVERSY

Quantum Corp. v. Rodime PLC, 65 F.3d 1577, 36 U.S.P.Q.2d 1162 (Fed. Cir. 1995) - REEXAMINATION, 35 US.C. 305

Quantum Corp. v. Sony Corp., 16 U.S.P.Q.2d 1447 (Cal. 1990) - JURISDICTION, 35 U.S.C. §271, USE

Quantum Corp. v. Tandon Corp., 18 U.S.P.Q.2d 1597 (Cal. 1991) - REISSUE

Quantum Corporation v. Tandon Corporation, 940 F.2d 642 (Fed. Cir. 1991) - BIFURCATION

Quantum Corp. v. Western Digital Corp., 15 U.S.P.Q.2d 1062 (Cal. 1990) - FOREIGN ASSOCIATE

Ex parte Quattlebaum and Noffsinger, 84 U.S.P.Q. 377 (PO Bd. App. 1948) - PROCESS

Ex parte Quayle, 25 U.S.P.Q. 74 (Commr. Patents 1935) - QUAYLE

The Quikrete Companies Inc. v. Nomix Corp., 874 F. Supp. 1362, 33 U.S.P.Q.2d 1032 (Ga. 1993) - INEQUITABLE CONDUCT

-R-

Racal-Vadic, Inc. v. Universal Data Systems, 207 U.S.P.Q. 902 (Ala. 1980) - CONVERSION, NUMBER OF REFERENCES, TEACH AWAY FROM

Racing Strollers Inc. v. TRI Industries Inc., 878 F.2d 1418, 11 U.S.P.Q.2d 1300 (Fed. Cir. 1989) - DESIGN APPLICATION, 35 U.S.C. §120

Radio Corp. of America v. Andrea, 15 F. Supp. 685, 30 U.S.P.Q. 194 (E.D. N.Y. 1936), modified, 90 F.2d 612, 34 U.S.P.Q. 312 (2d Cir. 1937) - EXPERIMENTAL USE

Radix Corp. v. Samuels, 13 U.S.P.Q.2d 1689 (D.C. 1989) - DE NOVO

Railex Corporation v. Joseph Guss & Sons, Inc., 40 F.R.D. 119, 148 U.S.P.Q. 640 (D.C. 1966) - JURY TRIAL, MORTGAGED PATENT

Railroad Dynamics, Inc. v. A. Stucki Co., 579 F. Supp. 353, 218 U.S.P.Q. 618 (Pa. 1983) - BEST MODE, COPYING, EXAMINATION, FIELD OF SEARCH, PRESUMPTION OF ADMINISTRATIVE REGULARITY, PRESUMPTION OF VALIDITY, PRIOR ART, SEARCH RECORD

Railroad Dynamics, Inc. v. A. Stucki Co., 727 F.2d 1506, 220 U.S.P.Q. 929 (Fed. Cir.) *cert. denied*, 469 U.S. 871 (1984) - JURY TRIAL, SUPPLEMENTAL DECLARATION OR OATH

In re Rainer, Redding, Hitov, Sloan, and Stewart, 305 F.2d 505, 134 U.S.P.Q. 343 (C.C.P.A. 1962) - CLAIM, REFERENCE, TIME

Raines v. Switch Manufacturing, 44 U.S.P.Q.2d 1195 (Cal. 1997) - *NOERR-PENNINGTON* DOCTRINE *Raleigh v. Tandy Corp.*, 45 U.S.P.Q.2d 1715 (Cal. 1997) - EXTRINSIC EVIDENCE

Ralph W. McKee and Harold Perpall v. Graton & Knight Co., 87 F.2d 262, 32 U.S.P.Q. 89 (4th Cir. 1937) - ANTICIPATION

Ralston Purina Company v. Far-Mar-Co, Inc., 586 F. Supp. 1176, 222 U.S.P.Q. 863 (Kan. 1984) - EXPERT OPINION, TEST, TESTING, USE

Ramos v. Boehringer Manheim Corp., 861 F. Supp. 1064, 33 U.S.P.Q.2d 1172 (Fla. 1994) - DOCTRINE OF EQUIVALENTS, INFRINGEMENT

Ramp Research and Development Inc. v. Structural Panels Inc., 977 F. Supp. 1169, 43 U.S.P.Q.2d 1432 (Fla. 1997) - REASONABLE ROYALTY

In re Randol and Redford, 425 F.2d 1268, 165 U.S.P.Q. 586 (C.C.P.A. 1970) - MODIFICATION

Randomex Inc. v. Scopus Corp., 849 F.2d 585, 7 U.S.P.Q.2d 1050 (Fed. Cir. 1988) - BEST MODE, TRADEMARK

Rapata v. Hershberger and Rickey, 140 U.S.P.Q. 66 (Comm'r 1961) - PUBLIC USE PROCEEDING

In re Rarey and Kennedy, 480 F.2d 1345, 178 U.S.P.Q. 463 (C.C.P.A. 1973) - CONJECTURE, REASON

Ex parte Raske, 28 U.S.P.Q.2d 1304 (B.P.A.I. 1993) - EXAMINER'S ANSWER, STATE OF THE ART

In re Ratti, 270 F.2d 810, 123 U.S.P.Q. 349 (C.C.P.A. 1959) - PROGRESS

Ray v. Lehman, 55 F.3d 606, 34 U.S.P.Q.2d 1786 (Fed. Cir. 1995) - MAINTENANCE FEE

Ex parte Raychem Corp., 25 U.S.P.Q.2d 1265 (B.P.A.I. 1992) - COMBINING REFERENCES, NEW GROUND OF REJECTION, REDUCTION IN REFERENCES, REEXAMINATION, 35 U.S.C. §103

Ex parte Razavi, 194 U.S.P.Q. 175 (PTO Bd. App. 1973) - SAME INVENTION, 35 U.S.C. §102(d)

RCA Corp. v. Data General Corp., 701 F. Supp. 456, 8 U.S.P.Q.2d 1305 (Del. 1988) - MEMORANDUM, PUBLICATION

The Read Corp. v. Freiday, 38 U.S.P.Q.2d 1220 (Fed. Cir. 1995 - *unpublished*) - LOST PROFITS

The Read Corp. v. Portec Inc., 970 F.2d 816, 23 U.S.P.Q.2d 1426 (Fed. Cir. 1992) - DAMAGES, EQUIVALENCY, INFRINGEMENT

Ex parte Remark, 15 U.S.P.Q.2d 1498 (B.P.A.I. 1990) - LIKE

Rengo Co. Ltd. v. Molins Machine Co., Inc., 657 F.2d 535, 211 U.S.P.Q. 303 (3d Cir. 1981) - NEGATIVE RULES OF INVENTION

Renishaw plc v. Marposs Societa' per Azioni, 48 U.S.P.Q.2d 1117 (Fed. Cir. 1998) - CLAIM INTERPRETATION, DEFINITION, DICTIONARY

In re Renstrom, 174 F.2d 140, 81 U.S.P.Q. 390 (C.C.P.A. 1949) - DIFFERENCE, STRUCTURAL DIFFERENCE, UNEXPECTED RESULTS

R.E. Phelon Co. v. Wabash Inc., 640 F. Supp. 1383, 1 U.S.P.Q.2d 1680 (Ind. 1986) - ON SALE

Research Corp. v. Gourmet's Delight Mushroom Co., Inc., 560 F. Supp. 811, 219 U.S.P.Q. 1023 (Pa. 1983) - ATTORNEY-CLIENT PRIVILEGE, INEQUITABLE CONDUCT

Research Corporation v. Pfister Associated Growers, Inc., 318 F. Supp. 1405, 168 U.S.P.Q. 206 (Ill. 1970) - BAD FAITH, REPRESENTATION, SETTLEMENT

Research Institute for Medicine and Chemistry Inc. v. Wisconsin Alumni Research Foundation Inc., 114 F.R.D. 672, 1 U.S.P.Q.2d 1929 (Wis. 1986) - CASE OR CONTROVERSY, DECLARATORY JUDGMENT

In re Reuter, Vickery, and Everett, 651 F.2d 751, 210 U.S.P.Q. 249 (C.C.P.A. 1981) - CORROBORATION, CREDIBILITY, OPINION

Rex Chainbelt Inc. v. Harco Products, Inc., 512 F.2d 993, 185 U.S.P.Q. 10 (9th Cir. 1975) - IMPLIED LICENSE, LABEL LICENSE, LICENSE, SHERMAN ACT, TYING ARRANGEMENT

Rexnord, Inc. v. The Laitram Corporation, 229 U.S.P.Q. 370 (Wis. 1986) - IRREPARABLE HARM, PRELIMINARY INJUNCTION

Rexnord Inc. v. Laitram Corp., 6 U.S.P.Q.2d 1817 (Wis. 1988) - DAMAGES, ENTIRE-MARKET-VALUE RULE, INFRINGEMENT, LOST PROFITS, MARKET VALUE RULE, UNPATENTED COMPONENTS

Rey-Bellet and Spiegelberg v. Engelhardt v. Schindler, 493 F.2d 1380, 181 U.S.P.Q. 453 (C.C.P.A. 1974) - CONCEPTION, DILIGENCE, REDUCTION TO PRACTICE, ROUTINE, TESTING

Reynolds Metals Company v. Aluminum Company of America, 457 F. Supp. 482, 198 U.S.P.Q. 529 (Ind. 1978) - RESULT, 35 U.S.C. §102(a)

Rheem Manufacturing Co. v. Johnson Heater Corp., 370 F. Supp. 806, 181 U.S.P.Q. 442 (Minn. 1974) - DECLARATORY JUDGMENT

Rhône-Poulenc Agrochime S.A. v. Biagro Western Sales Inc., 35 U.S.P.Q.2d 1203 (Cal. 1994) - EFFECTIVE, INDEFINITENESS

Rhone-Poulenc S.A. v. Dann, 507 F.2d 261, 184 U.S.P.Q. 196 (4th Cir. 1974) - CANCELLATION, LIMIT, NEW MATTER, TUMOR

Rhone-Poulenc Specialties Chimique v. SCM Corp., 769 F.2d 1569, 226 U.S.P.Q. 873 (Fed. Cir. 1985) - ARBITRATION

In re Riat, DeMontmollin, and Koller, 327 F.2d 685, 140 U.S.P.Q. 471 (C.C.P.A. 1964) - BREADTH, DYESTUFF, OPEN-ENDED CLAIM, RESIDUE

In re Rice, 481 F.2d 1316, 178 U.S.P.Q. 478 (C.C.P.A. 1973) - ASSERTION, HINDSIGHT

Richardson v. Suzuki Motor Co., 868 F.2d 1226, 9 U.S.P.Q.2d 1913 (Fed. Cir. 1989) - ABUSE OF DISCRETION, ADVISORY, ANTICIPATION, APPROPRIATION,

Rockwell International Corp v. United States, 147 F.3d 1358, 47 U.S.P.Q.2d 1027 (Fed. Cir. 1998) - ENABLING PRIOR ART

Ex parte Rodgers, 27 U.S.P.Q.2d 1738 (B.P.A.I. 1992) - EXPANDED PANEL, REEXAMINATION

Rohm and Haas Co. v. Brotech Corp., 815 F. Supp. 793, 26 U.S.P.Q.2d 1800 (Del. 1993) - ATTORNEY-CLIENT PRIVILEGE

Rohm and Haas Co. v. Brotech Corp., 127 F.3d 1089, 44 U.S.P.Q.2d 1459 (Fed. Cir. 1997) - EXPERT TESTIMONY

Rohm and Haas Company v. Commissioner of Patents, 387 F. Supp. 673, 177 U.S.P.Q. 625 (D.C. 1973) - IMPROPER MARKUSH, MARKUSH, UNITY OF INVENTION, 35 U.S.C. §131

Rohm & Haas Co. v. Crystal Chemical Co., 722 F.2d 1156, 220 U.S.P.Q. 289 (Fed. Cir. 1983) - CONDUCT, FRAUD, MISDEED, MISREPRESENTATION

Rohm and Haas Company v. Dawson Chemical Company, Inc., 214 U.S.P.Q. 56 (Tex. 1981) - ATTORNEY-CLIENT PRIVILEGE, FRAUD, PRIVILEGE, WORK-PRODUCT DOCTRINE

Rohm & Haas Co. v. Dawson Chemical Co., Inc., 557 F. Supp, 739, 217 U.S.P.Q. 515 (Tex. 1983) - CONCEPTION, CONTINUATION-IN-PART APPLICATION, DIVISION, FILE WRAPPER, LEXICOGRAPHER, PRESUMPTION OF VALIDITY, STAPLE ARTICLE OF COMMERCE

Rohm and Haas Company v. Gottschalk, 504 F.2d 259, 183 U.S.P.Q. 257 (DC 1974) - DISTINCT, WITHDRAWAL

Rohm and Haas Company v. International Trade Commission, 554 F.2d 462, 193 U.S.P.Q. 693 (C.C.P.A. 1977) - STANDING

Rohm and Haas Company v. Mobil Oil Corporation, 525 F. Supp. 1298, 212 U.S.P.Q. 354 (Del. 1981) - PROTESTOR

Rohm and Haas Company v. Owens-Corning Fiberglas Corporation, 196 U.S.P.Q. 726 (Ala. 1977) - SPECIFIC MODE

Ex parte Rohrer, 20 U.S.P.Q.2d 1460 (B.P.A.I. 1991) - ESTOPPEL

Roper Corp. v. Litton Systems, Inc., 757 F.2d 1266, 225 U.S.P.Q. 345 (Fed. Cir. 1985) - PRELIMINARY INJUNCTION

In re Rose, 220 F.2d 459, 105 U.S.P.Q. 237 (C.C.P.A. 1955) - CLAIM, SIZE, WEIGHT

Rosemount Inc. v. Beckman Instruments, Inc., 569 F. Supp. 934, 218 U.S.P.Q. 881 (Cal. 1983) - DEFINING CLAIMED SUBJECT MATTER, MEANING, MISJOINDER, SELECTION

Rosemount, Inc. v. Beckman Instruments, Inc., 727 F.2d 1540, 221 U.S.P.Q. 1 (Fed. Cir. 1984) - GAME

Rosemount Inc. v. U.S. International Trade Commission, 910 F.2d 819, 15 U.S.P.Q.2d 1569 (Fed. Cir. 1990) - PRESUMPTION, REASON, 19 U.S.C. §1337(a)

In re Rosenberg, 15 U.S.P.Q.2d 1751 (Commr. Patents & Trademarks 1990) - UNSIGNED DECLARATION

In re Rosenberger and Brandt, 386 F.2d 1015, 156 U.S.P.Q. 24 (C.C.P.A. 1967) - TEACH AWAY FROM

In re Rosicky, 276 F.2d 656, 125 U.S.P.Q. 341 (C.C.P.A. 1960) - 35 U.S.C. §102(e)

In re Ross and Davis, 305 F.2d 878, 134 U.S.P.Q. 320 (C.C.P.A. 1962) - BURDEN

Roton Barrier Inc. v. The Stanley Works, 79 F.3d 1112, 37 U.S.P.Q.2d 1816 (Fed. Cir. 1996) - VALIDITY

In re Rouffet, 149 F.3d 1350, 47 U.S.P.Q.2d 1453 (Fed. Cir. 1998) - COMBINING REFERENCES, INVENTION, MOTIVATION

In re Rousso, 222 F.2d 729, 106 U.S.P.Q. 99 (C.C.P.A. 1955) - DESIGN

Rowe v. Dror, 112 F.3d 473, 42 U.S.P.Q.2d 1550 (Fed. Cir. 1997) - 37 C.F.R. §1.633(a) , CLAIM INTERPRETATION, COPYING CLAIMS, EXAMINATION, JEPSON, JUDICIAL PRECEDENT, PREAMBLE

Rowley v. Tresenberg, 37 Fed. Supp. 90 (N.Y. 1941) - DESIGN

Royer v. Coup, 146 U.S. 524 (1892) - CLAIM CONSTRUCTION

Rubbermaid Commercial Products Inc. v. Contico International Inc., 836 F. Supp. 1247, 29 U.S.P.Q.2d 1574 (Va. 1993) - DESIGN PATENT INFRINGEMENT

Rubenstein v. Schmidt, 133 U.S.P.Q. 91 (Comm'r of Patents 1962) - LEGISLATIVE INTENT

Rubenstein v. Schmidt, 145 U.S.P.Q. 613 (Commr. Patents 1965) - ACQUIESCENCE, CANCELLATION, COLLATERAL ESTOPPEL, COPYING CLAIMS, RES JUDICATA

Ex parte Rubin, 5 U.S.P.Q.2d 1461 (B.P.A.I. 1987) - CANCER, COMBINATION IN-VENTION, COMPOSITION, CONCEPT, DISCLOSURE, OBJECTIVE TRUTH, OBVIOUSNESS, PROBLEM, STATEMENT IN THE SPECIFICATION, TEACH-ING, TRUTH, UNBELIEVABLE, 35 U.S.C. §101, UTILITY

In re Ruff and Dukeshire, 256 F.2d 590, 118 U.S.P.Q. 340 (C.C.P.A. 1958) - BORCHERDT DOCTRINE, EQUIVALENCE, EQUIVAALENTS, MARKUSH, REDUCTION IN SCOPPE, SUBSTITUTION OF EQUIVALENTS

In re Rundell, 48 F.2d 958, 9 U.S.P.Q. 220 (C.C.P.A. 1931) - AUTOMATIC

In re Ruscetta and Jenny, 255 F.2d 687, 118 U.S.P.Q. 101 (C.C.P.A. 1958) - ANTE-DATING A REFERENCE, APPLICANT'S PUBLICATION, APPLICANT'S RIGHTS, CASE, 37 C.F.R. §1.131, CONTINUATION-IN-PART APPLICATION, DECISION, FOREIGN, PRECEDENT, REFERENCE, SPECIES, STATUTORY BAR

In re Ruschig, Aumüller, Korger, Wagner, Scholz, and Bänder, 343 F.2d 965, 145 U.S.P.Q. 274 (C.C.P.A. 1965) - BUSINESS, COMPOUND, INVENTION, PRODUCT, PRODUCT CLAIM, PROPERTIES, PROPERTY, PROTECTION, SELECTION, VALUE

In re Russell, Jarrett, Bruno, and Remper, 193 U.S.P.Q. 680 (Comm'r of Patents and Trademarks 1975) - CONVERSION, DILIGENCE

Russell William Ltd. v. ABC Display & Supply Inc., 11 U.S.P.Q.2d 1812 (N.Y. 1989) - PRELIMINARY INJUNCTION

Russo v. Baxter Healthcare Corp., 140 F.3d 6, 46 U.S.P.Q.2d 1239 (1ˢᵗ Cir. 1998) - DISCLOSURE, NOVELTY

RustEvader Corp. v. Cowatch, 842 F. Supp. 171, 29 U.S.P.Q.2d 1076 (Penn. 1993) - 28 U.S.C. §1338

Ryco Inc. v. Ag-Bag Corp., 857 F.2d 1418, 8 U.S.P.Q.2d 1323 (Fed. Cir. 1988) - ANALO-GOUS ART, IMPROVEMENT, LOST PROFITS, OBVIOUSNESS, SUPERI-ORITY, WILLFUL

Ryko Manufacturing Co. v. Nu-Star Inc., 950 F.2d 714, 21 U.S.P.Q.2d 1053 (Fed. Cir. 1991) - NEXUS, RELEVANT ART, SECONDARY CONSIDERATIONS, SUMMARY JUDGMENT, SYNERGISM

-S-

In re Sabatino and Orlando, 480 F.2d 911, 178 U.S.P.Q. 357 (C.C.P.A. 1973) - SUPPORT

SAB Industri AB v. The Bendix Corporation, 199 U.S.P.Q. 95 (Va. 1978) - CONVERSION, FALSE OATH, REISSUE

Ex parte Sachs, 9 U.S.P.Q. 446 (PO Bd. App. 1931) - DISTINCT

Sachs v. Wadsworth, 48 F.2d 928, 9 U.S.P.Q. 252 (C.C.P.A. 1931) - REDUCTION TO PRACTICE

Saes Getters S.P.A. v. Ergenics Inc., 17 U.S.P.Q.2d 1581 (N.J. 1990) - INEQUITABLE CONDUCT

In re Saether, 492 F.2d 849, 181 U.S.P.Q. 36 (C.C.P.A. 1974) - CHARACTERISTIC, LIMITATION, PRODUCT BY PROPERTIES, PURPOSE, SELECTION

Saga International Inc. v. John D. Brush & Co., 984 F. Supp. 1283, 44 U.S.P.Q.2d 1947 (Cal. 1997) - RULE 65 (d)

Sage Products Inc. v. Devon Industries Inc., 148 F.R.D. 213, 28 U.S.P.Q.2d 1149 (Ill. 1993) CONSOLIDATION, RULE 42(a)

Sage Products Inc. v. Devon Industries Inc., 880 F. Supp. 718, 35 U.S.P.Q.2d 1321 (Cal. 1994) - BURDEN, CLAIM INTERPRETATION, SUMMARY JUDGMENT

Saginaw Products Corp. v. Eastern Airlines, Inc., 196 U.S.P.Q. 129 (Mich. 1977) - DAMAGES

In re Salem, Butterworth, and Ryan, 553 F.2d 676, 193 U.S.P.Q. 513 (C.C.P.A. 1977) - CONSTRUCTION, DEFINITION, DICTIONARY, DISCLOSURE, EVIDENCE, ENCYCLOPEDIA, JUDICIAL NOTICE, ORDINARY SKILL, PICK AND CHOOSE, REASON

In re Salmon, 705 F.2d 1579 217 U.S.P.Q. 981 (Fed. Cir. 1983) - DESIGN

In re Samour, 571 F.2d 559, 197 U.S.P.Q. 1 (C.C.P.A. 1978) - ANTICIPATION, ENABLING DISCLOSURE, FORMULA, REFERENCE, 35 U.S.C. §102(b)

Sampson v. Ampex Corporation, 463 F.2d 1042, 174 U.S.P.Q. 417 (2d Cir. 1972) - PRIOR APPLICATION

Sands v. Bonazoli, Kimball, and Palmer, 223 U.S.P.Q. 450 (PTO Bd. Pat. Int. 1983) - CORROBORATION, DERIVATION

Sandvik Aktiebolag v. E.J. Co., 121 F.3d 669, 43 U.S.P.Q.2d 1620 (Fed. Cir. 1997) - RECONSTRUCTION

Sandvik Aktiebolag v. Samuels, 20 U.S.P.Q.2d 1879 (D.C. 1991) - APPEAL, EXAMINER

San Haun New Materials High Tech Inc. v. ITC, 48 U.S.P.Q.2d 1865 (Fed. Cir. 1998) - CONSENT ORDER, DAMAGES

San Marino Electronic Corp. v. George J. Meyer Manufacturing Co., 155 U.S.P.Q. 617 (Cal. 1967) - GRANT-FORWARD CLAUSE, LICENSE

Sanofi, S.A. v. Med-Tech Veterinarian Products, Inc., 565 F. Supp. 931, 220 U.S.P.Q. 416 (N.J. 1983) - ASSIGNMENT, EXCLUSIVE LICENSE, IMPLIED LICENSE, LICENSE, LICENSE RECORDATION, RECONSTRUCTION

In re Sarett, 327 F.2d 1005, 140 U.S.P.Q. 474 (C.C.P.A. 1964) - DOMINANT OR DOMINATING CLAIM, DOMINATION, DOUBLE PATENTING, READABILITY, SAME INVENTION, SPECIES

Sargent v. Hall & Safe Lock Co., 114 U.S. 63 (1885) - CLAIM CONSTRUCTION, CLAIM LIMITATION, COMBINATION, DISCLAIMER

In re Sarkar, 575 F.2d 870, 197 U.S.P.Q. 788 (C.C.P.A. 1978) - SEAL RECORD

In re Sarkar, 588 F.2d 1330, 200 U.S.P.Q. 132 (C.C.P.A. 1978) - TRADE SECRET

Sarkisian v. Winn-Proof Corporation, 203 U.S.P.Q. 60 (Or. 1978) - OBVIOUSNESS

Sarkisian v. Winn-Proof Corp., 662 F.2d 596, 213 U.S.P.Q. 912 (9th Cir. 1981) - SKEPTICISM

Sarkisian v. Winn-Proof Corp., 696 F.2d 1313, 217 U.S.P.Q. 702 (9th Cir. 1983) - SECONDARY CONSIDERATIONS

In re Sasse, 629 F.2d 675 (C.C.P.A. 1980) - PRESUMPTION OF ENABLEMENT

Saturn Manufacturing, Inc. v. Williams Patent Crusher & Pulverizer Co., 713 F.2d 1347, 219 U.S.P.Q. 533 (Fed. Cir. 1983) - INDUSTRY ACCEPTANCE

In re Saunders and Gemeinhardt, 444 F.2d 599, 170 U.S.P.Q. 213 (C.C.P.A. 1971) - 37 C.F.R. §1.132, CRITICAL, EVIDENCE, REDUCTION IN SCOPE, "REGARDS" TEST, RETREAT

Scandiamant Aktiebolag v. Commissioner of Patents, 509 F.2d 463, 184 U.S.P.Q. 201 (D.C. Cir. 1974) - CRITICAL, LANGUAGE, RANGE

In re Scarborough, 500 F.2d 560, 182 U.S.P.Q. 298 (C.C.P.A. 1974) - ARGUMENT, COPENDING PATENT, ENABLEMENT

Ex parte Schaefer, 171 U.S.P.Q. 110 (PO Bd. App. 1970) - OMISSION OF ELEMENT OR STEP

Schaper Manufacturing Co. v. U.S. International Trade Commission, 717 F.2d 1368, 219 U.S.P.Q. 665 (Fed. Cir. 1983) - INDUSTRY

In re Schaub, Bernady, and Weiss, 537 F.2d 509, 190 U.S.P.Q. 324 (C.C.P.A. 1976) - ANTEDATING A REFERENCE, 37 C.F.R. §1.131, ESTER

In re Schechter and LaForge, 205 F.2d 185, 98 U.S.P.Q. 144 (C.C.P.A. 1953) - ALLOWED CLAIM, CLAIM, INSECTICIDE, RELATIONSHIP, SYNTHETIC

Scheffer v. Shanks, 207 U.S.P.Q. 211 (Comm'r of Patents and Trademarks 1979) - FOREIGN PATENT APPLICATION

Schendel v. Curtis, 83 F.3d 1399, 38 U.S.P.Q.2d 1743 (Fed. Cir. 1996) - RULE OF REASON

Ex parte Scherberich and Pfeifer, 201 U.S.P.Q. 397 (PTO Bd. App. 1977) - ARYL, BREADTH, DEFINING CLAIMED SUBJECT MATTER, HETEROCYCLIC

Ex parte Schier, 21 U.S.P.Q.2d 1016 (B.P.A.I. 1991) - 37 C.F.R. §1.192(c)(5), CLAIMS, STAND OR FALL TOGETHER

Schiessle v. Stephens, 717 F.2d 417 (7th Cir. 1983) - DISQUALIFICATION

In re Schirmer, 480 F.2d 1342, 178 U.S.P.Q. 483 (C.C.P.A. 1973) - CRITICALITY, PARAMETERS, ROUTINE, STEPS, TEMPERATURE

In re Schlittler and Uffer, 234 F.2d 882, 110 U.S.P.Q. 304 (C.C.P.A. 1956) - ABANDONED APPLICATION, CONCEPTION, DISCLOSURE, KNOWLEDGE, MANUSCRIPT, PUBLICATION, REDUCTION TO PRACTICE

In re Schmidt, 293 F.2d 274, 130 U.S.P.Q. 404 (C.C.P.A. 1961) - ERROR, SAME INVENTOR, 35 U.S.C. §116, 35 U.S.C. §256

Schmidt v. Reynolds, 140 U.S.P.Q. 118 (D.C. 1963) - ASSIGNEE, ATTORNEY, AU-
THORITY, 37 C.F.R. §1.313, WITHDRAW FROM ISSUE

Schmitt and Panouse v. Babcock and Herr, 377 F.2d 994, 153 U.S.P.Q. 719 (C.C.P.A.
1967) - PRIORITY

In re Schneider and Stuart, 481 F.2d 1350, 179 U.S.P.Q. 46 (C.C.P.A. 1973) - DRAWING

Schneider (USA) Inc. v. Cordis Corp., 29 U.S.P.Q.2d 1072 (Minn. 1993) - CROWDED
ART, DOCTRINE OF EQUIVALENTS

Schneider (USA) Inc. v. C.R. Bard Inc., 18 U.S.P.Q.2d 1076 (Mass. 1990) - INEQUITA-
BLE CONDUCT, SUMMARY JUDGMENT

Schneider (Europe) AG v. SciMed Life Systems Inc., 28 U.S.P.Q.2d 1225 (Minn. 1993) -
LICENSEE, NONEXCLUSIVE

Schnick v. Fenn, 277 F.2d 935, 125 U.S.P.Q. 567 (C.C.P.A. 1960) - REDUCTION TO
PRACTICE

Scholl, Inc. v. S.S. Kresge Co., 193 U.S.P.Q. 695 (Ill. 1977) - COPYING

Scholle Corp. v. Blackhawk Molding Co., 133 F.3d 1469, 45 U.S.P.Q.2d 1468 (Fed. Cir.
1998) - EQUITABLE ESTOPPEL

In re Schrader, 22 F.3d 290, 30 U.S.P.Q.2d 1455 (Fed. Cir. 1994) - PROCESS,
PROGRAM

Schrag v. Strosser, 21 U.S.P.Q.2d 1025 (B.P.A.I. 1991) - CONFIDENTIALITY AGREE-
MENT, PUBLIC USE

The Schriber-Schroth Company v. The Cleveland Trust Company, 311 U.S. 211, 47
U.S.P.Q. 345 (1940) - CLAIM CONSTRUCTION, DISCLAIMER, FILE WRAP-
PER ESTOPPEL

Ex parte Schundehutte and Trautner, 184 U.S.P.Q. 697 (PO Bd. App. 1974) - IN-
TENDED USE

In re Schuyler, 119 U.S.P.Q. 97 (Comm'r 1957) - ASSIGNEE, 37 C.F.R. §1.47(b),
OWNERSHIP, REISSUE, 35 U.S.C. §118

In re Schwartz and Paul, 147 U.S.P.Q. 394 (Comm'r 1960) - 35 U.S.C. §116

Schwarzkopf Development Corp. v. Ti Coating Inc., 7 U.S.P.Q.2d 1557 (N.Y. 1988) -
CASE OR CONTROVERSY

S.C. Johnson & Son, Inc. v. Carter-Wallace, Inc., 614 F. Supp. 1278, 225 U.S.P.Q. 1022
(N.Y. 1985) - AVAILABILITY OF PRIOR ART, FAILURE OF OTHERS, FOR-
BEARANCE FROM INFRINGEMENT, INCENTIVE, INVENTION, PER-
FORMANCE, PRIOR ART, PROPERTIES, SECONDARY CONSIDERATIONS,
UNEXPECTED PROPERTIES

S.C. Johnson & Son, Inc. v. Carter-Wallace, Inc., 781 F.2d 198, 228 U.S.P.Q. 367 (Fed.
Cir. 1986) - ATTORNEY'S FEES

Scosche Industries Inc. v. Visor Gear Inc., 121 F.3d 675, 43 U.S.P.Q.2d 1659 (Fed. Cir.
1997) - CONSENT JUDGMENT, INEQUITABLE CONDUCT, INTENT, ISSUE
PRECLUSION

Ex parte Scott, 54 U.S.P.Q. 148 (PO Bd. App. 1941) - COMPOUND, MULTIPLICITY

Scovill Manufacturing Company v. Sunbeam Corporation, 179 U.S.P.Q. 833 (Del. 1973) -
ON SALE

Ex parte Scott, 54 U.S.P.Q. 148 (PO Bd. App. 1941) - FORMULA

Scott v. Finney, 34 F.3d 1058, 32 U.S.P.Q.2d 1115 (Fed. Cir. 1994) - REDUCTION TO
PRACTICE

BOARD (BOARD OF APPEALS), CHALLENGE, CONTRADICT, ERROR, OPINION, STATEMENT BY THE BOARD

Semiconductor Energy Laboratory Co. v. Samsung Electronics Co., 4 F. Supp. 2d 477, 46 U.S.P.Q.2d 1874 (Va. 1998) - COMBINATION, CUMULATIVE, EXAMINER, INEQUITABLE CONDUCT

Seminole Tribe of Florida v. Florida, 517 U.S. 44 (1996) - STATES' IMMUNITY

Semmler v. American Honda Motor Co., 990 F. Supp. 967, 44 U.S.P.Q.2d 1553 (Ohio 1997) - EQUIVALENCY, INDEFINITENESS, INTERCHANGEABILITY, PROSECUTION HISTORY ESTOPPEL

Sensonics Inc. v. Aerosonic Corp., 81 F.3d 1566, 38 U.S.P.Q.2d 1551 (Fed. Cir. 1996) - DAMAGES

Serco Services Co. L.P. v. Kelley Co. Inc., 31 U.S.P.Q.2d 1795 (Tex. 1994) - DECLARATORY JUDGMENT

Serco Services Co. L.P. v. Kelley Co. Inc., 51 F.3d 1037, 34 U.S.P.Q.2d 1217 (Fed. Cir. 1995) - DECLARATORY JUDGMENT

In re SGS-Thomson Microelectronics Inc., 60 F.3d 839, 35 U.S.P.Q.2d 1572 (Fed. Cir. 1995 - unpublished) - JURY TRIAL

Shackelton v. J. Kaufman Iron Works, Inc., 689 F.2d 334, 217 U.S.P.Q. 98 (2d Cir. 1982) - SECONDARY CONSIDERATIONS

In re Shaffer, 229 F.2d 476, 108 U.S.P.Q. 326 (C.C.P.A. 1956) - COMBINING REFERENCES, PROBLEM

Shaked v. Taniguchi, 21 U.S.P.Q.2d 1285 (B.P.A.I. 1990) - INTERFERENCE, PRELIMINARY MOTION, REEXAMINATION

Shaked v. Taniguchi, 21 U.S.P.Q.2d 1288 (Commr. Patents & Trademarks 1990) - INTERFERENCE, REEXAMINATION

Shamrock Technologies Inc. v. Medical Sterilization Inc., 903 F.2d 789, 14 U.S.P.Q.2d 1728 (Fed. Cir. 1990) - ASSIGNMENT, ASSIGNOR ESTOPPEL, PRIVITY, SUMMARY JUDGMENT

Shamrock Technologies Inc. v. Precision Micron Powders Inc., 20 U.S.P.Q.2d 1797 (N.Y. 1991) - 35 U.S.C. §271(g)

Shatterproof Glass Corp. v. Guardian Glass Co., 322 F. Supp. 854, 168 U.S.P.Q. 212 (Mich. 1970) - EXCEPTIONAL

Shattuck v. Hoegl, 523 F.2d 509, 187 U.S.P.Q. 1 (2d Cir. 1975) - DISCOVERY

Ex parte Shea, 171 U.S.P.Q. 383 (PTO Bd. App. 1970) - APPROXIMATELY

Shearing v. Iolab Corp., 975 F.2d 1541, 24 U.S.P.Q.2d 1133 (Fed. Cir. 1992) - JMOL

Shelcore, Inc. v. CBS, Inc., 220 U.S.P.Q. 459 (N.J. 1983) - COLLATERAL ESTOPPEL, INVENTORSHIP, RES JUDICATA

Ex parte Shelton, 92 U.S.P.Q. 374 (PTO Bd. App. 1950) - APPROXIMATELY

Ex parte Shelton, 172 U.S.P.Q. 319 (PO Bd. App. 1971) - MULTIPLICITY

Ex parte Shepard and Gushue, 188 U.S.P.Q. 536 (PTO Bd. App. 1974) - DIRECTION, ELEMENT

In re Sherwood, 613 F.2d 809, 204 U.S.P.Q. 537 (C.C.P.A. 1980) - BEST MODE

In re Shetty, 566 F.2d 81, 195 U.S.P.Q. 753 (C.C.P.A. 1977) - ETHYLENE, INHERENCY, OBVIOUSNESS

In re Shibata, 203 U.S.P.Q. 780 (Commr. Patents & Trademarks 1979) - CONVERSION

Shindelar v. Holderman, Gaeddert, Ratzlaff, Pruitt, and Lohrentz, 628 F.2d 1337, 207 U.S.P.Q. 112 (C.C.P.A. 1980) - CROSS-APPEAL

Shipp v. Scott School Township, 54 F.2d 1019, 12 U.S.P.Q. 5 (7th Cir. 1931) - LATE CLAIMING

In re Shirouchi and Urade, 204 U.S.P.Q. 511 (PTO Solicitor 1978) - CERTIFICATE OF CORRECTION, 37 C.F.R. §1.323

In re Sichert, 566 F.2d 1154, 196 U.S.P.Q. 209 (C.C.P.A. 1977) - DIRECTION, INTERPRETATION, PREDICTABILITY, UNDUE EXPERIMENTATION, 21 U.S.C. §372(d)

Ex parte Siebach, 151 U.S.P.Q. 62 (PO Bd. App. 1966) - PLURAL CLAIMS

Ex parte Siegmund and Cole, 156 U.S.P.Q. 477 (PO Bd. App. 1967) - ANTECEDENT SUPPORT, DRAWING, *EXPRESSIS VERBIS, IPSIS VERBIS*

Siemens-Elema A.B. v. Puriton Bennett Corp., 13 U.S.P.Q.2d 1804 (Cal. 1989) - PRINTED PUBLICATION

Sierra On Line, Inc. v. Phoenix Software, Inc., 739 F.2d 1415 (9th Cir. 1984) - PRELIMINARY INJUNCTION

Sig Swiss Industrial Co. v. Fres-Co System USA Inc., 22 U.S.P.Q.2d 1601 (Pa. 1992) - ADVICE OF COUNSEL, ATTORNEY-CLIENT PRIVILEGE, EQUITABLE ESTOPPEL

Silvestri and Johnson v. Grant and Alburn, 496 F.2d 593, 181 U.S.P.Q. 706 (C.C.P.A. 1974) - ACCIDENTAL, ANTICIPATION, CHANGE IN FORM, CONCEPTION, COPYING CLAIMS, NOVELTY, RECOGNITION, REDUCTION TO PRACTICE

Ex parte Simons, 86 U.S.P.Q. 336 (PO Bd. App. 1949) - REACTION PRODUCT

Ex parte Singh, 17 U.S.P.Q.2d 1714 (B.P.A.I. 1990) - DOUBT, ENABLEMENT, PREDICTABILITY, STATEMENT

Sinko Tool & Manufacturing Co. v. Automatic Devices Corp., 157 F.2d 974, 71 U.S.P.Q. 199 (2d Cir. 1946) - REDUCTION TO PRACTICE

Site Microsurgical Systems Inc. v. The Cooper Companies Inc., 797 F. Supp. 333, 24 U.S.P.Q.2d 1463 (Del. 1992) - ENTIRE MARKET VALUE RULE

Ex parte Sizto, 9 U.S.P.Q.2d 2081 (B.P.A.I. 1988) - COMMENSURATE IN SCOPE, ENABLEMENT

Skil Corporation v. Lucerne Products, Inc., 684 F.2d 346, 216 U.S.P.Q. 371 (6th Cir. 1982) - FOREIGN PATENTS AND PROCEEDINGS

Ex parte Skinner, 2 U.S.P.Q.2d 1788 (B.P.A.I. 1986) - ALLEGATION, COMBINING REFERENCES, FUNCTIONAL LIMITATION, INHERENCY, POSSIBILITY, PROBABILITY, REASON, REASONABLE, SCIENTIFIC REASONING, SUGGESTION, TEACHING

In re Skoll, 523 F.2d 1392, 187 U.S.P.Q. 481 (C.C.P.A. 1975) - ACID, COMBINING REFERENCES, ESTOPPEL, INDEFINITENESS, INORGANIC, ORGANIC MARKUSH, SKILLED IN THE ART

In re Skrivan, 427 F.2d 801, 166 U.S.P.Q. 85 (C.C.P.A. 1970) - BREADTH, CLAIM LIMITATION, DEFINITION, DOUBLE PATENTING, SKILL OF THE ART, TERMINAL DISCLAIMER

Ex parte Skuballa, 12 U.S.P.Q.2d 1570 (B.P.A.I. 1989) - COMPOSITION, DOSAGE, MULTIPLE UTILITIES, PHARMACEUTICAL, USE, UTILITY

In re Slayter, 276 F.2d 408, 125 U.S.P.Q. 345 (C.C.P.A. 1960) - ANTICIPATION

Slimfold Manufacturing Co. Inc. v. Kinkead Industries Inc., 810 F.2d 1113, 1 U.S.P.Q.2d 1563 (Fed. Cir. 1987) - IDENTICAL, REISSUE

Slimfold Manufacturing Co. Inc. v. Kinkead Industries Inc., 932 F.2d 1453, 18 U.S.P.Q.2d 1842 (Fed. Cir. 1991) - ATTORNEY'S FEES, DESIGNING AROUND, DOCTRINE OF EQUIVALENTS, FRAUD ON A PATENT, SUBSTANTIAL

Slimmery International Inc. v. Stauffer-Meiji Inc., 6 U.S.P.Q.2d 1671 (Mo. 1987) - PREAMBLE

Slip Track Systems Inc. v. Metal Lite Inc., 48 U.S.P.Q.2d 1055 (Fed. Cir. 1998) - ANTE-DATING A REFERENCE, REEXAMINATION, STAY

In re Slocombe, 510 F.2d 1398, 184 U.S.P.Q. 740 (C.C.P.A. 1975) - CATALYSIS, 37 C.F.R. §1.132

Smeeth v. Fox Copper & Bronze Co., 130 F. 455 (3d Cir. 1904) - THREATENED INFRINGEMENT

Ex parte Smith, 43 U.S.P.Q. 157 (PTO Bd. App. 1937) - SUBSTANTIALLY

Smith v. Diamond, 209 U.S.P.Q. 1091 (D.C. 1981) - ATTORNEY, INVENTOR, RE-VIVAL, UNAVOIDABLE DELAY

Smith v. Goodyear Dental Vulcanite Co., 93 U.S. 486 (1877) - MATERIAL

Smith v. M&B Sales & Manufacturing, 13 U.S.P.Q.2d 2002 (Cal. 1990) - DESIGN

Smith v. Whitman Saddle Company, 148 U.S. 674 (1893) - DESIGN

In re Smith and Hubin, 481 F.2d 910, 178 U.S.P.Q. 620 (C.C.P.A. 1973) - DESCRIP-TION, POLYMER, SUPPORT

SmithKline Diagnostics, Inc. v. Helena Laboratories Corp., 859 F.2d 878, 8 U.S.P.Q.2d 1468 (Fed. Cir. 1988) - ALL-CLAIMS RULE, INEQUITABLE CONDUCT, MARKING

SmithKline Diagnostics. Inc. v. Helena Laboratories Corp., 12 U.S.P.Q.2d 1375 (Tex. 1989) - DAMAGES

SmithKline Diagnostics Inc. v. Helena Laboratories Corp., 926 F.2d 1161, 17 U.S.P.Q.2d 1922 (Fed. Cir. 1991) - DAMAGES, ROYALTY

Smith International, Inc. v. Hughes Tool Co., 718 F.2d 1573, 219 U.S.P.Q. 686 (Fed. Cir.), cert. denied, 464 U.S. 996, 220 U.S.P.Q. 385 (1983) - INJUNCTIVE RELIEF

Smith International, Inc. v. Hughes Tool Co., 759 F.2d 1572, 225 U.S.P.Q. 889 (Fed. Cir. 1985) - LAW-OF-THE-CASE DOCTRINE

Ex parte Smolka and Schwuger, 207 U.S.P.Q. 232 (PTO Bd. App. 1980) - ABAN-DONED APPLICATION, DEFENSIVE PUBLICATION, EFFECTIVE DATE, REFERENCE, 35 U.S.C. §102(e)

In re Smythe and Shamos, 480 F.2d 1376, 178 U.S.P.Q. 279 (C.C.P.A. 1973) - ADVAN-TAGE, DESCRIPTION, DISCLOSURE, FUNCTION, INHERENCY, INHER-ENT, INOPERATIVE, NEW MATTER, OMISSION OF ELEMENT OR STEP, SUPPORT, THEORY

Ex parte Snook, 119 U.S.P.Q. 255 (PO Bd. App. 1954) - PARTS

Sofamor Danek Group Inc. v. Depuy-Motech Inc., 74 F.3d 1216, 37 U.S.P.Q.2d 1529 (Fed. Cir. 1996) - FUNCTION/WAY/RESULT

Solarex Corp. v. Advanced Photovoltaic Systems Inc., 34 U.S.P.Q.2d 1234 (Del. 1995) - PUBLIC

Solder Removal Company v. United States International Trade Commission, 582 F.2d 628,

199 U.S.P.Q. 129 (C.C.P.A. 1978) - BURDEN, GOING FORWARD, PRESUMPTION OF VALIDITY, SUBSTANTIAL EVIDENCE, 35 U.S.C. §282

Solomon v. Greco, 18 U.S.P.Q.2d 1917 (N.Y. 1990) - FILE WRAPPER ESTOPPEL

Ex parte Solomons and Scammell, 201 U.S.P.Q. 42 (PTO Bd. App. 1978) - CONTINUATION APPLICATION, CONTINUING APPLICATION, DEPOSIT, PLANT

In re Soni, 54 F.3d 746, 34 U.S.P.Q.2d 1684 (Fed. Cir. 1995) - POLYMER, STATEMENT IN THE SPECIFICATION, UNEXPECTED RESULTS

Sonoco Products Co. v. Mobil Oil Corp., 15 U.S.P.Q.2d 1186 (S.C. 1989) - CLEAR AND CONVINCING, BURDEN, DEFERENCE, PTO

Sonoco Products Co. v. Durabag Co. Inc., 30 U.S.P.Q.2d 1295 (Cal. 1994) - ERROR, RECAPTURE RULE, SAME INVENTION

Sonoco Products Co. v. Mobil Oil Corp., 15 U.S.P.Q.2d 1186 (S.C. 1989) - EXAMINER, VALIDITY

South Corp. v. United States, 690 F.2d 1368, 215 U.S.P.Q. 657 (Fed. Cir. 1982) - CAFC

Southern Research Institute v. Griffin Corp., 938 F.2d 1761, 19 U.S.P.Q.2d 1761 (11th Cir. 1991) - ADMINISTRATIVE PROCEDURE ACT, 35 U.S.C. §207, 35 U.S.C. §209

Southwall Technologies Inc. v. Cardinal IG Co., 54 F.3d 1570, 34 U.S.P.Q.2d 1673 (Fed. Cir. 1995) - INFRINGEMENT, PROSECUTION HISTORY ESTOPPEL

Southwire Co. v. Essex Group, Inc., 570 F. Supp. 643, 219 U.S.P.Q. 1053 (Ill. 1983) - ATTORNEY-CLIENT PRIVILEGE

In re Spada, 911 F.2d 705, 15 U.S.P.Q.2d 1655 (Fed. Cir. 1990) - HYBRID, 35 U.S.C. §102/103

In re Spears, 223 F.2d 956, 106 U.S.P.Q. 290 (C.C.P.A. 1955) - USE

Special Metals Corporation v. Teledyne Industries, Inc., 215 U.S.P.Q. 698 (N.C. 1982) - FILE WRAPPER ESTOPPEL

Specialty Composites v. Cabot Corp., 845 F.2d 981, 6 U.S.P.Q.2d 1601 (Fed. Cir. 1988) - COPYING, OBJECTIVE EVIDENCE, SKILLED IN THE ART, TEACH AWAY FROM, UNEXPECTED RESULTS

Spectra-Physics Inc. v. Coherent Inc., 827 F.2d 1524, 3 U.S.P.Q.2d 1737 (Fed. Cir. 1987) - KNOWN

Spectronics Corp. v. H.B. Fuller Co. Inc., 940 F.2d 631, 19 U.S.P.Q.2d 1545 (Fed. Cir. 1991) - CONTROVERSY, INTERVENING RIGHTS

Ex parte Spence, 82 U.S.P.Q. 449 (PO Bd. App. 1946) - LATE CLAIMING

Sperry v. State of Florida, 378 U.S. 378, 137 U.S.P.Q. 578 (1965) - PATENT APPLICATION, 35 U.S.C. §112

In re Spiller, 500 F.2d 1170, 182 U.S.P.Q. 614 (C.C.P.A. 1974) - 37 C.F.R. §1.131

In re Spina, 975 F.2d 854, 24 U.S.P.Q.2d 1142 (Fed. Cir. 1992) - COPYING CLAIMS, DESCRIPTION

Spindelfabrik Suesson-Schurr Stahlecker & Grill GmbH v. Schubert & Salzer Maschinenfabrik Aktiengesellschaft, 829 F.2d 1075, 4 U.S.P.Q. 1044 (Fed. Cir. 1987), *cert. denied*, 108 S. Ct. 1022 (1988) - OPINION OF COUNSEL, WILLFUL

Spindelfabrik Suessen-Schurr, Stahlecker & Grill GmbH v. Schubert & Salzer Maschinenfabrik Aktiengesellschaft, 903 F.2d 1568, 14 U.S.P.Q.2d 1913 (Fed. Cir. 1990) - CONTEMPT

Spiner and Hoffman v. Pierce, 177 U.S.P.Q. 709 (PO Bd. Pat. Int. 1972) - ABAN-

DONED, COMMERCIALIZE, DERIVATION, DILIGENCE, FUNDING, STIP-ULATION, 35 U.S.C. §102(g)

Splendor Form Brassiere, Inc. v. Rapid-American Corporation, 187 U.S.P.Q. 151 (N.Y. 1975) - GENERIC CLAIM

In re Sporck, 301 F.2d 686, 133 U.S.P.Q. 360 (C.C.P.A. 1962) - ASSERTION, CHANGE, DOUBT, IMPROVEMENT, INGENUITY, RECONSTRUCTION, SIMPLICITY

Spound v. Mohasco Industries, Inc., 186 U.S.P.Q. 183 (Mass. 1975) - EXTENSION, PATENT OFFICE LICENSE, RETROACTIVE LICENSE

Square Liner 360°, Inc. v. Chisum, 215 U.S.P.Q. 1110 (Minn. 1981) - DAMAGES, NUMBER

Square Liner 360°, Inc. v. Chisum, 691 F.2d 362, 216 U.S.P.Q. 666 (8th Cir. 1982) - RECAPTURE

Squires v. Corbett, 560 F.2d 424, 194 U.S.P.Q. 513 (C.C.P.A. 1977) - COUNT, RIGHT TO MAKE

SRI International Inc. v. Advanced Technological Laboratories Inc., 127 F.3d 1462, 44 U.S.P.Q.2d 1422 (Fed. Cir. 1997) - ENHANCEMENT OF DAMAGES, NOTICE, OPINION OF COUNSEL, WILLFUL INFRINGEMENT

SRI International v. Matsushita Electric Corp. of America, 775 F.2d 1107, 227 U.S.P.Q. 577 (Fed. Cir. 1985) - CLAIM CONSTRUCTION, GIST, REVERSE DOCTRINE OF EQUIVALENTS, SKILLED IN THE ART, SPECIFICATION

SSIH Equipment, S.A. v. United States International Trade Commission, 713 F.2d 746, 218 U.S.P.Q. 678 (Fed. Cir. 1983) - INEQUITABLE CONDUCT

Staeger v. Commissioner of Patents and Trademarks, 189 U.S.P.Q. 272 (D.C. 1976) - 35 U.S.C. §118

Staehelin v. Secher, 24 U.S.P.Q.2d 1513 (B.P.A.I. 1992) - CONCEPTION, REDUCTION TO PRACTICE

Ex parte Stalego, 839 O.G. 828 (PO Bd. App. 1966) - CANCELED SUBJECT MAT-TER, COPENDING PATENT, REFERENCE

Ex parte Stalego, 154 U.S.P.Q. 52 (Bd. App. 1966) - CANCELLATION

Stambler v. Diebold Inc., 11 U.S.P.Q.2d 1709 (N.Y. 1988), *aff'd*, 11 U.S.P.Q.2d 1715 (Fed. Cir. 1989) - LACHES, SILENCE

Standal's Patents Ltd. v. Weyerhauser Co., 2 U.S.P.Q.2d 1185 (Or. 1986) - CLASS ACTION

Standard Havens Products Inc. v. Gencor Industries, Inc., 897 F.2d 511, 13 U.S.P.Q.2d 2029 (Fed. Cir. 1990) - STAY

Standard Havens Products Inc. v. Gencor Industries Inc., 953 F.2d 1360, 21 U.S.P.Q.2d 1321 (Fed. Cir. 1991) - ANTICIPATION, LOST PROFITS, NEW TRIAL

Standard Havens Products Inc. v. Gencor Industries Inc., 810 F. Supp. 1072, 25 U.S.P.Q.2d 1949 (Mo. 1993) - BLONDER-TONGUE DOCTRINE, REEXAMINATION

Standard Havens Inc. v. Manbeck, 762 F. Supp. 1349, 21 U.S.P.Q.2d 1635 (Mo. 1991) - JURISDICTION, MANDAMUS

Standard Oil Company v. American Cyanamid Company, 585 F. Supp. 1481, 224 U.S.P.Q. 210 (La. 1984) - RELATIVE TERM, SOLUBLE

The Standard Oil Company v. American Cyanamid Co., 774 F.2d 448, 227 U.S.P.Q. 293

(Fed. Cir. 1985) - HYPOTHETICAL PERSON, INVENTOR, OBVIOUSNESS, ORDINARY SKILL

Standard Oil Company (Indiana) v. Montecatini Edison S.p.A.; Phillips Petroleum Company v. E.I. du Pont de Nemours & Co.; E.I. du Pont de Nemours & Co. v. Montecatini Edison S.p.A., 342 F. Supp. 125, 174 U.S.P.Q. 7 (Del. 1972) - 28 U.S.C. §1338(a)

Standard Oil Company of Indiana v. Montedison S.p.A., 398 F. Supp. 420, 187 U.S.P.Q. 549 (Del. 1975) - ISSUE

Standard Oil Company (Indiana) v. Montedison, S.p.A.; Phillips Petroleum Company v. Montedison, S.p.A.; E.I. du Pont de Nemours & Company v. Montedison, S.p.A., 494 F. Supp. 370, 207 U.S.P.Q. 298 (Del. 1980) - 35 U.S.C. §146

Standard Oil Co. v. Nippon Shokubai Kagaku Kogyo, 754 F.2d 345, 224 U.S.P.Q. 863 (Fed. Cir. 1985) - 35 U.S.C. §286

Standard Packaging Corporation v. Curwood, Inc., 365 F. Supp. 134, 180 U.S.P.Q. 235 (Ill. 1973) - EXAMINER

Ex parte Standish, 10 U.S.P.Q.2d 1454 (B.P.A.I. 1988) - COMMERCIAL SUCCESS

Stanford Telecommunications Inc. v. U.S. District Court for the Northern District of California, 11 U.S.P.Q.2d 1480 (9th Cir. 1989) - JURISDICTION

In re Stanley and Lowe, 214 F.2d 151, 102 U.S.P.Q. 234 (C.C.P.A. 1954) - DOUBLE PATENTING, GENERIC INVENTION, IMPROVEMENT

The Stanley Works v. Haeger Potteries, Inc., 35 F.R.D. 551, 142 U.S.P.Q. 256 (Ill. 1964) - JOINT LICENSING, MUTUAL INTEREST

Stansbury v. Bond, 482 F.2d 968, 179 U.S.P.Q. 88 (C.C.P.A. 1973) - AMBIGUITY, COUNT

Stark v. Advanced Magnetics Inc., 29 F.3d 1570, 31 U.S.P.Q.2d 1290 (Fed. Cir. 1994) - CONVERSION

Stark v. Advanced Magnetics Inc., 894 F. Supp. 555, 36 U.S.P.Q.2d 1764 (Mass. 1995) - MANDATE RULE, 35 U.S.C. §256

Stark v. Advanced Magnetics Inc., 119 F.3d 1551, 43 U.S.P.Q.2d 1321 (Fed. Cir. 1997) - 35 U.S.C. §256

Starobin v. United States, 662 F.2d 747, 213 U.S.P.Q. 449 (U.S. Cl. Ct. 1981) - STATUTE OF LIMITATIONS, 28 U.S.C. §2501

State Industries, Inc. v. A.O. Smith Corporation, 751 F.2d 1226, 224 U.S.P.Q. 418 (Fed. Cir. 1985) - PATENT PENDING

State Industries Inc. v. Mor-Flo Industries Inc., 948 F.2d 1573, 20 U.S.P.Q.2d 1738 (Fed. Cir. 1991) - APPEAL, CLEAR ERROR, DAMAGES, FINDING, FRIVOLOUS, LAW-OF-THE-CASE DOCTRINE, 35 U.S.C. §284, 35 U.S.C. §285

State Street Bank & Trust Co. v. Signature Financial Group Inc., 149 F.3d 1368, 47 U.S.P.Q.2d 1596 (Fed. Cir. 1998) - METHOD OF DOING BUSINESS, SOFTWARE

In re Stattmann, 146 F.2d 290, 64 U.S.P.Q. 245 (C.C.P.A. 1944) - APPARATUS

Status Time Corp. v. Sharp Electronics Corp., 95 F.R.D. 27, 217 U.S.P.Q. 438 (N.Y. 1982) - FOREIGN ASSOCIATE, PRIVILEGE

Stauffer Chemical Company v. Monsanto Company, 623 F. Supp. 148, 227 U.S.P.Q. 401 (Mo. 1985) - ADVICE OF COUNSEL, ATTORNEY-CLIENT PRIVILEGE, PATENT OFFICE LICENSE, PRIVILEGE, WORK-PRODUCT PRIVILEGE

Steelcase, Inc. v. Delwood Furniture Co., Inc., 578 F.2d 74, 199 U.S.P.Q. 69 (5th Cir. 1978) - MOSITA

Steelcase Inc. v. Haworth Inc., 41 U.S.P.Q.2d 1468 (Cal. 1996) - TRANSFER, 28 U.S.C. §1404(a)

In re Steele, Mills, and Leis, 305 F.2d 859, 134 U.S.P.Q. 292 (C.C.P.A. 1962) - ASSUMPTION

Ex parte Steigerwald, 131 U.S.P.Q. 73 (Bd. App. 1961) - SUCH AS

In re Steinhauer and Valenta, 410 F.2d 411, 161 U.S.P.Q. 595 (C.C.P.A. 1969) - BREADTH, MIXTURE, POSITION, RING

Stein Industries Inc. v. Jarco Industries Inc., 40 U.S.P.Q.2d 1955 (N.Y. 1966) - OBVIOUSNESS

In re Stemniski, 444 F.2d 581, 170 U.S.P.Q. 343 (C.C.P.A. 1971) - ANALOG, ENABLING DISCLOSURE, FORMULA, HOMOLOGY, OBVIOUSNESS, REFERENCE, STRUCTURAL OBVIOUSNESS, 35 U.S.C. §102(b), USE

In re Stempel, 241 F.2d 755, 113 U.S.P.Q. 77 (C.C.P.A. 1957) - REFERENCE, 37 C.F.R. §1.131

In re Stephens, Benvau, and Benvau, 529 F.2d 1343, 188 U.S.P.Q. 659 (C.C.P.A. 1976) - 37 C.F.R. §1.71(b), CRITICAL, GENUS, GIST, NON-CRITICAL, SUPPORT, WORKING EXAMPLE

In re Steppan, Rebenstock, and Neugebauer, 394 F.2d 1013, 156 U.S.P.Q. 143 (C.C.P.A. 1967) - CONDENSATE, REACTION PRODUCT

Sterling Drug Inc. v. Watson, 135 F. Supp. 173, 108 U.S.P.Q. 37 (D.C. 1955) - ISOLATED

Ex parte Stern, 13 U.S.P.Q.2d 1379 (B.P.A.I. 1987) - DEEM

Ex parte Stevens, 16 U.S.P.Q.2d 1379 (B.P.A.I. 1990) - CANCER

In re Stevens, 212 F.2d 197, 101 U.S.P.Q. 284 (C.C.P.A. 1954) - ADJUSTABILITY

Stevens v. Schmid and Kirbach, 406 F.2d 776, 160 U.S.P.Q. 623 (C.C.P.A. 1969) - TRANSLATION

Stevenson v. International Trade Commission, 612 F.2d 546, 204 U.S.P.Q. 276 (C.C.P.A. 1979) - BREADTH, CCPA, REDUCTION TO PRACTICE

In re Stewart, 222 F.2d 747, 106 U.S.P.Q. 115 (C.C.P.A. 1955) - UNDISCLOSED PROPERTY, UNEXPECTED RESULTS

Stewart-Warner Corp. v. The City of Pontiac, Michigan, 717 F.2d 269, 219 U.S.P.Q. 1162 (6th Cir. 1983) - CLAIM, CONSTRUCTION

Sticker Industrial Supply Corp. v. Blaw-Knox Co., 405 F.2d 90, 160 U.S.P.Q. 177 (7th Cir. 1968) - CROSS-REFERENCE

Stoddard (see *A.F. Stoddard & Company, Ltd. v. Dann*)

Stoller v. Ford Motor Co., 18 U.S.P.Q.2d 1545 (Fed. Cir. 1991) - SUMMARY JUDGMENT

In re Strahilevitz, 668 F.2d 1229, 212 U.S.P.Q. 561 (C.C.P.A. 1982) - BREADTH, COPENDING PATENT, ENABLEMENT, EXAMPLE, NEW ARGUMENT, NEW RATIONALE, STANDARD OF REVIEW, SKILL OF THE ART

Stranco Inc. v. Atlantes Chemical Systems Inc., 15 U.S.P.Q.2d 1704 (Tex. 1990) - CONTINUATION-IN-PART APPLICATION, DEFERENCE, DIFFERENCE, DUE CARE, FILE WRAPPER ESTOPPEL, MODIFICATION, PREAMBLE, PREJUDGMENT INTEREST, PRESUMPTION OF VALIDITY, UTILITY, WILLFUL INFRINGEMENT

Stratoflex, Inc. v. Aeroquip Corporation, 561 F. Supp. 618, 218 U.S.P.Q. 231 (Mich. 1982) - OBVIOUSNESS

St. Regis Paper Company v. Royal Industries, 186 U.S.P.Q. 83 (Cal. 1974) - MISREPRE-
SENTATION, OATH

Ex parte Strijland, 26 U.S.P.Q.2d 1259 (B.P.A.I. 1992) - ICON

In re Striker, 182 U.S.P.Q. 507 (PO Solicitor 1973) - ATTORNEY, 37 C.F.R. §1.47(b),
EXCLUSIVE LICENSEE, PROPRIETARY

Ex parte Strobel and Catino, 160 U.S.P.Q. 352 (PO Bd. App. 1968) - DIRECTION,
SHOTGUN

Strojirenstvi v. Toyoda, 2 U.S.P.Q.2d 1222 (Commr. Patents & Trademarks 1986) - CON-
FLICT OF INTEREST

In re Stryker, 435 F.2d 1340, 168 U.S.P.Q. 372 (C.C.P.A. 1971) - ANTEDATING A
REFERENCE, COMMENSURATE IN SCOPE, CORROBORATION

Stryker Corp. v. Davol Inc., 10 F. Supp. 2d 841, 47 U.S.P.Q.2d 1740 (Mich. 1998) -
INFRINGEMENT

Stryker Corp. v. Intermedics Orthopedics Inc., 145 F.R.D. 298, 24 U.S.P.Q.2d 1676 (N.Y.
1992) - ATTORNEY-CLIENT PRIVILEGE

Stryker Corp. v. Intermedics Orthopedics Inc., 40 U.S.P.Q.2d 1065 (Fed. Cir. 1996) -
CLEARLY ERRONEOUS

Stryker Corp. v. Intermedics Orthopedics Inc., 42 U.S.P.Q.2d 1935 (N.Y. 1997) - AT-
TORNEY'S FEES

Stryker Corp. v. Zimmer Inc., 741 F. Supp. 509, 17 U.S.P.Q.2d 1945 (N.J. 1990) -
SILENCE

Ex parte Stubbs, 58 F.2d 447, 13 U.S.P.Q. 358 (C.C.P.A. 1932) - TRANSITORY

Studiengesellschaft Kohle, m.b.H. v. Dart Indus., Inc., 726 F.2d 724, 220 U.S.P.Q. 841
(Fed. Cir. 1984) - ANTICIPATION

Studiengesellschaft Kohle mbH v. Eastman Kodak Co., 450 F. Supp. 1211, 197 U.S.P.Q.
164 (Tex. 1977) - CATALYST, DOUBLE PATENTING

Studiengesellschaft Kohle mbH v. Hercules Inc., 748 F. Supp. 247, 18 U.S.P.Q.2d 1773
(Del. 1990) - FRAUDULENT CONCEALMENT, UNKNOWABLE

Studiengesellschaft Kohle mbH v. Northern Petrochemical Co., 784 F.2d 351, 228
U.S P.Q. 837 (Fed. Cir. 1986) - DOUBLE PATENTING, SAME INVENTION,
STATUTORY CLASS

Studiengesellschaft Kohle m.b.H. v. Shell Oil Co., 112 F.3d 1561, 42 U.S.P.Q.2d 1674
(Fed. Cir. 1997) - COMBINING PRIORITY APPLICATIONS, DAMAGES, ES-
TOPPEL, INVALID CLAIM, LEAR TEST, 35 U.S.C. §120 , VALIDITY

Sturtevant v. Van Remortel, 38 U.S.P.Q.2d 1134 (N.Y. 1995) - CONCEPTION, INVEN-
TOR, MOTION TO DISMISS

Sturzinger v. Commissioner of Patents, 377 F. Supp. 1284, 181 U.S.P.Q. 436 (D.C. 1974) -
FILING DATE, STOLEN

In re The Successor in Interest to Walter Andersen, 743 F.2d 1578, 223 U.S.P.Q. 378 (Fed.
Cir. 1984) - DOUBT, REEXAMINATION

Ex parte Sudilovsky, 21 U.S.P.Q.2d 1702 (B.P.A.I. 1991) - WORKING EXAMPLE

Suh v. Hoefle, 23 U.S.P.Q.2d 1321 (B.P.A.I. 1991) - INTERFERENCE,
OBVIOUSNESS, SKILL OF THE ART

In re Sulkowski, 487 F.2d 920, 180 U.S.P.Q. 46 (C.C.P.A. 1973) - DESCRIPTION,
DISCLOSURE, DNA, FORMULA, INHERENT, NAMING, NEW MATTER,
PRODUCT, RECOGNITION, SUPPORT

Sulkowski v. Houlihan, 179 U.S.P.Q. 685 (PO Bd. Pat. Intf. 1973) - ANTICIPATION, CONCEPTION, DESCRIPTION, DISCLOSURE, DNA, FORMULA, INHERENT,NAMING, NEW MATTER, PRODUCT, RECOGNITION, SUPPORT

Sulkowski v. Metlesics and Sternbach v. Houlihan, 179 U.S.P.Q. 687 (PO Bd. Pat. Intf. 1973) - SUBSTITUTED COUNT

Sumitomo Electric Industries Ltd. v. Corning Glass Works, 8 U.S.P.Q.2d 1453 (N.Y. 1988) - PROTECTIVE ORDER

Summagraphics Corp. v. Sanders Associates Inc., 19 U.S.P.Q.2d 1859 (Conn. 1991) - DISQUALIFICATION

In re Sun, 31 U.S.P.Q.2d 1451 (Fed. Cir. 1993 - *unpublished*) - AFFIDAVIT, 37 C.F.R. §1.107(b), CHALLENGE

Sun-Flex Co. Inc. v. Softview Computer Products Corp., 750 F. Supp. 962, 18 U.S.P.Q.2d 1171 (Ill. 1990) - INEQUITABLE CONDUCT

Sun Studs Inc. v. ATA Equipment Leasing Inc., 882 F.2d 1583, 11 U.S.P.Q.2d 1479 (Fed. Cir. 1989) - DIRECTED VERDICT

Sun Studs Inc. v. ATA Equipment Leasing Inc., 17 U.S.P.Q.2d 1768 (Or. 1990) - COSTS

Super Sack Manufacturing Corp. v. Chase Packaging Corp., 37 U.S.P.Q.2d 1394 (Tex. 1995) - DISMISSAL

In re Sureau, Kremer, and Dupre, 373 F.2d 1002, 153 U.S.P.Q. 66 (C.C.P.A. 1967) - KNOWN, 35 U.S.C. §112

Surgical Laser Technologies Inc. v. Heraeus Laseronics Inc., 34 U.S.P.Q.2d 1226 (Pa. 1995) - CONSENT DECREE, RULE 8(c), SUMMARY JUDGMENT, WAIVER

Surgical Laser Technologies Inc. v. Surgical Laser Products Inc., 25 U.S.P.Q.2d 1806 (Pa. 1992) - RECONSTRUCTION

In re Surrey, 370 F.2d 349, 151 U.S.P.Q. 724 (C.C.P.A. 1966) - CAN, PROPHETIC EXAMPLES, PECULATION, UTILITY

In re Sus and Schaefer, 306 F.2d 494, 134 U.S.P.Q. 301 (C.C.P.A. 1962) - APPLICANT'S RIGHTS, ARYL, BREADTH, COMMENSURATE IN SCOPE, LIMIT, PATENT LAWS, PROTECTION, SUBSTITUTED

In re Susi, 440 F.2d 442, 169 USPQ 423 (CCPA 1971) - SELECTION

In re Suska, 589 F.2d 527, 200 U.S.P.Q. 497 (C.C.P.A. 1979) - CONCEALMENT

In re Swartzel, 60 F.3d 843, 36 U.S.P.Q.2d 1510 (Fed. Cir. 1995) - DIVISIONAL DOCTRINE

In re Swentzel, 219 F.2d 216, 104 U.S.P.Q. 343 (C.C.P.A. 1955) - ASSERTION, SHOWING

In re Swinehart and Sfiligoj, 439 F.2d 210, 169 U.S.P.Q. 226 (C.C.P.A. 1971) - POINT OF NOVELTY, FUNCTIONAL, LANGUAGE, 35 U.S.C. §112

Switzer and Ward v. Slockman and Brady, 333 F.2d 935, 142 U.S.P.Q. 226 (C.C.P.A. 1964) - COPYING CLAIMS

Sybron Transition Corp. v. Nixon, Hargrave, Devans & Doyle, 770 F. Supp. 803, 21 U.S.P.Q.2d 1515 (N.Y. 1991) - ASSIGNEE ESTOPPEL

Sylgab Steel & Wire Corp. v. Imoco-Gateway Corp., 357 F. Supp. 657, 178 U.S.P.Q. 22 (Ill. 1973) - BEST MODE

Symbol Technologies Inc. v. Metrologic Instruments Inc., 771 F. Supp. 1390, 21 U.S.P.Q.2d 1481 (N.J. 1991) - DELAY, TORT

Symbol Technologies Inc. v. Opticon Inc., 935 F.2d 1569, 19 U.S.P.Q.2d 1241 (Fed. Cir.

1991) - CLAIM INTERPRETATION, CONSONANCE, DOUBLE PATENTING, ENABLEMENT, EXPERT, EXPERT TESTIMONY, INFRINGEMENT, INTENT TO DECEIVE, MEANS PLUS FUNCTION, NEGLIGENCE, OPINION, REFERENCE, RESTRICTION, TESTIMONY, UNITY OF INVENTION

Ex parte Symons, 134 U.S.P.Q. 74 (PO Bd. App. 1962) - DOUBLE PATENTING, 35 U.S.C. §100(b)

Syntex Pharmaceuticals International Ltd. v. K-Line Pharmaceuticals Ltd., 905 F.2d 1525, 15 U.S.P.Q.2d 1239 (Fed. Cir. 1990) - SUMMARY JUDGMENT

Syntex (U.S.A.) Inc. v. Paragon Optical Inc., 7 U.S.P.Q.2d 1001 (Ariz. 1987) - CONSISTING ESSENTIALLY OF, DOCTRINE OF EQUIVALENTS, FILE WRAPPER ESTOPPEL, RECAPTURE

Syntex (U.S.A.) Inc. v. U.S Patent and Trademark Office, 882 F.2d 1570, 11 U.S.P.Q.2d 1866 (Fed. Cir. 1989) - BPAI, REEXAMINATION

Synthetic Industries (Texas) Inc. v. Forta Fiber, Inc., 590 F. Supp. 1574, 224 U.S.P.Q. 955 (Pa. 1984) - CHANGE, CLAIM LIMITATION, CONTINUATION-IN-PART APPLICATION, DESCRIPTION, RANGE

Systematic Tool & Machine Co. v. Walter Kidde & Co., Inc., 390 F. Supp. 178, 185 U.S.P.Q. 281 (Pa. 1975) - COPYING

In re Szajna and Lump, 422 F.2d 443, 164 U.S.P.Q. 632 (C.C.P.A. 1970) - REEXAMINATION

-T-

In re Taborsky, 502 F.2d 775, 183 U.S.P.Q. 50 (C.C.P.A. 1974) - MODIFICATION

Tabuchi and Abe v. Nubel, Fitts, and Lorenzo, 559 F.2d 1183, 194 U.S.P.Q. 521 (C.C.P.A. 1977) - DEPOSITORY, SCREENING, STRAIN, UNDUE EXPERIMENTATION

In re Taggart, 115 U.S.P.Q. 413 (Comm'r 1957) - 37 C.F.R. §1.84

In re Application of Takao, 17 U.S.P.Q.2d 1155 (Commr. Patents & Trademarks 1990) - DILIGENCE, REVIVAL, TERMINAL DISCLAIMER

In re Talbott, 443 F.2d 1397, 170 U.S.P.Q. 281 (C.C.P.A. 1971) - 35 U.S.C. §102(d), 35 U.S.C. §172

Tanabe Seiyaku Co. v. U.S. International Trade Commission, 41 U.S.P.Q.2d 1976 (Fed. Cir. 1997) - DOCTRINE OF EQUIVALENTS, FOREIGN, INFRINGEMENT

Tandon Corp. v. U.S. International Trade Commission, 831 F.2d 1017, 4 U.S.P.Q.2d 1283 (Fed. Cir. 1987) - CLAIM CONSTRUCTION, CLAIM DIFFERENTIATION, MULTIPLICITY

In re Tangsrud, 184 U.S.P.Q. 746 (Comm'r 1973) - PRIORITY, 35 U.S.C. 119

Tank Insulation International Inc. v. Insultherm Inc., 104 F.3d 83, 41 U.S.P.Q.2d 1545 (5th Cir. 1997) - COMPULSORY COUNTERCLAIM

Ex parte Tanksley, 37 U.S.P.Q.2d 1382 (B.P.A.I. 1994) - CLAIM, SEARCH, 35 U.S.C. §112

Tapco Products Co. v. Van Mark Products Corp., 446 F.2d 420, 170 U.S.P.Q. 550 (6th Cir. 1971) - APPROPRIATE, BENEFIT, THEORY

Tapia v. Micheletti v. Wignall, Shelton, and Klee, 202 U.S.P.Q. 123 (PTO Bd. App. 1976) - CONCEPTION, INTRODUCTION, KNOWLEDGE

Ex parte Taras and Randall, 126 U.S.P.Q. 418 (PO Bd. App. 1959) - SOLVENT

In re Tatincloux and Guy, 228 F.2d 238, 108 U.S.P.Q. 125 (C.C.P.A. 1955) - SIMULTANEOUS

Taub, Wendler, and Slates v. Rausser and Oliveto, 145 U.S.P.Q. 497 (PO Bd. Pat. Int. 1964) - DILIGENCE

Ex parte Taylor, 167 U.S.P.Q. 637 (PO Bd. App. 1970) - NUCLEUS

Taylor v. Anderson, 234 U.S. 74 (1914) - ARISE UNDER PATENT LAWS

Taylor v. Brackman, 208 U.S.P.Q. 275 (PTO Bd. Pat. Int. 1979) - CONJECTURE

Taylor Engines, Inc. v. All Steel Engines, Inc., 192 F.2d 171, 92 U.S.P.Q. 35 (9th Cir. 1951) - 35 U.S.C. §261

T.D. Williamson Inc. v. Laymon, 723 F. Supp. 587, 13 U.S.P.Q.2d 1417 (Okla. 1989) - AVAILABILITY, BUT-FOR RULE OR TEST, INDUCE, PANDUIT TEST, SUBSTITUTE, SECOND LOWEST BIDDER, 35 U.S.C. §271

In re Teague, 254 F.2d 145, 117 U.S.P.Q. 284 (C.C.P.A. 1958) - AT LEAST, CONSTRUCTION, ONE

Tec-Air Inc. v. Nippondenso Manufacturing USA Inc., 33 U.S.P.Q.2d 1451 (Ill. 1994) - DISCOVERY, DISMISSAL, IMPROPER CONDUCT, SANCTIONS

Technical Development Corp. v. United States, 202 Ct. Cl. 237, 179 U.S.P.Q. 180 (Ct. Cl. 1973) - EVIDENCE

Technicon Instruments Corp. v. Alpkem Corp., 866 F.2d 417, 9 U.S.P.Q.2d 1540 (Fed. Cir. 1989) - INVALID PATENT, SHERMAN ACT, STIPULATION

Technimark Inc. v. Crellin Inc., 49 U.S.P.Q.2d 1134 (N.C. 1998) - DEDICATION

Technitrol, Incorporated v. Control Data Corporation, 164 U.S.P.Q. 552 (Md. 1970) - *IN REM*

Tee-Pak, Inc. v. St. Regis Paper Company, 491 F.2d 1193, 181 U.S.P.Q. 75 (6th Cir. 1974) - REISSUE

Teets v. Chromalloy Gas Turbine Corp., 83 F.3d 403, 38 U.S.P.Q.2d 1695 (Fed. Cir. 1996) - EMPLOYEE

Telectronics Pacing Systems Inc. v. Ventritex Inc., 19 U.S.P.Q.2d 1960 (Cal. 1991) - 35 U.S.C. §271

Telectronics Pacing Systems Inc. v. Ventritex Inc., 982 F.2d 1520, 25 U.S.P.Q.2d 1196 (Fed. Cir. 1992) - DECLARATORY JUDGMENT, SUMMARY JUDGMENT

Tenax Corp. v. Tensar Corp., 19 U.S.P.Q.2d 1881 (Md. 1991) - NEW TRIAL, PREJUDGMENT INTEREST, RIGHTS, WILLFUL INFRINGEMENT

Tennant Co. v. Hako Minuteman Inc., 22 U.S.P.Q.2d 1161 (Ill. 1991) - AMENDMENT, ESTOPPEL, FAILURE OF OTHERS

Tenneco Resins, Inc. v. Reeves Bros., Inc., 752 F.2d 630, 224 U.S.P.Q. 536 (Fed. Cir. 1985) - AMEND COMPLAINT

In re Tenney, Frank, and Knox, 254 F.2d 619, 117 U.S.P.Q. 348 (C.C.P.A. 1958) - GEBRAUCHSMUSTER, MICROFILM, PRINTED PUBLICATION

Texas Instruments Inc. v. Cypress Semiconductor Corp., 90 F.3d 1558, 39 U.S.P.Q.2d 1481 (Tex. 1995), aff'd 39 U.S.P.Q.2d 1492 (Fed. Cir. 1996) - JMOL, SUBSTANTIAL

Texas Instruments Inc. v. Cypress Semiconductor Corp., 90 F.3d 1558, 39 U.S.P.Q.2d 1492 (Fed. Cir. 1996) - CAFC, COLLATERAL ESTOPPEL, DIRECTED VERDICT, DOCTRINE OF EQUIVALENTS, ITC, SUBSTANTIAL

Texas Instruments, Inc. v. U.S. International Trade Commission, 805 F.2d 1558, 231 U.S.P.Q. 833 (Fed. Cir. 1986) - APPROPRIATION, BREADTH, COMBINATION,

DESCRIPTION, EQUIVALENCE, EQUIVALENTS, FRAUD ON A PATENT, FUNCTION, FUTURE DISCOVERIES, INFRINGEMENT, MEANS, SKILLED IN THE ART, SPECIFIC EXAMPLE

Texas Instruments, Inc. v. U.S. International Trade Commission, 846 F.2d 1369, 6 U.S.P.Q.2d 1886 (Fed. Cir. 1988) - PIONEER INVENTION

Texas Instruments Inc. v. International Trade Commission, 988 F.2d 1165, 26 U.S.P.Q.2d 1018 (Fed. Cir. 1993) - DOCTRINE OF EQUIVALENTS, LONG-FELT NEED, PROSECUTION HISTORY ESTOPPEL, TARIFF ACT, WHEREBY

Tezuka v. Wilson, 224 U.S.P.Q. 1030 (PTO Bd. Pat. Int. 1984) - COPYING CLAIMS

Theeuwes v. Bogentoft, 2 U.S.P.Q.2d 1378 (Comm'r 1986) - MOTION TO ADD OR SUBSTITUTE

Ex parte Thelin, 152 U.S.P.Q. 624 (PO Bd. App. 1966) - CANCELED SUBJECT MATTER, CONCEPTION, KNOWLEDGE, 35 U.S.C. §154

Thermalloy Inc. v. Aavid Engineering Inc., 39 U.S.P.Q.2d 1457 (N.H. 1996) - BROADEN, CLAIM CONSTRUCTION, REEXAMINATION, REISSUE

Therma-Tru Corp. v. Peachtree Doors Inc., 44 F.3d 988, 33 U.S.P.Q.2d 1274 (Fed. Cir. 1995) - DISCRETIONARY RULING, FINDINGS, INEQUITABLE CONDUCT, INTENT, JURY *Thermos Co. v. Starbucks Corp.*, 48 U.S.P.Q.2d 1310 (Ill. 1998) - SETTLEMENT

THK America Inc. v. Nippon Seiko K.K., 141 F.R.D. 463, 21 U.S.P.Q.2d 1705 (Ill. 1991) - MAGISTRATE JUDGE, 28 U.S.C. §636

THK America Inc. v. NSK Co. Ltd., 157 F.R.D. 637, 33 U.S.P.Q.2d 1248 (Ill. 1993) - ATTORNEY-CLIENT PRIVILEGE, ESTOPPEL, LACHES

Thomas & Betts Corp. v. Panduit Corp., 138 F.3d 277, 46 U.S.P.Q.2d 1026 (7th Cir. 1998) - LANHAM ACT, PATENT ACT, TRADEMARK

Thomas, Draber, Schmidt, and Eue v. Eiken, Rohr, Zech, and Wuerzer, 219 U.S.P.Q. 900 (PTO Bd. Pat. Intf. 1983) - PHARMACEUTICAL

In re Thompson and Ihde, 545 F.2d 1290, 192 U.S.P.Q. 275 (C.C.P.A. 1976) - ECONOMICS

In re Thuau, 135 F.2d 344, 57 U.S.P.Q. 324 (C.C.P.A. 1943) - COMPOSITION, OLD COMBINATION, THUAU DOCTRINE, USE

Thyssen Plastik Anger KG v. Induplas, Inc., 195 U.S.P.Q. 534 (P.R. 1977) - BEST MODE, BLOCK DIAGRAM, CONVENTIONAL

In re Tiffin and Erdman, 443 F.2d 394, 170 U.S.P.Q. 88 (C.C.P.A. 1971) - COMPARATIVE TEST DATA, EFFECTIVE DATE, EVIDENCE, OBVIOUSNESS

Tights, Inc. v. Kayser-Roth Corp. 442 F. Supp. 159, 196 U.S.P.Q. 750 (N.C. 1977) - ROYALTY

The Tillotson Manufacturing Company v. Textron, Inc., 337 F.2d 833, 143 U.S.P.Q. 268 (6th Cir. 1964) - CONFUSING

Titanium Metals Corp. of America v. Mossinghoff, 603 F. Supp. 87, 225 U.S.P.Q. 673 (D.C. 1984) - ADMINISTRATIVE REGULARITY, EXPERIMENTATION, INDEPENDENT EXPERT, OPINION, PTO, STANDARD FOR REVERSAL, 35 U.S.C. §145

Ex parte Titone, 177 U.S.P.Q. 731 (PO Bd. App. 1971) - BOARD (BOARD OF APPEALS)

T.J. Smith v. Consolidated Medical Equipment, Inc., 821 F.2d 646, 3 U.S.P.Q.2d 1316 (Fed. Cir. 1987) - PRELIMINARY INJUNCTION

Tol-O-Matic, Inc. v. Proma Produkt-Und Mktg. Gesellschaft m.b.H., 945 F.2d 1546 20 U.S.P.Q.2d 1332 (Fed. Cir. 1991) - INEQUITABLE CONDUCT, PLEADINGS, STANDARD OF REVIEW

Tomar Electronics Inc. v. Whelen Technologies Inc., 819 F. Supp. 871, 25 U.S.P.Q.2d 1464 (Ariz. 1992) - VENUE

In re Tomlinson, Hall, and Geigle, 363 F.2d 928, 150 U.S.P.Q. 623 (C.C.P.A. 1966) - OBVIOUS TO TRY OR EXPERIMENT

Tompkins v. Quigg, 6 U.S.P.Q.2d 1400 (D.C. 1987) - JURY TRIAL

Tone Brothers Inc. v. Sysco Corp., 28 F.3d 1192, 31 U.S.P.Q.2d 1321 (Fed. Cir. 1994) - DESIGN

The Toro Company v. L. R. Nelson Corporation, 524 F. Supp. 586, 213 U.S.P.Q. 207 (Ill. 1981) - FUNCTION, MEANS PLUS FUNCTION

The Toro Co. v. McCulloch Corp., 898 F. Supp. 679, 35 U.S.P.Q.2d 1622 (Minn. 1995) - 35 U.S.C. §287(a)

Total Containment Inc. v. Buffalo Environmental Products Corp., 35 U.S.P.Q.2d 1385 (Va. 1995) - ASSIGNOR ESTOPPEL, CIRCUMSTANTIAL EVIDENCE, INDUCEMENT, PATENTABILITY STANDARD

Total Containment Inc. v. Environ Products Inc., 33 U.S.P.Q.2d 1316 (Pa. 1994) - ASSIGNOR, INTERLOCUTORY ORDER, STATE OF THE ART

Total Containment Inc. v. Environ Products Inc., 34 U.S.P.Q.2d 1254 (Pa. 1995) - AMEND, ASSIGNOR ESTOPPEL, EQUITY

Toter Inc. v. City of Visalia, 44 U.S.P.Q.2d 1312 (Cal. 1997) - CLAIM INTERPRETATION

Towne v. Eisner, 245 U.S. 418 (1918) - WORD

Townsend Co. v. M.S.L. Industries, 150 U.S.P.Q. 237 (Ill. 1966) - ATTORNEY'S FEES

Township of Franklin Sewerage Authority v. Middlesex County Utilities Authority, 787 F.2d 117 (3d Cir.), *cert. denied*, 479 U.S. 828 (1986) - PRELIMINARY IONJUNCTION

TP Laboratories Inc. v. Professional Positioners, Inc., 724 F.2d 965, 220 U.S.P.Q. 577 (Fed. Cir. 1984) - EXPERIMENTAL USE, PERSUASION

TP Orthodontics Inc. v. Professional Positioners Inc., 17 U.S.P.Q.2d 1497 (Wis. 1990) - DAMAGES

Transco Products Inc. v. Performance Contracting Inc., 792 F. Supp. 594, 23 U.S.P.Q.2d 1691 (Ill. 1992) - CROWDED ART, DOCTRINE OF EQUIVALENTS

Transco Products Inc. v. Performance Contracting Inc., 821 F. Supp. 537, 28 U.S.P.Q.2d 1739 (Ill. 1993) - BEST MODE, CONTINUATION APPLICATION, NEW MATTER

Transco Products Inc. v. Performance Contracting Inc., 38 F.3d 551, 32 U.S.P.Q.2d 1077 (Fed. Cir. 1994) - BEST MODE

Transducer Patents Co. v. Renegotiation Board, 485 F.2d 26, 179 U.S.P.Q. 398 (9th Cir. 1973) - ASSIGNMENT, RECAPTURE

Transmatic Inc. v. Gulton Industries Inc., 835 F. Supp. 1026, 29 U.S.P.Q.2d 1541 (Mich. 1993) - DOCTRINE OF EQUIVALENTS, JURY TRIAL

Transmatic Inc. v. Gulton Industries Inc., 53 F.3d 1270, 35 U.S.P.Q.2d 1035 (Fed. Cir. 1995) - CONSTITUTIONAL QUESTION, DAMAGES, STANDARD OF REVIEW

-*U*-

Ultradent Products Inc. v. Life-Like Cosmetics Inc., 39 U.S.P.Q.2d 1969 (Utah 1996) - ANTICIPATION, MARKET SHARE

UMC Electronics Co. v. United States, 816 F.2d 647, 2 U.S.P.Q.2d 1465 (Fed. Cir. 1987) - ON SALE

UMC Industries, Inc. v. Seaborg, 439 F.2d 953, 169 U.S.P.Q. 325 (9th Cir. 1971) - ATOMIC ENERGY COMMISSION, 42 U.S.C. §2182

Underwater Devices Incorporated v. Morrison-Knudsen Company, Inc., 717 F.2d 1380, 219 U.S.P.Q. 569 (Fed. Cir. 1983) - BIFURCATION, DUE CARE, DUTY OF POTENTIAL INFRINGERS, FILE HISTORY, INFRINGEMENT OPINION, NEW TRIAL, OPINION, PROOF, VALIDITY OPINION

Underwood v. Gerber, 149 U.S. 224 (1893) - DOUBLE PATENTING, SAME DATE

Unidynamics Corp. v. Automatic Products International Ltd., 48 U.S.P.Q.2d 1099 (Fed. Cir. 1998) - DESIGN

Union Carbide Corporation v. Air Products & Chemicals, Inc., 202 U.S.P.Q. 43 (N.Y. 1978) - COUNTERCLAIM, DECLARATORY JUDGMENT, FEDERAL QUESTION, STATE COURT

Union Carbide Corp. v. American Can Co., 724 F.2d 1567, 220 U.S.P.Q. 584 (Fed. Cir. 1984) - SUMMARY JUDGMENT MOTION

Union Carbide Corp. v. Borg-Warner Corp., 550 F.2d 355, 193 U.S.P.Q. 1 (6th Cir. 1977) - BEST MODE

Union Carbide Corporation v. The Dow Chemical Company, 213 U.S.P.Q. 128 (Tex. 1981) - LENGTHY PROSECUTION

Union Carbide Corp. v. Terancon Corp., 682 F. Supp. 535, 6 U.S.P.Q.2d 1847 (Ga. 1988) - EXPERT TESTIMONY

Union Carbide Corp. v. Tarancon Corp., 742 F. Supp. 565, 15 U.S.P.Q.2d 1833 (Ga. 1990) - TRADE SECRET

Union Tool Co. v. Wilson, 259 U.S. 107 (1922) - IMPLIED LICENSE, INFRINGEMENT

Unique Concepts Inc. v. Manuel, 930 F.2d 573, 18 U.S.P.Q.2d 1654 (7th Cir. 1991) - JURISDICTION

Uniroyal, Inc. v. Rudkin-Wiley Corp., 837 F.2d 1044, 5 U.S.P.Q.2d 1434 (Fed. Cir.), *cert. denied*, 488 U.S. 825 (1988) - COMBINING REFERENCES, EXPERIMENTATION, EXPERT OPINION, MOSAIC, OBVIOUSNESS, OBVIOUS TO TRY OR EXPERIMENT, OPTIMIZE, ORDINARY SKILL, PARAMETERS, PREDICTABILITY, REASON, RETROSPECTIVE RECONSTRUCTION, ROUTINEEXPERIMENTATION, SCIENTIFIC PRINCIPLE, SUGGESTION, TEACHING

Uniroyal Inc. v. Rudkin-Wiley Corp., 721 F. Supp. 128, 13 U.S.P.Q.2d 1192 (Conn. 1989) - ATTORNEY'S FEES, DAMAGES, OPINION, WILLFUL

Unisplay S.A. v. American Electronic Sign Co., 69 F.3d 512, 36 U.S.P.Q.2d 1540 (Fed. Cir. 1995) - MAXIMUM RECOVERY RULE, REASONABLE ROYALTY

Unisys Corp. v. Commissioner of Patents and Trademarks, 39 U.S.P.Q.2d 1842 (D.C. 1993) - COMMISSIONER'S DECISION, STANDARD, SUPPLEMENTAL PRELIMINARY STATEMENT

United Carbon Co. v. Binney & Smith Co., 317 U.S. 228, 55 U.S.P.Q. 381 (1942) - ACCURACY, DEFINITION

United National Insurance Co. v. Bradleys' Electric Inc., 35 U.S.P.Q.2d 1559 (Tex. 1995)

-𝑣-

In re Vaeck, 947 F.2d 488, 20 U.S.P.Q.2d 1438 (Fed. Cir. 1991) - COMBINING REFER-
ENCES, DISCLOSURE, SUCCESS

Valmet Paper Machinery Inc. v. Beloit Corp., 868 F. Supp. 1085, 32 U.S.P.Q.2d 1794
(Wis. 1994) - ASSIGNMENT, STANDING

Valmet Paper Machinery Inc. v. Beloit Corp., 39 U.S.P.Q.2d 1878 (Wis. 1995) - INJUNC-
TION, NEW TRIAL

Valmont Industries, Inc. v. Reinke Manufacturing Co., 14 U.S.P.Q.2d 1374 (Neb. 1990) -
ENABLEMENT, INTERVENING RIGHTS

Valmont Industries Inc. v. Reinke Manufacturing Co. Inc., 983 F.2d 1039, 25 U.S.P.Q.2d
1451 (Fed. Cir. 1993) - DOCTRINE OF EQUIVALENTS, EQUIVALENTS

Valutron N.V. v. NCR Corp., 33 U.S.P.Q.2d 1986 (Ohio 1992), *affirmed* (Fed. Cir. 1993),
cert. denied (S.Ct. 1994) - DILATORY CONDUCT, ECONOMICS, FINANCIAL
INABILITY, INFRINGEMENT, LACHES, NEGOTIATIONS, SUCCESSOR IN
INTEREST

Vancil and Jenkins v. Arata, 202 U.S.P.Q. 58 (PTO Bd. Pat. Int. 1977) - CONCEPTION

Ex parte Vanderhye, 217 U.S.P.Q. 266 (PTO Bd. App. 1982) - COMPARATIVE TEST
DATA

In re Van Geuns, 946 F.2d 845, 20 U.S.P.Q.2d 1291 (Fed. Cir. 1991) - INTERFERENCE

In re Van Geuns, 988 F.2d 1181, 26 U.S.P.Q.2d 1057 (Fed. Cir. 1993) - CLAIMS CORRE-
SPONDING TO COUNT, COUNT, PATENTABILITY, TOGETHER

Vas-Cath Inc. v. Mahurkar, 745 F. Supp. 517, 17 U.S.P.Q.2d 1353 (Ill. 1990) - COLLAT-
ERAL ESTOPPEL, FOREIGN, FOREIGN PATENTS AND PROCEEDINGS,
PRECLUSION, PRIORITY

Vas-Cath v. Mahurkar, 935 F.2d 1559, 19 U.S.P.Q.2d 1111 (Fed. Cir. 1991) - DESCRIP-
TION, DISCLOSURE, DRAWINGS, SUMMARY JUDGMENT

Vaupel Textimaschinen KG v. Meccanica Euro Italia s.p.a., 944 F.2d 870, 20 U.S.P.Q.2d
1045 (Fed. Cir. 1991) - LACHES, PATENT

Vectra Fitness Inc. v. TNWK Corp., 49 U.S.P.Q.2d 1144 (Fed. Cir. 1998) - DIS-
CLAIMER, REISSUE

Vehicular Technologies Corp. v. Titan Wheel International Inc., 141 F.3d 1084, 46
U.S.P.Q.2d 1257 (Fed. Cir. 1998) - ADVANTAGE, "ALL ADVANTAGES" RULE,
DOCTRINE OF EQUIVALENTS

VE Holding Corp. v. Johnson Gas Appliance Co., 917 F.2d 1574, 16 U.S.P.Q.2d 1614
(Fed. Cir. 1990), *cert. denied*, 111 S.Ct. 1315 (1991) - RESIDE, 21 U.S.C. §372(d),
28 U.S.C. §1400(b)

Velo-Bind, Incorporated v. Minnesota Mining & Manufacturing Company, 647 F.2d 965,
211 U.S.P.Q. 926 (9th Cir. 1981) - SUBCOMBINATION

In re Venner and Bowser, 262 F.2d 91, 120 U.S.P.Q. 192 (C.C.P.A. 1958) - AUTOMATE,
MECHANIZE

Verdegaal Brothers Inc. v. Union Oil Company of California, 814 F.2d 628, 2 U.S.P.Q.2d
1051 (Fed. Cir. 1987) - ANTICIPATION, INHERENCY

Viam Corp. v. Iowa Export-Import Trading Co., 38 U.S.P.Q.2d 1833 (Fed. Cir. 1996) -
PERSONAL JURISDICTION

Ex parte Vibber, 144 U.S.P.Q. 278 (PO Bd. App. 1959) - INTEGRAL, SEPARATE

Victus Ltd. v. Collezione Europa U.S.A. Inc., 48 U.S.P.Q.2d 1145 (N.C. 1998) - IN-FRINGEMENT, PATENTABLY DISTINCT INVENTIONS

Vieau v. Japax, Inc., 823 F.2d 1510, 3 U.S.P.Q.2d 1094 (Fed. Cir. 1987) - BURDEN, DIRECTED VERDICT, SUBSTANTIAL EVIDENCE, VALIDITY

View Engineering Inc. v. Robotic Vision Systems Inc., 42 U.S.P.Q.2d 1956 (Fed. Cir. 1997) - RULE 11, SANCTIONS

In re Vincent, 135 F.2d 936, 57 U.S.P.Q. 557 (C.C.P.A. 1943) - HYBRID

Virginia Panel Corp. v. MAC Panel Co., 133 F.3d 860, 45 U.S.P.Q.2d 1225 (Fed. Cir. 1997) - PATENT MISUSE

Viskase Corp. v. American National Can Co., 979 F. Supp. 697, 45 U.S.P.Q.2d 1675 (Ill. 1997) - PERJURED TESTIMONY, RULE 60 (b)(3)

Vista Manufacturing Inc. v. Trac-Four Inc., 131 F.R.D. 134, 15 U.S.P.Q.2d 1345 (Ind. 1990) - RULE 11

Vitronics Corp. v. Conceptronic Inc., 90 F.3d 1576, 39 U.S.P.Q.2d 1573 (Fed. Cir. 1996) - CLAIM CONSTRUCTION, EXTRINSIC EVIDENCE

Vitronics Corp. v. Conceptronic Inc., 44 U.S.P.Q.2d 1536 (N.H. 1977) - ASSIGNOR

Vogel v. Jones, 443 F.2d 257, 170 U.S.P.Q. 188 (3rd Cir. 1971) - NONRESIDENT DE-FENDANT, RULE 34, RULE 35, RULE 45, 28 U.S.C. §1391(e), 35 U.S.C. §24

Vogel v. Jones, 346 F. Supp. 1005, 175 U.S.P.Q. 152 (D.C. 1972) - DISCOVERY, TRIAL DE NOVO

In re Vogel and Vogel, 422 F.2d 438, 164 U.S.P.Q. 619 (C.C.P.A. 1970) - CLAIM, SAME INVENTION, SCOPE, SUPPORT

Voisin v. Collier, 18 U.S.P.Q.2d 1169 (Commr. Patents & Trademarks 1989) - INTERFERENCE

In re Von Bramer and Ruggles, 127 F.2d 149, 53 U.S.P.Q. 345 (C.C.P.A. 1942); overruled - ENABLING DISCLOSURE

Ex parte Vollheim, Troger, and Lippert, 191 U.S.P.Q. 407 (PTO Bd. App. 1975) - CATA-LYSIS, COMPRISE, COMPRISING, CONDITIONS, INEFFECTIVE, OBJEC-TIVE ENABLEMENT

Vornado Air Circulation Systems Inc. v. Duracraft Corp., 58 F.3d 1498, 35 U.S.P.Q.2d 1332 (10th Cir. 1995) - PATENT

In re Voss, 557 F.2d 812, 194 U.S.P.Q. 267 (C.C.P.A. 1977) - BENEFIT, BURDEN, SUF-FICIENCY OF DISCLOSURE, 35 U.S.C. §102(b), 35 U.S.C. §112, 35 U.S.C. §120

-W-

In re Wadlinger, Kerr, and Rosinski, 496 F.2d 1200, 181 U.S.P.Q. 826 (C.C.P.A. 1974) - REISSUE

In re Wagner and Folkers, 371 F.2d 877, 152 U.S.P.Q. 552 (C.C.P.A. 1967) - KIND, POSITION, STRUCTURAL SIMILARITY, SUBSTITUTION

Wagoner and Protzman v. Barger and Haggerty, 463 F.2d 1377, 175 U.S.P.Q. 85 (C.C.P.A. 1972) - CONSTRUCTIVE REDUCTION TO PRACTICE

Wahl v. Rexnord, Inc., 624 F.2d 1169, 206 U.S.P.Q. 865 (C.C.P.A. 1980) - DESIGN

Wahl Instruments Inc. v. Acvious Inc., 950 F.2d 1575, 21 U.S.P.Q.2d 1123 (Fed. Cir. 1991) - BEST MODE, TRADEMARK

Wahpeton Canvas Co. v. Frontier Inc., 870 F.2d 1546, 10 U.S.P.Q.2d 1201 (Fed. Cir. 1989) - DEPENDENT CLAIM, RULE 49, VERDICT

Wahpeton Canvas Co. South Dakota Inc. v. Bremer, 893 F. Supp. 863, 35 U.S.P.Q.2d 1001 (Iowa 1995) - REPAIR

In re Waite and Allport, 168 F.2d 104, 77 U.S.P.Q. 586 (C.C.P.A. 1948) - CHANGE, CRITICAL, CRITICALITY, PROPORTIONS

In re Wakefield and Foster, 422 F.2d 897, 164 U.S.P.Q. 636 (C.C.P.A. 1970) - BREADTH, CLAIM, DEFINITENESS, DEFINITION, EXCLUDING PRIOR ART, MULTIPLICITY, NEGATIVE LIMITATION, OBSCURE, SYNTHETIC, UNNECESSARY, 35 U.S.C. §112

Waldemar Link, GmbH & Co. v. Osteonics Corp., 32 F.3d 556, 31 U.S.P.Q.2d 1855 (Fed. Cir. 1994) - AMENDMENT AFTER FINAL

Walker v. New Mexico & So. Pac. R. Co., 165 U.S. 593 (1897) - SEVENTH AMENDMENT

Walker Process Equipment, Inc. v. Food Machinery & Chemical Corp., 382 U.S. 172, 147 U.S.P.Q. 404 (1965) - ANTITRUST, MISUSE, SHERMAN ACT

Walker Process Equipment, Inc. v. FMC Corp., 356 F.2d 449, 148 U.S.P.Q. 308 (7th Cir.), cert. denied, 385 U.S. 824, 151 U.S.P.Q. 758 (1966) - DECLARATORY JUDGMENT

Wallace Clarke & Co. v. Acheson Industries, Inc., 532 F.2d 846, 190 U.S.P.Q. 321 (2d Cir. 1976) - CONSENT JUDGMENT, RES JUDICATA

In re Walles, Tousignant, and Houtman, 366 F.2d 786, 151 U.S.P.Q. 185 (C.C.P.A. 1966) - CARRIER, COMBINATION, COMPOSITION, DOUBLE PATENTING, INTENDED USE, INVENTION, PREAMBLE, SAME INVENTION, SOLVENT

In re Walter, 618 F.2d 758, 205 U.S.P.Q. 397 (C.C.P.A. 1980) - ALGORITHM, COMPUTER-ARTS INVENTION, FORM OVER SUBSTANCE, MEANS PLUS FUNCTION, NUMBER CRUNCHING, POINT OF NOVELTY, PROCESS

In re The Successor in Interest to Walter Andersen, 743 F.2d 1578, 223 U.S.P.Q. 378 (Fed. Cir. 1984) - DOUBT, REEXAMINATION

In re Wands, 858 F.2d 731, 8 U.S.P.Q.2d 1400 (Fed. Cir. 1988) - DEPOSIT, ENABLEMENT, EXPERIMENTATION, SCREENING, UNDUE EXPERIMENTATION

Wang Laboratories Inc. v. Applied Computer Sciences Inc., 958 F.2d 355, 22 U.S.P.Q.2d 1055 (Fed. Cir. 1992) - JUDICIAL ESTOPPEL

Wang Laboratories Inc. v. Mitsubishi Electronics America Inc., 29 U.S.P.Q.2d 1481 (Cal. 1993) - IRREPARABLE HARM

Wang Laboratories Inc. v. Mitsubishi Electronics America Inc., 30 U.S.P.Q.2d 1241 (Cal. 1993) - GENUINE, MATERIAL, PRIOR ART

Wang Laboratories Inc. v. Mitsubishi Electronics America Inc., 32 U.S.P.Q.2d 1641 (Cal. 1994) - BEST MODE, DECLARATION, EXPERT, SUMMARY JUDGMENT

Wang Laboratories Inc. v. Mitsubishi Electronics America Inc., 103 F.3d 1571, 41 U.S.P.Q.2d 1263 (Fed. Cir. 1997) - IMPLIED LICENSE

Wang Laboratories Inc. v. Toshiba Corp., 762 F. Supp. 1246, 19 U.S.P.Q.2d 1779 (Va. 1991) - DISQUALIFICATION

Wang Laboratories Inc. v. Toshiba Corp., 793 F. Supp. 676, 23 U.S.P.Q.2d 1953 (Va. 1992) - MOOT, SETTLEMENT

Wang Laboratories Inc. v. Toshiba Corp., 993 F.2d 858, 26 U.S.P.Q.2d 1767 (Fed. Cir. 1993) - DIRECTED VERDICT, FILE WRAPPER ESTOPPEL, ROYALTY

Wanlass v. Fedders Corp., 145 F.3d 1461, 47 U.S.P.Q.2d 1097 (Fed. Cir. 1998) - LACHES

Wanlass v. General Electric Co., 148 F.3d 1334, 46 U.S.P.Q.2d 1915 (Fed. Cir. 1998) - ECONOMIC PREJUDICE, EVIDENTIARY PREJUDICE, LACHES

In re Warmerdam, 33 F.3d 1354, 31 U.S.P.Q.2d 1754 (Fed. Cir. 1994) - ALGORITHM, COMPARING, COMPUTING, CROSS-CORRELATING, DETERMINING, IDENTIFYING, INITIALIZING, MODIFYING, NONSTATUTORY, SELECTING, TESTING

Warner-Jenkinson Co. v. Hilton Davis Chemical Co., 520 U.S. 17, 41 U.S.P.Q.2d 1865 (S.Ct. 1997) - DOCTRINE OF EQUIVALENTS, PROSECUTION HISTORY ESTOPPEL

Washburn v. Gould, 29 F. Cas. 312 (C.C.D. Mass. 1844) - WORD

Waterloo Furniture Components Ltd. v. Haworth Inc., 798 F. Supp. 489, 25 U.S.P.Q.2d 1138 (Ill. 1992) - MEANS

Waterman v. Mackenzie, 138 U.S. 252 (1891) - ASSIGNEE, ASSIGNMENT, RIGHT TO EXCLUDE

Water Technologies Corp. v. Calco, Ltd., 850 F.2d 660, 7 U.S.P.Q.2d 1097 (Fed. Cir.), *cert. denied*, 488 U.S. 968 (1988) - JUDICIAL ESTOPPEL

Water Technologies Corp. v. Calco Ltd., 714 F. Supp. 899, 11 U.S.P.Q.2d 1410 (Ill. 1989) - ATTORNEY'S FEES, DOUBT, PREJUDGMENT INTEREST, ROYALTY

In re Watkinson, 900 F.2d 230, 14 U.S.P.Q.2d 1407 (Fed. Cir. 1990) - MARKUSH, RECAPTURE RULE, REISSUE

In re Watson, 517 F.2d 465, 186 U.S.P.Q. 11 (C.C.P.A. 1975) - FEDERAL REGISTER, SAFETY

Watson, Commissioner of Patents v. Bruns, 239 F.2d 948, 111 U.S.P.Q. 325 (D.C. Cir. 1956) - 37 C.F.R. §1.196(b), NEW GROUND OF REJECTION

In re Way, 514 F.2d 1057, 185 U.S.P.Q. 580 (C.C.P.A. 1975) - CONJECTURE, SHOWING

In re Waymouth and Koury, 489 F.2d 1297, 180 U.S.P.Q. 453 (C.C.P.A. 1974) - NEW GROUND OF REJECTION

In re Waymouth and Koury, 499 F.2d 1273, 182 U.S.P.Q. 290 (C.C.P.A. 1974) - CRITICAL, EXPERIMENTATION, KIND, RANGE, SELECTION, UNEXPECTED RESULTS

Wayne-Gossard Corp. v. Moretz Hosiery, Inc., 539 F.2d 986, 191 U.S.P.Q. 543 (4th Cir. 1976) - INTERVENING RIGHTS

In re Webb, 916 F.2d 1553, 16 U.S.P.Q.2d 1433 (Fed. Cir. 1990) - DECISION, 35 U.S.C. 171

Webcraft Technologies, Inc. v. Alden Press, Inc., 228 U.S.P.Q. 182 (Ill. 1985) - CERTIFICATION, CLASS ACTION, VENUE

In re Weber, Soder, and Boksay, 580 F.2d 455, 198 U.S.P.Q. 328 (C.C.P.A. 1978) - APPLICANT'S RIGHTS, JOINDER OF INVENTION, MISJOINDER, RESTRICTION, UNITY OF INVENTION

Webster Loom Co. v. Elias S. Higgins, 105 U.S. (15 Otto.) 580 (1882) - DISCLOSURE, ECONOMICS, INVENTION, KNOWN, WELL KNOWN

We Care Inc. v. Ultra-Mark International Corp., 14 U.S.P.Q.2d 1804 (Minn. 1989) - INJUNCTIVE RELIEF, RIGHT TO EXCLUDE

Weil v. Fritz, Evans, and Cooke, 572 F.2d 856, 196 U.S.P.Q. 600 (C.C.P.A. 1978) - CONVERSION, INTERFERENCE, OATH

In re Weiler, 790 F.2d 1576, 229 U.S.P.Q. 673 (Fed. Cir. 1986) - ERROR, INTENT TO CLAIM

In re Weiskopf, 210 F.2d 287, 100 U.S.P.Q. 383 (C.C.P.A. 1954) - ANALOGOUS ART, EXTENSION OF MONOPOLY

In re Welstead, 463 F.2d 1110, 174 U.S.P.Q. 449 (C.C.P.A. 1972) - NARROWING CLAIM, NEW MATTER, REDUCTION IN SCOPE

In re Wertheim, 541 F.2d 257, 191 U.S.P.Q. 90 (C.C.P.A. 1976) - ANTECEDENT SUPPORT, ANTEDATING A REFERENCE, DESCRIPTION, IPSIS VERBIS, POSSESSION

In re Wertheim and Mishkin, 646 F.2d 527, 209 U.S.P.Q. 554 (C.C.P.A. 1981) - CO-PENDING PATENT

In re Wesseler, 367 F.2d 838, 151 U.S.P.Q. 339 (C.C.P.A. 1966) - ERROR, REISSUE, STATUTORY CONSTRUCTION

Western Electric Co. Inc. v. Piezo Technology Inc., 15 U.S.P.Q.2d 1401 (Fla. 1990) - EQUITABLE DEFENSES, LACHES, WILLFUL INFRINGEMENT

Western Water Management Inc. v. Brown, 40 F.3d 105, 33 U.S.P.Q.2d 2014 (5th Cir. 1994) - AFFIDAVIT

Ex parte Westfahl, 136 U.S.P.Q. 265 (PO Bd. App. 1962) - ALKYL, AROMATIC, ARYL, ESTER, FREE, HETEROCYCLIC, INDEFINITENESS, POLY-NUCLEAR, SUBSTITUTED

Westinghouse v. Boyden Power Brake Co., 170 U.S. 537 (1897) - EQUIVALENTS

West Interactive Corp. v. First Data Resources Inc., 972 F.2d 1295, 23 U.S.P.Q.2d 1927 (Fed. Cir. 1992) - CONTROVERSY, DECLARATORY JUDGMENT

Westmoreland Specialty Co. v. Hogan, 167 F. 327 (3d Cir. 1909) - MATERIAL

Ex parte Westphal, 26 U.S.P.Q.2d 1858 (B.P.A.I. 1992) - DISCLOSURE, REDUCTION IN SCOPE

Ex parte Westphal, Meiser, Eue, and Hack, 223 U.S.P.Q. 630 (PTO Bd. App. 1983) - TEST

Westvaco Corp. v. International Paper Co., 991 F.2d 735, 26 U.S.P.Q.2d 1353 (Fed. Cir. 1993) - DESIGNING AROUND, OPINION OF COUNSEL

Westwood Chemical, Inc. v. Dow Corning Corporation, 189 U.S.P.Q. 649 (Mich. 1975) - INFRINGEMENT

Westwood Chemical, Inc. v. United States, 525 F.2d 1367, 186 U.S.P.Q. 383 (U.S. Ct. Cl. 1975) - ADVANTAGE, CLAIM, CLASS, COLLATERAL ESTOPPEL, ESTOPPEL, INVENTION

Westwood Pharmaceuticals Inc. v. Quigg, 13 U.S.P.Q.2d 2067 (D.C. 1989) - STATUTORY CONSTRUCTION

Wetmore v. Miller, 477 F.2d 960, 177 U.S.P.Q. 699 (C.C.P.A. 1973) - COPYING CLAIMS

Ex parte Wettstein, Vischer, Meystre, Kahnt, and Neher, 140 U.S.P.Q. 187 (P.O. Bd. App. 1962) - CROSS-REFERENCE, ENABLEMENT, NEW MATTER

Wham-O Mfg. Co. v. All-American Yo-Yo Corporation, 377 F. Supp. 993, 181 U.S.P.Q.

Williams v. The Administrator of the National Aeronautics and Space Administration, 175 U.S.P.Q. 5 (C.C.P.A. 1972) - PROOF, REDUCTION TO PRACTICE

Williams v. The Gillette Co., 887 F. Supp. 181, 36 U.S.P.Q.2d 1374 (Ill. 1995) - RES JUDICATA

Williams Service Group Inc. v. O.B. Cannon & Son Inc., 859 F. Supp. 1521, 33 U.S.P.Q.2d 1705 (Pa. 1994) - CANDOR, ENABLEMENT, EXAMINER, EXPERT, FIELD OF SEARCH, HINDSIGHT, ORDINARY SKILL, PRIOR ART, SCOPE, SEARCH RECORD

In re Willis, 537 F.2d 513, 190 U.S.P.Q. 327 (C.C.P.A. 1976) - MANDATE, REEXAMINATION, REVIVAL, TERMINATION OF PROCEEDINGS

Willis Brothers, Inc. v. Ocean Scallops, Inc., 356 F. Supp. 1151, 176 U.S.P.Q. 53 (N.C. 1972) - BEST EFFORTS, DUE DILIGENCE, DUTY TO USE, EXCLUSIVE LICENSE, EXCLUSIVE LICENSEE, EXPLOIT

In re Wilson, 424 F.2d 1382, 165 U.S.P.Q. 494 (C.C.P.A. 1970) - TERM

Wilson v. Goldmark, 172 F.2d 575, 80 U.S.P.Q. 508 (C.C.P.A. 1949) - DILIGENCE

Wilson Sporting Coods Co. v. David Geoffrey & Associates, 904 F.2d 676, 14 U.S.P.Q.2d 1942 (Fed. Cir. 1990) - DEPENDENT CLAIM, DOCTRINE OF EQUIVALENTS, FRAUD ON A PATENT, INFRINGEMENT

Winans v. New York and Erie R. Co., 62 U.S. (21 How.) 88 (1859) - EXPERT TESTIMONY

Winning Ways Inc. v. Holloway Sportswear Inc., 37 U.S.P.Q.2d 1462 (Kan. 1995) - TRADE DRESS

In re Winslow, 365 F.2d 1017, 151 U.S.P.Q. 48 (1966) - SELECTION, 35 U.S.C. §103

Winter v. Banno, 229 U.S.P.Q. 212 (B.P.A.I. 1985) - BENZYL VS. PHENYL, OBVIOUS TO TRY OR EXPERIMENT, PHENYL VS. BENZYL

Ex parte Winters, 11 U.S.P.Q.2d 1387 (B.P.A.I. 1989) - COMMENSURATE IN SCOPE, COMPARATIVE TEAST DATA, DESCRIPTION, SPECULATION

In re Wiseman and Kovac, 596 F.2d 1019, 201 U.S.P.Q. 658 (C.C.P.A. 1979) - ARGUMENT, CAUSE, DEFECT, PHAIR DOCTRINE, PROBLEM

In re Witco Corp., 14 U.S.P.Q.2d 1557 (T.T.A.B. 1990) - DESIGN, TRADEMARK

W.L. Gore & Associates Inc. v. C. R. Bard Inc., 761 F. Supp. 376, 19 U.S.P.Q.2d 1621 (N.J. 1991) - CONSENT DECREE

W.L. Gore & Associates Inc. v. C.R. Bard Inc., 977 F.2d 558, 24 U.S.P.Q.2d 1451 (Fed. Cir. 1992) - CONSENT ORDER

W.L. Gore & Assoc., Inc. v. Garlock Inc., 721 F.2d 1540, 220 U.S.P.Q. 303 (Fed. Cir. 1983) *cert. denied*, 469 U.S. 851 (1984) - CRITICAL, DISCLOSURE, EARLY DISCLOSURE, FIRST TO FILE, HINDSIGHT, MOSAIC, PREDICTABILITY, PRODUCT OF A COMMERCIALIZED PROCESS, PUBLIC USE, SECRET, SUPPRESSION, TEACH AWAY FROM, UNDUE EXPERIMENTATION

W.L. Gore & Associates Inc. v. Garlock Inc., 842 F.2d 1275, 6 U.S.P.Q.2d 1277 (Fed. Cir. 1988) - CLAIM CONSTRUCTION, CONSTRUCTION OF CLAIMS, EMINENT DOMAIN, INFRINGEMENT, INJUNCTION, LAW-OF-THE-CASE DOCTRINE, OPINION, UNITED STATES GOVERNMENT

W.L. Gore & Associates Inc. v. International Medical Prosthetics Research Associates Inc., 16 U.S.P.Q.2d 1241 (Ariz. 1990) - ROYALTY, TEST METHOD

W.L. Gore & Associates Inc. v. International Medical Prosthetics Research Associates Inc., 975 F.2d 858, 24 U.S.P.Q.2d 1195 (Fed. Cir. 1992) - FINAL, RULE 54(b)

W.L. Gore & Associates, Inc. v. Oak Materials Group, Inc., 424 F. Supp. 700, 192 U.S.P.Q. 687 (Del. 1976) - DISCLAIMER

Wm. T. Burnett & Co. Inc. v. Cumulus Fibres Inc., 825 F. Supp. 734, 27 U.S.P.Q.2d 1953 (N.C. 1993) - PRELIMINARY MOTION, 35 U.S.C. §146

Wokas v. Dresser Industries Inc., 978 F. Supp. 839, 45 U.S.P.Q.2d 1600 (Ind. 1997) - NOTICE

Ex parte Wolf, 65 U.S.P.Q. 527 (PO Bd. App. 1945) - CANCELLATION

In re Wolfrum and Gold, 486 F.2d 588, 179 U.S.P.Q. 620 (C.C.P.A. 1973) - BOUNDS, PLURAL INVENTIONS, RESTRICTION, UNITY OF INVENTION, 35 U.S.C. §112

Ex parte Wolters and Kuypers, 214 U.S.P.Q. 735 (PTO Bd. App. 1979) - ASSUMPTION, DISCLOSURE, KIT, OBVIOUSNESS, WELL KNOWN

Wommack v. Durham Pecan Company, 715 F.2d 962, 219 U.S.P.Q. 1153 (5th Cir. 1983) - SHOP RIGHT

Wood v. Eames, 1880 C.D. 106, 17 O.G. 512 (Comm'r Pat. 1880) - TIE

In re Wood and Eversole, 599 F.2d 1032, 202 U.S.P.Q. 171 (C.C.P.A. 1979) - ANALOGOUS ART

In re Wood, Whittaker, Stirling, and Ohta, 582 F.2d 638, 199 U.S.P.Q. 137 (C.C.P.A. 1978) - ARGUMENT, SPECIFICATION, STATEMENT, STATEMENT IN THE SPECIFICATION

Woodard v. Sage Products, Inc., 818 F.2d 841, 2 U.S.P.Q.2d 1649 (Fed. Cir. 1987) - PRECEDENT

Woodland Trust v. Flowertree Nursery Inc., 148 F.3d 1368, 47 U.S.P.Q.2d 1363 (Fed. Cir. 1998) - 35 U.S.C. §102(b)

Work v. Bier, 106 F.R.D. 45, 226 U.S.P.Q. 657 (D.C. 1985) - FOREIGN DEPOSITION, HAGUE EVIDENCE CONVENTION, INTERFERENCE

Worldtronics International Inc. v. Ever Splendor Enterprise Co., 969 F. Supp. 1136, 44 U.S.P.Q.2d 1447 (Ill. 1997) - LONG-ARM STATUTE

World-Wide Volkswagen Corp. v. Woodson, 444 U.S. 286 (1980) - STREAM OF COMMERCE

In re Worrest, 201 F.2d 930, 96 U.S.P.Q. 381 (C.C.P.A. 1953) - ALTERNATIVE, AGGREGATION, INTERCHANGEABLE

W.R. Grace & Co.-Conn. v. Viskase Corp., 21 U.S.P.Q.2d 1121 (Ill. 1991) - ATTORNEY-CLIENT PRIVILEGE

In re Wright, 569 F.2d 1124, 193 U.S.P.Q. 332 (C.C.P.A. 1977) - DRAWING

In re Wright, 848 F.2d 1216, 6 U.S.P.Q.2d 1959 (Fed. Cir. 1988) - OBVIOUSNESS, PROBLEM, PROPERTIES, PROPERTY

In re Wright, 866 F.2d 422, 9 U.S.P.Q.2d 1649 (Fed. Cir. 1989) - DESCRIPTION

Wright Medical Technology Inc. v. Osteonics Corp., 914 F. Supp. 1524, 38 U.S.P.Q.2d 1573 (Tenn. 1995) - DECLARATORY JUDGMENT

Ex parte Wu, 10 U.S.P.Q.2d 2031 (B.P.A.I. 1988) - OPTIONALLY, SUCH AS, 35 U.S.C. §112

Wu v. Wang, 129 F.3d 1237, 44 U.S.P.Q.2d 1641 (Fed. Cir. 1997) - ADVERSE PARTY, INTERFERENCE

In re Wyer, 655 F.2d 221, 210 U.S.P.Q. 790 (C.C.P.A. 1981) - FOREIGN PATENT APPLICATION, PRINTED PUBLICATION

In re Wynne and Cousen, 255 F.2d 956, 118 U.S.P.Q. 306 (C.C.P.A. 1958) - PATENTABILITY

-X-

Xilinx Inc. v. Altera Corp., 33 U.S.P.Q.2d 1149 (Cal. 1994) - CLEAN HANDS, DUTY TO DISCLOSE, INTENT TO DECEIVE, RULE 9(b)

-y-

Ex parte Yale and Bernstein, 119 U.S.P.Q. 256 (PO Bd. App. 1958) - FREE, PURE

In re Yale, 434 F.2d 666, 168 U.S.P.Q. 46 (C.C.P.A. 1970) - ERROR, MISPRINT, TYPOGRAPHICAL ERROR

In re Yale, Sowinski, and Bernstein, 347 F.2d 995, 146 U.S.P.Q. 400 (C.C.P.A. 1965) - CONCESSION, DISCLAIMER

In re Yamamoto, 740 F.2d 1569, 222 U.S.P.Q. 934 (C.C.P.A. 1984) - CLAIM CONSTRUCTION, UNPATENTED CLAIM

In re Yan, 463 F.2d 1348, 175 U.S.P.Q. 96 (C.C.P.A. 1972) - EVIDENCE

In re Yang and Olsen, 177 U.S.P.Q. 88 (PO Solicitor 1973) - ACCESS, INCORPORATE BY REFERENCE, 35 U.S.C. §122

In re Yardley, 493 F.2d 1389, 181 U.S.P.Q. 331 (C.C.P.A. 1974) - CONTRACT, DESIGN, EXCLUSIVE RIGHT

In re Yarn Processing Patent Litigation, 177 U.S.P.Q. 514 (Fla. 1973) - FOREIGN ASSOCIATE, PRIVILEGE

In re Yates, 663 F.2d 1054, 211 U.S.P.Q. 1149 (C.C.P.A. 1981) - OPTIMIZE, ROUTINE EXPERIMENTATION

YBM Magnex Inc. v. International Trade Commission, 145 F.3d 1317, 46 U.S.P.Q.2d 1843 (Fed. Cir. 1998) - DISCLOSURE WITHOUT CLAIMING, UNCLAIMED DISCLOSURE

Yetter Manufacturing Co. v. Hiniker Co., Inc., 213 U.S.P.Q. 119 (Minn. 1981) - CANON 4, CLASSIFICATION

York Products Inc. v. Central Tractor Farm & Family Center, 40 U.S.P.Q.2d 1619 (Fed. Cir. 1996) - SUBSTANTIALLY

Ex parte Yoshino and Takasu, 227 U.S.P.Q. 52 (B.P.A.I. 1985) - KNOWLEDGE ABROAD, PRIOR ART, 35 U.S.C. §102(f)

In re Youmans, 142 U.S.P.Q. 447 (Comm'r 1960) - DRAWING

Young v. Dworkin, 489 F.2d 1277, 180 U.S.P.Q. 388 (C.C.P.A. 1974) - CONCEALMENT

Young v. Young, Baker, and Canaday v. Giffard, 119 U.S.P.Q. 470 (Comm'r of Pat. 1955) - ASSIGNEE, ELECTION

Young Engineers, Inc. v. United States Int'l Trade Comm'n, 721 F.2d 1305, 219 U.S.P.Q. 1142 (Fed. Cir. 1983) - SCOPE

In re Young, Young, and Guest, 173 F.2d 239, 81 U.S.P.Q. 139 (C.C.P.A. 1949) - CLASSIFICATION

In re Yuan, 188 F.2d 377, 89 U.S.P.Q. 324 (C.C.P.A. 1951) - MENTAL STEPS

Yuasa Battery Co. v. Commissioner of Patents and Trademarks, 3 U.S.P.Q.2d 1143 (D.C. 1987) - REEXAMINATION

Yukiyo Ltd. v. Watanabe, 111 F.3d 883, 42 U.S.P.Q.2d 1474 (Fed. Cir. 1997) - BRIEF, CD-ROM

-Z-

Zacharin v. United States, 38 U.S.P.Q.2d 1826 (U.S. Ct. Fed. Cl. 1996) - GOVERNMENT

In re Zahn, 617 F.2d 261, 204 U.S.P.Q. 988 (C.C.P.A. 1980) - DESIGN, DOTTED LINES, 35 U.S.C. §171

Ex parte Zbornik and Peterson, 109 U.S.P.Q. 508 (PO Bd. App. 1956) - METHOD

Zeneca Limited v. Novopharm Limited, 38 U.S.P.Q.2d 1585 (Md. 1996) - MOOTNESS, SETTLEMENT, VACATUR

Zeneca Ltd. v. Pharmachemie B.V., 42 U.S.P.Q.2d 1212 (Md. 1996) - PERSONAL JURISDICTION

Zenith Controls Inc. v. Automatic Switch Company, 648 F. Supp. 1497, 2 U.S.P.Q.2d 1025 (Ill. 1986) - DUTY TO DISCLOSE

Zenith Electronics Corp. v. ExZec Inc., 32 U.S.P.Q.2d 1959 (Ill. 1994) - CORPORATE OFFICER, INDUCE, 35 U.S.C. §271(b)

Zenith Labs. Inc. v. Bristol-Myers Squibb Co., 24 U.S.P.Q.2d 1652 (N.J. 1992), *aff'd in pertinent part*, 19 F.3d 1418, 30 U.S.P.Q.2d 1285 (Fed. Cir. 1994), *cert. denied*, 115 S.Ct. 500 (1994) - PRO-DRUG

Zenith Lab., Inc. v. Bristol-Myers Squibb Co., 19 F.3d 1418, 30 U.S.P.Q.2d 1285 (Fed. Cir.), *cert. denied*, 115 S.Ct. 500 (1994) - CONVERSION (*in situ* or *in vivo*), ESTOPPEL

In re Zenitz, 333 F.2d 924, 142 U.S.P.Q. 158 (C.C.P.A. 1964) - COMPARATIVE TEST DATA, COPENDING PATENT, INHERENT, SAFETY, PHARMACEUTICAL, UNDISCLOSED PROPERTY, UNEXPECTED RESULTS

In re Zickendraht, 319 F.2d 225, 138 U.S.P.Q. 22 (C.C.P.A. 1963) - EXPIRATION

Ziegler v. Phillips Petroleum Company, 483 F.2d 858, 177 U.S.P.Q. 481 (5th Cir. 1973) - CATALYST, CHEMICAL, CONSISTING ESSENTIALLY OF, CONSTRUCTION, DOCTRINE OF EQUIVALENTS, EXAMPLE

In re Ziegler, Breil, Holzkamp, and Martin, 347 F.2d 642, 146 U.S.P.Q. 76 (C.C.P.A. 1966) - ANTEDATING A REFERENCE, REFERENCE, SAME INVENTION, SPECIES, SUPPORT

In re Zletz, 893 F.2d 319, 13 U.S.P.Q.2d 1320 (Fed. Cir. 1989) - 37 C.F.R. §1.131, CLAIM INTERPRETATION, LOST COUNT, MEANING, UNPATENTED CLAIM

ZMI Corp. v. Cardiac Resuscitator Corp., 844 F.2d 1576, 6 U.S.P.Q.2d 1557 (Fed. Cir. 1988) - EXCLUDE, FILE WRAPPER, LEXICOGRAPHER, PROSECUTION HISTORY, THREE-PRONGED ANALYSIS

In re Zonenstein, 172 F.2d 599, 80 U.S.P.Q. 522 (C.C.P.A. 1949) - DESIGN

In re Zurko, 142 F.3d 1447, 46 U.S.P.Q.2d 1691 (Fed. Cir. 1998 - *in banc*) - ADMINISTRATIVE PROCEDURE ACT, CAFC, CLEARLY ERRONEOUS, PTO, PTO HISTORY, STANDARD OF REVIEW, *STARE DECISIS*